P9-BEE-191

Illustrative Student Essays

How Maupassant Uses Setting in "The Necklace" to Show the Character of Mathilde, 36, 45

The Plot of Eudora Welty's "A Worn Path," 122

Shirley Jackson's Dramatic Point of View in "The Lottery," 167

The Character of Minnie Wright in Glaspell's "A Jury of Her Peers," 218

The Setting of Conrad's "The Secret Sharer," 271

Conflict and Suspense in Hardy's "The Three Strangers," 318

Frank O'Connor's Control of Tone and Style in "First Confession," 370

Symbols of Light and Darkness in Porter's "The Jilting of Granny Weatherall," 421

The Allegory of Hawthorne's "Young Goodman Brown," 425

D. H. Lawrence's "The Horse Dealer's Daughter" as an Expression of the Idea that Loving Commitment is Essential in Life, 488

Fiction Research Essay: The Structure of Katherine Mansfield's "Miss Brill," 614

An Explication of Thomas Hardy's "The Man He Killed," 649

Diction and Character in Robinson's "Richard Cory," 681

The Character of the Duke in Browning's "My Last Duchess," 721

Imagery in T. S. Eliot's "Preludes," 754

A Study of Shakespeare's Metaphors in Sonnet 30: "When to the Sessions of Sweet Silent Thought," 796

The Speaker's Attitudes in Sharon Olds's "The Planned Child," 836

Rhyme, Rhythm, and Sound in Browning's "Porphyria's Lover," 887

The Rhymes and Repeated Words in Christina Rossetti's "Echo," 892

Form and Meaning in George Herbert's "Virtue," 935

Symbolism in Oliver's "Wild Geese," 978

Myth and Meaning in Dorothy Parker's "Penelope," 1018

Poetry Research Essay: "Beat! Beat! Drums!" and "I Hear America Singing": Two Whitman Poems Spanning the Civil War, 1197

Eugene O'Neill's Use of Negative Descriptions and Stage Directions in *Before Breakfast* as a Means of Revealing Character, 1259

The Problem of Hamlet's Apparent Delay, 1490

Setting as Symbol and Comic Structure in *A Midsummer Night's Dream*, 1609

Realism and Nonrealism in Tom's Triple Role in *The Glass Menagerie*, 1743

Welles' *Citizen Kane*: Whittling a Giant Down to Size, 1767

Drama Research Essay: The Ghost in *Hamlet*, 1840

The Treatment of Responses to War in Amy Lowell's "Patterns" and Wilfred Owen's "Anthem for Doomed Youth," 1883

Literary Treatments of the Conflicts Between Private and Public Life, 1887

Research Coverage

Bibliography—Setting up a Bibliography, 596

Computer-Aided Research, 598

Creative and Original Research, 605

Documenting Your Work, 607

Drama: Research Essay on Drama (Chapter 28A), 1839

Drama Research Essay: The Ghost in *Hamlet*, 1840

Endnotes, 609

Fiction: Research Essay on Fiction (Chapter 10A), 594

Fiction Research Essay: The Structure of Mansfield's "Miss Brill," 614

Footnotes, 609

MLA Documentation—Appendix I: MLA, 1905

Online Library Services, 597

Outlining: Strategies for Organizing Ideas in Your Research Essay, 611

Paraphrasing, 599

Plagiarism, 612

Poetry: Research Essay on Poetry (Chapter 22A), 1195

Poetry Research Essay: "Beat! Beat! Drums!" and "I Hear America Singing": Two Whitman Poems Spanning the Civil War, 1197

Taking Notes, 599

Topic— Selecting a Topic, 594

Why Do You Need This New Edition?

If you are wondering why you should buy this new edition of *Literature*, here are 7 good reasons!

❶ NEW MLA Document Maps: These visual representations help students locate key information for frequently cited sources such as books and Web sites.

❷ NEW Visualizing Genres: Fiction, poetry, and drama each feature a section devoted to images that represent key literary principles or visual-based media within the genre. In fiction, a comic strip and graphic novel are featured; in poetry, shaped poetry is highlighted; and in drama, two different production photos of *Hamlet* are used to compare and contrast different staging techniques.

❸ NEW Design: The entire book has been redesigned to make key features and selections easier to find and read.

❹ NEW Fiction Selections: Eleven new works, including James Baldwin, "Sonny's Blues," Joyce Carol Oates, "Where Are You Going, Where Have You Been?" and Ernest Hemingway, "Hills Like White Elephants."

❺ NEW Poetry Selections: Forty-five new works, including Pablo Neruda, "If You Forget Me," Gwendolyn Brooks, "The Mother," and Yusef Komunyakaa, "Facing It."

❻ NEW Drama Selection: August Wilson, *Fences*

❼ NEW Poetic Careers: Four varied poetic careers are now highlighted:

- **Emily Dickinson,** including "Because I could not stop for Death."

- **Robert Frost,** including "Stopping by Woods on a Snowy Evening."

- **Langston Hughes,** including "Harlem 1951."

- **Sylvia Plath,** including "Daddy."

Literature

Literature

An Introduction to Reading and Writing

NINTH EDITION

Edgar V. Roberts

Emeritus, Lehman College
The City University of New York

Longman

New York San Francisco Boston
London Toronto Sydney Tokyo Singapore Madrid
Mexico City Munich Paris Cape Town Hong Kong Montreal

Senior Acquisitions Editor: Vivian Garcia
Executive Marketing Manager: Joyce Nilsen
Senior Supplements Editor: Donna Campion
Production Manager: Savoula Amanatidis
Project Coordination, Text Design, and Electronic Page Makeup: Nesbitt Graphics, Inc.
Cover Design Manager: John Callahan
Cover Image: Mark Klein/New England Rural Images
Pearson Image Resource Center/Photo Researcher: Teri Stratford
Image Permission Coordinator: Craig Jones
Senior Manufacturing Buyer: Dennis J. Para
Printer and Binder: Quebecor World Book Services—Taunton
Cover Printer: Lehigh-Phoenix Color Corporation

For permission to use copyrighted material, grateful acknowledgment is made to the copyright holders on pp. 1979–1987, which are hereby made part of this copyright page.

Library of Congress Cataloging-in-Publication Data
Roberts, Edgar V.

  Literature : an introduction to reading and writing / Edgar V.
Roberts. -- 9th ed.
    p. cm.
  ISBN 978-0-13-604099-6 (student edition) -- ISBN 978-0-13-604102-3
(marketing sampler)
  1. Literature. 2. Exposition (Rhetoric) 3. Literature--Collections. 4.
College readers. 5. Report writing. I. Title.
  PN45.R575 2009
  808'.0668--dc22

                          2008042727

Longman
is an imprint of

ISBN-13: 978-0-13-604099-6
ISBN-10: 0-13-604099-3

www.pearsonhighered.com   1 2 3 4 5 6 7 8 9 10—QWT—11 10 09 08

Brief Contents

Detailed Contents
Topical and Thematic Contents
Preface

ix
xlix
lxi

PART I

The Process of Reading, Responding to, and Writing About Literature
1

PART II

Reading and Writing About Fiction
55

1 FICTION: AN OVERVIEW
56

2 POINT OF VIEW: THE POSITION OR STANCE OF THE WORK'S NARRATOR OR SPEAKER
127

3 CHARACTERS: THE PEOPLE IN FICTION
173

4 SETTING: THE BACKGROUND OF PLACE, OBJECTS, AND CULTURE IN STORIES
224

5 STRUCTURE: THE ORGANIZATION OF STORIES
275

6 TONE AND STYLE: THE WORDS THAT CONVEY ATTITUDES IN FICTION
324

7 SYMBOLISM AND ALLEGORY: KEYS TO EXTENDED MEANING
375

8 IDEA OR THEME: THE MEANING AND THE MESSAGE IN FICTION
432

9 A CAREER IN FICTION: FOUR STORIES BY EDGAR ALLAN POE WITH CRITICAL READINGS FOR RESEARCH
493

10 SEVEN STORIES FOR ADDITIONAL ENJOYMENT AND STUDY
543

10A WRITING A RESEARCH ESSAY ON FICTION
594

PART III

Reading and Writing About Poetry
623

11 MEETING POETRY: AN OVERVIEW
624

12 WORDS: THE BUILDING BLOCKS OF POETRY   653

13 CHARACTERS AND SETTING: WHO, WHAT,
        WHERE, AND WHEN IN POETRY   686

14 IMAGERY: THE POEM'S LINK TO THE SENSES   726

15 FIGURES OF SPEECH, OR METAPHORICAL
        LANGUAGE: A SOURCE OF DEPTH AND RANGE IN POETRY   760

16 TONE: THE CREATION OF ATTITUDE IN POETRY   800

17 PROSODY: SOUND, RHYTHM, AND RHYME IN POETRY   841

18 FORM: THE SHAPE OF POEMS   897

19 SYMBOLISM AND ALLUSION: WINDOWS
        TO WIDE EXPANSES OF MEANING   940

20 MYTHS: SYSTEMS OF SYMBOLIC ALLUSION IN POETRY   983

21 FOUR MAJOR AMERICAN POETS: EMILY DICKINSON,
        ROBERT FROST, LANGSTON HUGHES, AND SYLVIA PLATH   1023

22 ONE HUNDRED SIXTEEN POEMS FOR ADDITIONAL
        ENJOYMENT AND STUDY   1103

22A WRITING A RESEARCH ESSAY ON POETRY   1195

PART IV
Reading and Writing About Drama   1203

23 THE DRAMATIC VISION: AN OVERVIEW   1204

24 THE TRAGIC VISION: AFFIRMATION THROUGH LOSS   1265

25 THE COMIC VISION: RESTORING THE BALANCE   1496

26 VISIONS OF DRAMATIC REALITY AND NONREALITY:
        VARYING THE IDEA OF DRAMA AS IMITATION   1614

27 DRAMATIC VISION ON FILM: FROM THE SILVER
        SCREEN TO THE WORLD OF DIGITAL FANTASY   1748

28 HENRICK IBSEN AND THE REALISTIC PROBLEM PLAY:
        A DOLLHOUSE   1773

28A WRITING A RESEARCH ESSAY ON DRAMA   1839

PART V
Special Writing Topics About Literature

1853

29 CRITICAL APPROACHES IMPORTANT IN THE STUDY OF LITERATURE   1854

30 COMPARISON-CONTRAST AND EXTENDED COMPARISON-CONTRAST: LEARNING BY SEEING LITERARY WORKS TOGETHER   1876

31 TAKING EXAMINATIONS ON LITERATURE   1893

Appendixes

I MLA RECOMMENDATIONS FOR DOCUMENTING SOURCES   1905

II BRIEF BIOGRAPHIES OF POETS IN PART III   1916

GLOSSARY OF IMPORTANT KEY TERMS   1955

Credits   1979
Index of Authors, Titles, and First Lines   1988

Detailed Contents

Topical and Thematic Contents   xlix

Preface   lxi

PART I

The Process of Reading, Responding to, and Writing About Literature   1

WHAT IS LITERATURE, AND WHY DO WE STUDY IT?   3

Types of Literature: The Genres   3

Reading Literature and Responding to It Actively   5

🍁 **GUY DE MAUPASSANT**   *The Necklace*   5
To go to a ball, Mathilde Loisel borrows a necklace from a rich friend, but her rhapsodic evening has unforeseen consequences.

Reading and Responding in a Computer File or Notebook   12

Sample Notebook Entries on Maupassant's "The Necklace"   14

MAJOR STAGES IN THINKING AND WRITING ABOUT LITERARY TOPICS: DISCOVERING IDEAS, PREPARING TO WRITE, MAKING AN INITIAL DRAFT OF YOUR ESSAY, AND COMPLETING THE ESSAY   18

Writing Does Not Come Easily—for Anyone   18   •   *The Goal of Writing: To Show a Process of Thought*   19

Discovering Ideas ("Brainstorming")   20

Study the Characters in the Work   21   •   *Determine the Work's Historical Period and Background*   23   •   *Analyze the Work's Economic and Social Conditions*   23   •   *Explain the Work's Major Ideas*   24   •   *Describe the Work's Artistic Qualities*   24   •   *Explain Any Other Approaches That Seem Important*   25

Preparing to Write   25

Build Ideas from Your Original Notes   25   •   Trace Patterns of Action and Thought   26

The Need for the Actual Physical Process of Writing   27

Raise and Answer Your Own Questions   27   •   Put Ideas Together Using a Plus-Minus, Pro-Con, or Either-Or Method   28   •   Originate and Develop Your Thoughts Through Writing   29

Making an Initial Draft of Your Essay   29

Base Your Essay on a Central Idea, Argument, or Statement   29

The Need for a Sound Argument in Essays About Literature   31

Create a Thesis Sentence as Your Guide to Organization   31   •   Begin Each Paragraph with a Topic Sentence   32   •   Select Only One Topic—No More—for Each Paragraph   32

Referring to the Names of Authors   33

Use Your Topic Sentences as the Arguments for Your Paragraph Development   33

The Use of Verb Tenses in the Discussion of Literary Works   34

Develop an Outline as the Means of Organizing Your Essay   35

Illustrative Student Essay (First Draft): How Setting in "The Necklace" Is Related to the Character of Mathilde   36

Completing the Essay: Developing and Strengthening Your Essay Through Revision   38

Make Your Own Arrangement of Details and Ideas   38   •   Use Literary Material as Evidence to Support Your Argument   38   •   Always Keep to Your Point; Stick to It Tenaciously   39   •   Check Your Development and Organization   41   •   Try to Be Original   41   •   Write with Specific Readers as Your Intended Audience   42   •   Use Exact, Comprehensive, and Forceful Language   43   •   Illustrative Student Essay (Improved Draft): How Maupassant Uses Setting in "The Necklace" to Show the Character of Mathilde   45   •   Commentary on the Essay   48   •   Essay Commentaries   48

A Summary of Guidelines   49

Writing Topics About the Writing Process   49

A SHORT GUIDE TO THE USE OF REFERENCES AND QUOTATIONS IN ESSAYS ABOUT LITERATURE   50

Integrate Passages and Ideas into Your Essay   50

Distinguish Your Thoughts from Those of Your Author   50

Integrate Material by Using Quotation Marks   51

Blend Quotations into Your Own Sentences   51

Indent Long Quotations and Set Them in Block Format   52

Use an Ellipsis to Show Omissions   53

Use Square Brackets to Enclose Words That You Add Within Quotations   53

Be Careful Not to Overquote   53

Preserve the Spellings in Your Source   54

PART II

Reading and Writing About Fiction   55

1   FICTION: AN OVERVIEW   56

Modern Fiction   57

The Short Story   58

Elements of Fiction I: Verisimilitude and Donnée   58

Elements of Fiction II: Character, Plot, Structure, and Idea or Theme   60

Elements of Fiction III: The Writer's Tools   62

Visualizing Fiction: Cartoons, Graphic Narratives, Graphic Novels   63

Dan Piraro, *Bizarro*   65   •   Art Spiegelman, from *Maus*   65

STORIES FOR STUDY   71

 AMBROSE BIERCE   *An Occurrence at Owl Creek Bridge*   71
A condemned man dreams of escape, freedom, and family.

 EDWIDGE DANTICAT   *Night Talkers*   77
Through an evil act, a man learns goodness.

WILLIAM FAULKNER   *A Rose for Emily*   89
Even seemingly ordinary people hide deep and bizarre mysteries.

TIM O'BRIEN   *The Things They Carried*   95
During the Vietnam War, American soldiers carry not only their weighty equipment but many memories.

NEW **LUIGI PIRANDELLO**   *War*   105
During World War I in Italy, the loss of a loved one outweighs all rationalizations for the conflict.

ALICE WALKER *Everyday Use*   **108**

Mrs. Johnson, with her daughter Maggie, is visited by her citified daughter Dee, whose return home is accompanied by surprises.

 EUDORA WELTY *A Worn Path*   **114**

Phoenix Jackson, a devoted grandmother, walks a worn path on a mission of great love.

Plot: The Motivation and Causality of Fiction   **119**

Writing About the Plot of a Story   **121**   •   *Illustrative Student Essay: The Plot of Eudora Welty's "A Worn Path"*   **123**

Writing Topics About Plot in Fiction   **125**

2   POINT OF VIEW: THE POSITION OR STANCE OF THE WORK'S NARRATOR OR SPEAKER   **127**

An Exercise in Point of View: Reporting an Accident   **128**

Conditions That Affect Point of View   **130**

Point of View and Opinions   **130**

Determining a Work's Point of View   **131**

Mingling Points of View   **134**

Point of View and Verb Tense   **134**

Summary: Guidelines for Points of View   **135**

STORIES FOR STUDY   **136**

 RAYMOND CARVER *Neighbors*   **137**

Bill and Arlene Miller are looking after the apartment of the Stones, their neighbors, whose life seems to be brighter and fuller than theirs.

 SHIRLEY JACKSON *The Lottery*   **140**

What would it be like if the prize at a community-sponsored lottery were not the cash that people ordinarily hope to win?

 LORRIE MOORE *How to Become a Writer*   **146**

There is more to becoming a writer than simply sitting down at a table and beginning to write.

 JOYCE CAROL OATES *The Cousins*   **150**

What are the obstacles to friendship between close relatives who have lived their lives totally apart from each other?

Writing About Point of View 164 • 📄 *Illustrative Student Essay: Shirley Jackson's Dramatic Point of View in "The Lottery"* 167

Writing Topics About Point of View 171

3 CHARACTERS: THE PEOPLE IN FICTION   173

Character Traits 173

How Authors Disclose Character in Literature 175

Types of Characters: Round and Flat 177

Reality and Probability: Verisimilitude 179

STORIES FOR STUDY *180*

 NEW **RAYMOND CARVER** *Cathedral* **180**
A husband and wife receive a blind visitor who affects the man's way of seeing things.

 SUSAN GLASPELL *A Jury of Her Peers* **189**
In a small farmhouse kitchen, the wives of men investigating a murder discover significant evidence that forces them to make an urgent decision.

 KATHERINE MANSFIELD *Miss Brill* **202**
Miss Brill goes to the park for a pleasant afternoon, but she does not find what she was expecting.

 AMY TAN *Two Kinds* **205**
Jing-Mei leads her own kind of life despite the wishes and hopes of her mother.

 MARK TWAIN *Luck* **213**
A faithful follower describes an English general who was knighted for military brilliance.

Writing About Character 216 • 📄 *Illustrative Student Essay: The Character of Minnie Wright in Glaspell's "A Jury of Her Peers"* 219

Writing Topics About Character 222

4 SETTING: THE BACKGROUND OF PLACE, OBJECTS, AND CULTURE IN STORIES   224

What Is Setting? 224

The Literary Uses of Setting 225

STORIES FOR STUDY 228

 SANDRA CISNEROS   *The House on Mango Street*   **228**
"I knew then that I had to have a house."

 JOSEPH CONRAD   *The Secret Sharer*   **230**
What goes on in the mind of a person, insecure in his own position, when he makes a difficult moral judgment which may prove disastrous?

 JOANNE GREENBERG   *And Sarah Laughed*   **253**
The wife and mother in a family of hearing-impaired people learn to understand and appreciate their difficulties.

 JAMES JOYCE   *Araby*   **262**
An introspective boy learns much about himself when he tries to keep a promise.

 CYNTHIA OZICK   *The Shawl*   **266**
Can a mother in a Nazi concentration camp save her starving and crying baby?

Writing About Setting   269   •   📄 *Illustrative Student Essay: The Setting of Conrad's "The Secret Sharer"*   271

Writing Topics About Setting   274

5 STRUCTURE: THE ORGANIZATION OF STORIES   **275**

Formal Categories of Structure   275

Formal and Actual Structure   277

STORIES FOR STUDY 278

 RALPH ELLISON   *Battle Royal*   **278**
An intelligent black student, filled with hopes and dreams, is treated with monstrous indignity.

 THOMAS HARDY   *The Three Strangers*   **287**
The natives of Higher Crowstairs make a major decision about right and wrong even though they are more concerned about other matters.

 JAMAICA KINCAID   *What I Have Been Doing Lately*   **300**
Life develops from the repetition and recirculation of dreams and fantasies.

 JOYCE CAROL OATES   *Where Are You Going, Where Have You Been?*   **302**
A teenage girl is visited by an aggressive stranger who does not accept "no" for an answer.

TOM WHITECLOUD   *Blue Winds Dancing*   *313*
A Native American student leaves college in California to spend Christmas in his hometown in Wisconsin.

Writing About Structure in a Story   *317*   •   📄 *Illustrative Student Essay: Conflict and Suspense in Hardy's "The Three Strangers"*   *319*

Writing Topics About Structure   *323*

6   TONE AND STYLE: THE WORDS THAT CONVEY ATTITUDES IN FICTION   **324**

Diction: The Writer's Choice and Control of Words   *324*

Tone, Irony, and Style   *328*

Tone, Humor, and Style   *329*

STORIES FOR STUDY   331

KATE CHOPIN   *The Story of an Hour*   *331*
Louise Mallard is shocked and grieved by news that her husband has been killed, but she is about to have an even greater shock.

WILLIAM FAULKNER   *Barn Burning*   *333*
A young country boy grows in awareness, conscience, and individuality despite his hostile father.

ERNEST HEMINGWAY   *Hills Like White Elephants*   *344*
While waiting for a train, a man and woman reluctantly discuss an urgent situation.

ALICE MUNRO   *The Found Boat*   *347*
After winter snows have melted in a small Canadian community, young people start making discoveries about themselves.

FRANK O'CONNOR   *First Confession*   *354*
Jackie as a young man tells about his first childhood experience with confession.

DANIEL OROZCO   *Orientation*   *359*
A new employee is introduced to the rather unusual and surprising situations in the office.

JOHN UPDIKE   *A & P*   *363*
As a checkout clerk at the A & P near the local beaches, Sammy learns about the consequences of a difficult choice.

Writing About Tone and Style 367 • 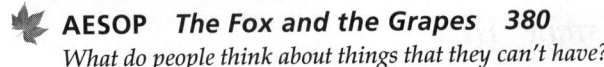 *Illustrative Student Essay:*
Frank O'Connor's Control of Tone and Style in "First Confession" 370

Writing Topics About Tone and Style 374

7 SYMBOLISM AND ALLEGORY: KEYS TO EXTENDED MEANING   375

Symbolism 375

Allegory 377

Fable, Parable, and Myth 378

Allusion in Symbolism and Allegory 379

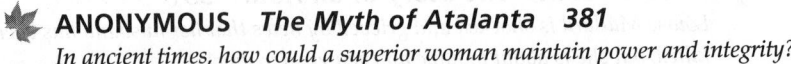 **STORIES FOR STUDY** 380

AESOP *The Fox and the Grapes* 380
What do people think about things that they can't have?

ANONYMOUS *The Myth of Atalanta* 381
In ancient times, how could a superior woman maintain power and integrity?

ANITA SCOTT COLEMAN *Unfinished Masterpieces* 382
Worthiness cannot rise when it is depressed by poverty and inequality.

NATHANIEL HAWTHORNE *Young Goodman Brown* 385
In colonial Salem, Goodman Brown has a bewildering encounter that changes his outlook on life.

FRANZ KAFKA *A Hunger Artist* 393
Public interest wanes even in a unique person.

LUKE *The Parable of the Prodigal Son* 399
Is there any limit to what a person can do to make divine forgiveness impossible?

GABRIEL GARCÍA MARQUEZ *A Very Old Man with Enormous Wings* 400
How do simple villagers respond to a miraculous visitor who appears in their town?

KATHERINE ANNE PORTER *The Jilting of Granny Weatherall* 405
As the end nears, Granny Weatherall has her memories and is surrounded by her loving adult children.

JOHN STEINBECK   *The Chrysanthemums*   *411*
As a housewife on a small ranch, Elisa Allen experiences changes to her sense of self-worth.

Writing About Symbolism and Allegory   417   •   📄 *Illustrative Student Essay (Symbolism): Symbols of Light and Darkness in Porter's "The Jilting of Granny Weatherall"*   421   •   📄 *Second Illustrative Student Essay (Allegory): The Allegory of Hawthorne's "Young Goodman Brown"*   425

Writing Topics About Symbolism and Allegory   430

8 IDEA OR THEME: THE MEANING AND THE MESSAGE IN FICTION   432

Ideas and Assertions   432

Ideas and Issues   432

Ideas and Values   433

The Place of Ideas in Literature   434

How to Find Ideas   435

STORIES FOR STUDY   *438*

 NEW **JAMES BALDWIN**   *Sonny's Blues*   *438*
A devoted brother describes how his brother, Sonny, is hurt by racial prejudice, and how Sonny finds fulfillment through love of music.

 TONI CADE BAMBARA   *The Lesson*   *457*
When a group of children visits a toy store for the wealthy, some of them draw conclusions about society and themselves.

 ANTON CHEKHOV   *The Lady with the Dog*   *462*
Bored with life, Dmitri Gurov meets Anna Sergeyevna and discovers previously unknown emotions and extremely new problems.

 D. H. LAWRENCE   *The Horse Dealer's Daughter*   *471*
Dr. Jack Fergusson and Mabel Pervin find, in each other's love, a new reason for being.

 AMÉRICO PAREDES   *The Hammon and the Beans*   *482*
Is American liberty restricted to people of only one group, or is it for everyone?

Writing About a Major Idea in Fiction   486   •   📄 *Illustrative Student Essay: D. H. Lawrence's "The Horse Dealer's Daughter" as an Expression of the Idea that Loving Commitment is Essential in Life*   488

Writing Topics About Ideas   492

9 A CAREER IN FICTION: FOUR STORIES BY EDGAR ALLAN POE WITH CRITICAL READINGS FOR RESEARCH   493

POE'S LIFE AND CAREER   493

Poe's Work as a Journalist and Writer of Fiction   494

Poe's Reputation   496

Bibliographic Sources   497

Writing Topics About Poe   498

FOUR STORIES BY EDGAR ALLAN POE (CHRONOLOGICALLY ARRANGED)

The Fall of the House of Usher (1839)   499

The Masque of the Red Death (1842)   510

The Black Cat (1843)   513

The Cask of Amontillado (1846)   519

Edited Selections from Criticism of Poe's Stories   523

1. Poe's Irony   523   •   2. The Narrators of "The Cask of Amontillado" and "The Fall of the House of Usher"   524   •   3. "The Fall of the House of Usher"   526   •   4. "The Black Cat" and "The Tell-Tale Heart"   527   •   5. "The Masque of the Red Death"   527   •   6. Symbolism in "The Masque of the Red Death"   527   •   7. "The Masque of the Red Death" as Representative of a "Diseased Age"   528   •   8. Sources and Analogues of "The Cask of Amontillado"   528   •   9. Poe's Idea of Unity and "The Fall of the House of Usher"   536   •   10. The Narrators of "The Cask of Amontillado" and "The Black Cat"   537   •   11. Poe, Women, and "The Fall of the House of Usher"   540   •   12. The Deceptive Narrator of "The Black Cat"   541

10 SEVEN STORIES FOR ADDITIONAL ENJOYMENT AND STUDY   543

JOHN CHIOLES   Before the Firing Squad   543
During World War II, in Nazi-occupied Greece, a young German soldier learns the importance of personal obligations.

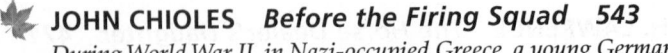 **STEPHEN CRANE   The Open Boat   548**
In this story of survival, the narrator tells of "the subtle brotherhood of men that was here established on the seas."

ANDRE DUBUS   The Curse   563
A man who has witnessed a gang attack on a defenseless woman experiences deep anguish and self-reproach.

CHARLOTTE PERKINS GILMAN *The Yellow Wallpaper* **566**
Who is the woman who is trying to emerge from behind the yellow wallpaper?

FLANNERY O'CONNOR *A Good Man Is Hard to Find* **576**
"The grandmother didn't want to go to Florida. She wanted to visit some of her connections in east Tennessee. . . ."

TILLIE OLSEN *I Stand Here Ironing* **586**
"My wisdom came too late."

PETRONIUS *(Gaius Petronius Arbiter)* *The Widow of Ephesus* **591
A young widow learns what it takes to save her newly found love.

10A WRITING A RESEARCH ESSAY ON FICTION   **594**

Selecting a Topic **594**

Setting Up a Bibliography **596**

Online Library Services **597**

Important Considerations About Computer-Aided Research **598**

Taking Notes and Paraphrasing Material **599**

Being Creative and Original While Doing Research **605**

Documenting Your Work **607**

Strategies for Organizing Ideas in Your Research Essay **611**

Plagiarism: An Embarrassing but Vital Subject—and a Danger to be Overcome **612**

Illustrative Student Essay Using Research: The Structure of Katherine Mansfield's "Miss Brill" **614**

Writing Topics About How to Undertake a Research Essay **622**

PART III

Reading and Writing About Poetry   **623**

11 MEETING POETRY: AN OVERVIEW   **624**

The Nature of Poetry **624**

 BILLY COLLINS *Schoolsville* **624**

 **LISEL MUELLER** *Hope* **626**

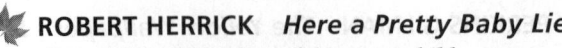 **ROBERT HERRICK   *Here a Pretty Baby Lies*   627**
Do not disturb the sleep of this sweet child.

Poetry of the English Language   628

How to Read a Poem   629

Studying Poetry   631

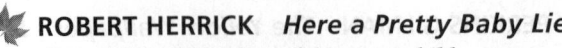 **ANONYMOUS   *Sir Patrick Spens*   631**

POEMS FOR STUDY   634

NEW **GWENDOLYN BROOKS   *The Mother*   634**

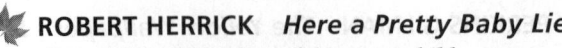 **EMILY DICKINSON   *Because I Could Not Stop for Death*   635**

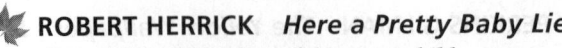 **ROBERT FRANCIS   *Catch*   636**

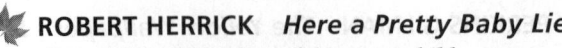 **ROBERT FROST   *Stopping by Woods on a Snowy Evening*   637**

 THOMAS HARDY   *The Man He Killed*   637

 JOY HARJO   *Eagle Poem*   638

 RANDALL JARRELL   *The Death of the Ball Turret Gunner*   639

NEW **BEN JONSON   *On My First Daughter*   640**

 EMMA LAZARUS *The New Colossus*   640

 LOUIS MACNEICE   *Snow*   641

 JIM NORTHRUP   *Ogichidag*   642

 NAOMI SHIHAB NYE   *Where Children Live*   642

 WILLIAM SHAKESPEARE   *Sonnet 55: Not Marble, Nor the Gilded Monuments*   643

 PERCY BYSSHE SHELLEY   *To — ["Music, When Soft Voices Die"]*   644

 ELAINE TERRANOVA   *Rush Hour*   644

Writing a Paraphrase of a Poem   645   •   📄 Illustrative Student Paraphrase: A Paraphrase of Thomas Hardy's "The Man He Killed"   646
Writing an Explication of a Poem   647   •   📄 Illustrative Student Essay: An Explication of Thomas Hardy's "The Man He Killed"   649

Writing Topics About the Nature of Poetry   652

12 WORDS: THE BUILDING BLOCKS OF POETRY 653

Choice of Diction: Specific and Concrete, General and Abstract 653

Levels of Diction 654

Special Types of Diction 655

Syntax 656

Decorum: The Matching of Subject and Word 657

Denotation and Connotation 658

ROBERT GRAVES *The Naked and the Nude* **660**
Word choices have profound effects on our perceptions.

POEMS FOR STUDY 661

WILLIAM BLAKE *The Lamb* **661**

ROBERT BURNS *Green Grow the Rashes, O* **662**

LEWIS CARROLL *Jabberwocky* **663**

HAYDEN CARRUTH *An Apology for Using the Word "Heart" in Too Many Poems* **664**

E. E. CUMMINGS *next to of course god america i* **665**

JOHN DONNE *Holy Sonnet 14: Batter My Heart, Three-Personed God* **666**

RICHARD EBERHART *The Fury of Aerial Bombardment* **667**

BART EDELMAN *Chemistry Experiment* **667**

THOMAS GRAY *Sonnet on the Death of Richard West* **668**

JANE HIRSHFIELD *The Lives of the Heart* **669**

A. E. HOUSMAN *Loveliest of Trees, the Cherry Now* **670**

CAROLYN KIZER *Night Sounds* **671**

DENISE LEVERTOV *Of Being* **672**

NEW **EUGENIO MONTALE** *English Horn (Corno Inglese)* **672**

NEW **JUDITH ORTIZ [COFER]** *Latin Women Pray* **673**

HENRY REED *Naming of Parts* **674**

EDWIN ARLINGTON ROBINSON *Richard Cory* **675**

THEODORE ROETHKE *Dolor* **676**

STEPHEN SPENDER   *I Think Continually of Those Who Were Truly Great*   676

WALLACE STEVENS   *Disillusionment of Ten O'Clock*   677

MARK STRAND   *Eating Poetry*   677

WILLIAM WORDSWORTH   *Daffodils (I Wandered Lonely as a Cloud)*   678

Writing About Diction and Syntax in Poetry   679   •   📄 *Illustrative Student Essay: Diction and Character in Robinson's "Richard Cory"*   681

Writing Topics About the Words of Poetry   684

13   CHARACTERS AND SETTING: WHO, WHAT, WHERE, AND WHEN IN POETRY   686

Characters in Poetry   686

ANONYMOUS   *Western Wind, When Wilt Thou Blow?*   687

ANONYMOUS   *Bonny George Campbell*   687

BEN JONSON   *Drink to Me, Only, with Thine Eyes*   689

BEN JONSON   *To the Reader*   690

Setting and Character in Poetry   692

LISEL MUELLER   *Alive Together*   692

POEMS FOR STUDY   694

MATTHEW ARNOLD   *Dover Beach*   694

WILLIAM BLAKE   *London*   695

ELIZABETH BREWSTER   *Where I Come From*   696

ROBERT BROWNING   *My Last Duchess*   697

WILLIAM COWPER   *The Poplar Field*   699

NEW ALLEN GINSBERG   *A Further Proposal*   699

LOUISE GLÜCK   *Snowdrops*   700

THOMAS GRAY   *Elegy Written in a Country Churchyard*   701

THOMAS HARDY   *The Ruined Maid*   704

DORIANNE LAUX   *The Life of Trees*   705

🍁 C. DAY LEWIS   *Song*   707

🍁 ᴺᴱᗯ ROBERT LOWELL   *Memories of West Street and Lepke*   707

🍁 CHRISTOPHER MARLOWE   *The Passionate Shepherd to His Love*   709

🍁 JOYCE CAROL OATES   *Loving*   710

🍁 SIR WALTER RALEGH   *The Nymph's Reply to the Shepherd*   711

🍁 CHRISTINA ROSSETTI   *A Christmas Carol*   712

🍁 JANE SHORE   *A Letter Sent to Summer*   713

🍁 WILLIAM WORDSWORTH   *Lines Composed a Few Miles Above Tintern Abbey*   714

🍁 JAMES WRIGHT   *A Blessing*   717

Writing About Character and Setting in Poetry   718   •   📄 *Illustrative Student Essay:* The Character of the Duke in Browning's "My Last Duchess" 721

Writing Topics About Character and Setting in Poetry   725

14   IMAGERY: THE POEM'S LINK TO THE SENSES   726

Responses and the Writer's Use of Detail   726

The Relationship of Imagery to Ideas and Attitudes   727

Types of Imagery   727

🍁 JOHN MASEFIELD   *Cargoes*   728
What do cargo-bearing ships tell us about the past and the present?

🍁 WILFRED OWEN   *Anthem for Doomed Youth*   729

🍁 ELIZABETH BISHOP   *The Fish*   730

POEMS FOR STUDY   733

🍁 ELIZABETH BARRETT BROWNING   *Sonnets from the Portuguese, Number 14: If Thou Must Love Me*   733

🍁 SAMUEL TAYLOR COLERIDGE   *Kubla Khan*   734

🍁 T. S. ELIOT   *Preludes*   735

SUSAN GRIFFIN   *Love Should Grow Up Like a Wild Iris in the Fields*   737

THOMAS HARDY   *Channel Firing*   738

GEORGE HERBERT   *The Pulley*   740

GERARD MANLEY HOPKINS   *Spring*   740

A. E. HOUSMAN   *On Wenlock Edge*   741

DENISE LEVERTOV   *A Time Past*   742

THOMAS LUX   *The Voice You Hear When You Read Silently*   743

NEW EUGENIO MONTALE   *Buffalo (Buffalo)*   744

NEW MARIANNE MOORE   *The Fish*   745

NEW PABLO NERUDA   *Every Day You Play*   746

EZRA POUND   *In a Station of the Metro*   747

NEW MIKLÓS RADNÓTI   *Forced March*   748

FRIEDRICH RÜCKERT   *If You Love for the Sake of Beauty*   749

WILLIAM SHAKESPEARE   *Sonnet 130: My Mistress' Eyes Are Nothing Like the Sun*   749

JAMES TATE *Dream On*   750

NEW DAVID WOJAHN   *"It's Only Rock and Roll, but I Like It": The Fall of Saigon*   751

Writing About Imagery   752   •   📄 Illustrative Student Essay: Imagery in T. S. Eliot's "Preludes"   754

Writing Topics About Imagery in Poetry   758

15   FIGURES OF SPEECH, OR METAPHORICAL LANGUAGE: A SOURCE OF DEPTH AND RANGE IN POETRY   760

Metaphors and Similes: The Major Figures of Speech   760

Characteristics of Metaphorical Language   762

JOHN KEATS   *On First Looking into Chapman's Homer*   762

Vehicle and Tenor   763

Other Figures of Speech   764

JOHN KEATS   *Bright Star*   765
A distant star is a guide for constancy in love.

JOHN GAY   *Let Us Take the Road*   767

POEMS FOR STUDY   768

JACK AGÜEROS   *Sonnet for You, Familiar Famine*   768

WILLIAM BLAKE   *The Tyger*   769

ROBERT BURNS   *A Red, Red Rose*   770

JOHN DONNE   *A Valediction: Forbidding Mourning*   771

JOHN DRYDEN   *A Song for St. Cecilia's Day*   772

ABBIE HUSTON EVANS   *The Iceberg Seven-Eighths Under*   774

THOMAS HARDY   *The Convergence of the Twain*   775

JOY HARJO   *Remember*   777

JOHN KEATS   *To Autumn*   778

MAURICE KENNY   *Legacy*   779

JANE KENYON   *Let Evening Come*   780

HENRY KING   *Sic Vita*   781

NEW ROBERT LOWELL   *Skunk Hour*   781

JUDITH MINTY   *Conjoined*   783

NEW PABLO NERUDA   *If You Forget Me*   784

MARGE PIERCY   *A Work of Artifice*   785

MURIEL RUKEYSER   *Looking at Each Other*   786

WILLIAM SHAKESPEARE   *Sonnet 18: Shall I Compare Thee to a Summer's Day?*   787

WILLIAM SHAKESPEARE   *Sonnet 30: When to the Sessions of Sweet Silent Thought*   787

ELIZABETH TUDOR, QUEEN ELIZABETH I   *On Monsieur's Departure*   788

MONA VAN DUYN   *Earth Tremors Felt in Missouri*   789

WALT WHITMAN   *Facing West from California's Shores*   790

🍁 **WILLIAM WORDSWORTH**   *London, 1802*   790

🍁 **SIR THOMAS WYATT**   *I Find No Peace*   791

> *Writing About Figures of Speech*   792   •   📄 *Illustrative*
> *Student Paragraph:* Wordsworth's Use of Overstatement in
> "London, 1802"   795   •   📄 *Illustrative Student Essay:* A Study of
> Shakespeare's Metaphors in Sonnet 30: "When to the Sessions of Sweet Silent
> Thought"   796

> *Writing Topics About Figures of Speech in Poetry*   798

16   TONE: THE CREATION OF ATTITUDE IN POETRY   800

Tone, Choice, and Response   800

🍁 **CORNELIUS WHUR**   *The First-Rate Wife*   801

Tone and the Need for Control   802

🍁 **WILFRED OWEN**   *Dulce et Decorum Est*   802

Tone and Common Grounds of Assent   803

Tone in Conversation and Poetry   804

Tone and Irony   804

🍁 **THOMAS HARDY**   *The Workbox*   805

Tone and Satire   807

🍁 **ALEXANDER POPE**   *Epigram from the French*   807

The speaker presents a stinging and ironic insult.

🍁 **ALEXANDER POPE**   *Epigram, Engraved on the Collar
of a Dog Which I Gave to His Royal Highness*   808

POEMS FOR STUDY   808

🍁 **WILLIAM BLAKE**   *On Another's Sorrow*   809

🍁 **JIMMY CARTER**   *I Wanted to Share My
Father's World*   810

🍁 **LUCILLE CLIFTON**   *homage to my hips*   811

🍁 **BILLY COLLINS**   *The Names*   812

🍁 **E. E. CUMMINGS**   *she being Brand /-new*   813

BART EDELMAN   *Trouble*   814

MARI EVANS   *I Am a Black Woman*   815

SEAMUS HEANEY   *Mid-Term Break*   817

WILLIAM ERNEST HENLEY   *When You Are Old*   817

NEW   DAVID IGNATOW   *The Bagel*   818

NEW   YUSEF KOMUNYAKAA   *Facing It*   819

ABRAHAM LINCOLN   *My Childhood's Home*   820

NEW   PAT MORA   *La Migra*   821

SHARON OLDS   *The Planned Child*   822

ROBERT PINSKY   *Dying*   823

ALEXANDER POPE   from *Epilogue to the Satires Dialogue I*   824

SALVATORE QUASÍMODO   *Auschwitz*   825

ANNE RIDLER   *Nothing Is Lost*   827

THEODORE ROETHKE   *My Papa's Waltz*   828

JANE SHORE   *A Letter Sent to Summer*   829

JONATHAN SWIFT   *A Description of the Morning*   830

DAVID WAGONER   *My Physics Teacher*   830

C. K. WILLIAMS   *Dimensions*   831

WILLIAM WORDSWORTH   *The Solitary Reaper*   832

WILLIAM BUTLER YEATS   *When You Are Old*   833

Writing About Tone in Poetry   834   •   Illustrative Student Essay: The Speaker's Attitudes in Sharon Olds's "The Planned Child"   836

Writing Topics About Tone in Poetry   839

17   PROSODY: SOUND, RHYTHM, AND RHYME IN POETRY   841

Important Definitions for Studying Prosody   841

Segments: Individually Meaningful Sounds   843

Poetic Rhythm   844

The Major Metrical Feet   845

Special Meters   848

Substitution   848

Accentual Strong-Stress, and "Sprung" Rhythms   849

The Caesura: The Pause Creating Variety and Natural Rhythms in Poetry   849

Segmental Poetic Devices   851

Rhyme: The Duplication and Similarity of Sounds   852

Rhyme and Meter   853

Rhyme Schemes   856

POEMS FOR STUDY   856

GWENDOLYN BROOKS   *We Real Cool*   857

ROBERT BROWNING   *Porphyria's Lover*   858

EMILY DICKINSON   *To Hear an Oriole Sing*   859

JOHN DONNE   *The Sun Rising*   860

T. S. ELIOT   *Macavity: The Mystery Cat*   861

RALPH WALDO EMERSON   *Concord Hymn*   863

ISABELLA GARDNER   *At a Summer Hotel*   863

ROBERT HERRICK   *Upon Julia's Voice*   864

GERARD MANLEY HOPKINS   *God's Grandeur*   864

JOHN HALL INGHAM   *George Washington*   865

PHILIP LEVINE   *A Theory of Prosody*   866

HENRY WADSWORTH LONGFELLOW   *The Sound of the Sea*   866

HERMAN MELVILLE   *Shiloh: A Requiem*   867

OGDEN NASH   *Very Like a Whale*   868

EDGAR ALLAN POE   *Annabel Lee*   869

EDGAR ALLAN POE   *The Bells*   870

ALEXANDER POPE   *From An Essay on Man Epistle I*   873

WYATT PRUNTY   *March*   875

🍁 EDWIN ARLINGTON ROBINSON *Miniver Cheevy 876*

NEW CHRISTINA ROSSETTI *Echo 877*

🍁 WILLIAM SHAKESPEARE *Sonnet 73: That Time of Year Thou May'st in Me Behold 878*

🍁 PERCY BYSSHE SHELLEY *Ode to the West Wind 878*

🍁 ALFRED, LORD TENNYSON *From Idylls of the King: The Passing of Arthur 881*

🍁 DAVID WAGONER *March for a One-Man Band 882*

Writing About Prosody 883

Referring to Sounds in Poetry 886

📄 *First Illustrative Student Essay:* Rhyme, Rhythm, and Sound in Browning's "Porphyria's Lover" 887 • 📄 *Second Illustrative Student Essay:* The Rhymes and Repeated Words in Christina Rossetti's "Echo" 892

Writing Topics About Rhythm and Rhyme in Poetry 895

18 FORM: THE SHAPE OF POEMS   897

Closed-Form Poetry 897

🍁 WILLIAM WORDSWORTH Fragment from *The Prelude 898*

🍁 ALEXANDER POPE Fragment from *The Rape of the Locke 898*

🍁 ALFRED, LORD TENNYSON *The Eagle 899*

🍁 JOHN MILTON Fragment from *Lycidas 902*

🍁 ANONYMOUS *Spun in High, Dark Clouds 903*

🍁 WILLIAM SHAKESPEARE *Sonnet 116: Let Me Not to the Marriage of True Minds 904*

No matter what happens, true love does not change.

Open-Form Poetry 905

🍁 WALT WHITMAN *Reconciliation 906*

Visualizing Poetry: Poetry and Artistic Expression: Visual Poetry, Concrete Poetry, and Prose Poems 907

🍁 E. E. CUMMINGS *Buffalo Bill's Defunct 908*

NEW GEORGE HERBERT *Colossians 3:3 (Our Life is Hid With Christ in God)* 909

GEORGE HERBERT *Easter Wings* 910

CHARLES HARPER WEBB *The Shape of History* 911

JOHN HOLLANDER *Swan and Shadow* 912

WILLIAM HEYEN *Mantle* 913

MAY SWENSON *Women* 914

CAROLYN FORCHÉ *The Colonel* 915

POEMS FOR STUDY 916

ELIZABETH BISHOP *One Art* 916

BILLY COLLINS *Sonnet* 917

JOHN DRYDEN *To the Memory of Mr. Oldham* 918

ROBERT FROST *Desert Places* 918

ALLEN GINSBERG *A Supermarket in California* 919

NIKKI GIOVANNI *Nikki-Rosa* 920

ROBERT HASS *Museum* 921

GEORGE HERBERT *Virtue* 922

JOHN KEATS *Ode to a Nightingale* 923

CLAUDE McKAY *In Bondage* 925

JOHN MILTON *On His Blindness (When I Consider How My Light Is Spent)* 926

DUDLEY RANDALL *Ballad of Birmingham* 927

THEODORE ROETHKE *The Waking* 928

GEORGE WILLIAM RUSSELL (Æ) *Continuity* 929

PERCY BYSSHE SHELLEY *Ozymandias* 929

DYLAN THOMAS *Do Not Go Gentle into That Good Night* 930

JEAN TOOMER *Reapers* 931

PHYLLIS WEBB *Poetics Against the Angel of Death* 931

 WILLIAM CARLOS WILLIAMS *The Dance 932*

Writing About Form in Poetry 933 • *Illustrative Student Essay: Form and Meaning in George Herbert's "Virtue" 935*

Writing Topics About Poetic Form 938

19 SYMBOLISM AND ALLUSION: WINDOWS TO WIDE EXPANSES OF MEANING 940

Symbolism and Meanings 940

 VIRGINIA SCOTT *Snow 942*
Tradition of place gives permanence to life.

The Function of Symbolism in Poetry 943

Allusions and Meaning 945

Studying for Symbols and Allusions 946

 POEMS FOR STUDY 947

 EMILY BRONTË *No Coward Soul Is Mine 948*

 AMY CLAMPITT *Beach Glass 949*

 ARTHUR HUGH CLOUGH *Say Not the Struggle Nought Availeth 950*

 PETER DAVISON *Delphi 951*

 JOHN DONNE *The Canonization 952*

 STEPHEN DUNN *Hawk 954*

 ISABELLA GARDNER *Collage of Echoes 955*

NEW DAN GEORGAKIS *Hiroshima Crewman 955*

 LOUISE GLÜCK *Celestial Music 956*

 JORIE GRAHAM *The Geese 957*

 THOMAS HARDY *In Time of "The Breaking of Nations" 958*

 GEORGE HERBERT *The Collar 959*

 JOSEPHINE JACOBSEN *Tears 960*

 ROBINSON JEFFERS *The Purse-Seine 961*

 JOHN KEATS *La Belle Dame Sans Merci: A Ballad 963*

X. J. KENNEDY   *Old Men Pitching Horseshoes*   965

TED KOOSER   *Year's End*   965

PHILIP LARKIN   *Next, Please*   966

DAVID LEHMAN   *Venice Is Sinking*   967

ANDREW MARVELL   *To His Coy Mistress*   968

MARY OLIVER   *Wild Geese*   969

NEW GARY SNYDER   *Milton by Firelight*   970

JUDITH VIORST   *A Wedding Sonnet for the Next Generation*   971

WALT WHITMAN   *A Noiseless Patient Spider*   972

RICHARD WILBUR   *Year's End*   973

WILLIAM BUTLER YEATS   *The Second Coming*   974

Writing About Symbolism and Allusion in Poetry   975   •   Illustrative
Student Essay: Symbolism in Oliver's "Wild Geese"   978

Writing Topics About Symbolism and Allusion in Poetry   981

20   MYTHS: SYSTEMS OF SYMBOLIC ALLUSION IN POETRY   983

Mythology as an Explanation of How Things Are   983

Mythology and Literature   986

WILLIAM BUTLER YEATS   *Leda and the Swan*   988
We have the power to live, but do we have the knowledge?

MONA VAN DUYN   *Leda*   989
Has the story of Leda been understood and properly told by male poets?

Six Poems Related to the Myth of Odysseus   990

POEMS FOR STUDY   991

LOUISE GLÜCK   *Penelope's Song*   991

W. S. MERWIN   *Odysseus*   992

DOROTHY PARKER   *Penelope*   993

LINDA PASTAN   *The Suitor*   993

ALFRED, LORD TENNYSON   *Ulysses*   994

PETER ULISSE   *Odyssey: 20 Years Later*   996

Six Poems Related to the Myth of Icarus   997

POEMS FOR STUDY   997

BRIAN ALDISS   *Flight 063*   997

W. H. AUDEN   *Musée des Beaux Arts*   998

EDWARD FIELD   *Icarus*   999

MURIEL RUKEYSER   *Waiting for Icarus*   1000

ANNE SEXTON   *To a Friend Whose Work Has Come to Triumph*   1001

WILLIAM CARLOS WILLIAMS   *Landscape with the Fall of Icarus*   1002

Four Poems Related to the Myth of Orpheus   1003

POEMS FOR STUDY   1003

EDWARD HIRSCH   *The Swimmers*   1004

RAINER MARIA RILKE   *The Sonnets to Orpheus, 1.19*   1004

MARK STRAND   *Orpheus Alone*   1005

ELLEN BRYANT VOIGT   *Song and Story*   1007

Three Poems Related to the Myth of the Phoenix   1008

POEMS FOR STUDY   1008

AMY CLAMPITT   *Berceuse*   1009

DENISE LEVERTOV   *Hunting the Phoenix*   1009

MAY SARTON   *The Phoenix Again*   1010

Two Poems Related to the Myth of Oedipus   1011

POEMS FOR STUDY   1011

MURIEL RUKEYSER   *Myth*   1012

JOHN UPDIKE   *On the Way to Delphi*   1012

Three Poems Related to the Myth of Pan   *1013*

POEMS FOR STUDY   1013

🍁 E. E. CUMMINGS   *in Just-*   *1014*

🍁 JOHN CHIPMAN FARRAR   *Song for a Forgotten Shrine to Pan*   *1015*

NEW ROBERT FROST   *Pan with Us*   *1015*

Writing About Myths in Poetry   1016   •   📄 Illustrative Student Essay: Myth and Meaning in Dorothy Parker's "Penelope"   *1018*

Writing Topics About Myths in Poetry   1022

21   FOUR MAJOR AMERICAN POETS: EMILY DICKINSON, ROBERT FROST, LANGSTON HUGHES, AND SYLVIA PLATH   1023

EMILY DICKINSON'S LIFE AND WORK   **1023**

Writing Topics About the Poetry of Emily Dickinson   1028

POEMS BY EMILY DICKINSON (ALPHABETICALLY ARRANGED)   1028

🍁 *After Great Pain, a Formal Feeling Comes (J341, F372)*   *1029*

🍁 *Because I Could Not Stop for Death (J712, F479) (Included in Chapter 11, p. 635)*

🍁 *The Bustle in a House (J1078, F1108)*   *1030*

🍁 *The Heart Is the Capital of the Mind (J1354, F1381)*   *1030*

🍁 *I Cannot Live with You (J640, F706)*   *1030*

🍁 *I Died for Beauty – But Was Scarce (J449, F448)*   *1031*

🍁 *I Dwell in Possibility (F466, J657)*   *1032*

🍁 *I Felt a Funeral in My Brain (J280, F340)*   *1032*

🍁 *I Heard a Fly Buzz – When I Died (J465, F491)*   *1033*

🍁 *I Like to See It Lap the Miles (J585, F383)*   *1033*

🍁 *I'm Nobody! Who Are You? (J288, F260)*   *1033*

🍁 *I Never Lost as Much but Twice (J49, F39)*   *1034*

🍁 *I Taste a Liquor Never Brewed (J214, F207)*   *1034*

Much Madness Is Divinest Sense (J435, F620)   1034

My Life Closed Twice Before Its Close (J1732, F1773)   1035

My Triumph Lasted Till the Drums (J1227, F1212)   1035

One Need Not Be a Chamber – To Be Haunted (J670, F407)   1035

Safe in Their Alabaster Chambers (J216, F124)   1036

Some Keep the Sabbath Going to Church (J324, F236)   1036

The Soul Selects Her Own Society (J303, F409)   1037

Success Is Counted Sweetest (J67, F112)   1037

Tell All the Truth but Tell It Slant (J1129, F1263)   1037

There's a Certain Slant of Light (J258, F320)   1037

To Hear an Oriole Sing (J526, F402) (Included in Chapter 17 p. 859)

Wild Nights – Wild Nights! (J249, F269)   1038

Edited Selections from Criticism of Dickinson's Poems   1038

1. From "Orthodox Modernisms"   1039 • 2. "The Landscape of the Spirit" 1044 • 3. From "The American Plain Style"   1048 • 4. From "The Histrionic Imagination"   1050 • 5. From "The Gothic Mode"   1053

ROBERT FROST'S LIFE AND WORK   1058

Writing Topics About the Poetry of Robert Frost   1062

POEMS BY ROBERT FROST (CHRONOLOGICALLY ARRANGED)   1063

The Tuft of Flowers (1913)   1063

NEW *Pan with Us (in Chapter 20, p. 1015)*

Mending Wall (1914)   1065

Birches (1915)   1066

The Road Not Taken (1915)   1067

"Out, Out—" (1916)   1067

The Oven Bird (1916)   1068

Fire and Ice (1920)   1068

🍁 *Stopping by Woods on a Snowy Evening (1923)*
    (In Chapter 11, p. 637)

🍁 *Misgiving (1923)*   1069

🍁 *Nothing Gold Can Stay (1923)*   1069

🍁 *Acquainted with the Night (1928)*   1069

🍁 *Desert Places (1936) (In Chapter 18, p. 918)*

🍁 *Design (1936)*   1070

🍁 *The Silken Tent (1936)*   1070

🍁 *The Gift Outright (1941)*   1071

🍁 *A Considerable Speck (1942)*   1071

🍁 *Take Something Like a Star (1943)*   1072

LANGSTON HUGHES' LIFE AND WORK   1072

Writing Topics About the Poetry of Langston Hughes   1075

POEMS OF LANGSTON HUGHES (ALPHABETICALLY ARRANGED)   1076

NEW *Bad Man*   1076

NEW *Cross*   1077

NEW *Dead in There*   1077

NEW *Dream Variations*   1078

🍁 *Harlem*   1078

🍁 *Let America Be America Again*   1078

NEW *Madam and Her Madam*   1080

🍁 *Negro*   1081

🍁 *The Negro Speaks of Rivers*   1082

NEW *125th Street*   1082

NEW *Po' Boy Blues*   1082

NEW *Silhouette*   1083

NEW *Subway Rush Hour*   1083

🍁 *Theme for English B*   1083

NEW *The Weary Blues*   1084

SYLVIA PLATH'S LIFE AND WORK   1085

Writing Topics About the Poetry of Sylvia Plath   1089

POEMS OF SYLVIA PLATH (ALPHABETICALLY ARRANGED)   1090

NEW *Ariel   1090*

NEW *The Colossus   1091*

NEW *Cut   1092*

NEW *Daddy   1093*

NEW *Edge   1095*

NEW *The Hanging Man   1096*

NEW *Lady Lazarus   1096*

Last Words   1098

Metaphors   1099

Mirror   1099

NEW *The Rival   1100*

NEW *Song for a Summer's Day   1100*

Tulips   1101

22   ONE HUNDRED SIXTEEN POEMS FOR ADDITIONAL ENJOYMENT AND STUDY   1103

MAYA ANGELOU   *My Arkansas   1106*

ANONYMOUS (NAVAJO)   *Healing Prayer from the Beautyway Chant   1106*

ANONYMOUS   *Lord Randal   1107*

MARGARET ATWOOD   *Variation on the Word Sleep   1108*

W. H. AUDEN   *The Unknown Citizen   1109*

WENDELL BERRY   *Another Descent   1109*

LOUISE BOGAN   *Women   1110*

ARNA BONTEMPS   *A Black Man Talks of Reaping   1110*

ANNE BRADSTREET   *To My Dear and Loving Husband   1111*

GWENDOLYN BROOKS *Primer for Blacks* 1111

ELIZABETH BARRETT BROWNING *Sonnets from the Portuguese: Number 43, How Do I Love Thee* 1113

ROBERT BROWNING *Soliloquy of the Spanish Cloister* 1113

WILLIAM CULLEN BRYANT *To Cole, the Painter, Departing for Europe* 1115

GEORGE GORDON, LORD BYRON *The Destruction of Sennacherib* 1116

NEW GEORGE GORDON, LORD BYRON *She Walks in Beauty* 1116

LEONARD COHEN *"The killers that run . . ."* 1117

BILLY COLLINS *Days* 1118

FRANCES CORNFORD *From a Letter to America on a Visit to Sussex: Spring 1942* 1118

STEPHEN CRANE *Do Not Weep, Maiden, for War Is Kind* 1119

ROBERT CREELEY *"Do you think . . ."* 1120

E. E. CUMMINGS *if there are any heavens* 1121

CARL DENNIS *The God Who Loves You* 1121

JOHN DONNE *The Good Morrow* 1122

JOHN DONNE *Holy Sonnet 10: Death Be Not Proud* 1123

JOHN DONNE *A Hymn to God the Father* 1123

PAUL LAURENCE DUNBAR *Sympathy [I Know What the Caged Bird Feels]* 1124

T. S. ELIOT *The Love Song of J. Alfred Prufrock* 1124

JAMES EMANUEL *The Negro* 1128

LYNN EMANUEL *Like God* 1128

CHIEF DAN GEORGE *The Beauty of the Trees* 1130

NIKKI GIOVANNI *Woman* 1130

NEW NIKKI GIOVANNI *Poetry* 1131

MARILYN HACKER *Sonnet Ending with a Film Subtitle* 1132

DANIEL HALPERN   *Snapshot of Hué*   1132

DANIEL HALPERN   *Summer in the Middle Class*   1133

H. S. (SAM) HAMOD   *Leaves*   1134

FRANCES E. W. HARPER   *She's Free!*   1135

MICHAEL S. HARPER   *Called*   1135

ROBERT HASS   *Spring Rain*   1136

ROBERT HAYDEN   *Those Winter Sundays*   1137

ROBERT HERRICK   *To the Virgins, to Make Much of Time*   1137

WILLIAM HEYEN   *The Hair: Jacob Korman's Story*   1138

A. D. HOPE   *Advice to Young Ladies*   1138

GERARD MANLEY HOPKINS   *Pied Beauty*   1139

GERARD MANLEY HOPKINS   *The Windhover*   1140

CAROLINA HOSPITAL   *Dear Tia*   1140

ROBINSON JEFFERS   *The Answer*   1141

DONALD JUSTICE   *On the Death of Friends in Childhood*   1141

JOHN KEATS   *Ode on a Grecian Urn*   1142

GALWAY KINNELL   *After Making Love We Hear Footsteps*   1144

NEW KATHERINE LARSON   *Statuary*   1144

IRVING LAYTON   *Rhine Boat Trip*   1145

LI-YOUNG LEE   *A Final Thing*   1146

ALAN P. LIGHTMAN   *In Computers*   1147

LIZ LOCHHEAD   *The Choosing*   1148

AUDRE LORDE   *Every Traveler Has One Vermont Poem*   1149

AMY LOWELL   *Patterns*   1149

ARCHIBALD MACLEISH   *Ars Poetica*   1152

HEATHER McHUGH   *Lines*   1153

CLAUDE McKAY   *The White City*   1153

W. S. MERWIN   *Listen*   1154

EDNA ST. VINCENT MILLAY   *What Lips My Lips Have Kissed, and Where, and Why*   1154

N. SCOTT MOMADAY   *The Bear*   1155

NEW MARIANNE MOORE   *Poetry*   1155

LISEL MUELLER   *Monet Refuses the Operation*   1156

HOWARD NEMEROV   *Life Cycle of Common Man*   1157

JIM NORTHRUP   *wahbegan*   1158

MARY OLIVER   *Ghosts*   1159

SIMON ORTIZ   *A Story of How a Wall Stands*   1161

NEW DOROTHY PARKER   *Résumé*   1162

LINDA PASTAN   *Ethics*   1162

LINDA PASTAN   *Marks*   1162

MOLLY PEACOCK   *Desire*   1163

MARGE PIERCY   *The Secretary Chant*   1163

EDGAR ALLAN POE   *The Raven*   1164

JOHN CROWE RANSOM   *Bells for John Whiteside's Daughter*   1166

JOHN RAVEN   *Assailant*   1167

ADRIENNE RICH   *Diving into the Wreck*   1167

ALBERTO RÍOS   *The Vietnam Wall*   1169

LUIS OMAR SALINAS   *In a Farmhouse*   1170

SONIA SANCHEZ   *rite on: white america*   1171

CARL SANDBURG   *Chicago*   1172

SIEGFRIED SASSOON   *Dreamers*   1172

GJERTRUD SCHNACKENBERG   *The Paperweight*   1173

ALAN SEEGER   *I Have a Rendezvous with Death*   1173

BRENDA SEROTTE   *My Mother's Face*   1174

WILLIAM SHAKESPEARE   *Sonnet 29: When in Disgrace with Fortune and Men's Eyes*   1175

WILLIAM SHAKESPEARE   *Sonnet 146: Poor Soul, the Center of My Sinful Earth*   1175

KARL SHAPIRO   *Auto Wreck*   1175

LESLIE MARMON SILKO   *Where Mountain Lion Lay Down with Deer*   1176

STEVIE SMITH   *Not Waving But Drowning*   1177

GARY SOTO   *Oranges*   1178

WILLIAM STAFFORD   *Traveling Through the Dark*   1179

GERALD STERN   *Burying an Animal on the Way to New York*   1179

WALLACE STEVENS   *The Emperor of Ice-Cream*   1180

MAY SWENSON   *Question*   1180

DYLAN THOMAS   *A Refusal to Mourn the Death, by Fire, of a Child in London*   1181

DANIEL TOBIN   *My Uncle's Watch*   1182

CHASE TWICHELL   *Blurry Cow*   1183

JOHN UPDIKE   *Perfection Wasted*   1183

TINO VILLANUEVA   *Day-Long Day*   1184

JUDITH VIORST   *True Love*   1185

SHELLY WAGNER   *The Boxes*   1185

ALICE WALKER   *Revolutionary Petunias*   1186

EDMUND WALLER   *Go, Lovely Rose*   1187

BRUCE WEIGL   *Song of Napalm*   1188

PHILLIS WHEATLEY   *On Being Brought from Africa to America*   1189

WALT WHITMAN   *Beat! Beat! Drums!*   1189

WALT WHITMAN   *Dirge for Two Veterans*   1190

WALT WHITMAN   *Full of Life Now*   1191

🍁 WALT WHITMAN   *I Hear America Singing*   1191

🍁 JOHN GREENLEAF WHITTIER   *The Bartholdi Statue*   1191

🍁 RICHARD WILBUR   *April 5, 1974*   1192

🍁 WILLIAM CARLOS WILLIAMS   *The Red Wheelbarrow*   1193

🍁 WILLIAM BUTLER YEATS   *The Wild Swans at Coole*   1193

🍁 PAUL ZIMMER   *The Day Zimmer Lost Religion*   1194

22A WRITING A RESEARCH ESSAY ON POETRY

Topics to Discover in Research   1195   •   📄 *Illustrative Student Essay Written with the Aid of Research: "Beat! Beat! Drums!" and "I Hear America Singing": Two Whitman Poems Spanning the Civil War*   **1196**

PART IV
Reading and Writing About Drama   1203

23   THE DRAMATIC VISION: AN OVERVIEW   1204

Drama as Literature   1204

Performance: The Unique Aspect of Drama   1211

Drama from Ancient Times to Our Own: Tragedy, Comedy, and Additional Forms   1215

🍁 ANONYMOUS   *The Visit to the Sepulcher (Visitatio Sepulchri)*   1217
How do the Three Marys respond to the news told by the angel?

Visualizing Plays: Imagining Dramatic Scenes and Actions   1221

PLAYS FOR STUDY   1225

🍁 EDWARD ALBEE   *The Sandbox*   1225
Mommy and Daddy take Grandma to a beach, but they plan more than relaxing in the sun.

🍁 SUSAN GLASPELL   *Trifles*   1232
In a farmhouse kitchen, the wives of lawmen investigating a murder discover details that compel them to make an urgent decision.

🍁 BETTY KELLER   *Tea Party*   1245
How do two aged ladies try to invite other people to come in and visit?

EUGENE O'NEILL *Before Breakfast* *1249*

What happens to people facing disappointment, anger, alienation, and lost hope?

Writing About the Elements of Drama *1256*

Referring to Plays and Parts of Plays *1259*

📄 *Illustrative Student Essay: Eugene O'Neill's Use of Negative Descriptions and Stage Directions in* Before Breakfast *as a Means of Revealing Character* *1260*

Writing Topics About the Elements of Drama *1264*

24 THE TRAGIC VISION: AFFIRMATION THROUGH LOSS   1265

The Origins of Tragedy *1265*

The Ancient Athenian Competitions in Tragedy *1267*

The Origin of Tragedy in Brief 1268

Aristotle and the Nature of Tragedy *1270*

Aristotle's View of Tragedy in Brief 1274

Irony in Tragedy *1275*

The Ancient Athenian Audience and Theater *1276*

Ancient Greek Tragic Actors and Their Costumes *1278*

Performance and the Formal Organization of Greek Tragedy *1279*

PLAYS FOR STUDY *1281*

 SOPHOCLES *Oedipus the King* *1281*
Can anyone, even a powerful king, evade destiny or his own character?

Renaissance Drama and Shakespeare's Theater *1318*

 WILLIAM SHAKESPEARE *The Tragedy of Hamlet, Prince of Denmark* *1322*
An initial act of evil is like an infestation.

Tragedy from Shakespeare to Arthur Miller *1421*

Death of a Salesman: *Tragedy, Symbolism, and Broken Dreams* *1422*

 ARTHUR MILLER *Death of a Salesman* *1424*
With all his hopes unfulfilled, Willy Loman still clings to his dreams.

Writing About Tragedy   1486   •   📄 *Illustrative Student Essay: The Problem of Hamlet's Apparent Delay*   1490

Writing Topics About Tragedy   1494

25   THE COMIC VISION: RESTORING THE BALANCE   1496

The Origins of Comedy   1496

Comedy from Roman Times to the Renaissance   1499

The Patterns, Characters, and Language of Comedy   1500

Types of Comedy   1502

PLAYS FOR STUDY   1504

🍁 **WILLIAM SHAKESPEARE   *A Midsummer Night's Dream*   1504**
The problems of lovers are resolved through the magic of the natural world, not through custom and law.

The Life and Theater of Molière   1559

Love Is the Doctor (L'Amour Médecin): *A Comic Farce*   1561

🍁 **MOLIÈRE (Jean Baptiste Poguelin)   *Love Is the Doctor* (*L'Amour Médecin*)   1563**
Things go along other paths than the ones Monsieur Sganarelle chooses

Comedy Since Shakespeare and Molière   1580

🍁 **ANTON CHEKHOV   *The Bear, A Joke in One Act*   1581**
A bachelor and a widow meet and immediately berate each other, but their lives are about to undergo great change.

🍁 **BETH HENLEY   *Am I Blue*   1591**
Two young but uncertain souls regain some of the certainty they were losing.

Writing About Comedy   1606   •   📄 *Illustrative Student Essay: Setting as Symbol and Comic Structure in Shakespeare's* A Midsummer Night's Dream   1609

Writing Topics About Comedy   1612

26   VISIONS OF DRAMATIC REALITY AND NONREALITY: VARYING THE IDEA OF DRAMA AS IMITATION   1614

Realism and Nonrealism in Drama   1614

Elements of Realistic and Nonrealistic Drama   1617

PLAYS FOR STUDY   1619

Langston Hughes Biography   1619

Hughes and the African American Theater After 1920   1620

Hughes's Career as a Dramatist   1620

Mulatto and the Reality of the Southern Black Experience   1621

 **LANGSTON HUGHES   *Mulatto   1622***
On a Southern plantation in the 1930s, a young man tries to assert his rights, but there are those who will not grant him any rights at all.

 **TENNESSEE WILLIAMS   *The Glass Menagerie   1643***
Tom would like to escape the memory of his home life, in which he finds only confusion and entrapment.

August Wilson Biography   1692

The Background of Fences   1693

NEW **AUGUST WILSON   *Fences   1695***
Troy Maxson, who as a young athlete could knock baseballs over fences, has led a life enclosed by other fences.

Writing About Realistic and Nonrealistic Drama   1740   •   📄 Illustrative Student Essay: Realism and Nonrealism in Tom's Triple Role in The Glass Menagerie   1743

Writing Topics About Dramatic Reality and Nonreality   1746

27   DRAMATIC VISION ON FILM: FROM THE SILVER SCREEN TO THE WORLD OF DIGITAL FANTASY   1748

A Thumbnail History of Film   1748

Stage Plays and Film   1749

DVD Technology and Film Study   1750

The Aesthetics of Film   1751

The Techniques of Film   1751

TWO FILM SCENES FOR STUDY   1756

 **ORSON WELLES AND HERMAN J. MANKIEWICZ   *Shot 71 from the Shooting Script of Citizen Kane   1756***
Two friends recognize their irreconcilable differences.

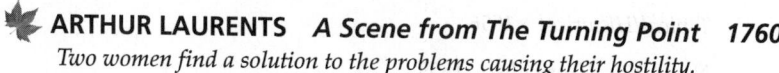 **ARTHUR LAURENTS   *A Scene from The Turning Point   1760***
Two women find a solution to the problems causing their hostility.

Writing About Film   1766   •   📄 *Illustrative Student Essay:* Welles's
Citizen Kane: *Whittling a Giant Down to Size*   1768

Writing Topics About Film   1772

28   HENRIK IBSEN AND THE REALISTIC PROBLEM PLAY: *A DOLLHOUSE*   1773

Ibsen's Life and Early Work   1773

Ibsen's Major Prose Plays   1774

A Dollhouse: *Ibsen's Best-Known Problem Play*   1775

Ibsen's Symbolism in A Dollhouse   1775

A Dollhouse *as a "Well-Made Play"*   1775

The Timeliness and Dramatic Power of A Dollhouse   1776

Bibliographic Studies   1776

 HENRIK IBSEN   *A Dollhouse (Et Dukkehjem)*   1777
*In their seemingly perfect household, Nora and Torvald discover the severe
differences between them.*

Edited Selections from Criticism of Ibsen's A Dollhouse *and Other Plays*
1825

1. Freedom, Truth, and Society—Rhetoric and Reality   1825   •   *2. Ibsen's
Feminist Characters*   1830   •   *3. "A Marxist Approach to* A Doll House*"*
1835

28A   WRITING A RESEARCH ESSAY ON DRAMA   1839

Topics to Discover in Research   1839   •   📄 *Illustrative Student Essay
Written with the Aid of Research: The Ghost in* Hamlet   1840

PART V

Special Writing Topics About Literature   1853

29   CRITICAL APPROACHES IMPORTANT IN THE STUDY OF LITERATURE   1854

Moral/Intellectual   1855

Topical/Historical   1856

New Critical/Formalist   1859

Structuralist *1861*

Feminist Criticism/Gender Studies/Queer Theory *1863*

Economic Determinist/Marxist *1866*

Psychological/Psychoanalytic *1867*

Archetypal/Symbolic/Mythic *1869*

Deconstructionist *1871*

Reader-Response *1873*

30 COMPARISON-CONTRAST AND EXTENDED COMPARISON-CONTRAST: LEARNING BY SEEING LITERARY WORKS TOGETHER   1876

Guidelines for the Comparison-Contrast Method *1877*

The Extended Comparison-Contrast Essay *1880*

Citing References in a Longer Comparison-Contrast Essay *1881*

Writing a Comparison-Contrast Essay *1881* • 📄 *Illustrative Student Essay (Two Works): The Treatment of Responses to War in Amy Lowell's "Patterns" and Wilfred Owen's "Anthem for Doomed Youth"* *1883* 📄 *Illustrative Student Essay (Extended Comparison-Contrast): Literary Treatments of the Conflicts Between Private and Public Life* *1887*

Writing Topics for Comparison and Contrast *1892*

31 TAKING EXAMINATIONS ON LITERATURE   1893

Answer the Questions That Are Asked *1893*

Systematic Preparation *1895*

Two Basic Types of Questions About Literature *1898*

APPENDIXES

I. MLA RECOMMENDATIONS FOR DOCUMENTING SOURCES   1905

II. BRIEF BIOGRAPHIES OF THE POETS IN PART III   1916

A GLOSSARY OF IMPORTANT LITERARY TERMS   1955

Credits   1979

Index of Authors, Titles, and First Lines   1988

Topical and Thematic Contents

For analytical purposes, the following lists of topical and thematic contents groups the selections into twenty-six categories. The idea is that the topical categories will facilitate a thematic and focused study and comparison of a number of works (see Chapter 30). Obviously each of the works brings out many other issues than are suggested by the topics. For comparison, however, the topics invite analyses based on specific issues. Thus, the category "Women" suggests that the listed works may profitably be examined for what they have to say about the lives and problems specifically of women, just as the category "Men" suggests a concentration on the lives and problems specifically of men. The topical headings are suggestive only; they are by no means intended to mandate interpretations or approaches. For emphasis, I will repeat this, and also I will italicize, underline, and boldface it: _**The topical headings are suggestive only; they are by no means intended to mandate interpretations or approaches.**_ I have accordingly assigned a number of works to two and sometimes even more categories. Ibsen's _A Dollhouse,_ for example, is not easily classified within a single category.

Because entries for the topical and thematic contents are to be as brief as possible, I use only the last names of authors and artists, although for authors with the same last names (e.g., Phyllis Webb, Charles Harper Webb; Beth Henley, W. E. Henley; Flannery O'Connor, Frank O'Connor), I supply the complete name. In listing works I shorten a number of longer titles. Thus I refer to _Let America_ (Hughes) rather than _Let America Be America Again,_ and to _That Time of Year_ (Shakespeare) rather than _That Time of Year Thou May'st in Me Behold,_ and so on, using such recognizable short titles rather than the full titles that appear in the regular table of contents, in the text itself, and in the index. Of course, some titles are already brief, such as _Reconciliation_ (Whitman), _Eating Poetry_ (Strand), _Edge_ (Plath), and _A Worn Path_ (Welty). Obviously, such titles are included in their entirety.

Continued from the earlier editions are references to works of art that are included in the plates. I hope that these will be usefully consulted for comparative purposes and that such comparisons will enhance the discussions of the various topics.

AMERICA IN PEACE, WAR, AND TRIBULATION

Stories

Baldwin, **Sonny's Blues** 438
Bierce, **An Occurrence** 71
Oates, **The Cousins** 150
O'Brien, **The Things They Carried** 95
Paredes, **The Hammon and the Beans** 482
Updike, **A & P** 363
Welty, **A Worn Path** 114
Whitecloud, **Blue Winds Dancing** 313

Poems

Agüeros, **Sonnet for . . . Famine** 768
Anonymous, **Healing Prayer** 1106
Berry, **Another Descent** 1109
Bryant, **To Cole, the Painter** 1115
Collins, **The Names** 812
Dickinson, **I Like to See It Lap** 1033
Dickinson, **My Triumph Lasted** 1035
Dunn, **Hawk** 954
Emerson, **Concord Hymn** 863
Frost, **The Gift Outright** 1071
Frost, **Take Something like a Star** 1072
George, **Beauty of the Trees** 1130
Harjo, **Remember** 777
Hass, **Spring Rain** 1136
Hospital, **Dear Tia** 1140
Hughes, **Let America** 1078
Hughes, **125th Street** 1082
Ingham, **George Washington** 865
Komunyakaa, **Facing It** 819
Lazarus, **New Colossus** 640
Lincoln, **My Childhood's Home** 820
Lorde, **Every Traveler** 1149
Lowell, **Memories of West Street** 707
Melville, **Shiloh: A Requiem** 867
Momaday, **The Bear** 1155
Mora, **La Migra** 821
Silko, **Where Mountain Lion** 1176
Terranova, **Rush Hour** 644
Walker, **Revolutionary Petunias** 1186
Whitman, **Facing West** 790
Whitman, **I Hear America Singing** 1191
Whittier, **The Bartholdi Statue** 1191
Wright, **A Blessing** 717

Plays

Glaspell, **Trifles** 1233
Miller, **Death of a Salesman** 1424
Wilson, **Fences** 1692

Art

Bierstadt, **Sierra Nevada** I–4
Cole, **The Oxbow** I–4
Heade, **Approaching Storm** I–2
Hopper, **Automat** I–6

ART, LANGUAGE, AND IMAGINATION

Stories

Bierce, **An Occurrence** 71
Carver, **Cathedral** 180
Moore, **How to Become a Writer** 146
Oates, **The Cousins** 150
Porter, **Jilting of Granny Weatherall** 405

Poems

Bryant, **To Cole the Painter** 1115
Carroll, **Jabberwocky** 663
Carruth, **Apology** 664
Coleridge, **Kubla Khan** 734
Collins, **Sonnet** 917
Dickinson, **I Taste a Liquor** 1034
Francis, **Catch** 636
Giovanni, **Poetry** 1131
Graves, **Naked and the Nude** 660
Hass, **Museum** 921
Keats, **Chapman's Homer** 762
Keats, **Ode on a Grecian Urn** 1142
Keats, **Ode to a Nightingale** 923
Lightman, **In Computers** 1147
Lux, **The Voice You Hear** 743
Montale, **English Horn** 672
Moore, **Poetry** 1155
Pope, **Epigram from the French** 807
Shakespeare, **Not Marble** 643
Shelley, **To—** 644
Spender, **I Think Continually** 676
Strand, **Eating Poetry** 677
Webb, **Poetics** 931
Williams, **The Dance** 932
Wordsworth, **London, 1802** 790

Art

Léger, **The City** I–8

CONFORMITY AND REBELLION

Stories

Chopin, **Story of an Hour** 331
Conrad, **The Secret Sharer** 230
Gilman, **The Yellow Wallpaper** 567

O'Connor, **First Confession** 354
Tan, **Two Kinds** 205
Whitecloud, **Blue Winds Dancing** 313

Poems

Cummings, **next to of course god** 665
Dickinson, **Some Keep the Sabbath** 1036
Lochhead, **The Choosing** 1148
Nemerov, **Life Cycle** 1157
Pound, **In a Station** 747
Stevens, **Disillusionment** 677
Walker, **Revolutionary Petunias** 1186

Plays

Henley, **Am I Blue** 1591
Ibsen, **A Dollhouse** 1775
Wilson, **Fences** 1692

Art

Goya, **The Colossus** I–13
Whistler, **The White Girl** I–11

DEATH

Stories

Bierce, **An Occurrence** 71
Chopin, **Story of an Hour** 331
Faulkner, **A Rose for Emily** 89
Crane, **The Open Boat** 548
Jackson, **The Lottery** 140
O'Brien, **The Things They Carried** 95
O'Connor, **A Good Man Is** 576
Ozick, **The Shawl** 266
Pirandello, **War** 105
Poe, **The Black Cat** 513
Poe, **House of Usher** 499
Porter, **Jilting of Granny Weatherall** 405

Poems

Anonymous, **Sir Patrick Spens** 631
Cummings, **Buffalo Bill's** 908
Dickinson, **Because I Could Not Stop** 635
Dickinson, **The Bustle in a House** 1030
Dickinson, **I Heard a Fly Buzz** 1033
Dickinson, **Alabaster Chambers** 1036
Donne, **Death Be Not Proud** 1123
Dryden, **Memory of Mr. Oldham** 918
Frost, **"Out, Out—"** 1067
Gray, **Death of Richard West** 668
Hardy, **Convergence of the Twain** 775
Heaney, **Mid-Term Break** 817
Herrick, **Here a Pretty Baby** 627

Heyen, **The Hair** 1138
Jarrell, **Ball Turret Gunner** 639
Jeffers, **The Purse-Seine** 961
Jonson, **On My First Daughter** 640
Kenyon, **Let Evening Come** 780
Lowell, **Patterns** 1149
Melville, **Shiloh: A Requiem** 867
Northrup, **wahbegan** 1158
Pinsky, **Dying** 823
Plath, **Edge** 1095
Plath, **Last Words** 1098
Radnóti, **Forced March** 748
Ransom, **John Whiteside's Daughter** 1166
Robinson, **Richard Cory** 675
Rossetti, **Echo** 877
Shakespeare, **Poor Soul** 1175
Shapiro, **Auto Wreck** 1175
Thomas, **Do Not Go Gentle** 930
Webb, **Poetics** 931
Whitman, **Dirge for Two Veterans** 1190

Plays

Albee, **The Sandbox** 1224
Miller, **Death of a Salesman** 1424
O'Neill, **Before Breakfast** 1248
Shakespeare, **Hamlet** 1322

Art

David, **Death of Socrates** I–10
Goya, **The Colossus** I–13
Picasso, **Guernica** I–9

ENDINGS AND BEGINNINGS

Stories

Baldwin, **Sonny's Blues** 438
Bierce, **An Occurrence** 71
Chioles, **Before the Firing Squad** 543
Conrad, **The Secret Sharer** 230
Gilman, **The Yellow Wallpaper** 566
Hemingway, **Hills Like White Elephants** 344
Lawrence, **Horse Dealer's Daughter** 471
Oates, **The Cousins** 150
Orozco, **Orientation** 359
Whitecloud, **Blue Winds Dancing** 313

Poems

Bishop, **One Art** 916
Brewster, **Where I Come From** 696
Brooks, **The Mother,** 634
Dickinson, **I Never Lost as Much** 1034

Glück, **Snowdrops**   700
Herrick, **Here a Pretty Baby Lies**   627
Housman, **On Wenlock Edge**   741
Levertov, **A Time Past**   742
Parker, **Résumé**   1162
Plath, **Ariel**   1090
Rossetti, **Echo**   877
Updike, **Perfection Wasted**   1183
Webb, **Poetics**   931
Whitman, **Facing West**   790
Whitman, **Full of Life Now**   1191

Plays

Albee, **The Sandbox**   1224
Ibsen, **A Dollhouse**   1775
O'Neill, **Before Breakfast**   1249

Art

Anonymous, **Hercules**   I–14
David, **Death of Socrates**   I–10

FAITH AND DOUBT

Stories

Crane, **The Open Boat**   548
Hawthorne, **Young Goodman Brown**   385
Luke, **The Prodigal Son**   399
O'Connor, **First Confession**   354
Pirandello, **War**   105
Porter, **Jilting of Granny Weatherall**   405
Tan, **Two Kinds**   205

Poems

Anonymous, **Healing Prayer**   1106
Arnold, **Dover Beach**   694
Brontë, **No Coward Soul Is Mine**   948
Browning, R., **Soliloquy**   1113
Davison, **Delphi**   951
Dickinson, **My Life Closed Twice**   1035
Dickinson, **Some Keep the Sabbath**   1036
Dickinson, **Certain Slant of Light**   1037
Frost, **Misgiving**   1069
Herbert, **The Collar**   959
Herbert, **Colossians III.3**   909
Hirshfield, **Lives of the Heart**   669
Kizer, **Night Sounds**   671
Larkin, **Next, Please**   966
Laux, **The Life of Trees**   705
Shakespeare, **Poor Soul**   1175
Shakespeare, **When to the Sessions**   787
Whitman, **Noiseless Patient Spider**   972
Williams, **Dimensions**   831
Zimmer, **Zimmer Lost Religion**   1194

Plays

Shakespeare, **Hamlet**   1322
Wilson, **Fences**   1692

Art

Bierstadt, **Sierra Nevada**   I–4
David, **Death of Socrates**   I–10

FIDELITY AND LOYALTY

Stories

Bierce, **An Occurrence**   71
Greenberg, **And Sarah Laughed**   253
Luke, **The Prodigal Son**   399
O'Brien, **The Things They Carried**   95
Ozick, **The Shawl**   266
Porter, **Jilting of Granny Weatherall**   405

Poems

Cummings, **if there are any heavens**   1121
Cummings, **next to of course god**   665
Edelman, **Chemistry Experiment**   667
Hardy, **The Man He Killed**   637
Hayden, **Those Winter Sundays**   1137
Ingham, **George Washington**   865
Jarrell, **Ball Turret Gunner**   639
Minty, **Conjoined**   783
Neruda, **If You Forget Me**   784
Owen, **Anthem for Doomed Youth**   729
Poe, **Annabel Lee**   869
Sassoon, **Dreamers**   1172
Viorst, **A Wedding Sonnet**   971
Weigl, **Song of Napalm**   1188

Plays

Ibsen, **A Dollhouse**   1775
Shakespeare, **Midsummer Night**   1504

Art

David, **Death of Socrates**   I–10

GOD, INSPIRATION, AND HUMANITY

Stories

Coleman, **Unfinished Masterpieces**   382
Crane, **The Open Boat**   548
Luke, **The Prodigal Son**   399

O'Connor, **First Confession**   354
Porter, **Jilting of Granny Weatherall**   405

Poems

Arnold, **Dover Beach**   694
Blake, **The Tyger**   769
Brontë, **No Coward Soul Is Mine**   948
Dennis, **The God Who Loves You**   1121
Dickinson, **I Dwell in Possibility**   1032
Donne, **A Hymn to God**   1123
Glück, **Celestial Music**   956
Harjo, **Eagle Poem**   638
Harjo, **Remember**   777
Herbert, **The Collar**   959
Herbert, **Easter Wings**   910
Herbert, **The Pulley**   740
Herbert, **Virtue**   922
Hopkins, **God's Grandeur**   864
King, **Sic Vita**   781
Levertov, **Of Being**   672
Ortiz (Cofer), **Latin Women Pray**   673
Pope, **An Essay on Man**   873
Shakespeare, **Poor Soul**   1175
Wordsworth, **The Solitary Reaper**   832
Yeats, **Leda and the Swan**   988

Plays

Anonymous, **Visit to the Sepulcher**   1217
Wilson, **Fences**   1692

Art

Bierstadt, **Sierra Nevada**   I–4
Léger, **The City**   I–8
Renoir, **The Umbrellas**   I–12

HOPE AND RENEWAL

Stories

Baldwin, **Sonny's Blues**   438
Conrad, **The Secret Sharer**   230
Greenberg, **And Sarah Laughed**   253
Lawrence, **Horse Dealer's Daughter**   471
Welty, **A Worn Path**   114
Whitecloud, **Blue Winds Dancing**   313

Poems

Berry, **Another Descent**   1109
Clough, **Say Not the Struggle**   950
Collins, **Days**   1118
Collins, **The Names**   812
Donne, **Death Be Not Proud**   1123

Emanuel, **Like God**   1128
Evans, **Iceberg**   774
Frost, **Take Something like a Star**   1072
George, **Beauty of the Trees**   1130
Hughes, **125th Street**   1082
Ignatow, **The Bagel**   818
Lazarus, **The New Colossus**   640
Levertov, **Of Being**   672
Merwin, **Listen**   1154
Mueller, **Hope**   626
Neruda, **Every Day You Play**   746
Ridler, **Nothing Is Lost**   827
Schnackenberg, **The Paperweight**   1173
Scott, **Snow**   942
Whitman, **Full of Life Now**   1191
Whittier, **The Bartholdi Statue**   1191
Wilbur, **Year's End**   973

Plays

Anonymous, **Visit to the Sepulcher**   1217
Shakespeare, **Midsummer Night**   1504

Art

Brueghel, **Peasants' Dance**   I–8
Herkomer, **Hard Times**   I–6

HUSBANDS AND WIVES

Stories

Carver, **Cathedral**   180
Chopin, **Story of an Hour**   331
Gilman, **The Yellow Wallpaper**   566
Glaspell, **A Jury of Her Peers**   189
Hawthorne, **Young Goodman Brown**   385
Poe, **The Black Cat**   513
Steinbeck, **The Chrysanthemums**   411

Poems

Anonymous, **George Campbell**   687
Bradstreet, **To My . . . Husband**   1111
Browning, **Do I Love Thee**   1113
Browning, **If Thou Must**   733
Browning, **My Last Duchess**   697
Frost, **The Silken Tent**   1070
Hacker, **Sonnet**   1132
Hardy, **The Workbox**   805
Kinnell, **After Making Love**   1144
Pastan, **Marks**   1162
Poe, **Annabel Lee**   869
Viorst, **A Wedding Sonnet**   971
Whur, **First-Rate Wife**   801

Plays

Albee, **The Sandbox**   1224
Glaspell, **Trifles**   1231
Ibsen, **A Dollhouse**   1775
O'Neill, **Before Breakfast**   1248

Art

Hopper, **Automat**   I–6
Renoir, **The Umbrellas**   I–12

THE INDIVIDUAL AND SOCIETY

Stories

Bambara, **The Lesson**   457
Conrad, **The Secret Sharer**   230
Greenberg, **And Sarah Laughed**   253
Hemingway, **Hills like White Elephants**   344
Oates, **Where Are You Going**   302
O'Connor, **A Good Man Is**   576
Welty, **A Worn Path**   114

Poems

Agüeros, **Sonnet for You**   768
Auden, **The Unknown Citizen**   1109
Blake, **London**   695
Blake, **On Another's Sadness**   809
Dickinson, **Much Madness**   1034
Dickinson, **The Soul Selects**   1037
Field, **Icarus**   999
Frost, **The Tuft of Flowers**   1063
Hope, **Advice**   1138
Hughes, **Theme for English B**   1083
Komunyakaa, **Facing It**   819
Milton, **On His Blindness**   926
Mora, **La Migra**   821
Nemerov, **Life Cycle**   1157
Pope, **Epigram . . . on the Collar**   808
Pope, **from Epilogue to the Satires**   824
Sandburg, **Chicago**   1172
Spender, **I Think Continually**   676
Whitman, **Full of Life Now**   1191
Williams, **The Dance**   932

Plays

Hughes, **Mulatto**   1619
Wilson, **Fences**   1692

Art

Brueghel, **Peasants' Dance**   I–8
Léger, **The City**   I–8

INNOCENCE AND EXPERIENCE

Stories

Bambara, **The Lesson**   457
Dubus, **The Curse**   563
Joyce, **Araby**   262
Oates, **The Cousins**   150
Tan, **Two Kinds**   205
Twain, **Luck**   213

Poems

Blake, **The Lamb**   661
Blake, **On Another's Sorrow**   809
Blake, **The Tyger**   769
Carter, **My Father's World**   810
Cummings, **she being Brand**   813
Eliot, **Preludes**   735
Frost, **Acquainted with the Night**   1069
Frost, **Desert Places**   918
Griffin, **Love Should Grow Up**   737
Lincoln, **My Childhood's Home**   820
Roethke, **Dolor**   676
Russell, **Continuity**   929

Plays

Shakespeare, **Hamlet**   1322
Sophocles, **Oedipus**   1281

Art

Brueghel, **Peasants' Dance**   I–8
Whistler, **The Little White Girl**   I–11

LIFE'S VALUES, CONDUCT, AND MEANING

Stories

Aesop, **Fox and the Grapes**   380
Chopin, **Story of an Hour**   331
Conrad, **The Secret Sharer**   230
Hemingway, **Hills Like White Elephants**   344
Luke, **The Prodigal Son**   399
Maupassant, **The Necklace**   5
O'Connor, **First Confession**   354

Poems

Brewster, **Where I Come From**   696
Dickinson, **After Great Pain**   1029
Dickinson, **I Dwell in Possibility**   1032
Frost, **Birches**   1066

Frost, **A Considerable Speck**   1071
Frost, **Fire and Ice**   1068
Frost, **Mending Wall**   1065
Frost, **The Road Not Taken**   1067
Frost, **Stopping by Woods**   637
Frost, **Tuft of Flowers**   1063
Graham, **The Geese**   957
Halpern, **Snapshot of Hué**   1132
Hamod, **Leaves**   1134
Hardy, **The Man He Killed**   637
Hughes, **Silhouette**   1083
Jacobsen, **Tears**   960
Jeffers, **The Answer**   1141
Keats, **Bright Star**   765
Levertov, **A Time Past**   742
Lightman, **In Computers**   1147
Longfellow, **Sound of the Sea**   866
Oliver, **Wild Geese**   969
Shakespeare, **When in Disgrace**   1175
Shelley, **Ozymandias**   929
Spender, **I Think Continually**   676
Swenson, **Question**   1180
Swift, **A Description**   830
Tennyson, **Ulysses**   994
Updike, **Perfection Wasted**   1183
Wagoner, **My Physics Teacher**   830
Whitman, **Facing West**   790
Williams, **Dimensions**   831

Plays

Ibsen, **A Dollhouse**   1775
Miller, **Death of a Salesman**   1424
Shakespeare, **Hamlet**   1322

Art

Bierstadt, **Sierra Nevada**   I–4
Cole, **The Oxbow**   I–4

LOVE AND COURTSHIP

Stories

Anonymous, **Myth of Atalanta**   381
Chekhov, **Lady with the Dog**   462
Faulkner, **A Rose for Emily**   89
Joyce, **Araby**   262
Lawrence, **Horse Dealer's Daughter**   471
Munro, **The Found Boat**   347

Poems

Atwood, **Variation . . . Sleep**   1108
Browning, E., **How Do I Love**   1113
Burns, **A Red, Red Rose**   770
Cummings, **she being Brand**   813

Frost, **The Silken Tent**   1070
Marvell, **To His Coy Mistress**   968
Neruda, **Every Day You Play**   746
Neruda, **If You Forget Me**   784
Plath, **Song for a Summer's Day**   1100
Poe, **Annabel Lee**   869
Queen Elizabeth I, **Departure**   788
Rukeyser, **Looking at Each Other**   786
Shakespeare, **Let Me Not**   904
Shakespeare, **Shall I Compare Thee**   787
Wyatt, **I Find No Peace**   791

Plays

Chekhov, **The Bear**   1581
Henley, **Am I Blue**   1591
Molière, **Love Is the Doctor**   1563
Shakespeare, **Midsummer Night**   1504

Art

Brueghel, **Peasants' Dance**   I–8
Boucher, **Madame de Pompadour**   I–5
Renoir, **The Umbrellas**   I–12

MEN

Stories

Baldwin, **Sonny's Blues**   438
Bierce, **An Occurrence**   71
Chopin, **Story of an Hour**   331
Conrad, **The Secret Sharer**   230
Ellison, **Battle Royal**   278
Hemingway, **Hills Like White Elephants**   344
Lawrence, **Horse Dealer's Daughter**   471
Luke, **The Prodigal Son**   399
Steinbeck, **The Chrysanthemums**   411

Poems

Anonymous, **Sir Patrick Spens**   631
Auden, **The Unknown Citizen**   1109
Cummings, **Buffalo Bill's**   907
Frost, **Birches**   1066
Ingham, **George Washington**   865
Hughes, **Bad Man**   1076
Jarrell, **Ball Turret Gunner**   639
Robinson, **Richard Cory**   675
Seeger, **Rendezvous with Death**   1173
Spender, **I Think Continually**   676

Plays

Chekhov, **The Bear**   1581
Glaspell, **Trifles**   1231

Ibsen, **A Dollhouse**   1775
Wilson, **Fences**   1692

Art

Anonymous, **Hercules**   I–14
Claude, **Harbour at Sunset**   I–3
Brueghel, **Landscape**   I–7

NATURE AND HUMANITY

Stories

Crane, **The Open Boat**   548
Hardy, **The Three Strangers**   287
Munro, **The Found Boat**   347
Steinbeck, **The Chrysanthemums**   411
Welty, **A Worn Path**   114
Whitecloud, **Blue Winds Dancing**   313

Poems

Berry, **Another Descent**   1109
Bishop, **The Fish**   730
Cowper, **The Poplar Field**   699
Evans, **Iceberg**   774
Frost, **Misgiving**   1069
Frost, **Pan with Us**   1015
Hass, **Spring Rain**   1136
Hollander, **Swan and Shadow**   912
Hopkins, **Spring**   740
Hopkins, **God's Grandeur**   864
Housman, **Loveliest of Trees**   670
Keats, **To Autumn**   778
Laux, **The Life of Trees**   705
Longfellow, **Sound of the Sea**   866
Momaday, **The Bear**   1155
Moore, **The Fish**   745
Oliver, **Ghosts**   1159
Oliver, **Wild Geese**   969
Plath, **Song for a Summer's Day**   1100
Stafford, **Traveling**   1179
Stern, **Burying an Animal**   1179
Tennyson, **The Eagle**   899
Whitman, **Noiseless Patient Spider**   972
Wordsworth, **Daffodils**   678
Wordsworth, **Solitary Reaper**   832
Wright, **A Blessing**   717

Play

Albee, **The Sandbox**   1227

Art

Bierstadt, **Sierra Nevada**   I–4
Cole, **The Oxbow**   I–4
Heade, **Approaching Storm**   I–2

PARENTS AND CHILDREN

Stories

Luke, **The Prodigal Son**   399
Ozick, **The Shawl**   266
Pirandello, **War**   105
Porter, **Jilting of Granny Weatherall**   405
Tan, **Two Kinds**   205

Poems

Brooks, **The Mother**   634
Carter, **I Wanted to Share**   810
Cummings, **if there are any heavens**   1121
Hamod, **Leaves**   1134
Hayden, **Those Winter Sundays**   1137
Jonson, **On My First Daughter**   640
Mueller, **Alive Together**   692
Nye, **Where Children Live**   642
Olds, **The Planned Child**   822
Pastan, **Marks**   1162
Plath, **Daddy**   1093
Roethke, **My Papa's Waltz**   828
Serotte, **My Mother's Face**   1174
Wagner, **The Boxes**   1185

Plays

Albee, **The Sandbox**   1227
Henley, **Am I Blue**   1591
Miller, **Death of a Salesman**   1424
Wilson, **Fences**   1692

Art

Anonymous, **Hercules**   I–14
Herkomer, **Hard Times**   I–6
Renoir, **The Umbrellas**   I–12

PAST AND PRESENT

Stories

Faulkner, **A Rose for Emily**   89
Jackson, **The Lottery**   140
Oates, **The Cousins**   150
Porter, **Jilting of Granny Weatherall**   405
Whitecloud, **Blue Winds Dancing**   313

Poems

Brewster, **Where I Come From**   696
Clampitt, **Beach Glass**   949
Cowper, **The Poplar Field**   699
Dennis, **The God Who Loves You**   1121
Farrar, **Forgotten Shrine to Pan**   1015

Frost, **Nothing Gold Can Stay** 1069
Gray, **Sonnet** 668
Housman, **On Wenlock Edge** 741
Keats, **Ode on a Grecian Urn** 1142
Layton, **Rhine Boat Trip** 1145
Levertov, **A Time Past** 742
Lochhead, **The Choosing** 1148
Rossetti, **Echo** 877
Shakespeare, **Shall I Compare Thee** 787
Shakespeare, **That Time of Year** 878
Shakespeare, **When to the**
   Sessions 787
Silko, **Where Mountain Lion** 1176
Webb, **The Shape of History** 911
Whitman, **Full of Life Now** 1191

Plays

Hughes, **Mulatto** 1619
Sophocles, **Oedipus the King** 1281

Art

Boucher, **Madame de Pompadour** I–5
Brueghel, **Peasants' Dance** I–8
Hopper, **Automat** I–6

RACE, ETHNICITY, AND NATIONALITY

Stories

Baldwin, **Sonny's Blues** 438
Bambara, **The Lesson** 457
Coleman, **Unfinished Masterpieces** 382
Danticat, **Night Talkers** 77
Ellison, **Battle Royal** 278
Ozick, **The Shawl** 266
Paredes, **The Hammon and the Beans** 482
Whitecloud, **Blue Winds Dancing** 313

Poems

Bontemps, **A Black Man Talks** 1110
Dunbar, **Sympathy** 1124
Emanuel, **The Negro** 1128
Evans, **I Am a Black Woman** 815
Giovanni, **Nikki-Rosa** 920
Hamod, **Leaves** 1134
Harper, **She's Free!** 1135
Hughes, **Harlem** 1078
Hughes, **125th Street** 1082
Hughes, **Silhouette** 1083
Hughes, **The Negro Speaks** 1082
Hughes, **Theme for English B** 1083

Lorde, **Every Traveler** 1149
McKay, **In Bondage** 925
McKay, **The White City** 1153
Randall, **Ballad of Birmingham** 927
Raven, **Assailant** 1167
Salinas, **In a Farmhouse** 1170
Sanchez, **rite on** 1171
Toomer, **Reapers** 931

Plays

Hughes, **Mulatto** 1619
Wilson, **Fences** 1692

REALITY AND UNREALITY

Stories

Bierce, **An Occurrence** 71
Carver, **Cathedral** 180
Gilman, **The Yellow Wallpaper** 566
Hawthorne, **Young Goodman Brown** 385
Jackson, **The Lottery** 140
Maupassant, **The Necklace** 5
Oates, **Where Are You Going** 302
Orozco, **Orientation** 359
Poe, **Masque of the Red Death** 510

Poems

Collins, **Schoolsville** 624
Creeley, **Do You Think . . .** 1120
Cummings, **next to of course god** 665
Dickinson, **I Felt a Funeral** 1032
Glück, **Snowdrops** 700
Hardy, **Convergence of the Twain** 775
Ignatow, **The Bagel** 818
Parker, **Résumé,** 1162
Plath, **Mirror** 1099
Poe, **Annabel Lee** 869
Smith, **Not Waving** 1177
Stevens, **Dillusionment** 677
Strand, **Eating Poetry** 677
Swift, **Description** 830
Van Duyn, **Earth Tremors** 789

Plays

Albee, **The Sandbox** 1227
Miller, **Death of a Salesman** 1424

Art

Bierstadt, **Sierra Nevada** I–4
Herkomer, **Hard Times** I–6

RECONCILIATION AND UNDERSTANDING

Stories

Baldwin, **Sonny's Blues**   438
Chioles, **Before the Firing Squad**   543
Conrad, **The Secret Sharer**   230
Greenberg, **And Sarah Laughed**   253
Luke, **The Prodigal Son**   399
Maupassant, **The Necklace**   5
Paredes, **The Hammon and the Beans**   482
Porter, **Jilting of Granny Weatherall**   405
Tan, **Two Kinds**   205

Poems

Blake, **On Another's Sorrow**   809
Cummings, **if there are any heavens**   1121
Dickinson, **I Dwell in Possibility**   1032
Edelman, **Trouble**   814
Glück, **Celestial Music**   956
Henley, **When You Are Old**   817
Hirshfield, **Lives of the Heart**   669
Housman, **On Wenlock Edge**   741
Kenny, **Legacy**   779
Kenyon, **Let Evening Come**   780
Lehman, **Venice Is Sinking**   967
Plath, **Edge**   1085
Rilke, **To Orpheus: 1.19**   1004
Russell, **Continuity**   929
Tate, **Dream On**   750
Whitman, **Reconciliation**   906

Play

Sophocles, **Oedipus the King**   1281

Art

Bierstadt, **Sierra Nevada**   I–4
Brueghel, **Landscape**   I–7
Claude, **Harbour at Sunset**   I–3

SALVATION AND DAMNATION

Stories

Danticat, **Night Talkers**   77
Dubus, **The Curse**   563
Hawthorne, **Young Goodman Brown**   385
Luke, **The Prodigal Son**   399
O'Connor, **A Good Man Is**   576
O'Connor, **First Confession**   354
Paredes, **The Hammon and the Beans**   482
Poe, **Masque of the Red Death**   510

Poems

Brontë, **No Coward Soul Is Mine**   948
Dickinson, **I Heard a Fly Buzz**   1033
Dickinson, **Some Keep the Sabbath**   1036
Donne, **Batter My Heart**   666
Donne, **Death Be Not Proud**   1123
Frost, **Fire and Ice**   1068
Frost, **Desert Places**   918
Frost, **Misgiving**   1069
Longfellow, **Sound of the Sea**   866
Masefield, **Cargoes**   728
Plath, **Last Words**   1098
Ridler, **Nothing Is Lost**   827
Shakespeare, **Poor Soul**   1175
Tate, **Dream On**   750
Webb, **Poetics**   931

Art

Brueghel, **Landscape**   I–7
Goya, **The Colossus**   I–13

WAR AND VIOLENCE

Stories

Chioles, **Before the Firing Squad**   543
Dubus, **The Curse**   563
O'Brien, **The Things They Carried**   95
Ozick, **The Shawl**   266
Pirandello, **War**   105

Poems

Cohen, **"The killers that run . . ."**   1117
Cornford, **Letter**   1118
Crane, **Do Not Weep, Maiden**   1119
Dickinson, **My Triumph Lasted**   1035
Eberhart, **Fury of Aerial**   667
Forché, **The Colonel**   915
Gay, **Let Us Take the Road**   767
Georgakas, **Hiroshima Crewman**   955
Hardy, **Breaking of Nations**   958
Hardy, **Channel Firing**   738
Hardy, **The Man He Killed**   637
Heyen, **The Hair**   1138
Jarrell, **Ball Turret Gunner**   639
Layton, **Rhine Boat Trip**   1145
Melville, **Shiloh: A Requiem**   867
Northrup, **Ogichidag**   642
Northrup, **Wahbegan**   1158
Owen, **Doomed Youth**   729
Owen, **Dulce et Decorum Est**   802
Quasimodo, **Auschwitz**   825
Radnóti, **Forced March**   748

Randall, **Ballad of Birmingham**   927
Reed, **Naming of Parts**   674
Sassoon, **Dreamers**   1172
Seeger, **Rendezvous with Death**   1173
Terranova, **Rush Hour**   644
Thomas, **Refusal to Mourn**   1181
Weigl, **Song of Napalm**   1188
Whitman, **Beat! Beat! Drums!**   1189
Whitman, **Dirge for Two Veterans**   1190
Whitman, **Reconciliation**   906
Yeats, **The Second Coming**   974

Play

Hughes, **Mulatto**   1619

Art

Goya, **The Colossus**   I–13
Picasso, **Guernica**   I–9

WOMEN

Stories

Anonymous, **Myth of Atalanta**   381
Chopin, **Story of an Hour**   331
Hemingway, **Hills Like White Elephants**   344
Maupassant, **The Necklace**   5
Munro, **The Found Boat**   347
Oates, **The Cousins**   150
Porter, **Jilting of Granny Weatherall**   405
Steinbeck, **The Chrysanthemums**   411
Walker, **Everyday Use**   108

Poems

Bogan, **Women**   1110
Browning, R., **My Last Duchess**   697
Clifton, **homage to my hips**   811
Giovanni, **Woman**   1130
Hacker, **Sonnet**   1132
Hope, **Advice to Young Ladies**   1138
Hughes, **Madam and Her Madam**   1080
Larson, **Statuary**   1144
Lowell, **Patterns**   1149
Minty, **Conjoined**   783
Piercy, **Secretary Chant**   1163
Piercy, **A Work of Artifice**   785
Plath, **Lady Lazarus**   1096
Plath, **Metaphors**   1099
Queen Elizabeth I, **Departure**   788
Swenson, **Women**   914
Terranova, **Rush Hour**   644
Whur, **First-Rate Wife**   801

Plays

Ibsen, **A Dollhouse**   1775
Glaspell, **Trifles**   1233
Keller, **Tea Party**   1244

Art

Boucher, **Madame de Pompadour**   I–5
Hopper, **Automat**   I–6
Renoir, **The Umbrellas**   I–12
Whistler, **The Little White Girl**   I–11

WOMEN AND MEN

Stories

Chopin, **Story of an Hour**   331
Gilman, **The Yellow Wallpaper**   566
Hemingway, **Hills Like White Elephants**   344
Lawrence, **Horse Dealer's Daughter**   471
Munro, **The Found Boat**   347
Oates, **Where Are You Going**   302
Steinbeck, **The Chrysanthemums**   411

Poems

Atwood, **Variation . . . sleep**   1108
Browning, E., **How Do I Love**   1113
Browning, R., **My Last Duchess**   697
Dickinson, **I Cannot Live with You**   1030
Dickinson, **Wild Nights**   1038
Donne, **The Canonization**   952
Donne, **The Good Morrow**   1122
Donne, **Valediction**   771
Frost, **The Silken Tent**   1070
Ginsberg, **A Further Proposal**   699
Griffin, **Love Should Grow**   737
Henley, **When You Are Old**   817
Keats, **La Belle Dame**   963
Kooser, **Year's End**   965
Marlowe, **Passionate Shepherd**   709
Minty, **Conjoined**   783
Neruda, **If You Forget Me**   784
Oates, **Loving**   710
Pastan, **Marks**   1162
Peacock, **Desire**   1163
Plath, **Song for a Summer's Day**   1100
Ralegh, **The Nymph's Reply**   711
Rückert, **If You Love . . .**   749
Terranova, **Rush Hour**   644
Swenson, **Women**   914
Viorst, **A Wedding Sonnet**   971
Waller, **Go, Lovely Rose**   1187

Whur, **The First-Rate Wife**   801
Yeats, **When You Are Old**   833

Plays
Henley, **Am I Blue**   1591
Shakespeare, **Midsummer Night**   1504
Wilson, **Fences**   1692

Art
Herkomer, **Hard Times**   I–6
Hopper, **Automat**   I–6

YOUTH AND AGE

Stories
Ellison, **Battle Royal**   278
Faulkner, **Barn Burning**   333
Joyce, **Araby**   262
O'Connor, **First Confession**   354
Paredes, **The Hammon and the Beans**   482
Porter, **Jilting of Granny Weatherall**   405

Poems
Brooks, **The Mother**   634
Collins, **Schoolsville**   624
Frost, **Birches**   1066
Frost, **Nothing Gold Can Stay**   1069
Henley, **When You Are Old**   817
Heyen, **Mantle**   913
Housman, **Loveliest of Trees**   670
Housman, **On Wenlock Edge**   741
Plath, **Mirror**   1099
Plath, **Song for a Summer's Day**   1100
Shakespeare, **That Time of Year**   878
Whitman, **Full of Life**   1191
Yeats, **When You Are Old**   833

Plays
Albee, **The Sandbox**   1227
Henley, **Am I Blue**   1591
Keller, **Tea Party**   1244
Miller, **Death of a Salesman**   1424

Art
Anonymous, **Hercules**   I–14
David, **The Death of Socrates**   I–10
Herkomer, **Hard Times**   I–6
Hopper, **Automat**   I–6

Preface

In the seventeenth century, John Dryden used the phrase "Here is God's Plenty" when he described Chaucer's *Canterbury Tales*. The same, I think, is applicable to the more than 500 separate works contained in this anthology. But the book is more than a collection. Its bedrock idea is that actual student writing deepens student understanding and appreciation of great literature. Many former students who long ago left our classrooms remember many works well because they once wrote essays about them in our literature-and-composition classes. To adapt a phrase from Joseph Joubert (1754–1824), it is axiomatic that students learn twice when they write about literature, for as they develop their thinking and writing skills they also solidify their understanding of what they have read. If speaking makes us ready, as Bacon said, writing makes us exact, and writing is therefore essential in the study of literature, or of any other discipline. It is the finished product of reading and thinking. *Literature: An Introduction to Reading and Writing* is dedicated to this idea.

Because writing reinforces reading so strongly, the ninth edition presents more than fifty illustrative writing examples embodying the strategies and methods described in the various chapters and appendixes. These full essays and paragraphs are intended as specimens to illustrate what students *might* do (not what they *must* do) with a particular topic. The goal of the essays is to show that the creation of thought does not take place until writers are able to fuse their reading responses with particular topics and issues (e.g., the symbolism in a poem, the main idea in a story, the use of stage directions in a play).

The illustrative essays are comparatively short and not as long as some instructors might assign, on the grounds that when responding to longer assignments about literature, many of our students, alas, inflate their papers with needless summary. It is clear that without a guiding, argumentative point, we don't have thought, and that without thought we cannot have a good essay. A simple summary of a work does not qualify as good writing.

In the major chapters, following each of the illustrative essays, there are analytical discussions (titled "Commentary on the Essay") that point out how the topics have served as the basis of the writer's thought. Graphically, the format of underlining thesis and topic sentences in the illustrative essays is a way of emphasizing the connections, and the format is thus a complementary way of fulfilling an essential aim of the book.

A logical extension (and a major hope) of this combined approach is that the techniques students acquire in studying literature as a reading and also a writing undertaking will help them in every course they may ever take, and in whatever professions or occupations they may follow. Students will always *read*—if not the authors contained here, then other authors, and certainly newspapers, letters, legal documents, memoranda, directions, instructions, magazine articles, technical and nontechnical reports, business proposals, Internet communications, and much more. Although as students advance into their working years they may never again need to write about topics such as setting, imagery, or symbolism, they will certainly always find a future need to *write*.

Most of the works anthologized in this edition are by American, British, and Canadian authors, but there has also been an increase in the number of ancient and medieval writers, along with later writers who lived in or came from Australia, France, Germany, Hungary, Italy, Norway, Poland, Russia, and South America, with authors who represent the diverse backgrounds of African American, American Indian, Latino, and Chinese cultures. In total, 299 authors are represented here, including eight anonymous authors. Slightly below sixty-one percent of the authors—180—were born after 1900. Of the eighty-three writers born since 1935, forty-two are women, or just slightly above fifty percent. If one counts only the number of authors born since the ending of World War II (1945), the percentage of women writers rises close to sixty percent.

The ninth edition includes a total of 519 separate works—fifty-nine stories, 440 poems (including some short portions of very long poems), and eighteen plays. Each work is suitable for discussion either alone or in comparison with other works. Eleven stories, one play, and forty-five poems are added here that were not included in the eighth edition. For purposes of analytical comparison, the works in two genres by seven writers are included—specifically Crane, Glaspell, Hughes, Oates, Poe, Shakespeare, and Updike. In addition, there are two plays by Shakespeare—a tragedy and a comedy—and there are two or more poems by a number of poets. A new feature, for more intensive study, is the addition of an increased number of poems in Chapter 21, "Four Major American Poets." To the twenty-five poems of Dickinson in this edition, and the eighteen by Frost, both of whom were represented in the eighth edition in detail, there are ten new poems by Hughes and nine by Plath, thus bringing the number of Hughes's poems to fifteen, and of Plath's to thirteen.

An additional feature is new in the ninth edition. This is the "visualizing" sections on fiction, poetry, and drama, which are to be found in Chapters 1, 11, and 23. Commentators have often observed that today's students are more visually oriented than students of the past—most likely because of the ever-present influence of television and computers in the home, and also because of the many other graphic forms in which the American public is introduced to facts and ideas. This aspect of our culture is often deplored, but it seems more fruitful to accept it as a fact of life and then go ahead to bring it to bear on the imaginative reading of literary works. What is important here is the development of the capacity

> to think,
>
> to follow through on ideas,
>
>   and
>
> to imagine—

in short, to exercise the mind totally in the interpretation of literature, and in any intellectual endeavor that our students will ever undertake. The study of fiction in the ninth edition is augmented by a discussion about the relationship between graphic narratives and verbal narratives. In poetry, the connection is made between traditional closed-form poetry, on the one hand, and visual poetry and prose poems, on the other. Of the three genres, the study of drama has traditionally been the most visual, for students can make connections between their own reading and the experiences they have had with plays on the stage or on film. The idea of these parallel sections is to provide students with an additional armament in their comprehension, their thought, and their emotional responses.

A Brief Overview of the Ninth Edition

The ninth edition reaffirms a principle to which *Literature: An Introduction to Reading and Writing* is dedicated—flexibility. The earlier editions have been used for introduction-to-literature courses, genre courses, and both composition and composition-and-literature courses. Adaptability and flexibility have been the keys to this variety. Instructors can use the book for classroom discussions, panel discussions, essay- or paragraph-length writing and study assignments, and questions for special topics not covered in class.

FICTION.   The "Reading and Writing About Fiction" section, the first in the book following the Introduction, consists of eleven chapters. Chapter 1 presents a general introduction to fiction, and Chapters 2 through 8—the topical chapters vital in each section of the book—introduce students to important subjects such as structure, character, point of view, symbolism, and idea. Chapter 9 includes four stories by Edgar Allan Poe, and for intensive study these are accompanied by a number of critical readings on Poe. Chapter 10 contains seven stories for additional enjoyment and study.

Readers will note that some of the eleven newly added stories are classic—such as those by Baldwin, Conrad, Crane, and Hemingway. The new stories complement the forty-eight stories that are retained from the eighth edition, such as those by Bierce, Faulkner, Gilman, Hawthorne, Joyce, Lawrence, Porter, and Twain.

Following Chapter 10 is Chapter 10A, the eleventh of the fiction chapters, which is devoted to research connected with fiction. Parallel discussions are Chapters 22A and 28A, which are about research in poetry and drama. These chapters have been added to reflect increased emphasis in research in the college teaching of literature, as noted by many observers of current practices in American colleges. Note that in Chapter 10A there is an extensive discussion of plagiarism and its avoidance. There has been great demand for this discussion on behalf of students, for as emphasis is placed on studying literature with the aid of research, comparable emphasis must also be placed on the judicious and ethical use of secondary sources.

POETRY.   The thirteen poetry chapters are arranged similarly to the fiction chapters. Chapter 11 is introductory. Chapters 12 through 20 deal with topics such as diction, imagery, tone, and symbolism. Chapter 21 presents the possibility of more intensive study of four major American poets, consisting of extensive selections by Dickinson, Frost, Hughes, and Plath. Chapter 22 contains 116 poems for additional enjoyment and study. Chapter 22A is the companion of Chapters 10A and 28A. Brief biographies of the anthologized poets are included in a separate section at the back of the book.

Poetry selections range from late medieval times to contemporary works, including poems published in the early years of the twenty-first century. Representative poets are Wyatt, Queen Elizabeth I, Shakespeare, Donne, Dryden, Pope, Wordsworth, Keats, Tennyson, Hopkins, Pound, Yeats, Eliot, Layton, Amy Lowell, Nye, and Clifton. Forty-five poems are new to the ninth edition. They represent a variety of poets, most of whom are widely recognized. Ginsberg, Hughes, Ignatow, Komunyakaa, Robert Lowell, Eugenio Montale, Mora, Neruda, Radnóti, Snyder, and Plath come readily to mind. Along with the poems included for the first time, the ninth edition retains 394 poems that were included in the eighth edition. The writers of two of these—Lincoln and Carter—were American presidents. Recent poets with many distinctions are Agüeros, Forché, Harjo, Hirshfield, Hospital, and Peacock. Of special note is the inclusion here of a number of nineteenth-century poets who were chosen for poems illustrating noteworthy aspects of American life. These are Bryant, Emerson, Ingham, Lincoln, Melville, and Whittier. (See the first category in the Topical and Thematic Table of Contents).

DRAMA. The drama section contains eighteen titles. New in the ninth edition is the critically acclaimed play *Fences* by August Wilson. Eight of the longer plays that were in the eighth edition have been kept in the ninth because of their independent significance (*Death of a Salesman, A Dollhouse, The Glass Menagerie, Hamlet, Love Is the Doctor, A Midsummer Night's Dream, Mulatto, Oedipus the King*). The total of full-length plays is now nine. These representative full plays make the ninth edition useful for instructors who wish to illustrate the history of drama. In an anthology of this scope, the nine shorter works (*The Sandbox, Am I Blue, The Bear, Before Breakfast, Tea Party, Visitatio Sepulchri,* and *Trifles,* together with the two film scenes—from *Citizen Kane* and *The Turning Point*) are valuable not only in themselves but also because they may be covered in no more than one or two classroom periods. The shorter plays may be enlivened by having parts read aloud and acted by students. Indeed, the anonymous *Visitatio Sepulchri* and Keller's *Tea Party* are brief enough to permit both classroom reading and discussion in a single period.

Additional Features

TABLE OF CONTENTS. The table of contents lists all the works and major chapter discussion heads in the book. A feature that has been well received are the many accompanying sentences that contain brief descriptions or impressions of the stories, plays, and a number of poems. It is hoped that these guiding sentences and questions will continue to interest students in approaching, anticipating, and reading the works.

TOPICAL AND THEMATIC TABLE OF CONTENTS. To make the ninth edition as flexible as possible, I have continued the topical and thematic table of contents, which is organized around a number of topics, such as *Hope and Renewal; Women; Men; Women and Men; Conformity and Rebellion; Endings and Beginnings; Innocence and Experience;* and *Race, Ethnicity, and Nationality.* Under these topics, generous numbers of stories, poems, and plays (and also comparable works of art) are listed (many in a number of categories), to aid in the study and comparison of topical or thematic units.

A special word seems still in order for the category *America in Peace, War, and Tribulation,* which is included first in the topical and thematic table of contents. After the attacks on the United States on September 11, 2001, it is fitting that a category of uniquely American topics be included for student analysis and discussion. Obviously there cannot be a full and comprehensive examination of the background and thought to be considered in extensive courses in American Literature, but a selection of works that bear on American life and values seems now to be deeply important. Some works in the category reflect an idealized America, but many also shed light on problems and issues that the United States has faced in the past and is continuing to face today. A few of the works concern our country at its beginning; some reflect the life of the frontier and the Civil War; others introduce issues of minority culture; still others introduce subjects such as war, misfortune, personal anguish, regret, healing, relationships between parents and children, the symbolic value of work, nostalgia, love, prejudice, and reverence for the land. It is my hope that students will study the listed works broadly, as general human issues that also deal with the complexity of life in the United States today.

QUESTIONS. Following each anthologized selection in the detailed chapters are study questions designed to help students in their exploration and understanding of literature. Some of these questions are factual and may be answered quickly. Others provoke extended thought and classroom discussion, and may also serve for both in-class and out-of-class writing assignments. At the ends of twenty chapters I include a number of more general assignments, offering students writing topics about character, symbolism, tragedy, etc. Many of these are comparison-contrast topics, and a number of them—at least one in each chapter—are assignments requiring creative writing (for example, "Write a poem," or "Compose a short scene"). Unique about these topics is that students are asked not only to write creatively and argue cogently, but also to analyze their own creative processes.

DATES. To place the various works in historical context, I provide the life dates for all authors, to the degree that these dates have been established. Because some contemporary authors are private and elusive, however, it has proved necessary to make a very small number of estimates of their dates. All the authors, except for the anonymous ones, are listed chronologically (and also alphabetically) on the inside covers. Along with the title of each anthologized work, I include its date of publication. Sometimes, however, a work was not published until long after the author actually wrote it, as with most of Emily Dickinson's poems. In such cases I have included the date of composition, if known.

NUMBERING.   For convenient reference, I have adopted a regular style of numbering the selections by fives:

Stories:	*Every fifth paragraph.*
Poems:	*Every fifth line.*
Poetic plays:	*Every fifth line, starting at 1 with each new scene and act.*
Prose plays:	*Every fifth speech, starting at 1 with each new scene and act.*

GLOSSES AND EXPLANATORY FOOTNOTES.   For poetry and poetic plays, brief marginal glosses are provided wherever they are needed. When a fuller explanation is required—for stories, poems and plays—I supply explanatory footnotes. Words and phrases that are footnoted or glossed are highlighted by a raised degree sign (°). Footnotes are located according to line, paragraph, or speech numbers.

GLOSSARY.   In the introductory discussions in the various chapters, significant terms and concepts are boldfaced. These are gathered alphabetically and explained briefly in the extensive glossary following the appendixes, with references locating page numbers in the text where the terms are considered more fully. Although the glossary is based on the chapters of the ninth edition, it is in fact comprehensive enough to be useful for general purposes.

BOXED DISCUSSIONS WITHIN THE CHAPTERS.   In a number of chapters, separately boxed and shaded sections signal brief but essential discussions of a number of significant matters. The topics chosen for this treatment—such as the use of tenses in discussing a work, the use of authorial names, explanations of how to refer to parts of plays, and the concept of decorum—were based on the recommendations of instructors and students. Users of previous editions have found these boxed discussions interesting and helpful.

SPECIAL WRITING TOPICS.   In the ninth edition I have retained the section titled "Special Writing Topics About Literature," which follows the drama section. This section contains three chapters (29–31) that at one time were appendixes, but that on the advice of many readers are now presented as a major section of the book. These chapters are arranged for emphasis on recent critical theory together with practical guides for writing comparison-contrast essays on literature and taking examinations on literature.

PHOTOGRAPHS AND ART REPRODUCTIONS.   To encourage the comparison of literary art with fine art and photography, a number of art reproductions and photographs are included, some within the chapters, and many in a full-color insert. Most of these artworks are considered directly in the introductions to the various chapters. I hope that the reproductions, together with others that instructors might wish to add during the course of teaching, will encourage comparison-and-contrast discussions and essays about the relationship of literature and art. As already noted, the Topical and Thematic Table of Contents lists relevant artworks along with literary works.

DRAMATIZATIONS ON VIDEOTAPE AND DVD. To strengthen the connections between fiction and drama, a number of stories are included that are available on videocassettes and also DVDs, which can be used as teaching tools for support and interpretation. References to a number of the available dramatizations are included in the Instructor's Manual. In the introductions to many of the plays there is a listing of many of the cassette and DVD versions that can be brought into the classroom.

Revisions

There is little throughout the ninth edition that has not been reexamined, revised, or rewritten. Extensive revisions have been made in the general introduction, the introductions to all the genres, and especially the introductory sections on Dickinson, Frost, Hughes, and Plath, together with innumerable changes and, I hope, improvements throughout the text.

The two appendixes have also been changed and updated. Many of the current MLA recommendations for documenting electronic sources, for example, are helpfully illustrated in Appendix I. The poet biographies in Appendix II have been updated to include new poets and up-to-date information. The glossary has been amended and rewritten throughout, as it has been improved regularly throughout the various editions of *Literature: An Introduction to Reading and Writing*.

In all the chapter discussions, the feature of subheads as sentences rather than topics has been retained from past editions. It is my hope that clearly defining headings will enable students to assimilate the following content easily. Of special importance in each of the main chapters are the sections "Questions for Discovering Ideas" and "Strategies for Organizing Ideas," which have been revised in light of the continuing goal to help students focus on their writing assignments.

Reading and Writing Now and in the Future

The more effectively students write about literature when taking their literature courses, the better they will be able to write later on—no matter what the topic. It is axiomatic that the power to analyze problems and make convincing written and oral presentations is a major characteristic of leadership and success in all fields. To acquire the skills of disciplined reading and strong writing is therefore the best possible preparation that students can make for the future, whatever it may hold.

While I stress the value of the ninth edition as a teaching tool, I also emphasize that literature is to be enjoyed and loved. Sometimes we neglect the truth that study and delight are complementary, and that intellectual stimulation and emotional enjoyment develop not only from the immediate responses of pleasure, involvement, and sympathy, but also from the understanding, contemplation, and confidence generated by knowledge and developing skill. I therefore hope that the selections in the ninth edition of *Literature: An Introduction to Reading and Writing* will teach students about humanity; about their own perceptions, feelings, and lives; and about the timeless patterns of human existence. I hope they will take delight in such discoveries and become engaged as they make them. I see the book as a stepping-stone to lifelong understanding, future achievement, and never-ending joy in great literature.

Supplementary Material for Instructors and Students

An extensive package of supplements accompanies the ninth edition of *Literature: An Introduction to Reading and Writing* for both instructors and students. Any one of the student supplements is available at no additional cost when packaged, except where noted. To create a package, contact your local Arts & Sciences Softside representative.

Instructor Materials

INSTRUCTOR'S MANUAL (0-13-604100-0). This comprehensive Instructor's Manual prepares you to teach any of the works contained in the text and also helps you in making assignments and comparing individual works with other works. Each of the chapters in the manual begins with introductory remarks and interpretive comments about the works (stories, poems, plays) within the chapter of the book. These are followed by detailed suggestions for discussing every study question. The Instructor's Manual also provides detailed discussion of works contained in the book, reviews of videotape and DVD performances of a number of stories in the book, and references to audio clips of poetry. Writing assignments and workshops with suggested guidelines for student editors help students to write about literature effectively.

THE LONGMAN ELECTRONIC TESTBANK FOR LITERATURE—CD ROM VERSION (0-321-14314-0). This testbank features various objective questions on the major works of fiction, short fiction, poetry, and drama. A versatile and handy resource, this easy-to-use testbank can be used for all quizzing and testing needs. This product is also available in print.

MYLITERATURELAB FACULTY TEACHING GUIDE (0-321-33213-X). This helpful resource gives instructors step-by-step advice for integrating the features of MyLiteratureLab into their classroom, including detailed instructions in how to use Exchange, an electronic instructor/peer feedback tool.

TEACHING LITERATURE ONLINE, SECOND EDITION (0-321-10618-0). Concise and practical, *Teaching Literature Online* provides instructors with strategies and advice for incorporating elements of computer technology into the literature classroom. Offering a range of information and examples, this manual provides ideas and activities for enhancing literature courses with the help of technology.

Technology/Multimedia

The following supplements represent technology that is book-specific to Roberts, *Literature*, Ninth Edition.

COMPANION WEB SITE. The Companion Web Site offers a multitude of resources at <www.pearsonhighered.com/roberts>. Here you will find a chapter-by-chapter guide to this text, as well as online quizzes that include instant scoring. The Web site also features author bios, annotated links for further study, a literary walking tour, and an interactive timeline. There is also an abundance of Web links to research specific authors, famous works written during numerous literary periods, and online literary journals. Students are invited to practice their writing about literature with writing activities, essay questions, writing workshops that show multiple drafts of student papers with commentary on each draft, and exclusive *Writers on Writing* interview videos.

LITERARY VISIONS PROGRAM. Literary Visions is a video instructional series on literary analysis for college and high school classrooms and adult learners. Noted critics, authors, scholars, and actors enliven this exploration of literature and literary analysis. Dramatizations, readings, and discussions build skills in critical thinking and writing. Illuminating excerpts of short fiction, poetry, plays, and essays—both classic and contemporary—highlight standard literary forms and devices including plot, myth, setting, and character. This course, containing twenty-six half-hour videocassettes, can be used as a complete college-level course; as supplementary material in courses in literature, composition, poetry, or drama, or those focusing on specific topics and genres within literature; as an offering for adult or continuing education students; as an important addition to library video collections; and as enrichment material for advanced high school curricula. For more information, visit <www.learner.org/resources/series41.html>.

Our *Literary Visions Study Guide,* an accompanying study guide for the Literary Visions program, contains information about lessons, objectives, goals, lesson assignments, a viewing guide, formal and informal writing exercises, self-tests, additional reading activities, and an overview of each video lesson. Several of the works covered in the videos and study guide are found in the ninth edition of *Literature: An Introduction to Reading and Writing.* This study guide is available at an additional cost.

The following supplements represent generic technology supplements that work with any of our introductory literature anthologies.

MYLITERATURELAB (WWW.MYLITERATURELAB.COM). MyLiteratureLab is a Web-based, state-of-the-art, interactive learning system designed to enhance introductory literature courses. It adds a whole new dimension to the study of literature with Longman Lectures, which are evocative, richly illustrated audio readings that include advice on how to read, interpret, and write about literary works from our own roster of Longman authors. This powerful program also features Diagnostic Tests, Interactive Readings with clickable prompts, student sample papers, Literature Timelines, Avoiding Plagiarism research aid, Grade Tracker, and Exchange, an electronic instructor/peer feedback tool.

ART OF LITERATURE CD-ROM (0-13-189103-0). This CD-ROM offers your students an extensive and interactive reference featuring video and audio clips of dramatic reenactments of selections, including Ernest Hemingway's "A Clean, Well-Lighted Place" and Gwendolyn Brooks' "We Real Cool." In-depth sections for fiction, poetry, and drama offer further analysis and interactive activities for selected works; Visuals for Study provide artwork related to literature pieces and photos of featured artists, and other literary resources.

VIDEO PROGRAM.   For qualified adopters, an impressive selection of videotapes is available to enrich students' experience of literature. Contact your local representative. You may find your local representative by going to www.pearsonhighered.com and clicking *Find Your Rep.*

Course-Related Supplements

PENGUIN DISCOUNT NOVEL PROGRAM.   In cooperation with Penguin Group USA, Pearson is proud to offer a variety of Penguin paperbacks at a significant discount— almost sixty percent off the retail price—when packaged with any Pearson title. To review the list of titles available for other disciplines, visit the Pearson/Penguin Group USA Web site at www.pearsonhighered.com/penguin.

Sourcebooks Shakespeare

Pearson Education, in conjunction with Sourcebooks, Inc., proudly offers The Sourcebooks Shakespeare. This revolutionary new book and CD format offers the complete text of the play with rich illustrations and extensive explanatory and production notes. An accompanying audio CD, narrated by acclaimed actor Sir Derek Jacobi, features recordings of key scenes from memorable productions to allow students to compare different interpretations of the play and its characters. One Sourcebooks Shakespeare title may be packaged at no additional cost with Roberts, *Literature: An Introduction to Reading and Writing*, Ninth Edition. Contact your local Pearson sales consultant for the package ISBN. Visit www.pearsonhighered.com/english for a complete list of the Sourcebooks Shakespeare titles.

ANALYZING LITERATURE: A GUIDE FOR STUDENTS, SECOND EDITION (0-321-09338-0). This supplement provides critical reading strategies, writing advice, and sample student papers to help students interpret and discuss literary works from a variety of genres. Suggestions for collaborative activities and online research topics are also featured as well as numerous exercises and writing assignments.

EVALUATING A PERFORMANCE (0-321-09541-3).   Written by Michael L. Greenwald and perfect for the student assigned to review a local production, this supplement offers specific prompts and suggestions for evaluating a production. Designed to look like a Playbill, it provides students with a convenient place to record their evaluation of the play's acting, directing, staging, lighting, costuming, and so on.

A GLOSSARY OF LITERARY AND CRITICAL TERMS (0-321-12691-2).   Written by Heidi Jacobs, this easy-to-use glossary includes definitions, explanations, and examples for over a hundred literary and critical terms that students commonly encounter in their readings or hear in their lectures and class discussions. In addition to basic terms related to form and genre, the glossary also includes terms and explanations related to literary history, criticism, and theory.

THE LONGMAN LITERATURE TIMELINE (0-321-14315-9). Prepared by Heidi L. M. Jacobs, this laminated four-page timeline provides students with a chronological overview of major literary works. In addition, the timeline lists major sociocultural and political events to provide students with historical and contextual insights into the impact historical events have had on writers and their works and vice versa.

RESPONDING TO LITERATURE: A WRITER'S JOURNAL (0-321-09542-1). This spiral-bound journal, by Daniel Kline, provides students with their own space for recording their reactions to the literature they read. Guided writing prompts, suggested writing assignments, and overviews of literary terms provide students with the tools and ideas they need for responding to fiction, poetry, and drama.

WHAT EVERY STUDENT SHOULD KNOW ABOUT CITING SOURCES WITH MLA DOCU- MENTATION (0-321-44737-9). Michael Greer's brief guide provides specific instructions on writing and documenting in Modern Language Association (MLA) style. It offers a comprehensive listing of in-text and works-cited models for a wide variety of print, electronic, and online sources. Also included are frequently asked questions about MLA style and guidelines for formatting research papers.

WHAT EVERY STUDENT SHOULD KNOW ABOUT AVOIDING PLAGIARISM (0-321-44689-5). Written by Linda Stern, this brief guide teaches students to take plagiarism seriously and understand its consequences. Here, source usage methods—summary, paraphrase and quotation—are explained with examples. The most common types of plagiarism are discussed, from simple mistakes such as forgetting to use quotation marks when using someone else's exact words, to wholesale fraudulence, such as purchasing student papers from online sites and claiming them as one's own work. A brief essential guide to citing sources using both MLA and APA documentation styles is also included.

WHAT EVERY STUDENT SHOULD KNOW ABOUT RESEARCHING ONLINE (0-321-44531-7). David Munger and Shireen Campbell have written this brief guide that teaches students how to conduct research in the first place they will look: the Web. It provides details on how to use search engines and databases, how to evaluate sources, how to document borrowed materials, and how to avoid online plagiarism. Annotated screenshots of Web pages show students where to locate the information they need to create a proper citation; numerous examples of correctly cited online and electronic sources are also provided.

Acknowledgments

As this book goes into its ninth edition, I wish to acknowledge the many people who at various times have offered helpful advice, information, and suggestions. To name them, as Dryden says in *Absalom and Achitophel*, is to praise them. They are Professors Eileen Allman, Peggy Cole, David Bady, Andrew Brilliant, Rex Butt, Stanley Coberly, Betty L. Dixon, Elizabeth Keats Flores, Alice Griffin, Loren C. Gruber, Robert Halli, Leslie Healey, Catherine Heath, Rebecca Heintz, Karen Holt, Claudia Johnson, Matthew Marino, Edward Martin, Evan Matthews, Pearl McHaney, Daniel McNamarra, Ruth Milberg-Kaye, Nancy K. Miller, JoAnna

Stephens Mink, Ervin Nieves, Glen Nygreen, Michael Paull, Norman Prinsky, Bonnie Ronson, Dan Rubey, Margaret Ellen Sherwood, Beverly J. Slaughter, Donald Tuthill, Keith Walters, Chloe Warner, Scott Westrem, Mardi Valgemae, Matthew Winston, and Ruth Zerner, and also Christel Bell, Linda Bridgers, Catherine Davis, Jim Freund, Edward Hoeppner, Anna F. Jacobs, Eleanor Tubbs, Brooke Mitchell, April Roberts, David Roberts, Gary Brown, Diane Foster, Braden Welborn, and Eve Zarin. I give special recognition and thanks to Ann Marie Radaskiewicz and to Professor Robert Zweig. The skilled assistance of Jonathan Roberts has been essential and invaluable at every stage of all the editions.

A number of other people have provided sterling guidance for the preparation of the ninth edition. They are Catherine Heath and Gary Brown of Victoria College; Brian Boyle, Prairie State College; Angie Macri, Pulaski Technical College; Dorothy Minor, Tulsa Community College, NEC; Mary L. Simpson, Central Texas College; Brenda Cornell, Central Texas College; Crystal Clark, Columbus State Community College; Evelyn Beck, Piedmont Technical College; Joshua Dickson, Jefferson Community College; Howard Kerner, Polk Community College; Jim Richey, Tyler Junior College; Emily Cosper, Delgado Community College; David Plumb, Broward College; Diana Gatz, St. Petersburg College; Joseph Couch, Montgomery College; Mark Coley, Tarrant County College; and Bente Videbaek, Stony Brook University.

I wish especially to thank Vivian Garcia, Senior Acquisitions Editor. She has been eminently creative, cheerful, helpful, and obliging during the time we have worked together. To Stephanie Magean, whose copy editing of the manuscript has been inestimably fine, I offer an extra salute of gratitude. Additional thanks are reserved for Lois Lombardo, our production editor, who has devoted great knowledge, intelligence, diligence, good humor, and skill to the many tasks needed to bring a book of this size to fruition. Thanks are also due to Mary Dalton-Hoffman for her superb work on securing permissions, Rona Tuccillo for research into the various photographs and illustrations, and to Joyce Nilsen, Executive Marketing Manager, Savoula Amanatidis, Production Manager, Donna DeBenedictis, Managing Editor, Dennis Para, Senior Manufacturing Buyer, and to Heather Vomero, Editorial Assistant. I also thank Carrie Brandon, Maggie Barbieri, Nancy Perry, Alison Reeves, Kate Morgan Jackson, Bill Oliver, and Paul O'Connell, earlier Prentice Hall English editors, for their imagination and foresight, and also for their patience with me and for their support over the years. Of major importance was the work of Ray Mullaney, Editor-in-Chief, Development, for his pioneering work with the text and for his continued support. I am also grateful to Gina Sluss, Barbara Muller, Marlane Miriello, Viqi Wagner, and Anne Marie Welsh for their work on earlier editions of the book.

Special acknowledgment is due to my associate, Professor Henry E. Jacobs (1946–1986) of the University of Alabama. His energy and creativity were essential in planning, writing, and bringing out the first edition of *Literature: An Introduction to Reading and Writing* back in 1986, but "fate and gloomy night" intervened to prevent our working together on subsequent revisions. *Vale.*

—EDGAR V. ROBERTS

Part I

The Process of Reading, Responding to, and Writing About Literature

The chapters that follow introduce a number of analytical approaches important in the study of literature, along with guidance for writing informative and well-focused essays based on these approaches. The chapters will help you fulfill two goals of composition and English courses: (1) to write good essays and (2) to understand and assimilate great works of literature.

The premise of this book is that no educational process is complete until you can apply what you study. That is, you have not learned something—really *learned* it— *until you talk or write about it.* This does not mean that you retell a story, state an undeveloped opinion, or describe an author's life, but rather that you deal directly with intellectual and artistic issues about individual works. The need to write requires you to strengthen your understanding and knowledge through the recognition of where your original study might have fallen short. Thus, it is easy for you to read the chapter on point of view (Chapter 2), and it is also easy to read Shirley Jackson's story "The Lottery." Your grasp of point of view as a concept will not be complete, however, nor will your appreciation of the technical artistry of this story be complete, until you have prepared yourself to write about the technique. As you do so, you will need to reread parts of the work, study your notes, and apply your knowledge to the problem at hand; you must check facts, grasp relationships, develop insights, and try to express yourself with as much exactness and certainty as possible.

Primarily, then, this book aims to help you improve your writing skills through the use of literature as subject matter. After you have finished a number of essays derived from the chapters ahead, you will be able to approach just about any literary work with the confidence that you can understand it and write about it.

What Is Literature, and Why Do We Study It?

We use the word **literature,** in a broad sense, to mean compositions that tell stories, dramatize situations, express emotions, and analyze and advocate ideas. Before the invention of writing thousands of years ago, literary works were necessarily spoken or sung, and they were retained only as long as living people continued to repeat them. In some societies, the oral tradition of literature still exists, with many poems and stories designed exclusively for spoken delivery. Even in our modern age of writing, printing, and electronic communication, much literature is still heard aloud rather than read silently. Parents delight their children with stories and poems read aloud; poets and storywriters read their works directly before live audiences; plays and scripts are interpreted on stages and before movie and television cameras for the benefit of a vast public.

No matter how we assimilate literature, we gain much from it. In truth, readers often cannot explain why they enjoy reading, for goals and ideals are not easily articulated. There are, however, areas of general agreement about the value of systematic and extensive reading.

Literature helps us grow, both personally and intellectually. It opens doors for us. It stretches our minds. It develops our imagination, increases our understanding, and enlarges our power of sympathy. It helps us see beauty in the world around us. It links us with the cultural, philosophical, and religious world of which we are a part. It enables us to recognize human dreams and struggles in different places and times. It helps us develop mature sensibility and compassion for all living beings. It nurtures our ability to appreciate the beauty of order and arrangement—gifts that are also bestowed by a well-structured song, a beautifully painted canvas, or a skillfully-chiseled statue. It enables us to see worthiness in the aims of all people. It exercises our emotions through interest, concern, sympathy, tension, excitement, regret, fear, laughter, and hope. It encourages us to assist creative and talented people who need recognition and support. Through our cumulative experience in reading, literature shapes our goals and values by clarifying our own identities—both positively, through acceptance of the admirable in human beings, and negatively, through rejection of the sinister. It enables us to develop perspectives on events occurring locally and globally, and thereby it gives us understanding and control. It is one of the shaping influences of life. It makes us human.

Types of Literature: The Genres

Literature may be classified into four categories or *genres:* (1) prose fiction, (2) poetry, (3) drama, and (4) nonfiction prose. Usually the first three are classified as **imaginative literature.**

3

The genres of imaginative literature have much in common, but they also have distinguishing characteristics. **Prose fiction,** or **narrative fiction,** includes **myths, parables, romances, novels,** and **short stories.** Originally, *fiction* meant anything made up, crafted, or shaped, but today the word refers to prose stories based in the imaginations of authors. The essence of fiction is **narration,** the relating or recounting of a sequence of events or actions. Fictional works usually focus on one or a few major characters who change and grow (in their ability to make decisions, their awareness or insight, their intellect, their attitude toward others, their sensitivity, and their moral capacity) as a result of how they deal with other characters and how they attempt to solve their problems. Although fiction, like all imaginative literature, can introduce true historical details, it is not real history, for its main purpose is to interest, stimulate, instruct, and divert, not to create a precise historical record.

If prose is expansive, **poetry** tends toward brevity. It offers us high points of emotion, reflection, thought, and feeling in what the English poet Wordsworth called "narrow room[s]." Yet in this context, it expresses the most powerful and deeply felt experiences of human beings, often awakening deep responses of welcome recognition: "Yes, I know what that's like. I would feel the same way. That's exactly right." Poems make us think, make us reflect, and generally instruct us. They can also stimulate us, surprise us, make us laugh or cry, inspire us, exalt us. Many poems become our lifelong friends, and we visit them again and again for insight, understanding, laughter, or the quiet reflection of joy or sorrow.

Poetry's power lies not only in its words and thoughts, but also in its music, using rhyme and a variety of rhythms to intensify its emotional impact. Although poems themselves vary widely in length, individual lines are often short because poets distill the greatest meaning and imaginative power from their words through rhetorical devices such as **imagery** and **metaphor.** Though poetry often requires many **formal** and **metrical** restrictions, it is paradoxically the very restrictiveness of poetry that provides poets with great freedom. Traditionally important poetic forms include the fourteen-line **sonnet,** as well as **ballads, blank verse, couplets, elegies, epigrams, hymns, limericks, odes, quatrains, songs** or **lyrics, tercets** or **triplets, villanelles,** and the increasingly popular **haiku.** Many songs or lyrics have been set to music, and some were written expressly for that purpose. Some poems are long and discursive, like many poems by the American poet Walt Whitman. **Epic poems,** such as those by Homer and Milton, contain thousands of lines. Since the time of Whitman, many poets have abandoned rhymes and regular rhythms in favor of **free verse,** a far-ranging type of poetry growing out of content and the natural rhythms of spoken language.

Drama is literature designed for stage or film presentation by people—actors—for the benefit and delight of other people—an audience. The essence of drama is the development of **character** and **situation** through **speech** and **action.** Like fiction, drama may focus on a single character or a small number of characters, and it enacts fictional (and sometimes historical) events as if they were happening right before our eyes. The audience therefore is a direct witness to the ways in which characters are influenced and changed by events and by other characters. Although most modern plays use prose **dialogue** (the conversation of two or more characters), on the principle that the language of drama should resemble the language of ordinary people as much as possible, many plays from the past, such as those of ancient Greece and Renaissance England, are in poetic form.

Nonfiction prose consists of news reports, feature articles, essays, editorials, textbooks, historical and biographical works, and the like, all of which describe or interpret facts and present judgments and opinions. The goal of nonfiction prose is to present truths and conclusions about the factual world. Imaginative literature, although also grounded in facts, is less concerned with the factual record than with the revelation of truths about life and human nature. Recently another genre has been emphasized within the category of nonfiction prose. This is **creative nonfiction,** a type of literature that is technically nonfiction, such as essays, articles, diaries, and journals, but which nevertheless introduces carefully structured form, vivid examples, relevant quotations, and highly creative and imaginative insights.

Reading Literature and Responding to It Actively

Sometimes we find it difficult, after we have finished reading a work, to express thoughts about it and to answer pointed questions about it. But more active and thoughtful reading gives us the understanding to develop well-considered answers. Obviously, we need to follow the work and to understand its details, but just as importantly, we need to respond to the words, get at the ideas, and understand the implications of what is happening. We rely on our own fund of knowledge and experience to verify the accuracy and truth of situations and incidents, and we try to articulate our own emotional responses to the characters and their problems.

To illustrate such active responding, we will examine "The Necklace" (1884), by the French writer Guy de Maupassant. "The Necklace" is one of the best known of all stories, and it is included here with marginal notes like those that any reader might make during original and follow-up readings. Many notes, particularly at the beginning, are *assimilative;* that is, they record details about the action. But as the story progresses, the marginal comments are more concerned with conclusions about the story's meaning. Toward the end, the comments are full rather than minimal; they result not only from first responses but also from considered thought. Here, then, is Maupassant's "The Necklace."

GUY DE MAUPASSANT (1850–1893)

Henri-René-Albert-Guy de Maupassant (1850–1893) is considered one of the major nineteenth-century French naturalist writers. Scion of an aristocratic Norman family, he received his baccalaureate degree from a lycée at Le Havre, after which he began studying law. When the Franco–Prussian War broke out, he served in the French army, including battlefield duty. After leaving the military he became a minor bureaucrat, first in the Ministry of Marine and then in the Ministry of Education (also the workplace of Loisel, the husband of "The Necklace").

As a youth Maupassant was an energetic oarsman, swimmer, and boatman—a power that he also devoted to his career as a writer. During the 1870s in Paris, he had regularly submitted his literary efforts to the novelist Gustave Flaubert (1821–1880), a family friend who regarded him as a son and whose criticism both improved and encouraged him. In Maupassant's thirties, after the death of his mentor Flaubert, his career flourished. His first published volume was a collection of poems (Des Vers, 1880), which he had to withdraw after it created a scandal and a lawsuit because of its sexual openness. After this time, until his death in 1893, he produced thirty volumes—novels, poems, articles, travel books, and three hundred short stories. In addition to "The Necklace," a few of his better-known stories are "The Ball of Fat," "Mademoiselle Fifi," and "A Piece of String."

Maupassant was a meticulous writer, devoting much attention to the reality of everyday existence (hence his status as a naturalist writer). A number of his stories are about events occurring during the Franco–Prussian War. Some are about life among bureaucrats, some about peasant life in Normandy, and a large number, including "The Necklace," about Parisian life. His major stories are characterized by strong irony; human beings are influenced by forces they cannot control, and their wishes are often frustrated by their own defects. Under such circumstances, Maupassant's characters exhibit varying degrees of weakness, hypocrisy, vanity, insensitivity, callousness, and even cruelty, but those who are victimized are viewed with understanding and sympathy.

The Necklace (1884)

Translated by Edgar V. Roberts

She was one of those pretty and charming women, born, as if by an error of destiny, into a family of clerks and copyists. She had no dowry, no prospects, no way of getting known, courted, loved, married by a rich and distinguished man. She finally settled for a marriage with a minor clerk in the Ministry of Education.

"She" is pretty but poor, and has no chance in life unless she marries. Without connections, she has no entry into high society and marries an insignificant clerk.

She was a simple person, without the money to dress well, but she was as unhappy as if she had gone through bankruptcy, for women have neither rank nor race. In place of high birth or important family connections, they can rely only on their beauty, their grace, and their charm. Their inborn finesse, their elegant taste, their engaging personalities, which are their only power, make working-class women the equals of the grandest ladies.

She is unhappy.

A view of women who have no chance for an independent life and a career. In 1884, women had nothing more than this. Sad.

She suffered constantly, feeling herself destined for all delicacies and luxuries. She suffered because of her grim apartment with its drab walls, threadbare furniture, ugly curtains. All such things, which most other women in her situation would not even have noticed, tortured her and filled her with despair. The sight of the young country girl who did her simple housework awakened in her only a sense of desolation and lost hopes. She daydreamed of large, silent anterooms, decorated with oriental tapestries and lighted by high bronze floor lamps, with two elegant valets in short culottes dozing in large armchairs under the effects of forced-air heaters. She imagined large drawing rooms draped in the most expensive silks, with fine end tables on which were placed knick-knacks of inestimable value. She dreamed of the perfume of dainty private rooms, which were designed only for intimate tête-à-têtes with the closest friends, who because of their achievements and fame would make her the envy of all other women.

She suffers because of her cheap belongings, wanting expensive things. She dreams of wealth and of how other women would envy her if she could display finery. But such luxuries are unrealistic and unattainable for her.

When she sat down to dinner at her round little table covered with a cloth that had not been washed for three days, in front of her husband who opened the kettle while declaring ecstatically, "Ah, good old beef stew! I don't know anything better," she dreamed of expensive banquets with shining placesettings, and wall hangings portraying ancient heroes and exotic birds in an enchanted forest. She imagined a gourmet-prepared main course carried on the most exquisite trays and served on the most beautiful dishes, with whispered gallantries which she would hear with a sphinxlike smile as she dined on the pink meat of a trout or the delicate wing of a quail.

Her husband's taste is for plain things, while she dreams of expensive gourmet food. He has adjusted to his status. She has not.

She had no decent dresses, no jewels, nothing. And she loved nothing but these; she believed herself born only for these. She burned with the desire to please, to be envied, to be attractive and sought after.

She lives for her unrealistic dreams, and these increase her frustration.   5

She had a rich friend, a comrade from convent days, whom she did not want to see anymore because she suffered so much when she returned home. She would weep for the entire day afterward with sorrow, regret, despair, and misery.

She even thinks of giving up a rich friend because she is so depressed after visiting her.

Well, one evening, her husband came home glowing and carrying a large envelope.

A new section in the story.

"Here," he said, "this is something for you."

She quickly tore open the envelope and took out a card engraved with these words:

> The CHANCELLOR OF EDUCATION *and*
>
> MRS. GEORGE RAMPONNEAU
>
> *request that*
>
> MR. AND MRS. LOISEL
>
> *do them the honor of coming to dinner*
>
> *at the Ministry of Education*
>
> *on the evening of January 8.*

An invitation to dinner at the Ministry of Education. A big plum.

Instead of being delighted, as her husband had hoped, she threw the invitation spitefully on the table, muttering:

It only upsets her.   10

"What do you expect me to do with this?"

"But honey, I thought you'd be glad. You never get to go out, and this is a special occasion! I had a lot of trouble getting the invitation. Everyone wants one. The demand is high and not many clerks get invited. Everyone important will be there."

Loisel really doesn't understand her. He can't sympathize with her unhappiness.

She looked at him angrily and stated impatiently:

"What do you want me to wear to go there?"

He had not thought of that. He stammered:

She declares that she hasn't anything to wear.   15

"But your theater dress. That seems nice to me . . ."

He stopped, amazed and bewildered, as his wife began to cry. Large tears fell slowly from the corners of her eyes to her mouth. He said falteringly:

He tries to persuade her that her theater dress might do for the occasion.

"What's wrong? What's the matter?"

But with a strong effort she had recovered, and she answered calmly as she wiped her damp cheeks:

"Nothing, except that I have nothing to wear and therefore can't go to the party. Give your invitation to someone else at the office whose wife will have nicer clothes than mine."

    20

Distressed, he responded:

"Well, all right, Mathilde. How much would a new dress cost, something you could use at other times, but not anything fancy?"

Her name is Mathilde.

He volunteers to pay for a new dress.

She thought for a few moments, adding things up and thinking also of an amount that she could ask without getting an immediate refusal and a frightened outcry from the frugal clerk.

Finally she responded tentatively:

She is manipulating him.

25   "I don't know exactly, but it seems to me that I could get by on four hundred francs."

He blanched slightly at this, because he had set aside just that amount to buy a shotgun for Sunday lark-hunts the next summer with a few friends in the Plain of Nanterre.

The dress will cost him his next summer's vacation. (He doesn't seem to have included her in his plans.)

However, he said:

"All right, you've got four hundred francs, but make it a pretty dress."

As the day of the party drew near, Mrs. Loisel seemed sad, uneasy, anxious, even though her gown was all ready. One evening her husband said to her:

A new section, the third in the story. The day of the party is near. Tension is mounting.

30   "What's the matter? You've been acting funny for several days."

She answered:

"It's awful, but I don't have any jewels to wear, not a single gem, nothing to dress up my outfit. I'll look like a beggar. I'd almost rather not go to the party."

Now she complains that she doesn't have any nice jewelry. She is manipulating him again.

He responded:

"You can wear a corsage of cut flowers. This year it's all the rage. For only ten francs you can get two or three gorgeous roses."

35   She was not convinced.

"No . . . there's nothing more humiliating than looking shabby in the company of rich women."

She has a good point, but there seems to be no way out.

But her husband exclaimed:

"God, but you're silly! Go to your friend Mrs. Forrestier, and ask her to lend you some jewelry. You know her well enough to do that."

He proposes a solution: Borrow jewelry from Mrs. Forrestier, who is apparently the rich friend mentioned earlier.

She uttered a cry of joy:

40   "That's right. I hadn't thought of that."

The next day she went to her friend's house and described her problem.

Mrs. Forrestier went to her mirrored wardrobe, took out a large jewel box, opened it, and said to Mrs. Loisel:

"Choose, my dear."

She saw bracelets, then a pearl necklace, then a Venetian cross of finely worked gold and gems. She tried on the jewelry in front of a mirror, and hesitated, unable to make up her mind about each one. She kept asking:

Mathilde has her choice of her friend's jewels.

45   "Do you have anything else?"

"Certainly. Look to your heart's content. I don't know what you'd like best."

Suddenly she found a superb diamond necklace in a black satin box, and her heart throbbed with desire for it. Her hands shook as she picked it up. She fastened it around her neck, watched it gleam at her throat, and looked at herself ecstatically.

Then she asked, haltingly and anxiously:

"Could you lend me this, nothing but this?"

"Why yes, certainly."

She jumped up, hugged her friend joyfully, then hurried away with her treasure.

The day of the party came. Mrs. Loisel was a success. She was prettier than anyone else, stylish, graceful, smiling and wild with joy. All the men saw her, asked her name, sought to be introduced. All the important administrators stood in line to waltz with her. The Chancellor himself eyed her.

She danced joyfully, passionately, intoxicated with pleasure, thinking of nothing but the moment, in the triumph of her beauty, in the glory of her success, on cloud nine with happiness made up of all the admiration, of all the aroused desire, of this victory so complete and so sweet to the heart of any woman.

She did not leave until four o'clock in the morning. Her husband, since midnight, had been sleeping in a little empty room with three other men whose wives had also been enjoying themselves.

He threw, over her shoulders, the shawl that he had brought for the trip home—a modest everyday wrap, the poverty of which contrasted sharply with the elegance of her evening gown. She felt it and hurried away to avoid being noticed by the other women who luxuriated in rich furs.

Loisel tried to hold her back:

"Wait a minute. You'll catch cold outdoors. I'll call a cab."

But she paid no attention and hurried down the stairs. When they reached the street they found no carriages. They began to look for one, shouting at cabmen passing by at a distance.

They walked toward the Seine, desperate, shivering. Finally, on a quay, they found one of those old night-going buggies that are seen in Paris only after dark, as if they were ashamed of their wretched appearance in daylight.

It took them to their door, on the Street of Martyrs, and they sadly climbed the stairs to their flat. For her, it was finished. As for him, he could think only that he had to begin work at the Ministry of Education at ten o'clock.

She took the shawl off her shoulders, in front of the mirror, to see herself once more in her glory. But suddenly she cried out. The necklace was no longer around her neck!

Her husband, already half undressed, asked:

"What's wrong?"

She turned toward him frantically:

"I . . . I . . . I no longer have Mrs. Forrestier's necklace."

He stood up, bewildered:

"What! . . . How! . . . It's not possible!"

Marginal notes:

A "superb" diamond necklace. This is what the story has been building up to.

This is what she wants, just this.

50

She leaves with the "treasure" Things might be looking up for her.

A new section.

The party. Mathilde is a huge success.

Another judgment about women. Does the author mean that only women want to be admired? Don't men want admiration, too?

Loisel, with other husbands, is bored, while the wives are literally having a ball.

Ashamed of her shabby   55 everyday shawl, she rushes away to avoid being seen. She is forced back into the reality of her true situation. Her glamour is gone.

A comedown after the nice evening. They take a wretched-looking buggy home.

"Street of Martyrs" Is this   60 name significant?

Loisel is down-to-earth.

SHE HAS LOST THE NECKLACE!

65

And they looked in the folds of the gown, in the folds of the shawl, in the pockets, everywhere. They found nothing.

He asked:

70 "You're sure you still had it when you left the party?"

"Yes. I checked it in the vestibule of the Ministry."

"But if you'd lost it in the street, we would've heard it fall. It must be in the cab."

"Yes, probably. Did you notice the number?"

"No. Did you see it?"

75 "No."

Overwhelmed, they looked at each other. Finally, Loisel got dressed again:

"I'm going out to retrace all our steps," he said, "to see if I can find the necklace that way."

And he went out. She stayed in her evening dress, without the energy to get ready for bed, stretched out in a chair, drained of strength and thought.

Her husband came back at about seven o'clock. He had found nothing.

80 He went to Police Headquarters and to the newspapers to announce a reward. He went to the small cab companies, and finally he followed up even the slightest hopeful lead.

She waited the entire day, in the same enervated state, in the face of this frightful disaster.

Loisel came back in the evening, his face pale and haggard. He had found nothing.

"You'll have to write to your friend," he said, "that you broke a clasp on her necklace and that you're having it fixed. That'll give us time to look around."

She wrote as he dictated.

85 By the end of the week they had lost all hope.

And Loisel, looking five years older, declared:

"We'll have to see about replacing the jewels."

The next day they took the case which had contained the necklace and went to the jeweler whose name was inside. He looked at his books:

"I wasn't the one, Madam, who sold the necklace. I only made the case."

90 Then they went from jeweler to jeweler, searching for a necklace like the other one, racking their memories, both of them sick with worry and anguish.

In a shop in the Palais-Royal, they found a necklace of diamonds that seemed to them exactly like the one they were looking for. It was priced at forty thousand francs. They could buy it for thirty-six thousand.

They got the jeweler to promise not to sell it for three days. And they made an agreement that he would buy it back for thirty-four thousand francs if the original was recovered before the end of February.

Loisel had saved eighteen thousand francs that his father had left him. He would have to borrow the rest.

Marginal notes:

They can't locate it. It seems to be lost. What a horrible feeling. What a comedown.

He goes out to search for the necklace.

But is unsuccessful.

He really tries. He's doing his best.

Loisel's plan to explain delaying the return. He takes charge, is resourceful.

Things are hopeless.

Note that Loisel does not even suggest that they explain things to Mrs. Forrestier.

They hunt for a replacement.

A new diamond necklace will cost 36,000 francs, a monumental amount.

They make a deal with the jeweler. (Is Maupassant hinting that things might work out for them?)

It will take all of Loisel's inheritance . . .

He borrowed, asking a thousand francs from one, five hundred from another, five louis° here, three louis there. He wrote promissory notes, undertook ruinous obligations, did business with finance companies and the whole tribe of loan sharks. He compromised himself for the remainder of his days, risked his signature without knowing whether he would be able to honor it; and, terrified by anguish over the future, by the black misery that was about to descend on him, by the prospect of all kinds of physical deprivations and moral tortures, he went to get the new necklace, and put down thirty-six thousand francs on the jeweler's counter.

Mrs. Loisel took the necklace back to Mrs. Forrestier, who said with an offended tone:

"You should have brought it back sooner; I might have needed it."

She did not open the case, as her friend feared she might. If she had noticed the substitution, what would she have thought? What would she have said? Would she not have taken her for a thief?

Mrs. Loisel soon discovered the horrible life of the needy. She did her share, however, completely, heroically. That horrifying debt had to be paid. She would pay. They dismissed the maid; they changed their address; they rented an attic flat.

She learned to do the heavy housework, dirty kitchen jobs. She washed the dishes, wearing away her manicured fingernails on greasy pots and encrusted baking dishes. She handwashed dirty linen, shirts, and dish towels that she hung out on the line to dry. Each morning, she took the garbage down to the street, and she carried up water, stopping at each floor to catch her breath. And, dressed in cheap house dresses, she went to the fruit dealer, the grocer, the butcher's, with her basket under her arms, haggling, insulting, defending her measly cash penny by penny.

They had to make installment payments every month, and, to buy more time, to refinance loans.

The husband worked evenings to make fair copies of tradesmen's accounts, and late into the night he made copies at five cents a page.

And this life lasted ten years.

At the end of ten years, they had paid back everything—everything—including the extra charges imposed by loan sharks and the accumulation of compound interest.

Mrs. Loisel looked old now. She had become the strong, hard, and rude woman of poor households. Her hair unkempt, with uneven skirts and rough, red hands, she spoke loudly, washed floors with large buckets of water. But sometimes, when her husband was at work, she sat down near the window, and she dreamed of that evening so long ago, of that party, where she had been so beautiful and so admired.

°*louis:* a gold coin worth twenty francs.

. . . plus another 18,000 francs that must be borrowed at enormous rates of interest.

Mrs. Forrestier is offended 95 *and complains about Mathilde's delay.*

Is this enough justification for not telling the truth? It seems to be for the Loisels.

A new section, the fifth.

They suffer to repay their debts. Mathilde accepts a cheap attic flat, and does all the heavy housework herself to save on domestic help.

She pinches pennies and haggles with the local merchants.

They struggle to meet 100 *payments.*

Mr. Loisel moonlights to make extra money.

For ten years they struggle, but they endure.

Another new section, the sixth of the story.

The Loisels have successfully paid back the loans. They have been quite virtuous.

105   What would life have been like if she had not lost that necklace? Who knows? Who knows? Life is so peculiar, so uncertain. How little a thing it takes to destroy you or to save you!

Well, one Sunday, when she had gone for a stroll along the Champs-Elysées to relax from the cares of the week, she suddenly noticed a woman walking with a child. It was Mrs. Forrestier, still youthful, still beautiful, still attractive.

Mrs. Loisel felt moved. Would she speak to her? Yes, certainly. And now that she had paid, she could tell all. Why not?

She walked closer.

"Hello, Jeanne."

110   The other gave no sign of recognition and was astonished to be addressed so familiarly by this working-class woman. She stammered:

"But . . . Madam! . . . I don't know. . . . You must have made a mistake."

"No. I'm Mathilde Loisel."

Her friend cried out:

"Oh! . . . My poor Mathilde, you've changed so much."

115   "Yes. I've had some tough times since I saw you last; in fact hardships . . . and all because of you! . . ."

"Of me . . . how so?"

"You remember the diamond necklace that you lent me to go to the party at the Ministry of Education?"

"Yes. What then?"

"Well, I lost it."

120   "How, since you gave it back to me?"

"I returned another exactly like it. And for ten years we've been paying for it. You understand this wasn't easy for us, who have nothing. . . . Finally it's over, and I'm damned glad."

Mrs. Forrestier stopped her.

"You say that you bought a diamond necklace to replace mine?"

"Yes, you didn't notice it, eh? It was exactly like yours."

125   And she smiled with proud and childish joy.

Mrs. Forrestier, deeply moved, took both her hands.

"Oh, my poor Mathilde! But mine was only costume jewelry. At most, it was worth only five hundred francs! . . ."

Mrs. Loisel (why does the narrator not say "Mathilde"?) is roughened and aged by the work. But she has behaved "heroically" (paragraph 98) and has shown her mettle.

The point of the story? Small, uncertain things shape our lives; we hang by a thread.

The seventh part of the story, a scene on the Champs-Elysées. Mathilde sees Jeanne Forrestier for the first time in the previous ten years.

Jeanne notes Mathilde's changed appearance.

Mathilde tells Jeanne everything.

SURPRISE! The lost necklace was not made of real diamonds, and the Loisels have slaved for no reason at all. But hard work and sacrifice probably brought out better qualities in Mathilde than she otherwise might have shown. Is this the point of the story? Look again at paragraph 105.

Reading and Responding in a Computer File or Notebook

The marginal comments printed with "The Necklace" demonstrate the active reading-responding process you should apply to everything you read. Use the margins in your text similarly to record your comments and questions, but plan also to record your more lengthy responses in a notebook, on note cards, on separate sheets of paper, or in a computer file. Be careful not to lose anything; keep all your notes. As you progress from work to work, you will find that your written or saved comments will be immensely important to you as your record, or journal, of your first impressions together with your more carefully considered and expanded thoughts.

In keeping your notebook, your objective should be to learn assigned works inside and out and then to say perceptive things about them. To achieve this goal, you need to read the work more than once. Develop a good note-taking system so that as you read, you will create a "memory bank" of your own knowledge. You can make withdrawals from this fund of ideas when you begin to write. As an aid in developing your own procedures for reading and "depositing" your ideas, you may wish to begin with the following guidelines for reading. Of course, you will want to modify these suggestions and add to them as you become a more experienced and disciplined reader.

GUIDELINES FOR READING

1. **Observations for basic understanding**
   a. Explain words, situations, and concepts. Write down words that are new or not immediately clear. Use your dictionary, and record the relevant meanings in your notebook. Write down special difficulties so that you can ask your instructor about them.
   b. Determine what is happening in the work. For a story or play, where do the actions take place? What do they show? Who is involved? Who is the major figure? Why is he or she major? What relationships do the characters have with one another? What concerns do the characters have? What do they do? Who says what to whom? How do the speeches advance the action and reveal the characters? For a poem, what is the situation? Who is talking, and to whom? What does the speaker say about the situation? Why does the poem end as it does and where it does?

2. **Notes on first impressions**
   a. Make a record of your reactions and responses. What did you think was memorable, noteworthy, funny, or otherwise striking? Did you worry, get scared, laugh, smile, feel a thrill, learn a great deal, feel proud, find a lot to think about?
   b. Describe interesting characterizations, events, techniques, and ideas. If you like a character or an idea, explain what you like, and do the same for characters and ideas you don't like. Is there anything else in the work that you especially like or dislike? Are parts easy or difficult to understand? Why? Are there any surprises? What was your reaction to them? Be sure to use your own words when writing your explanations.

3. **Development of ideas and enlargement of responses**
   a. Trace developing patterns. Make an outline or a scheme: What conflicts appear? Do these conflicts exist between people, groups, or ideas? How are the conflicts resolved? Is one force, idea, or side the winner? How do you respond to the winner or to the loser?
   b. Write expanded notes about characters, situations, and actions. What explanations need to be made about the characters? What is the nature of the situations (e.g., young people discover a damaged boat, and themselves, in the spring; a prisoner tries to hide her baby from cruel guards, and so on)?

What is the nature of the actions (e.g., a mother and daughter go shopping, a series of strangers intrude upon the celebration of a christening, a woman is told that her husband has been killed in a train wreck, a group of children are taken to a fashionable toy store, and so on)? What are the people like, and what are their habits and customs? What sort of language do they use?

c. Memorize important, interesting, and well-written passages. Copy them in full on note cards, and keep these in your pocket or purse. When walking to class, riding public transportation, or otherwise not occupying your time, learn them by heart. Please take memorization seriously.

d. Always write down questions that come up during your reading. You may raise these in class, and trying to write out your own answers will also aid your own study.

Sample Notebook Entries on Maupassant's "The Necklace"

The following entries demonstrate how you can use the foregoing guidelines in your first thoughts about a work. You should try to develop enough observations and responses to be useful later, both for additional study and for developing essays. Notice that the entries are not only comments but also questions.

Early in the story, Mathilde seems to be spoiled. She and her husband are not well off, but she is unable to face her own situation.

She is a dreamer but seems harmless. Her daydreams about a fancy home, with all the expensive belongings, are not unusual. It would be unusual to find people who do not have such dreams.

She is embarrassed by her husband's taste for plain food. The storyteller contrasts her taste for trout and quail with Loisel's cheaper favorites.

When the Loisels get the invitation to the ball, Mathilde becomes difficult. Her wish for an expensive dress (the cost of Loisel's shotgun) creates a problem, and she creates another problem by wanting to wear fine jewelry.

Her change in character can be related to the places in the story: the Street of Martyrs, the dinner party scene, the attic flat. Also she fills the places she daydreams about with the most expensive things she can imagine.

Her success at the party shows that she has the charm the storyteller talks about in paragraph 2. She seems never to have had any other chance to exert her power.

The worst part of her personality is shown in rushing away from the party because she is ashamed of her ordinary and shabby shawl, which she had worn because the time of the story is January. It is Mathilde's unhappiness and unwillingness to adjust to her modest means that cause the financial downfall of the Loisels. This disaster is her fault.

Borrowing the money to replace the necklace shows that both Loisel and Mathilde have a strong sense of honor. Making up the loss is good, even if it destroys them financially.

There are some nice touches, like Loisel's seeming to be five years older (paragraph 86) and his staying with the other husbands of women enjoying themselves (paragraph 54). These are well done.

It's too bad that Loisel and Mathilde don't confess to Jeanne that the jewels are lost. Their pride or their honor stops them—or perhaps their fear of being accused of theft.

Their ten years of slavish work (paragraphs 98-102) show how they have come down in life. Mathilde does all her work by hand, so she really does pitch in and is, as the narrator says, heroic.

The attic flat is important. Mathilde becomes loud and frumpy when living there (paragraph 99), but she also develops strength. She does what she has to. The earlier apartment and the elegance of her imaginary rooms had brought out her limitations.

The setting of the Champs-Elysées also reflects her character, for she feels free there to tell Jeanne about the disastrous loss and the ten years of sacrifice (paragraph 121), producing the surprise ending. A curious point: Is it likely that Mathilde would not have had any contact with Mrs. Forrestier during that ten-year period?

The narrator's statement "How little a thing it takes to destroy you or to save you!" (paragraph 105) is full of thought. The necklace is little, and it makes a gigantic problem. This creates the story's irony.

Questions: Is this story more about the surprise ending or about the character of Mathilde? Is she to be condemned or admired? Does the outcome stem from the little things that make us or break us, as the narrator suggests, or from the difficulty of rising above one's economic class, which seems true, or both? What do the speaker's remarks about women's status mean? (Remember, the story was published in 1884.) This probably isn't relevant, but wouldn't Jeanne, after hearing about the substitution, give the full value of the necklace to the Loisels (or at least return the necklace to them), and wouldn't they then be pretty well off?

These are reasonable—and also fairly full—remarks and observations about "The Necklace." Use your notebook or journal similarly for all reading assignments. If your assignment is simply to learn about a work, general notes like these should be enough. If you are preparing for a test, you might write pointed observations more in line with what is happening in your class, and also write and answer your own questions (see Chapter 31, "Taking Examinations on Literature"). If you have a writing assignment, observations like these can help you focus more closely on your topic—such as character, idea, or setting. Whatever your purpose, always take good notes, and put in as many details and responses as you can. The notes will be invaluable to you as a mind refresher and as a wellspring of thought.

Major Stages in Thinking and Writing About Literary Topics: Discovering Ideas, Preparing to Write, Making an Initial Draft of Your Essay, and Completing The Essay

Finished writing is the sharpened, focused expression of thought and study. It begins with the search for something to say—an idea. Not all ideas are equal; some are better than others, and getting good ideas is an ability that you will develop the more you think and write. As you discover ideas and explain them in words, you will also improve your perceptions and increase your critical faculties.

In addition, because literature itself contains the subject material (though not in a systematic way) of philosophy, religion, psychology, sociology, and politics, learning to analyze literature and to write about it will also improve your capacity to deal with these and other disciplines.

Writing Does Not Come Easily—for Anyone

A major purpose of your being in college, of which your composition and literature course is a vital part, is to develop your capacity to think and to express your thoughts clearly and fully. However, the process of creating a successfully argued essay—the actual process itself of writing—is not automatic. Writing begins in uncertainty and hesitation, and it becomes certain and confident—accomplished—only as a result of great care, applied thought, a certain amount of experimentation, the passage of time, and much effort. When you read complete, polished, well-formed pieces of writing, you might assume, as many of us do, that the writers wrote their successful versions the first time they tried and never needed to make any changes and improvements at all. In an ideal world, perhaps, something like this could happen, but not in this one.

If you could see the early drafts of writing you admire, you would be surprised and startled—and also encouraged—to see that good writers are also human and that what they first write is often uncertain, vague, tangential, tentative, incomplete, and messy. Good writers do not always like their first drafts; nevertheless, they work with their efforts and build upon them. They reconsider their ideas and try to restate them, discard some details, add others, chop paragraphs in half and reassemble the parts elsewhere, throw out much (and then maybe recover some of it), revise or completely rewrite sentences, change words, correct misspellings, sharpen expressions, and add new material to tie all the parts together in a smooth, natural flow.

The Goal of Writing: To Show a Process of Thought

As you approach the task of writing, you should constantly realize that your goal should always be to *explain* the work you are analyzing. You should never be satisfied simply to restate the events in the work. Too often students fall easily into a pattern of retelling a story or play, or of summarizing the details of a poem. But nothing could be further from what is expected from good writing. **Good writing should be the embodiment of your thought; it should show your thought in action.** Thinking is an active process that does not happen accidentally. Thinking requires that you develop ideas, draw conclusions, exemplify them and support them with details, and connect everything in a coherent manner. Your goal should constantly be to explain the results of your thinking—your ideas, your play of mind over the materials of a work, your insights, your conclusions.

Approach each writing assignment in light of the following objectives: You should consider your reader as a person who has read the work, just as you have done. This person knows what is in the work, and therefore does not need you to restate what she or he already knows. Instead, your reader wants to learn from you what to think about it. Therefore, always, your task as a writer is to explain something about the work, to describe the thoughts that you can develop about it. Let us consider again Maupassant's "The Necklace." We have recognized that the main character, Mathilde Loisel, is a young Parisian housewife who is married to a minor clerk in the Ministry of Education. We know this, but if we are reading an essay about the story we will want to learn more. Let us then suppose that a first goal of one of your paragraphs is to explain the deep dissatisfaction Mathilde feels in the early part of the story. Your paragraph might go as follows:

> In the early part of the story Maupassant establishes that Mathilde is deeply dissatisfied with her life. Her threadbare furniture and drab walls are a cause of her unhappiness. Under these circumstances her daydreams of beautiful rooms staffed by "elegant valets," together with a number of rooms for intimate conversations with friends, multiply her dissatisfaction. The meager meals that she shares with her husband make her imagine sumptuous banquets that she feels are rightfully hers by birth but that are denied her because of her circumstances. The emphasis in these early scenes of the story is always on Mathilde's discontentment and frustration.

Notice that this paragraph does not simply go over the story's events, but rather refers to the events in order to explain to us, as readers, the causes for Mathilde's unhappiness. The paragraph illustrates your process of thought. Here is another way in which you might use a thought to connect the same materials:

> In the early part of the story Maupassant emphasizes the economic difficulty of Mathilde's life. The threadbare furniture and ugly curtains, for example, highlight that there is no money to purchase better things. The same sparseness of existence is shown by the meager meals that she shares with her husband. With the capacity to appreciate better things, Mathilde is forced by circumstances to make do with worse. Her dreams of sumptuous banquets are therefore natural, given her level of frustration with the life around her. In short, her unhappiness is an understandable consequence of her aversion to her plain and drab apartment and the tightness of money.

Here the details are substantially the same as in the first paragraph, but they are unified by a different idea—namely, the economic constraints of Mathilde's life. What is important is that neither paragraph tells only the details. Instead the paragraphs illustrate the goal of writing with a purpose. Whenever you write, you should always be trying, as in these examples, to use a dominating thought or thoughts to shape the details in the work you are analyzing.

For both practiced and beginning writers alike, there are four stages of thinking and writing, and in each of these there are characteristic activities. In the beginning stage, writers try to find the details and thoughts that seem to be right for eventual inclusion in what they are hoping to write. The next (or middle) stage is characterized by written drafts, or sketches—ideas, sentences, paragraphs. An advanced stage of writing is the forming and ordering of what has previously been done—the creation and determination of a final essay. Although these stages occur in a natural order, they are not separate and distinct, but merge with each other and in effect are fused together. However, when you think you are close to finishing your essay, you may find that you are not as close as you might have thought. You are now in the finishing or completing stage, when you need to include something else, something more, something different, and something to make things complete. At this point you can easily re-create an earlier stage to discover new details and ideas. You might say that your work is always tentative until you regard it as finished or until you need to turn it in.

Discovering Ideas ("Brainstorming")

With the foregoing general goal in mind, let us assume that you have read the work about which you are to write and have made notes and observations on which you are planning to base your thought. You are now ready to consider and plan what to include in your essay. This earliest stage of writing is unpredictable and somewhat frustrating because you are on a search. You do not know quite what you want, for you are reaching out for ideas and you are not yet sure what they are and what you might say about them. This process of searching and discovery, sometimes also called **brainstorming,** requires you to examine any and every subject that your mind can produce.

Just as you are trying to reach for ideas, however, you also should try to introduce purpose and resolution into your thought. You have to zero in on something specific, and develop your ideas through this process. Although what you first write may seem indefinite, the best way to help your thinking is to put your mind, figuratively, into specific channels or grooves, and then to confine your thoughts within these boundaries. What matters is to get your mind going on a particular topic and to get your thoughts down on paper or onto a computer screen. Once you can see your thoughts in front of you, you can work with them and develop them. The drawing on the next page can be helpful to you as an illustration of the various facets of a literary work, or ways of talking about it.

Consider the work you have read—story, poem, play—as the central circle, from which a number of points, like the rays of a star, shine out, some of them prominently, others less so. These points, or rays, are the various subjects, or topics,

that you might decide to select in exploration, discovery, and discussion. Because some elements in a work may be more significant than others, the points are not all equal in size. Notice also that the points grow larger as they get nearer to the work, suggesting that once you select a point of discussion you may amplify that point with details and your own observations about the work.

You can consider literary works in many ways, but for now, as a way of getting started, you might choose to explore (1) the work's characters, (2) its historical period and background, (3) the social and economic conditions it depicts, (4) its major ideas, (5) any of its artistic qualities, or (6) any additional ideas that seem important to you.[1] These topics, of course, have many subtopics, but any one of them can help you in the concentration you will need for beginning your essay (and also for classroom discussion). All you need is one topic, just one; don't try everything at the same time. Let us see how our illustration can be revised to account for these topics. In the drawing on the next page the number of points is reduced to illustrate the points or approaches we have just raised (with an additional and unnamed point to represent all the other approaches that might be used for other studies). These points represent your ways of discovering ideas about the work.

Study the Characters in the Work

You do not need to be a professional psychologist to discuss the persons or characters that you find in a work (see also Chapter 3). You need to raise only issues about the characters and what they do and what they represent. What are the

---

[1]Together with additional topics, these critical approaches are discussed in more detail in Chapter 29.

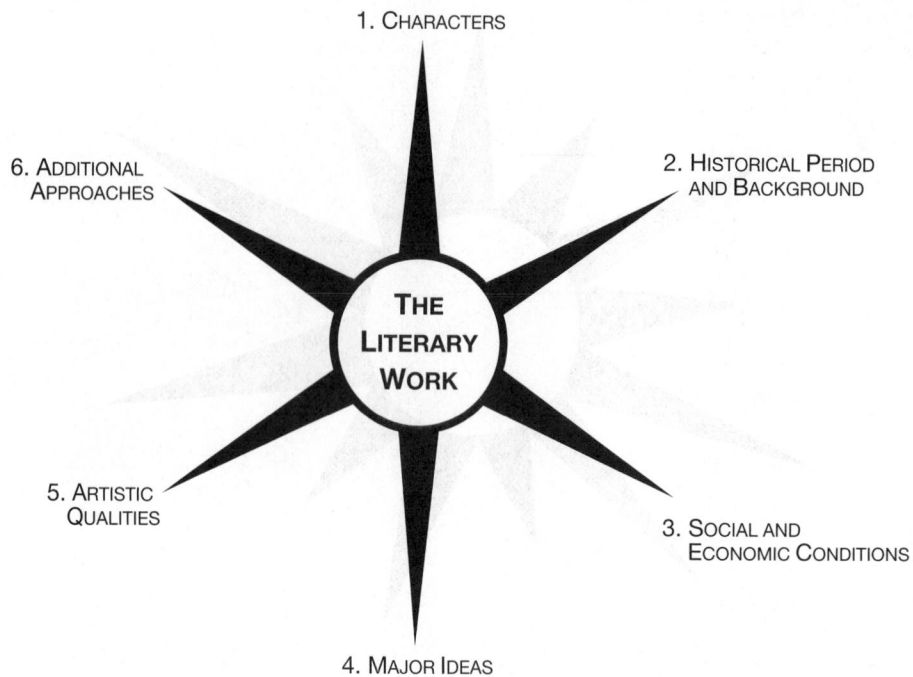

1. Characters

6. Additional Approaches

2. Historical Period and Background

THE LITERARY WORK

5. Artistic Qualities

3. Social and Economic Conditions

4. Major Ideas

characters like at the beginning of the work? What happens to them? Do they do anything that causes them to change, and how are they changed? Are the changes for good or for bad? Why do the characters do the things they do? What do they do correctly? What do they do incorrectly? Why? For example, Mathilde is wrong not to tell Jeanne about the lost necklace. Such an immediate admission of truth would save her and her husband ten years of hardship and deprivation. But Mathilde does not tell the truth. Why not? What do we learn about her character because she avoids or ignores this admission? Is her avoidance understandable? Why?

In discussing character, you might also wish to raise the issue of whether the characters in the work do or do not do what might normally be expected from people in their circumstances. Do they correspond to type? The idea here is that certain attitudes and behaviors are typical of people at particular stages of life (e.g., children behaving like children, lovers dealing with their relationship, a young couple coping with difficult finances). Thus we might ask questions about whether the usual circumstances experienced by the characters affect them, either by limiting them in some way or by freeing them. What attitudes seem typical of the characters? How do these attitudes govern what the characters do, or do not do? For example, one of the most typical circumstances of life is marriage. According to the positive and ideal type of marriage, a husband and wife should be forthcoming with each other; they should tell each other things and should not conceal what is on their minds. If they have problems, they should discuss them and try to solve them together. In "The Necklace" we see that Mathilde and Loisel do not show these desired qualities, and their absence of communication can be seen as an element in their financial catastrophe. However, during their long years of trouble they work together; they eventually exhibit the quality of honesty, and in this respect they fulfill their role, or type, as a married couple.

An analysis of typical attitudes themselves can also furnish you with material for discussion. For example, Mathilde, who is a member of the lower commercial class, has attitudes that are more appropriate to the upper or leisure class. She cannot bridge this gap, and her frustration causes her to nag her husband to give her enough money to live out her dream, if only for a moment.

Determine the Work's Historical Period and Background

An obvious topic is the historical circumstances of the work. When was the work written? How well does it portray details about life at the time it appeared? What is historically unique about it? To what degree does it help you learn something about the past that you did not previously know? What actions in the work are like or unlike actions going on at the present time? What truthfulness to life do you discover in the work? In "The Necklace," for example, which was published more than a century ago, Mathilde's duty is to stay at home as a housewife—a traditional role—while her husband is the family breadwinner. After the loss of the necklace she can no longer afford domestic help, and she is compelled to do all her own housework and her own shopping. She has none of today's home conveniences—no dishwasher, microwave, refrigerator or car. Her husband, a clerk or secretary-copyist, spends his workday copying business records by hand, for at the period of the story there were few typewriters and absolutely no word processors. Discussing matters like these might also help you with works written during modern times, because our own assumptions, artifacts, and habits will bear analysis and discussion.

Analyze the Work's Economic and Social Conditions

Closely related to the historical period, an obvious topic to pursue in many works is the economic and social condition of the characters. To what level of life, economically, do the characters belong? How are events in the work related to their condition? How does their money, or lack of it, limit what they do? How do their economic circumstances either restrict or liberate their imaginations? How do their jobs and their apparent income determine their way of life? If we ask some of these questions about "The Necklace," as we have seen, we find that Mathilde and her husband are greatly burdened by their lack of money, and also that their obligation to repay their huge loan drives them into economic want and sacrifice.

An important part of the economic and social analysis of literature is the consideration of female characters and what it means to be a woman. This is the feminist analysis of literature, which asks questions like these: What role is Mathilde compelled to take as a result of her sex and family background? How does Jeanne's way of life contrast with that of Mathilde? What can Mathilde do with her life? To what degree is she limited by her role as a housewife? Does she have any chance of an occupation outside the home? How does her economic condition cause her to yearn for better things? What causes her to borrow the necklace? What is her contribution, as a woman, to the repayment of the loans? Should

Mathilde's limited life in "The Necklace" be considered as a political argument for greater freedom for women? Once you start asking questions like these, you will find that your thinking is developing along with your ideas for writing.

The feminist approach to the interpretation of literature has been well established, and it will usually provide you with a way to discuss a work. It is also possible, of course, to analyze what a work says about the condition of being a man, or being a child. Depending on the work, many of the questions important in a feminist approach are not dissimilar to those you might use if you are dealing with childhood or male adulthood.

One of the most important social and economic topics is that of race and ethnicity. What happens in the work that seems to occur mainly because of the race of the characters? Is the author pointing out any deprivations, any absence of opportunity, any oppression? What do the characters do under such circumstances? Do they succeed or not? Are they negative? Are they angry? Are they resolute and determined? Your aim in an inquiry of this type should be to concentrate on actions and ideas in the work that are clearly related to race.

Explain the Work's Major Ideas

One of the major ways of focusing on a work is to zero in on various ideas and values or issues to be discovered there. What ideas might we gain from the story of the lengthy but needless sacrifice and drudgery experienced by Mathilde and her husband? An obvious and acceptable idea is presented by the speaker— namely, that even the smallest, most accidental incident can cause immense consequences. This is an idea that we might expand and illustrate in an entire essay. Here are some other ideas that we might also pursue, all of them based on the story's actions:

- Many actions have unforeseeable and uncontrollable consequences.
- Lack of communication is a major cause of hardship.
- Adversity brings out a character's good qualities.
- Mutual effort enables people to overcome difficulties.

These ideas are all to be found in Maupassant's story. In other works, of course, we may find comparable ideas, in addition to other major ideas and issues.

Describe the Work's Artistic Qualities

A work's artistic qualities provide many possible topics for studying, but basically here you may consider matters such as the work's plan or organization and the author's narrative method, writing style, or poetic techniques. In "The Necklace," we thus observe that almost the entire story develops with Mathilde at the center (narrative method; see also Chapter 2, on point of view). At first, the story brings us close to Mathilde, for we are told of her dissatisfaction and impatience with her surroundings. As the story progresses, the storyteller/speaker presents her person and actions more objectively and also more distantly. Another artistic approach would be to determine the story's pattern of development—how, chronologically, the loss of the necklace brings financial misfortune to the Loisels. We might also look for the author's inclusion of symbols in the story, such as the name of the street where the Loisels originally live, their move to an attic flat, or the roughness of Mathilde's hands as a result of her constant housework. There are many other ways to consider the formal aspects of a literary work.

Explain Any Other Approaches That Seem Important

Additional ways of looking at a work such as "The Necklace" might occur to you beyond those just described. One reader might raise the issue that the story's speaker seems to exhibit a particularly patronizing attitude toward women. He draws attention to Mathilde's joy because of the party, and generalizes about how her "victory" was so "sweet to the heart of any woman" (paragraph 53). A writer might want to make more of this attitude. Another aspect of the story might be the way in which Mathilde's physical appearance undergoes change as a result of her dismissing the maid and taking on the household chores herself. Still another aspect is the attitude of Loisel and his relationship with Mathilde, which seems rather distant. The story tells nothing about his reactions to the misfortune beyond how he pitches in to restore the borrowed money, almost to the point of enslaving himself to the task. Would he never have uttered any reproachful words toward his wife? The point here is that additional ideas may suggest themselves to you, and that you should keep yourself open to explore and discuss any of these other ways of seeing and thinking.

Preparing to Write

By this time you will already have been focusing on your topic and will have assembled much that you can put into your essay. You should now aim to develop paragraphs and sketches of what you will eventually include. You should think constantly of the point or argument you want to develop, but invariably digressions will occur, together with other difficulties—false starts, dead ends, total cessation of thought, digressions, despair, hopelessness, and general frustration. Remember, however, that it is important just to start. Jump right in and start writing anything at all—no matter how unacceptable your first efforts may seem— and force yourself to deal with the materials. The writing down of ideas does not commit you. You should not think that these first ideas are untouchable and holy just because you have written them on paper or on your computer screen. You can throw them out in favor of new ideas, you can make cross-outs and changes, and you can move paragraphs or even sections around as you wish. However, if you do not start writing, your first thoughts will remain locked in your mind and you will have nothing to work with. You must learn to accept the uncertainties in the writing process and make them work *for* you rather than *against* you.

Build Ideas from Your Original Notes

You need to get your mind going by mining your notebook or computer file for useful things you have already written. Thus, let us use an observation in our original set of notes—"The attic flat is important"—in reference to the poorer rooms where Mathilde and her husband live while they are paying back their creditors. With such a note as a start, you might develop a number of ideas to support an argument about Mathilde's character, as in the following:

> The attic flat is important. Early in the story, in her apartment, Mathilde is dreamy and impractical. She seems delicate, but after losing the necklace, she is delicate no longer. She becomes a worker after they move to the flat. She does a lot more when living there.
>
> In the flat, Mathilde has to sacrifice. She gives up her servant, washes greasy pots, climbs stairs carrying buckets of water, sloshes water around to clean floors, and does all the clothes washing by hand.
>
> When living in the flat she gets stronger, but she also becomes loud and common. She argues with shopkeepers to get the lowest prices. She stops caring for herself. There is a reversal here, from incapable and well groomed to capable but coarse.

In this way, even in an assertion as basic as "The attic flat is important," the process of putting together details is a form of concentrated thought that leads you creatively forward. You can express thoughts and conclusions that you could not express at the beginning. Such an exercise in stretching your mind leads you to put elements of the work together in ways that create ideas for good essays.

Trace Patterns of Action and Thought

You can also discover ideas by making a list or scheme for the story or main idea. What conflicts appear? Do these conflicts exist between people, groups, or ideas? How does the author resolve them? Is one force, idea, or side the winner? Why? How do you respond to the winner or to the loser? Using this method, you might make a list similar to this one:

> At the beginning, Mathilde is a fish out of water. She dreams of wealth, but her life is drab and her husband is dull.
>
> Fantasies make her even more dissatisfied; she punishes herself by thinking of a wealthy life.
>
> When the Loisels get the dinner invitation Mathilde pouts and whines. Her husband feels discomfort when she manipulates him into buying her an expensive party dress.
>
> Her world of daydreams hurts her real life when her desire for wealth causes her to borrow the necklace. Losing the necklace is just plain bad luck.

These arguments all focus on Mathilde's character, but you may wish to trace other patterns you find in the story. If you start planning an essay about another pattern, be sure to account for all the actions and scenes that relate to your topic. Otherwise, you may miss a piece of evidence that could lead you to new conclusions.

THE NEED FOR THE ACTUAL PHYSICAL PROCESS OF WRITING

Thinking and writing are interdependent processes. If you don't get your thoughts into words that are visible to you on a paper or computer screen, your thinking will be impeded. It is therefore vital for you to use the writing process as the most significant means of developing your ideas. If you are doing an assignment in class—tests, or impromptu essays—write your initial responses on a single side of your paper. This strategy will enable you to spread your materials out to get an actual physical overview of them when you begin writing. Everything will be open to you; none of your ideas will be hidden on the other side of the paper.

Outside of class, however, when you are at home or otherwise able to use a computer, your machine is an indispensable tool for your writing. It will help you develop ideas, for it quickly enables you to eliminate unworkable thoughts and to replace them with others. You can move sentences and paragraphs into new contexts, test how they look, and move them somewhere else if you choose.

In addition, the ability to print initial and tentative stages of writing makes rewriting easier. Using the printed draft, you can make additional notes, corrections, and suggestions for further development. With the marked-up draft as a guide, you can go back to the word processor and fill in your changes and improvements, repeating this procedure as often as you can. You can also make edits directly to your draft and track changes to see your edits versus your original draft. This facility makes the machine an incentive for improvement, right up to your final draft.

Word processing also helps you in the final preparation of your essays. Studies have shown that errors and awkward sentences are frequently found at the bottoms of handwritten pages. The reason is that writers hesitate to make improvements when they get near the end of a page because they shun the dreariness of starting the page over. Word processors eliminate this difficulty completely. Changes can be made anywhere in the draft, at any time, without any ill effect on the final appearance of your essay.

Regardless of your writing method, you should always remember that unwritten thought is incomplete thought. You cannot lay everything out at once on the word processor's screen. You can see only a small part of what you are writing. Therefore, somewhere in your writing process, you need to prepare a complete draft of what you have written. A clean, readable draft permits you to gather everything together and to make even more improvements through revision.

Raise and Answer Your Own Questions

A habit you should always cultivate is to raise your own questions, and try to answer them yourself as you consider your reading. The guidelines for reading (pp. 13–14) will help you formulate questions, but you can raise additional questions like these:

- What is happening as the work unfolds? How does an action at the beginning of the work bring about later actions and speeches?

- Who are the main characters? What seems unusual or different about what they do in the work?
- What conclusions can you draw about the work's actions, scenes, and situations? Explain these conclusions.
- What are the characters and speakers like? What do they do and say about themselves, their goals, the people around them, their families, their friends, their work, and the general circumstances of their lives?
- What kinds of words do the characters use: formal or informal words, slang or profanity?
- What literary conventions and devices have you discovered, and how do these affect the work? (When an author addresses readers directly, for example, that is a convention; when a comparison is used, that is a device, which might be either a metaphor or a simile.)

Of course, you can raise other questions as you reread the piece, or you can be left with one or two major questions that you decide to pursue.

Put Ideas Together Using a Plus-Minus, Pro-Con, or Either-Or Method

A common and very helpful method of discovering ideas is to develop a set of contrasts: plus-minus, pro-con, either-or. Let us suppose a plus-minus method of considering the following question about Mathilde: Should she be "admired" (plus) or "condemned" (minus)?

PLUS: ADMIRED?	MINUS: CONDEMNED?
After she cries when they get the invitation, she recovers with a "strong effort"—maybe she doesn't want her husband to feel bad.	She wants to be envied and admired only for being attractive and intriguing, not for more important qualities. She seems spoiled and selfish.
She scores a great victory at the dance. She really does have the power to charm and captivate.	She wastes her time in daydreaming about things she can't have, and she whines because she is unhappy.
Once she loses the necklace, she and her husband become poor and deprived. But she does "her share . . . completely, heroically" (paragraph 98) to make up for the loss.	Even though the Loisels live poorly, Mathilde manipulates her husband into giving her more money than they can afford for a party dress.
Even when she is poor, she dreams about that marvelous, shining moment at the great ball. This is pathetic, because Mathilde gets worse than she deserves.	She assumes that her friend Jeanne would think her a thief if she admitted losing the necklace. Shouldn't she have had more confidence in Jeanne?
At the end, after everything is paid back, and her reputation is secure, Mathilde confesses the loss to Jeanne.	She becomes loud and coarse and haggles about pennies, thus undergoing a cheapening of her person and manner.

By putting contrasting observations side by side in this way, you will find that ideas will start to come naturally and will be helpful to you when you begin writing, regardless of how you finally organize your essay. It is possible, for example, that you might develop either column as the argumentative basis of an essay, or you might use your notes to support the idea that Mathilde is too complex to be either wholly admired or wholly condemned. You might also want to introduce an entirely new topic of development—for example, that Mathilde should be pitied rather than condemned or admired. In short, arranging materials in the plus-minus pattern is a powerful way to discover ideas—a truly helpful habit of promoting thought—that can lead to ways of development that you do not at first realize.

Originate and Develop Your Thoughts Through Writing

You should always write down what you are thinking for, as a principle, *unwritten thought is incomplete thought.* Make a practice of writing your observations about the work, in addition to any questions that occur to you. This is an exciting step in preliminary writing because it can be useful when you write later drafts. You will discover that looking at what you have written can not only enable you to correct and improve the writing you have done but also lead you to recognize that you need more. The process goes just about like this: "Something needs to be added here—important details that my reader will not have noticed, new support for my argument, a new idea that has just occurred to me, a significant connection to link my thoughts." If you follow such a process, you will be using your own written ideas to create new ideas. You will be advancing your own abilities as a thinker and writer.

The processes just described of searching for ideas, or brainstorming, are useful for you at any stage of composition. Even when you are fairly close to finishing your essay, you might suddenly recognize that you need to add something more (or subtract something you don't like). When that happens, you may return to the discovery or brainstorming process to initiate and develop new ideas and new arguments.

Making an Initial Draft of Your Essay

As you use the brainstorming and focusing techniques, you are also in fact beginning your essay. You will need to revise your ideas as connections among them become clearer and as you reexamine the work to discover details to support the argument you are making. By this stage, however, you already have many of the raw materials you need for developing your topic.

Base Your Essay on a Central Idea, Argument, or Statement

By definition, an essay *is an organized, connected, and fully developed set of paragraphs that expand on a* **central idea, central argument,** or **central statement.** All parts of an essay should contribute to the reader's understanding of the idea.

To achieve unity and completeness, each paragraph refers to the argument and demonstrates how selected details from the work relate to it and support it. The central idea helps you control and shape your essay, just as it also provides guidance for your reader.

A successful essay about literature is a brief but thorough (not exhaustive) examination of a literary work in light of topics like those we have already raised—from character, background, and economic conditions to circumstances of gender, major ideas, artistic qualities, and any additional topic such as point of view and symbolism. Central ideas or arguments might be (1) that a character is strong and tenacious, or (2) that the story shows the unpredictability of action, or (3) that the point of view makes the action seem "distant and objective," or (4) that a major symbol governs the actions and thoughts of the major characters. In essays on these topics, all materials must be tied to such central ideas or arguments. Thus, it is a fact that Mathilde in "The Necklace" endures ten years of slavish work and sacrifice as she and her husband accumulate enough money to repay their monumental debt. This we know, but it is not relevant to an essay on her character unless you connect it by a central argument showing how it demonstrates one of her major traits—her growing strength and perseverance.

Look through all of your ideas for one or two that catch your eye for development. In all the early stages of preliminary writing, the chances are that you have already discovered at least a few ideas that are more thought provoking, or more important, than the others.

Once you choose an idea you think you can work with, write it as a complete sentence that is essential to the argument of your essay. A simple phrase such as "setting and character" does not focus thought the way a sentence does. The following sentence moves the topic toward new exploration and discovery because it combines a topic with an outcome: "The setting of 'The Necklace' reflects Mathilde's character." You can choose to be even more specific: "Mathilde's strengths and weaknesses are reflected in the real and imaginary places in 'The Necklace.'"

Now that you have phrased a single, central idea or argument for your essay, you have also established a guide by which you can accept, reject, rearrange, and change the ideas you have been planning to develop. You can now draft a few paragraphs (which you may base on some of the sketches you have already made; always use as much as you can of your early observations) to see whether your idea seems valid, or you can decide that it would be more helpful to make an outline or a list before you do more writing. In either case, you should use your notes for evidence to connect to your central idea. If you need to bolster your argument with more supporting details and ideas, go once again to the techniques of discovery and brainstorming.

Using the central idea that the changes in the story's settings reflect Mathilde's character might produce a paragraph like the following, which presents an argument about her negative qualities:

The original apartment in the Street of Martyrs and the dream world of wealthy places both show negative sides of Mathilde's character. The real-life apartment, though livable, is shabby. The furnishings all bring out her discontent. The shabbiness

THE NEED FOR A SOUND ARGUMENT IN ESSAYS ABOUT LITERATURE

As you write about literature, you should always try to connect your explanations to a specific argument; that is, you are writing about a specific work, but you are trying to prove—or argue—or demonstrate—a point or idea about it. This book provides you with a number of separate subjects relating to the study of literature. As you select one of these and begin writing, however, you are not to explain just that such-and-such a story has a character who changes and grows, or that such-and-such a poem contains the thought that nature creates great beauty. Rather, you should assert the importance of your topic to the work as a whole in relation to a specific point or argument. One example of an argument might be that a story's first-person point of view permits readers to draw their own conclusions about the speaker's character. Another argument might be that the poet's thought is shown in a poem's details about the bustling sounds and sights of animals in springtime.

Let us therefore repeat and stress that your writing *should always have an argumentative edge*—a goal of demonstrating the truth of your conclusions and clarifying and illuminating your idea about the topic and also about the work. It is here that the accuracy of your choices of details from the work, the soundness of your conclusions, and the cumulative weight of your evidence are essential. You cannot allow your main ideas to rest on one detail alone, but must support your conclusions by showing that the bulk of material leads to them and that they are linked in a reasonable chain of fact and logic. It is such clarification that is the goal of argumentation.

makes her think only of luxuriousness, and having one servant girl causes her to dream of having many servants. The luxury of her dream life heightens her unhappiness with what she actually has.

In such a preliminary draft, in which the purpose is to connect details and thoughts to the major idea, many details from the story are used in support. In the final draft, this kind of support is essential.

Create a Thesis Sentence as Your Guide to Organization

With your central idea or argument as your focus, you can decide which of the earlier observations and ideas can be developed further. Your goal is to establish a number of major topics to support your argument and to express them in a **thesis sentence** or **thesis statement**—an organizing sentence that contains the major topics you plan to treat in your essay. Suppose you choose three ideas from your discovery stage of development. If you put the central idea at the left and the list of topics at the right, you have the shape of the thesis sentence. Note that the first two topics below are taken from the discovery paragraph.

CENTRAL IDEA	**TOPICS**
The setting of "The Necklace" reflects Mathilde's character.	1. First apartment
	2. Dream-life mansion rooms
	3. Attic flat

This arrangement leads to the following thesis statement or thesis sentence.

> Mathilde's character growth is connected to her first apartment, her dream-life mansion rooms, and her attic flat.

You can revise the thesis sentence at any stage of the writing process if you find that you do not have enough evidence from the work to support it. Perhaps a new topic will occur to you, and you can include it, appropriately, as a part of your thesis sentence.

As we have seen, the central idea or central argument is the *glue* of the essay. The thesis sentence lists the parts to be fastened together—that is, the topics in which the central idea is to be demonstrated and argued. To alert your readers to your essay's structure, the thesis sentence is usually placed at the end of the introductory paragraph, just before the body of the essay.

As you write your first draft, you need to support the points of your thesis sentence with your notes and discovery materials. You can alter, reject, and rearrange ideas and details as you wish, as long as you change your thesis sentence to account for the changes (a major reason why many writers write their introductions last). The thesis sentence just shown contains three topics (it could be two, or four, or more) to be used in forming the body of the essay.

Begin Each Paragraph with a Topic Sentence

Just as the organization of the *entire essay* is based on the thesis, the form of each *paragraph* is based on its **topic sentence**—an assertion about how a topic from the predicate of the thesis statement supports the argument contained or implied in the central idea. The first topic in our example is the relationship of Mathilde's character to her first apartment, and the resulting paragraph should emphasize this relationship. If your topic is the coarsening of her character during the ten-year travail, you can then form a topic sentence by connecting the trait with the location, as follows:

> The attic flat reflects the coarsening of Mathilde's character.

Beginning with this sentence, the paragraph will present details that argue how Mathilde's rough, heavy housework changes her behavior, appearance, and general outlook.

Select Only One Topic—No More—for Each Paragraph

You should treat each separate topic in a single paragraph—one topic, one paragraph. However, if a topic seems especially difficult, long, and heavily detailed, you can divide it into two or more subtopics, each receiving a separate paragraph of its own—two or more subtopics, two or more separate paragraphs. Should you

REFERRING TO THE NAMES OF AUTHORS

As a general principle, for both men and women writers, you should regularly include the author's *full name* in the *first sentence* of your essay. Here are model first sentences.

> Shirley Jackson's "The Lottery" is a story featuring both suspense and horror.

> "The Lottery," by Shirley Jackson, is a story featuring both suspense and horror.

For all later references, use only last names, such as *Jackson, Maupassant, Lawrence,* or *Porter.* However, for the "giants" of literature, you should use the last names exclusively. In referring to writers like Shakespeare and Dickinson, for example, there is no need to include *William* or *Emily.*

In spite of today's informal standards, never use an author's first name alone, as in "*Shirley* skillfully creates suspense and horror in 'The Lottery.'" Also, do not use a courtesy title before the names of dead authors, such as "*Ms.* Jackson's 'The Lottery' is a suspenseful horror story," or "*Mr.* Shakespeare's idea is that information is uncertain." Use the last names alone.

As with all conventions, of course, there are exceptions. If you are referring to a childhood work of a writer, the first name might be appropriate, but be sure to shift to the last name when referring to the writer's mature works. If your writer has a professional or a noble title, such as "*Lord* Byron" or "*Queen* Elizabeth," it is not improper to use the title. Even then, however, the titles are commonly omitted for males, so that most references to Lord Byron and Alfred, Lord Tennyson, should be simply to "Byron" and "Tennyson."

Referring to living authors is somewhat problematical. Some journals and newspapers often use the courtesy titles *Mr.* and *Ms.* in their reviews. However, scholarly journals, which are likely to remain on library shelves and Web sites for many decades, follow the general principle of beginning with the entire name and then using only the last name for later references.

make this division, your topic then is really a section, and each paragraph in the section should have its own topic sentence.

Use Your Topic Sentences as the Arguments for Your Paragraph Development

Once you create a topic sentence, you can use it to focus your observations and conclusions. Let us see how our topic about the attic flat can be developed in a paragraph of argument:

> The attic flat reflects the coarsening of Mathilde's character. Maupassant emphasizes the burdens Mathilde endures to save money, such as mopping floors, cleaning greasy and encrusted pots and pans, taking out the garbage, and washing clothes and dishes by hand. This work makes her rough and coarse, an effect also shown by her giving up care of her hair and hands, wearing the cheapest dresses possible, haggling with the local shopkeepers, and becoming loud and penny-pinching. If at the beginning she is delicate and attractive, at the end she is unpleasant and coarse.

THE USE OF VERB TENSES IN THE DISCUSSION OF LITERARY WORKS

Literary works spring into life with each and every reading. You may thus assume that everything happening takes place in the present, and when writing about literature you should use the *present tense of verbs*. It is correct to say, "Mathilde and her husband *work* and *economize* [not *worked* and *economized*] for ten years to pay off the 18,000-franc loan they *take out* [not *took out*] to pay for the lost necklace."

When you consider an author's ideas, the present tense is also proper, on the principle that the words of an author are just as alive and current today (and tomorrow) as they were at the moment of writing, even if this same author might have been dead for hundreds or even thousands of years.

Because it is incorrect to shift tenses inappropriately, you may encounter a problem when you refer to actions that have occurred prior to the time of the main action. An instance is Bierce's "An Occurrence at Owl Creek Bridge" (Chapter 1), in which the main character, a Southern gentleman during the Civil War, is about to be hanged by Union soldiers because he tried to sabotage a strategically important bridge. The story emphasizes the relationship between cause (the attempted sabotage, occurring in the past) and effect (the punishment, occurring in the present). In discussing such a narrative it is important to keep details in order, and thus you can introduce the past tense as long as you make the relationship clear between past and present, as in this example: "Farquhar *is actually hanged* [present tense] by the Union soldiers. But his perceptions *turn him* [present tense] toward the past, and his final thoughts *dwell* [present tense] on the life and happiness he *knew* [past tense] at his own home with his dearest wife." This intermingling of past and present tenses is correct because it corresponds to the pattern of time brought out in the story.

A problem also arises when you introduce historical or biographical details about a work or author. It is appropriate to use the *past tense* for such details if they genuinely do belong to the past. Thus it is correct to state, "Shakespeare *lived* from 1564 to 1616," or that "Shakespeare *wrote* his tragedy *Hamlet* in about 1600–1601." It is also permissible to mix past and present tenses when you are treating historical facts about a literary work and are also considering it as a living text. Of prime importance is to keep things straight. Here is an example showing how past tenses (in bold) and present tenses (in italic) may be used when appropriate:

> Because *Hamlet* **was** first **performed** in about 1601, Shakespeare most probably **wrote** it shortly before this time. In the play, a tragedy, Shakespeare *treats* an act of vengeance, but more importantly he *demonstrates* the difficulty of ever learning the exact truth. The hero, Prince Hamlet, *is* the focus of this difficulty, for the task of revenge *is assigned* to him by the Ghost of his father. Though the Ghost *claims* that his brother, Claudius, *is* his murderer, Hamlet *is* not able to verify this claim.

Here, the historical details are in the past tense, while all details about the play *Hamlet*, including Shakespeare as the creating author whose ideas and words are still alive, are in the present.

As a general principle, you will be right most of the time if you use the present tense exclusively for literary details and the past tense for historical details. When in doubt, however, *consult your instructor*.

Here, details from the story are introduced to provide support for the topic sentence. All the subjects—the hard work, the lack of personal care, the wearing of cheap dresses, and the haggling with the shopkeepers—are introduced not to retell the story but rather to exemplify the argument the writer is making about Mathilde's character.

Develop an Outline as the Means of Organizing Your Essay

So far we have been creating a de facto **outline**—that is, a skeletal plan of organization. Some writers never use any outline but prefer informal lists of ideas; others always rely on outlines; still others insist that they cannot make an outline until they have finished writing. And then there are those writers who simply hate outlines. Regardless of your preference, your final essay should have a tight structure. Therefore, you should use a guiding outline to develop and shape your essay.

The outline we focus on here is the **analytical sentence outline.** This type is easier to create than it sounds. It consists of (1) an introduction, including the central idea and the thesis sentence, together with (2) topic sentences that are to be used in each paragraph of the body, followed by (3) a conclusion. When applied to the subject we have been developing, such an outline looks like this:

TITLE: *How Setting in "The Necklace" Is Connected to Mathilde's Character*

1. **Introduction**
   a. *Central idea*: Maupassant uses setting to show Mathilde's character.
   b. *Thesis statement*: Her character growth is brought out by her first apartment, her daydreams about elegant rooms in a mansion, and her attic flat.
2. **Body:** *Topic sentences* a, b, and c (and d, e, and f, if necessary)
   a. Details about her first apartment explain her dissatisfaction and depression.
   b. Her daydreams about mansion rooms are like the apartment because they too make her unhappy.
   c. The attic flat reflects the coarsening of her character.
3. **Conclusion** *Topic sentence*: All details in the story, particularly the setting, are focused on the character of Mathilde.

The *conclusion* may be a summary of the body; it may evaluate the main idea; it may briefly suggest further points of discussion; or it may be a reflection on the details of the body.

The illustrative essays included throughout this book are organized according to the principles of the analytical sentence outline. To emphasize the shaping effect of these outlines, all central ideas, thesis sentences, and topic sentences are underlined. In your own writing, you can underline or italicize these "skeletal" sentences as a check on your organization. Unless your instructor requires such markings, however, remove them in your final drafts.

Illustrative Student Essay (First Draft)

The following illustrative essay is a first draft of the subject we have been developing. It follows our outline, and it includes details from the story in support of the various topics. It is by no means, however, as good a piece of writing as it could be. The draft omits a topic, some additional details, and some new insights that are included in the second draft, which follows later (pp. 45–48). It therefore reveals the need to make improvements through additional brainstorming and discovery-prewriting techniques. The handwritten comments are like those that an instructor might make to help in the improvement of the essay.

> Underlined sentences in this paper *do not* conform to MLA style and are used solely as teaching tools to emphasize the central idea, thesis sentence, and topic sentences throughout the paper.

Deal 1

James Deal

Professor Smith

English 102

16 April 2008

How Setting in "The Necklace" Is Related

to the Character of Mathilde

Explain what setting is used for?

Does Mathilde's character grow or change?

More specific word needed

       In "The Necklace" Guy de Maupassant does not give much detail about the setting. He does not even describe the necklace itself, which is the central object in his plot, but he says only that it is "superb" (paragraph 47). Rather, he uses the setting to reflect the character of the central figure, Mathilde Loisel.* All his details are presented to bring out her traits. Her character growth is related to her first apartment, her dream-life mansion rooms, and her attic flat.†   [1]

Explain her reaction to this

Dissatisfaction is with husband or her life?

       Details about her first apartment explain her dissatisfaction and depression. The walls are "drab," the furniture "threadbare," and the curtains "ugly" (paragraph 3). There is only a simple country girl to do the housework. The tablecloth is not changed daily, and the best dinner dish is beef stew. Mathilde has no evening clothes, only a theater dress that she does not like. These details show her dissatisfaction about her life with her low-salaried husband.   [2]

*Central idea
†Thesis sentence

Deal 2

[3]   Her dream-life images of wealth are like the apartment because they too make her unhappy. In her daydreams about life in a mansion, the rooms are large, filled with expensive furniture and bric-a-brac, and draped in silk. She imagines private rooms for intimate talks, and big dinners with delicacies like trout and quail. With dreams of such a rich home, she feels even more despair about her modest apartment on the Street of Martyrs in Paris.

Be more specific about her dream world

Quote from story?

[4]   The attic flat reflects the coarsening of Mathilde's character. Maupassant emphasizes the burdens she endures to save money, such as mopping floors, cleaning greasy and encrusted pots and pans, taking out the garbage, and washing clothes and dishes by hand. This work makes her rough and coarse, a fact also shown by her giving up care of her hair and hands, wearing the cheapest dresses possible, haggling with local shopkeepers, and becoming loud and penny-pinching. If at the beginning she is delicate and attractive, at the end she is unpleasant and coarse.

Perhaps a paragraph about her walk on the Champs-Elysees

What else does the attic flat indicate about Mathilde? (Her work ethic?)

[5]   Maupassant focuses everything in the story, including the setting, on the character of Mathilde. He does not add anything extra. Thus he says little about the big party scene, but emphasizes the necessary detail that Mathilde was a great "success" (paragraph 52). It is this detail that brings out some of her early attractiveness and charm, despite her more usual frustration and unhappiness. Thus in "The Necklace," Maupassant uses setting as a means to his end—the story of Mathilde and her unnecessary sacrifice.

Any other details that highlight Mathilde's character?

Good first draft. Work on more specific topic sentences and more details in body paragraphs. Make sure details in body paragraphs are related to topic sentences. You may wish to include another paragraph about the walk on the Champs-Elysees.

Deal 3

Work Cited

Maupassant, Guy de. "The Necklace." Literature: An Introduction to Reading and Writing. Ed. Edgar V. Roberts. 9th ed. New York: Pearson Longman, 2009. 5–12.

Completing the Essay: Developing and Strengthening Your Essay Through Revision

After finishing your first draft, like this one, you may wonder what more you can do. Things may seem to be complete as they are, and that's it. You have read the work several times, have used discovering and brainstorming techniques to establish ideas to write about, have made an outline of your ideas, and have written a full draft. How can you do better?

The best way to begin is to observe that a major mistake writers make when writing about literature is to do no more than retell a story or summarize an idea. Retelling a story shows only that you have read it, not that you have thought about it. Writing a good essay requires you to arrange a pattern of argument and thought.

Make Your Own Arrangement of Details and Ideas

One way to escape the trap of summarizing stories and to set up a pattern of development is to stress your own order when referring to parts of a work. Rearrange details to suit your own central idea or argument. It is often important to write first about the conclusion or middle. Should you find that you have followed the chronological order of the work instead of stressing your own order, you can use one of the preliminary writing techniques to figure out new ways to connect your materials. The principle is that you should introduce details about the work *only* to support the points you wish to make. Details for the sake of detail are unnecessary.

Use Literary Material as Evidence to Support Your Argument

When you write, you are like a detective using clues as evidence for building a case, or a lawyer citing evidence to support an argument. Your goal is to convince your readers of your knowledge and the reasonableness of your conclusions. It is vital to use evidence convincingly so that your readers can follow your ideas. Let us look briefly at two drafts of a new example to see how writing can be improved by the pointed use of details. These are from drafts of an essay on the character of Mathilde.

PARAGRAPH 1

The major flaw of Mathilde's character is that she seems to be isolated, locked away from other people. She and her husband do not talk to each other much, except about external things. He speaks about his liking for beef stew, and she states that she cannot accept the big invitation because she has no nice dresses. Once she gets the dress, she complains because she has no jewelry. Even when borrowing the necklace from Jeanne

PARAGRAPH 2

The major flaw of Mathilde's character is that she is withdrawn and uncommunicative, apparently unwilling or unable to form an intimate relationship. For example, she and her husband do not talk to each other much, except about external things such as his taste for beef stew and her lack of a party dress and jewelry. With such an uncommunicative marriage, one might suppose that she would be more open with her close friend,

Forrestier, she does not say much. When she and her husband discover that the necklace is lost, they simply go over the details, and Loisel dictates a letter of explanation, which Mathilde writes in her own hand. Even when she meets Jeanne on the Champs-Elysées, Mathilde does not say a great deal about her life but only goes through enough details about the loss and replacement of the necklace to make Jeanne exclaim about the needlessness of the ten-year sacrifice.

Jeanne Forrestier, but Mathilde does not say much even to her. This flaw hurts her greatly, because if she were more open she might have explained the loss and avoided the horrible sacrifice. This lack of openness, along with her self-indulgent dreaminess, is her biggest defect.

A comparison of these paragraphs shows that the first has more words than the second (157 compared to 120) but that it is more appropriate for a rough than a final draft because the writer does little more than retell the story. Paragraph 1 is cluttered with details that do not support any conclusions. If you try to find what it says about Maupassant's actual use of Mathilde's solitary traits in "The Necklace," you will get little help. The writer needs to revise the paragraph by eliminating details that do not support the central idea.

On the other hand, the details in paragraph 2 actually do support the declared topic. Phrases such as "for example," "with such," and "this lack" show that the writer of paragraph 2 has assumed that the audience knows the story and now wants to read an argument in support of a particular interpretation. Paragraph 2 therefore guides readers by connecting the details to the topic. It uses these details as evidence, *not* as a retelling of actions. By contrast, paragraph 1 recounts a number of relevant actions *but does not connect them to the topic.* More details, of course, could have been added to the second paragraph, but they are unnecessary because the paragraph develops the argument with the details used. Good writing has many qualities, but one of the most important is shown in a comparison of the two paragraphs: *In good writing, no details are included unless they are used as supporting evidence in a pattern of thought and argument.*

Always Keep to Your Point; Stick to It Tenaciously

To show another distinction between first- and second-draft writing, let us consider a third example. The following unrevised paragraph, in which the writer assumes an audience that is interested in the relationship of economics to literature, is drawn from an essay about the idea of economic determinism in Maupassant's "The Necklace." In this paragraph the writer is trying to argue the point that economic circumstances underlie a number of incidents in the story. The idea is to assert that Mathilde's difficulties result not from her character traits but rather from her financial restrictions.

More important than chance in governing life is the idea that people are controlled by economic circumstances. Mathilde, as is shown at the story's opening, is born poor. Therefore she doesn't get the right doors opened for her, and she settles down to marriage with a minor clerk, Loisel. With a vivid imagination and a burning desire for luxury, seeming to be born only for a life of ease and wealth, she finds that her poor home brings out her daydreams of expensive surroundings. She taunts her husband when he brings the big invitation, because she does not have a suitable (that is, "expensive") dress. Once she gets the dress it is jewelry she lacks, and she borrows that and loses it. The loss of the necklace means great trouble because it forces the Loisels to borrow heavily and to struggle financially for ten years.

This paragraph begins with an effective topic sentence, indicating that the writer has a good plan. The remaining part, however, shows how easily writers can be diverted from their objective. The flaw is that the material of the paragraph, while accurate, is not clearly connected to the topic. Once the second sentence is under way, the paragraph gets lost in a retelling of events, and the promising topic sentence is forgotten. The paragraph therefore shows that the use of detail alone will not support an intended meaning or argument. *As a writer, you must do the connecting yourself, and make sure that all relationships are explicitly clear.* This point cannot be overstressed.

Let us see how the problem can be treated. If the ideal paragraph can be schematized with line drawings, we might say that the paragraph's topic should be a straight line, moving toward and reaching a specific goal (the topic or argument of the paragraph), with an exemplifying line moving away from the straight line briefly to bring in evidence but returning to the line to demonstrate the relevance of each new fact. Thus, the ideal scheme looks like this, with a straight line touched a number of times by an undulating line:

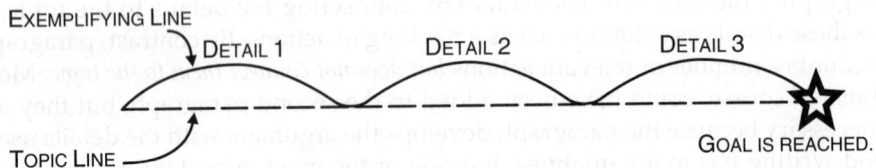

Notice that the exemplifying line, fluctuating to illustrate how documentation or exemplification is to be used, always returns to the topic line. A visual scheme for the faulty paragraph on "The Necklace," however, looks like this, with the line never returning but flying out into space.

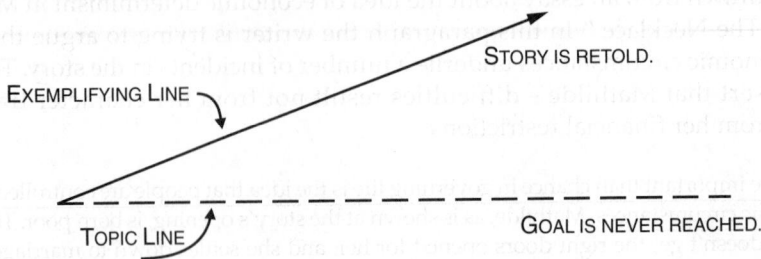

How might the faulty paragraph be improved? The best way is to remind the reader again and again of the topic and to use examples from the text in support.

As our model wavy-line diagram indicates, each time a topic is mentioned, the undulating line merges with the straight, or central-idea line. This relationship of argument to illustrative examples should prevail no matter what subject you write about, and you have to be tenacious in forming these connecting relationships. If you are analyzing *point of view*, for example, you should keep connecting your material to the speaker, or narrator, and the same applies to topics such as character, idea, or setting. According to this principle, we might revise the paragraph on economic determinism in "The Necklace" as follows. (Parts of sentences stressing the relationship of the examples to the topic sentence are underlined.)

> *More important than chance in governing life is the idea that people are controlled by economic circumstances.* As illustration, the speaker begins by emphasizing that Mathilde, the main character, is born poor. Therefore she doesn't get the right doors opened for her, and she settles down to marriage with a minor clerk, Loisel. In keeping with the idea, her vivid imagination and burning desire for luxury feed on her weakness of character as she feels deep unhappiness and depression because of the contrast between her daydreams of expensive surroundings and the poor home she actually has. These straitened economic circumstances inhibit her relationship with her husband, and she taunts him when he brings the big invitation because she does not have a suitable (that is, "expensive") dress. As a merging of her unrealistic dream life with actual reality, her borrowing of the necklace suggests the impossibility of overcoming economic restrictions. In the context of the idea, the ten-year sacrifice to pay for the lost necklace demonstrates that being poor keeps people down, destroying their dreams and their hopes for a better life.

The paragraph now successfully develops the argument promised by the topic sentence. While it has also been lengthened, the length has been caused not by inessential detail but by phrases and sentences that give form and direction. You might object that if you lengthened all your paragraphs in this way, your essays would grow too bulky. The answer is to reduce the number of major points and paragraphs, on the theory that *it is better to develop a few topics pointedly than to develop many pointlessly.* Revising for the purpose of strengthening central and topic ideas requires that you either throw out some topics or else incorporate them as subpoints in the topics you keep. To control your writing in this way can result only in improvement.

Check Your Development and Organization

It bears repeating over and over again that the first requirement of a good essay is to introduce a central idea or argument and then stick to it. Another major step toward excellence is to make your central idea expand and grow. The word *growth* is a metaphor describing the disclosure of ideas that were not at first noticeable, together with the expression of original, new, and fresh interpretations.

Try to Be Original

In everything you write, now and in the future, you should always try to be original. You might claim that originality is impossible because you are writing about someone else's work. "The author has said everything," might be the argument, "and therefore I can do little more than follow the story." This claim rests on the mistaken assumption that you have no choice in selecting material and no opportunity to have individual thoughts and make original contributions.

But you do have choices and opportunities to be original. You really do. One obvious area of originality is the development and formulation of your central idea. For example, a natural first response to "The Necklace" is "The story is about a woman who loses a borrowed necklace and endures hardship to help pay for it." But this response does not promise an argument because it refers only to events in the story and not to any idea. You can point the sentence toward an argument, however, if you call the hardship "needless." Just this word alone demands that you explain the differences between needed and unneeded hardships, and your application of these differences to the heroine's plight would produce an original essay. Even better and more original insights could result if the topic of the budding essay were to connect the dreamy, withdrawn traits of the main character to her misfortunes. A resulting central idea might be "People themselves create their own difficulties." Such an argument would require you to define not only the personal but also the representative nature of Mathilde's experiences, an avenue of exploration that could produce much in the way of a fresh, original essay about "The Necklace."

You can also develop your ability to treat your subject originally if you plan the body of the essay to build up to what you think is your most important and incisive idea. As examples of such planning, the following brief outline suggests how a central idea can be widened and expanded:

ARGUMENT: *Mathilde Grows as a Character in "The Necklace"*

1. She has normal daydreams about a better life.
2. In trying to make her daydreams seem real, she takes a risk but then loses.
3. She develops by facing her mistake and working hard to correct it.

The list shows how you can enlarge a subject if you treat your exemplifying details in an increasing order of importance. In this case, the order moves from Mathilde's habit of daydreaming to her growing strength of character. The pattern shows how you can meet two primary standards of excellence in writing—organization and growth.

Clearly, you should always try to develop your central idea or argument. Constantly adhere to your topic, and constantly develop it. Nurture it and make it grow. Admittedly, in a short essay you will be able to move only a short distance with an idea or argument, but you should never be satisfied to leave the idea exactly where you found it. To the degree that you can learn to develop your ideas, you will receive recognition for increasingly original writing.

Write with Specific Readers as Your Intended Audience

Whenever you write, you must decide how much detail to discuss. Usually you base this decision on your judgment of your readers. For example, if you assume that they have not read the work, you will need to include a short summary as background. Otherwise, they may not understand your argument.

Consider, too, whether your readers have any special interests or concerns. If they are particularly interested in politics, sociology, religion, or psychology, for example, you may need to select and develop your materials along one of these lines.

Your instructor will let you know who your audience is. Usually, it will be your instructor or your fellow students. They will be familiar with the work and will not expect you to retell a story or summarize an argument. Rather, they will want you to explain and interpret the work in the light of your main assertions about it. Thus, you can omit details that do not exemplify and support your argument, even if these details are important parts of the work. What you write should always be based on your developing idea together with your assessment of your readers.

Use Exact, Comprehensive, and Forceful Language

In addition to being original, organized, and well-developed, the best writing is exact, comprehensive, and forceful. At any stage of the composition process, you should try to correct and improve your earliest sentences and paragraphs, which usually need to be rethought, reworded, and rearranged.

Try to make your sentences meaningful. First, ask yourself whether your sentences mean what you really intend, or whether you can make them more exact and therefore stronger. For example, consider these two sentences from essays about "The Necklace":

1. It seems as though the main character's dreams of luxury cause her to respond as she does in the story.
2. This incident, although it may seem trivial or unimportant, has substantial significance in the creation of the story; by this I mean the incident that occurred is essentially what the story is all about.

These sentences are inexact and vague and therefore are unhelpful. Neither of them goes anywhere. Sentence 1 is satisfactory up to the verb *cause*, but then it falls apart because the writer has lost sight of an argumentative or thematic purpose. It would be better to describe what the response *is* rather than to say nothing more than that some kind of response *exists*. To make the sentence more exact, we might try the following revision.

Mathilde's dreams of luxury make her dissatisfied with her own possessions, and therefore she goes beyond her financial means to attend the big party.

With this revision, the writer could readily go on to consider the relationship of the early part of the story to the later parts. Without the revision, it is not clear where the writer might go.

Sentence 2 is vague because the writer has lost all contact with the main thread of argument. If we adopt the principle of trying to be exact, however, we can create more meaning and more promise:

The accidental loss of the necklace, which is trivial though costly, supports the narrator's claim that major turns in life are produced not by earthshaking events but rather by minor ones.

In addition to working for exactness, try to make sentences—all sentences, but particularly thesis and topic sentences—complete and comprehensive. Consider the following sentence:

> The idea in "The Necklace" is that Mathilde and her husband work hard to pay for the lost necklace.

Although this sentence promises to describe an idea, it does no more than state the story's major action. It needs additional rethinking and rephrasing to make it more comprehensive, as in these two revisions:

1. In "The Necklace" Maupassant brings out the importance of overcoming mistakes through hard work and responsibility.
2. Maupassant's surprise ending in "The Necklace" symbolizes the need for always being truthful.

Both new sentences are connected to the action described by the original phrasing, "Mathilde and her husband work hard to pay for the lost necklace," although they point toward differing treatments. The first sentence concerns the virtue shown by the Loisels in their sacrifice. Because the second sentence includes the word *symbolizes*, an essay stemming from it would stress the Loisels' mistake in not confessing the loss. In dealing with the symbolic meaning of their failure, an essay developed along the lines of the second sentence would focus on the negative sides of their characters, and an essay developed from the first sentence would stress their positive sides. Both of the revised sentences, therefore, are more comprehensive than the original sentence and thus would help a writer get on the track toward a thoughtful and analytical essay.

Of course, creating fine sentences is never easy, but as a mode of improvement, you might use some self-testing mechanisms:

- *For story materials.* Always relate the materials to a point or argument. Do not say simply, "Mathilde works constantly for ten years to help pay off the debt." Instead, blend the material into a point, like this: "Mathilde's ten-year effort shows her resolution to overcome the horror of indebtedness," or "Mathilde's ten-year effort brings out her strength of character."
- *For responses and impressions.* Do not say simply, "The story's ending left me with a definite impression." What are you giving your readers with a sentence like this? They want to know what your impression is, and therefore you need to describe it, as in the following: "The story's ending surprised me and also made me sympathetic to the major character," or "The story's ending struck me with the idea that life is unpredictable and unfair."
- *For ideas.* Make the idea clear and direct. Do not say, "Mathilde lives in a poor household," but rather refer to the story to bring out an idea, as follows: "Mathilde's story shows that economic deprivation hurts a person's quality of life."
- *For critical commentary.* Do not be satisfied with a statement such as "I found 'The Necklace' interesting." All right, the story is interesting, but what does that tell us? Instead, try to describe *what* was interesting and *why* it was interesting, as in this sentence: "I found 'The Necklace' interesting because it shows how chance and bad luck may disrupt or even destroy people's lives."

Good writing begins with attempts, like these, to rephrase sentences to make them really say something. If you always name and pin down descriptions, responses, and judgments, no matter how difficult the task seems, your sentences can be strong and forceful because you will be making them exact and comprehensive.

Illustrative Student Essay (Improved Draft)

If you refer again to the first draft of the essay about Maupassant's use of setting to illustrate Mathilde's character (pp. 36–37), you might notice that several parts of the draft need extensive reworking and revising. For example, paragraph 2 contains a series of short, unconnected comments; and the last sentence of that paragraph implies that Mathilde's dissatisfaction relates mainly to her husband rather than to her general circumstances. Paragraph 4 focuses too much on Mathilde's coarseness and not enough on her sacrifice and cooperation. The first draft also ignores the fact that the story ends in another location—the fashionable Parisian street the Champs-Elysées, where Maupassant continues to demonstrate the nature of Mathilde's character. Finally, there is not enough support in this draft for the contention (in paragraph 5) that everything in the story is related to the character of Mathilde.

To discover how these issues can be more fully considered, the following revision of the earlier draft creates more introductory detail, includes an additional paragraph, and reshapes each of the paragraphs to stress the relationship of the central idea or argument to the topics of the various paragraphs. Within the limits of a short assignment, the essay illustrates all the principles of organization and unity that we have been discussing here.

> Underlined sentences in this paper *do not* conform to MLA style and are used solely as teaching tools to emphasize the central idea, thesis sentence, and topic sentences throughout the paper.

Deal 1

James Deal

Professor Smith

English 102

16 April 2008

How Maupassant Uses Setting in "The Necklace" to Show the

Character of Mathilde

In "The Necklace" Guy de Maupassant uses setting to reflect the character   [1]

and development of the main character, Mathilde Loisel.* As a result, his

*Central idea.

setting is not particularly vivid or detailed. He does not even describe the ill-fated necklace--the central object in the story--but states only that it is "superb" (paragraph 47). In fact he includes descriptions of setting only if they illuminate qualities about Mathilde. Her changing character can be connected to the first apartment, the dream-life mansion rooms, the attic flat, and a fashionable public street.†

[2]   Details about the modest apartment of the Loisels on the Street of Martyrs indicate Mathilde's peevish lack of adjustment to life. Though everything is serviceable, she is unhappy with the "drab" walls, "threadbare" furniture, and "ugly" curtains (paragraph 3). She has domestic help, but she wants more servants than the simple country girl who does the household chores in the apartment. Her embarrassment and dissatisfaction are shown by details of her irregularly cleaned tablecloth and the plain and inelegant beef stew that her husband adores. Even her best theater dress, which is appropriate for apartment life but which is inappropriate for more wealthy surroundings, makes her unhappy. All these details of the apartment establish that Mathilde's major trait at the story's beginning is maladjustment. She therefore seems unpleasant and unsympathetic.

[3]   Like the real-life apartment, the impossibly wealthy setting of her daydreams about owning a mansion strengthens her unhappiness and her avoidance of reality. All the rooms of her fantasies are large and expensive, draped in silk and filled with nothing but the best furniture and bric-a-brac. Maupassant gives us the following description of her dream world:

> She imagined a gourmet-prepared main course carried on the most exquisite trays and served on the most beautiful dishes, with whispered gallantries that she would hear with a sphinxlike smile as she dined on the pink meat of a trout or the delicate wing of a quail.
> (paragraph 4)

With such impossible dreams, her despair is complete. Ironically, this despair, together with her inability to live with reality, brings about her undoing. It makes her agree to borrow the necklace (which is just as unreal as her

† Thesis sentence.

Deal 3

daydreams of wealth), and losing the necklace drives her into the reality of giving up her apartment and moving into the attic flat.

<u>Also ironically, the attic flat is related to the coarsening of her character while at the same time it brings out her best qualities of hard work and honesty</u>. Maupassant emphasizes the drudgery of the work Mathilde endures to maintain the flat, such as walking up many stairs, washing floors with large buckets of water, cleaning greasy and encrusted pots and pans, taking out the garbage, washing clothes by hand, and haggling loudly with local shopkeepers. All this reflects her coarsening and loss of sensibility, also shown by her giving up hair and hand care and by wearing cheap dresses. The work she performs, however, makes her heroic (paragraph 98). As she cooperates to help her husband pay back the loans, her dreams of a mansion fade, and all she has left is the memory of her triumphant appearance at the Minister of Education's party. Thus the attic flat brings out her physical change for the worse at the same time that it also brings out her psychological change for the better. **[4]**

<u>Her walk on the Champs-Elysées illustrates another combination of traits--self-indulgence and frankness</u>. The Champs-Elysées is the most fashionable street in Paris, and her walk to it is similar to her earlier indulgences in her daydreams of upper-class wealth. But it is on this street where she meets Jeanne, and it is her frankness in confessing to Jeanne that makes her completely honest. While the walk thus serves as the occasion for the story's concluding surprise and irony, Mathilde's being on the Champs-Elysées is totally in character, in keeping with her earlier reveries about luxury. **[5]**

<u>Other details in the story also have a similar bearing on Mathilde's character</u>. For example, the story presents little detail about the party scene beyond the statement that Mathilde is a great "success" (paragraph 52)--a judgment that shows her ability to shine if given the chance. After she and Loisel accept the fact that the necklace cannot be found, Maupassant includes details about the Parisian streets, about the visits to loan sharks, and about the **[6]**

Deal 4

jewelry shops in order to bring out Mathilde's sense of honesty and pride as she "heroically" prepares to live her new life of poverty. Thus, in "The Necklace," Maupassant uses setting to highlight Mathilde's maladjustment, her needless misfortune, her loss of youth and beauty, and finally her growth as a responsible human being.

Deal 5

Work Cited

Maupassant, Guy de. "The Necklace." Literature: An Introduction to Reading and Writing. Ed. Edgar V. Roberts. 9th ed. New York: Pearson Longman, 2009, 5–12.

Commentary on the Essay

Several improvements to the first draft are seen here. The language of paragraph 2 has been revised to show more clearly the inappropriateness of Mathilde's dissatisfaction. In paragraph 3, the irony of the story is brought out, and the writer has connected the details to the central idea in a richer pattern of ideas, showing the effects of Mathilde's despair. Paragraph 5—new in the improved draft—includes additional details about how Mathilde's walk on the Champs-Elysées is related to her character. In paragraph 6, the fact that Mathilde is able "to shine" at the dinner party is interpreted according to the central idea. Finally, the conclusion is now much more specific, summarizing the change in Mathilde's character rather than saying simply that the setting reveals "her needless misfortune." In short, the second draft reflects the complexity of "The Necklace" better than the first draft. Because the writer has revised the first-draft ideas about the story, the final essay is tightly structured, insightful, and forceful.

Essay Commentaries

Throughout this book, the illustrative essays are followed by short commentaries that show how the essays embody the chapter instructions and guidelines. For each essay that has a number of possible approaches, the commentary points out which one is used; and when an essay uses two or more approaches, the commentary makes this fact clear. In addition, each commentary singles out one of the paragraphs for more detailed analysis of its argument and use of detail. The commentaries will hence help you develop the insights necessary to use the essays as aids in your own study and writing.

A Summary of Guidelines

To sum up, follow these guidelines whenever you write about a story or any kind of literature:

- Do not simply retell the story or summarize the work. Bring in story materials only when you can use them as support for your central idea or argument.
- Throughout your essay, keep reminding your reader of your central idea.
- Within each paragraph, make sure that you stress your topic idea.
- Develop your subject. Make it bigger than it was when you began.
- Always make your statements exact, comprehensive, and forceful.
- And this bears repeating: Do not simply retell the story or summarize the work.

Writing Topics About the Writing Process

1. Write a brainstorming paragraph on the topic of anything in a literary work that you find especially good or interesting. Write as the thoughts occur to you; do not slow yourself down in an effort to make your writing seem perfect. You can make corrections and improvements later.

2. Using marginal and notebook notations, together with any additional thoughts, describe the way in which the author of a particular work has expressed important ideas and difficulties.

3. Create a plus-minus table to list your responses about a character or ideas in a work.

4. Raise questions about the actions of characters in a story or play in order to determine the various customs and manners of the society out of which the work is derived.

5. Analyze and explain the way in which the conflicts in a story or play are developed. What pattern or patterns do you find? Determine the relationship of the conflicts to the work's development, and fashion your idea of this relationship as an argument for a potential essay.

6. Basing your ideas on your marginal and notebook notations, select an idea and develop a thesis sentence from it, using your idea and a list of possible topics for an argument or central idea for an essay.

7. Using the thesis sentence you write for exercise 6, develop a brief analytical sentence outline that could help you in writing a full essay.

A Short Guide to the Use of References and Quotations in Essays About Literature

In establishing evidence for the points you make in your essays and essay examinations, you constantly need to refer to various parts of stories, plays, and poems. You also need to include shorter and longer quotations and to keep the time sequences straight within the works you are writing about. In addition, you may need to refer to biographical and historical details that have a bearing on the work or works you are studying. So that your own writing may flow as accurately and naturally as possible, you must be able to integrate these references and distinctions of time clearly and easily.

Integrate Passages and Ideas into Your Essay

Your essays should reflect your own thought as you study and analyze the characteristics, ideas, and qualities of an author's work. In a typical discussion of literature, you constantly need to introduce brief summaries, quotations, general interpretations, observations, and independent applications of everything you are discussing. It is not easy to keep these various elements integrated and to keep confusion from arising.

Distinguish Your Thoughts from Those of Your Author

Often a major problem is that it is hard for your reader to figure out when *your* ideas have stopped and your *author's* have begun. You must therefore arrange your sentences to make the distinctions clear, but you must also blend your materials so that your reader may follow you easily. Let us see an example of how such problems may be handled. Here, the writer being discussed is the Victorian poet Matthew Arnold (1822–1888). The passage moves from reference to Arnold's ideas to the essay writer's independent application of the ideas.

> [1] In his poem "Dover Beach," Arnold states that in past times religious faith was accepted as absolute truth. [2] To symbolize this idea he refers to the ocean, which surrounds all land, and the surf, which constantly rushes onto the earth's shores. [3] According to this symbolism, religious ideas are as vast as the ocean and as regular as the surf, and these ideas at one time constantly and irresistibly replenished people's lives. [4] Arnold's symbol of the flowing ocean changes, however, to a symbol of the ebbing ocean, thus illustrating his idea that belief and religious certainty were falling away. [5] It is this personal sense of spiritual emptiness that Arnold is associating with his own times, because what he describes, in keeping with the symbolism, is that in the present time the "drear" shoreline has been left vacant by the "melancholy long withdrawing roar" of retreat and reduction (lines 25–27).

This specimen paragraph combines but also separates paraphrase, interpretation, and quotation, and it thereby eliminates any possible confusion about the origin of the ideas and also about who is saying what. In the first three sentences the writer uses the phrases "Arnold states," "To symbolize this idea," and "According to this symbolism" to show clearly that interpretation is to follow. Although the fourth sentence marks a new direction of Arnold's ideas, it continues to separate restatement from interpretation. The fifth sentence indicates, through the phrase "in keeping with the symbolism," what seems to the writer to be the major idea of "Dover Beach."

Integrate Material by Using Quotation Marks

It is often necessary, and also interesting, to use short quotations from your author to illustrate and reinforce your ideas and interpretations. Here the problem of separating your thoughts from the author's is solved by quotation marks. In such an internal quotation, you may treat prose and poetry in the same way. If a poetic quotation extends from the end of one line to the beginning of another, however, indicate the line break with a virgule (/), and use a capital letter to begin the next line, as in the following:

> In "Lines Written in Early Spring" Wordsworth describes a condition in which his speaker is united with the surrounding natural world. Nature is a combination of the "thousand blended notes" of joyful birds (line 1) and the sights of "budding twigs" (line 17) and the "periwinkle" (line 10). In the exact words of the speaker, these "fair works" directly "link / The human soul that through me ran" (lines 5 and 6).

Blend Quotations into Your Own Sentences

The use of internal quotations still creates the problem of blending materials, however, for quotations should never be brought in unless you prepare your reader for them in some way. *Do not*, for example, use quotations in the following manner:

> Wordsworth states that his woodland grove is filled with the sounds of birds, the sights of flowers, and the feeling of the light wind, making for the thought that creatures of the natural world take pleasure in life. "The birds around me hopped and played."

This abrupt quotation throws the reader off balance because it is not blended into the previous sentence. It is necessary to prepare the reader to move from your discussion to the quotation, as in the following revision:

> Wordsworth claims that his woodland scene is made joyful by the surrounding flowers and the gentle breeze, causing his speaker, who states that "The birds around me hopped and played," to conclude that the natural world has resulted from a "holy plan" created by Nature.

Here the quotation is made an actual part of the sentence. This sort of blending is satisfactory, provided that the quotation is brief.

Indent Long Quotations and Set Them in Block Format

You can follow a general rule for incorporating quotations in your writing: Do not quote within a sentence any passage longer than twenty or twenty-five words (but consult your instructor, for the allowable number of words may vary). Quotations of greater length demand so much separate attention that they interfere with your own sentence. It is possible but not desirable to conclude one of your sentences with a quotation, but you should never make an extensive quotation in the *middle* of a sentence. By the time you finish such an unwieldy sentence, your reader will have lost sight of how it began. When your quotation is long, you should make a point of introducing it and setting it off separately as a block.

The physical layout of block quotations should be this: Double-space the quotation (like the rest of your essay), and indent it ten spaces from your left margin to distinguish it from your own writing. You might use fewer spaces for longer lines of poetry, but the standard should always be to create a balanced, neat page. After the quotation, resume your own discourse at the left margin or with a new paragraph. Do not leave extra lines of space above or below the quotation. Here is a specimen, from an essay about Wordsworth's "Lines Written in Early Spring":

> In "Lines Written in Early Spring" Wordsworth develops an idea that the world of nature is linked directly to the moral human consciousness. He speaks of no religious systems or books of moral values. Instead, he derives his ideas directly from his experience, assuming that the world was made for the joy of the living creatures in it, including human beings ("man"), and that anyone disturbing that power of joy is violating "Nature's holy plan" itself. Wordsworth's moral criticism, in other words, is derived from his faith in the integrity of creation:
>
>> If this belief from heaven be sent,
>> If such be Nature's holy plan,
>> Have I not reason to lament
>> What man has made of man?
>> (lines 21–24)
>
> The concept that morality and life are joined is the most interesting and engaging aspect of the poem. It seems to encourage a live-and-let-live attitude toward others, however, not an active program of direct outreach and help.

When quoting lines of poetry, always remember to quote them *as lines*. Do not run them together as though they were continuous prose. When you create such block quotations, as in the preceding example, you do *not* need quotation marks.

Today, computer usage is the established means of preparing papers, and therefore computer styling has become prominent in the handling of the matters discussed here. If you have style features in your menu, such as "Poem Text" or "Quotation," each of which sets block quotations apart from "Normal" text, you may certainly make use of the features. Be sure to explain to your instructor what you are doing, however, to make sure that your computer's features correspond to the styles that are required for your class.

Use an Ellipsis to Show Omissions

Whether your quotation is long or short, you will often need to change some of the material in it to conform to your own sentence requirements. You might wish to omit something from the quotation that is not essential to your point or to the flow of your sentence. Indicate such omissions with an ellipsis (three spaced periods), as follows (from an essay about Bierce's "An Occurrence at Owl Creek Bridge"):

> Under the immediate threat of death, Farquhar's perceptions are sharpened and heightened. In actuality there is "swirling water . . . racing madly beneath his feet," but it is his mind that is racing swiftly, and he accordingly perceives that a "piece of dancing driftwood . . . down the current" moves so slowly that he believes the stream is "sluggish."

If your quotation is very brief, however, do not use ellipses as they might be more distracting than helpful. For example, do not use them in a quotation like this:

> Keats asserts that ". . . a thing of beauty . . ." always gives joy.

Instead, make your quotation without the ellipses:

> Keats asserts that "a thing of beauty" always gives joy.

Use Square Brackets to Enclose Words That You Add Within Quotations

If you add words of your own to integrate the quotation into your own train of discourse or to explain words that may seem obscure, put square brackets around these words, as in the following passage:

> In "Lines Written in Early Spring," Wordsworth refers to a past experience of extreme happiness, in which Nature seemed to "link/The human soul that through . . . [him] ran." He is describing a state of mystical awareness in which "pleasant thoughts/Bring [him] sad thoughts," and make him "lament" moral and political cruelty (lines 2–8).

Be Careful Not to Overquote

A word of caution: *Do not use too many quotations.* You will be judged on your own thought and on the continuity and development of your own essay. It is tempting to include many quotations on the theory that you need to use examples from the text to illustrate and support your ideas. Naturally, it is important to introduce examples, but you should understand that too many quotations can disturb the flow of your own thought. If your essay consists of many illustrations linked together by no more than your introductory sentences, how much thinking have you actually shown? Try, therefore, to create your own discussion, using appropriate examples to connect your thought to the text or texts you are analyzing.

Preserve the Spellings in Your Source

Always reproduce your source exactly. Sometimes the works of British authors may include words like *tyre, defence, honour,* and *labour*. Duplicate these as you find them. Although most anthologies, such as this one, modernize the spelling of older writers, you may often encounter "old-spelling" editions in which all words—such as *entring, Shew, beautie, ore* (for "over"), *witte* (for "wit"), *specifick, 'twas, guaranty* (for "guarantee"), or *determin'd*—are spelled and capitalized exactly as they were centuries ago. Your principle should be *to duplicate everything exactly as you find it*, even if this means spelling words like *achieve* as *atchieve, music* as *Musick,* or *joke* as *joak*. A student once changed the word *an* to "and" in the construction "an I were" in a Shakespeare play. The result was misleading, because in introductory clauses *an* really meant *if* (or *and if*) and not *and*. Difficulties like this one are rare, but you can avoid them if you reproduce the text as you find it. Should you think that something is either misspelled or confusing as it stands, you may do one of two things:

1. Clarify or correct the confusing word or phrase within brackets, as in the following:

   In 1714, fencing was considered a "Gentlemany [i.e., gentlemanly] subject."

2. Use the word *sic* (Latin for *thus*, meaning "It is this way in the text") in brackets immediately after the problematic word or obvious mistake:

   He was just "finning [sic] his way back to health" when the next disaster struck.

Part II

Reading and Writing
About Fiction

Chapter 1

Fiction: An Overview

Fiction originally meant anything *made up* or *shaped*. As we understand the word today, it refers to *short or long prose stories*—and it has retained this meaning since 1599, the first year for which we have a record for it in print. Fiction is distinguished from the works it imitates, such as *historical accounts, reports, biographies, autobiographies, letters,* and *personal memoirs* and *meditations*. Although fiction often resembles these forms, it has a separate identity because it originates not in historical facts but in the imaginative and creative powers of the author. Writers of fiction may include historically accurate details, but their overriding goal is to tell a story and say something significant about life.

The essence of fiction, as opposed to drama, is **narration,** the recounting or telling of a sequence of events or actions. The earliest works of fiction relied almost exclusively on narration, with speeches or dialogue being reported rather than quoted directly. Much recent fiction includes extended passages of dialogue, thereby becoming more *dramatic* even though narration is still the primary mode.

Fiction is rooted in ancient legends and **myths.** Local priests told stories about their gods and heroes, as shown in some of the narratives of ancient Egypt. In the course of history, traveling storytellers would appear in a court or village to entertain listeners with tales of adventure in faraway countries. Although many of these were fictionalized accounts of events and people who may not ever have existed, they were largely accepted as fact or history. An especially long tale, an **epic,** was recited during a period of days. To aid their memories and to impress and entertain their listeners, the storytellers chanted their tales in poetry, often accompanying themselves on a stringed instrument.

Legends and epics also reinforced the local religions and power structures. Myths of gods like Zeus and Athena (Greece), Jupiter and Minerva (Rome), and Baal and Ishtar (Mesopotamia) abounded, together with stories of famous men and women like Achilles, Aeneas, Atalanta, David, Helen of Troy, Hercules, Joseph, Odysseus, Oedipus, Penelope, Ruth, Romulus and Remus, and Utu-Napishtim. The ancient Macedonian king and general Alexander the Great (356–323 BCE) developed many of his ideas about nobility and valor from *The Iliad,* Homer's epic about the Trojan War—and, we might add, from discussing the epic with his tutor, the philosopher Aristotle.

Perhaps nowhere is the moralistic-argumentative aspect of ancient storytelling better illustrated than in the **fables** of Aesop, a Greek who wrote in the sixth century BCE, and in the parables of Jesus as told in the Gospels of the New Testament (see Chapter 7). In these works, a short narrative provides an illustration of a religious, philosophic, or psychological conclusion.

Starting about eight hundred years ago, storytelling in Western civilization was developed to a fine art by writers such as Marie de France, a Frenchwoman who wrote in

England near the end of the twelfth century, Giovanni Boccaccio (Italian, 1313–1375), and Geoffrey Chaucer (English, c. 1340–1400). William Shakespeare (1564–1616) drew heavily on history and legend for the stories and characters in his plays.

Modern Fiction

Fiction as we understand the word today did not begin to flourish until the seventeenth and eighteenth centuries, when an alteration in the perception of human nature developed. For many centuries the idea had prevailed that human beings were in a fallen moral state—a state of "total depravity"—and that by themselves they needed the controlling hands of monarchy and church to keep them moral, peaceful, and pious. During the Renaissance, however, thinkers began to claim that humanity should be viewed within a perspective of greater and broader latitude. Some people were fallen, yes, but many others were not; and they could become moral through their own efforts without the control of political and moral authorities. It was this analysis that underlay the development of the democratic theory of government that has been accepted in much of modern society.

In literature, it thus became possible to view human beings of all social stations and ways of life as important literary topics. As one writer put it in 1709, human nature is by no means simple, for it is governed by many complex motives such as "passion, humor, caprice, zeal, faction, and a thousand other springs."[1] Observations such as this were the basis of the individual and psychological concerns that characterize fiction today. Indeed, fiction is strong because it is so real and personal. Characters have both first and last names; the countries and cities in which they live are visualized as real places, with real influences on the inhabitants; and their actions and interactions are like those that readers themselves have experienced, could experience, or could readily imagine themselves experiencing.

Along with attention to character, fiction is also concerned with the significance of place or environment on the lives of people. In the simplest sense, location is a backdrop or setting within which characters speak, move, and act. But more broadly, environment comprises the social, economic, and political conditions that affect the outcomes of people's lives. Fiction is primarily about the interactions among people, but it also involves these larger interactions—either directly or indirectly. Indeed, a typical work of fiction includes many forces, both small and large, that influence the ways in which characters meet and deal with their problems.

The first true works of fiction in Europe, however, were less concerned with society or politics than adventure. These were the lengthy Spanish and French **romances** of the sixteenth and seventeenth centuries. In English the word **novel** was borrowed from French and Italian to describe these works and to distinguish them from medieval and classical romances as something that was *new* (the meaning of *novel*). In England the word *story* was used along with *novel* in reference to the new literary form.

The increased levels of education and literacy in the eighteenth century facilitated the development of fiction. During the times of Shakespeare and John Dryden

---

[1] Anthony Ashley Cooper, Third Earl of Shaftesbury, "Sensus Communis," III, 3.

(1631–1700), the only way a writer could make a living from writing was either to be a member of the nobility or have a subsidy from a member of the nobility, or else to have a play accepted at a theater and then receive either a direct payment or the proceeds of an "author's benefit." The paying audiences, however, were limited to people who lived within a short distance of the theater or who had the leisure and money to stay in town and attend the plays during the theater season.

Once great numbers of people could read for themselves, the paying audience for literature expanded. A writer could write a novel and receive money for it from a publisher, who would then profit from a wide sale. Readers could start reading the book when they wished, and they would finish it when it was convenient to do so. Reading a novel could even be a social event, for people would gather together and read to each other as a means of sharing the reading experience. Quite often, as tastes for fiction developed, the writers would publish monthly installments of their novels. When the mail brought these new episodes and chapters, the principal activity would quickly focus on circles of listeners, who would listen eagerly while an expressive reader would bring the stories to life. Often these episodes would extend for many months, and the fiction-consuming public would discuss the latest experiences, and speculate about what would be happening next. With this wider audience of people whom authors would never see or know, it became possible for writers to develop a legitimate career out of their trade. Lengthy fictional stories had arrived as a major genre of literature.

The Short Story

Because novels were long, they took a long time to read—hours, days, even weeks. The early nineteenth-century American writer Edgar Allan Poe (1809–1849) addressed this problem and developed a theory of the **short story,** which he described in a review of Nathaniel Hawthorne's *Twice-Told Tales*. Poe was convinced that "worldly interests" prevented people from gaining the "totality" of comprehension and response that he believed reading should provide. A short, concentrated story (he called it "a brief prose tale" that could be read at a single sitting) was ideal for producing such a strong impression.

In the wake of the taste for short fiction after Poe, many writers have worked in the form. Today, stories are printed in many periodicals, such as *Harper's Magazine*, *The Atlantic Monthly*, and *Zoetrope*, and in many collections, such as *American Short Story Masterpieces*. Some of the better-established writers—William Faulkner, Ernest Hemingway, Shirley Jackson, Flannery O'Connor, Joyce Carol Oates, John Updike, Alice Walker, and Eudora Welty, to name only a small number—have published their stories in separate volumes.

Elements of Fiction I: Verisimilitude and *Donnée*

Fiction, along with drama, has a basis in **realism** or **verisimilitude.** That is, the situations or characters, although they are the invention of writers, are similar to those that many human beings experience, know, or think. Even fantasy, the creation of events that are dreamlike or fantastic, is anchored in the real world, however remotely. This connection of art and life has led some critics to label fiction, and also drama, as an art of imitation. Shakespeare's Hamlet states that an actor attempts to portray real human beings in realistic situations (to "hold a mirror up to Nature").

The same may also be said about writers of fiction, with the provisos that reality is not easily defined and that authors can follow many paths in imitating it. What matters in fiction is the way in which authors establish the ground rules for their works, whether with realistic or nonrealistic characters, places, actions, and physical and chemical laws. The assumption that authors make about the nature of their story material is called a postulate or a premise—what the American novelist Henry James called a *donnée* (something given). The *donnée* of some stories is to resemble the everyday world as much as possible. Eudora Welty's "A Worn Path" is such a story. In it we follow the difficult walk of an elderly woman as she goes from home to a medical office in Natchez, Mississippi, and we also learn of the virtually hopeless futility of her mission. The events of the story are not uncommon; they could happen in life just as Welty presents them.

Once a *donnée* is established, it governs the directions in which the story moves. Jackson's "The Lottery" (Chapter 2), for example, contains a premise or *donnée* that may be phrased like this: "Suppose that a small, ordinary town held a lottery in which the prize was not something good but instead was something bad." Everything in Jackson's story follows from this premise. At first we seem to be reading about innocent actions in a rural American community. By the end, however, in accord with the premise, the story enters the realm of nightmare.

In such ways authors may lead us into remote, fanciful, and symbolic levels of reality, as in Gilman's "The Yellow Wallpaper" (Chapter 10), in which we readers become drawn in to the disoriented world of a narrator who has totally lost her grip on the actuality of the situations around her. In Poe's "The Masque of the Red Death" (Chapter 9), the phantasmagoric *donnée* is that Death may assume a human but sinister shape. Literally nothing is out of bounds as long as the author makes clear the premise for the action.

Scenes and actions such as these, which are not realistic in our ordinary sense of the word, are normal in stories *as long as they follow the author's own stated or implied ground rules.* You may always judge a work by the standard of whether it is consistent with the premise, or the *donnée*, created by the writer.

In addition to referring to various levels of reality, the word *donnée* may also be taken more broadly. In *futuristic* and *science fiction*, for example, there is an assumption or *donnée* of certain situations and technological developments (e.g., interstellar space travel) that are not presently in existence. In a *love story*, the *donnée* is that two people meet and overcome an obstacle of some sort (usually not a serious one) on the way to fulfilling their love. Interesting variations of the love story are James Joyce's "Araby" (Chapter 4), D. H. Lawrence's "The Horse Dealer's Daughter" (Chapter 8), and Alice Munro's "The Found Boat" (Chapter 6).

There are, of course, other types. A *growth* or *apprenticeship story*, for example, is about the development of a major character, such as Jackie in Frank O'Connor's "First Confession" (Chapter 6). In the *detective story*, a mysterious event is posited, and then an individual draws conclusions from the available evidence, as in Susan Glaspell's "A Jury of Her Peers" (Chapter 3), in which the correct detective work is done by two women, not by the legally authorized police investigators.

In addition to setting levels of reality and fictional types, authors may use other controls or springboards as their *données*. Sometimes an initial situation may be the springboard of the narrative, such as the orientation speech in Daniel Orozco's "Orientation" (Chapter 6). Or the key may be a pattern of behavior, such as the boy's reactions to the people around him in O'Connor's "First Confession," or the solution of a mystery about a community icon, as in Faulkner's "A Rose for Emily." A shaping force, or *donnée*, always guides the actions, and often a number of such controls operate at the same time.

Elements of Fiction II: Character, Plot, Structure, and Idea or Theme

Works of fiction share a number of common elements. For reference here, the more significant ones are *character*, *plot*, *structure*, and *idea* or *theme*.

Character Brings Fiction to Life

Stories, like plays, are about characters, who are *not* real people but who are nevertheless *like* real people. A **character** may be defined as a reasonable facsimile of a human being, with all the good and bad traits of being human. Most stories are concerned with characters who are facing a major problem that develops from misunderstanding, misinformation, unfocused ideals and goals, difficult situations, troubled relationships, and generally challenging situations. The characters may win, lose, or tie. They may learn and be the better for the experience or may miss the point and be unchanged.

As we have stated, modern fiction has accompanied the development of a psychological interest in human beings. Psychology itself has grown out of the philosophical and religious idea that people have many inborn capacities—some of them good and others bad. People encounter many problems in their lives, and they make many mistakes; they expend much effort in coping and adjusting. But they nevertheless are important and interesting and are therefore worth writing about, whether male or female; young or old; white, black, tan, or yellow; rich or poor; worker or industrialist; traveler or resident; doctor, librarian, mother, daughter, homemaker, prince, ship captain, bartender, or army lieutenant.

The range of fictional characters is vast: A married couple struggling to repay an enormous debt, a young man learning about the nature of his desires, a woman recalling many conflicts with her mother, two close relatives speculating about the loss of their past, a woman surrounded by her insensitive and self-seeking brothers, a man making triumphs out of his blunders, an unmarried couple dealing with the serious issue of what to do about the possibility of future childbirth, a woman feverishly recollecting her long experience without a man whom she had loved—all these, and more, may be found in fiction just as they may also be found in all levels and conditions of life. Because we all share the same capacities for concern, involvement, sympathy, happiness, sorrow, exhilaration, and disappointment,

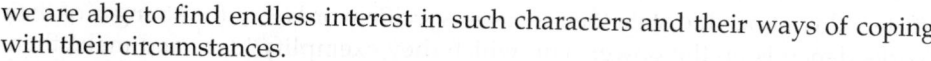

we are able to find endless interest in such characters and their ways of coping with their circumstances.

Plot Is the Plan of Fiction

Fictional characters, who are drawn from life, go through a series of lifelike actions or incidents, which make up the story. In a well-done story, all the actions or incidents, speeches, thoughts, and observations are linked together to make up an entirety, sometimes called an **organic unity.** The essence of this unity is the development and resolution of a **conflict**—or conflicts—in which the **protagonist,** or central character, is engaged. The interactions of causes and effects as they develop sequentially or chronologically make up the story's **plot.** (See the section on writing on pp. 119–125) That is, a story's actions follow one another in time as the protagonist meets and tries to overcome opposing forces. Sometimes plot has been compared to a story's *map, scheme,* or *blueprint.*

Often the protagonist's struggle is directed against another character—an **antagonist.** Just as often, however, the struggle may occur between the protagonist and opposing groups, forces, ideas, and choices—all of which make up a collective antagonist. The conflict may be carried out wherever human beings spend their lives, such as a kitchen, a hotel, a railway station bar, a restaurant, a town square, a schoolroom, an ordinary living room, a church, an exclusive store, a vacation resort, a café, or a battlefield. The conflict may also take place internally, within the mind of the protagonist.

Structure Is the Knitting Together of Fiction

Structure refers to the way a story is assembled. Chronologically, all stories are similar because they move from beginning to end in accord with the time needed for *causes* to produce *effects.* But authors choose many different ways to put their stories together. Some stories are told in straightforward sequential order, and a description of the plot of such stories is identical to a description of the structure. Other stories, however, may get pieced together through out-of-sequence and widely separated episodes, speeches, secondhand reports, vague recollections, accidental discoveries, dreams, nightmares, periods of delirium, fragments of letters, overheard conversations, and the like. In such stories, the plot and the structure diverge widely. Therefore, in dealing with the structure of stories, we emphasize not chronological order but the actual *arrangement* and *development* of the stories as they unfold, part by part. Usually we study an entire story, but we may also direct our attention toward the structure of a smaller aspect of arrangement such as an episode or passage of dialogue.

Idea or Theme Is the Vivifying Thought of Fiction

The word **idea** refers to the result or results of general and abstract thinking. A **theme** is an enactment or embodiment of an idea—an idea in movement, a recurrent idea. Often the two words are used interchangeably. Either directly or indirectly, fiction embodies ideas and **themes** that underlie and give life to stories and novels.

Writers do not need to state their ideas in specific words, but the strength of their works depends on the power with which they exemplify ideas and make them clear. Thus, writers of comic works are committed to the idea that human difficulties can be treated with humor. More serious works often show characters in the throes of difficult moral choices—the idea being that in a losing situation the only winners are those who maintain honor and self-respect. Mystery and suspense stories develop from the idea that problems have solutions, although the solutions at first may seem remote or impossible. Even stories written for entertainment alone, some of which may at first seem devoid of ideas, stem out of an idea or position that the work itself makes clear. Writers may deal with the triumphs and defeats of life, the admirable and the despicable, the humorous and the pathetic; but whatever their goal, they are always expressing ideas about human experience. We may therefore raise questions such as these as we look for ideas in fiction:

- What does this mean?
- Why does the author include it?
- What idea or ideas does it show?
- Why is it significant?

Many works can be discussed in terms of the *issues* that they raise. An **issue** may involve a work's characters in direct or implicit argument or opposition, and it may also bring out crucially important moments of decision about matters of private or public concern. In addition to the issues that the characters face, the works themselves may be considered for their more general issues.

Fictional ideas can also be considered as major themes that tie individual works together. Often an author makes the theme obvious, as in the Aesop fable in which a man uses an ax to kill a fly on another man's forehead. The theme of this fable might loosely be expressed in the sentence "The cure should not be worse than the disease." A major theme in Maupassant's "The Necklace" (p. 5) is that people may be destroyed or saved by the most minor of unforeseeable but sometimes unlucky events.

The process of determining and describing the themes or ideas in stories is never complete; there is always another theme that we can discuss, another issue that may be explored. Thus in Maupassant's "The Necklace," we might note the additional themes that adversity brings out worth, that telling the truth is better than concealing it, that envy often produces ill fortune, that people may build their lives on incorrect assumptions, and that good fortune is never recognized until it is lost. Indeed, one of the ways in which we judge stories is to determine the degree to which they embody a number of valid and important ideas.

Elements of Fiction III: The Writer's Tools

Narration Creates the Sequence and Logic of Fiction

Writers have a number of modes of presentation, or "tools," that they use in their stories. The principal tool (and the heart of fiction) is **narration,** the reporting of actions in sequential order. The object of narration is to *render* the story, to make it clear and to bring it alive to the reader's imagination through the movement of sentences through time. Unlike works of painting and sculpture, the reading and comprehension of a narration cannot be done in a single view. Jacques-Louis David's painting "The Death of Socrates" (p. I–10), for example, is like a narrative because it tells a story—an actual historical occurrence. As related by Plato in the dialogue *Phaedo,* Socrates takes the cup of hemlock, which he will drink as the means of carrying out his own execution. David does include details that tell the story visually. In the rear of the painting some of Socrates' friends have said good-bye and are sorrowfully mounting stairs to leave. Two of the remaining men hold their heads in grief, and two turn toward a wall in despair. The jailer avoids looking at Socrates as he offers the cup of hemlock. Also, on the bed are the unlocked manacles that might have held Socrates, thus emphasizing that he was, all the time, free to walk away had he so chosen. In fact, however, it is only the moment just before Socrates drinks the hemlock that David is able to capture in his painting. As a contrast, the writer of a narrative may include details about the many events leading up to and following such a moment, for a narration moves in a continuous line, from word to word, scene to scene, action to action, and speech to speech. As a result of this chronological movement, the reader's comprehension must necessarily also be chronological.

VISUALIZING FICTION

Cartoons, Graphic Narratives, Graphic Novels

David's painting is in the artistic tradition of "History Painting," which portrays a famous subject, such as *The Death of Socrates,* or *The Thracian Girl Carrying the Head of Orpheus on His Lyre* (see p. I–10, and I–1). A closely connected type of painting is "Genre Painting," which features scenes of ordinary life, such as Brueghel's *Peasants' Dance* (see p. I–8). A modern popular development of such art is the single line-drawn cartoon together with a caption, brought to perfection by the many cartoonists who provided comic panels for *The New Yorker* and also the innumerable other publications that have flourished right up to the present time. The point about most of the cartoons is that they are based in narrative, as are the history and genre painting traditions. In no more than a single picture drawing, clever cartoonists supply the graphic means by which viewers are able to infer how a situation has developed, and how it will conclude.

Whereas the painting traditions featured realistic or semirealistic visions of humanity, however, the cartoonists developed caricatures in their portrayal of their human and animal subjects. One of the many cartoons done for *The New Yorker* by Charles Addams (1912–1988), shows the Addams family, in their characteristically ghoulish garb and appearance, high on a terraced area of their ghostly house, preparing to pour boiling oil down on a group of Christmas choristers. One may easily imagine both the history and future of this event. The Addams cartoons, in this comically macabre vein, were so popular that a series of films and TV programs were successfully developed that dramatized various actions of the family. One of the most popular of modern cartoonists has been Gary Larson (b. 1950), who created thousands of panels for "The Far Side," the title of the syndicated cartoons he drew to popular acclaim from 1980 to 1995. Many of Larson's devoted followers expressed great regret when he gave up these cartoons. As his narrative technique, Larson created a situation that is easily followed because of both the various signs and also demonstrative actions of his characters, many of whom are not just caricatures of doughy and distorted human beings, but also of alien travelers, cows, ducks, dogs, snakes, spiders, ocean monsters, bears, deer, rhinoceroses, and comparable creatures. Even though there is no more than just a single picture in the typical Larson cartoon, Larson skillfully supplies a comic caption and the artistic narrative details from which readers may easily infer both the beginning and the ending.

Closely connected to the single panel cartoon, another major popular mode of narrative presentation is the comic strip, which became a part of regular daily newspapers in the twentieth century. Usually the comics were printed in three or four panels during each day of the week, and then on Sundays there was a color strip, usually involving as many as a dozen narrative cartoon panels. Often there was a continuous story in these strips that held the interest of readers for a number of months. From 1933 until 1987, for example, a strip featuring "Brick Bradford" continued regularly. The story, mainly science fiction, was played out both on a global and universal scale. One interesting adventure involved Brick and company taking a trip in a uniquely compressing and expanding spaceship, which reduced them to such an infinitely small degree that they could engage in an adventure on one of the atoms within the eye of a Lincoln-head penny. Other extremely popular comics featured Dick Tracy, a prominent detective concerned with solving crimes and capturing criminals (still regularly published), and *Terry and the Pirates* (1934–1973), a strip that took its readers to those wars in Asia that led up to and included American involvement in the Pacific Theater of operations during World War II. So popular were these comic strips that quarterly publications were soon issued, in which crime fighters like Superman, Batman, and The Specter would be the heroes of as many as four separate and complete adventure narratives.

Following World War II, many writers, collaborating with cartoonists, went beyond the traditional comic book limitations and started to adapt the comic book format for more serious and systematic novels. Well-known literary works first reached many readers through this medium, and many readers became so interested that they actually went on to read and appreciate the originals. In addition, many writers and cartoonists worked to create new graphically based works, often called "graphic novels." Perhaps the most famous of these is *Maus,* by Art Spiegelman, the winner of a Special Pulitzer Prize award in 1992. *Maus* is a work in the comic/graphic format that describes the horror and brutality of the German concentration camps, as witnessed by his father, during World War II (see p. 66). The form has proliferated and has reached the level of its own narrative/dramatic type. A number of separate "Sin City yarns" by Frank Miller (b. 1957), for example, has been used as the basis for popular films. In 2007, a graphic novel originally by Miller, with Lynn Varley, was *300,* which was made into a film dramatizing the story of the ancient battle between Greeks and Persians at Thermopylae.

DAN PIRARO Cartoon from *Bizarro*

Dan Piraro is a multitalented and prize-winning cartoonist, who was born in the latter twenti-eth century and educated in Oklahoma. He was especially artistic, and when working in the ad-vertising department at Neiman-Marcus he would sketch out unique cartoons that fascinated and entertained his co-workers. With such material, he successfully began syndicating his work in 1985, just five years after Gary Larson first syndicated his The Far Side. *Piraro named his cartoons* Bizarro *because of the closeness in sound to his own name, and also because of the ob-vious closeness to the Italian word* bizzarro *and our own word* bizarre. *His devoted followers, who look forward eagerly to his daily* Bizarro *cartoons which appear in many newspapers throughout the country, have termed his work as "surreal," "ascerbic," "oddball," and "off the wall." In addition to being a cartoonist, Piraro has also developed his skills as a speaker and a showman. He continues to do fine art, and to date has published eleven separate books, two of which are the recent* The Three Little Pigs Buy the White House *(2004) and* Bizarro and Other Strange Manifestations of the Art of Dan Piraro *(2006).*

QUESTIONS

1. How does Piraro establish the narrative situation of this cartoon? On what very fa-mous work of art does the drawing depend? What is the narrative in the original work? What is the narrative in Piraro's cartoon? How is the cartoon narrative particu-larly modern?

2. Why would the cartoon not be as funny as it is if we did not recognize the original from which the cartoon is derived?

3. On the basis of the contrast between the story in the cartoon and the story in the origi-nal to which it alludes, what principles of humor can you develop and describe?

ART SPIEGELMAN Page from *Maus*

Art Spiegelman (b. 1948) was born in Sweden and came to the United States with his parents. When in high school, he became fascinated with the art of cartooning and made that his profes-sion. For more than twenty years he worked at designing popular products, including such things as candy wrappers. He also spent a number of years teaching at the School for Visual Arts in New York, and he founded a comic magazine, Raw. *His most accomplished work is his graphic novel* Maus, *a page of which is included here as an illustration of the subject and tech-nique. Another of Spiegelman's honors was a Guggenheim Fellowship.*

Style Is the Author's Skill in Bringing Language to Life

The medium of fiction and of all literature is language, and the manipulation of language—the style—is a primary skill of the writer. A mark of a good style is the use of active verbs and nouns that are specific and concrete. Even with the most

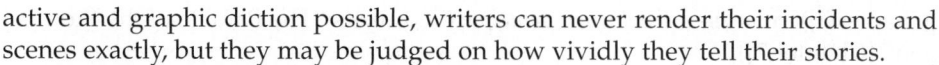

active and graphic diction possible, writers can never render their incidents and scenes exactly, but they may be judged on how vividly they tell their stories.

Point of View Guides What We See and Understand in Fiction

One of the most important ways in which writers knit their stories together, and also an important way in which they try to interest and engage readers, is through the careful control of **point of view**—the *voice* of the story, the speaker who does the narrating. It is the way the story establishes authenticity, either in reality or unreality. It may be regarded as the story's *focus*, the *angle of vision* from which things are not only seen and reported but also judged.

Basically, there are two kinds of point of view, but there are many, many variations, sometimes obvious and sometimes subtle. In the first-person point of view, a fictitious observer tells us what he or she saw, heard, concluded, and thought. This viewpoint is characterized by the use of the pronoun *I*, as the speaker refers to his or her position as an observer or commentator. The speaker or narrator—terms that are interchangeable—may sometimes seem to be the author speaking directly using an authorial voice. More often, however, the speaker is an independent character—a persona with characteristics that separate her or him from the author.

In common with all narrators, the first-person narrator establishes a clearly defined relationship to the story's events. Some narrators are deeply engaged in the action and are major movers; others are only minor participants or observers; still others have had nothing to do with the action but are transmitting the reports of others who were more fully involved. Sometimes the narrator uses the *we* pronoun if he or she is or has been part of a group that has witnessed the action or participated in it. Often, too, the narrator might use *we* when referring to ideas and interpretations shared with the reader or listener—the idea being to draw readers into the story as much as possible.

The third-person point of view uses third-person pronouns (*she, he, it, they, her, him, them,* etc.).[2] The third-person point of view may be (1) **limited,** with the focus being on one particular character and what he or she does, says, hears, thinks, and otherwise experiences; (2) **omniscient,** with the possibility that the activities and thoughts of all the characters are open and fully known by the speaker; or (3) **dramatic, or objective,** in which the story is confined *only* to the reporting of actions and speeches, with no commentary and no revelation of the thoughts of any of the characters unless the characters themselves express their thoughts dramatically.

Understanding point of view usually requires subtlety of perception—indeed, it may be one of the most difficult of all concepts in the study of fiction. In fuller perspective, therefore, we may think of it as the *total position* from which things are viewed, understood, and communicated. The position might be simply physical: *Where was the speaker located when the events occurred? Does the speaker give us a close or distant view of the events?* The position might also be personal or philosophical: *Do the events illustrate a personal opinion* (Maupassant's "The Necklace" [Part I p. 6]), *embody a philosophical judgment* (Hawthorne's "Young Goodman Brown"

---

[2] The possibilities of a second-person point of view are discussed in Chapter 2, p. 132.

[Chapter 7]), or *argue a theological principle* (St. Luke's "The Parable of the Prodigal Son" [Chapter 7])?

Point of view is one of the major ways by which authors make fiction vital. By controlling point of view, an author helps us make reasonable inferences about the story's actions. Authors use point of view to raise some of the same questions in fiction that perplex us in life. We need to evaluate what fictional narrators as well as real people tell us, for what they say is affected by their limitations, attitudes, opinions, and degree of candidness. The first-person narrator of James Joyce's "Araby" (Chapter 4) describes a series of boyhood incidents leading up to his memory that he had deceived himself with vain desires. In other words, he emphasizes what he considers to be his own shortcomings. But we might also realize that this narrator is unwittingly showing that it was not he who was at fault, but rather the religious and moral structure of which he was a part. For readers, the perception of a fictional point of view can be as complex as life itself, and it may be as difficult—in fiction as in life—to evaluate our sources of information.

Description Creates the World of Fiction

Together with narration, a vital aspect of fiction is **description**—those words that cause readers to imagine or re-create the scenes and actions of a story. Description can be both physical (places and persons) and psychological (an emotion or set of emotions). Because excessive description sometimes interrupts or postpones a story's actions, many writers include only as much as is necessary to provide locations for what is happening in the story.

Mood and atmosphere are important aspects of descriptive writing, and to the degree that descriptions are evocative, they may reach the level of **metaphor** and **symbolism**. These characteristics of fiction are a property of all literature, and you will also encounter them whenever you read poems and plays.

Dialogue Creates Interactions Among Fictional Characters

Another major tool of the writer of fiction is **dialogue.** By definition, dialogue is the conversation of two people, but more than two characters may also participate. It is of course the major medium of the playwright, and it is one of the means by which fiction writers bring vividness and dramatic tension to their stories. Straight narration and description can do no more than make a secondhand assertion ("hearsay") that a character's thoughts and responses exist, but dialogue makes everything firsthand and real.

Dialogue is hence a means of *showing* or *actualizing* rather than *reporting*. If characters feel pain or declare love, their own words may be taken as the expression of what is on their minds. Some dialogue may be terse and minimal. Other dialogue may be expanded, depending on the situation, the personalities of the characters, and the author's intent. Dialogue may concern any topic, including everyday and practical matters, personal feelings, reactions to the past, future plans, changing thoughts, sudden realizations, and ideas—be they political, social, philosophical, or religious.

The language of dialogue indicates the intelligence, articulateness, educational levels, or emotional states of the speakers. Hence the author might use *grammatical mistakes, faulty pronunciation,* or *slang* to show a character of limited or disadvantaged background or a character who is trying to be seen in that light. *Dialect* shows the region from which the speaker comes, just as *accent* indicates a place of national origin. *Jargon* and *cliché* suggest self-inflation or intellectual limitations—usually reasons for laughter. The use of *private or intimate expressions* clearly shows people who are close to each other emotionally. Speech that is interrupted by *voiced pauses* (for example, "er," "ah," "um," "y'know") or speech characterized by *inappropriate words* might show a character who is unsure or not in control. There are many possibilities in dialogue, but no matter what qualities you find, writers include dialogue to enable you to know their characters better.

Tone and Irony Guide Our Perceptions of Fictional Works

In every story we may consider **tone**—the ways in which authors convey attitudes toward readers and also toward the work's subjects. One of the major components of tone—**irony**—refers to language and situations that seem to reverse normal expectations. *Word choice* is the characteristic of **verbal irony,** in which what is meant is usually the opposite of what is said, as when we *mean* that people are doing badly even though we *say* that they are doing well. Broader forms of irony are situational and dramatic. **Situational irony** refers to circumstances in which bad things happen to good people, or in which rewards are not earned because forces beyond human comprehension seem to be in total control, making the world seem arbitrary and often absurd. In **dramatic irony** characters have only a nonexistent, partial, incorrect, or misguided understanding of what is happening to them, while both readers and other characters understand the situation more fully. Readers hence become concerned about the characters and hope that the characters will develop understanding quickly enough to avoid the problems bedeviling them and the pitfalls endangering them.

Symbolism and Allegory Relate Fiction to the Larger World

In literature broadly, as in fiction narrowly, even apparently ordinary things may be seen as **symbols**—everyday objects, occurrences, speeches, actions, and characters that may be understood to have meaning (or meanings) in excess of their obvious function and texture. Some symbols are widely recognized and therefore are considered as **cultural** or **universal.** Water, flowers, jewels, aspects of topography, the sun, certain stars, the flag, altars, and minarets are examples of cultural symbols. Other symbols are **contextual;** that is, they take on symbolic meaning only in their individual works, as when in Maupassant's "The Necklace" (Part I), Mathilde and her husband move into an attic flat so that they may save money. This action may be taken as representative or symbolic of their loss of economic and social status.

When a complete story, in addition to maintaining its own narrative integrity, can be applied point by point to a parallel set of situations, it is an **allegory.** Many stories are not complete allegories, however, even though they may contain sections having allegorical parallels. For instance, the Loisels' long servitude in Maupassant's "The Necklace" is similar to the lives and activities of many people who perform tasks for mistaken or meaningless reasons. "The Necklace," therefore, has allegorical overtones even though it is not, in totality, an allegory.

Commentary Provides Us with an Author's Thoughts

Writers may also include **commentary,** analysis, or interpretation, in the expectation that readers need insight into the characters and their actions. When fiction was new, authors often expressed such commentary directly. Henry Fielding (1707–1754) divided his novels into "books" and included a chapter of personal and philosophical commentary at the beginning of each of these. In the next century, George Eliot (1819–1880) included many extensive passages of commentary in her novels.

Later writers have kept commentary at a minimum, preferring instead to concentrate on direct action and dialogue, thereby allowing readers to draw their own conclusions about meaning. In first-person narrations, however, we may expect the narrators to make their own personal comments. Such observations may be accepted at face value, but we should recognize that anything the speakers say is also a mode of character disclosure and therefore just as much a part of the total story as the narrative incidents.

The Elements Together Are Present in Works of Fiction

These, then, are the major tools of fiction, which authors usually employ simultaneously in their works. Thus the story may be told by a character who is a witness, and thus it has a *first-person point of view.* The major *character,* the *protagonist,* goes through a series of actions as a result of a carefully arranged *plot.* Because of this plot, together with the author's chosen method of *narration,* the story will follow a certain kind of arrangement, or *structure,* such as a straightforward sequence or a disjointed series of episodes. The action may demonstrate the story's *theme* or central *idea.* The writer's *style* may be manifested in ironic expressions. The description of the character's actions may reveal *irony of situation,* while at the same time this situation is made vivid through *dialogue* in which the character is a participant. Because the plight of the character is like the plight of many persons in the world, this character may be considered as a *symbol,* and the various actions of his story may be considered as an *allegory.*

Throughout each story we read, no matter what characteristics we are considering, it is most important to realize that a work of fiction is an entirety, a unity. Any reading of a story should be undertaken not to break things down into parts but to understand and assimilate the work *as a whole.* The separate analysis of various topics is thus a *means* to that end, *not* the end itself. The study of fiction, like the study of all literature, is designed to foster our growth and to increase our understanding of the human condition.

Stories for Study

Ambrose Bierce . . . . An Occurrence at Owl Creek Bridge, 71

Edwidge Danticat . . . . Night Talkers, 77

William Faulkner . . . . A Rose for Emily, 89

Tim O'Brien . . . . The Things They Carried, 95

Luigi Pirandello . . . . War, 106

Alice Walker . . . . Everyday Use, 108

Eudora Welty . . . . A Worn Path, 114

AMBROSE BIERCE (1842–1914?)

Bierce was a native of Ohio, the youngest of nine children in the highly religious family of a poor farmer. When the Civil War began, he enlisted in the Union army as a drummer boy and rose to the rank of major by the war's end. After the war he went to San Francisco to begin a career in journalism. At various times he report- ed, edited, and wrote reviews for papers such as the San Francisco Examiner *and the* San Francisco News-Letter. *After he mar- ried, he and his wife spent five years in England, but eventually she left him and their two children died—events that had an em- bittering effect on him. In 1913 he traveled to Mexico, and nothing further is known about him; he is presumed to have died in revolutionary fighting there in 1914. Bierce published his first story in 1871 and later published two volumes of stories:* In the Midst of Life *(1892, originally published in 1891 as* Tales of Soldiers and Civilians, *which included "An Occurrence at Owl Creek Bridge"), and* Can Such Things Be? *(1893). He is perhaps best known for his sometimes cynical* The Devil's Dictionary *(1911). He favored the short story as a form over the novel on much the same grounds as Poe—namely, that the story could be designed to produce a single effect. He believed that fiction should be realistic and should build to concluding twists and surprises—goals that are seen in "An Occurrence at Owl Creek Bridge." His complete works, which he edited himself, appeared in twelve vol- umes from 1909 to 1912.*

An Occurrence at Owl Creek Bridge (1891)

A man stood upon a railroad bridge in northern Alabama, looking down into the swift water twenty feet below. The man's hands were behind his back, the wrists bound with a cord. A rope closely encircled his neck. It was attached to a stout cross-timber above his head and the slack fell to the level of his knees. Some loose boards laid upon the sleepers supporting the metals of the railway supplied a footing for him and his executioners—two private soldiers of the Federal army, directed by a sergeant who in civil life may have been a deputy sheriff. At a short remove upon the same temporary platform was an officer in the uniform of his rank, armed. He was a captain. A sentinel at each end of the bridge stood with his rifle in the position known as "support," that is to say, vertical in front of the left shoulder, the hammer resting on the forearm thrown straight across the chest—a formal and unnatural position, enforcing an erect carriage of the body. It did not appear to be the duty of these two men to know what was occurring at the center of the bridge; they merely blockaded the two ends of the foot planking that traversed it.

Beyond one of the sentinels nobody was in sight; the railroad ran straight away into a forest for a hundred yards, then, curving, was lost to view. Doubtless there was an outpost farther along. The other bank of the stream was open ground—a gentle acclivity topped with a stockade of vertical tree trunks, loopholed for rifles, with a single embrasure through which protruded the muzzle of a brass cannon commanding the bridge. Midway of the slope between the bridge and fort were the spectators—a single company of infantry in line, at "parade rest," the butts of the rifles on the ground, the barrels inclining slightly backward against the right shoulder, the hands crossed upon the stock. A lieutenant stood at the right of the line, the point of his sword upon the ground, his left hand resting upon his right. Excepting the group of four at the center of the bridge, not a man moved. The company faced the bridge, staring stonily, motionless. The sentinels, facing the banks of the stream, might have been statues to adorn the bridge. The captain stood with folded arms, silent, observing the work of his subordinates, but making no sign. Death is a dignitary who when he comes announced is to be received with formal manifestations of respect, even by those most familiar with him. In the code of military etiquette silence and fixity are forms of deference.

The man who was engaged in being hanged was apparently about thirty-five years of age. He was a civilian, if one might judge from his habit, which was that of a planter. His features were good—a straight nose, firm mouth, broad forehead, from which his long, dark hair was combed straight back, falling behind his ears to the collar of his well-fitting frock coat. He wore a mustache and pointed beard, but no whiskers; his eyes were large and dark gray, and had a kindly expression which one would hardly have expected in one whose neck was in the hemp. Evidently this was no vulgar assassin. The liberal military code makes provision for hanging many kinds of persons, and gentlemen are not excluded.

The preparations being complete, the two private soldiers stepped aside and each drew away the plank upon which he had been standing. The sergeant turned to the captain, saluted and placed himself immediately behind that officer, who in turn moved apart one pace. These movements left the condemned man and the sergeant standing on the two ends of the same plank, which spanned three of the cross-ties of the bridge. The end upon which the civilian stood almost, but not quite, reached a fourth. This plank had been held in place by the weight of the captain; it was now held by that of the sergeant. At a signal from the former the latter would step aside, the plank would tilt and the condemned man go down between two ties. The arrangement commended itself to his judgment as simple and effective. His face had not been covered nor his eyes bandaged. He looked a moment at his "unsteadfast footing," then let his gaze wander to the swirling water of the stream racing madly beneath his feet. A piece of dancing driftwood caught his attention and his eyes followed it down the current. How slowly it appeared to move! What a sluggish stream!

5 He closed his eyes in order to fix his last thoughts upon his wife and children. The water, touched to gold by the early sun, the brooding mists under the banks at some distance down the stream, the fort, the soldiers, the piece of driftwood—all had distracted him. And now he became conscious of a new disturbance. Striking through the thought of his dear ones was a sound which he could neither ignore nor understand, a sharp, distinct, metallic percussion like the stroke of a blacksmith's hammer upon the anvil; it had the same ringing quality. He wondered what it was, and whether immeasurably distant or near by—it seemed both. Its recurrence was regular, but as slow as the tolling of a death knell. He awaited each stroke with impatience and—he knew not why—apprehension. The intervals of silence grew progressively longer; the delays became maddening. With their greater infrequency the sounds increased in strength and sharpness. They hurt his ear like the thrust of a knife; he feared he would shriek. What he heard was the ticking of his watch.

He unclosed his eyes and saw again the water below him. "If I could free my hands," he thought, "I might throw off the noose and spring into the stream. By diving I could evade the bullets and, swimming vigorously, reach the bank, take to the woods and get away home. My home, thank God, is as yet outside their lines; my wife and little ones are still beyond the invader's farthest advance."

As these thoughts, which have here to be set down in words, were flashed into the doomed man's brain rather than evolved from it the captain nodded to the sergeant. The sergeant stepped aside.

II

Peyton Farquhar was a well-to-do planter, of an old and highly respected Alabama family. Being a slave owner and like other slave owners a politician he was naturally an original secessionist and ardently devoted to the Southern cause. Circumstances of an imperious nature, which it is unnecessary to relate here, had prevented him from taking service with the gallant army that had fought the disastrous campaigns ending with the fall of Corinth,° and he chafed under the inglorious restraint, longing for the release of his energies, the larger life of the soldier, the opportunity for distinction. That opportunity, he felt, would come, as it comes to all in war time. Meanwhile he did what he could. No service was too humble for him to perform in aid of the South, no adventure too perilous for him to undertake if consistent with the character of a civilian who was at heart a soldier, and who in good faith and without too much qualification assented to at least a part of the frankly villainous dictum that all is fair in love and war.

One evening while Farquhar and his wife were sitting on a rustic bench near the entrance to his grounds, a gray-clad soldier rode up to the gate and asked for a drink of water. Mrs. Farquhar was only too happy to serve him with her own white hands. While she was fetching the water her husband approached the dusty horseman and inquired eagerly for news from the front.

"The Yanks are repairing the railroads," said the man, "and are getting ready for another   10
advance. They have reached the Owl Creek bridge, put it in order and built a stockade on the north bank. The commandant has issued an order, which is posted everywhere, declaring that any civilian caught interfering with the railroad, its bridges, tunnels or trains will be summarily hanged. I saw the order."

"How far is it to the Owl Creek bridge?" Farquhar asked.

"About thirty miles."

"Is there no force on this side of the creek?"

"Only a picket post half a mile out, on the railroad, and a single sentinel at this end of the bridge."

"Suppose a man—a civilian and student of hanging—should elude the picket post and   15
perhaps get the better of the sentinel," said Farquhar, smiling, "what could he accomplish?"

The soldier reflected. "I was there a month ago," he replied, "I observed that the flood of last winter had lodged a great quantity of driftwood against the wooden pier at this end of the bridge. It is now dry and would burn like tow."

The lady had now brought the water, which the soldier drank. He thanked her ceremoniously, bowed to her husband and rode away. An hour later, after nightfall, he repassed the plantation, going northward in the direction from which he had come. He was a Federal scout.

III

As Peyton Farquhar fell straight downward through the bridge he lost consciousness and was as one already dead. From this state he was awakened—ages later, it seemed to him— by the pain of a sharp pressure upon his throat, followed by a sense of suffocation. Keen,

---

° *Corinth:* In the northeast corner of Mississippi, near the Alabama state line, Corinth was the site of a battle in 1862 won by the Union army.

poignant agonies seemed to shoot from his neck downward through every fiber of his body and limbs. These pains appeared to flash along well-defined lines of ramification and to beat with an inconceivably rapid periodicity. They seemed like streams of pulsating fire heating him to an intolerable temperature. As to his head, he was conscious of nothing but a feeling of fulness—of congestion. These sensations were unaccompanied by thought. The intellectual part of his nature was already effaced; he had power only to feel, and feeling was torment. He was conscious of motion. Encompassed in a luminous cloud, of which he was now merely the fiery heart, without material substance, he swung through unthinkable arcs of oscillation, like a vast pendulum. Then all at once, with terrible suddenness, the light about him shot upward with the noise of a loud plash; a frightful roaring was in his ears, and all was cold and dark. The power of thought was restored; he knew that the rope had broken and he had fallen into the stream. There was no additional strangulation; the noose about his neck was already suffocating him and kept the water from his lungs. To die of hanging at the bottom of a river!—the idea seemed to him ludicrous. He opened his eyes in the darkness and saw above him a gleam of light, but how distant, how inaccessible! He was still sinking, for the light became fainter and fainter until it was a mere glimmer. Then it began to grow and brighten, and he knew that he was rising toward the surface—knew it with reluctance, for he was now very comfortable. "To be hanged and drowned," he thought, "that is not so bad; but I do not wish to be shot. No; I will not be shot; that is not fair."

He was not conscious of an effort, but a sharp pain in his wrist apprised him that he was trying to free his hands. He gave the struggle his attention, as an idler might observe the feat of a juggler, without interest in the outcome. What splendid effort—what magnificent, what superhuman strength! Ah, that was a fine endeavor! Bravo! The cord fell away; his arms parted and floated upward; the hands dimly seen on each side in the growing light. He watched them with a new interest as first one and then the other pounced upon the noose at his neck. They tore it away and thrust it fiercely aside, its undulations resembling those of a water snake. "Put it back, put it back!" He thought he shouted these words to his hands, for the undoing of the noose had been succeeded by the direst pang that he had yet experienced. His neck ached horribly; his brain was on fire; his heart, which had been fluttering faintly, gave a great leap, trying to force itself out at his mouth. His whole body was racked and wrenched with an insupportable anguish! But his disobedient hands gave no heed to the command. They beat the water vigorously with quick, downward strokes, forcing him to the surface. He felt his head emerge; his eyes were blinded by the sunlight; his chest expanded convulsively, and with a supreme and crowning agony his lungs engulfed a great draught of air, which instantly he expelled in a shriek!

20   He was now in full possession of his physical senses. They were indeed, preternaturally keen and alert. Something in the awful disturbance of his organic system had so exalted and refined them that they made record of things never before perceived. He felt the ripples upon his face and heard their separate sounds as they struck. He looked at the forest on the bank of the stream, saw the individual trees, the leaves and the veining of each leaf—saw the very insects upon them: the locusts, the brilliant-bodied flies, the gray spiders stretching their webs from twig to twig. He noted the prismatic colors in all the dewdrops upon a million blades of grass. The humming of the gnats that danced above the eddies of the stream, the beating of the dragon flies' wings, the strokes of the water-spiders' legs, like oars which had lifted their boat—all these made audible music. A fish slid along beneath his eyes and he heard the rush of its body parting the water.

He had come to the surface facing down the stream; in a moment the visible world seemed to wheel slowly round, himself the pivotal point, and he saw the bridge, the fort, the soldiers upon the bridge, the captain, the sergeant, the two privates, his executioners. They were in silhouette against the blue sky. They shouted and gesticulated, pointing at him. The captain had drawn his pistol, but did not fire; the others were unarmed. Their movements were grotesque and horrible, their forms gigantic.

Suddenly he heard a sharp report and something struck the water smartly within a few inches of his head, spattering his face with spray. He heard a second report, and saw one of the sentinels with his rifle at his shoulder, a light cloud of blue smoke rising from the muzzle. The man in the water saw the eye of the man on the bridge gazing into his own through the sights of the rifle. He observed that it was a gray eye and remembered having read that gray eyes were keenest, and that all famous marksmen had them. Nevertheless, this one had missed.

A counter-swirl had caught Farquhar and turned him half round; he was again looking into the forest on the bank opposite the fort. The sound of a clear, high voice in a monotonous singsong now rang out behind him and came across the water with a distinctness that pierced and subdued all other sounds, even the beating of the ripples in his ears. Although no soldier, he had frequented camps enough to know the dread significance of that deliberate, drawling, aspirated chant; the lieutenant on shore was taking a part in the morning's work. How coldly and pitilessly—with what an even, calm intonation, presaging, and enforcing tranquility in the men—with what accurately measured intervals fell those cruel words:

"Attention, company! . . . Shoulder arms! . . . Ready! . . . Aim! . . . Fire!"

Farquhar dived—dived as deeply as he could. The water roared in his ears like the voice   25 of Niagara, yet he heard the dulled thunder of the volley and, rising again toward the surface, met shining bits of metal, singularly flattened, oscillating slowly downward. Some of them touched him on the face and hands, then fell away, continuing their descent. One lodged between his collar and neck; it was uncomfortably warm and he snatched it out.

As he rose to the surface, gasping for breath, he saw that he had been a long time under water; he was perceptibly farther down stream—nearer to safety. The soldiers had almost finished reloading; the metal ramrods flashed all at once in the sunshine as they were drawn from the barrels, turned in the air, and thrust into their sockets. The two sentinels fired again, independently and ineffectually.

The hunted man saw all this over his shoulder; he was now swimming vigorously with the current. His brain was as energetic as his arms and legs; he thought with the rapidity of lightning.

"The officer," he reasoned, "will not make that martinet's error a second time. It is as easy to dodge a volley as a single shot. He has probably already given the command to fire at will. God help me, I cannot dodge them all!"

An appalling plash within two yards of him was followed by a loud, rushing sound, *diminuendo*, which seemed to travel back through the air to the fort and died in an explosion which stirred the very river to its deeps! A rising sheet of water curved over him, fell down upon him, blinded him, strangled him! The cannon had taken a hand in the game. As he shook his head free from the commotion of the smitten water he heard the deflected shot humming through the air ahead, and in an instant it was cracking and smashing the branches in the forest beyond.

"They will not do that again," he thought; "the next time they will use a charge of grape.   30 I must keep my eye upon the gun; the smoke will apprise me—the report arrives too late; it lags behind the missile. That is a good gun."

Suddenly he felt himself whirled round and round—spinning like a top. The water, the banks, the forests, the now distant bridge, fort and men—all were commingled and blurred. Objects were represented by their colors only; circular horizontal streaks of color— that was all he saw. He had been caught in a vortex and was being whirled on with a velocity of advance and gyration that made him giddy and sick. In a few moments he was flung upon the gravel at the foot of the left bank of the stream—the southern bank—and behind a projecting point which concealed him from his enemies. The sudden arrest of his motion, the abrasion of one of his hands on the gravel, restored him, and he wept with delight. He dug his fingers into the sand, threw it over himself in handfuls and audibly blessed it. It looked like diamonds, rubies, emeralds; he could think of nothing beautiful which it did not resemble. The trees upon the bank were giant garden plants; he noted a definite order in their arrangement, inhaled the fragrance of their blooms. A strange, roseate light shone through the spaces among their trunks and the wind made in their branches the music of æolian harps. He had no wish to perfect his escape—was content to remain in that enchanting spot until retaken.

A whiz and rattle of grapeshot among the branches high above his head roused him from his dream. The baffled cannoneer had fired him a random farewell. He sprang to his feet, rushed up the sloping bank, and plunged into the forest.

All that day he traveled, laying his course by the rounding sun. The forest seemed interminable; nowhere did he discover a break in it, not even a woodman's road. He had not known that he lived in so wild a region. There was something uncanny in the revelation.

By nightfall he was fatigued, footsore, famishing. The thought of his wife and children urged him on. At last he found a road which led him in what he knew to be the right direction. It was as wide and straight as a city street, yet it seem untraveled. No fields bordered it, no dwelling anywhere. Not so much as the barking of a dog suggested human habitation. The black bodies of the trees formed a straight wall on both sides, terminating on the horizon in a point, like a diagram in a lesson in perspective. Overhead, as he looked up through this rift in the wood, shone great golden stars looking unfamiliar and grouped in strange constellations. He was sure they were arranged in some order which had a secret and malign significance. The wood on either side was full of singular noises, among which—once, twice, and again—he distinctly heard whispers in an unknown tongue.

35   His neck was in pain and lifting his hand to it found it horribly swollen. He knew that it had a circle of black where the rope had bruised it. His eyes felt congested; he could no longer close them. His tongue was swollen with thirst; he relieved its fever by thrusting it forward from between his teeth into the cold air. How softly the turf had carpeted the untraveled avenue—he could no longer feel the roadway beneath his feet!

Doubtless, despite his suffering, he had fallen asleep while walking, for now he sees another scene—perhaps he has merely recovered from a delirium. He stands at the gate of his own home. All is as he left it, and all bright and beautiful in the morning sunshine. He must have traveled the entire night. As he pushes open the gate and passes up the wide white walk, he sees a flutter of female garments; his wife, looking fresh and cool and sweet, steps down from the veranda to meet him. At the bottom of the steps she stands waiting, with a smile of ineffable joy, an attitude of matchless grace and dignity. Ah, how beautiful she is! He springs forward with extended arms. As he is about to clasp her he feels a stunning blow upon the back of the neck; a blinding white light blazes all about him with a sound like the shock of a cannon—then all is darkness and silence!

Peyton Farquhar was dead; his body, with a broken neck, swung gently from side to side beneath the timbers of the Owl Creek bridge.

QUESTIONS

1. What is the situation in the story? What did Farquhar do to deserve his execution?
2. Describe the various shifts in the story's point of view, particularly as indicated in paragraphs 5 and 37. How does Bierce make you aware of Farquhar's heightened consciousness?
3. According to Farquhar's perception of time, how long does it take him to get home after his escape (see paragraphs 33 and 36)?

4. What evidence can you find to indicate that Farquhar is experiencing great pain, despite his feelings that he is escaping?

5. What is the effect of the shift into the present tense in paragraph 36?

EDWIDGE DANTICAT (b. 1969)

Danticat is a native of Haiti and came to this country in 1981, when she was twelve, to live with her parents in Brooklyn. It was then that she started learning English even though at home she and her parents continued to speak the Creole of their native Haiti. She was educated at Barnard College and Brown University. Her first novel, Breath, Eyes, Memory *(1994), was selected for the Oprah Winfrey Book Club and was therefore assured wide circulation and recognition. Her collection of stories* Krik? Krak! *appeared in 1995, and* The Farming of Bones *was published in 1998. Most recently she has published* Behind the Mountains *(2002) and* The Dew Breaker *(2004).*

Night Talkers (2002)

He thought that the mountain would kill him, that he would never see the other side. He had been walking for two hours when suddenly he felt a sharp pain in his side. He tried some breathing exercises he remembered from medical shows on television, but it was hard to concentrate. All he could think of, besides the pain, was his roommate Michel, who'd had an emergency appendectomy a few weeks before in New York. What if he was suddenly stricken with appendicitis, here on top of a mountain, deep in the Haitian countryside, where the closest village seemed like a grain of sand in the valley below?

Hugging his midsection, he took cover from the scorching midday sun under a tall, arched, wind-deformed tree. He slid down onto his back, over the grainy pebbled soil, and closed his eyes, shutting out, along with the indigo sky, the sloping hills and craggy mountains that made up the rest of his journey.

He was on his way to visit his aunt Estina, his father's older sister, whom he'd not seen since he'd moved to New York six years before. He had lost his parents to the dictatorship when he was a boy, and his aunt Estina had raised him in the capital. After he'd moved to New York, she had returned to her home in the mountains, where she had always taken him during school holidays. This was the first time he was going to her village, as he had come to think of it, without her. If she were with him, she would have made him start his journey earlier in the day. They would have boarded a camion at the bus depot in Port-au-Prince before dawn and started climbing the mountain at sunrise to avoid sunstroke at high noon. If she knew he was coming, she would have hired him a mule and sent a child to accompany him, a child who would have known all the shortcuts to her village. She also would have advised him to wear a sun hat and bring more than the two bottles of water he'd consumed hours ago.

But no, he wanted to surprise her. However, the only person he was surprising was himself, by getting lost and nearly passing out and possibly lying there long enough to draw a few mountain vultures to come pick his skeleton clean.

When he finally opened his eyes, the sun was beating down on his face in pretty, symmetrical designs. Filtered through the long upturned branches of what he recognized as a giant saguaro cactus, the sunrays had patterned themselves into hearts, starfishes, and circles looped around one another.

5

He reached over and touched the cactus's thick trunk, which felt like a needle-filled pin-cushion or a field of dry grass. The roots were close to the soil, which his aunt Estina had once told him were designed to collect as much rainwater as possible. Further up along the spine, on the stem, was a tiny cobalt flower. He wanted to pluck it and carry it with him the rest of the way, but his aunt would scold him if she knew what he had done. Cactus flowers bloomed only for a few short days, then withered and died. He should let the cactus enjoy its flower for this brief time, his aunt would say.

The pain in his midsection had subsided, so he decided to get up and continue his walk until he reached his destination. There were many paths to his aunt's house, and seeing the lone saguaro had convinced him that he was on one of them.

He soon found himself in a village where a girl was pounding a pestle into a mortar, forming a small crater in the ground beneath the mortar as a group of younger children watched.

The girl stopped her pounding as soon as she saw him, causing the other children to turn their almost identical brown faces toward him.

10 "Bonjou, cousins," he said, remembering the childhood greeting his aunt had taught him. When he was a boy, in spite of the loss of his parents, he had thought himself part of a massive family, every child his cousin and every adult his aunt or uncle.

"Bonjou," the children replied.

"Ki jan ou ye?" How are you? the oldest girl added, distinguishing herself.

"Could I have some water, please?" he said to the oldest girl, determining that she was indeed the one in charge.

The girl turned her pestle over to the next oldest child and ran into the limestone house as he dropped his backpack on the ground and collapsed on the front gallery. The ground felt chilly against his bare legs, as though he had stumbled into a cold stream.

15 As one of the younger boys ran off behind the house, the other children settled down on the ground next to him, some of them reaching over and stroking his backpack.

The oldest girl came back with a glass in one hand and an earthen jar in the other. He watched as she poured the water, wondering if it, like her, was a mirage fabricated by his intense thirst. When she handed him the water, he drank it faster than it took her to pour him another glass, then another and another, until the earthen jar was clearly empty.

She asked if he wanted more.

"No," he replied. "Mèsi anpil."° Thank you.

The girl went back into the house to put the earthen jar and glass away. The children were staring up at him, too coy to question him and too curious not to stare. When the girl returned, she went back to her spot behind the mortar and pestle and just stood there as though she no longer knew what to do.

20 An old man carrying a machete and a sisal knapsack walked up to the bamboo gate that separated the road from the house. The boy who had run off earlier was at his side.

"How are you, konpê?"° the old man asked.

"Uncle," he said, "I was dying of thirst until your granddaughter here gave me some water to drink."

"My granddaughter?" the old man laughed. "She's my daughter. Do you think I look that old?"

He looked old, with a grizzly salt-and-pepper beard and a face full of folds and creases that seemed to map out every road he had traveled in his life.

25 The old man reached over and grabbed one of three wooden poles that held up the front of the house. He stood there for a while, saying nothing, catching his breath. After the children

---

° *Mèsi anpil:* I am full. I've had enough.
° *konpê:* i.e., French "copain," companion, friend, chum.

had brought him a calabash filled with water—the glass was obviously reserved for strangers—and two chairs for him and the stranger, he lit his pipe and exhaled a fragrant cloud of fresh tobacco and asked, "Where are you going, my son?"

"I am going to see my aunt, Estina Estème," he replied. "She lives in Beau Jour."

The old man removed the pipe from his mouth and reached up to scratch his beard.

"Estina Estème? The same Estina Estème from Beau Jour?"

"The same," he said, growing hopeful that he was not too far from his aunt's house.

"You say she is your aunt?"   30

"She is," he replied. "You know her?"

"Know her?" the old man retorted. "There are no strangers in these mountains. My grandfather Nozial and her grandfather Osnac were cousins. Who was your father?"

"My father was Maxo Jean Osnac," he said.

"The one who was killed in that explosion?" the old man asked. "He only had one boy. The mother died too, didn't she? Estina nearly died in that explosion too. Only the boy came out whole."

"I am the boy," he said, an egg-sized lump growing in his throat.   35

He didn't expect to be talking about these things so soon. He had prepared himself for only one conversation about his parents' death, the one he would inevitably have with his aunt.

The children moved a few inches closer to him, their eyes beaming as though they were being treated to a frightening folktale in the middle of the day.

"Even after all these years," the old man said, "I am sad for you. So you are that young man who used to come here with Estina, the one who left for New York some years back?"

The old man looked him up and down, as if searching for burn marks on his body, then ordered the children to retreat.

"Shoo," he commanded. "This is no talk for young ears."   40

The children quickly vanished, the oldest girl resuming her work with the mortar and pestle.

Rising from his chair, the old man said, "Come, I will take you to Estina Estème." Estina Estème lived in a valley between two lime-green mountains and a giant waterfall, which was constantly spraying a fine mist over the banana grove that surrounded her one-room house and the teal mausoleum that harbored the bones of her forebears. Her nephew recognized the house as soon as he saw it. It had not changed much, the sloped tin roof and the wooden frame intact. His aunt's banana grove seemed to have flourished, however. It was greener and denser than he remembered; her garden was packed with orange and avocado trees, a miracle given the barren mountain range he had just traveled through.

When he entered his aunt's yard, he was greeted by a flock of hens and roosters, which scattered quickly, seeking shelter on top of the family mausoleum.

He rushed to the front porch, where an old faded skirt and blouse were drying on the wooden railing. The door was open, so he ran into the house, leaving behind the old man and a small group of neighbors whom the old man had enticed into following them by announcing as he passed their houses that he had with him Estina Estème's only nephew.

In the small room was his aunt's cot, covered with a pale blue sheet. Nearby was a cal-   45
abash filled with water, within easy reach so she could drink from it at night without leaving her bed. Under the cot was her porcelain chamber pot and baskets filled with her better dresses and a few Sunday hats and shoes.

The old man peeked in to ask, "She's not here?"

"No," he replied. "She is not."

He was growing annoyed with the old man, even though he was now certain that he would have never found his aunt's house so quickly without his help.

When he walked out of the house, he found himself facing a dozen or so more people gathered in his aunt's yard. He scanned the faces and recognized some, but could not recall their names. Many in the group were nudging each other, whispering while pointing at him. Others called out, "Dany, don't you know me anymore?"

50   He walked over and kissed the women, shook hands with the men, and patted the children's heads.

"Please, where is my aunt?" he asked of the entire crowd.

"She will soon be here," a woman replied. "We sent for her."

Once he knew his aunt was on her way, he did his best to appear interested in catching up. Many in the crowd complained that once he got to New York, he forgot about them, never sending the watch or necklace or radio he had promised. Surprised that they had taken his youthful pledges so seriously, he made feeble excuses: "It's not so easy to earn money in New York . . . I thought you had moved to the capital . . . I didn't know your address."

"Where would we have gone?" one of the men rebutted. "We were not so lucky as you."

55   He was glad when he heard his aunt's voice, calling his name from the back of the crowd. The crowd parted and she appeared, pudgy yet graceful in a drop-waist dress. Her face was round and full, her few wrinkles more like tribal marks than signs of old age. Two people were guiding her by the elbows. As they were leading her to him, she pulled herself away and raised her hands in front of her, searching for him in the breeze. He had to remind himself once more that she was blind, had been since the day of the fire that had taken his parents' life.

The crowd moved back a few feet as he ran into her arms. She held him tightly, angling her head to kiss the side of his face.

"Dany, is it you?" She patted his back and shoulders to make sure.

"I brought him here for you," the old man said.

"Old Zo, why is it that you're always mixed up in everything?" she asked, joking.

60   "True to my name," the old man replied, "I am a bone that fits every stew."

The crowd laughed.

"Let's go in the house, Da," his aunt said. "It's hot out here."

As they started for her front door, he took her hand and tried to guide her, but found himself an obstacle in her path and let go. Once they were inside, she felt her way to her cot and sat down on the edge.

"Sit with me, Da," she said. "You have made your old aunt a young woman again."

65   "How are you?" He sat down next to her. "Truly?"

"Truly fine," she said. "Did Popo tell you different?"

For many years now, he had been paying a boyhood friend in Port-au-Prince, Popo, to come and check on her once a month. He would send Popo money to buy her whatever she needed, and Popo would in turn call him in New York to brief him on how she was doing.

"No," he said, "Popo didn't tell me anything."

"Then why did you come?" she asked. "I am not unhappy to see you, but you just dropped out of the sky, there must be a reason."

70   She felt for his face, found it, and kissed it for what seemed like a hundredth time since he'd seen her. "Were you sent back?" she asked. "We have a few boys here in the village who have been sent back. Many don't even speak Creole° anymore. They come here because this is the only place they have any family. There's one boy not far from here. I'll take you to visit him. You can speak to him, one American to another."

"You still go on your visits?" he asked.

° *Creole:* a local Haitian dialect.

"When they came to fetch me, I was with a girl in labor," she said.

"Still a midwife?"

"Helping the midwife," she replied. "You know I know every corner of these mountains. If a new tree grows, I learn where it is. Same with children. A baby's still born the same way it was when I had sight."

"I meant to come sooner," he said, watching her join and separate her fingers randomly, 75
effortlessly, like tree branches brushing against each other in a gentle breeze.

"I know," she said. "But why didn't you send word that you were on your way?"

"You're right," he said. "I didn't just drop out of the sky. I came because I wanted to tell you something."

"What is it, Da?" she asked, weaving and unweaving her fingers. "Are you finally getting married?"

"No," he said. "That's not it. I found him. I found him in New York, the man who killed Papa and Manman° and took your sight."

Why the old man chose that exact moment to come through the door he will never know. 80
Perhaps it was chance, serendipity, or maybe simply because the old man was a nosy pain in the ass. But just then Old Zo appeared in the doorway, pushing the mortar-and-pestle girl ahead of him with a covered plate of food in her hand.

"We brought you something to refresh you," he told Dany.

His aunt seemed neither distressed nor irritated by the interruption. She could have sent Old Zo and the girl away, but she didn't. Instead she told them to put their offering down on an old table in the corner. The girl quietly put the plate down and backed out of the room, avoiding Dany's eyes.

"I hope you're both hungry," the old man said, not moving from his spot. "Everyone is going to bring you something."

Clusters of food-bearing people streamed in and out of the house all afternoon. He and his aunt would sample each plate, then share the rest with the next visitor, until everyone in the valley had tasted at least one of their neighbor's dishes.

By the time all the visitors had left and he and his aunt were alone together, it was dark 85
and his aunt showed no interest in hearing what he had to say. Instead she offered him her cot, and he talked her into letting him have the sisal mat that she had laid out on the floor for herself.

She fell asleep much more quickly than he did. Mid-dream, she laughed, paid compliments, made promises, or gave warnings. "Listen, don't go too far. Come back soon. What a strong baby! I'll make you a dress. I'll make you coffee." Then she sat up in her cot to scold herself—"Estina, you are waking the boy"—before drifting once again into the movie in her head.

In the dark, listening to his aunt conduct entire conversations in her sleep, he realized that aside from blood, she and he shared nocturnal habits. They were both night talkers. He too spoke his dreams aloud in the night, in his sleep, to the point of sometimes jolting himself awake with the sound of his own voice. Usually he could only remember the very last words he spoke, but a lingering sensation remained that he had been talking, laughing, and at times crying all night long.

His aunt was already awake by the time he got up the next morning. With help from Old Zo's daughter, who seemed to have been rented out to his aunt for the duration of his visit, she had already set up breakfast on the small table brought out to the front gallery from inside the house. His aunt seemed fidgety, almost anxious, as if she had been waiting for him to rise for hours.

° *Manman:* Mama.

"Go wash yourself, Da," she said, handing him a towel. "I'll be waiting for you here."

90   Low shrubs covered in dew brushed against his ankles as he made his way down a trail toward the stream at the bottom of the fall. The water was freezing cold when he slipped in, but he welcomed the sensation of having almost every muscle in his body contract, as if to salute the dawn.

Had his father ever bathed in this stream? Had his parents bathed here together when they'd come to stay with his aunt? Had they enjoyed it, or had they wished for warmer waters and more privacy?

A group of women were coming down the path with calabashes and plastic jugs balanced on top of their heads. They would bathe, then fill their containers farther up, closer to the fall. He remembered spending hours as a boy watching the women bathe topless, their breasts flapping against their chests as they soaped and scrubbed themselves with mint and parsley sprigs, as if to eradicate every speck of night dust from their skin.

When he got back to his aunt's house, he had a visitor. It was a boy named Claude, a deportee. Claude was sitting next to his aunt, on the top step in front of the house; he was dipping his bread in the coffee that Old Zo's daughter had just made.

"I sent for Claude," his aunt announced. "Claude understands Creole and is learning to speak bit by bit, but he has no one to speak English to. I would like you to talk with him."

95   It was awkward at first, especially with the giant, overly muscular Claude looking so absolutely thrilled to see him, yet trying to hide it with a restrained smile and an overly firm handshake. Both of Claude's brawny arms were covered with tattoos from his shoulders down to his wrists, his skin a collaged canvas of Chinese characters plus kings and queens from a card deck: One-Eyed Jack, Hector, Lancelot, Judith, Rachel, Argine and Palas, they were all there, carved into his coal-black skin in blue ink. His hands were large too, his fingers long, thick, callused, perhaps the hands of a killer.

"What's up?" Claude stood up only to sit down again. "How you doing?"

Claude was probably in his late teens—too young, it seemed, to have been expatriated twice, from both his native country and his adopted land. Dany sat down on the step next to Claude as Old Zo's daughter handed him a cup of coffee and a piece of bread.

"How long you been here?" he asked Claude.

"Too long, man," Claude replied, "but I guess it could be worse. I could be down in the city, in Port, eating crap and sleeping on the street. Everyone here's been really cool to me, especially your aunt. She's kind of taken me under her wing. When I first got here, I thought I would get stoned. I mean I thought people would throw rocks at me, man, not the other kind of stoned. I mean, coming out of New York, then being in prison in Port for like three months because no one knew what to do with me, then finally my moms, who didn't speak to me for like the whole time I was locked up, came to Port and hooked me up with some family up here."

100   His aunt was leaning forward with both hands holding up her face, her white hair braided like a crown of gardenias around her head. She was listening to them speak, like someone trying to capture the indefinable essence of a great piece of music. Watching her face, the pleasure she was taking in the unfamiliar words, made him want to talk even more, find something drawn-out to say, tell a story of some kind, even recite some poetry, if only he knew any.

"So you're getting by all right?" he asked Claude.

"It took a lot of getting used to, but I'm settling in," Claude replied. "I got a roof over my head and it's quiet as hell here. No trouble worth a damn to get into. It's cool that you've come back to see your aunt, man. Some of the folks around here told me she had someone back in New York. I had a feeling when she'd ask me to speak English for her, it was because she really wanted to hear somebody else's voice, maybe yours. It's real cool that you didn't forget her, that you didn't forget your folks. I really wish I had stayed in touch more with my people, you know, then it wouldn't be so weird showing up here like I did. These people don't even know me, man. They've never seen my face before, not even in pictures. They still took me in, after everything I did, because my moms told them I was their blood. I look at them and I see nothing of me, man, blank, nada, but they look at me and they say he has so-and-so's nose and his grandmother's forehead, or some shit like that. It's like a puzzle, man, a weird-ass kind of puzzle. I am the puzzle and these people are putting me back together, telling me things about myself and my family that I never knew or gave a fuck about. Man, if I had run into these people back in Brooklyn, I would have laughed my ass off at them. I would have called them backward-ass peasants. But here I am, man, one of those backwardass peasants myself."

His aunt was engrossed, enthralled by Claude's speech, smiling at times while the morning sunrays danced across her eyes, never penetrating her pupils. He was starting to think of his aunt's eyes as a strange kind of prism, one that consumed light rather than reflected it.

"I can't honestly say I love it here, man"—Claude seemed to be wrapping up—"but it's worked out all right for me. It saved my life. I am at peace here and my family seems to have made peace with me. I came around, man. I can honestly say I was reformed in prison. I would have been a better citizen than most if they hadn't deported me."

"You still have a chance," Dany said, not believing it himself. "You can do something   105
with your life. Maybe you're back here for a reason, to make things better."

He was growing tired of Claude, tired of what he considered his lame excuses and an apparent lack of remorse for whatever it was he had done.

"How long will you be staying?" Claude asked.

"A while," Dany said.

"Is there anything you want to do?" Claude asked. "I know the area pretty well now. I take lots of walks to clear my head. I could show you around."

"I know where things are," Dany said. "And if I don't remember, my aunt can—"   110

"It's just with her not being able to see—"

"She can see, in her own way—"

"All right, cool, my man. I was just trying to be helpful."

Even with the brusque way their conversation ended, Claude seemed happy as he left. He had gotten his chance to speak English and tell his entire life story in the process.

After Claude's departure, Old Zo's daughter came up and took the empty coffee cup   115
from Dany's hand. She lingered in front of him for a minute, her palm accidentally brushing against his fingertips. At times she seemed older than she looked. Maybe she was twenty, twenty-five, but she looked twelve. He wondered what her story was. Were those children he had seen in Old Zo's yard hers? Did she have a husband? Was he in the city? Dead?

She hesitated before stepping away, as though she gave too much thought to every move she made. When she finally walked away, Dany's aunt asked him, "Do you know why Claude was in prison?"

"He didn't say."

"Do you know what his people say?"

"What do his people say?"

"They say he killed his father."   120

That night, Dany dreamed that he was having the conversation he'd come to have with his aunt. They were sitting on the step where he and Claude had spoken. He began the conversation by recalling with his aunt the day his parents died.

He was six years old and his father was working as a driver for a family in Port-au-Prince. The morning of the fire, his father had rushed home to tell his mother and aunt, who was visiting from Beau Jour, that his father's employer's family home had been burned down, but not before the family had escaped and gone into hiding. His father thought they should leave for Beau Jour, for the people who were looking for his employer might think his workers were hiding him. His parents and Estina were throwing a few things in a knapsack when his father told him to go out in the yard and watch out for any strangers. He was watching the street carefully, for even then he felt that he had never been given such an important job. That's when a very large man came up and threw two grenades in quick succession at his house. Before he could even turn his head, the house was on fire, pieces of wood and cement chunks flying everywhere. The man got back in his car, a black German DKW—he remembered it very well because it was the same type of car many of the military men drove and his father had pointed out to him that he should avoid those cars as much as possible—and drove away, but not before Dany got a good look at the man's large round face, a widow's peak dipping into the middle of his forehead.

A few moments later, his aunt came crawling out of the house, unable to see. His parents never came out.

He dreamed his aunt saying, "Yes this is how it happened," then urging him to elaborate on what he had begun to tell her before Old Zo had walked into the room. "You said you saw that same man in New York? Are you sure it was him?"

125   "Yes," he replied. "He is a barber now."

The man who had killed his parents was calling himself Albert Bienaimé:° these days. He had a wife and a grown daughter, both of whom seemed unaware of his past. Some men he had met at work told him that Albert Bienaimé was renting a room in the basement of his house, where they also lived. When he went to Albert Bienaimé's barbershop to ask about the room, he recognized Albert Bienaimé as the same man who had thrown the grenades at his parents' house. When he asked Albert Bienaimé where he was from, Albert Bienaimé said that he was from the mountains somewhere above Jacmel and had never lived in a city before moving to New York.

"You see," the dream aunt said, "he may not be the one."

He took the empty room in Albert Bienaimé's basement. He couldn't sleep for months, spending his weekends in nightclubs to pass the time. He visited Albert Bienaimé's barbershop regularly for haircuts, in order to observe him and reassure himself that he was indeed the same man who had thrown the explosives at his house. Finally, two nights ago, when Albert Bienaimé's wife was away at a religious retreat—he looked for such opportunities all the time and hadn't found one until then—he climbed the splintered steps to the first floor, then made his way with a flashlight to Albert Bienaimé's bedroom.

"What did you do?" the dream aunt asked.

130   He stood there and listened to Albert Bienaimé breathing. Albert Bienaimé was snoring, each round of snores beginning in a low groan and ending in a high-pitched shrill. He lowered his face toward Albert Bienaimé's widow's peak, hoping Albert Bienaimé would wake up and be startled to death. Even when he was a boy, he had heard about how some of the military people, like Albert Bienaimé, would choke their prisoners in their sleep, watching their faces swell and their eyes bulge out of their heads. He was certain when he'd come up the stairs that he was going to kill Albert Bienaimé. He thought of pressing a pillow down on Albert Bienaimé's face, but something stopped him. It wasn't fear, because he was feeling bold, fearless. It wasn't pity; he was too angry to feel pity. It was something else, something less measurable. Perhaps it was the dread of being wrong, of harming the wrong man, of making the wrong woman a widow and the wrong child an orphan. At that moment, all he wanted to do was run as far away from Albert Bienaimé as possible, leave and never come back. He left Albert Bienaimé's room and went down to the basement, booking himself on the next available flight to Port-au-Prince and knowing he would never be coming back. Even though he knew he

---

° *Bienaimé:* "well loved."

wouldn't be able to return on his expired visa, he wanted to see Beau Jour again. He needed to see his aunt. He needed to see a place where perhaps his parents had been happy.

Dany woke himself with the sound of his own voice reciting his story. His aunt was awake too, sitting up on her cot.

"Da, were you dreaming your parents?" she asked. "You were calling their names."

"Was I?" He would have thought he was calling Albert Bienaimé's name.

"You were calling your parents," she said, "just this instant."

He was still back there, in the yard, waiting for his parents to come out of that burning   135
house, in the room with Albert Bienaimé, wishing he could watch Albert Bienaimé die. His aunt's voice was just an echo of things he could no longer hear, his mother's voice praying, his father's voice laughing.

"I am sorry I woke you," he said, wiping the sweat off his forehead with the backs of his hands.

"I should have let you continue telling me what you came here to say. It's like walking up these mountains and losing something precious halfway. For you it would be no problem walking back, because you are still young and strong, but for me it would take a lot more time and effort."

He heard the cot squeak as she lay back down.

"I understand," he said.

She went back to sleep, whispering something under her breath, then growing com-   140
pletely silent. When he woke up the next morning, she was dead.

It was Old Zo's daughter who let out the first cry, announcing the death to the entire valley. Sitting near the body, on the edge of his aunt's cot, Dany was doubled over with an intense bellyache. Old Zo's daughter took over immediately, brewing him some tea while waiting for their neighbors to arrive.

The tea did nothing for him. He was not expecting it to. Part of him was grateful for the pain, for the physically agonizing diversion it was providing him.

Soon after Old Zo's daughter's cry, a few of the village women began to arrive. It was only then that he learned Old Zo's daughter's name, at least her nickname, Ti Fanm (Little Woman),° which the others kept shouting as they badgered her with questions.

"What happened, Ti Fanm?"

"Ti Fanm, did she die in her sleep?"   145

"Did she fall, Ti Fanm?"

"Ti Fanm, did she suffer?"

"Ti Fanm, she wasn't even sick."

"She was old," Ti Fanm said in a firm and mature voice. "It can happen like that."

They did not bother asking him anything. He wouldn't have known how to answer any-   150
way. After he and his aunt had spoken in the middle of the night, he thought she had fallen asleep. When he woke up in the morning, even later than he had the day before, she was still lying there, her eyes shut, her hands resting on her belly, her fingers intertwined. He tried to find her pulse, but she had none. He lowered his face to her nose and felt no breath. Then he walked out of the house and found Ti Fanm, sitting on the steps, waiting to cook his breakfast. The pain was already starting in his stomach. Ti Fanm came in and performed her own investigation, then let out that cry, a cry as loud as any siren he had heard on the streets of New York or the foghorns that blew occasionally from the harbor near the house where he had lived with his parents as a boy.

His aunt's house was filled with people now, each of them taking turns examining his aunt's body for signs of life, and when finding none immediately assigning themselves,

---

° *Ti Fanm:* a shortened form of "petite femme," or "little woman."

and each other, tasks related to her burial. One group ran off to get purple curtains, to hang shroudlike over the front door to show that this was a household in mourning. Another group went off to fetch an unused washbasin to bathe the corpse. Others were searching through the baskets beneath his aunt's cot for an appropriate dress to change her into after her bath. Another went looking for a carpenter to build her coffin.

The men assigned themselves to him and his pain.

"He is in shock," they said.

"Can't you see he's not able to speak?"

155   "He's not even looking at her. He's looking at the floor."

"He has a stomachache," Ti Fanm intercepted.

She brought him some warm salted coffee, which he drank in one gulp.

"He should lie down," one of the men said.

"But where?" Another rebutted. "Not next to her."

160   "He must have known she was going to die." He heard Old Zo's voice rising above the others. "He came just in time. Blood calls blood. She made him come so he could see her before she died. It would have been sad if she had died behind his back, especially since he never buried his parents."

They were speaking about him as though he couldn't understand, as if he were solely an English-speaker, like Claude. Perhaps this was the only way they could think of to console him right then, to offer him solace.

He wished that his stomach would stop hurting, that he could rise from the edge of the cot and take control of the situation, or at least participate in the preparations, but all he wanted to do was lie down next to his aunt, rest his head on her chest, and wrap his arms around her, the way he had done when he was a little boy. He wanted to close his eyes until he could wake up from this unusual dream where everyone was able to speak except the two of them. By midday he felt well enough to join Old Zo and some of the men, who were opening up a slot in the family mausoleum. He was in less pain now, but was still uncomfortable and moved slower than the others.

The women were inside the house, bathing his aunt's body and changing her into a blue dress he had sent her through Popo. He had seen it in a store window in Brooklyn and had chosen it for her, remembering that blue was her favorite color. The wrapping was still intact; she had never worn it.

Once the slot was opened, Old Zo announced that a Protestant minister would be coming by the next morning to say a prayer during the burial. Old Zo had wanted to transport the body to a church in the next village for a full service, but he didn't want his aunt to travel so far, only to return to her own yard to be buried.

165   "The coffin is almost ready," Old Zo said. "She will be able to rest in it during the wake."

He had always been perplexed by the mixture of jubilation and sorrow that was part of Beau Jour's wakes, by the fact that some of the participants played cards and dominoes while others served tea and wept. But what he had always enjoyed was the time carved out for the mourners to tell stories about the deceased, singular tales of first or last encounters, which could either make him holler with laughter or have his stomach spasms return as his grief grew.

The people of his aunt's village were telling such stories about her now. They told of how she once tried to make coffee and filtered dirt through her coffee pouch even though she was able to deliver twins without any trouble. They told of how as a young woman she had embroidered a trousseau that she carried everywhere with her, thinking it would attract a husband. They spoke of her ambition, of her wanting to be a baby seamstress, so she could make clothes for the very same children she was ushering into the world. If he could have managed it, he would have spoken of her sacrifices, of the fact that she had spent most of her life trying to keep him safe. He would have told of how he hadn't wanted to leave her, to go to New York, but she had insisted that he go so he would be as far away as possible from the people who had murdered his parents.

Claude arrived at the wake just as it was winding down, at a time when everyone was too tired to do anything but sit, stare, and moan, when through sleepy eyes the reason for the all-night gathering had become all too clear, when the purple shroud blowing from the doorway into the night breeze could no longer be ignored.

"I am so sorry, man," Claude said. "I was in Port today and when I came back my people told me. I am truly sorry, man. Your aunt was such good people. One of a kind, really. I am so sorry."

Claude moved forward, as if to hug him, Claude's broad shoulders towering over his   170
head. Dany stepped back, moving away, cringing. Perhaps it was what his aunt had told him, about Claude's having killed his father, but he did not want Claude to touch him.

Claude got the message and walked away, drifting toward a group of men who were nodding off at a table near the porch railing.

When he walked back inside the house, he found a small group of women sitting near the open coffin, keeping watch over his aunt. He was still unable to look at her in the coffin for too long. He envied these women the six years they had spent with her while he was gone. He dragged his sisal mat, the one he had been sleeping on these last two nights, to a corner as far away from the coffin as he could get, coiled himself into a ball, and tried to fall asleep.

It could happen like that, Ti Fanm had said. A person his aunt's age could fall asleep talking and wake up dead. He wouldn't have believed it if he hadn't seen it for himself. Death was supposed to be either quick and furious or drawn-out and dull, after a long illness. His aunt had chosen a middle ground. Perhaps Old Zo was right.

Blood calls blood. Perhaps she had summoned him here so he could at last witness a peaceful death and see how it was meant to be mourned. Perhaps Albert Bienaimé was not his parents' murderer after all, but just a phantom who'd shown up to escort him back here. He didn't know what to believe anymore.

He could not fall asleep, not with the women keeping watch over his aunt's body being   175
so close by. Not with Ti Fanm coming over every hour with a cup of tea, which was supposed to cure his bellyaches forever.

He didn't like her nickname, was uncomfortable using it. It was too generic, as though she was one of many from a single mold, with no distinctive traits of her own.

"What is your name?" he asked when she brought him her latest brew.

She seemed baffled, as though she were thinking he might need a stronger infusion, something to calm his nerves and a memory aid, too.

"Ti Fanm," she replied.

"Non," he said, "your true name, your full name."   180

"Alice Denise Auguste," she said.

The women who were keeping watch over his aunt were listening to their conversation, cocking their heads ever so slightly in their direction.

"How old are you?" he asked.

"Thirty," she said.

"Thank you," he said.

"You're deserving," she said, using an old-fashioned way of acknowledging his grat-   185
itude.

She was no longer avoiding his eyes, as though his grief and stomach ailment and the fact that he had asked her real name had rendered them equals.

He got up and walked outside, where many of his aunt's neighbors were sleeping on mats on the porch. There was a full moon overhead and a calm in the air that he was not expecting. In the distance he could hear the waterfall, a sound that, once you got used to it, you never paid much attention to. He walked over to the mausoleum, removed his shirt, and began to wipe the mausoleum with it, starting at the base and working his way up toward the headstone. It was clean already. The men had done a good job removing the leaves, pebbles, and dust that had accumulated on it while they were opening his aunt's slot, but he wanted to make sure it was spotless, that every piece of debris that had fallen on it since was gone.

"Need help?" Claude asked from a few feet away.

190   He must have been sleeping somewhere on the porch with the others before he saw Dany.

Dany threw his dusty shirt on the ground, climbed up on one of the mausoleum ledges, and sat down. He had wanted to do something, anything, to keep himself occupied until dawn.

"I'm sorry," Dany said, "for earlier."

"I understand," Claude said. "I'd be a real asshole if I got pissed off at you for anything you did or said to me at a time like this. You're in pain, man. I get that."

"I don't know if I'd call it pain," Dany said. "There's no word yet for it. No one has thought of a word yet."

195   "I know, man," Claude said. "It's a real bitch."

In spite of his huge muscles and oversized tattoos, Claude seemed oddly defenseless, like a refugee lost at sea, or a child looking for his parents in a supermarket aisle. Or maybe that's just how Dany wanted to see him, to make him seem more normal, less frightening.

"I hear you killed your father," Dany said.

The words sounded less severe coming out of his mouth than they did rolling around in his head.

"Can I sit?" Claude asked, pointing to a platform on the other side of the headstone.

200   Dany nodded.

"Yes, I killed my old man," Claude said. "Everyone here knows that shit by now. I wish I could say it was an accident. I wish I could say he was a bastard who beat the crap out of me and forced me to defend myself. I wish I could tell you I hated him, never loved him, didn't give a fuck about him at all. I was fourteen and strung out on shit. He came into my room and took the shit. It wasn't just my shit. It was shit I was hustling for someone else. I was really fucked up and wanted the shit back. I had a gun I was using to protect myself out on the street. I threatened him with it. He wouldn't give my shit back, so I shot him."

There was even less sorrow in Claude's voice than Dany had been able to muster over these past twenty-four hours. Dany was still numb, even as tears rolled down Claude's face; he had never known how to grieve or help others grieve. It was as though his parents' death had paralyzed that instinct in him.

"I am sorry," he said, feeling that someone should also think of a better word for this type of commiseration.

"Sorry?" Claude wiped the tears from his face with a quick swipe of his hand. "I am the luckiest fucker alive. I have done something really bad that now makes me want to live my life like a fucking angel. If I hadn't been a minor, I would have been locked up for the rest of my life. And if the prisons in Port had had more room, or if the police down there was worth a damn, I'd be in a small cell with a thousand people right now, not sitting here talking to you. Even with everything I've done, with everything that's happened to me, I am the luckiest fucker on this goddamned planet. Someone, somewhere, must be looking out for my ass."

205   It would be an hour or so before dawn. The moon was already fading, slipping away, on its way someplace else.

The only thing he could think to do for his aunt now was to get Claude to speak and speak and speak, which wouldn't be so hard, since Claude was already one of them, a member of their tribe. Claude was a night talker, one of those who spoke their nightmares out loud, to themselves, except Claude was also able to speak his nightmares to others, in the daytime, even when the moon had completely vanished and the sun had come out.

QUESTIONS

1. What is meant by "night talkers"? Who are the night talkers in the story? Why is the story titled "Night Talkers"?

2. Why has Dany returned to Haiti? Whom has he come to see? What has happened earlier, before Dany went to live in New York? How does Albert Bienaimé figure into Dany's life?

3. What is the significance of Estina's skepticism about Albert Bienaimé's involvement in the death of Dany's parents and in her loss of sight? What is the significance of Estina's death in the middle of the night?

4. Who is Claude? What crime has he committed, and under what circumstances? Describe the attitudes he expresses in his speech in paragraph 204. In what way is Claude's crime parallel with that of Albert Bienaimé?

WILLIAM FAULKNER (1897–1962)

Faulkner spent his childhood in Mississippi and became one of the foremost American novelists of the twentieth century. He twice received the Pulitzer Prize for Fiction (in 1955 and 1963), and he also received the Nobel Prize in Literature (in 1949). Throughout his extensive fiction about the special world that he named "Yoknapatawpha County," which is modeled on his own home area in Oxford, Mississippi, he treats life in the Southern United States as a symbol of humankind generally, emphasizing the decline of civilization and culture in the wake of the Civil War. Emily Grierson in "A Rose for Emily" is representative of this decline, for she maintains the appearances of status long after the substance is past. It is not unusual to find degraded, sullen, disturbed, and degenerate characters in Faulkner's fiction.

🍁 A Rose for Emily (1931)

) southern gothic.
gothic, romance

I

When Miss Emily Grierson died, our whole town went to her funeral; the men through a sort of respectful affection for a fallen monument, the women mostly out of curiosity to see the inside of her house, which no one save an old manservant—a combined gardener and cook—had seen in at least ten years.

It was a big, squarish frame house that had once been white, decorated with cupolas and spires and scrolled balconies in the heavily lightsome style of the seventies, set on what had once been our most select street. But garages and cotton gins had encroached and obliterated even the august names of that neighborhood; only Miss Emily's house was left, lifting its stubborn and coquettish decay above the cotton wagons and the gasoline pumps—an eyesore among eyesores. And now Miss Emily had gone to join the representatives of those august names where they lay in the cedar-bemused cemetery among the ranked and anonymous graves of Union and Confederate soldiers who fell at the battle of Jefferson.

Alive, Miss Emily had been a tradition, a duty, and a care; a sort of hereditary obligation upon the town, dating from that day in 1894 when Colonel Sartoris, the mayor—he who fathered the edict that no Negro woman should appear on the streets without an apron—remitted her taxes, the dispensation dating from the death of her father on into perpetuity. Not that Miss Emily would have accepted charity. Colonel Sartoris invented an involved tale to the effect that Miss Emily's father had loaned money to the town, which the town, as a matter of business, preferred this way of repaying. Only a man of Colonel Sartoris' generation and thought could have invented it, and only a woman could have believed it.

When the next generation, with its more modern ideas, became mayors and aldermen, this arrangement created some little dissatisfaction. On the first of the year they mailed her a tax notice. February came, and there was no reply. They wrote her a formal letter, asking her to call at the sheriff's office at her convenience. A week later the mayor wrote her himself, offering to call or to send his car for her, and received in reply a note on paper of an archaic shape, in a thin, flowing calligraphy in faded ink, to the effect that she no longer went out at all. The tax notice was also enclosed, without comment.

5   They called a special meeting of the Board of Aldermen. A deputation waited upon her, knocked at the door through which no visitor had passed since she ceased giving china-painting lessons eight or ten years earlier. They were admitted by the old Negro into a dim hall from which a stairway mounted into still more shadow. It smelled of dust and disuse—a close, dank smell. The Negro led them into the parlor. It was furnished in heavy, leather-covered furniture. When the Negro opened the blinds of one window, they could see that the leather was cracked; and when they sat down, a faint dust rose sluggishly about their thighs, spinning with slow motes in the single sun-ray. On a tarnished gilt easel before the fireplace stood a crayon portrait of Miss Emily's father.

They rose when she entered—a small, fat woman in black, with a thin gold chain descending to her waist and vanishing into her belt, leaning on an ebony cane with a tarnished gold head. Her skeleton was small and spare; perhaps that was why what would have been merely plumpness in another was obesity in her. She looked bloated, like a body long submerged in motionless water, and of that pallid hue. Her eyes, lost in the fatty ridges of her face, looked like two small pieces of coal pressed into a lump of dough as they moved from one face to another while the visitors stated their errand.

She did not ask them to sit. She just stood in the door and listened quietly until the spokesman came to a stumbling halt. Then they could hear the invisible watch ticking at the end of the gold chain.

Her voice was dry and cold. "I have no taxes in Jefferson. Colonel Sartoris explained it to me. Perhaps one of you can gain access to the city records and satisfy yourselves."

"But we have. We are the city authorities, Miss Emily. Didn't you get a notice from the sheriff, signed by him?"

10   "I received a paper, yes," Miss Emily said. "Perhaps he considers himself the sheriff . . . I have no taxes in Jefferson."

"But there is nothing on the books to show that, you see. We must go by the—"

"See Colonel Sartoris. I have no taxes in Jefferson."

"But, Miss Emily—"

"See Colonel Sartoris." (Colonel Sartoris had been dead almost ten years.) "I have no taxes in Jefferson. Tobe!" The Negro appeared. "Show these gentlemen out."

II

15   So she vanquished them, horse and foot, just as she had vanquished their fathers thirty years before about the smell. That was two years after her father's death and a short time after her sweetheart—the one we believed would marry her—had deserted her. After her father's death she went out very little; after her sweetheart went away, people hardly saw her at all. A few of

the ladies had the temerity to call, but were not received, and the only sign of life about the place was the Negro man—a young man then—going in and out with a market basket.

"Just as if a man—any man—could keep a kitchen properly," the ladies said; so they were not surprised when the smell developed. It was another link between the gross, teeming world and the high and mighty Griersons.

A neighbor, a woman, complained to the mayor, Judge Stevens, eighty years old.

"But what will you have me do about it, madam?" he said.

"Why, send her word to stop it," the woman said. "Isn't there a law?"

"I'm sure that won't be necessary," Judge Stevens said. "It's probably just a snake or a   20
rat that nigger of hers killed in the yard. I'll speak to him about it."

The next day he received two more complaints, one from a man who came in diffident deprecation. "We really must do something about it, Judge. I'd be the last one in the world to bother Miss Emily, but we've got to do something." That night the Board of Aldermen met—three graybeards and one younger man, a member of the rising generation.

"It's simple enough," he said. "Send her word to have her place cleaned up. Give her a certain time to do it in, and if she don't . . ."

"Dammit, sir," Judge Stevens said, "will you accuse a lady to her face of smelling bad?"

So the next night, after midnight, four men crossed Miss Emily's lawn and slunk about the house like burglars, sniffing along the base of the brickwork and at the cellar openings while one of them performed a regular sowing motion with his hand out of a sack slung from his shoulder. They broke open the cellar door and sprinkled lime there, and in all the outbuildings. As they recrossed the lawn, a window that had been dark was lighted and Miss Emily sat in it, the light behind her, and her upright torso motionlesss as that of an idol. They crept quietly across the lawn and into the shadow of the locusts that lined the street. After a week or two the smell went away.

That was when people had begun to feel really sorry for her. People in our town, remem-   25
bering how old lady Wyatt, her great-aunt, had gone completely crazy at last, believed that the Griersons held themselves a little too high for what they really were. None of the young men were quite good enough for Miss Emily and such. We had long thought of them as a tableau, Miss Emily a slender figure in white in the background, her father a spraddled silhouette in the foreground, his back to her and clutching a horsewhip, the two of them framed by the back flung front door. So when she got to be thirty and was still single, we were not pleased exactly, but vindicated; even with insanity in the family she wouldn't have turned down all of her chances if they had really materialized.

When her father died, it got about that the house was all that was left to her; and in a way, people were glad. At last they could pity Miss Emily. Being left alone, and a pauper, she had become humanized. Now she too would know the old thrill and the old despair of a penny more or less.

The day after his death all the ladies prepared to call at the house and offer condolence and aid, as is our custom. Miss Emily met them at the door, dressed as usual and with no trace of grief on her face. She told them that her father was not dead. She did that for three days, with the ministers calling on her, and the doctors, trying to persuade her to let them dispose of the body. Just as they were about to resort to law and force, she broke down, and they buried her father quickly.

We did not say she was crazy then. We believed she had to do that. We remembered all the young men her father had driven away, and we knew that with nothing left, she would have to cling to that which had robbed her, as people will.

III

She was sick for a long time. When we saw her again, her hair was cut short, making her look like a girl, with a vague resemblance to those angels in colored church windows—sort of tragic and serene.

30   The town had just let the contracts for paving the sidewalks, and in the summer after her father's death they began the work. The construction company came with niggers and mules and machinery, and a foreman named Homer Barron, a Yankee—a big, dark, ready man, with a big voice and eyes lighter than his face. The little boys would follow in groups to hear him cuss the niggers, and the niggers singing in time to the rise and fall of picks. Pretty soon he knew everybody in town. Whenever you heard a lot of laughing anywhere about the square, Homer Barron would be in the center of the group. Presently we began to see him and Miss Emily on Sunday afternoons driving in the yellow-wheeled buggy and the matched team of bays from the livery stable.

At first we were glad that Miss Emily would have an interest, because the ladies all said, "Of course a Grierson would not think seriously of a Northerner, a day laborer." But there were still others, older people, who said that even grief could not cause a real lady to forget *noblesse oblige* without calling it *noblesse oblige*. They just said, "Poor Emily. Her kinsfolk should come to her." She had some kin in Alabama; but years ago her father had fallen out with them over the estate of old lady Wyatt, the crazy woman, and there was no communication between the two families. They had not even been represented at the funeral.

And as soon as the old people said, "Poor Emily," the whispering began. "Do you suppose it's really so?" they said to one another. "Of course it is. What else could. . . ." This behind their hands; rustling of craned silk and satin behind jalousies closed upon the sun of Sunday afternoon as the thin, swift clop-clop-clop of the matched team passed: "Poor Emily."

She carried her head high enough—even when we believed that she was fallen. It was as if she demanded more than ever the recognition of her dignity as the last Grierson; as if it had wanted that touch of earthiness to reaffirm her imperviousness. Like when she bought the rat poison, the arsenic. That was over a year after they had begun to say "Poor Emily," and while the two female cousins were visiting her.

"I want some poison," she said to the druggist. She was over thirty then, still a slight woman, though thinner than usual, with cold, haughty black eyes in a face the flesh of which was strained across the temples and about the eyesockets as you imagine a light-house-keeper's face ought to look. "I want some poison," she said.

35   "Yes, Miss Emily. What kind? For rats and such? I'd recom—"

"I want the best you have. I don't care what kind."

The druggist named several. "They'll kill anything up to an elephant. But what you want is—"

"Arsenic," Miss Emily said. "Is that a good one?"

"Is . . . arsenic? Yes, ma'am. But what you want—"

40   "I want arsenic."

The druggist looked down at her. She looked back at him, erect, her face like a strained flag. "Why, of course," the druggist said. "If that's what you want. But the law requires you to tell what you are going to use it for."

Miss Emily just stared at him, her head tilted back in order to look him eye for eye, until he looked away and went and got the arsenic and wrapped it up. The Negro delivery boy brought her the package; the druggist didn't come back. When she opened the package at home there was written on the box, under the skull and bones: "For rats."

IV

So the next day we all said, "She will kill herself"; and we said it would be the best thing. When she had first begun to be seen with Homer Barron, we had said, "She will marry him." Then we said, "She will persuade him yet," because Homer himself had remarked— he liked men, and it was known that he drank with the younger men in the Elks' Club— that he was not a marrying man. Later we said, "Poor Emily" behind the jalousies as they passed on Sunday afternoon in the glittering buggy, Miss Emily with her head high and Homer Barron with his hat cocked and a cigar in his teeth, reins and whip in a yellow glove.

Then some of the ladies began to say that it was a disgrace to the town and a bad example to the young people. The men did not want to interfere, but at last the ladies forced the Baptist minister—Miss Emily's people were Episcopal—to call upon her. He would never divulge what happened during that interview, but he refused to go back again. The next Sunday they again drove about the streets, and the following day the minister's wife wrote to Miss Emily's relations in Alabama.

So she had blood-kin under her roof again and we sat back to watch developments. At 45 first nothing happened. Then we were sure that they were to be married. We learned that Miss Emily had been to the jeweler's and ordered a man's toilet set in silver, with the letters H. B. on each piece. Two days later we learned that she had bought a complete outfit of men's clothing, including a nightshirt, and we said, "They are married." We were really glad. We were glad because the two female cousins were even more Grierson than Miss Emily had ever been.

So we were not surprised when Homer Barron—the streets had been finished some time since—was gone. We were a little disappointed that there was not a public blowing-off, but we believed that he had gone on to prepare for Miss Emily's coming, or to give her a chance to get rid of the cousins. (By that time it was a cabal, and we were all Miss Emily's allies to help circumvent the cousins.) Sure enough, after another week they departed. And, as we had expected all along, within three days Homer Barron was back in town. A neighbor saw the Negro man admit him at the kitchen door at dusk one evening.

And that was the last we saw of Homer Barron. And of Miss Emily for some time. The Negro man went in and out with the market basket, but the front door remained closed. Now and then we would see her at a window for a moment, as the men did that night when they sprinkled the lime, but for almost six months she did not appear on the streets. Then we knew that this was to be expected too; as if that quality of her father which had thwarted her woman's life so many times had been too virulent and too furious to die.

When we next saw Miss Emily, she had grown fat and her hair was turning gray. During the next few years it grew grayer and grayer until it attained an even pepper-and-salt iron gray, when it ceased turning. Up to the day of her death at seventy-four it was still that vigorous iron-gray, like the hair of an active man.

From that time on her front door remained closed, save for a period of six or seven years, when she was about forty, during which she gave lessons in china-painting. She fitted up a studio in one of the downstairs rooms, where the daughters and granddaughters of Colonel Sartoris' contemporaries were sent to her with the same regularity and in the same spirit that they were sent to church on Sundays with a twenty-five-cent piece for the collection plate. Meanwhile her taxes had been remitted.

Then the newer generation became the backbone and the spirit of the town, and the 50 painting pupils grew up and fell away and did not send their children to her with boxes of color and tedious brushes and pictures cut from the ladies' magazines. The front door closed upon the last one and remained closed for good. When the town got free postal delivery, Miss Emily alone refused to let them fasten the metal numbers above her door and attach a mailbox to it. She would not listen to them.

Daily, monthly, yearly we watched the Negro grow grayer and more stooped, going in and out with the market basket. Each December we sent her a tax notice, which would be returned by the post office a week later, unclaimed. Now and then we would see her in one of the downstairs windows—she had evidently shut up the top floor of the house—like the carven torso of an idol in a niche, looking or not looking at us, we could never tell which. Thus she passed from generation to generation—dear, inescapable, impervious, tranquil, and perverse.

And so she died. Fell ill in the house filled with dust and shadows, with only a doddering Negro man to wait on her. We did not even know she was sick; we had long since given up trying to get any information from the Negro. He talked to no one, probably not even to her, for his voice had grown harsh and rusty, as if from disuse.

She died in one of the downstairs rooms, in a heavy walnut bed with a curtain, her gray head propped on a pillow yellow and moldy with age and lack of sunlight.

V

The Negro met the first of the ladies at the front door and let them in, with their hushed, sibilant voices and their quick, curious glances, and then he disappeared. He walked right through the house and out the back and was not seen again.

The two female cousins came at once. They held the funeral on the second day, with the town coming to look at Miss Emily beneath a mass of bought flowers, with the crayon face of her father musing profoundly above the bier and the ladies sibilant and macabre; and the very old men—some in their brushed Confederate uniforms—on the porch and the lawn, talking of Miss Emily as if she had been a contemporary of theirs, believing that they had danced with her and courted her perhaps, confusing time with its mathematical progression, as the old do, to whom all the past is not a diminishing road but, instead, a huge meadow which no winter ever quite touches, divided from them now by the narrow bottleneck of the most recent decade of years.

Already we knew that there was one room in that region above stairs which no one had seen in forty years, and which would have to be forced. They waited until Miss Emily was decently in the ground before they opened it.

The violence of breaking down the door seemed to fill this room with pervading dust. A thin, acrid pall as of the tomb seemed to lie everywhere upon this room decked and furnished as for a bridal: upon the valance curtains of faded rose color, upon the rose-shaded lights, upon the dressing table, upon the delicate array of crystal and the man's toilet things backed with tarnished silver, silver so tarnished that the monogram was obscured. Among them lay a collar and tie, as if they had just been removed, which, lifted, left upon the surface a pale crescent in the dust. Upon a chair hung the suit, carefully folded; beneath it the two mute shoes and the discarded socks.

The man himself lay in the bed.

For a long while we just stood there, looking down at the profound and fleshless grin. The body had apparently once lain in the attitude of an embrace, but now the long sleep that outlasts love, that conquers even the grimace of love, had cuckolded him. What was left of him, rotted beneath what was left of the nightshirt, had become inextricable from the bed in which he lay; and upon him and upon the pillow beside him lay that even coating of the patient and biding dust.

Then we noticed that in the second pillow was the indentation of a head. One of us lifted something from it, and leaning forward, that faint and invisible dust dry and acrid in the nostrils, we saw a long strand of iron-gray hair.

QUESTIONS

1. Who is Emily Grierson? What was the former position of her family in the town? What has happened to Emily after her father died? What are her economic circumstances? How does the deputation of alderman from the town of Jefferson treat her?

2. How do we learn about Emily? How do reports and rumors about her create the narrative of her life?

3. What has happened between Emily and Homer Barron? What is the significance, if any, of the fact that Homer is from the North?

4. Describe the plot of "A Rose for Emily." What contrasts and oppositions are developed in the story?

5. How does Faulkner shape the story's events to make Emily mysterious or enigmatic? In what ways does the ending come as a surprise?

TIM O'BRIEN (B. 1946)

William Timothy O'Brien was born in Minnesota and attended Macalester College in St. Paul. He saw duty in Vietnam during some of the more controversial times of that conflict, and after returning home he did graduate study, worked as a reporter, and became a writer. Among the works he has regularly published since the 1970s are If I Die in a Combat Zone, Box Me Up and Ship Me Home *(1973);* Northern Lights *(1974);* Going After Cacciato *(1978);* The Things They Carried *(1990), and* July, July *(2002). In his stories, which interweave fiction and autobiography, he realistically treats both the horrors of the Vietnam War and the ways in which returning veterans and their loved ones adjust to life after returning home. Because he portrays the lives and feelings of combat soldiers so well, he has been called one of the best American writers about war.*

🍁 The Things They Carried (1990)

First Lieutenant Jimmy Cross carried letters from a girl named Martha, a junior at Mount Sebastian College in New Jersey. They were not love letters, but Lieutenant Cross was hoping, so he kept them folded in plastic at the bottom of his rucksack. In the late afternoon, after a day's march, he would dig his foxhole, wash his hands under a canteen, unwrap the letters, hold them with the tips of his fingers, and spend the last hour of light pretending. He would imagine romantic camping trips into the White Mountains in New Hampshire. He would sometimes taste the envelope flaps, knowing her tongue had been there. More than anything, he wanted Martha to love him as he loved her, but the letters were mostly chatty, elusive on the matter of love. She was a virgin, he was almost sure. She was an English major at Mount Sebastian, and she wrote beautifully about her professors and roommates and midterm exams, about her respect for Chaucer and her great affection for Virginia Woolf. She often quoted lines of poetry; she never mentioned the war, except to say, Jimmy, take care of yourself. The letters weighed 10 ounces. They were signed Love, Martha, but Lieutenant Cross understood that Love was only a way of signing and did not mean what he sometimes pretended it meant. At dusk, he would carefully return the letters to his rucksack. Slowly, a bit distracted, he would get up and move among his men, checking the perimeter, then at full dark he would return to his hole and watch the night and wonder if Martha was a virgin.

The things they carried were largely determined by necessity. Among the necessities or near-necessities were P-38 can openers, pocket knives, heat tabs, wristwatches, dog tags, mosquito repellent, chewing gum, candy, cigarettes, salt tablets, packets of Kool-Aid, lighters, matches, sewing kits, Military Payment Certificates, C rations, and two or three canteens of water. Together, these items weighed between 15 and 20 pounds, depending upon a man's habits or rate of metabolism. Henry Dobbins, who was a big man, carried extra rations; he was especially fond of canned peaches in heavy syrup over pound cake. Dave Jensen, who practiced field hygiene, carried a toothbrush, dental floss, and several hotel-sized bars of soap he'd stolen on R&R in Sydney, Australia. Ted Lavender, who was scared, carried tranquilizers until he was shot in the head outside the village of Than Khe in mid-April. By necessity, and because it was SOP, they all carried steel helmets that weighed 5 pounds including the liner and camouflage cover. They carried the standard fatigue jackets and trousers. Very few carried underwear. On their feet they carried jungle boots—2.1 pounds—and Dave Jensen carried three pairs of socks and a can of Dr. Scholl's foot powder as a precaution against trench foot. Until he was shot, Ted Lavender carried six or seven ounces of premium dope, which for him was a necessity. Mitchell Sanders, the RTO, carried condoms. Norman Bowker carried a diary. Rat Kiley carried comic books. Kiowa, a devout Baptist, carried an illustrated New Testament that had been presented to him by his father, who taught Sunday school in Oklahoma City, Oklahoma. As a hedge against bad times, however, Kiowa also carried his grandmother's distrust of the white man, his grandfather's old hunting hatchet. Necessity dictated. Because the land was mined and booby-trapped, it was SOP for each man to carry a steel-centered, nylon-covered flak jacket, which weighed 6.7 pounds, but which on hot days seemed much heavier. Because you could die so quickly, each man carried at least one large compress bandage, usually in the helmet band for easy access. Because the nights were cold, and because the monsoons were wet, each carried a green plastic poncho that could be used as a raincoat or groundsheet or makeshift tent. With its quilted liner, the poncho weighed almost two pounds, but it was worth every ounce. In April, for instance, when Ted Lavender was shot, they used his poncho to wrap him up, then to carry him across the paddy, then to lift him into the chopper that took him away.

They were called legs or grunts.

To carry something was to hump it, as when Lieutenant Jimmy Cross humped his love for Martha up the hills and through the swamps. In its intransitive form, to hump meant to walk, or to march, but it implied burdens far beyond the intransitive.

5   Almost everyone humped photographs. In his wallet, Lieutenant Cross carried two photographs of Martha. The first was a Kodacolor snapshot signed Love, though he knew better. She stood against a brick wall. Her eyes were gray and neutral, her lips slightly open as she stared straight-on at the camera. At night, sometimes, Lieutenant Cross wondered who had taken the picture, because he knew she had boyfriends, because he loved her so much, and because he could see the shadow of the picture-taker spreading out against the brick wall. The second photograph had been clipped from the 1968 Mount Sebastian yearbook. It was an action shot—women's volleyball—and Martha was bent horizontal to the floor, reaching, the palms of her hands in sharp focus, the tongue taut, the expression frank and competitive. There was no visible sweat. She wore white gym shorts. Her legs, he thought, were almost certainly the legs of a virgin, dry and without hair, the left knee cocked and carrying her entire weight, which was just over one hundred pounds. Lieutenant Cross remembered touching that left knee. A dark theater, he remembered, and the movie was *Bonnie and Clyde*, and Martha wore a tweed skirt, and during the final scene, when he touched her knee, she turned and looked at him in a sad, sober way that made him pull his hand back, but he would always remember the feel of the tweed skirt and the knee beneath it and the sound of the gunfire that killed Bonnie and Clyde, how embarrassing it was, how slow and oppressive. He remembered kissing her good night at the dorm door. Right then, he thought, he should've done something brave. He should've carried her up the stairs to her room and tied her to the bed and touched that left knee all night long. He should've risked it. Whenever he looked at the photographs, he thought of new things he should've done.

What they carried was partly a function of rank, partly of field specialty.

As a first lieutenant and platoon leader, Jimmy Cross carried a compass, maps, code books, binoculars, and a .45-caliber pistol that weighed 2.9 pounds fully loaded. He carried a strobe light and the responsibility for the lives of his men.

As an RTO, Mitchell Sanders carried the PRC-25 radio, a killer, 26 pounds with its battery.

As a medic, Rat Kiley carried a canvas satchel filled with morphine and plasma and malaria tablets and surgical tape and comic books and all the things a medic must carry, including M&M's for especially bad wounds, for a total weight of nearly 20 pounds.

As a big man, therefore a machine gunner, Henry Dobbins carried the M-60, which weighed 23 pounds unloaded, but which was almost always loaded. In addition, Dobbins carried between 10 and 15 pounds of ammunition draped in belts across his chest and shoulders.

As PFCs or Spec 4s, most of them were common grunts and carried the standard M-16 gas-operated assault rifle. The weapon weighed 7.5 pounds unloaded, 8.2 pounds with its full 20-round magazine. Depending on numerous factors, such as topography and psychology, the riflemen carried anywhere from 12 to 20 magazines, usually in cloth bandoliers, adding on another 8.4 pounds at minimum, 14 pounds at maximum. When it was available, they also carried M-16 maintenance gear—rods and steel brushes and swabs and tubes of LSA oil—all of which weighed about a pound. Among the grunts, some carried the M-79 grenade launcher, 5.9 pounds unloaded, a reasonably light weapon except for the ammunition, which was heavy. A single round weighed 10 ounces. The typical load was 25 rounds. But Ted Lavender, who was scared, carried 34 rounds when he was shot and killed outside Than Khe, and he went down under an exceptional burden, more than 20 pounds of ammunition, plus the flak jacket and helmet and rations and water and toilet paper and tranquilizers and all the rest, plus the unweighed fear. He was dead weight. There was no twitching or flopping. Kiowa, who saw it happen, said it was like watching a rock fall, or a big sandbag or something—just boom, then down—not like the movies where the dead guy rolls around and does fancy spins and goes ass over teakettle—not like that, Kiowa said, the poor bastard just flat-fuck fell. Boom. Down. Nothing else. It was a bright morning in mid-April. Lieutenant Cross felt the pain. He blamed himself. They stripped off Lavender's canteens and ammo, all the heavy things, and Rat Kiley said the obvious, the guy's dead, and Mitchell Sanders used his radio to report one U.S. KIA and to request a chopper. Then they wrapped Lavender in his poncho. They carried him out to a dry paddy, established security, and sat smoking the dead man's dope until the chopper came. Lieutenant Cross kept to himself. He pictured Martha's smooth young face, thinking he loved her more than anything, more than his men, and now Ted Lavender was dead because he loved her so much and could not stop thinking about her. When the dustoff arrived, they carried Lavender aboard. Afterward they burned Than Khe. They marched until dusk, then dug their holes, and that night Kiowa kept explaining how you had to be there, how fast it was, how the poor guy just dropped like so much concrete. Boom-down, he said. Like cement.

In addition to the three standard weapons—the M-60, M-16, and M-79—they carried whatever presented itself, or whatever seemed appropriate as a means of killing or staying alive. They carried catch-as-catch-can. At various times, in various situations, they carried M-14s and CAR-15s and Swedish Ks and grease guns and captured AK-47s and Chi-Coms and RPGs and Simonov carbines and black market Uzis and .38-caliber Smith & Wesson handguns and 66 mm LAWs and shotguns and silencers and blackjacks and bayonets and C-4 plastic explosives. Lee Strunk carried a slingshot; a weapon of last resort, he called it. Mitchell Sanders carried brass knuckles. Kiowa carried his grandfather's feathered hatchet. Every third or fourth man carried a Claymore antipersonnel mine—3.5 pounds with its firing device. They all carried fragmentation grenades—14 ounces each. They all carried at least one M-18 colored smoke grenade—24 ounces. Some carried CS or tear gas grenades. Some carried white phosphorus grenades. They carried all they could bear, and then some, including a silent awe for the terrible power of the things they carried.

• • •

In the first week of April, before Lavender died, Lieutenant Jimmy Cross received a good-luck charm from Martha. It was a simple pebble, an ounce at most. Smooth to the touch, it was a milky white color with flecks of orange and violet, oval-shaped, like a miniature egg. In the accompanying letter, Martha wrote that she had found the pebble on the Jersey shoreline, precisely where the land touched water at high tide, where things came together but also separated. It was this separate-but-together quality, she wrote, that had inspired her to pick up the pebble and to carry it in her breast pocket for several days, where it seemed weightless, and then to send it through the mail, by air, as a token of her truest feelings for him. Lieutenant Cross found this romantic. But he wondered what her truest feelings were, exactly, and what she meant by separate-but-together. He wondered how the tides and waves had come into play on that afternoon along the Jersey shoreline when Martha saw the pebble and bent down to rescue it from geology. He imagined bare feet. Martha was a poet, with the poet's sensibilities, and her feet would be brown and bare, the toenails unpainted, the eyes chilly and somber like the ocean in March, and though it was painful, he wondered who had been with her that afternoon. He imagined a pair of shadows moving along the strip of sand where things came together but also separated. It was phantom jealousy, he knew, but he couldn't help himself. He loved her so much. On the march, through the hot days of early April, he carried the pebble in his mouth, turning it with his tongue, tasting sea salt and moisture. His mind wandered. He had difficulty keeping his attention on the war. On occasion he would yell at his men to spread out the column, to keep their eyes open, but then he would slip away into daydreams, just pretending, walking barefoot along the Jersey shore, with Martha, carrying nothing. He would feel himself rising. Sun and waves and gentle winds, all love and lightness.

What they carried varied by mission.

15   When a mission took them to the mountains, they carried mosquito netting, machetes, canvas tarps, and extra bug juice.

If a mission seemed especially hazardous, or if it involved a place they knew to be bad, they carried everything they could. In certain heavily mined AOs, where the land was dense with Toe Poppers and Bouncing Betties, they took turns humping a 28-pound mine detector. With its headphones and big sensing plate, the equipment was a stress on the lower back and shoulders, awkward to handle, often useless because of the shrapnel in the earth, but they carried it anyway, partly for safety, partly for the illusion of safety.

On ambush, or other night missions, they carried peculiar little odds and ends. Kiowa always took along his New Testament and a pair of moccasins for silence. Dave Jensen carried night-sight vitamins high in carotene. Lee Strunk carried his slingshot; ammo, he claimed, would never be a problem. Rat Kiley carried brandy and M&M's candy. Until he was shot, Ted Lavender carried the starlight scope, which weighed 6.3 pounds with its aluminum carrying case. Henry Dobbins carried his girlfriend's panty-hose wrapped around his neck as a comforter. They all carried ghosts. When dark came, they would move out single file across the meadows and paddies to their ambush coordinates, where they would quietly set up the Claymores and lie down and spend the night waiting.

Other missions were more complicated and required special equipment. In mid-April, it was their mission to search out and destroy the elaborate tunnel complexes in the Than Khe area south of Chu Lai. To blow the tunnels, they carried one-pound blocks of pentrite high explosives, four blocks to a man, 68 pounds in all. They carried wiring, detonators, and battery-powered clackers. Dave Jensen carried earplugs. Most often, before blowing the tunnels, they were ordered by higher command to search them, which was considered bad news, but by and large they just shrugged and carried out orders. Because he was a big man, Henry Dobbins was excused from tunnel duty. The others would draw numbers. Before Lavender died there were 17 men in the platoon, and whoever drew the number 17 would strip off his gear and crawl in headfirst with a flashlight and Lieutenant Cross's .45-caliber pistol. The rest of them would fan out as security. They would sit down or kneel, not facing the hole, listening to the ground beneath them, imagining cobwebs and ghosts, whatever was down there—the tunnel walls squeezing in—how the flashlight seemed impossibly heavy in the hand and how it was tunnel vision in the very strictest sense, compression in all ways, even time, and how you had to wiggle in—ass and elbows—a swallowed-up feeling—and how you found yourself worrying about odd things: Will your flashlight go dead? Do rats carry rabies? If you screamed, how far would the sound carry? Would your buddies hear it? Would they have the courage to drag you out? In some respects, though not many, the waiting was worse than the tunnel itself. Imagination was a killer.

On April 16, when Lee Strunk drew the number 17, he laughed and muttered something and went down quickly. The morning was hot and very still. Not good, Kiowa said. He looked at the tunnel opening, then out across a dry paddy toward the village of Than Khe. Nothing moved. No clouds or birds or people. As they waited, the men smoked and drank Kool-Aid, not talking much, feeling sympathy for Lee Strunk but also feeling the luck of the draw. You win some, you lose some, said Mitchell Sanders, and sometimes you settle for a rain check. It was a tired line and no one laughed.

Henry Dobbins ate a tropical chocolate bar. Ted Lavender popped a tranquilizer and   20
went off to pee.

After five minutes, Lieutenant Jimmy Cross moved to the tunnel, leaned down, and examined the darkness. Trouble, he thought—a cave-in maybe. And then suddenly, without willing it, he was thinking about Martha. The stresses and fractures, the quick collapse, the two of them buried alive under all that weight. Dense, crushing love. Kneeling, watching the hole, he tried to concentrate on Lee Strunk and the war, all the dangers, but his love was too much for him, he felt paralyzed, he wanted to sleep inside her lungs and breathe her blood and be smothered. He wanted her to be a virgin and not a virgin, all at once. He wanted to know her. Intimate secrets: Why poetry? Why so sad? Why that grayness in her eyes? Why so alone? Not lonely, just alone—riding her bike across campus or sitting off by herself in the cafeteria—even dancing, she danced alone—and it was the aloneness that filled him with love. He remembered telling her that one evening. How she nodded and looked away. And how, later, when he kissed her, she received the kiss without returning it, her eyes wide open, not afraid, not a virgin's eyes, just flat and uninvolved.

Lieutenant Cross gazed at the tunnel. But he was not there. He was buried with Martha under the white sand at the Jersey shore. They were pressed together, and the pebble in his mouth was her tongue. He was smiling. Vaguely, he was aware of how quiet the day was, the sullen paddies, yet he could not bring himself to worry about matters of security. He was beyond that. He was just a kid at war, in love. He was twenty-four years old. He couldn't help it.

A few moments later Lee Strunk crawled out of the tunnel. He came up grinning, filthy but alive. Lieutenant Cross nodded and closed his eyes while the others clapped Strunk on the back and made jokes about rising from the dead.

Worms, Rat Kiley said. Right out of the grave. Fuckin' zombie.

The men laughed. They all felt great relief.   25

Spook city, said Mitchell Sanders.

Lee Strunk made a funny ghost sound, a kind of moaning, yet very happy, and right then, when Strunk made that high happy moaning sound, when he went *Ahhooooo*, right then Ted Lavender was shot in the head on his way back from peeing. He lay with his mouth open. The teeth were broken. There was a swollen black bruise under his left eye. The cheekbone was gone. Oh shit, Rat Kiley said, the guy's dead. The guy's dead, he kept saying, which seemed profound—the guy's dead. I mean really.

•   •   •

The things they carried were determined to some extent by superstition. Lieutenant Cross carried his good-luck pebble. Dave Jensen carried a rabbit's foot. Norman Bowker, otherwise a very gentle person, carried a thumb that had been presented to him as a gift by Mitchell Sanders. The thumb was dark brown, rubbery to the touch, and weighed four ounces at most. It had been cut from a VC corpse, a boy of fifteen or sixteen. They'd found him at the bottom of an irrigation ditch, badly burned, flies in his mouth and eyes. The boy wore black shorts and sandals. At the time of his death he had been carrying a pouch of rice, a rifle and three magazines of ammunition.

You want my opinion, Mitchell Sanders said, there's a definite moral here.

30   He put his hand on the dead boy's wrist. He was quiet for a time, as if counting a pulse, then he patted the stomach, almost affectionately, and used Kiowa's hunting hatchet to remove the thumb.

Henry Dobbins asked what the moral was.

Moral?

You know. *Moral.*

Sanders wrapped the thumb in toilet paper and handed it across to Norman Bowker. There was no blood. Smiling, he kicked the boy's head, watched the flies scatter, and said, It's like with that old TV show—Paladin. Have gun, will travel.

35   Henry Dobbins thought about it.

Yeah, well, he finally said. I don't see no moral.

There it *is*, man.

Fuck off.

They carried USO stationery and pencils and pens. They carried Sterno, safety pins, trip flares, signal flares, spools of wire, razor blades, chewing tobacco, liberated joss sticks and statuettes of the smiling Buddha, candles, grease pencils, *The Stars and Stripes*, fingernail clippers, Psy Ops leaflets, bush hats, bolos, and much more. Twice a week, when the resupply choppers came in, they carried hot chow in green mermite cans and large canvas bags filled with iced beer and soda pop. They carried plastic water containers, each with a two-gallon capacity. Mitchell Sanders carried a set of starched tiger fatigues for special occasions. Henry Dobbins carried Black Flag insecticide. Dave Jensen carried empty sandbags that could be filled at night for added protection. Lee Strunk carried tanning lotion. Some things they carried in common. Taking turns, they carried the big PRC-77 scrambler radio, which weighed 30 pounds with its battery. They shared the weight of memory. They took up what others could no longer bear. Often, they carried each other, the wounded or weak. They carried infections. They carried chess sets, basketballs, Vietnamese-English dictionaries, insignia of rank, Bronze Stars and Purple Hearts, plastic cards imprinted with the Code of Conduct. They carried diseases, among them malaria and dysentery. They carried lice and ringworm and leeches and paddy algae and various rots and molds. They carried the land itself—Vietnam, the place, the soil—a powdery orange-red dust that covered their boots and fatigues and faces. They carried the sky. The whole atmosphere, they carried it, the humidity, the monsoons, the stink of fungus and decay, all of it, they carried gravity. They moved like mules. By daylight they took sniper fire, at night they were mortared, but it was not battle, it was just the endless march, village to village, without purpose, nothing won or lost. They marched for the sake of the march. They plodded along slowly, dumbly, leaning forward against the heat, unthinking, all blood and bone, simple grunts, soldiering with their legs, toiling up the hills and down into the paddies and across the rivers and up again and down, just humping, one step and then the next and then another, but no volition, no will, because it was automatic, it was anatomy, and the war was entirely a matter of posture and carriage, the hump was everything, a kind of inertia, a kind of emptiness, a dullness of desire and intellect and conscience and hope and human sensibility. Their principles were in their feet. Their calculations were biological. They had no sense of strategy or mission.

They searched the villages without knowing what to look for, not caring, kicking over jars of rice, frisking children and old men, blowing tunnels, sometimes setting fires and sometimes not, then forming up and moving on to the next village, then other villages, where it would always be the same. They carried their own lives. The pressures were enormous. In the heat of early afternoon, they would remove their helmets and flak jackets, walking bare, which was dangerous but which helped ease the strain. They would often discard things along the route of march. Purely for comfort, they would throw away rations, blow their Claymores and grenades, no matter, because by nightfall the resupply choppers would arrive with more of the same, then a day or two later still more, fresh watermelons and crates of ammunition and sunglasses and woolen sweaters—the resources were stunning—sparklers for the Fourth of July, colored eggs for Easter—it was the great American war chest—the fruits of science, the smokestacks, the canneries, the arsenals at Hartford, the Minnesota forests, the machine shops, the vast fields of corn and wheat—they carried like freight trains; they carried it on their backs and shoulders—and for all the ambiguities of Vietnam, all the mysteries and unknowns, there was at least the single abiding certainty that they would never be at a loss for things to carry.

After the chopper took Lavender away, Lieutenant Jimmy Cross led his men into the village of Than Khe. They burned everything. They shot chickens and dogs, they trashed the village well, they called in artillery and watched the wreckage, then they marched for several hours through the hot afternoon, and then at dusk, while Kiowa explained how Lavender died, Lieutenant Cross found himself trembling.

He tried not to cry. With his entrenching tool, which weighed five pounds, he began digging a hole in the earth.

He felt shame. He hated himself. He had loved Martha more than his men, and as a consequence Lavender was now dead, and this was something he would have to carry like a stone in his stomach for the rest of the war.

All he could do was dig. He used his entrenching tool like an ax, slashing, feeling both love and hate, and then later, when it was full dark, he sat at the bottom of his foxhole and wept. It went on for a long while. In part, he was grieving for Ted Lavender, but mostly it was for Martha, and for himself, because she belonged to another world, which was not quite real, and because she was a junior at Mount Sebastian College in New Jersey, a poet and a virgin and uninvolved, and because he realized she did not love him and never would.

Like cement, Kiowa whispered in the dark. I swear to God—boom, down. Not a word.

I've heard this, said Norman Bowker.

A pisser, you know? Still zipping himself up. Zapped while zipping.

All right, fine. That's enough.

Yeah, but you had to see it, the guy just—

I *heard*, man. Cement. So why not shut the fuck *up*?

Kiowa shook his head sadly and glanced over at the hole where Lieutenant Jimmy Cross sat watching the night. The air was thick and wet. A warm dense fog had settled over the paddies and there was the stillness that precedes rain.

After a time Kiowa sighed.

One thing for sure, he said. The lieutenant's in some deep hurt. I mean that crying jag—the way he was carrying on—it wasn't fake or anything, it was real heavy-duty hurt. The man cares.

Sure, Norman Bowker said.

Say what you want, the man does care.

We all got problems.

Not Lavender.

No, I guess not, Bowker said. Do me a favor, though.

Shut up?

That's a smart Indian. Shut up.

60   Shrugging, Kiowa pulled off his boots. He wanted to say more, just to lighten up his sleep, but instead he opened his New Testament and arranged it beneath his head as a pillow. The fog made things seem hollow and unattached. He tried not to think about Ted Lavender, but then he was thinking how fast it was, no drama, down and dead, and how it was hard to feel anything except surprise. It seemed unchristian. He wished he could find some great sadness, or even anger, but the emotion wasn't there and he couldn't make it happen. Mostly he felt pleased to be alive. He liked the smell of the New Testament under his cheek, the leather and ink and paper and glue, whatever the chemicals were. He liked hearing the sounds of night. Even his fatigue, it felt fine, the stiff muscles and the prickly awareness of his own body, a floating feeling. He enjoyed not being dead. Lying there, Kiowa admired Lieutenant Jimmy Cross's capacity for grief. He wanted to share the man's pain, he wanted to care as Jimmy Cross cared. And yet when he closed his eyes, all he could think was Boom-down, and all he could feel was the pleasure of having his boots off and the fog curling in around him and the damp soil and the Bible smells and the plush comfort of night.

After a moment Norman Bowker sat up in the dark.

What the hell, he said. You want to talk, *talk*. Tell it to me.

Forget it.

No, man, go on. One thing I hate, it's a silent Indian.

65   For the most part they carried themselves with poise, a kind of dignity. Now and then, however, there were times of panic, when they squealed or wanted to squeal but couldn't, when they twitched and made moaning sounds and covered their heads and said Dear Jesus and flopped around on the earth and fired their weapons blindly and cringed and sobbed and begged for the noise to stop and went wild and made stupid promises to themselves and to God and to their mothers and fathers, hoping not to die. In different ways, it happened to all of them. Afterward, when the firing ended, they would blink and peek up. They would touch their bodies, feeling shame, then quickly hiding it. They would force themselves to stand. As if in slow motion, frame by frame, the world would take on the old logic—absolute silence, then the wind, then sunlight, then voices. It was the burden of being alive. Awkwardly, the men would reassemble themselves, first in private, then in groups, becoming soldiers again. They would repair the leaks in their eyes. They would check for casualties, call in dust-offs, light cigarettes, try to smile, clear their throats and spit and begin cleaning their weapons. After a time someone would shake his head and say, No lie. I almost shit my pants, and someone else would laugh, which meant it was bad, yes, but the guy had obviously not shit his pants, it wasn't that bad, and in any case nobody would ever do such a thing and then go ahead and talk about it. They would squint into the dense, oppressive sunlight. For a few moments, perhaps, they would fall silent, lighting a joint and tracking its passage from man to man, inhaling, holding in the humiliation. Scary stuff, one of them might say. But then someone else would grin or flick his eyebrows and say, Roger-dodger, almost cut me a new asshole, *almost*.

There were numerous such poses. Some carried themselves with a sort of wistful resignation, others with pride or stiff soldierly discipline or good humor or macho zeal. They were afraid of dying but they were even more afraid to show it.

They found jokes to tell.

They used a hard vocabulary to contain the terrible softness. *Greased* they'd say. *Offed, lit up, zapped while zipping*. It wasn't cruelty, just stage presence. They were actors. When someone died, it wasn't quite dying, because in a curious way it seemed scripted, and because they had their lines mostly memorized, irony mixed with tragedy, and because they called it by other names, as if to encyst and destroy the reality of death itself. They kicked corpses. They cut off thumbs. They talked grunt lingo. They told stories about Ted Lavender's supply of tranquilizers, how the poor guy didn't feel a thing, how incredibly tranquil he was.

There's a moral here, said Mitchell Sanders.

They were waiting for Lavender's chopper, smoking the dead man's dope. 70

The moral's pretty obvious, Sanders said, and winked. Stay away from drugs. No joke, they'll ruin your day every time.

Cute, said Henry Dobbins.

Mind blower, get it? Talk about wiggy. Nothing left, just blood and brains.

They made themselves laugh.

There it is, they'd say. Over and over—there it is, my friend, there it is—as if the repetition 75 itself were an act of poise, a balance between crazy and almost crazy, knowing without going, there it is, which meant be cool, let it ride, because Oh yeah, man, you can't change what can't be changed, there it is, there it absolutely and positively and fucking well *is*.

They were tough.

They carried all the emotional baggage of men who might die. Grief, terror, love, longing—these were intangibles, but the intangibles had their own mass and specific gravity, they had tangible weight. They carried shameful memories. They carried the common secret of cowardice barely restrained, the instinct to run or freeze or hide, and in many respects this was the heaviest burden of all, for it could never be put down, it required perfect balance and perfect posture. They carried their reputations. They carried the soldier's greatest fear, which was the fear of blushing. Men killed, and died, because they were embarrassed not to. It was what had brought them to the war in the first place, nothing positive, no dreams of glory or honor, just to avoid the blush of dishonor. They died so as not to die of embarrassment. They crawled into tunnels and walked point and advanced under fire. Each morning, despite the unknowns, they made their legs move. They endured. They kept humping. They did not submit to the obvious alternative, which was simply to close the eyes and fall. So easy, really. Go limp and tumble to the ground and let the muscles unwind and not speak and not budge until your buddies picked you up and lifted you into the chopper that would roar and dip its nose and carry you off to the world. A mere matter of falling, yet no one ever fell. It was not courage, exactly; the object was not valor. Rather, they were too frightened to be cowards.

By and large they carried these things inside, maintaining the masks of composure. They sneered at sick call. They spoke bitterly about guys who had found release by shooting off their own toes or fingers. Pussies, they'd say. Candy-asses. It was fierce, mocking talk, with only a trace of envy or awe, but even so the image played itself out behind their eyes.

They imagined the muzzle against flesh. So easy: squeeze the trigger and blow away a toe. They imagined it. They imagined the quick, sweet pain, then the evacuation to Japan, then a hospital with warm beds and cute geisha nurses.

And they dreamed of freedom birds. 80

At night, on guard, staring into the dark, they were carried away by jumbo jets. They felt the rush of takeoff. *Gone!* they yelled. And then velocity—wings and engines—a smiling stewardess—but it was more than a plane, it was a real bird, a big sleek silver bird with feathers and talons and high screeching. They were flying. The weights fell off; there was nothing to bear. They laughed and held on tight, feeling the cold slap of wind and altitude, soaring, thinking *It's over, I'm gone!*—they were naked, they were light and free—it was all lightness, bright and fast and buoyant, light as light, a helium buzz in the brain, a giddy bubbling in the lungs as they were taken up over the clouds and the war, beyond duty, beyond gravity and mortification and global entanglements—*Sin loi!* they yelled. *I'm sorry, motherfuckers, but I'm out of it, I'm goofed, I'm on a space cruise, I'm gone!*—and it was a restful,

unencumbered sensation, just riding the light waves, sailing that big silver freedom bird over the mountains and oceans, over America, over the farms and great sleeping cities and cemeteries and highways and the golden arches of McDonald's, it was flight, a kind of fleeing, a kind of falling, falling higher and higher, spinning off the edge of the earth and beyond the sun and through the vast, silent vacuum where there were no burdens and where everything weighed exactly nothing—*Gone!* they screamed. *I'm sorry but I'm gone!*—and so at night, not quite dreaming, they gave themselves over to lightness, they were carried, they were purely borne.

On the morning after Ted Lavender died, First Lieutenant Jimmy Cross crouched at the bottom of his foxhole and burned Martha's letters. Then he burned the two photographs. There was a steady rain falling, which made it difficult, but he used heat tabs and Sterno to build a small fire, screening it with his body, holding the photographs over the tight blue flame with the tips of his fingers.

He realized it was only a gesture. Stupid, he thought. Sentimental, too, but mostly just stupid.

Lavender was dead. You couldn't burn the blame.

85   Besides, the letters were in his head. And even now, without photographs, Lieutenant Cross could see Martha playing volleyball in her white gym shorts and yellow T-shirt. He could see her moving in the rain.

When the fire died out, Lieutenant Cross pulled his poncho over his shoulders and ate breakfast from a can.

There was no great mystery, he decided.

In those burned letters Martha had never mentioned the war, except to say, Jimmy, take care of yourself. She wasn't involved. She signed the letters Love, but it wasn't love, and all the fine lines and technicalities did not matter. Virginity was no longer an issue. He hated her. Yes, he did. He hated her. Love, too, but it was a hard, hating kind of love.

The morning came up wet and blurry. Everything seemed part of everything else, the fog and Martha and the deepening rain.

90   He was a soldier, after all.

Half smiling, Lieutenant Jimmy Cross took out his maps. He shook his head hard, as if to clear it, then bent forward and began planning the day's march. In ten minutes, or maybe twenty, he would rouse the men and they would pack up and head west, where the maps showed the country to be green and inviting. They would do what they had always done. The rain might add some weight, but otherwise it would be one more day layered upon all the other days.

He was realistic about it. There was that new hardness in his stomach. He loved her but he hated her.

No more fantasies, he told himself.

Henceforth, when he thought about Martha, it would be only to think that she belonged elsewhere. He would shut down the daydreams. This was not Mount Sebastian, it was another world, where there were no pretty poems or midterm exams, a place where men died because of carelessness and gross stupidity. Kiowa was right. Boom-down, and you were dead, never partly dead.

95   Briefly, in the rain, Lieutenant Cross saw Martha's gray eyes gazing back at him.

He understood.

It was very sad, he thought. The things men carried inside. The things men did or felt they had to do.

He almost nodded at her, but didn't.

Instead he went back to his maps. He was now determined to perform his duties firmly and without negligence. It wouldn't help Lavender, he knew that, but from this point on he would comport himself as an officer. He would dispose of his good-luck pebble. Swallow it, maybe, or use Lee Strunk's slingshot, or just drop it along the trail. On the march he would impose strict field discipline. He would be careful to send out flank security, to prevent straggling or bunching up, to keep his troops moving at the proper pace and at the proper interval. He would insist on clean weapons. He would confiscate the remainder of Lavender's dope. Later in the day, perhaps, he would call the men together and speak to them plainly. He would accept the blame for what had happened to Ted Lavender. He would be a man about it. He would look them in the eyes, keeping his chin level, and he would issue the new SOPs in a calm, impersonal tone of voice, a lieutenant's voice, leaving no room for argument or discussion. Commencing immediately, he'd tell them, they would no longer abandon equipment along the route of march. They would police up their acts. They would get their shit together, and keep it together, and maintain it neatly and in good working order. He would not tolerate laxity. He would show strength, distancing himself.

Among the men there would be grumbling, of course, and maybe worse, because their days would seem longer and their loads heavier, but Lieutenant Jimmy Cross reminded himself that his obligation was not to be loved but to lead. He would dispense with love; it was not now a factor. And if anyone quarreled or complained, he would simply tighten his lips and arrange his shoulders in the correct command posture. He might give a curt little nod. Or he might not. He might just shrug and say, Carry on, then they would saddle up and form into a column and move out toward the villages west of Than Khe.

100

QUESTIONS

1. What do we learn about Lieutenant Jimmy Cross? How do we learn about him? Why does he blame himself for Lavender's death? How does Kiowa misinterpret his emotions? How do his concerns unify the story? What other unifying elements does the story contain?

2. What is the effect of the repetitions in the story (the constant descriptions of how much things weigh, the regular need to carry things, the way in which Lavender died)?

3. Why is Mitchell Sanders unable to put into words the moral of the dead man's thumb? How would you describe the moral?

4. Analyze paragraph 39. Discuss the various burdens the men of the platoon must carry. What bearing does this paragraph have upon other parts of the story?

LUIGI PIRANDELLO (1867–1936)

Pirandello was born in southern Sicily into a wealthy family. At first he was home schooled, but eventually went to high school in Palermo, the capital of Sicily. Later he attended the University of Palermo and the University of Rome, but then he went to Bonn, Germany (the birth city of Beethoven), where he gained a doctorate in humanities in 1891. His resources failed because of a disastrous flood in the family's Sicilian sulfur mine, and he was left mainly to his own resources as a teacher and writer. His marriage, which produced three children, proved disastrous as his wife eventually was declared insane and had to be institutionalized. Pirandello's early years were taken up mainly with the writing of stories and dramas. One of his three sons fought in World War I, and survived, unlike the son in the story "War." Eventually Pirandello developed a masterly career as a dramatist, his best known and highly original play being Six Characters in Search of an Author *in*

1921. With the support of Benito Mussolini, the Prime Minister and Dictator of Italy—support that many claimed was highly controversial because of Mussolini's later alliance with Adolf Hitler—Pirandello became well known internationally. In 1934, he was awarded the Nobel Prize in Literature.

War (1919)

The passengers who had left Rome by the night express had had to stop until dawn at the small station of Fabriano in order to continue their journey by the small old-fashioned local joining the main line with Sulmona.

At dawn, in a stuffy and smoky second-class carriage in which five people had already spent the night, a bulky woman in deep mourning was hoisted in—almost like a shapeless bundle. Behind her, puffing and moaning, followed her husband—a tiny man, thin and weakly, his face death-white, his eyes small and bright and looking shy and uneasy.

Having at last taken a seat he politely thanked the passengers who had helped his wife and who had made room for her; then he turned round to the woman trying to pull down the collar of her coat, and politely inquired:

"Are you all right, dear?"

5 The wife, instead of answering, pulled up her collar again to her eyes, so as to hide her face.

"Nasty world," muttered the husband with a sad smile.

And he felt it his duty to explain to his traveling companions that the poor woman was to be pitied, for the war was taking away from her her only son, a boy of twenty to whom both had devoted their entire life, even breaking up their home at Sulmona to follow him to Rome, where he had to go as a student, then allowing him to volunteer for war with an assurance, however, that at least for six months he would not be sent to the front and now, all of a sudden, receiving a wire saying that he was due to leave in three days' time and asking them to go and see him off.

The woman under the big coat was twisting and wriggling, at times growling like a wild animal, feeling certain that all those explanations would not have aroused even a shadow of sympathy from those people who—most likely—were in the same plight as herself. One of them, who had been listening with particular attention, said:

"You should thank God that your son is only leaving now for the front. Mine has been sent there the first day of the war. He has already come back twice wounded and been sent back again to the front."

10 "What about me? I have two sons and three nephews at the front," said another passenger.

"Maybe, but in our case it is our only son," ventured the husband.

"What difference can it make? You may spoil your only son with excessive attentions, but you cannot love him more than you would all your other children if you had any. Paternal love is not like bread that can be broken into pieces and split amongst the children in equal shares. A father gives all his love to each one of his children without discrimination, whether it be one or ten, and if I am suffering now for my two sons, I am not suffering half for each of them but double."

"True . . . true . . . " sighed the embarrassed husband, "but suppose (of course we all hope it will never be your case) a father has two sons at the front and he loses one of them, there is still one left to console him . . . while . . ."

"Yes," answered the other, getting cross, "a son left to console him but also a son left for whom he must survive, while in the case of the father of an only son if the son dies the father can die too and put an end to his distress. Which of the two positions is the worse? Don't you see how my case would be worse than yours?"

"Nonsense," interrupted another traveler, a fat, red-faced man with bloodshot eyes of   15
the palest gray.

He was panting. From his bulging eyes seemed to spurt inner violence of an uncontrolled vitality which his weakened body could hardly contain.

"Nonsense," he repeated, trying to cover his mouth with his hand so as to hide the two missing front teeth. "Nonsense. Do we give life to our children for our own benefit?"

The other travelers stared at him in distress. The one who had had his son at the front since the first day of the war sighed: "You are right. Our children do not belong to us, they belong to the Country. . . ."

"Bosh," retorted the fat traveler. "Do we think of the Country when we give life to our children? Our sons are born because . . . well, because they must be born and when they come to life they take our own life with them. This is the truth. We belong to them but they never belong to us. And when they reach twenty they are exactly what we were at their age. We too had a father and mother, but there were so many other things as well . . . girls, cigarettes, illusions, new ties . . . and the Country, of course, whose call we would have answered—when we were twenty—even if father and mother had said no. Now at our age, the love of our Country is still great, of course, but stronger than it is the love for our children. Is there any one of us here who wouldn't gladly take his son's place at the front if he could?"

There was a silence all round, everybody nodding as to approve.   20

"Why then," continued the fat man, "shouldn't we consider the feelings of our children when they are twenty? Isn't it natural that at their age they should consider the love for their Country (I am speaking of decent boys, of course) even greater than the love for us? Isn't it natural that it should be so, as after all they must look upon us as upon old boys who cannot move any more and must stay at home? If Country exists, if Country is a natural necessity, like bread, of which each of us must eat in order not to die of hunger, somebody must go to defend it. And our sons go, when they are twenty, and they don't want tears, because if they die, they die inflamed and happy (I am speaking, of course, of decent boys). Now, if one dies young and happy, without having the ugly sides of life, the boredom of it, the pettiness, the bitterness of disillusion . . . what more can we ask for him? Everyone should stop crying; everyone should laugh, as I do . . . or at least thank God—as I do—because my son, before dying, sent me a message saying that he was dying satisfied at having ended his life in the best way he could have wished. That is why, as you see, I do not even wear mourning. . . ."

He shook his light fawn coat as to show it; his livid lip over his missing teeth was trembling, his eyes were watery and motionless, and soon after he ended with a shrill laugh which might well have been a sob.

"Quite so . . . quite so . . ." agreed the others.

The woman who, bundled in a corner under her coat, had been sitting and listening had—for the last three months—tried to find in the words of her husband and her friends something to console her in her deep sorrow, something that might show her how a mother should resign herself to send her son not even to death but to a probably dangerous life. Yet not a word had she found amongst the many which had been said . . . and her grief had been greater in seeing that nobody—as she thought—could share her feelings.

But now the words of the traveler amazed and almost stunned her. She suddenly realized that it wasn't the others who were wrong and could not understand her, but herself who could not rise up to the same height of those fathers and mothers willing to resign themselves, without crying, not only to the departure of their sons but even to their death.   25

She lifted her head, she bent over from her corner trying to listen with great attention to the details which the fat man was giving to his companions about the way his son had fallen as a hero, for his King and his Country, happy and without regrets. It seemed to her that she had stumbled into a world she had never dreamt of, a world so far unknown to her and she was so pleased to hear everyone joining in congratulating that brave father who could so stoically speak of his child's death.

Then suddenly, just as if she had heard nothing of what had been said and almost as if waking up from a dream, she turned to the old man, asking him:

"Then . . . is your son really dead?"

Everybody stared at her. The old man, too, turned to look at her, fixing his great, bulging, horribly watery light gray eyes, deep in her face. For some little time he tried to answer, but words failed him. He looked and looked at her, almost as if only then—at that silly, incongruous question—he had suddenly realized at last that his son was really dead—gone forever—forever. His face contracted, became horribly distorted, then he snatched in haste a handkerchief from his pocket and, to the amazement of everyone, broke into harrowing, heart-rending, uncontrollable sobs.

QUESTIONS

1. Explain the means by which Pirandello develops the narrative structure of the story. Why does he include so much conversation? What might the story be like if it had been carried out exclusively through description?

2. Describe the thoughts about death expressed by the "fat, red-faced man with bloodshot eyes." How does this man seem to be defending the need for battlefield deaths? How do his true thoughts emerge in the story? How does he seem to be contradictory?

3. What do you think is the story's major idea, as it develops in the discussion by the passengers? Why does Pirandello choose the man who seems least appealing as the one to whom the ultimate sacrifice has happened?

4. In paragraph 28, why does the woman who is "bundled in a corner under her coat" ask the simple question of the fat man? Why is it she who asks the question, and not one of the other passengers?

ALICE WALKER (b. 1944)

Walker was born in Georgia and attended Sarah Lawrence College, graduating in 1965. In addition to teaching at Yale, Wellesley, and other schools, she has edited and published fiction, poetry, and biography, and she received a Guggenheim Fellowship in 1977. Her main hobby is gardening. For her collection of poems Revolutionary Petunias *(1973), she received a Wall Book Award nomination. Her best-known novel,* The Color Purple *(1982), was made into a movie that won an Academy Award in 1985. Her most recent novel is* By the Light of My Father's Smile *(1998).*

 Everyday Use (1973)

for your grandmama

I will wait for her in the yard that Maggie and I made so clean and wavy yesterday afternoon. A yard like this is more comfortable than most people know. It is not just a yard. It is like an extended living room. When the hard clay is swept clean as a floor and the fine sand around the edges lined with tiny, irregular grooves, anyone can come and sit and look up into the elm tree and wait for the breezes that never come inside the house.

Maggie will be nervous until after her sister goes: she will stand hopelessly in corners, homely and ashamed of the burn scars down her arms and legs, eying her sister with a mixture of envy and awe. She thinks her sister has held life always in the palm of one hand, that "no" is a word the world never learned to say to her.

You've no doubt seen those TV shows° where the child who has "made it" is confronted, as a surprise, by her own mother and father, tottering in weakly from backstage. (A pleasant surprise, of course: What would they do if parent and child came on the show only to curse out and insult each other?) On TV mother and child embrace and smile into each other's faces. Sometimes the mother and father weep, the child wraps them in her arms and leans across the table to tell how she would not have made it without their help. I have seen these programs.

Sometimes I dream a dream in which Dee and I are suddenly brought together on a TV program of this sort. Out of a dark and soft-seated limousine I am ushered into a bright room filled with many people. There I meet a smiling, gray, sporty man like Johnny Carson who shakes my hand and tells me what a fine girl I have. Then we are on the stage and Dee is embracing me with tears in her eyes. She pins on my dress a large orchid, even though she has told me once that she thinks orchids are tacky flowers.

In real life I am a large, big-boned woman with rough, man-working hands. In the winter I wear flannel nightgowns to bed and overalls during the day. I can kill and clean a hog as mercilessly as a man. My fat keeps me hot in zero weather. I can work outside all day, breaking ice to get water for washing; I can eat pork liver cooked over the open fire minutes after it comes steaming from the hog. One winter I knocked a bull calf straight in the brain between the eyes with a sledge hammer and had the meat hung up to chill before nightfall. But of course all this does not show on television. I am the way my daughter would want me to be: a hundred pounds lighter, my skin like an uncooked barley pancake. My hair glistens in the hot bright lights. Johnny Carson has much to do to keep up with my quick and witty tongue. 5

But that is a mistake, I know even before I wake up. Who ever knew a Johnson with a quick tongue? Who can even imagine me looking a strange white man in the eye? It seems to me I have talked to them always with one foot raised in flight, with my head turned in whichever way is farthest from them. Dee, though. She would always look anyone in the eye. Hesitation was no part of her nature.

"How do I look, Mama?" Maggie says, showing just enough of her thin body enveloped in pink skirt and red blouse for me to know she's there, hidden by the door.

"Come out into the yard," I say.

Have you ever seen a lame animal, perhaps a dog run over by some careless person rich enough to own a car, sidle up to someone who is ignorant enough to be kind to him? That is the way my Maggie walks. She has been like this, chin on chest, eyes on ground, feet in shuffle, ever since the fire that burned the other house to the ground.

Dee is lighter than Maggie, with nicer hair and a fuller figure. She's a woman now, though sometimes I forget. How long ago was it that the other house burned? Ten, twelve years? Sometimes I can still hear the flames and feel Maggie's arms sticking to me, her hair smoking and her dress falling off her in little black papery flakes. Her eyes seemed stretched open, blazed open by the flames reflected in them. And Dee, I see her standing off 10

° *TV shows:* In the early days of television, a popular show was *This Is Your Life*, which the narrator describes exactly here.

under the sweet gum tree she used to dig gum out of; a look of concentration on her face as she watched the last dingy gray board of the house fall in toward the red-hot brick chimney. Why don't you do a dance around the ashes? I'd wanted to ask her. She had hated the house that much.

I used to think she hated Maggie, too. But that was before we raised the money, the church and me, to send her to Augusta° to school. She used to read to us without pity; forcing words, lies, other folks' habits, whole lives upon us two, sitting trapped and ignorant underneath her voice. She washed us in a river of make-believe, burned us with a lot of knowledge we didn't necessarily need to know. Pressed us to her with the serious way she read, to shove us away at just the moment, like dimwits, we seemed about to understand.

Dee wanted nice things. A yellow organdy dress to wear to her graduation from high school; black pumps to match a green suit she'd made from an old suit somebody gave me. She was determined to stare down any disaster in her efforts. Her eyelids would not flicker for minutes at a time. Often I fought off the temptation to shake her. At sixteen she had a style of her own: and knew what style was.

I never had an education myself. After second grade the school was closed down. Don't ask me why: in 1927 colored asked fewer questions than they do now. Sometimes Maggie reads to me. She stumbles along good-naturedly, but can't see well. She knows she is not bright. Like good looks and money, quickness passed her by. She will marry John Thomas (who has mossy teeth in an earnest face) and then I'll be free to sit here and I guess just sing church songs to myself. Although I never was a good singer. Never could carry a tune. I was always better at a man's job. I used to love to milk till I was hooked in the side° in '49. Cows are soothing and slow and don't bother you, unless you try to milk them the wrong way.

I have deliberately turned my back on the house. It is three rooms, just like the one that burned, except the roof is tin; they don't make shingle roofs any more. There are no real windows, just some holes cut in the sides, like the portholes on a ship, but not round and not square, with rawhide holding the shutters up on the outside. This house is in a pasture, too, like the other one. No doubt when Dee sees it she will want to tear it down. She wrote me once that no matter where we "choose" to live, she will manage to come see us. But she will never bring her friends. Maggie and I thought about this and Maggie asked me, "Mama, when did Dee ever *have* any friends?"

15   She has a few. Furtive boys in pink shirts hanging about on washday after school. Nervous girls who never laughed. Impressed with her they worshiped the well-turned phrase, the cute shape, the scalding humor that erupted like bubbles in lye. She read to them.

When she was courting Jimmy T she didn't have much time to pay to us, but turned all her faultfinding power on him. He *flew* to marry a cheap city girl from a family of ignorant flashy people. She hardly had time to recompose herself.

When she comes I will meet—but there they are!

Maggie attempts to make a dash for the house, in her shuffling way, but I stay her with my hand. "Come back here," I say. And she stops and tries to dig a well in the sand with her toe.

It is hard to see them clearly through the strong sun. But even the first glimpse of leg out of the car tells me it is Dee. Her feet were always neat-looking, as if God himself had shaped them with a certain style. From the other side of the car comes a short, stocky man. Hair is all over his head a foot long and hanging from his chin like a kinky mule tail. I hear Maggie suck in her breath. "Uhnnnh," is what it sounds like. Like when you see the wriggling end of a snake just in front of your foot on the road. "Uhnnnh."

° *Augusta:* city in eastern Georgia, the location of Paine College.
° *hooked in the side:* kicked by a cow.

Dee next. A dress down to the ground, in this hot weather. A dress so loud it hurts my   20
eyes. There are yellows and oranges enough to throw back the light of the sun. I feel my
whole face warming from the heat waves it throws out. Earrings gold, too, and hanging
down to her shoulders. Bracelets dangling and making noises when she moves her arm up
to shake the folds of the dress out of her armpits. The dress is loose and flows, and as she
walks closer, I like it. I hear Maggie go "Uhnnnh" again. It is her sister's hair. It stands
straight up like the wool on a sheep. It is black as night and around the edges are two long
pigtails that rope about like small lizards disappearing behind her ears.

"Wa-su-zo-Tean-o!"° she says, coming on in that gliding way the dress makes her move.
The short stocky yellow with the hair to his navel is all grinning and he follows up with
"Asalamalakim,° my mother and my sister!" He moves to hug Maggie but she falls back,
tight up against the back of my chair. I feel her trembling there and when I look up I see the
perspiration falling off her chin.

"Don't get up," says Dee. Since I am stout it takes something of a push. You can see me
trying to move a second or two before I make it. She turns, showing white heels through
her sandals, and goes back to the car. Out she peeks next with a Polaroid. She stoops down
quickly and lines up picture after picture of me sitting there in front of the house with Maggie cowering behind me. She never takes a shot without making sure the house is included.
When a cow comes nibbling around the edge of the yard she snaps it and me and Maggie
and the house. Then she puts the Polaroid in the back seat of the car, and comes up and kisses
me on the forehead.

Meanwhile Asalamalakim is going through motions with Maggie's hand. Maggie's
hand is as limp as a fish, and probably as cold, despite the sweat, and she keeps trying to
pull it back. It looks like Asalamalakim wants to shake hands but wants to do it fancy. Or
maybe he don't know how people shake hands. Anyhow, he soon gives up on Maggie.

"Well," I say, "Dee."

"No, Mama," she says. "Not 'Dee,' Wangero Leewanika Kemanjo!"   25

"What happened to 'Dee'?" I wanted to know.

"She's dead," Wangero said. "I couldn't bear it any longer, being named after the people
who oppress me."

"You know as well as me you was named after your aunt Dicie," I said. Dicie is my sister. She named Dee. We called her "Big Dee" after Dee was born.

"But who was *she* named after?" asked Wangero.

"I guess after Grandma Dee," I said.   30

"And who was she named after?" asked Wangero.

"Her mother," I said, and saw Wangero was getting tired. "That's about as far back as I
can trace it," I said. Though, in fact, I probably could have carried it back beyond the Civil
War through the branches.

"Well," said Asalamalakim, "there you are."

"Uhnnnh," I heard Maggie say.

"There I was not," I said, "before 'Dicie' cropped up in our family, so why should I try to   35
trace it that far back?"

He just stood there grinning, looking down on me like somebody inspecting a Model A°
car. Every once in a while he and Wangero sent eye signals over my head.

"How do you pronounce this name?" I asked.

"You don't have to call me by it if you don't want to," said Wangero.

° *Wa-su-zo-Tean-o:* greeting used by black Muslims.
° *Asalamalakim:* Muslim salutation meaning "Peace be with you."
° *Model A car:* the Ford car that replaced the Model T in the late 1920s. The Model A was proverbial for its
quality and durability.

"Why shouldn't I?" I asked. "If that's what you want us to call you, we'll call you."

40   "I know it might sound awkward at first," said Wangero.

"I'll get used to it," I said. "Ream it out again."

Well, soon we got the name out of the way. Asalamalakim had a name twice as long and three times as hard. After I tripped over it two or three times he told me to just call him Hakim-a-barber. I wanted to ask him was he a barber, but I didn't really think he was, so I didn't ask.

"You must belong to those beef-cattle peoples down the road," I said. They said "Asala-malakim" when they met you, too, but they didn't shake hands. Always too busy: feeding the cattle, fixing the fences, putting up salt-lick shelters,° throwing down hay. When the white folks poisoned some of the herd the men stayed up all night with rifles in their hands. I walked a mile and a half just to see the sight.

Hakim-a-barber said, "I accept some of their doctrines, but farming and raising cattle is not my style." (They didn't tell me, and I didn't ask, whether Wangero (Dee) had really gone and married him.)

45   We sat down to eat and right away he said he didn't eat collards and pork was unclean. Wangero, though, went on through the chitlins and corn bread, the greens and everything else. She talked a blue streak over the sweet potatoes. Everything delighted her. Even the fact that we still used the benches her daddy made for the table when we couldn't afford to buy chairs.

"Oh, Mama!" she cried. Then turned to Hakim-a-barber. "I never knew how lovely these benches are. You can feel the rump prints," she said, running her hands underneath her and along the bench. Then she gave a sigh and her hand closed over Grandma Dee's butter dish. "That's it!" she said. "I knew there was something I wanted to ask you if I could have." She jumped up from the table and went over in the corner where the churn stood, the milk in it clabber° by now. She looked at the churn and looked at it.

"This churn top is what I need," she said. "Didn't Uncle Buddy whittle it out of a tree you all used to have?"

"Yes," I said.

"Uh huh," she said happily. "And I want the dasher, too."

50   "Uncle Buddy whittle that, too?" asked the barber.

Dee (Wangero) looked up at me.

"Aunt Dee's first husband whittled the dash," said Maggie so low you almost couldn't hear her. "His name was Henry, but they called him Stash."

"Maggie's brain is like an elephant's," Wangero said, laughing. "I can use the churn top as a centerpiece for the alcove table," she said, sliding a plate over the churn, "and I'll think of something artistic to do with the dasher."

When she finished wrapping the dasher the handle stuck out. I took it for a moment in my hands. You didn't even have to look close to see where hands pushing the dasher up and down to make butter had left a kind of sink in the wood. In fact, there were a lot of small sinks; you could see where thumbs and fingers had sunk into the wood. It was beautiful light yellow wood, from a tree that grew in the yard where Big Dee and Stash had lived.

55   After dinner Dee (Wangero) went to the trunk at the foot of my bed and started rifling through it. Maggie hung back in the kitchen over the dishpan. Out came Wangero with two quilts. They had been pieced by Grandma Dee and then Big Dee and me had hung them on the quilt frames on the front porch and quilted them. One was in the Lone Star pattern. The

---

° *salt-lick shelters:* shelters built to prevent rain from dissolving the large blocks of rock salt set up on poles for cattle.

° *clabber:* curdled, turned sour.

other was Walk Around the Mountain. In both of them were scraps of dresses Grandma Dee had worn fifty and more years ago. Bits and pieces of Grandpa Jarrell's Paisley shirts. And one teeny faded blue piece, about the size of a penny matchbox, that was from Great Grandpa Ezra's uniform that he wore in the Civil War.

"Mama," Wangero said sweet as a bird. "Can I have these old quilts?"

I heard something fall in the kitchen, and a minute later the kitchen door slammed.

"Why don't you take one or two of the others?" I asked, "These old things was just done by me and Big Dee from some tops your grandma pieced before she died."

"No," said Wangero. "I don't want those. They are stitched around the borders by machine."

"That'll make them last better," I said.

"That's not the point," said Wangero. "These are all pieces of dresses Grandma used to wear. She did all this stitching by hand. Imagine!" She held the quilts securely in her arms, stroking them.

"Some of the pieces, like those lavender ones, come from old clothes her mother handed down to her," I said, moving up to touch the quilts. Dee (Wangero) moved back just enough so that I couldn't reach the quilts. They already belonged to her.

"Imagine!" she breathed again, clutching them closely to her bosom.

"The truth is," I said, "I promised to give them quilts to Maggie, for when she marries John Thomas."

She gasped like a bee had stung her.

"Maggie can't appreciate these quilts!" she said. "She'd probably be backward enough to put them to everyday use."

"I reckon she would," I said. "God knows I been saving 'em for long enough with nobody using 'em. I hope she will!" I didn't want to bring up how I had offered Dee (Wangero) a quilt when she went away to college. Then she had told me they were old-fashioned, out of style.

"But they're *priceless!*" she was saying now, furiously; for she has a temper. "Maggie would put them on the bed and in five years they'd be in rags. Less than that!"

"She can always make some more," I said. "Maggie knows how to quilt."

Dee (Wangero) looked at me with hatred. "You just will not understand. The point is these quilts, *these* quilts!"

"Well," I said, stumped. "What would *you* do with them?"

"Hang them," she said. As if that was the only thing you *could* do with quilts.

Maggie by now was standing in the door. I could almost hear the sound her feet made as they scraped over each other.

"She can have them, Mama," she said, like somebody used to never winning anything, or having anything reserved for her. "I can 'member Grandma Dee without the quilts."

I looked at her hard. She had filled her bottom lip with checkerberry snuff and it gave her face a kind of dopey, hangdog look. It was Grandma Dee and Big Dee who taught her how to quilt herself. She stood there with her scarred hands hidden in the folds of her skirt. She looked at her sister with something like fear but she wasn't mad at her. This was Maggie's portion. This was the way she knew God to work.

When I looked at her like that something hit me in the top of my head and ran down to the soles of my feet. Just like when I'm in church and the spirit of God touches me and I get happy and shout. I did something I never had done before: hugged Maggie to me, then dragged her on into the room, snatched the quilts out of Miss Wangero's hands and dumped them into Maggie's lap. Maggie just sat there on my bed with her mouth open.

"Take one or two of the others," I said to Dee.

But she turned without a word and went out to Hakim-a-barber.

"You just don't understand," she said, as Maggie and I came out to the car.

80   "What don't I understand?" I wanted to know.

"Your heritage," she said. And then she turned to Maggie, kissed her, and said, "You ought to try to make something of yourself, too, Maggie. It's really a new day for us. But from the way you and Mama still live you'd never know it."

She put on some sunglasses that hid everything above the tip of her nose and her chin.

Maggie smiled; maybe at the sunglasses. But a real smile, not scared. After we watched the car dust settle I asked Maggie to bring me a dip of snuff. And then the two of us sat there just enjoying, until it was time to go in the house and go to bed.

QUESTIONS

1. Describe the narrator. Who is she? What is she like? Where and how does she live? What kind of life has she had? How does the story bring out her judgments about her two daughters?

2. Describe the narrator's daughters. How are they different physically and mentally? How have their lives been different?

3. Why did Dee change her name to "Wangero"? How is this change important, and how is it reflected in her attitude toward the family artifacts?

4. Describe the importance of the phrase "everyday use" (paragraph 66). How does this phrase highlight the conflicting values in the story?

EUDORA WELTY (1909–2001)

One of the major Southern writers, Welty was born in Jackson, Mississippi. She attended the Mississippi State College for Women and the University of Wisconsin, and she began her writing career during the Great Depression. By 1943 she had published two major story collections, Curtain of Green *(1941, including "A Worn Path") and* The Wide Net *(1943). She is the author of many stories and was awarded the Pulitzer Prize in 1973 for her short novel* The Optimist's Daughter *(1972). "A Worn Path" received an O. Henry Award in 1941.*

A Worn Path° (1941)

It was December—a bright frozen day in the early morning. Far out in the country there was an old Negro woman with her head tied in a red rag, coming along a path through the pinewoods. Her name was Phoenix Jackson. She was very old and small and she walked slowly in the dark pine shadows, moving a little from side to side in her steps, with the balanced heaviness and lightness of a pendulum in a grandfather clock. She carried a thin, small cane made from an umbrella, and with this she kept tapping the frozen earth in front of her. This made a grave and persistent noise in the still air, that seemed meditative like the chirping of a solitary little bird.

° "A Worn Path," from *A Curtain of Green and Other Stories*, Copyright 1941 and renewed 1969 by Eudora Welty, reprinted by permission of Harcourt, Inc.

She wore a dark striped dress reaching down to her shoe tops, and an equally long apron of bleached sugar sacks, with a full pocket: all neat and tidy, but every time she took a step she might have fallen over her shoelaces, which dragged from her unlaced shoes. She looked straight ahead. Her eyes were blue with age. Her skin had a pattern all its own of numberless branching wrinkles and as though a whole little tree stood in the middle of her forehead, but a golden color ran underneath, and the two knobs of her cheeks were illuminated by a yellow burning under the dark. Under the rag her hair came down on her neck in the frailest of ringlets, still black, and with an odor like copper.

Now and then there was a quivering in the thicket. Old Phoenix said, "Out of my way, all you foxes, owls, beetles, jack rabbits, coons and wild animals! . . . Keep out from under these feet, little bob-whites. . . . Keep the big wild hogs out of my path. Don't let none of those come running my direction. I got a long way." Under her small black-freckled hand her cane, limber as a buggy whip, would switch at the brush as if to rouse up any hiding things.

On she went. The woods were deep and still. The sun made the pine needles almost too bright to look at, up where the wind rocked. The cones dropped as light as feathers. Down in the hollow was the mourning dove—it was not too late for him.

The path ran up a hill. "Seem like there is chains about my feet, time I get this far," she   5
said, in the voice of argument old people keep to use with themselves. "Something always take a hold of me on this hill—pleads I should stay."

After she got to the top she turned and gave a full, severe look behind her where she had come. "Up through pines," she said at length. "Now down through oaks."

Her eyes opened their widest, and she started down gently. But before she got to the bottom of the hill a bush caught her dress.

Her fingers were busy and intent, but her skirts were full and long, so that before she could pull them free in one place they were caught in another. It was not possible to allow the dress to tear. "I in the thorny bush," she said. "Thorns, you doing your appointed work. Never want to let folks pass, no sir. Old eyes thought you was a pretty little *green* bush."

Finally, trembling all over, she stood free, and after a moment dared to stoop for her cane.

"Sun so high!" she cried, leaning back and looking, while the thick tears went over her   10
eyes. "The time getting all gone here."

At the foot of this hill was a place where a log was laid across the creek.

"Now comes the trial," said Phoenix.

Putting her right foot out, she mounted the log and shut her eyes. Lifting her skirt, leveling her cane fiercely before her, like a festival figure in some parade, she began to march across. Then she opened her eyes and she was safe on the other side.

"I wasn't as old as I thought," she said.

But she sat down to rest. She spread her skirts on the bank around her and folded her   15
hands over her knees. Up above her was a tree in a pearly cloud of mistletoe. She did not dare to close her eyes, and when a little boy brought her a plate with a slice of marble-cake on it she spoke to him. "That would be acceptable," she said. But when she went to take it there was just her own hand in the air.

So she left that tree, and had to go through a barbed-wire fence. There she had to creep and crawl, spreading her knees and stretching her fingers like a baby trying to climb the steps. But she talked loudly to herself: she could not let her dress be torn now, so late in the day, and she could not pay for having her arm or leg sawed off if she got caught fast where she was.

At last she was safe through the fence and risen up out in the clearing. Big dead trees, like black men with one arm, were standing in the purple stalks of the withered cotton field. There sat a buzzard.

"Who you watching?"

In the furrow she made her way along.

20 "Glad this is not the season for bulls," she said, looking sideways, "and the good Lord made his snakes to curl up and sleep in the winter. A pleasure I don't see no two-headed snake coming around that tree, where it come once. It took a while to get by him, back in the summer."

She passed through the old cotton and went into a field of dead corn. It whispered and shook and was taller than her head. "Through the maze now," she said, for there was no path.

Then there was something tall, black, and skinny there, moving before her.

At first she took it for a man. It could have been a man dancing in the field. But she stood still and listened, and it did not make a sound. It was as silent as a ghost.

"Ghost," she said sharply, "who be you the ghost of? For I have heard of nary death close by."

25 But there was no answer—only the ragged dancing in the wind.

She shut her eyes, reached out her hand, and touched a sleeve. She found a coat and inside that an emptiness, cold as ice.

"You scarecrow," she said. Her face lighted. "I ought to be shut up for good," she said with laughter. "My senses is gone. I too old, I the oldest people I ever know. Dance, old scarecrow," she said, "while I dancing with you."

She kicked her foot over the furrow, and with mouth drawn down, shook her head once or twice in a little strutting way. Some husks blew down and whirled in steamers about her skirts.

Then she went on, parting her way from side to side with the cane, through the whispering field. At last she came to the end, to a wagon track where the silver grass blew between the red ruts. The quail were walking around like pullets, seeming all dainty and unseen.

30 "Walk pretty," she said. "This is the easy place. This the easy going."

She followed the track, swaying through the quiet bare fields, through the little strings of trees silver in their dead leaves, past cabins silver from weather, with the doors and windows boarded shut, all like old women under a spell sitting there. "I walking in their sleep," she said, nodding her head vigorously.

In a ravine she went where a spring was silently flowing through a hollow log. Old Phoenix bent and drank. "Sweet-gum makes the water sweet," she said, and drank more. "Nobody know who made this well, for it was here when I was born."

The track crossed a swampy part where the moss hung as white as lace from every limb. "Sleep on, alligators, and blow your bubbles." Then the track went into the road.

Deep, deep the road went down between the high green-colored banks. Overhead the live-oaks met, and it was as dark as a cave.

35 A black dog with a lolling tongue came up out of the weeds by the ditch. She was meditating, and not ready, and when he came at her she only hit him a little with her cane. Over she went in the ditch, like a little puff of milkweed.

Down there, her sense drifted away. A dream visited her, and she reached her hand up, but nothing reached down and gave her a pull. So she lay there and presently went to talking. "Old woman," she said to herself, "that black dog come up out of the weeds to stall you off, and now there he sitting on his fine tail smiling at you."

A white man finally came along and found her—a hunter, a young man, with his dog on a chain.

"Well, Granny!" he laughed. "What are you doing there?"

"Lying on my back like a June-bug waiting to be turned over, mister," she said, reaching up her hand.

40 He lifted her up, gave her a swing in the air, and set her down. "Anything broken, Granny?"

"No sir, them old dead weeds is springy enough," said Phoenix, when she had got her breath. "I thank you for your trouble."

"Where do you live, Granny?" he asked, while the two dogs were growling at each other.
"Away back yonder, sir, behind the ridge. You can't even see it from here."

"On your way home?"

"No sir, I goin to town."

"Why, that's too far! That's as far as I walk when I come out myself, and I get something for my trouble." He patted the stuffed bag he carried, and there hung down a little closed claw. It was one of the bob-whites, with its beak hooked bitterly to show it was dead. "Now you go on home, Granny!"

"I bound to go to town, mister," said Phoenix. "The time come around."

He gave another laugh, filling the whole landscape. "I know you old colored people! Wouldn't miss going to town to see Santa Claus!"

But something held old Phoenix very still. The deep lines in her face went into a fierce and different radiation. Without warning, she had seen with her own eyes a flashing nickel fall out of the man's pocket onto the ground.

"How old are you, Granny?" he was saying.

"There is no telling, mister," she said, "no telling."

Then she gave a little cry and clapped her hands and said, "Git on away from here, dog! Look! Look at that dog!" She laughed as if in admiration. "He ain't scared of nobody. He a big black dog." She whispered, "Sic him!"

"Watch me get rid of that cur," said the man. "Sic him, Pete! Sic him!"

Phoenix heard the dogs fighting, and heard the man running and throwing sticks. She even heard a gunshot. But she was slowly bending forward by that time, further and further forward, the lids stretched down over her eyes, as if she were doing this in her sleep. Her chin was lowered almost to her knees. The yellow palm of her hand came out from the fold of her apron. Her fingers slid down and along the ground under the piece of money with the grace and care they would have in lifting an egg from under a setting hen. Then she slowly straightened up, she stood erect, and the nickel was in her apron pocket. A bird flew by. Her lips moved. "God watching me the whole time. I come to stealing."

The man came back, and his own dog panted about them. "Well, I scared him off that time," he said, and then he laughed and lifted his gun and pointed it at Phoenix.

She stood straight and faced him.

"Doesn't the gun scare you?" he said, still pointing it.

"No sir. I seen plenty go off closer by, in my day, and for less than what I done," she said, holding utterly still.

He smiled, and shouldered the gun. "Well, Granny," he said, "you must be a hundred years old, and scared of nothing. I'd give you a dime if I had any money with me. But you take my advice and stay home, and nothing will happen to you."

"I bound to go on my way, mister," said Phoenix. She inclined her head in the red rag. Then they went in different directions, but she could hear the gun shooting again and again over the hill.

She walked on. The shadows hung from the oak trees to the road like curtains. Then she smelled wood-smoke, and smelled the river, and she saw a steeple and the cabins on their steep steps. Dozens of little black children whirled around her. There ahead was Natchez shining. Bells were ringing. She walked on.

In the paved city it was Christmas time. There were red and green electric lights strung and crisscrossed everywhere, and all turned on in the daytime. Old Phoenix would have been lost if she had not distrusted her eyesight and depended on her feet to know where to take her.

She paused quietly on the sidewalk where people were passing by. A lady came along in the crowd, carrying an armful of red-, green-, and silver-wrapped presents; she gave off perfume like the red roses in hot summer, and Phoenix stopped her.

"Please, missy, will you lace up my shoe?" She held up her foot.

65 "What do you want, Grandma?"

"See my shoe," said Phoenix. "Do all right for out in the country, but wouldn't look right to go in a big building."

"Stand still then, Grandma," said the lady. She put her packages down on the sidewalk beside her and laced and tied both shoes tightly.

"Can't lace 'em with a cane," said Phoenix. "Thank you, missy. I doesn't mind asking a nice lady to tie up my shoe, when I gets out on the street."

Moving slowly and from side to side, she went into the big building, and into a tower of steps, where she walked up and around and around until her feet knew to stop.

70 She entered a door, and there she saw nailed up on the wall the document that had been stamped with the gold seal and framed in the gold frame, which matched the dream that was hung up in her head.

"Here I be," she said. There was a fixed and ceremonial stiffness over her body.

"A charity case, I suppose," said an attendant who sat at the desk before her.

But Phoenix only looked above her head. There was sweat on her face, the wrinkles in her skin shone like a bright net.

"Speak up, Grandma," the woman said, "What's your name? We must have your history, you know. Have you been here before? What seems to be the trouble with you?"

75 Old Phoenix only gave a twitch to her face as if a fly were bothering her.

"Are you deaf?" cried the attendant.

But then the nurse came in.

"Oh, that's just old Aunt Phoenix," she said. "She doesn't come for herself—she has a little grandson. She makes these trips just as regular as clockwork. She lives away back off the Old Natchez Trace." She bent down. "Well, Aunt Phoenix, why don't you just take a seat? We won't keep you standing after your long trip." She pointed.

The old woman sat down, bolt upright in the chair.

80 "Now, how is the boy?" asked the nurse.

Old Phoenix did not speak.

"I said, how is the boy?"

But Phoenix only waited and stared straight ahead, her face very solemn and withdrawn into rigidity.

"Is his throat any better?" asked the nurse. "Aunt Phoenix, don't you hear me? Is your grandson's throat any better since the last time you came for the medicine?"

85 With her hands on her knees, the old woman waited, silent, erect, and motionless, just as if she were in armor.

"You mustn't take up our time this way, Aunt Phoenix," the nurse said. "Tell us quickly about your grandson, and get it over. He isn't dead, is he?"

At last there came a flicker and then a flame of comprehension across her face, and she spoke.

"My grandson. It was my memory had left me. There I sat and forgot why I made my long trip."

"Forgot?" the nurse frowned. "After you came so far?"

90 Then Phoenix was like an old woman begging a dignified forgiveness for waking up frightened in the night. "I never did go to school, I was too old at the Surrender," she said in a soft voice. "I'm an old woman without an education. It was my memory fail me. My little grandson, he is just the same, and I forgot it in the coming."

"Throat never heals, does it?" said the nurse, speaking in a loud, sure voice to old Phoenix. By now she had a card with something written on it, a little list. "Yes. Swallowed lye. When was it—January—two, three years ago—"

Phoenix spoke unasked now. "No missy, he not dead, he just the same. Every little while his throat begin to close up again, and he not able to swallow. He not get his breath. He not able to help himself. So the time come around, and I go on another trip for the soothing medicine."

"All right. The doctor said as long as you came to get it, you could have it," said the nurse. "But it's an obstinate case."

"My little grandson, he sit up there in the house all wrapped up, waiting by himself," Phoenix went on. "We is the only two left in the world. He suffer and it don't seem to put him back at all. He got a sweet look. He going to last. He wear a little patch quilt and peep out holding his mouth open like a little bird. I remembers so plain now. I not going to forget him again, no, the whole enduring time. I could tell him from all the others in creation."

"All right." The nurse was trying to hush her now. She brought her a bottle of medicine. "Charity," she said, making a check mark in a book. 95

Old Phoenix held the bottle close to her eyes, and then carefully put it into her pocket. "I thank you," she said.

"It's Christmas time, Grandma," said the attendant. "Could I give you a few pennies out of my purse?"

"Five pennies is a nickel," said Phoenix stiffly. 100

"Here's a nickel," said the attendant.

Phoenix rose carefully and held out her hand. She received the nickel and then fished the other nickel out of her pocket and laid it beside the new one. She stared at her palm closely, with her head on one side.

Then she gave a tap with her cane on the floor.

"This is what come to me to do," she said, "I going to the store and buy my child a little windmill they sells, made out of paper. He going to find it hard to believe there such a thing in the world. I'll march myself back where he waiting, holding it straight up in this hand."

She lifted her free hand, gave a little nod, turned around, and walked out of the doctor's 105 office. Then her slow step began on the stairs, going down.

QUESTIONS

1. From the description of Phoenix, what do you conclude about her economic condition? How do you know that she has taken the path through the woods before? Is she accustomed to being alone? What do you make of her speaking to animals, and of her imagining a boy offering her a piece of cake? What does her speech show about her education and background?

2. Describe the plot of the story. With Phoenix as the protagonist, what are the obstacles ranged against her? How might Phoenix be considered to be in the grip of large and indifferent social and political forces?

3. Comment on the meaning of this dialogue between Phoenix and the hunter:

   "Doesn't the gun scare you?" he said, still pointing it.
   "No, sir. I seen plenty go off closer by, in my day, and for less than what I done," she said, holding utterly still.

4. A number of responses might be made to this story, among them admiration for Phoenix, pity for her and her grandson and for the downtrodden generally, anger at her impoverished condition, and apprehension about her approaching senility. Do you share in any of these responses? Do you have any others?

Plot: The Motivation and Causality of Fiction

Stories are made up mostly of actions or incidents that follow one another in chronological order. The same is also true of life, but there is a major difference. Fiction must make sense even though life itself does not always seem to make sense at all. Finding a sequential or narrative order is therefore only a first step in our consideration of fiction. What we depend on for the sense or meaning of fiction is **plot**—the elements governing the unfolding of the actions.

The English novelist E. M. Forster, in *Aspects of the Novel*, presents a memorable illustration of plot. To illustrate a bare set of actions, he proposes the following: "The king died, and then the queen died." Forster points out, however, that this sequence does not form a plot because it lacks *motivation* and *causation*; it is too much like life itself to be fictional. Thus he introduces motivation and causation in his next example: "The king died, and then the queen died of grief." The phrase "of grief" shows that one thing (grief) controls or overcomes another (the normal desire to live), and motivation and causation enter the sequence to form a plot. In a well-plotted story or play, one thing precedes or follows another not simply because time ticks away, but more importantly because *effects* follow *causes*. In a good work of fiction, nothing is irrelevant or accidental; everything is related and causative.

Determining the Conflicts in a Story

The controlling impulse in a connected pattern of causes and effects is **conflict**, which refers to people or circumstances that a character must face and try to overcome. Conflicts bring out extremes of human energy, causing characters to engage in the decisions, actions, responses, and interactions that make up fictional literature.

In its most elemental form, a conflict is the opposition of two people. Their conflict may take the shape of anger, hatred, envy, argument, avoidance, political or moral opposition, gossip, lies, fighting, and many other actions and attitudes. Conflicts may also exist between groups, although conflicts between individuals are more identifiable and therefore more suitable for stories. Conflicts may also be abstract—for example, when an individual opposes larger forces such as natural objects, ideas, modes of behavior, or public opinion. A difficult or even impossible *choice*—a dilemma—is a natural conflict for an individual person. A conflict may also be brought out in ideas and opinions that clash. In short, conflict shows itself in many ways.

DIRECTLY RELATING CONFLICT TO DOUBT, TENSION, AND INTEREST.   Conflict is the major element of plot because opposing forces arouse *curiosity*, cause *doubt*, create *tension*, and produce *interest*. The same responses are the lifeblood of athletic competition. Consider which kind of athletic event is more interesting: (1) One team gets so far ahead that the outcome is no longer in doubt, or (2) both teams are so evenly matched that the outcome is uncertain until the final seconds. Obviously, games are uninteresting—as games—unless they develop as contests between teams of comparable strength. The same principle applies to conflicts in stories and dramas. There should be uncertainty about a protagonist's success or failure. Unless there is doubt, there is no tension, and without tension there is no interest.

FINDING THE CONFLICTS TO DETERMINE THE PLOT.   To see a plot in operation, let us build on Forster's description. Here is a simple plot for a story of our own: "John and Jane meet, fall in love, and get married." This sentence contains a plot

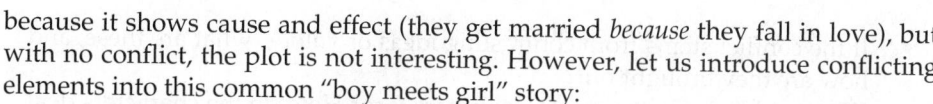

because it shows cause and effect (they get married *because* they fall in love), but with no conflict, the plot is not interesting. However, let us introduce conflicting elements into this common "boy meets girl" story:

> John and Jane meet in college and fall in love. They go together for a number of years and plan to marry, but a problem arises. Jane first wants to establish herself in a career, and after marriage she wants to be an equal contributor to the family. John understands Jane's wishes for equality, but he wants to get married first and let her finish her studies and have her career after they have children. Jane believes that John's plan is unacceptable because she thinks of it as a trap from which she might not escape. As they discuss their options they find themselves increasingly more irritated and unhappy with each other. Finally they bring their plans to an end, and they part in both anger and sorrow. Their love is not dead, however, but both go on to marry someone else and build separate lives and careers. In their new lives, neither is totally happy even though they like and respect their spouses. The years pass, and, after children and grandchildren, Jane and John meet again. He is now divorced and she is a widow. Because their earlier conflict is no longer a barrier, they rekindle their love, marry, and try to make up for the past. Even their new happiness, however, is tinged with regret and reproach because of their earlier conflicts, their unhappy decision to part, their lost years, and their increasing age.

Here we find a true plot because our original "boy meets girl" topic now contains a major conflict from which a number of related complications develop. These complications embody disagreements, choices, arguments, and ill feelings that produce tension, uncertainty, rupture, and regret. When we learn that John and Jane finally join together at the end we might still find the story painful to contemplate because it does not give us a "happily ever after" ending. Nevertheless, the story makes sense—as a story—because its plot brings out the plausible consequences of the understandable aims and hopes of John and Jane during their long relationship. It is the imposition of necessary causes and effects upon a series of events in time that creates the story's plot.

WRITING ABOUT THE PLOT OF A STORY

An essay about plot is an analysis of the story's conflict and its developments. The organization of your essay should not be modeled on sequential sections and principal events, however, because these invite only a retelling of the story. Instead, the organization is to be developed from the important elements of conflict. As you look for ideas about plot, try to answer the following questions.

Questions for Discovering Ideas

*   Who are the major and minor characters, and how do their characteristics put them in conflict? How can you describe the conflict or conflicts?
*   How does the story's action grow out of the major conflict?

- If the conflict stems from contrasting ideas or values, what are these, and how are they brought out?
- What problems do the major characters face? How do the characters deal with these problems?
- How do the major characters achieve (or not achieve) their major goal(s)? What obstacles do they overcome? What obstacles overcome them or alter them?
- At the end, are the characters successful or unsuccessful, happy or unhappy, satisfied or dissatisfied, changed or unchanged, enlightened or ignorant? How has the resolution of the major conflict produced these results?

Strategies for Organizing Ideas

To keep your essay brief, you need to be selective. Rather than detailing everything a character does, for example, stress the major elements in his or her conflict. Such an essay on Eudora Welty's "A Worn Path" might emphasize Phoenix as she encounters the various obstacles both in the woods and in town. When there is a conflict between two major characters, the obvious approach is to focus equally on both. For brevity, however, emphasis might be placed on just one. Thus, an essay on the plot of "A Rose for Emily" might stress the details about Emily's life that make her the central participant in the story's conflict.

In addition, the plot may be analyzed more broadly in terms of impulses, goals, values, issues, and historical perspectives. Thus, you might emphasize the elements of chance working against Mathilde in Maupassant's "The Necklace" (Part I p. 6) as a contrast to her dreams about wealth. A discussion of the plot of Poe's "The Masque of the Red Death" (Chapter 9) might stress the haughtiness of Prospero, the major character, because the plot could not develop without his egotism.

The conclusion may contain a brief summary of the points you have made. It is also a fitting location for a brief consideration of the effect or *impact* produced by the conflict. Additional ideas might focus on whether the author has arranged actions and dialogue to direct your favor toward one side or the other, or whether the plot is possible or impossible, serious or comic, fair or unfair, powerful or indifferent, and so on.

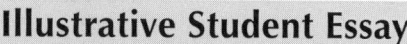

Illustrative Student Essay

Underlined sentences in this paper *do not* conform to MLA style and are used solely as teaching tools to emphasize the central idea, thesis sentence, and topic sentences throughout the paper.

Getty 1

Beth Getty

Professor Farmer

English 214

12 March 2008

The Plot of Eudora Welty's "A Worn Path"°

At first, the complexity of Eudora Welty's plot in "A Worn Path" is not   [1]
clear. The main character is Phoenix Jackson, an old, poor, and frail woman; the
story seems to be no more than a record of her walk to Natchez through the
woods from her rural home. By the story's end, however, the plot is clear: It
consists of the brave attempts of a courageous, valiant woman to carry on
against overwhelming forces.* Her determination despite the great odds against
her gives the story its impact. The powers ranged against her are old age,
poverty, environment, and illness.†

Old age as a silent but overpowering antagonist is shown in signs of   [2]
Phoenix's increasing senility. Not her mind but her feet tell her where to find
the medical office in Natchez. Despite her inner strength, she is unable to
explain her errand when the nursing attendant asks her. Instead she sits dumbly
and unknowingly for a time, until "a flame of comprehension" comes across
her face (paragraph 87, p. 118). Against the power of advancing age, Phoenix is
slowly losing. The implication is that soon she will lose entirely.

An equally crushing opponent is her poverty. She cannot afford to ride to   [3]
town, but must walk. She has no money, and acquires her ten cents for the
paper windmill by stealing and begging. The "soothing medicine" she gets for
her grandson (paragraph 92, p. 118) is given to her out of charity. Despite the

°This story appears on page 114.
*Central idea.
†Thesis sentence.

Getty 2

boy's need for advanced medical care, she has no money to provide it, and the story therefore shows that her guardianship is doomed.

Closely connected to her poverty is the way through the woods, which during her walk seems to be an almost active opponent. The long hill tires her, the thorn bush catches her clothes, the log endangers her balance as she crosses the creek, and the barbed-wire fence threatens to puncture her skin. Another danger on her way is the stray dog, which topples her over. Apparently not afraid, however, Phoenix carries on a cheerful monologue: [4]

> Out of my way, all you foxes, owls, beetles, jack rabbits, coons and wild animals! . . . Keep out from under these feet, little bobwhites. . . . Keep the big wild hogs out of my path. Don't let none of these come running my direction. I got a long way.
>
> (115, paragraph 3)

She prevails for the moment as she enters Natchez, but all the hazards of her walk are still there, waiting for her to return.

The force against Phoenix which shows her plight most clearly and pathetically is her grandson's incurable illness. His condition highlights her helplessness, for she is his only support. Her difficulties would be enough for one person alone, but with the grandson the odds against her are doubled. Despite her care, there is nothing anyone can do for the grandson but take the long worn path to get something to help him endure his pain. [5]

This brief description of the conflicts in "A Worn Path" only hints at the story's power. Welty layers the details to bring out the full range of the conditions against Phoenix, who cannot win despite her determination and devotion. The most hopeless fact, the condition of the invalid grandson, is not revealed until she reaches the medical office, and this delayed final revelation makes one's heart go out to her. The plot is strong because it is so real, and Phoenix is a pathetic but memorable protagonist struggling against overwhelming odds. [6]

Getty 3

Work Cited

Welty, Eudora. "A Worn Path." Literature: An Introduction to Reading and
     Writing. Ed. Edgar V. Roberts. 9th ed. New York: Pearson Longman, 2009.
     114–19.

Commentary on the Essay

The strategy of this essay is to explain the elements of plot in "A Worn Path" selectively, without duplicating the story's narrative order. Thus the third aspect of conflict, the woods, might be introduced first if the story's narrative order were to be followed, but it is deferred while the more personal elements of old age and poverty are considered. It is important to note that the essay does not deal with the story's other characters as part of Phoenix's conflict. Rather Phoenix's antagonist takes the shape of impersonal and unconquerable forces, like her grandson's illness.

Paragraph 1 briefly describes how one's first impressions are changed because of what happens at the end of the story. The thesis statement anticipates the body by listing the four topics about to be treated. Paragraph 2 concerns Phoenix's old age; paragraph 3 her poverty; paragraph 4 the woods; and paragraph 5 her grandson's illness. The concluding paragraph (6) points out that in this set of conflicts the protagonist cannot win, except as she lives out her duty and her devotion to help her grandson. Continuing the theme of the introduction, the last paragraph also accounts for the power of the plot: By building up to Phoenix's personal strength against unbeatable forces, the story evokes sympathy and admiration.

Writing Topics About Plot in Fiction

1. Suppose that someone has told you that "The Things They Carried" is too detailed and realistic to be considered a story. Explain to this person why the assertion should be considered wrong. What elements of narrative, character, plot, point of view, idea, and description justify calling "The Things They Carried" a story?

2. Consider the illustrative essay on the plot of Welty's "A Worn Path." How well does the essay organize the details about the story's plot? Do you accept the arguments in the essay? What other details and arguments can you think of that might explain Welty's plot more fully?

3. In "War," by Pirandello, why is the father whose son is dead made so initially unappealing? What effect on the plot of the story is made plain by the apparent nature of his character?

4. How do the separate sections of "An Occurrence at Owl Creek Bridge" affect the story's plot? Why is the second section a "flashback" of events that occurred before the actual story is taking place? Why is this flashback necessary to your understanding of the plot?

5. Write contrasting paragraphs about a character (whom you know or about whom you have read). In the first, try to make your reader like the character. In the second, try to create a hostile response to the character. Write an additional paragraph explaining the ways in which you tried to create these opposite responses. How fair would it be for a reader to dislike your negative paragraph even though your hostile portrait is successful?

6. Write a brief episode or story that takes place in a historical period you believe you know well, being as factually accurate as you can. Introduce your own fictional characters as important "movers and shakers," and deal with their public or personal affairs or both. You may model your characters and episodes on historical persons, but you are free to exercise your imagination completely and construct your own characters.

Chapter 2

Point of View: The Position or Stance of the Work's Narrator or Speaker

The term **"point of view"** refers to the **speaker, narrator, persona,** or **voice** created by authors to tell stories, make observations, present arguments, and express personal attitudes and judgments. Literally, point of view deals with how action and dialogue have been seen and heard. How does the speaker learn about the situation? Is the speaker a participant in the situation, or no more than a witness, either close or distant? How close to the action is she or he? How much does the speaker know? How accurate and complete are his or her reports? Is the speaker also involved in what happened? How thoroughly? Did he or she see everything, miss anything? How much did she or he understand? Point of view involves not only the speaker's actual position as an observer and recorder but also the ways in which the speaker's social, political, and mental circumstances affect the narrative. For this reason, point of view is one of the most complex and subtle aspects of literary study.

The underlying issue of point of view is epistemological: How do we acquire information? How can we verify its authenticity? How can we trust those who explain the world to us? What is their authority? Are they partial or impartial? What is their interest in telling us things? How reliable are their explanations? What physical and psychological positions might affect, or even distort, what they are saying? Do they have anything to hide? When they speak, are they trying to justify themselves to any degree?

Bear in mind that authors try not only to make their works vital and interesting but also to bring their presentations alive. The presentation is similar to a dramatic performance: In a play, the actors are always themselves, but as they perform their roles they impersonate and temporarily become the characters they act. In fictional works, not only do authors impersonate or pretend to be characters who do the talking, but also they create these characters. One such character is Jackie, the narrator of Frank O'Connor's "First Confession" (Chapter 6), who is telling about events that occurred when he was a child. Because he is the subject as well as the narrator, he has firsthand knowledge of the actions, even though he also says things indicating that he, as an adult, has not fully assimilated his childhood experience. Another speaking character is Francie of Lorrie Moore's "How to Become a Writer" (this chapter). On the pretext of giving advice to a budding writer, Francie seems to be describing some of the more ironically comic and also serious episodes of her own writing career. Francie is the one we read and hear, but Moore is the one supplying the words because Francie is a literary creation. In Poe's "The Masque of the Red Death" (Chapter 9), we constantly hear the speaker's voice and are influenced not only by his narration but also by his attitudes.

Because of the ramifications of creating a narrative voice, point of view may also be considered as the centralizing or guiding intelligence in a work—the mind that filters the fictional experience and presents only the most important details to create the maximum impact. It may be compared to the perspectives utilized by painters. As we note in Chapter 5 (p. 275), Claude Lorrain's painting *Harbour at Sunset* (p. I–3) puts all the buildings, ships, landscape, and foreground figures into the perspective of the distant sun's mysterious glow. Comparable paintings are Renoir's *The Umbrellas* and Whistler's *The Little White Girl, Symphony in White, No. 2,* both of which stress color— blue by Renoir and white by Whistler (pp. I–12 and I–11). The girl and her white dress occupy half of Whistler's painting, just as Renoir's umbrellas direct our eyes to the bustling dark blue that unites the foreground figures with the hidden world beyond. Thus, Renoir and Whistler connect life with color, while Claude suggests that human activities are minor in the perspective of the vast universe. (His human figures are small, and some are distant; indeed, he often hired other painters to do his figures.) The way reality is presented in each of the paintings—the point of view or guiding intelligence of the painter—determines our understanding of artistic ideas. Similarly, the point of view fashioned by the author of a literary work determines how we read, respond, and understand.

An Exercise in Point of View: Reporting an Accident

As an exercise to show that point of view is derived from lifelike situations, let us imagine that there has been an auto accident. Two cars, driven by Alice and Bill, have collided, and the after-crash scene is represented in the drawing. How might this accident be described? What would Alice say? What would Bill say?

Now assume that Frank, who is Bill's best friend, and Mary, who knows neither Bill nor Alice, were witnesses. What might Frank say about who was responsible? What might Mary say? Additionally, assume that you are a reporter for a local newspaper and are sent to report on the accident. You know none of the people involved. How will your report differ from the other reports? Finally, to what degree are all the statements designed to persuade listeners and readers that the details and claims made in the respective reports are true?

The likely differences in the various reports may be explained by reference to point of view. Obviously, because both Alice and Bill are deeply involved—each of them is a major participant or what may be called a **major mover**—they will likely arrange their words to make themselves seem blameless. Frank, because he is Bill's best friend, will report things in Bill's favor. Mary will favor neither Alice nor Bill, but let us assume that she did not look up to see the colliding cars until she heard the crash. Thus, she did not see the accident happening but saw only the immediate aftereffects. Amid all this mixture of partial and impartial views of the action, to whom should we attribute the greatest reliability?

Each person's report will have the "hidden agenda" of making herself or himself seem honest, objective, intelligent, impartial, and thorough. Thus, although both Alice and Bill may be truthful to the best of their abilities, their reports will not be reliable because they both have something to gain from avoiding responsibility for the accident. Also, Frank may be questionable as a witness because he is Bill's

friend and may report things to Bill's advantage. Mary could be reliable, but she did not see everything; therefore she is unreliable not because of motivation but rather because of her location as a witness. Most likely, your account as an impartial reporter will be the most reliable and objective of all, because your major interest is to learn all the details and to report the truth accurately, with no concern about the personal interests of either Alice or Bill.

As you can see, the ramifications of describing actions are far-reaching, and the consideration of the various interests and situations is subtle. Indeed, of all the aspects of literature, point of view is the most complex because it is so much like life itself. On the one hand, point of view is intertwined with the many interests and wishes of humanity at large; on the other, it is linked to the enormous difficulty of uncovering and determining truth.

Conditions That Affect Point of View

As this exercise in observation and expression demonstrates, point of view depends on two major factors. The first factor, as we have seen, is the physical situation of the narrator, or speaker, as an observer. How do the speaker's characteristics emerge from the narration? What are his or her qualifications or limitations as an observer? The second factor is the speaker's intellectual and emotional position. How might the speaker gain or lose from what takes place in the story? Are the speaker's observations and words colored by these interests? Does he or she have any persuasive purpose beyond being a straightforward recorder or observer? What values does the speaker impose upon the action?

In a story, as in many poems using narrative, authors take into account all these subtleties. For example, O'Connor's narrator, Jackie, in "First Confession" (Chapter 6) tells about boyhood family problems and his first experience with the sacrament of confession, but he has not yet fully separated himself from some of his youthful antagonisms. Whitecloud's speaker in "Blue Winds Dancing" (Chapter 5) is filled with misgivings about the life he leaves and relief about the life to which he is returning. These narrators show their own involvement and concern about the events they describe. The speaker in Jackson's "The Lottery," however, does not seem personally involved in the actions. This narrator listens, sees, and reports, but does not express deep involvement in the events of the story's country village. As readers, we need to develop our understanding of how such differing modes of presentation create the effects of these and all other stories and narrative poems.

Point of View and Opinions

Because point of view is often popularly understood to mean ideas, opinions, or beliefs, it must be stressed that the term is not directly synonymous with any of these. Point of view refers to a work's mode of narration—comprising narrator, language, audience, and perceptions of events and characters—whereas opinions and beliefs are thoughts and ideas that may or may not have anything to do with a narration. One may grant, however, that the position from which people see and understand things (e.g., established positions of political party, religion, social philosophy, and morality) has a most definite bearing on how they think and therefore on their opinions and beliefs. Opinions also affect how people view reality, and opinions affect, if not control, what they say about their perceptions of the world around them. Therefore, opinions stem out of point of view and at the same time have an influence on point of view. A four-star general and a buck private will have different things to say about what happens on a wartime battlefield.

For our purposes in this chapter, however, a discussion of point of view should emphasize how the narration and dramatic situation of a work create and shape the work. If ideas seem to be particularly important in a story, your objective should be not to analyze and discuss the ideas as ideas, but rather to consider whether and how these ideas affect what the narrator concludes and says about the story's actions and situations.

Determining a Work's Point of View

In your reading you will encounter a wide variety of points of view. To begin your analysis, first determine the work's grammatical voice (i.e., first, second, or third person). Then study the ways in which the subject, characterization, dialogue, and form interact with the point of view.

In the First-Person Point of View, the Narrator Tells about Events He or She Has Personally Witnessed

If the voice of the work is an "I," the author is using the **first-person point of view**—the impersonation of a fictional narrator or speaker who may be named or unnamed. In our hypothetical accident reports, both Alice and Bill are first-person speakers who are named. Similarly, the narrator of O'Connor's "First Confession," Jackie, is named and identified. By contrast, the narrator of Poe's "The Masque of the Red Death" (Chapter 9) is an unnamed speaker. In Twain's "Luck" (Chapter 3), there are two unnamed first-person speakers (the first "I" introduces the second "I").

First-person speakers report events as though they have acquired their knowledge in a number of ways:

- What they themselves have done, said, heard, and thought (firsthand experience).
- What they have observed others doing and saying (firsthand witness).
- What others have said to them or otherwise communicated to them (secondhand testimony and hearsay).
- What they are able to infer or deduce from the information they have discovered (inferential information).
- What they are able to conjecture about how a character or characters might think and act, given their knowledge of a situation (conjectural, imaginative, or intuitive information).

FIRST-PERSON SPEAKERS COME IN MANY VARIETIES.   Of all the points of view, the first person is the most independent of the author, because the first-person speaker may have a unique identity, with name, job, and economic and social position—a life separate totally from that of the author. Often, however, the author creates a more anonymous but still independent first-person speaker, as with the unnamed speaker-narrator of Poe's "The Masque of the Red Death" (Chapter 9). There are also situations in which an "I" speaker is pluralized by "we" when the first person includes other characters. Such a first-person plural point of view lends reliability to the narrative, as in Ellison's "Battle Royal" (Chapter 5), because the characters included as "we," even if they are sometimes unidentified by the speaker, may be considered additional witnesses.

SOME FIRST-PERSON SPEAKERS ARE RELIABLE, AND OTHERS ARE UNRELIABLE.   When you encounter a first-person narrative (whether a story or narrative poem), determine the narrator's position and ability, prejudices or self-interest, and judgment of his or her readers or listeners. Most first-person speakers describing their own experiences are to be accepted as **reliable** and authoritative. But sometimes first-person speakers are **unreliable** because they may have interests or limitations that lead them to mislead, distort, or even lie. There is reason, for example, to question Jackie's reliability as the speaker of O'Connor's "First Confession" (Chapter 6). As an adult he is describing the events within his family and his after-school preparation sessions prior to his attending his first confession; but he is giving us his childhood memories, and he is not including the potential views of those in his family about the ways in which things happened. Whether first-person speakers are reliable or unreliable, however, they are one of the means by which authors confer an authentic, lifelike aura to their works.

In the Second-Person Point of View, the Narrator Is Speaking to Someone Else Who Is Addressed as "You"

The **second-person point of view,** the least common of the points of view, and the most difficult for authors to manage, offers two major possibilities. In the first, a narrator (almost necessarily a first-person speaker) tells a listener what he or she has done and said at a past time. The actions might be a simple retelling of events, as when a parent tells a child about something the child did during infancy, or when a doctor tells a patient with amnesia about events before the causative injury. Also, the actions might also be subject to dispute and interpretation, as when a prosecuting attorney describes a crime for which a defendant is on trial or when a spouse lists grievances against an alienated spouse in a custody or divorce case. Still another situation of the second-person point of view might occur when an angry person accuses the listener of a betrayal or some other wrong. In such instances, it is worth bearing in mind that the point of view may possibly be considered first person rather than second, for the speaker is likely to be speaking subjectively about his or her own perception or analysis of the listener's actions. It is also worth bearing in mind that the second-person point of view in such instances may be totally wrong, and possibly also totally wrongheaded.

The second possibility is equally complex. Some narrators are obviously addressing a "you" but are instead referring mainly to themselves—and to listeners only tangentially—in preference to an "I." In addition, some narrators follow the usage—not uncommon in colloquial speech—of the indefinite "you." In this point of view, the "you" refers not only to a specific listener, who may or may not be present, but also to anyone at all, or maybe, and above all, to the speaker himself/herself. In this way the writer avoids the more formal use of such words as *one, a person,* or *people.* (Incidentally, the selection of *you* is non–gender-specific because it eliminates the need for the pronouns *he, she; she/he; he/she;* or *he or she.*) An ingenious employment of the second-person point of view is seen in Lorrie Moore's "How to Become a Writer" (this chapter). What we find on the pages is an informal, personal discussion in which the speaker uses "you" frequently, as though she is giving advice to any aspiring writers who are able to hear her. More subtly, however, we infer that the speaker is masking personal experience, some of it painful, behind her jokes, puns, and sometimes flippant "advice."

In the Third-Person Point of View, the Speaker Emphasizes the Actions and Speeches of Others

If events in the work are described in the third person (*he, she, it, they*), the author is using the **third-person point of view.** It is not always easy to characterize the voice in this point of view. Sometimes the speaker uses an "I," as in Poe's "The Masque of the Red Death" (Chapter 9), and this "I" may seemingly be identical with the author, but at other times the author creates a distinct **authorial voice** that may be included at times within the voice of the narrator, as in Hawthorne's "Young Goodman Brown" (Chapter 7). There are three variants of the third-person point of view: (1) *dramatic or objective,* (2) *omniscient,* and (3) *limited omniscient.*

THE DRAMATIC OR OBJECTIVE POINT OF VIEW IS THE BASIC METHOD OF NARRATION.
The most direct presentation of action and dialogue is the dramatic or objective point of view (also called *third-person objective*). It is the basic method of rendering action and speech that all the points of view share. The narrator of the dramatic point of view is an unidentified speaker who reports things in a way that is analogous to a hovering or tracking video camera or to what some critics have called "a fly on the wall (or tree)." Somehow, the narrator is always on the spot—in rooms, forests, village squares, moving vehicles, or even in outer space—to tell us what is happening and what is being said.

The dramatic presentation is limited only to what is said and what happens. The writer does not overtly draw conclusions or make interpretations, because the premise of the dramatic point of view is that readers, like a jury, can form their own interpretations if they are shown the right evidence. Jackson's "The Lottery"—a powerful example of the dramatic point of view—is an objective story about a bizarre public occasion in a small town. We, the readers, draw many conclusions about the story (such as that the people are tradition bound, insensitive, cruel, and so on), but because of the dramatic point of view Jackson does not state any of these conclusions for us.

THE NARRATOR OF THE OMNISCIENT POINT OF VIEW CAN SEE ALL, KNOW ALL, AND POTENTIALLY DISCLOSE ALL.
The third-person point of view is **omniscient** (all-knowing) when the speaker not only presents action and dialogue but also, at times, reports the thoughts and reactions of the characters. In our everyday real world, we never know, nor can we ever know, what other people are thinking. For practical purposes, their minds are closed to us. However, we always make assumptions about the thoughts of others, and these assumptions are the basis of the omniscient point of view. Authors use it freely but judiciously to explain responses, thoughts, feelings, and plans—an additional dimension that aids in the development of character. For example, in Maupassant's "The Necklace" (Part I),

the speaker takes an omniscient stance to explain the responses and thoughts of the major character and also, though in just a short passage, of her husband. Even in an omniscient point of view story, however, relatively little description is actually devoted to the thoughts of the characters, for most of the narration must necessarily be taken up with dramatic third-person descriptions.

THE NARRATOR OR SPEAKER IN THE LIMITED OR LIMITED-OMNISCIENT POINT OF VIEW FOCUSES ON THOUGHTS AND DEEDS OF A MAJOR CHARACTER.   More common than the omniscient and dramatic points of view is the **limited third person** or **limited omniscient third person,** in which the author concentrates on or limits the narration to the actions and thoughts of a major character. In our accident case (p. 128), Frank, being Bill's friend, would be sympathetic to Bill. Thus Frank's report of the collision would likely be third-person limited, with Bill as the center of interest. Depending on whether a narration focuses on action or motivation, the limited third-person narrator may explore the mentality of the major character either lightly or in depth. The name given to the central figure on whom the third-person omniscient point of view is focused is the **point-of-view character.** Thus, Peyton Farquhar in "An Occurrence at Owl Creek Bridge" (Chapter 1) and Miss Brill in Mansfield's "Miss Brill" (Chapter 3) are both point-of-view characters. Almost everything in these stories is there because the point-of-view characters see it, hear it, respond to it, think about it, imagine it entirely, do it or share in it, try to control it, or are controlled by it.

Mingling Points of View

In some works, authors mingle points of view in order to imitate reality. For example, many first-person narrators use various types of the third-person point of view during much of their narration. Authors also vary points of view to sustain interest, create suspense, or put the burden of response entirely upon readers. For example, Bierce in "An Occurrence at Owl Creek Bridge" (Chapter 1) keeps our attention focused on the reactions of the major character, Peyton Farquhar, until the last paragraph of the story, when there is a shift to a dramatic point of view as Farquhar is hanging from the bridge. This shift in point of view is an almost brutal pronouncement that none of Farquhar's hopes could ever have come true. A comparable but contrasting change in point of view occurs at the end of Hawthorne's "Young Goodman Brown" (Chapter 7), where the narrator objectively summarizes Brown's loveless and bleak life after his nightmare about evil.

Point of View and Verb Tense

As discussed in this chapter, point of view refers to the ways narrators and speakers perceive and report actions and speeches. In the broadest sense, however, point of view may be considered as a total way of rendering truth, and for this reason the tense chosen by the narrators is important. Most narratives rely on the past tense: The actions happened in the past, and they are now over.

The introduction of dialogue, however, even in a past-tense narration, dramatically brings the story into the present. Such dramatic rendering is accomplished by the dialogue concluding Maupassant's "The Necklace," for example, which emphasizes the irony of Mathilde's sacrifices during the previous ten years.

The narrator of a past-tense narrative may also introduce present-tense commentary during the narration—a strong means of signifying the importance of past events. Examples are in O'Connor's "First Confession" (Chapter 6), in which the narrator Jackie makes personal comments about the events he is describing, and in Mark Twain's "Luck" (Chapter 3), where the second narrator expresses amazement over the mistakes of the main character. In addition, as noted in Chapter 7, the narrators of parables and fables use past-tense narratives as vehicles for teaching current lessons in philosophy and religion.

In recent years a number of writers have used the present tense as their principal time reference. With the present tense, the narrative story or poem is rendered as a virtual drama that is unfolded moment by moment, as in "Blue Winds Dancing" (Chapter 5) when Whitecloud uses the present tense to emphasize the immediate experience of the narrator as he returns home.

Some writers intermingle tenses to show how time itself can be blended within the human mind, because our consciousness never exists only in the present but instead is a composite made up of past memories cresting upon a never-ending wave carrying us into the future. Thus at the end of Bierce's "An Occurrence at Owl Creek Bridge," the past-tense narration shifts into the present tense to demonstrate the vividness of the main character's perceptions just before his death.

Summary: Guidelines for Point of View

The following guidelines summarize and further classify the types of points of view. Use them to distinguish differences and shades of variation in stories and poems.

1. First Person (*I, my, mine, me,* and sometimes *we, our,* and *us*). First-person speakers are involved to at least some degree in the actions of the work. Such narrators may have (1) complete understanding, (2) partial or incorrect understanding, (3) no understanding at all, or (4) complete understanding with the motive to mislead or lie. Although the first three of these narrators probably tell the truth and are therefore **reliable,** they may also sometimes be **unreliable.** The only way to determine their reliability is to study the story closely. Obviously, the narrator of the fourth type—the one who misleads or lies—is by nature unreliable, but nevertheless the mode might possibly be accepted (although critically) on matters of detail. The three types of first-person speakers are these:

    a. *A Major Participant*
       i. Who tells his or her own story and thoughts as a major mover.
      ii. Who tells a story about others and also about herself or himself as one of the major movers.

    iii. Who tells a story mainly about others, and about himself or herself only tangentially.

   b. *A Minor Participant*, who tells a story about events experienced and witnessed.

   c. *A Nonparticipating But Identifiable Speaker*, who learns about events in other ways (e.g., listening to participants through direct conversation, overhearing conversation, examining documents, hearing news reports, and also rumors, imagining what might have occurred). The narrative of such a speaker is a combination of fact and conjectural reconstruction.

2. Second Person (*you*, or possibly *thou*). This is a point of view that authors use frequently enough to justify our knowing about it. Its premise is that the speaker knows more about the actions of a character (the "you") than the character himself or herself. It is used when the speaker (e.g., lawyer, spouse, friend, sports umpire, psychologist, parent, angry person) talks directly to the other person and explains this other person's past actions and statements. More generally, and in a colloquial and informal style, the speaker may also use "you" to mean himself or herself, the reader, or anyone at all.

3. Third Person (*she, he, it, they*). The speaker is outside the action and is mainly a reporter of actions and speeches. Some speakers may have unique and distinguishing traits even though no separate identity is claimed for them ("the unnamed third-person narrator"). Other third-person speakers who are not separately identified may represent the words and views of the authors themselves ("the authorial voice").

   a. *A Dramatic or Third-Person Objective Narrator.* The objective narrator reports only what can be seen and heard. The thoughts of characters are included only if they are spoken or written (dialogue, reported or overheard conversation, letters, reports, etc.).

   b. *An Omniscient Narrator.* The omniscient speaker sees all, knows all, and can report all. When necessary, the omniscient narrator can reveal the inner workings of the minds of any or all of a story's characters. Even on omniscient speaker, however, makes a mostly dramatic third-person presentation.

   c. *A Limited, or Limited Omniscient Narrator.* This narrator focuses on the actions, responses, thoughts, and feelings of a single major character. Although the resulting narration may concentrate on the major character's actions, it may also probe deeply within the mind of this character.

Stories for Study

Raymond Carver. . . . . Neighbors, 137

Shirley Jackson . . . . The Lottery, 140

Lorrie Moore . . . . How to Become a Writer, 146

Joyce Carol Oates . . . . The Cousins, 150

RAYMOND CARVER (1938–1988)

Originally from Oregon, Carver lived in Washington and spent much of his adult life in California. He studied at Chico State and at the Iowa Writers' Workshop. After doing blue-collar jobs for a time, he worked as an editor and then, finally, as a teacher. His collections include Will You Please Be Quiet, Please? *(1976) and* Cathedral *(1983).* Where I'm Calling From *(1988) collects earlier stories and adds a number of new ones.* Short Cuts *(1993) is a selection of ten stories that were woven together into a film (1993) by Robert Altman. Carver is considered a master of minimalism—that is, fiction that stresses only the essentials of action and description. Generally, his writing is economical, stripped to the bone. Many of his characters seem unusual if not odd or even cruel. For example, one of his brief stories, "Popular Mechanics," takes little more than a single page to depict how a couple breaking up is also about to break up (literally) their child. "Neighbors" is taken from* Where I'm Calling From.

 # Neighbors (1988)

Bill and Arlene Miller were a happy couple. But now and then they felt they alone among their circle had been passed by somehow, leaving Bill to attend to his bookkeeping duties and Arlene occupied with secretarial chores. They talked about it sometimes, mostly in comparison with the lives of their neighbors, Harriet and Jim Stone. It seemed to the Millers that the Stones lived a fuller and brighter life. The Stones were always going out for dinner, or entertaining at home, or traveling about the country somewhere in connection with Jim's work.

The Stones lived across the hall from the Millers. Jim was a salesman for a machine-parts firm and often managed to combine business with pleasure trips, and on this occasion the Stones would be away for ten days, first to Cheyenne, then on to St. Louis to visit relatives. In their absence, the Millers would look after the Stones' apartment, feed Kitty, and water the plants.

Bill and Jim shook hands beside the car. Harriet and Arlene held each other by the elbows and kissed lightly on the lips.

"Have fun," Bill said to Harriet.

"We will," said Harriet. "You kids have fun too."   5

Arlene nodded.

Jim winked at her. "Bye, Arlene. Take good care of the old man."

"I will," Arlene said.

"Have fun," Bill said.

"You bet," Jim said, clipping Bill lightly on the arm. "And thanks again, you guys."   10

The Stones waved as they drove away, and the Millers waved too.

"Well, I wish it was us," Bill said.

"God knows, we could use a vacation," Arlene said. She took his arm and put it around her waist as they climbed the stairs to their apartment.

After dinner Arlene said, "Don't forget. Kitty gets liver flavor the first night." She stood in the kitchen doorway folding the handmade tablecloth that Harriet had bought for her last year in Santa Fe.

Bill took a deep breath as he entered the Stones' apartment. The air was already heavy   15
and it was vaguely sweet. The sunburst clock over the television said half past eight. He remembered when Harriet had come home with the clock, how she had crossed the hall to

show it to Arlene, cradling the brass case in her arms and talking to it through the tissue paper as if it were an infant.

Kitty rubbed her face against his slippers and then turned onto her side, but jumped up quickly as Bill moved to the kitchen and selected one of the stacked cans from the gleaming drainboard. Leaving the cat to pick at her food, he headed for the bathroom. He looked at himself in the mirror and then closed his eyes and then looked again. He opened the medicine chest. He found a container of pills and read the label—*Harriet Stone. One each day as directed*—and slipped it into his pocket. He went back to the kitchen, drew a pitcher of water, and returned to the living room. He finished watering, set the pitcher on the rug, and opened the liquor cabinet. He reached in back for the bottle of Chivas Regal. He took two drinks from the bottle, wiped his lips on his sleeve, and replaced the bottle in the cabinet.

Kitty was on the couch sleeping. He switched off the lights, slowly closing and checking the door. He had the feeling he had left something.

"What kept you?" Arlene said. She sat with her legs turned under her, watching television.

"Nothing. Playing with Kitty," he said, and went over to her and touched her breasts.

20   "Let's go to bed, honey," he said.

The next day Bill took only ten minutes of the twenty-minute break allotted for the afternoon and left at fifteen minutes before five. He parked the car in the lot just as Arlene hopped down from the bus. He waited until she entered the building, then ran up the stairs to catch her as she stepped out of the elevator.

"Bill! God, you scared me. You're early," she said.

He shrugged. "Nothing to do at work," he said.

She let him use her key to open the door. He looked at the door across the hall before following her inside.

25   "Let's go to bed," he said.

"Now?" She laughed. "What's gotten into you?"

"Nothing. Take your dress off." He grabbed for her awkwardly, and she said, "Good God, Bill."

He unfastened his belt.

Later they sent out for Chinese food, and when it arrived they ate hungrily, without speaking, and listened to records.

30   "Let's not forget to feed Kitty," she said.

"I was just thinking about that," he said. "I'll go right over."

*   *   *

He selected a can of fish flavor for the cat, then filled the pitcher and went to water. When he returned to the kitchen, the cat was scratching in her box. She looked at him steadily before she turned back to the litter. He opened all the cupboards and examined the canned goods, the cereals, the packaged foods, the cocktail and wine glasses, the china, the pots and pans. He opened the refrigerator. He sniffed some celery, took two bites of cheddar cheese, and chewed on an apple as he walked into the bedroom. The bed seemed enormous, with a fluffy white bedspread draped to the floor. He pulled out a nightstand drawer, found a half-empty package of cigarettes and stuffed them into his pocket. Then he stepped to the closet and was opening it when the knock sounded at the front door.

He stopped by the bathroom and flushed the toilet on his way.

"What's been keeping you?" Arlene said. "You've been over here more than an hour."

35   "Have I really?" he said.

"Yes, you have," she said.

"I had to go to the toilet," he said.

"You have your own toilet," she said.

"I couldn't wait," he said.

That night they made love again.   40

In the morning he had Arlene call in for him. He showered, dressed, and made a light breakfast. He tried to start a book. He went out for a walk and felt better. But after a while, hands still in his pockets, he returned to the apartment. He stopped at the Stones' door on the chance he might hear the cat moving about. Then he let himself in at his own door and went to the kitchen for the key.

Inside it seemed cooler than his apartment, and darker too. He wondered if the plants had something to do with the temperature of the air. He looked out the window, and then he moved slowly through each room considering everything that fell under his gaze, carefully, one object at a time. He saw ashtrays, items of furniture, kitchen utensils, the clock. He saw everything. At last he entered the bedroom, and the cat appeared at his feet. He stroked her once, carried her into the bathroom, and shut the door.

He lay down on the bed and stared at the ceiling. He lay for a while with his eyes closed, and then he moved his hand under his belt. He tried to recall what day it was. He tried to remember when the Stones were due back, and then he wondered if they would ever return. He could not remember their faces or the way they talked and dressed. He sighed and with effort rolled off the bed to lean over the dresser and look at himself in the mirror.

He opened the closet and selected a Hawaiian shirt. He looked until he found Bermudas, neatly pressed and hanging over a pair of brown twill slacks. He shed his own clothes and slipped into the shorts and the shirt. He looked in the mirror again. He went to the living room and poured himself a drink and sipped it on his way back to the bedroom. He put on a blue shirt, a dark suit, a blue and white tie, black wing-tip shoes. The glass was empty and he went for another drink.

In the bedroom again, he sat on a chair, crossed his legs, and smiled, observing himself   45
in the mirror. The telephone rang twice and fell silent. He finished the drink and took off the suit. He rummaged through the top drawers until he found a pair of panties and a brassiere. He stepped into the panties and fastened the brassiere, then looked through the closet for an outfit. He put on a black and white checkered skirt and tried to zip it up. He put on a burgundy blouse that buttoned up the front. He considered her shoes, but understood they would not fit. For a long time he looked out the living-room window from behind the curtain. Then he returned to the bedroom and put everything away.

He was not hungry. She did not eat much, either. They looked at each other shyly and smiled. She got up from the table and checked that the key was on the shelf and then she quickly cleared the dishes.

He stood in the kitchen doorway and smoked a cigarette and watched her pick up the key.

"Make yourself comfortable while I go across the hall," she said. "Read the paper or something." She closed her fingers over the key. He was, she said, looking tired.

He tried to concentrate on the news. He read the paper and turned on the television. Finally he went across the hall. The door was locked.

"It's me. Are you still there, honey?" he called.   50

After a time the lock released and Arlene stepped outside and shut the door. "Was I gone so long?" she said.

"Well, you were," he said.

"Was I?" she said. "I guess I must have been playing with Kitty."

He studied her, and she looked away, her hand still resting on the doorknob.

"It's funny," she said. "You know—to go in someone's place like that."   55

He nodded, took her hand from the knob, and guided her toward their own door. He let them into their apartment.

"It *is* funny," he said.

He noticed white lint clinging to the back of her sweater, and the color was high in her cheeks. He began kissing her on the neck and hair and she turned and kissed him back.

"Oh, damn," she said. "Damn, damn," she sang, girlishly clapping her hands. "I just remembered. I really and truly forgot to do what I went over there to do. I didn't feed Kitty or do any watering." She looked at him. "Isn't that stupid?"

60 "I don't think so," he said. "Just a minute. I'll get my cigarettes and go back with you."

She waited until he had closed and locked their door, and then she took his arm at the muscle and said, "I guess I should tell you. I found some pictures."

He stopped in the middle of the hall. "What kind of pictures?"

"You can see for yourself," she said, and she watched him.

"No kidding." He grinned. "Where?"

65 "In a drawer," she said.

"No kidding," he said.

And then she said, "Maybe they won't come back," and was at once astonished at her words.

"It could happen," he said. "Anything could happen."

"Or maybe they'll come back and . . ." but she did not finish.

70 They held hands for the short walk across the hall, and when he spoke she could barely hear his voice.

"The key," he said. "Give it to me."

"What?" she said. She gazed at the door.

"The key," he said. "You have the key."

"My God," she said, "I left the key inside."

75 He tried the knob. It was locked. Then she tried the knob. It would not turn. Her lips were parted, and her breathing was hard, expectant. He opened his arms and she moved into them.

"Don't worry," he said into her ear. "For God's sake, don't worry."

They stayed there. They held each other. They leaned into the door as if against a wind, and braced themselves.

QUESTIONS

1. Who is the speaker of "Neighbors"? On whom is the speaker's attention directed?

2. Who are the Millers? Do they seem normal at first? As the story progresses, do they seem to get odd? What happens to them?

3. Should the story be considered as realistic fiction, or would it be more appropriate to consider it as an illustration of life's absurdities?

SHIRLEY JACKSON (1919–1965)

Jackson was a native of California. She graduated from Syracuse University in New York and lived much of her life in Vermont. Although her life was short, she was a successful writer of novels, short stories, biographies, and children's fiction. Her stories often depict unusual, unreal, or bizarre events in common settings, of which "The Lottery" is a major example. She wrote the story in only two hours and submitted it to the New Yorker without major revisions. When it was published many readers raised questions about how to interpret the conclusion. Jackson steadfastly refused to explain, leaving readers to decide for themselves.

🍁 The Lottery (1948)

The morning of June 27th was clear and sunny, with the fresh warmth of a full summer day; the flowers were blossoming profusely and the grass was richly green. The people of the village began to gather in the square, between the post office and the bank, around ten o'clock; in some towns there were so many people that the lottery took two days and had to be started on June 26th, but in this village, where there were only about three hundred people, the whole lottery took less than two hours, so it could begin at ten o'clock in the morning and still be through in time to allow the villagers to get home for noon dinner.

The children assembled first, of course. School was recently over for the summer, and the feeling of liberty sat uneasily on most of them; they tended to gather together quietly for a while before they broke into boisterous play, and their talk was still of the classroom and the teacher, of books and reprimands. Bobby Martin had already stuffed his pockets full of stones, and the other boys soon followed his example, selecting the smoothest and roundest stones; Bobby and Harry Jones and Dickie Delacroix—the villagers pronounced this name "Dellacroy"—eventually made a great pile of stones in one corner of the square and guarded it against the raids of the other boys. The girls stood aside, talking among themselves, looking over their shoulders at the boys, and the very small children rolled in the dust or clung to the hands of their older brothers or sisters.

Soon the men began to gather, surveying their own children, speaking of planting and rain, tractors and taxes. They stood together, away from the pile of stones in the corner, and their jokes were quiet and they smiled rather than laughed. The women, wearing faded house dresses and sweaters, came shortly after their menfolk. They greeted one another and exchanged bits of gossip as they went to join their husbands. Soon the women, standing by their husbands, began to call to their children, and the children came reluctantly, having to be called four or five times. Bobby Martin ducked under his mother's grasping hand and ran, laughing, back to the pile of stones. His father spoke up sharply, and Bobby came quickly and took his place between his father and his oldest brother.

The lottery was conducted—as were the square dances, the teen-age club, the Halloween program—by Mr. Summers, who had time and energy to devote to civic activities. He was a round-faced, jovial man and he ran the coal business, and people were sorry for him, because he had no children and his wife was a scold. When he arrived in the square, carrying the black wooden box, there was a murmur of conversation among the villagers, and he waved and called, "Little late today, folks." The postmaster, Mr. Graves, followed him, carrying a three-legged stool, and the stool was put in the center of the square and Mr. Summers set the black box down on it. The villagers kept their distance, leaving a space between themselves and the stool, and when Mr. Summers said, "Some of you fellows want to give me a hand?" there was a hesitation before two men, Mr. Martin and his oldest son, Baxter, came forward to hold the box steady on the stool while Mr. Summers stirred up the papers inside it.

The original paraphernalia for the lottery had been lost long ago, and the black box now resting on the stool had been put into use even before Old Man Warner, the oldest man in town, was born. Mr. Summers spoke frequently to the villagers about making a new box, but no one liked to upset even as much tradition as was represented by the black box. There was a story that the present box had been made with some pieces of the box that had preceded it, the one that had been constructed when the first people settled down to make a village here. Every year, after the lottery, Mr. Summers began talking again about a new box, but every year the subject was allowed to fade off without anything's being done. The black box grew shabbier each year; by now it was no longer completely black but splintered badly along one side to show the original wood color, and in some places faded or stained.

Mr. Martin and his oldest son, Baxter, held the black box securely on the stool until Mr. Summers had stirred the papers thoroughly with his hand. Because so much of the ritual had been forgotten or discarded, Mr. Summers had been successful in having slips of paper substituted for the chips of wood that had been used for generations. Chips of wood, Mr. Summers had argued, had been all very well when the village was tiny, but now that the population was more than three hundred and likely to keep on growing, it was necessary to use something that would fit more easily into the black box. The night before the lottery, Mr. Summers and Mr. Graves made up the slips of paper and put them in the box, and it was then taken to the safe of Mr. Summers' coal company and locked up until Mr. Summers was ready to take it to the square next morning. The rest of the year, the box was put away, sometimes one place, sometimes another; it had spent one year in Mr. Graves's barn and another year underfoot in the post office, and sometimes it was set on a shelf in the Martin grocery and left there.

There was a great deal of fussing to be done before Mr. Summers declared the lottery open. There were the lists to make up—of heads of families, heads of households in each family, members of each household in each family. There was the proper swearing-in of Mr. Summers by the postmaster, as the official of the lottery; at one time, some people remembered, there had been a recital of some sort, performed by the official of the lottery, a perfunctory, tuneless chant that had been rattled off duly each year; some people believed that the official of the lottery used to stand just so when he said or sang it, others believed that he was supposed to walk among the people, but years and years ago this part of the ritual had been allowed to lapse. There had been, also, a ritual salute, which the official of the lottery had had to use in addressing each person who came up to draw from the box, but this also had changed with time, until now it was felt necessary only for the official to speak to each person approaching. Mr. Summers was very good at all this; in his clean white shirt and blue jeans, with one hand resting carelessly on the black box, he seemed very proper and important as he talked interminably to Mr. Graves and the Martins.

Just as Mr. Summers finally left off talking and turned to the assembled villagers, Mrs. Hutchinson came hurriedly along the path to the square, her sweater thrown over her shoulders, and slid into place in the back of the crowd. "Clean forgot what day it was," she said to Mrs. Delacroix, who stood next to her, and they both laughed softly. "Thought my old man was out back stacking wood," Mrs. Hutchinson went on, "and then I looked out the window and the kids was gone, and then I remembered it was the twenty-seventh and came a-running." She dried her hands on her apron, and Mrs. Delacroix said, "You're in time, though. They're still talking away up there."

Mrs. Hutchinson craned her neck to see through the crowd and found her husband and children standing near the front. She tapped Mrs. Delacroix on the arm as a farewell and began to make her way through the crowd. The people separated good-humoredly to let her through; two or three people said, in voices just loud enough to be heard across the crowd, "Here comes your Missus, Hutchinson," and "Bill, she made it after all." Mrs. Hutchinson reached her husband, and Mr. Summers, who had been waiting, said cheerfully, "Thought we were going to have to get on without you, Tessie." Mrs. Hutchinson said, grinning, "Wouldn't have me leave m'dishes in the sink, now, would you, Joe?," and soft laughter ran through the crowd as the people stirred back into position after Mrs. Hutchinson's arrival.

10   "Well, now," Mr. Summers said soberly, "guess we better get started, get this over with, so's we can go back to work. Anybody ain't here?"

"Dunbar," several people said. "Dunbar, Dunbar."

Mr. Summers consulted his list. "Clyde Dunbar," he said. "That's right. He's broke his leg, hasn't he? Who's drawing for him?"

"Me, I guess," a woman said, and Mr. Summers turned to look at her. "Wife draws for her husband," Mr. Summers said. "Don't you have a grown boy to do it for you, Janey?"

Although Mr. Summers and everyone else in the village knew the answer perfectly well, it was the business of the official of the lottery to ask such questions formally. Mr. Summers waited with an expression of polite interest while Mrs. Dunbar answered.

"Horace's not but sixteen yet," Mrs. Dunbar said regretfully. "Guess I gotta fill in for the old man this year."

"Right," Mr. Summers said. He made a note on the list he was holding. Then he asked, 15 "Watson boy drawing this year?"

A tall boy in the crowd raised his hand. "Here," he said. "I'm drawing for m'mother and me." He blinked his eyes nervously and ducked his head as several voices in the crowd said things like "Good fellow, Jack," and "Glad to see your mother's got a man to do it."

"Well," Mr. Summers said, "guess that's everyone. Old Man Warner make it?"

"Here," a voice said, and Mr. Summers nodded.

A sudden hush fell on the crowd as Mr. Summers cleared his throat and looked at the list. "All ready?" he called. "Now, I'll read the names—heads of families first—and the men come up and take a paper out of the box. Keep the paper folded in your hand without looking at it until everyone has had a turn. Everything clear?"

The people had done it so many times that they only half listened to the directions; most 20 of them were quiet, wetting their lips, not looking around. Then Mr. Summers raised one hand high and said, "Adams." A man disengaged himself from the crowd and came forward. "Hi, Steve," Mr. Summers said, and Mr. Adams said, "Hi, Joe." They grinned at one another humorlessly and nervously. Then Mr. Adams reached into the black box and took out a folded paper. He held it firmly by one corner as he turned and went hastily back to his place in the crowd, where he stood a little apart from his family, not looking down at his hand.

"Allen," Mr. Summers said. "Anderson. . . . Bentham."

"Seems like there's no time at all between lotteries any more," Mrs. Delacroix said to Mrs. Graves in the back row. "Seems like we got through with the last one only last week."

"Time sure goes fast," Mrs. Graves said.

"Clark . . . Delacroix."

"There goes my old man," Mrs. Delacroix said. She held her breath while her husband 25 went forward.

"Dunbar," Mr. Summers said, and Mrs. Dunbar went steadily to the box while one of the women said, "Go on, Janey," and another said, "There she goes."

"We're next," Mrs. Graves said. She watched while Mr. Graves came around from the side of the box, greeted Mr. Summers gravely, and selected a slip of paper from the box. By now, all through the crowd there were men holding the small folded papers in their large hands, turning them over and over nervously. Mrs. Dunbar and her two sons stood together, Mrs. Dunbar holding the slip of paper.

"Harburt. . . . Hutchinson."

"Get up there, Bill," Mrs. Hutchinson said, and the people near her laughed.

"Jones." 30

"They do say," Mr. Adams said to Old Man Warner, who stood next to him, "that over in the north village they're talking of giving up the lottery."

Old Man Warner snorted. "Pack of crazy fools," he said. "Listening to the young folks, nothing's good enough for *them*. Next thing you know, they'll be wanting to go back to living in caves, nobody work any more, live *that* way for a while. Used to be a saying about 'Lottery in June, corn be heavy soon.' First thing you know, we'd all be eating stewed chickweed and acorns. There's *always* been a lottery," he added petulantly. "Bad enough to see young Joe Summers up there joking with everybody."

"Some places have already quit lotteries," Mrs. Adams said.

"Nothing but trouble in *that*," Old Man Warner said stoutly. "Pack of young fools."

35   "Martin." And Bobby Martin watched his father go forward. "Overdyke. . . . Percy."
"I wish they'd hurry," Mrs. Dunbar said to her older son. "I wish they'd hurry."
"They're almost through," her son said.
"You get ready to run tell Dad," Mrs. Dunbar said.
Mr. Summers called his own name and then stepped forward precisely and selected a slip from the box. Then he called, "Warner."
40   "Seventy-seventh year I been in the lottery," Old Man Warner said as he went through the crowd. "Seventy-seventh time."
"Watson." The tall boy came awkwardly through the crowd. Someone said, "Don't be nervous, Jack," and Mr. Summers said, "Take your time, son."
"Zanini."

After that, there was a long pause, a breathless pause, until Mr. Summers, holding his slip of paper in the air, said, "All right, fellows." For a minute, no one moved, and then all the slips of paper were opened. Suddenly, all the women began to speak at once, saying, "Who is it?" "Who's got it?" "Is it the Dunbars?" "Is it the Watsons?" Then the voices began to say, "It's Hutchinson. It's Bill," "Bill Hutchinson's got it."
"Go tell your father," Mrs. Dunbar said to her older son.
45   People began to look around to see the Hutchinsons. Bill Hutchinson was standing quiet, staring down at the paper in his hand. Suddenly, Tessie Hutchinson shouted to Mr. Summers, "You didn't give him time enough to take any paper he wanted. I saw you. It wasn't fair!"
"Be a good sport, Tessie," Mrs. Delacroix called, and Mrs. Graves said, "All of us took the same chance."
"Shut up, Tessie," Bill Hutchinson said.
"Well, everyone," Mr. Summers said, "that was done pretty fast, and now we've got to be hurrying a little more to get done in time." He consulted his next list. "Bill," he said, "you draw for the Hutchinson family. You got any other households in the Hutchinsons?"
"There's Don and Eva," Mrs. Hutchinson yelled. "Make *them* take their chance!"
50   "Daughters draw with their husbands' families, Tessie," Mr. Summers said gently. "You know that as well as anyone else."
"It wasn't *fair*," Tessie said.
"I guess not, Joe," Bill Hutchinson said regretfully. "My daughter draws with her husband's family, that's only fair. And I've got no other family except the kids."
"Then, as far as drawing for families is concerned, it's you," Mr. Summers said in explanation, "and as far as drawing for households is concerned, that's you, too. Right?"
"Right," Bill Hutchinson said.
55   "How many kids, Bill?" Mr. Summers asked formally.
"Three," Bill Hutchinson said. "There's Bill, Jr., and Nancy, and little Dave. And Tessie and me."
"All right, then," Mr. Summers said. "Harry, you got their tickets back?"
Mr. Graves nodded and held up the slips of paper. "Put them in the box, then," Mr. Summers directed. "Take Bill's and put it in."
"I think we ought to start over," Mrs. Hutchinson said, as quietly as she could. "I tell you it wasn't *fair*. You didn't give him time enough to choose. *Every*body saw that."
60   Mr. Graves had selected the five slips and put them in the box, and he dropped all the papers but those onto the ground, where the breeze caught them and lifted them off.
"Listen, everybody," Mrs. Hutchinson was saying to the people around her.
"Ready, Bill?" Mr. Summers asked, and Bill Hutchinson, with one quick glance around at his wife and children, nodded.

"Remember," Mr. Summers said, "take the slips and keep them folded until each person has taken one. Harry, you help little Dave." Mr. Graves took the hand of the little boy, who came willingly with him up to the box. "Take a paper out of the box, Davy," Mr. Summers said. Davy put his hand into the box and laughed. "Take just *one* paper," Mr. Summers said. "Harry, you hold it for him." Mr. Graves took the child's hand and removed the folded paper from the tight fist and held it while little Dave stood next to him and looked up at him wonderingly.

"Nancy next," Mr. Summers said. Nancy was twelve, and her school friends breathed heavily as she went forward, switching her skirt, and took a slip daintily from the box. "Bill, Jr.," Mr. Summers said, and Billy, his face red and his feet over-large, nearly knocked the box over as he got a paper out. "Tessie," Mr. Summers said. She hesitated for a minute, looking around defiantly, and then set her lips and went up to the box. She snatched a paper out and held it behind her.

"Bill," Mr. Summers said, and Bill Hutchinson reached into the box and felt around, 65 bringing his hand out at last with the slip of paper in it.

The crowd was quiet. A girl whispered, "I hope it's not Nancy," and the sound of the whisper reached the edges of the crowd.

"It's not the way it used to be," Old Man Warner said clearly. "People ain't the way they used to be."

"All right," Mr. Summers said. "Open the papers. Harry, you open little Dave's."

Mr. Graves opened the slip of paper and there was a general sigh through the crowd as he held it up and everyone could see that it was blank. Nancy and Bill, Jr., opened theirs at the same time, and both beamed and laughed, turning around to the crowd and holding their slips of paper above their heads.

"Tessie," Mr. Summers said. There was a pause, and then Mr. Summers looked at Bill 70 Hutchinson, and Bill unfolded his paper and showed it. It was blank.

"It's Tessie," Mr. Summers said, and his voice was hushed. "Show us her paper, Bill."

Bill Hutchinson went over to his wife and forced the slip of paper out of her hand. It had a black spot on it, the black spot Mr. Summers had made the night before with the heavy pencil in the coal-company office. Bill Hutchinson held it up, and there was a stir in the crowd.

"All right, folks," Mr. Summers said. "Let's finish quickly."

Although the villagers had forgotten the ritual and lost the original black box, they still remembered to use stones. The pile of stones the boys had made earlier was ready; there were stones on the ground with the blowing scraps of paper that had come out of the box. Mrs. Delacroix selected a stone so large she had to pick it up with both hands and turned to Mrs. Dunbar. "Come on," she said. "Hurry up."

Mrs. Dunbar had small stones in both hands, and she said, gasping for breath, "I can't 75 run at all. You'll have to go ahead and I'll catch up with you."

The children had stones already, and someone gave little Davy Hutchinson a few pebbles.

Tessie Hutchinson was in the center of a cleared space by now, and she held her hands out desperately as the villagers moved in on her. "It isn't fair," she said. A stone hit her on the side of the head.

Old Man Warner was saying, "Come on, come on, everyone." Steve Adams was in the front of the crowd of villagers with Mrs. Graves beside him.

"It isn't fair, it isn't right," Mrs. Hutchinson screamed, and then they were upon her.

QUESTIONS

1. Describe the point of view of the story. What seems to be the position from which the narrator sees and describes the events? How much extra information does the narrator provide?

2. What would the story be like if it were done with an omniscient point of view? With the first person? Could the story be as suspenseful as it is? In what other ways might the story be different with another point of view?

3. Does the conclusion of "The Lottery" seem to come as a surprise? In retrospect, what hints earlier in the story tell about what is to come?

4. A scapegoat, in the ritual of purification described in the Old Testament, was an actual goat that was released into the wilderness after having been ceremonially heaped with the "iniquities" of the people (Leviticus 16:22). What traces of such a ritual are suggested in "The Lottery"? Can you think of any other kinds of rituals that are retained today even though their purpose is now remote or even nonexistent?

5. Is "The Lottery" a horror story or a surprise story, or neither or both? Explain.

LORRIE MOORE (b. 1957)

Lorrie Moore, a Professor of English at the University of Wisconsin at Madison, has been internationally acclaimed, and her fiction has been heralded for its combination of wry humor, deep feeling, and impending tragedy. She was born in upstate New York and received an M.A. from Cornell. Following her first collection of stories, Self-Help *(1985), from which "How to Become a Writer" is taken, she published her first novel,* Anagrams *(1986). A later novel was* Who Will Run the Frog Hospital *(1994). In 1991 she published* Like Life, *a collection of eight stories taking its title from the last story, a grim portrait of life in a polluted, deteriorating future. In 2000 she published* The Forgotten Helper, *a "Christmas Story," and in 2007 her story collection* Pepsi Hotel *was published. She has received awards from the National Endowment for the Humanities, the Rockefeller Foundation, and the Rea Award for the Short Story. For her story collection* People Like That Are the Only People Here *(1997), she received the O Henry Award. Her collection* Birds of America *was nominated for the 1999 National Book Critics Circle Fiction Prize. In 2006 she was elected to the American Academy of Arts and Letters.*

🍁 How to Become a Writer (1985)

First, try to be something, anything, else. A movie star/astronaut. A movie star/missionary. A movie star/kindergarten teacher. President of the World. Fail miserably. It is best if you fail at an early age—say, fourteen. Early, critical disillusionment is necessary so that at fifteen you can write long haiku sequences about thwarted desire. It is a pond, a cherry blossom, a wind brushing against sparrow wing leaving for mountain. Count the syllables. Show it to your mom. She is tough and practical. She has a son in Vietnam and a husband who may be having an affair. She believes in wearing brown because it hides spots. She'll look briefly at your writing, then back up at you with a face blank as a donut. She'll say: "How about emptying the dishwasher?" Look away. Shove the forks in the fork drawer. Accidentally break one of the freebie gas station glasses. This is the required pain and suffering. This is only for starters.

In your high school English class look only at Mr. Killian's face. Decide faces are important. Write a villanelle about pores. Struggle. Write a sonnet. Count the syllables: nine, ten, eleven, thirteen. Decide to experiment with fiction. Here you don't have to count syllables. Write a short story about an elderly man and woman who accidentally shoot each other in the head, the result of an inexplicable malfunction of a shotgun which appears mysteriously in their living room one night. Give it to Mr. Killian as your final project. When you get it back, he has written on it: "Some of your images are quite nice, but you have no sense of plot." When you are home, in the privacy of your own room, faintly scrawl in pencil beneath his black-inked comments: "Plots are for dead people, pore-face."

Take all the babysitting jobs you can get. You are great with kids. They love you. You tell them stories about old people who die idiot deaths. You sing them songs like "Blue Bells of Scotland," which is their favorite. And when they are in their pajamas and have finally stopped pinching each other, when they are fast asleep, you read every sex manual in the house, and wonder how on earth anyone could ever do those things with someone they truly loved. Fall asleep in a chair reading Mr. McMurphy's *Playboy*. When the McMurphys come home, they will tap you on the shoulder, look at the magazine in your lap, and grin. You will want to die. They will ask you if Tracey took her medicine all right. Explain, yes, she did, that you promised her a story if she would take it like a big girl and that seemed to work out just fine. "Oh, marvelous," they will exclaim.

Try to smile proudly.

Apply to college as a child psychology major. 5

As a child psychology major, you have some electives. You've always liked birds. Sign up for something called "The Ornithological Field Trip." It meets Tuesdays and Thursdays at two. When you arrive at Room 134 on the first day of class, everyone is sitting around a seminar table talking about metaphors. You've heard of these. After a short, excruciating while, raise your hand and say diffidently, "Excuse me, isn't this Bird-watching One-oh-one?" The class stops and turns to look at you. They seem to all have one face—giant and blank as a vandalized clock. Someone with a beard booms out, "No, this is Creative Writing." Say: "Oh—right," as if perhaps you knew all along. Look down at your schedule. Wonder how the hell you ended up here. The computer, apparently, has made an error. You start to get up to leave and then don't. The lines at the registrar this week are huge. Perhaps you should stick with this mistake. Perhaps your creative writing isn't all that bad. Perhaps it is fate. Perhaps this is what your dad meant when he said, "It's the age of computers, Francie, it's the age of computers."

Decide that you like college life. In your dorm you meet many nice people. Some are smarter than you. And some, you notice, are dumber than you. You will continue, unfortunately, to view the world in exactly these terms for the rest of your life.

The assignment this week in creative writing is to narrate a violent happening. Turn in a story about driving with your Uncle Gordon and another one about two old people who are accidentally electrocuted when they go to turn on a badly wired desk lamp. The teacher will hand them back to you with comments: "Much of your writing is smooth and energetic. You have, however, a ludicrous notion of plot." Write another story about a man and a woman who, in the very first paragraph, have their lower torsos accidentally blitzed away by dynamite. In the second paragraph, with the insurance money, they buy a frozen yogurt stand together. There are six more paragraphs. You read the whole thing out loud in class. No one likes it. They say your sense of plot is outrageous and incompetent. After class someone asks you if you are crazy.

Decide that perhaps you should stick to comedies. Start dating someone who is funny, someone who has what in high school you called a "really great sense of humor" and what now your creative writing class calls "self-contempt giving rise to comic form."

Write down all of his jokes, but don't tell him you are doing this. Make up anagrams of his old girlfriend's name and name all of your socially handicapped characters with them. Tell him his old girlfriend is in all of your stories and then watch how funny he can be, see what a really great sense of humor he can have.

10   Your child psychology advisor tells you you are neglecting courses in your major. What you spend the most time on should be what you're majoring in. Say yes, you understand.

In creative writing seminars over the next two years, everyone continues to smoke cigarettes and ask the same things: "But does it work?" "Why should we care about this character?" "Have you earned this cliché?" These seem like important questions.

On days when it is your turn, you look at the class hopefully as they scour your mimeographs for a plot. They look back up at you, drag deeply, and then smile in a sweet sort of way.

You spend too much time slouched and demoralized. Your boyfriend suggests bicycling. Your roommate suggests a new boyfriend. You are said to be self-mutilating and losing weight, but you continue writing. The only happiness you have is writing something new, in the middle of the night, armpits damp, heart pounding, something no one has yet seen. You have only those brief, fragile, untested moments of exhilaration when you know: you are a genius. Understand what you must do. Switch majors. The kids in your nursery project will be disappointed, but you have a calling, an urge, a delusion, an unfortunate habit. You have, as your mother would say, fallen in with a bad crowd.

Why write? Where does writing come from? These are questions to ask yourself. They are like: Where does dust come from? Or: Why is there war? Or: If there's a God, then why is my brother now a cripple?

15   These are questions that you keep in your wallet, like calling cards. These are questions, your creative writing teacher says, that are good to address in your journals but rarely in your fiction.

The writing professor this fall is stressing the Power of the Imagination. Which means he doesn't want long descriptive stories about your camping trip last July. He wants you to start in a realistic context but then to alter it. Like recombinant DNA. He wants you to let your imagination sail, to let it grow big-bellied in the wind. This is a quote from Shakespeare.

Tell your roommate your great idea, your great exercise of imaginative power: a transformation of Melville to contemporary life. It will be about monomania and the fish-eat-fish world of life insurance in Rochester, New York. The first line will be "Call me Fishmeal," and it will feature a menopausal suburban husband named Richard, who because he is so depressed all the time is called "Mopey Dick" by his witty wife Elaine. Say to your roommate: "Mopey Dick, get it?" Your roommate looks at you, like a buddy, and puts an arm around your burdened shoulders. "Listen, Francie," she says, slow as speech therapy. "Let's go out and get a big beer."

The seminar doesn't like this one either. You suspect they are beginning to feel sorry for you. They say: "You have to think about what is happening. Where is the story here?"

The next semester the writing professor is obsessed with writing from personal experience. You must write from what you know, from what has happened to you. He wants deaths, he wants camping trips. Think about what has happened to you. In three years there have been three things: you lost your virginity; your parents got divorced; and your brother came home from a forest ten miles from the Cambodian border with only half a thigh, a permanent smirk nestled into one corner of his mouth.

About the first you write: "It created a new space, which hurt and cried in a voice that 20 wasn't mine, 'I'm not the same anymore, but I'll be okay.'"

About the second you write an elaborate story of an old married couple who stumble upon an unknown land mine in their kitchen and accidentally blow themselves up. You call it: "For Better or for Liverwurst."

About the last you write nothing. There are no words for this. Your typewriter hums. You can find no words.

At undergraduate cocktail parties, people say, "Oh, you write? What do you write about?" Your roommate, who has consumed too much wine, too little cheese, and no crackers at all, blurts: "Oh, my god, she always writes about her dumb boyfriend."

Later on in life you will learn that writers are merely open, helpless texts with no real understanding of what they have written and therefore must half-believe anything and everything that is said of them. You, however, have not yet reached this stage of literary criticism. You stiffen and say, "I do not," the same way you said it when someone in the fourth grade accused you of really liking oboe lessons and your parents really weren't just making you take them.

Insist you are not very interested in any one subject at all, that you are interested in the 25 music of language, that you are interested in—in—syllables, because they are the atoms of poetry, the cells of the mind, the breath of the soul. Begin to feel woozy. Stare into your plastic wine cup.

"Syllables?" you will hear someone ask, voice trailing off, as they glide slowly toward the reassuring white of the dip.

Begin to wonder what you do write about. Or if you have anything to say. Or if there even is such a thing as a thing to say. Limit these thoughts to no more than ten minutes a day; like sit-ups, they can make you thin.

You will read somewhere that all writing has to do with one's genitals. Don't dwell on this. It will make you nervous.

Your mother will come visit you. She will look at the circles under your eyes and hand you a brown book with a brown briefcase on the cover. It is entitled: *How to Become a Business Executive.* She has also brought the *Names for Baby* encyclopedia you asked for; one of your characters, the aging clown-school teacher, needs a new name. Your mother will shake her head and say: "Francie, Francie, remember when you were going to be a child psychology major?"

Say: "Mom, I like to write." 30

She'll say: "Sure you like to write. Of course. Sure you like to write."

Write a story about a confused music student and title it: "Schubert Was the One with the Glasses, Right?" It's not a big hit, although your roommate likes the part where the two violinists accidentally blow themselves up in a recital room. "I went out with a violinist once," she says, snapping her gum.

Thank god you are taking other courses. You can find sanctuary in nineteenth-century ontological snags and invertebrate courting rituals. Certain globular mollusks have what is called "Sex by the Arm." The male octopus, for instance, loses the end of one arm when placing it inside the female body during intercourse. Marine biologists call it "Seven Heaven." Be glad you know these things. Be glad you are not just a writer. Apply to law school.

From here on in, many things can happen. But the main one will be this: you decide not to go to law school after all, and, instead, you spend a good, big chunk of your adult life telling people how you decided not to go to law school after all. Somehow you end up writing again. Perhaps you go to graduate school. Perhaps you work odd jobs and take writing courses at night. Perhaps you are working on a novel and writing down all the clever remarks and intimate personal confessions you hear during the day. Perhaps you are losing your pals, your acquaintances, your balance.

35   You have broken up with your boyfriend. You now go out with men who, instead of whispering "I love you," shout: "Do it to me, baby." This is good for your writing.

Sooner or later you have a finished manuscript more or less. People look at it in a vaguely troubled sort of way and say, "I'll bet becoming a writer was always a fantasy of yours, wasn't it?" Your lips dry to salt. Say that of all the fantasies possible in the world, you can't imagine being a writer even making the top twenty. Tell them you were going to be a child psychology major. "I bet," they always sigh, "you'd be great with kids." Scowl fiercely. Tell them you're a walking blade.

Quit classes. Quit jobs. Cash in old savings bonds. Now you have time like warts on your hands. Slowly copy all of your friends' addresses into a new address book.

Vacuum. Chew cough drops. Keep a folder full of fragments.

> An eyelid darkening sideways.
> World as conspiracy.
> Possible plot? A woman gets on a bus.
> Suppose you threw a love affair and nobody came.

At home drink a lot of coffee. At Howard Johnson's order the cole slaw. Consider how it looks like the soggy confetti of a map: where you've been, where you're going—"You Are Here," says the red star on the back of the menu.

40   Occasionally a date with a face blank as a sheet of paper asks you whether writers often become discouraged. Say that sometimes they do and sometimes they do. Say it's a lot like having polio.

"Interesting," smiles your date, and then he looks down at his arm hairs and starts to smooth them, all, always, in the same direction.

QUESTIONS

1. To whom does the "you" in the story refer? How strong a case may be made that the "you" refers really to "I," and that Francie is actually telling a story about herself?

2. In light of the title, how adequate are Francie's "directions" for becoming a writer?

3. Describe some of the comic elements of the story. What serious ideas about the development of a writer's profession undergird the story's humor?

JOYCE CAROL OATES (b. 1938)

A superabundantly productive and richly acclaimed author of more than thirty novels—some under pseudonyms—and many collections of stories, books of poems, and collections of criticism, Joyce Carol Oates attended a one-room school as a child, and went on to receive her higher education at Syracuse University and the University of Wisconsin. She began her teaching career at the University of Detroit and currently, in addition to various guest positions, is Distinguished Professor in the Humanities at Princeton University. Just a few of her many novels are With Shuddering Fall *(1964),* Angel of Light *(1981),* Solstice *(1985),* Foxfire *(1993),* Middle Age: A Romance *(2001),* Missing Mom *(2005), and* Black Girl/White Girl *(2006). Recent story collections are* Faithless: Tales of Transgression *(2001),* I Am No One You Know *(2004), and*

High Lonesome: Selected Stories, 1966–2006 *(2006). Among her many awards and distinctions are a Guggenheim Fellowship, the Continuing Achievement Award of the O. Henry Award Prize Stories series, a National Book Award, and the Chicago Tribune Literary Prize, not to mention three nominations for the Pulitzer Prize.*

 The Cousins (2004)

Lake Worth, Florida
September 14, 1998

Dear Professor Morgenstern,

How badly I wish that I could address you as "Freyda"! But I don't have the right to such familiarity.

I have just read your memoir. I have reason to believe that we are cousins. My maiden name is "Schwart" (not my father's actual name, I think it was changed at Ellis Island in 1936),° but my mother's maiden name was "Morgenstern" and all her family was from Kaufbeuren as yours were. We were to meet in 1941 when we were small children, you and your parents and sister and brother were coming to live with my parents, my two brothers, and me in Milburn, New York. But the boat that was carrying you and other refugees, the *Marea*,° was turned back by U.S. Immigration at New York Harbor.

(In your memoir you speak so briefly of this. You seem to recall a name other than *Marea*. But I am sure that *Marea* was the name, for it seemed so beautiful to me like music. You were so young of course. So much would happen afterward, you would not remember this. By my calculation you were 6, and I was 5.)

All these years I had not known that you were living! I had not known that there were survivors in your family. It was told to us by my father that there were not. I am so happy for you and your success. To think that you were living in the U.S. since 1956 is a shock to me. That you were a college student in New York City while I was living (my first marriage, not a happy one) in upstate New York! Forgive me, I did not know of your previous books, though I would be intrigued by 'biological anthropology," I think! (I have nothing of your academic education, I'm so ashamed. Not only not college but I did not graduate from high school.)

Well, I am writing in the hope that we might meet. Oh very soon, Freyda! Before it's too late.

I am no longer your 5-year-old cousin dreaming of a new "sister" (as my mother promised) who would sleep with me in my bed and be with me always.

Your "lost" cousin,
Rebecca

°*Ellis Island in 1936:* In actuality, the German liner *S.S. St Louis*, with 930 Jewish refugee passengers aboard, first reached Havana, Cuba, in May 1936, but only a few refugees were allowed entrance to Cuba. The *St. Louis* then went to New York, where no refugees at all were to be allowed. From Rebecca's description a little later we learn that she was born while the ship was anchored in the New York Harbor. We may infer that the birth of Rebecca, who, being born in the United States, was automatically a citizen, made it possible for her family to stay here, and we conclude that they went through immigration procedures at Ellis Island. But in early June 1936, the *St. Louis* was forced to return most of the refugees to Europe, where they were dispersed to a number of separate countries. Those who were sent to England survived, but the others eventually were sent to Nazi concentration and extermination camps.
°*the Marea:* This reference indicates that the *Marea* was turned back. The result was that it was not until 1956 that Freyda was allowed entry and citizenship in the United States.

Lake Worth, Florida
September 15, 1998

Dear Professor Morgenstern,

I wrote to you just the other day. Now I see to my embarrassment that I may have sent the letter to a wrong address. If you are "on sabbatical leave" from the University of Chicago, as it says on the dust jacket of your memoir. I will try again with this, care of your publisher.

I will enclose the same letter. Though I feel it is not adequate, to express what is in my heart.

Your "lost" cousin,
Rebecca

P.S. Of course I will come to you, wherever & whenever you wish, Freyda!

Lake Worth, Florida
October 2, 1998

Dear Professor Morgenstern,

I wrote to you last month but I'm afraid that my letters were misaddressed. I will enclose these letters here, now that I know you are at the "Institute for Advanced Research" at Stanford University, Palo Alto, California.

It's possible that you have read my letters and were offended by them. I know, I am not a very good writer. I should not have said what I did about the Atlantic crossing in 1941, as if you would not know these facts for yourself. I did not mean to correct you, Professor Morgenstern, regarding the name of the very boat you and your family were on in that nightmare time!

In an interview with you reprinted in the Miami newspaper I was embarrassed to read that you have received so much mail from "relatives" since the memoir. I smiled to read where you said, "Where were all these relatives in America when they were needed?"

Truly we were here, Freyda! In Milburn, New York, on the Erie Canal.

Your cousin,
Rebecca

Palo Alto, CA
1 November 1998

Dear Rebecca Schward,

Thank you for your letter and for your response to my memoir. I have been deeply moved by the numerous letters I've received since the publication of *Back from the Dead: A Girlhood* both in the United States and abroad, and truly wish that I had time to reply to each of these individually and at length.

Sincerely,
FM
Freyda Morgenstern
Julius K. Tracey '48 Distinguished
Professor of Anthropology,
University of Chicago

Lake Worth, Florida
November 5, 1998

Dear Professor Morgenstern,

I'm very relieved now, I have the correct address! I hope that you will read this letter. I think you must have a secretary who opens your mail and sends back replies. I know, you are amused (annoyed?) by so many now claiming to be relatives of "Freyda Morgenstern."

Especially since your television interviews. But I feel very strongly, I am your true cousin. For I was the (only) daughter of Anna Morgenstern. I believe that Anna Morgenstern was the (only) sister of your mother, Sara, a younger sister. For many weeks my mother spoke of her sister, Sara, coming to live with us, your father and your Elzbieta, who was older than you by 3 or 4 years, and your brother, Leon, who was also older than you, not by so much.

We had photographs of you. I remember so clearly how your hair was so neatly plaited and how pretty you were, a "frowning girl" my mother said of you, like me. We did look alike then, Freyda, though you were much prettier of course. Elzbieta was blonde with a plump face. Leon was looking happy in the photograph, a sweet-seeming boy of maybe 8. To read that your sister and brother died in such a terrible way in "Theresienstadt"° was so sad. My mother never recovered from the shock of that time, I think. She was so hoping to see her sister again. When the *Marea* was turned back in the harbor, she gave up hope. My father did not allow her to speak German, only English, but she could not speak English well, if anyone came to the house she would hide. She did not speak much afterward to any of us and was often sick. She died in May 1949.

Reading this letter I see that I am giving a wrong emphasis, really! I never think of these long-ago things.

It was seeing your picture in the newspaper, Freyda! My husband was reading the *New York Times* & called me to him saying wasn't it strange, here was a woman looking enough like his wife to be a sister, though in fact you & I do not look so much alike, in my opinion, not any longer, but it was a shock to see your face, which is very like my mother's face as I remember it.

And then your name, *Freyda Morgenstern.*

At once I went out & purchased *Back from the Dead: A Girlhood.* I have not read any Holocaust memoirs out of a dread of what I would learn. Your memoir I read sitting in the car in the parking lot of the bookstore not knowing the time, how late it was, until my eyes could not see the pages. I thought, "It's Freyda! It's her! My sister I was promised." Now I am 62 years old, and so lonely in this place of retired wealthy people who look at me & think that I am one of them.

I am not one to cry. But I wept on many pages of your memoir though I know (from your interviews) you wish not to hear such reports from readers & have only contempt for "cheap American pity." I know, I would feel the same way. You are right to feel that way. In Milburn I resented the people who felt sorry for me as the "gravedigger's daughter" (my father's employment) more than the others who did not give a damn if the Schwarts lived or died.

I am enclosing my picture, taken when I was a girl of 16. It is all I have of those years. (I look very different now, I'm afraid!) How badly I wish I could send you a picture of my mother, Anna Morgenstern, but all were destroyed in 1949.

Your cousin,
Rebecca

Palo Alto, CA
16 November 1998

Dear Rebecca Schwart,

Sorry not to have replied earlier. I think yes it is quite possible that we are "cousins" but at such a remove it's really an abstraction, isn't it?

I am not traveling much this year, trying to complete a new book before my sabbatical ends. I am giving fewer "talks" and my book tour is over, thank God. (The venture into

---

°*Theresienstadt:* a Nazi concentration camp in what was then Czechoslovakia.

memoir was my first and will be my last effort at non-academic writing. It was far too easy, like opening a vein.) So I don't quite see how it would be feasible for us to meet at the present time.

Thank you for sending your photograph. I am returning it.

Sincerely,
FM

Lake Worth, Florida
November 20, 1998

Dear Freyda,

Yes, I am sure we are "cousins"! Though like you I don't know what "cousins" can mean.

I have no living relatives, I believe. My parents have been dead since 1949 & I know nothing of my brothers, whom I have not glimpsed in many years.

I think you despise me as your "American cousin." I wish you could forgive me for that. I am not sure how "American" I am, though I was not born in Kaufbeuren as you were but in New York Harbor in May 1936.° (The exact day is lost. There was no birth certificate or it was lost.) I mean, I was born on the refugee boat! In a place of terrible filth, I was told.

It was a different time then, 1936. The war had not begun & people of our kind were allowed to "emigrate" if they had money.

My brothers, Herschel & Augustus, were born in Kaufbeuren & of course both our parents. My father called himself "Jacob Schwart" in this country. (This is a name I have never spoken to anyone who knows me now. Not to my husband of course.) I knew little of my father except he had been a printer in the old world (as he called it with scorn) and at one time a math teacher in a boys' school. Until the Nazis forbade such people to teach. My mother, Anna Morgenstern, was married very young. She played piano, as a girl. We would listen to music on the radio sometime if Pa was not home. (The radio was Pa's.)

Forgive me, I know you are not interested in any of this. In your memoir you spoke of your mother as a record keeper for the Nazis, one of those Jewish "administrators" helping in the transport of Jews.° You are not sentimental about family. There is something so craven to it, isn't there. I respect the wishes of one who wrote *Back from the Dead*, which is so critical of your relatives & Jews & Jewish history & beliefs as of postwar "amnesia." I would not wish to dissuade you of such a true feeling, Freyda!

I have no true feelings myself, I mean that others can know.

Pa said you were all gone. Like cattle sent back to Hitler, Pa said. I remember his voice lifting, NINE HUNDRED SEVENTY-SIX REFUGEES, I am sick still hearing that voice.

Pa said for me to stop thinking about my cousins! They were not coming. They were *gone.*

Many pages of your memoir I have memorized, Freyda. And your letters to me. In your words, I can hear your voice. I love this voice so like my own. My secret voice I mean, that no one knows.

I will fly to California, Freyda. Will you give me permission? "Only say the word & my soul shall be healed."

Your cousin,
Rebecca

°*in May 1936:* This is the reference to the birth of Rebecca.

°*helping in the transport of Jews:* In the Nazi concentration camps, a number of Jewish prisoners served the Germans in various administrative capacities. These were called "Kapos," and they were known for their arbitrariness and brutality. Freyda, in the letter dated September 23, indicates that her mother was not a Kapo.

Lake Worth, Florida
November 21, 1998

Dear Freyda,

I am so ashamed, I mailed you a letter yesterday with a word misspelled: "dissuade." And I spoke of no living relatives, I meant no one remaining from the Schwart family. (I have a son from my first marriage, he is married with two children.)

I have bought other books of yours. *Biology: A History, Race and Racism: A History.* How impressed Jacob Schwart would be, the little girl in the photographs was never gone but has so very far surpassed him!

Will you let me come to see you in Palo Alto, Freyda? I could arrive for one day, we might have a meal together & I would depart the next morning. This is a promise.

Your (lonely) cousin,
Rebecca

Lake Worth, Florida
November 24, 1998

Dear Freyda,

An evening of your time is too much to ask, I think. An hour? An hour would not be too much, would it? Maybe you could talk to me of your work, anything in your voice would be precious to me. I would not wish to drag you into the cesspool of the past, as you speak of it so strongly. A woman like yourself capable of such intellectual work & so highly regarded in your field has no time for maudlin sentiment, I agree.

I have been reading your books. Underlining & looking up words in the dictionary. (I love the dictionary, it's my friend.) So exciting to consider How does science demonstrate the genetic basis of behavior?

I have enclosed a card here for your reply. Forgive me I did not think of this earlier.

Your cousin,
Rebecca

Palo Alto, CA
24 November 1998

Dear Rebecca Schwart,

Your letters of Nov. 20 & 21 are interesting. But the name "Jacob Schwart" means nothing to me, I'm afraid. There are numerous "Morgensterns" surviving. Perhaps some of these are your cousins, too. You might seek them out if you are lonely.

As I believe I have explained, this is a very busy time for me. I work much of the day and am not feeling very sociable in the evening. "Loneliness" is a problem engendered primarily by the too-close proximity of others. One excellent remedy is work.

Sincerely,
FM

P.S. I believe you have left phone messages for me at the Institute. As my assistant has explained to you, I have no time to answer such calls.

Lake Worth, Florida
November 27, 1998

Dear Freyda,

Our letters crossed! We both wrote on Nov. 24, maybe it's a sign.

It was on impulse I telephoned. "If I could hear her voice"—the thought came to me.

You have hardened your heart against your "American cousin." It was courageous in the memoir to state so clearly how you had to harden your heart against so much, to survive. Americans believe that suffering makes saints of us, which is a joke. Still I realize you have no time for me in your life now. There is no "purpose" to me.

Even if you won't meet me at this time, will you allow me to write to you? I will accept it if you do not reply. I would only wish that you might read what I write, it would make me so happy (yes, less lonely!), for then I could speak to you in my thoughts as I did when we were girls.

Your cousin,
Rebecca

P.S. In your academic writing you refer so often to "adaptation of species to environment." If you saw me, your cousin, in Lake Worth, Florida, on the ocean just south of Palm Beach, so very far from Milburn, N.Y., and from the "old world," you would laugh.

Palo Alto, CA
1 December 1998

Dear Rebecca Schwart,

My tenacious American cousin! I'm afraid it is no sign of anything, not even "coincidence," that our letters were written on the same day and that they "crossed."

This card. I admit I am curious at the choice. It happens this is a card on my study wall. (Did I speak of this in the memoir? I don't think so.) How do you happen to come into possession of this reproduction of Caspar David Friedrich's *Sturzacker*—you have not been to the museum in Hamburg, have you?° It's rare that any American even knows the name of this artist much esteemed in Germany.

Sincerely,
FM

Lake Worth, Florida
4 December 1998

Dear Freyda,

The post card of Caspar David Friedrich was given to me, with other cards from the Hamburg museum, by someone who traveled there. (In fact my son, who is a pianist. His name would be known to you, it's nothing like my own.)

I chose a card to reflect your soul. As I perceive it in your words. Maybe it reflects mine also. I wonder what you will think of this new card, which is German also but uglier.

Your cousin,
Rebecca

Palo Alto, CA
10 December 1998

Dear Rebecca,

Yes I like this ugly Nolde.° Smoke black as pitch and the Elbe like molten lava. You see into my soul, don't you! Not that I have wished to disguise myself.

So I return *Towboat on the Elbe* to my tenacious American cousin. THANK YOU but please do not write again. And do not call. I have had enough of you.

FM

°*Sturzacker:* Caspar David Friedrich (1774–1840), one of the best known German Romantic artists, painted the *Sturzacker* (a freshly plowed field) in 1825. It hangs in the Hamburg Kunsthalle, in Germany.
°*Nolde:* Emil Nolde (1867–1956), one of the best-known German Expressionists. His *Hamburg, Free Port* (1910) resembles the painting described here.

Palo Alto, CA
11 December 1998/2:00 A.M.

Dear "Cousin"!

Your 16-yr-old photo I made a copy of. I like that coarse mane of hair and the jaws so solid. Maybe the eyes were scared, but we know how to hide that, don't we cousin.

In the camp I learned to stand tall. I learned to be big. As animals make themselves bigger, it can be a trick to the eye that comes true. I guess you were a "big" girl, too.

I have always told the truth. I see no reason for subterfuge. I despise fantasizing. I have made enemies "among my kind" you can be sure. When you are "back from the dead" you do not give a damn for others' opinions & believe me, that has cost me in this so-called "profession" where advancement depends upon ass-kissing and its sexual variants not unlike the activities of our kindred primates.

Bad enough my failure to behave as a suppliant female through my career. In the memoir I take a laughing tone speaking of graduate studies at Columbia in the late 1950s. I did not laugh much then. Meeting my old enemies, who had wished to crush an impious female at the start of her career, not only female but a Jew & a refugee Jew from one of the camps, I looked them in the eye, I never flinched, but they flinched, the bastards. I took my revenge where & when I could. Now those generations are dying out, I am not pious about their memories. At conferences organized to revere them, Freyda Morgenstern is the "savagely witty" truth-teller.

In Germany, where history was so long denied, *Back from the Dead* has been a bestseller for five months. Already it has been nominated for two major awards. Here is a joke, and a good one, yes?

In this country, no such reception. Maybe you saw the "good" reviews. Maybe you saw the one full-page ad my cheapskate publisher finally ran in the *New York Review of Books*. There have been plenty of attacks. Worse even than the stupid attacks to which I have become accustomed in my "profession."

In the Jewish publications, & in Jewish-slanted publications, such shock/dismay/ disgust. A Jewish woman who writes so without sentiment of mother & other relatives who "perished" in Theresienstadt. A Jewish woman who speaks so coldly & "scientifically" of her "heritage." As if the so-called Holocaust is a "heritage." As if I have not earned my right to speak the truth as I see it and will continue to speak the truth, for I have no plans to retire from research, writing, teaching, & directing doctoral students for a long time. (I will take early retirement at Chicago, these very nice benefits, & set up shop elsewhere.)

This piety of the Holocaust! I laughed, you used that word so reverentially in one of your letters. I never use this word that slides off American tongues now like grease. One of the hatchet-reviewers called Morgenstern a traitor giving solace to the enemy (which enemy? there are many) by simply stating & restating, as I will each time I am asked, that the "holocaust" was an accident in history as all events in history are accidents. There is no purpose to history as to evolution, there is no goal or progress. Evolution is the term given to what is. The pious fantasizers wish to claim that the Nazis' genocidal campaign was a singular event in history, that it has elevated us above history. This is bullshit, I have said so & will continue to say so. There are many genocides, as long as there has been mankind. History is an invention of books. In biological anthropology we note that the wish to perceive "meaning" is one trait of our species among many. But that does not posit "meaning" in the world. If history did exist it is a great river/cesspool into which countless small streams & tributaries flow. In one direction. Unlike sewage it cannot back up. It cannot be "tested"—"demonstrated." It simply is. If the individual streams dry up, the river disappears. There is no "river-destiny." There are merely accidents in time. The scientist notes that without sentiment or regret.

Maybe I will send you these ravings, my tenacious American cousin. I'm drunk enough, in a festive mood!

Your (traitor) cousin,
FM

Lake Worth, Florida
15 December 1998

Dear Freyda,

How I loved your letter, that made my hands shake. I have not laughed in so long. I mean, in our special way.

It's the way of hatred. I love it. Though it eats you from the inside out. (I guess.)

It's a cold night here, a wind off the Atlantic. Florida is often wet-cold. Lake Worth/Palm Beach are very beautiful & very boring. I wish you might come here & visit, you could spend the rest of the winter, for it's often sunny of course.

I take your precious letters with me in the early morning walking on the beach. Though I have memorized your words. Until a year ago I would run, run, run for miles! At the rain-whipped edge of a hurricane I ran. To see me, my hard-muscled legs & straight back-bone, you would never guess I was not a young woman.

So strange that we are in our sixties, Freyda! Our baby-girl dolls have not aged a day.

(Do you hate it, growing old? Your photographs show such a vigorous woman. You tell yourself, "Every day I live was not meant to be" & there's happiness in this.)

Freyda, in our house of mostly glass facing the ocean you would have your own "wing." We have several cars, you would have your own car. No questions asked where you went. You would not have to meet my husband, you would be my precious secret.

Tell me you will come, Freyda! After the New Year would be a good time. When you finish your work each day we will go walking on the beach together. I promise we would not have to speak.

Your loving cousin,
Rebecca

Lake Worth, Florida
17 December 1998

Dear Freyda,

Forgive my letter of the other day, so pushy & familiar. Of course you would not wish to visit a stranger.

I must make myself remember: though we are cousins, we are strangers.

I was reading again *Back from the Dead*. The last section, in America. Your three marriages—"ill-advised experiments in intimacy/lunacy." You are very harsh & very funny, Freyda! Unsparing to others as to yourself.

My first marriage too was blind in love & I suppose "lunacy." Yet without it, I would not have my son.

In the memoir you have no regret for your "misbegotten fetuses" though for the "pain and humiliation" of the abortions illegal at the time. Poor Freyda! In 1957 in a filthy room in Manhattan you nearly bled to death, at that time I was a young mother so in love with my life. Yet I would have come to you, if I had known.

Though I know that you will not come here, yet I hold out hope that, suddenly yes you might! To visit, to stay as long as you wish. Your privacy would be protected.

I remain the tenacious cousin,
Rebecca

Lake Worth, Florida
New Year's Day 1999

Dear Freyda,

I don't hear from you, I wonder if you have gone away? But maybe you will see this. "If Freyda sees this even to toss away . . ."

I am feeling happy & hopeful. You are a scientist & of course you are right to scorn such feelings as "magical" & "primitive," but I think there can be a newness in the New Year. I am hoping this is so.

My father, Jacob Schwart, believed that in animal life the weak are quickly disposed of, we must hide our weakness always. You & I knew that as children. But there is so much more to us than just the animal, we know that, too.

Your loving cousin,
Rebecca

Palo Alto, CA
19 January 1999

Rebecca:

Yes I have been away. And I am going away again. What business is it of yours?

I was coming to think you must be an invention of mine. My worst weakness. But here on my windowsill propped up to stare at me is "Rebecca, 1952." The horse-mane hair & hungry eyes.

Cousin, you are so faithful! It makes me tired. I know I should be flattered, few others would wish to pursue "difficult" Professor Morgenstern now I'm an old woman. I toss your letters into a drawer, then in my weakness I open them. Once, rummaging through Dumpster trash I retrieved a letter of yours. Then in my weakness I opened it. You know how I hate weakness!

Cousin, no more.
FM

Lake Worth, Florida
23 January 1999

Dear Freyda,

I know! I am sorry.

I shouldn't be so greedy. I have no right. When I first discovered that you were living, last September, my thought was only "My cousin Freyda Morgenstern, my lost sister, she is alive! She doesn't need to love me or even know me or give a thought to me. It's enough to know that she did not perish and has lived her life."

Your loving cousin,
Rebecca

Palo Alto, CA
30 January 1999

Dear Rebecca,

We make ourselves ridiculous with emotions at our age, like showing our breasts. Spare us, please!

No more would I wish to meet you than I would wish to meet myself. Why would you imagine I might want a "cousin"—"sister"—at my age? I would like it that I have no living relatives any longer, for there is no obligation to think *Is he/she still living?*

Anyway, I'm going away. I will be traveling all spring. I hate it here. California suburban boring & without a soul. My "colleagues/friends" are shallow opportunists to whom I appear to be an opportunity.

I hate such words as "perish." Does a fly "perish," do rotting things "perish," does your enemy "perish"? Such exalted speech makes me tired.

Nobody "perished" in the camps. Many "died"—"were killed." That's all.

I wish I could forbid you to revere me. For your own good, dear cousin. I see that I am your weakness, too. Maybe I want to spare you.

If you were a graduate student of mine, though! I would set you right with a swift kick in the rear.

Suddenly there are awards & honors for Freyda Morgenstern. Not only the memoirist but the "distinguished anthropologist" too. So I will travel to receive them. All this comes too late of course. Yet like you I am a greedy person, Rebecca. Sometimes I think my soul is in my gut! I am one who stuffs herself without pleasure, to take food from others.

Spare yourself. No more emotion. No more letters!

FM

Chicago, IL

29 March 1999

Dear Rebecca Schwart,

Have been thinking of you lately. It has been a while since I've heard from you. Unpacking things here & came across your letters & photograph. How stark-eyed we all looked in black-and-white! Like x-rays of the soul. My hair was never so thick & splendid as yours, my American cousin.

I think I must have discouraged you. Now, to be frank, I miss you. It has been two months nearly since you wrote. These honors & awards are not so precious if no one cares. If no one hugs you in congratulations. Modesty is beside the point & I have too much pride to boast to strangers.

Of course, I should be pleased with myself: I sent you away. I know, I am a "difficult" woman. I would not like myself for a moment. I would not tolerate myself. I seem to have lost one or two of your letters, I'm not sure how many, vaguely I remember you saying you & your fam ily lived in upstate New York, my parents had arranged to come stay with you? This was in 1941? You provided facts not in my memoir. But I do remember my mother speaking with such love of her younger sister, Anna. Your father changed his name to "Schwart" from—what? He was a math teacher in Kaufbeuren? My father was an esteemed doctor. He had many non-Jewish patients who revered him. As a young man he had served in the German army in the first war, he'd been awarded a Gold Medal for Bravery & it was promised that such a distinction would protect him while other Jews were being transported. My father disappeared so abruptly from our lives, immediately we were transported to that place, for years I believed he must have escaped & was alive somewhere & would contact us. I thought my mother had information she kept from me. She was not quite the Amazon-mother of *Back from the Dead* . . . Well, enough of this! Though evolutionary anthropology must scour the past relentlessly, human beings are not obliged to do so.

It's a blinding-bright day here in Chicago, from my aerie on the 52nd floor of my grand new apartment building I look out upon the vast inland sea Lake Michigan. Royalties from the memoir have helped me pay for this, a less "controversial" book would not have earned. Nothing more is needed, yes?

Your cousin,

Freyda

Lake Worth, Florida

April 3, 1999

Dear Freyda,

Your letter meant much to me. I'm so sorry not to answer sooner. I make no excuses. Seeing this card I thought, "For Freyda!"

Next time I will write more. Soon I promise.

Your cousin,
Rebecca

Chicago, IL
22 April 1999

Dear Rebecca,

Rec'd your card. Am not sure what I think of it. Americans are ga-ga for Joseph Cornell° as they are for Edward Hopper.° What is *Lanner Waltzes*? Two little-girl doll figures riding the crest of a wave & in the background an old-fashioned sailing ship with sails billowing? "Collage"? I hate riddle-art. Art is to see, not to *think*.

Is something wrong, Rebecca? The tone of your writing is altered, I think. I hope you are not playing coy, to take revenge for my chiding letter of January. I have a doctoral student, a bright young woman not quite so bright as she fancies herself, who plays such games with me at the present time, at her own risk! I hate games, too.

(Unless they are my own.)

Your cousin,
Freyda

Chicago, IL
6 May 1999

Dear Cousin:

Yes, I think you must be angry with me! Or you are not well.

I prefer to think that you are angry. That I did insult you in your American soft heart. If so, I am sorry. I have no copies of my letters to you & don't recall what I said. Maybe I was wrong. When I am coldly sober, I am likely to be wrong. When drunk, I am likely to be less wrong.

Enclosed here is a stamped addressed card. You need only check one of the boxes: [ ] angry [ ] not well.

Your cousin,
Freyda

P.S. This Joseph Cornell Pond reminded me of you, Rebecca. A doll-girl playing her fiddle beside a murky inlet.

Lake Worth, Florida
September 19, 1999

Dear Freyda,

How strong & beautiful you were, at the awards ceremony in Washington! I was there, in the audience at the Folger Library. I made the trip just for you.

All of the writers honored spoke very well. But none so witty & unexpected as "Freyda Morgenstern," who caused quite a stir.

I'm ashamed to say, I could not bring myself to speak to you. I waited in line with so many others for you to sign *Back from the Dead* & when my turn came you were beginning to tire. You hardly glanced at me, you were vexed at the girl assistant fumbling the book. I did no more than mumble, "Thank you," & hurried away.

I stayed just one night in Washington, then flew home. I tire easily now, it was a mad thing to do. My husband would have prevented me if he'd known where I was headed.

°*Joseph Cornell:* (1903–1972), American artist. His *Lanner Waltzes* hangs in the Smithsonian American Art Museum. *Lanner Waltzes* refers to waltz music by the Austrian composer Josef Lanner (1801–1843), who in his day was as famous as Johann Strauss, Sr. (1804–1849).
°*Edward Hopper:* (1882–1967), American realist painter. (See p. I–6 for his painting, *Automat*.)

During the speeches you were restless onstage, I saw your eyes wandering. I saw your eyes on me. I was sitting in the third row of the theater. Such an old, beautiful little theater in the Folger Library. I think there must be so much beauty in the world we haven't seen. Now it is almost too late we yearn for it.

I was the gaunt-skull woman with the buzz cut. The heavy dark glasses covering half my face. Others in my condition wear gaudy turbans or gleaming wigs. Their faces are bravely made up. In Lake Worth/Palm Beach there are many of us. I don't mind my baldie head in warm weather & among strangers, for their eyes look through me as if I am invisible. You stared at me at first & then looked quickly away & afterward I could not bring myself to address you. It wasn't the right time, I had not prepared you for the sight of me. I shrink from pity & even sympathy is a burden. I had not known that I would make the reckless trip until that morning, for so much depends upon how I feel each morning, it's not predictable.

I had a present to give to you, I changed my mind & took away again feeling like a fool. Yet the trip was wonderful for me, I saw my cousin so close! Of course I regret my cowardice now it's too late.

You asked about my father. I will tell you no more than that I do not know my father's true name. "Jacob Schwart" was what he called himself & so I was "Rebecca Schwart," but that name was lost long ago. I have another more fitting American name, & I have also my husband's last name, only to you, my cousin, am I identified as "Rebecca Schwart."

Well, I will tell you one more thing: in May 1949 my father who was the gravedigger murdered your aunt Anna and wished to murder me but failed, he turned the shotgun onto himself & killed himself when I was 13 struggling with him for the gun & my strongest memory of that time was his face in the last seconds & what remained of his face, his skull & brains & the warmth of his blood splattered onto me.

I have never told anyone this, Freyda. Please do not speak of it to me, if you write again.

Your cousin
Rebecca

(I did not intend to write such an ugly thing, when I began this letter.)

Chicago, IL
23 September 1999

Dear Rebecca,

I'm stunned. That you were so close to me—and didn't speak.

And what you tell me of—. What happened to you at age 13.

I don't know what to say. Except yes I am stunned. I am angry, & hurt. Not at you, I don't think I am angry at you but at myself.

I've tried to call you. There is no "Rebecca Schwart" in the Lake Worth phone direc tory. Of course, you've told me there is no "Rebecca Schwart." Why in hell have you never told me your married name? Why are you so coy? I hate games, I don't have time for games.

Yes I am angry with you. I am upset & angry you are not well. (You never returned my card. I waited & waited & you did not.)

Can I believe you about "Jacob Schwart"! We conclude that the ugliest things are likely to be true.

In my memoir that isn't so. When I wrote it, 54 yrs later it was a text I composed of words chosen for "effect." Yes there are true facts in *Back from the Dead*. But facts are not "true" unless explained. My memoir had to compete with other memoirs of its type & so had to be "original." I am accustomed to controversy, I know how to tweak noses. The memoir makes light of the narrator's pain & humiliation. It's true, I did not feel that I would be one of those to die; I was too young, & ignorant, & compared to others I was healthy. My big blonde sister Elzbieta the relatives so admired, looking like a German girl-doll, soon lost all that hair & her bowels turned to bloody suet. Leon died trampled to death, I would learn afterward. What I say of my mother, Sara Morgenstern, is truthful only at the start. She was not a kapo but one hoping to cooperate with the Nazis to help her family (of course) & other Jews. She was a good organizer & much trusted but never so strong as the memoir has her. She did not say those cruel things, I have no memory of anything anyone said to me except orders shouted by authorities. All the quiet spoken words, the very breath of our lives together, was lost. But a memoir must have spoken words, & a memoir must breathe life.

I am so famous now—infamous! In France this month I am a new bestseller. In the U.K. (where they are outspoken anti-Semites, which is refreshing!) my word is naturally doubted yet still the book sells.

Rebecca, I must speak with you. I will enclose my number here. I will wait for a call. Past 10:00 P.M. of any night is best, I am not so cold-sober & nasty.

Your cousin,
Freyda

P.S. Are you taking chemotherapy now? What is the status of your condition? Please answer.

Lake Worth, Florida
October 8

Dear Freyda,

Don't be angry with me, I have wanted to call you. There are reasons I could not but maybe I will be stronger soon & I promise, I will call.

It was important for me to see you, and hear you. I am so proud of you. It hurts me when you say harsh things about yourself, I wish you would not. "Spare us"—yes?

Half the time I am dreaming & very happy. Just now I was smelling snakeroot. Maybe you don't know what snakeroot is, you have lived always in cities. Behind the gravedigger's stone cottage in Milburn there was a marshy place where this tall plant grew. The wildflowers were as tall as five feet. They had many small white flowers that look like frost. Very powdery, with a strange strong smell. The flowers were alive with bees humming so loudly it seemed like a living thing. I was remembering how waiting for you to come from over the ocean I had two dolls—Maggie, who was the prettiest doll, for you, and my doll, Minnie, who was plain & battered but I loved her very much. (My brother Herschel found the dolls at the Milburn dump. We found many useful things at the dump!) For hours I played with Maggie & Minnie & you, Freyda. All of us chattering away. My brothers laughed at me. Last night I dreamt of the dolls that were so vivid to me I had not glimpsed in 57 yrs. But it was strange, Freyda, you were not in the dream. I was not, either.

I will write some other time. I love you.

Your cousin,
Rebecca

Chicago, IL
12 October

Dear Rebecca,

Now I am angry! You have not called me & you have not given me your telephone number & how can I reach you? I have your street address but only the name "Rebecca Schwart." I am so busy, this is a terrible time. I feel as if my head is being broken by a mallet. Oh I am very angry at you, cousin!

Yet I think I should come to Lake Worth, to see you.

Should I?

QUESTIONS

1. Describe the nature of the narration in this story. Who are the speakers? How do you learn about them? What is the advantage, to the writer, of having each person describe aspects of the story?

2. To the best of your ability, describe the story that is actually being told here. What has happened? Who are the cousins? What sort of relationship have they had? How does Rebecca learn about her cousin Freyda? Why does she start the correspondence?

3. What sort of person is Freyda? How do we learn about her? What is she like, as a person? Is she "difficult," as she says of herself? Is she blunt? Is she unkind? What is happening to her life as she writes her letters over the year-long passage of time in the story? What changes does she undergo in the course of the story? Why are her final words so tentative, so unlike her earlier statements?

4. What sort of person is Rebecca? Why is she so sensitive? Is her self-assessment justified in the course of the story? What is happening to her during the time of the story? What positive aspects of her develop, as seen in her letters to her cousin?

5. Which character, Rebecca or Freyda, seems more fully portrayed in the story? Which seems more desirable, as a character? Why? What is the basis for your conclusions?

6. What do you learn, by Freyda's own words, about the nature of her book, *Back from the Dead*? Is everything in the book accurate? What reasons might Freyda have had for arranging truths in the book, and for introducing fictions?

WRITING ABOUT POINT OF VIEW

In your essay about point of view, you should explain how point of view contributes to making the work exactly as it is. As you prepare to write, therefore, consider language, authority and opportunity for observation, the involvement or detachment of the speaker, the selection of detail, interpretive commentaries, and narrative development. The following questions will help you get started.

Questions for Discovering Ideas

- How is the narration made to seem real or probable? Are the actions and speeches reported authentically, as they might be seen and reported in life?

- Is the narrator/speaker identifiable? What are the narrator's qualifications as an observer? How much of the story seems to result from the imaginative or creative powers of the narrator?

- How does the narrator/speaker perceive the time of the actions? If the predominant tense is the past, what relationship, if any, does the narrator establish between the past and the present (e.g., providing explanations, making conclusions)? If the tense is present, what effect does this tense have on your understanding of the story?

- To what extent does the point of view make the work interesting and effective?

FIRST-PERSON POINT OF VIEW

- What situation prompts the speaker to tell the story or explain the situation? What does the story tell us about the experience and interests of the narrator/speaker?
- Is the speaker talking to the reader, a listener, or herself? How does her audience affect what she is saying? Is the level of language appropriate to her and the situation? How much does she tell about herself?
- To what degree is the narrator involved in the action (i.e., as a major participant or major mover, minor participant, or nonparticipating observer)? Does he make himself the center of humor or admiration? How? Does he seem aware of changes he undergoes?
- Does the speaker criticize other characters? Why? Does she seem to report fairly and accurately what others have told her?
- How reliable is the speaker? Does the speaker seem to have anything to hide? Does it seem that he may be using the story for self-justification or exoneration? What effect does this complexity have on the story?

SECOND-PERSON POINT OF VIEW

- What situation prompts the use of the second person? How does the speaker acquire the authority to explain things to the listener? How directly involved is the listener? What is the relationship between the speaker and listener? If the listener is indefinite, why does the speaker choose to use "you" as the basis of the narration?

THIRD-PERSON POINT OF VIEW

- Does the author speak in an authorial voice, or does it seem that the author has adopted a special but unnamed voice for the work?
- What is the speaker's level of language (e.g., formal and grammatical, informal or intimate and ungrammatical)? Are actions, speeches, and explanations made fully or sparsely?
- From what apparent vantage point does the speaker report action and speeches? Does this vantage point make the characters seem distant or close? How much sympathy does the speaker express for the characters?
- To what degree is your interest centered on a particular character? Does the speaker give you thoughts and responses of this character (limited third person)?
- If the work is third-person omniscient, how extensive is this omniscience (e.g., all the characters or just a few)? Generally, what limitations or freedoms can be attributed to this point of view?
- What special kinds of knowledge does the narrator assume that the listeners or readers possess (e.g., familiarity with art, religion, politics, history, navigation, music, current or past social conditions)?
- How much dialogue is used in the story? Is the dialogue presented directly, as dramatic speech, or indirectly, as past-tense reports of speeches? What is your perception of the story's events as a result of the use of dialogue?

TENSE

- What tense is used predominantly throughout the story? If a single tense is used throughout (e.g., present, past), what is the effect of this constant use of tense?
- Does the story demonstrate a mixture of tenses? Why are the tenses mixed? What purpose is served by these variations? What is the effect of this mixture?
- Is any special use made of the future tense? What is the effect of this use on the present and past circumstances of the characters?

Organizing Your Essay About Point of View

Throughout your essay, you should develop your analysis of how the point of view determines such aspects as situation, form, general content, and language. The questions in the preceding section should help you decide how the point of view interacts with these other elements.

Begin by briefly stating the major influence of the point of view on the work. (*Examples:* "The omniscient point of view permits many insights into the major character," or "The first-person point of view makes the work seem like an exposé of backroom political deals.") How does the point of view make the work interesting and effective? How will your analysis support your central idea?

A fruitful and imaginative way to build your analysis and argument is to explore how changing the point of view might affect the presentation of the story. Let us consider Welty's "A Worn Path" (Chapter 1), which limits its third-person point of view to the circumstances of Phoenix Jackson, whose walk to Natchez is a mission of mercy for her invalid grandson. With the third-person limited focus as we have it, we derive just enough information about Phoenix to understand and sympathize deeply with her plight. If she herself were the narrator, however, we would get not an objective but rather a personalized view of her circumstances—and also perhaps a scattered and unfocused one—and the story would not be as powerful as it is. (Or it might become powerful through different means.) Two stories that would be vastly different if told from alternative perspectives are Carver's "Neighbors" and Tan's "Two Kinds" (Chapter 3). Just suppose—for a moment—that "Neighbors" were to have been written in the first person, not the third person, as though Bill or Arlene Miller were telling the story. Either speaker would likely dilute the narration and make himself or herself seem definitely limited intellectually when attempting to explain the unusual if not strange behavior once the Stones have left the Millers in charge. Or, suppose that "Two Kinds," which is the first-person narration of Jing-Mei, were rather to be told in the first person by Jing-Mei's mother. Certainly the mother would explain her ambitions for her daughter fully and reasonably, and Jing-Mei herself would not be as comprehensible to readers as she is in the story as we have it.

You can see that this alternative approach to point of view requires creative imagination, for to carry it out you must, as it were, invade the author's space and speculate about the results of a point of view that the author did not choose. Considering such hypothetical alternative points of view deeply, however, will greatly enhance your analytical and critical abilities.

In your conclusion, evaluate the success of the point of view. Is it consistent, effective, truthful? What does it contribute to the nature and quality of the story? What particular benefits does the writer gain or lose (if anything) as a result of the point of view?

Illustrative Student Essay

Underlined sentences in this paper *do not* conform to MLA style and are used solely as teaching tools to emphasize the central idea, thesis sentence, and topic sentences throughout the paper.

Garcia 1

Ashley Garcia

Professor Sutton

English 220

21 November 2008

Shirley Jackson's Dramatic Point of View in "The Lottery"°

The dramatic point of view in Shirley Jackson's "The Lottery" is   [1]

essential to her success in rendering horror in the midst of the ordinary.* The

story, however, is not only about horror: It may also be called a surprise

story, an allegory, or a portrayal of human insensitivity and cruelty. But the

validity of all other claims for "The Lottery" hinges on the author's control

over point of view to make the events develop out of a seemingly everyday,

matter-of-fact situation--a control that could not be easily maintained with

°This story appears on pages 141–45.
*Central Idea.

another point of view. <u>The success of Jackson's point of view is achieved</u> <u>through her characterization, selection of details, and diction.</u>†

[2]   Because of the dramatic point of view, <u>Jackson succeeds in presenting</u> <u>the villagers as ordinary folks attending a normal, festive event--in contrast</u> <u>to the horror of their real purpose.</u> The contrast depends on Jackson's speaker, who is emotionally uninvolved and who tells only enough about the three hundred townsfolk and their customs to permit the conclusion that they are normal, common people. The principal character is a local housewife, Tessie Hutchinson, but the speaker presents little about her except that she is just like everyone else--an important characteristic when she, like any other person being singled out for punishment, objects not to the lottery itself but to the "unfairness" of the drawing. The same commonness applies also to the other characters, whose brief conversations are recorded but not analyzed. This detached, reportorial method of making the villagers seem common and one-dimensional is fundamental to Jackson's dramatic point of view, and the cruel twist of the ending depends on the method.

[3]   <u>While there could be much description, Jackson's speaker omits some</u> <u>of the important details to conceal the lottery's horrifying purpose.</u> For example, the speaker presents enough information about the lottery to permit readers to understand its rules but does not disclose the grim prize for the "winner." The short saying "Lottery in June, corn be heavy soon" is mentioned as a remnant of a long-forgotten ritual, but the speaker does not explain anything more about this connection with scapegoatism and human sacrifice (paragraph 32). None of these references seems unusual as the narrator first presents them, and it is only the conclusion that reveals, in reconsideration, their shocking ghastliness.

[4]   <u>Without doubt, a point of view other than the dramatic would spoil</u> <u>Jackson's concluding horror because it would require more explanatory</u> <u>detail.</u> A first-person speaker, for example, would not be credible without

---

†Thesis sentence.

explaining the situation and revealing feelings that would give away the ending. Such an "I" speaker would need to say something like "The little boys gathered rocks but seemed not to be thinking about their forthcoming use in the stoning." But how would such detail affect the reader's response to the terrifying conclusion? Similarly, an omniscient narrator would need to include details about people's reactions (how could he or she be omniscient otherwise?). A more suitable alternative might be a limited omniscient point of view confined to, say, a stranger in town or one of the local children. But any intelligent stranger would be asking "giveaway" questions, and any child but a tiny tot would know about the lottery's sinister outcome. Either hypothetical point-of-view character would therefore require revealing the information too soon. The only conclusion is that Jackson's point of view--the dramatic--is best for this story. Because it permits her naturally to hold back crucial details, it is essential for the suspenseful delay of horror.

<u>Appropriate both to the suspenseful ending and also to the simple</u>   [5]
<u>character of the villagers is the speaker's language.</u> The words are accurate and descriptive but not elaborate. When Tessie Hutchinson appears, for example, she dries "her hands on her apron" (paragraph 8)--words that define her role as a housewife. Most of these simple, bare words may be seen as part of Jackson's technique of withholding detail to delay the reader's understanding. A prime example is the pile of stones, which is in truth a thoughtless and cruel preparation for the stoning, yet this conclusion cannot be drawn from the easy words describing it (141, paragraph 2):

> Bobby Martin had already stuffed his pockets full of stones, and the
> other boys soon followed his example, selecting the smoothest and
> roundest stones; Bobby and Harry Jones and Dickie Delacroix--the
> villagers pronounced this name "Dellacroy"--eventually made a great
> pile of stones in one corner of the square and guarded it against the
> raids of the other boys.

Both the nicknames and the connotation of boyhood games divert attention and obscure the horrible purpose of the stones. Even at the end, the speaker

Garcia 4

uses the word "pebbles" to describe the stones given to Tessie's son Davy
(paragraph 76). The implication is that Davy is playing a game, not
participating in the ritual stoning of his own mother!

[6]   Such masterly control over point of view is a major cause of Jackson's
success in "The Lottery." Her narrative method is to establish the appearance
of everyday, uneventful reality, which she maintains up to the beginning of
the last scene. She is so successful that a reader's first response to the stoning
is "Such an event could not take place among such common, earthy folks."
Yet it is this reality that validates Jackson's vision. Horror is not to be found
on moors and in haunted castles but among everyday people like Jackson's
three hundred villagers. Without her control of the dramatic point of view,
there could be little of this power of suggestion, and it would not be possible
to claim such success for the story.

Garcia 5

Work Cited

Jackson, Shirley. "The Lottery." Literature: An Introduction to Reading and
Writing. Ed. Edgar V. Roberts. 9th ed. New York: Pearson Longman, 2009.
141–45.

Commentary on the Essay

The strategy of this essay is to argue for the importance of Jackson's dramatic
point of view in building toward the shocking ending. Words of tribute throughout the essay are "success," "control," "essential," "appropriate," and "masterly."
The introductory paragraph sets out three areas for exploration in the body: character, detail, and diction.

The body begins with paragraph 2, in which the aim is not to present a full
character study (since the essay is not about character but point of view), but rather
to discuss the ways in which the dramatic point of view enables the characters to be

rendered. The argument of the paragraph is that the villagers are to be judged not as complete human beings but as "ordinary folks."

The second part of the body (paragraphs 3 and 4) emphasizes that the sparseness of detail permitted by the dramatic point of view aids Jackson in deferring conclusions about the horror of the drawing. Paragraph 4, which continues the topic of paragraph 3, shows how talking about alternative points of view may aid understanding of the story's actual point of view (see paragraph 4). The material for the paragraph is derived from notes speculating about whether Jackson's technique of withholding detail to build toward the concluding horror (the topic of paragraph 3) could be maintained with differing points of view. A combination of analysis and imagination is therefore at work in the paragraph.

The third section of the body (paragraph 5) emphasizes the idea that the flat, colorless diction defers awareness of what is happening; therefore the point of view is vital in the story's surprise and horror. The concluding paragraph (6) emphasizes the way in which general response to the story, and also its success, are conditioned by the detached, dramatic point of view.

Writing Topics About Point of View

1. Write a short narrative from the first-person point of view of one of these characters:

   a. Mathilde Loisel in "The Necklace" (Part I): How I ruined ten years of my life by not telling the truth.

   b. Old Man Warner in "The Lottery" (this chapter): People ain't the way they used to be.

   c. Faith in "Young Goodman Brown" (Chapter 7): I don't understand why my husband is so sour and sullen all the time.

   d. Bill Miller in "Neighbors" (this chapter): I am finding it fascinating to spend time in the apartment of the Stones.

2. Consider the narrative of "Neighbors" as an argument. How can you describe the argument? Is Carver arguing that people are civilized as long as they are being watched or instead that people, when unchecked, are irrational and uncivilized? What does the locked door signify in either argument?

3. How would Hawthorne's story "Young Goodman Brown" (Chapter 7) be affected if told by a narrator with different knowledge, different interests, and different purposes for telling the story, such as the narrators of "A Worn Path" (Chapter 1), Bierce's "An Occurrence at Owl Creek Bridge" Chapter 1), and the second narrator of Mark Twain's "Luck" (Chapter 3)?

4. Recall a childhood occasion on which you were punished. Write an explanation of the punishment as though you were the adult who was in the position of punishing you. Be sure to consider your childhood self objectively, in the third person. Present things from the viewpoint of the adult, and try to

determine how the adult would have learned about your action, judged it, and decided on your punishment.

5. Write an essay about the proposition that people often have something to gain when they speak, and that therefore we need to be critical about what others tell us. Are they trying to change our judgments and opinions? Are they telling the truth? Are they leaving out any important details? Are they trying to sell us something? In your discussion, you may strengthen your ideas by referring to stories that you have been reading.

6. In the reference section of your library, find two books on literary terms and concepts. How completely and clearly do these works explain the concept of point of view? With the aid of these books, together with the materials in this chapter, describe the interests and views of the narrators in Moore's "How to Become a Writer," Bierce's "An Occurrence at Owl Creek Bridge," or another story of your choice. You should also consult *Google,* under "Glossary of Literary Terms," to see some of the many online resources available to you.

Chapter 3

Characters: The People in Fiction

Writers of fiction create narratives that enhance and deepen our understanding of human character and human life. In our own day, under the influences of such pioneers as Freud (1856–1939), Jung (1875–1961), and Skinner (1904–1990), the science of psychology has influenced both the creation and the study of literature. It is well known that Freud buttressed some of his psychological conclusions by referring to literary works, especially plays by Shakespeare. Widely known classic films such as *Spellbound* (1945) and *The Snake Pit* (1948) have popularized the relationships between literary character and psychology. Without doubt, the presentation and understanding of character is one of the major aims of fiction (and literature generally).

In literature, a **character** is a verbal representation of a human being. Through action, speech, description, and commentary, authors portray characters who are worth caring about, cheering for, and even loving, although there are also characters you may laugh at, dislike, or even hate.

In a story or play emphasizing a major character, you may expect that each action or speech, no matter how small, is part of a total presentation of the complex combination of both the inner and the outer self that constitutes a human being. Whereas in life things may "just happen," in literature all actions, interactions, speeches, and observations are deliberate. Thus, you read about important actions like a long period of work and sacrifice (Maupassant's "The Necklace" in Part I), the uncertain relationship between a husband and wife (Carver's "Cathedral" in this chapter), acts of defiance and retribution (Poe's "The Masque of the Red Death" in Chapter 9), or a young man's poignant dream of freedom (Bierce's "An Occurrence at Owl Creek Bridge" in Chapter 1). By making such actions interesting, authors help you understand and appreciate not only their major characters but also life itself.

Character Traits

In studying a literary character, try to determine the character's outstanding *traits*. A **trait** is a quality of mind or habitual mode of behavior that is evident in both positive and negative ways, such as supplying moral support to friends and loved ones, being a person on whom people always rely, listening to the thoughts and problems of others, avoiding eye contact, never repaying borrowed money, taking the biggest portions, or always thinking oneself the center of attention. Similarly, artists utilize elements such as facial characteristics and expressions to convey

"Bust of Lorenzo de Medici," Florentine, fifteenth or sixteenth century, probably after a model by Andrea del Verrocchio and Orsino Benintendi. (*Photograph © Board of Trustees, National Gallery of Art, Washington, D.C. Samuel H. Kress Collection.*)

their judgments about the characteristics of their human subjects. If we study the facial expression of the bust of Lorenzo de' Medici by Andrea del Verrocchio (c. 1435–1488), for example, we can see that Verrocchio is presenting a negative view of his subject. Lorenzo's firm mouth, his fixed stare, and his closely knit eyebrows suggest a high degree of pride and ruthlessness.

Sometimes, of course, the traits we encounter are minor and therefore negligible, but often a trait may be a person's *primary* characteristic (not only in fiction but also in life). Thus, characters may be ambitious or lazy, serene or anxious, aggressive or fearful, thoughtful or inconsiderate, open or secretive, confident or self-doubting, kind or cruel, quiet or noisy, visionary or practical, careful or careless, impartial or biased, straightforward or underhanded, "winners" or "losers," and so on.

With this sort of list, to which you may add at will, you can analyze and develop conclusions about character. For example, Mathilde in Maupassant's "The Necklace" (Part I) indulges in thoughts of unattainable wealth and comfort, and is so swept up in her dreams that she scorns the comparatively good life she has with her reliable but dull husband. It is fair to say that this denial of reality is her major trait. It is also a major weakness, because Maupassant shows that her dream life harms her real life. Comparably, the character Miss Brill in Mansfield's "Miss Brill" (this chapter) is totally taken up by her overriding imaginary perceptions of her surroundings. All the actions she witnesses are filtered through these perceptions, and hence she seems disconnected from her true circumstances. A contrast between a mother's dreams and a daughter's realism is brought out by Amy Tan in "Two Kinds" (this chapter). By similarly analyzing the thoughts, actions, and speeches of the literary characters you encounter, you can also draw conclusions about their nature and their qualities.

Distinguishing Between Circumstances and Character Traits

When you study a fictional person, distinguish between circumstances and character, for circumstances have value *only if you show that they demonstrate important traits*. Thus, if our good friend Sam wins a lottery, let us congratulate him on his luck; but the win does not say much about his *character*—not much, that is, unless you also point out that for years he has been regularly spending hundreds of dollars each week for lottery tickets. In other words, making the effort to win a lottery *is* a character trait but winning (or losing) *is not*.

Or, let us suppose that an author stresses the neatness of one character and the sloppiness of another. If you accept the premise that people care for their appearance according to choice—and that choices develop from character—you can use these details to make conclusions about a person's self-esteem or the lack of it. In short, when reading about characters in literature, look beyond circumstances, actions, and appearances, and attempt to determine what these things show about character. Always try to get from the outside to the inside, for it is the internal qualities of character that determine external behavior.

How Authors Disclose Character in Literature

Basically, authors rely on five ways of bringing characters to life. Remember that you must use your own knowledge and experience to make judgments about the qualities of the characters.

The Actions of Characters Reveal Their Qualities

What characters *do* is our best clue to understanding what they *are*. For example, taking care of an apartment belonging to a neighbor who has gone on a trip is part of ordinary existence for most people who do it, and it shows little about their characters except a desire to be helpful (this, in itself, may be an unusual trait). But when Bill and Arlene Miller of Carver's "Neighbors" (Chapter 2) agree to take care of the apartment of the Stones, their neighbors, they cease being ordinary but somewhat strange folks and begin indulging in all their incipient neuroses. By contrast, in Tan's "Two Kinds," the narrator Jing-Mei, after her turbulent childhood opposition to her mother's influences, reaches an emotional reconciliation when playing the piano her mother had bought for her and given to her.

Like ordinary people, fictional characters do not necessarily understand why they do what they do, or think what they think. Nevertheless, their actions and thoughts provide insights into their characters. Miss Brill, of Mansfield's "Miss Brill" (this chapter), is alone on a Sunday afternoon, always alone, and she goes to a nearby public park to enjoy the passing crowds—her only weekly excitement. She eavesdrops on people sitting nearby, and draws silent conclusions about others, thus vicariously sharing in their lives. She even supposes that all those in the park are actors, along with herself, performing in a massive drama of life. Her unrealistic daydreams reveal her habitual solitude and pathetic vulnerability.

Actions may also signal qualities such as naiveté, weakness, deceit, a scheming personality, strong inner conflicts, sudden comprehension, or other growth or change. In Hardy's "The Three Strangers" (Chapter 5), the fact that the natives of Higher Crowstairs withhold their cooperation from the governmental forces trying to bring Timothy Summers to the gallows indicates a collective strength of character. The narrator of Carver's "Cathedral" (this chapter) undergoes a development of understanding when he and a blind visitor share in sketching a religious building and also when he closes his eyes in sympathy with his guest.

The Author's Descriptions Tell Us About Characters

Appearance and environment reveal much about a character's social and economic status, and they also tell us about character traits. Although Mathilde's dreams in Maupassant's "The Necklace" (Part 1) are unrealizable and destructive, they also bring about her character strength that emerges in the story. A somewhat comparable situation occurs in Carver's "Neighbors" (Chapter 2). In this story the unusual actions which the Millers go through in the apartment of the Stones indicates their weak grip on their own characters. With nothing to inhibit them, they unconsciously take over their new but temporary quarters, and begin living the lives of the Stones, of whom they are obviously jealous.

What Characters Say Reveals What They Are Like

Although the speeches of most characters are functional—essential to keeping the action moving along—they provide material from which you may draw conclusions. When the second traveler of Hawthorne's "Young Goodman Brown" (Chapter 7) speaks, for example, he reveals his devious and deceptive nature even though ostensibly he appears friendly. Jackie's parents and sister in O'Connor's "First Confession" (Chapter 6) speak angrily to Jackie, the intransigent child who is the story's narrator. Their anger suggests that they have little interest in Jackie's thoughts or concerns, but view their world through nothing more than stultifyingly ordinary eyes. It is because of the unsympathetic nature of his family that Jackie is so refreshed by the priest, who shows enough interest in Jackie to listen to him.

Often, characters use speech to obscure their motives. The traveling pot mender in Steinbeck's "The Chrysanthemums" (Chapter 7) is deceptive and guileful. His sole aim is to have Elisa give him some work to do, and we may consequently believe nothing of what he says. The Federal scout in Bierce's "An Occurrence at Owl Creek Bridge" (Chapter 1) is masquerading as a Confederate soldier, and in speaking with the major character Farquhar, who is a landowner and a Confederate loyalist, he speaks confidentially but deceivingly. The result of the scout's lies is that Farquhar is fooled into believing that he will be safe if he sabotages the bridge at Owl Creek.

What Others Say Tells Us About a Character

By studying what characters say about each other, you can enhance your understanding not only of the character being discussed but also about the characters doing the talking. For example, the narrator's father in Chioles's "Before the Firing Squad" (Chapter 10) speaks to his young son about not being too friendly with Fritz, who is still a teenager but who is also a member of the occupying German army. The father's summary is this: "He's the enemy." This oversimplified characterization of Fritz is belied at the story's end, when Fritz, at obvious personal risk, preserves the lives of the narrator, his family, and other villagers.

Ironically, speeches often indicate something other than what the speakers intend, perhaps because of prejudice, stupidity, or foolishness. Nora, in O'Connor's "First Confession" (Chapter 6) tells about Jackie's lashing out at her with a butter knife, but in effect she describes the boy's individuality just as she also discloses her own spitefulness.

The Author, Speaking as a Storyteller or an Observer, May Present Judgments about Characters

What the author, speaking as a work's authorial voice, says about a character is usually accurate, and the authorial voice can be accepted factually. However, when the authorial voice interprets actions and characteristics, as in Hawthorne's "Young Goodman Brown" (Chapter 7), the author himself or herself assumes the role of a reader or critic, whose opinions are therefore open to question. For this reason, authors frequently avoid interpretations and devote their skill to arranging events and speeches so that readers can draw their own conclusions.

Types of Characters: Round and Flat

No writer can present an entire life history of a protagonist, nor can each character in a story get "equal time" for development. Accordingly, some characters grow to be full and alive, while others remain shadowy. The British novelist and critic E. M. Forster, in *Aspects of the Novel*, calls the two major types "round" and "flat."

Round Characters Are Three-Dimensional and Lifelike

The basic trait of **round characters** is that we are told enough about them to permit the conclusion that they are three-dimensional, rounded, authentic, memorable, original, and true to life. They are the centers of our attention in most works of fiction. Their roundness and fullness are characterized by both individuality and unpredictability. It is true that, like all human beings, round characters have inherent qualities that the circumstances of a story bring out, and therefore their full realization as characters is directly connected to the stories in which they live their lives. Mabel, of Lawrence's "The Horse Dealer's Daughter" (Chapter 8), is a round character. She has spent her life taking care of her father and his affairs, but following her father's death she sees no value in continuing to live. It is when she becomes aware of a favorable change in her life that she becomes restored. Along with her new direction, however, she also anticipates new complications, and it is this complexity of response that especially marks the roundness and fullness of her character.

A complementary quality about round characters is that they are **dynamic.** Dynamic characters *recognize, change with,* or *adjust to* circumstances. Such changes may be shown in (1) an action or actions, (2) the realization of new strength and therefore the affirmation of previous decisions, (3) the acceptance of new conditions and the need for making changes, (4) the discovery of unrecognized truths, or (5) the reconciliation of the character to adverse conditions. A case in point is Farquhar in "An Occurrence at Owl Creek Bridge" (Chapter 1). Although he is a "well-to-do" Southern planter during the Civil War, for a number of reasons he has not been called to service in the Confederate Army. His life as a planter and slaveowner is stable, and would continue so; but when he learns about the possibility of dynamiting the bridge, he goes ahead and does it. By this action he undergoes change and growth; he is dynamic.

This is not to say that only round characters are dynamic, for less significant characters in a story may also undergo alteration as their circumstances change, as with Carol, Eva's good friend, in Munro's "The Found Boat" (Chapter 6). Carol shares in Eva's developing growth as an adolescent approaching the point of becoming a woman. Usually, dynamic character growth is good, but such growth, under some conditions, may bring a dynamic character to ruin—a situation, as we have just seen, experienced by Farquhar in "An Occurrence at Owl Creek Bridge."

Because a round character plays a major role in a story, he or she is often called the **hero** or **heroine.** Some round characters are not particularly heroic, however, so it is preferable to use the more neutral word **protagonist** (the "first actor"). The protagonist is central to the action, moves against an **antagonist** (the "opposing actor"), and exhibits the ability to adapt to new situations.

Flat Characters Are Simple and One-Dimensional

Unlike round characters, **flat characters** are not complex, but are simple and one-dimensional. They may have no more than a single role to perform in a story, or they may be associated with no more than a single dominating idea. Most flat characters end pretty much where they begin, and for this reason we may think of them as **static,** not dynamic. Often their absence of growth or development results from lack of knowledge or understanding, or even from stupidity or insensitivity. Flat characters are not worthless in fiction, however, for they highlight the development of the round characters. In Joyce's "Araby" (Chapter 4), there is little if any growth in Mangan's sister, and yet her presence is the major reason for the narrator's attitudes; and he travels to the Saturday night bazaar in order to please her.

Usually, flat characters are minor (e.g., relatives, acquaintances, functionaries), but not all minor characters are necessarily flat. Sometimes flat characters are prominent in certain types of literature, such as cowboy, police, and detective stories, where the focus is less on character than on performance. Such characters might be lively and engaging, even though they do not undergo significant change and development. They must be strong, tough, and clever enough to perform recurring tasks such as solving a crime, boxing with the major character, overcoming a villain, or finding a treasure. The term **stock character** is often used to describe characters in these repeating situations. To the degree that stock characters have many common traits, they are **representative** of their class or group. Such characters, with variations in names, ages, and sexes, have been constant in literature since the ancient Greeks. Some regular stock or representative characters are the insensitive father, the interfering mother, the sassy younger sister or brother, the greedy politician, the harassed boss, the resourceful cowboy or detective, the overbearing or henpecked husband, the submissive or nagging wife, the absent-minded professor, the angry police captain, the lovable drunk, and the town do-gooder.

Stock characters are usually also flat as long as they do no more than perform their roles and exhibit conventional and nonindividual traits. Because they possess no attitudes except those of their class, they are often called **stereotype characters,** or characters who all seem to have been cast in the same mold.

When authors bring characters into strong focus, however, no matter what roles they perform, the characters emerge from flatness and move into roundness. For example, Louise Mallard of Chopin's "The Story of an Hour" (Chapter 6) is a traditional housewife, and if she were no more than that she would be flat and stereotypical. After receiving the news that her husband has died, however, the roundness of her character emerges because of her sudden and unexpected exhilaration at the prospect of being widowed and free. A comparable character is Francie, the speaker of Lorrie Moore's "How to Become a Writer" (Chapter 2). Under the guise of giving instructions for undertaking the profession of writing, Francie demonstrates characteristic linguistic ability and wittiness. Of equal importance is that she also reveals a number of incidents in her personal and family life that have evoked both grief and disappointment. We may conclude that such experiences in effect have caused the adaptation and character growth that have made her the writer that she is. In sum, the ability to grow and develop and adjust to changing circumstances makes characters round and dynamic. Absence of these traits makes characters flat and static.

Reality and Probability: Verisimilitude

Characters in fiction should be true to life. Therefore their actions, statements, and thoughts must all be what human beings are *likely* to do, say, and think under the conditions presented in the literary work. This is the standard of **verisimilitude, probability,** or **plausibility.** One may readily admit that there are people *in life* who perform tasks or exhibit characteristics that are difficult or seemingly impossible (such as always leading the team to victory, always getting A+'s on every test, always being cheerful and helpful, or always understanding the needs of others). However, such characters in fiction would not be true to life because they do not fit within normal or usual behavior.

You should therefore distinguish between what characters may *possibly* do and what they *most frequently* or *most usually* do. Thus, in Maupassant's "The Necklace" (Part I), it is possible that Mathilde could be truthful and tell her friend Jeanne Forrestier about the lost necklace. In light of Mathilde's pride and concept of self-respect, however, it is more in character for her and her husband to hide the loss and borrow money for a replacement, even though they endure disastrous financial hardship for ten years. Granted the possibilities of the story (either self-sacrifice or the admission of fault or of a possible crime), the decision she makes with her husband is the more *probable* one.

Nevertheless, probability does not rule out surprise or even exaggeration. In Katherine Anne Porter's "The Jilting of Granny Weatherall" (Chapter 7), the accomplishments of Granny—such as fencing a hundred acres of farmland all by herself—do not seem impossible even if they do seem unlikely. But we learn that when she was young she became compulsively determined to overcome the ignominy of having been betrayed and jilted by her fiancé. It is therefore probable, or at least not improbable, that she would be capable of the heavy labor of building the fence.

Writers render probability of character in many ways. Works that attempt to mirror life—realistic, naturalistic, or "slice of life" stories like Joyce's "Araby" (Chapter 4)—set up a pattern of ordinary, everyday probability. Less realistic conditions establish different frameworks of probability, in which characters are *expected* to be unusual, as in Hawthorne's "Young Goodman Brown" (Chapter 7). Because a major way of explaining this story is that Brown is having a nightmarish psychotic trance, his bizarre and unnatural responses are probable. Equally probable is the way the doctors explain Louise Mallard's sudden death at the end of Chopin's "The Story of an Hour" (Chapter 6), even though their smug analysis is totally and comically wrong.

You might also encounter works containing *supernatural* figures, such as the second traveler in "Young Goodman Brown" and the unannounced guest in Poe's "The Masque of the Red Death" (Chapter 9). You may wonder whether such characters are probable or improbable. Usually, gods and goddesses embody qualities of the best and most moral human beings, and devils like Hawthorne's guide take on attributes of the worst. However, you might remember that the devil is often given dashing and engaging qualities so that he can deceive gullible sinners and then drag them screaming into the fiery pits of hell. The friendliness of Brown's guide is therefore not an improbable trait. In judging characters of this or any other type, your best criteria are probability, consistency, and believability.

Stories for Study

Raymond Carver . . . . Cathedral, 180
Susan Glaspell . . . . A Jury of Her Peers, 189
Katherine Mansfield . . . . Miss Brill, 202
Amy Tan . . . . Two Kinds, 205
Mark Twain . . . . Luck, 213

RAYMOND CARVER (1938–1988)

For a brief biographical note about Carver, see Chapter 2, page 137. "Cathedral," which has been called a high point in Carver's development as a writer, is taken from the collection Cathedral *(1983).*

ᴺᴱᵂ Cathedral (1983)

This blind man, an old friend of my wife's, he was on his way to spend the night. His wife had died. So he was visiting the dead wife's relatives in Connecticut. He called my wife from his in-laws'. Arrangements were made. He would come by train, a five-hour trip, and my wife would meet him at the station. She hadn't seen him since she worked for him one summer in Seattle ten years ago. But she and the blind man had kept in touch. They made tapes and mailed them back and forth. I wasn't enthusiastic about his visit. He was no one I knew. And his being blind bothered me. My idea of blindness came from the movies. In the movies, the blind moved slowly and never laughed. Sometimes they were led by seeing-eye dogs. A blind man in my house was not something I looked forward to.

That summer in Seattle she had needed a job. She didn't have any money. The man she was going to marry at the end of the summer was in officers' training school. He didn't have any money, either. But she was in love with the guy, and he was in love with her, etc. She'd seen something in the paper: HELP WANTED—*Reading to Blind Man*, and a telephone number. She phoned and went over, was hired on the spot. She'd worked with this blind man all summer. She read stuff to him, case studies, reports, that sort of thing. She helped him organize his little office in the county social-service department. They'd become good friends, my wife and the blind man. How do I know these things? She told me. And she told me something else. On her last day in the office, the blind man asked if he could touch her face. She agreed to this. She told me he touched his fingers to every part of her face, her nose—even her neck! She never forgot it. She even tried to write a poem about it. She was always trying to write a poem. She wrote a poem or two every year, usually after something really important had happened to her.

When we first started going out together, she showed me the poem. In the poem, she recalled his fingers and the way they had moved around over her face. In the poem, she talked about what she had felt at the time, about what went through her mind when the blind man touched her nose and lips. I can remember I didn't think much of the poem. Of course, I didn't tell her that. Maybe I just don't understand poetry. I admit it's not the first thing I reach for when I pick up something to read.

Anyway, this man who'd first enjoyed her favors, the officer-to-be, he'd been her childhood sweetheart. So okay. I'm saying that at the end of the summer she let the blind man run his hands over her face, said good-bye to him, married her childhood etc., who was now a commissioned officer, and she moved away from Seattle. But they'd kept in touch, she and the blind man. She made the first contact after a year or so. She called him up one night from an Air Force base in Alabama. She wanted to talk. They talked. He asked her to send a tape and tell him about her life. She did this. She sent the tape. On the tape, she told the blind man about her husband and about their life together in the military. She told the blind man she loved her husband but she didn't like it where they lived and she didn't like it that he was part of the military-industrial thing. She told the blind man she'd written a poem and he was in it. She told him that she was writing a poem about what it was like to be an Air Force officer's wife. The poem wasn't finished yet. She was still writing it. The blind man made a tape. He sent her the tape. She made a tape. This went on for years. My wife's officer was posted to one base and then another. She sent tapes from Moody AFB, McGuire, McConnell, and finally Travis, near Sacramento, where one night she got to feeling lonely and cut off from people she kept losing in that moving-around life. She got to feeling she couldn't go it another step. She went in and swallowed all the pills and capsules in the medicine chest and washed them down with a bottle of gin. Then she got into a hot bath and passed out.

But instead of dying, she got sick. She threw up. Her officer—why should he have a name? he was the childhood sweetheart, and what more does he want?—came home from somewhere, found her, and called the ambulance. In time, she put it all on a tape and sent

5

the tape to the blind man. Over the years, she put all kinds of stuff on tapes and sent the tapes off lickety-split. Next to writing a poem every year, I think it was her chief means of recreation. On one tape, she told the blind man she'd decided to live away from her officer for a time. On another tape, she told him about her divorce. She and I began going out, and of course she told her blind man about it. She told him everything, or so it seemed to me. Once she asked me if I'd like to hear the latest tape from the blind man. This was a year ago. I was on the tape, she said. So I said okay, I'd listen to it. I got us drinks and we settled down in the living room. We made ready to listen. First she inserted the tape into the player and adjusted a couple of dials. Then she pushed a lever. The tape squeaked and someone began to talk in this loud voice. She lowered the volume. After a few minutes of harmless chitchat, I heard my own name in the mouth of this stranger, this blind man I didn't even know! And then this: "From all you've said about him, I can only conclude—" But we were interrupted, a knock at the door, something, and we didn't ever get back to the tape. Maybe it was just as well. I'd heard all I wanted to.

Now this same blind man was coming to sleep in my house.

"Maybe I could take him bowling," I said to my wife. She was at the draining board doing scalloped potatoes. She put down the knife she was using and turned around.

"If you love me," she said, "you can do this for me. If you don't love me, okay. But if you had a friend, any friend, and the friend came to visit, I'd make him feel comfortable." She wiped her hands with the dish towel.

"I don't have any blind friends," I said.

10   "You don't have *any* friends," she said. "Period. Besides," she said, "goddamn it, his wife's just died! Don't you understand that? The man's lost his wife!"

I didn't answer. She'd told me a little about the blind man's wife. Her name was Beulah. Beulah! That's a name for a colored woman.

"Was his wife a Negro?" I asked.

"Are you crazy?" my wife said. "Have you just flipped or something?" She picked up a potato. I saw it hit the floor, then roll under the stove. "What's wrong with you?" she said. "Are you drunk?"

"I'm just asking," I said.

15   Right then my wife filled me in with more detail than I cared to know. I made a drink and sat at the kitchen table to listen. Pieces of the story began to fall into place.

Beulah had gone to work for the blind man the summer after my wife had stopped working for him. Pretty soon Beulah and the blind man had themselves a church wedding. It was a little wedding—who'd want to go to such a wedding in the first place?—just the two of them, plus the minister and the minister's wife. But it was a church wedding just the same. It was what Beulah had wanted, he'd said. But even then Beulah must have been carrying the cancer in her glands. After they had been inseparable for eight years—my wife's word, *inseparable*—Beulah's health went into a rapid decline. She died in a Seattle hospital room, the blind man sitting beside the bed and holding on to her hand. They'd married, lived and worked together, slept together—had sex, sure—and then the blind man had to bury her. All this without his having ever seen what the goddamned woman looked like. It was beyond my understanding. Hearing this, I felt sorry for the blind man for a little bit. And then I found myself thinking what a pitiful life this woman must have led. Imagine a woman who could never see herself as she was seen in the eyes of her loved one. A woman who could go on day after day and never receive the smallest compliment from her beloved. A woman whose husband could never read the expression on her face, be it misery or something better. Someone who could wear makeup or not—what difference to him? She could, if she wanted, wear green eye-shadow around one eye, a straight pin in her nostril, yellow slacks, and purple shoes, no matter. And then to slip off into death, the blind man's hand on her hand, his blind eyes streaming tears—I'm imagining now—her last thought maybe this: that he never even knew what she looked like, and she on an express to the grave. Robert was left with a small insurance policy and a half of a twenty-peso Mexican coin. The other half of the coin went into the box with her. Pathetic.

So when the time rolled around, my wife went to the depot to pick him up. With nothing to do but wait—sure, I blamed him for that—I was having a drink and watching the TV when I heard the car pull into the drive. I got up from the sofa with my drink and went to the window to have a look.

I saw my wife laughing as she parked the car. I saw her get out of the car and shut the door. She was still wearing a smile. Just amazing. She went around to the other side of the car to where the blind man was already starting to get out. This blind man, feature this, he was wearing a full beard! A beard on a blind man! Too much, I say. The blind man reached into the backseat and dragged out a suitcase. My wife took his arm, shut the car door, and, talking all the way, moved him down the drive and then up the steps to the front porch. I turned off the TV. I finished my drink, rinsed the glass, dried my hands. Then I went to the door.

My wife said, "I want you to meet Robert. Robert, this is my husband. I've told you all about him." She was beaming. She had this blind man by his coat sleeve.

The blind man let go of his suitcase and up came his hand.

I took it. He squeezed hard, held my hand, and then he let it go.   20

"I feel like we've already met," he boomed.

"Likewise," I said. I didn't know what else to say. Then I said, "Welcome. I've heard a lot about you." We began to move then, a little group, from the porch into the living room, my wife guiding him by the arm. The blind man was carrying his suitcase in his other hand. My wife said things like, "To your left here, Robert. That's right. Now watch it, there's a chair. That's it. Sit down right here. This is the sofa. We just bought this sofa two weeks ago."

I started to say something about the old sofa. I'd liked that old sofa. But I didn't say anything. Then I wanted to say something else, small-talk, about the scenic ride along the Hudson. How going *to* New York, you should sit on the right-hand side of the train, and coming *from* New York, the left-hand side.

"Did you have a good train ride?" I said. "Which side of the train did you sit on, by the   25
way?"

"What a question, which side!" my wife said. "What's it matter which side?" she said.

"I just asked," I said.

"Right side," the blind man said. "I hadn't been on a train in nearly forty years. Not since I was a kid. With my folks. That's been a long time. I'd nearly forgotten the sensation. I have winter in my beard now," he said. "So I've been told, anyway. Do I look distinguished, my dear?" the blind man said to my wife.

"You look distinguished, Robert," she said. "Robert," she said. "Robert, it's just so good to see you."

My wife finally took her eyes off the blind man and looked at me. I had the feeling she   30
didn't like what she saw. I shrugged.

I've never met, or personally known, anyone who was blind. This blind man was late forties, a heavy-set, balding man with stooped shoulders, as if he carried a great weight there. He wore brown slacks, brown shoes, a light-brown shirt, a tie, a sports coat. Spiffy. He also had this full beard. But he didn't use a cane and he didn't wear dark glasses. I'd always thought dark glasses were a must for the blind. Fact was, I wished he had a pair. At first glance, his eyes looked like anyone else's eyes. But if you looked close, there was something different about them. Too much white in the iris, for one thing, and the pupils seemed to move around in the sockets without his knowing it or being able to stop it. Creepy. As I stared at his face, I saw the left pupil turn in toward his nose while the other made an effort to keep in one place. But it was only an effort, for that eye was on the roam without his knowing it or wanting it to be.

I said, "Let me get you a drink. What's your pleasure? We have a little of everything. It's one of our pastimes."

"Bub, I'm a Scotch man myself," he said fast enough in this big voice.

"Right," I said. Bub! "Sure you are. I knew it."

35 He let his fingers touch his suitcase, which was sitting alongside the sofa. He was taking his bearings. I didn't blame him for that.

"I'll move that up to your room," my wife said.

"No, that's fine," the blind man said loudly. "It can go up when I go up."

"A little water with the Scotch?" I said.

"Very little," he said.

40 "I knew it," I said.

He said, "Just a tad. The Irish actor, Barry Fitzgerald? I'm like that fellow. When I drink water, Fitzgerald said, I drink water. When I drink whiskey, I drink whiskey." My wife laughed. The blind man brought his hand up under his beard. He lifted his beard slowly and let it drop.

I did the drinks, three big glasses of Scotch with a splash of water in each. Then we made ourselves comfortable and talked about Robert's travels. First the long flight from the West Coast to Connecticut, we covered that. Then from Connecticut up here by train. We had another drink concerning that leg of the trip.

I remembered having read somewhere that the blind didn't smoke because, as speculation had it, they couldn't see the smoke they exhaled. I thought I knew that much and that much only about blind people. But this blind man smoked his cigarette down to the nubbin and then lit another one. This blind man filled his ashtray and my wife emptied it.

When we sat down at the table for dinner, we had another drink. My wife heaped Robert's plate with cube steak, scalloped potatoes, green beans. I buttered him up two slices of bread. I said, "Here's bread and butter for you." I swallowed some of my drink. "Now let us pray," I said, and the blind man lowered his head. My wife looked at me, her mouth agape. "Pray the phone won't ring and the food doesn't get cold," I said.

45 We dug in. We ate everything there was to eat on the table. We ate like there was no tomorrow. We didn't talk. We ate. We scarfed. We grazed that table. We were into serious eating. The blind man had right away located his foods, he knew just where everything was on his plate. I watched with admiration as he used his knife and fork on the meat. He'd cut two pieces of meat, fork the meat into his mouth, and then go all out for the scalloped potatoes, the beans next, and then he'd tear off a hunk of buttered bread and eat that. He'd follow this up with a big drink of milk. It didn't seem to bother him to use his fingers once in a while, either.

We finished everything, including half a strawberry pie. For a few moments, we sat as if stunned. Sweat beaded on our faces. Finally, we got up from the table and left the dirty plates. We didn't look back. We took ourselves into the living room and sank into our places again. Robert and my wife sat on the sofa. I took the big chair. We had us two or three more drinks while they talked about the major things that had come to pass for them in the past ten years. For the most part, I just listened. Now and then I joined in. I didn't want him to think I'd left the room, and I didn't want her to think I was feeling left out. They talked of things that had happened to them—to them!—these past ten years. I waited in vain to hear my name on my wife's sweet lips: "And then my dear husband came into my life"—something like that. But I heard nothing of the sort. More talk of Robert. Robert had done a little of everything, it seemed, a regular blind jack-of-all-trades. But most recently he and his wife had had an Amway distributorship, from which, I gathered, they'd earned their living, such as it was. The blind man was also a ham radio operator. He talked in his loud voice about conversations he'd had with fellow operators in Guam, in the Philippines, in Alaska, and even in Tahiti. He said he'd have a lot of friends there if he ever wanted to go visit those places. From time to time, he'd turn his blind face toward me, put his hand under his beard, ask me something. How long had I been in my present position? (Three years.) Did I like my work? (I didn't.) Was I going to stay with it? (What were the options?) Finally, when I thought he was beginning to run down, I got up and turned on the TV.

My wife looked at me with irritation. She was heading toward a boil. Then she looked at the blind man and said, "Robert, do you have a TV?"

The blind man said, "My dear, I have two TVs. I have a color set and a black-and-white thing, an old relic. It's funny, but if I turn the TV on, and I'm always turning it on, I turn on the color set. It's funny, don't you think?"

I didn't know what to say to that. I had absolutely nothing to say to that. No opinion. So I watched the news program and tried to listen to what the announcer was saying.

"This is a color TV," the blind man said. "Don't ask me how, but I can tell." 50

"We traded up a while ago," I said.

The blind man had another taste of this drink. He lifted his beard, sniffed it, and let it fall. He leaned forward on the sofa. He positioned his ashtray on the coffee table, then put the lighter to his cigarette. He leaned back on the sofa and crossed his legs at the ankles.

My wife covered her mouth, and then she yawned. She stretched. She said, "I think I'll go upstairs and put on my robe. I think I'll change into something else. Robert, you make yourself comfortable," she said.

"I'm comfortable," the blind man said.

"I want you to feel comfortable in this house," she said. 55

"I am comfortable," the blind man said.

After she'd left the room, he and I listened to the weather report and then to the sports roundup. By that time, she'd been gone so long I didn't know if she was going to come back. I thought she might have gone to bed. I wished she'd come back downstairs. I didn't want to be left alone with a blind man. I asked him if he wanted another drink, and he said sure. Then I asked if he wanted to smoke some dope with me. I said I'd just rolled a number. I hadn't, but I planned to do so in about two shakes.

"I'll try some with you," he said.

"Damm right," I said. "That's the stuff."

"I got our drinks and sat down on the sofa with him. Then I rolled us two fat numbers. 60 I lit one and passed it. I brought it to his fingers. He took it and inhaled.

"Hold it as long as you can," I said. I could tell he didn't know the first thing.

My wife came back downstairs wearing her pink robe and her pink slippers.

"What do I smell?" she said.

"We thought we'd have us some cannabis," I said.

My wife gave me a savage look. Then she looked at the blind man and said, "Robert, 65 I didn't know you smoked."

He said, "I do now, my dear. There's a first time for everything. But I don't feel anything yet."

"This stuff is pretty mellow," I said. "This stuff is mild. It's dope you can reason with," I said. "It doesn't mess you up."

"Not much it doesn't, bub," he said, and laughed.

My wife sat on the sofa between the blind man and me. I passed her the number. She took it and toked and then passed it back to me. "Which way is this going?" she said. Then she said, "I shouldn't be smoking this. I can hardly keep my eyes open as it is. That dinner did me in. I shouldn't have eaten so much."

"It was the strawberry pie," the blind man said. "That's what did it," he said, and he 70 laughed his big laugh. Then he shook his head.

"There's more strawberry pie," I said.

"Do you want some more, Robert?" my wife said.

"Maybe in a little while," he said.

We gave our attention to the TV. My wife yawned again. She said, "Your bed is made up when you feel like going to bed, Robert. I know you must have had a long day. When you're ready to go to bed, say so." She pulled his arm. "Robert?"

75   He came to and said, "I've had a real nice time. This beats tapes, doesn't it?"

I said, "Coming at you," and I put the number between his fingers. He inhaled, held the smoke, and then let it go. It was like he'd been doing it since he was nine years old.

"Thanks, bub," he said. "But I think this is all for me. I think I'm beginning to feel it," he said. He held the burning roach out for my wife.

"Same here," she said. "Ditto. Me, too." She took the roach and passed it to me. "I may just sit here for a while between you two guys with my eyes closed. But don't let me bother you, okay? Either one of you. If it bothers you, say so. Otherwise, I may just sit here with my eyes closed until you're ready to go to bed," she said. "Your bed's made up, Robert, when you're ready. It's right next to our room at the top of the stairs. We'll show you up when you're ready. You wake me up now, you guys, if I fall asleep." She said that and then she closed her eyes and went to sleep.

The news program ended. I got up and changed the channel. I sat back down on the sofa. I wished my wife hadn't pooped out. Her head lay across the back of the sofa, her mouth open. She'd turned so that her robe slipped away from her legs, exposing a juicy thigh. I reached to draw her robe back over her, and it was then that I glanced at the blind man. What the hell! I flipped the robe open again.

80   "You say when you want some strawberry pie," I said.

"I will," he said.

I said, "Are you tired? Do you want me to take you up to your bed? Are you ready to hit the hay?"

"Not yet," he said. "No, I'll stay up with you, bub. If that's all right. I'll stay up until you're ready to turn in. We haven't had a chance to talk. Know what I mean? I feel like me and her monopolized the evening." He lifted his beard and he let it fall. He picked up his cigarettes and his lighter.

"That's all right," I said. Then I said, "I'm glad for the company."

85   And I guess I was. Every night I smoked dope and stayed up as long as I could before I fell asleep. My wife and I hardly ever went to bed at the same time. When I did go to sleep, I had these dreams. Sometimes I'd wake up from one of them, my heart going crazy.

Something about the church and the Middle Ages was on the TV. Not your run-of-the-mill TV fare. I wanted to watch something else. I turned to the other channels. But there was nothing on them, either. So I turned back to the first channel and apologized.

"Bub, it's all right," the blind man said. "It's fine with me. Whatever you want to watch is okay. I'm always learning something. Learning never ends. It won't hurt me to learn something tonight. I got ears," he said.

We didn't say anything for a time. He was leaning forward with his head turned at me, his right ear aimed in the direction of the set. Very disconcerting. Now and then his eyelids drooped and then they snapped open again. Now and then he put his fingers into his beard and tugged, like he was thinking about something he was hearing on the television.

On the screen, a group of men wearing cowls was being set upon and tormented by men dressed in skeleton costumes and men dressed as devils. The men dressed as devils wore devil masks, horns, and long tails. This pageant was part of a procession. The Englishman who was narrating the thing said it took place in Spain once a year. I tried to explain to the blind man what was happening.

90   "Skeletons," he said. "I know about skeletons," he said, and he nodded.

The TV showed this one cathedral. Then there was a long, slow look at another one. Finally, the picture switched to the famous one in Paris, with its flying buttresses and its spires reaching up to the clouds. The camera pulled away to show the whole of the cathedral rising above the skyline.

There were times when the Englishman who was telling the thing would shut up, would simply let the camera move around the cathedrals. Or else the camera would tour the countryside, men in fields walking behind oxen. I waited as long as I could. Then I felt I had to say something. I said, "They're showing the outside of this cathedral now. Gargoyles. Little statues carved to look like monsters. Now I guess they're in Italy. Yeah, they're in Italy. There's paintings on the walls of this one church."

"Are those fresco paintings, bub?" he asked, and he sipped from his drink.

I reached for my glass. But it was empty. I tried to remember what I could remember. "You're asking me are those frescoes?" I said. "That's a good question. I don't know."

The camera moved to a cathedral outside Lisbon. The differences in the Portuguese   95
cathedral compared with the French and Italian were not that great. But they were there. Mostly the interior stuff. Then something occurred to me, and I said, "Something has occurred to me. Do you have any idea what a cathedral is? What they look like, that is? Do you follow me? If somebody says cathedral to you, do you have any notion what they're talking about? Do you know the difference between that and a Baptist church, say?"

He let the smoke dribble from his mouth. "I know they took hundreds of workers fifty or a hundred years to build," he said. "I just heard the man say that, of course. I know generations of the same families worked on a cathedral. I heard him say that, too. The men who began their life's work on them, they never lived to see the completion of their work. In that wise, bub, they're no different from the rest of us, right?" He laughed. Then his eyelids drooped again. His head nodded. He seemed to be snoozing. Maybe he was imagining himself in Portugal. The TV was showing another cathedral now. This one was in Germany. The Englishman's voice droned on. "Cathedrals," the blind man said. He sat up and rolled his head back and forth. "If you want the truth, bub, that's about all I know. What I just said. What I heard him say. But maybe you could describe one to me? I wish you'd do it. I'd like that. If you want to know, I really don't have a good idea."

I stared hard at the shot of the cathedral on the TV. How could I even begin to describe it? But say my life depended on it. Say my life was being threatened by an insane guy who said I had to do it or else.

I stared some more at the cathedral before the picture flipped off into the countryside. There was no use. I turned to the blind man and said, "To begin with, they're very tall." I was looking around the room for clues. "They reach way up. Up and up. Toward the sky. They're so big, some of them, they have to have these supports. To help hold them up, so to speak. These supports are called buttresses. They remind me of viaducts, for some reason. But maybe you don't know viaducts, either? Sometimes the cathedrals have devils and such carved into the front. Sometimes lords and ladies. Don't ask me why this is," I said.

He was nodding. The whole upper part of his body seemed to be moving back and forth.

"I'm not doing so good, am I?" I said.   100

He stopped nodding and leaned forward on the edge of the sofa. As he listened to me, he was running his fingers through his beard. I wasn't getting through to him, I could see that. But he waited for me to go on just the same. He nodded, like he was trying to encourage me. I tried to think what else to say. "They're really big," I said. "They're massive. They're built of stone. Marble, too, sometimes. In those olden days, when they built cathedrals, men wanted to be close to God. In those olden days, God was an important part of everyone's life. You could tell this from their cathedral-building. I'm sorry," I said, "but it looks like that's the best I can do for you. I'm just no good at it."

"That's all right, bub," the blind man said. "Hey, listen. I hope you don't mind my asking you. Can I ask you something? Let me ask you a simple question, yes or no. I'm just curious and there's no offense. You're my host. But let me ask if you are in any way religious? You don't mind my asking?"

I shook my head. He couldn't see that, though. A wink is the same as a nod to a blind man. "I guess I don't believe in it. In anything. Sometimes it's hard. You know what I'm saying?"

"Sure, I do," he said.

105 "Right," I said.

The Englishman was still holding forth. My wife sighed in her sleep. She drew a long breath and went on with her sleeping.

"You'll have to forgive me," I said. "But I can't tell you what a cathedral looks like. It just isn't in me to do it. I can't do any more than I've done."

The blind man sat very still, his head down, as he listened to me.

I said, "The truth is, cathedrals don't mean anything special to me. Nothing. Cathedrals. They're something to look at on late-night TV. That's all they are."

110 It was then that the blind man cleared his throat. He brought something up. He took a handkerchief from his back pocket. Then he said, "I get it, bub. It's okay. It happens. Don't worry about it," he said. "Hey, listen to me. Will you do me a favor? I got an idea. Why don't you find us some heavy paper? And a pen. We'll do something. We'll draw one together. Get us a pen and some heavy paper. Go on, bub, get the stuff," he said.

So I went upstairs. My legs felt like they didn't have any strength in them. They felt like they did after I'd done some running. In my wife's room I looked around. I found some ballpoints in a little basket on her table. And then I tried to think where to look for the kind of paper he was talking about.

Downstairs, in the kitchen, I found a shopping bag with onion skins in the bottom of the bag. I emptied the bag and shook it. I brought it into the living room and sat down with it near his legs. I moved some things, smoothed the wrinkles from the bag, spread it out on the coffee table.

The blind man got down from the sofa and sat next to me on the carpet.

He ran his fingers over the paper. He went up and down the sides of the paper. The edges, even the edges. He fingered the corners.

115 "All right," he said. "All right, let's do her."

He found my hand, the hand with the pen. He closed his hand over my hand. "Go ahead, bub, draw," he said. "Draw. You'll see. I'll follow along with you. It'll be okay. Just begin now like I'm telling you. You'll see. Draw," the blind man said.

So I began. First I drew a box that looked like a house. It could have been the house I lived in. Then I put a roof on it. At either end of the roof, I drew spires. Crazy.

"Swell," he said. "Terrific. You're doing fine," he said. "Never thought anything like this could happen in your lifetime, did you, bub? Well, it's a strange life, we all know that. Go on now. Keep it up."

I put in windows with arches. I drew flying buttresses. I hung great doors. I couldn't stop. The TV station went off the air. I put down the pen and closed and opened my fingers. The blind man felt around over the paper. He moved the tips of his fingers over the paper, all over what I had drawn, and he nodded.

120 "Doing fine," the blind man said.

I took up the pen again, and he found my hand. I kept at it. I'm no artist. But I kept drawing just the same.

My wife opened up her eyes and gazed at us. She sat up on the sofa, her robe hanging open. She said, "What are you doing? Tell me, I want to know."

I didn't answer her.

The blind man said, "We're drawing a cathedral. Me and him are working on it. Press hard," he said to me. "That's right. That's good," he said. "Sure. You got it, bub, I can tell. You didn't think you could. But you can, can't you? You're cooking with gas now. You know what I'm saying? We're going to really have us something here in a minute. How's the old arm?" he said. "Put some people in there now. What's a cathedral without people?"

My wife said, "What's going on? Robert, what are you doing? What's going on?"   125

"It's all right," he said to her. "Close your eyes now," the blind man said to me.

I did it. I closed them just like he said.

"Are they closed?" he said. "Don't fudge."

"They're closed," I said.

"Keep them that way," he said. He said, "Don't stop now. Draw."   130

So we kept on with it. His fingers rode my fingers as my hand went over the paper. It was like nothing else in my life up to now.

Then he said, "I think that's it. I think you got it," he said. "Take a look. What do you think?"

But I had my eyes closed. I thought I'd keep them that way for a little longer. I thought it was something I ought to do.

"Well?" he said. "Are you looking?"

My eyes were still closed. I was in my house. I knew that. But I didn't feel like I was in-   135
side anything.

"It's really something," I said.

QUESTIONS

1. Who is the speaker/narrator of "Cathedral"? How much do we learn about his character? Would you describe the home life of the speaker and his wife as interesting or dull, and why? What is his attitude toward his wife's former employer, Robert, who is visiting his home? How does Robert first seem when he first appears? What is the speaker's response to being called "Bub"?

2. Why does the speaker continually refer to Robert as the "blind man," rather than by name? What change is detectable in the speaker's attitudes toward Robert at the end of the story? Why does the speaker keep his eyes closed at the very end? What change seems to have happened to him?

3. Describe the character of the speaker's wife. What connection does she have with Robert? How does Robert's visit affect her attitude toward the speaker, her husband?

4. What connection can you perceive between the story's title and the principal action? What might be considered symbolic about the title? Why does the speaker describe the various cathedrals of Europe that are shown and discussed on the TV program?

SUSAN GLASPELL (1882–1948)

For a brief biography and photo, see Chapter 23, page 1231.

 ## A Jury of Her Peers° (1917)

When Martha Hale opened the storm-door and got a cut of the north wind, she ran back for her big woolen scarf. As she hurriedly wound that round her head her eye made a scandalized

---

°Glaspell's play *Trifles*, with which this story may be compared, appears in Chapter 23.

sweep of her kitchen. It was no ordinary thing that called her away—it was probably further from ordinary than anything that had ever happened in Dickson County. But what her eye took in was that her kitchen was in no shape for leaving: her bread all ready for mixing, half the flour sifted and half unsifted.

She hated to see things half done; but she had been at that when the team from town stopped to get Mr. Hale, and then the sheriff came running in to say his wife wished Mrs. Hale would come too—adding, with a grin, that he guessed she was getting scary and wanted another woman along. So she had dropped everything right where it was.

"Martha!" now came her husband's impatient voice. "Don't keep folks waiting out here in the cold."

She again opened the storm-door, and this time joined the three men and the one woman waiting for her in the big two-seated buggy.

5   After she had the robes tucked around her she took another look at the woman who sat beside her on the back seat. She had met Mrs. Peters the year before at the county fair, and the thing she remembered about her was that she didn't seem like a sheriff's wife. She was small and thin and didn't have a strong voice. Mrs. Gorman, sheriff's wife before Gorman went out and Peters came in, had a voice that somehow seemed to be backing up the law with every word. But if Mrs. Peters didn't look like a sheriff's wife, Peters made it up in looking like a sheriff. He was to a dot the kind of man who could get himself elected sheriff— a heavy man with a big voice, who was particularly genial with the law-abiding, as if to make it plain that he knew the difference between criminals and non-criminals. And right there it came into Mrs. Hale's mind, with a stab, that this man who was so pleasant and lively with all of them was going to the Wrights' now as a sheriff.

"The country's not very pleasant this time of year," Mrs. Peters at last ventured, as if she felt they ought to be talking as well as the men.

Mrs. Hale scarcely finished her reply, for they had gone up a little hill and could see the Wright place now, and seeing it did not make her feel like talking. It looked very lonesome this cold March morning. It had always been a lonesome-looking place. It was down in a hollow, and the poplar trees around it were lonesome-looking trees. The men were looking at it and talking about what had happened. The county attorney was bending to one side of the buggy, and kept looking steadily at the place as they drew up to it.

"I'm glad you came with me," Mrs. Peters said nervously, as the two women were about to follow the men in through the kitchen door.

Even after she had her foot on the door-step, her hand on the knob, Martha Hale had a moment of feeling she could not cross that threshold. And the reason it seemed she couldn't cross it now was simply because she hadn't crossed it before. Time and time again it had been in her mind, "I ought to go over and see Minnie Foster"—she still thought of her as Minnie Foster, though for twenty years she had been Mrs. Wright. And then there was always something to do and Minnie Foster would go from her mind. But *now* she could come.

10   The men went over to the stove. The women stood close together by the door. Young Henderson, the county attorney, turned around and said, "Come up to the fire, ladies."

Mrs. Peters took a step forward, then stopped. "I'm not—cold," she said.

And so the two women stood by the door, at first not even so much as looking around the kitchen.

The men talked for a minute about what a good thing it was the sheriff had sent his deputy out that morning to make a fire for them, and then Sheriff Peters stepped back from the stove, unbuttoned his outer coat, and leaned his hands on the kitchen table in a way that seemed to mark the beginning of official business. "Now, Mr. Hale," he said in a sort of semi-official voice, "before we move things about, you tell Mr. Henderson just what it was you saw when you came here yesterday morning."

The county attorney was looking around the kitchen.

"By the way," he said, "has anything been moved?" He turned to the sheriff. "Are things   15
just as you left them yesterday?"

Peters looked from cupboard to sink; from that to a small worn rocker a little to one side
of the kitchen table.

"It's just the same."

"Somebody should have been left here yesterday," said the county attorney.

"Oh—yesterday," returned the sheriff, with a little gesture as of yesterday having been
more than he could bear to think of. "When I had to send Frank to Morris Center for that
man who went crazy—let me tell you. I had my hands full *yesterday*. I knew you could get
back from Omaha by today, George, and as long as I went over everything here myself—"

"Well, Mr. Hale," said the county attorney, in a way of letting what was past and gone   20
go, "tell just what happened when you came here yesterday morning."

Mrs. Hale, still leaning against the door, had that sinking feeling of the mother whose
child is about to speak a piece. Lewis often wandered along and got things mixed up in a
story. She hoped he would tell this straight and plain, and not say unnecessary things that
would just make things harder for Minnie Foster. He didn't begin at once, and she noticed
that he looked queer—as if standing in that kitchen and having to tell what he had seen
there yesterday morning made him almost sick.

"Yes, Mr. Hale?" the county attorney reminded.

"Harry and I had started to town with a load of potatoes," Mrs. Hale's husband began.

Harry was Mrs. Hale's oldest boy. He wasn't with them now, for the very good reason
that those potatoes never got to town yesterday and he was taking them this morning, so he
hadn't been home when the sheriff stopped to say he wanted Mr. Hale to come over to the
Wright place and tell the county attorney his story there, where he could point it all out.
With all Mrs. Hale's other emotions came the fear now that maybe Harry wasn't dressed
warm enough—they hadn't any of them realized how that north wind did bite.

"We come along this road," Hale was going on, with a motion of his hand to the road   25
over which they had just come, "and as we got in sight of the house I says to Harry, 'I'm
goin' to see if I can't get John Wright to take a telephone.' You see," he explained to Henderson, "unless I can get somebody to go in with me they won't come out this branch road except for a price *I* can't pay. I'd spoke to Wright about it once before; but he put me off,
saying folks talked too much anyway, and all he asked was peace and quiet—guess you
know about how much he talked himself. But I thought maybe if I went to the house and
talked about it before his wife, and said all the women-folks liked the telephones, and that
in this lonesome stretch of road it would be a good thing—well, I said to Harry that that
was what I was going to say—though I said at the same time that I didn't know as what his
wife wanted made much difference to John—"

Now there he was!—saying things he didn't need to say. Mrs. Hale tried to catch her
husband's eye, but fortunately the county attorney interrupted with:

"Let's talk about that a little later, Mr. Hale. I do want to talk about that, but I'm anxious
now to get along to just what happened when you got here."

When he began this time, it was very deliberately and carefully:

"I didn't see or hear anything. I knocked at the door. And still it was all quiet inside. I knew
they must be up—it was past eight o'clock. So I knocked again, louder, and I thought I heard
somebody say, 'Come in.' I wasn't sure—I'm not sure yet. But I opened the door—this door,"
jerking a hand toward the door by which the two women stood, "and there, in that rocker"—
pointing to it—"sat Mrs. Wright."

Everyone in the kitchen looked at the rocker. It came into Mrs. Hale's mind that that   30
rocker didn't look in the least like Minnie Foster—the Minnie Foster of twenty years before.
It was a dingy red, with wooden rungs up the back, and the middle rung was gone, and the
chair sagged to one side.

"How did she—look?" the county attorney was inquiring.

"Well," said Hale, "she looked—queer."

"How do you mean—queer?"

As he asked it he took out a note-book and pencil. Mrs. Hale did not like the sight of that pencil. She kept her eye fixed on her husband, as if to keep him from saying unnecessary things that would go into that note-book and make trouble.

35 Hale did speak guardedly, as if the pencil had affected him too.

"Well, as if she didn't know what she was going to do next. And kind of—done up."

"How did she seem to feel about your coming?"

"Why, I don't think she minded—one way or other. She didn't pay much attention. I said, 'Ho' do, Mrs. Wright? It's cold, ain't it?' And she said. 'Is it?'—and went on pleatin' at her apron.

"Well, I was surprised. She didn't ask me to come up to the stove, or to sit down, but just set there, not even lookin' at me. And so I said: 'I want to see John.'

40 "And then she—laughed. I guess you would call it a laugh.

"I thought of Harry and the team outside, so I said, a little sharp, 'Can I see John?' 'No,' says she—kind of dull like. 'Ain't he home?' says I. Then she looked at me. 'Yes,' says she, 'he's home.' 'Then why can't I see him?' I asked her, out of patience with her now. ''Cause he's dead' says she, just as quiet and dull—and fell to pleatin' her apron. 'Dead?' says I, like you do when you can't take in what you've heard.

"She just nodded her head, not getting a bit excited, but rockin' back and forth.

"'Why—where is he?' says I, not knowing *what* to say.

"She just pointed upstairs—like this"—pointing to the room above.

45 "I got up, with the idea of going up there myself. By this time I—didn't know what to do. I walked from there to here; then I says: 'Why, what did he die of?'

"'He died of a rope around his neck,' says she; and just went on pleatin' at her apron."

Hale stopped speaking, and stood staring at the rocker, as if he were still seeing the woman who had sat there the morning before. Nobody spoke; it was as if every one were seeing the woman who had sat there the morning before.

"And what did you do then?" the county attorney at last broke the silence.

"I went out and called Harry. I thought I might—need help. I got Harry in, and we went upstairs." His voice fell almost to a whisper. "There he was—lying over the—"

50 "I think I'd rather have you go into that upstairs," the county attorney interrupted, "where you can point it all out. Just go on now with the rest of the story."

"Well, my first thought was to get that rope off. It looked—"

He stopped, his face twitching.

"But Harry, he went up to him, and he said. 'No, he's dead all right, and we'd better not touch anything.' So we went downstairs.

"She was still sitting that same way. 'Has anybody been notified?' I asked. 'No,' says she, unconcerned.

55 "'Who did this, Mrs. Wright?' said Harry. He said it businesslike, and she stopped pleatin' at her apron. 'I don't know,' she says. 'You don't *know*?' says Harry. 'Weren't you sleepin' in the bed with him?' 'Yes,' says she, 'but I was on the inside.' 'Somebody slipped a rope round his neck and strangled him, and you didn't wake up?' says Harry. 'I didn't wake up,' she said after him.

"We may have looked as if we didn't see how that could be, for after a minute she said, 'I sleep sound.'

"Harry was going to ask her more questions, but I said maybe that weren't our business; maybe we ought to let her tell her story first to the coroner or the sheriff. So Harry went fast as he could over to High Road—the Rivers' place, where there's a telephone."

"And what did she do when she knew you had gone for the coroner?" The attorney got his pencil in his hand all ready for writing.

"She moved from that chair to this one over here"—Hale pointed to a small chair in the corner—"and just sat there with her hands held together and looking down. I got a feeling that I ought to make some conversation, so I said I had come in to see if John wanted to put in a telephone; and at that she started to laugh, and then she stopped and looked at me—scared."

At the sound of a moving pencil the man who was telling the story looked up. 60

"I dunno—maybe it wasn't scared," he hastened: "I wouldn't like to say it was. Soon Harry got back, and then Dr. Lloyd came, and you, Mr. Peters, and so I guess that's all I know that you don't."

He said that last with relief, and moved a little, as if relaxing. Everyone moved a little. The county attorney walked toward the stair door.

"I guess we'll go upstairs first—then out to the barn and around there."

He paused and looked around the kitchen.

"You're convinced there was nothing important here?" he asked the sheriff. "Nothing 65 that would—point to any motive?"

The sheriff too looked all around, as if to re-convince himself.

"Nothing here but kitchen things," he said, with a little laugh for the insignificance of kitchen things.

The county attorney was looking at the cupboard—a peculiar, ungainly structure, half closet and half cupboard, the upper part of it being built in the wall, and the lower part just the old-fashioned kitchen cupboard. As if its queerness attracted him, he got a chair and opened the upper part and looked in. After a moment he drew his hand away sticky.

"Here's a nice mess," he said resentfully.

The two women had drawn nearer, and now the sheriff's wife spoke. 70

"Oh—her fruit," she said, looking to Mrs. Hale for sympathetic understanding. She turned back to the county attorney and explained: "She worried about that when it turned so cold last night. She said the fire would go out and her jars might burst."

Mrs. Peters' husband broke into a laugh.

"Well, can you beat the woman! Held for murder, and worrying about her preserves!"

The young attorney set his lips.

"I guess before we're through with her she may have something more serious than pre- 75
serves to worry about."

"Oh, well," said Mrs. Hale's husband, with good-natured superiority, "women are used to worrying over trifles."

The two women moved a little closer together. Neither of them spoke. The county attorney seemed suddenly to remember his manners—and think of his future.

"And yet," said he, with the gallantry of a young politician, "for all their worries, what would we do without the ladies?"

The women did not speak, did not unbend. He went to the sink and began washing his hands. He turned to wipe them on the roller towel—whirled it for a cleaner place.

"Dirty towels! Not much of a housekeeper, would you say, ladies?" 80

He kicked his foot against some dirty pans under the sink.

"There's a great deal of work to be done on a farm," said Mrs. Hale stiffly.

"To be sure. And yet"—with a little bow to her—"I know there are some Dickson County farm-houses that do not have such roller towels." He gave it a pull to expose its full length again.

"Those towels get dirty awful quick. Men's hands aren't always as clean as they might be."

"Ah, loyal to your sex, I see," he laughed. He stopped and gave her a keen look. "But 85
you and Mrs. Wright were neighbors. I suppose you were friends, too."

Martha Hale shook her head.

"I've seen little enough of her of late years. I've not been in this house—it's more than a year."

"And why was that? You didn't like her?"

"I liked her well enough," she replied with spirit. "Farmers' wives have their hands full, Mr. Henderson. And then—" She looked around the kitchen.

90 "Yes?" he encouraged.

"It never seemed a very cheerful place," said she, more to herself than to him.

"No," he agreed; "I don't think anyone would call it cheerful. I shouldn't say she had the home-making instinct."

"Well, I don't know as Wright had, either," she muttered.

"You mean they didn't get on very well?" he was quick to ask.

95 "No; I don't mean anything," she answered, with decision. As she turned a little away from him, she added: "But I don't think a place would be any the cheerfuller for John Wright's bein' in it."

"I'd like to talk to you about that a little later, Mrs. Hale," he said. "I'm anxious to get the lay of things upstairs now."

He moved toward the stair door, followed by the two men.

"I suppose anything Mrs. Peters does'll be all right?" the sheriff inquired. "She was to take in some clothes for her, you know—and a few little things. We left in such a hurry yesterday."

The county attorney looked at the two women whom they were leaving alone there among the kitchen things.

100 "Yes—Mrs. Peters," he said, his glance resting on the woman who was not Mrs. Peters, the big farmer woman who stood behind the sheriff's wife. "Of course Mrs. Peters is one of us," he said, in a manner of entrusting responsibility. "And keep your eye out, Mrs. Peters, for anything that might be of use. No telling; you women might come upon a clue to the motive—and that's the thing we need."

Mr. Hale rubbed his face after the fashion of a showman getting ready for a pleasantry.

"But would the women know a clue if they did come upon it?" he said; and, having delivered himself of this, he followed the others through the stair door.

The women stood motionless and silent, listening to the footsteps, first upon the stairs, then in the room above them.

Then, as if releasing herself from something strange, Mrs. Hale began to arrange the dirty pans under the sink, which the county attorney's disdainful push of the foot had deranged.

105 "I'd hate to have men comin' into my kitchen," she said testily—"snoopin' round and criticizin'."

"Of course it's no more than their duty," said the sheriff's wife, in her manner of timid acquiescence.

"Duty's all right," replied Mrs. Hale bluffly; "but I guess that deputy sheriff that come out to make the fire might have got a little of this on." She gave the roller towel a pull. "Wish I'd thought of that sooner! Seems mean to talk about her for not having things slicked up, when she had to come away in such a hurry."

She looked around the kitchen. Certainly it was not "slicked up." Her eye was held by a bucket of sugar on a low shelf. The cover was off the wooden bucket, and beside it was a paper bag—half full.

Mrs. Hale moved toward it.

110 "She was putting this in there," she said to herself—slowly.

She thought of the flour in her kitchen at home—half sifted, half not sifted. She had been interrupted, and had left things half done. What had interrupted Minnie Foster? Why had that work been left half done? She made a move as if to finish it,—unfinished things always bothered her,—and then she glanced around and saw that Mrs. Peters was watching her—and she didn't want Mrs. Peters to get that feeling she had got of work begun and then—for some reason—not finished.

"It's a shame about her fruit," she said, and walked toward the cupboard that the county attorney had opened, and got on the chair, murmuring: "I wonder if it's all gone."

It was a sorry enough looking sight, but "Here's one that's all right," she said at last. She held it toward the light. "This is cherries, too." She looked again. "I declare I believe that's the only one."

With a sigh, she got down from the chair, went to the sink, and wiped off the bottle.

"She'll feel awful bad, after all her hard work in the hot weather. I remember the after-   115
noon I put up my cherries last summer."

She set the bottle on the table, and, with another sigh, started to sit down in the rocker. But she did not sit down. Something kept her from sitting down in that chair. She straightened—stepped back, and, half turned away, stood looking at it, seeing the woman who had sat there "pleatin' at her apron."

The thin voice of the sheriff's wife broke in upon her: "I must be getting those things from the front-room closet." She opened the door into the other room, started in, stepped back. "You coming with me, Mrs. Hale?" she asked nervously. "You—you could help me get them."

They were soon back—the stark coldness of that shut-up room was not a thing to linger in.

"My!" said Mrs. Peters, dropping the things on the table and hurrying to the stove.

Mrs. Hale stood examining the clothes the woman who was being detained in town had   120
said she wanted.

"Wright was close!"° she exclaimed, holding up a shabby black skirt that bore the marks of much making over. "I think maybe that's why she kept so much to herself. I s'pose she felt she couldn't do her part; and then, you don't enjoy things when you feel shabby. She used to wear pretty clothes and be lively—when she was Minnie Foster, one of the town girls, singing in the choir. But that—oh, that was twenty years ago."

With a carefulness in which there was something tender, she folded the shabby clothes and piled them at one corner of the table. She looked up at Mrs. Peters, and there was something in the other woman's look that irritated her.

"She don't care," she said to herself. "Much difference it makes to her whether Minnie Foster had pretty clothes when she was a girl."

Then she looked again, and she wasn't so sure; in fact, she hadn't at any time been per-fectly sure about Mrs. Peters. She had that shrinking manner, and yet her eyes looked as if they could see a long way into things.

"This all you was to take in?" asked Mrs. Hale.   125

"No," said the sheriff's wife; "she said she wanted an apron. Funny thing to want," she ventured in her nervous little way, "for there's not much to get you dirty in jail, goodness knows. But I suppose just to make her feel more natural. If you're used to wearing an apron—. She said they were in the bottom drawer of this cupboard. Yes—here they are. And then her little shawl that always hung on the stair door."

She took the small gray shawl from behind the door leading upstairs, and stood a minute looking at it.

Suddenly Mrs. Hale took a quick step toward the other woman.

"Mrs. Peters!"

"Yes, Mrs. Hale?"   130

"Do you think she—did it?"

A frightened look blurred the other thing in Mrs. Peters' eyes.

"Oh, I don't know," she said, in a voice that seemed to shrink away from the subject.

°*close:* that is, frugal, tightfisted.

"Well, I don't think she did," affirmed Mrs. Hale stoutly. "Asking for an apron, and her little shawl. Worryin' about her fruit."

135 "Mr. Peters says—." Footsteps were heard in the room above; she stopped, looked up, then went on in a lowered voice: "Mr. Peters says—it looks bad for her. Mr. Henderson is awful sarcastic in a speech, and he's going to make fun of her saying she didn't—wake up."

For a moment Mrs. Hale had no answer. Then, "Well, I guess John Wright didn't wake up—when they was slippin' that rope under his neck," she muttered.

"No, it's *strange*," breathed Mrs. Peters. "They think it was such a—funny way to kill a man."

She began to laugh; at sound of the laugh, abruptly stopped.

"That's just what Mr. Hale said," said Mrs. Hale, in a resolutely natural voice. "There was a gun in the house. He says that's what he can't understand."

140 "Mr. Henderson said, coming out, that what was needed for the case was a motive. Something to show anger—or sudden feeling."

"Well, I don't see any signs of anger around here," said Mrs. Hale, "I don't—" She stopped. It was as if her mind tripped on something. Her eye was caught by a dish-towel in the middle of the kitchen table. Slowly she moved toward the table. One half of it was wiped clean, the other half messy. Her eyes made a slow, almost unwilling turn to the bucket of sugar and the half empty bag beside it. Things begun—and not finished.

After a moment she stepped back, and said, in that manner of releasing herself:

"Wonder how they're finding things upstairs? I hope she had it a little more redd up° up there. You know,"—she paused, and feeling gathered,—"it seems kind of *sneaking*: locking her up in town and coming out here to get her own house to turn against her!"

"But, Mrs. Hale," said the sheriff's wife, "the law is the law."

145 "I s'pose 'tis," answered Mrs. Hale shortly.

She turned to the stove, saying something about that fire not being much to brag of. She worked with it a minute, and when she straightened up she said aggressively:

"The law is the law—and a bad stove is a bad stove. How'd you like to cook on this?"— pointing with the poker to the broken lining. She opened the oven door and started to express her opinion of the oven; but she was swept into her own thoughts, thinking of what it would mean, year after year, to have that stove to wrestle with. The thought of Minnie Foster trying to bake in that oven—and the thought of her never going over to see Minnie Foster—.

She was startled by hearing Mrs. Peters say: "A person gets discouraged—and loses heart."

The sheriff's wife had looked from the stove to the sink—to the pail of water which had been carried in from outside. The two women stood there silent, above them the footsteps of the men who were looking for evidence against the woman who had worked in that kitchen. That look of seeing into things, of seeing through a thing to something else, was in the eyes of the sheriff's wife now. When Mrs. Hale next spoke to her, it was gently:

150 "Better loosen up your things, Mrs. Peters. We'll not feel them when we go out."

Mrs. Peters went to the back of the room to hang up the fur tippet she was wearing. A moment later she exclaimed, "Why, she was piecing a quilt," and held up a large sewing basket piled high with quilt pieces.

Mrs. Hale spread some of the blocks on the table.

"It's a log-cabin pattern," she said, putting several of them together, "Pretty, isn't it?"

They were so engaged with the quilt that they did not hear the footsteps on the stairs. Just as the stair door opened Mrs. Hale was saying:

155 "Do you suppose she was going to quilt it or just knot it?"

The sheriff threw up his hands.

°*redd up*: neat.

"They wonder whether she was going to quilt it or just knot it!"

There was a laugh for the ways of women, a warming of hands over the stove, and then the county attorney said briskly:

"Well, let's go right out to the barn and get that cleared up."

"I don't see as there's anything so strange," Mrs. Hale said resentfully, after the outside door had closed on the three men—"our taking up our time with little things while we're waiting for them to get the evidence. I don't see as it's anything to laugh about."

"Of course they've got awful important things on their minds," said the sheriff's wife apologetically.

They returned to an inspection of the block for the quilt. Mrs. Hale was looking at the fine, even sewing, and preoccupied with thoughts of the woman who had done that sewing, when she heard the sheriff's wife say, in a queer tone:

"Why, look at this one."

She turned to take the block held out to her.

"The sewing," said Mrs. Peters, in a troubled way, "All the rest of them have been so nice and even—but—this one. Why, it looks as if she didn't know what she was about!"

Their eyes met—something flashed to life, passed between them; then, as if with an effort, they seemed to pull away from each other. A moment Mrs. Hale sat there, her hands folded over that sewing which was so unlike all the rest of the sewing. Then she had pulled a knot and drawn the threads.

"Oh, what are you doing, Mrs. Hale?" asked the sheriff's wife, startled.

"Just pulling out a stitch or two that's not sewed very good," said Mrs. Hale mildly.

"I don't think we ought to touch things," Mrs. Peters said, a little helplessly.

"I'll just finish up this end," answered Mrs. Hale, still in that mild, matter-of-fact fashion.

She threaded a needle and started to replace bad sewing with good. For a little while she sewed in silence. Then, in that thin, timid voice, she heard:

"Mrs. Hale!"

"Yes, Mrs. Peters?"

"What do you suppose she was so—nervous about?"

"Oh, I don't know," said Mrs. Hale, as if dismissing a thing not important enough to spend much time on. "I don't know as she was—nervous. I sew awful queer sometimes when I'm just tired."

She cut a thread, and out of the corner of her eye looked up at Mrs. Peters. The small, lean face of the sheriff's wife seemed to have tightened up. Her eyes had that look of peering into something. But next moment she moved, and said in her thin, indecisive way:

"Well, I must get those clothes wrapped. They may be through sooner than we think. I wonder where I could find a piece of paper—and string."

"In that cupboard, maybe," suggested to Mrs. Hale, after a glance around.

One piece of the crazy sewing remained unripped. Mrs. Peter's back turned, Martha Hale now scrutinized that piece, compared it with the dainty, accurate sewing of the other blocks. The difference was startling. Holding this block made her feel queer, as if the distracted thoughts of the woman who had perhaps turned to it to try and quiet herself were communicating themselves to her.

Mrs. Peters' voice roused her.

"Here's a bird-cage," she said. "Did she have a bird, Mrs. Hale?"

"Why, I don't know whether she did or not." She turned to look at the cage Mrs. Peters was holding up. "I've not been here in so long." She sighed. "There was a man round last year selling canaries cheap—but I don't know as she took one. Maybe she did. She used to sing real pretty herself."

Mrs. Peters looked around the kitchen.

"Seems kind of funny to think of a bird here." She half laughed—an attempt to put up a barrier. "But she must have had one—or why would she have a cage? I wonder what happened to it."

185 "I suppose maybe the cat got it," suggested Mrs. Hale, resuming her sewing.

"No; she didn't have a cat. She's got that feeling some people have about cats—being afraid of them. When they brought her to our house yesterday, my cat got in the room, and she was real upset and asked me to take it out."

"My sister Bessie was like that," laughed Mrs. Hale.

The sheriff's wife did not reply. The silence made Mrs. Hale turn round. Mrs. Peters was examining the bird-cage.

"Look at this door," she said slowly. "It's broke. One hinge has been pulled apart."

190 Mrs. Hale came nearer.

"Looks as if someone must have been—rough with it."

Again their eyes met—startled, questioning, apprehensive. For a moment neither spoke nor stirred. Then Mrs. Hale, turning away, said brusquely:

"If they're going to find any evidence, I wish they'd be about it. I don't like this place."

"But I'm awful glad you came with me, Mrs. Hale." Mrs. Peters put the bird-cage on the table and sat down. "It would be lonesome for me—sitting here alone."

195 "Yes, it would, wouldn't it?" agreed Mrs. Hale, a certain determined naturalness in her voice. She had picked up the sewing, but now it dropped in her lap, and she murmured in a different voice: "But I tell you what I *do* wish, Mrs Peters. I wish I had come over sometimes when she was here. I wish—I had."

"But of course you were awful busy, Mrs. Hale. Your house—and your children."

"I could've come," retorted Mrs. Hale shortly. "I stayed away because it weren't cheerful—and that's why I ought to have come. I"—she looked around—"I've never liked this place. Maybe because it's down in a hollow and you don't see the road. I don't know what it is, but it's a lonesome place, and always was. I wish I had come over to see Minnie Foster sometimes. I can see now—" She did not put it into words.

"Well, you mustn't reproach yourself," counseled Mrs. Peters. "Somehow, we just don't see how it is with other folks till—something comes up."

"Not having children makes less work," mused Mrs. Hale, after a silence, "but it makes a quiet house—and Wright out to work all day—and no company when he did come in. Did you know John Wright, Mrs. Peters?"

200 "Not to know him. I've seen him in town. They say he was a good man."

"Yes—good," conceded John Wright's neighbor grimly. "He didn't drink, and kept his word as well as most, I guess, and paid his debts. But he was a hard man, Mrs. Peters. Just to pass the time of day with him—." She stopped, shivered a little. "Like a raw wind that gets to the bone." Her eye fell upon the cage on the table before her, and she added, almost bitterly: "I should think she would've wanted a bird!"

Suddenly she leaned forward, looking intently at the cage. "But what do you s'pose went wrong with it?"

"I don't know," returned Mrs. Peters; "unless it got sick and died."

But after she said it she reached over and swung the broken door. Both women watched it as if somehow held by it.

205 "You didn't know—her?" Mrs. Hale asked, a gentler note in her voice.

"Not till they brought her yesterday," said the sheriff's wife.

"She—come to think of it, she was kind of like a bird herself. Real sweet and pretty, but kind of timid and—fluttery. How—she—did—change."

That held her for a long time. Finally, as if struck with a happy thought and relieved to get back to everyday things, she exclaimed:

"Tell you what, Mrs. Peters, why don't you take the quilt in with you? It might take up her mind."

"Why, I think that's a real nice idea, Mrs. Hale," agreed the sheriff's wife, as if she too   210
were glad to come into the atmosphere of a simple kindness. "There couldn't possibly be
any objection to that, could there? Now, just what will I take? I wonder if her patches are in
here—and her things?"

They turned to the sewing basket.

"Here's some red," said Mrs. Hale, bringing out a roll of cloth. Underneath that was a
box. "Here, maybe her scissors are in here—and her things." She held it up. "What a pretty
box! I'll warrant that was something she had a long time ago—when she was a girl."

She held it in her hand a moment; then, with a little sigh, opened it.

Instantly her hand went to her nose.

"Why—!"   215

Mrs. Peters drew nearer—then turned away.

"There's something wrapped up in this piece of silk," faltered Mrs. Hale.

"This isn't her scissors," said Mrs. Peters, in a shrinking voice.

Her hand not steady, Mrs. Hale raised the piece of silk. "Oh, Mrs. Peters!" she cried.
"It's—"

Mrs. Peters bent closer.   220

"It's the bird," she whispered.

"But, Mrs. Peters!" cried Mrs. Hale. "*Look* at it! Its *neck*—look at its neck! It's all—other
side *to.*"

She held the box away from her.

The sheriff's wife again bent closer.

"Somebody wrung its neck," said she, in a voice that was slow and deep.   225

And then again the eyes of the two women met—this time clung together in a look of
dawning comprehension, of growing horror. Mrs. Peters looked from the dead bird to the
broken door of the cage. Again their eyes met. And just then there was a sound at the outside door.

Mrs. Hale slipped the box under the quilt pieces in the basket, and sank into the chair
before it. Mrs. Peters stood holding to the table. The county attorney and the sheriff came in
from outside.

"Well, ladies," said the county attorney, as one turning from serious things to little pleasantries, "have you decided whether she was going to quilt it or knot it?"

"We think," began the sheriff's wife in a flurried voice, "that she was going to—knot it."

He was too preoccupied to notice the change that came in her voice on that last.   230

"Well, that's very interesting, I'm sure," he said tolerantly. He caught sight of the bird-
cage. "Has the bird flown?"

"We think the cat got it," said Mrs. Hale in a voice curiously even.

He was walking up and down, as if thinking something out.

"Is there a cat?" he asked absently.

Mrs. Hale shot a look up at the sheriff's wife.

"Well, not *now*," said Mrs. Peters. "They're superstitious, you know; they leave."   235

She sank into her chair.

The county attorney did not heed her. "No sign at all of anyone having come in from the
outside," he said to Peters, in the manner of continuing an interrupted conversation. "Their
own rope. Now let's go upstairs again and go over it, piece by piece. It would have to have
been someone who knew just the—"

The stair door closed behind them and their voices were lost.

The two women sat motionless, not looking at each other, but as if peering into some-   240
thing and at the same time holding back. When they spoke now it was as if they were afraid
of what they were saying, but as if they could not help saying it.

"She liked the bird," said Martha Hale, low and slowly. "She was going to bury it in that
pretty box."

"When I was a girl," said Mrs. Peters, under her breath, "my kitten—there was a boy took a hatchet, and before my eyes—before I could get there—" She covered her face an instant. "If they hadn't held me back I would have"—she caught herself, looked upstairs where footsteps were heard, and finished weakly—"hurt him."

Then they sat without speaking or moving.

"I wonder how it would seem," Mrs. Hale at last began, as if feeling her way over strange ground—"never to have had any children around?" Her eyes made a slow sweep of the kitchen, as if seeing what that kitchen had meant through all the years. "No, Wright wouldn't like the bird," she said after that—"a thing that sang. She used to sing. He killed that too." Her voice tightened.

245   Mrs. Peters moved uneasily.

"Of course we don't know who killed the bird."

"I knew John Wright," was Mrs. Hale's answer.

"It was an awful thing was done in this house that night, Mrs. Hale," said the sheriff's wife. "Killing a man while he slept—slipping a thing round his neck that choked the life out of him."

Mrs. Hale's hand went out to the bird cage.

250   "His neck. Choked the life out of him."

"We don't *know* who killed him," whispered Mrs. Peters wildly. "We don't *know.*"

Mrs. Hale had not moved. "If there had been years and years of—nothing, then a bird to sing to you, it would be awful—still—after the bird was still."

It was as if something within her not herself had spoken, and it found in Mrs. Peters something she did not know as herself.

"I know what stillness is," she said, in a queer, monotonous voice. "When we homesteaded in Dakota, and my first baby died—after he was two years old—and me with no other then—"

255   Mrs. Hale stirred.

"How soon do you suppose they'll be through looking for the evidence?"

"I know what stillness is," repeated Mrs. Peters, in just that same way. Then she too pulled back. "The law has got to punish crime, Mrs. Hale," she said in her tight little way.

"I wish you'd seen Minnie Foster," was the answer, "when she wore a white dress with blue ribbons, and stood up there in the choir and sang."

The picture of that girl, the fact that she had lived neighbor to that girl for twenty years, and had let her die for lack of life, was suddenly more than she could bear.

260   "Oh, I *wish* I'd come over here once in a while!" she cried. "That was a crime! Who's going to punish that?"

"We mustn't take on," said Mrs. Peters, with a frightened look toward the stairs.

"I might 'a' *known* she needed help! I tell you, it's *queer*, Mrs. Peters. We live close together, and we live far apart. We all go through the same things—it's all just a different kind of the same thing! If it weren't—why do you and I *understand?* Why do we *know*—what we know this minute?"

She dashed her hand across her eyes. Then, seeing the jar of fruit on the table, she reached for it and choked out:

"If I was you I wouldn't *tell* her her fruit was gone! Tell her it *ain't*. Tell her it's all right—all of it. Here—take this in to prove it to her! She—she may never know whether it was broke or not."

265   She turned away.

Mrs. Peters reached out for the bottle of fruit as if she were glad to take it—as if touching a familiar thing, having something to do, could keep her from something else. She got up, looked about for something to wrap the fruit in, took a petticoat from the pile of clothes she had brought from the front room, and nervously started winding that round the bottle.

"My!" she began, in a high; false voice, "it's a good thing the men couldn't hear us! Getting all stirred up over a little thing like a—dead canary." She hurried over that. "As if that could have anything to do with—with—My, wouldn't they *laugh?*"

Footsteps were heard on the stairs.

"Maybe they would," muttered Mrs. Hale—"maybe they wouldn't."

"No, Peters," said the county attorney incisively; "it's all perfectly clear, except the rea-   270
son for doing it. But you know juries when it comes to women. If there was some definite thing—something to show. Something to make a story about. A thing that would connect up with this clumsy way of doing it."

In a covert way Mrs. Hale looked at Mrs. Peters. Mrs. Peters was looking at her. Quickly they looked away from each other. The outer door opened and Mr. Hale came in.

"I've got the team° round now," he said. "Pretty cold out there."

"I'm going to stay here awhile by myself," the county attorney suddenly announced. "You can send Frank out for me, can't you?" he asked the sheriff. "I want to go over every-thing. I'm not satisfied we can't do better."

Again, for one brief moment, the two women's eyes found one another.

The sheriff came up to the table.   275

"Did you want to see what Mrs. Peters was going to take in?"

The county attorney picked up the apron. He laughed.

"Oh, I guess they're not very dangerous things the ladies have picked out."

Mrs. Hale's hand was on the sewing basket in which the box was concealed. She felt that she ought to take her hand off the basket. She did not seem able to. He picked up one of the quilt blocks which she had piled on to cover the box. Her eyes felt like fire. She had a feel-ing that if he took up the basket she would snatch it from him.

But he did not take it up. With another little laugh, he turned away, saying: 280

"No; Mrs. Peters doesn't need supervising. For that matter, a sheriff's wife is married to the law. Ever think of it that way, Mrs. Peters?"

Mrs. Peters was standing beside the table. Mrs. Hale shot a look up at her; but she could not see her face. Mrs. Peters had turned away. When she spoke, her voice was muffled.

"Not—just that way," she said.

"Married to the law!" chuckled Mrs. Peters' husband. He moved toward the door into the front room, and said to the county attorney:

"I just want you to come in here a minute, George. We ought to take a look at these   285
windows."

"Oh—windows," said the county attorney scoffingly.

"We'll be right out, Mr. Hale," said the sheriff to the farmer, who was still waiting by the door.

Hale went to look after the horses. The sheriff followed the county attorney into the other room. Again—for one final moment—the two women were alone in that kitchen.

Martha Hale sprang up, her hands tight together, looking at that other woman, with whom it rested. At first she could not see her eyes, for the sheriff's wife had not turned back since she turned away at that suggestion of being married to the law. But now Mrs. Hale made her turn back. Her eyes made her turn back. Slowly, unwillingly, Mrs. Peters turned her head until her eyes met the eyes of the other woman. There was a moment when they held each other in a steady, burning look in which there was no evasion nor flinching. Then Martha Hale's eyes pointed the way to the basket in which was hidden the thing that would make certain the conviction of the other woman—that woman who was not there and yet who had been there with them all through that hour.

°*team:* team of horses pulling the buggy in which the group had come.

290 For a moment Mrs. Peters did not move. And then she did it. With a rush forward, she threw back the quilt pieces, got the box, tried to put it in her handbag. It was too big. Desperately she opened it, started to take the bird out. But there she broke—she could not touch the bird. She stood there helpless, foolish.

There was the sound of a knob turning in the inner door. Martha Hale snatched the box from the sheriff's wife, and got it in the pocket of her big coat just as the sheriff and the county attorney came back into the kitchen.

"Well, Henry," said the county attorney facetiously, "at least we found out that she was not going to quilt it. She was going to—what is it you call it, ladies?"

Mrs. Hale's hand was against the pocket of her coat.

"We call it—knot it, Mr. Henderson."

QUESTIONS

1. Who is the central character? That is, on whom does the story focus?
2. Describe the differences between Mrs. Hale and Mrs. Peters, in terms of their status, backgrounds, and comparative strengths of character.
3. Why do the two women not voice their conclusions about the murderer? How does Glaspell show that they both know the murderer's identity, the reasons, and the method? Why do they both "cover up" at the story's conclusion?

KATHERINE MANSFIELD (1888–1923)

"Katherine Mansfield" was the pen name of Kathleen Mansfield Beauchamp Murry. She was brought up in a prosperous household in New Zealand, and in the early years of the twentieth century she went to England to study at Queen's College. An accomplished cellist, she had been a serious student of music, but she was discouraged from that profession by her father. She then turned to writing. Before she was thirty she realized that she was afflicted with tuberculosis, and spent many of her remaining years desperately seeking a cure. Without the benefit of modern antibiotics, however, her doom was sealed, and she succumbed to the disease in her thirty-fifth year. During her lifetime her collections were In a German Pension *(1911),* Bliss and Other Stories *(1920), and* The Garden Party and Other Stories *(1922), which included "Miss Brill." Her posthumous collections were* The Dove's Nest *(1923) and* Something Childish *(1924). Her husband and literary executor, the critic John Middleton Murry, arranged for a number of other publications after her death, including her letters and selections from her journals.*

Miss Brill (1920)

Although it was so brilliantly fine—the blue sky powdered with gold and great spots of light like white wine splashed over the Jardins Publiques°—Miss Brill° was glad that she had decided on her fur. The air was motionless, but when you opened your mouth there was just a faint chill, like a chill from a glass of iced water before you sip, and now and again a leaf came drifting—from nowhere, from the sky. Miss Brill put up her hand and touched her fur. Dear little thing! It was nice to feel it again. She had taken it out of its box that afternoon,

---

°*Jardins Publiques:* public gardens or park. The setting of the story is apparently a French seaside town.
°*Miss Brill:* Brill is the name of a common deep-sea flatfish.

shaken out the moth-powder, given it a good brush, and rubbed the life back into the dim little eyes. "What has been happening to me?" said the sad little eyes. Oh, how sweet it was to see them snap at her again from the red eiderdown! . . . But the nose, which was of some black composition, wasn't at all firm. It must have had a knock, somehow. Never mind—a little dab of black sealing-wax when the time came—when it was absolutely necessary. . . . Little rogue! Yes, she really felt like that about it. Little rogue biting its tail just by her left ear. She could have taken it off and laid it on her lap and stroked it. She felt a tingling in her hands and arms, but that came from walking, she supposed. And when she breathed, something light and sad—no, not sad, exactly—something gentle seemed to move in her bosom.

There were a number of people out this afternoon, far more than last Sunday. And the band sounded louder and gayer. That was because the Season had begun. For although the band played all the year round on Sundays, out of season it was never the same. It was like someone playing with only the family to listen; it didn't care how it played if there weren't any strangers present. Wasn't the conductor wearing a new coat, too? She was sure it was new. He scraped with his foot and flapped his arms like a rooster about to crow, and bandsmen sitting in the green rotunda blew out their cheeks and glared at the music. Now there came a little "flutey" bit—very pretty!—a little chain of bright drops. She was sure it would be repeated. It was; she lifted her head and smiled.

Only two people shared her "special" seat: a fine old man in a velvet coat, his hands clasped over a huge carved walking-stick, and a big old woman, sitting upright, with a roll of knitting on her embroidered apron. They did not speak. This was disappointing, for Miss Brill always looked forward to the conversation. She had become really quite expert, she thought, at listening as though she didn't listen, at sitting in other people's lives just for a minute while they talked round her.

She glanced, sideways, at the old couple. Perhaps they would go soon. Last Sunday, too, hadn't been as interesting as usual. An Englishman and his wife, he wearing a dreadful Panama hat and she button boots. And she'd gone on the whole time about how she ought to wear spectacles; she knew she needed them; but that it was no good getting any; they'd be sure to break and they'd never keep on. And he'd been so patient. He'd suggested everything—gold rims, the kind that curved round your ears, little pads inside the bridge. No, nothing would please her. "They'll always be sliding down my nose!" Miss Brill had wanted to shake her.

The old people sat on the bench, still as statues. Never mind, there was always the crowd to watch. To and fro, in front of the flower-beds and the band rotunda, the couples and groups paraded, stopped to talk, to greet, to buy a handful of flowers from the old beggar who had his tray fixed to the railings. Little children ran among them, swooping and laughing; little boys with big white silk bows under their chins, little girls, little French dolls, dressed up in velvet and lace. And sometimes a tiny staggerer came suddenly rocking into the open from under the trees, stopped, stared, as suddenly sat down "flop," until its small high-stepping mother, like a young hen, rushed scolding to its rescue. Other people sat on the benches and green chairs, but they were nearly always the same, Sunday after Sunday, and—Miss Brill had often noticed—there was something funny about nearly all of them. They were odd, silent, nearly all old, and from the way they stared they looked as though they'd just come from dark little rooms or even—even cupboards!

Behind the rotunda the slender trees with yellow leaves down drooping and through them just a line of sea, and beyond the blue sky with gold-veined clouds.

Tum-tum-tum tiddle-um! tiddle-um! tum tiddle-um tum ta! blew the band.

Two young girls in red came by and two young soldiers in blue met them, and they laughed and paired and went off arm-in-arm. Two peasant women with funny straw hats passed, gravely, leading beautiful smoke-coloured donkeys. A cold, pale nun hurried by. A beautiful woman came along and dropped her bunch of violets, and a little boy ran after to hand them to her, and she took them and threw them away as if they'd been poisoned. Dear me! Miss Brill didn't know whether to admire that or not! And now an ermine toque° and a gentleman in grey met just in front of her. He was tall, stiff, dignified and she was wearing the ermine toque she'd bought when her hair was yellow. Now everything, her hair, her face, even her eyes, was the same colour as the shabby ermine, and her hand, in its cleaned glove, lifted to dab her lips, was a tiny yellowish paw. Oh, she was so pleased to see him— delighted! She rather thought they were going to meet that afternoon. She described where she'd been—everywhere, here, there, along by the sea. The day was so charming—didn't he agree? And wouldn't he, perhaps? . . . But he shook his head, lighted a cigarette, slowly breathed a great deep puff into her face, and, even while she was still talking and laughing, flicked the match away and walked on. The ermine toque was alone; she smiled more brightly than ever. But even the band seemed to know what she was feeling and played more softly, played tenderly, and the drum beat, "The Brute! The Brute!" over and over. What would she do? What was going to happen now? But as Miss Brill wondered, the er- mine toque turned, raised her hand as though she'd seen some one else, much nicer, just over there, and pattered away. And the band changed again and played more quickly, more gaily than ever, and the old couple on Miss Brill's seat got up and marched away, and such a funny old man with long whiskers hobbled along in time to the music and was nearly knocked over by four girls walking abreast.

Oh, how fascinating it was! How she enjoyed it! How she loved sitting here, watching it all! It was like a play. It was exactly like a play. Who could believe the sky at the back wasn't painted? But it wasn't till a little brown dog trotted on solemn and then slowly trotted off, like a little "theatre" dog, a little dog that had been drugged, that Miss Brill discovered what it was that made it so exciting. They were all on the stage. They weren't only the au- dience, not only looking on; they were acting. Even she had a part and came every Sunday. No doubt somebody would have noticed if she hadn't been there; she was part of the per- formance after all. How strange she'd never thought of it like that before! And yet it ex- plained why she made such a point of starting from home at just the same time each week—so as not to be late for the performance—and it also explained why she had quite a queer, shy feeling at telling her English pupils how she spent her Sunday afternoons. No wonder! Miss Brill nearly laughed out loud. She was on the stage. She thought of the old in- valid gentleman to whom she read the newspaper four afternoons a week while he slept in the garden. She had got quite used to the frail head on the cotton pillow, the hollowed eyes, the open mouth and the high pinched nose. If he'd been dead she mightn't have noticed for weeks; she wouldn't have minded. But suddenly he knew he was having the paper read to him by an actress! "An actress!" The old head lifted; two points of light quivered in the old eyes. "An actress—are ye?" And Miss Brill smoothed the newspaper as though it were the manuscript of her part and said gently: "Yes, I have been an actress for a long time."

10   The band had been having a rest. Now they started again. And what they played was warm, sunny, yet there was just a faint chill—a something, what was it?—not sadness—no, not sadness—a something that made you want to sing. The tune lifted, lifted, the light shone; and it seemed to Miss Brill that in another moment all of them, all the whole compa- ny, would begin singing. The young ones, the laughing ones who were moving together, they would begin, and the men's voices, very resolute and brave, would join them. And then she too, she too, and the others on the benches—they would come in with a kind of accompaniment—something low, that scarcely rose or fell, something so beautiful— moving. . . . And Miss Brill's eyes filled with tears and she looked smiling at all the other

---

°*ermine toque:* close-fitting hat made of the white fur of an ermine; here the phrase stands for the woman wearing the hat.

members of the company. Yes, we understand, we understand, she thought—though what they understood she didn't know.

Just at the moment a boy and girl came and sat down where the old couple had been. They were beautifully dressed; they were in love. The hero and heroine, of course, just arrived from his father's yacht. And still soundlessly singing, still with that trembling smile, Miss Brill prepared to listen.

"No, not now," said the girl, "Not here, I can't."

"But why? Because of that stupid old thing at the end there?" asked the boy. "Why does she come here at all—who wants her? Why doesn't she keep her silly old mug at home?"

"It's her fu-fur which is so funny," giggled the girl. "It's exactly like a fried whiting."

"Ah, be off with you!" said the boy in an angry whisper. Then: "Tell me, ma petite chérie—"   15

"No, not here," said the girl, "Not *yet*."

On her way home she usually bought a slice of honeycake at the baker's. It was her Sunday treat. Sometimes there was an almond in her slice, sometimes not. It made a great difference. If there was an almond it was like carrying home a tiny present—a surprise—something that might very well not have been there. She hurried on the almond Sundays and struck the match for the kettle in quite a dashing way.

But to-day she passed the baker's by, climbed the stairs, went into the little dark room—her room like a cupboard—and sat down on the red eiderdown. She sat there for a long time. The box that the fur came out of was on the bed. She unclasped the necklet quickly; quickly, without looking, laid it inside. But when she put the lid on she thought she heard something crying.

QUESTIONS

1. Describe the scene in which the action of this story occurs.

2. What details about the life of Miss Brill do we learn from the story? What sort of life does she live? How often does she come to the park? How is her life comparable to the lives of the old people sitting on the benches as described in paragraph 5?

3. Miss Brill observes a number of people who are walking in the park, and she overhears some of their conversations. Why does Mansfield described these scenes, or vignettes, in so detailed a way?

4. What is the significance of the young couple near the story's end? What is Miss Brill's response to them? What is happening to Miss Brill as the story ends?

AMY TAN (b. 1952)

Amy Tan was born in Oakland, California, several years after her parents had left their native China to settle in the San Francisco Bay Area. Early in her life she exhibited talent as a writer, winning a first prize for essay writing at the age of eight. Her family endured the untimely deaths of her father and brother in 1967 and 1968, and the remaining family spent time afterward in Switzerland. She attended a number of U.S. colleges, including San Jose State University, where she graduated with honors in 1972 and received an M.A. in 1973. After graduating she did freelance business writing for companies such as IBM and Pacific Bell. By 1985 she had decided to devote herself to the writing of fiction, and she launched her career in 1986 with the publication of her first short story, "End Game." In 1989 her The Joy Luck Club, *an interlinked collection of stories, was published and enjoyed forty weeks on the* New York Times *best-sellers list. Her other major books are* The Kitchen God's Wife *(1991),* The Hundred Secret Senses *(1995), and* The Bonesetter's Daughter *(2001), which had been earlier excerpted for publication in* The New Yorker. *Tan has also written two children's books,* The Moon Lady *(1992) and* SAGWA The Chinese Siamese Cat *(1994). She collaborates with the novelist Stephen King and the humorist Dave Barry in a "literary garage band, the Rock Bottom Remainders," which raises money for literacy causes and also for groups devoted to First Amendment rights. In the fall of 2008, The San Francisco Opera was scheduled to perform the world première of* The Bone Setter's Daughter, *an opera based on Tan's novel. Stewart Wallace is the composer, and Tan is the librettist. "Two Kinds" is taken from* The Joy Luck Club.

🍁 Two Kinds (1989)

My mother believed you could be anything you wanted to be in America. You could open a restaurant. You could work for the government and get good retirement. You could buy a house with almost no money down. You could become rich. You could become instantly famous.

"Of course you can be prodigy, too," my mother told me when I was nine. "You can be best anything. What does Auntie Lindo know? Her daughter, she is only best tricky."

America was where all my mother's hopes lay. She had come here in 1949 after losing everything in China: her mother and father, her family home, her first husband, and two daughters, twin baby girls. But she never looked back with regret. There were so many ways for things to get better.

We didn't immediately pick the right kind of prodigy. At first my mother thought I could be a Chinese Shirley Temple. We'd watch Shirley's old movies on TV as though they were training films. My mother would poke my arm and say, "*Ni kan*"—You watch. And I would see Shirley tapping her feet, or singing a sailor song, or pursing her lips into a very round O while saying, "Oh my goodness."

5   "*Ni kan*," said my mother as Shirley's eyes flooded with tears. "You already know how. Don't need talent for crying!"

Soon after my mother got this idea about Shirley Temple, she took me to a beauty training school in the Mission district and put me in the hands of a student who could barely hold the scissors without shaking. Instead of getting big fat curls, I emerged with an uneven mass of crinkly black fuzz. My mother dragged me off to the bathroom and tried to wet down my hair.

"You look like Negro Chinese," she lamented, as if I had done this on purpose.

The instructor of the beauty training school had to lop off these soggy clumps to make my hair even again. "Peter Pan is very popular these days," the instructor assured my mother. I now had hair the length of a boy's, with straight-across bangs that hung at a slant two inches above my eyebrows. I liked the haircut and it made me actually look forward to my future fame.

In fact, in the beginning, I was just as excited as my mother, maybe even more so. I pictured this prodigy part of me as many different images, trying each one on for size. I was a dainty ballerina girl standing by the curtains, waiting to hear the right music that would send me floating on my tiptoes. I was like the Christ child lifted out of the straw manger, crying with holy indignity. I was Cinderella stepping from her pumpkin carriage with sparkly cartoon music filling the air.

10   In all of my imaginings, I was filled with a sense that I would soon become *perfect*. My mother and father would adore me. I would be beyond reproach. I would never feel the need to sulk for anything.

But sometimes the prodigy in me became impatient. "If you don't hurry up and get me out of here, I'm disappearing for good," it warned. "And then you'll always be nothing."

• • •

Every night after dinner, my mother and I would sit at the Formica kitchen table. She would present new tests, taking her examples from stories of amazing children she had read in *Ripley's Believe It or Not*, or *Good Housekeeping, Reader's Digest*, and a dozen other magazines she kept in a pile in our bathroom. My mother got these magazines from people whose houses she cleaned. And since she cleaned many houses each week, we had a great assortment. She would look through them all, searching for stories about remarkable children.

The first night she brought out a story about a three-year-old boy who knew the capitals of all the states and even most of the European countries. A teacher was quoted as saying the little boy could also pronounce the names of the foreign cities correctly.

"What's the capital of Finland?" my mother asked me, looking at the magazine story.

All I knew was the capital of California, because Sacramento was the name of the street   15
we lived on in Chinatown. "Nairobi!" I guessed, saying the most foreign word I could think of. She checked to see if that was possibly one way to pronounce "Helsinki"before showing me the answer.

The tests got harder—multiplying numbers in my head, finding the queen of hearts in a deck of cards, trying to stand on my head without using my hands, predicting the daily temperatures in Los Angeles, New York, and London.

One night I had to look at a page from the Bible for three minutes and then report everything I could remember. "Now Jehoshaphat had riches° and honor in abundance and . . . that's all I remember, Ma," I said.

And after seeing my mother's disappointed face once again, something inside of me began to die. I hated the tests, the raised hopes and failed expectations. Before going to bed that night, I looked in the mirror above the bathroom sink and when I saw only my face staring back— and that it would always be this ordinary face—I began to cry. Such a sad, ugly girl! I made high-pitched noises like a crazed animal, trying to scratch out the face in the mirror.

And then I saw what seemed to be the prodigy side of me—because I had never seen that face before. I looked at my reflection, blinking so I could see more clearly. The girl staring back at me was angry, powerful. This girl and I were the same. I had new thoughts, willful thoughts, or rather thoughts filled with lots of won'ts. I won't let her change me, I promised myself. I won't be what I'm not.

So now on nights when my mother presented her tests, I performed listlessly, my head   20
propped on one arm. I pretended to be bored. And I was. I got so bored I started counting the bellows of the foghorns out on the bay while my mother drilled me in other areas. The sound was comforting and reminded me of the cow jumping over the moon. And the next day, I played a game with myself, seeing if my mother would give up on me before eight bellows. After a while I usually counted only one, maybe two bellows at most. At last she was beginning to give up hope.

Two or three months had gone by without any mention of my being a prodigy again. And then one day my mother was watching *The Ed Sullivan Show*° on TV. The TV was old and the sound kept shorting out. Every time my mother got halfway up from the sofa to adjust the set, the sound would go back on and Ed would be talking. As soon as she sat down, Ed would go silent again. She got up, the TV broke into loud piano music. She sat down. Silence. Up and down, back and forth, quiet and loud. It was like a stiff embraceless dance between her and the TV set. Finally she stood by the set with her hand on the sound dial.

°*Now Jehoshaphat had riches:* Jing-Mei had been told to report on the Hebrew monarch Jehoshaphat as narrated in the eighteenth chapter of II Chronicles.
°*The Ed Sullivan Show:* Ed Sullivan (1902–1974), originally a newspaper columnist, hosted this popular variety television show from 1948 to 1971.

She seemed entranced by the music, a little frenzied piano piece with this mesmerizing quality, sort of quick passages and then teasing lilting ones before it returned to the quick playful parts.

"*Ni kan*," my mother said, calling me over with hurried hand gestures, "Look here."

I could see why my mother was fascinated by the music. It was being pounded out by a little Chinese girl, about nine years old, with a Peter Pan haircut. The girl had the sauciness of a Shirley Temple. She was proudly modest like a proper Chinese child. And she also did this fancy sweep of a curtsy, so that the fluffy skirt of her white dress cascaded slowly to the floor like the petals of a large carnation.

25   In spite of these warning signs, I wasn't worried. Our family had no piano and we couldn't afford to buy one, let alone reams of sheet music and piano lessons. So I could be generous in my comments when my mother bad-mouthed the little girl on TV.

"Play note right, but doesn't sound good! No singing sound," complained my mother.

"What are you picking on her for?" I said carelessly. "She's pretty good. Maybe she's not the best, but she's trying hard." I knew almost immediately I would be sorry I said that.

"Just like you," she said. "Not the best. Because you not trying." She gave a little huff as she let go of the sound dial and sat down on the sofa.

The little Chinese girl sat down also to play an encore of "Anitra's Dance" by Grieg.° I remember the song, because later on I had to learn how to play it.

30   Three days after watching *The Ed Sullivan Show*, my mother told me what my schedule would be for piano lessons and piano practice. She had talked to Mr. Chong, who lived on the first floor of our apartment building. Mr. Chong was a retired piano teacher and my mother had traded housecleaning services for weekly lessons and a piano for me to practice on every day, two hours a day, from four until six.

When my mother told me this, I felt as though I had been sent to hell. I whined and then kicked my foot a little when I couldn't stand it anymore.

"Why don't you like me the way I am? I'm *not* a genius! I can't play the piano. And even if I could, I wouldn't go on TV if you paid me a million dollars!" I cried.

My mother slapped me. "Who ask you be genius?" she shouted. "Only ask you be you best. For you sake. You think I want you be genius? Hnnh! What for! Who ask you!"

"So ungrateful," I heard her mutter in Chinese. "If she had as much talent as she has temper, she would be famous now."

35   Mr. Chong, whom I secretly nicknamed Old Chong, was very strange, always tapping his fingers to the silent music of an invisible orchestra. He looked ancient in my eyes. He had lost most of the hair on top of his head and he wore thick glasses and had eyes that always looked tired and sleepy. But he must have been younger than I thought, since he lived with his mother and was not yet married.

I met Old Lady Chong once and that was enough. She had this peculiar smell like a baby that had done something in its pants. And her fingers felt like a dead person's, like an old peach I once found in the back of the refrigerator; the skin just slid off the meat when I picked it up.

I soon found out why Old Chong had retired from teaching piano. He was deaf. "Like Beethoven!" he shouted to me. "We're both listening only in our head!" And he would start to conduct his frantic silent sonatas.

Our lessons went like this. He would open the book and point to different things, explaining their purpose: "Key! Treble! Bass! No sharps or flats! So this is C major! Listen now and play after me!"

°*"Anitra's Dance" by Grieg*: a portion of the suite composed for Ibsen's *Peer Gynt* by Norwegian composer Edvard Grieg (1843–1907).

And then he would play the C scale a few times, a simple chord, and then, as if inspired by an old, unreachable itch, he gradually added more notes and running trills and a pounding bass until the music was really something quite grand.

I would play after him, the simple scale, the simple chord, and then I just played some nonsense that sounded like a cat running up and down on top of garbage cans. Old Chong smiled and applauded and then said, "Very good! But now you must learn to keep time!"   40

So that's how I discovered that Old Chong's eyes were too slow to keep up with the wrong notes I was playing. He went through the motions in half-time. To help me keep rhythm, he stood behind me, pushing down on my right shoulder for every beat. He balanced pennies on top of my wrists so I would keep them still as I slowly played scales and arpeggios. He had me curve my hand around an apple and keep that shape when playing chords. He marched stiffly to show me how to make each finger dance up and down, staccato like an obedient little soldier.

He taught me all these things, and that was how I also learned I could be lazy and get away with mistakes, lots of mistakes. If I hit the wrong notes because I hadn't practiced enough, I never corrected myself. I just kept playing in rhythm. And Old Chong kept conducting his own private reverie.

So maybe I never really gave myself a fair chance. I did pick up the basics pretty quickly, and I might have become a good pianist at that young age. But I was so determined not to try, not to be anybody different that I learned to play only the most earsplitting preludes, the most discordant hymns.

Over the next year, I practiced like this, dutifully in my own way. And then one day I heard my mother and her friend Lindo Jong both talking in a loud bragging tone of voice so others could hear. It was after church, and I was leaning against the brick wall wearing a dress with stiff white petticoats. Auntie Lindo's daughter, Waverly, who was about my age, was standing farther down the wall about five feet away. We had grown up together and shared all the closeness of two sisters squabbling over crayons and dolls. In other words, for the most part, we hated each other. I thought she was snotty. Waverly Jong had gained a certain amount of fame as "Chinatown's Littlest Chinese Chess Champion."

"She bring home too many trophy," lamented Auntie Lindo that Sunday. "All day she   45
play chess. All day I have no time do nothing but dust off her winnings." She threw a scolding look at Waverly, who pretended not to see her.

"You lucky you don't have this problem," said Auntie Lindo with a sigh to my mother.

And my mother squared her shoulders and bragged: "Our problem worser than yours. If we ask Jing-Mei wash dish, she hear nothing but music. It's like you can't stop this natural talent."

And right then, I was determined to put a stop to her foolish pride.

A few weeks later, Old Chong and my mother conspired to have me play in a talent show which would be held in the church hall. By then, my parents had saved up enough to buy me a secondhand piano, a black Wurlitzer spinet with a scarred bench. It was the showpiece of our living room.

For the talent show, I was to play a piece called "Pleading Child" from Schumann's   50
Scenes from Childhood.° It was a simple, moody piece that sounded more difficult than it was. I was supposed to memorize the whole thing, playing the repeat parts twice to make the piece sound longer. But I dawdled over it, playing a few bars and then cheating, looking up to see what notes followed. I never really listened to what I was playing. I daydreamed about being somewhere else, about being someone else.

°*Scenes from Childhood: Scenes from Childhood*, or *Kinderszenen* (1836), is one of the best-known works for piano by Robert Schumann (1810–1856).

The part I liked to practice best was the fancy curtsy: right foot out, touch the rose on the carpet with a pointed foot, sweep to the side, left leg bends, look up and smile.

My parents invited all the couples from the Joy Luck Club to witness my debut. Auntie Lindo and Uncle Tin were there. Waverly and her two older brothers had also come. The first two rows were filled with children both younger and older than I was. The littlest ones got to go first. They recited simple nursery rhymes, squawked out tunes on miniature violins, twirled Hula Hoops, pranced in pink ballet tutus, and when they bowed or curtsied, the audience would sigh in unison, "Awww," and then clap enthusiastically.

When my turn came, I was very confident. I remember my childish excitement. It was as if I knew, without a doubt, that the prodigy side of me really did exist. I had no fear whatsoever, no nervousness. I remember thinking to myself, This is it! This is it! I looked out over the audience, at my mother's blank face, my father's yawn. Auntie Lindo's stiff-lipped smile, Waverly's sulky expression. I had on a white dress layered with sheets of lace, and a pink bow in my Peter Pan haircut. As I sat down I envisioned people jumping to their feet and Ed Sullivan rushing up to introduce me to everyone on TV.

And I started to play. It was so beautiful. I was so caught up in how lovely I looked that at first I didn't worry how I would sound. So it was a surprise to me when I hit the first wrong note and I realized something didn't sound quite right. And then I hit another and another followed that. A chill started at the top of my head and began to trickle down. Yet I couldn't stop playing, as though my hands were bewitched. I kept thinking my fingers would adjust themselves back, like a train switching to the right track. I played this strange jumble through two repeats, the sour notes staying with me all the way to the end.

When I stood up, I discovered my legs were shaking. Maybe I had just been nervous and the audience, like Old Chong, had seen me go through the right motions and had not heard anything wrong at all. I swept my right foot out, went down on my knee, looked up and smiled. The room was quiet, except for Old Chong, who was beaming and shouting, "Bravo! Bravo! Well done!" But then I saw my mother's face, her stricken face. The audience clapped weakly, and as I walked back to my chair, with my whole face quivering as I tried not to cry, I heard a little boy whisper loudly to his mother, "That was awful," and the mother whispered back, "Well, she certainly tried."

And now I realized how many people were in the audience, the whole world it seemed. I was aware of eyes burning into my back. I felt the shame of my mother and father as they sat stiffly throughout the rest of the show.

We could have escaped during intermission. Pride and some strange sense of honor must have anchored my parents to their chairs. And so we watched it all: the eighteen-year-old boy with a fake mustache who did a magic show and juggled flaming hoops while riding a unicycle. The breasted girl with white makeup who sang from *Madama Butterfly*° and got honorable mention. And the eleven-year-old boy who won first prize playing a tricky violin song that sounded like a busy bee.°

After the show, the Hsus, the Jongs, and the St. Clairs from the Joy Luck Club came up to my mother and father.

"Lots of talented kids," Auntie Lindo said vaguely, smiling broadly.

"That was somethin' else," said my father, and I wondered if he was referring to me in a humorous way, or whether he even remembered what I had done.

Waverly looked at me and shrugged her shoulders. "You aren't a genius like me," she said matter-of-factly. And if I hadn't felt so bad, I would have pulled her braids and punched her stomach.

°*Madama Butterfly:* The girl probably sang "Un Bel Di," the signature soprano aria from the opera *Madama Butterfly* by Giacomo Puccini (1858–1924).
°*busy bee:* probably the well-known "Flight of the Bumblebee" by Nikolay Rimsky-Korsakov (1844–1908).

But my mother's expression was what devastated me: a quiet, blank look that said she had lost everything. I felt the same way, and it seemed as if everybody were now coming up, like gawkers at the scene of an accident, to see what parts were actually missing. When we got on the bus to go home, my father was humming the busy-bee tune and my mother was silent. I kept thinking she wanted to wait until we got home before shouting at me. But when my father unlocked the door to our apartment, my mother walked in and then went to the back, into the bedroom. No accusations. No blame. And in a way, I felt disappointed. I had been waiting for her to start shouting, so I could shout back and cry and blame her for all my misery.

I assumed my talent-show fiasco meant I never had to play the piano again. But two days later, after school, my mother came out of the kitchen and saw me watching TV.

"Four clock," she reminded me as if it were any other day. I was stunned, as though she were asking me to go through the talent-show torture again. I wedged myself more tightly in front of the TV.

"Turn off TV," she called from the kitchen five minutes later.   65

I didn't budge. And then I decided. I didn't have to do what my mother said anymore. I wasn't her slave. This wasn't China. I had listened to her before and look what happened. She was the stupid one.

She came out from the kitchen and stood in the arched entryway of the living room. "Four clock," she said once again, louder.

"I'm not going to play anymore," I said nonchalantly. "Why should I? I'm not a genius."

She walked over and stood in front of the TV. I saw her chest was heaving up and down in an angry way.

"No!" I said, and I now felt stronger, as if my true self had finally emerged. So this was   70 what had been inside me all along.

"No! I won't!" I screamed.

She yanked me by the arm, pulled me off the floor, snapped off the TV. She was frighteningly strong, half pulling, half carrying me toward the piano as I kicked the throw rugs under my feet. She lifted me up and onto the hard bench. I was sobbing by now, looking at her bitterly. Her chest was heaving even more and her mouth was open, smiling crazily as if she were pleased I was crying.

"You want me to be someone that I'm not!" I sobbed. "I'll never be the kind of daughter you want me to be!"

"Only two kinds of daughters," she shouted in Chinese. "Those who are obedient and those who follow their own mind! Only one kind of daughter can live in this house. Obedient daughter!"

"Then I wish I wasn't your daughter. I wish you weren't my mother," I shouted. As I   75 said these things I got scared. It felt like worms and toads and slimy things crawling out of my chest, but it also felt good, as if this awful side of me had surfaced, at last.

"Too late change this," said my mother shrilly.

And I could sense her anger rising to its breaking point. I wanted to see it spill over. And that's when I remembered the babies she had lost in China, the ones we never talked about. "Then I wish I'd never been born!" I shouted. "I wish I were dead! Like them."

It was as if I had said the magic words. Alakazam!—and her face went blank, her mouth closed, her arms went slack, and she backed out of the room, stunned, as if she were blowing away like a small brown leaf, thin, brittle, lifeless.

It was not the only disappointment my mother felt in me. In the years that followed, I failed her so many times, each time asserting my own will, my right to fall short of expectations. I didn't get straight As. I didn't become class president. I didn't get into Stanford. I dropped out of college.

80   For unlike my mother, I did not believe I could be anything I wanted to be. I could only be me.

And for all those years, we never talked about the disaster at the recital or my terrible accusations afterward at the piano bench. All that remained unchecked, like a betrayal that was now unspeakable. So I never found a way to ask her why she had hoped for something so large that failure was inevitable.

And even worse, I never asked her what frightened me the most: Why had she given up hope?

For after our struggle at the piano, she never mentioned my playing again. The lessons stopped. The lid to the piano was closed, shutting out the dust, my misery, and her dreams.

So she surprised me. A few years ago, she offered to give me the piano, for my thirtieth birthday. I had not played in all those years. I saw the offer as a sign of forgiveness, a tremendous burden removed.

85   "Are you sure?" I asked shyly. "I mean, won't you and Dad miss it?"

"No, this your piano," she said firmly. "Always your piano. You only one can play."

"Well, I probably can't play anymore," I said. "It's been years."

"You pick up fast," said my mother, as if she knew this was certain. "You have natural talent. You could been genius if you want to."

"No I couldn't."

90   "You just not trying," said my mother. And she was neither angry nor sad. She said it as if to announce a fact that could never be disproved. "Take it," she said.

But I didn't at first. It was enough that she had offered it to me. And after that, every time I saw it in my parents' living room, standing in front of the bay windows, it made me feel proud, as if it were a shiny trophy I had won back.

Last week I sent a tuner over to my parents' apartment and had the piano reconditioned, for purely sentimental reasons. My mother had died a few months before and I had been getting things in order for my father, a little bit at a time. I put the jewelry in special silk pouches. The sweaters she had knitted in yellow, pink, bright orange—all the colors I hated—I put those in moth-proof boxes. I found some old Chinese silk dresses, the kind with little slits up the sides. I rubbed the old silk against my skin, then wrapped them in tissue and decided to take them home with me.

After I had the piano tuned, I opened the lid and touched the keys. It sounded even richer than I remembered. Really, it was a very good piano. Inside the bench were the same exercise notes with handwritten scales, the same secondhand music books with their covers held together with yellow tape.

I opened up the Schumann book to the dark little piece I had played at the recital. It was on the left-hand side of the page, "Pleading Child." It looked more difficult than I remembered. I played a few bars, surprised at how easily the notes came back to me.

95   And for the first time, or so it seemed, I noticed the piece on the right-hand side. It was called "Perfectly Contented." I tried to play this one as well. It had a lighter melody but the same flowing rhythm and turned out to be quite easy. "Pleading Child" was shorter but slower; "Perfectly Contented" was longer, but faster. And after I played them both a few times, I realized they were two halves of the same song.

QUESTIONS

1. What major characteristics about the narrator, Jing-Mei, are brought out in the story?
2. Describe the relationship between Jing-Mei and her mother. Why does Jing-Mei resist all efforts to develop her talents?

3. Characterize the mother. To what degree is she sympathetic? Unsympathetic? At the story's end, how does Jing-Mei feel about her mother?

4. What general details about the nature of first- and second-generation immigrants are presented in the story?

MARK TWAIN (1835–1910)

Mark Twain (born Samuel Clemens) is one of the literary giants of nineteenth- and early-twentieth-century America. Largely because of his use of colloquial and regional English in Huckleberry Finn, *he was acknowledged by Hemingway as a founder of American literature. He was born in Missouri and spent much of his youth as a Mississippi River pilot, Confederate soldier, journalist, and miner. In 1863 he adopted "Mark Twain" as his nom de plume. His most famous works are the novels* Tom Sawyer *(1876) and* Huckleberry Finn *(1884–1885).* Huckleberry Finn *is today the subject of controversy for characterizations some people consider racist, even though more than a century has passed since its publication. "Luck" is a brief story (Twain calls it a "sketch") illustrating Twain's art of comic debunking, a characteristic that he also shows in works such as* The Innocents Abroad *and the short critical essay "Fenimore Cooper's Literary Offenses." The technique in "Luck" is to present an inside, private view of a person of high reputation and in effect to show that "the emperor has no clothes."*

🍁 Luck[1] (1891)

It was at a banquet in London in honor of one of the two or three conspicuously illustrious English military names of this generation. For reasons which will presently appear, I will withhold his real name and titles and call him Lieutenant-General Lord Arthur Scoresby, Y.C., K.C.B., etc., etc. What a fascination there is in a renowned name! There sat the man, in actual flesh, whom I had heard of so many thousands of times since that day, thirty years before, when his name shot suddenly to the zenith from a Crimean battlefield,° to remain forever celebrated. It was food and drink to me to look, and look, and look at that demigod; scanning, searching, noting: the quietness, the reserve, the noble gravity of his countenance; the simple honesty that expressed itself all over him; the sweet unconsciousness of his greatness—unconsciousness of the hundreds of admiring eyes fastened upon him, unconsciousness of the deep, loving, sincere worship welling out of the breasts of those people and flowing toward him.

The clergyman at my left was an old acquaintance of mine—clergyman now, but had spent the first half of his life in the camp and field and as an instructor in the military school at Woolwich. Just at the moment I have been talking about a veiled and singular light glimmered in his eyes and he leaned down and muttered confidentially to me—indicating the hero of the banquet with a gesture:

"Privately—he's an absolute fool."

This verdict was a great surprise to me. If its subject had been Napoleon, or Socrates, or Solomon, my astonishment could not have been greater. Two things I was well aware of:

---

[1]This is not a fancy sketch. I got it from a clergyman who was an instructor at Woolwich forty years ago, and who vouched for its truth. [Twain's note.]
°*Crimean battlefield:* In the Crimean War (1853–1856), England was one of the allies that fought against Russia.

that the Reverend was a man of strict veracity and that his judgment of men was good. Therefore I knew, beyond doubt or question, that the world was mistaken about this hero: he *was* a fool. So I meant to find out, at a convenient moment, how the Reverend, all solitary and alone, had discovered the secret.

5   Some days later the opportunity came, and this is what the Reverend told me:

About forty years ago I was an instructor in the military academy at Woolwich. I was present in one of the sections when young Scoresby underwent his preliminary examination. I was touched to the quick with pity, for the rest of the class answered up brightly and handsomely, while he—why, dear me, he didn't know *anything*, so to speak. He was evidently good, and sweet, and lovable, and guileless; and so it was exceedingly painful to see him stand there, as serene as a graven image, and deliver himself of answers which were veritably miraculous for stupidity and ignorance. All the compassion in me was aroused in his behalf. I said to myself, when he comes to be examined again he will be flung over, of course; so it will be simply a harmless act of charity to ease his fall as much as I can. I took him aside and found that he knew a little of Caesar's history; and as he didn't know anything else, I went to work and drilled him like a galley-slave on a certain line of stock questions concerning Caesar which I knew would be used. If you'll believe me, he went through with flying colors on examination day! He went through on that purely superficial "cram," and got compliments too, while others, who knew a thousand times more than he, got plucked. By some strangely lucky accident—an accident not likely to happen twice in a century—he was asked no question outside of the narrow limits of his drill.

It was stupefying. Well, all through his course I stood by him, with something of the sentiment which a mother feels for a crippled child; and he always saved himself—just by miracle, apparently.

Now, of course, the thing that would expose him and kill him at last was mathematics. I resolved to make his death as easy as I could; so I drilled him and crammed him, and crammed him and drilled him, just on the line of questions which the examiners would be most likely to use, and then launched him on his fate. Well, sir, try to conceive of the result: to my consternation, he took the first prize! And with it he got a perfect ovation in the way of compliments.

Sleep? There was no more sleep for me for a week. My conscience tortured me day and night. What I had done I had done purely through charity, and only to ease the poor youth's fall. I never had dreamed of any such preposterous results as the thing that had happened. I felt as guilty and miserable as Frankenstein. Here was a wooden-head whom I had put in the way of glittering promotions and prodigious responsibilities, and but one thing could happen: he and his responsibilities would all go to ruin together at the first opportunity.

10   The Crimean War had just broken out. Of course there had to be a war, I said to myself. We couldn't have peace and give this donkey a chance to die before he is found out. I waited for the earthquake. It came. And it made me reel when it did come. He was actually gazetted to a captaincy in a marching regiment! Better men grow old and gray in the service before they climb to a sublimity like that. And who could ever have foreseen that they would go and put such a load of responsibility on such green and inadequate shoulders? I could just barely have stood it if they had made him a cornet; but a captain—think of it! I thought my hair would turn white.

Consider what I did—I who so loved repose and inaction. I said to myself, I am responsible to the country for this, and I must go along with him and protect the country against him as far as I can. So I took my poor little capital that I had saved up through years of work and grinding economy, and went with a sigh and bought a cornetcy in his regiment, and away we went to the field.

And there—oh, dear, it was awful. Blunders?—why he never did anything *but* blunder. But, you see, nobody was in the fellow's secret. Everybody had him focused wrong, and necessarily misinterpreted his performance every time. Consequently they took his idiotic blunders for inspirations of genius. They did, honestly! His mildest blunders were enough to make a man in his right mind cry; and they did make me cry—and rage and rave, too, privately. And the thing that kept me always in a sweat of apprehension was the fact that every fresh blunder he made increased the luster of his reputation! I kept saying to myself, he'll get so high that when discovery does finally come it will be like the sun falling out of the sky.

He went right along, up from grade to grade, over the dead bodies of his superiors, until at last, in the hottest moment of the battle of—down went our colonel, and my heart jumped into my mouth, for Scoresby was next in rank! Now for it, said I: we'll all land in Sheol in ten minutes, sure.

The battle was awfully hot; the allies were steadily giving way all over the field. Our regiment occupied a position that was vital; a blunder now must be destruction. At this crucial moment, what does this immortal fool do but detach the regiment from its place and order a charge over a neighboring hill where there wasn't a suggestion of an enemy! "There you go!" I said to myself; "this *is* the end at last."

And away we did go, and were over the shoulder of the hill before the insane movement could be discovered and stopped. And what did we find? An entire and unsuspected Russian army in reserve! And what happened? We were eaten up? That is necessarily what would have happened in ninety-nine cases out of a hundred. But no; those Russians argued that no single regiment would come browsing around there at such a time. It must be the entire English army, and that the sly Russian game was detected and blocked, so they turned tail, and away they went, pell-mell, over the hill and down into the field, in wild confusion, and we after them; they themselves broke the solid Russian center in the field, and tore through, and in no time there was the most tremendous rout you ever saw, and the defeat of the allies was turned into a sweeping and splendid victory! Marshall Canrobert looked on, dizzy with astonishment, admiration, and delight; and sent right off for Scoresby, and hugged him, and decorated him on the field in presence of all the armies!

And what was Scoresby's blunder that time? Merely the mistaking his right hand for his left—that was all. An order had come to him to fall back and support our right; and, instead, he fell *forward* and went over the hill to the left. But the name he won that day as a marvelous military genius filled the world with his glory, and that glory will never fade while history books last.

He is just as good and sweet and lovable and unpretending as a man can be, but he doesn't know enough to come in when it rains. Now that is absolutely true. He is the supremest ass in the universe; and until half an hour ago nobody knew it but himself and me. He has been pursued, day by day and year by year, by a most phenomenal astonishing luckiness. He has been a shining soldier in all our wars for a generation; he has littered his whole military life with blunders, and yet has never committed one that didn't make him a knight or a baronet or a lord or something. Look at his breast; why, he is just clothed in domestic and foreign decorations. Well, sir, every one of them is the record of some shouting stupidity or other; and, taken together, they are proof that the very best thing in all this world that can befall a man is to be born lucky. I say again, as I said at the banquet, Scoresby's an absolute fool.

QUESTIONS

1. Describe Twain's style as a writer of narrative prose. What kinds of detail does he present? Does he give you enough detail about the battle during the Crimean War, for example, to justify an assertion that he describes action vividly? Or does he confine his detail to illuminate the life of Scoresby?

2. What elements in the story are amusing? How does the development of humor depend on Twain's arrangement of words?

3. Study the first paragraph. What does Twain intend after the "look, and look, and look" phrase? Why do you think he begins the story with such a description, which might even be called heroic? Contrast this paragraph with paragraph 12, where the word *blunder* is repeated.

4. Who begins the story? Who finally tells it? How does the second narrator learn about Scoresby? How does he summarize Scoresby's career?

WRITING ABOUT CHARACTER

Usually your topic will be a major character in a story or drama, although you might also study one or more minor characters. After your customary overview, begin taking notes. List as many traits as you can, and also determine how the author presents details about the character through actions, appearances, speeches, comments by others, or authorial explanations. If you discover unusual traits, determine what they show. The following suggestions and questions will help you get started.

Questions for Discovering Ideas

- Who is the major character? What do you learn about this character from his or her actions and speeches? From the speeches and actions of other characters? How else do you learn about the character?
- How important is the character to the work's principal action? Which characters oppose the major character? How do the major character and the opposing antagonist(s) interact? What effects do these interactions create?
- What actions bring out important traits of the main character? To what degree does the character simply respond to events? To what degree does he or she create and influence events?
- Describe the main character's actions: Are they good or bad, intelligent or stupid, deliberate or spontaneous? How do they help you understand her or him? What do they show about the character as a person?
- Describe and explain the traits, both major and minor, of the character you plan to discuss. To what extent do the traits permit you to judge the character? What is your judgment?
- What descriptions (if any) of how the character looks do you discover in the story? What does this appearance demonstrate about him or her?
- In what ways is the character's major trait a strength—or a weakness? As the story progresses, to what degree does the trait become more (or less) prominent?
- How does the character recognize, change with, or adjust to circumstances? Is the character round and dynamic, or flat and passive?
- If the character you are analyzing is flat or passive, and minor, what function does he or she perform in the story (for example, by doing a task or by bringing out qualities of the major character)?

- If the character is a stereotype, to what type does he or she belong? To what degree does the character stay in the stereotypical role or rise above it? How?
- What do any of the other characters do, say, or think to give you understanding of the character you are analyzing? What does the character say or think about himself or herself? What does the storyteller or narrator say? How valid are these comments and insights? How helpful are they in providing insights into the character?
- Is the character lifelike or unreal? Consistent or inconsistent? Believable or not believable?

Strategies for Organizing Ideas

Sometimes when you have begun discussing a character you may find it easy to lapse into doing no more than presenting details of action without tying the actions to the character's traits and qualities. This is a trap to be avoided. Remember always to connect the actions and circumstances directly to characteristics—in other words to the *character* of the character. Do not be satisfied just to say what the character is doing, but tell your reader what the actions show about the character *as a person*—as a living, breathing individual with particular distinctness and unique identity. Always keep these thoughts in your mind when you discuss a literary character.

In your developing essay, identify the character you are studying, and refer to noteworthy problems in determining this character's qualities. Use your central idea and thesis statement to form for the body of your essay. Consider one of the following approaches to organize your ideas.

1. *Develop a central trait or major characteristic,* such as "a determination to preserve her children despite the constant threats around her" (Rosa of Ozick's "The Shawl" in Chapter 4) or "the habit of remaking the world through one's own eyes alone" (Miss Brill in Mansfield's "Miss Brill" in this Chapter). This kind of structure should be organized to show how the work brings out the trait. For example, one story might use selected speeches and actions to bring the character to life (the mother in Tan's "Two Kinds" in this chapter). Another story might employ the character's speeches and actions alone (Tessie Hutchinson of Jackson's "The Lottery" in Chapter 2). Studying the trait thus enables you to focus on the ways in which the author presents the character, and it also enables you to focus on separate parts of the work.

2. *Explain a character's growth or change.* This type of essay describes a character's traits at the work's beginning and then analyzes changes or developments. It is important to stress the actual alterations as they emerge, but at the same time to avoid retelling the story. Additionally, you should not only describe the changing traits but also analyze how they are brought out within the work (such as the unnamed narrator's drawing of a cathedral in Carver's "Cathedral" in this chapter, the dream of Goodman Brown in Chapter 7, or Mathilde Loisel's ten-year economic ordeal in Part I).

3. *Organize your essay around a number of important but separate events, objects, or characteristics.* Most major characters exhibit not just one but many separate traits and qualities. Thus, for example, Updike's Sammy of "A & P" (Chapter 6), appears at first to be just an ordinary young man. He seems lively but does not show any more than ordinary postadolescent interests and ordinary views on life. When a key incident occurs in the grocery store, however, he suddenly illustrates his capacity to make a significant moral gesture. His character might be studied on the basis of the separate characteristics he shows—provided, of course, that they are connected within the essay. (See the illustrative essay that follows here for this type of development.)

4. *Organize your essay around central actions, objects, or quotations that reveal primary characteristics.* Key incidents may stand out (such as falling inadvertently into a ditch), along with objects closely associated with the character being analyzed (such as a falling hair ribbon). There may be important quotations spoken by the character or by someone else in the work. Show how such elements serve as signposts or guides to understanding the character.

5. *Develop qualities of a flat character or characters.* If the character is flat (such as Eva's friend in Munro's "The Found Boat" in Chapter 6, or Jackie's sister in Frank O'Connor's "First Confession" in Chapter 6, or the nurses in the medical station in Welty's "A Worn Path" in Chapter 1), you might develop topics such as the function and relative significance of the character, the group the character represents, the relationship of the flat character to the round ones, the importance of this relationship, and any additional qualities or traits. For a flat character, you should explain the circumstances or characteristics that keep the character from seeming round and full, as well as the importance of these shortcomings in the author's presentation of character.

In your conclusion, show how the character's traits are related to the work as a whole. If the person was good but came to a bad end, does this misfortune make him or her seem especially worthy? If the person suffers, does the suffering suggest any attitudes about the class or type of which he or she is a part? Or does it illustrate the author's general view of human life? Or both? Do the characteristics explain why the person helps or hinders other characters? How does your essay help to clear up things that you did not understand on your first reading?

Illustrative Student Essay

Underlined sentences in this paper *do not* conform to MLA style and are used solely as teaching tools to emphasize the central idea, thesis sentence, and topic sentences throughout the paper.

Hernandez 1

Ali Hernandez

Professor Lee

English 12B

17 October 2008

The Character of Minnie Wright in Glaspell's "A Jury of Her Peers"

Minnie Wright is Susan Glaspell's major character in "A Jury of Her   [1]
Peers." She is the center, the focus, of the story. We do not learn about her firsthand, however, because she is not an actual speaking and acting character.
Rather, we get all our information from the speeches of the actual characters in
the story, who talk about her constantly. Lewis Hale, a neighboring farmer, tells
about Minnie's behavior after the body of her husband, John, was found
strangled, in bed. Mrs. Martha Hale, Hale's wife, tells about Minnie's young
womanhood and about how she became alienated from her nearest neighbors
because of John's stingy and unfriendly ways. Both Mrs. Hale and Mrs. Peters,
the Sheriff's wife, make observations about Minnie based on the condition of
her kitchen. <u>From this information we get a full portrait of Minnie, who has
changed from passivity to destructive assertiveness.</u>* <u>Her change in character is
indicated by her clothing, her dead canary, and her unfinished patchwork quilt.</u>†

<u>The clothes that Minnie wore in the past and has worn in the present</u>   [2]
<u>indicate her character as a person of charm who has withered under neglect and
contempt.</u> Martha Hale mentions Minnie's attractive and colorful dresses as a
young woman, even recalling a "white dress with blue ribbons" (200,
paragraph 258). Martha also recalls that Minnie, when young, was "sweet and
pretty, but kind of timid and--fluttery" (198, paragraph 207). In the light of
these recollections, Martha observes that Minnie had changed, and changed for

---

*Central idea.
†Thesis sentence.

Hernandez 2

the worse, during her dreary years of marriage with John Wright, who is characterized as a "raw wind that gets to the bone" (198, paragraph 201). As more evidence for Minnie's acceptance of her drab life, Mrs. Peters says that Minnie asks for no more than an apron and shawl when under arrest in the sheriff's home. This modest and shabby clothing, as contrasted with the colorful dresses of her youth, suggests her suppression of spirit.

[3]   It is the discovery of her dead canary that clearly marks the emergence of Minnie's rage to the point of actually killing her miserable husband. We learn that she, who when young had been in love with music, had endured her cheerless farm home for thirty years. During this time her husband's contempt made her life solitary, cheerless, unmusical, and depressingly impoverished. But her buying the canary (197, paragraph 182) suggests the reemergence of her love of song, just as it also suggests her growth toward self-assertion. That her husband (obviously her husband) had wrung the bird's neck may thus be seen as the cause not only of her immediate sorrow (shown by the dead bird in a "pretty box" (199, paragraph 212) but also of the anger that marks her change from a stock, obedient wife to a person angry enough to commit murder.

[4]   Like her love of song, her unfinished quilt indicates her creativity. In thirty years on the farm, never having had children, she has had nothing creative to do except for needlework like the quilt. Martha Hale comments on the beauty of Minnie's log-cabin design (196, paragraph 153), and Mrs. Peters draws attention to the pieces in the sewing basket (196, paragraph 151). The inference is that even though Minnie's life has been bleak, she has been able to indulge her characteristic love of color and form--and also of warmth, granted the purpose of a quilt.

[5]   Ironically, the quilt also shows Minnie's creativity in committing her act of murder. Both Mrs. Hale and Mrs. Peters interpret the breakdown of her stitching on the quilt as signs of distress about the dead canary and also of her nervousness in planning revenge. Further, even though nowhere in the story is it said that John is strangled with a quilting knot, this conclusion is inescapable. Both Mrs. Hale and Mrs. Peters agree that Minnie probably intended to knot the quilt rather than sew it in a quilt stitch, and Glaspell pointedly causes the men to learn this detail

Hernandez 3

also, even though they scoff at it and ignore it, thus showing their incompetence at recognizing evidence (197, paragraph 157). In other words, we learn that Minnie's only outlet for creativity--needlework--had enabled her to perform the murder in the only way she could, by strangling John with a slip-proof quilting knot. Even though her plan for the murder is deliberate--Mrs. Peters observes that the arrangement of the rope was "strange" and a "funny way to kill" (196, paragraph 137)--Minnie is not cold or remorseless. Her passivity after the crime demonstrates that planning to evade guilt, beyond simple denial, is not in her character. She is not so diabolically creative that she plans or even understands the irony of her having used a quilting knot to kill her husband (remember that he killed the bird by wringing its neck). Glaspell, however, makes the irony plain.

It is important to stress once more that we learn about Minnie from others. Nevertheless, Minnie is fully realized, round, and poignant. For the greater part of her adult life, she patiently endured her drab and colorless marriage even though it was so cruelly different from her youthful expectations. In the dreary surroundings of the Wright farm, she suppressed her grudges, just as she suppressed her prettiness, creativity, and love of color and beauty. In short, she had been nothing more than a flat character. The killing of the canary, however, causes her to change and to destroy her husband in an assertive rejection of her stock role as the suffering wife. She is a patient woman whose patience finally reaches the breaking point.

[6]

Hernandez 4

Work Cited

Glaspell, Susan. "A Jury of Her Peers." Literature: An Introduction to Reading and Writing. Ed. Edgar V. Roberts. 9th ed. New York: Pearson Longman, 2009. 189–202.

Commentary on the Essay

The strategy of this essay is to support the central idea that Minnie Wright is a round, developing character. Hence the essay illustrates one of the types described in strategy 3 on page 218. Other plans of organization could also have been chosen, such as the qualities of acquiescence, fortitude, and potential for anger (strategy 1); the change in Minnie from submission to vengefulness (strategy 2); or the reported actions of Minnie's singing, knotting quilts, and sitting in the kitchen on the morning after the murder (another way to use strategy 3).

Because Minnie does not appear in the story but is described only in the words of the major characters, the introductory paragraph of the illustrative essay deals with the way readers learn about her. The essay thus highlights how Glaspell uses strategies 2 and 4 in the introductory section of this chapter (see pp. 217–18) as the ways of rendering the story's main character, while omitting strategies 1, 3, and 5.

The essay's argument is developed through inferences made from details in the story—namely, Minnie's clothing (paragraph 2), her canary (paragraph 3), and her quilt (paragraphs 4 and 5). The concluding paragraph summarizes a number of these details, and it also considers how Minnie transcends the stock qualities of her role as a farm wife and gains roundness of character as a result of this emergence.

As a study in composition, paragraph 3 demonstrates how discussion of a specific character trait, together with related details, can contribute to the essay's main argument. The trait is Minnie's love of music (shown by her canary). The connecting details, selected from study notes, are her isolation as a farm wife, her lack of pretty clothing, the contemptibility of her husband, her grief when putting the dead bird into the box, and the loss of music in her life. In short, the paragraph weaves together enough material to show the relationship between Minnie's trait of loving music and the crisis of her developing anger—a change that marks her as a round character.

Writing Topics About Character

1. Compare the ways in which actions (or speeches, or the comments of others) are used to bring out the character traits of Jing-Mei in "Two Kinds" (this chapter), Jackie in "First Confession" (Chapter 6), the narrator's wife in "Cathedral" (this chapter), and Miss Brill in "Miss Brill" (this chapter).

2. Write a brief essay comparing the changes or developments of two major or *round* characters in stories included in this chapter or elsewhere in the book. You might deal with issues such as what the characters are like at the beginning; what conflicts they confront, deal with, or avoid; what qualities are brought out that signal the characters' changes or developments; and so on.

3. Compare the qualities and functions of two or more flat characters (e.g., Mangan's sister in Joyce's "Araby" in Chapter 4, the father and Old Chong in Tan's "Two Kinds," in this chapter, the hunter in "A Worn Path" in Chapter 1). How

do the flat characters bring out qualities of the major characters? What do you discover about their own character traits?

4. Using Scoresby (in Twain's "Luck" in this chapter), the narrator of "Battle Royal" (Chapter 5), and Jing-Mei (in Tan's "Two Kinds" in this chapter) as examples, describe the effects of circumstance on character. Under the rubric "circumstance" you may consider elements such as education, family, economic and social status, cultural background, and geographic isolation.

5. Compare the parent-child relationships in "Two Kinds," "War" (Chapter 1), and "First Confession" (Chapter 6).

6. Topics for argument or brief essays:

a. It often seems that fictional characters are under stress and also that they lead lives of great difficulty. How true is this claim? To what degree do the difficulties that characters experience bring out either good or bad qualities, or both?

b. Develop this argument: To our friends and close relatives, we are round, but to ourselves and most other people, we are flat.

7. Write a brief story about an important decision you have made (e.g., choosing a school, beginning or leaving a job, declaring a major, starting or ending a friendship). Show how your qualities of character (to the extent that you understand yourself), together with your experiences, have gone into the decision. You may write more comfortably if you give yourself another name and describe your actions in the third person.

Chapter 4

Setting: The Background of Place, Objects, and Culture in Stories

Like all human beings, literary characters do not exist in isolation. Just as they become human by interacting with other characters, they gain identity because of their cultural and political allegiances, their possessions, their jobs, and where they live, and move, and have their being. They are usually involved deeply with their environments, and their surroundings are causes of much of their motivation and many of their possible conflicts. Plays, stories, and narrative poems must therefore necessarily include descriptions of places, objects, and backgrounds—the setting.

What Is Setting?

Setting is the natural, manufactured, political, cultural, and temporal environment, including everything that characters know, own, and otherwise experience. Characters may be either helped or hurt by their surroundings, and they may oppose each other and even fight about possessions and goals. Further, as characters speak with each other, they reveal the degree to which they share the customs and ideas of their times.

Three Basic Types of Settings

Settings may be indoor places that are either private or public, together with all outdoor places. In addition, we may also consider historical and cultural circumstances as a vital aspect of setting.

PUBLIC AND PRIVATE PLACES, TOGETHER WITH VARIOUS POSSESSIONS, ARE IMPORTANT IN FICTION, AS IN LIFE. To reveal or highlight qualities of character, and also to make literature lifelike, authors include many details about objects and places of human manufacture, construction, and maintenance. Houses, both interiors and exteriors, are common, as are streets, alleys, public parks, park benches, garden paths, fences, confessionals, offices, hallways, steamships, sailboats, terraces, cemeteries, railway cars, trolley cars, historical landmarks, grocery stores, recital rooms, bridges, and the like. In addition, writers include references to objects such as walking sticks, baseballs, books, phonograph records, necklaces, money, guns, shawls, clocks, wallpaper, or hair ribbons. In Maupassant's "The Necklace" (Part I), the loss of a comfortable home brings out the best in the major character by causing her to adjust to her economic reversal, whereas in Lawrence's "The Horse

Dealer's Daughter" (Chapter 8), such a loss leads a major character to depression and attempted suicide.

Objects also enter directly into fictional action and character. The lives of the men in O'Brien's "The Things They Carried" (Chapter 1) depend on the myriad objects they must carry on their military missions. Trying on the neighbors' clothes is an indication of intense if not morbid peculiarity in Carver's "Neighbors" (Chapter 2). A falling hair ribbon reveals the inadequate relationship between Brown and Faith in Hawthorne's "Young Goodman Brown" (Chapter 7).

OUTDOOR PLACES ARE SCENES OF MANY FICTIONAL ACTIONS.   The natural world is an obvious location for the action of many narratives and plays. It is therefore important to note natural surroundings (hills, shorelines, valleys, mountains, meadows, fields, trees, lakes, streams), living creatures (birds, dogs, horses, sharks, snakes), and also the times, seasons, and conditions in which things happen (morning or night, summer or winter, sunlight or cloudiness, wind or calmness, rain or shine, sunlight or darkness, summer or winter, snowfall or blizzard, heat or cold)—any or all of which may influence and interact with character, motivation, and conduct.

CULTURAL AND HISTORICAL CIRCUMSTANCES ARE OFTEN IMPORTANT IN FICTION.   Just as physical setting influences characters, so do historical and cultural conditions and assumptions. The broad cultural setting of Jackson's "The Lottery" (Chapter 2) is built on the persistence of a primitive belief despite the sophistication of our own modern and scientific age. The brutal oppressiveness and obscene concentration-camp conditions in Ozick's "The Shawl" (this chapter) cause the major character to conceal a small child as the only way to keep that child alive. In Mansfield's "Miss Brill" (Chapter 3), we see that the shabbiness of a favorite article of clothing suggests the isolation of the principal character.

The Literary Uses of Setting

Authors use setting to create meaning, just as painters include backgrounds and objects to render ideas. For example, the contrasting settings of François Boucher's portrait *Madame de Pompadour* (p. I–5), Edward Hopper's *Automat* (p. I–6), and Whistler's *The Little White Girl, Symphony in White, No. 2* (p. I–11) demonstrate how the same subject—a single female figure—can show divergent views of human life, one elegant and pampered, another ordinary and forlorn, and one alone and bored.

Writers manipulate literary locations in a comparable way. For example, in Hawthorne's "Young Goodman Brown" (Chapter 7), a woodland path that is difficult to follow and filled with obstacles is a major topographical feature. The path is of course no more than ordinary, granted the time and circumstances of the story, but it also conveys the idea that life is difficult, unpredictable, treacherous, deceiving, and mysterious. Similarly, in O'Brien's "The Things They Carried" (Chapter 1), the constant attention to details indicates the exceedingly difficult and dangerous lives that were led by American soldiers during the Vietnam War.

The Setting Is Usually Essential and Vital in the Story

To study the setting in a narrative (or play), discover the important details and then try to explain their function. Depending on the author's purpose, the amount of detail may vary. Poe provides many graphic and also impressionistic details in "The Masque of the Red Death" (Chapter 9) so that we can follow, almost visually, the bizarre action at the story's end. In some works the setting is so intensely present, like the various Dublin scenes in Joyce's "Araby" (Chapter 4), that it is almost literally an additional participant in the action.

Setting Augments a Work's Realism and Credibility

One of the major purposes of literary setting is to establish **realism,** or **verisimilitude.** As the description of location and objects becomes particular and detailed, the events of the work become more believable. Maupassant places "The Necklace" (Part I) in real locations in late-nineteenth-century Paris, and for this reason the story has all the semblance of having actually happened. Even futuristic, symbolic, and fantastic stories, as well as ghost stories, seem more believable if they include places and objects from everyday experience. Hawthorne's "Young Goodman Brown" (Chapter 7) is such a story, as is Poe's "The Masque of the Red Death" (Chapter 9). Although these stories are by no means realistic, their credibility is enhanced because they take place in settings that have a basis in the world of reality.

Setting May Accentuate Qualities of Character

Setting may intersect with character as a means by which authors underscore the influence of place, circumstance, and time on human growth and change. Whitecloud's progressive settings in "Blue Winds Dancing" (Chapter 5), from California to Wisconsin, explain the disillusionment and also the fear that possesses the narrator, and also help us understand why he longed so deeply for home and the comfort provided to him by once again being with his family. (A blending of setting and character as seen in Maupassant's "The Necklace" is explored in the two drafts of the illustrative essay in Part I.)

The ways that characters respond and adjust to the world around them can reveal their qualities. Peyton Farquhar's scheme to escape from his fate, even when it is literally dangling in front of him, suggests that he is a character of great strength but also of powerful imagination (Bierce's "An Occurrence at Owl Creek Bridge" in Chapter 1). In contrast, Goodman Brown's Calvinistic religious conviction that human beings are inclined to evil, which is confirmed to him by his nightmarish encounter, indicates the weakness and gullibility of his character (Hawthorne's "Young Goodman Brown" in Chapter 7).

Setting Is a Means by Which Authors Structure and Shape Their Works

Authors often use setting as one of the means of organizing their stories, as in Maupassant's "The Necklace." The story's final scene is believable because Mathilde leaves her impoverished home to take a nostalgic stroll on the Champs-Elysées, the most fashionable street in Paris. Without this change of setting, she could not have encountered Jeanne Forrestier again, for their usual ways of life would have in fact separated them. In short, the structure of the story depends on a normal and natural change of scene.

Another organizational application of place, time, and object is a **framing** or **enclosing setting,** when an author opens with a particular description and then returns to the same setting at the end. An example is Steinbeck's "The Chrysanthemums" (Chapter 7), which begins with the major character tending her flowers and ends with her seeing the destruction of some of these same flowers that she had given away. A comparable use of framing occurs in Welty's "A Worn Path" (Chapter 1), in which the walking trips taken by the main character open and close the story—to the town and then away from the town. By such means, framing creates a formal completeness, just as it may underscore the author's depiction of the human condition.

Various Settings May Be Symbolic

If the scenes and materials of setting are highlighted or emphasized, they also may be taken as symbols through which the author expresses ideas. Such an emphasis is made in Ozick's "The Shawl," in which the shawl has the ordinary function of providing cover and warmth for a baby. Because it is so prominent, however, the shawl also symbolizes the attempt to preserve future generations; and because its loss also produces a human loss, it symbolizes the helplessness of the victims in Nazi extermination camps during World War II. In O'Brien's "The Things They Carried" (Chapter 1), the constant references to the weights of the objects symbolize how the men's lives depend on their own resources—their carried burdens.

Setting Is Used in the Creation of Atmosphere and Mood

Most actions *require* no more than a functional description of setting. Thus, taking a walk in a forest needs just the statement that there are many, or few, trees. However, if you find descriptions of shapes, light and shadows, animals, wind, and sounds, you may be sure that the author is creating an **atmosphere** or **mood** for the action (as in Gilman's "The Yellow Wallpaper" in Chapter 10 and Joyce's "Araby" in Chapter 4). There are many ways to develop moods. Descriptions of bright colors (red, orange, yellow) may contribute to a mood of happiness. The same colors in dim or eerie light, like the rooms in Poe's "The Masque of the Red Death" (Chapter 9), invoke gloom or augment hysteria. References to smells and sounds bring the setting to life further by asking additional sensory responses from the reader. The setting of a story in a small town or large city, in green or snow-covered fields, or in middle-class or lower-class residences may evoke responses to these places that contribute to the work's atmosphere.

Setting May Underscore a Work's Irony

Just as setting may reinforce character and theme, so it may establish expectations that are the opposite of what occurs. At the beginning of "The Lottery"

(Chapter 2), for example, Jackson describes the plainness and folksiness of the assembling townspeople—details that make the conclusion ironic, for it is these same everyday folks who bring about the final horror. Irony is also a motif in Chopin's "The Story of an Hour" (Chapter 6) inasmuch as the major characters in the story are unable to prevent the final outcome, even though their intentions aim toward the opposite result. The ironic use of setting is by no means limited only to fiction, because it may also be significantly important in plays and poems. The case of dueling pistols in Chekhov's *The Bear* (Chapter 25) brings out the developing love between Smirnov and Mrs. Popov, for instead of separating these characters through death, the pistols bring them into passionate direct contact. Thomas Hardy creates a heavily ironic situation in the poem "Channel Firing" (Chapter 14) when the noise of large guns at sea "wakens" the skeletons buried in an English churchyard. The irony is that those engaged in the gunnery practice, if "red war" gets "yet redder," will soon be numbered among the skeletons in the graveyard.

 ## Stories for Study

Sandra Cisneros . . . . The House on Mango Street, 228
Joseph Conrad . . . . The Secret Sharer, 230
Joanne Greenberg . . . . And Sarah Laughed, 253
James Joyce . . . . Araby, 262
Cynthia Ozick . . . . The Shawl, 266

SANDRA CISNEROS (b. 1954)

Cisneros, a Mexican-American, was born in Illinois and was educated there. Her higher education was at Loyola University and the University of Iowa Writers' Workshop. She has been a "poet in the schools" in addition to teaching and also working as a college recruiter. She has held two NEA fellowships, and in 2005 she received a prestigious MacArthur Foundation Fellowship. The House on Mango Street, *which includes the title story included here, was the first of her books. It was first published in 1983 and reissued in 1991. Its audience has extended beyond readers of English, for it has been translated into eleven languages and has made her one of the widest selling and best known Hispanic authors in the United States. Her* Woman Hollering Creek and Other Stories *was published in 1991, and her poetry volume* Loose Woman: Poems *appeared in 1994. She published* Hairs/Pelitos, *a book for small children, in 1997. In 2002 she published her second novel,* Caramelo, *which is based on the immigrant lives of her father and other members of her family.*

 ## The House on Mango Street (1983)

We didn't always live on Mango Street. Before that we lived on Loomis on the third floor, and before that we lived on Keeler. Before Keeler it was Paulina, and before that I can't remember.

But what I remember most is moving a lot. Each time it seemed there'd be one more of us. By the time we got to Mango Street we were six—Mama, Papa, Carlos, Kiki, my sister Nenny and me.

The house on Mango Street is ours and we don't have to pay rent to anybody or share the yard with the people downstairs or be careful not to make too much noise and there isn't a landlord banging on the ceiling with a broom. But even so, it's not the house we'd thought we'd get.

We had to leave the flat on Loomis quick. The water pipes broke and the landlord wouldn't fix them because the house was too old. We had to leave fast. We were using the washroom next door and carrying water over in empty milk gallons. That's why Mama and Papa looked for a house, and that's why we moved into the house on Mango Street, far away, on the other side of town.

They always told us that one day we would move into a house, a real house that would be ours for always so we wouldn't have to move each year. And our house would have running water and pipes that worked. And inside it would have real stairs, not hallway stairs, but stairs inside like the houses on T.V. And we'd have a basement and at least three washrooms so when we took a bath we didn't have to tell everybody. Our house would be white with trees around it, a great big yard and grass growing without a fence. This was the house Papa talked about when he held a lottery ticket and this was the house Mama dreamed up in the stories she told us before we went to bed.

But the house on Mango Street is not the way they told it at all. It's small and red with tight little steps in front and windows so small you'd think they were holding their breath. Bricks are crumbling in places, and the front door is so swollen you have to push hard to get in. There is no front yard, only four little elms the city planted by the curb. Out back is a small garage for the car we don't own yet and a small yard that looks smaller between the two buildings on either side. There are stairs in our house, but they're ordinary hallway stairs, and the house has only one washroom, very small. Everybody has to share a bedroom—Mama and Papa, Carlos and Kiki, me and Nenny. 5

Once when we were living on Loomis, a nun from my school passed by and saw me playing out front. The laundromat downstairs had been boarded up because it had been robbed two days before and the owner had painted on the wood YES WE'RE OPEN so as not to lose business.

Where do you live? she asked.

There, I said pointing up to the third floor.

You live *there*?

There. I had to look to where she pointed—the third floor, the paint peeling, wooden bars Papa had nailed on the windows so we wouldn't fall out. You live *there*? The way she said it made me feel like nothing. *There*. I lived *there*. I nodded. 10

I knew then I had to have a house. A real house. One I could point to. But this isn't it. The house on Mango Street isn't it. For the time being, Mama says. Temporary, says Papa. But I know how those things go.

QUESTIONS

1. Why is the speaker concerned with the nature of the houses she has lived in? What feeling does she show about these houses?

2. Describe the house on Mango Street. How does the condition of this house and the other houses explain the economic circumstances of the speaker's family?

3. What is the speaker like as a character? How do you learn about her? How much do you learn?

JOSEPH CONRAD (1857–1924)

Joseph Conrad (Teodor Jósef Konrad Korzeniowski), whose parents were Polish, was born in Ukraine. His parents died when he was quite young, and at the age of 16 he embarked on a career as a sailor, shipping aboard English sailing vessels. At this same time he began studying English, a learning task which occupied him for five years while he was plying his trade as a seaman. Ultimately he rose to become a ship's captain and frequently traveled to many distant areas of the world, including the Far East, in the business of international trade. Throughout his life he spoke English with a Polish accent, but his command of written English, as readers of "The Secret Sharer" will quickly discover, was masterly. He maintained that he might never have become a writer if he had not been able to write in English. In ill health, he left the sailing profession in 1895, and at that point he took up an entirely new career as a writer in his adopted language, having published his first novel, Almayer's Folly. *From this time until his death twenty-nine years later, he regularly produced novels, as well as personal reminiscences and observations on "life and letters." His best-known novels are* Lord Jim *(1900) and* Nostromo *(1904). His best-known tale, or lengthy short story, is* Heart of Darkness *(1902). This work received great attention in the second half of the twentieth century because of Francis Ford Coppola's movie* Apocalypse Now *(1979), which is an adaptation of* Heart of Darkness *as the details of the story are applied to American involvement in the Vietnam War.*

The Secret Sharer (1912)

1

On my right hand there were lines of fishing stakes resembling a mysterious system of half-submerged bamboo fences, incomprehensible in its division of the domain of tropical fishes, and crazy of aspect as if abandoned forever by some nomad tribe of fishermen now gone to the other end of the ocean; for there was no sign of human habitation as far as the eye could reach. To the left a group of barren islets, suggesting ruins of stone walls, towers, and block-houses, had its foundations set in a blue sea that itself looked solid, so still and stable did it lie below my feet; even the track of light from the westering sun shone smoothly, without that animated glitter which tells of an imperceptible ripple. And when I turned my head to take a parting glance at the tug which had just left us anchored outside the bar, I saw the straight line of the flat shore joined to the stable sea, edge to edge, with a perfect and unmarked closeness, in one leveled floor half brown, half blue under the enormous dome of the sky. Corresponding in their insignificance to the islets of the sea, two small clumps of trees, one on each side of the only fault in the impeccable joint, marked the mouth of the river Meinam° we had just left on the first preparatory stage of our homeward journey; and, far back on the inland level, a larger and loftier mass, the grove surrounding the great Paknam pagoda, was the only thing on which the eye could rest from the vain task of exploring the monotonous sweep of the horizon. Here and there gleams as of a few scattered pieces of silver marked the windings of the great river; and on the nearest of them, just within the bar, the tug steaming right into the land became lost to my sight, hull

---

°The locations Conrad describes in the story are all real, although many have been renamed since his time. The river Meinam, or Mae Nam, is the Chao Phraya River, which empties into the Gulf of Siam (now the Gulf of Thailand), where the story's action begins. The "great Paknam" Pagoda is the Phra Samut Chedi Pagoda. The location of the ship at the story's end is near the island Kaôh Rüng (Koh-ring), near Cambodia (Cambodje), many miles to the southeast of where the story begins (see paragraphs 295, 318).

and funnel and masts, as though the impassive earth had swallowed her up without an effort, without a tremor. My eye followed the light cloud of her smoke, now here, now there, above the plain, according to the devious curves of the stream, but always fainter and farther away, till I lost it at last behind the miter-shaped hill of the great pagoda. And then I was left alone with my ship, anchored at the head of the Gulf of Siam.

She floated at the starting point of a long journey, very still in an immense stillness, the shadows of her spars flung far to the eastward by the setting sun. At that moment I was alone on her decks. There was not a sound in her—and around us nothing moved, nothing lived, not a canoe on the water, not a bird in the air, not a cloud in the sky. In this breathless pause at the threshold of a long passage we seemed to be measuring our fitness for a long and arduous enterprise, the appointed task of both our existences to be carried out, far from all human eyes, with only sky and sea for spectators and for judges.

There must have been some glare in the air to interfere with one's sight, because it was only just before the sun left us that my roaming eyes made out beyond the highest ridge of the principal islet of the group something which did away with the solemnity of perfect solitude. The tide of darkness flowed on swiftly; and with tropical suddenness a swarm of stars came out above the shadowy earth, while I lingered yet, my hand resting lightly on my ship's rail as if on the shoulder of a trusted friend. But, with all that multitude of celestial bodies staring down at one, the comfort of quiet communion with her was gone for good. And there were also disturbing sounds by this time—voices, footsteps forward; the steward flitted along the main deck, a busily ministering spirit; a hand bell tinkled urgently under the poop deck. . . .

I found my two officers waiting for me near the supper table, in the lighted cuddy.° We sat down at once, and as I helped the chief mate, I said:

"Are you aware that there is a ship anchored inside the islands? I saw her mastheads above the ridge as the sun went down."   5

He raised sharply his simple face, overcharged by a terrible growth of whisker, and emitted his usual ejaculations: "Bless my soul, sir! You don't say so!"

My second mate was a round-cheeked, silent young man, grave beyond his years, I thought; but as our eyes happened to meet I detected a slight quiver on his lips. I looked down at once. It was not my part to encourage sneering on board my ship. It must be said, too, that I knew very little of my officers. In consequence of certain events of no particular significance, except to myself, I had been appointed to the command only a fortnight before. Neither did I know much of the hands forward. All these people had been together for eighteen months or so, and my position was that of the only stranger on board. I mention this because it has some bearing on what is to follow. But what I felt most was my being a stranger to the ship; and if truth must be told, I was somewhat of a stranger to myself. The youngest man on board (barring the second mate), and untried as yet by a position of the fullest responsibility, I was willing to take the adequacy of the others for granted. They had simply to be equal to their tasks: but I wondered how far I should turn out faithful to that ideal conception of one's own personality every man sets up for himself secretly.

Meantime the chief mate, with an almost visible effect of collaboration on the part of his round eyes and frightful whiskers, was trying to evolve a theory of the anchored ship. His dominant trait was to take all things into earnest consideration. He was of a painstaking turn of mind. As he used to say, he "liked to account to himself" for practically everything that came in his way, down to a miserable scorpion he had found in his cabin a week before. The why and the wherefore of that scorpion—how it got on board and came to select his room rather than the pantry (which was a dark place and more what a scorpion would be partial to), and how on earth it managed to drown itself in the inkwell of his writing desk—had exercised him infinitely. The ship within the islands was much more easily

---

°*cuddy:* a small mess hall next to the ship's kitchen.

accounted for; and just as we were about to rise from the table he made his pronouncement. She was, he doubted not, a ship from home lately arrived. Probably she drew too
much water to cross the bar except at the top of spring tides. Therefore she went into the
natural harbor to wait for a few days in preference to remaining in an open roadstead.

"That's so," confirmed the second mate, suddenly, in his slightly hoarse voice. "She
draws over twenty feet. She's the Liverpool ship *Sephora*° with a cargo of coal. Hundred
and twenty-three days from Cardiff."

10   We looked at him in surprise.

"The tugboat skipper told me when he came on board for your letters, sir," explained
the young man. "He expects to take her up the river the day after tomorrow."

After thus overwhelming us with the extent of his information he slipped out of the
cabin. The mate observed regretfully that he "could not account for that young fellow's
whims." What prevented him telling us all about it at once, he wanted to know.

I detained him as he was making a move. For the last two days the crew had had plenty
of hard work, and the night before they had very little sleep. I felt painfully that I—a
stranger—was doing something unusual when I directed him to let all hands turn in without setting an anchor. I proposed to keep on deck myself till one o'clock or thereabouts. I
would get the second mate to relieve me at that hour.

"He will turn out the cook and the steward at four," I concluded, "and then give you a
call. Of course at the lightest sign of any sort of wind we'll have the hands up and make a
start at once."

15   He concealed his astonishment. "Very well, sir." Outside the cuddy he put his head in
the second mate's door to inform him of my unheard-of caprice to take a five hours' anchor
watch on myself. I heard the other raise his voice incredulously:

"What? The captain himself?" Then a few more murmurs, a door closed, then another. A
few moments later I went on deck.

My strangeness, which had made me sleepless, had prompted that unconventional
arrangement, as if I had expected in those solitary hours of the night to get on terms with
the ship of which I knew nothing, manned by men of whom I knew very little more. Fast
alongside a wharf, littered like any ship in port with a tangle of unrelated things, invaded
by unrelated shore people, I had hardly seen her yet properly. Now, as she lay cleared for
sea, the stretch of her main deck seemed to me very fine under the stars. Very fine, very
roomy for her size, and very inviting. I descended the poop and paced the waist, my mind
picturing to myself the coming passage through the Malay Archipelago, down the Indian
Ocean, and up the Atlantic. All its phases were familiar enough to me, every characteristic,
all the alternatives which were likely to face me on the high seas—everything! . . . except
the novel responsibility of command. But I took heart from the reasonable thought that the
ship was like other ships, the men like other men, and that the sea was not likely to keep
any special surprises expressly for my discomfiture.

Arrived at that comforting conclusion, I bethought myself of a cigar and went below to get
it. All was still down there. Everybody at the after end of the ship was sleeping profoundly. I
came out again on the quarter-deck, agreeably at ease in my sleeping suit on that warm
breathless night, barefooted, a glowing cigar in my teeth, and, going forward, I was met by
the profound silence of the fore end of the ship. Only as I passed the door of the forecastle I
heard a deep, quiet, trustful sigh of some sleeper inside. And suddenly I rejoiced in the great
security of the sea as compared with the unrest of the land, in my choice of that untempted

---

°*Sephora*: the Greek version of the biblical name Zipporah, who was the wife of Moses. A puzzling story in Exodus (24–26) indicates that she saved her husband from the Lord's anger—the reason for which is not disclosed—
by circumcising one of her sons. We may presume here that the ship had been named *Sephora* as a symbol of
safety and good luck.

life presenting no disquieting problems, invested with an elementary moral beauty by the absolute straightforwardness of its appeal and by the singleness of its purpose.

The riding light in the fore-rigging burned with a clear, untroubled, as if symbolic, flame, confident and bright in the mysterious shades of the night. Passing on my way aft along the other side of the ship, I observed that the rope side ladder, put over, no doubt, for the master of the tug when he came to fetch away our letters, had not been hauled in as it should have been. I became annoyed at this, for exactitude in small matters is the very soul of discipline. Then I reflected that I had myself peremptorily dismissed my officers from duty, and by my own act had prevented the anchor watch being formally set and things properly attended to. I asked myself whether it was wise ever to interfere with the established routine of duties even from the kindest of motives. My action might have made me appear eccentric. Goodness only knew how that absurdly whiskered mate would "account" for my conduct, and what the whole ship thought of that informality of their new captain. I was vexed with myself.

Not from compunction certainly, but, as it were mechanically, I proceeded to get the ladder in myself. Now a side ladder of that sort is a light affair and comes in easily, yet my vigorous tug, which should have brought it flying on board, merely recoiled upon my body in a totally unexpected jerk. What the devil! . . . I was so astounded by the immovableness of that ladder that I remained stock-still, trying to account for it to myself like that imbecile mate of mine. In the end, of course, I put my head over the rail.   20

The side of the ship made an opaque belt of shadow on the darkling glassy shimmer of the sea. But I saw at once something elongated and pale floating very close to the ladder. Before I could form a guess a faint flash of phosphorescent light, which seemed to issue suddenly from the naked body of a man, flickered in the sleeping water with the elusive, silent play of summer lightning in a night sky. With a gasp I saw revealed to my stare a pair of feet, the long legs, a broad livid back immersed right up to the neck in a greenish cadaverous glow. One hand, awash, clutched the bottom rung of the ladder. He was complete but for the head. A headless corpse! The cigar dropped out of my gaping mouth with a tiny plop and a short hiss quite audible in the absolute stillness of all things under heaven. At that I suppose he raised up his face, a dimly pale oval in the shadow of the ship's side. But even then I could only barely make out down there the shape of his black-haired head. However, it was enough for the horrid, frost-bound sensation which had gripped me about the chest to pass off. The moment of vain exclamations was past, too. I only climbed on the spare spar and leaned over the rail as far as I could, to bring my eyes nearer to that mystery floating alongside.

As he hung by the ladder, like a resting swimmer, the sea lightning played about his limbs at every stir; and he appeared in it ghastly, silvery, fishlike. He remained as mute as a fish, too. He made no motion to get out of the water, either. It was inconceivable that he should not attempt to come on board, and strangely troubling to suspect that perhaps he did not want to. And my first words were prompted by just that troubled incertitude.

"What's the matter?" I asked in my ordinary tone, speaking down to the face upturned exactly under mine.

"Cramp," it answered, no louder. Then slightly anxious, "I say, no need to call anyone."

"I was not going to," I said.   25

"Are you alone on deck?"

"Yes."

I had somehow the impression that he was on the point of letting go the ladder to swim away beyond my ken—mysterious as he came. But, for the moment, this being appearing as if he had risen from the bottom of the sea (it was certainly the nearest land to the ship) wanted only to know the time. I told him. And he, down there, tentatively:

"I suppose your captain's turned in?"

"I am sure he isn't," I said.   30

He seemed to struggle with himself, for I heard something like the low, bitter murmur of doubt. "What's the good?" His next words came out with a hesitating effort.

"Look here, my man. Could you call him out quietly?"

I thought the time had come to declare myself.

"*I am the captain.*"

35   I heard a "By Jove!" whispered at the level of the water. The phosphorescence flashed in the swirl of the water all about his limbs, his other hand seized the ladder.

"My name's Leggatt."

The voice was calm and resolute. A good voice. The self-possession of that man had somehow induced a corresponding state in myself. It was very quietly that I remarked:

"You must be a good swimmer."

"Yes. I've been in the water practically since nine o'clock. The question for me now is whether I am to let go this ladder and go on swimming till I sink from exhaustion, or—to come on board here."

40   I felt this was no mere formula of desperate speech, but a real alternative in the view of a strong soul. I should have gathered from this that he was young; indeed, it is only the young who are ever confronted by such clear issues. But at this time it was pure intuition on my part. A mysterious communication was established already between us two—in the face of that silent darkened tropical sea. I was young, too; young enough to make no comment. The man in the water began suddenly to climb up the ladder, and I hastened away from the rail to fetch some clothes.

Before entering the cabin I stood still, listening in the lobby at the foot of the stairs. A faint snore came through the closed door of the chief mate's room. The second mate's door was on the hook, but the darkness in there was absolutely soundless. He, too, was young and could sleep like a stone. Remained the steward, but he was not likely to wake up before he was called. I got a sleeping suit out of my room and, coming back on deck, saw the naked man from the sea sitting on the main hatch, glimmering white in the darkness, his elbows on his knees and his head in his hands. In a moment he had concealed his damp body in a sleeping suit of the same gray-stripe pattern as the one I was wearing and followed me like my double on the poop. Together we moved right aft, barefooted, silent.

"What is it?" I asked in a deadened voice, taking the lighted lamp out of the binnacle, and raising it to his face.

"An ugly business."

He had rather regular features; a good mouth; light eyes under somewhat heavy, dark eyebrows; a smooth, square forehead; no growth on his cheeks; a small, brown mustache, and a well-shaped, round chin. His expression was concentrated, meditative, under the inspecting light of the lamp I held up to his face; such as a man thinking hard in solitude might wear. My sleeping suit was just right for his size. A well-knit young fellow of twenty-five at most. He caught his lower lip with the edge of white, even teeth.

45   "Yes," I said, replacing the lamp in the binnacle. The warm, heavy tropical night closed upon his head again.

"There's a ship over there," he murmured.

"Yes, I know. The *Sephora*. Did you know of us?"

"Hadn't the slightest idea. I am the mate of her—" He paused and corrected himself. "I should say I was."

"Aha! Something wrong?"

50   "Yes. Very wrong indeed. I've killed a man."

"What do you mean? Just now?"

"No, on the passage. Weeks ago. Thirty-nine south. When I say a man—"

"Fit of temper," I suggested, confidently.

The shadowy, dark head, like mine, seemed to nod imperceptibly above the ghostly gray of my sleeping suit. It was, in the night, as though I had been faced by my own reflection in the depths of a somber and immense mirror.

"A pretty thing to have to own up for a Conway boy,"° murmured my double, dis-   55
tinctly.

"You're a Conway boy?"

"I am," he said, as if startled. Then, slowly . . . "Perhaps you too—"

It was so; but being a couple of years older I had left before he joined. After a quick interchange of dates a silence fell; and I thought suddenly of my absurd mate with his terrific whiskers and the "Bless my soul—you don't say so" type of intellect. My double gave me an inkling of his thoughts by saying:

"My father's a parson in Norfolk. Do you see me before a judge and jury on that charge? For myself I can't see the necessity. There are fellows that an angel from heaven—And I am not that. He was one of those creatures that are just simmering all the time with a silly sort of wickedness. Miserable devils that have no business to live at all. He wouldn't do his duty and wouldn't let anybody else do theirs. But what's the good of talking! You know well enough the sort of ill-conditioned snarling cur—"

He appealed to me as if our experiences had been as identical as our clothes. And I knew   60
well enough the pestiferous danger of such a character where there are no means of legal repression. And I knew well enough also that my double there was no homicidal ruffian. I did not think of asking him for details, and he told me the story roughly in brusque, disconnected sentences. I needed no more. I saw it all going on as though I were myself inside that other sleeping suit.

"It happened while we were setting a reefed foresail, at dusk. Reefed foresail! You understand the sort of weather. The only sail we had left to keep the ship running; so you may guess what it had been like for days. Anxious sort of job, that. He gave me some of his cursed insolence at the sheet. I tell you I was overdone with this terrific weather that seemed to have no end to it. Terrific, I tell you—and a deep ship. I believe the fellow himself was half crazed with funk. It was no time for gentlemanly reproof, so I turned round and felled him like an ox. He up and at me. We closed just as an awful sea made for the ship: All hands saw it coming and took to the rigging, but I had him by the throat, and went on shaking him like a rat, the men above us yelling, 'Look out! look out!' Then a crash as if the sky had fallen on my head. They say that for over ten minutes hardly anything was to be seen of the ship—just the three masts and a bit of the forecastle head and of the poop all awash driving along in a smother of foam. It was a miracle that they found us, jammed together behind the forebits. It's clear that I meant business, because I was holding him by the throat still when they picked us up. He was black in the face. It was too much for them. It seems they rushed us aft together, gripped as we were, screaming 'Murder!' like a lot of lunatics, and broke into the cuddy. And the ship running for her life, touch and go all the time, any minute her last in a sea fit to turn your hair gray only a-looking at it. I understand that the skipper, too, started raving like the rest of them. The man had been deprived of sleep for more than a week, and to have this sprung on him at the height of a furious gale nearly drove him out of his mind. I wonder they didn't fling me overboard after getting the carcass of their precious shipmate out of my fingers. They had rather a job to separate us, I've been told. A sufficiently fierce story to make an old judge and a respectable jury sit up a bit. The first thing I heard when I came to myself was the maddening howling of that endless gale, and on that the voice of the old man. He was hanging on to my bunk, staring into my face out of his sou'wester.

°*Conway boy:* a graduate of the Conway Merchant Marine Academy at Conway, in north Wales.

"'Mr. Leggatt, you have killed a man. You can act no longer as chief mate of this ship.'"

His care to subdue his voice made it sound monotonous. He rested a hand on the end of the skylight to steady himself with, and all that time did not stir a limb, so far as I could see. "Nice little tale for a quiet tea party," he concluded in the same tone.

One of my hands, too, rested on the end of the skylight; neither did I stir a limb, so far as I knew. We stood less than a foot from each other. It occurred to me that if old "Bless my soul—you don't say so" were to put his head up the companion and catch sight of us, he would think he was seeing double, or imagine himself come upon a scene of weird witch-craft; the strange captain having a quiet confabulation by the wheel with his own gray ghost. I became very much concerned to prevent anything of the sort. I heard the other's soothing undertone.

65   "My father's a parson in Norfolk," it said. Evidently he had forgotten he had told me this important fact before. Truly a nice little tale.

"You had better slip down into my stateroom now," I said, moving off stealthily. My double followed my movements; our bare feet made no sound; I let him in, closed the door with care, and, after giving a call to the second mate, returned on deck for my relief.

"Not much sign of any wind yet," I remarked when he approached.

"No, sir. Not much," he assented, sleepily, in his hoarse voice, with just enough defer-ence, no more, and barely suppressing a yawn.

"Well, that's all you have to look out for. You have got your orders."

70   "Yes, sir."

I paced a turn or two on the poop and saw him take up his position face forward with his elbow in the rat-lines of the mizzen-rigging before I went below. The mate's faint snor-ing was still going on peacefully. The cuddy lamp was burning over the table on which stood a vase with flowers, a polite attention from the ships' provision merchant—the last flowers we should see for the next three months at the very least. Two bunches of bananas hung from the beam symmetrically, one on each side of the rudder casing. Everything was as before in the ship—except that two of her captain's sleeping suits were simultaneously in use, one motionless in the cuddy, the other keeping very still in the captain's stateroom.

It must be explained here that my cabin had the form of the capital letter L, the door being within the angle and opening into the short part of the letter. A couch was to the left, the bed-place to the right; my writing desk and the chronometers table faced the door. But anyone opening it, unless he stepped right inside, had no view of what I call the long (or vertical) part of the letter. It contained some lockers surmounted by a bookcase; and a few clothes, a thick jacket or two, caps, oilskin coat, and such like, hung on hooks. There was at the bottom of that part a door opening into my bathroom, which could be entered also di-rectly from the saloon. But that way was never used.

The mysterious arrival had discovered the advantage of this particular shape. Entering my room, lighted strongly by a big bulkhead lamp swung on gimbals above my writing desk, I did not see him anywhere till he stepped out quietly from behind the coats hung in the recessed part.

"I heard somebody moving about, and went in there at once," he whispered.

75   I, too, spoke under my breath.

"Nobody is likely to come in here without knocking and getting permission."

He nodded. His face was thin and the sunburn faded, as though he had been ill. And no wonder. He had been, I heard presently, kept under arrest in his cabin for nearly seven weeks. But there was nothing sickly in his eyes or in his expression. He was not a bit like me, really; yet, as we stood leaning over my bed-place, whispering side by side, with our dark heads together and our backs to the door, anybody bold enough to open it stealthily would have been treated to the uncanny sight of a double captain busy talking in whispers with his other self.

"But all this doesn't tell me how you came to hang on to our side ladder," I inquired, in the hardly audible murmurs we used, after he had told me something more of the proceedings on board the *Sephora* once the bad weather was over.

"When we sighted Java Head I had had time to think all those matters out several times over. I had six weeks of doing nothing else, and with only an hour or so every evening for a tramp on the quarter-deck."

He whispered, his arms folded on the side of my bed-place, staring through the open port. And I could imagine perfectly the manner of this thinking out—a stubborn if not a steadfast operation; something of which I should have been perfectly incapable.

80

"I reckoned it would be dark before we closed with the land," he continued, so low that I had to strain my hearing, near as we were to each other, shoulder touching shoulder almost. "So I asked to speak to the old man. He always seemed very sick when he came to see me—as if he could not look me in the face. You know, that foresail saved the ship. She was too deep to have run long under bare poles. And it was I that managed to set it for him. Anyway, he came. When I had him in my cabin—he stood by the door looking at me as if I had the halter around my neck already—I asked him right away to leave my cabin door unlocked at night while the ship was going through Sunda Straits. There would be the Java coast within two or three miles, off Angier Point. I wanted nothing more. I've had a prize for swimming my second year in the Conway."

"I can believe it," I breathed out.

"God only knows why they locked me in every night. To see some of their faces you'd have thought they were afraid I'd go about at night strangling people. Am I a murdering brute? Do I look it? By Jove! if I had been he wouldn't have trusted himself like that into my room. You'll say I might have chucked him aside and bolted out, there and then—it was dark already. Well, no. And for the same reason I wouldn't think of trying to smash the door. There would have been a rush to stop me at the noise, and I did not mean to get into a confounded scrimmage. Somebody else might have got killed—for I would not have broken out only to get chucked back, and I did not want any more of that work. He refused, looking more sick than ever. He was afraid of the men, and also of that old second mate of his who had been sailing with him for years—a gray-headed old humbug; and his steward, too, had been with him devil knows how long—seventeen years or more—a dogmatic sort of loafer who hated me like poison, just because I was the chief mate. No chief mate ever made more than one voyage in the *Sephora*, you know. Those two old chaps ran the ship. Devil only knows what the skipper wasn't afraid of (all his nerve went to pieces altogether in that hellish spell of bad weather we had)—of what the law would do to him—of his wife, perhaps. Oh, yes! she's on board. Though I don't think she would have meddled. She would have been only too glad to have me out of the ship in any way. The 'brand of Cain' business, don't you see. That's all right. I was ready enough to go off wandering on the face of the earth—and that was price enough to pay for an Abel of that sort. Anyhow, he wouldn't listen to me. 'This thing must take its course. I represent the law here.' He was shaking like a leaf. 'So you won't?' 'No!' 'Then I hope you will be able to sleep on that,' I said, and turned my back on him. 'I wonder that you can,' cries he, and locks the door.

"Well, after that, I couldn't. Not very well. That was three weeks ago. We have had a slow passage through the Java Sea; drifted about Carimata for ten days. When we anchored here they thought, I suppose, it was all right. The nearest land (and that's five miles) is the ship's destination; the consul would soon set about catching me; and there would have been no object in bolting to these islets there. I don't suppose there's a drop of water on them. I don't know how it was, but tonight that steward, after bringing me my supper, went out to let me eat it, and left the door unlocked. And I ate it—all there was, too. After I had finished I strolled out on the quarter-deck. I don't know that I meant to do anything. A breath of fresh air was all I wanted, I believe. Then a sudden temptation came over me. I kicked off my slippers and was in the water before I had made up my mind fairly. Somebody heard the splash and they raised an awful hullabaloo. 'He's gone! Lower the boats! He's committed suicide! No, he's swimming.' Certainly I was swimming. It's not so easy for a swimmer like me to commit suicide by drowning. I landed on the nearest islet before the boat left the ship's side. I heard them pulling about in the dark, hailing, and so on, but after a bit they gave up. Everything quieted down and the anchorage became as still as death. I sat down on a stone and began to think. I felt certain they would start searching for me at daylight. There was no place to hide on those stony things—and if there had been, what would have been the good? But now I was clear of that ship, I was not going back. So after a while I took off my clothes, tied them up in a bundle with a stone inside, and dropped them in the deep water on the outer side of the islet. That was suicide enough for me. Let them think what they liked, but I didn't mean to drown myself. I meant to swim till I sank—but that's not the same thing. I struck out for another of these little islands, and it was from that one that I first saw your riding light. Something to swim for. I went on easily, and on the way I came upon a flat rock a foot or two above water. In the daytime, I dare say, you might make it out with a glass from your poop. I scrambled up on it and rested myself for a bit. Then I made another start. That last spell must have been over a mile."

85   His whisper was getting fainter and fainter, and all the time he stared straight out through the porthole, in which there was not even a star to be seen. I had not interrupted him. There was something that made comment impossible in his narrative, or perhaps in himself; a sort of feeling, a quality, which I can't find a name for. And when he ceased, all I found was a futile whisper. "So you swam for our light?"

"Yes—straight for it. It was something to swim for. I couldn't see any stars low down because the coast was in the way, and I couldn't see the land, either. The water was like glass. One might have been swimming in a confounded thousand feet deep cistern with no place for scrambling out anywhere; but what I didn't like was the notion of swimming round and round like a crazed bullock before I gave out; and as I didn't mean to go back . . . No. Do you see me being hauled back, stark naked, off one of these little islands by the scruff of the neck and fighting like a wild beast? Somebody would have got killed for certain, and I did not want any of that. So I went on. Then your ladder—"

"Why didn't you hail the ship?" I asked, a little louder.

He touched my shoulder lightly. Lazy footsteps came right over our heads and stopped. The second mate had crossed from the other side of the poop and might have been hanging over the rail, for all we knew.

"He couldn't hear us talking—could he?" My double breathed into my very ear, anxiously.

90   His anxiety was an answer, a sufficient answer, to the question I had put to him. An answer containing all the difficulty of that situation. I closed the porthole quietly, to make sure. A louder word might have been overheard.

"Who's that?" he whispered then.

"My second mate. But I don't know much more of the fellow than you do."

And I told him a little about myself. I had been appointed to take charge while I least expected anything of the sort, not quite a fortnight ago. I didn't know either the ship or the people. Hadn't had the time in port to look about me or size anybody up. And as to the crew, all they knew was that I was appointed to take the ship home. For the rest, I was almost as much of a stranger on board as himself, I said. And at the moment I felt it most acutely. I felt that it would take very little to make me a suspect person in the eyes of the ship's company.

He had turned about meantime; and we, the two strangers in the ship, faced each other in identical attitudes.

"Your ladder—" he murmured, after a silence. "Who'd have thought of finding a ladder   95
hanging over at night in a ship anchored out here! I felt just then a very unpleasant faintness. After the life I've been leading for nine weeks, anybody would have got out of condition. I wasn't capable of swimming round as far as your rudder chains. And, lo and behold!
there was a ladder to get hold of. After I gripped it I said to myself, 'What's the good?'
When I saw a man's head looking over I thought I would swim away presently and leave
him shouting—in whatever language it was. I didn't mind being looked at. I—I liked it.
And then you speaking to me so quietly—as if you had expected me—made me hold on a
little longer. It had been a confounded lonely time—I don't mean while swimming. I was
glad to talk a little to somebody that didn't belong to the *Sephora*. As to asking for the captain, that was a mere impulse. It could have been no use, with all the ship knowing about
me and the other people pretty certain to be round here in the morning. I don't know—I
wanted to be seen, to talk with somebody, before I went on. I don't know what I would
have said . . . 'Fine night, isn't it?' or something of the sort."

"Do you think they will be round here presently?" I asked with some incredulity.

"Quite likely," he said, faintly

He looked extremely haggard all of a sudden. His head rolled on his shoulders.

"H'm. We shall see then. Meantime get into that bed," I whispered. "Want help? There."

It was a rather high bed-place with a set of drawers underneath. This amazing swimmer   100
really needed the lift I gave him by seizing his leg. He tumbled in, rolled over on his back,
and flung one arm across his eyes. And then, with his face nearly hidden, he must have
looked exactly as I used to look in that bed. I gazed upon my other self for a while before
drawing across carefully the two green serge curtains which ran on a brass rod. I thought
for a moment of pinning them together for greater safety, but I sat down on the couch, and
once there I felt unwilling to rise and hunt for a pin. I would do it in a moment. I was extremely tired, in a peculiarly intimate way, by the strain of stealthiness, by the effort of
whispering and the general secrecy of this excitement. It was three o'clock by now and I
had been on my feet since nine, but I was not sleepy; I could not have gone to sleep. I sat
there, fagged out, looking at the curtains, trying to clear my mind of the confused sensation
of being in two places at once, and greatly bothered by an exasperating knocking in my
head. It was a relief to discover suddenly that it was not in my head at all, but on the outside of the door. Before I could collect myself the words "Come in" were out of my mouth,
and the steward entered with a tray, bringing in my morning coffee. I had slept, after all,
and I was so frightened that I shouted, "This way! I am here, steward," as though he had
been miles away. He put down the tray on the table next the couch and only then said, very
quietly, "I can see you are here, sir." I felt him give me a keen look, but I dared not meet his
eyes just then. He must have wondered why I had drawn the curtains of my bed before
going to sleep on the couch. He went out, hooking the door open as usual.

I heard the crew washing decks above me. I knew I would have been told at once if there
had been any wind. Calm, I thought, and I was doubly vexed. Indeed, I felt dual more than
ever. The steward reappeared suddenly in the doorway. I jumped up from the couch so
quickly that he gave a start.

"What do you want here?"

"Close your port, sir—they are washing decks."

"It is closed," I said, reddening.

"Very well, sir." But he did not move from the doorway and returned my stare in an ex-   105
traordinary, equivocal manner for a time. Then his eyes wavered, all his expression
changed, and in a voice unusually gentle, almost coaxingly:

"May I come in to take the empty cup away, sir?"

"Of course!" I turned my back on him while he popped in and out. Then I unhooked and
closed the door and even pushed the bolt. This sort of thing could not go on very long. The

cabin was as hot as an oven, too. I took a peep at my double, and discovered that he had not moved, his arm was still over his eyes; but his chest heaved; his hair was wet; his chin glistened with perspiration. I reached over him and opened the port.

"I must show myself on deck," I reflected.

Of course, theoretically, I could do what I liked, with no one to say nay to me within the whole circle of the horizon; but to lock my cabin door and take the key away I did not dare. Directly I put my head out of the companion [,] I saw the group of my two officers, the second mate barefooted, the chief mate in long india-rubber boots, near the break of the poop, and the steward halfway down the poop ladder talking to them eagerly. He happened to catch sight of me and dived, the second ran down on the main deck shouting some order or other, and the chief mate came to meet me, touching his cap.

110   There was a sort of curiosity in his eye that I did not like. I don't know whether the steward had told them that I was "queer" only, or downright drunk, but I know the man meant to have a good look at me. I watched him coming with a smile which, as he got into point-blank range, took effect and froze his very whiskers. I did not give him time to open his lips.

"Square the yards by lifts and braces before the hands go to breakfast."

It was the first particular order I had given on board that ship; and I stayed on deck to see it executed, too. I had felt the need of asserting myself without loss of time. That sneering young cub got taken down a peg or two on that occasion, and I also seized the opportunity of having a good look at the face of every foremast man as they filed past me to go to the after braces. At breakfast time, eating nothing myself, I presided with such frigid dignity that the two mates were only too glad to escape from the cabin as soon as decency permitted; and all the time the dual working of my mind distracted me almost to the point of insanity. I was constantly watching myself, my secret self, as dependent on my actions as my own personality, sleeping in that bed, behind that door which faced me as I sat at the head of the table. It was very much like being mad, only it was worse because one was aware of it.

I had to shake him for a solid minute, but when at last he opened his eyes it was in the full possession of his senses, with an inquiring look.

"All's well so far," I whispered. "Now you must vanish into the bathroom."

115   He did so, as noiseless as a ghost, and I then rang for the steward, and facing him boldly, directed him to tidy up my stateroom while I was having my bath— "and be quick about it." As my tone admitted of no excuses, he said, "Yes, sir," and ran off to fetch his dustpan and brushes. I took a bath and did most of my dressing, splashing, and whistling softly for the steward's edification, while the secret sharer of my life stood drawn up bolt upright in that little space, his face looking very sunken in daylight, his eyelids lowered under the stern, dark line of his eyebrows drawn together by a slight frown.

When I left him there to go back to my room the steward was finished dusting. I sent for the mate and engaged him in some insignificant conversation. It was, as it were, trifling with the terrific character of whiskers; but my object was to give him an opportunity for a good look at my cabin. And then I could at last shut, with a clear conscience, the door of my stateroom and get my double back into the recessed part. There was nothing else for it. He had to sit still on a small folding stool, half smothered by the heavy coats hanging there. We listened to the steward going into the bathroom out of the saloon, filling the water bottles there, scrubbing the bath, setting things to rights, whisk, bang, clatter—out again into the saloon—turn the key—click. Such was my scheme for keeping my second self invisible. Nothing better could be contrived under the circumstances. And there we sat; I at my writing desk ready to appear busy with some papers, he behind me, out of sight of the door. It would not have been prudent to talk in daytime; and I could not have stood the excitement of that queer sense of whispering to myself. Now and then, glancing over my shoulder, I saw him far back there, sitting rigidly on the low stool, his bare feet close together, his arms folded, his head hanging on his breast—and perfectly still. Anybody would have taken him for me.

I was fascinated by it myself. Every moment I had to glance over my shoulder. I was looking at him when a voice outside the door said:

"Beg pardon, sir."

"Well!" . . . I kept my eyes on him, and so, when the voice outside the door announced, "There's a ship's boat coming our way, sir," I saw him give a start—the first movement he had made for hours. But he did not raise his bowed head.

"All right. Get the ladder over."

I hesitated. Should I whisper something to him? But what? His immobility seemed to have been never disturbed. What could I tell him he did not know already? . . . Finally I went on deck.

120

2

The skipper of the *Sephora* had a thin red whisker all round his face, and the sort of complexion that goes with hair of that color; also the particular, rather smeary shade of blue in the eyes. He was not exactly a showy figure; his shoulders were high, his stature but middling—one leg slightly more bandy than the other. He shook hands, looking vaguely around. A spiritless tenacity was his main characteristic, I judged. I behaved with a politeness which seemed to disconcert him. Perhaps he was shy. He mumbled to me as if he were ashamed of what he was saying; gave his name (it was something like Archbold—but at this distance of years I hardly am sure), his ship's name, and a few other particulars of that sort, in the manner of a criminal making a reluctant and doleful confession. He had had terrible weather on the passage out—terrible—terrible—wife aboard, too.

By this time we were seated in the cabin and the steward brought in a tray with a bottle and glasses. "Thanks! No." Never took liquor. Would have some water, though. He drank two tumblerfuls. Terrible thirsty work. Ever since daylight had been exploring the islands round his ship.

"What was that for—fun?" I asked, with an appearance of polite interest.

"No!" He sighed. "Painful duty."

125

As he persisted in his mumbling and I wanted my double to hear every word, I hit upon the notion of informing him that I regretted to say I was hard of hearing.

"Such a young man, too!" he nodded, keeping his smeary blue, unintelligent eyes fastened upon me. What was the cause of it—some disease? he inquired, without the least sympathy and as if he thought that, if so, I'd got no more than I deserved.

"Yes; disease," I admitted in a cheerful tone which seemed to shock him. But my point was gained, because he had to raise his voice to give me his tale. It is not worth while to record that version. It was just over two months since all this had happened, and he had thought so much about it that he seemed completely muddled as to its bearings, but still immensely impressed.

"What would you think of such a thing happening on board your own ship? I've had the *Sephora* for these fifteen years. I am a well-known shipmaster."

He was densely distressed—and perhaps I should have sympathized with him if I had been able to detach my mental vision from the unsuspected sharer of my cabin as though he were my second self. There he was on the other side of the bulkhead, four or five feet from us, no more, as we sat in the saloon. I looked politely at Captain Archbold (if that was his name), but it was the other I saw, in a gray sleeping suit, seated on a low stool, his bare feet close together, his arms folded, and every word said between us falling into the ears of his dark head bowed on his chest.

130

"I have been at sea now, man and boy, for seven-and-thirty years, and I've never heard of such a thing happening in an English ship. And that it should be my ship. Wife on board, too."

I was hardly listening to him.

"Don't you think," I said, "that the heavy sea which, you told me, came aboard just then might have killed the man? I have seen the sheer weight of a sea kill a man very neatly, by simply breaking his neck."

"Good God!" he uttered, impressively, fixing his smeary blue eyes on me. "The sea! No man killed by the sea ever looked like that." He seemed positively scandalized at my suggestion. And as I gazed at him, certainly not prepared for anything original on his part, he advanced his head close to mine and thrust his tongue out at me so suddenly that I couldn't help starting back.

135   After scoring over my calmness in this graphic way he nodded wisely. If I had seen the sight, he assured me, I would never forget it as long as I lived. The weather was too bad to give the corpse a proper sea burial. So next day at dawn they took it up on the poop, covering its face with a bit of bunting; he read a short prayer, and then, just as it was, in its oilskins and long boots, they launched it amongst those mountainous seas that seemed ready every moment to swallow up the ship herself and the terrified lives on board of her.

"That reefed foresail saved you," I threw in.

"Under God—it did," he exclaimed fervently. "It was by a special mercy, I firmly believe, that it stood some of those hurricane squalls."

"It was the setting of that sail which—" I began.

"God's own hand in it," he interrupted me. "Nothing less could have done it. I don't mind telling you that I hardly dared give the order. It seemed impossible that we could touch anything without losing it, and then our last hope would have been gone."

140   The terror of that gale was on him yet. I let him go on for a bit, then said, casually—as if returning to a minor subject:

"You were very anxious to give up your mate to the shore people, I believe?"

He was. To the law. His obscure tenacity on that point had in it something incomprehensible and a little awful; something, as it were, mystical, quite apart from his anxiety that he should not be suspected of "countenancing any doings of that sort." Seven-and-thirty virtuous years at sea, of which over twenty of immaculate command, and the last fifteen in the *Sephora*, seemed to have laid him under some pitiless obligation.

"And you know," he went on, groping shamefacedly amongst his feelings, "I did not engage that young fellow. His people had some interest with my owners. I was in a way forced to take him on. He looked very smart, very gentlemanly, and all that. But do you know—I never liked him, somehow. I am a plain man. You see, he wasn't exactly the sort for the chief mate of a ship like the *Sephora*."

I had become so connected in thoughts and impressions with the secret sharer of my cabin that I felt as if I, personally, were being given to understand that I, too, was not the sort that would have done for the chief mate of a ship like the *Sephora*. I had no doubt of it in my mind.

145   "Not at all the style of man. You understand," he insisted, superfluously, looking hard at me.

I smiled urbanely. He seemed at a loss for a while.

"I suppose I must report a suicide."

"Beg pardon?"

"Suicide! That's what I'll have to write to my owners directly I get in."

150   "Unless you manage to recover him before tomorrow," I assented, dispassionately. . . . "I mean, alive."

He mumbled something which I really did not catch, and I turned my ear to him in a puzzled manner. He fairly bawled:

"The land—I say, the mainland is at least seven miles off my anchorage."

"About that."

My lack of excitement, of curiosity, of surprise, of any sort of pronounced interest, began to arouse his distrust. But except for the felicitous pretense of deafness I had not tried to pretend anything. I had felt utterly incapable of playing the part of ignorance properly, and therefore was afraid to try. It is also certain that he had brought some ready-made suspicions with him, and that he viewed my politeness as a strange and unnatural phenomenon. And yet how else could I have received him? Not heartily! That was impossible for psychological reasons, which I need not state here. My only object was to keep off his inquiries. Surlily? Yes, but surliness might have provoked a point-blank question. From its novelty to him and from its nature, punctilious courtesy was the manner best calculated to restrain the man. But there was the danger of his breaking through my defense bluntly. I could not, I think, have met him by a direct lie, also for psychological (not moral) reasons. If he had only known how afraid I was of his putting my feeling of identity with the other to the test! But, strangely enough—(I thought of it only afterward)—I believe that he was not a little disconcerted by the reverse side of that weird situation, by something in me that reminded him of the man he was seeking—suggested a mysterious similitude to the young fellow he had distrusted and disliked from the first.

However that might have been, the silence was not very prolonged. He took another oblique step.   155

"I reckon I had no more than a two-mile pull to your ship. Not a bit more."

"And quite enough, too, in this awful heat," I said.

Another pause full of mistrust followed. Necessity, they say, is mother of invention, but fear, too, is not barren of ingenious suggestions. And I was afraid he would ask me point-blank for news of my other self.

"Nice little saloon, isn't it?" I remarked, as if noticing for the first time the way his eyes roamed from one closed door to the other. "And very well fitted out, too. Here, for instance," I continued reaching over the back of my seat negligently and flinging the door open, "is my bathroom."

He made an eager movement, but hardly gave it a glance. I got up, shut the door of the   160
bathroom, and invited him to have a look round, as if I were very proud of my accommodation. He had to rise and be shown round, but he went through the business without any raptures whatever.

"And now we'll have a look at my stateroom," I declared, in a voice as loud as I dared to make it, crossing the cabin to the starboard side with purposely heavy steps.

He followed me in and gazed around. My intelligent double had vanished. I played my part.

"Very convenient—isn't it?"

"Very nice. Very comf. . . ." He didn't finish, and went out brusquely as if to escape from some unrighteous wiles of mine. But it was not to be. I had been too frightened not to feel vengeful; I felt I had him on the run, and I meant to keep him on the run. My polite insistence must have had something menacing in it, because he gave in suddenly. And I did not let him off a single item; mate's room, pantry, storerooms, the very sail locker which was also under the poop—he had to look into them all. When at last I showed him out on the quarter-deck he drew a long, spiritless sigh, and mumbled dismally that he must really be going back to his ship now. I desired my mate, who had joined us, to see to the captain's boat.

The man of whiskers gave a blast on the whistle which he used to wear hanging round   165
his neck, and yelled, *"Sephora* away!" My double down there in my cabin must have heard,

and certainly could not feel more relieved than I. Four fellows came running out from somewhere forward and went over the side, while my own men, appearing on deck too, lined the rail. I escorted my visitor to the gangway ceremoniously, and nearly overdid it. He was a tenacious beast. On the very ladder he lingered, and in that unique, guiltily conscientious manner of sticking to the point:

"I say . . . you . . . you don't think that—"

I covered his voice loudly:

"Certainly not. . . . I am delighted. Good-by."

I had an idea of what he meant to say, and just saved myself by the privilege of defective hearing. He was too shaken generally to insist, but my mate, close witness of that parting, looked mystified and his face took on a thoughtful cast. As I did not want to appear as if I wished to avoid all communication with my officers, he had the opportunity to address me.

170   "Seems a very nice man. His boat's crew told our chaps a very extraordinary story, if what I am told by the steward is true. I suppose you had it from the captain, sir?"

"Yes. I had a story from the captain."

"A very horrible affair—isn't it, sir?"

"It is."

"Beats all these tales we hear about murders in Yankee ships."

175   "I don't think it beats them. I don't think it resembles them in the least."

"Bless my soul—you don't say so! But of course I've no acquaintance whatever with American ships, not I, so I couldn't go against your knowledge. It's horrible enough for me. . . . But the queerest part is that these fellows seemed to have some idea the man was hidden aboard here. They had really. Did you ever hear of such a thing?"

"Preposterous—isn't it?"

We were walking to and fro athwart the quarter-deck. No one of the crew forward could be seen (the day was Sunday), and the mate pursued:

"There was some little dispute about it. Our chaps took offense. 'As if we would harbor a thing like that,' they said. 'Wouldn't you like to look for him in our coal hole?' Quite a tiff. But they made it up in the end. I suppose he did drown himself. Don't you, sir?"

180   "I don't suppose anything."

"You have no doubt in the matter, sir?"

"None whatever."

I left him suddenly. I felt I was producing a bad impression, but with my double down there it was most trying to be on deck. And it was almost as trying to be below. Altogether a nerve-trying situation. But on the whole I felt less torn in two when I was with him. There was no one in the whole ship whom I dared take into my confidence. Since the hands had got to know his story, it would have been impossible to pass him off for anyone else, and an accidental discovery was to be dreaded now more than ever. . . .

The steward being engaged in laying the table for dinner, we could talk only with our eyes when I first went down. Later in the afternoon we had a cautious try at whispering. The Sunday quietness of the ship was against us; the stillness of air and water around her was against us; the elements, the men were against us—everything was against us in our secret partnership; time itself—for this could not go on forever. The very trust in Providence was, I suppose, denied to his guilt. Shall I confess that this thought cast me down very much? And as to the chapter of accidents which counts for so much in the book of success, I could only hope that it was closed. For what favorable accident could be expected?

185   "Did you hear everything?" were my first words as soon as we took up our position side by side, leaning over my bed-place.

He had. And the proof of it was his earnest whisper, "The man told you he hardly dared to give the order."

I understood the reference to be to that saving foresail.

"Yes. He was afraid of it being lost in the setting."

"I assure you he never gave the order. He may think he did, but he never gave it. He stood there with me on the break of the poop after the maintopsail blew away, and whimpered about our last hope—positively whimpered about it and nothing else—and the night coming on! To hear one's skipper go on like that in such weather was enough to drive any fellow out of his mind. It worked me up into a sort of desperation. I just took it into my hands and went away from him, boiling, and—But what's the use telling you? *You* know! . . . Do you think that if I had not been pretty fierce with them I should have got the men to do anything? Not it! The bosun perhaps? Perhaps! It wasn't a heavy sea—it was a sea gone mad! I suppose the end of the world will be something like that; and a man may have the heart to see it coming once and be done with it—but to have to face it day after day—I don't blame anybody. I was precious little better than the rest. Only—I was an officer of that old coal-wagon, anyhow—"

"I quite understand," I conveyed that sincere assurance into his ear. He was out of breath with whispering; I could hear him pant slightly. It was all very simple. The same strung-up force which had given twenty-four men a chance, at least, for their lives, had, in a sort of recoil, crushed an unworthy mutinous existence.   190

But I had no leisure to weigh the merits of the matter—footsteps in the saloon, a heavy knock. "There's enough wind to get under way with, sir." Here was the call of a new claim upon my thoughts and even upon my feelings.

"Turn the hands up," I cried through the door. "I'll be on deck directly."

I was going out to make the acquaintance of my ship. Before I left the cabin our eyes met—the eyes of the only two strangers on board. I pointed to the recessed part where the little campstool awaited him and laid my finger on my lips. He made a gesture—somewhat vague—a little mysterious, accompanied by a faint smile, as if of regret.

This is not the place to enlarge upon the sensations of a man who feels for the first time a ship move under his feet to his own independent word. In my case they were not unalloyed. I was not wholly alone with my command; for there was that stranger in my cabin. Or rather, I was not completely and wholly with her. Part of me was absent. That mental feeling of being in two places at once affected me physically as if the mood of secrecy had penetrated my very soul. Before an hour had elapsed since the ship had begun to move, having occasion to ask the mate (he stood by my side) to take a compass bearing of the Pagoda, I caught myself reaching up to his ear in whispers. I say I caught myself, but enough had escaped to startle the man. I can't describe it otherwise than by saying that he shied. A grave, preoccupied manner, as though he were in possession of some perplexing intelligence, did not leave him henceforth. A little later I moved away from the rail to look at the compass with such a stealthy gait that the helmsman noticed it—and I could not help noticing the unusual roundness of his eyes. These are trifling instances, though it's to no commander's advantage to be suspected of ludicrous eccentricities. But I was also more seriously affected. There are to a seaman certain words, gestures, that should in given conditions come as naturally, as instinctively as the winking of a menaced eye. A certain order should spring on to his lips without thinking; a certain sign should get itself made, so to speak, without reflection. But all unconscious alertness had abandoned me. I had to make an effort of will to recall myself back (from the cabin) to the conditions of the moment. I felt that I was appearing an irresolute commander to those people who were watching me more or less critically.

And, besides, there were the scares. On the second day out, for instance, coming off the deck in the afternoon (I had straw slippers on my bare feet) I stopped at the open pantry door and spoke to the steward. He was doing something there with his back to me. At the sound of my voice he nearly jumped out of his skin, as the saying is, and incidentally broke a cup.   195

"What on earth's the matter with you?" I asked, astonished.

He was extremely confused. "Beg your pardon, sir. I made sure you were in your cabin."

"You see I wasn't."

"No, sir. I could have sworn I had heard you moving in there not a moment ago. It's most extraordinary, very sorry, sir.

200   I passed on with an inward shudder. I was so identified with my secret double that I did not even mention the fact in those scanty, fearful whispers we exchanged. I suppose he had made some slight noise of some kind or other. It would have been miraculous if he hadn't at one time or another. And yet, haggard as he appeared, he looked always perfectly self-controlled, more than calm—almost invulnerable. On my suggestion he remained almost entirely in the bathroom, which, upon the whole, was the safest place. There could be really no shadow of an excuse for anyone ever wanting to go in there, once the steward had done with it. It was a very tiny place. Sometimes he reclined on the floor, his legs bent, his head sustained on one elbow. At others I would find him on the campstool, sitting in his gray sleeping suit and with his cropped dark hair like a patient, unmoved convict. At night I would smuggle him into my bed-place, and we would whisper together, with the regular footfalls of the officer of the watch passing and repassing over our heads. It was an infinitely miserable time. It was lucky that some tins of fine preserves were stowed in a locker in my stateroom; hard bread I could always get hold of; and so he lived on stewed chicken, *paté de foie gras*, asparagus, cooked oysters, sardines—on all sorts of abominable sham delicacies out of tins. My early morning coffee he always drank; and it was all I dared do for him in that respect.

Every day there was the horrible maneuvering to go through so that my room and then the bathroom should be done in the usual way. I came to hate the sight of the steward, to abhor the voice of that harmless man. I felt that it was he who would bring on the disaster of discovery. It hung like a sword over our heads.

The fourth day out, I think (we were working down the east side of the Gulf of Siam, tack for tack, in light winds and smooth water)—the fourth day, I say, of this miserable juggling with the unavoidable, as we sat at our evening meal, that man, whose slightest movement I dreaded, after putting down the dishes ran up on deck busily. This could not be dangerous. Presently he came down again; and then it appeared that he had remembered a coat of mine which I had thrown over a rail to dry after having been wetted in a shower which had passed over the ship in the afternoon. Sitting stolidly at the head of the table I became terrified at the sight of the garment on his arm. Of course he made for my door. There was no time to lose.

"Steward," I thundered. My nerves were so shaken that I could not govern my voice and conceal my agitation. This was the sort of thing that made my terrifically whiskered mate tap his forehead with his forefinger. I had detected him using that gesture while talking on deck with a confidential air to the carpenter. It was too far to hear a word, but I had no doubt that this pantomime could only refer to the strange new captain.

"Yes, sir," the pale-faced steward turned resignedly to me. It was this maddening course of being shouted at, checked without rhyme or reason, arbitrarily chased out of my cabin, suddenly called into it, sent flying out of his pantry on incomprehensible errands, that accounted for the growing wretchedness of his expression.

205   "Where are you going with that coat?"

"To your room, sir."

"Is there another shower coming?"

"I'm sure I don't know, sir. Shall I go up again and see, sir?"

"No! never mind."

210   My object was attained, as of course my other self in there would have heard everything that passed. During this interlude my two officers never raised their eyes off their respective plates; but the lip of that confounded cub, the second mate, quivered visibly.

I expected the steward to hook my coat on and come out at once. He was very slow about it; but I dominated my nervousness sufficiently not to shout after him. Suddenly I became aware (it could be heard plainly enough) that the fellow for some reason or other was opening the door of the bathroom. It was the end. The place was literally not big enough to swing a cat in. My voice died in my throat and I went stony all over. I expected to hear a yell of surprise and terror, and made a movement, but had not the strength to get on my legs. Everything remained still. Had my second self taken the poor wretch by the throat? I don't know what I would have done next moment if I had not seen the steward come out of my room, close the door, and then stand quietly by the sideboard.

Saved, I thought. But, no! Lost! Gone! He was gone!

I laid my knife and fork down and leaned back in my chair. My head swam. After a while, when sufficiently recovered to speak in a steady voice, I instructed my mate to put the ship round at eight o'clock himself.

"I won't come on deck," I went on. "I think I'll turn in, and unless the wind shifts I don't want to be disturbed before midnight. I feel a bit seedy."

"You did look middling bad a little while ago," the chief mate remarked without showing any great concern. — 215

They both went out, and I stared at the steward clearing the table. There was nothing to be read on that wretched man's face. But why did he avoid my eyes I asked myself. Then I thought I should like to hear the sound of his voice.

"Steward!"

"Sir!" Startled as usual.

"Where did you hang up that coat?"

"In the bathroom, sir." The usual anxious tone. "It's not quite dry yet, sir." — 220

For some time longer I sat in the cuddy. Had my double vanished as he had come? But of his coming there was an explanation, whereas his disappearance would be inexplicable. . . . I went slowly into my dark room, shut the door, lighted the lamp, and for a time dared not turn round. When at last I did I saw him standing bolt upright in the narrow recessed part. It would not be true to say I had a shock, but an irresistible doubt of his bodily existence flitted through my mind. Can it be, I asked myself, that he is not visible to other eyes than mine? It was like being haunted. Motionless, with a grave face, he raised his hands slightly at me in a gesture which meant clearly, "Heavens! what a narrow escape!" Narrow indeed. I think I had come creeping quietly as near insanity as any man who has not actually gone over the border. That gesture restrained me, so to speak.

The mate with the terrific whiskers was now putting the ship on the other tack. In the moment of profound silence which follows upon the hands going to their stations I heard on the poop his raised voice: "Hard alee!" and the distant shout of the order repeated on the maindeck. The sails, in that light breeze, made but a faint fluttering noise. It ceased. The ship was coming round slowly; I held my breath in the renewed stillness of expectation; one wouldn't have thought that there was a single living soul on her decks. A sudden brisk shout, "Mainsail haul!" broke the spell, and in the noisy cries and rush overhead of the men running away with the main brace we two, down in my cabin, came together in our usual position by the bed-place.

He did not wait for my question. "I heard him fumbling here and just managed to squat myself down in the bath," he whispered to me. "The fellow only opened the door and put his arm in to hang the coat up. All the same—"

"I never thought of that," I whispered back, even more appalled than before at the closeness of the shave, and marveling at that something unyielding in his character which was carrying him through so finely. There was no agitation in his whisper. Whoever was being driven distracted, it was not he. He was sane. And the proof of his sanity was continued when he took up the whispering again.

225   "It would never do for me to come to life again."

It was something that a ghost might have said. But what he was alluding to was his old captain's reluctant admission of the theory of suicide. It would obviously serve his turn—if I had understood at all the view which seemed to govern the unalterable purpose of his action.

"You must maroon me as soon as ever you can get amongst these islands off the Cambodje shore," he went on.

"Maroon you! We are not living in a boy's adventure tale," I protested. His scornful whispering took me up.

"We aren't indeed! There's nothing of a boy's tale in this. But there's nothing else for it. I want no more. You don't suppose I am afraid of what can be done to me? Prison or gallows or whatever they may please. But you don't see me coming back to explain such things to an old fellow in a wig and twelve respectable tradesmen, do you? What can they know whether I am guilty or not—or of *what* I am guilty, either? That's my affair. What does the Bible say? 'Driven off the face of the earth.'° Very well. I am off the face of the earth now. As I came at night so I shall go."

230   "Impossible!" I murmured. "You can't."

"Can't? . . . Not naked like a soul on the Day of Judgment. I shall freeze on to this sleeping suit. The Last Day is not yet—and, . . . you have understood thoroughly. Didn't you?"

I felt suddenly ashamed of myself. I may say truly that I understood—and my hesitation in letting that man swim away from my ship's side had been a mere sham sentiment, a sort of cowardice.

"It can't be done now till next night," I breathed out. "The ship is on the offshore tack and the wind may fail us."

"As long as I know that you understand," he whispered. "But of course you do. It's a great satisfaction to have got somebody to understand. You seem to have been there on purpose." And in the same whisper, as if we two whenever we talked had to say things to each other which were not fit for the world to hear, he added, "It's very wonderful."

235   We remained side by side talking in our secret way—but sometimes silent or just exchanging a whispered word or two at long intervals. And as usual he stared through the port. A breath of wind came now and again into our faces. The ship might have been moored in dock, so gently and on an even keel she slipped through the water, that did not murmur even at our passage, shadowy and silent like a phantom sea.

At midnight I went on deck, and to my mate's great surprise put the ship round on the other tack. His terrible whiskers flitted round me in silent criticism. I certainly should not have done it if it had been only a question of getting out of that sleepy gulf as quickly as possible. I believe he told the second mate, who relieved him, that it was a great want of judgment. The other only yawned. That intolerable cub shuffled about so sleepily and lolled against the rails in such a slack, improper fashion that I came down on him sharply.

"Aren't you properly awake yet?"

"Yes, sir! I am awake."

"Well, then, be good enough to hold yourself as if you were. And keep a lookout. If there's any current we'll be closing with some islands before daylight."

240   The east side of the gulf is fringed with islands, some solitary, others in groups. On the blue background of the high coast they seem to float on silvery patches of calm water, arid and gray, or dark green and rounded like clumps of evergreen bushes, with the larger ones, a mile or two long, showing the outlines of ridges, ribs of gray rock under the dark mantle of matted leafage. Unknown to trade, to travel, almost to geography, the manner of life they harbor is an unsolved secret. There must be villages—settlements of fishermen at least—on

---

°*face of the earth:* a common Biblical phrase; see Deuteronomy 6:15 or Jeremiah 28:16.

the largest of them, and some communication with the world is probably kept up by native craft. But all forenoon, as we headed for them, fanned along by the faintest of breezes, I saw no sign of man or canoe in the field of the telescope I kept on pointing at the scattered group.

At noon I gave no orders for a change of course, and the mate's whiskers became much concerned and seemed to be offering themselves unduly to my notice. At last I said:

"I am going to stand right in. Quite in—as far as I can take her."

The stare of extreme surprise imparted an air of ferocity also to his eyes, and he looked truly terrific for a moment.

"We're not doing well in the middle of the gulf," I continued, casually. "I am going to look for the land breezes tonight."

"Bless my soul! Do you mean, sir, in the dark amongst the lot of all them islands and reefs and shoals?"   245

"Well—if there are any regular land breezes at all on this coast one must get close in-shore to find them, mustn't one?"

"Bless my soul!" he exclaimed again under his breath. All that afternoon he wore a dreamy, contemplative appearance which in him was a mark of perplexity. After dinner I went into my stateroom as if I meant to take some rest. There we two bent our dark heads over a half-unrolled chart lying on my bed.

"There," I said. "It's got to be Koh-ring. I've been looking at it ever since sunrise. It has got two hills and a low point. It must be inhabited. And on the coast opposite there is what looks like the mouth of a biggish river—with some town, no doubt, not far up. It's the best chance for you that I can see.

"Anything. Koh-ring let it be."

He looked thoughtfully at the chart as if surveying chances and distances from a lofty   250
height—and following with his eyes his own figure wandering on the blank land of Cochin China, and then passing off that piece of paper clean out of sight into uncharted regions. And it was as if the ship had two captains to plan her course for her. I had been so worried and restless running up and down that I had not had the patience to dress that day. I had remained in my sleeping suit, with straw slippers and a soft floppy hat. The closeness of the heat in the gulf had been most oppressive, and the crew were used to see me wandering in that airy attire.

"She will clear the south point as she heads now," I whispered into his ear. "Goodness only knows when, though, but certainly after dark. I'll edge her in to half a mile, as far as I may be able to judge in the dark—"

"Be careful," he murmured, warningly—and I realized suddenly that all my future, the only future for which I was fit, would perhaps go irretrievably to pieces in any mishap to my first command.

I could not stop a moment longer in the room. I motioned him to get out of sight and made my way on the poop. That unplayful cub had the watch. I walked up and down for a while thinking things out, then beckoned him over.

"Send a couple of hands to open the two quarter-deck ports," I said, mildly.

He actually had the impudence, or else so forgot himself in his wonder at such an in-   255
comprehensible order, as to repeat:

"Open the quarter-deck ports! What for, sir?"

"The only reason you need concern yourself about is because I tell you to do so. Have them open wide and fastened properly."

He reddened and went off, but I believe made some jeering remark to the carpenter as to the sensible practice of ventilating a ship's quarter-deck. I know he popped into the mate's cabin to impart the fact to him because the whiskers came on deck, as it were by chance, and stole glances at me from below—for signs of lunacy or drunkenness, I suppose.

A little before supper, feeling more restless than ever, I rejoined, for a moment, my second self. And to find him sitting so quietly was surprising, like something against nature, inhuman.

260 I developed my plan in a hurried whisper.

"I shall stand in as close as I dare and then put her round. I shall presently find means to smuggle you out of here into the sail locker, which communicates with the lobby. But there is an opening, a sort of square for hauling the sails out, which gives straight on the quarter-deck and which is never closed in fine weather, so as to give air to the sails. When the ship's way is deadened in stays and all the hands are aft at the main braces you shall have a clear road to slip out and get overboard through the open quarter-deck port. I've had them both fastened up. Use a rope's end to lower yourself into the water so as to avoid a splash—you know. It could be heard and cause some beastly complication."

He kept silent for a while, then whispered, "I understand."

"I won't be there to see you go," I began with an effort. "The rest . . . I only hope I have understood, too."

"You have. From first to last," and for the first time there seemed to be a faltering, something strained in his whisper. He caught hold of my arm, but the ringing of the supper bell made me start. He didn't, though; he only released his grip.

265 After supper I didn't come below again till well past eight o'clock. The faint, steady breeze was loaded with dew; and the wet, darkened sails held all there was of propelling power in it. The night, clear and starry, sparkled darkly, and the opaque, lightless patches shifting slowly against the low stars were the drifting islets. On the port bow there was a big one more distant and shadowily imposing by the great space of sky it eclipsed.

On opening the door I had a back view of my very own self looking at a chart. He had come out of the recess and was standing near the table.

"Quite dark enough," I whispered.

He stepped back and leaned against my bed with a level, quiet glance. I sat on the couch. We had nothing to say to each other. Over our heads the officer of the watch moved here and there. Then I heard him move quickly. I knew what that meant. He was making for the companion; and presently his voice was outside my door.

"We are drawing in pretty fast, sir. Land looks rather close."

270 "Very well," I answered. "I am coming on deck directly."

I waited till he was gone out of the cuddy, then rose. My double moved too. The time had come to exchange our last whispers, for neither of us was ever to hear each other's natural voice.

"Look here!" I opened a drawer and took out three sovereigns.° "Take this, anyhow. I've got six and I'd give you the lot, only I must keep a little money to buy some fruit and vegetables for the crew from native boats as we go through Sunda Straits."

He shook his head.

"Take it," I urged him, whispering desperately. "No one can tell what—"

275 He smiled and slapped meaningly the only pocket of the sleeping jacket. It was not safe, certainly. But I produced a large old silk handkerchief of mine, and tying the three pieces of gold in a corner, pressed it on him. He was touched, I suppose, because he took it at last and tied it quickly round his waist under the jacket, on his bare skin.

Our eyes met; several seconds elapsed, till, our glances still mingled, I extended my hand and turned the lamp out. Then I passed through the cuddy, leaving the door of my room wide open. "Steward!"

He was still lingering in the pantry in the greatness of his zeal, giving a rub-up to a plated cruet stand the last thing before going to bed. Being careful not to wake up the mate, whose room was opposite, I spoke in an undertone.

°*sovereigns:* gold coins worth a pound each.

He looked round anxiously. "Sir!"

"Can you get me a little hot water from the galley?"

"I am afraid, sir, the galley fire's been out for some time now."   280

"Go and see."

He fled up the stairs.

"Now," I whispered, loudly, into the saloon—too loudly, perhaps, but I was afraid I couldn't make a sound. He was by my side in an instant—the double captain slipped past the stairs—through the tiny dark passage . . . a sliding door. We were in the sail locker, scrambling on our knees over the sails. A sudden thought struck me. I saw myself wandering barefooted, bareheaded, the sun beating on my dark poll. I snatched off my floppy hat and tried hurriedly in the dark to ram it on my other self. He dodged and fended off silently. I wonder what he thought had come to me before he understood and suddenly desisted. Our hands met gropingly, lingered united in a steady, motionless clasp for a second. . . . No word was breathed by either of us when they separated.

I was standing quietly by the pantry door when the steward returned.

"Sorry, sir. Kettle barely warm. Shall I light the spirit lamp?"   285

"Never mind."

I came out on deck slowly. It was not a matter of conscience to shave the land as close as possible—for now he must go overboard whenever the ship was put in stays. Must! There could be no going back for him. After a moment I walked over to leeward and my heart flew into my mouth at the nearness of the land on the bow. Under any other circumstances I would not have held on a minute longer. The second mate had followed me anxiously.

I looked on till I felt I could command my voice.

"She will weather," I said then in a quiet tone.

"Are you going to try that, sir?" he stammered out incredulously.   290

I took no notice of him and raised my tone just enough to be heard by the helmsman.

"Keep her good full."

"Good full, sir."

The wind fanned my cheek, the sails slept, the world was silent. The strain of watching the dark loom of the land grow bigger and denser was too much for me. I had shut my eyes—because the ship must go closer. She must! The stillness was intolerable. Were we standing still?

When I opened my eyes the second view started my heart with a thump. The black southern hill of Koh-ring seemed to hang right over the ship like a towering fragment of the everlasting night. On that enormous mass of blackness there was not a gleam to be seen, not a sound to be heard. It was gliding irresistibly toward us and yet seemed already within reach of the hand. I saw the vague figures of the watch grouped in the waist, gazing in awed silence.   295

"Are you going on, sir?" inquired an unsteady voice at my elbow.

I ignored it. I had to go on.

"Keep her full. Don't check her way. That won't do now," I said warningly.

"I can't see the sails very well," the helmsman answered me, in strange, quavering tones.

Was she close enough? Already she was, I won't say in the shadow of the land, but in the very blackness of it, already swallowed up as it were, gone too close to be recalled, gone from me altogether.   300

"Give the mate a call," I said to the young man who stood at my elbow still as death. "And turn all hands up."

My tone had a borrowed loudness reverberated from the height of the land. Several voices cried out together. "We are all on deck, sir."

Then stillness again, with the great shadow gliding closer, towering higher, without a light, without a sound. Such a hush had fallen on the ship that she might have been a bark of the dead floating in slowly under the very gate of Erebus.

"My God! Where are we?"

305   It was the mate moaning at my elbow. He was thunderstruck, and as it were deprived of the moral support of his whiskers. He clapped his hands and absolutely cried out, "Lost!"

"Be quiet," I said sternly.

He lowered his tone, but I saw the shadowy gesture of his despair. "What are we doing here?"

"Looking for the land wind."

He made as if to tear his hair, and addressed me recklessly.

310   "She will never get out. You have done it, sir. I knew it'd end in something like this. She will never weather, and you are too close now to stay. She'll drift ashore before she's round. O my God!"

I caught his arm as he was raising it to batter his poor devoted head, and shook it violently.

"She's ashore already," he wailed, trying to tear himself away. "Is she? . . . Keep good full there!"

"Good full, sir," cried the helmsman in a frightened, thin, childlike voice.

I hadn't let go the mate's arm and went on shaking it. "Ready about, do you hear? You go forward"—shake—"and stop there"—shake—"and hold your noise"—shake—"and see these head sheets properly overhauled"—shake, shake—shake.

315   And all the time I dared not look toward the land lest my heart should fail me. I released my grip at last and he ran forward as if fleeing for dear life.

I wondered what my double there in the sail locker thought of this commotion. He was able to hear everything—and perhaps he was able to understand why, on my conscience, it had to be thus close—no less. My first order "Hard alee!" reechoed ominously under the towering shadow of Koh-ring as if I had shouted in a mountain gorge. And then I watched the land intently. In that smooth water and light wind it was impossible to feel the ship coming-to. No! I could not feel her. And my second self was making now ready to slip out and lower himself overboard. Perhaps he was gone already? . . .

The great black mass brooding over our very mastheads began to pivot away from the ship's side silently. And now I forgot the secret stranger ready to depart, and remembered only that I was a total stranger to the ship. I did not know her. Would she do it? How was she to be handled?

I swung the mainyard and waited helplessly. She was perhaps stopped, and her very fate hung in the balance, with the black mass of Koh-ring like the gate of the everlasting night towering over her taffrail. What would she do now? Had she way on her yet? I stepped to the side swiftly, and on the shadowy water I could see nothing except a faint phosphorescent flash revealing the glassy smoothness of the sleeping surface. It was impossible to tell—and I had not learned yet the feel of my ship. Was she moving? What I needed was something easily seen, a piece of paper, which I could throw overboard and watch. I had nothing on me. To run down for it I didn't dare. There was no time. All at once my strained, yearning stare distinguished a white object floating within a yard of the ship's side. White on the black water. A phosphorescent flash passed under it. What was that thing? . . . I recognized my own floppy hat. It must have fallen off his head . . . and he didn't bother. Now I had what I wanted—the saving mark for my eyes. But I hardly thought of my other self, now gone from the ship, to be hidden forever from all friendly faces, to be a fugitive and a vagabond on the earth, with no brand of the curse on his sane forehead to stay a slaying hand . . . too proud to explain.

And I watched the hat—the expression of my sudden pity for his mere flesh. It had been meant to save his homeless head from the dangers of the sun. And now—behold—it was saving the ship, by serving me for a mark to help out the ignorance of my strangeness. Ha! It was drifting forward, warning me just in time that the ship had gathered sternway.

320   "Shift the helm," I said in a low voice to the seaman standing still like a statue.

The man's eyes glistened wildly in the binnacle light as he jumped round to the other side and spun round the wheel.

I walked to the break of the poop. On the overshadowed deck all hands stood by the forebraces waiting for my order. The stars ahead seemed to be gliding from right to left. And all was so still in the world that I heard the quiet remark "She's round," passed in a tone of intense relief between two seamen.

"Let go and haul."

The foreyards ran round with a great noise, amidst cheery cries. And now the frightful whiskers made themselves heard giving various orders. Already the ship was drawing ahead. And I was alone with her. Nothing! no one in the world should stand now between us, throwing a shadow on the way of silent knowledge and mute affection, the perfect communion of a seaman with his first command.

Walking to the taffrail, I was in time to make out, on the very edge of a darkness thrown by a towering black mass like the very gateway of Erebus—yes, I was in time to catch an evanescent glimpse of my white hat left behind to mark the spot where the secret sharer of my cabin and of my thoughts, as though he were my second self, had lowered himself into the water to take his punishment: a free man, a proud swimmer striking out for a new destiny. 325

QUESTIONS

1. Analyze the first three paragraphs of the story. What is the purpose of all the details of setting? How might a person claim that Conrad's great attention to detail is overdone?

2. Who is the narrator? What sort of person is he? Why does he determine to help Leggatt? Why does the Captain constantly think of Leggatt as his double? What do the Captain and Leggatt have in common?

3. How do the details of the Captain's cabin enable the Captain to conceal Leggatt successfully?

4. What details does the story provide about the techniques of sailing and handling ships in a storm? Why do you think Conrad provided these details?

5. What moral issue must the Captain deal with as he learns Leggatt's story and then decides to help Leggatt? Compare this issue with the issues confronted by Fritz in "Before the Firing Squad" (Chapter 10) and Sammy in "A & P" (Chapter 6). What possibilities of choice are available to the characters? How important are the consequences of those choices? Which character faces the most difficult decision?

JOANNE GREENBERG (b. 1932)

Greenberg, a resident of Colorado, graduated from American University in Washington and also attended the University of London. Under the pseudonym "Hannah Green," she achieved wide recognition in 1964 with the novel I Never Promised You a Rose Garden, *which describes the struggles of a teenage girl against schizophrenia. In 1977, the story was made into a successful film, featuring Kathleen Quinlan. Greenberg's fiction reflects her deep concern for "problems of the less fortunate." She is a member of the National Association for the Deaf and has taught sign language. As a writer she has been prolific, producing nearly a dozen novels. An early*

novel in which she considered life among the deaf was In This Sign *(1970). Other works are* Where the Road Goes *(1998),* A Season of Delight *(2004), and* Appearances *(2006). "And Sarah Laughed" is taken from her collection* Rites of Passage *(1972).*

NEW And Sarah Laughed° (1972)

She went to the window every fifteen minutes to see if they were coming. They would be taking the new highway cutoff; it would bring them past the south side of the farm; past the unused, dilapidated outbuildings instead of the orchards and fields that were now full and green. It would look like a poor place to the new bride. Her first impression of their farm would be of age and bleached-out, dried-out buildings on which the doors hung open like a row of gaping mouths that said nothing.

All day, Sarah had gone about her work clumsy with eagerness and hesitant with dread, picking up utensils to forget them in holding, finding them two minutes later a surprise in her hand. She had been planning and working ever since Abel wrote to them from Chicago that he was coming home with a wife. Everything should have been clean and orderly. She wanted the bride to know as soon as she walked inside what kind of woman Abel's mother was—to feel, without a word having to be said, the house's dignity, honesty, simplicity, and love. But the spring cleaning had been late, and Alma Yoder had gotten sick—Sarah had had to go over to the Yoders and help out.

Now she looked around and saw that it was no use trying to have everything ready in time. Abel and his bride would be coming any minute. If she didn't want to get caught shedding tears of frustration, she'd better get herself under control. She stepped over the pile of clothes still unsorted for the laundry and went out on the back porch.

The sky was blue and silent, but as she watched, a bird passed over the fields crying. The garden spread out before her, displaying its varying greens. Beyond it, along the creek, there was a row of poplars. It always calmed her to look at them. She looked today. She and Matthew had planted those trees. They stood thirty feet high now, stately as figures in a procession. Once—only once and many years ago—she had tried to describe in words the sounds that the wind made as it combed those trees on its way west. The little boy to whom she had spoken was a grown man now, and he was bringing home a wife. Married. . . .

5   Ever since he had written to tell them he was coming with his bride, Sarah had been going back in her mind to the days when she and Matthew were bride and groom and then mother and father. Until now, it hadn't seemed so long ago. Her life had flowed on past her, blurring the early days with Matthew when this farm was strange and new to her and when the silence of it was sharp and bitter like pain, not dulled and familiar like an echo of old age.

Matthew hadn't changed much. He was a tall, lean man, but he had had a boy's spareness then. She remembered how his smile came, wavered and went uncertainly, but how his eyes had never left her. He followed everything with his eyes. Matthew had always been a silent man; his face was expressionless and his body stiff with reticence, but his eyes had sought her out eagerly and held her and she had been warm in his look.

Sarah and Matthew had always known each other—their families had been neighbors. Sarah was a plain girl, a serious "decent" girl. Not many of the young men asked her out, and when Matthew did and did again, her parents had been pleased. Her father told her that Matthew was a good man, as steady as any woman could want. He came from honest, hardworking people and he would prosper any farm he had. Her mother spoke shyly of how his eyes woke when Sarah came into the room, and how they followed her. If she married him, her life would be full of the things she knew and loved, an easy, familiar world

---

°*And Sarah Laughed:* See Genesis 18:12.

with her parents' farm not two miles down the road. But no one wanted to mention the one thing that worried Sarah: the fact that Matthew was deaf. It was what stopped her from saying yes right away; she loved him, but she was worried about his deafness. The things she feared about it were the practical things: a fall or a fire when he wouldn't hear her cry for help. Only long after she had put those fears aside and moved the scant two miles into his different world, did she realize that the things she had feared were the wrong things.

Now they had been married for twenty-five years. It was a good marriage—good enough. Matthew was generous, strong, and loving. The farm prospered. His silence made him seem more patient, and because she became more silent also, their neighbors saw in them the dignity and strength of two people who do not rail against misfortune, who were beyond trivial talk and gossip; whose lives needed no words. Over the years of help given and meetings attended, people noticed how little they needed to say. Only Sarah's friend Luita knew that in the beginning, when they were first married, they had written yearning notes to each other. But Luita didn't know that the notes also were mute. Sarah had never shown them to anyone, although she kept them all, and sometimes she would go up and get the box out of her closet and read them over. She had saved every scrap, from questions about the eggs to the tattered note he had left beside his plate on their first anniversary. He had written it when she was busy at the stove and then he'd gone out and she hadn't seen it until she cleared the table.

The note said: "I love you derest wife Sarah. I pray you have happy day all day your life."

When she wanted to tell him something, she spoke to him slowly, facing him, and he took the words as they formed on her lips. His speaking voice was thick and hard to understand and he perceived that it was unpleasant. He didn't like to use it. When he had to say something, he used his odd, grunting tone, and she came to understand what he said. If she ever hungered for laughter from him or the little meaningless talk that confirms existence and affection, she told herself angrily that Matthew talked through his work. Words die in the air; they can be turned one way or another, but Matthew's work prayed and laughed for him. He took good care of her and the boys, and they idolized him. Surely that counted more than all the words—words that meant and didn't mean—behind which people could hide.

Over the years she seldom noticed her own increasing silence, and there were times when his tenderness, which was always given without words, seemed to her to make his silence beautiful.

She thought of the morning she had come downstairs feeling heavy and off balance with her first pregnancy—with Abel. She had gone to the kitchen to begin the day, taking the coffeepot down and beginning to fill it when her eye caught something on the kitchen table. For a minute she looked around in confusion. They had already laid away what the baby would need: diapers, little shirts and bedding, all folded away in the drawer upstairs, but here on the table was a bounty of cloth, all planned and scrimped for and bought from careful, careful study of the catalogue—yards of patterned flannel and plissé, coat wool and bright red corduroy. Sixteen yards of yellow ribbon for bindings. Under the coat wool was cloth Matthew had chosen for her; blue with a little gray figure. It was silk, and there was a card on which was rolled precisely enough lace edging for her collar and sleeves. All the long studying and careful planning, all in silence.

She had run upstairs and thanked him and hugged him, but it was no use showing delight with words, making plans, matching cloth and figuring which pieces would be for the jacket and which for sleepers. Most wives used such fussing to tell their husbands how much they thought of their gifts. But Matthew's silence was her silence too.

When he had left to go to the orchard after breakfast that morning, she had gone to their room and stuffed her ears with cotton, trying to understand the world as it must be to him, with no sound. The cotton dulled the outside noises a little, but it only magnified all the noises in her head. Scratching her cheek caused a roar like a downpour of rain; her own voice was like thunder. She knew Matthew could not hear his own voice in his head. She could not be deaf as he was deaf. She could not know such silence ever.

15   So she found herself talking to the baby inside her, telling it the things she would have told Matthew, the idle daily things: Didn't Margaret Amson look peaked in town? Wasn't it a shame the drugstore had stopped stocking lump alum—her pickles wouldn't be the same.

Abel was a good baby. He had Matthew's great eyes and gentle ways. She chattered to him all day, looking forward to his growing up, when there would be confidences between them. She looked to the time when he would have his own picture of the world, and with that keen hunger and hope she had a kind of late blooming into a beauty that made people in town turn to look at her when she passed in the street holding the baby in the fine clothes she had made for him. She took Abel everywhere, and came to know a pride that was very new to her, a plain girl from a modest family who had married a neighbor boy. When they went to town, they always stopped over to see Matthew's parents and her mother.

Mama had moved to town after Pa died. Of course they had offered to have Mama come and live with them, but Sarah was glad she had gone to a little place in town, living where there were people she knew and things happening right outside her door. Sarah remembered them visiting on a certain spring day, all sitting in Mama's new front room. They sat uncomfortably in the genteel chairs, and Abel crawled around on the floor as the women talked, looking up every now and then for his father's nod of approval. After a while he went to catch the sunlight that was glancing off a crystal nut dish and scattering rainbow bands on the floor. Sarah smiled down at him. She too had a radiance, and, for the first time in her life, she knew it. She was wearing the dress she had made from Matthew's cloth—it became her and she knew that too, so she gave her joy freely as she traded news with Mama.

Suddenly they heard the fire bell ringing up on the hill. She caught Matthew's eye and mouthed, "Fire engines," pointing uphill to the firehouse. He nodded.

In the next minutes there was the strident, off-key blare as every single one of Arcadia's volunteer firemen—his car horn plugged with a matchstick and his duty before him—drove hellbent for the firehouse in an ecstasy of bell and siren. In a minute the ding-ding-ding-ding careened in deafening, happy privilege through every red light in town.

20   "Big bunch of boys!" Mama laughed. "You can count two Saturdays in good weather when they don't have a fire, and that's during the hunting season!"

They laughed. Then Sarah looked down at Abel, who was still trying to catch the wonderful colors. A madhouse of bells, horns, screaming sirens had gone right past them and he hadn't cried, he hadn't looked, he hadn't turned. Sarah twisted her head sharply away and screamed to the china cats on the whatnot shelf as loud as she could, but Abel's eyes only flickered to the movement and then went back to the sun and its colors.

Mama whispered, "Oh, my dear God!"

Sarah began to cry bitterly, uncontrollably, while her husband and son looked on, confused, embarrassed, unknowing.

The silence drew itself over the season and the seasons layered into years. Abel was a good boy; Matthew was a good man.

25   Later, Rutherford, Lindsay, and Franklin Delano came. They too were silent. Hereditary nerve deafness was rare, the doctors all said. The boys might marry and produce deaf children, but it was not likely. When they started to school, the administrators and teachers told her that the boys would be taught specially to read lips and to speak. They would not be "abnormal," she was told. Nothing would show their handicap, and with training no one

need know that they were deaf. But the boys seldom used their lifeless voices to call to their friends; they seldom joined games unless they were forced to join. No one but their mother understood their speech. No teacher could stop all the jumping, turning, gum-chewing schoolboys, or remember herself to face front from the blackboard to the sound-closed boys. The lip-reading exercises never seemed to make plain differences—"man," "pan," "began."

But the boys had work and pride in the farm. The seasons varied their silence with colors—crows flocked in the snowy fields in winter, and tones of golden wheat darkened across acres of summer wind. If the boys couldn't hear the bedsheets flapping on the washline, they could see and feel the autumn day. There were chores and holidays and the wheel of birth and planting, hunting, fishing, and harvest. The boys were familiar in town; nobody ever laughed at them, and when Sarah met neighbors at the store, they praised her sons with exaggerated praise, well meant, saying that no one could tell, no one could really tell unless they knew, about the boys not hearing.

Sarah wanted to cry to these kindly women that the simple orders the boys obeyed by reading her lips were not a miracle. If she could ever hear in their long-practiced robot voices a question that had to do with feelings and not facts, and answer it in words that rose beyond the daily, tangible things done or not done, *that* would be a miracle.

Her neighbors didn't know that they themselves confided to one another from a universe of hopes, a world they wanted half lost in the world that was; how often they spoke pitting inflection against meaning to soften it, harden it, make a joke of it, curse by it, bless by it. They didn't realize how they wrapped the bare words of love in gentle humor or wild insults that the loved ones knew were ways of keeping the secret of love between the speaker and the hearer. Mothers lovingly called their children crow-bait, mouse-meat, devils. They predicted dark ends for them, and the children heard the secrets beneath the words, heard them and smiled and knew, and let the love said-unsaid caress their souls. With her own bitter knowledge Sarah could only thank them for well-meaning and return to silence.

Standing on the back porch now, Sarah heard the wind in the poplars and she sighed. It was getting on to noon. Warm air was beginning to ripple the fields. Matthew would be ready for lunch soon, but she wished she could stand out under the warm sky forever and listen to birds stitching sounds into the endless silence. She found herself thinking about Abel again, and the bride. She wondered what Janice would be like. Abel had gone all the way to Chicago to be trained in drafting. He had met her there, in the school. Sarah was afraid of a girl like that. They had been married quickly, without family or friends or toasts or gifts or questions. It hinted at some kind of secret shame. It frightened her. That kind of girl was independent and she might be scornful of a dowdy mother-in-law. And the house was still a mess.

From down the road, dust was rising. Matthew must have seen it too. He came over the rise and toward the house walking faster than usual. He'd want to slick his hair down and wash up to meet the stranger his son had become. She ran inside and bundled up the unsorted laundry, ran upstairs and pulled a comb through her hair, put on a crooked dab of lipstick, banged her shin, took off her apron and saw a spot on her dress, put the apron on again and shouted a curse to all the disorder she suddenly saw around her. 30

Now the car was crunching up the thin gravel of the driveway. She heard Matthew downstairs washing up, not realizing that the bride and groom were already at the house. Protect your own, she thought, and ran down to tell him. Together they went to the door and opened it, hoping that at least Abel's familiar face would comfort them.

They didn't recognize him at first, and he didn't see them. He and the tiny bride might have been alone in the world. He was walking around to open the door for her, helping her out, bringing her up the path to the house, and all the time their fingers and hands moved

and spun meanings at which they smiled and laughed; they were talking somehow, painting thoughts in the air so fast with their fingers that Sarah couldn't see where one began
and the other ended. She stared. The school people had always told her that such finger-
talk set the deaf apart. It was abnormal; it made freaks of them. . . . How soon Abel had accepted someone else's strangeness and bad ways. She felt so dizzy she thought she was
going to fall, and she was more bitterly jealous than she had ever been before.

The little bride stopped before them appealingly and in her dead, deaf-rote voice, said,
"Ah-am pliizd to meet'ou." Sarah put out her hand dumbly and it was taken and the girl's
eyes shone. Matthew smiled, and this time the girl spoke and waved her hands in time to
her words, and then gave Matthew her hand. So Abel had told that girl about Matthew's
deafness. It had never been a secret, but Sarah felt somehow betrayed.

They had lunch, saw the farm, the other boys came home from their summer school and
met Janice. Sarah put out cake and tea and showed Abel and Janice up to the room she had
made ready for them, and all the time the two of them went on with love-talk in their fingers; the jokes and secrets knitted silently between them, fears told and calmed, hopes spoken and echoed in the silence of a kitchen where twenty-five years of silence had imprisoned
her. Always they would stop and pull themselves back to their good manners, speaking or
writing polite questions and answers for the family; but in a moment or two, the talk would
flag, the urgent hunger would overcome them and they would fight it, resolutely turning
their eyes to Sarah's mouth. Then the signs would creep into their fingers, and the joy of talk
into their faces, and they would fall before the conquering need of their communion.

35 　　Sarah's friend Luita came the next day, in the afternoon. They sat over tea with the
kitchen window open for the cool breeze and Sarah was relieved and grateful to hold to a
familiar thing now that her life had suddenly become so strange to her. Luita hadn't
changed at all, thank God—not the hand that waved her tea cool or the high giggle that
broke into generous laughter.

"She's darling!" Luita said after Janice had been introduced, and, thankfully, had left
them. Sarah didn't want to talk about her, so she agreed without enthusiasm.

Luita only smiled back. "Sarah, you'll never pass for pleased with a face like that."

"It's just—just her ways," Sarah said. "She never even wrote to us before the wedding,
and now she comes in and—and changes everything. I'll be honest, Luita, I didn't want Abel
to marry someone who was deaf. What did we train him for, all those special classes? . . . *not*
to marry another deaf person. And she hangs on him like a wood tick all day . . ." She didn't
mention the signs. She couldn't.

Luita said, "It's just somebody new in the house, that's all. She's important to you, but a
stranger. Addie Purkhard felt the same way and you know what a lovely girl Velma turned
out to be. It just took time. . . . She's going to have a baby, did she tell you?"

40 　　"Baby? Who?" Sarah cried, feeling cold and terrified.

"Why, *Velma*. A baby due about a month after my Dolores'."

It had never occurred to Sarah that Janice and Abel could have a baby. She wanted to stop
thinking about it and she looked back at Luita whose eyes were glowing with something joyful that had to be said. Luita hadn't been able to see beyond it to the anguish of her friend.

Luita said, "You know, Sarah, things haven't been so good between Sam and me. . . ."
She cleared her throat. "You know how stubborn he is. The last few weeks, it's been like a
whole new start for us. I came over to tell you about it because I'm so happy, and I had to
share it with you."

She looked away shyly, and Sarah pulled herself together and leaned forward, putting
her hand on her friend's arm. "I'm so happy for you. What happened?"

45 　　"It started about three weeks ago—a night that neither of us could get to sleep. We hadn't
been arguing; there was just that awful coldness, as if we'd both been frozen stiff. One of us
started talking—just lying there in the dark. I don't even know who started, but pretty soon

we were telling each other the most secret things—things we never could have said in the light. He finally told me that Dolores having a baby makes him feel old and scared. He's afraid of it, Sarah, and I never knew it, and it explains why he hates to go over and see them, and why he argues with Ken all the time. Right there beside me he told me so many things I'd forgotten or misunderstood. In the dark it's like thinking out loud—like being alone and yet together at the same time. I love him so and I came so close to forgetting it. . . ."

Sarah lay in bed and thought about Luita and Sam sharing their secrets in the dark. Maybe even now they were talking in their flower-papered upstairs room, moving against the engulfing seas of silence as if in little boats, finding each other and touching and then looking out in awe at the vastness all around them where they might have rowed alone and mute forever. She wondered if Janice and Abel fingered those signs in the dark on each other's body. She began to cry. There was that freedom, at least; other wives had to strangle their weeping.

When she was cried out, she lay in bed and counted all the good things she had: children, possessions, acres of land, respect of neighbors, the years of certainty and success. Then she conjured the little bride, and saw her standing in front of Abel's old car as she had at first—with nothing; all her virtues still unproven, all her fears still forming, and her bed in another woman's house. Against the new gold ring on the bride's finger, Sarah threw all the substance of her years to weigh for her. The balance went with the bride. It wasn't fair! The balance went with the bride because she had put that communion in the scales as well, and all the thoughts that must have been given and taken between them. It outweighed Sarah's twenty-five years of muteness; outweighed the house and barn and well-tended land, and the sleeping family keeping their silent thoughts.

The days went by. Sarah tortured herself with elaborate courtesy to Janice and politeness to the accomplice son, but she couldn't guard her own envy from herself and she found fault wherever she looked. Now the silence of her house was throbbing with her anger. Every morning Janice would come and ask to help, but Sarah was too restless to teach her, so Janice would sit for a while waiting and then get up and go outside to look for Abel. Then Sarah would decide to make coleslaw and sit with the chopping bowl in her lap, smashing the chopper against the wood with a vindictive joy that she alone could hear the sounds she was making, that she alone knew how savage they were and how satisfying.

At church she would see the younger boys all clean and handsome, Matthew greeting friends, Janice demure and fragile, and Abel proud and loving, and she would feel a terrible guilt for her unreasonable anger; but back from town afterwards, and after Sunday dinner, she noticed as never before how disheveled the boys looked, how ugly their hollow voices sounded. Had Matthew always been so patient and unruffled? He was like one of his own stock, an animal, a dumb animal.

Janice kept asking to help and Sarah kept saying there wasn't time to teach her. She was amazed when Matthew, who was very fussy about his fruit, suggested to her that Janice might be able to take care of the grapes and, later, work in the orchard.

"I haven't time to teach her!"

"Ah owill teeech Ja-nuss," Abel said, and they left right after dinner in too much of a hurry.

Matthew stopped Sarah when she was clearing the table and asked why she didn't like Janice. Now it was Sarah's turn to be silent, and when Matthew insisted, Sarah finally turned on him. "You don't understand," she shouted. "You don't understand a thing!" And she saw on his face the same look of confusion she had seen that day in Mama's fussy front room when she had suddenly begun to cry and could not stop. She turned away with the

50

plates, but suddenly his hand shot out and he struck them to the floor, and the voice he couldn't hear or control rose to an awful cry, "Ah ahm dehf! Ah ahm dehf!" Then he went out, slamming the door without the satisfaction of its sound.

If a leaf fell or a stalk sprouted in the grape arbor, Janice told it over like a set of prayers. One night at supper, Sarah saw the younger boys framing those dumb-signs of hers, and she took them outside and slapped their hands. "*We* don't do that!" she shouted at them, and to Janice later she said, "Those . . . signs you make—I know they must have taught you to do that, but out here . . . well, it isn't our way."

55   Janice looked back at her in a confusion for which there were no words.

It was no use raging at Janice. Before she had come there had never been anything for Sarah to be angry about. . . . What did they all expect of her? Wasn't it enough that she was left out of a world that heard and laughed without being humiliated by the love-madness they made with their hands? It was like watching them undressing.

The wind cannot be caught. Poplars may sift it, a rising bird can breast it, but it will pass by and no one can stop it. She saw the boys coming home at a dead run now, and they couldn't keep their hands from taking letters, words, and pictures from the fingers of the lovers. If they saw an eagle, caught a fish, or got scolded, they ran to their brother or his wife, and Sarah had to stand in the background and demand to be told.

One day Matthew came up to her and smiled and said, "Look." He put out his two index fingers and hooked the right down on the left, then the left down gently on the right. "Fwren," he said, "Ja-nuss say, fwren."

To Sarah there was something obscene about all those gestures, and she said, "I don't like people waving their hands around like monkeys in a zoo!" She said it very clearly so that he couldn't mistake it.

60   He shook his head violently and gestured as he spoke. "Mouth eat; mouth kiss, mouth tawk! Fin-ger wohk; fin-ger tawk. E-ah" (and he grabbed his ear, violently), "e-ah dehf. *Mihn*," (and he rapped his head, violently, as if turning a terrible impatience against himself so as to spare her) "*mihn not* dehf!"

Later she went to the barn after something and she ran into Lindsay and Franklin Delano standing guilty, and when she caught them in her eye as she turned, she saw their hands framing signs. They didn't come into the house until it was nearly dark. Was their hunger for those signs so great that only darkness could bring them home? They weren't bad boys, the kind who would do a thing just because you told them not to. Did their days have a hunger too, or was it only the spell of the lovers, honey-honeying to shut out a world of moving mouths and silence?

At supper she looked around the table and was reassured. It could have been any farm family sitting there, respectable and quiet. A glance from the father was all that was needed to keep order or summon another helping. Their eyes were lowered, their faces composed. The hands were quiet. She smiled and went to the kitchen to fix the shortcake she had made as a surprise.

When she came back, they did not notice her immediately. They were all busy talking. Janice was telling them something and they all had their mouths ridiculously pursed with the word. Janice smiled in assent and each one showed her his sign and she smiled at each one and nodded, and the signers turned to one another in their joy, accepting and begging acceptance. Then they saw Sarah standing there; the hands came down, the faces faded.

She took the dinner plates away and brought in the dessert things, and when she went back to the kitchen for the cake, she began to cry. It was beyond envy now; it was too late for measuring or weighing. She had lost. In the country of the blind, Mama used to say, the one-eyed man is king. Having been a citizen of such a country, she knew better.

In the country of the deaf, the hearing man is lonely. Into that country a girl had come who, with a wave of her hand, had given the deaf ears for one another, and had made Sarah the deaf one.

Sarah stood, staring at her cake and feeling for that moment the profundity of the silence which she had once tried to match by stuffing cotton in her ears. Everyone she loved was in the other room, talking, sharing, standing before the awful, impersonal heaven and the unhearing earth with pictures of his thoughts, and she was the deaf one now. It wasn't "any farm family," silent in its strength. It was a yearning family, silent in its hunger, and a demure little bride had shown them all how deep the hunger was. She had shown Sarah that her youth had been sold into silence. She was too old to change now. 65

An anger rose in her as she stared at the cake. Why should they be free to move and gesture and look different while she was kept in bondage to their silence? Then she remembered Matthew's mute notes, his pride in Abel's training, his face when he had cried, "I am deaf!" over and over. She had actually fought that terrible yearning, that hunger they all must have had for their own words. If they could all speak somehow, what would the boys tell her?

She knew what she wanted to tell them. That the wind sounds through the poplar trees, and people have a hard time speaking to one another even if they aren't deaf. Luita and Sam had to have a night to hide their faces while they spoke. It suddenly occurred to her that if Matthew made one of those signs with his hands and she could learn that sign, she could put her hands against his in the darkness, and read the meaning—that if she learned those signs she could hear him. . . .

She dried her eyes hurriedly and took in the cake. They saw her and the hands stopped, drooping lifelessly again; the faces waited mutely. Silence. It was a silence she could no longer bear. She looked from face to face. What was behind those eyes she loved? Didn't everyone's world go deeper than chores and bread and sleep?

"I want to talk to you," she said. "I want to talk, to know what you think." She put her hands out before her, offering them.

Six pairs of eyes watched her. 70

Janice said, "Mo-ther."

Eyes snapped away to Janice; thumb was under lip: the Sign.

Sarah followed them. "Wife," she said, showing her ring.

"Wife," Janice echoed, thumb under lip to the clasp of hands.

Sarah said, "I love. . . ." 75

Janice showed her and she followed hesitantly and then turned to Matthew to give and to be received in that sign.

QUESTIONS

1. Characterize Sarah. What do we learn about her character from the way she cares for her surroundings and tends to her tasks?

2. What kinds of detail about the appearance and circumstances of the farm appear in the story? Why are these details included?

3. Why does Greenberg not disclose right away that Matthew is deaf? Why does she withhold the same detail about Abel? How does Sarah respond when she learns that Abel is deaf?

4. What attitudes toward deafness and communication does Janice, with her mastery of sign language, bring out in Sarah? To what degree may her attitudes be considered a crisis? How does Sarah respond to the crisis? Why?

JAMES JOYCE (1882–1941)

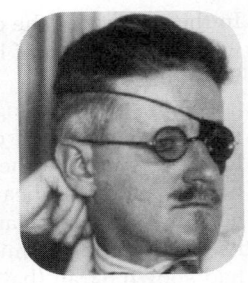

Joyce, one of the greatest twentieth-century writers, was born in Ireland and received a vigorous and thorough education there. He left Ireland in 1902 and spent most of the rest of his life in Switzerland and France. His best-known works are Dubliners *(1914),* A Portrait of the Artist as a Young Man *(1914–1915),* Ulysses *(1922), and* Finnegans Wake *(1939). Much of his work has been called "fictionalized autobiography," a quality shown in "Araby," which is selected from* Dubliners. *As a young child, Joyce had lived on North Richmond Street, just like the narrator of the story. The bazaar that the narrator visits actually did take place in Dublin, from May 14 to 19, 1894, when Joyce was the same age as the narrator. It was called "Araby in Dublin" and was advertised as a "Grand Oriental Fete."*

 Araby (1914)

North Richmond Street,° being blind,° was a quiet street except at the hour when the Christian Brothers' School set the boys free. An uninhabited house of two storeys stood at the blind end, detached from its neighbours in a square ground. The other houses of the street, conscious of decent lives within them, gazed at one another with brown imperturbable faces.

The former tenant of our house, a priest, had died in the back drawing room. Air, musty from having long been enclosed, hung in all the rooms, and the waste room behind the kitchen was littered with old useless papers. Among these I found a few paper-covered books, the pages of which were curled and damp: *The Abbott,* by Walter Scott, *The Devout Communicant°* and *The Memoirs of Vidocq.°* I liked the last best because its leaves were yellow. The wild garden behind the house contained a central apple-tree and a few straggling bushes under one of which I found the late tenant's rusty bicycle-pump. He had been a very charitable priest; in his will he had left all his money to institutions and the furniture of his house to his sister.

When the short days of winter came dusk fell before we had well eaten our dinners. When we met in the street the houses had grown sombre. The space of sky above us was the colour of ever-changing violet and towards it the lamps of the street lifted their feeble lanterns. The cold air stung us and we played till our bodies glowed. Our shouts echoed in the silent street. The career of our play brought us through the dark muddy lanes behind the houses where we ran the gauntlet of the rough tribes from the cottages, to the back doors of the dark dripping gardens where odours arose from the ashpits, to the dark odorous stables where a coachman smoothed and combed the horse or shook music from the buckled harness. When we returned to the street light from the kitchen windows had filled the areas. If my uncle was seen turning the corner we hid in the shadow until we had seen him safely housed. Or if Mangan's sister came out on the doorstep to call her brother in to his tea we watched her from our shadow peer up and down the street. We waited to see whether she would remain or go in and, if she remained, we left our shadow and walked up to Mangan's steps resignedly. She was waiting for us, her figure defined by the light from the half-opened door. Her brother always teased her before he obeyed and I stood by

---

°*North Richmond Street:* name of a real street in Dublin on which Joyce lived as a boy.
°*blind:* dead-end street.
°*The Devout Communicant:* a book of meditations by Pacificus Baker, published 1873.
°*The Memoirs of Vidocq:* published 1829, the story of François Vidocq, a Parisian chief of detectives.

the railings looking at her. Her dress swung as she moved her body and the soft rope of her hair tossed from side to side.

Every morning I lay on the floor in the front parlor watching her door. The blind was pulled down within an inch of the sash so that I could not be seen. When she came out on the doorstep my heart leaped. I ran to the hall, seized my books and followed her. I kept her brown figure always in my eye and, when we came near the point at which our ways diverged, I quickened my pace and passed her. This happened morning after morning. I had never spoken to her, except for a few casual words, and yet her name was like a summons to all my foolish blood.

Her image accompanied me even in places the most hostile to romance. On Saturday   5
evenings when my aunt went marketing I had to go to carry some of the parcels. We walked through the flaring street, jostled by drunken men and bargaining women, amid the curses of labourers, the shrill litanies of shop-boys who stood on guard by the barrels of pigs' cheeks, the nasal chanting of street singers, who sang a *come-all-you* about O'Donovan Rossa,° or a ballad about the troubles in our native land. These noises converged in a single sensation of life for me: I imagined that I bore my chalice safely through the throng of foes. Her name sprang to my lips at moments in strange prayers and praises which I myself did not understand. My eyes were often full of tears (I could not tell why) and at times a flood from my heart seemed to pour itself out into my bosom. I thought little of the future. I did not know whether I would ever speak to her or not or, if I spoke to her, how I could tell her of my confused adoration. But my body was like a harp and her words and gestures were like fingers running upon the wires.

One evening I went into the back drawing-room in which the priest had died. It was a dark rainy evening and there was no sound in the house. Through one of the broken panes I heard the rain impinge upon the earth, the fine incessant needles of water playing in the sodden beds. Some distant lamp or lighted window gleamed below me. I was thankful that I could see so little. All my senses seemed to desire to veil themselves and, feeling that I was about to slip from them, I pressed the palms of my hands together until they trembled, murmuring: *O love! O love!* many times.

At last she spoke to me. When she addressed the first words to me I was so confused that I did not know what to answer. She asked me was I going to *Araby.*° I forget whether I answered yes or no. It would be a splendid bazaar, she said; she would love to go.

—And why can't you? I asked.

While she spoke she turned a silver bracelet round and round her wrist. She could not go, she said, because there would be a retreat° that week in her convent. Her brother and two other boys were fighting for their caps and I was alone at the railings. She held one of the spikes, bowing her head towards me. The light from the lamp opposite our door caught the white curve of her neck, lit up her hair that rested there and, falling, lit up the hand upon the railing. It fell over one side of her dress and caught the white border of a petticoat, just visible as she stood at ease.

—It's well for you, she said.   10

—If I go, I said, I will bring you something.

What innumerable follies laid waste my waking and sleeping thoughts after that evening! I wished to annihilate the tedious intervening days. I chafed against the work of school. At night in my bedroom and by day in the classroom her image came between me and the page I strove to read. The syllables of the word *Araby* were called to me through the silence in

---

°*O'Donovan Rossa:* popular ballad about Jeremiah O'Donovan (1831–1915), a leader in the movement to free Ireland from English control. He was called "Dynamite Rossa."
°*Araby:* the bazaar held in Dublin from May 14 to 19, 1894.
°*retreat:* a special time set aside for concentrated religious instruction, discussion, and prayer.

which my soul luxuriated and cast an Eastern enchantment over me. I asked for leave to go to the bazaar on Saturday night. My aunt was surprised and hoped it was not some Freemason° affair. I answered few questions in class. I watched my master's face pass from amiability to sternness; he hoped I was not beginning to idle. I could not call my wandering thoughts together. I had hardly any patience with the serious work of life which, now that it stood between me and my desire, seemed to me child's play, ugly monotonous child's play.

On Saturday morning I reminded my uncle that I wished to go to the bazaar in the evening. He was fussing at the hall-stand, looking for the hatbrush, and answered me curtly:

—Yes, boy, I know.

15   As he was in the hall I could not go into the front parlour and lie at the window. I left the house in bad humour and walked slowly towards the school. The air was pitilessly raw and already my heart misgave me.

When I came home to dinner my uncle had not yet been home. Still, it was early. I sat staring at the clock for some time and, when its ticking began to irritate me, I left the room. I mounted the staircase and gained the upper part of the house. The high cold empty gloomy rooms liberated me and I went from room to room singing. From the front window I saw my companions playing below in the street. Their cries reached me weakened and indistinct and, leaning my forehead against the cool glass, I looked over at the dark house where she lived. I may have stood there for an hour, seeing nothing but the brown-clad figure cast by my imagination, touched discreetly by the lamplight at the curved neck, at the hand upon the railing and at the border below the dress.

When I came downstairs again I found Mrs. Mercer sitting at the fire. She was an old garrulous woman, a pawnbroker's widow, who collected used stamps for some pious purpose. I had to endure the gossip of the tea-table. The meal was prolonged beyond an hour and still my uncle did not come. Mrs. Mercer stood up to go: she was sorry she couldn't wait any longer, but it was after eight o'clock and she did not like to be out late, as the night air was bad for her. When she had gone I began to walk up and down the room, clenching my fists. My aunt said:

—I'm afraid you may put off your bazaar for this night of Our Lord.

At nine o'clock I heard my uncle's latchkey in the halldoor. I heard him talking to himself and heard the hall-stand rocking when it had received the weight of his overcoat. I could interpret these signs. When he was midway through his dinner I asked him to give me the money to go to the bazaar. He had forgotten.

20   —The people are in bed and after their first sleep now, he said.

I did not smile. My aunt said to him energetically:

—Can't you give him the money and let him go? You've kept him late enough as it is.

My uncle said he was very sorry he had forgotten. He said he believed in the old saying: *All work and no play makes Jack a dull boy*. He asked me where I was going and, when I had told him a second time he asked me did I know *The Arab's Farewell to his Steed*.° When I left the kitchen he was about to recite the opening lines of the piece to my aunt.

I held a florin° tightly in my hand as I strode down Buckingham Street towards the station. The sight of the streets thronged with buyers and glaring with gas recalled to me the purpose of my journey. I took my seat in a third-class carriage of a deserted train. After an intolerable delay the train moved out of the station slowly. It crept onward among ruinous houses and over the twinkling river. At Westland Row Station a crowd of people pressed to the carriage doors; but the porters moved them back, saying that it was a special train for

---

°*Freemason*: and therefore Protestant.
°*The Arab's Farewell to his Steed*: poem by Caroline Norton (1808–1877).
°*florin*: a two-shilling coin in the 1890s (when the story takes place), worth perhaps twenty dollars in today's money.

the bazaar. I remained alone in the bare carriage. In a few minutes the train drew up beside an improvised wooden platform. I passed out on to the road and saw by the lighted dial of a clock that it was ten minutes to ten. In front of me was a large building which displayed the magical name.

I could not find any sixpenny entrance and, fearing that the bazaar would be closed, I passed in quickly through a turnstile, handing a shilling to a weary-looking man. I found myself in a big hall girdled at half its height by a gallery. Nearly all the stalls were closed and the greater part of the hall was in darkness. I recognized a silence like that which pervades a church after a service. I walked into the centre of the bazaar timidly. A few people were gathered about the stalls which were still open. Before a curtain, over which the words *Café Chantant* were written in coloured lamps, two men were counting money on a salver. I listened to the fall of the coins. 25

Remembering with difficulty why I had come I went over to one of the stalls and examined porcelain vases and flowered tea-sets. At the door of the stall a young lady was talking and laughing with two young gentlemen. I remarked their English accents and listened vaguely to their conversation.

—O, I never said such a thing!

—O, but you did!

—O, but I didn't!

—Didn't she say that? 30

—Yes I heard her.

—O, there's a . . . fib!

Observing me the young lady came over and asked me did I wish to buy anything. The tone in her voice was not encouraging; she seemed to have spoken to me out of a sense of duty. I looked humbly at the great jars that stood like eastern guards at either side of the dark entrance to the stall and murmured:

—No, thank you.

The young lady changed the position of one of the vases and went back to the two young men. They began to talk of the same subject. Once or twice the young lady glanced at me over her shoulder. 35

I lingered before her stall, though I knew my stay was useless, to make my interest in her wares seem the more real. Then I turned away slowly and walked down the middle of the bazaar. I allowed the two pennies to fall against the sixpence in my pocket. I heard a voice call from one end of the gallery that the light was out. The upper part of the hall was now completely dark.

Gazing up into the darkness I saw myself as a creature driven and derided by vanity; and my eyes burned with anguish and anger.

QUESTIONS

1. Describe what you consider to be the story's major idea.

2. How might the bazaar, "Araby," be considered symbolically in the story? To what extent does this symbol embody the story's central idea?

3. Consider the attitude of the speaker toward his home as indicated in the first paragraph. Why do you think the speaker uses the word *blind* to describe the dead-end street? What relationship exists between the speaker's pain at the end of the story to the ideas in the first paragraph?

4. Who is the narrator? About how old is he at the time of the story? About how old when he tells the story? What effect is produced by this difference in age between narrator-as-character and narrator-as-storyteller?

CYNTHIA OZICK (b. 1928)

Ozick has published three novels, Trust *(1966),* The Cannibal Galaxy *(1983), and* The Messiah of Stockholm *(1987); three short-story collections,* The Pagan Rabbi *(1971),* Bloodshed *(1976), and* Levitation *(1982); and frequent essays and reviews, among which is the collection* Fame and Folly *(1996). Among her many recognitions and awards, she serves on the Board of Advisers of the* American Poetry Review. *Her 1990 novella "Puttermesser Paired" was the first story featured in* Prize Stories 1992: The O. Henry Awards, *edited by William Abrahams. "The Shawl," first published in the* New Yorker *in 1980, was republished in* The Shawl *in 1989, with a companion story describing the heroine's experiences in the United States after surviving the death camp. "The Shawl" was also adapted as a play in 1996.*

The Shawl (1980)

Stella, cold, cold the coldness of hell. How they walked on the roads together, Rosa with Magda curled up between sore breasts, Magda wound up in the shawl. Sometimes Stella carried Magda. But she was jealous of Magda. A thin girl of fourteen, too small, with thin breasts of her own, Stella wanted to be wrapped in a shawl, hidden away, asleep, rocked by the march, a baby, a round infant in arms. Magda took Rosa's nipple, and Rosa never stopped walking, a walking cradle. There was not enough milk; sometimes Magda sucked air; then she screamed. Stella was ravenous. Her knees were tumors on sticks, her elbows chicken bones.

Rosa did not feel hunger; she felt light, not like someone walking but like someone in a faint, in trance, arrested in a fit, someone who is already a floating angel, alert and seeing everything, but in the air, not there, not touching the road. As if teetering on the tips of her fingernails. She looked into Magda's face through a gap in the shawl: a squirrel in a nest, safe, no one could reach her inside the little house of the shawl's windings. The face, very round, a pocket mirror of a face: but it was not Rosa's bleak complexion, dark like cholera, it was another kind of face altogether, eyes blue as air, smooth feathers of hair nearly as yellow as the Star sewn into Rosa's coat. You could think she was one of *their* babies.

Rosa, floating, dreamed of giving Magda away in one of the villages. She could leave the line for a minute and push Magda into the hands of any woman on the side of the road. But if she moved out of line they might shoot. And even if she fled the line for half a second and pushed the shawl-bundle at a stranger, would the woman take it? She might be surprised, or afraid; she might drop the shawl, and Magda would fall out and strike her head and die. The little round head. Such a good child, she gave up screaming, and sucked now only for the taste of the drying nipple itself. The neat grip of the tiny gums. One mite of a tooth tip sticking up in the bottom gum, how shining, an elfin tombstone of white marble gleaming there. Without complaining, Magda relinquished Rosa's teats, first the left, then the right; both were cracked, not a sniff of milk. The duct crevice extinct, a dead volcano, blind eye, chill hole, so Magda took the corner of the shawl and milked it instead. She sucked and sucked, flooding the threads with wetness. The shawl's good flavor, milk of linen.

It was a magic shawl, it could nourish an infant for three days and three nights. Magda did not die, she stayed alive, although very quiet. A peculiar smell, of cinnamon and almonds, lifted out of her mouth. She held her eyes open every moment, forgetting how to blink or nap, and Rosa and sometimes Stella studied their blueness. On the road they raised one burden of a leg after another and studied Magda's face. "Aryan," Stella said, in a voice grown as thin as a string; and Rosa thought how Stella gazed at Magda like a young cannibal. And the time that Stella said "Aryan," it sounded to Rosa as if Stella had really said "Let us devour her."

But Magda lived to walk. She lived that long, but she did not walk very well, partly because   5
she was only fifteen months old, and partly because the spindles of her legs could not hold up
her fat belly. It was fat with air, full and round. Rosa gave almost all her food to Magda, Stella
gave nothing; Stella was ravenous, a growing child herself, but not growing much. Stella did
not menstruate. Rosa did not menstruate. Rosa was ravenous, but also not; she learned from
Magda how to drink the taste of a finger in one's mouth. They were in a place without pity, all
pity was annihilated in Rosa, she looked at Stella's bones without pity. She was sure that Stella
was waiting for Magda to die so she could put her teeth into the little thighs.

Rosa knew Magda was going to die very soon; she should have been dead already, but she
had been buried away deep inside the magic shawl, mistaken there for the shivering mound of
Rosa's breasts; Rosa clung to the shawl as if it covered only herself. No one took it away from
her. Magda was mute. She never cried. Rosa hid her in the barracks, under the shawl, but she
knew that one day someone would inform; or one day someone, not even Stella, would steal
Magda to eat her. When Magda began to walk Rosa knew that Magda was going to die very
soon, something would happen. She was afraid to fall asleep; she slept with the weight of her
thigh on Magda's body; she was afraid she would smother Magda under her thigh. The
weight of Rosa was becoming less and less; Rosa and Stella were slowly turning into air.

Magda was quiet, but her eyes were horribly alive, like blue tigers. She watched.
Sometimes she laughed—it seemed a laugh, but how could it be? Magda had never seen
anyone laugh. Still, Magda laughed at her shawl when the wind blew its corners, the bad
wind with pieces of black in it, that made Stella's and Rosa's eyes tear. Magda's eyes were
always clear and tearless. She watched like a tiger. She guarded her shawl. No one could
touch it; only Rosa could touch it. Stella was not allowed. The shawl was Magda's own
baby, her pet, her little sister. She tangled herself up in it and sucked on one of the corners
when she wanted to be very still.

Then Stella took the shawl away and made Magda die.

Afterward Stella said: "I was cold."

And afterward she was always cold, always. The cold went into her heart: Rosa saw that   10
Stella's heart was cold. Magda flopped onward with her little pencil legs scribbling this way
and that, in search of the shawl; the pencils faltered at the barracks opening, where the light
began. Rosa saw and pursued. But already Magda was in the square outside the barracks, in
the jolly light. It was the roll-call arena. Every morning Rosa had to conceal Magda under the
shawl against a wall of the barracks and go out and stand in the arena with Stella and hundreds of others, sometimes for hours, and Magda, deserted, was quiet under the shawl, sucking on her corner. Every day Magda was silent, and so she did not die. Rosa saw that today
Magda was going to die, and at the same time a fearful joy ran into Rosa's two palms, her fingers were on fire, she was astonished, febrile: Magda, in the sunlight, swaying on her pencil
legs, was howling. Ever since the drying up of Rosa's nipples, ever since Magda's last
scream on the road, Magda had been devoid of any syllable; Magda was a mute. Rosa believed that something had gone wrong with her vocal cords, with her windpipe, with the
cave of her larynx; Magda was defective, without a voice; perhaps she was deaf; there might
be something amiss with her intelligence; Magda was dumb. Even the laugh that came
when the ash-stippled wind made a clown out of Magda's shawl was only the air-blown
showing of her teeth. Even when the lice, head lice and body lice, crazed her so that she became as wild as one of the big rats that plundered the barracks at daybreak looking for carrion,
she rubbed and scratched and kicked and bit and rolled without a whimper. But now Magda's
mouth was spilling a long viscous rope of clamor.

"Maaaa—"

It was the first noise Magda had ever sent out from her throat since the drying up of
Rosa's nipples.

"Maaaa . . . aaa!"

Again! Magda was wavering in the perilous sunlight of the arena, scrabbling on such pitiful little bent shins. Rosa saw. She saw that Magda was grieving for the loss of her shawl, she saw that Magda was going to die. A tide of commands hammered in Rosa's nipples: Fetch, get, bring! But she did not know which to go after first, Magda or the shawl. If she jumped out into the arena to snatch Magda up, the howling would not stop, because Magda would still not have the shawl; but if she ran back into the barracks to find the shawl, and if she found it, and if she came after Magda holding it and shaking it, then she would get Magda back, Magda would put the shawl in her mouth and turn dumb again.

15   Rosa entered the dark. It was easy to discover the shawl. Stella was heaped under it, asleep in her thin bones. Rosa tore the shawl free and flew—she could fly, she was only air—into the arena. The sunheat murmured of another life, of butterflies in summer. The light was placid, mellow. On the other side of the steel fence, far away, there were green meadows speckled with dandelions and deep-colored violets; beyond them, even farther, innocent tiger lilies, tall, lifting their orange bonnets. In the barracks they spoke of "flowers," of "rain": excrement, thick turd-braids, and the slow stinking maroon waterfall that slunk down from the upper bunks, the stink mixed with a bitter fatty floating smoke that greased Rosa's skin. She stood for an instant at the margin of the arena. Sometimes the electricity inside the fence would seem to hum; even Stella said it was only an imagining, but Rosa heard real sounds in the wire: grainy sad voices. The farther she was from the fence, the more clearly the voices crowded at her. The lamenting voices strummed so convincingly, so passionately, it was impossible to suspect them of being phantoms. The voices told her to hold up the shawl, high; the voices told her to shake it, to whip with it, to unfurl it like a flag. Rosa lifted, shook, whipped, unfurled. Far off, very far, Magda leaned across her air-fed belly, reaching out with the rods of her arms. She was high up, elevated, riding someone's shoulder. But the shoulder that carried Magda was not coming toward Rosa and the shawl, it was drifting away, the speck of Magda was moving more and more into the smoky distance. Above the shoulder a helmet glinted. The light tapped the helmet and sparkled it into a goblet. Below the helmet a black body like a domino and a pair of black boots hurled themselves in the direction of the electrified fence. The electric voices began to chatter wildly. "Maa-maa, maaamaaa," they all hummed together. How far Magda was from Rosa now, across the whole square, past a dozen barracks, all the way on the other side! She was no bigger than a moth.

All at once Magda was swimming through the air. The whole of Magda traveled through loftiness. She looked like a butterfly touching a silver vine. And the moment Magda's feathered round head and her pencil legs and balloonish belly and zigzag arms splashed against the fence, the steel voices went mad in their growling, urging Rosa to run and run to the spot where Magda had fallen from her flight against the electrified fence; but of course Rosa did not obey them. She only stood, because if she ran they would shoot, and if she tried to pick up the sticks of Magda's body they would shoot, and if she let the wolf's screech ascending now through the ladder of her skeleton break out, they would shoot; so she took Magda's shawl and filled her own mouth with it, stuffed it in and stuffed it in, until she was swallowing up the wolf's screech and tasting the cinnamon and almond depth of Magda's saliva; and Rosa drank Magda's shawl until it dried.

QUESTIONS

1. Describe how Ozick presents the setting. Why do you not receive a clear picture of how things look? Why does Ozick present the details as she does?

2. In paragraph 15, what is on the other side of the fence? Explain Ozick's description here. Why does Ozick include these details so close to the story's end?

3. What character is the center of interest in "The Shawl"? Why is she being treated as she is? What are her impressions of the conditions and circumstances around her? What are her responses to her hunger and deprivation?

4. Explain the function of the more unpleasant and brutal details. What do you need to know about the circumstances of the story to respond to these details?

WRITING ABOUT SETTING

In preparing to write about setting, determine the number and importance of locations, artifacts, and customs. Ask questions like the following:

- How extensive are the visual descriptions? Does the author provide such vivid and carefully arranged detail about surroundings that you could draw a map or plan? Or is the scenery vague and difficult for you to reconstruct imaginatively? In either case, why?
- What connections, if any, are apparent between locations and characters? Do the locations bring characters together, separate them, facilitate their privacy, make intimacy and conversation difficult?
- How fully are objects described? How vital are they to the action? How important are they in the development of the plot or idea? How are they connected to the mental states of the characters?
- How important to plot and character are shapes, colors, times of day, clouds, storms, light and sun, seasons of the year, and conditions of vegetation?
- Are the characters poor, moderately well off, or rich? How does their economic condition affect what happens to them, and how does it affect their actions and attitudes?
- What cultural, religious, and political conditions are brought out in the story? How do the characters accept and adjust to these conditions? How do the conditions affect the characters' judgments and actions?
- What is the state of houses, furniture, and objects (e.g., polished and new, old and worn, ragged and torn)? What connections can you find between these conditions and the outlook and behavior of the characters?
- How important are sounds or silences? To what degree is music or other sound important in the development of character and action?
- Do characters respect or mistreat the environment? If there is an environmental connection, how central is it to the story?
- What conclusions do you think the author expects you to draw as a result of the neighborhood, culture, and larger world of the story?

Strategies for Organizing Ideas

Begin by making a brief description of the setting or scenes of the work, specifying the amount and importance of detail. Choosing one of the approaches in the following list, describe the approach you plan to develop. As you gather material for your essay, however, you may need to combine your major approach with one or more of the others. Whatever approach for development you choose, be sure to consider setting not as an end in itself but rather as illustration and evidence for claims you are making about the particular story.

1. *Setting and action.* Explore the importance of setting in the work. How extensively is the setting described? Are locations essential or incidental to the actions? Does the setting serve as part of the action (e.g., places of flight or concealment;

public places where people meet openly, or hidden places where they meet privately; natural or environmental conditions; seasonal conditions such as searing heat or numbing cold; customs and conventions)? Do any objects cause inspiration, difficulty, or conflict (such as a bridge, a farm, a walking stick, a necklace, a fence, a hair ribbon, a frozen lake, a bizarre party, a hat floating in water)? How directly do these objects influence the action?

2. *Setting and organization.* How is the setting connected to the various parts of the work? Does it undergo any changes as the action develops? Why are some parts of the setting more important than others? Is the setting used as a structural frame or enclosure for the story? Describe the effect and purpose of such a structural use of setting. How do objects such as money, appliances, property, or physical location (e.g., a subway platform, a prison camp, a winter scene on a lake) influence the characters? How do descriptions made at the start become important in the action later on?

3. *Setting and character.* (For examples of this approach, see the two drafts of the illustrative essay in Part I.) Analyze the degree to which setting influences and interacts with character. Are the characters happy or unhappy where they live? Do they get into discussions or arguments about their home environments? Do they want to stay or leave? Do the economic, philosophical, religious, or ethnic aspects of the setting make the characters undergo changes? What jobs do the characters perform because of their ways of life? What freedoms or restraints do these jobs cause? How does the setting influence their decisions, transportation, speech habits, eating habits, attitudes about love and honor, and general behavior?

4. *Setting and atmosphere.* To what extent does setting contribute to mood? Does the setting go b d the minimum needed for action or character? How do descriptive words paint verbal pictures and evoke moods through references to colors, shapes, sounds, smells, or tastes? Does the setting establish a mood, say, of joy or hopelessness, plenty or scarcity? What is the effect of daylight or nighttime upon events in the story? Do the locations and activities of the characters suggest permanence or impermanence (like returning home, creating figures out of mud, repairing a battered boat, perceiving ocean currents, being confined within a room)? Are things warm and pleasant, or cold and harsh? What connection do you find between the atmosphere and the author's expressed or apparent thoughts about existence?

5. *Setting and other aspects of the story.* Does the setting reinforce the story's meaning? Does it establish irony about the circumstances and ideas in the story? If you choose this approach, consult the introductory paragraph in "The Literary Uses of Setting" earlier in this chapter. If you are interested in writing about the symbolic implications of a setting, consult Chapter 7.

To conclude, summarize your major points or write about related aspects of setting that you have not considered. Thus, if your essay treats the relationship of setting and action, your conclusion might mention connections of the setting with character or atmosphere. You might also point out whether your central idea about setting also applies to other major aspects of the story.

Illustrative Student Essay

Underlined sentences in this paper *do not* conform to MLA style and are used solely as teaching tools to emphasize the central idea, thesis sentence, and topic sentences throughout the paper.

Jani 1

Sonal Jani

Professor Addas

English 200

1 March 2008

The Setting of Conrad's "The Secret Sharer"°

In "The Secret Sharer" Joseph Conrad makes his setting an integral and [1] inseparable part of his action and ideas.* The story is a sea story, which could not exist without the many details about the ocean, ships, currents, cabins, and men who sail. While some of Conrad's ideas about guilt, human sympathies, and the connection of divinity to human beings may be vague, the physical details about the setting are completely realized. The integration of setting and story can be followed in details about the Captain's cabin and the ocean itself and also in Conrad's suggestions that human affairs are linked to large, cosmic forces.†

The Captain's cabin is an essential part of the story's main action because it [2] enables the Captain, the story's speaker, successfully to conceal Leggatt, the stowaway. The tension resulting from the near-discoveries by the steward depends on Conrad's detailed descriptions of the cabin (see, for example, 236, paragraphs 71–72). It is described as having the shape of an "L," with the door on "the short part of the letter" (236, paragraph 71). Because the "vertical" part is not visible to anyone entering, and because the coats, the curtained bunk, and the bathroom all furnish concealment, Leggatt can avoid the steward's searching eyes. Further, the noise made by sailors walking on the deck above the cabin permits the Captain and Leggatt to speak together without being overheard, and therefore the plans for the escape can be safely communicated between the two men.

°**This story appears on pages 230–53.**
***Central idea.**
†**Thesis sentence.**

Jani 2

[3]   While it is obvious that a sea story takes the presence of the ocean for granted, the ocean is, for the story's purposes, equally as important as the cabin. It was during a severe storm that Leggatt decided to "reef" the sail that saved his ship, the Sephora. It was the disobedient sailor's insults, probably brought about by fear of the storm, that enraged Leggatt and made him strangle this sailor. Thus the ocean itself produces both a good and a bad result, and it is the bad result that causes Leggatt to flee the Sephora. When he escapes he swims to the Captain's ship at night, thus connecting the two men, who otherwise would never have met. When Leggatt leaves the Captain's ship at the end of the story, he does so by going into the sea from a rope hung from the sail locker, and, because the Captain wishes to keep Leggatt as safe as possible, he steers too close to shore. Therefore the potential shallowness of the ocean becomes an immediate danger to the Captain, who risks his entire career (which could "go irretrievably to pieces") on the chance that he will not run aground (249, paragraph 252).

[4]   While the setting of ocean and cabin helps create the story's adventure and tension, the descriptions also form part of Conrad's religious and philosophic setting. At the beginning, for example, we read the Captain's words:

> In this breathless pause at the threshold of a long passage we seemed to be measuring our fitness for a long and arduous enterprise, the appointed task . . . to be carried out, far from all human eyes, with only sky and sea for spectators and for judges. (231, paragraph 2)

When the captain of the Sephora agrees that Leggatt's reefing of the sail saved his ship, he asserts that "God's own hand" was "in it. . . . Nothing less could have done it" (242, paragraph 139). In reflecting on Leggatt's both saving the Sephora and strangling the sailor, the Captain draws the following paradoxical conclusion:

> The same strung-up force which had given twenty-four men a chance, at least, for their lives, had, in a sort of recoil, crushed an unworthy mutinous existence. (245, paragraph 190)

Jani 3

At the end of the story, when the Captain's hat floating on the water enables him to save his ship by turning around (252, paragraph 319), it seems clear that the setting, through the currents of water, is intended to suggest cosmic approval of the Captain's decision to help Leggatt.

An additional merging of setting and story should be mentioned in conclusion. This concerns the character of the Captain, the unnamed narrator. In his role as narrator, the Captain's observations about the sea, the sky, and the things the ship will encounter on the way back to England all show him as a clear-sighted man who understands the sea and the forces that control it. It is his knowledge of the danger of the sea during storms that makes possible his own personal "verdict" acquitting Leggatt for having strangled the mutinous sailor. Conrad's setting in this instance is so vital to the story that it becomes the very material of the Captain's morality, and it is this morality that causes the central decision around which all the events in the story turn. Because of details such as this one, it is no exaggeration to say that Conrad's setting and his story are totally connected and integrated.

[5]

Jani 4

Work Cited

Conrad, Joseph. "The Secret Sharer." Literature: An Introduction to Reading and Writing. Ed. Edgar V. Roberts. 9th ed. New York: Pearson Longman, 2009. 230–53.

Commentary on the Essay

This essay focuses on the connection between Conrad's setting and the action and ideas of the story. With this emphasis, the essay illustrates some of the aspects of strategy 1 described on pages 269–70. In showing the connection between setting, character, and ideas, it illustrates strategies 1 and 3.

The introductory paragraph indicates the closeness of setting and story, and lays out the areas to be developed in the essay. Paragraph 2 is developed with details showing the importance of the Captain's cabin. Paragraph 3 presents details about the relationship of the ocean to the story: in storm as a cause of Leggatt's good and bad actions, in calm and night as a link between the Captain and Leggatt, and in shallow water as a means of safety for Leggatt but as a threat to the Captain and the ship. Paragraph 4 presents details about the larger, cosmic aspects of the setting, for Conrad's story is not only about physical details but about the unseen forces that control human beings. The concluding paragraph illustrates the significance that knowledge of the ocean plays in the moral decision—and hence in the character—of the Captain.

Writing Topics About Setting

1. Compare and contrast how details of setting establish qualities and traits of the following female characters: Sarah of "And Sarah Laughed," Stella of "The Shawl" (this chapter), the speaker of "The House on Mango Street," and Miss Brill of "Miss Brill" (Chapter 3). To add to your comparison, you might discuss how the painters Boucher, Hopper, and Whistler portray background and dress to highlight the character of their female subjects (see pp. I–5, I–6, and I–11).

2. In what ways might we say that both "The Masque of the Red Death" (Chapter 9) and "The Shawl" (this chapter) are inseparable from their settings? To answer this question, consider the relationship of character to place and circumstance. How could the actions of the stories happen without the locations in which they occur?

3. Consider the significance of place and character in "A Rose for Emily" (Chapter 1) or "Araby" (this chapter).

4. Choose one story included in this chapter and rewrite a page or two, taking the characters out of their setting and placing them in an entirely new setting or in the setting of another story (you choose). Then write a brief analysis dealing with questions like these: How do you think your characters would be affected by their new settings? Do you make them change slowly or rapidly? Why? As a result of your rewriting, what can you conclude about the uses of setting in fiction?

5. Write a short narrative as though it is part of a story (which you may also wish to write for the assignment), using option (a) and/or (b).

   a. Relate a natural setting or type of day to a mood—for example, a nice day to happiness and satisfaction, or a cold, cloudy, rainy day to sadness. Or create irony by relating the nice day to sadness or the rainy day to happiness.

   b. Indicate how an object or circumstance becomes the cause of conflict or reconciliation (such as the shawl in "The Shawl" in this chapter or the newly tuned piano in "Two Kinds" in Chapter 3).

6. Locate two books or internet sources on the career of Edgar Allan Poe. On the basis of information you find in these sources, write a brief account of Poe's use of setting and place to evoke atmosphere and to bring out qualities of human character.

Chapter 5

Structure: The Organization of Stories

Structure refers to the ways in which writers arrange materials in accord with the general ideas and purposes of their works. Unlike plot, which is focused on conflict or conflicts, structure defines the layouts of works—the ways the story, play, or poem is shaped. Structure is about matters such as placement, balance, recurring themes, true and misleading conclusions, suspense, and the imitation of models or forms such as reports, letters, conversations, or confessions. A work might be divided into numbered sections or parts, or it might begin in a countryside (or one state) and conclude in a city (or another state), or it might develop a relationship between two people from their first introduction to their falling in love.

The importance of structure may be seen graphically in the art of the painter. As an example, the painting *Harbour at Sunset* (p. I–3), by the French painter Claude Lorrain (1600–1682), pictures a lifelike scene comprising a harbor, ships, boats, buildings, and a shore on which people are working, chatting, transacting business, and fighting. Near the horizon, the distant and glowing sun bathes the scene in light and therefore the source of all the human activities. This structuring of figures and background brings out contrasts between human beings, human artifacts and nature, and human existence and the cosmos. Claude's painting suggests that, despite temporary human concerns, the source of life is like the sun—remote, vast, mysterious, and beautiful. In fiction, we find that organization and structure highlight many similar contrasts. To study structure is to study these arrangements and the purposes for which they are made.

Formal Categories of Structure

Many aspects of structure are common to all genres of literature. Particularly for stories and plays, however, the following aspects form a skeleton, a pattern of development.

The Exposition Provides the Materials Necessary to Put the Plot into Operation

Exposition is the laying out, the putting forth, of the materials in the story—the main characters, their backgrounds, their characteristics, interests, goals, limitations, potentials, and basic assumptions. Exposition may not be limited to the beginning of the work, where it is most expected, but may be found anywhere. Thus, intricacies, twists, turns, false leads, blind alleys, surprises, and other quirks may be introduced to interest, intrigue, perplex, mystify, and please readers. Whenever something new arises, to the degree that it is new it is a part of exposition.

The Complication Marks the Beginning and the Growth of the Conflict

The **complication** is the onset and development of the major conflict—the plot. The major participants are the protagonist and antagonist, together with whatever ideas and values they represent, such as good or evil, freedom or oppression, independence or dependence, love or hate, intelligence or stupidity, and knowledge or ignorance.

The Crisis Marks the Decisions Made to End the Conflict

The **crisis** (the Greek word for *judgment* or *separation*—a separating, distinguishing, or turning point) marks that part of the action where the conflict reaches its greatest tension. During the crisis, a decision or an action is undertaken to resolve the complication or complications, and therefore the crisis is that point at which uncertainty and anxiety are greatest. Usually the crisis is followed closely by the next stage, the *climax*. In fact, the two often occur so near each other that they are considered the same.

The Climax Is the Conclusion of the Conflict

Because the **climax** (the Greek word for *ladder*) is a consequence of the crisis, it is the story's *high point* (from the idea of a ladder) and may take the shape of an action, a decision, an affirmation or denial, or an illumination or realization. It is the logical conclusion of the preceding actions; no new major developments follow it. In most stories, the climax occurs at the end or close to it. For example, in Oates's "The Cousins" (Chapter 2), the climax occurs when it becomes clear that the indifferent cousin is newly concerned to receive attention. Previously in the story, it has seemed that she does not need the burden of her cousin's letters, but the shift in her attitude is the story's high point, which demonstrates that her apparent annoyance has changed to her need to connect with her cousin.

The Resolution or Dénouement Finishes the Work and Releases the Tension

The **resolution** (the Latin word for *untying* or *releasing*) or **dénouement** (the French word for *untying* or *undoing*) is the completing of the story or play after the climax; for once the climax has occurred, the work's tension and uncertainty are finished, and most authors conclude quickly to avoid losing their readers' interest. For instance, Poe ends "The Masque of the Red Death" (Chapter 9) by asserting that the "illimitable" power of the Red Death has overcome the earth and all its occupants. In other words, after the story's major conflicts are finished, the dénouement brings the work to a satisfying and rapid ending.

Formal and Actual Structure

The structure just described is a *formal* one, an ideal pattern that moves directly from beginning to end. Few narratives and dramas follow this pattern exactly, however. A mystery story might hold back crucial details of exposition (because the goal is to mystify); a suspense story might keep the protagonist ignorant but provide readers with abundant details in order to maximize concern and tension about the outcome.

More realistic, less "artificial" stories might also contain structural variations. For example, Welty's "A Worn Path" (Chapter 1) produces a *double take* because of unique structuring. During most of the story the major character, Phoenix, seems to be in conflict with age, poverty, and environment. At the end, however, the story brings out an additional difficulty—a new conflict that enlarges our responses to include not just concern but also heartfelt anguish. "A Worn Path" is just one example of how a structural variation maximizes the impact of a work.

There are many other possible variants in structure. One of these is called **flashback,** or **selective recollection,** in which present circumstances are explained by the selective introduction of past events. The moment at which the flashback is introduced may be a part of the resolution of the plot, and the flashback might lead you into a moment of climax but then go from there to develop the details that are more properly part of the exposition. Let us again consider our brief story about John and Jane (Chapter 1) and use the flashback method of structuring the story:

> Jane is now old, and a noise outside causes her to remember the argument that forced her to part with John many years before. They were deeply in love, but their disagreement about her wishes for a career and equality split them apart. Then she pictures in her mind the years she and John have spent happily together after they married. She then contrasts her present happiness with her memory of her earlier, less happy marriage, and from there she recalls her youthful years of courtship with John before their disastrous conflict developed. Then she looks over at John, reading in a chair, and smiles. John smiles back, and the two embrace. Even then, Jane has tears on her cheeks.

In this structure the action begins and remains in the present. Important parts of the past flood the protagonist's memory in flashback, though not in the order in which they happened. Memory might be used structurally in other ways. An example is Katherine Anne Porter's "The Jilting of Granny Weatherall" (Chapter 7), an intense story that is developed within the dying perceptions of an aged woman, Granny Weatherall. As she passes in and out of delirium on her deathbed, we follow her recollection of major events in her life, such as being jilted on her wedding day, remarrying and bringing up her children, enduring her long widowhood, losing a favorite daughter, and retaining her lifelong obligation to her church. In short, this story builds its chronology through a series of apparently disconnected but closely unified flashbacks.

Each narrative or drama has its own unique structure. Some stories may be organized according to simple geography, as in Whitecloud's "Blue Winds Dancing" (a ride from California to Wisconsin in this chapter) and Munro's "The Found Boat" (from a spring flood to an exploration on and beside a river in Chapter 6). Parts or scenes might be carried on through conversations, as in Carver's "Neighbors"

(Chapter 2), or through a period of dying fantasy, as in Ambrose Bierce's "An Occurrence at Owl Creek Bridge" (Chapter 1). Additionally, parts of a work may be set out as fragments of conversation, as in St. Luke's "The Parable of the Prodigal Son" (Chapter 7), or as a ceremony, as in Hawthorne's "Young Goodman Brown" (Chapter 7), or as an announcement of a party, as in "The Necklace" (Part I). The possible variations in literary structures are infinite.

Stories for Study

Ralph Ellison . . . . Battle Royal, 278

Thomas Hardy . . . . The Three Strangers, 287

Jamaica Kincaid. . . . . What I Have Been Doing Lately, 300

Joyce Carol Oates . . . Where Are You Going, Where Have You Been?, 302

Tom Whitecloud . . . . Blue Winds Dancing, 313

RALPH ELLISON (1914–1994)

Ellison was born in Oklahoma seven years after it became a state. As a youth he was attracted to music, particularly jazz; and at one point he planned on becoming a classical music composer, his ideal being Richard Wagner, the giant among nineteenth century German operatic composers. In 1933 Ellison went to Alabama's Tuskegee Institute, but after three years he left for New York with a plan to become a sculptor. Once in New York, he met Richard Wright, and with Wright's encouragement and influence he began writing essays and stories for magazines such as New Challenge *and* New Masses. *Before he published* Invisible Man *in 1952, his best known works were the stories "King of the Bingo Game" and "Flying Home." With* Invisible Man, *which won a National Book Award in 1953, his work became widely read and taught. In 1964 he published* Shadow and Act, *a collection of essays, and in 1985 he published* Going to the Territory, *a book of essays and interviews. In later years he held a chair in humanities at New York University. His works published posthumously are* The Collected Essays of Ralph Ellison *(1995),* Flying Home and Other Stories *(1996), and the novel* Juneteenth *(1999).*

Battle Royal (1952)

It goes a long way back, some twenty years. All my life I had been looking for something, and everywhere I turned someone tried to tell me what it was. I accepted their answers too, though they were often in contradiction and even self-contradictory. I was naïve. I was looking for myself and asking everyone except myself questions which I, and only I, could answer. It took me a long time and much painful boomeranging of my expectations to achieve a realization everyone else appears to have been born with: That I am nobody but myself. But first I had to discover that I am an invisible man!

And yet I am no freak of nature, nor of history. I was in the cards, other things having been equal (or unequal) eighty-five years ago. I am not ashamed of my grandparents for having been slaves. I am only ashamed of myself for having at one time been ashamed. About eighty-five years ago they were told that they were free, united with others of our country in everything pertaining to the common good, and, in everything social, separate like the fingers of the hand.

And they believed it. They exulted in it. They stayed in their place, worked hard, and brought up my father to do the same. But my grandfather is the one. He was an odd old guy, my grandfather, and I am told I take after him. It was he who caused the trouble. On his deathbed he called my father to him and said, "Son, after I'm gone I want you to keep up the good fight. I never told you, but our life is a war and I have been a traitor all my born days, a spy in the enemy's country ever since I gave up my gun back in the Reconstruction. Live with your head in the lion's mouth. I want you to overcome 'em with yeses, undermine 'em with grins, agree 'em to death and destruction, let 'em swoller you till they vomit or bust wide open." They thought the old man had gone out of his mind. He had been the meekest of men. The younger children were rushed from the room, the shades drawn and the flame of the lamp turned so low that it sputtered on the wick like the old man's breathing. "Learn it to the young uns," he whispered fiercely; then he died.

But my folks were more alarmed over his last words than over his dying. It was as though he had not died at all, his words caused so much anxiety. I was warned emphatically to forget what he had said and, indeed, this is the first time it has been mentioned outside the family circle. It had a tremendous effect upon me, however. I could never be sure of what he meant. Grandfather had been a quiet old man who never made any trouble, yet on his deathbed he had called himself a traitor and a spy, and he had spoken of his meekness as a dangerous activity. It became a constant puzzle which lay unanswered in the back of my mind. And whenever things went well for me I remembered my grandfather and felt guilty and uncomfortable. It was as though I was carrying out his advice in spite of myself. And to make it worse, everyone loved me for it. I was praised by the most lily-white men of the town. I was considered an example of desirable conduct—just as my grandfather had been. And what puzzled me was that the old man had defined it as *treachery*. When I was praised for my conduct I felt a guilt that in some way I was doing something that was really against the wishes of the white folks, that if they had understood they would have desired me to act just the opposite, that I should have been sulky and mean, and that that really would have been what they wanted, even though they were fooled and thought they wanted me to act as I did. It made me afraid that some day they would look upon me as a traitor and I would be lost. Still I was more afraid to act any other way because they didn't like that at all. The old man's words were like a curse. On my graduation day I delivered an oration in which I showed that humility was the secret, indeed, the very essence of progress. (Not that I believed this—how could I, remembering my grandfather?—I only believed that it worked.) It was a great success. Everyone praised me and I was invited to give the speech at a gathering of the town's leading white citizens. It was a triumph for our whole community.

It was in the main ballroom of the leading hotel. When I got there I discovered that it was on the occasion of a smoker, and I was told that since I was to be there anyway I might as well take part in the battle royal to be fought by some of my schoolmates as part of the entertainment. The battle royal came first.

All of the town's big shots were there in their tuxedoes, wolfing down the buffet foods, drinking beer and whiskey and smoking black cigars. It was a large room with a high ceiling. Chairs were arranged in neat rows around three sides of a portable boxing ring. The fourth side was clear, revealing a gleaming space of polished floor. I had some misgivings over the battle royal, by the way. Not from a distaste for fighting, but because I didn't care too much for the other fellows who were to take part. They were tough guys who seemed to have no grandfather's curse worrying their minds. No one could mistake their toughness. And besides, I suspected that fighting a battle royal might detract from the dignity of

5

my speech. In those pre-invisible days I visualized myself as a potential Booker T. Washington.° But the other fellows didn't care too much for me either, and there were nine of them. I felt superior to them in my way, and I didn't like the manner in which we were all crowded together into the servants' elevator. Nor did they like my being there. In fact, as the warmly lighted floors flashed past the elevator we had words over the fact that I, by taking part in the fight, had knocked one of their friends out of a night's work.

We were led out of the elevator through a rococo hall into an anteroom and told to get into our fighting togs. Each of us was issued a pair of boxing gloves and ushered out into the big mirrored hall, which we entered looking cautiously about us and whispering, lest we might accidentally be heard above the noise of the room. It was foggy with cigar smoke. And already the whiskey was taking effect. I was shocked to see some of the most important men of the town quite tipsy. They were all there—bankers, lawyers, judges, doctors, fire chiefs, teachers, merchants. Even one of the more fashionable pastors. Something we could not see was going on up front. A clarinet was vibrating sensuously and the men were standing up and moving eagerly forward. We were a small tight group, clustered together, our bare upper bodies touching and shining with anticipatory sweat; while up front the big shots were becoming increasingly excited over something we still could not see. Suddenly I heard the school superintendent, who had told me to come, yell, "Bring up the shines gentlemen! Bring up the little shines!"

We were rushed up to the front of the ballroom, where it smelled even more strongly of tobacco and whiskey. Then we were pushed into place. I almost wet my pants. A sea of faces, some hostile, some amused, ringed around us, and in the center, facing us, stood a magnificent blonde—stark naked. There was dead silence. I felt a blast of cold air chill me. I tried to back away, but they were behind me and around me. Some of the boys stood with lowered heads, trembling. I felt a wave of irrational guilt and fear. My teeth chattered, my skin turned to goose flesh, my knees knocked. Yet I was strongly attracted and looked in spite of myself. Had the price of looking been blindness, I would have looked. The hair was yellow like that of a circus kewpie doll, the face heavily powdered and rouged, as though to form an abstract mask, the eyes hollow and smeared a cool blue, the color of a baboon's butt. I felt a desire to spit upon her as my eyes brushed slowly over her body. Her breasts were firm and round as the domes of East Indian temples, and I stood so close as to see the fine skin texture and beads of pearly perspiration glistening like dew around the pink and erected buds of her nipples. I wanted at one and the same time to run from the room, to sink through the floor, or go to her and cover her from my eyes and the eyes of the others with my body; to feel the soft thighs, to caress her and destroy her, to love her and murder her, to hide from her, and yet to stroke where below the small American flag tattooed upon her belly her thighs formed a capital V. I had a notion that of all in the room she saw only me with her impersonal eyes.

And then she began to dance, a slow sensuous movement; the smoke of a hundred cigars clinging to her like the thinnest of veils. She seemed like a fair bird-girl girdled in veils calling to me from the angry surface of some gray and threatening sea. I was transported. Then I became aware of the clarinet playing and the big shots yelling at us. Some threatened us if we looked and others if we did not. On my right I saw one boy faint. And now a man grabbed a silver pitcher from a table and stepped close as he dashed ice water upon him and stood him up and forced two of us to support him as his head hung and moans issued from his thick bluish lips. Another boy began to plead to go home. He was the largest of the group, wearing dark red fighting trunks much too small to conceal the erection which projected from him as though in answer to the insinuating low-registered moaning of the clarinet. He tried to hide himself with his boxing gloves.

°Booker T. Washington (1856–1915) was born a slave, but ultimately he became widely recognized as an educator, and served as president of the Tuskeegee Institute.

And all the while the blonde continued dancing, smiling faintly at the big shots who watched her with fascination, and faintly smiling at our fear. I noticed a certain merchant who followed her hungrily, his lips loose and drooling. He was a large man who wore diamond studs in a shirtfront which swelled with the ample paunch underneath, and each time the blonde swayed her undulating hips he ran his hand through the thin hair of his bald head and, with his arms upheld, his posture clumsy like that of an intoxicated panda, wound his belly in a slow and obscene grind. This creature was completely hypnotized. The music had quickened. As the dancer flung herself about with a detached expression on her face, the men began reaching out to touch her. I could see their beefy fingers sink into her soft flesh. Some of the others tried to stop them and she began to move around the floor in graceful circles, as they gave chase, slipping and sliding over the polished floor. It was mad. Chairs went crashing, drinks were spilt, as they ran laughing and howling after her. They caught her just as she reached a door, raised her from the floor, and tossed her as college boys are tossed at a hazing, and above her red, fixed-smiling lips I saw the terror and disgust in her eyes, almost like my own terror and that which I saw in some of the other boys. As I watched, they tossed her twice and her soft breasts seemed to flatten against the air and her legs flung widely as she spun. Some of the more sober ones helped her to escape. And I started off the floor, heading for the anteroom with the rest of the boys.

Some were still crying and in hysteria. But as we tried to leave we were stopped and ordered to get into the ring. There was nothing to do but what we were told. All ten of us climbed under the ropes and allowed ourselves to be blindfolded with broad bands of white cloth. One of the men seemed to feel a bit sympathetic and tried to cheer us up as we stood with our backs against the ropes. Some of us tried to grin. "See that boy over there?" one of the men said. "I want you to run across at the bell and give it to him right in the belly. If you don't get him, I'm going to get you. I don't like his looks." Each of us was told the same. The blindfolds were put on. Yet even then I had been going over my speech. In my mind each word was as bright as flame. I felt the cloth pressed into place, and frowned so that it would be loosened when I relaxed. 10

But now I felt a sudden fit of blind terror. I was unused to darkness. It was as though I had suddenly found myself in a dark room filled with poisonous cottonmouths. I could hear the bleary voices yelling insistently for the battle royal to begin.

"Get going in there!"

"Let me at that big nigger!"

I strained to pick up the school superintendent's voice, as though to squeeze some security out of that slightly more familiar sound.

"Let me at those black sonsabitches!" someone yelled. 15

"No, Jackson, no!" another voice yelled. "Here, somebody, help me hold Jack."

"I want to get at that ginger-colored nigger. Tear him limb from limb," the first voice yelled.

I stood against the ropes trembling. For in those days I was what they called ginger-colored, and he sounded as though he might crunch me between his teeth like a crisp ginger cookie.

Quite a struggle was going on. Chairs were being kicked about and I could hear voices grunting as with a terrific effort. I wanted to see, to see more desperately than ever before. But the blindfold was as tight as a thick skinpuckering scab and when I raised my gloved hands to push the layers of white aside a voice yelled, "Oh, no you don't, black bastard! Leave that alone!"

"Ring the bell before Jackson kills him a coon!" someone boomed in the sudden silence. And I heard the bell clang and the sound of the feet scuffling forward. 20

A glove smacked against my head. I pivoted, striking out stiffly as someone went past, and felt the jar ripple along the length of my arm to my shoulder. Then it seemed as though all nine of the boys had turned upon me at once. Blows pounded me from all sides while I struck out as best I could. So many blows landed upon me that I wondered if I were not the only blindfolded fighter in the ring, or if the man called Jackson hadn't succeeded in getting me after all.

Blindfolded, I could no longer control my motions. I had no dignity. I stumbled about like a baby or a drunken man. The smoke had become thicker and with each new blow it seemed to sear and further restrict my lungs. My saliva became like hot bitter glue. A glove connected with my head, filling my mouth with warm blood. It was everywhere. I could not tell if the moisture I felt upon my body was sweat or blood. A blow landed hard against the nape of my neck. I felt myself going over, my head hitting the floor. Streaks of blue light filled the black world behind the blindfold. I lay prone, pretending that I was knocked out, but felt myself seized by hands and yanked to my feet. "Get going, black boy! Mix it up!" My arms were like lead, my head smarting from blows. I managed to feel my way to the ropes and held on, trying to catch my breath. A glove landed in my midsection and I went over again, feeling as though the smoke had become a knife jabbed into my guts. Pushed this way and that by the legs milling around me, I finally pulled erect and discovered that I could see the black, sweat-washed forms weaving in the smoky-blue atmosphere like drunken dancers weaving to the rapid drum-like thuds of blows.

Everyone fought hysterically. It was complete anarchy. Everybody fought everybody else. No group fought together for long. Two, three, four, fought one, then turned to fight each other, were themselves attacked. Blows landed below the belt and in the kidney, with the gloves open as well as closed, and with my eye partly opened now there was not so much terror. I moved carefully, avoiding blows, although not too many to attract attention, fighting from group to group. The boys groped about like blind, cautious crabs crouching to protect their midsections, their heads pulled in short against their shoulders, their arms stretched nervously before them, with their fists testing the smoke-filled air like the knobbed feelers of hypersensitive snails. In one corner I glimpsed a boy violently punching the air and heard him scream in pain as he smashed his hand against a ring post.

For a second I saw him bent over holding his hand, then going down as a blow caught his unprotected head. I played one group against the other, slipping in and throwing a punch then stepping out of range while pushing the others into the melee to take the blows blindly aimed at me. The smoke was agonizing and there were no rounds, no bells at three minute intervals to relieve our exhaustion. The room spun round me, a swirl of lights, smoke, seating bodies surrounded by tense white faces. I bled from both nose and mouth, the blood spattering upon my chest.

25   The men kept yelling, "Slug him, black boy! Knock his guts out!"

"Uppercut him! Kill him! Kill that big boy!"

Taking a fake fall, I saw a boy going down heavily beside me as though we were felled by a single blow, saw a sneaker-clad foot shoot into his groin as the two who had knocked him down stumbled upon him. I rolled out of range, feeling a twinge of nausea.

The harder we fought the more threatening the men became. And yet, I had begun to worry about my speech again. How would it go? Would they recognize my ability? What would they give me?

I was fighting automatically and suddenly I noticed that one after another of the boys was leaving the ring. I was surprised, filled with panic, as though I had been left alone with an unknown danger. Then I understood. The boys had arranged it among themselves. It was the custom for the two men left in the ring to slug it out for the winner's prize. I discovered this too late. When the bell sounded two men in tuxedoes leaped into the ring and removed the blindfold. I found myself facing Tatlock, the biggest of the gang. I felt sick at my stomach. Hardly had the bell stopped ringing in my ears than it clanged again and I saw him moving swiftly toward me. Thinking of nothing else to do I hit him smash on the nose. He kept coming, bringing the rank sharp violence of stale sweat. His face was a black blank of a face, only his eyes alive—with hate of me and aglow with a feverish terror from what had happened to us all. I became anxious. I wanted to deliver my speech and he came at me as though he meant to beat it out of me. I smashed him again and again, taking his blows as they came. Then on a sudden impulse I struck him lightly and as we clinched, I whispered, "Fake like I knocked you out, you can have the prize."

"I'll break your behind," he whispered hoarsely.

"For *them?*"   30

"For *me*, sonofabitch!"

They were yelling for us to break it up and Tatlock spun me half around with a blow, and as a joggled camera sweeps in a reeling scene, I saw the howling red faces crouching tense beneath the cloud of blue-gray smoke. For a moment the world wavered, unraveled, flowed, then my head cleared and Tatlock bounced before me. That fluttering shadow before my eyes was his jabbing left hand. Then falling forward, my head against his damp shoulder, I whispered,

"I'll make it five dollars more."

"Go to hell!"   35

But his muscles relaxed a trifle beneath my pressure and I breathed, "Seven!"

"Give it to your ma," he said, ripping me beneath the heart.

And while I still held him I butted him and moved away. I felt myself bombarded with punches. I fought back with hopeless desperation. I wanted to deliver my speech more than anything else in the world, because I felt that only these men could judge truly my ability, and now this stupid clown was ruining my chances. I began fighting carefully now, moving in to punch him and out again with my greater speed. A lucky blow to his chin and I had him going too—until I heard a loud voice yell, "I got my money on the big boy."

Hearing this, I almost dropped my guard. I was confused: Should I try to win against the voice out there? Would not this go against my speech, and was not this a moment for humility, for nonresistance? A blow to my head as I danced about sent my right eye popping like a jack-in-the-box and settled my dilemma. The room went red as I fell. It was a dream fall, my body languid and fastidious as to where to land, until the floor became impatient and smashed up to meet me. A moment later I came to. An hypnotic voice said FIVE emphatically. And I lay there, hazily watching a dark red spot of my own blood shaping itself into a butterfly, glistening and soaking into the soiled gray world of the canvas.

When the voice drawled TEN I was lifted up and dragged to a chair. I sat dazed. My eye   40
pained and swelled with each throb of my pounding heart and I wondered if now I would be allowed to speak. I was wringing wet, my mouth still bleeding. We were grouped along the wall now. The other boys ignored me as they congratulated Tatlock and speculated as to how much they would be paid. One boy whimpered over his smashed hand. Looking up front, I saw attendants in white jackets rolling the portable ring away and placing a small square rug in the vacant space surrounded by chairs. Perhaps, I thought, I will stand on the rug to deliver my speech.

Then the M.C. called to us, "Come on up here boys and get your money."

We ran forward to where the men laughed and talked in their chairs, waiting. Everyone seemed friendly now.

"There it is on the rug," the man said. I saw the rug covered with coins of all dimensions and a few crumpled bills. But what excited me, scattered here and there, were the gold pieces.

"Boys, it's all yours," the man said. "You get all you grab."

"That's right, Sambo," a blond man said, winking at me confidentially.   45

I trembled with excitement, forgetting my pain. I would get the gold and the bills, I thought. I would use both hands. I would throw my body against the boys nearest me to block them from the gold.

"Get down around the rug now," the man commanded, "and don't anyone touch it until I give the signal."

"This ought to be good," I heard.

As told, we got around the square rug on our knees. Slowly the man raised his freckled hand as we followed it upward with our eyes.

50   I heard, "These niggers look like they're about to pray!"

Then, "Ready," the man said. "Go!"

I lunged for a yellow coin lying on the blue design of the carpet, touching it and sending a surprised shriek to join those rising around me. I tried frantically to remove my hand but could not let go. A hot, violent force tore through my body, shaking me like a wet rat. The rug was electrified. The hair bristled up on my head as I shook myself free. My muscles jumped, my nerves jangled, writhed. But I saw that this was not stopping the other boys. Laughing in fear and embarrassment, some were holding back and scooping up the coins knocked off by the painful contortions of the others. The men roared above us as we struggled.

"Pick it up, goddamnit, pick it up!" someone called like a bass-voiced parrot. "Go on, get it!"

I crawled rapidly around the floor, picking up the coins, trying to avoid the coppers and to get greenbacks and the gold. Ignoring the shock by laughing, as I brushed the coins off quickly, I discovered that I could contain the electricity—a contradiction, but it works. Then the men began to push us onto the rug. Laughing embarrassedly, we struggled out of their hands and kept after the coins. We were all wet and slippery and hard to hold. Suddenly I saw a boy lifted into the air, glistening with sweat like a circus seal, and dropped, his wet back landing flush upon the charged rug, heard him yell and saw him literally dance upon his back, his elbows beating a frenzied tattoo upon the floor, his muscles twitching like the flesh of a horse stung by many flies. When he finally rolled off, his face was gray and no one stopped him when he ran from the floor amid booming laughter.

55   "Get the money," the M.C. called. "That's good hard American cash!"

And we snatched and grabbed, snatched and grabbed. I was careful not to come too close to the rug now, and when I felt the hot whiskey breath descend upon me like a cloud of foul air I reached out and grabbed the leg of a chair. It was occupied and I held on desperately.

"Leggo, nigger! Leggo!"

The huge face wavered down to mine as he tried to push me free. But my body was slippery and he was too drunk. It was Mr. Colcord, who owned a chain of movie houses and "entertainment palaces." Each time he grabbed me I slipped out of his hands. It became a real struggle. I feared the rug more than I did the drunk, so I held on, surprising myself for a moment by trying to topple him upon the rug. It was such an enormous idea that I found myself actually carrying it out. I tried not to be obvious, yet when I grabbed his leg, trying to tumble him out of the chair, he raised up roaring with laughter, and, looking at me with soberness dead in the eye, kicked me viciously in the chest. The chair leg flew out of my hand. I felt myself going and rolled. It was as though I had rolled through a bed of hot coals. It seemed a whole century would pass before I would roll free, a century in which I was scared through the deepest levels of my body to the fearful breath within me and the breath seared and heated to the point of explosion. It'll all be over in a flash, I thought as I rolled clear. It'll all be over in a flash.

But not yet, the men on the other side were waiting, red faces swollen as though from apoplexy as they bent forward in their chairs. Seeing their fingers coming toward me I rolled away as a fumbled football rolls off the receiver's fingertips, back into the coals. That time I luckily sent the rug sliding out of place and heard the coins ringing against the floor and the boys scuffling to pick them up and the M.C. calling, "All right, boys, that's all. Go get dressed and get your money."

60   I was limp as a dish rag. My back felt as though it had been beaten with wires.

When we had dressed the M.C. came in and gave us each five dollars, except Tatlock, who got ten for being last in the ring. Then he told us to leave. I was not to get a chance to deliver my speech, I thought. I was going out into the dim alley in despair when I was stopped and told to go back. I returned to the ballroom, where the men were pushing back their chairs and gathering in groups to talk.

The M.C. knocked on a table for quiet. "Gentlemen," he said, "we almost forgot an important part of the program. A most serious part, gentlemen. This boy was brought here to deliver a speech which he made at his graduation yesterday. . . ."

"Bravo!"

"I'm told that he is the smartest boy we've got out there in Greenwood. I'm told that he knows more big words than a pocket-sized dictionary."

Much applause and laughter.

"So now, gentlemen, I want you to give him your attention." 65

There was still laughter as I faced them, my mouth dry, my eye throbbing. I began slowly, but evidently my throat was tense, because they began shouting, "Louder! Louder!"

"We of the younger generation extol the wisdom of that great leader and educator," I shouted, "who first spoke these flaming words of wisdom: 'A ship lost at sea for many days suddenly sighted a friendly vessel. From the mast of the unfortunate vessel was seen a signal: "Water, water; we die of thirst!" The answer from the friendly vessel came back: "Cast down your bucket where you are." The captain of the distressed vessel, at last heeding the injunction, cast down his bucket, and it came up full of fresh sparkling water from the mouth of the Amazon River.' And like him I say, and in his words, 'To those of my race who depend upon bettering their condition in a foreign land, or who underestimate the importance of cultivating friendly relations with the Southern white man, who is his next-door neighbor, I would say: "Cast down your bucket where you are"—cast it down in making friends in every manly way of the people of all races by whom we are surrounded. . . ."

I spoke automatically and with such fervor that I did not realize that the men were still talking and laughing until my dry mouth, filling up with blood from the cut, almost strangled me. I coughed, wanting to stop and go to one of the tall brass, sand-filled spittoons to relieve myself, but a few of the men, especially the superintendent, were listening and I was afraid. So I gulped it down, blood, saliva and all, and continued. (What powers of endurance I had during those days! What enthusiasm! What a belief in the rightness of things!) I spoke even louder in spite of the pain. But still they talked and still they laughed, as though deaf with cotton in dirty ears. So I spoke with greater emotional emphasis. I closed my ears and swallowed blood until I was nauseated. The speech seemed a hundred times as long as before, but I could not leave out a single word. All had to be said, each memorized nuance considered, rendered. Nor was that all. Whenever I uttered a word of three or more syllables a group of voices would yell for me to repeat it. I used the phrase "social responsibility" and they yelled:

"What's the word you say, boy?" 70

"Social responsibility," I said.

"What?"

"Social . . . "

"Louder."

". . . responsibility." 75

"More!"

"Respon—"

"Repeat!"

"—sibility."

The room filled with the uproar of laughter until, no doubt, distracted by having to gulp 80 down my blood, I made a mistake and yelled a phrase I had often seen denounced in newspaper editorials, heard debated in private.

"Social . . ."

"What?" they yelled.

". . . equality—"

The laughter hung smokelike in the sudden stillness. I opened my eyes, puzzled. Sounds of displeasure filled the room. The M.C. rushed forward. They shouted hostile phrases at me. But I did not understand.

85   A small dry mustached man in the front row blared out, "Say that slowly, son!"

"What sir?"

"What you just said!"

"Social responsibility, sir," I said.

"You weren't being smart, were you, boy?" he said, not unkindly.

90   "No, sir!"

"You sure that about 'equality' was a mistake?"

"Oh, yes, sir," I said. "I was swallowing blood."

"Well, you had better speak more slowly so we can understand. We mean to do right by you, but you've got to know your place at all times. All right, now, go on with your speech."

I was afraid. I wanted to leave but I wanted also to speak and I was afraid they'd snatch me down.

95   "Thank you, sir," I said, beginning where I had left off, and having them ignore me as before.

Yet when I finished there was a thunderous applause. I was surprised to see the superintendent come forth with a package wrapped in white tissue paper, and, gesturing for quiet, address the men.

"Gentlemen, you see that I did not overpraise this boy. He makes a good speech and some day he'll lead his people in the proper paths. And I don't have to tell you that that is important in these days and times. This is a good, smart boy, and so to encourage him in the right direction, in the name of the Board of Education I wish to present him a prize in the form of this . . ."

He paused, removing the tissue paper and revealing a gleaming calfskin brief case.

". . . in the form of this first-class article from Shad Whitmore's shop."

100   "Boy," he said, addressing me, "take this prize and keep it well. Consider it a badge of office. Prize it. Keep developing as you are and some day it will be filled with important papers that will help shape the destiny of your people."

I was so moved that I could hardly express my thanks. A rope of bloody saliva forming a shape like an undiscovered continent drooled upon the leather and I wiped it quickly away. I felt an importance that I had never dreamed.

"Open it and see what's inside," I was told.

My fingers a-tremble, I complied, smelling the fresh leather and finding an official-looking document inside. It was a scholarship to the state college for Negroes. My eyes filled with tears and I ran awkwardly off the floor.

I was overjoyed; I did not even mind when I discovered that the gold pieces I had scrambled for were brass pocket tokens advertising a certain make of automobile.

105   When I reached home everyone was excited. Next day the neighbors came to congratulate me. I even felt safe from grandfather, whose deathbed curse usually spoiled my triumphs. I stood beneath his photograph with my brief case in hand and smiled triumphantly into his stolid black peasant's face. It was a face that fascinated me. The eyes seemed to follow everywhere I went.

That night I dreamed I was at a circus with him and that he refused to laugh at the clowns no matter what they did. Then later he told me to open my brief case and read what was inside and I did, finding an official envelope stamped with the state seal; and inside the envelope I found another and another, endlessly, and I thought I would fall of weariness. "Them's years," he said. "Now open that one." And I did and in it I found an engraved document containing a short message in letters of gold. "Read it," my grandfather said. "Out loud."

"To Whom It May Concern," I intoned. "Keep This Nigger-Boy Running."

I awoke with the old man's laughter ringing in my ears.

(It was a dream I was to remember and dream again for many years after. But at the time I had no insight into its meaning. First I had to attend college.)

QUESTIONS

1. Describe the narrator. How old is he? What are the circumstances that lead him to the "gathering of the town's leading white citizens"? What conclusions do you draw about the mental and moral qualities of these citizens?

2. What is the significance of the advice given by the narrator's grandfather? What is the connection between the narrator's dream and the grandfather's advice?

3. What is a battle royal? What is the narrator's attitude toward the battle in which he is to participate? Why does he have this attitude? To what indignities are the boys subjected as a result of their appearance before the assembled townsmen? In what way is the female dancer's plight like that of the boys?

4. Describe how the story's structure underlies the story's attack on racism.

5. What special indignities are imposed on the narrator? Why does he have difficulty in delivering his speech? Why is he reminded that "you've got to know your place at all times" (paragraph 93)?

THOMAS HARDY (1840–1928)

Hardy was born in Dorsetshire, in southwest England, which he called "Wessex" in his novels and poems. He began a career as an architect but gave it up to become a novelist. In 1898, after he had published his stories and more than a dozen novels, including Tess of the D'Urbervilles, The Return of the Native, *and* Jude the Obscure, *he gave up novels and devoted himself to poetry. Before his death in 1928, he had published eight volumes of verse, which were collected and published posthumously in 1931.*

 ## The Three Strangers (1888)

Among the few features of agricultural England which retain an appearance but little modified by the lapse of centuries may be reckoned the high, grassy and furzy downs, coombs, or ewe-leases, as they are indifferently called, that fill a large area of certain counties in the south and southwest. If any mark of human occupation is met with hereon, it usually takes the form of the solitary cottage of some shepherd.

Fifty years ago such a lonely cottage stood on such a down, and may possibly be standing there now. In spite of its loneliness, however, the spot, by actual measurement, was not more than five miles from a county-town. Yet that affected it little. Five miles of irregular upland, during the long inimical seasons, with their sleets, snows, rains, and mists, afford withdrawing space enough to isolate a Timon or a Nebuchadnezzar;° much less, in fair weather, to please that less repellent tribe, the poets, philosophers, artists, and others who "conceive and meditate of pleasant things."

°*Timon or Nebuchadnezzar:* Both were proverbial for their solitude. The ancient Greek Timon was disappointed because he did not receive the advancement he expected, and he therefore withdrew from society totally. Nebuchadnezzar was the Babylonian king who, suffering from the delusion that he was an ox, was driven away from society to eat with beasts (Daniel 4).

Some old earthen camp or barrow, some clump of trees, at least some starved fragment of ancient hedge is usually taken advantage of in the erection of these forlorn dwellings. But, in the present case, such a kind of shelter had been disregarded. Higher Crowstairs, as the house was called, stood quite detached and undefended. The only reason for its precise situation seemed to be the crossing of two footpaths at right angles hard by, which may have crossed there and thus for a good five hundred years. Hence the house was exposed to the elements on all sides. But, though the wind up here blew unmistakably when it did blow, and the rain hit hard whenever it fell, the various weathers of the winter season were not quite so formidable on the coomb as they were imagined to be by dwellers on low ground. The raw rimes° were not so pernicious as in the hollows, and the frosts were scarcely so severe. When the shepherd and his family who tenanted the house were pitied for their sufferings from the exposure, they said that upon the whole they were less inconvenienced by "wuzzes and flames" (hoarses and phlegms) than when they had lived by the stream of a snug neighboring valley.

The night of March 28, 182–, was precisely one of the nights that were wont to call forth these expressions of commiseration. The level rainstorm smote walls, slopes, and hedges like the clothyard shafts° of Senlac and Crécy.° Such sheep and outdoor animals as had no shelter stood with their buttocks to the winds; while the tails of little birds trying to roost on some scraggy thorn were blown inside-out like umbrellas. The gable-end of the cottage was stained with wet, and the eavesdroppings flapped against the wall. Yet never was commiseration for the shepherd more misplaced. For that cheerful rustic was entertaining a large party in glorification of the christening of his second girl.

The guests had arrived before the rain began to fall, and they were all now assembled in the chief or living room of the dwelling. A glance into the apartment at eight o'clock on this eventful evening would have resulted in the opinion that it was as cozy and comfortable a nook as could be wished for in boisterous weather. The calling of its inhabitant was proclaimed by a number of highly polished sheep crooks without stems that were hung ornamentally over the fireplace, the curl of each shining crook varying from the antiquated type engraved in the patriarchal pictures of old family Bibles to the most approved fashion of the last local sheep-fair. The room was lighted by half a dozen candles having wicks only a trifle smaller than the grease which enveloped them, in candlesticks that were never used but at high-days, holy-days, and family feasts. The lights were scattered about the room, two of them standing on the chimney piece. This position of candles was in itself significant. Candles on the chimney piece always meant a party.

On the hearth, in front of a back-brand to give substance, blazed a fire of thorns, that crackled "like the laughter of the fool."°

Nineteen persons were gathered here. Of these, five women, wearing gowns of various bright hues, sat in chairs along the wall; girls shy and not shy filled the window-bench; four men, including Charley Jake the hedge-carpenter, Elijah New the parish-clerk, and John Pitcher, a neighboring dairyman, the shepherd's father-in-law, lolled in the settle; a young man and maid, who were blushing over tentative *pourparlers*° on a life-companionship, sat beneath the corner-cupboard; and an elderly engaged man of fifty or upward moved restlessly about from spots where his betrothed was not to the spot where she was. Enjoyment was pretty general, and so much the more prevailed in being unhampered by conventional

---

°*rimes:* coatings of frost.
°*clothyard shafts:* thirty-six-inch arrows.
°*Senlac and Crécy:* battlefields in France where, in the middle ages, armies of English bowmen had defeated numerically superior French forces.
°*like the laughter of the fool:* Ecclesiastes 7:6.
°*pourparler:* a conversation held prior to negotiation.

restrictions. Absolute confidence in each other's good opinion begat perfect ease, while the finishing stroke of manner, amounting to a truly princely serenity, was lent to the majority by the absence of any expression or trait denoting that they wished to get on in the world, enlarge their minds, or do any eclipsing thing whatever—which nowadays so generally nips the bloom and *bonhomie* of all except the two extremes of the social scale.

Shepherd Fennel had married well, his wife being a dairyman's daughter from a vale at a distance, who brought fifty guineas in her pocket and kept them there, till they should be required for ministering to the needs of a coming family. This frugal woman had been somewhat exercised as to the character that should be given to the gathering. A sit-still party had its advantages; but an undisturbed position of ease in chairs and settles was apt to lead on the men to such an unconscionable deal of toping that they would sometimes fairly drink the house dry. A dancing-party was the alternative; but this, while avoiding the foregoing objection on the score of good drink, had a counterbalancing disadvantage in the matter of good victuals, the ravenous appetites engendered by the exercise causing immense havoc in the buttery. Shepherdess Fennel fell back upon the intermediate plan of mingling short dances with short periods of talk and singing, so as to hinder any ungovernable rage in either. But this scheme was entirely confined to her own gentle mind: the shepherd himself was in the mood to exhibit the most reckless phases of hospitality.

The fiddler was a boy of those parts, about twelve years of age, who had a wonderful dexterity in jigs and reels, though his fingers were so small and short as to necessitate a constant shifting for the high notes, from which he scrambled back to the first position with sounds not of unmixed purity of tone. At seven the shrill tweedle-dee of this youngster had begun, accompanied by a booming ground-bass from Elijah New, the parish-clerk, who had thoughtfully brought with him his favorite musical instrument, the serpent. Dancing was instantaneous, Mrs. Fennel privately enjoining the players on no account to let the dance exceed the length of a quarter of an hour.

But Elijah and the boy, in the excitement of their position, quite forgot the injunction. Moreover, Oliver Giles, a man of seventeen, one of the dancers, who was enamored of his partner, a fair girl of thirty-three rolling years, had recklessly handed a new crown-piece to the musicians, as a bribe to keep going as long as they had muscle and wind. Mrs. Fennel, seeing the steam begin to generate on the countenances of her guests, crossed over and touched the fiddler's elbow and put her hand on the serpent's mouth. But they took no notice, and fearing she might lose her character of genial hostess if she were to interfere too markedly, she retired and sat down helpless. And so the dance whizzed on with cumulative fury, the performers moving in their planet-like courses, direct and retrograde, from apogee to perigee, till the hand of the well-kicked clock at the bottom of the room had traveled over the circumference of an hour.

While these cheerful events were in course of enactment within Fennel's pastoral dwelling, an incident having considerable bearing on the party had occurred in the gloomy night without. Mrs. Fennel's concern about the growing fierceness of the dance corresponded in point of time with the ascent of a human figure to the solitary hill of Higher Crowstairs from the direction of the distant town. This personage strode on through the rain without a pause, following the little-worn path which, further on in its course, skirted the shepherd's cottage.

It was nearly the time of full moon, and on this account, though the sky was lined with a uniform sheet of dripping cloud, ordinary objects out of doors were readily visible. The sad, wan light revealed the lonely pedestrian to be a man of supple frame; his gait suggested that he had somewhat passed the period of perfect and instinctive agility, though not so far as to be otherwise than rapid of motion when occasion required. At a rough guess, he might have been about forty years of age. He appeared tall, but a recruiting sergeant, or other person accustomed to the judging of men's heights by the eye, would have discerned that this was chiefly owing to his gauntness, and that he was not more than five-feet eight or nine.

10

Notwithstanding the regularity of his tread, there was caution in it, as in that of one who mentally feels his way; and despite the fact that it was not a black coat nor a dark garment of any sort that he wore, there was something about him which suggested that he naturally belonged to the black-coated tribes of men. His clothes were of fustian,° and his boots hobnailed, yet in his progress he showed not the mud-accustomed bearing of hobnailed and fustianed peasantry.

By the time that he had arrived abreast of the shepherd's premises the rain came down, or rather came along, with yet more determined violence. The outskirts of the little settlement partially broke the force of wind and rain, and this induced him to stand still. The most salient of the shepherd's domestic erections was an empty sty at the forward corner of his hedgeless garden, for in these latitudes the principle of masking the homelier features of your establishment by a conventional frontage was unknown. The traveler's eye was attracted to this small building by the pallid shine of the wet slates that covered it. He turned aside, and, finding it empty, stood under the pent-roof for shelter.

15   While he stood, the boom of the serpent within the adjacent house, and the lesser strains of the fiddler, reached the spot as an accompaniment to the surging hiss of the flying rain on the sod, its louder beating on the cabbage-leaves of the garden, on the eight or ten beehives just discernible by the path, and its dripping from the eaves into a row of buckets and pans that had been placed under the walls of the cottage. For at Higher Crowstairs, as at all such elevated domiciles, the grand difficulty of housekeeping was an insufficiency of water; and a casual rainfall was utilized by turning out, as catchers, every utensil that the house contained. Some queer stories might be told of the contrivances for economy in suds and dishwaters that are absolutely necessitated in upland habitations during the droughts of summer. But at this season there were no such exigencies; a mere acceptance of what the skies bestowed was sufficient for an abundant store.

At last the notes of the serpent ceased and the house was silent. This cessation of activity aroused the solitary pedestrian from the reverie into which he had elapsed, and, emerging from the shed, with an apparently new intention, he walked up the path to the house-door. Arrived here, his first act was to kneel down on a large stone beside the row of vessels, and to drink a copious draught from one of them. Having quenched his thirst, he rose and lifted his hand to knock, but paused with his eye upon the panel. Since the dark surface of the wood revealed absolutely nothing, it was evident that he must be mentally looking through the door, as if he wished to measure thereby all the possibilities that a house of this sort might include, and how they might bear upon the question of his entry.

In his indecision he turned and surveyed the scene around. Not a soul was anywhere visible. The garden path stretched downward from his feet, gleaming like the track of a snail; the roof of the little well (mostly dry), the well-cover, the top rail of the garden-gate, were varnished with the same dull liquid glaze; while, far away in the vale, a faint whiteness of more than usual extent showed that the rivers were high in the meads. Beyond all this winked a few bleared lamplights through the beating drops—lights that denoted the situation of the county-town from which he had appeared to come. The absence of all notes of life in that direction seemed to clinch his intentions, and he knocked at the door.

Within, a desultory chat had taken the place of movement and musical sound. The hedge-carpenter was suggesting a song to the company, which nobody just then was inclined to undertake, so that the knock afforded a not unwelcome diversion.

"Walk in!" said the shepherd, promptly.

20   The latch clicked upward, and out of the night our pedestrian appeared upon the door-mat. The shepherd arose, snuffed two of the nearest candles, and turned to look at him.

°*fustian:* a thick, coarse cloth.

Their light disclosed that the stranger was dark in complexion and not unprepossessing as to feature. His hat, which for a moment he did not remove, hung low over his eyes, without concealing that they were large, open, and determined, moving with a flash rather than a glance round the room. He seemed pleased with his survey, and, baring his shaggy head, said, in a rich, deep voice: "The rain is so heavy friends, that I ask leave to come in and rest awhile."

"To be sure, Stranger," said the shepherd. "And faith, you've been lucky in choosing your time, for we are having a bit of a fling for a glad cause—though, to be sure, a man could hardly wish that glad cause to happen more than once a year. "

"Nor less," spoke up a woman. "For 'tis best to get your family over and done with, as soon as you can, so as to be all the earlier out of the fag o't."

"And what may be this glad cause?" asked the stranger.

"A birth and christening," said the shepherd.   25

The stranger hoped his host might not be made unhappy either by too many or too few of such episodes and, being invited by a gesture to a pull at the mug, he readily acquiesced. His manner, which, before entering, had been so dubious, was now altogether that of a careless and candid man.

"Late to be traipsing athwart this coomb—hey?" said the engaged man of fifty. "Late it is, Master, as you say.—I'll take a seat in the chimney corner, if you have nothing to urge against it, Ma'am; for I am a little moist on the side that was next the rain."

Mrs. Shepherd Fennel assented, and made room for the self-invited comer, who, having got completely inside the chimney corner, stretched out his legs and arms with the expansiveness of a person quite at home.

"Yes, I am rather cracked in the vamp," he said freely, seeing that the eyes of the shepherd's wife fell upon his boots, "and I am not well fitted either. I have had some rough times lately, and have been forced to pick up what I can get in the way of wearing, but I must find a suit better fit for working-days when I reach home."

"One of hereabouts?" she inquired.   30

"Not quite that—further up the country."

"I thought so. And so be I; and by your tongue you come from my neighborhood."

"But you would hardly have heard of me," he said quickly. "My time would be long before yours, Ma'am, you see."

This testimony to the youthfulness of his hostess had the effect of stopping her cross-examination.

"There is only one thing more wanted to make me happy," continued the newcomer,   35
"and that is a little baccy, which I am sorry to say I am out of."

"I'll fill your pipe," said the shepherd.

"I must ask you to lend me a pipe likewise."

"A smoker, and no pipe about 'ee?"

"I have dropped it somewhere on the road."

The shepherd filled and handed him a new clay pipe, saying, as he did so, "Hand me   40
your baccy-box—I'll fill that too, now I am about it."

The man went through the movement of searching his pockets.

"Lost that too?" said his entertainer, with some surprise.

"I am afraid so," said the man with some confusion. "Give it to me in a screw of paper." Lighting his pipe at the candle with a suction that drew the whole flame into the bowl, he resettled himself in the corner and bent his looks upon the faint steam from his damp legs, as if he wished to say no more.

Meanwhile the general body of guests had been taking little notice of this visitor by reason of an absorbing discussion in which they were engaged with the band about a tune for the next dance. The matter being settled, they were about to stand up when an interruption came in the shape of another knock at the door.

45   At sound of the same the man in the chimney corner took up the poker and began stirring the brands as if doing it thoroughly were the one aim of his existence; and a second time the shepherd said, "Walk in!" In a moment another man stood upon the straw-woven door-mat. He too was a stranger.

This individual was one of a type radically different from the first. There was more of the commonplace in his manner, and a certain jovial cosmopolitanism sat upon his features. He was several years older than the first arrival, his hair being slightly frosted, his eyebrows bristly, and his whiskers cut back from his cheeks. His face was rather full and flabby, and yet it was not altogether a face without power. A few grog-blossoms marked the neighborhood of his nose. He flung back his long drab greatcoat, revealing that beneath it he wore a suit of cinder-gray shade throughout, large heavy seals, of some metal or other that would take a polish, dangling from his fob as his only personal ornament. Shaking the water drops from his low-crowned glazed hat, he said, "I must ask for a few minutes' shelter, comrades, or I shall be wetted to my skin before I get to Casterbridge."

"Make yourself at home, Master," said the shepherd, perhaps a trifle less heartily than on the first occasion. Not that Fennel had the least tinge of niggardliness in his composition; but the room was far from large, spare chairs were not numerous, and damp companions were not altogether desirable at close quarters for the women and girls in their bright-colored gowns.

However, the second comer, after taking off his greatcoat, and hanging his hat on a nail in one of the ceiling-beams as if he had been specially invited to put it there, advanced and sat down at the table. This had been pushed so closely into the chimney corner, to give all available room to the dancers, that its inner edge grazed the elbow of the man who had ensconced himself by the fire; and thus the two strangers were brought into close companionship. They nodded to each other by way of breaking the ice of unacquaintance, and the first stranger handed his neighbor the family mug—a huge vessel of brown ware, having its upper edge worn away like a threshold by the rub of whole generations of thirsty lips that had gone the way of all flesh, and bearing the following inscription burnt upon its rotund side in yellow letters:

THERE IS NO FUN

UNTIL i CUM

The other man, nothing loath, raised the mug to his lips, and drank on, and on, and on—till a curious blueness overspread the countenance of the shepherd's wife, who had regarded with no little surprise the first stranger's free offer to the second of what did not belong to him to dispense.

"I knew it!" said the toper to the shepherd with much satisfaction. "When I walked up your garden before coming in, and saw the hives all of a row, I said to myself, 'Where there's bees there's honey, and where there's honey there's mead.' But mead of such a truly comfortable sort as this I really didn't expect to meet in my older days." He took yet another pull at the mug, till it assumed an ominous elevation.

50   "Glad you enjoy it!" said the shepherd, warmly.

"It is goodish mead," assented Mrs. Fennel, with an absence of enthusiasm which seemed to say that it was possible to buy praise for one's cellar at too heavy a price. "It is trouble enough to make—and really I hardly think we shall make any more. For honey sells well, and we ourselves can make shift with a drop o' small mead° and metheglin° for common use from the comb-washings."

°*mead:* an alcoholic drink made from honey.
°*metheglin:* a cheaper drink made, with spices, from the water rinsed from the honeycomb after the better honey was extracted. See paragraph 54.

"Oh, but you'll never have the heart!" reproachfully cried the stranger in cinder-gray, after taking up the mug a third time and setting it down empty. "I love mead, when 'tis old like this, as I love to go to church o' Sundays, or to relieve the needy any day of the week."

"Ha, ha, ha!" said the man in the chimney corner, who, in spite of the taciturnity induced by the pipe of tobacco, could not or would not refrain from this slight testimony to his comrade's humor.

Now the old mead of those days, brewed of the purest first-year or maiden honey, four pounds to the gallon—with its due complement of white of eggs, cinnamon, ginger, cloves, mace, rosemary, yeast, and processes of working, bottling, and cellaring—tasted remarkably strong; but it did not taste so strong as it actually was. Hence, presently, the stranger in cinder-gray at the table, moved by its creeping influence, unbuttoned his waistcoat, threw himself back in his chair, spread his legs, and made his presence felt in various ways.

"Well, well, as I say," he resumed, "I am going to Casterbridge, and to Casterbridge I   55
must go. I should have been almost there by this time; but the rain drove me into your dwelling, and I'm not sorry for it."

"You don't live in Casterbridge?" said the shepherd.

"Not as yet; though I shortly mean to move there."

"Going to set up in trade, perhaps?"

"No, no," said the shepherd's wife. "It is easy to see that the gentleman is rich, and don't want to work at anything."

The cinder-gray stranger paused, as if to consider whether he would accept that defini-   60
tion of himself. He presently rejected it by answering, "Rich is not quite the word for me, Dame. I do work, and I must work. And even if I only get to Casterbridge by midnight I must begin work there at eight tomorrow morning. Yes, heat or wet, blow or snow, famine or sword, my day's work tomorrow must be done."

"Poor man! Then, in spite o' seeming, you be worse off than we," replied the shepherd's wife.

"'Tis the nature of my trade, men and maidens. 'Tis the nature of my trade more than my poverty. . . . But really and truly I must up and off, or I shan't get a lodging in the town." However, the speaker did not move, and directly added, "There's time for one more draught of friendship before I go; and I'd perform it at once if the mug were not dry."

"Here's a mug o' small," said Mrs. Fennel. "Small, we call it, though to be sure 'tis only the first wash o' the combs."

"No," said the stranger, disdainfully. "I won't spoil your first kindness by partaking o' your second."

"Certainly not," broke in Fennel. "We don't increase and multiply every day, and I'll fill   65
the mug again." He went away to the dark place under the stairs where the barrel stood. The shepherdess followed him.

"Why should you do this?" she said, reproachfully, as soon as they were alone. "He's emptied it once, though it held enough for ten people; and now he's not contented wi' the small, but must needs call for more o' the strong! And a stranger unbeknown to any of us. For my part, I don't like the look o' the man at all."

"But he's in the house, my honey; and 'tis a wet night, and a christening. Daze it, what's a cup of mead more or less? There'll be plenty more next bee-burning."

"Very well—this time, then," she answered, looking wistfully at the barrel. "But what is the man's calling, and where is he one of, that he should come in and join us like this?"

"I don't know. I'll ask him again."

The catastrophe of having the mug drained dry at one pull by the stranger in cinder-gray   70
was effectually guarded against this time by Mrs. Fennel. She poured out his allowance in a small cup, keeping the large one at a discreet distance from him. When he had tossed off his portion the shepherd renewed his inquiry about the stranger's occupation.

The latter did not immediately reply, and the man in the chimney corner, with sudden demonstrativeness, said, "Anybody may know my trade—I'm a wheelwright."

"A very good trade for these parts," said the shepherd.

"And anybody may know mine—if they've the sense the find it out," said the stranger in cinder-gray.

"You may generally tell what a man is by his claws," observed the hedge-carpenter, looking at his own hands. "My fingers be as full of thorns as an old pincushion is of pins."

75 The hands of the man in the chimney corner instinctively sought the shade, and he gazed into the fire as he resumed his pipe. The man at the table took up the hedge-carpenter's remark, and added smartly, "True; but the oddity of my trade is that, instead of setting a mark upon me, it sets a mark upon my customers."

No observation being offered by anybody in elucidation of this enigma, the shepherd's wife once more called for a song. The same obstacles presented themselves as at the former time—one had no voice, another had forgotten the first verse. The stranger at the table, whose soul had now risen to a good working temperature, relieved the difficulty by exclaiming that, to start the company, he would sing himself. Thrusting one thumb into the armhold of his waistcoat, he waved the other hand in the air, and, with an extemporizing gaze at the shining sheepcrooks above the mantelpiece, began:

> O my trade it is the rarest one,
>> Simple shepherds all—
> My trade is a sight to see;
> For my customers I tie, and take them up on high,
> And waft 'em to a far countree!

The room was silent when he had finished the verse—with one exception, that of the man in the chimney corner, who at the singer's word, "Chorus!" joined him in a deep bass voice of musical relish:

> And waft 'em to a far countree!

Oliver Giles, John Pitcher the dairyman, the parish-clerk, the engaged man of fifty, the row of young women against the wall, seemed lost in thought not of the gayest kind. The shepherd looked meditatively on the ground, the shepherdess gazed keenly at the singer, and with some suspicion; she was doubting whether this stranger were merely singing an old song from recollection, or was composing one there and then for the occasion. All were as perplexed at the obscure revelation as the guests at Belshazzar's Feast,° except the man in the chimney corner, who quietly said, "Second verse, stranger," and smoked on.

The singer thoroughly moistened himself from his lips inward, and went on with the next stanza as requested:

> My tools are but common ones,
>> Simple shepherds all—
> My tools are no sight to see:
> A little hempen string, and a post whereon to swing,
> Are implements enough for me!

Shepherd Fennel glanced round. There was no longer any doubt that the stranger was answering his question rhythmically. The guests one and all started back with suppressed exclamations. The young woman engaged to the man of fifty fainted halfway, and would have proceeded, but finding him wanting in alacrity for catching her she sat down trembling.

80 "Oh, he's the!" whispered the people in the background, mentioning the name of an ominous public officer. "He's come to do it! 'Tis to be at Casterbridge jail tomorrow—the

---

°*Belshazzar's Feast:* The famous handwriting on the wall, predicting the downfall of the ancient Babylonian kingdom, happened at this feast (Daniel 5).

man for sheep-stealing—the poor clockmaker we heard of, who used to live at Shottsford and had no work to do—Timothy Summers, whose family were astarving, and so he went out of Shottsford by the highroad, and took a sheep in open daylight, defying the farmer and the farmer's wife and the farmer's lad, and every man jack among 'em. He" (and they nodded toward the stranger of the deadly trade) "is come from up the country to do it because there's not enough to do in his own county-town, and he's got the place here now our own county-man's dead; he's going to live in the same cottage under the prison wall."

The stranger in cinder-gray took no notice of this whispered string of observations, but again wetted his lips. Seeing that his friend in the chimney corner was the only one who reciprocated his joviality in any way, he held out his cup toward that appreciative comrade, who also held out his own. They clinked together, the eyes of the rest of the room hanging upon the singer's actions. He parted his lips for the third verse; but at that moment another knock was audible upon the door. This time the knock was faint and hesitating.

The company seemed scared; the shepherd looked with consternation toward the entrance, and it was with some effort that he resisted his alarmed wife's deprecatory glance, and uttered for the third time the welcoming words, "Walk in!"

The door was gently opened, and another man stood upon the mat. He, like those who had preceded him, was a stranger. This time it was a short, small personage, of fair complexion, and dressed in a decent suit of dark clothes.

"Can you tell me the way to—?" he began: when, gazing round the room to observe the nature of the company among whom he had fallen, his eyes lighted on the stranger in cinder-gray. It was just at the instant when the latter, who had thrown his mind into his song with such a will that he scarcely heeded the interruption, silenced all whispers and inquiries by bursting into his third verse:

> Tomorrow is my working day,
> Simple shepherds all—
> Tomorrow is a working day for me:
> For the farmer's sheep is slain, and the lad who did it ta'en,
> And on his soul may God ha' merc-y!

The stranger in the chimney corner, waving cups with the singer so heartily that his mead splashed over on the hearth, repeated in his bass voice as before:

> And on his soul may God ha' merc-y!

All this time the third stranger had been standing in the doorway. Finding now that he did not come forward or go on speaking, the guests particularly regarded him. They noticed to their surprise that he stood before them the picture of abject terror—his knees trembling, his hand shaking so violently that the door-latch by which he supported himself rattled audibly: his white lips were parted, and his eyes fixed on the merry officer of justice in the middle of the room. A moment more and he had turned, closed the door, and fled.

"What a man can it be?" said the shepherd.

The rest, between the awfulness of their late discovery and the odd conduct of this third visitor, looked as if they knew not what to think, and said nothing. Instinctively they withdrew further and further from the grim gentleman in their midst, whom some of them seemed to take for the Prince of Darkness° himself, till they formed a remote circle, an empty space of floor being left between them and him—

> . . . circulus, cujus centrum diabolus.°

°*Prince of Darkness*: i.e., the Devil.
°*circulus . . . diabolus*: a circle, of which the devil is the center. A reference to the claim that when people danced in a circle, they endangered their souls because the devil was in control at the center.

The room was so silent—though there were more than twenty people in it—that nothing could be heard but the patter of the rain against the window-shutters, accompanied by the occasional hiss of a stray drop that fell down the chimney into the fire, and the steady puffing of the man in the corner, who had now resumed his pipe of long clay.

The stillness was unexpectedly broken. The distant sound of a gun reverberated through the air—apparently from the direction of the county-town.

"Be jiggered!" cried the stranger who had sung the song, jumping up.

90   "What does that mean?" asked several.

"A prisoner escaped from the jail—that's what it means. "

All listened. The sound was repeated, and none of them spoke but the man in the chimney corner, who said quietly, "I've often been told that in this county they fire a gun at such times; but I never heard it till now."

"I wonder if it is *my* man?" murmured the personage in cinder-gray.

"Surely it is!" said the shepherd involuntarily. "And surely we've zeed him! That little man who looked in at the door by now, and quivered like a leaf when he zeed ye and heard your song!"

95   "His teeth chattered, and the breath went out of his body," said the dairyman.

"And his heart seemed to sink within him like a stone," said Oliver Giles.

"And he bolted as if he'd been shot at," said the hedge-carpenter.

"True—his teeth chattered, and his heart seemed to sink; and he bolted as if he'd been shot at," slowly summed up the man in the chimney corner.

"I didn't notice it," remarked the hangman.

100   "We were all awondering what made him run off in such a fright," faltered one of the women against the wall, "and now 'tis explained!"

The firing of the alarm-gun went on at intervals, low and sullenly, and their suspicions became a certainty. The sinister gentleman in cinder-gray roused himself. "Is there a constable here?" he asked, in thick tones. "If so, let him step forward."

The engaged man of fifty stepped quavering out from the wall, his betrothed beginning to sob on the back of the chair.

"You are a sworn constable?"

"I be, Sir."

105   "Then pursue the criminal at once, with assistance, and bring him back here. He can't have gone far."

"I will, Sir, I will—when I've got my staff. I'll go home and get it, and come sharp here, and start in a body."

"Staff!—never mind your staff; the man'll be gone!"

"But I can't do nothing without my staff—can I, William, and John, and Charles Jake? No; for there's the king's royal crown apainted on en in yaller and gold, and the lion and the unicorn, so as when I raise en up and hit my prisoner, 'tis made a lawful blow thereby. I wouldn't 'tempt to take up a man without my staff—no, not I. If I hadn't the law to gie me courage, why, instead o' my taking up him he might take up me!"

"Now, I'm a king's man myself, and can give you authority enough for this," said the formidable officer in gray. "Now then, all of ye, be ready. Have ye any lanterns?"

110   "Yes—have ye any lanterns? I demand it!" said the constable.

"And the rest of you able-bodied—"

"Able-bodied men—yes—the rest of ye!" said the constable.

"Have you some good stout staves and pitchforks—"

"Staves and pitchforks—in the name o' the law! And take 'em in yer hands and go in quest, and do as we in authority tell ye!"

115   Thus aroused, the men prepared to give chase. The evidence was, indeed, though circumstantial, so convincing, that but little argument was needed to show the shepherd's

guests that after what they had seen it would look very much like connivance if they did not instantly pursue the unhappy third stranger, who could not as yet have gone more than a few hundred yards over such uneven country.

A shepherd is always well provided with lanterns; and, lighting these hastily, and with hurdle-staves in their hands, they poured out of the door, taking a direction along the crest of the hill, away from the town, the rain having fortunately a little abated.

Disturbed by the noise, or possibly by unpleasant dreams of her baptism, the child who had been christened began to cry heart-brokenly in the room overhead. These notes of grief came down through the chinks of the floor to the ears of the women below, who jumped up one by one, and seemed glad of the excuse to ascend and comfort the baby, for the incidents of the last half-hour greatly oppressed them. Thus in the space of two or three minutes the room on the ground-floor was deserted quite.

But it was not for long. Hardly had the sound of footsteps died away when a man returned round the corner of the house from the direction the pursuers had taken. Peeping in at the door, and seeing nobody there, he entered leisurely. It was the stranger of the chimney corner, who had gone out with the rest. The motive of his return was shown by his helping himself to a cut piece of skimmer cake that lay on a ledge beside where he had sat, and which he had apparently forgotten to take with him. He also poured out half a cup more mead from the quantity that remained, ravenously eating and drinking these as he stood. He had not finished when another figure came in just as quietly—his friend in cinder-gray.

"Oh—you here?" said the latter, smiling. "I thought you had gone to help in the capture." And this speaker also revealed the object of his return by looking solicitously round for the fascinating mug of old mead.

"And I thought you had gone," said the other, continuing his skimmer-cake with some effort.   120

"Well, on second thoughts, I felt there were enough without me," said the first confidentially, "and such a night as it is, too. Besides, 'tis the business o' the Government to take care of its criminal—not mine."

"True; so it is. And I felt as you did, that there were enough without me."

"I don't want to break my limbs running over the humps and hollows of this wild country."

"Nor I neither, between you and me."

"These shepherd-people are used to it—simple-minded souls, you know, stirred up to   125
anything in a moment. They'll have him ready for me before the morning, and no trouble to me at all."

"They'll have him, and we shall have saved ourselves all labor in the matter."

"True, true. Well, my way is to Casterbridge; and 'tis as much as my legs will do to take me that far. Going the same way?"

"No, I am sorry to say! I have to get home over there" (he nodded indefinitely to the right), "and I feel as you do, that it is quite enough for my legs to do before bedtime."

The other had by this time finished the mead in the mug, after which, shaking hands heartily at the door, and wishing each other well, they went their several ways.

In the meantime the company of pursuers had reached the end of the hog's-back eleva-   130
tion which dominated this part of the down. They had decided on no particular plan of action; and, finding that the man of the baleful trade was no longer in their company, they seemed quite unable to form any such plan now. They descended in all directions down the hill, and straightway several of the party fell into the snare set by Nature for all misguided midnight ramblers over this part of the cretaceous formation. The "lanchets," or flint slopes, which belted the escarpment at intervals of a dozen yards, took the less cautious ones unawares, and losing their footing on the rubbly steep they slid sharply downward,

the lanterns rolling from their hands to the bottom, and there lying on their sides till the horn was scorched through.

When they had again gathered themselves together, the shepherd, as the man who knew the country best, took the lead, and guided them round these treacherous inclines. The lanterns, which seemed rather to dazzle their eyes and warn the fugitive than to assist them in the exploration, were extinguished, due silence was observed; and in this more rational order they plunged into the vale. It was a grassy, briery, moist defile, affording some shelter to any person who had sought it; but the party perambulated it in vain, and ascended on the other side. Here they wandered apart, and after an interval closed together again to report progress. At the second time of closing in they found themselves near a lonely ash, the single tree on this part of the coomb, probably sown there by a passing bird some fifty years before. And here, standing a little to one side of the trunk, as motionless as the trunk itself appeared the man they were in quest of, his outline being well defined against the sky beyond. The band noiselessly drew up and faced him.

"Your money or your life!" said the constable sternly to the still figure.

"No, no," whispered John Pitcher. "'Tisn't our side ought to say that. That's the doctrine of vagabonds like him, and we be on the side of the law."

"Well, well," replied the constable, impatiently; "I must say something, mustn't I? and if you had all the weight o' this undertaking upon your mind, perhaps you'd say the wrong thing, too!—Prisoner at the bar, surrender in the name of the Father—the Crown, I mane!"

135   The man under the tree seemed now to notice them for the first time, and, giving them no opportunity whatever for exhibiting their courage, he strolled slowly toward them. He was, indeed, the little man, the third stranger; but his trepidation had in a great measure gone.

"Well, travelers," he said, "did I hear you speak to me?"

"You did; you've got to come and be our prisoner at once!" said the constable. "We arrest 'ee on the charge of not biding in Casterbridge jail in a decent proper manner to be hung tomorrow morning. Neighbors, do your duty, and seize the culprit!"

On hearing the charge, the man seemed enlightened, and, saying not another word, resigned himself with preternatural civility to the search-party, who, with their staves in their hands, surrounded him on all sides, and marched him back toward the shepherd's cottage.

It was eleven o'clock by the time they arrived. The light shining from the open door, a sound of men's voices within, proclaimed to them as they approached the house that some new events had arisen in their absence. On entering they discovered the shepherd's living-room to be invaded by two officers from Casterbridge jail, and a well-known magistrate who lived at the nearest county-seat, intelligence of the escape having become generally circulated.

140   "Gentlemen," said the constable, "I have brought back your man—not without risk and danger; but everyone must do his duty! He is inside this circle of able-bodied persons, who have lent me useful aid, considering their ignorance of Crown work.—Men, bring forward your prisoner!" And the third stranger was led to the light.

"Who is this?" said one of the officials.

"The man," said the constable.

"Certainly not," said the turnkey; and the first corroborated his statement.

"But how can it be otherwise?" asked the constable. "Or why was he so terrified at sight o' the singing instrument of the law who sat there?" Here he related the strange behavior of the third stranger on entering the house during the hangman's song.

145   "Can't understand it," said the officer coolly. "All I know is that it is not the condemned man. He's quite a different character from this one; a gauntish fellow, with dark hair and

eyes, rather good-looking, and with a musical bass voice that if you heard it once you'd never mistake as long as you lived."

"Why, souls—'twas the man in the chimney corner!"

"Hey—what?" said the magistrate, coming forward after inquiring particulars from the shepherd in the background. "Haven't you got the man after all?"

"Well, Sir," said the constable, "he's the man we were in search of, that's true; and yet he's not the man we were in search of. For the man we were in search of was not the man we wanted, Sir, if you understand my everyday way; for 'twas the man in the chimney corner!"

"A pretty kettle of fish altogether!" said the magistrate. "You had better start for the other man at once."

The prisoner now spoke for the first time. The mention of the man in the chimney corner seemed to have moved him as nothing else could do. "Sir," he said, stepping forward to the magistrate, "take no more trouble about me. The time is come when I may as well speak. I have done nothing; my crime is that the condemned man is my brother. Early this afternoon I left home at Shottsford to tramp it all the way to Casterbridge jail to bid him farewell. I was benighted, and called here to rest and ask the way. When I opened the door I saw before me the very man, my brother, that I thought to see in the condemned cell at Casterbridge. He was in this chimney corner; and jammed close to him, so that he could not have got out if he had tried, was the executioner who'd come to take his life, singing a song about it and not knowing that it was his victim who was close by, joining in to save appearances. My brother looked a glance of agony at me, and I know he meant, 'Don't reveal what you see; my life depends on it.' I was so terror-struck that I could hardly stand, and, not knowing what I did, I turned and hurried away." 150

The narrator's manner and tone had the stamp of truth, and his story made a great impression on all around. "And do you know where your brother is at the present time?" asked the magistrate.

"I do not. I have never seen him since I closed this door."

"I can testify to that, for we've been between ye ever since," said the constable.

"Where does he think to fly to?—what is his occupation?"

"He's a watch-and-clock-maker, Sir." 155

"'A said 'a was a wheelwright—a wicked rogue," said the constable.

"The wheels of clocks and watches he meant, no doubt," said Shepherd Fennel. "I thought his hands were palish for's trade."

"Well, it appears to me that nothing can be gained by retaining this poor man in custody," said the magistrate; "your business lies with the other, unquestionably."

And so the little man was released off-hand; but he looked nothing the less sad on that account, it being beyond the power of magistrate or constable to raze out the written troubles in his brain, for they concerned another whom he regarded with more solicitude than himself. When this was done, and the man had gone his way, the night was found to be so far advanced that it was deemed useless to renew the search before the next morning.

Next day, accordingly, the quest for the clever sheep-stealer became general and keen, to all appearance at least. But the intended punishment was cruelly disproportioned to the transgression, and the sympathy of a great many country-folk in that district was strongly on the side of the fugitive. Moreover, his marvelous coolness and daring in hob-and-nobbing with the hangman, under the unprecedented circumstances of the shepherd's party, won their admiration. So that it may be questioned if all those who ostensibly made themselves so busy in exploring woods and fields and lanes were quite so thorough when it came to the private examination of their own lofts and outhouses. Stories were afloat of a mysterious figure being occasionally seen in some old overgrown trackway or other, remote from turnpike roads, but when a search was instituted in any of these suspected quarters nobody was found. Thus the days and weeks passed without tidings. 160

In brief, the bass-voiced man of the chimney corner was never recaptured. Some said that he went across the sea, others that he did not, but buried himself in the depths of a populous city. At any rate, the gentleman in cinder-gray never did his morning's work at Casterbridge, nor met anywhere at all, for business purposes, the genial comrade with whom he had passed an hour of relaxation in the lonely house on the coomb.

The grass has long been green on the graves of Shepherd Fennel and his frugal wife; the guests who made up the christening party have mainly followed their entertainers to the tomb; the baby in whose honor they all had met is a matron in the sere and yellow leaf. But the arrival of the three strangers at the shepherd's that night, and the details connected therewith, is a story as well-known as ever in the country about Higher Crowstairs.

QUESTIONS

1. Describe the appearances of conflicts in this story. Which conflicts are real?
2. Describe the reasons for which the narrator tells so much about the people of Higher Crowstairs. How are these descriptions related to the story's major conflict?
3. Why does the author withhold the identities of the various strangers? How does this delay condition your attitudes toward the first stranger?
4. What kind of story might "The Three Strangers" be, structurally, if the first stranger were named and identified when he first enters the cottage, before the entrance of the other strangers?

JAMAICA KINCAID (b. 1949)

Jamaica Kincaid was born and educated in Antigua in the West Indies and now lives in Vermont. Her stories and novels are usually set in her native Antigua and often concern mother-daughter relationships, as in "Girl," one of her best-known (and very brief) stories. At the Bottom of the River *(1983), from which "What I Have Been Doing Lately" is taken, was her first collection of stories. Novels are* Annie John *(1985),* A Small Place *(1988),* Lucy *(1990), and more recently* The Autobiography of My Mother *(1996). Although some critics are concerned that Kincaid's fiction contains less action than situation, all agree that she superbly renders the speech rhythms and simple, primal concerns of her native islands.*

🍁 What I Have Been Doing Lately (1983)

What I have been doing lately: I was lying in bed and the doorbell rang. I ran downstairs. Quick. I opened the door. There was no one there. I stepped outside. Either it was drizzling or there was a lot of dust in the air and the dust was damp. I stuck out my tongue and the drizzle or the damp dust tasted like government school ink. I looked north. I looked south. I decided to start walking north. While walking north, I noticed that I was barefoot. While walking north, I looked up and saw the planet Venus. I said, "It must be almost morning." I saw a monkey in a tree. The tree had no leaves. I said, "Ah, a monkey. Just look at that. A monkey." I walked for I don't know how long before I came up to a big body of water. I wanted to get across it but I couldn't swim. I wanted to get across it but it would take me years to build a bridge. Years passed and then one would take me I didn't know how long to build a bridge. Years passed and then one day, feeling like it, I got into my boat and rowed across. When I got to the other side, it was noon and my shadow was small and fell beneath me. I set out on a path that stretched out straight ahead. I passed a house, and a dog was sitting on the verandah but it looked the other way when it saw me coming. I passed a boy tossing a ball in the air but the boy looked the other way when he saw me coming. I walked and I walked but I couldn't tell if I walked a long time because my feet didn't feel as if they would drop off. I turned around to see what I had left behind me but nothing was familiar. Instead of the straight path, I saw hills. Instead of the boy with his ball, I saw tall flowering trees. I looked up and the sky was without clouds and seemed near, as if it were the ceiling in my house and, if I stood on a chair, I could touch it with the tips of my fingers. I turned around and looked ahead of me again. A deep hole had opened up before me. I looked in. The hole was deep and dark and I couldn't see the bottom. I thought, What's down there?, so on purpose I fell in. I fell and I fell, over and over, as if I were an old suitcase. On the sides of the deep hole I could see things written, but perhaps it was in a foreign language because I couldn't read them. Still I fell, for I don't know how long. As I fell I began to see that I didn't like the way falling made me feel. Falling made me feel sick and I missed all the people I had loved. I said, I don't want to fall anymore, and I reversed myself. I was standing again on the edge of the deep hole. I looked at the deep hole and I said, You can close up now, and it did. I walked some more without knowing distance. I only knew that I passed through days and nights, I only knew that I passed through rain and shine, light and darkness. I was never thirsty and I felt no pain. Looking at the horizon, I made a joke for myself: I said, "The earth has thin lips," and I laughed.

Looking at the horizon again, I saw a lone figure coming toward me, but I wasn't frightened because I was sure it was my mother. As I got closer to the figure, I could see that it wasn't my mother, but still I wasn't frightened because I could see that it was a woman.

When this woman got closer to me, she looked at me hard and then she threw up her hands. She must have seen me somewhere before because she said, "It's you. Just look at that. It's you. And just what have you been doing lately?"

I could have said, "I have been praying not to grow any taller."

I could have said, "I have been listening carefully to my mother's words, so as to make a good imitation of a dutiful daughter."   5

I could have said, "A pack of dogs, tired from chasing each other all over town, slept in the moonlight."

Instead, I said, What I have been doing lately: I was lying in bed on my back, my hands drawn up, my fingers interlaced lightly at the nape of my neck. Someone rang the doorbell. I went downstairs and opened the door but there was no one there. I stepped outside. Either it was drizzling or there was a lot of dust in the air and the dust was damp. I stuck out my tongue and the drizzle or the damp dust tasted like government school ink. I looked north and I looked south. I started walking north. While walking north, I wanted to move fast, so I removed the shoes from my feet. While walking north, I looked up and saw the planet Venus and I said, "If the sun went out, it would be eight minutes before I would know it." I saw a monkey sitting in a tree that had no leaves and I said, "A monkey. Just look at that. A monkey." I picked up a stone and I threw it at the monkey. The monkey, seeing the stone, quickly moved out of its way. Three times I threw a stone at the monkey and three times it moved away. The fourth time I threw the stone, the monkey caught it and threw it back at me. The stone struck me on my forehead over my right eye, making a deep gash. The gash healed immediately but now the skin on my forehead felt false to me. I walked for I don't know how long before I came to a big body of water. I wanted to get across, so when the boat came I paid my fare. When I got to the other side, I saw a lot of people sitting on the beach and they were having a picnic. They were the most beautiful people I had ever seen. Everything about them was black and shiny. Their skin was black and shiny. Their shoes were black and shiny. Their hair was black and shiny. The clothes they wore were black and shiny. I could hear them laughing and chatting and I said, I would like to be with these people, so I started to walk toward them, but when I got up close to them I saw that they weren't at a picnic and they weren't beautiful and they weren't chatting and laughing. All around me was black mud and the people all looked as if they had been made up out of the black mud. I looked up and saw that the sky seemed far away and nothing I could stand on would make me able to touch it with my fingertips. I thought, If only I could get out of this, so I started to walk. I must have walked for a long time because my feet hurt and felt as if they would drop off. I thought, If only just around the bend I would see my house and inside my house I would find my bed, freshly made at that, and in the kitchen I would find my mother or anyone else that I loved making me a custard. I thought, If only it was a Sunday and I was sitting in a church and I had just heard someone sing a psalm. I felt very sad so I sat down. I felt so sad that I rested my head on my own knees and smoothed my own head. I felt so sad I couldn't imagine feeling any other way again. I said, I don't like this. I don't want to do this anymore. And I went back to lying in bed, just before the doorbell rang.

QUESTIONS

1. Is the story told as if it were real or a dream? Why is the dreamlike quality introduced? How soon do you learn that the dreamlike narration has begun?
2. To what level of existence do the various descriptions and actions belong? In what ways do the actions and descriptions exceed everyday reality? Why does the author not introduce specific elements that might be considered appropriate in a world of dreams or in a future world?
3. Structurally, why does the story become repetitive at paragraph 7? What differences are there between the second narration and the first? Why does the story end with the third sound of the doorbell? What is the meaning of the repetitive actions?
4. Should this work be considered a story at all? What makes it a story? In what ways is it unlike a story?

JOYCE CAROL OATES (b. 1938)

For a brief biographical note about Oates, see Chapter 2, page 150.

 ## Where Are You Going, Where Have You Been? (1970)

For Bob Dylan

Her name was Connie. She was fifteen and she had a quick nervous giggling habit of craning her neck to glance into mirrors, or checking other people's faces to make sure her own was all right. Her mother, who noticed everything and knew everything and who hadn't much reason any longer to look at her own face, always scolded Connie about it. "Stop gawking at yourself, who are you? You think you're so pretty?" she would say. Connie would raise her eyebrows at these familiar complaints and look right through her mother, into a shadowy vision of herself as she was right at that moment: she knew she was pretty and that was everything. Her mother had been pretty once too, if you could believe those old snapshots in the album, but now her looks were gone and that was why she was always after Connie.

"Why don't you keep your room clean like your sister? How've you got your hair fixed—what the hell stinks? Hair spray? You don't see your sister using that junk."

Her sister June was twenty-four and still lived at home. She was a secretary in the high school Connie attended, and if that wasn't bad enough—with her in the same building—she was so plain and chunky and steady that Connie had to hear her praised all the time by her mother and her mother's sisters. June did this, June did that, she saved money and helped clean the house and cooked and Connie couldn't do a thing, her mind was all filled with trashy daydreams. Their father was away at work most of the time and when he came home he wanted supper and he read the newspaper at supper and after supper he went to bed. He didn't bother talking much to them, but around his bent head Connie's mother kept picking at her until Connie wished her mother was dead and she herself was dead and it was all over. "She makes me want to throw up sometimes," she complained to her friends. She had a high, breathless, amused voice which made everything she said sound a little forced, whether it was sincere or not.

There was one good thing: June went places with girl friends of hers, girls who were just as plain and steady as she, and so when Connie wanted to do that her mother had no objections. The father of Connie's best girl friend drove the girls the three miles to town and left them off at a shopping plaza, so that they could walk through the stores or go to a movie, and when he came to pick them up again at eleven he never bothered to ask what they had done.

They must have been familiar sights, walking around that shopping plaza in their shorts   5
and flat ballerina slippers that always scuffed the sidewalk, with charm bracelets jingling on their thin wrists; they would lean together to whisper and laugh secretly if someone passed by who amused or interested them. Connie had long dark blond hair that drew anyone's eye to it, and she wore part of it pulled up on her head and puffed out and the rest of it she let fall down her back. She wore a pull-over jersey blouse that looked one way when she was at home and another way when she was away from home. Everything about her had two sides to it, one for home and one for anywhere that was not home: her walk that could be childlike and bobbing, or languid enough to make anyone think she was hearing music in her head, her mouth which was pale and smirking most of the time, but bright and pink on these evenings out, her laugh which was cynical and drawling at home—"Ha, ha, very funny"—but high-pitched and nervous anywhere else, like the jingling of the charms on her bracelet.

Sometimes they did go shopping or to a movie, but sometimes they went across the highway, ducking fast across the busy road, to a drive-in restaurant where older kids hung out. The restaurant was shaped like a big bottle, though squatter than a real bottle, and on its cap was a revolving figure of a grinning boy who held a hamburger aloft. One night in mid-summer they ran across, breathless with daring, and right away someone leaned out a car window and invited them over, but it was just a boy from high school they didn't like. It made them feel good to be able to ignore him. They went up through the maze of parked and cruising cars to the bright-lit, fly-infested restaurant, their faces pleased and expectant as if they were entering a sacred building that loomed out of the night to give them what haven and what blessing they yearned for. They sat at the counter and crossed their legs at the ankles, their thin shoulders rigid with excitement, and listened to the music that made everything so good: the music was always in the background like music at a church service, it was something to depend upon.

A boy named Eddie came in to talk with them. He sat backwards on his stool, turning himself jerkily around in semi-circles and then stopping and turning again, and after a while he asked Connie if she would like something to eat. She said she did and so she tapped her friend's arm on her way out—her friend pulled her face up into a brave droll look—and Connie said she would meet her at eleven, across the way. "I just hate to leave her like that," Connie said earnestly, but the boy said that she wouldn't be alone for long. So they went out to his car and on the way Connie couldn't help but let her eyes wander over the windshields and faces all around her, her face gleaming with a joy that had nothing to do with Eddie or even this place; it might have been the music. She drew her shoulders up and sucked in her breath with the pure pleasure of being alive, and just at that moment she happened to glance at a face just a few feet from hers. It was a boy with shaggy black hair, in a convertible jalopy painted gold. He stared at her and then his lips widened into a grin. Connie slit her eyes at him and turned away, but she couldn't help glancing back and there he was still watching her. He wagged a finger and laughed and said, "Gonna get you, baby," and Connie turned away again without Eddie noticing anything.

She spent three hours with him, at the restaurant where they ate hamburgers and drank Cokes in wax cups that were always sweating, and then down an alley a mile or so away, and when he left her off at five to eleven only the movie house was still open at the plaza. Her girl friend was there, talking with a boy. When Connie came up the two girls smiled at each other and Connie said, "How was the movie?" and the girl said, "*You* should know." They rode off with the girl's father, sleepy and pleased, and Connie couldn't help but look at the darkened shopping plaza with its big empty parking lot and its signs that were faded and ghostly now, and over at the drive-in restaurant where cars were still circling tirelessly. She couldn't hear the music at this distance.

Next morning June asked her how the movie was and Connie said, "So-so."

10 She and that girl and occasionally another girl went out several times a week that way, and the rest of the time Connie spent around the house—it was summer vacation—getting in her mother's way and thinking, dreaming, about the boys she met. But all the boys fell back and dissolved into a single face that was not even a face, but an idea, a feeling, mixed up with the urgent insistent pounding of the music and the humid night air of July. Connie's mother kept dragging her back to the daylight by finding things for her to do or saying, suddenly, "What's this about the Pettinger girl?"

And Connie would say nervously, "Oh, her. That dope." She always drew thick clear lines between herself and such girls, and her mother was simple and kindly enough to believe her. Her mother was so simple, Connie thought, that it was maybe cruel to fool her so much. Her mother went scuffling around the house in old bedroom slippers and complained over the telephone to one sister about the other, then the other called up and the two of them complained about the third one. If June's name was mentioned her mother's tone was approving, and if Connie's name was mentioned it was disapproving. This did not really mean she disliked Connie and actually Connie thought that her mother preferred her to June because she was prettier, but the two of them kept up a pretense of exasperation, a sense that they were tugging and struggling over something of little value to either of them. Sometimes, over coffee, they were almost friends, but something would come up—some vexation that was like a fly buzzing suddenly around their heads—and their faces went hard with contempt.

One Sunday Connie got up at eleven—none of them bothered with church—and washed her hair so that it could dry all day long, in the sun. Her parents and sister were going to a barbecue at an aunt's house and Connie said no, she wasn't interested, rolling her eyes to let her mother know just what she thought of it. "Stay home alone then," her mother said sharply. Connie sat out back in a lawn chair and watched them drive away, her father quiet and bald, hunched around so that he could back the car out, her mother with a look that was still angry and not at all softened through the windshield, and in the back seat poor old June all dressed up as if she didn't know what a barbecue was, with all the running yelling kids and the flies. Connie sat with her eyes closed in the sun, dreaming and dazed with the warmth about her as if this were a kind of love, the caresses of love, and her mind slipped over onto thoughts of the boy she had been with the night before and how nice he had been, how sweet it always was, not the way someone like June would suppose but sweet, gentle, the way it was in movies and promised in songs; and when she opened her eyes she hardly knew where she was, the back yard ran off into weeds and a fence-line of trees and behind it the sky was perfectly blue and still. The asbestos "ranch house" that was now three years old startled her—it looked small. She shook her head as if to get awake.

It was too hot. She went inside the house and turned on the radio to drown out the quiet. She sat on the edge of her bed, barefoot, and listened for an hour and a half to a program called XYZ Sunday Jamboree, record after record of hard, fast, shrieking songs she sang along with, interspersed by exclamations from "Bobby King": "An' look here you girls at Napoleon's—Son and Charley want you to pay real close attention to this song coming up!"

And Connie paid close attention herself, bathed in a glow of slow-pulsed joy that seemed to rise mysteriously out of the music itself and lay languidly about the airless little room, breathed in and breathed out with each gentle rise and fall of her chest.

After a while she heard a car coming up the drive. She sat up at once, startled, because it [15] couldn't be her father so soon. The gravel kept crunching all the way in from the road—the driveway was long—and Connie ran to the window. It was a car she didn't know. It was an open jalopy, painted a bright gold that caught the sunlight opaquely. Her heart began to pound and her fingers snatched at her hair, checking it, and she whispered "Christ, Christ," wondering how bad she looked. The car came to a stop at the side door and the horn sounded four short taps as if this were a signal Connie knew.

She went into the kitchen and approached the door slowly, then hung out the screen door, her bare toes curling down off the step. There were two boys in the car and now she recognized the driver: he had shaggy, shabby black hair that looked crazy as a wig and he was grinning at her.

"I ain't late, am I?" he said.

"Who the hell do you think you are?" Connie said.

"Toldja I'd be out, didn't I?"

"I don't even know who you are." [20]

She spoke sullenly, careful to show no interest or pleasure, and he spoke in a fast bright monotone. Connie looked past him to the other boy, taking her time. He had fair brown hair, with a lock that fell onto his forehead. His sideburns gave him a fierce, embarrassed look, but so far he hadn't even bothered to glance at her. Both boys wore sunglasses. The driver's glasses were metallic and mirrored everything in miniature.

"You wanta come for a ride?" he said.

Connie smirked and let her hair fall loose over one shoulder.

"Don'tcha like my car? New paint job," he said. "Hey."

"What?"

"You're cute." [25]

She pretended to fidget, chasing flies away from the door.

"Don'tcha believe me, or what?" he said.

"Look, I don't even know who you are," Connie said in disgust.

"Hey, Ellie's got a radio, see. Mine's broke down." He lifted his friend's arm and showed [30] her the little transistor the boy was holding, and now Connie began to hear the music. It was the same program that was playing inside the house.

"Bobby King?" she said.

"I listen to him all the time. I think he's great."

"He's kind of great," Connie said reluctantly.

"Listen, that guy's great. He knows where the action is."

Connie blushed a little, because the glasses made it impossible for her to see just what [35] this boy was looking at. She couldn't decide if she liked him or if he was just a jerk, and so she dawdled in the doorway and wouldn't come down or go back inside. She said, "What's all that stuff painted on your car?"

"Can'tcha read it?" He opened the door very carefully, as if he was afraid it might fall off. He slid out just as carefully, planting his feet firmly on the ground, the tiny metallic world in his glasses slowing down like gelatine hardening and in the midst of it Connie's bright green blouse. "This here is my name, to begin with," he said. ARNOLD FRIEND was written in tarlike black letters on the side, with a drawing of a round grinning face that reminded Connie of a pumpkin, except it wore sunglasses. "I wanta introduce myself, I'm Arnold Friend and that's my real name and I'm gonna be your friend, honey, and inside the car's Ellie Oscar, he's kinda shy." Ellie brought his transistor radio up to his shoulder and balanced it there. "Now these numbers are a secret code, honey," Arnold Friend explained. He read off the numbers 33, 19, 17 and raised his eyebrows at her to see what she thought of that, but she didn't think much of it. The left rear fender had been smashed and around it was written, on the gleaming gold background: DONE BY CRAZY WOMAN DRIVER. Connie had to laugh at that. Arnold Friend was pleased at her laughter and looked up at her. "Around the other side's a lot more—you wanta come and see them?"

"No."

"Why not?"

"Why should I?"

40 "Don'tcha wanta see what's on the car? Don'tcha wanta go for a ride?"

"I don't know."

"Why not?"

"I got things to do."

"Like what?"

45 "Things."

He laughed as if she had said something funny. He slapped his thighs. He was standing in a strange way, leaning back against the car as if he were balancing himself. He wasn't tall, only an inch or so taller than she would be if she came down to him. Connie liked the way he was dressed, which was the way all of them dressed: tight faded jeans stuffed into black, scuffed boots, a belt that pulled his waist in and showed how lean he was, and a white pull-over shirt that was a little soiled and showed the hard small muscles of his arms and shoulders. He looked as if he probably did hard work, lifting and carrying things. Even his neck looked muscular. And his face was a familiar face, somehow: the jaw and chin and cheeks slightly darkened, because he hadn't shaved for a day or two, and the nose long and hawk-like, sniffing as if she were a treat he was going to gobble up and it was all a joke.

"Connie, you ain't telling the truth. This is your day set aside for a ride with me and you know it," he said, still laughing. The way he straightened and recovered from his fit of laughing showed that it had been all fake.

"How do you know what my name is?" she said suspiciously.

"It's Connie."

"Maybe and maybe not."

50 "I know my Connie," he said, wagging his finger. Now she remembered him even better, back at the restaurant, and her cheeks warmed at the thought of how she sucked in her breath just at the moment she passed him—how she must have looked to him. And he had remembered her. "Ellie and I come out here especially for you," he said. "Ellie can sit in back. How about it?"

"Where?"

"Where what?"

"Where're we going?"

55 He looked at her. He took off the sunglasses and she saw how pale the skin around his eyes was, like holes that were not in shadow but instead in light. His eyes were chips of broken glass that catch the light in an amiable way. He smiled. It was as if the idea of going for a ride somewhere, to some place, was a new idea to him.

"Just for a ride, Connie sweetheart."

"I never said my name was Connie," she said.

"But I know what it is. I know your name and all about you, lots of things," Arnold Friend said. He had not moved yet but stood still leaning back against the side of his jalopy. "I took a special interest in you, such a pretty girl, and found out all about you like I know your parents and sister are gone somewheres and I know where and how long they're going to be gone, and I know who you were with last night, and your best girl friend's name is Betty. Right?"

He spoke in a simple lilting voice, exactly as if he were reciting the words to a song. His smile assured her that everything was fine. In the car Ellie turned up the volume on his radio and did not bother to look around at them.

"Ellie can sit in the back seat," Arnold Friend said. He indicated his friend with a casual   60
jerk of his chin, as if Ellie did not count and she should not bother with him.

"How'd you find out all that stuff?" Connie said.

"Listen: Betty Schultz and Tony Fitch and Jimmy Pettinger and Nancy Pettinger," he said, in a chant. "Raymond Stanley and Bob Hutter—"

"Do you know all those kids?"

"I know everybody."

"Look, you're kidding. You're not from around here."   65

"Sure."

"But—how come we never saw you before?"

"Sure you saw me before," he said. He looked down at his boots, as if he were a little offended. "You just don't remember."

"I guess I'd remember you," Connie said.

"Yeah?" He looked up at this, beaming. He was pleased. He began to mark time with the   70
music from Ellie's radio, tapping his fists lightly together. Connie looked away from his smile to the car, which was painted so bright it almost hurt her eyes to look at it. She looked at that name, ARNOLD FRIEND. And up at the front fender was an expression that was familiar—MAN THE FLYING SAUCERS. It was an expression kids had used the year before, but didn't use this year. She looked at it for a while as if the words meant something to her that she did not yet know.

"What're you thinking about? Huh?" Arnold Friend demanded. "Not worried about your hair blowing around in the car, are you?"

"No."

"Think I maybe can't drive good?"

"How do I know?"

"You're a hard girl to handle. How come?" he said. "Don't you know I'm your friend?   75
Didn't you see me put my sign in the air when you walked by?"

"What sign?"

"My sign." And he drew an X in the air, leaning out toward her. They were maybe ten feet apart. After his hand fell back to his side the X was still in the air, almost visible. Connie let the screen door close and stood perfectly still inside it, listening to the music from her radio and the boy's blend together. She stared at Arnold Friend. He stood there so stiffly relaxed, pretending to be relaxed, with one hand idly on the door handle as if he were keeping himself up that way and had no intention of ever moving again. She recognized most things about him, the tight jeans that showed his thighs and buttocks and the greasy leather boots and the tight shirt, and even that slippery friendly smile of his, that sleepy dreamy smile that all the boys used to get across ideas they didn't want to put into words. She recognized all this and also the singsong way he talked, slightly mocking, kidding, but serious and a little melancholy, and she recognized the way he tapped one fist against the other in homage to the perpetual music behind him. But all these things did not come together.

She said suddenly, "Hey, how old are you?"

His smile faded. She could see then that he wasn't a kid, he was much older—thirty, maybe more. At this knowledge her heart began to pound faster.

80 "That's a crazy thing to ask. Can'tcha see I'm your own age?"

"Like hell you are."

"Or maybe a coupla years older, I'm eighteen."

"Eighteen?" she said doubtfully.

He grinned to reassure her and lines appeared at the corners of his mouth. His teeth were big and white. He grinned so broadly his eyes became slits and she saw how thick the lashes were, thick and black as if painted with a black tarlike material. Then he seemed to become embarrassed, abruptly, and looked over his shoulder at Ellie. "*Him*, he's crazy," he said. "Ain't he a riot, he's a nut, a real character." Ellie was still listening to the music. His sunglasses told nothing about what he was thinking. He wore a bright orange shirt unbuttoned halfway to show his chest, which was a pale, bluish chest and not muscular like Arnold Friend's. His shirt collar was turned up all around and the very tips of the collar pointed out past his chin as if they were protecting him. He was pressing the transistor radio up against his ear and sat there in a kind of daze, right in the sun.

85 "He's kinda strange," Connie said.

"Hey, she says you're kinda strange! Kinda strange!" Arnold Friend cried. He pounded on the car to get Ellie's attention. Ellie turned for the first time and Connie saw with shock that he wasn't a kid either—he had a fair, hairless face, cheeks reddened slightly as if the veins grew too close to the surface of his skin, the face of a forty-year-old baby. Connie felt a wave of dizziness rise in her at this sight and she stared at him as if waiting for something to change the shock of the moment, make it all right again. Ellie's lips kept shaping words, mumbling along, with the words blasting in his ear.

"Maybe you two better go away," Connie said faintly.

"What? How come?" Arnold Friend cried. "We come out here to take you for a ride. It's Sunday." He had the voice of the man on the radio now. It was the same voice, Connie thought. "Don'tcha know it's Sunday all day and honey, no matter who you were with last night today you're with Arnold Friend and don't you forget it!—Maybe you better step out here," he said, and this last was in a different voice. It was a little flatter, as if the heat was finally getting to him.

"No. I got things to do."

90 "Hey."

"You two better leave."

"We ain't leaving until you come with us."

"Like hell I am—"

"Connie, don't fool around with me. I mean, I mean, don't fool *around*," he said, shaking his head. He laughed incredulously. He placed his sunglasses on top of his head, carefully, as if he were indeed wearing a wig, and brought the stems down behind his ears. Connie stared at him, another wave of dizziness and fear rising in her so that for a moment he wasn't even in focus but was just a blur, standing there against his gold car, and she had the idea that he had driven up the driveway all right but had come from nowhere before that and belonged nowhere and that everything about him and even about the music that was so familiar to her was only half real.

95 "If my father comes and sees you—"

"He ain't coming. He's at the barbecue."

"How do you know that?"

"Aunt Tillie's. Right now they're—uh—they're drinking. Sitting around," he said vaguely, squinting as if he were staring all the way to town and over to Aunt Tillie's backyard. Then the vision seemed to get clear and he nodded energetically. "Yeah. Sitting around. There's your sister in a blue dress, huh? And high heels, the poor sad bitch—nothing like you, sweetheart! And your mother's helping some fat woman with the corn, they're cleaning the corn—husking the corn—"

"What fat woman?" Connie cried.

"How do I know what fat woman. I don't know every goddam fat woman in the   100
world!" Arnold Friend laughed.

"Oh, that's Mrs. Hornby. . . . Who invited her?" Connie said. She felt a little light-headed. Her breath was coming quickly.

"She's too fat. I don't like them fat. I like them the way you are, honey," he said, smiling sleepily at her. They stared at each other for a while, through the screen door. He said softly, "Now what you're going to do is this: you're going to come out that door. You're going to sit up front with me and Ellie's going to sit in the back, the hell with Ellie, right? This isn't Ellie's date. You're my date. I'm your lover, honey."

"What? You're crazy—"

"Yes, I'm your lover. You don't know what that is but you will," he said. "I know that too. I know all about you. But look: it's real nice and you couldn't ask for nobody better than me, or more polite. I always keep my word. I'll tell you how it is, I'm always nice at first, the first time. I'll hold you so tight you won't think you have to try to get away or pretend anything because you'll know you can't. And I'll come inside you where it's all secret and you'll give in to me and you'll love me—"

"Shut up! You're crazy!" Connie said. She backed away from the door. She put her hands   105
against her ears as if she'd heard something terrible, something not meant for her. "People don't talk like that, you're crazy," she muttered. Her heart was almost too big now for her chest and its pumping made sweat break out all over her. She looked out to see Arnold Friend pause and then take a step toward the porch lurching. He almost fell. But, like a clever drunken man, he managed to catch his balance. He wobbled in his high boots and grabbed hold of one of the porch posts.

"Honey?" he said. "You still listening?"

"Get the hell out of here!"

"Be nice, honey. Listen."

"I'm going to call the police—"

He wobbled again and out of the side of his mouth came a fast spat curse, an aside not   110
meant for her to hear. But even this "Christ!" sounded forced. Then he began to smile again. She watched this smile come, awkward as if he were smiling from inside a mask. His whole face was a mask, she thought wildly, tanned down onto his throat but then running out as if he had plastered makeup on his face but had forgotten about his throat.

"Honey—? Listen, here's how it is. I always tell the truth and I promise you this: I ain't coming in that house after you."

"You better not! I'm going to call the police if you—if you don't—"

"Honey," he said, talking right through her voice, "honey, I'm not coming in there but you are coming out here. You know why?"

She was panting. The kitchen looked like a place she had never seen before, some room she had run inside but which wasn't good enough, wasn't going to help her. The kitchen window had never had a curtain, after three years, and there were dishes in the sink for her to do—probably—and if you ran your hand across the table you'd probably feel something sticky there.

"You listening, honey? Hey?"   115

"—going to call the police—"

"Soon as you touch the phone I don't need to keep my promise and can come inside. You won't want that."

She rushed forward and tried to lock the door. Her fingers were shaking. "But why lock it," Arnold Friend said gently, talking right into her face. "It's just a screen door. It's just nothing." One of his boots was at a strange angle, as if his foot wasn't in it. It pointed out to the left, bent at the ankle. "I mean, anybody can break through a screen door and glass and wood and iron or anything else if he needs to, anybody at all and specially Arnold Friend. If the place got lit up with a fire honey you'd come running out into my arms, right into my arms and safe at home—like you knew I was your lover and'd stopped fooling around. I don't mind a nice shy girl but I don't like no fooling around." Part of those words were spoken with a slight rhythmic lilt, and Connie somehow recognized them—the echo of a song from last year, about a girl rushing into her boyfriend's arms and coming home again—

Connie stood barefoot on the linoleum floor, staring at him. "What do you want?" she whispered.

120   "I want you," he said.

"What?"

"Seen you that night and thought, that's the one, yes sir. I never needed to look any more."

"But my father's coming back. He's coming to get me. I had to wash my hair first—" She spoke in a dry, rapid voice, hardly raising it for him to hear.

"No, your daddy is not coming and yes, you had to wash your hair and you washed it for me. It's nice and shining and all for me, I thank you, sweetheart," he said, with a mock bow, but again he almost lost his balance. He had to bend and adjust his boots. Evidently his feet did not go all the way down; the boots must have been stuffed with something so that he would seem taller. Connie stared out at him and behind him Ellie in the car, who seemed to be looking off toward Connie's right, into nothing. This Ellie said, pulling the words out of the air one after another as if he were just discovering them, "You want me to pull out the phone?"

125   "Shut your mouth and keep it shut," Arnold Friend said, his face red from bending over or maybe from embarrassment because Connie had seen his boots. "This ain't none of your business."

"What—what are you doing? What do you want?" Connie said. "If I call the police they'll get you, they'll arrest you—"

"Promise was not to come in unless you touch that phone, and I'll keep that promise," he said. He resumed his erect position and tried to force his shoulders back. He sounded like a hero in a movie, declaring something important. He spoke too loudly and it was as if he were speaking to someone behind Connie. "I ain't made plans for coming in that house where I don't belong but just for you to come out to me, the way you should. Don't you know who I am?"

"You're crazy," she whispered. She backed away from the door but did not want to go into another part of the house, as if this would give him permission to come through the door. "What do you . . . You're crazy, you . . ."

"Huh? What're you saying, honey?"

130   Her eyes darted everywhere in the kitchen. She could not remember what it was, this room.

"This is how it is, honey: you come out and we'll drive away, have a nice ride. But if you don't come out we're gonna wait till your people come home and then they're all going to get it."

"You want that telephone pulled out?" Ellie said. He held the radio away from his ear and grimaced, as if without the radio the air was too much for him.

"I toldja shut up, Ellie," Arnold Friend said, "you're deaf, get a hearing aid, right? Fix yourself up. This little girl's no trouble and's gonna be nice to me, so Ellie keep to yourself, this ain't your date—right? Don't hem in on me. Don't hog. Don't crush. Don't bird dog. Don't trail me," he said in a rapid meaningless voice, as if he were running through all the expressions he'd learned but was no longer sure which one of them was in style, then rushing on to new ones, making them up with his eyes closed, "Don't crawl under my fence, don't squeeze in my chipmunk hole, don't sniff my glue, suck my popsicle, keep your own greasy fingers on yourself!" He shaded his eyes and peered in at Connie, who was backed against the kitchen table. "Don't mind him honey he's just a creep. He's a dope. Right? I'm the boy for you and like I said you come out here nice like a lady and give me your hand, and nobody else gets hurt, I mean, your nice old bald-headed daddy and your mummy and your sister in her high heels. Because listen: why bring them in this?"

"Leave me alone," Connie whispered.

"Hey, you know that old woman down the road, the one with the chickens and stuff— 135 you know her?"

"She's dead!"

"Dead? What? You know her?" Arnold Friend said.

"She's dead—"

"Don't you like her?"

"She's dead—she's—she isn't here any more—" 140

"But don't you like her, I mean, you got something against her? Some grudge or something?" Then his voice dipped as if he were conscious of a rudeness. He touched the sunglasses perched on top of his head as if to make sure they were still there. "Now you be a good girl."

"What are you going to do?"

"Just two things, or maybe three," Arnold Friend said. "But I promise it won't last long and you'll like me that way you get to like people you're close to. You will. It's all over for you here, so come on out. You don't want your people in any trouble, do you?"

She turned and bumped against a chair or something, hurting her leg, but she ran into the back room and picked up the telephone. Something roared in her ear, a tiny roaring, and she was so sick with fear that she could do nothing but listen to it—the telephone was clammy and very heavy and her fingers groped down to the dial but were too weak to touch it. She began to scream into the phone, into the roaring. She cried out, she cried for her mother, she felt her breath start jerking back and forth in her lungs as if it were something Arnold Friend were stabbing her with again and again with no tenderness. A noisy sorrowful wailing rose all about her and she was locked inside it the way she was locked inside the house.

After a while she could hear again. She was sitting on the floor with her wet back against 145 the wall.

Arnold Friend was saying from the door, "That's a good girl. Put the phone back."

She kicked the phone away from her.

"No, honey. Pick it up. Put it back right."

She picked it up and put it back. The dial tone stopped.

"That's a good girl. Now come outside." 150

She was hollow with what had been fear, but what was now just an emptiness. All that screaming had blasted it out of her. She sat, one leg cramped under her, and deep inside her brain was something like a pinpoint of light that kept going and would not let her relax. She thought, I'm not going to see my mother again. She thought, I'm not going to sleep in my bed again. Her bright green blouse was all wet.

Arnold Friend said, in a gentle-loud voice that was like a stage voice, "The place where you came from ain't there any more, and where you had in mind to go is cancelled out. This place you are now—inside your daddy's house—is nothing but a cardboard box I can knock down any time. You know that and always did know it. You hear me?"

She thought, I have got to think. I have to know what to do.

"We'll go out to a nice field, out in the country here where it smells so nice and it's sunny," Arnold Friend said. "I'll have my arms around you so you won't need to try to get away and I'll show you what love is like, what it does. The hell with this house! It looks solid all right," he said. He ran a fingernail down the screen and the noise did not make Connie shiver, as it would have the day before. "Now put your hand on your heart, honey. Feel that? That feels solid too but we know better, be nice to me, be sweet like you can be-cause what else is there for a girl like you but to be sweet and pretty and give in?—and get away before her people come back?"

155   She felt her pounding heart. Her hand seemed to enclose it. She thought for the first time in her life that it was nothing that was hers, that belonged to her, but just a pounding, living thing inside this body that wasn't really hers either.

    "You don't want them to get hurt," Arnold Friend went on. "Now get up, honey. Get up all by yourself."

    She stood up.

    "Now turn this way. That's right. Come over here to me—Ellie, put that away, didn't I tell you? You dope. You miserable creepy dope," Arnold Friend said. His words were not angry but only part of an incantation. The incantation was kindly. "Now come out through the kitchen to me honey and let's see a smile, try it, you're a brave sweet little girl and now they're eating corn and hotdogs cooked to bursting over an outdoor fire, and they don't know one thing about you and never did and honey you're better than them because not a one of them would have done this for you."

    Connie felt the linoleum under her feet; it was cool. She brushed her hair back out of her eyes. Arnold Friend let go of the post tentatively and opened his arms for her, his elbows pointing in toward each other and his wrists limp, to show that this was an embarrassed embrace and a little mocking, he didn't want to make her self-conscious.

160   She put out her hand against the screen. She watched herself push the door slowly open as if she were safe back somewhere in the other doorway, watching this body and this head of long hair moving out into the sunlight where Arnold Friend waited.

    "My sweet little blue-eyed girl," he said, in a half-sung sigh that had nothing to do with her brown eyes but was taken up just the same by the vast sunlit reaches of the land behind him and on all sides of him, so much land that Connie had never seen before and did not recognize except to know that she was going to it.

QUESTIONS

1. Is this story realistic or fantastic, or a combination of the two? How much fantasy is apparent in the ostensibly realistic level of the story, and how much realism is apparent when the story becomes more and more of a fantasy? At what point does the story shift from everyday realism to the unusual? How does the latter part of the story become less and less realistic? How should this part be described? Is there any way, at the story's beginning, to anticipate what is going to be happening at the end? Explain.

2. Describe the characteristics of Arnold Friend. Why does Oates connect him with the blackness of tar and tarlike substance? What do you make out of his apparent ability to know about Connie's family, and about people at the party with the family? What do you make of his wobbling in his boots (paragraphs 105, 124), and his seeming to speak to someone, unseen, behind Connie?

3. Describe Connie. Is she unusual at all? What happens to her perceptions of her situation as she stands within the kitchen and Arnold Friend stands outside? Why does she leave the house with Arnold at the end?

4. Why does Arnold Friend speak so coarsely and angrily to his companion, Ellie? What does Ellie represent? How can Arnold Friend be construed not as realistic but demonic? If he is symbolic, what does he symbolize?

TOM WHITECLOUD (1914–1972)

Thomas St. Germain Whitecloud was born in New York City. However, he spent much of his youth on the Lac du Flambeau Indian Reservation near Woodruff, Wisconsin, the town mentioned in paragraph 20 of "Blue Winds Dancing." After attending colleges in New Mexico and California, he received his degree in medicine from Tulane University. He lived in Louisiana and Texas throughout his medical career, and at the time of his death he was a consultant for the Texas Commission on Alcoholism and Drug Abuse for Indians. "Blue Winds Dancing," which can be considered as either a story or a fictionalized autobiographical fragment, received a prize in 1938 from both Scribner's Magazine, *in which it was published, and the Phi Beta Kappa National Honor Society.*

🍁 Blue Winds Dancing (1938)

There is a moon out tonight. Moon and stars and clouds tipped with moonlight. And there is a fall wind blowing in my heart. Ever since this evening, when against a fading sky I saw geese wedge southward. They were going home. . . . Now I try to study, but against the pages I see them again, driving southward. Going home.

Across the valley there are heavy mountains holding up the night sky, and beyond the mountains there is home. Home, and peace, and the beat of drums, and blue winds dancing over snowfields. The Indian lodge will fill with my people, and our gods will come and sit among them. I should be there then. I should be at home.

But home is beyond the mountains, and I am here. Here where fall hides in the valleys, and winter never comes down from the mountains. Here where all the trees grow in rows; the palms stand stiffly by the roadsides, and in the groves the orange trees line in military rows, and endlessly bear fruit. Beautiful, yes: there is always beauty in order, in rows of growing things! But it is the beauty of captivity. A pine fighting for existence on a windy knoll is much more beautiful.

In my Wisconsin, the leaves change before the snows come. In the air there is the smell of wild rice and venison cooking; and when the winds come whispering through the forests, they carry the smell of rotting leaves. In the evenings, the loon calls, lonely; and birds sing their last songs before leaving. Bears dig roots and eat late fall berries, fattening for their long winter sleep. Later, when the first snows fall, one awakens in the morning to find the world white and beautiful and clean. Then one can look back over his trail and see the tracks following. In the woods there are tracks of deer and snowshoe rabbits, and long streaks where partridges slide to alight. Chipmunks make tiny footprints on the limbs and one can hear squirrels busy in hollow trees, sorting acorns. Soft lake waves wash the shores, and sunsets burst each evening over the lakes, and make them look as if they were afire.

That land which is my home! Beautiful, calm—where there is no hurry to get anywhere, no driving to keep up in a race that knows no ending and no goal. No classes where men talk and talk and then stop now and then to hear their own words come back to them from the students. No constant peering into the maelstrom of one's mind; no worries about grades and honors; no hysterical preparing for life until that life is half over; no anxiety about one's place in the thing they call Society. 5

I hear again the ring of axes in deep woods, the crunch of snow beneath my feet. I feel again the smooth velvet of ghost-birch bark. I hear the rhythm of the drums. . . . I am tired. I am weary of trying to keep up this bluff of being civilized. Being civilized means trying to do everything you don't want to, never doing anything you want to. It means dancing to the strings of custom and tradition; it means living in houses and never knowing or caring who is next door. These civilized white men want us to be like them—always dissatisfied—getting a hill and wanting a mountain.

Then again, maybe I am not tired. Maybe I'm licked. Maybe I am just not smart enough to grasp these things that go to make up civilization. Maybe I am just too lazy to think hard enough to keep up.

Still, I know my people have many things that civilization has taken from the whites. They know how to give; how to tear one's piece of meat in two and share it with one's brother. They know how to sing—how to make each man his own songs and sing them; for their music they do not have to listen to other men singing over a radio. They know how to make things with their hands, how to shape beads into design and make a thing of beauty from a piece of birch bark.

But we are inferior. It is terrible to have to feel inferior; to have to read reports of intelligence tests, and learn that one's race is behind. It is terrible to sit in classes and hear men tell you that your people worship sticks of wood—that your gods are all false, that the Manitou forgot your people and did not write them a book.

10   I am tired. I want to walk again among the ghost-birches. I want to see the leaves turn in autumn, the smoke rise from the lodgehouses, and to feel the blue winds. I want to hear the drums; I want to hear the drums and feel the blue whispering winds.

There is a train wailing into the night. The trains go across the mountains. It would be easy to catch a freight. They will say he has gone back to the blanket; I don't care. The dance at Christmas. . . .

A bunch of bums warming at a tiny fire talk politics and women and joke about the Relief and the WPA and smoke cigarettes. These men in caps and overcoats and dirty overalls living on the outskirts of civilization are free, but they pay the price of being free in civilization. They are outcasts. I remember a sociology professor lecturing on adjustment to society; hobos and prostitutes and criminals are individuals who never adjusted, he said. He could learn a lot if he came and listened to a bunch of bums talk. He would learn that work and a woman and a place to hang his hat are all the ordinary man wants. These are all he wants, but other men are not content to let him want only these. He must be taught to want radios and automobiles and a new suit every spring. Progress would stop if he did not want these things. I listen to hear if there is any talk of communism or socialism in the hobo jungles. There is none. At best there is a sort of disgusted philosophy about life. They seem to think there should be a better distribution of wealth, or more work, or something. But they are not rabid about it. The radicals live in the cities.

I find a fellow headed for Albuquerque, and talk road-talk with him. "It is hard to ride fruit cars. Bums break in. Better to wait for a cattle car going back to the Middle West, and ride that." We catch the next east-bound and walk the tops until we find a cattle car. Inside, we crouch near the forward wall, huddle, and try to sleep. I feel peaceful and content at last. I am going home. The cattle car rocks. I sleep.

Morning and the desert. Noon and the Salton Sea, lying more lifeless than a mirage under a somber sun in a pale sky. Skeleton mountains rearing on the skyline, thrusting out of the desert floor, all rock and shadow and edges. Desert. Good country for an Indian reservation. . . .

15   Yuma and the muddy Colorado. Night again, and I wait shivering for the dawn.

Phoenix. Pima country. Mountains that look like cardboard sets on a forgotten stage. Tucson, Papago country. Giant cacti that look like petrified hitchhikers along the highways. Apache country. At El Paso my road-buddy decides to go on to Houston. I leave him, and head north to the mesa country. Las Cruces and the terrible Organ Mountains, jagged peaks that instill fear and wondering. Albuquerque. Pueblos along the Rio Grande.

On the boardwalk there are some Indian women in colored sashes selling bits of pottery. The stone age offering its art to the twentieth century. They hold up a piece and fix the tourist with black eyes until, embarrassed, he buys or turns away. I feel suddenly angry that my people should have to do such things for a living. . . .

Santa Fe trains are fast, and they keep them pretty clean of bums. I decide to hurry and ride passenger coaltenders. Hide in the dark, judge the speed of the train as it leaves, and then dash out, and catch it. I hug the cold steel wall of the tender and think of the roaring fire in the engine ahead, and of the passengers back in the dining car reading their papers over hot coffee. Beneath me there is a blur of rails. Death would come quick if my hands should freeze and I fall. Up over the Sangre De Cristo range, around cliffs and through canyons to Denver. Bitter cold here, and I must watch out for Denver Bob. He is a railroad bull who has thrown bums from fast freights. I miss him. It is too cold, I suppose. On north to the Sioux country.

Small towns lit for the coming Christmas. On the streets of one I see a beam-shouldered young farmer gazing into a window filled with shining silver toasters. He is tall and wears a blue shirt buttoned, with no tie. His young wife by his side looks at him hopefully. He wants decorations for his place to hang his hat to please his woman. . . .

Northward again. Minnesota, and great white fields of snow; frozen lakes, and dawn running into dusk without noon. Long forests wearing white. Bitter cold, and one night the northern lights. I am nearing home.

I reach Woodruff at midnight. Suddenly I am afraid, now that I am but twenty miles ⟨20⟩ from home. Afraid of what my father will say, afraid of being looked on as a stranger by my own people. I sit by a fire and think about myself and all other young Indians. We just don't seem to fit in anywhere—certainly not among the whites, and not among the older people. I think again about the learned sociology professor and his professing. So many things seem to be clear now that I am away from school and do not have to worry about some man's opinion of my ideas. It is easy to think while looking at dancing flames.

Morning, I spend the day cleaning up, and buying some presents for my family with what is left of my money. Nothing much, but a gift is a gift, if a man buys it with his last quarter. I wait until evening, then start up the track toward home.

Christmas Eve comes in on a north wind. Snow clouds hang over the pines, and the night comes early. Walking along the railroad bed, I feel the calm peace of snowbound forests on either side of me. I take my time; I am back in a world where time does not mean so much now. I am alone; alone but not nearly so lonely as I was back on the campus at school. Those are never lonely who love the snow and the pines; never lonely when the pines are wearing white shawls and snow crunches coldly underfoot. In the woods I know there are the tracks of deer and rabbit; I know that if I leave the rails and go into the woods I shall find them. I walk along feeling glad because my legs are light and my feet seem to know that they are home. A deer comes out of the woods ahead of me, and stands silhouetted on the rails. The North, I feel, has welcomed me home. I watch him and am glad that I do not wish for a gun. He goes into the woods quietly, leaving only the design of his tracks in the snow. I walk on. Now and then I pass a field, white under the night sky, with houses at the far end. Smoke comes from the chimneys of the houses, and I try to tell what sort of wood each is burning by the smoke; some burn pine, others aspen, others tamarack. There is one from which comes black coal smoke that rises lazily and drifts out over the tops of the trees. I like to watch houses and try to imagine what might be happening in them.

Just as a light snow begins to fall I cross the reservation boundary; somehow it seems as though I have stepped into another world. Deep woods in a white-and-black winter night. A faint trail leading to the village.

The railroad on which I stand comes from a city sprawled by a lake—a city with a million people who walk around without seeing one another; a city sucking the life from all the country around; a city with stores and police and intellectuals and criminals and movies and apartment houses; a city with its politics and libraries and zoos.

Laughing, I go into the woods. As I cross a frozen lake I begin to hear the drums. Soft in the night the drums beat. It is like the pulse beat of the world. The white line of the lake ends at a black forest, and above the trees the blue winds are dancing.

I come to the outlying houses of the village. Simple box houses, etched black in the night. From one or two windows soft lamplight falls on the snow. Christmas here, too, but it does not mean much; not much in the way of parties and presents. Joe Sky will get drunk. Alex Bodidash will buy his children red mittens and a new sled. Alex is a Carlisle man, and tries to keep his home up to white standards. White standards. Funny that my people should be ever falling farther behind. The more they try to imitate whites the more tragic the result. Yet they want us to be imitation white men. About all we imitate well are their vices.

The village is not a sight to instill pride, yet I am not ashamed; one can never be ashamed of his own people when he knows they have dreams as beautiful as white snow on a tall pine.

Father and my brother and sister are seated around the table as I walk in. Father stares at me for a moment, then I am in his arms, crying on his shoulder. I give them the presents I have brought, and my throat tightens as I watch my sister save carefully bits of red string from the packages. I hide my feelings by wrestling with my brother when he strikes my shoulder in token of affection. Father looks at me, and I know he has many questions, but he seems to know why I have come. He tells me to go alone to the lodge, and he will follow.

I walk along the trail to the lodge, watching the northern lights forming in the heavens. White waving ribbons that seem to pulsate with the rhythm of the drums. Clean snow creaks beneath my feet, and a soft wind sighs through the trees, singing to me. Everything seems to say, "Be happy! You are home now—you are free. You are among friends—we are your friends; we, the trees, and the snow, and the lights." I follow the trail to the lodge. My feet are light, my heart seems to sing to the music, and I hold my head high. Across white snow fields blue winds are dancing.

Before the lodge door I stop, afraid, I wonder if my people will remember me. I wonder— "Am I Indian, or am I white?" I stand before the door a long time. I hear the ice groan on the lake, and remember the story of the old woman under the ice, trying to get out, so she can punish some runaway lovers. I think to myself, "If I am white I will not believe that story; If I am Indian, I will know that there is an old woman under the ice." I listen for a while, and I know that there is an old woman under the ice. I look again at the lights, and go in.

Inside the lodge there are many Indians. Some sit on benches around the walls, others dance in the center of the floor around a drum. Nobody seems to notice me. It seems as though I were among a people I have never seen before. Heavy women with long hair. Women with children on their knees—small children that watch with intent black eyes the movements of the dancers, whose small faces are solemn and serene. The faces of the old people are serene, too, and their eyes are merry and bright. I look at the old men. Straight, dressed in dark trousers and beaded velvet vests, wearing soft moccasins. Dark, lined faces intent on the music. I wonder if I am at all like them. They dance on, lifting their feet to the rhythm of the drums swaying lightly, looking upward. I look at their eyes, and am startled at the rapt attention to the rhythm of the music.

The dance stops. The men walk back to the walls, and talk in low tones or with their hands. There is little conversation, yet everyone seems to be sharing some secret. A woman looks at a small boy wandering away, and he comes back to her.

Strange, I think and then remember. These people are not sharing words—they are sharing a mood. Everyone is happy. I am so used to white people that it seems strange so many people could be together without someone talking. These Indians are happy because they are together, and because the night is beautiful outside, and the music is beautiful. I try hard to forget school and white people, and be one of these—my people. I try to forget everything but the night, and it is a part of me that I am one with my people and we are all a part of something universal. I watch eyes, and see now that the old people are speaking to me. They nod slightly, imperceptibly, and their eyes laugh into mine. I look around the room. All the eyes are friendly; they all laugh. No one questions my being here. The drums begin to beat again, and I catch the invitation in the eyes of the old men. My feet begin to lift to the rhythm, and I look out beyond the walls into the night and see the lights. I am happy. It is beautiful. I am home.

QUESTIONS

1. Describe the first section of the story in terms of the structure. Could a case be made that this first section contains its own crisis and climax and that the rest of the story is really a resolution?

2. What do you learn in the first section about the conflict in the attitudes of the narrator? What is his attitude about "civilization"? What values make him think this way? If he is the protagonist, who or what is the antagonist?

3. What does the narrator mean by saying, "I am alone; alone but not nearly so lonely as I was back on the campus at school" (paragraph 22)?

4. What is meant by the dancing of the blue winds—what kind of wisdom? What is the place for such wisdom in today's computerized, industrialized society?

WRITING ABOUT STRUCTURE IN A STORY

Your essay should concern arrangement and shape. In form, the essay should not restate or summarize the part-by-part unfolding of the narrative or argument. Rather, it should explain why things are where they are: "Why is this here and not there?" is the fundamental question you need to answer. Thus it is possible to begin with a consideration of a work's crisis, and then to consider how the exposition and complication have built up to it. A vital piece of information, for example, might have been withheld in the story's earlier exposition (as in Ambrose Bierce's "An Occurrence at Owl Creek Bridge" in Chapter 1 and Faulkner's "A Rose for Emily" in Chapter 1) and introduced only at or near the conclusion. Therefore the crisis might be heightened because there would have been less suspense if the detail had been introduced earlier. Consider the following questions in planning to write about the story's structure.

Questions for Discovering Ideas

- If spaces or numbers divide the story into sections or parts, what structural importance do these parts have?
- If there are no marked divisions, what major sections can you find? (You might make divisions according to places where actions occur, various times of day, changing weather, or increasingly important events.)
- If the story departs in major ways from the formal structure of exposition, complication, crisis, climax, and resolution, what purpose do these departures serve?

- What variations in chronological order, if any, appear in the story (for example, gaps in the time sequence; flashbacks or selective recollection)? What effects are achieved by these variations?
- Does the story delay any crucial details of exposition? Why? What effect is achieved by the delay?
- Where does an important action or a major section (such as the climax) begin? End? How is it related to the other formal structural elements, such as the crisis? Is the climax an action, a realization, or a decision? To what degree does it relieve the work's tension? What is the effect of the climax on your understanding of the characters involved in it? How is this effect related to the arrangement of the climax?

Strategies for Organizing Ideas

Your essay should show why an entire story is arranged the way it is—to reveal the nature of a character's situation, to create surprise, or to evoke sympathy, reveal nobility (or depravity) of character, unravel apparently insoluble puzzles, express philosophical or political values, or bring out maximum humor. You might also, however, explain the structure of no more than a part of the story, such as the climax or the complication.

The essay is best developed in concert or agreement with what the work contains. The location of scenes is an obvious organizing element. Thus, essays on the structure of Hawthorne's "Young Goodman Brown" (Chapter 7) and Whitecloud's "Blue Winds Dancing" (this chapter) might be based on the fact that both take place outdoors (a dark forest for one and a series of railway locations and a winter scene for the other). Similarly, an essay might explore the structure of Maupassant's "The Necklace" (Part I) by contrasting the story's indoor and outdoor locations. Similarly, in Hardy's "The Three Strangers" (this chapter) there is a regular series of contrasts between the raw weather outdoors and the warm companionship indoors, and an essay might trace the structural importance of these.

Other ways to consider structure may be derived from a work's notable aspects, such as the growing suspense of Jackson's "The Lottery" (Chapter 2) or the revelations about the "sinfulness" of Goodman Brown's father and neighbors in Hawthorne's "Young Goodman Brown" (Chapter 7).

The conclusion should highlight the main parts of your essay. You may also deal briefly with the relationship of structure to the plot. If the work you have analyzed departs from chronological order, you might explain the causes and effects of this departure. Your aim should be to focus on the success of the work as it has been brought about by the author's choices in development.

Illustrative Student Essay

Underlined sentences in this paper *do not* conform to MLA style and are used solely as teaching tools to emphasize the central idea, thesis sentence, and topic sentences throughout the paper.

Flores 1

Jeannette Flores

Professor Iacovelli

English 120

29 November 2008

Conflict and Suspense in Hardy's "The Three Strangers"°

Thomas Hardy's "The Three Strangers" is a finely woven story of   [1]
conflict and suspense. The suspense is essential to the conflict, which builds
from an opposition of right and wrong when applied to criminal justice.
Hardy controls the structure to develop this opposition, namely that the letter
of the law is insignificant when compared with the spirit of the law.* The
application of strict legality in Hardy's story is made to seem wrong, while
understanding and forgiveness, even in an apparently illegal context, is made
to seem right. As the basis of this idea, Hardy builds the story toward a major
incident that presents a conflict for his Wessex shepherds between (1) duty
toward law and (2) duty toward a human being who has been legally
condemned but whose crime has been extenuated. Hardy develops his
conflict and brings out his idea by showing the lives of his country people
positively, by portraying his hangman negatively, and by creating suspense
about his first stranger, who is the legally condemned "criminal."†

Although readers may not be aware of it during the early part of the story,   [2]
Hardy arranges events to demonstrate a generous and broad view of right and
wrong. The first one-sixth of the story is an exposition of the way of life of the
natives of Higher Crowstairs, who are shown to be warm and human. But in the
service of his idea, Hardy is actually building up one side of the conflict by
demonstrating that his natives are such nice, ordinary peasant folk that their

°**This story appears on pages 287–300.**
*****Central idea.**
†**Thesis sentence.**

Flores 2

judgments on matters of life and death are to be trusted. This is the positive side of Hardy's narrative argument.

[3]   When Hardy does engage both sides of the conflict--a complication occurring about midway through the story--by introducing the second stranger (the hangman), he has already established the grounds for his case, but he solidifies his argument by negatively presenting this ghoulish figure as brash, selfish, and obnoxious. When the natives learn of the second stranger's identity as the hangman, they are startled "with suppressed exclamations" (294, paragraph 79). The exclamations apparently take the form that if men such as the hangman are associated with the letter of the law, the natives--along with the reader--will prefer the spirit even if the spirit may lead people to support technically illegal actions. This reaction could not be sustained if the crime of the escaped criminal had been a violent one, but the "crime" was really the theft of a sheep to feed his starving family (295, paragraph 80). One may grant that Hardy is mitigating the crime here, but the conflict is not between right when it is right, and wrong when it is wrong, but rather between legality when it is wrong and illegality when it is right. As Hardy structures the events in the story, it is not possible to disagree with the consensus of the natives that the intended hanging of the thief "was cruelly disproportioned to the transgression" (299, paragraph 160), for even if a reader wanted to disagree with Hardy's argument on legal grounds, the emotional thrust of the story leads toward extenuation.

[4]   Critical to this extenuation is Hardy's creation of suspense about the identity of the first stranger as Timothy Summers, the escaped prisoner. Because throughout the story readers have assented to the values and way of life of Shepherd Fennel and his guests, Hardy's crisis and climax forestall an exclusively legalistic reaction. Hardy puts Summers before the eyes of both country folk and readers as a brave and witty human being, not as a depraved fugitive who has just escaped hanging. The revelation at the end therefore causes a second view of Summers. In retrospect, readers join the natives in admiring this first stranger's "marvelous coolness and daring in hob-and-nobbing

Flores 3

with the hangman" (299, paragraph 160) and consequently would be indignant if such a person were actually to be hanged. As a result of Hardy's judicious withholding and disclosing of detail, he leads readers to deny the law when it is used unfairly.

Related to the major conflict in the story are a number of lesser but still important conflicts. At crucial points, for example, Hardy establishes that the natives living marginally "in the country about Higher Crowstairs" (300, paragraph 162) are uneasy and fearful of the law. When they realize that the second stranger is the hangman, they recoil from him, and one of them begins trembling (294, paragraph 79). Hardy invites readers to conclude that the natives view the conviction of Summers as a threat also to themselves. In a comic vein, Hardy contrasts the law with the ineptness of the shepherds who are called upon to enforce it (296–98, paragraphs 106–134). He makes the law so remote from their lives that when they actually make an arrest--of the third stranger--they use words more appropriate to criminals or to priests (298, paragraphs 132–34). As an ironic dénouement of the story, Hardy tells us that the shepherds, resisting the legal but troubling hangman and magistrate, diligently search for Summers everywhere but where they know he can be found (299, paragraph 160). [5]

In addition, Hardy includes other little but human contrasts in order to develop sympathy for the folk and therefore to strengthen his argument and tighten his structure. Although the Fennels have twenty guests in their home, Mrs. Fennel is alarmed about giving them too much food and drink, and she is disturbed when the hangman selfishly depletes her store of mead. There is a small family disagreement on this score. Another minor and amusing conflict is set up by Hardy when Mrs. Fennel asks the musicians to stop playing, but they continue because they have been bribed by the amorous shepherd, Oliver Giles. There are also some noticeable contrasts in age among couples. Beyond these contrasts or opposites, which are vital to the story's structure, the technique of suspense is a conflict in itself, for it guides readers to consider and evaluate elements of the story a second time. [6]

Flores 4

These are all conflicts that Hardy employs in developing his major conflict between the right of the spirit of the law and the wrong of the letter of the law in "The Three Strangers."

Flores 5

Work Cited

Hardy, Thomas. "The Three Strangers." Literature: An Introduction to Reading and Writing. Ed. Edgar V. Roberts. 9th ed. New York: Pearson Longman, 2009. 287–300.

Commentary on the Essay

Essays about either plot (Chapter 1) or structure are concerned with the conflicts of the story, but the essay on plot concentrates on the opposing forces whereas the essay on structure focuses on the placement and arrangement of the story's details. Notice here that an essay on structure, like an essay on plot, does not simply retell the story event by event. That is not the concern of analytical writing. Instead, essays on both plot and structure explain the *conflict* (for plot) and the *arrangement and layout* (for structure). In both essays, the writer's assumption is that the reader has read the story, and therefore there is no need to retell it.

As expressed in paragraph 1, this essay focuses on how Hardy structures character and action in "The Three Strangers" to achieve a contrast between right and wrong. The discussion of all events leading to the people's exoneration of the fugitive is seen not as narrative but as a contributing part of Hardy's argument. The essay thus argues that the parts of the story are placed where they are because they are aspects of Hardy's own argument. To emphasize this aim, words and phrases are introduced, such as "arranges events," "engage both sides of the conflict," "structures the events," "creation of suspense," "establishes," and "in order to develop sympathy." All these expressions are intended as reminders that the subject of the essay is the way in which Hardy structures the story.

In the body, paragraph 2 explains how Hardy introduces the natives and their guests at the Fennels' cottage to illustrate their qualities of warmth and humanity. Paragraph 3 stresses the negative reaction of the country folk when they learn that the second stranger is the hangman. Together, then, paragraphs 2 and 3 explain the underlying causes of Hardy's arrangement of the narrative.

In paragraph 4 the essay deals with Hardy's delay in identifying the fugitive. This delay allows Hardy to elaborate on his positive picture of the country folk and their values, and it also helps him in persuading readers of the story to concur in the decision for justice that the natives make. Paragraph 5 states that other conflicts in the story show that the natives are uneasy with the law and fearful of it—attitudes that reinforce their decision to favor the first stranger. The last paragraph argues that additional "but human" contrasts are placed so as to augment Hardy's favorable portraits of the Fennels and their guests.

Writing Topics About Structure

1. What kind of story might Hardy's "The Three Strangers" (this chapter) be, structurally, if the first stranger were identified when he first appears, before the second stranger (the unnamed hangman) enters and starts to dominate the Christening party? What is gained, structurally, by the fact that the third stranger does not enter until late in the story?

2. Compare the structuring of the interior scenes in Conrad's "The Secret Sharer" (Chapter 4) and Hardy's "The Three Strangers" (this chapter). How do these scenes bring out the various conflicts of the stories? How does the presence of characters in the individual rooms contribute to the organization of the stories? What is the relationship of these characters to the major actions of the stories?

3. Compare Tan's "Two Kinds" (Chapter 3) and Whitecloud's "Blue Winds Dancing" (this chapter) as stories about clashing racial and social values. What are the comparative values? How do the narrators react to the values and ideas to which they object? How do the stories develop, structurally, as a result of their reactions?

4. Consider the surprises in Hardy's "The Three Strangers," Maupassant's "The Necklace" (Part I), Faulkner's "A Rose for Emily" (Chapter 1), Bierce's "An Occurrence at Owl Creek Bridge" (Chapter 1), and Chopin's "The Story of an Hour" (Chapter 6). How much preparation is made, structurally, for these surprises? In retrospect, to what degree are the surprises not surprises at all but rather necessary outcomes of the preceding parts of the works?

5. Consider those aspects of Whitecloud's "Blue Winds Dancing" (this chapter) that seem socially and politically significant. You might consider questions about the ability of a young minority student to flourish when removed from the security he gained from his home, about the values that the narrator has questioned in the courses he has been taking, or about why he does not speak about any friendships he might have made at school. What are the implications of this story for minority assimilation into the country's dominant culture, even today, granted that the story was written in the late 1930s?

6. Select a circumstance in your life that caused you doubt, difficulty, and conflict. Making yourself anonymous (give yourself a fictitious name and put yourself in a fictitious location), write a brief story about the occasion, stressing how your conflict began, how it affected you, and how you resolved it. You might choose to begin your story in the present tense and introduce details in flashback.

Chapter 6

Tone and Style: The Words That Convey Attitudes in Fiction

Tone refers to the methods by which writers and speakers reveal attitudes or feelings—toward the material, toward their readers, and toward the general situation they are describing or analyzing. It is an aspect of all spoken and written statements, whether serious analyses of political campaigns, earnest declarations of love, requests to pass a dinner dish, descriptions of social or athletic events, letters from students asking parents for money, or official government notices threatening penalties if fines and taxes are not paid. The attitudes expressed in each of these situations are usually readily apparent. When we speak about tone here, we refer to a variety of similar and dissimilar attitudes, but, in addition, and more importantly, we stress those modes of expression that create and shape those attitudes.

Although tone is a vast subject that can involve large matters of action and situation, in this chapter we will treat the interconnectedness of tone with **style**—the ways in which writers assemble words to tell the story, to develop the argument, to dramatize the play, or to compose the poem. Sometimes style is distinguished from content, but actually style is best considered as the choice of words in the *service* of content. The written expression of an action or scene, in other words, cannot be separated from the action or scene itself, nor can it be separated from the impressions and attitudes it creates.

By reading a story carefully, we may deduce the author's attitude or attitudes toward the subject matter and toward readers. In "The Story of an Hour," for example, Kate Chopin sympathetically portrays a young wife's secret wishes for freedom, just as Chopin also sardonically reveals the unwitting smugness that often pervades men's relationships with women.

Words and subject matter may also indicate the writer's assessment of readers. When Hawthorne's woodland guide in "Young Goodman Brown" (Chapter 7) refers to "King Philip's War," for example, Hawthorne clearly assumes that his readers know that this war in seventeenth-century New England was notoriously cruel and inhumane. In this way he indicates respect for the knowledge of his readers, and he also assumes that they will assent to his interpretation. Authors always make such considerations about readers by implicitly complimenting them on their capacity to recognize and understand the ways in which materials are presented.

Diction: The Writer's Choice and Control of Words

Control over style and tone is highly individual, because all authors put words uniquely together to fit the specific circumstances of specific works. We may therefore speak of the *style* of Ernest Hemingway and the *style* of Alice Munro, even though both writers adapt words to situations. An author may have a distinct style for narrative and descriptive passages but a very different style for dialogue.

The essential aspect of style is **diction,** the writer's selection of words. First, words must be accurate and comprehensive, so that all actions, scenes, and ideas are perfectly understandable to readers. If a writer's work is effective—if it portrays an action graphically and clearly, explains ideas accurately, and indicates the conditions of human relationships among the major characters—we may confidently say that the words are right. Additionally, right words bear the burden of controlling the ways in which readers respond to the material. Thus, a passage of action should verbally create the action and the place or places in which things happen, and it should also cause readers to be interested and involved. Similarly, explanatory or reflective passages should be clear but should also pique the curiosity and satisfy the understanding of readers. In short, the writer should make all efforts to control the work's tone.

Formal, Neutral, and Informal Diction Create Unique Effects

As a guide to the types of words authors use to control tone, a major classification of diction can be made according to three degrees of formality or informality: **formal** or *high,* **neutral** or *middle,* and **informal** or *low.*

Formal or *high* diction bestows major importance to the characters and actions being described. It consists of standard and also "elegant" words (frequently polysyllabic), correct word order, and the absence of contractions. The sentence "It is I," for example, is formal, for this expression is more "elegant" and grammatically correct than most American speakers normally now prefer. An example of formal diction may be seen in the narrative sections of Hawthorne's "Young Goodman Brown (Chapter 7)."

Neutral or *middle* diction is ordinary, everyday standard vocabulary, shunning longer words and using contractions when necessary. The sentence "It's me" is an example of what many American speakers naturally say in preference to the formal "It is I." Neutral words may be thought of as clear window glass, while words in the formal or high style are more decorative, like stained glass. Neutral diction is appropriate for stories about everyday, ordinary people going through situations they encounter or can imagine encountering in their lives. Generally, today's writers favor neutral diction as a means of putting their characters in a light that is normal and appropriate but also respectful. In Alice Munro's "The Found Boat" we see neutral, middle diction.

Nobody said a word this time, they all bent and stripped themselves. Eva, naked first, started running across the field, and then all the others ran, all five of them running bare through the knee-high hot grass, running towards the river. Not caring now about being caught but in fact leaping and yelling to call attention to themselves, if there was anybody to hear or see. They felt as if they were going to jump off a cliff and fly. They felt that something was happening to them different from anything that had happened before, and it had to do with the boat, the water, the sunlight, the dark ruined station, and each other. They thought of each other now hardly as names or people, but as echoing shrieks, reflections, all bold and white and loud and scandalous, and as fast as arrows. They went running without a break into the cold water and when it came almost to the tops of their legs they fell on it and swam. It stopped their noise. Silence, amazement, came over them in a rush. They dipped and floated and separated, sleek as mink. (353, paragraph 87)

The words of this passage are ordinary and easy. They are centered directly on the subject and do not draw attention to themselves. In an almost ritualistic way, the paragraph describes young people running impetuously toward a river and diving in. This action can be seen as sexually symbolic, but Munro's diction focuses on the experience itself, and the words are neither analytical nor clinical. If her intention had been to create searching psychological scrutiny, she might have used formal or high words from the language of psychology (*libido, urge, sublimation,* and so on). Instead, she uses words that could have been in the vocabularies of the characters themselves, who would have used comparable words to express their sensations. Hence they feel "as if they were going to jump off a cliff and fly," and in their excitement they think "that something was happening to them different from anything that had happened before." These neutral, middle words enable us to focus on the excitement of the situation rather than on deeper psychological significance. Munro therefore does not instruct us so much as she causes us to be amused and happy about the young people cavorting on the field and in the water.

Informal or *low* diction may range from *colloquial*—the language of relaxed, common activities—to the level of *substandard* or *slang* expressions. A person speaking to a close friend uses diction that would not be appropriate in public and formal situations and even in some social situations. Informal or low diction is thus appropriate for some narrative dialogue, depending, of course, on individual speakers. It is also a natural choice for stories told in the first-person point of view as though the speaker is talking directly to sympathetic and relaxed close friends— "pals." The following sentence from Bambara's "The Lesson" (Chapter 8) illustrates informal, low diction.

And school suppose to let up in summer I heard, but she don't never let up.

Note the ungrammatical "don't never," a double negative often used in informal or low speech but frowned upon in writing. Note also that the *d* has been dropped in the participle "suppose," that the word "is" before "suppose" is omitted, and that "I heard" follows and does not precede the clause "And school suppose to let up in summer." The purpose of these substandard usages is clearly to establish the voice of the speaker, Sylvia, and to encourage us to listen attentively to her story.

Authors Use Specific-General and Concrete-Abstract Language to Guide Readers to Perceptions of Numbers and Qualities

Another aspect of language is its degree of explicitness. **Specific** refers to words that bring to mind images from the real world. "My dog Teddie is barking" is specific. **General** statements refer to broad classes, such as "All people like pets" and "Dogs make good pets." There is an ascending order of generality from (1) very specific, to (2) less specific, to (3) general, as though the words themselves are climbing a ladder. Thus *peach* is a specific fruit. *Fruit* is specific but more general because it may also include apples, oranges, and all other fruits. *Dessert* is a still more general word, which can include all sweets, including fruits and peaches, and also other confections, such as ice cream. *Food* is more general yet, for it is a comprehensive word that describes everything we eat.

While *specific-general* refers to categories, *concrete-abstract* refers to qualities or conditions. **Concrete** words describe qualities of immediate perception. If you say, "Ice cream is cold," the word *cold* is concrete because it describes a condition that you can feel, just as you can taste ice cream's *sweetness* and feel its *creamy* texture in your mouth. **Abstract** words refer to broader and less palpable qualities; they may therefore apply to many separate things. If we describe ice cream as *good*, our word is abstract because *good* is far removed from ice cream itself and conveys no descriptive information about it. A vast number of things may be *good*, just as they may be *bad, fine, "cool," excellent*, and so on.

Usually, narrative and descriptive writing features specific and concrete words that are intended to help us visualize actions, scenes, and objects, for with more specificity and concreteness there is less ambiguity. Because exactness and vividness are goals of most fiction, specific and concrete words are the fiction writer's basic tools, with general and abstract words being used sparingly.

The point, however, is not that abstract and general words have no place at all, but rather that *words should be appropriate in the context*. Good writers control style in the interests of tone as well as description. Observe, for example, Hemingway's diction in "Hills Like White Elephants" (page 344). This brief story takes place at a railway station in Spain, and it consists largely of conversation between the "American and the girl with him" as they are waiting for a train. The two speak idly about details of the day, the appearance of the nearby hills, and the drinks they are having as they wait. The language here is all quite specific, but at a certain point the specifics bring out an obvious issue of contention the two had been discussing before the story opens. About a third of the way through the story, the man speaks about an operation that is "not really an operation at all." It is clear that the operation he wants "Jig" (the woman's nickname) to have is an abortion. In the rest of the story, the dialogue takes a more negative turn. Even when he says that he doesn't want her to go through with it unless she wants it, she understands his words as an expression of the anger her refusal would cause. Her many questions about their relationship after such an operation indicate her apprehensiveness not only about the procedure but also her increasing disappointment in the American. The height of the American's generalized view of abortion is his claim to have known "lots of people that have done it." Her response, at the same level of generalization, but with cutting irony, marks the height of their dispute: "So have I," said the girl. "And afterward they were all so happy." Through such passages, mixing appropriate specific details with general observations, Hemingway skillfully points readers toward great understanding of the life these two characters have shared together.

Authors Use Denotation and Connotation to Control Meaning and Suggestion

Another way to understand the connection of style and tone is to study the author's management of *denotation* and *connotation*. **Denotation** is a limiting term, referring to what a word means, and **connotation** is a broader word, referring to what the word suggests. For example, if a person in a social situation behaves in ways that are *friendly, warm, polite,* or *cordial,* these words are different in tone because they have different connotations. Similarly, both *cat* and *kitten* are close to each other denotatively, but *kitten* connotes more playfulness and cuteness than *cat.* Consider the connotations of words describing physical appearance. It is one thing to call a person *thin,* for example, but another to use such words as *skinny, gaunt, scrawny,* and *skeletal,* and still something else to say *fit, trim, svelte, slim,* and *slender.*

Through the careful choice of words, not only for denotation but also for connotation, writers control tone even though they might be describing similar or even identical situations. Let us look briefly at Cynthia Ozick's opening paragraph of "The Shawl" (Chapter 4).

> Stella, cold, cold the coldness of hell. How they walked on the roads together, Rosa with Magda curled up between sore breasts, Magda wound up in the shawl. Sometimes Stella carried Magda. But she was jealous of Magda. A thin girl of fourteen, too small, with thin breasts of her own, Stella wanted to be wrapped in a shawl, hidden away, asleep, rocked by the march, a baby, a round infant in arms. Magda took Rosa's nipple, and Rosa never stopped walking, a walking cradle. There was not enough milk; sometimes Magda sucked air; then she screamed. Stella was ravenous. Her knees were tumors on sticks, her elbows chicken bones.

This short but complex paragraph conveys a grisly close-up experience of horror during the enforced death marches of Nazi prisoners during the closing months of World War II. Many of the words here would be totally appropriate to the peaceful mothering and nurturing of an infant, but in the context of the paragraph these words dissolve into the bleakness and despair described in the passage. Stella, the thin fourteen-year-old girl who is forced to walk while carrying her infant sister, is "ravenous," a word suggesting her desperation for food, rather than "hungry," a word that connotes normal life in which meals are taken for granted. In addition, because of the march and her starved condition her knees have come to resemble "tumors on sticks" and her elbows are "chicken bones." Babies cry all the time, and the word *cry* would describe a baby under normal circumstances, but this paragraph conveys the unspeakably cruel treatment of innocent prisoners, and therefore Magda, Rosa's baby, "screamed." The brief discussion of these words shows how an author's skillful use of connotation shapes the tone of individual passages and, beyond that, of entire works.

Tone, Irony, and Style

The capacity to have more than one attitude toward someone or something is a uniquely human trait. We know that people are not perfect, but we love a number of them anyway. Therefore we speak to them not only with love and praise but also with banter and criticism. On occasion, you may have given mildly insulting greeting cards to your loved ones, not to affront them but to amuse them. You share smiles and laughs at these negative words on your cards, but at the same time you remind your loved ones of your affection.

The word **irony,** specifically **verbal irony,** describes such contradictory statements, in which one thing is said and the opposite is meant. There are important types of verbal irony. In **understatement** the expression does not fully describe the importance of a situation, and therefore makes its point by implication. For example, in Bierce's "An Occurrence at Owl Creek Bridge" (Chapter 1), the condemned man, Farquhar, contemplates the apparatus designed by the soldiers to hang him. After considering the method, Farquhar's response is described by the narrator: "The arrangement commended itself to his judgment as simple and effective" (page 72, paragraph 4). These words would be appropriate for ordinary machinery, perhaps, but because the apparatus is soon to cause Farquhar's death, the understated observation is ironic.

By contrast, in **hyperbole** or **overstatement,** the words are far in excess of the situation, and readers or listeners therefore understand that the true meaning is considerably less than what is said. An example is the priest's exaggerated dialogue with Jackie in "First Confession" (this chapter). Though the priest makes incongruously hyperbolic comments on Jackie's plans for slaughtering his grandmother, readers automatically know he means no such thing. The gulf between what is said and what is meant creates smiles and chuckles.

Often verbal irony is ambiguous, having double meaning or **double entendre.** Midway through "Young Goodman Brown" (Chapter 7), for example, the woodland guide leaves Brown alone while stating, "[W]hen you feel like moving again, there is my staff to help you along" (page 388, paragraph 40). The word "staff" is ambiguous, for it refers to the staff that resembles a serpent (page 386, paragraph 13). The word therefore suggests that the devilish guide is leaving Brown not only with a real staff but also with the spirit of evil (unlike the divine "staff" of Psalm 23:4 that gives comfort). Ambiguity of course may be used in relation to any topic. Quite often double-entendre is used in statements about sexuality, and on such occasions it is intended for the amusement of listeners or readers.

Tone, Humor, and Style

A major aspect of tone is humor and laughter. Everyone likes to laugh, and shared laughter is part of good human relationships. As common and enjoyable as laughter is, however, not many people can adequately explain why some things are funny. Even when reasons for laughter are analyzed and explained, it always seems that they do not answer all our questions. Explanation, however, is a goal worthy of pursuit. It seems that a common element in laughter is that it depends on our seeing something familiar in a new light, or encountering something surprisingly new or unique. It also seems that whenever we laugh—perhaps in the company of our friends or as a result of our reading or looking at films and television shows—we likely find that laughter is most often unplanned, personal, idiosyncratic, and unpredictable.

A primary ingredient in humor is something to laugh at—a person, thing, situation, custom, habit of speech or dialect, or arrangement of words. But once we have this ingredient we must also have *disproportion* or *incongruity;* that is, something happens or is said that violates what we might normally expect. It is such jarring juxtapositions that provide the comic newness prompting the occasion of laughter. In O'Connor's "First Confession" (this chapter), we might expect that Mrs. Ryan's discourse about enduring the agonizing pain of hellfire for all eternity might have made Jackie, the narrator, fearful. But is this what happens? Let us look:

> She lit a candle, took out a new half-crown [a valuable coin], and offered it to the first boy who would hold one finger—only one finger!—in the flame for five minutes by the school clock. Being always very ambitious I was tempted to volunteer, but I thought it might look greedy. Then she asked were we afraid of holding one finger—only one finger!—in a little candle flame for five minutes and not afraid of burning all over in roasting hot furnaces for all eternity. "All eternity! Just think of that! A whole lifetime goes by and it's nothing, not even a drop in the ocean of your sufferings." The woman was really interesting about hell, but my attention was all fixed on the half-crown. . . . (355, paragraph 5)

Jackie's response shows that Mrs. Ryan's challenge has not even dented his boyhood problems, which have nothing to do with eternal punishment. For him, punishment is a matter of things happening day by day: the "flaking" administered by his father and also the family disruptions caused by his grandmother. Eternity, for him as a little boy, is not even a remote concern. It is comparable incongruities in Jackie's responses that characterize the comic method in O'Connor's story. Situations producing laughter in most other works are not dissimilar to the situation of "First Confession," as in Orozco's "Orientation" (this chapter), in which a situation that we might expect to produce fear and alarm is treated by the speaker as though it is nothing extraordinary at all.

In addition, the language itself may be exploited for incongruity. A well-known example is the traditional stand-up comedian's statement, "One day I was walking in the local shopping mall, and I turned into a drugstore." Here the comedian causes laughter through the ambiguous meaning of "turned into," thus verbally changing an ordinary walk into a miraculously comic event. Another verbal incongruity is this one: "Barking loudly, I was awakened by my dog." Here the humor depends on the juggling of grammar: the modifier "barking loudly" is misplaced, and the resulting sentence seems to say incongruously that the speaker, and not the dog, is barking. A real-life speaker, who will be nameless here, once stated that he had trouble understanding the *"congregation* of verbs," not quite catching up to the word *conjugation*. Here the inadvertent pun creates the humor of the sentence. We laugh *at* the pun, and we also laugh *at* the speaker whose verbal mistake has produced the pun. The same speaker also described the grammatical parts of speech as "nouns, verbs, and *proverbs*." We conclude that he intended to say (maybe) either *pronouns* or *adverbs*, but somehow his understanding slipped and he created a comic incongruity. If we discover such verbal errors in a story, the author is controlling tone by directing humor against the speaker and his or her language, for the amusement of both readers and author alike.

It is such flashes of insight, or sudden revelations like these, that create the newness and spontaneity underlying humor. Indeed, the task of the writer is to develop ordinary materials to that point when spontaneity brings us to the explosiveness of laughter. This is not to say that works that you already know are not spontaneous or new. You can read O'Connor's "First Confession" and laugh, and read it again and laugh again, because even though you know what happens, the story shapes your acceptance of how Jackie maintains his natural innocence despite the fact that the older people around him, except for the priest, are pushing him to accept their own fears and anxieties. Jackie's experience is and always will be comic—and new—because it is so incongruous and so spontaneous.

Stories for Study

Kate Chopin . . . . The Story of an Hour, 331
William Faulkner. . . . . Barn Burning, 333
Ernest Hemingway. . . . . Hills Like White Elephants, 344
Alice Munro . . . . The Found Boat, 348
Frank O'Connor. . . . . First Confession, 354
Daniel Orozco . . . . Orientation, 359
John Updike . . . . A & P, 363

KATE CHOPIN (1851–1904)

Born in St. Louis, Missouri, Chopin lived in Louisiana from the time of her marriage until 1882. After her husband's death she returned to St. Louis and began to write. She published two collections of stories based on the life she had known back in Louisiana: Bayou Folk *(1894) and* A Night in Acadie *(1897). However, she became best known for her major novel,* The Awakening *(1899), which aroused negative reactions because it mentioned taboo subjects like adultery and miscegenation. Indeed, the critical disapproval was so intense that Chopin published no further works, even though she was at the height of her literary power and lived five years after the controversy.*

 ## The Story of an Hour (1894)

Knowing that Mrs. Mallard was afflicted with a heart trouble, great care was taken to break to her as gently as possible the news of her husband's death.

It was her sister Josephine who told her, in broken sentences: veiled hints that revealed in half concealing. Her husband's friend Richards was there, too, near her. It was he who had been in the newspaper office when intelligence of the railroad disaster was received, with Brently Mallard's name leading the list of "killed." He had only taken the time to assure himself of its truth by a second telegram, and had hastened to forestall any less careful, less tender friend in bearing the sad message.

She did not hear the story as many women have heard the same, with a paralyzed inability to accept its significance. She wept at once, with sudden, wild abandonment, in her sister's arms. When the storm of grief had spent itself she went away to her room alone. She would have no one follow her.

There stood, facing the open window, a comfortable, roomy armchair. Into this she sank, pressed down by a physical exhaustion that haunted her body and seemed to reach into her soul.

She could see in the open square before her house the tops of trees that were all aquiver with the new spring life. The delicious breath of rain was in the air. In the street below a peddler was crying his wares. The notes of a distant song which some one was singing reached her faintly, and countless sparrows were twittering in the eaves.

5

There were patches of blue sky showing here and there through the clouds that had met and piled one above the other in the west facing her window.

She sat with her head thrown back upon the cushion of the chair, quite motionless, except when a sob came up into her throat and shook her, as a child who has cried itself to sleep continues to sob in its dreams.

She was young, with a fair, calm face, whose lines bespoke repression and even a certain strength. But now there was a dull stare in her eyes, whose gaze was fixed away off yonder on one of those patches of blue sky. It was not a glance of reflection, but rather indicated a suspension of intelligent thought.

There was something coming to her and she was waiting for it, fearfully. What was it? She did not know; it was too subtle and elusive to name. But she felt it, creeping out of the sky, reaching toward her through the sounds, the scents, the color that filled the air.

10   Now her bosom rose and fell tumultuously. She was beginning to recognize this thing that was approaching to possess her, and she was striving to beat it back with her will—as powerless as her two white slender hands would have been.

When she abandoned herself a little whispered word escaped her slightly parted lips. She said it over and over under her breath: "free, free, free!" The vacant stare and the look of terror that had followed it went from her eyes. They stayed keen and bright. Her pulses beat fast, and the coursing blood warmed and relaxed every inch of her body.

She did not stop to ask if it were or were not a monstrous joy that held her. A clear and exalted perception enabled her to dismiss the suggestion as trivial.

She knew that she would weep again when she saw the kind, tender hands folded in death; the face that had never looked save with love upon her, fixed and gray and dead. But she saw beyond that bitter moment a long procession of years to come that would belong to her absolutely. And she opened and spread her arms out to them in welcome.

There would be no one to live for during those coming years; she would live for herself. There would be no powerful will bending hers in that blind persistence with which men and women believe they have a right to impose a private will upon a fellow-creature. A kind intention or a cruel intention made the act seem no less a crime as she looked upon it in that brief moment of illumination.

15   And yet she had loved him—sometimes. Often she had not. What did it matter! What could love, the unsolved mystery, count for in face of this possession of self-assertion which she suddenly recognized as the strongest impulse of her being!

"Free! Body and soul free!" she kept whispering.

Josephine was kneeling before the closed door with her lips to the keyhole, imploring for admission. "Louise, open the door! I beg; open the door—you will make yourself ill. What are you doing, Louise? For heaven's sake open the door."

"Go away. I am not making myself ill." No; she was drinking in a very elixir of life through that open window.

Her fancy was running riot along those days ahead of her. Spring days, and summer days, and all sorts of days that would be her own. She breathed a quick prayer that life might be long. It was only yesterday she had thought with a shudder that life might be long.

20   She arose at length and opened the door to her sister's importunities. There was a feverish triumph in her eyes, and she carried herself unwittingly like a goddess of Victory. She clasped her sister's waist, and together they descended the stairs. Richards stood waiting for them at the bottom.

Some one was opening the front door with a latchkey. It was Brently Mallard who entered, a little travel-stained, composedly carrying his grip-sack and umbrella. He had been far from the scene of the accident, and did not even know there had been one. He stood amazed at Josephine's piercing cry: at Richards' quick motion to screen him from the view of his wife.

But Richards was too late.

When the doctors came they said she had died of heart disease—of joy that kills.

QUESTIONS

1. What do we learn about Louise's husband? How has he justified her responses? How are your judgments about him controlled by the context of the story?

2. Analyze the tone of paragraph 5. How is the imagery here (and in the following paragraphs) appropriate for her developing mood?

3. What is the apparent attitude of the narrator toward the institution of marriage, and what elements of tone make this apparent?

4. What do Louise's sister and Richards have in common? How do their attitudes contribute to the irony of the story?

5. Consider the tone of the last paragraph. What judgment is being made about how men view their importance to women?

WILLIAM FAULKNER (1897–1962)

For a brief biographical note about Faulkner, see Chapter 1, page 89.

 Barn Burning (1939)

The store in which the Justice of the Peace's court was sitting smelled of cheese. The boy, crouched on his nail keg at the back of the crowded room, knew he smelled cheese, and more; from where he sat he could see the ranked shelves close-packed with the solid, squat, dynamic shapes of tin cans whose labels his stomach read, not from the lettering which meant nothing to his mind but from the scarlet devils and the silver curve of fish—this, the cheese which he knew he smelled and the hermetic meat° which his intestines believed he smelled coming in intermittent gusts momentary and brief between the other constant one, the smell and sense just a little of fear because mostly of despair and grief, the old fierce pull of blood. He could not see the table where the Justice sat and before which his father and his father's enemy (*our enemy* he thought in that despair; *ourn! mine and his both! He's my father!*) stood, but he could hear them, the two of them that is, because his father had said no word yet:

"But what proof have you, Mr. Harris?"

"I told you. The hog got into my corn. I caught it up and sent it back to him. He had no fence that would hold it. I told him so, warned him. The next time I put the hog in my pen. When he came to get it I gave him enough wire to patch up his pen. The next time I put the hog up and kept it. I rode down to his house and saw the wire I gave him still rolled on to the spool in his yard. I told him he could have the hog when he paid me a dollar pound fee. That evening a nigger came with the dollar and got the hog. He was a strange nigger. He said, 'He say to tell you wood and hay kin burn.' I said, 'What?' 'That what he say to tell you,' the nigger said. 'Wood and hay kin burn.' That night my barn burned. I got the stock out but I lost the barn."

"Where is the nigger? Have you got him?"

"He was a strange nigger, I tell you. I don't know what became of him."

"But that's not proof. Don't you see that's not proof?"

5

°*hermetic meat: canned meat.*

"Get that boy up here. He knows." For a moment the boy thought too that the man meant his older brother until Harris said. "Not him. The little one. The boy," and, crouching, small for his age, small and wiry like his father, in patched and faded jeans even too small for him, with straight, uncombed, brown hair and eyes gray and wild as storm scud, he saw the men between himself and the table part and become a lane of grim faces, at the end of which he saw the Justice, a shabby, collarless, graying man in spectacles, beckoning him. He felt no floor under his bare feet; he seemed to walk beneath the palpable weight of the grim turning faces. His father, stiff in his black Sunday coat donned not for the trial but for the moving, did not even look at him. *He aims for me to lie,* he thought, again with that frantic grief and despair. *And I will have to do hit.*

"What's your name, boy?" the Justice said.

"Colonel Sartoris Snopes," the boy whispered.

10   "Hey?" the Justice said. "Talk louder. Colonel Sartoris? I reckon anybody named for Colonel Sartoris in this country can't help but tell the truth, can they?" The boy said nothing. *Enemy! Enemy!* he thought; for a moment he could not even see, could not see that the Justice's face was kindly nor discern that his voice was troubled when he spoke to the man named Harris: "Do you want me to question this boy?" But he could hear, and during those subsequent long seconds there was absolutely no sound in the crowded little room save that of quiet and intent breathing it was as if he had swung outward at the end of a grape vine, over a ravine, and at the top of the swing had been caught in a prolonged instant of mesmerized gravity, weightless in time.

"No!" Harris said violently, explosively. "Damnation! Send him out of here!" Now time, the fluid world, rushed beneath him again, the voices coming to him again through the smell of cheese and sealed meat, the fear and despair and the old grief of blood:

"This case is closed. I can't find against you, Snopes, but I can give you advice. Leave this country and don't come back to it."

His father spoke for the first time, his voice cold and harsh, level, without emphasis: "I aim to. I don't figure to stay in a country among people who . . ." he said something unprintable and vile, addressed to no one.

"That'll do," the Justice said, "Take your wagon and get out of this country before dark. Case dismissed."

15   His father turned, and he followed the stiff black coat, the wiry figure walking a little stiffly, from where a Confederate provost's man's musket ball had taken him in the heel on a stolen horse thirty years ago, followed the two backs now, since his older brother had appeared from somewhere in the crowd, no taller than the father but thicker, chewing tobacco steadily, between the two lines of grim-faced men and out of the store and across the worn gallery and down the sagging steps and among the dogs and half-grown boys in the mild May dust, where as he passed a voice hissed:

"Barn burner!"

Again he could not see, whirling; there was a face in a red haze, moonlike, bigger than the full moon, the owner of it half again his size, he leaping in the red haze toward the face, feeling no blow, feeling no shock when his head struck the earth, scrabbling up and leaping again, feeling no blow this time either and tasting no blood, scrabbling up to see the other boy in full flight and himself already leaping into pursuit as his father's hand jerked him back, the harsh, cold voice speaking above him: "Go get in the wagon."

It stood in a grove of locusts and mulberries across the road. His two hulking sisters in their Sunday dresses and his mother and her sister in calico and sunbonnets were already in it, sitting on and among the sorry residue of the dozen and more movings which even the boy could remember—the battered stove, the broken beds and chairs, the clock inlaid with mother-of-pearl, which would not run, stopped at some fourteen minutes past two o'clock of a dead and forgotten day and time, which had been his mother's dowry. She was crying, though when she saw him she drew her sleeve across her face and began to descend from the wagon. "Get back," the father said.

"He's hurt, I got to get some water and wash his . . ."

"Get back in the wagon." his father said. He got in too, over the tail-gate. His father mounted to the seat where the older brother already sat and struck the gaunt mules two savage blows with the peeled willow, but without heat. It was not even sadistic; it was exactly that same quality which in later years would cause his descendants to over-run the engine before putting a motor car into motion, striking and reining back in the same movement. The wagon went on, the store with its quiet crowd of grimly watching men dropped behind; a curve in the road hid it. *Forever* he thought. *Maybe he's done satisfied now, now that he has . . .* stopping himself, not to say it aloud even to himself. His mother's hand touched his shoulder.

"Does hit hurt?" she said.

"Naw," he said. "Hit don't hurt. Lemme be."

"Can't you wipe some of the blood off before hit dries?"

"I'll wash tonight," he said. "Lemme be, I tell you."

The wagon went on. He did not know where they were going. None of them ever did or ever asked, because it was always somewhere, always a house of sorts waiting for them a day or two days or even three days away. Likely his father had already arranged to make a crop on another farm before he. . . . Again he had to stop himself. He (the father) always did. There was something about his wolflike independence and even courage when the advantage was at least neutral which impressed strangers, as if they got from his latent ravening ferocity not so much a sense of dependability as a feeling that his ferocious conviction in the rightness of his own actions would be of advantage to all whose interest lay with his.

That night they camped, in a grove of oaks and beeches where a spring ran. The nights were still cool and they had a fire against it, of a rail lifted from a nearby fence and cut into lengths—a small fire, neat, niggard almost, a shrewd fire; such fires were his father's habit and custom always, even in freezing weather. Older, the boy might have remarked this and wondered why not a big one; why should not a man who had not only seen the waste and extravagance of war, but who had in his blood an inherent prodigality with material not his own, have burned everything in sight? Then he might have gone a step farther and thought that that was the reason; that niggard blaze was the living fruits of nights passed during those four years in the woods hiding from all men, blue or grey, with his strings of horses (captured horses, he called them). And older still, he might have divined the true reason: that the element of fire spoke to some deep mainspring of his father's being, as the element of steel or of powder spoke to other men, as the one weapon for the preservation of integrity, else breath were not worth the breathing, and hence to be regarded with respect and used with discretion.

But he did not think this now and he had seen those same niggard blazes all his life. He merely ate his supper beside it and was already half asleep over his iron plate when his father called him, and once more he followed the stiff back, the stiff and ruthless limp, up the slope and on to the starlit road where, turning, he could see his father against the stars but without face or depth—a shape black, flat, and bloodless as though cut from tin in the iron folds of the frockcoat which had not been made for him, the voice harsh like tin and without heat like tin:

"You were fixing to tell them. You would have told him." He didn't answer. His father struck him with the flat of his hand on the side of the head, hard but without heat, exactly as he had struck the two mules at the store, exactly as he would strike either of them with any stick in order to kill a horse fly, his voice still without heat or anger: "You're getting to be a man. You got to learn. You got to learn to stick to your own blood or you ain't going to have any blood to stick to you. Do you think either of them, any man there this morning, would? Don't you know all they wanted was a chance to get at me because they knew I had them beat? Eh?" Later, twenty years later, he was to tell himself, "If I had said they wanted only truth, justice, he would have hit me again." But now he said nothing. He was not crying. He just stood there. "Answer me," his father said.

"Yes," he whispered. His father turned.

30   "Get on to bed. We'll be there tomorrow."

Tomorrow they were there. In the early afternoon the wagon stopped before a paintless two-room house identical almost with the dozen others it had stopped before even in the boy's ten years, and again, as on the other dozen occasions, his mother and aunt got down and began to unload the wagon, although his two sisters and his father and brother had not moved.

"Likely hit ain't fitten for hawgs," one of the sisters said.

"Nevertheless, fit it will and you'll hog it and like it," his father said. "Get out of them chairs and help your Ma unload."

The two sisters got down, big, bovine, in a flutter of cheap ribbons; one of them drew from the jumbled wagon bed a battered lantern, the other a worn broom. His father handed the reins to the older son and began to climb stiffly over the wheel. "When they get unloaded, take the team to the barn and feed them." Then he said, and at first the boy thought he was still speaking to his brother: "Come with me."

35   "Me?" he said.

"Yes," his father said. "You."

"Abner," his mother said. His father paused and looked back—the harsh level stare beneath the shaggy, graying, irascible brows.

"I reckon I'll have a word with the man that aims to begin tomorrow owning me body and soul for the next eight months."

They went back up the road. A week ago—or before last night, that is—he would have asked where they were going, but not now. His father had struck him before last night but never before had he paused afterward to explain why; it was as if the blow and the following calm, outrageous voice still rang, repercussed, divulging nothing to him save the terrible handicap of being young, the light weight of his few years, just heavy enough to prevent his soaring free of the world as it seemed to be ordered but not heavy enough to keep footed solid in it, to resist it and try to change the course of its events.

40   Presently he could see the grove of oaks and cedars and the other flowering trees and shrubs where the house would be, though not the house yet. They walked beside a fence massed with honeysuckle and Cherokee roses and came to a gate swinging open between two brick pillars, and now, beyond a sweep of drive, he saw the house for the first time and at that instant he forgot his father and the terror and despair both, and even when he remembered his father again (who had stopped) the terror and despair did not return. Because, for all the twelve movings, they had sojourned until now in a poor country, a land of small farms and fields and houses, and he had never seen a house like this before. *Hit's big as a courthouse* he thought quietly, with a surge of peace and joy whose reason he could not have thought into words, being too young for that: *They are safe from him. People whose lives are a part of this peace and dignity are beyond his touch, he no more to them than a buzzing wasp: capable of stinging for a little moment but that's all; the spell of this peace and dignity rendering even the barns and stable and cribs which belong to it impervious to the puny flames he might contrive . . .* this, the peace and joy, ebbing for an instant as he looked again at the stiff black back, the stiff and implacable limp of the figure which was not dwarfed by the house, for the reason that it had never looked big anywhere and which now, against the serene columned backdrop, had more than ever that impervious quality of something cut ruthlessly from tin, depthless, as though, sidewise to the sun, it would cast no shadow. Watching him, the boy remarked the absolutely undeviating course which his father held and saw the stiff foot

come squarely down in a pile of fresh droppings where a horse had stood in the drive and which his father could have avoided by a simple change of stride. But it ebbed only for a moment, though he could not have thought this into words either, walking on in the spell of the house, which he could even want but without envy, without sorrow, certainly never with that ravening and jealous rage which unknown to him walked in the ironlike black coat before him: *Maybe he will feel it too. Maybe it will even change him now from what maybe he couldn't help but be.*

They crossed the portico. Now he could hear his father's stiff foot as it came down on the boards with clocklike finality, a sound out of all proportion to the displacement of the body it bore and which was not dwarfed either by the white door before it, as though it had attained to a sort of vicious and ravening minimum not to be dwarfed by anything—the flat, wide, black hat, the formal coat of broadcloth which had once been black but which had now that friction-glazed greenish cast of the bodies of old house flies, the lifted sleeve which was too large, the lifted hand like a curled claw. The door opened so promptly that the boy knew the Negro must have been watching them all the time, an old man with neat grizzled hair, in a linen jacket, who stood barring the door with his body, saying "Wipe yo foots, white man, fo you come in here. Major ain't home nohow."

"Get out of my way, nigger," his father said, without heat too, flinging the door back and the Negro also and entering, his hat still on his head. And now the boy saw the prints of the stiff foot on the doorsill and saw them appear on the pale rug behind the machinelike deliberation of the foot which seemed to bear (or transmit) twice the weight which the body compassed. The Negro was shouting "Miss Lula! Miss Lula!" somewhere behind them, then the boy, deluged as though by a warm wave by a suave turn of carpeted stair and a pendant glitter of chandeliers and a mute gleam of gold frames, heard the swift feet and saw her too, a lady—perhaps he had never seen her like before either—in a gray, smooth gown with lace at the throat and an apron tied at the waist and the sleeves turned back, wiping cake or biscuit dough from her hands with a towel as she came up the hall, looking not at his father at all but at the tracks on the blond rug with an expression of incredulous amazement.

"I tried," the Negro cried. "I tole him to . . ."

"Will you please go away?" she said in a shaking voice. "Major de Spain is not at home. Will you please go away?"

His father had not spoken again. He did not speak again. He did not even look at her. He just stood stiff in the center of the rug, in his hat, the shaggy iron-gray brows twitching slightly above the pebble-colored eyes as he appeared to examine the house with brief deliberation. Then with the same deliberation he turned; the boy watched him pivot on the good leg and saw the stiff foot drag round the arc of the turning, leaving a final long and fading smear. His father never looked at it, he never once looked down at the rug. The Negro held the door. It closed behind them, upon the hysteric and indistinguishable woman-wail. His father stopped at the top of the steps and scraped his boot clean on the edge of it. At the gate he stopped again. He stood for a moment, planted stiffly on the stiff foot, looking back at the house. "Pretty and white, ain't it?" he said. "That's sweat. Nigger sweat. Maybe it ain't white enough yet to suit him. Maybe he wants to mix some white sweat with it." 45

Two hours later the boy was chopping wood behind the house within which his mother and aunt and the two sisters (the mother and aunt, not the two girls, he knew that; even at this distance and muffled by walls the flat loud voices of the two girls emanated an incorrigible idle inertia) were setting up the stove to prepare a meal, when he heard the hooves and saw the linen-clad man on a fine sorrel mare, whom he recognized even before he saw the rolled rug in front of the Negro youth following on a fat bay carriage horse—a suffused, angry face vanishing, still at full gallop, beyond the corner of the house where his father and brother were sitting in the two tilted chairs; and a moment later, almost before he could have put the axe down, he heard the hooves again and watched the sorrel mare go back out of the yard, already galloping again. Then his father began to shout one of the sisters' names, who presently emerged backward from the kitchen door dragging the rolled rug along the ground by one end while the other sister walked behind it.

"If you ain't going to tote, go on and set up the wash pot," the first said.

"You, Sarty!" the second shouted. "Set up the wash pot!" His father appeared at the door, framed against that shabbiness, as he had been against that other bland perfection, impervious to either, the mother's anxious face at his shoulder.

"Go on," the father said. "Pick it up." The two sisters stooped, broad, lethargic; stooping, they presented an incredible expanse of pale cloth and a flutter of tawdry ribbons.

50   "If I thought enough of a rug to have to git hit all the way from France I wouldn't keep hit where folks coming in would have to tromp on hit," the first said. They raised the rug.

"Abner," the mother said. "Let me do it."

"You go back and git dinner," his father said. "I'll tend to this."

From the woodpile through the rest of the afternoon the boy watched them, the rug spread flat in the dust beside the bubbling wash pot, the two sisters stooping over it with that profound and lethargic reluctance, while the father stood over them in turn, implacable and grim, driving them though never raising his voice again. He could smell the harsh homemade lye they were using; he saw his mother come to the door once and look toward them with an expression not anxious now but very like despair; he saw his father turn, and he fell to with the axe and saw from the corner of his eye his father raise from the ground a flattish fragment of field stone and examine it and return to the pot, and this time his mother actually spoke: "Abner. Abner. Please don't. Please, Abner."

Then he was done too. It was dusk; the whippoorwills had already begun. He could smell coffee from the room where they would presently eat the cold food remaining from the mid-afternoon meal, though when he entered the house he realized they were having coffee again because there was a fire on the hearth, before which the rug now lay spread over the backs of the two chairs. The tracks of his father's foot were gone. Where they had been were now long, water-cloudy scoriations resembling the sporadic course of a Lilliputian mowing machine.

55   It still hung there while they ate the cold food and then went to bed, scattered without order or claim up and down the two rooms, his mother in one bed, where his father would later lie, the older brother in the other, himself, the aunt, and the two sisters on pallets on the floor. But his father was not in bed yet. The last thing the boy remembered was the depthless, harsh silhouette of the hat and coat bending over the rug and it seemed to him that he had not even closed his eyes when the silhouette was standing over him, the fire almost dead behind it, the stiff foot prodding him awake. "Catch up the mule," his father said.

When he returned with the mule his father was standing in the black door, the rolled rug over his shoulder. "Ain't you going to ride?" he said.

"No. Give me your foot."

He bent his knee into his father's hand, the wiry, surprising power flowed smoothly, rising, he rising with it, on to the mule's bare back (they had owned a saddle once; the boy could remember it though not when or where) and with the same effortlessness his father swung the rug up in front of him. Now in the starlight they retraced the afternoon's path, up the dusty road rife with honeysuckle, through the gate and up the black tunnel of the drive to the lightless house, where he sat on the mule and felt the rough warp of the rug drag across his thighs and vanish.

"Don't you want me to help?" he whispered. His father did not answer and now he heard again that stiff foot striking the hollow portico with that wooden and clocklike deliberation, that outrageous overstatement of the weight it carried. The rug, hunched, not flung (the boy could tell that even in the darkness) from his father's shoulder, struck the angle of wall and floor with a sound unbelievably loud, thunderous, then the foot again, unhurried and enormous; a light came on in the house and the boy sat, tense, breathing steadily and quietly and just a little fast, though the foot itself did not increase its beat at all, descending the steps now; now the boy could see him.

"Don't you want to ride now?" he whispered. "We kin both ride now," the light within   60 the house altering now, flaring up and sinking. *He's coming down the stairs now,* he thought. He had already ridden the mule up beside the horse block; presently his father was up behind him and he doubled the reins over and slashed the mule across the neck, but before the animal could begin to trot the hard, thin arm came round him, the hard, knotted hand jerking the mule back to a walk.

In the first red rays of the sun they were in the lot, putting plow gear on the mules. This time the sorrel mare was in the lot before he heard it at all, the rider collarless and even bareheaded, trembling, speaking in a shaking voice as the woman in the house had done, his father merely looking up once before stooping again to the hame he was buckling, so that the man on the mare spoke to his stooping back:

"You must realize you have ruined that rug. Wasn't there anybody here, any of your women . . ." He ceased, shaking, the boy watching him, the older brother leaning now in the stable door, chewing, blinking slowly and steadily at nothing apparently. "It cost a hundred dollars. But you never had a hundred dollars. You never will. So I'm going to charge you twenty bushels of corn against your crop. I'll add it in your contract and when you come to the commissary you can sign it. That won't keep Mrs. de Spain quiet but maybe it will teach you to wipe your feet off before you enter her house again."

Then he was gone. The boy looked at his father, who still had not spoken or even looked up again, who was now adjusting the logger-head in the hame.

"Pap," he said. His father looked at him—the inscrutable face, the shaggy brows beneath which the gray eyes glinted coldly. Suddenly the boy went toward him, fast, stopping as suddenly. "You done the best you could!" he cried. "If he wanted hit done different why didn't he wait and tell you how? He won't git no twenty bushels! He won't git none! We'll get hit and hide hit! I kin watch . . ."

"Did you put the cutter back in that straight stock like I told you?"   65

"No, sir," he said.

"Then go do it."

That was Wednesday. During the rest of that week he worked steadily, at what was within his scope and some which was beyond it, with an industry that did not need to be driven nor even commanded twice; he had this from his mother, with the difference that some at least of what he did he liked to do, such as splitting wood with the half-size axe which his mother and aunt had earned, or saved money somehow, to present him with at Christmas. In company with the two older women (and on one afternoon even one of the sisters), he built pens for the shoat and the cow which were a part of his father's contract with the landlord, and one afternoon, his father being absent, gone somewhere on one of the mules, he went to the field.

They were running a middle buster now, his brother holding the plow straight while he handled the reins, and walking beside the straining mule, the rich black soil shearing cool and damp against his bare ankles, he thought *Maybe this is the end of it. Maybe even that twenty bushels that seems hard to have to pay for just a rug will be a cheap price for him to stop forever and always from being what he used to be;* thinking, dreaming now, so that his brother had to speak sharply to him to mind the mule: *Maybe he even won't collect the twenty bushels. Maybe it will all add up and balance and vanish—corn, rug, fire; the terror and grief, the being pulled two ways like between two teams of horses—gone, done with forever and ever.*

70 Then it was Saturday; he looked up from beneath the mule he was harnessing and saw his father in the black coat and hat. "Not that," his father said. "The wagon gear." And then, two hours later, sitting in the wagon bed behind his father and brother on the seat, the wagon accomplished a final curve, and he saw the weathered paintless store with its tattered tobacco- and patent-medicine posters and the tethered wagons and saddle animals below the gallery. He mounted the gnawed steps behind his father and brother, and there again was the lane of quiet, watching faces for the three of them to walk through. He saw the man in spectacles sitting at the plank table and he did not need to be told this was a Justice of the Peace; he sent one glare of fierce, exultant, partisan defiance at the man in collar and cravat now, whom he had seen but twice in his life, and that on a galloping horse, who now wore on his face an expression not of rage but of amazed unbelief which the boy could not have known was at the incredible circumstance of being sued by one of his own tenants, and came and stood against his father and cried at the Justice: "He ain't done it! He ain't burnt . . ."

"Go back to the wagon," his father said.

"Burnt?" the Justice said. "Do I understand this rug was burned too?"

"Does anybody here claim it was?" his father said. "Go back to the wagon." But he did not, he merely retreated to the rear of the room, crowded as that other had been, but not to sit down this time, instead, to stand pressing among the motionless bodies, listening to the voices:

"And you claim twenty bushels of corn is too high for the damage you did to the rug?"

75 "He brought the rug to me and said he wanted the tracks washed out of it. I washed the tracks out and took the rug back to him."

"But you didn't carry the rug back to him in the same condition it was in before you made the tracks on it."

His father did not answer, and now for perhaps half a minute there was no sound at all save that of breathing, the faint, steady suspiration of complete and intent listening.

"You decline to answer that, Mr. Snopes?" Again his father did not answer. "I'm going to find against you, Mr. Snopes. I'm going to find that you were responsible for the injury to Major de Spain's rug and hold you liable for it. But twenty bushels of corn seems a little high for a man in your circumstances to have to pay. Major de Spain claims it cost a hundred dollars. October corn will be worth about fifty cents. I figure that if Major de Spain can stand a ninety-five-dollar loss on something he paid cash for, you can stand a five-dollar loss you haven't earned yet. I hold you in damages to Major de Spain to the amount of ten bushels of corn over and above your contract with him, to be paid to him out of your crop at gathering time. Court adjourned."

It had taken no time hardly, the morning was but half begun. He thought they would return home and perhaps back to the field, since they were late, far behind all other farmers. But instead his father passed on behind the wagon, merely indicating with his hand for the older brother to follow with it, and crossed the road toward the blacksmith shop opposite, pressing on after his father, overtaking him, speaking, whispering up at the harsh, calm face beneath the weathered hat: "He won't git no ten bushels neither. He won't git one. We'll . . ." until his father glanced for an instant down on him, the face absolutely calm, the grizzled eyebrows tangled above the cold eyes, the voice almost pleasant, almost gentle:

80 "You think so? Well, we'll wait till October anyway."

The matter of the wagon—the setting of a spoke or two and the tightening of the tires—did not take long either, the business of the tires accomplished by driving the wagon into the spring branch behind the shop and letting it stand there, the mules nuzzling into the water from time to time, and the boy on the seat with the idle reins, looking up the slope and through the sooty tunnel of the shed where the slow hammer rang and where his father sat on an upended cypress bolt, easily, either talking or listening, still sitting there when the boy brought the dripping wagon up out of the branch and halted it before the door.

"Take them on to the shade and hitch," his father said. He did so and returned. His father and the smith and a third man squatting on his heels inside the door were talking, about crops and animals; the boy, squatting too in the ammoniac dust and hoof-parings and scales of rust, heard his father tell a long and unhurried story out of the time before the birth of the older brother even when he had been a professional horse-trader. And then his father came up beside him where he stood before a tattered last year's circus poster on the other side of the store, gazing rapt and quiet at the scarlet horses, the incredible poisings and convolutions of tulle and tights and the painted leers of comedians, and said, "It's time to eat."

But not at home. Squatting beside his brother against the front wall, he watched his father emerge from the store and produce from a paper sack a segment of cheese and divided it carefully and deliberately into three with his pocket knife and produce crackers from the same sack. They all three squatted on the gallery and ate slowly, without talking; then in the store again, they drank from a tin dipper tepid water smelling of the cedar bucket and of living beech trees. And still they did not go home. It was a horse lot this time, a tall rail fence upon and along which men stood and sat and out of which one by one horses were led, to be walked and trotted and then cantered back and forth along the road while the slow swapping and buying went on and the sun began to slant westward, they—the three of them—watching and listening, the older brother with his muddy eyes and his steady inevitable tobacco, the father commenting now and then on certain of the animals, to no one in particular.

It was after sundown when they reached home. They ate supper by lamplight, then, sitting on the doorstep, the boy watched the night fully accomplish, listening to the whippoorwills and the frogs, when he heard his mother's voice: "Abner! No! No! Oh, God, Oh, God, Abner!" and he rose, whirled, and saw the altered light through the door where a candle stub now burned in a bottle neck on the table and his father, still in the hat and coat, at once formal and burlesque as though dressed carefully for some shabby and ceremonial violence, emptying the reservoir of the lamp back into the five-gallon kerosene can from which it had been filled, while the mother tugged at his arm until he shifted the lamp to the other hand and flung her back, not savagely or viciously, just hard, into the wall, her hands flung out against the wall for balance, her mouth open and in her face the same quality of hopeless despair as had been in her voice. Then his father saw him standing in the door.

"Go to the barn and get that can of oil we were oiling the wagon with," he said. The boy did not move. Then he could speak.   85

"What . . ." he cried. "What are you . . ."

"Go get that oil," his father said. "Go."

Then he was moving, running, outside the house, toward the stable: this the old habit, the old blood which he had not been permitted to choose for himself, which had been bequeathed him willy nilly and which had run for so long (and who knew where, battening on what of outrage and savagery and lust) before it came to him. *I could keep on,* he thought. *I could run on and on and never look back, never need to see his face again. Only I can't. I can't,* the rusted can in his hand now, the liquid sloshing in it as he ran back to the house and into it, into the sound of his mother's weeping in the next room, and handed the can to his father.

"Ain't you going to even send a nigger?" he cried. "At least you sent a nigger before!"

This time his father didn't strike him. The hand came even faster than the blow had, the   90
same hand which had set the can on the table with almost excruciating care flashing from the can toward him too quick for him to follow it, gripping him by the back of his shirt and on to tiptoe before he had seen it quit the can, the face stooping at him in breathless and frozen ferocity, the cold, dead voice speaking over him to the older brother who leaned against the table, chewing with that steady, curious, sidewise motion of cows:

"Empty the can into the big one and go on. I'll catch up with you."

"Better tie him up to the bedpost," the brother said.

"Do like I told you," the father said. Then the boy was moving, his bunched shirt and the hard, bony hand between his shoulder-blades, his toes just touching the floor, across the room and into the other one, past the sisters sitting with spread heavy thighs in the two chairs over the cold hearth, and to where his mother and aunt sat side by side on the bed, the aunt's arms about the mother's shoulders.

"Hold him," the father said. The aunt made a startled movement. "Not you," the father said. "Lennie. Take hold of him. I want to see you do it." His mother took him by the wrist. "You'll hold him better than that. If he gets loose don't you know what he is going to do? He will go up yonder." He jerked his head toward the road. "Maybe I'd better tie him."

95   "I'll hold him," his mother whispered.

"See you do then." Then his father was gone, the stiff foot heavy and measured upon the boards, ceasing at last.

Then he began to struggle. His mother caught him in both arms, he jerking and wrenching at them. He would be stronger in the end, he knew that. But he had not time to wait for it. "Lemme go!" he cried. "I don't want to have to hit you!"

"Let him go!" the aunt said. "If he don't go, before God, I am going up there myself!"

"Don't you see I can't?" his mother cried. "Sarty! Sarty! No! No! Help me, Lizzie!"

100   Then he was free. His aunt grasped at him but it was too late. He whirled, running, his mother stumbled forward on to her knees behind him, crying to the nearer sister: "Catch him, Net! Catch him!" But that was too late too, the sister (the sisters were twins, born at the same time, yet either of them now gave the impression of being, encompassing as much living meat and volume and weight as any other two of the family) not yet having begun to rise from the chair, her head, face, alone merely turned, presenting to him in the flying instant an astonishing expanse of young female features untroubled by any surprise even, wearing only an expression of bovine interest. Then he was out of the room, out of the house, in the mild dust of the starlit road and the heavy rifeness of honeysuckle, the pale ribbon unspooling with terrific slowness under his running feet, reaching the gate at last and turning in, running, his heart and lungs drumming, on up the drive toward the lighted house, the lighted door. He did not knock, he burst in, sobbing for breath, incapable for the moment of speech; he saw the astonished face of the Negro in the linen jacket without knowing when the Negro had appeared.

"De Spain!" he cried, panted. "Where's . . ." then he saw the white man too emerging from a white door down the hall. "Barn!" he cried. "Barn!"

"What?" the white man said. "Barn?"

"Yes!" the boy cried. "Barn!"

"Catch him!" the white man shouted.

105   But it was too late this time too. The Negro grasped his shirt, but the entire sleeve, rotten with washing, carried away, and he was out that door too and in the drive again, and had actually never ceased to run even while he was screaming into the white man's face.

Behind him the white man was shouting. "My horse! Fetch my horse!" and he thought for an instant of cutting across the park and climbing the fence into the road, but he did not know the park nor how high the vine-massed fence might be and he dared not risk it. So he ran on down the drive, blood and breath roaring; presently he was in the road again though he could not see it. He could not hear either: the galloping mare was almost upon him before he heard her, and even then he held his course, as if the very urgency of his wild grief and need must in a moment more find him wings, waiting until the ultimate instant to hurl himself aside and into the weed-choked roadside ditch as the horse thundered past and on, for an instant in furious silhouette against the stars, the tranquil early summer night sky which, even before the shape of the horse and rider vanished, strained abruptly and violently upward: a long, swirling roar incredible and soundless, blotting the stars, and he springing up and into the road again, running again, knowing it was too late yet still running even after he heard the shot and, an instant later, two shots, pausing now without knowing he had ceased to run, crying "Pap! Pap!," running again before he knew he had begun to run, stumbling, tripping over something and scrabbling up again without ceasing to run, looking backward over his shoulder at the glare as he got up, running on among the invisible trees, panting, sobbing, "Father! Father!"

At midnight he was sitting on the crest of a hill. He did not know it was midnight and he did not know how far he had come. But there was no glare behind him now and he sat now, his back toward what he had called home for four days anyhow, his face toward the dark woods which he would enter when breath was strong again, small, shaking steadily in the chill darkness, hugging himself into the remainder of his thin, rotten shirt, the grief and despair now no longer terror and fear but just grief and despair. *Father. My father*, he thought. "He was brave!" he cried suddenly, aloud but not loud, no more than a whisper: "He was! He was in the war! He was in Colonel Sartoris' cav'ry!" not knowing that his father had gone to that war a private in the fine old European sense, wearing no uniform, admitting the authority of and giving fidelity to no man or army or flag, going to war as Malbrouck° himself did: for booty—it meant nothing and less than nothing to him if it were enemy booty or his own.

The slow constellations wheeled on. It would be dawn and then sun-up after a while and he would be hungry. But that would be tomorrow and now he was only cold, and walking would cure that. His breathing was easier now and he decided to get up and go on, and then he found that he had been asleep because he knew it was almost dawn, the night almost over. He could tell that from the whippoorwills. They were everywhere now among the dark trees below him, constant and inflectioned and ceaseless, so that, as the instant for giving over to the day birds drew nearer and nearer, there was no interval at all between them. He got up. He was a little stiff, but walking would cure that too as it would the cold, and soon there would be the sun. He went on down the hill, toward the dark woods within which the liquid silver voices of the birds called unceasing—the rapid and urgent beating of the urgent and quiring heart of the late spring night. He did not look back.

QUESTIONS

1. Discuss the style and tone of the final paragraph of "Barn Burning." What does it tell you about Sarty's location and the time of day? How do Faulkner's descriptions suggest that Sarty is embarking on a new phase of his life? Why does Faulkner conclude the paragraph—and the story—with the sentence "He did not look back"?

2. In the Bible, 2 Samuel, Chapter 2 and 3, Abner, the cousin of King Saul, is a powerful commander, warrior, and king maker. He is loyal to the son of King Saul and fights against the supporters of King David. Abner's death makes it possible for David to become uncontested ruler. Why do you think that Faulkner chose the name Abner for the father of the Snopes family? What actions of Abner Snopes make him seem heroic? Antiheroic? Why?

3. When and where is the story occurring? How does Faulkner convey this information to you?

4. Describe the characters of Sarty's mother and sisters. What do you learn about them? To what extent do any of them exhibit growth or development?

5. At the story's end, who is the rider of the horse? Who fires the three shots? Why does Faulkner not tell us the result of the shooting? (In Book I of *The Hamlet*, Faulkner explains that Abner and his other son, Flem, escape.)

°*Malbrouck:* hero of an old French ballad (*Malbrouck s'en va-t-en guerre*). The original Malbrouck, the English Duke of Marlborough (1650–1722) had been accused of profiteering during the War of the Spanish Succession (1702–1713).

ERNEST HEMINGWAY° (1899–1961)

Hemingway was born in Illinois. During World War I he served in the Ambulance Corps in France, where he was wounded. In the 1920s he published The Sun Also Rises *(1926) and* A Farewell to Arms *(1929), and the resulting critical fame made him a major literary celebrity. He developed a sparse style, in keeping with the elemental, stark lives of the characters he depicted. "Hills Like White Elephants," from the collection* Men Without Women *(1927), typifies that pared, annealed style. Of particular note in this story is the way in which Hemingway, by carefully controlling the various speeches of his two characters without providing any extra prose guidance, enables readers clearly to identify the speakers and to follow their interests about the topics of concern.*

 ## Hills Like White Elephants (1927)

The hills across the valley of the Ebro° were long and white. On this side there was no shade and no trees and the station was between two lines of rails in the sun. Close against the side of the station there was the warm shadow of the building and a curtain, made of strings of bamboo beads, hung across the open door into the bar, to keep out flies. The American and the girl with him sat at a table in the shade, outside the building. It was very hot and the express from Barcelona would come in forty minutes. It stopped at this junction for two minutes and went on to Madrid.

"What should we drink?" the girl asked. She had taken off her hat and put it on the table.

"It's pretty hot," the man said.

"Let's drink beer."

5   "Dos cervezas," the man said into the curtain.

"Big ones?" a woman asked° from the doorway.

"Yes. Two big ones."

The woman brought two glasses of beer and two felt pads. She put the felt pads and the beer glasses on the table and looked at the man and the girl. The girl was looking off at the line of hills. They were white in the sun and the country was brown and dry.

"They look like white elephants," she said.

10   "I've never seen one," the man drank his beer.

"No, you wouldn't have."

"I might have," the man said. "Just because you say I wouldn't have doesn't prove anything."

The girl looked at the bead curtain. "They've painted something on it," she said. "What does it say?"

"Anis del Toro. It's a drink."

15   "Could we try it?"

The man called "Listen" through the curtain. The woman came out from the bar.

°Hills Like White Elephants by Ernest Hemingway is reprinted with the permission of Scribner, an imprint of Simon & Schuster Adult Publishing Group, from *The Short Stories of Ernest Hemingway*. Copyright 1927 by Charles Scribner's Sons. Copyright renewed © 1955 by Ernest Hemingway. All rights reserved.
°*Ebro*: a river in Spain.
°*a woman asked*: The waitress speaks in Spanish. The American man understands Spanish, but the girl does not. The man therefore translates for her throughout the story, when necessary.

"Four reales."°

"We want two Anis del Toro."

"With water?"

"Do you want it with water?"

"I don't know," the girl said. "Is it good with water?"   20

"It's all right."

"You want them with water?" asked the woman.

"Yes, with water."

"It tastes like licorice," the girl said and put the glass down.

"That's the way with everything."   25

"Yes," said the girl. "Everything tastes of licorice. Especially all the things you've waited so long for, like absinthe."

"Oh, cut it out."

"You started it," the girl said. "I was being amused. I was having a fine time."

"Well, let's try and have a fine time."   30

"All right. I was trying. I said the mountains looked like white elephants. Wasn't that bright?"

"That was bright."

"I wanted to try this new drink. That's all we do, isn't it—look at things and try new drinks?"

"I guess so."

The girl looked across at the hills.   35

"They're lovely hills," she said. "They don't really look like white elephants. I just meant the coloring of their skin through the trees."

"Should we have another drink?"

"All right."

The warm wind blew the bead curtain against the table.

"The beer's nice and cool," the man said.

"It's lovely," the girl said.   40

"It's really an awfully simple operation, Jig," the man said. "It's not really an operation at all."

The girl looked at the ground the table legs rested on.

"I know you wouldn't mind it, Jig. It's really not anything. It's just to let the air in."

The girl did not say anything.   45

"I'll go with you and I'll stay with you all the time. They just let the air in and then it's all perfectly natural."

"Then what will we do afterward?"

"We'll be fine afterward. Just like we were before."

"What makes you think so?"

"That's the only thing that bothers us. It's the only thing that's made us unhappy."   50

The girl looked at the bead curtain, put her hand out and took hold of two of the strings of beads.

"And you think then we'll be all right and be happy."

"I know we will. You don't have to be afraid. I've known lots of people that have done it."

"So have I," said the girl. "And afterward they were all so happy."

"Well," the man said, "if you don't want to you don't have to. I wouldn't have you do it   55
if you didn't want to. But I know it's perfectly simple."

"And you really want to?"

"I think it's the best thing to do. But I don't want you to do it if you don't really want to."

°*reales:* A *real* was a silver Spanish coin.

"And if I do it you'll be happy and things will be like they were and you'll love me?"

"I love you now. You know I love you."

60   "I know. But if I do it, then it will be nice again if I say things are like white elephants, and you'll like it?"

"I'll love it. I love it now but I just can't think about it. You know how I get when I worry."

"If I do it you won't ever worry?"

"I won't worry about that because it's perfectly simple."

"Then I'll do it. Because I don't care about me."

65   "What do you mean?"

"I don't care about me."

"Well, I care about you."

"Oh, yes. But I don't care about me. And I'll do it and then everything will be fine."

"I don't want you to do it if you feel that way."

70   The girl stood up and walked to the end of the station. Across, on the other side, were fields of grain and trees along the banks of the Ebro. Far away, beyond the river, were mountains. The shadow of a cloud moved across the field of grain and she saw the river through the trees.

"And we could have all this," she said. "And we could have everything and every day we make it more impossible."

"What did you say?"

"I said we could have everything."

"We can have everything."

75   "No, we can't."

"We can have the whole world."

"No, we can't."

"We can go everywhere."

"No, we can't. It isn't ours any more."

80   "It's ours."

"No, it isn't. And once they take it away, you never get it back."

"But they haven't taken it away."

"We'll wait and see."

"Come on back in the shade," he said. "You mustn't feel that way."

85   "I don't feel any way," the girl said. "I just know things."

"I don't want you to do anything that you don't want to do—"

"Nor that isn't good for me," she said. "I know. Could we have another beer?"

"All right. But you've got to realize—"

"I realize," the girl said. "Can't we maybe stop talking?"

90   They sat down at the table and the girl looked across at the hills on the dry side of the valley and the man looked at her and at the table.

"You've got to realize," he said, "that I don't want you to do it if you don't want to. I'm perfectly willing to go through with it if it means anything to you."

"Doesn't it mean anything to you? We could get along."

"Of course it does. But I don't want anybody but you. I don't want any one else. And I know it's perfectly simple."

"Yes, you know it's perfectly simple."

95   "It's all right for you to say that, but I do know it."

"Would you do something for me now?"

"I'd do anything for you."

"Would you please please please please please please please stop talking?"

He did not say anything but looked at the bags against the wall of the station. There were labels on them from all the hotels where they had spent nights.

100   "But I don't want you to," he said, "I don't care anything about it."

"I'll scream," the girl said.

The woman came out through the curtains with two glasses of beer and put them down on the damp felt pads. "The train comes in five minutes," she said.

"What did she say?" asked the girl.

"That the train is coming in five minutes."

The girl smiled brightly at the woman, to thank her. 105

"I'd better take the bags over to the other side of the station," the man said. She smiled at him.

"All right. Then come back and we'll finish the beer."

He picked up the two heavy bags and carried them around the station to the other tracks. He looked up the tracks but could not see the train. Coming back, he walked through the barroom, where people waiting for the train were drinking. He drank an Anis at the bar and looked at the people. They were all waiting reasonably for the train. He went out through the bead curtain. She was sitting at the table and smiled at him.

"Do you feel better?" he asked.

"I feel fine," she said. "There's nothing wrong with me. I feel fine." 110

QUESTIONS

1. Who are the major characters in this story? What is the principal problem that they are facing? What does "Jig" want to do? What does "the American" want her to do?

2. What are her responses to his wishes? In what ways can you determine what her wishes are? What is happening to her judgment about the American?

3. Describe Hemingway's handling of the dialogue. Stylistically, how does Hemingway make it plain who is speaking, without the many "he said" and "she said" statements that you might find in other stories?

4. Why does the American stop in the station barroom to have another Anis, to which "Jig" has voiced what seems to be an objection?

5. What evidence do you find in the dialogue about the relationship between the American and "Jig" before the story has opened? Explain Hemingway's use of irony in Jig's speeches after paragraph 53. How do the speeches of Jig and the American let you know about their attitudes toward the future of their relationship? How does Jig seem to be growing psychologically as the story unfolds? How believable is her final statement, that she "feels fine"?

ALICE MUNRO (b. 1931)

Munro, who is a writer almost exclusively of short stories, grew up in Western Ontario, twenty miles east of Lake Huron—the approximate geographic locale of "The Found Boat." She received her higher education at the University of Western Ontario, after which she married and moved to British Columbia, where she began her writing career. Her first collection was Dance of the Happy Shades *(1968), followed three years later by the novelistic* Lives of Girls and Women. *Later volumes are* Something I've Been Meaning to Tell You *(1974),* The Beggar Maid *(1978),* The Moons of Jupiter *(1982),* The Progress of Love *(1986),* Friend of My Youth *(1990),* Open Secrets *(1995),* Selected Stories *(1997),* The Love of a Good Woman *(1998),* Hateship, Friendship, Courtship, Loveship, Marriage: Stories *(2002),* Runaway *(2004),* The View from Castle Rock *(2006), and* Carried Away *(2006, 2008). Her stories are mainly regional and have a realistic basis in her own experiences. The stories are not autobiographical, however; her characters and*

their actions develop out of her powerful imagination and strong sympathy and compassion. Recipient of Canada's Governor-General's Award for her very first work, she has merited additional honors throughout her full and distinguished career. Among her honors is the 1999 National Book Critics Circle Fiction Prize for The Love of a Good Woman. *In 2004* The New York Times *named* Runaway *one of the ten best books of 2004. In 2005* Time *named her one of the world's most influential people.*

🍁 The Found Boat (1974)

At the end of Bell Street, McKay Street, Mayo Street, there was the Flood. It was the Wawanash River, which every spring overflowed its banks. Some springs, say one in every five, it covered the roads on that side of town and washed over the fields, creating a shallow choppy lake. Light reflected off the water made everything bright and cold, as it is in a lakeside town, and woke or revived in people certain vague hopes of disaster. Mostly during the late afternoon and early evening, there were people straggling out to look at it, and discuss whether it was still rising, and whether this time it might invade the town. In general, those under fifteen and over sixty-five were most certain that it would.

Eva and Carol rode out on their bicycles. They left the road—it was the end of Mayo Street, past any houses—and rode right into a field, over a wire fence entirely flattened by the weight of the winter's snow. They coasted a little way before the long grass stopped them, then left their bicycles lying down and went to the water.

"We have to find a log and ride on it," Eva said.

"Jesus, we'll freeze our legs off."

5   "Jesus, we'll freeze our legs off!" said one of the boys who were there too at the water's edge. He spoke in a sour whine, the way boys imitated girls although it was nothing like the way girls talked. These boys—there were three of them—were all in the same class as Eva and Carol at school and were known to them by name (their names being Frank, Bud and Clayton), but Eva and Carol, who had seen and recognized them from the road, had not spoken to them or looked at them or, even yet, given any sign of knowing they were there. The boys seemed to be trying to make a raft, from lumber they had salvaged from the water.

Eva and Carol took off their shoes and socks and waded in. The water was so cold it sent pain up their legs, like blue electric sparks shooting through their veins, but they went on, pulling their skirts high, tight behind and bunched so they could hold them in front.

"Look at the fat-assed ducks in wading."

"Fat-assed fucks."

Eva and Carol, of course, gave no sign of hearing this. They laid hold of a log and climbed on, taking a couple of boards floating in the water for paddles. There were always things floating around in the Flood—branches, fence-rails, logs, road signs, old lumber; sometimes boilers, washtubs, pots and pans, or even a car seat or stuffed chair, as if somewhere the Flood had got into a dump.

10   They paddled away from shore, heading out into the cold lake. The water was perfectly clear, they could see the brown grass swimming along the bottom. Suppose it was the sea, thought Eva. She thought of drowned cities and countries. Atlantis. Suppose they were riding in a Viking boat—Viking boats on the Atlantic were more frail and narrow than this log on the Flood—and they had miles of clear sea beneath them, then a spired city, intact as a jewel irretrievable on the ocean floor.

"This is a Viking boat," she said. "I am the carving on the front." She stuck her chest out and stretched her neck, trying to make a curve, and she made a face, putting out her tongue. Then she turned and for the first time took notice of the boys.

"Hey, you sucks!" she yelled at them. "You'd be scared to come out here, this water is ten feet deep!"

"Liar," they answered without interest, and she was.

They steered the log around a row of trees, avoiding floating barbed wire, and got into a little bay created by a natural hollow of the land. Where the bay was now, there would be a pond full of frogs later in the spring, and by the middle of summer there would be no water visible at all, just a low tangle of reeds and bushes, green, to show that mud was still wet around their roots. Larger bushes, willows, grew around the steep bank of this pond and were still partly out of the water. Eva and Carol let the log ride in. They saw a place where something was caught.

It was a boat, or part of one. An old rowboat with most of one side ripped out, the board   15
that had been the seat just dangling. It was pushed up among the branches, lying on what would have been its side, if it had a side, the prow caught high.

Their idea came to them without consultation, at the same time:

"You guys! Hey, you guys!"

"We found you a boat!"

"Stop building your stupid raft and come and look at the boat!"

What surprised them in the first place was that the boys really did come, scrambling   20
overland, half running, half sliding down the bank, wanting to see.

"Hey, where?"

"Where is it. I don't see no boat."

What surprised them in the second place was that when the boys did actually see what boat was meant, this old flood-smashed wreck held up in the branches, they did not understand that they had been fooled, that a joke had been played on them. They did not show a moment's disappointment, but seemed as pleased at the discovery as if the boat had been whole and new. They were already barefoot, because they had been wading in the water to get lumber, and they waded in here without a stop, surrounding the boat and appraising it and paying no attention even of an insulting kind to Eva and Carol who bobbed up and down on their log. Eva and Carol had to call to them.

"How do you think you're going to get it off?"

"It won't float anyway."   25

"What makes you think it will float?"

"It'll sink. Glub-blub-blub, you'll all be drownded."

The boys did not answer, because they were too busy walking around the boat, pulling at it in a testing way to see how it could be got off with the least possible damage. Frank, who was the most literate, talkative and inept of the three, began referring to the boat as *she*, an affectation which Eva and Carol acknowledged with fish-mouths of contempt.

"She's caught two places. You got to be careful not to tear a hole in her bottom. She's heavier than you'd think."

It was Clayton who climbed up and freed the boat, and Bud, a tall fat boy, who got the   30
weight of it on his back to turn it into the water so that they could half float, half carry it to shore. All this took some time. Eva and Carol abandoned their log and waded out of the water. They walked overland to get their shoes and socks and bicycles. They did not need to come back this way but they came. They stood at the top of the hill, leaning on their bicycles. They did not go on home, but they did not sit down and frankly watch, either. They stood more or less facing each other, but glancing down at the water and at the boys struggling with the boat, as if they had just halted for a moment out of curiosity, and staying longer than they intended, to see what came of this unpromising project.

About nine o'clock, or when it was nearly dark—dark to people inside the houses, but not quite dark outside—they all returned to town, going along Mayo Street in a sort of procession. Frank and Bud and Clayton came carrying the boat, upside-down, and Eva and Carol walked behind, wheeling their bicycles. The boys' heads were almost hidden in the darkness of the overturned boat, with its smell of soaked wood, cold swampy water. The girls could look ahead and see the street lights in their tin reflectors, a necklace of lights climbing Mayo Street, reaching all the way up to the standpipe. They turned onto Burns Street heading for Clayton's house, the nearest house belonging to any of them. This was not the way home for Eva or for Carol either, but they followed along. The boys were perhaps too busy carrying the boat to tell them to go away. Some younger children were still out playing, playing hopscotch on the sidewalk though they could hardly see. At this time of year the bare sidewalk was still such a novelty and delight. These children cleared out of the way and watched the boat go by with unwilling respect; they shouted questions after it, wanting to know where it came from and what was going to be done with it. No one answered them. Eva and Carol as well as the boys refused to answer or even look at them.

The five of them entered Clayton's yard. The boys shifted weight, as if they were going to put the boat down.

"You better take it round to the back where nobody can see it," Carol said. That was the first thing any of them had said since they came into town.

The boys said nothing but went on, following a mud path between Clayton's house and a leaning board fence. They let the boat down in the back yard.

35   "It's a stolen boat, you know," said Eva, mainly for the effect. "It must've belonged to somebody. You stole it."

"You was the ones who stole it then," Bud said, short of breath. "It was you seen it first."

"It was you took it."

"It was all of us then. If one of us gets in trouble then all of us does."

"Are you going to tell anybody on them?" said Carol as she and Eva rode home, along the streets which were dark between the lights now and potholed from winter.

40   "It's up to you, I won't if you won't."

"I won't if you won't."

They rode in silence, relinquishing something, but not discontented.

The board fence in Clayton's back yard had every so often a post which supported it, or tried to, and it was on these posts that Eva and Carol spent several evenings sitting, jauntily but not very comfortably. Or else they just leaned against the fence while the boys worked on the boat. During the first couple of evenings neighborhood children attracted by the sound of hammering tried to get into the yard to see what was going on, but Eva and Carol blocked their way.

"Who said you could come in here?"

45   "Just us can come in this yard."

These evenings were getting longer, the air milder. Skipping was starting on the sidewalks. Further along the street there was a row of hard maples that had been tapped. Children drank the sap as fast as it could drip into the buckets. The old man and woman who owned the trees, and who hoped to make syrup, came running out of the house making noises as if they were trying to scare away crows. Finally, every spring, the old man would come out on his porch and fire his shotgun into the air, and then the thieving would stop.

None of those working on the boat bothered about stealing sap, though all had done so last year.

The lumber to repair the boat was picked up here and there, along back lanes. At this time of year things were lying around—old boards and branches, sodden mitts, spoons flung out with the dishwater, lids of pudding pots that had been set in the snow to cool, all the debris that can sift through and survive winter. The tools came from Clayton's cellar—left over, presumably, from the time when his father was alive—and though they had nobody to advise them the boys seemed to figure out more or less the manner in which boats are built, or rebuilt. Frank was the one who showed up with diagrams from books and *Popular Mechanics* magazines. Clayton looked at these diagrams and listened to Frank read the instructions and then went ahead and decided in his own way what was to be done.

Bud was best at sawing. Eva and Carol watched everything from the fence and offered criticism and thought up names. The names for the boat that they thought of were: Water Lily, Sea Horse, Flood Queen, and Caro-Eve, after them because they had found it. The boys did not say which, if any, of these names they found satisfactory.

The boat had to be tarred. Clayton heated up a pot of tar on the kitchen stove and brought it out and painted slowly, his thorough way, sitting astride the overturned boat. The other boys were sawing a board to make a new seat. As Clayton worked, the tar cooled and thickened so that finally he could not move the brush any more. He turned to Eva and held out the pot and said, "You can go in and heat this on the stove."

Eva took the pot and went up the back steps. The kitchen seemed black after outside, but   50
it must be light enough to see in, because there was Clayton's mother standing at the ironing board, ironing. She did that for a living, took in wash and ironing.

"Please may I put the tar pot on the stove?" said Eva, who had been brought up to talk politely to parents, even wash-and-iron ladies, and who for some reason especially wanted to make a good impression on Clayton's mother.

"You'll have to poke up the fire then," said Clayton's mother, as if she doubted whether Eva would know how to do that. But Eva could see now, and she picked up the lid with the stove-lifter, and took the poker and poked up a flame. She stirred the tar as it softened. She felt privileged. Then and later. Before she went to sleep a picture of Clayton came to her mind; she saw him sitting astride the boat, tar-painting, with such concentration, delicacy, absorption. She thought of him speaking to her, out of his isolation, in such an ordinary peaceful taking-for-granted voice.

On the twenty-fourth of May, a school holiday in the middle of the week, the boat was carried out of town, a long way now, off the road over fields and fences that had been repaired, to where the river flowed between its normal banks. Eva and Carol, as well as the boys, took turns carrying it. It was launched in the water from a cow-trampled spot between willow bushes that were fresh out in leaf. The boys went first. They yelled with triumph when the boat did float, when it rode amazingly down the river current. The boat was painted black, and green inside, with yellow seats, and a strip of yellow all the way around the outside. There was no name on it, after all. The boys could not imagine that it needed any name to keep it separate from the other boats in the world.

Eva and Carol ran along the bank, carrying bags full of peanut butter-and-jam sandwiches, pickles, bananas, chocolate cake, potato chips, graham crackers stuck together with corn syrup and five bottles of pop to be cooled in the river water. The bottles bumped against their legs. They yelled for a turn.

"If they don't let us they're bastards," Carol said, and they yelled together. "We found it!   55
We found it!"

The boys did not answer, but after a while they brought the boat in, and Carol and Eva came crashing, panting down the bank.

"Does it leak?"

"It don't leak yet."

"We forgot a bailing can," wailed Carol, but nevertheless she got in, with Eva, and Frank pushed them off, crying. "Here's to a Watery Grave!"

And the thing about being in a boat was that it was not solidly bobbing, like a log, but   60
was cupped in the water, so that riding in it was not like being on something in the water, but like being in the water itself. Soon they were all going out in the boat in mixed-up turns, two boys and a girl, two girls and a boy, a girl and a boy, until things were so confused it was impossible to tell whose turn came next, and nobody cared anyway. They went down the river—those who weren't riding, running along the bank to keep up. They passed under two bridges, one iron, one cement. Once they saw a big carp just resting, it seemed to smile at them, in the bridge-shaded water. They did not know how far they had gone on the river, but things had changed—the water had got shallower, and the land flatter. Across an

open field they saw a building that looked like a house, abandoned. They dragged the boat up on the bank and tied it and set out across the field.

"That's the old station," Frank said. "That's Pedder Station." The others had heard this name but he was the one who knew, because his father was the station agent in town. He said that this was a station on a branch line that had been torn up, and that there had been a sawmill here, but a long time ago.

Inside the station it was dark, cool. All the windows were broken. Glass lay in shards and in fairly big pieces on the floor. They walked around finding the larger pieces of glass and tramping on them, smashing them, it was like cracking ice on puddles. Some partitions were still in place, you could see where the ticket window had been. There was a bench lying on its side. People had been here, it looked as if people came here all the time, though it was so far from anywhere. Beer bottles and pop bottles were lying around, also cigarette packages, gum and candy wrappers, the paper from a loaf of bread. The walls were covered with dim and fresh pencil and chalk writings and carved with knives.

I LOVE RONNIE COLES
I WANT TO FUCK
KILROY WAS HERE
RONNIE COLES IS AN ASS-HOLE
WHAT ARE YOU DOING HERE?
WAITING FOR A TRAIN
DAWNA MARY-LOU BARBARA JOANNE

It was exciting to be inside this large, dark, empty place, with the loud noise of breaking glass and their voices ringing back from the underside of the roof. They tipped the old beer bottles against their mouths. That reminded them that they were hungry and thirsty and they cleared a place in the middle of the floor and sat down and ate the lunch. They drank the pop just as it was, lukewarm. They ate everything there was and licked the smears of peanut butter and jam off the bread-paper in which the sandwiches had been wrapped.

They played Truth or Dare.

65 "I dare you to write on the wall, I am a Stupid Ass, and sign your name."

"Tell the truth—what is the worst lie you ever told?"

"Did you ever wet the bed?"

"Did you ever dream you were walking down the street without any clothes on?"

"I dare you to go outside and pee on the railway sign."

70 It was Frank who had to do that. They could not see him, even his back, but they knew he did it, they heard the hissing sound of his pee. They all sat still, amazed, unable to think of what the next dare would be.

"I dare everybody," said Frank from the doorway. "I dare—Everybody."

"What?"

"Take off all our clothes."

Eva and Carol screamed.

75 "Anybody who won't do it has to walk—has to *crawl*—around this floor on their hands and knees."

They were all quiet, till Eva said, almost complacently, "What first?"

"Shoes and socks."

"Then we have to go outside, there's too much glass here."

They pulled off their shoes and socks in the doorway, in the sudden blinding sun. The field before them was bright as water. They ran across where the tracks used to go.

80 "That's enough, that's enough," said Carol. "Watch out for thistles!"

"Tops! Everybody take off their tops!"

"I won't! We won't, will we, Eva?"

But Eva was whirling round and round in the sun where the track used to be. "I don't care, I don't care! Truth or Dare! Truth or Dare!"

She unbuttoned her blouse as she whirled, as if she didn't know what her hand was doing, she flung it off.

Carol took off hers. "I wouldn't have done it, if you hadn't!"   85

"Bottoms!"

Nobody said a word this time, they all bent and stripped themselves. Eva, naked first, started running across the field, and then all the others ran, all five of them running bare through the knee-high hot grass, running towards the river. Not caring now about being caught but in fact leaping and yelling to call attention to themselves, if there was anybody to hear or see. They felt as if they were going to jump off a cliff and fly. They felt that something was happening to them different from anything that had happened before, and it had to do with the boat, the water, the sunlight, the dark ruined station, and each other. They thought of each other now hardly as names or people, but as echoing shrieks, reflections, all bold and white and loud and scandalous, and as fast as arrows. They went running without a break into the cold water and when it came almost to the tops of their legs they fell on it and swam. It stopped their noise. Silence, amazement, came over them in a rush. They dipped and floated and separated, sleek as mink.

Eva stood up in the water her hair dripping, water running down her face. She was waist deep. She stood on smooth stones, her feet fairly wide apart, water flowing between her legs. About a yard away from her Clayton also stood up, and they were blinking the water out of their eyes, looking at each other. Eva did not turn or try to hide; she was quivering from the cold of the water, but also with pride, shame, boldness, and exhilaration.

Clayton shook his head violently, as if he wanted to bang something out of it, then bent over and took a mouthful of river water. He stood up with his cheeks full and made a tight hole of his mouth and shot the water at her as if it was coming out of a hose, hitting her exactly, first one breast and then the other. Water from his mouth ran down her body. He hooted to see it, a loud self-conscious sound that nobody would have expected, from him. The others looked up from wherever they were in the water and closed in to see.

Eva crouched down and slid into the water, letting her head go right under. She swam,   90
and when she let her head out, downstream, Carol was coming after her and the boys were already on the bank, already running into the grass, showing their skinny backs, their white, flat buttocks. They were laughing and saying things to each other but she couldn't hear, for the water in her ears.

"What did he do?" said Carol.

"Nothing."

They crept in to shore. "Let's stay in the bushes till they go," said Eva. "I hate them anyway. I really do. Don't you hate them?"

"Sure," said Carol, and they waited, not very long, until they heard the boys still noisy and excited coming down to the place a bit upriver where they had left the boat. They heard them jump in and start rowing.

"They've got all the hard part, going back," said Eva, hugging herself and shivering vi-   95
olently. "Who cares? Anyway. It never was our boat."

"What if they tell?" said Carol.

"We'll say it's all a lie."

Eva hadn't thought of this solution until she said it, but as soon as she did she felt almost light-hearted again. The ease and scornfulness of it did make them both giggle, and slapping themselves and splashing out of the water they set about developing one of those fits of laughter in which, as soon as one showed signs of exhaustion, the other would snort and start up again, and they would make helpless—soon genuinely helpless—faces at each other and bend over and grab themselves as if they had the worst pain.

QUESTIONS

1. Consider the details used in passages of description in the story. What kinds of details are included?

2. What is the level of diction in the dialogue of the story? From the dialogue, what do you learn about the various speakers?

3. Study paragraph 10. What does the paragraph tell you about Eva as a limited-point-of-view center of interest? How?

4. Consider the last paragraph in the story as a paragraph of action. What verbs are used, and how well do they help you visualize and imagine the sounds of the scene? What is the effect of the verb "snort"?

5. From the lifestyle and artifacts mentioned, what do you learn about the time of the events and the economic level of the town? What is the effect of the facts that it is early springtime, that the water is still cold, but that in May the water is swimmable? What are the implications for summer?

FRANK O'CONNOR (1903–1966)

Frank O'Connor, the nom de plume of Michael O'Donovan, was an only child of poor parents in County Cork, Ireland. He began writing when young, and for a time he was a director of Ireland's national theater. His output as a writer was considerable, with sixty-seven stories appearing in the posthumous Collected Stories *of 1981. A meticulous writer, he was constantly revising his work. "First Confession," for example, went through a number of stages before the final version included here.*

First Confession (1951)

All the trouble began when my grandfather died and my grandmother—my father's mother—came to live with us. Relations in the one house are a strain at the best of times, but, to make matters worse, my grandmother was a real old countrywoman and quite unsuited to the life in town. She had a fat, wrinkled old face, and, to Mother's great indignation, went round the house in bare feet—the boots had her crippled, she said. For dinner she had a jug of porter° and a pot of potatoes with—sometimes—a bit of salt fish, and she poured out the potatoes on the table and ate them slowly, with great relish, using her fingers by way of a fork.

Now, girls are supposed to be fastidious, but I was the one who suffered most from this. Nora, my sister, just sucked up to the old woman for the penny she got every Friday out of the old-age pension, a thing I could not do. I was too honest, that was my trouble; and when I was playing with Bill Connell, the sergeant-major's son, and saw my grandmother steering up the path with the jug of porter sticking out from beneath her shawl I was mortified. I made excuses not to let him come into the house, because I could never be sure what she would be up to when we went in.

When Mother was at work and my grandmother made the dinner I wouldn't touch it. Nora once tried to make me, but I hid under the table from her and took the bread-knife with me for protection. Nora let on to be very indignant (she wasn't, of course, but she knew Mother saw through her, so she sided with Gran) and came after me. I lashed out at

---

°*porter:* a dark-brown beer.

her with the bread-knife, and after that she left me alone. I stayed there till Mother came in from work and made my dinner, but when Father came in later Nora said in a shocked voice: "Oh, Dadda, do you know what Jackie did at dinner-time?" Then, of course, it all came out; Father gave me a flaking; Mother interfered, and for days after that he didn't speak to me and Mother barely spoke to Nora. And all because of that old woman! God knows, I was heart-scalded.

Then, to crown my misfortune, I had to make my first confession and communion. It was an old woman called Ryan who prepared us for these. She was about the one age with Gran; she was well-to-do, lived in a big house on Montenotte, wore a black cloak and bonnet, and came every day to school at three o'clock when we should have been going home, and talked to us of hell. She may have mentioned the other place as well, but that could only have been by accident, for hell had the first place in her heart.

She lit a candle, took out a new half-crown, and offered it to the first boy who would   5
hold one finger—only one finger!—in the flame for five minutes by the school clock. Being always very ambitious I was tempted to volunteer, but I thought it might look greedy. Then she asked were we afraid of holding one finger—only one finger!—in a little candle flame for five minutes and not afraid of burning all over in roasting hot furnaces for all eternity. "All eternity! Just think of that! A whole lifetime goes by and it's nothing, not even a drop in the ocean of your sufferings." The woman was really interesting about hell, but my attention was all fixed on the half-crown. At the end of the lesson she put it back in her purse. It was a great disappointment; a religious woman like that, you wouldn't think she'd bother about a thing like a half-crown.

Another day she said she knew a priest who woke one night to find a fellow he didn't recognize leaning over the end of his bed. The priest was a bit frightened—naturally enough—but he asked the fellow what he wanted, and the fellow said in a deep, husky voice that he wanted to go to confession. The priest said it was an awkward time and wouldn't it do in the morning, but the fellow said that last time he went to confession, there was one sin he kept back, being ashamed to mention it, and now it was always on his mind. Then the priest knew it was a bad case, because the fellow was after making a bad confession and committing a mortal sin. He got up to dress, and just then the cock crew in the yard outside, and—lo and behold!—when the priest looked round there was no sign of the fellow, only a smell of burning timber, and when the priest looked at his bed didn't he see the print of two hands burned in it? That was because the fellow had made a bad confession. This story made a shocking impression on me.

But the worst of all was when she showed us how to examine our conscience. Did we take the name of the Lord, our God, in vain? Did we honour our father and our mother? (I asked her did this include grandmothers and she said it did.) Did we love our neighbours as ourselves? Did we covet our neighbour's goods? (I thought of the way I felt about the penny that Nora got every Friday.) I decided that, between one thing and another, I must have broken the whole ten commandments, all on account of that old woman, and so far as I could see, so long as she remained in the house I had no hope of ever doing anything else.

I was scared to death of confession. The day the whole class went I let on to have a toothache, hoping my absence wouldn't be noticed; but at three o'clock, just as I was feeling safe, along comes a chap with a message from Mrs. Ryan that I was to go to confession myself on Saturday and be at the chapel for communion with the rest. To make it worse, Mother couldn't come with me and sent Nora instead.

Now, that girl had ways of tormenting me that Mother never knew of. She held my hand as we went down the hill, smiling sadly and saying how sorry she was for me, as if she were bringing me to the hospital for an operation.

"Oh, God help us!" she moaned. "Isn't it a terrible pity you weren't a good boy? Oh,   10
Jackie, my heart bleeds for you! How will you ever think of all your sins? Don't forget you have to tell him about the time you kicked Gran on the shin."

"Lemme go!" I said, trying to drag myself free of her. "I don't want to go to confession at all."

"But sure, you'll have to go to confession, Jackie," she replied in the same regretful tone. "Sure, if you didn't the parish priest would be up to the house, looking for you. 'Tisn't, God knows, that I'm not sorry for you. Do you remember the time you tried to kill me with the bread-knife under the table? And the language you used to me? I don't know what he'll do with you at all, Jackie. He might have to send you up to the bishop."

I remember thinking bitterly that she didn't know the half of what I had to tell—if I told it. I knew I couldn't tell it, and understood perfectly why the fellow in Mrs. Ryan's story made a bad confession; it seemed to me a great shame that people wouldn't stop criticizing him. I remember that steep hill down to the church, and the sunlit hillsides beyond the valley of the river, which I saw in the gaps between the houses like Adam's last glimpse of Paradise.°

Then, when she had manœuvered me down the long flight of steps to the chapel yard, Nora suddenly changed her tone. She became the raging malicious devil she really was.

15   "There you are!" she said with a yelp of triumph, hurling me through the church door. "And I hope he'll give you the penitential psalms, you dirty little caffler."

I knew then I was lost, given up to eternal justice. The door with the coloured-glass panels swung shut behind me, the sunlight went out and gave place to deep shadow, and the wind whistled outside so that the silence within seemed to crackle like ice under my feet. Nora sat in front of me by the confession box. There were a couple of old women ahead of her, and then a miserable-looking poor devil came and wedged me in at the other side, so that I couldn't escape even if I had the courage. He joined his hands and rolled his eyes in the direction of the roof, muttering aspirations in an anguished tone, and I wondered had he a grandmother too. Only a grandmother could account for a fellow behaving in that heartbroken way, but he was better off than I, for he at least could go and confess his sins; while I would make a bad confession and then die in the night and be continually coming back and burning people's furniture.

Nora's turn came, and I heard the sound of something slamming, and then her voice as if butter wouldn't melt in her mouth, and then another slam, and out she came. God, the hypocrisy of women! Her eyes were lowered, her head was bowed, and her hands were joined very low down on her stomach, and she walked up the aisle to the side altar looking like a saint. You never saw such an exhibition of devotion, and I remembered the devilish malice with which she had tormented me all the way from our door, and wondered were all religious people like that, really. It was my turn now. With the fear of damnation in my soul I went in, and the confessional door closed of itself behind me.

It was pitch-dark and I couldn't see the priest or anything else. Then I really began to be frightened. In the darkness it was a matter between God and me, and He had all the odds. He knew what my intentions were before I even started; I had no chance. All I had ever been told about confession got mixed up in my mind, and I knelt to one wall and said: "Bless me, father, for I have sinned; this is my first confession." I waited for a few minutes, but nothing happened, so I tried it on the other wall. Nothing happened there either. He had me spotted all right.

It must have been then that I noticed the shelf at about one height with my head. It was really a place for grown-up people to rest their elbows, but in my distracted state I thought it was probably the place you were supposed to kneel. Of course, it was on the high side and not very deep, but I was always good at climbing and managed to get up all right. Staying up was the trouble. There was room only for my knees, and nothing you could get a grip on but a sort of wooden moulding a bit above it. I held on to the moulding and repeated

---

°*Adam's last glimpse of Paradise:* Genesis 3:23–24.

the words a little louder, and this time something happened all right. A slide was slammed back; a little light entered the box, and a man's voice said: "Who's there?"

"'Tis me, father," I said for fear he mightn't see me and go away again. I couldn't see him   20
at all. The place the voice came from was under the moulding, about level with my knees, so I took a good grip of the moulding and swung myself down till I saw the astonished face of a young priest looking up at me. He had to put his head on one side to see me, and I had to put mine on one side to see him, so we were more or less talking to one another upside-down. It struck me as a queer way of hearing confessions, but I didn't feel it my place to criticize.

"Bless me, father, for I have sinned; this is my first confession," I rattled off all in one breath, and swung myself down the least shade more to make it easier for him.

"What are you doing up there?" he shouted in an angry voice, and the strain the politeness was putting on my hold of the moulding, and the shock of being addressed in such an uncivil tone, were too much for me. I lost my grip, tumbled, and hit the door an unmerciful wallop before I found myself flat on my back in the middle of the aisle. The people who had been waiting stood up with their mouths open. The priest opened the door of the middle box and came out, pushing his biretta back from his forehead; he looked something terrible. Then Nora came scampering down the aisle.

"Oh, you dirty little caffler!" she said. "I might have known you'd do it. I might have known you'd disgrace me. I can't leave you out of my sight for one minute."

Before I could even get to my feet to defend myself she bent down and gave me a clip across the ear. This reminded me that I was so stunned I had even forgotten to cry, so that people might think I wasn't hurt at all, when in fact I was probably maimed for life. I gave a roar out of me.

"What's all this about?" the priest hissed, getting angrier than ever and pushing Nora   25
off me. "How dare you hit the child like that, you little vixen?"

"But I can't do my penance with him, father," Nora cried, cocking an outraged eye up to him.

"Well, go and do it, or I'll give you some more to do," he said, giving me a hand up. "Was it coming to confession you were, my poor man?" he asked me.

"'Twas, father," said I with a sob.

"Oh," he said respectfully, "a big hefty fellow like you must have terrible sins. Is this your first?"

"'Tis, father," said I.   30

"Worse and worse," he said gloomily. "The crimes of a lifetime. I don't know will I get rid of you at all today. You'd better wait now till I'm finished with these old ones. You can see by the looks of them they haven't much to tell."

"I will, father," I said with something approaching joy.

The relief of it was really enormous. Nora stuck out her tongue at me from behind his back, but I couldn't even be bothered retorting. I knew from the very moment that man opened his mouth that he was intelligent above the ordinary. When I had time to think, I saw how right I was. It only stood to reason that a fellow confessing after seven years would have more to tell than people that went every week. The crimes of a lifetime, exactly as he said. It was only what he expected, and the rest was the cackle of old women and girls with their talk of hell, the bishop, and the penitential psalms. That was all they knew. I started to make my examination of conscience, and barring the one bad business of my grandmother it didn't seem so bad.

The next time, the priest steered me into the confession box himself and left the shutter back the way I could see him get in and sit down at the further side of the grille from me.

"Well, now," he said, "what do they call you?"

"Jackie, father," said I.   35

"And what's a-trouble to you, Jackie?"

"Father," I said, feeling I might as well get it over while I had him in good humour, "I had it all arranged to kill my grandmother."

He seemed a bit shaken by that, all right, because he said nothing for quite a while.

40 "My goodness," he said at last, "that'd be a shocking thing to do. What put that into your head?"

"Father," I said, feeling very sorry for myself, "she's an awful woman."

"Is she?" he asked. "What way is she awful?"

"She takes porter, father," I said, knowing well from the way Mother talked of it that this was a mortal sin, and hoping it would make the priest take a more favourable view of my case.

"Oh, my!" he said, and I could see he was impressed.

45 "And snuff, father," said I.

"That's a bad case, sure enough, Jackie," he said.

"And she goes round in her bare feet, father," I went on in a rush of self-pity, "and she knows I don't like her, and she gives pennies to Nora and none to me, and my da sides with her and flakes me, and one night I was so heart-scalded I made up my mind I'd have to kill her."

"And what would you do with the body?" he asked with great interest.

"I was thinking I could chop that up and carry it away in a barrow I have," I said.

50 "Begor, Jackie," he said, "do you know you're a terrible child?"

"I know, father," I said, for I was just thinking the same thing myself. "I tried to kill Nora too with a bread-knife under the table, only I missed her."

"Is that the little girl that was beating you just now?" he asked.

"'Tis, father."

"Someone will go for her with a bread-knife one day, and he won't miss her," he said rather cryptically. "You must have great courage. Between ourselves, there's a lot of people I'd like to do the same to but I'd never have the nerve. Hanging is an awful death."

55 "Is it, father?" I asked with the deepest interest—I was always very keen on hanging. "Did you ever see a fellow hanged?"

"Dozens of them," he said solemnly. "And they all died roaring."

"Jay!" I said.

"Oh, a horrible death!" he said with great satisfaction. "Lots of fellows I saw killed their grandmothers too, but they all said 'twas never worth it."

He had me there for a full ten minutes talking, and then walked out the chapel yard with me. I was genuinely sorry to part with him, because he was the most entertaining character I'd ever met in the religious line. Outside, after the shadow of the church, the sunlight was like the roaring of waves on a beach; it dazzled me; and when the frozen silence melted and I heard the screech of trams on the road my heart soared. I knew now I wouldn't die in the night and come back, leaving marks on my mother's furniture. It would be a great worry to her, and the poor soul had enough.

60 Nora was sitting on the railing, waiting for me, and she put on a very sour puss when she saw the priest with me. She was made jealous because a priest had never come out of the church with her.

"Well," she asked coldly, after he left me, "what did he give you?"

"Three Hail Marys," I said.

"Three Hail Marys," she repeated incredulously. "You mustn't have told him anything."

"I told him everything," I said confidently.

65 "About Gran and all?"

"About Gran and all."

(All she wanted was to be able to go home and say I'd made a bad confession.)

"Did you tell him you went for me with the bread-knife?" she asked with a frown.

"I did to be sure."

"And he only gave you three Hail Marys?"

"That's all."

She slowly got down from the railing with a baffled air. Clearly, this was beyond her. As we mounted the steps back to the main road she looked at me suspiciously.

"What are you sucking?" she asked.

"Bullseyes."

"Was it the priest gave them to you?"

"'Twas."

"Lord God," she wailed bitterly, "some people have all the luck! 'Tis no advantage to anybody trying to be good. I might just as well be a sinner like you."

70

75

QUESTIONS

1. Describe Jackie as a narrator. What is the level of his language? To whom does he seem to be speaking or writing? What elements of language do you find in the story that seem characteristically Irish?

2. Describe Jackie's character. How old do you think he is at the time of the narration? Is there evidence that he has grown as a person since the time of the story's events? Do you think his attitudes have changed about his grandmother? His parents? His sister? Mrs. Ryan? The priest?

3. Is Jackie's confession a "good" one? Whose religion seems more appealing, Mrs. Ryan's or the priest's?

4. To what degree do the relationships within Jackie's family seem either ordinary or unusual?

5. "First Confession" is a funny story. What contributions are made to the humor by the situations? The language?

DANIEL OROZCO (b. c. 1957)

Orozco is a native of San Francisco. He studied at the University of Washington, where he earned a master's degree in fine arts. He also studied at Stanford University, where he was a Scowcroft and L'Heureux Fiction Fellow, and also a Jones Lecturer in Fiction in the Creative Writing Program. In 2005 he was a MacDowell Colony Fellow. He has become a prolific writer of stories, having published in collections such as The Best American Short Stories, The Best American Mystery Stories, *the* Pushcart Prize Anthology *of 2005,* Harper's Magazine, Zoetrope: All Story, Story Quarterly, *and* McSweeney's. *His story "Samoza's Dream" was one of the finalists in the competition for a 2006 National Magazine Award in fiction. He currently teaches creative writing at the University of Idaho. "Orientation," one of his best-known stories, first appeared in* The Seattle Review. *It was chosen by Jane Smiley for* The Best American Short Stories, 1995.

 ## Orientation (1994)

Those are the offices and these are the cubicles. That's my cubicle there, and this is your cubicle. This is your phone. Never answer your phone. Let the Voicemail System answer it. This is your Voicemail System Manual. There are no personal phone calls allowed. We do, however, allow for emergencies. If you must make an emergency phone call, ask your supervisor first. If you can't find your supervisor, ask Phillip Spiers, who sits over there. He'll check with Clarissa Nicks, who sits over there. If you make an emergency phone call without asking, you may be let go.

These are your IN and OUT boxes. All the forms in your IN box must be logged in by the date shown in the upper left-hand corner, initialed by you in the upper right-hand corner, and distributed to the Processing Analyst whose name is numerically coded in the lower left-hand corner. The lower right-hand corner is left blank. Here's your Processing Analyst Numerical Code Index. And here's your Forms Processing Procedures Manual.

You must pace your work. What do I mean? I'm glad you asked that. We pace our work according to the eight-hour workday. If you have twelve hours of work in your IN box, for example, you must compress that work into the eight-hour day. If you have one hour of work in your IN box, you must expand that work to fill the eight hour day. That was a good question. Feel free to ask questions. Ask too many questions, however, and you may be let go.

That is our receptionist. She is a temp. We go through receptionists here. They quit with alarming frequency. Be polite and civil to the temps. Learn their names, and invite them to lunch occasionally. But don't get close to them, as it only makes it more difficult when they leave. And they always leave. You can be sure of that.

5   The men's room is over there. The women's room is over there. John LaFountaine, who sits over there, uses the women's room occasionally. He says it is accidental. We know better, but we let it pass. John LaFountaine is harmless, his forays into the forbidden territory of the women's room simply a benign thrill, a faint blip on the dull flat line of his life.

Russell Nash, who sits in the cubicle to your left, is in love with Amanda Pierce, who sits in the cubicle to your right. They ride the same bus together after work. For Amanda Pierce, it is just a tedious bus ride made less tedious by the idle nattering of Russell Nash. But for Russell Nash, it is the highlight of his day. It is the highlight of his life. Russell Nash has put on forty pounds, and grows fatter with each passing month, nibbling on chips and cookies while peeking glumly over the partitions at Amanda Pierce, and gorging himself at home on cold pizza and ice cream while watching adult videos on TV.

Amanda Pierce, in the cubicle to your right, has a six-year-old son named Jamie, who is autistic. Her cubicle is plastered from top to bottom with the boy's crayon artwork—sheet after sheet of precisely drawn concentric circles and ellipses, in black and yellow. She rotates them every other Friday. Be sure to comment on them. Amanda Pierce also has a husband, who is a lawyer. He subjects her to an escalating array of painful and humiliating sex games, to which Amanda Pierce reluctantly submits. She comes to work exhausted and freshly wounded each morning, wincing from the abrasions on her breasts, or the bruises on her abdomen, or the second-degree burns on the backs of her thighs.

But we're not supposed to know any of this. Do not let on. If you let on, you may be let go.

Amanda Pierce, who tolerates Russell Nash, is in love with Albert Bosch, whose office is over there. Albert Bosch, who only dimly registers Amanda Pierce's existence, has eyes only for Ellie Tapper, who sits over there. Ellie Tapper, who hates Albert Bosch, would walk through fire for Curtis Lance. But Curtis Lance hates Ellie Tapper. Isn't the world a funny place? Not in the ha-ha sense, of course.

10   Anika Bloom sits in that cubicle. Last year, while reviewing quarterly reports in a meeting with Barry Hacker, Anika Bloom's left palm began to bleed. She fell into a trance, stared into her hand, and told Barry Hacker when and how his wife would die. We laughed it off. She was, after all, a new employee. But Barry Hacker's wife is dead. So unless you want to know exactly when and how you'll die, never talk to Anika Bloom.

Cohn Heavey sits in that cubicle over there. He was new once, just like you. We warned him about Anika Bloom. But at last year's Christmas Potluck, he felt sorry for her when he saw that no one was talking to her. Cohn Heavey brought her a drink. He hasn't been himself since. Cohn Heavey is doomed. There's nothing he can do about it, and we are powerless to help him. Stay away from Cohn Heavey. Never give any of your work to him. If he asks to do something, tell him you have to check with me. If he asks again, tell him I haven't gotten back to you.

This is the Fire Exit. There are several on this floor, and they are marked accordingly. We have a Floor Evacuation Review every three months, and an Escape Route Quiz once a month. We have our Biannual Fire Drill twice a year, and our Annual Earthquake Drill once a year. These are precautions only. These things never happen.

For your information, we have a comprehensive health plan. Any catastrophic illness, any unforeseen tragedy is completely covered. All dependents are completely covered. Larry Bagdikian, who sits over there, has six daughters. If anything were to happen to any of his girls, or to all of them, if all six were to simultaneously fall victim to illness or injury—stricken with a hideous degenerative muscle disease or some rare toxic blood disorder, sprayed with semiautomatic gunfire while on a class field trip, or attacked in their bunk beds by some prowling nocturnal lunatic—if any of this were to pass, Larry's girls would all be taken care of. Larry Bagdikian would not have to pay one dime. He would have nothing to worry about.

We also have a generous vacation and sick leave policy. We have an excellent disability insurance plan. We have a stable and profitable pension fund. We get group discounts for the symphony, and block seating at the ballpark. We get commuter ticket books for the bridge. We have Direct Deposit. We are all members of Costco.

This is our kitchenette. And this, this is our Mr. Coffee. We have a coffee pool, into which we each pay two dollars a week for coffee, filters, sugar, and CoffeeMate. If you prefer Cremora or half-and-half to CoffeeMate, there is a special pool for three dollars a week. If you prefer Sweet'n Low to sugar, there is a special pool for two-fifty a week. We do not do decaf. You are allowed to join the coffee pool of your choice, but you are not allowed to touch the Mr. Coffee. 15

This is the microwave oven. You are allowed to heat food in the microwave oven. You are not, however, allowed to cook food in the microwave oven.

We get one hour for lunch. We also get one fifteen-minute break in the morning, and one fifteen-minute break in the afternoon. Always take your breaks, if you skip a break, it is gone forever. For your information, your break is a privilege, not a right. If you abuse the break policy, we are authorized to rescind your breaks. Lunch, however, is a right, not a privilege. If you abuse the lunch policy, our hands will be tied, and we will be forced to look the other way. We will not enjoy that.

This is the refrigerator. You may put your lunch in it. Barry Hacker, who sits over there, steals food from this refrigerator. His petty theft is an outlet for his grief. Last New Year's Eve, while kissing his wife, a blood vessel burst in her brain. Barry Hacker's wife was two months pregnant at the time, and lingered in a coma for half a year before dying. It was a tragic loss for Barry Hacker. He hasn't been himself since. Barry Hacker's wife was a beautiful woman. She was also completely covered. Barry Hacker did not have to pay one dime. But his dead wife haunts him. She haunts all of us. We have seen her, reflected in the monitors of our computers, moving past our cubicles. We have seen the dim shadow of her face in our photocopies. She pencils herself in the receptionist's appointment book, with the notation: To see Barry Hacker. She has left messages in the receptionist's Voicemail box, messages garbled by the electronic chirrups and buzzes in the phone line, her voice echoing from an immense distance within the ambient hum. But the voice is hers. And beneath her voice, beneath the tidal whoosh of static and hiss, the gurgling and crying of a baby can be heard.

In any case, if you bring a lunch, put a little something extra in the bag for Barry Hacker. We have four Barrys in this office. Isn't that a coincidence?

This is Matthew Payne's office. He is our Unit Manager, and his door is always closed. We have never seen him, and you will never see him. But he is here. You can be sure of that. He is all around us. 20

This is the Custodian's Closet. You have no business in the Custodian's Closet.

And this, this is our Supplies Cabinet. If you need supplies, see Curtis Lance. He will log you in on the Supplies Cabinet Authorization Log, then give you a Supplies Authorization Slip. Present your pink copy of the Supplies Authorization Slip to Ellie Tapper. She will log you in on the Supplies Cabinet Key Log, then give you the key. Because the Supplies Cabinet is located outside the Unit Manager's office, you must be very quiet. Gather your supplies quietly. The Supplies Cabinet is divided into four sections. Section One contains letterhead stationery, blank paper and envelopes, memo and note pads, and so on. Section Two contains pens and pencils and typewriter and printer ribbons, and the like. In Section Three we have erasers, correction fluids, transparent tapes, glue sticks, et cetera. And in Section Four we have paper clips and push pins and scissors and razor blades. And here are the spare blades for the shredder. Do not touch the shredder, which is located over there. The shredder is of no concern to you.

Gwendolyn Stich sits in that office there. She is crazy about penguins, and collects penguin knickknacks: penguin posters and coffee mugs and stationery, penguin stuffed animals, penguin jewelry, penguin sweaters and T-shirts and socks. She has a pair of penguin fuzzy slippers she wears when working late at the office. She has a tape cassette of penguin sounds which she listens to for relaxation. Her favorite colors are black and white. She has personalized license plates that read PEN GWEN. Every morning, she passes through all the cubicles to wish each of us a good morning. She brings Danish on Wednesdays for Hump Day morning break, and doughnuts on Fridays for TGIF afternoon break. She organizes the Annual Christmas Potluck, and is in charge of the Birthday List. Gwendolyn Stich's door is always open to all of us. She will always lend an ear, and put in a good word for you; she will always give you a hand, or the shirt off her back, or a shoulder to cry on. Because her door is always open, she hides and cries in a stall in the women's room. And John LaFountaine—who, enthralled when a woman enters, sits quietly in his stall with his knees to his chest—John LaFountaine has heard her vomiting in there. We have come upon Gwendolyn Stich huddled in the stairwell, shivering in the updraft, sipping a Diet Mr. Pibb and hugging her knees. She does not let any of this interfere with her work. If it interfered with her work, she might have to be let go.

Kevin Howard sits in that cubicle over there. He is a serial killer, the one they call the Carpet Cutter, responsible for the mutilations across town. We're not supposed to know that, so do not let on. Don't worry. His compulsion inflicts itself on strangers only, and the routine established is elaborate and unwavering. The victim must be a white male, a young adult no older than thirty, heavyset, with dark hair and eyes, and the like. The victim must be chosen at random, before sunset, from a public place; the victim is followed home, and must put up a struggle; et cetera. The carnage inflicted is precise: the angle and direction of the incisions; the layering of skin and muscle tissue; the rearrangement of the visceral organs; and so on. Kevin Howard does not let any of this interfere with his work. He is, in fact, our fastest typist. He types as if he were on fire. He has a secret crush on Gwendolyn Stich, and leaves a red-foil-wrapped Hershey's Kiss on her desk every afternoon. But he hates Anika Bloom, and keeps well away from her. In his presence, she has uncontrollable fits of shaking and trembling. Her left palm does not stop bleeding.

25   In any case, when Kevin Howard gets caught, act surprised. Say that he seemed like a nice person, a bit of a loner, perhaps, but always quiet and polite.

This is the photocopier room. And this, this is our view. It faces southwest. West is down there, toward the water. North is back there. Because we are on the seventeenth floor, we are afforded a magnificent view. Isn't it beautiful? It overlooks the park, where the tops of those trees are. You can see a segment of the bay between those two buildings there. You can see the sun set in the gap between those two buildings over there. You can see this building reflected in the glass panels of that building across the way. There. See? That's you, waving. And look there. There's Anika Bloom in the kitchenette, waving back.

Enjoy this view while photocopying. If you have problems with the photocopier, see Russell Nash. If you have any questions, ask your supervisor. If you can't find your supervisor, ask Phillip Spiers. He sits over there. He'll check with Clarissa Nicks. She sits over there. If you can't find them, feel free to ask me. That's my cubicle. I sit in there.

QUESTIONS

1. What is the situation throughout this story? Who is talking? To whom is he talking? Does the listener have any chance to comment on the speaker's discourse?

2. In the first four paragraphs, is there anything unusual about the speaker's language? What does Orozco have the speaker say in paragraph 5 that alerts you to the unusual nature of the persons in the office?

3. Is there anything funny about the situations of fellow employees in the office? If not, how does one account for the fact that the story is comic? How do the speaker's controlled descriptions of the plights of the various office workers contribute to the story's comic tone?

4. Why is Kevin Howard the last one to be described by the speaker? Of what is Kevin guilty? What might the story be like if Kevin Howard had been mentioned first? Describe the comic technique of paragraph 25.

JOHN UPDIKE (b. 1932)

Updike was born and reared in Pennsylvania during the Great Depression. His parents were diligent about his education, and in 1950 he received a scholarship for study at Harvard, graduating in 1954. He worked for The New Yorker *for two years before deciding to devote himself exclusively to his own writing, but since then he has remained a frequent contributor of stories and poems to that magazine. In 1959, he published his first story collection,* The Same Door, *and his first novel,* The Poorhouse Fair. *In 1960, with* Rabbit, Run, *he began his extensive* Rabbit *chronicles. In 1981 he received the Pulitzer Prize for* Rabbit Is Rich. *His collected poems were published in 1993, and he is continually productive in writing new stories and poems. Today he is considered one of the best of America's major writers of fiction and poetry.*

🍁 A & P° (1961)

In walks these three girls in nothing but bathing suits. I'm in the third checkout slot, with my back to the door, so I don't see them until they're over by the bread. The one that caught my eye first was the one in the plaid green two-piece. She was a chunky kid, with a good tan and a sweet broad soft-looking can with those two crescents of white just under it, where the sun never seems to hit, at the top of the backs of her legs. I stood there with my hand on a box of HiHo crackers trying to remember if I rang it up or not. I ring it up again and the customer starts giving me hell. She's one of these cash-register-watchers, a witch about fifty with rouge on her cheekbones and no eyebrows, and I know it made her day to trip me up. She'd been watching cash registers for fifty years and probably never seen a mistake before.

By the time I got her feathers smoothed and her goodies into a bag—she gives me a little snort in passing, if she'd been born at the right time they would have burned her over in Salem—by the time I get her on her way the girls had circled around the bread and were coming back, without a pushcart, back my way along the counters, in the aisle between the checkouts and the Special bins. They didn't even have shoes on. There was this chunky one,

---

°*A & P:* the Great Atlantic and Pacific Tea Company, a large grocery chain established in 1859 and still flourishing in 18 states, with more than 800 A & P stores in the United States and 200 in Canada.

with the two-piece—it was bright green and the seams on the bra were still sharp and her belly was still pretty pale so I guessed she just got it (the suit)—there was this one, with one of those chubby berry-faces, the lips all bunched together under her nose, this one, and a tall one, with black hair that hadn't quite frizzed right, and one of these sunburns right across under the eyes, and a chin that was too long—you know, the kind of girl other girls think is very "striking" and "attractive" but never quite makes it, as they very well know, which is why they like her so much—and then the third one, that wasn't quite so tall. She was the queen. She kind of led them, the other two peeking around and making their shoulders round. She didn't look around, not this queen, she just walked straight on slowly, on these long white prima-donna legs. She came down a little hard on her heels, as if she didn't walk in her bare feet that much, putting down her heels and then letting the weight move along to her toes as if she was testing the floor with every step, putting a little deliberate extra action into it. You never know for sure how girls' minds work (do you really think it's a mind in there or just a little buzz like a bee in a glass jar?) but you got the idea she had talked the other two into coming in here with her, and now she was showing them how to do it, walk slow and hold yourself straight.

She had on a kind of dirty-pink—beige, maybe, I don't know—bathing suit with a little nubble all over it and, what got me, the straps were down. They were off her shoulders looped loose around the cool tops of her arms, and I guess as a result the suit had slipped a little on her, so all around the top of the cloth there was this shining rim. If it hadn't been there you wouldn't have known there could have been anything whiter than those shoulders. With the straps pushed off, there was nothing between the top of the suit and the top of her head except just *her*, this clean bare plane of the top of her chest down from the shoulder bones like a dented sheet of metal tilted in the light. I mean, it was more than pretty.

She had sort of oaky hair that the sun and salt had bleached, done up in a bun that was unraveling, and a kind of prim face. Walking into the A & P with your straps down, I suppose it's the only kind of face you *can* have. She held her head so high her neck, coming up out of those white shoulders, looked kind of stretched, but I didn't mind. The longer her neck was, the more of her there was.

5   She must have felt in the corner of her eye me and over my shoulder Stokesie in the second slot watching, but she didn't tip. Not this queen. She kept her eyes moving across the racks, and stopped, and turned so slow it made my stomach rub the inside of my apron, and buzzed to the other two, who kind of huddled against her for relief, and then they all three of them went up the cat-and-dog-food-breakfast-cereal-macaroni-rice-raisins-seasonings-spreads-spaghetti soft-drinks-crackers-and-cookies aisle. From the third slot I look straight up this aisle to the meat counter, and I watched them all the way. The fat one with the tan sort of fumbled with the cookies, but on second thought she put the package back. The sheep pushing their carts down the aisle—the girls were walking against the usual traffic (not that we have one-way signs or anything)—were pretty hilarious. You could see them, when Queenie's white shoulders dawned on them, kind of jerk, or hop, or hiccup, but their eyes snapped back to their own baskets and on they pushed. I bet you could set off dynamite in an A & P and the people would by and large keep reaching and checking oatmeal off their lists and muttering "Let me see, there was a third thing, began with A, asparagus, no ah, yes, applesauce!" or whatever it is they do mutter. But there was no doubt, this jiggled them. A few houseslaves in pin curlers even looked around after pushing their carts past to make sure what they had seen was correct.

You know, it's one thing to have a girl in a bathing suit down on the beach, where what with the glare nobody can look at each other much anyway, and another thing in the cool of the A & P, under the fluorescent lights, against all those stacked packages, with her feet paddling along naked over our checkerboard green-and-cream rubber-tile floor.

"Oh Daddy," Stokesie said beside me. "I feel so faint."

"Darling," I said. "Hold me tight." Stokesie's married, with two babies chalked up on his fuselage already, but as far as I can tell that's the only difference. He's twenty-two, and I was nineteen this April.

"Is it done?" he asks, the responsible married man finding his voice. I forgot to say he thinks he's going to be manager some sunny day, maybe in 1990 when it's called the Great Alexandrov and Petrooshki° Tea Company or something.

What he meant was, our town is five miles from the beach, with a big summer colony   10
out on the Point, but we're right in the middle of town, and the women generally put on a shirt or shorts or something before they get out of the car into the street. And anyway these are usually women with six children and varicose veins mapping their legs and nobody, including them could care less. As I say, we're right in the middle of town, and if you stand at our front doors you can see two banks and the Congregational church and the newspaper store and three real-estate offices and about twenty-seven old freeloaders tearing up Central Street because the sewer broke again. It's not as if we're on the Cape,° we're north of Boston and there's people in this town haven't seen the ocean for twenty years.

The girls had reached the meat counter and were asking McMahon something. He pointed, they pointed, and they shuffled out of sight behind a pyramid of Diet Delight peaches. All that was left for us to see was old McMahon patting his mouth and looking after them sizing up their joints. Poor kids, I began to feel sorry for them, they couldn't help it.

Now here comes the sad part of the story, at least my family says it's sad, but I don't think it's so sad myself. The store's pretty empty, it being Thursday afternoon, so there was nothing much to do except lean on the register and wait for the girls to show up again. The whole store was like a pinball machine and I didn't know which tunnel they'd come out of. After a while they come around out of the far aisle, around the light bulbs, records at discount of the Caribbean Six or Tony Martin Sings or some such gunk you wonder they waste the wax on, sixpacks of candy bars, and plastic toys done up in cellophane that fall apart when a kid looks at them anyway. Around they come, Queenie still leading the way, and holding a little gray jar in her hand. Slots Three through Seven are unmanned and I could see her wondering between Stokes and me, but Stokesie with his usual luck draws an old party in baggy gray pants who stumbles up with four giant cans of pineapple juice (what do these bums *do* with all that pineapple juice? I've often asked myself) so the girls come to me. Queenie puts down the jar and I take it into my fingers icy cold. Kingfish Fancy Herring Snacks in Pure Sour Cream: 49¢. Now her hands are empty, not a ring or a bracelet, bare as God made them, and I wonder where the money's coming from. Still with that prim look she lifts a folded dollar bill out of the hollow at the center of her nubbed pink top. The jar went heavy in my hand. Really, I thought that was so cute.

Then everybody's luck begins to run out. Lengel comes in from haggling with a truck full of cabbages on the lot and is about to scuttle into that door marked MANAGER behind which he hides all day when the girls touch his eye. Lengel's pretty dreary, teaches Sunday school and the rest, but he doesn't miss that much. He comes over and says, "Girls, this isn't the beach."

Queenie blushes, though maybe it's just a brush of sunburn I was noticing for the first time, now that she was so close. "My mother asked me to pick up a jar of herring snacks." Her voice kind of startled me, the way voices do when you see the people first, coming out so flat and dumb yet kind of tony, too, the way it ticked over "pick up" and "snacks." All of a sudden I slid right down her voice into her living room. Her father and the other men were standing around in ice-cream coats and bow ties and the women were in sandals picking up herring snacks on toothpicks off a big glass plate and they were all holding drinks

---

°*Great Alexandrov and Petrooshki:* apparently a reference to the possibility that someday Russia might rule the United States.
°*the Cape:* Cape Cod, the southeastern area of Massachusetts, a place of many resorts and beaches.

the color of water with olives and sprigs of mint in them. When my parents have somebody over they get lemonade and if it's a real racy affair Schlitz in tall glasses with "They'll Do It Every Time"° cartoons stenciled on.

15   "That's all right," Lengel said. "But this isn't the beach." His repeating this struck me as funny, as if it had just occurred to him, and he had been thinking all these years the A & P was a great big dune and he was the head lifeguard. He didn't like my smiling—as I say he doesn't miss much—but he concentrates on giving the girls that sad Sunday-school-superintendent stare.

Queenie's blush is no sunburn now, and the plump one in plaid, that I liked better from the back—a really sweet can—pipes up, "We weren't doing any shopping. We just came in for the one thing."

"That makes no difference," Lengel tells her, and I could see from the way his eyes went that he hadn't noticed she was wearing a two-piece before. "We want you decently dressed when you come in here."

"We *are* decent," Queenie says suddenly, her lower lip pushing, getting sore now that she remembers her place, a place from which the crowd that runs the A & P must look pretty crummy. Fancy Herring Snacks flashed in her very blue eyes.

"Girls, I don't want to argue with you. After this come in here with your shoulders covered. It's our policy." He turns his back. That's policy for you. Policy is what the kingpins want. What the others want is juvenile delinquency.

20   All this while, the customers had been showing up with their carts but, you know, sheep, seeing a scene, they had all bunched up on Stokesie, who shook open a paper bag as gently as peeling a peach, not wanting to miss a word. I could feel in the silence everybody getting nervous, most of all Lengel, who asks me, "Sammy, have you rung up their purchase?"

I thought and said "No" but it wasn't about that I was thinking. I go through the punches, 4, 9, GROC, TOT—it's more complicated than you think, and after you do it often enough, it begins to make a little song, that you hear words to, in my case "Hello (*bing*) there, you (*gung*) hap-py *pee*-pul (*splat*)!"—the *splat* being the drawer flying out. I uncrease the bill, tenderly as you may imagine, it just having come from between the two smoothest scoops of vanilla I had ever known were there, and pass a half and a penny into her narrow pink palm, and nestle the herrings in a bag and twist its neck and hand it over, all the time thinking.

The girls, and who'd blame them, are in a hurry to get out, so I say "I quit" to Lengel quick enough for them to hear, hoping they'll stop and watch me, their unsuspected hero. They keep right on going, into the electric eye; the door flies open and they flicker across the lot to their car, Queenie and Plaid and Big Tall Goony-Goony (not that as raw material she was so bad), leaving me with Lengel and a kink in his eyebrow.

"Did you say something, Sammy?"

"I said I quit."

25   "I thought you did."

"You didn't have to embarrass them."

"It was they who were embarrassing us."

I started to say something that came out "Fiddle-de-doo." It's a saying of my grandmother's, and I know she would have been pleased.

"I don't think you know what you're saying," Lengel said.

30   "I know you don't," I said. "But I do." I pull the bow at the back of my apron and start shrugging it off my shoulders. A couple customers that had been heading for my slot begin to knock against each other, like scared pigs in a chute.

°"*They'll Do It Every Time*": syndicated daily and Sunday cartoon created by Jimmy Hatlo.

Lengel sighs and begins to look very patient and old and gray. He's been a friend of my parents for years. "Sammy, you don't want to do this to your Mom and Dad," he tells me. It's true, I don't. But it seems to me that once you begin a gesture it's fatal not to go through with it. I fold the apron, "Sammy" stitched in red on the pocket, and put it on the counter, and drop the bow tie on top of it. The bow tie is theirs, if you've ever wondered. "You'll feel this for the rest of your life," Lengel says, and I know that's true, too, but remembering how he made that pretty girl blush makes me so scrunchy inside I punch the No Sale tab and the machine whirs "pee-pul" and the drawer splats out. One advantage to this scene taking place in summer, I can follow this up with a clean exit, there's no fumbling around getting your coat and galoshes, I just saunter into the electric eye in my white shirt that my mother ironed the night before, and the door heaves itself open, and outside the sunshine is skating around on the asphalt.

I look around for my girls, but they're gone, of course. There wasn't anybody but some young married screaming with her children about some candy they didn't get by the door of a powder-blue Falcon° station wagon. Looking back in the big windows, over the bags of peat moss and aluminum lawn furniture stacked on the pavement, I could see Lengel in my place in the slot, checking the sheep through. His face was dark gray and his back stiff, as if he'd just had an injection of iron, and my stomach kind of fell as I felt how hard the world was going to be to me hereafter.

QUESTIONS

1. From Sammy's language, what do you learn about his view of himself? About his educational and class level? The first sentence, for example, is grammatically incorrect in standard English but not uncommon in colloquial English. Point out and explain similar passages.

2. Consider the first eleven paragraphs as exposition, in which you learn about the location, the issues, and the participants in the story's conflict. Is there anything inessential in this section? Do you learn enough to understand the story? How might someone other than Sammy present the material?

3. How do you learn that Sammy is an experienced "girl watcher"? What does *he think* he thinks about most girls? To what degree is this estimate inconsistent with what he finally does after the girls leave?

4. Why does Sammy say "I quit" so abruptly? What does he mean when he says that the world is going to be hard to him after his experience at the A & P?

WRITING ABOUT TONE AND STYLE

The task of writing about tone and style is to identify attitudes that you find in the work and then to explain how attitudes are made obvious by the author's style. How do words describing characters, scenes, thoughts, and actions indicate attitude? In Poe's "The Masque of the Red Death" (Chapter 9), for example, do the descriptions of the dimly lit rooms evoke fear or tension, or do they seem exaggerated? Depending on the story, your devising and answering such questions will help you understand an author's control over tone.

°*Falcon:* small car that had recently been introduced by the Ford Motor Company.

Questions for Discovering Ideas

- Use a dictionary to discover the meaning of any words you do not immediately know. Are there any unusual words? Any especially difficult or uncommon ones? Do any of the words distract you as you read?
- How strongly do you respond to the story? What words bring out your interest, concern, indignation, fearfulness, anguish, amusement, or sense of affirmation?
- Does the diction seem unusual or noteworthy, such as words in dialect, polysyllabic words, or foreign words or phrases that the author assumes you know? Are there any especially connotative or emotive words? What do these words suggest concerning the author's apparent assumptions about readers?
- Can you easily visualize and imagine the situations described by the words? If you find it easy, or hard, to what degree does your success or difficulty stem from the level of diction?
- For passages describing action, how vivid are the words? How do they help you picture the action? How do they hold your attention?
- For passages describing exterior or interior scenes, how specific are the words? How much detail does the writer provide? Should there be more or fewer words? How vivid are the descriptions? How successfully does the author locate scenes spatially? How many words are devoted to colors, shapes, sizes, and so on? What is the effect of such passages?
- For passages of dialogue, what does the level of speech indicate about the characters? How do a person's speeches help to establish her or his character? For what purposes does the author use formal or informal diction? How much slang (low or informal language) do you find? Why is it there? How does dialogue shape your responses to the characters and to the actions?
- What role does the narrator/speaker play in your attitudes toward the story material? Does the speaker seem intelligent/stupid, friendly/unfriendly, sane/insane, or idealistic/pragmatic?
- What verbal irony do you find in the story? How is the irony connected to philosophies of marriage, family, society, politics, religion, or morality? How do you think you are expected to respond to the irony?
- Did anything in the story make you laugh? What placement of words brought out the humor? Explain how the word arrangement caused your laughter.

Strategies for Organizing Ideas

Begin with a careful reading, noting particularly those elements of language that convey attitudes. How does the author establish the dominant moods of the story (e.g., the humor of "First Confession," the tension in "Hills Like White Elephants" both in this chapter)? Some possibilities are the use or misuse of language, the exposé of a pretentious speaker, the use of exact and specific descriptions, the isolation of a major character, the failure of plans, and the continuance of naiveté in a disillusioned world.

Here are some of the things to discuss:

1. *How is the work's tone affected by situation, characters, action, and audience?* Does the speaker directly address any person or group? What attitude is expressed (love, respect, condescension, confidentiality, confidence, etc.)? What is the basic situation in the story? Do you find instances of verbal irony? What do these show (optimism or pessimism, for example)? How is the situation of the story controlled to shape your responses? That is, can actions, situations, or characters be seen as expressions of attitude, or as embodiments of certain favorable or unfavorable ideas or positions? What sort of person is the narrator or persona? Why does the narrator speak exactly as he or she does? How is the narrator's character manipulated to show apparent authorial attitude and to elicit reader response? Does the story promote respect, admiration, dislike, or other feelings about character or situation? How?

2. *What do diction and descriptions contribute to the tone?* Your concern here is not to analyze descriptions or diction for themselves alone, but to relate these matters to attitude. *For descriptions*: Do descriptions of natural scenery and conditions (snowstorms, cold, rain, ice, intense sunlight) complement or oppose the circumstances of the characters? Are there any systematic references to colors, sounds, or noises that collectively reflect an attitude? *For diction*: Do connotative meanings of words control response in any way? Does the diction require readers to have a large or technical vocabulary? Do speech patterns or the use of dialect evoke attitudes about speakers or their condition of life? Is the level of diction formal, middle, or informal? Do you find any substandard or slang expressions? What effect do these create? Are there unusual or particularly noteworthy expressions? If so, what attitudes do these show?

3. *To what degree does the story contain humor?* Is the story funny? How funny, how intense? How is the humor achieved? How does the language bring out the incongruity of funny situations? Are the objects of laughter still respected or loved even though the story's treatment of them causes amusement?

4. *How does the expression of ideas shape the work's tone?* Are any ideas advocated, defended mildly, or attacked? How does the author clarify his or her attitude toward these ideas—directly, by statement, or indirectly, through understatement, overstatement, or a character's speeches? In what ways does the story assume agreement between author and readers? What common religious views can you find? What political views, moral and behavioral standards, and so on?

In concluding, first summarize your main points and then go on to definitions, explanations, or afterthoughts, together with ideas reinforcing earlier points. To what extent has your analysis increased or reinforced your appreciation of the author's technique? Does the passage take on added importance as a result of your study? Is there anything else in the work comparable to the content, words, or ideas you have discussed in the passage?

NUMBERING YOUR PASSAGE FOR EASY REFERENCE

To focus on specifics of style and tone, the assignment visualized here is to analyze a passage—either short or long—from a story. After you have selected a passage, include a copy at the beginning of your essay, as in the student essay below. For your reader's convenience, number the sentences in the passage, and use these numbers when you refer to them. To focus your essay, either single out one aspect of style and tone, or discuss everything, depending on the length of the assignment. Be sure to consider relationships that you can discover between tone and *levels of diction, specific and general words, concrete and abstract words, denotation and connotation, irony,* and *humor.*

Illustrative Student Essay

Underlined sentences in the paper *do not* conform to MLA style and are used solely as teaching tools to emphasize the central idea, thesis sentence, and topic sentences throughout the paper.

Torres 1

Elizabeth Torres

Professor Moorehouse

English 20

15 November 2008

Frank O'Connor's Control of Tone and Style in "First Confession"*

[1] Nora's turn came, and I heard the sound of something slamming, and then her voice as if butter wouldn't melt in her mouth, and then another slam, and out she came. [2] God, the hypocrisy of women! [3] Her eyes were lowered, her head was bowed, and her hands were joined very low down on her stomach, and she walked up the aisle to the side altar looking like a saint. [4] You never saw such an exhibition of devotion, and I remembered the devilish malice with which she had tormented me all the way from our door, and wondered were all religious people like that, really. [5] It was my turn now. [6] With the fear of damnation in my soul I went in, and the confessional door closed of itself behind me.

*This story appears on pages 354–59.

Torres 2

This paragraph from O'Connor's "First Confession" appears midway in [1]
the story. It is transitional, coming between Jackie's "heartscalded" memories
of family troubles and his happier memory of the confession itself. Though
mainly narrative, the passage is punctuated by Jackie's recollections of disgust
with his sister and fear of eternal punishment for his childhood "sins." It is the
controlled contrast of these attitudes that creates the humor of the passage.* In
all respects--brevity, word level, concreteness, and grammatical control--the
passage is typical of the story's humor.†

The actions and responses of the paragraph are described briefly and [2]
accurately. The first four sentences convey Jackie's exaggerated reactions to
Nora's confession. Sentence 1 describes his recollections of her voice in the
confessional, and the tone of sentence 3 makes his judgment clear about the
hypocrisy of her pious appearance when she leaves for the altar. Each of these
descriptive sentences is followed by Jackie's angry reactions, at which readers
smile, at least, if they do not laugh. This depth of feeling is transformed to "fear
of damnation" at the beginning of sentence 6, which describes Jackie's own
entry into the confessional, with the closing door suggesting that he is being
shut off from the world and thrown into hell. In other words, the paragraph
succinctly presents the sounds, reactions, sights, and confusion of the scene
itself, all of which furnish readers with a brief and comic drama.

The humorous action of the passage is augmented by O'Connor's neutral [3]
level of diction, which enables readers to concentrate fully on Jackie's
responses. Jackie is recalling an unpleasant childhood memory, and the neutral,
middle diction enables readers both to sympathize with him and to be amused
by him. His words are neither unusual nor difficult. What could be more
ordinary, for example, than "butter," "slam," "out," "hands," "joined," "low,"
"people," and "closed"? Even Jackie's moral and religious words fall within the
vocabulary of ordinary discussions about sin and punishment: "hypocrisy,"
"exhibition," "devilish," "malice," "tormented," and "damnation." In the
passage, therefore, the diction accurately conveys Jackie's vision of the

*Central idea.
†Thesis sentence.

Torres 3

oppressive religious forces which he dislikes, and which he also exaggerates. Readers follow these words easily and with amusement.

[4]   Additionally, the words of the paragraph are appropriate to Jackie's boyhood anger because they are specific and concrete. When he tells about Nora going into the confessional, he says specifically that he "heard the sound of something slamming," followed by the sound of Nora's "voice," "another slam," and then her appearance as "she came" out of the confessional. Equally specific, and equally comic, is his description of Nora's appearance as she leaves. Readers can easily visualize her "bowed" head, her "lowered" eyes, and her prayerful hands, and are amused by the scene just as Jackie, as a child, was annoyed by it. In addition to these specific descriptions, sentences 2 and 4 contain Jackie's angry responses, which also provoke amusement. Sentence 4 presents the greater number of connotative abstractions--first the "exhibition of devotion," and second the "devilish malice with which she had tormented me." But these define Jackie's childhood conclusions about his sister, not his adult ones, and their incongruity furnishes readers with a realistic basis for laughter.

[5]   A major element contributing to Jackie's remembrance of his boyhood attitudes is the control over grammar that O'Connor gives to him. At the time of the narrative Jackie is presumably no longer angry, even though as a child he felt misunderstood and unfairly treated. He therefore does not need to recall his story in angry outbursts, despite his exclamation about the "hypocrisy of women," but rather he presents details with grammatical correctness. The very first sentence, for example, contains three parallel grammatical direct objects ("sound," "voice," "slam"), thereby using a minimal number of words while still detailing the major sounds of Nora's confession. The grammar of the third sentence illustrates the swiftness and sparseness of O'Connor's (and Jackie's) narrative style. The first three parallel clauses are each made up of four words ("her eyes were lowered," "her head was bowed," and "her hands were joined"). These clauses give Jackie the opportunity to introduce his sarcastic and amusing phrase "looking like a saint" at the end to express his disgust over his sister's "hypocrisy." This control shapes the developing comedy of the paragraph.

Torres 4

[6]

In all respects, the passage shows the right use of words and exactly the right tone. Jackie's accurate descriptions are mixed with his expressions of childhood emotions--all important aspects of O'Connor's good humor. In retrospect, Jackie's anger and disgust were unnecessary, but they were important to him as a child--so much so that his exaggerations make him the center of the story's comedy. The words that O'Connor skillfully puts in Jackie's mouth (or on his page) enable readers to share this particular experience of a first confession but to do so while smiling. Jackie's bittersweetmemories are successfully rendered and made comic through O'Connor's control over style and tone.

Torres 5

Work Cited

O'Connor, Frank. "First Confession." Literature: An Introduction to Reading and Writing. Ed. Edgar V. Roberts. 9th ed. New York: Pearson Longman, 2009. 354–59.

Commentary on the Essay

Paragraph 1 demonstrates how a passage being studied may be related to the entire work of which it is a part. The central idea connects the story's comic tone to O'Connor's control over situation and diction. Throughout the essay, the connection of style and humor are emphasized. The thesis sentence presents four topics that the essay will develop. Any one of these topics, if necessary, could also be treated separately.

In the body of the essay, the writer stresses the way O'Connor creates the story's tone by the careful manipulation of words and expressions. Paragraph 2 indicates O'Connor's verbal economy in describing the actions and reactions of the passage. Paragraph 3 deals with the level of diction, noting that the words are appropriate both to the action and to Jackie's anger when recollecting it. In paragraph 4 the topic is O'Connor's use of specific and concrete diction, a quality that makes for easy visualization of the details. This paragraph also considers the small number of abstract and general words that appear in O'Connor's sentences 2 and 4.

Paragraph 5 connects O'Connor's grammatical control with the speaker's recollected boyhood anger. Examples of parallelism are three direct objects in sentence 1 and the first three clauses in sentence 3. Paragraph 6, the conclusion of the essay, summarizes the means by which O'Connor uses style to create the comedy of Jackie and his recollected feelings.

Writing Topics About Tone and Style

1. In "First Confession," the adult narrator is describing events that happened to him as a child. To what degree has this narrator, Jackie, separated himself from his childish emotions? What does he say that might be considered residual childhood responses? What effect, if any, do such comments create? For an additional dimension to this topic, you might compare Jackie as a narrator with the unnamed narrator of Joyce's "Araby" (Chapter 4).

2. Munro's "The Found Boat" (this chapter), and Gilman's "The Yellow Wallpaper" (Chapter 10) probe the psychological makeup of the major characters. Write an essay about the nature and effect of the language of character depiction in these stories.

3. In "Hills Like White Elephants" (this chapter), how does Hemingway's style shape your responses to the two main characters? How much description do you find in the story? How much dialogue?

4. Consider a short story in which the narrator is the central character (for example, "The Lesson" in Chapter 8, "First Confession" in this chapter, "How to Become a Writer" in Chapter 2, and "Blue Winds Dancing" in Chapter 5). Write an essay showing how the language of the narrator affects your attitudes toward him or her (that is, your sympathy for the narrator, your interest in the narrative, your feelings toward the other characters and what they do). Be sure to emphasize the relationship between the language of the narrators and the attitudes they demonstrate and elicit.

5. In "Barn Burning" (this chapter), how does Faulkner make it plain that Sarty's father and brother do not trust Sarty? Why do they have this attitude? On what evidence is their distrust confirmed? As a reader, does their attitude make you like Sarty more or less? Why?

6. How does Chopin convey attitudes toward the marital role of women and men in "The Story of an Hour" (this chapter)? Consider Louise's reactions to the news that her husband has been killed, and also consider Josephine's responses.

7. Write two brief character sketches, or a description of an action, to be included in a longer story. Make the first favorable, and the second negative. Analyze your word choices in the contrasting accounts: What kinds of words do you select, and on what principles do you select them? What kinds of words might you select if you wanted to create a neutral account? On the basis of your answers, what can you conclude about the development of a fiction writer's style?

8. In your school library or online, consult the most recent copy of the *MLA International Bibliography of Books and Articles on the Modern Languages and Literatures*, and make a short list of books and articles on Kate Chopin, Ernest Hemingway, Alice Munro, or Frank O'Connor (just one, not all). Consult at least two of the works, and with these, together with your own insights, write a short description of the writer's irony (comic or serious) and social criticism.

Chapter 7

Symbolism and Allegory: Keys to Extended Meaning

Symbolism and **allegory,** like metaphors and similes (see Chapter 19) are modes that expand meaning. They are literary devices developed from the connections that real-life people make between their own existence and particular objects, places, or occurrences, through either experience or reading: A young woman might recall a number of childhood difficulties with her mother, but realize that her mother acted out of love. A college student might remember the quiet satisfaction of returning home after a turbulent time spent away at a distant university. A war veteran might recall the crushing burdens that he and his fellow soldiers carried in combat. An elderly woman on her deathbed might consider the value of her life even though she sustained a crushing disappointment when she was young. The significance of details like these can be meaningful not just at a single moment but also throughout an entire lifetime. Merely bringing them to mind or speaking about them unlocks their meanings, implications, and consequences. It is as though the reference alone can be the equivalent of pages of explanation and analysis.

From this principle, both symbolism and allegory are derived. By highlighting details as *symbols*, and stories or parts of stories as *allegories*, writers expand their meaning while keeping their works within reasonable lengths.

Symbolism

The words **symbol** and **symbolism** are derived from the Greek word meaning "to throw together" (*syn*, "together," and *ballein*, "to throw"). A symbol creates a direct meaningful equation between (1) a specific object, scene, character, or action and (2) ideas, values, persons, or ways of life. In effect, a symbol is a *substitute* for the elements being signified, much as the flag stands for the ideals of the nation.

In painting and sculpture, symbols are easily recognized, for to tell a story visually, the artist must make every object count. In the anonymous fresco *Hercules and the Infant Telephus* from ancient Herculaneum (p. I–14), for example, the painter has depicted a crucial event in the life of the mythical hero Hercules—the choice he had to make early in his life between pleasure or toil. By symbolically turning his head away from the seated figure representing Pleasure, Hercules is rejecting the life of ease that she symbolizes. Instead, his life will be one of work, hardship, battle, victory, and glory, as symbolized by the lion, the eagle, and the sheaf of arrows. The image of his child, Telephus, whom he later abandons and who is being suckled by a donkey, symbolizes Hercules' insensitivity, verging on cruelty, which became a part of his single-minded existence as a warrior and hero.

When we first encounter a symbol in a story (also in poems and plays), it may seem to carry no more weight than its surface or obvious meaning. It can be a description of a character, an object, a place, an action, or a situation, and it may function normally and usefully in this capacity. What makes a symbol symbolic, however, is its capacity to signify additional levels of meaning—major ideas, simple or complex emotions, or philosophical or religious qualities or values. There are two types of symbols—*cultural* and *contextual*.

Cultural Symbols Are Derived from Our Cultural and Historical Heritage

Many symbols are *generally* or *universally* recognized and are therefore **cultural** (also called **universal**). They embody ideas and emotions that writers and readers share as heirs of the same historical and cultural tradition. When using cultural symbols, a writer assumes that readers already know what the symbols represent. An example is the character Sisyphus of ancient Greek myth. As a punishment for trying to overcome death not just once but twice, Sisyphus is doomed by the underworld gods to roll a large boulder up a high hill forever. Just as he gets the boulder to the top, it rolls down, and then he is fated to roll it up again—and again—and again—because the boulder always rolls back. The plight of Sisyphus has been interpreted as a symbol of the human condition: In spite of constant struggle, a person rarely if ever completes anything. Work must always be done over and over from day to day and from generation to generation, and the same problems confront humanity throughout all time. Because of such fruitless effort, life seems to have little or no meaning. Nevertheless, there is hope: People who confront their tasks, as Sisyphus does, stay involved and active, and their tasks make their lives meaningful. A writer referring to Sisyphus would expect us to understand that this ancient mythological figure symbolizes these conditions.

Similarly, ordinary water, because living creatures cannot live without it, is recognized as a symbol of life. It has this meaning in the ceremony of baptism, and it conveys this meaning and dimension in a variety of literary contexts. Thus, a spouting fountain might symbolize optimism (as upwelling, bubbling life), and a stagnant pool might symbolize the pollution and diminution of life. Water is also a universal symbol of sexuality, and its condition or state can symbolize various romantic relationships. For instance, stories in which lovers meet near a turbulent stream, a roaring waterfall, a mud puddle, a beach with high breakers, a stormy sea, a calm lake, or a wide and gently flowing river symbolically represent love relationships that range from uncertainty to serenity.

Contextual Symbols Are Symbolic Only in Individual Works

Objects and descriptions that are not universal symbols can be symbols *only if they are made so within individual works*. These are **contextual, private,** or **authorial** symbols. Unlike cultural symbols, contextual symbols derive their meanings from the context and circumstances of individual works. For example, the standing clock in Poe's "The Masque of the Red Death" (Chapter 9) is a large timepiece that in the story symbolizes not only the passage of time but also the sinister forces of death. Similarly, Elisa's chrysanthemums in Steinbeck's "The Chrysanthemums" (this chapter) seem at first nothing more than prized flowers. As the story progresses, however, they gain symbolic significance. The traveling tinsmith's apparent interest in them is the wedge he uses to wheedle a small mending job from Elisa. Her description of the care needed in planting and tending them suggests that they symbolize her kindness, love, orderliness, femininity, and motherliness.

Like Poe's clock, Steinbeck's chrysanthemums are a major contextual symbol. But there is not necessarily any carryover of symbolic meaning. In other stories, clocks and flowers are not symbolic unless the authors of these stories deliberately give them a symbolic charge. Further, if they are symbolic, they can be given different meanings than in the Poe and Steinbeck stories.

Determine What Is Symbolic (and Not Symbolic)

In determining whether a particular object, action, or character is a symbol, you need to judge the importance that the author gives to it. If the element is prominent and also maintains a constancy of meaning, you can justify interpreting it as a symbol. In Coleman's "Unfinished Masterpieces" (this chapter), we are told about how as a child, Dora Johns made things "out of mud." These little figures—"dolls and toys, flying birds and trotting horses, frisking dogs and playing kittens"—are remembered by the narrator as "drying in the sun," but they are intensely fragile. When wet, their shapes can be destroyed by a touch, and when dry they can fall and break. Although these figures are made of ordinary mud, they symbolize the suppressing of talent among minorities. It is the importance that Coleman gives to Dora's shaped figures that invests them with symbolic meaning. Importance is therefore a key to the determination of symbolism, as at the end of Welty's "A Worn Path" (Chapter 1). Phoenix, Welty's major character, plans to spend all her money—ten cents—for a toy windmill for her sick grandson. Readers will note that the windmill is small and fragile, like Phoenix's life and that of her grandson, but that she wants to give the boy a little happiness despite their poor and hopeless circumstances. For these reasons the windmill is a contextual or authorial symbol of Phoenix's loving character, bravery, generous nature, and touching existence.

Allegory

An **allegory** is like a symbol because it transfers and broadens meaning. The term is derived from the Greek word *allegorein* (from *allos*, "other" and *agoreuein*, "to speak in public"), which means "to say something beyond what is commonly understood." Allegory, however, is more sustained than symbolism. An allegory is to a symbol as a motion picture is to a still picture. In form, an allegory is a complete and self-sufficient narrative, but it also signifies another series of conditions or events. Although some stories are allegories from beginning to end, many stories that are not allegories nevertheless may contain brief sections or episodes that are *allegorical*. Allegories are often concerned with morality and especially with religion, but we may also find political and social allegories. To the degree that literary works are true not only because of the lives of their main characters but also because of life generally, we might maintain that much literature may be considered allegorical even though the authors did not plan their works as allegories.

Understand the Applications and Meaning of Allegory

Allegories and the allegorical method are more than literary exercises. Without question, readers and listeners learn and memorize stories and tales more easily than moral lessons, and therefore allegory is a favorite method of teaching morality. In addition, thought and expression have not always been free and safe, as we hope they are today in the United States. At times in other nations, under sometimes repressive political systems, the threat of censorship and the danger of political or economic reprisal have prompted authors to express their views indirectly in the form of allegory rather than to name names and write openly, thereby risking political prosecution, accusations of libel, or even bodily harm. Hence, the double meanings of many allegories are based not just in the literary form but also in the reality of circumstances in our difficult world.

In studying allegory, determine whether all or part of a work can have an extended, allegorical meaning. The popularity of George Lucas's film *Star Wars* and its sequels (in videotape and newly refurbished re-releases on DVD) and also its "prequel" (*The Phantom Menace*), for example, is attributable at least partly to its being an allegory about the conflict between good and evil. Obi Wan Kenobi (intelligence) assists Luke Skywalker (heroism, boldness) and instructs him in "the Force" (moral or religious faith). Thus armed and guided, Skywalker opposes the powers of Darth Vader (evil) to rescue the Princess Leia (purity and goodness) with the aid of the latest spaceships and weaponry (technology). The story has produced a set of popular adventure films, accompanied by dramatic music and ingenious visual and sound effects. With the obvious allegorical overtones, however, it stands for any person's quest for self-fulfillment.

To apply a part of the allegory more specifically, consider that for a time the evil Vader imprisons Skywalker and that Skywalker must exert all his skill and strength to get free and overcome Vader. In the allegorical application of the episode, this imprisonment may be taken to signify those moments of doubt, discouragement, and depression that people experience while trying to better themselves through education, work, self-improvement, friendship, marriage, and so on.

Almost from the beginning of recorded literature, similar heroic deeds have been represented in allegorical forms. From ancient Greece, the allegorical hero Jason sails the *Argo* to distant lands to gain the Golden Fleece (those who take risks are rewarded). From Anglo-Saxon England, the hero Beowulf saves King Hrothgar's throne by killing the monster Grendel and his even more monstrous mother (victory comes to those who rely on the forces of good). From seventeenth-century England, Bunyan's *The Pilgrim's Progress* tells how the hero Christian overcomes difficulties and temptations while traveling from this world to the next (belief, perseverance, and resistance to temptation save the faithful). As long as the parallel connections are close and consistent, such as those mentioned here, an allegorical interpretation is valid.

Fable, Parable, and Myth

Closely related to symbolism and allegory in the ability to extend and expand meaning are three additional forms—*fable, parable,* and *myth.*

A Fable Is a Short Tale with a Pointed Moral

The **fable** (from the Latin word *fabula*, a story or narration) is an old, brief, and popular form. Often but not always, fables are about animals that possess human traits (such fables are called **beast fables**). Past collectors and editors of fables have attached "morals" or explanations to the brief stories, as is the case with Aesop, the most enduringly popular of fable writers. Tradition has it that Aesop was a slave who composed fables in ancient Greece. His fable "The Fox and the Grapes" signifies the trait of belittling things we cannot have. Other popular contributions to the fable tradition include Walt Disney's "Mickey Mouse," Walt Kelly's "Pogo," and Berke Breathed's "Bloom County." The adjective *fabulous* refers to the collective body of fables of all sorts, even though the word is often overused as little more than a routine term of approval.

A Parable Is a Short Narrative Illustrating a Religious Concept

A **parable** (from the Greek word *parabolé*, a "setting beside" or comparison) is a short, simple story with a moral or religious thrust. Parables are most often associated with Jesus, who used them to embody unique religious insights and truths. For example, his parables "The Prodigal Son" and "The Good Samaritan," as recorded by Luke, are interpreted to show God's understanding, forgiveness, concern, and love.

A Myth Is a Tale with Social, Political, Religious, or Philosophical Meanings

A **myth** (from the Greek word *muthos*, a "story" or "plot") is a traditional story that embodies and codifies the religious, philosophical, and cultural values of the civilization in which it is composed. Usually the central figures of mythical stories are heroes, gods, and demigods, such as the ancient figures Aeneas, Zeus, Hera, Prometheus, Athena, Dionysus, Sisyphus, Oedipus, Atalanta, Hercules, and Venus. Most myths are of course fictional, but some are based in historical truth. They are by no means confined to the past, for the word *myth* can also refer to abstractions and ideas that people today hold collectively, such as the concept of never-ending economic growth or the idea that the earth can endlessly sustain all human exploitation and activities with no adverse effects. Sometimes the words *myth* and *mythical* are used with the meaning "fanciful" or "untrue." Such disparagement is misleading because the truths of mythology are not to be found literally in the myths themselves but rather in their symbolic and allegorical interpretations.

Allusion in Symbolism and Allegory

Cultural or universal symbols and allegories often **allude** to other works from our cultural heritage, such as the Bible, ancient history and literature, and works of the British and American traditions. Sometimes understanding a story may require knowledge of history and current politics.

If the meaning of a symbol is not immediately clear to you, you will need a dictionary or other reference work. The scope of your college dictionary will surprise you. If you cannot find an entry there, however, try one of the major print or online encyclopedias, or ask your reference librarian, who can direct you to helpful books or online references. A few excellent guides, which are frequently reprinted, are *The Oxford Companion to Classical Literature* (ed. M. C. Howatson and Ian Chilvers); *The Oxford Companion to English Literature* (ed. Margaret Drabble); *Benét's Reader's Encyclopedia*, 4th Edition; Timothy Gantz's *Early Greek Myth: A Guide to Literary and Artistic Sources*; Barry B. Powell's *Classical Myth* (with translations by Herbert M. Howe); and Richmond Y. Hathorn's *Greek Mythology*. Most of these books are regularly reprinted.

Useful aids in finding biblical references are *Cruden's Complete Concordance*, which in various editions has been a reliable guide since 1737 (yes, 1737), and *Strong's Exhaustive Concordance of the Bible*, which has been revised and expanded regularly—and renamed (as *The Strongest Strong's Exhaustive Concordance of the Bible*)—since it was first published in 1890. These concordances list all the major words used in the Bible (usually the King James Version), so you can easily locate the chapter and verse of any and all biblical passages. If you still have trouble after using sources like these, be sure to see your instructor.

Stories for Study

Aesop . . . . The Fox and the Grapes, 380

Anonymous . . . . The Myth of Atalanta, 381

Anita Scott Coleman . . . . Unfinished Masterpieces, 382

Nathaniel Hawthorne . . . . Young Goodman Brown, 385

Franz Kafka . . . . A Hunger Artist, 393

Luke . . . . The Parable of the Prodigal Son, 399

Gabriel García Marquez . . . . A Very Old Man with Enormous Wings, 400

Katherine Anne Porter . . . . The Jilting of Granny Weatherall, 405

John Steinbeck . . . . The Chrysanthemums, 411

AESOP (c. 620 BCE–560 BCE)

Not much is known about the ancient fabulist Aesop. According to tradition, he was a freed slave who lived from about 620 to 560 BCE Aristotle claimed that he had been a public defender, but there is no other evidence that he existed at all. In fact, versions of some of the fables were known a millennium before his time. Aesop might therefore be considered as much a collector as a creator of fables.

 ## The Fox and the Grapes (c. 6th C. BCE)

From a painting by Diego Velasquez (1599–1660)

A hungry Fox came into a vineyard where there hung delicious clusters of ripe Grapes; his mouth watered to be at them; but they were nailed up to a trellis so high, that with all his springing and leaping he could not reach a single bunch. At last, growing tired and disappointed, "Let who will take them!" says he, "they are but green and sour; so I'll e'en let them alone."

QUESTIONS

1. How much do you learn about the characteristics of the fox? How are these character-istics related to the moral or message of the fable?
2. What is the conflict in the fable? What is the resolution?
3. In your own words, explain the meaning of the fable. Is the "sour grapes" explanation a satisfactory excuse, or is it a rationalization for failure?
4. From your reading of "The Fox and the Grapes," explain the characteristics of the fable as a type of literature.

ANONYMOUS

The story of Atalanta is an anonymous myth that was known throughout both the ancient Greek and Roman worlds. Because communication in ancient times was uncertain, there were varia-tions in some of the details of the story, such as the names of Atalanta's father and her suitors. However, there was general agreement about the details of her story, which was told by many dif-ferent writers, such as Apollodorus, Aelian, and Pacuvius. The best-known ancient text of the story appears in Ovid's Metamorphoses. *The story included here is slightly adapted from the brief but comprehensive version by Richmond Y. Hathorn (Greek Mythology, 1977).*

 ## The Myth of Atalanta (5th–1st C. BCE)

There was once a man from Arcadia, in southern Greece, who hoped very much for a son, and when his wife gave birth to a daughter, he abandoned the child in the woods. A she-bear that lived there suckled the baby, until some hunters chanced on the child and reared it, calling it Atalanta [i.e., "the invincible one"]. Atalanta grew up to be a true daughter of the wilderness, an incomparable hunter, being instructed by the Goddess of the Hunt, Artemis, herself. Atalanta was a runner who could outrace any man, and a skillful wrestler, on one occasion defeating the hero Peleus at Pelias' funeral games. She tried also to go on the expedition with the Argonauts to recover the Golden Fleece, but she was turned away by Jason, who was afraid of the trouble a beautiful young woman might cause in a crew of young men.

Then Atalanta took part in the hunting of the Calydonian Boar, falling in love with the Calydonian Prince Meleager and being loved in return. But as this love brought about Me-leager's death and as Atalanta was already inclined toward celibacy because of her alle-giance to Artemis, she resolved on leading a solitary manless life henceforth, especially because the oracle at Delphi warned her that marriage would cause her whole nature to be changed. So when she gave birth to Meleager's child on her way back from Calydon to Ar-cadia, she kept it a secret and exposed the baby boy on Mount Parthenion. This child, called Parthenopaeous, was found by the same shepherds who had found and reared Tele-phus (the son of Hercules and the Princess Auge), and he grew up to be Telephus' com-panion in early adventures. Eventually Parthenopaeous met his death in the war of the Seven against Thebes.

Meanwhile Atalanta had returned to her old hunting haunts, fighting off attacks of satyrs and discouraging the proposals of mortal men by stipulating that each suitor should complete with her in a race, in which she would be armed with a spear. The condition was that if she overtook her opponent she might stab him to death. And in this way she had disposed of three suitors, cutting off their heads and displaying them beside the racecourse.

There was a young Arcadian named Milanion, who hated women as much as Atalanta hated men, and who was as fond of the chase as she was. He encountered Atalanta frequently during his hunts, and imperceptibly he fell in love with her. More and more he put himself in her way, until he was faithfully following her around, carrying her hunting-nets and enduring her endless disdain. Once when a centaur, Hylaeus, whom Atalanta had rejected, attacked her in anger, Milanion intervened, receiving the blows of the centaur's club and even being wounded by one of the centaur's arrows while protecting Atalanta with his body. Atalanta killed the man-beast, and then nursed the injured Milanion back to health, her feeling for him growing warmer all the while.

5   Still there was no way of winning Atalanta short of defeating her in the footrace; so in spite of all her discouragements Milanion challenged her. But before the day of the race he prayed to Aphrodite, the Goddess of Love, for aid, and the Goddess plucked three golden apples from the Garden of the Hesperides and instructed him in their use. When the race had begun and Atalanta was drawing near, Milanion dropped one golden apple and the young woman stopped to pick it up. Again she drew near, and again he dropped an apple, the Goddess causing them to weigh heavily in Atalanta's bosom. So when the third apple was dropped and picked up, Milanion was able to reach the goal unscathed and to claim Atalanta as his bride.

But in the flush of his victory and her willing defeat they both forgot to give thanks to Aphrodite. The Goddess punished them by inflicting a rage of lust on both of them, so that they lost all control of themselves. Passing by a sanctuary of Cybele, the Great Mother of Gods, they fell immediately to lovemaking in the holy grotto near the holy temple. They behaved with such abandon that the very statues averted their eyes. The Great Mother was incensed and thought of killing them at once, but instead she changed Milanion into a Lion and Atalanta into a lioness and made them the team that draws her chariot.

QUESTIONS

1. What abilities does Atalanta have? How does she try to preserve her independence?

2. Why does Atalanta vow to shun men? What causes her to change her mind? What finally happens to her?

3. Consider the symbolic significance of Atalanta's name, the golden apples, the chopping off of the heads of slow-running suitors, the father's abandonment of Atalanta, the exposure of the infant Parthenopaeus, the battle with the centaur, the way in which Atalanta loses the race, and the lovemaking in the holy grotto of the Great Mother of Gods.

ANITA SCOTT COLEMAN (1890–1960)

Coleman, a writer of stories, poems, and essays, was born in Mexico and educated in New Mexico. Her mother had been a slave who had been bought out of slavery by her father. She published mainly in magazines. "Unfinished Masterpieces," for example, was published in Crisis: A Record of the Darker Races, *the magazine begun in 1910 that heralded the development of the Harlem Renaissance.*

🍁 Unfinished Masterpieces (1927)

There are days which stand out clearly like limpid pools beside the dusty road; when your thoughts, crystal clear as water, are pinioned in loveliness like star-points. Solitary days, which come often, if you are given to browsing in fields of past adventure; or rarely, if you are seldom retrospective; and not at all, if you are too greatly concerned with rushing onward to a nebulous future. Days whereupon your experiences glimmer before you waveringly like motion-pictures and the people you have known stroll through the lanes of memory, arrayed in vari-colored splendor or in amusing disarray. Days like these are to be revered, for they have their humors and their whimsicalities. Hurry your thoughts and the gathering imageries take flight. Perplexity but makes the lens of introspection blur. And of annoyance beware, for it is an evil vapor that disseminates and drowns the visions in the sea of grim realities. Such days must be cultivated. Scenes for their reception must be set. Cushions perhaps, and warmth of fire. Above all, the warmth of sweet content. Ease and comfort, comfort and ease and moods of receptivity. Then hither, come hither the places and the people we have known, the associations that withstand time's effacements. Backward ho, through the mazes of the past.

STOP! "Why howdy, Dora Johns." Darling playmate of my child-years. With wooly hair a length too short for even pigtails. Mud-spatters upon your funny black face. Mud-spatters all over your dress and your little black hands mud-spattered too.

Why? What? Come on and see. And lo! I am a child again.

Hand in hand, unmindful of her muddy ones, we skip around the old ramshackle house, back to the furthest corner of an unkempt yard, impervious to the tin cans, the ash-heap, the litter, the clutter that impedes our way, our eyes upon, our thoughts bent upon one small clean-swept corner, where there is mud. More mud and water in a battered tin can. And row after row of mud. No, not mud—not merely mud, but things made out of mud. Row on row, drying in the sun.

Carefully, I sit down, doubling up, to be as small as possible, for only this corner where   5
mud things are drying is clean and corners are seldom, if ever, quite large enough. Besides, I must not touch the things made out of mud. If the dried ones fall, they break. If the moist ones are molested, be it with ever so gentle a finger, they lose their shape. Moreover I must not disturb Dora.

Her little hands are busied with the mud. Little moulder's fingers are deftly plying their skill. Her child's face is alight. What has splashed her grave child's face with such a light? I wondered. I wonder now. The glitter of brittle talent, a gleam of sterling genius or the glow from artistic fires burning within the soul of a little black child?

Little Dora shaping figures out of mud. Vases and urns, dolls and toys, flying birds and trotting horses, frisking dogs and playing kittens, marvelous things out of mud. Crying aloud as though dealt a blow if one of the dried mud-figures is broken. Working in mud for endless hours, while the neighbor children play. Their hilarious merriment dropping like bombs into the quiet of our clean-swept corner. Deadly missiles seeking to find a mark. The insistent halloes of futile mirth forever bubbling on the other side of a highboard fence. The dividing fence and upon one side the clean-swept corner and the row on row of mud things drying in the sun. And Dora seeming not to heed the seething bubbles upon the other side, shaping, shaping marvelous things out of mud.

Yet, Oh Dora, now that the day is ours, will you not say, "When did the bombs of futile mirth strike their target? When did the tin-cans and the rags and the old ash-heap crowd you out from your clean-swept corner? What rude hand caused the dried mud shapes to fall and break? Who set a ruthless foot in the midst of your damp mud things?" Or were you too plastic, as plastic as your mud? You dare not tell. Only this you can whisper into the mists of our today. You are one of the Master's unfinished shapes which He will some day gather to mould anew into the finished masterpiece.

A lump of mud. Now, there is a sobriquet for you—you funny, funny man. Mr. William Williams. I saw you but once. We chanced to meet in the home of a mutual friend. I thought you so very funny then. Uncouth and very boorish, but ever, when these pageants of the past, these dumb shows of inarticulate folks arise before me upon retrospective days, you appear garbed in the tatters of pathos.

10   "I am fifty-one years old," you kept repeating. How pitiful those fifty-one years are. You wear a child's simplicity, the sort that is so sad to see upon a man. Fifty-one and penniless. Fifty-one and possessed of naught else but the clothing you wore. Fifty-one and no place on earth you might call home. You confessed to being a vagabond though "bum" was the term you used and you were very proud of your one accomplishment, an ability to avoid all labour.

    "I've given no man a full day's honest work in all my fifty-one years," you boasted. "I gambles. I ain't no cotton-pickin' nigger." Your one and only boast after holding life, the fathomless fountain of eternal possibilities, in your possession for fifty-one priceless years.

    Nevertheless you have lived and so intensely. You held us against our will. Clustered around you, listening to you talk. Relating clippings as it were from the scrap-book of your life.

    Tales of the road, of the only places you knew. Roads leading away from plantations where the cotton waited to be picked by numberless "cotton-pickin' niggers." Roads leading to pool halls and gambling dens. Roads beginning and roads ending in "riding the roads," carrying backward and forward, here and yon through the weird goblin land of the South's black belt.

    With a hardened casualness you told stories that revolted and at the same time cheered us with an all sufficing glow of thankfulness that life had spared us the sordidness of yours. Offhandily, you gave us humorous skits that tempered our laughter with wishes that we might know at least a bit of such a droll existence as had been yours. With magical words you painted pictures so sharply they cut scars upon our hearts. You drew others so filled with rollicking delight their gladsomeness was contagious. With the nonchalance of a player shuffling cards you flipped your characters before us, drawn directly from the cesspool of your contacts, and spellbound we listened.

15   Someone remarked how wonderful you talked and you replied, "Once, I sorter wanted to write books. Once, I uster read a heaps. See times when I was broke and nobody would stake me for a game. I'd lay around and read. I've read the Bible through and through and every Police Gazette I could lay my hands on. Yes, suh, I've read a heap. And I've wished a lot'er times I'd sense enough to write a book."

    Lump of mud. Containing the you, the splendid artist in you, the soul of you, the unfinished you in the ungainly lump of you, awaiting the gathering-up to be molded anew into the finished masterpiece.

    What a day! Here is my friend at whose fire-side I have lingered beholding Mr. William Williams, great lump of mud. To be sure, she also is an unfinished production. Though it is apparent that the Master had all but done when she slipped from his hands and dropped to earth to lie groping like the rest of us thereon.

    Let us sit here together, friend, and enjoy this day.

    I shall try to discover what recent gift you have given to the poor the while you are quietly stitching upon the garments, linens and scarlet, with which to clothe your household. Sit here and smile with the welcoming light in your eyes, knowing that your door is open to such as William Williams and Dora Johns, the Dora who is become as the mud beneath one's feet. Kind mistress of the widely opened door where white and black, rich and poor, of whatever caste or creed may enter and find comfort and ease and food and drink.

QUESTIONS

1. What talents do Dora and William possess? Why have they not lived up to their talents? What has kept them down? Why are they "unfinished masterpieces"?

2. How may Dora and William be seen as symbols? What do they symbolize?

3. Characterize the narrator. What attitude does she exhibit toward the lack of fulfillment of the major characters (see particularly paragraph 19)? How might the story have been different if the narrator had shown hostility, for example, or extreme bitterness?

NATHANIEL HAWTHORNE (1804–1864)

Hawthorne, a friend and associate of the fourteenth president of the United States, Franklin Pierce, is one of the great American writers of the nineteenth century. His most famous work is The Scarlet Letter *(1850), the sale of which gave him a degree of independence. During the administration of President Pierce (1853–1857), Hawthorne served as American consul in Liverpool, England, and this opportunity enabled him to travel extensively in Europe. Throughout his writing there runs a conflict between freedom and conventionality, with those choosing freedom sometimes suffering from the guilt that their choice brings. "Young Goodman Brown," which is one of the early stories that he included in* Twice-Told Tales *(1837, 1842), embodies this conflict.*

🍁 Young Goodman Brown (1835)

Young Goodman Brown came forth at sunset, into the street of Salem village,° but put his head back, after crossing the threshold, to exchange a parting kiss with his young wife. And Faith, as the wife was aptly named, thrust her own pretty head into the street, letting the wind play with the pink ribbons of her cap, while she called to Goodman Brown.

"Dearest heart," whispered she, softly and rather sadly, when her lips were close to his ear, "prithee, put off your journey until sunrise, and sleep in your own bed tonight. A lone woman is troubled with such dreams and such thoughts, that she's afeared of herself, sometimes. Pray, tarry with me this night, dear husband, of all nights in the year!"

"My love and my Faith," replied young Goodman Brown, "of all nights in the year, this one night must I tarry away from thee. My journey, as thou callest it, forth and back again, must needs be done 'twixt now and sunrise. What, my sweet, pretty wife, dost thou doubt me already, and we but three months married!"

"Then God bless you!" said Faith with the pink ribbons, "and may you find all well, when you come back."

"Amen!" cried Goodman Brown. "Say thy prayers, dear Faith, and go to bed at dusk, and no harm will come to thee."   5

So they parted; and the young man pursued his way, until, being about to turn the corner by the meeting-house, he looked back and saw the head of Faith still peeping after him, with a melancholy air, in spite of her pink ribbons.

"Poor little Faith!" thought he, for his heart smote him. "What a wretch am I, to leave her on such an errand! She talks of dreams, too. Methought, as she spoke, there was trouble in her face, as if a dream had warned her what work is to be done tonight. But no, no! 't would kill her to think it. Well; she's a blessed angel on earth; and after this one night, I'll cling to her skirts and follow her to Heaven."

°*Salem village:* in Massachusetts, about fifteen miles north of Boston. The time of the story is the late seventeenth or early eighteenth century.

With this excellent resolve for the future, Goodman Brown felt himself justified in making more haste on his present evil purpose. He had taken a dreary road, darkened by all the gloomiest trees of the forest, which barely stood aside to let the narrow path creep through, and closed immediately behind. It was all as lonely as could be; and there is this peculiarity in such a solitude, that the traveller knows not who may be concealed by the innumerable trunks and the thick boughs overhead; so that, with lonely footsteps, he may yet be passing through an unseen multitude.

"There may be a devilish Indian behind every tree," said Goodman Brown to himself; and he glanced fearfully behind him, as he added, "What if the devil himself should be at my very elbow!"

10   His head being turned back, he passed a crook of the road, and looking forward again, beheld the figure of a man, in grave and decent attire, seated at the foot of an old tree. He arose at Goodman Brown's approach, and walked onward, side by side with him.

"You are late, Goodman Brown," said he. "The clock of the Old South° was striking, as I came through Boston; and that is full fifteen minutes agone."

"Faith kept me back awhile," replied the young man, with a tremor in his voice, caused by the sudden appearance of his companion, though not wholly unexpected.

It was now deep dusk in the forest, and deepest in that part of it where these two were journeying. As nearly as could be discerned, the second traveller was about fifty years old, apparently in the same rank of life as Goodman Brown, and bearing a considerable resemblance to him, though perhaps more in expression than features. Still, they might have been taken for father and son. And yet, though the elder person was as simply clad as the younger, and as simple in manner too, he had an indescribable air of one who knew the world, and would not have felt abashed at the governor's dinner-table, or in King William's° court, were it possible that his affairs should call him thither. But the only thing about him that could be fixed upon as remarkable, was his staff, which bore the likeness of a great black snake, so curiously wrought, that it might almost be seen to twist and wriggle itself like a living serpent. This, of course, must have been an ocular deception, assisted by the uncertain light.

"Come, Goodman Brown!" cried his fellow-traveller, "this is a dull pace for the beginning of a journey. Take my staff, if you are so soon weary."

15   "Friend," said the other, exchanging his slow pace for a full stop, "having kept covenant by meeting thee here, it is my purpose now to return whence I came. I have scruples, touching the matter thou wot'st of.°

"Sayest thou so?" replied he of the serpent, smiling apart. "Let us walk on, nevertheless, reasoning as we go, and if I convince thee not, thou shalt turn back. We are but a little way in the forest, yet."

"Too far, too far!" exclaimed the goodman, unconsciously resuming his walk. "My father never went into the woods on such an errand, nor his father before him. We have been a race of honest men and good Christians, since the days of the martyrs.° And shall I be the first of the name of Brown that ever took this path and kept—"

"Such company, thou wouldst say," observed the elder person, interrupting his pause. "Well said, Goodman Brown! I have been as well acquainted with your family as ever a one among the Puritans; and that's no trifle to say. I helped your grandfather, the constable, when he lashed the Quaker woman so smartly through the streets of Salem. And it was I that brought your father a pitch-pine knot, kindled at my own hearth, to set

---

°*Old South:* The Old South Church, in Boston, is still there.
°*King William:* William III was king of England from 1688 to 1701 (the time of the story). William IV was king from 1830 to 1837 (the period when Hawthorne wrote the story).
°*thou wot'st:* you know.
°*days of the martyrs:* the martyrdoms of Protestants in England during the reign of Queen Mary (1553–1558).

fire to an Indian village, in King Philip's war.° They were my good friends, both; and many a pleasant walk have we had along this path, and returned merrily after midnight. I would fain be friends with you, for their sake."

"If it be as thou sayest," replied Goodman Brown, "I marvel they never spoke of these matters. Or, verily, I marvel not, seeing that the least rumor of the sort would have driven them from New England. We are a people of prayer, and good works to boot, and abide no such wickedness."

"Wickedness or not," said the traveller with twisted staff, "I have a very general ac- 20 quaintance here in New England. The deacons of many a church have drunk the commun- ion wine with me; the selectmen, of divers towns, make me their chairman; and a majority of the Great and General Court are firm supporters of my interest. The governor and I, too—but these are state secrets."

"Can this be so!" cried Goodman Brown, with a stare of amazement at his undisturbed companion. "Howbeit, I have nothing to do with the governor and council; they have their own ways, and are no rule for a simple husbandman like me. But, were I to go on with thee, how should I meet the eye of that good old man, our minister, at Salem village? Oh, his voice would make me tremble, both Sabbath-day and lecture-day!"°

Thus far, the elder traveller had listened with due gravity, but now burst into a fit of ir- repressible mirth, shaking himself so violently, that his snakelike staff actually seemed to wriggle in sympathy.

"Ha! ha! ha!" shouted he, again and again; then composing himself, "Well, go on, Good- man Brown, go on; but, prithee, don't kill me with laughing!"

"Well, then, to end the matter at once," said Goodman Brown, considerably nettled, "there is my wife, Faith. It would break her dear little heart; and I'd rather break my own!"

"Nay, if that be the case," answered the other, "e'en go thy ways, Goodman Brown. I would 25 not, for twenty old women like the one hobbling before us, that Faith should come to any harm."

As he spoke, he pointed his staff at a female figure on the path, in whom Goodman Brown recognized a very pious and exemplary dame, who had taught him his catechism in youth, and was still his moral and spiritual adviser, jointly with the minister and Deacon Gookin.

"A marvel, truly, that Goody° Cloyse should be so far in the wilderness, at nightfall!" said he. "But, with your leave, friend, I shall take a cut through the woods, until we have left this Christian woman behind. Being a stranger to you, she might ask whom I was con- sorting with, and whither I was going."

"Be it so," said his fellow-traveller. "Betake you to the woods, and let me keep the path."

Accordingly, the young man turned aside, but took care to watch his companion, who advanced softly along the road, until he had come within a staff's length of the old dame. She, meanwhile, was making the best of her way, with singular speed for so aged a woman, and mumbling some indistinct words, a prayer, doubtless, as she went. The traveller put forth his staff, and touched her withered neck with what seemed the serpent's tail.

"The devil!" screamed the pious old lady.

"Then Goody Cloyse knows her old friend?" observed the traveller, confronting her, and 30 leaning on his writhing stick.

°*King Philip's war:* This war (1675–1676), infamous for the atrocities committed by the New England settlers, re- sulted in the suppression of Indian tribal life and prepared the way for unlimited settlement of New England by European immigrants. "Philip" was the English name of Chief Metacomet of the Wampanoag tribe.
°*Sabbath-day and lecture-day:* "Sabbath-day" is Sunday. "Lecture-day" refers to Thursday lectures on biblical and moral topics.
°*Goody:* shortened form of "goodwife," a respectful name for a married woman of low rank. A "Goody Cloyse" was one of the women sentenced to execution by Hawthorne's great-grandfather, Judge John Hathorne.

"Ah, forsooth, and is it your worship, indeed?" cried the good dame. "Yea, truly is it, and in the very image of my old gossip,° Goodman Brown, the grandfather of the silly fellow that now is. But, would your worship believe it? My broomstick hath strangely disappeared, stolen, as I suspect, by that unhanged witch, Goody Cory,° and that, too, when I was all anointed with the juice of smallage and cinquefoil and wolf's-bane—"°

"Mingled with fine wheat and the fat of a new-born babe," said the shape of old Goodman Brown.

"Ah, your worship knows the recipe," cried the old lady, cackling aloud. "So, as I was saying, being all ready for the meeting, and no horse to ride on, I made up my mind to foot it; for they tell me there is a nice young man to be taken into communion tonight. But now your good worship will lend me your arm, and we shall be there in a twinkling."

35
"That can hardly be," answered her friend. "I will not spare you my arm, Goody Cloyse, but here is my staff, if you will."

So saying, he threw it down at her feet, where, perhaps, it assumed life, being one of the rods which its owner had formerly lent to the Egyptian Magi.° Of this fact, however, Goodman Brown could not take cognizance. He had cast up his eyes in astonishment, and looking down again, beheld neither Goody Cloyse nor the serpentine staff, but his fellow-traveller alone, who waited for him as calmly as if nothing had happened.

"That old woman taught me my catechism!" said the young man; and there was a world of meaning in this simple comment.

They continued to walk onward, while the elder traveller exhorted his companion to make good speed and persevere in the path, discoursing so aptly, that his arguments seemed rather to spring up in the bosom of his auditor, than to be suggested by himself. As they went he plucked a branch of maple, to serve for a walking-stick, and began to strip it of the twigs and little boughs, which were wet with evening dew. The moment his fingers touched them, they became strangely withered and dried up, as with a week's sunshine. Thus the pair proceeded, at a good free pace, until suddenly, in a gloomy hollow of the road, Goodman Brown sat himself down on the stump of a tree, and refused to go any farther.

"Friend," said he, stubbornly, "my mind is made up. Not another step will I budge on this errand. What if a wretched old woman do choose to go to the devil, when I thought she was going to Heaven! Is that any reason why I should quit my dear Faith, and go after her?"

40
"You will think better of this by and by," said his acquaintance, composedly. "Sit here and rest yourself a while; and when you feel like moving again, there is my staff to help you along."

Without more words, he threw his companion the maple stick, and was as speedily out of sight as if he had vanished into the deepening gloom. The young man sat a few moments by the roadside, applauding himself greatly, and thinking with how clear a conscience he should meet the minister, in his morning walk, nor shrink from the eye of good old Deacon Gookin. And what calm sleep would be his, that very night, which was to have been spent so wickedly, but purely and sweetly now, in the arms of Faith! Amidst these pleasant and praiseworthy meditations, Goodman Brown heard the tramp of horses along the road, and deemed it advisable to conceal himself within the verge of the forest, conscious of the guilty purpose that had brought him thither, though now so happily turned from it.

On came the hoof-tramps and the voices of the riders, two grave old voices, conversing soberly as they drew near. These mingled sounds appeared to pass along the road, within a few yards of the young man's hiding-place; but owing, doubtless, to the depth of the gloom, at that particular spot, neither the travellers nor their steeds were visible. Though

---

° *gossip:* from "good sib" or "good relative."
°*Goody Cory:* name of a woman who was also sent to execution by Judge Hathorne.
°*smallage and cinquefoil and wolf's-bane:* plants commonly used by witches in making ointments.
°*lent to the Egyptian Magi:* See Exodus 7:10–12.

their figures brushed the small boughs by the wayside, it could not be seen that they intercepted, even for a moment, the faint gleam from the strip of bright sky, athwart which they must have passed. Goodman Brown alternately crouched and stood on tiptoe, pulling aside the branches, and thrusting forth his head as far as he durst, without discerning so much as a shadow. It vexed him the more, because he could have sworn, were such a thing possible, that he recognized the voices of the minister and Deacon Gookin, jogging° along quietly, as they were wont to do, when bound to some ordination or ecclesiastical council. While yet within hearing, one of the riders stopped to pluck a switch.

"Of the two, reverend Sir," said the voice like the deacon's, "I had rather miss an ordination dinner than to-night's meeting. They tell me that some of our community are to be here from Falmouth and beyond, and others from Connecticut and Rhode Island; besides several of the Indian powwows,° who, after their fashion, know almost as much deviltry as the best of us. Moreover, there is a goodly young woman to be taken into communion."

"Mighty well, Deacon Gookin!" replied the solemn old tones of the minister. "Spur up, or we shall be late. Nothing can be done, you know, until I get on the ground."

The hoofs clattered again, and the voices, talking so strangely in the empty air, passed   45
on through the forest, where no church had ever been gathered, nor solitary Christian prayed. Whither, then, could these holy men be journeying, so deep into the heathen wilderness? Young Goodman Brown caught hold of a tree, for support, being ready to sink down on the ground, faint and over-burthened with the heavy sickness of his heart. He looked up to the sky, doubting whether there really was a Heaven above him. Yet, there was the blue arch, and the stars brightening in it.

"With Heaven above, and Faith below, I will yet stand firm against the devil!" cried Goodman Brown.

While he still gazed upward, into the deep arch of the firmament, and had lifted his hands to pray, a cloud, though no wind was stirring, hurried across the zenith, and hid the brightening stars. The blue sky was still visible, except directly overhead, where this black mass of cloud was sweeping swiftly northward. Aloft in the air, as if from the depths of the cloud, came a confused and doubtful sound of voices. Once, the listener fancied that he could distinguish the accents of town's people of his own, men and women, both pious and ungodly, many of whom he had met at the communion-table, and had seen others rioting at the tavern. The next moment, so indistinct were the sounds, he doubted whether he had heard aught but the murmur of the old forest, whispering without a wind. Then came a stronger swell of those familiar tones, heard daily in the sunshine, at Salem village, but never, until now, from a cloud at night. There was one voice, of a young woman, uttering lamentations, yet with an uncertain sorrow, and entreating for some favor, which, perhaps, it would grieve her to obtain. And all the unseen multitude, both saints and sinners, seemed to encourage her onward.

"Faith!" shouted Goodman Brown, in a voice of agony and desperation; and the echoes of the forest mocked him, crying—"Faith! Faith!" as if bewildered wretches were seeking her, all through the wilderness.

The cry of grief, rage, and terror was yet piercing the night, when the unhappy husband held his breath for a response. There was a scream, drowned immediately in a louder murmur of voices fading into far-off laughter, as the dark cloud swept away, leaving the clear and silent sky above Goodman Brown. But something fluttered lightly down through the air, and caught on the branch of a tree. The young man seized it and beheld a pink ribbon.

"My Faith is gone!" cried he, after one stupefied moment. "There is no good on earth,   50
and sin is but a name. Come, devil! for to thee is this world given."

°*jogging:* riding a horse at a slow trot.
°*powwow:* a Narragansett Indian word describing a priest or cult leader who led ritual ceremonies of dance, incantation, and magic.

And maddened with despair, so that he laughed loud and long, did Goodman Brown grasp his staff and set forth again, at such a rate, that he seemed to fly along the forest path, rather than to walk or run. The road grew wilder and drearier, and more faintly traced, and vanished at length, leaving him in the heart of the dark wilderness, still rushing onward, with the instinct that guides mortal man to evil. The whole forest was peopled with frightful sounds; the creaking of the trees, the howling of wild beasts, and the yell of Indians; while, sometimes, the wind tolled like a distant church bell, and sometimes gave a broad roar around the traveller, as if all Nature were laughing him to scorn. But he was himself the chief horror of the scene, and shrank not from its other horrors.

"Ha! ha! ha!" roared Goodman Brown, when the wind laughed at him. "Let us hear which will laugh loudest! Think not to frighten me with your deviltry! Come witch, come wizard, come Indian powwow, come devil himself! and here comes Goodman Brown. You may as well fear him as he fear you!"

In truth, all through the haunted forest, there could be nothing more frightful than the figure of Goodman Brown. On he flew, among the black pines, brandishing his staff with frenzied gestures, now giving vent to an inspiration of horrid blasphemy, and now shouting forth such laughter, as set all the echoes of the forest laughing like demons around him. The fiend in his own shape is less hideous than when he rages in the breast of man. Thus sped the demoniac on his course, until, quivering among the trees, he saw a red light before him, as when the felled trunks and branches of a clearing have been set on fire, and throw up their lurid blaze against the sky, at the hour of midnight. He paused, in a lull of the tempest that had driven him onward, and heard the swell of what seemed a hymn, rolling solemnly from a distance, with the weight of many voices. He knew the tune. It was a familiar one in the choir of the village meeting-house. The verse died heavily away, and was lengthened by a chorus, not of human voices, but of all the sounds of the benighted wilderness, pealing in awful harmony together. Goodman Brown cried out; and his cry was lost to his own ear, by its unison with the cry of the desert.

In the interval of silence, he stole forward, until the light glared full upon his eyes. At one extremity of an open space, hemmed in by the dark wall of the forest, arose a rock, bearing some rude, natural resemblance either to an altar or a pulpit, and surrounded by four blazing pines, their tops aflame, their stems untouched, like candles at an evening meeting. The mass of foliage, that had overgrown the summit of the rock, was all on fire, blazing high into the night, and fitfully illuminating the whole field. Each pendent twig and leafy festoon was in a blaze. As the red light arose and fell, a numerous congregation alternately shone forth, then disappeared in shadow, and again grew, as it were, out of the darkness, peopling the heart of the solitary woods at once.

55   "A grave and dark-clad company!" quoth Goodman Brown.

In truth, they were such. Among them, quivering to-and-fro, between gloom and splendor, appeared faces that would be seen, next day, at the council-board of the province, and others which, Sabbath after Sabbath, looked devoutly heavenward, and benignantly over the crowded pews, from the holiest pulpits in the land. Some affirm that the lady of the governor was there. At least, there were high dames well known to her, and wives of honored husbands, and widows a great multitude, and ancient maidens, all of excellent repute, and fair young girls, who trembled lest their mothers should espy them. Either the sudden gleams of light, flashing over the obscure field, bedazzled Goodman Brown, or he recognized a score of the church members of Salem village, famous for their especial sanctity. Good old Deacon Gookin had arrived, and waited at the skirts of that venerable saint, his reverend pastor. But, irreverently consorting with these grave, reputable, and pious people, these elders of the church, these chaste dames and dewy virgins, there were men of dissolute lives and women of spotted fame, wretches given over to all mean and filthy vice, and suspected even of horrid crimes. It was strange to see, that the good shrank not from the wicked, nor were the sinners abashed by the saints. Scattered, also, among their pale-faced enemies, were the Indian priests, or powwows, who had often scared their native forest with more hideous incantations than any known to English witchcraft.

"But, where is Faith?" thought Goodman Brown; and, as hope came into his heart, he trembled.

Another verse of the hymn arose, a slow and mournful strain, such as the pious love, but joined to words which expressed all that our nature can conceive of sin, and darkly hinted at far more. Unfathomable to mere mortals is the lore of fiends. Verse after verse was sung, and still the chorus of the desert swelled between, like the deepest tone of a mighty organ. And, with the final peal of that dreadful anthem, there came a sound, as if the roaring wind, the rushing streams, the howling beasts, and every other voice of the unconverted wilderness were mingling and according with the voice of guilty man, in homage to the prince of all. The four blazing pines threw up a loftier flame, and obscurely discovered shapes and visages of horror on the smoke-wreaths, above the impious assembly. At the same moment, the fire on the rock shot redly forth, and formed a glowing arch above its base, where now appeared a figure. With reverence be it spoken, the apparition bore no slight similitude, both in garb and manner, to some grave divine of the New England churches.

"Bring forth the converts!" cried a voice, that echoed through the field and rolled into the forest.

At the word, Goodman Brown stepped forth from the shadow of the trees, and approached the congregation, with whom he felt a loathful brotherhood, by the sympathy of all that was wicked in his heart. He could have well-nigh sworn, that the shape of his own dead father beckoned him to advance, looking downward from a smoke-wreath, while a woman, with dim features of despair, threw out her hand to warn him back. Was it his mother? But he had no power to retreat one step, nor to resist, even in thought, when the minister and good old Deacon Gookin seized his arms, and led him to the blazing rock. Thither came also the slender form of a veiled female, led between Goody Cloyse, that pious teacher of the catechism, and Martha Carrier, who had received the devil's promise to be queen of hell. A rampant hag was she! And there stood the proselytes, beneath the canopy of fire.   60

"Welcome, my children," said the dark figure, "to the communion of your race! Ye have found, thus young, your nature and your destiny. My children, look behind you!"

They turned; and flashing forth, as it were, in a sheet of flame, the fiend-worshippers were seen; the smile of welcome gleamed darkly on every visage.

"There," resumed the sable form, "are all whom ye have reverenced from youth. Ye deemed them holier than yourselves, and shrank from your own sin, contrasting it with their lives of righteousness and prayerful aspirations heavenward. Yet, here are they all, in my worshipping assembly! This night it shall be granted you to know their secret deeds; how hoary-bearded elders of the church have whispered wanton words to the young maids of their households; how many a woman, eager for widow's weeds, has given her husband a drink at bedtime, and let him sleep his last sleep in her bosom; how beardless youths have made haste to inherit their father's wealth; and how fair damsels—blush not, sweet ones!—have dug little graves in the garden, and bidden me, the sole guest, to an infant's funeral. By the sympathy of your human hearts for sin, ye shall scent out all the places—whether in church, bed-chamber, street, field, or forest—where crime has been committed, and shall exult to behold the whole earth one stain of guilt, one mighty blood-spot. Far more than this! It shall be yours to penetrate, in every bosom, the deep mystery of sin, the fountain of all wicked arts, and which inexhaustibly supplies more evil impulses than human power—than my power, at its utmost!—can make manifest in deeds. And now, my children, look upon each other."

They did so; and, by the blaze of the hell-kindled torches, the wretched man beheld his Faith, and the wife her husband, trembling before that unhallowed altar.

65   "Lo! there ye stand, my children," said the figure, in a deep and solemn tone, almost sad, with its despairing awfulness, as if his once angelic nature° could yet mourn for our miserable race. "Depending upon one another's hearts, ye had still hoped that virtue were not all a dream! Now are ye undeceived!—Evil is the nature of mankind. Evil must be your only happiness. Welcome, again, my children, to the communion of your race!"

    "Welcome!" repeated the fiend-worshippers, in one cry of despair and triumph.

    And there they stood, the only pair, as it seemed, who were yet hesitating on the verge of wickedness, in this dark world. A basin was hollowed, naturally, in the rock. Did it contain water, reddened by the lurid light? or was it blood? or, perchance, a liquid flame? Herein did the Shape of Evil dip his hand, and prepare to lay the mark of baptism upon their foreheads, that they might be partakers of the mystery of sin, more conscious of the secret guilt of others, both in deed and thought, than they could now be of their own. The husband cast one look at his pale wife, and Faith at him. What polluted wretches would the next glance show them to each other, shuddering alike at what they disclosed and what they saw!

    "Faith! Faith!" cried the husband. "Look up to Heaven, and resist the Wicked One!"

    Whether Faith obeyed, he knew not. Hardly had he spoken, when he found himself amid calm night and solitude, listening to a roar of the wind, which died heavily away through the forest. He staggered against the rock, and felt it chill and damp, while a hanging twig, that had been all on fire, besprinkled his cheek with the coldest dew.

70   The next morning, young Goodman Brown came slowly into the street of Salem village staring around him like a bewildered man. The good old minister was taking a walk along the grave-yard, to get an appetite for breakfast and meditate his sermon, and bestowed a blessing, as he passed, on Goodman Brown. He shrank from the venerable saint, as if to avoid an anathema. Old Deacon Gookin was at domestic worship, and the holy words of his prayer were heard through the open window. "What God doth the wizard pray to?" quoth Goodman Brown. Goody Cloyse, that excellent old Christian, stood in the early sunshine, at her own lattice, catechising a little girl, who had brought her a pint of morning's milk. Goodman Brown snatched away the child, as from the grasp of the fiend himself. Turning the corner by the meetinghouse, he spied the head of Faith, with the pink ribbons, gazing anxiously forth, and bursting into such joy at the sight of him that she skipt along the street, and almost kissed her husband before the whole village. But Goodman Brown looked sternly and sadly into her face, and passed on without a greeting.

    Had Goodman Brown fallen asleep in the forest, and only dreamed a wild dream of a witch-meeting?

    Be it so, if you will. But, alas! it was a dream of evil omen for young Goodman Brown. A stern, a sad, a darkly meditative, a distrustful, if not a desperate man did he become, from the night of that fearful dream. On the Sabbath day, when the congregation were singing a holy psalm, he could not listen, because an anthem of sin rushed loudly upon his ear, and drowned all the blessed strain. When the minister spoke from the pulpit, with power and fervid eloquence, and with his hand on the open Bible, of the sacred truths of our religion, and of saint-like lives and triumphant deaths, and of future bliss or misery unutterable, then did Goodman Brown turn pale, dreading lest the roof should thunder down upon the gray blasphemer and his hearers. Often, awaking suddenly at midnight, he shrank from the bosom of Faith, and at morning or eventide, when the family knelt down in prayer, he scowled, and muttered to himself, and gazed sternly at his wife, and turned away. And when he had lived long, and was borne to his grave, a hoary corpse, followed by Faith, an aged woman, and children and grandchildren, a goodly procession, besides neighbors not a few, they carved no hopeful verse upon his tombstone; for his dying hour was gloom.

°*once angelic nature:* Lucifer ("light bearer"), another name for the Devil, led the traditional revolt of the angels and was thrown into hell as his punishment. See Isaiah 14:12–15.

QUESTIONS

1. Near the end of the story the narrator asks the following: "Had Goodman Brown fallen asleep in the forest, and only dreamed a wild dream of a witch-meeting?" What is the answer? If Goodman Brown's visions come out of his own dreams (mind, subconscious), what do they tell us about him?

2. Is Goodman Brown round or flat? To what extent is he a symbolic "everyman" or representative of humankind?

3. Consider Hawthorne's use of symbolism, such as sunset and night, the walking sticks, the witches' sabbath, the marriage to Faith, and the vague shadows amid the darkness, together with other symbols that you may find.

4. What details establish the two settings? What characterizes Salem? The woods? Why might we be justified in seeing the forest as a symbolic setting?

5. To what extent are the people, objects, and events in Goodman Brown's adventure invested with enough *consistent* symbolic resonance to justify calling his episode in the woods an allegory? Consider Brown's wife, Faith, as an allegorical figure. What do you make of Brown's statements "I'll cling to her skirts and follow her to Heaven" (paragraph 7) and "Faith kept me back awhile" (paragraph 12)? In this same light, consider the other characters Brown meets in the forest, the sunset, the walk into the forest, and the staff "which bore the likeness of a great black snake" (paragraph 13).

FRANZ KAFKA (1883–1924)

Kafka was a Jewish writer who lived in Czechoslovakia but wrote in German. He published little during his lifetime, leaving a number of works unfinished. In Nazi Germany his works were forbidden because he was Jewish, and as a result he was not known by Germans until after 1950. His works were also forbidden in Stalinist Russia, for the same reason. In Britain and the United States, however, he received wide attention after 1930, largely because of the translations of Willa and Edwin Muir.

Kafka is associated with literature that focuses on the uncertain, the irrational, the alienated, the unreal, and the bizarre elements of human existence, and his life has often been subject to the studies of psychoanalysts. His situations or données are usually surreal, and his development of them follows turns of narrative that are both weird and nightmarish. For example, a man is a defendant in a trial that never seems to end in his posthumous The Trial *(1925). In perhaps the most famous of his stories, "The Metamorphosis" (1915), the hero discovers one day that he has turned into an enormous insect, and the story deals with the difficulties in the family and at work that result from this transformation. Such narratives so reflect uncertainty and so distort reality that the word "Kafkaesque" has been taken into our language as a description of impossible bureaucracy and unending personal difficulties. In this respect "A Hunger Artist" ("Ein Hungerkünstler") is representative of his work.*

🍁 A Hunger Artist (1924)

Translated by Willa and Edwin Muir

During these last decades the interest in professional fasting has markedly diminished. It used to pay very well to stage such great performances under one's own management, but today that is quite impossible. We live in a different world now. At one time the whole town took a lively interest in the hunger artist; from day to day of his fast the excitement mounted;

everybody wanted to see him at least once a day; there were people who bought season tickets for the last few days and sat from morning till night in front of his small barred cage; even in the nighttime there were visiting hours, when the whole effect was heightened by torch flares; on fine days the cage was set out in the open air, and then it was the children's special treat to see the hunger artist; for their elders he was often just a joke that happened to be in fashion, but the children stood openmouthed, holding each other's hands for greater security, marveling at him as he sat there pallid in black tights, with his ribs sticking out so prominently, not even on a seat but down among straw on the ground, sometimes giving a courteous nod, answering questions with a constrained smile, or perhaps stretching an arm through the bars so that one might feel how thin it was, and then again withdrawing deep into himself, paying no attention to anyone or anything, not even to the all-important striking of the clock that was the only piece of furniture in his cage, but merely staring into vacancy with half-shut eyes, now and then taking a sip from a tiny glass of water to moisten his lips.

Besides casual onlookers there were also relays of permanent watchers selected by the public, usually butchers, strangely enough, and it was their task to watch the hunger artist day and night, three of them at a time, in case he should have some secret recourse to nourishment. This was nothing but a formality, instituted to reassure the masses, for the initiates knew well enough that during his fast the artist would never in any circumstances, not even under forcible compulsion, swallow the smallest morsel of food; the honor of his profession forbade it. Not every watcher, of course, was capable of understanding this, there were often groups of night watchers who were very lax in carrying out their duties and deliberately huddled together in a retired corner to play cards with great absorption, obviously intending to give the hunger artist the chance of a little refreshment, which they supposed he could draw from some private hoard. Nothing annoyed the artist more than such watchers; they made him miserable; they made his fast seem unendurable; sometimes he mastered his feebleness sufficiently to sing during their watch for as long as he could keep going, to show them how unjust their suspicions were. But that was of little use; they only wondered at his cleverness in being able to fill his mouth even while singing. Much more to his taste were the watchers who sat close up to the bars, who were not content with the dim night lighting of the hall but focused him in the full glare of the electric pocket torch given them by the impresario. The harsh light did not trouble him at all, in any case he could never sleep properly, and he could always drowse a little, whatever the light, at any hour, even when the hall was thronged with noisy onlookers. He was quite happy at the prospect of spending a sleepless night with such watchers; he was ready to exchange jokes with them, to tell them stories out of his nomadic life, anything at all to keep them awake and demonstrate to them again that he had no eatables in his cage and that he was fasting as not one of them could fast. But his happiest moment was when the morning came and an enormous breakfast was brought them, at his expense, on which they flung themselves with the keen appetite of healthy men after a weary night of wakefulness. Of course there were people who argued that this breakfast was an unfair attempt to bribe the watchers, but that was going rather too far, and when they were invited to take on a night's vigil without a breakfast, merely for the sake of the cause, they made themselves scarce, although they stuck stubbornly to their suspicions.

Such suspicions, anyhow, were a necessary accompaniment to the profession of fasting. No one could possibly watch the hunger artist continuously, day and night, and so no one could produce first-hand evidence that the fast had really been rigorous and continuous; only the artist himself could know that, he was therefore bound to be the sole completely satisfied spectator of his own fast. Yet for other reasons he was never satisfied; it was not perhaps mere fasting that had brought him to such skeleton thinness that many people had regretfully to keep away from his exhibitions, because the sight of him was too much for them, perhaps it was dissatisfaction with himself that had worn him down. For he alone knew, what no other initiate knew, how easy it was to fast. It was the easiest thing in the world. He made no secret of this, yet people did not believe him; at the best they set him down as modest; most of them, however, thought he was out for publicity or else was some kind of cheat who found it easy to fast because he had discovered a way of making it easy, and then had the impudence to admit the fact, more or less. He had to put up with all that, and in the course of time had got used to it, but his inner dissatisfaction always rankled, and never yet, after any term of fasting—this must be granted to his credit—had he left the cage of his own free will. The longest period of fasting was fixed by his impresario at forty days, beyond that term he was not allowed to go, not even in great cities, and there was good reason for it, too. Experience had proved that for about forty days the interest of the public could be stimulated by a steadily increasing pressure of advertisement, but after that the town began to lose interest, sympathetic support began notably to fall off; there were of course local variations as between one town and another or one country and another, but as a general rule forty days marked the limit. So on the fortieth day the flower-bedecked cage was opened, enthusiastic spectators filled the hall, a military band played, two doctors entered the cage to measure the results of the fast, which were announced through a megaphone, and finally two young ladies appeared, blissful at having been selected for the honor, to help the hunger artist down the few steps leading to a small table on which was spread a carefully chosen invalid repast. And at this very moment the artist always turned stubborn. True, he would entrust his bony arms to the outstretched helping hands of the ladies bending over him, but stand up he would not. Why stop fasting at this particular moment, after forty days of it? He had held out for a long time, an illimitably long time; why stop now, when he was in his best fasting form, or rather, not yet quite in his best fasting form? Why should he be cheated of the fame he would get for fasting longer, for being not only the record hunger artist of all time, which presumably he was already, but for beating his own record by a performance beyond human imagination, since he felt that there were no limits to his capacity for fasting? His public pretended to admire him so much, why should it have so little patience with him; if he could endure fasting longer, why shouldn't the public endure it? Besides, he was tired, he was comfortable sitting in the straw, and now he was supposed to lift himself to his full height and go down to a meal the very thought of which gave him a nausea that only the presence of the ladies kept him from betraying, and even that with an effort. And he looked up into the eyes of the ladies who were apparently so friendly and in reality so cruel, and shook his head, which felt too heavy on its strengthless neck. But then there happened yet again what always happened. The impresario came forward, without a word—for the band made speech impossible—lifted his arms in the air above the artist, as if inviting Heaven to look down upon its creature here in the straw, this suffering martyr, which indeed he was, although in quite another sense; grasped him around the emaciated waist, with exaggerated caution, so that the frail condition he was in might be appreciated; and committed him to the care of the blenching ladies, not without secretly giving him a shaking so that his legs and body tottered and swayed. The artist now submitted completely; his head lolled on his breast as if it had landed there by chance; his body was hollowed out; his legs in a spasm of self-preservation clung close to each other at the knees, yet scraped on the ground as if it were not really solid ground, as if they were only trying to find solid ground; and the whole weight of his body, a featherweight after all, relapsed onto one of the ladies, who, looking around for help and panting a little—this post of honor was not at all what she had expected it to be—first stretched her neck as far as she could to keep her face at least free from contact with the artist, then finding this impossible, and her more fortunate companion not coming to her aid but merely holding extended in her own trembling hand the little bunch of knucklebones that was the artist's, to the great delight of the spectators burst into tears and had to be replaced by an attendant who had long been stationed in readiness. Then came the food, a little of which the impresario managed to get between the artist's lips, while he sat in a kind of half-fainting trance, to the accompaniment of cheerful patter designed to distract the public's attention from the artist's condition; after that, a toast was drunk to the public, supposedly prompted by a whisper from the artist in the impresario's ear; the band confirmed it with a mighty flourish, the spectators melted away, and no one had any cause to be dissatisfied with the proceedings, no one except the hunger artist himself, he only, as always.

So he lived for many years, with small regular intervals of recuperation, in visible glory, honored by the world, yet in spite of that troubled in spirit, and all the more troubled because no one would take his trouble seriously. What comfort could he possibly need? What more could he possibly wish for? And if some goodnatured person, feeling sorry for him, tried to console him by pointing out that his melancholy was probably caused by fasting, it could happen, especially when he had been fasting for some time, that he reacted with an outburst of fury and to the general alarm began to shake the bars of his cage like a wild animal. Yet the impresario had a way of punishing these outbreaks which he rather enjoyed putting into operation. He would apologize publicly for the artist's behavior, which was only to be excused, he admitted, because of the irritability caused by fasting; a condition hardly to be understood by well-fed people; then by natural transition he went on to mention the artist's equally incomprehensible boast that he could fast for much longer than he was doing; he praised the high ambition, the good will, the great self-denial undoubtedly implicit in such a statement; and then quite simply countered it by bringing out photographs, which were also on sale to the public, showing the artist on the fortieth day of a fast lying in bed almost dead from exhaustion. This perversion of the truth, familiar to the artist though it was, always unnerved him afresh and proved too much for him. What was a consequence of the premature ending of his fast was here presented as the cause of it! To fight against this lack of understanding, against a whole world of nonunderstanding, was impossible. Time and again in good faith he stood by the bars listening to the impresario, but as soon as the photographs appeared he always let go and sank with a groan back onto his straw, and the reassured public could once more come close and gaze at him.

5   A few years later when the witnesses of such scenes called them to mind, they often failed to understand themselves at all. For meanwhile the aforementioned change in public interest had set in; it seemed to happen almost overnight; there may have been profound causes for it, but who was going to bother about that; at any rate the pampered hunger artist suddenly found himself deserted one fine day by the amusement-seekers, who went streaming past him to other more-favored attractions. For the last time the impresario hurried him over half Europe to discover whether the old interest might still survive here and there; all in vain; everywhere, as if by secret agreement, a positive revulsion from professional fasting was in evidence. Of course it could not really have sprung up so suddenly as all that, and many premonitory symptoms which had not been sufficiently remarked or suppressed during the rush and glitter of success now came retrospectively to mind, but it was now too late to take any countermeasures. Fasting would surely come into fashion again at some future date, yet that was no comfort for those living in the present. What, then, was the hunger artist to do? He had been applauded by thousands in his time and could hardly come down to showing himself in a street booth at village fairs, and as for adopting another profession, he was not only too old for that but too fanatically devoted to fasting. So he took leave of the impresario, his partner in an unparalleled career, and hired himself to a large circus; in order to spare his own feelings he avoided reading the conditions of his contract.

A large circus with its enormous traffic in replacing and recruiting men, animals, and apparatus can always find a use for people at any time, even for a hunger artist, provided of course that he does not ask too much, and in this particular case anyhow it was not only the artist who was taken on but his famous and long-known name as well; indeed considering the peculiar nature of his performance, which was not impaired by advancing age, it could not be objected that here was an artist past his prime, no longer at the height of his professional skill, seeking a refuge in some quiet corner of a circus; on the contrary, the hunger artist averred that he could fast as well as ever, which was entirely credible, he even alleged that if he were allowed to fast as he liked, and this was at once promised him without more ado, he could astound the world by establishing a record never yet achieved, a statement that certainly provoked a smile among the other professionals, since it left out of account the change in public opinion, which the hunger artist in his zeal conveniently forgot.

He had not, however, actually lost his sense of the real situation and took it as a matter of course that he and his cage should be stationed, not in the middle of the ring as a main attraction, but outside, near the animal cages, on a site that was after all easily accessible. Large and gaily painted placards made a frame for the cage and announced what was to be seen inside it. When the public came thronging out in the intervals to see the animals, they could hardly avoid passing the hunger artist's cage and stopping there for a moment, perhaps they might even have stayed longer had not those pressing behind them in the narrow gangway, who did not understand why they should be held up on their way toward the excitements of the menagerie, made it impossible for anyone to stand gazing quietly for any length of time. And that was the reason why the hunger artist, who had of course been looking forward to these visiting hours as the main achievement of his life, began instead to shrink from them. At first he could hardly wait for the intervals; it was exhilarating to watch the crowds come streaming his way, until only too soon—not even the most obstinate self-deception, clung to almost consciously, could hold out against the fact—the conviction was borne in upon him that these people, most of them, to judge from their actions, again and again, without exception, were all on their way to the menagerie. And the first sight of them from the distance remained the best. For when they reached his cage he was at once deafened by the storm of shouting and abuse that arose from the two contending factions, which renewed themselves continuously, of those who wanted to stop and stare at him—he soon began to dislike them more than the others—not out of real interest but only out of obstinate self-assertiveness, and those who wanted to go straight on to the animals. When the first great rush was past, the stragglers came along, and these, whom nothing could have prevented from stopping to look at him as long as they had breath, raced past with long strides, hardly even glancing at him, in their haste to get to the menagerie in time. And all too rarely did it happen that he had a stroke of luck, when some father of a family fetched up before him with his children, pointed a finger at the hunger artist, and explained at length what the phenomenon meant, telling stories of earlier years when he himself had watched similar but much more thrilling performances, and the children, still rather uncomprehending, since neither inside nor outside school had they been sufficiently prepared for this lesson—what did they care about fasting?—yet showed by the brightness of their intent eyes that new and better times might be coming. Perhaps, said the hunger artist to himself many a time, things would be a little better if his cage were set not quite so near the menagerie, that made it too easy for people to make their choice, to say nothing of what he suffered from the stench of the menagerie, the animals' restlessness by night, the carrying past of raw lumps of flesh for the beasts of prey, the roaring at feeding times, which depressed him continually. But he did not dare to lodge a complaint with the management; after all, he had the animals to thank for the troops of people who passed his cage, among whom there might always be one here and there to take an interest in him, and who could tell where they might schedule him if he called attention to his existence and thereby to the fact that, strictly speaking, he was only an impediment on the way to the menagerie.

A small impediment, to be sure, one that grew steadily less. People grew familiar with the strange idea that they could be expected, in times like these, to take an interest in a hunger artist, and with this familiarity the verdict went out against him. He might fast as much as he could, and he did so; but nothing could save him now; people passed him by. Just try to explain to anyone the art of fasting! Anyone who has no feeling for it cannot be made to understand it. The fine placards grew dirty and illegible, they were torn down; the little notice board telling the number of fast days achieved, which at first was changed carefully every day, had long stayed at the same figure, for after the first few weeks even this small task seemed pointless to the staff; and so the artist simply fasted on and on, as he had once dreamed of doing, and it was no trouble to him, just as he had always foretold, but no one counted the days, no one, not even the artist himself, knew what records he was already breaking, and his heart grew heavy. And when once in a while some leisurely passer-by stopped, made merry over the old figure on the board, and spoke of swindling, that was in its way the stupidest lie ever invented by indifference and inborn malice, since it was not the hunger artist who was cheating, he was working honestly, but the world was cheating him of his reward.

Many more days went by, however, and that too came to an end. An overseer's eye fell on the cage one day and he asked the attendants why this perfectly good cage should be left standing there unused with dirty straw inside it; nobody knew, until one man, helped out by the notice board, remembered about the hunger artist. They poked into the straw with sticks and found him in it. "Are you still fasting?" asked the overseer, "when on earth do you mean to stop?" "Forgive me, everybody," whispered the hunger artist; only the overseer, who had his ear to the bars, understood him. "Of course," said the overseer, and tapped his forehead with a finger to let the attendants know what state the man was in, "we forgive you." "I always wanted you to admire my fasting," said the hunger artist. "We do admire it," said the overseer, affably. "But you shouldn't admire it," said the hunger artist. "Well then we don't admire it," said the overseer, "but why shouldn't we admire it?" "Because I have to fast, I can't help it," said the hunger artist. "What a fellow you are," said the overseer, "and why can't you help it?" "Because," said the hunger artist, lifting his head a little and speaking, with his lips pursed, as if for a kiss, right into the overseer's ear, so that no syllable might be lost, "because I couldn't find the food I liked. If I had found it, believe me, I should have made no fuss and stuffed myself like you or anyone else." These were his last words but in his dimming eyes remained the firm though no longer proud persuasion that he was still continuing to fast.

10   "Well, clear this out now!" said the overseer, and they buried the hunger artist, straw and all. Into the cage they put a young panther. Even the most insensitive felt it refreshing to see this wild creature leaping around the cage that had so long been dreary. The panther was all right. The food he liked was brought him without hesitation by the attendants; he seemed not even to miss his freedom; his noble body, furnished almost to the bursting point with all that it needed, seemed to carry freedom around with it too; somewhere in his jaws it seemed to lurk; and the joy of life streamed with such ardent passion from his throat that for the onlookers it was not easy to stand the shock of it. But they braced themselves, crowded around the cage, and did not want ever to move away.

QUESTIONS

1. Describe the plot and structure of "A Hunger Artist." What are the conflicts? How are they resolved? Explain the realistic details of the story. How do these contribute to the story's unusual subject matter?

2. Characterize the hunger artist as a person. What do you learn about him? What does he tell about why he first took to being a hunger artist? What is your response to the idea of seeing a man in a cage who is starving himself?

3. What does the hunger artist symbolize? How realistic and also symbolic is his career choice to become a hunger artist?

4. Consider the story as though it is a description of a spectator event. What does the presence of the panther indicate about public acclaim and public fickleness?

LUKE (1st c. CE)

Although little is known about Luke, evidence in Colossians, Philemon, and 2 Timothy indicates that a man named Luke was the "beloved physician" and traveling companion of the apostle Paul, who journeyed in the Mediterranean area during the middle of the first century CE Scholars indicate that Luke built his gospel from the Gospel of St. Mark and also from written sources known as "Q," some of which were also used by St. Matthew. Luke also relied on other sources that were available only to him. In addition to his gospel, Luke is also accepted as the author of the Acts of the Apostles.

🍁 The Parable of the Prodigal Son° (c. 90 CE)

¹¹ And he [Jesus] said, A certain man had two sons:

¹² And the younger of them said to *his* father, Father, give me the portion of goods that falleth to me. And he divided unto them *his* living.°

¹³ And not many days after the younger son gathered all together, and took his journey into a far country,° and there wasted his substance with riotous living.

¹⁴ And when he had spent all, there arose a mighty famine in that land; and he began to be in want.

¹⁵ And he went and joined himself to a citizen of that country; and he sent him into his fields to feed swine.°

¹⁶ And he would fain have filled his belly with the husks° that the swine did eat: and no man gave unto him.

¹⁷ And when he came to himself, he said, How many hired servants of my father's have bread enough and to spare, and I perish with hunger!

¹⁸ I will arise and go to my father, and will say unto him, Father, I have sinned against heaven, and before thee.

¹⁹ And am no more worthy to be called thy son: make me as one of thy hired servants.

²⁰ And he arose, and came to his father. But when he was yet a great way off, his father saw him, and had compassion, and ran, and fell on his neck, and kissed him.

²¹ And the son said unto him, Father, I have sinned against heaven, and in thy sight, and am no more worthy to be called thy son.

²² But the father said to his servants, Bring forth the best robe, and put *it* on him; and put a ring on his hand, and shoes on *his* feet:

²³ And bring hither the fatted calf,° and kill *it*; and let us eat, and be merry:

²⁴ For this my son was dead, and is alive again; he was lost, and is found. And they began to be merry.

°Luke 15:11–32
°*divided . . . his living:* one-third of the father's estate; the son had to renounce all further claim.
°*far country:* countries of the Jewish dispersal, or diaspora, in the areas bordering the Mediterranean Sea.
°*feed swine:* in Jewish custom, pigs were unclean.
°*husks:* pods of the carob tree, the eating of which was thought to be penitential.
°*fatted calf:* grain-fed calf.

²⁵ Now his elder son was in the field: and as he came and drew nigh to the house, he heard music and dancing.

²⁶ And he called one of the servants, and asked what these things meant.

²⁷ And he said unto him, Thy brother is come; and thy father hath killed the fatted calf, because he hath received him safe and sound.

²⁸ And he was angry, and would not go in: therefore came his father out, and intreated him.

²⁹ And he answering said to *his* father, Lo, these many years do I serve thee, neither transgressed I at any time thy commandment: and yet thou never gavest me a kid, that I might make merry with my friends:

³⁰ But as soon as this thy son was come, which hath devoured thy living with harlots, thou hast killed for him the fatted calf.

³¹ And he said unto him, Son, thou art ever with me, and all that I have is thine.

³² It was meet° that we should make merry, and be glad: for this thy brother was dead, and is alive again: and was lost, and is found.

QUESTIONS

1. Describe the character of the Prodigal Son. Is he flat or round, representative or individual? Why is it necessary that the character be considered representatively, even though he has individual characteristics?

2. What is the plot? What is the antagonism against which the Prodigal Son contends? Why is it necessary that the brother resent the brother's return?

3. What is the resolution of the parable? Why is there no "they lived happily ever after" ending?

4. Using verse numbers, analyze the structure of the parable. What determines your division of the parts? Do these parts coincide with the development of the plot? Describe the relationship of plot to structure in the parable.

5. What is the point of view here? How does the emphasis shift with verse 22?

6. On the basis of the fact that there are many characteristics here of many stories you have read, write a description of the parable as a type of literature.

GABRIEL GARCÍA MÁRQUEZ (b. 1928)

Gabriel José García Márquez, a native of Colombia, is one of the major and most successful South American writers, even though during his twenties and thirties he struggled against poverty and lack of recognition. It was not until 1967 that he published his One Hundred Years of Solitude, *still his most famous work, for which he was awarded the Nobel Prize for Literature in 1982. In recent years he has achieved national popular attention because* One Hundred Years of Solitude *was selected and publicized through Oprah Winfrey's Book Club. Recent works are his* Strange Pilgrims: Twelve Stories of Love and Other Demons *(1995),* Collected Stories *(1999),* Living to Tell the Tale *(2003), and* Chronicle of a Death Foretold *(English translation, 2003). Two of the major influences on his writing were the works of Kafka and Faulkner. He was particularly impressed with Faulkner's creation and development of the fictional world and history of Yoknapatawpha County, based on Faulkner's area of northern Mississippi.*

°*meet:* appropriate.

🍁 A Very Old Man with Enormous Wings (1971)

Translated by Gregory Rabassa

A Tale for Children

On the third day of rain they had killed so many crabs inside the house that Pelayo had to cross his drenched courtyard and throw them into the sea, because the newborn child had a temperature all night and they thought it was due to the stench. The world had been sad since Tuesday. Sea and sky were a single ash gray thing and the sands of the beach, which on March nights glimmered like powdered light, had become a stew of mud and rotten shellfish. The light was so weak at noon that when Pelayo was coming back to the house after throwing away the crabs, it was hard for him to see what it was that was moving and groaning in the rear of the courtyard. He had to go very close to see that it was an old man, a very old man, lying face down in the mud, who, in spite of his tremendous efforts, couldn't get up, impeded by his enormous wings.

Frightened by that nightmare, Pelayo ran to get Elisenda, his wife, who was putting compresses on the sick child, and he took her to the rear of the courtyard. They both looked at the fallen body with mute stupor. He was dressed like a ragpicker. There were only a few faded hairs left on his bald skull and very few teeth in his mouth, and his pitiful condition of a drenched great-grandfather had taken away any sense of grandeur he might have had. His huge buzzard wings, dirty and half-plucked, were forever entangled in the mud. They looked at him so long and so closely that Pelayo and Elisenda very soon overcame their surprise and in the end found him familiar. Then they dared speak to him, and he answered in an incomprehensible dialect with a strong sailor's voice. That was how they skipped over the inconvenience of the wings and quite intelligently concluded that he was a lonely castaway from some foreign ship wrecked by the storm. And yet, they called in a neighbor woman who knew everything about life and death to see him, and all she needed was one look to show them their mistake.

"He's an angel," she told them. "He must have been coming for the child, but the poor fellow is so old that the rain knocked him down."

On the following day everyone knew that a flesh-and-blood angel was held captive in Pelayo's house. Against the judgment of the wise neighbor woman, for whom angels in those times were the fugitive survivors of a celestial conspiracy, they did not have the heart to club him to death. Pelayo watched over him all afternoon from the kitchen, armed with his bailiff's club, and before going to bed he dragged him out of the mud and locked him up with the hens in the wire chicken coop. In the middle of the night, when the rain stopped, Pelayo and Elisenda were still killing crabs. A short time afterward the child woke up without a fever and with a desire to eat. Then they felt magnanimous and decided to put the angel on a raft with fresh water and provisions for three days and leave him to his fate on the high seas. But when they went out into the courtyard with the first light of dawn, they found the whole neighborhood in front of the chicken coop having fun with the angel, without the slightest reverence, tossing him things to eat through the openings in the wire as if he weren't a supernatural creature but a circus animal.

Father Gonzaga arrived before seven o'clock, alarmed at the strange news. By that time onlookers less frivolous than those at dawn had already arrived and they were making all kinds of conjectures concerning the captive's future. The simplest among them thought that he should be named mayor of the world. Others of sterner mind felt that he should be promoted to the rank of five-star general in order to win all wars. Some visionaries hoped that he could be put to stud in order to implant on earth a race of winged wise men who could take charge of the universe. But Father Gonzaga, before becoming a priest, had been a robust woodcutter. Standing by the wire, he reviewed his catechism in an instant and asked them to

5

open the door so that he could take a close look at that pitiful man who looked more like a huge decrepit hen among the fascinated chickens. He was lying in a corner drying his open wings in the sunlight among the fruit peels and breakfast leftovers that the early risers had thrown him. Alien to the impertinences of the world, he only lifted his antiquarian eyes and murmured something in his dialect when Father Gonzaga went into the chicken coop and said good morning to him in Latin. The parish priest had his first suspicion of an imposter when he saw that he did not understand the language of God or know how to greet His ministers. Then he noticed that seen close up he was much too human: he had an unbearable smell of the outdoors, the back side of his wings was strewn with parasites and his main feathers had been mistreated by terrestrial winds, and nothing about him measured up to the proud dignity of angels. Then he came out of the chicken coop and in a brief sermon warned the curious against the risks of being ingenuous. He reminded them that the devil had the bad habit of making use of carnival tricks in order to confuse the unwary.° He argued that if wings were not the essential element in determining the difference between a hawk and an airplane, they were even less so in the recognition of angels. Nevertheless, he promised to write a letter to his bishop so that the latter would write to his primate so that the latter would write to the Supreme Pontiff° in order to get the final verdict from the highest courts.

His prudence fell on sterile hearts. The news of the captive angel spread with such rapidity that after a few hours the courtyard had the bustle of a marketplace and they had to call in troops with fixed bayonets to disperse the mob that was about to knock the house down. Elisenda, her spine all twisted from sweeping up so much marketplace trash, then got the idea of fencing in the yard and charging five cents admission to see the angel.

The curious came from far away. A traveling carnival arrived with a flying acrobat who buzzed over the crowd several times, but no one paid any attention to him because his wings were not those of an angel but, rather, those of a sidereal bat. The most unfortunate invalids on earth came in search of health: a poor woman who since childhood had been counting her heartbeats and had run out of numbers; a Portuguese man who couldn't sleep because the noise of the stars disturbed him; a sleepwalker who got up at night to undo the things he had done while awake; and many others with less serious ailments. In the midst of that shipwreck disorder that made the earth tremble, Pelayo and Elisenda were happy with fatigue, for in less than a week they had crammed their rooms with money and the line of pilgrims waiting their turn to enter still reached beyond the horizon.

The angel was the only one who took no part in his own act. He spent his time trying to get comfortable in his borrowed nest, befuddled by the hellish heat of the oil lamps and sacramental candles that had been placed along the wire. At first they tried to make him eat some mothballs, which, according to the wisdom of the wise neighbor woman, were the food prescribed for angels. But he turned them down, just as he turned down the papal lunches that the penitents brought him, and they never found out whether it was because he was an angel or because he was an old man that in the end he ate nothing but eggplant mush. His only supernatural virtue seemed to be patience. Especially during the first days, when the hens pecked at him, searching for the stellar parasites that proliferated in his wings, and the cripples pulled out feathers to touch their defective parts with, and even the most merciful threw stones at him, trying to get him to rise so they could see him standing. The only time they succeeded in arousing him was when they burned his side with an iron for branding steers, for he had been motionless for so many hours that they thought he was dead. He awoke with a start, ranting in his hermetic language and with tears in his eyes, and he flapped his wings a couple of times, which brought on a whirlwind of chicken dung and lunar dust and a gale of panic that did not seem to be of this world. Although many

---

°*He . . . the unwary:* See *Hamlet* 2.2.573–78, for a further explanation of this power of the devil.
°*Supreme Pontiff:* one of the titles of the Pope.

thought that his reaction had been one not of rage but of pain, from then on they were careful not to annoy him, because the majority understood that his passivity was not that of a hero taking his ease but that of a cataclysm in repose.

Father Gonzaga held back the crowd's frivolity with formulas of maidservant inspiration while awaiting the arrival of a final judgment on the nature of the captive. But the mail from Rome showed no sense of urgency. They spent their time finding out if the prisoner had a navel, if his dialect had any connection with Aramaic, how many times he could fit on the head of a pin, or whether he wasn't just a Norwegian with wings. Those meager letters might have come and gone until the end of time if a providential event had not put an end to the priest's tribulations.

It so happened that during those days, among so many other carnival attractions, there 10 arrived in town the traveling show of the woman who had been changed into a spider for having disobeyed her parents. The admission to see her was not only less than the admission to see the angel, but people were permitted to ask her all manner of questions about her absurd state and to examine her up and down so that no one would ever doubt the truth of her horror. She was a frightful tarantula the size of a ram and with the head of a sad maiden. What was most heart-rending, however, was not her outlandish shape but the sincere affliction with which she recounted the details of her misfortune. While still practically a child she had sneaked out of her parents' house to go to a dance, and while she was coming back through the woods after having danced all night without permission, a fearful thunderclap rent the sky in two and through the crack came the lightning bolt of brimstone that changed her into a spider. Her only nourishment came from the meatballs that charitable souls chose to toss into her mouth. A spectacle like that, full of so much human truth and with such a fearful lesson, was bound to defeat without even trying that of a haughty angel who scarcely deigned to look at mortals. Besides, the few miracles attributed to the angel showed a certain mental disorder, like the blind man who didn't recover his sight but grew three new teeth, or the paralytic who didn't get to walk but almost won the lottery, and the leper whose sores sprouted sunflowers. Those consolation miracles, which were more like mocking fun, had already ruined the angel's reputation when the woman who had been changed into a spider finally crushed him completely. That was how Father Gonzaga was cured forever of his insomnia and Pelayo's courtyard went back to being as empty as during the time it had rained for three days and crabs walked through the bedrooms.

The owners of the house had no reason to lament. With the money they saved they built a two-story mansion with balconies and gardens and high netting so that crabs wouldn't get in during the winter, and with iron bars on the windows so that angels wouldn't get in. Pelayo also set up a rabbit warren close to town and gave up his job as bailiff for good, and Elisenda bought some satin pumps with high heels and many dresses of iridescent silk, the kind worn on Sunday by the most desirable women in those times. The chicken coop was the only thing that didn't receive any attention. If they washed it down with creolin° and burned tears of myrrh° inside it every so often, it was not in homage to the angel but to drive away the dungheap stench that still hung everywhere like a ghost and was turning the new house into an old one. At first, when the child learned to walk, they were careful that he not get too close to the chicken coop. But then they began to lose their fears and got used to the smell, and before the child got his second teeth he'd gone inside the chicken coop to play, where the wires were falling apart. The angel was no less standoffish with him than with other mortals, but he tolerated the most ingenious infamies with the patience of a dog who had no illusions. They both came down with chicken pox at the same time.

°*creolin:* a creosote based disinfectant.
°*myrrh:* a fragrant plant resin used in making incense and perfume; also one of the gifts of the Wise Men to the Christ Child (Matthew 2:11).

The doctor who took care of the child couldn't resist the temptation to listen to the angel's heart, and he found so much whistling in the heart and so many sounds in his kidneys that it seemed impossible for him to be alive. What surprised him most, however, was the logic of his wings. They seemed so natural on that completely human organism that he couldn't understand why other men didn't have them too.

When the child began school it had been some time since the sun and rain had caused the collapse of the chicken coop. The angel went dragging himself about here and there like a stray dying man. They would drive him out of the bedroom with a broom and a moment later find him in the kitchen. He seemed to be in so many places at the same time that they grew to think that he'd been duplicated, that he was reproducing himself all through the house, and the exasperated and unhinged Elisenda shouted that it was awful living in that hell full of angels. He could scarcely eat and his antiquarian eyes had also become so foggy that he went about bumping into posts. All he had left were the bare cannulae° of his last feathers. Pelayo threw a blanket over him and extended him the charity of letting him sleep in the shed, and only then did they notice that he had a temperature at night, and was delirious with the tongue twisters of an old Norwegian. That was one of the few times they became alarmed, for they thought he was going to die and not even the wise neighbor woman had been able to tell them what to do with dead angels.

And yet he not only survived his worst winter, but seemed improved with the first sunny days. He remained motionless for several days in the farthest corner of the courtyard, where no one would see him, and at the beginning of December° some large, stiff feathers began to grow on his wings, the feathers of a scarecrow, which looked more like another misfortune of decrepitude. But he must have known the reason for those changes, for he was quite careful that no one should notice them, that no one should hear the sea chanteys that he sometimes sang under the stars. One morning Elisenda was cutting some bunches of onions for lunch when a wind that seemed to come from the high seas blew into the kitchen. Then she went to the window and caught the angel in his first attempts at flight. They were so clumsy that his fingernails opened a furrow in the vegetable patch and he was on the point of knocking the shed down with the ungainly flapping that slipped on the light and couldn't get a grip on the air. But he did manage to gain altitude. Elisenda let out a sigh of relief, for herself and for him, when she saw him pass over the last houses, holding himself up in some way with the risky flapping of a senile vulture. She kept watching him even when she was through cutting the onions and she kept on watching until it was no longer possible for her to see him, because then he was no longer an annoyance in her life but an imaginary dot on the horizon of the sea.

QUESTIONS

1. Describe the plot of "A Very Old Man with Enormous Wings." What are the supernatural occurrences in the story? Is the angel a success or a failure at doing his job as an angel? How might the angel be interpreted symbolically?

2. Does the angel meet common notions of angelic characteristics? How do the family chickens treat him? What is the judgment of the doctor who examines him? What does he finally do?

3. What is the speaker's view of the angel? What vocabulary does he use to describe the angel?

4. Why is the work subtitled "A Tale for Children"?

°*cannulae:* the hollow, tubular parts of feathers.
°*December:* In South America, summer begins not in June but in December.

5. Describe the work's comic and satiric aspects—Father Gonzaga's conclusions about the angel's inability to understand Latin, for example, and the father's description of the procedure to secure a papal pronouncement about the angel's nature. Other topics might be Pelayo's attempts to exploit the angel for economic gain, or the fall-off of public interest in the angel.

KATHERINE ANNE PORTER (1890–1980)

Porter was a native of Texas but made her home in many places during her life, spending considerable time in Mexico and Germany. She established her reputation with her early collections Flowering Judas *(1930) and* Pale Horse, Pale Rider *(1939), which gained praise for her analyses and insights into human character. A later collection of stories was* The Leaning Tower *(1944). Her major novel,* Ship of Fools, *appeared in 1962 and was made into a motion picture. She was awarded the Pulitzer Prize for Fiction and also the National Book Award in 1966 for her* The Collected Stories. *"The Jilting of Granny Weatherall" first appeared in* Flowering Judas.

 ## The Jilting of Granny Weatherall (1930)

She flicked her wrist neatly out of Doctor Harry's pudgy careful fingers and pulled the sheet up to her chin. The brat ought to be in knee breeches. Doctoring around the country with spectacles on his nose! "Get along now, take your schoolbooks and go. There's nothing wrong with me."

Doctor Harry spread a warm paw like a cushion on her forehead where the forked green vein danced and made her eyelids twitch. "Now, now, be a good girl, and we'll have you up in no time."

"That's no way to speak to a woman nearly eighty years old just because she's down. I'd have you respect your elders, young man."

"Well, Missy, excuse me." Doctor Harry patted her cheek. "But I've got to warn you, haven't I? You're a marvel, but you must be careful or you're going to be good and sorry."

"Don't tell me what I'm going to be. I'm on my feet now, morally speaking. It's Cornelia. I had to go to bed to get rid of her."   5

Her bones felt loose, and floated around in her skin, and Doctor Harry floated like a balloon around the foot of the bed. He floated and pulled down his waistcoat and swung his glasses on a cord. "Well, stay where you are, it certainly can't hurt you."

"Get along and doctor your sick," said Granny Weatherall. "Leave a well woman alone. I'll call for you when I want you. . . . Where were you forty years ago when I pulled through milk-leg and double pneumonia? You weren't even born. Don't let Cornelia lead you on," she shouted, because Doctor Harry appeared to float up to the ceiling and out. "I pay my own bills, and I don't throw my money away on nonsense!"

She meant to wave good-by, but it was too much trouble. Her eyes closed of themselves, it was like a dark curtain drawn around the bed. The pillow rose and floated under her, pleasant as a hammock in a light wind. She listened to the leaves rustling outside the window. No, somebody was swishing newspapers: no, Cornelia and Doctor Harry were whispering together. She leaped broad awake, thinking they whispered in her ear.

"She was never like this, *never* like this!" "Well, what can we expect?" "Yes, eighty years old. . . ."

10   Well, and what if she was? She still had ears. It was like Cornelia to whisper around doors. She always kept things secret in such a public way. She was always being tactful and kind. Cornelia was dutiful; that was the trouble with her. Dutiful and good: "So good and dutiful," said Granny, "that I'd like to spank her." She saw herself spanking Cornelia and making a fine job of it.

"What'd you say, Mother?"

Granny felt her face tying up in hard knots.

"Can't a body think, I'd like to know?"

"I thought you might want something."

15   "I do. I want a lot of things. First off, go away and don't whisper."

She lay and drowsed, hoping in her sleep that the children would keep out and let her rest a minute. It had been a long day. Not that she was tired. It was always pleasant to snatch a minute now and then. There was always so much to be done, let me see: tomorrow.

Tomorrow was far away and there was nothing to trouble about. Things were finished somehow when the time came; thank God there was always a little margin over for peace: then a person could spread out the plan of life and tuck in the edges orderly. It was good to have everything clean and folded away, with the hair brushes and tonic bottles sitting straight on the white embroidered linen: the day started without fuss and the pantry shelves laid out with rows of jelly glasses and brown jugs and white stone-china jars with blue whirligigs and words painted on them: coffee, tea, sugar, ginger, cinnamon, allspice: and the bronze clock with the lion on top nicely dusted off. The dust that lion could collect in twenty-four hours! The box in the attic with all those letters tied up, well she'd have to go through that tomorrow. All those letters—George's letters and John's letters and her letters to them both—lying around for the children to find afterwards made her uneasy. Yes, that would be tomorrow's business. No use to let them know how silly she had been once.

While she was rummaging around she found death in her mind and it felt clammy and unfamiliar. She had spent so much time preparing for death there was no need for bringing it up again. Let it take care of itself now. When she was sixty she had felt very old, finished, and went around making farewell trips to see her children and grandchildren, with a secret in her mind: This is the very last of your mother, children! Then she made her will and came down with a long fever. That was all just a notion like a lot of other things, but it was lucky too, for she had once for all got over the idea of dying for a long time. Now she couldn't be worried. She hoped she had better sense now. Her father had lived to be one hundred and two years old and had drunk a noggin of strong hot toddy on his last birthday. He told the reporters it was his daily habit, and he owed his long life to that. He had made quite a scandal and was very pleased about it. She believed she'd just plague Cornelia a little.

"Cornelia! Cornelia!" No footsteps, but a sudden hand on her cheek. "Bless you, where have you been?"

20   "Here, mother."

"Well, Cornelia, I want a noggin of hot toddy."

"Are you cold, darling?"

"I'm chilly, Cornelia. Lying in bed stops the circulation. I must have told you that a thousand times."

Well, she could just hear Cornelia telling her husband that Mother was getting childish and they'd have to humor her. The thing that most annoyed her was that Cornelia thought she was deaf, dumb, and blind. Little hasty glances and tiny gestures tossed around her and over her head saying, "Don't cross her, let her have her way, she's eighty years old," and she sitting there as if she lived in a thin glass cage. Sometimes Granny almost made up her mind to pack up and move back to her own house where nobody could remind her every minute that she was old. Wait, wait, Cornelia, till your own children whisper behind your back!

In her day she had kept a better house and had got more work done. She wasn't too old 25
yet for Lydia to be driving eighty miles for advice when one of the children jumped the
track, and Jimmy still dropped in and talked things over: "Now, Mammy, you've a good
business head, I want to know what you think of this? . . ." Old Cornelia couldn't change
the furniture around without asking. Little things, little things! They had been so sweet
when they were little. Granny wished the old days were back again with the children
young and everything to be done over. It had been a hard pull, but not too much for her.
When she thought of all the food she had cooked, and all the clothes she had cut and
sewed, and all the gardens she had made—well, the children showed it. There they were,
made out of her, and they couldn't get away from that. Sometimes she wanted to see John
again and point to them and say, Well, I didn't do so badly, did I? But that would have to
wait. That was for tomorrow. She used to think of him as a man, but now all the children
were older than their father, and he would be a child beside her if she saw him now. It
seemed strange and there was something wrong in the idea. Why, he couldn't possibly recognize her. She had fenced in a hundred acres once, digging the post holes herself and
clamping the wires with just a negro boy to help. That changed a woman. John would be
looking for a young woman with the peaked Spanish comb in her hair and the painted fan.
Digging post holes changed a woman. Riding country roads in the winter when women
had their babies was another thing: sitting up nights with sick horses and sick negroes and
sick children and hardly ever losing one. John, I hardly ever lost one of them! John would
see that in a minute, that would be something he could understand, she wouldn't have to
explain anything!

It made her feel like rolling up her sleeves and putting the whole place to rights again.
No matter if Cornelia was determined to be everywhere at once, there were a great many
things left undone on this place. She would start tomorrow and do them. It was good to be
strong enough for everything, even if all you made melted and changed and slipped under
your hands, so that by the time you finished you almost forgot what you were working for.
What was it I set out to do? she asked herself intently, but she could not remember. A fog
rose over the valley, she saw it marching across the creek swallowing the trees and moving
up the hill like an army of ghosts. Soon it would be at the near edge of the orchard, and then
it was time to go in and light the lamps. Come in children, don't stay out in the night air.

Lighting the lamps had been beautiful. The children huddled up to her and breathed
like little calves waiting at the bars in the twilight. Their eyes followed the match and
watched the flame rise and settle in a blue curve, then they moved away from her. The lamp
was lit, they didn't have to be scared and hang on to mother any more. Never, never, never
more. God, for all my life I thank Thee. Without Thee, my God, I could never have done it.
Hail, Mary, full of grace.

I want you to pick all the fruit this year and see that nothing is wasted. There's always
someone who can use it. Don't let good things rot for want of using. You waste life when
you waste good food. Don't let things get lost. It's bitter to lose things. Now, don't let me
get to thinking, not when I am tired and taking a little nap before supper. . . .

The pillow rose about her shoulders and pressed against her heart and the memory was
being squeezed out of it: oh, push down the pillow, somebody: it would smother her if she
tried to hold it. Such a fresh breeze blowing and such a green day with no threats in it. But
he had not come, just the same. What does a woman do when she has put on the white veil
and set out the white cake for a man and he doesn't come? She tried to remember. No, I
swear he never harmed me but in that. He never harmed me but in that . . . and what if he
did? There was the day, the day, but a whirl of dark smoke rose and covered it, crept up and
over into the bright field where everything was planted so carefully in orderly rows. That
was hell, she knew hell when she saw it. For sixty years she had prayed against remembering him and against losing her soul in the deep pit of hell, and now the two things were

mingled in one and the thought of him was a smoky cloud from hell that moved and crept in her head when she had just got rid of Doctor Harry and was trying to rest a minute. Wounded vanity, Ellen, said a sharp voice in the top of her mind. Don't let your wounded vanity get the upper hand of you. Plenty of girls get jilted. You were jilted, weren't you. Then stand up to it. Her eyelids wavered and let in streamers of blue-gray light like tissue paper over her eyes. She must get up and pull the shades down or she'd never sleep. She was in bed again and the shades were not down. How could that happen? Better turn over, hide from the light, sleeping in the light gave you nightmares. "Mother, how do you feel now?" and a stinging wetness on her forehead. But I don't like having my face washed in cold water!

30   Hapsy? George? Lydia? Jimmy? No, Cornelia, and her features were swollen and full of little puddles. "They're coming, darling, they'll all be here soon." Go wash your face, child, you look funny.

Instead of obeying, Cornelia knelt down and put her head on the pillow. She seemed to be talking but there was no sound. "Well, are you tongue-tied? Whose birthday is it? Are you going to give a party?"

Cornelia's mouth moved urgently in strange shapes. "Don't do that, you bother me, daughter."

"Oh, no, Mother, Oh, no . . ."

Nonsense. It was strange about children. They disputed your every word. "No what, Cornelia?"

35   "Here's Doctor Harry."

"I won't see that boy again. He just left five minutes ago."

"That was this morning, Mother. It's night now. Here's the nurse."

"This is Doctor Harry, Mrs. Weatherall. I never saw you look so young and happy!"

"Ah, I'll never be young again—but I'd be happy if they'd let me lie in peace and get rested."

40   She thought she spoke up loudly, but no one answered. A warm weight on her forehead, a warm bracelet on her wrist, and a breeze went on whispering, trying to tell her something. A shuffle of leaves in the everlasting hand of God. He blew on them and they danced and rattled. "Mother, don't mind, we're going to give you a little hypodermic." "Look here, daughter, how do ants get in this bed? I saw sugar ants yesterday." Did you send for Hapsy too?

It was Hapsy she really wanted. She had to go a long way back through a great many rooms to find Hapsy standing with a baby on her arm. She seemed to herself to be Hapsy also, and the baby on Hapsy's arm was Hapsy and himself and herself, all at once, and there was no surprise in the meeting. Then Hapsy melted from within and turned flimsy as gray gauze and the baby was a gauzy shadow, and Hapsy came up close and said, "I thought you'd never come," and looked at her very searchingly and said, "You haven't changed a bit!" They leaned forward to kiss, when Cornelia began whispering from a long way off, "Oh, is there anything you want to tell me? Is there anything I can do for you?"

Yes, she had changed her mind after sixty years and she would like to see George. I want you to find George. Find him and be sure to tell him I forgot him. I want him to know I had my husband just the same and my children and my house like any other woman. A good house too and a good husband that I loved and fine children out of him. Better than I hoped for even. Tell him I was given back everything he took away and more. Oh, no, oh, God, no, there was something else besides the house and the man and the children. Oh, surely they were not all? What was it? Something not given back. . . . Her breath crowded down under her ribs and grew into a monstrous frightening shape with cutting edges; it bored up into her head, and the agony was unbelievable: Yes, John, get the doctor now, no more talk, my time has come.

When this one was born it should be the last. The last. It should have been born first, for it was the one she had truly wanted. Everything came in good time. Nothing left out, left over. She was strong, in three days she would be as well as ever. Better. A woman needed milk in her to have her full health.

"Mother, do you hear me?"

"I've been telling you—"

"Mother, Father Connolly's here."

"I went to Holy Communion only last week. Tell him I'm not so sinful as all that."

"Father just wants to speak to you."

He could speak as much as he pleased. It was like him to drop in and inquire about her soul as if it were a teething baby, and then stay on for a cup of tea and a round of cards and gossip. He always had a funny story of some sort, usually about an Irishman who made his little mistakes and confessed them, and the point lay in some absurd thing he would blurt out in the confessional showing his struggles between native piety and original sin. Granny felt easy about her soul. Cornelia, where are your manners? Give Father Connolly a chair. She had her secret comfortable understanding with a few favorite saints who cleared a straight road to God for her. All as surely signed and sealed as the papers for the new Forty Acres. Forever . . . heirs and assigns forever. Since the day the wedding cake was not cut, but thrown out and wasted. The whole bottom dropped out of the world, and there she was blind and sweating with nothing under her feet and the walls falling away. His hand had caught her under the breast, she had not fallen, there was the freshly polished floor with the green rug on it, just as before. He had cursed like a sailor's parrot and said, "I'll kill him for you." Don't lay a hand on him, for my sake leave something to God. "Now, Ellen, you must believe what I tell you . . ."

So there was nothing, nothing to worry about any more, except sometimes in the night one of the children screamed in a nightmare, and they both hustled out shaking and hunting for the matches and calling, "There, wait a minute, here we are!" John, get the doctor now. Hapsy's time has come. But there was Hapsy standing by the bed in a white cap. "Cornelia, tell Hapsy to take off her cap. I can't see her plain."

Her eyes opened very wide and the room stood out like a picture she had seen somewhere. Dark colors with the shadow rising towards the ceiling in long angles. The tall black dresser gleamed with nothing on it but John's picture, enlarged from a little one, with John's eyes very black when they should have been blue. You never saw him, so how do you know how he looked? But the man insisted the copy was perfect, it was very rich and handsome. For a picture, yes, but it's not my husband. The table by the bed had a linen cover and a candle and a crucifix. The light was blue from Cornelia's silk lampshades. No sort of light at all, just frippery. You had to live forty years with kerosene lamps to appreciate honest electricity. She felt very strong and she saw Doctor Harry with a rosy nimbus around him.

"You look like a saint, Doctor Harry, and I vow that's as near as you'll ever come to it."

"She's saying something."

"I heard you, Cornelia. What's all this carrying-on?"

"Father Connolly's saying—"

Cornelia's voice staggered and bumped like a cart in a bad road. It rounded corners and turned back again and arrived nowhere. Granny stepped up in the cart very lightly and reached for the reins, but a man sat beside her and she knew him by his hands, driving the cart. She did not look in his face, for she knew without seeing, but looked instead down the road where the trees leaned over and bowed to each other and a thousand birds were singing a Mass. She felt like singing too, but she put her hand in the bosom of her dress and pulled out a rosary, and Father Connolly murmured Latin in a very solemn voice and tickled her feet. My God, will you stop that nonsense? I'm a married woman. What if he did run away and leave me to face the priest by myself? I found another a whole world better. I wouldn't have exchanged my husband for anybody except St. Michael himself, and you may tell him that for me with a thank you in the bargain.

Light flashed on her closed eyelids, and a deep roaring shook her. Cornelia, is that lightning? I hear thunder. There's going to be a storm. Close all the windows. Call the children in . . . "Mother, here we are, all of us." "Is that you, Hapsy?" "Oh, no, I'm Lydia. We drove as fast as we could." Their faces drifted above her, drifted away. The rosary fell out of her hands and Lydia put it back. Jimmy tried to help, their hands fumbled together, and Granny closed two fingers around Jimmy's thumb. Beads wouldn't do, it must be something alive. She was so amazed her thoughts ran round and round. So, my dear Lord, this is my death and I wasn't even thinking about it. My children have come to see me die. But I can't, it's not time. Oh, I always hated surprises. I wanted to give Cornelia the amethyst set—Cornelia, you're to have the amethyst set, but Hapsy's to wear it when she wants, and, Doctor Harry, do shut up. Nobody sent for you. Oh, my dear Lord, do wait a minute. I meant to do something about the Forty Acres, Jimmy doesn't need it and Lydia will later on with that worthless husband of hers. I meant to finish the altar cloth and send six bottles of wine to Sister Borgia for her dyspepsia. I want to send six bottles of wine to Sister Borgia, Father Connolly, now don't let me forget.

Cornelia's voice made short turns and tilted over and crashed. "Oh, Mother, oh, Mother, oh, Mother. . . ."

"I'm not going, Cornelia. I'm taken by surprise. I can't go."

60   You'll see Hapsy again. What about her? "I thought you'd never come." Granny made a long journey outward, looking for Hapsy. What if I don't find her? What then? Her heart sank down and down, there was no bottom to death, she couldn't come to the end of it. The blue light from Cornelia's lampshade drew into a tiny point in the center of her brain, it flickered and winked like an eye, quietly it fluttered and dwindled. Granny lay curled down within herself, amazed and watchful, staring at the point of light that was herself; her body was now only a deeper mass of shadow in an endless darkness and this darkness would curl around the light and swallow it up. God, give a sign!

For the second time there was no sign. Again no bridegroom and the priest in the house. She could not remember any other sorrow because this grief wiped them all away. Oh, no, there's nothing more cruel than this—I'll never forgive it. She stretched herself with a deep breath and blew out the light.

QUESTIONS

1. What are Granny's circumstances in the story? What is happening to her? How do we learn about her and her past life? What evidence do you see in the story that Granny is hallucinating and becoming delirious?

2. What sort of person is Granny? Would you call her admirable? Why or why not? In what way is light symbolic in the story? In what ways is Granny associated with light? Would it be fair to claim that Granny has been a giver of light during her life?

3. What is the meaning of "jilting" as it applies to Granny? To what degree does Granny feel "jilted" at the end of her life? How has jilting colored and symbolized her life? How has she lived to overcome it?

4. Explain the story's point of view. (See also Chapter 2.) To what degree does the narrator enter Granny's mind to explain what is happening to her?

5. Who is Hapsy? What is the significance of Hapsy to Granny? What has apparently happened to Hapsy?

JOHN STEINBECK (1902–1968)

Steinbeck was born in Salinas, California, and for a time attended Stanford University. In the 1920s, while working at jobs such as surveying, picking fruit, and hatching trout, he began his writing career. A number of stories and novels preceded his best-known novel, The Grapes of Wrath *(1939), for which he was awarded the Pulitzer Prize in 1940. He received the Nobel Prize in Literature in 1962. His fiction, often set in rural areas, features a realistic and pessimistic view of life. A number of his novels have been made into films, the best known of which is* The Grapes of Wrath. *His home in Salinas is open to the visiting public.*

 ## The Chrysanthemums (1937)

The high grey-flannel fog of winter closed off the Salinas Valley° from the sky and from all the rest of the world. On every side it sat like a lid on the mountains and made of the great valley a closed pot. On the broad, level land floor the gang plows bit deep and left the black earth shining like metal where the shares had cut. On the foothill ranches across the Salinas River, the yellow stubble fields seemed to be bathed in pale cold sunshine, but there was no sunshine in the valley now in December. The thick willow scrub along the river flamed with sharp and positive yellow leaves.

It was a time of quiet and of waiting. The air was cold and tender. A light wind blew up from the southwest so that the farmers were mildly hopeful of a good rain before long; but fog and rain do not go together.

Across the river, on Henry Allen's foothill ranch there was little work to be done, for the hay was cut and stored and the orchards were plowed up to receive the rain deeply when it should come. The cattle on the higher slopes were becoming shaggy and rough-coated.

Elisa Allen, working in her flower garden, looked down across the yard and saw Henry, her husband, talking to two men in business suits. The three of them stood by the tractor shed, each man with one foot on the side of the little Fordson.° They smoked cigarettes and studied the machines as they talked.

Elisa watched them for a moment and then went back to her work. She was thirty-five.   5
Her face was lean and strong and her eyes were as clear as water. Her figure looked blocked and heavy in her gardening costume, a man's black hat pulled low down over her eyes, clodhopper shoes, a figured print dress almost completely covered by a big corduroy apron with four big pockets to hold the snips, the trowel and scratcher, the seeds and the knife she worked with. She wore heavy leather gloves to protect her hands while she worked.

She was cutting down the old year's chrysanthemum stalks with a pair of short and powerful scissors. She looked down toward the men by the tractor shed now and then. Her face was eager and mature and handsome; even her work with the scissors was over-eager, over-powerful. The chrysanthemum stems seemed too small and easy for her energy.

She brushed a cloud of hair out of her eyes with the back of her glove, and left a smudge of earth on the cheek in doing it. Behind her stood the neat white farm house with red geraniums close-banked around it as high as the windows. It was a hard-swept looking little house, with hard-polished windows, and a clean mud-mat on the front steps.

Elisa cast another glance toward the tractor shed. The strangers were getting into their Ford coupe. She took off a glove and put her strong fingers down into the forest of new

---

°*Salinas Valley:* in Monterey County, California, about 50 miles south of San Jose.
°*Fordson:* a tractor manufactured by the Ford Motor Company, with large steel-lugged rear wheels.

green chrysanthemum sprouts that were growing around the old roots. She spread the leaves and looked down among the close-growing stems. No aphids were there, no sowbugs or snails or cutworms. Her terrier fingers destroyed such pests before they could get started.

Elisa started at the sound of her husband's voice. He had come near quietly, and he leaned over the wire fence that protected her flower garden from cattle and dogs and chickens.

10 "At it again," he said. "You've got a strong new crop coming."

Elisa straightened her back and pulled on the gardening glove again. "Yes. They'll be strong this coming year." In her tone and on her face there was a little smugness.

"You've got a gift with things," Henry observed. "Some of those yellow chrysanthemums you had this year were ten inches across. I wish you'd work out in the orchard and raise some apples that big."

Her eyes sharpened. "Maybe I could do it, too. I've a gift with things, all right. My mother had it. She could stick anything in the ground and make it grow. She said it was having planters' hands that knew how to do it."

"Well, it sure works with flowers," he said.

15 "Henry, who were those men you were talking to?"

"Why, sure, that's what I came to tell you. They were from the Western Meat Company. I sold those thirty head of three-year-old steers. Got nearly my own price, too."

"Good," she said. "Good for you."

"And I thought," he continued, "I thought how it's Saturday afternoon, and we might go to Salinas for dinner at a restaurant, and then to a picture show—to celebrate, you see."

"Good," she repeated. "Oh, yes. That will be good."

20 Henry put on his joking tone. "There's fights tonight. How'd you like to go to the fights?"

"Oh, no," she said breathlessly. "No, I wouldn't like fights."

"Just fooling, Elisa. We'll go to a movie. Let's see. It's two now. I'm going to take Scotty and bring down those steers from the hill. It'll take us maybe two hours. We'll go in town about five and have dinner at the Cominos Hotel. Like that?"

"Of course I'll like it. It's good to eat away from home."

"All right, then. I'll go get up a couple of horses."

25 She said, "I'll have plenty of time to transplant some of these sets, I guess."

She heard her husband calling Scotty down by the barn. And a little later she saw the two men ride up the pale yellow hillside in search of the steers.

There was a little square sandy bed kept for rooting the chrysanthemums. With her trowel she turned the soil over and over, and smoothed it and patted it firm. Then she dug ten parallel trenches to receive the sets. Back at the chrysanthemum bed she pulled out the little crisp shoots, trimmed off the leaves of each one with her scissors and laid it on a small orderly pile.

A squeak of wheels and plod of hoofs came from the road. Elisa looked up. The country road ran along the dense bank of willows and cottonwoods that bordered the river, and up this road came a curious vehicle, curiously drawn. It was an old springwagon, with a round canvas top on it like the cover of a prairie schooner. It was drawn by an old bay horse and a little grey-and-white burro. A big stubble-bearded man sat between the cover flaps and drove the crawling team. Underneath the wagon, between the hind wheels, a lean and rangy mongrel dog walked sedately. Words were painted on the canvas in clumsy, crooked letters. "Pots, pans, knives, sisors, lawn mores. Fixed." Two rows of articles and the triumphantly definitive "Fixed" below. The black paint had run down in little sharp points beneath each letter.

Elisa, squatting on the ground, watched to see the crazy, loose-jointed wagon pass by. But it didn't pass. It turned into the farm road in front of her house, crooked old wheels skirling and squeaking. The rangy dog darted from between the wheels and ran ahead.

Instantly the two ranch shepherds flew out at him. Then all three stopped, and with stiff and quivering tails, with taut straight legs, with ambassadorial dignity, they slowly circled, sniffing daintily. The caravan pulled up to Elisa's wire fence and stopped. Now the newcomer dog, feeling outnumbered, lowered his tail and retired under the wagon with raised hackles and bared teeth.

The man on the wagon seat called out. "That's a bad dog in a fight when he gets started." 30
Elisa laughed. "I see he is. How soon does he generally get started?"

The man caught up her laughter and echoed it heartily. "Sometimes not for weeks and weeks," he said. He climbed stiffly down, over the wheel. The horse and the donkey dropped like unwatered flowers.

Elisa saw that he was a very big man. Although his hair and beard were greying, he did not look old. His worn black suit was wrinkled and spotted with grease. The laughter had disappeared from his face and eyes the moment his laughing voice ceased. His eyes were dark and they were full of the brooding that gets in the eyes of teamsters and of sailors. The calloused hands he rested on the wire fence were cracked, and every crack was a black line. He took off his battered hat.

"I'm off my general road, ma'am," he said. "Does this dirt road cut over across the river to the Los Angeles highway?"

Elisa stood up and shoved the thick scissors in her apron pocket. "Well, yes, it does, but it 35 winds around and then fords the river. I don't think your team could pull through the sand."

He replied with some asperity, "It might surprise you what them beasts can pull through."

"When they get started?" she asked.

He smiled for a second. "Yes. When they get started."

"Well," said Elisa, "I think you'll save time if you go back to the Salinas road and pick up the highway there."

He drew a big finger down the chicken wire and made it sing. "I ain't in any hurry, 40 ma'am. I go from Seattle to San Diego and back every year. Takes all my time. About six months each way. I aim to follow nice weather."

Elisa took off her gloves and stuffed them in the apron pocket with the scissors. She touched the under edge of her man's hat, searching for fugitive hairs. "That sounds like a nice kind of a way to live," she said.

He leaned confidentially over the fence. "Maybe you noticed the writing on my wagon. I mend pots and sharpen knives and scissors. You got any of them things to do?"

"Oh, no," she said quickly. "Nothing like that." Her eyes hardened with resistance.

"Scissors is the worst thing," he explained. "Most people just ruin scissors trying to sharpen 'em, but I know how. I got a special tool. It's a little bobbit kind of thing, and patented. But it sure does the trick."

"No. My scissors are all sharp." 45

"All right, then. Take a pot," he continued earnestly, "a bent pot, or a pot with a hole. I can make it like new so you don't have to buy no new ones. That's saving for you."

"No," she said shortly. "I tell you I have nothing like that for you to do."

His face fell to an exaggerated sadness. His voice took on a whining undertone. "I ain't had a thing to do today. Maybe I won't have no supper tonight. You see I'm off my regular road. I know folks on the highway clear from Seattle to San Diego. They save their things for me to sharpen up because they know I do it so good and save them money."

"I'm sorry," Elisa said irritably. "I haven't anything for you to do."

His eyes left her face and fell to searching the ground. They roamed about until they came 50 to the chrysanthemum bed where she had been working. "What's them plants, ma'am?"

The irritation and resistance melted from Elisa's face. "Oh, those are chrysanthemums, giant whites and yellows. I raise them every year, bigger than anybody around here."

"Kind of a long-stemmed flower? Looks like a quick puff of colored smoke?" he asked.

"That's it. What a nice way to describe them."

"They smell kind of nasty till you get used to them," he said.

55   "It's a good bitter smell," she retorted, "not nasty at all."

He changed his tone quickly. "I like the smell myself."

"I had ten-inch blooms this year," she said.

The man leaned farther over the fence. "Look. I know a lady down the road a piece, has got the nicest garden you ever seen. Got nearly every kind of flower but no chrysantheums. Last time I was mending a copper-bottom washtub for her (that's hard job but I do it good), she said to me, 'If you ever run acrost some nice chrysanthemums I wish you'd try to get me a few seeds.' That's what she told me."

Elisa's eyes grew alert and eager. "She couldn't have known much about chrysanthemums. You can raise them from seed, but it's much easier to root the little sprouts you see there."

60   "Oh," he said. "I s'pose I can't take none to her, then."

"Why yes you can," Elisa cried. "I can put some in damp sand, and you can carry them right along with you. They'll take root in the pot if you keep them damp. And then she can transplant them."

"She'd sure like to have some, ma'am. You say they're nice ones?"

"Beautiful," she said. "Oh, beautiful." Her eyes shone. She tore off the battered hat and shook out her dark pretty hair. "I'll put them in a flower pot, and you can take them right with you. Come into the yard."

While the man came through the picket gate Elisa ran excitedly along the geranium-bordered path to the back of the house. And she returned carrying a big red flower pot. The gloves were forgotten now. She kneeled on the ground by the starting bed and dug up the sandy soil with her fingers and scooped it into the bright new flower pot. Then she picked up the little pile of shoots she had prepared. With her strong fingers she pressed them into the sand and tamped around them with her knuckles. The man stood over her. "I'll tell you what to do," she said. "You remember so you can tell the lady."

65   "Yes, I'll try to remember."

"Well, look. These will take root in about a month. Then she must set them out, about a foot apart in good rich earth like this, see?" She lifted a handful of dark soil for him to look at. "They'll grow fast and tall. Now remember this. In July tell her to cut them down, about eight inches from the ground."

"Before they bloom?" he asked.

"Yes, before they bloom." Her face was tight with eagerness. "They'll grow right up again. About the last of September the buds will start."

She stopped and seemed perplexed. "It's the budding that takes the most care," she said hesitantly. "I don't know how to tell you." She looked deep into his eyes, searchingly. Her mouth opened a little, and she seemed to be listening. "I'll try to tell you," she said. "Did you ever hear of planting hands?"

70   "Can't say I have, ma'am."

"Well, I can only tell you what it feels like. It's when you're picking off the buds you don't want. Everything goes right down into your fingertips. You watch your fingers work. They do it themselves. You can feel how it is. They pick and pick the buds. They never make a mistake. They're with the plant. Do you see? Your fingers and the plant. You can feel that, right up your arm. They know. They never make a mistake. You can feel it. When you're like that you can't do anything wrong. Do you see that? Can you understand that?"

She was kneeling on the ground looking up at him. Her breast swelled passionately.

The man's eyes narrowed. He looked away self-consciously. "Maybe I know," he said. "Sometimes in the night in the wagon there—"

Elisa's voice grew husky. She broke in on him. "I've never lived as you do, but I know what you mean. When the night is dark—why, the stars are sharp-pointed, and there's quiet. Why, you rise up and up! Every pointed star gets driven into your body. It's like that. Hot and sharp and—lovely."

Kneeling there, her hand went out toward his legs in the greasy black trousers. Her hes- 75 itant fingers almost touched the cloth. Then her hand dropped to the ground. She crouched low like a fawning dog.

He said, "It's nice, just like you say. Only when you don't have no dinner, it ain't."

She stood up then, very straight, and her face was ashamed. She held the flower pot out to him and placed it gently in his arms. "Here. Put it in your wagon, on the seat, where you can watch it. Maybe I can find something for you to do."

At the back of the house she dug in the can pile and found two old and battered alu- minum saucepans. She carried them back and gave them to him. "Here, maybe you can fix these."

His manner changed. He became professional. "Good as new I can fix them." At the back of his wagon he set a little anvil, and out of an oily tool box dug a small machine ham- mer. Elisa came through the gate to watch him while he pounded out the dents in the ket- tles. His mouth grew sure and knowing. At a difficult part of the work he sucked his under-lip.

"You sleep right in the wagon?" Elisa asked. 80

"Right in the wagon, ma'am. Rain or shine. I'm dry as a cow in there."

"It must be nice," she said. "It must be very nice. I wish women could do such things."

"It ain't the right kind of a life for a woman."

Her upper lip raised a little, showing her teeth. "How do you know? How can you tell?" she said.

"I don't know ma'am," he protested. "Of course I don't know. Now here's your kettles, 85 done. You don't have to buy no new ones."

"How much?"

"Oh, fifty cents'll do. I keep my prices down and my work good. That's why I have all them satisfied customers up and down the highway."

Elisa brought him a fifty-cent piece from the house and dropped it in his hand. "You might be surprised to have a rival some time. I can sharpen scissors, too. And I can beat the dents out of little pots. I could show you what a woman might do."

He put his hammer back in the oily box and shoved the little anvil out of sight. "It would be a lonely life for a woman, ma'am, and a scarey life, too, with animals creeping under the wagon all night." He climbed over the single-tree, steadying himself with a hand on the burro's white rump. He settled himself in the seat, picked up the lines. "Thank you kindly, ma'am," he said. "I'll do like you told me; I'll go back and catch the Salinas road."

"Mind," she called, "if you're long in getting there, keep the sand damp." 90

"Sand, ma'am? . . . Sand? Oh, sure. You mean round the chrysanthemums. Sure I will." He clucked his tongue. The beasts leaned luxuriously into their collars. The mongrel dog took his place between the back wheels. The wagon turned and crawled out the entrance road and back the way it had come, along the river.

Elisa stood in front of her wire fence watching the slow progress of the caravan. Her shoulders were straight, her head thrown back, her eyes half-closed, so that the scene came vaguely into them. Her lips moved silently, forming the words "Good-bye—good-bye." Then she whispered, "That's a bright direction. There's a glowing there." The sound of her whisper startled her. She shook herself free and looked about to see whether anyone had been listening. Only the dogs had heard. They lifted their heads toward her from their sleeping in the dust, and then stretched out their chins and settled asleep again. Elisa turned and ran hurriedly into the house.

In the kitchen she reached behind the stove and felt the water tank. It was full of hot water from the noonday cooking. In the bathroom she tore off her soiled clothes and flung them into the corner. And then she scrubbed herself with a little block of pumice, legs and thighs, loins and chest and arms, until her skin was scratched and red. When she had dried herself she stood in front of a mirror in her bedroom and looked at her body. She tightened her stomach and threw out her chest. She turned and looked over her shoulder at her back.

After a while she began to dress, slowly. She put on her newest under-clothing and her nicest stockings and the dress which was the symbol of her prettiness. She worked carefully on her hair, pencilled her eyebrows and rouged her lips.

Before she was finished she heard the little thunder of hoofs and the shouts of Henry and his helper as they drove the red steers into the corral. She heard the gate bang shut and set herself for Henry's arrival.

His step sounded on the porch. He entered the house calling "Elisa, where are you?"

"In my room, dressing. I'm not ready. There's hot water for your bath. Hurry up. It's getting late."

When she heard him splashing in the tub, Elisa laid his dark suit on the bed, and shirt and socks and tie beside it. She stood his polished shoes on the floor beside the bed. Then she went to the porch and sat primly and stiffly down. She looked toward the river road where the willow-line was still yellow with frosted leaves so that under the high grey fog they seemed a thin band of sunshine. This was the only color in the grey afternoon. She sat unmoving for a long time. Her eyes blinked rarely.

Henry came banging out of the door, shoving his tie inside his vest as he came. Elisa stiffened and her face grew tight. Henry stopped short and looked at her. "Why—why, Elisa. You look so nice!"

"Nice? You think I look nice? What do you mean by 'nice'?"

Henry blundered on. "I don't know. I mean you look different, strong and happy."

"I am strong? Yes, strong. What do you mean 'strong'?"

He looked bewildered. "You're playing some kind of a game," he said helplessly. "It's a kind of a play. You look strong enough to break a calf over your knee, happy enough to eat it like watermelon."

For a second she lost her rigidity. "Henry! Don't talk like that. You didn't know what you said." She grew complete again. "I'm strong," she boasted. "I never knew before how strong."

Henry looked down toward the tractor shed, and when he brought his eyes back to her, they were his own again. "I'll get out the car. You can put on your coat while I'm starting."

Elisa went into the house. She heard him drive to the gate and idle down his motor, and then she took a long time to put on her hat. She pulled it here and pressed it there. When Henry turned the motor off she slipped into her coat and went out.

The little roadster bounced along on the dirt road by the river, raising the birds and driving the rabbits into the brush. Two cranes flapped heavily over the willow-line and dropped into the river-bed.

Far ahead on the road Elisa saw a dark speck. She knew.

She tried not to look as they passed it, but her eyes would not obey. She whispered to herself sadly. "He might have thrown them off the road. That wouldn't have been much trouble, not very much. But he kept the pot," she explained. "He had to keep the pot. That's why he couldn't get them off the road."

The roadster turned a bend and she saw the caravan ahead. She swung full around toward her husband so she could not see the little covered wagon and the mismatched team as the car passed them.

In a moment it was over. The thing was done. She did not look back. She said loudly, to be heard above the motor, "It will be good, tonight, a good dinner."

"Now you're changed again," Henry complained. He took one hand from the wheel and patted her knee. "I ought to take you in to dinner oftener. It would be good for both of us. We get so heavy out on the ranch."

"Henry," she asked, "could we have wine at dinner?"

"Sure we could. Say! That will be fine."

She was silent for a little while; then she said, "Henry, at those prize fights, do the men hurt each other very much?"   115

"Sometimes a little, not often. Why?"

"Well, I've read how they break noses, and blood runs down their chests. I've read how the fighting gloves get heavy and soggy with blood."

He looked around at her. "What's the matter, Elisa? I didn't know you read things like that." He brought the car to a stop, then turned to the right over the Salinas River bridge.

"Do any women ever go to the fights?" she asked.

"Oh, sure, some. What's the matter, Elisa? Do you want to go? I don't think you'd like it, but I'll take you if you really want to go."   120

She relaxed limply in the seat. "Oh, no. No. I don't want to go. I'm sure I don't." Her face was turned away from him. "It will be enough if we can have wine. It will be plenty." She turned up her coat collar so he could not see that she was crying weakly—like an old woman.

QUESTIONS

1. What point of view is used in the story? What are the advantages of this point of view?
2. Consider the symbolism of the setting in this story with respect to the Salinas Valley, the time of year, and the description of the Allen house. What do these things tell us about Elisa Allen and her world?
3. To what extent is Steinbeck's description of Elisa in paragraphs 5 and 6 symbolic? What is she wearing? What do her clothes hide or suppress?
4. What do the chrysanthemums symbolize for Elisa? What do they symbolize *about* her? What role do these flowers play in her life?
5. How does Elisa's character or sense of self change during the episode in which she washes and dresses for dinner? To what extent is this washing-dressing episode symbolic? How would you explain the symbolism?
6. Consider the symbolic impact of Elisa's seeing the chrysanthemum sprouts at the roadside. What does her reaction tell us about her values?

WRITING ABOUT SYMBOLISM AND ALLEGORY

To discover possible parallels that determine the presence of symbolism or allegory, consider the following questions.

Questions for Discovering Ideas

SYMBOLISM

- What cultural or universal symbols can you discover in names, objects, places, situations, or actions in a work (e.g., the character Faith, the woods, and the walking stick in "Young Goodman Brown"; the lumps of mud in "Unfinished Masterpieces"; the bleakness of the weather in "The Chrysanthemums"; or the straying son in "The Parable of the Prodigal Son")?

- What contextual symbolism can be found in a work? What leads you to conclude that it is symbolic? What is being symbolized? How definite or direct is the symbolism? How systematically is it used? How necessary to the work is it? To what degree does it strengthen the work? How strongly does the work stand on its own without the reading for symbolism?
- Is it possible to make parallel lists to show how qualities of a particular symbol match the qualities of a character or action? Here is such a list for the toy windmill in Welty's "A Worn Path"(Chapter 1):

Qualities of the Windmill	Comparable Qualities in Phoenix and Her Life
1. Cheap	1. Poor, but she gives all her money for the windmill
2. Breakable	2. Old, and not far from death
3. A gift	3. Generous
4. Not practical	4. Needs relief from reality and practicality
5. Colorful	5. Needs something new and cheerful

ALLEGORY

- How clearly does the author point you toward an allegorical reading (i.e., through names and allusions, consistency of narrative, literary context)?
- How consistent is the allegorical application? Does the entire work, or only a part, embody the allegory? On what basis do you draw these conclusions?
- How complete is the allegorical reading? How might the allegory yield to a diagram such as the one shown below on Hawthorne's "Young Goodman Brown," which shows how characters, actions, objects, and ideas correspond allegorically?

Young Goodman Brown	Brown Himself	Citizens of the Village	The Forest Figure (Father), the Devil	Faith	The Forest Meeting	Retreat into Suspicion and Distrust
allegorical application to morality and faith	Potential for good	Culture and religious reinforcement	Forces of evil and deceit	Salvation and love; ideals to be rescued and preserved	Attack on ideals; incentive to disillusionment	Destruction of faith; doubt, spiritual negligence, loss of certainty, increase of gloom and suspicion
allegorical application to personal and general concerns	Individual in pursuit of goals	External support for personal strength and growth	Obstacles to overcome, or by which to be overcome	Personal involvement, steadiness, happiness, religious conviction	Susceptibility to deceit, lack of conviction, misunderstanding, misinterpretation of others	Failure, depression, discouragement, disappointment, bitterness

OTHER FORMS

- What enables you to identify the story as a parable or fable? What lesson or moral is either clearly stated or implicit?
- What mythological identification is established in the work? What do you find in the story (names, situations, etc.) that enables you to determine its mythological significance? How is the myth to be understood? What symbolic value does the myth have? What current and timeless application does it have?

Strategies for Organizing Ideas

Relate the central idea of your essay to the meaning of the major symbols or allegorical thrust of the story. An idea about "Young Goodman Brown," for example, is that fanaticism darkens and limits the human soul. An early incident in the story provides symbolic support for this idea. Specifically, when Goodman Brown enters the woods, he resolves "to stand firm against the devil," and he then looks up toward "Heaven above him." As he looks, a "black mass of cloud" appears to hide the "brightening stars" (page 389, paragraph 47). Within the limits of our central idea, the cloud can be seen as a symbol, just like the widening path or the night walk itself. Look for ways to make solid connections like this when you designate something as a symbol or allegory.

Also, your essay will need to include justifications for your symbols or allegorical parallels. In Poe's "The Masque of the Red Death" (Chapter 9), for example, Prince Prospero's seemingly impregnable "castellated abbey" is a line of defense against the plague. But the Red Death in a human shape easily invades the castle and conquers Prospero and his ill-fated guests. If you treat the abbey as a symbol, it is important to apply it to measures that people take (medicine, escapist activity, etc.) to keep death distant and remote. In the same way, in describing the allegorical elements in "Young Goodman Brown," you need to establish a comprehensive statement such as the following: People lose ideals and forsake principles not because they are evil but because they misunderstand the people around them (see the second illustrative essay that follows).

For the body of your essay there are a number of strategies for discussing symbolism and allegory. You might use one exclusively or a combination.

SYMBOLISM

If you want to write about symbolism, you might consider the following points:

1. *The meaning of a major symbol.* Identify the symbol and what it stands for. Then answer questions such as these: Is the symbol cultural or contextual? How do you decide? How do you derive your interpretation of the symbolic meaning? What is the extent of the meaning? Does the symbol undergo modification or new applications if it reappears in the work? How does the symbol affect your understanding of the work? Does the symbol bring out any ironies? How does the symbol add strength and depth to the work?

2. *The development and relationship of symbols.* For two or more symbols, consider issues such as these: How do the symbols connect with each other (like night and the cloud in "Young Goodman Brown" as symbols of a darkening mind)? What additional meanings do the symbols provide? (The windmill and the medicine in "A Worn Path," for example, are ironic because the windmill suggests cheer while the medicine suggests hopelessness.) Do the symbols control the form of the work? How? (For example, at the beginning of Steinbeck's "The Chrysanthemums" the barren wintry countryside is compared to a "closed pot," and at the ending Elisa learns that the tinsmith has dumped the earth out of the flower pot that she had given to him as a gift. In a similar vein, Joyce's "Araby" in Chapter 4 begins with the "blind" or dead-end street and ends with the darkness of the closed bazaar.) Can these comparable objects and conditions be viewed symbolically in relationship to the development of the two stories? Other issues are whether the symbols fit naturally or artificially into the context of the story or whether and how the writer's symbols create unique quality or excellence.

ALLEGORY

When writing about allegory, you might use one of the following approaches.

1. *The application and meaning of the allegory.* What is the subject of the story (allegory, fable, parable, myth)? How can it be more generally applied to ideas or to qualities of human character, not only of its own time but also of our own? What other versions of the story do you know, if any? Does it illustrate, either closely or loosely, particular philosophies or religious views? If so, what are these? How do you know?

2. *The consistency of the allegory.* Is the allegory used consistently throughout the story, or is it used intermittently? Explain and illustrate this use. Would it be correct to call your story allegorical rather than an allegory? Can you determine how parts of the story are introduced for their allegorical importance? Examples are the increasingly dark pathway leading to home in Bierce's "An Occurrence at Owl Creek Bridge" (Chapter 1), which indicates the weakening hold that Farquhar has on life, the shabby fur muff in Mansfield's "Miss Brill" (Chapter 3), which suggest the comparably dismal circumstances of Miss Brill herself, and the Champs Elysées, the fashionable Parisian street in Maupassant's "The Necklace" (Part I), which corresponds to Mathilde's constant temptation to live beyond her means.

In concluding, you might summarize main points, describe general impressions, explain the impact of the symbolic or allegorical methods, indicate personal responses, or suggest further lines of thought and application. You might also assess the quality and appropriateness of the symbolism or allegory (such as Hawthorne's "Young Goodman Brown" opening at sunset and closing in gloom).

Illustrative Student Essay (Symbolism)

Underlined sentences in this paper *do not* conform to MLA style and are used solely as teaching tools to emphasize the central idea, thesis sentence, and topic sentences throughout the paper.

Raj 1

Michael Raj

Professor Thomas

English 320

27 September 2008

Symbols of Light and Darkness in Porter's "The Jilting of Granny Weatherall"°

In Katherine Anne Porter's "The Jilting of Granny Weatherall," Ellen   **[1]**
Weatherall--Granny Weatherall--is lying on her deathbed, and things in the story are described as they are being filtered through her conscious and unconscious mind. For sixty of her eighty years Granny has been a tower of strength to those around her, but now she is succumbing to powerful strokes, climaxed by the "deep roaring" of the terminal, killing stroke (410, paragraph 57). As she gets closer and closer to her last moments she fades in and out of awareness, and she finally loses direct awareness of her adult children who are keeping vigil around her. Near the end, as she receives last rites from her priest, she does not understand what is happening to her (409, paragraph 56). While she sometimes makes at least some contact with those around her, her mind wanders and touches base with her lifelong beliefs, hopes, plans, fears, embarrassments, sorrows, intentions, and convictions. Her mental associations reveal her personality as a valiant and triumphant woman who has met and overcome the major obstacles and challenges of her life.

She has been constant in her religious duties, and religious concerns are   **[2]**
never far from her mind. For example, one of her last thoughts is that she wants to send six bottles of wine to a Sister Borgia (410, paragraph 57). In her delirium her thoughts touch on her gratefulness for her life of hard work and service, and also on her love for her children, even including a child, Hapsy,

°**This story appears on pages 405–10.**

Raj 2

whom she apparently lost in childbirth but whom she imagines as having lived to adulthood (Hapsy seems to be the "something not given back" that she tries to remember [408 paragraph 42]). Significantly, as Granny's thoughts "spread out the plan of life and tuck in the edges orderly" (406, paragraph 17) her memories are dominated by biblical symbols of light and darkness.* The symbols of light crystallize her convictions and ideals, while the symbols of darkness express her lifelong fears and anxieties.†

[3]   Light, whiteness, and brightness symbolize the security and inner peace that Granny has sought but not always found. Several times she recalls that during her lifetime she made a ceremony out of lighting the household lamps to dispel the darkness, thus acting out many actions reminiscent of the Bible, such as the books of Genesis and Exodus. She remembers that when fog began to move toward her house, "marching across the creek swallowing the trees and moving up the hill like an army of ghosts," her regular reaction was "to go in and light the lamps" (407, paragraph 26). She also remembers that "lighting the lamps had been beautiful" when her children were small (407, paragraph 27). After the rooms had been illuminated, the children would no longer be frightened: "they didn't have to be scared and hang on to mother any more. Never, never, never more" (407, paragraph 27). Furthermore, when Granny contemplates having chased the darkness of their fears away with light, she associates the light with divine protection and guidance. She likes strong, bright light, not the blue light shining from her daughter Cornelia's silk lampshades, which she believes are "[no] sort of light at all, just frippery" (409, paragraph 51). Although darkness has always loomed near her, Granny constantly found comfort in light and brightness, symbols that reflect her need for order and peace of mind.

[4]   In contrast, images of darkness, smoke, and fog suggest the fear, doubt, and instability that Granny associates with uncertainty and abandonment. We learn that at the age of twenty she experienced the most crushing event of her life. On the day of her intended marriage, her fiancé, George, jilted her at the altar. She was inconsolable, and "The whole bottom dropped out of the world,

---

*Central idea.
†Thesis sentence.

Raj 3

and there she was blind and sweating and nothing under her feet and the walls falling away" (409, paragraph 49). When she recalls this betrayal, dark images flow into her mind--disturbing symbols of horror and rejection: "There was the day, the day, but a whirl of dark smoke rose and covered it, crept up and over into the bright field. [. . .] That was hell, she knew hell when she saw it" (407, paragraph 29). Even her marriage with John, who died young and left her as a widow to rear their children, has not lessened her pain and regret. On her deathbed, after sixty years of "pray[ing] against remembering him [George] and against losing her soul in the deep pit of hell" (407, paragraph 29), another symbol of darkness indicates that she has never truly recovered from being rejected: "the thought of him was a smoky cloud from hell that moved and crept in her head" (408, paragraph 29). These symbols of darkness bring out the shattering anguish of Granny's memory.

At the end of the story, the combination of references to light and dark symbolizes the second "jilting" that Granny has experienced in her life. After Porter establishes that darkness symbolizes doubt and despair and that light symbolizes safety and security, she uses both symbols to show Granny's state of mind during her final moments. Granny visualizes a "point of light that was herself" which is being consumed by darkness (410, paragraph 60). Through repetition, Porter stresses the negative symbolism of darkness, for Granny's "body was now only a deeper mass of shadow in an endless darkness and this darkness would curl around the light and swallow it up" (410, paragraph 60). As the darkness overwhelms her, she cries out to God to give her a saving and healing sign of divine presence. But "[f]or the second time there was no sign" (410, paragraph 61)--a direct echo of Matthew 12:39 ("there shall no sign be given"). It is safe to assume that Granny feels the despair of darkness as she dies, for her thoughts of George as bridegroom merge with her thoughts of God as bridegroom, and she feels jilted by the second just as by the first. Despite her despair, however, the true status of her soul is demonstrated by what we have learned throughout the story about the energy and devotion of her life. Her achievement as the center of her family is summed up by her brief prayer

[5]

Raj 4

as she remembers lighting the lamps, which is to her the symbol of divine love: "God, for all my life I thank thee. Without Thee, my God, I could never have done it" (407, paragraph 27).

[6]   The symbols are of course not only symbols, but they also have a basis in the actual reality of light and darkness. Thus at one point Granny remarks that she should "hide from the light" and that "sleeping in the light gave you nightmares" (408, paragraph 29). It appears that here, at least, reality is more significant than symbolism. When Granny approaches the very end of the "hard pull" of her life, she despairs because of the "cruel" realization that she has received no divine sign. The last words of the story describe her last moment: "She stretched herself with a deep breath and blew out the light." This ending is final, and at first we might think that Granny's light is gone and that the darkness she feared has overcome her. Another biblical quotation, however, may put the two symbols into additional perspective, for we learn in Isaiah that in the long run both light and darkness are divine, for God says, "I form the light, and create darkness" (Isaiah 45:7). This is a dimension of Granny's life that goes beyond symbolism.

Raj 5

Work Cited

Porter, Katherine Anne. "The Jilting of Granny Weatherall." Literature: An Introduction to Reading and Writing. Ed. Edgar V. Roberts. 9th ed. New York: Pearson Longman, 2009. 405–10.

Commentary on the Essay About Symbolism

This essay illustrates the principles of analysis described in the second part of the guide for considering symbolism. Connection within the essay may be seen in the continuity of topic from paragraph 1 to paragraph 2, and also from paragraph 4 to paragraph 5. Additionally, some of the individual words and phrases providing continuity are "in contrast," "another," "despite," "however," and "not only . . . but also."

Paragraph 1 establishes the nature of the story and also the qualities of the major character, Granny Weatherall. Paragraph 2 introduces her religious outlook, and it also contains the central idea, about the significance of symbolic light and darkness in the story. The concluding thesis sentence indicates that the body of the essay will treat the meanings of both symbols.

In the body, paragraph 3 introduces the idea that both symbols are common in the Bible, and that therefore they are a natural function of Granny's religiosity. Paragraph 4 is in contrast to paragraph 3 because it explains that Granny was jilted at age twenty and that she has always associated this horrible memory with darkness. Paragraph 5 emphasizes that to Granny, the darkness seems to be victorious as she assumes that God has deserted her just as she had been jilted when she was young. Paragraph 6 concludes the essay by (1) treating the reality of light and dark in the story, thereby pointing out that the symbols are not consistently used symbolically, and (2) introducing the biblical idea that Granny is in divine hands, whether in lightness or darkness.

Second Illustrative Student Essay (Allegory)

Underlined sentences in this paper *do not* conform to MLA style and are used solely as teaching tools to emphasize the central idea, thesis sentence, and topic sentences throughout the paper.

Murphy 1

Heather Murphy

Professor Thomas

English 2B

5 February 2008

The Allegory of Hawthorne's "Young Goodman Brown"°

Nathaniel Hawthorne's "Young Goodman Brown" is a nightmarish narrative. [1] It allegorizes the process by which something good--religion--becomes a justification for intolerance and prejudice. The major character, Young Goodman Brown of colonial Salem, begins as a pious and holy person, but he takes a walk into a nearby darkening forest of suspicion. The process is portrayed by Hawthorne as something created by the devil himself, who leads Goodman Brown into the increasingly evil and sinful night. By the end of the allegory, Brown is transformed into an unforgiving, antisocial, dour, and dreary misanthrope.

°This story appears on pages 385–92.

Murphy 2

[2]   Hawthorne's choice of the story's location reminds us that it was in Salem, in the late seventeenth century, that religious zealousness became so extreme that a number of witch trials and public hangings took place solely on the basis of suspicion and false accusation. This setting indicates that Hawthorne's immediate allegorical target is the overzealous pursuit of religious principles. And so Goodman Brown's trip not only takes him into the gloom of night, but also marks a descent into the darkest dungeons of his soul.*

[3]   While the story presents Brown's embarkation into religious zealotry, Hawthorne's allegory may also be applied generally to the ways in which people uncritically follow *any* ideal which leads them to distrust and suspect others. The allegory thus applies to those who swallow political slogans, who believe in their own racial or ethnic superiority, or who justify super-patriotism and super-nationalism. Thus convinced of their own supremacy, people ignore the greater need for love, understanding, toleration, cooperation, and forgiveness. Hawthorne's allegory is a realistic portrait of how people get into such a mental state, with Goodman Brown as the major example. Such people push ahead even against their own good nature and background, and they become prejudiced through delusion and suspicion.†

[4]   Young Goodman Brown's pathway into the night is not a direct plunge, but first Hawthorne shows that Brown does not begin without good nature. Many times early in the story we learn that Brown has doubts about the "evil purpose" of his allegorical walk. At the very beginning, Faith calls him back and pleads with him to stay with her (385, paragraph 2), but even so, he leaves her. As he walks away he thinks of himself as "a wretch" for doing so (385, paragraph 7). He excuses himself with a promise that once the evening is over he will stick with Faith forever after--an "excellent resolve for the future," as the narrator ironically states (386, paragraph 8). When Goodman Brown is reproached by the devil for being late, he gives the excuse "Faith kept me back a while" (386, paragraph 12), a sentence of ironic double meaning. Once he has kept his appointment with the devil, he states his intention to go no farther

*Central idea.
†Thesis sentence.

Murphy 3

because he has "scruples" which remind him that "it is my purpose now
to return whence I came" (386, paragraph 15). When he refers to his
family's proud and virtuous heritage, the devil is amused by his naivety.
Even when Brown is standing before the altar of profanation deep within
the forest, he appeals to Faith, "Look up to Heaven, and resist the Wicked
One!" (392, paragraph 68). All this hesitation represents a true conscience
in Goodman Brown even though he ignores it as he progresses deeper
into the forest of sin. His failure--and failure it is--is his inability or
unwillingness to persist in making his own insight and conscience his
guides of conduct.

It is important to remember that Goodman Brown is favored by his   [5]
background, which should have kept him on a true path of goodness. Almost
as a claim of entitlement he cries out, "With Heaven above, and Faith below,
I will yet stand firm against the devil" (389, paragraph 46). He also cries out
for Faith even when he hears a voice resembling hers that is "uttering
lamentations" within the darkening woods (389, paragraph 47). When he
sees Faith's pink ribbon fluttering down, he exclaims, "My Faith is gone!"
(389, paragraph 50). These instances show allegorically that Goodman
Brown's previous way of life has given him proper spiritual guidance. Even
as he is tempted before the "unhallowed altar" (391, paragraph 64), he asks
the question "But, where is Faith?" as though he could reclaim his previous
innocence (391, paragraph 57). Just as he ignores his conscience, he also
ignores the power of his background, and it is this neglect that fuels his
change into the "demoniac" who abandons himself to "the instinct that
guides mortal man to evil" (390, paragraph 51).

Another major element in Goodman Brown's allegorical path to   [6]
darkness is that he persuades himself that virtually all the people he knows
have yielded their lives to sin. In the grips of this distorted view of others,
he believes not what he sees but what he thinks he is seeing. Thus he
witnesses the encounter between the devil and Goody Cloyse shortly after he
enters the forest, but what he sees is not the good woman who taught him his

Murphy 4

catechism but rather a witch who is bent on evil and who is friendly with
the devil. He ignores the fact that he too is friendly with the devil (the image
of his own father) and therefore, while ignoring the log in his own eye, he
condemns Goody Cloyse for the speck in hers. After his transformation,
when he walks back into his village from his allegorical walk into evil,
he "snatche[s] away" a child from Goody as though she were preaching the
words of the devil (392, paragraph 70). He cannot believe that others possess
goodness as long as he is convinced by the devil's words that "the whole
earth [is] one stain of guilt, one mighty blood-spot" (391, paragraph 63).
For this reason he condemns both his minister and Deacon Gookin, whose
conspiratorial voices he imagines that he overhears on the pathway through
the forest. In short, the process of Hawthorne's allegory about the growth
of harmful pietism demonstrates that travelers on the pathway to prejudice
accept suspicion and mistrust without trying to get at the whole truth
and without recognizing that judgment is not in human but rather is in
divine hands.

[7]   As Hawthorne allegorizes the development of religious discrimination
he makes clear that mistrust and suspicion form its basis. Certainly, as the
devil claims, human beings commit many criminal and depraved sins
(391, paragraph 63), but this does not mean that all human beings are equally
at fault, and that they are beyond love and redemption. The key for Goodman
Brown is that he exceeds his judgmental role and condemns others solely on
his own hasty conclusions. As long as he has faith he will not falter, but when
he leaves his faith, or believes that he has lost his faith, he is adrift and will
see only evil wherever he looks. For this reason he permits suspicion and
loathing to distort his previous love for his wife and neighbors, and he
becomes harsh and desperate. Hawthorne devotes the concluding paragraph of
the story to a brief summary of Brown's life after the fateful night. This
conclusion completes the allegorical cycle beginning with Brown's initiation
into evil and extending to his "dying hour" of "gloom" and his unhopeful
tombstone (392, paragraph 72).

Murphy 5

Hawthorne's "Young Goodman Brown" allegorizes the paradox of [8]
how noble beliefs become ignoble. Goodman Brown dies in gloom because
he believes that his wrong vision is true. His form of evil is the hardest
to stop because wrongdoers who are convinced of their own goodness
are beyond reach. In view of such self-righteous evil, whether cloaked in the
apparent virtues of Puritanism or of some other blindly rigorous doctrine,
Hawthorne writes, "the fiend in his own shape is less hideous than when
he rages in the breast of man" (390, paragraph 53). Young Goodman Brown
is one of the many who create darkness but are convinced that they alone
walk in light.

Murphy 6

Work Cited

Hawthorne, Nathaniel. "Young Goodman Brown." Literature: An Introduction
to Reading and Writing. Ed. Edgar V. Roberts. 9th ed. New York: Pearson
Longman, 2009. 385–92.

Commentary on the Essay About Allegory

This essay deals with a major idea in "Young Goodman Brown," and it therefore
illustrates the first approach described earlier (p. 419). Unity in the essay is
achieved by a number of means. For example, paragraph 2 extends a topic in paragraph 1. Also, a phrase in sentence 2 of paragraph 1 is echoed in sentence 1 of
paragraph 8. Making additional connections within the essay are individual
words such as "another," "while," "therefore," and the repetition of words
throughout the essay that are contained in the thesis sentence.

The first three paragraphs of the essay constitute an extended introduction
to the topics of paragraphs 4 through 8, for they establish "Young Goodman

Brown" as an allegory. Paragraph 1 briefly treats the allegorical nature of the narrative. Paragraph 2 relates the historical basis of the topic to Hawthorne's purpose in writing the story, and it concludes with the essay's central idea. Paragraph 3 broadens the scope of Hawthorne's allegory by showing that it includes zealousness wherever it might appear. Paragraph 3 also concludes with the essay's thesis sentence.

Paragraph 4, the first in the body, deals with an important aspect of the allegory, and one that makes it particularly relevant and timely even today—namely, that people of goodwill may become evil under the pretense of goodness. Similarly, paragraph 5 points out that such people usually come from good backgrounds and have benefited from good influences during their lives.

Paragraphs 6 and 7 locate the origins of evil in two major human qualities—first, the belief in one's own delusions; and second, the mental confusion that results from the conviction that appearance is more real and believable than reality itself. Paragraph 8 concludes the essay on the note that the finished "product"—a person who has become suspicious and misguided—demonstrates how good ideas, when pushed to the extreme by false imagination, can backfire.

Writing Topics About Symbolism and Allegory

1. Compare and contrast the symbolism in Munro's "The Found Boat" (Chapter 6), Porter's "The Jilting of Granny Weatherall," Coleman's "Unfinished Masterpieces," García Marquez's "A Very Old Man with Enormous Wings," and Steinbeck's "The Chrysanthemums." To what degree do the stories rely on contextual symbols? On universal symbols? On the basis of your comparison, what is the case for asserting that realism and fantasy are directly related to the nature of the symbolism employed by the writer?

2. Why do writers who advocate moral, philosophical, or religious issues frequently use symbolism or allegory? In treating this question, you might introduce references from "The Parable of the Prodigal Son," and Hawthorne's "Young Goodman Brown."

3. Write an essay on the allegorical method of one or more of the parables included in the Gospel of St. Luke, such as "The Bridegroom" (5:34–35), "The Garments and the Wineskins" (5:36–39), "The Sower" (8:4–15), "The Good Samaritan" (10:25–37), "The Prodigal Son" (15:11–32), "The Ox in the Well" (14:5–6), "The Watering of Animals on the Sabbath" (13:15–17), "The Rich Fool" (12:16–21), "Lazarus" (16:19–31), "The Widow and the Judge" (18:1–8), and "The Pharisee and the Publican" (18:9–14).

4. Write your own brief story using a widely recognized cultural symbol such as the flag (patriotism, love of country, a certain type of politics), water (life, sexuality, regeneration), or the population explosion (the end of life on earth). By arranging actions and dialogue, make clear the issues conveyed by your symbol, and also try to resolve conflicts the symbol might raise among your characters.

5. Write a brief story in which you develop your own contextual symbol. You might, for example, demonstrate how holding a job brings out character strengths that are not at first apparent or how neglecting to care for the inside or outside of a house indicates a character's decline. The principle is to take something that can at first seem normal and ordinary, then to make that thing symbolic as you develop your story.

6. Using the catalog system of your library, discover a recent critical-biographical book or books about Hawthorne. Explain what the book says about Hawthorne's uses of symbolism. To what extent does the book relate Hawthorne's symbolism to his religious and family heritage?

Chapter 8

Idea or Theme: The Meaning and the Message in Fiction

The word **idea** refers to the result or results of general and abstract thinking. Synonymous words are *concept, thought, opinion,* and *principle.* In literary study the consideration of ideas relates to *meaning, interpretation, explanation,* and *significance.* Although ideas are usually extensive and complex, separate ideas can be described by individual words such as *right, good, love, piety, liberty, causation, wilderness,* and, not surprisingly, *idea* itself.

Ideas and Assertions

Although single words alone can name ideas, we must put these words into operation in *sentences* or *assertions* before they can advance our understanding. Good operational sentences about ideas are not the same as ordinary conversational statements such as "It's a nice day." An observation of this sort may be true (depending on the weather), but it gives us no ideas and does not stimulate our minds. Rather, a sentence asserting an idea about a nice day should initiate a thought or argument about the day's quality, such as "A nice day requires light breezes, blue sky, a warm sun, and relaxation." Because this sentence makes an assertion about the word *nice,* it allows us to consider and develop the idea of a nice day.

In studying literature, always express ideas as assertions. For example, you might state that an idea in Lawrence's "The Horse Dealer's Daughter" is "love," but it would be difficult to discuss anything more unless you make an assertion that promises an argument, such as "This story demonstrates the idea that love is irresistible and irrational." This assertion would lead you to explain the unlikely love that bursts out in the story. Similarly, for Welty's "A Worn Path" (Chapter 1) an assertion like the following would advance further argument: "Phoenix embodies the idea that caring for others gives no reward but the continuation of the duty itself."

Although we have noted only one idea in these two works, most stories contain many ideas. When one of the ideas seems to be the major one, which recurs throughout the work, it is called the **theme.** In practice, the words *theme* and *major idea* are the same.

Ideas and Issues

A word that is often used as an equivalent to idea is **issue,** which may be defined as an open and unsettled point or concern about which there may be argument or contention. On political matters, issues are usually about what courses of action to take, such as whether a new bridge should be built, or whether more money should be spent on schools. Often, however, the issues revolve about the theoretical basis on which to proceed. To this extent, issues are very close in meaning to ideas. The nature of issue as a concept—because issues develop out of situations—is particularly helpful in the study of literature. Sometimes issues are not stated and we as readers make inferences from the work or works we are discussing. What do we find there? What do we take away from that work? Have we understood the issue properly? How do we define the issue as an idea? The answers to such questions frequently lead us directly into discussions of ideas. Chopin's "The Story of an Hour" (Chapter 6) deals with a woman's unexpected thoughts when she is (mistakenly) told that her husband has died, and through her thoughts the story raises the issue of what a woman's role should be in marriage. In Bambara's "The Lesson" (this chapter) we find the issue of economic inequality and political injustice. Here the idea is that economic inequality results in an unacceptably high human cost. (See the illustrative essay at the end of this chapter.)

Ideas and Values

Literature embodies **values** along with ideas. *Value*, of course, commonly refers to the price of something, but in the realm of ideas and principles, it is a standard of what is desired, sought, esteemed, and treasured. For example, *democracy* refers to our political system, but it is also a complex idea of representative government that we esteem most highly, and so also do we esteem concepts such as *honor, cooperation, generosity,* and *love*. A vital idea/value is *justice,* which, put most simply, involves equality before the law and also the fair evaluation of conduct that is deemed unacceptable or illegal. Literature embodies values along with ideas. This means that ideas imply that certain conditions and standards should be—or should not be—highly esteemed. For example, the idea of *justice* may be considered abstractly and broadly, as Plato does in his *Republic* when developing his concept of a just government. In comparison, justice is also a subject of Susan Glaspell's story "A Jury of Her Peers" (Chapter 3; see also the story's companion piece, the play *Trifles* in Chapter 23). Glaspell treats the value of justice very practically, as a problem that arises when two women, wives of men investigating a murder, discover circumstantial evidence in a dreary farm kitchen that a housewife has strangled her husband in his sleep. One of the women is familiar with the woman and the situation of her miserable marriage, and as a result both women together suppress the incriminating evidence. With the freedom of their opportunity, in other words, the women choose to exonerate the farm wife, while denying the validity of the strictly legal case against her. By their action they have engaged in their own "jury nullification," by which they find the farm wife not guilty. In their judgment, which they act on but do not discuss, justice is better served by suppressing the evidence they have found in preference to bringing it forward. The idea of justice underlying Glaspell's "A Jury of Her Peers," in short, also involves a deeply held value. A comparable situation is presented by Thomas Hardy in "The Three Strangers" (Chapter 5) in which a large number of neighbors collectively deny the guilt of a man who has been imprisoned for what legally is considered a major crime.

A graphic connection of ideas and values is seen in Picasso's massive painting *Guernica* (p. I–9). The painting superbly illustrates the agony of Guernica, the Spanish town bombed by Nazi planes in 1937. The agonized horse and the screaming man, the disembodied head and arms, the mother holding her dead infant—all convey the idea that war is an unspeakable crime against humanity. Picasso's condemnation of war and the man responsible for the slaughter at Guernica, Francisco Franco (1892–1975), is also clear. That Picasso wanted his values to be understood is confirmed by his instruction that the painting was not to be displayed in Spain until after Franco died.

The Place of Ideas in Literature

Because writers of poems, plays, and stories are usually not systematic philosophers, it is not appropriate to go "message hunting" as though their works contained nothing but ideas. Indeed, there is great benefit and pleasure to be derived from just savoring a work—getting engrossed in the story, following the patterns of narrative and conflict, getting to like the characters, understanding the work's implications and suggestions, and listening to the sounds of the author's words—to name only a few of the reasons for which literature is treasured.

Nevertheless, ideas are vital to understanding and appreciating not just fiction, but all literature. Writers have ideas and want to communicate them to you. For example, in "The Horse Dealer's Daughter" (this chapter) Lawrence tells the story of a man and a woman who fall unpredictably but impetuously in love. This love is unlikely but real, and the story is therefore effective, but the story is also provocative because it develops the idea that love has the power to override all other personal emotions and decisions. Paredes's narrator in "The Hammon and the Beans" (this chapter) tells the story of a little Mexican girl, with great potential but no opportunities at all, who dies from an undisclosed illness produced by her family's impoverishment and medical neglect. Through this event the story conveys the idea that massive humanitarian damage is a major result of economic deprivation. In these works, the ideas of the authors both underlie and connect the various narrative details.

Distinguish Between Ideas and Actions

As you analyze works for ideas, it is important to avoid the trap of confusing ideas and actions. Such a trap is contained in the following sentence about O'Connor's "First Confession" (Chapter 6): "The major character, Jackie, misbehaves at home and tries to stab his sister with a bread knife." This sentence successfully describes a major action in the story, but it does not express an *idea* that connects characters and events, and for this reason it obstructs understanding. Some possible connections might be achieved with sentences like these: "'First Confession' illustrates the idea that family life may produce anger and potential violence" or "'First Confession' shows that compelling children to accept authority may produce effects that are the opposite of adult intentions." A study based on these connecting formulations could be focused on ideas and would not be sidetracked into doing no more than retelling O'Connor's story.

Distinguish Between Ideas and Situations

You should also distinguish between ideas and situations. For example, in Joyce's "Araby" (Chapter 4) the narrator describes his frustration and embarrassment when he arrives late at the Araby bazaar in Dublin. This is a *situation*, but it is not the *idea* brought out by the situation. Joyce's idea here is rather that immature love causes unreal dreams and hopes that result in disappointment and self-reproach. If you are able to distinguish a story's various situations from the writer's major idea or ideas, you will be able to focus on ideas and therefore sharpen your own thinking.

How to Find Ideas

Ideas are not as obvious as characters or setting. To determine an idea, you need to consider the meaning of what you read and then to develop explanatory and comprehensive assertions. Your assertions need not be the same as those that others might make. People notice different things, and individual formulations vary. In Chopin's "The Story of an Hour" (Chapter 6), for example, an initial expression of some of the story's ideas might take any of the following forms: (1) Partners in even a good marriage can have ambivalent feelings about their lives together. (2) An unforeseen event can lead a wife to develop negative but previously unrecognized thoughts. (3) Even those closest to a person may never realize this person's innermost feelings. Although any one of these choices could be a basic idea in the study of "The Story of an Hour," they have in common the main character's surprising feelings of release when she is told that her husband has been killed in an accident. In discovering ideas, you should follow a similar process—making a number of formulations for an idea and then selecting one for further development.

As you read, be alert to the different ways in which authors convey ideas. One author might prefer an indirect way through a character's speeches, whereas another may prefer direct statements. In practice, authors can employ any or all the following methods.

1. *Study the authorial voice.* Although authors mainly render action, dialogue, and situation, they sometimes state ideas to guide us and deepen our understanding. In the second paragraph of Maupassant's "The Necklace" (Part I), for example, the authorial voice presents the idea that women have only charm and beauty to get on in the world. Ironically, Maupassant uses the story to show that for the major character Mathilde, nothing is effective, for her charm cannot prevent disaster. Hawthorne, in "Young Goodman Brown" (Chapter 7), expresses this powerful idea: "The fiend in his own shape is less hideous than when he rages in the breast of man" (390, paragraph 53). The narrator makes this statement just when the major character, Goodman Brown, is speeding through "the benighted wilderness" on his way to the satanic ritual. Although the idea is complex and will sustain extensive discussion, its essential aspect is that the causes of evil originate within human beings themselves, and the implication is that we alone are responsible for all our actions, whether good or evil.

2. *Study the first-person speaker.* First-person narrators or speakers frequently express ideas along with their depiction of actions and situations, and they also make statements from which you can make inferences about ideas. (See also Chapter 2, on point of view.) Because what they say is part of a dramatic presentation, they can be right or wrong, well-considered or thoughtless, good or bad, or brilliant or half-baked, depending on the speaker. A somewhat half-baked speaker, yet an interesting one, is Sammy, the narrator of Updike's "A & P" (Chapter 6), who seems engulfed in intellectual commonplaces, particularly in his insinuation about the intelligence of women. In his defense, however, Sammy *acts* on the worthy idea that people have private rights. If the speaker seems to possess limited understanding or inadequate consideration of what he or she is saying, like Jackie, sometimes, in Frank O'Connor's "First Confession" (Chapter 6), you may nevertheless still study and evaluate such a speaker's ideas. Jackie, for example, maintains some of his childhood attitudes even though at the time of the narration he is an older and presumably mature narrator. An especially mature narrator is the unnamed speaker of Whitecloud's "Blue Winds Dancing" (Chapter 5), who is honestly discouraged by his experiences at a large Western university, and he is deeply distressed by the ideas he has heard from his professor about the inferiority of Native American culture. The first-person narrator of Gilman's "The Yellow Wallpaper" (Chapter 10) is increasingly delusional, yet an idea we can derive from her speech and circumstances is that people with her illness need less harsh and more humane treatment. In Tan's "Two Kinds" (Chapter 3) the narrator describes the negative behavior that stemmed from her childhood conflicts with her mother. An idea that may be taken from this narration is that adult composure is reached only through tortuous childhood paths. If the speaker seems to possess incomplete or limited understanding of what he or she is saying, you may nevertheless still study and evaluate this speaker's ideas. In Bambara's "The Lesson," for example, the narrator, Sylvia, is a child who speaks the language of the streets but who nevertheless exhibits natural analytical skills befitting an astute political scientist.

3. *Study the statements made by characters.* In many stories, characters express their own views, which can be right or wrong, admirable or contemptible. When you consider such dramatic speeches, you must do considerable interpreting and evaluating yourself. The second stranger, the hangman, in Hardy's "The Three Strangers" (Chapter 5), expresses ideas about crime and punishment that are inflexibly unenlightened and unjust. It is clear that the peasant folk of Higher Crowstairs hold kinder and more humane ideas. Old Man Warner in Jackson's "The Lottery" (Chapter 2) states that the lottery is valuable even though we learn from the narrator that the beliefs underlying it have long been forgotten. Because Warner is a zealous and insistent person, however, his words show that outdated ideas continue to do harm even when there is strong reason to reevaluate and abandon them.

4. *Study the work's figurative language.* Figurative language is one of the major components of poetry, but it also abounds in prose fiction (see also Chapter 15). In Joyce's "Araby," for example (Chapter 4), the narrator uses a beautiful comparison to describe his youthful admiration for his friend Mangan's sister. He says that his body "was like a harp and her words and gestures were like fingers running upon the wires" (paragraph 5). A less complimentary figure is seen in D. H. Lawrence's "The Horse Dealer's Daughter." Lawrence develops the comparison through the Pervin family. Joe Pervin, one of Mabel's brothers, is demeaning himself by accepting his future role as no more than a subordinate worker for his future father-in-law. Lawrence's idea is that financial security alone involves the sacrifice of personal freedom, and so the comparison shows that Joe is no different from the great draft horses on the Pervin estate: "He [Joe] would marry and go into harness. His life was over, he would be a subject animal now" (472, paragraph 7).

5. *Study how characters stand for ideas.* Characters and their actions can often be equated with certain ideas and values. The power of Mathilde's story in Maupassant's "The Necklace" (Part I) emphasizes the idea that unrealizable dreams can invade and damage the real world. Two diverse or opposed characters can embody contrasting ideas, as with Louise and Josephine of Chopin's "The Story of an Hour" (Chapter 6). Each woman can be taken to represent differing views about the role of women in marriage. In effect, characters who stand for ideas can assume symbolic status, as in Hawthorne's "Young Goodman Brown" (Chapter 7) where the protagonist symbolizes the alienation accompanying zealousness, or in Ozick's "The Shawl" (Chapter 4), where the small child Magda embodies the vulnerability and helplessness of human beings in the face of dehumanizing state brutality. Such characters can be equated directly with particular ideas, and to talk about them is a shorthand way of talking about the ideas.

6. *Study the work itself as an embodiment of ideas.* One of the most important ways in which authors express ideas is to interlock them within all parts and aspects of the work. The art of painting is instructive here, for a painting can be taken in with a single view that comprehends all the aspects of color, form, action, and expression, which can also be considered separately. Thus, we may again refer to the broken and distorted figures in Picasso's Guernica (p. I–9), which can be viewed together, and which emphasize the idea that war is not noble, for it creates unspeakable horror and suffering for human beings, animals, and the earth itself. In the same way, when a work is considered in its totality, the various parts collectively can embody major ideas, as in Bierce's "An Occurrence at Owl Creek Bridge" (Chapter 1), where Bierce dramatizes the idea that under great stress the human mind operates with lightning speed. Most works represent ideas in a similar way. Even "escape literature," which ostensibly enables readers to forget immediate problems, contains conflicts between good and evil, love and hate, good spies and bad, earthlings and aliens, and so on. Such works *do* thereby embody ideas, even though their avowed intention is not to make readers think but rather to help them forget.

Stories for Study

James Baldwin. . . . . Sonny's Blues, 438

Toni Cade Bambara. . . . . The Lesson, 457

Anton Chekhov. . . . . The Lady with the Dog, 462

D. H. Lawrence . . . . The Horse Dealer's Daughter, 471

Américo Paredes . . . . The Hammon and the Beans, 482

JAMES BALDWIN (1924–1987)

James Baldwin was born in Harlem in the 1920s. He converted to Pentecostalism late in the 1930s, and for a time he preached regularly, even though he had taken no formal training in theology or the ministry. Abandoning his role as a preacher early in the 1940s, he began working for a railroad in New Jersey and did this work for a number of years. Until 1948 he continued living in the United States, but then he left for Europe, spending the remainder of his life there and in the Middle East. Though he lived abroad, he wrote about life among alienated blacks in America and was considered a primary writer voicing the concerns and aims of the Black Power movement of the time. His view about young black men is best described in his own words, namely that they "were growing up with . . . their heads [being] bumped abruptly against the low ceiling of their actual possibilities." His works detail the ways in which youths handled such difficulties. One way was to become lost in narcotics addiction, a way that is tried by Sonny of "Sonny's Blues." A more creative way, which is finally adopted by Sonny, is music. The masterly concluding paragraphs of this story are a stirring tribute to the power of Sonny's playing of the Blues to lift his soul out of the "battle that was occurring in him" and to reach a state of emotional transcendence.

 ## Sonny's Blues (1957)

I read about it in the paper, in the subway, on my way to work. I read it, and I couldn't believe it, and I read it again. Then perhaps I just stared at it, at the newsprint spelling out his name, spelling out the story. I stared at it in the swinging lights of the subway car, and in the faces and bodies of the people, and in my own face, trapped in the darkness which roared outside.

It was not to be believed and I kept telling myself that, as I walked from the subway station to the high school. And at the same time I couldn't doubt it. I was scared, scared for Sonny. He became real to me again. A great block of ice got settled in my belly and kept melting there slowly all day long, while I taught my classes algebra. It was a special kind of ice. It kept melting, sending trickles of ice water all up and down my veins, but it never got less. Sometimes it hardened and seemed to expand until I felt my guts were going to come spilling out or that I was going to choke or scream. This would always be at a moment when I was remembering some specific thing Sonny had once said or done.

When he was about as old as the boys in my classes his face had been bright and open, there was a lot of copper in it; and he'd had wonderfully direct brown eyes, and great gentleness and privacy. I wondered what he looked like now. He had been picked up, the evening before, in a raid on an apartment downtown, for peddling and using heroin.

I couldn't believe it: but what I mean by that is that I couldn't find any room for it anywhere inside me. I had kept it outside me for a long time. I hadn't wanted to know. I had had suspicions, but I didn't name them, I kept putting them away. I told myself that Sonny was wild, but he wasn't crazy. And he'd always been a good boy, he hadn't ever turned hard or evil or disrespectful, the way kids can, so quick, so quick, especially in Harlem. I didn't want to believe that I'd ever see my brother going down, coming to nothing, all that light in his face gone out, in the condition I'd already seen so many others. Yet it had happened and here I was, talking about algebra to a lot of boys who might, every one of them for all I knew, be popping off needles every time they went to the head. Maybe it did more for them than algebra could.

I was sure that the first time Sonny had ever had horse,° he couldn't have been much older than these boys were now. These boys, now, were living as we'd been living then, they were growing up with a rush and their heads bumped abruptly against the low ceiling of their actual possibilities. They were filled with rage. All they really knew were two darknesses, the darkness of their lives, which was now closing in on them, and the darkness of the movies, which had blinded them to that other darkness, and in which they now, vindictively, dreamed, at once more together than they were at any other time, and more alone.

When the last bell rang, the last class ended, I let out my breath. It seemed I'd been holding it for all that time. My clothes were wet—I may have looked as though I'd been sitting in a steam bath, all dressed up, all afternoon. I sat alone in the classroom a long time. I listened to the boys outside, downstairs, shouting and cursing and laughing. Their laughter struck me for perhaps the first time. It was not the joyous laughter which—God knows why—one associates with children. It was mocking and insular, its intent to denigrate. It was disenchanted, and in this, also, lay the authority of their curses. Perhaps I was listening to them because I was thinking about my brother and in them I heard my brother. And myself.

One boy was whistling a tune, at once very complicated and very simple, it seemed to be pouring out of him as though he were a bird, and it sounded very cool and moving through all that harsh, bright air, only just holding its own through all those other sounds.

I stood up and walked over to the window and looked down into the courtyard. It was the beginning of the spring and the sap was rising in the boys. A teacher passed through them every now and again, quickly, as though he or she couldn't wait to get out of that courtyard, to get those boys out of their sight and off their minds. I started collecting my stuff. I thought I'd better get home and talk to Isabel.

The courtyard was almost deserted by the time I got downstairs. I saw this boy standing in the shadow of a doorway, looking just like Sonny. I almost called his name. Then I saw that it wasn't Sonny, but somebody we used to know, a boy from around our block. He'd been Sonny's friend. He'd never been mine, having been too young for me, and, anyway, I'd never liked him. And now, even though he was a grown-up man, he still hung around that block, still spent hours on the street corners, was always high and raggy. I used to run into him from time to time and he'd often work around to asking me for a quarter or fifty cents. He always had some real good excuse, too, and I always gave it to him, I don't know why.

But now, abruptly, I hated him. I couldn't stand the way he looked at me, partly like a dog, partly like a cunning child. I wanted to ask him what the hell he was doing in the school courtyard.

He sort of shuffled over to me, and he said, "I see you got the papers. So you already know about it."

"You mean about Sonny? Yes, I already know about it. How come they didn't get you?"

He grinned. It made him repulsive and it also brought to mind what he'd looked like as a kid. "I wasn't there. I stay away from them people."

"Good for you." I offered him a cigarette and I watched him through the smoke. "You come all the way down here just to tell me about Sonny?"

"That's right." He was sort of shaking his head and his eyes looked strange, as though they were about to cross. The bright sun deadened his damp dark brown skin and it made his eyes look yellow and showed up the dirt in his kinked hair. He smelled funky. I moved a little away from him and I said, "Well, thanks. But I already know about it and I got to get home."

"I'll walk you a little ways," he said. We started walking. There were a couple of kids still loitering in the courtyard and one of them said goodnight to me and looked strangely at the boy beside me.

°*horse:* heroin.

"What're you going to do?" he asked me. "I mean, about Sonny?"

"Look. I haven't seen Sonny for over a year. I'm not sure I'm going to do anything. Anyway, what the hell *can* I do?"

"That's right," he said quickly, "ain't nothing you can do. Can't much help old Sonny no more, I guess."

20 It was what I was thinking and so it seemed to me he had no right to say it.

"I'm surprised at Sonny, though," he went on—he had a funny way of talking, he looked straight ahead as though he were talking to himself—"I thought Sonny was a smart boy, I thought he was too smart to get hung."

"I guess he thought so too," I said sharply, "and that's how he got hung. And how about you? You're pretty goddamn smart, I bet."

Then he looked directly at me, just for a minute. "I ain't smart," he said. "If I was smart, I'd have reached for a pistol a long time ago."

"Look. Don't tell *me* your sad story, if it was up to me, I'd give you one." Then I felt guilty—guilty, probably, for never having supposed that the poor bastard *had* a story of his own, much less a sad one, and I asked, quickly, "What's going to happen to him now?"

25 He didn't answer this. He was off by himself some place. "Funny thing," he said, and from his tone we might have been discussing the quickest way to get to Brooklyn, "when I saw the papers this morning, the first thing I asked myself was if I had anything to do with it. I felt sort of responsible."

I began to listen more carefully. The subway station was on the corner, just before us, and I stopped. He stopped, too. We were in front of a bar and he ducked slightly, peering in, but whoever he was looking for didn't seem to be there. The juke box was blasting away with something black and bouncy and I half watched the barmaid as she danced her way from the juke box to her place behind the bar. And I watched her face as she laughingly responded to something someone said to her, still keeping time to the music. When she smiled one saw the little girl, one sensed the doomed, still-struggling woman beneath the battered face of the semiwhore.

"I never *give* Sonny nothing," the boy said finally, "but a long time ago I come to school high and Sonny asked me how it felt." He paused, I couldn't bear to watch him, I watched the barmaid, and I listened to the music which seemed to be causing the pavement to shake. "I told him it felt great." The music stopped, the barmaid paused and watched the juke box until the music began again. "It did."

All this was carrying me some place I didn't want to go. I certainly didn't want to know how it felt. It filled everything, the people, the houses, the music, the dark, quicksilver barmaid, with menace; and this menace was their reality.

"What's going to happen to him now?" I asked again.

30 "They'll send him away some place and they'll try to cure him." He shook his head. "Maybe he'll even think he's kicked the habit. Then they'll let him loose"—he gestured, throwing his cigarette into the gutter. "That's all."

"What do you mean, that's *all*?"

But I knew what he meant.

"I *mean*, that's *all*." He turned his head and looked at me, pulling down the corners of his mouth. "Don't you know what I mean?" he asked, softly.

"How the hell *would* I know what you mean?" I almost whispered it, I don't know why.

35 "That's right," he said to the air, "how would *he* know what I mean?" He turned toward me again, patient and calm, and yet I somehow felt him shaking, shaking as though he were going to fall apart. I felt that ice in my guts again, the dread I'd felt all afternoon; and again I watched the barmaid, moving about the bar, washing glasses, and singing. "Listen. They'll let him out and then it'll just start all over again. That's what I mean."

"You mean—they'll let him out. And then he'll just start working his way back in again. You mean he'll never kick the habit. Is that what you mean?"

"That's right," he said, cheerfully. "*You* see what I mean."

"Tell me," I said at last, "why does he want to die? He must want to die, he's killing himself, why does he want to die?"

He looked at me in surprise. He licked his lips. "He don't want to die. He wants to live. Don't nobody want to die, ever."

Then I wanted to ask him—too many things. He could not have answered, or if he had, I could not have borne the answers. I started walking. "Well, I guess it's none of my business." 40

"It's going to be rough on old Sonny," he said. We reached the subway station. "This is your station?" he asked. I nodded. I took one step down. "Damn!" he said, suddenly. I looked up at him. He grinned again. "Damn it if I didn't leave all my money home. You ain't got a dollar on you, have you? Just for a couple of days, is all."

All at once something inside gave and threatened to come pouring out of me. I didn't hate him any more. I felt that in another moment I'd start crying like a child.

"Sure," I said. "Don't sweat." I looked in my wallet and didn't have a dollar, I only had a five. "Here," I said. "That hold you?"

He didn't look at it—he didn't want to look at it. A terrible closed look came over his face, as though he were keeping the number on the bill a secret from him and me. "Thanks," he said, and now he was dying to see me go. "Don't worry about Sonny. Maybe I'll write him or something."

"Sure," I said. "You do that. So long."

"Be seeing you," he said. I went on down the steps. 45

And I didn't write Sonny or send him anything for a long time. When I finally did, it was just after my little girl died, he wrote me back a letter which made me feel like a bastard. Here's what he said:

Dear brother,

You don't know how much I needed to hear from you. I wanted to write you many a time but I dug how much I must have hurt you and so I didn't write. But now I feel like a man who's been trying to climb up out of some deep, real deep and funky hole and just saw the sun up there, outside. I got to get outside.

I can't tell you much about how I got here. I mean I don't know how to tell you. I guess I was afraid of something or I was trying to escape from something and you know I have never been very strong in the head (smile). I'm glad Mama and Daddy are dead and can't see what's happened to their son and I swear if I'd known what I was doing I would never have hurt you so, you and a lot of other fine people who were nice to me and who believed in me.

I don't want you to think it had anything to do with me being a musician. It's more than that. Or maybe less than that. I can't get anything straight in my head down here and I try not to think about what's going to happen to me when I get outside again. Sometime I think I'm going to flip and *never* get outside and sometime I think I'll come straight back. I tell you one thing, though, I'd rather blow my brains out than go through this again. But that's what they all say, so they tell me. If I tell you when I'm coming to New York and if you could meet me, I sure would appreciate it. Give my love to Isabel and the kids and I was sure sorry to hear about little Gracie. I wish I could be like Mama and say the Lord's will be done, but I don't know it seems to me that trouble is the one thing that never does get stopped and I don't know what good it does to blame it on the Lord. But maybe it does some good if you believe it.

Your brother,
Sonny

Then I kept in constant touch with him and I sent him whatever I could and I went to meet him when he came back to New York. When I saw him many things I thought I had forgotten came flooding back to me. This was because I had begun, finally, to wonder about Sonny, about the life that Sonny lived inside. This life, whatever it was, had made him older and thinner and it had deepened the distant stillness in which he had always moved. He looked very unlike my baby brother. Yet, when he smiled, when we shook hands, the baby brother I'd never known looked out from the depths of his private life, like an animal waiting to be coaxed into the light.

50   "How you been keeping?" he asked me.

"All right. And you?"

"Just fine." He was smiling all over his face. "It's good to see you again."

"It's good to see you."

The seven years' difference in our ages lay between us like a chasm: I wondered if these years would ever operate between us as a bridge. I was remembering, and it made it hard to catch my breath, that I had been there when he was born; and I had heard the first words he had ever spoken. When he started to walk, he walked from our mother straight to me. I caught him just before he fell when he took the first steps he ever took in this world.

55   "How's Isabel?"

"Just fine. She's dying to see you."

"And the boys?"

"They're fine, too. They're anxious to see their uncle."

"Oh, come on. You know they don't remember me."

60   "Are you kidding? Of course they remember you."

He grinned again. We got into a taxi. We had a lot to say to each other, far too much to know how to begin.

As the taxi began to move, I asked, "You still want to go to India?"

He laughed. "You still remember that. Hell, no. This place is Indian enough for me."

"It used to belong to them," I said.

65   And he laughed again. "They damn sure knew what they were doing when they got rid of it."

Years ago, when he was around fourteen, he'd been all hipped on the idea of going to India. He read books about people sitting on rocks, naked, in all kinds of weather, but mostly bad, naturally, and walking barefoot through hot coals and arriving at wisdom. I used to say that it sounded to me as though they were getting away from wisdom as fast as they could. I think he sort of looked down on me for that.

"Do you mind," he asked, "if we have the driver drive alongside the park? On the west side—I haven't seen the city in so long."

"Of course not," I said. I was afraid that I might sound as though I were humoring him, but I hoped he wouldn't take it that way.

So we drove along, between the green of the park and the stony, lifeless elegance of hotels and apartment buildings, toward the vivid, killing streets of our childhood. These streets hadn't changed, though housing projects jutted up out of them now like rocks in the middle of a boiling sea. Most of the houses in which we had grown up had vanished, as had the stores from which we had stolen, the basements in which we had first tried sex, the rooftops from which we had hurled tin cans and bricks. But houses exactly like the houses of our past yet dominated the landscape, boys exactly like the boys we once had been found themselves smothering in these houses, came down into the streets for light and air and found themselves encircled by disaster. Some escaped the trap, most didn't. Those who got out always left something of themselves behind, as some animals amputate a leg and leave it in the trap. It might be said, perhaps, that I had escaped, after all, I was a school teacher; or that Sonny had, he hadn't lived in Harlem for years. Yet, as the cab moved uptown through streets which seemed, with a rush, to darken with dark people, and as I covertly studied Sonny's face, it came to me that what we both were seeking through our separate cab windows was that part of ourselves which had been left behind. It's always at the hour of trouble and confrontation that the missing member aches.

We hit 110th Street and started rolling up Lenox Avenue. And I'd known this avenue all my life, but it seemed to me again, as it had seemed on the day I'd first heard about Sonny's trouble, filled with a hidden menace which was its very breath of life.   70

"We almost there," said Sonny.

"Almost." We were both too nervous to say anything more.

We live in a housing project. It hasn't been up long. A few days after it was up it seemed uninhabitably new, now, of course, it's already rundown. It looks like a parody of the good, clean, faceless life—God knows the people who live in it do their best to make it a parody. The beat-looking grass lying around isn't enough to make their lives green, the hedges will never hold out the streets, and they know it. The big windows fool no one, they aren't big enough to make space out of no space. They don't bother with the windows, they watch the TV screen instead. The playground is most popular with the children who don't play at jacks, or skip rope, or roller skate, or swing, and they can be found in it after dark. We moved in partly because it's not too far from where I teach, and partly for the kids; but it's really just like the houses in which Sonny and I grew up. The same things happen, they'll have the same things to remember. The moment Sonny and I started into the house I had the feeling that I was simply bringing him back into the danger he had almost died trying to escape.

Sonny has never been talkative. So I don't know why I was sure he'd be dying to talk to me when supper was over the first night. Everything went fine, the oldest boy remembered him, and the youngest boy liked him, and Sonny had remembered to bring something for each of them; and Isabel, who is really much nicer than I am, more open and giving, had gone to a lot of trouble about dinner and was genuinely glad to see him. And she's always been able to tease Sonny in a way that I haven't. It was nice to see her face so vivid again and to hear her laugh and watch her make Sonny laugh. She wasn't, or, anyway, she didn't seem to be, at all uneasy or embarrassed. She chatted as though there were no subject which had to be avoided and she got Sonny past his first, faint stiffness. And thank God she was there, for I was filled with that icy dread again. Everything I did seemed awkward to me, and everything I said sounded freighted with hidden meaning. I was trying to remember everything I'd heard about dope addiction and I couldn't help watching Sonny for signs. I wasn't doing it out of malice. I was trying to find out something about my brother. I was dying to hear him tell me he was safe.

"Safe!" my father grunted, whenever Mama suggested trying to move to a neighborhood which might be safer for children. "Safe, hell! Ain't no place safe for kids, nor nobody."   75

He always went on like this, but he wasn't, ever, really as bad as he sounded, not even on weekends, when he got drunk. As a matter of fact, he was always on the lookout for "something a little better," but he died before he found it. He died suddenly, during a drunken weekend in the middle of the war, when Sonny was fifteen. He and Sonny hadn't ever got on too well. And this was partly because Sonny was the apple of his father's eye. It was because he loved Sonny so much and was frightened for him, that he was always fighting with him. It doesn't do any good to fight with Sonny. Sonny just moves back, inside himself, where he can't be reached. But the principal reason that they never hit it off is that they were so much alike. Daddy was big and rough and loud-talking, just the opposite of Sonny, but they both had—that same privacy.

Mama tried to tell me something about this, just after Daddy died. I was home on leave from the army.

This was the last time I ever saw my mother alive. Just the same, this picture gets all mixed up in my mind with pictures I had of her when she was younger. The way I always see her is the way she used to be on a Sunday afternoon, say, when the old folks were talking after the big Sunday dinner. I always see her wearing pale blue. She'd be sitting on the sofa. And my father would be sitting in the easy chair, not far from her. And the living room would be full of church folks and relatives. There they sit, in chairs all around the living room, and the night is creeping up outside, but nobody knows it yet. You can see the darkness growing against the windowpanes and you hear the street noises every now and again, or maybe the jangling beat of a tambourine from one of the churches close by, but it's real quiet in the room. For a moment nobody's talking, but every face looks darkening, like the sky outside. And my mother rocks a little from the waist, and my father's eyes are closed. Everyone is looking at something a child can't see. For a minute they've forgotten the children. Maybe a kid is lying on the rug, half asleep. Maybe somebody's got a kid in his lap and is absent-mindedly stroking the kid's head. Maybe there's a kid, quiet and big-eyed, curled up in a big chair in the corner. The silence, the darkness coming, and the darkness in the faces frightens the child obscurely. He hopes that the hand which strokes his forehead will never stop—will never die. He hopes that there will never come a time when the old folks won't be sitting around the living room, talking about where they've come from, and what they've seen, and what's happened to them and their kinfolk.

But something deep and watchful in the child knows that this is bound to end, is already ending. In a moment someone will get up and turn on the light. Then the old folks will remember the children and they won't talk any more that day. And when light fills the room, the child is filled with darkness. He knows that everytime this happens he's moved just a little closer to that darkness outside. The darkness outside is what the old folks have been talking about. It's what they've come from. It's what they endure. The child knows that they won't talk any more because if he knows too much about what's happened to *them,* he'll know too much too soon, about what's going to happen to *him.*

80   The last time I talked to my mother, I remember I was restless. I wanted to get out and see Isabel. We weren't married then and we had a lot to straighten out between us.

There Mama sat, in black, by the window. She was humming an old church song, *Lord, you brought me from a long ways off.*° Sonny was out somewhere. Mama kept watching the streets.

"I don't know," she said, "if I'll ever see you again, after you go off from here. But I hope you'll remember the things I tried to teach you."

"Don't talk like that," I said, and smiled. "You'll be here a long time yet."

She smiled, too, but she said nothing. She was quiet for a long time. And I said, "Mama, don't you worry about nothing. I'll be writing all the time, and you be getting the checks . . ."

85   "I want to talk to you about your brother," she said, suddenly. "If anything happens to me he ain't going to have nobody to look out for him."

"Mama," I said, "ain't nothing going to happen to you *or* Sonny. Sonny's all right. He's a good boy and he's got good sense."

"It ain't a question of his being a good boy," Mama said, "nor of his having good sense. It ain't only the bad ones, nor yet the dumb ones that gets sucked under." She stopped, looking at me. "Your Daddy once had a brother," she said, and she smiled in a way that made me feel she was in pain. "You didn't never know that, did you?"

"No," I said, "I never knew that," and I watched her face.

"Oh, yes," she said, "your Daddy had a brother." She looked out of the window again. "I know you never saw your Daddy cry. But *I* did—many a time, through all these years."

90   I asked her, "What happened to his brother? How come nobody's ever talked about him?" This was the first time I ever saw my mother look old.

°*Lord. . . ways off:* a line from the second stanza of the gospel hymn "Look Where He Brought Me From."

"His brother got killed," she said, "when he was just a little younger than you are now. I knew him. He was a fine boy. He was maybe a little full of the devil, but he didn't mean nobody no harm."

Then she stopped and the room was silent, exactly as it had sometimes been on those Sunday afternoons. Mama kept looking out into the streets.

"He used to have a job in the mill," she said, "and, like all young folks, he just liked to perform on Saturday nights. Saturday nights, him and your father would drift around to different places, go to dances and things like that, or just sit around with people they knew, and your father's brother would sing, he had a fine voice, and play along with himself on his guitar. Well, this particular Saturday night, him and your father was coming home from some place, and they were both a little drunk and there was a moon that night, it was bright like day. Your father's brother was feeling kind of good, and he was whistling to himself, and he had his guitar slung over his shoulder. They was coming down a hill and beneath them was a road that turned off from the highway. Well, your father's brother, being always kind of frisky, decided to run down this hill, and he did, with that guitar banging and clanging behind him, and he ran across the road, and he was making water behind a tree. And your father was sort of amused at him and he was still coming down the hill, kind of slow. Then he heard a car motor and that same minute his brother stepped from behind the tree, into the road, in the moonlight. And he started to cross the road. And your father started to run down the hill, he says he don't know why. This car was full of white men. They was all drunk, and when they seen your father's brother they let out a great whoop and holler and they aimed the car straight at him. They was having fun, they just wanted to scare him, the way they do sometimes, you know. But they was drunk. And I guess the boy, being drunk, too, and scared, kind of lost his head. By the time he jumped it was too late. Your father says he heard his brother scream when the car rolled over him, and he heard the wood of that guitar when it give, and he heard them strings go flying, and he heard them white men shouting, and the car kept on a-going and it ain't stopped till this day. And, time your father got down the hill, his brother weren't nothing but blood and pulp."

Tears were gleaming on my mother's face. There wasn't anything I could say.   95

"He never mentioned it," she said, "because I never let him mention it before you children. Your Daddy was like a crazy man that night and for many a night thereafter. He says he never in his life seen anything as dark as that road after the lights of that car had gone away. Weren't nothing, weren't nobody on that road, just your Daddy and his brother and that busted guitar. Oh, yes. Your Daddy never did really get right again. Till the day he died he weren't sure but that every white man he saw was the man that killed his brother."

She stopped and took out her handkerchief and dried her eyes and looked at me.

"I ain't telling you all this," she said, "to make you scared or bitter or to make you hate nobody. I'm telling you this because you got a brother. And the world ain't changed."

I guess I didn't want to believe this. I guess she saw this in my face. She turned away from me, toward the window again, searching those streets.

"But I praise my Redeemer," she said at last, "that He called your Daddy home before   100 me. I ain't saying it to throw no flowers at myself, but, I declare, it keeps me from feeling too cast down to know I helped your father get safely through this world. Your father always acted like he was the roughest, strongest man on earth. And everybody took him to be like that. But if he hadn't had *me* there—to see his tears!"

She was crying again. Still, I couldn't move. I said, "Lord, Lord, Mama, I didn't know it was like that."

"Oh, honey," she said, "there's a lot that you don't know. But you are going to find it out." She stood up from the window and came over to me. "You got to hold on to your brother," she said, "and don't let him fall, no matter what it looks like is happening to him and no matter how evil you gets with him. You going to be evil with him many a time. But don't you forget what I told you, you hear?"

"I won't forget," I said. "Don't you worry, I won't forget. I won't let nothing happen to Sonny."

My mother smiled as though she were amused at something she saw in my face. Then, "You may not be able to stop nothing from happening. But you got to let him know you's *there*."

105   Two days later I was married, and then I was gone. And I had a lot of things on my mind and I pretty well forgot my promise to Mama until I got shipped home on a special furlough for her funeral.

And, after the funeral, with just Sonny and me alone in the empty kitchen, I tried to find out something about him.

"What do you want to do?" I asked him.

"I'm going to be a musician," he said.

For he had graduated, in the time I had been away, from dancing to the juke box to finding out who was playing what, and what they were doing with it, and he had bought himself a set of drums.

110   "You mean, you want to be a drummer?" I somehow had the feeling that being a drummer might be all right for other people but not for my brother Sonny.

"I don't think," he said, looking at me very gravely, "that I'll ever be a good drummer. But I think I can play a piano."

I frowned. I'd never played the role of the older brother quite so seriously before, had scarcely ever, in fact, *asked* Sonny a damn thing. I sensed myself in the presence of something I didn't really know how to handle, didn't understand. So I made my frown a little deeper as I asked: "What kind of musician do you want to be?"

He grinned. "How many kinds do you think there are?"

"Be *serious*," I said.

115   He laughed, throwing his head back, and then looked at me. "I *am* serious."

"Well, then, for Christ's sake, stop kidding around and answer a serious question. I mean, do you want to be a concert pianist, you want to play classical music and all that, or—or what?" Long before I finished he was laughing again. "For Christ's *sake*, Sonny!"

He sobered, but with difficulty. "I'm sorry. But you sound so—*scared!*" and he was off again.

"Well, you may think it's funny now, baby, but it's not going to be so funny when you have to make your living at it, let me tell you *that*." I was furious because I knew he was laughing at me and I didn't know why.

"No," he said, very sober now, and afraid, perhaps, that he'd hurt me, "I don't want to be a classical pianist. That isn't what interests me. I mean"—he paused, looking hard at me, as though his eyes would help me to understand, and then gestured helplessly, as though perhaps his hand would help—"I mean, I'll have a lot of studying to do, and I'll have to study *everything*, but, I mean, I want to play *with*—jazz musicians." He stopped. "I want to play jazz," he said.

120   Well, the word had never before sounded as heavy, as real, as it sounded that afternoon in Sonny's mouth. I just looked at him and I was probably frowning a real frown by this time. I simply couldn't see why on earth he'd want to spend his time hanging around nightclubs, clowning around on bandstands, while people pushed each other around a dance floor. It seemed—beneath him, somehow. I had never thought about it before, had never been forced to, but I suppose I had always put jazz musicians in a class with what Daddy called "goodtime people."

"Are you *serious?*"

"Hell, *yes*, I'm serious."

He looked more helpless than ever, and annoyed, and deeply hurt.

I suggested, helpfully: "You mean—like Louis Armstrong?"°

His face closed as though I'd struck him. "No. I'm not talking about none of that old-time, down home crap." 125

"Well, look, Sonny, I'm sorry, don't get mad. I just don't altogether get it, that's all. Name somebody—you know, a jazz musician you admire."

"Bird."

"Who?"

"Bird! Charlie Parker!° Don't they teach you nothing in the goddamn army?"

I lit a cigarette. I was surprised and then a little amused to discover that I was trembling. 130 "I've been out of touch," I said. "You'll have to be patient with me. Now. Who's this Parker character?"

"He's just one of the greatest jazz musicians alive," said Sonny, sullenly, his hands in his pockets, his back to me. "Maybe *the* greatest," he added, bitterly, "that's probably why *you* never heard of him."

"All right," I said, "I'm ignorant. I'm sorry. I'll go out and buy all the cat's records right away, all right?"

"It don't," said Sonny, with dignity, "make any difference to me. I don't care what you listen to. Don't do me no favors."

I was beginning to realize that I'd never seen him so upset before. With another part of my mind I was thinking that this would probably turn out to be one of those things kids go through and that I shouldn't make it seem important by pushing it too hard. Still, I didn't think it would do any harm to ask: "Doesn't all this take a lot of time? Can you make a living at it?"

He turned back to me and half leaned, half sat, on the kitchen table. "Everything takes 135 time," he said, "and—well, yes, sure, I can make a living at it. But what I don't seem to be able to make you understand is that it's the only thing I want to do."

"Well, Sonny," I said, gently, "you know people can't always do exactly what they *want* to do—"

"*No*, I don't know that," said Sonny, surprising me. "I think people *ought* to do what they want to do, what else are they alive for?"

"You getting to be a big boy," I said desperately, "it's time you started thinking about your future."

"I'm thinking about my future," said Sonny, grimly. "I think about it all the time."

I gave up. I decided, if he didn't change his mind, that we could always talk about it 140 later. "In the meantime," I said, "you got to finish school." We had already decided that he'd have to move in with Isabel and her folks. I knew this wasn't the ideal arrangement because Isabel's folks are inclined to be dicty and they hadn't especially wanted Isabel to marry me. But I didn't know what else to do. "And we have to get you fixed up at Isabel's."

There was a long silence. He moved from the kitchen table to the window. "That's a terrible idea. You know it yourself."

"Do you have a *better* idea?"

He just walked up and down the kitchen for a minute. He was as tall as I was. He had started to shave. I suddenly had the feeling that I didn't know him at all.

°*Louis Armstrong:* (1901–1971), famous for his jazz trumpet and also for his scratchy voice.
°*Charlie Parker:* (1920–1955), nicknamed "Bird," legendary for his saxophone playing and also for his role in the creation of bebop.

He stopped at the kitchen table and picked up my cigarettes. Looking at me with a kind of mocking, amused defiance, he put one between his lips. "You mind?"

145   "You smoking already?"

He lit the cigarette and nodded, watching me through the smoke. "I just wanted to see if I'd have the courage to smoke in front of you." He grinned and blew a great cloud of smoke to the ceiling. "It was easy." He looked at my face. "Come on, now. I bet you was smoking at my age, tell the truth."

I didn't say anything but the truth was on my face, and he laughed. But now there was something very strained in his laugh. "Sure. And I bet that ain't all you was doing."

He was frightening me a little. "Cut the crap," I said. "We already decided that you was going to go and live at Isabel's. Now what's got into you all of a sudden?"

"*You* decided it," he pointed out. "*I* didn't decide nothing." He stopped in front of me, leaning against the stove, arms loosely folded. "Look, brother. I don't want to stay in Harlem no more, I really don't." He was very earnest. He looked at me, then over toward the kitchen window. There was something in his eyes I'd never seen before, some thoughtfulness, some worry all his own. He rubbed the muscle of one arm. "It's time I was getting out of here."

150   "Where do you want to *go*, Sonny?"

"I want to join the army. Or the navy, I don't care. If I say I'm old enough, they'll believe me."

Then I got mad. It was because I was so scared. "You must be crazy. You goddamn fool, what the hell do you want to go and join the *army* for?"

"I just told you. To get out of Harlem."

"Sonny, you haven't even finished *school*. And if you really want to be a musician, how do you expect to study if you're in the *army?*"

155   He looked at me, trapped, and in anguish. "There's ways. I might be able to work out some kind of deal. Anyway, I'll have the G.I. Bill when I come out."

"*If* you come out." We stared at each other. "Sonny, please. Be reasonable. I know the setup is far from perfect. But we got to do the best we can."

"I ain't learning nothing in school," he said. "Even when I go." He turned away from me and opened the window and threw his cigarette out into the narrow alley. I watched his back. "At least, I ain't learning nothing you'd want me to learn." He slammed the window so hard I thought the glass would fly out, and turned back to me. "And I'm sick of the stink of these garbage cans!"

"Sonny," I said, "I know how you feel. But if you don't finish school now, you're going to be sorry later that you didn't." I grabbed him by the shoulders. "And you only got another year. It ain't so bad. And I'll come back and I swear I'll help you do *whatever* you want to do. Just try to put up with it till I come back. Will you please do that? For me?"

He didn't answer and he wouldn't look at me.

160   "Sonny. You hear me?"

He pulled away. "I hear you. But you never hear anything *I* say."

I didn't know what to say to that. He looked out of the window and then back at me. "OK," he said, and sighed. "I'll try."

Then I said, trying to cheer him up a little, "They got a piano at Isabel's. You can practice on it."

And as a matter of fact, it did cheer him up for a minute. "That's right," he said to himself. "I forgot that." His face relaxed a little. But the worry, the thoughtfulness, played on it still, the way shadows play on a face which is staring into the fire.

165   But I thought I'd never hear the end of that piano. At first, Isabel would write me, saying how nice it was that Sonny was so serious about his music and how, as soon as he came in from school, or wherever he had been when he was supposed to be at school, he went

straight to that piano and stayed there until suppertime. And, after supper, he went back to that piano and stayed there until everybody went to bed. He was at the piano all day Saturday and all day Sunday. Then he bought a record player and started playing records. He'd play one record over and over again, all day long sometimes, and he'd improvise along with it on the piano. Or he'd play one section of the record, one chord, one change, one progression, then he'd do it on the piano. Then back to the record. Then back to the piano.

Well, I really don't know how they stood it. Isabel finally confessed that it wasn't like living with a person at all, it was like living with sound. And the sound didn't make any sense to her, didn't make any sense to any of them—naturally. They began, in a way, to be afflicted by this presence that was living in their home. It was as though Sonny were some sort of god, or monster. He moved in an atmosphere which wasn't like theirs at all. They fed him and he ate, he washed himself, he walked in and out of their door; he certainly wasn't nasty or unpleasant or rude, Sonny isn't any of those things; but it was as though he were all wrapped up in some cloud, some fire, some vision all his own; and there wasn't any way to reach him.

At the same time, he wasn't really a man yet, he was still a child, and they had to watch out for him in all kinds of ways. They certainly couldn't throw him out. Neither did they dare to make a great scene about that piano because even they dimly sensed, as I sensed, from so many thousands of miles away, that Sonny was at that piano playing for his life.

But he hadn't been going to school. One day a letter came from the school board and Isabel's mother got it—there had, apparently, been other letters but Sonny had torn them up. This day, when Sonny came in, Isabel's mother showed him the letter and asked where he'd been spending his time. And she finally got it out of him that he'd been down in Greenwich Village, with musicians and other characters, in a white girl's apartment. And this scared her and she started to scream at him and what came up, once she began—though she denies it to this day—was what sacrifices they were making to give Sonny a decent home and how little he appreciated it.

Sonny didn't play the piano that day. By evening, Isabel's mother had calmed down but then there was the old man to deal with, and Isabel herself. Isabel says she did her best to be calm but she broke down and started crying. She says she just watched Sonny's face. She could tell, by watching him, what was happening with him. And what was happening was that they penetrated his cloud, they had reached him. Even if their fingers had been a thousand times more gentle than human fingers ever are, he could hardly help feeling that they had stripped him naked and were spitting on that nakedness. For he also had to see that his presence, that music, which was life or death to him, had been torture for them and that they had endured it, not at all for his sake, but only for mine. And Sonny couldn't take that. He can take it a little better today than he could then but he's still not very good at it and, frankly, I don't know anybody who is.

The silence of the next few days must have been louder than the sound of all the music ever played since time began. One morning, before she went to work, Isabel was in his room for something and she suddenly realized that all of his records were gone. And she knew for certain that he was gone. And he was. He went as far as the navy would carry him. He finally sent me a postcard from some place in Greece and that was the first I knew that Sonny was still alive. I didn't see him any more until we were both back in New York and the war had long been over.

He was a man by then, of course, but I wasn't willing to see it. He came by the house from time to time, but we fought almost every time we met. I didn't like the way he carried himself, loose and dreamlike all the time, and I didn't like his friends, and his music seemed to be merely an excuse for the life he led. It sounded just that weird and disordered.

Then we had a fight, a pretty awful fight, and I didn't see him for months. By and by I looked him up, where he was living, in a furnished room in the Village, and I tried to make it up. But there were lots of people in the room and Sonny just lay on his bed, and he wouldn't come downstairs with me, and he treated these other people as though they were his family and I weren't. So I got mad and then he got mad, and then I told him that he might just as well be dead as live the way he was living. Then he stood up and he told me not to worry about him any more in life, that he *was* dead as far as I was concerned. Then he pushed me to the door and the other people looked on as though nothing were happening, and he slammed the door behind me. I stood in the hallway, staring at the door. I heard somebody laugh in the room and then the tears came to my eyes. I started down the steps, whistling to keep from crying, I kept whistling to myself, *You going to need me, baby, one of these cold, rainy days.*

I read about Sonny's trouble in the spring. Little Grace died in the fall. She was a beautiful little girl. But she only lived a little over two years. She died of polio and she suffered. She had a slight fever for a couple of days, but it didn't seem like anything and we just kept her in bed. And we would certainly have called the doctor, but the fever dropped, she seemed to be all right. So we thought it had just been a cold. Then, one day, she was up, playing, Isabel was in the kitchen fixing lunch for the two boys when they'd come in from school, and she heard Grace fall down in the living room. When you have a lot of children you don't always start running when one of them falls, unless they start screaming or something. And, this time, Grace was quiet. Yet, Isabel says that when she heard that *thump* and then that silence, something happened in her to make her afraid. And she ran to the living room and there was little Grace on the floor, all twisted up, and the reason she hadn't screamed was that she couldn't get her breath. And when she did scream, it was the worst sound, Isabel says, that she'd ever heard in all her life, and she still hears it sometimes in her dreams. Isabel will sometimes wake me up with a low, moaning, strangled sound and I have to be quick to awaken her and hold her to me and where Isabel is weeping against me seems a mortal wound.

I think I may have written Sonny the very day that little Grace was buried. I was sitting in the living room in the dark, by myself, and I suddenly thought of Sonny. My trouble made his real.

175   One Saturday afternoon, when Sonny had been living with us, or, anyway, been in our house, for nearly two weeks, I found myself wandering aimlessly about the living room, drinking from a can of beer, and trying to work up the courage to search Sonny's room. He was out, he was usually out whenever I was home, and Isabel had taken the children to see their grandparents. Suddenly I was standing still in front of the living room window, watching Seventh Avenue. The idea of searching Sonny's room made me still. I scarcely dared to admit to myself what I'd be searching for. I didn't know what I'd do if I found it. Or if I didn't.

On the sidewalk across from me, near the entrance to a barbecue joint, some people were holding an old-fashioned revival meeting. The barbecue cook, wearing a dirty white apron, his conked hair reddish and metallic in the pale sun, and a cigarette between his lips, stood in the doorway, watching them. Kids and older people paused in their errands and stood there, along with some older men and a couple of very tough-looking women who watched everything that happened on the avenue, as though they owned it, or were maybe owned by it. Well, they were watching this, too. The revival was being carried on by three sisters in black, and a brother. All they had were their voices and their Bibles and a tambourine. The brother was testifying and while he testified two of the sisters stood together, seeming to say, amen, and the third sister walked around with the tambourine outstretched and a couple of people dropped coins into it. Then the brother's testimony ended and the sister who had been taking up the collection dumped the coins into her palm and transferred them to the pocket of her long black robe. Then she raised both hands, striking the tambourine against the air, and then against one hand, and she started to sing. And the two other sisters and the brother joined in.

It was strange, suddenly, to watch, though I had been seeing these street meetings all my life. So, of course, had everybody else down there. Yet, they paused and watched and listened and I stood still at the window. *"Tis the old ship of Zion,"* they sang, and the sister with the tambourine kept a steady, jangling beat, *"it has rescued many a thousand!"* Not a soul under the sound of their voices was hearing this song for the first time, not one of them had been rescued. Nor had they seen much in the way of rescue work being done around them. Neither did they especially believe in the holiness of the three sisters and the brother, they knew too much about them, knew where they lived, and how. The woman with the tambourine, whose voice dominated the air, whose face was bright with joy, was divided by very little from the woman who stood watching her, a cigarette between her heavy, chapped lips, her hair a cuckoo's nest, her face scarred and swollen from many beatings, and her black eyes glittering like coal. Perhaps they both knew this, which was why, when, as rarely, they addressed each other, they addressed each other as Sister. As the singing filled the air the watching, listening faces underwent a change, the eyes focusing on something within; the music seemed to soothe a poison out of them; and time seemed, nearly, to fall away from the sullen, belligerent, battered faces, as though they were fleeing back to their first condition, while dreaming of their last. The barbecue cook half shook his head and smiled, and dropped his cigarette and disappeared into his joint. A man fumbled in his pockets for change and stood holding it in his hand impatiently, as though he had just remembered a pressing appointment further up the avenue. He looked furious. Then I saw Sonny, standing on the edge of the crowd. He was carrying a wide, flat notebook with a green cover, and it made him look, from where I was standing, almost like a schoolboy. The coppery sun brought out the copper in his skin, he was very faintly smiling, standing very still. Then the singing stopped, the tambourine turned into a collection plate again. The furious man dropped in his coins and vanished, so did a couple of the women, and Sonny dropped some change in the plate, looking directly at the woman with a little smile. He started across the avenue, toward the house. He has a slow, loping walk, something like the way Harlem hipsters walk, only he's imposed on this his own half-beat. I had never really noticed it before.

I stayed at the window, both relieved and apprehensive. As Sonny disappeared from my sight, they began singing again. And they were still singing when his key turned in the lock.

"Hey," he said.

"Hey, yourself. You want some beer?"   180

"No. Well, maybe." But he came up to the window and stood beside me, looking out. "What a warm voice," he said.

They were singing *If I could only hear my mother pray again!*

"Yes," I said, "and she can sure beat that tambourine."

"But what a terrible song," he said, and laughed. He dropped his notebook on the sofa and disappeared into the kitchen. "Where's Isabel and the kids?"

"I think they went to see their grandparents. You hungry?"   185

"No." He came back into the living room with his can of beer. "You want to come some place with me tonight?"

I sensed, I don't know how, that I couldn't possibly say no. "Sure. Where?"

He sat down on the sofa and picked up his notebook and started leafing through it. "I'm going to sit in with some fellows in a joint in the Village."

"You mean, you're going to play, tonight?"

"That's right." He took a swallow of his beer and moved back to the window. He gave   190
me a sidelong look. "If you can stand it."

"I'll try," I said.

He smiled to himself and we both watched as the meeting across the way broke up. The three sisters and the brother, heads bowed, were singing *God be with you till we meet again.*

The faces around them were very quiet. Then the song ended. The small crowd dispersed. We watched the three women and the lone man walk slowly up the avenue.

"When she was singing before," said Sonny, abruptly, "her voice reminded me for a minute of what heroin feels like sometimes—when it's in your veins. It makes you feel sort of warm and cool at the same time. And distant. And—and sure." He sipped his beer, very deliberately not looking at me. I watched his face. "It makes you feel—in control. Sometimes you've got to have that feeling."

"Do you?" I sat down slowly in the easy chair.

195 "Sometimes." He went to the sofa and picked up his notebook again. "Some people do."

"In order," I asked, "to play?" And my voice was very ugly, full of contempt and anger.

"Well"—he looked at me with great, troubled eyes, as though, in fact, he hoped his eyes would tell me things he could never otherwise say—"they *think* so. And *if* they think so—!"

"And what do *you* think?" I asked.

He sat on the sofa and put his can of beer on the floor. "I don't know," he said, and I couldn't be sure if he were answering my question or pursuing his thoughts. His face didn't tell me. "It's not so much to *play*. It's to *stand* it, to be able to make it at all. On any level." He frowned and smiled: "In order to keep from shaking to pieces."

200 "But these friends of yours," I said, "they seem to shake themselves to pieces pretty goddamn fast."

"Maybe." He played with the notebook. And something told me that I should curb my tongue, that Sonny was doing his best to talk, that I should listen. "But of course you only know the ones that've gone to pieces. Some don't—or at least they haven't *yet* and that's just about all *any* of us can say." He paused. "And then there are some who just live, really, in hell, and they know it and they see what's happening and they go right on. I don't know." He sighed, dropped the notebook, folded his arms. "Some guys, you can tell from the way they play, they on something *all* the time. And you can see that, well, it makes something real for them. But of course," he picked up his beer from the floor and sipped it and put the can down again, "they *want* to, too, you've got to see that. Even some of them that say they don't—*some*, not all."

"And what about you?" I asked—I couldn't help it. "What about you? Do *you* want to?"

He stood up and walked to the window and remained silent for a long time. Then he sighed. "Me," he said. Then: "While I was downstairs before, on my way here, listening to that woman sing, it struck me all of a sudden how much suffering she must have had to go through—to sing like that. It's *repulsive* to think you have to suffer that much."

I said: "But there's no way not to suffer—is there, Sonny?"

205 "I believe not," he said and smiled, "but that's never stopped anyone from trying." He looked at me. "Has it?" I realized, with this mocking look, that there stood between us, forever, beyond the power of time or forgiveness, the fact that I had held silence—so long!—when he had needed human speech to help him. He turned back to the window. "No, there's no way not to suffer. But you try all kinds of ways to keep from drowning in it, to keep on top of it, and to make it seem—well, like *you*. Like you did something, all right, and now you're suffering for it. You know?" I said nothing. "Well you know," he said, impatiently, "why *do* people suffer? Maybe it's better to do something to give it a reason, *any* reason."

"But we just agreed," I said "that there's no way not to suffer. Isn't it better, then, just to—take it?"

"But nobody just takes it," Sonny cried, "that's what I'm telling you! *Everybody* tries not to. You're just hung up on the *way* some people try—it's not *your* way!"

The hair on my face began to itch, my face felt wet. "That's not true," I said, "that's not true. I don't give a damn what other people do, I don't even care how they suffer. I just care how *you* suffer." And he looked at me. "Please believe me," I said, "I don't want to see you—die—trying not to suffer."

"I won't," he said, flatly, "die trying not to suffer. At least, not any faster than anybody else."

"But there's no need," I said, trying to laugh, "is there? in killing yourself."   210

I wanted to say more, but I couldn't. I wanted to talk about will power and how life could be—well, beautiful. I wanted to say that it was all within; but was it? or, rather, wasn't that exactly the trouble? And I wanted to promise that I would never fail him again. But it would all have sounded—empty words and lies.

So I made the promise to myself and prayed that I would keep it.

"It's terrible sometimes, inside," he said, "that's what's the trouble. You walk these streets, black and funky and cold, and there's not really a living ass to talk to, and there's nothing shaking, and there's no way of getting it out—that storm inside. You can't talk it and you can't make love with it, and when you finally try to get with it and play it, you realize *nobody's* listening. So *you've* got to listen. You got to find a way to listen."

And then he walked away from the window and sat on the sofa again, as though all the wind had suddenly been knocked out of him. "Sometimes you'll do *anything* to play, even cut your mother's throat." He laughed and looked at me. "Or your brother's." Then he sobered. "Or your own." Then: "Don't worry. I'm all right now and I think I'll *be* all right. But I can't forget—where I've been. I don't mean just the physical place I've been, I mean where I've *been*. And *what* I've been."

"What have you been, Sonny?" I asked.   215

He smiled—but sat sideways on the sofa, his elbow resting on the back, his fingers playing with his mouth and chin, not looking at me. "I've been something I didn't recognize, didn't know I could be. Didn't know anybody could be." He stopped, looking inward, looking helplessly young, looking old. "I'm not talking about it now because I feel *guilty* or anything like that—maybe it would be better if I did, I don't know. Anyway, I can't really talk about it. Not to you, not to anybody," and now he turned and faced me. "Sometimes, you know, and it was actually when I was most *out* of the world, I felt that I was in it, that I was *with* it, really, and I could play or I didn't really have to *play*, it just came out of me, it was there. And I don't know how I played, thinking about it now, but I know I did awful things, those times, sometimes, to people. Or it wasn't that I *did* anything to them—it was that they weren't real." He picked up the beer can; it was empty; he rolled it between his palms: "And other times—well, I needed a fix, I needed to find a place to lean, I needed to clear a space to *listen*—and I couldn't find it, and I—went crazy, I did terrible things to *me*, I was terrible *for* me." He began pressing the beer can between his hands, I watched the metal begin to give. It glittered, as he played with it, like a knife, and I was afraid he would cut himself, but I said nothing. "Oh well. I can never tell you. I was all by myself at the bottom of something, stinking and sweating and crying and shaking, and I smelled it, you know? *my* stink, and I thought I'd die if I couldn't get away from it and yet, all the same, I knew that everything I was doing was just locking me in with it. And I didn't know," he paused, still flattening the beer can, "I didn't know, I still *don't* know, something kept telling me that maybe it was good to smell your own stink, but I didn't think that *that* was what I'd been trying to do—and—who can stand it?" and he abruptly dropped the ruined beer can, looking at me with a small, still smile, and then rose, walking to the window as though it were the lodestone rock. I watched his face, he watched the avenue. "I couldn't tell you when Mama died—but the reason I wanted to leave Harlem so bad was to get away from drugs. And then, when I ran away, that's what I was running from—really. When I came back, nothing had changed, *I* hadn't changed, I was just—older." And he stopped, drumming with his fingers on the windowpane. The sun had vanished, soon darkness would fall. I watched his face. "It can come again," he said, almost as though speaking to himself. Then he turned to me. "It can come again," he repeated. "I just want you to know that."

"All right," I said, at last. "So it can come again. All right."

He smiled, but the smile was sorrowful. "I had to try to tell you," he said.

"Yes," I said. "I understand that."

220 "You're my brother," he said, looking straight at me, and not smiling at all.

"Yes," I repeated, "yes. I understand that."

He turned back to the window, looking out. "All that hatred down there," he said, "all that hatred and misery and love. It's a wonder it doesn't blow the avenue apart."

We went to the only nightclub on a short, dark street, downtown. We squeezed through the narrow, chattering, jam-packed bar to the entrance of the big room, where the bandstand was. And we stood there for a moment, for the lights were very dim in this room and we couldn't see. Then, "Hello, boy," said a voice and an enormous black man, much older than Sonny or myself, erupted out of all that atmospheric lighting and put an arm around Sonny's shoulder. "I been sitting right here," he said, "waiting for you."

He had a big voice, too, and heads in the darkness turned toward us.

225 Sonny grinned and pulled a little away, and said, "Creole, this is my brother. I told you about him."

Creole shook my hand. "I'm glad to meet you, son," he said, and it was clear that he was glad to meet me *there*, for Sonny's sake. And he smiled, "You got a real musician in *your* family," and he took his arm from Sonny's shoulder and slapped him, lightly, affectionately, with the back of his hand.

"Well. Now I've heard it all," said a voice behind us. This was another musician, and a friend of Sonny's, a coal-black, cheerful-looking man, built close to the ground. He immediately began confiding to me, at the top of his lungs, the most terrible things about Sonny, his teeth gleaming like a lighthouse and his laugh coming up out of him like the beginning of an earthquake. And it turned out that everyone at the bar knew Sonny, or almost everyone; some were musicians, working there, or nearby, or not working, some were simply hangers-on, and some were there to hear Sonny play. I was introduced to all of them and they were all very polite to me. Yet, it was clear that, for them, I was only Sonny's brother. Here, I was in Sonny's world. Or, rather: his kingdom. Here, it was not even a question that his veins bore royal blood.

They were going to play soon and Creole installed me, by myself, at a table in a dark corner. Then I watched them, Creole, and the little black man, and Sonny, and the others, while they horsed around, standing just below the bandstand. The light from the bandstand spilled just a little short of them and, watching them laughing and gesturing and moving about, I had the feeling that they, nevertheless, were being most careful not to step into that circle of light too suddenly: that if they moved into the light too suddenly, without thinking, they would perish in flame. Then, while I watched, one of them, the small, black man, moved into the light and crossed the bandstand and started fooling around with his drums. Then—being funny and being, also, extremely ceremonious— Creole took Sonny by the arm and led him to the piano. A woman's voice called Sonny's name and a few hands started clapping. And Sonny, also being funny and being ceremonious, and so touched, I think, that he could have cried, but neither hiding it nor showing it, riding it like a man, grinned, and put both hands to his heart and bowed from the waist.

Creole then went to the bass fiddle and a lean, very bright-skinned brown man jumped up on the bandstand and picked up his horn. So there they were, and the atmosphere on the bandstand and in the room began to change and tighten. Someone stepped up to the microphone and announced them. Then there were all kinds of murmurs. Some people at the bar shushed others. The waitress ran around, frantically getting in the last orders, guys and chicks got closer to each other, and the lights on the bandstand, on the quartet, turned to a kind of indigo. Then they all looked different there. Creole looked about him for the last time, as though he were making certain that all his chickens were in the coop, and then he—jumped and struck the fiddle. And there they were.

All I know about music is that not many people ever really hear it. And even then, on the rare occasions when something opens within, and the music enters, what we mainly hear, or hear corroborated, are personal, private, vanishing evocations. But the man who creates the music is hearing something else, is dealing with the roar rising from the void and imposing order on it as it hits the air. What is evoked in him, then, is of another order, more terrible because it has no words, and triumphant, too, for that same reason. And his triumph, when he triumphs, is ours. I just watched Sonny's face. His face was troubled, he was working hard, but he wasn't with it. And I had the feeling that, in a way, everyone on the bandstand was waiting for him, both waiting for him and pushing him along. But as I began to watch Creole, I realized that it was Creole who held them all back. He had them on a short rein. Up there, keeping the beat with his whole body, wailing on the fiddle, with his eyes half closed, he was listening to everything, but he was listening to Sonny. He was having a dialogue with Sonny. He wanted Sonny to leave the shoreline and strike out for the deep water. He was Sonny's witness that deep water and drowning were not the same thing—he had been there, and he knew. And he wanted Sonny to know. He was waiting for Sonny to do the things on the keys which would let Creole know that Sonny was in the water.

And, while Creole listened, Sonny moved, deep within, exactly like someone in torment. I had never before thought of how awful the relationship must be between the musician and his instrument. He has to fill it, this instrument, with the breath of life, his own. He has to make it do what he wants it to do. And a piano is just a piano. It's made out of so much wood and wires and little hammers and big ones, and ivory. While there's only so much you can do with it, the only way to find this out is to try; to try and make it do everything.

And Sonny hadn't been near a piano for over a year. And he wasn't on much better terms with his life, not the life that stretched before him now. He and the piano stammered, started one way, got scared, stopped; started another way, panicked, marked time, started again; then seemed to have found a direction, panicked again, got stuck. And the face I saw on Sonny I'd never seen before. Everything had been burned out of it, and, at the same time, things usually hidden were being burned in, by the fire and fury of the battle which was occurring in him up there.

Yet, watching Creole's face as they neared the end of the first set, I had the feeling that something had happened, something I hadn't heard. Then they finished, there was scattered applause, and then, without an instant's warning, Creole started into something else, it was almost sardonic, it was *Am I Blue*.° And, as though he commanded, Sonny began to play. Something began to happen. And Creole let out the reins. The dry, low, black man said something awful on the drums, Creole answered, and the drums talked back. Then the horn insisted, sweet and high, slightly detached perhaps, and Creole listened, commenting now and then, dry, and driving, beautiful and calm and old. Then they all came together again, and Sonny was part of the family again. I could tell this from his face. He seemed to have found, right there beneath his fingers, a damn brand-new piano. It seemed that he couldn't get over it. Then, for awhile, just being happy with Sonny, they seemed to be agreeing with him that brand-new pianos certainly were a gas.

Then Creole stepped forward to remind them that what they were playing was the blues. He hit something in all of them, he hit something in me, myself, and the music tightened and deepened, apprehension began to beat the air. Creole began to tell us what the blues were all about. They were not about anything very new. He and his boys up there

°*Am I Blue*: written by Harry Akst and Grant Clarke, from the film *On with the Show* (1929). See Beth Henley's play *Am I Blue*, Chapter 25.

were keeping it new, at the risk of ruin, destruction, madness, and death, in order to find new ways to make us listen. For, while the tale of how we suffer, and how we are delighted, and how we may triumph is never new, it always must be heard. There isn't any other tale to tell, it's the only light we've got in all this darkness.

235

And this tale, according to that face, that body, those strong hands on those strings, has another aspect in every country, and a new depth in every generation. Listen, Creole seemed to be saying, listen. Now these are Sonny's blues. He made the little black man on the drums know it, and the bright, brown man on the horn. Creole wasn't trying any longer to get Sonny in the water. He was wishing him Godspeed. Then he stepped back, very slowly, filling the air with the immense suggestion that Sonny speak for himself.

Then they all gathered around Sonny and Sonny played. Every now and again one of them seemed to say, amen. Sonny's fingers filled the air with life, his life. But that life contained so many others. And Sonny went all the way back, he really began with the spare, flat statement of the opening phrase of the song. Then he began to make it his. It was very beautiful because it wasn't hurried and it was no longer a lament. I seemed to hear with what burning he had made it his, with what burning we had yet to make it ours, how we could cease lamenting. Freedom lurked around us and I understood, at last, that he could help us to be free if we would listen, that he would never be free until we did. Yet, there was no battle in his face now. I heard what he had gone through, and would continue to go through until he came to rest in earth. He had made it his: that long line, of which we knew only Mama and Daddy. And he was giving it back, as everything must be given back, so that, passing through death, it can live forever. I saw my mother's face again, and felt, for the first time, how the stones of the road she had walked on must have bruised her feet. I saw the moon-lit road where my father's brother died. And it brought something else back to me, and carried me past it. I saw my little girl again and felt Isabel's tears again, and I felt my own tears begin to rise. And I was yet aware that this was only a moment, that the world waited outside, as hungry as a tiger, and that trouble stretched above us, longer than the sky.

Then it was over. Creole and Sonny let out their breath, both soaking wet, and grinning. There was a lot of applause and some of it was real. In the dark, the girl came by and I asked her to take drinks to the bandstand. There was a long pause, while they talked up there in the indigo light and after awhile I saw the girl put a Scotch and milk on top of the piano for Sonny. He didn't seem to notice it, but just before they started playing again, he sipped from it and looked toward me, and nodded. Then he put it back on top of the piano. For me, then, as they began to play again, it glowed and shook above my brother's head like the very cup of trembling.°

QUESTIONS

1. Who is the narrator of this story? What relationship does he have with the primary character, Sonny? Why does the narrator describe some of the details of his own life, in addition to details about Sonny?

2. How does Sonny attempt to leave Harlem? What is his reason for trying to leave? Describe the confrontation of the narrator and Sonny after the death of their mother. What does Sonny disclose about himself when this confrontation occurs?

3. What is the reason for the attention paid to the Pentecostal group of women on the street below the apartment? What remarks does Sonny make at this time that indicate the concerns that are seething within him? What has Sonny made of his life?

4. How does the concluding scene at the Greenwich Village nightclub serve as a climax of Sonny's story? How successfully does Baldwin describe the playing of the blues?

°See Isaiah 51, especially 51:17: "thou hast drunken the dregs of the cup of trembling, and wrung them out."

TONI CADE BAMBARA (1939–1995)

Bambara (an African tribal name that Toni Cade appropriated from an old manuscript) was brought up in Harlem and Bedford Stuyvesant in New York. She received a B.A. from Queens College and an M.A. in American Studies from the City College of New York. For a time she was a social worker, and later she taught at many schools, including Rutgers, Duke, and the Scribe Video Center in Philadelphia. She also collaborated in the writing of television documentaries, including a life of W. E. B. Du Bois. In her fiction she treats the subjects of the black and also the female experience. She avoids using this material for political purposes, however, even though the subjects could easily fall within the political realm. Instead, she deals with her characters on the human level, trying to offer her readers "nourishment." Story collections are Gorilla, My Love *(1972), from which "The Lesson" is taken, and* The Sea Birds Are Still Alive *(1977). Her novels are* The Salt Eaters *(1980) and* If Blessing Comes *(1987).*

The Lesson (1972)

Back in the days when everyone was old and stupid or young and foolish and me and Sugar were the only ones just right, this lady moved on our block with nappy hair and proper speech and no makeup. And quite naturally we laughed at her, laughed the way we did at the junk man who went about his business like he was some big-time president and his sorry-ass horse his secretary. And we kinda hated her too, hated the way we did the winos who cluttered up our parks and pissed on our handball walls and stank up our hallways and stairs so you couldn't halfway play hide-and-seek without a goddamn gas mask. Miss Moore was her name. The only woman on the block with no first name. And she was black as hell, cept for her feet, which were fish-white and spooky. And she was always planning these boring-ass things for us to do, us being my cousin, mostly, who lived on the block cause we all moved North the same time and to the same apartment then spread out gradual to breathe. And our parents would yank our heads into some kinda shape and crisp up our clothes so we'd be presentable for travel with Miss Moore, who always looked like she was going to church, though she never did. Which is just one of the things the grownups talked about when they talked behind her back like a dog. But when she came calling with some sachet she'd sewed up or some gingerbread she'd made or some book, why then they'd all be too embarrassed to turn her down and we'd get handed over all spruced up. She'd been to college and said it was only right that she should take responsibility for the young ones education, and she not even related by marriage or blood. So they'd go for it. Specially Aunt Gretchen. She was the main gofer in the family. You got some ole dumb shit foolishness you want somebody to go for, you send for Aunt Gretchen. She been screwed into the go-along for so long, it's a blood-deep natural thing with her. Which is how she got saddled with me and Sugar and Junior in the first place while our mothers were in a la-de-da apartment up the block having a good ole time.

So this one day Miss Moore rounds us all up at the mailbox and it's purdee° hot and she's knockin herself out about arithmetic. And school suppose to let up in summer I heard, but she don't never let up. And the starch in my pinafore scratching the shit outta me and

---

°*purdee:* pretty.

I'm really hating this nappy-head bitch and her goddamn college degree. I'd much rather go to the pool or to the show where it's cool. So me and Sugar leaning on the mailbox being surly, which is a Miss Moore word. And Flyboy checking out what everybody brought for lunch. And Fat Butt already wasting his peanut-butter-and-jelly sandwich like the pig he is. And Junebug punchin on Q.T.'s arm for potato chips. And Rosie Giraffe shifting from one hip to the other waiting for somebody to step on her foot or ask her if she from Georgia so she can kick ass, preferably Mercedes'. And Miss Moore asking us do we know what money is, like we a bunch of retards. I mean real money, she say, like it's only poker chips or Monopoly papers we lay on the grocer. So right away I'm tired of this and say so. And would much rather snatch Sugar and go to the Sunset and terrorize the West Indian kids and take their hair ribbons and their money too. And Miss Moore files that remark away for next week's lesson on brotherhood, I can tell. And finally I say we oughta get to the subway cause it's cooler and besides we might meet some cute boys. Sugar done swiped her mama's lipstick, so we ready.

So we heading down the street and she's boring us silly about what things cost and what our parents make and how much goes for rent and how money ain't divided up right in this country. And then she gets to the part about we all poor and live in the slums, which I don't feature. And I'm ready to speak on that, but she steps out in the street and hails two cabs just like that. Then she hustles half the crew in with her and hands me a five-dollar bill and tells me to calculate 10 percent tip for the driver. And we're off. Me and Sugar and Junebug and Flyboy hangin out the window and hollering to everybody, putting lipstick on each other cause Flyboy a faggot anyway, and making farts with our sweaty armpits. But I'm mostly trying to figure how to spend this money. But they all fascinated with the meter ticking and Junebug starts laying bets as to how much it'll read when Flyboy can't hold his breath no more. Then Sugar lays bets as to how much it'll be when we get there. So I'm stuck. Don't nobody want to go for my plan, which is to jump out at the next light and run off to the first bar-b-que we can find. Then the driver tells us to get the hell out cause we there already. And the meter reads eighty-five cents. And I'm stalling to figure out the tip and Sugar say give him a dime. And I decide he don't need it bad as I do, so later for him. But then he tries to take off with Junebug foot still in the door so we talk about his mama something ferocious. Then we check out that we on Fifth Avenue and everybody dressed up in stockings. One lady in a fur coat, hot as it is. White folks crazy.

"This is the place," Miss Moore say, presenting it to us in the voice she uses at the museum. "Let's look in the windows before we go in."

5 "Can we steal?" Sugar asks very serious like she's getting the ground rules squared away before she plays. "I beg your pardon," say Miss Moore, and we fall out. So she leads us around the windows of the toy store and me and Sugar screamin, "This is mine, that's mine, I gotta have that, that was made for me, I was born for that," till Big Butt drowns us out.

"Hey, I'm going to buy that there."

"That there? You don't even know what it is, stupid."

"I do so," he say punchin on Rosie Giraffe. "It's a microscope."

"Whatcha gonna do with a microscope, fool?"

10 "Look at things."

"Like what, Ronald?" ask Miss Moore. And Big Butt ain't got the first notion. So here go Miss Moore gabbing about the thousands of bacteria in a drop of water and the somethin-orother in a speck of blood and the million and one living things in the air around us is invisible to the naked eye. And what she say that for? Junebug go to town on that "naked" and we rolling. Then Miss Moore ask what it cost. So we all jam into the window smudgin it up and the price tag say $300. So then she ask how long'd take for Big Butt and Junebug to save up their allowances. "Too long," I say. "Yeh," adds Sugar, "outgrown it by that time." And Miss Moore say no, you never outgrow learning instruments. "Why, even medical students and interns and," blah, blah, blah. And we ready to choke Big Butt for bringing it up in the first damn place.

"This here costs four hundred eighty dollars," say Rosie Giraffe. So we pile up all over her to see what she pointin out. My eyes tell me it's a chunk of glass cracked with something heavy, and different-color inks dripped into the splits, then the whole thing put into a oven or something. But for $480 it don't make sense.

"That's a paperweight made of semi-precious stones fused together under tremendous pressure," she explains slowly, with her hands doing the mining and all the factory work.

"So what's a paperweight?" asks Rosie Giraffe.

"To weigh paper with, dumbbell," say Flyboy, the wise man from the East.   15

"Not exactly," say Miss Moore, which is what she say when you warm or way off too. "It's to weigh paper down so it won't scatter and make your desk untidy." So right away me and Sugar curtsy to each other and then to Mercedes who is more the tidy type.

"We don't keep paper on top of the desk in my class," say Junebug, figuring Miss Moore crazy or lyin one.

"At home, then," she say. "Don't you have a calendar and a pencil case and a blotter and a letter-opener on your desk at home where you do your homework?" And she know damn well what our homes look like cause she nosys around in them every chance she gets.

"I don't even have a desk," say Junebug. "Do we?"

"No. And I don't get no homework neither," says Big Butt.   20

"And I don't even have a home," say Flyboy like he do at school to keep the white folks off his back and sorry for him. Send this poor kid to camp posters, is his specialty.

"I do," says Mercedes. "I have a box of stationery on my desk and a picture of my cat. My godmother bought the stationery and the desk. There's a big rose on each sheet and the envelopes smell like roses."

"Who wants to know about your smelly-ass stationery," say Rosie Giraffe fore I can get my two cents in.

"It's important to have a work area all your own so that. . . ."

"Will you look at this sailboat, please," say Flyboy, cuttin her off and pointin to the thing   25
like it was his. So once again we tumble all over each other to gaze at this magnificent thing in the toy store which is just big enough to maybe sail two kittens across the pond if you strap them to the posts tight. We all start reciting the price tag like we in assembly. "Hand-crafted sailboat of fiberglass at one thousand one hundred ninety-five dollars."

"Unbelievable," I hear myself say and am really stunned. I read it again for myself just in case the group recitation put me in a trance. Same thing. For some reason this pisses me off. We look at Miss Moore and she lookin at us, waiting for I dunno what.

"Who'd pay all that when you can buy a sailboat set for a quarter at Pop's, a tube of glue for a dime, and a ball of string for eight cents? It must have a motor and a whole lot else besides," I say. "My sailboat cost me about fifty cents."

"But will it take water?" say Mercedes with her smart ass.

"Took mine to Alley Pond Park once," say Flyboy. "String broke. Lost it. Pity."

"Sailed mine in Central Park and it keeled over and sank. Had to ask my father for an-   30
other dollar."

"And you got the strap," laugh Big Butt. "The jerk didn't even have a string on it. My old man wailed on his behind."

Little Q.T. was staring hard at the sailboat and you could see he wanted it bad. But he too little and somebodyd just take it from him. So what the hell. "This boat for kids, Miss Moore?"

"Parents silly to buy something like that just to get all broke up," say Rosie Giraffe.

"That much money it should last forever," I figure.

"My father'd buy it for me if I wanted it."   35

"Your father, my ass," say Rosie Giraffe getting a chance to finally push Mercedes.

"Must be rich people shop here," say Q.T.

"You are a very bright boy," say Flyboy. "What was your first clue?" And he rap him on the head with the back of his knuckles, since Q.T. the only one he could get away with. Though Q.T. liable to come up behind you years later and get his licks in when you half expect it.

"What I want to know is," I says to Miss Moore though I never talk to her, I wouldn't give the bitch that satisfaction, "is how much a real boat costs? I figure a thousand'd get you a yacht any day."

40 "Why don't you check that out," she says, "and report back to the group?" Which really pains my ass. If you gonna mess up a perfectly good swim day least you could do is have some answers. "Let's go in," she say like she got something up her sleeve. Only she don't lead the way. So me and Sugar turn the corner to where the entrance is, but when we get there I kinda hang back. Not that I'm scared, what's there to be afraid of, just a toy store. But I feel funny, shame. But what I got to be shamed about? Got as much right to go in as anybody. But somehow I can't seem to get hold of the door, so I step away from Sugar to lead. But she hangs back too. And I look at her and she looks at me and this is ridiculous. I mean, damn, I have never ever been shy about doing nothing or going nowhere. But then Mercedes steps up and then Rosie Giraffe and Big Butt crowd in behind and shove, and next thing we all stuffed into the doorway with only Mercedes squeezing past us, smoothing out her jumper and walking right down the aisle. Then the rest of us tumble in like a glued-together jigsaw done all wrong. And people lookin at us. And it's like the time me and Sugar crashed into the Catholic church on a dare. But once we got in there and everything so hushed and holy and the candles and the bowin and the handkerchiefs on all the drooping heads, I just couldn't go through with the plan. Which was for me to run up to the altar and do a tap dance while Sugar played the nose flute and messed around in the holy water. And Sugar kept givin me the elbow. Then later teased me so bad I tied her up in the shower and turned it on and locked her in. And she'd be there till this day if Aunt Gretchen hadn't finally figured I was lyin about the boarder takin a shower.

Same thing in the store. We all walkin on tiptoe and hardly touchin the games and puzzles and things. And I watched Miss Moore who is steady watchin us like she waitin for a sign. Like Mama Drewery watches the sky and sniffs the air and takes note of just how much slant is in the bird formation. Then me and Sugar bump smack into each other, so busy gazing at the toys, 'specially the sailboat. But we don't laugh and go into our fat-lady bump-stomach routine. We just stare at that price tag. Then Sugar run a finger over the whole boat. And I'm jealous and want to hit her. Maybe not her, but I sure want to punch somebody in the mouth.

"Whatcha bring us here for, Miss Moore?"

"You sound angry, Sylvia. Are you mad about something?" Givin me one of them grins like she tellin a grown-up joke that never turns out to be funny. And she's lookin very closely at me like maybe she plannin to do my portrait from memory. I'm mad, but I won't give her that satisfaction. So I slouch around the store bein very bored and say, "Let's go."

Me and Sugar at the back of the train watchin the tracks whizzin by large then small then gettin gobbled up in the dark. I'm thinking about this tricky toy I saw in the store. A clown that somersaults on a bar then does chin-ups just cause you yank lightly at his leg. Cost $35. I could see me askin my mother for a $35 birthday clown. "You wanna who that costs what?" she'd say, cocking her head to the side to get a better view of the hole in my head. Thirty-five dollars could buy new bunk beds for Junior and Gretchen's boy. Thirty-five dollars and the whole household could go visit Granddaddy Nelson in the country. Thirty-five dollars would pay for the rent and the piano bill too. Who are these people that spend that much for performing clowns and $1000 for toy sailboats? What kinda work they do and how they live and how come we ain't in on it? Where we are is who we are. Miss

Moore always pointin out. But it don't necessarily have to be that way, she always adds then waits for somebody to say that poor people have to wake up and demand their share of the pie and don't none of us know what kind of pie she talking about in the first damn place. But she ain't so smart cause I still got her four dollars from the taxi and she sure ain't gettin it. Messin up my day with this shit. Sugar nudges me in my pocket and winks.

Miss Moore lines us up in front of the mailbox where we started from, seem like years ago, and I got a headache for thinkin so hard. And we lean all over each other so we can hold up under the draggy-ass lecture she always finishes us off with at the end before we thank her for borin us to tears. But she just looks at us like she readin tea leaves. Finally she say, "Well, what did you think of F.A.O. Schwarz?" 45

Rosie Giraffe mumbles, "White folks crazy."

"I'd like to go there again when I get my birthday money," says Mercedes, and we shove her out the pack so she has to lean on the mailbox by herself.

"I'd like a shower. Tiring day," say Flyboy.

Then Sugar surprises me by sayin, "You know, Miss Moore, I don't think all of us here put together eat in a year what that sailboat costs." And Miss Moore lights up like somebody goosed her. "And?" she say, urging Sugar on. Only I'm standin on her foot so she don't continue.

"Imagine for a minute what kind of society it is in which some people can spend on a toy what it would cost to feed a family of six or seven. What do you think?" 50

"I think," say Sugar pushing me off her feet like she never done before, cause I whip her ass in a minute, "that this is not much of a democracy if you ask me. Equal chance to pursue happiness means an equal crack at the dough, don't it?" Miss Moore is besides herself and I am disgusted with Sugar's treachery. So I stand on her foot one more time to see if she'll shove me. She shuts up, and Miss Moore looks at me, sorrowfully I'm thinkin. And somethin weird is goin on, I can feel it in my chest.

"Anybody else learn anything today?" lookin dead at me. I walk away and Sugar has to run to catch up and don't even seem to notice when I shrug her arm off my shoulder.

"Well, we got four dollars anyway," she says.

"Uh hunh."

"We could go to Hascombs and get half a chocolate layer and then go to the Sunset and still have plenty money for potato chips and ice cream sodas." 55

"Uh hunh."

"Race you to Hascombs," she say.

We start down the block and she gets ahead which is O.K. by me cause I'm going to the West End and then over to the Drive to think this day through. She can run if she want to and even run faster. But ain't nobody gonna beat me at nuthin.

QUESTIONS

1. Who is Miss Moore? Why does she take an interest in the neighborhood children? Where does she take them? How does she attempt to teach them?

2. Describe Sylvia, the narrator, as a character. Why does she keep $4 of the five-dollar bill given her by Miss Moore? What does she mean by "ain't nobody gonna beat me at nuthin" in the story's final paragraph?

3. Describe the level of language of the narrator. Is she writing the story or speaking it? How do you know?

4. Consider paragraphs 44–50. What ideas about equality and inequality are brought out in the story? Do you think the children will remember the "lesson" or that they will forget it? Why?

ANTON CHEKHOV (1860–1904)

For a brief biography and photo, see Chapter 25, page 1663.

 ## The Lady with the Dog (1899)

Translated by Constance Garnett

I

It was said that a new person had appeared on the sea-front: a lady with a little dog. Dmitri Dmitritch Gurov, who had by then been a fortnight at Yalta, and so was fairly at home there, had begun to take an interest in new arrivals. Sitting in Verney's pavilion, he saw, walking on the sea-front, a fair-haired young lady of medium height, wearing a beret; a white Pomeranian dog was running behind her.

And afterwards he met her in the public gardens and in the square several times a day. She was walking alone, always wearing the same beret, and always with the same white dog; no one knew who she was, and every one called her simply "the lady with the dog."

"If she is here alone without a husband or friends, it wouldn't be amiss to make her acquaintance," Gurov reflected.

He was under forty, but he had a daughter already twelve years old, and two sons at school. He had been married young, when he was a student in his second year, and by now his wife seemed half as old again as he. She was a tall, erect woman with dark eyebrows, staid and dignified, and, as she said of herself, intellectual. She read a great deal, used phonetic spelling, called her husband, not Dmitri, but Dimitri, and he secretly considered her unintelligent, narrow, inelegant, was afraid of her, and did not like to be with her at home. He had begun being unfaithful to her long ago—had been unfaithful to her often, and, probably on that account, almost always spoke ill of women, and when they were talked about in his presence, used to call them "the lower race."

5   It seemed to him that he had been so schooled by bitter experience that he might call them what he liked, and yet he could not get on for two days together without "the lower race." In the society of men he was bored and not himself, with them he was cold and uncommunicative; but when he was in the company of women he felt free, and knew what to say to them and how to behave; and he was at ease with them even when he was silent. In his appearance, in his character, in his whole nature, there was something attractive and elusive which allured women and disposed them in his favour; he knew that, and some force seemed to draw him, too, to them.

Experience often repeated, truly bitter experience, had taught him long ago that with decent people, especially Moscow people—always slow to move and irresolute—every intimacy, which at first so agreeably diversifies life and appears a light and charming adventure, inevitably grows into a regular problem of extreme intricacy, and in the long run the situation becomes unbearable. But at every fresh meeting with an interesting woman this experience seemed to slip out of his memory, and he was eager for life, and everything seemed simple and amusing.

One evening he was dining in the gardens, and the lady in the beret came up slowly to take the next table. Her expression, her gait, her dress, and the way she did her hair told him that she was a lady, that she was married, that she was in Yalta for the first time and alone, and that she was dull there. . . . The stories told of the immorality in such places as Yalta are to a great extent untrue; he despised them, and knew that such stories were for the most part made up by persons who would themselves have been glad to sin if they had been able; but when the lady sat down at the next table three paces from him, he remembered these tales of easy conquests, of trips to the mountains, and the tempting thought of a swift, fleeting love affair, a romance with an unknown woman, whose name he did not know, suddenly took possession of him.

He beckoned coaxingly to the Pomeranian, and when the dog came up to him he shook his finger at it. The Pomeranian growled: Gurov shook his finger at it again.

The lady looked at him and at once dropped her eyes.

"He doesn't bite," she said, and blushed.

"May I give him a bone?" he asked; and when she nodded he asked courteously, "Have you been long in Yalta?"

"Five days."

"And I have already dragged out a fortnight here."

There was a brief silence.

"Time goes fast, and yet it is so dull here!" she said, not looking at him.

"That's only the fashion to say it is dull here. A provincial will live in Belyov or Zhidra and not be dull, and when he comes here it's 'Oh, the dullness! Oh, the dust!' One would think he came from Grenada."

She laughed. Then both continued eating in silence, like strangers, but after dinner they walked side by side; and there sprang up between them the light jesting conversation of people who are free and satisfied, to whom it does not matter where they go or what they talk about. They walked and talked of the strange light on the sea: the water was of a soft warm lilac hue, and there was a golden streak from the moon upon it. They talked of how sultry it was after a hot day. Gurov told her that he came from Moscow, that he had taken his degree in Arts, but had a post in a bank; that he had trained as an opera-singer, but had given it up, that he owned two houses in Moscow. . . . And from her he learnt that she had grown up in Petersburg, but had lived in S—— since her marriage two years before, that she was staying another month in Yalta, and that her husband, who needed a holiday too, might perhaps come and fetch her. She was not sure whether her husband had a post in a Crown Department or under the Provincial Council—and was amused by her own ignorance. And Gurov learnt, too, that she was called Anna Sergeyevna.

Afterwards he thought about her in his room at the hotel—thought she would certainly meet him next day; it would be sure to happen. As he got into bed he thought how lately she had been a girl at school, doing lessons like his own daughter; he recalled the diffidence, the angularity, that was still manifest in her laugh and her manner of talking with a stranger. This must have been the first time in her life she had been alone in surroundings in which she was followed, looked at, and spoken to merely from a secret motive which she could hardly fail to guess. He recalled her slender, delicate neck, her lovely grey eyes.

"There's something pathetic about her, anyway," he thought, and fell asleep.

II

A week had passed since they had made acquaintance. It was a holiday. It was sultry indoors, while in the street the wind whirled the dust round and round, and blew people's hats off. It was a thirsty day, and Gurov often went into the pavilion, and pressed Anna Sergeyevna to have syrup and water or an ice. One did not know what to do with oneself.

In the evening when the wind had dropped a little, they went out on the groyne° to see the steamer come in. There were a great many people walking about the harbour; they had gathered to welcome some one, bringing bouquets. And two peculiarities of a well-dressed Yalta crowd were very conspicuous: the elderly ladies were dressed like young ones, and there were great numbers of generals.

°*groyne:* a pier, a breakwater.

Owing to the roughness of the sea, the steamer arrived late, after the sun had set, and it was a long time turning about before it reached the groyne. Anna Sergeyevna looked through her lorgnette at the steamer and the passengers as though looking for acquaintances, and when she turned to Gurov her eyes were shining. She talked a great deal and asked disconnected questions, forgetting next moment what she had asked; then she dropped her lorgnette in the crush.

The festive crowd began to disperse; it was too dark to see people's faces. The wind had completely dropped, but Gurov and Anna Sergeyevna still stood as though waiting to see some one else come from the steamer. Anna Sergeyevna was silent now, and sniffed the flowers without looking at Gurov.

"The weather is better this evening," he said. "Where shall we go now? Shall we drive somewhere?"

25 She made no answer.

Then he looked at her intently, and all at once put his arm round her and kissed her on the lips, and breathed in the moisture and the fragrance of the flowers; and he immediately looked round him, anxiously wondering whether any one had seen them.

"Let us go to your hotel," he said softly.

And both walked quickly.

The room was close and smelt of the scent she had bought at the Japanese shop. Gurov looked at her and thought: "What different people one meets in the world!" From the past he preserved memories of careless, good-natured women, who loved cheerfully and were grateful to him for the happiness he gave them, however brief it might be; and of women like his wife who loved without any genuine feeling, with superfluous phrases, affectedly, hysterically, with an expression that suggested that it was not love nor passion, but something more significant; and of two or three others, very beautiful, cold women, on whose faces he had caught a glimpse of a rapacious expression—an obstinate desire to snatch from life more than it could give, and these were capricious, unreflecting, domineering, unintelligent women not in their first youth, and when Gurov grew cold to them their beauty excited his hatred, and the lace on their linen seemed to him like scales.

30 But in this case there was still the diffidence, the angularity of inexperienced youth, an awkward feeling; and there was a sense of consternation as though some one had suddenly knocked at the door. The attitude of Anna Sergeyevna—"the lady with the dog"—to what had happened was somehow peculiar, very grave, as though it were her fall—so it seemed, and it was strange and inappropriate. Her face dropped and faded, and on both sides of it her long hair hung down mournfully; she mused in a dejected attitude like "the woman who was a sinner" in an old-fashioned picture.

"It's wrong," she said. "You will be the first to despise me now."

There was a water-melon on the table. Gurov cut himself a slice and began eating it without haste. There followed at least half an hour of silence.

Anna Sergeyevna was touching; there was about her the purity of a good, simple woman who had seen little of life. The solitary candle burning on the table threw a faint light on her face, yet it was clear that she was very unhappy.

"How could I despise you?" asked Gurov. "You don't know what you are saying."

35 "God forgive me," she said, and her eyes filled with tears. "It's awful."

"You seem to feel you need to be forgiven."

"Forgiven? No. I am a bad, low woman; I despise myself and don't attempt to justify myself. It's not my husband but myself I have deceived. And not only just now; I have been deceiving myself for a long time. My husband may be a good, honest man, but he is a flunkey! I don't know what he does there, what his work is, but I know he is a flunkey! I was twenty when I was married to him. I have been tormented by curiosity; I wanted something better. 'There must be a different sort of life,' I said to myself. I wanted to live!

To live, to live! . . . I was fired by curiosity . . . you don't understand it, but, I swear to God, I could not control myself; something happened to me: I could not be restrained. I told my husband I was ill, and came here. . . . And here I have been walking about as though I were dazed, like a mad creature; . . . and now I have become a vulgar, contemptible woman whom any one may despise."

Gurov felt bored already, listening to her. He was irritated by the naïve tone, by this remorse, so unexpected and inopportune; but for the tears in her eyes, he might have thought she was jesting or playing a part.

"I don't understand," he said softly. "What is it you want?"

She hid her face on his breast and pressed close to him.

"Believe me, believe me, I beseech you . . ." she said. "I love a pure, honest life, and sin is loathsome to me. I don't know what I am doing. Simple people say: 'The Evil One has beguiled me.' And I may say of myself now that the Evil One has beguiled me."

"Hush, hush! . . ." he muttered.

He looked at her fixed, scared eyes, kissed her, talked softly and affectionately, and by degrees she was comforted, and her gaiety returned; they both began laughing.

Afterwards when they went out there was not a soul on the sea-front. The town with its cypresses had quite a deathlike air, but the sea still broke noisily on the shore; a single barge was rocking on the waves, and a lantern was blinking sleepily on it.

They found a cab and drove to Oreanda.

"I found out your surname in the hall just now: it was written on the board—Von Diderits," said Gurov. "Is your husband a German?"

"No; I believe his grandfather was a German, but he is an Orthodox Russian himself."

At Oreanda they sat on a seat not far from the church, looked down at the sea, and were silent. Yalta was hardly visible through the morning mist; white clouds stood motionless on the mountain-tops. The leaves did not stir on the trees, grasshoppers chirruped, and the monotonous hollow sound of the sea rising up from below, spoke of the peace, of the eternal sleep awaiting us. So it must have sounded when there was no Yalta, no Oreanda here; so it sounds now, and it will sound as indifferently and monotonously when we are all no more. And in this constancy, in this complete indifference to the life and death of each of us, there lies hid, perhaps, a pledge of our eternal salvation, of the unceasing movement of life upon earth, of unceasing progress towards perfection. Sitting beside a young woman who in the dawn seemed so lovely, soothed and spellbound in these magical surroundings—the sea, mountains, clouds, the open sky—Gurov thought how in reality everything is beautiful in this world when one reflects: everything except what we think or do ourselves when we forget our human dignity and the higher aims of our existence.

A man walked up to them—probably a keeper—looked at them and walked away. And this detail seemed mysterious and beautiful, too. They saw a steamer come from Theodosia, with its lights out in the glow of dawn.

"There is dew on the grass," said Anna Sergeyevna, after a silence.

"Yes. It's time to go home."

They went back to the town.

Then they met every day at twelve o'clock on the sea-front, lunched and dined together, went for walks, admired the sea. She complained that she slept badly, that her heart throbbed violently; asked the same questions, troubled now by jealousy and now by the fear that he did not respect her sufficiently. And often in the square or gardens, when there was no one near them, he suddenly drew her to him and kissed her passionately. Complete idleness, these kisses in broad daylight while he looked round in dread of some one's seeing them, the heat, the smell of the sea, and the continual passing to and fro before him of idle, well-dressed, well-fed people, made a new man of him; he told Anna Sergeyevna how beautiful she was, how fascinating. He was impatiently passionate, he would not move a step away from her, while she was often pensive and continually urged him to confess that he did not respect her, did not love her in the least, and thought of her as nothing but a common woman. Rather late almost every evening they drove somewhere out of town, to Oreanda or to the waterfall; and the expedition was always a success, the scenery invariably impressed them as grand and beautiful.

They were expecting her husband to come, but a letter came from him, saying that there was something wrong with his eyes, and he entreated his wife to come home as quickly as possible. Anna Sergeyevna made haste to go.

55 "It's a good thing I am going away," she said to Gurov. "It's the finger of destiny!"

She went by coach and he went with her. They were driving the whole day. When she had got into a compartment of the express, and when the second bell had rung, she said: "Let me look at you once more . . . look at you once again. That's right."

She did not shed tears, but was so sad that she seemed ill, and her face was quivering. "I shall remember you . . . think of you," she said. "God be with you; be happy. Don't remember evil against me. We are parting forever—it must be so, for we ought never to have met. Well, God be with you."

60 The train moved off rapidly, its lights soon vanished from sight, and a minute later there was no sound of it, as though everything had conspired together to end as quickly as possible that sweet delirium, that madness. Left alone on the platform, and gazing into the dark distance, Gurov listened to the chirrup of the grasshoppers and the hum of the telegraph wires, feeling as though he had only just waked up. And he thought, musing, that there had been another episode or adventure in his life, and it, too, was at an end, and nothing was left of it but a memory. . . . He was moved, sad, and conscious of a slight remorse. This young woman whom he would never meet again had not been happy with him; he was genuinely warm and affectionate with her, but yet in his manner, his tone, and his caresses there had been a shade of light irony, the coarse condescension of a happy man who was, besides, almost twice her age. All the time she had called him kind, exceptional, lofty; obviously he had seemed to her different from what he really was, so he had unintentionally deceived her. . . .

Here at the station was already a scent of autumn; it was a cold evening.

"It's time for me to go north," thought Gurov as he left the platform. "High time!"

III

At home in Moscow everything was in its winter routine; the stoves were heated, and in the morning it was still dark when the children were having breakfast and getting ready for school, and the nurse would light the lamp for a short time. The frosts had begun already. When the first snow has fallen, on the first day of sledge-driving it is pleasant to see the white earth, the white roofs, to draw soft, delicious breath, and the season brings back the days of one's youth. The old limes and birches, white with hoar-frost, have a good-natured expression; they are nearer to one's heart than cypresses and palms, and near them one doesn't want to be thinking of the sea and the mountains.

Gurov was Moscow born; he arrived in Moscow on a fine frosty day, and when he put on his fur coat and warm gloves, and walked along Petrovka, and when on Saturday evening he heard the ringing of the bells, his recent trip and the places he had seen lost all charm for him. Little by little he became absorbed in Moscow life, greedily read three newspapers a day, and declared he did not read the Moscow papers on principle! He already felt a longing to go to restaurants, clubs, dinner-parties, anniversary celebrations, and he felt flattered at entertaining distinguished lawyers and artists, and at playing cards with a professor at the doctors' club. He could already eat a whole plateful of salt fish and cabbage.

65 In another month, he fancied, the image of Anna Sergeyevna would be shrouded in a mist in his memory, and only from time to time would visit him in his dreams with a touching smile as others did. But more than a month passed, real winter had come, and everything was

still clear in his memory as though he had parted with Anna Sergeyevna only the day before. And his memories glowed more and more vividly. When in the evening stillness he heard from his study the voices of his children, preparing their lessons, or when he listened to a song or the organ at the restaurant, or the storm howled in the chimney, suddenly everything would rise up in his memory: what had happened on the groyne, and the early morning with the mist on the mountains, and the steamer coming from Theodosia, and the kisses. He would pace a long time about his room, remembering it all and smiling; then his memories passed into dreams, and in his fancy the past was mingled with what was to come. Anna Sergeyevna did not visit him in dreams, but followed him about everywhere like a shadow and haunted him. When he shut his eyes he saw her as though she were living before him, and she seemed to him lovelier, younger, tenderer than she was; and he imagined himself finer than he had been in Yalta. In the evenings she peeped out at him from the bookcase, from the fireplace, from the corner—he heard her breathing, the caressing rustle of her dress. In the street he watched the women, looking for some one like her.

He was tormented by an intense desire to confide his memories to some one. But in his home it was impossible to talk of his love, and he had no one outside; he could not talk to his tenants nor to any one at the bank. And what had he to talk of? Had he been in love, then? Had there been anything beautiful, poetical, or edifying or simply interesting in his relations with Anna Sergeyevna? And there was nothing for him but to talk vaguely of love, of woman, and no one guessed what it meant; only his wife twitched her black eyebrows, and said:

"The part of a lady-killer does not suit you at all, Dimitri."

One evening, coming out of the doctors' club with an official with whom he had been playing cards, he could not resist saying:

"If only you knew what a fascinating woman I made the acquaintance of in Yalta!"

The official got into his sledge and was driving away, but turned suddenly and shouted: 70

"Dmitri Dmitritch!"

"What?"

"You were right this evening: the sturgeon was a bit too strong!"

These words, so ordinary, for some reason moved Gurov to indignation, and struck him as degrading and unclean. What savage manners, what people! What senseless nights, what uninteresting, uneventful days! The rage for card-playing, the gluttony, the drunkenness, the continual talk always about the same thing. Useless pursuits and conversations always about the same things absorb the better part of one's time, the better part of one's strength, and in the end there is left a life grovelling and curtailed, worthless and trivial, and there is no escaping or getting away from it—just as though one were in a madhouse or a prison.

Gurov did not sleep all night, and was filled with indignation. And he had a headache 75 all next day. And the next night he slept badly; he sat up in bed, thinking, or paced up and down his room. He was sick of his children, sick of the bank; he had no desire to go any-where or to talk of anything.

In the holidays in December he prepared for a journey, and told his wife he was going to Petersburg to do something in the interests of a young friend—and he set off for S——. What for? He did not very well know himself. He wanted to see Anna Sergeyevna and to talk with her—to arrange a meeting, if possible.

He reached S——in the morning, and took the best room at the hotel, in which the floor was covered with grey army cloth, and on the table was an inkstand, grey with dust and adorned with a figure on horseback, with its hat in its hand and its head broken off. The hotel porter gave him the necessary information; Von Diderits lived in a house of his own in Old Gontcharny Street—it was not far from the hotel: he was rich and lived in good style, and had his own horses; every one in the town knew him. The porter pronounced the name "Dridirits."

Gurov went without haste to Old Gontcharny Street and found the house. Just opposite the house stretched a long grey fence adorned with nails.

"One would run away from a fence like that," thought Gurov, looking from the fence to the windows of the house and back again.

80   He considered: today was a holiday, and her husband would probably be at home. And in any case it would be tactless to go into the house and upset her. If he were to send her a note it might fall into her husband's hands, and then it might ruin everything. The best thing was to trust to chance. And he kept walking up and down the street by the fence, waiting for the chance. He saw a beggar go in at the gate and dogs fly at him; then an hour later he heard a piano, and the sounds were faint and indistinct. Probably it was Anna Sergeyevna playing. The front door suddenly opened, and an old woman came out, followed by the familiar white Pomeranian. Gurov was on the point of calling to the dog, but his heart began beating violently, and in his excitement he could not remember the dog's name.

He walked up and down, and loathed the grey fence more and more, and by now he thought irritably that Anna Sergeyevna had forgotten him, and was perhaps already amusing herself with some one else, and that that was very natural in a young woman who had nothing to look at from morning till night but that confounded fence. He went back to his hotel room and sat for a long while on the sofa, not knowing what to do, then he had dinner and a long nap.

"How stupid and worrying it is!" he thought when he woke and looked at the dark windows: it was already evening. "Here I've had a good sleep for some reason. What shall I do in the night?"

He sat on the bed, which was covered by a cheap grey blanket, such as one sees in hospitals, and he taunted himself in his vexation:

"So much for the lady with the dog . . . so much for the adventure. . . . You're in a nice fix. . . ."

85   That morning at the station a poster in large letters had caught his eye. "The Geisha" was to be performed for the first time. He thought of this and went to the theatre.

"It's quite possible she may go to the first performance," he thought.

The theatre was full. As in all provincial theatres, there was a fog above the chandelier, the gallery was noisy and restless; in the front row the local dandies were standing up before the beginning of the performance, with their hands behind them; in the Governor's box the Governor's daughter, wearing a boa, was sitting in the front seat, while the Governor himself lurked modestly behind the curtain with only his hands visible; the orchestra was a long time tuning up; the stage curtain swayed. All the time the audience were coming in and taking their seats Gurov looked at them eagerly.

Anna Sergeyevna, too, came in. She sat down in the third row, and when Gurov looked at her his heart contracted, and he understood clearly that for him there was in the whole world no creature so near, so precious, and so important to him; she, this little woman, in no way remarkable, lost in a provincial crowd, with a vulgar lorgnette in her hand, filled his whole life now, was his sorrow and his joy, the one happiness that he now desired for himself, and to the sounds of the inferior orchestra, of the wretched provincial violins, he thought how lovely she was. He thought and dreamed.

A young man with small side-whiskers, tall and stooping, came in with Anna Sergeyevna and sat down beside her; he bent his head at every step and seemed to be continually bowing. Most likely this was the husband whom at Yalta, in a rush of bitter feeling, she had called a flunkey. And there really was in his long figure, his side-whiskers, and the small bald patch on his head, something of the flunkey's obsequiousness; his smile was sugary, and in his buttonhole there was some badge of distinction like the number on a waiter.

During the first intermission the husband went away to smoke; she remained alone in   90
her stall. Gurov, who was sitting in the stalls, too, went up to her and said in a trembling
voice, with a forced smile:

"Good-evening."

She glanced at him and turned pale, then glanced again with horror, unable to believe
her eyes, and tightly gripped the fan and the lorgnette in her hands, evidently struggling
with herself not to faint. Both were silent. She was sitting, he was standing, frightened by
her confusion and not venturing to sit down beside her. The violins and the flute began tuning up. He felt suddenly frightened; it seemed as though all the people in the boxes were
looking at them. She got up and went quickly to the door; he followed her, and both walked
senselessly along passages, and up and down stairs, and figures in legal, scholastic, and
civil service uniforms, all wearing badges, flitted before their eyes. They caught glimpses of
ladies, of fur coats hanging on pegs; the draughts blew on them, bringing a smell of stale tobacco. And Gurov, whose heart was beating violently, thought:

"Oh, heavens! Why are these people here and this orchestra! . . ."

And at that instant he recalled how when he had seen Anna Sergeyevna off at the station
he had thought that everything was over and they would never meet again. But how far
they were still from the end!

On the narrow, gloomy staircase over which was written "To the Amphitheatre," she   95
stopped.

"How you have frightened me!" she said, breathing hard, still pale and overwhelmed.
"Oh, how you have frightened me! I am half dead. Why have you come? Why?"

"But do understand, Anna, do understand . . ." he said hastily in a low voice. "I entreat
you to understand. . . ."

She looked at him with dread, with entreaty, with love; she looked at him intently, to
keep his features more distinctly in her memory.

"I am so unhappy," she went on, not heeding him. "I have thought of nothing but you
all the time; I live only in the thought of you. And I wanted to forget, to forget you; but why,
oh, why, have you come?"

On the landing above them two schoolboys were smoking and looking down, but that   100
was nothing to Gurov; he drew Anna Sergeyevna to him, and began kissing her face, her
cheeks, and her hands.

"What are you doing, what are you doing!" she cried in horror, pushing him away. "We
are mad. Go away to-day; go away at once. . . . I beseech you by all that is sacred, I implore
you. . . . There are people coming this way!"

Some one was coming up the stairs.

"You must go away," Anna Sergeyevna went on in a whisper. "Do you hear, Dmitri
Dmitritch? I will come and see you in Moscow. I have never been happy; I am miserable
now, and I never, never shall be happy, never! Don't make me suffer still more! I swear I'll
come to Moscow. But now let us part. My precious, good, dear one, we must part!"

She pressed his hand and began rapidly going downstairs, looking round at him, and
from her eyes he could see that she really was unhappy. Gurov stood for a little while, listened, then, when all sound had died away, he found his coat and left the theatre.

IV

And Anna Sergeyevna began coming to see him in Moscow. Once in two or three months   105
she left S——, telling her husband that she was going to consult a doctor about an internal
complaint—and her husband believed her, and did not believe her. In Moscow she stayed
at the Slaviansky Bazaar hotel, and at once sent a man in a red cap to Gurov. Gurov went to
see her, and no one in Moscow knew of it.

Once he was going to see her in this way on a winter morning (the messenger had come the evening before when he was out). With him walked his daughter, whom he wanted to take to school: it was on the way. Snow was falling in big wet flakes.

"It's three degrees above freezing-point, and yet it is snowing," said Gurov to his daughter. "The thaw is only on the surface of the earth; there is quite a different temperature at a greater height in the atmosphere."

"And why are there no thunderstorms in the winter, father?"

He explained that, too. He talked, thinking all the while that he was going to see her, and no living soul knew of it, and probably never would know. He had two lives: one, open, seen and known by all who cared to know, full of relative truth and of relative falsehood, exactly like the lives of his friends and acquaintances; and another life running its course in secret. And through some strange, perhaps accidental, conjunction of circumstances, everything that was essential, of interest and of value to him, everything in which he was sincere and did not deceive himself, everything that made the kernel of his life, was hidden from other people; and all that was false in him, the sheath in which he hid himself to conceal the truth—such, for instance, as his work in the bank, his discussions at the club, his "lower race," his presence with his wife at anniversary festivities—all that was open. And he judged of others by himself, not believing in what he saw, and always believing that every man had his real, most interesting life under the cover of secrecy and under the cover of night. All personal life rested on secrecy, and possibly it was partly on that account that civilised man was so nervously anxious that personal privacy should be respected.

110   After leaving his daughter at school, Gurov went on to the Slaviansky Bazaar. He took off his fur coat below, went upstairs, and softly knocked at the door. Anna Sergeyevna, wearing his favourite grey dress, exhausted by the journey and the suspense, had been expecting him since the evening before. She was pale; she looked at him, and did not smile, and he had hardly come in when she fell on his breast. Their kiss was slow and prolonged, as though they had not met for two years.

"Well, how are you getting on there?" he asked. "What news?"

"Wait; I'll tell you directly. . . . I can't talk."

She could not speak; she was crying. She turned away from him, and pressed her handkerchief to her eyes.

"Let her have her cry out. I'll sit down and wait," he thought, and he sat down in an arm-chair.

115   Then he rang and asked for tea to be brought him, and while he drank his tea she remained standing at the window with her back to him. She was crying from emotion, from the miserable consciousness that their life was so hard for them; they could only meet in secret, hiding themselves from people, like thieves! Was not their life shattered?

"Come, do stop!" he said.

It was clear to him that this love of theirs would not soon be over, that he could not see the end of it. Anna Sergeyevna grew more and more attached to him. She adored him, and it was unthinkable to say to her that it was bound to have an end some day; besides, she would not have believed it!

He went up to her and took her by the shoulders to say something affectionate and cheering, and at that moment he saw himself in the looking-glass.

His hair was already beginning to turn grey. And it seemed strange to him that he had grown so much older, so much plainer during the last few years. The shoulders on which his hands rested were warm and quivering. He felt compassion for this life, still so warm and lovely, but probably already not far from beginning to fade and wither like his own. Why did she love him so much? He always seemed to women different from what he was, and they loved in him not himself, but the man created by their imagination, whom they had been eagerly seeking all their lives; and afterwards, when they noticed their mistake, they loved him all the same. And not one of them had been happy with him. Time passed, he had made their acquaintance, got on with them, parted, but he had never once loved; it was anything you like, but not love.

And only now when his head was grey he had fallen properly, really in love—for the 120 first time in his life.

Anna Sergeyevna and he loved each other like people very close and akin, like husband and wife, like tender friends; it seemed to them that fate itself had meant them for one another, and they could not understand why he had a wife and she a husband; and it was as though they were a pair of birds of passage, caught and forced to live in different cages. They forgave each other for what they were ashamed of in their past, they forgave everything in the present, and felt that this love of theirs had changed them both.

In moments of depression in the past he had comforted himself with any arguments that came into his mind, but now he no longer cared for arguments; he felt profound compassion, he wanted to be sincere and tender. . . .

"Don't cry, my darling," he said. "You've had your cry; that's enough. . . . Let us talk now, let us think of some plan."

Then they spent a long while taking counsel together, talked of how to avoid the necessity for secrecy, for deception, for living in different towns and not seeing each other for long at a time. How could they be free from this intolerable bondage?

"How? How?" he asked, clutching his head. "How?" 125

And it seemed as though in a little while the solution would be found, and then a new and splendid life would begin; and it was clear to both of them that they had still a long, long road before them, and that the most complicated and difficult part of it was only just beginning.

QUESTIONS

1. Compare ideas about love in this story and in Lawrence's "The Horse Dealer's Daughter." What effect does love have on individuals? How does it affect Gurov? How does it affect Anna? How does the story differentiate between infatuation and love? Do the stories indicate that love solves problems, or that love creates problems?

2. Describe the structure of this story. How might it be divided into parts? What conflict is developed in the course of the story? Where is the crisis and climax?

3. What characteristics of Gurov are brought out in the story? How does he change as the story develops? In what way does his change mark an improvement in his character?

4. In what locations does the story take place? How might these locations be said to symbolize the relationship between Gurov and Anna? Of what importance is the dog?

D. H. LAWRENCE (1885–1930)

Lawrence was born in an English mining community, but he received a sufficient education to enable him to become a teacher and writer. He fictionalized the early years of his life in the novel Sons and Lovers *(1913). His most controversial work,* Lady Chatterley's Lover, *was printed privately in Italy in 1928 but was not published in an uncut version in the United States until the 1960s. He shocked his contemporaries with his emphasis on the importance of sexuality, an idea that is central to "The Horse Dealer's Daughter." He was afflicted with tuberculosis and lived in a number of warm, sunny places, including Italy, New Zealand, and New Mexico, in an attempt to restore his health. Nevertheless, his illness claimed him in 1930, when he was only forty-five years old.*

The Horse Dealer's Daughter (1922)

"Well, Mabel, and what are you going to do with yourself?" asked Joe, with foolish flippancy. He felt quite safe himself. Without listening for an answer, he turned aside, worked a grain of tobacco to the tip of his tongue, and spat it out. He did not care about anything, since he felt safe himself.

The three brothers and the sister sat round the desolate breakfast table, attempting some sort of desultory consultation. The morning's post had given the final tap to the family fortunes, and all was over. The dreary dining-room itself, with its heavy mahogany furniture, looked as it were waiting to be done away with.

But the consultation amounted to nothing. There was a strange air of ineffectuality about the three men, as they sprawled at table, smoking and reflecting vaguely on their own condition. The girl was alone, a rather short, sullen-looking young woman of twenty-seven. She did not share the same life as her brothers. She would have been good-looking, save for the impassive fixity of her face, "bulldog," as her brothers called it.

There was a confused tramping of horses' feet outside. The three men all sprawled round in their chairs to watch. Beyond the dark holly-bushes that separated the strip of lawn from the high-road, they could see a cavalcade of shire horses swinging out of their own yard, being taken for exercise. This was the last time. These were the last horses that would go through their hands. The young men watched with critical, callous look. They were all frightened at the collapse of their lives, and the sense of disaster in which they were involved left them no inner freedom.

5 Yet they were three fine, well-set fellows enough. Joe, the eldest, was a man of thirty-three, broad and handsome in a hot, flushed way. His face was red, he twisted his black moustache over a thick finger, his eyes were shallow and restless. He had a sensual way of uncovering his teeth when he laughed, and his bearing was stupid. Now he watched the horses with a glazed look of helplessness in his eyes, a certain stupor of downfall.

The great draught-horses swung past. They were tied head to tail, four of them, and they heaved along to where a lane branched off from the highroad, planting their great hoofs floutingly in the fine black mud, swinging their great rounded haunches sumptuously, and trotting a few sudden steps as they were led into the lane, round the corner. Every movement showed a massive, slumbrous strength, and a stupidity which held them in subjection. The groom at the head looked back, jerking the leading rope. And the cavalcade moved out of sight up the lane, the tail of the last horse, bobbed up tight and stiff, held out taut from the swinging great haunches as they rocked behind the hedges in a motionlike sleep.

Joe watched with glazed hopeless eyes. The horses were almost like his own body to him. He felt he was done for now. Luckily, he was engaged to a woman as old as himself, and therefore her father, who was steward of a neighbouring estate, would provide him with a job. He would marry and go into harness. His life was over, he would be a subject animal now.

He turned uneasily aside, the retreating steps of the horses echoing in his ears. Then, with foolish restlessness, he reached for the scraps of bacon-rind from the plates, and making a faint whistling sound, flung them to the terrier that lay against the fender. He watched the dog swallow them, and waited till the creature looked into his eyes. Then a faint grin came on his face, and in a high, foolish voice he said:

"You won't get much more bacon, shall you, you little b—?"

10 The dog faintly and dismally wagged its tail, then lowered its haunches, circled round, and lay down again.

There was another helpless silence at the table. Joe sprawled uneasily in his seat, not willing to go till the family conclave was dissolved. Fred Henry, the second brother, was erect, clean-limbed, alert. He had watched the passing of the horses with more *sang-froid.*° If he was an animal, like Joe, he was an animal which controls, not one which is controlled. He was master of any horse, and he carried himself with a well-tempered air of mastery. But he was not master of the situations of life. He pushed his coarse brown moustache upwards, off his lip, and glanced irritably at his sister, who sat impassive and inscrutable.

"You'll go and stop with Lucy for a bit, shan't you?" he asked. The girl did not answer.

"I don't see what else you can do," persisted Fred Henry.

"Go as a skivvy,"° Joe interpolated laconically.

The girl did not move a muscle.   15

"If I was her, I should go in for training for a nurse," said Malcolm, the youngest of them all. He was the baby of the family, a young man of twenty-two, with a fresh, jaunty *museau.*°

But Mabel did not take any notice of him. They had talked at her and round her for so many years, that she hardly heard them at all.

The marble clock on the mantel-piece softly chimed the half-hour, the dog rose uneasily from the hearthrug and looked at the party at the breakfast table. But still they sat on in ineffectual conclave.

"Oh, all right," said Joe suddenly, *à propos* of nothing. "I'll get a move on."

He pushed back his chair, straddled his knees with a downward jerk, to get them free, in   20
horsey fashion, and went to the fire. Still he did not go out of the room; he was curious to know what the others would do or say. He began to charge his pipe, looking down at the dog and saying, in a high, affected voice:

"Going wi' me? Going wi' me are ter? Tha'rt goin' further than tha counts on just now, dost hear?"

The dog faintly wagged its tail, the man stuck out his jaw and covered his pipe with his hands, and puffed intently, losing himself in the tobacco, looking down all the while at the dog, with an absent brown eye. The dog looked up at him in mournful distrust. Joe stood with his knees stuck out, in real horsey fashion.

"Have you had a letter from Lucy?" Fred Henry asked of his sister.

"Last week," came the neutral reply.

"And what does she say?"

There was no answer.   25

"Does she *ask* you to go and stop there?" persisted Fred Henry.

"She says I can if I like."

"Well, then, you'd better. Tell her you'll come on Monday."

This was received in silence.   30

"That's what you'll do then, is it?" said Fred Henry, in some exasperation.

But she made no answer. There was a silence of futility and irritation in the room. Malcolm grinned fatuously.

"You'll have to make up your mind between now and next Wednesday," said Joe loudly, "or else find yourself lodgings on the kerbstone."

The face of the young woman darkened, but she sat on immutable.

"Here's Jack Fergusson!" exclaimed Malcolm, who was looking aimlessly out of the   35
window.

"Where?" exclaimed Joe, loudly.

"Just gone past."

°*sang-froid:* unconcern (literally, cold blood).
°*skivvy:* British slang for housemaid.
°*museau:* French for nose, snout (muzzle).

"Coming in?"

Malcolm craned his neck to see the gate.

40   "Yes," he said.

There was a silence. Mabel sat on like one condemned, at the head of the table. Then a whistle was heard from the kitchen. The dog got up and barked sharply. Joe opened the door and shouted:

"Come on."

After a moment, a young man entered. He was muffled up in overcoat and a purple woolen scarf, and his tweed cap, which he did not remove, was pulled down on his head. He was of medium height, his face was rather long and pale, his eyes looked tired.

"Hello, Jack! Well, Jack!" exclaimed Malcolm and Joe. Fred Henry merely said "Jack!"

45   "What's doing?" asked the newcomer, evidently addressing Fred Henry.

"Same. We've got to be out by Wednesday—Got a cold?"

"I have—got it bad, too."

"Why don't you stop in?"

"*Me* stop in? When I can't stand on my legs, perhaps I shall have a chance." The young man spoke huskily. He had a slight Scotch accent.

50   "It's a knock-out, isn't it," said Joe boisterously, "if a doctor goes round croaking with a cold. Looks bad for the patients, doesn't it?"

The young doctor looked at him slowly.

"Anything the matter with *you*, then?" he asked, sarcastically.

"Not as I know of. Damn your eyes, I hope not. Why?"

"I thought you were very concerned about the patients, wondered if you might be one yourself."

55   "Damn it, no, I've never been patient to no flaming doctor, and hope I never shall be," returned Joe.

At this point Mabel rose from the table, and they all seemed to become aware of her existence. She began putting the dishes together. The young doctor looked at her, but did not address her. He had not greeted her. She went out of the room with the tray, her face impassive and unchanged.

"When are you off then, all of you?" asked the doctor.

"I'm catching the eleven-forty," replied Malcolm. "Are you goin' down wi' th' trap,° Joe?"

"Yes, I've told you I'm going down wi' th' trap, haven't I?"

60   "We'd better be getting her in then.—So long, Jack, if I don't see you before I go," said Malcolm, shaking hands.

He went out, followed by Joe, who seemed to have his tail between his legs.

"Well, this is the devil's own," exclaimed the doctor, when he was left alone with Fred Henry. "Going before Wednesday, are you?"

"That's the orders," replied the other.

"Where, to Northampton?"

65   "That's it."

"The devil!" exclaimed Fergusson, with quiet chagrin.

And there was silence between the two.

"All settled up, are you?" asked Fergusson.

"About."

70   There was another pause.

"Well, I shall miss yer, Freddy boy," said the young doctor.

°*trap*: small wagon.

"And I shall miss thee, Jack," returned the other.

"Miss you like hell," mused the doctor.

Fred Henry turned aside. There was nothing to say. Mabel came in again, to finish clearing the table.

"What are *you* going to do then, Miss Pervin?" asked Fergusson. "Going to your sister's, are you?"   75

Mabel looked at him with her steady, dangerous eyes, that always made him uncomfortable, unsettling his superficial ease.

"No," she said.

"Well, what in the name of fortune *are* you going to do? Say what you *mean* to do," cried Fred Henry, with futile intensity.

But she only averted her head, and continued her work. She folded the white tablecloth, and put on the chenille cloth.

"The sulkiest bitch that ever trod!" muttered her brother.   80

But she finished her task with perfectly impassive face, the young doctor watching her interestedly all the while. Then she went out.

Fred Henry stared after her, clenching his lips, his blue eyes fixing in sharp antagonism, as he made a grimace of sour exasperation.

"You could bray her into bits, and that's all you'd get out of her," he said, in a small, narrowed tone.

The doctor smiled faintly.

"What's she *going* to do then?" he asked.

"Strike me if *I* know!" returned the other.   85

There was a pause. Then the doctor stirred.

"I'll be seeing you to-night, shall I?" he said to his friend.

"Ay—where's it to be? Are we going over to Jessdale?"

"I don't know. I've got such a cold on me. I'll come round to the Moon and Stars, anyway."   90

"Let Lizzie and May miss their night for once, eh?"

"That's it—if I feel as I do now."

"All's one—"

The two young men went through the passage and down to the back door together. The house was large, but it was servantless now, and desolate. At the back was a small bricked house-yard, and beyond that a big square, gravelled fine and red, and having stables on two sides. Sloping, dank, winter-dark fields stretched away on the open sides.

But the stables were empty. Joseph Pervin, the father of the family, had been a man of no   95
education, who had become a fairly large horse dealer. The stables had been full of horses, there was a great turmoil and come-and-go of horses and of dealers and grooms. Then the kitchen was full of servants. But of late things had declined. The old man had married a second time, to retrieve his fortunes. Now he was dead and everything was gone to the dogs, there was nothing but debt and threatening.

For months, Mabel had been servantless in the big house, keeping the home together in penury for her ineffectual brothers. She had kept house for ten years. But previously, it was with unstinted means. Then, however brutal and coarse everything was, the sense of money had kept her proud, confident. The men might be foul-mouthed, the women in the kitchen might have bad reputations, her brothers might have illegitimate children. But so long as there was money, the girl felt herself established, and brutally proud, reserved.

No company came to the house, save dealers and coarse men. Mabel had no associates of her own sex, after her sister went away. But she did not mind. She went regularly to church, she attended to her father. And she lived in the memory of her mother, who had died when she was fourteen, and whom she had loved. She had loved her father, too, in a different way, depending upon him, and feeling secure in him, until at the age of fifty-four he married again. And then she had set hard against him. Now he had died and left them all hopelessly in debt.

She had suffered badly during the period of poverty. Nothing, however, could shake the curious sullen, animal pride that dominated each member of the family. Now, for Mabel, the end had come. Still she would not cast about her. She would follow her own way just the same. She would always hold the keys of her own situation. Mindless and persistent, she endured from day to day. Why should she think? Why should she answer anybody? It was enough that this was the end, and there was no way out. She need not pass any more darkly along the main street of the small town, avoiding every eye. She need not demean herself any more, going into the shops and buying the cheapest food. This was at an end. She thought of nobody, not even of herself. Mindless and persistent, she seemed in a sort of ecstasy to be coming nearer to her fulfilment, her own glorification, approaching her dead mother, who was glorified.°

In the afternoon she took a little bag, with shears and sponge and a small scrubbing brush, and went out. It was a grey, wintry day, with saddened, dark-green fields and an atmosphere blackened by the smoke of foundries not far off. She went quickly, darkly along the causeway, heeding nobody, through the town to the churchyard.

100   There she always felt secure, as if no one could see her, although as a matter of fact she was exposed to the stare of everyone who passed along under the churchyard wall. Nevertheless, once under the shadow of the great looming church, among the graves, she felt immune from the world, reserved within the thick churchyard wall as in another country.

Carefully she clipped the grass from the grave, and arranged the pinky-white, small chrysanthemums in the tin cross. When this was done, she took an empty jar from a neighbouring grave, brought water, and carefully, most scrupulously sponged the marble headstone and the coping-stone.

It gave her sincere satisfaction to do this. She felt in immediate contact with the world of her mother. She took minute pains, went through the park in a state bordering on pure happiness, as if in performing this task she came into a subtle, intimate connection with her mother. For the life she followed here in the world was far less real than the world of death she inherited from her mother.

The doctor's house was just by the church. Fergusson, being a mere hired assistant, was slave to the countryside. As he hurried now to attend to the outpatients in the surgery, glancing across the graveyard with his quick eye, he saw the girl at her task at the grave. She seemed so intent and remote, it was like looking into another world. Some mystical element was touched in him. He slowed down as he walked, watching her as if spell-bound.

She lifted her eyes, feeling him looking. Their eyes met. And each looked again at once, each feeling, in some way, found out by the other. He lifted his cap and passed on down the road. There remained distinct in his consciousness, like a vision, the memory of her face, lifted from the tombstone in the churchyard, and looking at him with slow, large, portentous eyes. It *was* portentous, her face. It seemed to mesmerise him. There was a heavy power in her eyes which laid hold of his whole being, as if he had drunk some powerful drug. He had been feeling weak and done before. Now the life came back into him, he felt delivered from his own fretted, daily self.

105   He finished his duties at the surgery as quickly as might be, hastily filling up the bottles of the waiting people with cheap drugs. Then, in perpetual haste, he set off again to visit several cases in another part of his round, before teatime. At all times he preferred to walk, if he could, but particularly when he was not well. He fancied the motion restored him.

The afternoon was falling. It was grey, deadened, and wintry, with a slow, moist, heavy coldness sinking in and deadening all the faculties. But why should he think or notice?

°*who was glorified:* See Romans 8:17, 30.

He hastily climbed the hill and turned across the dark-green fields, following the black cin-dertrack. In the distance, across a shallow dip in the country, the small town was clustered like smouldering ash, a tower, a spire, a heap of low, raw, extinct houses. And on the near-est fringe of the town, sloping into the dip, was Oldmeadow, the Pervins' house. He could see the stables and the outbuildings distinctly, as they lay towards him on the slope. Well, he would not go there many more times! Another resource would be lost to him, another place gone: the only company he cared for in the alien, ugly little town he was losing. Noth-ing but work, drudgery, constant hastening from dwelling to dwelling among the colliers and the iron-workers. It wore him out, but at the same time he had a craving for it. It was a stimulant to him to be in the homes of the working people, moving as it were through the innermost body of their life. His nerves were excited and gratified. He could come so near, into the very lives of the rough, inarticulate, powerfully emotional men and women. He grumbled, he said he hated the hellish hole. But as a matter of fact it excited him, the con-tact with the rough, strongly-feeling people was a stimulant applied direct to his nerves.

Below Oldmeadow, in the green, shallow, soddened hollow of fields, lay a square, deep pond. Roving across the landscape, the doctor's quick eye detected a figure in black pass-ing through the gate of the field, down towards the pond. He looked again. It would be Mabel Pervin. His mind suddenly became alive and attentive.

Why was she going down there? He pulled up on the path on the slope above, and stood staring. He could just make sure of the small black figure moving in the hollow of the fail-ing day. He seemed to see her in the midst of such obscurity, that he was like a clairvoyant, seeing rather with the mind's eye than with ordinary sight. Yet he could see her positively enough, whilst he kept his eye attentive. He felt, if he looked away from her, in the thick, ugly falling dusk, he would lose her altogether.

He followed her minutely as she moved, direct and intent, like something transmitted rather than stirring in voluntary activity, straight down the field towards the pond. There she stood on the bank for a moment. She never raised her head. Then she waded slowly into the water.

He stood motionless as the small black figure walked slowly and deliberately towards the centre of the pond, very slowly, gradually moving deeper into the motionless water, and still moving forward as the water got up to her breast. Then he could see her no more in the dusk of the dead afternoon. 110

"There!" he exclaimed. "Would you believe it?"

And he hastened straight down, running over the wet, soddened fields, pushing through the hedges, down into the depression of callous wintry obscurity. It took him several min-utes to come to the pond. He stood on the bank, breathing heavily. He could see nothing. His eyes seemed to penetrate the dead water. Yes, perhaps that was the dark shadow of her black clothing beneath the surface of the water.

He slowly ventured into the pond. The bottom was deep, soft clay, he sank in, and the water clasped dead cold round his legs. As he stirred he could smell the cold, rotten clay that fouled up into the water. It was objectionable in his lungs. Still, repelled and yet not heeding, he moved deeper into the pond. The cold water rose over his thighs, over his loins, upon his abdomen. The lower part of his body was all sunk in the hideous cold ele-ment. And the bottom was so deeply soft and uncertain, he was afraid of pitching with his mouth underneath. He could not swim, and was afraid.

He crouched a little, spreading his hands under the water and moving them round, try-ing to feel for her. The dead cold pond swayed upon his chest. He moved again, a little deeper, and again, with his hands underneath, he felt all around under the water. And he touched her clothing. But it evaded his fingers. He made a desperate effort to grasp it.

And so doing he lost his balance and went under, horribly, suffocating in the foul earthy water, struggling madly for a few moments. At last, after what seemed an eternity, he got 115 his footing, rose again into the air and looked around. He gasped, and knew he was in the world. Then he looked at the water. She had risen near him. He grasped her clothing, and drawing her nearer, turned to take his way to land again.

He went very slowly, carefully, absorbed in the slow progress. He rose higher, climbing out of the pond. The water was not only about his legs; he was thankful, full of relief to be out of the clutches of the pond. He lifted her and staggered on to the bank, out of the horror of wet, grey clay.

He laid her down on the bank. She was quite unconscious and running with water. He made the water come from her mouth, he worked to restore her. He did not have to work very long before he could feel the breathing begin again in her; she was breathing naturally. He worked a little longer. He could feel her live beneath his hands; she was coming back. He wiped her face, wrapped her in his overcoat, looked round into the dim, dark-grey world, then lifted her and staggered down the bank and across the fields.

It seemed an unthinkably long way, and his burden so heavy he felt he would never get to the house. But at last he was in the stable-yard, and then in the house-yard. He opened the door and went into the house. In the kitchen he laid her down on the hearthrug, and called. The house was empty. But the fire was burning in the grate.

Then again he kneeled to attend to her. She was breathing regularly, her eyes were wide open as if conscious, but there seemed something missing in her look. She was conscious in herself, but unconscious of her surroundings.

120 He ran upstairs, took blankets from a bed, and put them before the fire to warm. Then he removed her saturated, earthy-smelling clothing, rubbed her dry with a towel, and wrapped her naked in the blankets. Then he went into the dining-room, to look for spirits. There was a little whiskey. He drank a gulp himself, and put some into her mouth.

The effect was instantaneous. She looked full into his face, as if she had been seeing him for some time, and yet had only just become conscious of him.

"Dr. Fergusson?" she said.

"What?" he answered.

He was divesting himself of his coat, intending to find some dry clothing upstairs. He could not bear the smell of the dead, clayey water, and he was mortally afraid for his own health.

125 "What did I do?" she asked.

"Walked into the pond," he replied. He had begun to shudder like one sick, and could hardly attend to her. Her eyes remained full on him, he seemed to be going dark in his mind, looking back at her helplessly. The shuddering became quieter in him, his life came back in him, dark and unknowing, but strong again.

"Was I out of my mind?" she asked, while her eyes were fixed on him all the time.

"Maybe, for the moment," he replied. He felt quiet, because his strength had come back. The strange fretful strain had left him.

"Am I out of my mind now?" she asked.

130 "Are you?" he reflected a moment. "No," he answered truthfully, "I don't see that you are." He turned his face aside. He was afraid, now, because he felt dazed, and felt dimly that her power was stronger than his, in this issue. And she continued to look at him fixedly all the time. "Can you tell me where I shall find some dry things to put on?" he asked.

"Did you dive into the pond for me?" she asked.

"No," he answered. "I walked in. But I went in overhead as well."

There was silence for a moment. He hesitated. He very much wanted to go upstairs to get into dry clothing. But there was another desire in him. And she seemed to hold him. His will seemed to have gone to sleep, and left him, standing there slack before her. But he felt warm inside himself. He did not shudder at all, though his clothes were sodden on him.

"Why did you?" she asked.

"Because I didn't want you to do such a foolish thing," he said.   135

"It wasn't foolish," she said, still gazing at him as she lay on the floor, with a sofa cushion under her head. "It was the right thing to do. *I* knew best, then."

"I'll go and shift these wet things," he said. But still he had not the power to move out of her presence, until she sent him. It was as if she had the life of his body in her hands, and he could not extricate himself. Or perhaps he did not want to.

Suddenly she sat up. Then she became aware of her own immediate condition. She felt the blankets about her, she knew her own limbs. For a moment it seemed as if her reason were going. She looked round, with wild eye, as if seeking something. He stood still with fear. She saw her clothing lying scattered.

"Who undressed me?" she asked, her eyes resting full and inevitable on his face.

"I did," he replied, "to bring you round."   140

For some moments she sat and gazed at him awfully, her lips parted.

"Do you love me then?" she asked.

He only stood and stared at her, fascinated. His soul seemed to melt.

She shuffled forward on her knees, and put her arms round him, round his legs, as he stood there, pressing her breasts against his knees and thighs, clutching him with strange, convulsive certainty, pressing his thighs against her, drawing him to her face, her throat, as she looked up at him with flaring, humble eyes of transfiguration, triumphant in first possession.

"You love me," she murmured, in strange transport, yearning and triumphant and con-   145
fident. "You love me. I know you love me, I know."

And she was passionately kissing his knees, through the wet clothing, passionately and indiscriminately kissing his knees, his legs, as if unaware of everything.

He looked down at the tangled wet hair, the wild, bare, animal shoulders. He was amazed, bewildered, and afraid. He had never thought of loving her. He had never wanted to love her. When he rescued her and restored her, he was a doctor, and she was a patient. He had had no single personal thought of her. Nay, this introduction of the personal element was very distasteful to him, a violation of his professional honour. It was horrible to have her there embracing his knees. It was horrible. He revolted from it, violently. And yet—and yet—he had not the power to break away.

She looked at him again, with the same supplication of powerful love, and that same transcendent, frightening light of triumph. In view of the delicate flame which seemed to come from her face like a light, he was powerless. And yet he had never intended to love her. He had never intended. And something stubborn in him could not give way.

"You love me," she repeated, in a murmur of deep, rhapsodic assurance. "You love me."

Her hands were drawing him, drawing him down to her. He was afraid, even a little 150
horrified. For he had, really, no intention of loving her. Yet her hands were drawing him towards her. He put out his hand quickly to steady himself, and grasped her bare shoulder. A flame seemed to burn the hand that grasped her soft shoulder. He had no intention of loving her: his whole will was against his yielding. It was horrible—And yet wonderful was the touch of her shoulder, beautiful the shining of her face. Was she perhaps mad? He had a horror of yielding to her. Yet something in him ached also.

He had been staring away at the door, away from her. But his hand remained on her shoulder. She had gone suddenly very still. He looked down at her. Her eyes were now wide with fear, with doubt, the light was dying from her face, a shadow of terrible greyness was returning. He could not bear the touch of her eyes' question upon him, and the look of death behind the question.

With an inward groan he gave way, and let his heart yield towards her. A sudden gentle smile came on his face. And her eyes, which never left his face, slowly, slowly filled with tears. He watched the strange water rise in her eyes, like some slow fountain coming up. And his heart seemed to burn and melt away in his breast.

He could not bear to look at her any more. He dropped on his knees and caught her head with his arms and pressed her face against his throat. She was very still. His heart, which seemed to have broken, was burning with a kind of agony in his breast. And he felt her slow, hot tears wetting his throat. But he could not move.

He felt the hot tears wet his neck and the hollows of his neck, and he remained motionless, suspended through one of man's eternities. Only now it had become indispensable to have her face pressed close to him; he could never let her go again. He could never let her head go away from the close clutch of his arm. He wanted to remain like that for ever, with his heart hurting him in a pain that was also life to him. Without knowing, he was looking down on her damp, soft brown hair.

155 Then, as it were suddenly, he smelt the horrid stagnant smell of the water. And at the same moment she drew away from him and looked at him. Her eyes were wistful and unfathomable. He was afraid of them, and he fell to kissing her, not knowing what he was doing. He wanted her eyes not to have that terrible, wistful, unfathomable look.

When she turned her face to him again, a faint delicate flush was glowing, and there was again dawning that terrible shining of joy in her eyes, which really terrified him, and yet which he now wanted to see, because he feared the look of doubt still more.

"You love me?" she said, rather faltering.

"Yes." The word cost him a painful effort. Not because it wasn't true. But because it was too newly true, the *saying* seemed to tear open again his newly-torn heart. And he hardly wanted it to be true, even now.

She lifted her face to him, and he bent forward and kissed her on the mouth gently, with the one kiss that is an eternal pledge. And as he kissed her his heart strained again in his breast. He never intended to love her. But now it was over. He had crossed over the gulf to her, and all that he had left behind had shrivelled and become void.

160 After the kiss, her eyes again slowly filled with tears. She sat still, away from him, with her face drooped aside, and her hands folded in her lap. The tears fell very slowly. There was complete silence. He too sat there motionless and silent on the hearthrug. The strange pain of his heart that was broken seemed to consume him. That he should love her? That this was love! That he should be ripped open in this way!—Him, a doctor!—How they would all jeer if they knew!—It was agony to him to think they might know.

In the curious naked pain of the thought he looked again to her. She was sitting there drooped into a muse. He saw a tear fall, and his heart flared hot. He saw for the first time that one of her shoulders was quite uncovered, one arm bare, he could see one of her small breasts; dimly, because it had become almost dark in the room.

"Why are you crying?" he asked, in an altered voice.

She looked up at him, and behind her tears the consciousness of her situation for the first time brought a dark look of shame to her eyes.

"I'm not crying, really," she said, watching him half frightened.

165 He reached his hand, and softly closed it on her bare arm.

"I love you! I love you!" he said in a soft, low vibrating voice, unlike himself.

She shrank, and dropped her head. The soft, penetrating grip of his hand on her arm distressed her. She looked up at him.

"I want to go," she said. "I want to go and get you some dry things."

"Why?" he said. "I'm all right."

170 "But I want to go," she said. "And I want you to change your things."

He released her arm, and she wrapped herself in the blanket, looking at him rather frightened. And still she did not rise.

"Kiss me," she said wistfully.

He kissed her, but briefly, half in anger.

Then, after a second, she rose nervously, all mixed up in the blanket. He watched her in her confusion, as she tried to extricate herself and wrap herself up so that she could walk. He watched her relentlessly, as she knew.

And as she went, the blanket trailing, and as he saw a glimpse of her feet and her white 175
leg, he tried to remember her as she was when he had wrapped her in the blanket. But then he didn't want to remember, because she had been nothing to him then, and his nature revolted from remembering her as she was when she was nothing to him.

A tumbling muffled noise from within the dark house startled him. Then he heard her voice:—"There are clothes." He rose and went to the foot of the stairs, and gathered up the garments she had thrown down. Then he came back to the fire, to rub himself down and dress. He grinned at his own appearance, when he had finished.

The fire was sinking, so he put on coal. The house was now quite dark, save for the light of a street-lamp that shone in faintly from beyond the holly trees. He lit the gas with matches he found on the mantel-piece. Then he emptied the pockets of his own clothes, and threw all his wet things in a heap into the scullery. After which he gathered up her sodden clothes, gently, and put them in a separate heap on the copper-top in the scullery.

It was six o'clock on the clock. His own watch had stopped. He ought to be back to the surgery. He waited, and still she did not come down. So he went to the foot of the stairs and called:

"I shall have to go."

Almost immediately he heard her coming down. She had on her best dress of black voile, 180
and her hair was tidy, but still damp. She looked at him—and in spite of herself, smiled.

"I don't like you in those clothes," she said.

"Do I look a sight?" he answered.

They were shy of one another.

"I'll make you some tea," she said.

"No, I must go." 185

"Must you?" And she looked at him again with the wide, strained, doubtful eyes. And again, from the pain of his breast, he knew how he loved her. He went and bent to kiss her, gently, passionately, with his heart's painful kiss.

"And my hair smells so horrible," she murmured in distraction. "And I'm so awful, I'm so awful! Oh, no, I'm too awful." And she broke into bitter, heartbroken sobbing. "You can't want to love me, I'm horrible."

"Don't be silly, don't be silly," he said, trying to comfort her, kissing her, holding her in his arms. "I want you, I want to marry you, we're going to be married, quickly, quickly—tomorrow if I can."

But she only sobbed terribly, and cried.

"I feel awful. I feel awful. I feel I'm horrible to you." 190

"No, I want you, I want you," was all he answered blindly, with that terrible intonation which frightened her almost more than her horror lest he should *not* want her.

QUESTIONS

1. What idea is Lawrence illustrating by the breakup of the Pervin household?
2. What does the comparison of Joe Pervin and the draft horses mean with regard specifically to Joe, and generally to people without love?
3. What kind of person is Mabel? How do her brothers treat her? How does she feel about her brothers? What dilemma does she face as the story begins?
4. What effect does Mabel have on Fergusson as he watches her in her home, in the churchyard, and at the pond? What does this effect contribute to Lawrence's ideas about love?

5. What do Mabel and Fergusson realize as he revives and warms her? How do their responses signify their growth as characters?

6. Why does the narrator tell us at the story's end that Fergusson "had no intention of loving" Mabel? What idea does this repeated assertion convey?

7. In this story, there is an extensive exploration of the ambiguous feelings of both Fergusson and Mabel after they realize their love. Why does Lawrence explore these feelings so extensively?

AMÉRICO PAREDES (1915–1999)

Paredes was a Mexican-American storyteller, folklorist, essayist, and poet, closely identified with Mexican-Americans living in Texas, his native state. He received his Ph.D. at the University of Texas in 1956 and also taught there for many years. His dissertation was published in 1958 as With His Pistol in His Hand, *a study of an early-twentieth-century popular ballad about a fugitive, Gregorio Cortés. Deeply interested in the culture of the "lower border," he was one of the leaders of the Chicano movement in cultural-literary studies. He edited the* Journal of American Folklore *and also edited* Folklore and Culture on the Texas-Mexican Border *(1993). Among his honors was a Guggenheim Fellowship in 1962 and the Aztec Eagle medal from the Mexican government in 1991. "The Hammon and the Beans" was first published in the* Texas Observer *in 1963 and was republished in* The Hammon and the Beans and Other Stories *in 1994.*

🍁 The Hammon and the Beans (1963)

Once we lived in one of my grandfather's houses near Fort Jones.° It was just a block from the parade grounds, a big frame house painted a dirty yellow. My mother hated it, especially because of the pigeons that cooed all day about the eaves. They had fleas, she said. But it was a quiet neighborhood at least, too far from the center of town for automobiles and too near for musical, night-roaming drunks.

At this time Jonesville-on-the-Grande was not the thriving little city that it is today. We told off our days by the routine on the post. At six sharp the flag was raised on the parade grounds to the cackling of the bugles, and a field piece thundered out a salute. The sound of the shot bounced away through the morning mist until its echoes worked their way into every corner of town. Jonesville-on-the-Grande woke to the cannon's roar, as if to battle, and the day began.

At eight the whistle from the post laundry sent us children off to school. The whole town stopped for lunch with the noon whistle, and after lunch everybody went back to work when the post laundry said that it was one o'clock, except for those who could afford to be old-fashioned and took the siesta. The post was the town's clock, you might have said, or like some insistent elder person who was always there to tell you it was time.

At six the flag came down, and we went to watch through the high wire fence that divided the post from the town. Sometimes we joined in the ceremony, standing at salute until the sound of the cannon made us jump. That must have been when we had just studied about

---

°*Fort Jones:* The setting of Fort Jones and Jonesville-on-the-Grande in Texas is fictional. The story takes place in the mid-1920s, one of the most turbulent periods of Mexican history and only a few years after the deaths of two of the greatest heroes of the Mexican revolution—Pancho Villa (1877–1923) and Emiliano Zapata (c. 1879–1919).

George Washington in school, or recited "The Song of Marion's Men"° about Marion the Fox and the British cavalry that chased him up and down the broad Santee. But at other times we stuck out our tongues and jeered at the soldiers. Perhaps the night before we had hung at the edges of a group of old men and listened to tales about Aniceto Pizaña and the "border troubles,"° as the local paper still called them when it referred to them gingerly in passing.

It was because of the border troubles, ten years or so before, that the soldiers had come   5 back to old Fort Jones. But we did not hate them for that; we admired them even, at least sometimes. But when we were thinking about the border troubles instead of Marion the Fox we hooted them and the flag they were lowering, which for the moment was theirs alone, just as we would have jeered an opposing ball team, in a friendly sort of way. On these occasions even Chonita would join in the mockery, though she usually ran home at the stroke of six. But whether we taunted or saluted, the distant men in khaki uniforms went about their motions without noticing us at all.

The last word from the post came in the night when a distant bugle blew. At nine it was all right because all the lights were on. But sometimes I heard it at eleven when everything was dark and still, and it made me feel that I was all alone in the world. I would even doubt that I was me, and that put me in such a fright that I felt like yelling out just to make sure I was really there. But next morning the sun shone and life began all over again. With its whistles and cannon shots and bugles blowing. And so we lived, we and the post, side by side with the wire fence in between.

The wandering soldiers whom the bugle called home at night did not wander in our neighborhood, and none of us ever went into Fort Jones. None except Chonita. Every evening when the flag came down she would leave off playing and go down towards what was known as the "lower" gate of the post, the one that opened not on Main Street but against the poorest part of town. She went into the grounds and to the mess halls and pressed her nose against the screens and watched the soldiers eat. They sat at long tables calling to each other through food-stuffed mouths.

"Hey bud, pass the coffee!"

"Give me the ham!"

"Yeah, give me the beans!"   10

After the soldiers were through the cooks came out and scolded Chonita, and then they gave her packages with things to eat.

Chonita's mother did our washing, in gratefulness—as my mother put it— for the use of a vacant lot of my grandfather's which was a couple of blocks down the street. On the lot was an old one-room shack which had been a shed long ago, and this Chonita's father had patched up with flattened-out pieces of tin. He was a laborer. Ever since the end of the border troubles there had been a development boom in the Valley, and Chonita's father was getting his share of the good times. Clearing brush and building irrigation ditches he sometimes pulled down as much as six dollars a week. He drank a good deal of it up, it was true. But corn was just a few cents a bushel in those days. He was the breadwinner, you might say, while Chonita furnished the luxuries.

Chonita was a poet too. I had just moved into the neighborhood when a boy came up to me and said, "Come on! Let's go hear Chonita make a speech."

She was already on top of the alley fence when we got there, a scrawny little girl of about nine, her bare dirty feet clinging to the fence almost like hands. A dozen other kids were

---

°"*Song of Marion's Men*": a poem by William Cullen Bryant (1794–1878) about Colonel Francis Marion (c. 1732–1795), who was a leader of irregular guerrilla forces in South Carolina during the Revolutionary War. Because of his hit-and-run tactics, involving his hiding in the swamps near the "broad Santee" river in South Carolina, Marion was nicknamed the "Swamp Fox."

°*border troubles*: The most serious border incidents occurred in 1916, when Pancho Villa was responsible for deaths of Americans on both sides of the border. He made repeated raids into New Mexico and Texas.

there below her, waiting. Some were boys I knew at school; five or six were her younger brothers and sisters.

15   "Speech! Speech!" they all cried. "Let Chonita make a speech! Talk in English, Chonita!"

They were grinning and nudging each other except for her brothers and sisters, who looked up at her with proud serious faces. She gazed out beyond us all with a grand, distant air and then she spoke.

"Give me the hammon and the beans!" she yelled. "Give me the hammon and the beans!"

She leaped off the fence and everybody cheered and told her how good it was and how she could talk English better than the teachers at the grammar school.

I thought it was a pretty poor joke. Every evening almost, they would make her get up on the fence and yell, "Give me the hammon and the beans!" And everybody would cheer and make her think she was talking English. As for me, I would wait there until she got it over with so we could play at something else. I wondered how long it would be before they got tired of it all. I never did find out because just about that time I got the chills and fever, and when I got up and around Chonita wasn't there anymore.

20   In later years I thought of her a lot, especially during the thirties when I was growing up. Those years would have been just made for her. Many's the time I have seen her in my mind's eyes, in the picket lines demanding not bread, not cake, but the hammon and the beans. But it didn't work out that way.

One night Doctor Zapata came into our kitchen through the back door. He set his bag on the table and said to my father, who had opened the door for him, "Well, she is dead."

My father flinched. "What was it?" he asked.

The doctor had gone to the window and he stood with his back to us, looking out toward the light of Fort Jones. "Pneumonia, flu, malnutrition, worms, the evil eye," he said without turning around. "What the hell difference does it make?"

"I wish I had known how sick she was," my father said in a very mild tone. "Not that it's really my affair, but I wish I had."

25   The doctor snorted and shook his head.

My mother came in and I asked her who was dead. She told me. It made me feel strange but I did not cry. My mother put her arm around my shoulders. "She is in Heaven now," she said. "She is happy."

I shrugged her arm away and sat down in one of the kitchen chairs.

"They're like animals," the doctor was saying. He turned round suddenly and his eyes glistened in the light. "Do you know what that brute of a father was doing when I left? He was laughing! Drinking and laughing with his friends."

"There's no telling what the poor man feels," my mother said.

30   My father made a deprecatory gesture. "It wasn't his daughter anyway."

"No?" the doctor said. He sounded interested.

"This is the woman's second husband," my father explained. "First one died before the girl was born, shot and hanged from a mesquite limb. He was working too close to the tracks the day the Olmito train was derailed."

"You know what?" the doctor said. "In classical times they did things better. Take Troy, for instance. After they stormed the city they grabbed the babies by the heels and dashed them against the wall. That was more humane."

My father smiled. "You sound very radical. You sound just like your relative down there in Morelos."°

35   "No relative of mine," the doctor said. "I'm a conservative, the son of a conservative, and you know that I wouldn't be here except for that little detail."

°*Morelos*: the home state of Zapata.

"Habit," my father said. "Pure habit, pure tradition. You're a radical at heart."

"It depends on how you define radicalism," the doctor answered. "People tend to use words too loosely. A dentist could be called a radical, I suppose. He pulls up things by the roots."

My father chuckled.

"Any bandit in Mexico nowadays can give himself a political label," the doctor went on, "and that makes him respectable. He's a leader of the people."

"Take Villa, now—" my father began.

"Villa was a different type of man," the doctor broke in.

"I don't see any difference."

The doctor came over to the table and sat down. "Now look at it this way," he began, his finger in front of my father's face. My father threw back his head and laughed.

"You'd better go to bed and rest," my mother told me. "You're not completely well, you know."

So I went to bed, but I didn't go to sleep, not right away. I lay there for a long time while behind my darkened eyelids Emiliano Zapata's cavalry charged down to the broad Santee, where there were grave men with hoary hairs.° I was still awake at eleven when the cold voice of the bugle went gliding in and out of the dark like something that couldn't find its way back to wherever it had been. I thought of Chonita in Heaven, and I saw her in her torn and dirty dress, with a pair of bright wings attached, flying round and round like a butter-fly shouting, "Give me the hammon and the beans!"

Then I cried. And whether it was the bugle, or whether it was Chonita or what, to this day I do not know. But cry I did, and I felt much better after that.

QUESTIONS

1. How does Paredes establish the setting of the story? What is the significance of the fort? Of the "dirty yellow" paint? Of the vacant lot and the shack?

2. Is Chonita a round or flat character? To what extent does the author make her symbolic and representative?

3. What is the tone of the story (some possibilities: ironic, cynical, resigned, bitter, resentful)? What techniques does Paredes use to control the tone?

4. How does Doctor Zapata's attitude toward Chonita's death, and the words he uses to announce it, help to control the tone?

5. How does the tale of Chonita's brief life and her death fit into the political, social, and broadly human framework of the story?

6. Near the end of Bryant's "Song of Marion's Men" (lines 53–56) the following four lines appear:

> And lovely ladies greet our band [i.e., of soldiers]
> With kindliest welcoming,
> And smiles like those of summer,
> And tears like those of spring.

Contrast these lines with the narrator's vision of Chonita in heaven.

°*grave men with hoary hairs*: Cf. lines 49–52 of Bryant's "Song of Marion's Men":

Grave men there are by broad Santee,
    Grave men with hoary hairs;
Their hearts are all with Marion,
    For Marion are their prayers.

WRITING ABOUT A MAJOR IDEA IN FICTION

Most likely you will write about a major idea or theme, but you may also get interested in one of your story's other ideas. As you begin brainstorming and developing your first drafts, consider questions such as the following:

Questions for Discovering Ideas

GENERAL IDEAS

- What ideas do you discover in the work? How do you discover them (through action, character description, scenes, figurative language)?
- To what do the ideas pertain? To individuals themselves? To individuals and society? To religion? To social, political, or economic circumstances? To fairness? To inequality? To justice?
- How balanced are the ideas? If a particular idea is strongly presented, what conditions and qualifications are also presented (if any)? What contradictory ideas are presented?
- Are the ideas limited to members of any groups represented by the characters (age, race, nationality, personal status)? Or are the ideas applicable to general conditions of life? Explain.
- Which characters in their own right represent or embody ideas? How do their actions and speeches bring out these ideas?
- If characters state ideas directly, how persuasive is their expression, how intelligent and well considered? How germane are the ideas to the work? How germane to more general conditions?
- With children, young adults, or the old, how do the circumstances express or embody an idea?

A SPECIFIC IDEA

- What idea seems particularly important in the work? Why? How is it presented? Is it asserted directly, indirectly, dramatically, ironically? Does any one method predominate? Why?
- How pervasive in the work is the idea (throughout or intermittent)? To what degree is it associated with a major character or action? How does the structure of the work affect or shape your understanding of the idea?
- What value or values are embodied in the idea? Of what importance are the values to the work's meaning?
- How compelling is the idea? How could the work be appreciated without reference to any idea at all?

Strategies for Organizing Ideas

Narrative and dramatic elements have a strong bearing on ideas in well-written stories, poems, and plays. In this sense, an idea is like a key in music or like a continuous thread tying together actions, characters, statements, symbols, and dialogue. As readers, we can trace such threads throughout the entire fabric of the work.

As you write about ideas, you may find yourself relying most heavily on the direct statements of the authorial voice or on a combination of these and your interpretation of characters and action. Or you may focus exclusively on a first-person speaker and use his or her ideas to develop your analysis. Always make clear the sources of your details and distinguish the sources from your own commentary.

In your essay, your general goal is to describe an idea and show its importance in the story. Each separate work will invite its own approach, but here are a number of strategies you might use to organize your essay:

1. *Analyze the idea as it applies to character. Example*: "Chonita embodies the idea that life amid poverty leads to the loss of dignity and opportunity, and also to the loss of health and even to death itself" ("The Hammon and the Beans").

2. *Show how actions bring out the idea. Example*: "That Mabel and Dr. Fergusson fall in love rather than go their separate ways indicates Lawrence's idea that love literally rescues human lives."

3. *Show how dialogue and separate speeches bring out the idea. Example*: "The priest's responses to Jackie's confession embody the idea that kindness and understanding are the best means to encourage religious and philosophical commitment" ("First Confession" in Chapter 6).

4. *Show how the story's structure is determined by the idea. Example*: "The idea that horror can exist in ordinary things leads to a structure in which Jackson (in 'The Lottery,' Chapter 2) introduces seemingly commonplace people, builds suspense about an impending misfortune, and develops a conclusion of mob insensitivity and cruelty."

5. *Treat variations or differing manifestations of the idea. Example*: "The idea that zealousness leads to harm is shown in Brown's nightmarish distortion of reality, his rejection of others, and his dying gloom" ("Young Goodman Brown" in Chapter 7).

6. *Deal with a combination of these (together with any other significant aspect). Example*: "The idea in 'Araby' (Chapter 4) that devotion is complex and contradictory is shown in the narrator's romantic mission as a carrier of parcels, his outcries to love in the back room of his house, and his self-reproach and shame at the story's end." (Here the idea is traced through both speech and action.)

Your conclusion might begin with a summary, together with your evaluation of the validity or force of the idea. If you have been convinced by the author's ideas, you might say that the author has expressed the idea forcefully and convincingly, or else you might show the relevance of the idea to current conditions. If you are not persuaded by the idea, you should demonstrate its shortcomings or limitations. If you wish to mention a related idea, whether in the story you have studied or in some other story, you might introduce that here, but be sure to stress the connections.

Illustrative Student Essay

Underlined sentences in this paper *do not* conform to MLA style and are used solely as teaching tools to emphasize the central idea, thesis sentence, and topic sentences throughout the paper.

de los Reyes 1

Oscar de los Reyes

Professor Garcia

English 112

7 October 2008

D. H. Lawrence's "The Horse Dealer's Daughter" as an Expression of the Idea

That Loving Commitment Is Essential in Life.°

[1]   Lawrence's "The Horse Dealer's Daughter" is an unusual love story. We learn that the lovers--Mabel Pervin (who is "The Horse Dealer's Daughter") and Dr. Jack Fergusson--have known each other for many years but have never thought of themselves as lovers. It is not until after an almost catastrophic event that the two recognize that they love each other. Lawrence makes clear that this new love is about to bring new meaning and new direction to their lives. Most important about this love is that it fulfills Lawrence's idea that it is dedicated commitment that gives life meaning.* Lawrence brings out this idea first by showing characters with no sense of love or commitment and then by developing the two major characters whose lives are to be fulfilled by commitment.†

[2]   Negatively, at the story's beginning, Lawrence introduces his idea through the Pervin brothers, who have no sense of service or commitment and who therefore are leading obtuse, insensitive, somewhat cruel, and basically "ineffectual" lives (475, paragraph 96). It is true that Joe, the oldest brother, is planning to marry, and, one might assume, is also undertaking the promises and commitments that marriage brings. But Joe is seeking marriage only to receive a job from his future father-in-law. In other words, his only duty is to himself, and even though that is a commitment of sorts, it is only a limited one.

°For this story appears on pages 472–81.
*Central idea.
†Thesis sentence.

de los Reyes 2

In line with Lawrence's idea, Joe's life has little if any meaning. Lawrence's speaker dismisses Joe with the cutting words that he is not much better than the large draft horses on the Pervin farm, whose "stupidity . . . [holds] them in subjection" (472, paragraph 6).

Lawrence's first use of his major characters, Mabel Pervin and Dr. Jack Fergusson, also embodies the negative aspect of his idea that lack of service and commitment to others leaves people aimless and unfulfilled. When Jack first enters the story his eyes look "tired" (474, paragraph 43), and he is suffering from a severe cold. His social life seems to be confined to spending time at a nearby pub and drinking with one of the Pervin brothers, Fred Henry, and two women named "Lizzie and May" (475, paragraphs 90–91). These outward signs of illness and aimlessness suggest an inner lack of conviction and commitment. But nevertheless, Jack is a good doctor. He may sometimes think of himself as a "slave" to his patients (476, paragraph 103), but he is dedicated to his work and finds excitement in it (477, paragraph 106). Therefore he declares that he cannot take a brief rest from serving his patients even to overcome his cold (474, paragraph 49). Clearly he is committed to his profession, but the commitment that comes from love is lacking in his life. When he goes into the pond to rescue Mabel, it is as a professional, not as a committed lover. His action, however, will change him and point him in the path of completeness.

[3]

Mabel is in a position similar to Jack's. Lawrence introduces her as "a rather short, sullen-looking young woman" with an "impassive fixity of her face" (472, paragraph 3). Her brothers all seem to dislike her. Like Jack, she is living only half a life, even though she has gained some little meaning through service, of a sort, to others. In the past she has been "keeping the home together" for her father and her brothers as the family fortunes declined. As long as the family had had money, her life was adequate, even if the household to which she was committed was "brutal and coarse" in many ways (475, paragraph 96). But with the family now "hopelessly in debt," requiring the breakup of the household, her duties are vanishing, and this loss also brings the loss of the meaning that her service has brought to her (475–76, paragraphs 97–98).

[4]

de los Reyes 3

[5]   In line with the idea, Lawrence makes plain that Mabel's developing despair will end her existence and that Jack's rootlessness, if unchanged, will keep him incomplete. Mabel's situation is, of course, the more critical. After completing her chores at home, thus fulfilling all her obligations there, she sets about to care for the grave of her dead mother, to whom her commitment is total (476, paragraphs 98–101). Once she finishes this loving task, she has nowhere to go, nothing more to do, and she therefore walks purposefully to the nearby pond and enters it in an attempt to drown herself (477, paragraph 109). One can read her attempted suicide as a symbol of Lawrence's idea that once a person's commitments end, meaning is gone and life is, without dedicated love, over.

[6]   The paragraphs devoted by Lawrence to the interchanges of Mabel and Jack after he has rescued her from the pond demonstrate the interconnectedness of love and commitment. When he brings her to the shore he works "to restore her" (478, paragraph 117). After he carries her home--an arduous and difficult task--he disrobes her and wraps her in blankets to bring back warmth and life to her. At this point his commitment to her, however, is not to a loved one but to a patient. But when Mabel recovers, her first thought is to associate her nakedness with a newly discovered love for her. She asks him "Do you love me then?" (479, paragraph 142). Once she has extracted a declaration of love, her first wishes are an enactment of Lawrence's idea of the power of commitment. She wants to get him "dry things" and then to make him some tea (480, 481, paragraphs 170, 184). She has been awakened to a new life by a man who suddenly appears in a totally new light, and her response is immediately to begin the simple tasks that follow naturally from commitment. For his part, Jack demonstrates his newly found commitment by stating that he wants the two of them "to be married" (481, paragraph 188). The idea is that love is for the moment, but commitment is for the long term.

[7]   The major and most truthful aspect of Lawrence's idea is that the transformation to loving obligation is not easy but is both tentative and complex. Lawrence demonstrates this complexity by showing that both Mabel

de los Reyes 4

and Jack are uneasy and uncertain, for neither one can easily give up the past (even though Mabel was willing to give up everything when she tried suicide). When Jack expresses love for Mabel it is in a voice that is "unlike himself" (480, paragraph 166), and her response is to say "I feel I'm horrible to you" (481, paragraph 190). Difficult and fearful as the change to their new commitment is, however, it is leading them into the lives they have been designed for. Generally, people who evade such a change, like the Pervin brothers, may find life easy, but they are permanently incomplete because they lack the bravery of committed love shown by Mabel and Jack. Thus, Lawrence's idea in "The Horse Dealer's Daughter" emphasizes that a full life requires love and commitment, no matter how difficult, and that without such commitment lives can be lived only in the shadows.

de los Reyes 5

Work Cited

Lawrence, D. H. "The Horse Dealer's Daughter." Literature: An Introduction to Reading and Writing. Ed. Edgar V. Roberts. 9th ed. New York: Pearson Longman, 2009. 472–81.

Commentary on the Essay

This essay follows strategy 6 (pages 486–87) by showing how separate components of the story exhibit the idea's pervasiveness. Throughout, citations of characters, actions, and speeches, together with observations about the story's organization, are used as evidence for the various conclusions. Transitions between paragraphs are effected by words and phrases like "introduces," "similar," "after he has rescued her," and "the major and most truthful aspect," all of which emphasize the continuity of the topic.

The first paragraph asserts that the story's major action—the development of love between the major characters—brings out Lawrence's idea that commitment gives meaning to life. The idea is to be developed as it applies to characters without commitment and then to those who find it.

The argument of paragraphs 2 through 4 is to show how Lawrence brings out his idea negatively by demonstrating the shortcomings of characters, including the story's two major characters, who are living without commitment. The essay thus asserts that Joe is following a path of stupidity, Jack a life of rootlessness, and Mabel an action of suicide. These details are brought out in support of the essay's central idea or argument. Paragraphs 5 and 6 treat the positive aspects of the main idea, focusing on the renewing effect of commitment for both Jack and Mabel. The last paragraph pays tribute to Lawrence's idea by demonstrating that it is realistic and true to life because both Jack and Mabel discover that their new commitments are not made easily but require profound and even disturbing changes in their lives.

Writing Topics About Ideas

1. Compare two stories containing similar themes. *Examples*: Chekhov's "The Lady with the Dog" and Lawrence's "The Horse Dealer's Daughter," Ozick's "The Shawl" (Chapter 4) and Chioles's "Before the Firing Squad" (Chapter 10), Chopin's "The Story of an Hour" (Chapter 6) and Gilman's "The Yellow Wallpaper" (Chapter 10). For help in developing your essay, consult Chapter 30 on the technique of comparison-contrast.

2. Write an essay criticizing the ideas in a story in this anthology that you dislike or to which you are indifferent. With what statements in the story do you disagree? What actions? What characters? How do your own beliefs and values cause you to dislike the story's ideas? How might the story be changed to illustrate ideas with which you would agree?

3. Select an idea that particularly interests you, and write a story showing how characters may or may not live up to the idea. If you have difficulty getting started, try one of these possible ideas:
   a. Interest and enthusiasm are hard to maintain for long.
   b. People always want more than they have or need.
   c. The concerns of adults are different from those of children.
   d. Confronting another person about a grievance is awkward.
   e. Making a romantic or career decision is hard because it requires a change in life's directions.

4. Using books that you discover through the retrieval system in your college or local library, or works that you find online, search for discussions of only one of the following topics, and write a brief report on what you find.
   a. Nathaniel Hawthorne on the significance of religion, both good and bad.
   b. Ernest Hemingway on individualism and self-realization.
   c. James Joyce on the significance of religion.
   d. D. H. Lawrence on the power of the working classes.
   e. Cynthia Ozick on the Holocaust.
   f. The ideas underlying Poe's concept of the short story as a form.

Chapter 9

A Career in Fiction: Four Stories by Edgar Allan Poe with Critical Readings for Research

POE'S LIFE AND CAREER (1809–1849)

Edgar Poe was born in Boston in January 1809. His parents, who were actors, separated before he was a year old. Needing to make an independent living, his mother, Elizabeth Poe, went on an acting tour, taking Edgar, his infant sister, and his older brother along with her. Shortly before Poe's third birthday, Elizabeth died, and the three children were separated. Poe was rescued from a childhood of poverty when he was taken into foster care by John and Frances Allan of Richmond, Virginia, who were childless. The Allans did not make a formal adoption, but when Poe was christened he was given Allan as his middle name. In 1815 John Allan, who was an importer, took his family to England, where they spent five years and where Poe received his elementary education. In 1820 the Allans returned to America and Poe resumed his studies at a private school. He was successful both as a student and as an athlete, one of his noteworthy achievements being a broad jump of 21 feet, 6 inches, a schoolboy record at the time. In 1826, at the age of seventeen, he matriculated at the University of Virginia, which had recently been founded by Thomas Jefferson.

Although Poe was a natural student, personal problems—primarily an increasingly strained relationship with Allan—upset his studies. Within a year he left college and went to Boston, where he published his first volume of poetry in 1827 (Tamerlane and Other Poems). In the same year he joined the army and quickly gained the highest rank of noncommissioned officers, although he left the service in 1829. In 1830, during a truce with Allan following the death of Mrs. Allan, he was granted an appointment at the U.S. Military Academy. Unfortunately, he got into debt, and Allan refused to help him out despite having become wealthy as the result of an inheritance. In fact, Allan, who had quickly remarried and was beginning a new family, stopped supporting Poe and cut him out of his will entirely. In 1831, lacking the financial help that he needed to maintain his life as a cadet, Poe got himself expelled from West Point by deliberately refusing to follow orders. After this time he never again used Allan in his name even though he kept A as his middle initial. Now totally dependent on his own resources, he embarked on a career as a writer.

Despite his difficulties with Allan, Poe had been held in high esteem by his fellow West Point cadets, who took up a collection to subsidize the second edition of his poetry in 1832. In the following years, and throughout his career as a writer and editor, he struggled constantly against poverty. It was not that he did not work hard and prolifically. He was always writing reviews, criticism, lectures, poetry, and fiction, and he even tried his hand as a playwright. As with his college and West Point experiences, however, he was unable to stay anywhere for long. He also struggled against alcohol, and excessive drinking caused him to lose some of his positions, although at other times his jobs simply vanished through no fault of his own.

Early in his writing career he went to live in Baltimore with his aunt, Maria ("Muddy") Clemm, and her daughter Virginia ("Sissy"). In 1836, he and Sissy, who was then only thirteen, were married. Mrs. Clemm continued to live with the couple and also managed household affairs as Poe moved from city to city to take new editorial positions. The marriage lasted eleven years until Sissy died of tuberculosis in 1847, when the Poes were living in Fordham, New York (later incorporated into the Bronx). The house they lived in (the "Poe Cottage") still stands and is open to the public. A plan for repair and restoration of the "Cottage" was announced in 2008, to begin in 2009.

Although Sissy's death marked a low point in Poe's life, he continued his writing, reviewing, and lecturing. In September 1849, he went on an extended lecture tour, including Richmond, where he had been brought up, as one of his destinations. When there he proposed to Sarah Elmira Royster Shelton, a wealthy widow to whom he had been engaged when he was in his late teens. Elmira's father had objected to the first engagement, and now her three brothers and two children objected because they believed that Poe was an opportunistic drunkard who wanted to marry Elmira only for her money. Despite these objections, Elmira appears genuinely to have loved Poe (she wrote that he was "the dearest object on earth" *to her), and she accepted his proposal. The couple set a date in mid-October 1849 for the wedding.*

It seems clear that Poe was trying to build a new life. He had just taken an oath of sobriety, he was about to marry the sweetheart of his youth, his lectures were increasingly popular, and he was developing an idea for a new critical journal. He had also just received an offer of a short-term but lucrative editing job in Philadelphia. So on September 27, 1849, he left Richmond for the boat and train ride to Philadelphia, after which he was planning to go north to New York to bring Mrs. Clemm to Richmond for the wedding. However, he never reached his destination in Philadelphia, he never did the editing job, and five days after his departure from Richmond he was found in Baltimore in a drunken and incoherent state. He was no longer dressed in his traveling suit but instead was wearing cheap and worn clothing, and he no longer possessed any of the money he had been carrying (which may have been considerable). To this day, what had brought him to this condition is a mystery. Existing evidence is inconclusive and sometimes contradictory, but it seems that he may have been waylaid, robbed, beaten, and encouraged or forced to drink a huge amount of liquor. Although it does not seem that anyone made an attempt on his life, as some accounts would have it, it does appear that at some period during the unexplained lapse of time he was under the control of people who were hostile to him.

Whatever actually did happen, and for whatever reason, Poe was in grave condition on October 3, 1849, when he was found and taken to the Washington College Hospital (now Church Hospital) in Baltimore. Because he was delirious and sometimes comatose in the hospital, he was unable to tell anyone what had happened to him. He worsened, and on October 7 he died. The following day he was buried in Baltimore's Presbyterian Cemetery. The Baltimore Clipper *reported that he had died of "congestion of the brain." Since then a number of possible diagnoses have been offered, including acute alcoholic poisoning, hypoglycemia, head trauma, diabetic shock, and even rabies. According to recent scholarship, however, there "simply is not enough medical evidence at hand" to determine the exact cause of death.[1] What we can safely conclude is that Poe died abruptly under mysterious, suspicious, or even sinister circumstances just when his life and career seemed to be taking a new and positive turn.*

Poe's Work as a Journalist and Writer of Fiction

During his seventeen-year career as a writer, Poe did editorial work for a number of magazines in Richmond, Philadelphia, and New York, with the most important of his associations being the *Southern Literary Messenger, Burton's Magazine, Graham's Magazine,* the *Broadway Journal,* and the *New York Mirror.* He sometimes

---

[1]See John Evangelist Walsh, *Midnight Dreary: The Mysterious Death of Edgar Allan Poe* (New Brunswick: Rutgers UP, 1998), 179.

had a regular income, although the largest salary he ever received was $800 from his editorship at *Graham's Magazine* in 1841–1842. In 1845 he seemed on the way to success when he began running the *Broadway Journal*, but this publication ran out of money early in 1846 and he was once again in financial trouble.

Along with his uncertain career in journalism and editing, Poe steadily wrote fiction. As a theoretical critic, he provided a foundation for short fiction and paved the way for subsequent writers of short stories. His critical review of Hawthorne's *Twice-Told Tales* (1842) is accepted as his theory of fiction.[2] In it he tells us that the special aim of the writer of a short prose tale is to create a concentrated emotional impact. Assuming that the writing is of high quality, the impact is directly related to the brevity of the narrative, which Poe states should take the reader no more than a single sitting of an hour or perhaps two. As a practical fact of reading, he indicates, longer stories and novels diffuse the desired effect because time itself produces inevitable distractions and the need for personal business. Therefore Poe's concept of the story stresses the primacy of effect. The implication of his theory is that, to achieve maximum impact, stories should be based on swiftly moving situations and descriptions, intricate plotting, and moods of fear and horror.

As a practitioner of fiction, Poe was both original and creative. It is to him that we owe the genres of detective story, murder story, horror story, suspense story, and psychological story (sometimes overlapping in the same work). Although he apparently considered himself a poet first and a fiction writer second, his complete stories, or tales, total more than seventy. He sought to capture his readers' attention by freely including material from his wide reading and by using his vivid and often sensational and macabre imagination. Some of his better-known tales are *The Narrative of A. Gordon Pym* (one of his longest stories, sometimes called a novel, 1837), "The Fall of the House of Usher" (1839), "The Murders in the Rue Morgue" (1841), "A Descent into the Maelström" (1841), "The Pit and the Pendulum" (1842), "The Masque of the Red Death" (1842), "The Tell-Tale Heart" (1843), "The Gold Bug" (1843), "The Black Cat" (1843), "The Purloined Letter" (1844), and "The Cask of Amontillado" (1846). He also assembled many of his tales into two major collections: *Tales of the Grotesque and Arabesque* (1840) and *Tales* (1845).

Because Poe as a practicing writer followed his own theory of fiction, he does not seek to create full-blown, round character development in his tales, but instead he focuses on situations, actions, and his characters' responses. His subject matter varies widely: He includes faraway, exotic, and even lugubrious locations such as Paris, the sea, American islands, dreary and collapsible mansions, Gothic interiors, cellars, subterranean vaults, and mythological ends of the earth. Few of his characters fall within the spectrum of what we think of as normal, and a number who start out as normal take a turn into the unusual or bizarre. Some characters are driven by pride and/or guilt; some commit deranged and grisly crimes; some are dead, either recently or for centuries; some of the dead are revivified long enough to claim possession over the living. The actions in Poe's stories are uncanny and often weird, consisting of intricate punishments, self-destructiveness,

---

[2]See also page 58.

live burials, mysterious substitutions of personality, journeys into unknown regions, trips to the moon, total physical and psychological collapse, and strange and sometimes comic resurrections of the dead.

Poe's Reputation

During his lifetime, Poe was not highly regarded in the United States. Perhaps his lack of recognition resulted from his own combativeness, for he regularly alienated people who might have supported him. From time to time he was involved in lawsuits, literary quarrels, and even a fistfight. He accused Henry Wadsworth Longfellow, one of the major poets of the time, of plagiarism—certainly not a way to make himself popular and respected within the nineteenth-century American literary community. He achieved success to the degree that he won a few prizes for stories, but his chief recognition was the praise heaped upon his poem "The Raven" in 1845 (for which he received little money). In 1846 he received a letter from Elizabeth Barrett Browning congratulating him on the warm reception of his works in England, and in the same year he was commended by Nathaniel Hawthorne even though he had written negative criticism of some of Hawthorne's fiction. The highest public recognition Poe received in his lifetime was his representation in *Prose Writers of America* (1847), edited by his sometime friend, Rufus Griswold, who also was his literary executor.

After Poe died, the decline of his reputation was hastened by Griswold, who published a short but poisonous biography, most of which was later included in various editions of Poe's collected works. (Griswold stated in italics that *"few will be grieved by"* Poe's death, and that Poe *"had few or no friends."*) Before long the public perception of Poe was that he had been an alcoholic and brooding loner who wrote about characters beyond the fringes of sanity. Poe's works did not contradict this image, for many unsophisticated readers readily believed that some of his disturbed fictional and poetic narrators (such as those of "The Black Cat," "The Cask of Amontillado," and "The Tell-Tale Heart") were the writer himself in his own person.

His work therefore fell into relative obscurity except in France, where he was considered a brilliant and creative though eccentric visionary. In the United States his reputation as a writer was obscured by the more objectionable and unexplainable aspects of his life, principally his marriage to his thirteen-year-old cousin together with reports of alcoholism and drug addiction and the mysterious circumstances of his death. As his writings have become more available, and as the early opinions about him have been modified, his literary reputation has risen. He is seen today as a romantic who asserted the need for artistic individuality and integrity, and who in his works explored the exotic, the passionate, the puzzling, the intricate, the uncontrollable, the vengeful, and—in the face of human violence—the power of conscience. Because many of his works are unrealistic, grisly, and macabre, general readers often appreciate him for the shudder of sensational horror, while critics find ample materials for readings that are symbolic, allegorical, feminist, psychological, structuralist, and formalist. Today, of all nineteenth-century American writers of fiction, Poe is the most widely published and still the most widely read. His stature as a writer was fully acknowledged in 1986, when his name was placed in the Hall of Fame of American Authors.

Bibliographic Sources

The number of books and essays about Poe is vast. The standard edition of his works is the three-volume *Collected Works of Edgar Allan Poe* (1969–1978), edited by Thomas Olive Mabbott. The Library of America edition of Poe's *Poetry and Tales* and *Essays and Reviews* appeared in 1984 in two volumes. A convenient popular edition has been regularly available for the last sixty years in the Modern Library edition of *The Complete Tales and Poems of Edgar Allan Poe,* with an introduction by Hervey Allen (1938). This volume includes seventy-three stories and fifty-three poems. Another readily available edition is G. R. Thompson, ed., *Great Short Works of Edgar Allan Poe* (1970). A thoroughgoing edition of the stories is *The Short Fiction of Edgar Allan Poe: An Annotated Edition* (1976, rpt. 1990), edited by Stuart and Susan Levine. This volume also contains a comprehensive introduction, a useful arrangement of the stories, copious notes, and an excellent working bibliography. An interesting popular edition is *18 Best Stories by Edgar Allan Poe* (1965), edited by Vincent Price and Chandler Brossard, with an introduction by Vincent Price, a film actor who specialized in movie villains and starred in film adaptations of Poe stories. Price's introduction, though brief, is therefore of independent interest.

Biographies of Poe are Kenneth Silverman, *Edgar A. Poe: Mournful and Never-ending Remembrance* (1991); Jeffrey Meyers, *Edgar Allan Poe: His Life and Legacy* (1992); and Scott Peeples, *Edgar Allan Poe Revisited* (1998). Other excellent biographies are Arthur H. Quinn, *Edgar Allan Poe: A Critical Biography* (1941, rpt. 1998 with a new foreword by Shawn Rosenheim); and Edward Wagenknecht, *Edgar Allan Poe: The Man Behind the Legend* (1963). George E. Woodberry's biography, *Edgar Allan Poe,* originally published in 1885, was reprinted in 1980 with an introduction and evaluation by R. W. B. Lewis. To these biographies should be added John Evangelist Walsh, *Midnight Dreary: The Mysterious Death of Edgar Allan Poe* (1998), a study of the relevant evidence concerning Poe's death.

Significant criticism and background information may be found in Kenneth Silverman, ed., *New Essays on Poe's Major Tales* (1993); William L. Howarth, ed., *Twentieth Century Interpretations of Poe's Tales* (1971); Charles E. May, *Edgar Allan Poe: A Study of the Short Fiction* (1991); Vincent Buranelli, *Edgar Allan Poe* (1961); A. Robert Lee, ed., *Edgar Allan Poe: The Design of Order* (1987); Kevin J. Hayes, ed., *The Cambridge Companion to Edgar Allan Poe* (2002); Eric W. Carlson, ed., *Critical Essays on Edgar Allan Poe* (1987); Shawn Rosenheim and Stephen Rachman, eds., *The American Face of Edgar Allan Poe* (1995); J. R. Hammond, *An Edgar Allan Poe Companion* (1981); J. Gerald Kennedy, ed., *A Historical Guide to Edgar Allan Poe* (2001); Dawn B. Sova, *Edgar Allan Poe A to Z: The Essential Reference to His Life and Work* (2001); and Bonnie Szumski and Carol Prime, eds., *Readings on Edgar Allan Poe* (1998). Eric W. Carlson in *The Recognition of Edgar Allan Poe*

(1966) reprints essays and portions of essays selected to show the changes and growth of Poe's reputation from the time of his death through 1965, the year of publication. Louis Broussard, *The Measure of Poe* (1969), includes a fifty-nine-page bibliography, up to date through 1969, and Charles E. May includes a ten-page bibliography, up to date through 1991. These works are complemented by the selected bibliography provided by Peeples (pp. 196–203), which reflects criticism through 1998. In 1993 a video recording was issued with the title *Homage to Edgar Allan Poe*.

Foreign interest in Poe was pioneered by the nineteenth-century French poet Charles Baudelaire, whose *Edgar Allan Poe: Sa Vie et ses Ouvrages* of 1852 was reprinted in 1994. A recent Italian work on Poe is by Giorgio Ghidetti, *Poe, L'Eresia de un Americano Maledetto* (1989).

Poe's works have been the subject of many films and musical settings. In 1960, Roger Corman produced a film adaptation of "The Fall of the House of Usher," and he also made film versions of "The Black Cat" and "The Masque of the Red Death." More than one composer has adapted "The Fall of the House of Usher" as a musical drama. Claude Debussy worked for the last twenty-eight years of his life on an opera based on "The Fall of the House of Usher," but never finished it. Another of Poe's stories, "Ligeia," has also been set to music. As one might expect, composers writing music for Poe's works have found the poetry to be of equal or greater interest than the fiction. The most significant musical version of Poe is by Sergei Rachmaninoff (1873–1943), who composed "The Bells" in 1913 for soloists, chorus, and orchestra to a Russian adaptation of the poem by Konstantin Balmont. Rachmaninoff himself considered *The Bells* as one of his very best compositions. Two additional musical versions of Poe's poems are Norman Dello Joio's chorus *The Quest* (1991) and Paul Moravec's song cycle *Evensong* (1992). Dawn B. Sova describes many other existing film and musical versions under the titles of Poe's works.

Writing Topics About Poe

1. Poe's idea that fiction should create a single and clearly focused impression or impact on the reader.
2. Poe's explorations of the eerie and bizarre.
3. Poe's use of setting in one or more stories.
4. Poe's use of irony and humor.
5. Poe and psychology: the meaning of evil in the lives of his characters.
6. The inevitability of guilt and punishment following criminal and immoral behavior.
7. The social background of Poe's stories (the people and their ways of life, work habits, husband-wife relationships, involvement in the world at large).
8. Poe's use of symbolism and/or allegory.
9. Poe's use of dramatic dialogue and indirect discourse.
10. Poe's use of the first-person narrator.

Four Stories by Edgar Allan Poe (Chronologically Arranged)

The Fall of the House of Usher (1839) 499
The Masque of the Red Death (1842) 510
The Black Cat (1843) 513
The Cask of Amontillado (1846) 519

The Fall of the House of Usher (1839)

> Son coèur est un luth suspendu;
> Sitôt qu'on le touche il résonne.°
>
> —De Béranger

During the whole of a dull, dark, and soundless day in the autumn of the year, when the clouds hung oppressively low in the heavens, I had been passing alone, on horseback, through a singularly dreary tract of country; and at length found myself, as the shades of the evening drew on, within view of the melancholy House of Usher. I know not how it was—but, with the first glimpse of the building, a sense of insufferable gloom pervaded my spirit. I say insufferable; for the feeling was unrelieved by any of that half-pleasurable, because poetic, sentiment, with which the mind usually receives even the sternest natural images of the desolate or terrible. I looked upon the scene before me—upon the mere house, and the simple landscape features of the domain—upon the bleak walls—upon the vacant eye-like windows—upon a few rank sedges—and upon a few white trunks of decayed trees—with an utter depression of soul which I can compare to no earthly sensation more properly than to the after-dream of the reveller upon opium—the bitter lapse into everyday life—the hideous dropping off of the veil. There was an iciness, a sinking, a sickening of the heart—an unredeemed dreariness of thought which no goading of the imagination could torture into aught of the sublime. What was it—I paused to think—what was it that so unnerved me in the contemplation of the House of Usher? It was a mystery all insoluble; nor could I grapple with the shadowy fancies that crowded upon me as I pondered. I was forced to fall back upon the unsatisfactory conclusion, that while, beyond doubt, there are combinations of very simple natural objects which have the power of thus affecting us, still the analysis of this power lies among considerations beyond our depth. It was possible, I reflected, that a mere different arrangement of the particulars of the scene, of the details of the picture, would be sufficient to modify, or perhaps to annihilate its capacity for sorrowful impression; and, acting upon this idea, I reined my horse to the precipitous brink of a black and lurid tarn that lay in unruffled lustre by the dwelling, and gazed down—but with a shudder even more thrilling than before—upon the remodelled and inverted images of the grey sedge, and the ghastly tree-stems, and the vacant and eye-like windows.

Nevertheless, in this mansion of gloom I now proposed to myself a sojourn of some weeks. Its proprietor, Roderick Usher, had been one of my boon companions in boyhood; but many years had elapsed since our last meeting. A letter, however, had lately reached me in a distant part of the country—a letter from him—which, in its wildly importunate nature,

---

°*Son coeur . . . résonne:* a passage from the poem "Le Refus" by Pierre-Jean de Béranger (1780–1857): "His heart is a tightly strung lute; / It rings as soon as it is touched."

had admitted of no other than a personal reply. The MS gave evidence of nervous agitation. The writer spoke of acute bodily illness—of a mental disorder which oppressed him—and of an earnest desire to see me, as his best, and indeed his only personal friend, with a view of attempting, by the cheerfulness of my society, some alleviation of his malady. It was the manner in which all this, and much more, was said—it was the apparent heart that went with his request—which allowed me no room for hesitation; and I accordingly obeyed forthwith what I still considered a very singular summons.

Although, as boys, we had been even intimate associates, yet I really knew little of my friend. His reserve had been always excessive and habitual. I was aware, however, that his very ancient family had been noted, time out of mind, for a peculiar sensibility of temperament, displaying itself, through long ages, in many works of exalted art, and manifested, of late, in repeated deeds of munificent yet unobtrusive charity, as well as in a passionate devotion to the intricacies, perhaps even more than to the orthodox and easily recognizable beauties of musical science. I had learned, too, the very remarkable fact, that the stem of the Usher race, all time-honoured as it was, had put forth, at no period, any enduring branch; in other words, that the entire family lay in the direct line of descent, and had always, with very trifling and very temporary variation, so lain. It was this deficiency, I considered, while running over in thought the perfect keeping of the character of the premises with the accredited character of the people, and while speculating upon the possible influence which the one, in the long lapse of centuries, might have exercised upon the other—it was this deficiency, perhaps, of collateral issue, and the consequent undeviating transmission, from sire to son, of the patrimony with the name, which had, at length, so identified the two as to merge the original title of the estate in the quaint and equivocal appellation of the "House of Usher"—an appellation which seemed to include, in the minds of the peasantry who used it, both the family and the family mansion.

I have said that the sole effect of my somewhat childish experiment—that of looking down within the tarn—had been to deepen the first singular impression. There can be no doubt that the consciousness of the rapid increase of my superstition—for why should I not so term it?—served mainly to accelerate the increase itself. Such, I have long known, is the paradoxical law of all sentiments having terror as a basis. And it might have been for this reason only, that, when I again uplifted my eyes to the house itself, from its image in the pool, there grew in my mind a strange fancy—a fancy so ridiculous, indeed, that I but mention it to show the vivid force of the sensations which oppressed me. I had so worked upon my imagination as really to believe that about the whole mansion and domain there hung an atmosphere peculiar to themselves and their immediate vicinity—an atmosphere which had no affinity with the air of heaven, but which had reeked up from the decayed trees, and the grey wall, and the silent tarn—a pestilent and mystic vapour, dull, sluggish, faintly discernible, and leaden-hued.

5   Shaking off from my spirit what must have been a dream, I scanned more narrowly the real aspect of the building. Its principal feature seemed to be that of an excessive antiquity. The discoloration of ages had been great. Minute fungi overspread the whole exterior, hanging in a fine tangled web-work from the eaves. Yet all this was apart from any extraordinary dilapidation. No portion of the masonry had fallen; and there appeared to be a wild inconsistency between its still perfect adaptation of parts, and the crumbling condition of the individual stones. In this there was much that reminded me of the specious totality of old wood-work which has rotted for long years in some neglected vault, with no disturbance from the breath of the external air. Beyond this indication of extensive decay, however, the fabric gave little token of instability. Perhaps the eye of a scrutinizing observer might have discovered a barely perceptible fissure, which, extending from the roof of the building in front, made its way down the wall in a zigzag direction, until it became lost in the sullen waters of the tarn.

Noticing these things, I rode over a short causeway to the house. A servant in waiting took my horse, and I entered the Gothic archway of the hall. A valet, of stealthy step, thence conducted me, in silence, through many dark and intricate passages in my progress to the studio of his master. Much that I encountered on the way contributed, I know not how, to heighten the vague sentiments of which I have already spoken. While the objects around me—while the carvings of the ceilings, the sombre tapestries of the walls, the ebon blackness of the floors, and the phantasmagoric armorial trophies which rattled as I strode, were but matters to which, or to such as which, I had been accustomed from my infancy—while I hesitated not to acknowledge how familiar was all this—I still wondered to find how unfamiliar were the fancies which ordinary images were stirring up. On one of the staircases, I met the physician of the family. His countenance, I thought, wore a mingled expression of low cunning and perplexity. He accosted me with trepidation and passed on. The valet now threw open a door and ushered me into the presence of his master.

The room in which I found myself was very large and lofty. The windows were long, narrow, and pointed, and at so vast a distance from the black oaken floor as to be altogether inaccessible from within. Feeble gleams of encrimsoned light made their way through the trellised panes, and served to render sufficiently distinct the more prominent objects around; the eye, however, struggled in vain to reach the remoter angles of the chamber, or the recesses of the vaulted and fretted ceiling. Dark draperies hung upon the walls. The general furniture was profuse, comfortless, antique, and tattered. Many books and musical instruments lay scattered about, but failed to give any vitality to the scene. I felt that I breathed an atmosphere of sorrow. An air of stern, deep, and irredeemable gloom hung over and pervaded all.

Upon my entrance, Usher rose from a sofa on which he had been lying at full length, and greeted me with a vivacious warmth which had much in it, I at first thought, of an overdone cordiality—of the constrained effort of the ennuye man of the world. A glance, however, at his countenance, convinced me of his perfect sincerity. We sat down; and for some moments, while he spoke not, I gazed upon him with a feeling half of pity, half of awe. Surely, man had never before so terribly altered, in so brief a period, as had Roderick Usher! It was with difficulty that I could bring myself to admit the identity of the wan being before me with the companion of my early boyhood. Yet the character of his face had been at all times remarkable. A cadaverousness of complexion; an eye large, liquid, and luminous beyond comparison; lips somewhat thin and very pallid, but of a surpassingly beautiful curve; a nose of a delicate Hebrew model, but with a breadth of nostril unusual in similar formations; a finely moulded chin, speaking, in its want of prominence, of a want of moral energy; hair of a more than web-like softness and tenuity; these features, with an inordinate expansion above the regions of the temple, made up altogether a countenance not easily to be forgotten. And now in the mere exaggeration of the prevailing character of these features, and of the expression they were wont to convey, lay so much of change that I doubted to whom I spoke. The now ghastly pallor of the skin, and the now miraculous lustre of the eye, above all things startled and even awed me. The silken hair, too, had been suffered to grow all unheeded, and as, in its wild gossamer texture, it floated rather than fell about the face, I could not, even with effort, connect its Arabesque expression with any idea of simple humanity.

In the manner of my friend I was at once struck with an incoherence—an inconsistency; and I soon found this to arise from a series of feeble and futile struggles to overcome an habitual trepidancy—an excessive nervous agitation. For something of this nature I had indeed been prepared, no less by his letter, than by reminiscences of certain boyish traits, and by conclusions deduced from his peculiar physical conformation and temperament. His action was alternately vivacious and sullen. His voice varied rapidly from a tremulous indecision (when the animal spirits seemed utterly in abeyance) to that species of energetic concision—that abrupt, weighty, unhurried, and hollow-sounding enunciation—that leaden, self-balanced and perfectly modulated guttural utterance, which may be observed in the lost drunkard, or the irreclaimable eater of opium, during the periods of his most intense excitement.

10   It was thus that he spoke of the object of my visit, of his earnest desire to see me, and of the solace he expected me to afford him. He entered, at some length, into what he conceived to be the nature of his malady. It was, he said, a constitutional and a family evil, and one for which he despaired to find a remedy—a mere nervous affection, he immediately added, which would undoubtedly soon pass off. It displayed itself in a host of unnatural sensations. Some of these, as he detailed them, interested and bewildered me; although, perhaps, the terms, and the general manner of the narration had their weight. He suffered much from a morbid acuteness of the senses; the most insipid food was alone endurable; he could wear only garments of certain texture; the odours of all flowers were oppressive; his eyes were tortured by even a faint light; and there were but peculiar sounds, and these from stringed instruments, which did not inspire him with horror.

To an anomalous species of terror I found him a bounden slave. "I shall perish," said he, "I must perish in this deplorable folly. Thus, thus, and not otherwise, shall I be lost. I dread the events of the future, not in themselves, but in their results. I shudder at the thought of any, even the most trivial, incident, which may operate upon this intolerable agitation of soul. I have, indeed, no abhorrence of danger, except in its absolute effect—in terror. In this unnerved—in this pitiable condition—I feel that the period will sooner or later arrive when I must abandon life and reason together, in some struggle with the grim phantasm, FEAR."

I learned, moreover, at intervals, and through broken and equivocal hints, another singular feature of his mental condition. He was enchained by certain superstitious impressions in regard to the dwelling which he tenanted, and whence, for many years, he had never ventured forth—in regard to an influence whose suppositious force was conveyed in terms too shadowy here to be re-stated—an influence which some peculiarities in the mere form and substance of his family mansion, had, by dint of long sufferance, he said, obtained over his spirit—an effect which the physique of the grey walls and turrets, and of the dim tarn into which they all looked down, had, at length, brought about upon the morale of his existence.

He admitted, however, although with hesitation, that much of the peculiar gloom which thus afflicted him could be traced to a more natural and far more palpable origin—to the severe and long-continued illness—indeed to the evidently approaching dissolution—of a tenderly beloved sister—his sole companion for long years—his last and only relative on earth. "Her decease," he said, with a bitterness which I can never forget, "would leave him (him the hopeless and the frail) the last of the ancient race of the Ushers." While he spoke, the lady Madeline (for so was she called) passed slowly through a remote portion of the apartment, and, without having noticed my presence, disappeared. I regarded her with an utter astonishment not unmingled with dread—and yet I found it impossible to account for such feelings. A sensation of stupor oppressed me, as my eyes followed her retreating steps. When a door, at length, closed upon her, my glance sought instinctively and eagerly the countenance of the brother—but he had buried his face in his hands, and I could only perceive that a far more than ordinary wanness had overspread the emaciated fingers through which trickled many passionate tears.

The disease of the lady Madeline had long baffled the skill of her physicians. A settled apathy, a gradual wasting away of the person, and frequent although transient affections of a partially cataleptical character, were the unusual diagnosis. Hitherto she had steadily borne up against the pressure of her malady, and had not betaken herself finally to bed; but, on the closing in of the evening of my arrival at the house, she succumbed (as her brother told me at night with inexpressible agitation) to the prostrating power of the destroyer; and I learned that the glimpse I had obtained of her person would thus probably be the last I should obtain—that the lady, at least while living, would be seen by me no more.

15   For several days ensuing, her name was unmentioned by either Usher or myself: and during this period I was busied in earnest endeavours to alleviate the melancholy of my friend. We painted and read together; or I listened, as if in a dream, to the wild improvisations of his

speaking guitar. And thus, as a closer and still closer intimacy admitted me more unre-servedly into the recesses of his spirit, the more bitterly did I perceive the futility of all attempt at cheering a mind from which darkness, as if an inherent positive quality, poured forth upon all objects of the moral and physical universe, in one unceasing radiation of gloom.

I shall ever bear about me a memory of the many solemn hours I thus spent alone with the master of the House of Usher. Yet I should fail in any attempt to convey an idea of the exact character of the studies, or of the occupations, in which he involved me, or led me the way. An excited and highly distempered ideality threw a sulphurous lustre over all. His long improvised dirges will ring for ever in my ears. Among other things, I hold painfully in mind a certain singular perversion and amplification of the wild air of the last waltz of Von Weber. From the paintings over which his elaborate fancy brooded, and which grew, touch by touch, into vagueness at which I shuddered the more thrillingly, because I shud-dered knowing not why;—from these paintings (vivid as their images now are before me) I would in vain endeavour to educe more than a small portion which should lie within the compass of merely written words. By the utter simplicity, by the nakedness of his designs, he arrested and overawed attention. If ever mortal painted an idea, that mortal was Roder-ick Usher. For me at least—in the circumstances then surrounding me—there arose out of the pure abstractions which the hypochondriac contrived to throw upon his canvas, an in-tensity of intolerable awe, no shadow of which felt I ever yet in the contemplation of the certainly glowing yet too concrete reveries of Fuseli.

One of the phantasmagoric conceptions of my friend, partaking not so rigidly of the spirit of abstraction, may be shadowed forth, although feebly, in words. A small picture presented the interior of an immensely long and rectangular vault or tunnel, with low walls, smooth, white, and without interruption or device. Certain accessory points of the design served well to convey the idea that this excavation lay at an exceeding depth below the surface of the earth. No outlet was observed in any portion of its vast extent, and no torch, or other artificial source of light was discernible; yet a flood of intense rays rolled throughout, and bathed the whole in a ghastly and inappropriate splendour.

I have just spoken of that morbid condition of the auditory nerve which rendered all music intolerable to the sufferer, with the exception of certain effects of stringed instruments. It was, perhaps, the narrow limits to which he thus confined himself upon the guitar, which gave birth, in great measure, to the fantastic character of the performances. But the fervid fa-cility of his impromptus could not be so accounted for. They must have been, and were, in the notes, as well as in the words of his wild fantasias (for he not unfrequently accompanied him-self with rhymed verbal improvisations), the result of that intense mental collectedness and concentration to which I have previously alluded as observable only in particular moments of the highest artificial excitement. The words of one of these rhapsodies I have easily remem-bered. I was, perhaps, the more forcibly impressed with it, as he gave it, because, in the under or mystic current of its meaning, I fancied that I perceived, and for the first time, a full con-sciousness on the part of Usher, of the tottering of his lofty reason upon her throne. The verses, which were entitled "The Haunted Palace," ran very nearly, if not accurately, thus:

I

In the greenest of our valleys,
By good angels tenanted,
Once a fair and stately palace—
Radiant palace—reared its head.
In the monarch Thought's dominion—
It stood there!
Never seraph spread a pinion
Over fabric half so fair.

II

Banners yellow, glorious, golden,
On its roof did float and flow;
(This—all this—was in the olden
Time long ago)
And every gentle air that dallied,
In that sweet day,
Along the ramparts plumed and pallid,
A winged odour went away.

III

Wanderers in that happy valley
Through two luminous windows saw
Spirits moving musically
To a lute's well tuned law,
Round about a throne, where sitting
(Porphyrogene!)
In state his glory well befitting,
The ruler of the realm was seen.

IV

And all with pearl and ruby glowing
Was the fair palace door,
Through which came flowing, flowing, flowing
And sparkling evermore,
A troop of Echoes whose sweet duty
Was but to sing,
In voices of surpassing beauty,
The wit and wisdom of their king.

V

But evil things, in robes of sorrow,
Assailed the monarch's high estate;
(Ah, let us mourn, for never morrow
Shall dawn upon him, desolate!)
And, round about his home, the glory
That blushed and bloomed
Is but a dim-remembered story,
Of the old time entombed.

VI

And travellers now within that valley,
Through the red-litten windows, see
Vast forms that move fantastically
To a discordant melody;
While, like a rapid ghastly river,
Through the pale door,
A hideous throng rush out forever,
And laugh—but smile no more.

I well remember that suggestions arising from this ballad, led us into a train of thought wherein there became manifest an opinion of Usher's which I mention not so much on account of its novelty (for other men° have thought thus,) as on account of the pertinacity with which he maintained it. This opinion, in its general form, was that of the sentience of all vegetable things. But, in his disordered fancy, the idea had assumed a more daring character, and trespassed, under certain conditions, upon the kingdom of inorganization. I lack words to express the full extent, or the earnest abandon of his persuasion. The belief, however, was connected (as I have previously hinted) with the gray stones of the home of his forefathers. The conditions of the sentience had been here, he imagined, fulfilled in the method of collocation of these stones—in the order of their arrangement, as well as in that of the many fungi which overspread them, and of the decayed trees which stood around—above all, in the long undisturbed endurance of this arrangement, and in its reduplication in the still waters of the tarn. Its evidence—the evidence of the sentience—was to be seen, he said, (and I here started as he spoke,) in the gradual yet certain condensation of an atmosphere of their own about the waters and the walls. The result was discoverable, he added, in that silent, yet importunate and terrible influence which for centuries had moulded the destinies of his family, and which made him what I now saw him—what he was. Such opinions need no comment, and I will make none.

Our books—the books which, for years, had formed no small portion of the mental existence of the invalid—were, as might be supposed, in strict keeping with this character of phantasm. We pored together over such works as the Ververt et Chartreuse of Gresset; the Belphegor of Machiavelli; the Heaven and Hell of Swedenborg; the Subterranean Voyage of Nicholas Klimm by Holberg; the Chiromancy of Robert Flud, of Jean D'Indagine, and of De la Chambre; the Journey into the Blue Distance of Tieck; and the City of the Sun by Campanella. One favourite volume was a small octavo edition of the Directorium Inquisitorum, by the Dominican Eymeric de Gironne; and there were passages in Pomponius Mela, about the old African Satyrs and OEgipans, over which Usher would sit dreaming for hours. His chief delight, however, was found in the perusal of an exceedingly rare and curious book in quarto Gothic—the manual of a forgotten church—the *Vigiliae Mortuorum Secundum Chorum Ecclesiae Maguntinae.*°

I could not help thinking of the wild ritual of this work, and of its probable influence upon the hypochondriac, when, one evening, having informed me abruptly that the lady Madeline was no more, he stated his intention of preserving her corpse for a fortnight, (previously to its final interment), in one of the numerous vaults within the main walls of the building. The worldly reason, however, assigned for this singular proceeding, was one which I did not feel at liberty to dispute. The brother had been led to his resolution (so he told me) by consideration of the unusual character of the malady of the deceased, of certain obtrusive and eager inquiries on the part of her medical men, and of the remote and exposed situation of the burial-ground of the family. I will not deny that when I called to mind the sinister countenance of the person whom I met upon the staircase, on the day of my arrival at the house, I had no desire to oppose what I regarded as at best but a harmless, and by no means an unnatural, precaution.

At the request of Usher, I personally aided him in the arrangements for the temporary entombment. The body having been encoffined, we two alone bore it to its rest. The vault in

20

°Watson, Dr. Percival, Spallanzani, and especially the Bishop of Landaff.—See "Chemical Essays," vol. 5. [This is Poe's own note. He is citing these scientific and historical writers as support for his assertions.]

°*Our books . . . Maguntinae:* Poe's speaker characterizes the works of the writers contained in the paragraph as being "in keeping with this character of phantasm." This judgment is right; the works are about mysticism, utopias, travels to fantastic underworld countries, palmistry, and forest deities such as Pan. The concluding reference is to a 1500 publication describing ceremonies and prayers for the dead.

which we placed it (and which had been so long unopened that our torches, half smothered in its oppressive atmosphere, gave us little opportunity for investigation) was small, damp, and entirely without means of admission for light; lying, at great depth, immediately beneath that portion of the building in which was my own sleeping apartment. It had been used, apparently, in remote feudal times, for the worst purposes of a donjon-keep, and, in later days, as a place of deposit for powder, or some other highly combustible substance, as a portion of its floor, and the whole interior of a long archway through which we reached it, were carefully sheathed with copper. The door, of massive iron, had been, also, similarly protected. Its immense weight caused an unusually sharp grating sound, as it moved upon its hinges.

Having deposited our mournful burden upon tressels within this region of horror, we partially turned aside the yet unscrewed lid of the coffin, and looked upon the face of the tenant. A striking similitude between the brother and sister now first arrested my attention; and Usher, divining, perhaps, my thoughts, murmured out some few words from which I learned that the deceased and himself had been twins, and that sympathies of a scarcely intelligible nature had always existed between them. Our glances, however, rested not long upon the dead—for we could not regard her unawed. The disease which had thus entombed the lady in the maturity of youth, had left, as usual in all maladies of a strictly cataleptical character, the mockery of a faint blush upon the bosom and the face, and that suspiciously lingering smile upon the lip which is so terrible in death. We replaced and screwed down the lid, and, having secured the door of iron, made our way, with toil, into the scarcely less gloomy apartments of the upper portion of the house.

And now, some days of bitter grief having elapsed, an observable change came over the features of the mental disorder of my friend. His ordinary manner had vanished. His ordinary occupations were neglected or forgotten. He roamed from chamber to chamber with hurried, unequal, and objectless step. The pallor of his countenance had assumed, if possible, a more ghastly hue—but the luminousness of his eye had utterly gone out. The once occasional huskiness of his tone was heard no more; and a tremulous quaver, as if of extreme terror, habitually characterized his utterance. There were times, indeed, when I thought his unceasingly agitated mind was labouring with some oppressive secret, to divulge which he struggled for the necessary courage. At times, again, I was obliged to resolve all into the mere inexplicable vagaries of madness, for I beheld him gazing upon vacancy for long hours, in an attitude of the profoundest attention, as if listening to some imaginary sound. It was no wonder that his condition terrified—that it infected me. I felt creeping upon me, by slow yet certain degrees, the wild influences of his own fantastic yet impressive superstitions.

25   It was, especially, upon retiring to bed late in the night of the seventh or eighth day after the placing of the lady Madeline within the donjon, that I experienced the full power of such feelings. Sleep came not near my couch—while the hours waned and waned away. I struggled to reason off the nervousness which had dominion over me. I endeavoured to believe that much, if not all of what I felt, was due to the bewildering influence of the gloomy furniture of the room—of the dark and tattered draperies, which, tortured into motion by the breath of a rising tempest, swayed fitfully to and fro upon the walls, and rustled uneasily about the decorations of the bed. But my efforts were fruitless. An irrepressible tremor gradually pervaded my frame; and, at length, there sat upon my very heart an incubus of utterly causeless alarm. Shaking this off with a gasp and a struggle, I uplifted myself upon the pillows, and, peering earnestly within the intense darkness of the chamber, hearkened—I know not why, except that an instinctive spirit prompted me—to certain low and indefinite sounds which came, through the pauses of the storm, at long intervals, I knew not whence. Overpowered by an intense sentiment of horror, unaccountable yet unendurable, I threw on my clothes with haste (for I felt that I should sleep no

more during the night,) and endeavoured to arouse myself from the pitiable condition into which I had fallen, by pacing rapidly to and fro through the apartment.

I had taken but few turns in this manner, when a light step on an adjoining staircase arrested my attention. I presently recognized it as that of Usher. In an instant afterwards he rapped, with a gentle touch, at my door, and entered, bearing a lamp. His countenance was, as usual, cadaverously wan—but, moreover, there was a species of mad hilarity in his eyes—an evidently restrained hysteria in his whole demeanor. His air appalled me—but anything was preferable to the solitude which I had so long endured, and I even welcomed his presence as a relief.

"And you have not seen it?" he said abruptly, after having stared about him for some moments in silence—"you have not then seen it?—but, stay! you shall." Thus speaking, and having carefully shaded his lamp, he hurried to one of the casements, and threw it freely open to the storm.

The impetuous fury of the entering gust nearly lifted us from our feet. It was, indeed, a tempestuous yet sternly beautiful night, and one wildly singular in its terror and its beauty. A whirlwind had apparently collected its force in our vicinity; for there were frequent and violent alterations in the direction of the wind; and the exceeding density of the clouds (which hung so low as to press upon the turrets of the house) did not prevent our perceiving the lifelike velocity with which they flew careering from all points against each other, without passing away into the distance. I say that even their exceeding density did not prevent our perceiving this—yet we had no glimpse of the moon or stars—nor was there any flashing forth of the lightning. But the under surfaces of the huge masses of agitated vapor, as well as all terrestrial objects immediately around us, were glowing in the unnatural light of a faintly luminous and distinctly visible gaseous exhalation which hung about and enshrouded the mansion.

"You must not—you shall not behold this!" said I, shudderingly, to Usher, as I led him, with a gentle violence, from the window to a seat. "These appearances, which bewilder you, are merely electrical phenomena not uncommon—or it may be that they have their ghastly origin in the rank miasma of the tarn. Let us close this casement;—the air is chilling and dangerous to your frame. Here is one of your favourite romances. I will read, and you shall listen;—and so we will pass away this terrible night together."

The antique volume which I had taken up was the "Mad Trist" of Sir Launcelot   30 Canning;° but I had called it a favourite of Usher's more in sad jest than in earnest; for, in truth, there is little in its uncouth and unimaginative prolixity which could have had interest for the lofty and spiritual ideality of my friend. It was, however, the only book immediately at hand; and I indulged a vague hope that the excitement which now agitated the hypochondriac, might find relief (for the history of mental disorder is full of similar anomalies) even in the extremeness of the folly which I should read. Could I have judged, indeed, by the wild overstrained air of vivacity with which he hearkened, or apparently hearkened, to the words of the tale, I might well have congratulated myself upon the success of my design.

I had arrived at that well-known portion of the story where Ethelred, the hero of the Trist, having sought in vain for peaceable admission into the dwelling of the hermit, proceeds to make good an entrance by force. Here, it will be remembered, the words of the narrative run thus:

"And Ethelred, who was by nature of a doughty heart, and who was now mighty withal, on account of the powerfulness of the wine which he had drunken, waited no longer to hold

---

°The "Mad Trist" of Sir Launcelot Canning: There was no Sir Launcelot Canning, unlike the authors cited in paragraph 27. The "passages" from "Canning" read by the narrator to Usher were written by Poe himself.

parley with the hermit, who, in sooth, was of an obstinate and maliceful turn, but, feeling the rain upon his shoulders, and fearing the rising of the tempest, uplifted his mace outright, and, with blows, made quickly room in the plankings of the door for his gauntleted hand; and now pulling therewith sturdily, he so cracked, and ripped, and tore all asunder, that the noise of the dry and hollow-sounding wood alarmed and reverberated throughout the forest."

At the termination of this sentence I started, and for a moment, paused; for it appeared to me (although I at once concluded that my excited fancy had deceived me)—it appeared to me that, from some very remote portion of the mansion, there came, indistinctly, to my ears, what might have been, in its exact similarity of character, the echo (but a stifled and dull one certainly) of the very cracking and ripping sound which Sir Launcelot had so particularly described. It was, beyond doubt, the coincidence alone which had arrested my attention; for, amid the rattling of the sashes of the casements, and the ordinary commingled noises of the still increasing storm, the sound, in itself, had nothing, surely, which should have interested or disturbed me. I continued the story:

"But the good champion Ethelred, now entering within the door, was sore enraged and amazed to perceive no signal of the maliceful hermit; but, in the stead thereof, a dragon of a scaly and prodigious demeanour, and of a fiery tongue, which sate in guard before a palace of gold, with a floor of silver; and upon the wall there hung a shield of shining brass with this legend enwritten—

> Who entereth herein, a conqueror hath bin;
> Who slayeth the dragon, the shield he shall win;

And Ethelred uplifted his mace, and struck upon the head of the dragon, which fell before him, and gave up his pesty breath, with a shriek so horrid and harsh, and withal so piercing, that Ethelred had fain to close his ears with his hands against the dreadful noise of it, the like whereof was never before heard."

Here again I paused abruptly, and now with a feeling of wild amazement—for there could be no doubt whatever that, in this instance, I did actually hear (although from what direction it proceeded I found it impossible to say) a low and apparently distant, but harsh, protracted, and most unusual screaming or grating sound—the exact counterpart of what my fancy had already conjured up for the dragon's unnatural shriek as described by the romancer.

Oppressed, as I certainly was, upon the occurrence of the second and most extraordinary coincidence, by a thousand conflicting sensations, in which wonder and extreme terror were predominant, I still retained sufficient presence of mind to avoid exciting, by any observation, the sensitive nervousness of my companion. I was by no means certain that he had noticed the sounds in question; although, assuredly, a strange alteration had, during the last few minutes, taken place in his demeanor. From a position fronting my own, he had gradually brought round his chair, so as to sit with his face to the door of the chamber; and thus I could but partially perceive his features, although I saw that his lips trembled as if he were murmuring inaudibly. His head had dropped upon his breast—yet I knew that he was not asleep, from the wide and rigid opening of the eye as I caught a glance of it in profile. The motion of his body, too, was at variance with this idea—for he rocked from side to side with a gentle yet constant and uniform sway. Having rapidly taken notice of all this, I resumed the narrative of Sir Launcelot, which thus proceeded:

"And now, the champion, having escaped from the terrible fury of the dragon, bethinking himself of the brazen shield, and of the breaking up of the enchantment which was upon it, removed the carcass from out of the way before him, and approached valorously over the silver pavement of the castle to where the shield was upon the wall; which in sooth tarried not for his full coming, but fell down at his feet upon the silver floor, with a mighty great and terrible ringing sound."

No sooner had these syllables passed my lips, than—as if a shield of brass had indeed, at the moment, fallen heavily upon a floor of silver—I became aware of a distinct, hollow, metallic, and clangorous, yet apparently muffled reverberation. Completely unnerved, I leaped to my feet; but the measured rocking movement of Usher was undisturbed. I rushed to the chair in which he sat. His eyes were bent fixedly before him, and throughout his whole countenance there reigned a stony rigidity. But, as I placed my hand upon his shoulder, there came a strong shudder over his whole person; a sickly smile quivered about his lips; and I saw that he spoke in a low, hurried, and gibbering murmur, as if unconscious of my presence. Bending closely over him, I at length drank in the hideous import of his words.

"Not hear it?—yes, I hear it, and have heard it. Long—long—long—many minutes, many hours, many days, have I heard it—yet I dared not—oh, pity me, miserable wretch that I am!—I dared not—I dared not speak! We have put her living in the tomb! Said I not that my senses were acute? I now tell you that I heard her first feeble movements in the hollow coffin. I heard them—many, many days ago—yet I dared not—I dared not speak! And now—to-night—Ethelred—ha! ha!—the breaking of the hermit's door, and the death-cry of the dragon, and the clangour of the shield!—say, rather, the rending of her coffin, and the grating of the iron hinges of her prison, and her struggles within the coppered archway of the vault! Oh whither shall I fly? Will she not be here anon? Is she not hurrying to upbraid me for my haste? Have I not heard her footsteps on the stair? Do I not distinguish that heavy and horrible beating of her heart? Madman!" here he sprang furiously to his feet, and shrieked out his syllables, as if in the effort he were giving up his soul—"Madman! I tell you that she now stands without the door!"

As if in the superhuman energy of his utterance there had been found the potency of a spell—the huge antique panels to which the speaker pointed, threw slowly back, upon the instant, their ponderous and ebony jaws. It was the work of the rushing gust—but then without those doors there DID stand the lofty and enshrouded figure of the lady Madeline of Usher. There was blood upon her white robes, and the evidence of some bitter struggle upon every portion of her emaciated frame. For a moment she remained trembling and reeling to and fro upon the threshold,—then, with a low moaning cry, fell heavily inward upon the person of her brother, and in her violent and now final death-agonies, bore him to the floor a corpse, and a victim to the terrors he had anticipated.

From that chamber, and from that mansion, I fled aghast. The storm was still abroad in all its wrath as I found myself crossing the old causeway. Suddenly there shot along the path a wild light, and I turned to see whence a gleam so unusual could have issued; for the vast house and its shadows were alone behind me. The radiance was that of the full, setting, and blood-red moon which now shone vividly through that once barely discernible fissure of which I have before spoken as extending from the roof of the building, in a zigzag direction, to the base. While I gazed, this fissure rapidly widened—there came a fierce breath of the whirlwind—the entire orb of the satellite burst at once upon my sight—my brain reeled as I saw the mighty walls rushing asunder—there was a long tumultuous shouting sound like the voice of a thousand waters—and the deep and dank tarn at my feet closed sullenly and silently over the fragments of the "House of Usher."

QUESTIONS

1. Consider Poe's use of setting in "The Fall of the House of Usher." Which details (e.g., landscape, weather, descriptive details) seem realistic? What is the condition of the house, both outside and inside? What is the relationship between the house and the Usher family?

2. Should Poe's description be taken literally or symbolically, or both? Explain.

3. What is the relationship between the narrator and Roderick Usher? Why is the narrator not named? Is he as involved in the events of the story as the unnamed narrator of "The Black Cat" or the named narrator of "The Cask of Amontillado"?

4. In what ways is Madeline a double of Usher himself? Why is Usher unwilling or unable to rescue her from the burial vault? What is the meaning of her falling on him at the end and bringing about his death?

5. Why is Usher's poem included as a part of the story? How does the poem explain the condition of the Usher household?

 # The Masque of the Red Death (1842)

The "Red Death" had long devastated the country. No pestilence had ever been so fatal, or so hideous. Blood was its Avatar° and its seal—the redness and the horror of blood. There were sharp pains, and sudden dizziness, and then profuse bleeding at the pores, with dissolution. The scarlet stains upon the body and especially upon the face of the victim, were the pest ban which shut him out from the aid and from the sympathy of his fellow-men. And the whole seizure, progress, and termination of the disease, were the incidents of half an hour.

But the Prince Prospero° was happy and dauntless and sagacious. When his dominions were half depopulated, he summoned to his presence a thousand hale and light-hearted friends from among the knights and dames of his court, and with these retired to the deep seclusion of one of his castellated abbeys. This was an extensive and magnificent structure, the creation of the prince's own eccentric yet august taste. A strong and lofty wall girdled it in. This wall had gates of iron. The courtiers, having entered, brought furnaces and massy hammers and welded the bolts. They resolved to leave means neither of ingress nor egress to the sudden impulses of despair or of frenzy from within. The abbey was amply provisioned. With such precautions the courtiers might bid defiance to contagion. The external world could take care of itself. In the meantime it was folly to grieve, or to think. The prince had provided all the appliances of pleasure. There were buffoons, there were improvisatori, there were ballet-dancers, there were musicians, there was Beauty, there was wine. All these and security were within. Without was the "Red Death."

It was toward the close of the fifth or sixth month of his seclusion, and while the pestilence raged most furiously abroad, that the Prince Prospero entertained his thousand friends at a masked ball of the most unusual magnificence.

It was a voluptuous scene, that masquerade. But first let me tell of the rooms in which it was held. There were seven—an imperial suite. In many palaces, however, such suites form a long and straight vista, while the folding doors slide back nearly to the walls on either hand, so that the view of the whole extent is scarcely impeded. Here the case was very different; as might have been expected from the duke's love of the *bizarre*. The apartments were so irregularly disposed that the vision embraced but little more than one at a time. There was a sharp turn at every twenty or thirty yards, and at each turn a novel effect. To the right and left, in the middle of each wall, a tall and narrow Gothic window looked out upon a closed corridor which pursued the windings of the suite. These windows were of stained glass whose color varied in accordance with the prevailing hue of the decorations of the chamber into which it opened. That at the eastern extremity was hung, for example, in blue—and vividly blue were its windows. The second chamber was purple in its ornaments and tapestries, and here the panes were purple. The third was green throughout, and so were the casements. The fourth was furnished and lighted with orange—the fifth with

°*Avatar:* model, incarnation, manifestation.
°*Prospero:* that is, "prosperous." In Shakespeare's play *The Tempest*, the principal character is Prospero.

white—the sixth with violet. The seventh apartment was closely shrouded in black velvet tapestries that hung all over the ceiling and down the walls, falling in heavy folds upon a carpet of the same material and hue. But in this chamber only, the color of the windows failed to correspond with the decorations. The panes here were scarlet—a deep blood color. Now in no one of the seven apartments was there any lamp or candelabrum, amid the profusion of golden ornaments that lay scattered to and fro or depended from the roof. There was no light of any kind emanating from lamp or candle within the suite of chambers. But in the corridors that followed the suite, there stood, opposite to each window, a heavy tripod, bearing a brazier of fire, that projected its rays through the tinted glass and so glaringly illumined the room. And thus were produced a multitude of gaudy and fantastic appearances. But in the western or black chamber the effect of the fire-light that streamed upon the dark hangings through the blood-tinted panes was ghastly in the extreme, and produced so wild a look upon the countenances of those who entered, that there were few of the company bold enough to set foot within its precincts at all.

It was in this apartment, also, that there stood against the western wall, a gigantic clock   5 of ebony. Its pendulum swung to and fro with a dull, heavy, monotonous clang; and when the minute-hand made the circuit of the face, and the hour was to be stricken, there came from the brazen lungs of the clock a sound which was clear and loud and deep and exceedingly musical, but of so peculiar a note and emphasis that, at each lapse of an hour, the musicians of the orchestra were constrained to pause, momentarily, in their performance, to hearken to the sound; and thus the waltzers perforce ceased their evolutions; and there was a brief disconcert of the whole gay company; and, while the chimes of the clock yet rang, it was observed that the giddiest grew pale, and the more aged and sedate passed their hands over their brows as if in confused revery or meditation. But when the echoes had fully ceased, a light laughter at once pervaded the assembly; the musicians looked at each other and smiled as if at their own nervousness and folly, and made whispering vows, each to the other, that the next chiming of the clock should produce in them no similar emotion; and then, after the lapse of sixty minutes (which embrace three thousand and six hundred seconds of the Time that flies), there came yet another chiming of the clock, and then were the same disconcert and tremulousness and meditation as before.

But, in spite of these things, it was a gay and magnificent revel. The tastes of the duke were peculiar. He had a fine eye for colors and effects. He disregarded the *decora*° of mere fashion. His plans were bold and fiery, and his conceptions glowed with barbaric lustre. There are some who would have thought him mad. His followers felt that he was not. It was necessary to hear and see and touch him to be *sure* that he was not.

He had directed, in great part, the movable embellishments of the seven chambers, upon occasion of this great fête,° and it was his own guiding taste which had given character to the masqueraders. Be sure they were grotesque. There were much glare and glitter and piquancy and phantasm—much of what has been since seen in "Hernani."° There were arabesque figures with unsuited limbs and appointments. There were delirious fancies such as the madman fashions. There were much of the beautiful, much of the wanton, much of the *bizarre*, something of the terrible, and not a little of that which might have excited disgust. To and fro in the seven chambers there stalked, in fact, a multitude of dreams. And these—the dreams—writhed in and about, taking hue from the rooms, and causing the wild music of the orchestra to seem as the echo of their steps. And, anon, there strikes the ebony clock which stands in the hall of the velvet. And then, for a moment, all is still, and all is silent save the voice of the clock. The dreams are stiff-frozen as they stand. But the

---

°*decora:* schemes, patterns.
°*fête:* party, revel.
°*Hernani:* tragedy by Victor Hugo (1802–1885), featuring elaborate scenes and costumes.

echoes of the chime die away—they have endured but an instant—and a light, half-subdued laughter floats after them as they depart. And now again the music swells, and the dreams live, and writhe to and fro more merrily than ever, taking hue from the many-tinted windows through which stream the rays from the tripods. But to the chamber which lies most westwardly of the seven there are now none of the maskers who venture; for the night is waning away; and there flows a ruddier light through the blood-colored panes; and the blackness of the sable drapery appalls; and to him whose foot falls upon the sable carpet, there comes from the near clock of ebony a muffled peal more solemnly emphatic than any which reaches *their* ears who indulge in the more remote gaieties of the other apartments.

But these other apartments were densely crowded, and in them beat feverishly the heart of life. And the revel went whirlingly on, until at length there commenced the sounding of midnight upon the clock. And then the music ceased, as I have told; and the evolutions of the waltzers were quieted; and there was an uneasy cessation of all things as before. But now there were twelve strokes to be sounded by the bell of the clock; and thus it happened, perhaps that more of thought crept, with more of time, into the meditations of the thoughtful among those who revelled. And thus, too, it happened, perhaps, that before the last echoes of the last chime had utterly sunk into silence, there were many individuals in the crowd who had found leisure to become aware of the presence of a masked figure which had arrested the attention of no single individual before. And the rumor of this new presence having spread itself whisperingly around, there arose at length from the whole company a buzz, or murmur, expressive of disapprobation and surprise—then, finally, of terror, of horror, and of disgust.

In an assembly of phantasms such as I have painted, it may well be supposed that no ordinary appearance could have excited such sensation. In truth the masquerade license of the night was nearly unlimited; but the figure in question had out-Heroded Herod,° and gone beyond the bounds of even the prince's indefinite decorum. There are chords in the hearts of the most reckless which cannot be touched without emotion. Even with the utterly lost, to whom life and death are equally jests, there are matters of which no jest can be made. The whole company, indeed, seemed now deeply to feel that in the costume and bearing of the stranger neither wit nor propriety existed. The figure was tall and gaunt, and shrouded from head to foot in the habiliments of the grave. The mask which concealed the visage was made so nearly to resemble the countenance of a stiffened corpse that the closest scrutiny must have had difficulty in detecting the cheat. And yet all this might have been endured, if not approved, by the mad revellers around. But the mummer had gone so far as to assume the type of the Red Death. His vesture was dabbled in *blood*—and his broad brow, with all the features of the face, was besprinkled with the scarlet horror.

10   When the eyes of Prince Prospero fell upon this spectral image (which, with a slow and solemn movement, as if more fully to sustain its *rôle*, stalked to and fro among the waltzers) he was seen to be convulsed, in the first moment with a strong shudder either of terror or distaste; but, in the next, his brow reddened with rage.

"Who dares"—he demanded hoarsely of the courtiers who stood near him—"who dares insult us with this blasphemous mockery? Seize him and unmask him—that we may know whom we have to hang, at sunrise, from the battlements!"

It was in the eastern or blue chamber in which stood the Prince Prospero as he uttered these words. They rang throughout the seven rooms loudly and clearly, for the prince was a bold and robust man, and the music had become hushed at the waving of his hand.

It was in the blue room where stood the prince, with a group of pale courtiers by his side. At first, as he spoke, there was a slight rushing movement of this group in the direction of the intruder, who, at the moment was also near at hand, and now, with deliberate and stately step, made closer approach to the speaker. But from a certain nameless awe with which the

---

°*out-Heroded Herod:* quoted from Shakespeare's *Hamlet*, act 3, scene 2, line 13, in reference to extreme overacting.

mad assumptions of the mummer had inspired the whole party, there were found none who put forth hand to seize him; so that, unimpeded, he passed within a yard of the prince's person; and, while the vast assembly, as if with one impulse, shrank from the centres of the rooms to the walls, he made his way uninterruptedly, but with the same solemn and measured step which had distinguished him from the first, through the blue chamber to the purple—through the purple to the green—through the green to the orange—through this again to the white—and even thence to the violet, ere a decided movement had been made to arrest him. It was then, however, that the Prince Prospero, maddening with rage and the shame of his own momentary cowardice, rushed hurriedly through the six chambers, while none followed him on account of a deadly terror that had seized upon all. He bore aloft a drawn dagger, and had approached, in rapid impetuosity, to within three or four feet of the retreating figure, when the latter, having attained the extremity of the velvet apartment, turned suddenly and confronted his pursuer. There was a sharp cry—and the dagger dropped gleaming upon the sable carpet, upon which, instantly afterward, fell prostrate in death the Prince Prospero. Then, summoning the wild courage of despair, a throng of the revellers at once threw themselves into the black apartment, and, seizing the mummer, whose tall figure stood erect and motionless within the shadow of the ebony clock, gasped in unutterable horror at finding the grave cerements and corpse-like mask, which they handled with so violent a rudeness, untenanted by any tangible form.

And now was acknowledged the presence of the Red Death. He had come like a thief in the night.° And one by one dropped the revellers in the blood-bedewed halls of their revel, and died each in the despairing posture of his fall. And the life of the ebony clock went out with that of the last of the gay. And the flames of the tripods expired. And Darkness and Decay and the Red Death held illimitable dominion over all.

QUESTIONS

1. What is happening throughout the country in this story? What does the Prince's reaction to these events tell us about him?
2. How do the details of number, color, and lighting help create the atmosphere and mood of the story?
3. Why do the color and window of the last room disturb the revellers? To what extent does this last room reflect the plot and ideas of the story?
4. What single object is located in this last room? How is this object described? What effect does its sound have on the revellers? What do you think Poe is suggesting by this object and its effects?
5. How are the nobles dressed for the masquerade? Why is the "masked figure" remarkable? How does Prospero react to him?

The Black Cat (1843)

For the most wild, yet most homely narrative which I am about to pen, I neither expect nor solicit belief. Mad indeed would I be to expect it, in a case where my very senses reject their own evidence. Yet, mad am I not—and very surely do I not dream. But to-morrow I die, and to-day I would unburden my soul. My immediate purpose is to place before the world, plainly, succinctly, and without comment, a series of mere household events. In their consequences, these events have terrified—have tortured—have destroyed me. Yet I will not

---

°*thief in the night:* 2 Peter 3:10.

attempt to expound them. To me, they have presented little but Horror—to many they will seem less terrible than *barroques*. Hereafter, perhaps, some intellect may be found which will reduce my phantasm to the common-place—some intellect more calm, more logical, and far less excitable than my own, which will perceive, in the circumstances I detail with awe, nothing more than an ordinary succession of very natural causes and effects.

From my infancy I was noted for the docility and humanity of my disposition. My tenderness of heart was even so conspicuous as to make me the jest of my companions. I was especially fond of animals, and was indulged by my parents with a great variety of pets. With these I spent most of my time, and never was so happy as when feeding and caressing them. This peculiarity of character grew with my growth, and in my manhood, I derived from it one of my principal sources of pleasure. To those who have cherished an affection for a faithful and sagacious dog, I need hardly be at the trouble of explaining the nature or the intensity of the gratification thus derivable. There is something in the unselfish and self-sacrificing love of a brute, which goes directly to the heart of him who has had frequent occasion to test the paltry friendship and gossamer fidelity of mere *Man*.

I married early, and was happy to find in my wife a disposition not uncongenial with my own. Observing my partiality for domestic pets, she lost no opportunity of procuring those of the most agreeable kind. We had birds, gold-fish, a fine dog, rabbits, a small monkey, and *a cat*.

This latter was a remarkably large and beautiful animal, entirely black, and sagacious to an astonishing degree. In speaking of his intelligence, my wife, who at heart was not a little tinctured with superstition, made frequent allusion to the ancient popular notion, which regarded all black cats as witches in disguise. Not that she was ever *serious* upon this point—and I mention the matter at all for no better reason than that it happens, just now, to be remembered.

5   Pluto°—this was the cat's name—was my favorite pet and playmate. I alone fed him, and he attended me wherever I went about the house. It was even with difficulty that I could prevent him from following me through the streets.

Our friendship lasted, in this manner, for several years, during which my general temperament and character—through the instrumentality of the Fiend Intemperance—had (I blush to confess it) experienced a radical alteration for the worse. I grew, day by day, more moody, more irritable, more regardless of the feelings of others. I suffered myself to use intemperate language to my wife. At length, I even offered her personal violence. My pets, of course, were made to feel the change in my disposition. I not only neglected, but ill-used them. For Pluto, however, I still retained sufficient regard to restrain me from maltreating him, as I made no scruple of maltreating the rabbits, the monkey, or even the dog, when by accident, or through affection, they came in my way. But my disease grew upon me—for what disease is like Alcohol!—and at length even Pluto, who was now becoming old, and consequently somewhat peevish—even Pluto began to experience the effects of my ill temper.

One night, returning home, much intoxicated, from one of my haunts about town, I fancied that the cat avoided my presence. I seized him; when, in his fright at my violence, he inflicted a slight wound upon my hand with his teeth. The fury of a demon instantly possessed me. I knew myself no longer. My original soul seemed, at once, to take its flight from my body and a more than fiendish malevolence, gin-nurtured, thrilled every fibre of my frame. I took from my waistcoat-pocket a pen-knife, opened it, grasped the poor beast by the throat, and deliberately cut one of its eyes from the socket! I blush, I burn, I shudder, while I pen the damnable atrocity.

°*Pluto:* the Roman name of Hades, the ancient God of the Underworld.

When reason returned with the morning—when I had slept off the fumes of the night's debauch—I experienced a sentiment half of horror, half of remorse, for the crime of which I had been guilty; but it was, at best, a feeble and equivocal feeling, and the soul remained untouched. I again plunged into excess, and soon drowned in wine all memory of the deed.

In the meantime the cat slowly recovered. The socket of the lost eye presented, it is true, a frightful appearance, but he no longer appeared to suffer any pain. He went about the house as usual, but, as might be expected, fled in extreme terror at my approach. I had so much of my old heart left, as to be at first grieved by this evident dislike on the part of a creature which had once so loved me. But this feeling soon gave place to irritation. And then came, as if to my final and irrevocable overthrow, the spirit of PERVERSENESS. Of this spirit philosophy takes no account. Yet I am not more sure that my soul lives, than I am that perverseness is one of the primitive impulses of the human heart—one of the indivisible primary faculties, or sentiments, which give direction to the character of Man. Who has not, a hundred times, found himself committing a vile or a silly action, for no other reason than because he knows he should not? Have we not a perpetual inclination, in the teeth of our best judgment, to violate that which is *Law*, merely because we understand it to be such? This spirit of perverseness, I say, came to my final overthrow. It was this unfathomable longing of the soul *to vex itself*—to offer violence to its own nature—to do wrong for the wrong's sake only—that urged me to continue and finally to consummate the injury I had inflicted upon the unoffending brute. One morning, in cool blood, I slipped a noose about its neck and hung it to the limb of a tree;—hung it with the tears streaming from my eyes, and with the bitterest remorse at my heart;—hung it *because* I knew that it had loved me, and *because* I felt it had given me no reason of offence;—hung it *because* I knew that in so doing I was committing a sin—a deadly sin that would so jeopardize my immortal soul as to place it—if such a thing wore possible—even beyond the reach of the infinite mercy of the Most Merciful and Most Terrible God.

On the night of the day on which this cruel deed was done, I was aroused from sleep by the cry of fire. The curtains of my bed were in flames. The whole house was blazing. It was with great difficulty that my wife, a servant, and myself, made our escape from the conflagration. The destruction was complete. My entire worldly wealth was swallowed up, and I resigned myself thenceforward to despair. 10

I am above the weakness of seeking to establish a sequence of cause and effect, between the disaster and the atrocity. But I am detailing a chain of facts—and wish not to leave even a possible link imperfect. On the day succeeding the fire, I visited the ruins. The walls, with one exception, had fallen in. This exception was found in a compartment wall, not very thick, which stood about the middle of the house, and against which had rested the head of my bed. The plastering had here, in great measure, resisted the action of the fire—a fact which I attributed to its having been recently spread. About this wall a dense crowd were collected, and many persons seemed to be examining a particular portion of it with very minute and eager attention. The words "strange!" "singular!" and other similar expressions, excited my curiosity. I approached and saw, as if graven in *bas relief* upon the white surface, the figure of a gigantic *cat*. The impression was given with an accuracy truly marvellous. There was a rope about the animal's neck.

When I first beheld this apparition—for I could scarcely regard it as less—my wonder and my terror were extreme. But at length reflection came to my aid. The cat, I remembered, had been hung in a garden adjacent to the house. Upon the alarm of fire, this garden had been immediately filled by the crowd—by some one of whom the animal must have been cut from the tree and thrown, through an open window, into my chamber. This had probably been done with the view of arousing me from sleep. The falling of other walls had compressed the victim of my cruelty into the substance of the freshly-spread plaster; the lime of which, with the flames, and the *ammonia* from the carcass, had then accomplished the portraiture as I saw it.

Although I thus readily accounted to my reason, if not altogether to my conscience, for the startling fact just detailed, it did not the less fail to make a deep impression upon my fancy. For months I could not rid myself of the phantasm of the cat; and, during this period, there came back into my spirit a half-sentiment that seemed, but was not, remorse. I went so far as to regret the loss of the animal, and to look about me, among the vile haunts which I now habitually frequented, for another pet of the same species, and of somewhat similar appearance, with which to supply its place.

One night as I sat, half stupefied, in a den of more than infamy, my attention was suddenly drawn to some black object, reposing upon the head of one of the immense hogsheads of Gin, or of Rum, which constituted the chief furniture of the apartment. I had been looking steadily at the top of this hogshead for some minutes, and what now caused me surprise was the fact that I had not sooner perceived the object thereupon. I approached it, and touched it with my hand. It was a black cat—a very large one—fully as large as Pluto, and closely resembling him in every respect but one. Pluto had not a white hair upon any portion of his body; but this cat had a large, although indefinite splotch of white, covering nearly the whole region of the breast.

15   Upon my touching him, he immediately arose, purred loudly, rubbed against my hand, and appeared delighted with my notice. This, then, was the very creature of which I was in search. I at once offered to purchase it of the landlord; but this person made no claim to it—knew nothing of it—had never seen it before.

I continued my caresses, and, when I prepared to go home, the animal evinced a disposition to accompany me. I permitted it to do so; occasionally stooping and patting it as I proceeded. When it reached the house it domesticated itself at once, and became immediately a great favorite with my wife.

For my own part, I soon found a dislike to it arising within me. This was just the reverse of what I had anticipated; but—I know not how or why it was—its evident fondness for myself rather disgusted and annoyed. By slow degrees, these feelings of disgust and annoyance rose into the bitterness of hatred. I avoided the creature; a certain sense of shame, and the remembrance of my former deed of cruelty, preventing me from physically abusing it. I did not, for some weeks, strike, or otherwise violently ill use it; but gradually—very gradually—I came to look upon it with unutterable loathing, and to flee silently from its odious presence, as from the breath of a pestilence.

What added, no doubt, to my hatred of the beast, was the discovery, on the morning after I brought it home, that, like Pluto, it also had been deprived of one of its eyes. This circumstance, however, only endeared it to my wife, who, as I have already said, possessed, in a high degree, that humanity of feeling which had once been my distinguishing trait, and the source of many of my simplest and purest pleasures.

With my aversion to this cat, however, its partiality for myself seemed to increase. It followed my footsteps with a pertinacity which it would be difficult to make the reader comprehend. Whenever I sat, it would crouch beneath my chair, or spring upon my knees, covering me with its loathsome caresses. If I arose to walk it would get between my feet and thus nearly throw me down, or, fastening its long and sharp claws in my dress, clamber, in this manner, to my breast. At such times, although I longed to destroy it with a blow, I was yet withheld from so doing, partly by a memory of my former crime, but chiefly—let me confess it at once—by absolute dread of the beast.

20   This dread was not exactly a dread of physical evil—and yet I should be at a loss how otherwise to define it. I am almost ashamed to own—yes, even in this felon's cell, I am almost ashamed to own—that the terror and horror with which the animal inspired me, had been heightened by one of the merest chimaeras it would be possible to conceive. My wife had called my attention, more than once, to the character of the mark of white hair, of which I have spoken, and which constituted the sole visible difference between the strange

beast and the one I had destroyed. The reader will remember that this mark, although large, had been originally very indefinite; but, by slow degrees—degrees nearly imperceptible, and which for a long time my Reason struggled to reject as fanciful—it had, at length, assumed a rigorous distinctness of outline. It was now the representation of an object that I shudder to name—and for this, above all, I loathed, and dreaded, and would have rid myself of the monster *had I dared*—it was now, I say, the image of a hideous—of a ghastly thing—of the GALLOWS!—oh, mournful and terrible engine of Horror and of Crime—of Agony and of Death!

And now was I indeed wretched beyond the wretchedness of mere Humanity. And *a brute beast*—whose fellow I had contemptuously destroyed—*a brute beast* to work out for *me*—for me a man, fashioned in the image of the High God—so much of insufferable woe! Alas! neither by day nor by night knew I the blessing of Rest any more! During the former the creature left me no moment alone; and, in the latter, I started, hourly, from dreams of unutterable fear, to find the hot breath of *the thing* upon my face, and its vast weight—an incarnate Night-Mare that I had no power to shake off—incumbent eternally upon my *heart!*

Beneath the pressure of torments such as these, the feeble remnant of the good within me succumbed. Evil thoughts became my sole intimates—the darkest and most evil of thoughts. The moodiness of my usual temper increased to hatred of all things and of all mankind; while, from the sudden, frequent, and ungovernable outbursts of a fury to which I now blindly abandoned myself, my uncomplaining wife, alas! was the most usual and the most patient of sufferers.

One day she accompanied me, upon some household errand, into the cellar of the old building which our poverty compelled us to inhabit. The cat followed me down the steep stairs, and, nearly throwing me headlong, exasperated me to madness. Uplifting an axe, and forgetting, in my wrath, the childish dread which had hitherto stayed my hand, I aimed a blow at the animal which, of course, would have proved instantly fatal had it descended as I wished. But this blow was arrested by the hand of my wife. Goaded, by the interference, into a rage more than demoniacal, I withdrew my arm from her grasp and buried the axe in her brain. She fell dead upon the spot, without a groan.

This hideous murder accomplished, I set myself forthwith, and with entire deliberation, to the task of concealing the body. I knew that I could not remove it from the house, either by day or by night, without the risk of being observed by the neighbors. Many projects entered my mind. At one period I thought of cutting the corpse into minute fragments, and destroying them by fire. At another, I resolved to dig a grave for it in the floor of the cellar. Again, I deliberated about casting it in the well in the yard—about packing it in a box, as if merchandize, with the usual arrangements, and so getting a porter to take it from the house. Finally I hit upon what I considered a far better expedient than either of these. I determined to wall it up in the cellar—as the monks of the middle ages are recorded to have walled up their victims.

For a purpose such as this the cellar was well adapted. Its walls were loosely constructed, and had lately been plastered throughout with a rough plaster, which the dampness of the atmosphere had prevented from hardening. Moreover, in one of the walls was a projection, caused by a false chimney, or fireplace, that had been filled up, and made to resemble the red of the cellar. I made no doubt that I could readily displace the bricks at this point, insert the corpse, and wall the whole up as before, so that no eye could detect any thing suspicious. And in this calculation I was not deceived. By means of a crow-bar I easily dislodged the bricks, and, having carefully deposited the body against the inner wall, I propped it in that position, while, with little trouble, I re-laid the whole structure as it originally stood. Having procured mortar, sand, and hair, with every possible precaution, I prepared a plaster which could not be distinguished from the old, and with this I very carefully went over the new brickwork. When I had finished,

25

I felt satisfied that all was right. The wall did not present the slightest appearance of having been disturbed. The rubbish on the floor was picked up with the minutest care. I looked around triumphantly, and said to myself—"Here at least, then, my labor has not been in vain."

My next step was to look for the beast which had been the cause of so much wretchedness; for I had, at length, firmly resolved to put it to death. Had I been able to meet with it, at the moment, there could have been no doubt of its fate; but it appeared that the crafty animal had been alarmed at the violence of my previous anger, and forebore to present itself in my present mood. It is impossible to describe, or to imagine, the deep, the blissful sense of relief which the absence of the detested creature occasioned in my bosom. It did not make its appearance during the night—and thus for one night at least, since its introduction into the house, I soundly and tranquilly slept; aye, slept even with the burden of murder upon my soul!

The second and the third day passed, and still my tormentor came not. Once again I breathed as a freeman. The monster, in terror, had fled the premises forever! I should behold it no more! My happiness was supreme! The guilt of my dark deed disturbed me but little. Some few inquiries had been made, but these had been readily answered. Even a search had been instituted—but of course nothing was to be discovered. I looked upon my future felicity as secured.

Upon the fourth day of the assassination, a party of the police came, very unexpectedly, into the house, and proceeded again to make rigorous investigation of the premises. Secure, however, in the inscrutability of my place of concealment, I felt no embarrassment whatever. The officers bade me accompany them in their search. They left no nook or corner unexplored. At length, for the third or fourth time, they descended into the cellar. I quivered not in a muscle. My heart beat calmly as that of one who slumbers in innocence. I walked the cellar from end to end. I folded my arms upon my bosom, and roamed easily to and fro. The police were thoroughly satisfied and prepared to depart. The glee at my heart was too strong to be restrained. I burned to say if but one word, by way of triumph, and to render doubly sure their assurance of my guiltlessness.

"Gentlemen," I said at last, as the party ascended the steps, "I delight to have allayed your suspicions. I wish you all health, and a little more courtesy. By the bye, gentlemen, this—this is a very well constructed house." [In the rabid desire to say something easily, I scarcely knew what I uttered at all.]—"I may say an *excellently* well constructed house. These walls—are you going, gentlemen?—these walls are solidly put together;" and here, through the mere frenzy of bravado, I rapped heavily, with a cane which I held in my hand, upon that very portion of the brick-work behind which stood the corpse of the wife of my bosom.

30   But may God shield and deliver me from the fangs of the Arch-Fiend! No sooner had the reverberation of my blows sunk into silence, than I was answered by a voice from within the tomb!—by a cry, at first muffled and broken, like the sobbing of a child, and then quickly swelling into one long, loud, and continuous scream, utterly anomalous and inhuman—a howl—a wailing shriek, half of horror and half of triumph, such as might have arisen only out of hell, conjointly from the throats of the damned in their agony and of the demons that exult in the damnation.

Of my own thoughts it is folly to speak. Swooning, I staggered to the opposite wall. For one instant the party upon the stairs remained motionless, through extremity of terror and of awe. In the next, a dozen stout arms were toiling at the wall. It fell bodily. The corpse, already greatly decayed and clotted with gore, stood erect before the eyes of the spectators. Upon its head, with red extended mouth and solitary eye of fire, sat the hideous beast whose craft had seduced me into murder, and whose informing voice had consigned me to the hangman. I had walled the monster up within the tomb!

QUESTIONS

1. Does the first paragraph establish clarity or ambiguity about the narrator and the events he is about to describe? Explain.
2. What changes occur in the narrator's character? Is he sane? Are his explanations of the changes plausible and convincing? Why is the narrator not named?
3. What does the narrator, in considering what he does to Pluto, mean by "perverseness" (paragraph 9)? Why does Poe introduce the details about perverseness? In what ways should the house fire and the consequences be considered as punishment for the narrator's actions?
4. How does the second cat resemble the first? What does the gallows mark represent when it takes shape on the new cat (paragraph 20)?
5. When the narrator knocks on the wall (paragraph 20), should his action be considered a mark of arrogance or an admission of guilt? Explain.

 # The Cask of Amontillado (1846)

The thousand injuries of Fortunato I had borne as I best could; but when he ventured upon insult, I vowed revenge. You, who so well know the nature of my soul, will not suppose, however, that I gave utterance to a threat. *At length* I would be avenged; this was a point definitively settled—but the very definitiveness with which it was resolved, precluded the idea of risk. I must not only punish, but punish with impunity. A wrong is unredressed when retribution overtakes its redresser. It is equally unredressed when the avenger fails to make himself felt as such to him who has done the wrong.

It must be understood, that neither by word nor deed had I given Fortunato cause to doubt my good will. I continued, as was my wont, to smile in his face, and he did not perceive that my smile *now* was at the thought of his immolation.

He had a weak point—this Fortunato—although in other regards he was a man to be respected and even feared. He prided himself on his connoisseurship in wine. Few Italians have the true virtuoso spirit. For the most part their enthusiasm is adopted to suit the time and opportunity—to practice imposture upon the British and Austrian *millionaires*. In painting and gemmary, Fortunato, like his countrymen, was a quack—but in the matter of old wines he was sincere. In this respect I did not differ from him materially: I was skilful in the Italian vintages myself, and bought largely whenever I could.

It was about dusk, one evening during the supreme madness of the carnival season, that I encountered my friend. He accosted me with excessive warmth, for he had been drinking much. The man wore motley. He had on a tight-fitting parti-striped dress, and his head was surmounted by the conical cap and bells. I was so pleased to see him, that I thought I should never have done wringing his hand.

I said to him—"My dear Fortunato, you are luckily met. How remarkably well you are looking to-day! But I have received a pipe of what passes for Amontillado, and I have my doubts." 5

"How?" said he. "Amontillado? A pipe? Impossible! And in the middle of the carnival!"

"I have my doubts," I replied; "and I was silly enough to pay the full Amontillado price without consulting you in the matter. You were not to be found, and I was fearful of losing a bargain."

"Amontillado!"

"I have my doubts."

"Amontillado!"

"And I must satisfy them." 10

"Amontillado!"

"As you are engaged, I am on my way to Luchesi. If any one has a critical turn, it is he. He will tell me—"

"Luchesi cannot tell Amontillado from Sherry."

15   "And yet some fools will have it that his taste is a match for your own."

"Come, let us go."

"Whither?"

"To your vaults."

"My friend, no; I will not impose upon your good nature. I perceive you have an engagement. Luchesi—"

20   "I have no engagement;—come."

"My friend, no. It is not the engagement, but the severe cold with which I perceive you are afflicted. The vaults are insufferably damp. They are encrusted with nitre."

"Let us go, nevertheless. The cold is merely nothing. Amontillado! You have been imposed upon. And as for Luchesi, he cannot distinguish Sherry from Amontillado."

Thus speaking, Fortunato possessed himself of my arm. Putting on a mask of black silk, and drawing a *roquelaire*° closely about my person, I suffered him to hurry me to my palazzo.

There were no attendants at home; they had absconded to make merry in honor of the time. I had told them that I should not return until the morning, and had given them explicit orders not to stir from the house. These orders were sufficient, I well knew, to insure their immediate disappearance, one and all, as soon as my back was turned.

25   I took from their sconces two flambeaux, and giving one to Fortunato, bowed him through several suites of rooms to the archway that led into the vaults. I passed down a long and winding staircase, requesting him to be cautious as he followed. We came at length to the foot of the descent, and stood together on the damp ground of the catacombs of the Montresors.

The gait of my friend was unsteady, and the bells upon his cap jingled as he strode.

"The pipe," said he.

"It is farther on," said I; "but observe the white web-work which gleams from these cavern walls."

He turned towards me, and looked into my eyes with two filmy orbs that distilled the rheum of intoxication.

30   "Nitre?" he asked, at length.

"Nitre," I replied. "How long have you had that cough?"

"Ugh! ugh! ugh!—ugh! ugh! ugh!—ugh! ugh! ugh!—ugh! ugh! ugh!—ugh! ugh! ugh!"

My poor friend found it impossible to reply for many minutes.

"It is nothing," he said, at last.

35   "Come," I said, with decision, "we will go back; your health is precious. You are rich, respected, admired, beloved; you are happy, as once I was. You are a man to be missed. For me it is no matter. We will go back; you will be ill, and I cannot be responsible. Besides, there is Luchesi—"

"Enough," he said; "the cough is a mere nothing; it will not kill me. I shall not die of a cough."

"True—true," I replied; "and, indeed, I had no intention of alarming you unnecessarily— but you should use all proper caution. A draught of this Medoc will defend us from the damps."

Here I knocked off the neck of a bottle which I drew from a long row of its fellows that lay upon the mould.

°*roquelaire:* a type of cloak.

"Drink," I said, presenting him the wine.

He raised it to his lips with a leer. He paused and nodded to me familiarly, while his 40
bells jingled.

"I drink," he said, "to the buried that repose around us."

"And I to your long life."

He again took my arm, and we proceeded.

"These vaults," he said, "are extensive."

"The Montresors," I replied, "were a great and numerous family." 45

"I forget your arms."

"A huge human foot d'or, in a field azure; the foot crushes a serpent rampant whose fangs are imbedded in the heel."

"And the motto?"

"*Nemo me impune lacessit.*"°

"Good!" he said. 50

The wine sparkled in his eyes and the bells jingled. My own fancy grew warm with the Medoc. We had passed through walls of piled bones, with casks and puncheons intermingling, into the inmost recesses of the catacombs. I paused again, and this time I made bold to seize Fortunato by an arm above the elbow.

"The nitre!" I said: "see, it increases. It hangs like moss upon the vaults. We are below the river's bed. The drops of moisture trickle among the bones. Come, we will go back ere it is too late. Your cough—"

"It is nothing," he said; "let us go on. But first, another draught of the Medoc."

I broke and reached him a flagon of De Grave. He emptied it at a breath. His eyes flashed with a fierce light. He laughed and threw the bottle upwards with a gesticulation I did not understand.

I looked at him in surprise. He repeated the movement—a grotesque one. 55

"You do not comprehend?" he said.

"Not I," I replied.

"Then you are not of the brotherhood."

"How?"

"You are not of the masons." 60

"Yes, yes," I said, "yes, yes."

"You? Impossible! A mason?"

"A mason," I replied.

"A sign," he said.

"It is this," I answered, producing a trowel from beneath the folds of my *roquelaire*. 65

"You jest," he exclaimed, recoiling a few paces. "But let us proceed to the Amontillado."

"Be it so," I said, replacing the tool beneath the cloak, and again offering him my arm. He leaned upon it heavily. We continued our route in search of the Amontillado. We passed through a range of low arches, descended, passed on, and descending again, arrived at a deep crypt, in which the foulness of the air caused our flambeaux rather to glow than flame.

At the most remote end of the crypt there appeared another less spacious. Its walls had been lined with human remains, piled to the vault overhead, in the fashion of the great catacombs of Paris. Three sides of this interior crypt were still ornamented in this manner. From the fourth the bones had been thrown down, and lay promiscuously upon the earth, forming at one point a mound of some size. Within the wall thus exposed by the displacing of the bones, we perceived a still interior recess, in depth about four feet, in width three, in height six or seven. It seemed to have been constructed for no especial use in itself, but

---

°*Nemo me impune lacessit:* No one attacks me with impunity.

formed merely the interval between two of the colossal supports of the roof of the catacombs, and was backed by one of their circumscribing walls of solid granite.

It was in vain that Fortunato, uplifting his dull torch, endeavored to pry into the depths of the recess. Its termination the feeble light did not enable us to see.

70 "Proceed," I said; "herein is the Amontillado. As for Luchesi—"

"He is an ignoramus," interrupted my friend, as he stepped unsteadily forward, while I followed immediately at his heels. In an instant he had reached the extremity of the niche, and finding his progress arrested by the rock, stood stupidly bewildered. A moment more and I had fettered him to the granite. In its surface were two iron staples, distant from each other about two feet, horizontally. From one of these depended a short chain, from the other a padlock. Throwing the links about his waist, it was but the work of a few seconds to secure it. He was too much astounded to resist. Withdrawing the key I stepped back from the recess.

"Pass your hand," I said, "over the wall; you cannot help feeling the nitre. Indeed it is *very damp. Once more let me implore* you to return. No? Then I must positively leave you. But I must first render you all the little attentions in my power."

"The Amontillado!" ejaculated my friend, not yet recovered from his astonishment.

"True," I replied; "the Amontillado."

75 As I said these words I busied myself among the pile of bones of which I have before spoken. Throwing them aside, I soon uncovered a quantity of building stone and mortar. With these materials and with the aid of my trowel, I began vigorously to wall up the entrance of the niche.

I had scarcely laid the first tier of my masonry when I discovered that the intoxication of Fortunato had in a great measure worn off. The earliest indication I had of this was a low moaning cry from the depth of the recess. It was *not* the cry of a drunken man. There was then a long and obstinate silence. I laid the second tier, and the third, and the fourth; and then I heard the furious vibrations of the chain. The noise lasted for several minutes, during which, that I might hearken to it with the more satisfaction, I ceased my labors and sat down upon the bones. When at last the clanking subsided, I resumed the trowel, and finished without interruption the fifth, the sixth, and the seventh tier. The wall was now nearly upon a level with my breast. I again paused, and holding the flambeaux over the masonwork, threw a few feeble rays upon the figure within.

A succession of loud and shrill screams, bursting suddenly from the throat of the chained form, seemed to thrust me violently back. For a brief moment I hesitated—I trembled. Unsheathing my rapier, I began to grope with it about the recess: but the thought of an instant reassured me. I placed my hand upon the solid fabric of the catacombs, and felt satisfied. I reapproached the wall. I replied to the yells of him who clamored. I re-echoed—I aided—I surpassed them in volume and in strength. I did this, and the clamorer grew still.

It was now midnight, and my task was drawing to a close. I had completed the eighth, the ninth, and the tenth tier. I had finished a portion of the last and the eleventh; there remained but a single stone to be fitted and plastered in. I struggled with its weight; I placed it partially in its destined position. But now there came from out the niche a low laugh that erected the hairs upon my head. It was succeeded by a sad voice, which I had difficulty in recognizing as that of the noble Fortunato. The voice said—

"Ha! ha! ha!—he! he!—a very good joke indeed—an excellent jest. We will have many a rich laugh about it at the palazzo—he! he! he!—over our wine—he! he! he!"

80 "The Amontillado!" I said.

"He! he! he!—he! he! he!—yes, the Amontillado. But is it not getting late? Will not they be awaiting us at the palazzo, the Lady Fortunato and the rest? Let us be gone."

"Yes," I said, "let us be gone."

"For the love of God, Montresor!"

"Yes," I said, "for the love of God!"

But to these words I hearkened in vain for a reply. I grew impatient. I called aloud— 85
"Fortunato!"

No answer. I called again—

"Fortunato!"

No answer still. I thrust a torch through the remaining aperture and let it fall within. There came forth in return only a jingling of the bells. My heart grew sick—on account of the dampness of the catacombs. I hastened to make an end of my labor. I forced the last stone into its position; I plastered it up. Against the new masonry I re-erected the old rampart of bones. For the half of a century no mortal has disturbed them. *In pace requiescat!*°

QUESTIONS

1. In what ways is this story typical of Poe's theory of the brief prose tale? How would you describe the effect or effects of the story?

2. Describe Poe's use of setting in "The Cask of Amontillado" (e.g., the cap and bells, Fortunato's motley clothing, the interior recess in which Fortunato is pinioned, etc.).

3. To whom is Montresor, the narrator speaking? What is the purpose of his saying "May he rest in peace" at the story's end? Why is the nature of Fortunato's insult against Montresor not explained in detail?

4. What do you learn about Montresor from his description of revenge and from his family's coat of arms?

5. How does Montresor manipulate Fortunato so that Fortunato seems to be the originator of the trip to examine the Amontillado? Who is Luchesi? What does Fortunato think of him?

Edited Selections from Criticism of Poe's Stories

The following selections are intended to supply details and ideas for essays on Poe's stories. For a selective bibliography, consult the *Bibliographical Sources* section above (pp. 497–98), which may be augmented with your college library research facilities and the most recent volumes of the *MLA International Bibliography* available in your library's reference room. In the following selections the bracketed page numbers refer to the original pagination of the sources included here. Footnotes in the sources have been deleted.

1. Poe's Irony[3]

Poe's "serious" tales, clearly, are only apparently serious in the manner that they purport to be. The whole of Poe's Gothic fiction can be read not only as an ambivalent parody of the world of Gothic horror tales, but also as an extended grotesquerie of the human condition. Nothing quite works out for his heroes, even though they sometimes make superhuman efforts, and even though they are occasionally rescued from their predicaments. They undergo extended series of ironic

---

°*In pace requiescat:* May he rest in peace.
[3]Selections 1–5 are from G. R. Thompson, ed., *Great Short Works of Edgar Allan Poe* (New York: Harper, 1970).

reverses in fictional structures so ironically twisted that the form itself, even the very plot, approaches an absurd hoax perpetrated on the characters. The universe created in Poe's fiction is one in which the human mind tries vainly to perceive order and meaning. The universe is deceptive; its basic mode seems almost to be a constant shifting of appearances; reality is a flux variously interpreted, or even [37] created, by the individual human mind. In its deceptiveness, the universe of Poe's Gothic fiction seems not so much malevolent as mocking or "perverse." The universe is much like a gigantic hoax that God has played on man, an idea which is the major undercurrent of Poe's essay on the universe, *Eureka*. Thus, the hoax-like irony of Poe's technique has its parallel in the dramatic world in which his characters move.

The ultimate irony of this universe, however, is the "perversity" of man's own mind. The mind, and the mind only, seems to sustain Poe's heroes in their most desperate predicaments; yet in an instant the mind is capable of slipping into confusion, hysteria, madness—even while it seems most rational. From a more "Gothicist" point of view, Edward H. Davidson, without using the term *irony*, and without reading Poe's Gothic tales ironically or satirically, comes to much the same conclusion regarding Poe's universe. "Poe's nightmare universe," Davidson writes, "is one in which . . . people . . . are condemned to live as if they are in some long aftertime of belief and morality." The evildoer is driven by "some maggot in the brain" that leaves him a kind of "moral freak" in a universe that also has some fantastic defect in it. In Poe's universe, Davidson suggests, evil and suffering are "the capacity and measure of man to feel and to know"; pain is the basis of life, and death is the only release from his "grotesque condition of 'perversity.'"

This view of Poe's "perverse" universe is, I think, essentially correct. Poe's fiction developed from a basically satiric mode into an ironic mode in which a tragic reponse to the perversities of fortune and to the treacheries of one's own mind is contrasted by a near-comic perception of the absurdity of man's condition in the universe. Such a double perception, according to the German Ironists, leads, through art, to a momentary [38] transcendence of the dark chaos of the universe. If the artist (and through him the reader) can mock man's absurd condition at the same time that he feels it deeply, he transcends earthly or finite limits in an artistic paralleling of God's infinite perception. In Poe, however, such transcendence is always at the expense of the less perceptive mind. Poe plays a constant intellectual game with his readers; he tries to draw the reader into the "Gothic" world of the mind, but he is ready at any moment to mock the simplistic Gothic vision (under the trappings of which Poe saw man's real estrangement and isolation) that contemporary readers insisted on in the popular magazines.

2. The Narrators of "The Cask of Amontillado" and "The Fall of the House of Usher"

When we come to the tales, the comic and ironic side of Poe is clearer and more emphatic. And it is here, rather than among the poems, I believe, that we find the *great* works of Poe. (All of Poe's works, except his one novel, *Arthur Gordon Pym*, are "short.") His criticism, though historically interesting in its specificity and topicality, and the best of his time (barring only Coleridge's criticism), is valuable today mainly for its precise enunciation of principles of rational control over even the wildest materials—for its enunciation of a principle, not merely of "unity," but of "totality of effect." "If [the] very first sentence," Poe wrote in his 1847 review of Hawthorne's *Twice-Told Tales*, "tend not to the outbringing of this [19] effect, then in his very first step has [the artist] committed a blunder. In the whole composition there should be no word written of which the tendency, direct *or indirect*, is not to the pre-established design" [my italics]. This principle he observed in each and every one of his tales—and not only in the well-known gothic tales and detective stories, but also in the underrated comic and satiric tales, even though in these he was "slapping" (as he said in a letter to Joseph Snodgrass in 1841) "left & right at things in general."

In Poe's characteristically intricate, even involuted patterns of dramatic irony, the apparent narrative "voice" which pervades the surface atmosphere of the work is also seen within a qualifying frame. Several of the tales (for example "The Black Cat," "The Tell-Tale Heart," "Ligeia," "The Imp of the Perverse," "The Cask of Amontillado") involve a confessional element, wherein a first-person narrator, like Montresor, seems calmly or gleefully to recount horrible deeds, but which generally implies a listener to whom the agonized soul is revealing his torment. Especially revealing of the ironic structure thus achieved is Montresor in "The Cask of Amontillado." In the surface story, Montresor seems to be chuckling over his flawlessly executed revenge upon unfortunate "Fortunato" fifty years before. But a moment's reflection suggests that the indistinct "you" whom Montresor addresses in the first paragraph is probably his death-bed confessor—for if Montresor has murdered Fortunato fifty years before, he must now be some seventy to eighty years of age. None of this is explicitly stated; it is presented dramatically, and we get the double effect of feeling the coldly calculated murder at the same time that we see the larger point that Montresor, rather than having successfully taken his revenge "with impunity," as he says, has instead suffered a fifty-year's ravage of conscience. Likewise, many of Poe's [20] gothic tales seem to involve supernatural happenings; but insinuated into them, like clues in a detective story, are details which begin to construct dramatic frames around the narrative "voice" of the work. These dramatic frames suggest the elusiveness of the experience as the first-person narrator renders it. As in Henry James and Joseph Conrad, there is often in Poe a tale within a tale within a tale; and the meaning of the whole lies in the relationship of the various implied stories and their frames rather than in the explicit meaning given to the surface story by the dramatically involved narrator.

Only within the last ten to fifteen years have critics begun to examine Poe's narrators as characters in the total design of his tales and poems, and to suspect that even his most famous Gothic works—like "Usher" and "Ligeia"—have ironic double and triple perspectives playing upon them: supernatural from one point of view, psychological from another point of view, and often burlesque from yet a third. Not only is nearly half of Poe's fiction satiric and comic in an obvious way, but the Gothic tales contain within them satiric and comic elements thematically related to the macabre elements. Poe seems very carefully to have aimed at the ironic effect of touching his readers simultaneously on an archetypal emotional level of fear and on an (almost subliminal) level of intellectual and philosophical perception of the Absurd. The result in the Gothic tales, as in many of the poems, is a kind of ambivalent mockery. We can respond to Poe's scenes of horror or despair at the same time that we are aware of their caricatural quality.

3. "The Fall of the House of Usher"

Between 1838 and 1840, the middle years of his [34] career, Poe published three of his most famous Gothic stories: "Ligeia," "The Fall of the House of Usher," and "William Wilson." Like "Ligeia," the other two tales involve "doubles" and dramatize a weird universe as perceived by a subjective mind. "Usher," despite the supernatural atmosphere, can be read as the tale of the frenzied fantasies of *both* the narrator and Usher, fantasies engendered by a vague fear that something ominous *may* happen and by the disconnected, alien environment. The overriding theme is the mechanism of fear itself, which has perversely operated on Roderick Usher before the narrator arrives, and which operates on the narrator *through* Usher afterwards. When the narrator rides his horse up to the House of Usher and gazes at its leaden-eyed aspect and at the tarn, with its sickly white stems of dead plants sticking up through the stagnant water, he is immediately seized by a vague apprehension. Later in the tale, he remarks that the "mental disorder" and "hysteria" of his friend Roderick Usher "terrified" [35] and "infected" him: "I felt creeping upon me, by slow yet certain degrees, the wild influences of his own fantastic yet impressive superstitions." The narrator's confrontation with (and submission to) a mind gone mad is imaged in the facelike appearance of the House itself, with its leaden-hued eyelike windows and its zigzag crack down the middle, and in the wild "arabesque" face of Roderick Usher. The poem "The Haunted Palace," which Usher has composed, is also a symbolic, indeed allegorical, portrait of a facelike structure. The "face" of the palace changes when the "Monarch Thought" topples from his throne within, and the palace comes to resemble the face of Usher and his House as the narrator has described them. Moreover, when the narrator first looks down into the tarn, what he should see of course is his own face since he is on its very brink, but instead he sees the inverted image of the "face" of the House of Usher. His next action is to go inside and meet Usher face to face. Immediately, his attention is arrested by certain details of Usher's face; though he does not articulate the resemblances, as such, the narrator so describes the weblike hair of Usher that we are compelled to remember the webwork of fungi about the eaves of the House.

By the time the narrator "sees" the "return" of Madeline Usher from her grave, the themes of narcissism and inversion are so clear that the relevance of the absurdist interlude, "The Mad Trist of Sir Lancelot Canning" to the story as a whole (that is, to the dramatic situation of the narrator rather than merely to Roderick's "trist" with his twin sister) is obvious. The tale is the story of the "mad trist" of the twin, hysterical personalities of the narrator and Usher. Finally, we do not know for sure *what* has happened for, as our narrator flees "aghast" from the scene, the face of the House splits apart and sinks into that tarn which first merged the images of the faces of both the House and the narrator. The tale has long been hailed as a masterpiece of [36] gothic horror; it is also a masterpiece of dramatic irony and structural symbolism.

4. "The Black Cat" and "The Tell-Tale Heart"[4]

"The Tell-Tale Heart" (1843), a study in obsessive paranoia, is yet another story of the mind watching itself disintegrate under the stresses of delusion in an [40] alienated world. It is the perverse fortune of the narrator to become fearful of the grotesque eye of a kindly old man, whom he says he loves. With a double perversity, he gives himself away to the police at the moment of success. Yet the narrator is caught in a weird world in which [41] he loves the old man yet displays no real emotion toward him, in which he cannot let the "beloved" old man live and yet cannot kill him without remorse, in which he cannot expose his crime and yet must do so. Perhaps the final irony is that the apparent beating of his own heart which he mistakes as, first, the beating of the still-living heart of the old man, and which, second, seems to be an emblem of his own guilt (and which, finally, compels him to confess), may very well be initially the peculiar thumping sound of the wood-beetles gnawing at the walls. "The Black Cat" (1843) carries the same themes further and details more clearly the irrational desire, almost the ultimate irony, to act against oneself, with an ambiguous conclusion suggesting the agency of malevolent fortune at the same time that it suggests subconscious self-punishment. The major absurdist irony, perhaps, is that the murder which the narrator commits is the result of subconscious remorse over the *cat* he has previously mistreated.

5. "The Masque of the Red Death"

"The Masque of The Red Death" (1842), a tale of the supernatural visitation of Death himself, can [39] also be read as a tone poem about hysteria, engendered by mood and setting, with a sarcastic concluding echo from Pope's *Dunciad*. Prince Prospero's sinister stronghold, of course, contrasts directly with the enchanted island of his namesake, Prospero, the magician in Shakespeare's *The Tempest*. The ironic theme of Poe's tale focuses on the grimly perverse joke of Prospero's having walled *in* death in a frenetic attempt to wall it out.

6. Symbolism in "The Masque of the Red Death"[5]

[88] The symbolism of certain stories of Poe is rather clear, and it would be useless to insist upon it. For example, "The Masque of the Red Death" is "a parable of the inevitability and universality of death," "the human condition of man's fate, and the fate of the universe." The seven rooms are none other than the seven ages of man; the gigantic ebony clock with the "dull, heavy, monotonous clang" emphasizes the passage of time; and the spectre in the winding sheet smeared with blood is the personification of death, or "man's . . . self aroused and self-developed fear of his own mistaken concept of death."

---

[4]"The Tell-Tale Heart" is not included in this selection.
[5]From Georges Zayed, "Symbolism in Poe's Tales." *Readings on Edgar Allan Poe*, ed. Bonnie Szumski and Carol Prime (San Diego: Greenhaven Press, 1998) 110–119.

7. "The Masque of the Red Death" as Representative of a "Diseased Age"[6]

[118] More than once, in his dialogues or critical writings, Poe describes the earth-bound, time-bound rationalism of his age as a *disease*. And that is what the Red Death signifies. Prince Prospero's flight from the Red Death is the poetic imagination's flight from temporal and worldly consciousness into dream. The thousand dancers of Prince Prospero's costume ball are just what Poe says they are—"dreams" or "phantasms," veiled and vivid creatures of Prince Prospero's rapt imagination. Whenever there is a feast, or a carnival, or costume ball in Poe, we may be sure that a dream is in progress.

But what is the gigantic ebony clock? . . . In sleep, our minds may roam beyond the temporal world, but our hearts tick on, binding us to time and mortality. Whenever the ebony clock strikes, the dancers of Prince Prospero's dream grow momentarily pale and still, in half-awareness that they and their revel must have an end; it is as if a sleeper should half-awaken, and know that he has been dreaming, and then sink back into dreams again.

The figure in blood-dabbled grave-clothes, who stalks through the terrified company and vanishes in the shadow of the clock, is waking, temporal consciousness, and his coming means the death of dreams. He breaks up Prince Prospero's ball. . . . The final confrontation between Prince Prospero and the shrouded figure is like the terrible final meeting between William Wilson and his double. Recognizing his adversary as his own worldly and mortal self, Prince Prospero gives a cry of despair which is also Poe's cry of despair: despair at the realization that only by self-destruction could the poet fully free his soul from the trammels of this world.

Poe's aesthetic, Poe's theory of the nature of art, seems to me insane. To say that art should repudiate everything [119] human and earthly, and find its subject-matter at the flickering end of dreams, is hopelessly to narrow the scope and function of art. Poe's aesthetic points toward such impoverishments as *poésie pure* and the abstract expressionist movement in painting. And yet, despite his aesthetic, Poe is a great artist, and I would rest my case for him on his prose allegories of psychic conflict. In them, Poe broke wholly new ground, and they remain the best things of their kind in our literature. Poe's mind may have been a strange one; yet all minds are alike in their general structure; therefore we can understand him, and I think that he will have something to say to us as long as there is civil war in the palaces of men's minds.

8. Sources and Analogues of "The Cask of Amontillado"[7]

"The Cask of Amontillado" is a prime example of [93] Poe's ability to sculpt materials from popular literature and culture into a masterwork of terror. At once derivative and freshly individualistic, the tale enacts Poe's belief that "the truest and surest test of *originality* is the manner of handling a hackneyed subject."

---

[6]From Richard Wilbur, "Poe's Use of Allegory." *Readings on Edgar Allan Poe*, ed. Bonnie Szumski and Carol Prime (San Diego: Greenhaven Press, 1998) 82–91.
[7]From David S. Reynolds, "Poe's Art of Transformation: 'The Cask of Amontillado' in Its Cultural Context," *New Essays on Poe's Major Tales*, ed. Kenneth Silverman, (New York: Cambridge, 1993) 93–112.

It has long been surmised that this story of murderous revenge reflects Poe's vindictive hatred of two prominent New York literary figures, the author Thomas Dunn English and the newspaper editor Hiram Fuller. If "The Cask" is on some level, a retaliatory document, surely Poe could not have envisioned a more ghoulish type of retaliation. Seen against the background of the war of the literati, the narrator Montresor (Poe) gets back at his enemy Fortunato (English) for a recent insult, using their mutual friend Luchesi (Fuller) as a foil in his scheme. Although we know from the start that Montresor is bent on revenge, and we have ominous feelings as he takes his foe into the depths of his skeleton-filled wine vaults, the tale's atmosphere is deceptively convivial; the two connoisseurs banter and drink as they go in search of the cask of Amontillado (a fine Spanish sherry) Montresor says he has received. Only when Montresor lures Fortunato into a small niche, quickly chains up his stupefied victim, and proceeds to wall up the niche with bricks and mortar are we overwhelmed by the horrifying fact of live burial.

Poe's animus against the literati may have motivated the revenge theme, but it fails to account for specific details of plot, character, and imagery. For those we must look to the tale's popular cultural context. Poe was a great borrower, and he had an eye on the popular market. On one level, his terror tales were clearly designed [94] to cater to a public increasingly enamored of horror and sensationalism. Writing in the era of the crime-filled penny papers and mass-produced pamphlet novels, he was well aware of the demands of the sensation-loving public. His letters are peppered with excited boasts about some work of his that has made a "sensation" or a "hit." In his tale "The Psyche Zenobia," he had the editor of a popular magazine declare: "Sensations are the great thing after all. Should you ever be drowned or hung, be sure and make a note of your sensations—they will be worth to you ten guineas a sheet." Following the lead of the sensation mongers, Poe made use of some of the wildest situations imaginable.

One such situation was live burial. In "The Premature Burial" Poe wrote that *"no* event is so terribly well adapted to inspire the supremeness of bodily and of mental distress, as is burial before death," a topic that creates "a degree of appalling and intolerable horror from which the most daring imagination must recoil." The specific work which established the premise of "The Cask of Amontillado" was Joel Tyler Headley's "A Man Built in a Wall," first published in the *Columbian Magazine* in 1844 and collected in Headley's *Letters from Italy* (1845). Headley reports having visited an Italian church containing a niche in which was discovered the skeleton of a man who had been buried alive by a workman under the direction of the man's smirking archenemy. After a detailed description of the grotesque posture of the skeleton, suggesting an excruciatingly painful death, Headley recreates the murder:

> The workman began at the feet, and with his mortar and trowel built up with the same carelessness he would exhibit in filling any broken wall. The successful enemy stood leaning on his sword—a smile of scorn and revenge on his features—and watched the face of the man he hated, but no longer feared. . . . It was slow work fitting the pieces nicely, so as to close up the aperture with precision. . . . With care and precision the last stone was fitted in the narrow space—the trowel passed smoothly over it—a stifled groan as if from the centre of a rock, broke the stillness—one strong shiver and all was over. The agony had passed—revenge was satisfied, and a secret locked up for the great revelation day.

Several details in Headley's piece—the premise of live burial in a hidden niche, the careful placement of the bricks, the revenge motive, the victim's [95] agonized groaning and numbed stillness—anticipate "The Cask of Amontillado."

Also analogous to Poe's story is Honoré de Balzac's "La Grande Bretêche," an adaptation of which appeared in the *Democratic Review* in November 1843. Balzac describes a jealous husband who, on discovering that his wife's lover is hiding in her closet, has the closet walled up as the lady watches. Poe most likely also knew the story "Apropos of Bores" (*New York Mirror,* December 2, 1837), in which a man at a party tells of going with a porter into the vast wine vaults of Lincoln's Inn to view several pipes of Madeira that were stored there. They found the pipes in good condition but had a terrifying accident: When their candle was extinguished, they groped to the cellar door only to have the key break off in the lock. They impulsively decided to forget their sorrows by staving in a wine pipe and getting drunk in order to forget "the horrible death that awaits us." Giving up this impulse, they soberly faced the fact that their remains would not be discovered until all traces of identity were destroyed. We never learn the outcome of the tale, for the narrator and his listeners are called to tea before he is finished.

Another predecessor of Poe's tale, hitherto unacknowledged, was the sensational best-seller *The Quaker City; or The Monks of Monk Hall* (1845) by George Lippard, Poe's friend from his Philadelphia days. Monk Hall, a huge mansion where Philadelphia's prominent citizens gather in secret revels and debauchery, has below it a so-called "deadvault," a vast cellar with labyrinthine passages and hidden recesses. The cellar is anticipatory of the vast vault beneath Montresor's mansion in several ways: It is lined with countless skeletons, its walls are clammy with moisture, and it is the scene of live burial. One critic has called "absurd" Poe's notion in "Cask" of "an ossuary . . . gruesomely combined with the appurtenances of a wine cellar," but many of Poe's contemporary readers had been prepared for such an odd coupling by the description of Monk Hall, where not only are the wine cellar and dead-vault side-by-side but the dead-vault is littered with liquor bottles strewn amid the skeletons. In a scene that presages Montresor's long descent with his victim into the catacombs, Devil-Bug, the sadistic keeper of Monk Hall, slowly takes a victim, Luke Harvey, down an extensive staircase into the depths of the dead-vault. Hardly as subtle as Montresor, Devil-Bug mutters to his [96] victim, "I am a-goin' to bury you alive! D'ye hear that? I'm a-goin' to bury you alive! "Just as Montresor howls and laughs at the enchained Fortunato, so Devil-Bug takes noisy pleasure in the sufferings of his victim. "He shrieked forth a horrible peal of laughter, more like the howl of a hyena, than the sound of a human laugh." Unlike Montresor, Devil-Bug does not succeed in his murderous scheme; his intended victim escapes. Devil-Bug, however, is haunted by the vision of a previous murder victim, just as (according to one reading) Montresor is tortured by the recollection of his crime.

A larger cultural phenomenon that influenced Poe was the temperance movement, which produced a body of literature and lectures filled with the kinds of horrifying images that fascinated him. Poe's bouts with the bottle, leading eventually to his death, are well known. Less familiar is Poe's ambiguous relationship with the American temperance movement. In the 1830s Poe had befriended the Baltimore writer John Lofland, who delivered temperance lectures even though, like several other backsliding reformers of the period, he drank and took drugs in private. Another of Poe's acquaintances, Timothy Shay Arthur, wrote some of the most popular (and darkest) temperance tales of the day, including Six *Nights with the Washingtonians* (1842) and *Ten Nights in a Barroom* (1854). In the early 1840s, the rise of the Washingtonians—reformed drunkards who told grisly tales of alcoholism in an effort to frighten listeners into signing a pledge of abstinence— brought to temperance rhetoric a new sensationalism. Walt Whitman's novel *Franklin Evans* (1842), for example, written on commission for the Washingtonians, luridly depicts the ill results of alcohol, including shattered homes, infanticide, crushing poverty that leads to crime, and delirium tremens with its nightmare visions. Poe had direct association with the Washingtonians. In 1843, after a period of heavy drinking, he promised a temperance friend from whom he hoped to gain a political appointment that he would join the Washingtonians. Whether or not he did so at that time, he did join a related group, the Sons of Temperance, in the last year of his life. When on August 31,1849, the *Banner of Temperance* announced Poe's initiation [97] into the order, it said: "We trust his pen will sometimes be employed in its behalf. A vast amount of good might be accomplished by so pungent and forcible a writer."

What the *Banner of Temperance* neglected to say was that Poe had already written temperance fiction, or more precisely, his own version of what I would call dark temperance, a popular mode that left didacticism behind and emphasized the perverse results of alcoholism. Following the lead of many dark temperance writers who portrayed once-happy families ripped asunder by a husband's inebriety, Poe in "The Black Cat" (1843) dramatized alcohol's ravages on an initially peaceful couple. The narrator tells us that he had once been known for his docility and gentleness but that his character—"through the instrumentality of the Fiend Intemperance—had (I blush to confess it) experienced a radical alteration for the worse. I grew, day by day, more moody, more irritable, more regardless of the feelings of others." As in popular temperance literature, the first sip is followed by escalating pathological behavior. The narrator declares that "my disease grew upon me—for what disease is like Alcohol!" One night a "fiendish malevolence, gin-nurtured" impels him to cut out the eye of his cat with a penknife, a deed he tries unsuccessfully to drown in wine. Before long he has been driven by alcohol to paranoia and crime, even to the extent of murdering his wife.

"The Cask of Amontillado" also studies the diseased psyche associated with alcohol. Everything in the story revolves around alcohol obsession. The object of the descent into the vault is a pipe of wine. Both of the main characters are wine connoisseurs, as is their mentioned friend Luchesi. The narrator, Montresor, boasts, "I was skilful in the Italian vintages myself, and bought largely whenever I could." As for Fortunato, he is so vain about his knowledge of wine and so fixated on the supposed Amontillado that he goes willingly to his own destruction. When we meet him, we learn "he had been drinking much" in the carnival revelry, and as he walks unsteadily into the vault his eyes look like "two filmy orbs that distilled the rheum of intoxication." He gets drunker after sharing the bottle of Médoc that Montresor breaks open in the cellar, and even more so when he subsequently gulps down the flacon of De Grave (one of several puns that point to his fate). Fortunato's name has a double meaning: from his perspective he is "fortunate" [98] to have an opportunity to show off his expertise in wines; from the reader's viewpoint, it is his bad "fortune" to be sucked to doom by his overriding interest in liquor. Poe's contemporary readers, accustomed to dark temperance rhetoric, would have found special significance in the interweaving of alcohol and death images in passages like this:

> The wine sparkled in his eyes and the bells jingled. My own fancy grew warm with Medoc. We had passed through walls of piled bones, with casks and puncheons intermingling, into the inmost depths of the catacombs.

The jingling of the bells reminds us of the fool Fortunato has become because of his destructive obsession. The wine-instilled agitation of Montresor's fancy reflects his role in this devilish communion, while the intermingled casks and bones, besides recalling Lippard's Monk Hall, enhance the eerie dark temperance atmosphere. After Montresor chains Fortunato to the wall, their dialogue takes on a dreary circularity that shows once again the importance of alcohol obsession to the story. "The Amontillado!" exclaims the victim; "True, the Amontillado," replies the murderer. Even after he has been walled in, the hapless Fortunato, in a desperate attempt to pass off the situation as a joke, returns to the subject of drinking:

> "We will have many a rich laugh about it at the palazzo—he! he! he!—over our wine—he! he! he!"
> "The Amontillado!" I said.
> "He! he! he!—he! he! he!—yes, the Amontillado!"

The dark temperance mode gives the tale a grim inevitability and another cultural phenomenon—anti-Masonry—contributes to its black humor and mysterious aura. At the center of the story is a dialogue that shows Poe tapping into his contemporaries' concerns about the Masons, a private all-male order widely thought to be involved in heinous crime. After drinking the bottle of De Grave, Fortunato throws it upward with a grotesque gesture Montresor does not understand. [99]

> "You do not comprehend?" he said.
> "Not I," I replied.
> "Then you are not of the brotherhood."
> "How?"
> "You are not of the masons."
> "Yes, yes," I said, "yes, yes."
> "You? Impossible! A mason?"
> "A mason," I replied.
> "A sign," he said.
> "It is this," I answered, producing a trowel from beneath the fold of my *roquelaire*.
> "You jest," he exclaimed, recoiling a few paces. "But let us proceed to the Amontillado."

This marvelous moment of black humor has a range of historical associations rooted in the anti-Masonry mania that had swept America during Poe's apprentice period. The pun on "mason" (referring both to the fraternal order and to a worker in brick and stone) seems to have a specific historical referent. At the center of the Masonry controversy was one William Morgan, a brick-and-stone mason of Batavia, New York, who in 1826, after thirty years of membership in the Masons, was determined to publish a harsh exposé of the order but was silenced before he could, most likely by vindictive members of the order. Morgan's disappearance was wreathed in mystery. One night in September 1826 he was seized, gagged, and spirited away in a carriage to the Niagara frontier, where all trace of him was lost. The story spread that a group of Masons, viewing Morgan as a traitor, had drowned him in the Niagara River. (It is perhaps meaningful, in this context, that Montresor leads his victim "below the river bed.") Anti-Masonry sentiment snowballed and became a substantial political movement, peaking in the mid-1830s and then feeding into the ascendant Whig party. The Masonic order was viewed as undemocratic and as a tangible threat to American institutions. In particular, its oath, whereby members swore to uphold rational secular values (without reference to God or Christianity), was seen as sacrilegious. When Poe has Fortunato make a "grotesque" movement signaling membership in the order, he is introducing a sign that many of his readers would have regarded as demonic. When Montresor [100] gives the sign of the trowel, he is not only foretelling the story's climax but is also summoning up the associations of brick-and-stone masonry, murderous revenge, and mysterious disappearance surrounding American Masonry.

So central is the Masonic image that the tale has been interpreted as an enactment of the historical conflict between Catholics and Masons. In this reading, Fortunato's real crime is that he is a Mason, whereas Montresor, a Roman Catholic, assumes a perverted priestly function in his ritualistic murder of his Masonic foe. It should be pointed out, however, that in the predominantly evangelical Protestant America of Poe's day *both* Masons and Catholics were held suspect. If anti-Masonic feeling feeds into the portrait of Fortunato, anti-Catholic sentiment lies behind several of the grim images in the tale. In the 1830s and 1840s, American Protestant authors, fearful of the rapid growth of the Catholic church with the sudden flood of immigrants arriving from abroad, produced a large body of lurid literature aimed at exposing alleged depravity and criminality among Catholics. In 1838 one alarmed commentator wrote of the "tales of lust, and blood, and murder . . . with which the ultra protestant is teeming." Of special interest in connection with Poe's tale is Maria Monk's best-selling *Awful Disclosures of . . . the Hotel Dieu Nunnery at Montreal* (1836), which featured a huge cellar that served as both a torture chamber and a tomb, where priests had killed some 375 people and cast their remains into a lime pit. Whether or not Poe had Maria Monk and her ilk in mind when he concocted his tale of torture behind cellar walls, it is notable that he made use of Catholic images: The story is set during the *Carnivale,* a Catholic season just before Lent; Montresor's family motto about the heel crushing the serpent refers to Genesis 3:14 (the curse upon the serpent) and historically symbolizes the Church militant triumphing over the forces of evil; the early history of the Church is recalled when the underground passages are called "catacombs"; and the final words, *"In pace requiescat!"* are the last words of a requiem mass. The Catholic connection is further strengthened if we accept the idea that Poe derived the name Montresor from an old French Catholic family. Although not explicitly anti-Catholic, the tale combines religious [101] and criminal imagery in a way reminiscent of the anti-Catholic bestsellers of the day.

Though grounded in nineteenth-century American culture, "The Cask of Amontillado" transcends its time-specific referents because it is crafted in such a way that it remains accessible to generations of readers unfamiliar with such sources as anti-Catholicism, temperance, and live-burial literature. The special power of the tale can be understood if we take into account Poe's theories about fiction writing, developed largely in response to emerging forms of popular literature that aroused both his interest and his concern. On the one hand, as a literary professional writing for popular periodicals ("Cask" appeared in the most popular of all, *Godey's Lady's Book)* Poe had to keep in mind the demands of an American public increasingly hungry for sensation. On the other hand, as a scrupulous craftsman he was profoundly dissatisfied with the way in which other writers handled sensational topics. John Neal's volcanic, intentionally disruptive fiction seemed energetic but formless to Poe, who saw in it "no precision, no finish . . . —always an excessive force but little of refined art." Similarly, he wrote of the blackly humorous stories in Washington Irving's *Tales of a Traveller* that "the interest is subdivided and frittered away, and their conclusions are insufficiently *climacic* [sic]." George Lippard's *The Ladye Annabel,* a dizzying novel involving medieval torture and necrophilic visions, struck him as indicative of genius yet chaotic. A serial novel by Edward Bulwer-Lytton wearied him with its "continual and vexatious shifting of scene," while N. P. Willis's sensational play *Tortesa* exhibited "the great error" of *"inconsequence.* Underplot is piled on underplot," as Willis gives us "vast designs that terminate in nothing."

In his own fiction Poe tried to correct the mistakes he saw in other writers. The good plot, he argued, was that from which nothing can be taken without detriment to the whole. If, as he rightly pointed out, much sensational fiction of the day was digressive and directionless, his best tales were tightly unified. Of them all, "The Cask of Amontillado" perhaps most clearly exemplifies the unity he aimed for.

The tale's compactness becomes instantly apparent when we compare it with the popular live-burial [102] works mentioned earlier. Headley's journalistic "A Man Built in a Wall" begins with a long passage about a lonely Italian inn and ends with an account of the countryside around Florence; the interpolated story about the entombed man dwells as much on the gruesome skeleton as on the vindictive crime. Balzac's "La Grande Brêteche" is a slowly developing tale in which the narrator gets mixed accounts about an old abandoned mansion near the Loire; only in the second half of the story does he learn from his landlady that the mansion had been the scene of a live burial involving a husband's jealous revenge. The entombment in "Apropos of Bores" is purely accidental (two unlucky men find themselves trapped in a wine vault) and is reduced to frivolous chatter when the narrator breaks off at the climactic moment and his listeners crack jokes and disperse to tea. Closest in spirit to Poe, perhaps, is the "dead-vault" scene in Lippard's *The Quaker* City: There is the same ritualistic descent into an immense cellar by a sadistic murderer intent on burying his victim alive. Lippard, however, constantly interrupts the scene with extraneous descriptions (he's especially fascinated by the skeletons and caskets strewn around the cellar). In addition, this is just one of countless bloodcurdling scenes in a meandering novel lightyears distant, structurally, from Poe's carefully honed tale.

• • •

So tightly woven is "The Cask" that it may be seen as an effort at literary one-upsmanship on Poe's part, designed pointedly as a contrast to other, more casually constructed live-burial pieces. In his essays on popular literature, Poe expressed particular impatience with irrelevancies of plot or character. For instance, commenting on J. H. Ingraham's perfervid best-seller *Lafitte, the Pirate of the Gulf,* he wrote: "We are surfeited with unnecessary details. . . . Of outlines there are none. Not a dog yelps, unsung."

There is absolutely no excess in "The Cask of Amontillado." Every sentence points inexorably to the horrifying climax. In the interest of achieving unity, Poe purposely leaves several questions unanswered. The tale is remarkable for what it leaves out. What are the "thousand injuries" Montresor has suffered at the hands of Fortunato? In particular, what was the "insult" that has driven Montresor to the grisly extreme of murder by live burial? What personal misfortune is he referring to when he tells his foe, "you are happy, as once [103] I was"? Like a painter who leaves a lot of suggestive white canvas, Poe sketches character and setting lightly, excluding excess material. Even so simple a detail as the location of the action is unknown. Most assume the setting is Italy, but one commentator makes a good case for France. What do we know about the main characters? As discussed, both are bibulous and proud of their connoisseurship in wines. Fortunato, besides being a Mason, is "rich, respected, admired, beloved," and there is a Lady Fortunato who will miss him. Montresor is descended from "a great and numerous family" and is wealthy enough to sustain a palazzo, servants, and extensive wine vaults.

Other than that, Poe tells very little about the two. Both exist solely to fulfill the imperatives of the plot Poe has designed. Everything Montresor does and says furthers his strategy of luring his enemy to his death. Everything Fortunato does and says reveals the fatuous extremes his vanity about wines will lead him to. Though limited, these characters are not what E. M. Forster would call flat. They swiftly come alive before our eyes because Poe describes them with acute psychological realism. Montresor is a complex Machiavellian criminal, exhibiting a full range of traits from clever ingratiation to stark sadism. Fortunato, the dupe whose pride leads to his own downfall, nevertheless exhibits enough admirable qualities that one critic has seen him as a wronged man of courtesy and good will. The drama of the story lies in the carefully orchestrated interaction between the two. Poe directs our attention away from the merely sensational and toward the psychological.

Herein lies another key difference between the tale and its precursors. In none of the popular live-burial works is the *psychology* of revenge a factor. In Headley and Lippard, the victim is unconscious and thus incognizant of the murderer's designs; similarly, in Balzac there is no communication at all between the murderer and the entombed. In Poe, the relationship between the two is, to a large degree, the story. Montresor says at the start, murder is most successful if the victim is made painfully aware of what is happening: "A wrong is unredressed . . . when the avenger fails to make himself felt as such to him who has done the wrong." By focusing on the process of vanity falling prey to sly revenge, [104] Poe shifts attention to psychological subtleties ignored by the other live-burial writers.

9. Poe's Idea of Unity and "The Fall of the House of Usher"[8]

[15] One of Poe's most characteristic ideas is unity. This is the key to the philoso-phy of *Eureka* and the visionary dialogues; this is the essence of his contribution to the theory and practice of the short story. In his review of Hawthorne's *Twice-Told Tales* he speaks of the need for totality, for "a certain unique single *effect* to be wrought out": every word of a piece of fiction should contribute to the realization of this aim. Many critics have noticed the intensity of the concentration on unity in "Usher"—how the opening description of the House and the narrator's reactions lead swiftly and inevitably to the final catastrophe. It is perhaps instructive to see the story's structure as three sections of about equal length: paragraphs 1 to 14 in-troduce the House, the circumstances of the narrator's visit, and Roderick and Madeline Usher; the movement is of entrance, of the opening of doors (there is perhaps a pun on the family name when the valet "threw open a door and ush-ered me into the presence of his master"). The middle section, paragraphs 15 to 29, develops the narrator's initial impressions through the analysis of Roderick's aes-thetic ideas, and the application of his most abstract and intellectual madness to his relationship with his sister. The final part, paragraphs 30 to 47 logically com-pletes these themes by building rapidly to Madeline's reappearance and the si-multaneous collapse of both Ushers and their house. Here there is a final door-opening, as Madeline reels on the threshold; then the tarn finally "closes" over the fragments of the fallen house. As often in Poe's fiction, the protagonist (here the narrator and both Ushers combined) ends teetering on the verge of a supreme revelation that is also his destruction, an opening that mockingly also closes everything.

Poe attains an effect of structural symmetry by placing certain actions and im-ages only in [16] the first and third parts: the sullen tarn; the appearances of Made-line in the apartment; and the speeches of Roderick (there is little dialogue; Roderick speaks only twice at length, once early in the story to confirm his "intol-erable agitation of soul," and then at the end to announce, *"We have put her living in the tomb!"*).

This unity of structure is reinforced by the style. From the magnificent open-ing sentences to the end, Poe's language is highly charged with emotion, but at the same time, quite abstract: for instance, the narrator remarks at the beginning, "a sense of insufferable gloom pervaded my spirit." Instead of simple, direct descrip-tion, we experience the narrator's *sense* of things. *Pervaded* is also a key word, evoking the notorious "atmosphere" of the House, the "condensation" of "vapours" from the tarn. As Poe's note about "sentience" suggests, he seeks cred-ibility for his psychological claims by using the vocabulary of nineteenth century chemistry. *Pervaded* is also important in introducing the theme of *oppression*, which recurs throughout: something sinister presses down on the mind, anticipating the collapse of the House. Later the narrator says: "An irrepressible terror pervaded my frame; and, at length, there sat upon my very heart an incubus of utterly causeless alarm." *Frame* hints at the identity of the human body with the building,

---

[8]From Thomas Woodson, ed., *Twentieth-Century Interpretations of "The Fall of the House of Usher"* (Englewood Cliffs: Prentice Hall, 1969) 15–17.

as does the similarity of appearance between Roderick's head and the House, and the imagery of his poem, "The Haunted Palace." In fact, a close study of the story's style reveals a very high degree of recurrence of a rather small and special vocabulary. The effect of this stylistic narrowness is to bring together, almost to the verge of solipsism, the sensations of both Roderick and the narrator, and the "sentience" of Madeline and the House, Madeline being less a character than an object to be perceived.

Another peculiarity of Poe's diction is his emphasis on the negative. In the first paragraph alone we find, in addition to *insufferable,* these adjectives and verbs: *unrelieved, unredeemed, unnerved, insoluble,* and *unsatisfactory.* The story is full of words beginning with *un-* or *in-,* or ending in *-less,* and expressions containing *no, not, mere,* or *scarcely.* Poe uses these words to maintain an excited, exaggerated tone, but also to evoke the results of oppression on the mind: the nightmare of a vacant, featureless world—imaged by sinking beneath the surface of the tarn—a world where meaning and value have dissolved into nothingness. [17]

Through these devices Poe has made style his weapon to redeem, as William Hedges has put it, the sensational material of popular fiction for the analysis of the soul. In the speeches of Roderick Usher this style is speeded up, intensified, almost to the point of hysterical incoherence. This style is then counterpointed to the burlesque extravagance of the "Mad Trist" of Sir Launcelot Canning, which the narrator describes as a style of "uncouth and unimaginative prolixity," portentously empty of meaning (perhaps Poe's attempt to imitate the effect of the porter's knocking on the door in *Macbeth*).

10. The Narrators of "The Cask of Amontillado" and "The Black Cat"[9]

It goes without saying that Poe, like other creative men, is sometimes at the mercy of his own worst qualities. Yet the contention that he is fundamentally a bad or tawdry stylist appears to me to be rather facile and sophistical. It is based, ultimately, on the untenable and often unanalyzed assumption that Poe and his narrators are identical literary twins and that he must be held responsible for all their wild or perfervid utterances; their shrieks and groans are too often conceived as originating from Poe himself. I believe, on the contrary, that Poe's narrators possess a character and consciousness distinct from those of their creator. These protagonists, I am convinced, speak their own thoughts and are the dupes of their own passions. In short, Poe understands them far better than they can possibly understand themselves. Indeed, he often so designs his tales as to show his narrators' limited comprehension of their own problems and states of mind; the structure of many of Poe's stories clearly reveals an ironical and comprehensive intelligence critically and artistically ordering events so as to establish a vision of life and character which the narrator's very inadequacies help to "prove."

---

[9]From James W. Gargano, "The Question of Poe's Narrators," *The Recognition of Edgar Allan Poe,* ed. Eric W. Carlson (Ann Arbor: U of Michigan P, 1966) 308–16.

[310] The structure of Poe's stories compels realization that they are more than the effusions of their narrators' often disordered mentalities. Through the irony of his characters' self-betrayal and through the development and arrangement of his dramatic actions, Poe suggests to his readers ideas never entertained by the narrators. Poe intends his readers to keep their powers of analysis and judgment ever alert; he does not require or desire complete surrender to the experience of the sensations being felt by his characters. The point of Poe's technique, then, is not to enable us to lose ourselves in strange or outrageous emotions, but to see these emotions and those obsessed by them from a rich and thoughtful perspective. I do not mean to advocate that, while reading Poe, we should cease to feel; but feeling should be "simultaneous" with an analysis carried on with the composure and logic of Poe's great detective, Dupin. For Poe is not merely a Romanticist; he is also a chronicler of the consequences of the Romantic excesses which lead to psychic disorder, pain, and disintegration.

[313] Evidence of Poe's "seriousness" seems to me indisputable in "The Cask of Amontillado." Far from being his author's mouthpiece, the narrator, Montresor, is one of the supreme examples in fiction of a deluded rationalist who cannot glimpse the moral implications of his planned folly. Poe's fine ironic sense makes clear that Montresor, the stalker of Fortunato, is both a compulsive and pursued man; for in committing a flawless crime against another human being, he really (like Wilson and the protagonist in "The Tell-Tale Heart") commits the worst of crimes against himself. His reasoned, "cool" intelligence weaves an intricate plot which, while ostensibly satisfying his revenge, despoils him of humanity. His impeccably contrived murder, his weird mask of goodness in an enterprise of evil, and his abandonment of all his life-energies in one pet project of hate convict him of a madness which he mistakes for the inspiration of genius. The brilliant masquerade setting of Poe's tale intensifies the theme of Montresor's apparently successful duplicity; Montresor's ironic appreciation of his own deviousness seems further to justify his arrogance of intellect. But the greatest irony of all, to which Montresor is never sensitive, is that the "injuries" supposedly perpetrated by Fortunato are illusory and that the vengeance meant for the victim recoils upon Montresor himself. In immolating Fortunato, the narrator unconsciously calls him the "noble" Fortunato and confesses that his own "heart grew sick." Though Montresor attributes this sickness to "the dampness of the catacombs," it is clear that his crime has begun to "possess" him.

[314] We see that, after fifty years, it remains the obsession of his life; the meaning of his existence resides in the tomb in which he has, symbolically, buried himself. In other words, Poe leaves little doubt that the narrator has violated his own mind and humanity, that the external act has had its destructive inner consequences.

The same artistic integrity and seriousness of purpose evident in "The Cask of Amontillado" can be discovered in "The Black Cat." No matter what covert meanings one may find in this much-discussed story, it can hardly be denied that the nameless narrator does not speak for Poe. Whereas the narrator, at the beginning of his "confession," admits that he cannot explain the events which overwhelmed him, Poe's organization of his episodes provides an unmistakable clue to his protagonist's psychic deterioration. The tale has two distinct, almost parallel parts: in the first, the narrator's inner moral collapse is presented in largely symbolic narrative; in the second part, the consequences of his self-violation precipitate an act of murder, punishable by society. Each section of the story deals with an ominous cat, an atrocity, and an exposé of a "crime." In the first section, the narrator's house is consumed by fire after he has mutilated and subsequently hanged Pluto, his pet cat. Blindly, he refuses to grant any connection between his violence and the fire; yet the image of a hanged cat on the one remaining wall indicates that he will be haunted and hag-ridden by his deed. The sinister figure of Pluto, seen by a crowd of neighbors, is symbolically both an accusation and a portent, an enigma to the spectators but an infallible sign to the reader.

In the second section of "The Black Cat," the reincarnated cat goads the narrator into the murder of his wife. As in "William Wilson," "The Tell-Tale Heart," and "The Cask of Amontillado," the narrator cannot understand that his assault upon another person derives from his own moral sickness and unbalance. Like his confreres, too, he seeks psychic release and freedom in a crime which completes his torture. To the end of his life he is incapable of locating the origin of his evil and damnation within himself.

The theme of "The Black Cat" is complicated for many critics by the narrator's dogged assertion that he was pushed into evil and self-betrayal by the "imp of the perverse." [315] This imp is explained, by a man who, it must be remembered, eschews explanation, as a radical, motiveless, and irresistible impulse within the human soul. Consequently, if his self-analysis is accepted, his responsibility for his evil life vanishes. Yet, it must be asked if it is necessary to give credence to the words of the narrator. William Wilson, too, regarded himself as a "victim" of a force outside himself and Montresor speaks as if he has been coerced into his crime by Fortunato. The narrator in "The Black Cat" differs from Wilson in bringing to his defense a well-reasoned theory with perhaps a strong appeal to many readers. Still, the narrator's pat explanation is contradicted by the development of the tale, for instead of being pushed into crime, he pursues a life which makes crime inevitable. He cherishes the intemperate self-indulgence which blunts his powers of self-analysis; he is guided by his delusions to the climax of damnation. Clearly, Poe does not espouse his protagonist's theory any more than he approves of the specious rationalizations of his other narrators. Just as the narrator's well constructed house has a fatal flaw, so the theory of perverseness is flawed because it really explains nothing. Moreover, even the most cursory reader must be struck by the fact that the narrator is most "possessed and maddened" when he most proudly boasts of selfcontrol. If the narrator obviously cannot be believed at the end of the tale, what argument is there for assuming that he must be telling the truth when he earlier tries to evade responsibility for his "sin" by slippery rationalizations?

A close analysis of "The Black Cat" must certainly exonerate Poe of the charge of merely sensational writing. The final frenzy of the narrator, with its accumulation of superlatives, cannot be ridiculed as an example of Poe's style. The breakdown of the shrieking criminal does not reflect similar breakdown in the author. Poe, I maintain, is a serious artist who explores the neuroses of his characters with probing intelligence. He permits his narrator to revel and flounder in torment, but he sees beyond the torment to its causes.

In conclusion, then, the five tales I have commented on display Poe's deliberate craftsmanship and penetrating sense of irony. If my thesis is correct, Poe's narrators should not be construed as his mouthpieces; instead they should be regarded as expressing, in "charged" language indicative of their internal disturbances, their own peculiarly nightmarish visions. Poe, I contend, is conscious of the abnormalities of his narrators and does not condone the intellectual ruses through which they strive, only too earnestly, to justify themselves. In short, though his narrators are often febrile or demented. Poe is conspicuously "sane." They may be "decidedly primitive" or "wildly incoherent," but Poe, in his stories at least, is mature and lucid.

11. Poe, Women, and "The Fall of the House of Usher"[10]

[340] Like the Egyptians, Poe would preserve bodies so as to prolong their historical effects. Corpses, particularly female ones, are regularly revived in Poe's tales: Ligeia, Morella, Berenice, and Eleanora all revisit the scenes of their lives. Many readers of Poe have noted the prevalence of female deaths in his work. His dictum that "the death . . . of a beautiful woman is, unquestionably, the most poetical topic in the world" has long suggested both a personal obsession with lost women—stemming from the early loss of his mother, a loss then recapitulated in the death of his young wife—and an aesthetic misogyny working to delimit and destroy women. Yet however much Poe's stories and poems seem to propel and be propelled by the deaths of women, the morbidity of his treatment of women is regularly accompanied by the imagination of their regeneration. The horror, and sometimes solace, for the husbands, brothers, and lovers of these women [341] is that they cannot be extinguished: they return as indestructible forces to haunt their partners. At the same time, these resurrected women testify to the stories their partners tell; they verify the narratives about themselves. Their regenerate corpses thus embody a principle of preservation, safeguarding the consciousnesses in which they figure as memories and thus poetic subjects.

The misogyny in Poe's representations of women consists less in his death plots than in his revivification of women in service to the history of consciousness. Poe's necrophilic interest in women quite distinctively eschews their given generative power and their role in the perpetuation of the species. He fantasizes a self that is always and only self-transmitting. . . . In the tales, he assuages the fear of termination with the notion of succession through regeneration, a regeneration of women's bodies to prolong not themselves but men's minds. The ghoulishness of Poe's portrayal of women lies in this single-minded prohibition of female generativity in order to produce evidence of a particular existence.

The anthropological and androcentric function of such figures as Ligeia, Morella, Berenice, and Eleanora is also to supply a legibility, albeit a problematic one, to death. Their returns, like Madeline's, suggest an uncertainty, both hopeful and horrific, about death. On the one hand, bodies somehow survive death, but on the other hand, bodies seem subject to many forms of death, or to conditions that seem indistinguishable from death. Madeline suffers from catalepsy. The loss of consciousness and rigidification of the muscles caused by this disease make its sufferers likely candidates for premature burial. As Poe explains in "The Premature Burial," even "the most rigorous medical tests fail to establish any material

[10]From Gillian Brown, "The Poetics of Extinction," *The American Face of Edgar Allan Poe*, ed. Shawn Rosenheim and Stephen Rachman (Baltimore: Johns Hopkins UP, 1995.) 340–44.

distinction between the state of the sufferer and what we conceive of absolute death." Thus bodies in such states can be misread, and effectively murdered by misreading. Such fatal misreadings anticipate the eventuality of death, making it the result of human (mis)calculations. The horror of premature burial in "The Fall of the House of Usher" and other Poe tales ("Berenice," "The Cask of Amontillado," and "Loss of Breath") lies in the body's helplessness to govern interpretations of itself. Individual intention always exists [342] amidst other intentionalities, other agents. The consciousness that resurrected bodies signify is not just their own. Corpses in Poe, then, are always potential evidence of murder.

Murder narratives nicely serve Poe's anthropological purposes because they highlight the presence of some form of agency. When Madeline emerges from her premature interment, she reveals her brother's murderous mistake, literally scaring him to death. In her "now final death-agonies," she bears "him to the floor a corpse, and a victim to the terrors he had anticipated." He dies in a "struggle with the grim phantasm, FEAR," just as he had foreseen. Since Roderick's anticipation produces both deaths, the story of the extinction of his family reads as the record of his sensibility. Anticipation thus operates as an engine of transmission, disseminating the traces of human agency in death.

Not just any human agency: What survives is evidence of Roderick's consciousness, imprinted on his friend the narrator, who has shared his presentiments and aided Roderick in entombing Madeline.

12. The Deceptive Narrator of "The Black Cat"[11]

Like "The Tell-Tale Heart," "The Black Cat" is not so much a confession as it is a murderer's attempt to rationalize his crime. "What disease is like Alcohol!" the narrator cries, elsewhere referring to the "Fiend Intemperance" and the "demon" that "possessed me" in order to shift responsibility from himself to his illness. Temperance crusaders sought to change public opinion on alcoholism, to treat it as a disease rather than as a moral failing or vice of the alcoholic. But . . . the story undercuts the narrator's insistence that the demon alcohol made him do it; readers see that his entire story is built on implausibilities and lame excuses, and his crime is motivated by impulses more sinister than a weakness for drink. As with "The Tell-Tale Heart," we must read against the narrator of "The Black Cat," establish which parts of his testimony should be believed and which should not, and try to discover the deeper motivations for the crime.

Once again, the concept of doubling provides a means for making sense of the narrator's strange logic. The black cat that replaces Pluto is certainly a kind of doppelgänger: uncannily, he too is missing an eye, he too is loved by the wife, and he too torments the narrator. . . . I see both cats as doubles for the wife, in the narrator's mind, at least: . . . Whenever the narrator mentions his wife, a black cat is close by. He physically abuses [97] both wife and cat, he tells us, even before hanging Pluto, and when he does hang it, its image mysteriously appears, of all places, on the wall above the unhappy couple's bed. Immediately after the second cat became "a great

---

[11]From Scott Peeples, *Edgar Allan Poe Revisited*, Twayne's United States Authors Series No. 705. (New York: Twayne, 1998) 96–98.

favorite with my wife," he explains, "For my own part, I soon found a dislike to it arising within me": as soon he associates cat with wife, he begins to loathe the cat. It is his wife who calls his attention to the gallows shape of the white spot on the cat's breast—appropriately so, for the gallows not only reflects Pluto's fate but forecasts the narrator's punishment for killing his wife. Finally, he unknowingly walls up the living cat with the wife, so that the cat's crying leads the police to the wife and leads the narrator to the story's final image of the cat perched on the dead wife's head. Although the context makes clear that the narrator's literal reference is to the cat in the last sentence, one can imagine cat and wife converging in the narrator's mind when he says "I had walled the monster up within the tomb!"

But why would the narrator want to kill his wife? For the very reason he gives for killing Pluto: "[I] hung it *because* I knew that it had loved me." He describes his wife as tender, possessing "that humanity of feeling which had once been my distinguishing trait," so it is reasonable to assume she would be affectionate and loving toward him. When the cat "spring[s] upon my knees, covering me with its loathsome caresses," or follows him closely, the narrator "long[s] to destroy it with a blow"; this exaggerated reaction to the cat's behavior leads one to suspect that the cat's expressions of love remind him of his wife's. When he does destroy his wife with a blow, his nonchalance is chilling, in contrast with his reaction to the murder of Pluto, which he calls "a deadly sin that would so jeopardize my immortal soul as to place it—if such a thing were possible—even beyond the reach of the infinite mercy of the Most Merciful and Most Terrible God." Either this guilt actually stems from his decision at that moment to kill his wife, having already killed her surrogate, or . . . he actually does kill his wife at the point when he says he killed Pluto, and in his confession fabricates the incident on the cellar stairs and the existence of a second cat. In either case, he responds to killing the cat as he ought to respond to killing his wife, a sin that is deadly and unforgivable because of his wife's innocence, because she died for loving him.

Such a paradox—death as the penalty for love—seems consistent with the contradictions that make up the narrator's initial description of his story. [98] It is "wild, yet most homely." The incidents have presented "little but Horror," yet he also refers to it as "a series of mere household events" and believes it could be perceived as "an ordinary succession of very natural causes and effects." And although he does not expect to be believed, he tries hard to explain his behavior as the result of all-too-human perverse impulses and the disease of alcoholism. One can attribute these contradictions, like the crime itself, to the narrator's madness, but again the story's network of uncanny images and plot twists warrants some consideration of how these bizarre occurrences might also be "mere household events." What the narrator does is horrible, shocking, and yet perhaps his motivations are common to marriages and other intimate relationships. . . . The narrator's hidden hatred of his wife, his unwillingness to acknowledge that hatred, his displacement of it onto the family pet, and certainly his turning to alcohol could be categorized as common "household events." His ultimate response, of course, is "wild" and "horrible"—but equally frightening is the implication that his predicament is not so uncommon, that, like the perverse impulse to do wrong for wrong's sake, the fear of intimacy is "one of the primitive impulses of the human heart—one of the indivisible primary faculties, or sentiments, which give direction to the character of Man."

Chapter 10

Seven Stories for Additional Enjoyment and Study

John Chioles . . . . Before the Firing Squad, 543
Stephen Crane . . . . The Open Boat, 548
Andre Dubus . . . . The Curse, 563
Charlotte Perkins Gilman . . . . The Yellow Wallpaper, 567
Flannery O'Connor . . . . A Good Man Is Hard to Find, 577
Tillie Olsen . . . . I Stand Here Ironing, 586
Petronius (Gaius Petronius Arbiter) . . . . The Widow of Ephesus, 591

JOHN CHIOLES (b. 1940)

Chioles, a Greek American, is a professor of comparative literature at New York University. He spends half of his time in New York, and half in Athens. He is known for his Literary Theory *(1996) and* Aeschylus: Mythic Theater, Political Voice *(1995). He has translated a number of Greek writers, including Taktsis, Siotis, and Cavafy. With Dinos Siotis, he translated* Twenty Contemporary Greek Poets *(1979). He also wrote a description of the history, art, and architecture of Athens, titled* Athens, Capital City *(1985). In the early 1990s, with Alexander Damianikos, he developed audio cassettes on* Arab and Islam, Hellenism, *and* Reformation. *His moving story "Before the Firing Squad" was included in* The Available Press/PEN Short Story Collection, *with an introduction by Anne Tyler (1985).*

The time of "Before the Firing Squad" is World War II, about 1944, during the closing days of the German occupation of Greece. The physical setting is an area of the Peloponnesus in southern Greece, not far from the site of ancient Sparta. Chioles mentions the Arkadian Mountains and also the area of Mani to the south (paragraph 2). Mani is the middle of the three peninsulas forming the southern part of the Peloponnesus. (The historical ancient Sparta, also in the Peloponnesus, was known for the discipline and ferocity of its armies and for the fact that in the Peloponnesian War in the fifth century BCE *it defeated the forces of Athens.)*

 ## Before the Firing Squad (1985)

The sound at first was a low moan, and you knew the momentum would build as soon as the hand-cranked siren, managed by teenaged boys, would pick up speed. No matter where I was, my knees turned to jelly, my pulse quickened, instinctively I would look up the hill to the bell tower of the church feeling betrayed that I could not be up there; at least there, watching the crank turn, the sound didn't frighten me. But the watch at the bell tower was for the older boys. You had to be at least twelve. From atop, where the giant bell hung, the boys kept a lookout for movement of vehicles; on a clear day they could see seven kilometers in the distance, beyond the bend.

Their convoys came from the main road. The moment they turned the bend that brings you full face with the town, their approach would echo against the side of the mountain. A hollow reverberation. The siren had by then stopped, to be replaced now by the rumbling of their trucks and heavy artillery. A moan of a different kind. The boys would run from the bell tower down the narrow streets to their homes. In no time, the dissonance of the enemy, something as ugly, efficient, and foreign to these parts as the unclean death they brought, appeared and disappeared, taking away the sun, leaving behind clouds of dust. They rarely stopped. But if they did, it could only bring down the reign of terror on all our heads. Mostly, though, they rode through on their way to Mani, where they would embark on ships bound for North Africa. To that end, they would ride roughshod over the Arkadian Mountains. What interested them most was to make sure they passed through the towns and hamlets without incident or delay, ready to crush any attempt at interference.

Their garrison of twelve soldiers stationed in the town wore mustard-colored uniforms, not the sinister black kind worn by the ones in the convoys.° These soldiers seemed very young and curiously happy. Everyone said they spoke a softer kind of German, without the harsh sounds of those northern peoples; most of them knew ancient Greek even, and liked the lilting songs of Homer. Their weapons were limited and not always in evidence. The whole town was ready to swear that these youths had never fought even a skirmish, let alone been in a war. My father used to call them Hitler's boy-soldiers, sent to promote a peaceful occupation, playing on the conscience of the partisans, counting on their decency. And, a curious thing, these young soldiers were never ambushed; none of them died in the everyday activity along these mountains, the daily sabotaging of the main artery, the only asphalt road leading down to the sea. While killing was the order of the day during that spring—ten townspeople executed for the death of one dark-uniformed German—these twelve had become practically the mascots of the town.

"I don't want you talking to this Fritz so much," Father said one day. "Everybody treats him like one of us. It isn't right." All the nice Germans we called Fritz and all the mean ones Ludwig; except that Fritz was really the name of my friend.

5   "He's harmless," I said. "And sometimes he brings his ration of chocolate and biscuits to share."

"He's the enemy," Father retorted the way he did when he would have no more discussion.

But the siren prevented any further talk. They came late in the afternoon of that day. My father was caught unawares. One convoy had already passed earlier, and he had run to the mountain and back again. They rarely had more than one a day. His reflexes were so swift that he practically knocked me over when he jumped to his feet.

"Put your warm sweater on and let's go." He had never taken me with him before. Women and children never ran to the mountain. The siren was for the men, whether they were part of the road sabotage teams or not. My father often stayed in the mountains for days; we never knew what he did there. "Hurry, we have no time. We'll take the back way so Fritz will not spot us. Your mother will know I've taken you with me."

The small garrison, our German mascots, lived across the street from us. They had requisitioned the best two-storied house, using the ground floor as offices and the second floor as living quarters. They were fully aware of the siren, but they pretended it came from the partisan stronghold in the mountain. Some said they even welcomed it; it gave them time

---

°*mustard colored . . . black kind:* The mustard-colored uniforms are those of the regular German army. The black uniforms belong to the Waffen SS, whose members were infamous for their cruelty.

to put on battle outfits, grab their guns, and move, a fierce-looking patrol, along the road. They never asked about the men of each household; their frequent absences from home they were content to believe had to do with working in the fields and vineyards. So Fritz had never asked about my father. Much like any of my friends, he was shy in his presence and avoided passing by whenever it was obvious Father was at home. Often he would come over to show us photos of his parents and his sisters, tell my mother how homesick he was, express joy or sadness whenever he would receive mail from home. And always my mother would find something to give him by way of comfort, a bunch of grapes or chestnuts or a few raisins. But whenever Father was at home it was understood he would never come over. He seemed no more than a boy and was treated much like the rest of us.

"Run faster! They're getting greedy today, and they could be mean." As we ran through brush foliage I would scrape my legs and thought how nice it will be when I get to wear long trousers in another year or so.   10

"When we get on top I'll pick some wild tea leaves and chamomile buds for Mother. We don't have to come right back, do we?"

"We'll stay as long as we have to. Till they're gone." My father's furrowed brow told me this was not a usual run. The enemy was changing its routine; that meant everything would become unpredictable.

"Whoever is not alert, and doesn't expect the worst, will never know the unexpected when it comes his way," my father was saying to his friends when we reached the thick forest of pines. Below us, like ants in the distance, carefully covered heavy artillery rolled along the asphalt road. The atmosphere was highly charged. An unusually large number of people had taken to the mountain. The mood had changed as the sun went away and a cold mid-afternoon chill set in. All the world turned dark green and it smelled of rain, even the canvas covering the moving guns and trucks below took on the color of running oil in the absence of the sun.

"It's best to do nothing for a couple of days. They'll have patrols everywhere," one of the older men was saying to Father.

"We could've blown the far bridge yesterday. We should have been warned about this."   15
"Maybe this is only the beginning of moving out their heavy stuff. It's up to us."

My presence in this adult conversation went unnoticed. Yet I knew I should not be hearing what was being said. So I slipped away quietly. Nearby, some goats beat their grazing rhythm on the bushes; they made the acanthus bob up and down. I had no time to wonder why the goats seemed so nervous. Just then I stepped on a dried branch which flew up at me, my feet got tangled, and I came tumbling a good ten meters down the slope. Though I was stunned, I felt hardly any pain. But the fear was real, for I heard the pounding of a machine-gun and felt the whistle of bullets flying above my head. I stayed down, hardly breathing. The machine-gun, rattling but unable to pin down movement in the vast forest, moved on along a horizontal line, then stopped.

As the moan of the convoy became more distant, I felt my father's hand lifting me up. I was more ashamed than hurting. Not until I stood upright did I see the blood running down my leg and a whole patch of skin from my knee hanging upside down.

"It's nothing" my father said, and quickly used his handkerchief to patch it up.

"It doesn't hurt any," I said.   20

"It will. Why did you come this far? Didn't we say we never come into full view of the road?"

"I fell down."

"You'll be all right. I'm going to have to send you home with your cousins. Your mother should take care of that knee."

I said nothing but followed sheepishly the downward path, my father's handkerchief tied behind my left knee. He had made the knot too tight and I felt a numbing pain but did not let on to my older cousins. Father had whispered something to them, that they should take care of me, I guessed, so I did not want to show I needed looking after.

25   At home there was commotion; our window was open. Mother had been putting my baby sister to sleep; she had lit the oil lamp. Across the way, the German soldiers were playing phonograph records, their usual sad music. (Only, Fritz had told me many times that their music was not at all funereal as the townspeople thought—it was happy and exultant, he'd say; still, it sounded sad to me.) Nobody got wind that I limped into the house at dusk. Stealth was always my strong point.

    When Mother saw me, there was an uproar and a lot to answer for. I explained quickly, and, seeing that my wound was still bleeding, she softened her tone as to the mystery of my whereabouts all afternoon.

    "Here, sit down. Let's have a look."

    I clenched my teeth while she cleaned the whole knee with a sponge. It stung good and sharp now.

    "You must be starved, too. Fritz has brought you a surprise. Uncover that bowl on the table. It's all for you."

30   A bowl of food, rice with bits of chicken, cubed chunks of meat in a thick white soup. Never had I eaten anything so tasty before. It came from a fancy tin that my friend received on special occasions. If each of us had to cherish one memory of food that would make our taste buds water, Fritz's bowl of chicken with rice on that evening would be mine. I felt no pain from the leg while I ate to my heart's content, nor did I notice that he had come to the window, looking in, and already my mother had silently shown him my knee. In no time, he returned with a first-aid kit and set about to dress the wound. He spoke admonishingly to me in German, but also found the right phrases in Greek to let me know he was unhappy with me.

    "Children don't become partisans, you know." But his smile gave him away. He only meant I should be careful. Then he became serious again. Whenever he looked serious his eyebrows went from the straw color of his hair to a darker shade and he looked older. Even his eyes did not keep their blue but went dark like the sea.

    It seemed a cloud hung over the fate of the twelve German soldiers of our town. They would be transferred soon. They might be taken to the front lines. Everything was becoming very unpredictable, he was telling my mother. I had never seen Fritz so sad before. He hung his head low as he pulled out of his trouser pocket a letter he had just received from his mother. She lived, he told us, in a big city in his country that was being bombed constantly now, and they had even less to eat than we did.

    "I do not know if I will see them again."

    "You will, you will. All this will soon be over and you'll get to go home. You'll see," my mother consoled as best she could.

35   The next morning the news was out. The whole town became concerned. If they left, would they be replaced by the black-uniformed ones? What would be in store for us? The neighborhood around us began to treat them like departing friends; they offered them sweets, dried fruits and nuts, and whatever parting hospitality they could. In their turn, the boy-soldiers responded with moist eyes, uncertain, and very scared of the weeks ahead. My mother always said, remembering those last few hours, not one of them looked a day over sixteen.

    An old philosopher who dwelled along the dusty plains of Asia Minor once said there will come a Great Year whose summer will be a World Conflagration. That's just what happened to us that summer. On the very day they came to collect their soldiers and depart for good, they also set fire to nearly every house in the town.

    Activity along the mountains had been fierce lately. The far bridge had been blown up; so had the narrow pass beyond. The siren howled urgently at full speed on that day.

When they turned the bend they began to slow down, rolling into town at a snail's pace to cover for their foot soldiers, who darted off the road, torches in hand, setting fire to every house, every barn, every haystack in sight. That way they took a long time to get to us who lived near the square; but we had seen the smoke and the flames and we knew what was in store for us.

My mother refused to run away, hoping, with children in hand, she might at least save the house. But as the confusion around us got worse, the shooting in all directions, the trails of smoke, the terror-filled sounds of homes bursting open under the flame—no one could possibly be reasoned with, no one caught up in such careening panic. Every black Ludwig looked like a madman in passionate play with fire. During these terrible moments Fritz was nowhere to be seen.

We stood at the door of our house and watched the commotion all around us, until a burst from an automatic hit near our feet and we were routed and shown the way to the open space in the middle of the square. While she held the baby and I held on to her sleeve, my mother shuffled us to the gathering place. We never looked behind. But we knew. All around the square the trucks were moving slowly, never at rest, making a terrible din, which drowned out the cries of the dozen or so women and children huddled in the middle. We were shoved against them, and for the first time I saw a number of our town mascots, the boy-soldiers, armed to the teeth, some guarding us, some being given stern orders by an officer while others were already jumping onto the moving trucks with all their gear.

The officer pointed in our direction and began to scream an order to his subordinates. Three of them rushed over to our group and kneaded us all into a straight line. I saw to my horror that Fritz was one of them. His eyes were dark and furious, hardly anyone recognized him; his whole body and movements had taken on a different shape. I felt a crushing disappointment. He looked old now like the others.

Their mission accomplished, the three ran back to the officer. He gave them what seemed final instructions and climbed into the cab of his moving truck. The three raced to set up just ahead of us a machine-gun with tripod at the front of the barrel. One of them brought the ammunition, and I saw Fritz reach into the box and bring out a magazine, which he loaded onto the gun. Just then, whistles began blowing, those piercing kind they use at train platforms to signal an imminent departure. They didn't want to remain sitting targets for the partisans, so they had to make haste.

Suddenly the motors got louder; speed was only seconds away. Fritz, now arguing with the other two soldiers, appeared even more fierce. They were pushing to get behind the machine-gun, but he seemed to win out. While they rushed to jump on the trucks, he fell on his belly and hugged the gun, groping for the trigger. We were all frozen with fear. I searched for his eyes in utter disbelief. Time fled and backtracked toward me again. I was aware only that the trucks were moving faster, that Fritz was frozen in his place, his right hand now on the ground, too far from the latch of the trigger. Then in a flash he jumped up, lifted the gun from its tripod, and let it sing half across the sky, while in the same motion he chased the last truck, leaping headfirst into it. His torso, writhing wildly to get his weight into the truck, was the last thing I saw of Fritz, who had in those last dancerlike movements transformed his body once more into the boy that he really was, waving goodbye at us with his legs.

QUESTIONS

1. Describe the historical period and the time of action of "The Firing Squad."
2. What aspects of the story may be categorized as realistic?

3. Who is the narrator of the story? How old is he? How much does he understand? In what ways is he a contact between the Greek and the German forces?

4. Explain the irony in this story. What is the irony of the family's knowing Fritz, particularly in view of the story's conclusion?

5. What is the nature of the crisis and climax of this story?

STEPHEN CRANE (1871–1900)

Born in New Jersey, Stephen Crane began writing stories at the age of eight, and by the time he was sixteen he was helping his brothers write for newspapers. He attended a number of colleges but did not graduate. While at Syracuse University, he completed his first novel, Maggie: A Girl of the Streets, *which he published with borrowed money in 1893. During the remainder of his brief and turbulent life (he died of tuberculosis in 1900) he worked as a writer and war correspondent. He spent a year in the West, and two of his better-known stories, "The Bride Comes to Yellow Sky" and "The Blue Hotel," came out of this experience. His best-known novel,* The Red Badge of Courage, *was published in 1895. On January 1, 1897, Crane was a passenger aboard the* Commodore, *a ship that was carrying military cargo to Cuba. Crane was a war correspondent with a New York newspaper, assigned to send dispatches home about the revolution that was then going on in Cuba. Within a day after leaving the port of Jacksonville, Florida, the* Commodore *sank in the Atlantic Ocean, and Crane and three others escaped in a ten-foot long dinghy and managed to come ashore in Daytona Beach. Crane published a news report about the sinking and rescue on January 6, 1897, and half a year later he published "The Open Boat," which is a fictional version of his difficulties in getting to shore in the dinghy.*

 The Open Boat (1897)

A Tale Intended to Be After the Fact:
Being the Experience of Four Men from the Sunk Steamer Commodore

I

None of them knew the color of the sky. Their eyes glanced level, and were fastened upon the waves that swept toward them. These waves were of the hue of slate, save for the tops, which were of foaming white, and all of the men knew the colors of the sea. The horizon narrowed and widened, and dipped and rose, and at all times its edge was jagged with waves that seemed thrust up in points like rocks.

Many a man ought to have a bathtub larger than the boat which here rode upon the sea. These waves were most wrongfully and barbarously abrupt and tall, and each frothtop was a problem in small-boat navigation.

The cook squatted in the bottom, and looked with both eyes at the six inches of gunwale which separated him from the ocean. His sleeves were rolled over his fat forearms, and the two flaps of his unbuttoned vest dangled as he bent to bail out the boat. Often he said, "Gawd! that was a narrow clip." As he remarked it he invariably gazed eastward over the broken sea.

The oiler, steering with one of the two oars in the boat, sometimes raised himself suddenly to keep clear of water that swirled in over the stern. It was a thin little oar, and it seemed often ready to snap.

The correspondent, ° pulling at the other oar, watched the waves and wondered why he   5
was there.

The injured captain, lying in the bow, was at this time buried in that profound dejection and indifference which comes, temporarily at least, to even the bravest and most enduring when, willy-nilly, the firm fails, the army loses, the ship goes down. The mind of the master of a vessel is rooted deep in the timbers of her, though he command for a day or a decade; and this captain had on him the stern impression of a scene in the grays of dawn of seven turned faces, and later a stump of a topmast with a white ball on it, that slashed to and fro at the waves, went low and lower, and down. Thereafter there was something strange in his voice. Although steady, it was deep with mourning, and of a quality beyond oration or tears.

"Keep 'er a little more south, Billie," said he.

"A little more south, sir," said the oiler in the stern.

A seat in this boat was not unlike a seat upon a bucking broncho, and by the same token a broncho is not much smaller. The craft pranced and reared and plunged like an animal. As each wave came, and she rose for it, she seemed like a horse making at a fence outrageously high. The manner of her scramble over these walls of water is a mystic thing, and, moreover, at the top of them were ordinarily these problems in white water, the foam racing down from the summit of each wave requiring a new leap, and a leap from the air. Then, after scornfully bumping a crest, she would slide and race and splash down a long incline, and arrive bobbing and nodding in front of the next menace.

A singular disadvantage of the sea lies in the fact that after successfully surmounting   10
one wave you discover that there is another behind it just as important and just as nervously anxious to do something effective in the way of swamping boats. In a ten-foot dinghy one can get an idea of the resources of the sea in the line of waves that is not probable to the average experience which is never at sea in a dinghy. As each slaty wall of water approached, it shut all else from the view of the men in the boat, and it was not difficult to imagine that this particular wave was the final outburst of the ocean, the last effort of the grim water. There was a terrible grace in the move of the waves, and they came in silence, save for the snarling of the crests.

In the wan light the faces of the men must have been gray. Their eyes must have glinted in strange ways as they gazed steadily astern. Viewed from a balcony, the whole thing would doubtless have been weirdly picturesque. But the men in the boat had no time to see it, and if they had had leisure, there were other things to occupy their minds. The sun swung steadily up the sky, and they knew it was broad day because the color of the sea changed from slate to emerald green streaked with amber lights, and the foam was like tumbling snow. The process of the breaking day was unknown to them. They were aware only of this effect upon the color of the waves that rolled toward them.

In disjointed sentences the cook and the correspondent argued as to the difference between a life-saving station and a house of refuge. The cook had said: "There's a house of refuge just north of the Mosquito Inlet Light, and as soon as they see us they'll come off in their boat and pick us up."

"As soon as who see us?" said the correspondent.

"The crew," said the cook.

"Houses of refuge don't have crews," said the correspondent. "As I understand them,   15
they are only places where clothes and grub are stored for the benefit of shipwrecked people. They don't carry crews."

°*correspondent:* foreign correspondent, newspaper reporter.

"Oh, yes, they do," said the cook.

"No, they don't," said the correspondent.

"Well, we're not there yet, anyhow," said the oiler, in the stern.

"Well," said the cook, "perhaps it's not a house of refuge that I'm thinking of as being near Mosquito Inlet Light; perhaps it's a life-saving station."

20   "We're not there yet," said the oiler in the stern.

II

As the boat bounced from the top of each wave the wind tore through the hair of the hatless men, and as the craft plopped her stern down again the spray slashed past them. The crest of each of these waves was a hill, from the top of which the men surveyed for a moment a broad tumultuous expanse, shining and wind-riven. It was probably splendid, it was probably glorious, this play of the free sea, wild with lights of emerald and white and amber.

"Bully good thing it's an on-shore wind," said the cook. "If not, where would we be? Wouldn't have a show."

"That's right," said the correspondent.

The busy oiler nodded his assent.

25   Then the captain, in the bow, chuckled in a way that expressed humor, contempt, tragedy, all in one. "Do you think we've got much of a show now, boys?" said he.

Whereupon the three were silent, save for a trifle of hemming and hawing. To express any particular optimism at this time they felt to be childish and stupid, but they all doubtless possessed this sense of the situation in their minds. A young man thinks doggedly at such times. On the other hand, the ethics of their condition was decidedly against any open suggestion of hopelessness. So they were silent.

"Oh, well," said the captain, soothing his children, "we'll get ashore all right."

But there was that in his tone which made them think; so the oiler quoth, "Yes! if this wind holds."

The cook was bailing. "Yes! if we don't catch hell in the surf."

30   Canton-flannel gulls flew near and far. Sometimes they sat down on the sea, near patches of brown seaweed that rolled over the waves with a movement like carpets on a line in a gale. The birds sat comfortably in groups, and they were envied by some in the dinghy, for the wrath of the sea was no more to them than it was to a covey of prairie chickens a thousand miles inland. Often they came very close and stared at the men with black bead-like eyes. At these times they were uncanny and sinister in their unblinking scrutiny, and the men hooted angrily at them, telling them to be gone. One came, and evidently decided to alight on the top of the captain's head. The bird flew parallel to the boat and did not circle, but made short sidelong jumps in the air in chicken-fashion. His black eyes were wistfully fixed upon the captain's head. "Ugly brute," said the oiler to the bird. "You look as if you were made with a jacknife." The cook and the correspondent swore darkly at the creature. The captain naturally wished to knock it away with the end of the heavy painter, but he did not dare do it, because anything resembling an emphatic gesture would have capsized this freighted boat; and so, with his open hand, the captain gently and carefully waved the gull away. After it had been discouraged from the pursuit the captain breathed easier on account of his hair, and others breathed easier because the bird struck their minds at this time as being somehow gruesome and ominous.

In the meantime the oiler and the correspondent rowed. And also they rowed. They sat together in the same seat, and each rowed an oar. Then the oiler took both oars; then the correspondent took both oars; then the oiler; then the correspondent. They rowed and they rowed. The very ticklish part of the business was when the time came for the reclining one in the stern to take his turn at the oars. By the very last star of truth, it is easier to steal eggs from under a hen than it was to change seats in the dinghy. First the man in the stern slid his hand along the thwart and moved with care, as if he were of Sèvres.° Then the man in the rowing-seat slid his hand along the other thwart. It was all done with the most extraordinary care. As the two sidled past each other, the whole party kept watchful eyes on the coming wave, and the captain cried: "Look out, now! Steady, there!"

The brown mats of seaweed that appeared from time to time were like islands, bits of earth. They were travelling, apparently, neither one way nor the other. They were, to all intents, stationary. They informed the men in the boat that it was making progress slowly toward the land.

The captain, rearing cautiously in the bow after the dinghy soared on a great swell, said that he had seen the lighthouse at Mosquito Inlet. Presently the cook remarked that he had seen it. The correspondent was at the oars then, and for some reason he too wished to look at the lighthouse; but his back was toward the far shore, and the waves were important, and for some time he could not seize an opportunity to turn his head. But at last there came a wave more gentle than the others, and when at the crest of it he swiftly scoured the western horizon.

"See it?" said the captain.

"No," said the correspondent, slowly; "I didn't see anything."   35

"Look again," said the captain. He pointed. "It's exactly in that direction."

At the top of another wave the correspondent did as he was bid, and this time his eyes chanced on a small, still thing on the edge of the swaying horizon. It was precisely like the point of a pin. It took an anxious eye to find a lighthouse so tiny.

"Think we'll make it, Captain?"

"If this wind holds and the boat don't swamp, we can't do much else," said the captain.   40

The little boat, lifted by each towering sea and splashed viciously by the crests, made progress that in the absence of seaweed was not apparent to those in her. She seemed just a wee thing wallowing, miraculously top up, at the mercy of five oceans. Occasionally a great spread of water, like white flames, swarmed into her.

"Bail her, cook," said the captain, serenely.

"All right, Captain," said the cheerful cook.

III

It would be difficult to describe the subtle brotherhood of men that was here established on the seas. No one said that it was so. No one mentioned it. But it dwelt in the boat, and each man felt it warm him. They were a captain, an oiler, a cook, and a correspondent, and they were friends—friends in a more curiously iron-bound degree than may be common. The hurt captain, lying against the water-jar in the bow, spoke always in a low voice and calmly; but he could never command a more ready and swiftly obedient crew than the motley three of the dinghy. It was more than a mere recognition of what was best for the common safety. There was surely in it a quality that was personal and heart-felt. And after this devotion to the commander of the boat, there was this comradeship, that the correspondent, for instance, who had been taught to be cynical of men, knew even at the time was the best experience of his life. But no one said that it was so. No one mentioned it.

"I wish we had a sail," remarked the captain. "We might try my overcoat on the end of an oar, and give you two boys a chance to rest." So the cook and the correspondent held the mast and spread wide the overcoat; the oiler steered; and the little boat made good way with her new rig. Sometimes the oiler had to scull sharply to keep a sea from breaking into the boat, but otherwise sailing was a success.

°*Sèvres*: a town southwest of Paris that is famous for the manufacture of fine porcelain and china.

45   Meanwhile the lighthouse had been growing slowly larger. It had now almost assumed color, and appeared like a little gray shadow on the sky. The man at the oars could not be prevented from turning his head rather often to try for a glimpse of this little gray shadow.

At last, from the top of each wave, the men in the tossing boat could see land. Even as the lighthouse was an upright shadow on the sky, this land seemed but a long black shadow on the sea. It certainly was thinner than paper. "We must be about opposite New Smyrna,"° said the cook, who had coasted this shore often in schooners. "Captain, by the way, I believe they abandoned that life-saving station there about a year ago."

"Did they?" said the captain.

The wind slowly died away. The cook and the correspondent were not now obliged to slave in order to hold high the oar. But the waves continued their old impetuous swooping at the dinghy, and the little craft, no longer under way, struggled woundily over them. The oiler or the correspondent took the oars again.

Shipwrecks are apropos of nothing. If men could only train for them and have them occur when the men had reached pink condition, there would be less drowning at sea. Of the four in the dinghy none had slept any time worth mentioning for two days and two nights previous to embarking in the dinghy, and in the excitement of clambering about the deck of a foundering ship they had also forgotten to eat heartily.

50   For these reasons, and for others, neither the oiler nor the correspondent was fond of rowing at this time. The correspondent wondered ingenuously how in the name of all that was sane could there be people who thought it amusing to row a boat. It was not an amusement; it was a diabolical punishment, and even a genius of mental aberrations could never conclude that it was anything but a horror to the muscles and crime against the back. He mentioned to the boat in general how the amusement of rowing struck him, and the weary-faced oiler smiled in full sympathy. Previously to the foundering, by the way, the oiler had worked double watch in the engine-room of the ship.

"Take her easy now, boys," said the captain. "Don't spend yourselves. If we have to run a surf you'll need all your strength, because we'll sure have to swim for it. Take your time."

Slowly the land arose from the sea. From a black line it became a line of black and a line of white—trees and sand. Finally the captain said that he could make out a house on the shore. "That's the house of refuge, sure," said the cook. "They'll see us before long, and come out after us."

The distant lighthouse reared high. "The keeper ought to be able to make us out now, if he's looking through a glass," said the captain. "He'll notify the life-saving people."

"None of those other boats could have got ashore to give word of the wreck," said the oiler, in a low voice, "else the life-boat would be out hunting us."

55   Slowly and beautifully the land loomed out of the sea. The wind came again. It had veered from the north-east to the south-east. Finally a new sound struck the ears of the men in the boat. It was the low thunder of the surf on the shore. "We'll never be able to make the lighthouse now," said the captain. "Swing her head a little more north, Billie."

"A little more north, sir," said the oiler.

Whereupon the little boat turned her nose once more down the wind, and all but the oarsman watched the shore grow. Under the influence of this expansion doubt and direful apprehension were leaving the minds of the men. The management of the boat was still most absorbing, but it could not prevent a quiet cheerfulness. In an hour, perhaps, they would be ashore.

Their backbones had become thoroughly used to balancing in the boat, and they now rode this wild colt of a dinghy like circus men. The correspondent thought that he had been

---

°*New Smyrna:* on the East Coast of Florida.

drenched to the skin, but happening to feel in the top pocket of his coat, he found therein eight cigars. Four of them were soaked with seawater; four were perfectly scatheless. After a search, somebody produced three dry matches; and thereupon the four waifs rode impudently in their little boat and, with an assurance of an impending rescue shining in their eyes, puffed at the big cigars, and judged well and ill of all men. Everybody took a drink of water.

IV

"Cook," remarked the captain, "there don't seem to be any signs of life about your house of refuge."

"No," replied the cook. "Funny they don't see us!"   60

A broad stretch of lowly coast lay before the eyes of the men. It was of low dunes topped with dark vegetation. The roar of the surf was plain, and sometimes they could see the white lip of a wave as it spun up the beach. A tiny house was blocked out black upon the sky. Southward, the slim lighthouse lifted its little gray length.

Tide, wind, and waves were swinging the dinghy northward. "Funny they don't see us," said the men.

The surf's roar was here dulled, but its tone was nevertheless thunderous and mighty. As the boat swam over the great rollers the men sat listening to this roar. "We'll swamp sure," said everybody.

It is fair to say here that there was not a life-saving station within twenty miles in either direction; but the men did not know this fact, and in consequence they made dark and opprobrious remarks concerning the eyesight of the nation's life-savers. Four scowling men sat in the dinghy and surpassed records in the invention of epithets.

"Funny they don't see us."   65

The light-heartedness of a former time had completely faded. To their sharpened minds it was easy to conjure pictures of all kinds of incompetency and blindness and, indeed, cowardice. There was the shore of the populous land, and it was bitter and bitter to them that from it came no sign.°

"Well," said the captain, ultimately, "I suppose we'll have to make a try for ourselves. If we stay out here too long, we'll none of us have strength left to swim after the boat swamps."

And so the oiler, who was at the oars, turned the boat straight for the shore. There was a sudden tightening of muscles. There was some thinking.

"If we don't all get ashore," said the captain—"if we don't all get ashore, I suppose you fellows know where to send news of my finish?"

They then briefly exchanged some addresses and admonitions. As for the reflections of   70
the men, there was a great deal of rage in them. Perchance they might be formulated thus: "If I am going to be drowned—if I am going to be drowned—if I am going to be drowned, why, in the name of the seven mad gods who rule the sea, was I allowed to come thus far and contemplate sand and trees? Was I brought here merely to have my nose dragged away as I was about to nibble the sacred cheese of life? It is preposterous. If this old ninny-woman, Fate, cannot do better than this, she should be deprived of the management of men's fortunes. She is an old hen who knows not her intention. If she has decided to drown me, why did she not do it in the beginning and save me all this trouble? The whole affair is absurd.—But no; she cannot mean to drown me. She dare not drown me. She cannot drown me. Not after all this work." Afterward the man might have had an impulse to shake his fist at the clouds. "Just you drown me, now, and then hear what I call you!"

°*No sign:* See Matthew 12:38, 39.

The billows that came at this time were more formidable. They seemed always just about to break and roll over the little boat in a turmoil of foam. There was a preparatory and long growl in the speech of them. No mind unused to the sea would have concluded that the dinghy could ascend these sheer heights in time. The shore was still afar. The oiler was a wily surfman. "Boys," he said swiftly, "she won't live three minutes more, and we're too far out to swim. Shall I take her to sea again, Captain?"

"Yes; go ahead!" said the captain.

This oiler, by a series of quick miracles and fast and steady oarsmanship, turned the boat in the middle of the surf and took her safely to sea again.

There was a considerable silence as the boat bumped over the furrowed sea to deeper water. Then somebody in gloom spoke: "Well, anyhow, they must have seen us from the shore by now."

75   The gulls went in slanting flight up the wind toward the gray, desolate east. A squall, marked by dingy clouds and clouds brick-red like smoke from a burning building, appeared from the south-east.

"What do you think of those life-saving people? Ain't they peaches?"

"Funny they haven't seen us."

"Maybe they think we're out here for sport! Maybe they think we're fishin'. Maybe they think we're damned fools."

It was a long afternoon. A changed tide tried to force them southward, but wind and wave said northward. Far ahead, where coast-line, sea, and sky formed their mighty angle, there were little dots which seemed to indicate a city on the shore.

80   "St. Augustine?"

The captain shook his head. "Too near Mosquito Inlet."

And the oiler rowed, and then the correspondent rowed; then the oiler rowed. It was a weary business. The human back can become the seat of more aches and pains than are registered in books for the composite anatomy of a regiment. It is a limited area, but it can become the theatre of innumerable muscular conflicts, tangles, wrenches, knots, and other comforts.

"Did you ever like to row, Billie?" asked the correspondent.

"No," said the oiler; "hang it!"

85   When one exchanged the rowing-seat for a place in the bottom of the boat, he suffered a bodily depression that caused him to be careless of everything save an obligation to wiggle one finger. There was cold sea-water swashing to and fro in the boat, and he lay in it. His head, pillowed on a thwart, was within an inch of the swirl of a wave-crest, and sometimes a particularly obstreperous sea came inboard and drenched him once more. But these matters did not annoy him. It is almost certain that if the boat had capsized he would have tumbled comfortably upon the ocean as if he felt sure that it was a great soft mattress.

"Look! There's a man on the shore!"

"Where?"

"There! See 'im?"

"Yes, sure! He's walking along."

90   "Now he's stopped. Look! He's facing us!"

"He's waving at us!"

"So he is! By thunder!"

"Ah, now we're all right! Now we're all right! There'll be a boat out here for us in half an hour."

"He's going on. He's running. He's going up to that house there."

95   The remote beach seemed lower than the sea, and it required a searching glance to discern the little black figure. The captain saw a floating stick, and they rowed to it. A bath towel was by some weird chance in the boat, and, tying this on the stick, the captain waved it. The oarsman did not dare turn his head, so he was obliged to ask questions.

"What's he doing now?"

"He's standing still again. He's looking, I think.—There he goes again—toward the house.—Now he's stopped again."

"Is he waving at us?"

"No, not now; he was, though."

"Look! There comes another man!"   100

"He's running."

"Look at him go, would you!"

"Why, he's on a bicycle. Now he's met the other man. They're both waving at us. Look!"

"There comes something up the beach."

"What the devil is that thing?"   105

"Why, it looks like a boat."

"Why, certainly, it's a boat."

"No; it's on wheels."

"Yes, so it is. Well, that must be the life-boat. They drag them along shore on a wagon."

"That's the life-boat, sure."   110

"No, by God, it's—it's an omnibus."

"I tell you it's a life-boat."

"It is not! It's an omnibus. I can see it plain. See? One of the these big hotel omnibuses."

"By thunder, you're right. It's an omnibus, sure as fate. What do you suppose they are doing with an omnibus? Maybe they are going around collecting the life-crew, hey?"

"That's it, likely. Look! There's a fellow waving a little black flag. He's standing on the   115
steps of the omnibus. There come those other two fellows. Now they're all talking together. Look at the fellow with the flag. Maybe he ain't waving it!"

"That ain't a flag, is it? That's his coat. Why, certainly, that's his coat."

"So it is; it's his coat. He's taken it off and is waving it around his head. But would you look at him swing it!"

"Oh, say, there isn't any life-saving station there. That's just a winter-resort hotel omnibus that has brought over some of the boarders to see us drown."

"What's that idiot with the coat mean? What's he signalling, anyhow?"

"It looks as if he were trying to tell us to go north. There must be a life-saving station up   120
there."

"No; he thinks we're fishing. Just giving us a merry hand. See? Ah, there, Willie!"

"Well, I wish I could make something out of those signals. What do you suppose he means?"

"He don't mean anything; he's just playing."

"Well, if he'd just signal us to try the surf again, or to go to sea and wait, or go north, or go south, or go to hell, there would be some reason in it. But look at him! He just stands there and keeps his coat revolving like a wheel. The ass!"

"There come more people."   125

"Now there's quite a mob. Look! Isn't that a boat?"

"Where? Oh, I see where you mean. No, that's no boat."

"That fellow is still waving his coat."

"He must think we like to see him do that. Why don't he quit it? It don't mean anything."

"I don't know. I think he is trying to make us go north. It must be that there's a life-saving   130
station there somewhere."

"Say, he ain't tired yet. Look at 'im wave!"

"Wonder how long he can keep that up. He's been revolving his coat ever since he caught sight of us. He's an idiot. Why aren't they getting men to bring a boat out? A fishing boat—one of those big yawls—could come out here all right. Why don't he do something?"

"Oh, it's all right now."

"They'll have a boat out here for us in less than no time, now that they've seen us."

135   A faint yellow tone came into the sky over the low land. The shadows on the sea slowly deepened. The wind bore coldness with it, and the men began to shiver.

"Holy smoke!" said one, allowing his voice to express his impious mood, "If we keep on monkeying out here! If we've got to flounder out here all night!"

"Oh, we'll never have to stay here all night! Don't you worry. They've seen us now, and it won't be long before they'll come chasing out after us."

The shore grew dusky. The man waving a coat blended gradually into this gloom, and it swallowed in the same manner the omnibus and the group of people. The spray, when it dashed uproariously over the side, made the voyagers shrink and swear like men who were being branded.

"I'd like to catch the chump who waved the coat. I feel like socking him one, just for luck."

140   "Why? What did he do?"

"Oh, nothing, but then he seemed so damned cheerful."

In the meantime the oiler rowed, and then the correspondent rowed, and then the oiler rowed. Gray-faced and bowed forward, they mechanically, turn by turn, plied the leaden oars. The form of the lighthouse had vanished from the southern horizon, but finally a pale star appeared, just lifting from the sea. The streaked saffron in the west passed before the all-merging darkness, and the sea to the east was black. The land had vanished, and was expressed only by the low and drear thunder of the surf.

"If I am going to be drowned—if I am going to be drowned—if I am going to be drowned, why, in the name of the seven mad gods who rule the sea, was I allowed to come thus far and contemplate sand and trees? Was I brought here merely to have my nose dragged away as I was about to nibble the sacred cheese of life?"

The patient captain, drooped over the water-jar, was sometimes obliged to speak to the oarsman.

145   "Keep her head up! Keep her head up!"

"Keep her head, up, sir." The voices were weary and low.

This was surely a quiet evening. All save the oarsman lay heavily and listlessly in the boat's bottom. As for him, his eyes were just capable of noting the tall black waves that swept forward in a most sinister silence, save for an occasional subdued growl of a crest.

The cook's head was on a thwart, and he looked without interest at the water under this nose. He was deep in other scenes. Finally he spoke. "Billie," he murmured, dreamfully, "what kind of pie do you like best?"

V

"Pie!" said the oiler and the correspondent, agitatedly. "Don't talk about those things, blast you!"

150   "Well," said the cook, "I was just thinking about ham sandwiches, and—"

A night on the sea in an open boat is a long night. As darkness settled finally, the shine of the light, lifting from the sea in the south, changed to full gold. On the northern horizon a new light appeared, a small bluish gleam on the edge of the waters. These two lights were the furniture of the world. Otherwise there was nothing but waves.

Two men huddled in the stern, and distances were so magnificent in the dinghy that the rower was enabled to keep his feet partly warm by thrusting them under his companions. Their legs indeed extended far under the rowing-seat until they touched the feet of the captain forward. Sometimes, despite the efforts of the tired oarsman, a wave came piling into the boat, an icy wave of the night, and the chilling water soaked them anew. They would twist their bodies for a moment and groan, and sleep the dead sleep once more, while the water in the boat gurgled about them as the craft rocked.

The plan of the oiler and the correspondent was for one to row until he lost the ability, and then arouse the other from his sea-water couch in the bottom of the boat.

The oiler plied the oars until his head drooped forward and the overpowering sleep blinded him; and he rowed yet afterward. Then he touched a man in the bottom of the boat, and called his name. "Will you spell me for a little while?" he said meekly.

"Sure, Billie," said the correspondent, awaking and dragging himself to a sitting posi-   155
tion. They exchanged places carefully, and the oiler, cuddling down in the sea-water at the cook's side, seemed to go to sleep instantly.

The particular violence of the sea had ceased. The waves came without snarling. The obligation of the man at the oars was to keep the boat headed so that the tilt of the roller would not capsize her, and to preserve her from filling when the crests rushed past. The black waves were silent and hard to be seen in the darkness. Often one was almost upon the boat before the oarsman was aware.

In a low voice the correspondent addressed the captain. He was not sure that the captain was awake, although this iron man seemed to be always awake. "Captain, shall I keep her making for that light north, sir?"

The same steady voice answered him. "Yes. Keep it about two points off the port bow."

The cook had tied a life-belt around himself in order to get even the warmth which this clumsy cork contrivance could donate, and he seemed almost stove-like when a rower, whose teeth invariably chattered wildly as soon as he ceased his labor, dropped down to sleep.

The correspondent, as he rowed, looked down at the two men sleeping underfoot. The   160
cook's arm was around the oiler's shoulders, and, with their fragmentary clothing and haggard faces, they were the babes of the sea—a grotesque rendering of the old babes in the wood.

Later he must have grown stupid at his work, for suddenly there was a growling of water, and a crest came with a roar and a swash into the boat, and it was a wonder that it did not set the cook afloat in his life-belt. The cook continued to sleep, but the oiler sat up, blinking his eyes and shaking with the new cold.

"Oh, I'm awful sorry, Billie," said the correspondent, contritely.

"That's all right, old boy," said the oiler, and lay down again and was asleep.

Presently it seemed that even the captain dozed, and the correspondent thought that he was the one man afloat on all the oceans. The wind had a voice as it came over the waves, and it was sadder than the end.

There was a long, loud swishing astern of the boat, and a gleaming trail of phosphores-   165
cence, like blue flame, was furrowed on the black waters. It might have been made by a monstrous knife.

Then there came a stillness, while the correspondent breathed with open mouth and looked at the sea.

Suddenly there was another swish and another long flash of bluish light, and this time it was alongside the boat, and might almost have been reached with an oar. The correspondent saw an enormous fin speed like a shadow through the water, hurling the crystalline spray and leaving the long glowing trail.

The correspondent looked over his shoulder at the captain. His face was hidden, and he seemed to be asleep. He looked at the babes of the sea. They certainly were asleep. So, being bereft of sympathy, he leaned a little way to one side and swore softly into the sea.

But the thing did not then leave the vicinity of the boat. Ahead or astern, on one side or the other, at intervals long or short, fled the long sparkling streak, and there was to be heard the *whirroo* of the dark fin. The speed and power of the thing was greatly to be admired. It cut the water like a gigantic and keen projectile.

The presence of this biding thing did not affect the man with the same horror that it would   170
if he had been a picnicker. He simply looked at the sea dully and swore in an undertone.

Nevertheless, it is true that he did not wish to be alone with the thing. He wished one of his companions to awake by chance and keep him company with it. But the captain hung motionless over the water-jar, and the oiler and the cook in the bottom of the boat were plunged in slumber.

VI

"If I am going to be drowned—if I am going to be drowned—if I am going to be drowned, why, in the name of the seven mad gods who rule the sea, was I allowed to come thus far and contemplate sand and trees?"

During this dismal night, it may be remarked that a man would conclude that it was really the intention of the seven mad gods to drown him, despite the abominable injustice of it. For it was certainly an abominable injustice to drown a man who had worked so hard, so hard. The man felt it would be a crime most unnatural.° Other people had drowned at sea since galleys swarmed with painted sails, but still—

When it occurs to a man that nature does not regard him as important, and that she feels she would not maim the universe by disposing of him, he at first wishes to throw bricks at the temple, and he hates deeply the fact that there are no bricks and no temples. Any visible expression of nature would surely be pelleted with his jeers.

175 Then, if there be no tangible thing to hoot, he feels, perhaps, the desire to confront a personification and indulge in pleas, bowed to one knee, and with hands supplicant, saying, "Yes, but I love myself."

A high cold star on a winter's night is the word he feels that she says to him. Thereafter he knows the pathos of his situation.

The men in the dinghy had not discussed these matters, but each had, no doubt, reflected upon them in silence and according to his mind. There was seldom any expression upon their faces save the general one of complete weariness. Speech was devoted to the business of the boat.

To chime the notes of his emotion, a verse mysteriously entered the correspondent's head. He had even forgotten that he had forgotten this verse, but it suddenly was in his mind.

> A soldier of the Legion lay dying in Algiers;
> There was lack of woman's nursing, there was dearth of woman's tears;
> But a comrade stood beside him, and he took that comrade's hand,
> And he said, "I never more shall see my own, my native land."°

In his childhood the correspondent had been made acquainted with the fact that a soldier of the Legion lay dying in Algiers, but he had never regarded the fact as important. Myriads of his school-fellows had informed him of the soldier's plight, but the dinning had naturally ended by making him perfectly indifferent. He had never considered it his affair that a soldier of the Legion lay dying in Algiers, nor had it appeared to him as a matter for sorrow. It was less to him than the breaking of a pencilpoint.

180 Now, however, it quaintly came to him as a human, living thing. It was no longer merely a picture of a few throes in the breast of a poet, meanwhile drinking tea and warming his feet at the grate; it was an actuality—stern, mournful, and fine.

The correspondent plainly saw the soldier. He lay on the sand with his feet out straight and still. While his pale left hand was upon his chest in an attempt to thwart the going of his life, the blood came between his fingers. In the far Algerian distance, a city of low square forms was set against a sky that was faint with the last sunset hues. The correspondent, plying the oars and dreaming of the slow and slower movements of the lips of the soldier, was

---

°*most unnatural:* See *Hamlet,* 1.5.25, 28 (p. 1341–42)
°*A soldier of the Legion . . . native land:* freely quoted and shortened from Caroline Norton's poem, "Bingen on the Rhine" (1883).

moved by a profound and perfectly impersonal comprehension. He was sorry for the soldier of the Legion who lay dying in Algiers.

The thing which had followed the boat and waited had evidently grown bored at the delay. There was no longer to be heard the slash of the cutwater, and there was no longer the flame of the long trail. The light in the north still glimmered, but it was apparently no nearer to the boat. Sometimes the boom of the surf rang in the correspondent's ears, and he turned the craft seaward then and rowed harder. Southward, some one had evidently built a watch-fire on the beach. It was too low and too far to be seen, but it made a shimmering, roseate reflection upon the bluff in back of it, and this could be discerned from the boat. The wind came stronger, and sometimes a wave suddenly raged out like a mountain cat, and there was to be seen the sheen and sparkle of a broken crest.

The captain, in the bow, moved on his water-jar and sat erect. "Pretty long night," he observed to the correspondent. He looked at the shore. "Those life-saving people take their time."

"Did you see that shark playing around?"

"Yes, I saw him. He was a big fellow, all right."

"Wish I had known you were awake."

Later the correspondent spoke into the bottom of the boat.

"Billie!" There was a slow and gradual disentanglement.

"Billie, will you spell me?"

"Sure," said the oiler.

As soon as the correspondent touched the cold, comfortable sea-water in the bottom of the boat and had huddled close to the cook's life-belt he was deep in sleep, despite the fact that his teeth played all the popular airs. This sleep was so good to him that it was but a moment before he heard a voice call his name in a tone that demonstrated the last stages of exhaustion. "Will you spell me?"

"Sure, Billie."

The light in the north had mysteriously vanished, but the correspondent took his course from the wide-awake captain.

Later in the night they took the boat farther out to sea, and the captain directed the cook to take one oar at the stern and keep the boat facing the seas. He was to call out if he should hear the thunder of the surf. This plan enabled the oiler and the correspondent to get respite together. "We'll give those boys a chance to get into shape again," said the captain. They curled down and, after a few preliminary chatterings and trembles, slept once more the dead sleep. Neither knew they had bequeathed to the cook the company of another shark, or perhaps the same shark.

As the boat caroused on the waves, spray occasionally bumped over the side and gave them a fresh soaking, but this had no power to break their repose. The ominous slash of the wind and the water affected them as it would have affected mummies.

"Boys," said the cook, with the notes of every reluctance in his voice, "she's drifted in pretty close. I guess one of you had better take her to sea again." The correspondent, aroused, heard the crash of the toppled crests.

As he was rowing, the captain gave him some whisky-and-water, and this steadied the chills out of him. "If I ever get ashore and anybody shows me even a photograph of an oar—"

At last there was a short conversation.

"Billie!—Billie, will you spell me?"

"Sure," said the oiler.

VII

When the correspondent again opened his eyes, the sea and sky were each of the gray hue of the dawning. Later, carmine and gold was painted upon the waters. The morning appeared finally, in its splendor, with a sky of pure blue, and the sunlight flamed on the tips of the waves.

On the distant dunes were set many little black cottages, and a tall white windmill reared above them. No man, nor dog, nor bicycle appeared on the beach. The cottages might have formed a deserted village.

The voyagers scanned the shore. A conference was held in the boat. "Well," said the captain, "if no help is coming, we might better try a run through the surf right away. If we stay out here much longer we will be too weak to do anything for ourselves at all." The others silently acquiesced in this reasoning. The boat was headed for the beach. The correspondent wondered if none ever ascended the tall wind-tower, and if they never looked seaward. This tower was a giant, standing with its back to the plight of the ants. It represented in a degree, to the correspondent, the serenity of nature amid the struggles of the individual— nature in the wind, and nature in the vision of men. She did not seem cruel to him then, nor beneficent, nor treacherous, nor wise. But she was indifferent, flatly indifferent. It is, perhaps, plausible that a man in this situation, impressed with the unconcern of the universe, should see the innumerable flaws of life, and have them taste wickedly in his mind, and wish for another chance. A distinction between right and wrong seems absurdly clear to him, then, in this new ignorance of the grave-edge, and he understands that if he were given another opportunity he would mend his conduct and his words, and be better and brighter during an introduction or at a tea.

"Now, boys," said the captain, "she is going to swamp sure. All we can do is to work her in as far as possible, and then when she swamps, pile out and scramble for the beach. Keep cool now, and don't jump until she swamps sure."

205   The oiler took the oars. Over his shoulders he scanned the surf. "Captain," he said, "I think I'd better bring her about and keep her head-on to the seas and back her in."

"All right, Billie," said the captain. "Back her in." The oiler swung the boat then, and, seated in the stern, the cook and the correspondent were obliged to look over their shoulders to contemplate the lonely and indifferent shore.

The monstrous inshore rollers heaved the boat high until the men were again enabled to see the white sheets of water scudding up the slanted beach. "We won't get in very close," said the captain. Each time a man could wrest his attention from the rollers, he turned his glance toward the shore, and in the expression of the eyes during this contemplation there was a singular quality. The correspondent, observing the others, knew that they were not afraid, but the full meaning of their glances was shrouded.

As for himself, he was too tired to grapple fundamentally with the fact. He tried to coerce his mind into thinking of it, but the mind was dominated at this time by the muscles, and the muscles said they did not care. It merely occurred to him that if he should drown it would be a shame.

There were no hurried words, no pallor, no plain agitation. The men simply looked at the shore. "Now, remember to get well clear of the boat when you jump," said the captain.

210   Seaward the crest of a roller suddenly fell with a thunderous crash, and the long white comber came roaring down upon the boat.

"Steady now," said the captain. The men were silent. They turned their eyes from the shore to the comber and waited. The boat slid up the incline, leaped at the furious top, bounced over it, and swung down the long back of the wave. Some water had been shipped, and the cook bailed it out.

But the next crest crashed also. The tumbling, boiling flood of white water caught the boat and whirled it almost perpendicular. Water swarmed in from all sides. The correspondent had his hands on the gunwale at this time, and when the water entered at that place he swiftly withdrew his fingers, as if he objected to wetting them.

The little boat, drunken with this weight of water, reeled and snuggled deeper into the sea.

"Bail her out, cook! Bail her out!" said the captain.

215   "All right, Captain," said the cook.

"Now, boys, the next one will do for us sure," said the oiler. "Mind to jump clear of the boat."

The third wave moved forward, huge, furious, implacable. It fairly swallowed the dinghy, and almost simultaneously the men tumbled into the sea. A piece of life-belt had lain in the bottom of the boat, and as the correspondent went overboard he held this to his chest with his left hand.

The January water was icy, and he reflected immediately that it was colder than he had expected to find it off the coast of Florida. This appeared to his dazed mind as a fact important enough to be noted at the time. The coldness of the water was sad; it was tragic. This fact was somehow mixed and confused with his opinion of his own situation, so that it seemed almost a proper reason for tears. The water was cold.

When he came to the surface he was conscious of little but the noisy water. Afterward he saw his companions in the sea. The oiler was ahead in the race. He was swimming strongly and rapidly. Off to the correspondent's left, the cook's great white and corked back bulged out of the water; and in the rear the captain was hanging with his one good hand to the keel of the overturned dinghy.

There is a certain immovable quality to a shore, and the correspondent wondered at it   220
amid the confusion of the sea.

It seemed also very attractive; but the correspondent knew that it was a long journey, and he paddled leisurely. The piece of life-preserver lay under him, and sometimes he whirled down the incline of a wave as if he were on a handsled.

But finally he arrived at a place in the sea where travel was beset with difficulty. He did not pause swimming to inquire what manner of current had caught him, but there his progress ceased. The shore was set before him like a bit of scenery on a stage, and he looked at it and understood with his eyes each detail of it.

As the cook passed, much farther to the left, the captain was calling to him, "Turn over on your back, cook! Turn over on your back and use the oar."

"All right, sir." The cook turned on his back, and, paddling with an oar, went ahead as if he were a canoe.

Presently the boat also passed to the left of the correspondent, with the captain clinging   225
with one hand to the keel. He would have appeared like a man raising himself to look over a board fence if it were not for the extraordinary gymnastics of the boat. The correspondent marvelled that the captain could still hold to it.

They passed on nearer to shore—the oiler, the cook, the captain—and following them went the water-jar, bouncing gaily over the seas.

The correspondent remained in the grip of this strange new enemy—a current. The shore, with its white slope of sand and its green bluff topped with little silent cottages, was spread like a picture before him. It was very near to him then, but he was impressed as one who, in a gallery, looks at a scene from Brittany or Algiers.

He thought: "I am going to drown? Can it be possible? Can it be possible? Can it be possible?" Perhaps an individual must consider his own death to be the final phenomenon of nature.

But later a wave perhaps whirled him out of this small deadly current, for he found suddenly that he could again make progress toward the shore. Later still he was aware that the captain, clinging with one hand to the keel of the dinghy, had his face turned away from the shore and toward him, and was calling his name. "Come to the boat! Come to the boat!"

In his struggle to reach the captain and the boat, he reflected that when one gets prop-   230
erly wearied drowning must really be a comfortable arrangement—a cessation of hostilities accompanied by a large degree of relief; and he was glad of it, for the main thing in his mind for some moments had been horror of the temporary agony. He did not wish to be hurt.

Presently he saw a man running along the shore. He was undressing with most remarkable speed. Coat, trousers, shirt, everything flew magically off him.

"Come to the boat!" called the captain.

"All right, Captain." As the correspondent paddled, he saw the captain let himself down to bottom and leave the boat. Then the correspondent performed his one little marvel of the voyage. A large wave caught him and flung him with ease and supreme speed completely over the boat and far beyond it. It struck him even then as an event in gymnastics and a true miracle of the sea. An overturned boat in the surf is not a plaything to a swimming man.

The correspondent arrived in water that reached only to his waist, but his condition did not enable him to stand for more than a moment. Each wave knocked him into a heap, and the undertow pulled at him.

235

Then he saw the man who had been running and undressing, and undressing and running, come bounding into the water. He dragged ashore the cook, and then waded toward the captain; but the captain waved him away and sent him to the correspondent. He was naked—naked as a tree in winter; but a halo was about his head, and he shone like a saint. He gave a strong pull, and a long drag, and a bully heave at the correspondent's hand. The correspondent, schooled in the minor formulae, said, "Thanks, old man." But suddenly the man cried, "What's that?" He pointed a swift finger. The correspondent said, "Go."

In the shallows, face downward, lay the oiler. His forehead touched sand that was periodically, between each wave, clear of the sea.

The correspondent did not know all that transpired afterward. When he achieved safe ground he fell, striking the sand with each particular part of his body. It was as if he had dropped from a roof, but the thud was grateful to him.

It seems that instantly the beach was populated with men with blankets, clothes, and flasks, and women with coffee-pots and all the remedies sacred to their minds. The welcome of the land to the men from the sea was warm and generous; but a still and dripping shape was carried slowly up the beach, and the land's welcome for it could only be the different and sinister hospitality of the grave.

When it came night, the white waves paced to and fro in the moonlight, and the wind brought the sound of the great sea's voice to the men on the shore, and they felt that they could then be interpreters.

QUESTIONS

1. Describe the speaker of the story. What is his position for seeing and reporting the action? How freely does he add his own commentary to the action and to the four survivors on the boat?

2. What is the significance of the fragment of the poem "The Soldier of Algiers" by Caroline Norton? How does the recollection influence the thoughts of the correspondent?

3. Although the story of "The Open Boat" is deadly serious, what elements of humor do you find in the story? Why do you think they are introduced as often as they are? What is the characteristic situation that brings about the humor of the situations and the commentary? What elements of the speech of the characters are treated comically?

4. What philosophical conclusions does the speaker draw from the materials of the story? Why is the passage "If I am going to be drowned . . . contemplate sand and trees" repeated throughout the story? How does this passage pertain particularly to Billie, the oiler? What is meant by the concluding statement that the rescued men "could then be interpreters"?

ANDRE DUBUS (1936–1999)

Dubus was born in Louisiana and received degrees from McNeese State College and the University of Iowa. He taught at Bradford College in Massachusetts before he was struck and disabled by a speeding automobile. He lived northwest of Boston near the Merrimack River, an area he often employed as the setting in his ficiton. The stories in his Selected Stories *(1988), from which "The Curse" is taken, touch the darker areas of human existence, but nevertheless have a compelling force. In "They Now Live in Texas," for example, a woman sees a horror ghost movie on her VCR and then awaits her own demons. In another story, "Townies,"* a drifting, purposeless young man kills his girlfriend and then achieves a curious serenity as he waits for the police. Dubus's last short story collection was Dancing After Hours *(1996). He also worked in the longer form of the novella and published several novellas in* We Don't Live Here Anymore *(1984). He gained many honors, among them a Guggenheim Fellowship and a MacArthur Fellowship.*

 ## The Curse (1988)

Mitchell Hayes was forty-nine years old, but when the cops left him in the bar with Bob, the manager, he felt much older. He did not know what it was like to be very old, a shrunken and wrinkled man, but he assumed it was like this: fatigue beyond relieving by rest, by sleep. He also was not a small man: his weight moved up and down in the hundred and seventies and he was five feet, ten inches tall. But now his body seemed short and thin. Both stood at one end of the bar; he was a large blackhaired man, and there was nothing in front of him but an ash tray he was using. He looked at Mitchell at the cash register and said: "Forget it. You heard what Smitty said."

Mitchell looked away, at the front door. He had put the chairs upside down on the table. He looked from the door past Bob to the empty space of floor at the rear; sometimes people danced there, to the jukebox. Opposite Bob, on the wall behind the bar, was a telephone; Mitchell looked at it. He had told Smitty there were five guys and when he moved to the phone one of them stepped around the corner of the bar and shoved him: one hand against Mitchell's chest, and it pushed him backward; he nearly fell. That was when they were getting rough with her at the bar. When they took her to the floor Mitchell looked once at her sounds, then looked down at the duckboard he stood on, or at the belly or chest of a young man in front of him.

He knew they were not drunk. They had been drinking before they came to his place, a loud popping of motorcycles outside, then walking into the empty bar, young and sunburned and carrying helmets and wearing thick leather jackets in August. They stood in front of Mitchell and drank drafts. When he took their first order he thought they were on drugs and later, watching them, he was certain. They were not relaxed, in the way of most drinkers near closing time. Their eyes were quick, alert as wary animals, and they spoke loudly, with passion, but their passion was strange and disturbing, because they were only chatting, bantering. Mitchell knew nothing of the effects of drugs, so could not guess what was in their blood. He feared and hated drugs because of his work and because he was the stepfather of teenagers: a boy and a girl. He gave last call and served them and leaned against the counter behind him.

Then the door opened and the girl walked in from the night, a girl he had never seen, and she crossed the floor toward Mitchell. He stepped forward to tell her she had missed last call, but before he spoke she asked for change for the cigarette machine. She was young, he guessed nineteen to twenty-one, and deeply tanned and had dark hair. She was sober and wore jeans and a dark blue tee shirt. He gave her the quarters but she was standing between two of the men and she did not get to the machine.

5   When it was over and she lay crying on the cleared circle of floor, he left the bar and picked up the jeans and tee shirt beside her and crouched and handed them to her. She did not look at him. She lay the clothes across her breasts and what Mitchell thought of now as her wound. He left her and dialed 911, then Bob's number. He woke up Bob. Then he picked up her sneakers from the floor and placed them beside her and squatted near her face, her crying. He wanted to speak to her and touch her, hold a hand or press her brow, but he could not.

    The cruiser was there quickly, the siren coming east from town, then slowing and deepening as the car stopped outside. He was glad Smitty was one of them; he had gone to high school with Smitty. The other was Dave, and Mitchell knew him because it was a small town. When they saw the girl Dave went out to the cruiser to call for an ambulance, and when he came back he said two other cruisers had those scumbags and were taking them in. The girl was still crying and could not talk to Smitty and Dave. She was crying when a man and woman lifted her onto a stretcher and rolled her out the door and she vanished forever in a siren.

    Bob came in while Smitty and Dave were sitting at the bar drinking coffee and Smitty was writing his report; Mitchell stood behind the bar. Bob sat next to Dave as Mitchell said: "I could have stopped them, Smitty."

    "That's our job," Smitty said. "You want to be in the hospital now?"

    Mitchell did not answer. When Smitty and Dave left, he got a glass of Coke from the cobra and had a cigarette with Bob. They did not talk. Then Mitchell washed his glass and Bob's cup and they left, turning off the lights. Outside Mitchell locked the front door, feeling the sudden night air after almost ten hours of air conditioning. When he had come to work the day had been very hot, and now he thought it would not have happened in winter. They had stopped for a beer on their way somewhere from the beach; he had heard them say that. But the beach was not the reason. He did not know the reason, but he knew it would not have happened in winter. The night was cool and now he could smell trees. He turned and looked at the road in front of the bar. Bob stood beside him on the small porch.

10   "If the regulars had been here," Bob said.

    He turned and with his hand resting on the wooden rail he walked down the ramp to the ground. At his car he stopped and looked over its roof at Mitchell.

    "You take it easy," he said.

    Mitchell nodded. When Bob got in his car and left, he went down the ramp and drove home to his house on a street that he thought was neither good nor bad. The houses were small and there were old large houses used now as apartments for families. Most of the people had work, most of the mothers cared for their children, and most of the children were clean and looked like they lived in homes, not caves like some he saw in town. He worried about the older kids, one group of them anyway. They were idle. When he was a boy in a town farther up the Merrimack River, he and his friends committed every mischievous act he could recall on afternoons and nights when they were idle. His stepchildren were not part of that group. They had friends from the high school. The front porch light was on for him and one in the kitchen at the rear of the house. He went in the front door and switched off the porch light and walked through the living and dining rooms to the kitchen. He got a can of beer from the refrigerator, turned out the light, and sat at the table. When he could see, he took a cigarette from Susan's pack in front of him.

    Down the hall he heard Susan move on the bed then get up and he hoped it wasn't for the bathroom but for him. He had met her eight years ago when he had given up on ever marrying and having kids, then one night she came into the bar with two of her girl friends from work. She made six dollars an hour going to homes of invalids, mostly what she called her little old ladies, and bathing them. She got the house from her marriage, and child support the guy paid for a few months till he left town and went south. She came barefoot down the hall and stood in the kitchen doorway and said: "Are you all right?"

15   "No."

She sat across from him, and he told her. Very soon she held his hand. She was good. He knew if he had fought all five of them and was lying in pieces in a hospital bed she would tell him he had done the right thing, as she was telling him now. He liked her strong hand on his. It was a professional hand and he wanted from her something he had never wanted before: to lie in bed while she bathed him. When they went to bed he did not think he would be able to sleep, but she kneeled beside him and massaged his shoulders and rubbed his temples and pressed her hands on his forehead. He woke to the voices of Marty and Joyce in the kitchen. They had summer jobs, and always when they woke him he went back to sleep till noon, but now he got up and dressed and went to the kitchen door. Susan was at the stove, her back to him, and Marty and Joyce were talking and smoking. He said good morning, and stepped into the room.

"What are you doing up?" Joyce said.

She was a pretty girl with her mother's wide cheekbones and Marty was a tall good-looking boy, and Mitchell felt as old as he had before he slept. Susan was watching him. Then she poured him a cup of coffee and put it at his place and he sat, Marty said: "You getting up for the day?"

"Something happened last night. At the bar." They tried to conceal their excitement, but he saw it in their eyes. "I should have stopped it. I think I *could* have stopped it. That's the point. There were these five guys. They were on motorcycles but they weren't bikers. Just punks. They came in late, when everybody else had gone home. It was a slow night anyway. Everybody was at the beach."

"They rob you?" Marty said.

"No. A girl came in. Young. Nice looking. You know: just a girl, minding her business." [20]

They nodded, and their eyes were apprehensive.

"She wanted cigarette change, that's all. Those guys were on dope. Coke or something. You know: they were flying in place."

"Did they rape her?" Joyce said.

"Yes, honey."

"The *fuckers*." [25]

Susan opened her mouth then closed it and Joyce reached quickly for Susan's pack of cigarettes. Mitchell held his lighter for her and said: "When they started getting rough with her at the bar I went for the phone. One of them stopped me. He shoved me, that's all. I should have hit him with a bottle."

Marty reached over the table with his big hand and held Mitchell's shoulder.

"No, Mitch. Five guys that mean. And coked up or whatever. No way. You wouldn't be here this morning."

"I don't know. There was always a guy with me. But just one guy, taking turns." [30]

"Great," Joyce said. Marty's hand was on Mitchell's left shoulder; she put hers on his right hand.

"They took her to the hospital," he said. "The guys are in jail."

"They are?" Joyce said.

"I called the cops. When they left."

"You'll be a good witness," Joyce said. [35]

He looked at her proud face.

"At the trial," she said.

The day was hot but that night most of the regulars came to the bar. Some of the younger ones came on motorcycles. They were a good crowd: they all worked, except the retired ones and no one ever bothered the women, not even the young ones with their summer tans. Everyone talked about it: some had read the newspaper story, some had heard the story in town, and they wanted to hear it from Mitchell. He told it as often as they asked but he did not finish it because he was working hard and could not stay with any group of customers long enough.

He watched their faces. Not one of them, even the women, looked at him as if he had not cared enough for the girl, or was a coward. Many of them even appeared sympathetic, making him feel for moments that he was a survivor of something horrible, and when that feeling left him he was ashamed. He felt tired and old, making drinks and change, moving and talking up and down the bar. At the stool at the far end Bob drank coffee and whenever Mitchell looked at him he smiled or nodded and once raised his right fist, with the thumb up.

40 Reggie was drinking too much. He did that two or three times a month and Mitchell had to shut him off and Reggie always took it humbly. He was a big gentle man with a long brown beard. But tonight shutting off Reggie demanded from Mitchell an act of will, and when the eleven o'clock news came on the television and Reggie ordered another shot and a draft, Mitchell pretended not to hear him. He served the customers at the other end of the bar, where Bob was. He could hear Reggie calling: Hey Mitch; shot and a draft, Mitch. Mitchell was close to Bob now. Bob said softly: "He's had enough."

Mitchell nodded and went to Reggie, leaned closer to him so he could speak quietly, and said: "Sorry, Reggie. Time for coffee. I don't want you dead out there."

Reggie blinked at him.

"Okay, Mitch." He pulled some bills from his pocket and put them on the bar. Mitchell glanced at them and saw at least a ten dollar tip. When he rang up Reggie's tab the change was sixteen dollars and fifty cents, and he dropped the coins and shoved the bills into the beer mug beside the cash register. The mug was full of bills, as it was on most nights, and he kept his hand in there, pressing Reggie's into the others, and saw the sunburned young men holding her down on the floor and one kneeling between her legs, spread and held, and he heard their cheering voices and her screaming and groaning and finally weeping and weeping and weeping, until she was the siren crying then fading into the night. From the floor behind him, far across the room, he felt her pain and terror and grief, then her curse upon him. The curse moved into his back and spread down and up his spine, into his stomach and legs and arms and shoulders until he quivered with it. He wished he were alone so he could kneel to receive it.

QUESTIONS

1. What kind of violence occurs in "The Curse"? What is your response to the violence? What issues are brought out by the violent action?

2. What is Mitchell's attitude toward the reality that he was able to do nothing to prevent the violence? What do his friends tell him? How right are they about what he might have done? How justifiable is Mitchell's sense of guilt at the incident?

3. What is Mitchell's dilemma? Why does he think about things as he does at the story's end?

4. In what ways does it seem that Mitchell has been changed by his experiences in the story? How is such change justifiable? Inevitable?

CHARLOTTE PERKINS GILMAN (1860–1935)

Born in 1860, Gilman did not begin writing seriously until after the birth of her daughter in the 1880s, which was followed by her "nervous breakdown." Attempting to establish her independence, she left her husband in 1890 and went to California, where she launched what was to become a distinguished career as an advocate for women's rights. For many decades she lectured and wrote extensively, her touchstone work being Women and Economics *(1898), in which she championed the need for women's financial independence. Among her many writings were* Concerning Children

(1900), Human Work *(1904), and* His Religion and Hers *(1923). In the 1930s she became incurably ill, and with death facing her, she took her own life in 1935.*

 # The Yellow Wallpaper° (1892)

It is very seldom that mere ordinary people like John and myself secure ancestral halls for the summer.

A colonial mansion, a hereditary estate, I would say a haunted house and reach the height of romantic felicity—but that would be asking too much of fate!

Still I will proudly declare that there is something queer about it.

Else, why should it be let so cheaply? And why have stood so long untenanted?

John laughs at me, of course, but one expects that.   5

John is practical in the extreme. He has no patience with faith, an intense horror of superstition, and he scoffs openly at any talk of things not to be felt and seen and put down in figures.

John is a physician, and *perhaps*—(I would not say it to a living soul, of course, but this is dead paper and a great relief to my mind)—*perhaps* that is one reason I do not get well faster.

You see, he does not believe I am sick! And what can one do?

If a physician of high standing, and one's own husband, assures friends and relatives that there is really nothing the matter with one but temporary nervous depression—a slight hysterical tendency—what is one to do?

My brother is also a physician, and also of high standing, and he says the same thing.   10

So I take phosphates or phosphites—whichever it is—and tonics, and air and exercise, and journeys, and am absolutely forbidden to "work" until I am well again.

Personally, I disagree with their ideas.

Personally, I believe that congenial work, with excitement and change, would do me good. But what is one to do?

I did write for a while in spite of them; but it *does* exhaust me a good deal—having to be   15
so sly about it, or else meet with heavy opposition.

I sometimes fancy that in my condition, if I had less opposition and more society and stimulus—but John says the very worst thing I can do is to think about my condition, and I confess it always makes me feel bad.

So I will let it alone and talk about the house.

The most beautiful place! It is quite alone, standing well back from the road, quite three miles from the village. It makes me think of English places that you read about, for there are hedges and walls and gates that lock, and lots of separate little houses for the gardeners and people.

There is a *delicious* garden! I never saw such a garden—large and shady, full of box-bordered paths, and lined with long grape-covered arbors with seats under them.

There were greenhouses, but they are all broken now.   20

There was some legal trouble, I believe, something about the heirs and co-heirs; anyhow, the place has been empty for years.

That spoils my ghostliness, I am afraid, but I don't care—there is something strange about the house—I can feel it.

I even said so to John one moonlight evening, but he said what I felt was a draught, and shut the window.

°*The Yellow Wallpaper:* The story is based on the "rest cure" developed after the Civil War by the famous Philadelphia physician S. Weir Mitchell (1829–1914); see paragraph 83. The Mitchell treatment required confining the patient to a hospital, hotel, or some other remote residence. Once isolated, the patient was to have complete bed rest, increased food intake, iron supplements, exercise, and sometimes massage and electric shock therapy. Gilman had experienced Mitchell's "cure," and sent a copy of this story to him as criticism. After receiving the story Mitchell modified his methods.

I get unreasonably angry with John sometimes. I'm sure I never used to be so sensitive. I think it is due to this nervous condition.

25   But John says if I feel so I shall neglect proper self-control; so I take pains to control myself—before him, at least, and that makes me very tired.

I don't like our room a bit. I wanted one downstairs that opened onto the piazza and had roses all over the window, and such pretty old-fashioned chintz hangings! But John would not hear of it.

He said there was only one window and not room for two beds, and no near room for him if he took another.

He is very careful and loving, and hardly lets me stir without special direction.

I have a schedule prescription for each hour in the day; he takes all care from me, and so I feel basely ungrateful not to value it more.

30   He said he came here solely on my account, that I was to have perfect rest and all the air I could get. "Your exercise depends on your strength, my dear," said he, "and your food somewhat on your appetite; but air you can absorb all the time." So we took the nursery at the top of the house.

It is a big, airy room, the whole floor nearly, with windows that look all ways, and air and sunshine galore. It was nursery first, and then playroom and gymnasium, I should judge, for the windows are barred for little children, and there are rings and things in the walls.

The paint and paper look as if a boys' school had used it. It is stripped off—the paper— in great patches all around the head of my bed, about as far as I can reach, and in a great place on the other side of the room low down. I never saw a worse paper in my life. One of those sprawling, flamboyant patterns committing every artistic sin.

It is dull enough to confuse the eye in following, pronounced enough constantly to irritate and provoke study, and when you follow the lame uncertain curves for a little distance they suddenly commit suicide—plunge off at outrageous angles, destroy themselves in unheard-of contradictions.

The color is repellent, almost revolting: a smouldering unclean yellow, strangely faded by the slow-turning sunlight. It is a dull yet lurid orange in some places, a sickly sulphur tint in others.

35   No wonder the children hated it! I should hate it myself if I had to live in this room long.

There comes John, and I must put this away—he hates to have me write a word.

We have been here two weeks, and I haven't felt like writing before, since that first day.

I am sitting by the window now, up in this atrocious nursery, and there is nothing to hinder my writing as much as I please, save lack of strength.

John is away all day, and even some nights when his cases are serious.

40   I am glad my case is not serious!

But these nervous troubles are dreadfully depressing.

John does not know how much I really suffer. He knows there is no reason to suffer, and that satisfies him.

Of course it is only nervousness. It does weigh on me so not to do my duty in any way!

I meant to be such a help to John, such a real rest and comfort, and here I am a comparative burden already!

45   Nobody would believe what an effort it is to do what little I am able—to dress and entertain, and order things.

It is fortunate Mary is so good with the baby. Such a dear baby!

And yet I *cannot* be with him, it makes me so nervous.

I suppose John never was nervous in his life. He laughs at me so about this wallpaper!

At first he meant to repaper the room, but afterward he said that I was letting it get the better of me, and that nothing was worse for a nervous patient than to give way to such fancies.

He said that after the wallpaper was changed it would be the heavy bedstead, and then   50
the barred windows, and then that gate at the head of the stairs, and so on.

"You know the place is doing you good," he said, "and really, dear, I don't care to reno-
vate the house just for a three months' rental."

"Then do let us go downstairs," I said. "There are such pretty rooms there."

Then he took me in his arms and called me a blessed little goose, and said he would go
down to the cellar, if I wished, and have it whitewashed into the bargain.

But he is right enough about the beds and windows and things.

It is as airy and comfortable a room as anyone need wish, and, of course, I would not be   55
so silly as to make him uncomfortable just for a whim.

I'm really getting quite fond of the big room, all but that horrid paper.

Out of one window I can see the garden—those mysterious deep-shaded arbors, the riotous old-fashioned flowers, and bushes and gnarly trees.

Out of another I get a lovely view of the bay and a little private wharf belonging to the
estate. There is a beautiful shaded lane that runs down there from the house. I always fancy
I see people walking in these numerous paths and arbors, but John has cautioned me not to
give way to fancy in the least. He says that with my imaginative power and habit of story-
making, a nervous weakness like mine is sure to lead to all manner of excited fancies, and
that I ought to use my will and good sense to check the tendency. So I try.

I think sometimes that if I were only well enough to write a little it would relieve the
press of ideas and rest me.

But I find I get pretty tired when I try.   60

It is so discouraging not to have any advice and companionship about my work. When I
get really well, John says we will ask Cousin Henry and Julia down for a long visit; but he
says he would as soon put fireworks in my pillow-case as to let me have those stimulating
people about now.

I wish I could get well faster.

But I must not think about that. This paper looks to me as if it *knew* what a vicious influence it had!

There is a recurrent spot where the pattern lolls like a broken neck and two bulbous eyes
stare at you upside down.

I get positively angry with the impertinence of it and the everlastingness. Up and down   65
and sideways they crawl, and those absurd unblinking eyes are everywhere. There is one
place where two breadths didn't match, and the eyes go all up and down the line, one a little higher than the other.

I never saw so much expression in an inanimate thing before, and we all know how
much expression they have! I used to lie awake as a child and get more entertainment and
terror out of blank walls and plain furniture than most children could find in a toy-store.

I remember what a kindly wink the knobs of our big old bureau used to have, and there
was one chair that always seemed like a strong friend.

I used to feel that if any of the other things looked too fierce I could always hop into that
chair and be safe.

The furniture in this room is no worse than inharmonious, however, for we had to bring it
all from downstairs. I suppose when this was used as a playroom they had to take the nursery things out, and no wonder! I never saw such ravages as the children have made here.

The wallpaper, as I said before, is torn off in spots, and it sticketh closer than a   70
brother°—they must have had perseverance as well as hatred.

°*sticketh closer than a brother:* Proverbs 18:24.

Then the floor is scratched and gouged and splintered, the plaster itself is dug out here and there, and this great heavy bed, which is all we found in the room, looks as if it had been through the wars.

But I don't mind it a bit—only the paper.

There comes John's sister. Such a dear girl as she is, and careful of me! I must not let her find me writing.

She is a perfect and enthusiastic housekeeper, and hopes for no better profession. I verily believe she thinks it is the writing which made me sick!

But I can write when she is out, and see her a long way off from these windows.

There is one that commands the road, a lovely shaded winding road, and one that just looks off over the country. A lovely country, too, full of great elms and velvet meadows.

This wallpaper has a kind of sub-pattern in a different shade, a particularly irritating one, for you can only see it in certain lights, and not clearly then.

But in the places where it isn't faded and where the sun is just so—I can see a strange, provoking, formless sort of figure that seems to skulk about behind that silly and conspicuous front design.

There's sister on the stairs!

Well, the Fourth of July is over! The people are all gone, and I am tired out. John thought it might do me good to see a little company, so we just had Mother and Nellie and the children down for a week.

Of course I didn't do a thing. Jennie sees to everything now.

But it tired me all the same.

John says if I don't pick up faster he shall send me to Weir Mitchell° in the fall.

But I don't want to go there at all. I had a friend who was in his hands once, and she says he is just like John and my brother, only more so!

Besides, it is such an undertaking to go so far.

I don't feel as if it was worthwhile to turn my hand over for anything, and I'm getting dreadfully fretful and querulous.

I cry at nothing, and cry most of the time.

Of course I don't when John is here, or anybody else, but when I am alone.

And I am alone a good deal just now. John is kept in town very often by serious cases, and Jennie is good and lets me alone when I want her to.

So I walk a little in the garden or down that lovely lane, sit on the porch under the roses, and lie down up here a good deal.

I'm getting really fond of the room in spite of the wallpaper. Perhaps *because* of the wallpaper.

It dwells in my mind so!

I lie here on this great immovable bed—it is nailed down, I believe—and follow that pattern about by the hour. It is as good as gymnastics, I assure you. I start, we'll say, at the bottom, down in the corner over there where it has not been touched, and I determine for the thousandth time that I *will* follow that pointless pattern to some sort of a conclusion.

I know a little of the principle of design, and I know this thing was not arranged on any laws of radiation, or alternation, or repetition, or symmetry, or anything else that I ever heard of.

It is repeated, of course, by the breadths, but not otherwise.

Looked at in one way, each breadth stands alone; the bloated curves and flourishes—a kind of "debased Romanesque" with delirium tremens—go waddling up and down in isolated columns of fatuity.

°*Weir Mitchell:* See note on page 567.

But, on the other hand, they connect diagonally, and the sprawling outlines run off in great slanting waves of optic horror, like a lot of wallowing sea-weeds in full chase.

The whole thing goes horizontally, too, at least it seems so, and I exhaust myself trying to distinguish the order of its going in that direction.

They have used a horizontal breadth for a frieze, and that adds wonderfully to the confusion.

There is one end of the room where it is almost intact, and there, when the crosslights fade and the low sun shines directly upon it, I can almost fancy radiation after all—the interminable grotesque seems to form around a common center and rush off in headlong plunges of equal distraction.

It makes me tired to follow it. I will take a nap, I guess.

I don't know why I should write this.

I don't want to.

I don't feel able.

And I know John would think it absurd. But I *must* say what I feel and think in some way—it is such a relief!

But the effort is getting to be greater than the relief.

Half the time now I am awfully lazy, and lie down ever so much. John says I mustn't lose my strength, and has me take cod liver oil and lots of tonics and things, to say nothing of ale and wine and rare meat.

Dear John! He loves me very dearly, and hates to have me sick. I tried to have a real earnest reasonable talk with him the other day, and tell him how I wish he would let me go and make a visit to Cousin Henry and Julia.

But he said I wasn't able to go, nor able to stand it after I got there; and I did not make out a very good case for myself, for I was crying before I had finished.

It is getting to be a great effort for me to think straight. Just this nervous weakness, I suppose.

And dear John gathered me up in his arms, and just carried me upstairs and laid me on the bed, and sat by me and read to me till it tired my head.

He said I was his darling and his comfort and all he had, and that I must take care of myself for his sake, and keep well.

He says no one but myself can help me out of it, that I must use my will and self-control and not let any silly fancies run away with me.

There's one comfort—the baby is well and happy, and does not have to occupy this nursery with the horrid wallpaper.

If we had not used it, that blessed child would have! What a fortunate escape! Why, I wouldn't have a child of mine, an impressionable little thing, live in such a room for worlds.

I never thought of it before, but it is lucky that John kept me here after all; I can stand it so much easier than a baby, you see.

Of course I never mention it to them any more—I am too wise—but I keep watch for it all the same.

There are things in that wallpaper that nobody knows about but me, or ever will.

Behind that outside pattern the dim shapes get clearer every day.

It is always the same shape, only very numerous.

And it is like a woman stooping down and creeping about behind that pattern. I don't like it a bit. I wonder—I begin to think—I wish John would take me away from here!

It is so hard to talk with John about my case, because he is so wise, and because he loves me so.

But I tried it last night.

It was moonlight. The moon shines in all around just as the sun does.

125   I hate to see it sometimes, it creeps so slowly, and always comes in by one window or another.

    John was asleep and I hated to waken him, so I kept still and watched the moonlight on that undulating wallpaper till I felt creepy.

    The faint figure behind seemed to shake the pattern, just as if she wanted to get out.

    I got up softly and went to feel and see if the paper *did* move, and when I came back John was awake.

    "What is it, little girl?" he said. "Don't go walking about like that—you'll get cold."

130   I thought it was a good time to talk, so I told him that I really was not gaining here, and that I wished he would take me away.

    "Why, darling!" said he. "Our lease will be up in three weeks, and I can't see how to leave before.

    "The repairs are not done at home, and I cannot possibly leave town just now. Of course, if you were in any danger, I could and would, but you really are better, dear, whether you can see it or not. I am a doctor, dear, and I know. You are gaining flesh and color, your appetite is better, I feel really much easier about you."

    "I don't weigh a bit more," said I, "nor as much; and my appetite may be better in the evening when you are here but it is worse in the morning when you are away!"

    "Bless her little heart!" said he with a big hug. "She shall be as sick as she pleases! But now let's improve the shining hours by going to sleep, and talk about it in the morning!"

135   "And you won't go away?" I asked gloomily.

    "Why, how can I, dear? It is only three weeks more and then we will take a nice little trip of a few days while Jennie is getting the house ready. Really, dear, you are better!"

    "Better in body perhaps—" I began, and stopped short, for he sat up straight and looked at me with such a stern, reproachful look that I could not say another word.

    "My darling," said he, "I beg of you, for my sake and for our child's sake, as well as for your own, that you will never for one instant let that idea enter your mind! There is nothing so dangerous, so fascinating, to a temperament like yours. It is a false and foolish fancy. Can you not trust me as a physician when I tell you so?"

    So of course I said no more on that score, and we went to sleep before long. He thought I was asleep first, but I wasn't, and lay there for hours trying to decide whether that front pattern and the back pattern really did move together or separately.

140   On a pattern like this, by daylight, there is a lack of sequence, a defiance of law, that is a constant irritant to a normal mind.

    The color is hideous enough, and unreliable enough, and infuriating enough, but the pattern is torturing.

    You think you have mastered it, but just as you get well under way in following, it turns a back-somersault and there you are. It slaps you in the face, knocks you down, and tramples upon you. It is like a bad dream.

    The outside pattern is a florid arabesque, reminding one of a fungus. If you can imagine a toadstool in joints an interminable string of toadstools, budding and sprouting in endless convolutions—why, that is something like it.

    That is, sometimes!

145   There is one marked peculiarity about this paper, a thing nobody seems to notice but myself, and that is that it changes as the light changes.

    When the sun shoots in through the east window—I always watch for that first long, straight ray—it changes so quickly than I never can quite believe it.

    That is why I watch it always.

    By moonlight—the moon shines in all night when there is a moon—I wouldn't know it was the same paper.

    At night in any kind of light, in twilight, candlelight, lamplight, and worst of all by moonlight, it becomes bars! The outside pattern, I mean, and the woman behind it is as plain as can be.

I didn't realize for a long time what the thing was that showed behind, that dim sub-pattern, but now I am quite sure it is a woman. 150

By daylight she is subdued, quiet. I fancy it is the pattern that keeps her so still. It is so puzzling. It keeps me quiet by the hour.

I lie down ever so much now. John says it is good for me, and to sleep all I can.

Indeed he started the habit by making me lie down for an hour after each meal.

It is a very bad habit, I am convinced, for you see, I don't sleep.

And that cultivates deceit, for I don't tell them I'm awake—oh, no! 155

The fact is I am getting a little afraid of John.

He seems very queer sometimes, and even Jennie has an inexplicable look.

It strikes me occasionally, just as a scientific hypothesis, that perhaps it is the paper!

I have watched John when he did not know I was looking, and come into the room suddenly on the most innocent excuses, and I've caught him several times *looking at the paper*! And Jennie too. I caught Jennie with her hand on it once.

She didn't know I was in the room, and when I asked her in a quiet, a very quiet voice, 160 with the most restrained manner possible, what she was doing with the paper, she turned around as if she had been caught stealing, and looked quite angry—asked me why I should frighten her so!

Then she said that the paper stained everything it touched, that she had found yellow smooches on all my clothes and John's and she wished we would be more careful!

Did not that sound innocent? But I know she was studying that pattern, and I am determined that nobody shall find it out but myself.

Life is very much more exciting now than it used to be. You see, I have something more to expect, to look forward to, to watch. I really do eat better, and am more quiet than I was.

John is so pleased to see me improve! He laughed a little the other day, and said I seemed to be flourishing in spite of my wallpaper.

I turned it off with a laugh. I had no intention of telling him it was *because* of the 165 wallpaper—he would make fun of me. He might even want to take me away.

I don't want to leave now until I have found it out. There is a week more, and I think that will be enough.

I'm feeling so much better!

I don't sleep much at night, for it is so interesting to watch developments; but sleep a good deal during the daytime.

In the daytime it is tiresome and perplexing.

There are always new shoots on the fungus, and new shades of yellow all over it. I can-170 not keep count of them, though I have tried conscientiously.

It is the strangest yellow, that wallpaper! It makes me think of all the yellow things I ever saw—not beautiful ones like buttercups, but old, foul, bad yellow things.

But there is something else about that paper—the smell! I noticed it the moment we came into the room, but with so much air and sun it was not bad. Now we have had a week of fog and rain, and whether the windows are open or not, the smell is here.

It creeps all over the house.

I find it hovering in the dining-room, skulking in the parlor, hiding in the hall, lying in wait for me on the stairs.

It gets into my hair. 175

Even when I go to ride, if I turn my head suddenly and surprise it—there is that smell!

Such a peculiar odor, too! I have spent hours in trying to analyze it, to find what it smelled like.

It is not bad—at first—and very gentle, but quite the subtlest, most enduring odor I ever met.

In this damp weather it is awful. I wake up in the night and find it hanging over me.

It used to disturb me at first. I thought seriously of burning the house—to reach the smell. 180

But now I am used to it. The only thing I can think of that it is like is the *color* of the paper! A yellow smell.

There is a very funny mark on this wall, low down, near the mopboard. A streak that runs round the room. It goes behind every piece of furniture, except the bed, a long, straight, even *smooch,* as if it had been rubbed over and over.

I wonder how it was done and who did it, and what they did it for. Round and round and round—round and round and round—it makes me dizzy!

I really have discovered something at last.

185 Through watching so much at night, when it changes so, I have finally found out.

The front pattern *does* move—and no wonder! The woman behind shakes it!

Sometimes I think there are a great many women behind, and sometimes only one, and she crawls around fast, and her crawling shakes it all over.

Then in the very bright spots she keeps still, and in the very shady spots she just takes hold of the bars and shakes them hard.

And she is all the time trying to climb through. But nobody could climb through that pattern—it strangles so; I think that is why it has so many heads.

190 They get through and then the pattern strangles them off and turns them upside down, and makes their eyes white!

If those heads were covered or taken off it would not be half so bad.

I think that woman gets out in the daytime!

And I'll tell you why—privately—I've seen her!

I can see her out of every one of my windows!

195 It is the same woman, I know, for she is always creeping, and most women do not creep by daylight.

I see her in that long shaded lane, creeping up and down. I see her in those dark grape arbors, creeping all around the garden.

I see her on that long road under the trees, creeping along, and when a carriage comes she hides under the blackberry vines.

I don't blame her a bit. It must be very humiliating to be caught creeping by daylight!

I always lock the door when I creep by daylight. I can't do it at night, for I know John would suspect something at once.

200 And John is so queer now that I don't want to irritate him. I wish he would take another room! Besides, I don't want anybody to get that woman out at night but myself.

I often wonder if I could see her out of all the windows at once.

But, turn as fast as I can, I can only see out of one at a time.

And though I always see her, she *may* be able to creep faster than I can turn! I have watched her sometimes away off in the open country, creeping as fast as a cloud shadow in a wind.

If only that top pattern could be gotten off from the under one! I mean to try it, little by little.

205 I have found out another funny thing, but I shan't tell it this time! It does not do to trust people too much.

There are only two more days to get this paper off, and I believe John is beginning to notice. I don't like the look in his eyes.

And I heard him ask Jennie a lot of professional questions about me. She had a very good report to give.

She said I slept a good deal in the daytime.

John knows I don't sleep very well at night, for all I'm so quiet!

210 He asked me all sorts of questions, too, and pretended to be very loving and kind.

As if I couldn't see through him!

Still, I don't wonder he acts so, sleeping under this paper for three months.

It only interests me, but I feel sure John and Jennie are affected by it.

• • •

Hurrah! This is the last day, but it is enough. John is to stay in town over night, and won't be out until this evening.

Jennie wanted to sleep with me—the sly thing; but I told her I should undoubtedly rest better for a night all alone.   215

That was clever, for really I wasn't alone a bit! As soon as it was moonlight and that poor thing began to crawl and shake the pattern, I got up and ran to help her.

I pulled and she shook. I shook and she pulled, and before morning we had peeled off yards of that paper.

A strip about as high as my head and half around the room.

And then when the sun came and that awful pattern began to laugh at me, I declared I would finish it today!

We go away tomorrow, and they are moving all my furniture down again to leave things   220
as they were before.

Jennie looked at the wall in amazement, but I told her merrily that I did it out of pure spite at the vicious thing.

She laughed and said she wouldn't mind doing it herself, but I must not get tired.

How she betrayed herself that time!

But I am here, and no person touches this paper but Me—not *alive*!

She tried to get me out of the room—it was too patent! But I said it was so quiet and   225
empty and clean now that I believed I would lie down again and sleep all I could, and not to wake me even for dinner—I would call when I woke.

So now she is gone, and the servants are gone, and the things are gone, and there is nothing left but that great bedstead nailed down, with the canvas mattress we found on it.

We shall sleep downstairs tonight, and take the boat home tomorrow.

I quite enjoy the room, now it is bare again.

How those children did tear about here!

This bedstead is fairly gnawed!   230

But I must get to work.

I have locked the door and thrown the key down into the front path.

I don't want to go out, and I don't want to have anybody come in, till John comes.

I want to astonish him.

I've got a rope up here that even Jennie did not find. If that woman does get out, and   235
tries to get away, I can tie her!

But I forgot I could not reach far without anything to stand on!

This bed will *not* move!

I tried to lift and push it until I was lame, and then I got so angry I bit off a little piece at one corner—but it hurt my teeth.

Then I peeled off all the paper I could reach standing on the floor. It sticks horribly and the pattern just enjoys it! All those strangled heads and bulbous eyes and waddling fungus growths just shriek with derision!

I am getting angry enough to do something desperate. To jump out of the window   240
would be admirable exercise, but the bars are too strong even to try.

Besides I wouldn't do it. Of course not. I know well enough that a step like that is improper and might be misconstrued.

I don't like to *look* out of the windows even—there are so many of those creeping women, and they creep so fast.

I wonder if they all came out of that wallpaper as I did?

But I am securely fastened now by my well-hidden rope—you don't get *me* out in the road there!

I suppose I shall have to get back behind the pattern when it comes night, and that is hard!   245

It is so pleasant to be out in this great room and creep around as I please!

I don't want to go outside. I won't, even if Jennie asks me to.

For outside you have to creep on the ground, and everything is green instead of yellow.

But here I can creep smoothly on the floor, and my shoulder just fits in that long smooch around the wall, so I cannot lose my way.

250   Why, there's John at the door!

It is no use, young man, you can't open it!

How he does call and pound!

Now he's crying to Jennie for an axe.

It would be a shame to break down that beautiful door!

255   "John, dear!" said I in the gentlest voice. "The key is down by the front steps, under a plantain leaf!"

That silenced him for a few moments.

Then he said, very quietly indeed, "Open the door, my darling!"

"I can't," said I. "The key is down by the front door under a plantain leaf!" And then I said it again, several times, very gently and slowly, and said it so often that he had to go and see, and he got it of course, and came in. He stopped short by the door.

"What is the matter?" he cried. "For God's sake, what are you doing!"

260   I kept on creeping just the same, but I looked at him over my shoulder.

"I've got out at last," said I, "in spite of you and Jane. And I've pulled off most of the paper, so you can't put me back!"

Now why should that man have fainted? But he did, and right across my path by the wall, so that I had to creep over him every time!

QUESTIONS

1. Describe the point of view of "The Yellow Wallpaper." How consistent is the point of view? How is the story told? To whom does the narrator seem to be speaking? How does the narrator change as the story progresses?

2. How much time elapses in the story? How well does this passage of time explain what is happening to the narrator?

3. What is the narrator's connection to the room's wallpaper? What has she obviously been doing in the course of the story? What does this show about her mental condition?

4. How effectively can a case be made that the "treatment" the narrator receives is actually the cause of her mental disturbance, which is so evident at the story's end?

FLANNERY O'CONNOR (1925–1964)

Mary Flannery O'Connor, a Georgia native, graduated from the Women's College of Georgia and received a master of fine arts degree from the University of Iowa in 1947. She contracted lupus, a disorder of the immune system, and was an invalid for the last ten years of her life. Despite her illness, she wrote extensively, publishing two novels and many short stories. Her first collection was A Good Man Is Hard to Find, *in 1955. A posthumous collection,* Everything That Rises Must Converge, *was published in 1965, and* Complete Stories *appeared in 1971. Her works combine flat realism with grotesque situations; violence occurs without apparent reason or preparation. Many of her characters are odd, eccentric, and bizarre. Others, such as the Misfit in "A Good Man Is Hard to Find," are gratuitously cruel. Ironically, however, their cold and depraved actions highlight the need for religious awakening because they enable some of the characters, such as the grandmother in the following story, to achieve spiritual elevation.*

A Good Man Is Hard to Find (1955)

The grandmother didn't want to go to Florida. She wanted to visit some of her connections in east Tennessee and she was seizing at every chance to change Bailey's mind. Bailey was the son she lived with, her only son. He was sitting on the edge of his chair at the table, bent over the orange sports section of the *Journal.* "Now look here, Bailey," she said, "see here, read this," and she stood with one hand on her thin hip and the other rattling the newspaper at his bald head. "Here this fellow that calls himself The Misfit is aloose from the Federal Pen and headed toward Florida and you read here what it says he did to these people. Just you read it I wouldn't take my children in any direction with a criminal like that aloose in it. I couldn't answer to my conscience if I did."

Bailey didn't look up from his reading so she wheeled around then and faced the children's mother, a young woman in slacks, whose face was as broad and innocent as a cabbage and was tied round with a green head-kerchief that had two points on the top like rabbit's ears. She was sitting on the sofa, feeding the baby his apricots out of a jar. "The children have been to Florida before," the old lady said. "You all ought to take them somewhere else for a change so they would see different parts of the world and be broad. They never have been to east Tennessee."

The children's mother didn't seem to hear her but the eight-year-old boy, John Wesley, a stocky child with glasses, said, "If you don't want to go to Florida, why dontcha stay at home?" He and the little girl, June Star, were reading the funny papers on the floor.

"She wouldn't stay at home to be queen for a day," June Star said without raising her yellow head.

"Yes and what would you do if this fellow, The Misfit, caught you?" the grandmother asked.   5

"I'd smack his face," John Wesley said.

"She wouldn't stay at home for a million bucks." June Star said. "Afraid she'd miss something. She has to go everywhere we go."

"All right, Miss," the grandmother said. "Just remember that the next time you want me to curl your hair."

June Star said her hair was naturally curly.

The next morning the grandmother was the first one in the car, ready to go. She had her   10
big black valise that looked like the head of a hippopotamus in one corner, and underneath it she was hiding a basket with Pitty Sing, the cat, in it. She didn't intend for the cat to be left alone in the house for three days because he would miss her too much and she was afraid he might brush against one of the gas burners and accidentally asphyxiate himself. Her son, Bailey, didn't like to arrive at a motel with a cat.

She sat in the middle of the back seat with John Wesley and June Star on either side of her. Bailey and the children's mother and the baby sat in the front and they left Atlanta at eight forty-five with the mileage on the car at 55890. The grandmother wrote this down because she thought it would be interesting to say how many miles they had been when they got back. It took them twenty minutes to reach the outskirts of the city.

The old lady settled herself comfortably, removing her white cotton gloves and putting them up with her purse on the shelf in front of the back window. The children's mother still had on slacks and still had her head tied up in a green kerchief, but the grandmother had on a navy blue straw sailor hat with a bunch of white violets on the brim and a navy blue dress with a small white dot in the print. Her collar and cuffs were white organdy trimmed with lace and at her neckline she had pinned a purple spray of cloth violets containing a sachet. In case of an accident, anyone seeing her dead on the highway would know at once that she was a lady.

She said she thought it was going to be a good day for driving, neither too hot nor too cold, and she cautioned Bailey that the speed limit was fifty-five miles an hour and that the patrolmen hid themselves behind billboards and small clumps of trees and sped out after you before you had a chance to slow down. She pointed out interesting details of the scenery: Stone Mountain; the blue granite that in some places came up to both sides of the highway; the brilliant red clay banks slightly streaked with purple; and the various crops that made rows of green lacework on the ground. The trees were full of silver-white sunlight and the meanest of them sparkled. The children were reading comic magazines and their mother had gone back to sleep.

"Let's go through Georgia fast so we won't have to look at it much," John Wesley said.

15   "If I were a little boy," said the grandmother. "I wouldn't talk about my native state that way. Tennessee has the mountains and Georgia has the hills."

"Tennessee is just a hillbilly dumping ground," John Wesley said, "and Georgia is a lousy state too."

"You said it," June Star said.

"In my time," said the grandmother, folding her thin veined fingers, "children were more respectful of their native states and their parents and everything else. People did right then. Oh look at the cute little pickaninny!" she said and pointed to a Negro child standing in the door of a shack. "Wouldn't that make a picture, now?" she asked and they all turned and looked at the little Negro out of the back window. He waved.

"He didn't have any britches on," June said.

20   "He probably didn't have any," the grandmother explained. "Little niggers in the country don't have things like we do. If I could paint, I'd paint that picture," she said.

The children exchanged comic books.

The grandmother offered to hold the baby and the children's mother passed him over the front seat to her. She set him on her knee and bounced him and told him about the things they were passing. She rolled her eyes and screwed up her mouth and stuck her leathery thin face into his smooth bland one. Occasionally he gave her a faraway smile. They passed a large cotton field with five or six graves fenced in the middle of it, like a small island. "Look at the graveyard!" the grandmother said, pointing it out. "That was the old family burying ground. That belonged to the plantation."

"Where's the plantation?" John Wesley asked.

"Gone With the Wind," said the grandmother. "Ha. Ha."

25   When the children finished all the comic books they had brought, they opened the lunch and ate it. The grandmother ate a peanut butter sandwich and an olive and would not let the children throw the box and the paper napkins out the window. When there was nothing else to do they played a game by choosing a cloud and making the other two guess what shape it suggested. John Wesley took one the shape of a cow and June Star guessed a cow and John Wesley said, no, an automobile, and June Star said he didn't play fair, and they began to slap each other over the grandmother.

The grandmother said she would tell them a story if they would keep quiet. When she told a story, she rolled her eyes and waved her head and was very dramatic. She said once when she was a maiden lady she had been courted by a Mr. Edgar Atkins Teagarden from Jasper, Georgia. She said he was a very good-looking man and a gentleman and that he brought her a water melon every Saturday afternoon with his initials cut in it, E. A. T. Well, one Saturday, she said, Mr. Teagarden brought the watermelon and there was nobody at home and he left it on the front porch and returned in his buggy to Jasper, but she never got the watermelon, she said, because a nigger boy ate it when he saw the initials, E. A. T.! This story tickled John Wesley's funny bone and he giggled and giggled but June Star didn't think it was any good. She said she wouldn't marry a man that just brought her a watermelon on Saturday. The grandmother said she would have done well to marry Mr. Teagarden because he was a gentleman and had bought Coca-Cola stock when it first came out and that he had died only a few years ago, a very wealthy man.

They stopped at The Tower for barbecued sandwiches. The Tower was a part stucco and part wood filling station and dance hall set in a clearing outside of Timothy. A fat man named Red Sammy Butts ran it and there were signs stuck here and there on the building and for miles up and down the highway saying, TRY RED SAMMY'S FAMOUS BARBECUE. NONE LIKE FAMOUS RED SAMMY'S! RED SAM! THE FAT BOY WITH THE HAPPY LAUGH A VETERAN! SAMMY'S YOUR MAN!

Red Sammy was lying on the bare ground outside The Tower with his head under a truck while a gray monkey about a foot high, chained to a small chinaberry tree, chattered nearby. The monkey sprang back into the tree and got on the highest limb as soon as he saw the children jump out of the car and run toward him.

Inside, The Tower was a long dark room with a counter at one end and tables at the other and dancing space in the middle. They all sat down at a broad table next to the nickelodeon and Red Sam's wife, a tall burnt-brown woman with hair and eyes lighter than her skin, came and took their order. The children's mother put a dime in the machine and played "The Tennessee Waltz," and the grandmother said the tune always made her want to dance. She asked Bailey if he would like to dance but he only glared at her. He didn't have a naturally sunny disposition like she did and trips made him nervous. The grandmother's brown eyes were very bright. She swayed her head from side to side and pretended she was dancing in her chair. June Star said play something she could tap to so the children's mother put in another dime and played a fast number and June Star stepped out onto the dance floor and did her up routine.

"Ain't she cute?" Red Sam's wife said, leaning over the counter. "Would you like to come be my little girl?"   30

"No I certainly wouldn't," June Star said. "I wouldn't live in a broken-down place like this for a million bucks!" and she ran back to the table.

"Ain't she cute?" the woman repeated, stretching her mouth politely.

"Aren't you ashamed?" hissed her grandmother.

Red Sam came in and told his wife to quit lounging on the counter and hurry with these people's order. His khaki trousers reached just to his hip bones and his stomach hung over them like a sack of meal swaying under his shirt. He came over and sat down at a table nearby and let out a combination sigh and yodel, "You can't win," he said. "You can't win," and he wiped his sweating red face with a gray handkerchief. "These days you don't know who to trust," he said. "Ain't that the truth?"

"People are certainly not nice like they used to be," said the grandmother.   35

"Two fellers come in here last week," Red Sammy said, "driving a Chrysler. It was a old beat-up car but it was a good one and these boys looked all right to me. Said they worked at the mill and you know I let them fellers charge the gas they bought? Now why did I do that?"

"Because you're a good man!" the grandmother said at once.

"Yes'm, I suppose so," Red Sam said as if he were struck with the answer.

His wife brought the orders, carrying the five plates all at once without a tray, two in each hand and one balanced on her arm. "It isn't a soul in this green world of God's that you can trust," she said. "And I don't count anybody out of that, not nobody," she repeated, looking at Red Sammy.

"Did you read about that criminal, The Misfit, that's escaped?" asked the grandmother.   40

"I wouldn't be a bit surprised if he didn't attack this place right here," said the woman. "If he hears about it being here, I wouldn't be none surprised to see him. If he hears it's two cent in the cash register, I wouldn't be a tall surprised if he . . ."

"That'll do," Red Sam said, "Go bring these people their Co'Colas," and the woman went off to get the rest of the order.

"A good man is hard to find." Red Sammy said. "Everything is getting terrible. I remember the day you could go off and leave your screen door unlatched. Not no more."

He and the grandmother discussed better times. The old lady said that in her opinion Europe was entirely to blame for the way things were now. She said the way Europe acted you would think we were made of money and Red Sam said it was no use talking about it, she was exactly right. The children ran outside into the white sunlight and looked at the monkey in the lacy chinaberry tree. He was busy catching fleas on himself and biting each one carefully between his teeth as if it were a delicacy.

45   They drove off again into the hot afternoon. The grandmother took cat naps and woke up every few minutes with her own snoring. Outside of Toombsboro she woke up and re-called an old plantation that she had visited in this neighborhood once when she was a young lady. She said the house had six white columns across the front and that there was an avenue of oaks leading up to it and two little wooden trellis arbors on either side in front where you sat down with your suitor after a stroll in the garden. She recalled exactly which road to turn off to get to it. She knew that Bailey would not be willing to lose any time look-ing at an old house, but the more she talked about it, the more she wanted to see it once again and find out if the little twin arbors were still standing. "There was a secret panel in this house," she said craftily, not telling the truth but wishing that she were, "and the story went that all the family silver was hidden in it when Sherman° came through but it was never found . . ."

"Hey!" John Wesley said, "Let's go see it! We'll find it! We'll poke all the woodwork and find it! Who lives there? Where do you turn off at? Hey Pop, can't we turn off there?"

"We never have seen a house with a secret panel!" June Star shrieked, "Let's go to the house with the secret panel! Hey, Pop, can't we go see the house with the secret panel!"

"It's not far from here, I know," the grandmother said. "It wouldn't take over twenty minutes."

Bailey was looking straight ahead. His jaw was as rigid as a horseshoe. "No," he said.

50   The children began to yell and scream that they wanted to see the house with the secret panel. John Wesley kicked the back of the front seat and June Star hung over her mother's shoulder and whined desperately into her ear that they never had any fun even on their va-cation, and that they could never do what THEY wanted to do. The baby began to scream and John Wesley kicked the back of the seat so hard that his father could feel the blows in his kidney.

"All right!" he shouted, and drew the car to a stop at the side of the road. "Will you all shut up? Will you all just shut up for one second? If you don't shut up, we won't go anywhere."

"It would be very educational for them," the grandmother murmured.

"All right," Bailey said, "but get this: this is the only time we're going to stop for any-thing like this. This is the one and only time."

"The dirt road that you have to turn down is about a mile back," the grandmother di-rected. "I marked it when we passed."

55   "A dirt road," Bailey groaned.

After they had turned around and were headed toward the dirt road, the grandmother recalled other points about the house, the beautiful glass over the front doorway and the candle-lamp in the hall. John Wesley said that the secret panel was probably in the fireplace.

"You can't go inside this house," Bailey said. "You don't know who lives there."

"While you all talk to the people in front, I'll run around behind and get in a window," John Wesley suggested.

"We'll all stay in the car," his mother said.

60   They turned onto the dirt road and the car raced roughly along in swirl of pink dust. The grandmother recalled the times when there were no paved roads and thirty miles was a

---

°*Sherman:* William Tecumseh Sherman (1820–1892), Union general during the Civil War.

day's journey. The dirt road was hilly and there were sudden washes in it and sharp curves on dangerous embankments. All at once they would be on a hill, looking down over the blue tops of trees for miles around, then the next minute, they would be in a red depression with the dust-coated trees looking down on them.

"This place had better turn up in a minute," Bailey said, "or I'm going to turn around."

The road looked as if no one had traveled on it in months.

"It's not much farther," the grandmother said and just as she said it, a horrible thought came to her. The thought was so embarrassing that she turned red in the face and her eyes dilated and her feet jumped up, upsetting her valise in the corner. The instant the valise moved, the newspaper top she had over the basket under it rose with a smart and Pitty Sing, the cat, sprang onto Bailey's shoulder.

The children were thrown to the floor and their mother, clutching the baby, was thrown out the door onto the ground; the old lady was thrown into the front seat. The car turned over once and landed right-side-up in a gulch on the side of the road. Bailey remained in the driver's seat with the cat—gray-striped with a broad white face and an orange nose—clinging to his neck like a caterpillar.

As soon as the children saw they could move their arms and legs, they scrambled out of   65
the car, shouting, "We've had an ACCIDENT!" The grandmother was curled up under the dashboard, hoping she was injured so that Bailey's wrath would not come down on her all at once. The horrible thought she had had before the accident was that the house she had remembered so vividly was not in Georgia but in Tennessee.

Bailey removed the cat from his neck with both hands and flung it out the window against the side of a pine tree. Then he got out of the car and started looking for the children's mother. She was sitting against the side of the red gutted ditch, holding the screaming baby, but she only had a cut down her face and a broken shoulder. "We've had an ACCIDENT!" the children screamed in a frenzy of delight.

"But nobody's killed," June Star said with disappointment as the grandmother limped out of the car, her hat still pinned to her head but the broken front brim standing up at a jaunty angle and the violet spray hanging off the side. They all sat down in the ditch, except the children, to recover from the shock. They were all shaking.

"Maybe a car will come along," said the children's mother hoarsely.

"I believe I have injured an organ," said the grandmother, pressing her side, but no one answered her. Bailey's teeth were clattering. He had on a yellow sport shirt with bright blue parrots designed in it and his face was as yellow as the shirt. The grandmother decided that she would not mention that the house was in Tennessee.

The road was about ten feet above and they could see only the tops of the trees on the   70
other side of it. Behind the ditch they were sitting in there were more woods, tall and dark and deep. In a few minutes they saw a car some distance away on top of a hill, coming slowly as if the occupants were watching them. The grandmother stood up and waved both arms dramatically to attract their attention. The car continued to come on slowly, disappeared around a bend and appeared again, moving even slower, on top of the hill they had gone over. It was a big black battered hearse-like automobile. There were three men in it.

It came to a stop just over them and for some minutes, the driver looked down with a steady expressionless gaze to where they were sitting, and didn't speak. Then he turned his head and muttered something to the other two and they got out. One was a fat boy in black trousers and a red sweat shirt with a silver stallion embossed on the front of it. He moved around on the right side of them and stood staring, his mouth partly open in a kind of loose grin. The other had on khaki pants and a blue striped coat and a gray hat pulled down very low, hiding most of his face. He came around slowly on the left side. Neither spoke.

The driver got out of the car and stood by the side of it, looking down at them. He was an older man than the other two. His hair was just beginning to gray and he wore silver-rimmed spectacles that gave him a scholarly look. He had a long creased face and didn't have on any shirt or undershirt. He had on blue jeans that were too tight for him and was holding a black hat and a gun. The two boys also had guns.

"We've had an ACCIDENT!" the children screamed.

The grandmother had the peculiar feeling that the bespectacled man was someone she knew. His face was as familiar to her as if she had known him all her life but she could not recall who he was. He moved away from the car and began to come down the embankment, placing his feet carefully so that he wouldn't slip. He had on tan and white shoes and no socks, and his ankles were red and thin. "Good afternoon," he said. "I see you all had a little spill."

75   "We turned over twice!" said the grandmother.

"Oncet," he corrected. "We seen it happen. Try their car and see will it run, Hiram," he said quietly to the boy with the gray hat.

"What you got that gun for?" John Wesley asked. "Whatcha gonna do with that gun?"

"Lady," the man said to the children's mother, "would you mind calling them children to sit down by you? Children make me nervous. I want all you all to set down right together there where you're at."

"What are you telling us what to do for?" June Star asked.

80   Behind them the line of woods gaped like a dark, open mouth. "Come here," said their mother.

"Look here now," Bailey began suddenly, "we're in a predicament! We're in . . ."

The grandmother shrieked. She scrambled to her feet and stood staring. "You're The Misfit!" she said. "I recognized you at once."

"Yes'm," the man said, smiling slightly as if he were pleased in spite of himself to be known, "but it would have been better for all of you, lady, if you hadn't reckernized me."

Bailey turned his head sharply and said something to his mother that shocked even the children. The old lady began to cry and The Misfit reddened.

85   "Lady," he said, "don't you get upset: Sometimes a man says things he don't mean. I don't reckon he meant to talk to you thataway."

"You wouldn't shoot a lady, would you?" the grandmother said and removed a clean handkerchief from her cuff and began to slap at her eyes with it.

The Misfit pointed the toe of his shoe into the ground and made a little hole and then covered it up again. "I would hate to have to," he said.

"Listen," the grandmother almost screamed, "I know you're a good man. You don't look a bit like you have common blood. I know you must come from nice people!"

"Yes mam," he said, "finest people in the world." When he smiled he showed a row of strong white teeth. "God never made a finer woman than my mother and my daddy's heart was pure gold," he said. The boy with the red sweat shirt had come around behind them and was standing with his gun at his hip. The Misfit squatted down on the ground. "Watch them children, Bobby Lee," he said. "You know they make me nervous." He looked at the six of them huddled together in front of him and he seemed to be embarrassed as if he couldn't think if anything to say. "Ain't a cloud in the sky," he remarked, looking up at it. "Don't see no sun but don't see no cloud neither."

90   "Yes, it's a beautiful day," said the grandmother. "Listen," she said, "you shouldn't call yourself The Misfit because I know you're a good man at heart. I can just look at you and tell."

"Hush!" Bailey yelled. "Hush! Everybody shut up and let me handle this!" He was squatting in the position of a runner about to sprint forward but he didn't move.

"I pre-chate that, lady," The Misfit said and drew a little circle in the ground with the butt of his gun.

"It'll take a half a hour to fix this here car," Hiram called, looking over the raised hood of it.

"Well, first you and Bobby Lee get him and that little boy to step over yonder with you," The Misfit said, pointing to Bailey and John Wesley. "The boys want to ask you something," he said to Bailey. "Would you mind stepping back in them woods there with them?"

"Listen," Bailey began, "we're in a terrible predicament. Nobody realizes what this is," 95
and his voice cracked. His eyes were as blue and intense as the parrots in his shirt and he remained perfectly still.

The grandmother reached up to adjust her hat brim as if she were going to the woods with him but it came off in her hand. She stood staring at it and after a second she let it fall to the ground. Hiram pulled Bailey up by the arm as if he were assisting an old man. John Wesley caught hold of his father's hand and Bobby Lee followed. They went off toward the woods and just as they reached the dark edge. Bailey turned and supporting himself against a gray naked pine trunk, he shouted, "I'll be back in a minute, Mamma, wait on me!"

"Come back this instant!" his mother shrilled but they all disappeared into the woods.

"Bailey Boy!" the grandmother called in a tragic voice but she found she was looking at The Misfit squatting on the ground in front of her. "I just know you're a good man," she said desperately. "You're not a bit common!"

"Nome, I ain't a good man," The Misfit said after a second as if he had considered her statement carefully, "but I ain't the worst in the world neither. My daddy said I was different breed of dog from my brothers and sisters. 'You know,' Daddy said, 'it's some that can live their whole life out without asking about it and it's others has to know why it is, and this boy is one of the latters. He's going to be into everything!'" He put on his black hat and looked up suddenly and then away deep into the woods as if he were embarrassed again. "I'm sorry I don't have on a shirt before you ladies," he said, hunching his shoulders slightly. "We buried our clothes that we had on when we escaped and we're just making do until we can get better. We borrowed these from some folks we met," he explained.

"That's perfectly all right," the grandmother said. "Maybe Bailey has an extra shirt in his 100 suitcase."

"I'll look and see terrectly," the Misfit said.

"Where are they taking him?" the children's mother screamed.

"Daddy was a card himself," the Misfit said. "You couldn't put anything over on him. He never got in trouble with the Authorities though. Just had the knack of handling them."

"You could be honest too if you'd only try," said the grandmother. "Think how wonderful it would be to settle down and live a comfortable life and not have to think about somebody chasing you all the time."

The Misfit kept scratching in the ground with the butt of his gun as if he were thinking 105
about it. "Yes'm, somebody is always after you," he murmured.

The grandmother noticed how thin his shoulder blades were just behind his hat because she was standing up looking down on him. "Do you ever pray?" she asked.

He shook his head. All she saw was the black hat wiggle between his shoulder blades. "Nome," he said.

There was a pistol shot from the woods, followed closely by another. Then silence. The old lady's head jerked around. She could hear the wind move through the tree tops like a long satisfied insuck of breath. "Bailey Boy!" she called.

"I was a gospel singer for a while," The Misfit said. "I been most everything. Been in the arm service, both land and sea, at home and abroad, been twicet married, been an undertaker, been with the railroads, plowed Mother Earth, been in a tornado, seen a man burnt alive oncet," and he looked up at the children's mother and the little girl who were sitting close together, their faces white and their eyes glassy; "I even seen a woman flogged," he said.

"Pray, pray," the grandmother began, "pray, pray . . ."   110

"I never was a bad boy that I remember of," The Misfit said in an almost dreamy voice, "but somewheres along the line I done something wrong and got sent to the penitentiary. I was buried alive," and he looked up and held her attention to him by a steady stare.

"That's when you should have started to pray," she said. "What did you do to get sent to the penitentiary that first time?"

"Turn to the right, it was a wall," The Misfit said, looking up again at the cloudless sky. "Turn to the left, it was a wall. Look up it was a ceiling, look down it was a floor. I forgot what I done, lady. I set there and set there, trying to remember what it was I done and I ain't re-called it to this day. Oncet in a while, I would think it was coming to me, but it never come."

"Maybe they put you in by mistake," the old lady said vaguely.

115   "Nome," he said. "It wasn't no mistake. They had the papers on me."

"You must have stolen something," she said.

The Misfit sneered slightly. "Nobody had nothing I wanted," he said. "It was a head-doctor at the penitentiary said what I had done was kill my daddy but I know that for a lie. My daddy died in nineteen ought nineteen of the epidemic flu and I never had a thing to do with it. He was buried in the Mount Hopewell Baptist churchyard and you can go there and see for yourself."

"If you would pray," the old lady said, "Jesus would help you."

"That's right," The Misfit said.

120   "Well then, why don't you pray?" she asked trembling with delight suddenly.

"I don't want no hep," he said. "I'm doing all right by myself."

Bobby Lee and Hiram came ambling back from the woods. Bobby Lee was dragging a yellow shirt with bright blue parrots in it.

"Throw me that shirt, Bobby Lee," The Misfit said. The shirt came flying at him and landed on his shoulder and he put it on. The grandmother couldn't name what the shirt reminded her of. "No, lady," The Misfit said while he was buttoning it up. "I found out the crime don't mat-ter. You can do one thing or you can do another, kill a man or take a tire off his car, because sooner or later you're going to forget what it was you done and just be punished for it."

The children's mother had begun to make heaving noises as if she couldn't get her breath. "Lady," he asked, "would you and that little girl like to step off yonder with Bobby Lee and Hiram and join your husband?"

125   "Yes, thank you," the mother said faintly. Her left arm dangled helplessly and she was holding the baby, who had gone to sleep, in the other. "Hep that lady up, Hiram," The Mis-fit said as she struggled to climb out of the ditch, "and Bobby Lee, you hold onto that little girl's hand."

"I don't want to hold hands with him," June Star said. "He reminds me of a pig."

The fat boy blushed and laughed and caught her by the arm and pulled her off into the woods after Hiram and her mother.

Alone with The Misfit, the grandmother found that she had lost her voice. There was not a cloud in the sky nor any sun. There was nothing around her but woods. She wanted to tell him that he must pray. She opened and closed her mouth several times before anything came out. Finally she found herself saying, "Jesus, Jesus," meaning Jesus will help you, but the way she was saying it, it sounded as if she might be cursing.

"Yes'm," The Misfit said as if he agreed. "Jesus thown everything off balance. It was the same case with Him as with me except He hadn't committed any crime and they could prove I had committed one because they had the papers on me. Of course," he said, "they never shown me any papers. That's why I sign myself now. I said long ago, you get you a signature and sign everything you do and keep a copy of it. Then you'll know what you done and you can hold up the crime to the punishment and see do they match and in the end you'll have something to prove you ain't been treated right. I call myself The Misfit," he said, "because I can't make what all I done wrong fit what all I gone through in punishment."

There was a piercing scream from the woods, followed closely by a pistol report. "Does it seem right to you, lady, that one is punished a heap and another ain't punished at all?" 130

"Jesus!" the old lady cried. "You've got good blood! I know you wouldn't shoot a lady! I know you come from nice people! Pray! Jesus, you ought not to shoot a lady: I'll give you all the money I've got!"

"Lady," The Misfit said, looking beyond her far into the woods, "there never was a body that give the undertaker a tip."

There were two more pistol reports and the grandmother raised her head like a parched old turkey hen crying for water and called, "Bailey Boy, Bailey Boy!" as if her heart would break.

"Jesus was the only One that ever raised the dead," The Misfit continued, "and He shouldn't have done it. He thown everything off balance. If He did what He said then it's nothing for you to do but thow away everything and follow Him, and if He didn't, then it's nothing for you to do but enjoy the few minutes you got left the best way you can—by killing somebody or burning down his house or doing some other meanness to him. No pleasure but meanness," he said and his voice had become almost a snarl.

"Maybe He didn't raise the dead," the old lady mumbled, not knowing what she was saying and feeling so dizzy that she sank down in the ditch with her legs twisted under her. 135

"I wasn't there so I can't say He didn't." The Misfit said, "I wisht I had of been there," he said, hitting the ground with his fist. "It ain't right I wasn't there because if I had of been there I would of known. Listen lady," he said in a high voice, I had of been there I would of known and I wouldn't be like I am now." His voice seemed about to crack and the grandmother's head cleared for an instant. She saw the man's face twisted close to her own as if he were going to cry and she murmured, "Why you're one of my babies. You're one of my own children!" She reached out and touched him on the shoulder. The Misfit sprang back as if a snake had bitten him and shot her three times through the chest. Then he put his gun down on the ground and took off his glasses, and began to clean them.

Hiram and Bobby Lee returned from the woods and stood over the ditch, looking down at the grandmother who half sat and half lay in a puddle of blood with her legs crossed under her like a child's and her face smiling up at the cloudless sky.

Without his glasses, The Misfit's eyes were red-rimmed and pale and defenseless-looking. "Take her off and thow her where you thown the others," he said, picking up the cat that was rubbing itself against his leg.

"She was a talker, wasn't she?" Bobby Lee said, sliding down the ditch with a yodel.

"She would of been a good woman," The Misfit said, "if it had been somebody there to shoot her every minute of her life." 140

"Some fun!" Bobby Lee said.

"Shut up, Bobby Lee," The Misfit said. "It's no real pleasure in life."

QUESTIONS

1. Describe the story's point of view. On whom is the story focused? How appealing is this character as a focal point of attention?

2. What is the function of chance in the story's development? Describe some of the chances, or unlikelihoods, in the story? Why does O'Connor develop the story through the unfolding of these unlikelihoods?

3. Who is the Misfit? Why is he given this name? To what degree is he symbolic? What might he symbolize?

4. Some have called this story a religious allegory. How might it be considered allegorical? What might the story's violence be seen to symbolize?

TILLIE OLSEN (c. 1913–2007)

Tillie Olsen was born in 1912 or 1913 in Nebraska. Although she did not have an extensive formal education, she was the recipient of five honorary degrees and a number of other honors, including a Guggenheim Fellowship. Her early efforts at writing were tentative, and after the mid-1930s she put her career on hold while she devoted herself to her four daughters, "everyday jobs," and marriage. In the 1950s she resumed writing, lecturing, and advocating feminist and minority issues, all of which characterized her career. Her total output was not great, for her work was deliberate, careful, and slow. In 1974 she completed her long-developing novel, Yonnondio, From the Thirties, *which she had begun while in her teens (she had published a single chapter from the novel in 1934). The subject of the novel, which could be considered as a virtual life's work, is a working-class family during the depression years. "I Stand Here Ironing" is from her 1956 prize-winning collection* Tell Me a Riddle *(1961). If one judges the story as being related to Olsen's own experiences, it is visualized as happening in about 1951, when the narrator, the mother, is thirty-eight, and Emily, the daughter, is nineteen.*

🍁 I Stand Here Ironing (1953–1954)

I stand here ironing, and what you asked me moves tormented back and forth with the iron.

"I wish you would manage the time to come in and talk with me about your daughter. I'm sure you can help me understand her. She's a youngster who needs help and whom I'm deeply interested in helping."

"Who needs help." . . . Even if I came, what good would it do? You think because I am her mother I have a key, or that in some way you could use me as a key? She has lived for nineteen years. There is all that life that has happened outside of me, beyond me.

And when is there time to remember, to sift, to weigh, to estimate, to total? I will start and there will be an interruption and I will have to gather it all together again. Or I will become engulfed with all I did not do, with what should have been and what cannot be helped.

5   She was a beautiful baby. The first and only one of our five that was beautiful at birth. You do not guess how new and uneasy her tenancy in her now-loveliness. You did not know her all those years she was thought homely, or see her poring over her baby pictures, making me tell her over and over how beautiful she had been—and would be, I would tell her—and was now, to the seeing eye. But the seeing eyes were few or nonexistent. Including mine.

I nursed her. They feel that's important nowadays. I nursed all the children, but with her, with all the fierce rigidity of first motherhood, I did like the books then said. Though her cries battered me to trembling and my breasts ached with swollenness, I waited till the clock decreed.

Why do I put that first? I do not even know if it matters, or if it explains anything.

She was a beautiful baby. She blew shining bubbles of sound. She loved motion, loved light, loved color and music and textures. She would lie on the floor in her blue overalls patting the surface so hard in ecstasy her hands and feet would blur. She was a miracle to me, but when she was eight months old I had to leave her daytimes with the woman downstairs to whom she was no miracle at all, for I worked or looked for work and for Emily's father, who "could no longer endure" (he wrote in his good-bye note) "sharing want with us."

I was nineteen. It was the pre-relief, pre-WPA world of the depression. I would start running as soon as I got off the streetcar, running up the stairs, the place smelling sour, and awake or asleep to startle awake, when she saw me she would break into a clogged weeping that could not be comforted, a weeping I can hear yet.

After a while I found a job hashing at night so I could be with her days, and it was better. But it came to where I had to bring her to his family and leave her.

It took a long time to raise the money for her fare back. Then she got chicken pox and I had to wait longer. When she finally came, I hardly knew her, walking quick and nervous like her father, looking like her father, thin, and dressed in a shoddy red that yellowed her skin and glared at the pockmarks. All the baby loveliness gone.

She was two. Old enough for nursery school they said, and I did not know then what I know now—the fatigue of the long day, and the lacerations of group life in the kinds of nurseries that are only parking places for children.

Except that it would have made no difference if I had known. It was the only place there was. It was the only way we could be together, the only way I could hold a job.

And even without knowing, I knew. I knew the teacher that was evil because all these years it has curdled into my memory, the little boy hunched in the corner, her rasp, "why aren't you outside, because Alvin hits you? that's no reason, go out, scaredy." I knew Emily hated it even if she did not clutch and implore "don't go Mommy" like the other children, mornings.

She always had a reason why we should stay home. Momma, you look sick. Momma, I feel sick. Momma, the teachers aren't there today, they're sick. Momma, we can't go, there was a fire there last night. Momma, it's a holiday today, no school, they told me.

But never a direct protest, never rebellion. I think of our others in their three-, four-year-oldness—the explosions, the tempers, the denunciations, the demands—and I feel suddenly ill. I put the iron down. What in me demanded that goodness in her? And what was the cost, the cost to her of such goodness?

The old man living in the back once said in his gentle way: "You should smile at Emily more when you look at her." What *was* in my face when I looked at her? I loved her. There were all the acts of love.

It was only with the others I remembered what he said, and it was the face of joy, and not of care or tightness or worry I turned to them—too late for Emily. She does not smile easily, let alone almost always as her brothers and sisters do. Her face is closed and sombre, but when she wants, how fluid. You must have seen it in her pantomimes, you spoke of her rare gift for comedy on the stage that rouses a laughter out of the audience so dear they applaud and applaud and do not want to let her go.

Where does it come from, that comedy? There was none of it in her when she came back to me that second time, after I had had to send her away again. She had a new daddy now to learn to love, and I think perhaps it was a better time.

Except when we left her alone nights, telling ourselves she was old enough.

"Can't you go some other time, Mommy, like tomorrow?" she would ask. "Will it be just a little while you'll be gone? Do you promise?"

The time we came back, the front door open, the clock on the floor in the hall. She rigid awake. "It wasn't just a little while. I didn't cry. Three times I called you, just three times, and then I ran downstairs to open the door so you could come faster. The clock talked loud. I threw it away, it scared me what it talked."

She said the clock talked loud again that night I went to the hospital to have Susan. She was delirious with the fever that comes before red measles, but she was fully conscious all the week I was gone and the week after we were home when she could not come near the new baby or me.

She did not get well. She stayed skeleton thin, not wanting to eat, and night after night she had nightmares. She would call for me, and I would rouse from exhaustion to sleepily call back: "You're all right, darling, go to sleep, it's just a dream," and if she still called, in a sterner voice, "now go to sleep, Emily, there's nothing to hurt you." Twice, only twice, when I had to get up for Susan anyhow, I went in to sit with her.

25   Now when it is too late (as if she would let me hold and comfort her like I do the others) I get up and go to her at once at her moan or restless stirring. "Are you awake, Emily? Can I get you something?" And the answer is always the same: "No, I'm all right, go back to sleep, Mother."

They persuaded me at the clinic to send her away to a convalescent home in the country where "she can have the kind of food and care you can't manage for her, and you'll be free to concentrate on the new baby." They still send children to that place. I see pictures on the society page of sleek young women planning affairs to raise money for it, or dancing at the affairs, or decorating Easter eggs or filling Christmas stockings for the children.

They never have a picture of the children so I do not know if the girls still wear those gigantic red bows and the ravaged looks on the every other Sunday when parents can come to visit "unless otherwise notified"—as we were notified the first six weeks.

Oh it is a handsome place, green lawns and tall trees and fluted flower beds. High up on the balconies of each cottage the children stand, the girls in their red bows and white dresses, the boys in white suits and giant red ties. The parents stand below shrieking up to be heard and the children shriek down to be heard, and between them the invisible wall "Not To Be Contaminated by Parental Germs or Physical Affection."

There was a tiny girl who always stood hand in hand with Emily. Her parents never came. One visit she was gone. "They moved her to Rose Cottage" Emily shouted in explanation. "They don't like you to love anybody here."

30   She wrote once a week, the labored writing of a seven-year-old. "I am fine. How is the baby. If I write my leter nicly I will have a star. Love." There never was a star. We wrote every other day, letters she could never hold or keep but only hear read—once. "We simply do not have room for children to keep any personal possessions," they patiently explained when we pieced one Sunday's shrieking together to plead how much it would mean to Emily, who loved so to keep things, to be allowed to keep her letters and cards.

Each visit she looked frailer. "She isn't eating," they told us.

(They had runny eggs for breakfast or mush with lumps, Emily said later, I'd hold it in my mouth and not swallow. Nothing ever tasted good, just when they had chicken.)

It took us eight months to get her released home, and only the fact that she gained back so little of her seven lost pounds convinced the social worker.

I used to try to hold and love her after she came back, but her body would stay stiff, and after a while she'd push away. She ate little. Food sickened her, and I think much of life too. Oh she had physical lightness and brightness, twinkling by on skates, bouncing like a ball up and down up and down over the jump rope, skimming over the hill; but these were momentary.

35   She fretted about her appearance, thin and dark and foreign-looking at a time when every little girl was supposed to look or thought she should look a chubby blonde replica of Shirley Temple. The doorbell sometimes rang for her, but no one seemed to come and play in the house or be a best friend. Maybe because we moved so much.

There was a boy she loved painfully through two school semesters. Months later she told me how she had taken pennies from my purse to buy him candy. "Licorice was his favorite and I brought him some every day, but he still liked Jennifer better'n me. Why, Mommy?" The kind of question for which there is no answer.

School was a worry to her. She was not glib or quick in a world where glibness and quickness were easily confused with ability to learn. To her overworked and exasperated teachers she was an overconscientious "slow learner" who kept trying to catch up and was absent entirely too often.

I let her be absent, though sometimes the illness was imaginary. How different from my now-strictness about attendance with the others. I wasn't working. We had a new baby, I was home anyhow. Sometimes, after Susan grew old enough, I would keep her home from school, too, to have them all together.

Mostly Emily had asthma, and her breathing, harsh and labored, would fill the house with a curiously tranquil sound. I would bring the two old dresser mirrors and her boxes of collections to her bed. She would select beads and single earrings, bottle tops and shells, dried flowers and pebbles, old postcards and scraps, all sorts of oddments; then she and Susan would play Kingdom, setting up landscapes and furniture, peopling them with action.

Those were the only times of peaceful companionship between her and Susan. I have edged away from it, that poisonous feeling between them, that terrible balancing of hurts and needs I had to do between the two, and did so badly, those earlier years. 40

Oh there are conflicts between the others too, each one human, needing, demanding, hurting, taking—but only between Emily and Susan, no, Emily toward Susan that corroding resentment. It seems so obvious on the surface, yet it is not obvious. Susan, the second child, Susan, golden- and curly-haired and chubby, quick and articulate and assured, everything in appearance and manner Emily was not; Susan, not able to resist Emily's precious things, losing or sometimes clumsily breaking them; Susan telling jokes and riddles to company for applause while Emily sat silent (to say to me later: that was *my* riddle, Mother, I told it to Susan); Susan, who for all the five years' difference in age was just a year behind Emily in developing physically.

I am glad for that slow physical development that widened the difference between her and her contemporaries, though she suffered over it. She was too vulnerable for that terrible world of youthful competition, of preening and parading, of constant measuring of yourself against every other, of envy, "If I had that copper hair," "If I had that skin. . . ." She tormented herself enough about not looking like the others, there was enough of the unsureness, the having to be conscious of words before you speak, the constant caring— what are they thinking of me? without having it all magnified by the merciless physical drives.

Ronnie is calling. He is wet and I change him. It is rare there is such a cry now. That time of motherhood is almost behind me when the ear is not one's own but must always be racked and listening for the child cry, the child call. We sit for a while and I hold him, looking out over the city spread in charcoal with its soft aisles of light, "*Shoogily*," he breathes and curls closer. I carry him back to bed, asleep. *Shoogily*. A funny word, a family word, inherited from Emily, invented by her to say: *comfort*.

In this and other ways she leaves her seal, I say aloud. And startle at my saying it. What do I mean? What did I start to gather together, to try and make coherent? I was at the terrible, growing years. War years. I do not remember them well. I was working, there were four smaller ones now, there was not time for her. She had to help be a mother, a housekeeper, and shopper. She had to set her seal. Mornings of crisis and near hysteria trying to get lunches packed, hair combed, coats and shoes found, everyone to school or Child Care on time, the baby ready for transportation. And always the paper scribbled on by a smaller one, the book looked at by Susan then mislaid, the homework not done. Running out to that huge school where she was one, she was lost, she was a drop; suffering over the unpreparedness, stammering and unsure in her classes.

There was so little time left at night after the kids were bedded down. She would struggle over books, always eating (it was in those years she developed her enormous appetite that is legendary in our family) and I would be ironing, or preparing food for the next day, or writing V-mail to Bill, or tending the baby. Sometimes, to make me laugh, or out of her despair, she would imitate happenings or types at school. 45

I think I said once: "Why don't you do something like this in the school amateur show?" One morning she phoned me at work, hardly understandable through the weeping: "Mother, I did it. I won, I won; they gave me first prize; they clapped and clapped and wouldn't let me go."

Now suddenly she was Somebody, and as imprisoned in her difference as she had been in anonymity.

She began to be asked to perform at other high schools, even in colleges, then at city and statewide affairs. The first one we went to, I only recognized her that first moment when thin, shy, she almost drowned herself into the curtains. Then: Was this Emily? The control, the command, the convulsing and deadly clowning, the spell, then the roaring, stamping audience, unwilling to let this rare and precious laughter out of their lives.

Afterwards: You ought to do something about her with a gift like that—but without money or knowing how, what does one do? We have left it all to her, and the gift has as often eddied inside, clogged and clotted, as been used and growing.

50   She is coming. She runs up the stairs two at a time with her light graceful step, and I know she is happy tonight. Whatever it was that occasioned your call did not happen today.

"Aren't you ever going to finish the ironing, Mother? Whistler painted his mother in a rocker. I'd have to paint mine standing over an ironing board." This is one of her communicative nights and she tells me everything and nothing as she fixes herself a plate of food out of the icebox.

She is so lovely. Why did you want me to come in at all? Why were you concerned? She will find her way.

She starts up the stairs to bed. "Don't get me up with the rest in the morning." "But I thought you were having midterms." "Oh, those," she comes back in, kisses me, and says quite lightly, "in a couple of years when we'll all be atom-dead they won't matter a bit."

She has said it before. She *believes* it. But because I have been dredging the past, and all that compounds a human being is so heavy and meaningful in me, I cannot endure it tonight.

55   I will never total it all. I will never come in to say: She was a child seldom smiled at. Her father left me before she was a year old. I had to work her first six years when there was work, or I sent her home and to his relatives. There were years she had care she hated. She was dark and thin and foreign-looking in a world where the prestige went to blondeness and curly hair and dimples, she was slow where glibness was prized. She was a child of anxious, not proud, love. We were poor and could not afford for her the soil of easy growth. I was a young mother, I was a distracted mother. There were the other children pushing up, demanding. Her younger sister seemed all that she was not. There were years she did not want me to touch her. She kept too much in herself, her life was such she had to keep too much in herself. My wisdom came too late. She has much to her and probably little will come of it. She is a child of her age, of depression, of war, of fear.

Let her be. So all that is in her will not bloom—but in how many does it? There is still enough left to live by. Only help her to know—help make it so there is cause for her to know—that she is more than this dress on the ironing board, helpless before the iron.

QUESTIONS

1. Describe the point of view of "I Stand Here Ironing." What is the narrator doing at the time of the narrative? Why do the events of the story have to do with ironing?

2. Describe the realistic qualities of the narrator. What sort of relationship has she had with her daughter, Emily?

3. Describe the circumstances in America through which the narrator has lived, from 1932 through the next twenty years.

4. What is Emily like? How does she develop, as brought out in the story?

PETRONIUS (GAIUS PETRONIUS ARBITER) (d. 66 CE)

Historically, Petronius was a political figure in the court of the Roman emperor Nero (r. 54–68), who is best remembered for his reprisals against Roman Christians after the famous fire in Rome in 64 CE. Petronius served as an ambassador and also as a consul (an office conferring the right to introduce legal cases in the Roman Senate). For a time he enjoyed imperial favor as one of Nero's inner circle. However, he was accused of being part of a conspiracy against Nero, and he was then ordered by the emperor to commit suicide, which he had no choice but to do.

As a writer, Petronius is best known for his picaresque Satyricon, *a lengthy work of which only a small part has survived. "The Widow of Ephesus" is taken from this work, which consists of a series of episodes and stories held together by the adventures of Encolpius, the narrator, and a group of his friends as they travel from town to town in southern Italy. The story of the Widow appears after a brawl that occurs on board the ship of Lichas, a wealthy sea captain whom Encolpius had earlier robbed, and his woman friend Tryphena, a courtesan with whom Encolpius has earlier had a brief affair. Encolpius and his friends, one of whom is Eumolpus, an elderly poet and raconteur, fight against Lichas and his crew. After the brawl, there is general joyousness on the ship, and the combatants settle down to hear the story of the Ephesian Widow. The speaker or narrator is Encolpius, who quotes Eumolpus's story.*

The Widow of Ephesus (from *Satyricon*, Chs. 108–13) (65 CE)

An English version by Edgar V. Roberts

We shook hands, chatted happily, and sang loudly while the entire ship rang with our noise. Sea birds landed on the yard-arms, and Eumolpus, who was drinking too much wine, decided to amuse us with a few stories. He began by insulting women. He called them weak because he claimed they were impetuous in love and would neglect even their own children while having an illicit affair. Moreover, he said that no woman he had ever known had the moral strength to resist a handsome man. He insisted that he did not get his ideas from legend or from historical accounts about evil women. Rather, he himself had actually seen what he was talking about, and he offered to tell us a true story in illustration. We immediately urged him on, and gave him our complete attention. This is the tale he told:

"Once upon a time in the city of Ephesus, on the Coast of Asia Minor, there lived a virtuous woman whose marital fidelity was so famous that women came from far and near just to get a glimpse of her. In the course of time, her husband got sick and died, and the newly widowed lady, all by herself, arranged his funeral and burial. At the funeral she was not satisfied only to follow the cortege in the usual way, by tearing her hair and beating her breasts. No, she actually accompanied the dead body right into the tomb, and after the coffin was placed in the vault in the custom of the Greeks, she began a vigil beside it, weeping and wailing both day and night.

"She was so rigorous in her duty that she neglected to eat, and she therefore became weaker by the hour. Neither her parents nor her closest relatives could persuade her to return home. Even the local politicians and judges could not convince her. She snubbed them, and so, with their dignity ruffled, they gave up trying.

"By this time this most amazing woman was already in the fifth day of her fast, to the sorrow of everyone in town, who believed that she would die at any moment. At her side was her faithful handmaiden, who shed as many tears as the mournful Widow did. This maiden also attended to practical matters such as refueling and relighting the torch whenever it was about to go out. Through all the city of Ephesus, from one end to another, no one talked about anything else. All the people from richest to poorest acknowledged the Widow as the supreme example of wifely love and duty. They had never seen or heard of anyone like her.

5   "But regular business in Ephesus also went on, and one day the Provincial Governor sentenced some local hoodlums to be crucified in the grounds next to the tomb in which the Widow stood vigil. On the night of the crucifixion a soldier was stationed there to keep away all relatives or friends who might have wanted to steal the bodies in order to bury them properly.

    "As he stood guard, he saw the torchlight from the Widow's tomb, and he also heard her heartbreaking outcries. Now, curiosity is a weakness of humankind, and this soldier was typically human. He went down the stairs into the sepulchre to take a look. Imagine his shock at the sight of this pretty woman and the corpse of her husband! At first he thought he was seeing ghosts, or apparitions out of the Kingdom of Hades! But when he saw how the Widow mourned, and how she had scarred her face with her fingernails, he understood that she was near death. He therefore ran up to his station and got his supper, which he carried to her. He pleaded with the sorrowing woman to stop tearing herself apart with sobs. 'The same inescapable fate waits for all human beings,' he said, 'the final trip of all to the home of the dead.' He racked his brain for other customary words of condolence which are intended to heal the broken hearts of the bereaved.

    "But the Widow, who was upset rather than consoled by this unexpected stranger, only tore at her bosom more violently, ripping out some of her hair and throwing it on the corpse. The soldier then kept repeating his soothing words, while at the same time he tempted her with the tasty food and drink of his supper. The first to yield was the Widow's handmaiden, who, tempted by the aromatic bouquet of the wine, gratefully accepted his generous offer.

    "Brought back to life by the wine and the food, the handmaiden joined the soldier in his siege against the fortress of her mistress's self-sacrifice. She cried out, 'What good can it do anyone if you starve yourself to death, if you bury yourself alive, or if you yourself speed up your own last breath before your time has truly come? Remember what the poet Virgil said:

    Do you believe that ashes or buried ghosts can feel?°

My Lady, come back to life, please! Give up this crazy notion of wifely duty and, as long as you are able, enjoy the light of the sun once more. Even your dead husband, if he could speak, would advise you to get on with your life.'

    "Nobody is deaf when told to eat or to continue staying alive, and so the Widow, starving after her long fast, finally gave way. She refreshed herself with the food just as vigorously as her handmaiden had done.

10   "But everybody knows that one appetite follows another, and it should come as no surprise that the soldier began wooing the Widow with the same tempting words he had used to rescue her from starvation. Although she was unparalleled for modesty, she recognized that he was an unusually handsome young man. He was also persuasive, and in addition the Widow's handmaiden quoted another line of Virgil to help him in his cause:

    Would you hold out against a pleasure-giving passion?°

    "Why make the story last longer? This woman stopped resisting, and she accepted the young soldier's love just as she had accepted his food. They spent the night together—and

---

°*Do . . . feel: Aeneid* 4.34.
°*Would . . . passion: Aeneid* 4.38.

after that the next night, and the next, and the next. Naturally they kept the door of the tomb barred and bolted so that any strangers or friends passing by would conclude that the faithful wife had died upon the body of her husband.

"The soldier was enchanted both by the beauty of his new sweetheart and by their secret affair, and he bought her a few small presents out of his small pay. Every night, as soon as it was dark, he would steal away to the tomb with his gifts, and would stay there until morning.

"But one evening the parents of one of the crucified thieves took advantage of him. They watched him abandon his post to enjoy his night of love, and then they hurried to their son's cross, carried his body away, and had the final ceremony for the dead performed over it. When morning came and the soldier saw that the cross was empty, he fell into a cold sweat because he knew that the punishment for his dereliction of duty would be death. He told the Widow, and swore that he could not wait for the sentence of a court martial. He would, he said, commit suicide for his folly by falling on his sword. He then asked the Widow to put his body in the tomb after he was dead—as the final resting place not only her husband, but also for him, her lover. The Widow, however, was not only virtuous and dutiful, but she was also resourceful.

" 'No,' she cried, 'heaven forbid that I should be forced by bad luck to stand vigil at the same time beside the bodies of the only two men in the world that I ever loved. I would rather hang up a dead man on the cross than permit a living man to die.'

"After these words she told him to take her husband's corpse from the vault, carry it to   15
the empty cross, nail it to the cross, and hoist it up. The soldier readily agreed to this practical scheme, and the next day everyone in town was asking how on earth the dead man had been able to climb onto the cross!"

As Eumolpus was finishing his story, Tryphena blushed until her face was red, and she tried to hide her embarrassment. The sailors were so amused that they rolled on the deck with laughter. While they laughed, Lichas sternly declared that the Provincial Governor should not have permitted such a farce. Indeed, Lichas said that the Governor's duty was to have restored the husband's corpse to the tomb, and then to have executed the Widow herself on the cross.

QUESTIONS

1. Describe the situation of the narration in "The Widow of Ephesus." Who is the narrator? How does he acquire the information he relates in his story? Who listens to the narrator? What are their reactions to the tale?

2. Describe the character of the widow. How might her actions be interpreted as evidence of weakness? Conversely, how might they be shown as marks of strength?

3. What is the soldier like? What marks of character strength does he show?

4. Compare this story with Anton Chekhov's play *The Bear* (Chapter 25), which Chekhov adapted from "The Widow of Ephesus." In what way does Chekhov interpret the character of the widow and of the soldier?

Chapter 10A

Writing a Research Essay on Fiction

Broadly, **research** is systematic investigation, examination, and experimentation. It is the basic tool of intellectual inquiry for anyone working in any discipline—physics, chemistry, biology, psychology, anthropology, history, and literature, to name just a few disciplines. With research, and with the breakthroughs of knowledge that research brings, our understanding and our civilization grow; without research, they languish.

The major assumption of doing research is that the researcher is reaching out to find and master new areas of knowledge. With each assignment the researcher acquires not only the knowledge gained from the particular task but also the skills needed to undertake further research and thereby to gain further knowledge. Some research tasks are elementary, such as using a dictionary to discover the meaning of a word and thereby aiding the understanding of an important passage. Many people would not even call that research. More detailed research uses an array of resources: critical studies, biographies, introductions, bibliographies, and histories. When you begin a research task you usually have little or no knowledge about your topic, but with such resources you can acquire expert knowledge in a relatively short time.

Although research is the animating spark of all disciplines, our topic here is **literary research**—the systematic use of primary and secondary sources in studying a literary problem. In doing literary research, you consult not only individual works themselves (primary sources) but many other works that shed light on them and interpret them (secondary sources). Typical research tasks are to learn important facts about a work and about the period in which it was written; to learn about the lives, careers, and other works of authors; to discover and apply the comments and judgments of modern or earlier critics; to learn details that help explain the meaning of works; and to learn about critical and artistic taste.

Selecting a Topic

In most instances, your instructor assigns a research essay on a specific topic. Sometimes, however, the choice of a topic will be left in your hands. For such assignments, it is helpful to know the types of research essays you might find most congenial. Here are some possibilities:

1. **A particular work.** At first, this type of research essay is probably the most common one, as shown in the illustrative essay (p. 614). You might treat character (for example, "The Character of Louise in Chopin's 'The Story of an Hour'" or "The Question of Whether Young Goodman Brown Is a Hero or a dupe in

Hawthorne's 'Young Goodman Brown'") or tone and style, ideas, structure, form, and the like. A research paper on a single work is similar to an essay on the same work, except that the research paper takes into account more views and facts than those you are likely to have without the research.

2. **A particular author.** A project might focus on an idea or some facet of style, imagery, setting, or tone of the author, tracing the origins and development of the topic through a number of different stories, poems, or plays. Examples are "Hardy's Treatment of Local Country Folkways in His Short Stories" and "Faulkner's Use of the Yoknapatawpha Environment in His Stories." This type of essay is suitable for a number of shorter works, although it is also applicable for a single major work, such as a longer story, novel, or play.

3. **Comparison and contrast** (see Chapter 30). There are two types.
   a. *An idea or quality common to two or more authors.* Here you show points of similarity or contrast, or else you show how one author's work can be taken to criticize another's. A possible subject is "Contrasting Uses of Dialogue in Ellison's 'Battle Royal' and Tan's 'Two Kinds,'" or "The Theme of Love and Sexuality in Faulkner's 'A Rose for Emily,' Munro's 'The Found Boat,' and Joyce's 'Araby.'"
   b. *Different critical views of a particular work or body of works.* Sometimes much is to be gained from an examination of differing critical opinions on topics like "The Meaning of Poe's 'The Masque of the Red Death'" or "Various Views of Hawthorne's 'Young Goodman Brown.'" Such a study would attempt to determine the critical opinion and taste to which a work did or did not appeal, and it might also aim at conclusions about whether the work was in the advance or rear guard of its time.

4. **The influence of an idea, author, philosophy, political situation, or artistic movement on specific works of an author or authors.** An essay on influences can be specific and to the point, as in "Details of Twentieth-Century Native American Life as Reflected in Whitecloud's 'Blue Winds Dancing,'" or else it can be more abstract and critical, as in "The Influence of Traditional Religion on Hawthorne's 'Young Goodman Brown.'"

5. **The origin of a particular work or type of work.** Such an essay might examine an author's biography to discover the germination and development of a work—for example, "Poe's 'The Masque of the Red Death' or his Theory of the Short Story" or "Shaw's 'Act of Faith' and Its Relationship to Post–World War II Literature."

If you consider these types, an idea of what to write may come to you. Perhaps you have particularly liked one author or several authors. If so, you might start to think along the lines of types 1, 2, or 3. If you are interested in influences or origins, then type 4 or 5 may suit you better.

If you still cannot decide on a topic after rereading the works you have liked, then you should carry your search for a topic into your school library. Look up your author or authors in the library's retrieval system. Your first goal should be to find a relatively recent book-length critical study published by a university press. Look for a title indicating that the book is a general one dealing with the author's major works rather than just one work. Study those chapters relevant to the work or works you have chosen. Most writers of critical studies describe their purpose and plan in their introductions or first chapters, so begin with the first part of the book. If there is no separate chapter on your primary text, use the index as your guide to the relevant pages. Reading in this way will give you enough knowledge about the issues and ideas raised by the work to enable you to select a promising topic. Once you make your decision, you are ready to develop a working bibliography.

Setting Up a Bibliography

The best way to develop a working bibliography of books and articles is to begin by finding major critical studies of the writer or writers. Again, use a book or books published by university presses—maybe the books you used to determine your topic. Such books will contain comprehensive bibliographies. Be careful to read the chapters on your primary work or works and to look for the footnotes or endnotes, for often you can save time if you record the names of books and articles listed in these notes. Then refer to the bibliographies included at the ends of the books, and select likely looking titles. Now, look at the dates of publication of the scholarly books. Let us suppose that you have found three books, published in 2001, 2006, and 2007. Unless you are planning an extensive research assignment, you can safely assume that the writers of critical works will have done the selecting for you of important works published before the date of publication. These bibliographies will be reliable, and you can use them with confidence. Thus, the bibliography in a book published in 2007 will be complete up through about 2006, for the writer will have finished the manuscript a year or so before the book was published. But such bibliographies will not go up to the present. For that, you will need to search for works published after the most recent of the books.

Consult Bibliographical Guides

Fortunately for students doing literary research, the Modern Language Association (MLA) of America has been providing a complete bibliography of literary studies for years, not only in English and American literatures but also in the literatures of many foreign languages. This is the *MLA International Bibliography of Books and Articles on the Modern Languages and Literatures* ("*MLA Bibliography*"). The *MLA Bibliography* started achieving completeness in the late 1950s. By 1969 the project had grown so huge that it was published in many parts, which are bound together in library editions. In the latest volume, dated 2006, this comprehensive bibliography lists 20,213 books and articles that were published in the year 2006. In addition, following these numbered listings there is a second half of the bibliography, 970 pages long, containing a detailed subject index. University and college libraries have sets of the *MLA Bibliography* on open shelves or tables. The bibliography is also published on CD-ROM and on the Internet—formats accessible to you through your college library services. You will need to consult a librarian about Internet access.

In the traditional book format, the *MLA Bibliography* is conveniently organized by period and author. Should you be doing research about James Joyce, look him up in *Volume I* under the category "Irish literature/1900–1999," where there are 190 entries of works about him. In this same volume you will also find references to most other authors of works in English, such as Shakespeare (drama, poetry), Wordsworth (poetry), and Arnold (poetry). You will find most books and articles listed under the author's last name. Journal references are abbreviated, but a lengthy list explaining abbreviations appears at the beginning of the volume. Using the *MLA Bibliography* in the book format, begin with the most recent one and then go backward to your stopping point. If your library has computers dedicated to electronic versions of the bibliography, you can search by typing in the name of your author or subject. By whatever means you gain access to the bibliography, be sure to get the complete information—especially volume numbers and years of publication—for each article and book.

There are many other bibliographies useful for students doing literary research, such as the *Essay and General Literature Index,* the *Readers' Guide to Periodical Literature,* and various specific indexes. The *MLA Bibliography* contains far in excess of abundance, however, for your present research purposes. Remember that as you progress in your reading, the notes and bibliographies in the works you consult will also constitute an unfolding selective bibliography. For the illustrative research essay in this chapter, a number of entries were discovered not from bibliographies like those just listed but from the reference lists in critical books.

Your list will make up a fairly comprehensive search bibliography, which you can use when you physically enter the library to begin collecting and using materials. An additional convenience is that many associated libraries, such as state colleges and urban public libraries, have pooled their resources. Thus, if you use the services of a network of nearby county libraries, you can go to another library to use materials that are not accessible at your own college or branch. If distances are great, however, and your own library does not have a book that you think is important to your project, you can ask a librarian to get the book for you through the Interlibrary Loan Service. Usually, given time, the libraries will accommodate as many of your needs as they can.

You are now ready to find your sources and take notes. Make the maximum use of your college library. Call out the books themselves, the kind you can hold in your hands, and the relevant journals containing the articles in which you are interested. Read them, and make the best use you can of them.

Online Library Services

Through computer access, many college and university libraries are constantly connected to a vast array of local, national, and even international libraries, so that by using various online services, you can extend your research far beyond the capacities of your own library. You can use one of the computers in your library, or your own personal computer, to gain access to the catalogs of large research libraries, provided that you enter the correct information, are able and willing to follow the program codes, and are patient and persistent.

GAINING ACCESS TO BOOKS AND ARTICLES THROUGH THE INTERNET. At one time, many smaller schools did not have copies of all the books and scholarly periodicals containing the results and reports of research. Many students were therefore frustrated in their attempts to find all the works that they had listed on their working bibliographies. Times, however, have changed. You may now gain access to many sources that are not in your library, for many of the works you want to read, which are not in your school's library, are now directly available to you through computer, page by page. A major source is *Questia,* an electronic depository of books and articles which is likely available to you through your college library. In total, *Questia* contains 67,000 "full text" books, and more than 1.5 million articles. For students doing research on Hawthorne's short stories, for example, *Questia* claims to have more than 6,000 books and more than 1,300 scholarly articles. *EBSCOhost* is a multidisciplinary database that includes "MagillOnLiteraturePlus" which has plot summaries and analysis of fictional works; *EBSCOhost* also has "Book Index with Reviews" that includes excerpts of book reviews along with book summaries. *WilsonWeb* has databases in many disciplines and includes "Book Review Digest Plus," which has summaries of books as well as complete book reviews. *WilsonWeb* also has "Short Story Index" which indexes stories appearing in collections and periodicals since 1984. *Columbia Grangers World of Poetry* has references to many types of poetry.

Another major electronic source is *JSTOR* (i.e., *Journal Storage*), a scholarly journal archive. Most college and university libraries, and many high schools, subscribe to this service, and it is available to you as a registered student. It includes computerized copies of complete sets of more than 600 scholarly journals in the arts and sciences. By gaining the proper credentials available to you as a student, you will have access to virtually any item you have entered in your bibliography.

Still another vital research source is Google Scholar, which is in the process of duplicating the pages of many thousands of scholarly works. The service is available, like Questia and JSTOR, through your college library. In other words, these electronic book and article services are available right now to provide you with abundant materials that previously were not readily available to most students at American colleges and universities.

 IMPORTANT CONSIDERATIONS ABOUT COMPUTER-AIDED RESEARCH

You must always remind yourself that online catalogs, such as those you might select from other colleges and universities, and from private organizations, can give you only what has been entered into them. If one university library classifies a work under "criticism and interpretation" and another classifies it under "characters," a search of "criticism and interpretation" at the first library will find the work but the same search at the second will not. Sometimes the inclusion of an author's life dates immediately following the name might throw off your search. Typographic errors in the system will cause additional search problems, although many programs try to forestall such difficulties by providing "nearby" entries to enable you to determine whether incorrectly entered topics may in fact be helpful to you.

Also, if you use online services, be careful to determine the year when the computerization began. Many libraries have a recent commencement date—1978, for example, or 1985. For completeness, therefore, you would need assistance in finding catalog entries for items published before these years.

It is particularly important *to avoid the many and varied so-called "free essays" on literary topics that fill a number of today's extremely popular search engines.* These essays are written largely by people who are themselves just beginning, not by scholars who have studied particular topics for many years and who have become experts in their analyses. The reason for using books and articles approved by scholarly publishers is that the works have been *refereed* by authorities in the particular field. If these authorities, or referees, have recommended publication, you are entitled to expect that the breadth and depth of the critical analyses will be well considered and reliable. That is not the case with the innumerable "free essays" that you might find in more general and unrefereed entries in the search engine.

Just a few years ago, the broadness of scope that electronic searches provide for most undergraduate students doing research assignments was not possible; today, it is commonplace. Even with the astounding possibilities of electronic resources, however, it is still necessary to take out actual books and articles—and read them and take notes on them—before you can begin and complete a research essay. These days, electronic services can supply you with actual copies of many of the materials you are seeking, but they cannot do your reading, note taking, and writing. All that is still up to you, as it always has been for all students doing research.

Taking Notes and Paraphrasing Material

There are many ways of taking notes, but a few things are clear. Because your notes should facilitate, not hinder, your writing of the final research essay, you will need a systematic way of handling your notes. Notes should not be taken helter-skelter. Nor should they be written on the front and back of a notebook, with only one side showing and the other side being out of your sight. The best way is to develop a method whereby you will be able to see all your notes together, laid out on a table in front of you. You might type your notes into your computer—leaving space between them, printing them out, and then, after cutting the separate items on your printout, laying these notes side by side and group by group. If you are taking handwritten notes, you can achieve simultaneous viewability by using note cards. If you have never used cards before, you might profit from consulting any one of a number of handbooks and special workbooks on research.[1] The principal advantage of cards is the ease with which you can see them at a

---

[1]See Muriel Harris, *Prentice Hall Reference Guide to Grammar and Usage*, 5th ed. (Upper Saddle River: Prentice Hall, 2003) 283–301.

glance when you lay them out on a desk or other large surface. Cards are also sturdy and will easily maintain their physical integrity as you handle them and assign them to their relevant piles. As a result, cards—or notes taken from printouts from your computer—may be easily classified; they may be numbered and renumbered; shuffled; tried out in one place, rejected, and then used in another place (or thrown away); and arranged in order when you start to write.

Taking Complete and Accurate Notes

WRITE THE SOURCE OF EACH NOTE YOU TAKE.   Be especially diligent about writing the source of your information on each card or computer note. This may seem bothersome, but it is easier than going back to the library to locate the correct source after you have begun your essay. You can save time if you take the complete data on one card or computer file—a "master card" for that source—and then create an abbreviation for the separate notes you take from the source. Here is an example, which also includes the location where the reference was originally found (e.g., card or computer catalog, computer search, bibliography in a book, the *MLA Bibliography,* etc.). Observe that the author's last name goes first.

DONOVAN, JOSEPHINE, ED. FEMINIST	PN
Literary Criticism: Explorations	98
in Theory. 2nd ed. Lexington:	W64
UP of Kentucky. 1989	F4
DONOVAN	
CARD CATALOG, "WOMEN"	

If you take many notes from this book, the name "Donovan" will serve as identification. Be sure not to lose your master group of references because you will need them when you prepare your list of works cited. If you are working with a computer, record the complete bibliographical data in a computer file.

RECORD THE PAGE NUMBER FOR EACH NOTE.   It would be hard to guess how much exasperation has been caused by the failure to record page numbers in notes. Be sure to write the page number down first, before you begin to take your note, and, to be doubly sure, write the page number again at the end of your note. If the detail goes from one page to the next in your source, record the exact spot where the page changes, as in this example.

> HEILBRUN AND STIMSON, IN DONOVAN, pp. 63–64
>
> [63]After the raising of the feminist consciousness it is necessary to develop/ [64]"the growth of moral perception" through anger and the "amelioration of social inequities."

The reason for such care is that you may wish to use only a part of a note you have taken, and when there are two pages you will need to be accurate in locating what goes where.

RECORD ONLY ONE FACT OR OPINION ON A CARD OR COMPUTER ENTRY. Record only one major detail for each of your notes—one quotation, one paraphrase, one observation—never two or more. You might be tempted to fill up the entire notes with many separate but unrelated details, but such a try at economy often gets you in trouble because you might want to use some of the details in other places. If you have only one entry per note, you will avoid such problems and also retain the freedom you need.

USE QUOTATION MARKS FOR ALL QUOTED MATERIAL. In taking notes it is extremely important—vitally important, urgently important—to distinguish copied material from your own words. Always put quotation marks around every direct quotation you copy verbatim from a source. Make the quotation marks immediately, before you forget, so that you will always know that the words of your notes within quotation marks are the words of another writer.

Often, as you write your notes, you may use some of your own words and some of the words from your source. In cases like this you should be even more cautious. *Put quotation marks around every word that you take directly from the source, even if your note looks like a picket fence.* Later, when you begin writing your essay, your memory of what is yours and not yours will be dim, and if you use another's words in your own essay without proper acknowledgment, you are risking the charge of plagiarism. Much of the time, plagiarism is caused not by deliberate deception but rather by sloppy note taking.[2]

IF YOUR SOURCE IS LONG, MAKE A BRIEF AND ACCURATE PARAPHRASE. When you take notes, it is best to paraphrase the sources. A paraphrase is a restatement in your own words, and because of this it is actually a first step in the writing of your essay. A big problem in paraphrasing is to capture the idea in the source without copying the words in the source. The best way is to read and reread the passage you are noting. Turn over the book or journal—or turn away from your computer screen—and write out the idea in your own words as accurately as you can. Once you have completed this note, compare it with the original and make corrections to improve your thought and emphasis. Add a short quotation if you believe it is needed, but be sure to use quotation marks. If your paraphrase is too close to the original, throw out the note and write another one. This effort may have its own reward because often you may be able to transfer some or even all of your note, word for word, directly to the appropriate place in your research essay.

To see the problems of paraphrasing, let us look at a paragraph of criticism and then see how a student doing research might take notes on it. The paragraph

---

[2]See page 612 for a further discussion of plagiarism.

is by Richard F. Peterson, from an essay entitled "The Circle of Truth: The Stories of Katherine Mansfield and Mary Lavin," published in *Modern Fiction Studies* 24 (1978): 383–94. In the passage to be quoted, Peterson is considering the structures of two Mansfield stories, "Bliss" and "Miss Brill":

> "Bliss" and "Miss Brill" are flawed stories, but not because the truth they reveal about their protagonists is too brutal or painful for the tastes of the common reader. In each story, the climax of the narrative suggests an arranged reality that leaves a lasting impression, not of life, but of the author's cleverness. This strategy of arrangement for dramatic effect or revelation, unfortunately, is common in Katherine Mansfield's fiction. Too often in her stories a dropped remark at the right or wrong moment, a chance meeting or discovery, an intrusive figure in the shape of a fat man at a ball or in the Café de Madrid, a convenient death of a hired man or a stranger dying aboard a ship, or a *deus ex machina* in the form of two doves, a dill pickle, or a fly plays too much of a role in / [386] creating a character's dilemma or deciding the outcome of the narrative. 385–386

Because taking notes forces a shortening of this or any criticism, it also requires you to discriminate, judge, interpret, and select; good note taking is not easy. There are some things to guide you, however, when you go through the many sources you uncover.

THINK ABOUT THE PURPOSE OF YOUR RESEARCH.   You may not know exactly what you are "fishing for" when you start to take notes, for you cannot prejudge what your essay will contain. Research is a form of discovery. But soon you will notice subjects and issues that your sources constantly explore. If you can accept one of these as your major topic, or focus of interest, you can use that as your guide in all further note taking.

For example, suppose you start to take notes on criticism about Katherine Mansfield's "Miss Brill," and after a certain amount of reading, you decide to focus on the story's structure. This decision guides your further research and note taking. Thus, for example, Richard Peterson criticizes Mansfield's technique of arranging climaxes in her stories. With your topic being "structure," it would therefore be appropriate to write a note about Peterson's judgment. The following note is adequate as a brief reminder of the content in the passage:

> Peterson 385   structure: negative
>
> Peterson claims that Mansfield creates climaxes that are too artificial, too unlifelike, giving the impression not of reality but of Mansfield's own "cleverness." 385

Let us now suppose that you want a fuller note, in the expectation that you need not just Peterson's general idea but also some of his supporting detail. Such a note might look like this:

Peterson 385   structure: negative

Peterson thinks that "Bliss" and "Miss Brill" are "flawed" because they have contrived endings that give the impression "not of life but of" Mansfield's "cleverness." She arranges things artificially, according to Peterson, to cause the endings in many other stories. Some of these things are chance remarks, discoveries, or meetings, together with other unexpected or chance incidents and objects. These contrivances make their stories imperfect. 385

In an actual research essay, any part of this note would be useful. The words are almost all the note taker's own, and the few quotations are within quotation marks. Note that Peterson, the critic, is properly recognized as the source of the criticism, so you could adapt the note easily when you are doing your writing. The key here is that your note taking should be guided by your developing plan for your essay.

Note taking is part of your thinking and composing process. You may not always know whether you will be able to use each note that you take, and you will always exclude many notes when you write your essay. You will always find, however, that taking notes is easier once you have determined your purpose.

GIVE YOUR NOTES TITLES. To help plan and develop the various parts of your essay, write a title for each of your notes, as in the examples in this chapter. This practice is a form of outlining. Let us continue discussing the structure of Mansfield's "Miss Brill," the actual subject of the illustrative research essay (pp. 614–20). As you do your research, you discover that there is a divergence of critical thought about how the ending of the story should be understood. Here is a note about one of the diverging interpretations:

Daly 90   Last sentence of the story

Miss Brill's "complete" "identification" with the shabby fur piece at the very end may cause readers to conclude that she is the one in tears but bravely does not recognize this fact, and also to conclude that she may never use the fur in public again because of her complete defeat. Everything may be for "perhaps the very last time." 90

Notice that the title classifies the topic of the note. If you use such classifications, a number of like-titled cards or computer notes could form the basis for a section in your essay about how to understand the conclusion of "Miss Brill." Whether you use this note or not—and very often you may not, for it may not fit into your final plan for your essay—the topic itself will guide you in further study and note taking.

WRITE DOWN YOUR OWN ORIGINAL THOUGHTS, AND BE SURE TO MARK THEM AS YOUR OWN.   As you take notes, you will be acquiring your own observations and thoughts. Do not push these aside in your mind, on the chance of remembering them later, *but write them down immediately*. Often you may notice a detail that your source does not mention, or you may get a hint for an idea that the critic does not develop. Often, too, you may get thoughts that can serve as "bridges" between details in your notes or as introductions or concluding observations. Be sure to title your comments and also to mark them as your own thought. Here is such a note, which is about Katherine Mansfield's emphasis on the impoverished existence of her heroine, Miss Brill, and the many people inhabiting the park where the action of the story takes place:

My Own   About Miss Brill's "cupboard"

Mansfield's speaker avoids taking us to the homes of the other people in the park, as she does when we follow Miss Brill into her living quarters. Instead, she lets us know that the silent couple, the complaining wife and suffering husband, the unseen man rejected by the young woman dumping the flowers, the "ermine toque," and the funny gentleman, not to mention the many people resembling statues in the park, all return to loneliness and personal pain.

Observe that the substance of this note (also most of the language) is used as the basis for much of paragraph 10 in the illustrative essay. The point here is that as you make your own observations while doing your research, you are also free to develop materials that can go directly into your final essay.

CLASSIFY YOUR CARDS OR COMPUTER NOTES, AND GROUP THEM.   If you do a careful and thorough job of taking notes, your essay will already have been forming in your mind. The titles of your notes and cards will suggest areas to be developed as you do your planning and initial drafting. Once you have assembled a stack of materials derived from a reasonable number of sources (your instructor may have assigned an approximate number or a minimum number), you can sort them into groups according to the topics and titles. For the illustrative research essay, after some shuffling and retitling, the cards were assembled in the following groups:

General structure

Specific structures: season, time of day, levels of cruelty, Miss Brill's own "hierarchies" of unreality

The concluding paragraphs, especially the last sentence

If you look at the major sections of the illustrative essay, you will see that the topics are closely adapted from these groups of cards. In other words, the arrangement of the cards is an effective means of outlining and organizing a research essay. Be smart; do it this way.

MAKE LOGICAL ARRANGEMENTS OF THE NOTES AND CARDS IN EACH GROUP. There is still much to do with each group of cards or printed notes. You cannot use the details as they happen to fall randomly in your stack. You need to decide which notes are relevant. You might also need to retitle some cards and use them elsewhere. Those that remain will have to be arranged in a logical order for you to find use for them in your essay.

Once you have your notes or cards in order, you can write whatever comments or transitions are needed to move from detail to detail. Write this material directly on the cards and be sure to use a different color ink so that you can distinguish later between the original note and what you add. Here is an example of such a "developed" note, with quotation and commentary distinguished by different kinds of type:

Magalaner 39   Structure, general

Magalaner, using "Miss Brill" as an example, speaks of Mansfield's weaving "a myriad of threads into a rigidly patterned whole" in her stories. (39). *Some of these "threads" are the fall season, the time of day, examples of unkindness, the park bench sitters from the cupboards, and Miss Brill's stages of unreality. Each of these is separate, but all work together structurally to unify the story.*

By adding such commentary to your notes, you are also simplifying the writing of your first draft. In many instances, the note and whatever comments you make may be moved directly into the paper with minor adjustments (some of the content of this note appears in paragraph 6 of the illustrative essay, and almost all the topics introduced here are developed in paragraphs 9 to 14).

Being Creative and Original While Doing Research

You will not always transfer your notes directly into your essay. The major trap to avoid in a research paper is that your use of sources can become an end in itself and therefore a shortcut for your own thinking and writing. Often, students make the mistake of introducing details the way a master of ceremonies introduces performers in a variety show. This is unfortunate because it is the student whose essay will be judged, even though the sources, like the performers, do all the work. Thus, it is important to be creative and original in a research essay and to do your own thinking and writing, even though you are relying heavily on your sources. Here are five ways in which research essays may be original.

1. Your selection of material is original with you. In each major part of your essay you will include many details from your sources. To be creative you should select different but related details and avoid overlapping or repetition. Your completed essay will be judged on the basis of the thoroughness with which you make your points with different details (which in turn will represent the completeness of your research). Even though you are relying on published materials and cannot be original on that score, your selection can be original because you bring these materials together for the first time, and because you emphasize some details and minimize others. Inevitably, your assemblage of details from your sources will be unique and therefore original.

2. The development of your essay is yours alone. Your arrangement of various points is an obvious area of originality: One detail seems naturally to precede another, and certain conclusions stem from certain details. As you present the details, conclusions, and arguments from your sources, you can also add an original stamp by introducing supporting details different from those in the source material. You can also add your own emphasis to particular points—an emphasis that you do not find in your sources.

3. The words are yours and yours alone. Naturally, the words that you use will be original because they are yours. Your topic sentences, for example, will all be your own. As you introduce details and conclusions, you will need to write "bridges" to get yourself from point to point. These can be introductory remarks or transitions. In other words, as you write, you are not just stringing your notes together, but rather you are actively assembling and arranging your thoughts, based on your notes, in creative and unique ways.

4. Explaining and contrasting controversial views is an original presentation of material. Closely related to your selection is that in your research you may have found conflicting or differing views on a topic. If you make a point to describe and distinguish these views, and explain the reasons for the differences, you are presenting material originally.

5. Your own insights and positions are uniquely your own. There are three possibilities here, all related to how well you have learned the primary texts on which your research in secondary sources is based.

a. *Weave your own interpretations and ideas into your essay.* An important part of taking notes is to make your own points precisely when they occur to you. Often you can expand these as truly original parts of your essay. Your originality does not need to be extensive; it may consist of no more than a single insight. Here is such a card, which was written during research on the structure of "Miss Brill."

My Own   Miss Brill's unreality

In light of this hierarchical structure of unrealities, it is ironic that the boy and girl sit down next to her just when she is at the height of her fancy about her own importance. When she hears the girl's insults, the couple introduces objective reality to her with a vengeance, and she is plunged from rapture to pain.

The originality here is built around the contrast between Miss Brill's exhilaration and her rapid and cruel deflation. This observation is not unusual or startling, but it nevertheless represents original thought about the story. When modified and adapted (and put into full sentences with proper punctuation), the material of the card supplies much of paragraph 13 of the illustrative essay. You can see that your development of a "My Own" note card is an important part of the prewriting stage of a research essay.

b. *Filling gaps in the sources enables you to present original thoughts and insights.* As you read your secondary sources, you may realize that an obvious conclusion is not being made or that an important detail is not being stressed. Here is an area that you can develop on your own. Your conclusions may involve a particular interpretation or major point of comparison, or they may rest on a particularly important but understressed word or fact. For example, paragraphs 10 to 13 in the illustrative essay form an argument based on observations that critics have overlooked, or have not stressed, about the attitudes of the heroine of "Miss Brill." In your research, whenever you find such a critical "vacuum" (assuming that you cannot read all the articles about some of your topics, where your discovery may already have been made a number of times), it is right to include whatever is necessary to fill it.

c. *By disputing your sources with your own arguments, you are being original.* The originality of your disagreement is that you will be using details in a different way from that of the critic or critics whom you are disputing, and your conclusions will be your own. This area of originality is similar to the laying out of controversial critical views, except that you furnish one of the opposing views yourself. The approach is limited because it is difficult to find many substantive points of interpretation on which there are not already clearly delineated opposing views. Paragraph 13 of the illustrative research essay shows how a disagreement can lead to a different, if not original, interpretation.

Documenting Your Work

It is necessary and essential to acknowledge—to *document*—all sources from which you have quoted or paraphrased factual and interpretive information. Because of the need to avoid being challenged for plagiarism, this point cannot be overemphasized. As the means of documentation, various reference systems use parenthetical references, footnotes, or endnotes. Whatever system is used, documentation almost always includes a carefully prepared bibliography, or list of works cited.

We will first discuss the list of works cited and then review the two major reference systems for use in a research paper. Parenthetical references, preferred by the Modern Language Association (MLA) since 1984, are described in Joseph Gibaldi, *MLA Handbook for Writers of Research Papers*, 6th ed., 2003. Footnotes or endnotes, recommended by the MLA before 1984, are still required by many instructors.

Include All the Works You Have Used in a List of Works Cited (Bibliography)

The key to any reference system is a carefully prepared list of works cited that is included at the end of the essay. "Works cited" means exactly that; the list should include just those books and articles you have actually used in your essay. If, however, your instructor requires that you use footnotes or endnotes, you can extend your concluding list to be a complete bibliography both of works cited and also of works consulted but not actually used. Always, always, always, follow your instructor's directions.

The list of works cited should include the following information, in each entry, in the form indicated.

FOR A BOOK

- The author's name: last name first, followed by first name and middle name or initial. Period.
- The title, underlined. Period.
- The city of publication (not state or nation), colon; publisher (easily recognized abbreviations or key words can be used unless they seem awkward or strange; see the *MLA Handbook*, pp. 272–74), comma; year of publication. Period.

FOR AN ARTICLE

- The author's name: last name first, followed by first name and middle name or initial. Period.
- The title of the article in quotation marks. Period.
- The title of the journal or periodical, underlined, followed by the volume number in Arabic (not Roman) numbers with no punctuation, then the year of publication within parentheses. Colon. For a daily paper or weekly magazine, omit the parentheses and cite the date in the British style followed by a colon (day, month, year, as in 2 Feb. 2007). Inclusive page numbers (without any preceding p. or pp.). Period.

The works you are citing should be listed alphabetically according to the last names of authors, with unsigned articles included in the list alphabetically by titles. Bibliographical lists are begun at the left margin, with subsequent lines in a five-space hanging indentation, so that the key locating word—the author's last name or the first title word of an unsigned article—can be easily seen. Many unpredictable and complex combinations, including ways to describe works of art, musical or other performances, and films, are detailed extensively in the *MLA Handbook* (142–235). Here are two model entries:

BOOK:

Alpers, Antony. The Life of Katherine Mansfield. New York: Viking, 1980.

ARTICLE:

Hankin, Cheryl. "Fantasy and the Sense of an Ending in the Work of Katherine Mansfield." Modern Fiction Studies 24 (1978): 465–74.

Refer to Works Parenthetically as You Draw Details from Them

Within the text of your research essay, use parentheses in referring to works from which you are using facts and conclusions. This parenthetical citation system is recommended in the *MLA Handbook* (238–60), and its guiding principle is to provide documentation without asking readers to interrupt their reading to find footnotes or endnotes. Readers wanting to see the complete reference can easily find it in your list of works cited. With this system, you incorporate the author's last name and the relevant page number or numbers directly, whenever possible, into the body of your essay. If the author's name is mentioned in your discussion, you need to give only the page number or numbers in parentheses. Here are two examples, from a critical study of another author, the eighteenth-century poet Alexander Pope:

> Alexander Pope believed in the idea that the universe is a whole, a totally unified body, which provides a "viable benevolent system for the salvation of everyone who does good" (Kallich 24).

> Martin Kallich draws attention to Alexander Pope's belief in the idea that the universe is a whole, a totally unified body, which provides a "viable benevolent system for the salvation of everyone who does good" (24).

Use Footnotes and Endnotes—Formal and Traditional Reference Formats

The most formal system of documentation still widely used is that of footnotes (references at the bottom of each page) or endnotes (references listed numerically at the end of the essay). If your instructor wants you to use one of these formats, do the following: Make a note the first time you quote or refer to a source, with the details ordered as outlined below.

FOR A BOOK

- The author's name: first name or initials first, followed by middle name or initial, then last name. Comma.
- The title, underlined for a book, no punctuation. If you are referring to a work in a collection (article, story, poem) use quotation marks for that, but underline the title of the book. No punctuation, but use a comma after the title if an editor, translator, or edition number follows.
- The name of the editor or translator, if relevant. Abbreviate "editor" or "edited by" as "ed.," "editors" as "eds." Use "trans." for "translator" or "translated by." No punctuation, but use a comma if an edition number follows.
- The edition (if indicated), abbreviated thus: 2nd ed., 3rd ed., and so on. No additional punctuation.
- The publication facts, within parentheses, without any preceding or following punctuation, in the following order:

City (but not the state or nation) of publication, colon.

Publisher (clear abbreviations are acceptable and desirable), comma.

Year of publication.

- The page number(s) with no "p." or "pp.," for example, 5, 6–10, 15–19, 295–307, 311–16. Period. If you are referring to longer works, such as novels or longer stories with division or chapter numbers, include these numbers for readers who may be using an edition different from yours.

FOR A JOURNAL OR MAGAZINE ARTICLE

- The author: first name or initials first, followed by middle name or initial, then last name. Comma.
- The title of the article, in quotation marks. Comma.
- The name of the journal, underlined. No punctuation.
- The volume number, in Arabic letters. No punctuation.
- The year of publication within parentheses. Colon. For newspaper and journal articles, omit the parentheses, and include day, month, and year (in the British style: 21 May 2005). Colon.
- The page number(s) with no "p." or "pp.": 5, 6–10, 34–36, 98–102, 345–47. Period.

For later notes to the same work, use the last name of the author as the reference unless you are referring to two or more works by the same author. Thus, if you refer to only one work by, say, Thomas Hardy, the name Hardy will be enough for all later references. Should you be referring to other works by Hardy, however, you will also need to make a short reference to the specific works to distinguish them, such as Hardy, "The Three Strangers," and Hardy, "The Man He Killed."

Footnotes are placed at the bottom of each page, and endnotes are included on separate page(s) at the end of the essay. The first lines of both footnotes and endnotes should be paragraph indented, and continuing lines should be flush with the left margin. Both endnote and footnote numbers are set in a smaller font and positioned slightly above the line (as superior numbers) like this:[12]. You can single-space footnotes and endnotes and leave a line of space between them. *Most computer programs have specially designed and consecutively numbered footnote formats. These are generally acceptable, but be sure to consult your instructor.* (For more detailed coverage of footnoting practices, see *MLA Handbook*, 298–313.)

Sample Footnotes

In the examples below, book titles and periodicals are underlined.

---

[3] Blanche H. Gelfant, <u>Women Writing in America: Voices in Collage</u> (Hanover: UP of New England, for Dartmouth College, 1984) 110.

[1] Günter Grass, "Losses," <u>Granta</u> 42 (Winter 1992): 99.

[5] John O'Meara, "Hamlet and the Fortunes of Sorrowful Imagination: A Re-examination of the Genesis and Fate of the Ghost," <u>Cahiers Elisabéthains</u> 35 (1989): 21.

[8] Grass 104.

[15] Gelfant 141.

[21] O'Meara 17.

In principle, you do not need to repeat in a footnote or endnote any material you have already mentioned in your own discourse. For example, if you recognize the author and title of your source, then the footnote or endnote should give no more than the data about publication. Here is an example:

In <u>The Fiction of Katherine Mansfield</u>,[9] Marvin Magalaner points out that Mansfield was as skillful in the development of epiphanies (that is, the use of highly significant though perhaps unobtrusive actions or statements to reveal the depths of a particular character) as James Joyce himself, the "inventor" of the technique.

[9](Carbondale: Southern Illinois UP, 1971) 130.

Follow the Requirements for Documentation Set by Other Academic Disciplines

A variety of reference systems and style manuals have been adopted by certain disciplines (e.g., mathematics, medicine, psychology) to serve their own special needs. If you receive no instructions from your instructors in other courses, you can adapt the systems described here. If you need to use the documentation methods of other fields, however, use the *MLA Handbook* (316–17) for guidance about which style manual to select.

When in Doubt, Consult Your Instructor

As long as all you want from a reference is the page number of a quotation or paraphrase, the parenthetical system described briefly here—and detailed fully in the *MLA Handbook*—is the most suitable and convenient one you can use. However, you may wish to use footnotes or endnotes if you need to add more details, provide additional explanations, or refer your readers to other materials that you are not using. Whatever method you follow, you must always acknowledge sources properly. Remember that whenever you begin to write and cite references, you might forget a number of specific details about documentation, and you will certainly discover that you have many questions. Be sure, then, to ask your instructor, who is your final authority.

Strategies for Organizing Ideas in Your Research Essay

INTRODUCTION   In your research essay you may wish to expand your introduction more than usual because of the need to relate the problem of research to your topic. You may wish to bring in relevant historical or biographical information. You may also wish to summarize critical opinion or describe critical problems about your topic. The idea is to lead your reader into your topic by providing interesting and significant materials that you have found.

Because of the length of many research essays, some instructors require a topic outline, which is in effect a brief table of contents. Because the inclusion of an outline is a matter of the instructor's choice, be sure to learn whether your instructor requires it.

BODY AND CONCLUSION   As you write the body and conclusion of your research essay, its development will be governed by your choice of topic. Consult the relevant chapters in this book about what to include for whatever approach or approaches you select (setting, ideas, point of view, character, tone, etc.).

In length, the research essay can be anywhere from as few as two or three or as many as fifteen or thirty or more pages, depending on your instructor's assignment. Obviously, an essay on a single work will be shorter than one based on several. If you narrow the scope of your topic, as suggested in the approaches described at the beginning of this chapter, you can readily keep your essay within the assigned length. The following illustrative research essay, for example, illustrates approach 1 (page 594) by being limited to only one character in one story. Were you to write on characters in a number of other stories by Mansfield or any other writer (approach 2), you could limit your total number of pages by stressing comparative treatments and by avoiding excessive detail about problems pertaining to only one work.

Although you limit your topic yourself in consultation with your instructor, you may encounter problems because you will deal not with one source alone but with many. Naturally the sources will provide you with details and also trigger many of your ideas. The problem is to handle the many strands without piling on too many details, and also without being led into digressions. It is important therefore to keep your central idea foremost; the constant stressing of your central idea will help you both to select relevant materials and to reject irrelevant ones.

 PLAGIARISM: AN EMBARRASSING BUT VITAL SUBJECT—AND A DANGER TO BE OVERCOME

When you are using sources as the substance of many of the details in your essay, you run the risk of *plagiarism*—using the words and ideas of other writers without their consent and without acknowledgment. Recognizing the source means being clear about the identity of other authors, together with the name or names of the works from which one gets details and ideas. When there is no recognition, readers, and the intellectual world generally, are deceived. They assume that the material they are reading is the original work and the intellectual possession of the writer. When there is no recognition, the plagiarizing author is committing intellectual theft.

This is no small matter. In the world of publications, many people who have committed plagiarism have suffered irreparable damage to their credibility and reputations as writers and authorities. Some well-known writers have found it hard if not impossible to continue their careers, and all because of the wide knowledge of their plagiarism. It does not end there. A plagiarist might be open to legal actions, and might, if the situation is grave enough, be required to supply financial restitution to the author or authors whose work has been illegally appropriated. In schools and colleges, students who plagiarize may face academic discipline. Often the discipline is a failure for the course, but it might also include suspension and expulsion. It is not possible to predict all the ill consequences of committing an act of plagiarism.

It therefore bears constant awareness and emphasis that you need to distinguish between the sources you are using and your own work. Your readers will assume that everything you write is your own unless you indicate otherwise. Therefore, when blending your words with the ideas from sources, *be clear about proper acknowledgments*. Most commonly, if you are simply presenting details and facts, you can write straightforwardly and let parenthetical references suffice as your authority, as in the following sentence from the illustrative research essay:

> Marvin Magalaner, using "Miss Brill" as an example, speaks of Mansfield's weaving of "a myriad of threads into a rigidly patterned whole" (39). Also noting Mansfield's control over form, Cheryl Hankin suggests that Mansfield's structuring is perhaps more "instinctive" than deliberate (474).

Here there can be no question about plagiarism, for the names of the authors of the critical sources are fully acknowledged, the page numbers are specific, and the quotation marks clearly distinguish the words of the critics from the words of the essay writer. If you grant recognition as recommended here, no confusion can result about the authority underlying your essay. The linking words obviously belong to the writer of the essay, but the parenthetical references clearly indicate that the sentence is based on two sources.

If you use an interpretation unique to a particular writer, or if you rely on a significant quotation from your source, you should make your acknowledgment an essential part of your discussion, as in this sentence.

> Saralyn Daly, referring to Miss Brill as one of Mansfield's "isolatoes"—that is, solitary persons cut off from normal human contacts—fears that the couple's callous insults have caused Miss Brill to face the outside world with her fur piece "perhaps for the very last time" (88, 90).

Here the idea of the critic is singled out for special acknowledgment. If you recognize your sources in this way, no confusion can arise about how you have used them.

Please, always keep foremost in your mind that *the purpose of research is to acquire knowledge and details from which to advance your own thoughts and interpretations*. You should consider your research discoveries as a kind of springboard from which you can launch yourself into your own written work. In this way, research should be creative. A test of how you use research is to determine how well you move from the details you are using to the development of your own ideas. Once you have gone forth in this way, you are using research correctly and creatively. Plagiarism will then no more be even a remote issue for you.

Illustrative Student Essay Using Research

Underlined sentences in this paper *do not* conform to MLA style and are used solely as teaching tools to emphasize the central idea, thesis sentence, and topic sentences throughout the paper.

Use 1/2 inch top margin, 1 inch bottom and side margin; double-space throughout.

Outline

I. Introduction. The parallel structures of "Miss Brill"

II. Season and time as structure

III. Insensitive or cruel actions as structure

IV. Miss Brill's "hierarchy of unrealities" as structure

V. The story's conclusion

VI. Conclusion

Put identifying information in upper-left corner, double-space.

Use 1/2 inch top margin, 1 inch bottom and side margin; double-space throughout.

Delgado 1

Simone Delgado

Professor Leeshock

Composition 102

30 January 2008

In MLA style, the header has the student's last name and page number.

The Structure of Katherine Mansfield's "Miss Brill"°

[1]

In the story "Miss Brill," Mansfield creates an aging and emotionally vulnerable character, Miss Brill, whose good feelings are dashed when she overhears some cruel and shattering personal insults. <u>In accord with Miss Brill's emotional deflation, the story is developed through a parallel number of structures.</u>* This parallelling demonstrates Mansfield's power generally over tight narrative control. Marvin Magalaner, using "Miss Brill" as an example, speaks of Mansfield's weaving "a myriad of threads into a rigidly patterned

Center title one double-space below identifying information.

°This story appears on pages 202–05.
*Central idea

Delgado 2

whole" (39). Also noting Mansfield's control over form, Cheryl Hankin suggests that Mansfield's structuring is perhaps more "instinctive" than deliberate (474). Either of these observations is great praise for Mansfield. The complementary parallels, threads, stages, or "levels" of "unequal length" (Harmat uses the terms "niveaux" and "longueur inégale," 49, 51) are the fall season, the time of day, insensitive or cruel actions, Miss Brill's own unreal perceptions, and the final section or dénouement.[†]

In MLA style, put only the page number in parentheses when the author is named in the text.

An important aspect of structure in "Miss Brill" is Mansfield's use of the season of the year. Autumn, with its propulsion toward winter, is integral to the deteriorating life of the heroine. In the first paragraph, we learn that there is a "faint chill" in the air (is the word "chill" chosen to rhyme with "Brill"?), and this phrase is repeated in paragraph 10 (204). Thus the author establishes autumn and the approaching year's end as the beginning of the downward movement toward dashed hopes. This seasonal reference is also carried out when we read that "yellow leaves" are "down drooping" in the local Jardins Publiques (203, paragraph 6) and that leaves are drifting "now and again" from almost "nowhere, from the sky" (204, paragraph 1). It is the autumn cold that has caused Miss Brill to wear her shabby fur piece, which later the young girl considers the object of contempt. The chill, together with the fur, forms a structural setting for both the action and the mood of the story. Sewell notes that "Miss Brill" both begins and ends with the fur, which is the direct cause of the heroine's deep hurt at the conclusion (25).

[2]

Like the seasonal structuring, the times of day parallel Miss Brill's darkening existence. At the beginning, the speaker points out that the day is "brilliantly fine--the blue sky powdered with gold," and that the light is "like white wine." This figurative language suggests the brightness and crispness of full sunlight. In paragraph 6 (203), where we also learn of the yellow leaves, "the blue sky with gold-veined clouds" indicates that time has been passing as clouds accumulate during late afternoon. By the story's end, Miss Brill has returned in sadness to her "little dark room" (205, paragraph 18).

[3]

†Thesis sentence

Delgado 3

In other words, the time moves from day to evening, from light to darkness, as a virtual accompaniment to Miss Brill's emotional pain.

[4]   Mansfield's most significant structural device, which is not emphasized by critics, is the introduction of insensitive or cruel actions. It is as though the hurt felt by Miss Brill on the bright Sunday afternoon is also being felt by many others. Because she is the spectator who is closely related to Mansfield's narrative voice, Miss Brill is the filter through whom these negative examples reach the reader. Considering the patterns that emerge, one may conclude that Mansfield intends that the beauty of the day and the joyousness of the band be taken as an ironic contrast to the pettiness and insensitivity of the people in the park.

[5]   The first of these people are the silent couple on Miss Brill's bench (203, paragraph 3) and the incompatible couple of the week before (203, paragraph 4). Because these seem no more than ordinary, they do not at first appear to be part of the story's pattern of cruelty and rejection. But their incompatibility, suggested by their silence and one-way complaining, establishes a structural parallel with the young and insensitive couple who later insult Miss Brill. Thus the first two couples prepare the way for the third, and all show increasing insensitivity and cruelty.

[6]   Almost unnoticed as a second level of negation is the vast group of "odd, silent, nearly all old" people filling "the benches and green chairs" (203, paragraph 5). They seem to be no more than a normal part of the Sunday afternoon landscape. But these people are significant structurally because the "dark little rooms--or even cupboards" that Miss Brill associates with them also, ironically, describe the place where she lives (203, 205, paragraphs 5, 18). The reader may conclude from Miss Brill's quiet eavesdropping that she herself is one of these nameless and faceless ones who lead similarly dreary lives.

[7]   After Mansfield sets these levels for her heroine, she introduces characters experiencing additional rejection and cruelty. The beautiful woman who throws down the bunch of violets is the first of these (203, paragraph 8). The story does not explain the causes of this woman's scorn,

Delgado 4

and Miss Brill does not know what to make of the incident; but the woman's actions suggest that she has been involved in a relationship that has ended in anger and bitterness.

The major figure involved in rejection, who is important enough to be considered a structural double of Miss Brill, is the woman wearing the ermine toque (203, paragraph 8). It is clear that she, like Miss Brill, is one of "the lonely and isolated women in a hostile world" that Mansfield is so skillful in portraying (Gordon 6). This woman tries to please the "gentleman in grey," but this man insults her by blowing smoke in her face. It could be, as Peter Thorpe observes, that she is "obviously a prostitute" (661). But it is more likely that the "ermine toque" has had a broken relationship with the gentleman, or perhaps even no relationship. Being familiar with his Sunday habits, she comes to the park to meet him, as though by accident, to attempt to renew contact. After her rejection, her hurrying off to meet someone "much nicer" (there is no such person, for Mansfield uses the phrase "as though" to introduce "ermine toque's" departure) is her way of masking her hurt. Regardless of the exact situation, however, Mansfield makes it plain that the encounter demonstrates vulnerability, unkindness, and pathos, but also a certain amount of self defense.

Once Mansfield establishes this major incident, she introduces two additional examples of insensitivity. At the end of paragraph 8 (203), the hobbling old man "with long whiskers" is nearly knocked over by the group of four girls, who show arrogance if not contempt toward him. The final examples involve Miss Brill herself. These are her recollections of the apparent indifference of her students and of the old invalid "who habitually sleeps" when she reads to him.

Although "Miss Brill" is a brief story, Mansfield creates a large number of structural parallels to the sudden climax brought about by the boorishly insensitive young couple. The boy and girl do not appear until the very end, in other words (204, paragraph 11), but extreme insults like theirs have been fully anticipated in the story's earlier parts. Mansfield's speaker does not take us to the homes of the other people in the park, as she does when we

[8]

In MLA style, put author and page number in parentheses when the author is not named in the sentence.

[9]

[10]

Delgado 5

follow Miss Brill to her wretched room. Instead, the narrative invites us to conclude that the silent couple, the complaining wife and long-suffering husband, the unseen man rejected by the young woman, the "ermine toque," and the funny gentleman, not to mention the many silent and withdrawn people sitting like statues in the park, all return to loneliness and personal pain that are comparable to the feelings of Miss Brill.

[11] The intricacy of the structure of "Miss Brill" does not end here. Of great importance is the structural development of the protagonist herself. Peter Thorpe notes a "hierarchy of unrealities" that govern the reader's increasing awareness of Miss Brill's plight (661). By this measure, the story's actions progressively bring out Miss Brill's failures of perception and understanding--failures that in this respect make her like her namesake fish, the lowly brill (Gargano).

[12] These unrealities begin with Miss Brill's fanciful but harmless imaginings about her shabby fur piece. This beginning sets up the pattern of her pathetic inner life. When she imagines that the park band is a "single, responsive, and very sensitive creature" (Thorpe 661), we realize that she is unrealistically making too much out of a mediocre band of ordinary musicians. Although she cannot interpret the actions of the beautiful young woman with the violets, she does see the encounter between the "ermine toque" and the gentleman in grey as a vision of rejection. Her response is correct, but then her belief that the band's drumbeats are sounding out "The Brute! The Brute!" indicates her vivid overdramatization of the incident. The "top of the hierarchy of unrealities" (Thorpe 661) is her fancy that Miss Brill is an actor with a vital part in a gigantic drama played by all the people in the park. The most poignant aspect of this daydream is her unreal thought that someone would miss her if she were to be absent.

Quotation marks around phrases show that they appeared separately in the source.

[13] In light of this hierarchical structure of unrealities, it is ironic that the boy and girl sit down next to her just when she is at the height of her fancy about her own importance. When she hears the girl's insults, the couple has introduced objective reality to her with a vengeance, and she is plunged from rapture to pain.

Delgado 6

The concluding two paragraphs of "Miss Brill" hence form a rapid dénouement to reflect her loneliness and solitude.

Of unique importance in the structure of "Miss Brill" are these final two paragraphs, in which Miss Brill, all alone, returns to her wretched little room. Saralyn Daly, referring to Miss Brill as one of Mansfield's "isolatoes"--that is, solitary persons cut off from normal human contacts--fears that the couple's callous insults have caused Miss Brill to face the outside world with her fur piece "perhaps for the very last time" (88, 90). Sydney Kaplan adds a political dimension to Miss Brill's defeat, asserting that here and in other stories Mansfield is expressing "outrage" against "a society in which privilege is . . . marked by indifference" to situations like those of Miss Brill (192).

[14]

It is clear that Mansfield is asking readers to consider not only Miss Brill alone, but also her similarity to the many park inhabitants who are like her. Miss Brill's grim existence exemplifies a common personal pattern in which the old are destroyed "by loneliness and sickness, by fear of death, by the thoughtless energy of the younger world around them" (Zinman 457). More generally, Mansfield herself considered such negative situations as "the snail under the leaf," which implies that a gnawing fate is waiting for everyone, not just those who are old (Meyers 213). With such a crushing experience for the major character, "Miss Brill" may be fitted to the structuring of Mansfield's stories described by André Maurois: "moments of beauty suddenly broken by contact with ugliness, cruelty, or death" (342–43).

[15]

Delgado 7

Works Cited

Daly, Saralyn R. Katherine Mansfield. New York: Twayne, 1965.

Gargano, James W. "Mansfield's Miss Brill." Explicator 19. 2 (1960): item 10
    (one page, unnumbered).

In MLA style, the list of sources, called the "Works Cited," begins a new page. Double-space throughout.

Gordon, Ian A. "Katherine Mansfield: Overview." Reference Guide to English Literature, 2nd ed. Ed. D. L. Kirkpatrick. London: St. James Press, 1991 (found at <www.galenet.com>).

Hankin, Cheryl. "Fantasy and the Sense of an Ending in the Work of Katherine Mansfield." Modern Fiction Studies 24 (1978): 465–74.

Harmat, Andrée-Marie. "Essai D'Analyse Structurale d'une Nouvelle Lyrique Anglaise: 'Miss Brill' de Katherine Mansfield." Les Cahiers de la Nouvelle 1 (1983): 49–74.

Kaplan, Sydney Janet. Katherine Mansfield and the Origins of Modernist Fiction. Ithaca and London: Cornell UP, 1991.

McLaughlin, Ann L. "The Same Job: The Shared Writing Aims of Katherine Mansfield and Virginia Woolf." Modern Fiction Studies 24 (1978): 369–82.

Magalaner, Marvin. The Fiction of Katherine Mansfield. Carbondale: Southern Illinois UP, 1971.

---. The Short Stories of Katherine Mansfield. New York: Knopf, 1967.

Mansfield, Katherine. "Miss Brill." Literature: An Introduction to Reading and Writing. Ed. Edgar V. Roberts. 9th ed. New York: Pearson Longman, 2009. 202–05. Parenthetical page numbers to "Miss Brill" refer to pages in this book.

Maurois, André. Points of View from Kipling to Graham Greene. 1935. New York: Ungar, 1968.

Meyers, Jeffrey. Katherine Mansfield: A Darker View. 1978. New York: Cooper Square Press, 2002.

Sewell, Arthur. Katherine Mansfield: A Critical Essay. Auckland: Unicorn, 1936.

Thorpe, Peter. "Teaching 'Miss Brill.'" College English 23 (1962): 661–63.

Zinman, Toby Silverman. "The Snail Under the Leaf: Katherine Mansfield's Imagery." Modern Fiction Studies 24 (1978): 457–64.

List sources in alphabetical order.

Commentary on the Essay

This essay fulfills an assignment of 1500–2000 words, with ten to fifteen sources. (There are actually fifteen.) The bibliography was developed from a college library computer catalog, references in books of criticism (Magalaner, Daly); the *MLA International Bibliography*; the *Essay and General Literature Index*, and the Literature Resource Center available through Netscape and a county library system (www.wls.lib.ny.us). The sources themselves were found in a college library with selective holdings, in a local public library, and in online resources. There is only one rare source, an article (Harmat) obtained in photocopy through interlibrary loan from one of only two U.S. libraries holding the journal in which it appears. The location was made through the national Online Computer Library Center (OCLC). For most semester-long or quarter-long courses, you will probably not have time to add to your sources by such a method, but the article in question refers specifically to "Miss Brill," and it was therefore desirable to examine it.

The sources consist of books, articles, and chapters or portions of books. One article (Sewell) has been published as a separate short monograph. Also, one of the sources is the story "Miss Brill" itself (with locations made by paragraph and page numbers), together with a collection of her stories. The sources are used for facts, interpretations, reinforcement of conclusions, and general guidance and authority.

All necessary thematic devices, including overall organization and transitions, are unique to the illustrative essay. The essay also contains passages taking issue with certain conclusions in a few of the sources. Additional particulars about the handling of sources and developing a research essay are included in the discussion of note taking and related matters in this chapter.

The central idea of the essay (paragraph 1) is built out of this idea, explaining that the movement of emotions in the story is accompanied by an intricate and complementary set of structures. Paragraphs 2 through 13 examine various elements of the story for their structural relationship to Miss Brill's emotions.

Paragraphs 2 and 3 detail the structural uses of the settings of autumn and times of day, pointing out how they parallel her experiences.

The longest part, paragraphs 4 through 10, is based on an idea not found in the sources—that a number of characters are experiencing difficulties and cruelties such as those that befall Miss Brill. Paragraph 5 cites the three couples of the story, paragraph 6 the silent old people, and paragraph 7 the scornful woman with violets. Paragraph 8 is developed in disagreement with one of the sources, showing how an essay involving research may be original even though the sources form the basis of discussion. Paragraph 9 contains additional examples of insensitivity—two of them involving Miss Brill herself. Paragraph 10 summarizes the story's instances of insensitivity and cruelty, once again emphasizing parallels to Miss Brill's situation.

Paragraphs 11 through 13 of the essay are based on ideas about the story's structure found in one of the sources (Thorpe). It is hence more derivative than paragraphs 4 through 10. Paragraphs 14 and 15, the concluding paragraphs of the essay, are devoted to the story's dénouement and to the broader application of the story: Miss Brill is to be considered an example of the anonymous "isolatoes" who inhabit the park. Because they are comparable to Miss Brill, their lives are unlikely just as sad and anguishing as hers is.

The list of works cited is the basis of all references in the essay, in accord with the *MLA Handbook*. By locating these references, a reader might readily examine, verify, and study any of the ideas and details drawn from the sources and developed in the essay.

Writing Topics About How to Undertake a Research Essay

In beginning research on any of the following topics, follow the steps in research described in this chapter.

1. Common themes in a number of stories by Hawthorne, Poe, Hardy, or Mansfield (just one, not all).
2. Various critical views of a Hemingway story.
3. Hawthorne's use of religious and moral topic material.
4. Porter's exemplification of Granny Weatherall's strength of character.
5. Views about women in Chopin, Welty, Mansfield, or Steinbeck.
6. Poe's view of the short story as represented in "The Masque of the Red Death."

Part III

Reading and Writing About Poetry

Chapter 11

Meeting Poetry:
An Overview

Our words **poem** and **poetry** are derived from the Greek word *poiein*, "to create or make," the idea being that poetry is a created artifact, a structure that develops from the human imagination and that is expressed rhythmically in words. Although the word *poet* originally meant the writer of any kind of literature, we now use the word exclusively to mean a person who writes poems. *Poetry* and *poem* describe a wide variety of spoken and written forms, styles, and patterns, and also a wide variety of subjects. In light of this variety, we believe that the best way to understand poetry is to experience it—read it, study it, savor it, think about it, dream about it, learn it, memorize it, mull it over, talk about it with others, ask questions about it, enjoy it, love it. The more experience with poetry you have, the more you will develop your own ideas and definitions of just what poetry is, and the deeper will be your comprehension and the greater your appreciation.

The Nature of Poetry

We begin with a favorite poem based in the lives of students and teachers alike.

BILLY COLLINS (b. 1941)

 ## Schoolsville (1985)

Glancing over my shoulder at the past,
I realize the number of students I have taught
is enough to populate a small town.

I can see it nestled in a paper landscape,
5   chalk dust flurrying down in winter,
nights dark as a blackboard.

The population ages but never graduates.
On hot afternoons they sweat the final in the park
and when it's cold they shiver around stoves
10   reading disorganized essays out loud.
A bell rings on the hour and everybody zigzags
in the streets with their books.

624

I forgot all their last names first and their
first names last in alphabetical order.
But the boy who always had his hand up   15
is an alderman and owns the haberdashery.
The girl who signed her papers in lipstick
leans against the drugstore, smoking,
brushing her hair like a machine.

Their grades are sewn into their clothes   20
like references to Hawthorne.°   *i.e., The Scarlet Letter*
The A's stroll along with other A's.
The D's honk whenever they pass another D.

All the creative writing students recline
on the courthouse lawn and play the lute.   25
Wherever they go, they form a big circle.

Needless to say, I am the mayor.
I live in the white colonial at Maple and Main.
I rarely leave the house. The car deflates
in the driveway. Vines twirl around the porchswing.   30

Once in a while a student knocks on the door
with a term paper fifteen years late
or a question about Yeats or double-spacing.
And sometimes one will appear in a window pane
to watch me lecturing the wall paper,   35
quizzing the chandelier, reprimanding the air.

QUESTIONS

1. What recognizable school experiences does the poem mention? Why is "Schoolsville" the title?

2. Describe the speaker. How does he indicate affection for students?

3. What details indicate that the poem is fantasy and not reality? To what degree is the poem humorous?

4. Compare the details of this poem with those in Roethke's "Dolor" (Chapter 12). What similarities do you find in the choice and appropriateness of detail? What differences?

5. Each poem you read may help you understand, and therefore define, poetry. How might this poem help you begin making a definition?

"Schoolsville" reveals the variety and freedom of poetry. Unlike poems that are set out in strict line lengths, rhythms, and rhymes, "Schoolsville," though arranged in lines, does not follow measured rhythmical or rhyming patterns. The language is not difficult, the descriptions are straightforward, and the scenes seem both real and amusing. Many details—such as the "chalk dust flurrying down" like snow, "the girl who signed her papers in lipstick," and the students forming a circle when they meet—are genuinely funny. But the poem moves from apparent reality to something beyond reality. Unifying the poem is the fanciful idea that school life is, like life generally, at once comical, serious, memorable, and poignant.

We may contrast "Schoolsville" with the following poem, "Hope," by Lisel Mueller, which deals with a topic—hope—that is common to us all, a topic that governs both our present and future behavior. What is unique, however, is that the poet provides us with thoughts about the nature of hope that might never have occurred to us. In this sense the poem fulfills the creative goal of poetry to lead us and guide us.

LISEL MUELLER (b. 1924)

Hope (1976)

It hovers in dark corners
before the lights are turned on,
   it shakes sleep from its eyes
   and drops from mushroom gills,
5   it explodes in the starry heads
      of dandelions turned sages,
         it sticks to the wings of green angels
         that sail from the tops of maples.

It sprouts in each occluded°eye   *closed, blind*
10 of the many-eyed potato,
   it lives in each earthworm segment
   surviving cruelty,
      it is the motion that runs
      from the eyes to the tail of a dog,
15   it is the mouth that inflates the lungs
         of the child that has just been born.

It is the singular gift
we cannot destroy in ourselves,
the argument that refutes death,
20 the genius that invents the future,
all we know of God.

It is the serum which makes us swear
not to betray one another;
it is in this poem, trying to speak.

QUESTIONS

1. How does the poem illustrate the meaning of hope? How true or adequate are the specific locations where hope may be found? How do these locations provide the grounds for a broadened understanding of hope?
2. What does the poet mean by saying that hope is a "singular gift / we cannot destroy in ourselves" and that hope is a "serum" that prevents people from betraying each other?

3. According to the illustrations in the poem, how strong is the connection between hope and life? Can anything or anyone be without hope?

4. Why does the poet write "trying to speak" rather than "speaking" in the final line?

"Hope" demonstrates that poetry is inseparable from life and living. We regularly hope for fine weather, good luck, happier times, love, successful academic and athletic performance, more money, more and better friendships, successful and rewarding careers, and so on. But Mueller takes us on a new and unexpected trip. Her speaker reminds us that hope exists in common things around us where we have never even imagined it might be, such as the fluttering seeds ("angels") of maple trees, the expanding lungs of a newborn baby, and "the genius that invents the future." Hope may even be found in the blind eyes of a potato which, when planted in lowly garden dirt, possess an indomitable wish for growth. The poem makes these ordinary things extraordinary. Mueller even leaves us with a speculative and unusual conclusion, giving life to hope by stating that hope speaks simultaneously with poetry itself. All these connections, which Mueller naturally and easily creates for us, cause us to say yes, to agree that hope exists in every obscure and out-of-the-way part of existence. Like all good poetry, "Hope" leads us into thoughts which we have not only not considered, but which we have never even dreamed about.

We should always recognize that good poems, regardless of their topic, have similar power. To see this, let us look at another poem, by the seventeenth-century English poet Robert Herrick.

ROBERT HERRICK (1591–1664)

Here a Pretty Baby Lies (1648)

Here a pretty baby lies
Sung asleep with lullabies:
Pray be silent, and not stir
Th'easy earth that covers her.

QUESTIONS

1. What situation is described in this poem? To what degree is this situation either ordinary or unusual?

2. How does the final line change your perception of the first three lines? How does it change your response to the poem?

3. Consider the double meanings of the following words and phrases: "Here . . . lies"; "Sung asleep"; "lullabies"; "stir."

4. Compare this poem with Jonson's "On My First Daughter" (this chapter.)

Nothing in the first three lines of this short poem seems anything other than ordinary. A scene is described that takes place over and over again everywhere in the world. A baby is sleeping quietly, and we are told to make no sounds that would awaken her. But the last line hits us with a hammer, making us realize that nothing in the poem is what we understood at first. We immediately change our initial impressions and realize that the baby is not just sleeping but dead, lying not in a cradle but in a coffin; that the lullabies are not the lullabies sung by a loving mother but the religious songs sung at a funeral ceremony; and that the stirring is not just making noise but disturbing the still-loose earth that has just been shoveled onto the baby's grave. The effect of this very simple poem has been called overwhelming; it was overwhelming when it was first written in the seventeenth century, and it is still overwhelming.

The three poems we have just seen have much in common; they are serious, engaging, original, and powerful. The first, however, is amusing and slightly perplexing; the second is serious and thought-provoking; the third is sad and deeply moving. There are no other poems like them. Once we have read them, we will never forget them. Even if we never read them again (but we should), they will echo in our minds as time passes, sometimes with great power and impact, sometimes with less. In reading them again we may rediscover our original responses, and often we may have entirely new responses to them. In short, these poems live, and as long as we too live, they will be a permanent part of our minds.

Preliminary Ideas About Poetry

As "Schoolsville," "Hope," and "Here a Pretty Baby Lies" demonstrate, all good poems are unique, and all good poems broaden our comprehension and add layers to our understandings. Like living itself, the experience of poetry is a developing process, but nevertheless, it is possible to offer a number of preliminary statements as a guide to understanding. To begin with, poems are imaginative works expressed in words that are used with the utmost compression, force, and economy. Unlike prose, which is expansive if not exhaustive, many poems are brief. But poetry is also comprehensive, offering us high points of thought, feeling, reflection, and resolution. Poems may be formed in just about any coherent and developed shape, from a line of a single word to lines of twenty, thirty, or more words; and these lines may be organized into any number of repeating or nonrepeating patterns. Some poems make us think, give us new and unexpected insights, and generally instruct us. Other poems arouse our emotions, surprise us, amuse us, and inspire us. Ideally, reading and understanding poetry should prompt us to reexamine, reinforce, and reshape our ideas, our attitudes, our feelings, and our lives. Let us hear what Robert Frost concluded about poetry: "Read it a hundred times: it will forever keep its freshness as a metal keeps its fragrance. It can never lose its sense of a meaning that once unfolded by surprise as it went."[1] Always be prepared for the surprise, and be delighted when it appears.

Poetry of the English Language

Today, most nations of the world have their own literatures, including poetry, with their own unique histories and characteristics. In this anthology, however, we are concerned primarily, but not exclusively, with poetry in our own language by American, British, and Canadian poets.

---

[1]"The Figure a Poem Makes," in *Complete Poems of Robert Frost 1949* (New York: Holt, 1949) viii.

The earliest poems in English date back to the period of *Old English* (450–1100). Many of these early English poems reflect the influence of Christianity. Indeed, the most famous poem, the epic *Beowulf,* was probably interpreted as a Christian allegory even though it concerns the secular themes of adventure, courage, and war. Ever since the *Middle English* period (1100–1500), poets have written about many other subjects, although religious themes have remained important. Today, we find poetry on virtually all topics, including worship, music, love, society, sports, individuality, strong drink, sexuality, warfare, government, and politics; some poems treat special and unusual topics such as fishing, machines, buildings, computers, exotic birds, and car crashes.

In short, poetry is in a flourishing condition in all its many forms. Commonly held moral principles are instilled by the use of well-known brief poems, epigrams, rhymes, and jingles, such as "Work. / Don't shirk," "A good beginning / Is half the winning," and "A stitch in time / Saves nine." Many people, such as poets themselves and teachers, read poetry or parts of poems aloud in front of audiences of students, friends, families, and general audiences. Many others read poetry silently in private for their own benefit. Nursery rhymes are one of the important means by which children learn the vocabulary and rhythms of our language. Poems that are set to music and sung aloud are especially powerful. Francis Scott Key's "The Star-Spangled Banner," which he wrote during the Battle of Fort McHenry in the War of 1812, is our national anthem and is sung before sports competitions and many other events. More recently, musical groups like the Beatles and U2, along with singer Bruce Springsteen, have given poetic expression to ideas that huge masses of people have taken to heart. Ever since the 1960s, people devoted to civil rights have been unified and strengthened by the simple lyrics of "We Shall Overcome," not only in the United States but throughout the world. During the national crisis following the attacks on the World Trade Center and the Pentagon in 2001, many people turned to "America the Beautiful" and "God Bless America" as songs that stir the heart. The strength and vitality of poetry could be similarly documented time and time again.

How to Read a Poem

With poetry, as with any other literary form, the more effort we put into understanding, the greater will be our reward. Poems are often about subjects that we have never experienced directly. We have never met the poet, never had his or her exact experiences, and never thought about things in exactly the same way. To recapture the experience of the poem, we need to understand the language, ideas, attitudes, and frames of reference that bring the poem to life.

We must therefore read all poems carefully, thoughtfully, sympathetically. The economy and compression of poetry mean that every part of the poem must carry some of the impact and meaning, and thus every part repays careful attention. Try to interact with the poem. Do not expect the poem (or the poet) to do all the work. The poem contributes its language, imagery, rhythms, ideas, and all the other aspects that make it poetry; but you, the reader, will need to open your mind and your heart to the poem's impact. You have to use your imagination and let it happen.

There is no single technique for reading, absorbing, and appreciating poetry. In Chapter 1 we offer a number of guidelines for studying any work of literature (pp. 13–14). In addition to following the guidelines, read each poem more than once and keep in mind these objectives.

1. **Read straight through to get a general sense of the poem.** In this first reading, do not stop to puzzle out hard passages or obscure words; just read through from beginning to end. The poem is probably not as hard as you might at first think.

2. **Try to understand the poem's meaning and organization.** As you read and reread the poem, study these elements.

- *The title.* The title is almost always informative. The title of Collins's "Schoolsville" suggests that the poem will contain a somewhat flippant treatment of school life. The title of Frost's "Stopping by Woods on a Snowy Evening" suggests that the poem will present ideas derived from a natural scene of cold and darkness.

- *The speaker.* Poems are dramatic, having points of view just like prose fiction. First-person speakers talk from the "inside" because they are directly involved in the action (like the speaker in Collins's "Schoolsville"). Other speakers are "outside" observers demonstrating the third-person limited and omniscient points of view, as in the anonymous "Sir Patrick Spens" (see also Chapter 2 on point of view).

- *The meanings of all words, whether familiar or unfamiliar.* The words in many poems are immediately clear, as in Herrick's "Here a Pretty Baby Lies," but other poems may contain unfamiliar words and references that need looking up. You will need to consult dictionaries, encyclopedias, and other sources until you gain a grasp of the poem's content. If you have difficulty with meanings even after using your sources, ask your instructor.

- *The poem's setting and situation.* Some poems establish their settings and circumstances vividly. Frost's "Stopping by Woods on a Snowy Evening" (p. 637) describes an evening scene in which the speaker stops his sleigh by a woods so that he can watch snow falling amid the trees. Although not all poems are so clear, you should learn as much as you can about setting and situation in every poem you read.

- *The poem's basic form and development.* Some poems, like the anonymous "Sir Patrick Spens," are narratives; others, like Northrup's "Ogichidag," are personal statements; still others may be speeches to another person, like Herrick's "Here a Pretty Baby Lies." The poems may be laid out in a sonnet form or may develop in two-line sequences (couplets). They may contain stanzas, as in Mueller's "Hope," each unified by a particular action or thought. Try to determine the form and to trace the way in which the poem unfolds, part by part.

- *The poem's subject and theme.* The subject indicates the general or specific topic, while the theme refers to the idea or ideas that the poem explores. Jarrell's "The Death of the Ball Turret Gunner" announces its subject in the title. However, you must usually infer the theme. Jarrell's theme is the repulsive ugliness of war, the poignancy of untimely death, the callousness of the living toward the dead, and the suddenness with which war forces young people to face cruelty and horror.

3. Read the poem aloud, sounding each word clearly. Although this step may seem unnecessary, reading aloud will enable you to judge the effect of sound, rhythm, and rhyme. If you read Jarrell's "The Death of the Ball Turret Gunner" aloud, for example, you will notice the impact of rhyming *froze* with *hose* and the suggestion of the percussive sounds of cannon fire in the repeated and rhyming *l*, *a*, and *k* sounds of *black flak.* (For a more detailed consideration of sounds in poetry, see Chapter 17.)

4. Prepare a paraphrase of the poem, and make an explication of the ideas and themes. A paraphrase (discussed later in this chapter) is a restatement of the poem in your own words, which helps crystallize your understanding. An explication, which is both explanation and interpretation, goes beyond paraphrase to consider significance—either of brief passages or of the entire poem.

Studying Poetry

Let us now look in detail at a poem, in this case one that tells a story. It was composed as a song, or ballad, sometime during the late Middle Ages or early Renaissance, when most people got information about the outside world from strolling balladeers who sang the news to them (there were no newspapers, and besides, few people could read anyway). It tells a story that is probably true, or at least that is based on a real event.

ANONYMOUS

 ## Sir Patrick Spens (fifteenth century)

The king sits in Dumferline° town,	
Drinking the blood-red wine:	
"O where will I get a good sailor	
To sail this ship of mine?"	
Up and spoke an eldern° knight	*old, senior* 5
Sat° at the king's right knee:	*who sat*
"Sir Patrick Spens is the best sailor	
That sails upon the sea."	
The king has written a braid° letter	*large, commanding*
And signed it wi'° his hand,	*with* 10
And sent it to Sir Patrick Spens,	
Was° walking on the sand.	*who was*
The first line that Sir Patrick read,	
A loud laugh laughèd he;	
The next line that Sir Patrick read,	15
A tear blinded his eye.	

°1 *Dumferline:* a town on the Firth of Forth, in Scotland.

"O who is this has° done this deed,   who has
    This ill deed done to me,
To send me out this time o'° the year,   of
20   To sail upon the sea?

"Make haste, make haste, my merry men all,
    Our good ship sails the morn."°   in the morning
"O say not so, my master dear,
    For I fear a deadly storm.

25 Late late yestere'en° I saw the new moon   yesterday evening
    With the old moon in her arm,
And I fear, I fear, my dear master,
    That we will come to harm."

O our Scots nobles were right loath
30   To wet their cork-heeled shoon,°   shoes
But long ere a'° the play were played   all
    Their hats they swam aboon.°   about [in the water]

O long, long may their ladies sit
    Wi' their fans into their hand,
35 Or e'er they see Sir Patrick Spens
    Come sailing to the land.

O long, long may the ladies stand,
    Wi' their gold combs in their hair,
Waiting for their own dear lords,
40   For they'll see them no more.

Half o'er, half o'er to Aberdour°
    It's fifty fathom deep,
And there lies good Sir Patrick Spens,
    Wi' the Scots lords at his feet.

°41 *Aberdour:* Aberdeen, on the east coast of Scotland on the North Sea, about 80 miles north of Dumferline.

QUESTIONS

1. What action does the poem describe? Who are the principal individual figures? What groups of people are involved with and concerned about the action?
2. What do you learn about the principal figure, Sir Patrick Spens? Why does he follow the king's orders rather than his own judgment?
3. What conflicts do you find in the poem? Do they seem personal or political?
4. What emotions are conveyed in the last two stanzas? Since the poem does not explain why the king sends Sir Patrick and his men to sea, how might the emotions have been expressed more strongly?
5. Describe the poem's use of dialogue. How many people speak? How do the speeches assist in conveying the poem's action?

"Sir Patrick Spens" is a **narrative ballad**. A **narrative** tells a story, and the term **ballad** defines the poem's shape or form, which was originally a song for dancing (related to our word *ballet*). The first two stanzas set up the situation: The king needs a captain and crew to undertake a vital mission, and an old knight— one of the king's close advisers—suggests Sir Patrick Spens, who is obviously distinguished and reliable. The rest of the poem focuses on the feelings and eventual death of Sir Patrick and his men. The third stanza provides a transition from the king to Sir Patrick. The king orders Sir Patrick to embark on an important sea voyage, and Sir Patrick reads the order. At first he laughs—probably sardonically, because Sir Patrick's response is that an order to go to sea during an obvious time of danger is nothing more than a grim joke. But when he realizes that the order is real, he foresees disaster. Our sense of impending calamity is increased when we learn that Sir Patrick's crewmen are also frightened (lines 23–28).

The shipwreck, described in the eighth stanza, is presented with ironic understatement. There is no description of the storm or of the crew's panic, nor does the speaker describe the masts splitting or the ship sinking under the waves. Although these horrors are omitted, the floating hats are grim evidence of destruction and death. The remainder of the poem continues in this vein of understatement. In the ninth and tenth stanzas the focus shifts back to the land, and to the ladies who will wait a "long, long" time (forever) for Sir Patrick and his men to return. The poem ends with a vision of Sir Patrick and the "Scots lords" lying "fifty fathom deep."

On first reflection, "Sir Patrick Spens" tells a sad tale without complications. The subject seems to describe no more than Sir Patrick's drowning, along with his crew and the Scots noblemen. One might therefore claim that the poem does not have a clear theme. Even the irony of the floating hats and the waiting ladies is straightforward and unambiguous.

However, you might consider how the poem appeals to our imaginations through its suggestions of the contradictions and conflicts between authority and individuals. Sir Patrick knows the danger, yet he still obeys the king. In addition, in lines 5, 17–20, and 31, there is a suggestion of political infighting. The "eldern knight" is in effect responsible for dooming the ship. Moreover, the "play" being "played" suggests that a political game is happening beyond the grim game of the men caught in the deadly storm (if Sir Patrick knows the danger, would not the knight also know it, and would not this knight also know the consequences of choosing Sir Patrick?). These political motives are not spelled out, but they are implied. Thus the poem is not only a sad tale but also a poignant dramatization of how power operates, of how a loyal person responds to a tragic dilemma, and of the pitiful consequences of that response.

In reading poetry, then, let the poem be your guide. Get all the words, try to understand dramatic situations, follow the emotional cues the poet gives you, and try to explain everything that is happening. Let the poem trigger your imagination. If you find implications that you believe are important, as with the political overtones of "Sir Patrick Spens," use details from the poem to support your observations. Resist the temptation to "uncover" unusual or far-fetched elements in the poem (such as that hope is a tiny spirit that inhabits human beings, trees, and vegetables, or that the "man he killed" was literally the speaker's brother). Draw only those conclusions that the poem itself supports.

Poems for Study

Gwendolyn Brooks . . . . The Mother, 634
Emily Dickinson . . . . Because I Could Not Stop for Death, 635
Robert Francis . . . . Catch, 636
Robert Frost . . . . Stopping by Woods on a Snowy Evening, 637
Thomas Hardy . . . . The Man He Killed, 637
Joy Harjo . . . . Eagle Poem, 638
Randall Jarrell . . . . The Death of the Ball Turret Gunner, 639
Ben Jonson . . . . On My First Daughter, 640
Emma Lazarus . . . . The New Colossus, 640
Louis MacNeice. . . . . Snow, 641
Jim Northrup . . . . Ogichidag, 642
Naomi Shihab Nye. . . . . Where Children Live, 642
William Shakespeare. . . . . Sonnet 55: Not Marble, Nor the
Gilded Monuments, 643
Percy Bysshe Shelley . . . . To — ("Music, when Soft Voices Die"), 644
Elaine Terranova . . . . Rush Hour, 644

GWENDOLYN BROOKS (1917–2000)

 ### The Mother (1945)

Abortions will not let you forget.
You remember the children you got that you did not get,
The damp small pulps with a little or with no hair,
The singers and workers that never handled the air.
5   You will never neglect or beat
Them, or silence or buy with a sweet.
You will never wind up the sucking-thumb
Or scuttle off ghosts that come.
You will never leave them, controlling your luscious sigh,
10   Return for a snack of them, with gobbling mother-eye.

I have heard in the voices of the wind the voices of my dim killed children.
I have contracted. I have eased
My dim dears at the breasts they could never suck.
I have said, Sweets, if I sinned, if I seized
15   Your luck
And your lives from your unfinished reach,
If I stole your births and your names,
Your straight baby tears and your games,
Your stilted or lovely loves, your tumults, your marriages, aches, and your deaths,
20   If I poisoned the beginnings of your breaths,
Believe that even in my deliberateness I was not deliberate.
Though why should I whine,
Whine that the crime was other than mine?—
Since anyhow you are dead.
25   Or rather, or instead,

You were never made.
But that too, I am afraid,
Is faulty: oh, what shall I say, how is the truth to be said?
You were born, you had body, you died.
It is just that you never giggled or planned or cried.   30

Believe me, I loved you all.
Believe me, I knew you, though faintly, and I loved, I loved you
All.

QUESTIONS

1. Describe the circumstances of the speaker. Who is she? What is the topic of her narrative? What has happened to her? What thoughts and feelings does she express about her experiences? Why does she say "how is the truth to be said" (line 28)?
2. What is the topic of this poem? What moral and political issues does the poem raise?
3. What conclusions do you think the poet wants you to draw from this poem? What "pro" and "con" positions might be derived from the poem?
4. Considering this poem, discuss what topical material might be imposed on writers of poetry? What might be considered "poetic" subject matter?

EMILY DICKINSON (1830–1886)

For a photo, see Chapter 21, page 1023.

Because I Could Not Stop for Death (1890; c.1863)°

Because I could not stop for Death—
He kindly stopped for me—
The Carriage held but just Ourselves—
And Immortality.

We slowly drove—He knew no haste   5
And I had put away
My labor and my leisure too,
For His Civility—

We passed the School, where Children strove
At Recess—in the Ring—
We passed the Fields of Gazing Grain—   10
We passed the Setting Sun—

Or rather—He passed Us—
The Dews drew quivering and chill—
For only Gossamer,° my Gown—   *thin fabric*   15
My Tippet°—only Tulle°—   *cape, scarf; thin silk*

°first published, 1890; written c. 1863. You will see two dates given for many poems in the book.

We passed before a House that seemed
A Swelling of the Ground—
The Roof was scarcely visible—
20   The Cornice—in the Ground—

Since then—tis Centuries—and yet
Feels shorter than the Day
I first surmised the Horses' Heads
Were toward Eternity—

QUESTIONS

1. Who is the speaker, and what is she like? Why couldn't she stop for Death? What perspective does her present position give the poem?
2. In what unusual ways does the poem characterize death?
3. What does the carriage represent? Where is it headed? Who are the riders? What is meant by the things the carriage passes?
4. What is represented by the house in line 17? Why does the poet use the word "House" in preference to some other word?

ROBERT FRANCIS (1901–1987)

 Catch (1950)

Two boys uncoached are tossing a poem together,
Overhand, underhand, backhand, sleight of hand, every hand,
Teasing with attitudes, latitudes, interludes, altitudes,
High, make him fly off the ground for it, low, make him stoop,
5   Make him scoop it up, make him as-almost-as-possible miss it,
Fast, let him sting from it, now, fool him slowly,
Anything, everything tricky, risky, nonchalant,
Anything under the sun to outwit the prosy,
Over the tree and the long sweet cadence down,
10   Over his head, make him scramble to pick up the meaning,
And now, like a posy, a pretty one plump in his hands.

QUESTIONS

1. Describe the language of "Catch." How does the poet establish that there are two meanings to most of the words in the game of catch played by the "boys"?
2. How accurately does the poem describe a game of ordinary catch in which the participants are throwing a baseball? How interesting would a game of catch be if the participants stood still and merely threw the ball back and forth to each other? How interesting would poetry be if the poet did not create variety just as the catch players vary their throws?
3. How well does the analogy of the game of catch explain why poetry sometimes requires extra efforts of understanding?

ROBERT FROST (1874–1963)

For a photo, see Chapter 21, page 1058.

Stopping by Woods on a Snowy Evening (1923)

Whose woods these are I think I know.
His house is in the village though;
He will not see me stopping here
To watch his woods fill up with snow.

My little horse must think it queer   5
To stop without a farmhouse near
Between the woods and frozen lake
The darkest evening of the year.

He gives his harness bells a shake
To ask if there is some mistake.   10
The only other sound's the sweep
Of easy wind and downy flake.

The woods are lovely, dark and deep,
But I have promises to keep,
And miles to go before I sleep,   15
And miles to go before I sleep.

QUESTIONS

1. What do we learn about the speaker? Where is he? What is he doing?
2. What is the setting (place, weather, time) of this poem?
3. Why does the speaker want to watch the "woods fill up with snow"?
4. What evidence suggests that the speaker is embarrassed or self-conscious about stopping? Consider the words "though" in line 2 and "must" in line 5.
5. The last stanza offers two alternative attitudes and courses of action. What are they? Which does the speaker choose?

THOMAS HARDY (1840–1928)

For a photo, see Chapter 5, page 287.

The Man He Killed (1902)

"Had he and I but met
  By some old ancient inn,
We should have sat us down to wet
  Right many a nipperkin!°

half-pint cup

5   "But ranged as infantry,
    And staring face to face,
I shot at him as he at me,
    And killed him in his place.

    "I shot him dead because—
10   Because he was my foe.
Just so: my foe of course he was;
    That's clear enough; although

    "He thought he'd 'list,° perhaps,   *enlist*
    Off-hand like—just as I—
15 Was out of work—had sold his traps°—   *possessions*
    No other reason why.

    "Yes; quaint and curious war is!
    You shoot a fellow down
You'd treat if met where any bar is,
20   Or help to half-a-crown."°

———————————————
°20 *half-a-crown:* at the time, the equivalent of $20 or $30.

QUESTIONS

1. Who and what is the speaker? What do you learn about him from his language?
2. What situation and event is the speaker recalling and relating?
3. What is the effect produced by repeating the word "because" in lines 9 and 10 and using the word "although" in line 12?
4. What is the speaker's attitude toward his "foe" and toward what he has done?
5. What point, if any, does this poem make about war? How are this poem and Jarrell's "The Death of the Ball Turret Gunner" similar and different?

JOY HARJO (b. 1951)

 ### Eagle Poem (1990)

To pray you open your whole self
To sky, to earth, to sun, to moon
To one whole voice that is you.
And know there is more
5 That you can't see, can't hear,
Can't know except in moments
Steadily growing, and in languages
That aren't always sound but other
Circles of motion.
10 Like eagle that Sunday morning
Over Salt River. Circled in blue sky
In wind, swept our hearts clean

With sacred wings.
We see you, see ourselves and know
That we must take the utmost care
And kindness in all things.   15
Breathe in, knowing we are made of
All this, and breathe, knowing
We are truly blessed because we
Were born, and die soon within a   20
True circle of motion,
Like eagle rounding out the morning
Inside us.
We pray that it will be done
In beauty.   25
In beauty.

QUESTIONS

1. What is meant by the requirement that "to pray you open your whole self/To sky, to earth, to sun, to moon"? What is the meaning of lines 4–9?

2. Why is the eagle significant to the speaker? Of what importance is the figure that the eagle makes?

3. Why does the poet repeat the phrase "In beauty" at the poem's end?

RANDALL JARRELL (1914–1965)

 ## The Death of the Ball Turret Gunner° (1945)

From my mother's sleep I fell into the State
And I hunched in its belly till my wet fur froze.°
Six miles from earth, loosed from its dream of life,
I woke to black flak° and the nightmare fighters.
When I died they washed me out of the turret with a hose.   5

°*Ball Turret Gunner:* High-altitude bombers in World War II (1941–1945) contained a revolvable gun turret both at the top and at the bottom, from which a machine-gunner could shoot at attacking fighter planes. Gunners in these turrets were sometimes mutilated by the gunfire of attacking planes. 2 *froze:* The stratospheric below-zero temperatures caused the moisture in the gunner's breath to freeze as it contacted the collar of his flight jacket. 4 *flak:* the round, black explosions of antiaircraft shells fired at bombers from the ground, an acronym of the German word *Fliegerabwehrkanone.*

QUESTIONS

1. Who is the speaker? Where has he been, and what has he been doing? What has happened to him?

2. In the first line, what is the poet saying about the age of the speaker and the opportunities he had for living before he was killed? How may this line be read politically and polemically?

3. What is a turret? What is your response to the last line?

BEN JONSON (1573–1637)

 ## On My First Daughter° (1616)

Here lies, to each her parents' ruth,°
Mary, the daughter of their youth:
Yet all heaven's gifts, being heaven's due,
It makes the father less, to rue.°
5 At six month's end, she parted hence
With safety of her innocence;
Whose soul heaven's Queen (whose name she bears),
In comfort of her mother's tears,
Hath placed amongst her virgin-train:°
10 Where, while that severed° doth remain,
This grave partakes° the fleshly birth,
Which cover lightly, gentle earth.

°*On My First Daughter:* Jonson's infant daughter, Mary, died at the age of six months, but the year of her death is unknown. The poem was included in the 1616 edition of Jonson's *Epigrams*. 1 *ruth:* sadness, grief 3–4 *Yet . . . rue:* i.e., because all heaven's gifts are [still] owned by heaven, the child's death takes from me, her father, a cause of mourning. 7–9 *Whose soul . . . virgin-train:* i.e., to comfort the tears of her mother, the Queen of heaven, after whom [my daughter] was named, has placed her soul among her [Mary's] virgin-train. 10 *that severed:* the child's soul, which at death is separated from the body. 11 *partakes:* contains the infant's body [until the Resurrection].

QUESTIONS

1. What is the situation of this poem? How does the speaker reconcile himself to the death of his infant daughter?
2. Compare this poem with Herrick's "Here a Pretty Baby Lies" (p. 627).

EMMA LAZARUS (1849–1887)

 ## The New Colossus (1883)

Not like the brazen giant of Greek fame,°
With conquering limbs astride from land to land;
Here at our sea-washed, sunset gates shall stand
A mighty woman with a torch, whose flame
5 Is the imprisoned lightning, and her name
Mother of Exiles. From her beacon-hand
Glows world-wide welcome; her mild eyes command
The air-bridged harbor that twin cities frame.°

°1 *brazen giant of Greek fame:* the statue of Apollo that stood at the harbor of ancient Rhodes, an island in the Aegean Sea. Known as the "Colossus," it was sheathed in copper, and it was one of the seven wonders of the ancient world. 8 *The air-bridged harbor that twin cities frame:* "The air-bridged harbor that is framed by the twin cities [of New York and Newark, New Jersey]."

"Keep, ancient lands, your storied pomp!" cries she
With silent lips. "Give me your tired, your poor,
Your huddled masses yearning to breathe free,
The wretched refuse of your teeming shore.
Send these, the homeless, tempest-tossed to me,
I lift my lamp beside the golden door!"

10

QUESTIONS

1. Why does the poem open with the word "Not"? What argument is introduced by the use of this word and its contrast with the Statue of Liberty? How is this argument brought out throughout the sonnet? Why is this poem always associated with the Statue of Liberty?

2. What does "golden door" mean about the United States? Why does the poet use the name "Mother of Exiles" in reference to the statue? How is "golden" (line 14) to be contrasted with "brazen" (line 1)?

3. What is meant by the "New Colossus"? How does the poem present an optimistic view for the "huddled masses" that will come to the United States to "breathe free"?

LOUIS MACNEICE (1907–1963)

 ### Snow (1935)

The room was suddenly rich and the great bay-window was
Spawning snow and pink roses against it
Soundlessly collateral and incompatible:
World is suddener than we fancy it.

World is crazier and more of it than we think,   5
Incorrigibly plural. I peel and portion
A tangerine and spit the pips and feel
The drunkenness of things being various.

And the fire flames with a bubbling sound for world
Is more spiteful and gay than one supposes—   10
On the tongue on the eyes on the ears in the palms of one's hands—
There is more than glass between the snow and the huge roses.

QUESTIONS

1. Where is the speaker at the time of the poem? What is the contrast between the roses and the snow? Why is this contrast important?

2. What words describe snow in lines 1–3? What words in lines 4, 5, 6, 8, 10 describe the world generally? Why does the speaker choose these words rather than more descriptive ones?

3. What does the last line suggest?

4. What similarities and differences do you find between "Snow" and Frost's "Stopping by Woods on a Snowy Evening" (p. 637)?

JIM NORTHRUP (b. 1943)

 ## Ogichidag° (1993)

I was born in war, WW Two.
Listened as the old men told stories
of getting gassed in the trenches, WW One.
Saw my uncles come back from
5   Guadalcanal, North Africa,
and the Battle of the Bulge.
Memorized the war stories
my cousins told of Korea.
Felt the fear in their voices.
10   Finally it was my turn,
my brothers too.
Joined the marines in time
for the Cuban Missile Crisis.
Heard the crack of rifles
15   in the rice paddies south of Da Nang.
Watched my friends die there
then tasted the bitterness of
the only war America ever lost.
My son is now a warrior.
20   Will I listen to his war stories
or cry into his open grave?

°The title "Ogichidag" is the Ojibway word for "warriors."

QUESTIONS

1. What battles are mentioned in the poem, and over what period of time do these battles extend?

2. How does the speaker state that he learned about the battles? Why is this method of gaining knowledge important? What experience has the speaker had with war?

3. Why does the speaker finish the poem by referring to his son? In relationship to the poem's structure, why is the concluding question important?

NAOMI SHIHAB NYE (b. 1952)

 ## Where Children Live (1982)

Homes where children live exude a pleasant rumpledness,
like a bed made by a child, or a yard littered with balloons.

To be a child again one would need to shed details
till the heart found itself dressed in the coat with a hood.
5   Now the heart has taken on gloves and mufflers,
the heart never goes outside to find something to "do."
And the house takes on a new face, dignified.
No lost shoes blooming under bushes.

No chipped trucks in the drive.
10   Grown-ups like swings, leafy plants, slow-motion back and forth.
While the yard of a child is strewn with the corpses
of bottle-rockets and whistles,
anything whizzing and spectacular, brilliantly short-lived.

Trees in children's yards speak in clearer tongues.
15   Ants have more hope. Squirrels dance as well as hide.
The fence has a reason to be there, so children can go in and out.
Even when the children are at school, the yards glow
with the leftovers of their affection,
the roots of the tiniest grasses curl toward one another
20   like secret smiles.

QUESTIONS

1. How accurately does the poem present the "pleasant rumpledness" of children?
2. What is the speaker's view of the comparative dependence or independence of children? What does the speaker think of children?
3. Sometimes poems about children can be overly sentimental. How well does this poem present sentiment about children? Does it go too far, or is it about right?

WILLIAM SHAKESPEARE (1564–1616)

For a portrait, see Chapter 24, page 1322.

 ## Sonnet 55: Not Marble, Nor the Gilded Monuments (1609)

Not marble, nor the gilded monuments
Of princes, shall outlive this powerful rhyme;
But you shall shine more bright in these contents
Than unswept stone, besmeared with sluttish time.
5   When wasteful war shall statues overturn,
And broils root out the work of masonry,
Nor° Mars his° sword nor war's quick fire shall burn   *Neither, Mars's*
The living record of your memory.
'Gainst death and all-oblivious enmity
10   Shall you pace forth; your praise shall still find room
Even in the eyes of all posterity
That wear this world out to the ending doom.°   *Judgment Day*
So, till the judgment that yourself arise,
You live in this, and dwell in lovers' eyes.

QUESTIONS

1. Who is the speaker of the poem, and who is being addressed?
2. What powers of destruction does the speaker mention? What, according to the speaker, will survive these powers?

3. What does "the living record of your memory" (line 8) mean?

4. What is the poem's subject? Theme?

PERCY BYSSHE SHELLEY (1792–1822)

 To—("Music, When Soft Voices Die") (1824)

Music, when soft voices die,
Vibrates in the memory;
Odors, when sweet violets sicken,
Live within the sense they quicken.°   *make vibrantly alive*

5   Rose leaves, when the rose is dead,
Are heaped for the belovèd's bed;
And so thy thoughts,° when thou art gone,   *this shall also happen to thy thoughts*
Love itself shall slumber on.

QUESTIONS

1. What is the topic of this poem? What view of reality is the poet describing? What is the purpose of the words *die, sicken, dead,* and *art gone*? If music, odors, roses, and thoughts are no longer alive in actuality, in what sense do they continue to live?

2. What is meant by the phrase "shall slumber on" (line 8)? How can love slumber on, but not die? What is the connection between love slumbering and the memory of music, the sense of the odors of violets, and the heaping of rose leaves on the marriage bed?

3. In what way does the speaker praise the thoughts of the listener?

ELAINE TERRANOVA (b. 1939)

 Rush Hour (1995)

Odd, the baby's scabbed face peeking over
the woman's shoulder. The little girl
at her side with her arm in a cast,
wearing a plain taffeta party dress.
5   The woman herself who is in shorts and sunglasses
among commuters in the underground station. Her body
that sags and tenses at the same time.

The little girl has not once moved
to touch her or to be touched.
10   Even on the train, she never turns and says,
"Mommy." Sunlight bobs over her blond head
inclining toward the window. The baby
is excited now. "Loo, loo, loo, loo,"
he calls, a wet crescendo. "He's pulling
15   my hair," the little girl at last cries out.

A kind man comes up the aisle to see
the baby. He stares at those rosettes of blood
and wants to know what's wrong with him.
The woman says a dog bit him. "It must have been
a big dog, then." "Oh, no. A neighbor's little dog."   20
The man says, "I hope they put that dog to sleep."
The woman is nearly pleading. "It was an accident. He didn't
mean to do it." The conductor, taking tickets,

asks the little girl how she broke her arm.
But the child looks out to the big, shaded houses.   25
The woman says, "She doesn't like to talk
about that." No one has seen what is behind
her own dark glasses. She pulls the children to her.
Maybe she is thinking of the arm raised over them,   30
Its motion that would begin like a blessing.

QUESTIONS

1. What clues early in the poem indicate that the woman and her children are victims of domestic abuse?

2. Why does the mother not appeal for help when the two men, the "kind man" and the conductor, inquire about the injuries of the children? What is the irony of the raised arm in the last two lines? What is the pathos of the mother's situation?

3. Describe the attitude of the speaker telling the story of the poem. Why does the speaker do no more than describe details, and not actually rail against domestic abuse?

WRITING A PARAPHRASE OF A POEM

Paraphrasing is especially useful in the study of poetry. It fixes both the general shape and the details of a poem in your mind, and it also reveals the poetic devices at work. A comparison of the original poem with the paraphrase highlights the techniques and the language that make the poem effective.

To paraphrase a poem, rewrite it in prose, in your own words. Decide what details to include—a number that you determine partly by the length of the poem and partly by the total length of your paraphrase. When you deal with lyrics, sonnets, and other short poems, you may include all the details, and thus your paraphrase may be as long as the work, or longer. Paraphrases of long poems, however, will be shorter than the originals because some details must be summarized briefly while others may be cut entirely.

It is vital to make your paraphrase accurate and also to use *only your own words*. To make sure that your words are all your own, read through the poem several times. Then, put the poem out of sight and write your paraphrase. Once you have finished, check yourself both for accuracy and vocabulary. If you find that you have borrowed too many of the poem's words, choose other words that mean the same thing, or else use quotation marks to set off the original words (but do not overuse quotations).

Above all, remain faithful to the poem, but *avoid drawing conclusions and giving unnecessary explanations*. It would be wrong in a paraphrase of Jarrell's "The Death of the Ball Turret Gunner," for example, to state, "This poem makes a forceful argument against the brutal and wasteful deaths caused by war." This assertion states the poem's *theme*, but it *does not* describe the poem's actual content.

Organizing Your Paraphrase

The organization of your paraphrase should reflect the poem's form or development. Include material in the order in which it occurs. With short poems, organize your paraphrase to reflect the poem's development line by line or stanza by stanza. In paraphrasing Shakespeare's "Not Marble, Nor the Gilded Monuments," for example, you should deal with each four-line group in sequence and then consider the final couplet. With longer poems, look for natural divisions such as groups of related stanzas, verse paragraphs, or other possible organizational units. In every situation, the poem's shape should determine the form of your paraphrase.

Illustrative Student Paraphrase

A Paraphrase of Thomas Hardy's "The Man He Killed"°

[1]   If the man I killed had met me in a bar, we would have sat down together and had many drinks. But because we belonged to armies of warring foot soldiers lined up on a battlefield, we shot at each other, and my shot killed him.

[2]   The reason I killed him, I think, was that he and I were enemies--just that. But as I think of it, I realize that he had enlisted exactly as I did. Maybe he did it on a whim, or maybe he had lost his job and sold everything he owned. There was no other reason to enlist.

[3]   Being at war is unusual and strange. Instead of buying a man a drink, or helping him out with a little money, you have to kill him.

°**This poem appears on page 637.**

Commentary on the Paraphrase

Because Hardy's poem is short, the paraphrase attempts to include all its details. The organization closely follows the poem's development. Paragraph 1, for example, restates the contents of the first two stanzas. Paragraph 2 restates the third and fourth stanzas. Finally, the last paragraph separately paraphrases the last stanza, which contains the reflections made by the poem's "I" speaker. This paragraph concludes the paraphrase just as the last stanza concludes the poem.

Notice that the essay does not abstract details from the poem, such as "The dead man might have become a good friend in peacetime" in paraphrasing stanza 5; nor does it extend details, such as "We would have gotten acquainted, had drinks together, told many stories, and done a lot of laughing" for stanza 1 (both stanzas, however, actually do suggest these details). Although the paraphrase reflects the poem's strong antiwar sentiments, an interpretive sentence like "By his very directness, the narrator brings out the senselessness and brutality of warfare" would be out of place. What is needed is a short restatement of the poem to demonstrate the essay writer's understanding of the poem's content, and no more.

WRITING AN EXPLICATION OF A POEM

Explication goes beyond the assimilation required for a paraphrase and thus provides you with the opportunity to show your understanding. But there is no need to explain everything in the poem. A complete, or total, explication would theoretically require you to explain the meaning and implications of each word and every line—a technique that obviously would be exhaustive (and exhausting). It would also be self-defeating, for explicating everything would prohibit you from using your judgment and deciding what is important.

A more manageable and desirable technique is therefore the general explication, which devotes attention to the meaning of individual parts in relationship to the entire work, as in the discussion of "Sir Patrick Spens" (p. 633). You might think of a general explication as your explanation or "reading" of the poem. Because it does not require you to go into exhaustive detail, you will need to be selective and to consider only those details that are significant in themselves and vital to your own thematic development.

Questions for Discovering Ideas

- What does the title contribute to the reader's understanding?
- Who is speaking? Where is the speaker when the poem is happening?
- What is the situation? What has happened in the past, or what is happening in the present, that has brought about the speech?
- What difficult, special, or unusual words does the poem contain? What references need explaining? How does an explanation assist in the understanding of the poem?
- How does the poem develop? Is it a personal statement? Is it a story?
- What is the main idea of the poem? What details make possible the formulation of the main idea?

Strategies for Organizing Ideas

Your general explication demonstrates your ability to (1) follow the essential details of the poem (the same as in a paraphrase), (2) understand the issues and the meaning the poem reveals, (3) explain some of the relationships of content to technique, and (4) note and discuss especially important or unique aspects of the poem.

In your introduction, use your central idea to express a general view of the poem, which your essay will bear out. The discussion of the anonymous "Sir Patrick Spens" (p. 633) suggests some possible central ideas—namely, that (1) the poem highlights a conflict between self-preservation and obedience to authority, and (2) innocent people may be caught in political infighting. In the following illustrative student essay explicating Hardy's "The Man He Killed," the central idea is that war is senseless.

In the body of your essay, first explain the poem's content—not with a paraphrase but with a description of the poem's major organizing elements. Hence, if the speaker of the poem is "inside" the poem as a first-person involved "I," you do not need to reproduce this voice yourself in your description. Instead, *describe* the poem in your own words, with whatever brief introductory phrases you find necessary, as in the second paragraph of the illustrative essay that follows.

Next, explicate the poem in relation to your central idea. Choose *your own* order of discussion, depending on your topics. You should, however, keep stressing your central idea with each new topic. Thus, you might wish to follow your description by discussing the poem's meaning, or even by presenting two or more possible interpretations.

You might also wish to refer to significant techniques. For example, in the anonymous "Sir Patrick Spens," a noteworthy technique is the unintroduced quotations (i.e., quotations appearing without any "he said" or "quoth he" phrases) as the ballad writer's means of dramatizing the commands and responses of Sir Patrick and his doomed crew. You might also introduce special topics, such as the crewman who explains that there will be bad luck because the new moon has "the old moon in her arm" (line 26). Such a reference to superstition might include the explanation of the crewman's assumptions, the relationship of his uneasiness to the remainder of the poem, and also how the ballad writer keeps the narrative brief. In short, discuss those aspects of meaning and technique that bear upon your central idea.

In your conclusion, you may repeat your major idea to reinforce your essay's thematic structure. Because your essay is a general explication, there will parts of the poem that you will not have discussed. You might therefore mention what might be gained from an exhaustive discussion of various parts of the poem (do not, however, begin to exhaust any subject in the conclusion of your essay). The last stanza of Hardy's "The Man He Killed," for example, contains the words "quaint and curious" in reference to war. These words are unusual, particularly because the speaker might have chosen *hateful, senseless, destructive,* or other similarly descriptive words. Why did Hardy have his speaker make such a choice? With brief attention to such a problem, you may conclude your essay.

Illustrative Student Essay

Underlined sentences in this paper *do not* conform to MLA style and are used solely as teaching tools to emphasize the central idea, thesis sentence, and topic sentences throughout the paper.

Lagerstrom 1

Steven Lagerstrom

Prof. Bonner

English 110

22 Sept. 2008

An Explication of Thomas Hardy's "The Man He Killed"°

<u>Hardy's "The Man He Killed" deals with the senselessness of war.</u>*   [1]
It does this through a silent contrast between the needs of ordinary people, as represented by a young man--the speaker--who has killed an enemy soldier in battle, and the antihuman and unnatural deaths of war. <u>Of major note in this contrast are the speaker's circumstances, his language, his sense of identity with the dead man, and his concerns and wishes.</u>†

　　<u>The speaker begins by contrasting the circumstances of warfare with</u>   [2]
<u>those of peace.</u> He does not identify himself, but his speech reveals that he is common and ordinary--a person who enjoys drinking in a bar and who prefers friendship and helpfulness to violence. If he and the man he killed had met in an inn, he says, they would have shared many drinks; but because they met on a battlefield they shot at each other, and he killed the other man. The speaker tries to justify the killing but can produce no stronger reason than that the dead man was his "foe." Once he states this reason, he again thinks of the similarities between himself and the dead man, and then he concludes that warfare is "quaint and curious" (line 17) because it forces a man to kill another man whom he would have befriended if they had met during peacetime.

　　<u>To make the irony of warfare clear, the poem uses easy, everyday</u>   [3]
<u>language to bring out the speaker's ordinary qualities.</u> His manner of speech is conversational, as in "We should have sat us down" (line 3),

°**This poem appears on page 637.**
*****Central idea.**
†**Thesis sentence.**

Lagerstrom 2

"'list" (for "enlist," line 13), and his use of "you" in the last stanza. Also, his word choices, shown in words like "nipperkin," "traps," and "fellow" (lines 4, 15, and 18), are common and informal, at least in British usage. This language is important because it establishes that the speaker is an average man whom war has thrown into an unnatural role.

[4]   As another means of stressing the stupidity of war, the poem makes clear that the two men--the live soldier who killed and the dead soldier who was killed--were so alike that they could have been brothers or even twins. They had similar ways of life, similar economic troubles, similar wishes to help other people, and similar motives in enlisting in the army. Symbolically, the "man he killed" is the speaker himself, and hence the killing may be considered a form of suicide. The poem thus raises the question of why two people who are almost identical should be shoved into opposing battle lines in order to kill each other. This question is rhetorical, for the obvious answer is that there is no good reason.

[5]   Because the speaker (and also, very likely, the dead man) is shown as a person embodying the virtues of friendliness and helpfulness, Hardy's poem is a strong disapproval of war. Clearly, political reasons for violence as policy are irrelevant to the characters and concerns of the men who fight. They, like the speaker, would prefer to follow their own needs rather than remote and meaningless ideals. The failure of complex but irrelevant political explanations is brought out most clearly in the third stanza, in which the speaker tries to give a reason for shooting the other man. Hardy's use of punctuation--the dashes--stresses the fact that the speaker has no commitment to the cause he served when killing. Thus the speaker stops at the word "because--" and gropes for a reason (line 9). Not being articulate, he can say only "Because he was my foe. / Just so: my foe of course he was; / That's clear enough" (lines 10–12). These short bursts of words indicate that he cannot explain things to himself or to anyone else except in the most obvious and trite terms, and in apparent embarrassment he inserts "of course" as a way of emphasizing hostility even though he clearly felt none toward the man he killed.

Lagerstrom 3

A reading thus shows the power of the poem's dramatic argument. Hardy **[6]**
does not establish closely detailed reasons against war as a policy but rather
dramatizes the idea that all political arguments are unimportant in view of the
central and glaring brutality of war--killing. Hardy's speaker is not able to
express deep feelings; rather he is confused because he is an average sort who
wants only to live and let live and to enjoy a drink in a bar with friends. But this
very commonness stresses the point that everyone is victimized by war--both
those who die and those who kill. The poem is a powerful argument for peace
and reconciliation.

Lagerstrom 4

Work Cited

Hardy, Thomas. "The Man He Killed." Literature: An Introduction to Reading
   and Writing. Ed. Edgar V. Roberts. 9th ed. New York: Pearson Longman,
   2009. 637.

Commentary on the Essay

This explication begins by stating a central idea about "The Man He Killed," then
indicates the topics to follow that will develop the idea. Although nowhere does
the speaker state that war is senseless, the illustrative essay takes the position that
the poem embodies this idea. A more detailed examination of the poem's themes
might develop the idea by discussing the ways in which individuals are caught up
in social and political forces, or the contrast between individuality and the state. In
this essay, however, the simple statement of the idea is enough.

Paragraph 2 describes the major details of the poem, with guiding phrases like
"The speaker begins," "he says," and "he again thinks." Thus the paragraph goes
over the poem, like a paraphrase, but explains how things occur, as is appropriate
for an explication. Paragraph 3 is devoted to the speaker's words and idioms, with
the idea that his conversational manner is part of the poem's contrasting method of
argument. If these brief references to style were more detailed, this topic could be
more fully developed as an aspect of Hardy's implied argument against war.

Paragraph 4 extends paragraph 3 inasmuch as it points out the similarities of the speaker and the man he killed. If the situation were reversed, the dead man might say exactly the same things about the present speaker. This affinity underscores the suicidal nature of war. Paragraph 5 treats the style of the poem's fourth stanza. In this context, the treatment is brief. The last paragraph reiterates the main idea and concludes with a tribute to the poem as an argument.

The entire essay therefore represents a reading and explanation of the poem's high points. It stresses a particular interpretation and briefly shows how various aspects of the poem bear it out.

Writing Topics About The Nature of Poetry

1. Skim the titles of poems listed in the table of contents of this book. Judging by the subjects of these poems, describe and discuss the possible range of subject matter for poetry. What topics seem most suitable? Why? Do any topics seem to be ruled out? Why? What additional subject matter would you suggest as possible topics for poems?

2. How accurate is the proposition that poetry is a particularly compressed form of expression? To support your position, you might refer to poems such as Dickinson's "Because I Could Not Stop for Death," Francis's "Catch," Frost's "Stopping by Woods on a Snowy Evening," and Shelley's "Music, When Soft Voices Die."

3. Consider the subject of war as brought out in Jarrell's "The Death of the Ball Turret Gunner," Hardy's "The Man He Killed," and Northrop's "Ogichidag." What ideas are common to the poems? What ideas are distinct and unique? On the basis of your comparison, consider the use of poetry as a vehicle for the expression of moral and political ideas.

4. Write two poems of your own about your future plans. In one, assume that the world is stable and will go on forever. In the other, assume that a large asteroid is out of orbit and is hurtling toward earth at great speed, and a collision six months from now will bring untold destruction and may even end life on earth. After composing your poems, write a brief explanation of how and why they differ in terms of language, references, and attitudes toward friends, family, country, religion, and so on.

5. Consult the brief section on reader-response criticism in Chapter 29. Then write an essay about your responses to one poem, or a number of poems, in this chapter. Assume that your own experiences are valuable guides for your judgment. In the poems that you have read, what has had a bearing on your experiences? What in your own experiences has given you insights into the poems? Try to avoid being anecdotal; instead, try to find a relationship between your experiences and the poetry.

6. In the reference section of your library, find two books (anthologies, encyclopedias, introductions, dictionaries of literary terms) about the general subject of poetry. On the basis of how these two sources define and explain poetry, write a brief essay telling a person younger than you what to expect from the reading of poems.

Chapter 12

Words: The Building Blocks of Poetry

Words are the spoken and written signifiers of thoughts, objects, and actions. They are also the building blocks of both poetry and prose, but poetry is unique because by its nature it uses words with the utmost economy. The words of poetry create rhythm, rhyme, meter, and form. They define the poem's speaker, the characters, the setting, and the situation, and they also carry its ideas and emotions. For this reason, each poet searches for perfect and indispensable words, words that convey all the compressed meanings, overtones, and emotions that each poem requires, and also the words that sound right and look right.

Life—and poetry—might be simpler (but less interesting) if there were an exact one-to-one correspondence between words and the objects or ideas they signify. Such close correspondences exist in artificial language systems such as chemical equations and computer languages. This identical correlation, however, is not characteristic of English or any other natural language. Instead, words have the independent and glorious habit of attracting and expressing a vast array of different meanings.

Even if we have not thought much about language, most of us know that words are sometimes ambiguous, and that much literature is built on ambiguity. For instance, in Shakespeare's *Romeo and Juliet,* when Mercutio says, "Seek for me tomorrow and you shall find me a grave man," the joke works because *grave* has two separate meanings, both of which come into play. In reading poetry, we recognize that poets rejoice in this shifting and elusive but also rich nature of language.

Choice of Diction: Specific and Concrete, General and Abstract

Because poets always try to use only the exactly right words, they constantly make conscious and subconscious decisions about diction. One of the major categories of their choice is diction that is either specific and concrete or general and abstract.

Specific language refers to objects or conditions that can be perceived or imagined; **general language** signifies broad classes of persons, objects, and phenomena. **Concrete diction** describes conditions or qualities that are exact and particular; **abstract diction** refers to qualities that are rarefied and theoretical. In practice, poems using specific and concrete words tend to be visual, familiar, and compelling. By contrast, poems that use general and abstract words tend to be detached and cerebral, and they often deal with universal questions or emotions.

These distinctions become clear when we compare Housman's "Loveliest of Trees" and Eberhart's "The Fury of Aerial Bombardment." Many of the terms and images that Housman uses, such as "cherry . . . /hung with bloom" and "three-score years and ten," are specific and concrete; they evoke exact time and clear visualization. By contrast, Eberhart's terms, such as "infinite spaces" and "eternal truth," are general and abstract, and it is therefore hard to define them with clarity and exactness. This contrast, which by no means implies that Housman's poem is superior to Eberhart's, reflects differences in word choices for different objectives.

Most poets employ mixtures of words in these categories because in many poems they draw general observations and abstract conclusions from specific situations and concrete responses. They therefore interweave their words to fit their situations and ideas, as in Roethke's "Dolor," which uses specific and concrete words to define a series of abstract emotional states.

Levels of Diction

Like ordinary speakers and writers of prose, poets choose words from the category of the three levels of diction: high or formal, middle or neutral, and low or informal. Often, the high and middle levels are considered standard or "right," while low language is dismissed as substandard or "wrong." In poetry, however, none of the classes is more correct than any other, for what counts is that they all function according to the poet's wishes, from broadly formal and intellectual to ordinary and popular.

High or Formal Diction Is Elevated and Elaborate

High or **formal diction** exactly follows the rules of syntax, seeking accuracy of expression even if unusually elevated or complex words are brought into play. Beyond "correctness," formal language is characterized by complex words and a lofty tone. In general, formal diction freely introduces words of French, Latin, and Greek derivation, some of which are quite long, so some people might think that formal language is "difficult." Graves uses formal diction in "The Naked and the Nude" when the speaker asserts that the terms in the title are "By lexicographers construed / As synonyms that should express / The same deficiency of dress." The Latinate words stiffen and generalize the passage: We find *lexicographers* instead of *dictionary writers*, *construed* (from Latin) instead of *thought* (native English), *express* (from Latin) instead of *say* or *show* (native English), and *deficiency* (Latin) instead of *lack* (English). It is simply a fact that our language contains thousands of words that have descended to our language from French, Latin, or Greek and that many of these are long and abstract. But not all words of this sort are necessarily long, nor are they abstract and stiff. Many of our short words, for example, are French in origin, such as *class*, *face*, *fort*, *paint*, *bat*, *tend*, *gain*, *cap*, *trace*, *order*, and *very*. A college-level dictionary contains brief descriptions of word origins, or etymologies; as an exercise, you might trace the origins of a number of words in a poem.

Middle or Neutral Diction Stresses Simplicity

Middle or **neutral diction** maintains the correct language and word order of formal diction but avoids elaborate words and elevated tone, just as it avoids idioms, colloquialisms, contractions, slang, jargon, and fads of speech. For example, Emily

Dickinson's "Because I Could Not Stop for Death" (Chapter 11) is almost entirely in middle diction.

Low or Informal Diction Is the Language of Common, Everyday Use

Low or **informal diction** is relaxed and un-self-conscious, the language of people buying groceries, gasoline, and pizza, and of people who may just be "hanging out." Poems using informal diction include common and simple words, idiomatic expressions, substandard expressions, foreign expressions, slang, "swearwords" or "cusswords," grammatical "errors," and contractions. Informal diction is seen in Hardy's "The Man He Killed" (Chapter 11), in which the speaker uses words and phrases like "many a nipperkin," "He thought he'd 'list," and "off-hand like."

Special Types of Diction

Depending on their subjects and purposes, poets (and writers of prose) may wish to introduce four special types of diction into their poems: *idiom, dialect, slang,* and *jargon.*

Idiom Refers to Unique Forms of Diction and Word Order

The word *idiom,* originally meaning "making one's own," refers to words, phrases, and expressions that are common and acceptable in a particular language, even though they might, upon analysis, seem peculiar or illogical. Standard English idioms are so ingrained into our thought that we do not notice them. Poems automatically reflect these idioms. Thus, for example, a poet may "think *of*" an idea, speak of "living *in*" a house, talk of "going *out* to play," or describe a woman "lovely *as* chandeliers." Poets hardly have choices about such idioms as long as they are using standard English. Real choice occurs when poets select idioms that are unusual or even ungrammatical, as in phrases like "had he and I but met," "we was happy," and "except that You than He" (this last phrase is by Emily Dickinson). Idioms like these enable poets to achieve levels of ordinary and colloquial diction, depending on their purposes.

Dialect Refers to Regional and Group Usage and Pronunciation

Although we recognize English as a common language, in practice the language is made up of many habits of speech or **dialects** that are characteristic of many groups, regions, and nations. In addition to "general American," we can recognize many common dialects, such as Southern, Midwestern, New England, Brooklynese, American Black English, Yiddish English, and Texan, together with "upper" British, Cockney, Scottish, and Australian English. Dialect is concerned with whether we refer to a *pail* (general American) or a *bucket* (Southern); or sit down on a *sofa* (Eastern) or a *couch* (general American) or *davenport* (Midwestern); or drink *soda* (Eastern), *pop* (Midwestern), *soda pop* (a confused Midwesterner living in the East, or a confused Easterner living in the Midwest), or *tonic* (Bostonian). Burns's "Green Grow the Rashes, O" and Hardy's "The Ruined Maid" (Chapter 13) illustrate the poetic use of dialect.

Slang Refers to Informal and Substandard Vocabulary and Idiom

Much of the language that people use every day is **slang.** Usually, slang is impermanent, appearing among certain speakers and then vanishing. The use of the word *bad* to mean "good" illustrates how a new slang meaning can develop, and even stay for a time. This is not to say that slang is not persistent, for some of it is a significant part of our language. There is a continuous word stock of substandard or "impolite" words, some of which are so-called "four-letter" words, that everyone knows but speaks only privately. There are also innumerable slang expressions. For example, we have many slang phrases describing dying, such as *kick the bucket, croak, be wasted, sleep with the fishes, buy the farm, be disappeared, be whacked,* and *be offed.* A nonnative speaker of English, unfamiliar with our slang, would have difficulty understanding that a person who "kicked the bucket," "bought the farm," "croaked," or "was offed" had actually died.

Even though slang is a permanent part of our language, it is usually confined to colloquial or conversational levels. (Interestingly, people with perfect command of standard English regularly use slang in private among their friends and acquaintances.) If slang is introduced into a standard context, therefore, it mars and jars, as in Cummings's "Buffalo Bill's Defunct" (Chapter 18), where the speaker refers to Buffalo Bill as a "blueeyed boy." Because the poem deals with the universality of death, the phrase, which usually refers to a young man on the make, ironically underscores this intention.

Jargon Is the Special Language and Terminology of Groups

Particular groups develop **jargon**—specialized words and expressions that are usually employed by members of specific professions or trades, such as astronauts, doctors, lawyers, computer experts, plumbers, and football players. Without an initiation, people ordinarily cannot understand the special meanings. Although jargon at its worst befuddles rather than informs, it is significant when it becomes part of mainstream English or is used in literature. Poets may introduce jargon for special effects. For example, Paul Zimmer, in "The Day Zimmer Lost Religion" (Chapter 22), wryly uses the phrase "ready for Him now," a boxing expression that describes a fighter in top condition. Linda Pastan uses "gives me an A" and "I'm dropping out," both phrases from school life, to create comic effects in "Marks" (Chapter 22). Another poem employing jargon is Eberhart's "The Fury of Aerial Bombardment," which uses technical terms for firearms to establish the authenticity of the poem's references and therefore to reinforce the poem's judgments about warfare.

Syntax

Syntax refers to word order and sentence structure. Normal English word order is fixed in a *subject-verb-object* sequence. At the simplest level, we say, "A dog (*subject*) bites (*verb*) a man (*object*)." This order is so central to our communication that any change significantly affects meaning: "A dog bites a man" is not the same as "A man bites a dog."

DECORUM: THE MATCHING OF SUBJECT AND WORD

A vital literary concept is **decorum** ("beautiful," "appropriate"); that is, words and subjects should be in perfect accord—formal words for serious subjects, and informal words for low subjects and comedy. In Shakespeare's *A Midsummer Night's Dream,* for example, the nobles usually speak poetry and the "mechanicals" speak prose (Chapter 25). When the nobility are relaxed and in the forest, however, they also speak prose. Decorum governs such choices of language.

In the eighteenth century, English writers aimed to make their language as dignified as ancient Latin, which was the international language of discourse. They therefore asserted that only formal diction was appropriate for poetry; common life and colloquial language were excluded, except in drama and popular ballads. These rules of decorum required standard and elevated language rather than common words and phrases. The development of scientific terminology during the eighteenth century also influenced language. In the scientific mode, poets of the time used descriptive phrases, like "lowing herd" for cattle (Thomas Gray) and "finny prey" for fish (Alexander Pope). In this vein, Thomas Gray observed the dependence of color on light in the line "And cheerful fields resume their green attire" from the "Sonnet on the Death of Richard West."

Pope, one of the greatest eighteenth-century poets, maintained these rules of decorum—and also made fun of them—in his mock-epic poem *The Rape of the Lock,* and more fully in the mock-critical work *Peri Bathous, or The Art of Sinking in Poetry.* In *The Rape of the Lock,* he refers to a scissors as a "glittering forfex." Similarly, in the following couplet he elevates the simple act of pouring coffee.

> From silver spouts the grateful liquors glide,
> While China's earth receives the smoking tide.

After Wordsworth transformed poetic diction early in the nineteenth century, the topics and language of people of all classes, with a special stress on common folk, have become a feature of poetry. Poets have continued to follow rules of decorum, however, inasmuch as the use of colloquial diction and even slang is a necessary consequence of popular subject matter.

Much of the time, poets follow normal word order, as in "The Lamb," where Blake creates a simple, easy order in keeping with the poem's purpose of presenting a childlike praise of God. Many modern poets, such as Mark Strand, go out of their way to create ordinary, everyday syntax, on the theory that a poem's sentence structures should not get in the way of the reader's perceptions.

Yet, just as poets always explore the limits of ideas, so also do they sometimes explore the many possibilities of syntax, as in line 7 of Donne's "Batter My Heart": "Reason, Your viceroy in me, me should defend." In prose, this sentence would read "Reason, who is Your viceroy in me, should defend me." But note that Donne drops the "who is," and that he also puts the direct object "me" before and not after the verb. The resulting emphasis on the pronoun *me* is appropriate to the personal-divine relationship that is the topic of the sonnet. The alteration also meets the demand of the poem's rhyme scheme. A set of particularly noteworthy syntactic variations occurs in Roethke's "Dolor." The poet uses an irregular and idiosyncratic combination of objects, phrases, and appositives to create ambiguity and uncertainty, underscoring the idea that school and office routines are aimless and depressing.

Some of the other means by which poets shape word order to create emphasis are an aspect of **rhetoric. Parallelism** is the most easily recognized rhetorical device. A simple form of parallelism is **repetition,** as with the question "who made thee?" in Blake's "The Lamb." Through the use of the same grammatical forms, though in different words, parallelism produces lines or portions of lines that impress our minds strongly, as in this passage from Robinson's "Richard Cory," in which there are four parallel past-tense verbs (italicized here).

> So on we *worked*, and *waited* for the light,
> And *went* without the meat, and *cursed* the bread;

The final two lines of this poem demonstrate how parallelism may embody **antithesis**—a contrasting situation or idea that brings out surprise and climax:

> And Richard Cory, one calm summer night,
> *Went* home and *put* a bullet through his head.

A major quality of parallelism is the packing of words (the *economy* and *compression* of poetry), for by using a parallel structure the poet makes a single word or phrase function a number of times, with no need for repetition. The opening verb phrase "have known" in Roethke's "Dolor," though used once, controls six parallel direct objects. At the end of Donne's "Batter My Heart," parallelism (along with antithesis) permits Donne to omit the italicized words added and bracketed in the last line here.

> for I,
> Except° You enthrall° me, never shall be free,   *unless; enslave*
> Nor [*shall I*] ever [*be*] chaste, except You ravish me.

Note also that parallelism and antithesis make possible the unique *abba* ordering of these two lines, with the pattern "enthrall" (verb), "free" (adjective), "chaste" (adjective), "ravish" (verb). This rhetorical pattern is called **antimetabole,** or **chiasmus,** and is a common pattern of creating emphasis.

Denotation and Connotation

To achieve the maximum impact, poets depend not just on the simplest, most essential meanings of words, but also on the suggestions and associations that words bring to us. For this reason, control over denotation and connotation (see also Chapter 6) is so important that it has been called the very soul of the poet's art.

Denotation Refers to Standard, Most Commonly Recognized Meanings

The ordinary dictionary meaning of a word—**denotation**—indicates conventional correspondences between words and objects or ideas. Although we might expect denotation to be straightforward, most English words have multiple denotations. The noun *house*, for example, can refer to a *building*, a *family*, a *branch of Congress*, a *theater*, a *theater audience*, a *sorority* or *fraternity*, an *astrological classification*, or a *brothel*. Although context usually makes the denotation of *house* more specific, the various meanings confer a built-in ambiguity in this simple word.

Denotation presents problems, because with the passing of time new meanings emerge and old ones are shed. In poems written in the eighteenth century and earlier, there are many words that have changed so completely that a modern dictionary is not much help. In Marvell's "To His Coy Mistress" (Chapter 19), for example, the speaker asserts that his "vegetable love should grow/ Vaster than empires, and more slow." At first reading, "vegetable" may seem to refer to something like a giant, loving turnip. When we turn to a current dictionary, we discover that *vegetable* is an adjective meaning "plantlike"; but *plantlike love* does not get us much beyond *vegetable love*. A reference to the *Oxford English Dictionary (OED)*, however, tells us that *vegetable* was used as an adjective in the seventeenth century to mean "living or growing like a plant." Thus we find out that "vegetable love" means love that grows slowly but steadily larger.

Connotation Refers to a Word's Emotional, Psychological, Social, and Historical Overtones

The life of language, and the most difficult to control, is a result of **connotation.** Almost no word is without it. For instance, according to the dictionary, the words *childish* and *childlike* denote the state of being like a child. Nevertheless, they connote or imply different sets of characteristics. *Childish* suggests a person who is bratty, stubborn, immature, silly, and petulant, whereas *childlike* suggests that a person may be innocent, charming, and unaffected. These different meanings are based entirely on connotations, for the denotations make little distinction.

Connotation affects us in almost everything we hear and read. We constantly encounter the manipulation of connotation in advertising, for example, which could not exist without the controlled management of meaning. Such manipulation may be as simple as calling a *used car* a *pre-owned car* to avoid the negative connotations of *used*. On the other hand, the manipulation may be as sophisticated as the current use of the word *lite* or *light* to describe foods and drinks. In all such products, *lite* denotes "dietetic," "low-calorie," or even "weak." The distinction—and the selling point—is found in connotation. Imagine how difficult it would be to sell a drink called "dietetic beer" or "weak beer." *Light* and *lite*, however, carry none of the negative connotations and, instead, suggest products that are pleasant, sparkling, bright, and healthy.

Poets always try to make individual words carry as many appropriate and effective denotations and connotations as possible. Put another way, poets use *packed* or *loaded* words that carry a broad range of meaning and association. With this in mind, read the following poem by Robert Graves.

ROBERT GRAVES (1895–1985)

 ## The Naked and the Nude (1957)

For me, the naked and the nude
(By lexicographers° construed
As synonyms that should express
The same deficiency of dress
5   Or shelter) stand as wide apart
As love from lies, or truth from art.
Lovers without reproach will gaze
On bodies naked and ablaze;
The Hippocratic° eye will see
10   In nakedness, anatomy;
And naked shines the Goddess when
She mounts her lion among men.

The nude are bold, the nude are sly
To hold each treasonable eye.
15   While draping by a showman's trick
Their dishabille° in rhetoric,
They grin a mock-religious grin
Of scorn at those of naked skin.

The naked, therefore, who compete
20   Against the nude may know defeat;
Yet when they both together tread
The briary pastures of the dead,
By Gorgons° with long whips pursued,
How naked go the sometime nude!

°2 *lexicographers*: writers of dictionaries. 9 *Hippocratic*: medical; the adjective derives from Hippocrates (c. 460–377 BCE), the ancient Greek who is considered the "father of medicine." 16 *dishabille*: being carelessly or partly dressed. 23 *Gorgons*: mythological female monsters with snakes for hair.

QUESTIONS

1. How does the speaker explain the denotations and connotations of "naked" and "nude" in the first stanza? What is indicated by the fact that the word *naked* is derived from Old English *nacod*, while *nude* comes from Latin *nudus*?

2. What examples of "the naked" and "the nude" do the second and third stanzas provide? What do the examples have in common?

3. How do the connotations of words like "sly," "draping," "dishabille," "rhetoric," and "grin" contribute to the poem's ideas about "the nude"?

4. What does "briary pastures of the dead" mean in line 22?

This poem explores the connotative distinctions between the title words, *naked* and *nude*, which share a common denotation. The title also suggests that the poem is about human customs; for if the speaker were considering the words alone, he would say "naked" and "nude" instead of "*the* naked and *the* nude." The speaker's use of *the* signifies a double focus on both language and human perspectives. In the first five lines, the poem establishes that the two key words should be "synonyms that should express / The same deficiency of dress" (lines 3–4). By introducing elevated and complex words such as "lexicographers" and "construed," however, Graves implies that the connection between "the naked" and "the nude" is sophisticated and artificial.

In the rest of the poem, Graves develops this distinction, linking the word *naked* to virtues of love, truth, innocence, and honesty, while connecting *nude* to artifice, hypocrisy, and deceit. At the end, he visualizes a classical underworld in which all pretentiousness will disappear, and the nude will lose their sophistication and become merged with the naked. The implication is that artifice will vanish in the face of eternal reality. A thorough study of the words in the poem bears out the consistency of Graves's idea, not only about the two words in the title, but also about the accumulated layers of history, usage, and philosophy that weigh upon human life and thought.

Poems for Study

William Blake . . . . The Lamb, 661
Robert Burns . . . . Green Grow the Rashes, O, 662
Lewis Carroll . . . . Jabberwocky, 663
Hayden Carruth . . . . An Apology for Using the Word "Heart"
in Too Many Poems, 664
E. E. Cummings . . . . next to of course god america i, 665
John Donne. . Holy Sonnet 14: Batter My Heart, Three-Personed God, 666
Richard Eberhart . . . . The Fury of Aerial Bombardment, 667
Bart Edelman . . . . Chemistry Experiment, 667
Thomas Gray . . . . Sonnet on the Death of Richard West, 668
Jane Hirshfield . . . . The Lives of the Heart, 669
A. E. Housman . . . . Loveliest of Trees, the Cherry Now, 670
Carolyn Kizer. . . . . Night Sounds, 671
Denise Levertov . . . . Of Being, 672
Eugenio Montale. . . . . English Horn (Corno Inglese), 672
Judith Ortiz [Cofer]. . . . . Latin Women Pray, 673
Henry Reed. . . . . Naming of Parts, 674
Edwin Arlington Robinson . . . . Richard Cory, 675
Theodore Roethke. . . . . Dolor, 676
Stephen Spender . . . . I Think Continually of Those Who Were
Truly Great, 676
Wallace Stevens . . . . Disillusionment of Ten O'Clock, 677
Mark Strand . . . . Eating Poetry, 677
William Wordsworth . . . . . Daffodils (I Wandered Lonely as a Cloud), 678

WILLIAM BLAKE (1757–1827)

 ## The Lamb (1789)

Little Lamb, who made thee?
  Dost thou know who made thee?
Gave thee life & bid thee feed,
By the stream & o'er the mead;
Gave thee clothing of delight,
Softest clothing wooly bright;

5

Gave thee such a tender voice,
Making all the vales rejoice!
   Little Lamb who made thee?
10   Dost thou know who made thee?
   Little Lamb I'll tell thee,
   Little Lamb I'll tell thee!
He is called by thy name,
For he calls himself a Lamb:
15   He is meek & he is mild,
He became a little child:
I a child & thou a lamb,
We are called by his name.
   Little Lamb God bless thee.
20   Little Lamb God bless thee.

QUESTIONS

1. Who or what is the speaker in this poem? The listener? How are they related?

2. What is the effect of repetition in the poem?

3. How would you characterize the diction in this poem? High, middle, or low? Abstract or concrete? How is it consistent with the speaker?

4. What are the connotations of "softest," "bright," "tender," "meek," and "mild"? What do these words imply about the Creator?

5. Describe the characteristics of God imagined in this poem. Contrast the image here with the image of God in Donne's "Batter My Heart."

ROBERT BURNS (1759–1796)

 ## Green Grow the Rashes, O (1787)

1

There's naught but care on ev'ry han',°   *hand*
   In every hour that passes, O;
What signifies the life o'° man   *of*
   An' 'twere na° for the lasses, O?   *if it were not*
Chorus:
5 Green grow the rashes,° O;   *rushes*
Green grow the rashes, O;
The sweetest hours that e'er I spend
   Are spent among the lasses, O!

2

The war'ly° race may riches chase,   *worldly*
10   An' riches still may fly them, O;
An' tho' at last they catch them fast,
   Their hearts can ne'er enjoy them, O.
Chorus.

3

But gie me a cannie° hour at e'en,°   *give me a happy; evening*
   My arms about my dearie, O,
An' war'ly cares an' war'ly men   15
   May a' gae tapsalteerie,° O!   *all go topsy-turvy*
Chorus.

4

For you sae douce° ye sneer at this,   *so sober, so straitlaced*
   Ye're naught but senseless asses, O;
The wisest man the warl' e'er° saw,   *world ever*
   He dearly loved the lasses, O.   20
Chorus.

5

Auld Nature swears the lovely dears
   Her noblest work she classes, O;
Her prentice han'° she tried on man,   *apprentice hand*
   An' then she made the lasses, O.
Chorus.

QUESTIONS

1. Who is the speaker? What is he like? What is his highest value? How seriously do you take his pronouncements?
2. How does the speaker justify his feelings? How does he compare his interests with those of other people?
3. What is the speaker's explanation of the origins of men and women? How might this explanation have been received in 1787, the year of publication, when most people accepted the creation story as told in Genesis?

LEWIS CARROLL (1832–1898)

 ## Jabberwocky° (1871)

'Twas brillig, and the slithy toves
   Did gyre and gimble in the wabe;
All mimsy were the borogoves,
   And the mome raths outgrabe.

"Beware the Jabberwock, my son!   5
   The jaws that bite, the claws that catch!
Beware the Jubjub bird, and shun
   The frumious Bandersnatch!

°The poem "Jabberwocky," which appears in the first chapter of *Through the Looking Glass*, is full of nonsense words that Carroll made up with the sound (rather than the sense) in mind. Alice admits that the poem makes some sense even though she does not know the words: "It seems very pretty . . . but it's rather hard to understand! . . . Somehow it seems to fill my head with ideas—only I don't exactly know what they are!"

He took his vorpal sword in hand;
10   Long time the manxome foe he sought—
So rested he by the Tumtum tree,
    And stood awhile in thought.

And, as in uffish thought he stood,
    The Jabberwock, with eyes of flame,
15 Came whiffling through the tulgey wood,
    And burbled as it came!

One, two! One, two! And through and through
    The vorpal blade went snicker-snack!
He left it dead, and with its head
20   He went galumphing back.

"And hast thou slain the Jabberwock?
    Come to my arms, my beamish boy!
O frabjous day! Callooh! Callay!"
    He chortled in his joy.

25 'Twas brillig, and the slithy toves
    Did gyre and gimble in the wabe;
All mimsy were the borogoves,
    And the mome raths outgrabe.

QUESTIONS

1. Summarize in your own words the story that this poem tells.
2. Humpty Dumpty begins to explain or explicate this poem for Alice in Chapter 6 of *Through the Looking Glass*. He explains that "'brillig' means four o'clock in the afternoon— the time when you begin *broiling* things for dinner." He also explains that "'slithy' means 'lithe' and 'slimy.' 'Lithe' is the same as 'active.' You see it's like a portmanteau—there are two meanings packed into one word." Go through the poem and determine what combinations of words are packed into these portmanteau words. *Brillig*, for example, might be seen as a combination of *broiling*, *brilliant*, and *light*.

HAYDEN CARRUTH (1921–2008)

An Apology for Using the Word "Heart" in Too Many Poems (1959)

What does it mean? Lord knows; least of all I.
    Faced with it, schoolboys are shy,
And grown-ups speak it at moments of excess
    Which later seem more or less
5 Unfeasible. It is equivocal, sentimental,
    Debatable, really a sort of lentil—
Neither pea nor bean. Sometimes it's a muscle,
    Sometimes courage or at least hustle,
Sometimes a core or center, but mostly it's
10   A sound that slushily fits

The meters of popular songwriters without
   Meaning anything. It is stout,
Leonine, chicken, great, hot, warm, cold,
   Broken, whole, tender, bold,
Stony, soft, green, blue, red, white,
   Faint, true, heavy, light,   15
Open, down, shallow, etc. No wonder
   Our superiors thunder
Against it. And yet in spite of a million abuses
   The word survives; its uses   20
Are such that it remains virtually indispensable
   And, I think, defensible.
The Freudian terminology is awkward or worse,
   And suggests so many perverse
Etiologies that it is useless; but "heart" covers   25
   The whole business, lovers
To monks, i.e., the capacity to love in the fullest
   Sense. Not even the dullest
Reader misapprehends it, although locating
   It is a matter awaiting   30
Someone more ingenious than I. But given
   This definition, driven
Though it is out of a poet's necessity, isn't
   The word needed at present
As much as ever, if it is well written and said,   35
   With the heart and the head?

QUESTIONS

1. How much attention is given in this poem to the meanings of the word "heart"? How accurate are the definitions? Why does the poet title the poem "An Apology . . ."?

2. Would it be fair to describe some of the definitions as "flippant"? Why? How do we know that the poet is being serious?

3. Why does Carruth say, "Not even the dullest / Reader misapprehends it" [i.e., the word "heart"]? How true is this claim?

E. E. CUMMINGS (1894–1962)

 ## next to of course god america i (1926)

"next to of course god america i
love you land of the pilgrims' and so forth oh
say can you see by the dawn's early my
country 'tis of centuries come and go
and are no more what of it we should worry   5
in every language even deafanddumb
thy sons acclaim your glorious name by gorry
by jingo by gee by gosh by gum
why talk of beauty what could be more beaut-
iful than these heroic happy dead   10

who rushed like lions to the roaring slaughter
they did not stop to think they died instead
then shall the voice of liberty be mute?"

He spoke. And drank rapidly a glass of water

QUESTIONS

1. What is the form of this poem? What is the rhyme scheme? What does Cummings achieve by not using capitalization and punctuation?
2. Who is the speaker? What characteristics and capacities does he show? How do you respond to him?
3. What ideas does the poem bring out? In what ways does the speaker parody the speakers that one is likely to hear on the Fourth of July throughout the United States? What is Cummings saying not only about the speakers but also about the crowds that listen to such speeches?

JOHN DONNE (1572–1631)

 ## Holy Sonnet 14: Batter My Heart, Three-Personed God (1633)

Batter my heart, three-personed God; for You
As yet but knock, breathe, shine, and seek to mend;
That I may rise and stand, o'erthrow me, and bend
Your force to break, blow, burn and make me new.
5   I, like an usurped° town, to another due,   *conquered*
Labor to admit You, but Oh, to no end;
Reason, Your viceroy in me, me should defend,
But is captived, and proves weak or untrue.
Yet dearly I love You, and would be loved fain,°   *gladly*
10   But am betrothed unto Your enemy.
Divorce me, untie or break that knot again;
Take me to You, imprison me, for I,
Except You enthrall me, never shall be free,
Nor ever chaste, except you ravish me.

QUESTIONS

1. What kind of God is suggested by the words "batter," "knock," "overthrow," and "break"? What does "three-personed God" mean?
2. With which person of God might the verbs "knock" and "break" be associated? The verbs "breathe" and "blow"? The verbs "shine" and "burn"?
3. What is the effect of the altered word order at the ends of lines 7 and 9?
4. Explain the words "enthrall" (line 13) and "ravish" (line 14) to resolve the apparent paradox or contradiction in the last two lines.

RICHARD EBERHART (1904–2005)

 ## The Fury of Aerial Bombardment (1947)

You would think the fury of aerial bombardment
Would rouse God to relent; the infinite spaces
Are still silent. He looks on shock-pried faces.
History, even, does not know what is meant.

You would feel that after so many centuries   5
God would give man to repent; yet he can kill
As Cain could, but with multitudinous will,
No farther advanced than in his ancient furies.

Was man made stupid to see his own stupidity?
Is God by definition indifferent, beyond us all?   10
Is the eternal truth man's fighting soul
Wherein the Beast ravens in its own avidity?

Of Van Wettering I speak, and Averill,
Names on a list, whose faces I do not recall
But they are gone to early death, who late in school   15
Distinguished the belt feed lever from the belt holding pawl.

QUESTIONS

1. Who or what is the speaker in this poem? What does the last stanza tell you about him? (Eberhart was a gunnery instructor during World War II.)

2. What type and level of diction predominates in lines 1–12? What observations about God are made in these lines? Compare the image of God presented here with the one found in Donne's "Batter My Heart, Three-Personed God" and Blake's "The Lamb." What similarities or differences do you find?

3. How does the level and type of diction change in the last stanza? What is the effect of these changes? How is jargon used here?

4. Compare this poem with Thomas Hardy's "Channel Firing" (p. 738). How are the ideas in the poems similar?

BART EDELMAN (b. 1951)

 ## Chemistry Experiment (2001)

We listened intently to the professor,
Followed each one of her instructions,
Read through the textbook twice,
Wore lab coats and safety goggles,
Mixed the perfect chemical combinations   5
In the proper amounts and order.
It was all progressing smoothly;
We thought we were a complete success.
And then the flash of light,

10 The loud, perplexing explosion,
   The black rope of smoke,
   Rising freely above our singed hair.
   Someone in another lab down the hallway
   Phoned the local fire department
15 Which arrived lickety-split
   With the hazardous waste crew,
   And they assessed the accident,
   Deciding we were out of danger.
   It was the talk of the campus
20 For many weeks afterwards.
   We, however, became so disillusioned
   That we immediately dropped the course
   And slowly retreated from each other.
   The very idea we could have done
25 More damage than we actually did—
   Blown up ourselves and the building
   From the base of its foundation—
   Shook us, like nothing had before.
   And even now, years later,
30 When anyone still asks about you,
   I get this sick feeling in my stomach
   And wonder what really happened
   To all that elementary matter.

QUESTIONS

1. What events are recounted in this poem? How may the narrative be placed into sections? Who is the listener or implied reader of the poem?
2. What level of language is contained here? Study lines 13–18. How does the diction change here? Why?
3. Why does the poem end as it does? What connection does this conclusion have with the previous parts of the poem? Why might this incident have caused the participants to have lost contact with each other?

THOMAS GRAY (1716–1771)

 ## Sonnet on the Death of Richard West
(1742; 1775)

In vain to me the smiling mornings shine,
   And redd'ning Phoebus° lifts his golden fire;
The birds in vain their amorous descant° join,   *love songs*
   Or cheerful fields resume their green attire:°
5 These ears, alas! for other notes repine;
   A different object do these eyes require.

°2 *Phoebus:* Apollo, the Sun God 4 *resume their green attire:* During the darkness of night, the "cheerful fields" have no color, but in the light of the morning sun they become green again.

My lonely anguish melts no heart but mine,
  And in my breast the imperfect joys expire.
Yet morning smiles the busy race to cheer,
  And new-born pleasure brings to happier men;
The fields to all their wonted tribute bear;°   10
  To warm their little loves the birds complain:°
I fruitless mourn to him that cannot hear,
  And weep the more because I weep in vain.

°11 *The fields . . . bear:* The fields contribute their customary harvest to benefit all creation. 12 *complain:* sing love songs.

QUESTIONS

1. What is the poem's subject, the speaker or the dead friend? How effective is the poem as a lament or dirge?

2. Describe the poem's level of diction. Why does the speaker use phrases like "smiling mornings" (line 1), "redd'ning Phoebus" (2), "golden fire" (2), "resume their green attire" (4), and "notes" (5)? How common are these phrases? What is their effect?

3. Consider the syntax in lines 5, 6, 9, 10, 11, and 12. What is unusual about the word order in these lines? What is the effect of this word order?

4. In the 1800 Preface to *Lyrical Ballads*, William Wordsworth printed this poem. He italicized lines 6–8 and 13 and 14 and wrote, "It will easily be perceived, that the only part of this Sonnet which is of any value is the lines printed in Italics; it is equally obvious, that . . . the language of these lines does in no respect differ from that of prose." What does Wordsworth's criticism mean? To what degree is it justified?

JANE HIRSHFIELD (b. 1953)

 ## The Lives of the Heart (1997)

Are ligneous,° muscular, chemical.
Wear birch-colored feathers,
green tunnels of horse-tail reed.
Wear calcified spirals, Fibonnacian spheres.°   5
Are edible; are glassy; are clay; blue schist.°
Can be burned as tallow, as coal,
can be skinned for garnets, for shoes.
Cast shadows or light;
shuffle; snort; cry out in passion.   10
Are salt, are bitter,
tear sweet grass with their teeth.
Step silently into blue needle-fall at dawn.
Thrash in the net until hit.
Rise up as cities, as serpented magma, as maples,   15

°1 *Ligneous:* woody, and therefore easily ignited. 4 *Fibonnacian spheres:* after Leonardo Fibonnaci (d. 1250), who described a sequence of numbers in which each new number is the sum of the previous two numbers. The pattern of numbers is found as a basic structure in many plants. 5 *schist:* a metamorphic, heavily layed rock.

hiss lava-red into the sea.
Leave the strange kiss of their bodies
in Burgess Shale. Can be found, can be lost
can be carried, broken, sung.
Lie dormant until they are opened by ice,
20   by drought. Go blind in the service of lace.
Are starving, are sated, indifferent, curious, mad.
Are stamped out in plastic, in tin.
Are stubborn, are careful, are slipshod,
are strong on the blue backs of flies
25   on the black backs of cows.
Wander the vacant whale-roads,° the white thickets
heavy with slaughter.
Wander the fragrant carpets of alpine flowers.
Not one is not held in the arms of the rest, to blossom.
30   Not one is not given to ecstasy's lions.
Not one does not grieve.
Each of them opens and closes, closes and opens
the heavy gate—violent, serene, consenting, suffering it all.

°26 *whale-roads*: a figurative phrase in Old English poetry referring to the sea.

QUESTIONS

1. Describe the attributes of the lives of the heart as brought out through the language of the first five lines.

2. Is there anywhere that lives of the heart are not to be found on earth? What is meant by lines such as "Not one is not given to ecstasy's lions" and "Go blind in the service of lace"?

3. How does the repetitiveness in this poem affect your perception of the lives of the heart? Explain the effect of the many repetitions of words and phrases like "are," "can be," "Not one," and the repetitions of verbs like "step," "thrash," "rise up," "hiss," "lie," "wander," and "opens and closes."

4. Do you find this poem easy or difficult? Why?

5. Contrast this poem with Carruth's "An Apology for Using the Word 'Heart' in Too Many Poems."

A. E. HOUSMAN (1859–1936)

Loveliest of Trees, the Cherry Now
(1896)

Loveliest of trees, the cherry now
Is hung with bloom along the bough,
And stands about the woodland ride°   *path*
Wearing white for Eastertide.

5   Now, of my threescore years and ten,
Twenty will not come again,

And take from seventy springs a score,
It only leaves me fifty more.

And since to look at things in bloom
Fifty springs are little room,   10
About the woodland I will go
To see the cherry hung with snow.

QUESTIONS

1. How old is the speaker? How can you tell? Why does he assume he will live seventy years ("threescore years and ten")?

2. How would you describe the speaker's perception or sense of time? What is the effect of the words "only" (line 8) and "little" (line 10)?

3. What ideas about time, beauty, and life does this poem explore? What does it suggest about the way we should live?

CAROLYN KIZER (b. 1925)

 ## Night Sounds (1984)

Imitated from the Chinese

The moonlight on my bed keeps me awake;
Living alone now, aware of the voices of evening,
A child weeping at nightmares, the faint love-cries of a woman,
Everything tinged by terror or nostalgia.

No heavy, impassive back to nudge with one foot   5
While coaxing, "Wake up and hold me,"
When the moon's creamy beauty is transformed
Into a map of impersonal desolation.

But, restless in this mock dawn of moonlight
That so chills the spirit, I alter our history;   10
You were never able to lie quite peacefully at my side,
Not the night through. Always withholding something.

Awake before morning, restless and uneasy,
Trying not to disturb me, you would leave my bed
While I lay there rigidly, feigning sleep.   15
Still—the night was nearly over, the light not as cold
As a full cup of moonlight.

And there were the lovely times when, to the skies' cold *No*
You cried to me, *Yes!* Impaled me with affirmation.
Now when I call out in fear, not in love, there is no answer.   20
Nothing speaks in the dark but the distant voices,
A child with the moon in his face, a dog's hollow cadence.

QUESTIONS

1. To what degree may this poem be considered confessional? What is being confessed?
2. Who is the "you" of the poem? What has happened between the speaker and the "you"? With what contrasts does the speaker conclude the poem? How are these contrasts related to the relationship between the speaker and the "you"?
3. What situation and impressions are brought about by these words in the first stanza: "moonlight," "weeping," "nightmares," "tinged," "terror," "nostalgia"?
4. What is the effect of the participles in stanzas 1–4 ("living," "coaxing," "withholding," "trying," "feigning")?

DENISE LEVERTOV (1923–1997)

 Of Being (1997)

I know this happiness
Is provisional:

      the looming presences—
      great suffering, great fear—

5   withdraw only
      into peripheral vision:

but ineluctable this shimmering
of wind in the blue leaves:

this flood of stillness
10 widening the lake of sky:

this need to dance,
this need to kneel:

      this mystery:

QUESTIONS

1. What is meant by "this happiness / Is provisional"?
2. What is it that withdraws (line 5)? How does the poet connect withdrawing with the poem's title?
3. What do the words "peripheral vision," "ineluctable," "blue leaves," "flood of stillness," and "lake of sky" contribute to your understanding of the "mystery" with which the poem closes? What is noteworthy about these words?
4. Why does the poet end the poem with a colon rather than a period?

EUGENIO MONTALE (1896–1981)

 English Horn (Corno Inglese) (1916–1920)

Translated by Robert Zweig

The intent wind that plays tonight
—recalling a strong slashing of blades—
the instrument of dense trees and sweeps

the horizon of copper
where streaks of light are stretching,   5
like roaring kites in the sky
(Moving clouds, clear kingdoms
above! High Eldorados'°
partly shut doors!)
and the angry sea, which scale by scale,   10
changes color
launches a twisted horn
of spume towards land;
The wind that is born and dies
in the hour that slowly goes black—   15
if only, tonight, it could play you too
dissonant instrument,
heart.

°8 *Eldorados'*: Eldorados was a mythical city of great wealth, believed in the sixteenth century to be in South America.

QUESTIONS

1. What does the wind do in this poem? Why do you think the speaker wishes the wind to "play" her heart?
2. What are the images of the earth? What are the images of the sky? How are they different?
3. What lines indicate that the speaker is either satisfied or dissatisfied with with her life? What images help you to understand her feelings about herself?
4. What does the speaker mean by referring to Eldorados' doors as "partly shut"?
5. What is the meaning of the title, "Engish Horn (Corno Inglese)"?

JUDITH ORTIZ [COFER] (b. 1952)

 ## Latin Women Pray (1987)

Latin women pray
In incense sweet churches
They pray in Spanish to an Anglo God
With a Jewish heritage.
And this great White Father   5
Imperturbable in his marble pedestal
Looks down upon his brown daughters
Votive candles shining like lust
In his all seeing eyes
Unmoved by their persistent prayers.   10

Yet year after year
Before his image they kneel
Margarita Josefina Maria and Isabel
All fervently hoping
That if not omnipotent   15
At least he be bilingual

QUESTIONS

1. What is the situation described in this poem? Who are the women who pray? What do their names indicate about them? To what God do these women pray? Are they living in their native countries?

2. What words in the poem explain the contradiction implied by the speaker? What is conveyed by the term "Anglo" (line 3). What is conveyed by the terms "White Father" and "Jewish heritage" (lines 4 and 5).

3. What are votive candles? Why does the speaker state that they shine "like lust"? What does "lust" indicate in this context?

4. Describe the effect of the last line (16). In what way is the line comic? How does the line contrast with the previous part of the poem?

HENRY REED (1914–1986)

 ## Naming of Parts (1946)

To-day we have naming of parts. Yesterday,
We had daily cleaning. And to-morrow morning,
We shall have what to do after firing. But to-day,
To-day we have naming of parts. Japonica
5 Glistens like coral in all of the neighboring gardens,
    And to-day we have naming of parts.

This is the lower sling swivel. And this
Is the upper sling swivel, whose use you will see,
When you are given your slings. And this is the piling swivel,
10 Which in your case you have not got. The branches
Hold in the gardens their silent, eloquent gestures,
    Which in our case we have not got.

This is the safety-catch, which is always released
With an easy flick of the thumb. And please do not let me
15 See anyone using his finger. You can do it quite easy
If you have any strength in your thumb. The blossoms
Are fragile and motionless, never letting anyone see
    Any of them using their finger.

And this you can see is the bolt. The purpose of this
20 Is to open the breech, as you see. We can slide it
Rapidly backwards and forwards: we call this
Easing the spring. And rapidly backwards and forwards
The early bees are assaulting and fumbling the flowers:
    They call it easing the Spring.

25 They call it easing the Spring: it is perfectly easy
If you have any strength in your thumb: like the bolt,
And the breech, and the cocking-piece, and the point of balance,
Which in our case we have not got; and the almond-blossom

Silent in all of the gardens and the bees going backwards and forwards,
  For to-day we have naming of parts.   30

QUESTIONS

1. There may be two speakers in this poem, or one speaker repeating the words of another and adding his own thoughts. What two voices do you hear?
2. What is the setting? The situation? How do these affect the speaker?
3. How and why is jargon used in the poem? With what set of "parts" is the jargon initially associated? How does this change?
4. How are phrases like "easing the spring" (lines 22, 24, 25) and "point of balance" (27) used ambiguously? What is the effect of repetition?

EDWIN ARLINGTON ROBINSON (1869–1935)

 Richard Cory (1897)

Whenever Richard Cory went down town,
We people on the pavement looked at him:
He was a gentleman from sole to crown,
Clean favored, and imperially slim.
And he was always quietly arrayed,   5
And he was always human when he talked;
But still he fluttered pulses when he said,
'Good-morning,' and he glittered when he walked.

And he was rich—yes, richer than a king—
And admirably schooled in every grace: 10
In fine, we thought that he was everything
To make us wish that we were in his place.

So on we worked, and waited for the light,
And went without the meat, and cursed the bread;
And Richard Cory, one calm summer night,   15
Went home and put a bullet through his head.

QUESTIONS

1. What is the effect of using "down town," "pavement," "meat," and "bread" in connection with the people who admire Richard Cory?
2. What are the connotations and implications of the name "Richard Cory"? Of the word "gentleman"?
3. Why does the poet use "sole to crown" instead of "head to toe" and "imperially slim" instead of "very thin" to describe Cory?
4. What effect does repetition produce in this poem? Consider especially the six lines that begin with "And."
5. What positive characteristic does Richard Cory possess (at least from the perspective of the speaker) besides wealth?

THEODORE ROETHKE (1908–1963)

 Dolor (1943)

I have known the inexorable sadness of pencils,
Neat in their boxes, dolor of pad and paper-weight,
All the misery of manila folders and mucilage,
Desolation in immaculate public places,
5 Lonely reception room, lavatory, switchboard,
The unalterable pathos of basin and pitcher,
Ritual of multigraph, paper-clip, comma,
Endless duplication of lives and objects.
And I have seen dust from the walls of institutions,
10 Finer than flour, alive, more dangerous than silica,
Sift, almost invisible, through long afternoons of tedium,
Dropping a fine film on nails and delicate eyebrows,
Glazing the pale hair, the duplicate grey standard faces.

QUESTIONS

1. What does "dolor" mean? What words objectify the concept?
2. Why does "Dolor" not contain the fourteen lines usual in a sonnet?
3. What institutions, conditions, and places does the speaker associate with "dolor"? What do these have in common?
4. Describe the relationships of sentence structures and lines in "Dolor."

STEPHEN SPENDER (1909–1995)

 I Think Continually of Those Who Were Truly Great (1934)

I think continually of those who were truly great.
Who, from the womb, remembered the soul's history
Through corridors of light where the hours are suns,
Endless and singing. Whose lovely ambition
5 Was that their lips, still touched with fire,
Should tell of the spirit clothed from head to foot in song.
And who hoarded from the spring branches
The desires falling across their bodies like blossoms.

What is precious is never to forget
10 The delight of the blood drawn from ageless springs
Breaking through rocks in worlds before our earth;
Never to deny its pleasure in the simple morning light,
Nor its grave evening demand for love;
Never to allow gradually the traffic to smother
15 With noise and fog the flowering of the spirit.

QUESTIONS

1. How does this poem cause you to reconsider what is usually understood by the word "great"? What are the principal characteristics of people "who were truly great"?

2. Why does Spender use the words "were great" rather than "are great"? What difference, if any, does this distinction make to Spender's definition of greatness?

3. What is the meaning of phrases like "delight of the blood," "in worlds before our earth," "hours are suns," "still touched with fire"? What other phrases need similar thought and explanation?

4. How practical is the advice of the poem in the light of its definitions of "great" and "precious"? Why should the practicality or impracticality of these definitions probably not be considered in your judgment of the poem?

WALLACE STEVENS (1879–1955)

 ## Disillusionment of Ten O'Clock (1923)

The houses are haunted
By white night-gowns.
None are green,
Or purple with green rings,
Or green with yellow rings,   5
Or yellow with blue rings.
None of them are strange,
With socks of lace
And beaded ceintures.°   *belts*
People are not going   10
To dream of baboons and periwinkles.
Only, here and there, an old sailor,
Drunk and asleep in his boots,
Catches tigers
In red weather.   15

QUESTIONS

1. Is the "Ten O'Clock" here morning or night? How can you tell?

2. What do "haunted" and "white night-gowns" suggest about the people who live in the houses? What do the negative images in lines 3–9 suggest?

3. To whom are these people contrasted in lines 12–15?

4. What are the connotations of "socks with lace" and "beaded ceintures"? With which character in the poem would you associate these things?

5. What is the effect of using words and images like "baboons," "periwinkles," "tigers," and "red weather" in lines 11–15? Who will dream of these things?

6. Explain the term "disillusionment" and explore its relation to the point that this poem makes about dreams, images, and imagination.

MARK STRAND (b. 1934)

 ## Eating Poetry (1968)

Ink runs from the corners of my mouth.
There is no happiness like mine.
I have been eating poetry.

The librarian does not believe what she sees.
5   Her eyes are sad
and she walks with her hands in her dress.

The poems are gone.
The light is dim.
The dogs are on the basement stairs and coming up.

10 Their eyeballs roll,
their blond legs burn like brush.
The poor librarian begins to stamp her feet and weep.

She does not understand.
When I get on my knees and lick her hand,
15 She screams.

I am a new man.
I snarl at her and bark.
I romp with joy in the bookish dark.

QUESTIONS

1. In the first three lines, which words tell you the poem is not to be taken literally?
2. What is the serious topic of the poem? What words indicate its serious intent?
3. What is the comic topic? Which words tell you that the poem's action is comic?

WILLIAM WORDSWORTH (1770–1850)

 ### Daffodils (I Wandered Lonely as a Cloud) (1807; 1804)°

I wandered lonely as a cloud
That floats on high o'er vales and hills,
When all at once I saw a crowd,
A host, of golden daffodils;
5   Beside the lake, beneath the trees,
Fluttering and dancing in the breeze.

Continuous as the stars that shine
And twinkle on the milky way,
They stretched in never-ending line
10 Along the margin of a bay:
Ten thousand saw I at a glance,
Tossing their heads in sprightly dance.

The waves beside them danced; but they
Out-did the sparkling waves in glee:

°Wordsworth's note: "Written at Town-end, Grasmere. Daffodils grew and still grow on the margin of Ullswater, and probably may be seen to this day as beautiful in the month of March, nodding their golden heads beside the dancing and foaming waves." Wordsworth also pointed out that lines 21 and 22, the "best lines," were by his wife, Mary.

A poet could not but be gay,   15
In such a jocund° company:
I gazed—and gazed—but little thought   *cheerful, merry*
What wealth the show to me had brought:

For oft, when on my couch I lie
In vacant or in pensive mood,   20
They flash upon that inward eye
Which is the bliss of solitude;
And then my heart with pleasure fills,
And dances with the daffodils.

QUESTIONS

1. What is the occasion of the poem? Where was the speaker at the time he describes in the poem? What was he doing? What did he see?
2. What words does Wordsworth use to show the life and beauty of the flowers at the side of the lake? How successful are these word choices?
3. How important to the speaker is the memory of this experience?

WRITING ABOUT DICTION AND SYNTAX IN POETRY

Study your poem carefully, line by line, to gain a general sense of its meaning. Try to establish how diction and syntax may be connected to elements such as tone, character, and idea. As you develop your ideas, look for effective and consistent patterns of word choice, connotation, repetition, and syntactic patterns that help create and reinforce the conclusions you have drawn about the poem. Ask questions like these.

Questions for Discovering Ideas

- Who is the speaker? What is the speaker's profession or way of life? How does the speaker's background affect his or her power of observation? How does the background affect his or her level of speech?
- Who is the listener? How does the listener affect what the speaker says?
- What other characters are in the poem? How are their actions described? How accurate and fair do you think these descriptions are?
- Is the level of diction in the poem elevated, neutral, or informal; and how does this level affect your perception of the speaker, subject, and main idea or ideas?
- What patterns of diction or syntax do you discover in the poem? (*Example:* Consider words related to situation, action, setting, or particular characters.) How ordinary or unusual are these words? Which, if any, are unusual enough to warrant further examination?
- Does the poem contain many "loaded" or connotative words in connection with any single element, such as setting, speaker, or theme?

- Does the poem contain a large number of general and abstract or specific and concrete words? What is the effect of these choices?
- Does the poem contain dialect? Colloquialisms? Jargon? If so, how does this special diction shape your response to the poem?
- What is the nature of the poem's syntax? Is there any unusual word order? What seems to be the purpose or effect of syntactic variations?
- Has the poet used any striking patterns of sentence structure such as parallelism or repetition? If so, what is the effect?

Strategies for Organizing Ideas

When you narrow your examination to one or two specific areas of diction or syntax, you should list important words, phrases, and sentences. Begin grouping examples that work in similar ways or produce similar effects. Investigate the full range of meaning and effect that the examples produce. Eventually you may be able to develop the related examples as units or sections for your essay.

Your central idea should emerge from your investigation of the diction or syntax that you find most fruitful and interesting. Let the poem be your guide. Since diction and syntax contribute to the poem's impact and meaning, try to connect your thesis and examples to your other conclusions. If you are writing about Stevens's "Disillusionment of Ten O'Clock," for example, your central idea might assert that Stevens uses words describing colors (i.e., "white," "green," "purple," "yellow," "blue," "red") to contrast life's visual reality with the psychological "disillusionment" of the "houses," "People," and "old sailor." Such a formulation makes a clear connection of diction to meaning.

There are many different ways to organize your material. If you deal with only one aspect of diction, such as connotative words, you might treat these in the order in which they appear in the poem. When you deal with two or three different aspects of diction and syntax, however, you might devote a series of paragraphs to related examples of multiple denotation, then connotation, and finally jargon (assuming the presence of jargon in the poem). In such an instance, your organization would be controlled by the types of material under consideration rather than by the order in which the words occur.

Alternatively, you might deal with the impact of diction or syntax on a series of other elements, such as character, setting, or situation. Such an essay would focus on a single type of lexical or syntactic device (described earlier in this chapter) as it relates to these different elements in sequence. Thus, you might discuss the link between connotation and situation, character, and the basic situation of the poem. Whatever organization you select, keep in mind that each poem will suggest its own avenues of exploration and strategies of organization.

In your conclusion, summarize your ideas about the impact of the poem's diction or syntax. You might also consider the larger implications of your ideas in connection with the thoughts and emotions evoked by your reading.

Illustrative Student Essay

Underlined sentences in this paper *do not* conform to MLA style and are used solely as teaching tools to emphasize the central idea, thesis sentence, and topic sentences throughout the paper.

Fitzpatrick 1

Lionel Fitzpatrick

Professor Allen

English 1B

20 October 2008

Diction and Character in Robinson's "Richard Cory"°

In "Richard Corey," Edwin Arlington Robinson dramatizes the idea that   [1]
nothing can guarantee happiness. His example, and the central character in the
poem, is Richard Cory, a man who apparently has everything: wealth, status,
dignity, taste, and respect. Cory's suicide, however, reveals that these qualities
did not make him happy. By creating a gulf between Cory and the people of the
town who admire and envy him, Robinson sets us up for the surprising suicide
described in the last two lines. The distinction is produced through the words
that Robinson uses to demean the general populace and elevate the central
character.* The speaker and his or her fellow townspeople are associated with
words that indicate their ordinary existence, while Richard Cory is described in
terms of nobility and privilege.†

The poem focuses on Richard Cory as perceived by the townspeople, who   [2]
wish that they "were in his place" (line 12). Robinson skillfully employs words
about these common folk to suggest their poverty and low status. In the first
line, for example, the speaker places himself or herself and these other people
"down town." The phrase refers to a central business district, but here it also
carries the negative connotation of the word "down." The word implies that
Cory's journey to town seems to be a descent, and that the people constantly
live in this "down" condition. A similar instance of connotative diction is
"pavement" (line 2), which can mean "sidewalk," but can also mean "street" or

°This poem appears on page 675.
*Central idea.
†Thesis sentence.

Fitzpatrick 2

"roadbed." The net effect of the word "pavement" rather than "sidewalk" is to place the "people" even lower than Richard Cory--literally on the street.

[3]   In contrast to these few words suggesting the people's lowness, the poem contains many words that glowingly describe Cory's high status. Many words and phrases suggest nobility or royalty. These implications begin with the title of the poem and the name "Richard Cory." That the word "rich" is contained within "Richard" implies Cory's wealth and privilege. It is also the name of a number of English kings, most notably Richard the Lion Hearted ("Richard Coeur de Lion"). The name "Cory" is equally connotative. It clearly suggests the "Coeur," the heart, of the famous king, and it also reminds us of "core," the central or innermost part of anything. The name thus points toward Cory's singular position and significance. Through sound, "Cory" also suggest the English word "court"--that is, a place for kings and courtiers. The name "Richard Cory" thus begins an association through sound and implication that links the central character to kingship and elegance.

[4]   There are other similar words in the poem's first stanza. The speaker describes Richard Cory as "a gentleman from sole to crown" (line 3). "Gentleman" refers to a civilized and well-mannered individual, but it originally also meant a man of "high" or "noble" birth. The phrase "from sole to crown" is another way of saying "from head to toe," but it connotes a great deal more. "Sole" means both "the bottom of a shoe or foot" and "alone" or "singular." Thus, the word suggests Cory's isolation and separation from the common folk. The word is also a pun (and homophone) on "soul," implying that Cory's gentility is inward as well as outward. The final touch is the word "crown." In context, the term denotes the top of the head, but it also has connotations of aristocracy and royalty.

[5]   The speaker also describes Cory as "clean favored" and "imperially slim" (line 4). The word "imperially," like "crown," makes an explicit connection between Cory and emperors. "Clean favored," instead of the more common "good-looking," connotes crisp and untouched features. More to the point, the term "favored" also means "preferred," "elevated," "honored," and "privileged." "Imperially slim," instead of "thin," is equally connotative of wealth and status.

Fitzpatrick 3

While both terms denote the same physical condition, *slim* suggests elegance, wealth, and choice, whereas "thin" suggests poverty and necessity.

Although this type of diction is mostly in the first stanza, Robinson [6] sustains the link between Cory and royalty by using similar terms in the rest of the poem. In stanza two, for example, he uses "quietly arrayed" and "glittered." Both carry elevated and imperial connotations. "Arrayed" means "dressed," but it is also a word in the King James Bible that suggests elegant and heavenly clothing (see Matthew 6:29; Acts 12:21, Revelation 7:13). "Quietly" also suggests solitude and introversion. "Glittered" complements "quietly"; it connotes richness of dress and manner, suggesting that the man himself is g0olden. In the third stanza, the deliberate cliché "richer than a king" again clearly links Richard Cory to royalty. The speaker also notes that Cory was "schooled in every grace" (line 10). The phrase means that Cory was trained in manners and social niceties, but "grace" connotes privilege and nobility ("Your Grace") and also the idea of heavenly love and forgiveness ("God's Grace").

It is clear, then, that Robinson uses the effects of connotation to lower the [7] common folk and elevate the central character. The words linked to the speaker and the other townspeople have demeaning and negative implications. At the same time, the poet uses words and phrases about Cory that connote royalty and privilege. This careful manipulation of diction widens the gulf between Cory and the town. It also heightens our sense that Cory has aristocratic looks, manners, taste, and breeding. The network of associations built through this skillful diction makes the poem's ending powerfully shocking, and reinforces the poem's idea that appearance, wealth, and high status do not necessarily produce happiness.

Fitzpatrick 4

Work Cited

Robinson, Edwin Arlington. "Richard Cory." Literature: An Introduction to Reading and Writing. Ed. Edgar V. Roberts. 9th ed. New York: Pearson Longman, 2009. 675.

Commentary on the Essay

This essay deals with Robinson's use of connotative words to elevate the central character and demean the townspeople. The opening paragraph makes a general assertion about the poem's theme, connects character to this assertion, and argues that Robinson controls diction to make his distinctions.

The body of the essay, in five paragraphs, deals with the effects of a number of examples of word choice. The examples of connotative words are arranged to reflect partly the characters they define and partly the order in which they appear in the poem. Thus, paragraph 2 discusses the common people and the speaker in connection with two highly connotative terms: *down town* and *pavement*.

The next four paragraphs (3–6) focus on Richard Cory and words or phrases that suggest royalty and privilege. The examples or diction examined here are taken up in the order in which they appear in the poem. Thus, paragraph 3 considers Cory's name, and the fourth explores the effects of *gentleman* and *sole to crown*. Paragraphs 5 and 6 continue this process, examining instances of diction that sustain the association between Cory and nobility. Taken together, the four paragraphs devoted to this central character illustrate Robinson's consistent manipulation of diction both to ennoble and isolate Cory.

The conclusion reasserts that Robinson's diction not only contributes to Cory's isolation but also adds to the impact of his mysterious suicide. In this way, the words and phrases examined in the essay are linked to the poem's exploration of ideas about the human condition.

Writing Topics About the Words of Poetry

1. Using Eberhart's "The Fury of Aerial Bombardment" in this chapter, together with poems by Jarrell (Chapter 11) and Owen (Chapters 14, 16), study the words that these poets use to indicate the weapons and actions of warfare. In an essay, consider these questions: What shared details make the poems similar? What separate details make them different? How do the poets use word choices to make their points about war as action, tragedy, and horror?

2. Write an essay considering the sound qualities of the invented words in "Jabberwocky." Some obvious choices are "brillig," "frumious," "vorpal," and "manxome," but you are free to choose any or all of them. What is the relationship between the sound and apparent meaning of these words? What effect do the surrounding normal words and normal word order have on the special words? How does Carroll succeed in creating a narrative "structure," even though the key words are, on the surface, nonsense?

3. Compare and contrast Hirshfield's "The Lives of the Heart" and Carruth's "An Apology for Using the Word 'Heart' in Too Many Poems." What common idea about love do the poems share? What differences? How does each poet use the comparable topics to develop ideas unique to each poem?

4. Write a brief essay discussing the use of connotation in Cummings's "next to of course god america i," Ortiz's "Latin Women Pray," Levertov's "Of Being,"

and "Roethke's "Dolor." What particularities of meaning do the poets introduce? How does their control of connotation contribute to the various ideas
you discover in the poems?

5. Compare the words describing natural scenes in Gray's "Sonnet on the Death
   of Richard West" and Wordsworth's "Daffodils." Which poem seems more
   specific and direct in its depiction of Nature?

6. Write a short poem describing a violent crime and commenting on it. Then, assume that you are the "alleged perpetrator" of the crime, and write another
   poem on the same topic. Even though you describe the same situation, how
   do your words differ, and why have you made these different choices? Explain the other different word choices you have made. You might also discuss
   words that you considered using but rejected.

7. Find a book or books in your library about the works of Gray, Roethke,
   Robinson, Wordsworth, or another poet represented in this chapter. How fully
   do these sources discuss the style of these poets? Write a brief report explaining how the writers of the book or books deal with poetic diction.

Chapter 13

Characters and Setting: Who, What, Where, and When in Poetry

Poets, like other writers, bring their works alive through the interactions of fictional characters who experience love and hatred, pleasure and pain, and most of the other conditions and situations of life. Just as in fiction, poetic **characters** are defined by what they say, what they do, and how they react, and also by what other characters say about them. Not all poetry is narrative, however. Hence we will study character in poems in relation to someone or something else—such as the interactions of speakers with listeners or with the reader, the inner conflicts of a speaker discussing the state of his or her spirit, and conditions such as love, hate, acceptance, disagreement, emulation, decision making, and action—brought out in personal, social, and political life.

In addition, we will examine the **setting** of a poem as one of the major means of measuring character (see also Chapter 3). Poetic protagonists, like those in stories, are necessarily influenced by their possessions, the places they inhabit, the conditions of their lives, and the times in which they live. The period that people have spent in a relationship, their relative wealth or poverty, their surroundings, their social and economic circumstances—all have a bearing on their characters. Poems therefore abound with references to events and situations and also to objects, such as beaches, forests, battlefields, graveyards, coffee spoons, melons, museums, and paintings.

Characters in Poetry

The Speaker or Persona Is the Voice of the Poem

The most significant character in poetry is the **speaker,** also called the **persona** (plural *personae*, a term that comes from the Etruscan-Latin word meaning "mask"). In prose fiction, we also use *speaker* and *persona*, but we often prefer the word *narrator* because of the obvious role of storyteller. This distinction emphasizes the personal and psychological importance of poetic speakers. Sometimes the speaker is a distinct character, with individual traits and well-imagined circumstances, as in Browning's "My Last Duchess" (this chapter), Donne's "Batter My Heart, Three-Personed God" (Chapter 12), and Marlowe's "The Passionate Shepherd to His Love" (this chapter). In Dickinson's "Because I Could Not Stop for Death" (Chapter 11), the speaker is especially unique, for she states that she has been dead for hundreds of years and is now looking back from eternity to the occasion of her death.

Not all poetic speakers have separate identities, for some embody a position or stance that the poet selects to present detail or advance an argument. The poet is thus the undeniable speaker, but the voice we hear may be considered as a brief dramatization of the poet's personality or need. Donne in "Batter My Heart" (Chapter 12) adopts such a stance—a supplicant or penitent praying for divine favor. In this sonnet Donne is not creating a separate dramatic character in deep religious anguish, but is expressing his own hope and fear.

Expectedly, poets use many sorts of speakers to voice their poems. In the poetry included in these chapters, there are poems spoken by kings and dukes, husbands and wives, parents and children, lovers and killers, colonels and enlisted men, shepherds and secretaries, believers and nonbelievers, commoners and members of the aristocracy, and almost every other kind of person you can imagine. In addition, you meet speakers who are mythological heroes and heroines, dead people, skeletons, machines, philosophers, lovers, former slaves, and ghosts. In fact, speakers do not have to be human; they can be animals, clouds, buildings, computers, or whatever the poet's imagination may create.

INSIDE SPEAKERS USE THE FIRST-PERSON VOICE AND ARE INVOLVED IN THE POEM'S ACTIONS. A poetic speaker may be *inside* or *outside* the poem, depending on the **point of view** used by the poet (see Chapter 2). If the point of view is first person, the speaker is *inside* the poem. Here is such a poem, written by an unknown late medieval poet.

ANONYMOUS

 ## Western Wind, When Wilt Thou Blow? (fifteenth century?)

Western wind, when wilt thou blow?
The small rain down can rain?
Christ, if my love were in my arms,
And I in my bed again.

In this poem the "my" and "I" pronouns indicate that the speaker is *inside* the poem speaking in the first person, wishing for gentle spring rain ("small rain") and the renewal of life and love that is signaled by spring.

OUTSIDE SPEAKERS USE THE THIRD PERSON AND ARE OBJECTIVE ABOUT THE POEM'S ACTIONS. The speaker is *outside* the poem, however, if the third person is used. In such poems, the speaker is not involved with the action; he or she describes what is happening to others, as in this anonymous Scots ballad.

ANONYMOUS

 ## Bonny George Campbell (late sixteenth century)

High upon Highlands
  And low upon Tay,°

°2 *Tay*: Loch Tay, a lake in Perth County, in central Scotland, about sixty miles north of Glasgow.

Bonny George Campbell
    Rode out on a day.
5 But toom° came his saddle,   *empty*
    All bloody to see,
Oh, home came his good horse,
    But never came he.

Down came his old mother,
10   Greeting full sair°   *weeping full sore*
And down came his bonny wife,
    Wringing her hair.

Saddled, and bridled,
    And booted rode he;
15 And home came his good horse,
    But never came he.

"My meadow lies green,
    And my corn is unshorn,°   *grain is not harvested*
My barn is to build°   *yet to be built*
20   And my babe is unborn."

Saddled, and bridled,
    And booted rode he;
Toom home came the saddle,
    But never came he.

QUESTIONS

1. What can you conclude about the character, social status, way of life, and feelings of the three persons mentioned in the poem?

2. What has happened to Bonny George Campbell, and how do you know?

3. Who is the speaker of the fifth stanza? What effect has Campbell's absence had on this speaker?

In this ballad the speaker limits his or her perspective to the people left behind who loved Campbell. They do not know his fate beyond what they infer from the bloody saddle—nor do we, because the speaker does not tell us. However, the speaker does describe the effects of the loss upon Campbell's mother and wife, even quoting the wife's lamentation, because Campbell's absence has deprived her of husband and breadwinner. By avoiding entering the poem as an "I," the speaker maintains objectivity and lets the details speak for themselves.

ADDITIONAL INFORMATION ABOUT SPEAKERS MAY BE GAINED FROM OTHER DETAILS IN POEMS. There is a great deal more to learn about poetic speakers. An obvious place to begin is the title. Take, for example, Marlowe's "The Passionate Shepherd to His Love," which reveals that the speaker is a young shepherd and that he is passionately in love.

We can also learn from the speaker's diction. In Housman's "Loveliest of Trees" (Chapter 12), the speaker reveals that he is twenty years old, that he doesn't think his remaining fifty years (assuming a lifetime of seventy years, the biblical life expectancy) will give him enough time to experience and observe life fully, that he enjoys the flowering of spring, that he knows enough about church rituals to claim that the whiteness of cherry blossoms coincides with the liturgical color of white for Easter, and that he is meditative and somber rather than extroverted and hilarious. All this is quite a bit of information from so short a poem.

If we look at all poems with the same care, we will discover many other details. Grammatical forms and word levels may define the speaker's social class or educational level. Similarly, the selection of topics may indicate the speaker's emotional state, self-esteem, knowledge, attitudes, habits, hobbies, and much more.

The Person with Whom or to Whom the Speaker Is Talking Is the Listener

The second type of character in poetry is the **listener**—a person, not the reader, whom the speaker addresses directly and who is therefore "inside" the poem. Occasionally we find poems in the form of a **dialogue** between two persons, so that the characters are *both* speakers and listeners, as in Randall's "Ballad of Birmingham" (Chapter 18). Whatever the form, the speaker-listener relationship creates drama and tension. In effect, we as readers are an audience, hearing either conversational exchanges or one-way conversations. The speakers of course identify themselves with the "I" pronoun and address their listeners with the pronouns "thou-thy-thee" and "you-your-yours."

In some poems the listener is passive, merely hearing the speaker's words without response, as in Marlowe's "The Passionate Shepherd to His Love" and Glück's "Snowdrops." In a variation of this situation the listener may not be present, but may instead be the speaker's intended recipient. In this case the speaker is like a letter writer and the listener is the "addressee." Such a listener is the "thou-thee-thine" of Ben Jonson's well-known "Drink to Me, Only, with Thine Eyes."

BEN JONSON (1572–1637)

For a portrait, see Chapter 11, page 640. The following two poems are by Ben Jonson.

🍁 Drink to Me, Only, with Thine Eyes (1616)

Drink to me, only, with thine eyes,
  And I will pledge° with mine;   *drink a toast*
Or leave a kiss but in the cup,
  And I'll not look for wine.
The thirst that from the soul doth° rise   *does* 5
  Doth ask a drink divine:
But might I of Jove's nectar° sup
  I would not change° for thine.   *exchange it [i.e., nectar]*

°7 *Jove's nectar:* Jove, or Jupiter, was the principal Roman god. Nectar (a word meaning "overcoming death") was the drink of the gods; a human being who drank it would become immortal.

I sent thee, late,° a rosy wreath,   *lately, a short time ago*
10   Not so much honoring thee,
As giving it a hope, that there
    It could not withered be.
But thou thereon did'st only breathe,
    And sent'st it back to me:
15 Since when° it grows, and smells, I swear,   *that time, then*
    Not of itself, but thee.

QUESTIONS

1. Who is the speaker? What do you learn about him, his knowledge, his wit, and his concern for the listener?
2. What has the speaker sent to the listener? What did she do, and why is he still writing to her?
3. How can the poem be seen as an attempt to "top" the listener's disdain? Explain why the speaker seems just as interested in showing his wittiness as in complimenting the listener.

This poem demonstrates that the listener has not been passive; she has returned the speaker's gift and thus has spurned him. Therefore the poem may be seen at least partly as the speaker's attempt, by demonstrating his wit, to ingratiate himself with the listener. In similar poems involving a speaker and a silent listener, we should consider both the dramatic situation and the listener's stated and implied responses.

A related but distinct type of situation involving a listener is the **dramatic monologue,** in which the speaker talks directly to an on-the-spot listener whose reactions may directly affect the course of the poem. Browning's "My Last Duchess" is such a poem, in which the speaker, the duke, addresses an envoy of a "count," a "you" listener, who has been given the task of arranging financial terms about the dowry to be given by the count when the duke marries the count's daughter.

Ultimately, we as readers are the listeners of all poems. In this capacity we are the poet's uninvolved, outside audience. Thus, in poems like Hardy's "The Workbox" (Chapter 16) and Browning's "My Last Duchess" (this chapter), we are a virtual hearing and viewing audience; and in a poem like Housman's "Loveliest of Trees" (Chapter 12), we are outside listeners, eavesdropping as the speaker meditates on time, death, and beauty. Sometimes, however, the poet may address us directly in our role as readers, as in this brief dedicatory poem that Ben Jonson uses to begin his book of epigrams published in 1616.

🍁 To the Reader (1616)

Pray thee, take care, that tak'st my book in hand,
To read it well: that is, to understand.

In these two brief lines, Jonson establishes intimacy with us as readers by using the second-person singular pronoun *thee.* Although we are clearly outside the poem, Jonson invites us inside by asking us to read well and understand all his forthcoming poems. As much as a poet can, he therefore closes the distance that exists between poet and poem, on the one hand, and reader, on the other.

Only rarely do poets address us directly, as Jonson does. For this reason it is important to determine what is meant when a poet uses the "you" pronoun (see also Chapter 2). Sometimes the "you" suggests that we are on-the-spot listeners and even colleagues or chums of poetic speakers; but more often the "you" is a conversational way by which the speaker refers to himself or herself. Hardy's speaker in "The Man He Killed"(Chapter 11), for example, uses an indirect "you" in this way, and thereby he establishes our assent to the idea that war is "quaint and curious." Even when we are invited to become inside-listeners in this way, however, our responses do not enter the poem structurally, and therefore our role as spectators or witnesses does not change. We remain an audience of outside listeners.

Poems Are Sometimes Little Dramas with Major and Minor Participants

Because many poems are dramatic, they often involve a third type of character—major or minor participants. We learn about these characters from appearance, speech, action, and reaction. In the anonymous "Sir Patrick Spens" (Chapter 11), for example, we learn from Sir Patrick's outcry that he is distressed, but from his action that he is an obedient sea captain. In Hardy's "Channel Firing" (Chapter 14), we learn that the ages-old skeletons are sorry that they sacrificed personal enjoyment when they were alive, because their strict living did nothing to improve humankind.

Most poetic speakers are reliable reporters about the actions and characters of the major and minor participants. For example, the speaker-narrator of the anonymous "Sir Patrick Spens" is honest and straightforward, and his assessment of Sir Patrick is reliable. But we should also be aware that poetic speakers, as in all fiction, can have interests beyond those of reportorial accuracy. A speaker who uses language for distortion and intimidation is the duke in Browning's "My Last Duchess." His words make clear that he is a liar and that we must look beyond his distortions to learn the character of the duchess and the nature of their life together.

Not all participants, of course, are human. Poets frequently include descriptions of the animal and vegetable kingdom, such as swimmers (game fish, people [sometimes]), flyers (orioles, bluejays, swans, ravens, nightingales, larks), walkers and runners (bears, deer, horses, lambs, lions, woodchucks, tigers), and growers (petunias, roses, leaves, birch trees). Although some of these animals and vegetables are sometimes given character traits, as with the horse in Frost's "Stopping by Woods on a Snowy Evening" (Chapter 11), they are more often restricted to roles that are mainly pictorial or symbolic.

Setting and Character in Poetry

The people in poetry do not exist in a vacuum. When they speak and act, they reflect the time, place, thought, social conventions, and general circumstances of their lives. Love poetry, for example, is often mainly about desire, but it is also concerned with the ranges of emotion and responsibility that human beings experience through culture and environment. Religion, economic circumstances, leisure, chance, and the condition of the natural world may all enter into a lover's pronouncements. Thus, the speaker of Marlowe's "The Passionate Shepherd to His Love" daydreams about spending time in open nature with his love, sharing the songs of birds and the sights of "valleys, groves, hills, and fields." Here the setting of an Arcadian dream world— without work, want, or illness—reinforces his desire. Comparably, in Lisel Mueller's "Alive Together," we see another loving character reflecting on a more complex and tenuous world of chance, historical accident, and unpredictable opportunity.

LISEL MUELLER (b. 1924)

 Alive Together (1976)

Speaking of marvels, I am alive
together with you, when I might have been
alive with anyone under the sun,
when I might have been Abélard's woman°
5 or the whore of a Renaissance pope
or a peasant wife with not enough food
and not enough love, with my children
dead of the plague. I might have slept
in an alcove next to the man
10 with the golden nose,° who poked it
into the business of stars,
or sewn a starry flag°
for a general with wooden teeth.
I might have been the exemplary Pocahontas°
15 Or a woman without a name
Weeping in Master's bed
for my husband, exchanged for a mule,
my daughter, lost in a drunken bet.
I might have been stretched on a totem pole
20 to appease a vindictive god
or left, a useless girl-child,
to die on a cliff. I like to think

°4 *Abélard's woman*: Peter Abelard (1079–1142), a famous teacher at the University of Paris, fell in love with his student, Eloise (1101–1162). They married, but their relationship was forcibly ended by Eloise's uncle; nevertheless, their passion and frustrated love have become legendary. 9, 10: *man with the golden nose*: Tycho Brahe (1546–1602), the brilliant and methodical Swedish astronomer, lost the bridge of his nose in a duel, and afterwards always wore a metallic prosthesis. 12 *sewn a starry flag*: Betsy Ross (1752–1836) created the first American flag in 1776 after visiting George Washington (1732–1797), who had to use wooden false teeth for most of his adult life. 14 *Pocahontas*: Pocahontas (1595–1617), an American Indian princess, was famous as a friend of John Smith of the Jamestown plantation in Virginia. Eventually she converted to Christianity and married John Rolfe. (c. 1585–1622)

I might have been Mary Shelley°
in love with a wrongheaded angel,
or Mary's friend. I might have been you.
This poem is endless, the odds against us are endless,   25
our chances of being alive together
statistically nonexistent;
still we have made it, alive in a time
when rationalists in square hats°
and hatless Jehovah's Witnesses°   30
agree it is almost over,
alive with our lively children
who—but for endless ifs—
might have missed out on being alive   35
together with marvels and follies
and longings and lies and wishes
and error and humor and mercy
and journeys and voices and faces
and colors and summers and mornings   40
and knowledge and tears and chance.

°23 *Mary Shelley:* Mary Wollstonecraft Shelley (1797–1851), the author of *Frankenstein* (1818), was the second wife of poet Percy Bysshe Shelley (1792–1822), who was known for his radical views. 30 *rationalists in square hats:* a reference to the poem "Rationalists, wearing square hats," by Wallace Stevens (1879–1955), in which the idea is that most thinkers are limited by their inability to comprehend truths that might lie beyond the close confines of their observation. 31 *Jehovah's Witnesses:* a large religious denomination, founded in 1931, whose members believe that human civilization will be destroyed during a universal war—the Battle of Armageddon. Then, surviving true believers will live a life of peace and harmony.

QUESTIONS

1. Describe the speaker. What assumptions does she make about her immediate listener? What does the poet, Mueller, assume about the knowledge of her readers?
2. What is the nature of life and existence, as the speaker expresses it in lines 40 through 46?
3. Why does Mueller use the phrase "might have . . ." as often as she does in the poem?

This richly allusive poem shows the interaction of character and the vagaries of human history. Mueller's speaker, in contemplating the "marvels" of her life, considers how slight are the chances that she and her husband could ever have lived during the same period of time, could ever have met under favorable circumstances, and then could ever have been able to create and live a long, rich, eventful, and satisfying married life together.

As a general principle, settings in poetry readily bring out the ideas of characters who create and express personal, political, philosophical, and religious thoughts. Gray's "Elegy Written in a Country Churchyard" shows how important such thought can be when it is integrated into poetry. Here the approaching "darkness" causes the speaker to think of the "rude forefathers of the hamlet" in their churchyard graves. This thought leads him to speculate about how death cuts off those who are talented and potentially great. The interaction here is complex, interweaving character and history with natural and cultural situations and images. A poem similarly connecting character and setting is Wordsworth's "Lines Composed a Few Miles above Tintern Abbey (this chapter)." This poem, based on the relationship of the past, present, and future of the speaker to the natural scenes he describes, is a model of how poetic setting and character can be fused.

It is no exaggeration to say that setting interacts with character in endless numbers of ways. Thus in Browning's "My Last Duchess," the duke's display of valuable art creates a setting that exposes his greed and cruelty. In "London," Blake introduces bleak sights and anguished sounds that evoke a response of repulsion and rejection. As the representation of a philosophical judgment, the setting of Arnold's "Dover Beach" demonstrates changeability and impermanence. The speaker's solution is to establish personal fidelity as a fixture against change, dissolution, and brutality. To greater or lesser degrees, most poems offer similar connections of setting and character.

Poems for Study

Matthew Arnold .... Dover Beach, 694
William Blake .... London, 695
Elizabeth Brewster........................ Where I Come From, 696
Robert Browning .... My Last Duchess, 697
William Cowper .... The Poplar Field, 699
Allen Ginsberg........................... A Further Proposal, 699
Louise Glück .... Snowdrops, 700
Thomas Gray............. Elegy Written in a Country Churchyard, 701
Thomas Hardy........................... The Ruined Maid, 704
Dorianne Laux .... The Life of Trees, 705
C. Day Lewis .... Song, 707
Robert Lowell .... Memories of West Street and Lepke, 707
Christopher Marlowe........ The Passionate Shepherd to His Love, 709
Joyce Carol Oates.................................... Loving, 710
Sir Walter Ralegh .... The Nymph's Reply to the Shepherd, 711
Christina Rossetti........................... A Christmas Carol, 712
Jane Shore .... A Letter Sent to Summer, 713
William Wordsworth .... Lines Composed a Few Miles Above Tintern Abbey, 714
James Wright .... A Blessing, 717

MATTHEW ARNOLD (1822–1888)

 ### Dover Beach (1867; 1849)

The sea is calm tonight.
The tide is full, the moon lies fair
Upon the straits—on the French coast the light
Gleams and is gone; the cliffs of England stand,
5 Glimmering and vast, out in the tranquil bay.
Come to the window, sweet is the night air!
Only, from the long line of spray
Where the sea meets the moon-blanched land,
Listen! you hear the grating roar
10 Of pebbles which the waves draw back, and fling,

At their return, up the high strand,
Begin, and cease, and then again begin,
With tremulous cadence slow, and bring
The eternal note of sadness in.

Sophocles long ago
Heard it on the Aegean, and it brought
Into his mind the turbid ebb and flow
Of human misery; we   15
Find also in the sound a thought,
Hearing it by this distant northern sea.

The Sea of Faith
Was once, too, at the full, and round earth's shore
Lay like the folds of a bright girdle furled.
But now I only hear   20
Its melancholy, long, withdrawing roar,
Retreating, to the breath   25
Of the night wind, down the vast edges drear
And naked shingles° of the world.   beaches

Ah, love, let us be true
To one another! for the world, which seems   30
To lie before us like a land of dreams,
So various, so beautiful, so new,
Hath really neither joy, nor love, nor light,
Nor certitude, nor peace, nor help for pain;
And we are here as on a darkling plain
Swept with confused alarms of struggle and flight,   35
Where ignorant armies clash by night.

Handwritten annotations:

SEA

1. Sea = cyclical = 2,000 yr eras (cycle)

2. Appearance vs. Reality

3. Waves and Tides beyond Human control, as well as Human Misery

The Sea of Faith → Christian Faith

Ah, love, let us be true → They don't have anything except each other

RELIGION vs SCIENCE

QUESTIONS

1. What words and details establish the setting?

2. Where are the speaker and listener? What can they see? Hear?

3. What sort of movement may be topographically traced in the first six lines of the poem, so that the scene finally focuses on the speaker and the listener?

4. What is meant by comparing the English Channel to the Aegean Sea, and relating the Aegean surf to the thought of Sophocles?

5. What faith remains after the loss of religious faith? Defend the claim that the faith is the speaker's commitment to personal fidelity rather than love.

WILLIAM BLAKE (1757–1827)

For a portrait, see Chapter 12, page 661.

 ## London (1794)

I wander thro' each charter'd° street,
Near where the charter'd Thames does flow,

°1 *charter'd*: privileged, licensed, authorized.

And mark in every face I meet
Marks of weakness, marks of woe.

5 In every cry of every Man,
In every Infant's cry of fear,
In every voice, in every ban,°   public pronouncement
The mind-forg'd manacles I hear.

How the Chimney-sweeper's cry
10 Every blackning Church appalls;°
And the hapless Soldier's sigh
Runs in blood down Palace walls.

But most thro' midnight streets I hear
How the youthful Harlot's curse
15 Blasts the new-born Infant's tear,
And blights with plagues the Marriage hearse.

°10 *appalls:* weakens, makes pale, shocks.

QUESTIONS

1. What does London represent to the speaker? How do the persons who live there contribute to the poem's ideas about the state of humanity?
2. What sounds does the speaker mention as a part of the London scene? Characterize these sounds in relation to the poem's main idea.
3. Because of the tension in the poem between civilized activity (as represented in the chartering of the street and the river) and free human impulses, explain how the poem might be considered revolutionary.
4. The poem appeared in *Songs of Experience*, published in 1794. Explain the appropriateness of Blake's including the poem in a collection so named.

ELIZABETH BREWSTER (b. 1922)

 ## Where I Come From (1994)

People are made of places. They carry with them
hints of jungles or mountains, a tropic grace
or the cool eyes of sea-gazers. Atmosphere of cities
how different drops from them, like the smell of smog
5 or the almost-not-smell of tulips in the spring,
nature tidily plotted in little squares
with a fountain in the centre; museum smell,
art also tidily plotted with a guidebook;
or the smell of work, glue factories maybe,
10 chromium-plated offices; smell of subways
crowded at rush hours.

Where I come from, people
carry woods in their minds, acres of pine woods;
blueberry patches in the burned-out bush;
wooden farmhouses, old, in need of paint,   15
with yards where hens and chickens circle about,
clucking aimlessly; battered schoolhouses
behind which violets grow. Spring and winter
are the mind's chief seasons: ice and the breaking of ice.

A door in the mind blows open, and there blows   20
a frosty wind from fields of snow.

QUESTIONS

1. In what sense are people "made of places" (line 1)? What kinds of places does the poet describe in the first eleven lines?

2. How does the poem shift at the middle of line 11? Does it seem that the speaker presents a more favorable view of the area "Where I come from" than of the area described in the first eleven lines?

3. What is the sense of the final two lines? How are these lines connected to the earlier parts of the poem? What sense of self-criticism is apparent in these last two lines?

ROBERT BROWNING (1812–1889)

 ## My Last Duchess° (1842)

Ferrara

That's my last Duchess painted on the wall,
Looking as if she were alive. I call
That piece a wonder, now: Frà Pandolf's° hands
Worked busily a day, and there she stands.
Will't please you sit and look at her? I said   5
"Frà Pandolf" by design, for never read
Strangers like you that pictured countenance,
The depth and passion of its earnest glance,
But to myself they turned (since none puts by
The curtain I have drawn for you, but I)   10
And seemed as they would ask me, if they durst,°   *dared*
How such a glance came there; so, not the first
Are you to turn and ask thus. Sir, 'twas not
Her husband's presence only, called that spot
Of joy into the Duchess' cheek: perhaps   15
Frà Pandolf chanced to say "Her mantle laps
Over my lady's wrist too much," or "Paint
Must never hope to reproduce the faint

°The poem "My Last Duchess" is based on incidents in the life of Alfonso II, duke of Ferrara, whose first wife died in 1561. Some claimed she was poisoned. The duke negotiated his second marriage to the daughter of the count of Tyrol through an agent. 3 *Frà Pandolf:* an imaginary painter who is also a monk.

Half-flush that dies along her throat": such stuff
20 Was courtesy, she thought, and cause enough
For calling up that spot of joy. She had
A heart—how shall I say?—too soon made glad,
Too easily impressed; she liked whate'er
She looked on, and her looks went everywhere.
25 Sir, 'twas all one! My favor at her breast,
The dropping of the daylight in the West,
The bough of cherries some officious fool
Broke in the orchard for her, the white mule
She rode with round the terrace—all and each
30 Would draw from her alike the approving speech,
Or blush, at least. She thanked men—good! but thanked
Somehow—I know not how—as if she ranked
My gift of a nine-hundred-years-old name
With anybody's gift. Who'd stoop to blame
35 This sort of trifling? Even had you skill
In speech—(which I have not)—to make your will
Quite clear to such a one, and say, "Just this
Or that in you disgusts me; here you miss,
Or there exceed the mark"—and if she let
40 Herself be lessoned so, nor plainly set
Her wits to yours, forsooth, and made excuse
—E'en then would be some stooping; and I choose
Never to stoop. Oh sir, she smiled, no doubt,
Whene'er I passed her; but who passed without
45 Much the same smile? This grew; I gave commands;
Then all smiles stopped together. There she stands
As if alive. Will't please you rise? We'll meet
The company below, then. I repeat,
The Count your master's known munificence
50 Is ample warrant that no just pretense
Of mine for dowry will be disallowed;
Though his fair daughter's self, as I avowed
At starting, is my object. Nay, we'll go
Together down, sir. Notice Neptune,° though,
55 Taming a sea horse, thought a rarity,
Which Claus of Innsbruck° cast in bronze for me!

[handwritten annotations in margin:]
Possession
He doesn't confront her b/c it is below his dignity
He commanded to kill her
He is here on a marriage deal but it is about the girl
control. he is neptune, tried to tame her, now just a picture like statue

---

°54 *Neptune:* Roman god of the sea. 56 *Claus of Innsbruck:* an imaginary sculptor.

QUESTIONS

1. Who dominates the conversation in this poem? Who is the listener? What is the purpose of the "conversation"? Why does the speaker avoid dealing with the purpose until near the poem's end?

2. What third character does the speaker describe? In what ways are his descriptions accurate or inaccurate? What judgment do you think Browning wants you to make of the speaker? Why?

3. How does the speaker's language illustrate his attitude toward his own power? In light of this attitude, what do you think Browning's point is in the poem?

WILLIAM COWPER (1731–1800)

The Poplar Field (1782)

The poplars are felled,° farewell to the shade   cut down
And the whispering sound of the cool colonnade.
The winds play no longer, and sing in the leaves,
Nor Ouse° on his bosom their image receives.

Twelve years have elapsed since I last took a view   5
Of my favourite field and the bank where they grew,
And now in the grass behold they are laid,
And the tree is my seat that once lent me a shade.

The blackbird has fled to another retreat
Where the hazels afford him a screen from the heat,   10
And the scene where his melody charmed me before,
Resounds with his sweet-flowing ditty no more.

My fugitive years are all hasting away,
And I must ere long lie as lowly as they,
With a turf on my breast, and a stone at my head,   15
Ere another such grove shall arise in its stead.

'Tis a sight to engage me, if any thing can,
To muse on the perishing pleasures of man;
Though his life be a dream, his enjoyments, I see,
Have a being less durable even than he.   20

°4 *Ouse:* river in northern England, near which Cowper lived.

QUESTIONS

1. What situation does the speaker describe? How has the scene changed from what he knew twelve years before? Why does the speaker refer to the passage of time? What kind of person is he?
2. How has the situation affected the blackbird? Why does the speaker care?
3. How does the scene affect the speaker? What idea does he express about what has occurred?

ALLEN GINSBERG (1926–1997)

A Further Proposal (1947)

Come live with me and be my love,
And we will some old pleasures prove.
Men like me have paid in verse
This costly courtesy, or curse;

But I would bargain with my art   5
(As to the mind, now to the heart),

My symbols, images, and signs
Please me more outside these lines.

For your share and recompense,
10   You will be taught another sense:
The wisdom of the subtle worm
Will turn most perfect in your form.

Not that your soul need tutored be
By intellectual decree,
15   But graces that the mind can share
Will make you, as more wise, more fair,

Till all the world's devoted thought
Find all in you it ever sought,
And even I, of skeptic mind,
20   A Resurrection of a kind.

This compliment, in my own way,
For what I would receive, I pay;
Thus all the wise have writ thereof,
And all the fair have been their love.

QUESTIONS

1. How is this poem integrated with the other comparable poems in this chapter (by Marlowe, Lewis, Ralegh)? In what ways is this poem more "realistic" than the others?

2. In what ways might this poem be considered cynical? How may it be read as a criticism of the other poems?

3. What does the speaker mean by saying that he is pleased more "outside these signs" (line 8)? What does he mean by "For what I would receive, I pay" (line 22)?

LOUISE GLÜCK (b. 1943)

 Snowdrops (1992)

Do you know what I was, how I lived? You know
what despair is; then
winter should have meaning for you.

I did not expect to survive,
5   earth suppressing me. I didn't expect
to waken again, to feel
in damp earth my body
able to respond again, remembering
after so long how to open again
10   in the cold light
of earliest spring—

afraid, yes, but among you again
crying yes risk joy

in the raw wind of the new world.

QUESTIONS

1. How much does the speaker say about her previous condition? What does she say about how she has changed? What do you conclude has happened to make her change?
2. Why is the poem titled "Snowdrops"? What are snowdrops? How are the descriptions those that actual snowdrops might articulate, if they could actually speak?
3. What is the meaning of the phrase "yes risk joy" in line 12, even though the "new world" is filled with "raw wind"?
4. Compare this poem with Dickinson's "I Taste a Liquor Never Brewed" (Chapter 21).

THOMAS GRAY (1716–1771)

 ## Elegy Written in a Country Churchyard (1751)

The curfew tolls the knell of parting day,
    The lowing herd wind slowly o'er the lea,
The ploughman homeward plods his weary way,
    And leaves the world to darkness and to me.

Now fades the glimm'ring landscape on the sight,   5
    And all the air a solemn stillness holds,
Save where the beetle wheels his droning flight,
    And drowsy tinklings lull the distant folds;

Save that from yonder ivy-mantled tower
    The moping owl does to the moon complain   10
Of such as wand'ring near her secret bower
    Molest her ancient solitary reign.

Beneath those rugged elms, that yew-tree's shade,
    Where heaves the turf in many a mold'ring heap,
Each in his narrow cell forever laid,   15
    The rude forefathers of the hamlet sleep.

The breezy call of incense-breathing morn,
    The swallow twitt'ring from the straw-built shed,
The cock's shrill clarion, or the echoing horn,°   *hunting horn*
    No more shall rouse them from their lowly bed.   20

For them no more the blazing hearth shall burn,
    Or busy housewife ply her evening care;
No children run to lisp their sire's return,
    Or climb his knees the envied kiss to share.

25   Oft did the harvest to their sickle yield,
     Their furrow oft the stubborn glebe° has broke;   *church land*
  How jocund did they drive their team afield!
     How bowed the woods beneath their sturdy stroke!

  Let not Ambition mock their useful toil
30   Their homely joys, and destiny obscure;
  Nor Grandeur hear with a disdainful smile
     The short and simple annals of the poor.

  The boast of heraldry, the pomp of power,
     And all that beauty, all that wealth e'er gave,
35   Awaits alike th'inevitable hour.
     The paths of glory lead but to the grave.

  Nor you, ye proud, impute to these the fault,
     If mem'ry o'er their tomb no trophies raise,
  Where through the long-drawn aisle and fretted vault
40   The pealing anthem swells the note of praise.

  Can storied urn or animated bust
     Back to its mansion call the fleeting breath?
  Can Honor's voice provoke the silent dust,
     Or Flatt'ry soothe the dull cold ear of death?

45   Perhaps in this neglected spot is laid
     Some heart once pregnant with celestial fire;
  Hands that the rod of empire might have swayed,
     Or waked to ecstasy the living lyre.

  But Knowledge to their eyes her ample page
50   Rich with the spoils of time did ne'er unroll;
  Chill Penury repressed their noble rage,
     And froze the genial current of the soul.

  Full many a gem of purest ray serene,
     The dark unfathomed caves of ocean bear;
55   Full many a flower is born to blush unseen,
     And waste its sweetness on the desert air.

  Some village Hampden,° that with dauntless breast
     The little tyrant of his fields withstood;
  Some mute inglorious Milton here may rest,
60   Some Cromwell guiltless of his country's blood.

  Th'applause of list'ning senates to command,
     The threats of pain and ruin to despise,
  To scatter plenty o'er a smiling land,
     And read their hist'ry in a nation's eyes.

°57 *Hampden:* John Hampden (1594–1643), English statesman who defended the rights of the people against King Charles I and who died in the English Civil War of 1642–1646.

Their lot forbade: nor circumscribed alone   65
    Their growing virtues, but their crimes confined;
Forbade to wade through slaughter to a throne,
    And shut the gates of mercy on mankind,

The struggling pangs of conscious truth to hide,
    To quench the blushes of ingenuous shame,   70
Or heap the shrine of luxury and pride
    With incense kindled at the Muse's flame.

Far from the madding° crowd's ignoble strife,   *raving*
    Their sober wishes never learned to stray;
Along the cool sequestered vale of life   75
    They kept the noiseless tenor of their way.

Yet ev'n these bones from insult to protect
    Some frail memorial still erected nigh,
With uncouth° rhymes and shapeless sculpture decked,   *uneducated, unsophisticated*
    Implores the passing tribute of a sigh.   80

Their names, their years, spelt by th'unlettered Muse,
    The place of fame and elegy supply;
And many a holy text around she strews,
    That teach the rustic moralist to die.

For who to dumb forgetfulness a prey,   85
    This pleasing anxious being e'er resigned,
Left the warm precincts of the cheerful day,
    Nor cast one longing ling'ring look behind?

On some fond breast the parting soul relies,
    Some pious drops the closing eye requires;   90
Ev'n from the tomb the voice of Nature cries,
    Ev'n in our ashes live their wonted fires.

For thee, who mindful of th'unhonored dead
    Dost in these lines their artless tale relate;
If chance, by lonely contemplation led,   95
    Some kindred spirit shall inquire thy fate.

Haply some hoary-headed swain may say,
    "Oft have we seen him at the peep of dawn
Brushing with hasty steps the dews away
    To meet the sun upon the upland lawn.   100

"There, at the foot of yonder nodding beech
    That wreathes its old fantastic° roots so high,   *fancifully extravagant, grotesque*
His listless length at noontide would he stretch
    And pore upon the brook that babbles by.

"Hard by yon wood, now smiling as in scorn,   105
    Mutt'ring his wayward fancies he would rove,

Now drooping, woeful wan, like one forlorn,
　　Or crazed with care, or crossed in hopeless love.

"One morn I missed him on the 'customed hill,
110　　Along the heath and near his fav'rite tree;
Another came; nor yet beside the rill,
　　Nor up the lawn, nor at the wood was he;

"The next with dirges due in sad array
　　Slow through the church-way path we saw him borne.
115　Approach and read (for thou canst read) the lay,
　　Graved on the stone beneath you aged thorn."

THE EPITAPH

Here rests his head upon the lap of earth
　　A youth to fortune and to fame unknown;
Fair Science frowned not on his humble birth,
120　　And Melancholy marked him for her own.

Large was his bounty, and his soul sincere,
　　Heav'n did a recompense as largely send:
He gave to mis'ry all he had, a tear:
　　He gain'd from Heav'n ('twas all he wished) a friend.

125　No farther seek his merits to disclose,
　　Or draw his frailties from their dread abode
(There they alike in trembling hope repose),
　　The bosom of his Father and his God.

QUESTIONS

1. What is the time of day of the speaker's meditation? What is happening in nature as the poem opens? Whom is the speaker addressing?
2. Who are the people buried in the church graveyard? What point does Gray make about the contributions they might have made if they had not died?
3. How does Gray's use of sights and sounds complement the poem's mood?
4. Who is "thee" (line 93)? What happens to him? Why is he included in the poem?

THOMAS HARDY (1840–1928)

For a photo, see Chapter 5, page 287.

 ## The Ruined Maid (1866)

"O 'melia,° my dear, this does everything crown!;°　　　　　　　　　　*i.e., Amelia*
Who could have supposed I should meet you in Town?

°1 *does everything crown:* crowns everything; is a great surprise.

And whence such fair garments, such prosperi-ty"—
"O didn't you know I'd been ruined," said she.

—"You left us in tatters, without shoes or socks,   5
Tired of digging potatoes, and spudding up docks;°   *digging up weeds*
And now you've gay bracelets and bright feathers three!"
"Yes: that's how we dress when we're ruined," said she.

—"At home in the barton° you said 'thee' and 'thou,'
And 'thik oon,' and 'theäs oon,' and 't'other';° but now   10
Your talking quite fits 'ee° for high compa-ny!"—   *thee*
"Some polish is gained with one's ruin," said she.

—"Your hands were like paws then, your face blue and bleak
But now I'm bewitched by your delicate cheek,
And your little gloves fit as on any la-dy!"—   15
"We never do work when we're ruined," said she.

—"You used to call home-life a hag-ridden dream,
And you'd sigh, and you'd sock;° but at present you seem   *moan, groan*
To know not of megrims° or melancho-ly!"—   *migraine headaches*
"True. One's pretty lively when ruined," said she.   20

—"I wish I had feathers, a fine sweeping gown,
And a delicate face, and could strut about Town!"—
"My dear—a raw country girl, such as you be,
Cannot quite expect that. You ain't ruined," said she.

°9 *At home in the barton:* when you lived at home on the farm. 9–10 '*thee*' . . . '*t'other*': i.e., you spoke familiarly in the country dialect (using the second-person pronoun), saying "thik oon" for "that one" and "theäs oon" for "this one."

QUESTIONS

1. Who are the two speakers? How have they come together? What are their present economic circumstances? Who is 'melia (Amelia)? Does she seem to be bragging to the first speaker? Why has not the first speaker learned about 'melia earlier, before their encounter in town?

2. How aware of her situation is 'melia? Is she happy or unhappy about it? How completely has she shed her country habits of speech?

3. What double meaning does the word "ruined" have in this poem? To what extent does Hardy use the poem to challenge conventional moral judgments?

DORIANNE LAUX (b. 1952)

 ## The Life of Trees (2003)

The pines rub their great noise
Into the spangled dark.
They scratch their itchy boughs
Against the house and the mystery
of that moan translates   5
into drudgery of ownership: time

to drag the ladder from the shed,
climb onto the roof with a saw
between my teeth, cut those suckers down.
10 What's reality if not a long exhaustive
cringe from the blade,
the teeth. I want to sleep
and dream the life of trees, beings
from the muted world who care nothing
15 for Money, Politics, Power,
Will or Right, who want little from the night
but a few dead stars going dim, a white owl
lifting from their limbs, who want only
to sink their roots into the wet ground
20 and terrify the worms or shake
their bleary heads like fashion models
or old hippies. If they could speak,
they wouldn't, only hum some low
green note, roll their pinecones
25 down the empty streets and blame it,
with a shrug, on the cold wind.
During the day they sleep inside
their furry bark, clouds shredding
like ancient lace above their crowns.
30 Sun. Rain. Snow. Wind. They fear
Nothing but the Hurricane, and Fire,
that whipped bully who rises up
and becomes his own dead father.
Then the young ones bend and bend
35 and the old know they may not make it,
go down with the power lines sparking,
broken at the trunk. They fling
their branches, forked sacrifice
to the beaten earth. They do not pray.
40 If they make a sound it's eaten
by the wind. And though the stars
return they do not offer thanks,
only ooze a sticky sap from their roundish
concentric wounds, clap the water
45 from their needles, straighten their spines
and breathe, and breathe again.

QUESTIONS

1. What contrast does the poem develop between human and sylvan or arboreal life? In
   general terms, what kind of existence do trees represent? How accurately does the
   poem describe this existence?

2. In what way does the speaker seem to idealize the cares and interests of trees, in contrast to the tasks and duties of human beings? How does the final line, "breathe, and
   breathe again," represent a goal or duty from which human beings may benefit?

3. Why does the speaker say "What's reality if not a long exhaustive / cringe from the blade,
   / the teeth?" How does this description fit an idea of the reality facing human beings?

C. DAY LEWIS (1904–1972)

 ## Song (1935)

Come, live with me and be my love,
And we will all the pleasures prove
Of peace and plenty, bed and board,
That chance employment may afford.

I'll handle dainties on the docks   5
And thou shalt read of summer frocks:
At evening by the sour canals
We'll hope to hear some madrigals.

Care on thy maiden brow shall put
A wreath of wrinkles, and thy foot   10
Be shod with pain: not silken dress
But toil shall tire thy loveliness.

Hunger shall make thy modest zone
And cheat fond death of all but bone—
If these delights thy mind may move,   15
Then live with me and be my love.

QUESTIONS

1. What is the connection and contrast between this poem and Marlowe's "Passionate Shepherd to His Love"?
2. To what other poems in this chapter is this poem related? How?
3. Who is the speaker in this poem? The listener?
4. What is the effect of words like "chance employment" (line 4), "read" (line 6), and "hope" (line 8)?

ROBERT LOWELL (1917–1977)

 ## Memories of West Street° and Lepke (1959)

Only teaching on Tuesdays, book-worming
in pajamas fresh from the washer each morning,
I hog a whole house on Boston's
"hardly passionate Marlborough Street,"°
where even the man   5
scavenging filth in the back alley trash cans,
has two children, a beach wagon, a helpmate,
and is "a young Republican."
I have a nine months' daughter,

°The West Street Jail in lower Manhattan, where Lowell spent ten days in 1943 before being sent to a federal prison to serve a year's sentence as a conscientious objector (C.O.) for refusing to serve in the armed services during World War II (1941–1945). 4 *Marlborough Street:* in Boston, where Lowell had a house in the late 1950s, when he was writing this poem.

10 young enough to be my granddaughter.
Like the sun she rises in her flame-flamingo infants' wear.

These are the tranquilized *Fifties*,
and I am forty. Ought I to regret my seedtime?
I was a fire-breathing Catholic C.O.,
15 and made my manic statement,
telling off the state and president, and then
sat waiting sentence in the bull pen
beside a negro boy with curlicues
of marijuana in his hair.

20 Given a year,
I walked on the roof of the West Street Jail, a short
enclosure like my school soccer court,
and saw the Hudson River once a day
through sooty clothesline entanglements
25 and bleaching khaki tenements.
Strolling, I yammered metaphysics with Abramowitz,°
a jaundice-yellow ("it's really tan")
and fly-weight pacifist,
so vegetarian,
30 he wore rope shoes and preferred fallen fruit.
He tried to convert Bioff and Brown,
the Hollywood pimps, to his diet.
Hairy, muscular, suburban,
wearing chocolate double-breasted suits,
35 they blew their tops and beat him black and blue.

I was so out of things, I'd never heard
of the Jehovah's Witnesses.
"Are you a C.O.?" I asked a fellow jailbird.
"No," he answered, "I'm a J.W."
40 He taught me the "hospital tuck,"
and pointed out the T-shirted back
of *Murder Incorporated's* Czar Lepke,°
there piling towels on a rack,
or dawdling off to his little segregated cell full
45 of things forbidden to the common man:
a portable radio, a dresser, two toy American
flags tied together with a ribbon of Easter palm.
Flabby, bald, lobotomized,
he drifted in a sheepish calm,
50 where no agonizing reappraisal
jarred his concentration on the electric chair
hanging like an oasis in his air
of lost connections. . . .

°26–31 *Abramowitz, Bioff and Brown:* These men were also prisoners at the West Street Jail. 41 *Czar Lepke:*
Louis "Lepke" Buchalter (1897–1944), a notorious professional criminal, was convicted of two murders (though
he had been connected with as many as a hundred); he was executed in 1944. A reported conversation between
Lepke and Lowell took place. Lepke stated that he was in prison for killing, and Lowell responded that he was in
prison for refusing to kill.

QUESTIONS

1. Why is the poem titled "Memories of West Street and Lepke"? What observations does the speaker make about his experiences at the West-Street Prison?

2. Why does the speaker open the poem by noting his present residence on Marlborough Street in Boston? How does he characterize this neighborhood? How is it contrasted with the West-Street Prison?

3. What conclusions do you think you are expected to draw from "Memories of West Street and Lepke"?

CHRISTOPHER MARLOWE (1564–1593)

 ## The Passionate Shepherd to His Love (1599)

Come live with me and be my love,	
And we will all the pleasures prove°	*test, try out*
That valleys, groves, hills, and fields,	
Woods, or steepy mountain yields.	
And we will sit upon the rocks,	5
Seeing the shepherds feed their flocks,	
By shallow rivers to whose falls	
Melodious birds sing madrigals.	
And I will make thee beds of roses	
And a thousand fragrant posies,	10
A cap of flowers, and a kirtle°	*long dress*
Embroidered all with leaves of myrtle;	
A gown made of the finest wool	
Which from our pretty lambs we pull;	
Fair lined slippers for the cold,	15
With buckles of the purest gold;	
A belt of straw and ivy buds,	
With coral clasps and amber studs;	
And if these pleasures may thee move,	
Come live with me, and be my love.	20
The shepherds' swains° shall dance and sing	*lovers*
For thy delight each May morning:	
If these delights thy mind may move,	
Then live with me and be my love.	

QUESTIONS

1. Describe the speaker. What does he do? What is he like? What does he want?

2. Who is the listener? What is the relationship between speaker and listener?

3. What sort of life does the speaker offer the listener?
4. What is the speaker's understanding of reality?

JOYCE CAROL OATES (b. 1938)

For a photo, see Chapter 2, page 150.

Loving (1970)

A balloon of gauze around us,
sheerest gauze: it is a balloon of skin
around us, fine light-riddled skin,
invisible.

5   If we reach out to pinch its walls it floats from us—
it eludes us wetly, this sac.

It is warmed by a network of veins
fine as hairs and invisible.
The veins pulsate and expand to the width
10 of eyelashes.
In them blood floats weightless as color.
The warm walls sink upon us when we love
each other, and are blinded by the heavier skin
that closes over our eyes.

15 We are in here together.
Outside, people are walking in a landscape—
it is a city landscape, it is theirs.
Their shouts and laughter come to us in broken sounds.
Their strides take them everywhere in daylight.
20 If they turn suddenly toward us we draw back—
the skin shudders wetly, finely—
will we be torn into two people?

The balloon will grow up around us again
as if breathed out of us, moist and sticky and light
25 as skin, more perfect than our own skin,
invisible.

QUESTIONS

1. What does the speaker mean by a "balloon of gauze around us"? How does she define this balloon? What does she mean by "We are in here together" (line 15)?
2. Why does the speaker refer to veins and blood and "warm walls" in discussing the subject of loving? How common are these references to love? How appropriate is the language?

3. How would you characterize the speaker's attitudes about love? To what does the final stanza refer?

SIR WALTER RALEGH (1552–1618)

 ## The Nymph's Reply to the Shepherd (1600)

If all the world and love were young,
And truth in every shepherd's tongue,
These pretty pleasures might me move
To live with thee and be thy love.

Time drives the flocks from field to fold°   *fenced field*   5
When rivers rage and rocks grow cold,
And Philomel° becometh dumb;   *the nightingale*
The rest complains of cares to come.

The flowers do fade, and wanton fields
To wayward winter reckoning yields;   10
A honey tongue, a heart of gall,
Is fancy's spring, but sorrow's fall.

Thy gowns, thy shoes, thy beds of roses,
Thy cap, thy kirtle,° and thy posies°   *long dress; flowers and poems*
Soon break, soon wither, soon forgotten—   15
In folly ripe, in reason rotten.

Thy belt of straw and ivy buds,
Thy coral clasps and amber studs,
All these in me no means can move
To come to thee and be thy love.   20

But could youth last and love still° breed,   *always*
Had joys no date nor age no need,
Then these delights my mind might move
To live with thee and be thy love.

QUESTIONS

1. Who is the speaker? What do we learn about the speaker? Who is the listener?
2. How are the ideas of love and the world in this poem different from those in Marlowe's poem?
3. To what extent is this poem a parody (an imitation that makes fun) of Marlowe's poem? To what extent is it a refutation of Marlowe's poem?
4. Determine the steps of the speaker's logical argument in this poem.

CHRISTINA ROSSETTI (1830–1894)

 A Christmas Carol (1872)

In the bleak mid-winter
   Frosty wind made moan,
Earth stood hard as iron,
   Water like a stone;
5 Snow had fallen, snow on snow,
   Snow on snow,
In the bleak mid-winter
   Long ago.

Our God, Heaven cannot hold Him
10   Nor earth sustain;
Heaven and earth shall flee away
   When He comes to reign:
In the bleak mid-winter
   A stable-place sufficed°   *see Luke 2:7*
15 The Lord God Almighty
   Jesus Christ.

Enough for Him whom cherubim
   Worship night and day,
A breastful of milk
20   And a mangerful of hay;
Enough for Him whom angels
   Fall down before,
The ox and ass and camel
   Which adore.

25 Angels and archangels
   May have gathered there,
Cherubim and seraphim
   Throng'd the air,
But only His mother
30   In her maiden bliss
Worshipped the Beloved
   With a kiss.

What can I give Him,
   Poor as I am?
35 If I were a shepherd°   *see Luke 2:8–20*
   I would bring a lamb,
If I were a wise man°   *see Matthew 2:1–12*
   I would do my part,—
Yet what I can I give Him,
40   Give my heart.

QUESTIONS

1. Why does Rossetti stress the bitterness and bleakness of the winter setting in this poem?

2. Why does the speaker stress the simplicity of the birthplace of "The Lord God Almighty"? What is the origin and tradition of this setting?

3. How does the fourth stanza prepare you for the speaker's description of her own condition in the fifth stanza?

4. How are the objects considered gifts by the speaker a part of the setting traditionally associated with the birth of Jesus? How does the speaker's gift reveal her character and condition?

JANE SHORE (b. 1947)

 ### A Letter Sent to Summer (1977)

Oh summer if you would only come
with your big baskets of flowers,
dropping by like an old friend
just passing through the neighborhood!

5   If you came to my door disguised
as a thirsty biblical angel
I'd buy all your hairbrushes and magazines!
I'd be more hospitable
than any ancient king.

10   I'd personally carry your luggage in,
Your monsoons. Your squadrons of bugs,
Your plums and lovely melons.
Let the rose let out its long long sigh
And Desire return to the hapless rabbit.

15   This request is also in my own behalf.
Inside my head it is always snowing,
even when I sleep. When I wake up,
and still you have not arrived,
I curl back into my blizzard of linens.

20   Not like winter's buckets of whitewash.
Please wallpaper my bedroom
with leafy vegetables and farms.
If you knocked right now,
I would not interfere.
25   Start near the window.
Start right here.

QUESTIONS

1. Describe the speaker. What do you learn about her and how she is responding to the time of year?

2. Describe what summer means to the speaker. What attributes does she give to summer? What contrasts are brought out by references to "bugs" and "monsoons" in addition to "plums" and "the rose"?

3. What does the phrase "always snowing" contribute to your understanding of the speaker's yearning for summer?

WILLIAM WORDSWORTH (1770–1850)

For a portrait, see Chapter 12, page 678.

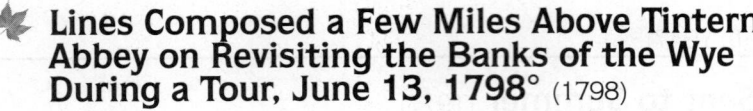

Lines Composed a Few Miles Above Tintern Abbey on Revisiting the Banks of the Wye During a Tour, June 13, 1798° (1798)

Five years have past; five summers, with the length
Of five long winters! and again I hear
These waters, rolling from their mountain-springs
With a soft inland murmur.—Once again
5   Do I behold these steep and lofty cliffs,
That on a wild secluded scene impress
Thoughts of more deep seclusion, and connect
The landscape with the quiet of the sky.
The day is come when I again repose

10 Here, under this dark sycamore, and view
These plots of cottage-ground, these orchard-tufts,
Which at this season, with their unripe fruits,
Are clad in one green hue, and lose themselves
'Mid groves and copses. Once again I see
15 These hedge-rows, hardly hedge-rows, little lines
Of sportive wood run wild; these pastoral farms,
Green to the very door; and wreaths of smoke
Sent up, in silence, from among the trees!
With some uncertain notice, as might seem
20 Of vagrant dwellers in the houseless woods,
Or of some Hermit's cave, where by his fire
The Hermit sits alone.
                         These beauteous forms,
Through a long absence, have not been to me
As is a landscape to a blind man's eye:
25 But oft, in lonely rooms, and 'mid the din
Of towns and cities, I have owed to them
In hours of weariness, sensations sweet,
Felt in the blood, and felt along the heart;
And passing even into my purer mind,
30 With tranquil restoration:—feelings too
Of unremembered pleasure: such, perhaps,
As have no slight or trivial influence

°Wordsworth first visited the valley of the Wye in southwest England in August 1793 at age twenty-three. On this second visit he was accompanied by his sister Dorothy (the "Friend" in line 115).

On that best portion of a good man's life,
His little, nameless, unremembered acts
Of kindness and of love. Nor less, I trust,   35
To them I may have owed another gift,
Of aspect more sublime; that blessed mood,
In which the burden of the mystery,
In which the heavy and the weary weight
Of all this unintelligible world,   40
Is lightened:—that serene and blessed mood,
In which the affections gently lead us on,—
Until, the breath of this corporeal frame
And even the motion of our human blood
Almost suspended, we are laid asleep   45
In body, and become a living soul:
While with an eye made quiet by the power
Of harmony, and the deep power of joy,
We see into the life of things.
                                        If this
Be but a vain belief, yet, oh!—how oft—   50
In darkness and amid the many shapes
Of joyless daylight; when the fretful stir
Unprofitable, and the fever of the world,
Have hung upon the beatings of my heart—
How oft, in spirit, have I turned to thee,   55
O sylvan Wye! thou wanderer thro' the woods,
How often has my spirit turned to thee!
And now, with gleams of half extinguished thought,
With many recognitions dim and faint,
    And somewhat of a sad perplexity,   60
The picture of the mind revives again:
While here I stand, not only with the sense
Of present pleasure, but with pleasing thoughts
That in this moment there is life and food
For future years. And so I dare to hope,   65
Though changed, no doubt, from what I was when first
I came among these hills; when like a roe
I bounded o'er the mountains, by the sides
Of the deep rivers, and the lonely streams,
Wherever nature led: more like a man   70
Flying from something that he dreads, than one
Who sought the thing he loved. For nature then
(The coarser pleasures of my boyish days,
And their glad animal movements all gone by)
To me was all in all.—I cannot paint   75
What then I was. The sounding cataract
Haunted me like a passion: the tall rock,
The mountain, and the deep and gloomy wood,
Their colours, and their forms, were then to me
An appetite; a feeling and a love,   80
That had no need of a remoter charm,
By thought supplied, nor any interest

Unborrowed from the eye.—That time is past,
And all its aching joys are now no more,
85   And all its dizzy raptures. Not for this
Faint I, nor mourn nor murmur; other gifts
Have followed; for such loss, I would believe,
Abundant recompense. For I have learned
To look on nature, not as in the hour
90   Of thoughtless youth; but hearing oftentimes
The still, sad music of humanity,
Nor harsh nor grating, though of ample power
To chasten and subdue. And I have felt
A presence that disturbs me with the joy
95   Of elevated thoughts; a sense sublime
Of something far more deeply interfused,
Whose dwelling is the light of setting suns,
And the round ocean, and the living air,
And the blue sky, and in the mind of man;
100 A motion and a spirit, that impels
All thinking things, all objects of all thought,
And rolls through all things. Therefore am I still
A lover of the meadows and the woods,
And mountains; and of all that we behold
105 From this green earth; of all the mighty world
Of eye, and ear,—both what they half create,
And what perceive; well pleased to recognize
In nature and the language of the sense,
The anchor of my purest thoughts, the nurse,
110 The guide, the guardian of my heart, and soul
Of all my moral being.
                                    Nor perchance,
If I were not thus taught, should I the more
Suffer my genial spirits to decay:
For thou art with me here upon the banks
115 Of this fair river; thou my dearest Friend,
My dear, dear Friend; and in thy voice I catch
The language of my former heart, and read
My former pleasures in the shooting lights
Of thy wild eyes. Oh! yet a little while
120 May I behold in thee what I was once,
My dear, dear Sister! and this prayer I make,
Knowing that Nature never did betray
The heart that loved her; 'tis her privilege,
Through all the years of this our life, to lead
125 From joy to joy: for she can so inform
The mind that is within us, so impress
With quietness and beauty, and so feed
With lofty thoughts, that neither evil tongues,
Rash judgments, nor the sneers of selfish men,
130 Nor greetings where no kindness is, nor all
The dreary intercourse of daily life,
Shall e'er prevail against us, or disturb
Our cheerful faith that all which we behold

Is full of blessings. Therefore let the moon
Shine on thee in thy solitary walk;
And let the misty mountain-winds be free   135
To blow against thee: and, in after years,
When these wild ecstasies shall be matured
Into a sober pleasure; when thy mind
Shall be a mansion for all lovely forms,
Thy memory be as a dwelling-place   140
For all sweet sounds and harmonies; oh! then,
If solitude, or fear, or pain, or grief,
Should be thy portion, with what healing thoughts
Of tender joy wilt thou remember me,
And these my exhortations! Nor, perchance—   145
If I should be where I no more can hear
Thy voice, nor catch from thy wild eyes these gleams
Of past existence—wilt thou then forget
That on the banks of this delightful stream
We stood together; and that I, so long   150
A worshipper of Nature, hither came
Unwearied in that service: rather say
With warmer love—oh! with far deeper zeal
Of holier love. Nor wilt thou then forget,
That after many wanderings, many years   155
Of absence, these steep woods and lofty cliffs,
And this green pastoral landscape, were to me
More dear, both for themselves and for thy sake!

QUESTIONS

1. What is the opening scene, and what meaning does the poet ascribe to it?
2. To the speaker, what is the relationship of remembered scenes and the growth of moral behavior?
3. What effect does the speaker believe the present will have on his future?
4. In lines 93–111, how successfully does the speaker make concrete his ideas about moral forces?
5. What is the power that the speaker attributes to nature? What is the "cheerful faith" of lines 133–134?

JAMES WRIGHT (1927–1980)

 A Blessing (1963)

Just off the highway to Rochester, Minnesota,
Twilight bounds softly forth on the grass.
And the eyes of those two Indian ponies
Darken with kindness.
They have come gladly out of the willows
To welcome my friend and me.   5
We step over the barbed wire into the pasture
Where they have been grazing all day, alone.
They ripple tensely, they can hardly contain their happiness

10   That we have come.
      They bow shyly as wet swans. They love each other.
      There is no loneliness like theirs.
      At home once more,
      They begin munching the young tufts of spring in the darkness.
15   I would like to hold the slenderer one in my arms.
      For she has walked over to me
      And nuzzled my left hand.
      She is black and white,
      Her mane falls wild on her forehead,
20   And the light breeze moves me to caress her long ear
      That is delicate as the skin over a girl's wrist.
      Suddenly I realize
      That if I stepped out of my body I would break
      Into blossom.

QUESTIONS

1. What has happened just before the poem opens? Account for the poet's use of the present tense in his descriptions.
2. Is the setting specific or general? What happens as the poem progresses?
3. What realization overtakes the speaker? How does this realization constitute a "blessing," and what does it show about his character?
4. Why is it necessary for the poet to include all the detail of the first twenty-one lines before the realization of the last three?

WRITING ABOUT CHARACTER AND SETTING IN POETRY

Writing about character and setting involves many of the same considerations whether you deal with prose fiction or poetry. You might therefore review the material on character presented in Chapter 3. However, there are some important differences between the two writing tasks. One of these is the way you find out about characters. In prose fiction, you can usually judge a character by the details about his or her actions, words, thoughts, appearance, and opinions. In poetry, the speaker is less likely to provide full details. Consequently, many conclusions must be inferred from the speaker's suggestions and hints.

Another difference between fiction and poetry concerns the types of character. Fiction presents a broad range of writing options: You may write about the protagonist, the antagonist, the narrator, or any of the incidental characters. In poetry you are usually limited to the speaker or to one of the characters described by the speaker (although you may sometimes be able to discuss the listener, too). In writing about Browning's "My Last Duchess," for example, you learn enough about both the duke and the duchess to write about either.

In planning and prewriting, you should determine as much as you can about the characters and their relationship to their situations—that is, to the action, emotion, ideas, setting, and other characters. Answering the following questions will help you to focus your ideas.

Questions for Discovering Ideas

ABOUT THE SPEAKER

- Who is the speaker? What is he or she doing? What does he or she say about himself or herself? About others?
- What conclusions can you draw about occurrences involving the speaker that took place before the poem begins?
- How reliable is the speaker as an observer and reporter? What knowledge enables the speaker to make judgments and opinions?
- What do the speaker's word choices reveal about his or her education and social standing? How does the language reveal his or her assumptions?
- What tone of voice is suggested in the speaker's presentation?
- How deeply is the speaker involved with the action of the poem? What connection does she or he make with the other characters? With the poem's actions?

ABOUT OTHER CHARACTERS

- How vividly does the poem describe action, appearance, emotions, responses, and ideas? How strong a picture do you get of any other character (characters)?
- How does each significant character respond to the surroundings described and implied in the poem?
- What is the character trying to gain or learn?
- How is the character affected by others, and how do others respond to her or to him?
- What degree of control does the character exert, and what does his or her effort tell you?
- How does the character speak and behave, and what do you learn from these words and actions?

Strategies for Organizing Ideas

When you write about a single character, formulate a central idea that focuses on his or her personality or status. If you are writing about the duke in Browning's "My Last Duchess," for example, your idea might be that he is arrogant, cruel, greedy, and power-mad. In writing about Sir Patrick Spens (Chapter 11), your idea would likely be about his self-sacrificing fidelity to the king. If the topic is a set of characters, the central idea should express a relationship or commonality among them. Thus the speaker of Lowell's "Memories of West Street and Lepke" suggests that his own presence in the "tranquillized Fifties" is not dissimilar to the "sheepish calm" of Lepke as he remembers him; and the characters described in Blake's "London" illustrate the withering effects of discriminatory law and religion.

Consider organizing your essay along the lines of one of the following approaches:

1. *Character as revealed by action.* Often the speaker describes himself or herself as a major character or major mover. What does the action reveal about this speaker? In Gray's "Elegy Written in a Country Churchyard," the speaker enters the churchyard at sunset, and his action causes him to think of life, glory, fame, fortune, and religious dedication. What do his speculations and conclusions reveal about his character? In Shore's "A Letter Sent to Summer," the speaker indicates that she would be willing to buy "hairbrushes and magazines" from Summer. What does this proposed action demonstrate?

In a parallel way, the speaker of Glück's "Snowdrops" is a newly animated early spring flower, the snowdrop, that has undergone a rebirth of life following the seeming death by burial in the earth during winter's cold. In addition, if we read the poem as a representation of human life, we may accept the speaker as a person describing recovery and renewal after an episode of great difficulty or depression corresponding to the cold and snow of winter. The poem's words describing the death and rebirth are "suppressing," "remembering," "earth," and "damp earth." What do these words, and the use of the words "yes risk joy" near the poem's end, indicate about the speaker's character and her relationship with the cyclical patterns of nature?

2. *Character as revealed by interaction.* Poems based in a dramatic situation yield best to this treatment. Browning's "My Last Duchess" (this chapter) is a fine example, as are Hardy's "Channel Firing" (Chapter 14) and Jonson's "Drink to Me, Only, with Thine Eyes" (this chapter). The situation in Arnold's "Dover Beach" is that the speaker is talking directly to a listener who is deeply close to him, his "love." What does the speaker's attitude toward the listener reveal about his character? In this and other poems, what do you learn about relationships and how they have affected the poetic characters?

3. *Character as revealed by circumstance or setting.* The essay based on the interrelationship of character and setting assumes that time, place, artifacts, money, family, culture, and history influence character and motivation, and also that individual and collective traits are developed as people try to control their surroundings. For instance, the speaker of Wright's "A Blessing" describes the thrill of becoming a witness of a roadside pasture, and at the end of the poem he feels as though he is about to "break / Into blossom." What enables him to reach this joyful conclusion? Why does he feel safe rather than frightened? Why does he believe in the benevolence of the two ponies, and, in turn, why do the ponies treat him with affection? What aspects of character enable him to step over the barbed wire without fear and to believe that the experience is really a "blessing"? Would such an experience have been possible at a more suspicious, less civilized time, when people stepping uninvited onto property might have been considered intruders and peppered with buckshot? In short, how has setting in the broadest sense merged with the speaker's character?

In dealing with the interrelationship of character and external situation, you might be able to organize the body of your essay by relying on certain aspects of the setting. Thus you might select the details about past, present, and future time in Gray's "Elegy Written in a Country Churchyard." Similarly, the details about the roaring surf and the dim lights in Arnold's "Dover Beach" can provide thematic links for a discussion of the speaker's sense of alienation, loss, and dedication. In such ways, you may use aspects of setting not only as topics to shed light on character but also to guide and shape your essay.

Whatever strategy you choose, remember that the organization of your essay will finally be determined by your poem. Each poem suggests its own avenues of exploration, directing your thought and organization.

In your conclusion you might summarize your major points about the character or characters, or you might tie your ideas into an assessment of the poem as a whole. Thus, you might briefly discuss the connection between character and character, character and environment, character and death, character and greed, character and love, and so on, and deal with these topics generally as you write your final sentences.

Illustrative Student Essay

Underlined sentences in this paper *do not* conform to MLA style and are used solely as teaching tools to emphasize the central idea, thesis sentence, and topic sentences throughout the paper.

Yen 1

Irene Yen

Prof. Rosen

English 103

21 November 2008

The Character of the Duke in Browning's "My Last Duchess"°

In this dramatic monologue, Browning skillfully develops the character of [1] his speaker, who holds the high position of Duke of Ferrara (in Italy) during the sixteenth century, a period of aristocratic absolutism. Because the duke is at the top of the political and social mountain, he exerts absolute control, whether for good or for bad. Browning's Duke is bad, and he is not just bad, but he is totally evil.* He reveals this evil in his one-way conversation with the listener, who is an envoy of a less powerful aristocrat, the count, whose daughter the

°This poem appears on page 697.
*Central idea.

Yen 2

Duke is claiming in marriage. The Duke's evil character is brought out by his indulgence in power, his intimidation of others, his manipulation of his dead wife, and his general contempt for others.†

[2]   The Duke's indulgence in power, the basis of his evil, is apparent in his use of indirect speech. On the surface, Browning makes him seem intelligent, civilized, and friendly. The Duke begins speaking by pointing out to his listener the beauty of a painting of his "last Duchess," but his entire speech--comprising the entire poem--reveals the horror of his self-indulgence. His indirect but threatening description of how he treated the duchess shows that he delights in evil. When he says "I gave commands; / Then all smiles stopped together" (lines 45–46), he is actually bragging about how he had the duchess killed. He is coldly horrible, the more so because he masks his evil with quiet words and a love of good art.

[3]   The Duke's intimidation of others is another of his horrible qualities. Early in the poem it seems that he is doing no more than telling about his dead wife, but the poem makes clear that he is intimidating both his listener--the Count's envoy--and also the Count, the listener's master. The last nine lines (48–56) indicate that his uninterrupted monologue should have been a dialogue in which he should have been negotiating the terms for the dowry he is to receive from the Count. The fact that he has talked only about how he got rid of his "last Duchess" shows his arrogance. Thus, there is no mention of dowry until lines 48–53, when the duke states that he will make a "just pretense" for a dowry which of course the Count will honor (for "just pretense," read a demand for all the Count's money and land). In addition, the Duke's commands, "Will't please you rise? We'll meet / The company below, then," indicate that the negotiation that never began is now over and that the envoy is totally in his power. This is intimidation of the most ruthless and inhuman sort.

[4]   The Duke's evil nature is also brought out in his description of the Duchess. If we study his words to determine what the Duchess was really like, we conclude that she was even-tempered and pleasant to all--the soul of graciousness and courtesy. In fact, it would be hard to say that she was anything

†Thesis sentence.

but perfect. But the Duke, rather than indicating pleasure with her, states that she was ungrateful because she was not submissive enough to him. He complains that the smile she gave to others was the same as the smile she gave to him (it probably was not; we may conclude that her smile to him probably covered fear):

> Oh sir, she smiled, no doubt,
>
> Whene'er I passed her; but who passed without
>
> Much the same smile? (lines 43–45)

These lines show that the Duke is a manipulator and that the poor Duchess was in an impossible situation. Very likely he would have complained also if she had smiled only at him and not at others--thereby leaving herself open to the Duke's perverted judgment that she did not show the graciousness toward others that he expected from his wife. No matter how good she was, there was no way for her to have pleased him. He would have manipulated her into an unfavorable position that would have justified his giving the "commands" to remove her.

Perhaps the worst of this monster's traits is the contempt he shows for people by thinking of them not as human beings but rather as things. Most notable is the way he thinks of the Duchess; he calls her painting a "piece" (line 3) to hang on a wall, looking "as if she were alive" (line 2). He does not even name her, or recognize her humanity by calling her "the *late* Duchess," and he speaks about the bronze statue of Neptune "taming a sea horse" (line 55) as being equal to her. This same contempt for people is shown in his claim that his interest in the Count's daughter is the "fair daughter's self" (line 52), while the rest of the poem makes clear that he wants only wealth and power out of the new marriage. Oddly, also, he seems to think of himself less as a person than as a "nine-hundred-years-old name" (line 33), and it is this intangible distinction that he prizes above his own humanity. In other words, he views even himself with contempt. [5]

Browning's Duke, then, is a person with absolute power but without the kindness and understanding to use it for anyone but himself. His complaints [6]

Yen 4

about the dead Duchess are meaningless, for they are no more than pretexts for
cruel self-indulgence. He is at the top of the power structure, and therefore he is
able to do what he wants without reprisal. People must defer to him and obey
him, but only because he makes everyone afraid. His intimidation, his
manipulation, his lust for power--all govern him, and leave him unable to look
at human beings as anything more than pawns in his game for control. He is an
example of the saying that absolute power corrupts absolutely, and his character
is therefore a frightening portrait of evil.

Yen 5

Work Cited

Browning, Robert. "My Last Duchess." Literature: An Introduction to Reading
and Writing. Ed. Edgar V. Roberts. 9th ed. New York: Pearson Longman,
2009. 697–98.

Commentary on the Essay

Because the subject of the discussion, the Duke, is the speaker, the essay is based
partially on details presented by him, but it is also partially based on interpretations. The principal subject matter is the interaction of the Duke and the subject of
the poem—the "last Duchess"—in addition to his interaction with the listener,
who is a representative of an inferior aristocrat, and whom he therefore treats with
contempt. Elements of setting are also introduced to illuminate the Duke's character: his works of art, his absolute power, his pride in his name and title, and his
wealth. The essay thus illustrates how character can be analyzed with reference to
(1) interactions between persons and persons and also (2) the connections of persons with their surroundings.

The central idea is that the Duke is evil. This point is made in paragraph 1,
with sufficient accompanying detail to explain that the Duke's position enables
him to exercise absolute power. Paragraph 2 discloses that indulgence in power is
one of his primary evil traits, while paragraphs 3, 4, and 5 bring out habits of intimidation, manipulation, and contempt. The final paragraph summarizes but

also asserts that the Duke's justifications for killing his wife are irrelevant to his real motives of greed and lust for power.

As the essay develops, transitions are effected by words such as "another," "also," "worst," and "then." The assertions in the essay are supported by references to specific details from the poem, quotations from the poem (with line numbers noted), and interpretations of details.

Writing Topics About Character and Setting in Poetry

1. Write an essay comparing the speakers of the "passionate shepherd" poems (by Marlowe, Ralegh, and Lewis). How are the speakers alike, and how are they different? How do their words and references indicate their characters? How do the speakers influence your judgments of the poems in which they appear?

2. Write an essay discussing the relationships between location, thought, and character as asserted in the poems by Arnold, Blake, Cowper, Hardy, and Shore. What importance do place and time have on the development of character? How do responses to time, historical period, and place influence ideas about how to live?

3. Consider Gray's "Elegy Written in a Country Churchyard," Rossetti's "A Christmas Carol," and Wright's "A Blessing" as poems embodying a type or types of religious experience. What common or similar circumstances occasion the religious reflections in the poems? What common ideas and conclusions do the poems express? Describe the nature of the speakers and discuss the ways in which their observations illustrate their qualities. What philosophical or sectarian differences do you find? On the basis of your study, explain typical patterns of religious experience. (For ideas about how to approach this topic, you may wish to consult Chapter 30 and also the section titled "Archetypal Criticism" in Chapter 29.)

4. Compare Laux's "The Life of Trees" and Brewster's "Where I Come From" as poems demonstrating the bearing that location and the world of nature have upon human character.

5. Write a short poem, biographical or autobiographical, showing how a certain time, place, or experience has shaped a present quality of character and/or a certain decision about life, friendships, and goals.

6. Use your library resources to locate two university press books about Robert Browning. Analyze the extent to which they discuss Browning's use of dramatic monologue. With the aid of what you discover, write a brief essay on Browning's use of the dramatic monologue as a means of disclosing character.

Chapter 14

Imagery: The Poem's Link to the Senses

In literature, **imagery** refers to words that trigger your imagination to recall and recombine images—memories or mental pictures of sights, sounds, tastes, smells, sensations of touch, and motions. The process is active and even vigorous, for when words or descriptions produce images, you are using your personal experiences with life and language to help you understand the works you are reading. In effect, you are re-creating the work *in your own way* through the controlled stimulation produced by the writer's words. Imagery is therefore one of the strongest modes of literary expression because it provides a channel to your active imagination, and along this channel, writers bring their works directly to you and into your consciousness.

For example, reading the word *lake* may bring to your mind your literal memory of a particular lake. Your mental picture—or image—may be a distant view of calm waters reflecting blue sky, a nearby view of gentle waves rippling in the wind, a close-up view of the sandy lake bottom from a boat, or an overhead view of a sun-drenched shoreline. Similarly, the words *rose, apple, hot dog, malted milk,* and *pizza* all cause you to recollect these objects, and, in addition, may cause you to recall their smells and tastes. Active and graphic words like *row, swim,* and *dive* stimulate you to picture moving images of someone performing these actions.

Responses and the Writer's Use of Detail

In studying imagery, we try to comprehend and explain our imaginative reconstruction of the pictures and impressions evoked by the work's images. We let the poet's words simmer and percolate in our minds. To get our imaginations stirring, we might follow a description by Samuel Taylor Coleridge in lines 37–41 of "Kubla Khan."

> A damsel with a dulcimer
> In a vision once I saw:
> It was an Abyssinian maid,
> And on her dulcimer she played
> Singing of Mount Abora.

We do not read about the color of the young woman's clothing or learn anything else about her appearance except that she is playing a stringed instrument, a dulcimer, and that she is singing a song about a mountain in a foreign, remote land. But Coleridge's image is enough. From it we can visualize a vivid, exotic picture of a young woman from a distant land singing, together with impressions of the loveliness of her song (even though we never hear it or understand it). The image lives.

The Relationship of Imagery to Ideas and Attitudes

Images do more than elicit impressions. By the *authenticating* effects of the vision and perceptions underlying them, they give you new ways of seeing the world and of strengthening your old ways of seeing it. Shakespeare, in Sonnet 116: "Let Me Not to the Marriage of True Minds" (Chapter 18), develops the idea that love provides people with consistency of purpose in their lives. Rather than stating the idea directly, he uses images of a landmark or lighthouse and also of a fixed star—sights with which we as his readers are familiar.

> . . . it [love] is an ever fixéd mark
> That looks on tempests and is never shaken;
> It is the star to every wandering bark°   boat, ship
> Whose worth's unknown, although his° height be taken.   its

These images form a link with readers that is clear and also verifiable by observation. Such uses of imagery comprise one of the strongest means by which writers reinforce ideas.

In addition, as you form mental pictures and impressions from a poet's images, you respond with appropriate attitudes and feelings. Thus the phrase "Beside the lake, beneath the trees," from Wordsworth's poem "Daffodils" (Chapter 12) prompts both the visualization of a wooded lakeshore and the related pleasantness of outdoor relaxation and happiness. A contrasting visualization is to be found in Hubert von Herkomer's painting *Hard Times* (p. I–6), in which all the images—the tired faces, the heavy load, the tools, the bleak road, the leafless trees—point toward the harsh life of the worker and his family, causing a response of sadness and sympathy. By using such imagery, artists and poets create sensory vividness, and they also influence and control our attitudes as readers.

Types of Imagery

Visual Imagery Is the Language of Sight

Human beings are visual. Sight is the most significant of our senses, for it is the key to our remembrance of other sense impressions. Therefore, the most frequently occurring literary imagery is to things we can visualize either exactly or approximately—**visual images.** In the three-stanza poem "Cargoes," John Masefield creates mental pictures or images of oceangoing merchant vessels from three periods of human history.

JOHN MASEFIELD (1878–1967)

 ## Cargoes (1902)

Quinquireme° of Nineveh° from distant Ophir,°
Rowing home to haven in sunny Palestine,
   With a cargo of ivory,
   And apes and peacocks,°
5 Sandalwood, cedarwood,° and sweet white wine.

Stately Spanish galleon coming from the Isthmus,°
Dipping through the Tropics by the palm-green shores,
   With a cargo of diamonds,
   Emeralds, amethysts,
10 Topazes, and cinnamon, and gold moidores.°

Dirty British coaster with a salt-caked smoke stack,
Butting through the Channel in the mad March days,
   With a cargo of Tyne coal,°
   Road-rails, pig-lead,
15 Firewood, iron-ware, and cheap tin trays.

°1 *quinquereme*: the largest of the ancient warships, although no wrecks have survived from antiquity. Very likely a quinquereme was powered by three tiers of oars and was named "quinquereme" because five men operated each vertical oar station. The top two oars were each taken by two men, while one man alone took the bottom oar. *Nineveh*: the capital of ancient Assyria, and an "exceeding great city" (Jonah 3:3). *Ophir*: Ophir probably was in Africa and was known for its gold (1 Kings 10:22; 1 Chron. 29:4). Masefield quotes from some of the biblical verses in his first stanza. 4 *apes and peacocks*: 1 Kings 10:22, and 2 Chron. 9:21. 5 *cedarwood*: 1 Kings 9:11. 6. *Isthmus*: the Isthmus of Panama. 10 *moidores*: coins used in Portugal and Brazil at the time the New World was being explored. 13 *Tyne coal*: coal from Newcastle upon Tyne, in northern England, proverbial for its coal production.

QUESTIONS

1. Consider the images of life during three periods of history: ancient Israel at the time of Solomon (c. 950 BCE), sixteenth-century Spain, and modern England. What do these images tell you about Masefield's interpretation of modern commercial life?
2. To what senses do most of the images refer (e.g., sight, taste)?
3. The poem contains no complete sentences. Why do you think Masefield included only verbals ("rowing," "dipping," "butting") to begin the second line of each stanza, rather than finite verbs?
4. In historical reality, the quinquereme was likely rowed by slaves, and the Spanish galleon likely carried riches stolen from Central American natives. How might these unpleasant details affect the impressions otherwise achieved in the first two stanzas?

Masefield's images are vivid as they stand and need no further amplification. For us to reconstruct them imaginatively, we do not need ever to have seen the ancient biblical lands or waters, or ever to have seen or handled the cheap commodities on a modern merchant ship. We have seen enough in our lives to *imagine* places and objects like these, and hence Masefield is successful in fixing his visual images in our minds.

Auditory Imagery Is the Language of Sound

Auditory images trigger our experiences with sound. For such images, let us consider Wilfred Owen's "Anthem for Doomed Youth," which is about the death of soldiers in warfare and the sorrow of their loved ones.

WILFRED OWEN (1893–1918)

 Anthem for Doomed Youth (1920)

What passing-bells° for these who die as cattle?
Only the monstrous anger of the guns.
Only the stuttering rifles' rapid rattle
Can patter out their hasty orisons.°   *prayers*
No mockeries for them from prayers or bells,   5
Nor any voice of mourning save the choirs—
The shrill, demented choirs of wailing shells;
And bugles calling for them from sad shires.°

What candles may be held to speed them all?
Not in the hands of boys, but in their eyes   10
Shall shine the holy glimmers of good-byes.
The pallor of girls' brows shall be their pall;
Their flowers the tenderness of patient minds,
And each slow dusk a drawing-down of blinds.

°1 *passing-bells:* church bells tolling upon the entry of a funeral cortege into a church cemetery. 8 *shires:* British counties.

QUESTIONS

1. What type of imagery predominates in the first eight lines? How does the imagery change in the last six lines?

2. Contrast the images of death at home and death on the battlefield. How does this contrast affect your experience and understanding of the poem?

3. Consider these images: "holy glimmers of good-byes," "pallor of girls' brows," "patient minds," "drawing-down of blinds." What relationship do the people defined by these images have to the doomed youth?

The poem begins with the question of "What passing-bells" may be tolled "for these who die as cattle." Owen's speaker is referring to the traditional tolling of a church bell to announce a burial. The images of these ceremonial sounds suggest a period of peace and order, when there is time to pay respect to the dead. But the poem points out that the only sound for those who have fallen in battle is the "rapid rattle" of "stuttering" rifles—not the solemn, dignified sounds of peace but the horrifying noises of war. Owen's auditory images evoke corresponding sounds in our imaginations, and they help us to experience the poem and to hate the uncivilized depravity of war.

Olfactory, Gustatory, and Tactile Imagery Refers to Smell, Taste, and Touch

In addition to sight and sound, you will find images from the other senses: smell, taste, and touch. Shakespeare includes an **olfactory image** of sweet perfumes in Sonnet 130: "My Mistress' Eyes Are Nothing Like the Sun," and the odor of roses is suggested in Burns's "A Red, Red Rose" (Chapter 15) and in Shelley's "Music, when soft voices die" (Chapter 11).

Gustatory images are also common, though less frequent than those referring to sight and sound. Lines 5 and 10 of Masefield's "Cargoes," for example, include images of "sweet white wine" and "cinnamon." Although the poem refers to these commodities as cargoes, the words themselves also register in our minds as gustatory images because they evoke our sense of taste.

Images of touch and texture—**tactile images**—are not as common, because touch is difficult to render except in terms of effects. The speaker of Amy Lowell's "Patterns" (Chapter 22), for example, uses tactile imagery when imagining a never-to-happen embrace with her fiancé, who we learn has been killed on a wartime battlefield. Her imagery in lines 51–52 records the effect of the embrace ("bruised"), whereas her internalized feelings are expressed in metaphors ("aching, melting"):

> And the buttons of his waistcoat bruised my body as he clasped me
> Aching, melting, unafraid.

Tactile images are not uncommon in love poetry, where references to touch and feeling are natural.

Kinetic and Kinesthetic Imagery Refers to Motion and Activity

References to movement are also images. Images of general motion are **kinetic** (remember that *motion pictures* may be called "cinema"; note the closeness of *kine* in *kinetic* and *cine* in *cinema*), whereas the term **kinesthetic** is applied to human or animal movement. Imagery of motion is closely related to visual images, for motion is most often seen. Masefield's "British coaster" is a visual image, but when it goes "Butting through the channel," this reference to motion makes it also kinetic. When Hardy's skeletons sit upright at the beginning of "Channel Firing," the image is **kinesthetic,** as is the action of Lowell's speaker in "Patterns," walking in the garden after hearing about her fiancé's death. Both types are seen at the conclusion of the following poem, Elizabeth Bishop's "The Fish."

ELIZABETH BISHOP (1911–1979)

 ### The Fish (1946)

I caught a tremendous fish
and held him beside the boat
half out of water, with my hook
fast in a corner of his mouth.

He didn't fight.   5
He hadn't fought at all.
He hung a grunting weight,
battered and venerable
and homely. Here and there
his brown skin hung in strips   10
like ancient wallpaper,
and its pattern of darker brown
was like wallpaper:
shapes like full-blown roses
stained and lost through age.   15
He was speckled with barnacles,
fine rosettes of lime,
and infested
with tiny white sea-lice,
and underneath two or three   20
rags of green weed hung down.
While his gills were breathing in
the terrible oxygen
—the frightening gills,
fresh and crisp with blood,   25
that can cut so badly—
I thought of the coarse white flesh
packed in like feathers,
the big bones and the little bones,
the dramatic reds and blacks   30
of his shiny entrails,
and the pink swim-bladder
like a big peony.
I looked into his eyes
which were far larger than mine   35
but shallower, and yellowed,
the irises backed and packed
with tarnished tinfoil
seen through the lenses
of old scratched isinglass.°   *a thin sheet of mica*   40
They shifted a little, but not
to return my stare.
—It was more like the tipping
of an object toward the light.
I admired his sullen face,   45
the mechanism of his jaw,
and then I saw
that from his lower lip
—if you could call it a lip—
grim, wet, and weaponlike,   50
hung five old pieces of fish-line,
or four and a wire leader
with the swivel still attached,
with all their five big hooks
grown firmly in his mouth.   55

A green line, frayed at the end
where he broke it, two heavier lines,
and a fine black thread
still crimped from the strain and snap
60 when it broke and he got away.
Like medals with their ribbons
frayed and wavering,
a five-haired beard of wisdom
trailing from his aching jaw.
65 I stared and stared
and victory filled up
the little rented boat,
from the pool of bilge
where oil had spread a rainbow
70 around the rusted engine
to the bailer rusted orange,
the sun-cracked thwarts,
the oarlocks on their strings,
the gunnels-until everything
75 was rainbow, rainbow, rainbow!
And I let the fish go.

QUESTIONS

1. Describe the poem's images of action (kinetic, kinesthetic). What is unusual about them?
2. What impression does the fish make upon the speaker? Is the fish beautiful? Ugly? Why is the fish described in such detail?
3. What do the "five old pieces of fish-line" indicate (line 51)?
4. How is the rainbow formed around the boat's engine? Why does the speaker refer to the "pool of bilge"? What does the rainbow mean to the speaker?
5. What right does the speaker have to keep the fish? Why does she choose to relinquish this right?

The kinetic images at the end of "The Fish" are those of victory filling the boat (difficult to visualize) and the oil spreading to make a rainbow in the bilgewater (easy to visualize). The kinesthetic images are readily imagined—the speaker's staring, observing, and letting the fish go—and they are vivid and real. The final gesture is the necessary outcome of the observed contrast between the deteriorating artifacts of human beings and the natural world of the fish, and it is a vivid expression of the right of the natural world to exist without human intervention. In short, Bishop's kinetic and kinesthetic images are designed to emphasize the need for freedom not only for human beings but for all the earth and animated nature.

The areas from which kinetic and kinesthetic imagery can be derived are too varied and unpredictable to describe. Occupations, trades, professions, businesses, recreational activities—all these might furnish images. One poet introduces references from gardening, another from money and banking, another from modern real estate developments, another from the falling of leaves in autumn, another from life in the jungle, another from life in the home. The freshness, newness, and surprise of much poetry result from the many and varied areas from which writers draw their images.

Poems for Study

Elizabeth Barrett Browning . . . . Sonnets from the Portuguese,
    Number 14: If Thou Must Love Me, 733
Samuel Taylor Coleridge . . . . Kubla Khan, 734
T. S. Eliot . . . . Preludes, 735
Susan Griffin . . . . . Love Should Grow Up Like a Wild Iris in the Fields, 737
Thomas Hardy . . . . Channel Firing, 738
George Herbert . . . . The Pulley, 740
Gerard Manley Hopkins . . . . Spring, 740
A. E. Housman . . . . On Wenlock Edge, 741
Denise Levertov . . . . A Time Past, 742
Thomas Lux . . . . The Voice You Hear When You Read Silently, 743
Eugenio Montale . . . . Buffalo (Buffalo), 744
Marianne Moore . . . . The Fish, 745
Pablo Neruda . . . . Every Day You Play, 746
Ezra Pound . . . . In a Station of the Metro, 747
Miklós Radnóti . . . . Forced March, 748
Friedrich Rückert . . . . If You Love for the Sake of Beauty, 749
William Shakespeare . . . . Sonnet 130: My Mistress' Eyes Are
    Nothing Like the Sun, 749
James Tate . . . . Dream On, 750
David Wojahn . . . . "It's Only Rock and Roll but I Like It":
    The Fall of Saigon, 751

ELIZABETH BARRETT BROWNING (1806–1861)

 ## Sonnets from the Portuguese, Number 14: If Thou Must Love Me (1850)

If thou must love me, let it be for nought
Except for love's sake only. Do not say
"I love her for her smile—her look—her way
Of speaking gently—for a trick of thought
That falls in well with mine, and certes° brought   *certainly*   5
A sense of pleasant ease on such a day"—
For these things in themselves, Belovèd, may
Be changed, or change for thee,- and love, so wrought,°   *created*
May be unwrought so. Neither love me for
Thine own dear pity's wiping my cheeks dry,—   10
A creature might forget to weep, who bore
Thy comfort long, and lose thy love thereby!
But love me for love's sake, that evermore
Thou mayst love on, through love's eternity.

QUESTIONS

1. Who is the speaker of this poem? Why might you conclude that the speaker is female?

2. What images does the speaker use to indicate possible causes for loving? What kinds of images are they? How does the speaker explain why they should be rejected?

3. How does the idea of lines 1, 13, and 14 build upon the ideas in the rest of the poem?

SAMUEL TAYLOR COLERIDGE (1772–1834)

 Kubla Khan (1816)

In Xanadu did Kubla Khan
A stately pleasure dome decree:
Where Alph,° the sacred river, ran
Through caverns measureless to man
5   Down to a sunless sea.
So twice five miles of fertile ground
With walls and towers were girdled round:
And there were gardens bright with sinuous rills,
Where blossomed many an incense-bearing tree;
10   And here were forests ancient as the hills,
Enfolding sunny spots of greenery.
But oh! that deep romantic chasm which slanted
Down the green hill athwart a cedarn cover!
A savage place! as holy and enchanted
15   As e'er beneath a waning moon was haunted
By woman wailing for her demon lover!
And from this chasm, with ceaseless turmoil seething,
As if this earth in fast thick pants were breathing,
A mighty fountain momently was forced:
20   Amid whose swift half-intermitted burst
Huge fragments vaulted like rebounding hail,
Or chaffy grain beneath the thresher's flail:
And 'mid these dancing rocks at once and ever
It flung up momently the sacred river.
25   Five miles meandering with a mazy motion
Through wood and dale the sacred river ran,
Then reached the caverns measureless to man,
And sank in tumult to a lifeless ocean:
And 'mid this tumult Kubla heard from far
30   Ancestral voices prophesying war!
The shadow of the dome of pleasure
Floated midway on the waves;
Where was heard the mingled measure
From the fountain and the caves.

°3 *Alph:* possibly a reference to the river Alpheus in Greece, as described by the ancient writers Virgil and Pausanras.

It was a miracle of rare device,   35
A sunny pleasure dome with caves of ice!

    A damsel with a dulcimer
    In a vision once I saw:
    It was an Abyssinian maid,
    And on her dulcimer she played
    Singing of Mount Abora.°   40
Could I revive within me
Her symphony and song,
To such a deep delight 'twould win me,
That with music loud and long,   45
I would build that dome in air,
That sunny dome! those caves of ice!
And all who heard should see them there,
And all should cry, Beware! Beware!
His flashing eyes, his floating hair!   50
Weave a circle round him thrice,
And close your eyes with holy dread,
For he on honeydew hath fed,
And drunk the milk of Paradise.

°41 *Mount Abora:* a mountain of Coleridge's imagination. But see John Milton's Paradise Lost, IV. 268–84.

QUESTIONS

1. How many of the poem's images might be sketched or visualized? Which ones would be panoramic landscapes? Which might be close-ups?

2. What is the effect of auditory images such as "wailing," "fast thick pants," "tumult," "ancestral voices prophesying war," and "mingled measure"?

3. When Coleridge was writing this poem, he was recalling it from a dream. At line 54 he was interrupted, and when he resumed he could write no more. How might an argument be made that the poem is finished?

4. How do lines 35–36 establish the pleasure dome as a place of mysterious oddity? What is the effect of the words "miracle" and "rare"? The effect of combining the images "sunny" and "caves of ice"?

5. Why does the speaker yearn for the power of the singing Abyssinian maid? What kinesthetic images end the poem? How are these images important in the speaker's desire to reconstruct the vision of the pleasure dome?

T. S. ELIOT (1888–1965)

 ## Preludes (1910)

I

The winter evening settles down
With smell of steaks in passageways.
Six o'clock.
The burnt-out ends of smoky days.

5 And now a gusty shower wraps
The grimy scraps
Of withered leaves about your feet
And newspapers from vacant lots;
The showers beat
10 On broken blinds and chimney-pots,
And at the corner of the street
A lonely cab-horse steams and stamps.
And then the lighting of the lamps.

II

The morning comes to consciousness
15 Of faint stale smells of beer
From the sawdust-trampled street
With all its muddy feet that press
To early coffee-stands.
With the other masquerades
20 That time resumes,
One thinks of all the hands
That are raising dingy shades
In a thousand furnished rooms.

III

You tossed a blanket from the bed,
25 You lay upon your back, and waited;
You dozed, and watched the night revealing
The thousand sordid images
Of which your soul was constituted;
They flickered against the ceiling.
30 And when all the world came back
And the light crept up between the shutters
And you heard the sparrows in the gutters,
You had such a vision of the street,
As the street hardly understands;
35 Sitting along the bed's edge, where
You curled the papers from your hair,
Or clasped the yellow soles of feet
In the palms of both soiled hands.

IV

His soul stretched tight across the skies
40 That fade behind a city block,
Or trampled by insistent feet
At four and five and six o'clock;
And short square fingers stuffing pipes,
And evening newspapers, and eyes
45 Assured of certain certainties,

The conscience of a blackened street
Impatient to assume the world.

    I am moved by fancies that are curled
Around these images, and cling:
The notion of some infinitely gentle   50
Infinitely suffering thing.

    Wipe your hand across your mouth, and laugh;
The worlds revolve like ancient women
Gathering fuel in vacant lots.

QUESTIONS

1. From what locations are the images in the first stanza derived? How do the images shift in the second stanza? What is the connection between the images in the second and third stanzas?

2. Who is the "you" in the third stanza? What images are associated with this listener?

3. Who is the "His" of the fourth stanza? How do the images develop in this stanza? What is meant particularly in the images of lines 46–47?

4. What is the nature of the bodily imagery in the poem? The urban imagery? What impressions do these images cause?

5. In lines 48–51, what does the speaker conclude? How do the last two unnumbered stanzas constitute a contrast of attitude?

SUSAN GRIFFIN (b. 1943)

 ## Love Should Grow Up Like a Wild Iris in the Fields (1972)

Love should grow up like a wild iris in the fields,
unexpected, after a terrible storm, opening a purple
mouth to the rain, with not a thought to the future,
ignorant of the grass and the graveyard of leaves
around, forgetting its own beginning. Love should   5
grow like a wild iris
but does not.
Love more often is to be found in kitchens at the dinner hour,
tired out and hungry, lingers over tables in houses where
the walls record movements; while the cook is probably angry,   10
and the ingredients of the meal are budgeted, while
a child cries feed me now and her mother not quite
hysterical says over and over, wait just a bit, just a bit.
Love should grow up in the fields like a wild iris
but never does   15
really startle anyone, was to be expected, was to be
predicted, is almost absurd, goes on from day to day, not quite
blindly, gets taken to the cleaners every fall, sings old

songs over and over, and falls on the same piece of rug that
20 never gets tacked down, gives up, wants to hide, is not
brave, knows too much, is not like an
iris growing wild but more like
staring into space
in the street
25 not quite sure
which door it was, annoyed about the sidewalk being
slippery, trying all the doors, thinking
if love wished the world to be well, it would be well.
Love should
30 grow up like a wild iris, but doesn't, it comes from
the midst of everything else, sees like the iris
of an eye, when the light is right,
feels in blindness and when there is nothing else is
tender, blinks, and opens
35 face up to the skies.

QUESTIONS

1. Contrast the locations of the images in the first seven lines and in the next eight. How do the ideas of the poet depend on this contrast in locations?

2. Note the difference in the mood of the verbs, from the "should" clause in the first six lines to the declarative present verb in line 7. Also, note the present tense verbs from lines 8–13, and then the "should" again in line 14. What is the effect of this differing use of verbs?

3. Trace the image of the wild iris throughout the poem. Why is the iris wild, and not cultivated? How does the iris grow? What is the effect of the change in the image of the iris from the flower to the eye (line 32)?

4. How is the sentence in lines 30–31 ("it comes from / the midst of everything else") related to the ideas and images in the rest of the poem?

THOMAS HARDY (1840–1928)

For a photo, see Chapter 5, page 287.

 ## Channel Firing (1914)

That night your great guns, unawares,
Shook all our coffins° as we lay,
And broke the chancel window-squares,
We thought it was the Judgment Day

°2 *coffins:* It has been common practice in England for hundreds of years to bury people in the floors or basements of churches.

And sat upright. While drearisome   5
Arose the howl of wakened hounds:
The mouse let fall the altar-crumb,
The worms drew back into the mounds,

The glebe° cow drooled. Till God called, "No;
It's gunnery practice out at sea   10
Just as before you went below;
The world is as it used to be:

"All nations striving strong to make
Red war yet redder. Mad as hatters
They do no more for Christés sake   15
Than you who are helpless in such matters.

"That this is not the judgment hour
For some of them's a blessed thing,
For if it were they'd have to scour
Hell's floor for so much threatening. . . .   20

"Ha, ha. It will be warmer when
I blow the trumpet (if indeed
I ever do; for you are men,
And rest eternal sorely need)."

So down we lay again. "I wonder,   25
Will the world ever saner be,"
Said one, "than when He sent us under
In our indifferent century!"

And many a skeleton shook his head.
"Instead of preaching forty year,"   30
My neighbor Parson Thirdly said,
"I wish I had stuck to pipes and beer."

Again the guns disturbed the hour,
Roaring their readiness to avenge,
As far inland as Stourton Tower,°   35
And Camelot,° and starlit Stonehenge.°

°9 *glebe*: a parcel of land adjoining and belonging to a church. Cows were grazed there to keep the grass short.
35 *Stourton Tower: a* tower commemorating King Alfred the Great's defeat of the Danes in 879 CE. 36 *Camelot*:
legendary seat of King Arthur's court. *Stonehenge: a* group of standing stones on Salisbury Plain, probably built as
a place of worship before 1000 BCE. Stonehenge is one of England's famous landmarks.

QUESTIONS

1. Who is the speaker in this poem? What is the setting? The situation?
2. To whom does the "your" in line 1 refer? The "our" in line 2?
3. What has awakened the speaker and his friends? What mistake have they made?
4. What three other voices are heard in the poem? How are their traits revealed?
5. What ideas about war and the nature of humanity does this poem explore?

GEORGE HERBERT (1593–1633)

 ## The Pulley (1633)

When God at first made man,
Having a glass of blessings standing by,
   "Let us," said he, "pour on him all we can.
Let the world's riches, which dispersed lie,
5   Contract into a span."°

   So strength first made a way;
Then beauty flowed, then wisdom, honor, pleasure.
   When almost all was out, God made a stay,
Perceiving that, alone of all his treasure,
10   Rest° in the bottom lay.

   "For if I should," said he,
"Bestow this jewel also on my creature,
   He would adore my gifts instead of me.
And rest in Nature, not the God of Nature;
15   So both should losers be.

   "Yet let him keep the rest,
But keep them with repining restlessness.
   Let him be rich and weary, that at least,
If goodness lead him not, yet weariness
20   May toss him to my breast."

°5 *into a span:* that is, within the control of human beings. 10 rest: (1) repose, security; (2) all that remains.

QUESTIONS

1. Describe the dramatic scene of the poem. Who is doing what?
2. What are the particular "blessings" that God confers on humanity, according to the speaker? Why should these be considered blessings?
3. Consider the image of the pulley as the means, or device (through "repining restlessness"), by which God compels people to become worshipful.
4. Analyze and discuss the meaning of the kinetic images signified by the words "pour," "flowed," "rest," and "toss."

GERARD MANLEY HOPKINS (1844–1889)

 ## Spring (1877)

Nothing is so beautiful as Spring—
   When weeds, in wheels, shoot long and lovely and lush;
   Thrush's eggs look little low heavens, and thrush
Through the echoing timber does so rinse and wring

The ear, it strikes like lightnings to hear him sing;   5
    The glassy peartree leaves and blooms, they brush
    The descending blue; that blue is all in a rush
With richness; the racing lambs too have fair their fling.

What is all this juice and all this joy?
    A strain of the earth's sweet being in the beginning   10
In Eden garden.— Have, get, before it cloy,
    Before it cloud, Christ, lord, and sour with sinning,
Innocent mind and Mayday in girl and boy,
    Most, O maid's child, thy choice and worthy the winning.

QUESTIONS

1. What images does the speaker mention as support for his first line, "Nothing is so beautiful as Spring"? Are these images those that you would normally expect? To what degree do they seem to be new or unusual?

2. What images of motion and activity do you find in the poem? Are these mainly static or dynamic? What do these suggest about the speaker's view of spring?

3. What is the relationship between "Eden garden" in line 11 and the scene described in lines 1–8? To what extent are spring and "Innocent mind and Mayday" a glimpse of the Garden of Eden?

4. Christ is mentioned in lines 12 and 14 (as "maid's child"). Do these references seal the poem off from readers who are not Christian? Why or why not?

A. E. HOUSMAN (1859–1936)

 ## On Wenlock Edge (1887)

On Wenlock Edge° the wood's in trouble;
His forest fleece the Wrekin° heaves;
The gale, it plies the saplings double,
And thick on Severn° snow the leaves.

'Twould° blow like this through holt and hanger°   5
When Uricon° the city stood;
'Tis the old wind in the old anger,
But then it threshed another wood.

Then, 'twas before my time, the Roman
At yonder heaving hill would stare;   10
The blood that warms an English yeoman,°
The thoughts that hurt him, they were there.

°1 *Wenlock Edge:* a range of high hills in western England, south of Birmingham. 2 *the Wrekin:* a volcano (now extinct) northwest of Birmingham. Housman suggests that the volcano is erupting, just one of the natural disturbances he describes in the first two stanzas. 4 *Severn:* a major river winding southward through the area toward Bristol. 5 *'Twould:* It would [back in Roman times]. 5 *holt and hanger:* woods and thick underbrush along a hillside or mountainside. 6 *Uricon:* Uriconium, a regional capital in western England during the Roman occupation from the first to the fifth centuries CE. 11 *yeoman:* a medieval English farmer who owned the land he farmed.

There, like the wind through woods in riot,
Through him the gale of life blew high;
15 The tree of man was never quiet—
Then 'twas the Roman, now 'tis I.

The gale, it plies the saplings double;
It blows so hard, 'twill soon be gone.
Today the Roman and his trouble
20 Are ashes under Uricon.

QUESTIONS

1. How extensively does the speaker stress the images of natural disturbances that are taking place on Wenlock Edge, with the wind, for example, plying the saplings double? Why does Housman repeat this line (line 3) in line 17?

2. What concerns of the ancient Roman in England are continued in the feelings of the speaker, who is inhabiting the same location as the Roman?

3. What is the view of history that the speaker develops in this poem? Is it a usual view of what we ordinarily think of as history? Why or why not? On what idea does the poem conclude?

DENISE LEVERTOV (1923–1997)

For a photo, see Chapter 12, page 672.

A Time Past (1975)

The old wooden steps to the front door
where I was sitting that fall morning
when you came downstairs, just awake,
and my joy at sight of you (emerging
into golden day—
5   the dew almost frost)
pulled me to my feet to tell you
how much I loved you:

those wooden steps
are gone now, decayed
10 replaced with granite,
hard, gray, and handsome.
The old steps live
only in me:
my feet and thighs
15 remember them, and my hands
still feel their splinters.
Everything else about and around that house
brings memories of others—of marriage,
of my son. And the steps do too: I recall
20 sitting there with my friend and her little son who died,
or was it the second one who lives and thrives?

And sitting there 'in my life,' often, alone or with my husband.
Yet that one instant,
your cheerful, unafraid, youthful, 'I love you too,'
the quiet broken by no bird, no cricket, gold leaves   25
spinning in silence down without
any breeze to blow them,
                        is what twines itself
in my head and body across those slabs of wood
that were warm, ancient, and now
wait somewhere to be burnt.   30

QUESTIONS

1. Describe the visual imagery of the poem. What tactile imagery is associated with the steps? What other images are part of the speaker's memory?

2. How is the image of the "old wooden steps" developed in the poem? What has happened to the wooden steps? What meaning may be derived from their having been replaced by the granite steps? How are these steps tied to the speaker's "time past"?

3. Why do you think the speaker expressly denies the recollection of any sounds of bird or cricket?

THOMAS LUX (b. 1946)

The Voice You Hear When You Read Silently (1997)

THE VOICE YOU HEAR WHEN YOU READ SILENTLY
is not silent, it is a speaking-
out-loud voice in your head: it is *spoken*,
a voice is *saying* it
as you read. It's the writer's words,   5
of course, in a literary sense
his or her "voice" but the sound
of that voice is the sound of *your* voice.
Not the sound your friends know
or the sound of a tape played back   10
but your voice
caught in the dark cathedral
of your skull, your voice heard
by an internal ear informed by internal abstracts
and what you know by feeling,   15
having felt. It is your voice
saying, for example, the word "barn"
that the writer wrote
but the "barn" you say
is a barn you know or knew. The voice   20
in your head, speaking as you read,
never says anything neutrally—some people
hated the barn they knew,
some people love the barn they know
so you hear the word loaded   25
and a sensory constellation

is lit: horse-gnawed stalls,
hayloft, black heat tape wrapping
a water pipe, a slippery
30   spilled *chirrr* of oats from a split sack,
the bony, filthy haunches of cows. . . .
And "barn" is only a noun—no verb
or subject has entered into the sentence yet!
The voice you hear when you read to yourself
35   is the clearest voice: you speak it
speaking to you.

QUESTIONS

1. What is meant by the "constellation" being lit when the reader reads a word, in this case "barn"? How does "constellation" explain the development of the barn image in lines 26–30?
2. Why is the "voice you hear when you read silently/ . . . not silent"?
3. Describe the meaning and associations of "the dark cathedral/of your skull" in lines 11–12. What is particularly significant about the use of "cathedral" in these lines?

EUGENIO MONTALE (1896–1981)

Buffalo (Buffalo)°(1929)

Translated by Robert Zweig

Gusting, a sweet inferno channeled
crowds of every color
in the loop of blaring megaphones.
The buses gushed out
5   into the evening.

On the churning gulf, heat evaporated
into smoke; down below, a shining arc
etched a current and the crowd was ready
at the passage. A black man
10   slumbered inside a ray of light
that cut the darkness; in a box, loose, easy women awaited
the ferry's landing. I said to myself:
Buffalo! —and the name worked.
                 I fell
15   into the limbo of the deafening voices of the blood where flashes
burn the sight like flickers of mirror.
I heard the dry crashes, and all around me
saw the curved, striped backs whirling
on the track.

°The Vélodrome Buffalo, a Parisian cycling racetrack, was the site of many world cycling records from 1893 until World War I, when it was replaced by an airplane factory. The Buffalo was named after Buffalo Bill Cody, whose Wild West show was performed there during the first year of its existence.

QUESTIONS

1. The setting of "Buffalo" is an indoor bicycle racetrack. Why do you think Montale chose this setting?

2. Is the description of this bicycle race objective or subjective? Which images can you cite to support your conclusion?

3. In Dante's "Inferno," a medieval Italian poem that greatly influenced Montale, a ferry takes Dante across a river into "hell." Might the ferry that the "loose, easy women" wait for be such a ferry? If so, how does that image help you to understand "Buffalo"?

4. What do you think is meant when the speaker says that uttering the word "Buffalo" worked? What did uttering that word do?

MARIANNE MOORE (1887–1972)

The Fish (1918)

wade
through black jade.
    Of the crow-blue mussel-shells, one keeps
    adjusting the ash-heaps;
        opening and shutting itself like   5

an
injured fan.
    The barnacles which encrust the side
    of the wave, cannot hide
        there for the submerged shafts of the   10

sun,
split like spun
    glass, move themselves with spotlight swiftness
    into the crevices—
        in and out, illuminating   15

the
turquoise sea
    of bodies. The water drives a wedge
    of iron through the iron edge
        of the cliff; whereupon the stars,   20

pink
rice-grains, ink-
    bespattered jelly fish, crabs like green
    lilies, and submarine
        toadstools, slide each on the other.   25

All
external
    marks of abuse are present on this
    defiant edifice—
        all the physical features of   30

ac-
cident—lack
    of cornice, dynamite grooves, burns, and
    hatchet strokes, these things stand
35   out on it; the chasm-side is

dead.
Repeated
    evidence has proved that it can live
    on what can not revive
40   its youth. The sea grows old in it.

QUESTIONS

1. Why is this poem titled "The Fish"? What actual fish does the poem describe? What images of other sea creatures do you find?

2. What action is described in this poem? In what ways may this poem be contrasted with Bishop's poem "The Fish"?

3. Describe the structure of rhymes in "The Fish." What pictorial image is suggested by the shapes of the stanzas and by the fact that most of the lines ending the stanzas extend grammatically to the next stanzas?

4. What idea does the speaker seem to be developing in the last three stanzas of the poem?

PABLO NERUDA (1904–1977)

Every Day You Play (1924)

Every day you play with the light of the universe.
Subtle visitor, you arrive in the flower and the water.
You are more than this white head that I hold tightly
as a cluster of fruit, every day, between my hands.

5   You are like nobody since I love you.
Let me spread you out among yellow garlands.
Who writes your name in letters of smoke among the stars of the south?
Oh let me remember you as you were before you existed.

Suddenly the wind howls and bangs at my shut window.
10   The sky is a net crammed with shadowy fish.
Here all the winds let go sooner or later, all of them.
The rain takes off her clothes.

The birds go by, fleeing.
The wind. The wind.
15   I can contend only against the power of men.
The storm whirls dark leaves
and turns loose all the boats that were moored last night to the sky.

You are here. Oh, you do not run away.
You will answer me to the last cry.
Cling to me as though you were frightened.   20
Even so, at one time a strange shadow ran through your eyes.

Now, now too, little one, you bring me honeysuckle,
and even your breasts smell of it.
While the sad wind goes slaughtering butterflies
I love you, and my happiness bites the plum of your mouth.   25

How you must have suffered getting accustomed to me,
my savage, solitary soul, my name that sends them all running.
So many times we have seen the morning star burn, kissing our eyes,
and over our heads the gray light unwind in turning fans.

My words rained over you, stroking you.   30
A long time I have loved the sunned mother-of-pearl of your body.
I go so far as to think that you own the universe.
I will bring you happy flowers from the mountains, bluebells,
dark hazels, and rustic baskets of kisses.

I want   35
to do with you what spring does with the cherry trees.

QUESTIONS

1. What is the situation of this poem? Who is talking to whom? What is their relationship?

2. Describe the nature of the images in this poem. What kinetic and kinesthetic images do you find? What is the effect of these images? What visual images do you find? What tactile images? Olfactory images? Gustatory images?

3. What reality is reflected in the poem's imagery? Analyze the images of lines 9–17, and their meaning.

4. What does the speaker mean by line 8, "Oh let me remember you as you were before you existed"?

EZRA POUND (1885–1972)

In a Station of the Metro° (1916)

The apparition of these faces in the crowd;
Petals on a wet, black bough.

°*Metro:* the Paris subway.

QUESTIONS

1. Is the image of the wet, black bough happy or sad? If the petals were on a tree in the sunlight, what would be the effect?

2. What is the meaning of the image suggested by "apparition"? Does it suggest a positive or negative view of human life?

3. This poem contains only two lines. Is it proper to consider it as a poem nevertheless? If it is not a poem, what is it?

MIKLÓS RADNÓTI (1909–1944)

 ### Forced March° (1944)

Translated by Zsuzsanna Ozsvath and Frederick Turner

Bor,° 15 September 1944

Crazy, he stumbles, flops, gets up,   and trudges on again.
He moves his ankles and his knees   like one wandering pain,
then sallies forth, as if a wing   lifted him where he went,
and when the ditch invites him in,   he dare not give consent,
5   and if you were to ask why not?   perhaps his answer is
a woman waits, a death more wise,   more beautiful than this.
Poor fool, the true believer: for weeks, above the rooves,
but for the scorching whirlwind,   nothing lives or moves:
the housewall's lying on its back,   the prune tree's smashed and bare;
10   even at home, when dark comes on,   the night is furred with fear.
Ah, if I could believe it!   that not only do I bear
what's worth the keeping in my heart,   but home is really there;
if it might be!—as once it was,   on a veranda old and cool,
where the sweet bee of peace would buzz,   prune marmalade would chill,
15   late summer's stillness sunbathe   in gardens half asleep,
fruit sway among the branches,   stark naked in the deep,
Fanni waiting at the fence   blonde by its rusty red,
and shadows would write slowly out   all the slow morning said—
but still it might yet happen!   The moon's so round today!
20   Friend, don't walk on. Give me a shout,   and I'll be on my way!

°In the late days of World War II, allied troops advanced into Germany from all directions. Because there were many prisoners in concentration and work camps in countries around Germany, the Nazis determined to hide the evidence. They therefore forced their prisoners, who were given little if any food, to endure agonizing marches to camps in and near Germany—distances of hundreds of miles. Evacuating the Bor area of Yugoslavia in September, 1944, the Germans forced a large number of Jewish laborers, one of whom was Radnóti, to walk to Hungary. "Forced March," one of his ten last poems, shows his reactions to the march, at the end of which he was shot to death and thrown into a mass grave. The poem was found in a small address book in the pocket of his raincoat after his body was exhumed in 1946. See also Cynthia Ozick's "The Shawl" (Chapter 4, page 266). *Bor:* A town in eastern Yugoslavia, about eighty miles southeast of Belgrade.

QUESTIONS

1. What is the purpose of the tactile images of tiredness and pain in lines 1–6?

2. What is the nature of the images in lines 7–10?

3. How does the poem's perspective shift at line 11? How do the images from lines 11–19 contribute to the speaker's mood, as shown in line 20? What do these lines tell you about human hope and strength?

FRIEDRICH RÜCKERT (1788–1866)

If You Love for the Sake of Beauty (1823)

Anonymous Translator

If you love for the sake of beauty, O never love me!
Love the sun, which has bright golden hair.
If you love for the sake of youth, O never love me!
Love the spring, which is reborn each year.
If you love for the sake of wealth, O never love me!   5
Love the mermaid, whose pearls are rich and clear.
If you love for the sake of love alone, O yes then, love me!
Love me as I love you—forever!

QUESTIONS

1. What is the poem's situation? Who is speaking? Who is the listener?
2. How do the images in lines 2, 4, and 6 exemplify the abstract concepts in lines 1, 3, and 5? How does the speaker use these images to reinforce his or her negative requests?
3. How may the final two lines be considered a climax of the poem?

WILLIAM SHAKESPEARE (1564–1616)

For a portrait, see Chapter 24, page 1322.

Sonnet 130: My Mistress' Eyes Are Nothing Like the Sun (1609)

My mistress' eyes are nothing like the sun;
Coral is far more red than her lips' red;
If snow be white, why then her breasts are dun;
If hairs be wires, black wires grow on her head.
I have seen roses damasked,° red and white,   *set in an elaborate bouquet*   5
But no such roses see I in her cheeks;
And in some perfumes is there more delight
Than in the breath that from my mistress reeks.
I love to hear her speak, yet well I know
That music hath a far more pleasing sound;   10
I grant I never saw a goddess go;
My mistress, when she walks, treads on the ground.
And yet, by heaven, I think my love as rare
As any she belied with false compare.

QUESTIONS

1. To what does the speaker negatively compare his mistress's eyes? Lips? Breasts? Hair? Cheeks? Breath? Voice? Walk? What kinds of images are created in these negative comparisons?

2. What conventional images does this poem ridicule? What sort of poem is Shakespeare mocking by using the negative images in lines 1–12?

3. In the light of the last two lines, do you think the speaker intends the images as insults? If not as insults, how should they be taken?

4. Are most of the images auditory, olfactory, visual, or kinesthetic? Explain.

5. What point does this poem make about love poetry? About human relationships? How does the imagery contribute to the development of both points?

JAMES TATE (b. 1943)

 Dream On (1998)

Some people go their whole lives
without ever writing a single poem.
Extraordinary people who don't hesitate
to cut somebody's heart or skull open.
5   They go to baseball games with the greatest of ease
and play a few rounds of golf as if it were nothing.
These same people stroll into a church
as if that were a natural part of life.
Investing money is second nature to them.
10   They contribute to political campaigns
that have absolutely no poetry in them
and promise none for the future.
They sit around the dinner table at night
and pretend as though nothing is missing.
15   Their children get caught shoplifting at the mall
and no one admits that it is poetry they are missing.
The family dog howls all night,
lonely and starving for more poetry in his life.
Why is it so difficult for them to see
20   that, without poetry, their lives are effluvial.
Sure, they have their banquets, their celebrations,
croquet, fox hunts, their seashores and sunsets,
their cocktails on the balcony, dog races,
and all that kissing and hugging, and don't
25   forget the good deeds, the charity work,
nursing the baby squirrels all through the night,
filling the birdfeeders all winter,
helping the stranger change her tire.
Still, there's that disagreeable exhalation
30   from decaying matter, subtle but ever present.
They walk around erect like champions.
They are smooth-spoken, urbane and witty.
When alone, rare occasion, they stare
into the mirror for hours, bewildered.
35   There was something they meant to say, but didn't:
"And if we put the statue of the rhinoceros
next to the tweezers, and walk around the room three times
learn to yodel, shave our heads, call

our ancestors back from the dead—"
poetrywise it's still a bust, bankrupt.   40
You haven't scribbled a syllable of it.
You're a nowhere man misfiring
the very essence of your life, flustering
nothing from nothing and back again.
The hereafter may not last all that long.   45
Radiant childhood sweetheart,
secret code of everlasting joy and sorrow,
fanciful pen strokes beneath the eyelids:
all day, all night meditation, knot of hope,
kernel of desire, pure ordinariness of life,   50
seeking, through poetry, a benediction
or a bed to lie down on, to connect, reveal,
explore, to imbue meaning on the day's extravagant labor.
And yet it's cruel to expect too much.
It's a rare species of bird   55
That refuses to be categorized.
Its song is barely audible.
It is like a dragonfly in a dream—
Here, then there, then here again,
Low-flying amber-wing darting upward   60
and then out of sight.
And the dream has a pain in its heart
the wonders of which are manifold,
or so the story is told.

QUESTIONS

1. Characterize the images from lines 3–20. What types of images, for the most part, are these? What part do they play in the poem's argument?

2. In lines 36–42 there is a different unit of imagery. What are the characteristics and purpose of these?

3. How does the speaker use images to characterize poetry from lines 55–64 (if we take the repetition of "it" in lines 55, 56, 58, and 59 as descriptions of poetry). How true is the idea that poetry is a dream with a pain in its heart (line 63)? What is the effect of the final line?

DAVID WOJAHN (b. 1953)

"It's Only Rock and Roll, but I Like It": The Fall of Saigon (1975; 1990)

The gutteral stammer of the chopper blades
Raising arabesques of dust, tearing leaves
From the orange trees lining the Embassy compound:
One chopper left, and a CBS cameraman leans
From inside its door, exploiting the artful   5
Mayhem. Somewhere a radio blares the Stones,
"I like it, like it, yes indeed. . . ." Carts full
Of files blaze in the yard. Flak-jacketed marines

Gunpoint the crowd away. The overloaded chopper strains
10   And blunders from the roof. An ice-cream-suited
Saigonese drops his briefcase; both hands
Now cling to the airborne skis. The camera gets
It all: the marine leaning out the copter bay,
His fists beating time. Then the hands giving way.

QUESTIONS

1. What actions are described in this poem? Why does the Saigonese man "cling to the airborne skis"? What happens to him?
2. Describe the poem's images of sound (auditory images). How many such images does the poem contain? What is their effect? What images of sight (visual) do you find? What other types of images?
3. Contrast the poem's title with its content.
4. Cumulatively, what is the relationship of the poem's images to the phrase "artful/Mayhem" in lines 5–6, and also to the poem's judgment about the American presence in Vietnam?

WRITING ABOUT IMAGERY

Questions for Discovering Ideas

In preparing to write, you should develop a set of thoughtful notes dealing with issues such as the following:

- What type or types of images prevail in the work? Visual (shapes, colors)? Auditory (sounds)? Olfactory (smells)? Tactile (touch and texture)? Gustatory (taste)? Kinetic or kinesthetic (motion)? Or is the imagery a combination?
- To what degree do the images reflect either the poet's actual observation or the poet's reading and knowledge of fields such as science or history?
- How well do the images stand out? How vivid are they? How does the poet make the images vivid?
- Within a group of images—say, visual or auditory—do the images pertain to one location or area rather than another (e.g., natural scenes rather than interiors, snowy scenes rather than grassy ones, loud and harsh sounds rather than quiet and soothing ones)?
- What explanation is needed for the images? (Images might be derived from the classics or the Bible, the Vietnam War or World War II, the behaviors of four-footed creatures or birds or fish, and so on.)
- What effect do the circumstances described in the poem (e.g., conditions of brightness or darkness, warmth or cold) have on your responses to the images? What purpose do you think the poet achieves by controlling these responses?
- How well are the images integrated within the poem's argument or development?

Answering questions like these will provide you with a sizable body of material that you can organize and then discuss in your essay.

Strategies for Organizing Ideas

Connect a brief overview of the poem to your plan for the body of your essay, noting perhaps that the writer uses images to strengthen ideas about war, character, or love or that the writer relies predominantly on images of sight, sound, and action. You might deal with just one of the following aspects, or you may combine your approaches, as you wish.

1. *Images suggesting ideas and/or moods.* Such an essay should emphasize the effects of the imagery. What ideas or moods are evoked by the images? (In this chapter the auditory images beginning Owen's "Anthem for Doomed Youth," for example, all point toward a condemnation of the brutality of war. The visual images in "Spring," by Hopkins, all point toward a sense of earthly and also divine growth and lushness.) Do the images promote approval or disapproval? Cheerfulness? Melancholy? Are the images drab, exciting, vivid? How? Why? Are they conducive to humor or surprise? How does the writer achieve these effects? Are the images consistent, or are they ambiguous? (The images in Masefield's "Cargoes" indicate first approval and then disapproval, with no ambiguity. By contrast, Shakespeare's images in "My Mistress' Eyes" might be construed as insults, but in context, they are really compliments [both in this chapter].)

2. *The types of images.* Here the emphasis is on the categories of images themselves. Is there a predominance of a particular type of image (e.g., visual or auditory), or is there a blending, as in Neruda's "Every Day You Play"? Is there a bunching of types at particular points in the poem or story? If so, why? Is there any shifting as the work develops (for example, in Owen's "Anthem for Doomed Youth" [this chapter] the auditory images first suggest loudness and harshness, but later auditory images describe quietness and sorrow)? Are the images appropriate, granted the nature and apparent intent of the work? Do they assist in making the ideas seem convincing? If any images seem inappropriate, is the inappropriateness intentional or inadvertent? What is the effect of the inappropriate imagery?

3. *Systems of images.* Here the emphasis should be on the areas from which the images are drawn. This is another way of considering the appropriateness of the imagery: Is there a pattern of similar or consistent images, such as dark and dreary urban scenes (Eliot's "Preludes" [this chapter]) or color and activity (Hopkins's "Spring" [this chapter])? Do all the images adhere consistently to a particular frame of reference, such as a sunlit garden (Lowell's "Patterns" [Chapter 22]), an extensive recreational forest and garden (Coleridge's "Kubla Khan"), a front stair (Levertov's "A Time Past"), or a forest at night (Blake's "The Tyger" [Chapter 15])? What is unusual or unique about the set of images? What unexpected or new responses do they produce?

Your conclusion, in addition to restating your major points, is the place for additional insights. It would not be proper to go too far in new directions here, but you might briefly take up one or more of the ideas that you have not developed in the body. In short, what have you learned from your study of imagery in the poem?

Illustrative Student Essay

Underlined sentences in this paper *do not* conform to MLA style and are used solely as teaching tools to emphasize the central idea, thesis sentence, and topic sentences throughout the paper.

Pugh 1

Mike Pugh

Professor Skaggs

English 101

14 January 2008

Imagery in T. S. Eliot's "Preludes"°

[1]   T. S. Eliot's poem "Preludes" offers a series of generally depressing images of life in modern cities.* The first stanza sets the scene by describing a wet, wintry urban street scene. The second stanza moves indoors to describe the actions of the residents "in a thousand furnished rooms" (line 23). The third stanza zooms in even closer to focus on one particular "you" (lines 24–38). Then the fourth stanza expands outward again to the action on the street. This alternation of images from outside to inside and then back to outside follows Eliot's use of specific images to communicate pessimistic ideas about modern urban life. Four types of images suggest Eliot's view that modern city dwellers are spiritually impoverished and that they suffer from a sense of meaninglessness.†

[2]   Numerous images of the human body focus on the commonness and antiheroism of most modern human beings. Eliot's speaker refers to human feet four different times (lines 7, 17, 37, 41)--not the mind, not the soul, but the feet. In the third stanza, the soles of a woman's feet are described as "yellow" (line 37), a color suggesting not health but sickness. And throughout the poem these feet are not marching heroically to a stirring martial tune, nor do they carry runners to victory, dance brilliantly to happy

°This poem appears on page 735.
*Central idea.
†Thesis sentence.

Pugh 2

music, walk purposefully with children in tow, or carry a political leader to a podium to deliver an important speech. No, these feet trudge through city streets as though they are just going through the motions: they "press" to "coffee-stands," presumably at lunch and break times (lines 17–18) and their only insistence occurs "At four and five and six o'clock" (line 42) when business closes for the day and people are in a rush to leave their purposeless jobs and get home to their equally purposeless lives. The feet are also destructive, for they not only trample the sawdust in the street (line 16), but in the fourth stanza they might somehow be thought to be trampling on a soul (lines 39–41).

Eliot's speaker zooms in on other specific parts of the body, too, including hands, fingers, eyes, and a mouth. The hands and fingers, like the feet, seem to be just going through the motions of raising shades or stuffing pipes (lines 21–22, 43). The eyes are "Assured of certain certainties" (line 45), a phrase which suggests that they focus only on the concrete and tangible world and avoid the consideration of faith and mystery. The mouth needs to be wiped (line 52) as though it is dirty--or perhaps foamy from beer. Such bodily images indicate that modern-day people are immersed in the physical world, and they also suggest that this focus amounts to a destructive anomie that is dulling their souls and making their lives meaningless.   **[3]**

While the bodily images suggest modern antiheroism, comparable images of dirt and squalor indicate that the world of cities is soiled and impoverished. Tree leaves are not fresh and green, but they are fallen and have become "grimy scraps" (line 6), blown by the wind, together with the pages of discarded newspapers of mindless headlines and news articles (line 8). The urban streets are "muddy" (line 17) and the shades in people's homes are "dingy" (line 22). The hands of a woman described in the third stanza are "soiled" (line 38). People wake up in the morning to the "faint stale smells of beer" (line 15) from the previous night's binging. All these images indicate a lack of cleanliness, and others stem from deterioration and neglect: The window blinds are "broken" (line 10), and even the songs of sparrows come from "the   **[4]** gutters" (line 32). In this dirty, squalid world, individual souls seem to have nowhere to go but down.

[5]   Not only is this environment filthy and tawdry, but also it is gloomy and unenlightened, and the city-dwellers' spiritual void is reflected in images of darkness. The first stanza begins in the darkness of an early winter evening (line 1), but even the relatively short days are described as "smoky" (line 4). Morning comes in the second and third stanzas, but in the third stanza the woman who rises from bed is disconcerted by the "thousand sordid images" (line 27) that have "flickered against the ceiling" during the night (line 29). The light of day has to creep "up between the shutters" (line 31), an image suggesting that it is uninvited and unwelcome.

[6]   A final set of images suggests that, in addition to being dirty, cheap, and dark, this urban world--both natural and human--is one of spiritual bankruptcy and enervation. The poem is set in winter (line 1), a cold, lifeless, and colorless season when the leaves have fallen from the branches to be blown about aimlessly on the streets and sidewalks. Evenings are described as the "burnt-out ends of smoky days" (line 4)--an image suggesting that human effort, day by day, amounts to no more than a foul-smelling cigarette butt. Twice, Eliot's speaker mentions vacant lots (lines 8, 54), an image conveying the idea that the outside world consists of both emptiness and wasted space scattered with undifferentiated litter. Such images of disuse and depletion are consistent with the poem's emphasis on spiritual stagnation.

[7]   These images are gloomy and hopeless, but the poem also contains slight signs--glimmers--of something more positive. In lines 46 and 47 the speaker introduces the image of the "conscience of a blackened street" which is "Impatient to assume the world." These lines do not make up a complete sentence, but rather form a fragment, and therefore the potentially positive associations and implications are tentative and maybe even illusory. Even so, the word "conscience" suggests something spiritual that may survive and even emerge despite the image of the "blackened street" on which people live. In addition, in the final stanza, Eliot's speaker explains, "I am moved by fancies

Pugh 4

that are curled / Around these images, and cling" (48–49). Specifically, they put
him in mind of "some infinitely gentle / Infinitely suffering thing" (50–51).
Something better, then, may be present, and may be redemptive through infinite
gentleness in the face of all the tawdriness of modern humanity. But the poet's
final words reflect the idea that his speaker has been given no more than a
fleeting image of a better world, and so the poem's negative images prevail. All
we can do, we are told, is to take what comes and not to expect too much, for
the world has always been like this, even from ancient times, revolving in its
orbit while people go about their tasks of daily survival and drudgery.

Pugh 5

Work Cited

Eliot, T. S. "Preludes." Literature: An Introduction to Reading and Writing. Ed.
Edgar V. Roberts. 9th ed. New York: Pearson Longman, 2009. 735.

Commentary on the Essay

This essay illustrates the third strategy for writing about imagery (p. 753), referring to the various locations that make up sets of images developed by Eliot in
"Preludes." This method permits the introduction of imagery drawn from identifiable visual classes, specifically, negative images of the human body and negative
images of street life and the time of day. The introductory paragraph of the essay
presents the central idea that Eliot uses his images to emphasize a gloomy view of
modern urban life. The thesis sentence indicates that the essay will discuss four
different types of images.

Paragraphs 2, 3, and 4 form a connected group stressing Eliot's use of images
which focus on various parts of the human body. In particular, paragraph 2 uses
the words "sickness," "trudge," "purposeless," and "destructive" to characterize
the negative mental pictures prompted by the images. Although the paragraph indicates downside responses to the images, it does not go beyond the limits of the
images themselves. The idea is that Eliot invites these responses.

Paragraph 5 stresses a second type of image in the poem—namely, images that refer to darkness and connect it to the psychological darkness and sordidness of individuals inhabiting the modern city.

The sixth paragraph demonstrates an additional class of image that denotes a whittling away of the human spirit. Here the images of winter, deciduous leaf fall, evening, and vacant lots are cited for the ways in which they cumulatively bring out this impression. The last paragraph deals with the images and thoughts about redemption brought out in the poem. The idea of the paragraph is that the images are so fleeting that they do not counterbalance the prevailing negative images of the rest of the poem.

Writing Topics About Imagery in Poetry

1. Compare the images of war in Owen's "Anthem for Doomed Youth" and Hardy's "Channel Firing" (both in this chapter). Describe the differing effects of the images. How are the images used? How effectively do these images aid in the development of the attitudes toward war expressed in each poem?

2. Basing your work on the poems in this chapter by Coleridge, Griffin and Hopkins, write an essay discussing the poetic use of images drawn from the natural world. What sorts of references do the poets make? What attitudes do they express about the details they select? What is the relationship between the images and religious views? What judgments about topics such as nature, God, humanity, and friendship do the poets show by their images?

3. Considering the imagery of Tate's "Dream On" (this chapter) write an essay explaining the nature and use of imagery in poetry. As you develop your thoughts, be sure to consider the different characteristics of Tate's images and to account for the impressions and ideas that they create. You may also wish to introduce references to images from other poems that are relevant to your points.

4. Write a comparison of the imagery in Elizabeth Browning's "If Thou Must Love Me" and Rückert's "If You Love for the Sake of Beauty"(pp. 733, 749). Even though the poems are on virtually identical subjects, how does the selection of images contribute toward making each poem distinct?

5. Write a poem describing one of these:
   a. Athletes who have just completed an exhausting run.
   b. Children getting out of school for the day.
   c. Your recollection of having been lost as a child.
   d. A cat that always sits down right on your schoolwork.
   e. A particularly good meal you had recently.
   f. The best concert you ever attended.
   g. Driving to work or school on a rainy or snowy day.

   Write an analysis of the images you selected for your poem, and explain your choices. What details stand out in your mind? What do you recall best—sight, smell, sound, action? What is the relationship between your images and the ideas you express in your poem?

6. Study the reproduction of Herkomer's painting *Hard Times* (p. I–6), then write an essay comparing and contrasting Herkomer's artistic techniques with Hopkins's poem "Spring" and Pound's "In a Station of the Metro," along with other poems that you may wish to include. What similarities and differences do you find in subject matter, treatment, arrangement, and general idea? On the basis of your comparison, what relationships do you perceive between poetic and painterly technique?

7. Use the retrieval system in your library or go online to research the topic of imagery in Shakespeare (see *imagery* or *style and imagery*). How many titles do you find? Over how many years have these works been published? Take out one of the books or articles, and write a brief report on your findings. What topics are discussed? What types of imagery are introduced? What relationship does the author make between imagery and content?

Chapter 15

Figures of Speech, or Metaphorical Language: A Source of Depth and Range in Poetry

Figures of speech, metaphorical language, figurative language, figurative devices, and rhetorical figures are terms describing organized patterns of comparison that deepen, broaden, extend, illuminate, and emphasize meaning. First and foremost, the use of figures of speech is a major characteristic by which great literature provides us with fresh and original ways of thinking, feeling, and understanding. Although figurative language is sometimes called "ornate," as though it were unnecessarily decorative, it is not uncommon in conversational speech, and it is essential in literary thought and expression. Unlike the writing of the social and "hard" sciences, imaginative literature is not direct and unambiguous, offering exact correspondences of words and things. Yes, literature presents specific and accurate descriptions and explanations, but it also moves in areas of implication and suggestiveness through the use of **figurative language,** which enables writers to amplify their ideas while still employing relatively small numbers of words. Such language is therefore a sine qua non in imaginative literature, particularly poetry, where it compresses thought, deepens understanding, and shapes response.

The two most important figures of speech, and the most easily recognized, are *metaphors* and *similes.* There are also many other metaphorical figures, some of which are *paradox, anaphora, apostrophe, personification, synecdoche* and *metonymy, pun* (or *paronomasia*), *synesthesia, overstatement,* and *understatement.* All these figures are modes of comparison, and they may be expressed in single words, phrases, clauses, or entire structures.

Metaphors and Similes: The Major Figures of Speech

A Metaphor Shows That Something Unknown Is Identical to Something Known

A **metaphor** (a "carrying out a change") equates known objects or actions with something that is unknown or to be explained (e.g., "Your words are music to my ears," "You are the sunshine of my life," "My life is a squirrel cage"). The equation of the metaphor not only explains and illuminates the thing—let us choose Judith Minty's concept of marital inseparability in "Conjoined"—but also offers distinctive and original and often startling ways of seeing it and thinking about it. Thus Minty draws her metaphor of a married couple from the joining of two onions under one onion skin. Here the metaphor is unique and surprising, and yet on examination it is right and natural, and also somewhat comic.

Metaphors are inseparable from language. In a heavy storm, for example, trees may be said to *bow* constantly as the wind blows against them. *Bow* is a metaphor because the word usually refers to performers' bending forward to acknowledge the applause of an audience and to indicate their gratitude for the audience's approval. The metaphor therefore asks us to equate our knowledge of theater life (something known) to a weather occurrence (something to be explained). A comparable reference to theater life creates one of the best-known metaphors to appear in Shakespeare's plays: "All the world's a stage, / And all the men and women merely players." Here, Shakespeare's character Jacques (JAY-queez) from Act 2, scene 7, of *As You Like It*, identifies human life exactly with stage life. In other words, the things said and done by stage actors are also said and done by living people in real life. It is important to recognize that Shakespeare's metaphor does not state that the world is *like* a stage but that it literally *is* a stage.

A Simile Shows That Something Unknown Is Similar to Something Known

A **simile** (a "showing of likeness or resemblance") illustrates the similarity or comparability of the known to something unknown or to be explained. Whereas a metaphor merges identities, a simile focuses on resemblances (e.g., "Your words are like music to me," "You are like sunshine in my life," "I feel like a squirrel in a cage"). Similes are distinguishable from metaphors because they are introduced by "like" with nouns and "as" (also "as if" and "as though") with clauses. If Minty had written that a married couple is like "The onion in my cupboard," her comparison would have been a simile.

Let us consider one of the best-known similes in poetry, from "A Valediction: Forbidding Mourning" by the Renaissance poet John Donne. This is a dramatic poem spoken by a lover about to go on a trip. His loved one is sorrowful, and he attempts to console her by claiming that even when he is gone, he will remain with her in spirit. The following stanza contains the famous simile embodying this idea.

> Our two souls therefore, which are one,
>   Though I must go, endure not yet
> A breach,° but an expansion   *break, separation*
>   Like gold to airy thinness beat.

The simile compares the souls of the speaker and his loved one to gold, a metal both valuable and malleable. By the simile, the speaker asserts that the impending departure will not be a separation but rather a thinning out, so that the relationship of the lovers will remain constant and rich, even as the distance between them increases. Because the comparison is introduced by *like*, the emphasis of the figurative language is on the similarity of the lovers' love to gold (which is always gold, even when it is thinned out by the goldsmith's hammer), not on the identification of the two.

Characteristics of Metaphorical Language

In language, the words **image** and **imagery** define words that stimulate the imagination and recall memories (images) of sights, sounds, tastes, smells, sensations of touch, and motions (see Chapter 14). Metaphors and similes go beyond literal imagery to introduce perceptions and comparisons that can be unusual, unpredictable, and surprising, as in Donne's simile comparing the lovers' relationship to gold. The comparison emphasizes the bond between the two lovers; the reference to gold shows how valuable the bond is; the unusual and original comparison is one of the elements that make the poem striking and memorable.

To see metaphorical language in further operation, let us take a commonly described condition—happiness. In everyday speech, we might use the sentence "She was happy" to state that a particular character was experiencing joy and excitement. The sentence is of course accurate, but it is not interesting. A more vivid way of saying the same thing is to use an image of action, such as "She jumped for joy." But another and better way of communicating joy is the following simile: "She felt as if she had just won the lottery." Because readers easily understand the disbelief, excitement, exhilaration, and delight that such an event would bring, they also understand—and feel—the character's happiness. It is the simile that evokes this perception and enables each reader to personalize the experience, for no simple description could help a reader comprehend the same degree of emotion.

As a parallel poetic example, let us look at John Keats's sonnet "On First Looking into Chapman's Homer," which Keats wrote soon after reading the translation of Homer's great epics *The Iliad* and *The Odyssey* by the Renaissance poet George Chapman. Keats, one of the greatest of all poets himself, describes his enthusiasm about Chapman's successful and exciting work.

JOHN KEATS (1795–1821)

 ### On First Looking into Chapman's Homer° (1816)

Much have I travell'd in the realms of gold,°   *the world of great art*
   And many goodly states and kingdoms seen:
   Round many western islands° have I been   *much ancient literature*
Which bards in fealty to Apollo° hold.
5 Oft of one wide expanse° had I been told   *epic poetry*
   That deep-brow'd Homer ruled as his demesne°;
   Yet did I never breathe its pure serene°   *realm, estate*
Till I heard Chapman speak out loud and bold:
Then felt I like some watcher of the skies
10   When a new planet swims into his ken°;   *range of vision*

°George Chapman (c. 1560–1634) published his translations of Homer's *Iliad* in 1612 and *Odyssey* in 1614–15. 4 *bards . . . Apollo*: writers who are sworn subjects of Apollo, the Greek god of light, music, poetry, prophecy, and the sun. 7 *serene*: a clear expanse of air; also grandeur, clarity; rulers were also sometimes called "serene majesty."

Or like stout Cortez° when with eagle eyes
  He star'd at the Pacific—and all his men
Look'd at each other with a wild surmise°—   *conjecture, supposition*
  Silent, upon a peak in Darien.

°11 *Cortez*: Hernando Cortès (1485–1547), a Spanish general and the conqueror of Mexico. Keats confuses him with Vasco de Balboa (c. 1475–1519), the first European to see the Pacific Ocean (in 1510) from Darien, an early name for the Isthmus of Panama.

As a first step in understanding the power of metaphorical language, we can briefly paraphrase the sonnet's content.

> I have enjoyed much art and read much poetry, and I have been told that Homer is the best writer of all. However, I did not appreciate his works until I first read them in Chapman's clear and forceful translation. This discovery was exciting and awe-inspiring.

If all Keats had written had been a paragraph like this one, we would pay little attention to it, for it conveys no excitement or wonder. But the last six lines of the sonnet contain two memorable similes ("like some watcher of the skies" and "like stout Cortez") that stand out and demand a special effort of imagination. To appreciate these similes fully, we need to imagine what it would be like to be an astronomer as he or she discovers a previously unknown planet, and what it would have been like to be one of the first European explorers to see the Pacific Ocean. As we imagine ourselves in these roles, we get a sense of the amazement, excitement, exhilaration, and joy that would accompany such discoveries. With that experience comes the realization that the world is far bigger and more astonishing than we had ever dreamed. Metaphorical language, therefore, makes strong demands on our creative imaginations. It bears repeating that as we develop our own mental pictures under the stimulation of metaphors and similes, we also develop appropriately associated attitudes and feelings. Let us consider once more how Keats's metaphor "realms of gold" invites us both to imagine brilliant and shining kingdoms and also to join Keats in valuing and loving not just poetry but all literature. The metaphorical "realms of gold" act upon our minds—liberating our imaginations, directing our understanding, and evoking our feelings. In such a way, reading and responding to the works of writers like Keats produces both mental and emotional experiences that were previously hidden to us. Poets constantly give us something new, and they increase our power to think and know. They enlarge us.

🍁 VEHICLE AND TENOR

To describe the relationship between a writer's ideas and the metaphors and similes chosen to objectify them, two useful terms have been coined by I. A. Richards (in *The Philosophy of Rhetoric* [1929]). First is the **vehicle,** or the specific words of the metaphor or simile. Second is the **tenor,** which is the totality of ideas and attitudes not only of the literary speaker but also of the author.

For example, the tenor of Donne's simile in "A Valediction: Forbidding Mourning" is the inseparable love and unbreakable connection of the two lovers; the vehicle is the hammering of gold "to airy thinness." Similarly, the tenor of the similes in the sestet of Keats's sonnet "On First Looking into Chapman's Homer" is awe and wonder; the vehicle is the description of astronomical and geographical discovery.

Other Figures of Speech

A Paradox Uses an Apparent Error or Contradiction to Reveal Truth

A **paradox** is "a thought beyond a thought," a figurative device through which something apparently wrong or contradictory is shown to be truthful and non-contradictory. The phrase "I, a child, very old" in Whitman's "Facing West from California's Shores" is a paradox. The obvious contradiction is that no one can be old and young at the same time, but this contradiction can be reconciled if we realize that even as people get older they still retain many of the qualities of children (such as enthusiasm and hope). Thus Whitman's contradiction is not contradictory (is this clause a paradox?) and the speaker may genuinely be "a child, very old." The second line of Sir Thomas Wyatt's sonnet "I Find No Peace" embodies two paradoxes. One opposes fear with hope, the other fire with ice: "I fear and hope, I burn and freeze like ice." These paradoxes reflect the contradictory states of people in love—wanting love ("hope," "burn"), but also being uncertain and unsure about the relationship ("fear," "freeze"). The paradoxes thus highlight the truth that love is a complex and often unsettling emotion.

Anaphora Provides Weight and Emphasis Through Repetition

Anaphora ("to carry again or repeat") is the repetition of the same word or phrase throughout a work or a section of a work in order to lend weight and emphasis. An example occurs in Blake's "The Tyger" (Chapter 15), when the interrogative word *what* is used five times to emphasize the mystery of evil (italics added).

> *What* the hammer? *what* the chain?
> In *what* furnace was thy brain?
> *What* the anvil? *what* dread grasp
> Dare its deadly terrors clasp?

Anaphora is the most obvious feature of Muriel Rukeyser's "Looking at Each Other," where the word *yes* begins each of the poem's twenty-five lines.

Apostrophe Creates the Drama of a Speaker Addressing an Audience

In an **apostrophe** (a "turning away," or redirection of attention) a speaker addresses a real or imagined listener who is not present. It is like a public speech, with readers as audience, and it therefore makes a poem dramatic. An apostrophe enables the speaker to develop ideas that might arise naturally on a public occasion, as in Wordsworth's sonnet "London, 1802," which is addressed to the long dead English poet Milton. In the following sonnet by Keats, "Bright Star," the speaker addresses a distant and inanimate star, yet through apostrophe he speaks as though the star has human understanding and divine power.

JOHN KEATS (1795–1822)

 Bright Star (1838; 1819)

Bright star! would I were steadfast as thou art—
   Not in lone splendor hung aloft the night,
And watching, with eternal lids apart,
   Like Nature's patient, sleepless eremite,°   *hermit, a holy presence*
The moving waters at their priestlike task   5
   Of pure ablution round earth's human shores,
Or gazing on the new soft-fallen mask
   Of snow upon the mountains and the moors;
No—yet still steadfast, still unchangeable,
   Pillowed upon my fair love's ripening breast,   10
To feel forever its soft fall and swell,
   Awake forever in a sweet unrest,
     Still, still to hear her tender-taken breath,
     And so live ever—or else swoon to death.

QUESTIONS

1. With what topic is the speaker concerned in this sonnet? How does he compare himself with the distant star?

2. What qualities does the speaker attribute specifically to the star? What role does he seem to assign to it? In light of this role, and the qualities needed to serve in it, how might the star be compared to a divine and benign presence?

3. In light of the emphasis on the words *forever* and *ever* in lines 11–14, how appropriate is the choice of the star as the subject of the apostrophe in the poem?

In this sonnet the speaker addresses the star as though it is a person or god, an object of adoration, and the poem is therefore like a petitional prayer. The star is idealized with qualities that the speaker wishes to establish in himself—namely, steadfastness, eternal watchfulness, and fidelity. The point of the apostrophe is thus to dramatize the speaker's yearning and to stress the permanence of space and eternity as contrasted with earthly impermanence.

Personification Is the Attribution of Human Traits to Abstractions or to Nonhuman Objects

A close neighbor of apostrophe is **personification,** another dramatic figurative device through which poets explore relationships to environment, ideals, and inner lives. In "Bright Star," as we have just seen, Keats personifies the star addressed by the speaker. Shakespeare's speaker in Sonnet 146, "Poor Soul, the Center of My Sinful Earth" (Chapter 22) personifies his own soul as he speaks of earthly and heavenly concerns. Other important uses of personification are seen in Shelley's "Ode to the West Wind" (Chapter 17) and also in Keats's "To Autumn" (this chapter) and "Ode on a Grecian Urn" (Chapter 22).

Synecdoche and Metonymy Transfer Meanings by Parts and Associations

These figures are close in purpose and effect. **Synecdoche** ("taking one thing out of another") is a device in which a part stands for the whole or a whole for a part, like the expression "all hands aboard," which describes the whole of a ship's crew by their hands, that part of them that performs work. **Metonymy** (a "transfer of name") substitutes one thing for another with which it is closely identified, as when "Hollywood" is used to mean the movie industry, or when "the White House" signifies the policies and activities of the American president. The purpose of both figures of speech is the creation of new insights and ideas, just like metaphors and similes.

Synecdoche is seen in Keats's "To Autumn," where the gourd and hazel shells, which are single instances of ripe produce, stand for the entire autumnal harvest. In Wordsworth's "London, 1802," the phrase "thy heart" (line 13) is a synecdoche in which a part—the heart—refers to the complete person. Metonymy is seen again in Keats's "To Autumn," when the "granary floor" (line 14), the place where grain is stored, bears the transferred meaning of the entire autumnal harvest.

Pun, or Paronomasia, Shows That Words with Similar or Identical Sounds Have Different Meanings

A **pun** ("a point or a puncture") or **paronomasia** ("something alongside a name") is wordplay stemming from the fact that words with different meanings have surprisingly similar or even identical sounds and that some individual words have surprisingly differing and even contradictory meanings. Because puns are sometimes considered outrageous and often require a little bit of thinking, people may groan when they hear them (even while they enjoy them). Also, because many puns seem to play only with sound, they have not always enjoyed critical acclaim. Good puns can always be relished because they work with sounds to reveal ideas. John Gay, for example, creates clever puns in the following song, sung chorally by the gang of thieves in *The Beggar's Opera* (1728), a play that, incidentally, marked the beginning of the modern musical comedy tradition.

JOHN GAY (1685–1732)

 Let Us Take the Road (1728)

Let us take the road.
  Hark! I hear the sound of coaches!
  The hour of attack approaches,
To your arms, brave boys, and load.
  See the ball I hold!°   *[holding up a bullet]*   5
  Let the chemists° toil like asses,   *alchemists*
  Our fire their fire surpasses,°   *Our [gun]fire is better than their [forge] fire.*
    And turns all our lead to gold.

QUESTIONS

1. What traits are shown by the singers of this poem? Why do they not seem frightening, despite their admission that they are holdup men?

2. Describe the puns in the poem. What kind of knowledge is needed to explain them fully? How many puns are there? How are they connected? Why do the puns seem both witty and outrageous?

Here "fire," "lead," and "gold" are puns. Lead was the "base" or "low" metal that the medieval alchemists ("chemists") tried to transform into ingots of gold, using the heat from their fires. The puns develop because the gang of cutthroats singing the song is about to go out to rob travelers at gunpoint. Hence their bullets are their lead, which they plan to transform into the gold coins they steal. Their fire is not the fire of alchemists, but rather pistol fire. Through these puns, Gay's villains charm us by their wit and delight in their villainy, even though in real life they would scare us to death.

Synesthesia Demonstrates the Oneness or Unity of Feelings

In **synesthesia** (the "bringing together of feelings") a poet describes a feeling or perception with words that usually refer to different or even opposite feelings or perceptions. Keats uses synesthesia extensively, as, for example, in the "Ode to a Nightingale" (Chapter 18), where a plot of ground is "melodious," a draught of wine tastes of "Dance, and Provençal song, and sunburnt mirth," and beaded bubbles are "winking at the brim" of a wine glass.

Overstatement and Understatement Are Means of Creating Emphasis

Two important devices creating emphasis are overstatement (or **hyperbole**), and understatement. **Overstatement,** also called the **overreacher,** is exaggeration for effect. In "London, 1802," for example, Wordsworth declares that England "is a fen/Of stagnant waters." That is, the country and its people collectively make up a stinking, polluted marsh, a muddy dump. What Wordsworth establishes by this overstatement is his judgment that England in 1802 was so morally and politically rotten that it needed a writer like Milton to unite the people around noble ideas.

In contrast with overstatement, **understatement** is the deliberate underplaying or undervaluing of a thing. One of the most famous poetic understatements is in Marvell's "To His Coy Mistress" (Chapter 19).

> The grave's a fine and private place,
> But none, I think, do there embrace.

Here Marvell, through understatement, wittily and grimly emphasizes the eternity of death by contrasting the motionless privacy of the grave with the active privacy of a trysting place.

Poems for Study

Jack Agüeros . . . . Sonnet for You, Familiar Famine, 768
William Blake . . . . The Tyger, 769
Robert Burns . . . . A Red, Red Rose, 770
John Donne. . . . . A Valediction: Forbidding Mourning, 771
John Dryden . . . . A Song for St. Cecilia's Day, 772
Abbie Huston Evans. . . . . The Iceberg Seven-Eighths Under, 774
Thomas Hardy . . . . The Convergence of the Twain, 775
Joy Harjo . . . . Remember, 777
John Keats . . . . To Autumn, 778
Maurice Kenny. . . . . Legacy, 779
Jane Kenyon . . . . Let Evening Come, 780
Henry King . . . . Sic Vita, 781
Robert Lowell. . . . . Skunk Hour, 781
Judith Minty. . . . . Conjoined, 783
Pablo Neruda . . . . If You Forget Me, 784
Marge Piercy. . . . . A Work of Artifice, 785
Muriel Rukeyser. . . . . Looking at Each Other, 786
William Shakespeare. . . . . Sonnet 18: Shall I Compare Thee
                                              to a Summer's Day? 787
William Shakespeare. . . . . Sonnet 30: When to the Sessions
                                              of Sweet Silent Thought, 787
Elizabeth Tudor, Queen Elizabeth I . . . . On Monsieur's Departure, 788
Mona Van Duyn. . . . . Earth Tremors Felt in Missouri, 789
Walt Whitman . . . . Facing West from California's Shores, 790
William Wordsworth . . . . London, 1802, 790
Sir Thomas Wyatt . . . . I Find No Peace, 791

JACK AGÜEROS (b. 1934)

 ## Sonnet for You, Familiar Famine (1996)

Nobody's waiting for any apocalypse to meet you, Famine!

We know you. There isn't a corner of our round world
where you don't politely accompany someone to bed each

night. In some families, you're the only one sitting
at the table when the dinner bell tolls. "He's not so   5
bad," say people who have plenty and easily tolerate you.
They argue that small portions are good for us, and
are just what we deserve. There's an activist side to
you, Famine. You've been known to bring down governments,
yet you never get any credit for your political reforms.   10

Don't make the mistake I used to make of thinking fat
people are immune to Famine. Famine has this other ugly
side. Famine knows that the more you eat the more you
long. That side bears his other frightening name, Emptiness.

QUESTIONS

1. What figure of speech does the poet use in this poem? What situation does the poem address?

2. What is the purpose of using this figure for the poem rather than a more direct analysis of the causes and effects of hunger?

3. What powers does the speaker attribute to Famine? How correct is his assessment of these powers?

WILLIAM BLAKE (1757–1827)

For a portrait, see Chapter 12, page 661.

🍁 The Tyger° (1794)

Tyger! Tyger! burning bright
In the forests of the night,
What immortal hand or eye
Could frame thy fearful symmetry?

In what distant deeps or skies   5
Burnt the fire of thine eyes?
On what wings dare he aspire?
What the hand, dare seize the fire?

And what shoulder, & what art,
Could twist the sinews of thy heart?   10
And when thy heart began to beat,
What dread hand? & what dread feet?

What the hammer? what the chain?
In what furnace was thy brain?
What the anvil? what dread grasp   15
Dare its deadly terrors clasp?

°"Tyger": refers not only to a tiger but also to any large, wild, ferocious cat.

When the stars threw down their spears,
And water'd heaven with their tears,
Did he smile his work to see?
20   Did he who made the Lamb make thee?

Tyger! Tyger! burning bright
In the forests of the night,
What immortal hand or eye
Dare frame thy fearful symmetry?

QUESTIONS

1. What do the associations of the image of "burning" suggest? Why is the burning done at night rather than day? What does night suggest?
2. Describe the kinesthetic images of lines 5–20. What ideas is Blake's speaker representing by these images? What attributes does the speaker suggest may belong to the blacksmith-type initiator of these actions?
3. Line 20 presents the kinesthetic image of a creator. What is implied about the mixture of good and evil in the world? What answer does the poem offer? Why does Blake phrase this line as a question rather than an assertion?
4. The sixth stanza repeats the first stanza with only one change of imagery of action. Contrast these stanzas, stressing the difference between "could" (line 4) and "dare" (24).

ROBERT BURNS (1759–1796)

For a portrait, see Chapter 12, page 662.

 ## A Red, Red Rose (1796)

O my Luve's like a red, red rose,
   That's newly sprung in June:
O my Luve's like the melodie
   That's sweetly play'd in tune.

5   As fair art thou, my bonnie lass,
   So deep in luve am I;
And I will luve thee still, my Dear,
   Till a'° the seas gang° dry.   *all; go*

Till a' the seas gang dry, my Dear,
10   And the rocks melt wi'° the sun: *with*
And I will luve thee still, my Dear,
   While the sands o'° life shall run.   *of*

And fare thee weel, my only Luve!
   And fare thee weel, awhile!
15   And I will come again, my Luve,
   Tho' it were ten thousand mile!

QUESTIONS

1. In light of the character and background of the speaker, do the two opening similes seem common or unusual? If they are just ordinary, does that fact diminish their value? How and why?

2. Describe the shift of listener envisioned after the first stanza. How are the last three stanzas related to the first?

3. Consider the metaphors concerning time and travel. How do the metaphors assist you in comprehending the speaker's character?

JOHNDONNE (1572–1631)

For a portrait, see Chapter 12, page 666.

A Valediction: Forbidding Mourning (1633)

As virtuous men pass mildly away,
  And whisper to their souls to go,
Whilst some of their sad friends do say
  The breath goes now, and some say, No;

So let us melt, and make no noise,   5
  No tear-floods, nor sigh-tempests move,
'Twere profanation of our joys
  To tell the laity° our love.

Moving of th'earth° brings harm and fears,   *earthquakes*
  Men reckon what it did and meant: 10
But trepidation° of the spheres,
  Though greater far, is innocent.

Dull sublunary lovers' love
  (Whose soul is sense°) cannot admit
Absence, because it doth remove   15
  Those things which elemented it.

But we by a love so much refined
  That our selves know not what it is,
Inter-assured of the mind,
  Care less, eyes, lips, and hands to miss.   20

Our two souls therefore, which are one,
  Though I must go, endure not yet
A breach, but an expansion
  Like gold to airy thinness beat.°

°7, 8 *profanation . . . laity:* as though the lovers are priests of love, whose love is a mystery. 11 *trepidation:* Before Sir Isaac Newton explained the precession of the equinoxes, it was assumed that the positions of heavenly bodies should be constant and perfectly circular. The clearly observable irregularities (caused by the slow wobbling of the earth's axis) were explained by the concept of *trepidation,* or a trembling or oscillation that occurred in the outermost of the spheres surrounding the earth. 14 *soul is sense:* lovers whose attraction is totally physical. 24 *gold to airy thinness beat:* a reference to the malleability of gold.

25 If they be two, they are two so
        As stiff twin compasses° are two;
    Thy soul, the fixt foot, makes no show
        To move, but doth, if th'other do.

    And though it in the center sit,
30   Yet when the other far doth roam,
    It leans and harkens after it,
        And grows erect, as that comes home.

    Such wilt thou be to me, who must
        Like th'other foot, obliquely run;
35 Thy firmness draws my circle just,°
        And makes me end where I begun.

°26 *compasses:* a compass used for drawing circles. 35 *just:* perfectly round.

QUESTIONS

1. What is the situation envisioned as the occasion for the poem? Who is talking to whom? What is their relationship?
2. What is the intention of the first two stanzas? What is the effect of the phrases "tear-floods" and "sigh-tempests"?
3. Describe the effect of the opening simile about men on their deathbeds.
4. What is the metaphor of the third stanza (lines 9–12)? In what sense might the "trepidation of the spheres" be less harmful than the parting of the lovers?
5. In lines 13–20 there is a comparison making the love of the speaker and his sweetheart superior to the love of average lovers. What is the basis for the speaker's claim?
6. What is the comparison begun by the word "refined" in line 17 and continued by the simile in line 24?

JOHN DRYDEN (1631–1700)

 A Song for St. Cecilia's Day° (1687)

I

    From harmony, from heavenly harmony
        This universal frame began:
        When Nature underneath a heap
            Of jarring atoms lay,
5   And could not heave her head,
    The tuneful voice was heard from high,
        "Arise, ye more than dead."
    Then cold, and hot, and moist, and dry°
    In order to their stations leap,
10   And Music's pow'r obey.

°St. Cecilia, the patron saint of music, was traditionally considered the creator of the pipe organ. In London after 1683, she was celebrated annually on November 22 by the performance of a poem set to orchestral and choral music. Dryden wrote two poems for the occasion: this one in 1687, and the longer "Alexander's Feast" in 1697. The best-known choral and orchestral version of the "Song for St. Cecilia's Day" is by Georg Frederic Handel. 8 *cold . . . dry:* Before the modern classification of elements, it was supposed that there were four "elements" having four primary qualities: earth = cold, fire = hot, water = moist, and air = dry.

From harmony, from heavenly harmony
    This universal frame began:
    From harmony to harmony
Through all the compass of the notes it ran,
The diapason° closing full in Man.°   15

II

What passion cannot Music raise and quell!
    When Jubal° struck the corded shell,
  His listening brethren stood around,
  And, wondering, on their faces fell
  To worship that celestial sound:
Less than a god they thought there could not dwell   20
    Within the hollow of that shell,
    That spoke so sweetly and so well.
What passion cannot Music raise and quell!

III

    The trumpet's loud clangor
      Excites us to arms   25
  With shrill notes of anger
    And mortal alarms.
  The double double double beat
    Of the thundering drum   30
Cries, "Hark! the foes come;
Charge, charge, 'tis too late to retreat."

IV

    The soft complaining flute
    In dying notes discovers
    The woes of hopeless lovers,   35
Whose dirge is whispered by the warbling lute.

V

    Sharp violins proclaim
Their jealous pangs, and desperation,
Fury, frantic indignation,
Depth of pains, and height of passion   40
    For the fair, disdainful dame.

VI

    But O! what art can teach,
    What human voice can reach
  The sacred organ's praise?
    Notes inspiring holy love,
Notes that wing their heavenly ways   45
    To mend the choirs above.

°15 *diapason:* the organ stop determining keys and chords; thus, metaphorically, the quality that created and shaped humankind. 15 *Man:* the human race. 17 *Jubal:* "the father of all such as handle the harp and organ" (Genesis 4:21).

VII

Orpheus° could lead the savage race
And trees unrooted left their place,
    Sequacious of the lyre;
50 But bright Cecilia raised the wonder higher:
When to her organ vocal breath was given,
An angel heard, and straight appeared,
      Mistaking earth for heaven.

Grand Chorus

55 As from the power of sacred lays
    The spheres began to move,
And sung the great Creator's praise
    To all the blessed above;
So, when the last and dreadful hour
60 This crumbling pageant shall devour
The trumpet shall be heard on high,
The dead shall live, the living die,
And Music shall untune the sky.°

°48 *Orpheus:* in Greek myth, the greatest of all musicians. His playing tamed wild animals, and trees uprooted themselves to go to hear him. (See Chapter 20.) 63 *And Music shall untune the sky:* The harmony of the sky (i.e., heavenly harmony) will be replaced eternally by musical harmony.

QUESTIONS

1. What is the central idea of "A Song for St. Cecilia's Day"? In light of this idea, what is the major attribute of the creator God (whom Dryden does not specifically mention)? Why does the angel mistake earth for heaven (stanza 7)? How is this example related to the poem's major idea?

2. Through what attribute is music related to the created universal order? How is music analogous to the ordering principles of creation? How long will music continue to exist? Why?

3. What powers are attributed to the various instruments? When is vocal music introduced? What is its effect?

4. Should Dryden's ideas in the poem be considered outdated? To what degree are the ideas still important and valid?

ABBIE HUSTON EVANS (1881–1983)

🍁 The Iceberg Seven-Eighths Under (1961)

Under the sky at night, stunned by our guesses,
We know incredibly much and incredibly little.
Wrapped in the envelope of gossamer air,
A clinging mote whirled round in a blizzard of stars,
5 A chaff-cloud of great suns that has not settled,

By the barn's black shoulder where the gibbous moon
Hangs low, no other light making a glimmer
In the dark country, hearing the breathing of cattle—
I do not need that anyone should tell me
Most real goes secret, sunken, nigh-submerged: 10
Yet does it dazzle with its least part showing,
Like the iceberg seven-eighths under.

QUESTIONS

1. How does the simile of the "iceberg seven-eighths under" explain the "Most real" that "goes secret"? In what way is this simile, together with line 11, an extension of the idea in line 2?
2. What metaphors does the poet use to describe the earth and the people ("We") on it?
3. Explain the contrast between the metaphors of night and darkness (lines 1, 6, 8) and the use of the word "dazzle" in line 11. How does the poem express awe about the visible universe?

THOMAS HARDY (1840–1928)

For a photo, see Chapter 5, page 287.

 ## The Convergence of the Twain (1912)

Lines on the Loss of the "Titanic"°

I

In a solitude of the sea
Deep from human vanity,
And the Pride of Life that planned her, stilly couches she.

II

Steel chambers, late the pyres
Of her salamandrine fires,°   5
Cold Currents thrid,° and turn to rhythmic tidal lyres.   *thread, instrumental strings*

III

Over the mirrors meant
To glass the opulent
The sea-worm crawls—grotesque, slimed, dumb, indifferent.

°*The Titanic:* The largest passenger ship in existence at the time, and considered unsinkable, was sunk after a collision with an iceberg on its maiden voyage in April 1912. The loss was particularly notable because some of the passengers were among the world's social elite, and 1,500 people died because there were not enough lifeboats for everyone. In 1985 the wreck of the ship was discovered on the ocean floor at a depth of 13,000 feet, and some of the ship's artifacts were recovered. The loss of the *Titanic* has become legendary. 4-5 *Steel chambers . . . salamandrine fires:* The idea here is that the "steel chambers" of the ship's furnaces were built to resist the high heat of the coal fires, much like the salamander of ancient myth, which could live through fire.

IV

    Jewels in joy designed
    To ravish the sensuous mind
Lie lightless, all their sparkles bleared and black and blind.

V

    Dim moon-eyed fishes near
    Gaze at the gilded gear
And query: "What does this vaingloriousness down here?"

VI

    Well: while was fashioning
    This creature of cleaving wing,
The Immanent Will that stirs and urges everything

VII

    Prepared a sinister mate
    For her—so gaily great—
A Shape of Ice, for the time far and dissociate.

VIII

    And as the smart ship grew
    In stature, grace, and hue,
In shadowy silent distance grew the Iceberg too.

IX

    Alien they seemed to be:
    No mortal eye could see
The intimate welding of their later history.

X

    Or sign that they were bent
    By paths coincident
On being anon twin halves of one august event.

XI

    Till the Spinner of the Years
    Said "Now!" And each one hears,
And consummation comes, and jars two hemispheres.

QUESTIONS

1. What human attributes does Hardy ascribe to the *Titanic?* What pronoun does he regularly use in reference to the ship? What is the name of this figure of speech?
2. What are the meanings of "vanity" (line 2), "Pride of Life" (line 3), and "vaingloriousness" (line 15) in relation to the speaker's judgment of the meaning of the *Titanic?*

3. Why does Hardy introduce the phrases "Spinner of the Years" (line 31) and "Immanent Will" (line 18)?

4. What is the idea of calling the iceberg the "sinister mate" of the *Titanic* (line 19)? What irony results from this phrase, and from the word "consummation" in the last line of the poem?

JOY HARJO (b. 1951)

For a photo, see Chapter 11, page 638.

 Remember (1983)

Remember the sky that you were born under,
know each of the star's stories.
Remember the moon, know who she is. I met her
in a bar once in Iowa City.
Remember the sun's birth at dawn, that is the   5
strongest point of time. Remember sundown
and the giving away to night.
Remember your birth, how your mother struggled
to give you form and breath. You are evidence of
her life, and her mother's, and hers.   10
Remember your father. He is your life, also.
Remember the earth whose skin you are:
red earth, black earth, yellow earth, white earth
brown earth, we are earth.
Remember the plants, trees, animal life who all have their   15
tribes, their families, their histories, too. Talk to them,
listen to them. They are alive poems.
Remember the wind. Remember her voice. She knows the
origin of this universe. I heard her singing Kiowa war
dance songs at the corner of Fourth and Central once.   20
Remember that you are all people and that all people
are you.
Remember that you are this universe and that this
universe is you.
Remember that all is in motion, is growing, is you.   25
Remember that language comes from this.
Remember the dance that language is, that life is.
Remember.

QUESTIONS

1. How many times is the word "remember" repeated in this poem? What is the name of this figure of speech? What is the effect of the repetitions?

2. Who is the speaker, and who is the listener? What is the apparent purpose of stating all the things that the listener is being asked to remember? What is the implication of the word "remember," inasmuch as many of the things designated for remembrance happened before the listener was alive or was old enough to have a memory?

3. What is meant by "the earth whose skin you are" in line 12? Explain the paradox of "you are all people and . . . all people / are you" in lines 21–22.

JOHN KEATS (1795–1821)

For a portrait, see this chapter, page 762.

 To Autumn (1820)

Season of mists and mellow fruitfulness!
   Close bosom-friend of the maturing sun;
Conspiring with him to load and bless
   With fruit the vines that round the thatch-eaves run;
5 To bend with apples the mossed cottage-trees,
   And fill all fruit with ripeness to the core;
     To swell the gourd, and plump the hazel shells
With a sweet kernel; to set budding more,
   And still more, later flowers for the bees,
10   Until they think warm days will never cease,
     For Summer has o'erbrimmed their clammy cells.

Who hath not seen thee oft amid thy store?
   Sometimes whoever seeks abroad may find
Thee sitting careless on a granary floor,
15   Thy hair soft-lifted by the winnowing wind,
Or on a half-reaped furrow sound asleep,
Drowsed with the fume of poppies, while thy hook
    Spares the next swath and all its twinèd flowers;
And sometimes like a gleaner thou dost keep
20   Steady thy laden head across a brook;
     Or by a cider-press, with patient look,
    Thou watchest the last oozings hours by hours.

Where are the songs of Spring? Ay, where are they?
   Think not of them, thou hast thy music too,—
25 While barrèd clouds bloom the soft-dying day,
   And touch the stubble-plains with rosy hue;
Then in a wailful choir the small gnats mourn
   Among the river sallows, borne aloft
    Or sinking as the light wind lives or dies;
30 And full-grown lambs loud bleat from hilly bourn;
   Hedge-crickets sing; and now with treble soft
The redbreast whistles from a garden-croft;
   And gathering swallows twitter in the skies.

QUESTIONS

1. How is personification used in the first stanza? How does it change in the second? What is the effect of such personification?

2. How does Keats structure the poem to accord with his apostrophe to autumn? That is, in what ways can the stanzas be distinguished by the type of discourse addressed to the season?

3. Analyze Keats's metonymy in the first stanza and synecdoche in the second. What effects does he achieve with these devices?

4. How, through the use of images, does Keats develop his idea that autumn is a season of "mellow fruitfulness"?

MAURICE KENNY (b. 1929)

 Legacy (1984)

my face is grass
　color of April rain;
arms, legs are the limbs
　of birch, cedar;
my thoughts are winds   5
　which blow;
pictures are in my mind
　are the climb uphill
　to dream in the sun;
　hawk feathers, and quills   10
　of porcupine running
　the edge of the stream
　which reflects stories
　of my many mornings
　and the dark faces of night   15
　mingled with victories
　of dawn and tomorrow;
corn of the fields and squash . . .
　the daughters of my mother
　who collect honey   20
　and all the fruits;
meadow and sky are the end of my day
　the stretch of my night
　yet the birth of my dust;
my wind is the breath of a fawn   25
　the cry of the cub
　the trot of the wolf
　whose print covers
　the tracks of my feet;
my word, my word,   30
　loaned
legacy, the obligation I hand
　to the blood of my flesh
　the sinew of the loins
to hold to the sun   35
and the moon
which direct the river
　that carries my song
　and the beat of the drum
to the fires of the village   40
　which endures.

QUESTIONS

1. Describe some of the paradoxes that Kenny explores in this poem. What do the paradoxes contribute to the speaker's explanation of his identity?

2. How can it be said that "meadow and sky are the end of my day / the stretch of my night / yet the birth of my dust" lines 22–24?

3. What is the speaker's legacy? How does it differ from what is usually thought of as a legacy?

4. Describe the content of the use of phrases and clauses beginning with "which" in this poem. What is the name of this repetitive usage? What is the effect in this poem?

JANE KENYON (1947–1995)

 ## Let Evening Come (1990)

Let the light of late afternoon
shine through chinks in the barn, moving
up the bales as the sun moves down.

Let the cricket take up chafing
5   as a woman takes up her needles
and her yarn. Let evening come.

Let dew collect on the hoe abandoned
in long grass. Let the stars appear
and the moon disclose her silver horn.

10   Let the fox go back to its sandy den.
Let the wind die down. Let the shed
go black inside. Let evening come.

To the bottle in the ditch, to the scoop
in the oats, to air in the lung
15   let evening come.

Let it come as it will, and don't
be afraid.° God does not leave us   *Matthew 28:10*
comfortless,° so let evening come.   *John 14:18*

QUESTIONS

1. This poem features the repetition of phrases beginning with the word *let*. What is this pattern called? How many such phrases does the poem contain? How does the pattern furnish strength to the poem?

2. What sorts of activities does the speaker associate with day? With night? How are these activities connected?

3. Describe the shift of topic in the last stanza. Does this shift occur logically or illogically from the earlier topic material of the poem? How does the final stanza seem to be an ordinary and necessary part of the activities described in the first five stanzas?

HENRY KING (1592–1669)

 ## Sic Vita° (1657)

Like to the falling of a star,
Or as the flights of eagles are,
Or like the fresh spring's gaudy hue,
Or silver drops of morning dew,
Or like a wind that chafes the flood,   5
Or bubbles which on water stood:
Even such is man, whose borrowed light
Is straight called in, and paid to night.
   The wind blows out, the bubble dies;
   The spring entombed in autumn lies: 10
   The dew dries up, the star is shot;
   The flight is past, and man forgot.

°Such is life (Latin).

QUESTIONS

1. How many similes do you find in lines 1–6? Describe the range of references; that is, from what sources are the similes derived? What do all these similes (and references) have in common?

2. Explain the two metaphors in lines 7–8. (One is brought out by the words "borrowed," "called in," and "paid," the other by "light" and "night.")

3. Explain the continuation in lines 9–12 of the similes in 1–6. Do you think that these last four lines are essential, or might the poem have been successfully concluded with line 8? Explain.

4. What point does this poem make about humanity? In what ways do the similes in the poem help explore these ideas and bring them to life?

ROBERT LOWELL (1917–1977)

 ## Skunk Hour (1959)

For Elizabeth Bishop°

Nautilus Island's° hermit
heiress still lives through winter in her Spartan cottage;
her sheep still graze above the sea.
Her son's a bishop. Her farmer
is first selectman in our village;   5
she's in her dotage.

Thirsting for
the hierarchic privacy
of Queen Victoria's century,

°For Elizabeth Bishop: Bishop and Lowell were friends. "Skunk Hour" is modeled on Bishop's "The Armadillo" (still in manuscript in 1958, published in 1965), which she dedicated to Lowell. He, reciprocally, dedicated "Skunk Hour" to her. 1 *Nautilus Island's:* Lowell had a summer house on Nautilus Island, Maine.

10 she buys up all
the eyesores facing her shore,
and lets them fall.

The season's ill—
we've lost our summer millionaire,
15 who seemed to leap from an L. L. Bean
catalogue. His nine-knot yawl
was auctioned off to lobstermen.
A red fox stain covers Blue Hill.°

And now our fairy
20 decorator brightens his shop for fall;
his fishnet's filled with orange cork,
orange, his cobbler's bench and awl;
there is no money in his work,
he'd rather marry.

25 One dark night,
my Tudor° Ford climbed the hill's skull;
I watched for love-cars. Lights turned down,
they lay together, hull to hull,
where the graveyard shelves on the town. . . .
30 My mind's not right.

A car radio bleats,
"Love, O careless Love°. . . ." I hear
my ill-spirit sob in each blood cell,
as if my hand were at its throat. . . .
35 I myself am hell;°
nobody's here—

only skunks, that search
in the moonlight for a bite to eat.
They march on their soles up Main Street:
40 white stripes, moonstruck eyes' red fire
under the chalk-dry and spar spire
of the Trinitarian Church.

I stand on top
of our back steps and breathe the rich air—
45 a mother skunk with her column of kittens swills the garbage pail.
She jabs her wedge-head in a cup
of sour cream, drops her ostrich tail,
and will not scare.

°18 *Blue Hill:* a small town near Bangor, Maine. 26 *Tudor:* a pun referring to a Two-Door Ford and to the Tudor ruling family in England, which was followed by the Stuart family in 1603. Queen Elizabeth was the last of the Tudor
monarchs. See her poem "On Monsieur's Departure" in this chapter. 32 *careless Love:* a traditional folk and blues
song: "Love, O love, O careless love, / You fly to my head like wine, / You've ruined the life of many a poor girl, / And
you nearly wrecked this life of mine." Singers like Bessie Smith, Pete Seeger, and Elvis Presley recorded this song,
which many other singers have freely adapted. 35 *I myself am hell:* quoted from Milton's *Paradise Lost*, 4.75.

QUESTIONS

1. What is the significance, if any, of the activities described by the speaker in lines 1–36? Are these ordinary or unusual activities? Why does the speaker state that he went looking for "love cars"? What is the importance of the speaker's noting that the lovers' lane is near the local graveyard?

2. In lines 30–36 the speaker makes observations about his mental condition. How does this section correspond to the idea of "confessional" poetry? (See Chapter 21, p. 1085.) Why does the speaker say "My mind's not right" in line 30 and "nobody's here" in line 36? Why does he quote John Milton's Satan by saying "I myself am hell" in line 35?

3. What is the poem's dominant tense? Why does Lowell use past tenses in the third and sixth stanzas?

4. Describe the meaning of the mother skunk and "column of kittens" in the last two stanzas. Why is it significant that the mother skunk "will not scare"? In what way may the mother skunk and her family be considered metaphorically?

JUDITH MINTY (b. 1937)

 Conjoined (1981)

a marriage poem

The onion in my cupboard, a monster, actually
two joined under one transparent skin:
each half-round, then flat and deformed
where it pressed and grew against the other.

An accident, like the two-headed calf rooted   5
in one body, fighting to suck at its mother's teats;
or like those other freaks, Chang and Eng,° twins
joined at the chest by skin and muscle, doomed
to live, even make love, together for sixty years.

Do you feel the skin that binds us   10
together as we move, heavy in this house?
To sever the muscle could free one,
but might kill the other. Ah, but men
don't slice onions in the kitchen, seldom see
what is invisible. We cannot escape each other.   15

°7 *Chang and Eng*: born in 1811, the original and most famous Siamese twins. Although they were never separated, they nevertheless fathered twenty-two children. They died in 1874.

QUESTIONS

1. What are the two things—the "us" and "we" of lines 10 and 11—that are conjoined? Since this is "a marriage poem," might they be the man and the woman? Why might they also be considered as the body and soul of the speaker; or the desire to be married and subordinated, on the one hand, and to be free and in control of destiny, on the other?

2. Explore the metaphor of the onion and the similes of the two-headed calf and the Siamese twins. Why do you think the poet introduces the words "monster," "accident," and "freaks" into these figures in lines 1, 5, and 7? In what sense do you believe that these words are applicable to the nature and plight of women?

3. Is it true that *all* "men / don't slice onions in the kitchen, seldom see / what is invisible" (lines 13–15)? Explain.

PABLO NERUDA (1904–1977)

 ## If You Forget Me (1952; 1963)

Translation by Donald S. Walsh

I want you to know
one thing.

You know how this is:
if I look
5 at the crystal moon, at the red branch
of the slow autumn at my window,
if I touch
near the fire
the impalpable ash
10 or the wrinkled body of the log,
everything carries me to you,
as if everything that exists,
aromas, light, metals,
were little boats
15 that sail
toward those isles of yours that wait for me.

Well, now,
if little by little you stop loving me
I shall stop loving you little by little.

20 If suddenly
you forget me
do not look for me,
for I shall already have forgotten you.

If you think it long and mad,
25 the wind of banners
that passes through my life,
and you decide
to leave me at the shore
of the heart where I have roots,
30 remember
that on that day,
at that hour,
I shall lift my arms

and my roots will set off
to seek another land.   35

But
if each day,
each hour,
you feel that you are destined for me
with implacable sweetness,   40
if each day a flower
climbs up to your lips to seek me,
ah my love, ah my own,
in me all that fire is repeated,
in me nothing is extinguished or forgotten,   45
my love feeds on your love, beloved,
and as long as you live it will be in your arms
without leaving mine.

QUESTIONS

1. What similes and metaphors do you discover in this poem? Explain the paradox in the last stanza.
2. What is the nature of the love the speaker expresses? How strongly and firmly does the speaker express his love? To what degree does he state that his love must be reciprocated to continue to exist?
3. Describe the development of the speaker's thought. Why does he introduce the metaphor that he might possibly lift up his roots "to seek another land"?

MARGE PIERCY (b. 1934)

 ## A Work of Artifice (1973)

The bonsai tree
in the attractive pot
could have grown eighty feet tall
on the side of a mountain
till split by lightning.   5
But a gardener
carefully pruned it.
It is nine inches high.
Every day as he
whittles back the branches   10
the gardener croons,
It is your nature
to be small and cozy,
domestic and weak;
how lucky, little tree,   15
to have a pot to grow in.
With living creatures
one must begin very early
to dwarf their growth:

20   the bound feet,
the crippled brain,
the hair in curlers,
the hands you
love to touch.

QUESTIONS

1. What is a bonsai tree? In what ways is it an apt metaphor for women? The tree "could have grown eighty feet tall." What would be the comparable growth and development of a woman?

2. What do you make of the gardener's song (lines 12–16)? If the bonsai tree were able to respond, would it accept the gardener's consolation? What conclusions about women's lives are implied by the metaphor of the tree?

3. How does the poem shift at line 17? To what extent do the next images (lines 20–24) embody women's lives? How are the images metaphorical?

MURIEL RUKEYSER (1913–1980)

Looking at Each Other (1978)

Yes, we were looking at each other
Yes, we knew each other very well
Yes, we had made love with each other many times
Yes, we had heard music together
5 Yes, we had gone to the sea together
Yes, we had cooked and eaten together
Yes, we had laughed often day and night
Yes, we fought violence and knew violence
Yes, we hated the inner and outer oppression
10 Yes, that day we were looking at each other
Yes, we saw the sunlight pouring down
Yes, the corner of the table was between us
Yes, bread and flowers were on the table
Yes, our eyes saw each other's eyes
15 Yes, our mouths saw each other's mouth
Yes, our breasts saw each other's breasts
Yes, our bodies entire saw each other
Yes, it was beginning in each
Yes, it threw waves across our lives
20 Yes, the pulses were becoming very strong
Yes, the beating became very delicate
Yes, the calling the arousal
Yes, the arriving the coming
Yes, there it was for both entire
25 Yes, we were looking at each other

QUESTIONS

1. What is the dramatic situation of the poem? What sort of listener is the speaker addressing?

2. Describe the rhetorical device at work here. How many different words are being repeated?

3. What is the effect of the repetitions? What is their relationship to the emotions and experiences that the speaker is describing?

WILLIAM SHAKESPEARE (1564–1616)

For a portrait, see Chapter 24, page 1322. The following two sonnets are by William Shakespeare.

 ## Sonnet 18: Shall I Compare Thee to a Summer's Day? (1609)

Shall I compare thee to a summer's day?	
Thou art more lovely and more temperate:	
Rough winds do shake the darling° buds of May,	*dear, cherished*
And summer's lease hath all too short a date:	
Sometime too hot the eye of heaven° shines	*the sun* 5
And often is his° gold complexion dimmed;	*its*
And every fair from fair sometime declines,	
By chance, or nature's changing course, untrimmed;	
But thy eternal summer shall not fade,	
Nor lose possession of that fair thou owest;°	*owns, possess* 10
Nor shall Death brag thou wander'st his shade,°	
When in eternal lines to time thou growest:	
So long as men can breathe, or eyes can see,	
So long lives this, and this gives life to thee.	

°11 *thou. . . shade:* you are wandering in Death's darkness.

QUESTIONS

1. What is the dramatic situation of the poem? Who is speaking to whom?

2. What do the metaphors in lines 1–8 assert? Why does the speaker emphasize life's brevity?

3. Describe the shift in topic beginning in line 9. How do these lines both deny and echo the subject of lines 1–8?

4. What relationship do the last two lines have to the rest of the poem? What is the meaning of "this" (line 14)? What sort of immortality does Shakespeare exalt in the sonnet?

 ## Sonnet 30: When to the Sessions of Sweet Silent Thought (1609)

When to the sessions° of sweet silent thought	*holding of court*
I summon° up remembrance of things past,	

°2 *summon:* to issue a summons to appear at a legal hearing.

I sigh the lack of many a thing I sought,
And with old woes new wail my dear time's waste:°
5 Then can I drown an eye (un-used to flow)
For precious friends hid in death's dateless° night,   endless
And weep afresh love's long since canceled° woe,   paid in full
And moan th'expense° of many a vanished sight.   cost, loss
Then can I grieve at grievances foregone,
10 And heavily° from woe to woe tell° o'er   sadly; count
The sad account of fore-bemoanéd moan,
Which I new pay, as if not paid before.
    But if the while I think on thee (dear friend)
    All losses are restored, and sorrows end.

°4 *old woes . . . waste:* revive old sorrows about lost opportunities and express sorrow for them again.

QUESTIONS

1. Explain the metaphor of "sessions" and "summon" in lines 1–2. Where are the "sessions" being held? What is a "summons" for remembrance?

2. What is the metaphor brought out by the word "canceled" in line 7? In what sense might a "woe" of love be canceled? Explain the metaphor of "expense" in line 8.

3. What type of transaction does Shakespeare refer to in the metaphor of lines 9–12? What understanding does the metaphor provide about the sadness and regret that a person feels about past mistakes and sorrows?

4. What role does the speaker assign to the "dear friend" of line 13 in relation to the metaphors of the poem?

ELIZABETH TUDOR, QUEEN ELIZABETH I (1533–1603)

 # On Monsieur's Departure (c. 1560; 1964)

I grieve° and dare not show my discontent,   I am unhappy
I love and yet am forced to seem to hate,
I do, yet dare not say I ever meant,
I seem stark mute but inwardly do prate.°   chatter endlessly
5   I am and not, I freeze and yet am burned,
    Since from myself another self I turned.

My care° is like my shadow in the sun,   loved one
Follows me flying, flies when I pursue it,
Stands and lies by me, doth what I have done.
10 His too familiar care° doth make me rue it.   alternativeness, love
    No means I find to rid him from my breast,
    Till by the end of things it be supprest.

Some gentler passion slide into my mind,
For I am soft and made of melting snow;
15 Or be more cruel, love, and so be kind.

Let me or float or sink, be high or low.
   Or let me live with some more sweet content.
   Or die and so forget what love ere meant.

QUESTIONS

1. What is the significance of "Monsieur's Departure"? How does this detail prompt the patterns of thought in the poem?

2. Explain the speaker's use of antithesis in the poem to explain her ambivalent situation. How seriously should we take the ideas in lines 12 and 18? Assuming that this is a deeply personal and private lyric, why, granted the speaker's royal status, does she express such contradictory feelings?

3. What is the meaning of the shadow simile in lines 7–10? How well does this comparison reveal her situation?

4. What is explained by the paradoxes in lines 5 and 15?

MONA VAN DUYN (1921–2004)

 ## Earth Tremors Felt in Missouri (1964)

The quake last night was nothing personal,
you told me this morning. I think one always wonders,
unless, of course, something is visible: tremors
that take us, private and willy-nilly, are usual.
But the earth said last night that what I feel,   5
you feel; what secretly moves you, moves me.
One small, sensuous catastrophe
makes inklings letters, spelled in a worldly tremble.

The earth, with others on it, turns in its course
as we turn toward each other, less than ourselves, gross,   10
mindless, more than we were. Pebbles, we swell
to planets, nearing the universal roll,
in our conceit even comprehending the sun,
whose bright ordeal leaves cool men woebegone.

QUESTIONS

1. In what ways is this poem intensely personal, a "confessional" poem? How does the poem develop materials that might be considered less personal and more public?

2. Why does the speaker equate herself and her listener with the earth? Granted that this metaphor is apt, what is then meant by "earth tremors," "quake last night," "Pebbles, we swell/to planets," and "comprehending the sun"?

3. What feelings are brought out in the last line through the words "ordeal" and "woebegone"?

4. Compare the use of the earth/person metaphor as it is used in this poem and in Donne's "The Good Morrow" (Chapter 22).

WALT WHITMAN (1819–1892)

Facing West from California's Shores (1860)

Facing west from California's shores,
Inquiring, tireless, seeking what is yet unfound,
I, a child, very old, over waves, towards the house of maternity,°
    the land of migrations, look afar,
Look off the shores of my Western sea, the circle almost circled;
5   For starting westward from Hindustan,° from the vales of Kashmir,
From Asia, from the north, from the God, the sage, and the hero,
From the south, from the flowery peninsulas° and the spice islands,°
Long having wandered since, round the earth having wandered
Now I face home again, very pleased and joyous.
10 (But where is what I started for so long ago?
And why is it yet unfound?)

°3 *house of maternity:* Asia, then considered the cradle of human civilization. 5 *Hindustan:* India. 7 *flowery peninsulas:* south India, south Burma, and the Maylay peninsula. 7 *spice islands:* the Molucca Islands of Indonesia.

QUESTIONS

1. What major paradox, or apparently contradictory situation, is described in this poem? How does the poet bring out this paradox? What has the speaker been seeking? Where has he looked for it?
2. Describe the meaning of the phrase "a child, very old"; "where is what I started for"; "the circle almost circled." In what ways are these phrases paradoxical?
3. Why does the speaker twice use the word "unfound" (lines 2, 11)? How might the word be considered a theme of the poem?

WILLIAM WORDSWORTH (1770–1850)

For a portrait, see Chapter 12, page 678.

London, 1802 (1802; 1807)

Milton! thou should'st be living at this hour:
England hath need of thee: she is a fen°   *bog, marsh*
Of stagnant waters: altar, sword, and pen,
Fireside, the heroic wealth of hall and bower,
5   Have forfeited their ancient English dower°   *widow's inheritance*
Of inward happiness. We are selfish men;
Oh! raise us up, return to us again;
And give us manners,° virtue, freedom, power.
Thy soul was like a star, and dwelt apart:
10 Thou hadst a voice whose sound was like the sea:
Pure as the naked heavens, majestic, free,
So didst thou travel on life's common way,
In cheerful godliness; and yet thy heart
The lowliest duties on herself did lay.

°8 *manners:* customs, moral codes of social and political conduct.

QUESTIONS

1. What is the effect of Wordsworth's apostrophe to Milton? What elements of Milton's career as a writer does Wordsworth emphasize?

2. In lines 3 and 4, the device of metonymy is used. How does Wordsworth judge the respective institutions represented by the details?

3. Consider the use of overstatement, or hyperbole, from lines 2–6. What effect does Wordsworth achieve by using the device as extensively as he does here?

4. What effect does Wordsworth make through his use of overstatement in his praise of Milton in lines 9–14? What does he mean by the metonymic references to "soul" (line 9) and "heart" (line 13)?

SIR THOMAS WYATT (1503–1542)

 ## I Find No Peace (1557)

I find no peace, and all my war is done,
  I fear and hope, I burn and freeze like ice;
  I fly above the wind yet can I not arise;
  And naught I have and all the world I season.
That looseth nor locketh holdeth me in prison,°   5
  And holdeth me not, yet I can scape° nowise;   *escape*
  Nor letteth me live nor die at my devise,°   *choice*
  And yet of death it giveth none occasion.
Without eyen° I see, and without tongue I plain;°   *eyes*
  I desire to perish, and yet I ask health;   10
  I love another, and thus I hate myself;
I feed me in sorrow, and laugh in all my pain.
  Likewise displeaseth me both death and life°
  And my delight is causer of this strife.

°5 *that . . . prison:* that is, "that which neither lets me go nor contains me holds me in prison." At the time of Wyatt, *-eth* was used for the third person singular present tense. 9 *plain:* express desires about love. 13 *Likewise . . . life:* literally, "it is displeasing to me, in the same way, both death and life." That is, "both death and life are equally distasteful to me."

QUESTIONS

1. What situation is the speaker reflecting upon? What metaphors and similes express his feelings? How successful are these figures?

2. How many paradoxes are in the poem? What is their cumulative effect? What is the topic of the paradoxes in lines 1–4? In lines 5–8? Why does the speaker declare that hating himself is a consequence of loving another? Why is it ironic that his "delight" is the "causer of this strife"?

3. To what extent do you think the paradoxes express the feelings of a person in love, particularly because in the sixteenth century, the free and unchaperoned meetings of lovers were not easily arranged?

WRITING ABOUT FIGURES OF SPEECH

Begin by determining the use, line by line, of metaphors, similes, or other rhetorical figures. Obviously, similes are the easiest figures to recognize because they introduce comparisons with the words *like* or *as*. Metaphors can be recognized because the topics are discussed not as themselves but as other topics. If the poems speak of falling leaves or law courts but the subjects involve memory or increasing age, you are looking at metaphors. Similarly, if the poet is addressing an absent person or a natural object, or if you find clear double meanings in words, you may have apostrophe, personification, or puns.

Questions for Discovering Ideas

- What figures of speech does the work contain? Where do they occur? Under what circumstances? How extensive are they?
- How do you recognize them? Are they signaled by a single word or phrase, such as "desert places" in Frost's "Desert Places" (Chapter 18); or are they more extensively detailed, as in Shakespeare's Sonnet 30, "When to the Sessions of Sweet Silent Thought"?
- How vivid are the figures? How obvious? How unusual? What kind of effort is needed to understand them in context?
- Structurally, how are the figures developed? How do they rise out of the situation envisioned in the poem? To what degree are the figures integrated into the poem's development of ideas? How do they relate to other aspects of the poem?
- Is one type of figure used in a particular section while another type predominates in another section? Why?
- If you have discovered a number of figures, what relationships can you find among them (such as the judicial and financial connections in Shakespeare's "When to the Sessions of Sweet Silent Thought")?
- How do the figures of speech broaden, deepen, or otherwise assist in making the ideas in the poem forceful?
- In general, how appropriate and meaningful are the figures of speech in the poem? What effect do the figures have on the poem's tone, and on your understanding and appreciation of the poem?

Strategies for Organizing Ideas

For this essay, you might choose one of two types of compositions. One is a full-length essay. The other, because some rhetorical figures may occupy only a small part of the poem, is a single paragraph. Let us consider the single paragraph first.

1. *A paragraph.* For a single paragraph you need only one topic, such as the hyperbole used in the opening of Wordsworth's sonnet "London, 1802." The goal is to deal with the single figure and its relationship to the poem's main idea. Thus the essay should describe the figure and discuss its meaning and implications. It is important to begin with a comprehensive topic sentence, such as one that explains the cleverness of the puns in Gay's "Let Us Take the Road," or the use of paradox in Wyatt's "I Find no Peace."

2. *A full-length essay.* One type of essay might examine just one figure, if the figure is pervasive enough in the poem to justify a full treatment. Most often, the poet's use of metaphors and similes is suitable for extensive discussion. A second type of essay might explore the meaning and effect of two or more figures, with the various parts of the body of the essay being taken up with each figure. The unity of this second kind of essay is achieved by the linking of a series of two or three different rhetorical devices to a single idea or emotion.

In the introduction, relate the quality of the figures to the general nature of the work. Thus, metaphors and similes of suffering might be appropriate to a religious, redemptive work, while those of sunshine, cheer, and flowers might be right for a romantic one. If there is any discrepancy between the metaphorical language and the topic, you could consider that contrast as a possible central idea, for it would clearly indicate the writer's ironic perspective. Suppose that the topic of the poem is love, but the figures put you in mind of darkness and cold: What might the poet be saying about the quality of love? You should also try to justify any claims that you make about the figures. For example, one of the similes in Coleridge's "Kubla Khan" (Chapter 14) compares the sounds of a "mighty fountain" to the breathing of the earth in "fast thick pants." How is this simile to be taken? As a reference to the animality of the earth? As a suggestion that the fountain, and the earth, are dangerous? Or simply as a comparison suggesting immense, forceful noise? How do you explain your answer or answers? Your introduction is the place to establish ideas and justifications of this sort.

The following approaches for discussing rhetorical figures are not mutually exclusive, and you may combine them as you wish. Most likely, your essay will bring in most of the following classifications.

1. *Interpret the meaning and effect of the figures.* Here you explain how the figures enable you to make an interpretation. In the second stanza of "A Valediction: Forbidding Mourning," for example, the following metaphor introduces church hierarchy and religious mystery to explain lovers and their love.

'Twere profanation of our joys
To tell the laity our love.

Here Donne emphasizes the mystical relationship of two lovers, drawing the metaphor from the religious tradition whereby any popular explanation of religious mysteries is considered a desecration. A directly explanatory approach, such as this, requires that metaphors, similes, or other figures be expanded and interpreted, including the explanation of necessary references and allusions.

2. *Analyze the frames of reference and their appropriateness to the subject matter.* Here you classify and locate the sources and types of the references and determine the appropriateness of these to the poem's subject matter. Ask questions similar to those you might ask in a study of imagery: Does the writer refer extensively to nature, science, warfare, politics, business, reading (e.g., Shakespeare's metaphor equating personal reverie with courtroom proceedings)? Does the metaphor seem appropriate? How? Why?

3. *Focus on the interests and sensibilities of the poet.* In a way this approach is like strategy 2, but the emphasis here is on what the selectivity of the writer might show about his or her vision and interests. You might begin by listing the figures in the poem and then determining the sources, just as you would do in discussing the sources of images generally. But then you should raise questions like the following: Does the writer use figures derived from one sense rather than another (i.e., sight, hearing, taste, smell, touch)? Does he or she record color, brightness, shadow, shape, depth, height, number, size, slowness, speed, emptiness, fullness, richness, drabness? Has the writer relied on the associations of figures of sense? Do metaphors and similes referring to green plants and trees, to red roses, or to rich fabrics, for example, suggest that life is full and beautiful, or do references to touch suggest amorous warmth? This approach is designed to help you draw conclusions about the author's taste or sensibility.

4. *Examine the effect of one figure on the other figures and ideas of the poem.* The assumption of this approach is that each literary work is unified and organically whole, so that each part is closely related and inseparable from everything else. Usually it is best to pick a figure that occurs at the beginning of the poem and then determine how this figure influences your perception of the rest of the poem. Your aim is to consider the relationship of part to parts and part to whole. The beginning of Donne's "A Valediction: Forbidding Mourning," for example, contains a simile comparing the parting of the speaker and his listener to the quiet dying of "virtuous men." What is the effect of this comparison upon the poem? To help you with questions like this, you might substitute a totally different detail, such as, here, the violent death of a condemned criminal, or the slaughter of a domestic animal, rather than the deaths of "virtuous men." Such suppositions, which would clearly be out of place, may help you understand and then explain the poet's figures of speech.

In your conclusion, summarize your main points, describe your general impressions, try to describe the impact of the figures, indicate your personal responses, or show what might further be done along the lines you have been developing. If you know other works by the same writer, or other works by other writers who use comparable or contrasting figures, you might explain the relationship of the other work or works to your present analysis.

Illustrative Student Paragraph

Wordsworth's Use of Overstatement in "London, 1802"°

Through overstatement in "London, 1802," Wordsworth emphasizes his tribute to Milton as a master of idealistic thought.* The speaker's claim that England is "a fen/Of stagnant waters" (lines 2–3) is overstated, as is the implication that people ("We") in England have no "manners, virtue, freedom, power" (lines 6, 8). With the overstatements, however, Wordsworth implies that the nation's well-being depends on the constant flow of creative thoughts by persons of great ideas. Because Milton was clearly the greatest of these, in the view of Wordsworth's speaker, the overstatements stress the need for leadership. Milton is the model, and the overstated criticism lays the foundation in the real political and moral world for the rebirth of another Milton. Thus, through overstatement, Wordsworth emphasizes Milton's importance and in this way pays tribute to him.

°**This poem appears on page 790.**
*****Central idea.**

Commentary on the Paragraph

This paragraph deals with a single rhetorical figure, in this case Wordsworth's overstatements in "London, 1802." Although most often the figure of speech will be fairly obvious, as this one in "London, 1802" is, prominence is not a requirement. In addition, there is no need to write an excessively long paragraph. The goal here is not to describe all the details of Wordsworth's overstatement, but to show how the figure affects his tribute to Milton. For this reason the paragraph illustrates clear and direct support of the major point.

Illustrative Student Essay

> Underlined sentences in this paper *do not* conform to MLA style and are used solely as teaching tools to emphasize the central idea, thesis sentence, and topic sentences throughout the paper.

Carter 1

David Carter

Professor Hernandez

English 1123

17 April 2008

A Study of Shakespeare's Metaphors in Sonnet 30:

"When to the Sessions of Sweet Silent Thought"°

[1]   In this sonnet Shakespeare's speaker stresses the sadness and regret of remembered experience, but he states that a person with these feelings may be cheered by the thought of a friend. His metaphors, cleverly used, create new and fresh ways of seeing personal life in this perspective.* He presents metaphors drawn from the public and business world of law courts, money, and banking or money-handling.†

[2]   The courtroom metaphor of the first four lines shows that memories of past experience are constantly present and influential. Like a judge commanding defendants to appear in court, the speaker "summon[s]" his memory of "things past" to appear on trial before him. This metaphor suggests that people are their own judges and that their ideals and morals are like laws by which they measure themselves. The speaker finds himself guilty of wasting his time in the past. Removing himself, however, from the strict punishment that a real judge might require, he does not condemn himself for his "dear time's waste," but instead laments it (line 4). The metaphor is thus used to indicate that a person's consciousness is made up just as much of self-doubt and reproach as by more positive qualities.

°This poem appears on page 787.
*Central idea.
†Thesis sentence.

Carter 2

With the closely related reference of money in the next group of four lines, [3]
Shakespeare shows that living is a lifelong investment and is inestimably
valuable for this reason. According to the money metaphor, living requires the
spending of emotions and commitment to others. When friends move away and
loved ones die, it is as though a fortune has been lost. Thus, the speaker's dead
friends are "precious" because he invested time and love in them, and the
"sights" that have "vanished" from his eyes make him "moan" because he went
to great "expense" for them (line 8).

Like the money metaphor, the metaphor of banking or money-handling in [4]
the next four lines emphasizes that memory is a bank in which life's
experiences are deposited. The full emotions surrounding experience are
recorded there, and may be withdrawn in moments of "sweet silent thought"
just as a depositor may withdraw money. Thus the speaker states that he counts
out the sad parts of his experience--his woe--just as a merchant or banker
counts money: "And heavily from woe to woe tell o'er" (line 10). Because
strong emotions still accompany his memories of past mistakes, the metaphor
extends to borrowing and the payment of interest. The speaker thus says that he
pays again with "new" woe the accounts that he had already paid with old woe.
The metaphor suggests that the past is so much a part of the present that a
person never stops feeling pain and regret.

The legal, financial, and money-handling metaphors combine in the last [5]
two lines to show how a healthy present life may overcome past regrets. The
"dear friend" being addressed in these lines has the resources (financial) to settle
all the emotional judgments that the speaker as a self-judge has made against
himself (legal). It is as though the friend is a rich patron who rescues him from
emotional bankruptcy (legal and financial) and the possible doom resulting from
the potential sentence of emotional misery and depression (legal).

In these metaphors, therefore, Shakespeare's references are drawn from [6]
everyday public and business actions, but his use of them is creative and
brilliant. In particular, the idea of line 8 ("And moan th'expense of many a
vanished sight") stresses that people spend much emotional energy in
preserving their friendships. Without such personal commitment, one cannot

Carter 3

have precious friends and loved ones. In keeping with this metaphor of

money and investment, one could measure life not in months or years, but in

the spending of emotion and involvement in personal relationships.

Shakespeare, by inviting readers to explore the values brought out by his

metaphors, gives new insights into the nature and value of life.

Carter 4

Work Cited

Shakespeare, William. "Sonnet 30: When to the Sessions of Sweet Silent

Thought." Literature: An Introduction to Reading and Writing. Ed. Edgar

V. Roberts. 9th ed. New York: Pearson Longman, 2009. 787.

Commentary on the Essay

This essay treats the three classes of metaphors that Shakespeare introduces in Sonnet 30. It thus illustrates the second strategy described on page 794. But the aim of the discussion is not to explore the extent and nature of the comparison between the metaphors and the personal situations described in the sonnet. Instead, the object is to explain how the metaphors develop Shakespeare's meaning. This essay therefore also illustrates the first strategy described on page 793.

In addition to providing a brief description of the sonnet, the introduction brings out the central idea and the thesis sentence. Paragraph 2 deals with the meaning of Shakespeare's courtroom metaphor. His money metaphor is explained in paragraph 3. Paragraph 4 considers the banking or money-handling figure. Paragraph 5 shows how Shakespeare's last two lines bring together the three strands of metaphor. The conclusion comments generally on the creativity of Shakespeare's metaphors, and it also amplifies the way in which the money metaphor leads toward an increased understanding of life.

Throughout the essay, transitions are brought about by the linking words in the topic sentences. In paragraph 3, for example, the words "closely related" and "next group" move the reader from paragraph 2 to the new content. In paragraph 4, the words effecting the transition are "like the money metaphor" and "the next four lines." The opening sentence of paragraph 5 refers collectively to the subjects of paragraphs 2, 3, and 4, thereby focusing them on the new topic of paragraph 5.

Writing Topics About Figures of Speech in Poetry

1. Study the simile of the "stiff twin compasses" in Donne's "A Valediction: Forbidding Mourning." Using such a compass or a drawing of one, write an essay that demonstrates the accuracy, or lack of it, of Donne's descriptions.

What light does the simile shed on the relationship of two lovers? How does it emphasize any or all of these aspects of love: closeness, immediacy, extent, importance, duration, intensity?

2. Consider some of the metaphors and similes in various poems in which you are interested. Write an essay that answers the following questions. How effective are the figures you select? (Examples: a rose [Burns], an iceberg [Evans], the sunken *Titanic* [Hardy], the summer's day [Shakespeare].) What insights do the figures provide within the contexts of their respective poems? How appropriate are they? Might they be expanded more fully, and if they were, what would be the effect?

3. Consider some of the other rhetorical figures in the poems of this chapter. Write an essay describing the importance of figures of speech in creating emphasis and in extending and deepening the ideas of poetry. Here are some possible topics, all on poems in this chapter.

    a. Paradox in Wyatt's "I Find No Peace" or Whitman's "Facing West from California's Shores."

    b. Paradox and apparent contradiction in Kenny's "Legacy."

    c. Metaphor in Minty's "Conjoined" or Piercy's "A Work of Artifice."

    d. Metaphor and simile in Evans's "The Iceberg Seven-eighths Under" or in Hardy's "The Convergence of the Twain."

    e. Anaphora in Rukeyser's "Looking at Each Other," Harjo's "Remember," or Kenyon's "Let Evening Come."

    f. A comparison of contrasts and paradoxes in Queen Elizabeth's "On Monsieur's Departure" and Wyatt's "I Find No Peace."

    g. Similes in King's "Sic Vita" or Donne's "A Valediction: Forbidding Mourning," personification in the poems by Wordsworth, Keats, or Agüeros; metonymy in Keats's "To Autumn."

4. Write a poem in which you create a governing metaphor or simile. Examples: "My girlfriend/boyfriend is like (a) an opening flower, (b) a difficult book, (c) an insoluble mathematical problem, (d) a bill that cannot be paid, (e) a slow-moving chess game." "Teaching a person how to do a particular job is like (a) shoveling heavy snow, (b) climbing a mountain during a landslide, (c) having someone force you underwater when you're gasping for breath." When you finish, describe the relationship between your comparison and the development and structure of your poem.

5. In your library's reference section, find the third edition of J. A. Cuddon's *A Dictionary of Literary Terms and Literary Theory* (1991) or some other dictionary of literary terms that you find under "list of literary terms" on *Google*. Study the entries for *metaphysical* and *conceit,* and write a brief report on these sections. You might attempt to answer questions like these: What is meant by the word *conceit*? What are some of the kinds of conceit the reference work discusses? What is a metaphysical conceit? Who are some of the writers considered metaphysical? In the "metaphysical" entry, of what importance is John Donne?

Chapter 16

Tone: The Creation of Attitude in Poetry

Tone, a term derived from the phrase *tone of voice,* describes the shaping of attitudes in poetry (see also Chapter 6, on tone and style in fiction). Each poet's choice of words governs the reader's responses, as do the participants and situations in the poem. In addition, the poet shapes responses through denotation and connotation, seriousness or humor, irony, metaphors, similes, understatement, overstatement, and other figures of speech (see Chapter 15). Of major importance is the poem's speaker. How much self-awareness does the speaker show? What is his or her background? What relationship does the speaker establish with listeners and readers? What does the speaker assume about the readers and about their knowledge? How do these assumptions affect the ideas and the diction?

To compare poetic tone with artistic tone, see the reproduction of Fernand Léger's painting *The City* (p. I-8). A viewer's response to the painting depends on the relationships of the various shapes to Léger's arrangement and color. The signs, stairs, pole, and human figures in the painting are all common in modern cities. By cutting them up or leaving them partially hidden, Léger creates an atmosphere suggesting that contemporary urban life is truncated, sinister, and even threatening.

The same control applies to poetic expression. The sentences must be just long enough to achieve the poet's intended effect—no shorter and no longer. In a conversational style there should be no formal words, just as in a formal style there should be no slang, no rollicking rhythms, and no frivolous rhymes—that is, unless the poet deliberately wants readers to be startled or shocked. In all the features that contribute to a poem's tone, the poet's consistency of intention is primary. Any unintentional deviations will cause the poem to sink and the poet to fail.

Tone, Choice, and Response

Remember that a major objective of poets is to stimulate, enrich, and inspire readers. Poets may begin their poems with a brief idea, a vague feeling, or a fleeting impression. Then, in the light of their developing design, they *choose* what to say—the form of their material and the words and phrases to express their ideas. The poem "Theme for English B" by Langston Hughes illustrates this process in almost outline form (see Chapter 21). Hughes's speaker lays out many interests that he shares with his intended reader, his English teacher, for the poem is imagined to be a response to a classroom assignment. In this way Hughes encourages all readers to accept his ideas of human equality.

In the long run, readers might not accept all the ideas in any poem, but the successful poem gains agreement—at least for a time—because the poet's control over tone is right. Each poem attempts to evoke total responses, which might be destroyed by any lapses in tone. Let us look at a poem in which the tone misses, and misses badly.

CORNELIUS WHUR (1782–1853)

 ## The First-Rate Wife (1837)

This brief effusion I indite,
   And my vast wishes send,
That thou mayst be directed right,
And have ere long within thy sight
   A most *enchanting* friend!   5

The *maiden* should have *lovely face*,
   And be of *genteel mien;*
If not, within thy dwelling place,
There may be vestige of disgrace,
   Not much admired—when seen.   10

Nor will thy dearest be complete
   Without *domestic* care;
If otherwise, howe'er discreet,
Thine eyes will very often meet
   What none desire to share!   15

And further still—thy future *dear*,
   Should have some *mental* ray;
If not, thou mayest drop a tear,
Because no *real sense* is there
   To charm life's dreary day!   20

QUESTIONS

1. What kind of person is the poem's speaker? What is the situation? What requirements does the speaker create for the "first-rate wife"?
2. Describe the poem's tone. How does the speaker's character influence the tone? In light of the tone, to what degree can the poem be considered insulting?
3. How might lines 14 and 15 be interpreted as a possible threat if the woman as a wife does not keep the house clean and straight?

In this poem the speaker is talking to a friend or associate and is explaining his requirements for a "first-rate wife." From his tone, he clearly regards getting married as little more than hiring a pretty housekeeper. In the phrase "some *mental* ray," for example, the word *some* does not mean "a great deal" but is more like "*at least* some," as though nothing more could be expected of a woman. Even allowing for the fact that the poem was written early in the nineteenth century and represents a benighted view of women and marriage, "The First-Rate Wife" offends most readers. Do you wonder why you've never heard of Cornelius Whur before?

Tone and the Need for Control

"The First-Rate Wife" demonstrates the need for the poet to be in control over all facets of the poem. The speaker must be aware of his or her situation and should not, like Whur's speaker, demonstrate any smugness or insensitivity, unless the poet is deliberately revealing the shortcomings of the speaker by dramatizing them for the reader's amusement, as E. E. Cummings does in the poem "next to of course god america i" (Chapter 12). In a poem with well-controlled tone, details and situations should be factually correct; observations should be logical and fair, and also comprehensive and generally applicable. The following poem, based on battlefield conditions in World War I, illustrates a masterly control over tone.

WILFRED OWEN (1893–1918)

Dulce et Decorum Est° (1920)

Bent double, like old beggars under sacks,
Knock-kneed, coughing like hags, we cursed through sludge,
Till on the haunting flares we turned our backs
And towards our distant rest began to trudge.
5 Men marched asleep. Many had lost their boots
But limped on, blood-shod. All went lame; all blind;
Drunk with fatigue; deaf even to the hoots
Of tired, outstripped Five-Nines° that dropped behind.

Gas!° GAS! Quick, boys!—An ecstasy of fumbling,
10 Fitting the clumsy helmets° just in time;
But someone still was yelling out and stumbling
And flound'ring like a man in fire or lime . . .
Dim, through the misty panes and thick green° light,
As under a green sea, I saw him drowning.

15 In all my dreams, before my helpless sight,
He plunges at me, guttering, choking, drowning.
If in some smothering dreams you too could pace
Behind the wagon that we flung him in.
And watch the white eyes writhing in his face,
20 His hanging face, like a devil's sick of sin;
If you could hear, at every jolt, the blood
Come gargling from the froth-corrupted lungs,
Obscene as cancer, bitter as the cud

°The Latin title is taken from Horace's *Odes*, Book 3, line 13: *Dulce et decorum est pro patria mori* ("It is sweet and honorable to die for the fatherland"). 8 *Five-Nines:* A "five-nine" was a 5.9-inch German high-explosive artillery shell that made a hooting sound before landing. 9 *Gas:* Chlorine gas was used as an antipersonnel weapon in 1915 by the Germans at Ypres, in Belgium. 10 *helmets:* Soldiers carried gas masks as normal battle equipment. 13 *thick green:* The deadly chlorine gas used in gas attacks has a greenish-yellow color.

Of vile, incurable sores on innocent tongues.—
My friend, you would not tell with such high zest
To children ardent for some desperate glory,
The old Lie: Dulce et decorum est
Pro patria mori.

25

QUESTIONS

1. What is the scene described in lines 1–8? What expressions does the speaker use to indicate his attitude toward the conditions?
2. What does the title of the poem mean? What attitude or conviction does it embody?
3. Does the speaker really mean "my friend" in line 25? In what tone of voice might this phrase be spoken?
4. What is the tonal relationship between the patriotic fervor of the Latin phrase and the images of the poem? How does the tonal contrast create the dominant tone of the poem?

The tone of "Dulce et Decorum Est" never lapses. The poet intends the description to evoke a response of horror and shock, for he contrasts the strategic goals of warfare with the speaker's personal experience of terror in battle. The speaker's language skillfully emphasizes first the dreariness and fatigue of warfare (with words like "sludge," "trudge," "lame," and "blind") and second the agony of violent death from chlorine gas (embodied in the participles "guttering," "choking," "drowning," "smothering," and "writhing"). With these details established, the concluding attack against the "glory" of war is difficult to refute, even if warfare is undertaken to defend or preserve one's country. Although the details about the agonized death may distress or discomfort a sensitive reader, they are not designed to do that alone but instead are integral to the poem's argument. Ultimately, it is the contrast between the high ideals of the Latin phrase and the ugliness of battlefield death that creates the dominant tone of the poem. The Latin phrase treats war and death in the abstract; the poem makes images of battle and death vividly real. The resultant tone is that of controlled bitterness and irony.

Tone and Common Grounds of Assent

Not all those reading Owen's poem will deny that war is sometimes necessary; the issues of politics and warfare are far too complex for that. But the poem does show another important aspect of tone—namely, the degree to which the poet judges and tries to control responses through the establishment of a *common ground of assent*. An appeal to a bond of commonly held interests, concerns, and assumptions is essential if a poet is to maintain an effective tone. Owen, for example, does not create arguments against the necessity of a just war. Instead, he bases the poem on realistic details about the choking, writhing, spastic death suffered by the speaker's comrade; and he appeals to emotions that everyone, pacifist and militarist alike, would feel—horror at the contemplation of violent death. Even assuming a widely divergent audience, in other words, the *tone* of the poem is successful because it is based on commonly acknowledged facts and commonly felt emotions. Knowing a poem like this one, even advocates of a strong military would need to defend their ideas on the grounds of *preventing* just such needless, ugly deaths. Owen carefully considers the responses of his readers, and he regulates speaker, situation, detail, and argument in order to make the poem acceptable for the broadest possible spectrum of opinion.

TONE IN CONVERSATION AND POETRY

Many readers think that tone is a subtle and difficult subject, but it is nevertheless true that in ordinary situations we master tone easily and expertly (see Chapter 6). We constantly use standard questions and statements that deal with tone, such as "What do you mean by that?" "What I'm saying is this . . . ," and "Did I hear you correctly?" together with other comments that extend to humor and, sometimes, to hostility. In poetry we do not have everyday speech situations; we have only the poems themselves and are guided by the materials they provide us. Some poems are straightforward and unambiguous, but in other poems feeling and mood are essential to our understanding. In Hardy's "The Workbox" (this chapter), for example, the husband's hand-made gift to his wife indicates not love but suspicion. Also, the husband's relentless linking of the dead man's coffin to the gift reveals his anger. Pope, in the passage from the "Epilogue to the Satires" (this chapter), satirically describes deplorable habits and customs of his English contemporaries in the 1730s. His concluding lines (of the passage and also of the poem) emphasize his scorn:

> Yet may this verse (if such a verse remain)
>
> Show there was one who held it in disdain.

Of course, poems may also reveal respect and wonder, as shown in the last six lines of Keats's "On First Looking into Chapman's Homer" (Chapter 15). By attending carefully to the details of such poems, you can draw conclusions about poetic tone that are as accurate as those you draw in normal speech situations.

Tone and Irony

Irony is a mode of indirection, a means of making a point by emphasizing a discrepancy or opposite (see also Chapter 6). Thus Owen uses the title "Dulce et Decorum Est" to emphasize that death in warfare is not sweet and honorable but rather demeaning and horrible. The title ironically reminds us of eloquent holiday speeches at the tombs of unknown soldiers, but as we have seen, it also reminds us of the reality of the agonized death of Owen's soldier. As an aspect of tone, therefore, irony is a powerful way of conveying attitudes, for it draws your attention to at least two ways of seeing a situation, enabling you not only to *understand* but also to *experience*. Poetry shares with fiction the various kinds of ironies that afflict human beings. These are *verbal irony*, *situational irony*, and *dramatic irony*.

Verbal Irony, through Word Selection, Emphasizes Ambiguities and Discrepancies

At almost any point in a poem, a poet may introduce the ironic effects of language itself—**verbal irony.** Cummings' poem "she being Brand/-new" is built on the double meanings derived from the procedures of breaking in a new car. Indeed, the entire poem is a virtuoso piece of double entendre. Another example of verbal irony occurs in Theodore Roethke's "My Papa's Waltz," in which the speaker uses the name of this graceful and stately dance to describe his childhood memories of his father's whirling him around the kitchen in wild, boisterous drunkenness.

Life's Anomalies and Uncertainties Underlie Situational Irony

Situational irony is derived from the discrepancies between the ideal and the actual. People would like to live their lives in terms of a standard of love, friendship, honor, success, and general excellence, but the irony is that the reality of their lives often falls far short of such standards. Whereas in fiction ironic situations emerge from extended narrative, in poetry such situations are usually at a high point or climax, and we must infer the narrative circumstances that have gone on before. Thomas Hardy, in "The Workbox," skillfully exploits an ironic situation between a husband and a wife.

THOMAS HARDY (1840–1928)

For a photo, see Chapter 5, page 287.

The Workbox (1914)

"See, here's the workbox, little wife,
 That I made of polished oak."
He was a joiner,° of village° life;   *cabinetmaker*
 She came of borough° folk.

He holds the present up to her   5
 As with a smile she nears
And answers to the profferer,
 "'Twill last all my sewing years!"

"I warrant it will. And longer too.
 'Tis a scantling° that I got   10
Off poor John Wayward's coffin, who
 Died of they knew not what.

"The shingled pattern that seems to cease
 Against your box's rim
Continues right on in the piece   15
 That's underground with him.

°3, 4 *village, borough:* An English village was small and rustic; a borough was larger and more sophisticated.
10 *scantling:* a small leftover piece of wood.

"And while I worked it made me think
    Of timber's varied doom:
One inch where people eat and drink,
20   The next inch in a tomb.

"But why do you look so white, my dear,
    And turn aside your face?
You knew not that good lad, I fear,
    Though he came from your native place?"

25 "How could I know that good young man,
    Though he came from my native town,
When he must have left far earlier than
    I was a woman grown?"

"Ah, no. I should have understood!
30   It shocked you that I gave
To you one end of a piece of wood
    Whose other is in a grave?"

"Don't, dear, despise my intellect.
    Mere accidental things
35 Of that sort never have effect
    On my imaginings."

Yet still her lips were limp and wan,
    Her face still held aside,
As if she had known not only John,
40   But known of what he died.

QUESTIONS

1. Who does most of the speaking? What does the speaker's tone show about the characters of the husband and the wife? What does the tone indicate about the poet's attitude toward them?

2. What do lines 21–40 indicate about the wife's knowledge of John and about her earlier relationship with him? Why does she deny such knowledge? What does the last stanza show about her? Why is John's death kept a mystery?

3. In lines 17–20, what irony is suggested by the fact that the wood was used both for John Wayward's coffin and the workbox?

4. Why is the husband's irony more complex than he realizes? What do his words and actions show about his character?

5. The narrator, or poet, speaks only in lines 3–7 and 37–40. How much of his explanation is essential? How much shows his attitude? How might the poem have been more effectively concluded?

"The Workbox" is a domestic drama of deception, cruelty, and sadness. The complex details are evidence of situational irony, that is, an awareness that human beings do not control their lives but are rather controlled by powerful forces—in this case by both death and earlier feelings and commitments. Beyond this domestic irony, Hardy also emphasizes symbolically the direct connection that death has with the living. As a result of the husband's gift made of the wood with which he has also made a coffin for the dead man, the wife will never escape being reminded of this man. Within the existence imagined in the poem, she will have to live with regret and the constant need to deny her true emotions, and her situation is therefore endlessly ironic.

Dramatic Irony Is Built on the Ignorance of Characters and the Greater Knowledge of Readers

In addition to the situational irony of "The Workbox," the wife's deception reveals that the husband is in a situation of **dramatic irony.** He does not know the circumstances of his wife's past, and he does not actually *know*—though he suspects—that his wife is not being truthful about her earlier relationship with the dead man; but the poem is sufficient to enable readers to draw the right conclusions. By emphasizing the wood, the husband is apparently trying to make his wife uncomfortable, even to the point of extracting a confession from her; but he has only his suspicions, and he therefore remains unsure of the truth and also of his wife's feelings. Because of these uncertainties, Hardy has deftly used dramatic irony to create a poem of great complexity and pathos.

Tone and Satire

Satire, a vital genre in the study of tone, is designed to expose human follies and vices. In method, a satiric poem may be bitter and vituperative, but often it employs humor and irony, on the grounds that anger turns readers away while a comic tone more easily wins interest and agreement. The speaker of a satiric poem may either attack folly and vice directly, or may dramatically embody the folly or vice himself or herself and thus serve as an illustration of the satiric subject. An example of the first type is the following short poem by Alexander Pope, in which the speaker directly attacks a listener who has claimed to be a poet but whom the speaker considers both a bad poet and a fool. The speaker cleverly uses insult as the method of attack.

ALEXANDER POPE (1688–1744)

For a portrait, see this chapter, page 824.

 ## Epigram from the French (1732)

Sir, I admit your general rule
That every poet is a fool:
But you yourself may serve to show it,
That every fool is not a poet.

QUESTIONS

1. What has the listener said before the poem begins? How does the speaker build on the listener's previous comment?
2. Considering this poem as a brief satire, describe the nature of satiric attack and the corresponding tone of attack.
3. Look at the pattern "poet," "fool," "fool," "poet." This is a rhetorical pattern (*a, b, b, a*) called *chiasmus* or *antimetabole*. What does the pattern contribute to the poem's effectiveness?

An example of the second type of satiric poem is another of Pope's epigrams, in which the speaker is an actual embodiment of the subject being attacked.

Epigram, Engraved on the Collar of a Dog Which I Gave to His Royal Highness (1738)

I am his Highness' dog at Kew:°   the royal palace near London
Pray tell me sir, whose dog are you?

QUESTIONS

1. Who or what is the subject of the satiric attack?
2. What attitude is expressed toward social pretentiousness?

Here the speaker is, comically, the king's dog, and the listener is an unknown dog. Pope's satire is directed not against canines, however, but against human beings who overemphasize the significance of social class. The first line ridicules those who claim social status that is derived, not earned. The second implies an unwillingness to recognize the listener until the question of rank is resolved. Pope, by using the dog as a speaker, reduces such snobbishness to an absurdity. A similar satiric poem attacking pretentiousness is "next to of course god america i" by Cummings (Chapter 12). In this poem the speaker voices a set of patriotic platitudes, and in doing so illustrates Cummings's satiric point that most speeches of this sort are empty-headed. Satiric tone may thus range widely, being sometimes objective, comic, and distant; sometimes deeply concerned and scornful; and sometimes dramatic, ingenuous, and revelatory. Always, however, the satiric mode aims toward confrontation and exposé.

Poems for Study

William Blake . . . . On Another's Sorrow, 809
Jimmy Carter . . . . I Wanted to Share My Father's World, 810
Lucille Clifton . . . . homage to my hips, 811
Billy Collins . . . . The Names, 812
E. E. Cummings . . . . she being Brand / -new, 813
Bart Edelman . . . . Trouble, 814
Mari Evans . . . . I Am a Black Woman, 815
Seamus Heaney . . . . Mid-Term Break, 817

William Ernest Henley . . . . When You Are Old, 817

David Ignatow . . . . The Bagel, 818

Yusef Komunyakaa . . . . Facing It, 819

Abraham Lincoln . . . . My Childhood's Home, 820

Pat Mora . . . . La Migra, 821

Sharon Olds . . . . The Planned Child, 822

Robert Pinsky . . . . Dying, 823

Alexander Pope . . . . from Epilogue to the Satires, Dialogue I, 824

Salvatore Quasímodo . . . . Auschwitz, 825

Anne Ridler . . . . Nothing Is Lost, 827

Theodore Roethke . . . . My Papa's Waltz, 828

Jane Shore . . . . A Letter Sent to Summer, 829

Jonathan Swift . . . . A Description of the Morning, 830

David Wagoner . . . . My Physics Teacher, 830

C. K. Williams . . . . Dimensions, 831

William Wordsworth . . . . The Solitary Reaper, 832

William Butler Yeats . . . . When You Are Old, 833

WILLIAM BLAKE (1757–1827)

For a portrait, see Chapter 12, page 661.

On Another's Sorrow (1789)

Can I see another's woe,
And not be in sorrow too.
Can I see another's grief,
And not seek for kind relief.

Can I see a falling tear,   5
And not feel my sorrows share,
Can a father see his child
Weep, nor be with sorrow filled.

Can a mother sit and hear,
An infant groan an infant fear—   10
No never can it be.
Never never can it be.

And can he who smiles on all
Hear the wren with sorrows small,
Hear the small birds grief & care   15
Hear the woes that infants bear—

And not sit beside the nest
Pouring pity in their breast,
And not sit the cradle near
Weeping tear on infants tear.   20

And not sit both night & day,
Wiping all our tears away.
O! no never can it be.
Never never can it be.

25   He doth give his joy to all.
He becomes an infant small.
He becomes a man of woe
He doth feel the sorrow too.

Think not, thou canst sigh a sigh,
30   And thy maker is not by.
Think not, thou canst weep a tear,
And thy maker is not near.

O! he gives to us his joy,
That our grief he may destroy
35   Till our grief is fled & gone
He doth sit by us and moan.

QUESTIONS

1. Describe the character of this poem's speaker. What is he like? What are the circumstances of the persons in need of sympathy?

2. Describe the tone of the poem. What connection with human suffering does the speaker establish with human sympathy and with the divine "maker"?

3. Why do you think Blake uses the word "maker" (line 32) rather than God? According to the poem, what are the continuing roles of the maker among human beings? What assurances do people in sorrow have from their belief in divinity?

JIMMY CARTER (b. 1924)

 ## I Wanted to Share My Father's World (1995)

This is a pain I mostly hide,
but ties of blood, or seed, endure,
and even now I feel inside
the hunger for his outstretched hand,
5   a man's embrace to take me in,
the need for just a word of praise.

I despised the discipline
he used to shape what I should be,
not owning up that he might feel
10   his own pain when he punished me.

I didn't show my need to him,
since his response to an appeal
would not have meant as much to me,
or been as real.

From those rare times when we did cross   15
the bridge between us, the pure joy
survives.
          I never put aside
the past resentments of the boy
until, with my own sons, I shared   20
his final hours, and came to see
what he'd become, or always was—
the father who will never cease to be
alive in me.

QUESTIONS

1. This poem is about the remembered attitudes of President Carter's speaker toward his father. What is the nature of these attitudes? To what degree are these attitudes of sons to fathers either usual or unusual? Why does the speaker state in line 1, "This is a pain I mostly hide"?

2. Why does the speaker use the words "despised" (line 7) and "resentments" (line 18)? Why does he mention "those rare times" in line 15?

3. What is the tone of the last stanza? Why does the speaker refer to going with his own sons to share the "final hours" of his father? What is the tone of the final two lines?

LUCILLE CLIFTON (b. 1936)

 homage to my hips (1987)

these hips are big hips
they need space to
move around in.
they don't fit into little
petty places, these hips   5
are free hips.
they don't like to be held back.
these hips have never been enslaved.
they go where they want to go.
they do what they want to do.   10
these hips are mighty hips.
these hips are magic hips.
i have known them
to put a spell on a man and
spin him like a top!   15

QUESTIONS

1. What is unusual about the subject matter? Considering that some people are embarrassed to mention their hips, what attitudes does the speaker express here?

2. How do the words "enslaved," "want to go," "want to do," "mighty," and "spell" define the poem's ideas about the relationship between mentality and physicality?

3. To what degree is this a comic poem? What about the subject and the diction makes the poem funny?

BILLY COLLINS (b. 1941)

For a photo, see Chapter 11, page 624.

 The Names° (2002)

Yesterday, I lay awake in the palm of the night.
A fine rain stole in, unhelped by any breeze,
And when I saw the silver glaze on the windows,
I started with A, with Ackerman, as it happened,
5   Then Baxter and Calabro,
Davis and Eberling, names falling into place
As droplets fell through the dark.

Names printed on the ceiling of the night.
Names slipping around a watery bend.
10   Twenty-six willows on the banks of a stream.

In the morning, I walked out barefoot
Among thousands of flowers
Heavy with dew like the eyes of tears,
And each had a name—
15   Fiori inscribed on a yellow petal
Then Gonzalez and Han, Ishikawa and Jenkins.

Names written in the air
And stitched into the cloth of the day.
A name under a photograph taped to a mailbox.
20   Monogram on a torn shirt,
I see you spelled out on storefront windows
And on the bright unfurled awnings of this city.
I say the syllables as I turn a corner—
Kelly and Lee,
25   Medina, Nardella, and O'Connor.
When I peer into the woods,
I see a thick tangle where letters are hidden
As in a puzzle concocted for children.
Parker and Quigley in the twigs of an ash,
30   Rizzo, Schubert, Torres, and Upton,
Secrets in the boughs of an ancient maple.

Names written in the pale sky.
Names rising in the updraft amid buildings.

Names silent in stone
35   Or cried out behind a door.
Names blown over the earth and out to sea.
In the evening—weakening light, the last swallows.

°This poem was read by Professor Collins before a joint session of the U.S. Congress held in New York City on September 6, 2002. It was first published earlier that day in the *New York Times*.

A boy on a lake lifts his oars.
A woman by a window puts a match to a candle,
And the names are outlined on the rose clouds—   40
Vanacore and Wallace,
(let X stand, if it can, for the ones unfound)
Then Young and Ziminsky, the final jolt of Z.

Names etched on the head of a pin.
One name spanning a bridge, another undergoing a tunnel.   45
A blue name needled into the skin.
Names of citizens, workers, mothers and fathers,
The bright-eyed daughter, the quick son.
Alphabet of names in green rows in a field.
Names in the small tracks of birds.   50
Names lifted from a hat
Or balanced on the tip of the tongue.
Names wheeled into the dim warehouse of memory.
So many names, there is barely room on the walls of the heart.

N.B. In light of the topic of this poem, questions seem superfluous.

E. E. CUMMINGS (1894–1962)

For a photo, see Chapter 12, page 665.

she being Brand / -new (1926)

she being Brand

-new;and you
know consequently a
little stiff i was
careful of her and (having   5

thoroughly oiled the universal
joint tested my gas felt of
her radiator made sure her springs were O.

K.)i went right to it flooded-the-carburetor cranked her

up, slipped the   10
clutch (and then somehow got into reverse she
kicked what
the hell) next
minute i was back in neutral tried and

again slo-wly;bare, ly nudg. ing (my   15

lev-er Right-
oh and her gears being in

A 1 shape passed
from low through
20 second-in-to-high like
greasedlightning) just as we turned the corner of Divinity

avenue i touched the accelerator and give

her the juice, good

                    (it

25 was the first ride and believe i we was
happy to see how nice she acted right up to
the last minute coming back down by the Public
Gardens i slammed on

the
30 internalexpanding
&
externalcontracting
brakes Bothatonce and

brought allofher tremB
35 -ling
to a:dead.

stand-
;Still)

QUESTIONS

1. How extensive is the verbal irony, the double entendre, in this poem? This poem is considered comic. Do you agree? Why or why not? This poem might also be considered sexist. Do you agree? Why or why not?

2. How do the spacing and alignment affect your reading of the poem? How does the unexpected and sometimes absent punctuation—such as in line 15, "again slo-wly;bare, ly nudg. ing (my"—contribute to the humor?

3. Can this poem in any respect be called off-color or bawdy? How might you refute such charges in light of the tone the speaker uses to equate a first sexual experience with the breaking in of a new car?

BART EDELMAN (b. 1951)

For a photo, see Chapter 12, page 667.

 ## Trouble (2005)

Everything pointed to trouble;
Danger and distress pranced
Topless on my wooden roof.

Misfortune grew in the garden
I tended day and night
I was afflicted by the urge   5
To do myself in,
But I was so out of it
I failed to plan ahead.
I eased into my hardship   10
Like a pair of black loafers,
Suddenly two sizes too small.
Soon I began to pity
My big, fat, flat feet.
Woe became my middle name,   15
I suffered from the heebie-jeebies
And Saint Vitus left the order
When he saw me dance;
Alas, it wasn't a pretty picture.
I found my meager little life   20
Lost any sense of decency.
I could smell disaster in the wind—
Hot air breathing down my back.
In other words . . .
I was hopelessly unable   25
To shoulder the burden I bore.
Then I simply gave up,
Drove to the hardware store,
Bought a gallon of Dutch Boy #157,
And painted myself into a corner,   30
Where I now live, rather comfortably,
Monopolizing every moment
I choose to spend with myself;
No more a victim of boredom—
A teller of tall tales.   35

QUESTIONS

1. How serious is this poem? How funny is it? Can it be both serious and funny? What does the diction contribute to the tone, particularly well-worn phrases such as "out of it" and "heebie jeebies"?

2. What situation is the speaker describing when he says at the beginning that "everything pointed to trouble" (i.e., he was suffering from malaise or maybe depression)? What is the tone of the descriptions in the poem?

3. On what situation does the poem close? What does the speaker mean by "painted myself into a corner"? How has the speaker solved his problems and ended his trouble?

MARI EVANS (b. 1923)

I Am a Black Woman (1970)

I am a black woman
the music of my song
some sweet arpeggio of tears

is written in a minor key
5   and I
can be heard humming in the night
Can be heard
    humming
in the night

10   I saw my mate leap screaming to the sea
and I / with these hands / cupped the lifebreath
from my issue in the canebreak
I lost Nat's swinging body° in a rain of tears

and heard my son scream all the way from Anzio°
15   for Peace he never knew . . . I

learned Da Nang° and Pork Chop Hill°
in anguish
Now my nostrils know the gas
and these trigger tire / d fingers
20   seek the softness in my warrior's beard
I
am a black woman
tall as a cypress
strong
25   beyond all definition still
defying place
and time
and circumstance
    assailed
30   impervious
        indestructible

Look
    on me and be
renewed

°13 *Nat's swinging body:* Nat Turner was hanged in 1831 for leading a slave revolt in Southampton, Virginia.
14 *Anzio:* seacoast town in Italy, the scene of fierce fighting between the Allies and the Germans in 1943 during World War II. 16 *Da Nang:* major American military base in South Vietnam, frequently attacked during the Vietnam War. *Pork Chop Hill:* site of a bloody battle between UN and Communist forces during the Korean War (1950–1953).

QUESTIONS

1. What attitude is indicated by the phrase "sweet arpeggio of tears"? How does "in a minor key" complete both the idea and the comparison?

2. What phrases and descriptions does the speaker use to indicate her attitudes of anguish, despair, pain, and indignation?

3. In the last fourteen lines, what contrasting attitude is expressed? How does the speaker make this attitude clear? On balance, is the poem optimistic or pessimistic? Why?

SEAMUS HEANEY (b. 1939)

 ## Mid-Term Break (1966)

I sat all morning in the college sick bay
Counting bells knelling classes to a close.
At two o'clock our neighbors drove me home.

In the porch I met my father crying—
He had always taken funerals in his stride—   5
And Big Jim Evans saying it was a hard blow.

The baby cooed and laughed and rocked the pram
When I came in, and I was embarrassed
By old men standing up to shake my hand

And tell me they were "sorry for my trouble,"   10
Whispers informed strangers I was the eldest,
Away at school, as my mother held my hand

In hers and coughed out angry tearless sighs.
At ten o'clock the ambulance arrived
With the corpse, stanched and bandaged by the nurses.   15

Next morning I went up into the room. Snowdrops
And candles soothed the bedside; I saw him
For the first time in six weeks. Paler now,

Wearing a poppy bruise on his left temple,
He lay in the four foot box as in his cot.   20
No gaudy scars, the bumper knocked him clear.

A four foot box, a foot for every year.

QUESTIONS

1. What is the situation of the poem? Who is the speaker? Why has he been called home?
   What are his responses to the circumstances at home?

2. How old was the speaker's brother at the time of the accident? How do you know?
   When you read line 19, what do you at first make of the "poppy bruise"?

3. Describe your responses to the last four lines of the poem the first time you read them.
   What clues in the earlier part of the poem prepare you for these final three lines? Do
   they sufficiently prepare you, or does the final line come as a surprise? Why is the
   poem unrhymed until the final two lines?

WILLIAM ERNEST HENLEY (1849–1903)

 ## When You Are Old (1888)

When you are old, and I am passed away—
Passed, and your face, your golden face, is gray—

I think whate'er the end, this dream of mine,
Comforting you, a friendly star will shine
5   Down the dim slope where still you stumble and stray.
So may it be: that so dead Yesterday,
No sad-eyed ghost but generous and gay,
May serve you memories like almighty wine,
            When you are old!
10 Dear Heart, it shall be so. Under the sway
Of death the past's enormous disarray
Lies hushed and dark. Yet though there come no sign,
Live on well pleased; immortal and divine
Love shall still tend you, as God's angels may,
15   When you are old.

QUESTIONS

1. Describe the organization of thought as it is affected by time. How much attention is given to a visualization of the old age of the listener? What does the speaker imagine will have happened to him? What consolation does the speaker believe the listener will have in this future period?

2. What comfort does the speaker say will justify the listener's living on "well pleased" (line 13)? What "shall still tend" the listener? Why does the speaker say "God's angels may" rather than "God's angels will"?

DAVID IGNATOW (1914–1987)

 ## The Bagel (1993)

I stopped to pick up the bagel
rolling away in the wind,
annoyed with myself
for having dropped it
5   as if it were a portent.
Faster and faster it rolled,
with me running after it
bent low, gritting my teeth,
and I found myself doubled over
10 and rolling down the street
head over heels, one complete somersault
after another like a bagel
and strangely happy with myself.

QUESTIONS

1. What situation does the speaker describe in this poem? Does it make sense? If it doesn't, what is the real situation that the speaker describes?

2. Considering the tone of the poem, how reasonable is it to conclude that some poems, like some activities, exist solely so that readers—and writer—might simply be made happy and be amused.

YUSEF KOMUNYAKAA (b. 1947)

NEW Facing It (1988)

My black face fades,
hiding inside the black granite.°
I said I wouldn't,
dammit: No tears.
I'm stone. I'm flesh.   5
My clouded reflection eyes me
like a bird of prey, the profile of night
slanted against morning. I turn
this way—the stone lets me go.
I turn that way—I'm inside   10
the Vietnam Veterans Memorial
again, depending on the light
to make a difference.
I go down the 58,022° names,
half-expecting to find   15
my own in letters like smoke.
I touch the name Andrew Johnson;
I see the booby trap's white flash.
Names shimmer on a woman's blouse
but when she walks away   20
the names stay on the wall.
Brushstrokes flash, a red bird's
wings cutting across my stare.
The sky. A plane in the sky.
A white vet's image floats   25
closer to me, then his pale eyes
look through mine. I'm a window.
He's lost his right arm
inside the stone. In the black mirror
a woman's trying to erase names: 30
No, she's brushing a boy's hair.

°2 *black granite:* The Vietnam Veterans Memorial Wall in Washington, D.C., designed by the sculptor Maya Lin
(b. 1959), and dedicated in 1982, is composed of polished black granite. Carved into the panels are lists of the
names of all the military personnel who died during the Vietnamese War. 14 *58, 002:* In 2007, the list had grown
to 58,256 names.

QUESTIONS

1. What sights and actions does the speaker describe in the poem? What does he see?
   Why does he state that his "black face" fades and is hiding inside the black granite?
   What is meant by the vet's having "lost his right arm / inside the stone" (lines 28–29)?

2. What other people are at the memorial? What is the significance of what they are
   doing?

3. Considering the actions of the speaker and the other visitors, how would you characterize the tone of the poem?

4. Compare this poem with "The Vietnam Wall" by Alberto Rios in Chapter 22.

ABRAHAM LINCOLN (1809–1865)

🍁 My Childhood's Home° (1844)

My childhood's home I see again,
    And sadden with the view;
And still, as memory crowds my brain,
    There's pleasure in it too.

5   O Memory! thou midway world
      'Twixt earth and paradise,
Where things decayed and loved ones lost
    In dreamy shadows rise,

And, freed from all that's earthly vile,
10   Seem hallowed, pure, and bright,
Like scenes in some enchanted isle
    All bathed in liquid light.

As dusky mountains please the eye
    When twilight chases day;
15   As bugle-notes that, passing by,
    In distance die away.

As leaving some grand waterfall,
    We, lingering, list its roar—
So memory will hallow all
20   We've known, but know no more.

Near twenty years have passed away
    Since here I bid farewell
To woods and fields, and scenes of play,
    And playmates loved so well.

25   Where many were, but few remain
    Of old familiar things;
But seeing them, to mind again
    The lost and absent brings.

The friends I left the parting day,
30   How changed, as time has sped!
Young childhood grown, strong manhood gray,
    And half of all are dead.

I hear the loved survivors tell
    How nought from death could save
35   Till every sound appears a knell,
    And every spot a grave.

°In 1844, while on a political campaign in Indiana, Lincoln visited the home where he had been raised and where his mother and sister were buried. The occasion prompted him to write this poem.

I range the fields with pensive tread
   And pace the hollow rooms,
And feel (companion of the dead)
   I'm living in the tombs.   40

QUESTIONS

1. How does Lincoln's speaker explain the importance of memory? How is the sentence "So memory will hallow all / We've known, but know no more" (lines 19–20) related to the descriptions and ideas that follow?

2. Do stanzas 6 and 7 seem exaggerated, self-indulgent, or sentimental? What seems to forestall this criticism of the ideas here?

3. What leads the speaker to the conclusion he makes in the last two lines?

PAT MORA (b. 1942)

 ## *La Migra*° (1993)

1

Let's play *La Migra*
I'll be the Border Patrol.
You be the Mexican maid.
I get the badge and sunglasses.
You can hide and run,   5
but you can't get away
because I have a jeep.
I can take you wherever
I want, but don't ask
questions because   10
I don't speak Spanish.
I can touch you wherever
I want but don't complain
too much because I've got
boots and kick—if I have to,   15
and I have handcuffs.
Oh, and a gun.
Get ready, get set, run.

2

Let's play *La Migra*.
You be the Border Patrol.   20
I'll be the Mexican woman.
Your jeep has a flat,

°border patrol, border guards, immigration police.

and you have been spotted
by the sun.
25   All you have is heavy: hat
glasses, badge, shoes, gun.
I know this desert,
where to rest,
where to drink.
30   Oh, I am not alone.
You hear us singing
and laughing with the wind,
Agua dulce brota aquí
aquí, aquí,° but since you
35   can't speak Spanish,
you do not understand.
Get ready.

°32–33 *Aqua . . . aquí:* "fresh water springs [are] here, here, here." The idea is that the Mexican woman can survive in the desert because she knows where to find fresh water, whereas the border patrolman does not.

QUESTIONS

1. Why does Mora create "La Migra" as a drama, with the first speaker being a border patrolman, and the second being the "Mexican woman"? What is gained by this arrangement?

2. How is the tone created in the first stanza? What kind of person is the border guard shown to be? What attitude toward him does Mora create? What current political concerns does this attitude address?

3. What is the tone of the second stanza? What resources does the Mexican woman have? What handicaps of the border guard does she point out? In terms of the poem's tone, what is the implication of the final line?

SHARON OLDS (b. 1942)

 ## The Planned Child (1996)

I hated the fact that they had planned me, she had taken
a cardboard out of his shirt from the laundry
as if sliding the backbone up out of his body,
and made a chart of the month and put
5   her temperature on it, rising and falling
to know the day to make me—I would have
liked to have been conceived in heat,
in haste, by mistake, in love, in sex,
not on cardboard, the little x on the
10   rising line that did not fall again.

But when a friend was pouring wine
and said that I seem to have been a child who had been wanted,
I took the wine against my lips
as if my mouth were moving along

that valved wall in my mother's body, she was   15
bearing down, and then breathing from the mask, and then
bearing down, pressing me out into
the world that was not enough for her without me in it,
not the moon, the sun, Orion
cartwheeling across the dark, not   20
the earth, the sea—none of it
was enough, for her, without me.

QUESTIONS

1. Who is the speaker? What is she like? What is she talking about? Why does she begin the poem talking about something she hated?

2. What change of attitudes is described by the poem? Why does the poem seem to require such a change?

3. What attitude is expressed in the concluding global, planetary, solar, and stellar references? Why does the speaker state that, to her mother, she has more value than this image?

4. What unique qualities of perception and expression does the speaker exhibit? Have you ever read a poem before in which details about conception and childbirth have been so prominent? Why are these details included in this poem?

ROBERT PINSKY (b. 1940)

 ## Dying (1984)

Nothing to be said about it, and everything—
The change of changes, closer or further away:
The Golden Retriever next door, Gussie, is dead,

Like Sandy, the Cocker Spaniel from three doors down
Who died when I was small; and every day   5
Things that were in my memory fade and die.

Phrases die out: first, everyone forgets
What doornails are; then after certain decades
As a dead metaphor, *"dead as a doornail"* flickers

And fades away. But someone I know is dying—   10
And though one might say glibly, "everyone is,"
The different pace makes the difference absolute.

The tiny invisible spores in the air we breathe,
That settle harmlessly on our drinking water
And on our skin, happen to come together,   15

With certain conditions on the forest floor,
Or even a shady corner of the lawn—
And overnight the fleshy, pale stalks gather,

The colorless growth without a leaf or flower;
20 And around the stalks, the summer grass keeps growing
With steady pressure, like the insistent whiskers

That grow between shaves on a face, the nails
Growing and dying from the toes and fingers
At their own humble pace, oblivious

25 As the nerveless moths, that live their night or two—
Though like a moth a bright soul keeps on beating,
Bored and impatient in the monster's mouth.

QUESTIONS

1. What details about death does the poem introduce? How are they connected in the poem's development? What is the effect of these details on the tone of the poem?

2. What is meant by line 12, "The different pace makes the difference absolute"? How strongly does this statement counter the phrase "everyone is" in line 11?

3. Up until line 25 this poem can be considered negative or even despairing. What is the effect of lines 26 and 27 on this negative tone? What is the meaning of the phrase "monster's mouth" in these last two lines?

ALEXANDER POPE (1685–1744)

from Epilogue to the Satires, Dialogue I Line 137–72 (1738)

Virtue may choose the high or low degree,
'Tis just alike to Virtue, and to me;
Dwell in a monk, or light upon a king,
140 She's still the same, beloved, contented thing.
Vice is undone, if she forgets her birth,
And stoops from angels to the dregs of earth:
But 'tis the Fall degrades her to a whore;
Let Greatness own her, and she's mean no more:°
145 Her birth, her beauty, crowds and courts confess,°
Chaste matrons praise her, and grave bishops bless:
In golden chains the willing world she draws,
And hers the gospel is, and hers the laws:
Mounts the tribunal, lifts her scarlet head,
150 And sees pale Virtue carted° in her stead!
Lo! at the wheels of her triumphal car,°   *carriage*
Old England's genius, rough with many a scar,
Dragged in the dust! his arms hang idly round,
His flag inverted trails along the ground!°

°144 *mean no more*: i.e., if the rich and powerful follow vice, vice is no longer low but fashionable. 145 *Her birth . . . confess*: i.e., under the dictates of fashion, both crowds and courts claim that Vice is both high-born and beautiful. 150 *carted*: It was an eighteenth-century punishment to display prostitutes in a cart; in addition, condemned criminals were carried in a cart from prison to Tyburn, in London, where they were hanged. 152–154 *Old England's genius . . . along the ground*: i.e., the spirit of England is humiliated by being tied to Vice's triumphal carriage and then dragged along the ground. The idea is that corrupt politicians have sacrificed England's defensive power for their own gain.

Our youth, all liveried o'er with foreign gold, 155
Before her dance; behind her crawl the old!
See thronging millions to the pagod° run,
And offer country, parent, wife, or son!
Hear her black trumpet through the land proclaim,
That "not to be corrupted is the shame." 160
In soldier, churchman, patriot, man in power,
'Tis avarice all, ambition is no more!
See, all our nobles begging to be slaves!
See, all our fools aspiring to be knaves!
The wit of cheats, the courage of a whore, 165
Are what ten thousand envy and adore.
All, all look up, with reverential awe,
On crimes that scape,° or triumph o'er the law: *escape*
While truth, worth, wisdom, daily they decry—
"Nothing is sacred now but villainy." 170
Yet may this verse (if such a verse remain)
Show there was one who held it in disdain.

°157 *pagod*: i.e., a pagoda, a symbol of how people have forsaken their own religion and adopted foreign religions.

QUESTIONS

1. The entire poem is in the form of a dialogue, in which these concluding lines are identified as being spoken by "P" (Pope). Should readers therefore take these lines as an expression of Pope's own ideas? In your answer, pay special attention to the final couplet.

2. Explain this poem as social satire. What is attacked? What evidence does the speaker advance to support his case that society has deserted virtue and religion?

3. Describe the poem's tone. What specific charges does the speaker make against the prevailing sociopolitical structure?

4. How timely is the poem? To what degree might such charges be advanced in our society today?

SALVATORE QUASÍMODO (1901–1968)

 ## Auschwitz° (1983)

Translated by Jack Bevan

Far from the Vistula,° along the northern plain,
love, in a death-camp there at Auschwitz:
on the pole's rust and tangled fencing, rain
funeral cold.
No tree, no birds in the grey air 5

°*Auschwitz* is the German name for the town of Oswiecim in southern Poland, site of the most notorious of the German concentration-extermination camps in World War II. There were two major camps—Auschwitz itself, a former Polish army camp, and nearby Birkenau, which contained many temporary barracks for worker-prisoners, together with gas chambers and crematoria for the extermination of hundreds of thousands of victims. 1 *Vistula*: The Vistula River rises in the northern Carpathian Mountains, south of Auschwitz.

or above our thought, but limp
pain that memory leaves
to its silence without irony or anger.
You ask no elegies or idylls: only
10 the meaning of our destiny, you, here,
hurt by the mind's war,
uncertain at the clear
presence of life. For life is here
in every No that seems a certainty:
15 here we shall hear the angel weep, the monster, hear
our future time
beating the hereafter that is here, forever
in motion, not an image
of dreams, of possible pity.
20 Here are the myths, the metamorphoses.
Lacking the name of symbols or a god,
they are history, earth places,
they are Auschwitz, love. How suddenly
the dear forms of Alpheus and Arethusa°
25 changed into shadow-smoke!

Out of that hell hung with a white
inscription "work will make you free"°
there came the endless smoke
of many thousand women thrust at dawn
30 out of the kennels up to the firing-wall,
or, screaming for mercy to water, choked,
their skeleton mouths under the jets of gas.

You, soldier, will find them in your annals
taking the forms of animals and rivers,
35 or are you too, now, ash of Auschwitz,
medal of silence?
Long tresses in glass urns can still be seen
bound up with charms, and an infinity
of ghostly little shoes and shawls of Jews:°
40 relics of a time of wisdom,
of man whose knowledge takes the shape of arms,
they are the myths, our metamorphoses.
Over the plains where love and sorrow
and pity rotted, there in the rain
45 a No inside us beat;
a No to death that died at Auschwitz
never from the pit of ashes
to show itself again.

°24 Alpheus and Arethusa: a river and fountain in Greece. In ancient mythology, Alpheus, who loved Arethusa, was transformed into the river (bearing his name) to be united with Arethusa, who was transformed into the fountain (bearing her name). 27 *work will make you free*: a translation of the large metal sign *Arbeit macht frei*, which crested the main gate of Auschwitz and is still on display there. A copy of the sign is displayed in the Holocaust Museum in Washington, D.C. 37–39 *Long tresses . . . shawls of Jews*: Today the barracks at Auschwitz house permanent displays that include the hair, shoes, eyeglasses, luggage, and clothing of thousands of the victims.

QUESTIONS

1. Compare the tone of the first ten lines with that of the last six. What differences do you notice? How does the idea of the last three lines answer the question posed in lines 9 and 10?

2. Even though the speaker is referring to the deadliest of all the camps, what does he mean by "For life is here / in every No that seems a certainty" (lines 13–14)?

3. In line 20 the speaker mentions ancient myths about metamorphoses or transformations. What type of metamorphosis is linked to the death camps in lines 26–42? What attitudes are brought out by this linkage?

ANNE RIDLER (1912–2001)

 Nothing Is Lost (1994)

Nothing is lost.
We are too sad to know that, or too blind;
Only in visited moments do we understand:
    It is not that the dead return—
        They are about us always, though unguessed.   5

    This penciled Latin verse
You dying wrote me, ten years past and more,
Brings you as much alive to me as the self you wrote it for,
    Dear father, as I read your words
        With no word but Alas.   10

    Lines in a letter, lines in a face
Are faithful currents of life: the boy has written
His parents across his forehead, and as we burn
    Our bodies up each seven years,
        His own past self has left no plainer trace.   15

    Nothing dies.
The cells pass on their secrets, we betray them
Unknowingly: in a freckle, in the way
    We walk, recall some ancestor,
        And Adam in the color of our eyes.   20

    Yes, on the face of the new born,
Before the soul has taken full possession,
There pass, as over a screen, in succession
    The images of other beings:
        Face after face looks out, and then is gone.   25

    Nothing is lost, for all in love survive.
I lay my cheek against his sleeping limbs
To feel if he is warm, and touch in him
    Those children whom no shawl could warm,
        No arms, no grief, no longing could revive.   30

Thus what we see, or know,
Is only a tiny portion, at the best,
Of the life in which we share; an iceberg's crest
   Our sunlit present, our partial sense,
35   With deep supporting multitudes below.

QUESTIONS

1. What is unusual about the phrase "nothing dies" (line 16)? How successfully does the poet explain and exemplify the idea?

2. In what ways does the "face of the new born" reflect the "images of other beings" (lines 21–24)? How might the "color of our eyes" demonstrate that we are descended from Adam (line 20)? How true is it that "all in love survive" (line 26)?

3. In what ways might this poem offer comfort to readers who believe strongly in the concept of their own uniqueness and originality?

THEODORE ROETHKE (1907–1963)

For a photo, see Chapter 12, page 676.

🍁 My Papa's Waltz (1942)

The whiskey on your breath
Could make a small boy dizzy;
But I hung on like death:
Such waltzing was not easy.

5   We romped until the pans
Slid from the kitchen shelf;
My mother's countenance
Could not unfrown itself.

The hand that held my wrist
10   Was battered on one knuckle;
At every step you missed
My right ear scraped a buckle.

You beat time on my head
With a palm caked hard by dirt,
15   Then waltzed me off to bed
Still clinging to your shirt.

QUESTIONS

1. What is the tone of the speaker's opening description of his father? What is the tone of the phrases "like death" and "such waltzing"?

2. What is the "waltz" the speaker describes? What is the tone of his words describing it in lines 5–15?

3. What does the reference to his "mother's countenance" contribute to the tone? What situation is suggested by the selection of the word "unfrown"?

4. What does the tone of the physical descriptions of the father contribute to your understanding of the speaker's attitude toward his childhood experiences as his father's dance partner?

JANE SHORE (b. 1947)

 ## A Letter Sent to Summer (1977)

Oh summer if you would only come
with your big baskets of flowers,
dropping by like an old friend
just passing through the neighborhood!

If you came to my door disguised   5
as a thirsty biblical angel
I'd buy all your hairbrushes and magazines!
I'd be more hospitable
than any ancient king.

I'd personally carry your luggage in,   10
Your monsoons. Your squadrons of bugs,
Your plums and lovely melons.
Let the rose let out its long long sigh
And Desire return to the hapless rabbit.

This request is also in my own behalf.   15
Inside my head it is always snowing,
even when I sleep. When I wake up,
and still you have not arrived,
I curl back into my blizzard of linens.

Not like winter's buckets of whitewash.   20
Please wallpaper my bedroom
with leafy vegetables and farms.
If you knocked right now,
I would not interfere.
Start near the window.   25
Start right here.

QUESTIONS

1. Describe the speaker. What do you learn about her and how she is responding to the time of year?

2. Describe what summer means to the speaker. What attributes does she give to summer? What contrasts are brought out by references to "bugs" and "monsoons" in addition to "plums" and "the rose"?

3. What does the phrase "always snowing" contribute to your understanding of the speaker's yearning for summer?

JONATHAN SWIFT (1667–1745)

A Description of the Morning (1709)

Now hardly here and there a hackney-coach
Appearing, showed the ruddy morn's approach.
Now Betty from her master's bed had flown,
And softly stole to discompose her own.
5 The slip-shod 'prentice from his master's door
Had pared the dirt, and sprinkled round the floor.
Now Moll had whirled her mop with dextrous airs,
Prepared to scrub the entry and the stairs.
The youth with broomy stumps began to trace
10 The kennel's edge,° where wheels had worn the place.
The small-coal man° was heard with cadence deep,   *charcoal seller*
Till drowned in shriller notes of chimney-sweep.
Duns° at his lordship's gate began to meet;   *bill collectors*
And brickdust Moll had screamed through half the street.
15 The turnkey° now his flock returning sees,
Duly let out a-nights to steal for fees.
The watchful bailiffs take their silent stands,
And schoolboys lag° with satchels in their hands.

°10 *kennel's edge:* that is, the edge of the gutter. Swift annotated this line "To find old Nails." 15 *turnkey:* an entrepreneur, operating a jail for profit, who allowed prisoners to go free at night so that they might bring him a night's booty to pay for the necessities provided them in jail. 18 *schoolboys lag:* cf. Shakespeare's *As You Like It,* 2.7.145–47.

QUESTIONS

1. What images of life in early-eighteenth-century London are presented in this poem? Who is "Betty"? Why is she discomposing her bed? Are such images to be considered ordinary, heroic, or antiheroic? Why?

2. Why does Swift conclude with the reference to "schoolboys" lagging "with satchels in their hands"? Why would it not have been preferable to conclude with reference to adult behavior?

3. How do you know that Swift's poem is satiric? What is being satirized?

DAVID WAGONER (b. 1926)

My Physics Teacher (1981)

He tried to convince us, but his billiard ball
Fell faster than his pingpong ball and thumped
To the floor first, in spite of Galileo.°
The rainbows from his prism skidded off-screen
5 Before we could tell an infra from an ultra.
His hand-cranked generator refused to spit
Sparks and settled for smoke. The dangling pith
Ignored the attractions of his amber wand,
No matter how much static he rubbed and dubbed

From the seat of his pants, and the housebrick   10
He lowered into a tub of water weighed
(Eureka!) more than the overflow.°

He believed in a World of Laws, where problems had answers,
Where tangible objects and intangible forces
Acting thereon could be lettered, numbered, and crammed   15
Through our tough skulls for lifetimes of homework.
But his only uncontestable demonstration
Came with our last class: he broke his chalk
On a formula, stooped to catch it, knocked his forehead
On the eraser-gutter, staggered slewfoot, and stuck   20
One foot forever into the wastebasket.

°3–12 *Galileo . . . overflow:* These lines describe classic classroom demonstrations in physics. Galileo first formulated
the law of uniform falling bodies. Newton explained that a prism divides light into the colors of the rainbow.
("Infra" refers to infrared light; "ultra" to ultraviolet.) Sparks leaping across the space between two wires graphically
demonstrate electrical generation and power. The motion of dried pith toward a charged piece of amber demonstrates the magnetic power of static electricity. Archimedes explained how the weight of a floating object is the
same as the weight of water it displaces, and also how the volume of an immersed object (not the weight) is the
same as the volume of displaced water. The physics teacher did not understand this distinction. (According to legend, Archimedes made this discovery when taking a bath, and then shouted *"Eureka!"* ["I have found it"].)

QUESTIONS

1. What idea underlies the physics teacher's use of classroom demonstrations? What is
   the speaker's apparent response to this idea?
2. What happens to these demonstrations? Why are these failures comic and farcical?
   What effect do the poem's farcical actions have upon the validity of the teacher's
   ideas?

C. K. WILLIAMS (b. 1936)

 Dimensions (1969)

There is a world somewhere else that is unendurable.
Those who live in it are helpless in the hands of the elements,
they are like branches in the deep woods in wind
that whip their leaves off and slice the heart of the night
and sob. They are like boats bleating wearily in fog.   5

But here, no matter what, we know where we stand.
We know more or less what comes next. We hold out.
Sometimes a dream will shake us like little dogs, a fever
hang on so we're not ourselves or love wring us out,
but we prevail, we certify and make sure, we go on.   10

There is a world that uses its soldiers and widows
for flour, its orphans for building stone, its legs for pens.
In that place, eyes are softened and harmless like God's
and all blend in the traffic of their tragedy and pass by

15 like people. And sometimes one of us, losing the way,
will drift over the border and see them there, dying,
laughing, being revived. When we come home, we are half way.
Our screams heal the torn silence. We are like scars.

QUESTIONS

1. Why should this poem be called ironic? Should the irony be called situational? Cosmic? Why?

2. What is intended by the poem's title? What is the implication of the first line? What irony does the line bring out? Describe the irony of the second stanza (lines 6–10).

3. What is meant by "losing the way" and drifting "over the border" (lines 15–16)? What is the meaning and the irony of the last three lines? What does it mean to be "like scars" (line 18)?

WILLIAM WORDSWORTH (1770–1850)

For a portrait, see Chapter 12, page 678.

 ## The Solitary Reaper (1807)

Behold her, single in the field,
Yon solitary Highland Lass!
Reaping and singing by herself;
Stop here, or gently pass!

5   Alone she cuts and binds the grain,
And sings a melancholy strain;
O listen! for the Vale profound
Is overflowing with the sound.

No Nightingale did ever chaunt
10 More welcome notes to weary bands
Of travelers in some shady haunt,
Among Arabian sands;
A voice so thrilling ne'er was heard
In springtime from the Cuckoo bird,
15 Breaking the silence of the seas
Among the farthest Hebrides.°

Will no one tell me what she sings?°
Perhaps the plaintive numbers flow
For old, unhappy, far-off things,
20 And battles long ago;

°16 *Hebrides:* a group of islands off the west coast of Scotland. 17 *Will . . . sings:* The speaker does not understand Scots Gaelic, the language in which the woman sings.

Or is it some more humble lay,
Familiar matter of today?
Some natural sorrow, loss, or pain,
That has been, and may be again?

Whate'er the theme, the Maiden sang   25
As if her song could have no ending;
I saw her singing at her work,
And o'er the sickle bending—

I listened, motionless and still;
And, as I mounted up the hill,   30
The music in my heart I bore,
Long after it was heard no more.

QUESTIONS

1. What is the scene described in the poem? Where is the speaker? What actions does he describe?

2. Why does the poet shift from present tense to the past tense at line 25? What is gained by this shift?

3. What speculations does the speaker make about the meaning of the woman's song? What conclusions does he make? What do you conclude from his observations?

WILLIAM BUTLER YEATS (1865–1939)

 ## When You Are Old (1893)

When you are old and grey and full of sleep,
And nodding by the fire, take down this book,
And slowly read, and dream of the soft look
Your eyes had once, and of their shadows deep;

How many loved your moments of glad grace,   5
And loved your beauty with love false or true,
But one man loved the pilgrim soul in you,
And loved the sorrows of your changing face;

And bending down beside the glowing bars,
Murmur, a little sadly, how Love fled   10
And paced upon the mountains overhead
And hid his face amid a crowd of stars.

QUESTIONS

1. What is the speaker of this poem like? How does the speaker describe himself?

2. To whom is the speaker speaking? What are you asked to conclude about the past relationship between the speaker and the listener?

3. Describe the dominant attitudes expressed by the speaker. What words might describe the poem's tone?

4. Compare the tone of this poem with that of Henley's "When You Are Old" (p. 817).

WRITING ABOUT TONE IN POETRY

Be careful to note those elements of the work that touch particularly on attitudes or authorial consideration. For example, you may be studying Hughes's "Theme for English B," where it is necessary to consider the force of the poet's claim for equality (see Chapter 21). How serious is the claim? Does the speaker's apparent matter-of-factness make him seem less than enthusiastic? Or does this tone indicate that equality is so fundamental a right that its realization should be an everyday part of life? Devising and answering such questions can help you understand the degree to which authors show control of tone. Similar questions apply when you study internal qualities such as style and characterization.

Questions for Discovering Ideas

- What is the speaker like? Is he or she intelligent, observant, friendly, idealistic, realistic, trustworthy? How do you think you should respond to the speaker's characteristics?
- Do all the speeches seem right for the speaker and situation? Are all descriptions appropriate, all actions believable?
- If the work is comic, at what is the comedy directed? At situations? At characters? At the speaker himself or herself? What is the poet's apparent attitude toward the comic objects?
- Does the writer ask you to (1) sympathize with those in misfortune, (2) rejoice with those who have found happiness, (3) lament the human condition, (4) become angry against unfairness and inequality, (5) admire examples of noble human behavior, or (6) have another appropriate emotional response?
- Do any words seem unusual or especially noteworthy, such as dialect, polysyllabic words, foreign words or phrases that the author assumes you know, or especially connotative words? What is the effect of such words on the poem's tone?

Strategies for Organizing Ideas

The goal of your essay is to examine all aspects bearing on the tone. Consider the following topics.

1. *The audience, situation, and characters.* Is any person or group directly addressed by the speaker? What attitude is expressed (love, respect, condescension, confidentiality, confidence, etc.)? What is the basic situation in the work? What is the nature of the speaker or persona? What is the relationship of the speaker to the material? What is the basis of the speaker's authority? Does the speaker give you the whole truth? Is he or she trying to withhold anything? Why? How is the speaker's character manipulated to show apparent authorial attitude and to stimulate responses? Do you find any of the various sorts of irony? If so, what does the irony show (optimism or pessimism, for example)? How is the situation controlled to shape your responses? That is, can actions, situations, or characters be seen as expressions of attitude or as embodiments of certain favorable or unfavorable ideas or positions? How does the work promote respect, admiration, dislike, or other feelings about character or situation?

2. *Descriptions and diction.* Your concern here is to relate attitudes to the poet's use of language and description. Are there any systematic references, such as to colors, sounds, noises, natural scenes, and so on, that collectively reflect an attitude? Do connotative meanings of words control response in any way? Is any special knowledge of references or unusual words expected of readers? What is the extent of this knowledge? Do speech or dialect patterns indicate attitudes about speakers or their condition of life? Are speech patterns normal and standard or slang and substandard? What is the effect of these patterns? Are there unusual or particularly noteworthy expressions? If so, what attitudes do these show? Does the author use verbal irony? To what effect?

3. *Humor.* Is the work funny? How funny, how intense? How is the humor achieved? Does the humor develop out of incongruous situations or language, or both? Is there an underlying basis of attack in the humor, or are the objects of laughter still respected or even loved despite having humor directed against them?

4. *Ideas.* Ideas may be advocated, defended mildly, attacked, or ridiculed. Which attitude is present in the work you have been studying? How does the poet make his or her attitude clear—directly, by statement, or indirectly, through understatement, overstatement, or the language of a character? In what ways does the work assume a common ground of assent between author and reader? That is, are there apparently common assumptions about religious views, political ideas, moral and behavioral standards, and so on? Are these common ideas readily acceptable, or is any concession needed by the reader to approach the work? For example, a major subject of Arnold's "Dover Beach" (Chapter 13) is that absolute belief in the truth of organized religion has been lost. This subject may not be important to everyone, but even an irreligious reader or a follower of another faith may find common ground in the poem's psychological situation or in the desire to learn as much as possible about so important an institution as religion.

5. *Unique characteristics.* Each work has unique properties that contribute to the tone. For example, Roethke's "My Papa's Waltz" is a brief narrative in which the speaker's recollected feelings about his father's boisterously drunken behavior must be inferred from understatement. Hardy's "Channel Firing" (Chapter 14) develops from the comic and absurd joke that the sounds of cannons being fired from ships at sea are so loud they could waken the dead. Be alert for such special circumstances in the poem you are considering, and as you plan and develop your essay, take them into account.

Your conclusion may summarize your main points and from there go on to any needed definitions, explanations, or afterthoughts, together with ideas reinforcing earlier points. If you have changed your mind or have made new realizations, briefly explain these. Finally, you might mention some other major aspect of the work's tone that you did not develop in the body.

Illustrative Student Essay

Underlined sentences in this paper *do not* conform to MLA style and are used solely as teaching tools to emphasize the central idea, thesis sentence, and topic sentences throughout the paper.

Regal 1

Willa Regal

Professor Tyler

English 102

18 May 2008

The Speaker's Attitudes in Sharon Olds's "The Planned Child"°

[1]
"The Planned Child" is unusual and striking because in it Sharon Olds deals so frankly with her speaker's concern about the circumstances of her conception and birth. Few people ever learn about how they were conceived, and even fewer ever think about it enough to criticize it, and yet the poem's details concern this topic. As unusual as such details are, however, <u>the poem's power results from the way the speaker traces the development of her attitudes towards her origins--from hate, to uncertainty, to acceptance.</u>* These attitudes <u>may be traced in the poem's two stanzas, its ordinary diction, and the way its use of the first-person pronoun indicates the speaker's importance.</u>†

[2]
<u>Olds's first stanza contrasts the speaker's hatred for planning and organization and her preference for disorganization.</u> The stanza is arresting, if not shocking, because in it the speaker goes into the past to describe her feelings about how her mother calculated ovulation times to insure conception. Rather than finding it comical that she owes her existence to the chart her mother made on a laundry cardboard, the speaker says she hated this planned record keeping. She explains this attitude because the planning, to her way of thinking, reduced her to little more than an X on a rising graph line and by implication, therefore, it seemed cold and impersonal. From the description the speaker makes of conception in lines 7 and 8, it seems that spontaneous and

°This poem appears on page 822.
*Central idea.
†Thesis sentence.

Regal 2

disorganized love by her parents would have created a warmer, more welcoming reason for her existence.

The second stanza is continuous with the first because it stems out of feelings occasioned by an unplanned but significant moment. A friend serves wine to the speaker and tells her that she seems to have been "a child who had been wanted" (line 12, italics added). This casual social event is symbolic (is it similar to an experience of communion?) because it gives the speaker a lifegiving insight into her existence. The conclusion of the poem is then devoted to the speaker's newly created feelings of involvement with her mother. She finds affection for her mother in the details of childbirth--bearing down, breathing, pressing, and the emergence into life of the speaker herself. The poem's climax is the speaker's apparently amazed realization that she herself was actually wanted. The X on the graph therefore was a means of achieving a far greater goal, for her mother valued her more than the world or the galaxy. As the speaker imagines her mother's lifegiving act, she imagines how loving it was, and therefore she senses her own importance. [3]

With such an unusual topic, one might expect a fair amount of abstract and medical diction, but such is not the case. Most of the words are flat and ordinary (e.g., "a friend was pouring wine"). Despite their simplicity, however, the diction confronts readers with direct physical details of planned conception and the labor of childbirth. The speaker refers matter-of-factly to a temperature chart, the birth canal, and breathing into a mask and bearing down during labor. Of major note is the intensity that Olds achieves through the selection of simple but strong verbs and verbals ("hated," "planned," "had taken," " sliding," "made," "pouring," "were moving," "bearing down," "breathing," "pressing," and "cartwheeling"). All these words fit the poet's aim to connect with one of life's first facts--being conceived and then delivered. [4]

As this basic detail indicates, the central figure of the poem is the speaker and her attitudes. This centrality is emphasized by the frequent use of the first person pronoun throughout the poem. A form of the pronoun appears twelve times, and the poem begins with "I" and concludes with "me." This number may not seem high in a personal poem of twenty-two lines, but it is [5]

Regal 3

high enough to support the idea that the poem is about attitudes toward self-realization. The poem explores some vital personal questions: Could the speaker love herself knowing that she was planned and not spontaneous? Not when these calculations seemed to result from nothing more than cold science. But could she love herself after learning that the calculations were preceded by love for her? Yes, and as a result the speaker makes inferences from this new information. She imagines that nothing in the world was more important to her mother than she. She therefore has more value than the earth and stars themselves, and this vision closes the poem on a strongly positive and affirmative note:

> not the moon, the sun, Orion
>
> cartwheeling across the dark, not
>
> the earth, the sea--none of it
>
> was enough, for her, without me. (lines 20-22)

[6]   Thus, an examination of "The Planned Child" reveals both the need and difficulty of self understanding. The poem is a confession of changing attitudes in the light of a growing sense of personal origin. Olds makes this point through the commonness and universality of details about birth. Yet the poem is not personal or egocentric because it is about the need of discovering who one is. Without this knowledge the poem's speaker is uncertain and hostile. But once she can see that she is part of a pattern of love and creativity, she becomes positive and assertive. The tone of "The Planned Child" reflects the speaker's growing confidence that results from her increased knowledge and awareness.

Regal 4

Work Cited

Olds, Sharon. "The Planned Child." Literature: An Introduction to Reading and
    Writing. Ed. Edgar V. Roberts. 9th ed. New York: Pearson Longman, 2009.
    822–23.

Commentary on the Essay

Because this essay embodies a number of approaches by which tone may be studied in any work (situation, diction, special characteristics), it is typical of many essays that use a combined approach. The central idea, expressed in the first paragraph, is that the dominant attitudes in "The Planned Child" are the speaker's change from hostility to certainty.

Paragraph 2 considers the poem's first section, in which the speaker explains why a preference for spontaneity caused her initial hatred of how she came into being (strategy 4, p. 835). Paragraph 3 shows how the explanation of a unique situation can be seen as a feature of tone (strategy 5, p. 835). The paragraph pursues the speaker's thoughts that develop from an unexpected comment from a friend. In this sense, a casual moment explains how the speaker's relative confusion shifts to the greater self-confidence and acceptance of her mother's labors to bring her into the world.

Paragraph 4 concerns the poem's treatment of the unusual subject matter through comparatively simple diction (strategy 1, p. 834). Words in the paragraph that indicate attitudes are "confronts," "matter-of-factly," "intensity," and "desire." Paragraph 5 considers how Olds's use of the first-person pronoun fits into the poem's recognition of the speaker's importance (strategy 2, p. 835). The paragraph asserts that the poem's positive conclusion is augmented by images on a planetary, solar, galactic, geographic, and marine scale (strategy 5).

The concluding paragraph points out that the speaker's concern with her origins is not simply a matter of egocentrism, but rather results from her need to connect with an attitude that is more human and loving than the act of planning at first seems to convey.

Writing Topics About Tone in Poetry

1. Consider Clifton's "homage to my hips," Cummings's "she being Brand/ -new," Hardy's "The Workbox," Whur's "The First-Rate Wife," and Henley's "When You Are Old" as poems about love. What similarities do you find? That is, do the poets state that love creates joy, satisfaction, distress, embarrassment, trouble? How does the tone of each of the poems enable you to draw your conclusions? What differences do you find in the ways the poets either control or do not control tone?

2. Consider these same poems from a feminist viewpoint (see Chapter 29). What importance and value do the poems give to women? How do they view women's actions? Generally, what praise or blame do the poems deserve because of their treatment of women?

3. a. Consider the tone of Roethke's "My Papa's Waltz." Some readers have concluded that the speaker is expressing fond memories of his childhood experiences with his father. Others believe that the speaker is ambiguous about the father and that he suppresses childhood pain as he describes the father's boisterousness in the kitchen. Basing your conclusion on the tone of the poem alone, how should the poem be interpreted?

b. From resources in your library or online, find two critical biographies about Theodore Roethke published by university presses. What do these works disclose about Roethke's childhood and his family, particularly his father? On the basis of what you learn, should your interpretation of the tone of "My Papa's Waltz" be changed or unchanged? Why?

4. Write a poem about a person or occasion that has made you either glad or angry. Try to create the same feelings in your reader, but create these feelings through your rendering of situation and your choices of the right words. (*Possible topics:* a social injustice; an unfair grade; a compliment you have received on a task well done; the landing of a good job; the winning of a game; a rise in the price of gasoline; a good book or movie.)

5. What judgments about modern city life do you think Léger conveys in his painting *The City* (p. I–8)? If the tone of paintings can be considered similar to poetic tone, in what ways is *The City* comparable to the presentation of detail in Eliot's "Preludes" (Chapter 14), Blake's "London" (Chapter 13), Sandburg's "Chicago" (Chapter 22), and Swift's "A Description of the Morning" (this chapter)—together with any other poems you wish to include?

6. How does Edelman establish a friendly relationship between the speaker and the reader in "Trouble"? In what way does this relationship create the tone of the poem?

7. Explain how the details and ideas in Ridler's "Nothing Is Lost" shape the poem's tone (this chapter). What is the effect of the stanzaic pattern and the rhymes on your understanding and on your responses to the poem's ideas? In terms of ideas and tone, how does this poem compare with Pinsky's "Dying" (this chapter)?

8. Quasímodo's "Auschwitz" (this chapter) concerns one of the twentieth century's central evils, the most abhorrent of the Nazi death camps, about which people have expressed anger, horror, indignation, outrage, disgust, hatred, and vengefulness. To what degree do you find these attitudes in Quasímodo's poem? How do such attitudes, or others, govern the poem's tone?

Chapter 17

Prosody: Sound, Rhythm, and Rhyme in Poetry

P **rosody** (the pronunciation or accent of a song or poem, a song set to music) is the general word describing the study of poetic sounds and rhythms. Common alternative words are **metrics, versification, mechanics of verse,** and the **music of poetry.** Most readers, when reading poetry aloud, interpret the lines and develop an appropriate speed and expressiveness of delivery—a proper *rhythm.* Indeed, some people think of rhythm and sound as the *music* of poetry because they convey musical rhythms and tempos. Like music, poetry often requires a regular beat. The tempo and loudness of poetry may vary freely, however, and a reader may stop at any time to repeat the sounds and to think about the words and ideas. It is the music of poetry that makes the speaking and hearing of poetry dramatic, exciting, and inspiring.

In considering prosody, we should recognize that poets, being especially attuned to language, blend words and ideas together so that "the *Sound* must seem an *Eccho* to the sense" (Pope, *An Essay on Criticism,* line 365. This spelling is authentic; don't be alarmed.). The consequence of this idea is that *prosodic technique cannot be separated from a poem's content.* For this reason, the study of prosody aims to determine how poets control their words so that the sound of a poem complements its expression of emotions and ideas.

Important Definitions for Studying Prosody

To understand and discuss prosody, you need to be able to explain the various sounds of both speech and poetry. Let us grant that the subject is technical, detailed, and also subtle, and as a result, the study of vocal production can take, and has taken, entire careers. A basic knowledge of spoken sound, however, will enable you to analyze that aspect of the poet's craft that pertains to qualities of pronunciation and rhythm.

Vowel Sounds Create the Flow of Poetic Speech

The continuous stream of speech, whether conversation, oratory, or poetry, is provided mainly by **vowel sounds.** A vowel (from the Latin word *vox,* or "voice") results from vibrations resonating in the space between the tongue and the top of the mouth. As our tongues go up or down or forward or backward, or as they curl or flatten out, and as our lips move synchronously with our tongues, we form vowels. Some vowels are "long," such as the *ee* sound in "flee," the *ay* sound in "pay," the *oh* sound in "open", and the *oo* sound in "food" and "fruit." Others are "short," such as the *ih* sound in "fit" and "sit," the *uh* sound in "fun" and "done," and the *eh* sound in "set" and "debt." Some vowels are called "front" (e.g., *see*, pl*a*y) and some are called "back" (kn*o*wing, m*oo*n), depending on the position of the tongue in the production of the sound. Some are rounded (h*o*pe, h*oo*p) because their production requires pursed lips, but more are unrounded (gr*ee*n, sw*i*m).

Many of our English vowel sounds are pronounced as a **schwa,** or minimal vowel sound, despite their spellings (e.g., the *e* in "th*e* boy," the *a* in "*a*lone"). Thus, "*a*bout," "stag*e*s," "rap*i*d," "nati*o*n," and "circ*u*s" contain the vowels *a, e, i, o,* and *u,* but all the italicized letters make the same *schwa* sound.

Of special importance is the **diphthong** (two voices, two sounds)—a meaningful sound that begins with one vowel sound and then is completed by the movement to another vowel sound. The three English diphthongs are the *aye* (as in *eye*) as in "try" and "appliance," the *ow* sound in "house" and " shout," and the *oy* sound in "foil" and "employ."

Consonant Sounds Are Meaningful Sounds Produced through the Creation of Vocal Obstructions in the Mouth

Consonant sounds ("sounds made at the same time [as vowels]") result from the touching and near touching of various parts of the mouth (lips, tongue, teeth, hard palate, soft palate), thus producing meaningful sounds obstructing the flow of vowel sounds. Some consonants might theoretically be prolonged (e.g., *m, h, sh*), while others are by nature no more than momentary (*t, k*). In combination, consonants and vowels make for understandable speech. The consonants are classified into three major groups:

1. *Stop sounds, also called* plosives, *are percussive and abrupt.* There are six **stop sounds,** which are made by the momentary stoppage and release of breath either when the lips touch each other (*p* and *b*), or when the tongue touches the hard palate (the *k* and *g* in *keep* and *gear*) or soft palate (the *k* and *g* in *cool* and *goal*), or when the tongue touches the alveolar ridge immediately above the teeth (*t* and *d*).

2. *Continuant sounds are smooth and flowing.* **Continuant sounds** are consonants produced by the steady release of the breath in conjunction with various positions of the tongue in relation to the lips, teeth, and palate, as in *n, ng, l, r, th* (as in *thorn*), *th* (as in *the*), *f, v, s, z, sh* (as in *sharp*), and *zh* (as in *pleasure*); or with the touching of the lower lip and upper teeth for the sounds *f* and *v*; or with the touching of both lips for the sound *m*. Two special sounds called **affricates** begin with the stops *t* and *d* and then become the continuants *sh* and *zh* (as in *chew* and *judge*).

3. *Semivowel sounds are more like consonants than vowels.* **Semivowel sounds** are midway between vowels and consonants, and they have in common that they move from an originating sound and then move to another vowel sound. They are *w* (as in *wagon, win, weather*), *y* (as in *yes, young, union*), and *h* (*hope, heap*).

Consonants may be either **voiced** *or* **voiceless.** Voiced consonants are produced with the vibration of the vocal chords (e.g., *b, d, g, v, z, zh*), whereas voiceless consonants are produced by the breath alone, for this reason being whispered sounds (e.g., *p, t, k, f, s, sh*). Among the semivowels, *w* and *y* are voiced, but *h* is voiceless. Any singer can sing the sound *z*, which is voiced; but not even the greatest singers, such as the late opera stars Beverly Sills and Luciano Pavarotti, could ever have sung an *s* sound, which is voiceless.

Nasal consonants require the stoppage of the breath in the mouth so that the sound can be released through the nose. The consonants, also called **nasals,** are *n*, *m*, and *ng* (as in su*n*, su*m*, and su*ng*). In English, the *n* and *m* sounds may begin and end words or may appear in the middle of a word, whereas the *ng* sound may appear in the middle or end but may not begin a word. The nasals affect the pronunciation of adjoining consonants, as in words like *mountain* and *student*, in which the *t* and *d* sounds are released nasally by most speakers of English. Adjoining consonants also affect the pronunciation of the nasal, as in words like *sink* and *Thanksgiving*, in which the palatal *k* sound causes the preceding nasal to be an *ng* sound, as in *sing* and *thing*, even though the sound is spelled with an *n* alone.

Segments: Individually Meaningful Sounds

Individual sounds in combination make up syllables and words, and separate words in combination make up lines of poetry. Syllables and words are made up of **segments**, or individually meaningful sounds (which linguists call **segmental phonemes**). In the word *tape*, there are three segments: *t*, *ay*, and *p*. When you hear these three sounds in order, you recognize the word *tape*, as distinguished from, say, *top* and *type*. It takes four alphabetical letters—*t*, *a*, and *pe*—to spell (or **graph**) *tape*, because the *t*, *a*, and *pe* create the three meaningful segments making up the word. Quite often, as with the final *pe* spelling of "tape," English uses more than one letter to spell or graph a segment. This happens all the time—so often, in fact, that we hardly notice the connection between sound and spelling. For example, in the word *enough*, there are four segments (*ee*, *n*, *uh*, *f*), although six letters are required for the correct spelling: *e*, *n*, *ou*, and *gh*. The last two segments (*u* and *f*) require two letters each (two letters forming one segment are called a *digraph*). In the word *through*, there are three segments but *seven* letters. In order for the *oo* segment in this word to be spelled correctly, it must have four letters (*ough*). Note, however, that in the word *flute*, the *oo* segment requires only one letter, *u*. When we study the effects of various segments in relationship to poetic rhythm, we deal with **sound;** usually our concern is with prosodic devices, such as **alliteration, assonance,** and **rhyme.**

When segments are meaningfully combined, they make up syllables and words. A **syllable,** in both prose and poetry, consists of a single meaningful strand of sound, such as the article *a* in "*a* table," the stem *lin* in "*lin*en," and the entire word *screech*. The article *a*, which is both a syllable and a word, has only one segment; *lin*, the first syllable of the two-syllable word "linen," contains three segments (*lin* does not occur alone in English except as an abbreviation, but it is used in combinations such as *lingerie, poplin,* and *linoleum*); *screech* is a complete word of one syllable consisting of the five segments *s*, *k*, *r*, *ee*, and *tch*. The past tense of *screech* (*screeched*) adds one meaningful sound at the end—*t*—and two letters, *ed*, but this additional sound does not create a new syllable. The understanding of what constitutes syllables is important because poetic rhythm is determined by the positions of heavily stressed and less heavily stressed syllables.

Distinguish between Spellings and the Actual Sounds of Words

It is important—vital—to understand the differences between spelling, or **graphics,** and pronunciation, or **phonetics.** Not all English sounds are spelled and pronounced in the same way, as we can see with the *p* sound in *tape* and *top.* Thus the letter *s* has three very different sounds in the words *sweet, sugar,* and *flows: s, sh* ("sharp"), and *z.* On the other hand, the words *shape, ocean, nation, sure, fissure, Eschscholtzia,* and *machine* use different combinations of letters to spell the *sh* sound.

Vowel sounds may also be spelled in different ways. The *ee* sound, for example, can be spelled *i* in *machine, ee* in *speed, ea* in *eat, e* in *even,* and *y* in *funny,* yet the vowel sounds in *eat, break,* and *bear* are not the same even though they are spelled the same. The *z* sound has an interesting variety of spellings, as in the *ss* in *business,* the *z* alone in *zinc,* and the *sth* in *asthma,* not to mention other various spellings. Remember this: With both consonants and vowel sounds, *do not mistake the spelling of a sound with the sound itself.*

Poetic Rhythm

Rhythm in speech is a combination of vocal speeds, rises and falls, starts and stops, vigor and slackness, and relaxation and tension. In ordinary speech and in prose, rhythm—as important as it is—is not as important as the flow of ideas. In poetry, rhythm is significant because poetry is emotionally charged, compact, and intense. Poets invite us to change speeds while reading—to slow down and linger over some words and sounds and to pass rapidly over others. They also invite us to give more-than-ordinary vocal stress or emphasis to certain syllables and less stress to others. The more intense syllables are called **heavy stress** syllables, and it is the heavy stresses that determine the **accent** or **beat** of a poetic line. The less intense syllables receive **light stress.** In traditional verse, poets select patterns called **feet,** which consist of a regularized relationship of heavy stresses to light stresses.

Scansion Is the Systematic Study of Poetic Rhythm

To study the patterns of versification in any poem, you **scan** the poem. The act of scanning—**scansion**—enables you to discover how the poem establishes a prevailing metrical pattern, and also how and why there are variations in the pattern.

DETERMINE STRESSES, OR BEATS.   In the scansion of a poem, it is important to use a commonly recognized notational system to record stresses or accents. A **heavy stress** or **primary stress** (also called an **accented syllable**) is indicated by a prime mark or acute accent ('), or it may be indicated by capital letters, as in "To BE or NOT to BE." A **light stress** (also called an **unaccented syllable**) is indicated by a bowl-like half circle called a **breve** (˘) or sometimes by a raised circle or degree sign (°). If you are using capital letters to indicate a heavy stress, use lowercase letters to indicate the light stress, as in "When I con-SID-er HOW my LIGHT is SPENT."

Because the capital-lowercase system is somewhat less difficult to manage than the accent system, we will use the capital letter system for illustrative purposes in this chapter, and recommend it for your use. To separate one foot from another, a **virgule** or **slash** (/) is used. Thus, the following line, from Coleridge's "The Rime of the Ancient Mariner," may be schematized formally in this way:

WA – ter, / WA - ter, / EV - ery WHERE,

Here the virgules or slashes show that the line contains two two-syllable feet followed by a single three-syllable foot.

DETERMINE THE METER OR MEASURE.   A major part of scansion is the determination of a poem's **meter,** or the number of feet in its lines. Lines containing five feet are **pentameter,** four are **tetrameter,** three are **trimeter,** two are **dimeter,** and one is **monometer.** To these may be added the less common line lengths **hexameter,** a six-foot line; **heptameter** or the **septenary,** seven feet; and **octameter,** eight feet. In terms of accent or beat, a trimeter line has three beats (heavy stresses), a pentameter line five beats, and so on.

The Major Metrical Feet

You are now ready to scan poems and to determine the patterns of metrical feet, which measure the relationships of syllables and stresses. In English the names of the feet are derived from Greek poetry. We may classify them as feet of two syllables, three syllables, and one syllable (or imperfect).

The Two-Syllable Foot

1. *Iamb (Light/Heavy).* The most important poetic foot in English is the **iamb** (a word of unknown origin), which contains a light stress followed by a heavy stress:

the WINDS

The iamb is the most important and most common foot, because it most nearly duplicates natural speech and at the same time elevates speech to poetry. It is the most versatile of English poetic feet, and it is capable of great variation. Even within the same line, iambic feet vary in intensity, thus supporting the shades of meaning designed by the poet. For example, in this line of iambic pentameter from Wordsworth's sonnet "The World Is Too Much with Us," each foot is unique:

The WINDS / that WILL / be HOWL - / ing AT / all HOURS, /

Even though "will" and "at" are both in normally heavy-stress positions in this line, they are not as strongly emphasized as "winds," "howl -," and "hours" (indeed, they are also less strong than "all," which is in the light-stress position in the concluding iamb). Such variability, approximating the stresses and rhythms of actual speech, makes the iamb suitable for both serious and light verse, and it therefore helps poets to focus attention on ideas and emotions. If they use iambic meter with skill, it never becomes monotonous, for it does not distract readers by drawing attention to its own rhythm.

2. *Trochee (Heavy/Light)*. The **trochee** (*running*), sometimes called the **choree** (*dancing*), consists of a heavy accent followed by a light:

FLOW - er

Rhythmically, most two-syllable English words are **trochaic** (tro-KAY-ick), as may be seen in words like *author, early, follow, major, morning, often, singing, snowfall, something, story, water, walking, willow,* and *window.* A major exception is seen in many two-syllable words beginning with prefixes, such as *sublime, because,* and *impel.* Another exception is found in two-syllable words that are borrowed from another language but are still pronounced as in the original language, as with *machine, technique, garage,* and *chemise,* all of which are recent importations from French, in which iambic accentuation prevails. Illustrating the strength of trochaic rhythm in English, however, the final stresses in many French words borrowed hundreds of years ago now regularly accent the next-to-last syllable, as with *apartment, cherry, expression, language, lesson, nation,* and *very.*

Because trochaic rhythm has often been called *falling, dying, light,* or *anticlimactic,* and because iambic rhythm has been called *rising, elevating, serious,* and *climactic,* poets have preferred the iambic foot. They therefore have arranged various place-ments of single- and multiple-syllable words, and have also used a variety of other means, so that the heavy-stress syllable is at the end of the foot, as in Shakespeare's

With - IN / his BEND - / ing SICK - / le's COM - / pass COME, /

in which three successive trochaic words (*bending, sickle's,* and *compass*) are arranged to match the iambic meter.

3. *Spondee (Heavy/Heavy)*. The **spondee** (originally the prevailing accent of music that was characteristically played during the pouring of libations or offerings)—also called a **hovering accent**—consists of two successive, equally heavy accents, as in "men's eyes" in Shakespeare's line

When IN / dis - GRACE / with FOR - /tune AND / MEN'S EYES

The spondee is mainly a substitute foot in English verse, because successive spon-dees inevitably become iambs or trochees. An entire poem written in spondees would be unlikely within traditional metrical patterns and ordinary English syn-tax (but see Brooks's poem "We Real Cool"). As a substitute foot, however, the spondee creates emphasis. A way that is often used to indicate the **spondaic foot** is to link the two syllables together with chevronlike marks like this:

MEN'S EYES

4. *Pyrrhic (Light/Light).* The **pyrrhic** (a foot, a war dance) consists of two unstressed syllables, even though one of them may be in a normally stressed position, as in "on their" in this line from Pope's *Pastorals* (4.5):

Now SLEEP - / ing FLOCKS / on their / SOFT FLEE - / ces LIE. /

The pyrrhic is made up of weakly accented words, such as prepositions (e.g., *on, to*) and articles (*the, a*). Like the spondee, it is a substitute foot for an iamb or a trochee. An entire poem could not be in pyrrhics because the pyrrhics, like spondees, would be resolved as trochees and iambs. As a substitute foot, however, the pyrrhic acts as a rhythmic catapult to move the reader swiftly to the next heavy-stress syllable, and therefore it undergirds the ideas conveyed by more important words.

The Three-Syllable Foot

1. *Dactyl (Heavy/Light/Light).* The **dactyl** (after the shape of a finger, which has a long joint and two shorter joints) has a heavy stress followed by two lights, as in this line from Swinburne:

GREEN as our / HOPE in it, / WHITE as our / FAITH in it. /

2. *Anapest (Light/Light/Heavy).* The **anapest** ("beaten back," *or* "turned around"; the reverse of a dactyl) consists of two light accents followed by a heavy accent, as in this line from Francis Scott Key:

by the DAWN'S / ear - ly LIGHT. /

The Imperfect Foot

A single stressed syllable (´) by itself, or an unstressed syllable (˘) by itself, creates an **imperfect foot.** There is nothing "imperfect" about an imperfect foot. Instead, the imperfect foot is a variant or substitute occurring in a poem in which one of the major feet forms the metrical pattern. The second line of Key's "The Star-Spangled Banner," for example, is anapestic, but it contains an imperfect foot at the end:

What so PROUD - / ly we HAILED / at the TWI- /light's last GLEAM- / ing. /

Some analysts of prosody would claim that the final syllable here is **catalectic** ("left off"). That is, the final foot, which consists of only one syllable, is missing a syllable.

You can see that there is nothing absolutely open and shut about prosodic analysis. What counts is that you make correct observations about poetic rhythms, not that you always perfectly use the language of prosodic analysis.

🍁 SPECIAL METERS

In many poems you will find meters other than those described above. Poets like Browning, Tennyson, Poe, and Swinburne introduce special or unusual meters. Other poets manipulate pauses or **caesurae** (discussed later) to create the effects of unusual meters. For these reasons, you should know about metrical feet, such as the following:

1. **Amphibrach** (short at both ends). A light, heavy, and light:

   Ah FEED me / and FILL me / with PLEAS - ure / (Swinburne)

2. **Amphimacer** (long at both ends) or **cretic** (originally, apparently, a song from the island of Crete). A heavy, light, and heavy:

   LOVE is BEST. / (Browning)

3. **Bacchius** or **Bacchic** (pertaining to Bacchus, the god of wine and conviviality). A light stress followed by two heavy stresses, as in the word "singing" in the following line:

   Some LATE LARK / [SING - ing] / (W. E. Henley)

4. **Dipodic Measure** (literally, "two feet" combining to make one) or **syzygy** (a yoking together), or **double duple** meter. Dipodic measure develops in longer lines when a poet submerges two regular feet under a stronger beat, so that a "galloping" or "rollicking" rhythm results. For example, the following line from Masefield's "Cargoes" (Chapter 14) may be scanned as trochaic hexameter, with the concluding foot being an iamb:

   QUIN - que / REME of / NIN- e- / VEH from / DIS-tant / o - PHIR, /

In reading, however, a stronger beat is superimposed, which makes one foot out of two—dipodic measure or syzygy:

   QUIN - quer - eme of / NIN - e - veh from / DIS – tant o –PHIR,

---

Substitution

Most regular poems (i.e., poems written according to the traditional rhythms of prosody) follow a formal pattern that may be analyzed according to the feet we have been describing here. Too much formal regularity, however, sometimes makes for monotony, and so for interest and emphasis (and also, especially, because of the natural rhythms of English speech), poets frequently alter and enlarge the regular patterns through the **substitution** of a dominant foot by a variant foot. Thus in an iambic line the poet may insert a spondee or an anapest and by this means may provide a wider and more conversational rhythmical range than the unvarying use of the poem's chosen pattern can achieve. As an example, the pattern of Jonathan Swift's "A Description of the Morning" (Chapter 16) is iambic pentameter (i.e., five iambs per line). However, Swift introduces a formal substitution at the beginning of the following line, describing how a group of creditors gathers at the door of an aristocrat who has not been paying his debts:

> DUNS at / his LORD- / ship's GATE / be - GAN / to MEET;

The first foot is a trochee, and the strong accent on *Duns* enables Swift to stress his comic assertion about His Lordship's financial embarrassment. Note also that the light accent on *at* enables the voice to move rapidly through *at his lord*. Thus, although the first two feet are a trochee and an iamb, the rhythmical effect is that of an imperfect foot followed by an anapest. This simple substitution helps Swift to emphasize and satirize the unglamorous side of London life early in the eighteenth century.

When studying rhythm, your main concern in noting substitutions is to determine the formal metrical pattern and then to analyze the variations on this pattern and their principal techniques and effects. Always try to show how these variations have enabled the poet to get points across and to achieve emphasis.

Accentual, Strong-Stress, and "Sprung" Rhythms

The foregoing descriptions of poetic feet will enable the analysis of most so-called traditional poetry. A number of poets, however, stretch the bounds of traditional feet, and use generally unmeasured rhythms derived from accentual or strong stresses. Such lines are historically linked to the poetry of Old English (see Chapter 11). At that time, each line was divided in two, with two major stresses, also alliterated, occurring in each half. In the nineteenth century, Gerard Manley Hopkins (1844–1889) developed what he called **sprung rhythm,** a rhythm in which the major stresses would be released or "sprung" from the line. The method is complex, but a primary characteristic is the placement together of one-syllable stressed words combined with alliteration (see below), as in this line from "Pied Beauty"(Chapter 22).

> With SWIFT, SLOW; SWEET, SOUR; a - DAZZ - le, DIM;

Here a number of single-syllable words create five major stresses, while one word (a – DAZZ – le) contributes a central stress together with a strong "d" alliteration to match the "d" of "dim." Many of Hopkins's lines combine alliteration and strong stresses in this way to create the same "springing" effect, or heavy emphasis.

A parallel instance of strongly stressed lines is seen in "We Real Cool" by Brooks. In this poem the effect is achieved by the exclusive use of monosyllabic stressed words combined with internal rhyme, repetition, and alliteration.

The Caesura: The Pause Creating Variety and Natural Rhythms in Poetry

Whenever we speak, we run words together rapidly, without apparent pauses. We do, however, stop briefly and almost unnoticeably between significant units or phrases. Intelligible conversation could not take place without these pauses, which, both grammatically and rhythmically, create separate units of meaning called **cadence groups.** In poetry using a regular meter, the cadence groups operate just as they do in prose to make ideas clear. That is, while we follow the poetic measures, we also pause briefly at the ends of phrases, and we pause longer, for emphasis, at the ends of sentences. In scansion, the name of these pauses, which linguists call *junctures,* is **caesura** (a "cutting off"), pluralized as **caesurae.** When writing out our scansion of a line, we use two diagonal slashes or **virgules** (//) to indicate a caesura, so that the caesura can be distinguished from the single virgule separating feet. Often the caesura coincides with the end of a foot, as at the end of the second iamb in this line by William Blake ("To Mrs. Anna Flaxman").

With HANDS / di - VINE // he MOV'D / the GEN - / tle SOD. /

The caesura, however, may fall within a foot, and there may be more than one in a line, as within the second and third iambs in this line by Ben Jonson (from a poem of praise about "Penshurst," an English country estate):

Thou ART / not, //PENS - / hurst, // BUILT / to EN - / vious SHOW. /

When a caesura ends a line, usually marked by a comma, semicolon, or period, that line is **end-stopped,** as in this famous line opening Keats's "Endymion":

A THING / of BEAU - / ty // IS / a JOY / for - EV - er. /

If a line has no punctuation at the end and the thought carries over to the next line, it is called **run-on.** A term also used to indicate run-on lines is **enjambement** (a straddling). The following passage, a continuation of the line from Keats, contains three run-on lines:

Its loveliness increases; // it will never
Pass into nothingness; // but still will keep
A bower quiet for us, // and a sleep
Full of sweet dreams, // . . .

It is important to recognize that the formal rhythms of poetry are superimposed on the rhythms of natural speech, creating a tension between the two. By manipulating the placement of caesurae—the pauses that develop naturally in speech—poets create many of the variant rhythms that are provided by formal substitution. If the poet ends a cadence group within a foot, the pause, or caesura, may cause us actually to *hear* trochees, amphibrachs, and other variant feet even though the line may scan correctly and regularly in the established meter. This type of *de facto* variation is **rhetorical substitution.** A noteworthy example in an iambic pentameter line is this one from the first epistle of Pope's *Essay on Man* (1.66):

His AC- / tions', // PAS-/sions', // BE-/ing's, // USE /and END. /

This is the second line in a "heroic" couplet, which theoretically requires that there should be only a single caesura following the fourth syllable. In this line, however, Pope provides us with great rhythmical variety. He uses not one but rather three caesurae, each of them producing an emphatic pause or juncture. Pope's line is regularly iambic, but the effect is different in actual reading or speaking. Because of the caesurae after the third, fifth, and seventh syllables, the rhythm produces an amphibrach, a trochee, another trochee, and an amphimacer. The effect is a skillful line containing two inner two-syllable feet, framed by two three-syllable feet, thus:

> His AC-tions', // PAS-sions', // BE-ing's, // USE and END.
> AMPHIBRACH   TROCHEE   TROCHEE   AMPHIMACER

The spoken substitutions effected by the caesurae in this regular line produce the effect of substitution—rhetorical substitution—and therefore tension and interest. Never believe that Pope did not know what he was doing with words and rhythms.

Segmental Poetic Devices

Once you have completed your analysis of rhythms, you should consider the segmental poetic devices in the poem. Usually these devices are used to create emphasis, but sometimes in context they may echo or imitate actions and objects. The segmental devices most common in poetry are *assonance, alliteration, onomatopoeia,* and *euphony and cacophony*.

Identical Vowel Sounds Create *Assonance*

Assonance is the repetition of identical *vowel* sounds in different words—for example, the short *i* in "swift Camilla skims" (Pope). It is a strong means of emphasis, as in the following line, where the *u* sound connects the two words *lull* and *slumber,* and the short *i* connects *him, in,* and *his:*

> And more, to lull him in his slumber soft. (Spenser)

Identical Consonant Sounds Create Alliteration

Like assonance, **alliteration** is a means of highlighting ideas by words containing the same consonant sound—for example, the repeated *m* in Spenser's "Mixed with a murmuring wind," or the *s* sound in Edmund Waller's praise of Oliver Cromwell, "Your never-failing sword made war to cease," which emphasizes the connection between the words *sword* and *cease.*

There are two kinds of alliteration. Most commonly, alliteration is regarded as the repetition of identical consonant sounds that begin syllables in close patterns—for example, in Pope's lines "Laborious, heavy, busy, bold, and blind," "While pensive poets painful vigils keep," and "brazen brainless brothers." When used judiciously, alliteration gives strength to ideas by emphasizing key words, but too much can cause comic and catastrophic consequences.

The second form of alliteration occurs when a poet repeats identical or similar consonant sounds that do not begin syllables but nevertheless create a pattern—for example, the z segment in the line "In these places freezing breezes easily cause sneezes," or the *m, b,* and *p* segments (all of which are made *bilabially*—that is, with both lips) in "The *m*iserably *m*umbling and *m*o*m*entously *m*urmuring *b*owler *p*ropels *p*egs and *p*ebbles in the *b*ubbling *p*ool." Such clearly designed patterns are hard to overlook.

Verbal Imitation of Real Sounds Is Onomatopoeia, or "Poetic Sound Effects"

Onomatopoeia is a blend of consonant and vowel sounds designed to *imitate* or *suggest* a situation or an action. It is made possible in poetry because many English words are **echoic** in origin; that is, they are verbal echoes of the actions they describe, such as *buzz, bump, slap,* and so on. In "The Bells," Poe uses such words to create onomatopoeia. Through the combined use of assonance and alliteration, he imitates the kinds of bells that he celebrates. Thus, wedding bells sound softly with "molten golden notes" (*o*), while alarm bells "clang and clash and roar" (*kl*). David Wagoner includes imitative words like *tweedledy, thump,* and *wheeze* to suggest the sounds of the music produced by the protagonist of his "March for a One-Man Band" (this chapter).

Pleasing Sounds Create Euphony, and Harsh Sounds Create Cacophony

Words describing smooth or jarring sounds, particularly those resulting from consonants, are euphony and cacophony. **Euphony** ("good sound") refers to words containing consonants that permit an easy and smooth flow of spoken sound. Although there is no rule that some consonants are inherently more pleasant than others, students of poetry often cite sounds like *m, n, ng, l, v,* and *z,* together with *w* and *y,* as being especially easy on the ears. The opposite of euphony is **cacophony** ("bad sound"), in which percussive and choppy sounds make for vigorous and noisy pronunciation, as in tongue twisters like "black bug's blood" and "shuffling shellfish fashioned by a selfish sushi chef." Obviously, unintentional cacophony is a mark of imperfect control. When a poet uses it and controls it for effect, however, as in Pope's "The *hoarse, rough verse* shou'd like the *Torrent* roar" (*An Essay on Criticism,* line 369), and in Coleridge's "Huge fragments vaulted like rebounding hail, / Or chaffy grain beneath the thresher's flail" ("Kubla Khan"), cacophony is a mark of poetic skill. Although poets generally aim at easily flowing, euphonious lines, cacophony does have a place, always depending on the poet's intention and subject matter.

Rhyme: The Duplication and Similarity of Sounds

Rhyme refers to words containing identical final syllables. One type of rhyme involves words with identical concluding vowel sounds, or assonance, as in *day, weigh, hey, bouquet, fiancé,* and *matinee.* A second type of rhyme is created by assonance combined with identical consonant sounds, as in *ache, bake, break,* and *opaque;* or *turn, yearn, fern, spurn,* and *adjourn;* or *apple* and *dapple,* or *fantastic* and *elastic.* Rhymes like these, because their rhyming sounds are identical, are called **exact rhymes.** It is important to note that rhymes result from *sound* rather than from spelling; words do not have to be spelled the same way or look alike to rhyme. All the words rhyming with *day,* for example, are spelled differently, but because they all contain the same *a* sound, they rhyme.

Rhyme, above all, gives delight and sustains interest, and it strengthens a poem's psychological impact. Through its network of similar sounds that echo and resonate in our minds, it promotes memory by clinching feelings and ideas. It has been an important aspect of poetry for hundreds of years, and, although many poets have shunned it because they find it restrictive and artificial, it is closely connected with how well particular poems move us or leave us flat. There are few restrictions on the types of words that poets may choose in making rhymes. Nouns may be rhymed with verbs, adjectives, adverbs, and other nouns or with any other rhyming word, regardless of part of speech.

Most often, rhymes are placed at the ends of lines. Two successive lines may rhyme, for example, or rhymes may appear in alternating lines. It is also possible to introduce rhyming words at intervals of four, five, or more lines. If rhyming sounds are too far away from each other, however, it is difficult for readers to re-call them and they therefore lose their effectiveness. Sometimes poets use rhyme within individual lines—**internal rhyme.** Poe uses internal rhyme effectively in the concluding stanzas of "Annabel Lee," where he rhymes the words *ever dissever; beams, dreams; rise, eyes;* and *tide* and *side.* Internal rhyme is not common, but you should be alert for it and make note of it when it occurs.

Poets who are skillful and original rhymers are able to create fresh, unusual, and surprising turns of thought. We can therefore judge poets on their use of rhyme. Often poets become quite creative rhymers, putting together words like *bent 'em* and *Tarentem* or *masterly* and *dastardly.* Some rhymers, whom an anony-mous sixteenth-century critic called a "rakehelly rout of ragged rhymers," are satisfied with easy rhymes, or **cliché rhymes,** like *trees* and *breeze* (a rhyme that Alexander Pope criticized in 1711 in *An Essay on Criticism,* lines 350–51). But good rhymes and good poets go together, in creative cooperation. The seven-teenth-century poet John Dryden, who wrote volumes of rhyming couplets, ac-knowledged that the need to find rhyming words inspired ideas he had not anticipated. In this sense, rhyme has been—and still is—a vital element of poetic creativity.

Rhyme and Meter

The effects of rhyme are closely bound to rhythm and meter. There is general agreement that rhymes coinciding with a strong accent are conducive to serious subjects. Commensurately, rhymes coinciding with syllables of light stress are ap-propriate for light and comic subject matter. There is no hard-and-fast rule about such matters, for the effects of rhyme always result from the poet's skill, regard-less of rhymes. There is enough truth in the observations, however, to warrant considering the relationship of rhyme and accent.

Rising Rhymes Form the Climaxing Syllables of Iambs and Anapests

The most significant type of **rising rhyme** is **iambic rhyme,** which utilizes one-syllable words in an iambic foot (like *the west* and *in rest, more strong* and *ere long*) and two-syllable words in which the accent falls on the second syllable (like *away* and *today, demand* and *command*). Such rhymes are also called **heavy-stress rhyme** or **accented rhyme.** Iambic rhyme is illustrated in the opening lines of Robert Frost's "Stopping by Woods on a Snowy Evening" (Chapter 11; italics added):

> Whose woods / these are / I think / I *KNOW.* //
> His house / is in / the vil - / lage *THOUGH;* //

Here, the rhyming sounds are produced by one-syllable words—*know* and *though*—that occur in the final heavy-stress positions of the lines. The rhyme climaxing a final syllable can also involve spondees, as in lines 9–12 of Shakespeare's "Sonnet 18: Shall I Compare Thee to a Summer's Day?" (Chapter 15; italics added):

> But thy eternal summer shall *not fade,*
> Nor lose possession of that fair *thou owest;*
> Nor shall Death brag thou wander'st in *his shade,*
> When in eternal lines to time *thou growest:*

Falling Rhymes Conclude with One or Two or More Lightly Stressed Syllables

Rhymes using words of two or more syllables, in which the heavy stress is followed by light syllables, are **trochaic rhyme** or **double rhyme** for two-syllable rhymes, and **dactylic rhyme** or **triple rhyme** for three-syllable rhymes. Less technically, these types of rhymes are also called **falling rhymes** or **dying rhymes,** because the intensity of pronunciation decreases on the light accent or accents following the heavy accent. Falling rhyme is seen in lines 2 and 4 of "Miniver Cheevy" by Edwin Arlington Robinson (italics added):

> Miniver Cheevy, child of scorn
>   Grew lean while he assailed the *seasons;*
> He wept that he was ever born,
>   And he had *reasons.*

Here the double rhyme reinforces the humor of the passage, thus helping to make Miniver Cheevy seem self-centered and pathetic.

Double rhymes can also be used to bring out irony or anticlimax, as in "a-dying" and "flying" in Browning's "Soliloquy of the Spanish Cloister" (Chapter 22):

> If I trip him just *a-dying,*
>   Sure of heaven as sure can be,
> Spin him round and send him *flying*
>   Off to hell, a Manichee?

Browning uses trochaic rhymes freely throughout this poem, including the rhyming of English and Latin words (e.g., "rose-acacia" and *"Plena gratiâ"*). The effect of such rhymes is to complement Browning's exposé of the anger and hypocrisy of the speaker, a monk, who condemns no one but himself as he inveighs against a saintly fellow monk.

Dactylic or **triple rhyme,** even more than trochaic rhyme, is light and often humorous, because it tends to minimize the subject matter and maximize the rhythm, as in Eliot's "Macavity: The Mystery Cat," where Eliot rhymes *Macavity* with *gravity*, *depravity*, and *suavity*. These are comic rhymes, totally in keeping with the nature of the poem's feline hero. Ogden Nash makes great use of such rhymes in "Very Like a Whale." There, among other ingenious and amusing rhymes, we see *better for* rhymed with *metaphor*, and *experience* with *Assyrians*. How many of us could be clever enough to create rhymes like these?

Variations in Rhyme Extend the Boundaries of Rhyming Poetry

Unlike poets writing in other languages (such as Italian, which offers virtually endless rhyming possibilities because most Italian words end in vowel sounds), English poets are limited in selecting rhymes because our language is short in identical word terminations. To compensate for this shortfall of English rhymes, a tradition has grown that many English words may be rhymed even if their sounds do not duplicate each other exactly.

Rhymes may therefore be created out of words with similar but not identical sounds—**inexact rhyme.** In most inexact rhymes, either the vowel segments are different while the consonants are the same, or vice versa. In addition to *inexact rhyme*, this type of rhyme is variously called **slant rhyme, near rhyme, half rhyme, off rhyme, analyzed rhyme**, or **suspended rhyme.** In employing slant rhyme, a poet can pair *bleak* with *broke* or *could* with *solitude*. Emily Dickinson uses slant rhyme extensively in "To Hear an Oriole Sing" (this chapter); in the second stanza of the poem she rhymes *bird, unheard*, and *crowd. Bird* and *unheard* form an exact rhyme, but the vowel and consonant shift in *crowd* produces a slant rhyme.

Another common variation is **eye rhyme** or **sight rhyme.** In eye rhyme, the sounds to be eye-rhymed are *identical in spelling* but *different in pronunciation*. Entire words may be eye-rhymed, so that *wind* (verb) may be joined to *wind* (noun), and *cóntest* (noun) may be used with *contést* (verb). In most eye rhymes, however, it is only the relevant parts of words that must be spelled identically. Thus *stove* may pair with *prove* and *above*, and *bough* may match *cough, dough, enough*, and *through*, despite all the differing pronunciations. The following lines contain eye rhyme:

> Although his claim was not to praise but *bury,*
> His speech for Caesar roused the crowd to *fury.*

The different pronunciations of *bury* and *fury* make clear the contrast between exact rhyme and eye rhyme. In exact rhyme, identical sound is crucial; spelling is usually the same but may be different as long as the sounds remain identical. In eye rhyme, the eye-rhyming patterns must be spelled identically but the sounds must be different.

An additional variation is **identical rhyme** (noted earlier); that is, the same words are placed into rhyming positions, such as *veil* and *veil* or *stone* and *stone.* Perhaps the most extreme variation is **vowel rhyme,** in which poets put words ending in vowels into rhyming positions, as in *day* and *sky* or *key* and *play.*

Rhyme Schemes

A **rhyme scheme** refers to a poem's pattern of rhyming sounds, which can be schematized by alphabetical letters. The first rhyming sounds, such as *love* and *dove*, are marked with an *a*; the next rhyming sounds, such as *swell* and *fell*, receive a *b*; the next sounds, such as *first* and *burst*, receive a *c*; and so on. Thus, a pattern of lines ending with the words *love, moon, thicket*; *dove, June, picket*; and *above, croon, wicket* can be schematized as *abc abc abc.*

To formulate a rhyme scheme or pattern, you include the meter and the number of feet in each line as well as the letters indicating rhymes. Here is such a formulation for a Shakespearean sonnet:

Iambic pentameter: *abab cdcd efef gg*

This scheme shows that all the lines in the poem are iambic, with five feet in each line. Spaces are used here to mark a stanzaic pattern of three 4-line units, or **quatrains,** and to separate this pattern with the concluding **couplet.** In each quatrain, the rhymes fall on the first and third, and the second and fourth, lines.

Should the number of feet in the lines of a poem or **stanza** vary, as in odes and songs, you need to show this fact by using a number in front of each letter:

Iambic: *4a3b4a3b5a5a4b*

This formulation shows an intricate pattern of rhymes and line lengths in a stanza of seven lines. The first, third, fifth, and sixth lines rhyme and vary from four to five feet. The second, fourth, and seventh lines also rhyme and vary from three to four feet.

The absence of a rhyme sound is indicated by an *x.* Thus, you formulate the rhyme scheme of **ballad measure** like this:

Iambic: *4x3a4x3a*

The formulation shows that the quatrain alternates iambic tetrameter (four feet) with iambic trimeter (three feet). In this ballad quatrain, only lines 2 and 4 rhyme; there is no end rhyme in lines 1 and 3.

Poems for Study

Gwendolyn Brooks . . . . We Real Cool, 857

Robert Browning . . . . Porphyria's Lover, 858

Emily Dickinson . . . . To Hear an Oriole Sing, 859

John Donne. . . . . The Sun Rising, 860

T. S. Eliot . . . . Macavity: The Mystery Cat, 861

Ralph Waldo Emerson . . . . Concord Hymn, 863
Isabella Gardner . . . . At a Summer Hotel, 863
Robert Herrick. . . . . Upon Julia's Voice, 864
Gerard Manley Hopkins . . . . God's Grandeur, 864
John Hall Ingham . . . . George Washington, 865
Philip Levine . . . . A Theory of Prosody, 866
Henry Wadsworth Longfellow. . . . . The Sound of The Sea, 866
Herman Melville . . . . Shiloh: a Requiem, 867
Ogden Nash. . . . . Very Like a Whale, 868
Edgar Allan Poe . . . . Annabel Lee, 869
Edgar Allan Poe . . . . The Bells, 870
Alexander Pope . . . . from An Essay on Man, Epistle I, 873
Wyatt Prunty. . . . . March, 875
Edwin Arlington Robinson . . . . Miniver Cheevy, 876
Christina Rossetti . . . . Echo, 877
William Shakespeare. . . . . Sonnet 73: That Time of Year Thou
                                                     May'st in Me Behold, 878
Percy Bysshe Shelley . . . . Ode to the West Wind, 878
Alfred, Lord Tennyson . . . . From Idylls of The King:
                                                      The Passing of Arthur, 881
David Wagoner . . . . March for a One-Man Band, 882

GWENDOLYN BROOKS (1917–2000)

 ## We Real Cool (1959)

The Pool Players.
Seven at the Golden Shovel.

We real cool. We
Left school. We

Lurk late. We
Strike straight. We

Sing sin. We
Thin gin. We

Jazz June. We
Die soon.

5

QUESTIONS

1. What is the major idea of the poem? Who is the speaker? How is the last sentence a climax? How is this sentence consistent with the declarations in lines 1–7? How is the poet's attitude made clear?

2. Describe the patterning of stresses in the poem. Explain the absence of light stresses. What method is employed to achieve the constant strong stresses?

ROBERT BROWNING (1812–1889)

For a photo, see Chapter 13, page 697.

 Porphyria's Lover° (1836)

The Rain set early in to-night,
    The sullen wind was soon awake,
It tore the elm-tops down for spite,
    And did its worst to vex the lake:
5   I listened with heart fit to break.
When glided in Porphyria; straight
    She shut the cold out and the storm,
And kneeled and made the cheerless grate
    Blaze up, and all the cottage warm;
10   Which done, she rose, and from her form
Withdrew the dripping cloak and shawl,
    And laid her soiled gloves by, untied
Her hat and let the damp hair fall,
    And, last, she sat down by my side
15   And called me. When no voice replied,
She put my arm about her waist,
    And made her smooth white shoulder bare,
And all her yellow hair displaced,
    And, stooping, made my cheek lie there,
20   And spread, o'er all, her yellow hair.
Murmuring how she loved me—she
    Too weak, for all her heart's endeavor,
To set its struggling passion free
    From pride, and vainer ties dissever,
25   And give herself to me forever,
But passion sometimes would prevail,
    Nor could to-night's gay feast restrain
A sudden thought of one so pale
    For love of her, and all in vain:
30   So, she was come through wind and rain.
Be sure I looked up at her eyes
    Happy and proud; at last I knew
Porphyria worshipped me: surprise
    Made my heart swell, and still it grew
35   While I debated what to do.
That moment she was mine, mine, fair,
    Perfectly pure and good: I found
A thing to do, and all her hair
    In one long yellow string I wound
40   Three times her little throat around
And strangled her. No pain felt she;

°When Browning published "Porphyria's Lover" in his *Dramatic Lyrics* of 1842, he grouped it with another poem under the title "Madhouse Cells."

I am quite sure she felt no pain.
As a shut bud that holds a bee,
  I warily oped her lids: again
  Laughed the blue eyes without a stain.
And I untightened next the tress   45
  About her neck; her cheek once more
Blushed bright beneath my burning kiss:
  I propped her head up as before
  Only, this time my shoulder bore   50
Her head, which droops upon it still:
  The smiling rosy little head,
So glad it has its utmost will,
  That all it scorned at once is fled,
  And I, its love, am gained instead!   55
Porphyria's love: she guessed not how
  Her darling one wish would be heard.
And thus we sit together now,
  And all night long we have not stirred,
  And yet God has not said a word!   60

QUESTIONS

1. What is the situation in this poem? Who is the speaker? Where is he at the time he is speaking? To whom is he speaking?

2. Who is Porphyria? What has happened after her meeting with the speaker?

3. Explain the speaker's mental state. What evidence do you find for asserting that he is unstable? What is his justification for strangling Porphyria?

4. Describe the pattern of rhymes in the poem. What is the prevailing metrical pattern? What variations seem consistent with the speaker's mental condition?

5. Why do you suppose Browning chose circumstances like these for the subject of a poem?

EMILY DICKINSON (1830–1886)

For a photo, see Chapter 21, page 1023.

 ## To Hear an Oriole Sing (F402, J526) (1891; c. 1862)

To hear an Oriole sing
May be a common thing–
Or only a divine.

It is not of the Bird
Who sings the same, unheard,
As unto Crowd–   5

The Fashion of the Ear
Attireth that it hear
In Dun, or fair–

10   So whether it be Rune,
       Or whether it be none
       Is of within.

       The "Tune is in the Tree–"
       The Skeptic–showeth me—
15   "No Sir! In Thee!"

QUESTIONS

1. What can you deduce about the speaker? The listener? Who speaks in line 13? To whom is line 15 addressed?

2. Formulate the rhyme scheme of this poem. How does it help subdivide the poem into cohesive units of thought? To what extent does it unify the poem?

3. Locate all the slant rhymes in this poem. What effect do these have on your reading and perception? How is the rhyme here like the oriole's song?

4. To what degree does rhyme reinforce meaning? Note especially the rhyme words in the final stanza.

JOHN DONNE (1572–1631)

For a portrait, see Chapter 12, page 666.

 ## The Sun Rising (1633)

       Busy old fool, unruly Sun,
       Why dost thou thus,
Through windows, and through curtains call on us?
Must to thy motions lovers' seasons run?
5   Saucy pedantic wretch, go chide
           Late school boys and sour prentices,°   *apprentices*
       Go tell Court-huntsmen, that the King will ride,
       Call country ants to harvest offices;°   *duties*
Love, all alike, no season knows, nor clime,°   *climate*
10 Nor hours, days, months, which are the rags of time.

       Thy beams, so reverend, and strong
       Why shouldst thou think?°
I could eclipse and cloud them with a wink,
But that I would not lose her sight so long;
15   If her eyes have not blinded thine,

°8 *Call . . . offices*: i.e., Notify the country's ants to carry out the duty of eating the harvest of grain and produce.
11, 12 *Thy beams . . . think?*: i.e., why shouldst thou think that thy beams are so reverend and strong?

Look, and tomorrow late, tell me,
   Whether both the Indias of spice and Mine°
Be where thou leftst them, or lie here with me.
Ask for those kings whom thou saw'st yesterday,
And thou shalt hear, All here in one bed lay.   20

   She'is° all States, and all Princes, I,
      Nothing else is.
Princes do but play us; compared to this,
All honor's mimic; all wealth alchemy.°
   Thou, sun, art half as happy'as° we,   25
      In that the world's contracted thus;
Thine age asks ease, and since thy duties be
   To warm the world, that's done in warming us.
Shine here to us, and thou art everywhere;
This bed thy center° is, these walls, thy sphere.   30

°17 *Indias of spice and Mine:* The India of "spice" is the East Indies; the India of "Mine" (gold) is the West Indies. 21 *She'is:* For scansion, these two words are to be considered one syllable ("shé's"). 24 *all wealth alchemy:* i.e., all wealth is false because it has been created by alchemists. 25 *happy'as:* to be scanned as a trochee ("háppyăz"). 30 *center:* the earth, around which the sun revolves (according to the Ptolemaic view of the solar system).

QUESTIONS

1. What is the speaker like? How deeply does he seem to be in love? How does he feel about love? What evidence do you find that the speaker has a good sense of humor?
2. To whom is the poem addressed? What is the speaker's attitude toward this listener?
3. What solar, seasonal, geographical, and political metaphors are developed in the poem?
4. What is the poem's rhyme scheme? What is the metrical norm of the lines? What variations on this norm do you find in the poem?

T. S. ELIOT (1888–1965)

For a photo, see Chapter 14, page 735.

 ## Macavity: The Mystery Cat (1939)

Macavity's a Mystery Cat: he's called the Hidden Paw—
For he's the master criminal who can defy the Law.
He's the bafflement of Scotland Yard, the Flying Squad's despair:
For when they reach the scene of the crime—*Macavity's not there!*

   Macavity, Macavity, there's no one like Macavity,   5
He's broken every human law, he breaks the law of gravity.
His powers of levitation would make a fakir stare,
And when you reach the scene of crime—*Macavity's not there!*
You may seek him in the basement, you may look up in the air—
But I tell you once and once again, *Macavity's not there!*   10

Macavity's a ginger cat, he's very tall and thin;
You would know him if you saw him, for his eyes are sunken in.
His brow is deeply lined with thought, his head is highly domed;
His coat is dusty from neglect, his whiskers are uncombed.
15 He sways his head from side to side, with movements like a snake;
And when you think he's half asleep, he's always wide awake.

Macavity, Macavity, there's no one like Macavity,
For he's a fiend in feline shape, a monster of depravity.
You may meet him in a by-street, you may see him in the square—
20 But when a crime's discovered, then *Macavity's not there!*

He's outwardly respectable. (They say he cheats at cards.)
And his footprints are not found in any file of Scotland Yard's.
And when the larder's looted, or the jewel-case is rifled,
Or when the milk is missing, or another Peke's been stifled,°
25 Or the greenhouse glass is broken, and the trellis past repair—
Ay, there's the wonder of the thing! *Macavity's not there!*

And when the Foreign Office find a Treaty's gone astray,
Or the Admiralty lose some plans and drawings by the way,
There may be a scrap of paper in the hall or on the stair—
30 But it's useless to investigate-*Macavity's not there!*
And when the loss has been disclosed, the Secret Service say:
"It *must* have been Macavity!"—but he's a mile away.
You'll be sure to find him resting, or a-licking of his thumbs,
Or engaging in doing complicated long division sums.

35 Macavity, Macavity, there's no one like Macavity,
There never was a Cat of such deceitfulness and suavity.
He always has an alibi, and one or two to spare:
At whatever time the deed took place—MACAVITY WASN'T THERE!
And they say that all the Cats whose wicked deeds are widely known
40 (I might mention Mungojerrie, I might mention Griddlebone)
Are nothing more than agents for the Cat who all the time
Just controls their operations: the Napoleon of Crime!

°24 *Peke's been stifled:* A Pekinese dog (a small animal, with silky hair) has been found dead.

QUESTIONS

1. What are some of Macavity's major "crimes" as a master criminal and "mystery cat"? How, if the "crimes" had been attributed to a human being, would they be grievous wrongs? Since they are attributed to a cat, how do they add to the comic qualities of the poem?

2. What is the basic metrical foot of the poem? How many feet are contained in each of the lines? What is the norm?

3. Once you begin reading and getting into the lines, what new kind of pattern emerges? How many major stresses appear in each line? In light of the nature of the poem, how is the dipodic rhythm appropriate?

RALPH WALDO EMERSON (1803–1882)

 ## Concord Hymn (1837)

Sung at the completion of the Battle Monument, July 4, 1837

By the rude bridge that arched the flood,
  Their flag to April's breeze unfurled,
Here once the embattled farmers stood,
  And fired the shot heard round the world.

The foe long since in silence slept;   5
  Alike the conqueror silent sleeps;
And Time the ruined bridge has swept
  Down the dark stream which seaward creeps.

On the green bank, by this soft stream,
  We set to-day a votive stone;   10
That memory may their deed redeem,
  When, like our sires, our sons are gone.

Spirit, that made those spirits dare
  To die, and leave their children free,
Bid Time and Nature gently spare   15
  The shaft we raise to them and thee.

QUESTIONS

1. Line 4 is one of the best-known lines of American poetry. Why is it so well-known? Discuss the rhythm of the line. Where are the heavy accents? What complication occurs in the phrase "heard round"?
2. Discuss line 7. What does Emerson do grammatically to get his idea across and also to create the verbal "swept" to rhyme with "slept"?
3. Describe Emerson's use of alliteration and assonance in the poem.

ISABELLA GARDNER (1915–1981)

 ## At a Summer Hotel (1979)

I am here with my bountiful womanful child
to be soothed by the sea not roused by these roses roving wild.
My girl is gold in the sun and bold in the dazzling water,
She drowses on the blond sand and in the daisy fields my daughter
dreams. Uneasy in the drafty shade I rock on the veranda   5
reminded of Europa Persephone Miranda.°

°6 *Europa Persephone Miranda:* Europa was a princess in Greek mythology who attracted the attention of Zeus, the king of the gods. He took the form of a bull and carried her over the sea to Crete. She bore him three sons. Persephone, in Greek mythology, was the daughter of Zeus and Demeter, the goddess of fertility. She attracted the attention of Hades, the god of the underworld, who forcibly carried her off and married her. Miranda is an innocent young woman in Shakespeare's play *The Tempest* who was exiled on an island for twelve years with her father, Prospero. One of his servants, the beastlike Caliban, attempted to rape her.

QUESTIONS

1. Why is the speaker "uneasy" (line 5)? How do the references to Europa, Persephone, and Miranda help define this uneasiness?
2. To what extent do alliteration and repetition unify the lines and make the sound echo sense? Note especially the *ful* sounds in line 1, the *s* and *r* sounds in line 2, and the *d* and *dr* sounds in lines 4–5.
3. What is the effect of internal rhyme in this poem?
4. What kind of rhyme (rising or falling, exact or slant) is in lines 1–2? To what extent does this rhyme highlight the poem's central idea? What rhyme is in lines 3–6? How does this rhyme affect the poem's tone and impact?

ROBERT HERRICK (1591–1674)

 ## Upon Julia's Voice (1648)

So smooth, so sweet, so silv'ry is thy voice,
As, could they hear, the damned would make no noise,
But listen to thee (walking in thy chamber)
Melting melodious words, to lutes of amber.

QUESTIONS

1. How do the words "silv'ry" and "amber" contribute to the praise of Julia's voice? How powerful does the speaker claim her voice is?
2. What is the "joke" of the poem? How can the praise of Julia's voice be interpreted as general praise for Julia herself?
3. How and where is alliteration used in the poem? Which of the alliterative sounds best complement the words praising the sweetness of Julia's voice?

GERARD MANLEY HOPKINS (1844–1889)

For a photo, see Chapter 14, page 740.

 ## God's Grandeur (1877)

The world is charged with the grandeur of God.
    It will flame out, like shining from shook foil;
    It gathers to a greatness, like the ooze of oil
Crushed. Why do men then now not reck his rod?°
5 Generations have trod, have trod, have trod;
    And all is seared with trade; bleared, smeared with toil;
    And wears man's smudge and shares man's smell: the soil
Is bare now, nor can foot feel, being shod.

°4 *reck his rod:* God as king holds a scepter, making official laws through scriptures which people ("men") disobey.

And for all this, nature is never spent;
   There lives the dearest freshness deep down things;
And though the last lights off the black West went
   Oh, morning, at the brown brink eastward, springs—
Because the Holy Ghost over the bent
    World broods with warm breast and with ah! bright wings.

10

QUESTIONS

1. What is the contrast between the assertions in lines 1–4 and 5–8 (the octave)? How do lines 9–14 (the sestet) develop out of this contrast?
2. Analyze Hopkins's use of alliteration. What alliterative patterns occur? How do these affect meter and emphasis? On the basis of your analysis, describe "sprung rhythm" as used by Hopkins.
3. What instances of assonance, repetitions, and internal rhyme do you find?

JOHN HALL INGHAM (1860–c.1931)

 ## George Washington (1900)

This was the man God gave us when the hour
Proclaimed the dawn of Liberty begun;
Who dared a deed and died when it was done
Patient in triumph, temperate in power,—
Not striving like the Corsican° to tower
To heaven, nor like great Philip's greater son°
To win the world and weep for worlds unwon,
Or lose the star to revel in the flower.
The lives that serve the eternal verities
Alone do mold mankind. Pleasure and pride
Sparkle awhile and perish, as the spray
Smoking across the crests of cavernous seas
Is impotent to hasten or delay
The everlasting surges of the tide.

5

10

°5 *Corsican:* Napoleon I (1769–1821), General and Emperor of France from 1804–1814. 7 *great Philip's greater son:* Alexander the Great, King of Macedonia (356–323 BCE.), who conquered all the known world in the short years of his reign. There was a tradition, derived from Plutarch's *Lives*, that Alexander wept because there were no more worlds for him to conquer.

QUESTIONS

1. For what reasons does the poet extol Washington? Explain the symbolism of line 8, "Or lose the star to revel in the flower." What is the sense of the simile in the last five lines of the poem?
2. Trace the patterning of alliteration and assonance in the poem. How effectively does the poet use these devices? Are they appropriate, or might some think they are overly obvious?
3. In line 3 there occurs a pattern called *consonance,* in which words have the same beginning and ending consonant sounds ("*dared* a *deed* and *died*"). Why do you think the poet includes this pattern here?

PHILIP LEVINE (b. 1928)

 ## A Theory of Prosody (1988)

When Nellie, my old pussy
cat, was still in her prime,
she would sit behind me
as I wrote, and when the line
5   got too long she'd reach
one sudden black foreleg down
and paw at the moving hand,
the offensive one. The first
time she drew blood I learned
10   it was poetic to end
a line anywhere to keep her
quiet. After all, many mornings
she'd gotten to the chair
long before I was even up.
15   Those nights I couldn't sleep
she'd come and sit in my lap
to calm me. So I figured
I owed her the short cat line.
She's dead now almost nine years,
20   and before that there was one
during which she faked attention
and I faked obedience.
Isn't that what it's about—
pretending there's an alert cat
25   who leaves nothing to chance.

QUESTIONS

1. Why is this poem comic? How effective a "theory of prosody" is contained in the poem? What is suggested by the syllable break in line 12? How seriously are we to take the final lines?

2. What is the relationship between the speaker and his cat, Nellie? How true is it that cats sitting at a table with their masters and mistresses sometimes take a swipe at what they are writing?

3. Compare this poem with Robert Frost's "A Considerable Speck" (Chapter 21). In what ways do the poets seem to be having a good time? Nevertheless, what truths about writing are they advancing in the poems?

HENRY WADSWORTH LONGFELLOW (1807–1882)

 ## The Sound of the Sea (1875)

The sea awoke at midnight from its sleep,
  And round the pebbly beaches far and wide
  I heard the first wave of the rising tide
Rush onward with uninterrupted sweep;
5   A voice out of the silence of the deep,

A sound mysteriously multiplied
  As of a cataract from the mountain's side,
Or roar of winds upon a wooded steep.
    So comes to us at times, from the unknown
      And inaccessible solitudes of being,   10
        The rushing of the sea-tides of the soul;
        And inspirations, that we deem our own,
    Are some divine foreshadowing and foreseeing
      Of things beyond our reason or control.

QUESTIONS

1. What is the analogy on which this poem is based? How does the form of the poem follow this analogy? Is the poem to be considered philosophical, mystical, or religious? Why does the poet conclude with the idea of "things beyond our reason or control"?

2. Describe the form of this poem, its rhyme scheme, and its use of rhyme.

3. What is the basic meter of the poem? Describe variations gained through substitution.

4. Describe the effects of alliteration and assonance in the poem. How do these prosodic devices complement the meanings of the affected words?

HERMAN MELVILLE (1819–1891)

 ## Shiloh: A Requiem° (1862)

Skimming lightly, wheeling still,
  The swallows fly low
Over the field in clouded days,
  The forest field of Shiloh—
Over the field where April rain   5
Solaced the parched one stretched in pain
Through the pause of night
That followed the Sunday fight
  Around the church of Shiloh—
The church so lone, the log-built one,   10
That echoed to many a parting groan
    And natural prayer
  Of dying foemen mingled there—
Foemen at morn, but friends at eve—
  Fame or country least their care: 15
(What like a bullet can undeceive!)
  But now they lie low,
While over them the swallows skim,
  And all is hushed at Shiloh.

°One of the earliest major battles of the Civil War, the Battle of Shiloh, in southwestern Tennessee, also called the Battle of Pittsburg Landing, took place in April 1862. It was a remarkably bloody but substantially indecisive conflict, with 10,000 casualties on each side.

QUESTIONS

1. Why is it difficult to determine the dominant meter in this poem? What do you think the dominant meter is? What types of metrical feet can you find here?

2. What connection can you make between the indeterminate meter and Melville's subject?

3. What rhymes does Melville create for "Shiloh"? What is the effect of these rhymes? What other rhymes does Melville introduce? How do these rhymes link together his ideas?

4. What irony is expressed in line 14: "Foemen at morn, but friends at eve"?

OGDEN NASH (1902–1971)

 Very Like a Whale° 1934

One thing that literature would be greatly the better for
Would be a more restricted employment by authors of simile and metaphor.
Authors of all races, be they Greeks, Romans, Teutons or Celts,
Can't seem just to say that anything is the thing it is but have to go out of their
     way to say that it is like something else.
What does it mean when we are told
That the Assyrian came down like a wolf on the fold?
In the first place, George Gordon Byron° had had enough experience
To know that it probably wasn't just one Assyrian, it was a lot of Assyrians.
However, as too many arguments are apt to induce apoplexy and thus hinder longevity,
We'll let it pass as one Assyrian for the sake of brevity.
Now then, this particular Assyrian; the one whose cohorts were gleaming in purple
     and gold,
Just what does the poet mean when he says he came down like a wolf on the fold?
In heaven and earth more than is dreamed of in our philosophy there are a great
     many things,
But I don't imagine that among them there is a wolf with purple and gold cohorts
     or purple and gold anythings.
No, no, Lord Byron, before I'll believe that this Assyrian was actually like a wolf
     I must have some kind of proof;
Did he run on all fours and did he have a hairy tail and a big red mouth and big
     white teeth and did he say Woof woof woof?
Frankly I think it very unlikely, and all you were entitled to say, at the very most,
Was that the Assyrian cohorts came down like a lot of Assyrian cohorts about to
     destroy the Hebrew host.
But that wasn't fancy enough for Lord Byron, oh dear me no, he had to invent a lot of
     figures of speech and then interpolate them.
With the result that whenever you mention Old Testament soldiers to people they say Oh
     yes, they're the ones that a lot of wolves dressed up in gold and purple ate them.
That's the kind of thing that's being done all the time by poets, from Homer to
     Tennyson;
They're always comparing ladies to lilies° and veal to venison.
How about the man who wrote,
Her little feet stole in and out like mice beneath her petticoat?°

Line numbers: 5 (at line "way to say..."), 10 (at "We'll let it pass..."), 15 (at "I must have some kind of proof"), 20 (at "yes, they're the ones...").

°See *Hamlet*, 3.2.358. 7 *George Gordon Byron:* See Byron, "The Destruction of Sennacherib" (Chapter 22), which Nash is satirizing in this poem. 22 *ladies to lilies:* See Burns, "A Red, Red Rose" (Chapter 15). 24 *little feet . . . petticoat:* In Sir John Suckling's "A Ballad upon a Wedding" (1641), the following lines appear: "Her feet beneath her petticoat / Like little mice stole in and out." Also in a poem by Robert Herrick complimenting the feet of Susanna Southwell (1648), he wrote: "Her pretty feet / Like snails did creep."

Wouldn't anybody but a poet think twice   25
Before stating that his girl's feet were mice?
Then they always say things like that after a winter storm
The snow is a white blanket. Oh it is, is it, all right then, you sleep under a six-inch
    blanket of snow and I'll sleep under a half-inch blanket of unpoetical blanket
    material and we'll see which one keeps warm.
And after that maybe you'll begin to comprehend dimly
What I meant by too much metaphor and simile.   30

QUESTIONS

1. How serious is Nash when he states that literature would be improved if poets would remove simile and metaphor from their works? How just is his "criticism" of metaphor in line 4?
2. Explain how Nash achieves humor in this poem. How does the ending of the first line indicate that the subject matter is to be considered with a smile?
3. Describe Nash's rhymes in this poem. What types of rhymes do you find here? In what ways are some of the rhymes comic? How original are Nash's rhymes?

EDGAR ALLAN POE (1809–1849)

For a portrait, see Chapter 9, page 493. The following two poems are by Edgar Allan Poe.

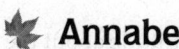 ## Annabel Lee (1849)

It was many and many a year ago,
   In a kingdom by the sea,
That a maiden there lived whom you may know
   By the name of Annabel Lee;
And this maiden she lived with no other thought   5
   Than to love and be loved by me.

She was a child and *I* was a child,
   In this kingdom by the sea,

But we loved with a love that was more than love—
   I and my Annabel Lee—   10
With a love that the wingéd seraphs of Heaven
   Coveted her and me.

And this was the reason that, long ago,
   In this kingdom by the sea,
A wind blew out of a cloud by night   15
   Chilling my Annabel Lee;
So that her high-born kinsmen came
   And bore her away from me,
To shut her up in a sepulchre
   In this kingdom by the sea.   20

The angels, not half so happy in Heaven,
    Went envying her and me:—
Yes! that was the reason (as all men know,
    In this kingdom by the sea)
25   That the wind came out of the cloud chilling
    And killing my Annabel Lee.

But our love it was stronger by far than the love
    Of those who were older than we—
    Of many far wiser than we—
30   And neither the angels in Heaven above
    Nor the demons down under the sea
    Can ever dissever my soul from the soul
    Of the beautiful Annabel Lee:—

For the moon never beams without bringing me dreams
35   Of the beautiful Annabel Lee;
And the stars never rise but I feel the bright eyes
    Of the beautiful Annabel Lee:
And so all the night-tide, I lie down by the side
Of my darling, my darling, my life and my bride
40   In her sepulchre there by the sea—
    In her tomb by the side of the sea.

QUESTIONS

1. How does the speaker explain the death of Annabel Lee? What is his attitude about the cause of her death? How does this judgment explain the actions he describes at the poem's end?

2. What basic meter does the poet establish in the poem? What variations do you find on this pattern?

3. Why do stanzas 3, 5, and 6 contain more lines than stanzas 1, 2, and 4? Why does stanza 5 contain seven lines, concluding with a dash?

4. Describe the poem's internal rhymes, repetitions, assonances, and alliterations. What is their effect? Why did Poe include them?

 **The Bells** (1849)

1

Hear the sledges with the bells—
    Silver bells!
What a world of merriment their melody foretells!
How they tinkle, tinkle, tinkle,
5   In the icy air of night!
While the stars that oversprinkle
All the heavens, seem to twinkle
    With a crystalline delight;

Keeping time, time, time,
   In a sort of Runic rhyme,
To the tintinnabulation that so musically wells   10
      From the bells, bells, bells, bells,
         Bells, bells, bells—
From the jingling and the tinkling of the bells.

2

Hear the mellow wedding bells—
      Golden bells!   15
What a world of happiness their harmony foretells!
   Through the balmy air of night
   How they ring out their delight!—
      From the molten-golden notes,
      And all in tune,   20
   What a liquid ditty floats
To the turtle-dove that listens, while she gloats
      On the moon!
   Oh, from out the sounding cells,
What a gush of euphony voluminously wells!   25
      How it swells!
      How it dwells
   On the Future!-how it tells
   Of the rapture that impels
   To the swinging and the ringing   30
   Of the bells, bells, bells—
Of the bells, bells, bells, bells,
      Bells, bells, bells—
To the rhyming and the chiming of the bells!   35

3

Hear the loud alarum bells—
      Brazen bells!
What a tale of terror, now, their turbulency tells!
   In the startled ear of night
   How they scream out their affright!   40
      Too much horrified to speak,
      They can only shriek, shriek,
         Out of tune,
In a clamorous appealing to the mercy of the fire,
In a mad expostulation with the deaf and frantic fire,   45
      Leaping higher, higher, higher,
      With a desperate desire,
      And a resolute endeavor
      Now—now to sit, or never,
By the side of the pale-faced moon,   50
      Oh, the bells, bells, bells!
      What a tale their terror tells
         Of Despair!
   How they clang, and clash, and roar!

55 What a horror they outpour
On the bosom of the palpitating air!
   Yet the ear, it fully knows,
     By the twanging
     And the clanging,
60   How the danger ebbs and flows;
   Yet the ear distinctly tells,
     In the jangling
     And the wrangling,
How the danger sinks and swells,
65 By the sinking or the swelling in the anger of the bells—
     Of the bells-
   Of the bells, bells, bells, bells,
     Bells, bells, bells—
In the clamor and the clangor of the bells!

4

70 Hear the tolling of the bells—
     Iron bells!
What a world of solemn thought their monody compels!
   In the silence of the night,
   How we shiver with affright
75 At the melancholy menace of their tone!
   For every sound that floats
   From the rust within their throats
     Is a groan.
     And the people—ah, the people—
80   They that dwell up in the steeple,
     All alone,
   And who tolling, tolling, tolling,
    In that muffled monotone,
Feel a glory in so rolling
85   On the human heart a stone—
   They are neither man nor woman—
   They are neither brute nor human—
     They are Ghouls:—
   And their king it is who tolls:-
90   And he rolls, rolls, rolls,
     Rolls
    A paean from the bells!
   And his merry bosom swells
     With the paean of the bells!
95   And he dances, and he yells;
Keeping time, time, time,
In a sort of Runic rhyme,
   To the paean of the bells—
   Of the bells:
100 Keeping time, time, time,
In a sort of Runic rhyme,
   To the throbbing of the bells—

Of the bells, bells, bells—
 To the sobbing of the bells;
Keeping time, time, time,
 As he knells, knells, knells,
In a happy Runic rhyme,
 To the rolling of the bells— 105
Of the bells, bells, bells:—
 To the tolling of the bells—
Of the bells, bells, bells, bells,
 Bells, bells, bells— 110
To the moaning and the groaning of the bells.

QUESTIONS

1. What kinds of bells does Poe extol in each of the stanzas? What metals and images does he associate with each type of bell? How appropriate are these? Why do you think the stanzas become progressively longer?

2. What segmental sounds does Poe utilize as imitative of the various bells? What differences in vowels are observable between the silver sledge bells, for example, and the brass ("brazen") alarum bells? Between the vowels describing the iron bells and the golden bells?

3. What is the effect of the repetition of the word "bells" throughout? What onomatopoeic effect is created by these repetitions?

4. Describe the pattern of rhymes in this poem.

ALEXANDER POPE (1685–1744)

For a portrait, see Chapter 16, page 824.

🍁 from *An Essay on Man, Epistle I, lines 17–90* (1734)

I. Say first, of God above, or man.° below,   *men; humanity*
What can we reason but from what we know?
Of man, what see we but his station here,
From which to reason, or to which refer?
Through worlds unnumbered though the God be known,   20
'Tis ours to trace him° only in our own.   *God*
He who through vast immensity can pierce,
See worlds on worlds compose one universe,
Observe how system into system runs,
What other planets circle other suns,   25
What varied being peoples every star,
May tell why Heaven has made us as we are.
But of this frame the bearings and the ties,
The strong connections, nice dependencies,
Gradations just, has thy pervading soul   30
Looked through? or can a part contain the whole?
 Is the great chain that draws all to agree,
And drawn supports, upheld by God, or thee?

35 II. Presumptuous man! the reason wouldst thou find,
  Why formed so weak, so little, and so blind?
  First, if thou canst, the harder reason guess,
  Why formed no weaker, blinder, and no less!
  Ask of thy mother earth, why oaks are made
40 Taller or stronger than the weeds they shade!
  Or ask of yonder argent fields above,
  Why Jove's satellites are less than Jove!
   Of systems possible, if 'tis confessed
  That wisdom infinite must form the best,
45 Where all must full or not coherent be,
  And all that rises, rise in due degree;
  Then, in the scale of reasoning life, 'tis plain,
  There must be, somewhere, such a rank as man:
  And all the question (wrangle e'er so long)
50 Is only this, if God has placed him wrong.
   Respecting man, whatever wrong we call,
  May, must be right, as relative to all.
  In human works, though labored on with pain,
  A thousand movements scarce one purpose gain;
55 In God's, one single can its end produce;
  Yet serves to second too some other use.
  So man, who here seems principal alone,
  Perhaps acts second to some sphere unknown,
  Touches some wheel, or verges to some goal;
60 'Tis but a part we see, and not a whole.
   When the proud steed shall know why main restrains.
  His fiery course, or drives him o'er the plains:
  When the dull ox, why now he breaks the clod,
  Is now a victim, and now Egypt's god:
65 Then shall man's pride and dullness comprehend
  His actions', passions', being's, use and end;
  Why doing, suffering, checked, impelled; and why
  This hour a slave, the next a deity.
   Then say not man's imperfect, Heaven in fault;
70 Say rather, man's as perfect as he ought:
  His knowledge measured to his state and place;
  His time a moment, and a point his space.
  If to be perfect in a certain sphere,
  What matter, soon or late, or here or there?
75 The blessed today is as completely so,
  As who began a thousand years ago.
   III. Heaven from all creatures hides the book of fate,
  All but the page prescribed, their present state;
  From brutes what men, from men what spirits know,
80 Or who could suffer being here below?
  The lamb thy riot dooms to bleed today,
  Had he thy reason, would he skip and play?
  Pleased to the last, he crops the flowery food,
  And licks the hand just raised to shed his blood.
85 Oh blindness to the future! kindly given,

That each may fill the circle marked by Heaven:
Who sees with equal eye, as God of all,
A hero perish, or a sparrow fall,
Atoms or systems into ruin hurled,
And now a bubble burst, and now a world.   90

QUESTIONS

1. What is the topic of the passage? How appropriate is it to present such material in the form of couplets? How does Pope use the couplet to develop his thought in the poem?

2. Analyze five or six of the couplets. On the basis of your study, what principles of the couplet does Pope follow? You might consider the average lengths of words and the use of iambs, caesurae, and end-stopped lines.

3. Describe Pope's use of rhyme. What types of words does he rhyme? How helpful are the rhymes in the emphasis of Pope's ideas?

WYATT PRUNTY (b. 1947)

 March (1998)

Seeing the March rain flood a field
Then runnel from sight, as the wind
Kicks up a bare-limbed fury of trees
And a single crow flies north-northeast
Into gray distances from which   5
One bruised cloud goes driven grimly
After another so the whole sky
Blunders in a stampede of shapes
So changeable they disprove shape,
And then the rain again, in which   10
The clouds come down but differently
This time, driven like nails blunted
And lost with hitting the ground
Till how many will it take
To fill the field then disappear,   15
As what we call a change in season
Blusters, or storms, or goes dead still
With us left standing underneath
To wonder or ignore such change
From overhead to sometimes underfoot   20
And going on regardless where we go,
Who we were, what we ever said or did.

QUESTIONS

1. Describe the grammatical structure of this poem. Why do you think the poet leaves the poem as a very long "sentence fragment" and does not create individual sentences as units? What is the relationship between this use of grammar and the poem's topic?

2. Consider the poem's last five lines. What point does the poet make about the world of rain and nature, on the one hand, and the world of human beings, on the other?

3. Describe the poet's use of alliteration (e.g., "flood a field") and assonance ("wind . . . kicks . . . limbed . . . single . . . Into . . . distances . . . which" etc.). How do these devices contribute to the energy of the poem?

EDWIN ARLINGTON ROBINSON (1869–1935)

For a photo, see Chapter 12, page 675.

 ## Miniver Cheevy (1910)

Miniver Cheevy, child of scorn,
   Grew lean while he assailed the seasons;
He wept that he was ever born,
   And he had reasons.

5   Miniver loved the days of old
   When swords were bright and steeds were prancing;
The vision of a warrior bold
   Would set him dancing.

Miniver sighed for what was not,
10   And dreamed, and rested from his labors;
He dreamed of Thebes° and Camelot,°
   And Priam's° neighbors.

Miniver mourned the ripe renown
   That made so many a name so fragrant;
15   He mourned Romance, now on the town,
   And Art, a vagrant.

Miniver loved the Medici,°
   Albeit he had never seen one;
He would have sinned incessantly
20   Could he have been one.

Miniver cursed the commonplace
   And eyed a khaki suit with loathing;
He missed the medieval grace
   Of iron clothing.

25   Miniver scorned the gold he sought,
   But sore annoyed was he without it;
Miniver thought, and thought, and thought,
   And thought about it.

°11 *Thebes*: a city in Greece prominent in Greek legend and mythology in connection with Cadmus and Oedipus. Camelot: legendary seat of the Round Table and capital of Britain during the reign of King Arthur. 12 *Priam's*: Priam was the king of Troy during the Trojan War. 17 *Medici*: wealthy Italian family that ruled Florence from the fifteenth to the eighteenth century. During the Renaissance, Lorenzo de'Medici was an important patron of the arts.

Miniver Cheevy, born too late,
  Scratched his head and kept on thinking;
Miniver coughed, and called it fate,
  And kept on drinking.   30

QUESTIONS

1. What is the speaker's attitude toward the central character? How does rhyme help define this attitude?

2. How does repetition reinforce the image of the central character and the speaker's attitude? Consider the beginning of each stanza and lines 27–28.

3. What rhyme predominates in lines 2 and 4 of each stanza? How does this rhyme help make sound echo sense?

CHRISTINA ROSSETTI (1830–1894)

For a portrait, see Chapter 13, page 712.

 ## Echo (1854)

Come to me in the silence of the night
  Come in the speaking silence of a dream;
Come with soft rounded cheeks and eyes as bright
    As sunlight on a stream;
      Come back in tears.   5
O memory, hope, love of finished years.

O dream how sweet, too sweet, too bitter sweet,
  Whose wakening should have been in paradise,
Where souls brimful of love abide and meet;
    Where thirsty longing eyes   10
      Watch the slow door
That opening, letting in, lets out no more.

Yet come to me in dreams, that I may live
  My very life again though cold in death;
Come back to me in dreams, that I may give   15
    Pulse for pulse, breath for breath:
      Speak low, lean low,
As long ago, my love, how long ago.

QUESTIONS

1. Why is this poem titled "Echo"? What kind of echoed experience does the speaker describe? What has happened that causes the speaker to state that past love is now a part of "finished years"? How does she suggest that she might relive this experience?

2. What words are echoed throughout the poem? Follow the patterning of the word "dream," for example, or "Come," or "love."

3. Describe the pattern of the poem's rhymes. What words are rhymed? What more can you say about them in terms of content, syllabication, and parts of speech?

WILLIAM SHAKESPEARE (1564–1616)

For a portrait, see Chapter 24, page 1322.

 ## Sonnet 73: That Time of Year Thou May'st in Me Behold (1609)

That time of year thou may'st in me behold
When yellow leaves, or none, or few, do hang
Upon those boughs which shake against the cold,
Bare ruined choirs,° where late the sweet birds sang.
5   In me thou see'st the twilight of such day
As after sunset fadeth in the west;
Which by and by black night doth take away,
Death's second self,° that seals up all in rest.
In me thou see'st the glowing of such fire,
10 That on the ashes of his° youth doth lie,   *its*
As the death-bed whereon it must expire,
Consumed with that which it was nourished by.°
This thou perceivest, which makes thy love more strong,
To love that well which thou must leave ere long.

°4 *choirs*: the part of a church just in front of the altar. 8 *Death's . . . self*: That is, night is a mirror image of death inasmuch as it brings the sleep of rest just as death brings the sleep of actual death. 12 *Consumed . . . by*: That is, the ashes of the fuel burned at the fire's height now prevent the fire from continuing, and in fact extinguish it.

QUESTIONS

1. Describe the content of lines 1–4, 5–8, and 9–12. What connects these three sections? How does the concluding couplet relate to the first twelve lines?
2. Analyze the iambic pentameter of the poem. Consider the spondees in lines 2 ("do hang"), 4 ("bare ru-" and "birds sang"), 5 ("such day"), 7 ("black night"), 8 ("death's sec-"), 9 ("such fire"), 10 ("doth lie"), 11 ("death-bed"), 13 ("more strong"), and 14 ("ere long"). What is the effect of these substitutions on the poem's ideas?
3. How does the enjambment of lines 1–3 and 5–6 permit these lines to seem to conclude *as lines* even though grammatically they carry over to form sentences?
4. In lines 2, 5, 6, and 9, where does Shakespeare place the caesurae? What relationship is there between the rhythms produced by these caesurae and the content of lines 1–12? In lines 13 and 14, how do the rising stressed caesurae relate to the content?

PERCY BYSSHE SHELLEY (1792–1822)

 ## Ode to the West Wind (1820)

I

O wild West Wind, thou breath of Autumn's being,
Thou, from whose unseen presence the leaves dead
Are driven, like ghosts from an enchanter fleeing,

Yellow, and black, and pale, and hectic° red,
Pestilence-stricken multitudes: O Thou,
Who chariotest to their dark wintry bed   5

The winged seeds, where they lie cold and low,
Each like a corpse within its grave, until
Thine azure sister of the Spring° shall blow

Her clarion o'er the dreaming earth, and fill   10
(Driving sweet buds like flocks to feed in air)
With living hues and odours plain and hill:

Wild Spirit, which art moving everywhere;
Destroyer and Preserver; hear, O hear!

II

Thou on whose stream, 'mid the steep sky's commotion,   15
Loose clouds like Earth's decaying leaves are shed,
Shook from the tangled boughs of Heaven and Ocean,

Angels of rain and lightning: there are spread
On the blue surface of thine aery surge,
Like the bright hair uplifted from the head   20

Of some fierce Maenad,° even from the dim verge
Of the horizon to the zenith's height,
The locks of the approaching storm. Thou Dirge

Of the dying year, to which this closing night
Will be the dome of a vast sepulchre,   25
Vaulted with all thy congregated might

Of vapours,° from whose solid atmosphere   *clouds*
Black rain and fire and hail will burst: O hear!

III

Thou who didst waken from his summer dreams
The blue Mediterranean, where he lay,   30
Lulled by the coil of his crystalline streams,

Beside a pumice isle in Baiae's bay,°
And saw in sleep old palaces and towers
Quivering within the wave's intenser day,
All overgrown with azure moss and flowers   35
So sweet, the sense faints picturing them! Thou
For whose path the Atlantic's level powers

°4 *hectic:* a tubercular fever that produced flushed cheeks. 9 *Spring:* the wind that will blow in the spring.
21 *Maenad:* a frenzied female worshipper of Dionysus, the god of wine and fertility in Greek mythology. 32 *Baiae's bay:* a bay of the Mediterranean Sea west of Naples, famous for the elaborate villas built on the shore by Roman emperors.

Cleave themselves into chasms, while far below
The sea-blooms and the oozy woods which wear
40 The sapless foliage of the ocean, know

Thy voice, and suddenly grow grey with fear,
And tremble and despoil themselves: O hear!

IV

If I were a dead leaf thou mightest bear;
If I were a swift cloud to fly with thee;
45 A wave to pant beneath thy power, and share

The impulse of thy strength, only less free
Than thou, O Uncontrollable! If even
I were as in my boyhood, and could be

The comrade of thy wanderings over Heaven,
50 As then, when to outstrip thy skiey speed
Scarce seemed a vision; I would ne'er have striven

As thus with thee in prayer in my sore need,
Oh! lift me as a wave, a leaf, a cloud!
I fall upon thorns of life! I bleed!

55 A heavy weight of hours has chained and bowed
One too like thee: tameless, and swift, and proud.

V

Make me thy lyre,° even as the forest is:
What if my leaves are falling like its own!
The tumult of thy mighty harmonies

60 Will take from both a deep, autumnal tone,
Sweet though in sadness. Be thou, Spirit fierce,
My spirit! Be thou me, impetuous one!

Drive my dead thoughts over the universe
Like withered leaves to quicken a new birth!
65 And, by the incantation of this verse,

Scatter, as from an unextinguished hearth
Ashes and sparks, my words among mankind!
Be through my lips to unawakened Earth

The trumpet of a prophecy! O Wind,
70 If Winter comes, can Spring be far behind?

°57 *lyre*: an Aeolian harp, a musical device that is sounded by the wind blowing across strings.

QUESTIONS

1. To what extent are the speaker's thoughts and feelings organized by the poem's five sections? What is the logical progression from section to section?
2. What aspect of the natural world does the wind affect in the first section of the poem? The second stanza? The third? What does the West Wind symbolize? Why does the speaker state, "Make me thy lyre"?
3. Formulate the structure (meter and rhyme scheme) of the stanzas. How many times (and where) is the *e* rhyme of the first stanza repeated as a rhyming sound? What is the effect of this repetition?
4. Describe Shelley's use of alliteration and assonance in the poem.

ALFRED, LORD TENNYSON (1809–1892)

 ### From *Idylls of the King: The Passing of Arthur,* Lines 344–93 (1869; 1842)

But, as he walked, King Arthur panted hard,
Like one that feels a nightmare on his bed   345
When all the house is mute. So sighed the King,
Muttering and murmuring at his ear, "Quick, quick!
I fear it is too late, and I shall die."
But the other swiftly strode from ridge to ridge,
Clothed with his breath, and looking, as he walked,   350
Larger than human on the frozen hills.
He heard the deep behind him, and a cry
Before. His own thought drove him like a goad.
Dry clashed his harness in the icy caves
And barren chasms, and all to left and right   355
The bare black cliff clanged round him, as he based
His feet on juts of slippery crag that rang
Sharp-smitten with the dint of armèd heels—
And on a sudden, lo! the level lake,
And the long glories of the winter moon.   360

Then saw they how there hove a dusky barge,
Dark as a funeral scarf from stem to stern,
Beneath them; and descending they were ware°   aware
That all the decks were dense with stately forms,
Black-stoled, black-hooded, like a dream—by these   365
Three Queens with crowns of gold; and from them rose
A cry that shivered to the tingling stars,
And, as it were one voice, an agony
Of lamentation, like a wind that shrills
All night in a waste land, where no one comes,   370
Or hath come, since the making of the world.

Then murmured Arthur, "Place me in the barge."
So to the barge they came. There those three Queens
Put forth their hands, and took the King, and wept.
But she, that rose the tallest of them all   375

And fairest, laid his head upon her lap,
And loosed the shattered casque,° and chafed his hands,   *helmet*
And called him by his name, complaining loud,
And dropping bitter tears against a brow
380 Striped with dark blood: for all his face was white
And colorless, and like the withered moon
Smote by the fresh beam of the springing east;
And all his greaves and cuisses° dashed with drops   *pieces of armor*
Of onset;° and the light and lustrous curls—   *blood*
385 That made his forehead like a rising sun
High from the dais—throne-were parched with dust:
Or, clotted into points and hanging loose,
Mixed with the knightly growth that fringed his lips.
So like a shattered column lay the King:
390 Not like that Arthur who, with lance in rest,
From spur to plume a star of tournament,
Shot through the lists at Camelot, and charged
Before the eyes of ladies and of kings.

QUESTIONS

1. How does Tennyson develop the mood of depression and loss associated with the dying of Arthur? What is the effect of the concluding simile?

2. Analyze the patterns of assonance and alliteration in the passage. What patterns are developed most extensively? What effects are thus achieved?

3. Describe Tennyson's use of onomatopoeia in lines 349–60, 369–71, and 380–83. What segments contribute to this effect?

DAVID WAGONER (b. 1926)

 ## March for a One-Man Band (1983)

He's *a boom a blat* in the uniform
Of an army *tweedledy* band *a toot*
Complete with medals *a honk* cornet
Against *a thump* one side of his lips
5 And the other stuck with *a sloop a tweet*
A whistle *a crash* on top of *a crash*
A helmet *a crash* a cymbal a drum
At his *bumbledy* knee and a *rimshot* flag
A click he stands at attention *a wheeze*
10 And plays the Irrational Anthem *bang*.

QUESTIONS

1. What attitude does the speaker convey about the one-man band? Why is the Anthem "Irrational" rather than "National"?

2. Describe the onomatopoeic effect of the italicized percussive words. What is the purpose of the rhythms that these words cause?

3. What ambiguity is suggested by the *bang* of line 10? How does this ambiguity make the poem seem more than simply an entertaining display of sounds?

WRITING ABOUT PROSODY

Because studying prosody requires specific details and descriptions, it is best to limit your study to a short poem or to a short passage from a long poem. A sonnet, a stanza of a lyric poem, or a fragment from a long poem will often be sufficient. If you choose a fragment, it should be self-contained, such as an entire speech or a short episode or scene.

The analysis of even a short poem, however, can grow long because of the need to describe word positions and stresses and also to determine the various effects. For this reason you do not have to exhaust your topic. Try to make your discussion representative of the prosody of your poem or passage.

Your first reading in preparation for your essay should be for comprehension. On second and third readings, make notes of sounds, accents, and rhymes by reading the poem aloud. To perceive sounds, one student helped herself by reading aloud in an exaggerated way in front of a mirror. If you have privacy or are not self-conscious, you might do the same. Let yourself go a bit. As you dramatize your reading (maybe even in front of fellow students), you will find that heightened levels of reading also accompany the poet's expression of important ideas. Mark these spots for later analysis and discussion so that you will be able to make strong assertions about the relationship of sound to sense.

What counts in your study of prosody is that your analyses be clear enough to provide help in developing your actual discussion. Carry out your study of the passage in the following way:

- Determine the formal pattern of feet. You may wish to use lowercase letters for light stresses and capital letters for heavy stresses, as in "And ON/a SUD-/den, LO!/the LEV -/el LAKE" (Tennyson). The capital letters really make the strong accents stand out. Or, you may wish to use a short acute accent or stress mark for heavily stressed syllables (') and the breve for unaccented or lightly stressed syllables (˘), as in "A˘nd ón / ˘a súd ' / d˘en Ló! / th˘e lév - / e˘l Láke." Use chevrons to mark spondees, as in

    his own / thought drove / him

- Indicate the separate feet by a diagonal slash or virgule (/). Indicate caesurae and end-of-line pauses by double virgules (//).
- Be sure to mark the formal and rhetorical substitutions that you discover.
- Do the same for alliteration, assonance, onomatopoeia, and rhyme. You might wish to use colored pencils to draw lines connecting the repeating sounds, for these effects will be close together in the poem, and your connections will dramatize this closeness.

Once you have analyzed the various effects in your poem and have recorded these on your work sheets and in your notes, you will be ready to formulate a central idea and organization. The focus of your essay should reflect the most significant features of prosody in relationship to some other element of the poem, such as speaker, tone, or ideas.

Strategies for Organizing Ideas

In preparing for your essay, try to establish ideas about the following. Above all, it is important to keep foremost the connections of prosody to the subject of the poem or passage you are studying.

Is there any characteristic, any particular rhythm, that might help to establish a character, as in Browning's "Porphyria's Lover" (see the first illustrative essay)? Are there varying rhythmic lengths that might create particular emphases on visual or auditory images, as Poe does in "The Bells"? Does the poet include, say, a number of monosyllabic words in close order to create an imitation of special speech patterns, as Brooks does in "We Real Cool"?

Can you find evidence that prosody is being used as an organizational element? In an Italian or Petrarchan sonnet, for example, the rhymes are important in tying together the development of ideas. In a Shakespearean sonnet there are three 4-line groups (quatrains), each containing the development of a particular idea or image or symbol, and the concluding two lines rhyme and at the same time create a "cap" or idea tying the previous ideas together. (This aspect of prosody is also important in the consideration of poetic form, described in Chapter 18.)

Can you show that the variation of dominant poetic feet is done in such a way that strong stresses fall on words that are therefore made especially important? This characteristic is of course a major aspect of poetry. In "The Sun Rising," for example, Donne begins with a trochaic substitution: "Busy old fool, . . ." This trochee creates what is in effect an opening outburst against the sun, as though it is a meddling Peeping Tom. It makes for humor at the beginning, and it also makes the poem dramatic and conversational—all of which Donne clearly intended.

In rhyming poems, what is the effect of the rhyme? What is the pattern of the rhymes? What is their effect on your perception of the merging of sound and idea? What sorts of words are rhymed—nouns, verbs, adjectives, a combination of these? Are the rhymes especially clever, as in Eliot's "Macavity: The Mystery Cat," or unusual, as in Gardner's "At a Summer Hotel"? Generally, what are the rhymes like? How do they "clinch" or connect ideas? What part does rhyme play in the poem's development?

Try to describe the poet's use of segmental (sound) devices, specifically assonance and alliteration. Hopkins uses alliteration powerfully in "God's Grandeur." One can find this device everywhere in the poem, but in line 2 it is especially noteworthy: "It will flame out, like shining from shook foil," in which the predominant *f* and *sh* continuants enable Hopkins to stress his simile about the grandeur of divine creation. A few lines later Hopkins uses assonance with similar power: "Why do men then now not reck his rod?" Alliteration aside, the *eh* sounds in "men," "then," and "reck" make the poem exemplary in the connections of prosody and topic.

What connection can you make between the general prosodic characteristics of the poem and the dominant mood or manner? The percussiveness of Wagoner's "March for a One-Man Band" is integral to his comic view of his boisterous subject. The rollicking rhythms of Eliot's "Macavity" are a fine example of the ways in which rhythms underscore the lightness and humor of the topic. The same is true of Nash's "Very Like a Whale," in which the rhythm is a major element in the comic tone, together with lines of varying length and clever and unexpected rhymes. The truncated line lengths of Levine's "A Theory of Prosody" are essential in the poem's comic minimization of some aspects of poetic theory.

What significance can you find in the ways in which the poet has put together elements like euphony, cacophony, and onomatopoeia? For example, it is difficult to overlook Tennyson's euphonious line "And the long glories of the winter moon." Tennyson creates onomatopoeia in describing a noble warrior climbing down a precipitous hill: "The bare black cliff clanged round him, . . ." Shelley in "Ode to the West Wind" creates cacophony in describing "old palaces and towers/Quivering within the wave's intenser day." How do poets create such effects?

After a brief description of the poem (perhaps saying that it is a sonnet, a two-stanza lyric, a dipodic burlesque poem, and so on), establish the scope of your essay. Your central idea will outline the thought that you wish to carry out through your prosodic analysis—for example, that regularity of meter is consistent with a happy, firm vision of love or life; or that frequent spondees emphasize the solidity of the speaker's wish to love; or that particular sounds echo some of the poem's actions.

Depending on your assignment, you should state in your introduction, beyond the essential details about the poem or passage, those aspects of prosody you plan to discuss. It might be all aspects of rhythm or sound, or perhaps just one, such as the poet's use of regular meter or a particular substitution, or alliteration, or assonance. It is possible, for example, to devote an entire essay to (1) regular meter; (2) one particular variation in meter, such as the anapest or spondee; (3) rhyme; (4) assonance; (5) alliteration; (6) euphony or cacophony; or (7) onomatopoeia. For brevity, the illustrative essay treats rhyme, rhythm, and segmental effects together.

The body of your essay may include all the following elements or just one, depending on your instructor's assignment.

1. *Rhythm.* Establish the formal metrical pattern. What is the dominant metrical foot and line length? Are some lines shorter than the pattern? What relationship do the variable lengths have with the subject matter? If the poem is a lyric or a sonnet, are important words and syllables successfully placed in stressed positions in order to achieve emphasis? Try to relate line lengths to exposition, development of ideas, and rising or falling emotions. It is also important to look for either repeating or varying metrical patterns as the subject matter reaches peaks or climaxes. Generally, deal with the relationship between the formal rhythmical pattern and the poet's ideas and attitudes.

When noting substitutions, analyze the formal variations and the principal effects of these. If you concentrate on only one substitution, describe any apparent pattern in its use—that is, its locations, recurrences, and effects on meaning.

2. *Segmental effects.* Here you might be discussing, collectively or separately, the use and effects of assonance, alliteration, onomatopoeia, cacophony, and euphony. Be sure to establish that the instances you choose really occur systematically enough in the poem to form a pattern. Illustrate sounds by including relevant words within parentheses. You might write separate paragraphs on alliteration, assonance, and any other seemingly important pattern. Also, because space is always at a premium, you might concentrate on only one noteworthy effect, like a certain pattern of assonance, rather than on everything. Throughout your discussion, always keep foremost the relationship between content and sound.

 REFERRING TO SOUNDS IN POETRY

To make illustrations clear, emphasize the sounds to which you are calling attention. If you use an entire word to illustrate a sound, underline or italicize only the sound, not the entire word, and put the word within quotation marks (for example, "The poet uses a t ['tip,' 'top,' and 'terrific']"). When you refer to entire words containing particular segments, however, underline or italicize these words (for example, "The poet uses a t in tip, top, and terrific," or "The poet uses a t in tip, top, and terrific).

---

3. *Rhyme.* Your discussion of rhyme should describe the major features of the poem's rhymes, specifically the scheme and variants, the lengths and rhythms of the rhyming words, and noteworthy segmental characteristics. In discussing the grammar of the rhymes, note the kinds of words (i.e., verbs, nouns, etc.) used for rhymes: Are they all the same? Does one form predominate? Is there variety? Can you determine the grammatical positions of the rhyming words? How may these characteristics be related to the idea or theme of the poem?

Another avenue of exploration might be to study the qualities of the rhyming words. Are the words specific? Concrete? Abstract? Are there any striking rhymes? Any surprises? Any rhymes that are particularly clever and witty? Do any rhymes give unique comparisons or contrasts? How?

Generally, note any striking or unique rhyming effects. Without becoming overly subtle or far-fetched, you can make valid and interesting conclusions. Do any sounds in the rhyming words appear in patterns of assonance or alliteration elsewhere in the poem? Do the rhymes contribute to onomatopoeia in the poem? Broadly, what aspects of rhyme are uniquely effective because they blend fully with the poem's thought and mood?

In your conclusion, try to develop a short evaluation of the poet's prosodic performance. If we accept the premise that poetry is designed not only to stimulate emotions but also to provide information and transfer attitudes, to what degree do the prosodic techniques of your poem contribute to these goals? Without going into excessive detail (and writing another essay), what more can you say here? What has been the value of your study to your understanding and appreciating the poem? If you think your analysis has helped you to develop new awareness of the poet's craft, it would be appropriate to state what you have learned.

First Illustrative Student Essay

Underlined sentences in this paper *do not* conform to MLA style and are used solely as teaching tools to emphasize the central idea, thesis sentence, and topic sentences throughout the paper.

Novoa 1

Cristina Novoa

Professor Damon

English 2202

11 May 2008

Rhyme, Rhythm, and Sound in Browning's "Porphyria's Lover"°

[1]

In Robert Browning's dramatic monologue "Porphyria's Lover," the "lover" is the murderously insane speaker. It is early in the morning, and he tells his listeners about the events of the night, his last night with Porphyria, a golden-haired beauty who had "come through wind and rain" (line 30) from a happy celebration to meet him for a romantic rendezvous. Incredibly, he says that he strangled her rather than accept her living love because that is the only way he could hold her without the fear of her ever leaving him. Further, he is able to rationalize murdering her by assuring his listeners that by this action he has given Porphyria her "utmost will" (line 53), her "darling one wish" (line 57), that she give herself to him forever instead of being diverted by her "pride, and vainer ties" (line 24). His belief in divine approval for this act is shown in his claim that "God has not said a word" against him (line 60), a particularly sick statement. The way he tells his tale is expressive of his extreme separation from reality.* Specifically, the rhymes, rhythms, and sounds within the poem all reflect the disturbance of this demented killer.†

[2]

Browning uses the rhymes of the poem to reflect the speaker's agitated state of mind. Although the four-stress iambic lines are not divided into stanzas, they are actually grouped into twelve sets of five by the rhyme scheme--ababb. While this grouping is symmetrical overall, the extra rhyming

°This poem appears on page 858.
*Central idea.
†Thesis sentence.

Novoa 2

line concluding each group skews what is otherwise a neatly alternating pattern of rhymes. This asymmetrical fifth line is consistent with how the speaker's ostensibly balanced and calm description of his grisly crime reveals the abnormal imbalances in his thought.

[3]   In addition, the rhyming sounds by themselves indicate the speaker's irrationality. For the most part, the rhyming sounds are separate and are unrepeated among the different groups of lines. Only two of the five-line groups include rhyming sounds that appear in a previous group: in the ninth group, the rhyming words "she" and "bee" (lines 41, 43) duplicate the sounds of "she" and "free" in the fifth group (lines 21, 23), and the rhyming words "pain," "again," and "stain" (lines 42, 44–45) echo the sixth group's "restrain," "vain," and "rain" (lines 27, 29–30). (This assumes that Browning pronounced "again" as a rhyming word with the others.) Significantly, the group that repeats rhyming sounds from previous groups is the one that contains the speaker's description of his killing Porphyria and then, in a particularly depraved action, lifting her eyelids and determining that her blue eyes were still laughing. The earlier groups that are linked through rhyme to this description are the ones in which he concludes that his love for her is "all in vain" (line 29) because she is "too weak" to cut the ties that bind her to whatever life she has had away from him (lines 22–25). Thus, the connection created by the rhyming sounds reinforces the cause-and-effect relationship between the speaker's deranged assessment of his wish to possess Porphyria totally and the act of murder that he believes has fulfilled his wish.

[4]   The meter, too, can be seen to reflect the speaker's troubled state. The poem's iambic tetrameter is not a "heroic" measure like iambic pentameter, but is a measure that seems more appropriate for satiric and more common subjects. The meter can be seen in the poem's first five lines:

> The RAIN / set EAR- / ly IN / to – NIGHT,
> The SUL- / len WIND / was SOON / a - WAKE,
> It TORE / the ELM- / tops DOWN / for SPITE,
> And DID / its WORST / to VEX / the LAKE:
> i LIST - / ened WITH / heart FIT / to BREAK.

Novoa 3

A number of lines in the poem, such as lines 41–45, vary this rhythm with spondees that may be taken as evidence of the speaker's inner turbulence when describing his actions. (Here only the spondees are marked):

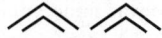
And strangled her. No pain felt she;

I am quite sure she felt no pain.

As a shut bud that holds a bee,

I warily oped her lids: again

Laughed the blue eyes without a stain.

The spondees here suggest a disruption of order, which is appropriate in light of the speaker's tortured admission that only after he has killed her is Porphyria "without a stain"--that is, pure.

Another notable group contains the lines in which he assumes the ability to read Porphyria's mind, and then states that no matter how strongly she was "murmuring" that she loved him, she nevertheless was too proud and too vain to give herself to him totally:

[5]

Murmuring how she loved me--she

Too weak, for all her heart's endeavor,

To set its struggling passion free

From pride, and vainer ties dissever,

And give herself to me forever. (lines 21–25)

In this group there is only one regular line, the middle one (line 23). The others show irregularity either through the use of spondees or, at the line ends, amphibrachs ("endeavor," "dissever," "forever"). It is clear that these are not just variations in rhythm, but that they show the speaker's weakened mental state.

Novoa 4

[6]   In addition, one may find in the poem a good deal of assonance and alliteration, usually on words and phrases in which the speaker's abnormality is specially brought out. Thus, in lines 36 and 37 we have alliteration on m and p sounds in "That moment she was mine, mine, fair, / Perfectly pure . . ." Under other circumstances, in other poems, alliteration is used as a way of emphasizing key words and ideas, but here the alliteration suggests the speaker's excitement when recalling his weird and diseased fantasy about possessing Porphyria. The same excitement and agitation can be seen in the use of the b alliteration in line 48. It should be stressed that here the speaker is confessing to outright necrophilia. After he has strangled Porphyria, opened her eyes, and loosened her hair, he kisses her, and he then states that she "Blushed bright beneath my burning kiss." These b sounds, which occur four times in the line, indicate the speaker's excitement when he describes his kiss. Earlier, he also has included words with stress on the b sound: "As a shut bud that holds a bee." In these same words, "shut bud," one may also find assonance on the "uh" sound. Assonance occurs again, on the "eh" sound, in lines 46–49: "next," "tress," "neck," and "head." This same assonance on eh occurs again in five lines of the next group (51 to 55). It appears that this killer is most expressive when his emotions are heightened by the memory of his diseased act.

[7]   The poem's subtle cacophony, too, reflects the speaker's mad, agitated frame of mind. This can be seen in the first five lines which, although they establish the regularity of the meter, contain words about the storm that better suggest the speaker's anger and hatred than an actual storm. Importantly, the sounds in a number of these words are percussive, and their cacophony suggests his agitation: "tore," "spite," "worst," "vex" (i.e., veks), "heart fit," and "break." This man is not shouting and raving, but he definitely is totally controlled by his abnormal compulsiveness. Thus, the hissing "s" sounds in a number of words in the first five lines suggest that the sounds of the words emerging into his consciousness to describe the wind and storm are like the raging tempest in his mind: "sullen," "soon," "tops," "spite," "worst," "vex" (i.e., veks), "listened."

Novoa 5

"Porphyria's Lover" is a masterly poem in which subject and style fuse [8]
together in a most meaningful way. The meter is for the most part regular, but it
contains variations that may be taken to highlight the speaker's disturbance. So
also is it with Browning's control over his use of segmental devices, which are
brought out in lines in which the speaker describes his insane act of murdering
his sweetheart, whose only mistake was to fall in love and be faithful. In
virtually every way, the poem's irregularities and variations complement the
speaker's delirium and also his moments of pathological exhilaration.

Novoa 6

Work Cited

Browning, Robert. "Porphyria's Lover." Literature: An Introduction to Reading
and Writing. Ed. Edgar V. Roberts. 9th ed. New York: Pearson Longman,
2009. 858–59.

Commentary on the Essay

This essay presents a relatively full treatment of the prosody of Browning's "Porphyria's Lover." It is to be understood that there could be further analysis of the poem's prosody. If such analysis did no more than lengthen the essay, however, without adding significantly to the conclusions, it would be superfluous.

Paragraph 1 is introductory and is concerned with establishing the poem's content—an essential purpose considering the extremity of the speaker's character. The central idea makes the connection between his madness and "the way he tells his tale." The discussion of prosody itself begins in paragraphs 2 and 3 with the description of the poem's rhymes. A principal idea here is that the fifth rhyming line of each five-line group, together with other characteristics of the rhyme, is to be construed as suggestive of the speaker's abnormal imbalances.

In paragraphs 4 and 5 the topic shifts to the poem's rhythms. Here, the use of the spondee and the uncommon amphibrach is to be considered not as substitutions inserted for emphasis or variety but rather as evidence of the disruptions in the speaker's thoughts. In paragraph 6 the topic is assonance and alliteration, which normally also are segmental elements that thrust individual words and lines into po-sitions of emphasis. Here, however, the devices are shown to indicate the speaker's excitement at the memory of possessing Porphyria and kissing her after killing her.

Paragraph 7 introduces the poem's "subtle cacophony" as made apparent in the first stanza, in which, even before we suspect the speaker of any wrongdoing, he describes the wind in words featuring sharp and painful sounds—words that can be interpreted to show that he is ascribing a malign influence to the rainstorm. The idea in the essay, here, is that the malignity is not a function of nature but rather of himself. Paragraph 8 is a summarizing statement speaking about the fus-ing together of subject and style and also asserting that the irregularities and vari-ations in the poem are consistent with the speaker's disturbed mind.

Of greatest importance for the clarity of the essay, there are many supporting examples. Some of these are embodied within the essay, and others are set off in block style, accurately marked, and numbered by line. In any essay about prosody, readers are likely to be unsure of the validity of the writer's observations unless such examples are provided and are clearly located within the poem.

Second Illustrative Student Essay

Underlined sentences in this paper *do not* conform to MLA style and are used solely as teaching tools to emphasize the central idea, thesis sentence, and topic sentences throughout the paper.

Vomero 1

Heather Vomero

Professor Garcia

English 220

3 March 2008

The Rhymes and Repeated Words in Christina Rossetti's "Echo"°

[1]   In the three-stanza lyric poem "Echo," Christina Rossetti uses rhyme as a way of saying that one might regain in dreams a love that is lost in reality.* As the real love is to the dream of love, so is an original sound to an echo. This symbolism underlies the poem's title and also Rossetti's unique use of rhyme. Aspects of her rhyme are the lyric pattern, the forms and qualities of the rhyming words, and the special use of repetition.†

°This poem appears on page 877.
*Central idea.
†Thesis sentence.

Vomero 2

<u>The rhyme pattern is simple, and, like rhyme generally, it may be</u>   [2]
<u>considered as a pattern of echoes.</u> Each stanza contains four lines of alternating rhymes concluded by a couplet, as follows:

Iambic: 5a, 5b, 5a, 3b, 2c, 5c.

There are nine separate rhymes throughout the poem, three in each stanza. Only two words are used for each rhyme, and no rhyme is used twice. Of the eighteen rhyming words, sixteen are one syllable long--almost all the rhymes. The remaining two words consist of two and three syllables. With such a great number of single-syllable words, the rhymes are all rising ones, on the accented halves of iambic feet, and the end-of-line emphasis is on simple words.

<u>The grammatical forms and positions of the rhyming words lend support</u>   [3]
<u>to the introspective subject matter.</u> Although there is variety, more than half the rhyming words are nouns. There are ten in all, and eight are placed as the objects of prepositions (e.g., "of a dream, "on a stream," "of finished years"). The nouns that are not the objects of prepositions are the subject and object of the same subordinate clause (lines 10 and 11). It seems clear that much of the poem's verbal energy occurs in the first parts of the lines, leaving the rhymes to occur in modifying elements, as in these lines(italics added):

Come to me in the silence of the night (line 1)

Yet come to me in dreams, that I may live (lines 13 and 14)

My very life again though cold in death; (14)

Most of the other rhymes are in similarly internalized positions. This careful arrangement is consistent with the speaker's emphasis on her yearning to relive her love within dreams.

<u>The qualities of the words are also consistent with the poem's emphasis on</u>   [4]
<u>the speaker's internal life.</u> Most of the rhyming words are impressionistic. Even the specific words--"stream," "tears," "eyes," "door," and "breathe"--reflect the speaker's mental condition. In this regard, the rhyming words of lines 1 and 3 are effective. These are "night" and "bright," which contrast the bleakness of the speaker's solitary condition with the vitality of her inner life.

Vomero 3

Another effective contrast is in lines 14 and 16, where "death" and "breath" are rhymed. This rhyme underscores the sad fact that even though the speaker's love has vanished, it lives in present memory just as an echo continues after the original sound is gone.

[5]   It is in emphasizing how memory echoes experience that Rossetti creates her special use of rhyming words. She creates an ingenious repetition of a number of words; these are the poem's echoes. The major echoing word is the verb "come," which appears as identical rhyme six times at the beginnings of lines in stanzas 1 and 3. Some of the other rhyming words are also repeated. The most notable is "dream," the rhyming word in line 2. Rossetti repeats the word in line 7 and uses the plural, "dreams," in lines 13 and 15. In line 7 the rhyming word "sweet" is the third use of that word, a climax of "how sweet, too sweet, too bitter sweet." Concluding the poem, Rossetti repeats "breath" (16), "low" (17), and the phrase "long ago" (18). These repeating identical rhymes justify the title "Echo," and they also stress the major idea that it is only in memory that experience has reality, even if dreams are no more than echoes.

[6]   Thus rhyme is not just ornamental in "Echo," but integral. The ease of Rossetti's rhymes, like the poem's diction generally, keeps the focus on regret and yearning rather than self-indulgence. As in all rhyming poems, Rossetti's rhymes emphasize the line-endings. The rhymes go beyond this effect, however, because they are used internally as identical rhymes of the terminal rhyming words. "Echo" is a poem in which rhyme is inseparable from meaning.

Vomero 4

Work Cited

Rossetti, Christina. "Echo." Literature: An Introduction to Reading and
    Writing. Ed. Edgar V. Roberts. 9th ed. New York: Pearson Longman,
    2009. 877.

Commentary on the Essay

This essay indicates how a single aspect of prosody—in this case, rhyme—can be the subject of an entire essay. Throughout, illustrative words are highlighted, and numbers are used to indicate the lines from which the illustrations are drawn. The introductory paragraph asserts that rhyme is vital in Rossetti's poem, particularly inasmuch as it also explains the title, "Echo." The thesis statement indicates the four topics to be developed in the body.

Paragraph 2 deals with the mechanical, mathematical aspects of the poem's rhymes. The high number of monosyllabic rhyming words is used to explain Rossetti's use of rising rhymes. Paragraph 3 treats the grammar of the rhymes. For example, an analysis and count reveal that there are ten rhyming nouns and three rhyming verbs. The verb of command *come* is mentioned to show that most of the rhyming words exist within groups modifying this word. The grammatical analysis is thus related to the internalized nature of the poem's subject.

Paragraph 4 emphasizes the impressionistic nature of the rhyming words and also points out two instances in which rhymes stress the contrast between real life and the speaker's introspective life. Paragraph 5 deals with how Rossetti repeats five of the poem's rhyming words. This repetition creates a pattern of echoes, in keeping with the poem's title.

The final paragraph concludes that Rossetti uses rhyme integrally within "Echo," not ornamentally. In addition, the point is emphasized that the internal rhymes or echoes are another facet of Rossetti's rhyming skill.

Writing Topics About Rhythm and Rhyme in Poetry

1. For Shakespeare's Sonnet 73, "That Time of Year Thou May'st in Me Behold," describe how Shakespeare creates iambics. What is the relationship of lightly accented syllables to the heavily accented ones? Where does Shakespeare use articles (*the*), pronouns (*this, his*), prepositions (*upon, against, of*), relative clause markers (*which, that*), and adverb clause markers (*as, when*) in relation to syllables of heavy stress? On the basis of this study, how would you characterize Shakespeare's control of the iambic foot?

2. Eliot's "Macavity: The Mystery Cat," Robinson's "Miniver Cheevy," Poe's "The Bells," and Nash's "Very Like a Whale," all include "falling" rhymes. What is the effect of this rhyming pattern in the poems? To what degree do the poems achieve seriousness despite the fact that falling rhyme is often used generally to complement humorous and light verse?

3. Compare the sounds used in Poe's "The Bells" with those of Wagoner's "March for a One-Man Band." What effects are achieved by each poet? What is the relationship in each poem between sound and content? Which poem do you prefer on the basis of sound? Why?

4. Analyze the rhymes in two of the following poems: Shakespeare's Sonnet No. 73, Hopkins's "God's Grandeur," Poe's "Annabel Lee," Shelley's "Ode to the West Wind," or the passage from Pope's "Essay on Man." What is interesting

or unique about the various rhyming words? What relationships can you discover between the rhymes and the topics of the poems?

5. Compare one of the rhyming poems with one of the nonrhyming poems included in this chapter. What differences in reading and sound can you discover as a result of the use or nonuse of rhyme? What benefits does rhyme give to the poem? What benefits does nonrhyme give?

6. Analyze Hardy's use of rhymes in "Channel Firing" (Chapter 14). What effects does Hardy create by using trochaic rhyme, like *hatters* and *matters*, and also by using dactylic rhyme, like *saner be* and *century*? What is the relationship of such rhymes to the heavy-stress rhymes in the poem?

7. Write a short poem of your own, using rhymes with trochaic words or dactylic words such as *computer, hermetic, scholastic, remarkable, along with me, inedible, moron, anxiously, emotion, fishing,* and so on. If you have trouble with exact rhymes, see what you can do with slant rhymes and eye rhymes. The idea is to use your ingenuity.

8. Using the topical index in your library or online, take out a book on prosody, such as Harvey Gross's *Sound and Form in Modern Poetry* (1968) or *The Structure of Verse* (1966), or Gay Wilson Allen's *American Prosody* (1935, reprinted 1966). Select a topic (e.g., formal or experimental prosody) or a poet (e.g., Arnold, Blake, Browning, Frost, Shakespeare), and write a summary of the ideas and observations that the writers make on your subject. What relationship do the writers make about prosody and the poet's ideas? How does prosody enter into the writer's thought and into the ways in which the poets emphasize ideas and images?

Chapter 18

Form: The Shape of Poems

B ecause poetry is compressed and highly rhythmical, it always exists under self-imposed restrictions, or conventions. Traditionally, many poets have chosen a variety of clearly recognizable shapes or forms—*closed-form poetry.* Since the middle of the nineteenth century, however, many poets have rejected regular patterns in favor of poems that appear more free and spontaneous—*open-form poetry.* Both terms refer to the structure and technique of the poems, not to the content or ideas.

Closed-Form Poetry

Closed-form poetry is written in specific and traditional patterns of lines produced through *line length, meter, rhyme,* and *line groupings.* In the closed form (and also in the open form), the **line** is, loosely, the poetic equivalent of the prose sentence. A prime characteristic of the closed-form line, as opposed to a sentence, is that its length should be measured or restricted. Various numbers of lines may be grouped together through rhyme and other means to form a **stanza,** which is the poetic equivalent of a paragraph in prose. Individual lines may coincide exactly with sentences, although quite often sentences stretch out over two or more lines. Stanzas consist of groups of lines that are both connected and also separated by developments of subject, idea, or expression of feeling.

Over the centuries English and American poets have appropriated and evolved many closed forms. Among the most important of these are *blank verse,* the *couplet,* the *tercet* or *triplet, terza rima,* the *villanelle,* the *quatrain,* the *sonnet,* the *song* or *lyric,* the *ode,* the *ballad,* the *elegy,* and *common measure* or the *hymnal stanza,* together with forms like *haiku,* the *epigram,* the *epitaph,* the *limerick,* the *clerihew,* and the *double dactyl.*

Blank Verse Consists of Five Unrhymed Iambic Lines

One of the most common closed forms in English is **blank verse,** or unrhymed iambic pentameter, which represents the adaptation and fusion of sentences to poetic form. The great advantage of blank verse is that it resembles normal speech but at the same time it maintains poetic identity. It is suitable for relatively short poems, but it may also extend for hundreds or even thousands of lines. It is the most adaptable line of English poetry. The master of blank verse is Shakespeare, who used it extensively in his plays. Since Shakespeare, poets of English have used blank verse again and again. Milton used it in his masterly long epic *Paradise Lost*. Wordsworth was fond of blank verse and used it in some of his best-known poems. Let us look at a passage from his autobiographical poem *The Prelude* (1850) to see his blank verse—which has been praised as "conversational," "flexible," and "majestic"—in action (for another example, see Chapter 13, p. 714).

> Wisdom and Spirit of the universe!
> Thou Soul that art the eternity of thought,
> That givest to forms and images a breath
> And everlasting motion, not in vain
> By day or star-light thus from my first dawn
> Of childhood didst thou intertwine for me
> The passions that build up our human soul;
> Not with the mean and vulgar works of man,
> But with high objects, with enduring things—
> With life and nature, purifying thus
> The elements of feeling and of thought,
> And sanctifying, by such discipline,
> Both pain and fear, until we recognize
> A grandeur in the beatings of the heart. (Book I, lines 401–414)

The development of these lines takes place through a simultaneous blending of line lengths and grammatical coherence. Wordsworth expresses his ideas enthusiastically within his chosen iambic rhythm, which is both restricting and liberating, and by this means he brings about the "majestic" elevation that is characteristic of his poetry.

The Couplet Consists of Two Lines Connected by Thought and Rhyme

The **couplet** contains two rhyming lines and is the shortest distinct closed form. The two lines are usually identical in length and meter. Some couplets are short. Even lines in monometer (one major stress), like "I sing / Each spring," can make up a couplet. However, most English couplets are in iambic tetrameter (four stresses) or iambic pentameter (five stresses), and they have been a regular feature of English poetry ever since Chaucer used them in the fourteenth century. In the seventeenth and eighteenth centuries, the iambic-pentameter couplet was considered appropriate for epic, or heroic, poetry. For this reason it is often called the **heroic couplet.** Because these centuries are considered the "neoclassic" age of literature, the form is also called the **neoclassic couplet.** It was used with consummate skill by John Dryden (1631–1700) and Alexander Pope (1688–1744).

Usually, the heroic couplet expresses a complete idea and is grammatically self-sufficient. It thrives on the rhetorical strategies of **parallelism** and **antithesis.** Look, for example, at these two couplets from "The Rape of the Lock," Pope's well-known mock-epic poem (1711):

> Here Britain's statesmen oft the fall foredoom
> Of foreign tyrants, and of nymphs at home;

Here thou, great Anna! whom three realms obey,
Dost sometimes counsel take—and sometimes tea.

These lines describe activities at Hampton Court, the royal palace and residence of Queen Anne (reigned 1701–1714). Notice that the first couplet allows Pope to link "Britain's statesmen" with two parallel but also antithetical events: the fall of nations and the "fall" of young women. Similarly, the second heroic couplet allows for the parallel and comic linking of royal meetings of state ("counsel") and teatime (in the early eighteenth century, *tea* was pronounced "tay"). The example thus demonstrates how the heroic couplet may contrast amusing and ironic actions and situations.

The Tercet or Triplet Consists of Three Lines

A three-line stanza is called a **tercet** or **triplet.** Tercets may be written in any uniform line length or meter and most commonly contain three rhymes (*aaa, bbb,* and so on), which are, in effect, short stanzas. The following poem by Tennyson is in iambic tetrameter triplets.

ALFRED, LORD TENNYSON (1809–1892)

For a photo, see Chapter 17, page 881.

 The Eagle (1851)

He clasps the crag with crooked hands;
Close to the sun in lonely lands,
Ring'd with the azure world, he stands.

The wrinkled sea beneath him crawls;
He watches from his mountain walls,
And like a thunderbolt he falls.

5

In the first tercet, we view the eagle as though at a distance. In the second, the perspective shifts, and we see through the eagle's eyes and follow his actions. In this tercet the verbs are active: the sea "crawls" and the eagle "falls." While the two tercets and the shift in perspective divide the poem, alliteration pulls things back together. This is especially true of the *k* sound in "clasps," "crag," "crooked," "close," and "crawls" and the *w* sound in "with," "world," "watches," and "walls."

TERZA RIMA.   There are two important variations on the tercet pattern, each requiring a high degree of ingenuity and control. The first tercet variation is **terza rima,** in which stanzas are interlocked through a pattern that requires the center termination in one tercet to be rhymed twice in the next: *aba bcb cdc ded,* and so on. You can see an example of terza rima in Shelley's "Ode to the West Wind" (Chapter 17).

THE VILLANELLE. The most complex variation of the tercet pattern is the **villanelle,** a nineteen-line form containing six tercets, rhymed *aba*, and concluded by four lines. The first and third lines of the first tercet are repeated alternately in subsequent tercets as a refrain, and they are also used in the concluding four lines. For examples see Elizabeth Bishop's "One Art," Theodore Roethke's "The Waking," and Dylan Thomas's "Do Not Go Gentle into That Good Night."

The Quatrain Is a Unit of Four Lines

The most common and adaptable stanzaic building block is the four-line **quatrain.** This stanza has been popular for hundreds of years and has lent itself to many variations. Like couplets and tercets, quatrains may be written in any line length and meter; even the line lengths within a quatrain may vary. The determining factor is the rhyme scheme, and even that is variable, depending on the form and the poet's aims. Quatrains may be rhymed *aaaa,* but they can also be rhymed *abab, abba, aaba,* or even *abcb.* Quatrains are basic components of many traditional closed forms, most notably ballads and sonnets, and they are significant in many religious hymns.

The Sonnet Is a Versatile Poem of Fourteen Lines

The **sonnet,** consisting of fourteen lines, is one of the most popular and durable closed poetic forms. Initially it was an Italian form (*sonnetto* means "little song") created by the medieval Italian poet Petrarch (1304–1374), who wrote collections or *cycles* of sonnets. The sonnet form as made famous by Petrarch is called the **Italian sonnet** or **Petrarchan sonnet** in Petrarch's honor. The form and style of Petrarchan sonnets were adapted to English poetry in the early sixteenth century, and with variations they have been used ever since. As a form, the Petrarchan sonnet is in iambic pentameter, and it contains two quatrains (the **octave**) and two tercets (the **sestet**). In structure and meaning, the octave presents a problem or situation that is resolved in the sestet, as in Milton's "On His Blindness." The rhyme scheme of the Petrarchan octave is fixed in an *abba, abba* pattern. The sestet offers a number of different rhyming possibilities, including *cdc cdc* and *cde cde.*

THE SHAKESPEAREAN SONNET OR ENGLISH SONNET. Shakespeare was the most original adapter of the sonnet tradition. Recognizing that there are fewer rhyming words in English than in Italian, he developed the **Shakespearean sonnet** or **English sonnet,** based on seven rhymes (in the pattern *abab cdcd efef gg*) rather than the five rhymes of the Italian sonnet. As indicated by the rhyme scheme, the Shakespearean sonnet contains three quatrains and a concluding couplet. The pattern of thought therefore shifts from the octave-sestet organization of the Italian sonnet to a four-part argument on a single thought or emotion. Each Shakespearean quatrain contains a separate development of the sonnet's central idea or problem, and the couplet provides a climax and resolution.

The Song or Lyric Is a Stanzaic Poem of Variable Measure and Length

The **song** or **lyric** is a stanzaic form that was originally designed to be sung to a repeating melody, although few lyrics today are written specifically for music. Even so, the line lengths and rhyme schemes of the first stanza are duplicated in subsequent stanzas, as though for repeated singing to the same tune. The stanzas of a lyric may be built from any combination of single lines, couplets, triplets, and quatrains. The line lengths may shift, and a great deal of metrical variation is common.

The lyric is one of the most adaptable and variable of all verse forms at the present time. In fact, the lyric is one of the forms most commonly used by contemporary poets. The form may be personal, public, philosophical, religious, and political, in addition to its use as a vehicle to express love and other emotions. There is theoretically no limit to the number of stanzas in a lyric, although there are usually no more than five or six. A. E. Housman's "Loveliest of Trees" (Chapter 12), for example, is a lyric made up of three quatrains containing two couplets each. It is in iambic tetrameter and it rhymes *aabb*. The second and third stanzas repeat the same pattern of rhyme, *ccdd eeff*. Lyrics often feature quite complex and ingenious stanzaic structures. Donne's "The Canonization" (Chapter 19) for instance, contains five stanzas, each of which follows the pattern *"iambic: 5a4b5b5a4c4c4c4a3a."* This nine-line stanza contains three different rhymes and three different line lengths. Nevertheless, the same intricate pattern is repeated in each of the five stanzas.

The Ode Is a Complex and Extensive Stanzaic Poem

The **ode** is a more variable stanzaic form than the lyric, with varying line lengths and intricate rhyme schemes. Usually the topics of odes are meditative and philosophical, but there is no set topic material, just as there is no set form. Some odes have repeating patterns, while others offer no duplication and introduce a new structure in each stanza. Poets have developed their own structures according to their needs. Keats's great odes were particularly congenial to his ideas, as in "Ode to a Nightingale," which consists of eight stanzas in iambic pentameter with the repeating form *ababcde3cde*. Although many odes have been set to music, most do not fit repeating melodies.

The Elegy is a Poem about Death and Its Meaning for the Living

The **elegy** ("lament," or "mournful song") has had a long and rich history in other languages extending back to ancient times, and it has defined a number of topics, but for our purposes it is a poem of lamentation. Usually the topic is the death of a specific person, but it is also generally concerned with mortality and the negative and tragic aspects of life. In English the most notable elegy is Milton's "Lycidas" (1638), which he wrote in observance of the death by drowning of a "learned friend" with whom he had gone to school. Milton also composed this poem as a **pastoral,** that is, a poem describing rural lives and concerns, with direct allegorical implications for the lives of city-dwellers. So that you may get a sense of this poem, here are the opening twenty-four lines.

Yet once more, O ye laurels, and once more
Ye myrtles brown, with ivy never sere,°   *dry, withered*
I come to pluck your berries° harsh and crude,   *to write this poem*
And with forced fingers rude,
5   Shatter your leaves before the mellowing year.
Bitter constraint, and sad occasion dear,
Compels me to disturb your season due;
For Lycidas is dead, dead ere his prime,
Young Lycidas, and hath° not left his peer: *who hath*
10   Who would not sing for Lycidas? he knew
Himself to sing, and build the lofty rhyme.
He must not float upon his watery bier
Unwept, and welter to the parching wind,
Without the meed° of some melodious tear.   *gift, honor*
15   Begin then, sisters° of the sacred well,   *the muses*
That from beneath the seat of Jove° doth spring,   *God (Jupiter)*
Begin, and somewhat loudly sweep the string.
Hence with denial vain, and coy excuse,
So may some gentle muse
20   With lucky° words favor my destined urn,   *providential, inspired*
And as he passes turn,
And bid fair peace be to my sable shroud.
For we were nursed upon the self-same hill,
Fed the same flock; by fountain, shade, and rill.°   *i.e., we went to the same school*

Today few people think of the traditional formalities of elegiac writing, and prefer to understand poems as elegies if they concern death, mortality, and grief. Thus, Collins's "The Names" (Chapter 16), Dryden's "To the Memory of Mr. Oldham" (this chapter) Pinsky's "Dying" (Chapter 16), Ransom's "Bells for John Whiteside's Daughter" (Chapter 22), Cummings' "Buffalo Bill's Defunct" (this chapter) and Dickinson's "The Bustle in a House" (Chapter 21), to name just a few poems in this book, might, broadly, all be considered elegies.

A Ballad Consists of Many Narrative Quatrains

The **ballad,** which fuses narrative description with dramatic dialogue, originated in folk literature and is one of the oldest closed forms in English poetry. Ballads consist of many quatrains in which lines of iambic tetrameter alternate with iambic trimeter. Normally, only the second and fourth lines of each stanza rhyme, in the pattern *xaxa xbxb xcxc* and so on. The ballad was designed for singing, like the anonymous "Sir Patrick Spens" (Chapter 11). Popular ballad tunes were used over and over again by later balladeers, often as many as forty and fifty times, or more, and many of the tunes have survived to the present day and are still well known—for example, the anonymous "Lord Randal" (Chapter 22). The music to folk ballads like "Greensleeves" and "Waly Waly" (not in this collection) has been known now for the past 400 years in both England and America, and many balladeers have written words to be sung to this music.

Common Measure, or the Hymnal Stanza, Is a Poem Consisting of a Number of Quatrains

Common measure, a quatrain form, is similar to the ballad stanza. It shares with the ballad the alternation of four-beat and three-beat iambic lines but adds a second rhyme to the first and third lines of each quatrain: *abab cdcd* and so on. Because the measure is often used in hymns, it is sometimes called the **hymnal stanza.** Many of Emily Dickinson's poems, including "Because I Could Not Stop for Death" (Chapter 11), are in common measure.

The Haiku Is a Complete Poem of Seventeen Syllables

The **haiku** originated in Japan, where it has been a favorite genre for hundreds of years. It traditionally imposes strict rules on the writer: (1) There should be three lines (a tercet) of five, seven, and five syllables per line, for a total of seventeen syllables. (2) The topic should be derived from nature. (3) The poem should embody a unique observation or insight. Today, English-language poets have adapted the haiku but have taken liberties with the subject matter and have often reduced the syllable count. Whether the traditional pattern is varied or not, however, the haiku must be short, simple, objective, clear, and (often) symbolic. The following anonymous haiku illustrates some of these qualities.

Spun in High, Dark Clouds

Spun in high, dark clouds,
Snow forms vast webs of white flakes
And drifts lightly down.

In the tradition of haiku, the subject is derived from nature, and the syllable pattern is 5–7–5. The central metaphor equates gathering snow with the webs of silkworms or spiders. To supply tension, the lines contrast "high" with "down" and "dark" with "white." Because of the enforced brevity, the diction is simple and, except for the word "forms," of English derivation (our word *form* is of Latin origin). In addition, most of the words are monosyllabic, and through this means the poem fills the seventeen-syllable form with sixteen words.

There Are Additional but Less Significant Closed-Form Types

Many other closed forms have enjoyed long popularity. One of these, the **epigram,** is a short and witty poem that usually makes a humorous or satiric point. Epigrams are two to four lines long and are often written in couplets. The form was developed by the Roman poet Martial (c. 40–103 CE) and has always been popular. Humorous and sometimes irreverent **epitaphs,** brief poems composed to mark the death of someone, can also be epigrams.

Another popular type is the **limerick,** a five-line form popularized by the English artist and humorist Edward Lear (1812–1888). Like the epigram, limericks are comic, their humor being reinforced by falling rhymes. Usually, they are bawdy.

Comic closed forms continue to be devised by enterprising writers. The **clerihew,** a two-couplet form invented in the late nineteenth century by Edmund Clerihew Bentley (1875–1956), is related to the epigram. A final illustration of closed-form humor is the **double dactyl,** devised in the 1960s by Anthony Hecht and Paul Pascal. The form is related to the epigram, limerick, and clerihew, and it has rules that govern the meter, line length, and specific topic material.

Poets Use the Closed Form to Shape and Polish Meaning

Although many contemporary poets consider closed forms restrictive and even stultifying, the closed form has always provided both a framework and a challenge for poets to express new and fresh ideas, attitudes, and feelings. Let us look at the way Shakespeare uses the sonnet form to shape thoughts and emotions:

WILLIAM SHAKESPEARE (1564–1616)

For a portrait, see Chapter 24, page 1322.

 Sonnet 116: Let Me Not to the Marriage of True Minds (1609)

Let me not to the marriage of true minds
Admit impediments.° Love is not love
Which alters when it alteration finds,
Or bends with the remover to remove:
5   Oh, no! it is an ever-fixéd mark,
That looks on tempests and is never shaken;
It is the star to every wandering bark,
Whose worth's unknown, although his height° be taken   *its altitude*
Love's not Time's fool,° though rosy lips and cheeks   *slave*
10 Within his° bending sickle's compass come;   *Time's*
Love alters not with his brief hours and weeks,
But bears it out even to the edge of doom.°   *the Last Judgment*
If this be error and upon me proved,
I never writ, nor no man ever loved.

°2 *impediments:* a reference to "The Order of Solemnization of Matrimony" in the Anglican Church's *Book of Common Prayer:* "I require that if either of you know of any impediment why ye may not be lawfully joined together in Matrimony, ye do now confess it."

QUESTIONS

1. Describe the restrictions of this closed form. How is the poem's argument structured by the form?
2. What is the poem's meter? Rhyme scheme? Structure?

3. Describe the varying ideas about love explored in the three quatrains.
4. What does the concluding couplet contribute to the poem's argument about love?

Even if we did not know that the poem is Shakespeare's, we would recognize it as a Shakespearean sonnet. It is in iambic pentameter and contains three quatrains and a concluding couplet, rhyming *abab cdcd efef gg*. The sonnet form provides the organization for the poem's argument—that real love is a "marriage of true minds" existing independent of earthly time and change. Each quatrain advances a new perspective on this idea.

This is not to say that Shakespeare exhausts the subject or that he wants to. The ideas in the third quatrain, for example, about how love transcends time, could be greatly expanded. A philosophical analysis of the topic might deal extensively with Platonic ideas about reality—whether it exists in *particulars* or *universals*. Similarly, the poem's very last line, if it were to become the topic of a prose discourse, might include the introduction of evidence about the poet's own writing, and also about many examples of human love. But the two lines are enough, granted the restrictions of the form, and more would be superfluous. One might add that most readers find Shakespeare's poem interesting and vital, while extensive philosophical discourses often drop into laps as readers fall asleep.

The closed poetic form therefore may be viewed as a complex consequence of poetic compression. No matter what form a poet chooses—couplet, sonnet, song, ballad, ode—that form imposes restrictions, and it therefore challenges and shapes the poet's thought. The poet of the closed form shares with all writers the need to make ideas seem logical and well supported, but the challenge of the form is to make all this happen *within the form itself*. The thought must be developed clearly and also fully, and there should be no lingering doubts once the poem is completed. The words must be the most fitting and exact ones that could be selected. When we look at good poems in the closed form, in short, we may be sure that they represent the ultimate degree of poetic thought, discipline, and skill.

Open-Form Poetry

Among the closed forms, as we have seen, the ode is the form that gives poets great opportunity for variability and expansion. The ode is thus the closed form that is most nearly related, in spirit, to **open-form poetry,** but the open form eliminates the restrictions of the closed form. Each open-form poem is unique and unpredictable. Poetry of this type was once termed **free verse** (from the French *vers libre*) to signify its liberation from regular metrics and its embrace of spoken rhythms. But open-form poetry is not therefore disorganized or chaotic. Open-form poets have instead created new and original ways to arrange words and lines—new ways to express thoughts and feelings, and new ways to order poetic experience.

Poets writing in the open form attempt to fuse form and content by stressing speechlike rhythms, creating a natural and easy-flowing word order, altering and varying line lengths according to the importance of ideas, and creating emphasis through the control of shorter and longer pauses. They often isolate individual words, phrases, and clauses as single lines, freely emphasize their ideas through the manipulation of spaces separating words and sentences, and sometimes even break up individual words in separate lines to highlight their importance. Sometimes they create poems that look exactly like prose and that are printed in blocks and paragraphs instead of stanzas or lines, as with "Museum" by Robert Hass. Such **prose poems** rely on a progression of images and the cadences of language.

Open-Form Poetry Is Free in Form and Variable in Content

An early example of open-form poetry is Walt Whitman's "Reconciliation" This poem was included in *Drum Taps*, a collection of fifty-three poems about the poet's reactions to Civil War battles in Virginia.

WALT WHITMAN (1819–1892)

For a photo, see Chapter 15, page 790.

 ## Reconciliation (1865, 1881)

Word over all, beautiful as the sky,
Beautiful that war and all its deeds of carnage must in time be utterly lost,
That the hands of the sisters Death and Night incessantly softly wash again, and ever
    again, this soiled world;
For my enemy is dead, a man divine as myself is dead,
5 I look where he lies white-faced and still in the coffin—I draw near,
Bend down and touch lightly with my lips the white face in the coffin.

QUESTIONS

1. How do individual lines, varying line lengths, punctuation, pauses, and cadences create rhythm and organize the images and ideas in this poem?
2. How do alliteration, assonance, and the repetition of words unify the poem and reinforce its content?
3. What is the "word" referred to in line 1? What does the speaker find "beautiful" about this "word" and the passage of time?
4. What instances of personification can you find? What do these personified figures do? What does the speaker do in lines 5–6? Why does he do this?

"Reconciliation" shows the power of open-form poetry. There is no dominant meter, rhyme scheme, or stanza pattern. Instead, Whitman uses individual lines and varying line lengths to organize and emphasize the images, ideas, and emotions. He also uses repetition, alliteration, and assonance to make internal line connections.

Without going into every aspect of the poem, one may note the unifying elements in the first few lines. The "word over all" (i.e., reconciliation, peace) is linked to the second line by the repetition of the words "beautiful" and "all," while "beautiful" is grammatically complemented by the clauses "that . . . lost" (line 2) and "That . . . world" (line 3). The reconciling word is thus connected to the image of the two personified figures, Death and Night, who "wash" war and carnage (bloodshed) out of "this soiled world."

In the third line, unity and emphasis are created through the repetition of "again" and the alliteration on the *ly* sound of "incessant**ly**" and "soft**ly**," the *s* sound in "**s**isters," "incessantly," "softly," and "soil'd," and the *d* sound in "han**ds**," "**D**eath," "soil'**d**," and "**W**orld." One may also note the unifying assonance patterns of *ih* in "**i**ts," "**i**n," "s**i**sters," "**i**ncessantly," and "th**i**s;" and *aye* in "sk**y**," "t**i**me," and "N**igh**t." The pauses, or junctures, of the line create internal rhythms that coincide with the thought, "That the hands // of the sisters // Death and Night // incessantly softly // wash again and ever again // this soiled world."

This selective analysis demonstrates that open-form poetry creates its own unity. While some of the unifying elements, such as alliteration and assonance, are also a property of closed-form poetry, many are unique to poetry of the open form, such as the repetitions, the reliance on grammatical structures, and the control of rhythms. The concept of the open form is that the topic itself shapes the number of lines, the line lengths, and the physical appearance on the page. Unity is there—development is there—but the open form demands that there be as many shapes and forms as there are topics.

VISUALIZING POETRY

Poetry and Artistic Expression: Visual Poetry, Concrete Poetry, and Prose Poems

Along with the fact that many poets have rejected traditional closed-form patterns, they have moved in new directions with the open form. The idea has been to allow poetry to follow a wide range of poetic shapes, including avenues of experimentation. Poets have continued to express ideas about the topics we usually associate with poetry—which really means just about everything—but in addition, they have imaginatively invented new looks for their poems on the actual page. Some poets may indulge in creative playfulness by fashioning visual surprises, thus focusing on the medium itself, in which each poem starts its life, waiting patiently for readers. In fact, some poets give almost as much attention to their visual arrangement of letters, words, lines, and white space as they do to the content of their poems. To draw attention to particular thoughts, many poets deliberately alter the spellings of certain words; or they may run a number of words together, without spaces between them, to set them apart; or they may abandon the traditional capitalization of each new line; or, for that matter, they may simply reject some or all capitalization. We may see some of these characteristics in E. E. Cummings's poem "Buffalo Bill's Defunct," in which Cummings uses stretched-out lines in contrast with shorter lines, runs successive words together, and varies the placement of line beginnings, all as the means of guiding readers to see, hear, and comprehend the poem in accordance with his wishes.

E. E. CUMMINGS (1894–1962)

For a photo, see Chapter 12, page 665.

Buffalo Bill's Defunct° (1923)

Buffalo Bill's
defunct
      who used to
      ride a watersmooth-silver
5   stallion
and break onetwothreefourfive pigeonsjustlikethat
                        Jesus
he was a handsome man
                and what i want to know is
10 how do you like your blueeyed boy
Mister Death

°The poem has no title; it is usually referred to as "Portrait" or by its first two lines. Buffalo Bill (William F. Cody, 1846–1917) was an American plainsman, hunter, army scout, sharpshooter, and showman whose Wild West show began touring the world in 1883; he became a symbol of the Wild West.

QUESTIONS

1. What is the effect of devoting a whole line to "Buffalo Bill's" (line 1), "defunct" (line 2), "stallion" (line 5), "Jesus" (line 7), and "Mister Death" (line 11)? How does this technique reflect and emphasize the content of the poem?
2. How does the typographical arrangement of line 6 contribute to the fusion of sound and sense? What other examples of this technique do you find?
3. Explain the denotations and connotations of *defunct*. What would be lost (or gained) by using the term *dead* or *deceased* instead?
4. To what extent is this poem a "portrait" of Buffalo Bill? What do we learn about him? Is the portrait respectful, mocking, or something in between?

Cummings's poem is in the tradition of earlier poetry that was very much like anagrams or puzzles. One interesting early type featured the weaving of words inside a poem, with the special words in effect doing double duty—being coherent and meaningful within a poem, and having a separate coherence and meaning themselves. Such examples, both integral and extraneous at the same time, are almost like a verbal game, which applies also to much later concrete poetry. In the following poem, by the early seventeenth-century poet George Herbert, the poem develops out of the biblical text in Colossians: "Set your affection on things above, not on things on the earth. For ye are dead, and your life is hid with Christ in God. When Christ, *who is* our life, shall appear, then shall ye also appear with him in glory" (3: 2–4). The idea of Paul, the writer of Colossians, is a complex one, and it is vital in Christian theology: that the human lifetime is short but only seemingly so, because eternal life is hidden to human beings and will not be recognized until the eventual return of Jesus. Within the poem, the sentence that Herbert creates is this: "My Life Is Hid In Him That Is My Treasure." This sentence descends, word by word and diagonally downward from left to right. The words of the descending sentence are boldfaced, capitalized, and italicized here.

GEORGE HERBERT (1593–1633)

 ## Colossians 3:3 (Our Life Is Hid with Christ in God) (1633)

MY words and thoughts do both express this notion,
That *LIFE* hath with the sun a double motion.
The first *IS* straight, and our diurnal friend,
The other *HID* and doth obliquely bend.
One life is wrapped *IN* flesh, and tends to earth: 5
The other winds towards *HIM,* whose happy birth
Taught me to live here so, *THAT* still one eye
Should aim and shoot at that which *IS* on high:
     Quitting with daily labor all *MY* pleasure,
     To gain at harvest an eternal *TREASURE.*   10

QUESTIONS

1. How is the Sun to be considered "our diurnal friend"? What is the distinction made in the poem between "straight" and "obliquely"?
2. What is the "double motion" that is embodied (a) in the lives of human beings, (b) in the poem itself, and also (c) in the line that descends within the poem? How does the form of the poem reinforce these ideas?

The "hidden" sentence is essential to the poem in two ways: it is integrated grammatically while at the same time it possesses its own separate coherence and meaning. It reminds us of the importance of the visual aspects of poetry. **Visual poetry,** also called **shaped verse** and sometimes **picture poetry,** is alive and well today. Within this form, poets not only emphasize the idea and emotion of their subjects but also fashion their poems into a generalized or pictorial shape on the page, using words, lines, and spaces. The Chinese have been producing such poetry for many generations, and there are surviving examples from ancient Greece. In the English Renaissance, many poets fashioned the lines of their poems to represent wings, altars, squares, triangles, stars, and the like. This type of poetry was often ingenious, and the figures were graphic extensions of traditional poetic images and symbols.

In writing about visual and concrete poems, you should seek correspondences between images and poetic ideas. Describe the shape of the poem and the figures it resembles. Determine how varying line lengths, the placement of individual words and phrases, and the use of space all contribute to the visual effect. A superb example of traditional visual poetry is "Easter Wings," also by George Herbert, which is a religious poem fashioned into two approximately equal shapes:

Easter Wings (1633)

Lord, who createdst man in wealth and store,°   *abundance*
    Though foolishly he lost the same,
        Decaying more and more
          Till he became
5   Most poor:
          With thee
        O let me rise
      As larks, harmoniously,
    And sing this day thy victories:
10 Then shall the fall° further the flight in me.

My tender age in sorrow did I begin:
    And still° with sicknesses and shame   *always, constantly*
        Thou didst so punish sin,
          That I became
15   Most thin.
          With thee
        Let me combine,
      And feel this day thy victory;°
    For, if I imp° my wing on thine,
20 Affliction shall advance the flight in me.

°2, 10 *foolishly he lost; fall . . .* Two references to the biblical account of how sin and death were introduced as a punishment for humankind after Adam and Eve disobeyed God in the Garden of Eden. 18 *victory:* I Corinthians 15:54–57. 19 *imp:* to repair a falcon's wing or tail by grafting on feathers.

QUESTIONS

1. What does the poem look like when viewed straight on? When viewed sideways, with the left side at the top? How do these two images echo and emphasize the poem's content?
2. How does the typographical arrangement echo the sense? In lines 5 and 15, for example, how are typography, shape, and meaning fused?
3. What do lines 1–5 tell you about humanity's spiritual history, according to Herbert? What do lines 11–15 tell you about the speaker's spiritual state? How are these parallel?

    In our own time, many poets have followed Herbert's precedent by creating shaped verse in which the visual image and the poetic meaning merge as separate aspects of one major idea. A unique shape for a recent poem is Charles Harper Webb's "The Shape of History." Let us see how Webb controls the lengths of lines to build his geometrical figure:

CHARLES HARPER WEBB (b. 1952)

 The Shape of History (1995)

Turning and turning in the widening gyre . . .°

Today's paper is crammed full of news: pages and pages on the Somalia
Famine, the Balkan Wars, Gays in the Military. On this date a year ago,
only 1/365 of "The Year's Top Stories" happened. *Time* magazine fits a
decade into one thin retrospective. Barely enough occurred a century
ago to fill one sub-chapter in a high school text. 500 years ago, one   5
or two things happened every 50 years. 5000 years ago, a city
was founded, a grain cultivated, a civilization toppled every
other century. Still farther back, the years march by in
groups like graduates at a big state university: 10,000 to
20,000 BC; 50,000–100,000 BC; 1–10 million BC.   10
Before that, things happened once an Era: Mam—
mals in the Cenozoic, Dinosaurs in the Meso-
zoic, Forests in the Paleozoic, Protozoans in
the Pre-Cambrian. Below that, at the
very base of time's twisting gyre, its   15
cornucopia, its ram's-horn trum-
pet, its tornado tracking across
eternity, came what Christians call Creation, astro-
physicists call the Big   20
Bang. Then, for tril-
lions of years,
nothing at
all.

°*Turning . . . gyre:* See line 1 of Yeats's "The Second Coming," Chapter 19, page 974

QUESTIONS

1. What shape does the poet give to history? How accurate is this shape?
2. How do the lengths of the first and final two lines graphically show how civilization has grown? What "top stories" are mentioned in the first few lines? How representative of modern news are these stories? How long will it take for such stories to be replaced by new, similar stories?
3. In the light of the epigraph by Yeats, what does the speaker apparently think will happen in the future?
4. Considering the content and the diminishing shape of the poem's twenty-four lines, what do you think is meant by "nothing at/all"?

A comparable visual poem is John Hollander's "Swan and Shadow." Notice that Hollander, in order to compose the top image and the bottom reflection he seeks, develops a creative pattern of lines and individual words. The pattern coheres grammatically, and it also functions constructively to create the visual picture, which is also three-dimensional. The connections here are skillful, and the finished poem shows a command over both poetic and graphic art.

JOHN HOLLANDER (b. 1929)

🍁 Swan and Shadow (1969)

```
                        Dusk
                     Above the
                  water hang the
                           loud
5                          flies
                        Here
                      O so
                     gray
                    then
10                  What              A pale signal will appear
                    When         Soon before its shadow fades
                    Where        Here in this pool of opened eye
                    In us    No Upon us As at the very edges
                 of where we take shape in the dark air
15                 this object bares its image awakening
                    ripples of recognition that will
                    brush darkness up into light
     even after this bird this hour both drift by atop the perfect sad instant now
                    already passing out of sight
20                 toward yet-untroubled reflection
                 this image bears its object darkening
                 into memorial shades Scattered bits of
                  light         No of water Or something across
                  water            Breaking up No Being regathered
25                soon             Yet by then a swan will have
                  gone                 Yes out of mind into what
                  vast
                  pale
                  hush
30               of a
                  place
                    past
            sudden dark as
                 if a swan
35                    sang
```

QUESTIONS

1. How effectively and consistently does the shape image reinforce the meaning?
2. What specific words, phrases, and lines are emphasized by the typographical arrangement? To what extent does this effect give added impact to the poem?
3. How well does the structure echo the verbal images of the poem?
4. Do you find Hollander's experiment with shaped verse as successful as Herbert's in "Easter Wings" If so, demonstrate how it succeeds. If not, explain why.

Many patterns of visual form may be variable and, sometimes, surprising. William Heyen creates a unique form in his poem "Mantle," about his reflections about the brilliant professional career of Mickey Mantle, who is fondly remembered by sports fans as one of the superior home-run sluggers in baseball history. Many students experience a great joy of discovery when they recognize the shape that Heyen is simulating here with his poetic stanzas.

WILLIAM HEYEN (b. 1940)

 ## Mantle° (1980)

      Mantle ran so hard, they said,
     he tore his legs to pieces,
       What is this but spirit?

     52 homers in '56, the triple crown.
   I was a high school junior, batting   5
      fourth behind him in a dream.

    I prayed for him to quit, before
his lifetime dropped below .300.
     But he didn't, and it did.

  He makes Brylcreem commercials now,   10
models with open mouths draped around him
   as they never were in Commerce, Oklahoma,

     where the sandy-haired, wide-shouldered boy
stood up against his barn,
     lefty for an hour (Ruth, Gehrig),   15

       then righty (DiMaggio),
    as his father winged them in,
    and the future blew toward him,

         now a fastball, now a slow
        curve hanging   20
         like a model's smile.

°Mickey Mantle (1931–1995), a Yankee outfielder from 1951–1968. A switch hitter, he hit eighteen World Series home runs (a record) and 536 career home runs. He was the American League's most valuable player in 1956, the year he won the triple crown (line 4).

QUESTIONS

1. Describe the shape of the poem, being careful to study the last stanza. Why is this shape appropriate for a famous baseball player?
2. How does the poet use Mantle as a symbol in this poem?
3. Who are Ruth, Gehrig, and DiMaggio? In what ways are they like Mantle?

Just as some visual art is abstract and suggestive, rather than pictorial, so also may be the forms created by writers of visual poems. Such a poem is May Swenson's "Women," which is suggestive of feminine rhythm and movement. It is almost as though the poem itself is a dancing and gently swaying figure.

MAY SWENSON (1919–1989)

Women (1968)

Women   Or they
   should be   should be
     pedestals   little horses
      moving   those wooden
5   pedestals   sweet
       moving   oldfashioned
       to the   painted
        motions   rocking
        of men   horses
10   the gladdest things in the toyroom
       The   feelingly
      pegs   and then
     of their   unfeelingly
    ears   To be
15   so familiar   joyfully
   and dear   ridden
  to the trusting   rockingly
fists   ridden until
To be chafed   the restored
20 egos dismount and the legs stride away
Immobile   willing
  sweetlipped   to be set
   sturdy   into motion
   and smiling   Women
25   women   should be
    should always   pedestals
    be waiting   to men

QUESTIONS

1. Is this poem an instance of closed-form, open-form, or visual poetry? In what different ways or sequences can it be read? How do the different sequences change the meaning?
2. How well does the image of the poem reinforce its meaning? Would the effect be different if the columns of words were straight instead of undulating?
3. To what extent do repetition and alliteration help to organize the poem and underscore its sense? Note especially *w*, *m*, *f*, *r*, and *s* sounds.
4. What does this poem *say* that women should be? Does it mean what it says? How are men characterized? In what way is this poem ironic?

Another and somewhat less graphic type of free verse is called the "prose poem." This phrase may seem like a contradiction in terms, but the idea that poets can write poems in the shape of prose is not surprising, granted that many modern poets are committed to principles of poetic freedom.[1] Some topics might possibly be more suitable to a prose form because they may seem less connected to poetry than to local or international news events, or they may involve the poet in

---

[1] See David Lehman, ed., *Great American Prose Poems: From Poe to the Present* (New York: Scribner, 2003).

reflections about politics, or about moral or religious matters. "Museum," by Robert Hass, is such a poem (p. 921), in which the speaker lays out a tranquil scene and draws an optimistic conclusion. But sometimes the subject may seem problematic, and therefore more appropriate for a less formal treatment than poetry might offer. Above all, however, the major characteristic of the prose poem is that it should have the compactness and intensity of poetry, even though on the page, from a distance, it may at first seem just like any ordinary prose paragraph. Carolyn Forché creates such poetic intensity in her prose poem "The Colonel."

CAROLYN FORCHÉ (b. 1950)

 ## The Colonel (1978)

What you have heard is true. I was in his house. His wife carried a tray of coffee and sugar. His daughter filed her nails, his son went out for the night. There were daily papers, pet dogs, a pistol on the cushion beside him. The moon swung bare on its black cord over the house. On the television was a cop show. It was in English. Broken bottles were embedded in the walls around the house to scoop the kneecaps from a man's legs or cut his hands to lace. 5 On the windows there were gratings like those in liquor stores. We had dinner, rack of lamb, good wine, a gold bell was on the table for calling the maid. The maid brought green mangoes, salt, a type of bread. I was asked how I enjoyed the country. There was a brief commercial in Spanish. His wife took everything away. There was some talk then of how difficult it had become to govern. The parrot said hello on the terrace. The colonel told it to 10 shut up, and pushed himself from the table. My friend said to me with eyes: say nothing. The colonel returned with a sack used to bring groceries home. He spilled many human ears on the table. They were like dried peach halves. There is no other way to say this. He took one of them in his hands, shook it in our faces, dropped it into a water glass. It came alive there. I am tired of fooling around he said. As for the rights of anyone, tell your people they 15 can go fuck themselves. He swept the ears to the floor with his arm and held the last of his wine in the air. Something for your poetry, no? he said. Some of the ears on the floor caught this scrap of his voice. Some of the ears on the floor were pressed to the ground.

QUESTIONS

1. Why does the poet use the prose poem form for this poem?
2. What is the character of the colonel? How can he be gracious, and then abusive, at the same time? What atrocities has he committed or ordered committed?
3. Why does the speaker include details about the walls about the house? What do the walls show about the mentality of those within the walls? Explain the meaning of the last sentence.

As you explore modern poems, you will regularly encounter many different forms. Most poems will appear to be no more than slight variations of traditional poetic lines, but many will stretch and alter normal and expected linear patterns. And some will aim at fusing words and pictures, such as those we have examined briefly here. Modern writers seek to explore ideas and to blend their new thoughts with the poetic medium of new and original patterns of development. In addition to the poets mentioned here, many other modern poets have worked similarly with free forms. Some of these poets, included elsewhere in this volume, are Allan Ginsberg, Robinson Jeffers, Marge Piercy, Alberto Rios, Sonya Sanchez, and C. K. Williams.

Poems for Study

Elizabeth Bishop .... One Art, 916
Billy Collins.. Sonnet, 917
John Dryden .... To the Memory of Mr. Oldham, 918
Robert Frost.. Desert Places, 918
Allen Ginsberg .... A Supermarket in California, 919
Nikki Giovanni.. Nikki-Rosa, 920
Robert Hass... Museum, 921
George Herbert.. Virtue, 922
John Keats .... Ode to a Nightingale, 923
Claude McKay .... In Bondage, 925
John Milton .... On His Blindness (When I Consider
                                            How My Light Is Spent), 926
Dudley Randall .... Ballad of Birmingham 927
Theodore Roethke .... The Waking, 928
George William Russell (Æ)......................... Continuity, 929
Percy Bysshe Shelley .... Ozymandias, 929
Dylan Thomas........... Do Not Go Gentle into That Good Night, 930
Jean Toomer....................................... Reapers, 931
Phyllis Webb .... Poetics Against the Angel of Death, 931
William Carlos Williams........................... The Dance, 932

ELIZABETH BISHOP (1911–1979)

 ## One Art (1976)

The art of losing isn't hard to master;
so many things seem filled with the intent
to be lost that their loss is no disaster.

Lose something every day. Accept the fluster
5   of lost door keys, the hour badly spent.
The art of losing isn't hard to master.

Then practice losing farther, losing faster;
places, and names, and where it was you meant
to travel. None of these will bring disaster.

10   I lost my mother's watch. And look! my last, or
next-to-last, of three loved houses went.
The art of losing isn't hard to master.

I lost two cities, lovely ones. And, vaster,
some realms I owned, two rivers, a continent.
15   I miss them, but it wasn't a disaster.

—Even losing you (the joking voice, a gesture
I love) I shan't have lied. It's evident

the art of losing's not too hard to master
though it may look like (*Write* it!) like disaster.

QUESTIONS

1. This poem is written in a traditional closed form called the *villanelle* (originally an Italian peasant song), which was developed in France during the Middle Ages. A villanelle is nineteen lines long. Fairly strict rules govern the length and structure of stanzas, the rhyme scheme, and the repetition of complete lines. Try to formulate these rules. For comparison, see Roethke's "The Waking" and Thomas's "Do Not Go Gentle into That Good Night."
2. On what idea is the poem based? What evidence does the speaker produce about losing? What feelings does she express about her losses?
3. How could the speaker have lost "two cities"? What other things has she lost that justify her claim that "the art of losing isn't hard to master"? What might she mean by having lost the "you" to whom the poem is addressed?

BILLY COLLINS (b. 1941)

For a photo, see Chapter 11, page 624.

 ## Sonnet (1999)

All we need is fourteen lines, well, thirteen now,
and after this next one just a dozen
to launch a little ship on love's storm-tossed seas,
then only ten more left like rows of beans.
How easily it goes unless you get Elizabethan   5
and insist the iambic bongos must be played
and rhymes positioned at the ends of lines,
one for every station of the cross.
But hang on here while we make the turn
into the final six where all will be resolved,   10
where longing and heartache will find an end,
where Laura will tell Petrarch to put down his pen,
take off those crazy medieval tights,
blow out the lights, and come at last to bed.

QUESTIONS

1. Why is this poem amusing? What makes it amusing?
2. What is the effect of lines 6 and 7? Why does the speaker refer to "every station of the cross" in line 8?
3. What is the "little ship" that is to be launched on "love's storm-tossed seas"? To what tradition of the sonnet form is this a reference?
4. Why does the poet conclude the poem with a description of a scene between Petrarch and Laura?

JOHN DRYDEN (1631–1700)

 ## To the Memory of Mr. Oldham° (1684)

Farewell, too little and too lately known,
Whom I began to think and call my own:
For sure our souls were near allied, and thine
Cast in the same poetic mold with mine.
5   One common note on either lyre did strike,
And knaves and fools we both abhorred alike.
To the same goal did both our studies drive;
The last set out the soonest did arrive.
Thus Nisus° fell upon the slipp'ry place,
10 While his young friend performed and won the race.
O early ripe! to thy abundant store
What could advancing age have added more?
It might (what nature never gives the young)
Have taught the numbers of thy native tongue.
15 But satire needs not those, and wit will shine
Through the harsh cadence of a rugged line;
A noble error, and but seldom made,
When poets are by too much force betrayed.
Thy gen'rous fruits, though gathered ere their prime,
20 Still showed a quickness; and maturing time
But mellows what we write to the dull sweets of rhyme.
Once more, hail and farewell;° farewell, thou young.
But ah too short, Marcellus° of our tongue;
Thy brows with ivy and with laurels° bound;
25 But fate and gloomy night encompass thee around.

°John Oldham (1653–1683) was a young poet whom Dryden admired. 9 *Nisus: a* character in Virgil's *Aeneid* who slipped in a pool of blood while running a race. thus allowing his best friend to win. 22 *hail and farewell:* an echo of the Latin phrase "ave atque vale"; see Catallus, *Odes,* 101.10. 23 *Marcellus:* a Roman general who was adopted by the Emperor Augustus as his successor but died at the age of twenty. 24 *laurels:* a plant sacred to Apollo, the Greek god of poetry; the traditional prize given to poets is a wreath of laurel.

QUESTIONS

1. What is the meter of this poem? Rhyme scheme? Closed form? How does the form control the tempo? Why is this tempo appropriate?
2. What does the speaker reveal about himself in lines 1–10? About Oldham? About his relationship with Oldham? What did the two have in common?
3. What is the effect of Dryden's frequent classical allusions? What pairs of rhyming words most effectively clinch ideas?

ROBERT FROST (1874–1963)

For a photo, see Chapter 21, page 1058.

Desert Places (1936)

Snow falling and night falling fast, oh, fast
In a field I looked into going past,

And the ground almost covered smooth in snow,
But a few weeds and stubble showing last.

The woods around it have it—it is theirs.   5
All animals are smothered in their lairs.
I am too absent-spirited to count;
The loneliness includes me unawares.

And lonely as it is that loneliness
Will be more lonely ere it will be less—   10
A blanker whiteness of benighted snow
With no expression, nothing to express.

They cannot scare me with their empty spaces
Between stars—on stars where no human race is.
I have it in me so much nearer home   15
To scare myself with my own desert places.

QUESTIONS

1. What is the meter? The rhyme scheme? The form?
2. What setting and situation are established in lines 1–4? What does the snow affect here? What does it affect in lines 5–8? In lines 9–12?
3. What different kinds of "desert places" is this poem about? Which kind is the most important? Most frightening?
4. How does the type of rhyme (rising or falling) change in the last stanza? How does this change affect the tone and impact of the poem?
5. How does the stanzaic pattern of this poem organize the progression of the speaker's thoughts, feelings, and conclusions?

ALLEN GINSBERG (1926–1997)

For a photo, see Chapter 13, page 699.

🍁 A Supermarket in California (1955)

What thoughts I have of you tonight, Walt Whitman,° for
I walked down the sidestreets under the trees with a headache
self-conscious looking at the full moon.
   In my hungry fatigue, and shopping for images, I went
into the neon fruit supermarket, dreaming of your   5
   enumerations!°
   What peaches and what penumbras! Whole families
shopping at night! Aisles full of husbands! Wives in the
avocados, babies in the tomatoes!—and you, Garcia Lorca,° what
were you doing down by the watermelons?   10
   I saw you, Walt Whitman, childless, lonely old grubber,
poking among the meats in the refrigerator and eyeing the grocery boys.

°1 *Walt Whitman:* American poet (1819–1892) who experimented with open forms and significantly influenced the development of twentieth-century poetry. 6 *enumerations:* Many of Whitman's poems contain long lists. 9 *Garcia Lorca:* Spanish surrealist poet and playwright (1896–1936) whose later poetry became progressively more like prose.

I heard you asking questions of each: Who killed the pork
chops? What price bananas? Are you my Angel?
15   I wandered in and out of the brilliant stacks of cans
following you, and followed in my imagination by the store detective.
    We strode down the open corridors together in our solitary
fancy tasting artichokes, possessing every frozen delicacy, and
never passing the cashier.

20   Where are we going, Walt Whitman? The doors close in
an hour. Which way does your beard point tonight?
    (I touch your book and dream of our odyssey in the supermarket
and feel absurd.)
    Will we walk all night through solitary streets? The trees
25 add shade to shade, lights out in the houses, we'll both be lonely.

    Will we stroll dreaming of the lost America of love past blue
automobiles in driveways, home to our silent cottage?
    Ah, dear father, graybeard, lonely old courage-teacher,
what America did you have when Charon° quit poling his ferry
30 and you got out on a smoking bank and stood watching the
boat disappear on the black waters of Lethe?°

°29 *Charon:* boatman in Greek mythology who ferried the souls of the dead across the river Styx into Hades, the underworld. 31 *Lethe:* the river of forgetfulness in Hades. The dead drank from this river and forgot their former lives.

QUESTIONS

1. Where is the speaker? What is he doing? What is his condition?
2. What effect is produced by placing Whitman and Lorca in the market?
3. To what extent do we find Whitman-like enumerations in this work? What is the effect of such enumerations?
4. Why is this a poem? What poetic devices are employed here? To what extent might it make more sense to consider this prose rather than poetry?

NIKKI GIOVANNI (b. 1943)

Nikki-Rosa (1968)

childhood remembrances are always a drag
if you're Black
you always remember things like living in Woodlawn°
with no inside toilet
5 and if you become famous or something
they never talk about how happy you were to have your mother
all to yourself and
how good the water felt when you got your bath from one of those
big tubs that folk in chicago barbecue in
10 and somehow when you talk about home
it never gets across how much you

°3 *Woodlawn:* a predominantly black suburb of Cincinnati, Ohio.

understood their feelings
as the whole family attended meetings about Hollydale
and even though you remember
your biographers never understand   15
your father's pain as he sells his stock
and another dream goes
and though you're poor it isn't poverty that
concerns you
and though they fought a lot   20
it isn't your father's drinking that makes any difference
but only that everybody is together and you
and your sister have happy birthdays and very good christmasses
and I really hope no white person ever has cause to write about me
because they never understand Black love is Black wealth and they'll   25
probably talk about my hard childhood and never understand that
all the while I was quite happy

QUESTIONS

1. To what extent do individual lines, caesurae, and cadences create a rhythm and reinforce the sense of this poem?
2. What points does the speaker make about childhood in general, the childhoods of
   blacks, and her own childhood?
3. What ideas about the ways in which whites understand or misunderstand blacks does
   this poem explore?

ROBERT HASS (b. 1941)

 ## Museum (1989)

On the morning of the Käthe Kollwitz° exhibit, a young man and woman come into the
museum restaurant. She is carrying a baby; he carries the air-freight edition of the Sunday
New York Times. She sits in a high-backed wicker chair, cradling the infant in her arms. He
fills a tray with fresh fruit, rolls, and coffee in white cups and brings it to the table. His hair
is tousled, her eyes are puffy. They look like they were thrown down into sleep and then   5
yanked out of it like divers coming up for air. He holds the baby. She drinks coffee, scans
the front page, butters a roll and eats it in their little corner in the sun. After a while, she
holds the baby. He reads the *Book Review* and eats some fruit. Then he holds the baby while
she finds the section of the paper she wants and eats fruit and smokes. They've hardly
exchanged a look. Meanwhile, I have fallen in love with this equitable arrangement, and   10
with the baby who cooperates by sleeping. All around them are faces Käthe Kollwitz
carved in wood of people with no talent or capacity for suffering who are suffering the
numbest kinds of pain: hunger, helpless terror. But this young couple is reading the Sunday
paper in the sun, the baby is sleeping, the green has begun to emerge from the rind of the
cantaloupe, and everything seems possible.

°1 *Käthe Kollwitz:* Kollwitz (1867–1945) was a German artist well known for her sculptures and engravings portraying the misery of poverty and war.

QUESTIONS

1. Does this poem contain material that you ordinarily think of as poetic? What seems "poetic"? "Unpoetic"? Why?
2. Why does Hass not present the poem in lines? On what principle (topical, grammatical) might you set it up in line form? How might its being in lines change the way you read it as well as see it?
3. How does the poem contrast the young couple and their baby with the art of Käthe Kollwitz?
4. In the light of this poem, how seriously should we take the final statement ("and everything seems possible")?

GEORGE HERBERT (1593–1633)

Virtue° (1633)

Sweet day, so cool, so calm, so bright,
The bridal of the earth and sky:
The dew shall weep thy fall tonight;
    For thou must die.

5 Sweet rose, whose hue, angry° and brave,°   *red; splendid*
Bids the rash° gazer wipe his eye:
Thy root is ever in its grave,
    And thou must die.

Sweet spring, full of sweet days and roses,
10 A box where sweets° compacted lie: *perfumes*
My music shows ye have your closes,°
    And all must die.

Only a sweet and virtuous soul,
Like seasoned timber, never gives;°
15 But though the whole world turn to coal,°
    Then chiefly lives.

°The title can allude to (a) divine Power operating both outside and inside an individual; (b) a characteristic quality or property; (c) conformity to divine and moral laws. 6 *rash:* eager or sympathetic. 11 *closes:* A *close* is the conclusion of a musical composition. 14 *never gives:* i.e., never gives in, never deteriorates and collapses (like rotted timber). 15 *turn to coal:* the burned-out residue of the earth after the universal fire on Judgment Day.

QUESTIONS

1. What is the rhyme scheme of this poem? The meter? The form?
2. What points does the speaker make about the day, the rose, spring, and the "sweet and virtuous soul"?

JOHN KEATS (1795–1821)

For a portrait, see Chapter 15, page 762.

 ## Ode to a Nightingale (1819)

1

My heart aches, and a drowsy numbness pains
   My sense, as though of hemlock° I had drunk,   *a poisonous herb*
Or emptied some dull opiate to the drains
   One minute past, and Lethe-wards° had sunk:
'Tis not through envy of thy happy lot,   5
   But being too happy in thine happiness,—
      That thou, light-winged Dryad° of the trees,
         In some melodious plot
      Of beechen green, and shadows numberless,
Singest of summer in full-throated ease.   10

2

O, for a draught of vintage! that hath been
   Cool'd a long age in the deep-delved earth,
Tasting of Flora° and the country green,
   Dance, and Provençal song, and sunburnt mirth!
O for a beaker full of the warm South,
   Full of the true, the blushful Hippocrene,°   15
      With beaded bubbles winking at the brim,
         And purple-stainèd mouth;
      That I might drink, and leave the world unseen,
And with thee fade away into the forest dim: 20

3

Fade far away, dissolve, and quite forget
   What thou among the leaves hast never known,
The weariness, the fever, and the fret
   Here, where men sit and hear each other groan;
Where palsy shakes a few, sad, last gray hairs,   25
   Where youth grows pale, and spectre-thin, and dies;
      Where but to think is to be full of sorrow
         And leaden-eyed despairs,
      Where Beauty cannot keep her lustrous eyes,
Or new Love pine at them beyond to-morrow.   30

°4 *Lethe-wards:* toward the river of forgetfulness in Hades, the underworld of Greek mythology. 7 *Dryad:* in Greek mythology, a semidivine tree spirit. 13 *Flora:* the Roman goddess of flowers. 16 *Hippocrene:* the fountain of the Muses on Mt. Helicon in Greek mytholoy; the phrase thus refers to both the waters of poetic inspiration and a cup of wine.

4

Away! away! for I will fly to thee,
   Not charioted by Bacchus° and his pards,°   *leopards*
But on the viewless wings of Poesy,°   *poetry*
   Though the dull brain perplexes and retards:
35 Already with thee! tender is the night,
      And haply the Queen-Moon is on her throne,
         Cluster'd around by all her starry Fays;°   *fairies*
            But here there is no light,
      Save what from heaven is with the breezes blown
40   Through verdurous glooms and winding mossy ways.

5

I cannot see what flowers are at my feet,
   Nor what soft incense hangs upon the boughs,
But, in embalmed° darkness, guess each sweet   *fragrant*
   Wherewith the seasonable month endows
45 The grass, the thicket, and the fruit-tree wild;
      White hawthorn, and the pastoral eglantine;°   *honeysuckle*
         Fast fading violets cover'd up in leaves;
            And mid-May's eldest child,
      The coming musk-rose, full of dewy wine,
50   The murmurous haunt of flies on summer eves.

6

Darkling° I listen; and, for many a time   *in the dark*
   I have been half in love with easeful Death,
Call'd him soft names in many a musèd rhyme,
   To take into the air my quiet breath;
55 Now more than ever seems it rich to die,
      To cease upon the midnight with no pain,
         While thou art pouring forth thy soul abroad
            In such an ecstasy!
      Still wouldst thou sing, and I have ears in vain—
60   To thy high requiem become a sod.

7

Thou wast not born for death, immortal Bird!
   No hungry generations tread thee down;
The voice I hear this passing night was heard
   In ancient days by emperor and clown:
65 Perhaps the self-same song that found a path

°32 *Bacchus:* the Greek god of wine. See Chapter 24.

Through the sad heart of Ruth,° when, sick for home,
  She stood in tears amid the alien corn;°   *wheat, grain*
    The same that oft-times hath
Charm'd magic casements, opening on the foam
  Of perilous seas, in faery lands forlorn.   70

8

Forlorn! the very word is like a bell
  To toll me back from thee to my sole self!
Adieu! the fancy° cannot cheat so well   *imagination*
  As she is fam'd to do, deceiving elf.
Adieu! adieu! thy plaintive anthem fades   75
  Past the near meadows, over the still stream,
    Up the hill-side; and now 'tis buried deep
      In the next valley-glades:
  Was it a vision, or a waking dream?
    Fled is that music:—Do I wake or sleep?   80

°66 *Ruth:* the widow of Boaz in the biblical Book of Ruth.

QUESTIONS

1. Formulate the structure (meter of each line and rhyme scheme) of the stanzas. What traditional form is employed here?
2. What is the speaker's mental and emotional state in stanza 1? What similes are employed to describe this condition?
3. What does the speaker want in stanza 2? Whom does he want to join? Why? From what aspects of the world (stanza 3) does he want to escape?
4. How do the speaker's mood and perspective change in stanza 4? How does he achieve this transition? What characterizes the world that the speaker enters in stanza 5? What senses are employed to describe this world?
5. What does the speaker establish about the nightingale's song in stanza 7? What does the song come to symbolize?

CLAUDE McKAY (1890–1948)

 ## In Bondage (1922)

I would be wandering in distant fields
Where man, and bird, and beast, live leisurely,
And the old earth is kind, and ever yields
Her goodly gifts to all her children free;
Where life is fairer, lighter, less demanding,   5
And boys and girls have time and space for play
Before they come to years of understanding—
Somewhere I would be singing, far away.
For life is greater than the thousand wars
Men wage for it in their insatiate lust,   10

And will remain like the eternal stars,
When all that shines to-day is drift and dust.

But I am bound with you in your mean graves,
O black men, simple slaves of ruthless slaves.

QUESTIONS

1. What is the meter of this poem? The rhyme scheme? The form? To what extent does the form organize the speaker's thoughts?
2. Lines 1–8 present a conditional (rather than actual) situation that the speaker desires. What word signals this nature? What is the speaker's wish?
3. What point does the speaker make about life in lines 9–12?
4. How does the couplet undermine the rest of the poem? What single word conveys this reversal? How effectively do the rhymes clinch the poem's meaning? What is the speaker telling us about the lives of African Americans?

JOHN MILTON (1608–1674)

 On His Blindness (When I Consider How My Light Is Spent)° (1655)

When I consider how my light is spent
  Ere half my days, in this dark world and wide,
  And that one talent° which is death to hide,
  Lodged with me useless, though my soul more bent
5 To serve therewith my Maker, and present
  My true account, lest he returning chide;
  "Doth God exact day-labor, light denied?"
  I fondly° ask; but Patience to prevent°   *foolishly; forestall*
That murmur, soon replies, "God doth not need
10   Either man's work or his own gifts; who best
  Bear his mild yoke, they serve him best. His state
Is kingly. Thousands at his bidding speed
  And post o'er land and ocean without rest;
  They also serve who only stand and wait."

°Milton began to go blind in the late 1640s and was completely blind by 1651. 3 *talent*: both a skill and a reference to the talents discussed in the parable in Matthew 25:14–30.

QUESTIONS

1. What is the meter of this poem? The rhyme scheme? The closed form?
2. To what extent do the two major divisions of this form organize the poem's ideas?
3. What problem is raised in the octave? What are the speaker's complaints? Who is the speaker in the sestet? How are the earlier conflicts resolved?
4. Explore the word *talent* and relate its various meanings to the poem as a whole.

DUDLEY RANDALL (1914–2000)

🍁 Ballad of Birmingham° (1966)

(On the bombing of a church in Birmingham, Alabama, 1963)

"Mother dear, may I go downtown
Instead of out to play,
And march the streets of Birmingham
In a Freedom March today?"

"No, baby, no, you may not go,   5
For the dogs are fierce and wild,
And clubs and hoses, guns and jails
Aren't good for a little child."

"But, mother, I won't be alone.
Other children will go with me,   10
And march the streets of Birmingham
To make our country free."

"No, baby, no, you may not go,
For I fear those guns will fire.
But you may go to church instead   15
And sing in the children's choir."

She has combed and brushed her night-dark hair,
And bathed rose petal sweet,
And drawn white gloves on her small brown hands,
And white shoes on her feet.   20

The mother smiled to know her child
Was in the sacred place,
But that smile was the last smile
To come upon her face.

For when she heard the explosion,   25
Her eyes grew wet and wild.
She raced through the streets of Birmingham
Calling for her child.

She clawed through bits of glass and brick,
Then lifted out a shoe   30
"Oh, here's the shoe my baby wore,
But, baby, where are you?"

°Four black children were killed when the 16th Street Baptist Church in Birmingham, Alabama, was bombed in 1963. A man was finally indicted for the murders in 1977 and convicted in 1982. There was an additional conviction in 2002.

QUESTIONS

1. Formulate the structure (meter, rhyme scheme, stanza form) of this poem. What traditional closed form is employed here?
2. Who is the speaker in stanzas 1 and 3? In stanzas 2 and 4? How are quotation and repetition employed to create tension?
3. What ironies do you find in the mother's assumptions? In the poem as a whole? In the society pictured in the poem?
4. Compare the poem to "Sir Patrick Spens" (p. 631). How are the structures of all three alike? To what extent do all three deal with the same type of subject matter?

THEODORE ROETHKE (1908–1963)

For a photo, see Chapter 12, page 676.

 ## The Waking (1953)

I wake to sleep, and take my waking slow.
I feel my fate in what I cannot fear.
I learn by going where I have to go.

We think by feeling. What is there to know?
5 I hear my being dance from ear to ear.
I wake to sleep, and take my waking slow.

Of those so close beside me, which are you?
God bless the Ground! I shall walk softly there,
And learn by going where I have to go.

10 Light takes the Tree; but who can tell us how?
The lowly worm climbs up a winding stair;
I wake to sleep, and take my waking slow.

Great Nature has another thing to do
To you and me; so take the lively air,
15 And, lovely, learn by going where to go.

This shaking keeps me steady. I should know.
What falls away is always. And is near.
I wake to sleep, and take my waking slow.
I learn by going where I have to go.

QUESTIONS

1. Compare the form of this poem with the poems by Bishop and Thomas in this chapter.
2. In what way or ways does the speaker "wake to sleep"? What other apparent contradictions does the speaker develop in this poem? Why might a reader conclude that the poem is positive rather than negative?
3. What does the speaker mean by saying that he learns "by going where I have to go"? In what way does "always" fall away (line 17)?

GEORGE WILLIAM RUSSELL ("Æ") (1867–1935)

 ## Continuity (1897)

No sign is made while empires pass.
The flowers and stars are still His care.
The constellations hid in grass,
The golden miracles in air.

Life in an instant will be rent   5
Where death is glittering blind and wild—
The Heavenly Brooding is intent
To that last instant on Its child.

It breathes the glow in brain and heart,
Life is made magical. Until   10
Body and spirit are apart
The Everlasting works Its will.

In that wild orchid that your feet
In their next falling shall destroy,
Minute and passionate and sweet   15
The Mighty Master holds His joy.

Though the crushed jewels droop and fade
The artist's labors will not cease,
And of the ruins shall be made
Some yet more lovely masterpiece.   20

QUESTIONS

1. Describe the form of this poem, including the number of stanzas, the regularity of the meter, and the variations that you find.
2. What is the nature of the topic matter of this poem? Is it more appropriate for a song or for a hymn? Would you consider the poem personal, or public?
3. What is the conceptualization of "The Mighty Master" in this poem? In particular, consider the ideas in lines 2, 12, 16, and 18.
4. Compare this poem with Hardy's "In Time of 'The Breaking of Nations'" (Chapter 19). What comparable ideas do you find in the two poems? What differing ideas?

PERCY BYSSHE SHELLEY (1792–1822)

Ozymandias (1818)

I met a traveller from an antique land,
Who said—"Two vast and trunkless legs of stone
Stand in the desert. . . . Near them, on the sand,
Half sunk, a shattered visage lies, whose frown,
And wrinkled lip, and sneer of cold command,   5

Tell that its sculptor well those passions read
Which yet survive, stamped on these lifeless things,
The hand that mocked them, and the heart that fed;
And on the pedestal, these words appear;
10   'My name is Ozymandias, King of Kings,
Look on my Works, ye Mighty, and despair!'
Nothing beside remains. Round the decay
Of that colossal Wreck, boundless and bare
The lone and level sands stretch far away."

QUESTIONS

1. What is the meter of this poem? The rhyme scheme? What traditional closed form is modified here? How do the modifications affect the poem?
2. To what extent are content and meaning shaped by the closed form? What is described in the octave? In the sestet?
3. Characterize Ozymandias (thought to be Ramses II, pharaoh of Egypt, who died in 1225 BCE) from the way he is portrayed in this poem.

DYLAN THOMAS (1914–1953)

 ## Do Not Go Gentle into That Good Night (1951)

Do not go gentle into that good night,
Old age should burn and rave at close of day;
Rage, rage against the dying of the light.

Though wise men at their end know dark is right,
5   Because their words had forked no lightning they
Do not go gentle into that good night.

Good men, the last wave by, crying how bright
Their frail deeds might have danced in a green bay,
Rage, rage against the dying of the light.

10   Wild men who caught and sang the sun in flight,
And learn, too late, they grieved it on its way,
Do not go gentle into that good night.

Grave men, near death, who see with blinding sight
Blind eyes could blaze like meteors and be gay,
15   Rage, rage against the dying of the light.

And you, my father, there on the sad height,
Curse, bless, me now with your fierce tears, I pray.
Do not go gentle into that good night.
Rage, rage against the dying of the light.

QUESTIONS

1. What conclusions do you make about the poem's speaker, listener, and situation?
2. What connotative words do you find here? Consider "dying," the "good" of "good night," "gentle," "Curse, bless, me now with your fierce tears, I pray," and "grave."
3. What five different kinds of men does the speaker discuss in stanzas 2–5? What do they have in common? Of what value are they to the speaker's father (line 16)?
4. Compare the form of this poem with the poems by Bishop and Roethke in this chapter.

JEAN TOOMER (1894–1967)

 ## Reapers (1923)

Black reapers with the sound of steel on stones
Are sharpening scythes. I see them place the hones
In their hip-pockets as a thing that's done,
And start their silent swinging, one by one.
Black horses drive a mower through the weeds,   5
And there, a field rat, startled, squealing bleeds,
His belly close to ground. I see the blade,
Blood-stained, continue cutting weeds and shade.

QUESTIONS

1. What is the poem's meter? The rhyme scheme? The form? What is the difference between Toomer's use of the form and Dryden's?
2. How do the images of this poem relate to each other? How does the image of the bleeding field rat and the "blood-stained" blade heighten the impact?
3. How does alliteration unify this poem and make sound echo sense? Note especially the *s* and *b* sounds and the phrase "silent swinging."

PHYLLIS WEBB (b. 1927)

 ## Poetics Against the Angel of Death° (1962)

I am sorry to speak of death again
(some say I'll have a long life)
but last night Wordsworth's 'Prelude' °
suddenly made sense—I mean the measure,
the elevated tone, the attitude   5
of private Man speaking to public men.
Last night I thought I would not wake again
but now with this June morning I run ragged to elude
the Great Iambic Pentameter
who is the Hound of Heaven° in our stress   10

°See Byron's "The Destruction of Sennacherib," stanza 3 (Chapter 22). 3 *Wordsworth's 'Prelude'*: See this chapter, page 898. 10 *Hound of Heaven (The)*: a long poem (1893) by Francis Thompson (1859–1907) about attempting to evade God's love.

because I want to die
writing Haiku
or, better,
long lines, clean and syllabic as knotted bamboo. Yes!

QUESTIONS

1. In the poem itself, what is meant by the "Angel of Death"?
2. What attitude does the speaker express about iambic pentameter? How does the speaker explain this attitude? How defensible is the attitude?
3. For what poetic forms does the speaker express a preference? Why? How does the form of this poem bear out the preference?

WILLIAM CARLOS WILLIAMS (1883–1963)

 The Dance (1944)

In Brueghel's° great picture, The Kermess,
the dancers go round, they go round and
around, the squeal and the blare and the
tweedle of bagpipes, a bugle and fiddles
5 tipping their bellies (round as the thick-sided
glasses whose wash they impound)
their hips and their bellies off balance
to turn them. Kicking and rolling about
the Fair Grounds, swinging their butts, those
10 shanks must be sound to bear up under such
rollicking measures, prance as the dance
in Brueghel's great picture, The Kermess.

°1 *Brueghel's:* Pieter Brueghel (c. 1525–1569), a Flemish painter. *Peasants' Dance (The Kermess)* shows peasants dancing in celebration of the anniversary of the founding of a church *(church mass)*. See page 1–8.

QUESTIONS

1. What effect is produced by repeating the first line as the last line?
2. How do repetition, alliteration, assonance, onomatopoeia, and internal rhyme affect the tempo, feeling, and meaning of the poem? How do the numerous participles (like "tipping," "kicking," "rolling") make sound echo sense?
3. What words are capitalized? What effect is produced by omitting the capital letters at the beginning of each line? How does this typographical choice reinforce the sound and the sense of the poem?
4. Most of the lines of this poem are run-on rather than end-stopped, and many of them end with fairly weak words such as *and, the, about,* and *such.* What effect is produced through these techniques?
5. How successful is Williams in making the words and sentence rhythms echo the visual rhythms in Brueghel's painting? Why is this open form more appropriate to the images of the poem than any closed form could be?

WRITING ABOUT FORM IN POETRY

An essay about form in poetry should demonstrate a relationship between a poem's sense and its form. Do not discuss form or shape in isolation, for such an essay would be no more than a detailed description. The first thing to do as you go about determining what you want to say is to examine the poem's main ideas. Consider the various elements that contribute to the poem's impact and effectiveness: the speaker, listener, setting, situation, diction, imagery, and rhetorical devices. Once you understand these, it will be easier to establish a connection between form and content.

You will find it helpful to prepare a work sheet that highlights the elements you are deciding that you wish to discuss. For closed forms, these elements will be rhyme scheme, meter, line lengths, and stanzaic patterns. They may also include significant words and phrases that connect stanzas. The work sheet for an open-form poem should indicate variables such as rhythm and phrases; the use of pauses; significant words that are isolated or emphasized through typography; patterns of repeated sounds, words, phrases, and images; and, if relevant, the relationship the poem's content and any special visual effects.

Questions for Discovering Ideas

CLOSED FORM

- What is the principal meter? Line length? Rhyme scheme? To what extent do these establish and/or reinforce the form?
- What is the form of each stanza or unit? How many stanzas or divisions does the poem contain? How does the poem establish a pattern? How does the pattern control the poem's developing content?
- What is the form of the poem (e.g., couplet, tercet, ballad, villanelle, sonnet)? In what ways is the poem traditional, and what variations does it introduce? What is the effect of the variations?
- How effectively does the structure create or reinforce the poem's internal logic? What topical, logical, or thematic progressions unite the various parts of the poem?
- To what extent does the form organize the images of the poem? How does the poet develop images within single units or stanzas? Do images recur in more than one section? What is the purpose and effect of this recurrence?
- To what extent does the form organize and bring out the poem's ideas or emotions?

OPEN FORM

- What does the poem look like on the page? What is the relationship of its shape to its meaning?
- How does the poet use variable line lengths, spaces, punctuation, capitalization, and the like to shape the poem? How do these variables contribute to the poem's sense and impact?
- What rhythms are built into the poem through language or typography? How are these relevant to the poem's content?

- What is the poem's progression of ideas, images, and/or emotions? How is the logic created and what does it contribute?
- How does form or typography isolate or unite, and thus emphasize, various words and phrases? What is the effect of such emphasis?
- What patterns do you discover of words and sounds? To what degree do the patterns create order and structure? How are they related to the sense of the poem?

Strategies for Organizing Ideas

In developing your central idea, you should illustrate the connections between form and meaning. For example, in planning an essay on Randall's "Ballad of Birmingham" you might develop your ideas according to the speeches that are a normal feature of the ballad form. The poem's first part is a dialogue between mother and child about the hazard of the local streets and the safety of the local church. In the second part, after the explosion, the mother runs toward the church and calls for her child, who, ironically, will never again engage with her in further dialogue. Another plan is needed for an essay on Williams's "The Dance"; such a plan might link the lively, bustling movement of the dancers pictured in Brueghel's painting "Peasants' Dance" (p. I–8) to the rhythms, repetitions, and run-on lines of the poem. Still another plan would be needed for a discussion of Heyen's "Mantle," the form of which requires enough stanzas of approximately equal length to make up the pattern of a pitched ball. (What is this pattern?)

Your introduction should contain general remarks about the poem, but it should, above that, focus on the connection between form and substance. Describe the ways in which structure and content interact together, with a brief listing of your specific topics.

Early in the body, describe the formal characteristics of your poem, using schemes and numbers (as in paragraph 2 of the illustrative student essay). With closed forms, your description should detail such standard features as the traditional form, meter, rhyme scheme, stanzaic structure, and number of stanzas. With open-form poetry, you should focus on the most striking and significant features of the verse (as in the brief discussion of Whitman's "Reconciliation" on pp. 906–07).

Be sure to integrate your discussion of both form and content. It may be that you have uncovered a good deal of information about technical features such as alliteration or rhyme, or you may wish to stress that words, phrases, and clauses develop a pattern of ideas. Remember that you are not making a paraphrase or a general explication, but instead are showing how the poet uses form—either an open or a closed one—in the service of meaning. The order in which you deal with your topics is entirely up to you.

The conclusion of your essay might contain additional relevant observations about shape or structure. It might also summarize your argument. Here, as in all essays about literature, make sure to reach an actual conclusion rather than simply a stopping point.

Illustrative Student Essay

Underlined sentences in this paper *do not* conform to MLA style and are used solely as teaching tools to emphasize the central idea, thesis sentence, and topic sentences throughout the paper.

Adams 1

Kimberly Adams

Professor Patter

English 102

20 February 2008

Form and Meaning in George Herbert's "Virtue"°

Herbert's devotional four-stanza poem "Virtue" (1633) contrasts the   [1]
mortality of worldly things with the immortality of the "virtuous soul." This is
not an uncommon topic in religious poetry and hymns, and there is nothing
unusual about this contrast. What is unusual, however, is the simplicity and
directness of Herbert's expressions and the way in which he integrates his ideas
within his stanzaic song pattern. Each part of the poem organizes the images
logically and underscores the supremacy of life over death.* Through control
over line and stanza groupings, rhyme scheme, and repeated sounds and words,
Herbert's stanzas create a structural and visual distinction between the "sweet"
soul and the rest of creation.†

Herbert's control over lines within the stanzas is particularly strong. Each   [2]
stanza follows the same *abab* rhyme scheme. Because some rhyme sounds and
words are repeated throughout the first three stanzas, however, the structure of
the poem can be formulated as 4a4b4a2b 4c4b4c2b 4d4b4d2b 4e4f4e2f. Each
stanza thus contains three lines of iambic tetrameter with a final line of iambic
dimeter--an unusual pattern that creates a unique emphasis. In the first three
stanzas, the dimeter lines repeat the phrase "must die," while in the last
stanza the contrast is made on the words "Then chiefly lives." These rhythms

°This poem appears on page 922.
*Central idea.
†Thesis sentence.

Adams 2

require a sensitive reading, and they powerfully underscore Herbert's idea that death is conquered by eternal life.

[3]   Like individual lines, Herbert's stanzaic structure provides the poem's pattern of organization and logic. The first stanza focuses on the image of the "Sweet day," comparing the day to "The bridal of the earth and sky" (line 2) and asserting that the day inevitably "must die." Similarly, the second stanza focuses on the image of a "Sweet rose" and asserts that it too "must die." The third stanza shifts to the image of "Sweet spring." Here the poet blends the images of the first two stanzas into the third by noting that the "Sweet spring" is "full of sweet days and roses" (line 9). The stanza concludes with the summarizing claim that "all must die." In this way, the third stanza is the climax of Herbert's imagery of beauty and mortality. The last stanza introduces a new image--"a sweet and virtuous soul"-- and an assertion that is contrasted with the ideas expressed in the previous three stanzas. Although the day, the rose, and the spring "must die," the soul "never" deteriorates, but "chiefly lives" even "though the whole world turn to coal" (line 15). With its key image of the "virtuous soul," this last stanza marks the logical conclusion of Herbert's argument. His pattern of organization allows this key image of permanence to be separated structurally from the images of impermanence.

[4]   This structural organization of images and ideas is repeated and reinforced by other techniques. Herbert's rhyme scheme, for example, links the first three stanzas while isolating the fourth. That the b rhyme is repeated at the ends of the second and fourth lines of each of the first three stanzas makes these stanzas into a complete unit. The fourth stanza, however is different in both content and rhyme. The stanza introduces the concept of immortality, and it also introduces entirely new rhymes, replacing the b rhyme with an f rhyme. Thus the rhyme scheme, by sound alone, parallels the poem's imagery and logic.

[5]   As a complement to the rhyming sounds, the poem also demonstrates organizing patterns of assonance. Most notable is the oo sound, which is repeated throughout the first three stanzas in the words "cool," "dew," "whose,"

Adams 3

"hue," "root," and "music." The oo sound might also have still been prominent in the word "thou," so that in the first three stanzas the oo, which is suggestive of a moan (certainly appropriate to things that die), is repeated eight times. In the last stanza there is a stress on the o sound, in "only," "soul," "though," "whole," and "coal." While oh may also be a moan, in this context it is more like an exclamation, in keeping with the triumph contained in the final line.

Herbert's repetition of key words and phrases also distinguishes the first three stanzas from the last stanza. Each of the first three stanzas begins with "sweet" and ends with "must die." These repetitions stress both the beauty and the mortality of worldly things. In the last stanza, however, this repetition is abandoned, just as the stress on immortality transcends mortality. The "Sweet" that begins each of the first three stanzas is replaced by "Only" (line 13). Similarly, "must die" is replaced with "chiefly lives." Both substitutions separate this final stanza from the three previous stanzas. More importantly, the shift in the verbal pattern emphasizes the transition from death to the virtuous soul's immortality. **[6]**

The lyric form of Herbert's "Virtue" provides an organizational pattern for the poem's images and ideas. At the same time, the stanzaic pattern and the rhyme scheme allow the poet to draw a strong distinction between the corruptible world and the immortal soul. The closed form of this poem is not arbitrary or incidental; it is an integral way of asserting the importance of the key image--the "sweet and virtuous soul." **[7]**

Adams 4

Work Cited

Herbert, George. "Virtue." Literature: An Introduction to Reading and Writing. Ed. Edgar V. Roberts. 9th ed. New York: Pearson Longman, 2009. 922.

Commentary on the Essay

The introductory paragraph establishes the groundwork of the essay—the treatment of form in relationship to content. The main idea is that each part of the poem represents a complete blending of image, logic, and meaning.

Paragraph 2, the first in the body, demonstrates how the poem's schematic formulation is integrated into Herbert's contrast of death and life. In this respect the paragraph demonstrates how a formal enumeration can be integrated within an essay's thematic development.

The focus of paragraph 3 is the organization of both images and ideas from stanza to stanza. Paragraph 4 begins with a transitional sentence that repeats part of the essay's central idea and, at the same time, connects it to paragraph 3. In the same way, paragraph 4 is closely tied to both paragraphs 1 and 3. The main topic here, the rhyme scheme of "Virtue," is introduced in the second sentence. This paragraph asserts that rhythm also reinforces the division between mortality and immortality. On much the same topic, paragraph 5 introduces Herbert's use of assonance, which can be seen as integral in the poem's blending of form and content.

Paragraph 6 takes up the last structural element described in the introduction—repeated key words and phrases. The idea is that these repetitions emphasize the distinction in the poem between mortality and immortality.

Paragraph 7, the conclusion, provides a brief overview and summation of the essay's argument. In addition, it concludes that form in "Virtue" is neither arbitrary nor incidental but rather an integral part of the poem's meaning.

Writing Topics About Poetic Form

1. Describe the use of the ode form as exemplified by Shelley's "Ode to the West Wind" (Chapter 17) and Keats's "Ode to a Nightingale" (this chapter). What patterns of regularity do you find? What differences do you find in the form and content of the poems? How do you account for these differences?

2. How do Cummings, Dryden, Randall, and Thomas use different forms to consider the subject of death (in "Buffalo Bill's Defunct," "To the Memory of Mr. Oldham," "Ballad of Birmingham," and "Do Not Go Gentle into That Good Night")? What differences in form and treatment do you find? What similarities do you find, despite these differences?

3. Consider the structural arrangement and shaping of the following works: Brueghel's painting *Peasants' Dance* (I–8), Hass's "Museum," Heyen's "Mantle," Hollander's "Swan and Shadow," Charles Harper Webb's "The Shape of History," and Williams's "The Dance." How do painter and poets utilize topic, arrangement, shape, and space to draw attention to their main ideas? How do the shaped and prose poems (Hass, Heyen, Hollander, and Webb) blend poetic and artistic techniques?

4. Compare and contrast the use of the villanelle by Bishop ("One Art"), Roethke ("The Waking"), and Thomas ("Do Not Go Gentle into That Good Night"). What topics do the poets develop? Why do the poets choose the

villanelle as their poetic form? What lines do they repeat? What is the effect of this repetition?

5. Compare the sonnets in this chapter by McKay, Shelley, Milton, and Collins. In what ways are the poetic forms of these poets similar? Different? How may Collins's poem be read as a commentary on the sonnet forms of the other poets?

6. Write a visual poem, and explain the principles on which you develop your lines. Here are some possible topics (just to get you started): a telephone, a cat, a dog, a car, a football, a snow shovel, a giraffe. After finishing your poem, write a short essay that considers the following and other questions: What are the strengths and limitations of the visual form, according to your experience? How does the form help make your poem serious or comic? How does it encourage creative language and original development of ideas?

7. Write a haiku. Be sure to fit your poem to the 5–7–5 pattern of syllables. What challenges and problems do you encounter in this form? Once you have completed your haiku (which, to be traditional, should be on a topic concerned with nature), try to cut the number of syllables to 4–5–4. Explain how you establish the first haiku pattern, and also explain how you go about cutting the total number of syllables. Be sure to explain what kinds of words you use (length, choice of diction, etc.).

8. Using an online reference system or regular card catalog, depending on availability in your college library, look up one of the following topics: "ballads, England," "concrete poetry," or "blank verse." How many references are included under these listings? What sorts of topics are included under the basic topic?

Chapter 19

Symbolism and Allusion: Windows to Wide Expanses of Meaning

Symbolism refers to the use of symbols in works of art and in all other forms of expression. As we note in Chapter 7, a **symbol** has meaning in and of itself, but it is also understood to represent something else, like the flag for the country or the school song for the school. Symbols occur in stories as well as in poems, but poetry relies more heavily on symbols because it is more concise and because it comprises more forms than fiction, which is restricted to narratives.

Most of the words we use every day are symbols, for they stand for various objects without actually being those objects. When we say *horse*, for example, or *tree*, or *run*, these words are symbols of horses and trees and people running. They direct our minds to real horses, real trees, and real actions in the real world that we have seen and can therefore easily imagine. In literature, however, symbolism implies a special relationship that expands our ordinary understanding of words, descriptions, and arguments.

Symbolism and Meanings

Symbolism goes beyond the close referral of word to thing; it is more like a window through which one can glimpse the extensive world outside. Because poetry is compact, its descriptions and portrayals of experience are brief. Symbolism is therefore one of its primary characteristics. It is a shorthand way of referring to extensive ideas or attitudes that otherwise would be inappropriate to include in the brief format of a poem. Thus Philip Larkin, in "Next, Please," uses the word "armada" as a symbol that is both apt and original (p. 966). His thought is that we do not find fulfillment in the present, but rather we look to the symbolic "armada of promises" and expectations that we constantly and habitually dream about for a better future. Like the Spanish Armada that attempted to overthrow the English government in 1588, Larkin's armada seems tiny and far removed from present reality, but as a symbol it suggests that human beings neglect the opportunities they have at the moment in favor of fixing their hopes on the promise of better things to happen—things that are defeated or that never even materialize. This idea could easily be developed through many more observations about the futility of unreal hope, but Larkin is more concerned to symbolize the idea than to amplify it.

Symbolism Extends Meaning Beyond Normal Connotation

The use of symbols is a way of moving outward, a means of extending and crystallizing information and ideas. For example, at the time of William Blake

(1757–1827), the word *tiger* meant both a large, wild cat and also the specific animal we know today as a tiger. The word's connotation therefore links it with wildness and predation. As a symbol in "The Tyger" (Chapter 15), however, Blake uses the animal as a stand-in for what he considers cosmic negativism—the savage, wild forces that undermine the progress of civilization. Thus the tiger as a symbol is more meaningful than either the denotation or the connotation of the word would indicate. A visual comparison can be made with Francisco Goya's painting "The Colossus" (I–13), in which the giant pugilistic figure above the tiny figures in the landscape represents the combination of anger, defiance, and ruthlessness that is unleashed and unchecked during times of war.[1]

Cultural or Universal Symbols Are Widely Recognized

Many symbols, wherever they are used, possess a ready-made, clearly agreed upon meaning. These are **cultural** or **universal symbols** (also discussed in Chapter 7). Many such symbols, like the tiger, are taken directly from nature. Other natural universal symbols are springtime and morning, which signify beginnings, growth, hope, optimism, and love. If such symbols were to be introduced into a poem about the suddenness and irrevocability of death, however, they would be ironic, for their presence would emphasize the contrast between death and life.

Cultural symbols are drawn from history and custom, such as the many Judeo-Christian religious symbols that appear in poetry. References to the lamb, Eden, Egyptian bondage, shepherds, exile, the Temple, blood, water, bread, the cross, and wine—all Jewish and/or Christian symbols—occur over and over again. Sometimes these symbols are prominent in a purely devotional context. In other contexts, however, they may be contrasted with symbols of warfare and corruption to show how extensively people neglect their moral and religious obligations.

Contextual, Private, or Authorial Symbols Are Operative as Symbols Only Within Individual Works

Symbols that are not widely or universally recognized are termed **contextual, private,** or **authorial symbols** (also discussed in Chapter 7). Some of these have a natural relationship with the objects and ideas being symbolized. Let us consider snow, which is cold and white and covers everything when it falls. A poet can exploit this quality and make snow a symbol. At the beginning of the long poem "The Waste Land," T. S. Eliot does exactly that; he refers to snow as a symbol of retreat from life, a withdrawal into an intellectual and moral hibernation. Another poem symbolizing snow is the following one. Here the poet refers to snow as both a literal and figurative link between the living and the dead.

---

[1]The attribution of "The Colossus" to Goya has recently been questioned.

VIRGINIA SCOTT (b. 1938)

 ### Snow (1977)

A doe stands at the roadside,
spirit of those who have lived here
and passed known through our memory.
The doe stands at the edge of the icy road,
5   then darts back into the woods.

Snow falling,
mother-spirit hovering,
white on the drops in the road and fields,
light from the windows
10   of the old house
brightening the snow.

Presences: mother,
grandmother,
here in their place
15   at the foot of *ben lomond*,°   *A Canadian mountain*
green trees black in the hemlock night.

The doe stands at the edge of the icy road,
then darts back into the woods.

Golden Grove, New Brunswick, Canada
January 5, 1977

QUESTIONS

1. How is snow described in the poem? How and where is it seen? As a symbol, what does it signify in relationship to the doe, the memory of other people, the mother-spirit, the old house, the light, the presences, the mountains, and the trees?
2. Explain the structural purpose for which the doe is mentioned three times in the poem, with lines 17 and 18 repeating 4 and 5. As a symbol, what do you think the doe signifies?
3. What are the relationships described in the poem between memory of the past and existence in the present? What does the symbolism contribute to your understanding of these relationships?

This poem describes a real circumstance at a real place at a real time; the poet has even provided an actual location and date, just as we do when writing a letter. We can therefore presume that the snow is real snow, falling in the evening just as lights go on in the nearby houses. This detail by itself would be sufficient as a realistic image, but as Scott develops the poem, the snow symbolizes the link between the speaker's memory of the past and perception of the present. The reality of the moment is suffused with the memory of the people—"mother, / grandmother"—who "lived here." The poet is meditating on the idea that individuals, though they may often be by themselves, like the speaker, are never alone as long as they have a vivid memory of the past. Symbolically, the past and present are always connected, just as the snow covers the scene.

At the poem's conclusion, the doe darting into the woods suggests a linking of present and future (i.e., as long as there are woods, does will dart into them). Both the snow and the deer are private and contextual symbols, for they are established and developed within the poem, and they do not have the same symbolic value elsewhere. Through the symbolism, therefore, the poet has converted a private moment into an idea of general significance.

Similarly, references to other ordinary materials may be symbolic if the poet emphasizes them sufficiently, as in Keats's "La Belle Dame Sans Merci," which opens and closes with the image of withered sedge, or grass. What might seem like nothing more than a natural detail becomes additionally important because it can be understood to symbolize the loss and bewilderment felt by people when loved ones seem to be faithless and destructive rather than loyal and supportive.

The meanings of symbols may be placed on a continuum of qualities from good to bad, high to low, favorable to unfavorable. For example, the sea-washed shore in Clampitt's "Beach Glass" (this chapter) is on the positive end, symbolizing the regular and eternal relationship of ocean and land. Cummings's old balloonman of "in Just-" (Chapter 20) is on the positive end, symbolizing the irresistible call of growth and sexuality. Outright horror is suggested by the symbol of the rough beast slouching toward Bethlehem in Yeats's "The Second Coming" (this chapter). Although this mythical beast shares the same traditional birthplace with Jesus, the commonality is ironic because the beast represents the extremes of anger, hatred, and brutality that in Yeats's judgment were dominant in modern national politics.

The Function of Symbolism in Poetry

Poets do not simply jam symbols into a poem artificially and arbitrarily. Rather, symbols are structurally important and meaningful first, and are secondarily symbolic. We therefore find symbols in single words, and also in actions, scenes and settings, characters and characterizations, and various situations.

Many Words are Automatically Symbolic

With general and universal symbols, a single word is often sufficient, as with references to the lamb, shepherd, cross, blood, bread, and wine; or to summer and winter; or to drought and flood, morning and night, heat and shade, storm and calm, or feast and famine. One of the most famous of all birds, the nightingale, is an example of a single word being instantly symbolic. Because of this bird's beautiful song, it symbolizes natural, unspoiled beauty as contrasted with the contrived attempts by human beings to create beauty. Keats refers to the bird in this way in his "Ode to a Nightingale" (Chapter 18), and his speaker compares human mortality with the virtually eternal beauty of this singer.

Another symbolic bird is the goose. Because migratory Canada geese fly south in the fall, they symbolize the loss of summer abundance, seasonal change, alteration, and loss, with accompanying feelings of regret and sorrow. Because they return north in the spring, however, they also symbolize regeneration, newness, anticipation, and hope. These contrasting symbolic values are important in Jorie Graham's "The Geese" and Mary Oliver's "Wild Geese." Graham emphasizes that the geese are "crossing" overhead but nevertheless that human affairs of "the everyday" continue despite the changes symbolized by the geese. In contrast, Oliver emphasizes geese as symbols of renewal, for the geese returning in spring suggest that "the world offers itself to your imagination."

Symbolism Is to Be Seen in Actions

Not only words but also actions may be presented as symbols. In Scott's "Snow," as we have just observed, the doe darting into the darkening woods symbolizes renewal and the mystery of life. In Hardy's "In Time of 'The Breaking of Nations,'" the action of the man plowing a field symbolizes the continued life and vitality of the folk, the people, despite the political wrangling and endless brutality that are constantly occurring in the world.

Symbolism Is to Be Seen in Settings and Scenes

While settings and scenes may be no more than just that—settings and scenes—the poet may develop them as symbols. We may note a symbolic setting in Wilbur's "Year's End." Wilbur draws our attention to a little dog, curled up as if sleeping, and its (presumable) owners, all of whom were killed by falling lava when the eruption of Mount Vesuvius destroyed Pompeii, the ancient Roman town in southern Italy, in 79 CE. In the poem's context, this scene symbolizes the incompleteness of human achievements, a condition not only of present life but also of ancient life. Keats, in "La Belle Dame Sans Merci," introduces the "elfin grot" (grotto) of the "lady in the meads." This grotto is an unreal, magical, womblike location symbolizing both the allure and the disappointment that on occasions characterize sexual attraction.

Symbolism Is to Be Seen in Characters

Poets also devise characters or people as symbols of ideas or values, like the speaker in Herbert's "The Collar" (this chapter). This speaker describes his fierce reluctance against committing himself to God's service, but his anger vanishes when he thinks he hears a soothingly divine voice calling "Child." In this way he himself becomes a symbol of devoted obedience. In Keats's "La Belle Dame Sans Merci" (this chapter), the "fairy's child" is a symbol of the mystery of love. The figures in Hardy's "In Time of 'The Breaking of Nations'" (this chapter) symbolize the power of average, ordinary people to endure even "Though Dynasties pass."

Symbolism Is to Be Seen in Situations

A poem's situations, circumstances, and conditions may also be symbolic. The position of the young gunner in the World War II bomber, six miles above the earth in Jarrell's "The Death of the Ball Turret Gunner" (Chapter 11), makes him vulnerable and helpless, and his death symbolizes the condition of humankind in the modern age of fear and anxiety, when life is threatened by global war and technologically expert destructiveness. In "she being Brand / -new" (Chapter 16), Cummings cleverly uses the situation of the speaker's breaking in a new automobile as the symbol of another kind of encounter involving the speaker.

Allusions and Meaning

Just as symbolism enriches meaning, so also does **allusion** (see also Chapter 7), that take the form of (1) unacknowledged brief quotations from other works and (2) references to historical events and any aspect of human culture—art, music, literature, and so on. The use of allusions is a means of connecting new literary works with the broader cultural tradition of which the works are a part. In addition, allusions presuppose a common bond of knowledge between the poet and the reader. On the one hand, poets making allusions compliment the past, and on the other, they salute readers able to discover how the meanings of the allusions are transformed in the new context.

Allusions Add Dimension to Poetry

An allusion carries with it the entire context of the work from which it is drawn. Perhaps the richest sources of references and stories are the King James Bible and the plays of Shakespeare. Keats introduces a biblical allusion in "Ode to a Nightingale" (Chapter 18), where he refers to the story of Ruth, who was "sick for home" while standing "in tears amid the alien corn." This allusion is particularly rich, because Ruth became the mother of Jesse. According to the Gospel of Matthew, it was from the line of Jesse that King David was born, and it was from the house of David that Jesus was born. Thus Keats's nightingale is not only a symbol of natural beauty, but through the biblical allusion it symbolizes regeneration and redemption, much in keeping with Keats's assertion that the bird is "not born for death." In Yeats's "The Second Coming," we encounter an allusion to Shakespeare's *Macbeth*. Yeats uses the phrase "blood-dimmed tide," which refers to Macbeth's soliloquy in the second act of *Macbeth*. In the play, after murdering Duncan, Macbeth asks if there is enough water in Neptune's ocean to wash the blood from his hands. His immediate, guilt-ridden response is that Duncan's blood will instead turn the green water to red (2.2.63–66). This image of crime being bloody enough to stain the ocean's water is thus the allusive context of Yeats's "blood-dimmed tide."

Once works become well known, as with the Bible and the plays of Shakespeare, they may in turn become a source of allusions for subsequent writers. Such a well-known work is Frost's "Stopping by Woods on a Snowy Evening" (Chapter 11), which contains an oft-quoted last line: "And miles to go before I sleep." This line is so universally recognized that it is now considered as a symbol of the need to complete tasks and fulfill obligations.

Allusions may be discovered in no more than a single word or phrase in a poem, provided that the expression is unusual enough or associative enough to bear the weight of the reference. Scott's "Snow," for example, speaks of "green trees black in the hemlock night." Of course, the word *hemlock* refers to a common evergreen tree observed by the speaker, but a distillation of hemlock was also the poison drunk by Socrates when the ancient Athenians executed him, as described in Plato's *Phaedo*.[2] Because of this association, any use of the word *hemlock* can be construed as

---

[2]See Jacques-Louis David's painting, *The Death of Socrates* (I–10).

an allusion to the death of Socrates and the abuse of legal authority. Another allusion to hemlock occurs in the beginning lines of "Ode to a Nightingale" (Chapter 18), in which Keats refers to hemlock. His speaker declares that a "drowsy numbness" has overtaken him "as though of hemlock . . . [he] had drunk." As the poem continues, we realize that Keats's allusion refers to the way in which death might open a new plane of existence for the speaker—a life of immortal beauty. Thus Keats builds the single-word allusion into new speculation about the possible nature of life and death.

Phrases, descriptions, and situations may also signal allusions, as in Josephine Jacobsen's "Tears," where the following sentence occurs: "Yet the globe is salt / with that savor." This is an allusion to the book of Matthew, 5:13: "Ye are the salt of the earth: but if the salt have lost his savour, wherewith shall it be salted?" This biblical passage refers to the need for believers to retain their faith, for without such faith they are "good for nothing, but to be cast out." However, Jacobsen is discussing something different—namely, the endlessness of grief as a condition of life, with the continuing facts of sorrow remaining on the earth as a silent legacy. By making this allusion, Jacobsen adds to her idea the implication that, throughout human history, sorrow and tears have been a result of the loss of faith and love in human relationships.

Allusions are therefore an important means by which poets broaden context and deepen meaning. The issues a poet raises in a new poem, in other words, are important not only there but are linked through allusion to issues raised earlier by other thinkers or brought out by previous events, places, or persons. With connections made through allusions, poets clarify their own ideas. Allusion is hence not literary "theft" but is rather a means of enrichment.

Studying for Symbols and Allusions

As you study poetry, remember that symbols and allusions do not come marked with special notice and fanfare. There will be no brass band to let you know. Your decision to call something symbolic must be based on the circumstances of the poem. Let us say that the poet introduces a major item of importance at a climactic part of the poem, or that the poet introduces a description that is unusual or noteworthy, such as the connection between "stony sleep" and the "rough beast" in Yeats's "The Second Coming." When such a connection occurs, the element may no longer be taken literally but should be read as a symbol.

Even after you have found a connection such as this, however, you will need to discover and understand symbolic meaning. For instance, in the context of Yeats's "The Second Coming," the phrase "rough beast" might refer to the person or persons hinted at in traditional interpretations of the New Testament as the "Antichrist." In a secular frame of reference, the associations of blankness and pitilessness suggest brutality and suppression. Still further, however, if the last hundred years had not been a period in which millions of people were persecuted and exterminated in military and secret police operations, even these associations might make the "rough beast" quizzical but not necessarily symbolic. But because of the rightness of the application, together with the traditional biblical associations, the figure clearly should be construed as a symbol of heartless persecution and brutality.

As you can see, the interpretation of a symbol requires that you consider, in some depth, the person, object, situation, or action being considered as symbolic. If the element can be seen as general and representative—characteristic of the condition of a large number of human beings—it assumes symbolic significance. As a rule, the more ideas that you can associate with the element, the more likely it is to be a symbol.

As for allusions, the identification of an allusion is usually simple. A word, situation, or phrase either is an allusion or it is not, and hence the matter is easily settled once a source is located. The problem comes in determining how the allusion affects the context of the poem you are reading. Thus we understand that in the poem "Snow," Scott alludes to Frost's "Desert Places" (Chapter 18) by borrowing Frost's phrase "Snow falling." Once this allusion is established, its purpose must still be learned. Thus, on the one hand, the allusion might mean that the situation in "Snow" is the same as in Frost's poem—namely, that the speaker is making observations about interior blankness—the "desert places" of the mind, or soul. On the other hand, the poet may be using the allusion in a new sense, and such is indeed the case. Whereas Frost uses the falling snow to suggest coldness of spirit, Scott uses it, more warmly, to connect the natural scene to the memory of family. In other words, once the presence of an allusion is established, the challenge of reading and understanding goes on.

Poems for Study

Emily Brontë . . . . No Coward Soul Is Mine, 948

Amy Clampitt. . . . . Beach Glass, 949

Arthur Hugh Clough . . . . Say Not the Struggle Nought Availeth, 950

Peter Davison . . . . Delphi, 951

John Donne . . . . The Canonization, 952

Stephen Dunn . . . . Hawk, 954

Isabella Gardner . . . . Collage of Echoes, 955

Dan Georgakis . . . . Hiroshima Crewman, 955

Louise Glück . . . . Celestial Music, 956

Jorie Graham . . . . The Geese, 957

Thomas Hardy . . . . In Time of "The Breaking of Nations," 958

George Herbert . . . . The Collar, 959

Josephine Jacobsen . . . . Tears, 960

Robinson Jeffers . . . . The Purse-Seine, 961

John Keats . . . . La Belle Dame Sans Merci: A Ballad, 963

X. J. Kennedy . . . . Old Men Pitching Horseshoes, 965

Ted Kooser . . . . Year's End, 965

Philip Larkin . . . . Next, Please, 966

David Lehman . . . . Venice Is Sinking, 967

Andrew Marvell . . . . To His Coy Mistress, 968

Mary Oliver . . . . Wild Geese, 969

Gary Snyder . . . . Milton by Firelight, 970

Judith Viorst . . . . A Wedding Sonnet for the Next Generation, 971

Walt Whitman . . . . A Noiseless Patient Spider, 972

Richard Wilbur . . . . Year's End, 973

William Butler Yeats . . . . The Second Coming, 974

EMILY BRONTË (1818–1848)

 # No Coward Soul Is Mine (1850; 1846)

No coward soul is mine,
No trembler in the world's storm-troubled sphere:
   I see Heaven's glories shine,
And faith shines equal, arming me from fear.

5   O God within my breast,
Almighty, ever-present Deity
   Life—that in me has rest,
As I—undying Life—have power in Thee!

    Vain are the thousand creeds
10 That move men's hearts, unutterably vain,
   Worthless as withered weeds,
Or idle froth amid the boundless main,°   *i.e, oceans throughout the world*

    To waken doubt in one
Holding so fast by Thine infinity;
15   So surely anchored on
The steadfast rock of immortality.

    With wide-embracing love
Thy spirit animates eternal years,
   Pervades and broods above,
20 Changes, sustains, dissolves, creates, and rears.

    Though earth and man were gone,
And suns and universes ceased to be,
   And Thou wert left alone,°   *if Thou were to be left (totally) alone*
Every existence would exist in Thee.

25   There is not room for Death,
Nor atom that his might could render void:
   Thou—THOU art Being and Breath,
And what THOU art may never be destroyed.

QUESTIONS

1. Why does the speaker assert in the first stanza that "No coward soul in mine"? Why does she raise this issue? Why might someone consider a soul like hers cowardly? Does the speaker make a convincing argument for the poem's first line?

2. Who is "God within my breast" of the poem? What connection or lack of connection does this "Thee/THOU/THY" have with the "thousand creeds / That move men's hearts" of lines 9 and 10?

3. In general, what is the breadth and scope of the symbolic references in this poem? Compare the symbolism of the "storm-troubled sphere" in stanza 1, and of the vanished world, suns, universes, and even humanity in stanza 6.

4. What is the meaning and connection of the symbols "withered weeds" (line 11) and "idle froth" (line 12)? To what extent does the speaker, in lines 9–12, seem to be denigrating conventional religious faiths? How does the grammatical connection between stanzas 3 and 4 help in the understanding of these stanzas?

5. What does the speaker apparently mean, in lines 23–24, by the statement "And Thou wert left alone, / Every existence would exist in Thee"?

6. Describe the symbolism implied in the word "arming" in the first stanza. Against what does the speaker need arming? Who or what is arming her soul? What do "infinity" (line 14) and "immortality" (line 16) contribute to her expressed sense of her own personal strength?

AMY CLAMPITT (1920–1994)

 Beach Glass (1983)

While you walk the water's edge,
turning over concepts
I can't envision, the honking buoy
serves notice that at any time
the wind may change,   5
the reef-bell clatters
its treble monotone, deaf as Cassandra°
to any note but warning. The ocean,
cumbered by no business more urgent
than keeping open old accounts   10
that never balanced,
goes on shuffling its millenniums
of quartz, granite, basalt.

       It behaves
toward the permutations of novelty—   15
driftwood and shipwreck, last night's
beer cans, spilt oil, the coughed-up
residue of plastic—with random
impartiality, playing catch or tag
or touch-last like a terrier,   20
turning the same thing over and over,
over and over. For the ocean, nothing
is beneath consideration.

°7 *Cassandra*: mythical Trojan prophetess who accurately foretold future disasters but whom no one believed.

The houses

25 of so many mussels and periwinkles
have been abandoned here, it's hopeless
to know which to salvage. Instead
I keep a lookout for beach glass—
amber of Budweiser, chrysoprase°

30 of Almadén and Gallo, lapis
by way of (no getting around it,
I'm afraid) Phillips'
Milk of Magnesia, with now and then a rare
translucent turquoise or blurred amethyst

35 of no known origin.

The process

goes on forever: they came from sand,
they go back to gravel,
along with the treasuries

40 of Murano,° the buttressed
astonishments of Chartres,°
which even now are readying
for being turned over and over as gravely
and gradually as an intellect

45 engaged in the hazardous
redefinitions of structures
no one has yet looked at.

°29 *chrysoprase*: a gold-green gemstone. 40 *Murano*: a Venetian island famous for its glass. 41 *Chartres*: the medieval cathedral of Chartres, France, which is unique because of the incredible beauty of its stained glass windows.

QUESTIONS

1. What is the symbolic idea of the poet's description of the buoy near the shore? How does the reference to Cassandra support the poem's meaning?

2. What life forms, now jetsam, does the speaker observe on the shore? What human artifacts have been cast ashore? Why does she choose to collect some of these artifacts? Why does she use words like "chrysoprase," "lapis," and "amethyst" in reference to these objects?

3. What is the meaning of the last stanza? What is the purpose of the poem's symbolic contrast between the beach glass and the glass from Murano and Chartres? What do these objects symbolize?

ARTHUR HUGH CLOUGH (1819–1861)

 ## Say Not the Struggle Nought Availeth (1849)

Say not the struggle nought availeth,
   The labour and the wounds are vain,
The enemy faints not, nor faileth,°   *See Isaiah 40:28–31*
   And as things have been they remain.°

°1–4 *Say . . . remain*: In more direct syntax, the title sentence may be construed as "Do not say that the struggle [of life] is of no value." Lines 2, 3, and 4 are each direct objects of the opening verb "Say not."

If hopes were dupes, fears may be liars; °   5
    It may be, in yon smoke concealed,
Your comrades chase e'en now the fliers,°   *soldiers in retreat*
    And, but for you, possess the field.°   *have control over the battlefield*

For while the tired waves, vainly breaking,
    Seem here no painful inch to gain,   10
Far back, through creeks and inlets making,
    Comes silent, flooding in, the main.°   *i.e., the ocean*

And not by eastern windows only,
    When daylight comes, comes in the light,
In front, the sun climbs slow, how slowly,   15
    But westward, look, the land is bright.

°5 *If hopes . . . liars*: i.e., If one grants that hope is unreal and therefore deceptive, one may also grant that fear is unreal and therefore equally deceptive.

QUESTIONS

1. How many separate symbols are there in this poem? From what topics are they drawn? Why does Clough allude to some of the words in Isaiah?

2. Consider this poem as a persuasive argument against feelings of personal depression and desolation. How does Clough use symbols as the basis of his argument that the listener should overcome his or her despair?

3. Why does Clough end the poem, in line 16, with the observation that the sun shining in the East illuminates the West? Why does Clough draw attention to the slowness of the ascendant sun? Additionally, to what degree might "westward" be considered as a symbol of immortality because it is the location of the setting sun?

PETER DAVISON (1928–2004)

 ## Delphi° (1964)

The crackle of parched grass bent by wind
Is the only music in the grove
Except the gush of the Pierian Spring.°
Eagles are often seen, but through a glass
Their naked necks declare them to be vultures.   5
The place is sacred with a sanctity
Now faded, like a kerchief washed too often.

°In ancient Greece, Delphi was the location of the Temple of Apollo, the home of the famous oracle. Fumes issuing from an underground opening, around which the temple was built, would overcome the priestess, always named Pythia, and she would then deliver prophecies to priests, who would then pass them on, in prose, to inquiring people who wished to know the future. These people of course would have previously made an offering to the Temple. 3 *Pierian Spring*: A famous spring near Delphi, on the western slope of Mount Olympus, sacred to the Muses. Consider Alexander Pope's lines from *An Essay on Criticism*: "A little learning is a dangerous thing; / Drink deep, or taste not, the Pierian Spring."

There lies the crevice where the priestesses
Hid in the crypt and drugged themselves and spoke
10   Until in later years the ruling powers
Bribed them to prophesy what was desired.
Till then the Greeks took pride in hopelessness
And, though they sometimes wrestled with their gods,°
They never won a blessing or a name
15   But only knowledge.
                         I shall never know myself
Enough to know what things I half believe
And, half believing, only half deny.

°13 *wrestled with their gods:* See Genesis 32:24–32.

QUESTIONS

1. What is the topic of this poem? Why is the poem titled "Delphi"?
2. What is the meaning of the final three lines? How do they relate to the previous part of the poem? Why does the speaker include them?
3. Explain the allusions to Delphi, the "crevice where the priestesses / Hid in the crypt," and the reference to Genesis in lines 13–15.

JOHN DONNE (1572–1631)

For a portrait, see Chapter 12, page 666.

The Canonization° (1633)

For Godsake hold your tongue, and let me love,
   Or chide my palsy, or my gout,
My five gray hairs, or ruin'd fortune flout,
   With wealth your state, your mind with Arts improve,°
5   Take you a course,° get you a place,°
      Observe His Honor,° or his grace,°
Or the King's real, or his stampèd face
   Contemplate,° what you will, approve,°
   So you will let me love.

10   Alas, alas, who's injured by my love?
   What merchant's ships have my sighs drown'd?
Who says my tears have overflow'd his ground?
   When did my colds a forward spring° remove?
      When did the heats which my veins fill°

°Canonization is the making of saints. 4 *With wealth . . . improve:* i.e., Improve your state with wealth and your mind with arts. 5 *Take you a course:* take up a career. *place:* a political appointment. 6 *His Honor:* any important courtier. *his grace:* a person of greatest eminence, such as a bishop or the king. 7, 8 *Or . . . contemplate:* i.e., Or contemplate either the king's real face (at court) or stamped face (on coins). 8 *What . . . approve:* Try anything you like (i.e., "Mind your own business"). 13 a *forward spring:* an early spring (season). 14 *the heats . . . fill:* i.e., "the heats (fevers) that fill my veins." Donne apparently wrote this line before the discovery of blood circulation was announced by William Harvey in 1616.

Add one more to the plaguy Bill?°   15
Soldiers find wars, and Lawyers find out still
    Litigious men, which quarrels move,
    Though she and I do love.

Call us what you will, we are made such by love;
    Call her one, me another fly,°   20
We'are Tapers° too, and at our own cost die,°   candles
    And we in us find the Eagle and the Dove.°
        The Phoenix riddle° hath more wit
        By us, we two, being one, are it.
So, to one neutral thing both sexes fit,   25
    We die and rise the same, and prove
    Mysterious° by this love.

We can die by it, if not live by love,
    And if unfit for tombs and hearse
Our legend be, it will be fit for verse;   30
    And if no piece of Chronicle we prove,
        We'll build in sonnets pretty rooms;
        As well a well wrought run becomes
The greatest ashes, as half-acre tombs,
    And by these hymns, all shall approve   35
    Us *Canoniz'd* for love:°

And thus invoke° us; "You whom reverend love   pray to saints
    Made one another's hermitage;°
You, to whom love was peace, that now is rage;
    Who did the whole world's soul extract, and drove   40
        Into the glasses of your eyes
        So made such mirrors, and such spies,
That they did all to you epitomize,°
    Countries, towns, courts: Beg from above
    A pattern of your love!"   45

°15 *plaguy Bill:* a regularly published list of deaths caused by the plague. 20 *fly:* a butterfly or moth (and apparently superficial and light-headed). 21 *at . . . die:* It was supposed that sexual climax shortened life. 22 *the Eagle and the Dove:* masculine and feminine symbols. 23 *Phoenix riddle:* In ancient times the phoenix, a mythical bird that lived for a thousand years, was supposed to die and rise five hundred years later from its own ashes; hence the phoenix symbolized immortality and the renewal of life and desire (See Chapter 20). 27 *Mysterious:* unknowable to anyone but God, and therefore quintessentially holy. 35, 36 *by these hymns . . . Canoniz'd for love:* The idea is that later generations will remember the lovers and elevate them to the sainthood of a religion of love. Because the lovers' love is recorded so powerfully in the speaker's poems ("sonnets" in line 33), these later generations will use the poems as hymns in their worship of love. 38 *Made . . . hermitage:* made a religious retreat for each other. 40–43 *Who did . . . epitomize:* An allusion to reputed alchemical processes, and therefore to be understood approximately like this: "Who extracted the whole world's soul and, through your eyes, assimilated this soul into yours, so that you, whose eyes saw and reflected each other, embodied the love and desire felt by all human beings."

QUESTIONS

1. What is the situation of the poem? Whom is the speaker addressing? Why does he begin as he does? How does he defend his love?
2. What symbols do you find in the poem? What are the symbols? What is being symbolized?

3. What mythic and religious mysteries are linked with sexual love in the third stanza? What does "canonization" mean? What canonizes and immortalizes the lovers? How does the "canonization" symbolize the poem's idea about the nature of love?

4. What will future lovers ask of these saints of love? Of what use will the speaker's poem be at that time? What do you think of the speaker's claim about love?

STEPHEN DUNN (b. 1939)

 ## Hawk (1989)

What a needy, desperate thing
to claim what's wild for oneself,
yet the hawk circling above the pines
looks like the same one I thought

5   might become mine after it crashed
into the large window and lay
one wing spread, the other loosely
tucked, then no, not dead, got up

dazed, and in minutes was gone.
10   Now once again
this is its sky, this its woods.
The tasty small birds it loves

have seen their God and know
the suddenness of such love
15   as we know lightning or flash flood.
If hawks can learn, this hawk learned

what's clear can be hard
down where the humans live,
and that the hunting isn't good
20   where the air is such a lie.

It glides above the pines and I
turn back into the room, the hawk book
open on the cluttered table
to Cooper's Hawk

25   and the unwritten caption
that to be wild
means nothing you do or have done
needs to be explained. ·

QUESTIONS

1. Why does the speaker consider the issue of owning or not owning the hawk that crashed into his window?

2. In what way is the hawk significant? How can a reader justify considering it as a symbol? What does the bird symbolize?

3. What is the meaning of the final four lines? How true are the lines? If "to be wild" needs no explanation, what does it mean, in contrast, to be civilized?

ISABELLA GARDNER (1915–1981)

 ## Collage of Echoes (1979)

I have no promises to keep
Nor miles to go before I sleep,°
For miles of years I have made promises
and (mostly) kept them.
    It's time I slept.
Now I lay me down to sleep°
With no promises to keep.
    My sleaves are ravelled°
    I have travelled.°

                                              5

°2 *miles to go before I sleep*: See Robert Frost, "Stopping by Woods on a Snowy Evening" (page 470), lines 13–16. 6 *Now I lay me down to sleep*: from the child's prayer: Now I lay me down to sleep; / I pray the Lord my soul to keep. / If I should die before I wake, / I pray the Lord my soul to take. 8 *My sleaves are ravelled*: See *Macbeth*, 11.2.37: "Sleep that knits up the ravelled sleave of care." 9 *I have travelled*: See Keats, "On First Looking into Chapman's Homer" (page 762).

QUESTIONS

1. Given the allusions in the poem, what do you conclude about the speaker's judgment of the reader's knowledge of literature?
2. How reliant is "Collage of Echoes" upon the contexts being echoed? How do the echoes assist in enabling enjoyment and appreciation of the poem?
3. In relation to the speaker's character as demonstrated in the poem, consider the phrases "(mostly) kept them," "With no promises to keep," and "My sleaves are ravelled." What do they show about the speaker's self-assessment? In what way might these phrases be considered comic?

DAN GEORGAKIS (b. 1938)

 ## ʰᵉʷ Hiroshima Crewman (1969)

Somewhere in California
his body humbled by a hair shirt,
a vow of silence on his lips,
a Hiroshima crewman tries to find a life.
If he should ever choose to break his peace,
he might speak of death by fire
no Nazi ordered; he might tell how
war produces many brands of Auschwitz soap and Dachau lampshade.

                                              5

QUESTIONS

1. Explain the meaning and purpose of the poem's title. In what way is a "hair shirt" symbolic? What does it symbolize?

2. Why is the principal figure called a "Hiroshima Crewman"? What has happened to him since August 6, 1945, the date of the atomic bombing of Hiroshima? What is the Crewman now doing, according to the poem?

3. Describe the symbolism of "death by fire" and "Auschwitz soap and Dachau lampshade." What are the human and political implications of this symbolism?

LOUISE GLÜCK (b. 1943)

For a photo, see Chapter 13, page 700.

🍁 Celestial Music (1990)

I have a friend who still believes in heaven.
Not a stupid person, yet with all she knows, she literally talks to god,
she thinks someone listens in heaven.
On earth, she's unusually competent.
5   Brave, too, able to face unpleasantness.

We found a caterpillar dying in the dirt, greedy ants crawling over it.
I'm always moved by weakness, by disaster, always eager to oppose vitality.
But timid, also, quick to shut my eyes.
Whereas my friend was able to watch, to let events play out
10   according to nature. For my sake, she intervened,
brushing a few ants off the torn thing, and set it down across the road.

My friend says I shut my eyes to god, that nothing else explains
my aversion to reality. She says I'm like the child who buries her head in the pillow
so as not to see, the child who tells herself
15   that light causes sadness—
My friend is like the mother. Patient, urging me
to wake up an adult like herself, a courageous person—

In my dreams, my friend reproaches me. We're walking
on the same road, except it's winter now;
20   she's telling me that when you love the world you hear celestial music:
look up, she says. When I look up, nothing.
Only clouds, snow, a white business in the trees
like brides leaping to a great height—
Then I'm afraid for her; I see her
25   caught in a net deliberately cast over the earth—

In reality, we sit by the side of the road, watching the sun set;
from time to time, the silence pierced by a birdcall.
It's this moment we're both trying to explain, the fact
that we're at ease with death, with solitude.
30   My friend draws a circle in the dirt; inside, the caterpillar doesn't move.

She's always trying to make something whole, something beautiful, an image
capable of life apart from her.
We're very quiet. It's peaceful sitting here, not speaking, the composition

fixed, the road turning suddenly dark, the air
going, cool, here and there the rocks shining and glittering—   35
it's this stillness that we both love.
The love of form is a love of endings.

QUESTIONS

1. What is the significance of the caterpillar at the poem's beginning? How might the caterpillar be taken as a symbol? What might it symbolize? What does the "celestial music" of line 20 signify? Why does the speaker not seem to hear it?

2. Why does the speaker describe the character of her friend? How does the speaker assert the differences she has with her friend? What does the setting sun symbolize in lines 26–37? How might it be symbolic that the speaker and her friend are sitting at the same side of the road?

3. Explain the poem's final line. What is the form that the speaker describes? Why might not the "love of endings" be the love of beginnings? Why is it necessary to love endings?

JORIE GRAHAM (b. 1954)

 ## The Geese (1980)

Today as I hang out the wash I see them again, a code
as urgent as elegant,
tapering with goals.
For days they have been crossing. We live beneath these geese

as if beneath the passage of time, or a most perfect heading.   5
Sometimes I fear their relevance.
Closest at hand,
between the lines,

the spiders imitate the paths the geese won't stray from,
imitate them endlessly to no avail: 10
things will not remain connected,
will not heal,

and the world thickens with texture instead of history,
texture instead of place.
Yet the small fear of the spiders   15
binds and binds

the pins to the lines, the line to the eaves, to the pincushion bush,
as if, at any time, things could fall further apart
and nothing could help them
recover their meaning. And if these spiders had their way,   20

chainlink over the visible world,
would we be in or out? I turn to go back in.
There is a feeling the body gives the mind
of having missed something, a bedrock poverty, like falling

25 without the sense that you are passing through one world,
that you could reach another
anytime. Instead the real
is crossing you,

your body an arrival
30 you know is false but can't outrun. And somewhere in between
these geese forever entering and
these spiders turning back

this astonishing delay, the everyday, takes place.

QUESTIONS

1. What is the dominant tense of the poem? What effect does this tense have on the speaker's conclusions?
2. What action does the speaker perform in the course of the poem? What is the relationship between this action and the final lines?
3. What do the geese symbolize? What do the spiders symbolize? How are these symbols contrasted?
4. The first half of this poem, particularly lines 11 and 18, is reminiscent of Yeats's "The Second Coming" (p. 974). In your judgment, what use does Graham make of this allusion?

THOMAS HARDY (1840–1928)

For a photo, see Chapter 5, page 287.

 ## In Time of "The Breaking of Nations"° (1916; 1915)

Only a man harrowing clods
   In a slow silent walk,
With an old horse that stumbles and nods
   Half asleep as they stalk.

5 Only thin smoke without flame
   From the heaps of couch grass:°   *quack grass*
Yet this will go onward the same
   Though Dynasties pass.

Yonder a maid and her wight°   *fellow*
10   Come whispering by;
War's annals will fade into night
   Ere their story die.

°See Jeremiah 51:20, "with you I break nations in pieces."

QUESTIONS

1. What does Hardy symbolize by the man, horse, smoke and couple? How realistic and vivid are these symbols? Are they universal or contextual?

2. How does Hardy show that the phrase "breaking of nations" is to be taken symbolically? What meaning is gained by the biblical allusion of this phrase?

3. Contrast the structure of stanza 1 with that of stanzas 2 and 3. How does the form of stanzas 2 and 3 enable Hardy to emphasize the main idea?

4. How does the speaker show his evaluation of the life of the common people? You might consider that at the time (1915), World War I was raging in Europe.

GEORGE HERBERT (1593–1633)

 ## The Collar° (1633)

I struck the board, and cry'd "No more;
    I will abroad!
What? shall I ever sigh and pine?
My lines and life are free; free as the road,
  Loose as the wind, as large as store,   5
    Shall I be still in suit?°
 Have I no harvest but a thorn°
 To let me blood, and not restore
What I have lost with cordial fruit?
    Sure there was wine   10
 Before my sighs did dry it: there was corn
  Before my tears did drown it.
 Is the year only lost to me?
  Have I no bays° to crown it?
No flowers, no garlands gay? all blasted?   15
    All wasted?
 Not so, my heart: but there is fruit,
    And thou hast hands.
 Recover all thy sight-blown age
On double pleasures: leave thy cold dispute   20
Of what is fit, and not; forsake thy cage;
    Thy rope of sands,
Which petty thoughts have made, and made to thee
  Good cable, to enforce and draw,
    And be thy law,   25
 While thou didst wink and wouldst not see.
    Away; take heed:
    I will abroad.
Call in thy death's head there: tie up thy fears.
    He that forbears   30

°*collar*: (a) the collar worn by a member of the clergy; (b) the collar of the harness of a draft animal such as a horse; (c) a restraint placed on prisoners; (d) a pun on *choler* (yellow bile), a bodily substance that was thought to cause quick rages. 6 *in suit*: waiting upon a person of power to gain favor or position. 7 *thorn*: See Mark 15:17. 14 *bays*: laurel crowns to signify victory and honor.

To suit° and serve his need,   *follow*
  Deserves his load."
But as I rav'd and grew more fierce and wild
  At every word,
35 Me thought I heard one calling, "Child:"
  And I replied, *"My Lord."*

QUESTIONS

1. What is the opening situation? Why is the speaker angry? Against what role in life is he complaining?
2. In light of the many possible meanings of *collar* (see note), explain the title as a symbol in the poem.
3. Explain the symbolism of the thorn (line 7), blood (line 8), wine (line 10), bays (line 14), flowers and garlands (line 15), cage (line 27), rope of sands (line 22), death's head (line 29), and the dialogue in lines 35 and 36.

JOSEPHINE JACOBSEN (1908–2003)

 ## Tears (1981)

Tears leave no mark on the soil
or pavement; certainly not in sand
or in any known rain forest;
never a mark on stone.
5 One would think that no one in Persepolis
or Ur° ever wept.

You would assume that, like Alice,°
we would all be swimming, buffeted
in a tide of tears.
10 But they disappear. Their heat goes.
Yet the globe is salt
with that savor.°

The animals want no part in this.
The hare both screams and weeps
15 at her death, one poet says.
The stag, at death, rolls round drops
down his muzzle; but, he is in
Shakespeare's forest.°

°5, 6 *Persepolis . . . Ur*: Persepolis was the capital city of ancient Persia (now Iran). Ur, on the Persian Gulf, was the capital city of the ancient Sumerian Empire. Today, both cities survive only in ruins. The Hebrew patriarch Abraham traveled from "Ur of the Chaldees" to settle in the land of Canaan, the "promised land." 7 *Alice*: in Lewis Carroll's *Alice's Adventures in Wonderland* (Ch. 2), Alice sheds tears, and then is reduced in size and almost drowns in her own teardrops. 11–12 *Yet . . . Savor*: Matthew 5:13. 14–18 *The hare . . . forest*: In the poem *Autumn* by James Thomson (1700–1748), lines 401–57, a cruel hunt of the hare and the stag is described. It is the stag who sheds "big round tears" and "groans in anguish" when dying. Jacobsen's allusion to Shakespeare—to whom Thomson is also alluding—is *As You Like It*, 2.1.29–43.

These cases are mythically rare.
No, it is the human being who persistently   20
weeps, in some countries, openly, in others, not.
Children who, even when frightened, weep most hopefully;
women, licensed weepers.°
Men, in secret, or childishly; or nobly.

Could tears not make a sea of their mass?   25
It could be salt and wild enough;
it could rouse storms and sink ships,
erode, erode its shores:
tears of rage, of love, of torture,
of loss. Of loss.   30

Must we see the future
in order to weep? Or the past?
Is that why the animals
refuse to shed tears?
But what of the present, the tears of the present?   35
The awful relief, like breath

after strangling? The generosity
of the verb "to shed"?
They are a classless possession
yet are not found in the museum   40
of even our greatest city.
Sometimes what was human, turns
into an animal, dry-eyed.

°23 *licensed weepers:* In certain countries, such as Greece, professional "weepers" weep and cry aloud at funerals.

QUESTIONS

1. What does the poem's major symbol, tears, mean? What significance does the poem attribute to tears? Why are tears sometimes disregarded?
2. How does the poem apply the symbol to various cultures and conditions?
3. How do tears differentiate human beings from animals? What is the symbolic value of this difference? In light of the contrast, what is the meaning of the last two lines?
4. Explain the poem's use of allusions (i.e., Persepolis, Ur, the New Testament, *Alice's Adventures in Wonderland*, professional mourners, Shakespeare).

ROBINSON JEFFERS (1887–1962)

 ## The Purse-Seine (1937)

1

Our sardine fishermen work at night in the dark of the moon;
         daylight or moonlight
They could not tell where to spread the net, unable to see the
         phosphorescence of the shoals of fish.

They work northward from Monterey, coasting Santa Cruz;
    off New Year's Point or off Pigeon Point
The look-out man will see some lakes of milk-color light on the seas's
    night-purple; he points, and the helmsman
Turns the dark prow, the motorboat circles the gleaming shoal and drifts out
5   her seine-net. They close the circle
And purse the bottom of the net, then with great labor haul it in.

2

                                     I cannot tell you
How beautiful the scene is, and a little terrible, then, when the crowded fish
Know they are caught, and wildly beat from one wall to the other of their closing destiny
    the phosphorescent
Water to a pool of flame, each beautiful slender body sheeted with flame, like a
10   live rocket
A comet's tail wake of clear yellow flame; while outside the narrowing
Floats and cordage of the net great sea-lions come up to watch, sighing in the dark; the
    vast walls of night
Stand erect to the stars.

3

                            Lately I was looking from a night mountain-top
On a wide city, the colored splendor, galaxies of light; how could I help but recall the
15   seine-net
Gathering the luminous fish? I cannot tell you how beautiful the city appeared, and a
    little terrible.
I thought, We have geared the machines and locked all together into interdependence;
    we have built the great cities; now
There is no escape. We have gathered vast populations incapable of free survival,
    insulated
From the strong earth, each person in himself helpless, on all dependent. The circle is
    closed, and the net
Is being hauled in. They hardly feel the cords drawing, yet they shine already. The
20   inevitable mass-disasters
Will not come in our time nor in our children's, but we and our children
Must watch the net draw narrower, government take all powers—or revolution, and
    the new government
Take more than all, add to kept bodies kept souls—or anarchy, the mass-disasters.

4

                    These things are Progress;
Do you marvel our verse is troubled or frowning, while it keeps its reason? Or it lets go,
25   lets the mood flow
In the manner of the recent young men into mere hysteria, splintered gleams, crackled
    laughter. But they are quite wrong.
There is no reason for amazement; surely one always knew that cultures decay, and life's
    end is death.

QUESTIONS

1. Describe how the purse-seine is used to haul in the sardines. What is the speaker's reaction to the scene as described in stanza 2?
2. How does the speaker explain that the purse-seine is a symbol? What does it symbolize? What do the sardines symbolize?
3. Compare the ideas of Jeffers with those of Yeats in "The Second Coming." Are the ideas of Jeffers more or less methodical?
4. Is the statement at the end to be taken as a fact or as a resigned acceptance of that fact? Does the poem offer any solution to the problem?
5. How can the sea-lions of line 12, and their sighs, be construed as a symbol?

JOHN KEATS (1795–1821)

For a portrait, see Chapter 15, page 762.

 ## La Belle Dame Sans Merci: A Ballad° (1820; 1819)

1

O what can ail thee, knight at arms,
  Alone and palely loitering?
The sedge has wither'd from the lake,
  And no birds sing.

2

O what can ail thee, knight at arms,   5
  So haggard and so woe-begone?
The squirrel's granary is full,
  And the harvest's done.

3

I see a lily on thy brow
  With anguish moist and fever dew,   10
And on dry cheeks a fading rose
  Fast withereth too.

4

I met a lady in the meads,°   *meadows*
  Full beautiful, a fairy's child;
Her hair was long, her foot was light,   15
  And her eyes were wild.

°"La Belle Dame Sans Merci" is French for "The beautiful lady without pity" (that is, "The heartless woman"). This is also the title of a medieval poem by Alain Chartier; Keats's poem bears no other relationship to the medieval poem, which was thought at the time to have been by Chaucer.

5

I made a garland for her head,
   And bracelets too, and fragrant zone;°   *belt*
She look'd at me as she did love,
20   And made sweet moan.

6

I set her on my pacing steed,
   And nothing else saw all day long,
For sidelong would she bend, and sing
   A fairy's song.

7

25 She found me roots of relish° sweet,   *magical potion*
   And honey wild, and manna° dew,   *See Exodus 16:14–36*
And sure in language strange she said—
   I love thee true.

8

She took me to her elfin grot,°   *grotto*
30   And there she wept, and sigh'd full sore,
And there I shut her wild wild eyes
   With kisses four.

9

And there she lullèd me asleep,
   And there I dream'd—Ah! woe betide!
35 The latest° dream I ever dream'd   *last*
   On the cold hill's side.

10

I saw pale kings, and princes too,
   Pale warriors, death pale were they all;
They cried—"La belle dame sans merci
40   Hath thee in thrall!"°   *slavery*

11

I saw their starv'd lips in the gloam
   With horrid warning gapèd wide,
And I awoke and found me here
   On the cold hill's side.

12

45 And this is why I sojourn here,
   Alone and palely loitering,
Though the sedge is wither'd from the lake,
   And no birds sing.

QUESTIONS

1. Who is the speaker of stanzas 1–3? Who speaks after that?
2. In light of the dreamlike content of the poem, how can the knight's experience be viewed as symbolic? What is being symbolized?
3. Consider "relish" (line 25), "honey" (line 26), and "manna" (line 26) as symbols. Are they realistic or mythical? What does the allusion to manna signify? What is symbolized by the "pale kings, and princes too" and "Pale warriors" (lines 37–38)?
4. Consider the poem's setting as symbols of the knight's state of mind.

X. J. KENNEDY (b. 1929)

 ## Old Men Pitching Horseshoes (1985)

Back in a yard where ringers groove a ditch,
These four in shirtsleeves congregate to pitch
Dirt-burnished iron. With appraising eye,
One sizes up a peg, hoists and lets fly—
A clang resounds as though a smith had struck   5
Fire from a forge. His first blow, out of luck,
Rattles in circles. Hitching up his face,
He swings, and weight once more inhabits space,
Thumbles as gently as a new-laid egg.
Extended iron arms surround their peg   10
Like one come home to greet a long-lost brother.
Shouts from one outpost. Mutters from the other.
Now changing sides, each withered pitcher moves
As his considered dignity behooves
Down the worn path of earth where August flies   15
And sheaves of air in warm distortions rise.
To stand ground, fling, kick dust with all the force
Of shoes still hammered to a living horse.

QUESTIONS

1. How does the poet indicate that the pitching of horseshoes is symbolic? As symbols, why are old men chosen rather than young men?
2. Discuss the effects of the words "congregate," "outpost," "withered," "sheaves," "kick dust," and "force." What do these words contribute to the poem's symbolism?
3. Compare the topic of this poem with the concluding lines of T. S. Eliot's "Preludes" (Chapter 14), especially the last two lines. How is the symbolism of these poems similar? Different?

TED KOOSER (b. 1939)

 ## Year's End (1985)

Now the seasons are closing their files
on each of us, the heavy drawers
full of certificates rolling back

into the tree trunks, a few old papers
5 flocking away. Someone we loved
has fallen from our thoughts,
making a little, glittering splash
like a bicycle pushed by a breeze.
Otherwise, not much has happened;
10 we fell in love again, finding
that one red feather in the wind.

QUESTIONS

1. What is the occasion of the poem? Why does the speaker use the pronouns "us," "we," "our," and "we" as references? Does he mean only himself? Does he mean others beside himself?

2. How might certificates roll back into tree trunks? What is the meaning of the speaker's mention of papers "flocking away"?

3. In line 10 the speaker says that "We fell in love again." In what way does the "one red feather in the wind" symbolize this action? Why doesn't the speaker talk sooner in the poem about falling in love?

4. Compare this poem with Wilbur's "Year's End" (this chapter) and Roethke's "Dolor" (Chapter 12). What do the poems have in common? In what ways is Kooser's "Year's End" unique?

PHILIP LARKIN (1922–1985)

 ## Next, Please (1955)

Always too eager for the future, we
Pick up bad habits of expectancy.
Something is always approaching; every day
Till then we say,

5 Watching from a bluff the tiny, clear,
Sparkling armada of promises draw near.
How slow they are! And how much time they waste,
Refusing to make haste!

Yet still they leave us holding wretched stalks
10 Of disappointment, for, though nothing balks
Each big approach, leaning with brasswork prinked,°   *adorned*
Each rope distinct.

Flagged, and the figurehead with golden tits
Arching our way, it never anchors; it's
15 No sooner present than it turns to past.
Right to the last

We think each one will heave to and unload
All good into our lives, all we are owed

For waiting so devoutly and so long.
But we are wrong: 20

Only one ship is seeking us, a black-
Sailed unfamiliar, towing at her back
A huge and birdless silence. In her wake
No waters breed or break.

QUESTIONS

1. What is the subject of the poem? The theme? What point does it make about time, expectation, human nature, and the way we live our lives?

2. What cliché does the extended metaphor that begins in the second stanza ironically revitalize and reverse? How does this metaphor make the total meaning of the poem clearer and more palpable?

3. How do meter, rhyme, and diction help create meaning? Consider, for example, the metrical variation in the fourth line of each stanza, rhyming pairs such as "waste-haste" and "wake-break," or words such as "bluff" and "armada."

4. Compare this poem to Marvell's "To His Coy Mistress." To what extent is "Next, Please" a *carpe diem* poem?

DAVID LEHMAN (b. 1948)

 ## Venice Is Sinking (2002)

In New York we defy
everything but gravity
but we're not sinking
unlike Venice we're level
though encircled with water   5
we travel underground in
trains going through tunnels
our grandparents built
in a way it's a miracle
when you think of any of   10
the ways any of us could
die in a day if some
apparatus we rely on
unthinkingly,
the elevator or the subway   15
or the good faith of motorists,
should fail—
think of it—
what are the odds
that we'd still be here   20
as we are

QUESTIONS

1. Why is the poem titled "Venice Is Sinking." In light of the title, why does the poet discuss New York throughout the poem? In what way can Venice be considered symbolic of New York, and also, generally, of all big cities?

2. Why does the poet discuss the "miracle" of New York? To what degree might New York symbolize the precariousness of existence? How is it significant that pedestrians are dependent on the "good faith of motorists"? Is it only the faith of motorists on whom we rely for our continued existence?

3. Why do you think the poet largely avoids punctuation and capitalization? How could this lack illustrate any ideas about the nature of modern life?

ANDREW MARVELL (1621–1678) *Assilogism: If... then*

🍁 To His Coy Mistress (1681)

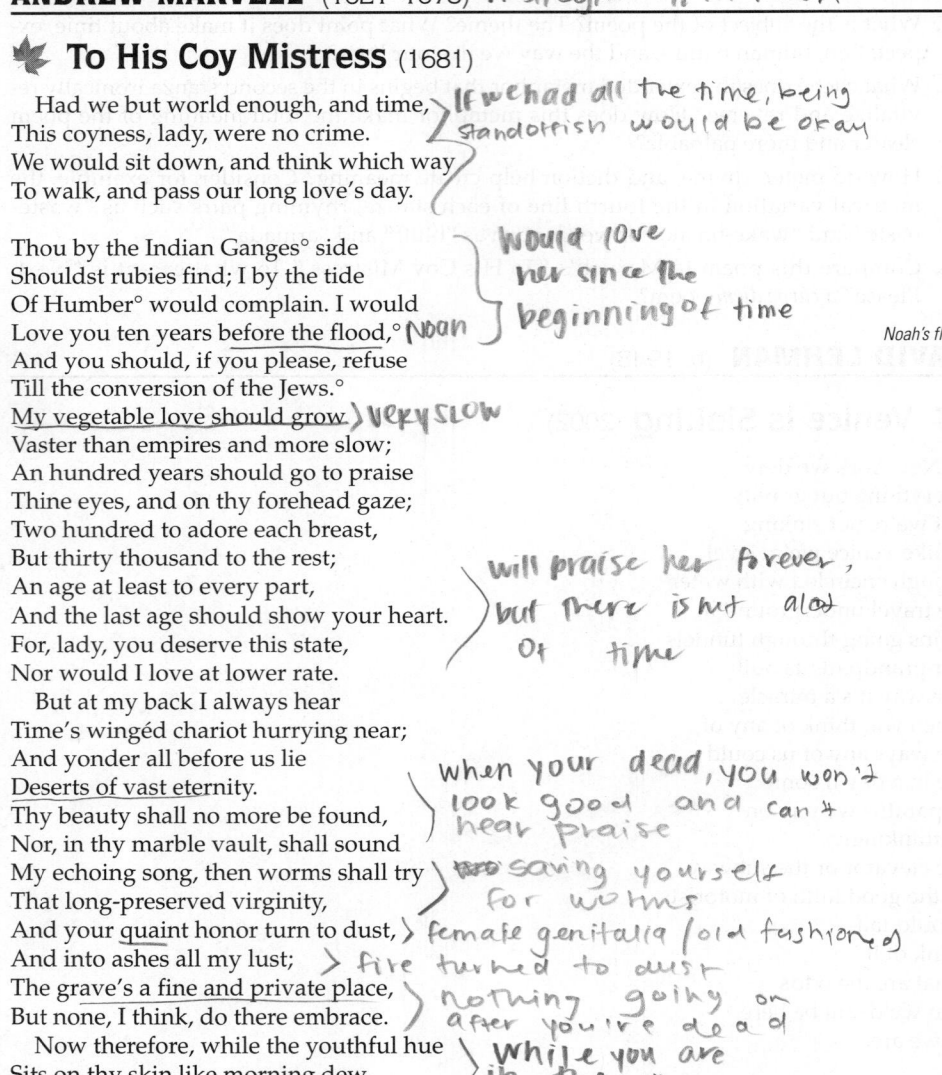

Had we but world enough, and time, *If we had all the time, being*
This coyness, lady, were no crime. *standoffish would be okay*
We would sit down, and think which way
To walk, and pass our long love's day.

5   Thou by the Indian Ganges° side *would love*
Shouldst rubies find; I by the tide *her since the*
Of Humber° would complain. I would *beginning of time*
Love you ten years before the flood,° *Noah*   Noah's flood
And you should, if you please, refuse
10 Till the conversion of the Jews.°
My vegetable love should grow *very slow*
Vaster than empires and more slow;
An hundred years should go to praise
Thine eyes, and on thy forehead gaze;
15 Two hundred to adore each breast,
But thirty thousand to the rest; *will praise her forever,*
An age at least to every part, *but there is but   alot*
And the last age should show your heart. *of   time*
For, lady, you deserve this state,
20 Nor would I love at lower rate.
    But at my back I always hear
Time's wingéd chariot hurrying near;
And yonder all before us lie
Deserts of vast eternity. *when your dead, you won't*
25 Thy beauty shall no more be found, *look good   and can't*
Nor, in thy marble vault, shall sound *hear praise*
My echoing song, then worms shall try *stop saving yourself*
That long-preserved virginity, *for worms*
30 And your quaint honor turn to dust, *female genitalia (old fashioned)*
And into ashes all my lust; *fire turned to dust*
The grave's a fine and private place, *nothing going on*
But none, I think, do there embrace. *after you're dead*
    Now therefore, while the youthful hue *while you are*
35 Sits on thy skin like morning dew, *in the morning*
And while thy willing soul transpires *of your life*

°5 *Ganges*: a large river than runs across most of India. 7 *Humber*: a small river that runs through northern England to the North Sea. 10 *Jews*: Traditionally, this conversion is supposed to occur just before the Last Judgment.

At every pore with instant fires,
Now let us sport us while we may,
And now, like <u>amorous birds of prey,</u>
Rather at once our time devour
Than languish in his slow-chapped° power.   slow-jawed   40
Let us roll all our strength and all
Our sweetness up into one ball,
And tear our pleasures with rough stife
Thorough° the iron gates of life: through
Thus, though we cannot make our sun   45
Stand still, yet we will make him run.

[handwritten annotations: contradiction to vegtable love / Let's live every moment / J. alfred Prufrock / can't stop time, but we can run with him / wim / Carp Diem = live, live, live!, seize life!]

QUESTIONS

1. In lines 1–20 the speaker sets up a hypothetical situation and the first part of a pseudo-logical proof: If *A* then *B*. What specific words indicate the logic of this section? What hypothetical situation is established?

2. How do geographic and biblical allusions affect our sense of time and place?

3. In lines 21–32 the speaker refutes the hypothetical condition set up in the first twenty lines. What word indicates that this is a refutation? How do symbols of death create and reinforce meaning here?

4. The last part of the poem (lines 33–46) presents the speaker's "logical" conclusion. What words indicate that this is a conclusion? What is the conclusion?

MARY OLIVER (b. 1935)

 ## Wild Geese (1986)

You do not have to be good.
You do not have to walk on your knees
for a hundred miles through the desert, repenting
You only have to let the soft animal of your body
    love what it loves.   5
Tell me about despair, yours, and I will tell you mine.
Meanwhile the world goes on.
Meanwhile the sun and the clear pebbles of the rain
are moving across the landscapes,   10
over the prairies and the deep trees,
the mountains and the rivers.
Meanwhile the wild geese, high in the clean blue air,
are heading home again.
Whoever you are, no matter how lonely,   15
the world offers itself to your imagination,
calls to you like the wild geese, harsh and exciting—
over and over announcing your place
in the family of things.

QUESTIONS

1. What idea is contained in the first five lines? What ideas are expressed in lines 6–12? In what ways are lines 13–17 a climax of the poem? How does this last section build on the poem's earlier parts?

2. What is symbolized by the references to "the sun and the clear pebbles of the rain," and so on, in lines 7–10? Do these symbols suggest futility or hope?

3. What do the wild geese symbolize (lines 11–12, 15)? How is the symbol of the geese a response to the poem's first six lines? How well would the words *acceptance, self-knowledge,* or *adjustment* describe the poem's ideas? What other words would be better or more suitable? Why?

GARY SNYDER (b. 1930)

 Milton by Firelight (1955)

Piute Creek, August 1955°

"O Hell, what doe mine eyes with grief behold?"°
Working with an old
Singlejack° miner, who can sense
The vein and cleavage
5   In the very guts of rock, can
Blast granite, build
Switchbacks° that last for years   *trails, or roads*
Under the beat of snow, thaw, mule-hooves.
What use, Milton, a silly story
10 Of our lost general parents,
eaters of fruit?°   *See 4.331–35 of Paradise Lost*

The Indian, the chainsaw boy,
And a string of six mules
Came riding down to camp
15 Hungry for tomatoes and green apples.
Sleeping in saddle-blankets
Under a bright night-sky
Han River slantwise° by morning.
Jays squall
20 Coffee boils

In ten thousand years the Sierras
Will be dry and dead, home of the scorpion.
Ice-scratched slabs and bent trees.
No paradise, no fall,
25 Only the weathering land

°*Piute Creek:* a creek and spring in the Sierra Nevada Mountains in Yosemite Park in California. During the summer of 1955, Snyder was working with a Yosemite trail crew, and became familiar with the tasks and tools of making hiking trails. 1 *O Hell!* . . . *behold:* from Milton's *Paradise Lost* (1667), Book 4, line 358. The line begins Satan's speech about his own fallen condition, which he contrasts with the prelapsarian state of paradise which Adam and Eve at that time enjoyed. It is in this speech that Satan plans to avenge his own fall by bringing both death and the loss of innocence to Adam and Eve, and, of course, to all of humanity. Snyder's speaker describes the biblical story made epic by Milton—which he calls "a silly story"—in lines 11–13 of this poem. 3 *Single-jack:* a wooden wedge that, when soaked with water, swells in size to split large rocks. 18 *Han River slantwise:* perhaps the meaning is that the men slept so soundly that when they woke, their eyes seemed to appear Asiatic, as though they were from the Han River area in Korea.

The wheeling sky,
Man, with his Satan
Scouring the chaos of the mind.
Oh Hell!

Fire down   30
Too dark to read, miles from a road
The bell-mare° clangs in the meadow
That packed dirt for a fill-in
Scrambling through loose rocks
On an old trail   35
All of a summer's day.

°32 *bell-mare:* pack trains in the West were led by a mare with a bell around her neck. The mules and horses of the train would obediently line up behind the bell and follow its sound wherever the bell-mare went. One of the many paintings of the West by Frederic Remington (1861–1909) is *The Bell Mare* (1904).

QUESTIONS

1. Why does the speaker contrast the future of the Sierra Nevada Mountains with human concerns about Satan? What is the purpose of the oath in line 28?

2. In Book 4 of *Paradise Lost,* Milton states that the home of Adam and Eve is totally clean and devoid of "Beast, Bird, Insect, or Worm." Why does Snyder draw attention to the future when the Sierras will be "home of the scorpion" (line 22)? What does the scorpion symbolize? In what other ways does Snyder criticize realistic and idealistic conceptions of human and earthly perfection?

3. In what way is the final line, "All of a summer's day," symbolic?

JUDITH VIORST (b. 1931)

 ## A Wedding Sonnet for the Next Generation (2000)

He might compare you to a summer's day,°
Declaring you're far fairer in his eyes.
She might, with depth and breadth and many sighs,
Count all the ways she loves you, way by way.°

He might say when you're old and full of sleep,   5
He'll cherish still the Pilgrim soul in you.°
She might—oh, there are poems so fine, so true,
To help you speak of love and vows to keep.

Words help. And you are writing your own poem.
It doesn't always scan or always rhyme.   10

°1 *summer's day:* See Shakespeare, "Shall I Compare Thee to a Summer's Day?" (Chapter 15). 3, 4 *She might . . . way by way:* See Elizabeth Barrett Browning, "How Do I Love Thee" (Chapter 22). 5, 6 *He might say . . . Pilgrim soul in you:* See Yeats, "When You Are Old" (Chapter 16).

It mingles images of the sublime
With plainer words: Respect. Trust. Comfort. Home.

How very rich is love's vocabulary
When friends, dear friends, best friends decide to marry.

QUESTIONS

1. Why does the poem speak of "the Next Generation" in the title? What is the form of the poem? Why do the first lines alternate between "he" and "she"?
2. What is the meaning and effect of the allusions in lines 1–6? Why does Viorst introduce these allusions? What assumptions does she make about her audience for this poem?
3. How does the poem change in the last six lines? How does the language shift in these lines?
4. What does it mean to say "you are writing your own poem"? How are the final two lines related to the previous parts of the poem?

WALT WHITMAN (1819–1892)

For a photo, see Chapter 15, page 790.

A Noiseless Patient Spider (1868)

A noiseless patient spider,
I marked where on a little promontory it stood isolated,
Marked how to explore the vacant vast surrounding,
It launched forth filament, filament, filament out of itself,
5 Ever unreeling them, ever tirelessly speeding them.

And you O my soul where you stand,
Surrounded, detached, in measureless oceans of space,
Ceaselessly musing, venturing, throwing, seeking the spheres
        to connect them,
Till the bridge you will need be formed, till the ductile anchor hold,
10 Till the gossamer thread you fling catch somewhere, O my soul.

QUESTIONS

1. The subject of the second stanza is seemingly unrelated to the subject of the first. How are these stanzas related?
2. In what way does the spider's web symbolize the soul and the poet's view of the isolation of human beings? How does the web symbolize the soul's ceaseless "musing . . . seeking" and the attempt "to connect"?
3. Explain why the second stanza is not a complete sentence. How might this grammatical feature be related to the spider's web? To the poet's idea that life requires striving but does not offer completeness?

RICHARD WILBUR (b. 1921)

Year's End (1950)

Now winter downs the dying of the year,
And Night is all a settlement of snow;
From the soft street the rooms of houses show
A gathered light, a shapen atmosphere,
Like frozen-over lakes whose ice is thin   5
And still allows some stirring down within.

I've known the wind by water banks to shake
The late leaves down, which frozen where they fell
And held in ice as dancers in a spell
Fluttered all winter long into a lake;   10
Graved on the dark in gestures of descent,
They seemed their own most perfect monument.

There was perfection in the death of ferns
Which laid their fragile cheeks against the stone
A million years. Great mammoths overthrown   15
Composedly have made their long sojourns,
Like palaces of patience, in the gray
And changeless lands of ice. And at Pompeii°

The little dog lay curled and did not rise
But slept the deeper as the ashes rose   20
And found the people incomplete, and froze
The random hands, the loose unready eyes
Of men expecting yet another sun
To do the shapely thing they had not done.

These sudden ends of time must give us pause.   25
We fray into the future, rarely wrought
Save in the tapestries of afterthought.
More time, more time. Barrages of applause
Come muffled from a buried radio.
The New-year bells are wrangling with the snow.   30

°18 *Pompeii*: the southern Italian Roman city covered by lava during the eruption of Mount Vesuvius in 79 CE. Many people and animals died trying to escape the lava flow and were covered over where they fell. Modern excavators created statues of these fallen figures by using plaster to fill in cavities left by their bodies. One of these was the "little dog" mentioned in line 19.

QUESTIONS

1. What natural and historical symbols does Wilbur introduce in the poem? What ideas do the symbols present about time and the use people make of time?

2. Describe Wilbur's use of two-word groups united by assonance and consonance in the poem (e.g., "*Pe*ople in*co*mplete," "*d*owns the *dy*ing," "*sti*ll . . . *sti*rring"). How effective are these groups in drawing your attention to Wilbur's meaning?

3. Describe the symbols in the final stanza ("fray into the future," "tapestries of after-thought," "muffled from a buried radio"). Why does the poem conclude with the symbols of "New-year bells" and "snow"?

4. Consider the meaning of line 25. How can this line be interpreted so that the poem may have either positive or negative views of human activity?

WILLIAM BUTLER YEATS (1865–1939)

For a photo, see Chapter 16, page 833. *—imagery: ocean, desert, death*

NEW The Second Coming° (1920; 1919) *)not of Christ, something else* *global impact of evil*

Turning and turning in the widening gyre°
The falcon cannot hear the falconer; *> Things falling apart*
Things fall apart; the center cannot hold; *) No order*
Mere anarchy is loosed upon the world,
5 The blood-dimmed tide° is loosed, and everywhere *)allusion to Macbeth*
The ceremony of innocence is drowned; *)Baptism (there will be no more)*
The best lack all conviction, while the worst
Are full of passionate intensity.
Surely some <u>revelation</u> is at hand; *)biblical allusion / "insight"*
10 Surely the Second Coming is at hand.
  The Second Coming! Hardly are those words out
  When a vast image out of *Spiritus Mundi*° *)a collective unconscious*
Troubles my sight; somewhere in sands of the desert *sphinx/Egypt*
A shape with lion body and the head of a man,° *) image of tyranny*
15 A gaze blank and <u>pitiless as the sun,</u> *personification*
Is moving its slow thighs, while all about it
Reel shadows of the indignant <u>desert birds.</u> *vultures*
The darkness drops again; but now I know *the last 2,000*
That twenty centuries of stony sleep *years have incubated*
20 Were vexed to nightmare by a rocking cradle, *the horrors to come*

(handwritten left margin: Foreshadow of what's coming)

°The phrase "second coming" has been traditionally used to refer to expectations of the return of Jesus for the salvation of believers, as described in the New Testament. The prophecies foretold that Christ's return would be preceded by famine, epidemics, wars between nations, and general civil disturbance. Yeats believed that human history could be measured in cycles of approximately 2,000 years (see line 19, "twenty centuries"). According to this system, the birth of Jesus ended the Greco-Roman cycle and in 1919, when Yeats wrote "The Second Coming," it appeared to him that the Christian period was ending and a new era was about to take its place. The New Testament expectation was that Jesus would reappear. Yeats, by contrast, holds that the disruptions of the twentieth century were preceding a takeover by the forces of evil. 1 *gyre*; a radiating spiral, cone, or vortex. Yeats used the intersecting of two of these shapes as a visual symbol of his cyclic theory. As one gyre spiraled and widened out, to become dissipated, one period of history would end; at the same time a new gyre, closer to the center, would begin and spiral in a reverse direction to the starting point of the old gyre. A drawing of this plan looks like this:

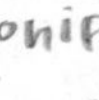

The falcon of line 2 is at the broadest, centrifugal point of one gyre, symbolically illustrating the end of a cycle. The "indignant desert birds" of line 17 "reel" in a tighter circle, symbolizing the beginning of the new age in the new gyre. 5 *blood-dimmed tide*: quotation from Shakespeare's Macbeth, 2.2.60–63. 12 *Spiritus Mundi*: literally, the spirit of the world, a collective human consciousness that furnished writers and thinkers with a common fund of images and symbols. Yeats referred to this collective repository as "a great memory passing on from generation to generation." 14 *lion body and the head of a man*: that is, the Sphinx, which in ancient Egypt symbolized the pharaoh as a spirit of the sun. Because of this pre-Christian origin, the reincarnation of a sphinx could therefore represent qualities associated in New Testament books like Revelation (11, 13, 17), Mark (13:14–20), and 2 Thessalonians (2:1–12) with a monstrous, superhuman, satanic figure.

And what rough beast, its hour come round at last,
Slouches towards <u>Bethlehem</u> to be born?

QUESTIONS   ˙ոilusion to
           pinnpide of jesus

1. Consider the following as symbols: the "gyre," the "falcon," the "blood-dimmed tide," the "ceremony of innocence," the "worst" who are "full of passionate intensity." What ideas and values do these symbolize in the poem?

2. Why does Yeats capitalize the phrase "Second Coming"? To what does this phrase refer? Explain the irony of Yeats's use of the phrase in this poem.

3. Contrast the symbols of the falcon of line 2 and the desert birds of line 17. Considering that these are realistically presented, how does the realism contribute to their identity as symbols?

4. What is symbolized by the sphinx being revealed as a "rough beast"? What is the significance of the beast's going "towards Bethlehem to be born"?

WRITING ABOUT SYMBOLISM AND ALLUSION IN POETRY

As you read the assigned poem, take careful and accurate notes, and make observations about the presence of symbols or allusions or both. Explanatory notes will help you establish basic information, but you also need to explain meanings and create interpretations in your own words. Use a dictionary for understanding words or phrases that require further study. For allusions, you might check out original sources to determine original contexts. Use the explanations supplied in your text, and ask your instructor when you need more information. Try to determine the ways in which your poem is similar to, or different from, the original work or source, and then determine the purpose served by the allusion.

Questions for Discovering Ideas

CULTURAL OR UNIVERSAL SYMBOLS

- What symbols that you can characterize as cultural or universal can you discover in names, objects, places, situations, or actions in the poem (e.g., nightingales, hemlock, a thorn, two lovers, Bethlehem)?
- How are these symbols used? What do they mean, both specifically, in the poem, and universally, in a broader context? What would the poem be like without the symbolic meaning?

CONTEXTUAL SYMBOLS

- What contextual symbols can you locate in the poem (e.g., withered sedge, a flock of birds, a doe running into a woods)? How are these symbols used specifically in the poem? What would the poem be like if the contextual symbol were not taken to be symbolic?
- What causes you to conclude that the symbols are truly symbolic? What is being symbolized? What do the symbols mean? How definite or direct is the symbolism?
- Is the symbolism used systematically throughout the poem, or is it used only once? How does the symbolism affect the poem's ideas or emotions?

ALLUSIONS

- Granted your knowledge of literature, science, geography, television, the Bible, film, popular culture, and other fields of knowledge, what allusions do you recognize?
- Do you find other references in these or other categories? What do the allusions mean in their original context? What do they mean within the poem?
- Do you see any possible allusions that you are not sure about? What help do you find in the explanatory notes in the text you are using? Consult a dictionary, such as *The Oxford Dictionary of Allusions,* or another reference work to discover the nature of these allusions. Refer also to Chapter 7. If you have questions, be sure to ask your reference librarian for assistance.

Strategies for Organizing Ideas

Begin with a brief description of the poem and of the symbolism or allusions in it. A symbol might be central to the poem, or an allusion might be introduced at a particularly important point. Your central idea might take you in a number of directions: You might conclude that the symbolism is based on objects like flowers and natural scenes, or that it stems out of an action or set of actions, or that it is developed from an initial situation such as a time of the day or year. The symbols may be universal or contextual; they may be applicable particularly to personal life or to political or social life. Allusions may emphasize the differences between your poem and the work or event to which the allusion refers, or they may highlight the circumstances of your poem. In addition, you might make a point that the symbols and/or allusions make the poem seem optimistic, or pessimistic, and so on.

Here are some possible approaches for your essay, which may be combined as need arises.

1. *The meaning of symbols or allusions.* This approach is the most natural one to take for an essay on symbolism or allusion. If you have discovered a symbol or symbols, or allusions, explain the meaning as best you can. What is the poem's major idea? How do you know that your interpretation is valid? How do the poem's symbols and allusions contribute to your interpretation? How pervasive, how applicable, are these devices? If you have discovered many symbols and allusions, which ones predominate? What do they mean? Why are some more important than others? What connects them with each other and with the poem's main ideas? How are you able to make conclusions about all this?

2. *The effect of symbols or allusions on the poem's form.* Here the goal is to determine how symbolism or allusion is related to the poetic structure. Where does the symbol occur? If it is early in the poem, how do the subsequent parts relate to the ideas borne by the symbol? What logical or chronological function does the symbol serve in the poem's development? Is the symbol repeated, and if so, to what effect? If the symbol is introduced later, has it been antici-pated earlier? How do you know? Can the symbol be considered climactic? What might the structure of the poem have been like if the symbolism had not been used? (Answering this question can help you judge how the symbol influences the poem's structure.) Many of these same questions might also be applied to an allusion or allusions. In addition, for an allusion, it is important to compare the contexts of the work you are studying and the original to determine how the poet uses the allusion as a part of the poem's form or structure.

3. *The relationship between the literal and the symbolic.* The object here is to describe the literal nature of the symbols, and then to determine their appro-priateness to the poem's context. If the symbol is part of a narrative, what is its literal function? If the symbol is a person, object, or setting, what physical as-pects are described? Are colors included? Shapes? Sizes? Sounds? In light of this description, how applicable is the symbol to the ideas it embodies? How appropriate is the literal condition to the symbolic condition? The answers to questions like these should lead not so much to a detailed account of the meaning of the symbols but rather to an account of their appropriateness to the topics and ideas of the poem.

4. *The implications and resonances of symbols and allusions.* This type of essay is more personal than the others, for it is devoted to the suggestions and associations—the "implications and resonances"—that the poem's symbols and allusions bring out. The object of the essay is to describe your own responses or chain of thinking that the poem sets in motion. You are therefore free to move in your own direction as long as you base your dis-cussion on the symbols and allusions in the poem. If the poet is speaking in general terms about the end of an era, for example, as with the symbol of the "rough beast" in Yeats's "The Second Coming" and the giant fishnets in Jeffers's "The Purse-Seine," then you could apply these symbols to your own thinking.

Your conclusion might contain a summary of your main points. If your poem is rich in symbols or allusions, you might also consider some of the ele-ments that you have not discussed in the body and try to tie these together with those you have already discussed. It would also be appropriate to intro-duce any new ideas you developed as a result of your study.

Illustrative Student Essay

Underlined sentences in this paper *do not* conform to MLA style and are used solely as teaching tools to emphasize the central idea, thesis sentence, and topic sentences throughout the paper.

Jani 1

Sonal Jani

Professor Barack

English 212

20 March 2008

Symbolism in Oliver's "Wild Geese"°

[1]   Mary Oliver's "Wild Geese" can be understood as an extended answer to the issue raised in its first line. This idea, to be refuted, is unusual--one might almost say startling--because it is stated so baldly: "You do not have to be good." It does not seem that many poems begin with a line like that. The rest of the poem is developed through a series of symbols asserting the idea that there is a more significant kind of goodness.* Oliver's argument is to shun traditional habits of contrition and repentance, and instead to emphasize that goodness exists in the animal and human spirit within oneself, and also everywhere in Nature. She assserts this idea first through a traditional but negative symbol, and second through a series of positive symbols of the natural world.†

[2]   The first symbol in the poem negatively symbolizes traditional but ineffective approaches to creating goodness within oneself. The picture is that of a hermit-like person actively suffering for contrition's sake:

You do not have to walk on your knees

for a hundred miles through the desert, repenting. (lines 2–3)

The notion of "repenting" symbolizes the tradition that human beings must endure punishment to atone for guilt and sins. The vision of knees in the desert

°**This poem appears on page 969.**
*Central Idea.
†**Thesis sentence.**

Jani 2

thus symbolizes the deeply ingrained idea that self-denial and suffering are
needed to achieve goodness and inner peace.

Before going on with the more detailed symbolism of the poem, Oliver   [3]
introduces another element of the presumed discussion the speaker is having
with a listener who has spoken before the poem begins, but who now just
listens. The idea is that goodness can be found within "the soft animal of
your body":

> You only have to let the soft animal of your body
>
> love what it loves. (lines 4,5)

It is not clear just what sort of animal is described, but the word "animal" is
based on the action of breathing, the essential characteristic of living beings.
The essence of life is therefore the "soft animal" (not a vicious animal) of the
self, which here symbolizes the ethics that are a consequence of love.

A second part of the poem begins with the seventh line, "Meanwhile the   [4]
world goes on." The idea here is that there is a larger existence than the one that
is defined by human concepts of goodness or repentance, guilt or despair. The
speaker's argument is carried out with a cumulative set of symbols derived from
the natural world. These are "the sun and the clear pebbles of the rain" which
are visualized as "moving across" the world--over "prairies," "deep trees,"
"mountains," and "rivers" (lines 8–11), all of which describe vast expanses of
land and wilderness. Because of their virtual infiniteness, these natural objects
make human concerns seem small and insignificant. Thus, as symbols, they
signify the need for a larger perspective and a more broad dedication than
human beings usually make.

In this context the poet introduces the symbol of "the wild geese, high   [5]
in the clean blue air" (line 12). The geese, part of the general symbol of the
world going on, are migrating homeward. The idea seems mystical, but
nevertheless the symbolism provides a clear analogy for human beings
living in our modern troubled and troubling civilization. We are part of the
universe, the world. We live here and belong here, just as the wild geese do.
We tend to forget our place here, however, as we lose perspective and

Jani 3

become enmeshed in cultural concerns which lead us only to guilt and loneliness (line 14). The need is to listen to the inner animal, the outer world, which has a strong pull on our imaginations, just as the wild geese symbolize a natural power that restores the world's creatures to home and to a sense of belonging.

[6]   The "world," in the symbolic fabric of Oliver's poem, is an active participant in the process. It "offers itself to your imagination, / calls to you like the wild geese, harsh and exciting--" (lines 15,16). The idea of the symbol is that we, like the wild geese, should let our imaginations follow the call. While people are traditionally preoccupied with despair, the sentient and nonsentient elements of nature are simply being. We could be like that if only we could perceive the symbolic meaning of the world around us. If we follow the morallity of the trees and the sun and the rain, we too will experience the strength of being a part of nature. Our morality will then flow to us as a matter of course because we will have acknowledged our place "in the family of things" (line 18) just as the geese return home to lead their lives in the landscapes of the world.

Jani 4

Work Cited

Oliver, Mary. "Wild Geese." Literature: An Introduction to Reading and
      Writing. Ed. Edgar V. Roberts. 9th ed. New York: Pearson Longman,
      2009. 969.

Commentary on the Essay

This essay conforms to the first strategy for writing about symbolism (p. 976) inasmuch as it involves a concentrated explanation of the symbolism in Oliver's "Wild Geese"—symbolism that is mainly drawn from the world of Nature.

The introduction briefly characterizes Oliver's confrontational opening line and goes on to assert that the rest of the poem is developed through a succession of symbols. The central idea is responsive to the opening line—namely, that the poem is to introduce symbols of "a more significant kind of goodness"—and the thesis sentence states that in the body there will be a discussion of a negative symbol and a set of more positive symbols.

Paragraphs 3 through 5 consider the meanings of the poem's three major symbols—the "soft animal" (3), rain, land, and wilderness (4), and the "wild geese" (5). The final paragraph deals with the issue of goodness and the different kind of "good" brought out in the poem's symbolism (that is, being part of the "family of things").

Writing Topics About Symbolism and Allusion in Poetry

1. Analyze the ways in which Keats, Herbert, and Jeffers use symbols to convey the fact and idea of capture and thralldom in "La Belle Dame Sans Merci," "The Collar," and "The Purse-Seine." What major symbols do the three poets use? How appropriate is each symbol in its respective poem? How do the poets use the symbols to focus on the problems they present in their poems?

2. Describe the differences in the ways in which Graham, Viorst, and Yeats use allusions in "The Geese," "A Wedding Sonnet for the Next Generation," and "The Second Coming." How completely can we understand these poems without an explanation of the allusions? How extensive should explanations be? To what extent does the allusiveness make the poems difficult? Challenging? Interesting? Enriching?

3. Compare the use of religious symbols in Donne's "The Canonization" and Herbert's "The Collar." What are the locations from which the poets draw their symbols? How do the symbols figure into the major ideas and arguments of the poems?

4. Describe the nature of the symbols in Hardy's "In Time of 'The Breaking of Nations'" and Whitman's "A Noiseless Patient Spider." What parallels in general topic matter do you discover? How do the poets make the poems diverge, despite the common qualities of the symbols?

5. Write a poem in which you develop a major symbol, as Jeffers does in "The Purse-Seine" and Cowper does in "The Poplar Field" (Chapter 13). To get yourself started, you might consider symbols like these:

   - A littered street or sidewalk
   - A new SUV, or an all-terrain vehicle, or a hybrid
   - Coffee-hour after religious services

- An athletic competition
- A computer
- The checkout counter at the neighborhood supermarket
- The family dog looking out a front window as the children leave for school
- A handgun

Write an essay describing the process of your creation. How do you begin? How much detail is necessary? How many conclusions do you need to bring out about your symbol? When do you think you have said enough? Too much? How do you decide?

6. Write a poem in which you make your own allusions to your own experiences, such as attending school, participating in an activity, joining a team, reading a book, identifying with a fictional or a movie character, recalling a passage from a popular song or a poem or story you have read, or going to a recent artistic or political event. What assumptions do you make about your reader when you bring out your allusions? How do you make the allusion (i.e., by a quotation, a name, a title, an indirect reference)? How does your allusion deepen your meaning? How does your allusion increase your own power of expression?

7. Write an essay describing the use of animals and birds as symbols in this chapter's poems by Graham, Jeffers, Oliver, and Whitman. How do the poets show the symbolic connection of the animals to human affairs? How faithfully do they consider the animals as animals?

8. From your library, take out a university press study of Yeats or Jeffers. How much detail is devoted in the study to either poet's use of symbols? How pervasively is symbolism employed by the poet? How does the poet use symbolism to express ideas about science or nationalism? What other use or uses does the poet make of symbolism?

Chapter 20

Myths: Systems of Symbolic Allusion in Poetry

Our word **myth** is derived from the Greek word *muthos* or *mythos*, meaning a story, narrative, or plot. Usually, we think of a myth as a story that deals with the relationships of gods to humanity (the myths of Prometheus or Odysseus), with battles among gods (the myth of Zeus and Chronos) or heroes (the myth of Achilles and Hector), or with heroic quests (the myth of Jason and the Argonauts). In addition, a myth may be a set of beliefs or assumptions among societies (the myth of the American frontier, the myth of endless progress, the myth of the Lorelei). **Mythology** refers collectively to stories and beliefs, either of one particular society (*Greek mythology*) or of a number of societies (*the mythology of the Ancient Near East*). A system of beliefs and religious or historical doctrine is a **mythos** (the *Islamic mythos* or the *Buddhist mythos*). Although we usually think that myths are ancient—and of course many are—the meanings of myths are not limited exclusively to the past. Old myths profoundly influence our modern consciousness, and they, together with new assumptions and mythical ways of seeing and understanding, continue not only to affect our daily lives but also to shape our local and national political policies.

Mythology as an Explanation of How Things Are

Throughout the ages, people have developed myths because they want to know who they are, where they have been, where they are going, how the world got the way it is, and whether anyone up there cares. Mythical stories and characters provide answers to such questions. They comprise narrative systems that explain the history, culture, religion, and collective psychology of individual societies and civilizations. They also satisfy our need to understand and humanize conditions that are otherwise unknown, mysterious, and frightening.

Although many myths originated in primitive times, they still today provide a wealth of material and allusion in literature and art. The world around us seems more rich, awesome, and divine when we know that many events, places, creatures, trees, and flowers are important in the beautiful stories and legends that we have inherited from the past.

Myths and the Sciences Are Not the Same

Myths and the sciences overlap, since both provide explanations for the universe. At the beginning of civilization, almost all the vital questions were answered by myths, such as those about gods, the creation of the earth and humanity, lightning and thunder, earthquakes and volcanoes, sexuality, birth, good, evil, and death.

As Western civilization became progressively more educated and sophisticated, particularly after the time of Copernicus (1473–1543), scientific discoveries replaced myths as the means of explaining the "how" of life and existence. Thus we understand today that lightning and thunder are produced by electrically charged clouds, not by the great and powerful gods Zeus and Thor hurling lightning bolts from the sky (but lightning is still not a thoroughly understood phenomenon). Wherever volcanoes erupt, we know that the cause is molten rock under great pressure deep within the earth's crust being vented violently through fissures in the volcano, not the anger of the Hawaiian goddess Pele.

Even though myths are not scientific, however, they should not be dismissed. It is true that we know an immense amount scientifically about *how* things happen, but in the last resort we do not really know *why* they happen. For instance, although physicists and theorists tell us an astoundingly great deal about the early stages of the universe and the development of galaxies, quasars, black holes, stars, the solar system, and our earth, they do not answer the imponderable religious and philosophical questions about causes that myths attempt to explain. It is interesting to observe that our discoveries of the moons circling the planets, such as the gas giants Jupiter and Saturn, are given names derived from mythology, such as Io, Callisto, and Ganymede—moons of Jupiter that were discovered by Galileo four hundred years ago.

Mythical Stories and Concepts Have Great Power

Myths are ingrained in our minds and in our speech. For example, we *know* with scientific certainty that we have daylight when our city or town faces the sun directly, and that we have night when we are turned away from the sun and are in the earth's shadow. Nevertheless, we continue to use the phrases "the sun rises" and "the sun sets" to explain day and night, as though we still believed the myth that the earth is flat and that the sun circles around it. Such mythically originated language is inseparable from our minds. Even the belief that science and technology can solve every earthly problem may be seen as a myth. Human beings, in short, are **mythopoeic**— that is, not only do we live with myths, but we habitually create them.

We should therefore realize that myths express truth symbolically even if mythical heroes and stories themselves are scientifically or historically no more than fabrications. The truths are not to be found in mythical lore itself but rather in what they show about our earthly existence. Thus, when we read about the problems of the ancient Theban king Oedipus, we can safely assume that the specific details of his life (if he actually ever did live) did not happen just as Sophocles dramatizes them in *Oedipus the King*. But we find in the play a powerful rendering of how human beings make mistakes and how they must pay for them. In short, the truth of the Oedipus myth is psychological, not literal and historical.

Myths Explain Our Circumstances in the World and the Universe

We can broaden our consideration by adding that myths also imply a special perspective about how people see their place and purpose. This kind of myth may be constructive and generative. Thus, at one time most North Americans accepted

the myth that Nature was limitless and hostile and in need of being conquered. With this concept in mind, settlers moved into every available corner of the land— to build, farm, create industries, and establish new ways of life. Without such an inspiring myth, people might have stayed put, and the nation would never have achieved its current prominence.

This is not to say that all myths are positive; indeed, some myths are destructive. Thus, the once-positive myth of hostile and inexhaustible Nature has led us into the massive problems we face today with environmental exploitation and degradation. There is need for a different myth—a myth declaring that the earth is no longer inimical and in need of taming, but rather that it is beautiful, tender, and fragile and is in need of preservation and conservation. The Ansel Adams photograph "Forest Floor, Yosemite Valley" is a visual embodiment of this more tolerant and loving myth of Nature.

Mythological Themes or Motifs Are Common to Many Cultures

Since myths address our human need to know, it is not surprising to find that many civilizations, separated by time and space, have parallel myths, such as the many stories accounting for the creation of the universe. The details of these myths are different, but the *patterns* are similar inasmuch as they all posit both an original time and act of creation and a creator god or gods who also take part in human history. The principal god is perceived as a shaper, a modeler, a divine artisan, who has fashioned the orderly systems we find in the world, such as life, daylight, ecological dependence, tides, warmth, fertility, harvests, morality, and social stability.

One of the most crucial of all myths involves sin, disobedience, and evil, which are usually blamed for winter, natural calamities, illness, and death. A corollary of the myth is that a god-hero or goddess-heroine must undergo a sacrifice to atone for sin and to ensure the renewed vitality of spring. In *The Golden Bough,* a massive collection and analysis of mythic stories, Sir James Frazer (1854–1941) compares a series of mythical death-renewal motifs. Among such sacrificed and reborn gods are Thammuz (Babylonia), Attis (Phrygia), Osiris (Egypt), and Adonis, Dionysus, and Persephone (Greece). Again, the specific myths take different forms, but they reflect the same mysteries, fears, and hopes.

Scholars and anthropologists like Frazer were among the first to observe the interrelationships among myths produced by diverse cultures. The Swiss psychoanalyst Carl Gustav Jung (1875–1961) offered an explanation for this duplication. He noticed that images, characters, and events similar to those in literature, mythology, and religion also occurred in the dreams of his patients. He termed these recurring images **archetypes** (from the Greek word meaning "model" or "first mold") and developed a theory that all human beings share a universal or collective unconsciousness. Even if Jung's theory is ignored, the fact remains that types of mythic creatures such as dragons and centaurs, archetypal mother-daughter and father-son stories, and narratives involving sacrifices, heroic quests, and trips to the underworld recur throughout various mythologies and pervade our literature.[1]

Mythology and Literature

When writing was invented approximately four to five thousand years ago, the first written works recorded oral mythologies; that is, the mythologies had already existed for long periods of time before they were written down. The ancient Greek poet Homer, for example (perhaps a mythical figure himself), told about the mythical gods and heroes of the Trojan War. Homer did not actually write (tradition says he was blind), but other writers learned, recorded, and transmitted his epics. The Latin writer Ovid (43 BCE–17 CE) knew a large body of mythology and wrote poetic stories based on it. The result of this assimilation of myth into poetry was a combination of literature and religion that served the double purpose of teaching and entertaining. In this way, poets throughout antiquity used mythology as a mine for ideas, images, and symbols.

Although almost two thousand years have passed since Ovid lived, writers and artists still rely on mythology. In every generation since the earliest Anglo-Saxon poems and legends, poets of English have retold and updated mythological stories. Indeed, most of the poems in this chapter are from the twentieth

[1]See also Chapter 29 for a further discussion of archetypes.

century. Modern poetry utilizing mythology, however, is no longer designed to reinforce the dominant religion. Instead, it uses mythology to link past and present, to dramatize important concerns, and to symbolize universal patterns of thought.

Most Western poets who use mythological material in their verse turn to long-standing bodies of myth, particularly those of Greco-Roman, Norse-Teutonic, and Judeo-Christian origin. These systems of mythology are **universal** or **public,** since they are part of a vast common heritage. Like *cultural symbols*, they make up a reservoir of material that all writers are free to employ.

References to Mythology Are Common in Poetry

When poets make references to a myth, as in poems like Tennyson's "Ulysses" and Parker's "Penelope," both of which refer to the myth of Odysseus (Ulysses), they assume that readers already understand something about the stories and characters. With these poems, readers are expected to know enough of Homer's *Odyssey* to recall that this hero fought in the Trojan War for ten years and then was forced to spend an additional ten years in attempting to return to Ithaca, the island kingdom that he ruled. In other words, during most of his reign he was a warrior and adventurer—an absentee ruler—but at the same time his queen, Penelope, stayed at home.

Although you might have enough background in mythology to understand a poet's mythological references, you may sometimes need to fill in or reinforce your knowledge. A good place to start is a dictionary or general encyclopedia, where you will find brief identifications of mythic figures and a key to further reading. Eventually you will want access to more detailed information. Excellent books that retell the stories of Greco-Roman mythology are Richmond Hathorn's *Greek Mythology*, M. C. Howatson's *The Oxford Companion to Classical Literature*, and Timothy Gantz's *Early Greek Myth: A Guide to Literary and Artistic Sources*. Bullfinch's *The Age of Fable* and Edith Hamilton's *Mythology* are respected traditional books. Charles Mills Gayley's *The Classic Myths in English Literature and in Art* has been a standard and revered book for more than a century. There are also many classical dictionaries, such as the *Oxford Classical Dictionary*, that are immensely useful. Early in the nineteenth century, John Keats learned much of his mythology from John Lemprière's *A Classical Dictionary: Containing A Copious Account of all The Proper Names Mentioned in Ancient Authors*. Many libraries have this book on their reference shelves and it can also be located through Google Scholar, and your use of it will both inform you and impress you with a sense of bibliographical history. Not all mythology is classical. Should you want to understand references to the myths of Paul Bunyan and Johnny Appleseed, for example, you would want a collection of American folktales. References to Odin, Thor, the Valkyries, or Loki should lead you to a collection of Norse-Teutonic mythology.

Myths Are Often Vital in Poetry

Let us look at a poem by William Butler Yeats that draws on Greco-Roman mythology:

WILLIAM BUTLER YEATS (1865–1939)

For a photo, see Chapter 16, page 833.

 ## Leda and the Swan (1924; 1923)

A sudden blow: the great wings beating still
Above the staggering girl, her thighs caressed
By the dark webs, her nape caught in his bill,
He holds her helpless breast upon his breast.

5 How can those terrified vague fingers push
The feathered glory from her loosening thighs?
And how can body, laid in that white rush,
But feel the strange heart beating where it lies?

A shudder in the loins engenders there
10 The broken wall, the burning roof and tower
And Agamemnon dead.
                                    Being so caught up,
So mastered by the brute blood of the air,
Did she put on his knowledge with his power
Before the indifferent beak could let her drop?

QUESTIONS

1. What mythic event does the poem retell? Who was Leda? The swan? Who were Leda's children? What events are alluded to in lines 10 and 11?
2. How is Leda described? What words suggest her helplessness? What phrases suggest the swan's mystery and divinity?
3. What question is raised in the last two lines? To what extent does the poem provide an answer to this question?

Yeats's sonnet focuses on a specific event of ancient Greek mythology: Zeus, king of the gods, having taken the form of a swan, raped Leda, a Spartan queen. According to the myth, this violent event was a starting point not only of Greek civilization but also of the angers and troubles of humanity in general. One of the children born of the rape was Helen of Troy, whose abduction by Paris precipitated the Trojan War. Yeats's phrase "The broken wall, the burning roof and tower" refers to the Greek destruction of Troy. Another child was Clytemnestra, married to Agamemnon, king of Mycenae and leader of the allied Greek forces. Because Agamemnon had sacrificed their daughter Iphigeneia as a part of the war effort, Clytemnestra vowed revenge and had him murdered when he returned home from the Trojan War.

After a graphic recounting of the swan's attack on Leda and a brief reference to the sack of Troy and Agamemnon's death, Yeats's concluding lines raise a central issue stemming from the myth. While Leda took on some of Zeus's divine power with the rape (through the process of childbearing), the poem asks whether she also "put on" some of his divine knowledge—whether she acquired Zeus's foreknowledge of the fall of Troy, the murder of Agamemnon, and, by extension, the subsequent events in history. Of course, the question is rhetorical and the answer is negative.

If all Yeats's poem did were to question the ancient myth in this way, it would be of limited interest for modern readers. But it does more than that; it directs our attention to concerns of today. Thus, we may conclude from Yeats's use of the myth that human beings, like Leda, do not have foreknowledge, but have only their own culture, experience, and intelligence as their guides. If divine beings exist, they have no interest in human affairs, but are rather uninvolved and "indifferent" (line 14). By extension the myth suggests that the burden of civilization is on human beings themselves and that if knowledge and power are ever to be combined for constructive goals, that blending must be a human achievement.

Yeats thus employs mythic material in this sonnet to raise a searching question about the natures of existence, knowledge, and power. The historical process is embodied in the rape, the children born out of it, and their troubles. As the central figure of the myth, Leda is the focal point of circumstances and concerns that have extended from the distant past to the present, and that will certainly extend into the future.

A poem of great interest because it is not only based on the ancient myth of Leda, but also is deliberately connected to "Leda and the Swan," is Mona Van Duyn's sixteen-line "Leda":

MONA VAN DUYN (1921–2004)

 ## Leda (1970)

> *"Did she put on his knowledge with his power*
> *Before the indifferent beak could let her drop?"*

Not even for a moment. He knew, for one thing, what he was.
When he saw the swan in her eyes he could let her drop.
In the first look of love men find their great disguise,
and collecting these rare pictures of himself was his life.

Her body became the consequence of his juice,   5
while her mind closed on a bird and went to sleep.
Later, with the children in school, she opened her eyes
and saw her own openness, and felt relief.

In men's stories her life ended with his loss.
She stiffened under the storm of his wings to a glassy shape,   10
stricken and mysterious and immortal. But the fact is,
she was not, for such an ending, abstract enough.

She tried for a while to understand what it was
that had happened, and then decided to let it drop.
She married a smaller man with a beaky nose,   15
And melted away in the storm of everyday life.

QUESTIONS

1. What relationship does this poem have to Yeats's "Leda and the Swan"?
2. Why does Van Duyn refer to "men's stories" in line 9? What sort of story is she telling in this poem? What use is she making here of the Leda myth? Why does she conclude the poem as she does?
3. Why does Van Duyn use sixteen lines for her poem, rather than casting it in the form of a sonnet? What rhyming pattern and repetitive pattern does she use in this poem?

Van Duyn quotes Yeats's final two lines, and the beginning of her poem is a direct answer to these lines. She puts the scene not in ancient classical times, but rather in the context of modern life, and the issues of the poem are the ways in which women's lives differ from men's. It is in such a way that Van Duyn has taken the original myth, alluded to the famous poem of Yeats, and added her own ideas to both ancient and modern treatments. As these poems demonstrate, mythology could hardly be more alive and vital in modern poetry.

Because myths thus embody recurring issues, they have great value for modern readers. Muriel Rukeyser's "Myth," for example (this chapter, p. 1012) uses the ancient myth about Oedipus to shed light amusingly on misperceptions about male-female relationships. Edward Field's "Icarus" (one of a number of Icarus poems we include in this chapter, p. 999) uses the ancient Icarus myth to decry the impact of modern society upon individuals. In these and in other poems based in mythology, you may look for such original ways in which poets receive something old and make it new. Myths do not belong only to the past but are alive and well in the present.

The poems in this chapter feature mythical material about Odysseus and Icarus, to which are added a number of poems based on other myths. Although the poems delve into ancient mythology for their subjects, they are remarkably different; each offers its own meaning, impact, and poetic experience. The poets shape their mythic material to illustrate and symbolize ideas about pride, daring, disillusionment, suffering, indignation, creativity, idealism, and indifference to the plights of others, and therefore the poems demonstrate how myths can be used for original effects in new poetic contexts. As you study the poems, consider these general questions along with the questions following the poems.

- How completely does the poem deal with the myth? What is included? What is excluded?
- What does the poet expect that you should know about the myth?
- How does the poet create a variation on the myth beyond the original?
- Why do modern poets treat mythical subjects?
- Do they simply interpret or reinterpret ancient stories, or do they use the ancient stories to shed light on modern circumstances? Why? How?

Six Poems Related to the Myth of Odysseus

Odysseus (Ulysses) was the mythical king of the island realm of Ithaca and one of the principal Greek generals in the Trojan War. He spent ten years fighting at Troy, and after the Greek victory he set sail for home. He encountered so many obstacles and delays, however, and his return took so long—an additional ten years—that adventure, traveling and lingering in places became a way of life with him. When he sailed near the Sirens, who lured sailors to death with the beauty of their songs, he resisted their attraction by having his crew tie him to the mast of his ship. For a year he was confined on the island of Aeaea by Circe, a sorceress. Circe turned his men into swine, but he escaped this transformation by taking a magical herb. For seven years he was held by the nymph Calypso on the island of Ogygia. There were many other adventures, all described in Homer's *Odyssey*.

During his long absence, his kingdom was entrusted to his wife and queen, Penelope. Penelope was dutiful and faithful, but she was besieged by crowds of suitors, each of whom sought to take over the Ithacan kingdom by marrying her, on the assumption that her husband was dead. She promised to accept one of the suitors when she finished making a shroud for her father-in-law. During the day she wove the shroud, but at night she unraveled her day's work, in this way delaying the need to fulfill her promise to remarry. By the time the suitors discovered her ruse, Odysseus had returned. With the help of his son Telemachus, he slaughtered all the suitors and restored himself as king.

Poems for Study

Louise Glück . . . . Penelope's Song, 991

W. S. Merwin . . . . Odysseus, 992

Dorothy Parker . . . . Penelope, 993

Linda Pastan . . . . The Suitor, 993

Alfred, Lord Tennyson . . . . Ulysses, 994

Peter Ulisse . . . . Odyssey: 20 Years Later, 996

LOUISE GLÜCK (b. 1943)

For a photo, see Chapter 13, page 700.

 ## Penelope's Song (1996)

Little soul, little perpetually undressed one,
do now as I bid you, climb
the shelf-like branches of the spruce tree;
wait at the top, attentive, like
a sentry or look-out. He will be home soon;   5
it behooves you to be
generous. You have not been completely
perfect either; with your troublesome body
you have done things you shouldn't
discuss in poems. Therefore   10
call out to him over the open water, over the bright water
with your dark song, with your grasping,
unnatural song—passionate,

like Maria Callas.° Who
15 wouldn't want you? Whose most demonic appetite
could you possibly fail to answer? Soon
he will return from wherever he goes in the meantime,
suntanned from his time away, wanting
his grilled chicken. Ah, you must greet him,
20 you must shake the boughs of the tree
to get his attention,
but carefully, carefully, lest
his beautiful face be marred
by too many falling needles.

°14 *Maria Callas:* Callas (1923–1977) was one of the best-known sopranos of the twentieth century, famous for her acting and her fiery interpretations of operatic heroines.

QUESTIONS

1. Who is the speaker of this poem? To whom is she speaking? What does she tell herself that she might not tell a companion or friend?
2. Describe your response to the poem if the speaker is Penelope, planning to welcome Odysseus after his twenty-year adventure in Troy and on the high seas.
3. Describe your response if the speaker is a modern woman planning to welcome her husband after he has spent Sunday afternoon seeing a professional football game. How does the poem seem to change under these circumstances?
4. If such were the circumstances, what use is Glück making of the Odysseus myth?

W. S. MERWIN (b. 1927)

🍁 Odysseus (1960)

Always the setting forth was the same,
Same sea, same dangers waiting for him
As though he had got nowhere but older.
Behind him on the receding shore
5 The identical reproaches, and somewhere
Out before him, the unravelling patience
He was wedded to. There were the islands
Each with its woman and twining welcome
To be navigated, and one to call "home."
10 The knowledge of all that he betrayed
Grew till it was the same whether he stayed
Or went. Therefore he went. And what wonder
If sometimes he could not remember
Which was the one who wished on his departure
15 Perils that he could never sail through,
And which, improbable, remote, and true,
Was the one he kept sailing home to?

QUESTIONS

1. What aspects of the Odysseus myth are evoked in this poem? What point does the poem make about Odysseus's experiences?

2. To what extent is Odysseus symbolic of a specific kind of life and attitude? How does our knowledge of Odysseus contribute to the impact and meaning of the poem?

3. Compare this poem with Parker's "Penelope." How is the same mythic material used toward different ends in these poems?

4. Compare this poem with Tennyson's "Ulysses." Explain how and why the same mythic figure can be used to convey such different ideas.

DOROTHY PARKER (1893–1967)

Penelope (1936)

In the pathway of the sun,
  In the footsteps of the breeze,
Where the world and sky are one,
  He shall ride the silver seas,
    He shall cut the glittering wave.   5
I shall sit at home, and rock;
Rise, to heed a neighbor's knock;
Brew my tea, and snip my thread;
Bleach the linen for my bed.
    They will call him brave.   10

QUESTIONS

1. How does the speaker describe her life? How is her life different from that of the male figure described in lines 1–5?

2. To what extent is Penelope a symbol? What does she symbolize? How does our knowledge of the myth deepen our response to this symbolism?

LINDA PASTAN (b. 1932)

The Suitor (1988)

There is always a story
that no one bothers to tell:
the younger son of a younger son,
hardly a suitor at all, sits
at the sharp edge of the table   5
among the boisterous men, not hungry
except for a glimpse of Penelope,
a woman wasted, he thinks—
those pale arms, that hair
a web she might have woven   10
around her own head.
Sometimes he tries to speak
to the son° who looks at him wonderingly,   *Telemachus*
but doesn't answer.
How could Odysseus have left?   15

he asks himself, but is grateful
for the chance to pretend
it could be him she'll choose.
He almost knows it must end badly,
20   though his will be a minor tributary
in that unplumbed sea
of wasted blood.

QUESTIONS

1. Why does Pastan choose a young man as the suitor of the poem? Who are the "boisterous men," and what is the suitor's relationship to them?

2. How does the suitor feel about Penelope? What does he have to gain by being a part of the suitors seeking her hand in marriage?

3. What will be the suitor's fate? Why does Pastan close on the note of "wasted blood"?

ALFRED, LORD TENNYSON (1809–1892)

For a photo, see Chapter 17, page 881.

 ## Ulysses (1842; 1833)

It little profits that an idle king,
By this still hearth, among these barren crags,
Matched with an aged wife, I mete and dole
Unequal laws° unto a savage race,   *rewards and punishments*
5   That hoard, and sleep, and feed, and know not me.
I cannot rest from travel; I will drink
Life to the lees.° All times I have enjoyed   *dregs*
Greatly, have suffered greatly, both with those
That loved me, and alone; on shore, and when
10   Through scudding drifts the rainy Hyades°
Vexed the dim sea. I am become a name;
For always roaming with a hungry heart
Much have I seen and known—cities of men
And manners, climates, councils, governments,
15   Myself not least, but honored of them all—
And drunk delight of battle with my peers,
Far on the ringing plains of windy Troy.
I am a part of all that I have met;
Yet all experience is an arch wherethrough
20   Gleams that untraveled world whose margin fades
Forever and forever when I move.
How dull it is to pause, to make an end,
To rust unburnished, not to shine in use!
As though to breathe were life! Life piled on life
25   Were all too little, and of one to me
Little remains; but every hour is saved

°10 *Hyades:* nymphs who were placed among the stars by Zeus, the king of the gods. The name means "rain," and the rising of the stars was thought to precede a storm.

From that eternal silence, something more,
A bringer of new things; and vile it were
For some three suns to store and hoard myself,
And this gray spirit yearning in desire   30
To follow knowledge like a sinking star,
Beyond the utmost bound of human thought.

    This is my son, mine own Telemachus,
To whom I leave the scepter and the isle°—
Well-loved of me, discerning to fulfill   35
This labor, by slow prudence to make mild
A rugged people, and through soft degrees
Subdue them to the useful and the good.
Most blameless is he, centered in the sphere
Of common duties, decent not to fail   40

In offices of tenderness, and pay
Meet° adoration to my household gods,   *appropriate*
When I am gone. He works his work, I mine.

    There lies the port; the vessel puffs her sail;
There gloom the dark, broad seas. My mariners,   45
Souls that have toiled, and wrought, and thought with me—
That ever with a frolic welcome took
The thunder and the sunshine, and opposed
Free hearts, free foreheads—you and I are old;
Old age hath yet his honor and his toil.   50
Death closes all; but something ere the end,
Some work of noble note, may yet be done,
Not unbecoming men that strove with Gods.
The lights begin to twinkle from the rocks;
The long day wanes; the slow moon climbs; the deep   55
Moans round with many voices. Come, my friends,
'Tis not too late to seek a newer world.
Push off, and sitting well in order smite
The sounding furrows; for my purpose holds
To sail beyond the sunset, and the baths   60
Of all the western stars, until I die.
It may be that the gulfs will wash us down;
It may be we shall touch the Happy Isles,°
And see the great Achilles,° whom we knew.

    Though much is taken, much abides; and though   65
We are not now that strength which in old days
Moved earth and heaven, that which we are, we are—
One equal temper of heroic hearts,
Made weak by time and fate, but strong in will
To strive, to seek, to find, and not to yield.   70

°34 *isle:* Ithaca, the island realm ruled by Odysseus 63 *Happy Isles:* the Elysian Fields, dwelling place of mortals who have been made immortal by the gods. 64 *Achilles:* Greek hero of the Trojan War who killed Hector and was in turn killed by Paris.

QUESTIONS

1. Who is the speaker of the poem? What is his attitude toward his life in Ithaca? What key phrases and adjectives in lines 1–5 establish this attitude?
2. Who is Telemachus? What is the speaker's attitude toward him? How are the speaker and Telemachus different?
3. What aspects of Ulysses are emphasized in this poem? To what extent does he become symbolic? What does he symbolize?

PETER ULISSE (b. 1944)

Odyssey: 20 Years Later (1995)

I battled Trojans with Odysseus.
Bludgeoning the eye of Polyphemus
I meandered past Scylla and Charybdis,
descended into Hades, outwitted Calypso.
5   I ate of the lotus, and forgot.
Twenty years I roamed—

Wandering Jew, Prodigal Son, opener
of doors in empty streets I
embraced strangers like a lover's quest,
10   searched for the beautiful which
alone
could make a life complete.
I released hands in bedrooms,
turned to St. Augustine

15   It is only now I feel the pull
of salmon swimming up current,
turtles drawn to Galapagos,
fowls finding a path through
a thousand mile sky,
20   only now I understand
Odyssey not as Cyclops, Sirens,
or unfavorable winds but

simply as
coming home.

QUESTIONS

1. Who is the "I" of line 1? How does this line reveal the identity of the "I"? How is this speaker different from the speaker of Tennyson's "Ulysses"? What do the final lines tell you about the speaker's and Odysseus's journeys?
2. Consider the speaker's description of having duplicated the actions performed by Odysseus and other ancient figures. What ideas does the speaker present about the repetitive or cyclical nature of human experience?
3. What autobiographical or confessional details are contained in lines 13–19? What educational experiences are alluded to in these lines?

Six Poems Related to the Myth of Icarus

Icarus was the son of Daedalus, the greatest master of applied science in ancient Greek myth. The story begins with Minos, king of Crete, who also ruled Athens and the rest of the Greek world. Each year (or, according to other versions of the story, every nine years) Minos compelled the Athenians to make a tribute of seven young people to be sacrificed to the Minotaur, an enormously powerful monster, half man and half bull, who was the source of Cretan military and political power. Needing to control the monster by confining him, Minos hired Daedalus to build an enclosure—a labyrinth—as a prison. Daedalus completed this job and then asked royal leave to return home, but Minos wanted to benefit further from the skills of Daedalus. Accordingly, Minos imprisoned Daedalus in the labyrinth together with his son, Icarus. Angered by the king's overbearing treatment, Daedalus got revenge by aiding the Athenian hero, Theseus, in killing the Minotaur and thereby in freeing Athens from the burden of the living tribute. Daedalus then exerted his great inventiveness to carry out an aerial escape from the labyrinth. He made two pairs of wings out of wax and feathers—one pair for himself and one for Icarus. Daedalus flew safely away and eventually made his home in Sicily. Icarus, however, flew too close to the sun. The wax melted and the wings fell apart. Icarus fell into the Icarian Sea (named after him), and he drowned.

Poems for Study

Brian Aldiss . . . . Flight 063, 997
W. H. Auden . . . . Musée des Beaux Arts, 998
Edward Field . . . . Icarus, 999
Muriel Rukeyser . . . . Waiting for Icarus, 1000
Anne Sexton . . . . . . To a Friend Whose Work Has Come to Triumph, 1001
William Carlos Williams . . . . Landscape with the Fall of Icarus, 1002

BRIAN ALDISS (b. 1925)

 Flight 063 (1994)

Why always speak of Icarus' fall?—
That legendary plunge
Amid a shower of tallow
And feathers and the poor lad's
Sweat? And that little splash   5
Which caught the eye of Brueghel°
While the sun remained
Aloof within its private zone?

°6 *Brueghel:* Pieter Brueghel (or Breughel) (c. 1525–1569) was a Flemish painter whose subjects included the Nativity ("the miraculous birth"), the Crucifixion ("the dreadful martyrdom"), and the fall of Icarus. His *Landscape with the Fall of Icarus* is reproduced on page I–7.

That fall remains
10   Suspended in the corporate mind.
Yet as our Boeing flies
High above the Arctic Circle

Into the sun's eye, think—
Before the fall the flight was.
15   (So with Adam—just before
The Edenic Fall, he had
That first taste of Eve.)

Dinner is served aboard Flight 063.
We eat from plastic trays, oblivious
20   To the stratosphere.

But Icarus—his cliff-top jump,
The leap of heart, the blue air scaled—
His glorious sense of life
Imperiled. Time
25   Fell far below, the everyday
Was lost in his ascent.

Up, up, he sailed, unheeding
Such silly limitations as
The melting point of wax.

QUESTIONS

1. What attitude toward Icarus does the speaker present (see lines 21–26)? What emotions
    does he attribute to Icarus during the beginning of the flight? What is the significance
    of line 14 ("Before the fall the flight was")?
2. What do the words "dinner" and "oblivious" suggest about modern attitudes toward
    flight?
3. Why does the speaker emphasize the word "think" (line 13)? Why is the melting point
    of wax a "silly" limitation?

W. H. AUDEN (1907–1973)

 Musée des Beaux Arts° (1940)

About suffering they were never wrong,
The Old Masters: how well they understood
Its human position; how it takes place
While someone else is eating or opening a window or just
        walking dully along;

°Museum of Fine Arts (French).

How, when the aged are reverently, passionately waiting   5
For the miraculous birth, there always must be
Children who did not specially want it to happen, skating
On a pond at the edge of the wood:
They never forgot
That even the dreadful martyrdom must run its course   10
Anyhow in a corner, some untidy spot
Where the dogs go on with their doggy life and the torturer's horse
Scratches its innocent behind on a tree.
In Brueghel's *Icarus*, for instance: how everything turns away
Quite leisurely from the disaster; the ploughman may   15
Have heard the splash, the forsaken cry,
But for him it was not an important failure; the sun shone
As it had to on the white legs disappearing into the green
Water; and the expensive delicate ship that must have seen
Something amazing, a boy falling out of the sky,   20
Had somewhere to get to and sailed calmly on.

QUESTIONS

1. What does the speaker say about the perceptions of the "Old Masters" to suffering? What use does Auden make of the Brueghel painting?

2. What concern do those close to Icarus's fall show toward the fall and the drowning? In the light of this concern, what ideas does the poem express about the ultimate importance of heroism and great occurrences?

3. Compare this poem with Frost's "Out, Out—" (Chapter 21). What does each poet indicate about the attitudes of people toward the suffering of others? Would you characterize these poems as painfully truthful? Ironic? Disillusioned?

EDWARD FIELD (b. 1924)

Icarus (1963)

Only the feathers floating around the hat
Showed that anything more spectacular had occurred
Than the usual drowning. The police preferred to ignore
The confusing aspects of the case,
And the witnesses ran off to a gang war.   5
So the report filed and forgotten in the archives read simply
"Drowned," but it was wrong: Icarus
Had swum away, coming at last to the city
Where he rented a house and tended the garden.

"That nice Mr. Hicks" the neighbors called him,   10
Never dreaming that the gray, respectable suit
Concealed arms that had controlled huge wings
Nor that those sad, defeated eyes had once
Compelled the sun. And had he told them
They would have answered with a shocked, uncomprehending stare.   15
No, he could not disturb their neat front yards;

Yet all his books insisted that this was a horrible mistake:
What was he doing aging in a suburb?
Can the genius of the hero fall
20   To the middling stature of the merely talented?

And nightly Icarus probes his wound
And daily in his workshop, curtains carefully drawn,
Constructs small wings and tries to fly
To the lighting fixture on the ceiling:
25   Fails every time and hates himself for trying.

He had thought himself a hero, had acted heroically,
And dreamt of his fall, the tragic fall of the hero;
But now rides commuter trains,
Serves on various committees,
30   And wishes he had drowned.

QUESTIONS

1. What twist on the Icarus myth occurs in this poem?
2. How does Field undercut the heroic myth of Icarus? What happens to Icarus after he rents a house and tends his garden? What does Icarus, the daily suburban commuter with "sad, defeated eyes," wish at the poem's end?
3. What level of language does Field use in this poem? How does this language complement the poem's antiheroic view of Icarus?

MURIEL RUKEYSER (1913–1980)

For a photo, see Chapter 15, page 786.

🍁 Waiting for Icarus (1973)

He said he would be back and we'd drink wine together
He said that everything would be better than before
He said we were on the edge of a new relation
He said he would never again cringe before his father
5   He said that he was going to invent full-time
He said he loved me that going into me
He said was going into the world and the sky
He said all the buckles were very firm
He said the wax was the best wax
10   He said Wait for me here on the beach
He said Just don't cry

I remember the gulls and the waves
I remember the islands going dark on the sea
I remember the girls laughing
15   I remember they said he only wanted to get away from me
I remember mother saying: Inventors are like poets,
                              a trashy lot

I remember she told me those who try out inventions are worse
I remember she added: Women who love such are the worst of all
I have been waiting all day, or perhaps longer.   20
I would have liked to try those wings myself.
It would have been better than this.

QUESTIONS

1. Who is speaking? How long has she been waiting for Icarus? When is she speaking? Does she know what has happened to Icarus?

2. In what ways is the speaker's narration a complaint? What does she complain about? How do her words bring ancient and modern circumstances to a common level?

3. To what degree is this poem humorous? What effect does Rukeyser's use of anaphora (see p. 764) have on the development of the poem?

ANNE SEXTON (1928–1974)

 ## To a Friend Whose Work Has Come to Triumph° (1962)

Consider Icarus, pasting those sticky wings on,
testing that strange little tug at his shoulder blade,
and think of that first flawless moment over the lawn
of the labyrinth. Think of the difference it made!
There below are the trees, as awkward as camels;   5
and here are the shocked starlings pumping past
and think of innocent Icarus who is doing quite well:
larger than a sail, over the fog and the blast
of the plushy ocean, he goes. Admire his wings!
Feel the fire at his neck and see how casually   10
he glances up and is caught, wondrously tunneling
into that hot eye. Who cares that he fell back to the sea?
See him acclaiming the sun and come plunging down
while his sensible daddy goes straight into town.

°The title alludes to and reverses the title of a poem by William Butler Yeats, "To a Friend Whose Work Has Come to Nothing" (1914).

QUESTIONS

1. Describe the contrast made in this poem between Icarus and Daedalus ("his sensible daddy"). What achievement does the speaker attribute to Icarus? Does the speaker seem to like or dislike Icarus?

2. In relation to line 12, what is the significance of the poem's title? In what sense has Icarus's life been a model for "Triumph"?

3. What tone is indicated by phrases like "sticky wings," "strange little tug," "awkward as camels," "plushy ocean," "hot eye," and "sensible daddy"?

WILLIAM CARLOS WILLIAMS (1883–1963)

For a photo, see Chapter 18, page 932.

 Landscape with the Fall of Icarus (1962)

According to Brueghel°
when Icarus fell
it was spring

a farmer was ploughing
5   his field
the whole pageantry

of the year was
awake tingling
near

10   the edge of the sea
concerned
with itself
sweating in the sun
that melted
15   the wings' wax
unsignificantly
off the coast
there was

a splash quite unnoticed
20   this was
Icarus drowning

°1 *Brueghel:* See the note for line 6 in Aldiss's "Flight 063" (p. 997). Also see I–7.

QUESTIONS

1. As the speaker presents the actual fall of Icarus as contained in Brueghel's painting, how significant is Icarus himself?

2. The poem is in tercets (three-line groups), and no line has more than four words. What is the effect of these sparse lines on the seriousness of Icarus's situation? Why does the poem not contain more detail?

3. Why does the speaker mention other things, specifically, the season, the farmer, the act of ploughing, the "tingling" pageant "of the year," and the shoreline—before he describes the splash in the last three lines?

4. Compare the view of Icarus in this poem with the views of Aldiss, Auden, Field, and Spender.

Four Poems Related to the Myth of Orpheus

In ancient Greece, Orpheus was considered a progenitor of art, culture, and music. His principal power was his music, for he was famous as the inventor of the lyre and also of song, and therefore he was revered as the originator of thought and order and as one of the creators of human civilization. When he played and sang, his music was so beautiful that he changed the course of rivers, deflected heavy thrown objects, and tamed wild animals. As a thinker and poet, he originated the practice of medicine, developed the skill and implements for literature and writing, and fashioned the knowledge and practice of agriculture. He also had prophetic powers, and for this reason he became the central figure in a number of mystical and secret religious cults.

Orpheus traveled with the Argonauts on the voyage of the *Argo* to gain the Golden Fleece. He was vital in the success of the mission, for his music was so beautiful that he saved the Argonauts from the Sirens, who otherwise would have attracted the men and then eaten them.

He was married to Eurydice, a dryad (a female spirit who lived among trees), who was bitten by a serpent and killed. In great bereavement, Orpheus went down into the Underworld—the kingdom of Hades, who was the god of the dead—in the hope that he could bring her back from death. Hades, along with his wife Persephone, was so favorably impressed by his music and by his love that he, as king of the Underworld, granted Orpheus the power to lead Eurydice back to life on earth. The proviso was that he not look at her on the return journey, for if he did, Eurydice would be lost to him permanently. Orpheus did indeed look back before the two reached the land of the living, and she was reclaimed by death.

In deep sorrow at his loss, Orpheus forsook most human activities except music. A group of Maenads celebrating the God Dionysus encountered him. They were angered because he no longer recognized the power of Dionysus, and in the madness of their rituals they tore him apart, literally, and threw his remains into the Hebrus River, in Thrace. Even though he was dismembered, his head floated on the water, and he still sang his customary beautiful songs. Also, his arms and hands still played the lyre. Eventually his remains came to rest on the Island of Lesbos, where a shrine to him was built. Nightingales sang regularly over his grave, and the Muses placed his lyre in the night sky. In the Underworld, his spirit was finally reunited with his dearest Eurydice. (See I-1.)

Poems for Study

Edward Hirsch . . . . The Swimmers, 1004

Rainer Maria Rilke . . . . The Sonnets to Orpheus: I.19, 1004

Mark Strand . . . . Orpheus Alone, 1005

Ellen Bryant Voigt . . . . Song and Story, 1007

EDWARD HIRSCH (b. 1950)

 ### The Swimmers (2005)

We warbled on the muddy banks
and waded up to our throats in the Delaware River

talking about Ovid washing himself in the Black Sea
and Paul Celan floating face down in the Seine.

5   We swam arm over arm through the green silt
and coasted along on our backs, marveling and mourning

for Shelley drowning off the shore at Viareggio
and Li Po tumbling drunkenly into the Yangtze.

These were the strokes we praised, weren't they,
10   the butterfly and the crawl, the lullabies

we crooned on the first warm day of summer
in honor of the non-swimmers, Crane and Berryman,°

in honor of Orpheus whose butchered head
is forever singing above the choppy waves.

°3–12 *Ovid . . . Berryman.* All these men were poets, and their deaths were all connected with water. Ovid (43 BCE–17 CE) died in exile in 17 CE at a town on the Black Sea during the reign of Augustus Caesar. Paul Celan (1920–1970) committed suicide in the Seine in April 1970. Percy Bysshe Shelley (1792–1822) died at sea when his boat capsized. Li Po, a Chinese poet of the eighth century CE, drowned when trying to embrace the moon's reflection in the Yangtze River. Hart Crane (1899–1932), committed suicide in 1932 by jumping from a ship into the Gulf of Mexico. John Berryman (1914–1972) leapt to his death from a Mississippi River bridge in Minneapolis in 1972.

QUESTIONS

1. Who are the "we" in this poem? What was the group collectively doing as they swam and waded in the Delaware River? Why do the drowned and dead poets come into the mind of the speaker?

2. Who are the swimmers and non-swimmers in the poem? Why does the speaker make a distinction between the two?

3. What do the drowned and dead poets have in common with Orpheus? In what sense are these writers still living, just as Orpheus is still living and "forever singing above the choppy waves"?

RAINER MARIA RILKE (1875–1926)

 ### The Sonnets to Orpheus: I.19 (1923)

Translated by Edgar V. Roberts

Though the world changes fast,
like shifting clouds,

with all things finished,
we fall home to ancient dust.

Far beyond this wavering uncertainty,   5
greater and more free,
your age-old song stays firm,
God with the lyre.

The lesson of suffering is unknown;
love is never understood;   10
and what we lose in Death

is not disclosed.
On earth, song alone
gives holiness and joy.

QUESTIONS

1. What does the poet mean by saying that the world changes fast? In the first quatrain, why does he contrast the fluctuating world and the ancient dust?

2. If the world is characterized by flux and change, what human possession is eternal? Why does the poet associate this possession with Orpheus?

3. With what topic are lines 9–12 concerned? How may the final two lines be understood as a contrast to these lines, and also as the poem's logical conclusion? What power is associated with Orpheus in these final two lines and throughout the poem?

MARK STRAND (b. 1934)

 ## Orpheus Alone (1989)

It was an adventure much could be made of: a walk
On the shores of the darkest known river,
Among the hooded, shoving crowds, by steaming rocks
And rows of ruined huts half buried in the muck;
Then to the great court with its marble yard   5
Whose emptiness gave him the creeps, and to sit there
In the sunken silence of the place and speak
Of what he had lost, what he still possessed of his loss,
And then, pulling out all the stops, describing her eyes,
Her forehead, where the golden light of evening spread,   10
The curve of her neck, the slope of her shoulders, everything
Down to her thighs and calves, letting the words come,
As if lifted from sleep, to drift upstream,
Against the water's will, where all the condemned
And pointless labor, stunned by his voice's cadence,   15
Would come to a halt, and even the crazed, disheveled
Furies, for the first time, would weep, and the soot-filled
Air would clear just enough for her, the lost bride,
To step through the image of herself and be seen in the light.

20 As everyone knows, this was the first great poem,
Which was followed by days of sitting around
In the houses of friends, with his head back, his eyes
Closed, trying to will her return, but finding
Only himself, again and again, trapped

25 In the chill of his loss, and, finally,
Without a word, taking off to wander the hills
Outside of town, where he stayed until he had shaken
The image of love and put in its place the world
As he wished it would be, urging its shape and measure

30 Into speech of such newness that the world was swayed,
And trees suddenly appeared in the bare place
Where he spoke and lifted their limbs and swept
The tender grass with the gowns of their shade,
And stones, weightless for once, came and set themselves there,

35 And small animals lay in the miraculous fields of grain
And aisles of corn, and slept. The voice of light
Had come forth from the body of fire, and each thing
Rose from its depths and shone as it never had.
And that was the second great poem,

40 Which no one recalls anymore. The third and greatest
Came into the world as the world, out of the unsayable,
Invisible source of all longing to be, it came
As things come that will perish, to be seen or heard
Awhile, like the coating of frost or the movement

45 Of wind, and then no more; it came in the middle of sleep
Like a door to the infinite, and, circled by flame,
Came again at the moment of waking, and sometimes,
Remote and small, it came as a vision with trees
By a weaving stream, brushing the bank

50 With their violet shade, with somebody's limbs
Scattered among the matted, mildewed leaves nearby,
With his severed head rolling under the waves,
Breaking the shifting columns of light into a swirl
Of slivers and flecks; it came in a language

55 Untouched by pity, in a poem, lavish and dark,
Where death is reborn and sent into the world as a gift,
So the future, with no voice of its own, or hope
Of ever becoming more than it will be, might mourn.

QUESTIONS

1. What are the three great and creative poems that the poet associates with "Orpheus Alone"? What powers does the poet attribute to Orpheus, or to the spirit of Orpheus? Why are these poems called poems, and not elements of creation?

2. Why does no one recall the second great poem? What has happened in the world to make this forgetfulness happen? Which of the poems do you think is the greatest poem?

3. Why must Eurydice be lost, and Orpheus be dismembered, for the three poems to come into existence? What qualities of human beings seem to require the sacrifice of other human beings so that progress and beauty may become a part of life?

ELLEN BRYANT VOIGT (b. 1943)

🍁 Song and Story (1992)

The girl strapped in the bare mechanical crib
does not open her eyes, does not cry out.
The glottal tube is taped into her face;
bereft of sound, she seems so far away.
But a box on the stucco wall, wired to her chest,   5
televises the flutter of her heart—
news from the pit—her pulse rapid and shallow,
a rising line, except when her mother sings,
outside the bars: whenever her mother sings
the line steadies into a row of waves,   10
song of the sea, song of the scythe

    old woman by the well, picking up stones
    old woman by the well, picking up stones

When Orpheus, beating rhythm with a spear
against the deck of the armed ship, sang   15
to steady the oars, he borrowed an old measure:
broadax striking oak, oak singing back,
the churn, the pump, the shuttle sweeping the warp
like the waves against the shore they were pulling toward.
The men at the oars saw only the next man's back.   20
They were living a story—the story of desire,
The rising line of ships at war or trade.
If the sky's dark fabric was pierced by stars,
they didn't see them; if dolphins leapt from the water,
they didn't see them. Sweat beaded their backs   25
like heavy dew. But whether they came to triumph
or defeat, music ferried them out
and brought them back, taking the dead and wounded
back to the wave-licked, smooth initial shore,
song of the locust, song of the broom   30

    old woman in the field, binding wheat
    old woman by the fire, grinding corn

When Orpheus, braiding rushes by the stream,
devised a song for the overlords of hell
to break the hearts they didn't know they had,   35
he drew one from the olive grove—
the raven's hinged wings from tree to tree,
whole flocks of geese crossing the ruffled sky,
the sun's repeated arc, moon in its wake:
this wasn't the music of pain. Pain has no music,   40
pain is a story: it starts,
Eurydice was taken from the fields.
She did not sing—you cannot sing in hell—
but in that viscous dark she heard the song
flung like a rope into the crater of hell,   45
song of the sickle, song of the hive

old woman by the cradle, stringing beads
old woman by the cradle, stringing beads

The one who can sing sings to the one who can't,
50   who waits in the pit, like Procne° among the slaves,
as the gods decide how all such stories end,
the story woven into the marriage gown,
or scratched with a stick in the dust around the well,
or written in blood in the box on the stucco wall—
55   look at the wall:
the song, rising and falling, sings in the heartbeat,
sings in the seasons, sings in the daily round—
even at night, deep in the murmuring wood—
listen—one bird, full-throated, calls to another,
60   *little sister*, frantic little sparrow° under the eaves.

°50–60 *Procne . . . frantic little sparrow*: Procne was married to Tereus, King of Thrace, who raped Procne's sister Philomela. To gain revenge against her husband, Procne went in disguise among the slaves of Tereus and then killed Itys, her son by Tereus, and served him to Tereus for dinner. Tereus was prevented from revenge against Procne because he was turned into a hoopoe, while Procne became a nightingale and Philomela became a swallow.

QUESTIONS

1. Why does the poem's first stanza contain the story of the girl strapped into the crib? What happens to the girl when her mother sings to her? What is the connection between this action and the subject of the poem, Orpheus?

2. What is the event in the life of Orpheus described in the second stanza? What attributes of Orpheus, and the theme of the poem, are brought out in this stanza?

3. What better known story about Orpheus is contained in the third stanza? How does Orpheus devise a song to break the hearts of the overlords of hell?

4. What is the purpose and effect of the two line groups between the stanzas? Why are these lines repetitious? Compare the effect of these lines and the concluding lines of Eliot's "Preludes" (Chapter 14).

Three Poems Related to the Myth of the Phoenix

In ancient myth, the Phoenix was a gold and red Arabian bird resembling an eagle. At the end of a long period—some accounts say five hundred years, others say fifteen hundred—the Phoenix would be mysteriously consumed by fire. A new Phoenix would then reconstitute itself from the ashes of the old, and a new life cycle would begin. According to the myth, this process continued indefinitely. Because of this constant renewal, many religions have considered the Phoenix story optimistically, as a symbol of life overcoming death.

Poems for Study

Amy Clampitt . . . . Berceuse, 1009
Denise Levertov . . . . Hunting the Phoenix, 1009
May Sarton . . . . The Phoenix Again, 1010

AMY CLAMPITT (1920–1994)

 ## Berceuse° (1982)

Listen to Gieseking° playing a Berceuse
of Chopin°—the mothwing flutter
light as ash, perishable as burnt paper—

and sleep, now the furnaces of Auschwitz°
are all out, and tourists go there.   5
The purest art has slept with turpitude,

we all pay taxes. Sleep. The day of waking
waits, cloned from the phoenix—
a thousand replicas in upright silos,

nurseries of the ultimate enterprise.   10
Decay will undo what it can, the rotten
fabric of our repose connives with doomsday.

Sleep on, scathed felicity. Sleep, rare
and perishable relic. Imagining's no shutter
against the absolute, incorrigible sunrise.   15

°A lullaby or cradle song. 1 *Gieseking:* Walter Gieseking (1895–1956), famous French pianist. 2 *Chopin:* Frédéric Chopin (1810–1849), Polish composer and pianist. 4 *Auschwitz:* World War II Nazi death camp near Kraków, Poland. See also Quasímodo's poem "Auschwitz" (p. 825).

QUESTIONS

1. In what ways is this poem pessimistic? How does the speaker contrast the best and worst aspects of human life?
2. What is meant by line 6? What irony is contained in the image of the phoenix (stanza 3)? What objects are replicated in the "upright silos"?
3. What are the "felicity" and "relic" of lines 13 and 14? Why should these "sleep" (see also line 7)? What is meant by the "absolute, incorrigible sunrise" of line 15?

DENISE LEVERTOV (1923–1997)

For a photo, see Chapter 12, page 672.

 ## Hunting the Phoenix (1987)

Leaf through discolored manuscripts,
make sure no words
lie thirsting, bleeding,
waiting for rescue. No:
old loves half—   5
articulated, moments forced
out of the stream of perception

to play 'statue,'
and never released—
10   they had no blood to shed.
You must seek
the ashy nest itself
if you hope to find
charred feathers, smouldering flightbones,
15   and a twist of singing flame
rekindling.

QUESTIONS

1. What use is Levertov making here of the phoenix myth? How does the poem's organization make the references to the phoenix clear?

2. What is the speaker referring to that might be recorded in "discolored manuscripts"? What might be the things that have "no blood to shed"?

3. Why, in the last six lines, does the speaker introduce a reference to "the ashy nest"? What is meant by the poem's advice to seek this nest? What is the promise if one does seek out the nest?

MAY SARTON (1912–1995)

 ## The Phoenix° Again (1988)

On the ashes of this nest
Love wove with deathly fire
The phoenix takes its rest
Forgetting all desire.

5   After the flame, a pause,
After the pain, rebirth.
Obeying nature's laws
The phoenix goes to earth.

You cannot call it old
10   You cannot call it young.
No phoenix can be told,
This is the end of song.

It struggles now alone
Against death and self-doubt,
15   But underneath the bone
The wings are pushing out.

And one cold starry night
Whatever your belief

°*Phoenix:* See the note to line 23 of John Donne's "The Canonization" (p. 952).

The phoenix will take flight
Over the seas of grief

To hear her thrilling song
To stars and waves and sky
For neither old nor young
The phoenix does not die.

QUESTIONS

1. What is the phoenix? What does it signify?
2. What significance does the phoenix have for the speaker? What personal situation does the speaker seem to be describing? Why does the speaker invoke the details of the phoenix's return to life after death?
3. Compare Sarton's use of the phoenix with the uses by Donne in "The Canonization" (p. 952) and Clampitt in "Berceuse" (p. 1009).

Two Poems Related to the Myth of Oedipus

For the story of Oedipus, see the introduction to *Oedipus the King* by Sophocles (Chapter 24)

The Great Sphinx, Gîza, Egypt. (Foto Marburg/Art Resource, New York, NY.)

Poems for Study

Muriel Rukeyser . . . . Myth, 1012

John Updike . . . . On the Way to Delphi, 1012

MURIEL RUKEYSER (1913–1980)

For a photo, see Chapter 15, page 786.

 Myth (1978)

Long afterward, Oedipus, old and blinded, walked the
roads.   He smelled a familiar smell.   It was
the Sphinx.   Oedipus said, "I want to ask one question.
Why didn't I recognize my mother?"   "You gave the
5   wrong answer," said the Sphinx.   "But that was what
made everything possible," said Oedipus.   "No," she said.
"When I asked, What walks on four legs in the morning,
two at noon, and three in the evening, you answered,
Man.   You didn't say anything about woman."
10   "When you say Man," said Oedipus, "you include women
too. Everyone knows that."   She said, "That's what
you think."

QUESTIONS

1. Who was Oedipus? The Sphinx? According to this poem, what was wrong with Oedipus's answer to the Riddle of the Sphinx?
2. What elements and techniques in this work allow you to consider it a poem?
3. What two myths and meanings of *myth* are embodied in the title?
4. To what extent does the poem's colloquial language revitalize the mythic material?

JOHN UPDIKE (b. 1932)

For a photo, see Chapter 6, page 363.

 On the Way to Delphi (1978)

Oedipus slew his father near this muddy field
the bus glides by as it glides by many another,
and Helicon° is real; the Muses hid and dwelled
on a hill, less than a mountain, that we could climb
5   if the bus would stop and give us the afternoon.

From these small sites, now overrun by roads and fame,
dim chieftains stalked into the world's fog and grew huge.
Where shepherds sang their mistaken kings, stray factories
mar with cement and smoke the lean geology
10   that wants to forget—*has* forgotten—the myths it bred.

°3 *Helicon:* a mountain in southwestern Greece. In ancient Greek mythology, Helicon was the home of the Nine Muses.

We pass some slopes where houses, low, of stone, blend in
like utterings on the verge of sleep—accretions scarce
distinguishable from scree,° on the uphill way rocks, rubble
to architecture and law. No men are visible.
All out: Parnassus.° The oracle's voice is wild.   15

°13 *scree:* piles of loose rock at the base of a mountain or hill. 15 *Parnassus:* a mountain sacred to Dionysus, Apollo, and the Muses. The geography of the poem indicates that the speaker's reflections take place on a tour bus ride from Athens north and west to Delphi, which is at the foot of Mount Parnassus.

QUESTIONS

1. What is the situation of the speaker of this poem? Where is he? What is he doing? What prompts his observations about Oedipus and the sacred mountains of ancient Greece?
2. Why does the speaker observe that the field is "muddy" near where Oedipus killed his father?
3. In the second stanza, what prompts the contrast between the present and the mythical past? What does it mean to say that modern people have forgotten the ancient myths? What is symbolic about the low houses that are similar to "scree"?

Three Poems Related to the Myth of Pan

Pan was the ancient Greek god of hunters, shepherds, country folk generally, and domestic animals. He was also a god of fertility and in this capacity was recognized for his lasciviousness. His name coincides with the Greek word meaning "all," and consequently he was sometimes given the attributes of a single, comprehensive, all-encompassing god. Because shepherds necessarily went far from home with their sheep—roaming woodlands, valleys, hills, and mountainsides—Pan was associated with distant, dangerous, and solitary locations, where shrines were built for him. Because of this association with shepherds and their life, he was visualized as having the body of a man but the horns, ears, thighs, tail, and legs of a goat. Shepherds, to divert themselves on their pastoral journeying, played a flute, called a syrinx, made up of seven reeds, and Pan was the reputed inventor of this instrument. He was called *Faunus* by the Romans, who celebrated a festival in his name each year in February (a month of purification). This was known as the *Lupercalia,* a festival held for general fertility. The festival also permitted a certain amount of license, for naked or lightly clad young men who held light whips cut from the skins of sacrificial goats would lash female spectators to ensure their fertility, all in the name of Pan or Faunus.

Poems for Study

E. E. Cummings . . . . in Just-, 1014
John Chipman Farrar . . . . Song for a Forgotten Shrine to Pan, 1015
Robert Frost. . . . . Pan with Us, 1015

E. E. CUMMINGS (1894–1962)

For a photo, see Chapter 12, page 665.

 ## in Just- (1923)

in Just-
spring   when the world is mud-
luscious the little
lame balloonman

5 whistles   far   and wee

and eddieandbill come
running from marbles and
piracies and it's
spring

10 when the world is puddle-wonderful

the queer
old balloonman whistles
far   and   wee
and bettyandisbel come dancing

15 from hop-scotch and jump-rope and

it's
spring
and
    the
20   goat-footed

balloonMan   whistles
far
and
wee

QUESTIONS

1. Who is the balloonman? What mythical figure does he represent? How do you know? What characteristics does this balloonman/balloonMan have? What does the balloon-man's whistle symbolize?

2. Besides the balloonman, there are four other characters in the poem. Who are they? Why does Cummings run their names together? What impulses are acting on these characters that are regarded as attributable to Pan?

3. Read the poem aloud. Taking into account the spacing and alignment, how does the physical arrangement on the page influence your perceptions not only of the poem's content but also of its rhythm?

4. Explain the following as symbols: "spring," "mud-luscious," "puddle-wonderful," and "hop-scotch."

Gustave Moreau (1826–1898), *Thracian Girl Carrying the Head of Orpheus on His Lyre*, 1865. Oil on wood, 60 5/8 x 39 1/8 in. (154 x 99.5 cm). Musée d'Orsay, Paris, France. Image courtesy of The Art Renewal Center.

The story of Orpheus is briefly summarized in Chapter 20 (p. 1003). Compare the *Thracian Girl* with Hirsch's "The Swimmers" (p. 1004) and Strand's "Orpheus Alone" (p. 1005).

❧ **Martin Johnson Heade (1819–1904),** *Approaching Storm: Beach Near Newport,* c. 1861–1862. Oil on canvas, 71.12 x 148.27 cm (28 x 58 3/8 in.). Courtesy of the Museum of Fine Arts, Boston. Gift of Maxim Karolik for the M. and M. Karolik Collection of American Paintings, 1815–1865. (45.889) Reproduced with permission. Photograph ©2007 Museum of Fine Arts, Boston. All Rights Reserved.

Heade's treatment of the ocean and shore may be compared with Arnold's "Dover Beach" (p. 694) and Longfellow's "The Sound of the Sea" (p. 866). Compare also with Cole's *View from Mount Holyoke* **and Bierstadt's** *Among the Sierra Nevada Mountains.*

🍁 Claude Lorrain (1600–1682), *Harbour at Sunset*, 1639. Oil on canvas. Louvre, Paris.
©Erich Lessing/Art Resource, New York.

Claude's *Harbour at Sunset* is discussed in Chapters 2 and 5 (pp. 128 and 275). Compare with Lynn Emanuel's "Like God" (p. 1128) and Plath's "Song for a Summer's Day" (p. 1100).

Thomas Cole (1801–1848), *View from Mount Holyoke, Northampton, Massachusetts, after a Thunderstorm—The Oxbow,* 1836. Oil on canvas, H. 51 1/2 in., W. 76 in. (130.8 x 193 cm). Signed and dated (lower left): T. Cole 1836. The Metropolitan Museum of Art, Gift of Mrs. Russell Sage, 1908. (08.228) Photograph ©1995 The Metropolitan Museum of Art.

***View from Mount Holyoke* may be compared with Evans', "The Iceberg Seven-Eighths Under" (p. 774) and Bryant's "To Cole, the Painter" (p. 1115).**

Albert Bierstadt (1830–1902), *Among the Sierra Nevada Mountains, California,* 1868. Oil on canvas, 71 x 120 in. (183 x 305 cm). ©Smithsonian American Art Museum, Washington D.C./Art Resource, New York.

Compare *Among the Sierra Nevada Mountains* with Wordsworth's "Tintern Abbey Lines" (p. 714), Hopkins's "Spring" (p. 740), and Chief Dan George's "The Beauty of the Trees" (p. 1130).

François Boucher (1703–1770), *Madame de Pompadour*, c. 1757. Paper on canvas, 60 x 45.5 cm. Louvre, Paris. ©Erich Lessing/Art Resource, New York.

This painting, along with Hopper's *Automat*, is discussed in Chapter 4 (p. 225). Compare with Frost's "The Silken Tent" (p. 1070), Joyce's "Araby" (p. 262), Browning's "My Last Duchess" (p. 697), and Whur's "The First-Rate Wife" (p. 801).

This painting along with Boucher's *Madame de Pompadour* is discussed in Chapter 4 (p. 225). Compare with Frost's "The Silken Tent" (p. 1070), Joyce's "Araby" (p. 262), Browning's "My Last Duchess" (p. 697), and Whur's "The First-Rate Wife" (p. 801).

***Hard Times* is discussed in Chapter 14 (p. 727). Compare *Hard Times* with Cowper's "The Poplar Field" (p. 699) and Whitecloud's "Blue Winds Dancing" (p. 313).**

🍁 Pieter Brueghel the Elder (c. 1525–1569), *Landscape with the Fall of Icarus*, c. 1554–1555. Musées Royaux des Beaux-Arts de Belgique, Brussels. ©Scala/Art Resource, New York.

Compare *Landscape with the Fall of Icarus* to Bierce's "An Occurrence at Owl Creek Bridge" (p. 71), Auden's "Musée des Beaux Arts" (p. 998), Sexton's "To a Friend Whose Work Has Come to Triumph" (p. 1001) and William Carlos Williams's "Landscape with the Fall of Icarus" (p. 1002).

Compare *Peasants' Dance* with William Carlos Williams's "The Dance" (p. 932) and Hardy's "The Three Strangers" (p. 287).

***The City* is discussed in Chapter 16 (p. 800). Compare with Frost's "The Tuft of Flowers" (p. 1063), Swift's "A Description of the Morning" (p. 830), and Sandburg's "Chicago" (p. 1172).**

Pablo Picasso (1881–1973), *Guernica*, 1937. Oil on canvas, 350 x 782 cm. Museo Nacional Centro de Arte Reina Sofia, Madrid, Spain. ©2006 Estate of Pablo Picasso/Artists Rights Society (ARS), New York. John Bigelow Taylor/Art Resource, New York.

Guernica is briefly discussed in Chapter 8 (p. 434). Compare *Guernica* with Pirandello's "War" (p. 106), Crane's "Do Not Weep" (p. 1119), Radnóti's "Forced March" (p. 748), Melville's "Shiloh: A Requiem" (p. 867), and Forché's "The Colonel" (p. 915).

Jacques-Louis David (1748–1825), *The Death of Socrates*, 1787. Oil on canvas. H. 51 in., W. 77 1/4 in. (129.5 x 196.2 cm). Signed and dated (lower left): L.D./MDCCLXXXVII; (on bench at right): L. David. The Metropolitan Museum of Art, Catharine Lorillard Wolfe Collection, Wolfe Fund, 1931. (31.45) Photograph ©1995 The Metropolitan Museum of Art.

The Death of Socrates is discussed in Chapter 1 (p. 63). Compare with Hardy's "The Convergence of the Twain" (p. 775), Amy Lowell's "Patterns" (p. 1149), and Thomas's "Do Not Go Gentle into that Good Night" (p. 930).

James Abbott McNeill Whistler (1834–1903), *The Little White Girl, Symphony in White, No. 2,* 1864. Oil on canvas, 76.5 x 51.1 cm. ©Tate Gallery, London/Art Resource, New York.

The Little White Girl is briefly discussed in Chapter 4 (p. 225).
Compare it with Joyce's "Araby" (p. 262) and Ransom's "Bells for John Whiteside's Daughter" (p. 1166).

🍁 **Auguste Renoir (1841–1919)**, *The Umbrellas,* c. 1881–1886. National Gallery, London.
©Art Resource, New York.

The Umbrellas shows a Parisian scene crowded with people. It may almost be considered an illustration of Maupassant's "The Necklace" (p. 6). Compare with "The Necklace" and also with Nye's "Where Children Live" (p. 642).

Francisco de Goya y Lucientes (1746–1828), *The Colossus*, 1808–1810. Oil on canvas, 116 x 105 cm. Museo del Prado, Madrid, Spain. ©Erich Lessing/Art Resource, New York.

***The Colossus*, which is discussed in Chapter 19 (p. 941), may be compared with "The New Colossus" by Emma Lazarus (p. 640), Whitman's "Dirge for Two Veterans" (p. 1190), Plath's "The Colossus" (p. 1091), and Eberhart's "The Fury of Aerial Bombardment" (p. 667).**

Hercules and the Infant Telephus. A Roman fresco from Herculaneum. Museo Archeologico Nazionale, Naples, Italy. (© Scala/Art Resource, New York)

This anonymous fresco from ancient Herculaneum is discussed in Chapter 7 (p. 375). Compare with Coleman's "Unfinished Masterpieces" (p. 382), Larkin's "Next, Please" (p. 966), and Graham's "The Geese" (p. 957).

 Theater of Dionysus, fourth century BCE Athens.

Ancient Greek theaters are described in Chapter 24 (pp. 1276–78).

 Anonymous Elizabethan Architect, The Reconstructed Globe Theater, London. Stage of the Globe Theater in London. Courtesy of April E. Roberts.

The new Globe's stage adheres to the original, with attributes such as its ceiling representing the *heavens* and the balcony area known as the *gallery* (pp. 1319–21).

🍁 **Anonymous Elizabethan Architect,** The Reconstructed Globe Theater, London. Interior of the Globe Theater in London. Courtesy of April E. Roberts.

Theaters of Shakespeare's day, particularly the Globe, are discussed in Chapter 24 (pp. 1319–22).

🍁 **Anonymous Elizabethan Architect,** The Reconstructed Globe Theater, London. Exterior of the Globe Theater in London. Courtesy of April E. Roberts.

Authentic reconstruction is based on sixteenth-century drawings and archaeological research (pp. 1322).

JOHN CHIPMAN FARRAR (1896–1974)

Song for a Forgotten Shrine to Pan (1919)

Come to me, Pan, with your wind-wild laughter,
  Where have you hidden your golden reed?
Pipe me a torrent of tune-caught madness,
  Come to me, Pan, in my lonely need

Where are the white-footed youths and the maidens,   5
  Garlanded, rosy-lipped, lyric with spring?
They tossed me poppies, tall lilies and roses
  And now but the winds their soft blown petals bring.

Where are the fauns and the nymphs and the satyrs?
  Where are the voices that sang in the trees?   10
Beauty has fled like a wind-startled nestling,
  Beauty, O Pan, and your sweet melodies.

Come to me! Come to me! God of mad music,
  Come to me, child of the whispering night.
Bring to all silences, torrents of music,   15
  People all shadows with garlands of light.

QUESTIONS

1. Why does the title indicate that the Shrine to Pan is "forgotten"? What does the speaker mean by "my lonely need" in line 4?
2. What attributes of Pan are brought out in the poem? Why does the speaker use the phrase "Come to me" five times in the poem? What does he yearn for?
3. Describe Farrar's use of dactyls and anapests in this poem. What rhythmical effects does he achieve? How do the rhythms seem to affect the speaker's thoughts about the god Pan?

ROBERT FROST (1874–1963)

For a photo, see Chapter 21, page 1058.

Pan with Us° (1913)

Pan came out of the woods one day—
His skin and his hair and his eyes were gray,
The gray of the moss of walls were they—
  And stood in the sun and looked his fill
  At wooded valley and wooded hill.   5

He stood in the zephyr, pipes in hand,
On a height of naked pasture land;

°See Matthew 1:23, "and they shall call his name Emmanuel, which being interpreted is, God with us."

In all the country he did command
    He saw no smoke and he saw no roof.
5   That was well! and he stamped a hoof.

His heart knew peace, for none came here
To this lean feeding, save once a year
Someone to salt the half-wild steer,
    Or homespun children with clicking pails
15   Who see so little they tell no tales.

He tossed his pipes, too hard to teach
A new-world song, far out of reach,
For a sylvan sign that the blue jay's screech
    And the whimper of hawks beside the sun
20   Were music enough for him, for one.

Times were changed from what they were:
Such pipes kept less of power to stir
The fruited bough of the juniper
    And the fragile bluets clustered there
25   Than the merest aimless breath of air.

They were pipes of pagan mirth,
And the world had found new terms of worth.
He laid him down on the sunburned earth
    And raveled a flower and looked away.
30   Play? Play?—What should he play?

QUESTIONS

1. What is the situation of the poem? What does Pan look like? What sort of god is he? How does modern life seem to him?

2. Why does Pan throw away his pipes? What is music enough for him? What, apparently, is the speaker's thought about what music would be enough? Explain the abruptness of the final line.

3. What does the speaker mean by stating that "Times were changed from what they were" (line 21)? Why does the poem end with a question? What is the issue raised by the question, concerning such things as modern taste/beliefs/religious faith? What answer might be advanced in answer to the question?

WRITING ABOUT MYTHS IN POETRY

An essay on myths in poetry will normally connect the mythic material in a poem to some other element, such as speaker, character, action, tone, setting, situation, imagery, form, or meaning. This approach suggests a two-part exploration of the poem, one concerned with its general sense and the other with the ways in which myths shape and control that sense.

As you study the poem, look for the ways in which myth enriches the poem and focuses its meaning. The following questions should be helpful to you.

Questions for Discovering Ideas

- To what extent does the title identify the mythic content of the poem and thus provide a key for understanding?
- How much of the poem's action, setting, and situation are borrowed from mythology? What is the significance of the action in the myth? What does this action symbolize? How does the poet reshape the action and its significance?
- To what extent does our understanding of the myth explain the poem's speaker, characters, situations, and ideas? What characters, including the speaker, are drawn from mythology?
- In what ways are these characters symbolic (see Chapter 19)? What aspects of this symbolism are carried into the poem? How does the poem either maintain or change the symbolism?
- How do the various formal elements of the poem, such as diction, rhyme, meter, and form, reshape the mythic material and affect the meaning and impact of the myth?
- How does the tone of the poem either reinforce or undercut the ideas and implications of the original myth? Cite specific words and phrases that lead you to your conclusions.
- Does the rhyme (if any) lead us to consider the mythic content as serious or comic?
- Generally, how does the mythic content help develop and clarify the poem?

Strategies for Organizing Ideas

A main challenge in writing about myths is to develop a focus or central idea. If, for example, you find that the poem retells a myth in order to make a point about history or society, you should fashion your major idea to reflect that connection. Similarly, if the poem employs a mythical speaker or character to convey ideas about war or heroism, your essay should focus on the links among myth, character, and those ideas.

When you formulate a central idea, draft it as a complete sentence that conveys the full scope of your ideas. It is not enough merely to assert that a given poem contains a great deal of mythic material. If you are writing about Yeats's "Leda and the Swan," for example, you might be tempted to form a central idea that argues, "Yeats's 'Leda and the Swan' retells the myth of Leda's rape by Zeus and the consequences of that event." That sentence does not tell the reader anything about the *way* the Leda myth works in the poem, nor does it provide a basis for any discussion beyond summary and paraphrase. A more effective formulation would be the following: "In Yeats's 'Leda and the Swan,' the myth of Leda's rape by Zeus and the consequences of that rape illustrate the process of history and also question the connection between knowledge and power." This sentence points to a specific connection between mythological content and the poem's effect, and it gives a shaping direction to the essay.

In your introductory paragraph or paragraphs, you should briefly summarize the significant parts of your poem's mythical elements, together with any noteworthy details about the poem's form or circumstances of composition. Your aim should be to focus on the poem (and the mythic material within the poem) rather than on the myth itself. Thus, you should link the mythical elements with other aspects of the poem and make assertions about the effects of this connection. To organize the body of your essay, you can employ various strategies like the following:

1. You might echo the organization of the poem, shaping the central paragraphs so as to reflect the poem's line-by-line or stanza-by-stanza logic.

2. You might choose an organization based on a series of different mythic elements or figures. For instance, if a poem alludes to Odysseus, to his wife, Penelope, or to his son, Telemachus, you might devote paragraphs to the way each figure shapes the poem's impact and meaning.

3. You might use the relevant elements of poetry as the focal points of organization. Thus, if you argue that diction, rhyme, and tone shape the mythological material to produce significant effects, you would deal with each element in turn.

To bring your essay to a convincing and assertive close, you might summarize your major points. At the same time, you might draw your reader's attention to the significance of your observations and to any further implications of the ways in which the myth is integrated into the poem you have studied.

Illustrative Student Essay

Underlined sentences in this paper *do not* conform to MLA style and are used solely as teaching tools to emphasize the central idea, thesis sentence, and topic sentences throughout the paper.

Cross 1

Karen Cross

Professor Lee

English 122

6 October 2008

Myth and Meaning in Dorothy Parker's "Penelope"°

[1]   Dorothy Parker's short lyric poem "Penelope" uses mythic allusion and symbolism to criticize conventional ideas about the roles of women and men. Her speaker is the mythic figure Penelope, the wife of King Odysseus of the

°**This poem appears on page 993.**

Cross 2

ancient realm of Ithaca. Not only is Penelope the speaker, but she is also the poem's major figure. <u>Parker uses Penelope to assert that society has consistently misjudged and undervalued women's lives.</u>* <u>Parker's assertions are brought out through the poem's title, its mythic resonance, its diction, and its view of the representative lives of both Odysseus and Penelope.</u>†

     <u>The key to the poem's use of myth is the title, "Penelope."</u> As the only place [2] where the poem's mythological speaker is named, the title alludes to Homer's *Odyssey,* which tells that Penelope endures a twenty-year wait while her husband is at war and at sea. Her seemingly endless wait is filled with trouble. Her palace is occupied by boorish suitors who assume that Odysseus is dead and that his kingship is vacant. They therefore demand that Penelope choose a new husband. Only Penelope and Telemachus, her son, cling to the hope that Odysseus is still alive. She keeps the arrogant suitors at bay by promising to marry one of them after she finishes weaving a shroud for Odysseus's father. To delay this event, she works at the loom by day and unravels the work by night.

     <u>Although the title refers directly to Penelope, the poem itself also deals with Odysseus.</u> Lines 1–5 evoke the king's adventures in Penelope's phrases [3] "He shall ride the silver seas" (line 4) and "He shall cut the glittering wave" (line 5). Because Odysseus is not identified by name but only by the pronoun "he," readers might see this male figure as a symbol of all men who choose to lead their principal lives outside the home. The adjectives "silver" and "glittering" connote splendor and glory, while the verbs "ride" and "cut" suggest resoluteness and boldness. In addition, the phrases "pathway of the sun" (line 1) and "footsteps of the breeze" (line 2) add romance and mystery. In the same lines, however, one may perceive that the wife is providing a subtle undercutting of her absent husband's heroism. The phrase "ride the silver seas," for example, suggests that some of the Homeric lines are clichés. The implication is that the glorified accounts of active heroes like Odysseus are both exaggerated and inaccurate.

*Central idea.
†Thesis sentence.

Cross 3

[4]   Just as this language has general implications for men, the language about Penelope herself is significant for women. In lines 6–9 she, as the speaker, contrasts the restrictions of her life with the freedom of male lives. Here we find no adjectives at all; the woman's existence is thus rendered factually, without adornment of any sort. In addition, the verbs represent passive and domestic activities: "sit," "rock," "rise," "brew," "snip," and "bleach." These last two verbs are especially effective. The phrase "snip my thread" (line 8) is the only allusion to Penelope's unhappy existence. It refers to her daring deception of the suitors through her nightly unraveling of the shroud. At the same time, "snip" is contrasted with the verb "cut" used earlier in the poem. While the words are synonyms, their connotations are different because "cut" implies violence, whereas "snip" suggests careful and delicate activity. "Bleach" is equally connotative. Although the word refers directly to "the linen for my bed," it is consistent with the view that the circumstances of Penelope's life are faded and colorless.

[5]   The poem's final line ironically clarifies Penelope's attitude toward the different roles of men and women. Penelope asserts, "They will call him brave." "They" refers to society, to the world at large, and to generations of readers who have admired Odysseus in Homer's Iliad and Odyssey. The meter of the line--a concluding spondee--places a great emphasis on the word "him," thus demonstrating the speaker's realization, and the poet's assertion, that society ignores or dismisses the quiet bravery of women. In myth and in life, the woman's role demands just as much courage and conviction as the man's.

[6]   "Penelope" thus employs mythic figures and events to criticize the historical perception of the roles of men and women. Odysseus, the mythical and typical male, is presented as a heroic figure, but he too is human, and his adventures are tinged with overdramatization. Parker's point is not to demean him, however, but rather to emphasize that women, too, have their own heroism. Biology and destiny may have traditionally confined women at home to keep house and to weave tapestries while men are granted the freedom to find adventure in far-off lands. But waiting at home while meeting domestic challenges takes courage too. Penelope and Odysseus lived at a time of the old

Cross 4

ways, but if Parker's poem is understood properly, it is time for new ways to

begin. Penelope is right to express annoyance and irony when considering the

judgment of history. Our knowledge of her courageous survival in Ithaca during

the absence of Odysseus adds significantly to the truth and depth of her feelings.

Cross 5

Work Cited

Dorothy Parker, "Penelope." Literature: An Introduction to Reading and

Writing. Ed. Edgar V. Roberts. 9th ed. New York: Pearson Longman,

2009. 993.

Commentary on the Essay

This essay shows how Parker uses the Penelope-Odysseus myth to shed new light on conventional attitudes about men and women. As a guide for one's own writing aims, therefore, the essay illustrates how the mythological material can lead to ideas for development.

Although the body of the essay follows the organization of the poem itself, it is not a summary of the poem. Thus, paragraph 2 focuses on the title, paragraph 3 on lines 1–5, paragraph 4 on lines 6–9, and paragraph 5 on the last line. Each of the paragraphs also advances a specific aspect of the essay's central idea. In paragraph 2, Penelope is identified and the relevant mythic material is reviewed. The information in this paragraph is logically necessary for the remainder of the essay.

In paragraph 3, the title and its mythic importance introduce Odysseus and the symbol of the heroic male. Here, the point is that Parker's diction for her speaker undercuts the active male image while seeming to glorify it. The first sentence of paragraph 4 provides a transition from Odysseus and heroic males to Penelope and the perceived passiveness of women. Again, the essay explores the way Parker's diction and mythic allusion demonstrate that there is more to the lives of women than is usually claimed. Paragraph 5 looks at the poem's final line in relation to the contrasted lives of "heroic" men and "passive" women. Here, the essay shows how tone and meter reveal the speaker's attitude toward these contrasting lives and society's misperception of them.

The conclusion goes quickly over the essay's basic points, and it emphasizes that the essay writer's interpretation of the ancient myth brings new light to a traditional problem. In paragraph 6 the writer concludes the essay with some brief comments that deal with the poem's ideas and their importance at the present time.

Writing Topics About Myth in Poetry

1. In Glück's "Penelope's Song," Merwin's "Odysseus," Parker's "Penelope," Pastan's "The Suitor," Tennyson's "Ulysses," and Ulisse's "Odyssey: 20 Years Later," the poets evoke the same myth but for different purposes. What are these purposes? What views do you find about adventure, domesticity, and sexuality? What attitudes toward figures in the myth (Odysseus, Penelope, Calypso, the Sirens, Circe) do the poets bring out? How do word choice, selection of detail, and point of view influence each poet's conclusions?

2. The myth of Icarus is used by Aldiss, Auden, Field, Rukeyser, Sexton, and Williams. Basing your conclusions on two or more of the poems in this group, what similarities and differences can you describe? How do the poets present the myth? How do they use the myth to create unusual or surprising endings, and to comment on contemporary but also permanent attitudes about life and the sufferings of others?

3. What point does Rukeyser's "Myth" make about both men and women and their attitudes toward each other? How does our knowledge of the Oedipus myth (see Sophocles' play *Oedipus the King* [Chapter 24] help clarify these aspects of the poem? In what respects is the poem contemporary?

4. Compare and contrast (a) the use of the phoenix myth by Clampitt, Levertov, and Sarton, or (b) the use of the mythology of the god Pan by Cummings, Farrar, and Frost.

5. The four poems by Hirsch, Rilke, Strand, and Voigt are all connected by the common topic of the myth of Orpheus. What is the common treatment of the Orpheus myth in these poems? What major differences can you perceive? How is each poem, though touching on a common topic, different?

6. In your library, choose a book on myths, such as Kenneth McLeish, *Myth: Myths and Legends of the World Explored* (1996), or Richard Erdoes and Alfonso Ortiz, *American Indian Myths and Legends* (1984). Select a story from among the many myths described there (e.g., Oedipus, Jason, Prometheus, Antigone, Sisyphus, Beaver stealing fire from the Pines, Coyote placing the stars, A Tale of Elder Brother). To these you might add biblical stories (e.g., the fight between God and Satan, Noah, Leviathan, Joseph and his brothers, the Hebrew captivity in Egypt, the Exodus, the Babylonian captivity) and other legends and actual historical stories (Robin Hood, Paul Bunyan, Davy Crockett, the Amistad event, the forty-niners, the Civil War, the Lone Ranger, the log cabin, the Rough Riders, etc.). Write a poem based on the story you choose. Try to present your own view about the importance, timeliness, intelligence, and truth of your story. What kinds of detail do you select? How do you give the figures mythic status? How do you make your own attitudes apparent by your arrangement of detail and your word choice?

Chapter 21

Four Major American Poets: Emily Dickinson, Robert Frost, Langston Hughes, and Sylvia Plath

In Chapters 11 through 20 we have considered poetry in terms of its elements and effects. In this chapter we present collections of poems by four major American poets: Emily Dickinson (1830–1886), Robert Frost (1874–1963), Langston Hughes (1902–1967), and Sylvia Plath (1932–1963). As both history and chance would have it, Dickinson, Frost, and Plath were New Englanders, although Plath spent four of her last six years living in England. Hughes was born and raised in the Midwest, but came to New York as an adult, and stayed. Dickinson is one of the most prominent poetic voices of the nineteenth century. Both Frost and Hughes are recognized as poetic giants of the twentieth century. Plath's poetic career was unfortunately cut short, but the posthumous edition of her poems received the honor of a Pulitzer Prize when it was published in 1982, almost twenty years after her death.

Although the poems included here comprise only a small part of the work of these poets, our hope is that there are enough poems to illustrate the typical concerns and major characteristics that are to be found in the study of their poetic careers.

EMILY DICKINSON'S LIFE AND WORK (1830–1886)

Emily Elizabeth Dickinson, who is acknowledged today as one of America's greatest poets, was born on December 10, 1830. She was raised in Amherst, Massachusetts, which in the nineteenth century was a small and tradition-bound town. Dominating the Dickinson family was Emily's father, Edward, a lawyer, a legislator, and a rigorous Calvinist, whose concept of life was stern religious observance and obedience to God's laws as derived from the Bible. Emily was taken to Sunday School, but late in her teens she declined to pronounce herself a believing Christian. She

spent a number of years at primary school and eventually studied classics at Amherst Academy. She also enrolled at the South Hadley Seminary for Women

Emily Dickinson's room at the family homestead in Amherst, Massachusetts, where she wrote much of her poetry.

(now Mount Holyoke College), but her parents withdrew her after a year because of ill health.[1]

During these years of childhood and youth, she led a normally active life. She saw many people, liked school and her teachers, wrote essays, acquired a number of good friends, gossiped, sang at the piano to her own accompaniment, treasured spring flowers, amused her friends with impromptu stories, studied theology, read Pope's *An Essay on Man*, did a good deal more reading, and planned to become the "Belle of Amherst" at the age of seventeen. She also began writing poetry, which consisted mainly of occasional verses and Valentines.

After leaving school she returned home. She was to spend the rest of her life there, sharing in family and household duties. In 1856 she won a second prize at the local fair for her recipe for Rye and Indian bread. She took occasional trips, including long stays in Boston in 1864 and 1865 to be treated

---

[1]It would appear that there are four reliable likenesses of Emily Dickinson. The first is a painting of her and her brother and sister, done by Otis A. Bullard in about 1840, showing Emily at the age of about nine. There is a silhouette of her at the age of about fourteen. The first and most reliable photo is a daguerreotype taken of her at about the age of sixteen. This is the photo that is always duplicated. Still another photograph has come to light that may show Dickinson at the age of about thirty to thirty-five. As yet the photo, an albumen print with Dickinson's name on the back, has not been authenticated, but it is fair to say that its resemblance to the authentic photo is uncanny. (See *The New Yorker*, May 22, 2000, pp. 30–31). This photo is included in Alfred Habegger, *My Wars Are Laid Away in Books* (2001), where all the likenesses are included. Habegger believes that the photo is authentic. Richard B. Sewall includes a photograph of a young woman as the frontispiece to the second volume of his *The Life of Emily Dickinson* (1974), and he duplicates this same photo on page 752 of the one-volume *Life* of 1980. On the back of the original is written "Emily Dickenson [sic] 1860" in an unknown hand, and the features of the portrayed woman are consistent with those in the daguerreotype of Dickinson at sixteen. Although it is tempting to consider this photograph genuine, the attribution has not been validated.

for an undisclosed eye ailment. Eventually, however, she stopped traveling altogether.

Although Dickinson had written poems since her school days, she did not devote herself to poetry until her late twenties—beginning in about 1858. After this time her poetic output expanded, almost miraculously. Many of her poems are quite short, consisting of no more than a single stanza, but some are much longer. No more than ten of them were published during her lifetime, mostly against her wishes. Instead, her "publication" consisted of making fair copies of the poems in handwriting that is quite difficult to read. In the privacy of her own room she put numbers of poems together in "fascicles," which consist of folded sheets of stationery bound with thread. These handwritten copies were for her eyes only, although she frequently sent copies in letters and also sent batches of poems to friends. The poems she didn't prepare carefully for her fascicles were kept in little packets. She locked away all these private literary treasures, which were discovered only after her death.

In total, 1,775 to 1,789 of her poems have been recovered. The figure 1,775 is the number of poems included by Thomas H. Johnson in *The Complete Poems of Emily Dickinson* (1955), the first major complete edition of Dickinson's poetry. The figure 1,789 is the number included by Ralph W. Franklin in *The Poems of Emily Dickinson: Variorum Edition* (1998). Both editions are based on exhaustive studies of all the documentary evidence available at the times when the editors were doing their research. Beyond these major scholarly editions, a number of brief poems have been mined from Dickinson's letters, and these were published, in 1993, as 498 new poems, on the theory that parts of the letters reach a succinctness and rhythm more characteristic of poetry than prose. These poems are short, some being no more than two lines long. If one accepts them as additional Dickinson poems, they bring the total count above 2,280.

Although a surprising amount of biographical information is available about Dickinson, the connections between events in her life and her poems are missing. For example, it seems obvious that a real and powerful sadness underlies the poignant conclusion of "I Cannot Live with You," just as a sense of personal inadequacy or reproach may have caused her to write "I Felt a Funeral in My Brain." We can only guess, however, about the specific situations, if any, that led her to write such poems.

Nevertheless, the general occasions inspiring some of her poems are clear. The world she lived in was small, and she found subjects in her surroundings: house, garden, yard, and village. A lowly snake is the topic of one of her poems—one of the few published when she was alive—as are butterflies, a singing oriole, and a vibrating hummingbird. She even wrote a poem about the railroad locomotives servicing her home town of Amherst. Sometimes no more than a recollection, a single word, a concept, or a paradox that arose from her own interior monologue enabled her to originate poems. Such inspirations account for topics such as a haunted mind, a memory, a state of solitude, the nature of truth and beauty, the condition of self-reliance, the angle of winter light. For one of the poems, "My Triumph Lasted Till the Drums," one may postulate a connection with her thoughts about the Civil War. She was at the height of her poetic power during this time, and she expresses feelings about the horrors of the war in these ironic lines: "A Bayonet's contrition / Is nothing to the Dead."

Dickinson's poems on death and dying probably had occasional sources also, even though these sources may be far removed from the time and circumstance of the poems. One of Dickinson's dearest childhood friends was Sophia Holland, who died in 1844. Perhaps the loss of Sophia was one of her memories when she wrote "I Never Lost as Much But Twice," and "The Bustle in a House," together with her other poems on death.

Much of her other poetry may have a similar if remote occasional origin. She wrote poems about love and the psychology of personal relationships, even though she never married or had a love affair that we know about. We may therefore wonder about the internal necessity that caused her to write poems like "Wild Nights–Wild Nights!" and "I Cannot Live with You," which portray states of sexual ecstasy and final renunciation. And what sorts of personal experience and introspection underlay such poems as "After Great Pain, a Formal Feeling Comes," "The Soul Selects Her Own Society," and "I Dwell in Possibility"?

In the absence of specific details linking her life to her poetry, therefore, the occasions of her poems must remain no more than peripherally relevant—themselves unseen, though in the effects they remain. We are left to conclude that her inspiration rose from within herself. She is a contemplative and personal poet, whether she herself is the omnipresent "I" of her poems or whether the "I" is an objective speaker to whom she assigns all the strength of her imagination and her dreams. This speaker possesses bright wit, clever and engaging playfulness, acute powers of observation, deep sensitivity, intense introspection, and tender responsiveness. She is alive, quick, and inventive. She enjoys riddles. She leads readers into new and unexplored regions of thought and feeling.

All these characteristics are to be discovered everywhere in her poetry. Her speaker expresses a vital joy and delirious energy in the quizzical poem "I Taste a Liquor Never Brewed," an insouciant bluffness in "Some Keep the Sabbath Going to Church," and overwhelming tenderness and regret at the end of "The Bustle in a House." In the last stanza of "I Cannot Live with You" she captures the deep anguish of a relationship that is ending.

> So We must meet apart –
> You there – I – here –
> With just the Door ajar
> That Oceans are – and Prayer –
> And that White Sustenance –
> Despair –

She is also reverent, and a number of poems introduce the topics of God, immortality, scripture, and the final judgment. But she is sometimes saucy and flippant about religion. Going to church on Sunday, for example, was expected of the dutiful Christian, but she explains why she prefers staying home with "a Bobolink for a Chorister."

> So instead of getting to Heaven, at last –
> I'm going, all along.

Undeniably, Dickinson's external daily life was uneventful. Her inner life was anything but uneventful, however, for she was always reflecting and thinking. What we know about her is that her inquiring and restless mind was the source of her compulsive poetic strength, and that her poetry expresses the vital personal feelings and psychological insights that emerged from her thoughts about life, love, death, Nature, and God. It is not possible to read her poems without revering her as a person and as a poet.

After Emily Dickinson died, in 1886, her sister, Lavinia, was astonished to find the many fascicles and packets of poems that she had left. Lavinia recognized the significance of this work and eventually turned much of it over to Thomas Higginson and Mabel L. Todd for editing and publication. They published three separate volumes of Dickinson's verse (in 1890, 1891, and 1896), each containing about a hundred poems. In these volumes, the editors eliminated slant rhymes, smoothed out the meter, revised those metaphors that struck them as outrageous, and regularized the punctuation.

These well-intentioned editorial "adjustments" remained intact until 1955, when the Harvard University Press published Thomas H. Johnson's three-volume complete edition. Johnson also published a single-volume edition of the poems in 1961 and, in addition, a paperback selection titled *Final Harvest: Emily Dickinson's Poems* (1961). Johnson's pioneering edition has been followed by the ambitious and comprehensive *The Poems of Emily Dickinson: Variorum Edition* in three volumes (Cambridge: Harvard UP, 1998), edited by Ralph W. Franklin, who also edited the facsimile edition of the handwritten poems, *The Manuscript Books of Emily Dickinson* (Cambridge: Harvard UP, 1981). Franklin's edition has also been published in one volume as *The Poems of Emily Dickinson: Reading Edition* (Cambridge: Harvard UP, 1999). The poems that have been extracted from Dickinson's letters were edited by William H. Shurr, with Anna Dunlap and Emily Grey Shurr, as *New Poems of Emily Dickinson* (Chapel Hill: U of North Carolina P, 1993).

Definitive biographies of Dickinson are Richard B. Sewall, *The Life of Emily Dickinson* (New York: Farrar, 1974; rpt. [Harvard UP] 1980; rpt. 1994); Alfred Habegger, *My Wars Are Laid Away in Books: The Life of Emily Dickinson* (New York: Random House, 2001); and Cynthia Griffin Wolff, *Emily Dickinson* (New York: Knopf, 1986). A useful book containing biographical, critical, and many other details is Jane Donahue Eberwein, ed., *An Emily Dickinson Encyclopedia* (Westport: Greenwood, 1998). The numbers of important critical studies are legion. Some of these are Albert J. Gelpi, *Emily Dickinson: The Mind of the Poet* (Cambridge: Harvard UP, 1966); Joanne F. Diehl, *Dickinson and the Romantic Imagination* (Princeton: Princeton UP, 1981); David Porter, *Dickinson, the Modern Idiom* (Cambridge: Harvard UP, 1981); Susan Juhasz, *The Undiscovered Continent: Emily Dickinson and the Space of the Mind* (Bloomington: U of Indiana P, 1983); Donna Dickenson, *Emily Dickinson* (Leamington Spa: Berg, 1985); Sharon Leder and Andrea Abbott, *The Language of Exclusion: The Poetry of Emily Dickinson and Christina Rossetti* (New York: Greenwood, 1987); Cristanne Miller, *Emily Dickinson: A Poet's Grammar* (Cambridge: Harvard UP, 1987); Joanne Dobson, *Dickinson and the Strategies of Reticence* (Bloomington: U of Indiana P, 1989); Paula Bennett, *Emily Dickinson: Woman Poet* (Iowa City: U of Iowa P, 1990); Gary Lee Stonum, *The Dickinson Sublime* (Madison: U of Wisconsin P, 1990); Joan Kirkby, *Emily Dickinson* (New York: St. Martin's, 1991); Judith Farr,

The Passion of Emily Dickinson (Cambridge: Harvard UP, 1992); Claudia Ottlinger, *The Death-Motif in the Poetry of Emily Dickinson and Christina Rossetti* (Frankfurt: Lang, 1996); and Paul Crumbley, *Inflections of the Pen: Dash and Voice in Emily Dickinson* (Lexington: U of Kentucky P, 1996).

Collections of essays on Dickinson are Paul J. Ferlazzo, ed., *Critical Essays on Emily Dickinson* (Boston: Hall, 1958, a historical collection); Richard B. Sewall, ed., *Emily Dickinson: A Collection of Critical Essays* (Englewood Cliffs: Prentice Hall, 1963); Judith Farr, ed., *Emily Dickinson: A Collection of Critical Essays* (Upper Saddle River: Prentice Hall, 1996); and Gudrun Grabher et al., eds. *The Emily Dickinson Handbook* (Amherst: U of Massachusetts P, 1998). One of the hour-long programs in the PBS *Voices and Visions* series (1987) features Dickinson's work.

Topics for Writing About the Poetry of Emily Dickinson

1. Dickinson's characteristic brevity in the explanation of situations and the expression of ideas.
2. Dickinson's use of personal but not totally disclosed subject matter.
3. Dickinson's use of imagery and symbolism: sources, types, meanings.
4. Dickinson's humor and irony.
5. Dickinson's ideas about love, separation, personal pain, war, death, faith, religion, science, the soul.
6. Dickinson's power as a poet.
7. Dickinson's poems as they appear on the page: the relationship of meaning to lines, stanzas, capitalization, punctuation, the use of the dash.
8. The structuring of a number of Dickinson's poems: subject, development, conclusions.
9. The character of the speaker in a number of Dickinson's poems: personality, things noticed, accuracy of conclusions. If there appears to be a listener in the poems, what effect does this listener have on the speaker?
10. Dickinson's verse forms and use of rhymes.
11. Themes of exhilaration, sorrow, pity, triumph, and regret in Dickinson.

Poems by Emily Dickinson (Alphabetically Arranged)

For ease in locating the selections included here, the poems are arranged alphabetically by the first significant word in the first line. There are two numbers following the title of each poem. The first number (e.g., J501) refers to the poem numbers in Thomas H. Johnson's *The Complete Poems of Emily Dickinson*. Critics since Johnson's edition have unanimously employed these numbers. The second number (e.g., F373) refers to the new numbering in Ralph W. Franklin's *The Poems of Emily Dickinson: Variorum Edition*. It would appear that future Dickinson criticism will need to include both numbers if the poem under discussion is to be properly identified, as with the following title: *After Great Pain, a Formal Feeling Comes (J341, F372).*

A single mark resembling a hyphen or short dash, following a brief space, was Dickinson's most-used punctuation. For this edition, this mark is represented by a "1/N" printed dash, thus: After great pain, a formal feeling comes –

After Great Pain, a Formal Feeling Comes (J341, F372) 1029
Because I Could Not Stop for Death (J712, F479)
  (See Chapter 11, p. 635)
The Bustle in a House (J1078, F1108). 1030
The Heart Is the Capital of the Mind (J1354, F1381) 1030
I Cannot Live with You (J640, F706). 1030
I Died for Beauty – But Was Scarce (J449, F448) 1031
I Dwell in Possibility (F466, J657). 1032
I Felt a Funeral in My Brain (J280, F340) 1032
I Heard a Fly Buzz – When I Died (J465, F591) 1033
I Like to See It Lap the Miles (J585, F383) 1033
I'm Nobody! Who Are You? (J288, F260). 1033
I Never Lost as Much but Twice (J49, F39) 1034
I Taste a Liquor Never Brewed (J214, F207). 1034
Much Madness Is Divinest Sense (J435, F620) 1034
My Life Closed Twice Before Its Close (J1732, F1773) 1035
My Triumph Lasted Till the Drums (J1227, F1212). 1035
One Need Not Be a Chamber – To Be Haunted (J670, F407) 1035
Safe in Their Alabaster Chambers (J216, F124) 1036
Some Keep the Sabbath Going to Church (J324, F236) 1036
The Soul Selects Her Own Society (J303, F409) 1037
Success Is Counted Sweetest (J67, F112) 1037
Tell All the Truth but Tell It Slant (J1129, F1263). 1037
There's a Certain Slant of Light (J258, F320). 1037
To Hear an Oriole Sing (J526, F402)
  (See Chapter 17, p. 859)
Wild Nights – Wild Nights! (J249, F269) 1038

After Great Pain, a Formal Feeling Comes (J341, F372) (1929, c.1862)

After great pain, a formal feeling comes –
The Nerves sit ceremonious, like Tombs –
The Stiff Heart questions 'was it He, that bore,'
And 'Yesterday, or Centuries before'?

The Feet, mechanical, go round –   5
A Wooden way
Of Ground, or Air, or Ought° –   *anything, nothing*
Regardless grown,
A Quartz contentment, like a stone –

This is the Hour of Lead –   10
Remembered, if outlived,
As Freezing persons, recollect the Snow –
First – Chill – then Stupor – then the letting go –

Because I Could Not Stop for Death (J712, F479)

(See Chapter 11, p. 635)

 ## The Bustle in a House (J1078, F1108) (1890, c.1865)

The Bustle in a House
The Morning after Death
Is solemnest of industries
Enacted upon Earth –

5 The Sweeping up the Heart
And putting Love away
We shall not want to use again
Until Eternity –

 ## The Heart Is the Capital of the Mind (J1354, F1381) (1929, c.1875)

The Heart is the Capital of the Mind –
The Mind is a single State –
The Heart and the Mind together make
A single Continent.

5 One – is the Population –
Numerous enough –
This ecstatic Nation
Seek – it is Yourself –

 ## I Cannot Live with You (J640, F706) (1890, c.1863)

I cannot live with You –
It would be Life –
And Life is over there –
Behind the Shelf

5 The Sexton keeps the Key to –
Putting up
Our Life – His Porcelain –
Like a Cup –

Discarded of the Housewife –
10 Quaint – or Broke –
A newer Sevres° pleases –   *a fine French porcelain*
Old Ones crack –

I could not die – with You –
For One must wait
15 To shut the Other's Gaze down –
You – could not –

And I – Could I stand by
And see You – freeze –
Without my Right of Frost –
Death's privilege?   20

Nor could I rise – with You –
Because Your Face
Would put out Jesus' –
That New Grace

Glow plain – and foreign   25
On my homesick eye –
Except that You than He
Shone closer by –

They'd judge Us – How –
For You – served Heaven – You know,   30
Or sought to –
I could not –

Because You saturated sight –
And I had no more eyes
For sordid excellence   35
As Paradise

And were You lost, I would be –
Though my name
Rang loudest
On the Heavenly fame –   40

And were You – saved –
And I – condemned to be
Where You were not
That self – were Hell to Me –

So We must meet apart –   45
You there – I – here –
With just the Door ajar
That Oceans are – and Prayer –
And that White Sustenance –
Despair –   50

I Died for Beauty – but Was Scarce (J449, F448) (1890, c.1862)

I died for Beauty – but was scarce
Adjusted in the Tomb
When One who died for Truth, was lain
In an adjoining Room –

                                                                               5
He questioned softly "Why I failed"?
"For Beauty," I replied –

"And I – for Truth – Themselves are One –
We Brethren, are," He said –

And so, as Kinsmen, met a Night –
10   We talked between the Rooms –
Until the Moss had reached our lips –
And covered up – Our names –

I Dwell in Possibility (F466, J657) (1929, c.1862)

I dwell in Possibility –
A fairer House than Prose –
More numerous of Windows –
Superior – for Doors –

5   Of Chambers as the Cedars –
Impregnable of eye –
And for an everlasting Roof
The Gambrels of the Sky –

Of Visitors – the fairest –
10   For Occupation – This –
The spreading wide my narrow Hands
To gather Paradise –

I Felt a Funeral in My Brain (J280, F340) (1896, c.1862)

I felt a Funeral, in my Brain,
And Mourners to and fro
Kept treading – treading – till it seemed
That Sense was breaking through –

5   And when they all were seated,
A Service, like a Drum –
Kept beating – beating – till I thought
My mind was going numb –

And then I heard them lift a Box
10   And creak across my Soul
With those same Boots of Lead, again,
Then Space – began to toll,

As all the Heavens were a Bell,
And Being, but an Ear,
15   And I, and Silence, some strange Race
Wrecked, solitary, here –

And then a Plank in Reason, broke,
And I dropped down, and down –
And hit a World, at every plunge,
20   And Finished knowing – then –

I Heard a Fly Buzz – When I Died (J465, F591) (1896, c.1863)

I heard a Fly buzz – when I died –
The Stillness in the Room
Was like the Stillness in the Air –
Between the Heaves of Storm –

The Eyes around – had wrung them dry –   5
And Breaths were gathering firm
For that last Onset – when the King
Be witnessed – in the Room –

I willed my Keepsakes – Signed away
What portion of me be   10
Assignable – and then it was
There interposed a Fly –

With Blue – uncertain – stumbling Buzz –
Between the light – and me –
And then the Windows failed – and then   15
I could not see to see –

 ## I Like to See It Lap the Miles (J585, F383) (1891, c.1862)

I like to see it lap the Miles –
And lick the Valleys up –
And stop to feed itself at Tanks –
And then – prodigious step

Around a Pile of Mountains –   5
And supercilious peer
In Shanties – by the sides of Roads –
And then a Quarry pare

To fit it's sides
And crawl between   10
Complaining all the while
In horrid – hooting stanza –
Then chase itself down Hill –

And neigh like Boanerges° –
Then – prompter than a Star   15
Stop – docile and omnipotent
At it's own stable door –

°14 *Boanerges:* a surname meaning "the sons of thunder" that appears in Mark 3:17.

 ## I'm Nobody! Who Are You? (J288, F260) (1891, c.1861)

I'm Nobody! Who are you?
Are you – Nobody – too?

Then there's a pair of us!
Don't tell! they'd banish us – you know!

5   How dreary – to be – Somebody!
How public – like a Frog –
To tell your name – the livelong June –
To an admiring Bog!

I Never Lost as Much but Twice (J49, F39) (1890; c.1858)

I never lost as much but twice –
And that was in the sod.
Twice have I stood a beggar
Before the door of God!

5   Angels – twice descending
Reimbursed my store –
Burglar! Banker – Father!
I am poor once more!

I Taste a Liquor Never Brewed (J214, F207)
(1861; c.1860)

I taste a liquor never brewed –
From Tankards scooped in Pearl –
Not all the Frankfort Berries°   *grapes*
Yield such an Alcohol!

5   Inebriate of Air – am I –
And Debauchee of Dew –
Reeling – thro endless summer days –
From inns of Molten Blue –

When "Landlords" turn the drunken Bee
10   Out of the Foxglove's door –
When Butterflies – renounce their "drams" –
I shall but drink the more!

Till Seraphs swing their Snowy Hats –
And Saints – to windows run –
15   To see the little Tippler
From Manzanilla° come

°16 *Manzanilla:* a pale sherry from Spain. Dickinson may also have been thinking of Manzanillo, a Cuban city known for rum.

Much Madness Is Divinest Sense (J435, F620) (1890; c.1863)

Much Madness is divinest Sense –
To a discerning Eye –
Much Sense – the starkest Madness –
'Tis the Majority

In this, as all, prevail –
Assent – and you are sane –
Demur – you're straightway dangerous –
And handled with a Chain –

5

My Life Closed Twice Before Its Close
(J1732, F1773) (1896)

My life closed twice before it's close;
It yet remains to see
If Immortality unveil
A third event to me,

So huge, so hopeless to conceive
As these that twice befell.
Parting is all we know of heaven,
And all we need of hell.

5

My Triumph Lasted Till the Drums
(J1227, F1212) (1935; c.1871)

My Triumph lasted till the Drums
Had left the Dead alone
And then I dropped my Victory
And chastened stole along
To where the finished Faces
Conclusion turned on me
And then I hated Glory
And wished myself were They.

5

What is to be is best descried
When it has also been –
Could Prospect taste of Retrospect
The Tyrannies of Men
Were Tenderer, diviner
The Transitive toward –
A Bayonet's contrition
Is nothing to the Dead.

10

15

One Need Not Be a Chamber – To Be Haunted
(J670, F407) (1891; c.1862)

One need not be a chamber – to be Haunted –
One need not be a House –
The Brain has Corridors – surpassing
Material Place –

Far safer, of a midnight meeting
External Ghost
Than it's interior confronting –
That cooler Host –

5

Far safer, through an Abbey gallop,
10   The Stones a'chase –
Than unarmed, one's a'self encounter –
In lonesome Place –

Ourself behind ourself, concealed –
Should startle most –
15   Assassin hid in our Apartment
Be Horror's least –

The Body – borrows a Revolver –
He bolts the Door –
O'erlooking a superior spectre –
20   Or More –

 ## Safe in Their Alabaster Chambers (J216, F124) (1862; c.1859)

Safe in their Alabaster Chambers –
Untouched by Morning –
And untouched by Noon –
Lie the meek members of the Resurrection –
5   Rafter of Satin – and Roof of Stone!

Grand go the Years – in the Crescent – above them –
Worlds scoop their Arcs –
And Firmaments – row –
Diadems – drop – and Doges° – surrender –
10   Soundless as dots – on a Disc of snow –

_____

°9 *Doges:* Rulers of Venice and Genoa, Italian city-states during the Renaissance.

 ## Some Keep the Sabbath Going to Church (J324, F236) (1864; c.1861)

Some keep the Sabbath going to Church –
I keep it, staying at Home –
With a Bobolink for a Chorister –
And an Orchard, for a Dome –

5   Some keep the Sabbath in Surplice –
I, just wear my Wings –
And instead of tolling the Bell, for Church,
Our little Sexton – sings.

God preaches, a noted Clergyman –
10   And the sermon is never long.
So instead of getting to Heaven, at last –
I'm going, all along.

 The Soul Selects Her Own Society (J303, F409) (1890; c.1862)

The Soul selects her own Society –
Then – shuts the Door –
To her divine Majority –
Present no more –

Unmoved – she notes the Chariots – pausing –   5
At her low Gate –
Unmoved – an Emperor be kneeling
Opon° her Mat –   *upon*

I've known her – from an ample nation –
Choose One –   10
Then – close the Valves of her attention –
Like Stone –

Success Is Counted Sweetest (J67, F112) (1864; c.1859)

Success is counted sweetest
By those who ne'er succeed.
To comprehend a nectar
Requires sorest need.

Not one of all the purple Host   5
Who took the Flag today
Can tell the definition
So clear of Victory

As he defeated – dying –
On whose forbidden ear   10
The distant strains of triumph
Burst agonized and clear!

Tell All the Truth but Tell It Slant (J1129, F1263)
(1945; c.1872)

Tell all the truth but tell it slant –
Success in Circuit lies
Too bright for our infirm Delight
The Truth's superb surprise
As Lightning to the Children eased   5
With explanation kind
The Truth must dazzle gradually
Or every man be blind –

There's a Certain Slant of Light (J258, F320) (1890; c.1862)

There's a certain Slant of light,
Winter Afternoons –

That oppresses, like the Heft
Of Cathedral Tunes –

5   Heavenly Hurt, it gives us –
We can find no scar,
But internal difference –
Where the Meanings, are –

None may teach it – Any –
10 'Tis the Seal Despair –
An imperial affliction
Sent us of the Air –

When it comes, the Landscape listens –
Shadows – hold their breath –
15 When it goes, 'tis like the Distance
On the look of Death –

To Hear an Oriole Sing (J526, F402)

(See Chapter 17, p. 859)

Wild Nights – Wild Nights! (J249, F269) (1891; c.1861)

Wild Nights – Wild Nights!
Were I with thee
Wild Nights should be
Our luxury!

5 Futile – the winds –
To a Heart in port –
Done with the Compass –
Done with the Chart!

Rowing in Eden –
10 Ah – the Sea!
Might I but moor – tonight –
In thee!

Edited Selections from Criticism of Dickinson's Poems

The following selections are intended to supply details and ideas for essays on Dickinson's poems. For a selective bibliography, consult the "Bibliographic Sources" section (p. 1027), which may be augmented with your college library catalogue and the most recent volumes of the *MLA International Bibliography* available in the reference room of your library. The bracketed page numbers refer to the original pagination of the sources included here. Footnotes in the sources have been omitted.

1. From "Orthodox Modernisms"[2]

Dickinson's power derives partly from a cluster of techniques, from certain [222] themes, and from tonal qualities that we consider modern and admire for their apparent newness. Her work is a catalogue of these modernisms, conventional to us now in their familiarity and so commonly known in her repertoire that a summary here will suffice. She possessed an intuitive knack for exploiting the capacity of language under certain distortions or tensions to arrest, illuminate, pierce, astonish. Her wonderfully engaging first lines range from the controlled audacity of flatness and understatement ("Before I got my eye put out") to marvelous lines of great syntactic pressure involving mystery, lure, expectation, and which play sophisticatedly with line-end novelty and grammatical deception.

The animated lexical selection that is the heart of her craft comprises violations sometimes of great daring. She surprised with her language and, when it was not so deliberately concocted as to be coy or patent, it brings off its risks and shocks in a modern way. A corpse in poem 287 [J287, F259] is "This Pendulum of snow" and death's finality is in "Decades of Arrogance." Elsewhere her lexical surprises manage a careful deflation and austerity that dehumanize, objectify, as in these sciential lines about a corpse:

> The busy eyes – congealed –
> It straightened – that was all . . .
> It multiplied indifference

Dry and hard, spare in a Poundian sense, this cold language forms into an analytical instrument of great accuracy. There is also word parading of the sort we now admire as well in Marianne Moore. In Dickinson's little known poem about a June [223] bug, the polysyllables thump against the single-syllable vernacular:

> From Eminence remote
> Drives ponderous perpendicular
>
> . . . .
> Depositing his Thunder
> He hoists abroad again –
> A Bomb upon the Ceiling
> Is an improving thing
> It keeps conjecture flourishing –   [J1128, F1150]

Dickinson interrupted nineteenth-century poetic discourse with a vernacular so direct it seemed crude to her first public. She disarmingly called it in poem 373 [J373, F575] "my simple speech" and "plain word." It was in fact flattened speech, a *talking* that was depoetizing; and an escape from pomposity. Into her poems and particularly into those outrageous first lines came a natural breath and diction that created the illusion and the impact of real speech acts. . . .

Most modern, perhaps, among Dickinson's techniques is her use of language [225] realms as constitutive elements in analytical structure. She makes the language

---

[2]From David Porter, *Dickinson: The Modern Idiom* (Cambridge: Harvard University Press, 1981), from the section entitled "Orthodox Modernisms."

medium itself objective and able to cut like a tool, managing this in at least three ways: vernacular diction inserted in formal language for its cross-cut effect; deploying Anglo-Saxon abruptness against the formalities of Latinate diction (this has been much noticed); and cleverly treating a subject with an alien lexical set. An instance of this last, as I have noted elsewhere, is characterizing God in the language of law or commerce. Dickinson, intuitively audacious in this, makes one language subset cut against and criticize another level of lexical selection, making a drama of language itself as if lexicons were themselves characters. Here is God silently measured by cold legalisms.

> I read my sentence – steadily –
> Reviewed it with my eyes,
> To see that I made no mistake
> In it's extremest clause –
> The Date, and manner, of the shame –
> And then the Pious Form
> That "God have mercy" on the Soul
> The Jury voted Him –   [J412, F432]

Besides such strategies of diction choice at which she was so adept, Dickinson employed other techniques that we call modern. As noted, she elided syntax (for various reasons), omitted transitions, and dropped structural and even syntactical copulas. This habit of withholding connective material produces curiously vexatious ways we now choose to see as modern: discontinuity of structure and story, and remystification of phenomena that seem simple and clear, and those extinguishings of meaning by which we experience complexity and feel the intractable quality of existence again. Beyond this, Dickinson's habitual brevity seems modern in its glimpses and incompleteness. These are notes raised to literature, notation as authentic response. Wayward in punctuation, the poems disregard nicety and neglect finish. They have an aura of spontaneity and the status of randomness, which, as when we look at impressionist or action painting, we find congenial and not a counterfeiting of sensation and reality. Like Hardy, but apparently less knowingly, her poetry was revolutionary because it avoided the jeweled line. It was more a making of the irregular line through a rough simplicity and by drastic reduction. Indeed, sometimes the print version of her manuscripts unavoidably makes a modern line disposition.

[226]

> And Life was not so
> Ample I
> Could finish – Enmity –   [J478, F763]

Her partial rhymes and the structural instability and shifts in poems contribute to this impatient art.

Dickinson's rift vision, the ability to make language cut into the disparities between concept and reality, between the expectation and the actuality—this creation in language of cruel parallax—effects a disruption and penetration that we also call modern. It appeals to our suspicion of wholeness and seamless compatible meaning. This effect is behind Harold Bloom's accurate observation that Dickinson, as much as any modern, made the visible world a little hard to see.

The several techniques emphasized here as modern are well known and often displayed as the true source of Dickinson's modernity. Yet we shall see that her modernity operated at a more fundamental level than this. For now it is clear that these several conventional modernisms, what have now become part of the technical orthodoxy of modernist verse in English, contribute to the powerful effect that is indubitably of our time: the estrangement from outer reality and the resistance of common words to definitive meaning. The estrangement is accomplished by the compact, unsustained, raw power of language at the surface of her clipped-off poems.

In her themes, as well, Dickinson is with the moderns. Her language, animated by her selective cleverness, together with the snapshot brevity of her hymn form, courted instability and change and spotted the vulnerability of settled states. This is why sunsets evoked some of her best imagistic effort. The spectacle of day's end was intensely, exaggeratedly visual, it was naturally associated with death, and it was recurrent novelty, change taking place before the eyes. The sunset was thus a visual allegory for what most centrally engaged this poet. [227]

Her preoccupation with change led to more desperate visions of mutability where the price of each moment of transport qualified every ecstasy, showing by her allegorical terms the furrow that threatens every glow. Unlike Emerson and Whitman, Dickinson brought into view with her strange and critical metaphors the opaque being of man, the "mysterious peninsula" as she called it, the unmanageable, excruciatingly sensitive, and needful portion that was her preoccupation.

She possessed a modernist knowledge of the mind's hidden places, what she called "That awful stranger Consciousness," terrifying to face. Equipped with her estranging language, she raised to the reader's awareness the intricate workings out of sight, careful not to "Mistake the Outside for the in" as she said. It is this interior life, in (for this recluse) the inevitable metaphor of the house, that is "haunted" and is the crucial spot where we enact our ignorance of ourselves and the world. Here is the "interior Confronting," where "Unarmed, one's a'self encounter." Now become an orthodox element of modern themes—what Irving Howe has called a modern fondness for the signs of psychic division—the interior life and the language to see it were the particular loci of Dickinson's attention. Encountering the self both dictated the strategies of her language and was the act in which her language had its circumstantial reflection.

"I felt a Funeral in my Brain" [J280, F340] is the first coolly targeted modern interior in American poetry, and it is handled adroitly with modernist attention not to moral judgment but to judgment-free description. There is no emotional slither, to use Pound's term, or didactic assertion as in other poems such as "Bound – a trouble / And lives can bear it!" or "A Weight with Needles on the pounds," but rather psychological interiority seen minutely. The funeral-in-the-brain poem, representative of a substantial cluster of Dickinson's works on psychic distress, manifested two generations in advance the doctrine of imagism that Pound defined as the transfer of a complex of emotions in an instant of time.

It was Dickinson diving into the wreck and her devastated speaker indeed "wrecked" in the poem. Assurance of diction and line is firm. The poem has structure and lexical cohesion of a high order for Dickinson, and it is this firmness that

[228] operates so effectively against the subject matter of instability and disintegration. It is a superb performance, thoroughly modernist in its dark vision clinically portrayed.

Such language . . . made visible a new category of psychic suffering. Minutely observant, its figure of the interior funeral sustained, the poem moves with impressive directness into its surrealist transformation at the line "Then Space – began to toll." The familiar terms make new equations: Heaven is a Bell, Being an ear, and Silence a strange Race, and the wreck itself an annihilating silence. The surreal landscape, haunted with Dickinson's sense of exclusion and ignorance, unfolds, at least to the somewhat redundant last stanza, with a sure finality of language and wholeness of vision. In its cold-blooded, unflinching way as well as in the interior location of its action, the poem is supremely modernist. From the broader view of the Dickinson canon, we see how her concern with the interior reflects an equally modern concern with intense self-consciousness extending even to self-torture and the poetry of breakdown. . . .

[229] The protomodernist image of the durable face of technological violence, of assault masked by dehumanized visages, is related in terror to another theme of Dickinson's that is hardly depictable by such momentary frissons. That is her vision of the *absence of an end*. I find this the most frightful of all Dickinson's modernist themes because it involves the pathological extremity of her familiar images such as this, of death in life, that ends an eight-line poem of utter inertness.

> I take my living place
> As one commuted led –
> A Candidate for Morning Chance
> But dated with the Dead.   [J1194, F1209]

The smell of nihilism rises from more than a few poems, sometimes in a complete flatness of tune where her theme is the loss that drains every gain: note the eight lines that tick off loss beginning "Finding is the first Act / The second, loss" [J870, F910]. Associated with this theme of lost purpose and the absence of an end is a fearful corollary: the prevention of ripeness, of completion and thereby of knowledge and identity. It is the vision we saw in "What ripeness after that": that is, a life of incompletion, of ignorance, of need without assuaging. It can stand for the quintessential modernist condition—until with Dickinson we find ourselves going deeper . . .

[230] Particular tones in Dickinson's poetry are also part of her commonly recognized modernism. Currents of doubt and the snowman moments give certain poems a psychological desperation that was unfamiliar to much nineteenth-century poetry. The sharply discrepant tone in poems, their directness of statement, and the audacity of their attack on conventional belief and easy-going piety are elements that would have given offense in her own time and so did not appear in the first editions of her poetry in the 1890s. Her colloquial and irreverently casual heresy at times ("It's easy to invent a Life"), her deliberate inelegance in a primitive offbeat diction ("It is simple to ache in the Bone or the Rind"), and the seemingly sophisticated skepticism in off-hand phrases ("Our Savior, by a Hair") combine to give a considerable portion of the poetry a discordant tone that undercuts the poetry of unquestioned assent with which her contemporaries filled the verse books of the day.

Satire and irreverence along a gamut from mild asides to bitter attack are also modernist elements that form part of our critical orthodoxy and the surfaces by which Dickinson can be labeled a modern. In the poem beginning "There's been a [231] Death, in the opposite house" [J389, F547] she creates a gentle satire on the impersonal organization that swings into action at a death, with its ritual movements and the professional mourners who take charge. In such verse of casual irreverence, the understatement and vernacular ease effectively counterpoint the regular common meter that arranges them. Deft lexical selection provides the edge that cuts in in the modern way. Her lines on the aurora borealis, where the common expectation would be for "paint" and "tint," Dickinson slips all askew by substituting "infection" and "taint":

> The North – Tonight . . .
> Infects my simple spirit
> With Taints of Majesty   [J290, F319]

She deflated a generically solemn occasion by unobtrusive negation and the one unexpected word "soldered":

> I've seen a Dying Eye
> Run round and round a Room . . .
> And then – be soldered down
> Without disclosing what it be
> 'Twere blessed to have seen   [J547, F648]

Her language pierced theological pomposities with strokes of marvelous wit, as here with out-of-place words from the public hall set off against Resurrection:

> No crowd that has occurred
> Exhibit – I suppose
> That General Attendance
> That Resurrection – does   [J515, F653]

Dickinson's modernist tones include the confessional one. She excelled in [232] creating a sense of private immediacy because, by the strategy of seemingly autobiographical speech acts, she reproduced in writing the speaking voice. Archibald MacLeish has written most knowingly on the unique voice by which we identify her. It is language signifying emotional experience close at hand that impresses us. The voice, quotation marks invisible, contradicts a reader's conscious awareness of the deliberately written text. This way in which Dickinson *did* speak out to strangers produces what we take to be an immediate proximity to the mind. The flattened conversational tone depoetizes experience and gives it a confessional authenticity of the sort we are familiar with in our own time.

> To Ache is human – not polite –
> The Film upon the eye
> Mortality's Old Custom –
> Just locking up – to Die   [J479, F458]

Toughness of attitude and candor couched in unstudied inelegance are further tonal qualities by which twentieth-century readers have assigned Dickinson to the origins of modernism along with Whitman. The blunt tones sound frequently along her lines, as here in this bald assertion that seems to have no poetic pretentions: "Men die – externally – / It is a truth – of Blood" [J531, F584].

Boldly secular content and skeptical tone quite disjunct from the orderly arrangement of the hymn form make an ironic combination. The poems produce that most modern of all attitudes, the ironicalization of experience. Beyond that, the disjunction and tonal qualities together effect a modernist estrangement, dissonance, and thus a critical perspective. Her bruskness deromanticizes, as in the moon poem that begins "I watched the Moon around the House." Dickinson's daring comes out most clearly if her moon is put alongside the famous protoimagist poem on the moon by T. E. Hulme. Dickinson's lines have in their more compact shape a greater bravado. It is part of what she shares with poets who followed her.

> like a Head – a Guillotine
> Slide carelessly away –
> like a Stemless Flower –
> Upheld in rolling Air –   [J629, F593]

[233]   The best summing up of these tonal qualities we now see as a modern set is in that phrase *the ironicalization of experience*. The tonal undercutting, the evasion of stock sincerity, the protective irreverence and throwaway understatement, thus making the hymn form play a different tune: all these effects, even if there were behind them no perspective of mind much more fundamental, would withal make Dickinson a modern. Neither sophisticated nor sustained, hers was a poetic cunning working by stealth of language and subversion of form to create surprise by strangeness. Out of these strategies came a disordering of experience, a new confession of our precarious status.

2. From "The Landscape of the Spirit"[3]

[14]   Dickinson's poems frequently assert her sense of the mind's actuality with images
[15]   of caverns and corridors [J777, F877; J670, F407], windows and doors [J303, F409; J657, F466], even cellars [J1182, F1234]. Because she took the mind to be her dwelling place, it is appropriate that she use these domestic figurative correspondences to describe it. Yet her poems using such architectural analogues go beyond pointing out how a mind might be like a house. They set out to show, as well, what happens in a mind that is as a house, so that the solidity that door and window frame provide grants substance both to the setting and to the events occurring within. The architectural vocabulary usually portrays the mind as an enclosed space, its confinement responsible for power, safety, yet fearful confrontation.

---

[3]From Suzanne Juhasz, *"The Undiscovered Continent": Emily Dickinson and the Space of the Mind* (Bloomington: Indiana University Press, 1983), from the chapter entitled "The Landscape of the Spirit."

Poem 303 [J303, F409] is a strong statement about the power of the self alone. The soul is shown living within a space defined by door, gate, and mat. The external world, with its nations and their rulers, is kept outside.

> The soul selects her own Society –
> Then – shuts the Door –
> To her divine Majority –
> Present no more –
>
> Unmoved – she notes the Chariots – pausing –
> At her low Gate –
> Unmoved – an Emperor be kneeling
> Upon her Mat –
>
> I've known her– from an ample nation –
> Choose One –
> Then – close the Valves of her attention –
> Like Stone –

Traditional ideas about power are reversed here. Not control over vast populations but the ability to construct a world for oneself comprises the greatest power, a god-like achievement, announces the opening stanza. Not only is the soul alone "divine," but it is also identified as "Society" and "Majority": the poem also challenges our ideas about what constitutes a social group. Consequently, the enclosed space of the soul's house is more than adequate for a queenly life, and ambassadors of the external world's glories, even emperors, can easily be scorned. Yet while the speaker claims her equality with those most powerful in the outer world—they may be emperors, but she is "divine Majority," at the same time she asserts her difference from them; for her domestic vocabulary of door, low gate and mat establishes her dwelling as not a grand palace but rather a simple house.

While associating power with the enclosed space of the mind, the poem also [16] implies how isolation is confinement, too. When the soul turns in upon her own concerns, she closes "the Valves of her attention – / Like Stone –."

Valves permit the flow of whatever they regulate in one direction only: here from outside to inside. Either of the halves of a double door or any of the leaves of a folding door are valves. Valves seen as doors reinforce the poem's house imagery, while their association with stone makes the walls separating soul from world so solid as to be, perhaps, prison-like.

Prison-like because they allow no escape from the kinds of conflict, the kinds of terror, even, that must occur within. Poem 670 [J670, F407] exaggerating the architectural vocabulary, compares the chambers of the mind to the haunted castle of gothic fiction, a stereotypical setting for horror.

> One need not be a Chamber – to be Haunted –
> One need not be a House –
> The Brain has Corridors – surpassing
> Material Place –

Far safer, of a Midnight Meeting
External Ghost
Than its interior Confronting –
That Cooler Host.

Far safer, through an Abbey gallop,
The stones a'chase –
Than Unarmed, one's a'self encounter –
In lonesome Place –

Ourself behind ourself, concealed –
Should startle most –
Assassin hid in our Apartment
Be Horror's least.

The Body – borrows a Revolver –
He bolts the Door –
O'erlooking a superior spectre –
Or More –

The poem assumes that the mind is substantial, possessing corridors and chambers, because it is the dwelling place of "oneself." The extended comparison that is developed, between two kinds of dwellings, two binds of hauntings, is for the purpose of dramatizing how there can be something more frightening than the most frightening situation usually imaginable.

[17]

Both the second and third stanzas begin with the same phrase: "Far safer." Safer are the supernatural events of gothic castles, meeting ghosts at midnight; we are warned about "interior confronting," the everyday moments of the mind, another lonesome place, when "one's a'self encounter." One clue to the degree of difference in horror is the word, "Unarmed." We come prepared to find ghosts in spooky old castles, but not in what Dickinson calls in another poem "That polar privacy / A soul admitted to itself" [J1695, F1696].

There is, in fact, no way one can be armed against this particular kind of ghost. The murderer seeking to kill the body can be vanquished—one can borrow a revolver, bolt the door. But this assassin is hidden within oneself—is oneself. There is no escape. As Dickinson comments in poem 894 [J894, F1076], "Of Consciousness, her awful Mate / The Soul cannot be rid."

In the final stanza [of poem J670, F407] the quintessence of this horror is revealed. The rhetoric of the poem has been dramatic as well as concrete. Two dramas, in fact, have been enacted and contrasted. The external self has been venturing into lonesome abbeys, discovering hidden assassins in her chamber, even as the internal self has become aware of the existence of the "Cooler Host." Now the two plots turn into one. The self, who is, after all, body and mind at once, bolts the door, only to discover that she has locked herself in with herself. Adventuring in the external world, one need not confront one's own consciousness. But when one turns from "Horror's least" to live in the mind, that "superior spectre" can never be avoided again.

Because consciousness is self-confrontation, it establishes a "society" within, of "ourself" with "ourself." To represent the conflict and struggle engendered here, poem 642 uses an architectural vocabulary that provides a setting, fortress, for a drama of siege and defense. Yet even as "One need not be a Chamber – to be Haunted –" constructs a comparison between external and internal ghost stories only to conflate them, so the following poem's distinctions between inner and outer, protagonist and antagonist, turn out to be fictions.

> Me from Myself – to banish –
> Had I Art –
> Impregnable my Fortress
> Unto All Heart –
>
> But since Myself – assault Me –
> How have I peace
> Except by subjugating
> Consciousness?
>
> And since We're mutual Monarch
> How this be
> Except by Abdication –
> Me – of Me – ?   [J642, F709]

[18]

The speaker of the poem "Myself" wishes for the ability to banish from her castle an enemy, called "Me." In the second stanza she admits to the complexity of the problem; more than skill is required to maintain the defense, because there is a profound connection between the combatants. Reversing their titles—"Me" is now the speaker, "Myself" the opponent—the poem acknowledges their interchangeability while at the same time continuing to deal with them as separate entities. The enemy is also identified as "Heart" in the first stanza, "Consciousness" in the second. That these are as much aspects of "Me" as they are of "Myself" the poem will not yet admit.

Although we know that the poem is discussing one person and not two, its dramatic fiction of attacker and attacked creates a situation that is surely war, albeit civil. When the dichotomy itself is collapsed in the final stanza, the effect is to intensify the situation, the pain, the impossibility of victory. "Mutual Monarch," the antagonists are revealed to be in actuality both within. There is nobody without. Without doesn't matter. Victory is impossible, is not a mere matter of "art," because enemy and friend are one. "Consciousness" is the self's awareness of itself and could be vanquished only through the annihilation of self, which would leave no victor, since no self is left. The very naming of the characters in this drama articulates and also anticipates this conclusion. If in stanza one the defender was Myself, the attacker, Me; and in stanza two the attacker was Myself, the defender, Me; in the final stanza they, as mutual Monarch, are "Me" and "Me."

The poem's structure dramatizes an experienced conflict. If the fictional dichotomy of within and without is necessary so that we might understand the problem, so is the final denial of the fiction, that we might better understand the conclusion: that self-consciousness means precisely the encounter of the self with itself, and that this is a perpetual struggle.

3. From "The American Plain Style"⁴

[143]   In a still broader sense of influence, the American idiom itself, in both its literary and daily forms, may have contributed to Dickinson's use of a style that is biblical in origin. By the mid-nineteenth-century Puritan "plain style" had become the language of self-expression, the trusted idiom in America, although—or perhaps because—it

[144]   had lost its bolstering doctrinal and political contexts. According to Perry Miller's "An American Language," the plain style's demand that one speak from personal knowledge and as comprehensibly as possible made it the natural mode of discourse for a people living "in the wilderness:" and, by the late eighteenth century, attempting to form a democracy. All American writers, he claims, have had to deal with the consequences of this wholesale adoption of the principles and techniques of plain style. Because of its pervasiveness, Dickinson would inevitably have used language to some extent within its dictates. For epistemological reasons also, Dickinson may have felt some affinity for this style. Miller describes the plain style as inherently "defiant"—a style that both proclaims authority for the word and places the word's authority in individuals' articulate examinations of the truth; the style encourages practical discourse on theoretical or spiritual truths. Hence, it can as easily be turned against the idea of an authoritative God as it can be used to support that idea. Authority of language lies with the "plainest" (that is, apparently most artless yet still most commanding) speaker. The Puritans kept the style's implicit defiance in check by subordinating their word to God's Word; the latter was the law that theirs attempted to interpret and reflect. Emerson, Miller claims, partially maintained this check on defiance through his romantic belief in Nature as the origin of language, while Thoreau released the defiance of this style in his prose, "glory[ing] in his participation in the community of sin."

   More covertly than Thoreau, Dickinson does the same. Her very disguise of defiance, however, may also stem in part from inherent characteristics of the plain style, which demands the simplicity reflected in its name but paradoxically also a kind of reticence that may prevent its complete message from being articulated. Ideally, the plain speaker "convey[s] the emphasis, the hesitancies, the searchings of language as it is spoken"; plainness lies in the apparent artlessness of the speaker's or writer's use of the word. Partly as a consequence, writers in the plain style leave much unsaid, and they claim that their discourse says even less than it does. Using words sparingly leaves much to implication, and making modest claims for a text may disguise the authority its author in fact feels. Thus the plain style frequently underplays its own importance and seriousness; even when it most anarchically expresses the perception of the individual, it maintains the guise of saying little, and that only matter-of-factly. Hence, while speaking "plain" truth, an individual may confound every

[145]   doctrine that the Puritans held true and believed the plain style must express. As Miller puts it: "The forthright method [plain style] proved to be . . . the most subversive power that the wicked could invoke against those generalities it had, long ago, been designed to protect." Through reticence, indirection, and disguised claims for the authority of her word, Dickinson manipulates characteristics of the plain use of

---

⁴From Christanne Miller, *Emily Dickinson: A Poet's Grammar* (Cambridge: Harvard University Press, 1987), from the section entitled "The American Plain Style."

language in poetry that contradict Puritan convictions about the individual's relation to God and His Word. The style that affirms God's truth for the Puritans, and denies that God's power is the only good (while still celebrating it) for Thoreau, becomes ironic with Dickinson: while appearing to affirm or naively question, she denies the trustworthiness of any superhuman power. . . .

It is in her attitude toward language and toward communication itself as much as in her characteristic manipulations of the word that Dickinson differs from her [146] contemporaries and predecessors who wrote in plain style. Like them, she emphasizes the bare force of the word, eschewing elaborate syntax, modifiers, and extended conceits. Like them, she tends to stress the word's direct mediation between the individual and the world (for them, God). Like them, but to an unusual extreme, she makes small claims for her writing: her poems are "a letter to the World"; she is often a girl, or (like) a daisy, bird, spider, or gnat. Even when she has volcanic power, she generally appears harmless and unimportant: "A meditative spot – / An acre for a Bird to choose / Would be the General thought –" [J1677, F1743]. Dickinson, however, senses a different need for both plainness and reticence from those who believe in a natural or divine law of language. The word has two faces for her. Its effect may be epiphanic and it may come to her as a "gift," revealing "That portion of the Vision" she could not find without the help of "Cherubim" [J1126, F1243]. This is the language of poetry, of pure communication, "Like signal esoteric sips / Of the communion Wine" [J1452, F1476], or a "word of Gold" [J430, F388]. At other times the word is all but meaningless—an "Opinion" [J797, F849], an empty term. In a letter to Bowles she writes: "The old words are *numb*– and there *a'nt* any *new* ones – Brooks – are useless – in *Freshettime* –" (L 252). Her trick as poet is to make the old words new. To do this, she trusts "Philology," not God or Nature, and when she succeeds in doing this she feels that she has been lucky.

To Dickinson's mind, success in speaking plainly, in creating a word "that breathes" [J1651, F1715] does not prove spiritual salvation or make her a candidate for fame, partly because her sense of moral superiority depends on overthrowing the notion that God or the world can save her. The economical use of the words of ordinary life gives language its power. Speaking indirectly or subversively disguises the poet's usurpation of moral judgment from divine or human law, and thus saves her to speak again. As Perry Miller suggests, in Dickinson's poetry the pull between plainness and reticence subverts the whole idea of plainness. Because her meanings are not plain, they cannot be expressed plainly despite her use of simple words; her plainest speech *is* that of indirection.

As this conception of language implies, for Dickinson there is no stable relation between spiritual truth, the facts of existence, and the terms of language. Names are not adequate to things, and the function of language is not primarily to name. Things are perceived and understood through their relations to the rest of the world and by the process of cumulative, even contradictory, definition rather than by categorization or labeling. Dickinson has greater affinity with the lexicographer, the scientist of language seeking to clarify each word's various meanings, than she does [148] with the Romantic *Ur*-poet Adam. Her language stresses the relation between object and its effects or relations in an active world; meaning, for her, is not fixed by rules or even by her own previous perception of the world. The principles of Dickinson's world do not have to do with immutable properties and distinctions.

Dickinson manifests her belief in the flux or instability of relationship in the narratives of her poems more obviously than in her use of language. For example, the figures of her poems often change positions relative to each other, or prove to be undifferentiable rather than separate identities. In "The Moon is distant from the Sea," first "She" is the moon and "He" the water, then she becomes "the distant Sea –" and his are the ordering "Amber Hands –" of light [J429, F387]; the "single Hound" attending the Soul proves to be "It's own identity." [J822, F817]; in an early poem, she and her playmate Tim turn out to be "I – 'Tim'– and – Me!" [J196, F231]. In a late poem, desired object, self, and "Messenger" are indistinguishable in both their presence and their absence; in a mockery of simplicity, all have the same name:

> We send the Wave to find the Wave –
> An Errand so divine,
> The Messenger enamored too,
> Forgetting to return,
> We make the wise distinction still,
> Soever made in vain,
> The sagest time to dam the sea is when the sea is gone –
>
> [J1604, F1643]

Although this poem may be read as an elaboration of a truism—that one must give to receive, or that some losses cannot be prevented—it also ironically suggests that distinguishing present and absent sea (loved "Wave" from our own) is "vain." The "wise distinction" persists in failing to recognize the absurdity of damming what is not there and cannot be kept anyway. We attempt to conserve only what we have already lost.

Similarly, in "The Sea said 'Come' to the Brook" [J1210, F1275], the grown Brook takes the same form and title as the Sea that wanted to keep it small, as if to prove that the existence of one sea does not prevent the growth of innumerable physically indistinguishable others. In the last stanza it is not immediately clear which "Sea" is which:

> The Sea said "Go" to the Sea –
> The Sea said "I am he
> You cherished"– "Learned Waters –
> Wisdom is stale – to Me"

In countless other poems, unspecified and multiply referential "it" or "this" is as meaningful a subject for speculation as any clearly delineated event or object. Metaphor serves as the primary tool of definition and explanation because it allows for the greatest flexibility in its reference to fact.

4. From "The Histrionic Imagination"[5]

[82]   Dickinson recognized, early in her career, the value of the dramatic monologue and learned to use it with skill. A well-known poem, dated about 1858 or 1859 when the

---

[5]From Elizabeth Phillips, *Emily Dickinson: Personae and Performance* (University Park: Pennsylvania State University Press, 1988), from the chapter entitled "The Histrionic Imagination."

apprenticeship was nearing its end, serves both as an example in which she has not quite mastered the form but is alert to its efficacy and as a work in which she draws on her own experience but changes it in the act of speaking about it.

> I never lost as much but twice,
> And that was in the sod.
> Twice have I stood a beggar
> Before the door of God!
>
> Angels – twice descending
> Reimbursed my store –
> Burglar! Banker – Father!
> I am poor once more!   [J49, F39]

The story line of the verse is addressed to an imagined interlocutor on the subject of the power of God; when the poet allows the speaker to address God directly, however, the break in point of view discloses that Dickinson has not yet learned to integrate narration and drama. The austerely restricted language of the narrative is right for the recollection of painful loss in contrast to the defiant and improvident moment when the persona forgets the unidentified listener and turns in line seven to revile God directly, but an experienced poet does not lose awareness of the audience assumed in a monologue even when the character being depicted rages on.   [83]

Despite the violation of point of view, or perhaps because of it, the supplicant's outburst continues to reverberate in our ears as we listen to the falling strain of a voice quickly regaining control and we believe we have overheard Emily Dickinson herself quarreling with God. When we find in a second poem, "Going to Heaven!" (#79, [J79, F128] c. 1859), that the persona, a young girl who both hopes to go and is glad she isn't going to heaven, says, "If you sh'd get there first / Save just a little place for me / Close to the two I lost –," we look elsewhere for the experiences about which *she* is talking in the angry indictment of God. Who, among the people she loved, we ask, died during Dickinson's childhood and youth? And what other personal loss is of the enormity of death? Because neither poem gives any clues, we search the biography for them.

There was more anguish in the life of young Emily Dickinson than "I never lost as much but twice" enumerates. She recalled, in a letter of March 28, 1846, to Abiah Root, whose schoolmate had just died, an experience of early sorrow. The opening words of the recollection prefigure the idiomatic cadence in which the poem begins. She wrote: "I have never lost but one friend near my age & with whom my thoughts & her own were the same. It was before you came to Amherst. My friend was Sophia Holland. She was too lovely for earth & she was transplanted from earth to heaven. . . . Then it seemed to me I should die too." Emily, who was fourteen at the time of the death of her friend in the spring of 1844, gave way to "a fixed melancholy," told no one the cause of her grief, and was not well. Her parents sent her to Boston, where she stayed with relatives for a month and her health improved so that her "spirits were better." In May 1846, her maternal grandfather, Joel Norcross, died; there is no record of how she felt about him, but she went again in August to Boston for her health. In May 1848, during her seventeenth year, Jacob Holt, a friend about whom she anxiously asked more than once in letters from Holyoke, died at the age of twenty-six; he wrote some rather commonplace poems, one of which she copied in her Bible. There were, also, other persons who are usually suggested as "the two" she lost in death. Since the emotions of loss became more complex as she matured, they well may be fused beyond one's ability to extricate them in the poem.

[84]   Leonard Humphrey, who was principal of the Amherst Academy in 1846–1847, Emily's last year there, died at the age of twenty-six in November 1850; reporting the death of her "master" to Abiah, Emily mourned but did not give way to melancholy: "my rebellious thoughts," she asserted, "are many." Thereafter, Ben Newton, who introduced her to Emerson's poetry in 1850, left Amherst for Worcester, married in 1851, and died at the age of thirty-two on March 24, 1853. He taught her to read, she said, and was, "the first of my own friends." Had she forgotten Sophia Holland, who has not counted in explanations of the poet's loss?

Additional comments in the letters seem to lend support to readers who identify "the two she lost as Humphrey and Newton (Or are they "three": Holt, Humphrey, and Newton?) Writing on April 25, 1862, to Higginson, the poet said: "When a little Girl, I had a friend who taught me Immortality – but venturing too near, himself – he never returned – Soon after, my Tutor, died– and for several years, my Lexicon was my only companion." As if she were explaining "I never lost as much but twice," which Higginson had not seen, she added: "Then I found one more – but he was not contented I be his scholar – so he left the Land." This remark causes further speculation about whether the final loss in the poem is a kind different from that "in the sod." Casual readers then want to hear a name such as Charles Wadsworth or Samuel Bowles, neither of whom had "left the land" before or during the year in which Dickinson made a final copy of the verse ending with the dramatic cry: "Burglar! Banker – Father! / I am poor once more!"

There is not only too much evidence but too much uncertainty about what to choose from it for ascertaining the specific provocations of the poem's dramatic script. Nevertheless, if the letters to Abiah Root began the account of the incremental sorrow that is Dickinson's subject, one can say the soliloquy depends on events that are autobiographical but is not a literal recording of any one among them. The poet was rather finding words to make emotions *sound* true.

The recurrent experience of separations and loss may well be the source of another poem, which is more lyrical than dramatic. The emphasis is again on emotions related to a life "closed twice," but beyond the term "parting" there is no evidence that permits one to identity the events to which the persona refers. If the experiences are personal, they have been transmuted into flawless lines:

> My life closed twice before its close –
> It yet remains to see
> If Immortality unveil
[85]   > A third event to me
>
> So huge, so hopeless to conceive
> As these that twice befell.
> Parting is all we know of heaven,
> And all we need of hell.   [J1732, F1773, n.d.]

Although there is no autograph copy or date of composition for this justly famous poem, it points up Dickinson's practice of trying out different aspects of a
theme in order to realize the perfection of form inherent in it. The poet ceased,
moreover, to be an amateur in exploiting the possibilities of the dramatic monologue, which became the genre for a number of equally memorable Dickinson
texts.

5. From "The Gothic Mode: 'Tis so appalling – it exhilarates –' "6

Emily Dickinson's gothic poems are perhaps her most startling challenge to the [87]
symbolic order. They are transgressive poems of great energy that explore taboo
states usually excluded from consideration. In these poems the speakers spare the
reader no excess in their relish of the macabre, as a selection of first lines suggests:
"As by the dead we love to sit" [J88, F78]; "Do People moulder equally, / They
bury, in the Grave?" [J432, F390] or "If I may have it, when it's dead." [J577, F431].
In many poems, the dead simply refuse to Lie down; witty, garrulous corpses relentlessly address the reader from deathbed or grave: "Twas just this time, last
year, I died" [J445, F344]; "I heard a Fly buzz – when I died –" [J465, F591], "I died
for Beauty –" [J449, F448]. In others the speaker confronts an unknown self and
experiences "A doubt if it be Us" [J859, F903].

The Gothic poems fall into three main categories: those in which the speaker
encounters unknown forces within the self; those in which the walking dead are
women and continue Dickinson's explorations of gender; and those in which
death is welcomed as a liberation from the confinements of the symbolic order.
These poems challenge the ideals and propriety of the social order; they are disturbing because they question the certainty and rightness of its interpretations of
the world. Madness suggests that there are forces within that are beyond its juris- [88]
diction; human identity is not ultimately fixed, coherent, controlled, knowable.
The dissolution of death is a permanent reminder of the fragility and artificiality
of the social order and its rigid conventions.

The nineteenth century saw the articulation of the idea of the unconscious and
Dickinson's poems participate in that impulse. Dickinson was acutely aware of
what Edward Young had referred to as "the stranger within thee." In his book
Night Thoughts (1742–1745), which was used as one of the textbooks at Amherst
Academy, Young writes that reason is but "a baffled counsellor": man looks within
and finds "an awful stranger." Dickinson was similarly aware of an alien aspect to
consciousness, writing in Poem 894: "Of Consciousness, her awful Mate / The
Soul cannot be rid –" [J894, F1076]. Sometimes consciousness was an oppressive
companion:

> I do not know the man so bold
> He dare in lonely Place
> That awful stranger Consciousness
> Deliberately face –   [J1323, F1325]

6From Joan Kirkby, *Emily Dickinson* (New York: St. Martin's Press, 1991), from the chapter entitled "The Gothic
Mode: 'Tis so appalling – it exhilarates.'"

Several poems explore the encounter of the self with a stranger within. In Poem 670 [J670, F407], the internal ghost is an awesome force to be reckoned with:

One need not be a Chamber – to be Haunted –
One need not be a House –
The Brain has Corridors – surpassing
Material Place –
Far safer, of a Midnight Meeting
External Ghost
Than its interior Confronting –
That Cooler Host.

[89]

Far safer, through an Abbey gallop,
The Stones a'chase –
Than Unarmed, one's a' self encounter –
In lonesome Place –

Ourself behind ourself, concealed –
Should startle most –
Assassin hid in our Apartment
Be Horror's least.

The Body – borrows a Revolver –
He bolts the Door–
O'erlooking a superior spectre –
Or More –

In this poem the mind itself is seen as more terrifying and dangerous than a haunted house; it has dark, unknown corridors surpassing "Material place." The encounter with one's concealed self is more dangerous than ghost, or graveyard, or assassin; they are "Horror's least." These could be fled on horseback, locked out or vanquished with revolver, but there is no escape from the self. Indeed the self hidden within the self is "a superior spectre –/Or More –," suggesting some terror greater than any hitherto conceived. The mind has within itself the potential for insurrection and dissolution. . . .

[98]   Dickinson's most famous Poem 712 [J712, F479] "Because I could not stop for Death –" deals with a similar moment in which a woman is severed from her chosen tasks and carried off by an anonymous gentleman called "Death." Once again the fair theme of love is associated with "a thought so mean." However, this poem makes explicit the fact that the advent of the gentleman caller is nothing short of death for the woman. While this poem is usually read as a poem about death, revealing Dickinson's playfully macabre vision of death as a gentleman caller, it is a poem that identifies the gentleman caller as death; for him woman is expected to put away both her labour and her leisure. Like the woman in Poem 732 [J732, F857] she is expected to rise "to His Requirement" and drop "The Playthings of Her Life / To take the honorable Work / Of Woman, and of Wife –."

Because I could not stop for Death –
He kindly stopped for me

The Carriage held but just Ourselves –
And Immortality.

We slowly drove – He knew no haste
And I had put away
My labor and my leisure too,
For His Civility –

We passed the School, where Children strove
At Recess – in the Ring –
We passed the Fields of Gazing Grain –
We passed the Setting Sun –

[99]

Or rather – He passed Us –
The Dews drew quivering and chill –
For only Gossamer, my Gown –
My Tippet – only Tulle –

We paused before a House that seemed
A Swelling of the Ground –
The Roof was scarcely visible –
The Cornice – in the Ground –

Since then – 'tis Centuries – and yet
Feels shorter than the Day
I first surmised the Horses' Heads
Were toward Eternity –

The first stanza suggests that the female speaker is so deeply engaged in her own life that she does not wish to stop, but it also suggests the passivity of female desire. Courting is a male prerogative; she must wait to be called upon, but once chosen a surrender that is both quick and total is expected. She must give up her work and her leisure "For His Civility." He has all the privileges of authority; he nominates the time of execution but is regarded as "kindly" and civil. That the death coach contains the new couple— "And Immortality"—suggests something of the enormous duration of the marriage journey. However, it also suggests that male authority extends into eternity; both earthly life and after life are in his hands; indeed that hypothesis underpins his authority here.

The second stanza highlights the slowness and solemnity of this journey to a bridal house that strongly resembles a grave. Like the anonymous "He" in Poem 315 [J315, F477] "He fumbles at your Soul," "He knew no haste." She is assumed to have no interest or activity separate from his. Rather like the woman in Poem [100] 273 [J273, F330] "He put the Belt around my life –," she begins to sense her "Lifetime folding up –." As the journey progresses the speaker becomes increasingly aware that she has lost all agency and volition. Like the woman in Poem 443 [J443, F522] her "ticking" has stopped. The fields of grain are "gazing" at her; the setting sun "passed Us." In her bridal finery she experiences a mortal chill: "For only Gossamer, my Gown – / My Tippet – only Tulle –." Indeed the fine silk veil around her neck is a kind of noose; like the bride in Poem 1072 [J1072, F194] she is "Born – Bridalled – Shrouded – / In a day –." The wedding house turns out to be her grave; it is lowly and scarcely undifferentiated from the ground. Since this deathly bridal day, it seems like" and "Eternity." Dickinson's poem suggests the eternity of death-in-life endured after marriage, what the woman in Poem 443 [J443, F522] refers to as "Miles on Miles of Nought–."

In this poem woman is interrupted from her independent activities and brought to a house that seems "A Swelling of the Ground," inevitably suggesting the house of biological destiny, the womb as tomb. There is the suggestion in the poem that female autonomy would threaten the existing order; a woman with her own work and her own leisure may be too busy "to stop" for connubial death. In Poem 1445 [J1445, F1470] "Death is the supple Suitor," images of death and courtship are intertwined in similar fashion; it is "a stealthy Wooing"; a coach carries the woman away to "Troth unknown" and "Kindred as responsive / As Porcelain."

Dickinson's most striking gothic poems are those in which the dead address the speaker from deathbed or grave. These poems bear out Gillian Beer's view that "Ghost stories are to do with the insurrection, not the resurrection of the dead. It is the element of "the insurrectionary" and "the uncontrollable" that confounds. It goes without saying that these poems are disconcerting. Death is the ultimate taboo and the corpse "the ultimate impurity," "the most sickening waste." Yet Dickinson's speakers provocatively play on graves, sit by the dead, wonder if corpses moulder equally. In drawing near the corpse, the object that marks the limit between life and death, Dickinson invokes a place that is outside the rule of the symbolic order. In these poems, death marks the dissolution of the social order and becomes an emblem of liberation from its oppressive and artificial conventions. The corpse highlights the frailty of the symbolic order. As Julia Kristeva writes, a "decaying body, lifeless, completely turned into dejection, blurred between the inanimate and the inorganic . . . the corpse represents fundamental pollution." It is "above all the opposite of the spiritual, of the symbolic, and of divine law."

[101]

In Poem 465 [J465, F591] Dickinson presents a speaker beyond the limit of the symbolic order; she has "Signed away / What portion of me be / Assignable –" and is henceforth to nature, a decomposing body subject only to the fly. The poem highlights the radical distance between the dying, who awaits the dissolution of the human into the undifferentiated matter of the corpse, and the living, who remain entirely bound up in the trappings of the social order, property, keepsakes, and the law of the father—"the King" who is to be "witnessed – in the Room –."

I heard a Fly buzz – when I died –
The Stillness in the Room
Was like the Stillness in the Air –
Between the Heaves of Storm –

The Eyes around – had wrung them dry –
And Breaths were gathering firm
For that last Onset – when the King
Be witnessed – in the Room–

I willed my Keepsakes – Signed away   [102]
What portion of me be
Assignable – and then it was
There interposed a Fly –

With Blue – uncertain stumbling Buzz –
Between the light – and me –
And then the Windows failed – and then
I could not see to see –   [J465, F591]

At the moment of death, the speaker's attention is deflected by the buzz of a fly, lowly earthly representative of physical decay. For the dying person that simple presence erases all other concerns, social and religious alike. However, the living reaffirm their allegiance to the symbolic order. They turn their attention away from the dying person and what is represented by death to an affirmation of their faith; they prepare themselves to witness God's presence in the room, his taking of the dying person.

While the living await the "King" and the re-inscription of the social order, the dying person awaits the fly and a decomposition of the self into corporeal waste. She has willed her keepsakes and signed away the portion of her with meaning in the social order, that is property, gender, social identity. The use of sign and assignable is significant in this context. In death the subject relinquishes the power to sign, to signify, to mark with characters, and to assign, to transfer or designate by writing. The corpse is outside the sign, outside the system of differences inscribed by the social order. The dead body is disconcertingly free of its rules, systems, distinctions and limits. In death there is also a dissolution of the gender-marked body. The corpse is an "it," as the speaker notes in Poem 389 [J389, F547] "There's been a Death, in the Opposite House":

Somebody flings a Mattress out –
The Children hurry by –
They wonder if *it* died – on that   [103]
I used to – when a Boy –

The buzzing fly blocks out the light of distinction and differentiation. The buzz of the fly is the antithesis of human language with its discrete units of modulated sounds. That the blue of the sky is transposed to the buzz of the fly suggests a further scrambling of the senses. Indeed the windows fail, which suggests a total breakdown of the social framing of experience. Windows are artificial barriers between inside and outside, nature and culture; windows frame and limit vision. However, in death the social framing of experience ends. There is darkness and a dissolution of all the restricting categories and hierarchies on which the social order is based.

A similar dynamics informs Poem 449 [J449, F448], which is Dickinson's witty retort to the closing lines of Keats' "Ode on a Grecian Urn": "Beauty is Truth, Truth Beauty, – that is all / Ye know on earth and all ye need to know." In Dickinson's poem death deposes pomp.

I died for Beauty – but was scarce
Adjusted in the Tomb

When One who died for Truth, was lain
In an adjoining Room –

He questioned softly "Why I failed"?
"For Beauty," I replied –
"And I – for Truth – Themself are One –
We Brethren, are," He said –

And so, as Kinsmen, met a Night –
We talked between the Rooms –
Until the Moss had reached our lips –
And covered up – our names –

[104]   The concepts and abstractions of the symbolic order avail for little here. The fact of physical decomposition overtakes the speaker practically in mid sentence. The moss covers up the speakers' names and makes the differences for which they died irrelevant. Each corpse has died as she thought in significance, for a large life ordering abstraction whose significance would continue after death. However, death marks the dissolution of the whole system of differences on which the social order is based. The moss like the fly signals the dissolution of the symbolic order as well as the decay of the body; the moss seals the lips, the locus of speech, and covers up "our names –."

ROBERT FROST'S LIFE AND WORK (1874–1963)

Robert Lee Frost published his first book of poems, *A Boy's Will*, when he was living in England in 1913. At this time he was unrecognized and unknown in the United States. Ezra Pound wrote that "it is a sinister thing that so American . . . a talent . . . should have to be exported before it can find due encouragement and recognition." Time, of course, made Frost the most visible and admired American poet of his day. He eventually received twenty-five honorary degrees and four Pulitzer Prizes. Although there was no officially recognized national poet until the 1980s, when the Poet Laureateships were established through the Library of Congress, he came as close as possible to being America's official poet when he read "The Gift Outright" at the inauguration of President John F. Kennedy in January 1961. Writing in 1999, Joyce Carol Oates stated, "Frost's influence is so pervasive in American poetry, like Whitman's, as to be beyond assessment."[7] His collected poetic works continue to earn him this recognition.

Although in his person, and in his poetry, Frost presented himself as the quintessential New Englander, he was born on March 26, 1874, in California,

---

[7] *American Poetry Review* 28.6 (1999): 9.

where he spent his first ten years of life. His father, William Frost, had gone to San Francisco to take a job with the *San Francisco Bulletin*, and he and his wife Belle had their two children there. When William died in 1885, Frost's mother returned east to Lawrence, Massachusetts, where Frost attended high school, studied classics, and began writing poetry. He graduated in 1892 as co-valedictorian with Elinor White, whom he married in 1895. After high school he attended Dartmouth College for seven weeks and then turned to newspaper work and teaching school. Two years after his marriage, he enrolled at Harvard (1897–1899), aiming at a specialty in classical literature. He had hoped to take courses with William James, but he was disappointed because James was on leave during the years of Frost's attendance. However, Frost was able to take a class taught by the famous philosopher George Santayana. Personal reasons, including an unwillingness to submit to rigorous academic discipline, led him to end his student days at Harvard without a degree.

The image that one gains of Frost at this time is that he had enormous capability, powerful energy, much anxiety and self-doubt, and uncertain focus. In later years he stated that his early interests inclined him toward a number of separate careers: archaeology, astronomy, farming, or teaching Latin. It does not seem that he had any vision of himself as the poet and man of letters he was to become. Even at the height of his fame he minimized his poetic achievement by telling an audience at Amherst College that all he ever wanted from his poetic career was to be successful in writing "a few little poems it'd be hard to get rid of. That's all I ask."[8]

Much of Frost's early uncertainty resulted from his need to support his growing family. He gravitated toward farming as a way of life that would take up his physical energies and also give him the chance to think and to write. Fortunately, he had a supportive grandfather, William Frost Sr., who backed up his grandfatherly affection with financial support. In 1900 William Senior gave Robert a farm in Derry, New Hampshire, and for the next twelve years the poet lived in Derry, raised chickens and apples, wrote poetry, and taught English, from 1906 to 1911, at Pinkerton Academy in Derry. His life was hard but satisfying, but, as he later said, he was "not much of a farmer." He preferred to sit up late at night reading and studying, and then sleeping until noon. He did not see it as his obligation to get up with the sun and then go about the endless tasks and chores needed for successful farming. He was also an unusual farmer because he had been acquiring an immense amount of erudition, including the study of Latin and Greek poets and large numbers of Shakespeare's sonnets. It was during this time in Derry, in the first decade of the twentieth century, that he wrote many of his most famous poems, either in completed form or in draft. He sent many of these poems to magazines, but he got no publications and many rejection slips.

By 1912 he was aching to devote himself to writing but was extremely discouraged about the way things were going. According to the terms of Grandfather Frost's gift, however, he was permitted to sell the farm and use the money for his

---

[8]*Amherst Alumni News* (April 1954), quoted in Jay Parini, *Robert Frost: A Life* (New York: Holt, 1999) p. 391.

own purposes. Because he believed that he might make a better start abroad, he decided to move to England, one of the many moves he was to make during his lifetime. He joked that he might live in poverty abroad without embarrassing his relatives and friends in the United States. Once he landed in England, his poetic career was energized. He found a publisher who liked his poems and put him under contract. Almost overnight he emerged from obscurity through the publication of his first two poetic volumes, *A Boy's Will* (1913) and *North of Boston* (1914), which were favorably reviewed and which started to earn him acclaim in the United States. He also met a number of emerging and established poets, including Pound, Eliot, and Yeats.

Just as in 1913 he had been anxious to move abroad, early in 1915 he was anxious to return home. In 1914, World War I had been declared, and he believed life would be better and safer in the United States. Once he got back he took up residence on a farm near Franconia, New Hampshire. His life after this time was one of increasing professional success together with a heavy burden of personal anxiety and grief. He and his wife lost two of their children in infancy. In addition, their daughter Marjorie died in 1934, and their son Carol, who suffered severe bouts of depression, committed suicide in 1940. Elinor herself died in 1938, and daughter Irma was institutionalized in 1949. In addition, Frost was constantly stretching his finances to help his remaining adult children as they attempted to create their own lives. There is no question that Frost, who was becoming the most celebrated poet of his generation, suffered intensely in private.

But it must be emphasized that his career as a poet flourished beyond his early hopes. In 1916 he published *Mountain Interval,* a book containing "The Road Not Taken," "Birches," and "Out, Out—." He soon was in constant demand as a teacher and speaker. Amherst College created the position of poet-in-residence for him, an honor that would continue for much of his life. He also regularly lectured at Michigan, Harvard, Yale, and Dartmouth. Stories abound about his brilliance in front of audiences, both large and small. Seminars that he began teaching in the afternoon would stretch late into the evening as he captivated his students with his insights and his immense knowledge. Moreover, when television blossomed as a medium after 1950, he enthusiastically widened his national audience. With his memorably rumpled appearance, white hair, and cultivated New England voice, he was interviewed on many early television shows, and as a result he became perhaps the most widely recognizable poet in the history of literature.

As he gained all these successes as a teacher and lecturer, his poetic output remained constant and regular. In 1923 he published *Selected Poems* and *New Hampshire. New Hampshire,* for which he won a Pulitzer Prize, contains some of his best-known work: "Stopping by Woods on a Snowy Evening," "Fire and Ice," and "Nothing Gold Can Stay." Throughout his career there were many additional collections. *West Running Brook* appeared in 1928, *Collected Poems* in 1930. Additional collections were *A Further Range* (1936), *A Witness Tree* (1942), *Steeple Bush* (1947), *Complete Poems* (1949), *Aforesaid* (1954), and *In the Clearing* (1962).

Early in his career and throughout his long public experience as a speaker and lecturer, Frost cultivated his persona as a philosophical, wry, and wise country poet. This is the friendly, avuncular voice we most regularly hear, the one that expresses knowledge and concern for the land, history, and human nature. Even with this genial persona, however, there are complicated undertones of wit and irony. There is also what Randall Jarrell called "The Other Frost," the often agonized and troubled spirit whose voice is heard in poems such as "Acquainted with the Night," "Desert Places," and "Fire and Ice."

Regardless of the voice we hear, Frost preferred traditional poetic forms and rhythms, and he disapproved of free verse so strongly that he once asserted that writing it was like playing tennis without a net. He possessed complete knowledge of traditional forms (he knew much Latin poetry by heart). We therefore find, in much of his poetry, that he uses conventional rhyme schemes and clear meters with traditional metrical substitutions, together with closed forms such as couplets, sonnets (with interesting varying rhyme patterns), terza rima, quatrains, stanzas, and blank verse (see Chapter 18). Tension in the poems is created through the contrast of traditional form and Frost's characteristic conversational style. His diction is informal, plain, and colloquial, and his phrases are simple and direct. He uses and refines the natural speech patterns and rhythms of New England, polishing the language of everyday life and blending speech and formal patterns into a compact and unique poetic texture.

Structurally, Frost's poems typically move in a smooth, uninterrupted flow from an event or an object, through a metaphor, to an idea. Within this pattern, he usually describes a complete event rather than a single vision. The heart of the process is image or metaphor. Frost's metaphors are sparse and careful; they are brought sharply into focus and skillfully interwoven within each poem. Frost himself saw metaphors as the beginning of the process. In *Education by Poetry* (1931) he states, "poetry begins in trivial metaphors, pretty metaphors, 'grace' metaphors, and goes on to the profoundest thinking that we have. Poetry provides the one permissible way of saying one thing and meaning another." In "The Figure a Poem Makes," a brief essay that he wrote as the Preface to *The Complete Poems of Robert Frost* of 1949, he goes on further to describe what to him was the poetic process: "The figure a poem makes. It begins in delight and ends in wisdom. The figure is the same as for love. No one can really hold that the ecstasy should be static and stand still in one place. It begins in delight, it inclines to the impulse, it assumes direction with the first line laid down, it runs a course of lucky events, and ends in a clarification of life—not necessarily a great clarification, such as sects and cults are founded on, but in a momentary stay against confusion."

Frost's poems are usually based in everyday life and rural settings. Poems are occasioned by flowers, stone fences, rain, snow, birch trees, falling leaves, a spider, a tree branch, birds, a hired man, a garden, children, wood chopping, apple picking, piano playing, sleigh riding, and hay cutting, to name just a few of Frost's topics. However, the Frostian poetic structure always moves from such subjects toward philosophical generalizations about life and death, survival and responsibility, and nature and humanity. As he said in "The Figure a Poem Makes," the "delight" of poetry "is in the surprise of remembering something I didn't know I knew."

One of Frost's major appeals is that his poems are easily accessible. They are by no means simplistic, however, but run deep, as may be seen in such poems as "The Road Not Taken" and "Misgiving." They are often complex and ambiguous, as in "Mending Wall," in which the philosophies of the speaker and his fence-repairing neighbor are memorably presented and contrasted. Readers often conclude that the speaker's wish to remove barriers is this poem's major idea, but the neighbor's argument for maintaining them is equally strong. Further, in "Desert Places" (Chapter 18) we are presented with a chilling view of the infinite desert within the human spirit. In "Acquainted with the Night," Frost's sophisticated urban speaker tells us of the night of the city and also presents hints about the dark night of the soul.

Frost's complete works are in Richard Poirier and Mark Richardson, eds., *Robert Frost: Collected Poems, Prose, and Plays* (1995), and in Edward Connery Lathem, ed., *The Poetry of Robert Frost: The Collected Poems* (1969, frequently reprinted), which is also available in a paperback edition (2002). Of great use is Edward Connery Lathem's *A Concordance to the Poetry of Robert Frost* (rpt. 1994). Twelve of Frost's lectures have been preserved in Reginald Cook, *Robert Frost, A Living Voice* (Amherst: U of Massachusetts P, 1974). The standard biography, although often hostile, is by Lawrance Thompson, in three volumes: *Robert Frost: The Early Years*; *The Years of Triumph*; and *The Later Years* (New York: Holt Rinehart, 1966–1977). The last volume was completed after Thompson's death by Roy H. Winnick. An excellent biography is Jay Parini, *Robert Frost: A Life* (New York: Holt, 1999).

Useful criticism includes George Nitchie, *Human Values in the Poetry of Robert Frost* (Durham: Duke UP, 1960); Reuben Brower, *The Poetry of Robert Frost: Constellations of Intention* (New York: Oxford UP, 1963); Philip L. Gerber, *Robert Frost* (Boston: Twayne, 1966, rpt. 1982); Richard Poirier, *Robert Frost: The Work of Knowing* (Palo Alto: Stanford UP, 1990); John Kemp, *Robert Frost and New England: The Poet as Regionalist* (Princeton: Princeton UP, 1979); Richard Wakefield, *Robert Frost and the Opposing Lights of the Hour* (New York: Lang, 1985); James Potter, *A Robert Frost Handbook* (University Park: Pennsylvania State UP, 1980); Harold Bloom, ed., *Robert Frost*, Bloom's Modern Critical Views (New York: Chelsea House, 2003; a collection of critical essays); George Monteiro, *Robert Frost and the New England Renaissance* (Lexington: UP of Kentucky, 1988); Judith Oster, *Toward Robert Frost: The Reader and the Poet* (Athens: U of Georgia P, 1991); George F. Bagby, *Frost and the Book of Nature* (Knoxville: U of Tennessee P, 1993); and Katherine Kearns, *Robert Frost and a Poetics of Appetite* (New York: Cambridge UP, 1994). One of the programs in the PBS *Voices and Visions* series (1987) features his work.

Writing Topics About the Poetry of Robert Frost

1. The nature of Frost's topics (situations, scenes, actions) and his use of them for observation, narration, and metaphor.

2. Frost's assessment of the human situation: work, love, death, choices, diminution of life, stoicism, keeping or not keeping boundaries.

3. Frost's speaker: character, experiences, recollections, and reflections. In developing his subjects, to what degree does the speaker take a possible listener into account?

4. Frost as a poet of ideas. His vision of the way things are or should be.

5. Frost as a "confessional" poet: misgivings, the admission of personal error and personal fears.

6. Frost's use of narration and description in his poetry.

7. The structuring of Frost's poems: situation, observation, and generalization.

8. Frost's poetic diction: level and relationship to topic; conversational style.

9. Poetic forms in Frost: rhythm, meter, rhyme, and line and stanza patterns.

10. Frost's wry humor.

Poems by Robert Frost (Chronologically Arranged)

The Tuft of Flowers (1913) 1063

Pan With Us
  (See Chapter 20, p. 1015)

Mending Wall (1914) 1065

Birches (1915) 1066

The Road Not Taken (1915) 1067

"Out, Out—" (1916) 1067

The Oven Bird (1916) 1068

Fire and Ice (1920). 1068

Stopping by Woods on a Snowy Evening (1923)
  (See Chapter 11, p. 637)

Misgiving (1923) 1069

Nothing Gold Can Stay (1923) 1069

Acquainted with the Night (1928). 1069

Desert Places (1936)
  (See Chapter 18, p. 918)

Design (1936). 1070

The Silken Tent (1936) 1070

The Gift Outright (1941). 1071

A Considerable Speck (1942) 1071

Take Something Like a Star (1943). 1072

The Tuft of Flowers (1913)

I went to turn the grass once after one
Who mowed it in the dew before the sun.

The dew was gone that made his blade so keen
Before I came to view the leveled scene

5   I looked for him behind an isle of trees;
I listened for his whetstone on the breeze.

But he had gone his way, the grass all mown,
And I must be, as he had been,—alone,

"As all must be," I said within my heart,
10   "Whether they work together or apart."

But as I said it, swift there passed me by
On noiseless wing a bewildered butterfly,

Seeking with memories grown dim o'er night
Some resting flower of yesterday's delight.

15   And once I marked his flight go round and round,
As where some flower lay withering on the ground.

And then he flew as far as eye could see,
And then on tremulous wing came back to me.

I thought of questions that have no reply,
20   And would have turned to toss the grass to dry.

But he turned first, and led my eye to look
At a tall tuft of flowers beside a brook,

A leaping tongue of bloom the scythe had spared
Beside a reedy brook the scythe had bared.

25   The mower in the dew had loved them thus,
By leaving them to flourish, not for us,

Nor yet to draw one thought of ours to him,
But from sheer morning gladness at the brim.

The butterfly and I had lit upon,
30   Nevertheless, a message from the dawn,

That made me hear the wakening birds around,
And hear his long scythe whispering to the ground,

And feel a spirit kindred to my own;
So that henceforth I worked no more alone;

35   But glad with him, I worked as with his aid,
And weary, sought at noon with him the shade.

And dreaming, as it were, held brotherly speech
With one whose thought I had not hoped to reach.

"Men work together," I told him from the heart,
"Whether they work together or apart."   40

 ## Pan with Us (1913)

(See Chapter 20, p. 1015)

 ## Mending Wall (1914)

Something there is that doesn't love a wall,
That sends the frozen-ground-swell under it,
And spills the upper boulders in the sun;
And makes gaps even two can pass abreast.
The work of hunters is another thing: 5
I have come after them and made repair
Where they have left not one stone on a stone,
But they would have the rabbit out of hiding,
To please the yelping dogs. The gaps I mean,
No one has seen them made or heard them made,   10
But at spring mending-time we find them there.
I let my neighbor know beyond the hill;
And on a day we meet to walk the line
And set the wall between us once again.
We keep the wall between us as we go.   15
To each the boulders that have fallen to each.
And some are loaves and some so nearly balls
We have to use a spell to make them balance:
'Stay where you are until our backs are turned!'
We wear our fingers rough with handling them.   20
Oh, just another kind of outdoor game,
One on a side. It comes to little more:
There where it is we do not need the wall:
He is all pine and I am apple orchard.
My apple trees will never get across   25
And eat the cones under his pines, I tell him.
He only says, "Good fences make good neighbors."
Spring is the mischief in me, and I wonder
If I could put a notion in his head:
"*Why* do they make good neighbors? Isn't it   30
Where there are cows? But here there are no cows."
Before I built a wall I'd ask to know
What I was walling in or walling out,
And to whom I was like to give offense.
Something there is that doesn't love a wall,   35
That wants it down. I could say "Elves" to him,
But it's not elves exactly, and I'd rather
He said it for himself. I see him there
Bringing a stone grasped firmly by the top

40 In each hand, like an old-stone savage armed.
He moves in darkness as it seems to me,
Not of woods only and the shade of trees.
He will not go behind his father's saying,
And he likes having thought of it so well
45 He says again, "Good fences make good neighbors."

🍁 Birches (1915)

When I see birches bend to left and right
Across the lines of straighter darker trees,
I like to think some boy's been swinging them.
But swinging doesn't bend them down to stay
5 As ice-storms do. Often you must have seen them
Loaded with ice a sunny winter morning
After a rain. They click upon themselves
As the breeze rises, and turn many-colored
As the stir cracks and crazes their enamel.
10 Soon the sun's warmth makes them shed crystal shells
Shattering and avalanching on the snow-crust—
Such heaps of broken glass to sweep away
You'd think the inner dome of heaven had fallen.
They are dragged to the withered bracken by the load,
15 And they seem not to break; though once they are bowed
So low for long, they never right themselves:
You may see their trunks arching in the woods
Years afterwards, trailing their leaves on the ground
Like girls on hands and knees that throw their hair
20 Before them over their heads to dry in the sun.
But I was going to say when Truth broke in
With all her matter-of-fact about the ice-storm
I should prefer to have some boy bend them
As he went out and in to fetch the cows—
25 Some boy too far from town to learn baseball,
Whose only play was what he found himself,
Summer or winter, and could play alone.
One by one he subdued his father's trees
By riding them down over and over again
30 Until he took the stiffness out of them,
And not one but hung limp, not one was left
For him to conquer. He learned all there was
To learn about not launching out too soon
And so not carrying the tree away
35 Clear to the ground. He always kept his poise
To the top branches, climbing carefully
With the same pains you use to fill a cup
Up to the brim, and even above the brim.
Then he flung outward, feet first, with a swish,
40 Kicking his way down through the air to the ground.
So was I once myself a swinger of birches.
And so I dream of going back to be.

It's when I'm weary of considerations,
And life is too much like a pathless wood
Where your face burns and tickles with the cobwebs   45
Broken across it, and one eye is weeping
From a twig's having lashed across it open.
I'd like to get away from earth awhile
And then come back to it and begin over.
May no fate willfully misunderstand me   50
And half grant what I wish and snatch me away
Not to return. Earth's the right place for love:
I don't know where it's likely to go better.
I'd like to go by climbing a birch tree,
And climb black branches up a snow-white trunk   55
Toward Heaven, till the tree could bear no more,
But dipped its top and set me down again.
That would be good both going and coming back.
One could do worse than be a swinger of birches.

 ## The Road Not Taken (1915)

Two roads diverged in a yellow wood,
And sorry I could not travel both
And be one traveler, long I stood
And looked down one as far as I could
To where it bent in the undergrowth;   5

Then took the other, as just as fair,
And having perhaps the better claim,
Because it was grassy and wanted wear;
Though as for that the passing there
Had worn them really about the same,   10

And both that morning equally lay
In leaves no step had trodden black.
Oh, I kept the first for another day!
Yet knowing how way leads on to way,
I doubted if I should ever come back.   15

I shall be telling this with a sigh
Somewhere ages and ages hence:
Two roads diverged in a wood, and I —
I took the one less traveled by,
And that has made all the difference.   20

 ## "Out, Out—" (1916)

The buzz saw snarled and rattled in the yard
And made dust and dropped stove-length sticks of wood,
Sweet-scented stuff when the breeze drew across it.
And from there those that lifted eyes could count
Five mountain ranges one behind the other   5

Under the sunset far into Vermont.
And the saw snarled and rattled, snarled and rattled,
As it ran light, or had to bear a load.
And nothing happened: day was all but done.
10 Call it a day, I wish they might have said
To please the boy by giving him the half hour
That a boy counts so much when saved from work.
His sister stood beside them in her apron
To tell them "Supper." At the word, the saw,
15 As if to prove saws knew what supper meant,
Leaped out at the boy's hand, or seemed to leap—
He must have given the hand. However it was,
Neither refused the meeting. But the hand!
The boy's first outcry was rueful laugh,
20 As he swung toward them holding up the hand
Half in appeal, but half as if to keep
The life from spilling. Then the boy saw all—
Since he was old enough to know, big boy
Doing a man's work, though a child at heart—
25 He saw all spoiled. "Don't let him cut my hand off—
The doctor, when he comes. Don't let him, sister!"
So. But the hand was gone already.
The doctor put him in the dark of ether.
He lay and puffed his lips out with his breath.
30 And then—the watcher at his pulse took fright.
No one believed. They listened at his heart.
Little—less—nothing!–and that ended it.
No more to build on there. And they, since they
Were not the one dead, turned to their affairs.

🍁 The Oven Bird (1916)

There is a singer everyone has heard,
Loud, a mid-summer and a mid-wood bird,
Who makes the solid tree trunks sound again.
He says that leaves are old and that for flowers
5 Mid-summer is to spring as one to ten.
He says the early petal-fall is past
When pear and cherry bloom went down in showers
On sunny days a moment overcast;
And comes that other fall we name the fall.
10 He says the highway dust is over all.
The bird would cease and be as other birds
But that he knows in singing not to sing.
The question that he frames in all but words
Is what to make of a diminished thing.

🍁 Fire and Ice (1920)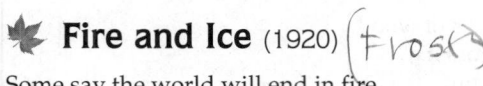

Some say the world will end in fire,
Some say in ice.

From what I've tasted of desire
I hold with those who favor fire.

[handwritten: passion will destroy you : ex) power money , land]

But if it had to perish twice,
I think I know enough of hate

[handwritten: hatred : racism, sexism, etc.]

To say that for destruction ice
Is also great
And would suffice.

[handwritten: under statement]

5

Stopping by Woods on a Snowy Evening (1923)

(See Chapter 11, p. 637)

Misgiving (1923)

All crying, "We will go with you, O Wind!"
The foliage follow him, leaf and stem;
But a sleep oppresses them as they go,
And they end by bidding him stay with them.

Since ever they flung abroad in spring   5
The leaves had promised themselves this flight,
Who now would fain seek sheltering wall,
Or thicket, or hollow place for the night.

And now they answer his summoning blast
With an ever vaguer and vaguer stir,   10
Or at utmost a little reluctant whirl
That drops them no further than where they were.

I only hope that when I am free
As they are free to go in quest
Of the knowledge beyond the bounds of life   15
It may not seem better to me to rest.

Nothing Gold Can Stay (1923)

Nature's first green is gold,
Her hardest hue to hold.
Her early leaf's a flower;
But only so an hour.
Then leaf subsides to leaf.   5
So Eden sank to grief,
So dawn goes down to day.
Nothing gold can stay.

Acquainted with the Night (1928)

I have been one acquainted with the night.
I have walked out in rain—and back in rain.
I have outwalked the furthest city light.

I have looked down the saddest city lane.
5   I have passed by the watchman on his beat
And dropped my eyes, unwilling to explain.

I have stood still and stopped the sound of feet
When far away an interrupted cry
Came over houses from another street,
10 But not to call me back or say good-by,
And further still at an unearthly height,
One luminary clock against the sky

Proclaimed the time was neither wrong nor right.
I have been one acquainted with the night.

 ## Desert Places (1936)

(See Chapter 18, p. 918)

 ## Design (1936)

I found a dimpled spider, fat and white,
On a white heal-all,° holding up a moth
Like a white piece of rigid satin cloth—
Assorted characters of death and blight
5   Mixed ready to begin the morning right,
Like the ingredients of a witches' broth—
A snow-drop spider, a flower like a froth,
And dead wings carried like a paper kite.

What had that flower to do with being white,
10 The wayside blue and innocent heal-all?
What brought the kindred spider to that height,
Then steered the white moth thither in the night?
What but design of darkness to appall?—
If design govern in a thing so small.

°2 *heal-all*: a flower, usually blue, thought to have healing powers.

 ## The Silken Tent (1936)

She is as in a field a silken tent
At midday when a sunny summer breeze
Has dried the dew and all its ropes relent,
So that in guys it gently sways at ease,
5   And its supporting central cedar pole,
That is its pinnacle to heavenward
And signifies the sureness of the soul,
Seems to owe naught to any single cord,
But strictly held by none, is loosely bound
10 By countless silken ties of love and thought
To everything on earth the compass round,

And only by one's going slightly taut
In the capriciousness of summer air
Is of the slightest bondage made aware.

The Gift Outright (1941)

The land was ours before we were the land's.
She was our land more than a hundred years
Before we were her people. She was ours
In Massachusetts, in Virginia,
But we were England's, still colonials,   5
Possessing what we still were unpossessed by,
Possessed by what we now no more possessed.
Something we were withholding made us weak
Until we found out that it was ourselves
We were withholding from our land of living,   10
And forthwith found salvation in surrender.
Such as we were we gave ourselves outright
(The deed of gift was many deeds of war)
To the land vaguely realizing westward,
But still unstoried, artless, unenhanced,   15
Such as she was, such as she would become.

A Considerable Speck (1942)

(Microscopic)

A speck that would have been beneath my sight
On any but a paper sheet so white
Set off across what I had written there.
And I had idly poised my pen in air
To stop it with a period of ink   5
When something strange about it made me think.
This was no dust speck by my breathing blown,
But unmistakably a living mite
With inclinations it could call its own.
It paused as with suspicion of my pen,   10
And then came racing wildly on again
To where my manuscript was not yet dry;
Then paused again and either drank or smelt —
With loathing, for again it turned to fly.
Plainly with an intelligence I dealt.   15
It seemed too tiny to have room for feet,
Yet must have had a set of them complete
To express how much it didn't want to die.
It ran with terror and with cunning crept.
It faltered: I could see it hesitate;   20
Then in the middle of the open sheet
Cower down in desperation to accept
Whatever I accorded it of fate.
I have none of the tenderer-than-thou

25   Collectivistic regimenting love
       With which the modern world is being swept
       But this poor microscopic item now!
       Since it was nothing I knew evil of
       I let it lie there till I hope it slept.
30   I have a mind myself and recognize
       Mind when I meet with it in any guise.
       No one can know how glad I am to find
       On any sheet the least display of mind.

🍁 Take Something Like a Star° (1943)

      O Star (the fairest one in sight),
      We grant your loftiness the right
      To some obscurity of cloud—
      It will not do to say of night,
5   Since dark is what brings out your light.
      Some mystery becomes the proud.
      But to be wholly taciturn
      In your reserve is not allowed.
      Say something to us we can learn
10   By heart and when alone repeat.
      Say something! And it says, "I burn,"
      But say with what degree of heat.
      Talk Fahrenheit, talk Centigrade.
      Use language we can comprehend.
15   Tell us what elements you blend.
      It gives us strangely little aid,
      But does tell something in the end.
      And steadfast as Keats' Eremite,
      Not even stooping from its sphere,
20   It asks a little of us here.
      It asks of us a certain height,
      So when at times the mob is swayed
      To carry praise or blame too far,
      We may take something like a star
25   To stay our minds on and be staid.

°Earlier versions of this poem used the title "Choose Something Like a Star."

LANGSTON HUGHES' LIFE AND WORK (1902–1967)

*For a discussion of Hughes and his work in drama,
see pages 1619–20.*

James Mercer Langston Hughes was born in Missouri in
1902. His childhood was characterized by uncertainty and
instability. When his parents became estranged, he was
cared for by his maternal grandmother, but he also lived

with friends of his parents and was moved, among other places, to Kansas, Illinois, and Ohio, where he received his primary and secondary schooling. He began writing early, and while in grade school in Lincoln, Illinois, he was declared class poet. Upon graduation from high school in Ohio, he lived for a year in Mexico. His father supported him when he promised to study engineering at Columbia, but he left after a year because he objected to the racism he perceived there. For a time after that he went from job to job without much purpose. At one point he was a seaman, then a cook in a nightclub in Paris, then a bouncer, and then a busboy in a hotel in Washington, DC. During those Washington years, Hughes worked for a brief time as an assistant to Dr. Carter G. Woodson, known today as the "father" of Black History, and the founder, in 1926, of what has become Black History Week, celebrated each year. It was in Washington that he submitted his earliest poems to the poet Vachel Lindsay (1879–1931), who was a resident of the hotel. Lindsay quickly became a champion of the increasing body of Hughes's poetry, and introduced the young man to various publishers. One of the earliest major results of this association was the publication of Hughes's first collection of poetry, *The Weary Blues*, in 1926, which included "The Negro Speaks of Rivers."

With such encouragement Hughes went back to school in earnest, graduating in 1929 from Lincoln University in Pennsylvania, from which he later received an honorary doctorate. In the wake of the stock market crash in 1929 and the Great Depression that followed, Hughes was hard put to make his living as a thinker and writer. It was also during this time that he became radicalized. He visited Haiti and Cuba, and as a result of his experiences there he attacked what he considered to be American imperialist foreign policy in the Caribbean area. He also translated the poetry of a number of Cuban and Haitian writers. He was able to spend a year in Soviet Russia, assisting in the preparation of a film exposing racial prejudice in the United States. He continued to write and publish, and soon he became recognized as one of the leading figures of the Harlem Renaissance—an energetic burst of African American literary creativity that also included Claude McKay and Jean Toomer. It has been observed that Hughes was the first African American to make his living as a writer. Make his living he did, but he was not a recipient of the public acclaim that created opulence for many subsequent writers.

During the following forty years of his writing career, Hughes was to write in every major literary genre, including translations, regular newspaper columns, and, in the late thirties, reports on the Spanish Civil War. He published a total of thirty-five books. Along with other early works were poems that he published in the *Crisis*, the official journal of the National Association for the Advancement of Colored People. In his first collection of short stories, *The Ways of White Folks* (1934), he fictionalized his disaffection with the condition of both southern and northern African Americans. One of the stories in this collection was "Father and Son," a version of the material that he turned into the two-act play *Mulatto,* which was produced at the Vanderbilt Theater in New York in October 1935. The play had a run of 373 performances, the record at that time for a Broadway play by an African American dramatist (see also Chapter 26, where *Mulatto* is included).

Hughes's own description of his calling as an author was to write about "Negro life in America." In addition to three short-story collections, he eventually published sixteen books of poems and two novels, together with twenty plays and texts for musical plays. He also edited a number of anthologies of the works of other African American writers, in addition to his constant production of articles and reviews. His total output was indeed voluminous. A few of his poetry collections, after *The Weary Blues* in 1926, were *The Dream Keeper* (1932), *Montage of a Dream Deferred* (1951), *The First Book of Jazz* (1955), and *Selected Poems* (1959). He published more than 860 poems during his lifetime.

His poetry develops from the idea of observing and celebrating Negro life in America. To achieve this goal, Hughes adopts a number of voices—not one voice, as in most of the poems of Dickinson and Frost, but a number of voices. His diction therefore is characterized by variety. Sometimes the words are straightforward and eloquent, as in "Let America Be America Again." We also encounter varieties of speech, from that of Hughes's beloved Harlem to the words to be found in the blues that Hughes also loved so dearly. In the poem "125th Street," he deals with the potentiality of blacks, who are both beautiful and capable. The underlying idea is that the American Dream has not been fulfilled for blacks, and that America, as a nation dedicated to equality, therefore remains unfulfilled and incomplete.

It is from such thinking that Hughes employs poetry, and literature generally, as a medium for political criticism. In "Negro" (1958), for example, Hughes asserts that Negroes, from the very beginnings of human history, have been enslaved and economically handicapped, and have suffered from all the cruelty that slavery and inequality have entailed. Thus, in the days of ancient Egypt, and Rome, the speaker's forbears were enslaved. In America, George Washington, the father of the country, kept slaves at Mount Vernon, just as Caesar had kept slaves on his estate in the first century BCE, and just as blacks, in inferior positions of heavy labor, made mortar so that the men who constructed the Woolworth Building in New York might practice their skills of craftsmanship, which they gained because of their racial privilege. In the nineteenth century, the age of colonialism, the men who exploited the Belgian Congo for profit also cruelly subjugated and exploited their slaves, just as in the twentieth-century agrarian South there was violent and cruel racial suppression—a topic Hughes more fully considers in the play *Mulatto* (see p. 1623). Hughes fills his poetry with the voices of modern African Americans who are the living heirs of this age-old inequality and prejudice. Thus the speaker of "The Weary Blues" is tired of life, and the speaker of "Po' Boy Blues" claims that "I's so weary / I wish I'd never been born." A more violent avenue of response is seen in the legendary poem "Harlem," in which the speaker considers the possibility that a "raisin in the sun" might "explode" (in violence against the cumulative suppression of centuries). A more subdued but ultimately more powerful response is that of education, which Hughes considers in "Theme for English B." Here, the speaker is a black who is obviously successful in the sphere of education. Even though this speaker recognizes his lack of equality, he is prepared to compete equally in the society that is producing resignation and possible violence among others of his race.

In looking at Hughes's poetry, then, we may discover the many aspects that typefied the experiences of being black in America. There are expressions of religious renunciation, feelings of personal unease, rationalizations for personal cruelty, observations about funerals (i.e., the death of a "cool bop daddy" [or "re-bop daddy"]), descriptions of the depraved horror of lynchings, anticipation of a future of equality, uneasiness about being castigated by angry parents, the irony of naming a movie theater after Lincoln but not after John Brown, the irony of uncontrolled population growth, a sense of personal loneliness, the excitement of Harlem night life, the beauties of jukebox love songs, and the difficulty of being both loving and nurturing. In short, we may find in the poetry of Hughes the reflections about life that he believed represented not only the voice but also the soul of his people.

The complete poems of Langston Hughes are contained in Arnold Rampersad, ed., *The Collected Poems of Langston Hughes* (New York: Knopf, 1994). Rampersad is the general editor of *The Collected Works of Langston Hughes* (Columbia, Mo.: Missouri UP), which is currently nearing completion. Hughes himself was involved in selecting the works for inclusion in *The Langston Hughes Reader: The Selected Writings of Langston Hughes* (New York: Braziller, 1958). This book is unique because it contains much introductory and explanatory commentary by Hughes. Biographies of Hughes include Milton Meltzer, *Langston Hughes* (New York: Crowell, 1968), and Arnold Rampersad, *The Life of Langston Hughes,* 2 vols. (Oxford: Oxford UP, 2002). Works of poetry criticism include Onwuchekwa Jemie, *Langston Hughes: An Introduction to the Poetry* (New York: Columbia, 1976); Steven C. Tracy, *Langston Hughes and the Blues* (Urbana: U of Illinois P, 1988, rpt 2001); and Harold Bloom, *Langston Hughes* (New York: Chelsea House, 2002). More general books of criticism of Hughes are Henry L. Gates, *Langston Hughes: Critical Perspectives Past and Present* (New York: Amistad, 1993); Harold Bloom, *Langston Hughes: Comprehensive Research and Study Guide* (New York: Chelsea House, 1999); Harold Bloom, *Langston Hughes* (New York: Chelsea House, 2007), and Steven C. Tracy, ed., *A Historical Guide to Langston Hughes* (Oxford: Oxford UP, 2004). This last volume contains a short biography of Hughes by R. Baxter Miller.

Writing Topics About the Poetry of Langston Hughes

1. Direct and indirect political implications in Hughes' poetry: social and political protest. Many of Hughes' poems reflect his concern with injustice in America and make reference to historical events. For instance, *The Negro Speaks of Rivers* makes reference to Abraham Lincoln's visit to New Orleans that influenced his decision to end slavery. Do you think that reading one of Hughes' poems may have an effect on how people think about this issue? Is there anything about America at the time Hughes was writing that you didn't know?

2. The dramatic use of speakers in the poems. Different individuals, different concerns, different voices, one poet.

3. Hughes's use of geographical place and regionalism in the poetry.

4. Hughes's diction in the poems: levels of diction, standard and substandard speech. Hughes often uses everyday speech, common words and slang. In which poems do you find this characteristic most predominant? How might the poems be different if they were written in standard English?

5. The treatment of racial cruelty in the poems. (For comparison on this topic you might also want to consider Hughes's *Mulatto*, on p. 1622.)

6. The connection of the blues to the content and to the points of view in the poems. Following the pattern of songs, such as Blues patterns in "Po' Boy Blues," many of the poems repeat lines, sometimes with slight variation. What is the effect of these repetitions? How are the lyrics of songs and poems different or the same?

7. "Weariness" and resignation as a recurring topic in the poems.

8. Hughes's ideas about what should be and what really exists. The ideal versus the actual in the poems.

9. The sense of humor in the poems. Laughing to keep from crying (which is the title of a collection of short stories published by Hughes in 1952).

Poems of Langston Hughes (Alphabetically Arranged)

Bad Man 1076
Cross. 1077
Dead in There 1077
Dream Variations 1078
Harlem. 1078
Let America Be America Again 1078
Madam and Her Madam 1080
Negro. 1081
The Negro Speaks of Rivers 1082
125th Street 1082
Po' Boy Blues. 1082
Silhouette 1083
Subway Rush Hour 1083
Theme for English B 1083
The Weary Blues 1084

 ## Bad Man (1927)

I'm a bad, bad man
Cause everybody tells me so.
I'm a bad, bad man.
Everybody tells me so.

I takes my meanness and ma licker
Everywhere I go.   5

I beats my wife an'
I beats ma side fall too.
Beats my wife an'
Beats my side gall too.   10
Don't know why I do it but
It keeps me from feelin' blue.

I'm so bad I
Don't even want to be good.
So bad, bad, bad I   15
Don't even want to be good.
I'm goin' to da devil an'
I wouldn't go to heaven if I could.

Cross (1925, 1926)

My old man's a white old man
And my old mother's black.
If ever I cursed my white old man
I take my curses back.
If ever I cursed my black old mother   5
And wished she were in hell,
I'm sorry for that evil wish
And now I wish her well.
My old man died in a fine big house.
My ma died in a shack.   10
I wonder where I'm going to die,
Being neither white nor black.

Dead in There (1951)

Sometimes
A night funeral
Going by
Carries home
A cool bop daddy.   5

Hearse and flowers
Guarantee
He'll never hype
Another paddy.

It's hard to believe,   10
But dead in there,
He'll never lay a
Hype nowhere!

15 He's my ace-boy,
    Gone away.
    Wake up and live!
    He used to say.

    Squares
    Who couldn't dig him,
20 Plant him now—
    Out where it makes
    No diff' no how.

 ## Dream Variations (1924, 1926)

    To fling my arms wide
    In some place of the sun,
    To whirl and to dance
    Till the white day is done.
5   Then rest at cool evening
    Beneath a tall tree
    While night comes on gently,
        Dark like me—
10 This is my dream!
    To fling my arms wide
    In the face of the sun,
    Dance! Whirl! Whirl!
    Till the quick day is done.
    Rest at pale evening . . .
15 A tall, slim tree . . .
    Night coming tenderly
        Black like me.

 ## Harlem (1951)

    What happens to a dream deferred?
    Does it dry up
    like a raisin in the sun?
    Or fester like a sore—
5   And then run?
    Does it stink like rotten meat?
    Or crust and sugar over—
    like a syrupy sweet?

    Maybe it just sags
10 like a heavy load.

    Or does it explode?

 ## Let America Be America Again (1936)

    Let America be America again.
    Let it be the dream it used to be.

Let it be the pioneer on the plain
Seeking a home where he himself is free.

(America never was America to me.)   5

Let America be the dream the dreamers dreamed—
Let it be that great strong land of love
Where never kings connive nor tyrants scheme
That any man be crushed by one above.

(It never was America to me.)   10

O, let my land be a land where Liberty
Is crowned with no false patriotic wreath,
But opportunity is real, and life is free,
Equality is in the air we breathe.

(There's never been equality for me,   15
Nor freedom in this "homeland of the free.")

Say who are you that mumbles in the dark?
And who are you that draws your veil across the stars?
I am the poor white, fooled and pushed apart,
I am the Negro bearing slavery's scars.   20
I am the red man driven from the land,
I am the immigrant clutching the hope I seek—
And finding only the same old stupid plan
Of dog eat dog, of mighty crush the weak.
I am the young man, full of strength and hope,   25
Tangled in that ancient endless chain
Of profit, power, gain, of grab the land!
Of grab the gold! Of grab the ways of satisfying need!
Of work the men! Of take the pay!
Of owning everything for one's own greed!   30

I am the farmer, bondsman to the soil.
I am the worker sold to the machine.
I am the Negro, servant to you all.
I am the people, worried, hungry, mean—
Hungry yet today despite the dream.   35
Beaten yet today—O, Pioneers!
I am the man who never got ahead,
The poorest worker bartered through the years.

Yet I'm the one who dreamt our basic dream
In the Old World while still a serf of kings,   40
Who dreamt a dream so strong, so brave, so true,
That even yet its mighty daring sings
In every brick and stone, in every furrow turned
That's made America the land it has become.
O, I'm the man who sailed those early seas   45

In search of what I meant to be my home—
For I'm the one who left dark Ireland's shore,
And Poland's plain, and England's grassy lea,
And torn from Black Africa's strand I came
50   To build a "homeland of the free."
The free?

A dream–
Still beckoning to me!

O, let America be America again—
55   The land that never has been yet—
And yet must be—
The land where every man is free.
The land that's mine—
The poor man's, Indian's, Negro's, ME—
60   Who made America,
Whose sweat and blood, whose faith and pain,
Whose hand at the foundry, whose plow in the rain,
Must bring back our mighty dream again.
Sure, call me any ugly name you choose—
65   The steel of freedom does not stain.
From those who live like leeches on the people's lives,
We must take back our land again,
America!

O, yes;
70   I say it plain,
America never was America to me,
And yet I swear this oath—
America will be!
An ever-living seed,
75   Its dream
Lies deep in the heart of me.

We, the people, must redeem
Our land, the mines, the plants, the rivers,
The mountains and the endless plain—
80   All, all the stretch of these great green states—
And make America again!

❈ Madam and Her Madam (1943, 1949)

I worked for a woman,
She wasn't mean—
But she had a twelve-room
House to clean.

5   Had to get breakfast,
Dinner, and supper, too—

Then take care of her children
When I got through.

Wash, iron, and scrub,
Walk the dog around—   10
It was too much,
Nearly broke me down.

I said, Madam,
Can it be
You trying to make a   15
Pack-horse out of me?

She opened her mouth.
She cried, Oh, no!
You know, Alberta,
I love you so!   20

I said, Madam,
That may be true—
But I'll be dogged
If I love you!

 Negro (1958)

I am a Negro:
    Black as the night is black,
    Black like the depths of my Africa.

I've been a slave:
    Caesar told me to keep his door-steps clean.   5
    I brushed the boots of Washington.

I've been a worker:
    Under my hand the pyramids arose.
    I made mortar for the Woolworth Building.

I've been a singer: 10
    All the way from Africa to Georgia
    I carried my sorrow songs.
    I made ragtime.

I've been a victim:
    The Belgians cut off my hands in the Congo.   15
    They lynch me still in Mississippi.

I am a Negro:
    Black as the night is black,
    Black like the depths of my Africa.

The Negro Speaks of Rivers (1926)

I've known rivers:
I've known rivers ancient as the world and older than the flow of human blood in
    human veins.

My soul has grown deep like the rivers.

I bathed in the Euphrates when dawns were young.
5   I built my hut near the Congo and it lulled me to sleep.

I looked upon the Nile and raised the pyraminds above it.
I heard the singing of the Mississippi when Abe Lincoln went down to New Orleans,
    and I've seen its muddy bosom turn all golden in the sunset.

I've known rivers:
Ancient, dusky rivers.

10 My soul has grown deep like the rivers.

 ## 125th Street (1951)

Face like a chocolate bar
Full of nuts and sweet.

Face like a jack-o'-lantern,
Candle inside.

5   Face like slice of melon
Grin that wide.

 ## Po' Boy Blues (1926, 1927)

When I was home de
Sunshine seemed like gold.
When I was home de
Sunshine seemed like gold.
5   Since I come up North de
Whole damn world's turned cold.

I was a good boy,
Never done no wrong.
Yes, I was a good boy,
10 Never done no wrong,
But this world is weary
An' de road is hard an' long.

I fell in love with
A gal I thought was kind.
15 Fell in love with
A gal I thought was kind.

She made me lose ma money
An' almost lose ma mind.

Weary, weary,
Weary early in de morn.   20
Weary, weary,
Early, early in de morn.
I's so weary
I wish I'd never been born.

 ## Silhouette (1936)

Southern gentle lady,
        Do not swoon.
They've just hung a black man
        In the dark of the moon.

        They've hung a black man   5
            To a roadside tree
        In the dark of the moon
            For the world to see
            How Dixie protects
        Its white womanhood.   10

Southern gentle lady
        Be good!
        Be good!

 ## Subway Rush Hour (1951)

Mingled
breath and smell
so close
mingled
black and white   5
so near
no room for fear.

Theme for English B (1959)

The instructor said,

    Go home and write
    a page tonight.
    And let that page come out of you—
    Then, it will be true.   5

I wonder if it's that simple?

I am twenty-two, colored, born in Winston-Salem.
I went to school there, then Durham, then here

to this college on the hill above Harlem.°
10 I am the only colored student in my class.
The steps from the hill lead down to Harlem,
through a park, then I cross St. Nicholas,
Eighth Avenue, Seventh, and I come to the Y,
the Harlem Branch Y, where I take the elevator
15 up to my room, sit down, and write this page:

It's not easy to know what is true for you or me
at twenty-two, my age. But I guess I'm what
I feel and see and hear. Harlem, I hear you:
hear you, hear me—we two—you, me talk on this page.
20 (I hear New York, too.) Me—who?

Well, I like to eat, sleep, drink, and be in love.
I like to work, read, learn, and understand life.
I like a pipe for a Christmas present,
or records—Bessie,° bop,° or Bach.°

25 I guess being colored doesn't make me not like
the same things other folks like who are other races.
So will my page be colored that I write?
Being me, it will not be white.
But it will be
30 a part of you, instructor.
You are white—
yet a part of me, as I am a part of you.
That's American.

Sometimes perhaps you don't want to be a part of me.
35 Nor do I often want to be a part of you.
But we are, that's true!
As I learn from you,
I guess you learn from me—
although you're older—and white—
40 and somewhat more free.

This is my page for English B.

°9 *college . . . Harlem:* a reference to Columbia University in the Columbia Heights section of New York City.
The other streets and buildings mentioned in lines 11–14 refer to specific places in the same vicinity. *24 Bessie:*
Bessie Smith (c. 1898–1937), American jazz singer, famed as the "Empress of the Blues." *bop:* a type of popular
music that was in vogue in the 1940s through the 1960s. *Bach:* Johann Sebastian Bach (1685–1750), German
composer, considered the master of the baroque style of music.

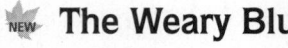 **The Weary Blues** (1923, 1926)

Droning a drowsy syncopated tune,
Rocking back and forth to a mellow croon,
    I heard a Negro play.
Down on Lenox Avenue the other night

By the pale dull pallor of an old gas light 5
   He did a lazy sway . . .
   He did a lazy sway . . .
To the tune o' those Weary Blues.
With his ebony hands on each ivory key
He made that poor piano moan with melody. 10
   O Blues!
Swaying to and fro on his rickety stool
He played that sad raggy tune like a musical fool.
   Sweet Blues!
Coming from a black man's soul. 15
   O Blues!
In a deep song voice with a melancholy tone
I heard that Negro sing, that old piano moan—
   "Ain't got nobody in all this world,
   Ain't got nobody but ma self. 20
   I's gwine to quit ma frownin'
   And put ma troubles on the shelf."
Thump, thump, thump, went his foot on the floor.
He played a few chords then he sang some more–
   "I got the Weary Blues 25
   And I can't be satisfied.
   Got the Weary Blues
   And can't be satisfied—
   I ain't happy no mo'
   And I wish that I had died." 30
And far into the night he crooned that tune.
The stars went out and so did the moon.
The singer stopped playing and went to bed
While the Weary Blues echoed through his head.
He slept like a rock or a man that's dead. 35

SYLVIA PLATH'S LIFE AND WORK (1932–1963)

Sylvia Plath is one of those poets about whom the life facts are integrally connected to her works. She is considered a "confessional" poet, the basis of whose work lies in her own personal experiences, with all their difficulties, uncertainties, and personal pain. Her confessions, however, are not intended as expressions of complaint or as descriptions of intimate details. Instead, she is confessional in that she attempts to demonstrate her relationship to the many unique and often adverse situations she encountered in life. In historical comparison, the *Confessions* of St. Augustine
(354–430) were composed to reveal the power and beneficence of God. John Bunyan (1628–88) wrote his *Grace Abounding to the Chief of Sinners* as testimony of the bountiful forgiveness of God. Jean-Jacques Rouseau (1712–78) wrote his autobiographical *Confessions,* perhaps partially to shock readers, but also to show the

particular links that together make up the whole person. One might add that in "Sonnet 146" (1609), Shakespeare's speaker considers the defects of his own soul, and urges rededication to spiritual pursuits (p. 1175).

In all these instances of confessional literature, confession itself is based in the admission of some sorts of transgression—usually in the form of self-indulgence— but the confession is also put in a wider context. As a twentieth-century confessional poet, Plath is ranked with fellow American poets Robert Lowell (one of Plath's teachers), Anne Sexton (a friend and confidante of Plath, and a fellow student in Lowell's class), D. W. Snodgrass, and John Berryman. Plath was a tormented soul, tortured at times, but she was a poet of great ability and brilliance, of extremes of happiness and depression—alternatively charming and blunt, but never dull. That her poems were not unrelievedly concerned with the negative aspects of confession may be seen in her "Song for a Summer's Day" and "Metaphors"—poems that would not seem unusual or special in the work of any other lyric poet. But in the poems Plath wrote during the final years of her life, we can see evidence of deeper discontent and anger. At times she refers to direct autobiographical details, or else she presents inferences based on such details. As a result, events of her brief life and lamentable death are definitely relevant to her poetry.

Sylvia Plath was born in 1932. Her father, Otto Plath, was a naturalized citizen whose native country was Germany. He was a professor at Boston University, an entomologist, and an authority on bees. Her mother, Aurelia Schober, was much younger than Otto, and was from Austria. She also eventually taught at Boston University. Plath's father was diabetic, but was in denial about his affliction. In 1940 he was hospitalized for a foot infection. The foot was amputated, but the infection was rampant. It metastasized and caused his death when Sylvia was just eight years old. It then fell to her mother, Aurelia, to take over the management of her household and children—Sylvia and her brother, Warren.

Sylvia was deeply grieved by her father's death, and upon being told of it, swore that she could no longer believe in God. One of her first responses was an unsuccessful and perhaps accidental suicide attempt when she was ten, using a razor blade to gash her throat. Her adolescent responses were less destructive, but there can be no doubt the loss of her father afflicted her deeply for the rest of her brief life. Her later experiences with insomnia, her frequent respiratory infections, and her depression perhaps had their own etiology, but the loss of her father was always there, undermining her struggle for normality. She compensated for her loss by becoming an exceedingly fine student, regularly receiving A's in her courses. As she achieved academic excellence and advancement, she also, at an early age, began sending her writings, primarily poems, to various publications, hoping for the national acceptance that would demonstrate that others recognized her precociousness. Throughout her school years she continued the arduous process of submission and publication, and by the time she matriculated at Smith College in 1952, she had developed an impressive list of academic prizes and local publications. She was tops in her high school graduating class, and she published essays, stories, and poems in publications like *Mademoiselle* and *The Christian Science Monitor*. Eventually she signed a contract with *The New Yorker* agreeing that she would give that magazine the right of first submission for any and all of her new poems.

Despite such successes, however, she regularly received rejection slips—not at all uncommon for beginning writers—and these weighed heavily upon her self-image. She became so despondent that she once again attempted suicide. In 1953, she hid herself in the crawl space under her mother's house, and swallowed almost the entire contents of a bottle of sleeping pills, many of which she fortunately regurgitated. She was, however, rendered unconscious. Everyone thought she had been abducted, and her disappearance made headlines in the Boston area. After a few days her brother heard her groaning under the house, and she was taken to the hospital for treatment and recovery. After that she underwent electric shock therapy, which in the 1950s was a standard medical treatment for depression and attempted suicide. She describes this experience in her well-received *The Bell Jar* early in 1963, and she also alludes to it in her poem "Lady Lazarus," which she wrote just four months before her actual suicide in February 1963:

> Dying
> Is an art, like everything else,
> I do it exceptionally well.
> > lines 43-45

She recovered, took heart, and went on to graduate from Smith *summa cum laude*. In 1955, as a new graduate, she applied for a Fulbright Scholarship for study in England. She won the award, and matriculated at Newnham College, Cambridge, for the year 1955–56, which was extended to 1956–57. The winning of a Fulbright was an inestimable honor for those who received it, but the allowances were quite low—just about $1450 for all the living expenses of an entire year. Needless to say, Sylvia was regularly hurting for money.

During her days at Cambridge, Plath met Ted Hughes, then a striving poet, who later became English Poet Laureate (1984–98). It was at this point that she decided to try achieving excellence through marriage and children. The two married in 1956, and their marriage continued for six years, two of which they spent in the United States after Sylvia had finished the period of her Fulbright Scholarship. When she became pregnant, the couple returned to England, where childbirth was paid for by the English National Health Service. Although the Hugheses had two children, born in 1960 and 1962, and although there were long periods of peace, tenderness, and constructive and peaceful cooperation between the two, their relationship also generated conflict and bitterness. Indeed, they once came to blows and scratches against each other. They separated in 1962. Sylvia became guardian of the children, and took up residence in rooms in a London house where William Butler Yeats had one time lived. Although she was encouraged by the connection with Yeats, she became unconquerably depressed during the bitterly cold winter of 1962–63. Early in the morning of February 11, 1963, in the throes of deep and final anguish, she sealed the cracks in the doors of the bedroom of her sleeping children, to protect them, and left milk and cookies for them. She went to her kitchen, and turned on the gas. Despite her intellectual power and desire to excel, she had never been able to escape the demon of depression. She died at the age of thirty—her life cut regrettably short, her full potential never to be realized or recognized.

When she died, Sylvia Plath had not yet gained a major reputation. Just a few weeks before her death, her novel *The Bell Jar* appeared. Although the work was well received, she had written it under a *nom de plume* ("Victoria Lucas") and she had not yet received the public recognition that was to follow. Ever since the 1960s, however, her reputation has been elevated posthumously to the point where some critics have called her one of the greatest poets of the twentieth century. The story of her life has also made her rather much of a *cause célèbre* of the feminist movement. The idea is that during her last years her star was falling just as the star of her husband was rising. And as she necessarily became enmeshed in the endless tasks of caring for her baby and her toddler, he looked elsewhere for companionship. After Plath's suicide, there were people who accused him of having brought about her death. On her gravestone, her married name, "Hughes," was chiseled out, and then was chiseled out again when a new stone was reinstalled over the grave. When Hughes, even as Poet Laureate, would have a speaking engagement in the thirty-five years after her death, hecklers would sometimes try to drown him out. He was never able to live down the circumstances of Plath's suicide.

Plath's poems, grounded as they are in her own experiences, do not necessarily make for easy reading, because they frequently describe reactions to specific details known by the speaker, but unknown by the reader. The result is that some of the poems seem obscure. Let us take the opening three lines from "Ariel," the poem that Plath wrote on her birthday, October 27, 1962: "Stasis in darkness. / Then the substanceless blue / Pour of tor and distances." As readers we accept these details as meaningful, even though the process of mind that produced the lines is not known. "Tor" is a venerable English word for a high hill, probably borrowed from the Celts, who lived in the land before the Angles and the Saxons took the country over militarily in the fifth century. "Pour" suggests figuratively how the hill emerges in the landscape of early morning as though it is being poured out to the viewer's eye. A further probe seems in order. A biographical detail is that "Ariel," the poem's title, was the name of a horse that Plath had ridden frequently in 1957, during the earlier and happier years of her marriage. It would appear that riding had given her a sense of freedom and fulfillment. In addition, Ariel is also a spirit/fairy that serves Prospero in Shakespeare's *The Tempest* (1611). At the play's end, when Prospero is bidding farewell to his magical powers, he gives Ariel his freedom. We may therefore conclude that the reference to Ariel is Plath's dominating image of a desire for release from restrictions and a wish for the freedom of rolling hills, far distances, and the endless blue of the air. Somewhere, one can find a better existence than the one we know here on earth, although, from the poem's last line, it could also be a "cauldron" that creates difficulty and causes other problems. And so "Ariel" the poem may be taken as an expression of yearning and not unmixed hope.

Comparably, one of Plath's best known confessional poems is "Daddy." It was only natural that she could not ever have totally overcome her grief at losing her father, despite all her compensating excellences during her adolescent and college years. When she and Ted Hughes became parents themselves, she became "Mommy" and he "Daddy." Most young parents, in delight at having their own children, rejoice in using these names for each other. It would therefore appear that when Plath wrote "Daddy," she was thinking of both Daddies together. She never was given the time to know her own father well, and may even have subconsciously condemned him for the neglect of his own illness and his consequent culpability for deserting the Plath family. Such a response is not unusual among survivors of a family loss. In addition to this grievance, she had profoundly loved and admired her children's Daddy, but he had caused her extreme anger, grief, and bitterness. She wrote the poem "Daddy" on October 12, 1962, just at the time when she and Hughes were undergoing what was appearing to be their final separation. In the poem, Plath's speaker castigates the Daddy virtually as a persecuting Nazi. Nothing even remotely like this was true, of course, but nevertheless the speaker talks of her anguish as though the details about Nazism were factual. Thus this major detail of the poem is fictional, but Plath's mental anguish was real, and her anger was real. It is for the power and the expression of such personal insights that Plath is today valued so highly as a lyric and confessional poet.

The most comprehensive edition of Plath's poems is Ted Hughes, ed, *The Collected Poems: Sylvia Plath*. (Cambridge: Harper and Row, 1981). The appearance of this volume in 1981 posthumously earned Plath the Pulitzer Prize for Poetry in 1982. Before she died, Plath planned a volume of "Ariel" poems. Her intended collection is included in *Ariel: The Restored Edition. A Facsimile of Plath's Manuscript, Reinstating Her Original Selection and Arrangements* (New York: Harper, 2005). Susan R. Van Dine's *Revising Life: Sylvia Plath's Ariel Poems* (Chapel Hill: U of North Carolina P, 1994) considers these poems. Plath's journals are published in *The Unabridged Journals of Sylvia Plath*, Karen V. Kukil, ed. (New York: Anchor Books, 2000), a very lengthy volume. Well-detailed biographies of Plath are Linda Wagner-Martin, *Sylvia Plath: A Biography* (New York: St. Martin's, 1988), and Anne Stevenson, *Bitter Fame: A Life of Sylvia Plath* (Boston: Houghton Mifflin, 1990). A blending of biography and criticism is Wagner-Martin's *Sylvia Plath: A Literary Life* (New York: Palgrave McMillan, 2003). Critical works are Tim Kendall, *Sylvia Plath: A Critical Study* (London: Faber, 2001), and Lynda K. Bundtzen, *The Other Ariel* (Amherst: U of Massachusetts P, 2001). A significant number of critical essays are included in Jo Gill, ed. *The Cambridge Companion to Sylvia Plath* (Cambridge: Cambridge UP, 2006). A detailed review of criticism on Plath is Claire Brennan, ed., *The Poetry of Sylvia Plath* (New York: Columbia UP, 2001).

Writing Topics About the Poetry of Sylvia Plath

1. Plath as a "confessional" poet. What is she confessing? How much is personal? How much seems objective description and discussion? What problems and concerns does she confess?

2. Plath's references to death in her poems. What is her attitude toward her own suicide attempts? What is the relationship of "Cut" to "Last Words" and to "Lady Lazarus"?

3. The problems of "Daddy." Who is the Daddy whom she addresses? What objective criticism does she make of Daddy? What do you make of the concluding lines? Why does Plath introduce references to Nazi cruelties, here and in "Lady Lazarus"?

4. Plath's use of comparisons. How expected are her comparisons? What causes the uniqueness and surprise of her best comparisons?

5. Plath's poetic rhythms. What use does she make of adjoining heavy accents (spondees)? What is the relationship of her rhythms to her ideas?

6. Her use of rhymes, assonance, and alliteration. How do these rhythms and sounds undergird her ideas?

7. Write an explication of any one of Plath's poems.

8. The meaning of "Mirror." Explain the concluding image.

9. Plath's more cheerful poems ("Metaphors," "Song for a Summer's Day"). What do these poems suggest about her thoughts about what most people probably think of about happiness?

Poems of Sylvia Plath (Alphabetically Arranged)

Ariel 1090
The Colossus 1091
Cut 1092
Daddy. 1093
Edge. 1095
The Hanging Man 1096
Lady Lazarus 1096
Last Words. 1098
Metaphors. 1099
Mirror. 1099
The Rival 1100
Song for a Summer's Day 1100
Tulips 1101

Note: The numbers preceding each of the poems that follow refer to the numerical system used by Ted Hughes in *The Collected Poems: Sylvia Plath* (New York: HarperCollins, 1981). The dates following some of the poems indicate the dates on which Plath either wrote the poems, or completed them.

 NEW **Ariel** (1962)

194
Stasis in darkness.
Then the substanceless blue
Pour of tor and distances.

God's lioness,
5   How one we grow,
Pivot of heels and knees!—The furrow

Splits and passes, sister to
The brown arc
Of the neck I cannot catch,

Nigger-eye   10
Berries cast dark
Hooks—

Black sweet blood mouthfuls,
Shadows.
Something else   15

Hauls me through air—
Thighs, hair;
Flakes from my heels.

White
Godiva, I unpeel—   20
Dead hands, dead stringencies.

And now I
Foam to wheat, a glitter of seas.
The child's cry

Melts in the wall.   25
And I
Am the arrow,

The dew that flies
Suicidal, at one with the drive
Into the red   30

Eye, the cauldron of morning.
                              27 October 1962

❧ᴺᴱᵂ The Colossus° (1959)

117
I shall never get you put together entirely,
Pieced, glued, and properly jointed.
Mule-bray, pig-grunt and bawdy cackles
Proceed from your great lips.
It's worse than a barnyard.   5

Perhaps you consider yourself an oracle,
Mouthpiece of the dead, or of some god or other.
Thirty years now I have labored
To dredge the silt from your throat.
I am none the wiser.   10

_____

°At the harbor of the Aegean island of Rhodes, the ancient Rhodians erected a gigantic statue of Apollo, the "Colossus," which was considered one of the seven wonders of the ancient world. When earthquakes later hit the city, the Colossus was destroyed. Modern marine archaeologists have discovered fragments of the statue in the harbor waters.

Scaling little ladders with gluepots and pails of lysol
I crawl like an ant in mourning
Over the weedy acres of your brow
To mend the immense skull-plates and clear
15   The bald, white tumuli° of your eyes.   *grave mounds*

A blue sky out of the Oresteia
Arches above us. O father, all by yourself
You are pithy and historical as the Roman Forum
I open my lunch on a hill of black cypress.
20   Your fluted bones and acanthine hair° are littered

In their old anarchy to the horizon-line.
It would take more than a lightning-stroke
To create such a ruin.
Nights, I squat in the cornucopia
25   Of your left ear, out of the wind.

Counting the red stars and those of plum-color.
The sun rises under the pillar of your tongue.
My hours are married to shadow.
No longer do I listen for the scrape of a keel
30   On the blank stones of the landing.

°20 *fluted bones and acanthine hair:* The design of ancient temple columns was not smooth, but rather fluted. In the Corinthian style, the most elaborate columnar design, capitals atop the fluted columns were modeled on the acanthus plant.

Cut (1962)

For Susan O'Neill Roe*

191
What a thrill –
My thumb instead of an onion.
The top quite gone
Except for a sort of a hinge

5   Of skin,
A flap like a hat,
Dead white.
Then that red plush.

Little pilgrim,
10   The Indian's axed your scalp.
Your turky wattle
Carpet rolls

Straight from the heart.
I step on it,

---

*Susan O'Neill Roe was Plath's nanny and babysitter.

Clutching my bottle   15
Of pink fizz.

A celebration, this is.
Out of a gap
A million soldiers run,
Redcoats, every one.   20

Whose side are they on?
O my
Homunculus,° I am ill.   *a tiny human being*
I have taken a pill to kill

The thin   25
Papery feeling.
Saboteur,
Kamikaze man—

The stain on your
Gauze Ku Klux Klan   30
Babushka
Darkens and tarnishes and when

The balled
Pulp of your heart
Confronts its small   35
Mill of silence

How you jump—
Trepanned° veteran,   *i.e., trephined, usually the result of an operation opening skull bone*
Dirty girl,
Thumb stump.   40
        24 October 1962

NEW **Daddy** (1962)

183
You do not do, you do not do
Any more, black shoe
In which I have lived like a foot
For thirty years, poor and white
Barely daring to breathe or Achoo.   5

Daddy, I have had to kill you.
You died before I had time—
Marble-heavy, a bag full of God,
Ghastly statue with one gray toe
Big as a Frisco seal   10

And a head in the freakish Atlantic
Where it pours bean green over blue

In the waters off beautiful Nauset.
I used to pray to recover you.
15   Ach, du.

In the German tongue, in the Polish town
Scraped flat by the roller
Of wars, wars, wars.
But the name of the town is common.
20   My Polack friend

Says there are a dozen or two.
So I never could tell where you
Put your foot, your root,
I never could talk to you.
25   The tongue stuck in my jaw.

It stuck in a barb wire snare.
Ich, ich, ich, ich,
I could hardly speak.
I thought every German was you.
30   And the language obscene

An engine, an engine
Chuffing me off like a Jew.
A Jew to Dachau, Auschwitz, Belsen.
I began to talk like a Jew.
35   I think I may well be a Jew.

The snows of the Tyrol, the clear beer of Vienna
Are not very pure or true.
With my gipsy ancestress and my weird luck
And my Taroc pack and my Taroc pack
40   I may be a bit of a Jew.

I have always been scared of *you*,
With your Luftwaffe, your gobbledygoo.
And your neat mustache
And your Aryan eye, bright blue.
45   Panzer-man, panzer-man, O You—

Not God but a swastika
So black no sky could squeak through.
Every woman adores a Fascist,
The boot in the face, the brute
50   Brute heart of a brute like you.

You stand at the blackboard, daddy,
In the picture I have of you,
A cleft in your chin instead of your foot
But no less a devil for that, no not
55   Any less the black man who

Bit my pretty red heart in two.
I was ten when they buried you.
At twenty I tried to die
And get back, back, back to you.
I thought even the bones would do.   60

But they pulled me out of the sack,
And they stuck me together with glue.
And then I knew what to do.
I made a model of you,
A man in black with a Meinkampf look   65

And a love of the rack and the screw.
And I said I do, I do.
So daddy, I'm finally through.
The black telephone's off at the root,
The voices just can't worm through.   70

If I've killed one man, I've killed two—
The vampire who said he was you
And drank my blood for a year,
Seven years, if you want to know.
Daddy, you can lie back now.   75

There's a stake in your fat black heart
And the villagers never liked you.
They are dancing and stamping on you.
They always *knew* it was you.
Daddy, daddy, you bastard, I'm through.   80

12 October 1962

 Edge (1963)

224
The woman is perfected.
Her dead

Body wears the smile of accomplishment,
The illusion of a Greek necessity

Flows in the scrolls of her toga,   5
Her bare

Feet seem to be saying:
We have come so far, it is over.

Each dead child coiled, a white serpent,
One at each little   10

Pitcher of milk, now empty.
She has folded

Them back into her body as petals
Of a rose close when the garden

15   Stiffens and odors bleed
From the sweet, deep throats of the night flower.

The moon has nothing to be sad about,
Staring from her hood of bone.

She is used to this sort of thing.
20   Her blacks crackle and drag.

                        5 February 1963

 ## The Hanging Man (1960)

123
By the roots of my hair some god got hold of me.
I sizzled in his blue volts like a desert prophet.

The nights snapped out of sight like a lizard's eyelid:
A world of bald white days in a shadeless socket.

5   A vulturous boredom pinned me in this tree.
If he were I, he would do what I did.

                        27 June 1960

 ## Lady Lazarus (1962)

198
I have done it again.
One year in every ten
I manage it—

A sort of walking miracle, my skin
5   Bright as a Nazi lampshade,
My right foot

A paperweight,
My face a featureless, fine
Jew linen.

10   Peel off the napkin
O my enemy.
Do I terrify?—

The nose, the eye pits, the full set of teeth?
The sour breath
15   Will vanish in a day.

Soon, soon the flesh
The grave cave ate will be
At home on me

And I a smiling woman.
I am only thirty.   20
And like the cat I have nine times to die.

This is Number Three.
What a trash
To annihilate each decade.

What a million filaments.   25
The peanut-crunching crowd
Shoves in to see

Them unwrap me hand and foot
The big strip tease.
Gentlemen, ladies   30

These are my hands
My knees.
I may be skin and bone,

Nevertheless, I am the same, identical woman.
The first time it happened I was ten.   35
It was an accident.

The second time I meant
To last it out and not come back at all.
I rocked shut

As a seashell.   40
They had to call and call
And pick the worms off me like sticky pearls.

Dying
Is an art, like everything else,
I do it exceptionally well.   45

I do it so it feels like hell.
I do it so it feels real.
I guess you could say I've a call.

It's easy enough to do it in a cell.
It's easy enough to do it and stay put.   50
It's the theatrical

Comeback in broad day
To the same place, the same face, the same brute
Amused shout:

55   "A miracle!"
    That knocks me out.
    There is a charge

    For the eyeing of my scars, there is a charge
    For the hearing of my heart—
60   It really goes.

    And there is a charge, a very large charge
    For a word or a touch
    Or a bit of blood

    Or a piece of my hair or my clothes.
65   So, so, Herr Doktor.
    So, Herr Enemy.

    I am your opus,
    I am your valuable,
    The pure gold baby

70   That melts to a shriek.
    I turn and burn.
    Do not think I underestimate your great concern.

    Ash, ash—
    You poke and stir.
75   Flesh, bone, there is nothing there—

    A cake of soap,
    A wedding ring,
    A gold filling.

    Herr God, Herr Lucifer
80   Beware
    Beware.

    Out of the ash
    I rise with my red hair
    And I eat men like air.
               23–29 October 1962

 ## Last Words (1961)

152
I do not want a plain box, I want a sarcophagus
With tigery stripes, and a face on it
Round as the moon, to stare up.
I want to be looking at them when they come
5   Picking among the dumb minerals, the roots
I see them already—the pale, star-distance faces.
Now they are nothing, they are not even babies.

Imagine them without fathers or mothers, like the first gods.
They will wonder if I was important.
I should sugar and preserve my days like fruit!   10
My mirror is clouding over –
A few more breaths, and it will reflect nothing at all.
The flowers and the faces whiten to a sheet.

I do not trust the spirit. It escapes like steam
In dreams, through mouth-hole or eye-hole. I can't stop it.   15
One day it won't come back. Things aren't like that.
They stay, their little particular lusters
Warmed by much handling. They almost purr.
When the soles of my feet grow cold,
The blue eye of my turquoise will comfort me.   20
Let me have my copper cooking pots, let my rouge pots
Bloom about me like night flowers, with a good smell.
They will roll me up in bandages, they will store my heart
Under my feet in a neat parcel.
I shall hardly know myself. It will be dark,   25
And the shine of these small things sweeter than the face of Ishtar.°

21 October, 1961

°26 *Ishtar.* In ancient Babylonian and Assyrian mythology, the principal goddess of fertility, love, and war.

Metaphors (1959)

102
I'm a riddle in nine syllables,
An elephant, a ponderous house,
A melon strolling on two tendrils.
O red fruit, ivory, fine timbers!
This loaf's big with its yeasty rising.   5
Money's new-minted in this fat purse.
I'm a means, a stage, a cow in calf.
I've eaten a bag of green apples,
Boarded the train there's no getting off.

20 March 1959

Mirror (1961)

154
I am silver and exact. I have no preconceptions.
Whatever I see, I swallow immediately.
Just as it is, unmisted by love or dislike
I am not cruel, only truthful—
The eye of a little god, four-cornered.   5
Most of the time I meditate on the opposite wall.
It is pink, with speckles. I have looked at it so long
I think it is a part of my heart. But it flickers.
Faces and darkness separate us over and over.

10   Now I am a lake. A woman bends over me.
     Searching my reaches for what she really is.
     Then she turns to those liars, the candles or the moon.
     I see her back, and reflect it faithfully
     She rewards me with tears and an agitation of hands.
15   I am important to her. She comes and goes.
     Each morning it is her face that replaces the darkness.
     In me she has drowned a young girl, and in me an old woman
     Rises toward her day after day, like a terrible fish.

                                                    23 October 1961

 ## The Rival (1961)

147
If the moon smiled, she would resemble you.
You leave the same impression
Of something beautiful, but annihilating.
Both of you are great light borrowers.
5   Her O-mouth grieves at the world; yours is unaffected,
     And your first gift is making stone out of everything.
     I wake to a mausoleum; you are here,
     Ticking your fingers on the marble table, looking for cigarettes,
     Spiteful as a woman, but not so nervous,
10   And dying to say something unanswerable.

     The moon, too, abases her subjects,
     But in the daytime she is ridiculous.
     Your dissatisfactions, on the other hand,
     Arrive through the mailslot with loving regularity,
15   White and blank, expansive as carbon monoxide.

     No day is safe from news of you,
     Walking about in Africa maybe, but thinking of me.
                                                    July 1961

 ## Song for a Summer's Day (1956)

12
Through fen and farmland walking
With my own country love
I saw slow flocked cows move
White hulks on their day's cruising;
5   Sweet grass sprang for their grazing.

     The air was bright for looking:
     Most far in blue, aloft,
     Clouds steered a burnished drift;
     Larks' nip and tuck arising
10   Came in for my love's praising.

Sheen of the noon sun striking
Took my heart as if
It were a green-tipped leaf
Kindled by my love's pleasing
Into an ardent blazing.   15

And so, together, talking,
Through Sunday's honey-air
We walked (and still walk there—
Out of the sun's bruising)
Till the night mists came rising.   20

 Tulips (1961)

142
The tulips are too excitable, it is winter here.
Look how white everything is, how quiet, how snowed-in.
I am learning peacefulness, lying by myself quietly
As the light lies on these white walls, this bed, these hands.
I am nobody; I have nothing to do with explosions.   5
I have given my name and my day-clothes up to the nurses
And my history to the anesthetist and my body to surgeons.

They have propped my head between the pillow and the sheet-cuff
Like an eye between two white lids that will not shut.
Stupid pupil, it has to take everything in.   10
The nurses pass and pass, they are no trouble,
They pass the way gulls pass inland in their white caps,
Doing things with their hands, one just the same as another,
So it is impossible to tell how many there are.

My body is a pebble to them, they tend it as water   15
Tends to the pebbles it must run over, smoothing them gently.
They bring me numbness in their bright needles, they bring me sleep.
Now I have lost myself I am sick of baggage—
My patent leather overnight case like a black pillbox,
My husband and child smiling out of the family photo;   20
Their smiles catch onto my skin, little smiling hooks.

I have let things slip, a thirty-year-old cargo boat
Stubbornly hanging on to my name and address.
They have swabbed me clear of my loving associations.
Scared and bare on the green plastic-pillowed trolley   25
I watched my tea set, my bureaus of linen, my books
Sink out of sight, and the water went over my head.
I am a nun now, I have never been so pure.

I didn't want any flowers, I only wanted
To lie with my hands turned up and be utterly empty.   30
How free it is, you have no idea how free—

The peacefulness is so big it dazes you,
And it asks nothing, a name tag, a few trinkets.
It is what the dead close on, finally; I imagine them
35 Shutting their mouths on it, like a Communion tablet.

The tulips are too red in the first place, they hurt me.
Even through the gift paper I could hear them breathe
Lightly, through their white swaddlings, like an awful baby.
Their redness talks to my wound, it corresponds.
40 They are subtle: they seem to float, though they weigh me down,
Upsetting me with their sudden tongues and their color,
A dozen red lead sinkers round my neck.

Nobody watched me before, now I am watched.
The tulips turn to me, and the window behind me
45 Where once a day the light slowly widens and slowly thins,
And I see myself, flat, ridiculous, a cut-paper shadow
Between the eye of the sun and the eyes of the tulips,
And I have no face, I have wanted to efface myself.
The vivid tulips eat my oxygen.

50 Before they came the air was calm enough,
Coming and going, breath by breath, without any fuss.
Then the tulips filled it up like a loud noise.
Now the air snags and eddies round them the way a river
Snags and eddies round a sunken rust-red engine.
55 They concentrate my attention, that was happy
Playing and resting without committing itself.

The walls, also, seem to be warming themselves.
The tulips should be behind bars like dangerous animals;
They are opening like the mouth of some great African cat,
60 And I am aware of my heart: it opens and closes
Its bowl of red blooms out of sheer love of me.
The water I taste is warm and salt, like the sea,
And comes from a country far away as health.

                                              18 March 1961

Chapter 22

One Hundred Sixteen Poems for Additional Enjoyment and Study

Maya Angelou . . . . My Arkansas, 1106

Anonymous (Navajo) . . . . Healing Prayer from the
Beautyway Chant, 1106

Anonymous . . . . Lord Randal, 1107

Margaret Atwood . . . . Variation on the Word *Sleep*, 1108

W. H. Auden . . . . The Unknown Citizen, 1108

Wendell Berry . . . . Another Descent, 1109

Louise Bogan . . . . Women, 1110

Arna Bontemps . . . . A Black Man Talks of Reaping, 1110

Anne Bradstreet . . . . To My Dear and Loving Husband, 1111

Gwendolyn Brooks . . . . Primer for Blacks, 1111

Elizabeth Barrett Browning . . . . Sonnets from the Portuguese:
Number 43, How Do I Love Thee?, 1113

Robert Browning . . . . Soliloquy of the Spanish Cloister, 1113

William Cullen Bryant . . . . To Cole, the Painter,
Departing for Europe, 1115

George Gordon, Lord Byron . . . . . . The Destruction of Sennacherib, 1116

George Gordon, Lord Byron . . . . She Walks in Beauty, 1116

Leonard Cohen . . . . "The killers that run . . .", 1117

Billy Collins . . . . Days, 1118

Frances Cornford . . . . From a Letter to America on a
Visit to Sussex: Spring 1942, 1118

Stephen Crane . . . . Do Not Weep, Maiden, for War Is Kind, 1119

Robert Creeley . . . . "Do you think . . .", 1120

E. E. Cummings . . . . if there are any heavens, 1121

Carl Dennis . . . . The God Who Loves You, 1121

John Donne . . . . The Good Morrow, 1122

John Donne . . . . Holy Sonnet 10: Death Be Not Proud, 1123

John Donne . . . . A Hymn to God the Father, 1123

Paul Laurence Dunbar . . . . Sympathy [I Know What the
Caged Bird Feels], 1124

T. S. Eliot . . . . The Love Song of J. Alfred Prufrock, 1124

James Emanuel . . . . The Negro, 1128

Lynn Emanuel . . . . Like God, 1128

Chief Dan George . . . . The Beauty of the Trees, 1130

Nikki Giovanni. . . . . Woman, 1130

Nikki Giovanni. . . . . Poetry, 1131

Marilyn Hacker . . . . Sonnet Ending with a Film Subtitle, 1132

Daniel Halpern . . . . Snapshot of Hué, 1132

Daniel Halpern. . . . . Summer in the Middle Class, 1133

H. S. (Sam) Hamod . . . . Leaves, 1134

Frances E. W. Harper . . . . She's Free!, 1135

Michael S. Harper . . . . Called, 1135

Robert Hass . . . . Spring Rain, 1136

Robert Hayden . . . . Those Winter Sundays, 1137

Robert Herrick. . . . . To the Virgins, to Make Much of Time, 1137

William Heyen . . . . The Hair: Jacob Korman's Story, 1138

A. D. Hope . . . . Advice to Young Ladies, 1138

Gerard Manley Hopkins . . . . Pied Beauty, 1139

Gerard Manley Hopkins. The Windhover, 1140

Carolina Hospital . . . . Dear Tia, 1140

Robinson Jeffers . . . . The Answer, 1141

Donald Justice . . . . On the Death of Friends in Childhood, 1141

John Keats . . . . Ode on a Grecian Urn, 1142

Galway Kinnell . . . . After Making Love We Hear Footsteps, 1144

Katherine Larson . . . . Statuary, 1144

Irving Layton . . . . Rhine Boat Trip, 1145

Li-Young Lee . . . . A Final Thing, 1146

Alan P. Lightman . . . . In Computers, 1147

Liz Lochhead . . . . The Choosing, 1148

Audre Lorde . . . . Every Traveler Has One Vermont Poem, 1149

Amy Lowell . . . . Patterns, 1149

Archibald Macleish . . . . Ars Poetica, 1152

Heather McHugh Lines,1153

Claude McKay . . . . The White City, 1153

W. S. Merwin . . . . Listen, 1154

Edna St. Vincent Millay . . . . What Lips My Lips Have Kissed,
and Where, and Why, 1154

N. Scott Momaday . . . . The Bear, 1155

Marianne Moore . . . . Poetry, 1155

Lisel Mueller . . . . Monet Refuses the Operation, 1156

Howard Nemerov . . . . Life Cycle of Common Man, 1157

Jim Northrup . . . . wahbegan, 1158

Mary Oliver . . . . Ghosts, 1159

Simon Ortiz . . . . A Story of How a Wall Stands, 1161

Dorothy Parker . . . . Résumé, 1162

Linda Pastan. . . . . Ethics, 1162

Linda Pastan. . . . . Marks, 1162

Molly Peacock . . . . Desire, 1163

Marge Piercy . . . . The Secretary Chant, 1163

Edgar Allan Poe. . . . . The Raven, 1164

John Crowe Ransom . . . . Bells for John Whiteside's Daughter, 1166
John Raven . . . . Assailant, 1167
Adrienne Rich . . . . Diving into the Wreck, 1167
Alberto Ríos. . . . . The Vietnam Wall, 1169
Luis Omar Salinas. . . . . In a Farmhouse, 1170
Sonia Sanchez . . . . rite on: white america, 1171
Carl Sandburg . . . . Chicago, 1172
Siegfried Sassoon . . . . Dreamers, 1172
Gjertrud Schnackenberg . . . . The Paperweight, 1173
Alan Seeger . . . . I Have a Rendezvous with Death, 1173
Brenda Serotte . . . . My Mother's Face, 1174
William Shakespeare . . . . Sonnet 29: When in Disgrace
with Fortune and Men's Eyes, 1175
William Shakespeare . . . . Sonnet 146: Poor Soul,
the Center of My Sinful Earth, 1175
Karl Shapiro . . . . Auto Wreck, 1176
Leslie Marmon Silko. . . . . Where Mountain
Lion Lay Down with Deer, 1176
Stevie Smith . . . . Not Waving But Drowning, 1177
Gary Soto . . . . Oranges, 1178
William Stafford . . . . Traveling Through the Dark, 1179
Gerald Stern . . . . Burying an Animal on the
Way to New York, 1179
Wallace Stevens . . . . The Emperor of Ice-Cream, 1180
May Swenson . . . . Question, 1180
Dylan Thomas . . . . A Refusal to Mourn, the Death,
by Fire, of a Child in London, 1181
Daniel Tobin. . . . . My Uncle's Watch, 1182
Chase Twichell . . . . Blurry Cow, 1183
John Updike . . . . Perfection Wasted, 1183
Tino Villanueva . . . . Day-Long Day, 1184
Judith Viorst . . . . True Love, 1185
Shelly Wagner . . . . The Boxes, 1185
Alice Walker . . . . Revolutionary Petunias, 1186
Edmund Waller . . . . Go, Lovely Rose, 1187
Bruce Weigl . . . . Song of Napalm, 1188
Phillis Wheatley. . . . . On Being Brought from Africa to America, 1189
Walt Whitman . . . . Beat! Beat! Drums!, 1189
Walt Whitman . . . . Dirge for Two Veterans, 1190
Walt Whitman . . . . Full of Life Now, 1191
Walt Whitman . . . . I Hear America Singing, 1191
John Greenleaf Whittier . . . . The Bartholdi Statue, 1192
Richard Wilbur . . . . April 5, 1974, 1192
William Carlos Williams . . . . The Red Wheelbarrow, 1193
William Butler Yeats. . . . . The Wild Swans at Coole, 1193
Paul Zimmer . . . . The Day Zimmer Lost Religion, 1194

MAYA ANGELOU (b. 1928)

 ## My Arkansas (1978)

There is a deep brooding
in Arkansas.
Old crimes like moss pend
from poplar trees.
5 The sullen earth°   Cf. Shakespeare, Sonnet 29, line 12 (p. 1175)
is much too
red for comfort.

Sunrise seems to hesitate
and in that second
10 lose its
incandescent aim, and
dusk no more shadows
than the noon.
The past is brighter yet.

15 Old hates and
ante-bellum° lace are rent
but not discarded.
Today is yet to come
in Arkansas.
20 It writhes. It writhes in awful
waves of brooding.

°16 *ante-bellum:* before the U.S. Civil War (1861–1865).

ANONYMOUS (NAVAJO)

 ## Healing Prayer from the Beautyway Chant
(traditional nineteenth century)

Out of the East, Beauty has come home,
Out of the South, Beauty has come home,
Out of the West, Beauty has come home,
Out of the North, Beauty has come home,
5 Out of the highest heavens and the lowest lands,
  Beauty has come home.
  Everywhere around us, Beauty has come home.
As we live each day, everything evil will leave us.
  We will be entirely healed,
10 Our bodies will exult in the fresh winds,
  Our steps will be firm.
As we live each day,
  Everything before us will be Beautiful;
  Everything behind us will be Beautiful;
15 Everything above us will be Beautiful;

Everything below us will be Beautiful;
Everything around us will be Beautiful;
All our thoughts will be Beautiful;
All our words will be Beautiful;
All our dreams will be Beautiful.   20
We will be forever restored, forever whole.
All things will be Beautiful forever.

ANONYMOUS

 ## Lord Randal (sixteenth century)

"Oh, where have you been, Lord Randal, my son?
Oh, where have you been, my handsome young man?"
"Oh, I've been to the wildwood; mother, make my bed soon,
I'm weary of hunting and I fain° would lie down."   *gladly*

"And whom did you meet there, Lord Randal, my son?   5
And whom did you meet there, my handsome young man?"
"Oh, I met with my true love; mother, make my bed soon,
I'm weary of hunting and I fain would lie down."

"What got you for supper, Lord Randal, my son?
What got you for supper, my handsome young man?"   10
"I got eels boiled in broth; mother, make my bed soon,
I'm weary of hunting and I fain would lie down."

"And who got your leavings, Lord Randal, my son?
And who got your leavings, my handsome young man?"
"I gave them to my dogs; mother, make my bed soon,   15
I'm weary of hunting and I fain would lie down."

"And what did your dogs do, Lord Randal, my son?
And what did your dogs do, my handsome young man?"
"Oh, they stretched out and died; mother, make my bed soon,
I'm weary of hunting and I fain would lie down."   20

"Oh, I fear you are poisoned, Lord Randal, my son,
Oh, I fear you are poisoned, my handsome young man."
"Oh, yes, I am poisoned; mother, make my bed soon,
For I'm sick at my heart and I fain would lie down."

"What will you leave your mother, Lord Randal, my son?   25
What will you leave your mother, my handsome young man?"
"My house and my lands; mother, make my bed soon,
For I'm sick at my heart and I fain would lie down."

"What will you leave your sister, Lord Randal, my son?
What will you leave your sister, my handsome young man?"   30

"My gold and my silver; mother, make my bed soon,
For I'm sick at my heart and I fain would lie down."

"What will you leave your brother, Lord Randal, my son?
What will you leave your brother, my handsome young man?"
35   "My horse and my saddle; mother, make my bed soon,
For I'm sick at my heart and I fain would lie down."

"What will you leave your true-love, Lord Randal, my son?
What will you leave your true-love, my handsome young man?"
"A halter to hang her; mother, make my bed soon,
40   For I'm sick at my heart and I want to lie down."

MARGARET ATWOOD (b. 1939)

 ## Variation on the Word *Sleep* (1981)

I would like to watch you sleeping,
which may not happen.
I would like to watch you,
sleeping. I would like to sleep
5   with you, to enter
your sleep as its smooth dark wave
slides over my head

and walk with you through that lucent
wavering forest of bluegreen leaves
10   with its watery sun & three moons
towards the cave where you must descend,
towards your worst fear

I would like to give you the silver
branch, the small white flower, the one
15   word that will protect you
from the grief at the center
of your dream, from the grief
at the center. I would like to follow
you up the long stairway
20   again & become
the boat that would row you back
carefully, a flame
in two cupped hands
to where your body lies
25   beside me, and you enter
it as easily as breathing in

I would like to be the air
that inhabits you for a moment
only. I would like to be that unnoticed
30   & that necessary.

W. H. AUDEN (1907–1973)

For a photo, see Chapter 20, page 998.

 ## The Unknown Citizen (1940)

(To JS/07/M/378
This Marble Monument Is Erected by the State)
He was found by the Bureau of Statistics to be
One against whom there was no official complaint,
And all the reports on his conduct agree
That, in the modern sense of an old-fashioned word, he was a saint,
For in everything he did he served the Greater Community.   5

Except for the War till the day he retired
He worked in a factory and never got fired,
But satisfied his employers, Fudge Motors Inc.
Yet he wasn't a scab° or odd in his views.   *strikebreaker*
For his Union reports that he paid his dues,   10
(Our report on his Union shows it was sound)
And our Social Psychology workers found
That he was popular with his mates° and liked a drink.   *co-workers*
The Press are convinced that he bought a paper every day
And that his reactions to advertisements were normal in every way.   15
Policies taken out in his name prove that he was fully insured,
And his Health-card shows he was once in hospital but left it cured.
Both Producers Research and High-Grade Living declare
He was fully sensible to the advantages of the Installment Plan
And had everything necessary to the Modern Man,   20
A phonograph, a radio, a car and a frigidaire.
Our researchers into Public Opinion are content
That he held the proper opinions for the time of year;
When there was peace, he was for peace; when there was war, he went.
He was married and added five children to the population,   25
Which our Eugenist says was the right number for a parent of his generation,
And our teachers report that he never interfered with their education.
Was he free? Was he happy? The question is absurd:
Had anything been wrong, we should certainly have heard.

WENDELL BERRY (b. 1934)

 ## Another Descent (1985)

Through the weeks of deep snow
we walked above the ground
on fallen sky, as though we did
not come of root and leaf, as though
we had only air and weather   5
for our difficult home.
            But now

as March warms, and the rivulets
run like birdsong on the slopes,
and the branches of light sing in the hills,
10   slowly we return to earth.

LOUISE BOGAN (1897–1970)

 ## Women (1923)

Women have no wilderness in them,
They are provident instead,
Content in the tight hot cell of their hearts
To eat dusty bread.

5   They do not see cattle cropping red winter grass,
They do not hear
Snow water going down under culverts
Shallow and clear.

They wait, when they should turn to journeys,
10   They stiffen, when they should bend.
They use against themselves that benevolence
To which no man is friend.

They cannot think of so many crops to a field
Or of clean wood cleft by an axe.
15   Their love is an eager meaninglessness
Too tense, or too lax.

They hear in every whisper that speaks to them
A shout and a cry.
20   As like as not, when they take life over their door-sills
They should let it go by.

ARNA BONTEMPS (1902–1973)

 ## A Black Man Talks of Reaping (1940)

I have sown beside all waters in my day.
I planted deep, within my heart the fear
that wind or fowl would take the grain away.
I planted safe against this stark, lean year.

5   I scattered seed enough to plant the land
in rows from Canada to Mexico
but for my reaping only what the hand
can hold at once is all that I can show.

Yet what I sowed and what the orchard yields
my brother's sons are gathering stalk and root;
small wonder then my children glean in fields
they have not sown, and feed on bitter fruit.

10

ANNE BRADSTREET (1612–1672)

 ## To My Dear and Loving Husband (1678)

If ever two were one, then surely we.
If ever man were loved by wife, then thee;
If ever wife was happy in a man,
Compare with me ye women if you can.
I prize thy love more than whole mines of gold,
Or all the riches that the East doth hold.
My love is such that rivers cannot quench,
Nor ought but love from thee give recompense.
Thy love is such I can no way repay;
The heavens reward thee manifold, I pray.
Then while we live, in love let's so persever,
That when we live no more we may live ever.

5

10

GWENDOLYN BROOKS (1917–2000)

For a photo, see Chapter 17, page 857.

 ## Primer for Blacks (1980)

Blackness
is a title,
is a preoccupation,
is a commitment Blacks
are to comprehend—
and in which you are
to perceive your Glory.

5

The conscious shout
of all that is white is
"It's Great to be white."
The conscious shout
of the slack in Black is
"It's Great to be white."
Thus all that is white
has white strength and yours.

10

15

The word Black
has geographic power,
pulls everybody in:
Blacks here—

20   Blacks there—
Blacks wherever they may be.
And remember, you Blacks, what they told you—
remember your Education:
"one Drop—one Drop
25   maketh a brand new Black."
     'Oh mighty Drop.
   ——And because they have given us kindly
so many more of our people.

Blackness
30   stretches over the land.
Blackness—
the Black of it,
the rust-red of it,
the milk and cream of it,
35   the tan and yellow-tan of it,
the deep-brown middle-brown high-brown of it,
the "olive" and ochre of it—
Blackness
marches on.

40   The huge, the pungent object of our prime out-ride
is to Comprehend,
to salute and to Love the fact that we are Black,
which *is* our "ultimate Reality,"
which is the lone ground
45   from which our meaningful metamorphosis,
from which our prosperous staccato,
group of individual, can rise.

Self-shriveled Blacks.
Begin with gaunt and marvelous concession:
50   YOU are our costume and our fundamental bone.

     All of you—
     You COLORED ones,
     you NEGRO ones,
those of you who proudly cry
55   "I'm half INDian"—
     those of you who proudly screech
     "I'VE got the blood of George WASHington in
       MY veins"—

ALL of you—
60   you proper Blacks,
you half-Blacks,
you wish-I-weren't Blacks,
Niggeroes and Niggerenes.

You.

ELIZABETH BARRETT BROWNING (1806–1861)

 ## Sonnets from the Portuguese: Number 43, How Do I Love Thee? (1850)

How do I love thee? Let me count the ways.
I love thee to the depth and breadth and height
My soul can reach, when feeling out of sight
For the ends of Being and ideal Grace.
I love thee to the level of every day's   5
Most quiet need, by sun and candlelight.
I love thee freely, as men strive for Right;
I love thee purely, as they turn from Praise.
I love thee with the passion put to use
In my old griefs, and with my childhood's faith.   10
I love thee with a love I seemed to lose
With my lost saints,—I love thee with the breath,
Smiles, tears, of all my life!—and, if God choose,
I shall but love thee better after death.

ROBERT BROWNING (1812–1889)

For a photo, see Chapter 13, page 697.

Soliloquy of the Spanish Cloister (1842)

1

Gr-r-r—there go, my heart's abhorrence!
    Water your damned flowerpots, do!
If hate killed men, Brother Lawrence,
    God's blood, would not mine kill you!
What? your myrtle bush wants trimming?   5
    Oh, that rose has prior claims—
Needs its leaden vase filled brimming?
    Hell dry you up with its flames!

2

At the meal we sit together:
    Salve tibi:° I must hear   *Hail to thee!*   10
Wise talk of the kind of weather,
    Sort of season, time of year:
Not a plenteous cork-crop: scarcely
    Dare we hope oak-galls, I doubt:
What's the Latin name for "parsley"?   15
    What's the Greek name for Swine's Snout?

3

Whew! We'll have our platter burnished,
    Laid with care on our own shelf!
With a fire-new spoon we're furnished,
20   And a goblet for ourself,
Rinsed like something sacrificial
    Ere 'tis fit to touch our chaps°   *jaws*
Marked with L. for our initial!
    (He-he! There his lily snaps!)

4

25 *Saint*, forsooth! While brown Dolores
    Squats outside the Convent bank
With Sanchicha, telling stories,
    Steeping tresses in the tank,
Blue-black, lustrous, thick like horsehairs,
30   —Can't I see his dead eye glow,
Bright as 'twere a Barbary corsair's?°   *pirate's*
    (That is, if he'd let it show!)

5

When he finishes refection,°   *dinner*
    Knife and fork he never lays
35 Cross-wise, to my recollection,
    As do I, in Jesu's praise.
I the Trinity illustrate,
    Drinking watered orange-pulp—
In three sips the Arian° frustrate;   *Anti-Trinitarian (a heretic)*
40   While he drains his at one gulp.

6

Oh, those melons? If he's able
    We're to have a feast! so nice!
One goes to the Abbot's table,
    All of us get each a slice.
45 How go on your flowers? None double?
    Not one fruit-sort can you spy?
Strange!—And I, too, at such trouble,
    Keep them close-nipped on the sly!

7

There's a great text in Galatians,°   *perhaps 3:10 or 5:19–21*
50   Once you trip on it, entails
Twenty-nine distinct damnations,
    One sure, if another fails:

If I trip him just a-dying,
    Sure of heaven as sure can be,
Spin him round and send him flying   55
    Off to hell, a Manichee?°   *heretic*

8

Or, my scrofulous° French novel   *pornographic*
    On gray paper with blunt type!
Simply glance at it, you grovel
    Hand and foot in Belial's° gripe: *the Devil* 60
If I double down its pages
    At the woeful sixteenth print,
When he gathers his greengages,
    Ope a sieve and slip it in't?

9

Or, there's Satan!—one might venture   65
    Pledge one's soul to him, yet leave
Such a flaw in the indenture°   *contract*
    As he'd miss till, past retrieve,
Blasted lay that rose-acacia
    We're so proud of! *Hy, Zy, Hine* . . .   70
'St, there's Vespers! *Plena gratia*°   *full of grace*
    Ave, Virgo!° Gr-r-r—you swine!   *Hail, Virgin!*

WILLIAM CULLEN BRYANT (1794–1878)

🍂 To Cole,° the Painter, Departing for Europe (1829)

Thine eyes shall see the light of distant skies;
    Yet, Cole! thy heart shall bear to Europe's strand
    A living image of our own bright land,
Such as upon thy glorious canvas lies;
Lone lakes—savannas where the bison roves—   5
    Rocks rich with summer garlands—solemn streams—
    Skies where the desert eagle wheels and screams—
Spring bloom and autumn blaze of boundless groves.

Fair scenes shall greet thee where thou goest—fair,
    But different—everywhere the trace of men,   10
    Paths, homes, graves, ruins, from the lowest glen
To where life shrinks from the fierce Alpine air.
    Gaze on them, till the tears shall dim thy sight,
    But keep that earlier, wilder image bright.

°See page I-4 for a painting by Thomas Cole (1801–1848).

GEORGE GORDON, LORD BYRON (1788–1824)

The following two poems are by George Gorden, Lord Byron.

 ## The Destruction of Sennacherib°(1815)

The Assyrian came down like the wolf on the fold,
And his cohorts were gleaming in purple and gold;
And the sheen of their spears was like stars on the sea,
When the blue wave rolls nightly on deep Galilee.

5 Like the leaves of the forest when summer is green,
That host with their banners at sunset were seen:
Like the leaves of the forest when autumn hath blown,
That host on the morrow lay withered and strown.

For the Angel of Death spread his wings on the blast,
10 And breathed in the face of the foe as he passed;
And the eyes of the sleepers waxed deadly and chill,
And their hearts but once heaved—and for ever grew still!

And there lay the steed with his nostril all wide,
But through it there rolled not the breath of his pride;
15 And the foam of his gasping lay white on the turf,
And cold as the spray of the rock-beating surf.

And there lay the rider distorted and pale,
With the dew on his brow, and the rust on his mail;
And the tents were all silent, the banners alone,
20 The lances unlifted, the trumpet unblown.

And the widows of Ashur° are loud in their wail,
And the idols are broke in the temple of Baal;°
And the might of the Gentile, unsmote by the sword,
Hath melted like snow in the glance of the Lord!

°Sennacherib was king of the ancient Near Eastern empire of Assyria from 705 to 681 BCE. He laid siege to Jerusalem in about 702 BCE, even though King Hezekiah had already rendered tribute to Assyria. According to 2 Kings 19:35–36, a miracle occurred to save the besieged Hebrews: "the angel of the Lord went out and smote . . . [185,000 Assyrian soldiers]; and when they [the Hebrews] arose early in the morning, behold, they [the Assyrians] were all dead corpses." See page 868 for Ogden Nash's parody of parts of this poem. 21 *Ashur:* the land of the Assyrians. 22 *Baal:* a god who supposedly controlled weather and storms.

 ## She Walks in Beauty (1815)

She walks in beauty, like the night
   Of cloudless climes and starry skies;
And all that's best of dark and bright
   Meet in her aspect and her eyes:
5 Thus mellow'd to that tender light
   Which heaven to gaudy day denies.

One shade the more, one ray the less,
    Had half impair'd the nameless grace
Which waves in every raven tress,
    Or softly lightens o'er her face;   10
Where thoughts serenely sweet express
    How pure, how dear their dwelling-place.

And on that cheek, and o'er that brow,
    So soft, so calm, yet eloquent,
The smiles that win, the tints that glow,   15
    But tell of days in goodness spent,
A mind at peace with all below,
    A heart whose love is innocent!

LEONARD COHEN (b. 1934)

"The killers that run . . ." (1972)

The killers that run
        the other countries
are trying to get us
to overthrow the killers
        that run our own   5
I for one
prefer the rule
        of our native killers
I am convinced
        the foreign killer   10
will kill more of us
than the old familiar killer does
        Frankly I don't believe
anyone out there
really wants us to solve   15
our social problems
        I base this all on how I feel
about the man next door
I just hope he doesn't
        get any uglier   20
Therefore I am a patriot
I don't like to see
        a burning flag
because it excites
the killers on either side   25
to unfortunate excess
which goes on gaily
        quite unchecked
until everyone is dead

BILLY COLLINS (b. 1941)

For a photo, see Chapter 11, page 624.

 ### Days (1995)

Each one *is* a gift, no doubt.
mysteriously placed in your waking hand
or set upon your forehead
moments before you open your eyes.

5　Today begins cold and bright,
the ground heavy with snow
and the thick masonry of ice,
the sun glinting off the turrets of clouds.

Through the calm eye of the window
10　everything is in its place
but so precariously
this day might be resting somehow

on the one before it,
all the days of the past stacked high
15　like the impossible tower of dishes
entertainers used to build on stage.

No wonder you find yourself
perched on the top of a tall ladder
hoping to add one more.
20　Just another Wednesday

you whisper,
then holding your breath,
place this cup on yesterday's saucer
without the slightest clink.

FRANCES CORNFORD (1886–1960)

 ### From a Letter to America on a Visit to Sussex: Spring 1942 (1942)

How simply violent things
Happen, is strange.
How strange it was to see
In the soft Cambridge sky our Squadron's wings,
5　And hear the huge hum in the familiar grey.
And it was odd today
On Ashdown Forest that will never change,
To find a gunner in the gorse, flung down,

Well-camouflaged, and bored and lion-brown.
A little further by those twisted trees   10
(As if it rose on humped preposterous seas
Out of a Book of Hours) up a bank
Like a large dragon, purposeful though drunk,
Heavily lolloped, swayed and sunk,
A tank.   15
All this because manoeuvres had begun.
But now, but soon,
At home on any usual afternoon,
High overhead
May come the Erinyes° winging   *the furies in Greek mythology*   20
Or here the boy may lie beside his gun,
His mud-brown tunic gently staining red,
While larks get on with their old job of singing.

STEPHEN CRANE (1871–1900)

 # Do Not Weep, Maiden, for War Is Kind (1896; 1895)

Do not weep, maiden, for war is kind.
Because your lover threw wild hands toward the sky
And the affrighted steed ran on alone,
Do not weep.
War is kind.   5

> Hoarse, booming drums of the regiment
> Little souls who thirst for fight,
> These men were born to drill and die
> The unexplained glory flies above them
> Great is the battle-god, great, and his kingdom—   10
> A field where a thousand corpses lie.

Do not weep, babe, for war is kind.
Because your father tumbled in the yellow trenches,
Raged at his breast, gulped and died,
Do not weep.   15
War is kind.

> Swift, blazing flag of the regiment
> Eagle with crest of red and gold,
> These men were born to drill and die
> Point for them the virtue of slaughter   20
> Make plain to them the excellence of killing
> And a field where a thousand corpses lie.

Mother whose head hung humble as a button
On the bright splendid shroud of your son,
Do not weep.   25
War is kind.

ROBERT CREELEY (1926–2005)

 "Do you think . . ." (1972)

Do you think that if
you once do what you want
to do you will want not to do it.

Do you think that if
5   there's an apple on the table
and somebody eats it, it
won't be there anymore.

Do you think that if
two people are in love with one another,
10   one or the other has got to be
less in love than the other at
some point in the otherwise happy relationship.

Do you think that if
you once take a breath, you're by
15   that committed to taking the next one
and so on until the very process of
breathing's an endlessly expanding need
almost of its own necessity forever.

Do you think that if
20   no one knows then whatever
it is, no one will know and
that will be the case, like
they say, for an indefinite
period of time if such time
25   can have a qualification of such time.

Do you know anyone,
really. Have you been, really,
much alone. Are you lonely,
now, for example. Does anything
30   really matter to you, really, or
has anything mattered. Does each
thing tend to be there, and then not
to be there, just as if that were it.

Do you think that if
35   I said, *I love you,* or anyone
said it, or you did. Do you
think that if you had all
such decisions to make and could
make them. Do you think that
40   if you did. That you really
would have to think it all into
reality, that world, each time, new.

E. E. CUMMINGS (1894–1962)

For a photo, see Chapter 12, page 665.

 if there are any heavens (1931)

if there are any heavens my mother will(all by herself)have
one.   It will not be a pansy heaven nor
a fragile heaven of lilies-of-the-valley but
it will be a heaven of blackred roses

my father will be (deep like a rose   5
tall like a rose)

standing near my

swaying over her
(silent)
with eyes which are really petals and see   10

nothing with the face of a poet really which
is a flower and not a face with
hands
which whisper
This is my beloved my   15

                         (suddenly in sunlight

he will bow,

& the whole garden will bow)

CARL DENNIS (b. 1939)

 The God Who Loves You (2001)

It must be troubling for the god who loves you
To ponder how much happier you'd be today
Had you been able to glimpse your many futures.
It must be painful for him to watch you on Friday evenings
Driving home from the office, content with your week—   5
Three fine houses sold to deserving families—
Knowing as he does exactly what would have happened
Had you gone to your second choice for college,
Knowing the roommate you'd have been allotted
Whose ardent opinions on painting and music   10
Would have kindled in you a lifelong passion.
A life thirty points above the life you're living
On any scale of satisfaction. And every point
A thorn in the side of the god who loves you.
You don't want that, a large-souled man like you   15
Who tries to withhold from your wife the day's disappointments

So she can save her empathy for the children.
And would you want this god to compare your wife
With the woman you were destined to meet on the other campus?
20   It hurts you to think of him ranking the conversation
You'd have enjoyed over there higher in insight
Than the conversation you're used to.
And think how this loving god would feel
Knowing that the man next in line for your wife
25   Would have pleased her more than you ever will
Even on your best days, when you really try.
Can you sleep at night believing a god like that
Is pacing his cloudy bedroom, harassed by alternatives
You're spared by ignorance? The difference between what is
30   And what could have been will remain alive for him
Even after you cease existing, after you catch a chill
Running out in the snow for the morning paper,
Losing eleven years that the god who loves you
Will feel compelled to imagine scene by scene
35   Unless you come to the rescue by imagining him
No wiser than you are, no god at all, only a friend
No closer than the actual friend you made at college,
The one you haven't written in months. Sit down tonight
And write him about the life you can talk about
40   With a claim to authority, the life you've witnessed,
Which for all you know is the life you've chosen.

JOHN DONNE (1572–1631)

For a portrait, see Chapter 12, page 666. The following three poems are by John Donne.

The Good Morrow (1633)

I wonder, by my troth, what thou and I
Did, till we loved! Were we not weaned till then,
But sucked on country pleasures, childishly?
Or snorted we in the seven sleepers' den?°
5   'Twas so; But this, all pleasures fancies be.
If ever any beauty I did see,
Which I desired, and got, t'was but a dream of thee.

And now good morrow to our waking souls,
Which watch not one another out of fear;
10   For love all love of other sights controls,°
And makes one little room an everywhere.
Let sea-discoverers to new worlds have gone,

°4 *seven sleepers' den*: a reference to the miraculous legend of the Seven Sleepers of Ephesus, in Asia Minor. Seven young nobles fled Ephesus to avoid religious persecution by the Emperor Decius (c. 250 CE). They took refuge in a cave and were sealed inside. They then slept for either 230 or 309 years, and they emerged praising God. After they died, their remains were taken to St. Victor's Church in Marseilles, France, where they were encrypted. 10 *For love . . . controls*: i.e., Love is so powerful that it eliminates fear and makes everything in the world worthy of love.

Let maps to other, worlds on worlds have shown,°
Let us possess one world; each hath one, and is one.

My face in thine eye, thine in mine appears,°   15
And true plain hearts do in the faces rest;
Where can we find two better hemispheres
Without sharp North, without declining West?
Whatever dies was not mixed equally;
If our two loves be one, or thou and I   20
Love so alike, that none do slacken, none can die.°

°13, 14 *let sea-discoverers . . . shown:* i.e., let sea-explorers discover new worlds, and let maps show other new worlds to other discoverers. 15 *My face . . . appears:* Each face is reflected in the pupils of the other lover's eyes. 19–21 *Whatever . . . can die:* Scholastic philosophy argued that elements that are united in perfect balance will never change or decay; hence, such a mixture cannot die. Donne's analogy suggests—humorously—that the love of the lovers is too pure to die, and that they may therefore go on making love forever.

Holy Sonnet 10: Death Be Not Proud (1633)

Death, be not proud, though some have callèd thee
Mighty and dreadful, for thou art not so;
For those whom thou think'st thou dost overthrow
Die not, poor Death, nor yet canst thou kill me.
From rest and sleep, which but thy pictures° be,   *imitations*   5
Much pleasure; then from thee much more must flow,
And soonest our best men with thee do go,
Rest of their bones, and soul's delivery.
Thou art slave to fate, chance, kings, and desperate men,
And dost with poison, war, and sickness dwell,   10
And poppy° or charms can make us sleep as well   *opium*
And better than thy stroke; why swell'st° thou then?   *puff up with pride*
One short sleep past, we wake eternally°   *i.e., we will live eternally*
And death shall be no more; Death, thou shalt die.

A Hymn to God the Father (1633)

Wilt Thou forgive that sin where I begun,
    Which is my sin, though it were done before?
Wilt Thou forgive those sins through which I run,
    And do them still, though still I do deplore?
        When Thou hast done, Thou hast not done,   5
            For I have more.

Wilt Thou forgive that sin by which I won
    Others to sin and made my sin their door?
Wilt Thou forgive that sin which I did shun
    A year or two, but wallowed in a score?
        When Thou hast done, Thou hast not done,
            For I have more.   10

I have a sin of fear, that when I have spun
　My last thread, I shall perish on the shore;
15　Swear by Thy Self, that at my death Thy sun
　Shall shine as it shines now and heretofore;
　　And, having done that, Thou hast done,
　　　I have no more.

PAUL LAURENCE DUNBAR (1872–1906)

 ## Sympathy (1895)

I know what the caged bird feels, alas!
When the sun is bright on the upland slopes;
When the wind stirs soft through the springing grass
And the river flows like a stream of glass;
5　When the first bird sings and the first bud opes,
And the faint perfume from its chalice steals—
I know what the caged bird feels!

I know why the caged bird beats his wing
Till its blood is red on the cruel bars;
10　For he must fly back to his perch and cling
When he fain would be on the bough a-swing;
And a pain still throbs in the old, old scars
And they pulse again with a keener sting—
I know why he beats his wing!

15　I know why the caged bird sings, ah me,
When his wing is bruised and his bosom sore,
When he beats his bars and would be free;
It is not a carol of joy or glee,
But a prayer that he sends from his heart's deep core,
20　But a plea, that upward to Heaven he flings—
I know why the caged bird sings!

T. S. ELIOT (1888–1965)

For a photo, see Chapter 14, page 735.

→ name: indicates
high Soaety.
pretentious

 ## The Love Song of J. Alfred Prufrock° (1915; 1911)

*S'io credesse che mia risposta fosse
A persona che mai tornasse al mondo,*

°The poem is a monologue spoken by Prufrock; the name is invented but suggests a businessman. The Italian epigraph is quoted from Dante's *Inferno* (Canto 27, lines 61–66) and is spoken by a man who relates his evil deeds to Dante because he assumes that Dante will never return to the world: "If I believed that my response were made to a person who would ever revisit the world, this flame would stand motionless. But since none has ever returned from this depth alive, if I hear the truth, I answer you without fear of exposure."

Questa fiamma staria senza piu scosse.
Ma per ciò che giammai di questo fondo
Non tornò vivo alcun, s'i'odo il vero,
Senza tema d'infamia ti rispondo.

[handwritten: trapped in a kind of hell (Dante) - but he is trapped in his hell of insecurity / inability to take risks]

Let us go then, you and I
When the evening is spread out against the sky
Like a patient etherized upon a table;   *[handwritten: knocked out]*
Let us go, through certain half-deserted streets,
The muttering retreats   5
Of restless nights in one-night cheap hotels   *[handwritten: sex]*
And sawdust restaurants with oyster shells;   *[handwritten: sex/aphrodisiacs]*

[handwritten: no feelings / knocked out]
[handwritten: blatant sexual imagery]

Streets that follow like a tedious argument
Of insidious intent
To lead you to an overwhelming question . . .   *[handwritten: asking the woman out.]*   10
Oh, do not ask, "What is it?"
Let us go and make our visit.   *[handwritten: they're going to a party]*

In the room the women come and go   *[handwritten: all talk / high society / maybe? maybe not. he's intimidated]*
Talking of Michelangelo.°

[handwritten in left margin: surrealism]

The yellow fog that rubs its back upon the windowpanes,   *[handwritten: dream-like]*   15
The yellow smoke that rubs its muzzle on the windowpanes   *[handwritten: dog? cat]*   *[handwritten: experience, fog surrealist]*
Licked its tongue into the corners of the evening,
Lingered upon the pools that stand in drains,
Let fall upon its back the soot that falls from chimneys,   *[handwritten: seemingly out of nowhere, but adds atmosphere]*
Slipped by the terrace, made a sudden leap,   20
And seeing that it was a soft October night,
Curled once about the house, and fell asleep.

And indeed there will be time   *[handwritten: -alluding to his coy mistress "carpe diem" poem]*
For the yellow smoke that slides along the street,   *[handwritten: -opposite b/c he cannot ask this woman out]*
Rubbing its back upon the windowpanes;   25
There will be time, there will be time°
To prepare a face to meet the faces that you meet;
There will be time to murder and create,
And time for all the works and days° of hands   *[handwritten: he is referring to his social skills]*
That lift and drop a question on your plate;   30
Time for you and time for me,
And time yet for a hundred indecisions,
And for a hundred visions and revisions,
Before the taking of a toast and tea.

°14 *Michelangelo:* one of the greatest Italian Renaissance painters and sculptors (1475–1564). The name suggests that the women are cultured, or at least pretending to be so. 26 *time:* an allusion to Andrew Marvell's "To His Coy Mistress" (p. 968). 29 *works and days:* an allusion to a long poem, *Works and Days,* by the Greek poet Hesiod in the eighth century BCE. It is the primary source of the myth of Pandora (i.e., one who receives "all gifts"), who was considered to be "the first mortal female that ever lived" (Lemprière). Hesiod claims that Zeus, who was enraged by the theft of fire by Prometheus, created womankind, symbolized by Pandora, as his revenge on mankind, and to this end he directed Hermes to give her "a shameless mind and a deceitful nature" (tr. Hugh G. Evelyn-White, *Works and Days* 57–59, 68). I thank Professor Donald Tuthill for his work and helpfulness in the writing of this note.

35   In the room the women come and go
      Talking of Michelangelo.

      And indeed there will be time
      To wonder, "Do I dare?" and, "Do I dare?"
      Time to turn back and descend the stair,
40   With a bald spot in the middle of my hair—
      (They will say: "How his hair is growing thin!")
      My morning coat, my collar mounting firmly to the chin,
      My necktie rich and modest, but asserted by a simple pin—
      (They will say: "But how his arms and legs are thin!")
45   Do I dare
      Disturb the universe?
      In a minute there is time
      For decisions and revisions which a minute will reverse.

      For I have known them all already, known them all—
50   Have known the evenings, mornings, afternoons,
      I have measured out my life with coffee spoons;
      I know the voices dying with a dying fall°
      Beneath the music from a farther room.
          So how should I presume?

55   And I have known the eyes already, known them all—
      The eyes that fix you in a formulated phrase,
      And when I am formulated, sprawling on a pin,
      When I am pinned and wriggling on the wall,
      Then how should I begin
60   To spit out all the butt-ends of my days and ways?
      And how should I presume?

      And I have known the arms already, known them all—
      Arms that are braceleted and white and bare
      (But in the lamplight, downed with light brown hair!)
65   Is it perfume from a dress
      That makes me so digress?
      Arms that lie along a table, or wrap about a shawl.
          And should I then presume?
          And how should I begin?

                    * * * * *

70   Shall I say, I have gone at dusk through narrow streets
      And watched the smoke that rises from the pipes
      Of lonely men in shirt-sleeves, leaning out of windows? . . .

      °52 *dying fall:* an allusion to a speech by Orsino in Shakespeare's *Twelfth Night* (1.1.4).

I should have been a pair of ragged claws)   *A little low crab/roach-like*
Scuttling across the floors of silent seas.)

* * * * *

And the afternoon, the evening, sleeps so peacefully!) *personification*   75
Smoothed by long fingers,
Asleep . . . tired . . . or it malingers,°
Stretched on the floor, here beside you and me.
Should I, after tea and cakes and ices,
Have the strength to force the moment to its crisis?) *very big deal to him*   80
But though I have wept and fasted, wept and prayed,   *John the*
Though I have seen my head (grown slightly bald) brought in upon a platter,°) *Baptist*
I am no prophet—and here's no great matter;   *Alfred is no*
I have seen the moment of my greatness flicker,   *his fear*   *John the*
And I have seen the eternal Footman hold my coat, and snicker,   *Baptist)* 85
And in short, I was afraid.

And would it have been worth it, after all,
After the cups, the marmalade, the tea,
Among the porcelain, among some talk of you and me,
Would it have been worth while,   90
To have bitten off the matter with a smile,
To have squeezed the universe into a ball°
To roll it toward some overwhelming question,
To say: "I am Lazarus,° come from the dead,   *If he asks and*
Come back to tell you all, I shall tell you all"—   *he totally misunderstands* 95
If one, setting a pillow by her head,   *her*
    Should say: "That is not what I meant at all.
    That is not it, at all."

And would it have been worth it, after all,
Would it have been worth while,   100
After the sunsets and the dooryards and the sprinkled streets,
After the novels, after the teacups, after the skirts that trail along the floor—
And this, and so much more?—
It is impossible to say just what I mean!
But as if a magic lantern threw the nerves in patterns on a screen: 105
Would it have been worth while
If one, setting a pillow or throwing off a shawl,
And turning toward the window, should say:
    "That is not it at all,   ) *She's uninterested*
    That is not what I meant, at all."   110

* * * * *

No! I am not Prince Hamlet,° nor was meant to be;
Am an attendant lord, one that will do   *He is a background*
To swell a progress,° start a scene or two,   *person*

°77 *malingers:* pretends to be ill. 82 *platter:* as was the head of John the Baptist; see Mark 6:17–28 and Matthew
14:3–11. 92 *ball:* another allusion to Marvell's "Coy Mistress." 94 *Lazarus:* See John 11:1–44. 111 *Prince Hamlet:* the
hero of Shakespeare's play *Hamlet*. 113 *swell a progress:* enlarge a royal procession.

Advise the prince; no doubt, an easy tool,   *→ a pleaser-things of others first*
115 Deferential, glad to be of use,
Politic, cautious, and meticulous;
Full of high sentence,° but a bit obtuse;
At times, indeed, almost ridiculous—
Almost, at times, the Fool.

120 I grow old . . . I grow old . . .   *not wanting to get wet*
I shall wear the bottoms of my trousers rolled.°

comb over
Shall I part my hair behind? Do I dare to eat a peach?   *fear of sex and messiness*
I shall wear white flannel trousers, and walk upon the beach.
I have heard the mermaids singing, each to each.   *sailers, sex, ocean*

125 I do not think that they will sing to me.

I have seen them riding seaward on the waves
Combing the white hair of the waves blown back   *dreams*   *his inade quay*
When the wind blows the water white and black.

We have lingered in the chambers of the sea
130 By sea-girls wreathed with seaweed red and brown
Till human voices wake us, and we drown.   *reality*

°117 *sentence*: ideals, opinions, sentiment. 121 *rolled*: a possible reference to pants cuffs, which were becoming fashionable in 1910.

JAMES EMANUEL (b. 1921)

 ## The Negro (1968)

Never saw him.
Never can.
Hypothetical,
Haunting man:

5 Eyes a-saucer,
Yessir bossir,
Dice a-clicking,
Razor flicking.

The-ness froze him
10 In a dance.
A-ness never
Had a chance.

LYNN EMANUEL (b. 1949)

 ## Like God (1998)

you hover above the page staring
down on a small town. By its roads
some scenery loafs in a hammock of
sleepy prose and here is a mongrel

loping and here is a train pulling into
a station in three long sentences and
here are the people in galoshes waiting.
But you know this story and it is not
about those travelers and their galoshes,
but about your life, so, like a diver
climbing over the side of a boat and
down into the ocean, you climb, sentence
by sentence, into this story on this page.

You have been expecting yourself
as the woman who purrs by in a dress
by Patou, and a porter manacled to
the luggage, and a matron bulky as
the *Britannia,* and there, haunting
her ankles like a piece of ectoplasm
that barks is, once again, that small
white dog from chapter twenty.
These are your fellow travelers and
you become part of their logjam of
images of hats and umbrellas and
Vuitton luggage, you are a face
behind or inside these faces, a
heartbeat in the volley of these
heartbeats, as you choose, out of all
the passengers, the journey of a man
with a mustache scented faintly with
Prince Albert. "He must be a secret
sensualist," you think and your awareness
drifts to his trench coat, worn, softened,
and flabby, a coat with a lobotomy, just
as the train arrives at a destination.

No, you would prefer another stop
in a later chapter where the climate is
affable and sleek. But most of
the passengers are disembarking, and
you did not choose to be in the story
of the white dress. You did not choose
the story of the matron whose bosom
is like the prow of a ship and who is
launched toward lunch at The Hotel Pierre,
or even the story of the dog-on-a-leash,
even though this is now your story:
the story of the man-who-had-to-
take-the-train and walk the dark road
described hurriedly by someone sitting
at the café so you could discover it,
although you knew all along it would
be there, you, who have been hovering
above this page, holding the book in
your hands, like God, reading.

CHIEF DAN GEORGE (1899–1981)

 ## The Beauty of the Trees (1974)

The beauty of the trees,
the softness of the air,
the fragrance of the grass,
   speaks to me.

5   The summit of the mountain,
the thunder of the sky,
the rhythm of the sea,
   speaks to me.

The faintness of the stars,
10 the freshness of the morning,
the dewdrop on the flower,
   speaks to me.

The strength of fire,
the taste of salmon,
15 the trail of the sun,
and the life that never goes away,
   they speak to me.

And my heart soars.

NIKKI GIOVANNI (b. 1943)

For a photo, see Chapter 18, page 920. The following two poems are by Nikki Giovanni.

 ## Woman (1978)

she wanted to be a blade
of grass amid the fields
but he wouldn't agree
to be the dandelion

5 she wanted to be a robin singing
through the leaves
but he refused to be
her tree

she spun herself into a web
10   and looking for a place to rest
turned to him
but he stood straight
declining to be her corner

she tried to be a book
but he wouldn't read   15
she turned herself into a bulb
but he wouldn't let her grow

she decided to become
a woman
and though he still refused   20
to be a man
she decided it was all
right

Poetry (1996)

poetry is motion graceful
as a fawn
gentle as a teardrop
strong like the eye
finding peace in a crowded room   5
we poets tend to think
our words are golden
though emotion speaks too
loudly to be defined
by silence   10
sometimes after midnight or just before
the dawn
we sit typewriter in hand
pulling loneliness around us
forgetting our lovers or children   15
who are sleeping
ignoring the weary wariness
of our own logic
to compare a poem
    no one understands it   20
it never says "love me" for poets are
beyond love
it never says "accept me" for poems seek not
acceptance but controversy
it only says "I am" and therefore   25
i concede that you are too

a poem is pure energy
horizontally contained
between the mind
of the poet and the ear of the reader   30
if it does not sing discard the ear
for poetry is song
if it does not delight discard

the heart for poetry is joy
35   if it does not inform then close
off the brain for it is dead
if it cannot heed the insistent message
that life is precious

which is all we poets
40   wrapped in our loneliness
are trying to say

MARILYN HACKER (b. 1942)

 ## Sonnet Ending with a Film Subtitle (1979)

For Judith Landry

Life has its nauseating ironies:
The good die young, as often has been shown;
Chaste spouses catch Venereal Disease;
And feminists sit by the telephone.
5   Last night was rather bleak, tonight is starker.
I may stare at the wall till half-past-one.
My friends are all convinced Dorothy Parker
Lives, but is not well, in Marylebone.°   *a district in London*
I wish that I could imitate my betters
10   And fortify my rhetoric with guns.
Some day we women all will break our fetters
And raise our daughters to be Lesbians.
(I wonder if the bastard kept my letters?)
Here follow untranslatable French puns.

DANIEL HALPERN (b. 1945)

The following two poems are by Daniel Halpern.

 ## Snapshot of Hué (1982)

For Robert Stone

They are riding bicycles on the other side
of the Perfume River.

A few months ago the bridges were down
and there was no one on the streets.

5   There were the telling piles on corners,
debris that contained a little of everything.

There was nothing not under cover—
even the sky remained impenetrable

day after day. And if you were seen
on the riverbank you were knocked down.   10

It is clear today. The litter in the streets
has been swept away. It couldn't have been

that bad, one of us said, the river barely moving,
the bicycles barely moving, the sun posted above.

 ## Summer in the Middle Class (1991)

All over America
it's suddenly
mid-July
We're chasing
our sons around   5
the yard
with balls and sticks
We are lumbering
because we are overweight
and a little older   10
being survivors
of the baby boom
making good the legacy
At sundown
a million barbecues ignite   15
as if from a single match
Webers
Crestlines
international hibachis
and the sad slabs of meat   20
begin to emerge
from their various marinades
the tables get set
and the mosquitoes awaken
for the evening meal   25

When they have finished
what is rightfully theirs
the children are removed
from the tables
and the adults open   30
another bottle or can of beer
The evenings are special
this time of year
the heat finally bearable
the coals a coolish grey   35

dying into themselves
It's what happens in unison
that makes America America
the lights going off
40   the fluorescent show
of t.v. coming on
and then
the total darkness

H. S. (SAM) HAMOD (b. 1936)

 ## Leaves (1973)

For Sally

Tonight, Sally and I are making stuffed
grapeleaves, we get out a package, it's
drying out, I've been saving it in the freezer, it's
one of the last things my father ever picked in this
5   life—they're over five years old
and up to now
we just kept finding packages of them in the
freezer, as if he were still picking them
somewhere packing them
10   carefully to send to us
making sure they didn't break into pieces.

                                * * *

"To my Dar Garnchildn
Davd and Lura
from Thr Jido"
15   twisted on tablet paper
between the lines
in this English lettering
hard for him even to print,
I keep this small torn record,
20   this piece of paper stays in the upstairs storage,
one of the few pieces of American
my father ever wrote. We find his Arabic letters
all over the place, even in the files we find
letters to him in English, one I found from Charles Atlas
25   telling him, in 1932,
"Of course, Mr. Hamod, you too can build
your muscles like mine . . ."

                                  * * *

Last week my mother told me, when I was
asking why I became a poet, "But don't you remember,

your father made up poems, don't you remember him   30
singing in the car as we drove—those were poems."
Even now, at night, I sometimes
get out the Arabic grammar book
though it seems so late.

FRANCES E. W. HARPER (1825–1911)

 ## She's Free! (1854)

How say that by law we may torture and chase
A woman whose crime is the hue of her face?—
With her step on the ice, and her arm on her child,
The danger was fearful, the pathway was wild. . . .
But she's free! yes, free from the land where the slave,   5
From the hand of oppression, must rest in the grave;
Where bondage and blood, where scourges and chains,
Have placed on our banner indelible stains. . . .

The bloodhounds have miss'd the scent of her way,
The hunter is rifled and foiled of his prey,
The cursing of men and clanking of chains   10
Make sounds of strange discord on Liberty's plains. . . .
Oh! poverty, danger and death she can brave,
For the child of her love is no longer a slave.

MICHAEL S. HARPER (b. 1938)

 ## Called (1975)

Digging the grave
through black dirt,
gravel and rocks
that will hold her down,
we speak of her heat   5
which has driven her out
over the highway
in her first year.

A fly glides from her mouth
as we take her four legs,   10
and the great white neck
muddled at the lakeside
bends gracefully into the arc
of her tongue, colorless, now,
and we set her in the bed   15
of earth and rock

which will hold her as the sun
sets over her shoulders.

You had spoken of her brother,
20 100 lbs or more,
and her slight frame
from the diet of chain
she had broken;
on her back
25 as the spade cools her brow
with black dirt, rocks,
sand, white tongue,
what pups does she hold
that are seeds unspayed
30 in her broken body;
what does her brother say
to the seed gone out over
the prairie, on the hunt
of the unreturned:
35 and what do we say
to the master of the dog dead,
heat, highway, this bed
on the shoulder
of the road west
40 where her brother called, calls

ROBERT HASS (b. 1941)

Spring Rain (1989)

Now the rain is falling, freshly, in the intervals between sunlight,

a Pacific squall started no one knows where, drawn east as the drifts of
warm air make a channel;

it moves its own way, like water or the mind,

5 and spills this rain passing over. The Sierras will catch it as last snow
flurries before summer, observed only by the wakened marmots at ten
thousand feet,

and we will come across it again as larkspur and penstemon sprouting
along a creek above Sonora Pass next August,

10 where the snowmelt will have trickled into Dead Man's Creek and the
creek spilled into the Stanislaus and the Stanislaus into the San Joaquin
and the San Joaquin into the slow salt marshes of the bay.

That's not the end of it: the gray jays of the mountains eat larkspur seeds,
which cannot propagate otherwise.

To simulate the process, you have to soak gathered seeds all night in the 15
acids of coffee

and then score them gently with a very sharp knife before you plant them
in the garden.

ROBERT HAYDEN (1913–1980)

 ### Those Winter Sundays (1962)

Sundays too my father got up early
and put his clothes on in the blueblack cold,
then with cracked hands that ached
from labor in the weekday weather made
banked fires blaze. No one ever thanked him. 5
I'd wake and hear the cold splintering, breaking,
When the rooms were warm, he'd call,
and slowly I would rise and dress,
fearing the chronic angers of that house,

Speaking indifferently to him, 10
who had driven out the cold
and polished my good shoes as well.
What did I know, what did I know
of love's austere and lonely offices?

ROBERT HERRICK (1591–1674)

 ### To the Virgins, to Make Much of Time (1648)

Gather ye rosebuds while ye may,
    Old time is still a-flying;
And this same flower that smiles today
    Tomorrow will be dying.

The glorious lamp of heaven, the sun, 5
    The higher he's a-getting,
The sooner will his race be run,
    And nearer he's to setting.

That age is best which is the first,
    When youth and blood are warmer; 10
But being spent, the worse, and worst
    Times still succeed the former.

Then be not coy, but use your time,
    And, while ye may, go marry;
For, having lost but once your prime, 15
    You may forever tarry.

WILLIAM HEYEN (b. 1940)

 ## The Hair: Jacob Korman's Story (1980)

Ten kilometers from Warsaw,
I arrived in Rembertow where
hundreds of Jews had lived
until the wheel turned: *Judenrein.*°   *cleansed; rid of Jews*

5   You think they let themselves be taken?
They would not fill the trucks.
Men were shot trying to pull guns
from the guards' hands.

and hands of dead women
10   clutched hair, hair of SS guards
blood-patched hair everywhere,
a *velt mit hor,* a field of hair

A. D. HOPE (1907–2000)

 ## Advice to Young Ladies (1970)

A.U.C.° 334: about this date
For a sexual misdemeanor, which she denied,
The vestal virgin Postumia was tried.
Livy records it among affairs of state.°

5   They let her off: it seems she was perfectly pure;
The charge arose because some thought her talk
Too witty for a young girl, her ways, her walk
Too lively, her clothes too smart to be demure.

The Pontifex Maximus, summing up the case,
10   Warned her in future to abstain from jokes,
To wear less modish and more pious frocks.
She left the court reprieved, but in disgrace.

What then? With her the annalist is less
Concerned than what the men achieved that year;
15   Plots, quarrels, crimes, with oratory to spare!
I see Postumia with her dowdy dress,

Stiff mouth and listless step; I see her strive
To give dull answers. She had to knuckle down.
A vestal virgin who scandalized that town
20   Had fair trial, then they buried her alive.

°1 A.U.C.: *ab urbe condita,* "from the founding of the city" (Latin); 334 years after the founding of ancient
Rome. 4 *Titus Livius: The History of Rome,* Vol. I. Electronic Text Center, U of Virginia Library. 4.44.

Alive, bricked up in suffocating dark,
A ration of bread, a pitcher if she was dry
Preserved the body they did not wish to die
Until her mind was quenched to the last spark.

How many the black maw has swallowed in its time!   25
Spirited girls who would not know their place.
Talented girls who found that the disgrace
Of being a woman made genius a crime;

How many others, who would not kiss the rod
Domestic bullying broke, or public shame?   30
Pagan or Christian, it was much the same:
Husbands, Saint Paul declared, rank next to God.

Livy and Paul, it may be, never knew
That Rome was doomed; each spoke of her with pride.
Tacitus, writing after both had died,   35
Showed that whole fabric rotten through and through.

Historians spend their lives and lavish ink
Explaining how great commonwealths collapse
From great defects of policy—perhaps
The cause is sometimes simpler than they think.   40

It may not seem so grave an act to break
Postumia's spirit as Galileo's, to gag
Hypatia° as crush Socrates, or drag
Joan as Giordano Bruno to the stake.

Can we be sure: Have more states perished, then,   45
For having shackled the enquiring mind,
Than those who, in their folly not less blind,
Trusted the servile womb to breed free men?

°43 *Hypatia:* Hypatia of Alexandria (c.370–415 CE). He was a scholar and teacher who was brutally murdered by a mob of religious fanatics.

GERARD MANLEY HOPKINS (1844–1889)

For a photo, see Chapter 14, page 740. The following two poems are by Gerard Manley Hopkins.

 ## Pied Beauty (1918, 1877)

Glory be to God for dappled things—
    For skies of couple-colour as a brinded° cow;
        For rose-moles all in stipple upon trout that swim;
Fresh-firecoal chestnut-falls;° finches' wings;

°2 *brinded:* brindled, that is, grey with dark spots. 4 *chestnut-falls:* the meat of a roasted chestnut.

5   Landscape plotted and pieced°—fold,° fallow,° and plough;
         And áll trádes, their gear and tackle and trim.

All things counter,° original, spare,° strange;
     Whatever is fickle, freckled (who knows how?)
         With swift, slow; sweet, sour; adazzle, dim;
10   He fathers-forth whose beauty is past change:
Praise him.

°5 *pieced:* divided into fields of different colors, depending on the crops or use. *fold:* an enclosed field for animals. *fallow:* a plowed but unplanted field. 7 *counter:* opposed, as in contrasting patterns. *spare:* rare.

 ## The Windhover° (1918, 1877)

To Christ Our Lord

I caught this morning morning's minion,° king-   *darling*
     dom of daylight's dauphin,° dapple-dawn-drawn Falcon, in his riding
         Of the rolling level underneath him steady air, and striding
High there, how he rung upon the rein of a wimpling wing
5   In his ecstasy! then off, off forth on swing,
         As a skate's heel sweeps smooth on a bow-bend: the hurl and gliding
         Rebuffed the big wind. My heart in hiding
Stirred for a bird,—the achieve of, the mastery of the thing!

Brute beauty and valour and act, oh, air, pride, plume, here
10   Buckle!° AND the fire that breaks from thee then, a billion   *join*
Times told lovelier, more dangerous. O my chevalier!°   *knight*
     No wonder of it: shéer plód makes plough down sillion°
Shine, and blue-beak embers, ah my dear,
     Fall, gall themselves, and gash gold-vermilion.

°The poem's title refers to a kestrel—or falcon—that glides or hovers in the wind. 2 *dauphin:* prince, heir to the throne of France. 12 *sillion:* the ridge of earth between two plowed furrows in a field.

CAROLINA HOSPITAL (b. 1957)

 ## Dear Tia (1988)

I do not write.
The years have frightened me away.
My life in a land so familiarly foreign,
a denial of your presence.
5   Your name is mine.
One black and white photograph of your youth,

all I hold on to.
One story of your past.

The pain comes not from nostalgia.
I do not miss your voice urging me in play,   10
your smile,
or your pride when others called you my mother.
I cannot close my eyes and feel your soft skin;
listen to your laughter;
smell the sweetness of your bath   15
I write because I cannot remember at all.

ROBINSON JEFFERS (1887–1962)

For a photo, see Chapter 19, page 961.

The Answer (1937)

Then what is the answer?—Not to be deluded by dreams.
To know that great civilizations have broken down into violence, and their tyrants come,
    many times before.
When open violence appears, to avoid it with honor or choose the least ugly faction;
    these evils are essential.
To keep one's own integrity, be merciful and uncorrupted and not wish for evil; and not
    be duped
By dreams of universal justice or happiness. These dreams will not be fulfilled.   5
To know this, and know that however ugly the parts appear the whole remains beautiful.
    A severed hand
Is an ugly thing, and man dissevered from the earth and stars and his history . . . for
    contemplation or in fact . . .

Often appears atrociously ugly. Integrity is wholeness, the greatest beauty is
Organic wholeness, the wholeness of life and things, the divine beauty of the universe.
    Love that, not man
Apart from that, or else you will share man's pitiful confusions, or drown in despair
    when his days darken.   10

DONALD JUSTICE (1925–2004)

On the Death of Friends in Childhood (1960)

We shall not ever meet them bearded in heaven,
Nor sunning themselves among the bald of hell;
If anywhere, in the deserted schoolyard at twilight,
Forming a ring, perhaps, or joining hands
In games whose very names we have forgotten,   5
Come, memory, let us seek them there in the shadows.

JOHN KEATS (1795–1821)

For a portrait, see Chapter 15, page 762.

 ## Ode on a Grecian Urn° (1820; 1819)

1

Thou still unravish'd bride of quietness,
   Thou foster-child of silence and slow time,
Sylvan historian, who canst thus express
A flowery tale more sweetly than our rhyme:
5 What leaf-fring'd legend° haunts about thy shape   *border and tale*
   Of deities or mortals, or of both,
     In Tempe° or the dales of Arcady?°
   What men or gods are these? What maidens loth?
What mad pursuit? What struggle to escape?
10   What pipes and timbrels? What wild ecstasy?

2

Heard melodies are sweet, but those unheard
   Are sweeter; therefore, ye soft pipes, play on;
Not to the sensual ear, but, more endear'd,
   Pipe to the spirit ditties of no tone:
15 Fair youth, beneath the trees, thou canst not leave
   Thy song, nor ever can those trees be bare;
     Bold lover, never, never canst thou kiss,
Though winning near the goal—yet, do not grieve;
     She cannot fade, though thou hast not thy bliss,
20   For ever wilt thou love, and she be fair!

3

Ah, happy, happy boughs! that cannot shed
   Your leaves, nor ever bid the spring adieu;
And, happy melodist, unwearied,
   For ever piping songs for ever new;
25 More happy love! more happy, happy love!
   For ever warm and still to be enjoy'd,
     For ever panting, and for ever young;
All breathing human passion far above,
     That leaves a heart high-sorrowful and cloy'd,
30   A burning forehead, and a parching tongue.

°The imaginary Grecian urn to which the poem is addressed combines design motifs from many different existing urns. This imaginary one is decorated with a border of leaves and trees, men (or gods) chasing women, a
young musician sitting under a tree, lovers, and a priest and congregation leading a heifer to sacrifice. 7 *Tempe:*
a beautiful rustic valley in Greece. *Arcady:* refers to the valleys of Arcadia, a state in ancient Greece known for
its beauty and peacefulness.

"The Krater of Thanagra," fourth century BCE, showing a wedding procession and musicians. National Archeological Museum, Athens, Greece. Alinari/Art Resource, NY.

4

Who are these coming to the sacrifice?
  To what green altar, O mysterious priest,
Lead'st thou that heifer lowing at the skies,
  And all her silken flanks with garlands drest?
What little town by river or sea shore,   35
  Or mountain-built° with peaceful citadel,   *built on a mountain*
    Is emptied of this folk, this pious morn?
And, little town, thy streets for evermore
  Will silent be; and not a soul to tell
    Why thou art desolate, can e'er return.   40

5

O Attic shape! Fair attitude! with brede°
  Of marble men and maidens overwrought,°
With forest branches and the trodden weed;
  Thou, silent form, dost tease us out of thought
45 As doth eternity: Cold Pastoral!
  When old age shall this generation waste,
Thou shalt remain, in midst of other woe
Than ours, a friend to man, to whom thou say'st,
"Beauty is truth, truth beauty,"—that is all
50 Ye know on earth, and all ye need to know.

braid, pattern
ornamented

GALWAY KINNELL (b. 1927)

 ## After Making Love We Hear Footsteps (1980)

For I can snore like a bullhorn
or play loud music
or sit up talking with any reasonably sober Irishman
and Fergus will only sink deeper
5 into his dreamless sleep, which goes by all in one flash,
but let there be that heavy breathing
or a stifled come-cry anywhere in the house
and he will wrench himself awake
and make for it on the run—as now, we lie together,
10 after making love, quiet, touching along the length of our bodies,
familiar touch of the long-married,
and he appears—in his baseball pajamas, it happens,
the neck opening so small
he has to screw them on, which one day may make him wonder
15 about the mental capacity of baseball players—
and flops down between us and hugs us and snuggles himself to sleep,
his face gleaming with satisfaction at being this very child.

In the half darkness we look at each other
and smile
20 and touch arms across his little, startlingly muscled body—
this one whom habit of memory propels to the ground of his making,
sleeper only the mortal sounds can sing awake,
this blessing love gives again into our arms.

KATHERINE LARSON (b. 1977)

 ## Statuary (2006)

The late cranes throwing
their necks to the wind stay
somewhere between

the place that rain begins
& the place that it ends   5
they seem to exist just there
above the horizon at least
I only see them that way
tossed up
against the gray October   10
light not heavy enough
for feet to be useful or
useless enough to make
gravity untie its string. I'm sick
of this stubbornness   15
but the earthworms
seem to think it all right
they move forward
& let the world pass
through them they eat   20
& eat at it, content to connect
everything through
the individual links
of their purple bodies to stay
one place would be death.   25
But somewhere between
the crane & the worm
between the days I pass through
& the days that pass
through me   30
is the mind. And memory
which outruns the body &
grief which arrests it.

IRVING LAYTON (1912–2006)

 # Rhine Boat Trip° (1977)

The castles on the Rhine
are all haunted
by the ghosts of Jewish mothers
looking for their ghostly children

And the clusters of grapes   5
in the sloping vineyards
are myriads of blinded eyes
staring at the blind sun

The tireless Lorelei:°
can never comb from their hair   10

°The title refers to the Rhine River, which flows through Germany. 9 *Lorelei:* legendary seductive nymphs
who lived in the cliffs overlooking the Rhine, and whose singing lured sailors to shipwreck.

the crimson beards
of murdered rabbis

However sweetly they sing
one hears only
15   the low wailing of cattle-cars°
moving invisibly across the land

15 *cattle-cars:* railroad cars designed to transport cattle but used by the Nazis to transport Jews from the cities
of Europe to extermination camps.

LI-YOUNG LEE (b. 1957)

 ## A Final Thing (1990)

I am that last, that
final thing, the body
in a white sheet listening,

the whole of me trained,
5   curled like one great ear on
a sound, a noise I know, a

woman talking
in another room,
the woman I love; and

10   though I can't hear
her words, by their voicing
I can guess

she is telling a story,

using a voice which speaks to another,
15   weighted with that other's attention,
and avowing it
by deepening in intention.

Rich with the fullness of what's declared,
this voice points
20   away from itself
to some place

in the hearer,
sends the hearer back
to himself
25   to find what he knows.

A saying full of hearing,
a murmuring full of telling

and compassion for the listener
and for what's told,

now interrupted by a second voice, 30

thinner, higher, uncertain,
Querying, it seems
an invitation to be met,
stirring anticipation, embodying
incompletion of time and the day. 35

My son, my first-born, and his mother
are involved in a story no longer only theirs,
for I am implicated,
all three of us now
clinging to expectancy, riding sound and air. 40

Will my first morning of heaven be this?
No. And this is not
my last morning on earth.
I am simply last
in my house 45

to waken, and the first
sound I hear
is the voice of one I love
speaking to one we love.
I hear it through the bedroom wall; 50

something, someday, I'll close my eyes to recall.

ALAN P. LIGHTMAN (b. 1948)

 ## In Computers (1982, 1981)

In the magnets of computers will
    be stored

Blend of sunset over wheat
    fields.
Low thunder of gazelle. 5
Light, sweet wind on high
    ground.
Vacuum stillness spreading from
    a thick snowfall.

Men will sit in rooms 10
upon the smooth, scrubbed earth
or stand in tunnels on the moon

and instruct themselves in how it
   was.
15 Nothing will be lost.
Nothing will be lost.

LIZ LOCHHEAD (b. 1947)

 ## The Choosing (1984)

We were first equal Mary and I
with same coloured ribbons in mouse-coloured hair
and with equal shyness,
we curtseyed to the lady councillor
5 for copies of Collins' Children's Classics.
First equal, equally proud.

Best friends too Mary and I
a common bond in being cleverest (equal)
in our small school's small class.
10 I remember
the competition for top desk
or to read aloud the lesson
at school service.
And my terrible fear
15 of her superiority at sums.
I remember the housing scheme
where we both stayed.
The same houses, different homes,
where the choices were made.
20 I don't know exactly why they moved,
but anyway they went.
Something about a three-apartment
and a cheaper rent.
But from the top deck of the high-school bus
25 I'd glimpse among the others on the corner
Mary's father, mufflered, contrasting strangely
with the elegant greyhounds by his side.
He didn't believe in high school education,
especially for girls,
30 or in forking out for uniforms.

Ten years later on a Saturday—
I am coming from the library—
sitting near me on the bus,
Mary
35 with a husband who is tall,
curly haired, has eyes
for no one else but Mary.
Her arms are round the full-shaped vase

that is her body.
Oh, you can see where the attraction lies   40
in Mary's life—
not that I envy her, really.

And I am coming from the library
with my arms full of books.
I think of those prizes that were ours for the taking   45
and wonder when the choices got made
we don't remember making.

AUDRE LORDE (1934–1992)

 ## Every Traveler Has One Vermont Poem (1986)

Spikes of lavender aster under Route 91
hide a longing or confession
"I remember when air was invisible"
from Chamberlin Hill down to Lord's Creek
tree mosses point the way home.   5

Two nights of frost
and already the hills are turning
curved green against the astonished morning
sneeze-weed and ox-eye daisies
nor caring I am a stranger   10
making a living choice.

Tanned boys I do not know
on their first proud harvest
wave from their father's tractor
one smiles as we drive past   15
the other hollers
nigger
into cropped and fragrant air.

AMY LOWELL (1874–1925)

 ## Patterns (1916)

I walk down the garden paths,
And all the daffodils
Are blowing, and the bright blue squills.
I walk down the patterned garden-paths
In my stiff, brocaded gown.   5
With my powdered hair and jewelled fan,
I too am a rare
Pattern. As I wander down
The garden paths.
My dress is richly figured,   10
And the train

Makes a pink and silver stain
On the gravel, and the thrift
Of the borders.
15   Just a plate of current fashion
Tripping by in high-heeled, ribboned shoes.
Not a softness anywhere about me,
Only whalebone° and brocade.
And I sink on a seat in the shade
20   Of a lime tree. For my passion
Wars against the stiff brocade.
The daffodils and squills
Flutter in the breeze
As they please.
25   And I weep;
For the lime-tree is in blossom
And one small flower has dropped upon my bosom.

And the plashing of waterdrops
In the marble fountain
30   Comes down the garden-paths.
The dripping never stops.
Underneath my stiffened gown
Is the softness of a woman bathing in a marble basin,
A basin in the midst of hedges grown
35   So thick, she cannot see her lover hiding,
But she guesses he is near,
And the sliding of the water
Seems the stroking of a dear
Hand upon her.
40   What is Summer in a fine brocaded gown!
I should like to see it lying in a heap upon the ground.
All the pink and silver crumpled up on the ground.

I would be the pink and silver as I ran along the paths,
And he would stumble after,
45   Bewildered by my laughter.
I should see the sun flashing from his sword-hilt and buckles on his shoes.
I would choose
To lead him in a maze along the patterned paths,
A bright and laughing maze for my heavy-booted lover.
50   Till he caught me in the shade,
And the buttons of his waistcoat bruised my body as he clasped me,
Aching, melting, unafraid.
With the shadows of the leaves and the sundrops,
And the plopping of the waterdrops,
55   All about us in the open afternoon—
I am very like to swoon

°18 *whalebone:* Baleen from whales was used to make corsets for women because it was strong and flexible, like an early plastic.

With the weight of this brocade,
For the sun sifts through the shade.

Underneath the fallen blossom
In my bosom,   60
Is a letter I have hid.
It was brought to me this morning by a rider from the Duke.
Madam, we regret to inform you that Lord Hartwell
Died in action Thursday se'nnight.°
As I read it in the white, morning sunlight,   65
The letters squirmed like snakes.
"Any answer, Madam," said my footman.
"No," I told him.
"See that the messenger takes some refreshment.

No, no answer."   70
And I walked into the garden,
Up and down the patterned paths,
In my stiff, correct brocade.
The blue and yellow flowers stood up proudly in the sun,
Each one.   75
I stood upright too,
Held rigid to the pattern
By the stiffness of my gown.
Up and down I walked.
Up and down.   80

In a month he would have been my husband.
In a month, here, underneath this lime,
We would have broken the pattern;
He for me, and I for him,
He as Colonel, I as Lady,   85
On this shady seat.
He had a whim
That sunlight carried blessing.
And I answered, "It shall be as you have said."
Now he is dead.   90

In Summer and In Winter I shall walk
Up and down
The patterned garden-paths
In my stiff, brocaded gown.
The squills and daffodils   95
Will give peace to pillared roses, and to asters, and to snow.
I shall go
Up and down,
In my gown.
Gorgeously arrayed,   100

°64 *se'nnight:* seven nights, hence a week ago.

Boned and stayed.
And the softness of my body will be guarded from embrace
By each button, hook, and lace.
For the man who should loose me is dead,
105 Fighting with the Duke in Flanders,°
In a pattern called a war.
Christ! What are patterns for?

°105 *Flanders:* A place of frequent warfare in Belgium. The speaker's clothing (lines 5, 6) suggests the time of the Duke of Marlborough's Flanders campaigns of 1702–1710. The Battle of Waterloo (1815) was also fought nearby under the Duke of Wellington. During World War I, fierce fighting against the Germans occurred in Flanders in 1914 and 1915, with great loss of life.

ARCHIBALD MACLEISH (1892–1982)

 ## Ars Poetica (1926)

A poem should be palpable and mute
As a globed fruit,

Dumb
As old medallions to the thumb,

5 Silent as the sleeve-worn stone
Of casement ledges where the moss has grown—

A poem should be wordless
As the flight of birds

* * *

A poem should be motionless in time
10 As the moon climbs.

Leaving, as the moon releases
Twig by twig the night-entangled trees,

Leaving, as the moon behind the winter leaves,
Memory by memory the mind—

15 A poem should be motionless in time
As the moon climbs.

* * *

A poem should be equal to:
Not true.

For all the history of grief
20 An empty doorway and a maple leaf

For love
The leaning grasses and two lights above the sea—

A poem should not mean
But be.

HEATHER MCHUGH (b. 1948)

 ### Lines (1981)

Some are waiting, some can't wait.
The stores are full of necessities.

The sun dies down, the graveyard
grows, the subway is a wind
instrument with so many stops, but   5
even the underground comes
to an end, and all those flights
of fancy birds settle for one
telephone wire, the one on which
just now, the man in utterly   10
unheard-of love has caught
the word goodbye. He puts
the receiver back in the cradle
and stands. Outside his window
an old man with a hearing-aid walks   15
without aim, happy just to be alive.

CLAUDE MCKAY (1890–1948)

 ### The White City (1922)

I will not toy with it nor bend an inch.
Deep in the secret chambers of my heart
I muse my life-long hate, and without flinch
I bear it nobly as I live my part.
My being would be a skeleton, a shell,   5
If this dark Passion that fills my every mood,
And makes my heaven in the white world's hell,
Did not forever feed me vital blood.
I see the mighty city through a mist—
The strident trains that speed the goaded mass,   10
The poles and spires and towers vapor-kissed,
The fortressed port through which the great ships pass,
The tides, the wharves, the dens I contemplate,
Are sweet like wanton loves because I hate.

W. S. MERWIN (b. 1927)

 Listen (1988)

Listen
with the night falling we are saying thank you
we are stopping on the bridges to bow from the railings
we are running out of the glass rooms
5   with our mouths full of food to look at the sky
and say thank you
we are standing by the water looking out
in different directions

back from a series of hospitals back from a mugging
10 after funerals we are saying thank you
after the news of the dead
whether or not we knew them we are saying thank you
looking up from tables we are saying thank you
in a culture up to its chin in shame
15 living in the stench it has chosen we are saying thank you
over telephones we are saying thank you
in doorways and in the backs of cars and in elevators
remembering wars and the police at the back door
and the beatings on stairs we are saying thank you
20 in the banks that use us we are saying thank you

with the animals dying around us
our lost feelings we are saying thank you
with the forests falling faster than the minutes
of our lives we are saying thank you
25 with the words going out like cells of a brain
with the cities growing over us like the earth
we are saying thank you faster and faster
with nobody listening we are saying thank you
we are saying thank you and waving
30 dark though it is

EDNA ST. VINCENT MILLAY (1892–1950)

 **What Lips My Lips Have Kissed,
and Where, and Why** (1923)

What lips my lips have kissed, and where, and why,
I have forgotten, and what arms have lain
Under my head till morning; but the rain
Is full of ghosts tonight, that tap and sigh
5   Upon the glass and listen for reply,
And in my heart there stirs a quiet pain
For unremembered lads that not again
Will turn to me at midnight with a cry.

Thus in the winter stands the lonely tree,
Nor knows what birds have vanished one by one,   10
Yet knows its boughs more silent than before:
I cannot say what loves have come and gone,
I only know that summer sang in me
A little while, that in me sings no more.

N. SCOTT MOMADAY (b. 1934)

 ## The Bear (1992)

What ruse of vision,
escarping the wall of leaves,
    rending incision
into countless surfaces,

    would cull and color   5
his somnolence, whose old age
    has outworn valor,
all but the fact of courage?

    Seen, he does not come,
move, but seems forever there,   10
    dimensionless, dumb
in the windless noon's hot glare.

    More scarred than others
these years since the trap maimed him,
    pain slants his withers,   15
drawing up the crooked limb.

    Then he is gone, whole,
without urgency, from sight,
    as buzzards control,
imperceptibly, their flight.   20

MARIANNE MOORE (1887–1972)

 ## Poetry° (1921)

I, too, dislike it: there are things that are important beyond all this fiddle.
    Reading it, however, with a perfect contempt for it, one discovers in
    it after all, a place for the genuine.
        Hands that can grasp, eyes
        that can dilate, hair that can rise   5
            if it must, these things are important not because a

---

°In the last edition of her *Collected Poems*, Moore deleted everything in this poem following "genuine" in line 3.

high-sounding interpretation can be put upon them but because they are
   useful. When they become so derivative as to become unintelligible,
     the same thing may be said for all of us, that we
10   do not admire what
         we cannot understand: the bat
          holding on upside down or in quest of something to

eat, elephants pushing, a wild horse taking a roll, a tireless wolf under
   a tree, the immovable critic twitching his skin like a horse that feels a
15   flea, the base-
       ball fan, the statistician—
       nor is it valid
         to discriminate against "business documents and

school-books"°; all these phenomena are important. One must make a distinction
20   however: when dragged into prominence by half poets, the result is not poetry,
   nor till the poets among us can be
       "literalists of
       the imagination"°—above
       insolence and triviality and can present

25 for inspection, "imaginary gardens with real toads in them," shall we have
   it. In the meantime, if you demand on the one hand,
       the raw material of poetry in
         all its rawness and
         that which is on the other hand
30   genuine, you are interested in poetry.

°18–19 *"business . . . school-books"*: The phrase is quoted from the Russian novelist Leo Tolstoy (1828–1910). Moore's original note cites a passage in Tolstoy's *Diaries* (1917), in which he discusses the difference between prose and poetry: "Where the boundary between prose and poetry lies, I shall never be able to understand. . . . Poetry is verse: prose is not verse. Or else poetry is everything with the exception of business documents and school books." 22–23 *"literalists of the imagination"*: Moore's original note refers to W. B. Yeats's discussion of William Blake in *Ideas of Good and Evil* (1903), where Yeats observes that Blake was "a too literal realist of imagination."

LISEL MUELLER (b. 1924)

 ## Monet Refuses the Operation° (1986)

Doctor, you say there are no halos
around the streetlights in Paris
and what I see is an aberration
caused by old age, an affliction.
5 I tell you it has taken me all my life
to arrive at the vision of gas lamps as angels,
to soften and blur and finally banish

°Claude Monet (1840–1926), the French painter often known as the "father" of impressionism, was plagued by cataracts during the last decades of his life, and he became increasingly blind. His eye doctor, Charles Coutela, performed surgery on his right eye in 1923, but afterward Monet was angry because he could no longer perceive color accurately. Though he was urged to undergo an operation on his left eye, he strongly refused.

the edges you regret I don't see,
to learn that the line I called the horizon
does not exist and sky and water,   10
so long apart, are the same state of being.
Fifty-four years before I could see
Rouen cathedral is built
of parallel shafts of sun,
and now you want to restore   15
my youthful errors: fixed
notions of top and bottom,
the illusion of three-dimensional space,
wisteria separate
from the bridge it covers.   20
What can I say to convince you
the Houses of Parliament dissolve
night after night to become
the fluid dream of the Thames?
I will not return to a universe   25
of objects that don't know each other,
as if islands were not the lost children
of one great continent. The World
is flux, and light becomes what it touches,
becomes water, lilies on water,   30
above and below water,
becomes lilac and mauve and yellow
and white and cerulean lamps,
small fists passing sunlight
so quickly to one another   35
that it would take long, streaming hair
inside my brush to catch it.
To paint the speed of light!
Our weighted shapes, these verticals,
burn to mix with air   40
and change our bones, skin, clothes
to gases. Doctor,
if only you could see
how heaven pulls earth into its arms
and how, infinitely the heart expands   45
to claim this world, blue vapor without end.

HOWARD NEMEROV (1920–1991)

 ## Life Cycle of Common Man (1960)

Roughly figured, this man of moderate habits,
This average consumer of the middle class,
Consumed in the course of his average life span
Just under half a million cigarettes,
Four thousand fifths of gin and about   5
A quarter as much vermouth; he drank

Maybe a hundred thousand cups of coffee,
And counting his parents' share it cost
Something like half a million dollars
10 To put him through life. How many beasts
Died to provide him with meat, belt and shoes
Cannot be certainly said.

But anyhow,
It is in this way that a man travels through time,
15 Leaving behind him a lengthening trail
Of empty bottles and bones, of broken shoes,
Frayed collars and worn out or outgrown
Diapers and dinnerjackets, silk ties and slickers.

Given the energy and security thus achieved,
20 He did . . .? What? The usual things, of course,
The eating, dreaming, drinking and begetting,
And he worked for the money which was to pay
For the eating, et cetera, which were necessary
If he were to go on working for the money, et cetera,
25 But chiefly he talked. As the bottles and bones
Accumulated behind him, the words proceeded
Steadily from the front of his face as he
Advanced into the silence and made it verbal.
Who can tally the tale of his words? A lifetime
30 Would barely suffice for their repetition;
If you merely printed all his commas the result
Would be a very large volume, and the number of times
He said "thank you" or "very little sugar, please,"
Would stagger the imagination. There were also
35 Witticisms, platitudes, and statements beginning
"It seems to me" or "As I always say."
Consider the courage in all that, and behold the man
Walking into deep silence, with the ectoplastic
Cartoon's balloon of speech proceeding
40 Steadily out of the front of his face, the words
Borne along on the breath which is his spirit
Telling the numberless tale of his untold Word
Which makes the world his apple, and forces him to eat.

JIM NORTHRUP (b. 1943)

 wahbegan°(1993)

Didja ever hear a sound
smell something
taste something
that brought you back

°The title "wahbegan" is an Ojibway name.

to Vietnam, instantly?   5
Didja ever wonder
when it would end?
It ended for my brother.
He died in the war
but didn't fall down   10
for fifteen tortured years.
His flashbacks are over,
another casualty whose name
will never be on the Wall.
Some can find peace   15
only in death.
The sound of his
family crying hurt.
The smell of the flowers
didn't comfort us.   20
The bitter taste
in my mouth
still sours me.
How about a memorial
for those who made it   25
through the war
but still died
before their time?

MARY OLIVER (b. 1935)

 ## Ghosts (1983)

1

Have you noticed?

2

Where so many millions of powerful bawling beasts
lay down on the earth and died
it's hard to tell now
what's bone, and what merely   5
was once.

The golden eagle, for instance,
has a bit of heaviness in him;
moreover the huge barns
seem ready, sometimes, to ramble off   10
toward deeper grass.

3

1805
near the Bitterroot Mountains:

a man named Lewis kneels down
15 on the prairie watching
a sparrow's nest cleverly concealed in the wild hyssop
and lined with buffalo hair. The chicks,
not more than a day hatched, lean
quietly into the thick wool as if
20 content, after all,
to have left the perfect world and fallen,
helpless and blind
into the flowered fields and the perils
of this one.

4

25 In the book of the earth it is written:
nothing can die.

In the book of the Sioux it is written:
they have gone away into the earth to hide.
Nothing will coax them out again
30 *but the people dancing.*

5

Said the old-timers:
the tongue
is the sweetest meat.

Passengers shooting from train windows
35 could hardly miss, they were
that many.

Afterward the carcasses
stank unbelievably, and sang with flies, ribboned
with slopes of white fat,
40 black ropes of blood—hellhunks
in the prairie heat.

6

Have you noticed? how the rain
falls soft as the fall
of moccasins. *Have you noticed?*
45 how the immense circles still,
stubbornly, after a hundred years,
mark the grass where the rich droppings
from the roaring bulls
fell to the earth as the herd stood
50 day after day, moon after moon
in their tribal circle, outwaiting
the packs of yellow-eyed wolves that are also
have you noticed? gone now.

7

Once only, and then in a dream,
I watched while, secretly
and with the tenderness of any caring woman,
a cow gave birth
to a red calf, tongued him dry and nursed him
in a warm corner
of the clear night
in the fragrant grass
in the wild domains
of the prairie spring, and I asked them,
in my dream I knelt down and asked them
to make room for me.

55

60

65

SIMON ORTIZ (b. 1941)

 # A Story of How a Wall Stands (1976)

> *At Aacqu there is a wall almost 400 years old which*
> *supports hundreds of tons of dirt and bones—it's a*
> *graveyard built on a steep incline—and it looks like*
> *it's about to fall down the incline but will not for a long time.*

My father, who works with stone,
says, "That's just the part you see,
the stones which seem to be
just packed in on the outside,"
and with his hands put the stone and mud
in place. "Underneath
what looks like loose stone,
there is stone woven together."
He ties one hand over the other,
fitting like the bones of his hands
and fingers. "That's what is
holding it together."

5

10

"It is built that carefully,"
he says, "the mud mixed
to a certain texture," patiently
"with the fingers," worked
in the palm of his hand. "So that
placed between the stones, they hold
together for a long, long time."

15

He tells me those things,
the story of them worked
with his fingers, in the palm
of his hands, working the stone
and the mud until they become
the wall that stands a long, long time.

20

25

DOROTHY PARKER (1893–1967)

 ### Résumé (1936)

Razors pain you;
Rivers are damp;
Acids stain you;
And drugs cause cramp.
5   Guns aren't lawful;
Nooses give;
Gas smells awful;
You might as well live.

LINDA PASTAN (b. 1932)

The following two poems are by Linda Pastan.

 ### Ethics (1980)

In ethics class so many years ago
our teacher asked this question every fall:
if there were a fire in a museum
which would you save, a Rembrandt painting
5   or an old woman who hadn't many
years left anyhow? Restless on hard chairs
caring little for pictures or old age
we'd opt one year for life, the next for art
and always half-heartedly. Sometimes
10 the woman borrowed my grandmother's face
leaving her usual kitchen to wander
some drafty, half-imagined museum.
One year, feeling clever, I replied
why not let the woman decide herself?
15 Linda, the teacher would report, eschews
the burdens of responsibility.
This fall in a real museum I stand
before a real Rembrandt, old woman,
or nearly so, myself. The colors
20 within this frame are darker than autumn,
darker even than winter—the browns of earth,
though earth's most radiant elements burn
through the canvas. I know now that woman
and painting and season are almost one
25 and all beyond saving by children.

 ### Marks (1978)

My husband gives me an A
for last night's supper,
an incomplete for my ironing,

a B plus in bed.
My son says I am average, 5
an average mother, but if
I put my mind to it
I could improve.
My daughter believes
in Pass/Fail and tells me 10
I pass. Wait 'til they learn
I'm dropping out.

MOLLY PEACOCK (b. 1947)

 ## Desire (1984)

It doesn't speak and it isn't schooled,
like a small foetal animal with wettened fur.
It is the blind instinct for life unruled,
visceral frankincense and animal myrrh.
It is what babies bring to kings, 5
an eyes-shut, ears-shut medicine of the heart
that smells and touches endings and beginnings
without the details of time's experienced *part-*
fit-into-part-fit-into-part. Like a paw,
it is blunt; like a pet who knows you 10
and nudges your knee with its snout—but more raw
and blinder and younger and more divine, too,
than the tamed wild—it's the drive for what is real,
deeper than the brain's detail: the drive to feel.

MARGE PIERCY (b. 1936)

For a photo, see Chapter 15, page 785.

 ## The Secretary Chant (1973)

My hips are a desk.
From my ears hang
chains of paper clips.
Rubber bands form my hair.
My breasts are wells of mimeograph ink. 5
My feet bear casters.
Buzz. Click.
My head is a badly organized file.
My head is a switchboard
where crossed lines crackle. 10
Press my fingers
and in my eyes appear
credit and debit.
Zing. Tinkle.

15 My navel is a reject button.
From my mouth issue canceled reams.
Swollen, heavy, rectangular
I am about to be delivered
of a baby
20 Xerox machine.
File me under W
because I wonce
was
a woman.

EDGAR ALLAN POE (1809–1849)

For a portrait, see Chapter 11, page 493.

 ## The Raven (1845)

Once upon a midnight dreary, while I pondered, weak and weary,
Over many a quaint and curious volume of forgotten lore—
While I nodded, nearly napping, suddenly there came a tapping,
As of some one gently rapping, rapping at my chamber door.
5 "Tis some visitor," I muttered, "tapping at my chamber door—
    Only this and nothing more."

Ah, distinctly I remember it was in the bleak December;
And each separate dying ember wrought its ghost upon the floor.
Eagerly I wished the morrow;—vainly I had sought to borrow
10 From my books surcease of sorrow—sorrow for the lost Lenore—
For the rare and radiant maiden whom the angels name Lenore—
    Nameless *here* for evermore.

And the silken, sad, uncertain rustling of each purple curtain
Thrilled me—filled me with fantastic terrors never felt before;
15 So that now, to still the beating of my heart, I stood repeating
"'Tis some visitor entreating entrance at my chamber door—
Some late visitor entreating entrance at my chamber door;—
    This it is and nothing more."

Presently my soul grew stronger; hesitating then no longer,
20 "Sir," said I, "or Madam, truly your forgiveness I implore;
But the fact is I was napping, and so gently you came rapping,
And so faintly you came tapping, tapping at my chamber door,
That I scarce was sure I heard you"—here I opened wide the door;
    Darkness there and nothing more.

25 Deep into that darkness peering, long I stood there wondering, fearing,
Doubting, dreaming dreams no mortal ever dared to dream before;
But the silence was unbroken, and the stillness gave no token,
And the only word there spoken was the whispered word, "Lenore!"
This I whispered, and an echo murmured back the word "Lenore!"
30   Merely this and nothing more.

Back into the chamber turning, all my soul within me burning,
Soon again I heard a tapping somewhat louder than before.
"Surely," said I, "surely that is something at my window lattice;
Let me see, then, what thereat is, and this mystery explore—
Let my heart be still a moment and this mystery explore;—   35
    'Tis the wind and nothing more!"

Open here I flung the shutter, when, with many a flirt and flutter
In there stepped a stately Raven of the saintly days of yore.
Not the least obeisance made he; not a minute stopped or stayed he;
But, with mien of lord or lady, perched above my chamber door—   40
Perched upon a bust of Pallas just above my chamber door—
    Perched, and sat, and nothing more.

Then this ebony bird beguiling my sad fancy into smiling,
By the grave and stern decorum of the countenance it wore,
"Though thy crest be shorn and shaven, thou," I said, "art sure no craven,   45
Ghastly grim and ancient Raven wandering from the Nightly shore—
Tell me what thy lordly name is on the Night's Plutonian shore!"
    Quoth° the Raven "Nevermore."   *said*

Much I marvelled this ungainly fowl to hear discourse so plainly,
Though its answer little meaning—little relevancy bore   50
For we cannot help agreeing that no living human being
Ever yet was blessed with seeing bird above his chamber door—
Bird or beast upon the sculptured bust above his chamber door,
    With such name as "Nevermore."

But the Raven, sitting lonely on the placid bust, spoke only   55
That one word, as if his soul in that one word he did outpour.
Nothing farther then he uttered—not a feather then he fluttered—
Till I scarcely more than muttered "Other friends have flown before—
On the morrow *he* will leave me, as my hopes have flown before."
    Then the bird said "Nevermore."   60

Startled at the stillness broken by reply so aptly spoken,
"Doubtless," said I, "what it utters is its only stock and store
Caught from some unhappy master whom unmerciful Disaster
Followed fast and followed faster till his songs one burden bore—
Till the dirges of his Hope that melancholy burden bore   65
    Of "Never—nevermore."

But the Raven still beguiling all my fancy into smiling,
Straight I wheeled a cushioned seat in front of bird and bust and door;
Then, upon the velvet sinking, I betook myself to linking
Fancy unto fancy, thinking what this ominous bird of yore—   70
What this grim, ungainly, ghastly, gaunt, and ominous bird of yore
    Meant in croaking "Nevermore."

This I sat engaged in guessing, but no syllable expressing
To the fowl whose fiery eyes now burned into my bosom's core;

75   This and more I sat divining, with my head at ease reclining
On the cushion's velvet lining that the lamp-light gloated o'er,
But whose velvet violet lining with the lamp-light gloating o'er,
    She shall press, ah, nevermore!

Then, methought, the air grew denser, perfumed from an unseen censer
80   Swung by Seraphim whose foot-falls tinkled on the tufted floor.
"Wretch," I cried, "thy God hath lent thee—by these angels he hath sent thee
Respite—respite and nepenthe° from thy memories of Lenore;
Quaff, oh quaff this kind nepenthe and forget this lost Lenore!"
    Quoth the Raven "Nevermore."

85   "Prophet!" said I, "thing of evil! prophet still, if bird or devil!—
Whether Tempter sent, or whether tempest tossed thee here ashore,
Desolate yet all undaunted, on this desert land enchanted—
On this home by Horror haunted—tell me truly, I implore—
Is there—*is* there balm in Gilead?°—tell me—tell me, I implore!"
90   Quoth the Raven "Nevermore."

"Prophet!" said I, "thing of evil!—prophet still, if bird or devil!
By that Heaven that bends above us—by that God we both adore
Tell this soul with sorrow laden if, within the distant Aidenn,°
It shall clasp a sainted maiden whom the angels name Lenore—
95   Clasp a rare and radiant maiden whom the angels name Lenore."
    Quoth the Raven "Nevermore."

"Be that word our sign of parting, bird or fiend!" I shrieked, upstarting—
"Get thee back into the tempest and the Night's Plutonian shore!
Leave no black plume as a token of that lie thy soul hath spoken!
100   Leave my loneliness unbroken!—quit the bust above my door!
Take thy beak from out my heart, and take thy form from off my door!"
    Quoth the Raven "Nevermore."

And the Raven, never flitting, still is sitting, *still* is sitting
On the pallid bust of Pallas just above my chamber door;
105   And his eyes have all the seeming of a demon's that is dreaming,
And the lamp-light o'er him streaming throws his shadow on the floor;
And my soul from out that shadow that lies floating on the floor
    Shall be lifted—nevermore!

°82 *nepenthe*: an ancient drug said to cure a person of grief. 89 *balm in Gilead*: Gilead was an ancient biblical region known for its physicians and healing balms; see Jeremiah 8:22. 93 *Aidenn*: Eden, the Garden of Eden. Poe apparently took the form from his reading in Arabic literature.

JOHN CROWE RANSOM (1888–1974)

Bells for John Whiteside's Daughter (1924)

There was such speed in her little body,
And such lightness in her footfall,

It is no wonder her brown study
Astonishes us all.

Her wars were bruited in our high window.   5
We looked among orchard trees and beyond
Where she took arms against her shadow,
Or harried unto the pond.

The lazy geese, like a snow cloud
Dripping their snow on the green grass,   10
Tricking and stopping, sleepy and proud,
Who cried in goose, Alas,

For the tireless heart within the little
Lady with rod that made them rise
From their noon apple-dreams and scuttle   15
Goose-fashion under the skies!

But now go the bells, and we are ready,
In one house we are sternly stopped
To say we are vexed at her brown study,
Lying so primly propped.   20

JOHN RAVEN (b. 1936)

 ## Assailant (1969)

He jumped me while I was asleep.
He was big and fat.
I been in many fights before,
but never one like that.
The only way I could survive,   5
was to get my hat . . .
His *name?*
Officers, I ain't talkin' 'bout no man;
I'm talkin' 'bout a rat!

ADRIENNE RICH (b. 1929)

 ## Diving into the Wreck (1973)

First having read the book of myths,
and loaded the camera,
and checked the edge of the knife-blade,
I put on
the body armor of black rubber   5
the absurd flippers
the grave and awkward mask.
I am having to do this
not like Cousteau with his

10   assiduous team
aboard the sun-flooded schooner
but here alone.

There is a ladder.
The ladder is always there
15   hanging innocently
close to the side of the schooner.
We know what it is for,
we who have used it.
otherwise
20   it is a piece of maritime floss
some sundry equipment.

I go down.
Rung after rung and still
the oxygen immerses me
25   the blue light
the clear atoms
of our human air.
I go down.
My flippers cripple me,
30   I crawl like an insect down the ladder
and there is no one
to tell me when the ocean
will begin.

First the air is blue and then
35   it is bluer and then green and then
black I am blacking out and yet
my mask is powerful
it pumps my blood with power
the sea is another story
40   the sea is not a question of power
I have to learn alone
to turn my body without force
in the deep element.

And now: it is easy to forget
45   what I came for
among so many who have always
lived here
swaying their crenellated fans
between the reefs
50   and besides
you breathe differently down here.

I came to explore the wreck.
The words are purposes.
The words are maps.
55   I came to see the damage that was done

and the treasures that prevail.
I stroke the beam of my lamp
slowly along the flank
of something more permanent
than fish or weed   60

the thing I came for:
the wreck and not the story of the wreck
the thing itself and not the myth
the drowned face always staring
toward the sun   65
the evidence of damage
worn by salt and sway into this threadbare beauty
the ribs of the disaster
curving their assertion
among the tentative haunters.   70

This is the place.
And I am here, the mermaid whose dark hair
streams black, the merman in his armored body.
We circle silently
about the wreck   75
we dive into the hold.
I am she: I am he

whose drowned face sleeps with open eyes
whose breasts still bear the stress
whose silver, copper, vermeil cargo lies   80
obscurely inside barrels
half-wedged and left to rot
we are the half-destroyed instruments
that once held to a course
the water-eaten log   85
the fouled compass

We are, I am, you are
by cowardice or courage
the one who find our way
back to this scene   90
carrying a knife, a camera
a book of myths
in which
our names do not appear.

ALBERTO RÍOS (b. 1952)

 ## The Vietnam Wall (1988)

I
Have seen it
And I like it. The magic,

The way like cutting onions
5 It brings water out of nowhere.
Invisible from one side, a scar
Into the skin of the ground
From the other, a black winding
Appendix line.
10   A dig.
          An archaeologist can explain.
The walk is slow at first,
Easy, a little black marble wall
Of a dollhouse,
15 A smoothness, a shine
The boys in the street want to give.
One name. And then more
Names, long lines, lines of names until
They are the shape of the U. N. Building
20 Taller than I am: I have walked
Into a grace.
And everything I expect has been taken away, like that, quick:
          The names are not alphabetized.
          They are in the order of dying,
25   An alphabet of—somewhere—screaming.
I start to walk out. I almost leave
But stop to look up names of friends,
My own name. There is somebody
Severiano Rios.
30 Little kids do not make the same noise
Here, junior high school boys don't run
Or hold each other in headlocks.
No rules, something just persists
Like pinching on St. Patrick's Day
35 Every year for no green.
          No one knows why.
Flowers are forced
Into the cracks
Between sections
40 Men have cried
At this wall.
I have
Seen them.

LUIS OMAR SALINAS (b. 1937)

 ## In a Farmhouse (1973)

Fifteen miles
out of Robstown
with the Texas sun
fading in the distance
5 I sit in the bedroom
profoundly,

animated by the day's work
in the cottonfields.

I made two dollars and
thirty cents today   10
I am eight years old
and I wonder
how the rest of the Mestizos°
do not go hungry
and if one were to die   15
of hunger
what an odd way
to leave for heaven.

°13 *Mestizos*: persons of mixed Spanish and Amerindian ancestry.

SONIA SANCHEZ (b. 1934)

🍁 rite on: white america (1970)

this country might have
been a pio
  neer land
once.
  but.   there ain't   5
no mo
     indians   blowing
custer's° mind
     with a different
image of america.   10
           this country
might have
       needed shoot/
outs/ daily/
      once.   15
       but there ain't
no mo real/ white/   allamerican
           bad/guys.
just
    u & me.   20
      blk/ and un/armed.
this country might have
been a pion
      eer land.   once.
         and it still is.   25
check out
    the falling
gun/shells   on our blk/tomorrows.

°8 *custer's*: General George Armstrong Custer (1839–1876) was killed in his "last stand" at the Little Bighorn in Montana during a battle with Sioux Indians.

CARL SANDBURG (1878–1967)

 # Chicago (1916)

Hog Butcher for the World,
Tool Maker, Stacker of Wheat,
Player with Railroads and the Nation's Freight Handler;
Stormy, husky, brawling,
5   City of the Big Shoulders:

They tell me you are wicked and I believe them, for I have
  seen your painted women under the gas lamps luring
  the farm boys.
And they tell me you are crooked and I answer: Yes, it is true I have seen the gunman
  kill and go free to kill again.
And they tell me you are brutal and my reply is: On the faces of women and children I
  have seen the marks of wanton hunger.
And having answered so I turn once more to those who sneer at this my city, and I give
  them back the sneer and say to them:
Come and show me another city with lifted head singing so proud to be alive and coarse
10   and strong and cunning.
Flinging magnetic curses amid the toil of piling job on job, here is a tall bold slugger set
  vivid against the little soft cities;
Fierce as a dog with tongue lapping for action, cunning as a savage pitted against the
  wilderness,
    Bareheaded,
    Shoveling,
15   Wrecking,
    Planning,
    Building, breaking, rebuilding,
Under the smoke, dust all over his mouth, laughing with white teeth,
Under the terrible burden of destiny laughing as a young man laughs,
20 Laughing even as an ignorant fighter laughs who has never lost a battle,
Bragging and laughing that under his wrist is the pulse, and under his ribs the heart of
  the people,
      Laughing!
Laughing the stormy, husky, brawling laughter of Youth, half-naked, sweating, proud to
  be Hog Butcher, Tool Maker, Stacker of Wheat, Player with Railroads and Freight
  Handler to the Nation.

SIEGFRIED SASSOON (1886–1967)

Dreamers (1918)

Soldiers are citizens of death's grey land,
  Drawing no dividend from time's to-morrows.
In the great hour of destiny they stand,
  Each with his feuds, and jealousies, and sorrows.

5 Soldiers are sworn to action; they must win
  Some flaming, fatal climax with their lives.

Soldiers are dreamers; when the guns begin
    They think of firelit homes, clean beds, and wives.

I see them in foul dug-outs, gnawed by rats,
    And in the ruined trenches, lashed with rain,   10
Dreaming of things they did with balls and bats,
    And mocked by hopeless longing to regain
Bank-holidays,° and picture shows, and spats,
    And going to the office in the train.

°13 *Bank-holidays:* legal holidays in Great Britain.

GJERTRUD SCHNACKENBERG (b. 1953)

 ## The Paperweight (1982)

The scene within the paperweight is calm,
A small white house, a laughing man and wife,
Deep snow. I turn it over in my palm
And watch it snowing in another life,

Another world, and from this scene learn what   5
It is to stand apart: she serves him tea
Once and forever, dressed from head to foot
As she is always dressed. In this toy, history

Sifts down through the glass like snow, and we
Wonder if her single deed tells much   10
Or little of the way she loves, and whether he
Sees shadows in the sky. Beyond our touch,

Beyond our lives, they laugh, and drink their tea.
We look at them just as the winter night
With its vast empty spaces bends to see   15
Our isolated little world of light,

Covered with snow, and snow in clouds above it,
And drifts and swirls too deep to understand.
Still I must try to think a little of it,
With so much winter in my head and hand.   20

ALAN SEEGER (1888–1916)

I Have a Rendezvous with Death (1916)

I have a rendezvous with Death
At some disputed barricade,
When Spring comes back with rustling shade

And apple blossoms fill the air—
5   I have a rendezvous with Death
When Spring brings back blue days and fair.

It may be he shall take my hand
And lead me into his dark land
And close my eyes and quench my breath—
10   It may be I shall pass him still.

I have a rendezvous with Death
On some scarred slope of battered hill,
When Spring comes round again this year
And the first meadow flowers appear.

15   God knows 'twere better to be deep
Pillowed in silk and scented down,
Where Love throbs out in blissful sleep,
Pulse nigh to pulse and breath to breath,
Where hushed awakenings are dear. . . .
20   But I've a rendezvous with Death
At midnight in some flaming town,
When Spring trips north again this year,
And I to my pledged word am true,
I shall not fail that rendezvous.

BRENDA SEROTTE (b. 1946)

 ## My Mother's Face (1991)

Dressing for work
I glanced in the mirror
startled to see my mother's face
white, with the mouth turned down
5   her red frizzled hair
wild in all directions.
She turned sideways
to study my dress
standing tiptoe like I do
10   craning her long neck
in a futile attempt to see my feet.
Then without warning, the tears
rolling from the outer corners down
past slightly pitted cheeks
15   past that inverted smile
into the cave of her bosom
which heaved a sigh so forlorn
so weighted with loss
that had I not been standing silent
20   I would have surely thought it was me.

WILLIAM SHAKESPEARE (1564–1616)

For a portrait, see Chapter 24, page 1322. The following two sonnets are by William Shakespeare.

Sonnet 29: When in Disgrace with Fortune and Men's Eyes (1609)

When, in disgrace with Fortune and men's eyes,
I all alone beweep my outcast state,
And trouble deaf heaven with my bootless° cries,   *futile, useless*
And look upon myself and curse my fate,
Wishing me like to one more rich in hope,   5
Featured like him, like him with friends possessed,
Desiring this man's art and that man's scope,
With what I most enjoy contented least;
Yet in these thoughts myself almost despising,
Haply I think on thee, and then my state,   10
Like to the lark at break of day arising
From sullen earth, sings hymns at heaven's gate;
For thy sweet love remembered such wealth brings
That then I scorn to change my state with kings.

Sonnet 146: Poor Soul, the Center of My Sinful Earth (1609)

Poor soul, the center of my sinful earth,
Thrall° to these rebel powers that thee array,°   *captive*
Why dost thou pine within and suffer dearth
Painting thy outward walls so costly gay?
Why so large cost having so short a lease,   5
Dost thou upon thy fading mansion spend?
Shall worms, inheritors of this excess,
Eat up thy charge? Is this thy body's end?
Then, soul, live thou upon thy servant's loss,°
And let that pine to aggravate thy store;°   10
Buy terms° divine in selling hours of dross°   *periods; refuse*
Within be fed, without be rich no more:
So shalt thou feed on Death, that feeds on men,
And Death once dead, there's no more dying then.

°2 *array:* surround or dress out, as in a military formation. 9 *thy servant's loss:* the loss of the body. 10 *let . . . store:* let the body ("that") dwindle ("pine") to increase ("aggravate") the riches ("store") of the soul.

KARL SHAPIRO (1913–2000)

Auto Wreck (1941)

Its quick soft silver bell beating, beating,
And down the dark one ruby flare

Pulsing out red light like an artery,
The ambulance at top speed floating down
5 Past beacons and illuminated clocks
Wings in a heavy curve, dips down,
And brakes speed, entering the crowd.
The doors leap open, emptying light;
Stretchers are laid out, the mangled lifted
10 And stowed into the little hospital.
Then the bell, breaking the hush, tolls once,
And the ambulance with its terrible cargo
Rocking, slightly rocking, moves away,
As the doors, an afterthought, are closed.
15 We are deranged, walking among the cops
Who sweep glass and are large and composed.
One is still making notes under the light.
One with a bucket douches ponds of blood
Into the street and gutter.
20 One hangs lanterns on the wrecks that cling,
Empty husks of locusts, to iron poles.
Our throats were tight as tourniquets,
Our feet were bound with splints, but now,
Like convalescents intimate and gauche,
25 We speak through sickly smiles and warn
With the stubborn saw of common sense,
The grim joke and the banal resolution.
The traffic moves around with care,
But we remain, touching a wound
30 That opens to our richest horror.
Already old, the question Who shall die?
Becomes unspoken Who is innocent?
For death in war is done by hands;
Suicide has cause and stillbirth, logic;
35 And cancer, simple as a flower, blooms.
But this invites the occult mind,
Cancels our physics with a sneer,
And spatters all we knew of dénouement
Across the expedient and wicked stones.

LESLIE MARMON SILKO (b. 1948)

 # Where Mountain Lion Lay Down with Deer (1974)

I climb the black rock mountain
stepping from day to day
        silently.
I smell the wind for my ancestors
5   pale blue leaves
       crushed wild mountain smell.

Returning
   up the gray stone cliff
   where I descended
       a thousand years ago.   10

Returning to faded black stone
   where mountain lion lay down with deer.
It is better to stay up here

            watching wind's reflection
            in tall yellow flowers.   15
The old ones who remember me are gone
       the old songs are all forgotten
and the story of my birth.
How I danced in snow-frost moonlight
     distant stars to the end of the Earth,   20
How I swam away
        in freezing mountain water
        narrow mossy canyon tumbling down
            out of the mountain
            out of the deep canyon stone   25

      down
          the memory
              spilling out
              into the world.

STEVIE SMITH (1902–1971)

 # Not Waving but Drowning (1957)

Nobody heard him, the dead man,
But still he lay moaning:
I was much further out than you thought
And not waving but drowning.

Poor chap, he always loved larking   5
And now he's dead
It must have been too cold for him his heart gave way,
They said.

Oh, no no no, it was too cold always
(Still the dead one lay moaning)   10
I was much too far out all my life
And not waving but drowning.

GARY SOTO (b. 1952)

 ## Oranges (1984)

The first time I walked
With a girl, I was twelve,
Cold, and weighted down
With two oranges in my jacket.
5   December. Frost cracking
Beneath my steps, my breath
Before me, then gone,
As I walked toward
Her house, the one whose
10 Porch light burned yellow
Night and day, in any weather.
A dog barked at me, until
She came out pulling
At her gloves, face bright
15 With rouge. I smiled,
Touched her shoulder, and led
Her down the street, across
A used car lot and a line
Of newly planted trees,
20 Until we were breathing
Before a drugstore. We
Entered, the tiny bell
Bringing a saleslady
Down a narrow aisle of goods.
25 I turned to the candies
Tiered like bleachers,
And asked what she wanted—
Light in her eyes, a smile
Starting at the corners
30 Of her mouth. I fingered
A nickel in my pocket,
And when she lifted a chocolate
That cost a dime,
I didn't say anything.
35 I took the nickel from
My pocket, then an orange,
And set them quietly on
The counter. When I looked up,
The lady's eyes met mine,
40 And held them, knowing
Very well what it was all
About.
            Outside,
A few cars hissing past,
45 Fog hanging like old
Coats between the trees.
I took my girl's hand

In mine for two blocks,
Then released it to let
Her unwrap the chocolate.   50
I peeled my orange
That was so bright against
The gray of December
That, from some distance,
Someone might have thought   55
I was making a fire in my hands.

WILLIAM STAFFORD (1914–1993)

 ## Traveling Through the Dark (1960)

Traveling through the dark I found a deer
dead on the edge of the Wilson River road.
It is usually best to roll them into the canyon:
that road is narrow; to swerve might make more dead.

By glow of the tail-light I stumbled back of the car   5
and stood by the heap, a doe, a recent killing;
she had stiffened already, almost cold.
I dragged her off; she was large in the belly.

My fingers touching her side brought me the reason—
her side was warm; her fawn lay there waiting,   10
alive, still, never to be born.
Beside that mountain road I hesitated.

The car aimed ahead its lowered parking lights;
under the hood purred the steady engine.
I stood in the glare of the warm exhaust turning red;   15
around our group I could hear the wilderness listen.
I thought hard for us all—my only swerving—,
then pushed her over the edge into the river.

GERALD STERN (b. 1925)

 ## Burying an Animal on the Way to New York (1977)

Don't flinch when you come across a dead animal lying on the road;
you are being shown the secret of life.
Drive slowly over the brown flesh;
you are helping to bury it.
If you are the last mourner there will be no caress   5
at all from the crushed limbs
and you will have to slide over the dark spot imagining
the first suffering all by yourself
Shreds of spirit and little ghost fragments will be spread out

10   for two miles above the white highway.
Slow down with your radio off and your window open
to hear the twittering as you go by.

WALLACE STEVENS (1879–1955)

For a photo, see Chapter 12, page 677.

 ## The Emperor of Ice-Cream (1923)

Call the roller of big cigars,
The muscular one, and bid him whip
In kitchen cups concupiscent curds.
Let the wenches dawdle in such dress
5   As they are used to wear, and let the boys
Bring flowers in last month's newspapers.
Let be be finale° of seem.
The only emperor is the emperor of ice-cream.
Take from the dresser of deal,°
Lacking the three glass knobs, that sheet
On which she embroidered fantails° once

And spread it so as to cover her face.
If her horny feet protrude, they come
To show how cold she is, and dumb.
15   Let the lamp affix its beam.
The only emperor is the emperor of ice-cream.

°7 *finale:* the grand conclusion. 9 *deal:* unfinished pine or fir used to make cheap furniture. 11 *fantails:* fantail pigeons.

MAY SWENSON (1919–1989)

For a photo, see Chapter 18, page 914.

 ## Question (1978)

Body my house
my horse my hound
what will I do
when you are fallen

5   Where will I sleep
How will I ride
What will I hunt

Where can I go
without my mount
10   all eager and quick

How will I know
in thicket ahead
is danger or treasure
when Body my good
bright dog is dead   15

How will it be
to lie in the sky
without roof or door
and wind for an eye

With cloud for shift   20
how will I hide?

DYLAN THOMAS (1914–1953)

For a photo, see Chapter 18, page 930.

 ## A Refusal to Mourn the Death, by Fire, of a Child in London (1946)

Never until the mankind making
Bird beast and flower
Fathering and all humbling darkness
Tells with silence the last light breaking
And the still hour   5
Is come of the sea tumbling in harness

And I must enter again the round
Zion of the water bead
And the synagogue of the ear of corn
Shall I let pray the shadow of a sound   10
Or sow my salt seed
In the least valley of sackcloth to mourn

The majesty and burning of the child's death.
I shall not murder
The mankind of her going with a grave truth   15
Nor blaspheme down the stations of the breath
With any further
Elegy of innocence and youth.

Deep with the first dead lies London's daughter,
Robed in the long friends,   20
The grains beyond age, the dark veins of her mother,
Secret by the unmourning water
Of the riding Thames.°
After the first death, there is no other.

°23 *Thames:* the river Thames, which flows through London.

DANIEL TOBIN (b. 1958)

 ## My Uncle's Watch (1999)

"Bist du Jude? Bist du Jude?" the SS   *Are you a Jew?*
officer repeated, like a schoolteacher
menacing a slow pupil, the camp for POWs
a train ride from Dachau. "Nicht Jude,"   *Not a Jew*
5   my uncle told him: "I'm not a Jew,"
his whole body braced while the cold eyes
probed the face of the watch he bought
on Hester Street before the war,
the jeweler's name still etched on the case
10   behind the steadily turning hands.

Christmas, my eleventh year, a quarter century later,
I watched his unbroken body
ease into the big Queen Anne chair
in my parents' house, the family crowded round,
15   the creche a tattered barracks under the tree.
He told how his captor twisted the watch
once around his finger,
then tossed it lightly in his lap,
an act, I know now, of unbounded mercy,
20   given Himmler's boast—"I say who is a Jew."

That was the year of other impossibilities:
men walking on the moon, my team winning the pennant,°
the bishop's question weighing on me like a threat
before my Confirmation. Come Easter,
25   the tall nun would enter the classroom,
black gown trailing to her nobbled shoes,°   *donated shoes*
her face framed like a mask
inside the peaked hood, and fire another:
"Who of you would give yourselves as ransom
30   for the rest if the Nazis came here now?"

No one answered, regimented behind our desks.
But I heard my friends' jeers of "Christ-killer" explode
from the schoolyard to the synagogue across the street,
the nuns' veiled slurs, the neighbors' brusque "Cheap as a Jew,"
35   and saw myself a little Jew-Christ marched alone
to the gas chamber—Christ of the ashen-haired comforter,
Christ of the lampshade—forgetting that God
is no hero, but a child for whom others are killed,

°21–22 *other impossibilities . . . pennant:* In 1969, the New York Mets, created just seven years before, won the National League pennant and also took the World Series. Also, in July 1969, Neil Armstrong and Buzz Aldrin were the first two human beings to walk on the moon.

so my uncle's watch could tick on his unslashed wrist
in time without end and without redemption.   40

CHASE TWICHELL (b. 1950)

 ## Blurry Cow (1983)

Two cows stand transfixed
by a trough of floating leaves,
facing as if into the camera,
black and white. One stamps
at the hot sting of a deerfly.   5

Seen from the window of a train,
the hoof lifts forever
over hay crosshatched by speed,
and the scales of the haunches
balance. The rest is lost: 10
the head a sudden slur of light,
the dog loping along the tracks
toward a farm yard
where a woman wavers
in her mirage of laundry.   15
A blurry cow, of all things,
strays into the mind's eye,
the afterimage
of this day on earth.

JOHN UPDIKE (b. 1932)

For a photo, see Chapter 6, page 363.

 ## Perfection Wasted (1990)

And another regrettable thing about death
is the ceasing of your own brand of magic,
which took a whole life to develop and market—
the quips, the witticisms, the slant
adjusted to a few, those loved ones nearest   5
the lip of the stage, their soft faces blanched
in the footlight glow, their laughter close to tears,
their tears confused with their diamond earrings,
their warm pooled breath in and out with your heartbeat,
their response and your performance twinned.   10
The jokes over the phone. The memories packed
in the rapid-access file. The whole act.
Who will do it again? That's it: no one;
imitators and descendants aren't the same.

TINO VILLANUEVA (b. 1941)

 ## Day-Long Day (1972)

> *Again the drag of pisca,° pisca . . . pisca . . .*
> *Daydreams border on sun-fed hallucinations,*
> *eyes and hands automatically discriminate*
> *whiteness of cotton from field of vision.*
> *Pisca, pisca.*
> > *"Un Hijo del Sol,"°*
> > *Genaro Gonzales°*

Third-generation timetable.
Sweat day-long dripping into open space;
sun blocks out the sky, suffocates the only breeze.
From el amo desgraciado,° a sentence:

5   "I wanna bale a day, and the boy here
don't hafta go to school."

* * *

In time-binding motion—
a family of sinews and backs,
row-trapped,
10   zigzagging through summer-long rows
of cotton: Lubbock by way of Wharton.°

"Está como si escupieran fuego,"° a mother moans
in sweat-patched jeans,
stooping
15   with unbending dreams.
"Estudia para que no seas burro como nosotros,"°
our elders warn, their gloves and cuffs
leaf-stained by seasons.

* * *

Bronzed and blurry-eyed by
20   the blast of degrees,
we blend into earth's rotation.
And sweltering toward Saturday, the
day-long day is sunstruck by 6:00 P.M.
One last chug-a-lug from a water jug
25   old as granddad.
Day-long sweat dripping into open space:
Wharton by way of Lubbock.

°*pisca:* picking cotton. *Un Hijo del Sol:* a Son of the Sun. *Genaro Gonzales:* Hispanic author, born in 1949. 4 *el amo desgraciado:* the despicable boss. 11 *Lubbock . . . Wharton:* cities on opposite sides of Texas. 12 *Está . . . fuego:* "It's as if they are spewing fire." 16 *Estudia . . . nosotros:* "Study so that you will not be a burro like us."

JUDITH VIORST (b. 1931)

For a photo, see Chapter 19, page 971.

 True Love° (1968)

It is true love because
I put on eyeliner and a concerto and make pungent observations about the great issues
        of the day
Even when there's no one here but him,
And because
I do not resent watching the Green Bay Packers   5
Even though I am philosophically opposed to football,
And because
When he is late for dinner and I know he must be either having an affair or lying dead
        in the middle of the street,
I always hope he's dead.

It's true love because   10
If he said quit drinking martinis but I kept drinking them and the next morning I
        couldn't get out of bed,
He wouldn't tell me he told me,
And because
He is willing to wear unironed undershorts
Out of respect for the fact that I am philosophically opposed to ironing,   15
And because
If his mother was drowning and I was drowning and he had to choose one of us to save,
He says he'd save me.

It's true love because
When he went to San Francisco on business while I had to stay home with the painters
        and the exterminator and the baby who was getting the chicken pox,   20
He understood why I hated him,
And because
When I said that playing the stock market was juvenile and irresponsible and then the
        stock I wouldn't let him buy went up twenty-six points,
I understood why he hated me,
And because   25
Despite cigarette cough, tooth decay, acid indigestion, dandruff, and other features of
        married life that tend to dampen the fires of passion,
We still feel something
We can call
True love.

°See Shakespeare's *A Midsummer Night's Dream*, 1.1.132: "The course of true love never did run smooth."

SHELLY WAGNER (b. 1950)

 The Boxes (1991)

When I told the police I couldn't find you,
they began a search that included everything—

even the boxes in the house:
the footlockers of clothes in the attic,
5   the hamper in the bathroom,
and the Chinese lacquered trunk by the sofa.
They made me raise every lid.
I told them you would never stay in a box,
not with all the commotion.
10   You would have jumped out,
found your flashlight
and joined the search.

Poor Thomas, taking these men
who don't know us
15   through our neighbors' garages
where you never played,
hoping they were right
and we were wrong
and he would find you and
20   snatch you home by the hand

so the police cars could
get out of our driveway
and the divers would
get out of our river
25   because it was certainly
past our bedtime.
We would double-bolt our doors
like always,
say longer prayers than usual
30   and go to bed. But during the night
I would have sat till morning
beside my sleeping boys.
But that's not what happened.
Thomas is still here, now older.
35   I still go to his room
when he is sleeping
just to look at him.
I still visit the cemetery,
not as often,
40   but the urge is the same:
to lie down on the grass,
put my arm around the hump of ground
and tell you, "Get out of this box!
Put a stop to this commotion. Come home.
45   You should be in bed."

ALICE WALKER (b. 1944)

 ## Revolutionary Petunias (1972)

Sammy Lou of Rue
sent to his reward

the exact creature who
murdered her husband,
using a cultivator's hoe   5
with verve and skill;
and laughed fit to kill
in disbelief
at the angry, militant
pictures of herself   10
the Sonneteers quickly drew:
not any of them people that
she knew.
A backwoods woman
her house was papered with   15
funeral home calendars and
faces appropriate for a Mississippi
Sunday School. She raised a George,
a Martha, a Jackie and a Kennedy. Also
a John Wesley Junior.°   20
"Always respect the word of God,"
she said on her way to she didn't
know where, except it would be by
electric chair, and she continued
"Don't yall forget to *water*   25
my purple petunias."

°18–20 *George . . . Junior:* The children are named after George and Martha Washington, Jackie and John
Fitzgerald Kennedy (1917–1963, thirty-fifth U.S. president), and John Wesley (1703–1791), English evangelical
preacher who founded Methodism.

EDMUND WALLER (1606–1687)

 ## Go, Lovely Rose (1645)

   Go, lovely rose!
Tell her that wastes her time and me
   That now she knows,
When I resemble° her to thee,   *compare*
How sweet and fair she seems to be.   5

   Tell her that's young,
And shuns to have her graces spied,
   That hadst thou sprung
In deserts, where no men abide,
Thou must have uncommended died.   10

   Small is the worth
Of beauty from the light retired;
   Bid her come forth,
Suffer herself to be desired,
And not blush so to be admired.   15

Then die! that she
The common fate of all things rare
    May read in thee;
How small a part of time they share
20 That are so wondrous sweet and fair.

BRUCE WEIGL (b. 1949)

 ## Song of Napalm (1985)

For My Wife

After the storm, after the rain stopped pounding,
We stood in the doorway watching horses
Walk off lazily across the pasture's hill.
We stared through the black screen,
5 Our vision altered by the distance
So I thought I saw a mist
Kicked up around their hooves when they faded
Like cut-out horses
Away from us.
10 The grass was never more blue in that light, more
Scarlet; beyond the pasture
Trees scraped their voices in the wind, branches
Criss-crossed the sky like barbed-wire
But you said they were only branches.

15 Okay. The storm stopped pounding.
I am trying to say this straight: for once
I was sane enough to pause and breathe
Outside my wild plans and after the hard rain
I turned my back on the old curses, I believed
20 They swung finally away from me . . .

But still the branches are wire
And thunder is the pounding mortar,
Still I close my eyes and see the girl
Running from her village, napalm
25 Stuck to her dress like jelly,
Her hands reaching for the no one
Who waits in waves of heat before her.

So I can keep on living,
So I can stay here beside you,
30 I try to imagine she runs down the road and wings
Beat inside her until she rises
Above the stinking jungle and her pain
Eases, and your pain, and mine.
But the lie swings back again.
35 The lie works only as long as it takes to speak

And the girl runs only so far
As the napalm allows
Until her burning tendons and crackling
Muscles draw her up
Into that final position   40
Burning bodies so perfectly assume. Nothing
Can change that; she is burned behind my eyes
And not your good love and not the rain-swept air
And not the jungle green
Pasture unfolding before us can deny it.   45

PHILLIS WHEATLEY (1754–1784)

 ## On Being Brought from Africa to America (1773)

'Twas mercy brought me from my *Pagan* land,
Taught my benighted soul to understand
That there's a God, that there's a *Saviour* too:
Once I redemption neither sought nor knew.
Some view our sable race with scornful eye,   5
"Their colour is a diabolic die."
Remember, *Christians*, *Negroes*, black as *Cain*,
May be refin'd, and join th' angelic train.

WALT WHITMAN (1819–1892)

For a photo, see Chapter 15, page 790. The following four poems are by Walt Whitman.

 ## Beat! Beat! Drums! (1861)

Beat! beat! drums!—blow! bugles! blow!
Through the windows—through doors—burst like a ruthless force,
Into the solemn church, and scatter the congregation,
Into the school where the scholar is studying;
Leave not the bridegroom quiet—no happiness must he have now with his bride,   5
Nor the peaceful farmer any peace, plowing his field or gathering his grain,
So fierce you whir and pound you drums—so shrill you bugles blow.

Beat! beat! drums!—blow! bugles! blow!
Over the traffic of cities—over the rumble of wheels in the streets;
Are beds prepared for sleepers at night in the houses? no sleepers must sleep in
        those beds,   10
No bargainers' bargains by day—no brokers or speculators—would they continue?
Would the talkers be talking? would the singer attempt to sing?
Would the lawyer rise in the court to state his case before the judge?
Beat! beat! drums—blow! bugles! blow!

Then rattle quicker, heavier drums—you bugles wilder blow.   15

Make no parley—stop for no expostulation,
Mind not the timid—mind not the weeper or prayer,
Mind not the old man beseeching the young man,
Let not the child's voice be heard, nor the mother's entreaties,

20   Make even the trestles to shake the dead where they lie awaiting the hearses,
So strong you thump O terrible drums—so loud you bugles blow.

🍁 Dirge for Two Veterans (1865)

The last sunbeam
Lightly falls from the finished Sabbath,
On the pavement here, and there beyond it is looking,
    Down a new-made double grave.

5   Lo, the moon ascending,
Up from the east the silvery round moon,
Beautiful over the house-tops, ghastly, phantom moon,
    Immense and silent moon.

I see a sad procession,
10   And I hear the sound of coming full-keyed bugles,
All the channels of the city streets they're flooding,
    As with voices and with tears.

I hear the great drums pounding
And the small drums steady whirring,
15   And every blow of the great convulsive drums,
    Strikes me through and through.

For the son is brought with the father,
(In the foremost ranks of the fierce assault they fell,
Two veterans son and father dropped together,
20   And the double grave awaits them.)

Now nearer blow the bugles,
And the drums strike more convulsive,
And the daylight o'er the pavement quite has faded,
    And the strong dead-march enwraps me.

25   In the eastern sky up-buoying,
The sorrowful vast phantom moves illumined,
('Tis some mother's large transparent face,
    In heaven brighter growing.)

O strong dead-march you please me!
30   O moon immense with your silvery face you soothe me!
O my soldiers twain! O my veterans passing to burial!
    What I have I also give you.

The moon gives you light,
And the bugles and the drums give you music,
And my heart, O my soldiers, my veterans,
    My heart gives you love.   35

Full of Life Now (1857)

Full of life now, compact, visible,
I, forty years old the eighty-third year of the States,
To one a century hence or any number of centuries hence,
To you yet unborn these, seeking you.

When you read these I that was visible am become invisible,   5
Now it is you, compact, visible, realizing my poems, seeking me,
Fancying how happy you were if I could be with you and become your comrade;
Be it as if I were with you. (Be not too certain but I am now with you.)

I Hear America Singing (1867)

I hear America singing, the varied carols I hear:
Those of mechanics—each one singing his, as it should be, blithe and strong;
The carpenter singing his, as he measures his plank or beam,
The mason singing his, as he makes ready for work, or leaves off work;
The boatman singing what belongs to him in his boat—the deckhand singing on the
    steamboat deck;   5
The shoemaker singing as he sits on his bench—the hatter singing as he stands;
The wood cutter's song—the ploughboy's on his way in the morning, or at noon
    intermissions, or at sundown;
The delicious singing of the mother—or of the young wife at work—or of the girl
    sewing or washing—
Each singing what belongs to him or her and to none else;
The day what belongs to the day—at night, the part of young fellows, robust, friendly,   10
Singing, with open mouths, their strong melodious songs.

JOHN GREENLEAF WHITTIER (1807–1892)

The Bartholdi Statue° (1886)

The land, that, from the rule of kings,
    In freeing us, itself made free,
Our Old World Slister, to us brings
    Her sculptured Dream of Liberty:

°The Statue of Liberty, by Frédéric Auguste Bartholdi (1834–1904) was dedicated in October 1886. The
Compte de Rochambeau (1725–1807) was a general commanding the French forces at Yorktown in 1781, and
his efforts were helpful and decisive in defeating the English.

5 Unlike the shapes on Egypt's sands
    Uplifted by the toil-worn slave,
On Freedom's soil with freemen's hands
    We rear the symbol free hands gave.

    O France, the beautiful! to thee
10   Once more a debt of love we owe:
In peace beneath thy Colors three,
    We hail a later Rochambeau!

Rise, stately Symbol! holding forth
    Thy light and hope to all who sit
15 In chains and darkness! Belt the earth
    With watch-fires from thy torch uplit!

Reveal the primal mandate still
    Which Chaos heard and ceased to be,
Trace on mid-air th'Eternal Will
20   In signs of fire: "Let Man be free!"

Shine far, shine free, a guiding light
    To Reason's ways and Virtue's aim,
A lightning-flash the wretch to smite
    Who shields his licence with thy name!

RICHARD WILBUR (b. 1921)

For a photo, see Chapter 19, page 973.

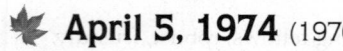 April 5, 1974 (1976)

The air was soft, the ground still cold.
In the dull pasture where I strolled
Was something I could not believe.
Dead grass appeared to slide and heave,
5 Though still too frozen-flat to stir,
And rocks to twitch, and all to blur.
What was this rippling of the land?
Was matter getting out of hand
And making free with natural law?
10 I stopped and blinked, and then I saw
A fact as eerie as a dream.
There was a subtle flood of steam
Moving upon the face of things.
It came from standing pools and springs
15 And what of snow was still around;
It came of winter's giving ground

So that the freeze was coming out,
As when a set mind, blessed by doubt,
Relaxes into mother-wit.
Flowers, I said, will come of it.   20

WILLIAM CARLOS WILLIAMS (1883–1963)

For a photo, see Chapter 18, page 932.

 ## The Red Wheelbarrow (1923)

so much depends
upon

a red wheel
barrow

glazed with rain   5
water

beside the white
chickens.

WILLIAM BUTLER YEATS (1865–1939)

For a photo, see Chapter 16, page 833.

 ## The Wild Swans at Coole (1919)

The trees are in their autumn beauty,
The woodland paths are dry,
Under the October twilight the water
Mirrors a still sky;
Upon the brimming water among the stones   5
Are nine-and-fifty swans.

The nineteenth autumn has come upon me
Since I first made my count;
I saw, before I had well finished,
All suddenly mount   10
And scatter wheeling in great broken rings
Upon their clamorous wings.

I have looked upon those brilliant creatures,
And now my heart is sore.
All's changed since I, hearing at twilight,   15

The first time on this shore,
The bell beat of their wings above my head,
Trod with a lighter tread.

Unwearied still, lover by lover,
20 They paddle in the cold
Companionable streams or climb the air;
Their hearts have not grown old;
Passion or conquest, wander where they will,
Attend upon them still.

25 But now they drift on the still water,
Mysterious, beautiful;
Among what rushes will they build,
By what lake's edge or pool
Delight men's eyes when I awake some day
30 To find they have flown away?

PAUL ZIMMER (b. 1934)

🍁 The Day Zimmer Lost Religion (1973)

The first Sunday I missed Mass on purpose
I waited all day for Christ to climb down
Like a wiry flyweight° from the cross and
Club me on my irreverent teeth, to wade into
5 My blasphemous gut and drop me like a
Red hot thurible,° the devil roaring in
Reserved seats until he got the hiccups.

It was a long cold way from the old days
When cassocked and surpliced° I mumbled Latin
10 At the old priest and rang his obscure bell.
A long way from the dirty wind that blew
The soot like venial sins° across the schoolyard
Where God reigned as a threatening,
One-eyed triangle high in the fleecy sky.

15 The first Sunday I missed Mass on purpose
I waited all day for Christ to climb down
Like the playground bully, the cuts and mice
Upon his face agleam, and pound me
Till my irreligious tongue hung out.
20 But of course He never came, knowing that
I was grown up and ready for Him now.

°3 *flyweight:* a boxer weighing less than 112 pounds. 6 *thurible:* a censer, a container in which incense is burned. 9 *cassocked and surpliced:* wearing the traditional garb of an altar boy during Mass. 12 *venial sins:* minor inadvertent sins.

Chapter 22A

Writing a Research Essay on Poetry

The end of the fiction section of this book, Chapter 10A (p. 594), contains a chapter on the use of research as the basis of an essay of term-paper length on fiction. Because the objects and goals of research are general, most of the materials in Chapter 10A are also essential for research projects in all the genres. It is therefore necessary to consult Chapter 10A for many relevant ways to engage in detailed research, which you can apply not only to writing about fiction but also to writing about both poetry and drama.

Here, however, our concern is to suggest a more limited use of research for the development of essays on the topic of poetry. Any of the essay assignments on poetry described in Chapters 11 to 16 can serve as the basic topic for the introduction of helpful research materials. Because of the general nature of research, the use of research for writing about poetry is not essentially different from research used in writing about fiction and drama.

Topics to Discover in Research

There are some general objectives in the use of research, but your goal should always be to discover materials that have a meaningful bearing on the poem or poems about which you are writing. Here are some things to look for:

- *The period of time when a poem was written, together with significant events.* In this chapter, the illustrative essay about Whitman cites the American Civil War (1861–65) as the dominating national event occurring at the time of the poems (pp. 1189 and 1191). Comparably, Hardy's "The Convergence of the Twain" Chapter 15, (p. 775) was written as a commentary on the sinking of the British liner *Titanic* in 1912. Emerson's "Concord Hymn" (Chapter 17, p. 863) was written for a ceremonial occasion sixty years after the Revolutionary War events described in the poem.
- *Social, natural, and/or political circumstances at the time of the poem.* What was the dominant political situation at the time? Who were the sorts of persons in political power? What attitudes were prevalent at the time with regard to the circumstances of nature? Wordsworth, for example, often creates an implicit comparison between the natural world at peace and negative human activities that are at odds with it. Pope, in the "Epilogue

to the Satires (Chapter 16, p. 824)," cites a general condition of moral laxity that he perceived in the social and political structure of England of his day.

- *Biographical details about a poet.* At what time in his or her life did the poet write a particular poem? What kind of work was he or she doing at the time, and which of the poet's particular concerns might be relevant to our understanding of the poem? Did the poet write anything about the poem in his or her personal correspondence? What was this? Are there any results of interviews with the poet that might be introduced to explain the poem? What were the poet's aims in creating a particular poem?
- *Specific or general thoughts by the poet that are relevant to the poem.* Sometimes there might be details about a poet's thoughts on the thinking and reading he or she was doing, or on works of art, or on religious or philosophical musings. Langston Hughes was deeply concerned about the circumstances of African Americans in the United States, and wrote many poems on this topic. Elaine Terranova was equally concerned with the condition of women and families, and her "Rush Hour" is an expression of this deep concern (Chapter 11, p. 664).

In planning your approach, you should aim at an essay that is relevant to the poem or poems you have chosen. Thus, your topic may be the nature of the poem's speaker, such as "The Character of Mueller's Speaker in 'Alive Together,'" or "Cummings's Use of the Speaker to Control Tone in 'if there are any heavens.'" Or it may be the poet's use of images, or metaphors, or symbols, such as "Shakespeare's Widely Varied Imagery in His Sonnets." Or you may want to write about a poet's use of allusions or the use of mythical materials. A rich field for discussion might be the comparison of poems or poets, such as "Uses of Description in Schnackenberg's 'The Paperweight' and Rich's 'Diving into the Wreck,'" or "The Topic of Death in Frost's 'Out, Out—' and Sassoon's 'Dreamers,'" or "The Treatment of Love and Sexuality by Peacock in 'Desire' and Donne in 'The Sun Rising.'" The possibilities are legion. Of even greater significance than your choice of topic—which should be basically the same whether you are using or not using research—is your integration of research discoveries into the development of your essay.

Illustrative Student Essay Written with the Aid of Research

Underlined sentences in this paper *do not* conform to MLA style and are used solely as teaching tools to emphasize the central idea, thesis sentence, and topic sentences throughout the paper.

Zweig 1

Micol Zweig

Professor Melvin

English 112 25

April 2008

Put identifying
information in
upper left corner,
double space.

"Beat! Beat! Drums!" and "I Hear America Singing":

Two Whitman Poems Spanning the Civil War°

Comparing two of Walt Whitman's poems, "Beat! Beat! Drums!" and   [1]

"I Hear America Singing," alongside the historical background informing

his writing, helps in the understanding of both poems.* Walt Whitman was

born in 1819, when American democracy was in its infancy. He held many

jobs as a young man; at various times he worked as a printer, editor, and

teacher, and in 1840 he even campaigned for future President Martin Van

Buren (Callow 365).

As a keen observer, Whitman took many notes about what he saw. He   [2]

started to write in celebration of America's potential. He wrote many poems

about the people and places of his immediate environment, and these poems

gave birth to his famous collection, Leaves of Grass (1855). Many critics have

pointed out that Whitman was uncertain about his poetic skills before he began

this collection. One critic remarks that "Whitman was not really a poet at all, but

a man of the people with his eyes open and his senses hungry for experience"

(Zweig 113). By the time of the Civil War in 1861, he had written many of his

best known poems, but the experience of war was to transform him.

In MLA style, put
author and page
number in
parentheses
when author is
not named in the
sentence.

His "Beat! Beat! Drums!" was written in 1861 at the beginning of the   [3]

Civil War. In this poem, Whitman expresses his disfavor of the war, claiming

that the pounding of the drums, which represents the fierceness of war itself, is

an egregious disruption of ordinary American life. His 1860 poem, "I Hear

America Singing"--also published again in Leaves of Grass after the war had

ended--serves as a sharp contrast to "Beat! Beat! Drums!" In this more

tranquil poem, music is transformed to symbolize peace. Both poems serve

as examples of how similar motifs may be used to exemplify very different

°These poems appear on pages 1189 and 1191.
*Central idea.

Zweig 2

In MLA style, the header has the student's last name and page number.

[4]

moods and tones. Whitman's tone and his use of musical imagery demonstrate the difference between America at peace and America at war.[†]

   Whitman's attitude towards the war was complex. As the war developed, he saw it as an opportunity for America to develop its own identity, but he also feared impending horrors of combat. "Beat! Beat! Drums!" reflects both the ominous nature of war and also the "patriotic fervor which swept the North" (Allen 75). In contrast, "I Hear America Singing" reflects the optimism in Whitman's poetry both before and after his many disturbing experiences during the war. "From the time Whitman visited his wounded brother George in Virginia in the spring of 1862 until the end of the war . . . he visited thousands of soldiers in army hospitals" (Allen 84). On these visits he sometimes saw people dying right in front of him, and he also saw piles of amputated limbs that were decaying in the sun. "Beat! Beat! Drums!" describes the high-pitched "ruthless force" (line 2) that he had perceived. "I Hear America Singing," although first written before the war, was republished at a time when Whitman's best work was behind him, when "there was not silence but sporadic effort, sparse and diminished" (Zweig 345). Seen in this light, "I Hear America Singing" can be seen as a looking back to earlier times in its vision of a whole nation singing as individuals--yet as one--and a looking forward to a hopeful future.

When citing poetry in MLA style, cite the line number for the poem.

[5]

   Though references to music form recurring images of sound in both poems, they are used in each to symbolize different states. In "Beat! Beat! Drums!" the blowing of the bugles and the beating of the drums are a warning of the terrible and all-encompassing aspects of war. In this poem, the speaker commands the fierce and pounding noises invoking the startling sound of drums and bugles to serve as a warning of impending war. "Beat! beat! drums!-- blow! bugles! blow!" (lines 1, 8, 14) is repeated every six to seven lines, punctuating the flow of disturbing imagery in the lines surrounding them. These repeated lines, with the exception of one word ("bugles") all have one syllable, making the lines themselves sound like the military rhythm of a snare drum which is a sharp contrast to the "varied carols" that each American

[†]**Thesis sentence.**

Zweig 3

possesses in "I Hear America Singing." While the sounds of "Beat! Beat! Drums!" attempt to unite and alert different people to the oncoming conflict, the music in "I Hear America Singing" focuses on the idea that differences are both the strength and hallmark of America. The speaker's admonition in "Beat! Beat! Drums!" to increase the intensity of sound--"Then rattle quicker, heavier drums--you bugles wilder blow" (line 15)--may be contrasted with the varied rhythms of "I Hear America Singing," which come together as "strong melodious songs" (line 11). This harmonious resolution of diverse songs sets a very different tone from the one at the end of "Beat! Beat! Drums!", when the speaker's command has been realized: "So strong you thump O terrible drums--so loud you bugles blow" (line 21). The symbolic sounds of both poems convey contrasting states of mind.

In each of the Whitman poems, images of sound emphasize tone and mood. [6]
"Beat! Beat! Drums!" conveys a tone of serious urgency. Where life had been going on peacefully before the outbreak of war, the drums and bugles "burst like a ruthless force" (line 2) through doors and windows, now rendering a peaceful existence impossible. These jarring sounds disrupt the studying scholar and "scatter the congregation" of "the solemn church" (line 3). The mood of the poem conveys hopelessness as the speaker wonders if life will be able to continue amidst the din. He asks, "would the talkers be talking? would the singer attempt to sing?" (line 13). "I hear America Singing" conveys the opposite tone, one of peaceful contentment and proud patriotism as the poet becomes an approving listener of the harmonies around him. There is a predominant feeling of optimism in this poem as the mechanics, carpenters, masons, and all others sing their respective songs. The reader gets a sense of America's strength and hope, unlike the lives of Americans during the disruption and strife of war, as all different types of people cheerfully sing "what belongs to him or her and none else" (line 9), and then at night these same people gather to sing melodiously together. "I Hear America Singing" stresses the individualism and optimism of a country emerging from the all-encompassing strife indicated by the incessant beating drums and blaring bugles of "Beat! Beat! Drums!"

Zweig 4

[7]   As the poet of American democracy Whitman wrote about the great events of his time. "Beat! Beat! Drums!" paints a disturbing picture for the reader, the image of an unstoppable army playing the shrieking music of destruction that affects everything in its path, leaving the bridegroom unhappy and the "peaceful farmer" without "any peace" (line 6). "I Hear America Singing" announces the significance of the individual--the "I" that is part of the melody of a large and prosperous nation at peace. In Walt Whitman's most famous and ambitious poem, "Song of Myself," the symbolic singing of "myself" announces the pride and exuberant presence of the speaker's ego amidst the diversity of a democratic nation. In "Beat! Beat! Drums!" and "I Hear America Singing" the images of sound are used to convey very different aspects of American life. While to some critics "Whitman's art as a poet" may be a matter of mystery (Van Doren xxiii) there is little doubt of his intense feelings about the Civil War and what he wrote about it. Reading the poems together, along with knowing about Whitman's life, brings greater meaning to each poem.

Zweig 5

Works Cited

In MLA style, the list of sources, called the works cited, begins a new page. Double space throughout.

Allen, Gay Wilson. A Reader's Guide to Walt Whitman. New York: Farrar, Straus, and Giroux, 1970.

Callow, Philip. From Noon to Starry Night; A Life of Walt Whitman. Chicago: Ivan R. Dee, 1992.

Doren, Mark Van, ed. The Portable Walt Whitman. New York: Viking, 1973.

List sources in alphabetical order.

Whitman, Walt. "Beat! Beat! Drums!" "I Hear America Singing." Literature: An Introduction to Reading and Writing. Ed. Edgar V. Roberts. 9th ed. New York: Pearson Longman, 2009. 1189, 1191.

Zweig, Paul. Walt Whitman: The Making of the Poet. New York: Basic, 1984.

Commentary on the Essay

The research objective of this essay is the introduction of biographical details as informational support for the topic of comparison and contrast. The opening paragraph, citing one research reference, places the two poems in the context of Whitman's life. In paragraph 2, the writer connects the poems to Whitman's unique qualities as an observer, citing a research reference in support of this capacity. In paragraph 3, the writer locates the poems in the time of the Civil War, pointing out how the poems deal with opposites of American life. Paragraph 4 introduces three research references that support the details of Whitman's actual Civil War experiences. Paragraphs 5 and 6, based on the texts of the two poems themselves, grow out of paragraph 4, for they deal with the opposing music of harshness, on the one hand, and "peaceful contentment and proud patriotism," on the other. In the final paragraph, 7, the writer introduces two additional research references, while stressing Whitman's intense feelings about the subject matter of the two poems.

Part IV

Reading and Writing About Drama

Chapter 23

The Dramatic Vision: An Overview

Drama has much in common with the other genres of literature. Like fiction, drama focuses on one or a few major characters who enjoy success or endure failure as they face challenges and deal with other characters. Many plays are written in prose, as is fiction, on the principle that the language of drama should resemble the language of life as much as possible. Drama is also like poetry because both genres develop situations through speech and action. Indeed, a great number of plays, particularly those of past ages, exist as poetry. The dramatists of ancient Athens employed intricate poetic forms in their plays. Many European plays from the Renaissance through the nineteenth century were written in blank verse or rhymed couplets, a tradition of poetic drama preserved by twentieth-century dramatists, such as Christopher Fry and T. S. Eliot.

As separate genres, however, drama, fiction, and poetry have major differences. Fiction is distinguished from drama because the essence of fiction is narration: the making known or relating or recounting of a sequence of events or actions—the actual telling of a story. Poetry is unlike both drama and fiction because it exists in many formal and informal shapes, and it is the shortest of the genres. Although we usually read poetry silently and alone, it is also frequently read aloud before groups. Unlike both fiction and poetry, drama is literature designed for impersonation by people—actors—for the benefit and delight of other people—an audience.

Drama as Literature

Drama is a unique genre because it can be presented and discussed both as literature—drama itself—and as performance—the production of plays in the theater. The major literary aspects of drama are the *text, language, characters, plot, structure, point of view, tone, symbolism,* and *theme* or *meaning.* All these elements have remained constant throughout the history of drama. In addition, drama written in poetic forms, such as Shakespeare's *Hamlet* (Chapter 24) and *A Midsummer Night's Dream* (Chapter 25), includes elements such as meter and rhyme.

The Text Is the Printed (or Handwritten) Play

The text of a play is a plan for bringing the play into action on the stage. The most notable features of the text are *dialogue, monologue,* and *stage directions.* **Dialogue** is the conversation of two or more characters. A **monologue** is spoken by a single character who is usually alone onstage. **Stage directions** are the playwright's

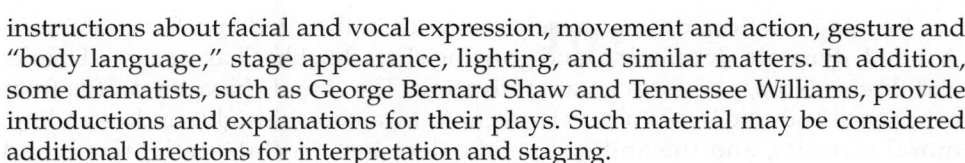

instructions about facial and vocal expression, movement and action, gesture and "body language," stage appearance, lighting, and similar matters. In addition, some dramatists, such as George Bernard Shaw and Tennessee Williams, provide introductions and explanations for their plays. Such material may be considered additional directions for interpretation and staging.

Language, Imagery, and Style Bring the Play to Life

What we learn about characters, relationships, and conflicts is conveyed in dramatic language. Through dialogue, and sometimes through soliloquy and aside, characters use language to reveal intimate details about their lives and their deepest thoughts—their loves, hatreds, hopes, and plans.

To bring such revelations before the audience, dramatists employ words that have wide-ranging connotations and that acquire many layers of meaning. Such is the case with the variations of the phrase "well liked" in Arthur Miller's *Death of a Salesman* (Chapter 24). Similarly, playwrights can introduce metaphors and symbols that contribute significantly to a play's meaning and impact. Again in *Death of a Salesman*, the abandoned auto trip and the imminence of an auto accident are central symbols.

Dramatists also make sure that the words of their characters fit the circumstances, the time, and the place of the play. Miller's Willy Loman speaks the language of modern America, and Shakespeare's Hamlet speaks Elizabethan blank verse, almost academic prose, and "one-liner" remarks. In addition, dramatists employ accents, dialects, idiom, jargon, and clichés to indicate character traits. The gravediggers in *Hamlet* speak in a Renaissance English lower-class dialect that distinguishes them from the aristocratic characters in the play.

Characters Talk Themselves Alive Through Speech and Action

Drama necessarily focuses on its **characters,** who are persons the playwright creates to embody the play's actions, ideas, and attitudes. Of course, characters are characters, no matter where we find them, and many of the character types that populate drama are also inhabitants of fiction. The major quality of characters in drama, however, is that they come alive through their speeches and actions. To understand them, we must listen to their words and watch and interpret how they react both to their circumstances and to the characters around them. They are also sometimes described and discussed by other characters, but primarily they are rendered dramatically.

Drama is not designed to present the full life stories of its characters. Rather, the plots of drama bring out intense and highly focused oppositions or conflicts in which the characters are engaged. In accord with such conflicts, most major dramatic characters are considered as *protagonists* and *antagonists*. The **protagonist** (the first or leading struggler or actor), usually the central character, is opposed by the **antagonist** (the one who struggles against). A classic conflict is seen in Shakespeare's *Hamlet,* in which Prince Hamlet, the protagonist, tries first to confirm and then to punish the crime committed by King Claudius, his uncle and the play's antagonist.

Just as in fiction, drama presents us with both *round* and *flat* characters. A **round, dynamic, developing,** and **growing character,** like Shakespeare's Hamlet and Ibsen's Nora, possesses great **motivation.** The round character profits from experience and undergoes a development in awareness, insight, understanding, moral capacity, and the ability to make decisions. A **flat, static, fixed,** and **unchanging character,** like Daddy in Albee's *The Sandbox,* does not undergo any change or growth. There is no rule, however, that flat characters must be dull. They can be charming, vibrant, entertaining, and funny, but even if they are memorable in these ways, they remain fixed and static.

Dramatic characters can also be considered as *realistic, nonrealistic, stereotyped* (or *stock*), *ancillary,* and *symbolic.* **Realistic characters** are designed to seem like individualized women and men; the dramatist gives them thoughts, desires, motives, personalities, and lives of their own. **Nonrealistic characters** are often undeveloped and symbolic. An interesting example is Torvald Helmer of Ibsen's *A Dollhouse* (Chapter 28). In terms of his assumptions and expectations, he is nonrealistic for most of the play, but he becomes sadly realistic when he recognizes the disastrous effects of his previous outlook on life and marriage. He is unique because he does not so much grow as undergo an almost instant change.

Throughout the ages, drama and other types of literature have relied on **stereotype** or **stock characters**—that is, unindividualized characters whose actions and speeches make them seem to have been taken from a mold. The general types developed in the comedy of ancient Athens and Rome, and in the drama of the Renaissance, are the *stubborn father,* the *romantic hero* and *heroine,* the *clever male servant,* the *saucy maidservant,* the *braggart soldier,* the *bumpkin,* the *trickster,* the *victim,* the *insensitive husband,* the *shrewish wife,* and the *lusty youth.* Modern drama continues these stereotypes, and it has also invented many of its own, such as the *private eye,* the *stupid bureaucrat,* the *corrupt politician,* the *independent pioneer,* the *kindly prostitute,* the *loner cowboy,* and the *town sheriff who never loses the draw in a showdown.*

There are also **ancillary characters** who set off or highlight the protagonist and who provide insight into the action. The first type, the **foil,** has been a feature of drama since its beginnings in ancient Athens. The foil is a character who is to be compared and contrasted with the protagonist. Laertes and Fortinbras are foils in *Hamlet.* Because of the play's circumstances, Laertes is swept into destruction along with Hamlet, whereas Fortinbras picks up the pieces and gets life moving again after the final death scene. The second type is the **choric figure,** who is loosely connected to the choruses of ancient drama. Usually the choric figure is a single character, often a confidant of the protagonist, such as Hamlet's friend Horatio. When the choric figure expresses ideas about the play's major issues and actions, he or she is called a **raisonneur** (the French word meaning "reasoner" [but also "quibbler"]) or **commentator.**

Any of the foregoing types of characters can also be **symbolic** in the context of individual plays. They can symbolize ideas, moral values, religious concepts, ways of life, or some other abstraction. For instance, Linda in *Death of a Salesman* symbolizes helplessness before destructive forces, whereas Fred Higgins in *Mulatto* (Chapter 26) symbolizes the cynicism, indifference, cruelty, and misuse of responsibility that accompany the concept of racial supremacy.

Action, Conflict, and Plot Make Up a Play's Development

Plays are made up of a series of sequential and related **actions** or **incidents.** The actions are connected by **chronology**—the logic of time—and the term given to the principles underlying this ordered chain of actions and reactions is **plot,** which is a connected plan or pattern of causation. The impulse controlling the connections is **conflict,** which refers to people or circumstances—the antagonist—that the protagonist tries to overcome. Most dramatic conflicts are vividly apparent because the clashes of wills and characters take place onstage, right in front of our eyes. Conflicts can also exist between groups, although conflicts between individuals are more identifiable and therefore more common in plays.

Dramatic plots can be simplified and schematized, but most of them are as complicated as life itself. Special complications result from a **double** or **multiple plot**— two or more different but related lines of action. Usually one of these plots is the **main plot,** but the **subplot** can be independently important and sometimes even more interesting. Such a situation occurs in *A Midsummer Night's Dream,* where the exploits of Bottom and the "mechanicals," which form just one of the four strands of plot, are so funny that they often steal the show in productions of the play.

Structure Is the Play's Pattern of Organization

The way a play is arranged or laid out is its **structure.** With variations, many traditional plays contain elements that constitute a structure of *five-stages:* (1) *exposition* or *introduction,* (2) *complication* and *development,* (3) *crisis* or *climax,* (4) *falling action,* and (5) *dénouement, resolution,* or *catastrophe.* In the nineteenth century, the German novelist and critic Gustav Freytag (1816–1895) visualized this pattern as a pyramid (though he used six elements rather than five). In the so-called **Freytag pyramid,** the exposition and complication lead up to a high point of tension—the crisis or climax—followed by the falling action and the catastrophe.

This pyramidal pattern of organization can be observed to greater or lesser degrees throughout many plays. Some plays follow the pattern closely, but often there is uncertainty about when one phase of the structure ends and the next one

The Freytag Pyramid

1.   Exposition or Introduction
2.   Complication and Development
3.   Crisis or Climax
4.   Falling Action
5.   Dénouement, Resolution, or Catastrophe

begins. In addition, words defining some of the stages are variable. Even though students of drama agree about the meaning of the first two stages, the terms for the final three are not used with precision. With these reservations, the Freytag pyramid is valuable in the analysis of dramatic plot structure.

1. *The **exposition** or **introduction** brings out everything we need to know to understand and follow what is to happen in the play.* In the first part of a drama, the dramatist introduces the play's background, characters, situations, and conflicts. Although exposition is occasionally presented through direct statements to the audience, the better method is to render it dramatically. Both major and minor characters thus perform the task of exposition through dramatic dialogue— describing situations, actions, and plans, and also explaining the traits and motives of other characters. In such a way, Sophocles provides expository material in the prologue to *Oedipus the King* (Chapter 24), featuring Oedipus, the Priest, and Creon. Eugene O'Neill in *Before Breakfast* dramatizes the exposition in the early actions and speeches of the major character, Mrs. Rowland. In *Hamlet*, Horatio's explanations to Barnardo and Marcellus provide vital information about circumstances in the Danish court.

2. *The **complication** and **development** mark the onset of the play's major conflicts.* In this second stage, also called the **rising action,** we see the beginning of difficulties that seem overwhelming and insoluble, as in *Hamlet*, where we learn in the exposition that the death of the king has occurred before the play opens. Complication develops as the characters try to learn answers to some of the following perplexing questions: Was the death a murder? If so, who did it? How was it done? How can the murderer be identified? Is the man suspected of the murder truly guilty? What should be done about the murder? What punishment should there be? In *A Midsummer Night's Dream*, less serious complications result from the development of issues like these: Can young lovers overcome parental opposition? Can a bumbling group of amateur actors successfully perform a play before the highest social group in the nation? Can a squabble among supernatural beings be brought to a peaceful conclusion?

3. *The **crisis** or **climax** is the culmination of the play's conflicts and complications— the intense moments of decision.* The uncertainty and anxiety of the complication lead to the third stage, the **crisis** ("turning point") or **climax** ("high point"). In this third stage, all the converging circumstances compel the hero or heroine to recognize what needs to be done to resolve the play's major conflict. Another way of considering the crisis or climax is to define it as that point in the play when uncertainty ends and inevitability begins, as when Hamlet vows vengeance after drawing conclusions about the king's reaction to the player scene.

4. *The **falling action**—a time of avoidance and delay—forms the downward slope of the pyramid, as complicating elements defer the play's conclusion.* In *Hamlet*, for example, a number of scenes make up the falling action: Hamlet's decision not to kill Claudius at prayer, Hamlet's departure for England, the gravedigger scene and the conflicts at Ophelia's grave, and the murderous conspiracy of Claudius and Laertes. In *Oedipus the King*, Oedipus continues to seek confirming evidence about the death of his father, although by the end of Episode 3—the climax—he has all the information he needs to determine that he himself is the murderer.

5. *The dénouement is the end, the logical outcome of what has gone before.* In the **dénouement** ("unraveling") or **resolution** ("untying"), also called the **catastrophe** ("overturning"), all tragic protagonists undergo suffering or death, all mysteries are explained, all conflicts are resolved, all mistakes are corrected, all dastardly schemes are defeated, all long-lost children are identified, all obstacles to love are overcome, all deserving characters are rewarded, and the play ends. In short, the function of the dénouement is to end complications and conflicts, not to create new ones. It is important to observe that the word *catastrophe* for the final dramatic stage should not necessarily be construed in the sense of a calamity, even though most tragic catastrophes are calamitous. It is probably best, however, to use the words *dénouement* and *resolution* as general descriptions of a play's final stage and to reserve *catastrophe* for tragedies.

Of great significance is that the various points of the pyramid define an abstract model that is applicable to most plays—tragedy, comedy, and tragicomedy alike. Since the time of Shakespeare, however, most dramatists writing in English have been concerned less with dramatic form than with dramatic effect. As a result, many plays in English do not perfectly follow the pattern charted in the Freytag pyramid. You should, therefore, be prepared for plays that conceal or delay essential parts of the exposition; create a number of separate crises and climaxes; confine the climax, falling action, and dénouement into a short space at the play's end; or modify the formal pattern in other significant ways.

Point of View Focuses on a Play's Major Character (or Characters) and Ideas

In fiction, **point of view** refers to the narrative *voice* of the story, the speaker or guiding intelligence through which the characters and actions are presented (see Chapter 2). In drama, the term refers generally to a play's **perspective** or focus— the ways in which dramatists direct attention to the play's characters and their concerns. In the theater, dramatists govern our responses visually by putting major characters onstage and keeping them there. That these characters are always speaking and moving before our eyes makes us devote our attention to them, become involved with them, and see things pretty much as they see things. For example, once the opening speeches of *Hamlet* are over, the play focuses directly on Hamlet and never wavers, even after he lies dead on the stage in the last act. In O'Neill's *Before Breakfast*, the entire play is a monologue spoken by Mrs. Rowland, and we therefore see things from her perspective even though we recognize her limitations and shortcomings.

The dramatist can also keep characters and issues in our minds by causing other characters to speak about them. Thus most of the speeches in Glaspell's *Trifles* are designed to shape our understanding of what Minnie Wright did to her husband on the lonely Wright farm, and why she did it. Because everyone is always talking about Minnie and her boorish but recently murdered husband, the play makes this perspective inescapable.

Tone or Atmosphere Creates Mood and Attitude

Playwrights have unique ways of conveying **tone** or **atmosphere** beyond those techniques used by poets and fiction writers (see Chapter 6). Some of these are vocal ranges, stage gestures (such as rolling one's eyes, throwing up one's hands, staring at another character, holding one's forehead in despair, jumping for joy, making side remarks, and staggering in grief). Even silence, intensive stares, and shifting glances can be effective means for creating moods and controlling attitudes.

Whereas the voices and actions of actors establish mood on the stage, we do not have these guides in reading. There are written guides, however, to dramatic tone: Sometimes a playwright uses stage directions as an indication of tone, as Ibsen does in *A Dollhouse*, directing the inflections of a speaker's voice with the stage direction that she is shaking her head when speaking. Similarly, Hughes suggests the mood of one of his characters in *Mulatto*, with the direction that he "runs" to his mother and hugs her "teasingly."

When such directions are absent—and usually they are—we need to take the diction, tempo, imagery, and context as clues to the tone of specific speeches and whole plays. In the opening scene of *Hamlet*, Shakespeare uses short and rapidly delivered sentences to create a mood of fearfulness, anxiety, and apprehensiveness. This opening passage anticipates the Ghost's forthcoming charge of murder against Claudius, and it also prepares us for the ominous events to come in the rest of the play.

One of the most common methods playwrights employ to control the tone of the play is **dramatic irony.** This type of **situational** (as opposed to **verbal**) irony refers to circumstances in which characters have only a partial, incorrect, or misguided understanding of what is happening, while both readers and other characters understand the situation completely. Readers hence become concerned about the characters and hope that they will develop understanding quickly enough to avoid the problems bedeviling them and the threats endangering them. The classic example of dramatic irony occurs in Sophocles's *Oedipus the King*: As Oedipus condemns the murderer of his father, he also condemns himself, though unwittingly.

Dramatists Frequently Introduce Symbolism and Allegory

In drama, as in fiction and poetry, the meaning of a **symbol** extends beyond its surface meaning (see Chapters 7 and 19). Dramatic symbols, which can be characters, settings, objects, actions, situations, or statements, can be either cultural or contextual. **Cultural** or **universal symbols**—such as crosses, flags, snakes, and flowers—are generally understood by the audience or reader regardless of the context in which they appear. In Act 5 of *Hamlet*, for example, we readily accept Yorick's skull as a symbol of death. **Contextual** or **private symbols** develop their impact only within the context of a specific play or even a particular scene. We often don't realize at first that such objects or actions are symbolic; they acquire symbolic meaning only through context and continued action. In the living room setting of Hughes's *Mulatto*, for instance, there is a vestibule "leading to the porch." There is nothing unusual about this location, but as the play develops we

realize that it symbolizes that the rights and privileges of whites on the plantation are denied to the African Americans who work there.

When a play offers consistent and sustained symbols that refer to general human experiences, that play can be construed as an **allegory,** or at least as being **allegorical.** For example, Ibsen's *A Dollhouse* can be considered allegorically as an expression of the shortcomings of any way of life in which a grown person is infantilized and therefore is prevented from realizing the mature and independent life that she is entitled to seek as an adult.

Subject and Theme Are the Complex of Ideas Presented by the Dramatist

Most playwrights do not aim to propagandize their audience, but they do nevertheless embody ideas in their plays. The aspects of humanity a playwright explores constitute the play's **subject.** Plays can be *about* love, religion, hatred, war, ambition, death, envy, or anything else that is part of the human condition.

The ideas that the play dramatizes make up the play's **theme** or meaning. A play might explore the idea that love will always find a way or that marriage can be destructive, that pride always leads to disaster, or that grief can be conquered through strength and a commitment to life. Full, evening-long plays can contain many thematic strands. Ibsen creates such complexity in *A Dollhouse,* in which he deals with themes of selfless devotion, egotism, pompousness, hypocrisy, betrayal, and women's self-determination. Even short plays can have complex themes, as in O'Neill's *Before Breakfast,* which explores the themes that anger can be stronger than love, that deceit is a consequence of alienation, and that despair and fear can conquer the normal wish to live.

Performance: The Unique Aspect of Drama

As we read and talk about drama, we should always remind ourselves that *plays are meant to be acted.* It is **performance** that makes a play immediate, exciting, and powerful. The elements of performance are the *actors,* the *director* and the *producer,* the *stage, sets* or *scenery, lighting, costumes* and *makeup,* and the *audience.*

Actors Bring the Play to Our Eyes and Ears

Actors are trained and have the experience to exert their intelligence, emotions, imaginations, voices, and bodies to make their characters real to us. Actors speak as they imagine the characters might speak—earnestly, eagerly, calmly, excitedly, prayerfully, exultantly, sorrowfully, or angrily. When they respond, they respond as they imagine the characters might respond—with surprise, expectation, approval, happiness, irony, acceptance, rejection, resignation, or resolution. When they move about the stage according to patterns called **blocking,** they move as they imagine the characters might move—slowly, swiftly, smoothly, hesitatingly, furtively, stealthily, or clumsily, and gesturing broadly or subtly. Actors also frequently engage in **stage business**—gestures or movements that make the play dynamic, spontaneous, and often funny.

The Director and the Producer Create and Support the Play's Production

In the theater, all aspects of performance are shaped and supervised by the **director** and the **producer.** The producer, the one with the money, is responsible for financing and arranging the production. Working closely with the producer is the director, who is the most significant member of the entire dramatic production. The director cooperates closely with the actors and guides them in speaking, responding, standing, and moving in ways that are consistent with his or her vision of the play. When a play calls for special effects (for example, the Ghost in *Hamlet*), both the producer and the director work with specialists, such as musicians, choreographers, and sound and lighting technicians to enhance and enliven the performance.

The *Stage* Is the Location of Both Speech and Action

Most modern theaters feature an interior **proscenium stage**—a picture-frame stage that is like a room with one wall missing so that the audience can look in on the action. In most proscenium stages, a large curtain representing the missing wall is usually opened and closed to indicate the beginning and ending of acts. Members of the audience who are seated centrally before the stage are close to the action, but people seated at the sides, to the rear, behind a tall person, or in the balcony are to greater or lesser degrees removed from the vital and up-close involvement that is desirable in good theater. There is no question that such remoteness is a built-in disadvantage of many proscenium stages.

Modern theater designers have therefore experimented with stage designs inspired by theaters of the past. One notable success has been to revive the shape of the ancient Greek amphitheater (with seats rising from the stage in an expanding half-circle), a structure employed in theaters like the Tyrone Guthrie in Minneapolis and the Shakespeare Festival Theatre in Ashland, Oregon. Because seats for the audience ascend in semicircular tiers around three sides of the stage, most of the audience is closer to the action—and better able to see—than in a theater with a proscenium stage. The audience is also, therefore, more closely involved in the dramatic action.

Like many other modern theaters, these theaters feature a **thrust stage** or **apron stage** (like the **platform stage** used in the time of Shakespeare), which enlarges the proscenium stage with an acting area projecting into the audience by twenty or more feet. It is on this apron that a good deal of the acting occurs. Closely related to the apron stage is **theater-in-the-round,** a stage open on all sides like a boxing ring, surrounded by the audience. Productions for both types of stages are especially lively because the actors usually enter and leave through the same doorways and aisles used by the audience.

Sets (Scenery) Create the Play's Location and Appearance

Most productions use **sets** (derived from the phrase "set scenes," i.e., fixed scenes) or **scenery** to establish the action in place and time, to underscore the ideas of the director, and to determine the level of reality of the production. Sets are constructed and decorated to indicate a specific place (a living room, a kitchen, a throne room, a forest, a graveyard) or a detached and indeterminate place with a specific atmosphere (an open plain, a vanished past, a nightmarish future). When we first see the stage at the beginning of a performance, it is the scenery that we see, bringing the play to life through walls, windows, stairways, furniture, furnishings, and painted locations.

In most proscenium stages, the sets establish a permanent location or **scene** resembling a framed picture. All characters enter this setting, and they leave once they have achieved their immediate purpose. Such a fixed scene is established in *Oedipus the King*, which is set entirely in front of the royal palace of ancient Thebes, and in *Before Breakfast*, set in the dreary kitchen of a New York apartment. Generally, one-act plays rely on a single setting and a short imagined time of action. Many full-length plays also confine the action to a single setting despite the longer imagined time during which the action takes place.

Because sets are usually elaborate and costly, many producers use single fixed-scene sets that are flexible and easily changed. Some productions employ a single, neutral set throughout the play and then mark scene changes with the physical introduction of movable **properties** (or **props**)—chairs, tables, beds, flower vases, hospital curtain-enclosures, trees, shovels, skulls, and so on. The use of props to mark separate scenes is a necessity in modern productions of plays that require constant scene changes, like *Hamlet*. Interestingly, many productions make scene changes an integral part of the drama by having costumed stage-hands, or even the actors themselves, carry props on and off the stage. In a 1995 New York production of *Hamlet*, for example, Hamlet himself (performed by Ralph Fiennes) carried in the chairs needed for the spectators of the player scene.

The constant changing of scenery is sometimes avoided by the use of a **unit set**—a series of platforms, rooms, stairs, and exits that form the locations for all the play's actions, as in Miller's *Death of a Salesman.* The movement of the characters from place to place within the unit set marks the shifting scenes and changing topics.

Like characters, the setting can be realistic or nonrealistic. A **realistic setting,** sometimes called a **naturalistic setting,** requires extensive construction and properties, for the object is to create as lifelike a stage as possible. In O'Neill's *Before Breakfast*, for example, the setting is a realistic copy of a tacky early-twentieth-century apartment kitchen. By contrast, a **nonrealistic setting** is nonrepresentational and often symbolic, as in the beach scene established in Albee's *The Sandbox.* Sometimes a realistic play can be made suggestive and expressive through the use of a nonrealistic setting.

Lighting Creates Clarity, Emphasis, and Mood

In ancient and medieval times, plays were performed in daylight, and hence no artificial illumination was required. With the advent of indoor theaters and evening performances, **lighting** became a necessity. At first, artificial lighting was provided by lanterns, candelabras, sconces, and torches (yes, some theaters burned down), and indirect lighting was achieved by reflectors and valances—all of which were used with great ingenuity and effect. Later, gaslight and limelight lamps replaced the earlier open flames.

The evolution of theater lighting reached its climax with the development of electric lights in the nineteenth century. Today, dramatic performances are enhanced by virtually all the technical features of our electronic age—including specialized lamps, color filters, spotlights, dimmers, and simulated fires. This dazzling technology, which employs hundreds or even thousands of lights of varying intensity in unlimited combination, is used to highlight individual characters, to isolate and emphasize various parts of the stage, to establish times, and generally to shape the moods of individual scenes. Lighting can also divide the stage or a unit set into different acting areas simply through the illumination of one section and the darkening of the rest, as in productions of plays like Albee's *The Sandbox*. The result is that lighting has become an integral element of set design, especially when the dramatist uses a **scrim** (a curtain that becomes transparent when illuminated from behind), which permits great variety in the portrayal of scenes and great rapidity in scene changes. In our day it is a rare stage indeed that does not contain an elaborate, computerized, and complicated (and expensive) lighting system.

Costumes and Makeup Establish the Nature and Appearance of the Actors

Actors make plays vivid by wearing **costumes** and using **makeup,** which help the audience understand a play's time period together with the occupations, mental outlooks, and socioeconomic conditions of the characters. Costumes, which include not only dress but also items such as jewelry, good-luck charms, swords, firearms, and canes, can be used realistically (farm women in plain clothes, a salesman in a business suit, a king in rich robes) or symbolically (a depressed character wearing black). Makeup usually enhances an actor's facial features, just as it can fix the illusion of youth or age or emphasize a character's joy or sorrow.

The Audience Responds to the Performance and Helps to Shape It

To be complete, plays require an interaction of actors and **audience.** Drama enacts fictional or historical events as if they were happening in the present, and members of the audience—whether spectators or readers—are direct witnesses to the dramatic action from start to finish. The audience most definitely has a creative impact on theatrical performances. Although audiences are made up of people who otherwise do not know each other, they have a common bond of interest in the play. Therefore, even though they are isolated by the darkness of the theater in which they sit, they respond communally. Their reactions (e.g., laughter, gasps, applause) provide instant feedback to the actors and thus continually influence the delivery and pace of the performance. For this reason, drama *in the theater* is the most immediate and accessible of the literary arts. There is no intermediary between the audience and the stage action—no narrator, as in prose fiction, and no speaker, as in poetry.

Drama from Ancient Times to Our Own: Tragedy, Comedy, and Additional Forms

Today, people interested in drama have more options than at any other time in human history. There is professional live theater in many major cities, and touring theatrical troupes reach areas with smaller populations. Many cities and towns have amateur community theaters, and so also do many schools and churches. Movie theaters and multiplexes are flourishing. Television has brought film versions of plays to the home screen, together with innumerable situation comedies (**"sitcoms"**), continuous narrative dramas (including **soap operas**), made-for-TV films, documentary dramas (**"docudramas"**), short skits on comedy shows, and many other types. All these different genres ultimately spring from the drama that was developed twenty-six hundred years ago in Athens, the leading ancient Greek city-state. Although subsequent centuries have produced many variations, the types the Athenians created are still as important today as they were then. They are tragedy and comedy.[1]

Tragedy and Comedy Originated in Ancient Greece

During the sixth century BCE, drama first arose from choral presentations the Athenians held during religious festivals celebrating Dionysus, the god of wine, conviviality, sexual vitality, ecstasy, fertility, and freedom. The choruses were made up of young men who sang or chanted lengthy songs that the Athenians called **dithyrambs;** the choruses also performed interpretive dance movements during the presentations. The dithyrambs were not dramatizations but rather recitations, which became dramatic when a member of the chorus was designated to step forward and impersonate a particular hero through the process of **acting.** Soon, additional men from the choruses took acting roles, and the focus of the performances shifted from the choral group to individual actors. Greek **tragedy** as we know it had come into being. It was this pattern of drama that during the fifth century BCE produced a golden age of tragedy. Most of the tragedies have been lost, and only a small but very significant number of plays by the three greatest Athenian dramatists—Aeschylus, Sophocles, and Euripides—have survived.

Not long after the emergence of tragedy, **comedy** became an additional feature of the festivals. Because the ancient Athenians encouraged free speech, at least for males, the comedy writers created a boisterous, lewd, and freely critical type of burlesque comedy that later critics called **Old Comedy.** The eleven surviving plays of the comic dramatist Aristophanes represent this tradition. In the fourth century BCE, after Athenian power and freedom had declined because of the debilitating Peloponnesian War at the end of the fifth century, this type of comedy was replaced by **Middle Comedy,** a more social, discreet, and international drama, and then by **New Comedy,** a type of play featuring the development of situation, plot, and character. The best-known writer of New Comedy was Menander, whose plays for centuries were thought to be totally lost. In the last hundred

---

[1]Fuller discussions of tragedy and comedy are presented in Chapters 24 and 25.

years, however, a number of fragments of his work have been discovered, including one play in its entirety.

Both of these Greek dramatic types have proved long lasting. The introduction of subject matter about loss in the earliest tragedies has led to today's common understanding that tragedy dramatizes an individual's fall from a secure and elevated position to social or personal defeat. Likewise, what we usually consider typical comedies are directly linked to the pattern of ancient New Comedy: plays that dramatize the regeneration of individuals who begin in insecurity and end with their overcoming troubles and anticipating happiness.

Tragedy and Comedy Were of Less Significance in Ancient Rome

The two Athenian dramatic forms were adopted by the Romans during the periods of the Republic (before 29 BCE) and the Empire (after 29 BCE). Although Republican Rome produced writers of note who created comedies (Plautus, c. 254–184 BCE, and Terence, c. 195 or 185–159 BCE), the only significant playwright of imperial times was the tragedian Seneca (4 BCE–65 CE), who wrote "closet dramas"—that is, plays designed to be read in private, household rooms, but not performed in public.

Ancient Drama Faded along with the Breakup of the Western Roman Empire

As the Roman Empire in Western Europe disintegrated in the fifth century CE, many of its institutions, including the theater, disintegrated with it. In the next five centuries, often called the "Dark Ages," Europe fell into feudalism, characterized by political decentralization and social fragmentation. The intellectuals of the period—most of them clergy—were creating Christian theology and establishing the growing church while abandoning the memories and records of the past, of which drama was a major element. As far as we know, there were no public theaters, no patrons able or willing to support public performances, no popular audiences with the money to pay for admission, no official permission by secular and religious authorities to perform plays, and no practicing dramatists—in short, there was no organized theater. It is hard to believe, however, that the human need for stories and fantasies did not remain. Tales and songs were unquestionably passed on from parents to children and community to community throughout these otherwise gloomy centuries.

Medieval Drama Developed as a Part of Church Services

When drama emerged hundreds of years after the fall of Rome, it had little to do with the Greek and Roman dramatic tradition, because it was a creation of the Christian church. It was at some point in the tenth century—approximately when the medieval period or Middle Ages were emerging from the Dark Ages—that the clergy started to realize the potentiality of dramatic presentations within the mass. It was then that the **trope**—a short dramatic interlude performed in conjunction with the mass, either with or without musical accompaniment—developed in the churches. Tropes were not considered as separate dramas, however, but became an integral part of regular services.

The earliest tropes were written for Easter rituals. The prototype of the Easter trope, which is included here, represented the discovery of the empty tomb as evidence of Christ's resurrection. This is the *Visitatio Sepulchri,* or *The Visit to the Sepulcher,* often known as the *Quem Quaeritis* ("Whom are you seeking") *trope.* This is considered the first European drama, from which all later medieval, renaissance, and modern dramas have developed. Authored by persons who are unknown and forever unknowable, the trope was in Latin and was chanted not for the people but for cloistered monks and priests. It was enacted many times both on the continent and the British Isles, and in later centuries it became a regular feature of Easter worship. It has survived in a variety of forms in medieval manuscripts. Some versions contain detailed directions about performance, and some are cast in a question-and-answer format.

Although the *Quem Quaeritis* trope was a part of ritual, it clearly involved impersonation—and therefore drama—to the degree that priests and monks represented the persons and scenes contained in the gospel accounts of the resurrection. The heart of the trope is that the Angel at the tomb announces the resurrection to the three Marys, who then leave to proclaim the news.

ANONYMOUS

 ## The Visit to the Sepulcher
(Visitatio Sepulchri) (tenth century CE)

[CAST OF CHARACTERS]

[The Angel at the Tomb]
[Mary the Mother of James the Younger and Joses]
[Mary Magdalene]
[Mary of Bethany, the Sister of Martha and Lazarus°]

[SCENE: *The Sepulcher in which Christ was entombed after the Crucifixion.* THE ANGEL, *dressed in white and holding a palm leaf, enters and sits beside a location curtained off to represent the tomb. Behind the curtain is a table or other surface representing a burial slab on which there is a linen sheet (i.e., the burial shroud supplied by Joseph of Aramathea). The three* MARYS *enter, carrying vessels [thuribles] as though they are intending to anoint Christ's body with aromatic oils and spices. At first they do not see the tomb, and they wander about until they do. Then they stop in front of the Angel.*]

ANGEL: Whom are you seeking in this Sepulcher, O followers of Christ?
THE THREE HOLY WOMEN: [*Speaking together.*] Jesus of Nazareth, who was crucified, O heavenly one.

°Although gospel accounts are in accord about the first two Marys, there is no agreement about the third woman, who is named Salome by Mark and Joanna by Luke. Neither of the gospel accounts of the Resurrection indicates that Mary of Bethany was the third Mary. Nevertheless, medieval tradition had it that there was a third Mary, and that she was Mary the sister of Lazarus and Martha, most likely on the authority of John 12:7, where Jesus implies that this Mary will be one of those to anoint his dead body.

ANGEL: [*Pulling back the curtain to show the empty tomb.*] He is not here. He has been resurrected, as was predicted. Go forth, tell everyone that he is risen. Spread the news!

THE THREE HOLY WOMEN: [*Kneeling and singing.*] Alleluia! Today Christ the Lord, the Son of God, the Mighty Lion, has been resurrected! Thanks be to God! Tell it to all the world!

ANGEL: Come and see the place where the Lord was laid.

[*The Three Holy Women examine the empty tomb and, with the Angel, display the burial shroud.*]

ANGEL: Alleluia! Alleluia! Hurry, tell the disciples that the Lord has risen! Alleluia! Alleluia! [*He exits, singing alleluias.*]

THE THREE HOLY WOMEN: [*Rejoicing, and singing in unison.*] The Lord, who hung on the tree for us, has risen from the grave! Alleluia!

[*They exit, joyfully repeating these lines.*]

QUESTIONS

1. What dramatic characteristics, as opposed to the obvious theology, do you find in this brief play?
2. Describe the play's dramatic actions. What sorts of movement would have been carried out? How extensive might have been the use of properties?
3. How do you imagine this play would have affected people attending the service in which it was performed?

Comparable Dramatic Ceremonies Followed the *Visitatio Sepulchri*

During the eleventh and twelfth centuries, the *Visit to the Sepulcher* ceremony became more elaborate, with additional characters and actions, such as the race by Peter and John to the tomb and Mary Magdalen's recognition of the risen Christ after having first confused him for a gardener. Some of the ceremonies, which were eventually performed before congregations, became extensive enough to require a lengthy performance. Historians of drama observe that this Easter ceremony was *dramatic liturgy* rather than *liturgical drama*, but any congregations present would likely have ignored this distinction. Instead they would have welcomed the ceremony as something totally new, dramatic, vital, and exciting.

In addition to the Easter pageantry, the church also developed special Christmas ceremonies, such as those for the Three Wise Men, the Shepherds, the scene at the stable, the ranting Herod, and the Slaughter of the Innocents (Innocents Day was December 28). These ceremonies were observed as regular parts of Easter and Christmas rituals for hundreds of years after their beginnings in the tenth century.

A New Kind of Drama, the Corpus Christi Play, Grew Independently of the Church

Growing out of the religious dramatic tradition, a full-blown religious and civic drama developed in the fourteenth century. This was the Corpus Christi (i.e., "Body of Christ") play, which evolved just as the drama of ancient Athens had developed out of religious festivals for the god Dionysus in the sixth century BCE.[2] The major expression of the new religious drama came during the celebration of Corpus Christi Day, a celebration of the doctrine of transubstantiation (i.e., during mass, Eucharistic bread and wine are believed to become miraculously transformed into the real body and blood of Christ). The Corpus Christi feast is observed on the first Thursday after Trinity Sunday, which itself is the first Sunday after Pentecost.

Corpus Christi Day regularly featured local processions devoted to the worship of the Eucharist, and in this way it brought religious celebration into the streets and before the public. Because the feast occurred at the end of the liturgical year, it coincided with the beginning of good weather. The winter and spring rains abated, daylight hours lengthened, short trips from country villages to nearby towns became possible, and people could spend an entire day outside and still be comfortable.

The goal of the new plays was to create a complete **cycle,** dramatizing the biblical accounts of world history from the Creation to Judgment Day. The plays were produced by local craft guilds, the members of whom were master tradesmen. Hence the plays were also known as *mysteries,* or *mystery plays.* Naturally, the guild masters wanted to boost the prestige of their towns and their own wealth and power. They therefore welcomed the customers and patrons who thronged to these annual religious celebrations. Although there were as yet no professional acting companies like the one that Shakespeare was to join in the late sixteenth century, the annual staging of the Corpus Christi plays required many participants. The planning by the local guilds was therefore complex and challenging; the result was an engaging and inspiring drama.

As the Corpus Christi feasts grew in importance, the plays became a highlight of town life in the early summer. By the fifteenth century as many as forty towns had their own cycles. Some were large and elaborate; some—probably those performed in the smaller towns—were modest. Often the performances took place not only on Corpus Christi Thursday but also on Friday and Saturday, thus creating an extensive religious and secular celebration. Although the texts of most of these plays have been lost, cycles from four towns have been preserved. These cycles, named after the towns that presented them, contain more than 150 plays.

English Replaced Latin as the Language of the Corpus Christi Plays

A major influence on the Corpus Christi drama—with profound implications for later drama—was the increasing importance of the English language at this time. During the two centuries following the Norman Conquest in 1066, the ruling and intellectual languages of England had been French and Latin. By the fourteenth century, however, things were changing: English had been enriched with close to 10,000 French words (a huge number of which we still retain) and was reasserting its role as the major language of England. More and more, the governing classes

---

[2]See page 1215.

were committed to England—having a centuries-long tradition there—and used English as the language of intellectual and political discourse. Native writers began looking with increased favor on English as a literary language. A new literature in English—including drama—was ripe for development.

Other Religious Dramas Originated after the Corpus Christi Plays

In the course of time, additional types of religious dramas were developed. One of these was the **miracle play,** a devotional dramatization of the lives of saints. In addition, the **morality play** was developed as a genre instructing the faithful in the proper way to lead a devotional life. The most famous of these, in about 1500, was *Everyman*, which even today retains a good deal of interest and power.

In the Renaissance, Ancient and Medieval Traditions Fused to Create a New Secular Drama

In the sixteenth century, drama became liberated from these religious foundations and began rendering the twists and turns of more secular human conflicts. It was also at this time that the drama of ancient Greece and Rome was rediscovered. Therefore, the performing tradition growing out of the medieval church was combined with the surviving ancient tragedies and comedies to create an entirely new drama that quickly reached its highest point in the plays of Shakespeare. In this way, tragedy and comedy, the forms originated by the Athenians, had a revival during the Renaissance in Europe.[3]

New Types of Drama Have Developed Since the Renaissance

Renaissance drama was by no means a copy of ancient forms, however, even though a number of sixteenth- and seventeenth-century playwrights, including Shakespeare, reworked many of the ancient plays. The plays of Renaissance England, and later the plays of the United States, offer mixtures of tragedy and comedy. For example, some of Shakespeare's comedies treat disturbing and potentially destructive topics, just as many of his tragedies include scenes that are farcical, witty, and ironic. When the patterns and emotions are truly mixed, the play is called a **tragicomedy,** a term first used by the Roman playwright Plautus. In many ways tragicomedy is the dominant form of twentieth-century drama.

Additional types of drama that evolved from tragedy and comedy include farce, melodrama, and social drama. The major purpose of **farce,** which was also a strong element in the Athenian Old Comedy, is to make audiences laugh. Typically, it is crammed full of extravagant dialogue, stage business, and slapstick, with

---

[3]The Renaissance revival of drama also transformed the theater into a business. Earlier drama had been a product of the church and religious life, but during the Renaissance, actors and theater people found that they could make a living in the theater. Although at first there was little money in acting and in writing plays, some of the theater managers were able to do quite well. Shakespeare himself was a theater manager as well as a dramatist and minor actor. He earned enough from his shares in the Globe Theatre to retire in 1611 and leave London to spend his remaining days in his native Stratford-upon-Avon.

exaggerated emotions and rapid extremes of action. The "mechanicals" in Shakespeare's *A Midsummer Night's Dream* offer us good examples of farcical action and speech.

Resembling tragedy but stepping back from tragic outcomes is **melodrama,** a form in which most situations and characters are so exaggerated that they seem ridiculous. In its pure form, melodrama brings characters to the brink of ruin but saves them through the superhuman resources of a hero who always arrives just in time to pay the mortgage, save the business, and rescue the heroine, while the grumbling villain flees the stage muttering "Curses, foiled again," or words, believe it or not, to this effect.

The nineteenth century saw the creation of a form of topical drama known as **social drama** (sometimes called **problem drama**), a type that still exists as serious drama today. This type of play explores social problems and the individual's place in society. The plays can be tragic, comic, or mixed. Examples of social drama are Ibsen's *A Dollhouse* and Hughes's *Mullato.*

Despite all these terms and types, keep in mind that classification is not the goal of reading or seeing plays. It is less important to identify the melodramatic elements in O'Neill's *Before Breakfast* or the absurdist elements in Albee's *The Sandbox* than it is to understand and share the experiences and ideas that each play offers.

VISUALIZING PLAYS

Imagining Dramatic Scenes and Actions

As we have noted, drama relies heavily on actors and directors to bring it to life. You might therefore ask why we bother to read plays without seeing them performed. The most obvious answer is that we may never get the chance actually to *see* a professional or amateur performance of a particular play. But we also read plays to familiarize ourselves with important literature. Plays are not simply maps to theatrical production; they are a significant and valuable part of our literary heritage. Dramas like Sophocles's *Oedipus the King,* Shakespeare's *Hamlet,* and Miller's *Death of a Salesman* have become cultural touchstones. Finally, we read plays in order to have the time to study and understand them. Only through reading do we have the opportunity to look at the parts that make up the whole and to determine how they fit together to create a moving and meaningful experience.

Reading a play, as opposed to attending a performance, carries both advantages and disadvantages. The major disadvantage is that we lack the immediacy of live theater. We do not see a majestic palace or a run-down living room, the rich robes of a king or the pathetic rags of a beggar, a vital and smiling young person or a tired and tearful old person. We do not hear the lovers flirting, the servants complaining, the soldiers boasting, the opponents threatening, the conspirators plotting; nor do we hear fanfares of trumpets or the sounds of a wedding ceremony or a funeral procession.

The primary advantage of reading is that we can consider each element in the play at length, and we can "stage" the play in our imagination and do our best to visualize it. Here are some major things for you to consider: In the theater, the action proceeds at the director's pace. You have no opportunity to turn back to an interesting scene or to reconsider an important speech. In addition, a performance always represents someone else's interpretation. The director and the actors have made choices that emphasize certain avenues of exploration, and thereby they have cut off others. Reading a play allows us to avoid these drawbacks—provided that we read attentively and with understanding. We can read at our own tempo, turn back and reread a particular speech or scene, or explore those implications or ideas that strike us as interesting.

Nevertheless, of the three types of imaginative literature, *drama is most particularly suited for your visual imagination*. Aids in visualization are readily available to help you in your study. At the present time there are many versions of plays that have been acted and recorded on tape and more recently on DVD. You may look at such commercial versions to stimulate your imagination and give you almost a director's view of how a play might be presented onstage. There are professional interpretations of *Oedipus the King*, *A Dollhouse*, *Fences*, and *Death of a Salesman* that you might consult. In addition, there are a great many versions of *Hamlet* on DVD. Looking at selected scenes from any of these performances will give you a sense of the choices made by various directors, and therefore you can achieve a heightened awareness of how you yourself might want the plays to look, and to sound.

As a specimen scene, we might consider Shakespeare's *Hamlet* 1.5, in which Hamlet sees and hears the Ghost for the first time as the Ghost describes his murder at the hand of Claudius—his brother and Hamlet's uncle. In addition, the Ghost charges Hamlet to avenge the murder. This scene is most crucial, and it might be called Hamlet's principal information scene, for it deeply affects his understanding and also his objectives during the play. When he first appears, he is sad and depressed, and is wearing black for mourning, as a result of his father's death and the quick remarriage of his mother with Claudius. But after the scene with the Ghost, who provides seemingly reliable testimony that Claudius is a murderer, Hamlet becomes a person consumed with the intention of gaining revenge. So the scene is pivotal, and you, or any reader, would want the scene to seem authentic and believable.

It's important to begin with a thought. Always begin with a thought: How do you think you yourself might demonstrate the scene's importance? How would you make the scenery look? How complete should everything in the scene be made to appear? That is, should the Ghost be totally visible, or should he perhaps be somewhat obscured, or should he be seen through a haze, in order to emphasize his ghostliness? What sorts of costumes would you use? How would you make the Elsinore walls and battlements seem like a place where significant truth is to be expressed? How would you show Hamlet's agitation when he first sees the Ghost? How would you show the ways in which Hamlet's encounter with the Ghost affects him? After the encounter, when Hamlet's companions rejoin him, how should he behave? How would you demonstrate his comments about the Ghost's voice under the stage? What do his words show about his mental state, and how should the actor in the role of Hamlet deliver these words?

For brief illustration here about how the Ghost's scene may be visualized, we might refer to six different DVD versions of the scene in productions featuring Kenneth Branagh, Ethan Hawke, Derek Jacobi, Kevin Kline, Laurence Olivier, and Campbell Scott.[4] Perhaps the most traditional setting of our scene is in the Olivier version of 1948, in black and white, that shows many stone walls and stairs, in which a good deal of smoke and fog obscures the scene and also surrounds the Ghost when the camera is focused on him. The Jacobi version, in color, uses a staging that is similar to this. Fog is also present in the Campbell Scott color version, in which the confrontation of Hamlet and the Ghost takes place on an ocean shore, with a mild surf, rather than high on the parapets of Elsinore. When Hamlet tells his companions that the Ghost can tunnel under the earth very rapidly, the Scott version realistically confirms this action, for the Ghost's hands actually appear at various places coming out of the beach sand, most startlingly when the hand clasps the sword on which all the men have sworn silence. A comparable and also more elaborate treatment is the Branagh version, where the scene is no longer on the battlements but in a snowy woods and underbrush, and the presence of the Ghost makes the entire earth seem to boil and smoke. The eyes of the Branagh Ghost are penetrating and mysteriously nonhuman, and when Hamlet asks his companions to swear, the Ghost's assenting command literally fractures the earth. The Ethan Hawke version is different from these because the action takes place within Hamlet's room in a New York apartment. When we first see the Ghost (acted by Sam Shepard), he is outside, on a terrace, appearing to be an ordinary businessman and looking out at the city. It is then that Hamlet lets him in through the door to his computer room. There is nothing ghostly here, as in the other versions, but all seems ordinary, and the room actually seems rather cluttered. Things are so ordinary, in fact, that the TV set in the room is on, and is showing a picture. Is the state of this messy computer room meant to suggest anything about Hamlet's mind?

The point here is that you can boost your own imaginative reconstruction of the scene, and any other scene in any other play, by considering what others have done. The key is your own reading and thinking. What were other viewers trying to do and to show? How might you want to do things differently? What other effects might be achieved? You will need to figure out what stage effects might be needed. What sorts of lighting would best bring out the scene? What would be the significance of spotlighting, if you were to use it? Think. What scenes might best be done in close-up? What sorts of stage movement might there be? A particularly tension-filled moment is created in the Jacobi version of the Ghost scene, for example, when Hamlet falls dangerously backward from a high stairway, seemingly heading toward severe injury, but his companions catch him and save him. What does that production gain by this action, which is not called for in the text of the play? Another question you might deal with concerns how the characters interact with each other, as when Hamlet, after returning from his encounter with the Ghost, tells his friends that "There's ne'er a villain dwelling in all Denmark / But he's an arrant knave" (1.5.124–25). Should

[4]*William Shakespeare's Hamlet: A Kenneth Branagh Film*, dir. Kenneth Branagh, perf. Kenneth Branagh, Julie Christie, Billy Crystal, and Derek Jacobi. Castle Rock Entertainment, 1996, 2007.

Hamlet, dir. and adapt. Michael Almerayda, perf. Ethan Hawke. Buena Vista Home Entertainment, 2000.

Hamlet, perf. Derek Jacobi. Ambrose Video Publishing, BBX & Time-Life Films, 1980.

William Shakespeare's Hamlet, dir. Kevin Kline and Kirk Browning, perf. Kevin Kline. Educational Broadcasting Corp, 1990.

Laurence Olivier's Hamlet, dir. Laurence Olivier, perf. Laurence Olivier. Two Cities Film Ltd., 1948, Criterion Collection 82, 2000.

Hamlet, dir. and adapt. Campbell Scott and Eric Simonson, perf. Cambell Scott. Artisan Entertainment, 2000.

(Scene from Olivier's *Hamlet*): The costuming of Sir Laurence Olivier's *Hamlet*, shown above is traditionally Shakespearean.

Horatio's response be spoken seriously, or comically? Other questions you can raise might concern whether some of the action, from *Hamlet* or any other play, should be cut for production.

You might also think about questions of costuming. One might expect to see a *Hamlet* production done in clothing that was customary at the time of Shakespeare, as in the Olivier and Jacobi versions. What is the effect of more recent costumes, as in the Branagh and Scott versions, or ordinary late twentieth-century everyday garb, as in the Hawke version? And you should also consider the modes of speech, and their effect on your imaginary production. The Olivier Ghost, for example, speaks as we might expect a ghost to speak, in deep tones, slowly. In the Branagh version, the Ghost's speech is accompanied by noisy wind of seemingly hurricane velocity. This is not so in the Jacobi version, in which this Ghost, who is angry about having been murdered, speaks rapidly and forcefully about the circumstances of his death. He is not happy, and he clearly wants Hamlet to be disturbed also. The Ghost in the Hawke version is more quietly conversational, in keeping with the interior in which the action takes place, and before he leaves he embraces Hamlet, his son, even if he is a Ghost and therefore, supposedly, nonsubstantial at the time of the action. Indeed, this ghost looks very substantial and very realistic.

In a word, try to use the advantages of reading and study, together with your own imagination. You have the time and freedom to read carefully, reflect deeply, and follow your thoughts. Think. Rely on whatever experiences you can

(Scene from Hawke's *Hamlet*): As seen in this production still, late twentieth-century costumes were used in Ethan Hawke's version of *Hamlet*.

gain from theatrical productions, movies, and recorded productions to enhance your reading. Stage the play as fully as you can in the theater of your mind. Become the director, producer, set designer, lighting technician, and costume designer, and pretend that you control all the actors. Build whatever mental presentations you like, dress your actors as you see fit, and move the characters across the stage of your mind. Enjoy.

Plays for Study

Edward Albee . . . . The Sandbox, 1225
Susan Glaspell . . . . Trifles, 1232
Betty Keller . . . . Tea Party, 1245
Eugene O'Neill . . . . Before Breakfast, 1249

EDWARD ALBEE (b. 1928)

Edward Albee, one of the leading American playwrights of the last half of the twentieth century, began life with many personal and educational handicaps. He was an adopted child whose adoptive mother alienated and eventually disowned him. As a boy he was moved in and out of various schools. Eventually, he studied at Trinity College in Hartford, Connecticut, but he left without a degree even though in 1997 the "alumni, faculty, students, and friends" of Trinity "proudly" congratulated him on having received the Kennedy Center Honors of 1996.

After leaving Trinity, Albee worked for many years at a variety of odd jobs, including three years delivering telegrams, but at the urging of the Pulitzer Prize winning playwright Thornton Wilder (1897–1975), he turned his talent to writing plays. He has been constantly productive ever since. His first play was The Zoo Story *(1958), a brief play that was premiered in 1959 in Berlin and published in 1960. This was followed by* The Sandbox *(1959),* The Death of Bessie Smith *(1960), and* The American Dream *(1961). His best-known play,* Who's Afraid of Virginia Woolf?, *appeared in 1962 and marks the pinnacle of his career. After a long and successful run in New York, it was awarded the 1963 Tony Award as best play. In 1966 it was made into a successful film featuring Richard Burton and Elizabeth Taylor, who won an Academy Award for her performance.*

Albee's work after Who's Afraid of Virginia Woolf *has met with mixed reactions.* Tiny Alice *(1964) was declared confusing and derivative, but* A Delicate Balance *(1966) and* Seascape *(1975) both won Pulitzer Prizes.* Listening, *which appeared in 1977, is unique in Albee's work because it was intended for radio, not the stage. Some of his later plays and adaptations had short lives in the theater.* The Lady from Dubuque *(1980) survived only twelve performances on Broadway, and negative reviews forced* The Man Who Had Three Arms *off the Broadway stage in 1983.*

Some of his more recent work has achieved more favorable recognition. In 1993–1994, the Signature Theater Company of New York presented a season-long set of Albee performances. One of them featured The Sandbox *as one of three one-act "sand plays," the others being* Box *(1968) and* Finding the Sun *(1983). Additionally, two of his other plays,* Three Tall Women *(1991, Pulitzer Prize in Drama for 1994) and* Fragments *(1994), were performed to great acclaim. In the last several years he has written* The Play about the Baby *(2001) and* The Occupant *(2002). He continues to write, and states that he has no plans to stop doing so.*

He claims that his plays are about "closings down"; that is, about how dreams never reach fulfillment, and how happiness—our greatest dream and our constant pursuit—is constantly beyond our grasp. Other descriptions of his work might include a pervasive sense of alienation, loss, uneasiness, fear, and uncertainty, mixed with a certain degree of humor. Although Albee is not easily categorized, he has introduced elements of the theater of the absurd into his work. His first play, The Zoo Story, *is in the absurdist manner, which is characterized by the stripping away of the conventions of behavior and accidents of personality. The idea is that life is, at bottom, irrational and meaningless. The title of one of his plays,* A Delicate Balance, *symbolizes the Albee view of existence: Any stability that we are lucky enough to achieve in life is no more than a stage of delicate balance, which can be toppled by distrust, bitterness, reproach, and anger that can strike with hurricane force at almost any time. If life seems happy, that happiness is only temporary, and to think otherwise is superficial and untrue.*

The Sandbox, *written in 1959 and first performed in New York in 1960, represents Albee's critique of the American family as an institution that is not constructive but destructive. His vacationing family consists of characters whom he presents in an absurdist frame of reference. Grandma, the protagonist, is in conflict with society, her family, and death. Only the last of these conflicts is resolved at the conclusion. Mommy and Daddy represent Albee's vision of the American family reduced to a bare-bones form. Plot, character, setting, and symbol all convey the judgment that modern lives and values are drab and, basically, dull and average. Albee provides his characters with absurd, banal, sometimes childish, and idiomatic speeches that are filled with specific and concrete words interspersed with clichés that bring the play to the level of ordinary life or, perhaps, somewhat below it. In effect, the characters dramatize their own bleak lives through their own words. Although the number of characters is small and the scene is restricted, there is a surprising amount of activity, which culminates in the unusual but surprisingly tender conclusion.*

The Sandbox (1959)

THE PLAYERS

The Young Man, 25, a good-looking, well-built boy in a bathing suit
Mommy, 55, a well-dressed, imposing woman
Daddy, 60, a small man; gray, thin
Grandma, 86, a tiny, wizened woman with bright eyes
The Musician, no particular age, but young would be nice

Note: When, in the course of the play, MOMMY and DADDY call each other by these names, there should be no suggestion of regionalism. These names are of empty affection and point up the presenility and vacuity of their characters.   0.1

The Scene: A bare stage, with only the following: Near the footlights, far stage-right, two simple chairs set side by side, facing the audience; near the footlights, far stage-left, a chair facing stage-right with a music stand before it; farther back, and stage-center, slightly elevated and raked, a large child's sandbox with a toy pail and shovel; the background is the sky, which alters from brightest day to deepest night.   0.2

At the beginning, it is brightest day; the YOUNG MAN is alone on stage, to the rear of the sandbox, and to one side. He is doing calisthenics until quite at the very end of the play. These calisthenics, employing the arms only, should suggest the beating and fluttering of wings. The YOUNG MAN is, after all, the Angel of Death.   0.3

MOMMY and DADDY enter from stage-left, MOMMY first.

MOMMY: [*Motioning to DADDY.*] Well, here we are; this is the beach.
DADDY: [*Whining.*] I'm cold.
MOMMY: [*Dismissing him with a little laugh.*] Don't be silly; it's as warm as toast. Look at that nice young man over there: *he* doesn't think it's cold. [*Waves to the YOUNG MAN.*] Hello.
YOUNG MAN: [*With an endearing smile.*] Hi!
MOMMY: [*Looking about.*] This will do perfectly . . . don't you think so, Daddy? There's   5
sand there . . . and the water beyond. What do you think, Daddy?
DADDY: [*Vaguely.*] Whatever you say, Mommy.
MOMMY: [*With the same little laugh.*] Well, of course . . . whatever I say. Then, it's settled, is it?
DADDY: [*Shrugs.*] She's *your* mother, not mine.
MOMMY: *I* know she's my mother. What do you take me for? [*A pause.*] All right, now; let's get on with it. [*She shouts into the wings, stage-left.*] You! Out there! You can come in now.

The MUSICIAN enters, seats himself in the chair, stage-left, places music on the music stand, is ready to play. MOMMY nods approvingly.

MOMMY: Very nice; very nice. Are you ready, Daddy? Let's go get Grandma.   10
DADDY: Whatever you say, Mommy.
MOMMY: [*Leading the way out, stage-left.*] Of course, whatever I say. [*To the MUSICIAN.*] You can begin now. [*The MUSICIAN begins playing; MOMMY and DADDY exit; the MUSICIAN, all the while playing, nods to the YOUNG MAN.*]
YOUNG MAN: [*With the same endearing smile.*] Hi!

After a moment, MOMMY and DADDY re-enter, carrying GRANDMA. She is borne in by their hands under her armpits; she is quite rigid; her legs are drawn up; her feet do not touch the ground; the expression on her ancient face is that of puzzlement and fear.

DADDY: Where do we put her?
MOMMY: [*The same little laugh.*] Wherever I say, of course. Let me see . . . well . . . all right, over   15
there . . . in the sandbox. [*Pause.*] Well, what are you waiting for, Daddy? . . . The sandbox!

Together they carry GRANDMA *over to the sandbox and more or less dump her in.*

GRANDMA: [*Righting herself to a sitting position; her voice a cross between a baby's laugh and cry.*] Ahhhhhh! Graaaaa!
DADDY: [*Dusting himself.*] What do we do now?
MOMMY: [*To the* MUSICIAN.] You can stop now.

The MUSICIAN *stops.*

[*Back to* DADDY.] What do you mean, what do we do now? We go over there and sit down, of course. [*To the* YOUNG MAN.] Hello there.
YOUNG MAN: [*Again smiling.*] Hi!

MOMMY *and* DADDY *move to the chairs, stage-right, and sit down. A pause.*

20   GRANDMA: [*Same as before.*] Ahhhhhh! Ah-haaaaaa! Graaaaaa!
DADDY: Do you think . . . do you think she's . . . comfortable?
MOMMY: [*Impatiently.*] How would I know?
DADDY: [*Pause.*] What do we do now?
MOMMY: [*As if remembering.*] We . . . wait. We . . . sit here . . . and we wait . . . that's what we do.
25   DADDY: [*After a pause.*] Shall we talk to each other?
MOMMY: [*With that little laugh; picking something off her dress.*] Well, you *can* talk, if you want to . . . if you can think of anything to *say* . . . if you can think of anything *new.*
DADDY: [*Thinks.*] No . . . I suppose not.
MOMMY: [*With a triumphant laugh.*] Of course not!
GRANDMA: [*Banging the toy shovel against the pail.*] Haaaaaa! Ah-haaaaaa!
30   MOMMY: [*Out over the audience.*] Be quiet, Grandma . . . just be quiet, and wait.

GRANDMA *throws a shovelful of sand at* MOMMY.

MOMMY: [*Still out over the audience.*] She's throwing sand at me! You stop that, Grandma; you stop throwing sand at Mommy! [*To* DADDY .] She's throwing sand at me.

DADDY *looks around at* GRANDMA, *who screams at him.*

GRANDMA: GRAAAAA!
MOMMY: Don't look at her. Just . . . sit here . . . be very still . . . and wait. [*To the* MUSICIAN.] You . . . uh . . . you go ahead and do whatever it is you do.

The MUSICIAN *plays.*

MOMMY *and* DADDY *are fixed, staring out beyond the audience.* GRANDMA *looks at them, looks at the* MUSICIAN, *looks at the sandbox, throws down the shovel.*

GRANDMA: Ah-haaaaaa! Graaaaaa! [*Looks for reaction; gets none. Now . . . directly to the audience.*] Honestly! What a way to treat an old woman! Drag her out of the house . . . stick her in a car . . . bring her out here from the city . . . dump her in a pile of sand . . . and leave her to set. I'm eighty-six years old! I was married when I was seventeen. To a farmer. He died when I was thirty. [*To the* MUSICIAN.] Will you stop that, please?

The MUSICIAN *stops playing.*

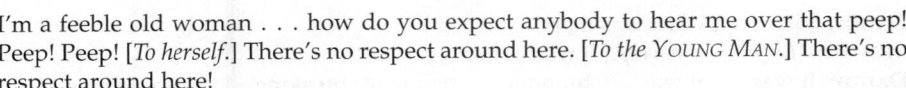

I'm a feeble old woman . . . how do you expect anybody to hear me over that peep! Peep! Peep! [*To herself.*] There's no respect around here. [*To the* YOUNG MAN.] There's no respect around here!

YOUNG MAN: [*Same smile.*] Hi!   35

GRANDMA: [*After a pause, a mild double-take, continues, to the audience.*] My husband died when I was thirty [*indicates Mommy*], and I had to raise that big cow over there all by my lonesome. You can imagine what *that* was like. Lordy! [*To the* YOUNG MAN.] Where'd they get *you*?

YOUNG MAN: Oh . . . I've been around for a while.

GRANDMA: I'll bet you have! Heh, heh, heh. Will you look at you!

YOUNG MAN: [*Flexing his muscles.*] Isn't that something? [*Continues his calisthenics.*]

GRANDMA: Boy, oh boy; I'll say. Pretty good.   40

YOUNG MAN: [*Sweetly.*] I'll say.

GRANDMA: Where ya from?

YOUNG MAN: Southern California.

GRANDMA: [*Nodding.*] Figgers; figgers. What's your name, honey?

YOUNG MAN: I don't know. . . .   45

GRANDMA: [*To the audience.*] Bright, too!

YOUNG MAN: I mean . . . I mean, they haven't given me one yet . . . the studio . . .

GRANDMA: [*Giving him the once-over.*] You don't say . . . you don't say. Well . . . uh, I've got to talk some more . . . don't you go 'way.

YOUNG MAN: Oh, no.

GRANDMA: [*Turning her attention back to the audience.*] Fine; fine. [*Then, once more, back to the*   50
YOUNG MAN.] You're . . . you're an actor, hunh?

YOUNG MAN: [*Beaming.*] Yes. I am.

GRANDMA: [*To the audience again; shrugs.*] I'm smart that way. *Anyhow,* I had to raise . . . *that* over there all by my lonesome; and what's next to her there . . . that's what she married. Rich? I tell you . . . money, money, money. They took me off the *farm* . . . which was real decent of them . . . and they moved me into the big town house with *them* . . . fixed a nice place for me under the stove . . . gave me an army blanket . . . and my own dish . . . my very own dish! So, what have I got to complain about? Nothing, of course. I'm not complaining. [*She looks up at the sky, shouts to someone off-stage.*] Shouldn't it be getting dark now, dear?

The lights dim; night comes on. The MUSICIAN *begins to play; it becomes deepest night. There are spots on all the players, including the* YOUNG MAN, *who is, of course, continuing his calisthenics.*

DADDY: [*Stirring.*] It's nighttime.

MOMMY: Shhhh. Be still . . . wait.

DADDY: [*Whining.*] It's so hot.   55

MOMMY: Shhhh. Be still . . . wait.

GRANDMA: [*To herself.*] That's better. Night. [*To the* MUSICIAN.] Honey, do you play all through this part?

The MUSICIAN *nods.*

Well, keep it nice and soft; that's a good boy.

The MUSICIAN *nods again; plays softly.*

That's nice.

There is an off-stage rumble.

Daddy: [*Starting.*] What was that?

Mommy: [*Beginning to weep.*] It was nothing.

60 **Daddy:** It was . . . it was . . . thunder . . . or a wave breaking . . . or something.

Mommy: [*Whispering, through her tears.*] It was an off-stage rumble . . . and you know what *that* means.

Daddy: I forget. . . .

Mommy: [*Barely able to talk.*] It means the time has come for poor Grandma . . . and I can't bear it!

Daddy: [*Vacantly.*] I . . . I suppose you've got to be brave.

65 **Grandma:** [*Mocking.*] That's right, kid; be brave. You'll bear up; you'll get over it.

Another off-stage rumble . . . louder.

Mommy: Ohhhhhhhhhh . . . poor Grandma . . . poor Grandma. . . .

Grandma: [*To* Mommy.] I'm fine! I'm all right! It hasn't happened yet!

A violent off-stage rumble. All the lights go out, save the spot on the Young Man; *the* Musician *stops playing.*

Mommy: Ohhhhhhhhhh . . . Ohhhhhhhhhh. . . .

Grandma: Don't put the lights up yet. . . . I'm not ready; I'm not quite ready. [*Silence.*] All right, dear . . . I'm about done.

The lights come up again, to brightest day; the Musician *begins to play.* Grandma *is discovered, still in the sandbox, lying on her side, propped up on an elbow, half covered, busily shoveling sand over herself.*

70 **Grandma:** I don't know how I'm supposed to do anything with this goddam toy shovel. . . .

Daddy: Mommy! It's daylight!

Mommy: [*Brightly.*] So it is! Well! Our long night is over. We must put away our tears, take off our mourning . . . and face the future. It's our duty.

Grandma: [*Still shoveling; mimicking*] . . . take off our mourning . . . face the future. . . . Lordy!

Mommy *and* Daddy *rise, stretch.* Mommy *waves to the* Young Man.

Young Man: [*With that smile.*] Hi!

Grandma *plays dead. (!)* Mommy *and* Daddy *go over to look at her; she is a little more than half buried in the sand; the toy shovel is in her hands, which are crossed on her breast.*

75 **Mommy:** [*Before the sandbox; shaking her head.*] Lovely! It's . . . it's hard to be sad . . . she looks . . . so happy. [*With pride and conviction.*] It pays to do things well. [*To the* Musician.] All right, you can stop now, if you want to. I mean, stay around for a swim, or something; it's all right with us. [*She sighs heavily.*] Well Daddy . . . off we go.

Daddy: Brave Mommy!

Mommy: Brave Daddy! [*They exit, stage-left.*]

Grandma: [*After they leave; lying quite still.*] It pays to do things well. . . . Boy, oh boy! [*She tries to sit up.*] . . . Well, kids. . . [*But she finds she can't.*] . . . I . . . I can't get up. I . . . can't move.

The Young Man *stops his calisthenics, nods to the* Musician, *walks over to* Grandma, *kneels down by the sandbox.*

GRANDMA: I . . . can't move. . . .

YOUNG MAN: Shhhhh . . . be very still. . . .   80

GRANDMA: I . . . I can't move. . . .

YOUNG MAN: Uh . . . ma'am; I . . . I have a line here.

GRANDMA: Oh, I'm sorry, sweetie; you go right ahead.

YOUNG MAN: I am . . . uh . . .

GRANDMA: Take your time, dear.   85

YOUNG MAN: [*Prepares; delivers the line like a real amateur.*] I am the Angel of Death. I am . . . uh . . . I am come for you.

GRANDMA: What . . . wha . . . [*Then, with resignation.*] . . . ohhh . . . ohhhh, I see.

The YOUNG MAN *bends over, kisses* GRANDMA *gently on the forehead.*

GRANDMA: [*Her eyes closed, her hands folded on her breast again, the shovel between her hands, a sweet smile on her face.*] Well . . . that was very nice, dear. . . .

YOUNG MAN: [*Still kneeling.*] Shhhhhh . . . be still. . . .

GRANDMA: What I meant was . . . you did that very well, dear. . . .   90

YOUNG MAN: [*Blushing.*] . . . oh . . .

GRANDMA: No; I mean it. You've got that . . . you've got a quality.

YOUNG MAN: [*With his endearing smile.*] Oh . . . thank you; thank you very much . . . ma'am.

GRANDMA: [*Slowly; softly—as the* YOUNG MAN *puts his hands on top of* GRANDMA'S] You're . . . you're welcome . . . dear.

Tableau. The MUSICIAN *continues to play as the curtain slowly comes down.*

                                                                           CURTAIN

QUESTIONS

1. Why does Mommy say, "This is the beach" (line 1)? What are the characters waiting for there?

2. Why does Albee indicate that Daddy is whining? What is the effect of Daddy's repetition of "Whatever you say, Mommy"?

3. How does Grandma "speak" to Mommy and Daddy? How does she speak to the audience and the Young Man? How do you account for this difference?

4. At the end of the play, just as in the opening scene directions (0.3 S.D.), Albee identifies the Young Man as the Angel of Death (speech 86). What else does the Young Man symbolize or represent? What does Grandma apparently think of him? How does he treat her?

5. What do the off-stage rumbles signify (57.1 S.D., 65.1 S.D., 67.1 S.D.)?

6. How do Mommy and Daddy react to Grandma's "death"? How would you characterize their language, both here and throughout the play?

7. How does Grandma react to the comments of Mommy and Daddy about her death? What does Grandma reveal about the way Mommy and Daddy deal with death?

GENERAL QUESTIONS

1. How does the setting, described at the play's beginning (0.2–3 S.D.) illustrate the play's level of reality? What props are realistic? Symbolic? Why is the play titled *The Sandbox*? What does the sandbox represent? What is your reaction when you realize what the sandbox is to be used for?

2. What is the realistic/nonrealistic effect of speeches such as Mommy's telling the Musician "You can come in now" (speech 9), Grandma's cuing of the lighting technician (speech 69), and the Young Man's statement that he has "a line here" (speech 82)?

3. Are the characters in the play interesting as characters? Why does Albee not give them names? What does each character symbolize?

4. *The Sandbox* is full of repetition. Characters repeat words and even whole lines two and sometimes three times. How does this repetition affect your understanding of character, meaning, and level of reality?

5. Is there anything unusual about the diction spoken by the characters? Do any of the characters voice any original thoughts? Why or why not? How would you describe the nature of their vocabulary?

6. How many different generations are presented in *The Sandbox*? Which characters represent each generation? Why does Grandma inveigh against Mommy? How does Grandma illustrate her feelings about how she has been treated in the home of Mommy and Daddy?

7. Almost every speech in this play is preceded by a stage direction, and stage directions are included within a number of speeches. What is the purpose of these directions? What might the play be like without them?

8. A student observed that *The Sandbox* at first seems strange and absurd but nevertheless that the concluding speeches are deeply moving. Is your reaction different or the same? Explain the growth or change of your responses to the play.

9. Compare the treatment of Death in this play with the treatments you find in Dickinson's "Because I Could Not Stop for Death" (p. 635), Pinsky's "Dying" (p. 823), Frost's "Out, Out—" (p. 1067), Porter's "The Jilting of Granny Weatherall" (p. 405), and any other relevant work of your choice in this book.

SUSAN GLASPELL (1882–1948)

Susan Glaspell, a writer of both plays and fiction, was a native of Iowa. She was educated at Drake University and the University of Chicago. In her thirties she moved to the Northeast and became interested in theater. Along with her husband, George Cook, she was a founder and director of the Provincetown Players of Cape Cod in 1914. The organization encouraged lesser-known young dramatists and was often experimental, but nevertheless it became successful enough to justify the opening of a second theater in New York. The first offerings of the theater were many one-act plays, featuring the earlier works of Glaspell herself, Eugene O'Neill, Edna Ferber, Edmund Wilson, and Edna St. Vincent Millay.

Glaspell wrote or coauthored over ten plays for the Provincetown Players, including Suppressed Desires *(1914),* Close the Book *(1917),* Women's Honor *(1918),* Tickless Time *(1918),* Bernice *(1919, her first full-length play),* The Inheritors *(1921), and* The Verge *(1921). After 1922, however, she gave up the theater and turned almost exclusively to fiction. The exception was* Alison's House *(1930), a play loosely based on the life and family of Emily Dickinson, for which she won a Pulitzer Prize.*

Glaspell deals with diverse topics in her drama, including misunderstood parentage, the effects of psychoanalysis, rejection of the machine age, the function and importance of honor, the tensions between political conservatives and liberals, and the onset of psychosis. Running through much of her work are strongly feminist ideas, based on a critique of the power—personal, social, and political—that men possess and that women are denied. Usually, Glaspell focuses on the negative and destructive effects that male–female relationships have on women, but she also stresses the ways in which women cope with their circumstances. To maintain character integrity and to preserve their domestic strength, they are forced into roles that are characterized not by direct but by indirect action.

Trifles, Glaspell's best-known drama, displays these characteristics. She wrote it in ten days for the Provincetown Players, who produced the play in 1916. Its inspiration was a murder trial she had covered while working as a reporter for a Des Moines newspaper before moving to the Northeast. In 1917 she refashioned the material for the short story "A Jury of Her Peers," with which *Trifles* can be compared (see p. 189). Although Glaspell preserves a considerable amount of dramatic dialogue in the story, the additions and changes she makes are indicative of the differences between drama and fiction.

Trifles concerns a murder investigation, but the play is not a mystery. Soon after the characters enter and go about their business, the two women characters begin to uncover the circumstances that reveal the killer and the nature of the crime. Once the facts are established, however, the action focuses on the significant details of motive. Indeed, the heart of the play consists of the contrasting ways in which the men and the women attempt to uncover and understand the motive. The men—the county attorney and the sheriff, accompanied by Hale—look for signs of violent rage, and they move onstage and offstage throughout the house in their search. The women—Mrs. Hale and Mrs. Peters—stay onstage and draw their conclusions from the ordinary, everyday details of a farm woman's kitchen. It is finally the women, not the men, who realize the true power that comes from understanding. Their realization—as well as their strength—leads them to their final decisions about how to judge the killer and treat the evidence.

The language that Glaspell gives to her characters is in keeping with the plain and simple lives the characters lead: simple, specific, and unadorned. Of the two groups, the women are more direct in the expression of their ideas. Once they realize the gravity of the situation they are exploring, however, they become indirect, but only because they fear to speak the words that describe the truths they have discovered. By contrast, the men usually talk convivially and smugly about the crime and their own roles in life, patronizingly among themselves about the women, and almost scornfully to the women about womanly concerns.

Trifles (1916)

CAST OF CHARACTERS

George Henderson, county attorney
Henry Peters, sheriff
Lewis Hale, a neighboring farmer
Mrs. Peters
Mrs. Hale

SCENE: *The kitchen in the now abandoned farmhouse of* JOHN WRIGHT, *a gloomy kitchen, and left without having been put in order—unwashed pans under the sink, a loaf of bread outside the bread-box, a dish-towel on the table—other signs of incompleted work. At the rear the outer door opens and the* SHERIFF *comes in followed by the* COUNTY ATTORNEY *and* HALE. *The* SHERIFF *and* HALE *are men in middle life, the* COUNTY ATTORNEY *is a young man; all are much bundled up and go at once to the stove. They are followed by the two women—the* SHERIFF'S *wife first; she is a slight wiry woman, a thin nervous face.* MRS. HALE *is larger and would ordinarily be called more comfortable looking, but she is disturbed now and looks fearfully about as she enters. The women have come in slowly, and stand close together near the door.*

The five principal actors arrive in the cold and bleak kitchen of the Wright farm at the beginning of Glaspell's *Trifles* in the original 1916 production, featuring Marjorie Vonnegut, Elinor M. Cox, John Kind, Arthur Hohl, and T. W. Gibson.

COUNTY ATTORNEY: [*Rubbing his hands.*] This feels good. Come up to the fire, ladies.

MRS. PETERS: [*After taking a step forward.*] I'm not—cold.

SHERIFF: [*Unbuttoning his overcoat and stepping away from the stove as if to mark the beginning of official business.*] Now, Mr. Hale, before we move things about, you explain to Mr. Henderson just what you saw when you came here yesterday morning.

COUNTY ATTORNEY: By the way, has anything been moved? Are things just as you left them yesterday?

5   SHERIFF: [*Looking about.*] It's just the same. When it dropped below zero last night I thought I'd better send Frank out this morning to make a fire for us—no use getting pneumonia with a big case on, but I told him not to touch anything except the stove—and you know Frank.

COUNTY ATTORNEY: Somebody should have been left here yesterday.

SHERIFF: Oh—yesterday. When I had to send Frank to Morris Center for that man who went crazy—I want you to know I had my hands full yesterday. I knew you could get back from Omaha by today and as long as I went over everything here myself—

COUNTY ATTORNEY: Well, Mr. Hale, tell just what happened when you came here yesterday morning.

HALE: Harry and I had started to town with a load of potatoes. We came along the road from my place and as I got here I said, "I'm going to see if I can't get John Wright to go in with me on a party telephone." I spoke to Wright about it once before and he put me off, saying folks talked too much anyway, and all he asked was peace and quiet—I guess you know about how much he talked himself; but I thought maybe if I went to the house and talked about it before his wife, though I said to Harry that I didn't know as what his wife wanted made much difference to John—

10   COUNTY ATTORNEY: Let's talk about that later, Mr. Hale. I do want to talk about that, but tell now just what happened when you got to the house.

HALE: I didn't hear or see anything; I knocked at the door, and still it was all quiet inside. I knew they must be up, it was past eight o'clock. So I knocked again, and I thought I heard somebody say, "Come in." I wasn't sure, I'm not sure yet, but I opened. the door—this door [*Indicating the door by which the two women are still standing.*] and there in that rocker—[*Pointing to it.*] sat Mrs. Wright.

[*They all look at the rocker.*]

COUNTY ATTORNEY: What—was she doing?

HALE: She was rockin' back and forth. She had her apron in her hand and was kind of—pleating it.

COUNTY ATTORNEY: And how did she—look?

HALE: Well, she looked queer. 15

COUNTY ATTORNEY: How do you mean—queer?

HALE: Well, as if she didn't know what she was going to do next. And kind of done up.

COUNTY ATTORNEY: How did she seem to feel about your coming?

HALE: Why, I don't think she minded—one way or other. She didn't pay much attention. I said, "How do, Mrs. Wright, it's cold, ain't it?" And she said, "Is it?"—and went on kind of pleating at her apron. Well, I was surprised; she didn't ask me to come up to the stove, or to set down, but just sat there, not even looking at me, so I said, "I want to see John." And then she—laughed. I guess you would call it a laugh. I thought of Harry and the team outside, so I said a little sharp: "Can't I see John?" "No," she says, kind o' dull like. "Ain't he home?" says I. "Yes," says she, "he's home." "Then why can't I see him?" I asked her, out of patience. "Cause he's dead," says she. "*Dead*?" says I. She just nodded her head, not getting a bit excited, but rockin' back and forth. "Why—where is he?" says I, not knowing what to say. She just pointed upstairs—like that. [*Himself pointing to the room above.*] I got up, with the idea of going up there. I walked from there to here—then I says, "Why, what did he die of?" "He died of a rope round his neck," says she, and just went on pleatin' at her apron. Well, I went out and called Harry. I thought I might—need help. We went upstairs and there he was lyin'—

COUNTY ATTORNEY: I think I'd rather have you go into that upstairs, where you can point it 20 all out. Just go on now with the rest of the story.

HALE: Well, my first thought was to get that rope off. It looked . . . [*Stops, his face twitches.*] . . . but Harry, he went up to him, and he said, "No, he's dead all right, and we'd better not touch anything." So we went back downstairs. She was still sitting that same way. "Has anybody been notified?" I asked. "No," says she, unconcerned. "Who did this, Mrs. Wright?" said Harry. He said it businesslike—and she stopped pleatin' of her apron. "I don't know," she says. "You don't *know*?" says Harry. "No," says she. "Weren't you sleepin' in the bed with him?" says Harry. "Yes," says she, "but I was on the inside." "Somebody slipped a rope round his neck and strangled him and you didn't wake up?" says Harry. "I didn't wake up," she said after him. We must 'a looked as if we didn't see how that could be, for after a minute she said, "I sleep sound." Harry was going to ask her more questions but I said maybe we ought to let her tell her story first to the coroner, or the sheriff, so Harry went fast as he could to Rivers' place, where there's a telephone.

COUNTY ATTORNEY: And what did Mrs. Wright do when she knew that you had gone for the coroner?

HALE: She moved from that chair to this one over here [*Pointing to a small chair in the corner.*] and just sat there with her hands held together and looking down. I got a feeling that I ought to make some conversation, so I said I had come in to see if John wanted to put in a telephone, and at that she started to laugh, and then she stopped and looked at me—scared. [*The* COUNTY ATTORNEY, *who has had his notebook out, makes a note.*] I dunno, maybe it wasn't scared. I wouldn't like to say it was. Soon Harry got back, and then Dr. Lloyd came, and you, Mr. Peters, and so I guess that's all I know that you don't.

COUNTY ATTORNEY: [*Looking around.*] I guess we'll go upstairs first—and then out to the barn and around there. [*To the* SHERIFF.] You're convinced that there was nothing important here—nothing that would point to any motive.

25 SHERIFF: Nothing here but kitchen things.

[*The* COUNTY ATTORNEY, *after again looking around the kitchen, opens the door of a cupboard closet. He gets up on a chair and looks on a shelf. Pulls his hand away, sticky.*]

COUNTY ATTORNEY: Here's a nice mess.

[*The women draw nearer.*]

MRS. PETERS: [*To the other woman.*] Oh, her fruit; it did freeze. [*To the* LAWYER.] She worried about that when it turned so cold. She said the fire'd go out and her jars would break.

SHERIFF: Well, can you beat the women! Held for murder and worryin' about her preserves.

COUNTY ATTORNEY: I guess before we're through she may have something more serious than preserves to worry about.

30 HALE: Well, women are used to worrying over trifles.

[*The two women move a little closer together.*]

COUNTY ATTORNEY: [*With the gallantry of a young politician.*] And yet, for all their worries, what would we do without the ladies? [*The women do not unbend. He goes to the sink, takes a dipperful of water from the pail and pouring it into a basin, washes his hands. Starts to wipe them on the roller towel, turns it for a cleaner place.*] Dirty towels! [*Kicks his foot against the pans under the sink.*] Not much of a housekeeper, would you say, ladies?

MRS HALE: [*Stiffly.*] There's a great deal of work to be done on a farm.

COUNTY ATTORNEY: To be sure. And yet [*With a little bow to her.*] I know there are some Dickson county farmhouses which do not have such roller towels.

[*He gives it a pull to expose its full length again.*]

MRS HALE: Those towels get dirty awful quick. Men's hands aren't always as clean as they might be.

35 COUNTY ATTORNEY: Ah, loyal to your sex, I see. But you and Mrs. Wright were neighbors. I suppose you were friends, too.

MRS HALE: [*Shaking her head.*] I've not seen much of her of late years. I've not been in this house—it's more than a year.

COUNTY ATTORNEY: And why was that? You didn't like her?

MRS HALE: I liked her all well enough. Farmers' wives have their hands full, Mr. Henderson. And then—

COUNTY ATTORNEY: Yes—?

40 MRS HALE: [*Looking about.*] It never seemed a very cheerful place.

COUNTY ATTORNEY: No—it's not cheerful. I shouldn't say she had the homemaking instinct.

MRS HALE: Well. I don't know as Wright had, either.

COUNTY ATTORNEY: You mean that they didn't get on very well?

MRS HALE: No, I don't mean anything. But I don't think a place'd be any cheerfuller for John Wright's being in it.

COUNTY ATTORNEY: I'd like to talk more of that a little later. I want to get the lay of things upstairs now.   45

[*He goes to the left, where three steps lead to a stair door.*]

SHERIFF: I suppose anything Mrs. Peters does'll be all right. She was to take in some clothes for her, you know, and a few little things. We left in such a hurry yesterday.

COUNTY ATTORNEY: Yes, but I would like to see what you take, Mrs. Peters, and keep an eye out for anything that might be of use to us.

MRS. PETERS: Yes, Mr. Henderson.

[*The women listen to the men's steps on the stairs, then look about the kitchen.*]

MRS HALE: I'd hate to have men coming into my kitchen, snooping around and criticising.

[*She arranges the pans under the sink which the Lawyer had shoved out of place.*]

MRS. PETERS: Of course it's no more than their duty.   50

MRS HALE: Duty's all right, but I guess that deputy sheriff that came out to make the fire might have got a little of this on. [*Gives the roller towel a pull.*] Wish I'd thought of that

The men are watching as Mr. Hale (Gregory Aldrich) gets in trouble with his wife, Mrs. Hale (June Thiele), in a 2004 student production of *Trifles*, directed by Rachel Blackwell, at the University of Alaska, Fairbanks.

sooner. Seems mean to talk about her for not having things slicked up when she had to come away in such a hurry.

Mrs. Peters: [*Who had gone to a small table in the left rear corner of the room, and lifted one end of a towel that covers a pan.*] She had bread set.

[*Stands still.*]

Mrs. Hale: [*Eyes fixed on a loaf of bread beside the breadbox, which is on a low shelf at the other side of the room. Moves slowly toward it.*] She was going to put this in there. [*Picks up loaf, then abruptly drops it. In a manner of returning to familiar things.*] It's a shame about her fruit. I wonder if it's all gone. [*Gets up on the chair and looks.*] I think there's some here that's all right, Mrs. Peters. Yes—here; [*Holding it toward the window.*] this is cherries, too. [*Looking again.*] I declare I believe that's the only one. [*Gets down, bottle in her hand. Goes to the sink and wipes it off on the outside.*] She'll feel awful bad after all her hard work in the hot weather. I remember the afternoon I put up my cherries last summer.

[*She puts the bottle on the big kitchen table, center of the room. With a sigh, is about to sit down in the rocking-chair. Before she is seated realizes what chair it is; with a slow look at it, steps back. The chair which she has touched rocks back and forth.*]

Mrs. Peters: Well, I must get those things from the front room closet. [*She goes to the door at the right, but after looking into the other room, steps back.*] You coming with me, Mrs. Hale? You could help me carry them.

[*They go in the other room; reappear, Mrs. Peters carrying a dress and skirt, Mrs. Hale following with a pair of shoes.*]

55 Mrs. Peters: My, it's cold in there.

[*She puts the clothes on the big table and hurries to the stove.*]

Mrs. Hale: [*Examining the skirt.*] Wright was close. I think maybe that's why she kept so much to herself. She didn't even belong to the Ladies Aid. I suppose she felt she couldn't do her part, and then you don't enjoy things when you feel shabby. She used to wear pretty clothes and be lively, when she was Minnie Foster, one of the town girls singing in the choir. But that—oh, that was thirty years ago. This all you was to take in?

Mrs. Peters: She said she wanted an apron. Funny thing to want, for there isn't much to get you dirty in jail, goodness knows. But I suppose just to make her feel more natural. She said they was in the top drawer in this cupboard. Yes, here. And then her little shawl that always hung behind the door. [*Opens stair door and looks.*] Yes, here it is.

[*Quickly shuts door leading upstairs.*]

Mrs. Hale: [*Abruptly moving toward her.*] Mrs. Peters?

Mrs. Peters: Yes, Mrs. Hale?

60 Mrs. Hale: Do you think she did it?

Mrs. Peters: [*In a frightened voice.*] Oh, I don't know.

Mrs. Hale: Well, I don't think she did. Asking for an apron and her little shawl. Worrying about her fruit.

Mrs. Peters: [*Starts to speak, glances up, where footsteps are heard in the room above. In a low voice.*] Mr. Peters says it looks bad for her. Mr. Henderson is awful sarcastic in a speech and he'll make fun of her sayin' she didn't wake up.

MRS. HALE: Well, I guess John Wright didn't wake when they was slipping that rope under his neck.

MRS. PETERS: No, it's strange. It must have been done awful crafty and still. They say it was such a—funny way to kill a man, rigging it all up like that.

MRS. HALE: That's just what Mr. Hale said. There was a gun in the house. He says that's what he can't understand.

MRS. PETERS: Mr. Henderson said coming out that what was needed for the case was a motive; something to show anger, or—sudden feeling.

MRS. HALE: [*Who is standing by the table.*] Well, I don't see any signs of anger around here. [*She puts her hand on the dish towel which lies on the table, stands looking down at table, one half of which is clean, the other half messy.*] It's wiped to here. [*Makes a move as if to finish work, then turns and looks at loaf of bread outside the breadbox. Drops towel. In that voice of coming back to familiar things.*] Wonder how they are finding things upstairs. I hope she had it a little more redd-up° up there. You know, it seems kind of *sneaking*. Locking her up in town and then coming out here and trying to get her own house to turn against her!

MRS. PETERS: But Mrs. Hale, the law is the law.

MRS. HALE: I s'pose 'tis. [*Unbuttoning her coat.*] Better loosen up your things,

MRS. PETERS: You won't feel them when you go out.

[*Mrs. Peters takes off her fur tippet,° goes to hang it on hook at back of room, stands looking at the under part of the small corner table.*]

MRS. PETERS: She was piecing a quilt.

[*She brings the large sewing basket and they look at the bright pieces.*]

MRS. HALE: It's log cabin pattern. Pretty, isn't it? I wonder if she was goin' to quilt it or just knot it?

[*Footsteps have been heard coming down the stairs. The* SHERIFF *enters followed by* HALE *and the* COUNTY ATTORNEY.]

SHERIFF: They wonder if she was going to quilt it or just knot it!

[*The men laugh; the women look abashed.*]

COUNTY ATTORNEY: [*Rubbing his hands over the stove.*] Frank's fire didn't do much up there, did it? Well, let's go out to the barn and get that cleared up.

[*The men go outside.*]

MRS. HALE: [*Resentfully.*] I don't know as there's anything so strange, our takin' up our time with little things while we're waiting for them to get the evidence. [*She sits down at the big table smoothing out a block with decision.*] I don't see as it's anything to laugh about.

MRS. PETERS: [*Apologetically.*] Of course they've got awful important things on their minds.

[*Pulls up a chair and joins* MRS. HALE *at the table.*]

°68 *redd-up*: neat, arranged in order. 71 S.D. *tippet*: scarflike garment of fur or wool for the neck and shoulders.

MRS. HALE: [*Examining another block.*] Mrs. Peters, look at this one. Here, this is the one she was working on, and look at the sewing! All the rest of it has been so nice and even. And look at this! It's all over the place! Why, it looks as if she didn't know what she was about!

[*After she has said this they look at each other, then start to glance back at the door. After an instant* MRS. HALE *has pulled at a knot and ripped the sewing.*]

MRS. PETERS: Oh, what are you doing, Mrs. Hale?

80 MRS. HALE: [*Mildly.*] Just pulling out a stitch or two that's not sewed very good. [*Threading a needle.*] Bad sewing always made me fidgety.
MRS. PETERS: [*Nervously.*] I don't think we ought to touch things.
MRS. HALE: I'll just finish up this end. [*Suddenly stopping and leaning forward.*] Mrs. Peters?
MRS. PETERS: Yes, Mrs. Hale?
MRS. HALE: What do you suppose she was so nervous about?

85 MRS. PETERS: Oh—I don't know. I don't know as she was nervous. I sometimes sew awful queer when I'm just tired. [*MRS. HALE starts to say something, looks at MRS. PETERS, then goes on sewing.*] Well I must get these things wrapped up. They may be through sooner than we think. [*Putting apron and other things together.*] I wonder where I can find a piece of paper, and string.
MRS. HALE: In that cupboard, maybe.
MRS. PETERS: [*Looking in cupboard.*] Why, here's a bird-cage. [*Holds it up.*] Did she have a bird, Mrs. Hale?
MRS. HALE: Why, I don't know whether she did or not—I've not been here for so long. There was a man around last year selling canaries cheap, but I don't know as she took one; maybe she did. She used to sing real pretty herself.
MRS. PETERS: [*Glancing around.*] Seems funny to think of a bird here. But she must have had one, or why would she have a cage? I wonder what happened to it?

90 MRS. HALE: I s'pose maybe the cat got it.
MRS. PETERS: No, she didn't have a cat. She's got that feeling some people have about cats—being afraid of them. My cat got in her room and she was real upset and asked me to take it out.
MRS. HALE: My sister Bessie was like that. Queer, ain't it?
MRS. PETERS: [*Examining the cage.*] Why, look at this door. It's broke. One hinge is pulled apart.
MRS. HALE: [*Looking too.*] Looks as if someone must have been rough with it.

95 MRS. PETERS: Why, yes.

[*She brings the cage forward and puts it on the table.*]

MRS. HALE: I wish if they're going to find any evidence they'd be about it. I don't like this place.
MRS. PETERS: But I'm awful glad you came with me, Mrs. Hale. It would be lonesome for me sitting here alone.
MRS. HALE: It would, wouldn't it? [*Dropping her sewing.*] But I tell you what I do wish, Mrs. Peters. I wish I had come over sometimes when she was here. I—[*Looking around the room.*]—wish I had.
MRS. PETERS: But of course you were awful busy, Mrs. Hale—your house and your children.

100 MRS. HALE: I could've come. I stayed away because it weren't cheerful—and that's why I ought to have come. I—I've never liked this place. Maybe because it's down in a

hollow and you don't see the road. I dunno what it is, but it's a lonesome place and always was. I wish I had come over to see Minnie Foster sometimes. I can see now—

[*Shakes her head.*]

MRS. PETERS: Well, you mustn't reproach yourself, Mrs. Hale. Somehow we just don't see how it is with other folks until—something comes up.

MRS. HALE: Not having children makes less work—but it makes a quiet house, and Wright out to work all day, and no company when he did come in. Did you know John Wright, Mrs. Peters?

MRS. PETERS: Not to know him; I've seen him in town. They say he was a good man.

MRS. HALE: Yes—good; he didn't drink, and kept his word as well as most, I guess, and paid his debts. But he was a hard man, Mrs. Peters. Just to pass the time of day with him— [*Shivers.*] Like a raw wind that gets to the bone. [*Pauses, her eye falling on the cage.*] I should think she would 'a wanted a bird. But what do you suppose went with it?

MRS. PETERS: I don't know, unless it got sick and died.   105

[*She reaches over and swings the broken door, swings it again, both women watch it.*]

MRS. HALE: You weren't raised round here, were you? [*MRS. PETERS shakes her head.*] You didn't know—her?

MRS. PETERS: Not till they brought her yesterday.

MRS. HALE: She—come to think of it, she was kind of like a bird herself—real sweet and pretty, but kind of timid and—fluttery. How—she—did—change. [*Silence; then as if struck by a happy thought and relieved to get back to everyday things.*] Tell you what, Mrs. Peters, why don't you take the quilt in with you? It might take up her mind.

MRS. PETERS: Why, I think that's a real nice idea, Mrs. Hale. There couldn't possibly be any objection to it, could there? Now, just what would I take? I wonder if her patches are in here—and her things.

[*They look in the sewing basket.*]

MRS. HALE: Here's some red. I expect this has got sewing things in it. [*Brings out a fancy box.*]   110
What a pretty box. Looks like something somebody would give you. Maybe her scissors are in here. [*Opens box. Suddenly puts her hand to her nose.*] Why— [*MRS. PETERS bends nearer, then turns her face away.*] There's something wrapped up in this piece of silk.

MRS. PETERS: Why, this isn't her scissors.

MRS. HALE: [*Lifting the silk.*] Oh, Mrs. Peters—it's—

[*Mrs. Peters bends closer.*]

MRS. PETERS: It's the bird.

MRS. HALE: [*Jumping up.*] But, Mrs. Peters—look at it! Its neck! Look at its neck! It's all—other side *to*.

MRS. PETERS: Somebody—wrung—its—neck.   115

[*Their eyes meet. A look of growing comprehension, of horror. Steps are heard outside. MRS. HALE slips box under quilt pieces, and sinks into her chair. Enter SHERIFF and COUNTY ATTORNEY. MRS. PETERS rises.*]

COUNTY ATTORNEY: [*As one turning from serious things to little pleasantries.*] Well, ladies, have you decided whether she was going to quilt it or knot it?

MRS. PETERS: We think she was going to—knot it.

COUNTY ATTORNEY: Well, that's interesting, I'm sure. [*Seeing the bird-cage.*] Has the bird flown?

MRS. HALE: [*Putting more quilt pieces over the box.*] We think the—cat got it.

120 **COUNTY ATTORNEY:** [*Preoccupied.*] Is there a cat?

[*MRS. HALE glances in a quick covert way at MRS. PETERS.*]

MRS. PETERS: Well, not *now.* They're superstitious, you know. They leave.

COUNTY ATTORNEY: [*To SHERIFF PETERS, continuing an interrupted conversation.*] No sign at all of anyone having come from the outside. Their own rope. Now let's go up again and go over it piece by piece. [*They start upstairs.*] It would have to have been someone who knew just the—

[*MRS. PETERS sits down. The two women sit there not looking at one another, but as if peering into something and at the same time holding back. When they talk now it is in the manner of feeling their way over strange ground, as if afraid of what they are saying, but as if they cannot help saying it.*]

MRS. HALE: She liked the bird. She was going to bury it in that pretty box.

MRS. PETERS: [*In a whisper.*] When I was a girl—my kitten—there was a boy took a hatchet, and before my eyes—and before I could get there—[*Covers her face an instant.*] If they hadn't held me back I would have—[*Catches herself, looks upstairs where steps are heard, falters weakly.*]—hurt him.

125 **MRS. HALE:** [*With a slow look around her.*] I wonder how it would seem never to have had any children around. [*Pause.*] No, Wright wouldn't like the bird—a thing that sang. She used to sing. He killed that, too.

MRS. PETERS: [*Moving uneasily.*] We don't know who killed the bird.

MRS. HALE: I knew John Wright.

MRS. PETERS: It was an awful thing was done in this house that night, Mrs. Hale. Killing a man while he slept, slipping a rope around his neck that choked the life out of him.

MRS. HALE: His neck. Choked the life out of him.

[*Her hand goes out and rests on the bird-cage.*]

130 **MRS. PETERS:** [*With rising voice.*] We don't know who killed him. We don't know.

MRS. HALE: [*Her own feeling not interrupted.*] If there'd been years and years of nothing, then a bird to sing to you, it would be awful—still, after the bird was still.

MRS. PETERS: [*Something within her speaking.*] I know what stillness is. When we homesteaded in Dakota, and my first baby died—after he was two years old, and me with no other then—

MRS. HALE: [*Moving.*] How soon do you suppose they'll be through, looking for the evidence?

MRS. PETERS: I know what stillness is. [*Pulling herself back.*] The law has got to punish crime, Mrs. Hale.

135 **MRS. HALE:** [*Not as if answering that.*] I wish you'd seen Minnie Foster when she wore a white dress with blue ribbons and stood up there in the choir and sang. [*A look around the room.*] Oh, I wish I'd come over here once in a while! That was a crime! That was a crime! Who's going to punish that?

MRS. PETERS: [*Looking upstairs.*] We mustn't—take on.

MRS. HALE: I might have known she needed help! I know how things can be—for women. I tell you, it's queer, Mrs. Peters. We live close together and we live far apart. We all go through the same things—it's all just a different kind of the same thing. [*Brushes her eyes, noticing the bottle of fruit, reaches out for it.*] If I was you I wouldn't tell her her fruit was gone. Tell her it *ain't*. Tell her it's all right. Take this in to prove it to her. She—she may never know whether it was broke or not.

MRS. PETERS: [*Takes the bottle, looks about for something to wrap it in; takes petticoat from the clothes brought from the other room, very nervously begins winding this around the bottle. In a false voice.*] My, it's a good thing the men couldn't hear us. Wouldn't they just laugh! Getting all stirred up over a little thing like a—dead canary. As if that could have anything to do with—with—wouldn't they *laugh*!

[*The men are heard coming down stairs.*]

MRS. HALE: [*Under her breath.*] Maybe they would—maybe they wouldn't.

COUNTY ATTORNEY: No, Peters, it's all perfectly clear except a reason for doing it. But you   140
know juries when it comes to women. If there was some definite thing. Something to show—something to make a story about—a thing that would connect up with this strange way of doing it—

[*The women's eyes meet for an instant. Enter HALE from outer door.*]

HALE: Well, I've got the team° around. Pretty cold out there.

COUNTY ATTORNEY: I'm going to stay here a while by myself. [*To the SHERIFF.*] You can send Frank out for me, can't you? I want to go over everything. I'm not satisfied that we can't do better.

SHERIFF: Do you want to see what Mrs. Peters is going to take in?

[*The COUNTY ATTORNEY goes to the table, picks up the apron, laughs.*]

COUNTY ATTORNEY: Oh, I guess they're not very dangerous things the ladies have picked out. [*Moves a few things about, disturbing the quilt pieces which cover the box. Steps back.*] No, Mrs. Peters doesn't need supervising. For that matter, a sheriff's wife is married to the law. Ever think of it that way, Mrs. Peters?

MRS. PETERS: Not—just that way.   145

SHERIFF: [*Chuckling.*] Married to the law. [*Moves toward the other room.*] I just want you to come in here a minute, George. We ought to take a look at these windows.

COUNTY ATTORNEY: [*Scoffingly.*] Oh, windows!

SHERIFF: We'll be right out, Mr. Hale.

[*HALE goes outside. The SHERIFF follows the COUNTY ATTORNEY into the other room. Then MRS. HALE rises, hands tight together, looking intensely at MRS. PETERS, whose eyes make a slow turn, finally meeting MRS. HALE's. A moment MRS. HALE holds her, then her own eyes point the way to where the box is concealed. Suddenly MRS. PETERS throws back quilt pieces and tries to put the box in the bag she is wearing. It is too big. She opens box, starts to take bird out, cannot touch it, goes to pieces, stands there helpless. Sound of a knob turning in the other room. MRS. HALE snatches the box and puts it in the pocket of her big coat. Enter COUNTY ATTORNEY and SHERIFF.*]

°141 *team*: team of horses.

County Attorney: [*Facetiously.*] Well, Henry, at least we found out that she was not going to quilt it. She was going to—what is it you call it, ladies?

150 Mrs. Hale: [*Her hand against her pocket.*] We call it—knot it, Mr. Henderson.

CURTAIN

QUESTIONS

1. How does the first entrance of the characters establish a distinction between the men and women in the play? What is suggested by the different reactions of the men and women to the frozen preserves?

2. What does Mr. Hale report to the County Attorney in his extended narrative? How observant is he? How accurate?

3. What is needed for a strong legal case against Minnie? What does the Sheriff conclude about the kitchen? What do his conclusions tell you about the men?

4. What are the women's conclusions about the bad sewing? What does Mrs. Hale do about it? At this point, what might she be thinking about the murder?

5. Of what importance are Mrs. Hale's descriptions (a) of Minnie as a young woman and (b) of the Wrights' marriage?

6. What do the women deduce from the broken birdcage and the dead bird? How are these symbolic, and what do they symbolize?

7. How did Minnie Wright murder her husband? What hints lead you to this solution? What information permits the women to make the right inferences about the crime and the method of strangulation?

8. What does Mrs. Hale do with the "trifles" of evidence? Why? How is her reaction to the evidence different from that of Mrs. Peters? What conflict develops between these women? How is it resolved?

9. Why does Mrs. Hale feel guilty about her relationship with Minnie Wright? To what degree does her guilt shape her decisions and actions?

GENERAL QUESTIONS

1. To what does the title of this play refer? How does this irony of the word trifles help shape the play's meaning?

2. What are the men like? Are they round characters or flat? How observant are they? What is their attitude toward their jobs? Toward their own importance? Toward the women and "kitchen things"?

3. What is Mrs. Hale like? How observant is she? What is her attitude toward the men and their work, and toward herself?

4. Some critics argue that Minnie is the play's most important character, even though she never appears onstage. Do you agree? Why do you think Glaspell did not make Minnie a speaking character?

5. How is symbolism employed to establish and underscore the play's meaning? Consider especially the birdcage, the dead bird, and the repeated assertion that Mrs. Wright was going to "knot" (tie) rather than "quilt" (sew) the quilt.

BETTY KELLER (b. 1930)

Betty Keller, a Canadian, has brought a wide variety of experience to her work for the theater, including such unlikely jobs as insurance adjuster, farmer, photographer's assistant, and prison matron. She served as a teacher for many theatrical workshops in Vancouver, including four years with Playhouse Holiday. *She taught drama and theater at the Windsor Secondary School in North Vancouver until 1974, the year she published* Improvisations in Creative Drama, *the collection of short plays and sketches from which* Tea Party *is selected. She also taught at Simon Fraser University and the University of British Columbia. She was the founder/producer of the western Canadian writers festival and workshop program* The Festival of the Written Arts *from 1983 to 1994. In addition to her work in drama, she has written biographical and historical works, including* Pauline: A Biography of Pauline Johnson *(1982);* Black Wolf: The Life of Ernest Thompson Seton *(1984);* On the Shady Side: Vancouver 1886–1914 *(1986);* Sea Silver: Inside British Columbia's Salmon Farming Industry *(1996);* Bright Seas and Pioneer Spirits: The Sunshine Coast *(1996);* Better the Devil You Know *(2001); and* A Stain upon the Sea: West Coast Salmon Farming *(2004).*

Brief as *Tea Party* is, it illustrates the power of drama to depict character and situation and to convey emotion. The main characters are two lonely elderly sisters who have outlived their friends and relatives and have no one except the people who occasionally come to their house to perform various services, such as delivering the paper and reading the meters. The sketch presents their plight deftly and succinctly, touching with great tenderness on the pathos of their loneliness.

Tea Party is too short to present difficult choices for the characters, and hence they hardly get the opportunity to go through the responses and changes that are found in full-length plays. Both Alma and Hester are individualized, however, as they carry on a minor controversy about names and dates from their long-vanished past. Beyond this, in Alma's last speech, which ends the dramatic sketch, one might find a hint of the awareness and recognition that we expect of round, developed characters. Even though the paperboy is not a speaking part, his unkindness to the sisters is shown clearly, and in this way Keller dramatizes the poignant situation of persons whom life has passed by. It is difficult to find a play that conveys so much of life and feeling in so short a span of time and action.

Tea Party (1974)

CHARACTERS

    Alma Evans: seventy-five years old, small and spare framed. Her clothing is simple but not outdated, her grey hair cut short and neat. She walks with the aid of a cane, although she would not be classed as a cripple.

    Hester Evans: seventy-nine years old. There is little to distinguish her physically from her sister, except perhaps a face a little more pinched and pain-worn. She sits in a wheelchair; but although her legs may be crippled, her mind certainly is not.

    The Boy: in his early teens, seen only fleetingly.

SCENE: *The sitting room of the Evans sisters' home. The door to the street is on the rear wall Upstage Left,° a large window faces the street Upstage Center. On the right wall is the door to the kitchen; on*

°Upstage Left: To visualize stage locations, assume that the stage directions are described from the viewpoint of an actor facing the audience. Thus "Right" is actually to the left of the audience, and "Left" is right. "Downstage" refers to the front of the stage, whereas "Upstage" is the back. The terms *down* and *up* were established at a time when stages were tilted toward the audience, so that spectators at floor level could have as complete a view as possible of the entire stage.

the left, a door to the remainder of the house. Downstage Left is an easy chair, Upstage Right a sofa, Downstage Right a tea trolley. The room is crowded with the knickknacks gathered by its inhabitants in three-quarters of a century of living.

[*At rise,* ALMA *is positioning* HESTER'S *wheelchair Upstage Left.* ALMA'S *cane is on* HESTER'S *lap.*]

HESTER: That's it.

[ALMA *takes her cane from* HESTER. *They both survey the room.*]

ALMA: I think I'll sit on the sofa . . . at the far end.
HESTER: Yes. That will be cosy. Then he can sit on this end between us.

[ALMA *sits on the Downstage Right end of the sofa. They both study the effect.*]

ALMA: But then he's too close to the door, Hester!

[HESTER *nods, absorbed in the problem.*]

5   **ALMA:** [*Moving to the Upstage Left end of sofa.*] Then I'd better sit here.
HESTER: But now he's too far away from me, Alma.

[*Alma stands; both of them study the room again.*]

ALMA: But if I push the tea trolley in front of you, he'll have to come to you, won't he?
HESTER: Oh, all right, Alma. You're sure it's today?
ALMA: [*Pushing the tea trolley laden with cups and napkins, etc. to Hester.*] The first Thursday of the month.
10   **HESTER:** You haven't forgotten the chocolate biscuits?°
ALMA: No dear, they're on the plate. I'll bring them in with the tea. [*Goes to the window, peering up the street to the Right.*]
HESTER: And cocoa?
ALMA: I remembered.
HESTER: You didn't remember for Charlie's visit.
15   **ALMA:** Charlie drinks tea, Hester. I didn't make cocoa for him because he drinks tea.
HESTER: Oh, he didn't stay last time anyway.
ALMA: It was a busy day. . . .
HESTER: Rushing in and out like that. I was going to tell him about father and the *Bainbridge* . . . and he didn't stay.
ALMA: What about the *Bainbridge?*
20   **HESTER:** Her maiden voyage out of Liverpool . . . when father was gone three months and we thought he'd gone down with her.
ALMA: That wasn't the *Bainbridge.*
HESTER: Yes, it was. It was the *Bainbridge.* I remember standing on the dock in the snow when she finally came in. That was the year I'd begun first form, and I could spell out the letters on her side.
ALMA: It was her sister ship, the *Heddingham.*
HESTER: The *Bainbridge.* You were too young to remember. Let's see, the year was . . .
25   **ALMA:** Mother often told the story. It was the *Heddingham* and her engine broke down off Cape Wrath beyond the Hebrides.

°10 *chocolate biscuits:* chocolate cookies.

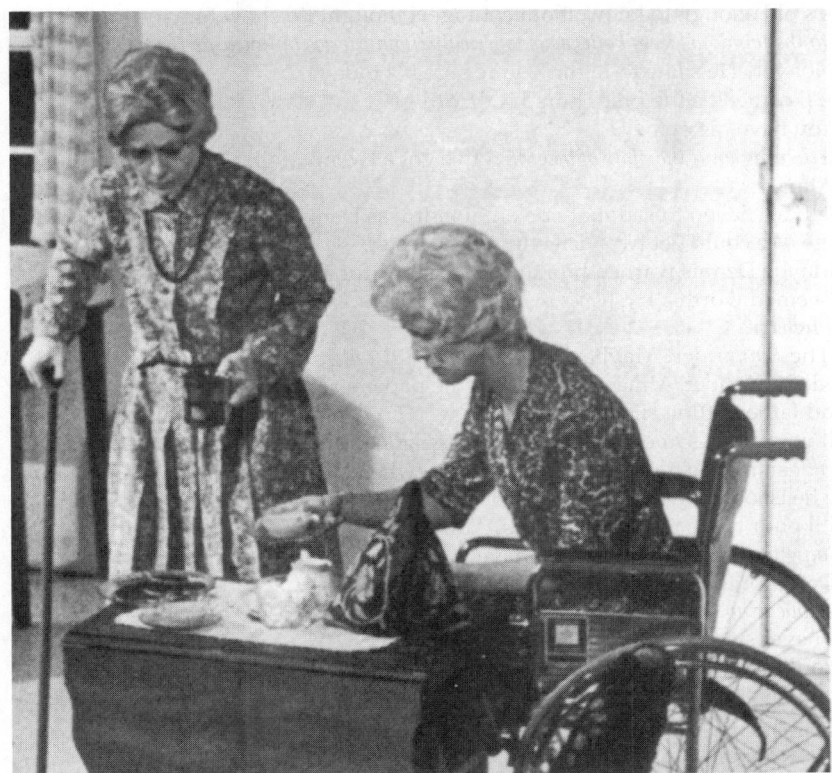

Alma (standing) and Hester (in the wheelchair) discuss what they will do if their newsboy comes in for some tea in Keller's *Tea Party*. The actors are Fran Burnside and Sandie McGinnis in the production by the Driftwood Players in February 1987.

HESTER: It was 1902 and you were just four years old.

ALMA: The *Heddingham*, and she limped into port on January the fifth.

HESTER: January the fourth just after nine in the morning, and we stood in the snow and watched the *Bainbridge* nudge the pier, and I cried and the tears froze on my cheeks.

ALMA: The *Heddingham*.

HESTER: Alma, mother didn't cry, you know. I don't think she ever cried. My memory of   30
names and places is sharp so that I don't confuse them as some others I could mention, but sometimes I can't remember things like how people reacted. But I remember that day. There were tears frozen on my cheeks but mother didn't cry.

ALMA: [*Nodding.*] She said he didn't offer a word of explanation. Just marched home beside her.

HESTER: [*Smiling.*] He never did say much. . . . Is he coming yet?

ALMA: No, can't be much longer though. Almost half past four.

HESTER: Perhaps you'd better bring in the tea. Then it will seem natural.

ALMA: Yes dear, I know. [*Exits out door Upstage Right.*] Everything's ready.   35

HESTER: What will you talk about?

ALMA: [*Re-entering with the teapot.*] I thought perhaps . . . [*Carefully putting down the teapot.*] . . . perhaps brother George!

HESTER: And the torpedo? No, Alma, he's not old enough for that story!

ALMA: He's old enough to know about courage. I thought I'd show him the medal, too. [*She goes to the window, peers both ways worriedly, then carries on towards the kitchen.*]

40 HESTER: Not yet? He's late to-night. You're sure it's today?

ALMA: He'll come. It's the first Thursday. [*Exit.*]

HESTER: You have his money?

ALMA: [*Returning with the plate of biscuits.*] I've got a twenty dollar bill, Hester.

HESTER: Alma!

45 ALMA: Well, we haven't used that one on him. It was Dennis, the last one, who always had change. We could get two visits this way, Hester.

HESTER: Maybe Dennis warned him to carry change for a twenty.

ALMA: It seemed worth a try. [*Goes to the window again.*] Are you going to tell him about the *Heddingham*?

HESTER: The *Bainbridge*. Maybe . . . or maybe I'll tell him about the day the Great War ended. Remember, Alma, all the noise, the paper streamers . . .

ALMA: And father sitting silent in his chair.

50 HESTER: It wasn't the same for him with George gone. Is he coming yet?

ALMA: No dear, maybe he's stopped to talk somewhere. [*Looking to the right.*] . . . No . . . no, there he is, on the Davis' porch now!

HESTER: I'll pour then. You get the cocoa, Alma.

ALMA: [*Going out.*] It's all ready, I just have to add hot water.

HESTER: Don't forget the marshmallows!

55 ALMA: [*Reappearing.*] Oh, Hester, what if he comes in and just sits down closest to the door? He'll never stay!

HESTER: You'll have to prod him along. For goodness sakes, Alma, get his cocoa!

[*Alma disappears.*]

HESTER: He must be nearly here. He doesn't go to the Leschynskis, and the Blackburns don't get home till after six.

ALMA: [*Returning with the cocoa.*] Here we are! Just in . . .

[*The Boy passes the window. There is a slapping sound as the newspaper lands on the porch. Alma and Hester look at the door and wait, hoping to hear a knock, but they both know the truth. Finally, Alma goes to the door, opens it and looks down at the newspaper.*]

ALMA: He's gone on by.

60 HESTER: You must have had the day wrong.

ALMA: No, he collected at the Davis'.

HESTER: [*After a long pause.*] He couldn't have forgotten us.

ALMA: [*Still holding the cocoa, she turns from the door.*] He's collecting at the Kerighan's now. [*She closes the door and stands forlornly.*]

HESTER: Well, don't stand there with that cocoa! You look silly. [*Alma brings the cocoa to the tea trolley.*] Here's your tea. [*Alma takes the cup, sits on the Upstage Left end of the sofa. There is a long silence.*]

65 HESTER: I think I'll save that story for the meter man.

ALMA: The *Heddingham*?

HESTER: The *Bainbridge*.

ALMA: [*After a pause.*] They don't read the meters for two more weeks.

Slow Blackout

QUESTIONS

1. What is the play's major conflict? The minor conflict?
2. Why do the two sisters discuss their seating arrangements for the paperboy? How do we learn that they have made these arrangements before?
3. What does Alma's plan for the twenty-dollar bill show about her? What does the discussion about both the money and the paperboys indicate about their own self-awareness?
4. How does controversy about the names *Bainbridge* and *Heddingham* help you understand the two sisters?

GENERAL QUESTIONS

1. How does Keller's description of the sets aid you in understanding the action? The normal tasks of the women? From the setting of this play, what are your conclusions about the relationship of objects and spatial arrangements to the action and development of drama?
2. Consider the women, particularly with regard to their age. In the light of their health and their isolation, how does *Tea Party* present the circumstances of the aged? How can the play be constructed as a sociological/political argument, with the elderly as the focus?

EUGENE O'NEILL (1888–1953)

Eugene O'Neill is one of America's great playwrights. He wrote more than forty plays and won three Pulitzer Prizes. He is still the only U.S. dramatist to have received the Nobel Prize for literature (1936).

O'Neill was born in New York, the son of a well-known actor, and was educated sporadically as his parents traveled from city to city on theatrical tours. Eventually he studied at Princeton, but he left to go to work, first in a mail-order house and then in Honduras, where he engaged in prospecting. He then began a brief career as a seaman, traveling on both sides of the Atlantic. He contracted tuberculosis in about 1912, and while in a sanitarium he began to write plays. Upon release he studied playwriting at Harvard, but by 1916 he had left to try his luck as a playwright with the Provincetown Players, the same company that Susan Glaspell had helped found and where she began her writing career. It was in 1916, the same year that Glaspell wrote Trifles, *that the Provincetown Players produced O'Neill's first drama,* Bound East for Cardiff.

O'Neill maintained a close connection with the Provincetown Players for several years, providing them with ten one-act plays between 1916 and 1920. Among these were Thirst *(1916),* Before Breakfast *(1916),* Fog *(1917),* The Long Voyage Home *(1917),* Ile *(1917), and* The Rope *(1917). His later (and longer) works include* The Emperor Jones *(1920),* Anna Christie *(1921),* Desire Under the Elms *(1924),* Strange Interlude *(1928),* Mourning Becomes Electra *(1931), and* The Iceman Cometh *(1946). O'Neill also wrote an autobiographical play,* Long Day's Journey into Night *(1936), that at his request was withheld until after his death. Staged on Broadway in 1956, it received the Pulitzer Prize in drama (O'Neill's third Pulitzer); it was later made into a film starring Katherine Hepburn.*

Before Breakfast, though one of O'Neill's earliest plays, shows his characteristic control of point of view, conflict, character, and setting. The play was first staged in December 1916 by the Provincetown Players in New York City's Greenwich Village (where Christopher Street, the address of the Rowlands' apartment, is located). The play contains little action, and yet it is charged with conflict. The plot is simple and straightforward—a wife onstage berates her offstage husband for twenty minutes. The conflict between them is long-standing and bitter, and it is resolved in the play's horrifying conclusion.

Above all, *Before Breakfast* illustrates O'Neill's skillful control over dramatic point of view. By giving Mrs. Rowland every word spoken on the stage, O'Neill causes the audience to understand everything as it is filtered through her mind. Indeed, the play is a bravura piece for a gifted actress. Because Mrs. Rowland dominates the stage so completely, it is tempting to see her character as one of constantly nagging spitefulness. It is to O'Neill's credit, however, that she is not without basic strength, and that her bitterness is not without cause. Alfred, the unseen and unheard offstage husband, has contributed to their estranged relationship.

Of particular note in indicating the impasse that the characters have reached are O'Neill's extensive stage directions describing the setting. We learn that the Rowlands' flat is in Greenwich Village, the traditional New York home of artists, poets, and actors. On the one hand, therefore, the flat suggests Alfred's artistic aspirations, but on the other, the poverty of the surroundings indicates the sad truth that such dreams cannot be sustained unless someone pays the rent.

The language of Mrs. Rowland, the only speaking character in the play, indicates both her lack of education and her intense dissatisfaction. Phrases such as "I got," "like I was," "liable" for "likely," and "sewing my fingers off" suggest that her knowledge of language has not been derived from education and study. Her speech also suggests the social gulf that originally separated her from Alfred, a gulf that they tried to bridge in their marriage but which now has opened up irretrievably. A number of other phrases embody the taunts that Mrs. Rowland directs at Alfred ("pawn, pawn, pawn," "like a man," "a fine life," "in trouble," etc.).

Before Breakfast (1916)

CHARACTERS

Mrs. Rowland, the wife
Mr. Alfred Rowland, the husband

0.1   SCENE. *A small room serving both as kitchen and dining room in a flat on Christopher Street, New York City. In the rear, to the right, a door leading to the outer hallway. On the left of the doorway, a sink, and a two-burner gas stove. Over the stove, and extending to the left wall, a wooden closet for dishes, etc. On the left, two windows looking out on a fire escape where several potted plants are dying of neglect. Before the windows, a table covered with oilcloth. Two cane-bottomed chairs are placed by the table. Another stands against the wall to the right of door in rear. In the right wall, rear, a doorway leading into a bedroom. Farther forward, different articles of a man's and a woman's clothing are hung on pegs. A clothes line is strung from the left corner, rear, to the right wall, forward.*

0.2   *It is about eight thirty in the morning of a fine, sunshiny day in the early fall.*

0.3   MRS. ROWLAND *enters from the bedroom, yawning, her hands still busy putting the finishing touches on a slovenly toilet by sticking hairpins into her hair which is bunched up in a drab-colored mass on top of her round head. She is of medium height and inclined to a shapeless stoutness, accentuated by her formless blue dress, shabby and worn. Her face is characterless, with small regular features and eyes of a nondescript blue. There is a pinched expression about her eyes and nose and her weak, spiteful mouth. She is in her early twenties but looks much older.*

She comes to the middle of the room and yawns, stretching her arms to their full length. Her 0.4
drowsy eyes stare about the room with the irritated look of one to whom a long sleep has not been a
long rest. She goes wearily to the clothes hanging on the right and takes an apron from a hook. She
ties it about her waist, giving vent to an exasperated "damn" when the knot fails to obey her clumsy
fingers. Finally gets it tied and goes slowly to the gas stove and lights one burner. She fills the coffee
pot at the sink and sets it over the flame. Then slumps down into a chair by the table and puts a hand
over her forehead as if she were suffering from headache. Suddenly her face brightens as though she
had remembered something, and she casts a quick glance at the dish closet; then looks sharply at the
bedroom door and listens intently for a moment or so.

MRS. ROWLAND: [*In a low voice.*] Alfred! Alfred! [*There is no answer from the next room and she*
   continues suspiciously in a louder tone.] You needn't pretend you're asleep. [*There is no*
   reply to this from the bedroom, and, reassured, she gets up from her chair and tiptoes cautiously
   to the dish closet. She slowly opens one door, taking great care to make no noise, and slides out,
   from their hiding place behind the dishes, a bottle of Gordon gin and a glass. In doing so she
   disturbs the top dish, which rattles a little. At this sound she starts guiltily and looks with sulky
   defiance at the doorway to the next room.]

   [*Her voice trembling.*] Alfred!

[*After a pause, during which she listens for any sound, she takes the glass and pours out a large*
drink and gulps it down; then hastily returns the bottle and glass to their hiding place. She closes the
closet door with the same care as she had opened it, and, heaving a great sigh of relief, sinks down
into her chair again. The large dose of alcohol she has taken has an almost immediate effect. Her fea-
tures become more animated, she seems to gather energy, and she looks at the bedroom door with a
hard, vindictive smile on her lips. Her eyes glance quickly about the room and are fixed on a man's
coat and vest which hang from a hook at right. She moves stealthily over to the open doorway and
stands there, out of sight of anyone inside, listening for any movement.]

   [*Calling in a half-whisper.*] Alfred!

Mrs. Rowland (Lona Leigh) attends to the coffee in the 2001 Provincetown Playhouse, New York City, production of
Before Breakfast, directed by Stephen Kennedy Murphy, lighting by Matthew E. Adelson, and sets by Roger Hanna.

[*Again there is no reply. With a swift movement she takes the coat and vest from the hook and returns with them to her chair. She sits down and takes the various articles out of each pocket but quickly puts them back again. At last, in the inside pocket of the vest, she finds a letter.*]

[*Looking at the handwriting—slowly to herself.*] Hmm! I knew it.

[*She opens the letter and reads it. At first her expression is one of hatred and rage, but as she goes on to the end it changes to one of triumphant malignity. She remains in deep thought for a moment, staring before her, the letter in her hands, a cruel smile on her lips. Then she puts the letter back in the pocket of the vest, and still careful not to awaken the sleeper, hangs the clothes up again on the same hook, and goes to the bedroom door and looks in.*]

5   [*In a loud, shrill voice.*] Alfred! [*Still louder.*] Alfred! [*There is a muffled, yawning groan from the next room.*] Don't you think it's about time you got up? Do you want to stay in bed all day? [*Turning around and coming back to her chair.*] Not that I've got any doubts about your being lazy enough to stay in bed forever. [*She sits down and looks out of the window, irritably.*] Goodness knows what time it is. We haven't even got any way of telling the time since you pawned your watch like a fool. The last valuable thing we had, and you knew it. It's been nothing but pawn, pawn, pawn, with you—anything to put off getting a job, anything to get out of going to work like a man.

[*She taps the floor with her foot nervously, biting her lips.*]

[*After a short pause.*] Alfred! Get up, do you hear me? I want to make that bed before I go out. I'm sick of having this place in a continual muss on your account. [*With a certain vindictive satisfaction.*] Not that we'll be here long unless you manage to get some money some place. Heaven knows I do my part—and more—going out to sew every day while you play the gentleman and loaf around bar rooms with that good-for-nothing lot of artists from the Square.°

[*A short pause during which she plays nervously with a cup and saucer on the table.*]

And where are you going to get money, I'd like to know? The rent's due this week and you know what the landlord is. He won't let us stay a minute over our time. You say you *can't* get a job. That's a lie and you know it. You never even look for one. All you do is moon around all day writing silly poetry and stories that no one will buy—and no wonder they won't. I notice I can always get a position, such as it is; and it's only that which keeps us from starving to death.

[*Gets up and goes over to the stove—looks into the coffee pot to see if the water is boiling; then comes back and sits down again.*]

You'll have to get money to-day some place. I can't do it all, and I won't do it all. You've got to come to your senses. You've got to beg, borrow, or steal it somewheres. [*With a contemptuous laugh.*] But where, I'd like to know? You're too proud to beg, and you've borrowed the limit, and you haven't the nerve to steal.

[*After a pause—getting up angrily.*] Aren't you up yet, for heaven's sake? It's just like you to go to sleep again, or pretend to. [*She goes to the bedroom door and looks in.*] Oh, you are up. Well, it's about time. You needn't look at me like that. Your airs don't fool me a bit any more. I know you too well—better than you think I do—you and your goings-on.

°6 *Square*: Washington Square, at the center of Greenwich Village in New York.

[*Turning away from the door—meaningly.*] I know a lot of things, my dear. Never mind what I know, now. I'll tell you before I go, you needn't worry. [*She comes to the middle of the room and stands there, frowning.*]

[*Irritably.*] Hmm! I suppose I might as well get breakfast ready—not that there's   10 anything much to get. [*Questioningly.*] Unless you have some money? [*She pauses for an answer from the next room which does not come.*] Foolish question! [*She gives a short, hard laugh.*] I ought to know you better than that by this time. When you left here in such a huff last night I knew what would happen. You can't be trusted for a second. A nice condition you came home in! The fight we had was only an excuse for you to make a beast of yourself. What was the use pawning your watch if all you wanted with the money was to waste it in buying drink?

[*Goes over to the dish closet and takes out plates, cups, etc., while she is talking.*]

Hurry up! It don't take long to get breakfast these days, thanks to you. All we got this morning is bread and butter and coffee; and you wouldn't even have that if it wasn't for me sewing my fingers off. [*She slams the loaf of bread on the table with a bang.*]

The bread's stale. I hope you'll like it. *You* don't deserve any better, but I don't see why *I* should suffer.

[*Going over to the stove.*] The coffee'll be ready in a minute, and you needn't expect me to wait for you.

[*Suddenly with great anger.*] What on earth are you doing all this time? [*She goes over to the door and looks in.*] Well, you're *almost* dressed at any rate. I expected to find you back in bed. That'd be just like you. How awful you look this morning! For heaven's sake, shave! You're disgusting! You look like a tramp. No wonder no one will give you a job. I don't blame them—when you don't even look halfway decent. [*She goes to the stove.*] There's plenty of hot water right here. You've got no excuse. [*Gets a bowl and pours some of the water from the coffee pot into it.*] Here.

[*He reaches his hand into the room for it. It is a sensitive hand with slender fingers. It trembles and some of the water spills on the floor.*]

[*Tauntingly.*] Look at your hand tremble! You'd better give up drinking. You can't stand it.   15 It's just your kind that get the D.T.'s. *That would be* the last straw! [*Looking down at the floor.*] Look at the mess you've made of this floor—cigarette butts and ashes all over the place. Why can't you put them on a plate? No, you wouldn't be considerate enough to do that. You never think of me. You don't have to sweep the room and that's all you care about.

[*Takes the broom and commences to sweep viciously, raising a cloud of dust. From the inner room comes the sound of a razor being stropped.*]°

[*Sweeping.*] Hurry up! It must be nearly time for me to go. If I'm late I'm liable to lose my position, and then I couldn't support you any longer. [*As an afterthought she adds sarcastically.*] And then you'd have to go to work or something dreadful like that. [*Sweeping under the table.*] What I want to know is whether you're going to look for a job today or not. You know your family won't help us any more. They've had enough of you, too. [*After a moment's silent sweeping.*] I'm about sick of all this life. I've a good notion to go home, if I wasn't too proud to let them know what a failure you've been—you, the millionaire Rowland's only son, the

---

°15. *S.D. stropped:* Alfred is using a leather strap to sharpen a straight razor, the kind barbers still use, with a very sharp steel blade that is hinged to a handle.

Harvard graduate, the poet, the catch of the town—Huh! [*With bitterness.*] There wouldn't be many of them now envy my catch if they knew the truth. What has our marriage been, I'd like to know? Even before your *millionaire* father died owing everyone in the world money, you certainly never wasted any of your time on your wife. I suppose you thought I'd ought to be glad you were *honorable* enough to marry me—after getting me into trouble. You were ashamed of me with your fine friends because my father's only a grocer, that's what you were. At least he's honest, which is more than any one could say about yours. [*She is sweeping steadily toward the door. Leans on her broom for a moment.*]

You hoped every one'd think you'd been forced to marry me, and pity you, didn't you? You didn't hesitate much about telling me you loved me, and making me believe your lies, before it happened, did you? You made me think you didn't want your father to buy me off as he tried to do. I know better now. I haven't lived with you all this time for nothing. [*Somberly.*] It's lucky the poor thing was born dead, after all. What a father you'd have been!

[*Is silent, brooding moodily for a moment—then she continues with a sort of savage joy.*]

But I'm not the only one who's got you to thank for being unhappy. There's one other, at least, and *she* can't hope to marry you now. [*She puts her head into the next room.*] How about Helen? [*She starts back from the doorway, half frightened.*]

Don't look at me that way! Yes, I read her letter. What about it? I got a right to. I'm your wife. And I know all there is to know, so don't lie. You needn't stare at me so. You can't bully me with your superior airs any longer. Only for me you'd be going without breakfast this very morning. [*She sets the broom back in the corner—whiningly.*] You never did have any gratitude for what I've done. [*She comes to the stove and puts the coffee into the pot.*] The coffee's ready. I'm not going to wait for you. [*She sits down in her chair again.*]

20 [*After a pause—puts her hand to her head—fretfully.*] My head aches so this morning. It's a shame I've got to go to work in a stuffy room all day in my condition. And I wouldn't if you were half a man. By rights I ought to be lying on my back instead of you. You know how sick I've been this last year; and yet you object when I take a little something to keep up my spirits. You even didn't want me to take that tonic I got at the drug store. [*With a hard laugh.*] I know you'd be glad to have me dead and out of your way; then you'd be free to run after all these silly girls that think you're such a wonderful, misunderstood person—this Helen and the others. [*There is a sharp exclamation of pain from the next room.*]

[*With satisfaction.*] There! I knew you'd cut yourself. It'll be a lesson to you. You know you oughtn't to be running around nights drinking with your nerves in such an awful shape. [*She goes to the door and looks in.*]

What makes you so pale? What are you staring at yourself in the mirror that way for? For goodness sake, wipe that blood off your face! [*With a shudder.*] It's horrible. [*In relieved tones.*] There, that's better. I never could stand the sight of blood. [*She shrinks back from the door a little.*] You better give up trying and go to a barber shop. Your hand shakes dreadfully. Why do you stare at me like that? [*She turns away from the door.*] Are you still mad at me about that letter? [*Defiantly.*] Well, I had a right to read it. I'm your wife. [*She comes to the chair and sits down again. After a pause.*]

I knew all the time you were running around with someone. Your lame excuses about spending the time at the library didn't fool me. Who is this Helen, anyway? One of those artists? Or does she write poetry, too? Her letter sounds that way. I'll bet she told you your things were the best ever, and you believed her, like a fool. Is she young and pretty? I was young and pretty, too, when you fooled me with your fine, poetic talk; but life with you would soon wear anyone down. What I've been through!

[*Goes over and takes the coffee off the stove.*] Breakfast is ready. [*With a contemptuous glance.*] Breakfast! [*Pours out a cup of coffee for herself and puts the pot on the table.*] Your coffee'll be cold. What are you doing—still shaving, for heaven's sake? You'd better give it up. One of these mornings you'll give yourself a serious cut. [*She cuts off bread and butters it. During the following speeches she eats and sips her coffee.*]

I'll have to run as soon as I've finished eating. One of us has got to work. [*Angrily.*] Are 25 you going to look for a job today or aren't you? I should think some of your fine friends would help you, if they really think you're so much. But I guess they just like to hear you talk. [*Sits in silence for a moment.*]

I'm sorry for this Helen, whoever she is. Haven't you got any feelings for other people? What will her family say? I see she mentions them in her letter. What is she going to do— have the child—or go to one of those doctors? That's a nice thing, I must say. Where can she get the money? Is she rich? [*She waits for some answer to this volley of questions.*]

Hmm! You won't tell me anything about her, will you? Much I care. Come to think of it, I'm not so sorry for her after all. She knew what she was doing. She isn't any schoolgirl, like I was, from the looks of her letter. Does she know you're married? Of course, she must. All your friends know about your unhappy marriage. I know they pity you, but they don't know my side of it. They'd talk different if they did.

[*Too busy eating to go on for a second or so.*]

This Helen must be a fine one, if she knew you were married. What does she expect, then? That I'll divorce you and let her marry you? Does she think I'm crazy enough for that—after all you've made me go through? I guess not! And you can't get a divorce from me and you know it. No one can say *I've* ever done anything wrong. [*Drinks the last of her cup of coffee.*]

She deserves to suffer, that's all I can say. I'll tell you what I think; I think your Helen is no better than a common street-walker, that's what I think. [*There is a stifled groan of pain from the next room.*]

Did you cut yourself again? Serves you right. [*Gets up and takes off her apron.*] Well, I've 30 got to run along. [*Peevishly.*] This is a fine life for me to be leading! I won't stand for your loafing any longer. [*Something catches her ear and she pauses and listens intently.*] There! You've overturned the water all over everything. Don't say you haven't. I can hear it dripping on the floor. [*A vague expression of fear comes over her face.*] Alfred! Why don't you answer me?

[*She moves slowly toward the room. There is the noise of a chair being overturned and something crashes heavily to the floor. She stands, trembling with fright.*]

Alfred! Alfred! Answer me! What is it you knocked over? Are you still drunk? [*Unable to stand the tension a second longer she rushes to the door of the bedroom.*] Alfred!

[*She stands in the doorway looking down at the floor of the inner room, transfixed with horror. Then she shrieks wildly and runs to the other door, unlocks it and frenziedly pulls it open, and runs shriek-ing madly into the outer hallway.*]

[*The curtain falls.*]

QUESTIONS

1. What does the setting tell you about the Rowlands?
2. How is Mrs. Rowland described in the opening stage directions? How does O'Neill use adjectives to shape your initial response to her? How does the rest of the play sustain or alter this image?
3. How does Mrs. Rowland speak to Alfred? What does she complain about? What does she accuse Alfred of being and doing?
4. What happened during Mrs. Rowland's premarital affair with Alfred? Why didn't she let Alfred's father "buy her off"?
5. Where is the play's crisis? Which character comes to a crisis? What leads you to conclude that the character and play have reached a crisis?
6. Mrs. Rowland precipitates the climax by discussing Alfred's affair. What do we learn about Helen? What pushes Alfred over the edge?

GENERAL QUESTIONS

1. How does the setting define the characters, their relationship, and their life? What details of setting are most significant?
2. Is Mrs. Rowland flat or round? Static or dynamic? Individualized or stereotyped? Why does she have no first name?
3. Why is Alfred Rowland kept off stage (except for his hand) and given no dialogue? How does this affect the play?
4. Alfred is presented from his wife's point of view. How accurate is this portrait? To what degree does Alfred justify his wife's accusations?
5. Why does O'Neill present the history of Alfred's family and his relationship with Mrs. Rowland out of chronological order? What is the effect of this method of presentation?

WRITING ABOUT THE ELEMENTS OF DRAMA

Although some aspects of drama, such as lighting and stage movement, are purely theatrical, drama shares a number of elements with fiction and poetry. The planning and the writing processes for essays about drama are therefore similar to those used for essays on the other genres. As you plan, select a play and an appropriate element or series of elements. It would be inappropriate, for example, to attempt an essay about character development in *Tea Party* (p. 1245), because this play is too short to probe the two characters deeply.

Once you select the play, choose a focus, which will be your central idea. For example, you might argue that a character is flat, static, nonrealistic, or symbolic of good or evil. Or, to assert relationships among elements, you might claim that a play's meaning is shaped and emphasized through setting or through conflict.

Topics for Discovering Ideas

PLOT, ACTION, CONFLICT. (See also Chapter 1.) In planning an essay on plot or structure, demonstrate how actions and conflicts unfold. In addition, link this concern to other dramatic elements, such as tone or theme. In general, this topic breaks down into three areas—conflict, plot, and structure. For conflict, determine what the conflicts are, which one is central, and how it is resolved. What kind of conflict is it? Does it suggest any general behavioral patterns? For plot, determine the separate stages of development. What is the climax? The dénouement? How are they anticipated or foreshadowed? In examining plot structures and patterns, determine whether the play has a subplot or second plot. If so, how is it related to the main plot? Is a significant pattern of action repeated? If so, what is the effect? To what extent do these parallel or repetitive patterns influence theme and meaning? How do they control your responses?

CHARACTERS. (See also Chapter 3.) Focus on a significant figure and formulate a central idea about his or her personality, function, or meaning. Is the character round or flat? Static or dynamic? Individualized or stereotyped? Realistic or nonrealistic? Symbolic? How is the character described in the stage directions? By other characters? By himself or herself? What does he or she do, think, say? What is the character's attitude toward the environment? The action? Other characters? Himself or herself? To what extent does he or she articulate and/or embody key ideas in the play?

POINT OF VIEW AND PERSPECTIVE. (See also Chapter 2.) In many plays, such as *Hamlet* (Chapter 24) and *Before Breakfast,* the playwright presents the action from the perspective of an individual character. The audience therefore sees things as this character sees the same things, influences them, and is influenced by them. When you deal with such a technique, consider how the perspective affects the play's structure and meaning. Why is this point of view useful or striking? What does it suggest about character? Theme? To what extent does your reaction to the play correspond with or diverge from this perspective?

Another feature of perspective is that characters may speak directly to the audience, in a *soliloquy,* or indirectly, in a *monologue.* In dealing with these perspectives, consider whether you sympathize with the character doing the speaking. What information does the character convey? What is he or she trying to prove? What is the tone of the speech? What do these devices contribute to your response? Generally, what does the perspective contribute to your understanding of the play?

SETTING, SETS, AND PROPS. (See also Chapter 4.) Normally, you will not write about setting and properties in isolation; such an essay would simply produce a detailed description of the setting(s) and objects. Instead, a discussion of setting in drama should be linked to another element, such as character, mood, or meaning. Such an essay will demonstrate the ways in which setting(s) and objects help establish the play's time, place, characters, lifestyle, values, or ideas.

When dealing with a single setting, pay close attention to the opening stage directions and any other directions or dialogue that describe the environment or objects. In plays with multiple settings, you will normally select one or two for examination. Ask yourself whether the setting is realistic or nonrealistic and to what extent it may be symbolic. What details and objects are specified? What do these tell you about the time, the place, and the characters and their way of life and values? To what extent does the setting contribute to the play's tone, atmosphere, impact, and meaning?

DICTION, IMAGERY, AND STYLE. (See also Chapters 6, 12, and 14.) As with setting, try to connect the devices of language to some other element, such as tone, character, or meaning. Investigate the play's levels of diction and types of dialect, jargon, slang, or clichés. To what extent do these techniques define the characters and support or undercut their ideas? What connotative words or phrases are repeated? Which are spoken at particularly significant moments? What striking or consistent threads of imagery, metaphor, tone, or meaning do you find? How do all these aspects of language shape your reaction?

TONE AND ATMOSPHERE. (See also Chapters 6, 12, and 16.) Try to deal with *how* the tone is established and *what* impact it has on the play's meaning. Seek those devices the playwright employs to control your attitudes toward individual characters, situations, and outcomes. Look for clues in stage directions, diction, imagery, rhetorical devices, tempo, and context. Is tone articulated directly? Or indirectly, through irony? Also try to establish the presence of dramatic irony: To what extent do you (as a reader or spectator) know more than many of the onstage characters?

SYMBOLISM AND ALLEGORY. (See also Chapters 7 and 19.) Try to determine the characters, objects, settings, situations, actions, words or phrases, and/or costumes that seem to be symbolic. What do they symbolize, and how do you know that they are symbolic? Are they universal or contextual? Is the symbolism extensive and consistent enough to form an allegorical system? If so, what are the two levels of meaning addressed by the allegory? To what extent does the symbolism or allegory shape the play's meaning and your responses to it?

THEME. (See also Chapter 8.) The questions and areas of concern listed above should help you in discussing theme. Try to connect theme with various other aspects of the play, such as character, conflict, action, setting, language, or symbolism. What key ideas does the play explore, and what aspects of the play convey these ideas most emphatically? In dealing with each topic and question, isolate the elements and devices that have the strongest impact on meaning.

Strategies for Organizing Ideas

For an essay on drama, you might choose from a number of strategies. If you are writing about loneliness and frustration in Keller's *Tea Party*, for example, you might select a number of objects or occurrences as the launching point for your discussion. Some of these might be the tea trolley and the sofa, the bringing in of the cocoa, or the paperboy's rapid movement past the window. In discussing the crimes of Claudius in Shakespeare's *Hamlet*, you might choose (1) the testimony of the Ghost to Hamlet, (2) Claudius's reaction to the players' scene, (3) his speech as he is praying, and (4) his poisoning of the cup, showing how these actions convincingly establish his villainy. For such essays, you might devote separate paragraphs to each element, or you might use two or more paragraphs for each element as you develop your ideas further.

Similar strategies can be found for every possible type of essay on drama. In dealing with character in Keller's *Tea Party*, for example, you might claim that a number of symbolic props help to establish and reinforce the characters of the two aged sisters and their loneliness. You might then use separate paragraphs to discuss these related symbols, such as Hester's wheelchair, the arrangement of the furniture, or the preparation for serving tea. Similarly, in writing about language in plays like Anton Chekhov's *The Bear* (Chapter 25), you would establish how the particular play connects qualities of speech to revelations about topics such as character and idea. Thus, Smirnov's constant use of exclamations, shouts, and profanity, at least until shortly before the play's end, establish his irascibility.

 ## REFERRING TO PLAYS AND PARTS OF PLAYS

Italicize or underline the titles of plays as you would do for book titles. In referring to speeches, assume that your reader may have a text different from yours. Therefore, provide the information necessary for finding the exact location, regardless of text.

In the body of your essay: For a play with act, scene, and line or speech numbers, refer to *Act* (Arabic numeral), *scene* (Arabic numeral), and *line* or *speech* number (Arabic numeral), separated by commas. For clarity, spell out these words: *Hamlet accuses his mother of offenses against his father in Act 3, scene 4, line 9*, or *Claudius defends his own status as king in Act 4, scene 5, lines 120–23*.

In direct quotations including block quotations (set apart from your own writing): Write the Arabic numbers in parentheses following the quotation, as in (*3.1.33*). Use periods to separate these numbers. When no word precedes the last number, this number is understood to refer to a line in a poetic play. If you are referring to speeches, however, it is best for you to make this fact clear. Thus, if you write "(2.2.speech 38)," you will leave no doubt in your reader's mind that you are referring to the second act, the second scene, and the thirty-eighth speech. The principle you should always follow is that your reference should leave no doubts in your reader's mind about what the numbers mean.

When a play is divided into acts but not scenes, or if the play contains only one act, spell out the details completely. Thus, in a play like *Death of a Salesman*, which contains two acts and an epilogue, you may refer to *Act 1, speech 348*, or *Epilogue, speech 5*. If the play contains no act numbers but only numbered scenes, spell things out similarly: *scene 1, speech 29*. When referring to a one-act play like *Tea Party*, use the speech number; e.g., *speech 60, speech 22*.

For stage directions: Use the line or speech number immediately preceding the direction, and abbreviate *stage direction* as *S.D.*, as in *scene 1, speech 16 S.D.* Your reader will then know that you are referring to the stage direction following speech 16 in scene 1. If there are stage directions at the opening of the play before the speeches begin (as in *Before Breakfast*), use a zero and then a decimal point followed by an Arabic numeral to refer to the paragraph of directions. Thus *0.3 S.D.* refers to the third paragraph of directions at the play's beginning.

For prefaces, scene directions, and casts of characters: Not all of the plays have prefatory material; but if there is a preface, refer to it as though you are considering a stage direction, as in *Miller reminds us to be "aware of towering angular shapes" in the introductory remarks to Act 1 (0.2 S.D.).*

For scene directions at the beginning of acts or scenes, use the most specific style to make the circumstances clear: *The scene directions for Act 1 of Ibsen's* A Dollhouse *describe the comfortable home of the Helmer family;* or *In the section marked "The Setting" beginning Act 1 of* Mulatto, *Hughes states that Colonel Norwood's living room is "long outdated" (0.2 S.D.).*

For the cast of characters, the same principle applies. Spell out what you mean, such as the *cast of characters*, the *Characters* list, or the *Dramatis Personae*, as in *"In the 'Cast of Characters' list of* Mulatto, *Hughes indicates that Colonel Norwood is a 'commanding' person."* The important thing about referring to parts of plays is that you be clear and exact. The guidance offered here will cover most situations, but complications and exceptions will occur. When they do, always ask your instructor what to do and what systems of reference to use.

Illustrative Student Essay

Underlined sentences in this paper *do not* conform to MLA style and are used solely as teaching tools to emphasize the central idea, thesis sentence, and topic sentences throughout the paper.

Cooper 1

Cameron Cooper

Professor Ortiz

English 129

6 April 2008

Eugene O'Neill's Use of Negative Descriptions and Stage Directions in <u>Before</u>

<u>Breakfast</u>° as a Means of Revealing Character

    In the one-act play <u>Before Breakfast</u>, O'Neill dramatizes the suicidal crisis   [1]

and climax of a worsening husband-wife relationship. The story of the

---

°This play appears on pages 1248–54.

Cooper 2

marriage is clear. Mrs. Rowland, when still a young girl, was naive and opportunistic. She seduced and then married Alfred Rowland, who she thought was the heir of his father's millions. Her resulting pregnancy ended in stillbirth. As if this were not enough, Alfred's father died not a millionaire, but a pauper. During the years of these disappointments, Mrs. Rowland has lost whatever pleasantness she once possessed and has descended into a state of personal neglect, alcoholism, and selfishness.[*] To bring out these traits early in the play, O'Neill relies on negative descriptions and stage directions.[†]

    The descriptions of Mrs. Rowland's personal neglect emphasize her loss of **[2]** self-esteem. The directions indicate that she has allowed her figure to become "a shapeless stoutness," and that she has piled her hair into a "drab-colored mass." This neglect of her physical person is capped off, according to O'Neill's description, by her blue dress, which is "shabby and worn" and "formless" (0.1 S.D.). Clearly, the shabbiness and excessive wear may result from poverty and thus show little about her character, but the formlessness of the dress indicates a characteristic lack of concern about appearance, also shown by her stoutness and her hair. This slovenliness shows how she wants to appear in public, because she is dressed and ready to go to work for the day. O'Neill's negative descriptions thus define her lack of self-respect.

    Similarly uncomplimentary, O'Neill's directions about her sneakiness reveal **[3]** her dependence on alcohol. A serious sign of distress, even though it might also be funny onstage, is the direction indicating that she takes out a bottle of gin that she keeps hidden in a "dish closet" (speech 1 S.D.). With this stage direction O'Neill symbolizes the weakest trait of the secret drinker, which he also shows in the direction that Mrs. Rowland brightens up once she has taken a stiff jolt of gin:

> The large dose of alcohol she has taken has an almost immediate effect. Her features become more animated, she seems to gather energy, and she looks at the bedroom with a hard, vindictive smile on her lips. (speech 1 S.D.)

[*]Central idea.
[†]Thesis sentence.

Cooper 3

It is safe to assume that these stage directions, on the morning of the play's action, would also have applied to her behavior on many previous mornings. In short, O'Neill is telling us that Mrs. Rowland is a secret alcoholic.

[4]   The furtiveness of her drinking also shows up in her search of Alfred's clothing, which also shows her selfishness and bitterness. When she methodically empties his pockets and uncovers the letter that we soon learn is from his mistress, the stage directions show that she unhesitatingly reads the letter. Then O'Neill directs the actress to form "a cruel smile on her lips" as she thinks about what to do with this new information (speech 4 S.D.). As with the drinking, we see Mrs. Rowland rifling through Alfred's things only this once, but the action suggests that this secretive prying is a regular feature of her life. However, it is her discovery on this morning--before breakfast--that is the key to the action, because her extensive monologue against her husband, which constitutes most of the play, allows her to vent all her hatred by reproaching him about his lack of work, his neglect of her, the time he spends with friends, and his love affair.

[5]   While O'Neill uses these stage directions and descriptions to convey Mrs. Rowland's unpleasantness, he provides balance in her speeches and additional actions. He makes her a master of harangue, but there is nothing either in the directions or in her speeches to indicate that she wants to drive Alfred to suicide. Indeed, her horror at his suicide is genuine--just as it concludes the play with an incredible shock. In addition, on the positive side, her speeches show that despite her alcoholism and anger she is actually functioning in the outside world--as a seamstress--and that it is she who provides the meager money on which the couple is living (speech 6). In addition, she is working despite the fact that she has been feeling ill for a period of time (speech 20). She also has enough concern for Alfred to bring him hot water for shaving (speech 14 S.D.).

[6]   It is clear that O'Neill wants us to conclude that if Mrs. Rowland were a supportive person, Alfred might not be the nervous alcoholic who cuts his throat in the bathroom. However, the play does not make clear that he ever could have been better, even with the maximum support of a perfect wife.

Cooper 4

Certainly, Mrs. Rowland is not supportive. The stage directions and speeches show that she is limited by her weakness and bitterness. With such defects of character, she has unquestionably never given Alfred any support at all, and probably never could. Everything that O'Neill tells us about her indicates that she is petty and selfish, and that she originally married Alfred expecting to receive and not to give.

    As things stand at the beginning of the play, then, Alfred is at the brink of   **[7]** despair, and Mrs. Rowland's bitter and reproachful speeches drive him to self-destruction. Despite all the malice that O'Neill attributes to her character through the stage descriptions and directions, however, it is not possible to say that she is the sole cause of Alfred's suicide. O'Neill shows that Mrs. Rowland is an unpleasant, spiteful, and messy whiner, but it is not possible to reach any further conclusions.

Cooper 5

Work Cited

Eugene O'Neill, Before Breakfast. Literature: An Introduction to Reading and
    Writing. Ed. Edgar V. Roberts. 9th ed. New York: Pearson Longman, 2009.
    1248–54.

Commentary on the Essay

This essay shows how dramatic conventions can be considered in reference to the analysis of character. Although the essay refers briefly to Mrs. Rowland's speeches, it stresses those descriptions and directions that O'Neill designs specifically for the actress performing the role. The essay thus indicates one way to discuss a play, as distinguished from a story or poem.

    The introductory paragraph contains enough of the story about Mrs. Rowland and her husband to help the reader make sense of the subsequent material about the stage directions and descriptions. Throughout the essay, paragraph transitions are effected by words such as *similarly, also, while,* and *then.*

Paragraph 2, the first of the body, deals with O'Neill's stage directions concerning Mrs. Rowland's slovenly appearance and personal care. Paragraphs 3 and 4 are concerned with directions about her behavior—first her excessive drinking and then her search of Alfred's clothing. Paragraph 5 briefly attempts to consider how O'Neill uses Mrs. Rowland's speeches and other actions to balance the totally negative portrait he builds up through the negative stage directions.

Paragraphs 6 and 7 close the essay. Paragraph 6 considers how the stage directions lead no further than the conclusion that the Rowland' marriage is a terrible one. Paragraph 7 continues the argument of paragraph 6, with the additional thought that O'Neill's stage directions do not justify concluding that Mrs. Rowland's spiteful character is the cause of her husband's suicide.

Writing Topics About the Elements of Drama

1. *Tea Party* might be considered sentimental, on the grounds that the two elderly characters are presented to evoke sympathy and anguish, not to resemble the life of real persons. Write an essay defending the play against this judgment, being sure to make references to Keller's characterizations and her development of character.

2. *Before Breakfast* is set in an apartment in Greenwich Village in Lower Manhattan around 1916. It was performed in Greenwich Village in December 1916. Write an essay that deals with the following questions.

   a. What do you make of this convergence of settings—artistic and realistic?

   b. What do you think O'Neill assumed about his original audience's reaction to the setting?

3. Write an essay on one of the following topics. Before you begin writing, you might read Chapter 29 for suggestions on how to proceed.

   a. The viewpoint of the men in *Trifles*.

   b. A feminist analysis of Mrs. Rowland in *Before Breakfast*.

   c. The two sisters as archetypal old people in *Tea Party*.

   d. The economic situation of the characters in *The Sandbox*.

4. On the basis of the plays included in this chapter, write an essay dealing with the characteristics of the dramatic form. Consider topics such as dialogue, monologue, soliloquy, action, vocal ranges, staging, comparative lengths of plays, pauses in speech, stage directions, laughter, seriousness, and the means by which the dramatists engage the audience in characters and situations.

5. Using the catalogue in your library, or online resources, look up the category *Drama—Criticism* or *Drama—History and Criticism*, whatever title your sources use. You will find a number of categories, such as the relationship of drama to (a) elements, (b) history, (c) origin, (d) philosophy, (e) production, (f) religion, (g) stagecraft, and (h) themes. Develop a short bibliography on one of these topics and take out two or three of the relevant books. Describe them briefly, and explain—and criticize if possible—the principal ideas in one of the chapters.

Chapter 24

The Tragic Vision: Affirmation Through Loss

ragedy is drama in which a major character undergoes a loss but also achieves illumination or a new perspective. It is considered the most elevated literary form because it concentrates affirmatively on the religious and cosmic implications of its major character's misfortunes. In ancient Greece, it originated as a key element in Athenian religious festivals during the decades before Athens became a major military, economic, and cultural power during the fifth century BCE.

Tragedy, however, was not religious in a sectarian sense. It did not dramatize religious doctrines and did not present a consistent religious view. To the Athenians, religion connected the past with the present and with the gods, and through this connection it served to enrich individuals, society, and the state.

Originally, tragedy in Athens was associated with the worship of Dionysus—one of the twelve principal gods who, it was thought, transformed human personality, freed people from care and grief, ensured their fertility, and provided them with joy. To elevate this god in the eyes of his fellow Athenians, the Athenian tyrant Peisistratus (ruled 560–527 BCE) added the worship of Dionysus to the regular religious festivals that the Athenians held in honor of their gods.[1]

The Origins of Tragedy

From the standpoint of drama, the most significant of these Dionysian festivals were the **Lenaia**—a short celebration held in January (the Greek month *Gamelion*)—and the **City Dionysia** (or **Great Dionysia**)—a weeklong event in March-April (*Elaphebolion*, the month of stags). In the sixth century BCE, ceremonies held during the festival of the City Dionysia began to include tragedy, although not in the form that has been transmitted to us. The philosopher and critic

---

[1]Ancient religion is difficult for us to comprehend fully because of our completely different religious traditions and the passage of 2,500 years of history. In its origins, Greek religion was local in nature—a by-product of the geographic isolation of the various Greek city-states. Collective public worship of a single god within centrally located religious buildings—like the churches, temples, and mosques we know today—did not then exist. Instead, the Greeks believed in many gods with varying powers and interests who could travel invisibly and at will from place to place within their dominions. Consequently the Greeks erected many separate local shrines and sanctuaries for their gods,, which were considered holy to particular gods and where people might place offerings and say prayers. (See Acts, 17:24, for a reference to such shrines in the Ancient Near East.) Throughout the Greek world there were apparently more than 300 shrines dedicated to Asclepius, the God of Healing and Medicine, where worshipers could pray individually for their ailments to be cured. In important city-states like Athens and Corinth, large temples were dedicated to gods, such as Zeus, Athena, and Apollo, whom leading citizens especially revered. Even then, the temples were not designed for mass worship, but rather were considered resident sanctuaries for the gods themselves. Therefore, the major space in the temples was a holy-of-holies reserved only for the god. To make public this essentially private worship, the Greek city-states held religious festivals such as the Athenian celebrations of Dionysus and Athena.

Aristotle (384–322 BCE), writing almost two hundred years after these events, claimed that the first tragedies developed from a choral ode called a **dithyramb**— an ode or song that was sung or chanted and also danced by large choruses of men at the festivals.[2] According to Aristole, the first tragedies were choral improvisations originating with "the authors of the Dithyramb" (*Poetics* IV.12, p.19).

The Stories of Tragedy Were Drawn from Tales of Prehistoric Times

From Aristotle's claim, we can conclude that tragedy soon took on the characteristics and conventions that elevated it. For subject matter, writers turned to well-known stories, or myths, or legends, about the heroes and demigods of the prehistoric period between the vanished age of bronze and the living age of iron. These myths described individual adventures and achievements, including epic explorations and battles that had taken place principally during the time of the Trojan War. Like the stories that we know from the Bible, the Greek myths illustrated divine-human relationships and also served as examples or models of heroic behavior. With few exceptions, these myths became the fixed tragic subject matter. Indeed, Aristotle called them the "received legends" that by his time in the fourth century BCE had become the "usual subjects of tragedy" (*Poetics* IX.8, p. 37).

The mythical heroes—many of whom were objects of cult worship—were kings, queens, princes, and princesses. They engaged in conflicts; they suffered; and, often, they died. Although they were great and noble, they were nevertheless human, and a common critical judgment is that they were dominated by **hubris** or **hybris** (arrogant pride, insolence, contemptuous violence), which was manifested in destructive actions such as deceit, subterfuge, lying, betrayal, revenge, cruelty, murder, suicide, patricide, infanticide, and self-mutilation. By truthfully demonstrating the faults of these heroes along with their greatness, the writers of tragedy also invoked philosophical and religious issues that provided meaning and value in the face of misfortune and suffering.

The Word Tragedy Underwent an Elevation in Meaning

One of the genuine puzzles about tragedy is the word itself, which combines the Greek words *tragos* ("goat") and *oide* ("ode" or "song")—a "goat ode" or "goat song." This meaning raises the question of how so unlikely a word is linked to the tragic form. One often-repeated answer is that the word was first applied to choral ceremonials performed at the ritual sacrifice of a goat. Another is that the word described a choral competition in which a goat was the prize.

A more persuasive recent answer is that the word **tragedy** stemmed from the word *tragoidoi*, or "billy goat singers," which was applied negatively to the young

---

[2]S. H. Butcher, *Aristotle's Theory of Poetry and Fine Art*, 4th ed. (New York: Dover, 1951) 19 (VI.12). All parenthetical references to Aristotle are from this edition, but see also Stephen Halliwell, *The Poetics of Aristotle: Translation and Commentary* (Chapel Hill: U of North Carolina P, 1987). The origin of the word *dithyramb* is obscure. Some ancient etymologists claimed that the word was derived from the legendary "double birth" of Dionysus. This derivation is based on the idea that dithyramb is a compound (*dis*, "two," and *thyra*, "door") referring to the myth that Zeus removed Dionysus from the womb of his mother, Semele, and then placed the fetus within his thigh. When Zeus removed Dionysus, the god had "come through the door" of birth twice. This derivation, however, has been disputed. For a description of the origin of comedy during the festivals for Dionysus, see Chapter 25.

men (*ephebes*) in the choruses.[3] The ephebes were military trainees between the ages of eighteen and twenty, and those trainees who were best at close-order drill were selected for their ability as chorus members to carry out precision dance movements. Because of their youth, however, they were still likened to young goats.[4] Indeed, tragedy was originally not called *tragodia* (tragedy) at all, but rather *tragoidoi*, as though the chorus members were more important than the speeches they recited. This explanation is consistent with the improvisatory origins of tragedy as explained by Aristotle. In the decades following its beginnings, the genre grew in importance, quality, and stature, and the word *tragedy* underwent the accompanying elevation that it still possesses.

Tragedy Evolved from a Choral Form to a Dramatic Form

Because the surviving Athenian plays are dominated by acting parts, modern readers sometimes conclude that the chorus parts annoyingly interrupt the main action. It may be surprising to recognize that in the beginning there were no individual actors at all, only choruses. The introduction of actors—and their eventual domination—was one of the improvisations that Aristotle associates with the evolution of tragedy. We can surmise that during a festival performance of a now unknown choral ode, the chorus leader stepped forward to deliver lines introducing and linking the choral speeches. Because of this special function, the new speaker—called a **hypocrites** (hoo-pock-rih-TAYSS), which became the word for actor—was soon separated and distinguished from the chorus.

The next essential step was impersonation, or the assuming of a dramatic role. The *hypocrites* would represent a hero, and the chorus would represent groups such as townspeople, worshipers, youths, or elders. With the commencement of such role-playing, genuine drama had begun. According to tradition, the first *hypocrites* or actor—and therefore the acknowledged founder of the acting profession—was the writer and choral leader Thespis, in about 536–533 BCE, during the reign of Peisistratus.

The Ancient Athenian Competitions in Tragedy

Once Thespis set the pattern of action involving actor and chorus, the writing of tragedies as a competition within the Dionysian festivals became institutionalized.

The Tragic Dramatists Competed for the Honor of Having Their Plays Performed

Early each summer, a number of dramatists vied for the honor of having their plays performed at the next City Dionysia, to be held the following spring. They

---

[3]For this argument, see John J. Winkler, "The Ephebes' Song: *Tragodia* and *Polis*," in John J. Winkler and Froma I. Zeitlin, eds., *Nothing to Do with Dionysos? Athenian Drama in Its Social Context* (Princeton: Princeton UP, 1990), pp. 20–62. For a discussion of the military nature of the ancient Greek city-state, see Paul Rahe, "The Martial Republics of Classical Greece," *The Wilson Quarterly*, vol. 17, no. 1 (Winter 1993): 58–70.

[4]There is nothing unusual about this comparison. In English a common everyday word for a child is *kid*, which is the standard word (along with *kit*) for a young goat and also other young animals.

THE ORIGIN OF TRAGEDY IN BRIEF

In the sixth century BCE, **tragedy** originated in Athens at the time of the City Dionysia, one of the major religious festivals held to celebrate Dionysus, a liberating god and one of the twelve major gods of the city. As a genre, tragedy first featured improvisations on a type of choral ode called a *dithyramb*. It then evolved, as Aristotle says, "by slow degrees" (*Poetics* IV.12, p. 19), developing new elements as they seemed appropriate and necessary.

One of the vital new elements was an emphasis on the misfortune or death of a major character.* This emphasis resulted not from a preconceived theoretical design, however, but rather from the reality of suffering in the lives of the heroic subjects. As writers of tragedy developed the cosmic and religious implications of such adversity, performances offered philosophic, religious, moral, and civic benefits, and therefore, presumably, simply attending the performance of a tragedy came to be regarded as the fulfillment of a religious obligation.

Because tragedy was originally linked to the choral dithyrambs, it is important to stress that *tragedy began as a dramatic form for choruses, not for actors*. Even after actors became dominant in the plays, the chorus was important enough for Aristotle to state that "the chorus should be regarded as one of the actors" (XVIII.7, p. 69).

---

*Although the tragic protagonist often dies at the play's end, the extant Athenian tragedies do not follow this pattern rigidly. It is true that the major figures suffer, and sometimes they die, but often they escape punishment entirely, and they may even receive divine pardon.

prepared three tragedies (a **trilogy**)[5] together with a **satyr play** (a boisterous burlesque) and submitted the four works to the Eponymous Archon, one of the city's two principal magistrates and the man for whom the year was named. The three best submissions were approved, or "given a chorus," for performance at the festival. On the last day of the festival, after the performances were over, the Archon awarded a prize to the tragic playwright voted best for that year. There was also a prize for the best writer of a comedy. The winner's prize was not money, but rather a crown of ivy and the glory of triumph.

The Three Greatest Athenian Tragic Playwrights Were Aeschylus, Sophocles, and Euripides

To gain the honor of victory during the centuries of the competitions, many writers of tragedy composed and submitted many plays. The total number must have

---

[5]In the earliest dramas, the trilogies shared a common subject, as may be seen in the *Oresteia* of Aeschylus, which is a cycle of three plays on the subject of the royal house of Agamemnon. But by the time of Sophocles and Euripides, connected trilogies were no longer required. Sophocles' *Oedipus the King* and *Oedipus at Colonus*, for example, were submitted at widely different times.

been exceedingly large, certainly in the high hundreds and likely in the thousands. Most of these have long since vanished because there were no more than a few copies of each play, all handwritten on perishable papyrus scrolls, and because there was no systematic and secure way of preserving the copies.

A small number of works by three tragic playwrights, however, have survived. These dramatists are **Aeschylus** (525–456 BCE), who added a second actor; **Sophocles** (c. 496–406 BCE), who added a third actor, created scene design, and enlarged the chorus from twelve to fifteen; and **Euripides** (c. 484–406 BCE). Although these three playwrights did not win prizes every time they entered the competitions, a consensus grew that they were the best, and by the middle of the fourth century BCE, their works were recognized as classics. Although tragedies seem to have been originally intended for only one performance—at the festival for which they competed—an exception was made for these three dramatists, whose tragedies were then performed repeatedly both in Athens and elsewhere in the Greek-speaking world.

The combined output of the three classic playwrights was slightly more than three hundred plays, of which three-fourths were tragedies and one-fourth were satyr plays. As many as eight hundred years after the end of the fifth century BCE, these plays, together with many other Greek tragedies, satyr plays, and comedies, were available to readers who could afford to buy copies or to pay scribes to copy them.[6] However, with the increasing dominance of Christianity, the plays fell into neglect because they were considered pagan and also because vellum or parchment, which made up the pages of the books (*codexes* or *codices*) that replaced papyrus scrolls, was enormously expensive and was reserved for Christian works. Most of the unique and priceless copies of Athenian plays were subsequently forgotten, burned, or thrown out with the garbage.

Thirty-Three Tragedies by the Three Great Athenian Tragedians Have Survived to the Present Day

The Greek dramatic tradition might have vanished entirely had it not been for the efforts of Byzantine scholars during the ninth century CE, when Constantinople became the center of a revival of interest in classical Greek language and literature. A primary characteristic of this revival was the copying and preservation of important texts—including those of the major Greek writers. We may conclude that the scholars and scribes copied as many of the plays as they could locate, and that they tried to shelter their copies in the supposedly secure monastery libraries.

However, security was impossible to maintain during those centuries. Fire, neglect, time, political destabilization, and pillage (such as the sack of Constantinople by Christian Crusaders in 1204) took an enormous toll on the Byzantine manuscript collections. Even so, seven tragedies by Aeschylus, seven by Sophocles,

---

[6]In the third century BCE, a complete hand-copied set of Greek plays was apparently deposited in the Egyptian Royal Library that formed a part of the Ptolemaic museum and palace of Alexandria, but at some point all the holdings were lost, thrown away, or destroyed, just as the palace and museum were destroyed. In modern Alexandria, the location of the ancient library is not exactly known. Current underwater explorations in the harbor of Alexandria may yet result, however, in increased knowledge about the location of the library. See Luciano Canfora, *The Vanished Library: A Wonder of the Ancient World* (Berkeley: U of California P, 1990).

and ten by Euripides somehow were saved from destruction.[7] Additionally, in the fourteenth century, a scholar named Demetrius Triclinius made a lucky find of scrolls containing nine more plays by Euripides (part of what was once a complete set), bringing the total of Euripidean plays to nineteen. Therefore, of all the hundreds upon hundreds of plays written by all the Greek tragic playwrights, only thirty-three still survive intact. These plays make up the complete Greek tragedy as we know it.[8]

There is, however, just a little more: Many ancient writers often quoted brief passages from plays that were not otherwise preserved, and these portions therefore still exist. Moreover, many collectors living in ancient Egypt owned copies of the plays, and not everything from these collections was lost. In recent centuries, papyrus and vellum fragments—some quite extensive—have been recovered by archaeologists from such unlikely locations as ancient Egyptian rubbish dumps, tombs, and the linings of coffins.[9]

Aristotle and the Nature of Tragedy

Because Aristotle's *Poetics* (*Peri Poietikes*), the first section of his major critical work, survives substantially intact from antiquity, he is in effect the Western world's first critic and aesthetician. From him, later critics derived the various "rules" of tragic composition. He also wrote a second part of the *Poetics* concerning comedy. This second work is lost, but enough fragments and summaries survive to permit a partial hypothetical reconstruction.[10] Aristotle also considered aspects of literature in parts of other philosophical works, principally the *Ethics* and the *Politics*. In addition he, along with his students, assembled a catalog of Greek tragedy from its beginnings to his own time (the *Didaskaliae*), even though much of this catalog did not survive antiquity. He was therefore able to base his criticism on virtually the entire body of Greek tragedy, including written copies of many plays, since lost, that he had probably never seen performed. No one before

---

[7]Many standard reference works contain the assertion that these twenty-four plays were selected by an unnamed Byzantine schoolmaster for use in the Byzantine schools, and that this anthology was widely adopted and exclusively used thereafter. This claim would explain why the anthologized plays were preserved while unanthologized plays were lost. L. D. Reynolds and N. G. Wilson, in their authoritative *Scribes and Scholars: A Guide to the Transmission of Greek and Latin Literature*, 3rd ed. (Oxford UP, 1991), question this hypothesis. They point out that there is no historical record that such an anthology was ever made, that modern scholars are in truth ignorant "of the origin of the selection," and that therefore "it is perhaps best to abandon the idea that a conscious act of selection by an individual was a primary factor in determining the survival of texts" (p. 54).

[8]The survival of Greek drama was under constant threat until the first printed editions were published at the beginning of the sixteenth century.

[9]There are some interesting leads that may yet yield additional copies of ancient texts. The finds from the excavations at Oxyrrhynchus, in Egypt, have been stored in boxes at the University of Oxford. Because they have been considered unreadable, they have lain neglected for more than a hundred years. The recent use of special ultraviolet light, however, has now made it possible for the first time to read and record the texts of the documents. It is possible that copies of ancient plays may be among the finds. In addition, a private library at the Villa of the Papyri in Herculaneum, in Italy, has been unrecoverable ever since 79 BCE, when it was buried beneath the pyroclastic flow from Vesuvius during the disastrous eruption that covered Pompeii and Herculaneum. Recent efforts have suggested that diligent archaeological work might yet produce copies of ancient manuscripts, possibly including copies of Greek plays. All this is yet for the future.

[10]See Richard Janko, trans., *Aristotle, Poetics I with the Tractatus Coislinianus, A Hypothetical Reconstruction of Poetics II, the Fragments of the On Poets* (Indianapolis: Hackett, 1987) pp. 47–55.

or after Aristotle has had more firsthand knowledge of Greek tragedy. His criticism is therefore especially valuable because it rests not only on his acute powers of observation, but also on his unique and encyclopedic knowledge.

As we have seen, Aristotle states that tragedy grew out of improvisations related to dithyrambic choral odes. He adds that once tragedy reached its "natural" or ideal form it stopped evolving (*Poetics* IV.12, p. 19). His observations are designed to explain the ideal characteristics of tragedy. Throughout the *Poetics* he stresses concepts of exactitude, proportion, appropriateness, and control. His famous definition of tragedy is in accord with these concepts. In the sixth chapter of the *Poetics*, he states that tragedy is "an imitation of an action that is serious, complete, and of a certain magnitude; in language embellished with each kind of artistic ornament, the several kinds being found in separate parts of the play; in the form of action, not of narrative; through pity and fear effecting the proper purgation of these emotions" (VI.2, p. 23).

To Aristotle, the Key to Tragedy Is the Concept of Catharsis

The last part of this definition—that purgation or **catharsis** is the end or goal of tragedy—crystallizes the earlier parts. In Aristotle's view, tragedy arouses the powerful emotions of pity and fear (*eleos* and *phobos*), and, through the experience of the drama, brings about a "proper purgation" or purification of these emotions. Originally, the word *catharsis* was a medical term, and therefore many interpreters argue that tragedy produces a therapeutic effect through an actual purging or "vomiting" of emotions—a sympathetic release of feelings that produces emotional relief and encourages psychological health. In other words, tragedy heals.

A complementary and equally compelling view is that tragic catharsis has a larger public and moral purpose. In this sense, Aristotle's description of tragedy is an implicit argument defending literature itself against the strong disapproval of his teacher, Plato.[11] Both master and pupil accepted the premise that human beings behave thoughtlessly and stupidly as a result of uncontrolled emotion. While in the grip of deep feelings, people cannot be virtuous and can do no good for others because they make bad decisions that produce bad personal, social, political, military, and moral results. Consequently, if individual temperance and public justice are to prevail, there is a universal need to moderate and regulate the emotions. Because Plato states that the emotionalism of literature is untrue, undignified, and unreasonable, he denies that literature can address this need.

But in the *Poetics* and in relevant parts of other works, Aristotle asserts that tragedy does indeed address the need, and does so through the process of catharsis. By arousing our dominant feelings of pity and fear, tragedy trains our emotions and *habituates* us to measure, shape, channel, and control our passions. Through catharsis, we develop a condition of poise and balance among emotional forces, and we achieve this balanced state harmlessly because the artistic context of tragedy gives us immunity from the personal damage that our deepest passions might produce in our actual lives. It is the habitual compassion for the plights of

---

[11]See Janko, especially pp. xvi–xx, and Butcher's discussion on pp. 245–251 of *Aristotle's Theory of Poetry and Fine Art.*

others that makes us part of our civic and national communities and that ultimately develops our greater humanity. Tragedy therefore is vital in the growth of personal and collective virtue, for people who regularly experience the emotional catharsis or regulation of tragedy will be led to measure and direct their loves and their hates, to pledge their loyalties sensibly, and to make balanced decisions and take balanced actions, both for themselves and for the public.

It is important to stress that Aristotle states that catharsis is also brought about by other literary genres, especially comedy and epic, and, in addition, by music. In other words, artistic works have in common that they cleanse or purify the emotions. It is through the continuous and renewed shaping and regulating of feelings—catharsis—that tragedy, like literature and art broadly, encourages and develops ethical sensibility, and therefore on philosophical, religious, and political grounds it is defensible and necessary.

The Tragic Plot Is Structured to Arouse and Shape Emotions

In the light of the concept of catharsis, Aristotle's description of the formal aspects and characteristics of tragedy can be seen as an outline of the ways in which these characteristics first arouse the emotions and then shape them.

THE TRAGIC PLOT REQUIRES THE REPRESENTATION OF A SINGLE MAJOR ACTION. Aristotle concedes that tragedy is not true in the sense that history is true. He therefore stresses that a tragic plot, or **muthos,** is not an exact imitation or duplication of life, but rather a **representation** or *mimesis.* The concept of representation acknowledges both the moral role of the writer and the artistic freedom needed to create works conducive to proper responses. A tragic plot therefore consists of a self-contained and concentrated single action. Anything outside this action, such as unrelated incidents in the life of the major character, is not to be contained in the play. The action of *Oedipus the King,* for example, is focused on Oedipus's determination as king of Thebes to free his city from the pestilence that is destroying it. Although other aspects of his life are introduced in the play's dialogue because they are relevant to the action, they are reported rather than dramatized. Only those incidents integral to the action are included in the play.

TRAGIC RESPONSES ARE BROUGHT TO A HEAD THROUGH REVERSAL, RECOGNITION, AND SUFFERING. Aristotle's discussion of the three major elements of tragic plot is particularly significant. The elements all appear near the conclusion of a tragic play because they are the probable and inevitable results of the early elements of exposition and complication. First is the "**reversal** of the situation" (*peripeteia*) from apparent good to bad, or a "change [usually also a surprise] by which the action veers round to its opposite," as in *Oedipus the King,* where the outcome is the reverse of what Oedipus intends and expects (XI.1, p. 41). Even if the outcome is unhappy—especially if it is unhappy—it is "the right ending" (XIII.6, p. 47) because it is the most tragic; that is, it evokes the greatest degree of pity and fear.

Second is "a change from ignorance to knowledge, producing love or hate between the persons destined by the poet for good or bad fortune." Aristotle calls this change *anagnorisis* or **recognition** (XI.2, p. 41). In the best and most powerful tragedies, according to him, the reversal and the recognition occur together and create surprise. Aristotle considers recognition to be the discovery of the true identity and involvement of persons, the establishment of guilt or innocence, and the revelation of previously unknown details, for "it is upon such situations that the issues of good or bad fortune will depend" (XI.4, p. 41). One might add that recognition is of major importance because ideally, upon discovering the truth, the protagonist acknowledges errors and accepts responsibility. In *Oedipus the King*, Oedipus finally recognizes his own guilt even though during most of the play he has been trying to escape it. He then becomes the agent of his own punishment. Because such recognition illustrates that human beings have the strength to preserve their integrity even in adversity, it is one of the elements making tragedy the highest of all literary forms.

Aristotle describes the third part of plot as a **"scene of suffering"** (*pathos*) that he defines as "a destructive or painful action, such as death on the stage, bodily agony, wounds, and the like" (XI.6, p. 43). He stresses that the destructive or painful action, including death, should be caused by "those who are near or dear to one another" (XIV.4, pp. 49–50). That is, violence should occur within a royal household or family rather than against a hostile foe. Because the trust, love, and protectiveness that one hopes for in a family is replaced by treachery, hate, and mayhem, the suffering of the tragic protagonist is one of the major ways in which tragedy arouses fear and pity.

Additional Aristotelian Tragic Requirements Are Seriousness, Completeness, and Artistic Balance

The first part of Aristotle's definition, asserting that a tragedy is "serious, complete, and of a certain magnitude," can be seen as a vital aspect of his analysis of how tragedy shapes responses. The term **serious,** meaning noble or elevated, concerns the play's tone and level of life, in contrast with the boisterousness and ribaldry of Athenian comedies. While comedy represents human character as less serious than it is, tragedy shows it as more serious (II.4, p. 13). Seriousness is also a consequence of the political and cosmological dimensions of the issues in which the heroic characters are engaged. By **complete,** we understand that a tragedy must be shaped and perfected into a logical and finished whole. The beginning, the middle, and the ending must be so perfectly placed that changing or removing any part would spoil the work's integrity (VII.2-3, p. 31). By stating that a tragedy should be of a "certain" or proportional **magnitude,** Aristotle refers to a balance of length and subject matter. The play should be short enough to "be easily embraced by the memory" and long enough to "admit of a change . . . from good fortune to bad" (VII.5–7, p. 33). In other words, everything is artistically balanced; nothing superfluous is included, and nothing essential is omitted.

For Aristotle, Appropriate Diction and Song Are Necessary in Tragedy

For modern readers, Aristotle's description of tragic structure is more easily understood than his discussion of tragic language. His statement about tragic poetry—that it is the "mere metrical arrangement of the words" (VI.4, p. 25)—is clear as far as it goes, for the plays themselves show that the tragic playwrights used poetic forms deliberately and exactly. As for **song** (*melos*), Aristotle's claim that it is "a term whose sense everyone understands" (VI.4, p. 25) is not illuminating. What is therefore significant about his discussion of verse and song is his statement that the "several kinds of artistic ornament are to be found in separate parts of the play" (VI.2, p. 23). That is, where verse is appropriate, the tragic playwrights include poetry as a means of elevating the drama; where music and song are appropriate, they include these to increase beauty and intensify the drama. As with the other aspects of tragedy, therefore, the most fitting standards of judgment are placement, balance, and appropriateness.

The Tragedy's Hero Is the Focus of Sympathetic Tragic Emotions

Aristotle's description of the tragic protagonist or hero, though not included in his definition of tragedy, is integral to the concept of catharsis and therefore to his description of tragedy. As with the other parts of his analysis, he demonstrates the exact effects and limits of the topic—the perfected balance of form necessary to bring about proper tragic responses. To this end, he states that we, as normally imperfect human beings, are able to sympathize with a "highly renowned and prosperous" protagonist because that protagonist is also imperfect—a person who exists between extremes, just "like ourselves" (XIII.2, p. 45). The misfortunes of this noble protagonist are caused not by "vice" or "depravity" but rather by "some great error or frailty" (XIII.4, p. 47). Aristotle's word for such shortcomings is *hamartia*, which is often translated as **tragic flaw**, and it is this flaw that makes the protagonist human—neither a saint nor a villain. If the protagonist were a saint (one who is "eminently good and just"), his or her suffering would be undeserved and unfair, and our pity would be overwhelmed by indignation and anger—not a proper tragic reaction. Nor could we pity a villain enduring adversity and pain, for we would judge the suffering to be deserved, and our primary response would then be satisfaction—also not a proper reaction. Therefore, an ideal tragedy is fine-tuned to control our emotions exactly, producing horror and fear because the suffering protagonist is a person like ourselves, and pity because the suffering far exceeds what the protagonist deserves.

 ARISTOTLE'S VIEW OF TRAGEDY IN BRIEF

Aristotle's definition of tragedy hinges on his idea that tragedy, as a dramatic form, is designed to evoke powerful emotions and thereby, through catharsis, to serve a salutary political, moral, and ethical purpose. The tragic incidents and plot must be artistically constructed to produce the "essential tragic effect" (VI.12, p. 27). Therefore Aristotle stresses that plot and incidents, arranged for this effect, form the end or goal—the "chief thing of all"—of tragedy (VI.10, p. 27).

Irony in Tragedy

Implicit in the excessiveness of tragic suffering is the idea that the universe is mysterious and often unfair and that unseen but powerful forces—fate, fortune, circumstances, and the gods—directly intervene in human life. Ancient Athenian belief was that the gods give rewards or punishments to suit their own purposes, which mortals cannot bring about, prevent, or understand. For example, in *Prometheus Bound* (attributed to Aeschylus), the god Hephaestus binds Prometheus to a rock in the Scythian Mountains as punishment for having given fire and technology to humankind. (A good deed produces suffering.) Conversely, in *Medea*, Euripides shows that the god Apollo permits Medea to escape after killing her own children. (A criminal deed produces reward.)

Situational and Cosmic Irony Are Essential in Tragedy

These examples illustrate the pervasiveness of **situational irony** and **cosmic irony** in tragedy. Characters find themselves in unforeseeable difficulties that are caused by others or that they themselves inadvertently cause. When they try to resolve these difficulties responsibly and nobly, their actions do not produce the desired results—this is consistent with Aristotle's idea of reversal—and usually things come out badly. For example, Oedipus brings suffering on himself just when he succeeds—and *because* he succeeds—in rescuing his city. Whether on the personal or cosmic level, therefore, there is no escape—no way to evade responsibility, and no way to change the unalterable laws that thrust human beings into such situations.

Situational irony and cosmic irony are not confined to ancient tragedies. Shakespeare's tragic hero Hamlet speaks about the "divinity that shapes our ends," thus expressing the unpredictability of hopes, plans, and achievements, and also the wisdom of resignation. In *Death of a Salesman* (this chapter), Miller's hero, Willy Loman, is gripped not so much by divine power as by time—the agent of destruction being the inexorable force of economic circumstances.

The Tragic Dilemma Confronts the Problem of Free Will Versus Fate

These ironies are connected to what is called the **tragic dilemma**—a situation that forces the tragic protagonist to make a difficult choice. The tragic dilemma has also been called a "lose-lose" situation. Thus, Oedipus cannot shirk his duty as king of Thebes because that would be ruinous. He therefore tries to eliminate his city's affliction, but that course is also ruinous. In other words, the choices posed in a tragic dilemma seemingly permit freedom of will, but the consequences of any choice demonstrate the inescapable fact that powerful forces, perhaps even fate or inevitability, baffle even the most reasonable and noble intentions. As Shakespeare's Hamlet states, "O cursèd spite, / That ever I was born to set it right" (1.5.188–89).

Dramatic Irony Focuses Attention on the Tragic Limitations of Human Vision and Knowledge

It is from a perspective of something like divinity that we as readers or spectators perceive the action of tragedies. We are like the gods because we always know more than the characters. Such dramatic irony permits us, for example, to know what Oedipus does not know: In defensive rage he killed his real father, and he himself is therefore his city's bane. Similar dramatic irony can be found in *Hamlet*, for we realize that Claudius murdered Hamlet's father while Hamlet himself has only unsubstantiated accusations of this truth. The underlying basis of **dramatic irony** in real life is of course that no one can know the future, and few if any can anticipate accident, illness, and all the social, economic, political, and military adversity that may invade and destroy our ways of life.

The Ancient Athenian Audience and Theater

Athenian audiences of the fifth century BCE, predominantly free men but also a small number of women, took their theater seriously. Indeed, as young men many citizens had taken active parts in the parades and choruses. Admission was charged for those able to pay, but subsidies allowed poorer people to attend as well. Rich Athenians, as a duty (*liturgeia*) to the state, underwrote the costs of the productions—except for three professional actors who were paid by the government. Each wealthy man, for his contribution, was known as a *choragos,* or choral sponsor. To gain public recognition, the choragos sometimes performed as the leader of the chorus.

Ancient Athenian Theater Originated in the Marketplace, or Agora

In the beginning, tragic performances were given specially designated space in the Athenian *agora,* or marketplace. In the center of the performing area was an altar dedicated to Dionysus, around which the choruses danced and chanted. Apparently, wooden risers must have been set up for the spectators around the performers.

Ancient Greek Plays Were Performed in the Athenian Theater of Dionysus

By the early fifth century BCE, a half-circular outdoor theater or amphitheater (a *theatron* was a "place for seeing") was constructed at the base of the southern hill of the Acropolis in the area sacred to Dionysus (see p. I–15). All later performances of Athenian tragedies were held at this **Theater of Dionysus,** which held as many as fourteen thousand people (the comic dramatist Aristophanes estimated that thirteen thousand were in attendance at one of his plays). In the earliest days of the theater, most spectators sat on the sloping ground, but eventually wooden and then stone benches were constructed in the rising semicircle, with more elegant seating for dignitaries in front. Although the theater was outdoors, the acoustics were sufficiently good to permit audiences to hear both the chorus and the actors, provided that the audience remained reasonably quiet during performances.

THE ORCHESTRA WAS THE FOCAL POINT OF BOTH SIGHT AND SOUND.   Centered at the base of the hill—the focus of attention—was a round area modeled on the space that had been used in the agora. This was the *orchestra* (or-KESS-tra) or "dancing place," which was about sixty-five feet in diameter. Here, each chorus sang its odes and performed its dance movements to the rhythm of a double-piped flute (*aulos*), an instrument that was also used to mark the step in military drill. In the center was a permanent altar.

THE SKENE WAS A VERSATILE BUILDING USED FOR BOTH ACTION AND ENTRANCES.   Behind the *orchestra* was a building for actors, costumes, and props called the *skene* (SKAY-nay, "tent"), from which is derived our modern word *scene*. Originally a tent or hut, the *skene* was later made of wood and decorated to provide backdrops for the various plays. Some theater historians argue that the stage itself was a wooden platform (*proskenion* [*pro-SKAY-nee-on*], the origin of the modern *proscenium*) in front of the *skene* to elevate the actors and set them off from the chorus. At the center of the *skene*, a double door for entrances and exits opened out to the stage and the *orchestra*. Through this door a large platform (*ekkyklyma* [eck-KEEK-lee-mah) could be rolled out to show interior scenes. There was no curtain.

The roof of the *skene* was sometimes used as a place of action (as in Aeschylus's *Agamemnon*). A *mechane* (*may-KAH-nay*), or crane, was also located there so that actors playing gods could be swung up, down, and around as a mark of divine power. It was this crane that inspired Menander to coin the phrase *theos apo mechanes,* or, in Latin, *deus ex machina* ("a god out of the machine"), terms that refer to an artificial and/or illogical action or device introduced at a play's end to bring otherwise impossible conflicts to a satisfactory solution.

THE ACTORS PERFORMED IN ALL STAGE AND ORCHESTRA AREAS, AND THE CHORUS PERFORMED IN THE ORCHESTRA.   The performing space for the actors was mainly in front of the *skene*. The space for the chorus was the entire *orchestra*. The chorus

The ancient theater at Epidaurus, Greece.

View of a modern production of Sophocles' *Oedipus at Colonus* at the Theater of Epidaurus. Note the size of the orchestra, the formation and gestures of the chorus (fifteen members, in masks, together with the choral leader), the central altar, the reconstructed *skene*, and the single actor on the proscenium.

entered the *orchestra*—and left it at the end of the play—along the aisles between the retaining wall of the hillside seats and the front of the *skene*. Each of these lateral walkways was known as a *parados* ("way in"), the name also given to the chorus's entry scene. The actors often used the *skene* for entrances and exits, but they were also free to use either of the walkways.

THE THEATER WAS REPAIRED AND RESTORED A NUMBER OF TIMES IN ANTIQUITY. In the centuries after it was built, the Theater of Dionysus was remodeled and restored a number of times. Aeschylus' trilogy the *Oresteia* was performed in 458 BCE, for example, not long after a renovation. The ruins that can be seen on the south slope of the Acropolis today are not those of the theater known by Sophocles, but rather those of a Roman restoration. A better sense of how the theater looked during the time of Sophocles can be gained from the Theater of Epidaurus, which during antiquity was considered one of the best Greek theaters and today remains in excellent condition.

Ancient Greek Tragic Actors and Their Costumes

The task of the three competing playwrights who had been "given a chorus" by the archon to stage their works during the **City Dionysia** (and later during the **Lenaia**) was to plan, choreograph, and direct the productions, usually with the aid of professionals. By performance time, the dramatists would already have spent many weeks preparing the three assigned actors and fifteen choristers. They also would have directed rehearsals for a small number of auxiliary chorus members and other silent extras taking roles such as servants and soldiers.

Costumes Distinguished the Actors from the Chorus

All these participants needed costumes. The chorus members were lightly clad, for ease of movement, and were apparently barefoot. The main actors wore the identifying costumes of tragedy—namely, sleeved robes, boots, and masks. Their robes were heavily decorated and embroidered. Their calf-high leather boots, called *kothornoi* or, in English, **buskins,** were like the elegant boots worn by the patron god Dionysus in painting and statuary. During the following centuries, the buskins became elevator shoes that made the tragic actors taller, in keeping with their heroic stature.

Masks Worn by Chorus and Actors Helped the Audience Recognize and Distinguish the Characters

A vital aspect of costuming was the use of conventionalized plaster and linen masks, which were designed to identify and delineate characters. These were of particular help for those in the audience who sat at increasing distances away and up from the orchestra and stage, and who therefore would have had trouble seeing facial expressions. As many as twenty-eight different kinds of masks were in use for the tragic productions. Each mask portrayed a distinct facial type and expression (e.g., king, queen, young woman or man, old woman or man, servant, shepherd). The choristers wore identical masks for their group roles. Apparently the masks covered the entire head, except for openings for seeing, breathing, and speaking. They included a high headdress and, when necessary, a beard.

The masks, along with costume changes, gave the actors great versatility. Each actor could assume a number of different roles simply by entering the *skene*, changing mask and costume, and reentering as a new character. Thus, in *Oedipus the King* a single actor could represent the seer Tiresias and later reappear as the Messenger. The masks even made it possible for two actors, or even all three, to perform as the same character in separate parts of the play if the need arose.

Performance and the Formal Organization of Greek Tragedy

On performance days, the competing playwrights staged their plays from morning to afternoon, first the tragedies, then the satyr plays (and after these, comedies by other writers). Because plays were performed with a minimum of scenery and props, dramatists used dialogue to establish times and locations. Each tragedy was performed in the order of the formally designated sections that modern editors have marked in the printed texts. It is therefore possible to describe the production of a play in terms of these structural divisions.

The First Part Was the Prologue, the Play's Exposition

There was considerable variety in the performance of the **prologue.** Sometimes it was given by a single actor, speaking as either a mortal or a god. In *Oedipus the King,*

Sophocles used all three actors for the prologue (Oedipus, the Priest, and Creon), speaking to themselves and also to the extras acting as the Theban populace.

The Second Part Was the Parados, the Entry of the Chorus into the Orchestra

The entrance of the chorus into the orchestra was the *parados*. Once in the orchestra, the chorus remained there until the play's end. Because they were required to project their voices to spectators in the top seats, they both sang and chanted their lines. They also moved rhythmically in a number of stanzaic *strophes* (turns), *antistrophes* (counterturns), and *epodes* (units following the songs). These dance movements, regulated by the rhythm of the *aulos* or flute as in a military drill, were done in straight-line formations of five or three, but we do not know whether the chorus stopped or continued moving when delivering their lines. After the *parados*, the choristers would necessarily have knelt or sat at attention, in this way focusing on the activities of the actors and, when necessary, responding as a group.

The Play's Principal Action Consisted of Four Epeisodia and Stasima

With the chorus as a model audience, the drama itself was developed in four full sections or acting units. The major part of each section was the **epeisodion, or episode.** Each episode featured the actors, who presented both action and speech, including swift one-line interchanges known as **stichomuthia, or stichomythy.**

When the episode ended, the actors withdrew.[12] The following second part of the acting section was called a *stasimon* (plural *stasima*), performed by the chorus in the *orchestra*. Like the *parados*, the *stasima* required dance movements, along with the chanting and singing of strophes, antistrophes, and epodes. The topics concerned the play's developing action, although over time the *stasima* became more general and therefore less integral to the play.

The Play Concluded with the Exodos

When the last of the four episode-*stasimon* sections had been completed, the *exodos* (literally, "a way out"), or the final section, commenced. It contained the resolution of the drama, the exit of the actors, and the last pronouncements, dance movements, and exit of the chorus.

The Role of the Chorus Was Diminished as Greek Tragedy Evolved

We know little about tragic structure at the very beginning of the form, but Athenian tragedies of the fifth century BCE followed the pattern just described. Aeschylus, whose works are the earliest surviving Athenian tragedies, lengthened the episodes, thus emphasizing the actors and diminishing "the importance of the Chorus" (*Poetics* IV.13, p. 19). Sophocles made the chorus even less important. Euripides, Sophocles's younger contemporary, concentrated on the episodes, making

---

[12]For example, at the end of the first episode of *Oedipus the King*, Oedipus goes into the *skene*—the palace— while a servant leads Tiresias off along the *parados*, thus indicating that he is leaving Thebes entirely.

the chorus almost incidental. In later centuries, dramatists dropped the choral sections completely, establishing the pattern for the five-act structure adopted by Roman dramatists and later by Renaissance dramatists.

Plays for Study

Sophocles . . . . Oedipus the King, 1282

William Shakespeare . . . . Hamlet, 1323

Arthur Miller. . . . . Death of a Salesman, 1424

SOPHOCLES (c. 496–406 BCE)

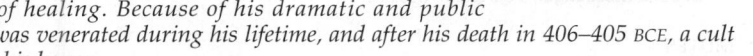

Sophocles was born between 500 and 494 BCE into an affluent Athenian family. He began acting and singing early, and he served as a choral leader in the celebrations for the defeat of the Persians at Marathon in 480 BCE. In 468 he won highest festival honors for the first play he submitted for competition, Triptolemos. *He wrote at least 120 plays, approximately 90 of them tragedies, and he won the prize a record 24 times. He was also an active citizen. He was twice elected general of his tribe, and he served as a priest in the cult of Asclepius, the god of healing. Because of his dramatic and public achievements, he was venerated during his lifetime, and after his death in 406–405 BCE, a cult was established in his honor.*

When *Oedipus the King* was first performed between 430 and 425 BCE, most of the audience would have known the general outlines of the story inasmuch as it was one of the "received legends" of tragedy: the antagonism of the gods Hephaestus and Hera toward Cadmus of Thebes (of whom Oedipus was a descendant); the prophecy that the Theban king Laius would be killed by his own son; the exposure of the newly born Oedipus on a mountainside; his rescue by a well-meaning shepherd; his youth spent as the adopted son of King Polybus and Queen Merope of Corinth; his trip to Delphi to learn his origins; his impetuous murder of Laius (a stranger to him); his solution of the Sphinx's riddle; his ascension as king of Thebes and his marriage to Queen Jocasta, his mother; his reign as king; the plague that afflicted Thebes; his attempts at restoration; and Jocasta's suicide when the truth of Oedipus's past is revealed.

Although these details were commonly known, there was disagreement about the outcome of Oedipus's life. One version told that he remarried, had four children with his new wife, reigned long and successfully, died in battle, and was finally worshiped as a hero. Sophocles, however, dramatizes a version—either borrowed or of his own creation—that tells of Oedipus's self-imposed punishment.

As we have said, Aristotle prized *Oedipus the King* so highly that he used it to illustrate many of his principles of tragedy. Of particular interest is that the play embodies the so-called three **unities,** which are implicit in the Poetics although Aristotle does not stress them. Sophocles creates *unity of place* by using the front of the royal palace of Thebes as the location for the entire action. He creates *unity of action* by dramatizing only those activities leading to Oedipus's recognition of the true scourge of the city. Finally, he creates *unity of time* because the stage or action time coincides with real-life time. In fact, the play's time is considerably shorter than the "single revolution of the sun" (*sic*) that Aristotle recommends as the proper period for a complete tragic action (V.4, p. 23). Above all, *Oedipus the King* meets Aristotle's requirements for one of the very best plays because of the skill with which Sophocles makes Oedipus's recognition of his guilt coincide exactly with the disastrous reversal of his fortunes (XI.2, p. 41).

Oedipus the King (430–425 BCE)

Translated by Thomas Gould

CHARACTERS

Oedipus,° The King of Thebes
Priest of Zeus, Leader of the Suppliants
Creon, Oedipus's Brother-in-law
Chorus, a Group of Theban Elders
Choragos, Spokesman of the Chorus
Tiresias, a blind Seer or Prophet
Jocasta, The Queen of Thebes
Messenger, from Corinth, once a Shepherd
Herdsman, once a Servant of Laius
Second Messenger, a Servant of Oedipus

MUTES

Suppliants, Thebans seeking Oedipus's help
Attendants, for the Royal Family
Servants, to lead Tiresias and Oedipus
Antigone, Daughter of Oedipus and Jocasta
Ismene, Daughter of Oedipus and Jocasta

[*The action takes place during the day in front of the royal palace in Thebes. There are two altars (left and right) on the Proscenium and several steps leading down to the Orchestra. As the play opens, Thebans of various ages who have come to beg Oedipus for help are sitting on these steps and in part of the Orchestra. These suppliants are holding branches of laurel or olive which have strips of wool° wrapped around them. Oedipus enters from the palace (the central door of the Skene).*]

PROLOGUE

OEDIPUS: My children, ancient Cadmus'° newest care,
why have you hurried to those seats, your boughs
wound with the emblems of the suppliant?
The city is weighed down with fragrant smoke,
with hymns to the Healer° and the cries of mourners.
I thought it wrong, my sons, to hear your words
through emissaries, and have come out myself,
I, Oedipus, a name that all men know.

5

°*Oedipus:* The name means "swollen foot." It refers to the mutilation of Oedipus's feet by his father, Laius, before the infant was sent to Mount Cithaeron to be put to death by exposure. 0.1 S.D. *wool:* Branches wrapped with wool are traditional symbols of prayer or supplication. 1 *Cadmus:* Oedipus's great-great-grandfather (although he does not know this) and the founder of Thebes. 5 *Healer:* Apollo, god of prophecy, light, healing, justice, purification, and destruction.

[OEDIPUS *addresses the* PRIEST.]

> Old man—for it is fitting that you speak
> for all—what is your mood as you entreat me,   10
> fear or trust? You may be confident
> that I'll do anything. How hard of heart
> if an appeal like this did not rouse my pity!
>
> PRIEST: You, Oedipus, who hold the power here,
> you see our several ages, we who sit   15
> before your altars—some not strong enough
> to take long flight, some heavy in old age,
> the priests, as I of Zeus,° and from our youths
> a chosen band. The rest sit with their windings
> in the markets, at the twin shrines of Pallas,°   20
> and the prophetic embers of Ismēnos.°
> Our city, as you see yourself, is tossed
> too much, and can no longer lift its head
> above the troughs of billows red with death.
> It dies in the fruitful flowers of the soil,   25
> it dies in its pastured herds, and in its women's
> barren pangs. And the fire-bearing god°
> has swooped upon the city, hateful plague,
> and he has left the house of Cadmus empty.
> Black Hades° is made rich with moans and weeping.   30
> Not judging you an equal of the gods,
> do I and the children sit here at your hearth,
> but as the first of men, in troubled times
> and in encounters with divinities.
> You came to Cadmus' city and unbound   35
> the tax we had to pay to the harsh singer,°
> did it without a helpful word from us,
> with no instruction; with a god's assistance
> you raised up our life, so we believe.
> Again now Oedipus, our greatest power,   40
> we plead with you, as suppliants, all of us,
> to find us strength, whether from a god's response,
> or learned in some way from another man.
> I know that the experienced among men
> give counsels that will prosper best of all.   45
> Noblest of men, lift up our land again!

°18 *Zeus:* father and king of the gods. 20 *Pallas:* Athena, goddess of wisdom, arts, crafts, and war. 21 *Ismēnos:* a reference to the temple of Apollo near the river Ismenos in Thebes. Prophecies were made here by "reading" the ashes of the altar fires. 27 *fire-bearing god:* contagious fever viewed as a god. 30 *Black Hades:* refers to both the underworld, where the spirits of the dead go, and the god of the underworld. 36 *harsh singer:* the Sphinx, a monster with a woman's head, a lion's body, and wings. The "tax" that Oedipus freed Thebes from was the destruction of all the young men who failed to solve the Sphinx's riddle and were subsequently devoured. The Sphinx always asked the same riddle: "What goes on four legs in the morning, two legs at noon, and three legs in the evening, and yet is weakest when supported by the largest number of feet?" Oedipus discovered the correct answer—man, who crawls in infancy, walks in his prime, and uses a stick in old age—and thus ended the Sphinx's reign of terror. The Sphinx destroyed herself when Oedipus answered the riddle. Oedipus's reward for freeing Thebes of the Sphinx was the throne and the hand of the recently widowed Jocasta.

Think also of yourself; since now the land
calls you its Savior for your zeal of old,
oh let us never look back at your rule
50   as men helped up only to fall again!
Do not stumble! Put our land on firm feet!
The bird of omen was auspicious then,
when you brought that luck; be that same man again!
The power is yours; if you will rule our country,
55   rule over men, not in an empty land.
A towered city or a ship is nothing
if desolate and no man lives within.
OEDIPUS: Pitiable children, oh I know, I know
the yearnings that have brought you. Yes, I know
60   that you are sick. And yet, though you are sick,
there is not one of you so sick as I.
For your affliction comes to each alone,
for him and no one else, but my soul mourns
for me and for you, too, and for the city.
65   You do not waken me as from a sleep,
for I have wept, bitterly and long,
tried many paths in the wanderings of thought,
and the single cure I found by careful search
I've acted on: I sent Menoeceus' son,
70   Creon, brother of my wife, to the Pythian
halls of Phoebus,° so that I might learn
what I must do or say to save this city.
Already, when I think what day this is,
I wonder anxiously what he is doing.
75   Too long, more than is right, he's been away.
But when he comes, then I shall be a traitor
if I do not do all that the god reveals.
PRIEST: Welcome words! But look, those men have signaled
that it is Creon who is now approaching!
80   **OEDIPUS:** Lord Apollo! May he bring Savior Luck,
a Luck as brilliant as his eyes are now!
PRIEST: His news is happy, it appears. He comes,
forehead crowned with thickly berried laurel.°
OEDIPUS: We'll know, for he is near enough to hear us.

[*Enter* CREON *along one of the Parados.*]

85   Lord, brother in marriage, son of Menoeceus!
What is the god's pronouncement that you bring?
CREON: It's good. For even troubles, if they chance
to turn out well, I always count as lucky.
OEDIPUS: But what was the response? You seem to say
90   I'm not to fear—but not to take heart either.
CREON: If you will hear me with these men present,
I'm ready to report—or go inside.

°70–71 *Pythian . . . Phoebus:* the temple of Phoebus Apollo's oracle or prophet at Delphi. 83 *laurel:* Creon is
wearing a garland of laurel leaves, sacred to Apollo.

[CREON *moves up the steps toward the palace.*]

OEDIPUS: Speak out to all! The grief that burdens me
    concerns these men more than it does my life.
CREON: Then I shall tell you what I heard from the god.   95
    The task Lord Phoebus sets for us is clear:
    drive out pollution sheltered in our land,
    and do not shelter what is incurable.
OEDIPUS: What is our trouble? How shall we cleanse ourselves?
CREON: We must banish or murder to free ourselves   100
    from a murder that blows storms through the city.
OEDIPUS: What man's bad luck does he accuse in this?
CREON: My Lord, a king named Laius ruled our land
    before you came to steer the city straight.
OEDIPUS: I know. So I was told—I never saw him.   105
CREON: Since he was murdered, you must raise your hand
    against the men who killed him with their hands.
OEDIPUS: Where are they now? And how can we ever find
    the track of ancient guilt now hard to read?
CREON: In our own land, he said. What we pursue,   110
    that can be caught; but not what we neglect.
OEDIPUS: Was Laius home, or in the countryside—
    or was he murdered in some foreign land?
CREON: He left to see a sacred rite, he said;   115
    He left, but never came home from his journey.
OEDIPUS: Did none of his party see it and report—
    someone we might profitably question?
CREON: They were all killed but one, who fled in fear,
    and he could tell us only one clear fact.
OEDIPUS: What fact? One thing could lead us on to more   120
    if we could get a small start on our hope.
CREON: He said that bandits chanced on them and killed him—
    with the force of many hands, not one alone.
OEDIPUS: How could a bandit dare so great an act—
    unless this was a plot paid off from here!   125
CREON: We thought of that, but when Laius was killed,
    we had no one to help us in our troubles.
OEDIPUS: It was your very kingship that was killed!
    What kind of trouble blocked you from a search?
CREON: The subtle-singing Sphinx asked us to turn   130
    from the obscure to what lay at our feet.
OEDIPUS: Then I shall begin again and make it plain.
    It was quite worthy of Phoebus, and worthy of you,
    to turn our thoughts back to the murdered man,
    and right that you should see me join the battle   135
    for justice to our land and to the god.
    Not on behalf of any distant kinships,
    it's for myself I will dispel this stain.
    Whoever murdered him may also wish
    to punish me—and with the selfsame hand.   140
    In helping him I also serve myself.
    Now quickly, children: up from the altar steps,

and raise the branches of the suppliant!
Let someone go and summon Cadmus' people:
145   say I'll do anything.

[*Exit an* ATTENDANT *along one of the Parados.*]

Our luck will prosper
if the god is with us, or we have already fallen.
PRIEST: Rise, my children; that for which we came,
he has himself proclaimed he will accomplish.
May Phoebus, who announced this, also come
150   as Savior and reliever from the plague.

[*Exit* OEDIPUS *and* CREON *into the Palace. The* PRIEST *and the* SUPPLIANTS *exit left and right along the Parados. After a brief pause, the* CHORUS *(including the* CHORAGOS*) enters the Orchestra from the Parados.*]

PARADOS

Strophe 1°
CHORUS: Voice from Zeus,° sweetly spoken, what are you
that have arrived from golden
Pytho° to our shining
Thebes? I am on the rack, terror
155   shakes my soul.
Delian Healer,° summoned by "i ē!"
I await in holy dread what obligation, something new
or something back once more with the revolving years,
you'll bring about for me.
160   Oh tell me, child of golden Hope,
deathless Response!

Antistrophe 1
I appeal to you first, daughter of Zeus,
deathless Athena,
and to your sister who protects this land,
165   Artemis,° whose famous throne is the whole circle
of the marketplace,
and Phoebus, who shoots from afar: i ō!
Three-fold defenders against death, appear!
If ever in the past, to stop blind ruin
170   sent against the city,
you banished utterly the fires of suffering,
come now again!

Strophe 2
Ah! Ah! Unnumbered are the miseries
I bear. The plague claims all

°151 *Strophe:* Strophe and antistrophe (line 162) are stanzaic units referring to movements, countermovements, and gestures that the Chorus performed while singing or chanting in the orchestra. See p. 1280. 151 *Voice from Zeus:* a reference to Apollo's prophecy. Zeus taught Apollo how to prophesy. 153 *Pytho:* Delphi. 156 *Delian Healer:* Apollo. 165 *Artemis:* goddess of virginity, childbirth, and hunting.

our comrades. Nor has thought found yet a spear   175
by which a man shall be protected. What our glorious
earth gives birth to does not grow. Without a birth
from cries of labor
    do the women rise.
One person after another   180
    you may see, like flying birds,
faster than indomitable fire, sped
to the shore of the god that is the sunset.°

Antistrophe 2

And with their deaths unnumbered dies the city.
Her children lie unpitied on the ground,   185
spreading death, unmourned.
Meanwhile young wives, and gray-haired mothers with them,
on the shores of the altars, from this side and that,
suppliants from mournful trouble,
    cry out their grief.   190
A hymn to the Healer shines,
the flute a mourner's voice.
Against which, golden goddess, daughter of Zeus,
    send lovely Strength.

Strophe 3

Cause raging Ares°—who,   195
    armed now with no shield of bronze,
burns me, coming on amid loud cries—
to turn his back and run from my land,
with a fair wind behind, to the great
    hall of Amphitritē,°   200
or to the anchorage that welcomes no one,
Thrace's troubled sea!
If night lets something get away at last,
    it comes by day.
Fire-bearing god . . .   205
    you who dispense the might of lightning,
Zeus! Father! Destroy him with your thunderbolt!

[*Enter* OEDIPUS *from the palace.*]

Antistrophe 3

Lycēan Lord!° From your looped
    bowstring, twisted gold,
I wish indomitable missiles might be scattered   210
and stand forward, our protectors; also fire-bearing
radiance of Artemis, with which
    she darts across the Lycian mountains.

°183 *god . . . sunset*: Hades, god of the underworld. 195 *Ares*: god of war and destruction. 200 *Amphitritē*: the Atlantic Ocean. 208 *Lycēan Lord*: Apollo.

215   I call the god whose head is bound in gold,
       with whom this country shares its name,
       Bacchus,° wine-flushed, summoned by "euoi!,"
           Maenads' comrade,
       to approach ablaze
           with gleaming . . . . . .
220   pine, opposed to that god-hated god.

EPISODE 1

OEDIPUS: I hear your prayer. Submit to what I say
       and to the labors that the plague demands
       and you'll get help and a relief from evils.
       I'll make the proclamation, though a stranger
225   to the report and to the deed. Alone,
       had I no key, I would soon lose the track.
       Since it was only later that I joined you,
       to all the sons of Cadmus I say this:
       whoever has clear knowledge of the man
230   who murdered Laius, son of Labdacus,
       I command him to reveal it all to me—
       nor fear if, to remove the charge, he must
       accuse himself: his fate will not be cruel—
       he will depart unstumbling into exile.
235   But if you know another, or a stranger,
       to be the one whose hand is guilty, speak:
       I shall reward you and remember you.
       But if you keep your peace because of fear,
       and shield yourself or kin from my command,
240   hear you what I shall do in that event:
       I charge all in this land where I have throne
       and power, shut out that man—no matter who—
       both from your shelter and all spoken words,
       nor in your prayers or sacrifices make
245   him partner, not allot him lustral° water.
       All men shall drive him from their homes: for he
       is the pollution that the god-sent Pythian
       response has only now revealed to me.
       In this way I ally myself in war
250   with the divinity and the deceased.°
       And this curse, too, against the one who did it,
       whether alone in secrecy, or with others:
       may he wear out his life unblest and evil!
       I pray this, too: if he is at my hearth
255   and in my home, and I have knowledge of him,
       may the curse pronounced on others come to me.
       All this I lay to you to execute,
       for my sake, for the god's, and for this land
       now ruined, barren, abandoned by the gods.

°245 *lustral*: purifying. 250 *the deceased*: Laius.

Even if no god had driven you to it,   260
you ought not to have left this stain uncleansed,
the murdered man a nobleman, a king!
You should have looked! But now, since, as it happens,
It's I who have the power that he had once,
and have his bed, and a wife who shares our seed,   265
and common bond had we had common children
(had not his hope of offspring had back luck—
but as it happened, luck lunged at his head);
because of this, as if for my own father,
I'll fight for him, I'll leave no means untried,   270
to catch the one who did it with his hand,
for the son of Labdacus, of Polydôrus,
of Cadmus before him, and of Agênor.°
This prayer against all those who disobey:
the gods send out no harvest from their soil,   275
nor children from their wives. Oh, let them die
victims of this plague, or of something worse.
Yet for the rest of us, people of Cadmus,
we the obedient, may Justice, our ally,
and all the gods, be always on our side!   280

CHORAGOS: I speak because I feel the grip of your curse:
    the killer is not *I*. Nor can I point
    to him. The one who set us to this search,
    Phoebus, should also name the guilty man.
OEDIPUS: Quite right, but to compel unwilling gods—   285
    no man has ever had that kind of power.
CHORAGOS: May I suggest to you a second way?
OEDIPUS: A second or a third—pass over nothing!
CHORAGOS: I know of no one who sees more of what
    Lord Phoebus sees than Lord Tiresias.   290
    My Lord, one might learn brilliantly from him.
OEDIPUS: Nor is this something I have been slow to do.
    At Creon's word I sent an escort—twice now!
    I am astonished that he has not come.
CHORAGOS: The old account is useless. It told us nothing.   295
OEDIPUS: But tell it to me. I'll scrutinize all stories.
CHORAGOS: He is said to have been killed by travelers.
OEDIPUS: I have heard, but the one who did it no one sees.
CHORAGOS: If there is any fear in him at all,
    he won't stay here once he has heard that curse.   300
OEDIPUS: He won't fear words: he had no fear when he did it.

[Enter TIRESIAS from the right, led by a SERVANT and two of Oedipus's ATTENDANTS.]

CHORAGOS: Look there! There is the man who will convict him!
    It's the god's prophet they are leading here.
    one gifted with the truth as no one else.
OEDIPUS: Tiresias, master of all omens—   305
    public and secret, in the sky and on the earth—

°272–73 *son . . . Agênor*: refers to Laius by citing his genealogy.

your mind, if not your eyes, sees how the city
lives with a plague, against which Thebes can find
no Saviour or protector, Lord, but you.
310   For Phoebus, as the attendants surely told you,
returned this answer to us: liberation
from the disease would never come unless
we learned without a doubt who murdered Laius—
put them to death, or sent them into exile.
315   Do not begrudge us what you may learn from birds
or any other prophet's path you know!
Care for yourself, the city, care for me,
care for the whole pollution of the dead!
We're in your hands. To do all that he can
320   to help another is man's noblest labor.
TIRESIAS: How terrible to understand and get
no profit from the knowledge! I knew this,
but I forgot, or I had never come.
OEDIPUS: What's this? You've come with very little zeal.
325   TIRESIAS: Let me go home! If you will listen to me,
You will endure your troubles better—and I mine.
OEDIPUS: A strange request, not very kind to the land
that cared for you—to hold back this oracle!
TIRESIAS: I see your understanding comes to you
330   inopportunely. So that won't happen to me . . .
OEDIPUS: Oh, by the gods, if you understand about this,
don't turn away! We're on our knees to you.
TIRESIAS: None of you understands! I'll never bring
my grief to light—will not speak of yours.
335   OEDIPUS: You know and won't declare it! Is your purpose
to betray us and to destroy this land?
TIRESIAS: I will grieve neither of us. Stop this futile
cross-examination. I'll tell you nothing!
OEDIPUS: Nothing? You vile traitor! You could provoke
340   a stone to anger! You still refuse to tell?
Can nothing soften you, nothing convince you?
TIRESIAS: You blamed anger in me—you haven't seen.
Can nothing soften you, nothing convince you?
OEDIPUS: Who wouldn't fill with anger, listening
345   to words like yours which now disgrace this city?
TIRESIAS: It will come, even if my silence hides it.
OEDIPUS: If it will come, then why won't you declare it?
TIRESIAS: I'd rather say no more. Now if you wish,
respond to that will all your fiercest anger!
350   OEDIPUS: Now I am angry enough to come right out
with this conjecture: you, I think, helped plot
the deed; you did it—even if your hand
cannot have struck the blow. If you could see,
I should have said the deed was yours alone.
355   TIRESIAS: Is that right! Then I charge you to abide
by the decree you have announced: from this day
say no word to either these or me,
for you are the vile polluter of this land!

OEDIPUS: Aren't you appalled to let a charge like that
    come bounding forth? How will you get away?   360
TIRESIAS: You cannot catch me. I have the strength of truth.
OEDIPUS: Who taught you this? Not your prophetic craft!
TIRESIAS: You did. You made me say it. I didn't want to.
OEDIPUS: Say what? Repeat it so I'll understand.
TIRESIAS: I made no sense? Or are you trying me?   365
OEDIPUS: No sense I understood. Say it again!
TIRESIAS: I say you are the murderer you seek.
OEDIPUS: Again that horror! You'll wish you hadn't said that.
TIRESIAS: Shall I say more, and raise your anger higher?
OEDIPUS: Anything you like! Your words are powerless.   370
TIRESIAS: You live, unknowing, with those nearest to you
    in the greatest shame. You do not see the evil.
OEDIPUS: You won't go on like that and never pay!
TIRESIAS: I can if there is any strength in truth.
OEDIPUS: In truth, but not in you! You have no strength,   375
    blind in your ears, your reason, and your eyes.
TIRESIAS: Unhappy man! Those jeers you hurl at me
    before long all these men will hurl at you.
OEDIPUS: You are the child of endless night; it's not
    for me or anyone who sees to hurt you.   380
TIRESIAS: It's not my fate to be struck down by you.
    Apollo is enough. That's his concern.
OEDIPUS: Are these inventions Creon's or your own?
TIRESIAS: No, your affliction is yourself, not Creon.
OEDIPUS: Oh success!—in wealth, kingship, artistry,   385
    in any life that wins much admiration—
    the envious ill will stored up for you!
    to get at my command, a gift I did not
    seek, which the city put into my hands,
    my loyal Creon, colleague from the start,   390
    longs to sneak up in secret and dethrone me.
    So he's suborned this fortuneteller—schemer!
    deceitful beggar-priest!—who has good eyes
    for gains alone, though in his craft he's blind.
    Where were your prophet's powers ever proved?   395
    Why, when the dog who chanted verse° was here,
    did you not speak and liberate this city?
    Her riddle wasn't for a man chancing by
    to interpret; prophetic art was needed,
    but you had none, it seems—learned from birds   400
    or from a god. I came along, yes I,
    Oedipus the ignorant, and stopped her—
    by using thought, not augury from birds.
    And it is I whom you may wish to banish,
    so you'll be close to the Creontian throne.   405
    You—and the plot's concocter—will drive out
    pollution to your grief; you look quite old
    or you would be the victim of that plot!

°396 *dog . . . verse:* the Sphinx.

CHORAGOS: It seems to us that this man's words were said
410   in anger, Oedipus, and yours as well.
           Insight, not angry words, is what we need,
           the best solution to the god's response.
TIRESIAS: You are the king, and yet I am your equal
           in my right to speak. In that I too am Lord,
415   for I belong to Loxias,° not you.
           I am not Creon's man. He's nothing to me.
           Hear this, since you have thrown my blindness at me:
           Your eyes can't see the evil to which you've come,
           nor where you live, nor who is in your house.
420   Do you know your parents? Now knowing, you are
           their enemy, in the underworld and here.
           A mother's and a father's double-lashing
           terrible-footed curse will soon drive you out.
           Now you can see, then you will stare into darkness.
425   What place will not be harbor to your cry,
           or what Cithaeron° not reverberate
           when you have heard the bride-song in your palace
           to which you sailed? Fair wind to evil harbor!
           Nor do you see how many other woes
430   will level you to yourself and to your children.
           So, at my message, and at Creon, too,
           splatter muck! There will never be a man
           ground into wretchedness as you will be.
OEDIPUS: Am I to listen to such things from him!
435   May you be damned! Get out of here at once!
           Go! Leave my palace! Turn around and go!

[*TIRESIAS begins to move away from* OEDIPUS.]

TIRESIAS: I wouldn't have come had you not sent for me.
OEDIPUS: I did not know you'd talk stupidity,
           or I wouldn't have rushed to bring you to my house.
440   TIRESIAS: Stupid I seem to you, yet to your parents
           who gave you natural birth I seemed quite shrewd.
OEDIPUS: Who? Wait! Who is the one who gave me birth?
TIRESIAS: This day will give you birth,° and ruin too.
OEDIPUS: What murky, riddling things you always say!
445   TIRESIAS: Don't you surpass us all at finding out?
OEDIPUS: You sneer at what you'll find has brought me greatness.
TIRESIAS: And that's the very luck that ruined you.
OEDIPUS: I wouldn't care, just so I saved the city.
TIRESIAS: In that case I shall go. Boy, lead the way!
450   OEDIPUS: Yes, let him lead you off. Here, underfoot,
           you irk me. Gone, you'll cause no further pain.
TIRESIAS: I'll go when I have said what I was sent for.
           Your face won't scare me. You can't ruin me.

°415 *Loxias:* Apollo. 426 *Cithaeron:* reference to the mountain on which Oedipus was to be exposed as an infant.
443 *give you birth:* that is, identify your parents.

I say to you, the man whom you have looked for
as you pronounced your curses, your decrees   455
on the bloody death of Laius—he is here!
A seeming stranger, he shall be shown to be
a Theban born, though he'll take no delight
in that solution. Blind, who once could see,
a beggar who was rich, through foreign lands   460
he'll go and point before him with a stick.
To his beloved children, he'll be shown
a father who is also brother; to the one
who bore him, son and husband; to his father,
his seed-fellow and killer. Go in   465
and think this out; and if you find I've lied,
say then I have no prophet's understanding!

[*Exit* TIRESIAS, *led by a* SERVANT. OEDIPUS *exits into the palace with his* ATTENDANTS.]

STASIMON 1

Strophe 1

CHORUS: Who is the man of whom the inspired
            rock of Delphi° said
         he has committed the unspeakable   470
            with blood-stained hands?
         Time for him to ply a foot
         mightier than those of the horses
            of the storm in his escape;
         upon him mounts and plunges the weaponed   475
         son of Zeus,° with fire and thunderbolts,
         and in his train the dreaded goddesses
         of Death, who never miss.

Antistrophe 1

         The message has just blazed,
            gleaming from the snows   480
         of Mount Parnassus: we must track
            everywhere the unseen man.
         He wanders, hidden by wild
         forests, up through caves
            and rocks, like a bull,   485
         anxious, with an anxious foot, forlorn.
         He puts away from him the mantic° words come from earth's
         navel,° at its center, yet these live
         forever and still hover round him.

Strophe 2

         Terribly he troubles me,
            the skilled interpreter of birds!°   490

°469 *rock of Delphi*: Apollo's oracle at Delphi. 476 *son of Zeus*: Apollo. 487 *mantic*: prophetic. 487–488 *earth's navel*: Delphi. 491 *interpreter of birds*: Tiresias. The Chorus is troubled by his accusations.

I can't assent, nor speak against him.
Both paths are closed to me.
I hover on the wings of doubt,
495   not seeing what is here nor what's to come.
What quarrel started in the house of Labdacus°
or in the house of Polybus,°
      either ever in the past
      or now, I never
500 heard, so that . . . with this fact for my touchstone
I could attack the public
      fame of Oedipus, by the side of the Labdaceans
an ally, against the dark assassination.

Antistrophe 2

No, Zeus and Apollo
505   understand and know things
mortal; but that another man
      can do more as a prophet than I can—
for that there is no certain test,
      though, skill to skill,
510 one man might overtake another.
No, never, not until
      I see the charges proved,
when someone blames him shall I nod assent.
For once, as we all saw, the winged maiden° came
515 against him: he was seen then to be skilled,
      proved, by that touchstone, dear to the people. So,
never will my mind convict him of the evil.

EPISODE 2

[Enter CREON *from the right door of the skene and speaks to the* CHORUS.*]*

CREON: Citizens, I hear that a fearful charge
    is made against me by King Oedipus!
520 I had to come. If, in this crisis,
    he thinks that he has suffered injury
    from anything that I have said or done,
    I have no appetite for a long life—
    bearing a blame like that! It's no slight blow,
525   the punishment I'd take from what he said:
    it's the ultimate hurt to be called traitor
    by the city, by you, by my own people!
CHORAGOS: The thing that forced that accusation out
    could have been anger, not the power of thought.
530 CREON: But who persuaded him that thoughts of mine
    had led the prophet into telling lies?
CHORAGOS: I do not know the thought behind his words.

°496 *house of Labdacus:* the line of Laius. 497 *Polybus:* Oedipus's foster father. 514 *winged maiden:* the Sphinx.

CREON: But did he look straight at you? Was his mind right
    when he said that I was guilty of this charge?
CHORAGOS: I have no eyes to see what rulers do.   535
    But here he comes himself out of the house.   ·

[*Enter OEDIPUS from the palace.*]

OEDIPUS: What? You here? And can you really have
    the face and daring to approach my house
    when you're exposed as its master's murderer
    and caught, too, as the robber of my kingship?   540
    Did you see cowardice in me, by the gods,
    or foolishness, when you began this plot?
    Did you suppose that I would not detect
    your stealthy moves, or that I'd not fight back?
    It's your attempt that's folly, isn't it—   545
    tracking without followers or connections,
    kingship which is caught with wealth and numbers?
CREON: Now wait! Give me as long to answer back!
    Judge me for yourself when you have heard me!
OEDIPUS: You're eloquent, but I'd be slow to learn   550
    from you, now that I've seen your malice toward me.
CREON: That I deny. Hear what I have to say.
OEDIPUS: Don't you deny it! You are the traitor here!
CREON: If you consider mindless willfulness
    a prized possession, you are not thinking sense.   555
OEDIPUS: If you think you can wrong a relative
    and get off free, you are not thinking sense.
CREON: Perfectly just, I won't say no. And yet
    what is this injury you say I did you?
OEDIPUS: Did you persuade me, yes or no, to send   560
    someone to bring that solemn prophet here?
CREON: And I still hold to the advice I gave.
OEDIPUS: How many years ago did your King Laius . . .
CREON: Laius! Do what? Now I don't understand.
OEDIPUS: Vanish—victim of a murderous violence?   565
CREON: That is a long count back into the past.
OEDIPUS: Well, was this seer then practicing his art?
CREON: Yes, skilled and honored just as he is today.
OEDIPUS: Did he, back then, ever refer to me?
CREON: He did not do so in my presence ever.   570
OEDIPUS: You did inquire into the murder then.
CREON: We had to, surely, though we discovered nothing.
OEDIPUS: But the "skilled" one did not say this then? Why not?
CREON: I never talk when I am ignorant.
OEDIPUS: But you're not ignorant of your own part.   575
CREON: What do you mean? I'll tell you if I know.
OEDIPUS: Just this: if he had not conferred with you
    he'd not have told about my murdering Laius.
CREON: If he said that, you are the one who knows.
    But now it's fair that you should answer me.   580
OEDIPUS: Ask on! You won't convict me as the killer.

CREON: Well then, answer. My sister is your wife?
OEDIPUS: Now there's a statement that I can't deny.
CREON: You two have equal power in this country?
585   OEDIPUS: She gets from me whatever she desires.
CREON: And I'm a third? The three of us are equals?
OEDIPUS: That's where you're treacherous to your kinship!
CREON: But think about this rationally, as I do.
        First look at this: do you think anyone
590   prefers the anxieties of being king
        to untroubled sleep—if he has equal power?
        I'm not the kind of man who falls in love
        with kingship. I am content with a king's power.
        And so would any man who's wise and prudent.
595   I get all things from you, with no distress;
        as king I would have onerous duties, too.
        How could the kingship bring me more delight
        than this untroubled power and influence?
        I'm not misguided yet to such a point
600   that profitable honors aren't enough.
        As it is, all wish me well and all salute;
        those begging you for something have me summoned,
        for their success depends on that alone.
        Why should I lose all this to become king?
605   A prudent mind is never traitorous.
        Treason's a thought I'm not enamored of;
        nor could I join a man who acted so.
        In proof of this, first go yourself to Pytho°
        and ask if I brought back the true response.
610   Then, if you find I plotted with that portent
        reader,° don't have me put to death by your vote
        only—I'll vote myself for my conviction.
        Don't let an unsupported thought convict me!
        It's not right mindlessly to take the bad
615   for good or to suppose the good are traitors.
        Rejecting a relation who is loyal
        is like rejecting life, our greatest love.
        In time you'll know securely without stumbling,
        for time alone can prove a just man just,
620   though you can know a bad man in a day.
CHORAGOS: Well said, to one who's anxious not to fall.
        Swift thinkers, Lord, are never safe from stumbling.
OEDIPUS: But when a swift and secret plotter moves
        against me, I must make swift counterplot.
625   If I lie quiet and await his move,
        he'll have achieved his aims and I'll have missed.
CREON: You surely cannot mean you want me exiled!
OEDIPUS: Not exiled, no. Your death is what I want!
CREON: If you would first define what envy is . . .
630   OEDIPUS: Are you still stubborn! Still disobedient?

°608 *Pytho*: Delphi. 610–611 *portent reader*: Apollo's oracle or prophet.

CREON: I see you cannot think!
OEDIPUS: For me I can.
CREON: You should for me as well!
OEDIPUS: But you're a traitor!
CREON: What if you're wrong?
OEDIPUS: Authority must be maintained.
CREON: Not if the ruler's evil.
OEDIPUS: Hear that, Thebes!
CREON: It is my city too, not yours alone!   635
CHORAGOS: Please don't, my Lords! Ah, just in time, I see
    Jocasta there, coming from the palace.
    With her help you must settle your quarrel.

[*Enter* JOCASTA *from the Palace.*]

JOCASTA: Wretched men! What has provoked this ill-
    advised dispute? Have you no sense of shame,   640
    with Thebes so sick, to stir up private troubles?
    Now go inside! And Creon, you go home!
    Don't make a general anguish out of nothing!
CREON: My sister, Oedipus your husband here
    sees fit to do one of two hideous things: 645
    to have me banished from the land—or killed!
OEDIPUS: That's right: I caught him, Lady, plotting harm
    against my person—with a malignant science.
CREON: May my life fail, may I die cursed, if I
    did any of the things you said I did!   650
JOCASTA: Believe his words, for the god's sake, Oedipus,
    in deference above all to his oath
    to the gods. Also for me, and for these men!

KOMMOS°

Strophe 1
CHORUS: Consent, with will and mind,
    my king, I beg of you!   655
OEDIPUS: What do you wish me to surrender?
CHORUS: Show deference to him who was not feeble in time past
    and is now great in the power of his oath!
OEDIPUS: Do you know what you're asking?
CHORUS: Yes.
OEDIPUS: Tell me then.
CHORUS: Never to cast into dishonored guilt, with an unproved   660
    assumption, a kinsman who has bound himself by curse.
OEDIPUS: Now you must understand, when you ask this,
    you ask my death or banishment from the land.

Strophe 2
CHORUS: No, by the god who is the foremost of all gods,
    the Sun! No! Godless,   665
        friendless, whatever death is worst of all,

°654 *Kommos:* a dirge or lament sung by the Chorus and one or more of the chief characters.

let that be my destruction, if this
     thought ever moved me!
But my ill-fated soul
670   this dying land
wears out—the more if to these older troubles
she adds new troubles from the two of you!
OEDIPUS: Then let him go, though it must mean my death,
    or else disgrace and exile from the land.
675   My pity is moved by your words, not by his—
    he'll only have my hate, wherever he goes.
CREON: You're sullen as you yield; you'll be depressed
    when you've passed through this anger. Natures like yours
    are hardest on themselves. That's as it should be.
OEDIPUS: Then won't you go and let me be?
680 CREON: I'll go.
    Though you're unreasonable, they know I'm righteous.

                                                [Exit CREON.]

Antistrophe 1

CHORUS: Why are you waiting, Lady?
    Conduct him back into the palace!
JOCASTA: I will, when I have heard what chanced.
685 CHORUS: Conjectures—words alone, and nothing based on thought.
    But even an injustice can devour a man.
JOCASTA: Did the words come from both sides?
CHORUS: Yes.
JOCASTA: What was said?
CHORUS: To me it seems enough! enough! the land already troubled,
690   that this should rest where it has stopped.
OEDIPUS: See what you've come to in your honest thought,
    in seeking to relax and blunt my heart?

Antistrophe 2

CHORUS: I have not said this only once, my Lord.
    That I had lost my sanity,
695   without a path in thinking—
be sure this would be clear
    if I put you away
who, when my cherished land
    wandered crazed
700 with suffering, brought her back on course.
    Now, too, be a lucky helmsman!
JOCASTA: Please, for the god's sake, Lord, explain to me
    the reason why you have conceived this wrath?
OEDIPUS: I honor you, not them,° and I'll explain
705   to you how Creon has conspired against me.
JOCASTA: All right, if that will explain how the quarrel started.
OEDIPUS: He says I am the murderer of Laius!

°704 *them:* the Chorus.

JOCASTA: Did he claim knowledge or that someone told him?

OEDIPUS: Here's what he did: he sent that vicious seer
   so he could keep his own mouth innocent.   710

JOCASTA: Ah then, absolve yourself of what he charges!
   Listen to this and you'll agree, no mortal
   is ever given skill in prophecy.
   I'll prove this quickly with one incident.
   It was foretold to Laius—I shall not say   715
   by Phoebus himself, but by his ministers—
   that when his fate arrived he would be killed
   by a son who would be born to him and me.
   And yet, so it is told, foreign robbers
   murdered him, at a place where three roads meet.   720
   As for the child I bore him, not three days passed
   before he yoked the ball-joints of its feet,°
   then cast it, by others' hands, on a trackless mountain.
   That time Apollo did not make our child
   a patricide, or bring about what Laius   725
   feared, that he be killed by his own son.
   That's how prophetic words determined things!
   Forget them. The things a god must track
   he will himself painlessly reveal.

OEDIPUS: Just now, as I was listening to you, Lady,   730
   what a profound distraction seized my mind!

JOCASTA: What made you turn around so anxiously?

OEDIPUS: I thought you said that Laius was attacked
   and butchered at a place where three roads meet.

JOCASTA: That is the story, and it is told so still.   735

OEDIPUS: Where is the place where this was done to him?

JOCASTA: The land's called Phocis, where a two-forked road
   comes in from Delphi and from Daulia.

OEDIPUS: And how much time has passed since these events?

JOCASTA: Just prior to your presentation here   740
   as king this news was published to the city.

OEDIPUS: Oh, Zeus, what have you willed to do to me?

JOCASTA: Oedipus, what makes your heart so heavy?

OEDIPUS: No, tell me first of Laius' appearance,
   what peak of youthful vigor he had reached.   745

JOCASTA: A tall man, showing his first growth of white.
   He had a figure not unlike your own.

OEDIPUS: Alas! It seems that in my ignorance
   I laid those fearful curses on myself.

JOCASTA: What is it, Lord? I flinch to see your face.   750

OEDIPUS: I'm dreadfully afraid the prophet sees.
   But I'll know better with one more detail.

JOCASTA: I'm frightened too. But ask: I'll answer you.

OEDIPUS: Was his retinue small, or did he travel
   with a great troop, as would befit a prince?   755

JOCASTA: There were just five in all, one a herald.
   There was a carriage, too, bearing Laius.

°722 *ball-joints of its feet*: the ankles.

OEDIPUS: Alas! Now I see it! But who was it,
    Lady, who told you what you know about this?
760 JOCASTA: A servant who alone was saved unharmed.
OEDIPUS: By chance, could he be now in the palace?
JOCASTA: No, he is not. When he returned and saw
    you had the power of the murdered Laius,
    he touched my hand and begged me formally
765   to send him to the fields and to the pastures,
    so he'd be out of sight, far from the city.
    I did. Although a slave, he well deserved
    to win this favor, and indeed far more.
OEDIPUS: Let's have him called back in immediately.
770 JOCASTA: That can be done, but why do you desire it?
OEDIPUS: I fear, Lady, I have already said
    too much. That's why I wish to see him now.
JOCASTA: Then he shall come; but it is right somehow
    that I, too, Lord, should know what troubles you.
775 OEDIPUS: I've gone so deep into the things I feared
    I'll tell you everything. Who has a right
    greater than yours, while I cross through this chance?
    Polybus of Corinth was my father,
    my mother was the Dorian Meropē.
780   I was first citizen, until this chance
    attacked me—striking enough, to be sure,
    but not worth all the gravity I gave it.
    This: at a feast a man who'd drunk too much
    denied, at the wine, I was my father's son.
785   I was depressed and all that day I barely
    held it in. Next day I put the question
    to my mother and father. They were enraged
    at the man who'd let this fiction fly at me.
    I was much cheered by them. And yet it kept
790   grinding into me. His words kept coming back.
    Without my mother's or my father's knowledge
    I went to Pytho. But Phoebus sent me away
    dishonoring my demand. Instead, other
    wretched horrors he flashed forth in speech.
795   He said that I would be my mother's lover,
    show offspring to mankind they could not look at,
    and be his murderer whose seed I am.°
    When I heard this, and ever since, I gauged
    the way to Corinth by the stars alone,
800   running to a place where I would never see
    the disgrace in the oracle's words come true.
    But I soon came to the exact location
    where, as you tell of it, the king was killed.
    Lady, here is the truth. As I went on,
805   when I was just approaching those three roads,
    a herald and a man like him you spoke of

°797 *be . . . am*: that is, murder my father.

came on, riding a carriage drawn by colts.
Both the man out front and the old man himself°
tried violently to force me off the road.
The driver, when he tried to push me off,   810
I struck in anger. The old man saw this, watched
me approach, then leaned out and lunged down
with twin prongs° at the middle of my head!
He got more than he gave. Abruptly—struck
once by the staff in this my hand—he tumbled   815
out, head first, from the middle of the carriage.
And then I killed them all. But if there is
a kinship between Laius and this stranger,
who is more wretched than the man you see?
Who was there born more hated by the gods?   820
For neither citizen nor foreigner
may take me in his home or speak to me.
No, they must drive me off. And it is I
who have pronounced these curses on myself!
I stain the dead man's bed with these my hands,   825
by which he died. Is not my nature vile?
Unclean?—if I am banished and even
in exile I may not see my own parents,
or set foot in my homeland, or else be yoked
in marriage to my mother, and kill my father,   830
Polybus, who raised me and gave me birth?
If someone judged a cruel divinity
did this to me, would he not speak the truth?
You pure and awful gods, may I not ever
see that day, may I be swept away   835
from men before I see so great and so
calamitous a stain fixed on my person!

CHORAGOS: These things seem fearful to us, Lord, and yet,
        until you hear it from the witness, keep hope!
OEDIPUS: That is the single hope that's left to me,   840
        to wait for him, that herdsman—until he comes.
JOCASTA: When he appears, what are you eager for?
OEDIPUS: Just this: if his account agrees with yours
        then I shall have escaped this misery.
JOCASTA: But what was it that struck you in my story?   845
OEDIPUS: You said he spoke of robbers as the ones
        who killed him. Now: if he continues still
        to speak of many, then I could not have killed him.
        One man and many men just do not jibe.
        But if he says one belted man, the doubt   850
        is gone. The balance tips toward me. I did it.
JOCASTA: No! He told it as I told you. Be certain.
        He can't reject that and reverse himself.
        The city heard these things, not I alone.

°808 *old man himself:* Laius. 812–813 *lunged . . . prongs:* Laius strikes Oedipus with a two-pronged horse goad
or whip.

855   But even if he swerves from what he said,
       he'll never show that Laius' murder, Lord,
       occurred just as predicted. For Loxias
       expressly said my son was doomed to kill him.
       The boy—poor boy—he never had a chance
860   to cut him down, for he was cut down first.
       Never again, just for some oracle
       will I shoot frightened glances right and left.
OEDIPUS: That's full of sense. Nonetheless, send a man
       to bring that farm hand here. Will you do it?
865 JOCASTA: I'll send one right away. But let's go in.
       Would I do anything against your wishes?

[*Exit* OEDIPUS *and* JOCASTA *through the central door into the palace.*]

STASIMON 2

Strophe 1

CHORUS: May there accompany me
       the fate to keep a reverential purity in what I say,
       in all I do, for which the laws have been set forth
870   and walk on high, born to traverse the brightest,
       highest upper air; Olympus° only
       is their father, nor was it
       mortal nature
       that fathered them, and never will
875   oblivion lull them into sleep;
       the god in them is great and never ages.

Antistrophe 1

       The will to violate, seed of the tyrant,
       if it has drunk mindlessly of wealth and power,
       without a sense of time or true advantage,
880   mounts to a peak, then
       plunges to an abrupt . . . destiny,
       where the useful foot
       is of no use. But the kind
       of struggling that is good for the city
885   I ask the god never to abolish.
       The god is my protector: never will I give that up.

Strophe 2

       But if a man proceeds disdainfully
           in deeds of hand or word
       and has no fear of Justice
890   or reverence for shrines of the divinities
       (may a bad fate catch him
           for his luckless wantonness!),
       if he'll not gain what he gains with justice
       and deny himself what is unholy,
895   or if he clings, in foolishness, to the untouchable

°871 *Olympus*: Mount Olympus, home of the gods, treated as a god.

(what man, finally, in such an action, will have strength
enough to fend off passion's arrows from his soul?),
if, I say, this kind of
        deed is held in honor—
why should I join the sacred dance?   900

Antistrophe 2
    No longer shall I visit and revere
            Earth's navel° the untouchable,
    nor visit Abae's° temple,
            or Olympia,°
    if the prophecies are not matched by events   905
            for all the world to point to.
    No, you who hold the power, if you are rightly called
    Zeus the king of all, let this matter not escape you
    and your ever-deathless rule,
        for the prophecies to Laius fade . . .   910
    and men already disregard them;
        nor is Apollo anywhere
            glorified with honors.
    Religion slips away.

EPISODE 3

[*Enter* JOCASTA *from the palace carrying a branch wound with wool and a jar of incense. She is attended by two women.*]

JOCASTA: Lords of the realm, the thought has come to me   915
        to visit shrines of the divinities
    with suppliant's branch in hand and fragrant smoke.
    For Oedipus excites his soul too much
    with alarms of all kinds. He will not judge
    the present by the past, like a man of sense.   920
    He's at the mercy of all terror-mongers.

[JOCASTA *approaches the altar on the right and kneels.*]

        Since I can do no good by counseling,
    Apollo the Lycēan!—you are the closest—
    I come a suppliant, with these my vows,
    for a cleansing that will not pollute him.   925
    For when we see him shaken we are all
    afraid, like people looking at their helmsman.

[*Enter a* MESSENGER *along one of the Parados. He sees* JOCASTA *at the altar and then addresses the* CHORUS.]

MESSENGER: I would be pleased if you would help me, stranger.
        Where is the palace of King Oedipus?
    Or tell me where he is himself, if you know.   930

°902 *Earth's navel*: Delphi. 903 *Abae*: a town in Phocis where there was another oracle of Apollo. 904 *Olympia*:
site of the oracle of Zeus.

CHORUS: This is his house, stranger. He is within.
This is his wife and mother of his children.
MESSENGER: May she and her family find prosperity,
if, as you say, her marriage is fulfilled.
935 JOCASTA: You also, stranger, for you deserve as much ·
for your gracious words. But tell me why you've come.
What do you wish? Or what have you to tell us?
MESSENGER: Good news, my Lady, both for your house and
husband.
940 JOCASTA: What is your news? And who has sent you to us?
MESSENGER: I come from Corinth. When you have heard my
news
you will rejoice, I'm sure—and grieve perhaps.
JOCASTA: What is it? How can it have this double power?
945 MESSENGER: They will establish him their king, so say
the people of the land of Isthmia°
JOCASTA: But is old Polybus not still in power?
MESSENGER: He's not, for death has clasped him in the tomb.
JOCASTA: What's this? Has Oedipus' father died?
950 MESSENGER: If I have lied then I deserve to die.
JOCASTA: Attendant! Go quickly to your master,
and tell him this.

[*Exit an* ATTENDANT *into the palace.*]

Oracles of the gods!
Where are you now? The man whom Oedipus
fled long ago, for fear that he should kill him—
955 he's been destroyed by chance and not by him!

[*Enter* OEDIPUS *from the palace.*]

OEDIPUS: Darling Jocasta, my beloved wife,
Why have you called me from the palace?
JOCASTA: First hear what this man has to say. Then see
what the god's grave oracle has come to now!
960 OEDIPUS: Where is he from? What is this news he brings me?
JOCASTA: From Corinth. He brings news about your father:
that Polybus is no more! that he is dead!
OEDIPUS: What's this, old man? I want to hear you say it.
MESSENGER: If this is what must first be clarified,
965 please be assured that he is dead and gone.
OEDIPUS: By treachery or by the touch of sickness?
MESSENGER: Light pressures tip agèd frames into their sleep.
OEDIPUS: You mean the poor man died of some disease.
MESSENGER: And of the length of years that he had tallied.
970 OEDIPUS: Aha! Then why should we look to Pytho's vapors,°
or to the birds that scream above our heads?°
If we could really take those things for guides,
I would have killed my father. But he's dead!

°946 *land of Isthmia*: Corinth, which is on an isthmus. 970 *Pytho's vapors*: the prophecies of the oracle at Delphi.
971 *birds . . . heads*: the prophecies derived from interpreting the flights of birds.

He is beneath the earth, and here am I,
who never touched a spear. Unless he died   975
of longing for me and I "killed" him that way!
No, in this case, Polybus, by dying, took
the worthless oracle to Hades with him.

JOCASTA: And wasn't I telling you that just now?

OEDIPUS: You were indeed. I was misled by fear.   980

JOCASTA: You should not care about this anymore.

OEDIPUS: I must care. I must stay clear of my mother's bed.

JOCASTA: What's there for man to fear? The realm of chance
    prevails. True foresight isn't possible.
    His life is best who lives without a plan.   985
    This marriage with your mother—don't fear it.
    How many times have men in dreams, too, slept
    with their own mothers! Those who believe such things
    mean nothing endure their lives most easily.

OEDIPUS: A fine, bold speech, and you are right, perhaps,   990
    except that my mother is still living,
    so I must fear her, however well you argue.

JOCASTA: And yet your father's tomb is a great eye.

OEDIPUS: Illuminating, yes. But I still fear the living.

MESSENGER: Who is the woman who inspires this fear?   995

OEDIPUS: Meropē, Polybus' wife, old man.

MESSENGER: And what is there about her that alarms you?

OEDIPUS: An oracle, god-sent and fearful, stranger.

MESSENGER: Is it permitted that another know?

OEDIPUS: It is. Loxias once said to me   1000
    I must have intercourse with my own mother
    and take my father's blood with these my hands.
    So I have long lived far away from Corinth.
    This has indeed brought much good luck, and yet,
    to see one's parents' eyes is happiest.   1005

MESSENGER: Was it for this that you have lived in exile?

OEDIPUS: So I'd not be my father's killer, sir.

MESSENGER: Had I not better free you from this fear,
    my Lord? That's why I came—to do you service.

OEDIPUS: Indeed, what a reward you'd get for that!   1010

MESSENGER: Indeed, this is the main point of my trip,
    to be rewarded when you get back home.

OEDIPUS: I'll never rejoin the givers of my seed!°

MESSENGER: My son, clearly you don't know what you're doing.

OEDIPUS: But how is that, old man? For the gods' sake, tell me!   1015

MESSENGER: If it's because of them you won't go home.

OEDIPUS: I fear that Phoebus will have told the truth.

MESSENGER: Pollution from the ones who gave you seed?

OEDIPUS: That is the thing, old man, I always fear.

MESSENGER: Your fear is groundless. Understand that.   1020

OEDIPUS: Groundless? Not if I was born their son.

MESSENGER: But Polybus is not related to you.

OEDIPUS: Do you mean Polybus was not my father?

°1013 *givers of my seed*: that is, my parents. Oedipus still thinks Meropē and Polybus are his parents.

MESSENGER: No more than I. We're both the same to you.

1025   OEDIPUS: Same? One who begot me and one who didn't?

MESSENGER: He didn't beget you any more than I did.

OEDIPUS: But then, why did he say I was his son?

MESSENGER: He got you as a gift from my own hands.

OEDIPUS: He loved me so, though from another's hands?

1030   MESSENGER: His former childlessness persuaded him.

OEDIPUS: But had you bought me, or begotten me?

MESSENGER: Found you. In the forest hallows of Cithaeron.

OEDIPUS: What were you doing traveling in that region?

MESSENGER: I was in charge of flocks which grazed those mountains.

1035   OEDIPUS: A wanderer who worked the flocks for hire?

MESSENGER: Ah, but that day. I was your savior, son.

OEDIPUS: From what? What was my trouble when you took me?

MESSENGER: The ball-joints of your feet might testify.

OEDIPUS: What's that? What makes you name that ancient trouble?

1040   MESSENGER: Your feet were pierced and I am your rescuer.

OEDIPUS: A fearful rebuke those tokens left for me!

MESSENGER: That was the chance that names you who you are.

OEDIPUS: By the gods, did my mother or my father do this?

MESSENGER: That I don't know. He might who gave you to me.

1045   OEDIPUS: From someone else? You didn't chance on me?

MESSENGER: Another shepherd handed you to me.

OEDIPUS: Who was he? Do you know? Will you explain!

MESSENGER: They called him one of the men of—was it Laius?

OEDIPUS: The one who once was king here long ago?

1050   MESSENGER: That is the one! The man was shepherd to him.

OEDIPUS: And is he still alive so I can see him?

MESSENGER: But you who live here ought to know that best.

OEDIPUS: Does any one of you now present know
    about the shepherd whom this man has named?

1055   Have you seen him in town or in the fields? Speak out!
    The time has come for the discovery!

CHORAGOS: The man he speaks of, I believe, is the same
    as the field hand you have already asked to see.
    But it's Jocasta who would know this best.

1060   OEDIPUS: Lady, do you remember the man we just
    now sent for—is that the man he speaks of?

JOCASTA: What? The man he spoke of? Pay no attention!
    His words are not worth thinking about. It's nothing.

OEDIPUS: With clues like this within my grasp, give up?

1065   Fail to solve the mystery of my birth?

JOCASTA: For the love of the gods, and if you love your life,
    give up this search! My sickness is enough.

OEDIPUS: Come! Though my mothers for three generations
    were in slavery, you'd not be lowborn!

1070   JOCASTA: No, listen to me! Please! Don't do this thing!

OEDIPUS: I will not listen; I will search out the truth.

JOCASTA: My thinking is for you—it would be best.

OEDIPUS: This "best" of yours is starting to annoy me.

JOCASTA: Doomed man! Never find out who you are!

OEDIPUS: Will someone go and bring that shepherd here?   1075
    Leave her to glory in her wealthy birth!
JOCASTA: Man of misery! No other name
    shall I address you by, ever again.

                  [*Exit JOCASTA into the palace after a long pause.*]

CHORAGOS: Why has your lady left, Oedipus,
    hurled by a savage grief? I am afraid   1080
    disaster will come bursting from this silence.
OEDIPUS: Let it burst forth! However low this seed
    of mine may be, yet I desire to see it.
    She, perhaps—she has a woman's pride—
    is mortified by my base origins.   1085
    But I who count myself the child of Chance,
    the giver of good, shall never know dishonor.
    She is my mother,° and the months my brothers
    who first marked out my lowness, then my greatness.
    I shall not prove untrue to such a nature   1090
    by giving up the search for my own birth.

STASIMON 3

Strophe

CHORUS: If I have mantic power
    and excellence in thought,
    by Olympus,
        you shall not, Cithaeron, at tomorrow's   1095
    full moon,
    fail to hear us celebrate you as the countryman
    of Oedipus, his nurse and mother,
    or fail to be the subject of our dance,
        since you have given pleasure   1100
    to our king.
Phoebus, whom we summon by "iē!,"
may this be pleasing to you!

Antistrophe

    Who was your mother, son?
    which of the long-lived nymphs   1105
    after lying with Pan,°
        the mountain roaming . . . Or was it a bride
    of Loxias?°
    For dear to him are all the upland pastures.
    Or was it Mount Cyllēnē's lord,°   1110
    or the Bacchic god,°
        dweller of the mountain peaks,
    who received you as a joyous find
    from one of the nymphs of Helicon,
    the favorite sharers of his sport?   1115

°1088 *She . . . mother*: Chance is my mother. 1106 *Pan*: god of shepherds and woodlands, half man and half goat. See page 1013. 1108 *Loxias*: Apollo. 1110 *Mount Cyllēnē's lord*: Hermes, messenger of the gods. 1111 *Bacchic god*: Dionysus.

EPISODE 4

OEDIPUS: If someone like myself, who never met him,
    may calculate—elders, I think I see
    the very herdsman we've been waiting for.
    His many years would fit that man's age,
1120   and those who bring him on, if I am right,
    are my own men. And yet, in real knowledge,
    you can outstrip me, surely: you've seen him.

[*Enter the old* HERDSMAN *escorted by two of Oedipus's* ATTENDANTS. *At first, the* HERDSMAN *will not look at* OEDIPUS.]

CHORAGOS: I know him, yes, a man of the house of Laius,
    a trusty herdsman if he ever had one.
1125 OEDIPUS: I ask you first, the stranger come from Corinth:
    is this the man you spoke of?
MESSENGER: That's he you see.
OEDIPUS: Then you, old man. First look at me! Now answer:
    did you belong to Laius' household once?
HERDSMAN: I did. Not a purchased slave but raised in the palace.
1130 OEDIPUS: How have you spent your life? What is your work?
HERDSMAN: Most of my life now I have tended sheep.
OEDIPUS: Where is the usual place you stay with them?
HERDSMAN: On Mount Cithaeron. Or in that district.
OEDIPUS: Do you recall observing this man there?
1135 HERDSMAN: Doing what? Which is the man you mean?
OEDIPUS: This man right here. Have you had dealings with him?
HERDSMAN: I can't say right away. I don't remember.
MESSENGER: No wonder, master. I'll bring clear memory
    to his ignorance. I'm absolutely sure
1140   he can recall it, the district was Cithaeron,
    he with a double flock, and I, with one,
    lived close to him, for three entire seasons,
    six months long, from spring right to Arcturus.°
    Then for the winter I'd drive mine to my fold,
1145   and he'd drive his to Laius' pen again.
    Did any of the things I say take place?
HERDSMAN: You speak the truth, though it's from long ago.
MESSENGER: Do you remember giving me, back then,
    a boy I was to care for as my own?
1150 HERDSMAN: What are you saying? Why do you ask me that?
MESSENGER: There, sir, is the man who was that boy!
HERDSMAN: Damn you! Shut your mouth! Keep your silence!
OEDIPUS: Stop! Don't you rebuke his words.
    Your words ask for rebuke far more than his.
1155 HERDSMAN: But what have I done wrong, most royal master?

°1143 *from spring right to Arcturus:* that is, from spring to early fall, when the summer star Arcturus (in the constellation Boötes) was no longer visible in the early evening sky. It did not rise at night again until early in the following spring.

OEDIPUS: Not telling of the boy of whom he asked.
HERDSMAN: He's ignorant and blundering toward ruin.
OEDIPUS: Tell it willingly—or under torture.
HERDSMAN: Oh god! Don't—I am old—don't torture me!
OEDIPUS: Here! Someone put his hands behind his back!   1160
HERDSMAN: But why? What else would you find out, poor man?
OEDIPUS: Did you give him the child he asks about?
HERDSMAN: I did. I wish that I had died that day!
OEDIPUS: You'll come to that if you don't speak the truth.
HERDSMAN: It's if I speak that I shall be destroyed.   1165
OEDIPUS: I think this fellow struggles for delay.
HERDSMAN: No, no! I said already that I gave him.
OEDIPUS: From your own home, or got from someone else?
HERDSMAN: Not from my own. I got him from another.
OEDIPUS: Which of these citizens? What sort of house?   1170
HERDSMAN: Don't—by the gods!—don't, master, ask me more!
OEDIPUS: It means your death if I must ask again.
HERDSMAN: One of the children of the house of Laius.
OEDIPUS: A slave—or born into the family?
HERDSMAN: I have come to the dreaded thing, and I shall say it.   1175
OEDIPUS: And I to hearing it, but hear I must.
HERDSMAN: He was reported to have been—his son.
    Your lady in the house could tell you best.
OEDIPUS: Because she gave him to you?
HERDSMAN: Yes, my lord.
OEDIPUS: What was her purpose?
HERDSMAN: I was to kill the boy.   1180
OEDIPUS: The child she bore?
HERDSMAN: She dreaded prophecies.
OEDIPUS: What were they?
HERDSMAN: The word was that he'd kill his parents.
OEDIPUS: Then why did you give him up to this old man?
HERDSMAN: In pity, master—so he would take him home,
    to another land. But what he did was save him   1185
    for this supreme disaster. If you are the one
    he speaks of—know your evil birth and fate!
OEDIPUS: Ah! All of it was destined to be true!
    Oh light, now may I look my last upon you,
    shown monstrous in my birth, in marriage monstrous,   1190
    a murderer monstrous in those I killed.

                         [*Exit* OEDIPUS, *running into the palace.*]

STASIMON 4

Strophe 1

CHORUS: Oh generations of mortal men,
    while you are living, I will
        appraise your lives at zero!
    What man   1195

comes closer to seizing lasting blessedness
than merely to seize its semblance,
and after living in this semblance, to plunge?
With your example before us,
1200   with your destiny, yours,
            suffering Oedipus, no mortal
can I judge fortunate.

Antistrophe 1

For he,° outranging everybody,
shot his arrow° and became the lord
1205   of wide prosperity and blessedness,
oh Zeus, after destroying
the virgin with the crooked talons,°
singer of oracles; and against death,
in my land, he arose a tower of defense.
1210   From which time you were called my king
and granted privileges supreme—in mighty
Thebes the ruling lord.

Strophe 2

But now—whose story is more sorrowful than yours?
Who is more intimate with fierce calamities,
1215   with labors, now that your life is altered?
Alas, my Oedipus, whom all men know:
one great harbor.°—
one alone sufficed for you,
as son and father,
1220   when you tumbled,° plowman° of the woman's chamber.
How, how could your paternal
            furrows, wretched man,
endure you silently so long.

Antistrophe 2

Time, all-seeing, surprised you living an unwilled life
1225   and sits from of old in judgment on the marriage, not a marriage,
where the begetter is the begot as well.
Ah, son of Laius . . . ,
would that—oh, would that
I had never seen you!
1230   I wail, my scream climbing beyond itself
from my whole power of voice. To say it straight:
            from you I got new breath—
but I also lulled my eye to sleep.°

°1203 *he*: Oedipus. 1204 *shot his arrow*: took his chances; made a guess at the Sphinx's riddle. 1207 *virgin . . . talons*: the Sphinx. 1217 *one great harbor*: metaphorical allusion to Jocasta's body. 1220 *tumbled*: were born and had sex. *plowman*: Plowing is used here as a sexual metaphor. 1233 *I . . . sleep*: I failed to see the corruption you brought.

EXODOS

[*Enter the* SECOND MESSENGER *from the palace.*]

SECOND MESSENGER: You who are first among the citizens,
    what deeds you are about to hear and see!   1235
    What grief you'll carry, if, true to your birth,
    you still respect the house of Labdacus!
    Neither the Ister nor the Phasis river
    could purify this house, such suffering
    does it conceal, or soon must bring to light—   1240
    willed this time, not unwilled. Griefs hurt worst
    which we perceive to be self-chosen ones.

CHORAGOS: They were sufficient, the things we knew before,
    to make us grieve. What can you add to those?

SECOND MESSENGER: The thing that's quickest said and quickest heard: 1245
    our own, our royal one, Jocasta's dead.

CHORAGOS: Unhappy queen! What was responsible?

SECOND MESSENGER: Herself. The bitterest of these events
    is not for you, you were not there to see,
    but yet, exactly as I can recall it,   1250
    you'll hear what happened to that wretched lady.
    She came in anger through the outer hall,
    and then she ran straight to her marriage bed,
    tearing her hair with the fingers of both hands.
    Then, slamming shut the doors when she was in,   1255
    she called to Laius, dead so many years,
    remembering the ancient seed which caused
    his death, leaving the mother to the son
    to breed again an ill-born progeny.
    She mourned the bed where she, alas, bred double—   1260
    husband by husband, children by her child.
    From this point on I don't know how she died,
    for Oedipus then burst in with a cry,
    and did not let us watch her final evil.
    Our eyes were fixed on him. Wildly he ran   1265
    to each of us, asking for his spear
    and for his wife—no wife: where he might find
    the double mother-field, his and his children's.
    He raved, and some divinity then showed him—
    for none of us did so who stood close by.   1270
    With a dreadful shout—as if some guide were leading—
    he lunged through the double doors; he bent the hollow
    bolts from the sockets, burst into the room,
    and there we saw her, hanging from above,
    entangled in some twisted hanging strands.   1275
    He saw, was stricken, and with a wild roar
    ripped down the dangling noose. When she, poor woman,
    lay on the ground, there came a fearful sight:
    he snatched the pins of worked gold from her dress,
    with which her clothes were fastened: these he raised   1280
    and struck into the ball-joints of his eyes.°

°1281 *ball-joints of his eyes:* his eyeballs. Oedipus blinds himself in both eyes at the same time.

He shouted that they would no longer see
the evils he had suffered or had done,
see in the dark those he should not have seen,
1285   and know no more those he once sought to know.
While chanting this, not once but many times
he raised his hand and struck into his eyes.
Blood from his wounded eyes poured down his chin,
not freed in moistening drops, but all at once
1290   a stormy rain of black blood burst like hail.
These evils, coupling them, making them one,
have broken loose upon both man and wife.
The old prosperity that they had once
was true prosperity, and yet today,
1295   mourning, ruin, death, disgrace, and every
evil you could name—not one is absent.
CHORAGOS: Has he allowed himself some peace from all this grief?
SECOND MESSENGER: He shouts that someone slide the bolts and show
to all the Cadmeians the patricide,
1300   his mother's—I can't say it, it's unholy—
so he can cast himself out of the land,
not stay and curse his house by his own curse.
He lacks the strength, though, and he needs a guide,
for his is a sickness that's too great to bear.
1305   Now you yourself will see: the bolts of the doors
are opening. You are about to see
a vision even one who hates must pity.

[*Enter the blinded* OEDIPUS *from the palace, led in by a household* SERVANT.]

CHORAGOS: This suffering sends terror through men's eyes,
terrible beyond any suffering
1310   my eyes have touched. Oh man of pain,
what madness reached you? Which god from far off,
surpassing in range his longest spring,
struck hard against your god-abandoned fate?
Oh man of pain,
1315   I cannot look upon you—though there's so much
I would ask you, so much to hear,
so much that holds my eyes—
so awesome the convulsions you send through me.
OEDIPUS: Ah! Ah! I am a man of misery.
1320   Where am I carried? Pity me! Where
is my voice scattered abroad on wings?
Divinity, where has your lunge transported me?
CHORAGOS: To something horrible, not to be heard or seen.

KOMMOS

Strophe 1
OEDIPUS: Oh, my cloud
1325   of darkness, abominable, unspeakable as it attacks me,
not to be turned away, brought by an evil wind!
Alas!

Again alas! Both enter me at once:
the sting of the prongs,° the memory of evils!
CHORUS: I do not marvel that in these afflictions   1330
you carry double griefs and double evils.

Antistrophe 1

OEDIPUS: Ah, friend,
so you at least are there, resolute servant!
Still with a heart to care for me, the blind man.
Oh! Oh!   1335
I know that you are there. I recognize
even inside my darkness, that voice of yours.
CHORUS: Doer of horror, how did you bear to quench
your vision? What divinity raised your hand?

Strophe 2

OEDIPUS: It was Apollo there, Apollo, friends,   1340
who brought my sorrows, vile sorrows to their perfection,
these evils that were done to me.
But the one who struck them with his hand,
that one was none but I, in wretchedness.
For why was I to see   1345
when nothing I could see would bring me joy?
CHORUS: Yes, that is how it was.
OEDIPUS: What could I see, indeed,
or what enjoy—what greeting
is there I could hear with pleasure, friends?   1350
Conduct me out of the land
as quickly as you can!
Conduct me out, my friends,
the man utterly ruined,
supremely cursed,   1355
the man who is by gods
the most detested of all men!
CHORUS: Wretched in disaster and in knowledge:
oh, I could wish you'd never come to know!

Antistrophe 2

OEDIPUS: May he be destroyed, whoever freed the savage shackles   1360
from my feet when I'd been sent to the wild pasture,
whoever rescued me from murder
and became my savior—
a bitter gift:
if I had died then,   1365
I'd not have been such grief to self and kin.
CHORUS: I also would have had it so.
OEDIPUS: I'd not have returned to be my father's
murderer; I'd not be called by men

°1329 *prongs*: refers to both the whip that Laius used and the two gold pins Oedipus used to blind himself.

1370
my mother's bridegroom.
Now I'm without a god,
     child of a polluted parent,
fellow progenitor with him
     who gave me birth in misery.

1375
If there's an evil that
     surpasses evils, that
has fallen to the lot of Oedipus.

CHORAGOS: How can I say that you have counseled well?
Better not to be than live a blind man.

1380
OEDIPUS: That this was not the best thing I could do—
don't tell me that, or advise me any more!
Should I descend to Hades and endure
to see my father with these eyes? Or see
my poor unhappy mother? For I have done,

1385
to both of these, things too great for hanging.
Or is the sight of children to be yearned for,
to see new shoots that sprouted as these did?
Never, never with these eyes of mine!
Nor city, nor tower, nor holy images

1390
of the divinities! For I, all-wretched,
most nobly raised—as no one else in Thebes—
deprived myself of these when I ordained
that all expel the impious one—god-shown
to be polluted, and the dead king's son!°

1395
Once I exposed this great stain upon me,
could I have looked on these with steady eyes?
No! No! And if there were a way to block
the source of hearing in my ears, I'd gladly
have locked up my pitiable body,

1400
so I'd be blind and deaf. Evils shut out—
that way my mind could live in sweetness.
Alas, Cithaeron,° why did you receive me?
Or when you had me, not killed me instantly?
I'd not have had to show my birth to mankind.

1405
Polybus, Corinth, halls—ancestral,
they told me—how beautiful was your ward,
a scar that held back festering disease!
Evil my nature, evil my origin.
You, three roads, and you, secret ravine,

1410
you oak grove, narrow place of those three paths
that drank my blood° from these my hands, from him
who fathered me, do you remember still
the things I did to you? When I'd come here,
what I then did once more? Oh marriages! Marriages!

1415
You gave us life and when you'd planted us
you sent the same seed up, and then revealed

°1392–94 *I . . . son*: Oedipus refers to his own curse against the murderer as well as his sins of patricide and incest. 1402 *Cithaeron*: the mountain on which the infant Oedipus was exposed. 1411 *my blood*: i.e., the blood of my father, Laius, and therefore my family's blood.

fathers, brothers, sons, and kinsman's blood,
and brides, and wives, and mothers, all the most
atrocious things that happen to mankind!
One should not name what never should have been.   1420
Somewhere out there, then, quickly, by the gods,
cover me up, or murder me, or throw me
to the ocean where you will never see me more!

[OEDIPUS *moves toward the* CHORUS *and they back away from him.*]

Come! Don't shrink to touch this wretched man!
Believe me, do not be frightened! I alone   1425
of all mankind can carry these afflictions.

[*Enter* CREON *from the palace with* ATTENDANTS.]

CHORAGOS: Tell Creon what you wish for. Just when we need him
he's here. He can act, he can advise you.
He's now the land's sole guardian in your place.
OEDIPUS: Ah! Are there words that I can speak to him?   1430
What ground for trust can I present? It's proved
that I was false to him in everything.
CREON: I have not come to mock you, Oedipus,
nor to reproach you for your former falseness.
You men, if you have no respect for sons   1435
of mortals, let your awe for the all-feeding
flames of lordly Hēlius° prevent
your showing unconcealed so great a stain,
abhorred by earth and sacred rain and light.
Escort him quickly back into the house!   1440
If blood kin only see and hear their own
afflictions, we'll have no impious defilement.
OEDIPUS: By the gods, you've freed me from one terrible fear,
so nobly meeting my unworthiness:
grant me something—not for me; for you!   1445
CREON: What do you want that you should beg me so?
OEDIPUS: To drive me from the land at once, to a place
where there will be no man to speak to me!
CREON: I would have done just that—had I not wished
to ask first of the god what I should do.   1450
OEDIPUS: His answer was revealed in full—that I,
the patricide, unholy, be destroyed.
CREON: He said that, but our need is so extreme,
it's best to have sure knowledge what must be done.
OEDIPUS: You'll ask about a wretched man like me?   1455
CREON: Is it not time you put your trust in the god?
OEDIPUS: But I bid you as well, and shall entreat you.
Give her who is within what burial
you will—you'll give your own her proper rites;
but me—do not condemn my fathers' land   1460
to have me dwelling here while I'm alive,

°1437 Hēlius: the sun.

but let me live on mountains—on Cithaeron
famed as mine, for my mother and my father,
while they yet lived, made it my destined tomb,
1465   and I'll be killed by those who wished my ruin!
And yet I know: no sickness will destroy me,
nothing will: I'd never have been saved
when left to die unless for some dread evil.
Then let my fate continue where it will!
1470   As for my children, Creon, take no pains
for my sons—they're men and they will never lack
the means to live, wherever they may be—
but my two wretched, pitiable girls,
who never ate but at my table, never
1475   were without me—everything that I
would touch, they'd always have a share of it—
please care for them! Above all, let me touch
them with my hands and weep aloud my woes!
Please, my Lord!
1480   Please, noble heart! Touching with my hands,
I'd think I held them as when I could see.

[*Enter* ANTIGONE *and* ISMENE *from the palace with* ATTENDANTS.]

What's this?
Oh gods! Do I hear, somewhere, my two dear ones
sobbing? Has Creon really pitied me
1485   and sent to me my dearest ones, my children?
Is that it?
CREON: Yes, I prepared this for you, for I knew
you'd feel this joy, as you have always done.
OEDIPUS: Good fortune, then, and, for your care, be guarded
1490   far better by divinity than I was!
Where are you, children? Come to me! Come here
to these my hands, hands of your brother, hands
of him who gave you seed, hands that made
these once bright eyes to see now in this fashion.

[*OEDIPUS embraces his daughters.*]

1495   He, children, seeing nothing, knowing nothing,
he fathered you where his own seed was plowed.
I weep for you as well, though I can't see you,
imagining your bitter life to come,
the life you will be forced by men to live.
1500   What gatherings of townsmen will you join,
what festivals, without returning home
in tears instead of watching holy rites?
And when you've reached the time for marrying,
where, children, is the man who'll run the risk
1505   of taking on himself the infamy
that will wound you as it did my parents?
What evil is not here? Your father killed

his father, plowed the one who gave him birth,
and from the place where he was sown, from there
he got you, from the place he too was born.   1510
These are the wounds: then who will marry you?
No man, my children. No, it's clear that you
must wither in dry barrenness, unmarried.

[*Oedipus addresses Creon.*]

Son of Menoeceus! You are the only father
left to them—we two who gave them seed   1515
are both destroyed: watch that they don't become
poor, wanderers, unmarried—they are your kin.
Let not my ruin be their ruin, too!
No, pity them! You see how young they are,
bereft of everyone, except for you.   1520
Consent, kind heart, and touch me with your hand!

[*Creon grasps Oedipus's right hand.*]

You, children, if you had reached an age of sense,
I would have counseled much. Now, pray you may live
always where it's allowed, finding a life
better than his was, who gave you seed.   1525
Creon: Stop this now. Quiet your weeping. Move away, into the house.
Oedipus: Bitter words, but I obey them.
Creon: There's an end to all things.
Oedipus: I have first this request.
Creon: I will hear it.
Oedipus: Banish me from my homeland.
Creon: You must ask that of the god.
Oedipus: But I am the gods' most hated man!
Creon: Then you will soon get what you want.   1530
Oedipus: Do you consent?
Creon: I never promise when, as now, I'm ignorant.
Oedipus: Then lead me in.
Creon: Come. But let your hold fall from your children.
Oedipus: Do not take them from me, ever!
Creon: Do not wish to keep all of the
power. You had power, but that power did not follow you through life.

[*Oedipus's daughters are taken from him and led into the palace by Attendants. Oedipus is led
into the palace by a Servant. Creon and the other Attendants follow. Only the Chorus remains.*]

Chorus: People of Thebes, my country, see: here is that Oedipus—   1535
he who "knew" the famous riddle, and attained the highest power,
whom all citizens admired, even envying his luck!
See the billows of wild troubles which he has entered now!
Here is the truth of each man's life: we must wait, and see his end,
scrutinize his dying day, and refuse to call him happy   1540
till he has crossed the border of his life without pain.

[*Exit the Chorus along each of the Parados.*]

QUESTIONS

1. *Prologue and Parados.* What is the situation in Thebes as the play begins? Why does Oedipus want to discover the murderer of Laius?
2. *Episode 1 and Stasimon 1.* When Tiresias refuses to speak, how is the reaction of Oedipus characteristic of him? What other examples of this behavior can you find?
3. When Tiresias does speak, he speaks the truth. Why doesn't Oedipus accept the story that Tiresias tells?
4. *Episode 2 and Stasimon 2.* Of what does Oedipus accuse Creon, and how does Creon defend himself? Is Creon convincing? Why or why not?
5. What does Jocasta have to say about oracles and prophecy? Why do you think she expresses this attitude? How do her views differ from those of the Chorus?
6. When does Oedipus begin to think that he himself is the murderer? What details lead him to this conclusion?
7. *Episode 3 and Stasimon 3.* Why does the news from the Messenger from Corinth at first seem good? How is the situation reversed?
8. *Episode 4 and Stasimon 4.* What do you make of the coincidences that the same Herdsman (a) saved the infant Oedipus from death, (b) was the lone survivor of the attack on Laius and also the sole witness to the attack, and (c) will provide testimony that will destroy Oedipus?
9. What moral does the Chorus express about the life and downfall of Oedipus?

GENERAL QUESTIONS

1. In *Oedipus the King,* the peripeteia, anagnorisis, and catastrophe all occur at the same moment. When is this moment? Who is most severely affected by it?
2. Sophocles describes Oedipus's life piecemeal, out of chronological order. Put the details into chronological order, and consider how you might dramatize them. Why does Sophocles's ordering of events make for an effective play? Be sure to emphasize some of the coincidences in the life and career of Oedipus.
3. What is the major conflict in the play? What other conflicts does Sophocles bring out? How is the complexity of the conflicts brought out by Sophocles?
4. In the light of your understanding of tragedy and the tragic hero, describe *Oedipus the King* as a tragedy.
5. Describe Sophocles's use of dramatic irony in the play.
6. Describe the functions of the Chorus and the Choragos. Explain the relationship of the choral odes to the play's actions.

Renaissance Drama and Shakespeare's Theater

In the early years of the English Renaissance, there was a flourishing native tradition of theater that had developed first within the church and then with the cooperation of the church.[13] The bridge from religious drama to the drama of the Renaissance was created in a number of ways. Of great importance was the growth of traveling dramatic professional companies, who performed their plays

---

[13]For an account of the medieval dramatic tradition, see Chapter 23, 1216–20.

in local inn yards—square or quadrangular spaces surrounded by the rooms of the inn. In addition, plays were performed at court, in the great rooms of aristocratic houses, in the law courts, and at universities.

Aside from this well-established performing tradition, the immediate influence on the creation of a new drama was the development of a taste for dramatic topics drawn from nonreligious sources. The earliest of such plays in the sixteenth century was the so-called **Tudor interlude,** named after the monarchs of the Tudor family who ruled England from 1485 to 1603. *Interlude* is a misnomer, for the plays were often quite long. The interludes, supported by the nobility, were tragedies, comedies, or historical plays that were performed by both professional actors and students. They sometimes featured abstract and allegorical characters and provided opportunities for both music and farcical action.

After the middle of the sixteenth century, the revival of ancient drama and culture came increasingly to the fore. The dominating influence was the Roman dramatist Seneca (4 BCE–65 CE), eight of whose tragedies, derived from Greek tragedy, had survived from antiquity. A vital quality of the Senecan tragedies was that they were violent and bloody, and thus they gave a classical precedent for the revenge and murder that were to be featured in the Elizabethan drama. Seneca became important not so much because he had written great works but rather because he had written in Latin. He could therefore be readily understood by a generation of new dramatists who had been schooled in Roman history, culture, language, and literature.

Shakespeare Became a Theatrical Entrepreneur as Well as a Writer

The first group of these Elizabethan playwrights included Christopher Marlowe, Thomas Kyd, Robert Greene, George Peele, Thomas Lodge, and John Lyly. These were the men whose plays William Shakespeare watched and acted in when he first arrived in London from Stratford-upon-Avon in the late 1580s. By 1594 he had joined the Lord Chamberlain's Men, the most popular of the London acting companies. He rose swiftly as both an actor and dramatist, and by 1599 he had become an active partner with the company (called the "King's Men" after the accession of James I in 1603) in a venture to construct a new theater, the Globe, within a stone's throw of the earlier theater, the Rose. It was for exclusive production at the Globe that Shakespeare wrote some of his greatest plays (including *Hamlet*) from 1599 to 1608, when the company began playing alternately at the outdoor Globe and the indoor Blackfriars (formerly a part of a monastery that had been adapted for theatrical presentations).

The Globe Was a Small But Versatile Theater That Strongly Influenced the Nature of Shakespeare's Plays

Compared with the massive Greek outdoor amphitheaters, the Globe was small. Some theater historians have calculated that it could have held an audience of as many as two to three thousand, although this estimate seems excessive, for half that number would have been extremely large. Moreover, we need not suppose that the theater was always filled to squeezing room only.

THE GLOBE WAS A "RING"-TYPE THEATER OPEN TO THE SKY. Recent archaeological excavations of the site of the Globe, together with a complete reconstruction based on the knowledge newly gained, show that it was a twenty-sided building. For practical purposes it was round—as it is shown in a contemporary drawing—and its outer diameter was approximately a hundred feet. From above, it would have resembled a ring, or, as Shakespeare called the type in *Henry V*, a "wooden O." Its central yard was open to the sky, a detail that it had appropriated from the confined areas of the inns. The **platform stage,** covered by a roof, was built thirty feet into the yard at the building's south side. Because of the uncertainty and capriciousness of English weather, the acting season extended from spring through fall. During the wettest and coldest months, the theater was not used.

THE GLOBE PROVIDED A NUMBER OF ACTING AREAS. This thrust stage was close to five feet high—probably lower in front (*downstage*) and higher in back (*upstage*). Actors could move anywhere on this stage to speak their lines. On the second level above the stage was a gallery for spectators, musicians, and actors (as in the balcony scene in Shakespeare's *Romeo and Juliet*). Actors might enter this gallery to deliver lines, and then they might also descend from there to the main stage. The area below the stage was called the *hell.* At center stage there was a trapdoor to the hell that was used for the entrances and exits of devils, monsters, and ghosts such as the Ghost of Hamlet's father. Downstage, holding up the protective roof, there were two columns. The ceiling of this roof, called the *heavens*, was decorated with colorful paintings. A hut on the roof itself contained machinery for lowering and raising actors who took the roles of fairies, witches, and gods. Behind the upstage area, which could be curtained off for interior scenes, there was a small and cramped *tiring house* and storage area where actors changed their costumes and waited for their cues. Two or three doors opened outward from the tiring house to the stage.

THERE WERE THREE LOCATIONS FOR THE AUDIENCE. The admission price permitted spectators into the ground area. Those who remained there stood during the entire performance and crowded as close as they could to the stage. These people, who were patronizingly called the *groundlings,* often endured rain and cold in addition to the discomfort of their need to stand. For additional charges, spectators could get out of bad weather by sitting in one of the three seating levels within the roofed galleries (part of the "O"). Those who could afford it paid still another charge for seats directly on the stage—a custom that continued in English theaters until the time of David Garrick in the eighteenth century.

THE GLOBE, LIKE OTHER ELIZABETHAN THEATERS, MANDATED ITS OWN PRODUCTION AND STAGE CONVENTIONS. Just as in the Athenian theater, there was no artificial lighting, and performances therefore took place in the afternoon. The plays were performed rapidly, without intermissions or indications of act and scene changes except for occasional rhymed couplets. With no curtain and no scenery, the exits and entrances of the actors indicated shifts in scene. This type of scene division produced swift changes in time and place and made for great fluidity and fast pacing.

The conditions of performance and the physical shape of the theater resulted in a number of theatrical conventions. The two columns supporting the stage roof, for example, were versatile. Sometimes they represented trees or the sides of buildings, and conventionally they were used as places of concealment and for eavesdropping. Time, place, and circumstances of weather were established through dialogue, as in the opening scene of *Hamlet* when Horatio speaks of "the morn, in russet mantle clad" (line 165), or in *As You Like It*, when Rosalind says, "This is the forest of Arden" (2.4.15).

The Globe's relatively small size and its thrust stage made for intimate performances. There was little separation of audience and actors, unlike the *orchestra* in Greek theaters that widened the distance between actors and spectators, or with the proscenium and curtain of many modern theaters. The groundlings surrounding the thrust stage at a typical Elizabethan performance were extremely close to the actors at all times. The close proximity of the groundlings and of those spectators who had paid to sit on the stage itself encouraged much interaction between actors and audience. This closeness led to two unique stage conventions. One of these, the **aside,** permitted a character to make brief remarks directly to the audience or to another character without the rest of the characters' hearing the words. In the other, the **soliloquy,** a character alone onstage described his or her thoughts or plans directly to the audience. For example, when Hamlet delivers his second soliloquy, he criticizes his emotional detachment from his father's murder and explains how he plans to test Claudius's guilt (2.2.524–580). Under such circumstances, members of the Elizabethan audience almost literally became additional members of the cast.

THE ACTORS FOLLOWED ESTABLISHED CONVENTIONS IN GESTURE AND COSTUME.
The actors in Shakespeare's day were legally bound to the company of which they were members. Without the protection of the company, they were considered "rogues and vagabonds." In England the actors were male, with adolescent boys performing the women's roles because women were excluded from the stage. The actors used no masks. Instead, they developed expressions and gestures that would seem to us, today, excessively stylized. The acting mannerisms sometimes seemed excessive to Shakespeare, too, as is indicated by Hamlet's instructions to the traveling actors. He tells them not to "saw the air too much with your hand" and not to "tear a passion to tatters, to very rags" (3.2.4–9).

The actors wore elaborate costumes to demonstrate the nature and status of the characters. Thus kings always wore robes and crowns, and they carried orbs and scepters. A fool (a type of comic and ironic commentator) wore a multicolored or *motley* costume, and clowns and "mechanicals" wore the common clothing of the humble classes, as with the "hempen homespuns" of *A Midsummer Night's Dream.* Ragged clothing indicated a reduction in circumstances, as in *King Lear,* and Ophelia's description of Hamlet's disordered clothing in the second act of *Hamlet* indicates the prince's disturbed mental condition (2.1.74–82). Whenever characters took on a disguise, as in *As You Like It*, this disguise was impenetrable to the other characters.

The New Globe Theater Has Been Built Near the Site of Shakespeare's Globe

Shakespeare's Globe burned in 1613. The rebuilt Globe that replaced it was torn down by the Puritans under Oliver Cromwell in 1664, on the grounds that drama encouraged vice and free thought. From then on the location was variously occupied by tenements, breweries, other buildings, and a road. In the late 1980s, however, archaeological excavations took place at the sites of both the Globe and the nearby Rose Theater, and the subsequent discoveries provided exciting new information about theaters and theatergoing in Shakespeare's day. A reconstruction of the Globe was undertaken and is now complete—not at the original location but close by. The original site could not be used because it was preempted by a protected building and a vital street leading to Southwark Bridge. Theatergoers in London are now able to attend performances of Shakespeare's plays in this new theater under conditions almost identical to those that Shakespeare's audiences and acting company knew, including, for the "groundlings," rain, wind, cold, and the discomfort of standing (see the photograph of the reconstruction of the Globe stage, p. I–15).[14]

WILLIAM SHAKESPEARE (1564–1616)

Shakespeare was born in 1564 in Stratford-upon-Avon, in western England. He attended the Stratford grammar school; he married in 1582, and he and his wife had three children. He left his family and moved to London sometime between 1585 and 1592. During this period he became a professional actor, and he also began writing plays and poems. Because the London theaters were closed during the plague years 1592–1594, he apparently worked at other jobs, about which we know nothing. By 1595, however, he was recognized as a major writer of comedies and tragedies. He soon became a member of the Lord Chamberlain's Men, the leading theatrical company, and, as we have seen, he became a shareholder in the new Globe Theatre in 1599. Fortunately, he realized good returns from the business venture and also from his plays, and he became moderately wealthy. He stopped writing for the stage in 1611, having written a total of thirty-seven plays, of which eleven were tragedies. He also collaborated in writing a few other plays. During his retirement he lived in his native Stratford. He died in 1616 and is buried next to the altar of Stratford's Trinity Church, beneath a bust and an inscribed gravestone.

When the Lord Chamberlain's Men first staged *Hamlet* in 1602 at the Globe, it was not the first time the story had been dramatized on the London stage. There is evidence that a play based on the Hamlet story, now lost, had been performed before 1589. Therefore, at least some of the theatergoers might have known the story.

Even if none of them knew the story, however, they would have known the tradition of **revenge tragedy.** The Elizabethans had been introduced to the drama of vengeance through the English translations of Seneca's tragedies during the 1570s and early 1580s. Another important precedent was Thomas Kyd's *Spanish Tragedy* (c. 1587), the first English play in the revenge tradition, which featured a hero who commits suicide. The major conventions of the genre were a ghost who calls for vengeance and a revenger who pretends to be insane at least part of the time. Above all, the tradition required that the revenger would also die, no matter how good a person or how just his cause.

Although Elizabethan audiences were prepared for *Hamlet* by the revenge formula, they could have anticipated neither a protagonist of Hamlet's likeableness

---

[14]See J. R. Mulryne and Margaret Shewring, eds., *Shakespeare's Globe Rebuilt* (Cambridge: Cambridge UP, 1997). Further information about the Globe Theatre may be found at the Shakespeare Globe Center, USA, <www.sgc.umd.edu>.

and complexity nor a play of such profundity. The earlier revengers were flat characters with a single fixation on righting wrongs through personal vengeance. Hamlet, however, is acutely aware of the political and moral corruption of the Danish court, and he reflects on the fallen state of humanity. Experiencing despair and guilt, he even contemplates suicide. He learns from his experiences and meditations, discovering that he must look beyond reason and philosophy for ways of coping with the world. He also develops patience and learns to trust in Providence, the "divinity that shapes our ends" (5.2.10).

The play itself demonstrates the far-reaching effects of evil, which branches inexorably outward from Claudius's initial act of murder. The evil ensnares innocent and guilty alike. Hamlet, the avenger, becomes the direct and indirect cause of deaths, and as a result, he in turn also becomes an object of revenge. By the play's end, all the major and two of the minor characters are dead: Polonius, Ophelia, Rosencrantz, Guildenstern, Gertrude, Claudius, Laertes, and, finally, Hamlet himself. The play's crowning irony is that Hamlet does not complete his vengeance because of the murder of his father, King Hamlet, as he originally sets out to do. Rather, he kills Claudius immediately upon learning that the king has murdered Gertrude, his mother.

In the centuries since Shakespeare wrote *Hamlet*, the play has remained among the most popular, most moving, and most effective plays in the world. It has been translated into scores of languages. Major actors from Shakespeare's day to ours—including Richard Burbage as the first Hamlet, and John Barrymore, Kenneth Branagh, Ralph Fiennes, Mel Gibson, Ethan Hawke, Derek Jacoby, Kevin Kline, Laurence Olivier, and Nicol Williamson—have starred in the role. Beyond the play's stage popularity, *Hamlet* has become one of the central documents of Western civilization. Somehow, most people know about Hamlet and are familiar with passages like "To be or not to be," "The play's the thing," and "The undiscovered country, from whose bourn / No traveler returns" even if they have never read the play or seen a live or filmed performance.

The Tragedy of Hamlet, Prince of Denmark (c. 1602)

*Edited by Alice Griffin**

CHARACTERS

Claudius, King of Denmark
Hamlet, Son to the former, and nephew to the present King
Polonius, Lord Chamberlain
Horatio, Friend to Hamlet
Laertes, Son to Polonius
Valtemand
Cornelius
Rosencrantz   } Courtiers
Guildenstern
Osric
A Gentleman
A Priest

---

*Professor Griffin's text for *Hamlet* was the Second Quarto (edition) published in 1604, with modifications based on the First Folio, published in 1623. Stage directions in those editions are printed here without brackets; added stage directions are printed within brackets. We have edited Griffin's notes for this text.

Marcellus ⎫
Barnardo ⎬ Officers
Francisco, a Soldier
Reynaldo, Servant to Polonius
Players
Two Clowns, gravediggers
Fortinbras, Prince of Norway
A Norwegian Captain
English Ambassadors
Gertrude, Queen of Denmark, mother to Hamlet
Ophelia, Daughter to Polonius
Ghost of Hamlet's Father
Lords, Ladies, Officers, Soldiers, Sailors, Messengers, Attendants

[SCENE: *Elsinore*]

ACT 1

Scene 1. [A platform on the battlements of the castle]

Enter BARNARDO *and* FRANCISCO, *two Sentinels.*

BARNARDO: Who's there?
FRANCISCO: Nay, answer me. Stand and unfold° yourself.
BARNARDO: Long live the king.
FRANCISCO: Barnardo?
5   BARNARDO: He.
FRANCISCO: You come most carefully upon your hour.
BARNARDO: 'Tis now struck twelve, get thee to bed Francisco.
FRANCISCO: For this relief much thanks, 'tis bitter cold, And I am sick at heart.
BARNARDO: Have you had quiet guard?
FRANCISCO: Not a mouse stirring.
10 BARNARDO: Well, good night:
         If you do meet Horatio and Marcellus,
         The rivals° of my watch, bid them make haste.°

Enter HORATIO *and* MARCELLUS.

FRANCISCO: I think I hear them. Stand ho, who is there?
HORATIO: Friends to this ground.
MARCELLUS: And liegemen° to the Dane°
FRANCISCO: Give you good night.
15 MARCELLUS: O, farewell honest soldier,
         Who hath relieved you?
FRANCISCO: Barnardo hath my place;
         Give you good night.   *Exit* FRANCISCO.
MARCELLUS: Holla, Barnardo!
BARNARDO: Say,
         What, is Horatio there?
HORATIO: A piece of him.
BARNARDO: Welcome Horatio, welcome good Marcellus.
20 HORATIO: What, has this thing appeared again tonight?

°2 *unfold:* reveal. 12 *rivals:* partners. 14 *liegemen:* subjects. *Dane:* King of Denmark.

BARNARDO: I have seen nothing.

MARCELLUS: Horatio says 'tis but our fantasy,°
    And will not let belief take hold of him,
    Touching this dreaded sight twice seen of us,
    Therefore I have entreated him along   25
    With us to watch the minutes of this night,
    That if again this apparition come,
    He may approve° our eyes and speak to it.

HORATIO: Tush, tush, 'twill not appear.

BARNARDO: Sit down awhile,
    And let us once again assail your ears,   30
    That are so fortified against our story,
    What we have two nights seen.

HORATIO: Well, sit we down,
    And let us hear Barnardo speak of this,

BARNARDO: Last night of all,
    When yon same star that's westward from the pole°   35
    Had made his course t'illume that part of heaven
    Where now it burns, Marcellus and myself,
    The bell then beating one—

Enter GHOST.

MARCELLUS: Peace, break thee off, look where it comes again.

BARNARDO: In the same figure like the king that's dead.   40

MARCELLUS: Thou art a scholar, speak to it Horatio.

BARNARDO: Looks a' not like the king? mark it Horatio.

HORATIO: Most like, it harrows me with fear and wonder.

BARNARDO: It would be spoke to.

MARCELLUS: Question it Horatio.

HORATIO: What art thou that usurp'st° this time of night,   45
    Together with that fair and warlike form,
    In which the majesty of buried Denmark°
    Did sometimes° march? by heaven I charge thee speak.

MARCELLUS: It is offended.

BARNARDO: See, it stalks away.

HORATIO: Stay, speak, speak, I charge thee speak.   *Exit* GHOST 50

MARCELLUS: 'Tis gone and will not answer.

BARNARDO: How now Horatio, you tremble and look pale,
    Is not this something more than fantasy?
    What think you on't?

HORATIO: Before my God I might not this believe,   55
    Without the sensible and true avouch°
    Of mine own eyes.

MARCELLUS: Is it not like the king?

HORATIO: As thou art to thyself.
    Such was the very armour he had on,
When he the ambitious Norway°combated: 60
    So frowned he once, when in an angry parle°

°22 *fantasy*: imagination. 28 *approve*: prove reliable. 35 *pole*: North Star. 45 *usurp'st*: wrongfully occupy (both the time and the shape of the dead king). 47 *buried Denmark*: the buried King of Denmark. 48 *sometimes*: formerly. 56 *sensible . . . avouch*: assurance of the truth of the senses. 60 *Norway*: King of Norway. 61 *parle*: parley, verbal battle.

He smote the sledded Polacks° on the ice.
'Tis strange.

MARCELLUS: Thus twice before, and jump° at this dead hour,
65   With martial stalk hath he gone by our watch.

HORATIO: In what particular thought to work, I know not,
But in the gross and scope° of mine opinion,
This bodes some strange eruption to our state.

MARCELLUS: Good now sit down, and tell me he that knows,
70   Why this same strict and most observant watch
So nightly toils the subject° of the land,
And why such daily cast of brazen cannon
And foreign mart,° for implements of war,
Why such impress° of shipwrights, whose sore° task
75   Does not divide the Sunday from the week,
What might be toward° that this sweaty haste
Doth make the night joint-labourer with the day,
Who is't that can inform me?

HORATIO: That can I.
At least the whisper goes so; our last king,
80   Whose image even but now appeared to us,
Was as you know by Fortinbras of Norway,
Thereto pricked on by a most emulate° pride,
Dared to the combat; in which our valiant Hamlet
(For so this side of our known world esteemed him)
85   Did slay this Fortinbras, who by a sealed compact,°
Well ratified by law and heraldy,°
Did forfeit (with his life) all those his lands
Which he stood seized° of, to the conqueror:
Against the which a moiety competent°
90   Was gagèd° by our King, which had returned
To the inheritance of Fortinbras,
Had he been vanquisher; as by the same co-mart,°
And carriage of the article designed,°
His fell to Hamlet; now sir, young Fortinbras,
95   Of unimprovèd mettle° hot and full,
Hath in the skirts° of Norway here and there
Sharked up° a list of lawless resolutes°
For food and diet to some enterprise
That hath a stomach° in't, which is no other,
100   As it doth well appear unto our state,
But to recover of us by strong hand
And terms compulsatory, those foresaid lands
So by his father lost; and this I take it,
Is the main motive of our preparations,

°62 *sledded Polacks:* Polish soldiers on sleds. 64 *jump:* just. 67 *gross and scope:* general view. 71 *toils the subject:* makes the subjects toil. 73 *mart:* trade. 74 *impress:* conscription. *sore:* difficult. 76 *toward:* forthcoming. 82 *emulate:* rivaling. 85 *compact:* treaty. 86 *law and heraldy:* heraldic law regulating combats. 88 *seized:* possessed. 89 *moiety competent:* equal amount. 90 *gagèd:* pledged. 92 *co-mart:* joint bargain. 93 *carriage . . . designed:* intent of the treaty drawn up. 95 *unimproved mettle:* untested (1) metal (2) spirit. 96 *skirts:* outskirts. 97 *Sharked up:* gathered up indiscriminately (as a shark preys). *lawless resolutes:* determined outlaws. 99 *stomach:* show of courage.

The source of this our watch, and the chief head°   105
Of this post-haste and romage° in the land.
BARNARDO: I think it be no other, but e'en so;
      Well may it sort° that this portentous figure
      Comes armèd through our watch so like the king
      That was and is the question of these wars.   110
HORATIO: A mote it is to trouble the mind's eye:
      In the most high and palmy° state of Rome,
      A little ere the mightest Julius fell,
      The graves stood tenantless, and the sheeted dead
      Did squeak and gibber in the Roman Streets,   115
      As stars with trains of fire,° and dews of blood,
      Disasters° in the sun; and the moist star,°
      Upon whose influence Neptune's empire stands,
      Was sick almost to doomsday with eclipse.
      And even the like precurse° of feared events,   120
      As harbingers preceding still° the fates
      And prologue to the omen° coming on,
      Have heaven and earth together demonstrated
      Unto our climatures° and countrymen.

Enter GHOST.

But soft, behold, lo where it comes again.   125
I'll cross° it though it blast me: *Spreads his arms.*
                        stay illusion,
If thou hast any sound or use of voice,
Speak to me.
If there be any good thing to be done
That may to thee do ease, and grace° to me,   130
Speak to me.
If thou art privy° to thy country's fate
Which happily° foreknowing may avoid,
O speak:
Or if thou hast uphoarded in thy life   135
Extorted treasure in the womb of earth,
For which they say you spirits oft walk in death,

                                                              The cock crows.

Speak of it, stay and speak. Stop it Marcellus.
MARCELLUS: Shall I strike it with my partisan?°
HORATIO: Do, if it will not stand
BARNARDO: 'Tis here.
HORATIO: 'Tis here.   140
MARCELLUS: 'Tis gone.   *Exit GHOST.*

°105 *head*: fountainhead. 106 *romage*: bustle (rummage). 108 *sort*: turn out. 112 *palmy*: triumphant. 116 *stars . . . fire*: meteors. 117 *Disasters*: unfavorable portents. *moist star*: moon. 120 *precurse*: portent. 121 *still*: always. 122 *omen*: disaster. 124 *climatures*: regions. 126 *cross*: (1) cross its path (2) spread my arms to make a cross of my body (to ward against evil). 130 *grace*: (1) honor (2) blessedness. 132 *art privy*: know secretly of. 133 *happily*: perhaps. 139 *partisan*: spear.

We do it wrong being so majestical,
To offer it the show of violence,
For it is as the air, invulnerable,
145   And our vain blows malicious mockery.°
BARNARDO: It was about to speak when the cock crew.°
HORATIO: And then it started like a guilty thing,
Upon a fearful summons; I have heard,
The cock that is the trumpet to the morn,
150   Doth with his lofty and shrill-sounding throat
Awake the god of day, and at his warning
Whether in sea or fire, in earth or air,°
Th'extravagant and erring° spirit hies°
To his confine, and of the truth herein
155   This present object made probation.°
MARCELLUS: It faded on the crowing of the cock.
Some say that ever 'gainst° that season comes
Wherein our Saviour's birth is celebrated
This bird of dawning singeth all night long,
160   And then they say no spirit dare stir abroad,
The nights are wholesome,° then no planets strike,°
No fairy takes,° nor witch hath power to charm,
So hallowed, and so gracious is that time.
HORATIO: So have I heard and do in part believe it.
165   But look, the morn in russet° mantle clad
Walks o'er the dew of yon high eastward hill:
Break we our watch up and by my advice
Let us impart what we have seen tonight
Unto young Hamlet, for upon my life
170   This spirit dumb to us, will speak to him:
Do you consent we shall acquaint him with it,
As needful in our loves,° fitting our duty?
MARCELLUS: Let's do't I pray, and I this morning know
Where we shall find him most convenient.   *Exeunt.°*

Scene 2. [A room of state in the castle]

Flourish.° Enter CLAUDIUS *King of Denmark,* GERTRUDE *the Queen, [members of the] Council: as*
POLONIUS; *and his son* LAERTES, HAMLET, *[*VALTEMAND *and* CORNELIUS*] cum aliis.°*

KING: Though yet of Hamlet our dear brother's death
The memory be green, and that it us befitted
To bear our hearts in grief, and our whole kingdom
To be contracted in one brow of woe,
5   Yet so far hath discretion fought with nature,°

°145 *malicious mockery:* mockery because they only imitate harm. 146 *cock crew:* (traditional signal for ghosts to return to their confines). 152 *sea . . . air:* the four elements (inhabited by spirits, each indigenous to a particular element). 153 *extravagant and erring:* going beyond its bounds (vagrant) and wandering. *hies:* hastens. 155 *made probation:* gave proof. 157 *'gainst:* just before. 161 *wholesome:* healthy (night air was considered unhealthy). *strike:* exert evil influence. 162 *takes:* bewitches. 165 *russet:* reddish. 172 *needful . . . loves:* urged by our friendship. 174 S.D.: *Exeunt:* all exit. 0.1 S.D.: *Flourish:* fanfare or trumpets. *cum aliis:* with others. 5 *nature:* natural impulse (of grief).

That we° with wisest sorrow think on him
Together with remembrance of ourselves:°
Therefore our sometime° sister,° now our queen,
Th'imperial jointress° to this warlike state,
Have we as 'twere with a defeated joy,   10
With an auspicious, and a dropping eye,°
With mirth in funeral, and with dirge in marriage,
In equal scale weighing delight and dole,
Taken to wife: nor have we herein barred
Your better wisdoms,° which have freely gone   15
With this affair along—for all, our thanks.
Now follows that you know, young Fortinbras,
Holding a weak supposal of our worth°
Or thinking by our late dear brother's death
Our state to be disjoint and out of frame,°   20
Colleaguèd° with this dream of his advantage,°
He hath not failed to pester us with message
Importing the surrender of those lands
Lost by his father, with all bands° of law,
To our most valiant brother—so much for him: 25
Now for ourself, and for this time of meeting,
Thus much the business is. We have here writ
To Norway, uncle of young Fortinbras—
Who impotent and bed-rid scarcely hears
Of this his nephew's purpose—to suppress   30
His further gait° herein, in that the levies,
The lists, and full proportions are all made
Out of his subject.° and we here dispatch
You good Cornelius, and you Valtemand,
For bearers of this greeting to old Norway,   35
Giving to you no further personal power
To business with the king, more than the scope
Of these delated° articles allow:
Farewell, and let your haste commend your duty.°
CORNELIUS, VALTEMAND: In that, and all things, will we show our duty.   40
KING: We doubt it nothing, heartily farewell.

                                                   Exeunt VALTEMAND and CORNELIUS.

And now Laertes what's the news with you?
You told us to some suit, what is't Laertes?
You cannot speak of reason to the Dane
And lose your voice;° what wouldst thou beg, Laertes,   45
That shall not be my offer, not thy asking?°

°6 *we*: royal plural. The King speaks not only for himself, but for his entire government. 7 *remembrance of our-selves*: reminder of our duties. 8 *sometime*: former. *sister*: sister-in-law. 9 *jointress*: widow who inherits the estate. 11 *auspicious* . . . *eye*: one eye happy, the other tearful. 14–15 *barred* . . . *wisdoms*: failed to seek and abide by your good advice. 18 *weak* . . . *worth*: low opinion of my ability in office. 20 *out of frame*: tottering. 21 *Colleaguèd*: supported. *advantage*: superiority. 24 *bands*: bonds. 31 *gait*: progress. 31–33 *levies* . . . *subject*: Taxes, conscriptions, and supplies are all obtained from his subjects. 38 *delated*: prescribed; defined. 39 *haste* . . . *duty*: prompt departure signify your respect. 45 *lose your voice*: speak in vain. 46 *offer* . . . *asking*: grant even before requested.

      The head is not more native° to the heart,
      The hand more instrumental to the mouth,
      Than is the throne of Denmark to thy father.
      What wouldst thou have, Laertes?

50 **LAERTES:**   My dread lord,
      Your leave and favour° to return to France,
      From whence, though willingly I came to Denmark
      To show my duty in your coronation,
      Yet now I must confess, that duty done,

55   My thoughts and wishes bend again toward France,
      And bow them to your gracious leave and pardon.°
KING: Have you your father's leave? What says Polonius?
POLONIUS: He hath my lord wrung from me my slow leave
      By laboursome petition, and at last

60   Upon his will I sealed my hard consent.°
      I do beseech you give him leave to go.
KING: Take thy fair hour Laertes, time be thine,
      And thy best graces spend it at thy will.
      But now my cousin° Hamlet, and my son—

65 **HAMLET:** [*Aside.*] A little more than kin,° and less than kind.°
KING: How is it that the clouds still hang on you?
HAMLET: Not so my lord, I am too much in the sun.°
QUEEN: Good Hamlet cast thy nighted colour° off
      And let thine eye look like a friend on Denmark,°

70   Do not for ever with thy vailèd° lids
      Seek for thy noble father in the dust,
      Thou know'st 'tis common, all that lives must die,
      Passing through nature to eternity.
HAMLET: Ay madam, it is common.°
QUEEN: If it be,

75   Why seems it so particular with thee?
HAMLET: Seems, madam? nay it is, I know not "seems."
      'Tis not alone my inky cloak, good mother,
      Nor customary suits of solemn black,
      Nor windy suspiration of forced breath,

80   No, nor the fruitful river in the eye,°
      Nor the dejected haviour° of the visage,
      Together with all forms, moods, shapes of grief,
      That can denote me truly: these indeed seem,
      For they are actions that a man might play,°

85   But I have that within which passes show,
      These but the trappings and the suits of woe.°

°47 *native:* related. 51 *leave and favour:* kind permission. 56 *pardon:* allowance. 60 *Upon . . . consent:* (1) At his request, I gave my grudging consent. (2) On the soft sealing wax of his (legal) will, I stamped my approval. 64 *cousin:* kinsman (used for relatives outside the immediate family). 65 *more than kin:* too much of a kinsman, being both uncle and stepfather. *less than kind:* (1) unkind because of being a kin (proverbial) and taking the throne from the former king's son (2) unnatural (as it was considered incest to marry the wife of one's dead brother). 67 *in the sun:* (1) in presence of the king (often associated metaphorically with the sun) (2) proverbial: "out of heaven's blessing into the warm sun" (3) of a "son." 68 *nighted colour:* black. 69 *Denmark:* the King of Denmark. 70 *vailèd:* downcast. 74 *common:* (1) general (2) vulgar. 79–80 *windy . . . eye:* (hyperbole used to describe exaggerated sighs and tears). 81 *haviour:* behavior. 84 *play:* act. 86 *trappings . . . woe:* outward, superficial costumes of mourning.

KING: 'Tis sweet and commendable in your nature Hamlet,
    To give these mourning duties to your father:
    But you must know your father lost a father,
    That father lost, lost his, and the survivor bound   90
    In filial obligation for some term
    To do obsequious sorrow:° but to persever
    In obstinate condolement,° is a course
    Of impious stubbornness, 'tis unmanly grief,
    It shows a will most incorrect to heaven,   95
    A heart unfortified, a mind impatient,
    An understanding simple and unschooled:
    For what we know must be, and is as common
    As any the most vulgar thing to sense,°
    Why should we in our peevish opposition   100
    Take it to heart? Fie, 'tis a fault to heaven,
    A fault against the dead, a fault to nature,
    To reason most absurd, whose common theme
    Is death of fathers, and who still° hath cried
    From the first corse,° till he that died today,   105
    "This must be so." We pray you throw to earth
    This unprevailing° woe, and think of us
    As of a father, for let the world take note
    You are the most immediate° to our throne,
    And with no less nobility of love   110
    Than that which dearest father bears his son,
    Do I impart toward you. For your intent
    In going back to school in Wittenberg,
    It is most retrograde° to our desire,
    And we beseech you, bend you° to remain   115
    Here in the cheer and comfort of our eye,
    Our chiefest courtier, cousin, and our son.
QUEEN: Let not thy mother lose her prayers Hamlet,
    I pray thee stay with us, go not to Wittenberg.
HAMLET: I shall in all my best obey you madam.   120
KING: Why 'tis a loving and a fair reply,
    Be as ourself in Denmark. Madam come,
    This gentle and unforced accord of Hamlet
    Sits smiling to my heart, in grace whereof,
    No jocund health that Denmark drinks today,   125
    But the great cannon to the clouds shall tell,
    And the king's rouse° the heaven shall bruit° again,
    Re-speaking earthly thunder; come away.

                          Flourish: Exeunt all but HAMLET.

°92 *do obsequious sorrow:* express sorrow befitting obsequies or funerals. 93 *condolement:* grief. 99 *As any . . . sense:* as the most ordinary thing the senses can perceive. 104 *still:* always. 105 *corse:* corpse (of Abel, also, ironically, the first fratricide). 107 *unprevailing:* useless. 109 *most immediate:* next in succession (though Danish kings were elected by the council, an Elizabethan audience might feel that Hamlet, not Claudius, should be king). 114 *retrograde:* movement (of planets) in a reverse direction. 115 *beseech . . . you:* hope you will be inclined. 127 *rouse:* toast that empties the wine cup. *bruit:* sound.

HAMLET: O that this too too sullied° flesh would melt,
130   Thaw and resolve itself into a dew,
        Or that the Everlasting had not fixed
        His canon° 'gainst self-slaughter. O God, God,
        How weary, stale, flat, and unprofitable
        Seem to me all the uses of this world!
135   Fie on't, ah fie, 'tis an unweeded garden
        That grows to seed, things rank° and gross in nature
        Possess it merely.° That it should come to this,
        But two months dead, nay not so much, not two,
        So excellent a king, that was to this
140   Hyperion° to a satyr,° so loving to my mother,
        That he might not beteem° the winds of heaven
        Visit her face too roughly—heaven and earth,
        Must I remember? why, she would hang on him
        As if increase of appetite had grown
145   By what it fed on,° and yet within a month—
        Let me not think on't: Frailty, thy name is woman—
        A little month or ere those shoes were old
        With which she followed my poor father's body
        Like Niobe° all tears, why she, even she—
150   O God, a beast that wants° discourse of reason
        Would have mourned longer—married with my uncle,
        My father's brother, but no more like my father
        Than I to Hercules: within a month,
        Ere yet the salt of most unrighteous° tears
155   Had left the flushing° in her gallèd° eyes,
        She married. O most wicked speed, to post°
        With such dexterity to incestuous° sheets:
        It is not, nor it cannot come to good,
        But break my heart, for I must hold my tongue.

Enter HORATIO, MARCELLUS and BARNARDO.

HORATIO: Hail to your lordship.
160   HAMLET: I am glad to see you well;
        Horatio, or I do forget my self.
HORATIO: The same my lord, and your poor servant ever.
HAMLET: Sir my good friend, I'll change° that name with you:
        And what make you from Wittenberg, Horatio?
165   Marcellus.
MARCELLUS: My good lord.
HAMLET: I am very glad to see you: good even, sir.

°129 *sullied:* tainted. 132 *canon:* divine edict. 136 *rank:* (1) luxuriant, excessive (2) bad-smelling. 137 *merely:* entirely. 140 *Hyperion:* god of the sun. *satyr:* part-goat, part-man woodland deity (noted for lust). 141 *beteem:* allow. 144–145 *As if . . . on:* as if the more she fed, the more her appetite increased. 149 *Niobe:* (who boasted of her children before Leto and was punished by their destruction; Zeus changed the weeping mother to a stone dropping continual tears). 150 *wants:* lacks. 154 *unrighteous:* (because untrue). 155 *flushing:* redness. *gallèd:* rubbed sore. 156 *post:* rush. 157 *incestuous:* (the church forbade marriage to one's brother's widow). 163 *change:* exchange (and be called your friend).

But what in faith make you from Wittenberg?
HORATIO: A truant disposition, good my lord.
HAMLET: I would not hear your enemy say so,   170
    Nor shall you do mine ear that violence
    To make it truster of your own report
    Against yourself. I know you are no truant,
    But what is your affair in Elsinore?
    We'll teach you to drink deep ere you depart.   175
HORATIO: My Lord, I came to see your father's funeral.
HAMLET: I prithee do not mock me, fellow student,
    I think it was to see my mother's wedding.
HORATIO: Indeed my lord it followed hard upon.
HAMLET: Thrift, thrift, Horatio, the funeral baked meats°   180
    Did coldly° furnish forth the marriage tables.
    Would I had met my dearest° foe in heaven
    Or ever I had seen that day Horatio.
    My father, methinks I see my father.
HORATIO: Where my lord?
HAMLET: In my mind's eye Horatio.   185
HORATIO: I saw him once, a' was a goodly° king.
HAMLET: A' was a man, take him for all in all,
    I shall not look upon his like again.
HORATIO: My lord, I think I saw him yesternight.
HAMLET: Saw? Who?   190
HORATIO: My lord, the king your father.
HAMLET: The king my father?
HORATIO: Season your admiration° for a while
    With an attent ear till I may deliver
    Upon the witness of these gentlemen
    This marvel to you.
HAMLET: For God's love let me hear!   195
HORATIO: Two nights together had these gentlemen,
    Marcellus and Barnardo, on their watch
    In the dead waste and middle of the night,
    Been thus encountered. A figure like your father
    Armed at point exactly, cap-a-pe,°   200
    Appears before them, and with solemn march,
    Goes slow and stately by them; thrice he walked
    By their oppressed° and fear-surprisèd eyes
    Within his truncheon's° length, whilst they distilled°
    Almost to jelly with the act of fear,   205
    Stand dumb and speak not to him; this to me
    In dreadful secrecy° impart they did,
    And I with them the third night kept the watch,
    Where as they had delivered, both in time,
    Form of the thing, each word made true and good,   210

°180 *funeral baked meats*: food prepared for the funeral. 181 *coldly*: when cold. 182 *dearest*: direst. 186 *goodly*: handsome. 192 *Season your admiration*: control your wonder. 200 *at point . . . cap-a-pe*: in every detail, head to foot. 203 *oppressed*: overcome by horror. 204 *truncheon*: staff (of office). *distilled*: dissolved. 207 *in dreadful secrecy*: as a dread secret.

The apparition comes: I knew your father,
These hands are not more like.

HAMLET: But where was this?

MARCELLUS: My lord upon the platform where we watch.

HAMLET: Did you not speak to it?

HORATIO: My lord I did,
215   But answer made it none, yet once methought
It lifted up it° head, and did address
Itself to motion° like as it would speak:
But even then the morning cock crew loud,
And at the sound it shrunk in haste away
And vanished from our sight.

220 HAMLET: 'Tis very strange.

HORATIO: As I do live my honoured lord 'tis true,
And we did think it writ down in our duty
To let you know of it.

HAMLET: Indeed indeed sirs, but this troubles me.
Hold you the watch tonight?

225 ALL: We do my lord.

HAMLET: Armed say you?

ALL: Armed my lord.

HAMLET: From top to toe?

ALL: My lord from head to foot.

HAMLET: Then saw you not his face.

230 HORATIO: O yes my lord, he wore his beaver° up.

HAMLET: What, looked he frowningly?

HORATIO: A countenance more in sorrow than in anger.

HAMLET: Pale, or red?

HORATIO: Nay, very pale.

HAMLET: And fixed his eyes upon you?

HORATIO: Most constantly.

235 HAMLET: I would I had been there.

HORATIO: It would have much amazed you.

HAMLET: Very like, very like, stayed it long?

HORATIO: While one with moderate haste might tell° a hundred.

MARCELLUS, BARNARDO: Longer, longer.

HORATIO: Not when I saw't.

240 HAMLET: His beard was grizzled,° no?

HORATIO: It was as I have seen it in his life,
A sable silvered.°

HAMLET: I will watch tonight;
Perchance 'twill walk again.

HORATIO: I warr'nt it will.

HAMLET: If it assume my noble father's person,
245   I'll speak to it though hell itself should gape
And bid me hold my peace;° I pray you all

°216 *it:* its. 216–217 *address . . . motion:* start to move. 230 *beaver:* visor. 238 *tell:* count. 240 *grizzled:* grey. 242 *A sable silvered:* black flecked with gray. 245–246 *though hell . . . peace:* despite the risk of hell (for speaking to a demon) warning me to be silent.

If you have hitherto concealed this sight
Let it be tenable° in your silence still,
And whatsoever else shall hap tonight,
Give it an understanding but no tongue.   250
I will requite your loves, so fare you well:
Upon the platform 'twixt eleven and twelve
I'll visit you.
ALL: Our duty to your honour.
HAMLET: Your loves, as mine to you:° farewell.   *Exeunt.* [HAMLET *remains.*]
My father's spirit (in arms) all is not well,   255
I doubt° some foul play, would the night were come;
Till then sit still my soul. Foul deeds will rise,
Though all the earth o'erwhelm them to men's eyes.   *Exit.*

Scene 3. [Polonius's chambers]

Enter LAERTES *and* OPHELIA *his sister.*

LAERTES: My necessaries are embarked, farewell,
And sister, as the winds give benefit
And convoy° is assistant, do not sleep
But let me hear from you.
OPHELIA: Do you doubt that?
LAERTES: For Hamlet, and the trifling of his favour,   5
Hold it a fashion, and a toy in blood,°
A violet in the youth of primy nature,°
Forward,° not permanent, sweet, not lasting,
The perfume and suppliance of° a minute,
No more.
OPHELIA: No more but so?
LAERTES: Think it no more.   10
For nature crescent° does not grow alone
In thews and bulk,° but as this temple waxes°
The inward service of the mind and soul
Grows wide withal.° Perhaps he loves you now,
And now no soil nor cautel° doth besmirch   15
The virtue of his will:° but you must fear,
His greatness weighed,° his will is not his own,
For he himself is subject to his birth:
He may not as unvalued persons° do,
Carve° for himself, for on his choice depends   20
The sanctity and health of this whole state,
And therefore must his choice be circumscribed
Unto the voice and yielding° of that body
Whereof he is the head. Then if he says he loves you,

°248 *tenable:* held, kept. 254 *Your loves . . . you:* offer your friendship (rather than duty) in exchange for mine.
256 *doubt:* fear. 3 *convoy:* conveyance. 6 *toy in blood:* whim of the passions. 7 *youth of primy nature:* early spring. 8
Forward: premature. 9 *suppliance of:* supplying diversion for. 11 *nature crescent:* man as he grows. 12 *thews and bulk:*
sinews and body. *temple waxes:* body grows (1 Cor. 6:19). 14 *withal:* at the same time. 15 *cautel:* deceit. 16 *will:* desire. 17 *weighed:* considered. 19 *unvalued persons:* common people. 20 *Carve:* choose (as does the one who carves
the food). 23 *voice and yielding:* approving vote.

25   It fits your wisdom so far to believe it
        As he in his particular act and place
        May give his saying deed,° which is no further
        Than the main voice of Denmark goes withal.
        Then weigh what loss your honour may sustain
30   If with too credent° ear you list° his songs,
        Or lose your heart, or your chaste treasure open
        To his unmast'red importunity.°
        Fear it Ophelia, fear it my dear sister,
        And keep you in the rear of your affection,
35   Out of the shot and danger of desire.
        The chariest° maid is prodigal enough
        If she unmask her beauty to the moon.
        Virtue itself 'scapes not calumnious strokes.
        The canker galls the infants° of the spring
40   Too oft before their buttons° be disclosed,
        And in the morn and liquid dew of youth
        Contagious blastments° are most imminent.
        Be wary then, best safety lies in fear,
        Youth to itself rebels,° though none else near.
45 **OPHELIA:** I shall the effect° of this good lesson keep
        As watchman to my heart: but good my brother,
        Do not as some ungracious° pastors do,
        Show me the steep and thorny way to heaven,
        Whiles like a puffed and reckless libertine
50   Himself the primrose path of dalliance treads,
        And recks not his own rede.°

Enter POLONIUS.

LAERTES: O fear me not,°
        I stay too long, but here my father comes:
        A double blessing is a double grace,
        Occasion smiles upon a second leave.°
55 **POLONIUS:** Yet here Laertes? aboard, aboard for shame,
        The wind sits in the shoulder of your sail,
        And you are stayed for: there, my blessing with thee,
        And these few precepts in thy memory
        Look thou character.° Give thy thoughts no tongue,
60   Nor any unproportioned thought his act:
        Be thou familiar, but by no means vulgar;°
        Those friends thou hast, and their adoption tried,°
        Grapple them unto thy soul with hoops of steel,
        But do not dull° thy palm with entertainment

°26–27 *in his . . . deed:* limited by personal responsibilities and rank, may perform what he promises. 30 *credent:* credulous. *list:* listen to. 31–32 *your chaste . . . importunity:* lose your virginity to his uncontrolled persistence. 36 *chariest:* most cautious. 39 *canker . . . infants:* cankerworm or caterpillar harms the young plants. 40 *buttons:* buds. 42 *blastments:* blights. 44 *to itself rebels:* lusts by nature. 45 *effect:* moral. 47 *ungracious:* lacking God's grace. 51 *recks . . . rede:* does not follow his own advice. *fear me not:* Don't worry about me. 54 *Occasion . . . leave:* opportunity favors a second leave-taking. 59 *character:* write, impress, imprint. 61 *vulgar:* indiscriminately friendly. 62 *adoption tried:* loyalty proved. 64 *dull:* get callouses on.

Of each new-hatched unfledged° comrade. Beware   65
Of entrance to a quarrel, but being in,
Bear't that th'opposèd may beware of thee.
Give every man thy ear, but few thy voice:
Take each man's censure,° but reserve thy judgment.
Costly thy habit° as thy purse can buy,   70
But not expressed in fancy,° rich, not gaudy,
For the apparel oft proclaims the man,
And they in France of the best rank and station,
Are of a most select and generous chief° in that:
Neither a borrower nor a lender be,   75
For loan oft loses both itself and friend,
And borrowing dulls the edge of husbandry;°
This above all, to thine own self be true
And it must follow as the night the day,
Thou canst not then be false to any man.   80
Farewell, my blessing season° this in thee.
LAERTES: Most humbly do I take my leave my lord.
POLONIUS: The time invites you, go, your servants tend.°
LAERTES: Farewell Ophelia, and remember well
    What I have said to you.
OPHELIA: 'Tis in my memory locked,   85
    And you yourself shall keep the key of it.
LAERTES: Farewell.   *Exit* LAERTES.
POLONIUS: What is't Ophelia he hath said to you?
OPHELIA: So please you, something touching the Lord Hamlet.
POLONIUS: Marry,° well bethought: 90
    'Tis told me he hath very oft of late
    Given private time to you, and you yourself
    Have of your audience been most free and bounteous.
    If it be so, as so 'tis put on me,
    And that in way of caution, I must tell you,   95
    You do not understand yourself so clearly
    As it behooves my daughter, and your honour.
    What is between you? give me up the truth.
OPHELIA: He hath my lord of late made many tenders°
    Of his affection to me.   100
POLONIUS: Affection, puh, you speak like a green girl
    Unsifted° in such perilous circumstance.
    Do you believe his tenders as you call them?
OPHELIA: I do not know my lord what I should think.
POLONIUS: Marry, I will teach you; think yourself a baby   105
    That you have ta'en these tenders° for true pay
    Which are not sterling.° Tender yourself more dearly,°

°65 *new-hatched unfledged:* new and untested. 69 *censure:* opinion. 70 *habit:* clothing. 71 *expressed in fancy:* so fantastic as to be ridiculous. 74 *select . . . chief:* judicious and noble eminence. 77 *husbandry:* thrift. 81 *season:* bring
to maturity. 83 *tend:* attend, wait. 90 *Marry:* (a mild oath, from "By the Virgin Mary"). 99 *tenders:* offers (see lines
106–9). 102 *Unsifted:* untested. 106 *tenders:* offers (of money). 107 *sterling:* genuine (currency). *Tender . . .
dearly:* hold yourself at a higher value.

Or (not to crack the wind of the poor phrase,
Running it thus°) you'll tender me a fool.°

110   OPHELIA: My lord he hath importuned me with love
In honourable fashion.

POLONIUS: Ay, fashion you may call it, go to, go to.

OPHELIA: And hath given countenance° to his speech, my lord,
With almost all the holy vows of heaven.

115   POLONIUS: Ay, springes° to catch woodcocks.° I do know
When the blood burns, how prodigal the soul
Lends the tongue vows: these blazes daughter,
Giving more light than heat, extinct in both,
Even in their promise, as it is a-making,°

120   You must not take for fire. From this time
Be something scanter of your maiden presence,
Set your entreatments at a higher rate
Than a command to parle;° for Lord Hamlet,
Believe so much in him that he is young,

125   And with a larger tether may he walk
Than may be given you: in few° Ophelia,
Do not believe his vows, for they are brokers°
Not of that dye which their investments° show,
But mere implorators° of unholy suits,

130   Breathing° like sanctified and pious bonds,°
The better to beguile. This is for all,
I would not in plain terms from this time forth
Have you so slander any moment leisure
As to give words or talk with the Lord Hamlet.

135   Look to't I charge you, come your ways.°

OPHELIA: I shall obey, my lord.   [*Exeunt.*]

Scene 4. [The platform on the battlements]

Enter HAMLET, HORATIO *and* MARCELLUS.

HAMLET: The air bites shrewdly,° it is very cold.

HORATIO: It is a nipping and an eager° air.

HAMLET: What hour now?

HORATIO: I think it lacks of twelve.

5   MARCELLUS: No, it is struck.

HORATIO: Indeed? I heard it not: it then draws near the season°
Wherein the spirit held his wont to walk.

A flourish of trumpets, and two pieces [of ordnance] go off.

°108–9 *crack . . . thus*: make the phrase lose its breath. 109 *tender . . . fool*: (1) make me look foolish (2) present me with a baby. 113 *countenance*: confirmation. 115 *springes*: snares. *woodcocks*: snipelike birds (believed to be stupid and therefore easily trapped). 118–19 *extinct . . . a-making*: losing both appearance, because of brevity, and substance, because of broken promises. 122–23 *Set . . . parle*: Don't rush to negotiate a surrender as soon as the besieger asks for a discussion of terms. 126 *few*: short. 127 *brokers*: (1) business agents (2) procurers. 128 *investments*: (1) business ventures (2) clothing. 129 *implorators*: solicitors. 130 *Breathing*: speaking softly. *bonds*: pledges. 135 *come your ways*: come along. 1 *shrewdly*: fiercely. 2 *eager*: sharp. 6 *season*: time, period.

What does this mean my lord?

HAMLET: The king doth wake° tonight and takes his rouse,°
    Keeps wassail° and the swagg'ring up-spring° reels: 10
    And as he drains his draughts of Rhenish° down,
    The kettle-drum and trumpet thus bray out
    The triumph of his pledge.°

HORATIO: Is it a custom?

HAMLET: Ay marry is't,
    But to my mind, though I am native here   15
    And to the manner born,° it is a custom
    More honoured in the breach than the observance.°
    This heavy-headed revel east and west
    Makes us traduced and taxed of° other nations:
    They clepe° us drunkards, and with swinish phrase   20
    Soil our addition,° and indeed it takes
    From our achievements, though performed at height,°
    The pith and marrow of our attribute.°
    So oft it chances in particular men,
    That for some vicious mole of nature° in them,   25
    As in their birth, wherein they are not guilty
    (Since nature cannot choose his origin),
    By the o'ergrowth of some complexion,°
    Oft breaking down the pales° and forts of reason,
    Or by some habit, that too much o'er-leavens°   30
    The form of plausive° manners—that these men,
    Carrying I say the stamp of one defect,
    Being nature's livery,° or fortune's star,°
    His virtues else be they as pure as grace,
    As infinite as man may undergo,   35
    Shall in the general censure° take corruption
    From that particular fault: the dram of evil
    Doth all the noble substance often doubt,
    To his own scandal.°

Enter GHOST.

HORATIO: Look my lord, it comes.

HAMLET: Angels and ministers of grace defend us: 40
    Be thou a spirit of health, or goblin damned,°
    Bring with thee airs from heaven, or blasts from hell,
    Be thy intents wicked, or charitable,

°9 *wake*: stay awake. *rouse*: drinks that empty the cup. 10 *Keeps wassail*: holds drinking bouts. *up-spring*: a vigorous German dance. 11 *Rhenish*: Rhine wine. 13 *triumph . . . pledge*: victory of emptying the cup with one draught. 16 *to . . . born*: accustomed to the practice since birth. 17 *More . . . observance*: better to break than to observe. 19 *traduced and taxed of*: defamed and taken to task by. 20 *clepe*: call. 20–21 *with swinish . . . addition*: blemish our reputation by comparing us to swine. 22 *at height*: to the maximum. 23 *attribute*: reputation. 25 *mole of nature*: natural blemish. 28 *o'er growth . . . complexion*: overbalance of one of the body's four humors or fluids believed to determine temperament. 29 *pales*: defensive enclosures. 30 *too much o'er-leavens*: excessively modifies (like too much leaven in bread). 31 *plausive*: pleasing. 33 *nature's livery*: marked by nature. *fortune's star*: destined by chance. 36 *general censure*: public opinion. 37–39 *the dram . . . scandal*: the minute quantity of evil often casts doubt upon his noble nature, to his shame. 41 *spirit . . . damned*: true ghost or demon from hell.

Thou com'st in such a questionable° shape,
45   That I will speak to thee. I'll call thee Hamlet,
King, father, royal Dane. O answer me,
Let me not burst in ignorance, but tell
Why thy canonized° bones hearsèd° in death
Have burst their cerements°? why the sepulchre,
50   Wherein we saw thee quietly interred
Hath oped his ponderous and marble jaws,
To cast thee up again? What may this mean
That thou, dead corse, again in complete steel
Revisits thus the glimpses of the moon,
55   Making night hideous, and we fools of nature°
So horridly to shake our disposition
With thoughts beyond the reaches of our souls,
Say why is this? wherefore? what should we do?   GHOST beckons HAMLET.
HORATIO: It beckons you to go away with it,
60   As if it some impartment did desire°
To you alone.
MARCELLUS: Look with what courteous action
It waves you to a more removèd ground,
But do not go with it.
HORATIO: No, by no means.
HAMLET: It will not speak, then I will follow it.
HORATIO: Do not my lord.
65   HAMLET: Why what should be the fear?
I do not set my life at a pin's fee,°
And for my soul, what can it do to that
Being a thing immortal as itself;
It waves me forth again, I'll follow it.
70   HORATIO: What if it tempt you toward the flood my lord,
Or to the dreadful summit of the cliff
That beetles o'er° his base into the sea,
And there assume some other horrible form
Which might deprive your sovereignty of reason,°
75   And draw you into madness? think of it,
The very place puts toys of desperation,°
Without more motive, into every brain
That looks so many fathoms to the sea
And hears it roar beneath.
HAMLET: It waves me still:
80   Go on, I'll follow thee.
MARCELLUS: You shall not go my lord.
HAMLET: Hold off your hands.
HORATIO: Be ruled, you shall not go.
HAMLET: My fate cries out,

°44 *questionable*: question-raising. 48 *canonized*: buried in accordance with church edict. *hearsèd*: entombed. 49 *cerements*: waxed cloth wrappings. 55 *fools of nature*: mocked by our natural limitations when faced with the supernatural. 60 *some . . . desire*: desired to impart something. 66 *fee*: value. 72 *beetles o'er*: overhangs. 74 *deprive . . . reason*: dethrone your reason from its sovereignty. 76 *toys of desperation*: desperate whims.

And makes each petty artire° in this body
As hardy as the Nemean lion's° nerve;°
Still am I called, unhand me gentlemen,   85
By heaven I'll make a ghost of him that lets° me:
I say away; go on, I'll follow thee.   *Exeunt* GHOST *and* HAMLET.
HORATIO: He waxes desperate° with imagination.
MARCELLUS: Let's follow, 'tis not fit thus to obey him.
HORATIO: Have after—to what issue will this come?   90
MARCELLUS: Something is rotten in the state of Denmark.
HORATIO: Heaven will direct it.
MARCELLUS: Nay, let's follow him.   *Exeunt.*

Scene 5. [Another part of the platform]

Enter GHOST *and* HAMLET.

HAMLET: Whither wilt thou lead me? Speak, I'll go no further.
GHOST: Mark me.
HAMLET: I will.
GHOST: My hour is almost come
When I to sulphurous and tormenting flames
Must render up myself.
HAMLET: Alas poor ghost.
GHOST: Pity me not, but lend thy serious hearing   5
To what I shall unfold.
HAMLET: Speak, I am bound° to hear.
GHOST: So art thou to revenge, when thou shalt hear.
HAMLET: What?
GHOST: I am thy father's spirit,
Doomed for a certain term to walk the night,   10
And for the day confined to fast in fires,
Till the foul crimes done in my days of nature°
Are burnt and purged away: but that I am forbid
To tell the secrets of my prison-house,
I could a tale unfold whose lightest word   15
Would harrow up thy soul, freeze thy young blood,
Make thy two eyes like stars start from their spheres,°
Thy knotted and combinèd locks to part,
And each particular hair to stand an° end,
Like quills upon the fretful porpentine:°   20
But this eternal blazon° must not be
To ears of flesh and blood; list, list, O list:
If thou didst ever thy dear father love—
HAMLET: O God!
GHOST: Revenge his foul and most unnatural murder.   25
HAMLET: Murder?

°83 *artire:* ligament. 84 *Nemean lion:* (killed by Hercules as one of his twelve labors). *nerve:* sinew. 86 *lets:* prevents. 88 *waxes desperate:* grows frantic. 6 *bound:* obliged by duty. 12 *crimes . . . nature:* sins committed during my life on earth. 17 *spheres:* (1) orbits (according to Ptolemy, each planet was confined to a sphere revolving around the earth) (2) sockets. 19 *an:* on. 20 *fretful porpentine:* angry porcupine. 21 *eternal blazon:* revelation about eternity.

GHOST: Murder most foul, as in the best it is,
　　　But this most foul, strange and unnatural.
HAMLET: Haste me to know't, that I with wings as swift
30　　　As meditation or the thoughts of love,
　　　May sweep to my revenge.
GHOST: I find thee apt,°
　　　And duller shouldst thou be than the fat° weed
　　　That rots itself in ease on Lethe wharf,°
　　　Wouldst thou not stir in this; now Hamlet hear,
35　　　'Tis given out, that sleeping in my orchard,°
　　　A serpent stung me, so the whole ear of Denmark
　　　Is by a forgèd process° of my death
　　　Rankly abused:° but know thou noble youth,
　　　The serpent that did sting thy father's life
　　　Now wears his crown.
40　HAMLET:　　　　　　　　O my prophetic soul!
　　　My uncle?
GHOST: Ay, that incestuous, that adulterate° beast,
　　　With witchcraft of his wit, with traitorous gifts,
　　　O wicked wit and gifts, that have the power
45　　　So to seduce; won to his shameful lust
　　　The will of my most seeming-virtuous queen;
　　　O Hamlet, what a falling-off was there,
　　　From me whose love was of that dignity
　　　That it went hand in hand, even with the vow
50　　　I made to her in marriage, and to decline
　　　Upon° a wretch whose natural gifts were poor
　　　To° those of mine;
　　　But virtue, as it never will be moved,
　　　Though lewdness court it in a shape of heaven,°
55　　　So lust, though to a radiant angle linked,
　　　Will sate itself in a celestial bed
　　　And prey on garbage.
　　　But soft, methinks I scent the morning air,
　　　Brief let me be; sleeping within my orchard,
60　　　My custom always of the afternoon,
　　　Upon my secure° hour thy uncle stole
　　　With juice of cursèd hebona° in a vial,
　　　And in the porches of my ears did pour
　　　The leperous° distilment, whose effect
65　　　Holds such an enmity with blood of man,
　　　That swift as quicksilver it courses through
　　　The natural gates and alleys of the body,
　　　And with a sudden vigour it doth posset°
　　　And curd, like eager° droppings into milk,
70　　　The thin and wholesome° blood; so did it mine,

°31 *apt:* ready. 32 *fat:* slimy. 33 *Lethe wharf:* the banks of Lethe (river in Hades from which spirits drank to forget their past lives). 35 *orchard:* garden. 37 *process:* account. 38 *abused:* deceived. 42 *adulterate:* adulterous. 50–51 *decline Upon:* descend to. 52 *To:* compared to. 54 *shape of heaven:* angelic appearance. 61 *secure:* unsuspecting. 62 *hebona:* poisonous sap of the ebony or henbane. 64 *leperous:* leprosy-causing. 68 *posset:* curdle. 69 *eager:* sour. 70 *wholesome:* healthy.

And a most instant tetter° barked about°
Most lazar°-like with vile and loathsome crust
All my smooth body.
Thus was I sleeping by a brother's hand,
Of life, of crown, of queen at once dispatched,   75
Cut off even in the blossoms of my sin,
Unhouseled, disappointed, unaneled,°
No reck'ning° made, but sent to my account°
With all my imperfections on my head;
O horrible, O horrible, most horrible!   80
If thou hast nature in thee bear it not,
Let not the royal bed of Denmark be
A couch for luxury° and damnèd incest.
But howsoever thou pursues this act,
Taint not thy mind, nor let thy soul contrive   85
Against thy mother aught,° leave her to heaven,
And to those thorns that in her bosom lodge
To prick and sting her. Fare thee well at once,
The glow-worm shows the matin° to be near
And 'gins to pale this uneffectual fire:°   90
Adieu, adieu, adieu, remember me.   *Exit.*
HAMLET: O all you host of heaven! O earth! what else?
And shall I couple° hell? O fie! Hold, hold my heart,
And you my sinews, grow not instant old,
But bear me stiffly up; remember thee?   95
Ay thou poor ghost, while memory holds a seat
In this distracted globe.° Remember thee?
Yea, from the table° of my memory
I'll wipe away all trivial fond° records,
All saws of books,° all forms, all pressures° past   100
That youth and observation copied there,
And thy commandment all alone shall live
Within the book and volume of my brain,
Unmixed with baser matter, yes by heaven:
O most pernicious woman!   105
O villain, villain, smiling damnèd villain!
My tables,° meet° it is I set it down
That one may smile, and smile, and be a villain,
At least I am sure it may be so in Denmark.
So uncle, there you are: now to my word,°   110
It is 'Adieu, adieu, remember me.'
I have sworn't.

°71 *tetter*: skin eruption. *barked about*: covered (like bark on a tree). 72 *lazar*: leper. 77 *Unhouseled . . . unaneled*: without final sacrament, unprepared (without confession) and lacking extreme unction (anointing). 78 *reck'ning*:(1) accounting (2) payment of my bill (3) confession and absolution. *account*: judgment. 83 *luxury*: lust. 86 *aught*: anything. 89 *matin*: dawn. 90 *'gins . . . fire*: his light becomes ineffective, made pale by day. 93 *couple*: engage in a contest against. 97 *distracted globe*: (his head). 98 *table*: tablet, "table-book." 99 *fond*: foolish. 100 *saws of books*: maxims (sayings) copied from books. *forms, all pressures*: ideas, impressions, meditations, etc. 107 *tables*: tablet; notepad. *meet*: fitting. 110 *word*: motto (to guide my actions).

Enter HORATIO and MARCELLUS.

HORATIO: My lord, my lord!
MARCELLUS: Lord Hamlet!
HORATIO: Heaven secure° him.
HAMLET: So be it.
115 MARCELLUS: Illo, ho, ho, my lord!
HAMLET: Hillo, ho, ho, boy, come° bird, come.
MARCELLUS: How is't my noble lord?
HORATIO: What news my lord?
HAMLET: O, wonderful!
HORATIO: Good my lord, tell it.
HAMLET: No, you will reveal it.
HORATIO: Not I my lord, by heaven.
120 MARCELLUS: Nor I my lord.
HAMLET: How say you then, would heart of man once think it?
     But you'll be secret?
BOTH: Ay, by heaven, my lord.
HAMLET: There's ne'er a villain dwelling in all Denmark
     But he's an arrant° knave.
125 HORATIO: There needs no ghost my lord, come from the grave
     To tell us this.
HAMLET: Why right, you are in the right,
     And so without more circumstance° at all
     I hold it fit that we shake hands and part,
     You, as your business and desire shall point you,
130 For every man hath business and desire
     Such as it is, and for my own poor part,
     Look you, I will go pray.
HORATIO: These are but wild and whirling words my lord.
HAMLET: I am sorry they offend you, heartily,
     Yes faith, heartily.
135 HORATIO: There's no offence my lord.
HAMLET: Yes by Saint Patrick, but there is Horatio,
     And much offence too: touching this vision here,
     It is an honest° ghost, that let me tell you:
     For your desire to know what is between us,
140 O'ermaster't as you may. And now good friends,
     As you are friends, scholars, and soldiers,
     Give me one poor request.
HORATIO: What is't, my lord? we will.
HAMLET: Never make known what you have seen tonight.
BOTH: My lord we will not.
HAMLET: Nay, but swear't.
145 HORATIO: In faith
     My lord, not I.
MARCELLUS: Nor I my lord, in faith.

°113 *secure*: protect. 116 *Hillo . . . come*: falconer's cry with which Hamlet replies to their calls. 124 *arrant*:
thoroughgoing. 127 *circumstance*: ceremony. 138 *honest*: true (not a devil in disguise).

HAMLET: Upon my sword.
MARCELLUS: We have sworn my lord already.
HAMLET: Indeed, upon my sword,° indeed.
GHOST: Swear.   *GHOST cries under the stage.*
HAMLET: Ha, ha, boy, say'st thou so, art thou there, truepenny°?   150
    Come on, you hear this fellow in the cellarage,
    Consent to swear.
HORATIO: Propose the oath my lord.
HAMLET: Never to speak of this that you have seen.
    Swear by my sword.
GHOST: [*Beneath.*] Swear.   155
HAMLET: Hic et ubique?° then we'll shift our ground:
    Come hither gentlemen,
    And lay your hands again upon my sword,
    Swear by my sword
    Never to speak of this that you have heard.   160
GHOST: [*Beneath.*] Swear by his sword.
HAMLET: Well said old mole, canst work i'th' earth so fast?
    A worthy pioner°—once more remove;° good friends.
HORATIO: O day and night, but this is wondrous strange.
HAMLET: And therefore as a stranger give it welcome.   165
    There are more things in heaven and earth Horatio,
    Than are dreamt of in your philosophy.
    But come,
    Here as before, never so help you mercy,
    How strange or odd some'er I bear myself,   170
    (As I perchance hereafter shall think meet
    To put an antic disposition on°)
    That you at such times seeing me, never shall
    With arms encumbere° thus, or this head-shake,
    Or by pronouncing of some doubtful phrase,   175
    As "Well, well, we know," or "We could an if we would,"
    Or "If we list° to speak," or "There be and if they might,"
    Or such ambiguous giving out, to note
    That you know aught of me; this do swear,
    So grace and mercy at your need help you.   180
GHOST: [*Beneath.*] Swear. [*They swear.*]
HAMLET: Rest, rest, perturbed spirit: so gentlemen,
    With all my love I do commend me to you,°
    And what so poor a man as Hamlet is,
    May do t'express his love and friending to you   185
    God willing shall not lack: let us go in together,
    And still° your fingers on your lips I pray.
    The time is out of joint: O cursèd spite,
    That ever I was born to set it right.
    Nay come, let's go together.   *Exeunt.*   190

°148 *sword*: (the cross-shaped hilt). 150 *truepenny*: old pal. 156 *Hic et ubique*: here and everywhere. 163 *pioner*: digger (army trencher). *remove*: move elsewhere. 172 *put . . . on*: assume a mad or grotesque behavior. 174 *encumbered*: folded. 177 *list*: please. 183 *commend . . . you*: put myself in your hands. 187 *still*: always.

ACT 2

Scene 1. [Polonius's chambers]

Enter old POLONIUS *with his man* REYNALDO.

POLONIUS: Give him this money, and these notes Reynaldo.
REYNALDO: I will my lord.
POLONIUS: You shall do marvellous° wisely, good Reynaldo,
    Before you visit him, to make inquire
    Of his behaviour.
5   REYNALDO: My lord, I did intend it.
POLONIUS: Marry, well said, very well said; look you sir,
    Inquire me first what Danskers° are in Paris,
    And how, and who, what means, and where they keep,°
    What company, at what expense, and finding
10   By this encompassment° and drift of question
    That they do know my son, come you more nearer
    Than your particular demands° will touch it,
    Take you as 'twere some distant knowledge of him,
    As thus, "I know his father, and his friends,
15   And in part him"—do you mark this, Reynaldo?
REYNALDO: Ay, very well my lord.
POLONIUS: "And in part him, but," you may say, "not well,
    But if't be he I mean, he's very wild,
    Addicted so and so;" and there put on him
20   What forgeries° you please, marry none so rank°
    As may dishonour him, take heed of that,
    But sir, such wanton, wild, and usual slips,
    As are companions noted and most known
    To youth and liberty.
25   REYNALDO: As gaming my lord.
POLONIUS: Ay, or drinking, fencing, swearing,
    Quarrelling, drabbing°—you may go so far.
REYNALDO: My lord, that would dishonour him.
POLONIUS: Faith no, as you may season it in the charge.°
    You must not put another scandal on him,
30   That he is open to incontinency,°
    That's not my meaning, but breathe his faults so quaintly°
    That they may seem the taints of° liberty,
    The flash and outbreak of a fiery mind,
    A savageness in unreclaimèd blood,°
35   Of general assault.°
REYNALDO: But my good lord—
POLONIUS: Wherefore° should you do this?
REYNALDO: Ay my lord,
    I would know that.

°3 *marvellous:* wonderfully. 7 *Danskers:* Danes. 8 *keep:* lodge. 10 *encompassment:* roundabout way. 12 *particular demands:* specific questions. 20 *forgeries:* inventions. *rank:* excessive. 26 *drabbing:* whoring. 28 *season . . . charge:* temper the charge as you make it. 30 *incontinency:* uncontrolled lechery. 31 *quaintly:* delicately. 32 *taints of:* blemishes due to. 34 *unreclaimèd blood:* unbridled passion. 35 *general assault:* attacking all (young men). 36 *Wherefore:* why.

POLONIUS: Marry sir, here's my drift,
    And I believe it is a fetch of warrant:°
    You laying these slight sullies on my son,   40
    As 'twere a thing a little soiled i'th' working,°
    Mark you, your party in converse, him you would sound,
    Having ever seen° in the prenominate crimes°
    The youth you breathe of guilty, be assured
    He closes with you in this consequence,°   45
    "Good sir," or so, or "friend," or "gentleman,"
    According to the phrase, or the addition°
    Of man and country.
REYNALDO: Very good my lord.
POLONIUS: And then sir, does a'° this, a' does, what was I
    about to say?   50
    By the mass I was about to say something,
    Where did I leave?
REYNALDO: At "closes in the consequence,"
    At "friend, or so, and gentleman."
POLONIUS: At "closes in the consequence," ay marry,
    He closes thus, "I know the gentleman,   55
    I saw him yesterday, or th'other day,
    Or then, or then, with such or such, and as you say,
    There was a' gaming, there o'ertook in's rouse,°
    There falling out at tennis," or perchance
    "I saw him enter such a house of sale,"   60
    Videlicet,° a brothel, or so forth. See you now,
    Your bait of falsehood takes this carp of truth,
    And thus do we of wisdom, and of reach,°
    With windlasses,° and with assays of bias,°
    By indirections find directions out: 65
    So by my former lecture and advice
    Shall you my son; you have me, have you not?
REYNALDO: My lord I have.
POLONIUS: God bye ye, fare ye well.
REYNALDO: Good my lord.
POLONIUS: Observe his inclination in yourself.°   70
REYNALDO: I shall my lord.
POLONIUS: And let him ply° his music.
REYNALDO: Well my lord.
POLONIUS: Farewell.

Exit REYNALDO.

Enter OPHELIA.

    How now Ophelia, what's the matter?

°39 *fetch of warrant*: trick guaranteed to succeed. 41 *working*: handling. 43 *Having ever seen*: if he has ever seen. *prenominate crimes*: aforenamed sins. 45 *closes . . . consequence*: comes to terms with you as follows. 47 *addition*: title, form of address. 49 *a'*: he. 58 *o'ertook in's rouse*: overcome by drunkenness. 61 *Videlicet*: namely. 63 *reach*: far-reaching knowledge. 64 *windlasses*: roundabout approaches. *assays of bias*: indirect attempts. 72 *ply*: practice.

OPHELIA: O my lord, my lord, I have been so affrighted.

75 **POLONIUS:** With what, i'th'name of God?

OPHELIA: My lord, as I was sewing in my closet,°
    Lord Hamlet with his doublet all unbraced,°
    No hat upon his head, his stockings fouled,
    Ungart'red, and down-gyvèd° to his ankle,

80   Pale as his shirt, his knees knocking each other,
    And with a look so piteous in purport°
    As if he had been loosèd out of hell
    To speak of horrors, he comes before me.

POLONIUS: Mad for thy love?

OPHELIA: My lord I do not know,
    But truly I do fear it.

85 **POLONIUS:**   What said he?

OPHELIA: He took me by the wrist, and held me hard,
    Then goes he to the length of all his arm,°
    And with his other hand thus o'er his brow,
    He falls to such perusal of my face

90   As° a' would draw it; long stayed he so,
    At last, a little shaking of mine arm,
    And thrice his head thus waving up and down,
    He raised a sigh so piteous and profound
    As it did seem to shatter all his bulk,°

95   And end his being; that done, he lets me go,
    And with his head over his shoulder turned
    He seemed to find his way without his eyes,
    For out adoors he went without their helps,
    And to the last bended their light on me.

POLONIUS: Come, go with me, I will go seek the king,
    This is the very ecstasy° of love,
    Whose violent property fordoes itself,°
    And leads the will to desperate undertakings
    As oft as any passion under heaven

105   That does afflict our natures: I am sorry.
    What, have you given him any hard words of late?

OPHELIA: No my good lord, but as you did command
    I did repel his letters, and denied
    His access to me.

POLONIUS: That hath made him mad.

110   I am sorry that with better heed and judgment
    I had not quoted° him. I feared he did but trifle
    And meant to wrack° thee, but beshrew my jealousy.°
    By heaven it is as proper to our age
    To cast beyond ourselves in our opinions,°

115   As it is common for the younger sort

°76 *closet*: private room. 77 *doublet all unbraced*: jacket all unfastened. 79 *down-gyvèd*: down around his ankles (like prisoners' fetters or gyves). 81 *purport*: expression. 87 *goes . . . arm*: holds me at arm's length. 90 *As*: as if. 94 *bulk*: body. 101 *ecstasy*: madness. 102 *Whose . . . itself*: that, by its violent nature, destroys the lover. 111 *quoted*: observed. 112 *wrack*: ruin. *beshrew my jealousy*: curse my suspicion. 113–14 *proper . . . opinions*: natural for old people to read more into something than is actually there.

To lack discretion; come, go we to the king,
This must be known, which being kept close, might move
More grief to hide, than hate to utter love.°   [*Exeunt.*]

Scene 2. [A room in the castle]

Flourish. Enter KING *and* QUEEN, ROSENCRANTZ *and* GUILDENSTERN, *cum aliis.*

KING: Welcome dear Rosencrantz and Guildenstern.
    Moreover° that we much did long to see you,
    The need we have to use you did provoke
    Our hasty sending. Something have you heard
    Of Hamlet's transformation—so call it.   5
    Sith° nor th'exterior nor the inward man
    Resembles that it was. What it should be,
    More than his father's death, that thus hath put him
    So much from th'understanding of himself,
    I cannot dream of: I entreat you both,   10
    That being of so young days° brought up with him,
    And sith so neighboured to his youth and haviour,
    That you vouchsafe your rest° here in our court
    Some little time, so by your companies
    To draw him on to pleasures, and to gather   15
    So much as from occasion you may glean,
    Whether aught to us unknown afflicts him thus,
    That opened° lies within our remedy.
QUEEN: Good gentlemen, he hath much talked of you,
    And sure I am, two men there are not living   20
    To whom he more adheres. If it will please you
    To show us so much gentry° and good will,
    As to expend your time with us awhile,
    For the supply and profit of our hope,
    Your visitation shall receive such thanks   25
    As fits a king's remembrance.
ROSENCRANTZ: Both your majesties
    Might by the sovereign power you have of us,
    Put your dread pleasures more into command
    Than to entreaty.
GUILDENSTERN: But we both obey,
    And here give up ourselves in the full bent,°   30
    To lay our service freely at your feet
    To be commanded.
KING: Thanks Rosencrantz, and gentle Guildenstern.
QUEEN: Thanks Guildenstern, and gentle Rosencrantz.
    And I beseech you instantly to visit   35
    My too much changèd son. Go some of you
    And bring these gentlemen where Hamlet is.

°117–18 *being kept . . . love:* if kept secret, might cause more grief than if we risked the king's displeasure.
2 *Moreover:* in addition to the fact. 6 *Sith:* since. 11 *of . . . days:* from your early days. 13 *vouchsafe your rest:* agree
to stay. 18 *opened:* discovered. 22 *gentry:* courtesy. 30 *in the full bent:* to the utmost (in archery, bending the bow).

GUILDENSTERN: Heavens make our presence and our practices°
    Pleasant and helpful to him.
QUEEN: Ay, amen.

                                  Exeunt ROSENCRANTZ *and* GUILDENSTERN.

Enter POLONIUS.

40   POLONIUS: Th'ambassadors from Norway my good lord,
        Are joyfully returned.
    KING: Thou still° hast been the father of good news.
    POLONIUS: Have I, my lord? Assure you, my good liege,
        I hold my duty as I hold my soul,
45   Both to my God and to my gracious king;
        And I do think, or else this brain of mine
        Hunts not the trail of policy° so sure
        As it hath used to do, that I have found
        The very cause of Hamlet's lunacy.
50   KING: O speak of that, that do I long to hear.
    POLONIUS: Give first admittance to th'ambassadors,
        My news shall be the fruit° to that great feast.
    KING: Thyself do grace to them, and bring them in.   *[Exit* POLONIUS.]
        He tells me my dear Gertrude, he hath found
55   The head and source of all your son's distemper.
    QUEEN: I doubt° it is no other but the main,
        His father's death and our o'erhasty marriage.
    KING: Well, we shall sift him.

Enter POLONIUS, VALTEMAND, *and* CORNELIUS.

                  Welcome, my good friends.
        Say Valtemand, what from our brother Norway?
60   VALTEMAND: Most fair return of greetings and desires;
        Upon our first,° he sent out to suppress
        His nephew's levies, which to him appeared
        To be a preparation 'gainst the Polack,
        But better looked into, he truly found
65   It was against your highness, whereat grieved
        That so his sickness, age, and impotence
        Was falsely borne in hand,° sends out arrests
        On Fortinbras, which he in brief obeys,
        Receives rebuke from Norway, and in fine,°
70   Makes vow before his uncle never more
        To give th'assay° of arms against your majesty:
        Whereon old Norway, overcome with joy,
        Gives him threescore thousand crowns in annual fee,
        And his commission to employ those soldiers
75   So levied (as before) against the Polack,
        With an entreaty herein further shown,
        That it might please you to give quiet pass°
        Through your dominions for this enterprise,

°38 *practices:* (1) actions (2) plots. 42 *still:* always. 47 *policy:* (1) politics (2) plots. 52 *fruit:* dessert. 56 *doubt:* suspect. 61 *first:* first presentation. 67 *borne in hand:* deceived. 69 *fine:* finishing. 71 *assay:* test. 77 *pass:* passage.

On such regards of safety and allowance
As therein are set down.
KING: It likes° us well,   [*Giving a paper.*]   80
And at our more considered time° we'll read,
Answer, and think upon this business:
Meantime, we thank you for your well-took labour,
Go to your rest, at night we'll feast together.
Most welcome home.   *Exeunt* AMBASSADORS.
POLONIUS: This business is well ended.   85
My liege and madam, to expostulate°
What majesty should be, what duty is,
Why day is day, night night, and time is time.
Were nothing but to waste night, day, and time.
Therefore since brevity is the soul of wit,°   90
And tediousness the limbs and outward flourishes,°
I will be brief. Your noble son is mad:
Mad call I it, for to define true madness,
What is't but to be nothing else but mad?
But let that go.
QUEEN: More matter, with less art.   95
POLONIUS: Madam, I swear I use no art at all:
That he is mad 'tis true: 'tis true, 'tis pity,
And pity 'tis 'tis true: a foolish figure,°
But farewell it, for I will use no art.
Mad let us grant him then, and now remains   100
That we find out the cause of this effect,
Or rather say, the cause of this defect,
For this effect defective comes by cause:
Thus it remains, and the remainder thus.
Perpend.°   105
I have a daughter, have while she is mine,
Who in her duty and obedience, mark,
Hath given me this, now gather and surmise.
[*Reads.*] "To the celestial, and my soul's idol, the most
beautified° Ophelia,"—   110
That's an ill phrase, a vile phrase, "beautified" is a vile
phrase, but you shall hear. Thus: [*Reads.*]
"In her excellent white bosom, these," &c.—
QUEEN: Came this from Hamlet to her?
POLONIUS: Good madam stay awhile, I will be faithful.   [*Reads.*]   115
"Doubt thou the stars are fire,
    Doubt that the sun doth move,°
Doubt° truth to be a liar,
    But never doubt I love.
O dear Ophelia, I am ill at these numbers, I have not   120
art to reckon° my groans, but that I love thee best, O
most best, believe it. Adieu.

°80 *likes:* pleases. 81 *at . . . time:* when time is available for consideration. 86 *expostulate:* discuss. 90 *wit:* understanding. 91 *tediousness . . . flourishes:* embellishments and flourishes cause tedium. 98 *figure:* rhetorical figure. 105 *Perpend:* consider. 110 *beautified:* beautiful. 117 *move:* (as it was believed to do, around the earth). 118 *Doubt:* suspect. 121 *reckon:* express in meter.

Thine evermore, most dear lady, whilst
this machine° is to° him, Hamlet."

125   This in obedience hath my daughter shown me,
And more above hath his solicitings,
As they fell out by time, by means, and place,
All given to mine ear.

KING: But how hath she
Received his love?

POLONIUS: What do you think of me?

130   KING: As of a man faithful and honourable.

POLONIUS: I would fain prove so. But what might you think
When I had seen this hot love on the wing,
As I perceived it (I must tell you that)
Before my daughter told me, what might you,
135   Or my dear majesty your queen here think,
If I had played the desk or table-book,°
Or given my heart a winking° mute and dumb,
Or looked upon this love with idle° sight,
What might you think? No, I went round to work,
140   And my young mistress this I did bespeak,
"Lord Hamlet is a prince out of thy star,°
This must not be:" and then I prescripts° gave her
That she should lock herself from his resort,°
Admit no messengers, receive no tokens:
145   Which done, she took the fruits of my advice,
And he repelléd, a short tale to make,
Fell into a sadness, then into a fast,
Thence to a watch,° thence into a weakness,
Thence to a lightness,° and by this declension,
150   Into the madness wherein now he raves,
And all we mourn for.

KING: Do you think 'tis this?

QUEEN: It may be, very like.

POLONIUS: Hath there been such a time, I would fain know that,
That I have positively said "'Tis so,"
When it proved otherwise?

155   KING: Not that I know.

POLONIUS: Take this, from this, if this be otherwise;

[*Points to his head and shoulder.*]

If circumstances lead me, I will find
Where truth is hid, though it were hid indeed
Within the center.

KING: How may we try° it further?

°124 *machine:* body. *to:* attached to. 136 *played . . . book:* kept it concealed as in a desk or personal notebook. 137 *given . . . winking:* had my heart shut its eyes to the matter. 138 *idle:* unseeing. 141 *out . . . star:* out of your sphere (above you in station). 142 *prescripts:* orders. 143 *resort:* company. 148 *watch:* sleeplessness. 149 *lightness:* lightheadedness. 159 *try:* test.

POLONIUS: You know sometimes he walks four hours together 160
    Here in the lobby.
QUEEN: So he does indeed.
POLONIUS: At such a time, I'll loose° my daughter to him.
    Be you and I behind an arras° then,
    Mark the encounter: if he love her not,
    And be not from his reason fall'n thereon, 165
    Let me be no assistant for a state,°
    But keep a farm and carters.
KING: We will try it.

Enter HAMLET reading on a book.

QUEEN: But look where sadly the poor wretch comes reading.
POLONIUS: Away, I do beseech you both away,
    I'll board him presently,° O give me leave.   *Exeunt KING and QUEEN.* 170
    How does my good Lord Hamlet?
HAMLET: Well, God-a-mercy.
POLONIUS: Do you know me, my lord?
HAMLET: Excellent well, you are a fishmonger.°
POLONIUS: Not I my lord. 175
HAMLET: Then I would you were so honest a man.
POLONIUS: Honest, my lord?
HAMLET: Ay sir, to be honest as this world goes, is to be one
    man picked out of ten thousand.
POLONIUS: That's very true, my lord. 180
HAMLET: For if the sun breed maggots° in a dead dog, being a good
    kissing carrion°—have you a daughter?
POLONIUS: I have my lord.
HAMLET: Let her not walk i'th'sun:° conception° is a blessing, but as
    your daughter may conceive, friend look to'it. 185
POLONIUS: [*Aside.*] How say you by that? Still harping on my daughter,
    yet he knew me not at first, a' said I was a fishmonger.
    A' is far gone, far gone, and truly in my youth, I suffered
    much extremity for love, very near this. I'll speak to him
    again. What do you read my lord? 190
HAMLET: Words, words, words.
POLONIUS: What is the matter my lord?
HAMLET: Between who?
POLONIUS: I mean the matter° that you read, my lord.
HAMLET: Slanders sir; for the satirical rogue says here, that old men 195
    have grey beards, that their faces are wrinkled, their eyes
    purging thick amber and plum-tree gum,° and that they
    have a plentiful lack of wit, together with most weak
    hams. All which sir, though I most powerfully and

°162 *loose*: (1) release (2) turn loose. 163 *arras*: hanging tapestry. 166 *assistant . . . state*: state official. 170 *board him presently*: approach him immediately. 174 *fishmonger*: (1) fish dealer (2) pimp. 181 *breed maggots*: (in the belief that the rays of the sun caused maggots to breed in dead flesh). 182 *kissing carrion*: piece of flesh for kissing. 184 *Let . . . sun*: (1) (proverbial: "out of God's blessing, into the warm sun") (2) because the sun is a breeder (3) don't let her go near me (with a pun on "sun" and "son"). *conception*: (1) understanding (2) pregnancy. 194 *matter*: (1) content (Polonius's meaning) (2) cause of a quarrel (Hamlet's interpretation). 197 *purging . . . gum*: exuding a viscous yellowish discharge.

200   potently believe, yet I hold it not honesty° to have it thus set
        down, for yourself sir shall grow old as I am: if like a crab
        you could go backward.
     POLONIUS: [*Aside.*] Though this be madness, yet there is method
        in't.
205   Will you walk out of the air° my lord?
     HAMLET: Into my grave.
     POLONIUS: [*Aside.*] Indeed that's out of the air; how pregnant°
        sometimes his replies are, a happiness° that often
        madness hits on, which reason and sanity could not so
210   prosperously° be delivered of. I will leave him, and
        suddenly contrive the means of meeting between him
        and my daughter. My honourable lord, I will most
        humbly take leave of you.
     HAMLET: You cannot sir take from me anything that I will more
215   willingly part withal: except my life, except my life,
        except my life.
     POLONIUS: Fare you well my lord.
     HAMLET: These tedious old fools.

Enter ROSENCRANTZ and GUILDENSTERN.

     POLONIUS: You go to seek the Lord Hamlet, there he is.
220   ROSENCRANTZ: [*To POLONIUS.*] God save you sir.   [*Exit POLONIUS.*]
     GUILDENSTERN: My honoured lord.
     ROSENCRANTZ: My most dear lord.
     HAMLET: My excellent good friends, how dost thou Guildenstern?
        Ah Rosencrantz, good lads, how do you both?
225   ROSENCRANTZ: As the indifferent° children of the earth.
     GUILDENSTERN: Happy, in that we are not over-happy:
        On Fortune's cap we are not the very button.°
     HAMLET: Nor the soles of her shoe?
     ROSENCRANTZ: Neither my lord.
230   HAMLET: Then you live about her waist, or in the middle of her
        favours?
     GUILDENSTERN: Faith, her privates° we.
     HAMLET: In the secret parts of Fortune? O most true, she is a
        strumpet.° What news?
235   ROSENCRANTZ: None my lord, but that the world's grown honest.
     HAMLET: Then is doomsday near: but your news is not true. Let me
        question more in particular: what have you my good
        friends, deserved at the hands of Fortune, that she sends
        you to prison hither?
240   GUILDENSTERN: Prison, my lord?
     HAMLET: Denmark's a prison.
     ROSENCRANTZ: Then is the world one.

°200 *honesty*: decency. 205 *out . . . air*: (in the belief that fresh air was bad for the sick). 207 *pregnant*: full of meaning. 208 *happiness*: aptness. 210 *prosperously*: successfully. 225 *indifferent*: ordinary. 227 *On Fortune's . . . button*: we are not at the height of our fortunes. 232 *privates*: (1) intimate friend (2) private parts. 234 *strumpet*: inconstant woman, giving favor to many.

HAMLET: A goodly one, in which there are many confines, wards,°
    and dungeons; Denmark being one o'th'worst.

ROSENCRANTZ: We think not so my lord.   245

HAMLET: Why then 'tis none to you; for there is nothing either good
    or bad, but thinking makes it so: to me it is a prison.

ROSENCRANTZ: Why then your ambition makes it one: 'tis too narrow for
    your mind.

HAMLET: O God, I could be bounded in a nutshell, and count   250
    myself a king of infinite space; were it not that I have bad
    dreams.

GUILDENSTERN: Which dreams indeed are ambition: for the very substance
    of the ambitious, is merely the shadow of a dream.

HAMLET: A dream itself is but a shadow.   255

ROSENCRANTZ: Truly, and I hold ambition of so airy and light a quality,
    that it is but a shadow's shadow.

HAMLET: Then are our beggars bodies, and our monarchs and
    outstretched heroes the beggars' shadows:° shall we to th'
    court? for by my fay,° I cannot reason.   260

BOTH: We'll wait upon° you.

HAMLET: No such matter. I will not sort° you with the rest of my
    servants: for to speak to you like an honest man, I am most
    dreadfully attended. But in the beaten way of friendship,
    what make you at Elsinore?   265

ROSENCRANTZ: To visit you my lord, no other occasion.

HAMLET: Beggar that I am, I am even poor in thanks, but I thank
    you, and sure dear friends, my thanks are too dear a
    halfpenny:° were you not sent for? is it your own inclining?
    is it a free° visitation? come, come, deal justly with me,   270
    come, come, nay speak.

GUILDENSTERN: What should we say my lord?

HAMLET: Anything but to th'purpose: you were sent for, and there
    is a kind of confession in your looks, which your modesties
    have not craft enough to colour: I know the good king and   275
    queen have sent for you.

ROSENCRANTZ: To what end my lord?

HAMLET: That you must teach me: but let me conjure° you, by the
    rights of our fellowship, by the consonancy of our youth,°
    by the obligation of our ever-preserved love, and by what   280
    more dear a better proposer can charge you withal,° be
    even and direct with me whether you were sent for or no.

ROSENCRANTZ: [*Aside to* GUILDENSTERN.] What say you?

HAMLET: Nay then, I have an eye of° you: If you love me,
    hold not off.   285

GUILDENSTERN: My lord, we were sent for.

HAMLET: I will tell you why, so shall my anticipation prevent° your

---

°243 *wards*: cells. 258–59 *Then are . . . shadows*: then beggars are the true substance and ambitious kings and heroes the elongated shadows of beggars' bodies (for only a real substance can cast a shadow). 260 *fay*: faith. 261
wait upon: attend. 262 *sort*: class. 268–69 *too dear a halfpenny*: worth not even a halfpenny (as I have no influence). 270 *free*: voluntary. 278 *conjure*: appeal to. 279 *consonancy . . . youth*: agreement in our ages. 281 *withal*:
with. 284 *of*: on. 287 *prevent*: forestall.

discovery,° and your secrecy to the king and queen moult
no feather.° I have of late, but wherefore I know not, lost all
290   my mirth, forgone all custom of exercises: and indeed it
goes so heavily with my disposition, that this goodly
frame the earth, seems to me a sterile promontory, this
most excellent canopy the air, look you, this brave°
o'erhanging firmament, this majestical roof fretted° with
295   golden fire,° why it appeareth nothing to me but a foul and
pestilent congregation of vapours.° What a piece of work is
a man! How noble in reason, how infinite in faculties,° in
form and moving, how express° and admirable in action,
how like an angel in apprehension, how like a god: the
300   beauty of the world; the paragon of animals; and yet to
me, what is this quintessence of dust? Man delights not
me, no, nor woman neither, though by your smiling, you
seem to say so.
ROSENCRANTZ: My lord, there was no such stuff in my thoughts.
305   HAMLET: Why did ye laugh then, when I said 'man delights not me'?
ROSENCRANTZ: To think, my lord, if you delight not in man, what lenten
entertainment° the players shall receive from you: we coted°
them on the way, and hither are they coming to offer you
service.
310   HAMLET: He that plays the king shall be welcome, his majesty shall
have tribute of me, the adventurous knight° shall use his
foil and target,° the lover shall not sigh gratis,° the humorous
man° shall end his part in peace,° the clown shall make
those laugh whose lungs are tickle o'th'sere,° and the lady
315   shall say her mind freely: or the blank verse shall halt° for't.
What players are they?
ROSENCRANTZ: Even those you were wont to take such delight in, the
tragedians of the city.
HAMLET: How chances it they travel? Their residence° both in
320   reputation and profit was better both ways.
ROSENCRANTZ: I think their inhibition comes by the means of the late innovation.°
HAMLET: Do they hold the same estimation they did when I was in
the city; are they so followed?
325   ROSENCRANTZ: No indeed are they not.
HAMLET: How comes it? Do they grow rusty?
ROSENCRANTZ: Nay, their endeavour keeps in the wonted pace; but there
is sir an aery° of children, like eyases,° that cry out on the

---

°288 *discovery:* disclosure. 288–89 *moult no feather:* change in no way. 293 *brave:* splendid. 294 *fretted:* ornamented with fretwork. 295 *golden fire:* stars. 296 *pestilent . . . vapours:* (clouds were believed to carry contagion). 297
faculties: physical powers. 298 *express:* well framed. 306–7 *lenten entertainment:* meager treatment. 307 *coted:*
passed. 311 *adventurous knight:* knight errant (a popular stage character). 312 *foil and target:* sword blunted for
stage fighting, and small shield. 312 *gratis:* (without applause). 312–13 *humorous man:* eccentric character with a
dominant trait, caused by an excess of one of the four humors, or bodily fluids. 313 *in peace:* without interruption.
314 *tickle o'th'sere:* attuned to respond to laughter, as the finely adjusted gunlock responds to the touch of the trigger (fr. hunting). 315 *halt:* limp (if she adds her own opinions and spoils the meter). 319 *residence:* i.e., in a city
theatre. 321–22 *inhibition . . . innovation:* i.e., they were forced out of town by a more popular theatrical fashion.
The following speeches allude to the "War of the Theatres" (1601–1602) between the child and adult acting
companies. 328 *aery:* nest. *eyases:* young hawks.

top of question,° and are most tyrannically° clapped for't:
these are now the fashion, and so berattle° the common　　330
stages° (so they call them) that many wearing rapiers° are
afraid of goose-quills,° and dare scarce come thither.

HAMLET: What, are they children? Who maintains 'em? How are
they escoted°? Will they pursue the quality no longer than
they can sing°? Will they not say afterwards if they should　　335
grow themselves to common players (as it is most like, if
their means are not better) their writers do them wrong, to
make them exclaim against their own succession°?

ROSENCRANTZ: Faith, there has been much to-do on both sides: and the
nation holds it no sin to tarre° them to controversy. There　　340
was for a while, no money bid for argument,° unless the
poet and the player went to cuffs in the question.°

HAMLET: Is't possible?

GUILDENSTERN: O there has been much throwing about of brains.

HAMLET: Do the boys carry it away°?　　345

ROSENCRANTZ: Ay, that they do my lord, Hercules and his load too.°

HAMLET: It is not very strange, for my uncle is king of Denmark,
and those that would make mows° at him while my father
lived, give twenty, forty, fifty, a hundred ducats apiece
for his picture in little.° 'Sblood,° there is something in this　　350
more than natural, if philosophy° could find it out.

A flourish for the PLAYERS.

GUILDENSTERN: There are the players.

HAMLET: Gentlemen, you are welcome to Elsinore: your hands,
come then, th'appurtenance° of welcome is fashion and
ceremony; let me comply with you in this garb,° lest my　　355
extent° to the players, which I tell you must show fairly
outwards, should more appear like entertainment than
yours.° You are welcome: but my uncle-father, and aunt-mother,
are deceived.

GUILDENSTERN: In what my dear lord?　　360

HAMLET: I am but mad north-north-west; when the wind is southerly,
I know a hawk from a handsaw.°

Enter POLONIUS.

POLONIUS: Well be with you, gentlemen.

°328–29 *that cry . . . question:* whose shrill voices can be heard above all others. 329 *tyrannically:* strongly. 330 *berattle:* berate. 330–31 *common stages:* public playhouses (the children's companies performed in private theatres). 331 *wearing rapiers:* (worn by gentlemen). 332 *goose-quills:* pens (of satirical dramatists who wrote for the children). 334 *escoted:* supported. 334–35 *pursue . . . sing:* continue acting only until their voices change. 338 *succession:* inheritance. 340 *tarre:* provoke. 341 *bid for argument:* paid for the plot of a proposed play. 342 *went . . . question:* came to blows on the subject. 345 *carry it away:* carry off the prize. 346 *Hercules . . . too:* (Shakespeare's own company at the Globe Theater, whose sign was Hercules carrying the globe of the world). 348 *mows:* mouths, grimaces. 350 *little:* a miniature. *'Sblood:* by God's blood. 351 *philosophy:* science. 354 *appurtenance:* accessory. 355 *comply . . . garb:* observe the formalities with you in this style. 356 *extent:* i.e., of welcome. 357–58 *should . . . yours:* should appear more hospitable than yours. 362 *I know . . . handsaw:* I can tell the difference between two things that are unlike ("hawk" = [1] bird of prey [2] mattock, pickaxe; "handsaw" = [1] hernshaw or heron bird [2] small saw).

HAMLET: Hark you Guildenstern, and you too, at each ear a hearer:
365   that great baby you see there is not yet out of his swaddling
    clouts.°
ROSENCRANTZ: Happily° he is the second time come to them, for they say
    an old man is twice a child.
HAMLET: I will prophesy, he comes to tell me of the players, mark
370   it.—You say right sir, a Monday morning, 'twas then
    indeed.
POLONIUS: My lord, I have news to tell you.
HAMLET: My lord, I have news to tell you. When Roscius° was an
    actor in Rome—
375 POLONIUS: The actors are come hither, my lord
HAMLET: Buz, buz.°
POLONIUS: Upon my honour.
HAMLET: Then came each actor on his ass—
POLONIUS: The best actors in the world, either for tragedy, comedy,
380   history, pastoral, pastoral-comical, historical-pastoral,
    tragical-historical, tragical-comical-historical-pastoral,
    scene individable,° or poem unlimited.° Seneca cannot be
    too heavy, nor Plautus° too light for the law of writ, and the
    liberty:° these are the only men.
385 HAMLET: O Jephthah,° judge of Israel, what a treasure hadst thou
POLONIUS: What a treasure had he, my lord?
HAMLET: Why
      'One fair daughter and no more,
        The which he lovèd passing° well.'
390 POLONIUS: [*Aside.*] Still on my daughter
HAMLET: Am I not i'th' right, old Jephthah?
POLONIUS: If you call me Jephthah my lord, I have a daughter that I
    love passing well.
HAMLET: Nay, that follows not.
395 POLONIUS: What follows then, my lord?
HAMLET: Why
        "As by lot, God wot,"
    and then you know
        "It came to pass, as most like° it was:"
400   the first row° of the pious chanson will show you more, for
    look where my abridgement° comes.

Enter four or five PLAYERS.

    You are welcome masters, welcome all. I am glad to see
    thee well: welcome, good friends. O my old friend, why
    thy face is valanced° since I saw thee last, com'st thou to
405   beard me in Denmark? What, my young lady° and

°365–66 *swaddling clouts:* strips of cloth binding a newborn baby. 367 *Happily:* perhaps. 373 *Roscius:* famous
Roman actor. 376 *Buz, buz:* (contemptuous). 382 *scene individable:* play observing the unities (time, place, action). *poem unlimited:* play ignoring the unities. 382–83 *Seneca, Plautus:* Roman writers of tragedy and comedy,
respectively. 383–84 *law . . . liberty:* "rules" regarding the unities and those exercising freedom from the unities.
385 *Jephthah:* (who was forced to sacrifice his only daughter because of a rash promise: Judges 11:29–39). 389
passing: surpassingly. 399 *like:* likely. 400 *row:* stanza. 401 *abridgement:* (the players who will cut short my song).
404 *valanced:* fringed with a beard. 405 *lady:* boy playing women's role.

mistress? by'r lady, your ladyship is nearer to heaven than
when I saw you last, by the altitude of a chopine.° Pray
God your voice, like a piece of uncurrent° gold, be not
cracked within the ring.° Masters, you are all welcome:
we'll e'en to't like French falconers, fly at any thing we see:°   410
we'll have a speech straight. Come give us a taste of your
quality: come, a passionate speech.

1. PLAYER: What speech, my good lord?

HAMLET: I heard thee speak me a speech once, but it was never
acted, or if it was, not above once, for the play I remember   415
pleased not the million, 'twas caviary to the general,° but it
was (as I received it, and others, whose judgments in such
matters cried in the top of mine°) an excellent play, well
digested in the scenes, set down with as much modesty as
cunning.° I remember one said there were no sallets.° In the   420
lines, to make the matter savoury, nor no matter in the
phrase that might indict the author of° affection, but called
it an honest method, as wholesome as sweet, and by very
much more handsome than fine:° one speech in't I chiefly
loved, 'twas Aeneas' tale to Dido, and thereabout of it   425
especially where he speaks of Priam's slaughter.° If it live in
your memory begin at this line, let me see, let me see:
       "The rugged Pyrrhus,° like th'Hyrcanian beast'°—   430
'tis not so: it begins with Pyrrhus—
       "The rugged Pyrrhus, he whose sable° arms,
Black as his purpose, did the night resemble
When he lay couched in th'ominous horse,°
Hath now this dread and black complexion smeared
With heraldy more dismal: head to foot
Now is he total gules,° horridly tricked°   435
With blood of fathers, mothers, daughters, sons,
Baked and impasted° with the parching° streets,
That lend a tyrannous and damnèd light
To their lord's murder. Roasted in wrath and fire,
And thus o'er-sizèd° with coagulate gore,   440
With eyes like carbuncles,° the hellish Pyrrhus
Old grandsire Priam seeks;"
So proceed you.

POLONIUS: 'Fore God, my lord, well spoken, with good accent and
good discretion.°   445

1. PLAYER: "Anon he finds him,
Striking too short at Greeks, his antique° sword,

°407 *chopine*: thick-soled shoe. 408 *uncurrent*: not legal tender. 409 *ring*: (1) ring enclosing the design on a gold
coin (to crack it within the ring [to steal the gold] made it "uncurrent") (2) sound. 410 *fly . . . see*: undertake any
difficulty. 416 *caviary . . . general*: like caviar, too rich for the general public. 418 *cried . . . mine*: spoke with
more authority than mine. 419–20 *modesty as cunning*: moderation as skill. 420 *sallets*: spicy bits. 422 *indict . . .
of*: charge . . . with. 424 *handsome than fine*: dignified than finely wrought. 426 *Priam's slaughter*: the murder of
the King of Troy (as told in the Aeneid). 428 *Pyrrhus*: son of Achilles. *Hyrcanian beast*: tiger noted for fierceness.
430 *sable*: black. 432 *horse*: the hollow wooden horse used by the Greeks to enter Troy. 435 *gules*: red. *horridly
tricked*: horribly decorated. 437 *impasted*: coagulated. *parching*: (because the city was on fire). 440 *o'er-sizèd*: covered over. 441 *carbuncles*: red gems. 445 *discretion*: interpretation. 447 *antique*: ancient.

Rebellious to his arm, lies where it falls,
Repugnant to command,° unequal matched,
450 Pyrrhus at Priam drives, in rage strikes wide,
But with the whiff and wind of his fell° sword,
Th'unnerved father falls: then senseless Ilium,°
Seeming to feel this blow, with flaming top
Stoops to his base; and with a hideous crash
455 Takes prisoner Pyrrhus' ear. For lo, his sword
Which was declining on the milky head
Of reverend Priam, seemed i'th'air to stick;
So as a painted° tyrant Pyrrhus stood,
And like a neutral to his will and matter,°
460 Did nothing:
But as we often see, against° some storm,
A silence in the heavens, the rack° stand still,
The bold winds speechless, and the orb° below
As hush as death, anon the dreadful thunder
465 Doth rend the region, so after Pyrrhus' pause,
A rousèd vengeance sets him new awork,
And never did the Cyclops'° hammers fall
On Mars's armour, forged for proof eterne,°
With less remorse than Pyrrhus' bleeding sword
470 Now falls on Priam.
Out, out, thou strumpet Fortune: all you gods,
In general synod° take away her power,
Break all the spokes and fellies from her wheel,°
And bowl the round nave° down the hill of heaven
475 As low as to the fiends."°

POLONIUS: This is too long.

HAMLET: It shall to the barber's with your beard; prithee say on: he's
for a jig, or a tale of bawdry, or he sleeps. Say on, come to
Hecuba.

480 **1. PLAYER:** "But who, ah woe, had seen the mobled° queen—"

HAMLET: "The mobled queen"?

POLONIUS: That's good, "mobled queen" is good.

1. PLAYER: "Run barefoot up and down, threat'ning the flames
With bissom rheum,° a clout° upon that head
485 Where late the diadem stood, and for a robe,
About her lank and all o'er-teemèd° loins,
A blanket in the alarm of fear caught up—
Who this had seen, with tongue in venom steeped,
'Gainst Fortune's state° would treason have pronounced;
490 But if the gods themselves did see her then,
When she saw Pyrrhus make malicious sport

°449 *Repugnant to command:* refusing to obey its commander. 451 *fell:* savage. 452 *senseless Ilium:* unfeeling Troy.
458 *painted:* pictured. 459 *like . . . matter:* unmoved by either his purpose or its achievement. 461 *against:* before.
462 *rack:* clouds. 463 *orb:* earth. 467 *Cyclops:* workmen of Vulcan, armorer of the gods. 468 *for proof eterne:* to be
eternally invincible. 472 *synod:* assembly. 473 *fellies . . . wheel:* curved pieces of the rim of the wheel that fortune
turns, representing a man's fortunes. 474 *nave:* hub. 475 *fiends:* i.e., of hell. 480 *mobled:* muffled in a scarf. 484
bissom rheum: binding tears. *clout:* cloth. 486 *o'er-teemèd:* worn out by excessive childbearing. 489 *state:* reign.

In mincing with his sword her husband's limbs,
The instant burst of clamour that she made,
Unless things mortal move them not at all,
Would have made milch° the burning eyes of heaven,   495
And passion in the gods."
POLONIUS: Look where° he has not turned° his colour, and has tears in's
    eyes, prithee no more.
HAMLET: 'Tis well, I'll have thee speak out the rest of this soon.
    Good my lord, will you see the players well bestowed,° do   500
    you hear, let them be well used, for they are the abstract°
    and brief chronicles° of the time; after your death you were
    better have a bad epitaph than their ill report while you
    live.
POLONIUS: My lord, I will use them according to their desert.°   505
HAMLET: God's bodkin° man, much better. Use every man after° his
    desert, and who shall 'scape whipping? Use them after
    you own honour and dignity: the less they deserve, the
    more merit is in your bounty. Take them in.
POLONIUS: Come sirs.   *Exeunt* POLONIUS *and* PLAYERS.   510
HAMLET: Follow him friends, we'll hear a play tomorrow; [*Stops the*
    FIRST PLAYER.] dost thou hear me, old friend, can you play
    The Murder of Gonzago?
1. PLAYER: Ay my lord.
HAMLET: We'll ha't tomorrow night. You could for a need° study a   515
    speech of some dozen or sixteen lines, which I would set
    down and insert in't, could you not?
1. PLAYER: Ay my lord.
HAMLET: Very well, follow that lord, and look you mock him not.

                                           [*Exit* FIRST PLAYER.]

[*To* ROSENCRANTZ *and* GUILDENSTERN.] My good friends, I'll   520
    leave you till night, you are welcome to Elsinore.
ROSENCRANTZ: Good my lord.

                          [*Exeunt* ROSENCRANTZ *and* GUILDENSTERN.]

HAMLET: Ay so, God bye to you.—Now I am alone.
    O what a rogue and peasant slave am I.
    Is it not monstrous that this player here,   525
    But in a fiction, in a dream of passion,°
    Could force his soul so to his own conceit°
    That from her working all his visage wanned,°
    Tears in his eyes, distraction in his aspect,
    A broken voice, and his whole function° suiting   530
    With forms° to his conceit; and all for nothing,

°495 *milch:* milky, moist. 497 *where:* whether. *turned:* changed. 500 *bestowed:* lodged. 501 *abstract:* summary (noun). 502 *brief chronicles:* history in brief. 505 *desert:* merit. 506 *God's bodkin:* God's little body, the communion wafer (an oath). *after:* according to. 515 *for a need:* if necessary. 526 *dream of passion:* portrayal of emotion. 527 *conceit:* imagination. 528 *wanned:* grew pale. 530 *function:* bearing. 531 *With forms:* in appearance.

For Hecuba!
What's Hecuba to him, or he to Hecuba,
That he should weep for her? what would he do,
535 Had he the motive and the cue for passion
That I have? he would drown the stage with tears,
And cleave the general ear° with horrid speech,
Make mad the guilty and appal the free,°
Confound° the ignorant, and amaze indeed
540 The very faculties of eyes and ears; yet I,
A dull and muddy-mettled° rascal, peak°
Like John-a-dreams, unpregnant of° my cause,
And can say nothing; no, not for a king,
Upon whose property and most dear life,
545 A damned defeat was made: am I a coward?
Who calls me villain, breaks my pate° across,
Plucks off my beard° and blows it in my face,
Tweaks me by the nose, gives me the lie i'th'throat
As deep as to the lungs,° who does me this?
550 Ha, 'swounds,° I should take it; for it cannot be
But I am pigeon-livered,° and lack gall
To make oppression bitter, or ere this
I should ha' fatted all the region kites°
With this slave's offal: bloody, bawdy villain,
555 Remorseless, treacherous, lecherous, kindless° villain!
O vengeance!
Why what an ass am I, this is most brave,°
That I, the son of a dear father murdered,
Prompted to my revenge by heaven and hell,
560 Must like a whore unpack my heart with words,
And fall a-cursing like a very drab,°
A scullion,° fie upon't, foh.
About, my brains; hum, I have heard,
That guilty creatures sitting at a play,
Have by the very cunning of the scene
565 Been struck so to the soul, that presently°
They have proclaimed their malefactions:
For murder, though it have no tongue, will speak
With most miraculous organ: I'll have these players
570 Play something like the murder of my father
Before mine uncle, I'll observe his looks,
I'll tent° him to the quick, if a' do blench°
I know my course. The spirit that I have seen
May be a devil, and the devil hath power
575 T'assume a pleasing shape, yea, and perhaps

°537 *general ear*: ears of all in the audience. 538 *free*: innocent. 539 *Confound*: confuse. 541 *muddy-mettled*: dull-spirited. *peak*: pine, mope. 542 *John-a-dreams*: a daydreaming fellow. *unpregnant of*: unstirred by. 546 *pate*: head. 547 *Plucks . . . beard*: (a way of giving insult). 548–49 *gives . . . lungs*: insults me by calling me a liar of the worst kind (the lungs being deeper than the throat). 550 *'swounds*: God's wounds. 551 *pigeon-livered*: meek and uncourageous. 553 *region kites*: vultures of the upper air. 555 *kindless*: unnatural. 557 *brave*: fine. 561 *drab*: whore. 562 *scullion*: kitchen wench. 566 *presently*: immediately. 572 *tent*: probe. *blench*: flinch.

Out of my weakness, and my melancholy,
As he is very potent with such spirits,
Abuses me to damn me; I'll have grounds
More relative than this: the play's the thing
Wherein I'll catch the conscience of the king.   *Exit.*   580

ACT 3

Scene 1. [A room in the castle]

Enter KING, QUEEN, POLONIUS, OPHELIA, ROSENCRANTZ, GUILDENSTERN, LORDS.

KING: And can you by no drift of conference°
    Get from him why he puts on this confusion,°
    Grating so harshly all his days of quiet
    With turbulent and dangerous lunacy?
ROSENCRANTZ: He does confess he feels himself distracted,   5
    But from what cause, a' will by no means speak.
GUILDENSTERN: Nor do we find him forward to be sounded,°
    But with a crafty madness keeps aloof
    When we would bring him on to some confession
    Of his true state.
QUEEN: Did he receive you well?   10
ROSENCRANTZ: Most like a gentleman.
GUILDENSTERN: But with much forcing of his disposition.°
ROSENCRANTZ: Niggard of question,° but of our demands
    Most free in his reply.
QUEEN: Did you assay° him
    To any pastime?   15
ROSENCRANTZ: Madam, it so fell out that certain players
    We o'er-raught° on the way: of these we told him,
    And there did seem in him a kind of joy
    To hear of it: they are here about the court,
    And as I think, they have already order   20
    This night to play before him.
POLONIUS: 'Tis most true,
    And he beseeched me to entreat your majesties
    To hear and see the matter.°
KING: With all my heart, and it doth much content me   25
    To hear him so inclined.
    Good gentlemen, give him a further edge,°
    And drive his purpose into these delights.
ROSENCRANTZ: We shall my lord.   [*Exeunt* ROSENCRANTZ *and* GUILDENSTERN.]
KING: Sweet Gertrude, leave us too,
    For we have closely° sent for Hamlet hither,   30
    That he, as 'twere by accident, may here

°1 *drift of conference*: turn of conversation. 2 *puts . . . confusion*: seems so distracted ("puts on" indicates the king's private suspicion that Hamlet is playing mad). 7 *forward . . . sounded*: disposed to be sounded out. 12 *forcing . . . disposition*: forcing himself to be so. 13 *Niggard of question*: unwilling to talk. 14 *assay*: tempt. 17 *o'er-raught*: overtook. 24 *matter*: i.e., of the play. 27 *give . . . edge*: encourage his keen interest. 30 *closely*: secretly.

Affront° Ophelia;
Her father and myself, lawful espials,°
Will so bestow° ourselves, that seeing unseen,
35   We may of their encounter frankly° judge,
And gather by him as he is behaved,
If't be th'affliction of his love or no
That thus he suffers for.

QUEEN: I shall obey you.
And for your part Ophelia, I do wish
40   That your good beauties be the happy cause
Of Hamlet's wildness, so shall I hope your virtues
Will bring him to his wonted° way again,
To both your honours.

OPHELIA: Madam, I wish it may.   [*Exit* QUEEN.]
POLONIUS: Ophelia, walk you here—Gracious,° so please you,
45   We will bestow ourselves—read on this book,°
That show of such an exercise° may colour°
Your loneliness; we are oft to blame in this,
'Tis too much proved,° that with devotion's visage
And pious action, we do sugar o'er
The devil himself.

50   KING: [*Aside.*] O 'tis too true,°
How smart a lash that speech doth give my conscience.
The harlot's cheek, beautied with plast'ring art,
Is not more ugly to° the thing that helps it,
Than is my deed to my most painted word:°
55   O heavy burden!

POLONIUS: I hear him coming, let's withdraw my lord.

                                                                Exeunt.

Enter HAMLET.
HAMLET: To be, or not to be, that is the question,
Whether 'tis nobler in the mind° to suffer
The slings and arrows of outrageous fortune,
60   Or to take arms against a sea of troubles,
And by opposing, end them: to die, to sleep,
No more; and by a sleep, to say we end
The heart-ache, and the thousand natural shocks
That flesh is heir to; 'tis a consummation
65   Devoutly to be wished. To die, to sleep,
To sleep, perchance to dream, ay there's the rub,°
For in that sleep of death what dreams may come

°32 *Affront:* meet face to face with. 33 *espials:* spies. 34, 45 *bestow:* place. 35 *frankly:* freely. 42 *wonted:* customary. 44 *Gracious:* i.e., Your Grace. 45 *book:* (of prayer). 46 *exercise:* religious exercise. *colour:* make plausible. 48 *'Tis . . . proved:* it is all too apparent. 50 *'tis too true:* (the king's first indication that he is guilty). 53 *to:* compared to. 52–54 *harlot's cheek . . . word:* just as the harlot's cheek is even uglier by contrast to the makeup that tries to beautify it, so my deed is uglier by contrast to the hypocritical words under which I hide it. 58 *nobler in the mind:* best, according to "sovereign" reason. 66 *rub:* obstacle.

When we have shuffled off this mortal coil°
Must give us pause—there's the respect°
That makes calamity of so long life:°   70
For who would bear the whips and scorns of time,
Th'oppressor's wrong, the proud man's contumely,°
The pangs of disprized love, the law's delay,°
The insolence of office,° and the spurns
That patient merit of th'unworthy takes,   75
When he himself might his quietus° make
With a bare bodkin;° who would fardels° bear,
To grunt and sweat under a weary life,
But that the dread of something after death,
The undiscovered° country, from whose bourn°   80
No traveler returns, puzzles the will,
And makes us rather bear those ills we have,
Than fly to others that we know not of.
Thus conscience does make cowards of us all,
And thus the native hue° of resolution   85
Is sicklied o'er with the pale cast of thought,
And enterprises of great pitch° and moment,°
With this regard° their currents turn awry,°
And lose the name of action. Soft you now,
The fair Ophelia—Nymph, in thy orisons°   90
Be all my sins remembered.

OPHELIA: Good my lord,
How does your honour for this many a day.°
HAMLET: I humbly thank you: well, well, well.
OPHELIA: My lord, I have remembrances of yours
That I have longèd long to re-deliver,   95
I pray you now receive them.
HAMLET: No, not I,
I never gave you aught.
OPHELIA: My honoured lord, you know right well you did,
And with them words of so sweet breath° composed
As made the things more rich: their perfume lost,   100
Take these again, for to the noble mind
Rich gifts wax° poor when givers prove unkind.
There my lord.
HAMLET: Ha, ha, are you honest°?
OPHELIA: My lord.   105
HAMLET: Are you fair°?
OPHELIA: What means your lordship?

°68 *mortal coil*: (1) turmoil of mortal life (2) coil of flesh encircling the body. 70 *makes calamity of so long life*: makes living long a calamity. 72 *contumely*: contempt. 73 *law's delay*: longevity of lawsuits. 74 *office*: officials. 76 *quietus*: settlement of his debt. 77 *bare bodkin*: mere dagger. *fardels*: burdens. 78 *undiscovered*: unknown, unexplored. *bourn*: boundary. 85 *native hue*: natural complexion. 87 *pitch*: height, excellence. *moment*: importance. 88 *regard*: consideration. *their currents turn awry*: change their course. 90 *orisons*: prayers (referring to her prayer book). 92 *this . . . day*: all these days. 99 *breath*: speech. 102 *wax*: grow. 104 *honest*: (1) chaste (2) truthful. 106 *fair*: (1) beautiful (2) honorable.

HAMLET: That if you be honest and fair, your honesty should admit
    no discourse to your beauty.°
110 OPHELIA: Could beauty my lord, have better commerce than with
    honesty?
HAMLET: Ay truly, for the power of beauty will sooner transform
    honesty° from what it is to a bawd,° than the force of
    honesty can translate beauty into his likeness. This was
115   sometime° a paradox, but now the time gives it proof. I did
    love you once.
OPHELIA: Indeed my lord, you made me believe so.
HAMLET: You should not have believed me, for virtue cannot so
120   inoculate our old stock, but we shall relish of it.° I loved you not.
OPHELIA: I was the more deceived.
HAMLET: Get thee to a nunnery,° why wouldst thou be a breeder of
    sinners? I am myself indifferent honest,° but yet I could
    accuse me of such things, that it were better my mother
125   had not borne me: I am very proud, revengeful, ambitious,
    with more offences at my beck,° than I have thoughts
    to put them in, imagination to give them shape, or time to
    act them in: what should such fellows as I do, crawling
    between earth and heaven? we are arrant° knaves all,
130   believe none of us, go thy ways to a nunnery. Where's
    your father?
OPHELIA: At home my lord.
HAMLET: Let the doors be shut upon him, that he may play the fool
    nowhere but in's own house. Farewell.
135 OPHELIA: O help him, you sweet heavens.
HAMLET: If thou dost marry, I'll give thee this plague° for thy dowry:
    be thou as chaste as ice, as pure as snow, thou shalt not
    escape calumny; get thee to a nunnery, go, farewell. Or if
    thou wilt needs marry, marry a fool, for wise men know
140   well enough what monsters° you make of them: to a nunnery
    go, and quickly too, farewell.
OPHELIA: O heavenly powers, restore him.
HAMLET: I have heard of your paintings too, well enough. God hath
    given you one face, and you make yourselves another: you
145   jig,° you amble, and you lisp,° you nick-name God's
    creatures, and make your wantonness your ignorance,° go to,
    I'll no more on't, it hath made me mad. I say we will have
    no moe° marriage. Those that are married already, all but
    one shall live, the rest shall keep as they are: to a nunnery,
150   go.
                                                   Exit HAMLET.

°108–9 *admit . . . beauty*: (1) not allow communication with your beauty (2) not allow your beauty to be used as
a trap (Hamlet may have overheard the Polonius–Claudius plot or spotted their movement behind the arras).
113 *honesty*: chastity. *bawd*: procurer, pimp. 115 *sometime*: once. 119 *inoculate . . . it*: change our sinful nature (as
a tree is grafted to improve it) but we will keep our old taste (as will the fruit of the grafted tree). 122 *nunnery*:
(1) cloister (2) slang for "brothel" (cf. "bawd" above). 123 *indifferent honest*: reasonably virtuous. 126 *beck*: beckoning. 129 *arrant*: absolute. 136 *plague*: curse. 140 *monsters*: horned cuckolds (men whose wives were unfaithful).
145 *jig*: walk in a mincing way. *lisp*: put on affected speech. 146 *make your . . . ignorance*: excuse your caprices as
being due to ignorance. 148 *moe*: more.

OPHELIA: O what a noble mind is here o'erthrown!
  The courtier's, soldier's, scholar's, eye, tongue, sword,
  Th'expectancy and rose° of the fair state,
  The glass° of fashion, and the mould of form,°
  Th'observed of all observers, quite quite down,   155
  And I of ladies most deject and wretched,
  That sucked the honey of his music vows,
  Now see that noble and most sovereign° reason
  Like sweet bells jangled, out of tune and harsh,
  That unmatched form and feature° of blown° youth   160
  Blasted with ecstasy,° O woe is me,
  T'have seen what I have seen, see what I see.

Enter KING *and* POLONIUS.

KING: Love? his affections° do not that way tend,
  Nor what he spake, though it lacked form a little,
  Was not like madness. There's something in his soul   165
  O'er which his melancholy sits on brood,
  And I do doubt,° the hatch and the disclose°
  Will be some danger; which for to prevent,
  I have in quick determination
  Thus set it down: he shall with speed to England,   170
  For the demand of our neglected° tribute:
  Haply° the seas, and countries different,
  With variable° objects, shall expel
  This something°-settled matter in his heart,
  Whereon his brains still beating puts him thus   175
  From fashion of himself.° What think you on't?
POLONIUS: It shall do well. But yet do I believe
  The origin and commencement of his grief
  Sprung from neglected° love. How now Ophelia?
  You need not tell us what Lord Hamlet said,   180
  We heard it all. My lord, do as you please,
  But if you hold it fit, after the play,
  Let his queen-mother all alone entreat him
  To show his grief, let her be round° with him,
  And I'll be placed (so please you) in the ear   185
  Of° all their conference. If she find° him not,
  To England send him: or confine him where
  Your wisdom best shall think.
KING: It shall be so,
  Madness in great ones must not unwatched go.   *Exeunt.*

°153 *expectancy and rose*: fair hope. 154 *glass*: mirror. *mould of form*: model of manners. 158 *sovereign*: (because it should rule). 160 *feature*: external appearance. *blown*: flowering. 161 *Blasted with ecstasy*: blighted by madness. 163 *affections*: emotions, afflictions. 166–67 *on brood . . . hatch . . . disclose*: (metaphor of a hen sitting on eggs). 167 *doubt*: fear. 171 *neglected*: (being unpaid). 172 *Haply*: perhaps. 173 *variable*: varied. 174 *something*: somewhat. 176 *fashion of himself*: his usual self. 179 *neglected*: unrequited. 184 *round*: direct. 185–86 *in the ear Of*: so as to overhear. 186 *find*: find out.

Scene 2. [A hall in the castle]

Enter HAMLET and three of the PLAYERS.

HAMLET: Speak the speech° I pray you as I pronounced it to you,
    trippingly on the tongue, but if you mouth it° as many of
    your players do, I had as lief the town-crier spoke my
    lines. Nor do not saw the air too much with your hand
5   thus, but use all gently, for in the very torrent, tempest,
    and as I may say, whirlwind of your passion, you must
    acquire and beget° a temperance that may give it smoothness.
    O it offends me to the soul, to hear a robustious°
    periwig-pated° fellow tear a passion to tatters, to very rags,
10   to split the ears of the groundlings,° who for the most part
    are capable of° nothing but inexplicable dumb shows° and
    noise: I would have such a fellow whipped for o'erdoing
    Termagant.° It out-herods Herod,° pray you avoid it.
    1. PLAYER: I warrant you honour.
15 **HAMLET:** Be not too tame neither, but let your own discretion be
    your tutor, suit the action to the word, the word to the
    action, with this special observance, that you o'erstep not
    the modesty° of nature: for any thing so o'erdone, is from°
    the purpose of playing, whose end both at the first, and
20   now, was and is, to hold as 'twere the mirror up to nature,
    to show virtue her own feature, scorn° her own image, and
    the very age and body of the time his form and pressure.°
    Now this overdone, or come tardy off,° though it make the
    unskilful° laugh, cannot but make the judicious grieve, the
25   censure of the which one,° must in your allowance°
    o'erweigh a whole theatre of others. O there be players
    that I have seen play, and heard others praise, and that
    highly (not to speak it profanely) that neither having
    th'accent of Christians, nor the gait of Christian, pagan,
30   nor man, have so strutted and bellowed, that I have
    thought some of nature's journeymen° had made men, and
    not made them well, they imitated humanity so
    abominably.
    1. PLAYER: I hope we have reformed that indifferently° with us, sir.
35 **HAMLET:** O reform it altogether, and let those that play your clowns
    speak no more than is set down for them,° for there be of
    them that will themselves laugh, to set on some quantity
    of barren° spectators to laugh too, though in the meantime,

---

°1 *the speech*: i.e., that Hamlet has inserted. 2 *mouth it*: deliver it slowly and overdramatically. 7 *acquire and beget*: achieve for yourself and instill in other actors. 8 *robustious*: boisterous. 9 *periwig-pated*: wig-wearing. 10 *groundlings*: audience who paid least and stood on the ground floor. 11 *capable of*: able to understand. *dumb shows*: pantomimed synopses of the action to follow. 13 *Termagant*: violent, ranting character in the guild or mystery plays. *out-herods Herod*: outdoes even Herod, King of Judea, who commanded the slaughter of the Innocents and who was a ranting tyrant in the Corpus Christi plays. See p. 1218. 18 *modesty*: moderation. *from*: away from. 21 *scorn*: that which should be scorned. 22 *age . . . pressure*: shape of the times in its accurate impression. 23 *come tardy off*: understated, underdone. 24 *unskilful*: unsophisticated. 25 *one*: the judicious. *allowance*: estimation. 31 *journeymen*: artisans working for others and not yet masters of their trades. 34 *indifferently*: reasonably well. 36 *speak no more . . . them*: stick to their lines. 38 *barren*: witless.

some necessary question° of the play be then to be considered:
that's villainous, and shows a most pitiful ambition   40
in the fool that uses it. Go make you ready.   *Exeunt* PLAYERS

Enter POLONIUS, ROSENCRANTZ, *and* GUILDENSTERN.

How now my lord, will the king hear this piece of work?
POLONIUS: And the queen too, and that presently.
HAMLET: Bid the players make haste.   *Exit* POLONIUS.
    Will you two help to hasten them?   45
ROSENCRANTZ: Ay my lord.   *Exeunt they two.*
HAMLET: What ho, Horatio!

Enter HORATIO.

HORATIO: Here sweet lord, at your service.
HAMLET: Horatio, thou art e'en as just° a man
    As e'er my conversation coped withal.°   50
HORATIO: O my dear lord.
HAMLET: Nay, do not think I flatter,
    For what advancement may I hope from thee,
    That no revenue hast but thy good spirits
    To feed and clothe thee? Why should the poor be flattered?
    No, let the candied° tongue lick° absurd pomp,   55
    And crook the pregnant° hinges of the knee
    Where thrift may follow fawning.° Dost thou hear,
    Since my dear soul was mistress of her choice,
    And could of men distinguish her election,°
    Sh'hath sealed° thee for herself, for thou hast been   60
    As one in suff'ring all that suffers nothing,
    A man that Fortune's buffets° and rewards
    Hast ta'en with equal thanks; and blest are those
    Whose blood° and judgment are so well co-mingled,
    That they are not a pipe for Fortune's finger   65
    To sound what stop° she please.° give me that man
    That is not passion's slave, and I will wear him
    In my heart's core, ay in my heart of heart,
    As I do thee. Something too much of this.
    There is a play tonight before the king,   70
    One scene of it comes near the circumstance
    Which I have told thee of my father's death.
    I prithee when thou seest that act afoot,
    Even with the very comment° of thy soul
    Observe my uncle: if his occulted° guilt   75
    Do not itself unkennel° in one speech,

°39 *question*: dialogue. 49 *just*: well balanced. 50 *coped withal*: had to do with. 55–57 *candied . . . fawning*: (metaphor of a dog licking and fawning for candy). 55 *candied*: flattering. *lick* pay court to. 56 *pregnant*: quick in motion. 56–57 *crook . . . fawning*: obsequiously kneel when personal profit may ensue. 59 *election*: choice. 60 *sealed*: confirmed. 62 *buffets*: blows. 64 *blood*: passions. 66 *sound . . . please*: play whatever tune she likes. *stop*: finger hole in wind instrument for varying the sound. 74 *very comment*: acutest observation. 75 *occulted*: hidden. 76 *unkennel*: force from hiding.

It is a damnèd ghost° that we have seen,
And my imaginations are as foul
As Vulcan's stithy,° give him heedful note,
80   For I mine eyes will rivet to his face,
And after we will both our judgments join
In censure of his seeming.°
HORATIO: Well my lord,
If a' steal aught the whilst this play is playing,
And 'scape detecting, I will pay° the theft.   *Sound a flourish.*
85   HAMLET: They are coming to the play. I must be idle,°
Get you a place.

*Enter Trumpets and Kettledrums, KING, QUEEN, POLONIUS, OPHELIA, ROSENCRANTZ, GUILDEN-
STERN, and other LORDS attendant, with his GUARD carrying torches. Danish March.*

KING: How fares° our cousin Hamlet?
HAMLET: Excellent i'faith, of the chameleon's dish: I eat the air,°
      promise-crammed, you cannot feed capons so.°
90   KING: I have nothing with° this answer Hamlet, these words are
      not mine.°
HAMLET: No, nor mine now. [*To* POLONIUS.] My lord, you played
      once i'th'university you say?
POLONIUS: That did I my lord, and was accounted a good actor.
95   HAMLET: What did you enact?
POLONIUS: I did enact Julius Caesar, I was killed i'th'Capitol, Brutus
      killed me.
HAMLET: It was a brute part of him to kill so capital a calf there. Be
      the players ready?
100   ROSENCRANTZ: Ay my lord, they stay upon your patience.°
QUEEN: Come hither my dear Hamlet, sit by me.
HAMLET: No, good mother, here's metal more attractive.°
POLONIUS: [*To the* KING.] O ho, do you mark that?
HAMLET: Lady, shall I lie in your lap?
105   OPHELIA: No my lord.
HAMLET: I mean, my head upon your lap?
OPHELIA: Ay my lord.
HAMLET: Do you think I meant country° matters?
OPHELIA: I think nothing my lord.
110   HAMLET: That's a fair thought to lie between maids' legs.
OPHELIA: What is, my lord?
HAMLET: Nothing.
OPHELIA: You are merry my lord.
HAMLET: Who, I?

°77 *damnèd ghost*: devil (not the ghost of my father). 79 *Vulcan's stithy*: the forge of the blacksmith of the gods.
82 *censure . . . seeming*: (1) judgment of his appearance (2) disapproval of his pretending. 84 *pay*: i.e., for. 85 *be
idle*: act mad. 87 *fares*: does, but Hamlet takes it to mean "eats" or "dines." 88 *eat the air*: the chamelion supposedly ate air, but Hamlet also puns on "heir." 89 *you cannot . . . so*: (1) even a capon cannot feed on air and your
promises (2) like a capon stuffed with food before being killed, I am stuffed (fed up) with your promises. 90
nothing with: nothing to do with. 91 *not mine*: not in answer to my question. 100 *stay . . . patience*: await your permission. 102 *metal more attractive*: (1) iron more magnetic (2) stuff ("mettle") more beautiful. 108 *country*: rustic, sexual (with a pun on a slang word for the female sexual organ).

Hamlet (played by Kevin Kline), Queen Gertrude (played by Dana Ivy), and Ophelia (played by Diane Venora) in the New York Shakespeare Festival production of *Hamlet* (1990), directed by Mr. Kline for the Public Broadcasting System.

OPHELIA: Ay my lord.   115
HAMLET: O God, your only jig-maker: what should a man do but be
    merry, for look you how cheerfully my mother looks, and
    my father died within's two hours.
OPHELIA: Nay, 'tis twice two months my lord.
HAMLET: So long? Nay then let the devil wear black, for I'll have a   120
    suit of sables,° O heavens, die two months ago, and not
    forgotten yet? Then there's hope a great man's memory
    may outlive his life half a year, but by'r lady° a' must build
    churches then, or else shall a' suffer not thinking on,° with

---

°121 *sables*: (1) rich fur (2) black mourning garb. 123 *by'r lady*: by Our Lady (the Virgin Mary). 124 *not thinking on*: being forgotten.

125   the hobby-horse,° whose epitaph is "For O, for O, the
        hobby-horse is forgot."

The trumpets sound. Dumb Show° follows. Enter a King and a Queen, very lovingly, the Queen em-
bracing him, and he her. She kneels and makes show of protestation unto him. He takes her up, and
declines his head upon her neck. He lies him down upon a bank of flowers; she seeing him asleep
leaves him: anon comes in another man, takes off his crown, kisses it, pours poison in the sleeper's
ears, and leaves him: the Queen returns, finds the King dead, and makes passionate action. The poi-
soner with some three or four mutes° comes in again, seeming to condole with her. The dead body is
carried away. The poisoner wooes the Queen with gifts: she seems harsh and unwilling awhile, but in
the end accepts his love.

                                                                           Exeunt.

OPHELIA: What means this, my lord?
HAMLET: Marry, this is miching mallecho,° it means mischief.
OPHELIA: Belike this show imports the argument° of the play.

Enter PROLOGUE.

130   HAMLET: We shall know by this fellow: the players cannot keep
                counsel,° they'll tell all.
        OPHELIA: Will a' tell us what this show meant?
        HAMLET: Ay, or any show that you will show him. Be not you ashamed to show, he'll not
135   shame to tell you what it means.
        OPHELIA: You are naught,° you are naught, I'll mark the play.
        PROLOGUE: For us and for our tragedy,
                Here stooping to your clemency,
                We beg your hearing patiently.   [*Exit.*]
140   HAMLET: Is this a prologue, or the posy° of a ring?
        OPHELIA: 'Tis brief, my lord.
        HAMLET: As woman's love.

Enter PLAYER KING and QUEEN.

        PLAYER KING: Full thirty times hath Phoebus' cart° gone round
                Neptune's salt wash,° and Tellus' orbèd ground,°
145   And thirty dozen moons with borrowed sheen
                About the world have times twelve thirties been,
                Since love our hearts, and Hymen° did our hands
                Unite commutual,° in most sacred bands.
        PLAYER QUEEN: So many journeys may the sun and moon
150   Make us again count o'er ere love be done,
                But woe is me, you are so sick of late,
                So far from cheer, and from your former state,
                That I distrust you:° yet though I distrust,

°125 *hobby-horse:* (1) character in the May games (2) slang for "prostitute." 126 S.D.: *Dumb Show:* pantomimed
synopsis of the action to follow. 126 S.D.: *mutes:* actors without speaking parts. 128 *miching mallecho:* skulking
mischief. 129 *imports the argument:* signifies the plot. 131 *counsel:* a secret. 136 *naught:* naughty, lewd. 140 *posy:*
motto (engraved in a ring). 143 *Phoebus' cart:* chariot of the sun. 144 *wash:* sea. *Tellus . . . ground:* the earth (Tellus was a Roman earth goddess). 147 *Hymen:* Roman god of marriage. 148 *commutual:* mutually. 153 *distrust you:*
am worried about you.

Discomfort you, my lord, it nothing must.
For women fear too much, even as they love,   155
And women's fear and love hold quantity,°
In neither aught, or in extremity:°
Now what my love is, proof° hath made you know,
And as my love is sized, my fear is so.
Where love is great, the littlest doubts are fear,   160
Where little fears grow great, great love grows there.
PLAYER KING: Faith, I must leave thee love, and shortly too,
My operant° powers their functions leave° to do,
And thou shalt live in this fair world behind,
Honoured, beloved, and haply° one as kind   165
For husband shalt thou—.
PLAYER QUEEN: O confound the rest:
Such love must needs be treason in my breast.
In second husband let me be accurst,
None wed the second, but who killed the first.
HAMLET: [Aside.] That's wormwood,° wormwood.   170
PLAYER QUEEN: The instances° that second marriage move°
Are base respects of thrift,° but none of love.
A second time I kill my husband dead,
When second husband kisses me in bed.
PLAYER KING: I do believe you think what now you speak,   175
But what we do determine, oft we break:
Purpose is but the slave to memory
Of violent birth but poor validity.°
Which now like fruit unripe sticks on the tree,
But fall unshaken when they mellow be.   180
Most necessary 'tis that we forget
To pay ourselves what to ourselves is debt.°
What to ourselves in passion we propose,
The passion ending, doth the purpose lose.
The violence of either grief or joy   185
Their own enactures° with themselves destroy:
Where joy most revels, grief doth most lament;
Grief joys, joy grieves, on slender accident.
This world is not for aye,° nor 'tis not strange
That even our loves should with our fortunes change: 190
For 'tis a question left us yet to prove,
Whether love lead fortune, or else fortune love.°
The great man down, you mark his favourite flies,
The poor advanced, makes friends of enemies:
And hitherto doth love on fortune tend,   195
For who not needs, shall never lack a friend,
And who in want a hollow friend doth try,
Directly seasons him° his enemy.

°156 *quantity:* proportion. 157 *In neither . . . extremity:* their love and fear are either absent or excessive. 158 *proof:* experience. 163 *operant:* vital. *leave:* cease. 165 *haply:* perhaps. 170 *wormwood:* bitter (like the herb). 171 *instances:* causes. *move:* motivate. 172 *respects of thrift:* consideration of profit. 178 *validity:* strength. 181–82 *Most . . . debt:* we are easy creditors to ourselves and forget our former promises (debts). 186 *enactures:* fulfillments. 189 *aye:* ever. 192 *fortune love:* fortune lead love. 198 *seasons him:* causes him to become.

But orderly to end where I begun,
200   Our wills and fates do so contrary run,
That our devices still° are overthrown,
Our thoughts are ours, their ends none of our own.
So think thou wilt no second husband wed,
But die thy thoughts when thy first lord is dead.
205   PLAYER QUEEN: Nor earth to me give food, nor heaven light,
Sport and repose lock from me day and night,
To desperation turn my trust and hope,
An anchor's° cheer in prison be my scope,
Each opposite that blanks° the face of joy,
210   Meet what I would have well, and it destroy,
Both here and hence° pursue me lasting strife,
If once a widow, ever I be wife.
HAMLET: If she should break it now.
PLAYER KING: 'Tis deeply sworn: sweet, leave me here awhile,
215   My spirits grow dull, and fain° I would beguile
The tedious day with sleep.   *Sleeps.*
PLAYER QUEEN: Sleep rock thy brain.
And never come mischance between us twain.   *Exit.*
HAMLET: Madam, how like you this play?
QUEEN: The lady doth protest too much methinks.
220   HAMLET: O but she'll keep her word.
KING: Have you heard the argument°? Is there no offence in't?
HAMLET: No, no, they do but jest, poison in jest, no offence
i'th'world.
KING: What do you call the play?
225   HAMLET: The Mouse-trap. Marry, how? Tropically:° this play is the
image of a murder done in Vienna: Gonzago is the duke's
name, his wife Baptista, you shall see anon, 'tis a knavish
piece of work, but what of that? Your majesty, and we
that have free° souls, it touches us not: let the galled jade
230   winch,° our withers are unwrung.°

Enter LUCIANUS.

This is one Lucianus, nephew to the king.
OPHELIA: You are as good as a chorus,° my lord.
HAMLET: I could interpret between you and your love, if I could see
the puppets dallying.
235   OPHELIA: You are keen my lord, you are keen.°
HAMLET: It would cost you a groaning to take off mine edge.
OPHELIA: Still better and worse.°
HAMLET: So you mistake° your husbands. Begin, murderer. Pox,°
leave thy damnable faces° and begin. Come, the croaking
240   raven doth bellow for revenge.

°201 *devices still*: plans always. 208 *anchor's*: hermit's. 209 *opposite that blanks*: contrary event that pales. 211 *here and hence*: in this world and the next. 215 *fain*: gladly. 221 *argument*: plot. 225 *Tropically*: figuratively. 229 *free*: innocent. 229–30 *galled jade winch*: chafed old horse wince (from its sores). 230 *withers are unwrung*: (1) shoulders are unchafed (2) consciences are clear. 232 *chorus*: actor who introduced the action. 235 *keen*: (1) sharp (Ophelia's meaning) (2) sexually excited (Hamlet's interpretation). 237 *better and worse*: better wit but a worse meaning, with a pun on "better" and "bitter." 238 *mistake*: mis-take. *Pox*: a plague on it. 239 *faces*: exaggerated facial expressions.

LUCIANUS: Thoughts black, hands apt, drugs fit, and time agreeing,
    Confederate season,° else no creature seeing,°
    Thou mixture rank, of midnight weeds collected,
    With Hecate's° ban° thrice blasted, thrice infected,
    Thy natural magic, and dire property,   245
    On wholesome° life usurps immediately.   *Pours the poison in his ears.*
HAMLET: A' poisons him i'th'garden for's estate, his name's Gonzago,
    the story is extant, and written in very choice
    Italian, you shall see anon how the murderer gets the love
    of Gonzago's wife.   250
OPHELIA: The king rises.
HAMLET: What, frighted with false fire°?
QUEEN: How fares my lord?
POLONIUS: Give o'er the play.
KING: Give me some light. Away!   *Exeunt all but* HAMLET *and* HORATIO.   255
ALL: Lights, lights, lights!
HAMLET: Why, let the stricken deer go weep,
        The hart ungallèd° play,°
    For some must watch while some must sleep,   260
        Thus runs the world away.
    Would not this° sir, and a forest of feathers,° if the rest of my
    fortunes turn Turk with° me, with two Provincial roses° on
    my razed° shoes, get me a fellowship° in a cry° of players?
HORATIO: Half a share.°
HAMLET: A whole one, I.   265
        For thou dost know, O Damon° dear,
        This realm dismantled was
    Of Jove° himself, and now reigns here
        A very very—pajock.°
HORATIO: You might have rhymed.°   270
HAMLET: O good Horatio, I'll take the ghost's word for a thousand
    pound. Didst perceive?
HORATIO: Very well my lord.
HAMLET: Upon the talk of the poisoning?
HORATIO: I did very well note him.   275

Enter ROSENCRANTZ *and* GUILDENSTERN.

HAMLET: Ah ha, come, some music. Come, the recorders.°
    For if the king like not the comedy,
    Why then belike he likes it not, perdy.°
    Come, some music.

°242 *Confederate . . . seeing*: no one seeing me except time, my confederate. 244 *Hecate*: goddess of witchcraft. *ban*: evil spell. 246 *wholesome*: healthy. 252 *false fire*: discharge of blanks (not gunpowder). 257–58 *deer . . . play*: (the belief that a wounded deer wept, abandoned by the others). 258 *ungallèd*: unhurt. 261 *this*: i.e., sample (of my theatrical talent). *feathers*: plumes (worn by actors). 262 *turn Turk with*: cruelly turn against. *Provincial roses*: rosettes named for Provins, France. 263 *razed*: slashed, decorated with cutouts. *fellowship*: partnership. *cry*: pack, troupe. 264 *share*: divisions of profits among members of a theatrical production company. 266 *Damon*: legendary ideal friend to Pythias. 268 *Jove*: (Hamlet's father). 269 *pajock*: peacock (associated with lechery). 270 *rhymed*: (used "ass" instead of "pajock"). 276 *recorders*: soft-toned woodwind instruments, similar to flutes. 278 *perdy*: by God (*pardieu*).

280   GUILDENSTERN: Good my lord, vouchsafe me a word with you.

HAMLET: Sir, a whole history.

GUILDENSTERN: The king, sir—

HAMLET: Ay sir, what of him?

GUILDENSTERN: Is in his retirement, marvellous distempered.

285   HAMLET: With drink sir?

GUILDENSTERN: No my lord, with choler.°

HAMLET: Your wisdom should show itself more richer to signify
    this to the doctor: for, for me to put him to his purgation,°
    would perhaps plunge him into more choler.

290   GUILDENSTERN: Good my lord, put your discourse into some frame,° and
    start not so wildly from my affair.

HAMLET: I am tame sir, pronounce.

GUILDENSTERN: The queen your mother, in most great affliction of spirit,
    hath sent me to you.

295   HAMLET: You are welcome.

GUILDENSTERN: Nay good my lord, this courtesy is not of the right breed.°
    If it shall please you to make me a wholesome° answer, I
    will do your mother's commandment: if not, your pardon°
    and my return shall be the end of my business.

300   HAMLET: Sir I cannot.

ROSENCRANTZ: What, my lord?

HAMLET: Make you a wholesome answer: my wit's diseased. But
    sir, such answer as I can make, you shall command, or
    rather as you say, my mother: therefore no more, but to

305   the matter. My mother you say.

ROSENCRANTZ: Then thus she says, your behaviour hath struck her into
    amazement and admiration.°

HAMLET: O wonderful son that can so 'stonish a mother. But is there
    no sequel at the heels of this mother's admiration? Impart.

310   ROSENCRANTZ: She desires to speak with you in her closet°
    ere you go to bed.

HAMLET: We shall obey, were she ten times our mother. Have you
    any further trade with us?

ROSENCRANTZ: My lord, you once did love me.

315   HAMLET: And do still, by these pickers and stealers.°

ROSENCRANTZ: Good my lord, what is your cause of distemper? You do
    surely bar the door upon your own liberty, if you deny
    your griefs to your friend.°

HAMLET: Sir, I lack advancement.

320   ROSENCRANTZ: How can that be, when you have the voice° of the king
    himself for your succession in Denmark?

HAMLET: Ay sir, but 'while the grass grows'°—the proverb is
    something musty. °

°286 *choler*: anger. 288 *purgation*: (1) purging of excessive bile (2) judicial investigations (3) purgatory. 290 *frame*: order. 296 *breed*: (1) species (2) manners. 297 *wholesome*: reasonable. 298 *pardon*: permission to depart. 307 *admiration*: wonder. 310 *closet*: private room, bedroom. 315 *pickers and stealers*: hands (from the prayer, "Keep my hands from picking and stealing"). 317–818 *deny . . . friend*: refuse to let your friend know the cause of your suffering. 320 *voice*: vote. 322 *while . . . grows*: (the proverb ends: "the horse starves"). 323 *something musty*: somewhat too old and trite (to finish).

Enter the PLAYERS *with recorders.*

O the recorders, let me see one. To withdraw° with you,
why do you go about to recover the wind of me,° as if you   325
would drive me into a toil°?
GUILDENSTERN: O my lord, if my duty be too bold, my love is too
unmannerly.°
HAMLET: I do not well understand that. Will you play
upon this pipe°?   330
GUILDENSTERN: My lord I cannot.
HAMLET: I pray you.
GUILDENSTERN: Believe me. I cannot.
HAMLET: I do beseech you.
GUILDENSTERN: I know no touch of it° my lord.   335
HAMLET: It is as easy as lying; govern these ventages° with your
fingers and thumb, give it breath with your mouth, and it
will discourse most eloquent music. Look you, these are
the stops.
GUILDENSTERN: But these cannot I command to any utt'rance of harmony,   340
I have not the skill.
HAMLET: Why look you now how unworthy a thing you make of
me: you would play upon me, you would seem to know
my stops, you would pluck out the heart of my mystery,
you would sound me from my lowest note to the top of my   345
compass.° and there is much music, excellent voice in this
little organ,° yet cannot you make it speak. 'Sblood, do you
think I am easier to be played on than a pipe? Call me what
instrument you will, though you can fret° me, you cannot
play upon me.   350

Enter POLONIUS.

God bless you sir.
POLONIUS: My lord, the queen would speak with you, and presently.
HAMLET: Do you see yonder cloud that's almost in shape of a camel?
POLONIUS: By th'mass and 'tis, like a camel indeed.
HAMLET: Methinks it is like a weasel.   355
POLONIUS: It is backed like a weasel.
HAMLET: Or like a whale?
POLONIUS: Very like a whale.
HAMLET: Then I will come to my mother by and by.°
[*Aside.*] They fool me to the top of my bent.°   360
I will come by and by.
POLONIUS: I will say so.   *Exit.*
HAMLET: "By and by" is easily said.
Leave me, friends.   [*Exeunt all but* HAMLET.]

°324 *withdraw*: speak privately. 325 *recover . . . me*: drive me toward the wind, as with a prey, to avoid its scent-
ing the hunter. 326 *toil*: snare. 327–28 *is too unmannerly*: makes me forget my good manners. 330 *pipe*: recorder.
335 *know . . . it*: have no skill at fingering it. 336 *ventages*: holes, stops. 346 *compass*: range. 347 *organ*: musical
instrument. 349 *fret*: (1) irritate (2) play an instrument that has "frets" or bars to guide the fingering. 359 *by and
by*: very soon. 360 *fool me . . . bent*: force me to play the fool to my utmost.

365   'Tis now the very witching time of night.
When churchyards yawn,° and hell itself breathes out
Contagion° to this world: now could I drink hot blood,
And do such bitter business as the day
Would quake to look on: soft, now to my mother—
370   O heart, lose not thy nature,° let not ever
The soul of Nero° enter this firm bosom,
Let me be cruel, not unnatural.
I will speak daggers to her, but use none:
My tongue and soul in this be hypocrites,°
375   How in my words somever she be shent,°
To give them seals,° never my soul consent.   *Exit.*

Scene 3. [A room in the castle]

Enter KING, ROSENCRANTZ, *and* GUILDENSTERN.

KING: I like him not, nor stands it safe with us
     To let his madness range. Therefore prepare you,
     I your commission will forthwith dispatch,°
     And he to England shall along with you:
5   The terms of our estate° may not endure
     Hazard so near's° as doth hourly grow
     Out of his brows.°
GUILDENSTERN: We will ourselves provide:°
     Most holy and religious fear it is
     To keep those many many bodies safe
10   That live and feed upon your majesty.
ROSENCRANTZ: The single and peculiar° life is bound
     With all the strength and armour of the mind
     To keep itself from noyance,° but much more
     That spirit, upon whose weal° depends and rests
15   The lives of many; the cess° of majesty
     Dies not alone, but like a gulf° doth draw
     What's near it, with it. O'tis a massy wheel
     Fixed on the summit of the highest mount,
     To whose huge spokes, ten thousand lesser things
20   Are mortised° and adjoined, which when it falls,
     Each small annexment, petty consequence,
     Attends° the boist'rous ruin. Never alone
     Did the king sigh, but with a general groan.
KING: Arm° you I pray you, to this speedy voyage,
25   For we will fetters put about this fear,
     Which now goes too free-footed.
ROSENCRANTZ: We will haste us.

Exeunt [ROSENCRANTZ *and* GUILDENSTERN.]

°366 *churchyards yawn*: graves open. 367 *Contagion*: (1) evil (2) diseases. 370 *nature*: natural affection. 371 *Nero*: (who killed his mother). 374 *My tongue . . . hypocrites*: I will speak cruelly but intend no harm. 375 *shent*: chastised. 376 *give them seals*: confirm them with action (as a legal "deed" is confirmed with a "seal"). 3 *forthwith dispatch*: immediately have prepared. 5 *terms . . . estate*: circumstances of my royal office. 6 *near's*: near us. 7 *brows*: effronteries. *provide*: prepare. 11 *peculiar*: individual. 13 *noyance*: harm. 14 *weal*: well-being. 15 *cess*: cessation, death. 16 *gulf*: whirlpool. 20 *mortised*: securely fitted. 22 *Attends*: accompanies. 24 *Arm*: prepare.

Enter POLONIUS.

POLONIUS: My lord, he's going to his mother's closet:
    Behind the arras I'll convey myself
    To hear the process.° I'll warrant she'll tax him home,
    And as you said, and wisely was it said,   30
    'Tis meet° that some more audience than a mother,
    Since nature makes them partial, should o'erhear
    The speech of vantage,° fare you well my liege,°
    I'll call upon you ere you go to bed,
    And tell you what I know.

KING: Thanks, dear my lord.   *Exit* [POLONIUS.]   35
    O my offence is rank, it smells to heaven,
    It hath the primal eldest curse° upon't,
    A brother's murder. Pray can I not,
    Though inclination be as sharp as will.°
    My stronger guilt defeats my strong intent,   40
    And like a man to double business bound,
    I stand in pause where I shall first begin,
    And both neglect; what if this cursèd hand
    Were thicker than itself with brother's blood,
    Is there not rain enough in the sweet heavens   45
    To wash it white as snow? Whereto serves mercy
    But to confront the visage of offence°?
    And what's in prayer but this two-fold force,
    To be forestallèd° ere we come to fall,
    Or pardoned being down? Then I'll look up,   50
    My fault is past. But O what form of prayer
    Can serve my turn? "Forgive me my foul murder":
    That cannot be, since I am still possessed
    Of those effects° for which I did the murder:
    My crown, mine own ambition, and my queen.   55
    May one be pardoned and retain th'offence?
    In the corrupted currents of this world,
    Offence's gilded hand may shove by justice,
    And oft 'tis seen the wicked prize itself
    Buys out the law;° but 'tis not so above,   60
    There is no shuffling,° there the action lies
    In his true nature,° and we ourselves compelled
    Even to the teeth and forehead of our faults°
    To give in evidence. What then? What rests°?
    Try what repentance can. What can it not?   65
    Yet what can it, when one can not repent?
    O wretched state? O bosom black as death!
    O limèd soul, that struggling to be free,

°29 *the process:* what proceeds. 31 *meet:* fitting. 33 *of vantage:* from an advantageous position. *liege:* lord. 37 *primal . . . curse:* curse of Cain. 39 *inclination . . . will:* my desire to pray is as strong as my determination to do so. 47 *confront . . . offence:* plead in man's behalf against sin (at the Last Judgment). 49 *forestallèd:* prevented. 54 *effects:* results. 59–60 *wicked . . . law:* fruits of the crime bribe the judge. 61 *shuffling:* evasion. 61–62 *action . . . nature.* (1) deed is seen in its true nature (2) legal action is sustained according to the truth. 63 *to the teeth . . . faults:* meeting our sins face to face. 64 *rests:* remains.

Art more engaged;° help, angels, make assay:°
70   Bow stubborn knees, and heart with strings of steel,
Be soft as sinews of the new-born babe,
All may be well.   [*He kneels.*]

Enter HAMLET.

HAMLET: Now might I do it pat,° now a' is a-praying,
And now I'll do't, [*Draws his sword.*] and so a' goes to heaven,
75   And so am I revenged: that would be scanned:°
A villain kills my father, and for that,
I his sole son, do this same villain send
To heaven.
Why, this is hire and salary, not revenge.
80   A' took my father grossly,° full of bread,°
With all his crimes° broad blown,° as flush° as May,
And how his audit° stands who knows save heaven,
But in our circumstance and course of thought,
'Tis heavy° with him: and am I then revenged
85   To take him in the purging of his soul,
when he is fit and seasoned° for his passage?
No.   [*Sheathes his sword.*]
Up sword, and know thou a more horrid hent,°
When he is drunk asleep, or in his rage,
90   Or in th'incestuous pleasure of his bed,
At game, a-swearing, or about some act
That has no relish° of salvation in't,
Then trip him that his heels may kick at heaven,
And that his soul may be as damned and black
95   As hell whereto it goes; my mother stays,
This physic° but prolongs thy sickly days   *Exit.*
KING: [*Rises.*] My words fly up, my thoughts remain below,
Words without thoughts never to heaven go.   *Exit.*

Scene 4. [The Queen's closet]

Enter QUEEN *and* POLONIUS.

POLONIUS: A' will come straight, look you lay home° to him,
Tell him his pranks have been too broad° to bear with,
And that your grace hath screened and stood between
Much heat° and him. I'll silence me° even here:
5   Pray you be round with him.
HAMLET: [*Within.*] Mother, mother, mother.

°68–69 *limèd . . . engaged*: like a bird caught in lime (a sticky substance spread on twigs as a snare), the soul in its struggle to clear itself only becomes more entangled. 69 *make assay*: I'll make an attempt. 73 *pat*: opportunely. 75 *would be scanned*: needs closer examination. 80 *grossly*: unpurified (by final rites). *bread*: self-indulgence. 81 *crimes*: sins. *broad blown*: in full flower. *flush*: lusty. 82 *audit*: account. 84 *heavy*: grievous. 86 *seasoned*: ready (prepared). 88 *horrid hent*: horrible opportunity ("hint") for seizure ("hent") by me. 92 *relish*: taste. 96 *physic*: (1) medicine (2) purgation of your soul by prayer. 1 *lay home*: thrust home; speak sharply. 2 *broad*: unrestrained. 4 *heat*: anger. *silence me*: hide in silence.

QUEEN: I'll war'nt you,
    Fear me not. Withdraw, I hear him coming.   [POLONIUS *hides behind the arras.*]

Enter HAMLET.

HAMLET: Now mother, what's the matter?
QUEEN: Hamlet, thou hast thy father much offended.
HAMLET: Mother, you have my father much offended.   10
QUEEN: Come, come, you answer with an idle° tongue.
HAMLET: Go, go, you question with a wicked tongue.
QUEEN: Why, how now Hamlet?
HAMLET: What's the matter now?
QUEEN: Have you forgot me?
HAMLET: No by the rood,° not so,
    You are the queen, your husband's brother's wife,   15
    And would it were not so, you are my mother.
QUEEN: Nay, then I'll set those to you that can speak.°
HAMLET: Come, come, and sit you down, you shall not budge,
    You go not till I set you up a glass°
    Where you may see the inmost part of you.   20
QUEEN: What wilt thou do? Thou wilt not murder me?
    Help, help, ho!
POLONIUS: [*Behind the arras.*] What ho! help, help, help!
HAMLET: How now, a rat? dead for a ducat,° dead.   *Kills* POLONIUS [*through the arras.*]

POLONIUS: O I am slain!
QUEEN: O me, what hast thou done?
HAMLET: Nay I know not,
    Is it the king?
QUEEN: O what a rash and bloody deed is this!
HAMLET: A bloody deed, almost as bad, good mother,
    As kill a king, and marry with his brother.   30
QUEEN: As kill a king?
HAMLET: Ay lady, it was my word.
    [*To* POLONIUS.] Thou wretched, rash, intruding fool, farewell,
    I took thee for thy better,° take thy fortune,
    Thou find'st to be too busy is some danger.   35
    [*To the* QUEEN.] Leave wringing of your hands, peace, sit you down,
    And let me wring your heart, for so I shall
    If it be made of penetrable stuff,
    If damnèd custom° have not brazed° it so,
    That it be proof° and bulwark against sense.°   40
QUEEN: What have I done, that thou dar'st wag thy tongue
    In noise so rude against me?
HAMLET: Such an act
    That blurs the grace and blush of modesty,
    Calls virtue hypocrite, takes off the rose°
    From the fair forehead of an innocent love   45

°11 *idle:* foolish. 14 *rood:* cross. 17 *speak:* i.e., to you as you should be spoken to. 19 *glass:* looking glass. 24 *for a ducat:* I wager a ducat (an Italian gold coin). 34 *thy better:* the king. 39 *custom:* habit. *brazed:* brass-plated (brazened). 40 *proof:* armor. *sense:* sensibility. 44 *rose:* (symbol of perfection and innocence).

And sets a blister there,° makes marriage vows
As false as dicers' oaths, O such a deed,
As from the body of contraction° plucks
The very soul and sweet religion makes
50 A rhapsody° of words; heaven's face does glow,°
Yea this solidity and compound mass°
With heated visage, as against the doom,°
Is thought-sick at the act.

QUEEN: Ay me, what act,
That roars so loud, and thunders in the index°?

55 HAMLET: Look here upon this picture, and on this,
The counterfeit presentment° of two brothers:
See what a grace was seated on this brow,
Hyperion's curls, the front° of Jove himself,
An eye like Mars, to threaten and command,
60 A station° like the herald Mercury,
New-lighted on a heaven-kissing hill,
A combination and a form indeed,
Where every god did seem to set his seal
To give the world assurance of a man.
65 This was your husband. Look you now what follows.
Here is your husband, like a mildewed ear,°
Blasting° his wholesome brother. Have you eyes?
Could you on this fair mountain leave to feed,°
And batten° on this moor? Ha! Have you eyes?
70 You cannot call it love, for at your age
The hey-day in the blood° is tame, it's humble,
And waits upon the judgment, and what judgment
Would step from this to this? Sense° sure you have
Else could you not have motion,° but sure that sense
75 Is apoplexed,° for madness would not err,
Nor sense to ecstasy was ne'er so thralled°
But it reserved some quantity of choice
To serve in such a difference.° What devil was't
That thus hath cozened you at hoodman-blind°?
80 Eyes without feeling, feeling without sight,
Ears without hands or eyes, smelling sans all,°
Or but a sickly part of one true sense
Could not so mope:° O shame, where is thy blush?
Rebellious hell,
85 If thou canst mutine° in a matron's bones,
To flaming youth let virtue be as wax

°46 *blister there*: (whores were punished by being branded on the forehead). 48 *body of contraction*: marriage contract. 50 *rhapsody*: (meaningless) mixture. *glow*: blush. 51 *solidity . . . mass*: solid earth, compounded of the four elements. 52 *against the doom*: expecting Judgment Day. 54 *index*: (1) table of contents (2) prologue. 56 *counterfeit presentment*: painted likeness. 58 *Hyperion*: Greek sun god. *front*: forehead. 60 *station*: bearing. 66 *ear*: i.e., of grain. 67 *Blasting*: blighting. 68 *leave to feed*: leave off feeding. 69 *batten*: gorge yourself. 70 *hey-day in the blood*: youthful passion. 73 *Sense*: perception by the senses. 74 *motion*: impulse. 75 *apoplexed*: paralyzed. 76 *sense . . . thralled*: sensibility was never so enslaved by madness. 78 *in . . . difference*: where the difference was so great. 79 *cozened . . . blind*: cheated you at blindman's bluff. 81 *sans all*: without the other senses. 83 *so mope*: be so dull. 85 *mutine*: rebel, mutiny.

And melt in her own fire. Proclaim no shame
When the compulsive° ardour gives the charge,°
Since frost itself as actively doth burn,
And reason panders will.°

QUEEN: O Hamlet, speak no more,   90
Thou turn'st my eyes into my very soul,
And there I see such black and grainèd° spots
As will not leave their tinct.°

HAMLET: Nay, but to live
In the rank sweat of an enseamèd° bed,
Stewed in corruption, honeying, and making love   95
Over the nasty sty.

QUEEN: O speak to me no more,
These words like daggers enter in mine ears,
No more, sweet Hamlet.

HAMLET: A murderer and a villain,
A slave that is not twentieth part the tithe°
Of your precedent lord, a vice° of kings,   100
A cutpurse° of the empire and the rule,
That from a shelf the precious diadem stole
And put it in his pocket.

QUEEN: No more.

HAMLET: A king of shreds and patches—

Enter the GHOST *in his night-gown.*°

Save me and hover o'er me with your wings,   105
You heavenly guards. What would your gracious figure?

QUEEN: Alas, he's mad.

HAMLET: Do you not come your tardy son to chide,
That lapsed in time and passion° lets go by
Th'important acting of your dread command?   110
O say!

GHOST: Do not forget: this visitation
Is but to whet thy almost blunted purpose.
But look, amazement on thy mother sits,
O step between her and her fighting soul,
Conceit° in weakest bodies strongest works,   115
Speak to her Hamlet.

HAMLET: How is it with you lady?

QUEEN: Alas, how is't with you,
That you do bend your eye on vacancy,°
And with th'incorporal° air do hold discourse?   120
Forth at your eyes your spirits° wildly peep,
And as the sleeping soldiers in th'alarm,
Your bedded° hairs, like life in excrements,°

°88 *compulsive:* compelling. *gives the charge:* attacks. 90 *panders will:* pimps for lust. 92 *grainèd:* dyed in grain, unfading. 93 *leave their tinct:* lose their color. 94 *enseamèd:* greasy. 99 *tithe:* one-tenth part. 100 *vice:* buffoon (like the character of Vice in the morality plays). 101 *cutpurse:* pickpocket. 104.1 S.D.: *night-gown:* dressing gown. 109 *lapsed . . . passion:* having let time elapse and passion cool. 116 *Conceit:* imagination. 119 *vacancy:* (she cannot see the ghost). 120 *incorporal:* bodiless. 121 *spirits:* vital forces. 123 *bedded:* lying flat. *excrements:* outgrowths (of the body).

Start up and stand an° end. O gentle son,
125 Upon the heat and flame of thy distemper
Sprinkle cool patience. Whereon do you look?
HAMLET: On him, on him, look you how pale he glares,
His form and cause conjoined, preaching to stones,
Would make them capable.° Do not look upon me,
130 Lest with this piteous action you convert
My stern effects,° then what I have to do
Will want° true colour,° tears perchance for blood.
QUEEN: To whom do you speak this?
HAMLET: Do you see nothing there?
QUEEN: Nothing at all, yet all that is I see.
HAMLET: Nor did you nothing hear?
135 QUEEN: No, nothing but ourselves.
HAMLET: Why look you there, look how it steals away,
My father in his habit as he lived,°
Look where he goes, even now out at the portal.   *Exit* [GHOST.]
QUEEN: This is the very coinage of your brain,
140 This bodiless creation ecstasy
Is very cunning in.°
HAMLET: Ecstasy?
My pulse as yours doth temperately keep time,
And makes as healthful music. It is not madness
That I have uttered; bring me to the test
145 And I the matter will re-word, which madness
Would gambol° from. Mother, for love of grace,
Lay not that flattering unction° to your soul,
That not your trespass but my madness speaks,
It will but skin and film the ulcerous place,
150 Whiles rank corruption mining° all within,
Infects unseen. Confess yourself to heaven,
Repent what's past, avoid what is to come,
And do not spread the compost° on the weeds
To make them ranker. Forgive me this my virtue,°
155 For in the fatness° of these pursy° times
Virtue itself of vice must pardon beg,
Yea curb and woo° for leave to do him° good.
QUEEN: O Hamlet, thou hast cleft my heart in twain.
HAMLET: O throw away the worser part of it,
160 And live the purer with the other half.
Good night, but go not to my uncle's bed,
Assume° a virtue if you have it not.
That monster custom, who all sense doth eat
Of habits evil,° is angel yet in this,
165 That to the use° of actions fair and good,

°124 *an*: on. 129 *capable*: i.e., of feeling pity. 130–31 *convert . . . effects*: transform my outward signs of sternness. 132 *want*: lack. *colour*: (1) complexion (2) motivation. 137 *habit . . . lived*: clothing he wore when alive. 140–41 *bodiless . . . cunning in*: madness (ecstasy) is very skillful in causing an affected person to hallucinate. 146 *gambol*: leap. 147 *unction*: salve. 150 *mining*: undermining. 153 *compost*: manure. 154 *virtue*: sermon on virtue. 155 *fatness*: grossness. *pursy*: flabby. 157 *curb and woo*: bow and plead. *him*: vice. 162 *Assume*: put on the guise of. 163–164 *all sense . . . evil*: confuses the sense of right and wrong in a habitué. 165 *use*: habit.

He likewise gives a frock or livery
That aptly° is put on. Refrain tonight,
And that shall lend a kind of easiness
To the next abstinence, the next more easy:
For use° almost can change the stamp° of nature,   170
And either . . . the° devil, or throw him out
With wondrous potency: once more good night,
And when you are desirous to be blessed,
I'll blessing beg of you. For this same lord,°
I do repent; but heaven hath pleased it so   175
To punish me with this, and this with me,
That I must be their scourge and minister.°
I will bestow° him and will answer well°
The death I gave him; so again good night.
I must be cruel only to be kind;   180
This bad begins, and worse remains behind.°
One word more, good lady.
QUEEN: What shall I do?
HAMLET: Not this by no means that I bid you do:
    Let the bloat° king tempt you again to bed,
    Pinch wanton on your cheek, call you his mouse,   185
    And let him for a pair of reechy° kisses,
    Or paddling in your neck with his damned fingers,
    Make you to ravel° all this matter out
    That I essentially am not in madness,
    But mad in craft. 'Twere good you let him know,   190
    For who that's but a queen, fair, sober, wise,
    Would from a paddock, from a bat, a gib,°
    Such dear concernings hide? who would do so?
    No, in despite of sense and secrecy,
    Unpeg the basket on the house's top,   195
    Let the birds fly, and like the famous ape,
    To try conclusions° in the basket creep,
    And break your own neck down.°
QUEEN: Be thou assured, if words be made of breath,
    And breath of life, I have no life to breathe   200
    What thou hast said to me.
HAMLET: I must to England, you know that.
QUEEN: Alack,
    I had forgot: 'tis so concluded on.
HAMLET: There's letters sealed, and my two school-fellows,
    Whom I will trust as I will adders fanged,   205
    They bear the mandate, they must sweep my way

°167 *aptly*: readily. 170 *use*: habit. *stamp*: form. 171 *either . . . the*: (word omitted, for which "tame," "curl," "lodge," and "quell" have been suggested). 173 *lord*: Polonius. 177 *their . . . minister*: heaven's punishment and agent of retribution. 178 *bestow*: stow away. *answer well*: assume full responsibility for. 181 *bad . . . behind*: is a bad beginning to a worse end to come. 184 *bloat*: bloated with dissipation. 186 *reechy*: filthy. 188 *ravel*: unravel. 192 *paddock, bat, gib*: toad, bat, tomcat ("familiars" or demons in animal shape that attend on witches). 195–198 *Unpeg . . . down*: (the story refers to an ape that climbs to the top of a house and opens a basket of birds; when the birds fly away, the ape crawls into the basket, tries to fly, and breaks his neck. The point is that if she gives away Hamlet's secret, she harms herself). 197 *try conclusions*: experiment.

And marshal me to knavery:° let it work,
For 'tis the sport to have the enginer°
Hoist with his own petar,° and't shall go hard
210 But I will delve one yard below their mines,
And blow them at the moon: O 'tis most sweet
When in one line two crafts directly meet.°
This man shall set me packing,°
I'll lug the guts into the neighbour room;
215 Mother good night indeed. This counsellor
Is now most still, most secret, and most grave,
Who was in life a foolish prating knave.
Come sir, to draw toward an end with you.
Good night mother.   *Exit* HAMLET *tugging in* POLONIUS.

ACT 4

Scene 1. [A room in the castle]

Enter KING *and* QUEEN *with* ROSENCRANTZ *and* GUILDENSTERN.

KING: There's matter in these sighs, these profound heaves,
You must translate, 'tis fit we understand them.
Where is your son?
QUEEN: Bestow this place on us° a little while.

Exeunt ROSENCRANTZ *and* GUILDENSTERN.

5   Ah mine own lord, what have I seen tonight!
KING: What, Gertrude? How does Hamlet?
QUEEN: Mad as the sea and wind when both contend
Which is the mightier, in his lawless fit,
Behind the arras hearing something stir,
10   Whips out his rapier, cries "A rat, a rat,"
And in this brainish apprehension° kills
The unseen good old man.
KING: O heavy deed!
It had been so with us° had we been there:
His liberty is full of threats to all,
15   To you yourself, to us, to every one.
Alas, how shall this bloody deed be answered?
It will be laid to us,° whose providence°
Should have kept short,° restrained, and out of haunt°
This mad young man; but so much was our love,
20   We would not understand what was most fit,
But like the owner of a foul disease,

°206–7 *sweep* . . . *knavery:* (like the marshal who went before a royal procession, clearing the way, so Rosencrantz and Guildenstern clear Hamlet's path to some unknown evil). 208 *enginer*: maker of war engines. 209 *Hoist* . . . *betar*: blown up by his own bomb. 212 *in one* . . . *meet*: the digger of the mine and the digger of the countermine meet halfway in their tunnels. 213 *packing*: (1) i.e., my bags (2) rushing away (3) plotting. 4 *Bestow* . . . *us*: leave us. 11 *brainish apprehension*: insane delusion. 13 *us*: me (royal plural). 17 *laid to us*: blamed on me. *providence*: foresight. 18 *short*: tethered by a short leash. *out of haunt*: away from others.

To keep it from divulging,° let it feed
Even on the pith of life: where is he gone?
QUEEN: To draw apart the body he hath killed,
    O'er whom his very madness, like some ore   25
    Among a mineral of metals base,°
    Shows itself pure: a' weeps for what is done.
KING: O Gertrude, come away:
    The sun no sooner shall the mountains touch,
    But we will ship him hence and this vile deed   30
    We must with all our majesty and skill
    Both countenance° and excuse. Ho Guildenstern!

Enter ROSENCRANTZ and GUILDENSTERN.

    Friends both, go join you with some further aid;
    Hamlet in madness hath Polonius slain,
    And from his mother's closet hath he dragged him.   35
    Go seek him out, speak fair, and bring the body
    Into the chapel; I pray you haste in this.   *[Exeunt Gentlemen.]*
    Come Gertrude, we'll call up our wisest friends,
    And let them know both what we mean to do
    And what's untimely done: [so haply slander,]   40
    Whose whisper o'er the world's diameter,
    As level° as the cannon to his blank°
    Transports his° poisoned shot, may miss our name,
    And hit the woundless° air. O come away,
    My soul is full of discord and dismay.   *Exeunt.*   45

Scene 2. [Another room in the castle]

Enter HAMLET.

HAMLET: Safely stowed.
    Gentlemen within: Hamlet, Lord Hamlet!
    But soft, what noise, who calls on Hamlet?
    O here they come.

Enter ROSENCRANTZ and GUILDENSTERN.

ROSENCRANTZ: What have you done my lord with the dead body?   5
HAMLET: Compounded it with dust whereto 'tis kin.
ROSENCRANTZ: Tell us where 'tis that we may take it thence,
    And bear it to the chapel.
HAMLET: Do not believe it.
ROSENCRANTZ: Believe what?   10
HAMLET: That I can keep your counsel° and not mine own.° Besides,
    to be demanded of° a sponge, what replication° should be
    made by the son of a king?
ROSENCRANTZ: Take you me for a sponge, my lord?

°22 *divulging*: being divulged. 25–26 *ore . . . base*: pure ore (such as gold) in a mine of base metal. 32 *countenance*: defend. 42 *As level*: with a straight aim. *blank*: white bull's-eye at the target's center. 43 *his*: slander's. 44 *woundless*: invulnerable. 11 *counsel*: (1) advice (2) secret. *keep . . . own*: follow your advice and not keep my own secret. 12 *demanded of*: questioned by. *replication*: reply to a charge.

15 HAMLET: Ay sir, that soaks up the king's countenance,° his rewards,
his authorities. But such officers do the king best service in
the end; he keeps them like an apple in the corner of his
jaw, first mouthed to be last swallowed: when he needs
what you have gleaned, it is but squeezing you, and
20 sponge, you shall be dry again.
ROSENCRANTZ: I understand you not my lord.
HAMLET: I am glad of it: a knavish speech sleeps in° a foolish ear.
ROSENCRANTZ: My lord, you must tell us where the body is, and go with
us to the king.
25 HAMLET: The body is with the king, but the king° is not with the
body. The king is a thing—
GUILDENSTERN: A thing my lord?
HAMLET: Of nothing, bring me to him. Hide fox, and all after.°   *Exeunt.*

Scene 3. [Another room in the castle]

Enter KING and two or three.

KING: I have sent to seek him, and to find the body:
How dangerous is it that this man goes loose,
Yet must not we put the strong law on him,
He's loved of the distracted multitude,°
5 Who like not in° their judgment, but their eyes,
And where 'tis so, th'offender's scourge° is weighed
But never the offence: to bear all° smooth and even,
This sudden sending him away must seem
Deliberate pause° diseases desperate grown,
10 By desperate appliance° are relieved,
Or not at all.

Enter ROSENCRANTZ and all the rest.

                  How now, what hath befallen?
ROSENCRANTZ: Where the dead body is bestowed my lord,
We cannot get from him.
KING: But where is he?
ROSENCRANTZ: Without, my lord, guarded,° to know your pleasure.
KING: Bring him before us.
15 ROSENCRANTZ: Ho, bring in the lord.

Enter HAMLET (guarded) and GUILDENSTERN.

KING: Now Hamlet, where's Polonius?
HAMLET: At supper.
KING: At supper? where?
HAMLET: Not where he eats, but where a' is eaten: a certain
20 convocation of politic° worms are e'en° at him. Your worm is your
only emperor for diet, we fat all creatures else to fat us,

°15 *countenance:* favor. 22 *sleeps in:* means nothing to. 25 *king . . . king:* Hamlet's father . . . Claudius. 28 *Hide fox . . . after:* (cry in a children's game, like hide-and-seek). 4 *distracted multitude:* confused mob. 5 *in:* according to. 6 *scourge:* punishment. 7 *bear all:* carry out everything. 9 *Deliberate pause:* considered delay. 10 *appliance:* remedy. 14 *guarded:* (Hamlet is under guard until he boards the ship). 20 *politic:* (1) statesmanlike (2) crafty. *e'en:* even now.

and we fat ourselves for maggots. Your fat king and your
lean beggar is but variable service,° two dishes but to one
table, that's the end.

KING: Alas, alas.   25

HAMLET: A man may fish with the worm that hath eat of a king, and
eat of the fish that hath fed of that worm.

KING: What dost thou mean by this?

HAMLET: Nothing but to show you how a king may go a progress°
through the guts of a beggar.   30

KING: Where is Polonius?

HAMLET: In heaven, send thither to see. If your messenger find him
not there, seek him i'th'other place yourself: but if indeed
you find him not within this month, you shall nose him as
you go up the stairs into the lobby.   35

KING: [*To* ATTENDANTS.] Go seek him there.

HAMLET: A' will stay till you come.   [*Exeunt.*]

KING: Hamlet, this deed, for thine especial safety—
Which we do tender,° as we dearly grieve
For that which thou hast done—must send thee hence   40
With fiery quickness. Therefore prepare thyself,
The bark is ready, and the wind at help,°
Th'associates tend,° and every thing is bent
For England.

HAMLET: For England.

KING: Ay Hamlet.

HAMLET: Good.

KING: So is it if thou knew'st our purposes.   45

HAMLET: I see a cherub° that sees them: but come, for England.
Farewell dear mother.

KING: Thy loving father, Hamlet.

HAMLET: My mother: father and mother is man and wife, man and
wife is one flesh, and so my mother: come, for England.   *Exit.* 50

KING: [*To* ROSENCRANTZ *and* GUILDENSTERN.]
Follow him at foot,° tempt him with speed aboard,
Delay it not, I'll have him hence tonight.
Away, for every thing is sealed and done
That else leans on° th'affair, pray you make haste.   [*Exeunt.*]
And England,° if my love thou hold'st at aught°—   55
As my great power thereof may give thee sense,
Since yet thy cicatrice° looks raw and red
After the Danish sword, and thy free awe
Pays homage° to us—thou mayst not coldly set°
Our sovereign process,° which imports at full   60
By letters congruing° to that effect,
The present° death of Hamlet. Do it England,

°23 *variable service*: different types of food. 29 *go a progress*: make a splendid royal journey from one part of the
country to another. 39 *tender*: cherish. 42 *at help*: helpful. 43 *tend*: wait. 46 *cherub*: (considered the watchmen of
heaven). 51 *at foot*: at his heels. 54 *leans on*: relates to. 55 *England*: King of England. *my love . . . aught*: you place
any value on my favor. 57 *cicatrice*: scar. 58–59 *free . . . homage*: awe which you, though free, still show by paying
homage. 59 *coldly set*: lightly estimate. 60 *process*: command. 61 *congruing*: agreeing. 62 *present*: immediate.

For like the hectic° in my blood he rages,
And thou must cure me; till I know 'tis done,
65   Howe'er my haps,° my joys were ne'er begun.   *Exit.*

Scene 4. [A plain in Denmark]

Enter FORTINBRAS *with his army over the stage.*

FORTINBRAS: Go captain, from me greet the Danish king,
        Tell him that by his license, Fortinbras
        Craves the conveyance° of a promised march
        Over his kingdom. You know the rendezvous:
5   If that his majesty would aught with us,
        We shall express our duty in his eye,°
        And let him know so.
CAPTAIN: I will do't, my lord.
FORTINBRAS: Go softly° on.   *Exit.*

Enter HAMLET, ROSENCRANTZ, [GUILDENSTERN,] *etc.*

HAMLET: Good sir whose powers° are these?
10   CAPTAIN: They are of Norway sir.
HAMLET: How purposed sir I pray you?
CAPTAIN: Against some part of Poland.
HAMLET: Who commands them sir?
CAPTAIN: The nephew to old Norway, Fortinbras.
15   HAMLET: Goes it against the main° of Poland sir,
        Or for some frontier?
CAPTAIN: Truly to speak, and with no addition,
        We go to gain a little patch of ground
        That hath in it no profit but the name.°
20   To pay five ducats, five, I would not farm it;
        Nor will it yield to Norway or the Pole
        A ranker° rate, should it be sold in fee.°
HAMLET: Why then the Polack never will defend it.
CAPTAIN: Yes, it is already garrisoned.
25   HAMLET: Two thousand souls, and twenty thousand ducats
        Will not debate the question of° this straw:°
        This is th'imposthume of much wealth and peace,°
        That inward breaks, and shows no cause without
        Why the man dies. I humbly thank you sir.
CAPTAIN: God bye you sir.   [*Exit.*]
30   ROSENCRANTZ: Will't please you go my lord?
HAMLET: I'll be with you straight, go a little before.

                                            [*Exeunt all but* HAMLET.]

        How all occasions do inform against me,
        And spur my dull revenge. What is a man
        If his chief good and market° of his time

°63 *hectic*: fever. 65 *haps*: fortunes. 3 *conveyance of*: escort for. 6 *in his eye*: face to face. 8 *softly*: slowly. 9 *powers*: troops. 15 *main*: body. 19 *name*: glory. 22 *ranker*: higher (as annual interest on the total). *in fee*: outright. 26 *debate . . . of*: settle the dispute over. *straw*: triviality. 27 *imposthume . . . peace*: swelling discontent (inner abscess) resulting from too much wealth and peace. 34 *market*: profit.

Be but to sleep and feed? a beast, no more: 35
Sure he that made us with such large discourse,°
Looking before and after,° gave us not
That capability and god-like reason
To fust° in us unused. Now whether it be
Bestial oblivion,° or some craven° scruple   40
Of thinking too precisely on th'event°—
A thought which quartered hath but one part wisdom,
And ever three parts coward—I do not know
Why yet I live to say "This thing's to do,"
Sith I have cause, and will, and strength, and means   45
To do't; examples gross° as earth exhort me:
Witness this army of such mass and charge,°
Led by a delicate and tender° prince,
Whose spirit with divine ambition puffed,
Makes mouths° at the invisible event,°   50
Exposing what is mortal, and unsure,
To all that fortune, death, and danger dare,
Even for an egg-shell. Rightly to be great,
Is not to stir without great argument,
But greatly to find quarrel in a straw   55
When honour's at the stake.° How stand I then
That have a father killed, a mother stained,
Excitements° of my reason, and my blood,
And let all sleep, while to my shame I see
The imminent death of twenty thousand men,   60
That for a fantasy and trick° of fame
Go to their graves like beds, fight for a plot
Whereon the numbers cannot try the cause,°
Which is not tomb enough and continent°
To hide the slain. O from this time forth,   65
My thoughts be bloody, or be nothing worth.   *Exit.*

Scene 5. [A room in the castle]

Enter QUEEN, HORATIO *and a* GENTLEMAN.

QUEEN: I will not speak with her.
GENTLEMAN: She is importunate, indeed distract,°
    Her mood will needs be° pitied.
QUEEN: What would she have?
GENTLEMAN: She speaks much of her father, says she hears
    There's tricks i'th'world, and hems,° and beats her heart,   5
    Spurns enviously at straws,° speaks things in doubt°
    That carry but half sense: her speech is nothing,

°36 *discourse:* power of reasoning. 37 *Looking . . . after:* seeing causes and effects. 40 *Bestial oblivion:* forgetfulness, as a beast forgets its parents. *craven:* cowardly. 41 *event:* outcome. 46 *gross:* obvious. 47 *charge:* expense. 48 *delicate and tender:* gentle and young. 50 *mouths:* faces. *event:* outcome. 53–56 *Rightly . . . stake:* the truly great do not fight without just cause ("argument"), but it is nobly ("greatly") done to fight even for a trifle if honor is at stake. 58 *Excitements:* incentives. 61 *fantasy and trick:* illusion and trifle. 63 *Whereon . . . cause:* too small to accommodate all the troops fighting for it. 64 *continent:* container. 2 *distract:* insane. 3 *will needs be:* needs to be. 5 *hems:* coughs. 6 *Spurns . . . straws:* reacts maliciously to trifles. *in doubt:* ambiguous.

Yet the unshapèd use of it doth move
The hearers to collection;° they aim° at it,
10 And botch° the words up fit to their own thoughts,
Which as her winks, and nods, and gestures yield them,
Indeed would make one think there might be thought,
Though nothing sure, yet much unhappily.
HORATIO: 'Twere good she were spoken with, for she may strew
15 Dangerous conjectures in ill-breeding minds.
QUEEN: Let her come in.   *Exit* GENTLEMAN.
    [*Aside.*] To my sick soul, as sin's true nature is;°
    Each toy° seems prologue to some great amiss,°
    So full of artless jealousy° is guilt,
20 It spills itself, in fearing to be spilt.

Enter OPHELIA, *distracted.*°

OPHELIA: Where is the beauteous majesty of Denmark?
QUEEN: How now Ophelia?
OPHELIA: [*Sings.*] How should I your true love know
                      From another one?
25   By his cockle hat and staff,°
                      And his sandal shoon.°
QUEEN: Alas sweet lady, what imports this song?
OPHELIA: Say you? nay, pray you mark.
         [*Sings.*] He is dead and gone, lady,
30   He is dead and gone,
                  At his head a grass-green turf,
                      At his heels a stone.
           O ho.
QUEEN: Nay but Ophelia—
OPHELIA: Pray you mark.
35   [*Sings.*] White his shroud as the mountain snow—

Enter KING.

QUEEN: Alas, look here my lord,
OPHELIA: [*Sings.*] Larded° all with sweet flowers,
            Which bewept to the ground did not go,
                With true-love showers.
40 KING: How do you, pretty lady?
OPHELIA: Well, God 'ild° you. They say the owl was a baker's
    daughter.° Lord, we know what we are, but know not what
    we may be. God be at your table.°
KING: Conceit° upon her father.
45 OPHELIA: Pray you let's have no words of this, but when they ask
    you what it means, say you this:
    [*Sings.*] Tomorrow is Saint Valentine's day,

_____

°9 *collection*: inference. *aim*: guess. 10 *botch*: patch. 17 *as sin's . . . is*: as is natural for the guilty. 18 *toy*: trifle. *amiss*: disaster. 19 *artless* jealousy: uncontrollable suspicion. 20 S.D.: *distracted*: insane. 25 *cockle hat and staff*: (marks of the pilgrim, the cockle shell symbolizing his journey to the shrine of St. James; the pilgrim was a common metaphor for the lover). 26 *shoon*: shoes. 37 *Larded*: trimmed. 41 *God 'ild*: God yield (reward). 41–42 *owl . . . daughter*: (in a medieval legend, a baker's daughter was turned into an owl because she gave Jesus short weight on a loaf of bread). 43 *God . . . table*: (a blessing at dinner). 44 *Conceit*: thinking.

All in the morning betime,°
And I a maid at your window
    To be your Valentine.   50
Then up he rose, and donned his clo'es,
    And dupped° the chamber door,
Let in the maid, that out a maid,
    Never departed more.
KING: Pretty Ophelia.   55
OPHELIA: Indeed, la, without an oath I'll make an end on't.
    [*Sings.*] By Gis° and by Saint Charity,
        Alack and fie for shame,
    Young men will do't, if they come to't,
        By Cock° they are to blame.   60
    Quoth she, Before you tumbled me,
        You promised me to wed.
    He answers. So would I ha' done, by yonder sun,
        An° thou hadst not come to my bed.
KING: How long hath she been thus?   65
OPHELIA: I hope all will be well. We must be patient, but I cannot
    choose but weep to think they would lay him i'th' cold
    ground. My brother shall know of it, and so I thank you
    for your good counsel. Come, my coach: good night   70
    ladies, good night. Sweet ladies, good night, good night.   [*Exit* OPHELIA.]
KING: Follow her close, give her good watch I pray you.   [*Exit* HORATIO.]
    O this is the poison of deep grief, it springs
    All from her father's death, and now behold:
    O Gertrude, Gertrude,
    When sorrows come, they come not single spies,   75
    But in battalions: first her father slain,
    Next, your son gone, and he most violent author
    Of his own just remove, the people muddied,°
    Thick and unwholesome in their thoughts and whispers
    For good Polonius' death: and we have done but greenly°   80
    In hugger-mugger° to inter him: poor Ophelia
    Divided from herself and her fair judgment,
    Without the which we are pictures or mere beasts,
    Last, and as much containing° as all these,
    Her brother is in secret come from France,   85
    Feeds on his wonder,° keeps himself in clouds,°
    And wants not buzzers° to infect his ear
    With pestilent speeches of his father's death,
    Wherein necessity, of matter beggared,
    Will nothing stick our person to arraign°   90
    In ear and ear:° O my dear Gertrude, this

°48 *betime*: early (because the first woman a man saw on Valentine's Day would be his true love). 52 *dupped*: opened. 57 *Gis*: contraction of "Jesus." 60 *Cock*: (vulgarization of "God" in oaths). 64 *An*: if. 78 *muddied*: stirred up. 80 *done but greenly*: acted like amateurs. 81 *hugger-mugger*: secret haste. 84 *containing*: i.e., cause for sorrow. 86 *Feeds . . . wonder*: sustains himself by wondering about his father's death. *clouds*: gloom, obscurity. 87 *wants not buzzers*: lacks not whispering gossips. 89–90 *Wherein . . . arraign*: in which the tellers, lacking facts, will not hesitate to accuse me. 91 *In ear and ear*: whispering from one ear to another.

Like to a murdering-piece° in many places
Gives me superfluous death.   *A noise within.*
QUEEN: Alack, what noise is this?
KING: Attend!   *Enter a* MESSENGER.
95   Where are my Switzers.° Let them guard the door.
      What is the matter?
MESSENGER.   Save yourself, my lord.
      The ocean, overpeering of his list,°
      Eats not the flats° with more impiteous haste
      Than young Laertes in a riotous head°
100   O'erbears your officers: the rabble call him lord,
      And as the world were now but to begin,
      Antiquity forgot, custom not known,
      The ratifiers and props of every word,
      They cry "Choose we, Laertes shall be king!"
105   Caps, hands, and tongues applaud it to the clouds,
      "Laertes shall be king, Laertes king!"   *A noise within.*
QUEEN: How cheerfully on the false trail they cry.
      O this is counter,° you false Danish dogs.
KING: The doors are broke.

Enter LAERTES *with others.*

110 LAERTES: Where is this king? Sirs, stand you all without.°
DANES: No, let's come in.
LAERTES: I pray you give me leave.°
DANES: We will, we will.   *[They retire.]*
LAERTES: I thank you, keep the door. O thou vile king,
      Give me my father.
QUEEN: Calmly, good Laertes.
115 LAERTES: That drop of blood that's calm proclaims me bastard,
      Cries cuckold° to my father, brands° the harlot
      Even here between the chaste unsmirchèd brows
      Of my true mother.
KING: What is the cause Laertes,
      That thy rebellion looks so giant-like?
120   Let him go Gertrude, do not fear° our person,
      There's such divinity° doth hedge a king,
      That treason can but peep to° what it would,
      Acts little of his° will. Tell me Laertes,
      Why thou art this incensed. Let him go Gertrude.
125   Speak man.
LAERTES: Where is my father?
KING: Dead.
QUEEN: But not by him.
KING: Let him demand his fill.
LAERTES: How came he dead? I'll not be juggled with.

°92 *murdering-piece*: small cannon shooting shrapnel, to inflict numerous wounds. 95 *Switzers*: Swiss guards.
97 *overpeering . . . list*: rising above its usual limits. 98 *flats*: lowlands. 99 *head*: armed force. 108 *counter*: following the
scent backward. 110 *without*: outside. 111 *leave*: i.e., to enter alone. 116 *cuckold*: betrayed husband. *brands*: (so har-
lots were punished). 120 *fear*: i.e., for. 121 *divinity*: divine protection. 122 *peep to*: strain to see. 123 *his*: treason's.

To hell allegiance, vows to the blackest devil,
Conscience and grace, to the profoundest pit. 130
I dare damnation: to this point I stand,
That both the worlds I give to negligence,°
Let come what comes, only I'll be revenged
Most throughly for my father.
KING: Who shall stay you?
LAERTES: My will, not all the world's:° 135
And for my means, I'll husband° them so well,
They shall go far with little.
KING: Good Laertes,
If you desire to know the certainty
Of your dear father, is't writ in your revenge
That swoopstake,° you will draw both friend and foe, 140
Winner and loser?
LAERTES: None but his enemies.
KING: Will you know them then?
LAERTES: To his good friends thus wide I'll ope my arms,
And like the kind life-rend'ring pelican,°
Repast them with my blood.
KING: Why now you speak 145
Like a good child, and a true gentleman.
That I am guiltless of your father's death,
And am most sensibly° in grief for it,
It shall as level° to your judgment 'pear
As day does to your eye. 150

[*A noise within.*]

[*Crowd shouts.*] Let her come in.
LAERTES: How now, what noise is that?

Enter OPHELIA.

O heat, dry up my brains, tears seven time salt,
Burn out the sense and virtue° of mine eye!
By heaven, thy madness shall be paid with weight,° 155
Till our scale turn the beam,° O rose of May,
Dear maid, kind sister, sweet Ophelia:
O heavens, is't possible a young maid's wits
Should be as mortal as an old man's life?
Nature is fine in love, and where 'tis fine, 160
It sends some previous instance of itself
after the thing it loves.°
OPHELIA: [*Sings.*] They bore him barefaced on the bier,
            Hey non nonny, nonny, hey nonny:

°132 *both . . . negligence:* I care nothing for this world or the next. 135 *world's:* i.e., will. 136 *husband:* economize.
140 *swoopstake:* sweeping in all the stakes in a game, both of winner and loser. 144 *pelican:* (the mother pelican
was believed to nourish her young with blood pecked from her own breast). 148 *sensibly:* feelingly. 149 *level:*
plain. 154 *sense and virtue:* feeling and power. 155 *with weight:* with equal weight. 156 *turn the beam:* outweigh the
other side. 160–62 *Nature . . . loves:* filial love that is so refined and pure sends some precious token (her wits)
after the beloved dead.

165   And in his grave rained many a tear—
          Fare you well my dove.
LAERTES: Hadst thou thy wits, and didst persuade revenge,
          It could not move thus.
OPHELIA: You must sing "adown adown," and you call him adown-a.
170   O how the wheel becomes it.° It is the false steward that
          stole his master's daughter.
LAERTES: This nothing's more than matter.°
OPHELIA: There's rosemary,° that's for remembrance, pray you love
          remember: and there is pansies, that's for thoughts.
175 **LAERTES:** A document° in madness, thoughts and remembrance
          fitted.°
OPHELIA: There's fennel for you, and columbines.° There's rue° for
          you, and here's some for me, we may call it herb of grace°
          o'Sundays: O, you must wear your rue with a difference.°
180   There's daisy,° I would give you some violets,° but they
          withered all when my father died: they say a' made a good
          end;
              [*Sings.*] For bonny sweet Robin is all my joy.
LAERTES: Thought and affliction, passion, hell itself,
185   She turns to favour and to prettiness.
OPHELIA: [*Sings.*] And will a' not come again,
              And will a' not come again?
                No, no, he is dead,
                Go to thy death-bed,
190   He never will come again.
              His beard was as white as snow,
              All flaxen was his poll,°
                He is gone, he is gone,
                And we cast away moan,
195   God ha' mercy on his soul.
          And of all Christian souls, I pray God. God bye you.

                                        Exit OPHELIA.

LAERTES: Do you see this, O God?
KING: Laertes, I must commune with your grief,
          Or you deny me right: go but apart,
200   Make choice of whom your wisest friends you will,
          And they shall hear and judge 'twixt you and me;
          If by direct or by collateral° hand
          They find us touched,° we will our kingdom give,
          Our crown, our life, and all that we call ours
205   To you in satisfaction; but if not,
          Be you content to lend your patience to us,

°170 *wheel becomes it*: refrain ("adown") suits the subject (Polonius's fall). 173 *There's rosemary*: (given to Laertes; she may be distributing imaginary or real flowers). 175 *document*: lesson. 175–76 *thoughts . . . fitted*: thoughts of revenge matched with remembrance of Polonius. 177 *fennel . . . columbines*: (given to the king, symbolizing flattery and ingratitude). *rue*: (given to the queen, symbolizing sorrow or repentance). 178 *herb of grace*: (because it symbolizes repentance). 179 *with a difference*: for a different reason (Ophelia's is for sorrow and the queen's for repentance). 180 *daisy*: (symbolizing dissembling). *violets*: (symbolizing faithfulness). 192 *flaxen . . . poll*: white was his head. 202 *collateral*: indirect. 203 *touched*: tainted with guilt.

And we shall jointly labour with your soul
To give it due content.
LAERTES: Let this be so.
His means of death, his obscure funeral,
No trophy,° sword, nor hatchment° o'er his bones,   210
No noble rite, nor formal ostentation,°
Cry° to be heard as 'twere from heaven to earth,
That I must call't in question.
KING: So you shall,
And where th'offence is, let the great axe fall.
I pray you go with me.   [*Exeunt.*]   215

Scene 6. [Another room in the castle]

Enter HORATIO *and others.*

HORATIO: What are they that would speak with me?
GENTLEMAN: Seafaring men sir, they say they have letters for you.
HORATIO: Let them come in.   [*Exit* ATTENDANT.]
      I do not know from what part of the world
      I should be greeted, if not from Lord Hamlet.   5

Enter SAILORS.

SAILOR: God bless you sir.
HORATIO: Let him bless thee too.
SAILOR: A'shall sir, an't please him. There's a letter for you sir, it
      came from th'ambassador that was bound for England, if
      your name be Horatio, as I am let to know it is.   10
HORATIO: [*Reads the letter.*] "Horatio, when thou shalt have
      overlooked° this, give these fellows some means to the king,
      they have letters for him. Ere we were two days old at sea,
      a pirate of very warlike appointment° gave us chase.
      Finding ourselves too slow of sail, we put on a compelled   15
      valour, and in the grapple° I boarded them. On the instant
      they got clear of our ship, so I alone became their prisoner.
      They have dealt with me like thieves of mercy,° but they
      knew what they did. I am to do a good turn for them. Let
      the king have the letters I have sent, and repair° thou to me   20
      with as much speed as thou wouldst fly death. I have
      words to speak in thine ear will make thee dumb, yet are
      they much too light for the bore° of the matter. These good
      fellows will bring thee where I am. Rosencrantz and
      Guildenstern hold their course for England. Of them I   25
      have much to tell thee. Farewell.
                  He that thou knowest thine, Hamlet."
      Come, I will give you way° for these your letters,
      And do't the speedier that you may direct me
      To him from whom you brought them.   *Exeunt.*   30

°210 *trophy:* memorial. *hatchment:* tablet displaying coat of arms. 211 *ostentation:* ceremony. 212 Cry: cry out. 12
overlooked: read over. 14 *appointment:* equipment. 16 *in the grapple:* when the pirate ship hooked onto ours. 18 *of
mercy:* merciful. 20 *repair:* come. 23 *bore:* size, caliber. 28 *way:* access (to the king).

Scene 7. [Another room in the castle]

Enter KING *and* LAERTES.

KING: Now must your conscience my acquittance seal,°
    And you must put me in your heart for friend,
    Sith you have heard and with a knowing ear,
    That he which hath your noble father slain
    Pursued my life.
5 LAERTES: It well appears: but tell me
    Why you proceeded not against these feats
    So crimeful and so capital in nature,
    As by your safety, greatness, wisdom, all things else,
    You mainly were stirred up.°
  KING: O for two special reasons,
10   Which may to you perhaps seem much unsinewed,°
    But yet to me they're strong. The queen his mother
    Lives almost by his looks, and for myself,
    My virtue or my plague, be it either which,
    She's so conjunctive° to my life and soul,
15   That as the star moves not but in his sphere,°
    I could not but by her. The other motive,
    Why to a public count° I might not go,
    Is the great love the general gender° bear him,
    Who dipping all his faults in their affection,
20   Would like the spring that turneth wood to stone,°
    Convert his gyves to graces,° so that my arrows,
    Too slightly timbered° for so loud a wind,
    Would have reverted to my bow again,
    And not where I had aimed them.
25 LAERTES: And so have I a noble father lost,
    A sister driven into desperate terms,°
    Whose worth, if praises may go back° again,
    Stood challenger on mount of all the age
    For her perfections.° But my revenge will come.
30 KING: Break not your sleeps for that, you must not think
    That we are made of stuff so flat and dull,
    That we can let our beard be shook with danger,
    And think it pastime. You shortly shall hear more,
    I loved your father, and we love ourself,
35   And that I hope will teach you to imagine—

Enter a MESSENGER *with letters.*

      How now. What news?

°1 *my acquittance seal*: confirm my acquittal. 9 *mainly . . . up*: were strongly urged. 10 *much unsinewed*: very weak. 14 *conjunctive*: closely allied. 15 *in his sphere*: (referring to the Ptolemaic belief that each planet, fixed in its own sphere, revolved around the earth). 17 *count*: accounting. 18 *general gender*: common people. 20 *the spring . . . stone*: (the baths of King's Newnham in Warwickshire were described as being able to turn wood into stone because of their high concentrations of lime). 21 *Convert . . . graces*: regard his fetters (had he been imprisoned) as honors. 22 *slightly timbered*: light-shafted. 26 *desperate terms*: madness. 27 *go back*: i.e., before her madness. 28–29 *challenger . . . perfections*: like a challenger on horseback, ready to defend against the world her claim to perfection.

MESSENGER: Letters my lord, from Hamlet.
These to your majesty, this to the queen.
KING: From Hamlet? Who brought them?
MESSENGER: Sailors my lord they say, I saw them not:
They were given me by Claudio, he received them   40
Of him that brought them.
KING: Laertes you shall hear them:
Leave us.   *Exit [MESSENGER]*
[*Reads*] "High and mighty, you shall know I am set naked° on
your kingdom. Tomorrow shall I beg leave to see your kingly
eyes, when I shall, first asking your pardon° thereunto,   45
recount the occasion of my sudden and more strange return.
                                        Hamlet."
What should this mean? Are all the rest come back?
Or is it some abuse,° and no such thing?
LAERTES: Know you the hand?
KING: 'Tis Hamlet's character.° "Naked,"   50
And in a postscript here he says "alone."
Can you devise me°?
LAERTES: I am lost in it my lord, but let him come,
It warms the very sickness in my heart
That I shall live and tell him to his teeth,   55
"Thus didest thou."
KING: If it be so Laertes—
As how should it be so? how otherwise?—
Will you be ruled by me?
LAERTES: Ay my lord,
So you will not o'errule me to a peace.
KING: To thine own peace: if he be now returned,   60
As checking at° his voyage, and that he means
No more to undertake it, I will work him
To an exploit, now ripe in my device,°
Under the which he shall not choose but fall:
And for his death no wind of blame shall breathe,   65
But even his mother shall uncharge the practice,°
And call it accident.
LAERTES: My lord, I will be ruled,
The rather if you could devise it so
That I might be the organ.°
KING: It falls right.
You have been talked of since your travel much,   70
And that in Hamlet's hearing, for a quality
Wherein they say you shine: your sum of parts°
Did not together pluck such envy from him
As did that one, and that in my regard
Of the unworthiest siege.°   75

°43 *naked*: without resources. 45 *pardon*: permission. 49 *abuse*: deception. 50 *character*: handwriting. 52 *devise me*: explain it. 61 *checking at*: altering the course of (when the falcon forsakes one quarry for another). 63 *ripe in my device*: already planned by me. 66 *uncharge the practice*: acquit the plot (of treachery). 69 *organ*: instrument. 72 *your sum of parts*: all your accomplishments. 75 *siege*: rank.

75 **LAERTES:**   What part is that my lord?

KING: A very riband° in the cap of youth,
    Yet needful too, for youth no less becomes°
    The light and careless livery° that it wears,
    Than settled age his sables° and his weeds°
80 Importing health and graveness; two months since,°
    Here was a gentleman of Normandy—
    I have seen myself, and served against the French,
    And they can° well on horseback—but this gallant
    Had witchcraft in't, he grew unto his seat,
85 And to such wondrous doing brought his horse,
    As had he been incorpsed and demi-natured°
    With the brave beast. So far he topped my thought,
    That I in forgery of° shapes and tricks
    Come short of what he did.

LAERTES: A Norman was't?

90 **KING:** A Norman.

LAERTES: Upon my life, Lamord.°

KING: The very same.

LAERTES: I know him well, he is the brooch° indeed
    And gem of all the nation.

KING: He made confession° of you,
95 And gave you such a masterly report
    For art and exercise in your defence,
    And for your rapier most especial,
    That he cried out 'twould be a sight indeed
    If one could match you; the scrimers° of their nation
100 He swore had neither motion, guard, nor eye,
    If you opposed them; sir this report of his
    Did Hamlet so envenom° with his envy,
    That he could nothing do but wish and beg
    Your sudden coming o'er to play with him.
    Now out of this—

105 **LAERTES:**   What out of this, my lord?

KING: Laertes, was your father dear to you?
    Or are you like the painting of a sorrow,
    A face without a heart?

LAERTES: Why ask you this?

KING: Not that I think you did not love your father.
110 But that I know love is begun by time,
    And that I see in passages of proof,°
    Time qualifies° the spark and fire of it:
    There lives within the very flame of love
    A kind of wick or snuff that will abate it,°
115 And nothing is at a like goodness still,°

°76 *riband*: decoration. 77 *becomes*: befits. 78 *livery*: clothing (denoting rank or occupation). 79 *sables*: fur-trimmed gowns. *weeds*: garments. 80 *since*: ago. 83 *can*: can do. 86 *incorpsed . . . natured*: made into one body, sharing half its nature. 88 *in forgery of*: imagining. 91 *Lamord*: a name meaning "death" in French. 92 *brooch*: ornament. 94 *confession*: report. 99 *scrimers*: fencers. 102 *envenom*: poison. 111 *passages of proof*: examples drawn from experience. 112 *qualifies*: weakens. 114 *snuff . . . it*: charred end of the wick that will diminish the flame. 115 *still*: always.

For goodness growing to a plurisy,°
Dies in his own too-much. That we would do
We should do when we would: for this "would"° changes,
And hath abatements and delays as many
As there are tongues, are hands, are accidents,   120
And then this "should"° is like a spendthrift sigh,
That hurts by easing,° but to the quick° of th'ulcer:
Hamlet comes back, what would you undertake
To show yourself in deed your father's son
More than in words?
LAERTES: To cut his throat i'th'church.   125
KING: No place indeed should murder sanctuarize,°
Revenge should have no bounds: but good Laertes,
Will you do this, keep close within your chamber:
Hamlet returned shall know you are come home,
We'll put on° those shall praise your excellence,   130
And set a double varnish on the fame
The Frenchman gave you, bring you in fine° together,
And wager on your heads; he being remiss,°
Most generous, and free from all contriving,
Will not peruse the foils, so that with ease,   135
Or with a little shuffling, you may choose
A sword unbated,° and in a pass of practice°
Requite him for your father.
LAERTES: I will do't,
And for the purpose, I'll anoint my sword.
I bought an unction° of a mountebank°   140
So mortal,° that but dip a knife in it,
Where it draws blood, no cataplasm° so rare,
Collected from all simples° that have virtue°
Under the moon,° can save the thing from death
That is but scratched withal: I'll touch my point   145
With this contagion, that if I gall° him slightly,
It may be death.
KING: Let's further think of this,
Weigh what convenience both of time and means
May fit us to our shape;° if this should fail,
And that our drift° look through° our bad performance,   150
'Twere better not assayed; therefore this project
Should have a back or second that might hold
If this did blast in proof,° soft, let me see,
We'll make a solemn wager on your cunnings°—

°116 *plurisy*: excess. 118 "*would*": will to act. 121 "*should*": reminder of one's duty. 121–22 *spendthrift . . . easing*:
A sigh which, though giving temporary relief, wastes life, as each sigh draws a drop of blood away from the heart
(a common Elizabethan belief). 126 *murder sanctuarize*: give sanctuary to murder. 130 *put on*: incite. 132 *in fine*:
finally. 133 *remiss*: easy-going. 137 *unbated*: not blunted (the edges and points were blunted for fencing). *pass of
practice*: (1) match for exercise (2) treacherous thrust. 140 *unction*: ointment. *mountebank*: quack doctor, medicine man. 141 *mortal*: deadly. 142 *cataplasm*: poultice. 143 *simples*: herbs. *virtue*: power (of healing). 144 *Under the
moon*: (when herbs were supposed to be collected to be most effective). 146 *gall*: scratch. 149 *shape*: plan.
150 *drift*: aim. *look through*: be exposed by. 153 *blast in proof*: fail when tested (as a bursting cannon). 154 *cunnings*:
skills.

155 I ha't:
When in your motion you are hot and dry,
As make your bouts more violent to that end,
And that he calls for drink, I'll have prepared him
A chalice for the nonce,° whereon but sipping,
160 If he by chance escape your venomed stuck,°
Our purpose may hold there; but stay, what noise?

Enter QUEEN.

How, sweet queen?
QUEEN: One woe doth tread upon another's heel,
So fast they follow; your sister's drowned, Laertes.
165 LAERTES: Drowned! O where?
QUEEN: There is a willow grows aslant a brook,
That shows his hoar° leaves in the glassy stream,
There with fantastic garlands did she make
Of crow-flowers,° nettles, daisies, and long purples,°
170 That liberal° shepherds give a grosser name,
But our cold° maids do dead men's fingers call them.
There on the pendent boughs her coronet weeds°
Clamb'ring to hang, an envious sliver° broke,
When down her weedy trophies and herself
175 Fell in the weeping brook: her clothes spread wide,
And mermaid-like awhile they bore her up,
Which time she chanted snatches of old tunes,
As one incapable of° her own distress,
Or like a creature native and induced
180 Unto° that element: but long it could not be
Till that her garments, heavy with their drink,
Pulled the poor wretch from her melodious lay
To muddy death.
LAERTES: Alas, then she is drowned?
QUEEN: Drowned, drowned.
185 LAERTES: Too much of water hast thou, poor Ophelia,
And therefore I forbid my tears; but yet
It is our trick, nature her custom holds,
Let shame say what it will; when these° are gone,
The woman will be out.° Adieu my lord,
190 I have a speech o'fire that fain would blaze,
But that this folly douts it.°   *Exit.*
KING: Let's follow, Gertrude,
How much I had to do to calm his rage;
Now fear I this will give it start again,
Therefore let's follow.   *Exeunt.*

°159 *nonce*: occasion. 160 *stuck*: thrust. 167 *hoar*: grey (on the underside). 169 *crow-flowers*: buttercups. *long purples*: spike-like early orchid. 170 *liberal*: libertine. 171 *cold*: chaste. 172 *coronet weeds*: garland of weeds. 173 *envious sliver*: malicious branch 178 *incapable of*: unable to understand. 179–180 *induced Unto*: endowed by nature to exist in. 188 *these*: i.e., tears. 189 *woman . . . out*: womanly habits will be out of me. 191 *folly douts it*: tears put it out.

ACT 5

Scene 1. [A churchyard]

Enter two CLOWNS°

1. CLOWN: Is she to be buried in Christian burial,° when she wilfully seeks her own
     salvation?°
2. CLOWN: I tell thee she is, therefore make her grave straight.° The
     crowner hath sat on her,° and finds it Christian burial.
1. CLOWN: How can that be, unless she drowned herself in her own   5
     defence?°
2. CLOWN: Why, 'tis found so.
1. CLOWN: It must be "se offendendo,"° it cannot be else: for here lies
     the point: if I drown myself wittingly, it argues an act,
     and an act hath three branches, it is to act, to do, and to   10
     perform; argal,° she drowned herself wittingly.
2. CLOWN: Nay, but hear you, Goodman Delver.
1. CLOWN: Give me leave: here lies the water, good. Here stands the
     man, good. If the man go to this water and drown himself,
     it is, will he nill he,° he goes, mark you that. But if the   15
     water come to him, and drown him, he drowns not
     himself. Argal, he that is not guilty of his own death, shortens not his own
     life.
2. CLOWN: But is this law?
1. CLOWN: Ay marry is't, crowner's quest° law.   20
2. CLOWN: Will you ha' the truth on't? If this had not been a
     gentlewoman, she would have been buried out o'Christian
     burial.
1. CLOWN: Why there thou say'st, and the more pity that great folk
     should have countenance° in this world to drown or hang   25
     themselves more than their even-Christen.° Come, my
     spade; there is no ancient gentlemen but gardeners,
     ditchers and grave-makers; they hold up Adam's profession.
2. CLOWN: Was he a gentleman?
1. CLOWN: A' was the first that ever bore arms.°   30
2. CLOWN: Why, he had none.
1. CLOWN: What, art a heathen? How dost thou understand the
     Scripture? The Scripture says Adam digged; could he dig
     without arms? I'll put another question to thee; if thou
     answerest me not to the purpose, confess thyself—   35
2. CLOWN: Go to.
1. CLOWN: What is he that builds stronger than either the mason, the
     shipwright, or the carpenter?
2. CLOWN: The gallows-maker, for that frame outlives a thousand
     tenants.   40

°0.2 S.D.: *clowns*: rustics. 1 *Christian burial*: consecrated ground within a churchyard (where suicides were not allowed burial). 2 *salvation*: i.e., "damnation." The gravediggers make a number of such "mistakes," later termed "malapropisms." 3 *straight*: straightaway, at once. 4 *crowner . . . her*: coroner has ruled on her case. 5–6 *her own defence*: (as self-defense justifies homicide, so may it justify suicide). 8 *"se offendendo"*: (he means *"se defendendo,"* in self-defense). 11 *argal*: (corruption of "ergo" = therefore). 15 *will he nill he*: will he or will he not (willy nilly). 20 *quest*: inquest. 25 *countenance*: privilege. 26 *even-Christen*: fellow Christian. 30 *arms*: (with a pun on "coat of arms").

1. CLOWN: I like thy wit well in good faith, the gallows does well, but how does it well? It does well to those that do ill. Now thou dost ill to say the gallows is built stronger than the church. Argal, the gallows may do well to thee.° To't

45 again, come.

2. CLOWN: "Who builds stronger than a mason, a shipwright, or a carpenter?"

1. CLOWN: Ay, tell me that, and unyoke.°

2. CLOWN: Marry, now I can tell.

50 **1. CLOWN:** To't.

2. CLOWN: Mass,° I cannot tell.

1. CLOWN: Cudgel thy brains no more about it, for your dull ass will not mend his pace with beating, and when you are asked this question next, say "a grave-maker:" the houses he makes last till doomsday. Go get thee to Yaughan,° and fetch me a stoup° of liquor.   [*Exit 2. Clown.*]

Enter HAMLET and HORATIO afar off.

1. CLOWN: [*Sings.*] In youth when I did love, did love,
                        Methought it was very sweet,
                  To contract oh the time for a° my behove,°
60   O methought there a was nothing a meet.°

HAMLET: Has this fellow no feeling of his business, that a'sings in grave-making?

HORATIO: Custom hath made it in him a property of easiness.°

HAMLET: 'Tis e'en so, the hand of little employment hath the

65   daintier sense.°

1. CLOWN: [*Sings.*] But age with his stealing steps
                  Hath clawed me in his clutch,
                  And hath shipped me intil° the land,
                  As if I had never been such.

                                                        [*Throws up a skull.*]

70 **HAMLET:** That skull had a tongue in it, and could sing once: how the knave jowls° it to the ground, as if'twere Cain's jaw-bone,° that did the first murder. This might be the pate of a politician, which this ass now o'erreaches;° one that would circumvent° God, might it not?

75 **HORATIO:** It might my lord.

HAMLET: Or of a courtier, which could say "Good morrow sweet lord, how dost thou good lord?" This might be my lord such-a-one, that praised my lord such-a-one's horse, when a'meant to beg it, might it not?

80 **HORATIO:** It might my lord.

HAMLET: Why e'en so, and now my Lady Worm's, chopless,° and knocked about the mazzard° with a sexton's spade; here's

---

°44 *to thee:* i.e., by hanging you. 48 *unyoke:* unharness (your wits, after this exertion). 51 *Mass:* by the mass. 55 *Yaughan:* probably a local innkeeper. 56 *stoup:* stein, drinking mug. 59 *oh, a:* (he grunts as he works). *behove:* benefit. 60 *meet:* suitable. 63 *Custom . . . easiness:* being accustomed to it has made him indifferent. 65 *daintier sense:* finer sensibility (being uncalloused). 68 *intil:* into. 71 *jowls:* casts (with obvious pun). *Cain's jaw-bone:* the jawbone of an ass with which Cain murdered Abel. 73 *o'erreaches:* (1) reaches over (2) gets the better of. 74 *would circumvent:* tried to outwit. 81 *chopless:* lacking the lower jaw. 82 *mazzard:* head.

fine revolution an° we had the trick° to see't. Did these
bones cost no more the breeding, but to play at loggets°
with them? Mine ache to think on't.   85

1. CLOWN: [*Sings.*] A pick-axe and a spade, a spade,
                           For and a shrouding sheet,
                           O a pit of clay for to be made
                           For such a guest is meet.°   [*Throws up another skull.*]   90
HAMLET: There's another: why may not that be the skull of a
     lawyer? Where be his quiddities° now, his quillets,° his
     cases, his tenures,° and his tricks? Why does he suffer this
     rude knave now to knock him about the sconce° with a
     dirty shovel, and will not tell him of his action of battery?
     Hum, this fellow might be in's time a great buyer of land,
     with his statutes,° his recognizances,° his fines,° his double   95
     vouchers,° his recoveries:° is this the fine° of his fines, and
     the recovery° of his recoveries, to have his fine pate full of
     fine dirt? Will his vouchers vouch him no more of his
     purchases, and double ones too, than the length and
     breadth of a pair of indentures?° The very conveyances° of   100
     his lands will scarcely lie in this box,° and must th'inheritor°
     himself have no more, ha?
HORATIO: Not a jot more my lord.
HAMLET: Is not parchment made of sheep-skins?
HORATIO: Ay my lord, and of calves'-skins too.   105
HAMLET: They are sheep and calves which seek out assurance° in
     that. I will speak to this fellow. Whose grave's this, sirrah?
1. CLOWN: Mine sir:
          [*Sings.*] O a pit of clay for to be made
                         For such a guest is meet.   110
HAMLET: I think it be thine indeed, for thou liest in't.
1. CLOWN: You lie out on't° sir, and therefore 'tis not yours; for my
     part I do not lie in't, and yet it is mine.
HAMLET: Thou dost lie in't, to be in't and say it is thine: 'tis for the
     dead, not for the quick,° therefore thou liest.   115
1. CLOWN: 'Tis a quick lie sir, 'twill away again from me to you.
HAMLET: What man dost thou dig it for?
1. CLOWN: For no man sir.
HAMLET: What woman then?
1. CLOWN: For none neither.   120
HAMLET: Who is to be buried in't?
1. CLOWN: One that was a woman sir, but rest her soul she's dead.
HAMLET: How absolute° the knave is, we must speak by the card,° or

---

°83 *an*: if. *trick*: knack. 84 *loggets*: game in which small pieces of wood were thrown at fixed stakes. 89 *meet*: fitting. 91 *quiddities*: subtle definition. *quillets*: minute distinctions. 92 *tenures*: property holdings. 93 *sconce*: head. 96 *statutes*: mortgages. *recognizances*: promissory bonds. 96–97 *fines, recoveries*: legal processes for transferring real estate. 97 *vouchers*: persons who vouched for a title to real estate. *fine*: end. 98 *recovery*: attainment. 100–101 *length . . . indentures*: contracts in duplicate, which spread out, would just cover his grave. 101 *conveyances*: deeds. 102 *box*: the grave. *inheritor*: owner. 107 *assurance*: (1) security (2) transfer of land. 113 *on*: of. 116 *quick*: living. 124 *absolute*: precise. *by the card*: exactly to the point (card on which compass points are marked).

125   equivocation° will undo us. By the lord, Horatio, this
       three years I have took note of it, the age is grown so
       picked,° that the toe of the peasant comes so near the heel of
       the courtier, he galls his kibe.° How long hast thou been
       grave-maker?

130 **1. Clown:** Of all the days i'th'year I came to't that day that our last
       king Hamlet overcame Fortinbras.

    Hamlet: How long is that since?

    1. Clown: Cannot you tell that? Every fool can tell that. It was the very
       day that young Hamlet was born: he that is mad and
135   sent into England.

    Hamlet: Ay marry, why was he sent into England?

    1. Clown: Why because a' was mad: a' shall recover his wits there, or
       if a' do not, 'tis no great matter there.

    Hamlet: Why?

140 **1. Clown:** 'Twill not be seen in him there, there the men are as mad
       as he.

    Hamlet: How came he mad?

    1. Clown: Very strangely they say.

    Hamlet: How strangely?

145 **1. Clown:** Faith, e'en with losing his wits.

    Hamlet: Upon what ground?

    1. Clown: Why here in Denmark: I have been sexton here man and
       boy thirty years.

    Hamlet: How long will a man lie i'th'earth ere he rot?

150 **1. Clown:** Faith, if a' be not rotten before a' die, as we have many
       pocky° corses nowadays that will scarce hold the laying in,
       a' will last you some eight year, or nine year. A tanner will
       last you nine year.

    Hamlet: Why he more than another?

155 **1. Clown:** Why sir, his hide is so tanned with his trade, that a' will
       keep out water a great while; and your water is a sore°
       decayer of your whoreson dead body. Here's a skull now:
       this skull hath lain you i'th'earth three-and-twenty years.

    Hamlet: Whose was it?

160 **1. Clown:** A whoreson mad fellow's it was, whose do you think it
       was?

    Hamlet: Nay, I know not.

    1. Clown: A pestilence on him for a mad rogue, a' poured a flagon of
       Rhenish° on my head once; this same skull sir, was sir,
165   Yorick's skull, the king's jester.

    Hamlet: This?

    1. Clown: E'en that.

    Hamlet: Let me see. [*Takes the skull.*] Alas poor Yorick, I knew him
       Horatio, a fellow of infinite jest, of most excellent fancy,°
170   he hath borne me on his back a thousand times: and now
       how abhorred in my imagination it is: my gorge rises at it.
       Here hung those lips that I have kissed I know not how

---

°125 *equivocation*: ambiguity. 127 *picked*: fastidious ("picky"). 128 *galls his kibe*: chafes the sore on the courtier's heel.
151 *pocky*: rotten (with venereal disease). 156 *sore*: grievous. 164 *Rhenish*: Rhine wine. 169 *fancy*: imagination.

Hamlet (Mel Gilson) contemplates the power of death while looking at the skull of the king's jester, Yorick, in the 1990 film production of *Hamlet*, directed by Franco Zeffirelli.

oft. Where be your gibes now? your gambols, your songs,
your flashes of merriment, that were wont to set the table
on a roar?° not one now to mock your own grinning? quite   175
chop-fallen?° Now get you to my lady's chamber, and tell
her, let her paint an inch thick, to this favour° she must
come. Make her laugh at that. Prithee Horatio, tell me one
thing.
HORATIO: What's that, my lord?   180
HAMLET: Dost thou think Alexander looked o' this fashion
    i'th'earth?
HORATIO: E'en so.
HAMLET: And smelt so? pah.   [*Puts down the skull.*]
HORATIO: E'en so my lord.   185
HAMLET: To what base uses we may return, Horatio. Why may not
    imagination trace the noble dust of Alexander, til a'find it
    stopping a bung-hole?°
HORATIO: 'Twere to consider too curiously,° to consider so.
HAMLET: No faith, not a jot, but to follow him thither with modesty°   190
    enough, and likelihood to lead it; as thus: Alexander died,
    Alexander was buried, Alexander returneth to dust, the

°175 *on a roar:* roaring with laughter. 176 *chop-fallen:* (1) lacking a lower jaw (2) dejected, "down in the mouth."
177 *favour:* appearance. 188 *bung-hole:* hole in a cask. 189 *curiously:* minutely. 190 *modesty:* moderation.

dust is earth, of earth we make loam,° and why of that loam
whereto he was converted, might they not stop a
195   beer-barrel?
        Imperious Caesar, dead and turned to clay,
        Might stop a hole to keep the wind away.
        O that that earth which kept the world in awe,
        Should patch a wall t'expel the winter's flaw.°
200   But soft, but soft awhile, here comes the king,
       The queen, the courtiers.

Enter KING, QUEEN, LAERTES, [*Doctor of Divinity*], *and a coffin, with Lords attendant.*

                 Who is this they follow?
   And with such maimèd° rites? This doth betoken
   The corse they follow did with desp'rate hand
   Fordo it° own life; 'twas of some estate.°
   Couch° we awhile, and mark.   [*They retire.*]
205 **HAMLET:**   That is Laertes,
   A very noble youth: mark.
LAERTES: What ceremony else?
DOCTOR: Her obsequies have been as far enlarged
   As we have warranty: her death was doubtful,°
210   And but that great command o'ersways the order,
   She should in ground unsanctified have lodged
   Til the last trumpet: for charitable prayers,
   Shards,° flints and pebbles should be thrown on her:
   Yet here she is allowed her virgin crants,°
215   Her maiden strewments,° and the bringing home
   Of° bell and burial.
LAERTES: Must there no more be done?
DOCTOR: No more be done:
   We should profane the service of the dead,
   To sing sage requiem° and such rest to her
   As to peace-parted souls.
220 **LAERTES:**   Lay her i'th'earth,
   And from her fair and unpolluted flesh
   May violets spring: I tell thee churlish priest,
   A minist'ring angel shall my sister be,
   When thou liest howling.
HAMLET: What, the fair Ophelia?
225 **QUEEN:** [*Scattering flowers.*] Sweets to the sweet, farewell.
   I hoped thou shouldst have been my Hamlet's wife:
   I thought thy bride-bed to have decked, sweet maid,
   And not have strewed thy grave.
LAERTES: O treble woe
   Fall ten times treble on that cursèd head
230   Whose wicked deed thy most ingenious sense°

°193 *loam:* a clay mixture used as plaster. 199 *flaw:* windy gusts. 202 *maimèd:* abbreviated. 204 *Fordo it:* destroy its.
estate: social rank. 205 *Couch:* hide. 209 *doubtful:* suspicious. 213 *Shards:* bits of broken pottery. 214 *crants:* garland.
215 *strewments:* flowers strewn on the grave. 215–16 *bringing home Of:* laying to rest with. 219 *sage requiem:*
solemn dirge. 230 *sense:* mind.

Deprived thee of. Hold off the earth awhile,
Till I have caught her once more in mine arms;   *Leaps in the grave.*
Now pile your dust upon the quick° and dead,
Till of this flat a mountain you have made
T'o'ertop old Pelion,° or the skyish head   235
Of blue Olympus.
HAMLET: [*Comes forward.*] What is he whose grief
    Bears such an emphasis? whose phrase of sorrow
    Conjures the wand'ring stars,° and makes them stand
    Like wonder-wounded hearers? This is I,   240
    Hamlet the Dane.   *HAMLET leaps in after LAERTES.*
LAERTES: [*Grapples with him.*] The devil take thy soul.
HAMLET: Thou pray'st not well,
    I prithee take thy fingers from my throat,
    For though I am not splenitive° and rash,   245
    Yet have I in me something dangerous,
    Which let thy wiseness fear; hold off thy hand.
KING: Pluck them asunder.
QUEEN: Hamlet, Hamlet!
ALL: Gentlemen!
HORATIO: Good my lord, be quiet.

          [*ATTENDANTS part them, and they come out of the grave.*]

HAMLET: Why, I will fight with him upon this theme   250
    Until my eyelids will no longer wag.
QUEEN: O my son, what theme?
HAMLET: I loved Ophelia, forty thousand brothers
    Could not with all their quantity of love
    Make up my sum. What wilt thou do for her?   255
KING: O he is mad, Laertes.
QUEEN: For love of God, forbear° him.
HAMLET: 'Swounds,° show me what thou't do:
    Woo't° weep? woo't fight? woo't fast? woo't tear thyself?
    Woo't drink up eisel?° eat a crocodile?°   260
    I'll do't. Dost thou come here to whine?
    To outface me with leaping in her grave?
    Be buried quick with her, and so will I.
    And if thou prate of mountains, let them throw
    Millions of acres on us, till our ground,   265
    Singeing his pate against the burning zone,°
    Make Ossa° like a wart. Nay, an thou'lt mouth,
    I'll rant as well as thou.
QUEEN: This is mere° madness,
    And thus awhile the fit will work on him:
    Anon as patient as the female dove   270

°233 *quick*: live. 235 *Pelion*: mountain (on which the Titans placed Mt. Ossa, to scale Mt. Olympus and reach the gods). 239 *Conjures . . . stars*: casts a spell over the planets. 245 *splenitive*: quick-tempered (anger was thought to originate in the spleen). 257 *forbear*: be patient with. 258 *'Swounds*: corruption of "God's wounds." 259 *Woo't*: wilt thou. 260 *eisel*: vinegar (thought to reduce anger and encourage melancholy). *crocodile*: (associated with hypocritical tears). 266 *burning zone*: sun's sphere. 267 *Ossa*: see note to line 235. 268 *mere*: absolute.

When that her golden couplets° are disclosed,
His silence will sit drooping.
HAMLET: Hear you sir,
What is the reason that you use me thus?
I loved you ever; but it is no matter.
275   Let Hercules himself do what he may,
The cat will mew, and dog will have his day.
KING: I pray thee good Horatio, wait upon him.   *Exit HAMLET.*
[*Aside to Laertes.*] Strengthen your patience in our last night's speech,   [*HORATIO follows.*]
We'll put the matter to the present push°—
280   Good Gertrude, set some watch over your son—
This grave shall have a living monument.°
An hour of quiet shortly shall we see,
Till then, in patience our proceeding be.   *Exeunt.*

Scene 2. [A hall in the castle]

Enter HAMLET and HORATIO.

HAMLET: So much for this sir, now shall you see the other;
You do remember all the circumstance.
HORATIO: Remember it my lord!
HAMLET: Sir, in my heart there was a kind of fighting
5   That would not let me sleep; methought I lay
Worse than the mutines in the bilboes.° Rashly—
And praised be rashness for it: let us know,
Our indiscretion sometimes serves us well
When our deep plots do pall,° and that should learn us
10   There's a divinity that shapes our ends,
Rough-hew them how we will—
HORATIO: That is most certain.
HAMLET: Up from my cabin,
My sea-gown° scarfed about me, in the dark
Groped I to find out them, had my desire,
15   Fingered° their packet, and in fine° withdrew
To mine own room again, making so bold,
My fears forgetting manners, to unseal
Their grand commission; where I found, Horatio—
Ah royal knavery—an exact command,
20   Larded° with many several sorts of reasons,
Importing Denmark's health, and England's too,
With ho, such bugs and goblins in my life,°
That on the supervise,° no leisure bated,°
No, not to stay° the grinding of the axe,
My head should be struck off.

°271 *golden couplets:* fuzzy yellow twin fledglings. 279 *present push:* immediate test. 281 *living monument:* (1) lasting tombstone (2) living sacrifice (Hamlet) to memorialize it. 6 *mutines . . . bilboes:* mutineers in shackles. 9 *pall:* fail. 13 *sea-gown:* short-sleeved knee-length gown worn by seamen. 15 *Fingered:* got my fingers on. *in fine:* to finish. 20 *Larded:* embellished. 22 *bugs . . . life:* imaginary evils attributed to me, like imaginary goblins ("bugs") meant to frighten children. 23 *supervise:* looking over (the commission). *leisure bated:* delay excepted. 24 *stay:* await.

HORATIO: Is't possible?

HAMLET: Here's the commission, read it at more leisure.   25
    But wilt thou hear now how I did proceed?

HORATIO: I beseech you.

HAMLET: Being thus be-netted round with villainies,
    Ere I could make a prologue to my brains,   30
    They had begun the play.° I sat me down,
    Devised a new commission, wrote it fair°—
    I once did hold it, as our statists° do,
    A baseness° to write fair, and laboured much
    How to forget that learning, but sir now   35
    It did me yeoman's° service: wilt thou know
    Th'effect of what I wrote?

HORATIO: Ay, good my lord.

HAMLET: An earnest conjuration° from the king,
    As England was his faithful tributary,
    As love between them like the palm might flourish,   40
    As peace should still her wheaten garland wear
    And stand a comma° 'tween their amities,
    And many such like "as'es"° of great charge,°
    That on the view and know of these contents,
    Without debatement further, more or less,   45
    He should those bearers put to sudden death,
    Not shriving° time allowed.

HORATIO: How was this sealed?

HAMLET: Why even in that was heaven ordinant,°
    I had my father's signet° in my purse,
    Which was the model° of that Danish seal: 50
    Folded the writ up in the form of th'other,
    Subscribed° it, gave't th'impression,° placed it safely,
    The changeling° never known: now the next day
    Was our sea-fight, and what to this was sequent
    Thou knowest already.   55

HORATIO: So Guildenstern and Rosencrantz go to't.

HAMLET: Why man, they did make love to this employment,°
    They are not near my conscience, their defeat
    Does by their own insinuation° grow:
    'Tis dangerous when the baser nature comes   60
    Between the pass° and fell° incensed points
    Of mighty opposites.

HORATIO: Why, what a king is this!

HAMLET: Does it not, think thee, stand me now upon°—
    He that hath killed my king, and whored my mother,

°30–31 *Ere . . . play*: Before I could outline the action in my mind, my brains started to play their part. 32 *wrote it fair*: wrote a finished (neat) copy, a "fair copy." 33 *statists*: statesmen. 34 *baseness*: mark of humble status. 36 *yeoman's*: (in the sense of "faithful"). 38 *conjuration*: entreaty (he parodies the rhetoric of such documents). 42 *comma*: connection. 43 *as'es*: (1) the "as" clauses in the commission (2) asses. *charge*: (1) weight (in the clauses) (2) burdens (on the asses). 47 *shriving*: confession and absolution. 48 *was heaven ordinant*: it was divinely ordained. 49 *signet*: seal. 50 *model*: replica. 52 *Subscribed*: signed. *impression*: i.e., of the seal. 53 *changeling*: substitute (baby imp left when an infant was spirited away). 57 *did . . . employment*: asked for it. 59 *insinuation*: intrusion. 61 *pass*: thrust. *fell*: fierce. 63 *stand . . . upon*: become incumbent upon me now.

65   Popped in between th'election° and my hopes,
      Thrown out his angle° for my proper° life,
      And with such cozenage°—is't not perfect conscience
      To quit° him with this arm? And isn't not to be damned,
      To let this canker of our nature° come
70   In further evil?
HORATIO: It must be shortly known to him from England
      What is the issue of the business there.
HAMLET: It will be short, the interim is mine,
      And a man's life's no more than to say "One."°
75   But I am very sorry good Horatio,
      That to Laertes I forgot myself;
      For by the image of my cause, I see
      The portraiture of his;° I'll court his favours:
      But sure the bravery° of his grief did put me
      Into a towering passion.
80 HORATIO: Peace, who comes here?

Enter young OSRIC.

OSRIC: Your lordship is right welcome back to Denmark.
HAMLET: I humbly thank you sir. [*Aside to Horatio.*] Dost know this
      water-fly?
HORATIO: No my good lord.
85 HAMLET: Thy state is the more gracious,° for 'tis a vice to know him:
      he hath much land, and fertile: let a beast be lord of beasts,
      and his crib shall stand at the king's mess;° 'tis a chough,°
      but as I say, spacious in the possession of dirt.
OSRIC: Sweet lord, if you lordship were at leisure, I should
90   impart a thing to you from his majesty.
HAMLET: I will receive it sir, with all diligence of spirit; put your
      bonnet° to his right use, 'tis for the head.
OSRIC: I thank your lordship, it is very hot.
HAMLET: No, believe me 'tis very cold, the wind is northerly.
95 OSRIC: It is indifferent° cold my lord indeed.
HAMLET: But yet methinks it is very sultry and hot for my
      complexion.°
OSRIC: Exceedingly, my lord, it is very sultry, as 'twere, I cannot
      tell how: but my lord, his majesty bade me signify to you
100   that a' has laid a great wager on your head. Sir, this is the
      matter—
HAMLET: [*Moves him to put on his hat.*] I beseech you remember—
OSRIC: Nay good my lord, for mine ease,° in good faith. Sir, here
      is newly come to court Laertes, believe me, an absolute
105   gentleman, full of most excellent differences,° of very soft

---

°65 *election*: (the Danish king was so chosen). 66 *angle*: fishing hook. *proper*: very own. 68 *quit*: repay, requite.
69 *canker of our nature*: cancer of humanity. 74 *to say "One"*: to score one hit in fencing. 77–78 *by the image . . .
his*: in the depiction of my situation, I see the reflection of his. 79 *bravery*: ostentation. 85 *gracious*: favorable.
86–87 *let a beast . . . mess*: An ass who owns enough property can eat with the king. 87 *chough*: chattering bird,
jackdaw. 92 *bonnet*: hat. 95 *indifferent*: reasonably. 97 *complexion*: temperament. 103 *for mine ease*: for my own
comfort. 105 *differences*: accomplishments.

society, and great showing: indeed to speak feelingly of
him, he is the card° or calendar of gentry: for you shall find
in him the continent of what part a gentleman would see.°

HAMLET: Sir, his definement° suffers no perdition° in you, though I
know to divide him inventorially would dozy°   110
th'arithmetic of memory, and yet but yaw neither, in
respect of his quick sail,° but in the verity of extolment,° I
take him to be a soul of great article,° and his infusion° of
such dearth and rareness, as to make true diction of him,
his semblable° is his mirror, and who else would trace° him,   115
his umbrage,° nothing more.°

OSRIC: Your lordship speaks most infallibly of him.

HAMLET: The concernancy° sir? why do we wrap the gentleman in
our more rawer breath?°

OSRIC: Sir?   120

HORATIO: Is't not possible to understand in another tongue?° You
will do't sir, really.

HAMLET: What imports the nomination° of this gentleman?

OSRIC: Of Laertes?

HORATIO: His purse is empty already, all's golden words are spent.   125

HAMLET: Of him, sir.

OSRIC: I know you are not ignorant—

HAMLET: I would you did sir, yet in faith if you did, it would not
much approve me.° Well, sir.

OSRIC: You are not ignorant of what excellence Laertes is—   130

HAMLET: I dare not confess that, lest I should compare with him in
excellence, but to know a man well were to know himself.°

OSRIC: I mean sir for his weapon, but in the imputation° laid on
him by them in his meed,° he's unfellowed.°

HAMLET: What's his weapon?   135

OSRIC: Rapier and dagger.

HAMLET: That's two of his weapons—but well.

OSRIC: The king sir, hath wagered with him six Barbary horses,
against which he has impawned,° as I take it, six French
rapiers and poniards,° with their assigns,° as girdle, hangers,°   140
and so. Three of the carriages° in faith are very dear to
fancy,° very responsive to the hilts, most delicate carriages,
and of very liberal conceit.°

°107 *card*: shipman's compass card. 108 *continent . . . see*: (continuing the marine metaphor) (1) geographical continent (2) all the qualities a gentleman would look for. 109–16 *Sir . . . more*: (Hamlet outdoes Osric in affected speech). 109 *definement*: description. *perdition*: loss. 110 *dozy*: dizzy. 111–12 *yaw . . . sail*: (1) moving in an unsteady course (as another boat would do, trying to catch up with Laertes' "quick sail") (2) staggering to one trying to list his accomplishments. 112 *in . . . extolment*: to praise him truthfully. 113 *article*: scope. *infusion*: essence. 114–16 *as to make . . . more*: to describe him truly I would have to employ his mirror to depict his only equal—himself, and who would follow him is only a shadow. 115 *semblable*: equal. *trace*: (1) describe (2) follow. 116 *umbrage*: shadow. 118 *concernancy*: relevance. 121 *Is't not . . . tongue*: Cannot Osric understand his own way of speaking when used by another? 123 *nomination*: naming. 128–129 *if you did . . . me*: If you found me to be "not ignorant," it would prove little (as you are no judge of ignorance). 132 *to know . . . himself*: to know a man well, one must first know oneself. 133 *imputation*: repute. 134 *meed*: worth. *unfellowed*: unequaled. 139 *impawned*: staked. 140 *poniards*: daggers. *assigns*: accessories. *girdle, hangers*: belt, straps attached thereto, from which swords were hung. 141 *carriages*: hangers. 141–42 *dear to fancy*: rare in design. 143 *liberal conceit*: elaborate conception.

HAMLET: What call you the carriages?

145 **HORATIO:** I knew you must be edified by the margent° ere you had
done.

OSRIC: The carriages sir, are the hangers.

HAMLET: The phrase would be more germane to the matter, if we
could carry a cannon by our sides: I would it might be
150 hangers till then, but on: six Barbary horses against six
French swords, their assigns, and three liberal-conceited
carriages—that's the French bet against the Danish. Why
is this all "impawned" as you call it?

OSRIC: The king sir, hath laid sir, that in a dozen passes between
155 yourself and him, he shall not exceed you three hits°; he
hath laid on twelve for nine, and it would come to
immediate trial, if your lordship would vouchsafe the
answer.°

HAMLET: How if I answer no?

160 **OSRIC:** I mean my lord, the opposition of your person in trial.

HAMLET: Sir, I will walk here in the hall; if it please his majesty, it is
the breathing time° of day with me; let the foils be brought,
the gentleman willing, and the king hold his purpose, I
will win for him an I can, if not, I will gain nothing but my
165 shame and the odd hits.

OSRIC: Shall I re-deliver you° e'en so?

HAMLET: To this effect sir, after what flourish your nature will.°

OSRIC: I commend° my duty to your lordship.

HAMLET: Yours, yours.   [*Exit OSRIC.*]

170 He does well to commend it himself, there are no tongues
else for's turn.°

HORATIO: This lapwing° runs away with the shell on his head.

HAMLET: A' did comply° sir, with his dug° before a' sucked it: thus
has he—and many more of the same bevy that I know the
175 drossy° age dotes on—only got the tune of the time, and
out of an habit of encounter,° a kind of yeasty collection,°
which carries them through and through the most fond
and winnowed° opinions; and do but blow them to their
trial, and bubbles are out.°

Enter a LORD.

180 **LORD:** My lord, his majesty commended him to you by young
Osric, who brings back to him that you attend him in
the hall. He sends to know if your pleasure hold to play
with Laertes, or that you will take longer time.

°145 *margent*: marginal note. 154–55 *laid . . . three hits*: wagered that in twelve bouts Laertes must win three more
than Hamlet. 158 *answer*: acceptance of the challenge (Hamlet interprets as "reply"). 162 *breathing time*: exercise
period. 166 *re-deliver you*: take back your answer. 167 *after . . . will*: embellished as you wish. 168 *commend*: offer
(Hamlet interprets as "praise"). 170–71 *no tongues . . . turn*: no others who would. 172 *lapwing*: (reported to be so
precocious that it ran as soon as hatched). 173 *comply*: observe the formalities of courtesy. *dug*: mother's breast.
175 *drossy*: frivolous. 176 *habit of encounter*: habitual association (with others as frivolous). *yeasty collection*: frothy
assortment of phrases. 177–78 *fond and winnowed*: trivial and considered. 178–79 *blow . . . out*: blow on them to
test them and they are gone.

HAMLET: I am constant to my purposes, they follow the king's
    pleasure, if his fitness speaks,° mine is ready: now or   185
    whensoever, provided I be so able as now.
LORD: The king, and queen, and all are coming down.
HAMLET: In happy time.
LORD: The queen desires you to use some gentle entertainment°
    to Laertes, before you fall to play.   190
HAMLET: She well instructs me.   *[Exit* LORD.]
HORATIO: You will lose this wager, my lord.
HAMLET: I do not think so, since we went into France, I have been in
    continual practice, I shall win at the odds; but thou
    wouldst not think how ill all's here about my heart: but it   195
    is no matter.
HORATIO: Nay good my lord—
HAMLET: It is but a foolery, but it is such a kind of gaingiving° as
    would perhaps trouble a woman.
HORATIO: If your mind dislike any thing, obey it. I will forestall their   200
    repair° hither, and say you are not fit.
HAMLET: Not a whit, we defy augury;° there is a special providence
    in the fall of a sparrow.° If it be now, 'tis not to come:
    if it be not to come, it will be now; if it be not now,
    yet it will come—the readiness is all. Since no man has   205
    aught of what he leaves, what is't to leave betimes?° let
    be.

A table prepared. Trumpets, Drums, and officers with cushions. Enter KING, QUEEN, *and all the
state,* [OSRIC], *foils, daggers, and* LAERTES.

KING: Come Hamlet, come and take this hand from me.
    [*Puts Laertes' hand into Hamlet's.*]
HAMLET: Give me your pardon sir, I have done you wrong,
    But pardon't as you are a gentleman.   210
    This presence knows, and you must needs have heard,
    How I am punished with a sore distraction.°
    What I have done
    That might your nature, honour, and exception°
    Roughly awake, I here proclaim was madness: 215
    Was't Hamlet wronged Laertes? never Hamlet.
    If Hamlet from himself be ta'en away,
    And when he's not himself, does wrong Laertes,
    Then Hamlet does it not, Hamlet denies it:
    Who does it then? his madness. If't be so,   220
    Hamlet is of the faction that is wronged,
    His madness is poor Hamlet's enemy.
    Sir, in this audience,
    Let my disclaiming from a purposed evil,

°185 *his fitness speaks:* it agrees with his convenience. 189 *gentle entertainment:* friendly treatment. 198 *gaingiving:* misgiving 201 *repair:* coming. 202 *augury:* omens. 202–3 *special . . . sparrow:* ("Are not two sparrows sold for a farthing? and one of them shall not fall on the ground without your Father": Matthew 10:29). 206 *betimes:* early (before one's time). 212 *sore distraction:* grievous madness. 214 *exception:* disapproval.

225   Free me so far in your most generous thoughts,
        That I have shot my arrow o'er the house
        And hurt my brother.°
LAERTES: I am satisfied in nature,
        Whose motive in this case should stir me most
        To my revenge, but in my terms of honour
230   I stand aloof, and will no reconcilement,
        Till by some elder masters of known honour
        I have a voice and precedent° of peace
        To keep my name ungored:° but till that time,
        I do receive your offered love, like love,
        And will not wrong it.
235 HAMLET: I embrace it freely,
        And will this brother's wager frankly° play.
        Give us the foils: come on.
LAERTES: Come, one for me.
HAMLET: I'll be your foil° Laertes, in mine ignorance
        Your skill shall like a star i'th' darkest night
        Stick fiery off° indeed.
240 LAERTES: You mock me sir.
HAMLET: No, by this hand.
KING: Give them the foils young Osric. Cousin° Hamlet,
        You know the wager.
HAMLET: Very well my lord.
        Your grace has laid the odds o'th'weaker side.
245 KING: I do not fear it, I have seen you both,
        But since he is bettered,° we have therefore odds.
LAERTES: This is too heavy: let me see another.°
HAMLET: This likes° me well, these foils have all a° length?
OSRIC: Ay my good lord.   *Prepare to play.*
250 KING: Set me the stoups° of wine upon that table:
        If Hamlet give the first or second hit,
        Or quit in answer of° the third exchange,
        Let all the battlements their ordnance fire.
        The king shall drink to Hamlet's better breath,
255   And in the cup an union° shall he throw,
        Richer than that which four successive kings
        In Denmark's crown have worn: give me the cups,
        And let the kettle° to the trumpet speak,
        The trumpet to the cannoneer without,
260   The cannons to the heavens, the heaven to earth,
        "Now the king drinks to Hamlet." Come begin.
        And you the judges bear a wary eye.   *Trumpets the while.*

°226–27 *That I have . . . brother:* (that it was accidental). 232 *voice and precedent:* opinion based on precedent.
233 *name ungored:* reputation uninjured. Laertes says that he cannot accept Hamlet's apology formally until he is
assured that his acceptance will not harm his honor or damage his reputation. 236 *frankly:* freely. 238 *foil:* (1) the
blunted sword with which they fence (2) leaf of metal set under a jewel to make it shine more brilliantly. 240
Stick fiery off: show in shining contrast. 242 *Cousin:* kinsman. 246 *bettered:* either (1) judged to be better, or (2)
better trained. 247 *another:* (the unbated and poisoned sword). 248 *likes:* pleases all. *a:* all the same. 250 *stoups:*
goblets. 252 *quit in answer of:* score a draw in. 255 *union:* large pearl. 258 *kettle:* kettledrum.

HAMLET: Come on sir.

LAERTES: Come my lord.   *They play.*

HAMLET: One.

LAERTES: No.

HAMLET: Judgment.

OSRIC: A hit, a very palpable hit.

Flourish. Drum, trumpets and shot. A piece° goes off.

LAERTES: Well, again.

KING: Stay, give me drink. Hamlet, this pearl is thine.   265

    Here's to thy health: give him the cup.

HAMLET: I'll play this bout first, set it by a while.

    Come.   *[They play.]*

        Another hit. What say you?

LAERTES: A touch, a touch, I do confess't.

KING: Our son shall win.   270

QUEEN: He's fat° and scant of breath.

    Here Hamlet, take my napkin,° rub thy brows.   *[She takes HAMLET's cup.]*

    The queen carouses° to thy fortune, Hamlet.

HAMLET: Good madam.

KING: Gertrude, do not drink.

QUEEN: I will my lord, I pray you pardon me.

KING: [*Aside.*] It is the poisoned cup, it is too late.   275

HAMLET: I dare not drink yet madam: by and by.

QUEEN: Come, let me wipe thy face.

LAERTES: [*To the King.*] My lord, I'll hit him now.

KING: I do not think't.

LAERTES: [*Aside.*] And yet 'tis almost 'gainst my conscience.

HAMLET: Come for the third Laertes, you do but dally,   280

    I pray you pass° with your best violence,

    I am afeard you make a wanton of me.°

LAERTES: Say you so? Come on.   *Play.*

OSRIC: Nothing neither way   *[They break off.]*

LAERTES: Have at you now.°   *[Wounds HAMLET.]*

In scuffling they change rapiers.

KING: Part them, they are incensed.   285

HAMLET: Nay, come again.   *[The QUEEN falls.]*

                        [HAMLET wounds LAERTES.]

OSRIC: Look to the queen there, ho!

HORATIO: They bleed on both side. How is it, my lord?

OSRIC: How is't, Laertes?

LAERTES: Why as a woodcock° to my own springe,° Osric,

    I am justly killed with mine own treachery.   290

HAMLET: How does the queen?

KING: She sounds° to see them bleed.

°264.1 S.D.: *piece:* i.e., a cannon. 270 *fat:* sweating (sweat was thought to be melted body fat). 271 *napkin:* handkerchief. 272 *carouses:* drinks. 281 *pass:* thrust. 282 *make a wanton of me:* are indulging me like a spoiled child. 285 *Have . . . now:* (the bout is over when Laertes attacks Hamlet and catches him off guard). 289 *woodcock:* snipe-like bird (believed to be foolish and therefore easily trapped). *springe:* trap. 291 *sounds:* swoons.

QUEEN: No, no, the drink, the drink, O my dear Hamlet,
    The drink, the drink, I am poisoned.   *[Dies.]*
HAMLET: O villainy! ho! let the door be locked,
295   Treachery, seek it out!
LAERTES: It is here Hamlet. Hamlet, thou art slain,
    No medicine in the world can do thee good,
    In thee there is not half an hour of life,
    The treacherous instrument is in thy hand,
300   Unbated° and envenomed. The foul practice°
    Hath turned itself on me, lo, here I lie
    Never to rise again: thy mother's poisoned:
    I can no more: the king, the king's to blame.
HAMLET: The point envenomed too:
305   Then venom, to thy work.   *Hurts the KING.*
ALL: Treason! treason!
KING: O yet defend me friends, I am but hurt.°
HAMLET: Here, thou incestuous, murderous, damnèd Dane,
    Drink off this potion: is thy union here?
    Follow my mother.   *KING dies.*
LAERTES: He is justly served,
310   It is a poison tempered° by himself:
    Exchange forgiveness with me, noble Hamlet,
    Mine and my father's death come not upon thee,°
    Nor thine on me.   *Dies.*
315 HAMLET: Heaven make thee free° of it, I follow thee.
    I am dead, Horatio; wretched queen, adieu.
    You that look pale, and tremble at this chance,
    That are but mutes,° or audience to this act,
    Had I but time, as this fell sergeant° Death
320   Is strict in his arrest, O I could tell you—
    But let it be; Horatio, I am dead,
    Thou livest, report me and my cause aright
    To the unsatisfied.°
HORATIO: Never believe it;
325   I am more an antique Roman° than a Dane:
    Here's yet some liquor left.
HAMLET: As thou'rt a man,
    Give me the cup, let go, by heaven I'll ha't.
    O God, Horatio, what a wounded name,
    Things standing thus unknown, shall live behind me.
330   If thou didst ever hold me in thy heart,
    Absènt thee from felicity awhile,
    And in this harsh world draw thy breath in pain
    To tell my story.   *A march afar off, and shot within.*
              What warlike noise is this?
OSRIC: Young Fortinbras with conquest come from Poland,
335   To th'ambassadors of England gives
    This warlike volley.

°300 *Unbated:* not blunted. *practice:* plot. 307 *but hurt:* only wounded. 311 *tempered:* mixed. 313 *come . . . thee:* are not to be blamed on you. 315 *free:* guiltless. 318 *mutes:* actors without speaking parts. 319 *fell sergeant:* cruel sheriff's officer. 323 *unsatisfied:* uninformed. 325 *antique Roman:* ancient Roman (who considered suicide honorable).

HAMLET: O I die Horatio,
 The potent poison quite o'er-crows° my spirit,
 I cannot live to hear the news from England,
 But I do prophesy th'election° lights
 On Fortinbras, he has my dying voice,°   340
 So tell him, with th'occurrents more and less°
 Which have solicited°—the rest is silence.   *Dies.*
HORATIO: Now cracks a noble heart: good night sweet prince,
 And flights of angels sing thee to thy rest.
 Why does the drum come hither?   345

Enter FORTINBRAS *and English Ambassadors, with drum, colours, and attendants.*

FORTINBRAS: Where is this sight?
HORATIO: What is it you would see?
 If aught of woe, or wonder, cease your search.
FORTINBRAS: This quarry cries on havoc.° O proud death,
 What feast is toward° in thine eternal cell,
 That thou so many princes at a shot   350
 So bloodily hast struck?
AMBASSADOR: The sight is dismal,
 And our affairs from England come too late;
 The ears° are senseless that should give us hearing,
 To tell him his commandment is fulfilled,
 That Rosencrantz and Guildenstern are dead: 355
 Where should we have our thanks?
HORATIO: Not from his mouth,
 Had it th'ability of life to thank you;
 He never gave commandment for their death;
 But since so jump° upon this bloody question,
 You from the Polack wars, and you from England   360
 Are here arrived, give order that these bodies
 High on a stage be placèd to the view,
 And let me speak to th'yet unknowing world
 How these things came about; so shall you hear
 Of carnal, bloody and unnatural acts,   365
 Of accidental judgments, casual° slaughters,
 Of deaths put on° by cunning and forced cause,°
 And in this upshot, purposes mistook,
 Fall'n on th'inventors' heads:° all this can I
 Truly deliver.
FORTINBRAS: Let us haste to hear it,   370
 And call the noblest to the audience.
 For me, with sorrow I embrace my fortune;
 I have some rights of memory° in this kingdom,
 Which now to claim my vantage° doth invite me.

°337 *o'er-crows*: overpowers, conquers. 339 *election*: (for king of Denmark). 340 *voice*: vote. 341 *occurrents more and less*: events great and small. 342 *solicited*: incited me. 348 *quarry . . . havoc*: heap of dead bodies proclaims slaughter done here. 349 *toward*: in preparation. 353 *ears*: (of Claudius). 359 *jump*: opportunely. 366 *casual*: unpremeditated. 367 *put on*: prompted by. *forced cause*: being forced to act in self-defense. 368–369 *purposes . . . heads*: plots gone wrong and destroying their inventors. 373 *of memory*: remembered. 374 *vantage*: advantageous position.

375 **HORATIO:** Of that I shall have also cause to speak,
And from his mouth whose voice will draw on more:°
But let this same° be presently performed,
Even while men's minds are wild,° lest more mischance
On° plots and errors happen.

FORTINBRAS: Let four captains
380   Bear Hamlet like a soldier to the stage,
For he was likely, had he been put on,°
To have proved most royal; and for his passage,°
The soldiers' music and the rite of war
Speak loudly for him:
385   Take up the bodies, such a sight as this,
Becomes the field, but here shows much amiss.
Go bid the soldiers shoot.

Exeunt marching: after the which a peal of ordnance are shot off.

QUESTIONS

1. *Act 1.* How do you learn in the first scene that something is wrong in Denmark?
2. In scene 2, how does Claudius appear? Does he seem rational? Good? A good administrator? A competent ruler? A loving husband and uncle?
3. What does Hamlet reveal about his own mental and psychological state in his first soliloquy?
4. Why do both Laertes and Polonius caution Ophelia about Hamlet's interest in her?
5. What does the Ghost tell Hamlet to do and not to do? Why does Hamlet believe he needs independent proof about the validity of the Ghost?
6. *Act 2.* Who is Polonius? What is his analysis of Hamlet's "madness"? What do his speeches show us about him?
7. Describe Hamlet's self-accusation in the "O What a Rogue" soliloquy (2.2.524–80). To what degree is his accusation justified?
8. *Act 3.* How do you react to Hamlet's treatment of Ophelia in Act 3, Scene 1? What evidence suggests that he knows he is being watched by Claudius and Polonius?
9. What does Hamlet think of Claudius's reaction to "The Murder of Gonzago"? Why does Claudius not react to the dumb-show before the play-within-a-play?
10. Why does Hamlet not kill Claudius when the King is at prayer?
11. Describe Hamlet's treatment of Gertrude during their confrontation in her private room? Is Hamlet justified in his treatment? Why does the Ghost appear here?
12. *Act 4.* How are Laertes's wishes for revenge like Hamlet's wishes for revenge?
13. How does Claudius plan to use Laertes's desire for vengeance against Hamlet? To what extent does Laertes allow himself to be used?
14. *Act 5.* Comic relief is a humorous episode designed to ease tension. How does the scene of the gravediggers qualify as comic relief? Why is comic relief appropriate at this point of the play? How does the scene broaden the play's themes?
15. Describe the lessons that Hamlet tells Horatio he has learned about life. How does this understanding show that Hamlet has changed? Why is it ironic?

°376 *draw on more:* influence more (votes). 377 *this same:* this telling of the story. 378 *wild:* upset. 379 *On:* on top of. 381 *put on:* i.e., put on the throne. 382 *passage:* i.e., to the next world.

16. How is Gertrude killed? Hamlet? Laertes? Claudius? Why does Hamlet insist that Horatio not commit suicide?

GENERAL QUESTIONS

1. Describe Claudius. Is he purely evil, or is he merely a flawed human being? Could the play also be called "The Tragedy of Claudius, King of Denmark"?

2. Characterize Horatio. Why does Hamlet trust and admire him? How is he different from Rosencrantz and Guildenstern? Are these characters round or flat? How can one justify Hamlet's arrangement for the deaths of R & G?

3. *Hamlet* is full of conflicts that oppose people to other people, to society, and to themselves. List all the conflicts you can find in the play. Decide which of these is the central conflict, and explain your choice.

4. What is the crisis of *Hamlet?* When does it occur? Whom does it affect? What is the catastrophe? The Resolution?

5. In Act 4, Claudius notes that "sorrows come . . . in battalions." By the end of the play these sorrows include the deaths of all the major characters except Horatio. To what degree can Claudius be held responsible for all the sorrows of the play? Which sorrows may be particularly traced to Hamlet?

6. How does Shakespeare demonstrate that *Hamlet* is a tragedy of the state as well as the individual? Is the condition of Denmark better or worse at the end of the play than at the beginning?

Tragedy from Shakespeare to Arthur Miller

Shakespeare's tragedies feature people of elevated station, such as kings, princes, dukes, and generals. When he creates characters of a lower status, he often treats them as comic, as we see in the gravediggers in *Hamlet* and the "hempen homespuns" in *A Midsummer Night's Dream.* This traditional distinction was based on the common assumption of the time that social order rested on the lives and trials of the elite and powerful. The magnitude of the deeds—and errors—of royalty was a primary element giving tragedy its larger dimensions. Yet it was to people of the lesser orders that the future belonged. They were to become the beneficiaries of belief in the dignity not just of the few, but of the many.

As long as monarchy and despotism remained the principal political systems in Europe, however, most writers of tragedy continued to draw their subject matter from activities of the noble persons. But one can see anticipations of things to come. In the eighteenth century, an interesting experiment in tragedy—and also therefore a play looking toward the future—was *The London Merchant* (1731) by George Lillo (1693–1739), which forsook socially superior characters altogether and instead dramatized the "history" of a young boy, the worker's apprentice George Barnwell, who makes an error that leads to theft, murder, arrest, and finally the gallows. Lillo's aim was primarily moral and exemplary—the play was just as much a sermon as a drama. The impact of *The London Merchant* was not that the human spirit is elevated through adversity or that human beings should stand in awe before the tragic potential of their acts; rather it was that audiences should avoid mistakes such as those made by Lillo's unfortunate protagonist. It was clear that writers of tragedy would ultimately need to face the problem of reconciling the treatment of ordinary people with the tragic ideal of human dignity and nobility.

In the late eighteenth century, a number of political revolutions began that continued into and throughout much of the twentieth. Most of these depended on the theory, or hope, that human beings are perfectible, but the political beliefs of modern democracy did not add to the tradition of tragedy until the mid-twentieth century with the emergence of the talent of Arthur Miller (1915–2005). Miller's tragic plays are drawn from the modern world as we know it. His characters are common people—those who live in modern cities, and who walk, drive, or take the bus to work; those who go to modern schools, succeed or fail there, and then go on to make their ordinary livings. These are the people we know and see every day, those whose lives and tragedies are the stuff of Miller's greatest play, *Death of a Salesman*, first performed in February, 1949. Miller's major character is indeed one of the workers, a salesman, and also a family man—Willy Loman.

Death of a Salesman: Tragedy, Symbolism, and Broken Dreams

In writing a tragedy about Willy's struggle and failure, Miller effectively redefines the nature of tragedy in modern times. In a *New York Times* essay published shortly after the Broadway opening, Miller argues that "the common man is as apt a subject for tragedy in its highest sense as kings were."[15] He asserts that tragedy springs from the individual's quest for a proper place in the world and from his or her readiness "to lay down . . . life, if need be, to secure . . . [a] sense of personal dignity." Willy is ordinary, the "low man." He is self-deluded, deceitful, unfaithful, and weak; he denies the truth when he is confronted with it. But Miller links Willy's defects with his quest for dignity: "the flaw or crack in the character is really . . . his inherent unwillingness to remain passive in the face of what he conceives to be a challenge to his dignity, his image of his rightful status." It is with great justice that Linda, Willy's wife, asserts to her sons that attention must be paid to so significant a person. In this sense, Miller meets the challenge of creating a modern character worthy of tragic elevation.

Miller's first title of the play was *The Inside of His Head*, and his initial visualization, "conceived half in laughter," was that of "an enormous face the height of the proscenium arch which would appear and then open up, and we would see the inside of a man's head."[16] Ironically, Miller saw the inside of Willy's head as "a mass of contradictions" that are embodied within the play as a function of two types of time and action: real and remembered. Willy's memory is always with him, shaping the way he reacts to the present. Sometimes past events even occur along with present action, as in Act 1 when Willy speaks with his dead brother, whom he is remembering at the same time that he is involved in a card game.

Like the acting of past events, the setting of *Death of a Salesman* is realistic but also symbolic. The play demonstrates the degree to which Miller relies on developments in the physical theater that took place between Shakespeare's day and our own. He adapts both the concepts of the picture-frame proscenium stage and the apron stage. The Loman house—set on the stage—is a framework with three rooms (or

---

[15]"Tragedy and the Common Man," *New York Times*, February 27, 1949, sec. 2. p. 1.
[16]Arthur Miller, "Introduction to the Collected Plays," *Arthur Miller's Collected Plays* (New York: Viking, 1957). p. 23.

Stage set for *Death of a Salesman*.

acting areas). The forestage and apron are used for all scenes away from the house and for memory scenes. The house is hemmed in by apartment houses and lit with an "angry glow of orange"—suggesting that Willy's present existence is urbanized and claustrophobic. When memory takes over, the apartment houses disappear (a technique of lighting), and the orange glow gives way to pastoral colors and the shadows of leaves—the setting for dreams about past times and receding hopes.

Death of a Salesman is very much about dreams, illusions, and self-deception. Willy's central illusion—is it his tragic flaw?—is the American dream of economic success gained by the merchandising of the self. The dream of being "well liked" is embodied in a series of smaller dreams (illusions, lies) that Willy has tried to instill in his sons. But reality destroys these dreams. Willy's expectation of a New York City job and a salary, for example, is wrecked by his disastrous encounter with his younger but unsympathetic boss. Only Linda escapes the tyranny of dreams. She serves and supports Willy completely, but she remains firmly planted in the real world of house payments, insurance premiums, and support for Willy.

At the end of the play, we are left with a number of questions about the degree to which Willy recognizes and understands the illusory nature of his dreams and his self-image. He does recognize that he has run out of lies, and that he has nothing left to sell. He also understands—according to Miller—his alienation from true values.

> Had Willy been unaware of his separation from values that endure he would have died contentedly while polishing his car. . . . But he was agonized by his awareness of being in a false position, so constantly haunted by the hollowness of all he had placed his faith in, so aware, in short, that he must somehow be filled with his spirit or fly apart, that he staked his life on the ultimate assertion.[17]

---

[17]*Ibid.*, pp. 34–35.

Yet even then, Willy is still gripped by delusion. He imagines that his insurance money will make Biff "magnificent," and he dreams that his funeral will be massive. Ironically, Biff has already abandoned the business world, and only five people come to the funeral. Miller's view of Willy's ambiguous life is perhaps expressed by Willy's two sons in the *Requiem* scene. Biff states that Willy's dreams, like his life, were illusory: "He had all the wrong dreams. All, all wrong" (*Requiem*, speech 16). Willy's other son, ironically named Happy, provides an alternative judgment about Willy: "[Willy] had a good dream. It's the only dream you can have—to come out number-one man" (*Requiem*, speech 25).

ARTHUR MILLER (1915–2005)

Arthur Aster Miller was born in New York in 1915 and educated at the University of Michigan, where he won a prize for a play he had written as an undergraduate. After graduation he wrote with the Federal Theater Project (part of President Roosevelt's New Deal). When that project lost funding, he wrote radio plays, a novel, and, during World War II, an account of military training. His first play, The Man Who Had All the Luck, *met little success on Broadway in 1944. After the war he quickly catapulted into fame as a dramatist with* All My Sons *(1947);* Death of a Salesman *(1949);* An Enemy of the People *(1951, an adaptation of Ibsen's play);* The Crucible *(1953); and* A View from the Bridge *(1955). Many of these combine his interests in family relationships and sociopolitical issues. For instance,* All My Sons *explores the character of Joe Keller, an industrialist and war profiteer who had allowed faulty engines to be installed in U.S. military aircraft during World War II. The play investigates Keller's guilt and his emerging realization that the airmen who died because of his defective engines were "all" his sons. Another of Miller's most important plays,* The Crucible, *reflects the suspicions and unfounded accusations rampant in the McCarthy era early in the 1950s.*

Miller's later work includes the screenplay The Misfits *(1961), the last film in which Marilyn Monroe, who was then his wife, starred; and the plays* After the Fall *(1964),* Incident at Vichy *(1964, made into a film in 1973 and done as a radio play in 2002),* The Price *(1968),* Fame *(1970),* The Reason Why *(1972),* The Creation of the World and Other Business *(1972),* The Archbishop's Ceiling *(1976),* The American Clock *(1980),* Playing for Time *(1985),* I Can't Remember Anything *(1987),* Clara *(1987), a filmscript titled* Everybody Wins *(1990),* The Ride Down Mount Morgan *(1991, London),* Broken Glass *(1994),* Some Kind of Love Story *(1998), and* Resurrection Blues *(2002, Minneapolis). In 1996* The Crucible *was revised and presented as a successful film, directed by Nicholas Hytner, with Daniel Day-Lewis, Winona Ryder, and Paul Scofield.*

 ## Death of a Salesman (1949)

CHARACTERS

Willy Loman
Linda, his wife
Biff ⎫
      ⎬ his sons
Happy ⎭
Uncle Ben
Charley
Bernard
The Woman

Howard Wagner
Jenny
Stanley
Miss Forsythe
Letta

The action takes place in WILLY LOMAN's *house and yard and in various places he visits in the New York and Boston of today.*

ACT 1

A melody is heard, played upon a flute. It is small and fine, telling of grass and trees and the horizon. The curtain rises.   0.1

Before us is the Salesman's house. We are aware of towering, angular shapes behind it, surround-   0.2
ing it on all sides. Only the blue light of the sky falls upon the house and forestage; the surrounding area shows an angry glow of orange. As more light appears, we see a solid vault of apartment houses around the small, fragile-seeming home. An air of the dream clings to the place, a dream rising out of reality. The kitchen at center seems actual enough, for there is a kitchen table with three chairs, and a refrigerator. But no other fixtures are seen. At the back of the kitchen there is a draped entrance, which leads to the living-room. To the right of the kitchen, on a level raised two feet, is a bedroom fur-nished only with a brass bedstead and a straight chair. On a shelf over the bed a silver athletic trophy stands. A window opens onto the apartment house at the side.

Behind the kitchen, on a level raised six and a half feet, is the boys' bedroom, at present barely vis- 0.3
ible. Two beds are dimly seen, and at the back of the room a dormer window. (This bedroom is above the unseen living-room.) At the left a stairway curves up to it from the kitchen.

The entire setting is wholly or, in some places, partially transparent. The roof-line of the house is 0.4
one-dimensional; under and over it we see the apartment buildings. Before the house lies an apron, curving beyond the forestage into the orchestra. This forward area serves as the back yard as well as the locale of all Willy's imaginings and of his city scenes. Whenever the action is in the present the actors observe the imaginary wall-lines, entering the house only through its door at the left. But in the scenes of the past these boundaries are broken, and characters enter or leave a room by stepping "through" a wall onto the forestage.

[*From the right,* WILLY LOMAN, *the Salesman, enters, carrying two large sample cases. The flute* 0.5
plays on. He hears but is not aware of it. He is past sixty years of age, dressed quietly. Even as he crosses the stage to the doorway of the house, his exhaustion is apparent. He unlocks the door, comes into the kitchen, and thankfully lets his burden down, feeling the soreness of his palms. A word-sigh escapes his lips—it might be "Oh, boy, oh, boy." He closes the door, then carries his cases out into the living-room, through the draped kitchen doorway.]

[LINDA, *his wife, has stirred in her bed at the right. She gets out and puts on a robe, listening. Most* 0.6
often jovial, she has developed an iron repression of her exceptions to WILLY's *behavior—she more than loves him, she admires him, as though his mercurial nature, his temper, his massive dreams and little cruelties, served her only as sharp reminders of the turbulent longings within him, longings which she shares but lacks the temperament to utter and follow to their end.*]

LINDA: [*hearing* WILLY *outside the bedroom, calls with some trepidation*] Willy!
WILLY: It's all right. I came back.
LINDA: Why? What happened? [*slight pause*] Did something happen, Willy?
WILLY: No, nothing happened.
LINDA: You didn't smash the car, did you?   5
WILLY: [*with casual irritation*] I said nothing happened. Didn't you hear me?
LINDA: Don't you feel well?

WILLY: I'm tired to the death. [*The flute has faded away. He sits on the bed beside her, a little numb.*] I couldn't make it. I just couldn't make it, Linda.

LINDA: [*very carefully, delicately*] Where were you all day? You look terrible.

10 WILLY: I got as far as a little above Yonkers.° I stopped for a cup of coffee. Maybe it was the coffee.

LINDA: What?

WILLY: [*after a pause*] I suddenly couldn't drive any more. The car kept going off onto the shoulder, y'know?

LINDA: [*helpfully*] Oh. Maybe it was the steering again. I don't think Angelo knows the Studebaker.

WILLY: No, it's me, it's me. Suddenly I realize I'm goin' sixty miles an hour and I don't remember the last five minutes. I'm—I can't seem to—keep my mind to it.

15 LINDA: Maybe it's your glasses. You never went for your new glasses.

WILLY: No, I see everything. I came back ten miles an hour. It took me nearly four hours from Yonkers.

LINDA: [*resigned*] Well, you'll just have to take a rest, Willy, you can't continue this way.

WILLY: I just got back from Florida.

LINDA: But you didn't rest your mind. Your mind is overactive, and the mind is what counts, dear.

20 WILLY: I'll start out in the morning. Maybe I'll feel better in the morning. [*She is taking off his shoes.*] These goddam arch supports are killing me.

LINDA: Take an aspirin. Should I get you an aspirin? It'll soothe you.

WILLY: [*with wonder*] I was driving along, you understand? And I was fine. I was even observing the scenery. You can imagine, me looking at scenery, on the road every week of my life. But it's so beautiful up there, Linda, the trees are so thick, and the sun is warm. I opened the windshield and just let the warm air bathe over me. And then all of a sudden I'm goin' off the road! I'm tellin' ya, I absolutely forgot I was driving. If I'd've gone the other way over the white line I might've killed somebody. So I went on again—and five minutes later I'm dreamin' again, and I nearly—[*He presses two fingers against his eyes.*] I have such thoughts, I have such strange thoughts.

LINDA: Willy, dear. Talk to them again. There's no reason why you can't work in New York.

WILLY: They don't need me in New York. I'm the New England man. I'm vital in New England.

25 LINDA: But you're sixty years old. They can't expect you to keep traveling every week.

WILLY: I'll have to send a wire to Portland. I'm supposed to see Brown and Morrison tomorrow morning at ten o'clock to show the line. Goddammit, I could sell them! [*He starts putting on his jacket.*]

LINDA: [*taking the jacket from him*] Why don't you go down to the place tomorrow and tell Howard you've simply got to work in New York? You're too accommodating, dear.

WILLY: If old man Wagner was alive I'd a been in charge of New York now! That man was a prince, he was a masterful man. But that boy of his, that Howard, he don't appreciate. When I went north the first time, the Wagner Company didn't know where New England was!

LINDA: Why don't you tell those things to Howard, dear?

30 WILLY: [*encouraged*] I will, I definitely will. Is there any cheese?

LINDA: I'll make you a sandwich.

WILLY: No, go to sleep. I'll take some milk. I'll be up right away. The boys in?

°10 *Yonkers:* Yonkers is immediately north of New York City, touching the city limits of the Bronx. Because Willy lives in Brooklyn, to the south, he got no more than thirty or thirty-five miles from home.

LINDA: They're sleeping. Happy took Biff on a date tonight.

WILLY: [*interested*] That so?

LINDA: It was so nice to see them shaving together, one behind the other, in the   35
bathroom. And going out together. You notice? The whole house smells of shaving
lotion.

WILLY: Figure it out. Work a lifetime to pay off a house. You finally own it, and there's
nobody to live in it.

LINDA: Well, dear, life is a casting off. It's always that way.

WILLY: No, no, some people—some people accomplish something. Did Biff say anything
after I went this morning?

LINDA: You shouldn't have criticized him, Willy, especially after he just got off the train. You
mustn't lose your temper with him.

WILLY: When the hell did I lose my temper? I simply asked him if he was making any   40
money. Is that a criticism?

LINDA: But, dear, how could he make any money?

WILLY: [*worried and angered*] There's such an undercurrent in him. He became a moody man.
Did he apologize when I left this morning?

LINDA: He was crestfallen, Willy. You know how he admires you. I think if he finds himself,
then you'll both be happier and not fight any more.

WILLY: How can he find himself on a farm? Is that a life? A farmhand? In the beginning,
when he was young, I thought, well, a young man, it's good for him to tramp around,
take a lot of different jobs. But it's more than ten years now and he has yet to make
thirty-five dollars a week!

LINDA: He's finding himself, Willy.   45

WILLY: Not finding yourself at the age of thirty-four is a disgrace!

LINDA: Shh!

WILLY: The trouble is he's lazy, goddammit!

LINDA: Willy, please!

WILLY: Biff is a lazy bum!   50

LINDA: They're sleeping. Get something to eat. Go on down.

WILLY: Why did he come home? I would like to know what brought him home.

LINDA: I don't know. I think he's still lost, Willy. I think he's very lost.

WILLY: Biff Loman is lost. In the greatest country in the world a young man with such—
personal attractiveness, gets lost. And such a hard worker. There's one thing about
Biff—he's not lazy.

LINDA: Never.   55

WILLY: [*with pity and resolve*] I'll see him in the morning; I'll have a nice talk with him. I'll get
him a job selling. He could be big in no time. My God! Remember how they used to
follow him around in high school? When he smiled at one of them their faces lit up.
When he walked down the street . . . [*He loses himself in reminiscences.*]

LINDA: [*trying to bring him out of it*] Willy, dear, I got a new kind of American-type cheese
today. It's whipped.

WILLY: Why do you get American when I like Swiss?

LINDA: I just thought you'd like a change—

WILLY: I don't want a change! I want Swiss cheese. Why am I always being contradicted?   60

LINDA: [*with a covering laugh*] I thought it would be a surprise.

WILLY: Why don't you open a window in here, for God's sake?

LINDA: [*with infinite patience*] They're all open dear.

WILLY: The way they boxed us in here. Bricks and windows, windows and bricks.

LINDA: We should've bought the land next door.   65

WILLY: The street is lined with cars. There's not a breath of fresh air in the neighborhood.
The grass don't grow any more, you can't raise a carrot in the back yard. They

should've had a law against apartment houses. Remember those two beautiful elm trees out there? When I and Biff hung the swing between them?

LINDA: Yeah, like being a million miles from the city.

WILLY: They should've arrested the builder for cutting those down. They massacred the neighborhood. [*lost*] More and more I think of those days, Linda. This time of year it was lilac and wisteria. And then the peonies would come out, and the daffodils. What fragrance in this room!

LINDA: Well, after all, people had to move somewhere.

70 WILLY: No, there's more people now.

LINDA: I don't think there's more people. I think—

WILLY: There's more people! That's what's ruining this country! Population is getting out of control. The competition is maddening! Smell the stink from that apartment house! And another one on the other side . . . How can they whip cheese?

[*On* WILLY's *last line,* BIFF *and* HAPPY *raise themselves up in their beds, listening.*]

LINDA: Go down, try it. And be quiet.

WILLY: [*turning to* LINDA, *guiltily*] You're not worried about me, are you, sweetheart?

75 BIFF: What's the matter?

HAPPY: Listen!

LINDA: You've got too much on the ball to worry about.

WILLY: You're my foundation and my support, Linda.

LINDA: Just try to relax, dear. You make mountains out of molehills.

80 WILLY: I won't fight with him any more. If he wants to go back to Texas, let him go.

LINDA: He'll find his way.

WILLY: Sure. Certain men just don't get started till later in life. Like Thomas Edison, I think. Or B. F. Goodrich.° One of them was deaf. [*He starts for the bedroom doorway.*] I'll put my money on Biff.

LINDA: And Willy—if it's warm Sunday we'll drive in the country. And we'll open the windshield, and take lunch.

WILLY: No, the windshields don't open on the new cars.

85 LINDA: But you opened it today.

WILLY: Me? I didn't. [*He stops.*] Now isn't that peculiar! Isn't that a remarkable—[*He breaks off in amazement and fright as the flute is heard distantly.*]

LINDA: What, darling?

WILLY: That is the most remarkable thing.

LINDA: What, dear?

90 WILLY: I was thinking of the Chevvy. [*slight pause*] Nineteen twenty-eight . . . when I had that red Chevvy—[*Breaks off.*] That funny? I coulda sworn I was driving that Chevvy today.

LINDA: Well, that's nothing. Something must've reminded you.

WILLY: Remarkable. Ts. Remember those days? The way Biff used to simonize that car? The dealer refused to believe there was eighty thousand miles on it. [*He shakes his head.*] Heh! [*to* LINDA] Close your eyes, I'll be right up. [*He walks out of the bedroom.*]

HAPPY: [*to* BIFF] Jesus, maybe he smashed up the car again!

LINDA: [*calling after* WILLY] Be careful on the stairs, dear! The cheese is on the middle shelf! [*She turns, goes over to the bed, takes his jacket, and goes out of the bedroom.*]

°82 *Thomas Edison, B. F. Goodrich*: Thomas A. Edison (1847–1931) was an American inventor who developed the electric light and the phonograph. Benjamin Franklin Goodrich (1841–1888) founded the B. F. Goodrich Rubber and Tire Company. It was Edison who suffered from deafness.

[*Light has risen on the boys' room. Unseen, WILLY is heard talking to himself, "Eighty thousand miles," and a little laugh. BIFF gets out of bed, comes downstage a bit, and stands attentively. BIFF is two years older than his brother HAPPY, well built, but in these days bears a worn air and seems less self-assured. He has succeeded less, and his dreams are stronger and less acceptable than HAPPY's. HAPPY is tall, powerfully made. Sexuality is like a visible color on him, or a scent that many women have discovered. He, like his brother, is lost, but in a different way, for he has never allowed himself to turn his face toward defeat and is thus more confused and hard-skinned, although seemingly more content.*]

HAPPY: [*getting out of bed*] He's going to get his license taken away if he keeps that up. I'm 95
    getting nervous about him, y'know, Biff?
BIFF: His eyes are going.
HAPPY: No, I've driven with him. He sees all right. He just doesn't keep his mind on it. I
    drove into the city with him last week. He stops at a green light and then it turns red
    and he goes. [*He laughs.*]
BIFF: Maybe he's color-blind.
HAPPY: Pop? Why he's got the finest eye for color in the business. You know that.
BIFF: [*sitting down on his bed*] I'm going to sleep. 100
HAPPY: You're not still sour on Dad, are you, Biff?
BIFF: He's all right, I guess.
WILLY: [*underneath them, in the living-room*] Yes, sir, eighty thousand miles—eighty-two
    thousand!
BIFF: You smoking? 105
HAPPY: [*holding out a pack of cigarettes*] Want one?
BIFF: [*taking a cigarette*] I can never sleep when I smell it.
WILLY: What a simonizing job, heh!
HAPPY: [*with deep sentiment*] Funny, Biff y'know? Us sleeping in here again? The old beds.
    [*He pats his bed affectionately.*] All the talk that went across those two beds, huh? Our
    whole lives.
BIFF: Yeah. Lotta dreams and plans.
HAPPY: [*with a deep and masculine laugh*] About five hundred women would like to know 110
    what was said in this room.

[*They share a soft laugh.*]

BIFF: Remember that big Betsy something—what the hell was her name—over on Bushwick
    Avenue?
HAPPY: [*combing his hair*] With the collie dog!
BIFF: That's the one. I got you in there, remember?
HAPPY: Yeah, that was my first time—I think. Boy, there was a pig! [*They laugh, almost
    crudely.*] You taught me everything I know about women. Don't forget that.
BIFF: I bet you forgot how bashful you used to be. Especially with girls. 115
HAPPY: Oh, I still am, Biff.
BIFF: Oh, go on.
HAPPY: I just control it, that's all. I think I got less bashful and you got more so. What
    happened, Biff? Where's the old humor, the old confidence? [*He shakes BIFF's knee. BIFF
    gets up and moves restlessly about the room.*] What's the matter?
BIFF: Why does Dad mock me all the time? 120
HAPPY: He's not mocking you, he—
BIFF: Everything I say there's a twist of mockery on his face. I can't get near him.
HAPPY: He just wants you to make good, that's all. I wanted to talk to you about Dad for a
    long time, Biff. Something's—happening to him. He—talks to himself.
BIFF: I noticed that this morning. But he always mumbled.

HAPPY: But not so noticeable. It got so embarrassing I sent him to Florida. And you know something? Most of the time he's talking to you.

125 BIFF: What's he say about me?

HAPPY: I can't make it out.

BIFF: What's he say about me?

HAPPY: I think the fact that you're not settled, that you're still kind of up in the air . . .

BIFF: There's one or two other things depressing him, Happy.

130 HAPPY: What do you mean?

BIFF: Never mind. Just don't lay it all to me.

HAPPY: But I think if you just got started—I mean—is there any future for you out there?

BIFF: I tell ya, Hap, I don't know what the future is. I don't know—what I'm supposed to want.

HAPPY: What do you mean?

135 BIFF: Well, I spent six or seven years after high school trying to work myself up. Shipping clerk, salesman, business of one kind or another. And it's a measly manner of existence. To get on that subway on the hot mornings in summer. To devote your whole life to keeping stock, or making phone calls, or selling or buying. To suffer fifty weeks of the year for the sake of a two-week vacation, when all you really desire is to be outdoors, with your shirt off. And always to have to get ahead of the next fella. And still—that's how you build a future.

HAPPY: Well, you really enjoy it on a farm? Are you content out there?

BIFF: [*with rising agitation*] Hap, I've had twenty or thirty different kinds of jobs since I left home before the war, and it always turns out the same. I just realized it lately. In Nebraska when I herded cattle, and the Dakotas, and Arizona, and now in Texas. It's why I came home now, I guess, because I realized it. This farm I work on, it's spring there now, see? And they've got about fifteen new colts. There's nothing more inspiring or—beautiful than the sight of a mare and a new colt. And it's cool there now, see? Texas is cool now, and it's spring. And whenever spring comes to where I am, I suddenly get the feeling, my God, I'm not gettin' anywhere! What the hell am I doing, playing around with horses, twenty-eight dollars a week! I'm thirty-four years old, I oughta be makin' my future. That's when I come running home. And now, I get here, and I don't know what to do with myself. [*after a pause*] I've always made a point of not wasting my life, and everytime I come back here I know that all I've done is to waste my life.

HAPPY: You're a poet, you know that, Biff? You're a—you're an idealist!

BIFF: No, I'm mixed up very bad. Maybe I oughta get married. Maybe I oughta get stuck into something. Maybe that's my trouble. I'm like a boy. I'm not married, I'm not in business, I just—I'm like a boy. Are you content, Hap? You're a success, aren't you? Are you content?

140 HAPPY: Hell, no!

BIFF: Why? You're making money, aren't you?

HAPPY: [*moving about with energy, expressiveness*] All I can do now is wait for the merchandise manager to die. And suppose I get to be merchandise manager? He's a good friend of mine, and he just built a terrific estate on Long Island. And he lived there about two months and sold it, and now he's building another one. He can't enjoy it once it's finished. And I know that's just what I would do. I don't know what the hell I'm workin' for. Sometimes I sit in my apartment—all alone. And I think of the rent I'm paying. And it's crazy. But then, it's what I always wanted. My own apartment, a car, and plenty of women. And still, goddammit, I'm lonely.

BIFF: [*with enthusiasm*] Listen, why don't you come out West with me?

HAPPY: You and I, heh?

BIFF: Sure, maybe we could buy a ranch. Raise cattle, use our muscles. Men built like we are   145
should be working out in the open.

HAPPY: [*avidly*] The Loman Brothers, heh?

BIFF: [*with vast affection*] Sure, we'd be known all over the counties!

HAPPY: [*enthralled*] That's what I dream about, Biff. Sometimes I want to just rip my clothes
off in the middle of the store and outbox that goddam merchandise manager. I mean I
can outbox, outrun, and outlift anybody in that store, and I have to take orders from
those common, petty sons-of-bitches till I can't stand it any more.

BIFF: I'm tellin' you, kid, if you were with me I'd be happy out there.

HAPPY: [*enthused*] See, Biff, everybody around me is so false that I'm constantly lowering   150
my ideals . . .

BIFF: Baby, together we'd stand up for one another, we'd have someone to trust.

HAPPY: If I were around you—

BIFF: Hap, the trouble is we weren't brought up to grub for money. I don't know how to do
it.

HAPPY: Neither can I!

BIFF: Then let's go!   155

HAPPY: The only thing is—what can you make out there?

BIFF: But look at your friend. Builds an estate and then hasn't the peace of mind to
live in it.

HAPPY: Yeah, but when he walks into the store the waves part in front of him. That's fifty-
two thousand dollars a year coming through the revolving door, and I got more in my
pinky finger than he's got in his head.

BIFF: Yeah, but you just said—

HAPPY: I gotta show some of those pompous, self-important executives over there that Hap   160
Loman can make the grade. I want to walk into the store the way he walks in. Then I'll
go with you, Biff. We'll be together yet, I swear. But take those two we had tonight.
Now weren't they gorgeous creatures?

BIFF: Yeah, yeah, most gorgeous I've had in years.

HAPPY: I get that any time I want, Biff. Whenever I feel disgusted. The only trouble is, it gets
like bowling or something. I just keep knockin' them over and it doesn't mean
anything. You still run around a lot?

BIFF: Naa. I'd like to find a girl—steady, somebody with substance.

HAPPY: That's what I long for.

BIFF: Go on! You'd never come home.   165

HAPPY: I would! Somebody with character, with resistance! Like Mom, y'know? You're
gonna call me a bastard when I tell you this. That girl Charlotte I was with tonight is
engaged to be married in five weeks. [*He tries on his new hat.*]

BIFF: No kiddin'!

HAPPY: Sure, the guy's in line for the vice-presidency of the store. I don't know what gets
into me, maybe I just have an overdeveloped sense of competition or something, but
I went and ruined her, and furthermore I can't get rid of her. And he's the third
executive I've done that to. Isn't that a crummy characteristic? And to top it all, I go to
their weddings! [*Indignantly, but laughing*] Like I'm not supposed to take bribes.
Manufacturers offer me a hundred-dollar bill now and then to throw an order their
way. You know how honest I am, but it's like this girl, see. I hate myself for it. Because
I don't want the girl, and, still, I take it and—I love it!

BIFF: Let's go to sleep.

HAPPY: I guess we didn't settle anything, heh?   170

BIFF: I just got one idea that I think I'm going to try.

HAPPY: What's that?

BIFF: Remember Bill Oliver?

HAPPY: Sure, Oliver is very big now. You want to work for him again?

175 **BIFF:** No, but when I quit he said something to me. He put his arm on my shoulder and he said, "Biff, if you ever need anything, come to me."

HAPPY: I remember that. That sounds good.

BIFF: I think I'll go to see him. If I could get ten thousand or even seven or eight thousand dollars I could buy a beautiful ranch.

HAPPY: I bet he'd back you. 'Cause he thought highly of you, Biff. I mean, they all do. You're well liked, Biff. That's why I say to come back here, and we both have the apartment. And I'm tellin' you, Biff, any babe you want . . .

BIFF: No, with a ranch I could do the work I like and still be something. I just wonder though. I wonder if Oliver still thinks I stole that carton of basketballs.

180 **HAPPY:** Oh, he probably forgot that long ago. It's almost ten years. You're too sensitive. Anyway, he didn't really fire you.

BIFF: Well, I think he was going to. I think that's why I quit. I was never sure whether he knew or not. I know he thought the world of me, though. I was the only one he'd let lock up the place.

WILLY: [below] You gonna wash the engine, Biff?

HAPPY: Shh!

[BIFF looks at HAPPY, who is gazing down, listening. WILLY is mumbling in the parlor.]

HAPPY: You hear that?

[They listen. WILLY laughs warmly.]

185 **BIFF:** [growing angry] Doesn't he know Mom can hear that?

WILLY: Don't get your sweater dirty, Biff!

[A look of pain crosses BIFF's face.]

HAPPY: Isn't that terrible! Don't leave again, will you? You'll find a job here. You gotta stick around. I don't know what to do about him, it's getting embarrassing.

WILLY: What a simonizing job!

BIFF: Mom's hearing that!

190 **WILLY:** No kiddin', Biff, you got a date? Wonderful!

HAPPY: Go on to sleep. But talk to him in the morning, will you?

BIFF: [reluctantly getting into bed] With her in the house. Brother!

HAPPY: [getting into bed] I wish you'd have a good talk with him.

[The light on their room begins to fade.]

BIFF: [to himself in bed] That selfish, stupid . . .

195 **HAPPY:** Sh . . . Sleep, Biff.

[Their light is out. Well before they have finished speaking, WILLY's form is dimly seen below in the darkened kitchen. He opens the refrigerator, searches in there, and takes out a bottle of milk. The apartment houses are fading out, and the entire house and surroundings become covered with leaves. Music insinuates itself as the leaves appear.]

WILLY: Just wanna be careful with those girls, Biff, that's all. Don't make any promises. No promises of any kind. Because a girl, y'know, they always believe what you tell 'em, and you're very young, Biff, you're too young to be talking seriously to girls.

[Light rises on the kitchen. WILLY, talking, shuts the refrigerator door and comes downstage to the kitchen table. He pours milk into a glass. He is totally immersed in himself, smiling faintly.]

WILLY: Too young entirely, Biff. You want to watch your schooling first. Then when you're all set, there'll be plenty of girls for a boy like you. [*He smiles broadly at a kitchen chair.*] That so? The girls pay for you? [*He laughs.*] Boy, you must really be makin' a hit.

[WILLY *is gradually addressing—physically—a point offstage, speaking through the wall of the kitchen, and his voice has been rising in volume to that of a normal conversation.*]

WILLY: I been wondering why you polish the car so careful. Ha! Don't leave the hubcaps, boys. Get the chamois to the hubcaps. Happy, use newspaper on the windows, it's the easiest thing. Show him how to do it, Biff! You see, Happy? Pad it up, use it like a pad. That's it, that's it, good work. You're doin' all right, Hap. [*He pauses, then nods in approbation for a few seconds, then looks upward.*] Biff, first thing we gotta do when we get time is clip that big branch over the house. Afraid it's gonna fall in a storm and hit the roof. Tell you what. We get a rope and sling her around, and then we climb up there with a couple of saws and take her down. Soon as you finish the car, boys, I wanna see ya. I got a surprise for you, boys.

BIFF: [*offstage*] Whatta ya got, Dad?

WILLY: No, you finish first. Never leave a job till you're finished—remember that. [*looking   200 toward the "big trees"*] Biff, up in Albany I saw a beautiful hammock. I think I'll buy it next trip, and we'll hang it right between those two elms. Wouldn't that be something? Just swingin' there under those branches. Boy, that would be . . .

[YOUNG BIFF *and* YOUNG HAPPY *appear from the direction* WILLY *was addressing.* HAPPY *carries rags and a pail of water.* BIFF, *wearing a sweater with a block "S," carries a football.*]

BIFF: [*pointing in the direction of the car offstage*] How's that, Pop, professional?

WILLY: Terrific. Terrific job, boys. Good work, Biff.

HAPPY: Where's the surprise, Pop?

WILLY: In the back seat of the car.

HAPPY: Boy! [*He runs off.*]   205

BIFF: What is it, Dad? Tell me, what'd you buy?

WILLY: [*laughing, cuffs him*] Never mind, something I want you to have.

BIFF: [*turns and starts off*] What is it, Hap?

HAPPY: [*offstage*] It's a punching bag!

BIFF: Oh, Pop!   210

WILLY: It's got Gene Tunney's° signature on it!

[HAPPY *runs onstage with a punching bag.*]

BIFF: Gee, how'd you know we wanted a punching bag?

WILLY: Well, it's the finest thing for the timing.

HAPPY: [*lies down on his back and pedals with his feet*] I'm losing weight, you notice, Pop?

WILLY: [*to* HAPPY] Jumping rope is good too.   215

BIFF: Did you see the new football I got?

WILLY: [*examining the ball*] Where'd you get a new ball?

BIFF: The coach told me to practice my passing.

WILLY: That so? And he gave you the ball, heh?

BIFF: Well, I borrowed it from the locker room. [*He laughs confidentially.*]   220

WILLY: [*laughing with him at the theft*] I want you to return that.

HAPPY: I told you he wouldn't like it!

°211 *Gene Tunney:* James Joseph Tunney (1898–1978), a boxer who won the heavyweight championship from Jack Dempsey in 1926 and retired undefeated in 1928.

BIFF: [*angrily*] Well, I'm bringing it back!

WILLY: [*stopping the incipient argument, to* HAPPY] Sure, he's gotta practice with a regulation ball, doesn't he? [*to* BIFF] Coach'll probably congratulate you on your initiative!

225 **BIFF:** Oh, he keeps congratulating my initiative all the time, Pop.

WILLY: That's because he likes you. If somebody else took that ball there'd be an uproar. So what's the report, boys, what's the report?

BIFF: Where'd you go this time, Dad? Gee we were lonesome for you.

WILLY: [*pleased, puts an arm around each boy and they come down to the apron*] Lonesome, heh?

BIFF: Missed you every minute.

230 **WILLY:** Don't say? Tell you a secret, boys. Don't breathe it to a soul. Someday I'll have my own business, and I'll never have to leave home any more.

HAPPY: Like Uncle Charley, heh?

WILLY: Bigger than Uncle Charley! Because Charley is not—liked. He's liked, but he's not—well liked.

BIFF: Where'd you go this time, Dad?

WILLY: Well, I got on the road, and I went north to Providence. Met the Mayor.

235 **BIFF:** The Mayor of Providence!

WILLY: He was sitting in the hotel lobby.

BIFF: What'd he say?

WILLY: He said, "Morning!" And I said, "You got a fine city here, Mayor." And then he had coffee with me. And then I went to Waterbury. Waterbury is a fine city. Big clock city, the famous Waterbury clock. Sold a nice bill there. And then Boston—Boston is the cradle of the Revolution. A fine city. And a couple of other towns in Mass., and on to Portland and Bangor and straight home!

BIFF: Gee, I'd love to go with you sometime, Dad.

240 **WILLY:** Soon as summer comes.

HAPPY: Promise?

WILLY: You and Hap and I, and I'll show you all the towns. America is full of beautiful towns and fine, upstanding people. And they know me, boys, they know me up and down New England. The finest people. And when I bring you fellas up, there'll be open sesame for all of us, 'cause one thing, boys: I have friends. I can park my car in any street in New England, and the cops protect it like their own. This summer, heh?

BIFF AND HAPPY: [*together*] Yeah! You bet!

WILLY: We'll take our bathing suits.

245 **HAPPY:** We'll carry your bags, Pop!

WILLY: Oh, won't that be something! Me comin' into the Boston stores with you boys carryin' my bags. What a sensation!

[BIFF *is prancing around, practicing passing the ball.*]

WILLY: You nervous, Biff, about the game?

BIFF: Not if you're gonna be there.

WILLY: What do they say about you in school, now that they made you captain?

250 **HAPPY:** There's a crowd of girls behind him everytime the classes change.

BIFF: [*taking* WILLY'*s hand*] This Saturday, Pop, this Saturday—just for you, I'm going to break through for a touchdown.

HAPPY: You're supposed to pass.

BIFF: I'm takin' one play for Pop. You watch me, Pop, and when I take off my helmet, that means I'm breakin' out. Then you watch me crash through that line!

WILLY: [*kisses* BIFF] Oh, wait'll I tell this in Boston!

[BERNARD *enters in knickers. He is younger than* BIFF, *earnest and loyal, a worried boy.*]

BERNARD: Biff, where are you? You're supposed to study with me today.   255

WILLY: Hey, looka Bernard. What're you lookin' so anemic about, Bernard?

BERNARD: He's gotta study, Uncle Willy. He's got Regents° next week.

HAPPY: [*tauntingly, spinning* BERNARD *around*] Let's box, Bernard!

BERNARD: Biff! [*He gets away from* HAPPY.] Listen, Biff, I heard Mr. Birnbaum say that if you don't start studyin' math he's gonna flunk you, and you won't graduate. I heard him!

WILLY: You better study with him, Biff. Go ahead now.   260

BERNARD: I heard him!

BIFF: Oh, Pop, you didn't see my sneakers! [*He holds up a foot* FOR WILLY *to look at.*]

WILLY: Hey, that's a beautiful job of printing!

BERNARD: [*wiping his glasses*] Just because he printed University of Virginia on his sneakers doesn't mean they've got to graduate him, Uncle Willy!

WILLY: [*angrily*] What're you talking about? With scholarships to three universities they're   265
gonna flunk him?

BERNARD: But I heard Mr. Birnbaum say—

WILLY: Don't be a pest, Bernard! [*to his boys*] What an anemic!

BERNARD: Okay, I'm waiting for you in my house, Biff.

[BERNARD *goes off. The* LOMANS *laugh.*]

WILLY: Bernard is not well liked, is he?

BIFF: He's liked, but he's not well liked.   270

HAPPY: That's right, Pop.

WILLY: That's just what I mean. Bernard can get the best marks in school, y'understand, but when he gets out in the business world, y'understand, you are going to be five times ahead of him. That's why I thank Almighty God you're both built like Adonises. Because the man who makes an appearance in the business world, the man who creates personal interest, is the man who gets ahead. Be liked and you will never want. You take me, for instance. I never have to wait in line to see a buyer. "Willy Loman is here!" That's all they have to know, and I go right through.

BIFF: Did you knock them dead, Pop?

WILLY: Knocked 'em cold in Providence, slaughtered 'em in Boston.

HAPPY: [*on his back, pedaling again*] I'm losing weight, you notice, Pop?   275

[LINDA *enters, as of old, a ribbon in her hair, carrying a basket of washing.*]

LINDA: [*with youthful energy*] Hello, dear!

WILLY: Sweetheart!

LINDA: How'd the Chevvy run?

WILLY: Chevrolet, Linda, is the greatest car ever built. [*to the boys*] Since when do you let your mother carry wash up the stairs?

BIFF: Grab hold there, boy!   280

HAPPY: Where to, Mom?

LINDA: Hang them up on the line. And you better go down to your friends, Biff. The cellar is full of boys. They don't know what to do with themselves.

BIFF: Ah, when Pop comes home they can wait!

WILLY: [*laughs appreciatively*] You better go down and tell them what to do, Biff.

BIFF: I think I'll have them sweep out the furnace room.   285

WILLY: Good work, Biff.

BIFF: [*goes through wall-line of kitchen to doorway at back and calls down*] Fellas! Everybody sweep out the furnace room! I'll be right down!

°257 *Regents*: a statewide high school proficiency examination administered in New York.

VOICES: All right! Okay, Biff.

BIFF: George and Sam and Frank, come out back! We're hangin' up the wash! Come on, Hap, on the double! [*He AND HAPPY carry out the basket.*]

290 **LINDA:** The way they obey him!

WILLY: Well, that's training, the training. I'm tellin' you, I was sellin' thousands and thousands, but I had to come home.

LINDA: Oh, the whole block'll be at that game. Did you sell anything?

WILLY: I did five hundred gross in Providence and seven hundred gross in Boston.

LINDA: No! Wait a minute, I've got a pencil. [*She pulls pencil and paper out of her apron pocket.*] That makes your commission . . . Two hundred—my God! Two hundred and twelve dollars!

295 **WILLY:** Well, I didn't figure it yet, but . . .

LINDA: How much did you do?

WILLY: Well, I—I did—about a hundred and eighty gross in Providence. Well, no—it came to—roughly two hundred gross on the whole trip.

LINDA: [*without hesitation*] Two hundred gross. That's . . . [*She figures.*]

WILLY: The trouble was that three of the stores were half closed for inventory in Boston. Otherwise I woulda broke records.

300 **LINDA:** Well, it makes seventy dollars and some pennies. That's very good.

WILLY: What do we owe?

LINDA: Well, on the first there's sixteen dollars on the refrigerator—

WILLY: Why sixteen?

LINDA: Well, the fan belt broke, so it was a dollar eighty.

305 **WILLY:** But it's brand new.

LINDA: Well, the man said that's the way it is. Till they work themselves in, y'know.

[*They move through the wall-line into the kitchen.*]

WILLY: I hope we didn't get stuck on that machine.

LINDA: They got the biggest ads of any of them!

WILLY: I know, it's a fine machine. What else?

310 **LINDA:** Well, there's nine-sixty for the washing machine. And for the vacuum cleaner there's three and a half due on the fifteenth. Then the roof, you got twenty-one dollars remaining.

WILLY: It don't leak, does it?

LINDA: No, they did a wonderful job. Then you owe Frank for the carburetor.

WILLY: I'm not going to pay that man! That goddam Chevrolet, they ought to prohibit the manufacture of that car!

LINDA: Well, you owe him three and a half. And odds and ends, comes to around a hundred and twenty dollars by the fifteenth.

315 **WILLY:** A hundred and twenty dollars! My God, if business don't pick up I don't know what I'm gonna do!

LINDA: Well, next week you'll do better.

WILLY: Oh, I'll knock 'em dead next week. I'll go to Hartford. I'm very well liked in Hartford. You know, the trouble is, Linda, people don't seem to take to me.

[*They move onto the forestage.*]

LINDA: Oh, don't be foolish.

WILLY: I know it when I walk in. They seem to laugh at me.

320 **LINDA:** Why? Why would they laugh at you? Don't talk that way, Willy.

[*WILLY moves to the edge of the stage. LINDA goes into the kitchen and starts to darn stockings.*]

WILLY: I don't know the reason for it, but they just pass me by. I'm not noticed.

LINDA: But you're doing wonderful, dear. You're making seventy to a hundred dollars a week.

WILLY: But I gotta be at it ten, twelve hours a day. Other men—I don't know—they do it easier. I don't know why—I can't stop myself—I talk too much. A man oughta come in with a few words. One thing about Charley. He's a man of few words, and they respect him.

LINDA: You don't talk too much, you're just lively.

WILLY: [*smiling*] Well, I figure, what the hell, life is short, a couple of jokes. [*to himself*]   325
I joke too much! [*The smile goes.*]

LINDA: Why? You're—

WILLY: I'm fat. I'm very—foolish to look at, Linda. I didn't tell you, but Christmas time I happened to be calling on F. H. Stewarts, and a salesman I know, as I was going in to see the buyer I heard him say something about—walrus. And I—I cracked him right across the face. I won't take that. I simply will not take that. But they do laugh at me. I know that.

LINDA: Darling . . .

WILLY: I gotta overcome it. I know I gotta overcome it. I'm not dressing to advantage, maybe.

LINDA: Willy, darling, you're the handsomest man in the world—   330

WILLY: Oh, no, Linda.

LINDA: To me you are. [*slight pause*] The handsomest.

[*From the darkness is heard the laughter of a woman. WILLY doesn't turn to it, but it continues through LINDA's lines.*]

LINDA: And the boys, Willy. Few men are idolized by their children the way you are.

[*Music is heard as behind a scrim, to the left of the house, The WOMAN, dimly seen, is dressing.*]

WILLY: [*with great feeling*] You're the best there is, Linda, you're a pal, you know that? On the road—on the road I want to grab you sometimes and just kiss the life outa you.

[*The laughter is loud now, and he moves into a brightening area at the left, where THE WOMAN has come from behind the scrim and is standing, putting on her hat, looking into a "mirror" and laughing.*]

WILLY: Cause I get so lonely—especially when business is bad and there's nobody to talk to.   335
I get the feeling that I'll never sell anything again, that I won't make a living for you, or a business, a business for the boys. [*He talks through THE WOMAN's subsiding laughter; THE WOMAN primps at the "mirror."*] There's so much I want to make for—

THE WOMAN: Me? You didn't make me, Willy. I picked you.

WILLY: [*pleased*] You picked me?

THE WOMAN: [*who is quite proper-looking, WILLY's age*] I did. I've been sitting at that desk watching all the salesmen go by, day in, day out. But you've got such a sense of humor, and we do have such a good time together, don't we?

WILLY: Sure, sure. [*He takes her in his arms.*] Why do you have to go now?

THE WOMAN: It's two o'clock . . .   340

WILLY: No, come on in! [*He pulls her.*]

THE WOMAN: . . . my sisters'll be scandalized. When'll you be back?

WILLY: Oh, two weeks about. Will you come up again?

THE WOMAN: Sure thing. You do make me laugh. It's good for me. [*She squeezes his arm, kisses him.*] And I think you're a wonderful man.

WILLY: You picked me, heh?   345

THE WOMAN: Sure. Because you're so sweet. And such a kidder.

WILLY: Well, I'll see you next time I'm in Boston.

THE WOMAN: I'll put you right through to the buyers.

WILLY: [*slapping her bottom*] Right. Well, bottoms up!

350 THE WOMAN: [*slaps him gently and laughs*] You just kill me, Willy. [*He suddenly grabs her and kisses her roughly.*] You kill me. And thanks for the stockings. I love a lot of stockings. Well, good night.

WILLY: Good night. And keep your pores open!

THE WOMAN: Oh, Willy!

[*THE WOMAN bursts out laughing, and LINDA's laughter blends in. THE WOMAN disappears into the dark. Now the area at the kitchen table brightens. LINDA is sitting where she was at the kitchen table, but now is mending a pair of her silk stockings.*]

LINDA: You are, Willy. The handsomest man. You've got no reason to feel that—

WILLY: [*coming out of THE WOMAN's dimming area and going over to LINDA*] I'll make it all up to you, Linda, I'll—

355 LINDA: There's nothing to make up, dear. You're doing fine, better than—

WILLY: [*noticing her mending*] What's that?

LINDA: Just mending my stockings. They're so expensive—

WILLY: [*angrily, taking them from her*] I won't have you mending stockings in this house! Now throw them out!

[*LINDA puts the stockings in her pocket.*]

BERNARD: [*entering on the run*] Where is he? If he doesn't study!

360 WILLY: [*moving to the forestage, with great agitation*] You'll give him the answers!

BERNARD I do, but I can't on a Regents! That's state exam! They're liable to arrest me!

WILLY: Where is he? I'll whip him, I'll whip him!

LINDA: And he'd better give back that football, Willy, it's not nice.

WILLY: Biff! Where is he? Why is he taking everything?

365 LINDA: He's too rough with the girls, Willy. All the mothers are afraid of him!

WILLY: I'll whip him!

BERNARD: He's driving the car without a license!

[*THE WOMAN's laugh is heard.*]

WILLY: Shut up!

LINDA: All the mothers—

370 WILLY: Shut up!

BERNARD: [*backing quietly away and out*] Mr. Birnbaum says he's stuck up.

WILLY: Get outa here!

BERNARD: If he doesn't buckle down he'll flunk math! [*He goes off.*]

LINDA: He's right, Willy, you've gotta—

375 WILLY: [*exploding at her*] There's nothing the matter with him! You want him to be a worm like Bernard? He's got spirit, personality . . .

[*As he speaks, LINDA, almost in tears, exits into the living-room. WILLY is alone in the kitchen, wilting and staring. The leaves are gone. It is night again, and the apartment houses look down from behind.*]

WILLY: Loaded with it. Loaded! What is he stealing? He's giving it back, isn't he? Why is he stealing? What did I tell him? I never in my life told him anything but decent things.

[*HAPPY in pajamas has come down the stairs; WILLY suddenly becomes aware of HAPPY's presence.*]

HAPPY: Let's go now, come on.

WILLY: [*sitting down at the kitchen table*] Huh! Why did she have to wax the floors herself? Everytime she waxes the floors she keels over. She knows that!

HAPPY: Shh! Take it easy. What brought you back tonight?

WILLY: I got an awful scare. Nearly hit a kid in Yonkers. God! Why didn't I go to Alaska   380 with my brother Ben that time! Ben! That man was a genius, that man was success incarnate! What a mistake! He begged me to go.

HAPPY: Well, there's no use in—

WILLY: You guys! There was a man started with the clothes on his back and ended up with diamond mines!

HAPPY: Boy, someday I'd like to know how he did it.

WILLY: What's the mystery? The man knew what he wanted and went out and got it! Walked into a jungle, and comes out, the age of twenty-one, and he's rich! The world is an oyster, but you don't crack it open on a mattress!

HAPPY: Pop, I told you I'm gonna retire you for life.   385

WILLY: You'll retire me for life on seventy goddam dollars a week? And your women and your car and your apartment, and you'll retire me for life! Christ's sake, I couldn't get past Yonkers today! Where are you guys, where are you? The woods are burning! I can't drive a car!

[*CHARLEY has appeared in the doorway. He is a large man, slow of speech, laconic, immovable. In all he says, despite what he says, there is pity, and now, trepidation. He has a robe over pajamas, slippers on his feet. He enters the kitchen.*]

CHARLEY: Everything all right?

HAPPY: Yeah, Charley, everything's . . .

WILLY: What's the matter?

CHARLEY: I heard some noise. I thought something happened. Can't we do something about   390 the walls? You sneeze in here, and in my house hats blow off.

HAPPY: Let's go to bed, Dad. Come on.

[*CHARLEY signals to HAPPY to go.*]

WILLY: You go ahead, I'm not tired at the moment.

HAPPY: [*to WILLY*] Take it easy, huh? [*He exits.*]

WILLY: What're you doin' up?

CHARLEY: [*sitting down at the kitchen table opposite WILLY*] Couldn't sleep good. I had a   395 heartburn.

WILLY: Well, you don't know how to eat.

CHARLEY: I eat with my mouth.

WILLY: No, you're ignorant. You gotta know about vitamins and things like that.

CHARLEY: Come on, let's shoot. Tire you out a little.

WILLY: [*hesitantly*] All right. You got cards?   400

CHARLEY: [*taking a deck from his pocket*] Yeah, I got them. Someplace. What is it with those vitamins?

WILLY: [*dealing*] They build up your bones. Chemistry.

CHARLEY: Yeah, but there's no bones in a heartburn.

WILLY: What are you talkin' about? Do you know the first thing about it?

CHARLEY: Don't get insulted.   405

WILLY: Don't talk about something you don't know anything about.

[*They are playing. Pause.*]

CHARLEY: What're you doin' home?

WILLY: A little trouble with the car.

CHARLEY: Oh, [*Pause*] I'd like to take a trip to California.
410 WILLY: Don't say.
CHARLEY: You want a job?
WILLY: I got a job, I told you that. [*after a slight pause*] What the hell are you offering me a job for?
CHARLEY: Don't get insulted.
WILLY: Don't insult me.
415 CHARLEY: I don't see no sense in it. You don't have to go on this way.
WILLY: I got a good job. [*slight pause*] What do you keep comin' in for?
CHARLEY: You want me to go?
WILLY: [*after a pause, withering*] I can't understand it. He's going back to Texas again. What the hell is that?
CHARLEY: Let him go.
420 WILLY: I got nothin' to give him, Charley, I'm clean, I'm clean.
CHARLEY: He won't starve. None a them starve. Forget about him.
WILLY: Then what have I got to remember?
CHARLEY: You take it too hard. To hell with it. When a deposit bottle is broken you don't get your nickel back.
WILLY: That's easy enough for you to say.
425 CHARLEY: That ain't easy for me to say.
WILLY: Did you see the ceiling I put up in the living-room?
CHARLEY: Yeah, that's a piece of work. To put up a ceiling is a mystery to me. How do you do it?
WILLY: What's the difference?
CHARLEY: Well, talk about it.
430 WILLY: You gonna put up a ceiling?
CHARLEY: How could I put up a ceiling?
WILLY: Then what the hell are you bothering me for?
CHARLEY: You're insulted again.
WILLY: A man who can't handle tools is not a man. You're disgusting.
435 CHARLEY: Don't call me disgusting, Willy.

[UNCLE BEN, *carrying a valise and an umbrella, enters the forestage from around the right corner of the house. He is a stolid man, in his sixties, with a mustache and an authoritative air. He is utterly certain of his destiny, and there is an aura of far places about him. He enters exactly as* WILLY *speaks.*]

WILLY: I'm getting awfully tired, Ben.

[BEN's *music is heard.* BEN *looks around at everything.*]

CHARLEY: Good, keep playing; you'll sleep better. Did you call me Ben?

[BEN *looks at his watch.*]

WILLY: That's funny. For a second there you reminded me of my brother Ben.
BEN: I only have a few minutes. [*He strolls, inspecting the place.* WILLY *and* CHARLEY *continue playing.*]
440 CHARLEY: You never heard from him again, heh? Since that time?
WILLY: Didn't Linda tell you? Couple of weeks ago we got a letter from his wife in Africa. He died.
CHARLEY: That so.
BEN: [*chuckling*] So this is Brooklyn, eh?
CHARLEY: Maybe you're in for some of his money.
445 WILLY: Naa, he had seven sons. There's just one opportunity I had with that man . . .

BEN: I must make a train, William. There are several properties I'm looking at in Alaska.

WILLY: Sure, sure! If I'd gone with him to Alaska that time, everything would've been totally different.

CHARLEY: Go on, you'd froze to death up there.

WILLY: What're you talking about?

BEN: Opportunity is tremendous in Alaska, William. Surprised you're not up there.   450

WILLY: Sure, tremendous.

CHARLEY: Heh?

WILLY: There was the only man I ever met who knew the answers.

CHARLEY: Who?

BEN: How are you all?   455

WILLY: [*taking a pot, smiling*] Fine, fine.

CHARLEY: Pretty sharp tonight.

BEN: Is Mother living with you?

WILLY: No, she died a long time ago.

CHARLEY: Who?   460

BEN: That's too bad. Fine specimen of a lady, Mother.

WILLY: [*to CHARLEY*] Heh?

BEN: I'd hoped to see the old girl.

CHARLEY: Who died?

BEN: Heard anything from Father, have you?   465

WILLY: [*unnerved*] What do you mean, who died?

CHARLEY: [*taking a pot*] What're you talkin' about?

BEN: [*looking at his watch*] William, it's half-past eight!

WILLY: [*As though to dispel his confusion he angrily stops CHARLEY's hand.*] That's my build!

CHARLEY: I put the ace—   470

WILLY: If you don't know how to play the game I'm not gonna throw my money away on you!

CHARLEY: [*rising*] It was my ace, for God's sake!

WILLY: I'm through, I'm through!

BEN: When did Mother die?

WILLY: Long ago. Since the beginning you never knew how to play cards.   475

CHARLEY: [*picks up the cards and goes to the door*] All right! Next time I'll bring a deck with five aces.

WILLY: I don't play that kind of game!

CHARLEY: [*turning to him*] You ought to be ashamed of yourself!

WILLY: Yeah?

CHARLEY: Yeah! [*He goes out.*]   480

WILLY: [*slamming the door after him*] Ignoramus!

BEN: [*as WILLY comes toward him through the wall-line of the kitchen*] So you're William.

WILLY: [*shaking BEN's hand*] Ben! I've been waiting for you so long! What's the answer? How did you do it?

BEN: Oh, there's a story in that.

[*LINDA enters the forestage, as of old, carrying the wash basket.*]

LINDA: Is this Ben?   485

BEN: [*gallantly*] How do you do, my dear.

LINDA: Where've you been all these years? Willy's always wondered why you—

WILLY: [*pulling BEN away from her impatiently*] Where is Dad? Didn't you follow him? How did you get started?

BEN: Well, I don't know how much you remember.

490 WILLY: Well, I was just a baby, of course, only three or four years old—

BEN: Three years and eleven months.

WILLY: What a memory, Ben!

BEN: I have many enterprises, William, and I have never kept books.

WILLY: I remember I was sitting under the wagon in—was it Nebraska?

495 BEN: It was South Dakota, and I gave you a bunch of wild flowers.

WILLY: I remember you walking away down some open road.

BEN: [*laughing*] I was going to find Father in Alaska.

WILLY: Where is he?

BEN: At that age I had a very faulty view of geography, William. I discovered after a few days that I was heading due south, so instead of Alaska, I ended up in Africa.

500 LINDA: Africa!

WILLY: The Gold Coast!

BEN: Principally diamond mines.

LINDA: Diamond mines!

BEN: Yes, my dear. But I've only a few minutes—

505 WILLY: No! Boys! Boys! [*YOUNG BIFF and HAPPY appear.*] Listen to this. This is your Uncle Ben, a great man! Tell my boys, Ben!

BEN: Why, boys, when I was seventeen I walked into the jungle, and when I was twenty-one I walked out. [*He laughs.*] And by God I was rich.

WILLY: [*to the boys*] You see what I been talking about? The greatest things can happen!

BEN: [*glancing at his watch*] I have an appointment in Ketchikan Tuesday week.

WILLY: No, Ben. Please tell about Dad. I want my boys to hear. I want them to know the kind of stock they spring from. All I remember is a man with a big beard, and I was in Mamma's lap, sitting around a fire, and some kind of high music.

510 BEN: His flute. He played the flute.

WILLY: Sure, the flute, that's right!

[*New music is heard, a high, rollicking tune.*]

BEN: Father was a very great and a very wild-hearted man. We would start in Boston, and he'd toss the whole family into the wagon, and then he'd drive the team right across the country; through Ohio, and Indiana, Michigan, Illinois, and all the Western states. And we'd stop in the towns and sell the flutes that he'd made on the way. Great inventor, Father. With one gadget he made more in a week than a man like you could make in a lifetime.

WILLY: That's just the way I'm bringing them up, Ben—rugged, well liked, all-around.

BEN: Yeah? [*to BIFF*] Hit that, boy—hard as you can. [*He pounds his stomach.*]

515 BIFF: Oh, no, sir!

BEN: [*taking boxing stance*] Come on, get to me! [*He laughs.*]

BIFF: Okay! [*He cocks his fists and starts in.*]

WILLY: Go to it, Biff! Go ahead, show him!

LINDA: [*to WILLY*] Why must he fight, dear?

520 BEN: [*sparring with BIFF*] Good boy! Good boy!

WILLY: How's that, Ben, heh?

HAPPY: Give him the left, Biff!

LINDA: Why are you fighting?

BEN: Good boy! [*suddenly comes in, trips BIFF, and stands over him, the point of his umbrella poised over BIFF's eye.*]

525 LINDA: Look out, Biff!

BIFF: Gee!

BEN: [*patting* BIFF'S *knee*] Never fight fair with a stranger, boy. You'll never get out of the jungle that way. [*taking* LINDA'S *hand and bowing*] It was an honor and a pleasure to meet you, Linda.

LINDA: [*withdrawing her hand coldly, frightened*] Have a nice—trip.

BEN: [*to* WILLY] And good luck with your—what do you do?

WILLY: Selling.   530

BEN: Yes. Well . . . [*He raises his hand in farewell to all.*]

WILLY: No, Ben, I don't want you to think . . . [*He takes* BEN'S *arm to show him.*] It's Brooklyn, I know, but we hunt too.

BEN: Really, now.

WILLY: Oh, sure, there's snakes and rabbits and—that's why I moved out here. Why, Biff can fell any one of these trees in no time! Boys! Go right over to where they're building the apartment house and get some sand. We're gonna rebuild the entire front stoop right now! Watch this, Ben!

BIFF: Yes, sir! On the double, Hap!   535

HAPPY: [*as he and* BIFF *run off*] I lost weight, Pop, you notice?

[CHARLEY *enters in knickers, even before the boys are gone.*]

CHARLEY: Listen, if they steal any more from that building the watchman'll put the cops on them!

LINDA: [*to* WILLY] Don't let Biff . . .

[BEN *laughs lustily.*]

WILLY: You shoulda seen the lumber they brought home last week. At least a dozen six-by-tens worth all kinds a money.

CHARLEY: Listen, if that watchman—   540

WILLY: I gave them hell, understand. But I got a couple of fearless characters there.

CHARLEY: Willy, the jails are full of fearless characters.

BEN: [*clapping* WILLY *on the back, with a laugh at* CHARLEY] And the stock exchange, friend!

WILLY: [*joining in* BEN'S *laughter*] Where are the rest of your pants?

CHARLEY: My wife bought them.   545

WILLY: Now all you need is a golf club and you can go upstairs and go to sleep. [*to* BEN] Great athlete! Between him and his son Bernard they can't hammer a nail!

BERNARD: [*rushing in*] The watchman's chasing Biff!

WILLY: [*angrily*] Shut up! He's not stealing anything!

LINDA: [*alarmed, hurrying off left*] Where is he? Biff, dear! [*She exits.*]

WILLY: [*moving toward the left, away from* BEN] There's nothing wrong. What's the matter   550
with you?

BEN: Nervy boy. Good!

WILLY: [*laughing*] Oh, nerves of iron, that Biff!

CHARLEY: Don't know what it is. My New England man comes back and he's bleedin', they murdered him up there.

WILLY: It's contacts, Charley, I got important contacts!

CHARLEY: [*sarcastically*] Glad to hear it, Willy. Come in later, we'll shoot a little casino. I'll   555
take some of your Portland money. [*He laughs at* WILLY *and exits.*]

WILLY: [*turning to* BEN] Business is bad, it's murderous. But not for me, of course.

BEN: I'll stop by on my way back to Africa.

WILLY: [*longingly.*] Can't you stay a few days? You're just what I need, Ben, because I—I have a fine position here, but I—well, Dad left when I was such a baby and I never had a chance to talk to him and I still feel—kind of temporary about myself.

BEN: I'll be late for my train.

[*They are at opposite ends of the stage.*] .

560 WILLY: Ben, my boys—can't we talk? They'd go into the jaws of hell for me, see, but I—

BEN: William, you're being first-rate with your boys. Outstanding, manly chaps!

WILLY: [*hanging on to his words*] Oh, Ben, that's good to hear! Because sometimes I'm afraid that I'm not teaching them the right kind of—Ben, how should I teach them?

BEN: [*giving great weight to each word, and with a certain vicious audacity*] William, when I walked into the jungle, I was seventeen. When I walked out I was twenty-one. And, by God, I was rich! [*He goes off into darkness around the right corner of the house.*]

WILLY: . . . was rich! That's just the spirit I want to imbue them with! To walk into a jungle! I was right! I was right! I was right!

[BEN *is gone, but* WILLY *is still speaking to him as* LINDA, *in her nightgown and robe, enters the kitchen, glances around for* WILLY, *then goes to the door of the house, looks out and sees him. Comes down to his left. He looks at her.*]

565 LINDA: Willy, dear? Willy?

WILLY: I was right!

LINDA: Did you have some cheese? [*He can't answer.*] It's very late, darling. Come to bed, heh?

WILLY: [*looking straight up*] Gotta break your neck to see a star in this yard.

LINDA: You coming in?

570 WILLY: Whatever happened to that diamond watch fob? Remember? When Ben came from Africa that time? Didn't he give me a watch fob with a diamond in it?

LINDA: You pawned it, dear. Twelve, thirteen years ago. For Biff's radio correspondence course.

WILLY: Gee, that was a beautiful thing. I'll take a walk.

LINDA: But you're in your slippers.

WILLY: [*starting to go around the house at the left*] I was right! I was! [*Half to* LINDA, *as he goes, shaking his head*] What a man! There was a man worth talking to. I was right!

575 LINDA: [*calling after* WILLY] But in your slippers, Willy!

[WILLY *is almost gone when* BIFF, *in his pajamas, comes down the stairs and enters the kitchen.*]

BIFF: What is he doing out there?

LINDA: Sh!

BIFF: God Almighty, Mom, how long has he been doing this?

LINDA: Don't, he'll hear you.

580 BIFF: What the hell is the matter with him?

LINDA: It'll pass by morning.

BIFF: Shouldn't we do anything?

LINDA: Oh, my dear, you should do a lot of things, but there's nothing to do, so go to sleep.

[HAPPY *comes down the stairs and sits on the steps.*]

HAPPY: I never heard him so loud, Mom.

585 LINDA: Well, come around more often; you'll hear him. [*She sits down at the table and mends the lining of* WILLY's *jacket.*]

BIFF: Why didn't you ever write me about this, Mom?

LINDA: How would I write to you? For over three months you had no address.

BIFF: I was on the move. But you know I thought of you all the time. You know that, don't you, pal?

LINDA: I know, dear, I know. But he likes to have a letter. Just to know that there's still a possibility for better things.

BIFF: He's not like this all the time, is he?   590

LINDA: It's when you come home he's always the worst.

BIFF: When I come home?

LINDA: When you write you're coming, he's all smiles, and talks about the future, and—
    he's just wonderful. And then the closer you seem to come, the more shaky he gets,
    and then, by the time you get here, he's arguing, and he seems angry at you. I think it's
    just that maybe he can't bring himself to—to open up to you. Why are you so hateful to
    each other? Why is that?

BIFF: [*evasively*] I'm not hateful, Mom.

LINDA: But you no sooner come in the door than you're fighting!   595

BIFF: I don't know why. I mean to change. I'm tryin', Mom, you understand?

LINDA: Are you home to stay now?

BIFF: I don't know. I want to look around, see what's doin'.

LINDA: Biff, you can't look around all your life, can you?

BIFF: I just can't take hold, Mom. I can't take hold of some kind of a life.   600

LINDA: Biff, a man is not a bird, to come and go with the springtime.

BIFF: Your hair . . . [*He touches her hair.*] Your hair got so gray.

LINDA: Oh, it's been gray since you were in high school. I just stopped dyeing it, that's all.

BIFF: Dye it again, will ya? I don't want my pal looking old. [*He smiles.*]

LINDA: You're such a boy! You think you can go away for a year and . . . You've got to get it   605
    into your head now that one day you'll knock on this door and there'll be strange
    people here—

BIFF: What are you talking about? You're not even sixty, Mom.

LINDA: But what about your father?

BIFF: [*lamely*] Well, I meant him, too.

HAPPY: He admires Pop.

LINDA: Biff, dear, if you don't have any feeling for him, then you can't have any feeling for   610
    me.

BIFF: Sure I can, Mom.

LINDA: No. You can't just come to see me, because I love him. [*with a threat, but only a threat,
    of tears*] He's the dearest man in the world to me, and I won't have anyone making him
    feel unwanted and low and blue. You've got to make up your mind now, darling,
    there's no leeway any more. Either he's your father and you pay him that respect, or
    else you're not to come here. I know he's not easy to get along with—nobody knows
    that better than me—but . . .

WILLY: [*from the left, with a laugh*] Hey, hey, Biffo!

BIFF: [*starting to go out after WILLY*] What the hell is the matter with him? [*HAPPY stops him.*]

LINDA: Don't—don't go near him!   615

BIFF: Stop making excuses for him! He always, always wiped the floor with you. Never had
    an ounce of respect for you.

HAPPY: He's always had respect for—

BIFF: What the hell do you know about it?

HAPPY: [*surlily*] Just don't call him crazy!

BIFF: He's got no character—Charley wouldn't do this. Not in his own house—spewing out   620
    that vomit from his mind.

HAPPY: Charley never had to cope with what he's got to.

BIFF: People are worse off than Willy Loman. Believe me, I've seen them!

LINDA: Then make Charley your father, Biff. You can't do that, can you? I don't say he's a
    great man. Willy Loman never made a lot of money. His name was never in the paper.
    He's not the finest character that ever lived. But he's a human being, and a terrible
    thing is happening to him. So attention must be paid. He's not to be allowed to fall into

his grave like an old dog. Attention, attention must be finally paid to such a person. You called him crazy—

BIFF: I didn't mean—

625 **LINDA:** No, a lot of people think he's lost his—balance. But you don't have to be very smart to know what his trouble is. The man is exhausted.

HAPPY: Sure!

LINDA: A small man can be just as exhausted as a great man. He works for a company thirty-six years this March, opens up unheard-of territories to their trademark, and now in his old age they take his salary away.

HAPPY: [*indignantly*] I didn't know that, Mom.

LINDA: You never asked, my dear! Now that you get your spending money someplace else you don't trouble your mind with him.

630 **HAPPY:** But I gave you money last—

LINDA: Christmas time, fifty dollars! To fix the hot water it cost ninety-seven fifty! For five weeks he's been on straight commission,° like a beginner, an unknown!

BIFF: Those ungrateful bastards!

LINDA: Are they any worse than his sons? When he brought them business, when he was young, they were glad to see him. But now his old friends, the old buyers that loved him so and always found some order to hand him in a pinch—they're all dead, retired. He used to be able to make six, seven calls a day in Boston. Now he takes his valises out of the car and puts them back and takes them out again and he's exhausted. Instead of walking he talks now. He drives seven hundred miles, and when he gets there no one knows him any more, no one welcomes him. And what goes through a man's mind, driving seven hundred miles home without having earned a cent? Why shouldn't he talk to himself? Why? When he has to go to Charley and borrow fifty dollars a week and pretend to me that it's his pay? How long can that go on? How long? You see what I'm sitting here and waiting for? And you tell me he has no character? The man who never worked a day but for your benefit? When does he get the medal for that? Is this his reward—to turn around at the age of sixty-three and find his sons, who he loved better than his life, one a philandering bum—

HAPPY: Mom!

635 **LINDA:** That's all you are, my baby! [*To* BIFF] And you! What happened to the love you had for him? You were such pals! How you used to talk to him on the phone every night! How lonely he was till he could come home to you!

BIFF: All right, Mom. I'll live here in my room, and I'll get a job. I'll keep away from him, that's all.

LINDA: No, Biff. You can't stay here and fight all the time.

BIFF: He threw me out of this house, remember that.

LINDA: Why did he do that? I never knew why.

640 **BIFF:** Because I know he's a fake and he doesn't like anybody around who knows!

LINDA: Why a fake? In what way? What do you mean?

BIFF: Just don't lay it all at my feet. It's between me and him—that's all I have to say. I'll chip in from now on. He'll settle for half my pay check. He'll be all right. I'm going to bed. [*He starts for the stairs.*]

LINDA: He won't be all right.

BIFF: [*turning on the stairs, furiously*] I hate this city and I'll stay here. Now what do you want?

°631 *straight commission:* refers to the fact that Willy is receiving no salary, only a commission (percentage) on the sales he makes.

LINDA: He's dying, Biff.   645

[*HAPPY turns quickly to her, shocked.*]

BIFF: [*after a pause*] Why is he dying?
LINDA: He's been trying to kill himself.
BIFF: [*with great horror*] How?
LINDA: I live from day to day.
BIFF: What're you talking about?   650
LINDA: Remember I wrote you that he smashed up the car again? In February?
BIFF: Well?
LINDA: The insurance inspector came. He said that they have evidence. That all these accidents in the last year—weren't—weren't—accidents.
HAPPY: How can they tell that? That's a lie.
LINDA: It seems there's a woman . . . [*She takes a breath as*]   655
BIFF: [*sharply but contained*] What woman?
LINDA: [*simultaneously*] . . . and this woman . . .
LINDA: What?
BIFF: Nothing. Go ahead.
LINDA: What did you say?   660
BIFF: Nothing. I just said what woman?
HAPPY: What about her?
LINDA: Well, it seems she was walking down the road and saw his car. She says that he wasn't driving fast at all, and that he didn't skid. She says he came to that little bridge, and then deliberately smashed into the railing, and it was only the shallowness of the water that saved him.
BIFF: Oh, no, he probably just fell asleep again.
LINDA: I don't think he fell asleep.   665
BIFF: Why not?
LINDA: Last month . . . [*with great difficulty*] Oh, boys, it's so hard to say a thing like this! He's just a big stupid man to you, but I tell you there's more good in him than in many other people. [*She chokes, wipes her eyes.*] I was looking for a fuse. The lights blew out, and I went down the cellar. And behind the fuse box—it happened to fall out—was a length of rubber pipe—just short.
HAPPY: No kidding?
LINDA: There's a little attachment on the end of it. I knew right away. And sure enough, on the bottom of the water heater there's a new little nipple on the gas pipe.
HAPPY: [*angrily*] That—jerk.   670
BIFF: Did you have it taken off?
LINDA: I'm—I'm ashamed to. How can I mention it to him? Every day I go down and take away that little rubber pipe. But, when he comes home, I put it back where it was. How can I insult him that way? I don't know what to do. I live from day to day, boys. I tell you, I know every thought in his mind. It sounds so old-fashioned and silly, but I tell you he put his whole life into you and you've turned your backs on him. [*She is bent over in the chair, weeping, her face in her hands.*] Biff, I swear to God! Biff, his life is in your hands!
HAPPY: [*to BIFF*] How do you like that damned fool!
BIFF: [*kissing her*] All right, pal, all right. It's all settled now. I've been remiss. I know that, Mom. But now I'll stay, and I swear to you, I'll apply myself. [*kneeling in front of her, in a fever of self-reproach*] It's just—you see, Mom, I don't fit in business. Not that I won't try. I'll try, and I'll make good.
HAPPY: Sure you will. The trouble with you in business was you never tried to please   675
people.

BIFF: I know, I—

HAPPY: Like when you worked for Harrison's. Bob Harrison said you were tops, and then you go and do some damn fool thing like whistling whole songs in the elevator like a comedian.

BIFF: [*against* HAPPY] So what? I like to whistle sometimes.

HAPPY: You don't raise a guy to a responsible job who whistles in the elevator!

680 LINDA: Well, don't argue about it now.

HAPPY: Like when you'd go off and swim in the middle of the day instead of taking the line around.

BIFF: [*his resentment rising*] Well, don't you run off? You take off sometimes, don't you? On a nice summer day?

HAPPY: Yeah, but I cover myself!

LINDA: Boys!

685 HAPPY: If I'm going to take a fade the boss can call any number where I'm supposed to be and they'll swear to him that I just left. I'll tell you something that I hate to say, Biff, but in the business world some of them think you're crazy.

BIFF: [*angered*] Screw the business world!

HAPPY: All right, screw it! Great, but cover yourself!

LINDA: Hap, Hap!

BIFF: I don't care what they think! They've laughed at Dad for years, and you know why? Because we don't belong in this nuthouse of a city! We should be mixing cement on some open plain, or—or carpenters. A carpenter is allowed to whistle!

[WILLY *walks in from the entrance of the house, at left.*]

690 WILLY: Even your grandfather was better than a carpenter. [*Pause. They watch him.*] You never grew up. Bernard does not whistle in the elevator, I assure you.

BIFF: [*as though to laugh* WILLY *out of it*] Yeah, but you do, Pop.

WILLY: I never in my life whistled in an elevator! And who in the business world thinks I'm crazy?

BIFF: I didn't mean it like that, Pop. Now don't make a whole thing out of it, will ya?

WILLY: Go back to the West! Be a carpenter, a cowboy, enjoy yourself!

695 LINDA: Willy, he was just saying—

WILLY: I heard what he said!

HAPPY: [*trying to quiet* WILLY] Hey, Pop, come on now . . .

WILLY: [*continuing over* HAPPY's *line*] They laugh at me, heh? Go to Filene's, go to the Hub, go to Slattery's,° Boston. Call out the name Willy Loman and see what happens! Big shot!

BIFF: All right, Pop.

700 WILLY: Big!

BIFF: All right!

WILLY: Why do you always insult me?

BIFF: I didn't say a word! [*to* LINDA] Did I say a word?

LINDA: He didn't say anything, Willy.

705 WILLY: [*going to the doorway of the living room*] All right, good night, good night.

LINDA: Willy, dear, he just decided . . .

WILLY: [*to* BIFF] If you get tired hanging around tomorrow, paint the ceiling I put up in the living-room.

BIFF: I'm leaving early tomorrow.

HAPPY: He's going to see Bill Oliver, Pop.

710 WILLY: [*interestedly*] Oliver? For what?

°698 *Filene's, the Hub, Slattery's:* department stores in New England.

BIFF: [*with reserve, but trying, trying*] He always said he'd stake me. I'd like to go into business, so maybe I can take him up on it.

LINDA: Isn't that wonderful?

WILLY: Don't interrupt. What's wonderful about it? There's fifty men in the City of New York who'd stake him. [*to BIFF*] Sporting goods?

BIFF: I guess so. I know something about it and—

WILLY: He knows something about it! You know sporting goods better than Spalding, for   715
God's sake! How much is he giving you?

BIFF: I don't know. I didn't even see him yet, but—

WILLY: Then what're you talkin' about?

BIFF: [*getting angry*] Well, all I said was I'm gonna see him, that's all!

WILLY: [*turning away*] Ah, you're counting your chickens again.

BIFF: [*starting left for the stairs*] Oh, Jesus, I'm going to sleep!   720

WILLY: [*calling after him*] Don't curse in this house!

BIFF: [*turning*] Since when did you get so clean?

HAPPY: [*trying to stop them*] Wait a . . .

WILLY: Don't use that language to me! I won't have it!

HAPPY: [*grabbing BIFF, shouts*] Wait a minute! I got an idea. I got a feasible idea. Come here,   725
Biff, let's talk this over now, let's talk some sense here. When I was down in Florida last
time, I thought of a great idea to sell sporting goods. It just came back to me. You and I,
Biff—we have a line, the Loman Line. We train a couple of weeks, and put on a couple
of exhibitions, see?

WILLY: That's an idea!

HAPPY: Wait! We form two basketball teams, see? Two waterpolo teams. We play each other.
It's a million dollars' worth of publicity. Two brothers, see? The Loman Brothers.
Displays in the Royal Palms—all the hotels. And banners over the ring and the
basketball court: "Loman Brothers." Baby, we could sell sporting goods!

WILLY: That is a one-million-dollar idea!

LINDA: Marvelous!

BIFF: I'm in great shape as far as that's concerned.   730

HAPPY: And the beauty of it is, Biff, it wouldn't be like a business. We'd be out playin' ball
again . . .

BIFF: [*enthused*] Yeah, that's . . .

WILLY: Million-dollar . . .

HAPPY: And you wouldn't get fed up with it, Biff. It'd be the family again. There'd be the
old honor, and comradeship, and if you wanted to go off for a swim or somethin'—
well, you'd do it! Without some smart cooky gettin' up ahead of you!

WILLY: Lick the world! You guys together could absolutely lick the civilized world.   735

BIFF: I'll see Oliver tomorrow. Hap, if we could work that out . . .

LINDA: Maybe things are beginning to—

WILLY: [*wildly enthused, to LINDA*] Stop interrupting! [*to BIFF*] But don't wear sport jacket and
slacks when you see Oliver.

BIFF: No, I'll—

WILLY: A business suit, and talk as little as possible, and don't crack any jokes.   740

BIFF: He did like me. Always liked me.

LINDA: He loved you!

WILLY: [*to LINDA*] Will you stop! [*to BIFF*] Walk in very serious. You are not applying for a
boy's job. Money is to pass. Be quiet, fine, and serious. Everybody likes a kidder, but
nobody lends him money.

HAPPY: I'll try to get some myself, Biff. I'm sure I can.

WILLY: I see great things for you kids. I think your troubles are over. But remember, start big   745
and you'll end big. Ask for fifteen. How much you gonna ask for?

BIFF: Gee, I don't know—

WILLY: And don't say "Gee." "Gee" is a boy's word. A man walking in for fifteen thousand dollars does not say "Gee!"

BIFF: Ten, I think, would be top though.

WILLY: Don't be so modest. You always started too low. Walk in with a big laugh. Don't look worried. Start off with a couple of your good stories to lighten things up. It's not what you say, it's how you say it—because personality always wins the day.

750 **LINDA:** Oliver always thought the highest of him—

WILLY: Will you let me talk?

BIFF: Don't yell at her, Pop, will ya?

WILLY: [*angrily*] I was talking, wasn't I?

BIFF: I don't like you yelling at her all the time, and I'm tellin' you, that's all.

755 **WILLY:** What're you, takin' over this house?

LINDA: Willy—

WILLY: [*turning on her*] Don't take his side all the time, godammit!

BIFF: [*furiously*] Stop yelling at her!

WILLY: [*suddenly pulling on his cheek, beaten down, guilt ridden*] Give my best to Bill Oliver— he may remember me.

[*He exits through the living-room doorway.*]

760 **LINDA:** [*her voice subdued*] What'd you have to start that for? [*BIFF turns away.*] You see how sweet he was as soon as you talked hopefully? [*She goes over to BIFF.*] Come up and say good night to him. Don't let him go to bed that way.

HAPPY: Come on, Biff, let's buck him up.

LINDA: Please, dear. Just say good night. It takes so little to make him happy. Come. [*She goes through the living-room doorway, calling upstairs from within the living-room.*] Your pajamas are hanging in the bathroom, Willy!

HAPPY: [*looking toward where LINDA went out*] What a woman! They broke the mold when they made her. You know that, Biff?

BIFF: He's off salary. My God, working on commission!

765 **HAPPY:** Well, let's face it: he's no hot-shot selling man. Except that sometimes, you have to admit, he's a sweet personality.

BIFF: [*deciding*] Lend me ten bucks, will ya? I want to buy some new ties.

HAPPY: I'll take you to a place I know. Beautiful stuff. Wear one of my striped shirts tomorrow.

BIFF: She got gray. Mom got awful old. Gee, I'm gonna go in to Oliver tomorrow and knock him for a—

HAPPY: Come on up. Tell that to Dad. Let's give him a whirl. Come on.

770 **BIFF:** [*steamed up*] You know, with ten thousand bucks, boy!

HAPPY: [*as they go into the living-room*] That's the talk, Biff, that's the first time I've heard the old confidence out of you! [*from within the living-room, fading off*] You're gonna live with me, kid, and any babe you want just say the word . . . [*The last lines are hardly heard. They are mounting the stairs to their parents' bedroom.*]

LINDA: [*entering her bedroom and addressing WILLY, who is in the bathroom. She is straightening the bed for him.*] Can you do anything about the shower? It drips.

WILLY: [*from the bathroom*] All of a sudden everything falls to pieces! Goddam plumbing, oughta be sued, those people. I hardly finished putting it in and the thing . . . [*His words rumble off.*]

LINDA: I'm just wondering if Oliver will remember him. You think he might?

775 **WILLY:** [*coming out of the bathroom in his pajamas*] Remember him? What's the matter with you, you crazy? If he'd've stayed with Oliver he'd be on top by now! Wait'll Oliver gets

a look at him. You don't know the average caliber any more. The average young man today—[*He is getting into bed*]—is got a caliber of zero. Greatest thing in the world for him was to bum around.

[*BIFF and HAPPY enter the bedroom. Slight pause.*]

WILLY: [*stops short, looking at BIFF*] Glad to hear it, boy.

HAPPY: He wanted to say good night to you, sport.

WILLY: [*to BIFF*] Yeah. Knock him dead, boy. What'd you want to tell me?

BIFF: Just take it easy, Pop. Good night. [*He turns to go.*]

WILLY: [*unable to resist*] And if anything falls off the desk while you're talking to him—like a 780 package or something—don't you pick it up. They have office boys for that.

LINDA: I'll make a big breakfast—

WILLY: Will you let me finish? [*to BIFF*] Tell him you were in the business in the West. Not farm work.

BIFF: All right, Dad.

LINDA: I think everything—

WILLY: [*going right through her speech*] And don't undersell yourself. No less than fifteen 785 thousand dollars.

BIFF: [*unable to bear him*] Okay. Good night, Mom. [*He starts moving.*]

WILLY: Because you got a greatness in you, Biff, remember that. You got all kinds a greatness . . . [*He lies back, exhausted.*]

[*BIFF walks out.*]

LINDA: [*calling after BIFF*] Sleep well, darling!

HAPPY: I'm gonna get married, Mom. I wanted to tell you.

LINDA: Go to sleep, dear. 790

HAPPY: [*going*] I just wanted to tell you.

WILLY: Keep up the good work. [*HAPPY exits.*] God . . . remember that Ebbets Field° game? The championship of the city?

LINDA: Just rest. Should I sing to you?

WILLY: Yeah. Sing to me. [*LINDA hums a soft lullaby.*] When that team came out—he was the tallest, remember?

LINDA: Oh, yes. And in gold. 795

[*BIFF enters the darkened kitchen, takes a cigarette, and leaves the house. He comes downstage into a golden pool of light. He smokes, staring at the night.*]

WILLY: Like a young god. Hercules—something like that. And the sun, the sun all around him. Remember how he waved to me? Right up from the field, with the representatives of three colleges standing by? And the buyers I brought, and the cheers when he came out—Loman, Loman, Loman! God Almighty, he'll be great yet. A star like that, magnificent, can never really fade away!

[*The light on WILLY is fading. The gas heater begins to glow through the kitchen wall, near the stairs, a blue flame beneath red coils.*]

LINDA: [*timidly*] Willy dear, what has he got against you?

WILLY: I'm so tired. Don't talk any more.

[*BIFF slowly returns to the kitchen. He stops, stares toward the heater.*]

LINDA: Will you ask Howard to let you work in New York?

°792 *Ebbets Field*: the baseball stadium of the Brooklyn Dodgers before they moved to Los Angeles in 1958. Biff had played there in a city championship football game. See 2.210 (page 1459).

800 **WILLY:** First thing in the morning. Everything'll be all right.

[*BIFF reaches behind the heater and draws out a length of rubber tubing. He is horrified and turns his head toward WILLY's room, still dimly lit, from which the strains of LINDA's desperate but monotonous humming rise.*]

WILLY: [*staring through the window into the moonlight*] Gee, look at the moon moving between the buildings!

[*BIFF wraps the tubing around his hand and quickly goes up the stairs.*]

ACT 2

[*Music is heard, gay and bright. The curtain rises as the music fades away. WILLY, in shirt sleeves, is sitting at the kitchen table, sipping coffee, his hat in his lap. LINDA is filling his cup when she can.*]

WILLY: Wonderful coffee. Meal in itself.
LINDA: Can I make you some eggs?
WILLY: No. Take a breath.
LINDA: You look so rested, dear.
5 **WILLY:** I slept like a dead one. First time in months. Imagine, sleeping till ten on a Tuesday morning. Boys left nice and early, heh?
LINDA: They were out of here by eight o'clock.
WILLY: Good work!
LINDA: It was so thrilling to see them leaving together. I can't get over the shaving lotion in this house!
WILLY: [*smiling*] Mmm—
10 **LINDA:** Biff was very changed this morning. His whole attitude seemed to be hopeful. He couldn't wait to get downtown to see Oliver.
WILLY: He's heading for a change. There's no question, there simply are certain men that take longer to get—solidified. How did he dress?
LINDA: His blue suit. He's so handsome in that suit. He could be a—anything in that suit!

[*WILLY gets up from the table. LINDA holds his jacket for him.*]

WILLY: There's no question, no question at all. Gee, on the way home tonight I'd like to buy some seeds.
LINDA: [*laughing*] That'd be wonderful. But not enough sun gets back there. Nothing'll grow any more.
15 **WILLY:** You wait, kid, before it's all over we're gonna get a little place out in the country, and I'll raise some vegetables, a couple of chickens . . .
LINDA: You'll do it yet, dear.

[*WILLY walks out of his jacket, LINDA follows him.*]

WILLY: And they'll get married, and come for a weekend. I'd build a little guest house. 'Cause I got so many fine tools, all I'd need would be a little lumber and some peace of mind.
LINDA: [*joyfully*] I sewed the lining . . .
WILLY: I could build two guest houses, so they'd both come. Did he decide how much he's going to ask Oliver for?
20 **LINDA:** [*getting him into the jacket*] He didn't mention it, but I imagine ten or fifteen thousand. You going to talk to Howard today?
WILLY: Yeah. I'll put it to him straight and simple. He'll just have to take me off the road.
LINDA: And Willy, don't forget to ask for a little advance, because we've got the insurance premium. It's the grace period now.

WILLY: That's a hundred . . . ?

LINDA: A hundred and eight, sixty-eight. Because we're a little short again.

WILLY: Why are we short?   25

LINDA: Well, you had the motor job on the car . . .

WILLY: That goddam Studebaker!

LINDA: And you got one more payment on the refrigerator . . .

WILLY: But it just broke again!

LINDA: Well, it's old, dear.   30

WILLY: I told you we should've bought a well-advertised machine. Charley bought a General Electric and it's twenty years old and it's still good, that son-of-a-bitch.

LINDA: But, Willy—

WILLY: Whoever heard of a Hastings refrigerator? Once in my life I would like to own something outright before it's broken! I'm always in a race with the junkyard! I just finished paying for the car and it's on its last legs. The refrigerator consumes belts like a goddam maniac. They time those things. They time them so when you finally paid for them, they're used up.

LINDA: [*buttoning up his jacket as he unbuttons it*] All told, about two hundred dollars would carry us, dear. But that includes the last payment on the mortgage. After this payment, Willy, the house belongs to us.

WILLY: It's twenty-five years!   35

LINDA: Biff was nine years old when we bought it.

WILLY: Well, that's a great thing. To weather a twenty-five year mortgage is—

LINDA: It's an accomplishment.

WILLY: All the cement, the lumber, the reconstruction I put in this house! There ain't a crack to be found in it any more.

LINDA: Well, it served its purpose.   40

WILLY: What purpose? Some stranger'll come along, move in, and that's that. If only Biff would take this house, and raise a family . . . [*He starts to go.*] Good-by, I'm late.

LINDA: [*suddenly remembering*] Oh, I forgot! You're supposed to meet them for dinner.

WILLY: Me?

LINDA: At Frank's Chop House on Forty-eighth near Sixth Avenue.

WILLY: Is that so! How about you?   45

LINDA: No, just the three of you. They're gonna blow you to a big meal!

WILLY: Don't say! Who thought of that?

LINDA: Biff came to me this morning, Willy, and he said, "Tell Dad, we want to blow him to a big meal." Be there six o'clock. You and your two boys are going to have dinner.

WILLY: Gee whiz! That's really somethin'. I'm gonna knock Howard for a loop, kid. I'll get an advance, and I'll come home with a New York job. Goddammit, now I'm gonna do it!

LINDA: Oh, that's the spirit, Willy!   50

WILLY: I will never get behind a wheel the rest of my life!

LINDA: It's changing, Willy, I can feel it changing!

WILLY: Beyond a question. G'by, I'm late. [*He starts to go again.*]

LINDA: [*calling after him as she runs to the kitchen table for a handkerchief*] You got your glasses?

WILLY: [*feels for them, then comes back in*] Yeah, yeah, got my glasses.   55

LINDA: [*giving him the handkerchief*] And a handkerchief.

WILLY: Yeah, handkerchief.

LINDA: And your saccharine?

WILLY: Yeah, my saccharine.

LINDA: Be careful on the subway stairs.   60

[*She kisses him, and a silk stocking is seen hanging from her hand. WILLY notices it.*]

WILLY: Will you stop mending stockings? At least while I'm in the house. It gets me nervous. I can't tell you. Please.

[*LINDA hides the stocking in her hand as she follows WILLY across the forestage in front of the house.*]

LINDA: Remember, Frank's Chop House.

WILLY: [*passing the apron*] Maybe beets would grow out there.

LINDA: [*laughing*] But you tried so many times.

65   **WILLY:** Yeah. Well, don't work hard today. [*He disappears around the right corner of the house.*]

LINDA: Be careful!

[*As WILLY vanishes, LINDA waves to him. Suddenly the phone rings. She runs across the stage and into the kitchen and lifts it.*]

LINDA: Hello? Oh, Biff! I'm so glad you called, I just . . . Yes, sure, I just told him. Yes, he'll be there for dinner at six o'clock, I didn't forget. Listen, I was just dying to tell you. You know that little rubber pipe I told you about? That he connected to the gas heater? I finally decided to go down the cellar this morning and take it away and destroy it. But it's gone! Imagine? He took it away himself, it isn't there! [*She listens.*] When? Oh, then you took it. Oh—nothing, it's just that I'd hoped he'd taken it away himself. Oh, I'm not worried, darling, because this morning he left in such high spirits, it was like the old days! I'm not afraid any more. Did Mr. Oliver see you? . . . Well, you wait there then. And make a nice impression on him, darling. Just don't perspire too much before you see him. And have a nice time with Dad. He may have big news too . . . That's right, a New York job. And be sweet to him tonight, dear. Be loving to him. Because he's only a little boat looking for a harbor. [*She is trembling with sorrow and joy.*] Oh, that's wonderful, Biff, you'll save his life. Thanks, darling. Just put your arm around him when he comes into the restaurant. Give him a smile. That's the boy . . . Good-by, dear . . . You got your comb? . . . That's fine. Good-by, Biff dear.

[*In the middle of her speech, HOWARD WAGNER, thirty-six, wheels in a small typewriter table on which is a wire-recording machine and proceeds to plug it in. This is on the left forestage. Light slowly fades on LINDA as it rises on HOWARD. HOWARD is intent on threading the machine and only glances over his shoulder as WILLY appears.*]

WILLY: Pst! Pst!

HOWARD: Hello, Willy, come in.

70   **WILLY:** Like to have a little talk with you, Howard.

HOWARD: Sorry to keep you waiting. I'll be with you in a minute.

WILLY: What's that, Howard?

HOWARD: Didn't you ever see one of these? Wire recorder.

WILLY: Oh. Can we talk a minute?

75   **HOWARD:** Records things. Just got delivery yesterday. Been driving me crazy, the most terrific machine I ever saw in my life. I was up all night with it.

WILLY: What do you do with it?

HOWARD: I bought it for dictation, but you can do anything with it. Listen to this. I had it home last night. Listen to what I picked up. The first one is my daughter. Get this. [*He flicks the switch and "Roll out the Barrel" is heard being whistled.*] Listen to that kid whistle.

WILLY: That is lifelike, isn't it?

HOWARD: Seven years old. Get that tone.

80   **WILLY:** Ts, ts. Like to ask a little favor if you . . .

[*The whistling breaks off, and the voice of HOWARD'S DAUGHTER is heard.*]

His Daughter: "Now you, Daddy."

Howard: She's crazy for me! [*Again the same song is whistled.*] That's me! Ha! [*He winks.*]

Willy: You're very good!

[*The whistling breaks off again. The machine runs silent for a moment.*]

Howard: Sh! Get this now, this is my son.

His Son: "The capital of Alabama is Montgomery; the capital of Arizona is Phoenix; the   85
    capital of Arkansas is Little Rock; the capital of California is Sacramento . . . " [*and on,
    and on*]

Howard: [*holding up five fingers*] Five years old, Willy!

Willy: He'll make an announcer some day!

His Son: [*continuing*] "The capital . . . "

Howard: Get that—alphabetical order! [*The machine breaks off suddenly.*] Wait a minute. The
    maid kicked the plug out.

Willy: It certainly is a—   90

Howard: Sh, for God's sake!

His Son: "It's nine o'clock, Bulova watch time. So I have to go to sleep."

Willy: That really is—

Howard: Wait a minute! The next is my wife.

[*They wait.*]

Howard's Voice: "Go on, say something." [*pause*] "Well, you gonna talk?"   95

His Wife: "I can't think of anything."

Howard's Voice: "Well, talk—it's turning."

His Wife: [*shyly, beaten*] "Hello." [*Silence*] "Oh, Howard, I can't talk into this . . . "

Howard: [*snapping the machine off*] That was my wife.

Willy: That is a wonderful machine. Can we—   100

Howard: I tell you, Willy, I'm gonna take my camera, and my bandsaw, and all my hobbies,
    and out they go. This is the most fascinating relaxation I ever found.

Willy: I think I'll get one myself.

Howard: Sure, they're only a hundred and a half. You can't do without it. Supposing you
    wanna hear Jack Benny,° see? But you can't be at home at that hour. So you tell the
    maid to turn the radio on when Jack Benny comes on, and this automatically goes on
    with the radio . . .

Willy: And when you come home you . . .

Howard: You can come home twelve o'clock, one o'clock, any time you like, and you get   105
    yourself a Coke and sit yourself down, throw the switch, and there's Jack Benny's
    program in the middle of the night!

Willy: I'm definitely going to get one. Because lots of time I'm on the road, and I think to
    myself, what I must be missing on the radio!

Howard: Don't you have a radio in the car?

Willy: Well, yeah, but who ever thinks of turning it on?

Howard: Say, aren't you supposed to be in Boston?

Willy: That's what I want to talk to you about, Howard. You got a minute?   110

[*He draws a chair in from the wing.*]

Howard: What happened? What're you doing here?

Willy: Well . . .

°103 *Jack Benny:* (1894–1974), vaudeville, radio, television, and movie comedian.

HOWARD: You didn't crack up again, did you?

WILLY: Oh, no. No . . .

115   HOWARD: Geez, you had me worried there for a minute. What's the trouble?

WILLY: Well, tell you the truth, Howard, I've come to the decision that I'd rather not travel any more.

HOWARD: Not travel! Well, what'll you do?

WILLY: Remember, Christmas time, when you had the party here? You said you'd try to think of some spot for me here in town.

HOWARD: With us?

120   WILLY: Well, sure.

HOWARD: Oh, yeah, yeah. I remember. Well, I couldn't think of anything for you, Willy.

WILLY: I tell ya, Howard. The kids are all grown up, y'know. I don't need much any more. If I could take home—well, sixty-five dollars a week, I could swing it.

HOWARD: Yeah, but Willy, see I—

WILLY: I tell ya why, Howard. Speaking frankly and between the two of us, y'know—I'm just a little tired.

125   HOWARD: Oh, I could understand that, Willy. But you're a road man, Willy, and we do a road business. We've only got a half-dozen salesmen on the floor here.

WILLY: God knows, Howard, I never asked a favor of any man. But I was with the firm when your father used to carry you up here in his arms.

HOWARD: I know that, Willy, but—

WILLY: Your father came to me the day you were born and asked me what I thought of the name of Howard, may he rest in peace.

HOWARD: I appreciate that, Willy, but there just is no spot here for you. If I had a spot I'd slam you right in, but I just don't have a single solitary spot.

[*He looks for his lighter.* WILLY *has picked it up and gives it to him. Pause.*]

130   WILLY: [*with increasing anger*] Howard, all I need to set my table is fifty dollars a week.

HOWARD: But where am I going to put you, kid?

WILLY: Look, it isn't a question of whether I can sell merchandise, is it?

HOWARD: No, but it's a business, kid, and everybody's gotta pull his own weight.

WILLY: [*desperately*] Just let me tell you a story, Howard—

135   HOWARD: 'Cause you gotta admit, business is business.

WILLY: [*angrily*] Business in definitely business, but just listen for a minute. You don't understand this. When I was a boy—eighteen, nineteen—I was already on the road. And there was a question in my mind as to whether selling had a future for me. Because in those days I had a yearning to go to Alaska. See, there were three gold strikes in one month in Alaska, and I felt like going out. Just for the ride, you might say.

HOWARD: [*barely interested*] Don't say.

WILLY: Oh, yeah, my father lived many years in Alaska. He was an adventurous man. We've got quite a little streak of self-reliance in our family. I thought I'd go out with my older brother and try to locate him, and maybe settle in the North with the old man. And I was almost decided to go, when I met a salesman in the Parker House.° His name was Dave Singleman. And he was eighty-four years old, and he'd drummed merchandise in thirty-one states. And old Dave, he'd go up to his room, y'understand, put on his green velvet slippers—I'll never forget—and pick up his phone and call the buyers, and without ever leaving his room, at the age of eighty-four, he made his living. And when I saw that, I realized that selling was the greatest career a man could want. 'Cause what could be more satisfying than to be able to go, at the age of eighty-four, into twenty or thirty different cities, and pick up a phone, and be remembered and loved and helped by so many different people? Do you

---

°138 *Parker House:* a hotel in Boston.

know? when he died—and by the way he died the death of a salesman, in his green velvet slippers in the smoker of the New York, New Haven and Hartford, going into Boston—when he died, hundreds of salesmen and buyers were at his funeral. Things were sad on a lotta trains for months after that. [*He stands up. Howard has not looked at him.*] In those days there was personality in it, Howard. There was respect, and comradeship, and gratitude in it. Today, it's all cut and dried, and there's no chance for bringing friendship to bear—or personality. You see what I mean? They don't know me any more.

HOWARD: [*moving away, to the right*] That's just the thing, Willy.

WILLY: If I had forty dollars a week—that's all I'd need. Forty dollars, Howard.   140

HOWARD: Kid, I can't take blood from a stone, I—

WILLY: [*desperation is on him now*] Howard, the year Al Smith° was nominated, your father came to me and—

HOWARD: [*starting to go off*] I've got to see some people, kid.

WILLY: [*stopping him*] I'm talking about your father! There were promises made across this desk! You mustn't tell me you've got people to see—I put thirty-four years into this firm, Howard, and now I can't pay my insurance! You can't eat the orange and throw the peel away—a man is not a piece of fruit! [*after a pause*] Now pay attention. Your father—in 1928 I had a big year. I averaged a hundred and seventy dollars a week in commissions.

HOWARD: [*impatiently*] Now, Willy, you never averaged—   150 · *(145)*

WILLY: [*banging his hand on the desk*] I averaged a hundred and seventy dollars a week in the year of 1928! And your father came to me—or rather, I was in the office here—it was right over this desk—and he put his hand on my shoulder—

HOWARD: [*getting up*] You'll have to excuse me, Willy, I gotta see some people. Pull yourself together. [*going out*] I'll be back in a little while.

[*On HOWARD's exit, the light on his chair grows very bright and strange.*]

WILLY: Pull myself together! What the hell did I say to him? My God, I was yelling at him! How could I! [*WILLY breaks off, staring at the light, which occupies the chair, animating it. He approaches this chair, standing across the desk from it.*] Frank, Frank, don't you remember what you told me that time? How you put your hand on my shoulder, and Frank . . . [*He leans on the desk and as he speaks the dead man's name he accidentally switches on the recorder, and instantly*]

HOWARD'S SON: " . . . of New York is Albany. The capital of Ohio is Cincinnati, the capital of Rhode Island is . . . " [*The recitation continues.*]

WILLY: [*leaping away with fright, shouting*] Ha! Howard! Howard! Howard!   150

HOWARD: [*rushing in*] What happened?

WILLY: [*pointing at the machine, which continues nasally, childishly, with the capital cities*] Shut it off! Shut it off!

HOWARD: [*pulling the plug out*] Look, Willy . . .

WILLY: [*pressing his hands to his eyes*] I gotta get myself some coffee. I'll get some coffee . . .

[*WILLY starts to walk out. HOWARD stops him.*]

HOWARD: [*rolling up the cord*] Willy, look . . .   155

WILLY: I'll go to Boston.

°142 *Al Smith:* Alfred E. Smith was governor of New York State (1919–1921, 1923–1929) and the Democratic presidential candidate defeated by Herbert Hoover in 1928.

HOWARD: Willy, you can't go to Boston for us.

WILLY: Why can't I go?

HOWARD: I don't want you to represent us. I've been meaning to tell you for a long time now.

160 WILLY: Howard, are you firing me?

HOWARD: I think you need a good long rest, Willy.

WILLY: Howard—

HOWARD: And when you feel better, come back, and we'll see if we can work something out.

WILLY: But I gotta earn money, Howard. I'm in no position to—

165 HOWARD: Where are your sons? Why don't your sons give you a hand?

WILLY: They're working on a very big deal.

HOWARD: This is no time for false pride, Willy. You go to your sons and you tell them that you're tired. You've got two great boys, haven't you?

WILLY: Oh, no question, no question, but in the meantime . . .

HOWARD: Then that's that, heh?

170 WILLY: All right, I'll go to Boston tomorrow.

HOWARD: No, no.

WILLY: I can't throw myself on my sons. I'm not a cripple!

HOWARD: Look, kid, I'm busy this morning.

WILLY: [grasping HOWARD'S ARM] Howard, you've got to let me go to Boston!

175 HOWARD: [hard, keeping himself under control] I've got a line of people to see this morning. Sit down, take five minutes, and pull yourself together, and then go home, will ya? I need the office, Willy [He starts to go, turns, remembering the recorder, starts to push off the table holding the recorder.] Oh, yeah. Whenever you can this week, stop by and drop off the samples. You'll feel better, Willy, and then come back and we'll talk. Pull yourself together, kid, there's people outside.

[HOWARD exits, pushing the table off left. WILLY stares into space, exhausted. Now the music is heard—BEN's music—first distantly, then closer. As WILLY speaks, BEN enters from the right. He carries valise and umbrella.]

WILLY: Oh, Ben, how did you do it? What is the answer? Did you wind up the Alaska deal already?

BEN: Doesn't take much time if you know what you're doing. Just a short business trip. Boarding ship in an hour. Wanted to say good-by.

WILLY: Ben, I've got to talk to you.

BEN: [glancing at his watch] Haven't much time, William.

180 WILLY: [crossing the apron to BEN] Ben, nothing's working out. I don't know what to do.

BEN: Now, look here, William. I've bought timberland in Alaska and I need a man to look after things for me.

WILLY: God, timberland! Me and my boys in those grand outdoors!

BEN: You've a new continent at your doorstep, William. Get out of these cities, they're full of talk and time payments and courts of law. Screw on your fists and you can fight for a fortune up there.

WILLY: Yes, yes! Linda, Linda!

[LINDA enters as of old, with the wash.]

185 LINDA: Oh, you're back?

BEN: I haven't much time.

WILLY: No, wait! Linda, he's got a proposition for me in Alaska.

LINDA: But you've got—[to BEN] He's got a beautiful job here.

WILLY: But in Alaska, kid, I could—

LINDA: You're doing well enough, Willy!   190

BEN: [*to LINDA*] Enough for what, my dear?

LINDA: [*frightened of BEN and angry at him*] Don't say those things to him! Enough to be happy right here, right now. [*to WILLY, while BEN laughs*] Why must everybody conquer the world? You're well liked, and the boys love you, and someday—[*to BEN*]—why old man Wagner told him just the other day that if he keeps it up he'll be a member of the firm, didn't he, Willy?

WILLY: Sure, sure. I am building something with this firm, Ben, and if a man is building something he must be on the right track, mustn't he?

BEN: What are you building? Lay your hand on it. Where is it?

WILLY: [*hesitantly*] That's true, Linda, there's nothing.   195

LINDA: Why? [*to BEN*] There's a man eighty-four years old—

WILLY: That's right, Ben, that's right. When I look at that man I say, what is there to worry about?

BEN: Bah!

WILLY: It's true, Ben. All he has to do is go into any city, pick up the phone, and he's making his living and you know why?

BEN: [*picking up his valise*] I've got to go.   200

WILLY: [*holding BEN back*] Look at this boy!

[*BIFF, in his high school sweater, enters carrying suitcase. HAPPY carries BIFF's shoulder guards, gold helmet, and football pants.*]

WILLY: Without a penny to his name, three great universities are begging for him, and from there the sky's the limit, because it's not what you do, Ben. It's who you know and the smile on your face! It's contacts, Ben, contacts! The whole wealth of Alaska passes over the lunch table at the Commodore Hotel,° and that's the wonder, the wonder of this country, that a man can end with diamonds here on the basis of being liked! [*He turns to BIFF*] And that's why when you get out on that field today it's important. Because thousands of people will be rooting for you and loving you. [*to BEN, who has again begun to leave*] And Ben! when he walks into a business office his name will sound out like a bell and all the doors will open to him! I've seen it, Ben, I've seen it a thousand times! You can't feel it with your hand like timber, but it's there!

BEN: Good-by, William.

WILLY: Ben, am I right? Don't you think I'm right? I value your advice.

BEN: There's a new continent at your doorstep, William. You could walk out rich. Rich! [*He is gone.*]   205

WILLY: We'll do it here, Ben! You hear me? We're gonna do it here!

[*YOUNG BERNARD rushes in. The gay music of the Boys is heard.*]

BERNARD: Oh, gee, I was afraid you left already!

WILLY: Why? What time is it?

BERNARD: It's half-past one!

WILLY: Well, come on, everybody! Ebbets Field next stop! Where's the pennants? [*He rushes through the wall-line of the kitchen and out into the dining-room.*]   210

°202 *Commodore Hotel*: a large hotel in New York City.

LINDA: [*to* BIFF] Did you pack fresh underwear?

BIFF: [*who has been limbering up*] I want to go!

BERNARD: Biff, I'm carrying your helmet, ain't I?

HAPPY: No, I'm carrying the helmet.

215 BERNARD: Oh, Biff, you promised me.

HAPPY: I'm carrying the helmet.

BERNARD: How am I going to get in the locker room?

LINDA: Let him carry the shoulder guards. [*She puts her coat and hat on in the kitchen.*]

BERNARD: Can I, Biff? 'Cause I told everybody I'm going to be in the locker room.

220 HAPPY: In Ebbets Field it's the clubhouse.

BERNARD: I meant the clubhouse. Biff!

HAPPY: Biff!

BIFF: [*grandly, after a slight pause.*] Let him carry the shoulder guards.

HAPPY: [*as he gives* BERNARD *the shoulder guards*] Stay close to us now.

[WILLY *rushes in with the pennants.*]

225 WILLY: [*handing them out*] Everybody wave when Biff comes out on the field. [*HAPPY and* BERNARD *run off.*] You set now, boy?

[*The music has died away.*]

BIFF: Ready to go, Pop. Every muscle is ready.

WILLY: [*at the edge of the apron*] You realize what this means?

BIFF: That's right, Pop.

WILLY: [*feeling* BIFF's *muscles*] You're comin' home this afternoon captain of the All-Scholastic Championship Team of the City of New York.

230 BIFF: I got it, Pop. And remember, pal, when I take off my helmet, that touchdown is for you.

WILLY: Let's go! [*He is starting out, with his arm around* BIFF, *when* CHARLEY *enters, as of old, in knickers.*] I got no room for you, Charley.

CHARLEY: Room? For what?

WILLY: In the car.

CHARLEY: You goin' for a ride? I wanted to shoot some casino.

WILLY: [*furiously*] Casino! [*incredulously*] Don't you realize what today is?

235 LINDA: Oh, he knows, Willy. He's just kidding you.

WILLY: That's nothing to kid about!

CHARLEY: No, Linda, what's goin' on?

LINDA: He's playing in Ebbets Field.

CHARLEY: Baseball in this weather?

240 WILLY: Don't talk to him. Come on, come on! [*He is pushing them out.*]

CHARLEY: Wait a minute, didn't you hear the news?

WILLY: What?

CHARLEY: Don't you listen to the radio? Ebbets Field just blew up.

WILLY: You go to hell! [CHARLEY *laughs. Pushing them out.*] Come on, come on! We're late.

245 CHARLEY: [*as they go*] Knock a homer, Biff, knock a homer!

WILLY: [*the last to leave, turning to* CHARLEY] I don't think that was funny, Charley. This is the greatest day of his life.

CHARLEY: Willy, when are you going to grow up?

WILLY: Yeah, heh? When this game is over, Charley, you'll be laughing out the other side of your face. They'll be calling him another Red Grange.° Twenty-five thousand a year.

°249 *Red Grange:* Harold Edward Grange (1903–1991), all-America halfback (1923–1925) at the University of Illinois.

CHARLEY: [*kidding*] Is that so?   250
WILLY: Yeah, that's so.
CHARLEY: Well, then, I'm sorry, Willy. But tell me something.
WILLY: What?
CHARLEY: Who is Red Grange?
WILLY: Put up your hands. Goddam you, put up your hands!   255

[*CHARLEY, chuckling, shakes his head and walks away, around the left corner of the stage. WILLY follows him. The music rises to a mocking frenzy.*]

WILLY: Who the hell do you think you are, better than everybody else? You don't know
   everything, you big, ignorant, stupid . . . . Put up your hands!

[*Light rises, on the right side of the forestage, on a small table in the reception room of CHARLEY's office. Traffic sounds are heard. BERNARD, now mature, sits whistling to himself. A pair of tennis rackets and an overnight bag are on the floor beside him.*]

WILLY: [*offstage*] What are you walking away for? Don't walk away! If you're going to say
   something say it to my face! I know you laugh at me behind my back. You'll laugh out
   of the other side of your goddam face after this game. Touchdown! Touchdown! Eighty
   thousand people! Touchdown. Right between the goal posts.

[*BERNARD is a quiet, earnest, but self-assured young man. WILLY's voice is coming from right upstage now. BERNARD lowers his feet off the table and listens. JENNY, his father's secretary, enters.*]

JENNY: [*distressed*] Say, Bernard, will you go out in the hall?
BERNARD: What is that noise? Who is it?
JENNY: Mr. Loman. He just got off the elevator.   260
BERNARD: [*getting up*] Who's he arguing with?
JENNY: Nobody. There's nobody with him. I can't deal with him any more, and your father
   gets all upset everytime he comes. I've got a lot of typing to do, and your father's
   waiting to sign it. Will you see him?
WILLY: [*entering*] Touchdown! Touch—[*He sees JENNY.*] Jenny, Jenny, good to see you. How're
   ya? Workin'? Or still honest?
JENNY: Fine. How've you been feeling?
WILLY: Not much any more, Jenny. Ha, ha! [*He is surprised to see the rackets.*]   265
BERNARD: Hello, Uncle Willy.
WILLY: [*almost shocked*] Bernard! Well, look who's here! [*He comes quickly, guiltily, to BERNARD
   and warmly shakes his hand.*]
BERNARD: How are you? Good to see you.
WILLY: What are you doing here?
BERNARD: Oh, just stopped off to see Pop. Get off my feet till my train leaves. I'm going to   270
   Washington in a few minutes.
WILLY: Is he in?
BERNARD: Yes, he's in his office with the accountants. Sit down.
WILLY: [*sitting down*] What're you going to do in Washington?
BERNARD: Oh, just a case I've got there, Willy.
WILLY: That so? [*Indicating the rackets*] You going to play tennis there?   275

BERNARD: I'm staying with a friend who's got a court.

WILLY: Don't say. His own tennis court. Must be fine people, I bet.

BERNARD: They are, very nice. Dad tells me Biff's in town.

WILLY: [*with a big smile*] Yeah, Biff's in. Working on a very big deal, Bernard.

280 **BERNARD:** What's Biff doing?

WILLY: Well, he's been doing very big things in the West. But he decided to establish himself here. Very big. We're having dinner. Did I hear your wife had a boy?

BERNARD: That's right. Our second.

WILLY: Two boys! What do you know!

BERNARD: What kind of a deal has Biff got?

285 **WILLY:** Well, Bill Oliver—very big sporting-goods man—he wants Biff very badly. Called him in from the West. Long distance, carte blanche, special deliveries. Your friends have their own private tennis court?

BERNARD: You still with the old firm, Willy?

WILLY: [*after a pause*] I'm—I'm overjoyed to see how you made the grade, Bernard, overjoyed. It's an encouraging thing to see a young man really—really—Looks very good for Biff—very—[*He breaks off, then*] Bernard—[*He is so full of emotion, he breaks off again.*]

BERNARD: What is it, Willy?

WILLY: [*small and alone*] What—what's the secret?

290 **BERNARD:** What secret?

WILLY: How—how did you? Why didn't he ever catch on?

BERNARD: I wouldn't know that, Willy.

WILLY: [*confidentially, desperately*] You were his friend, his boyhood friend. There's something I don't understand about it. His life ended after that Ebbets Field game. From the age of seventeen nothing good ever happened to him.

BERNARD: He never trained himself for anything.

295 **WILLY:** But he did, he did. After high school he took so many correspondence courses. Radio mechanics; television; God knows what, and never made the slightest mark.

BERNARD: [*taking off his glasses*] Willy, do you want to talk candidly?

WILLY: [*rising, faces* BERNARD] I regard you as a very brilliant man, Bernard. I value your advice.

BERNARD: Oh, the hell with the advice, Willy. I couldn't advise you. There's just one thing I've always wanted to ask you. When he was supposed to graduate, and the math teacher flunked him—

WILLY: Oh, that son-of-a-bitch ruined his life.

300 **BERNARD:** Yeah, but, Willy, all he had to do was go to summer school and make up that subject.

WILLY: That's right, that's right.

BERNARD: Did you tell him not to go to summer school?

WILLY: Me? I begged him to go. I ordered him to go!

BERNARD: Then why wouldn't he go?

305 **WILLY:** Why? Why! Bernard, that question has been trailing me like a ghost for the last fifteen years. He flunked the subject, and laid down and died like a hammer hit him!

BERNARD: Take it easy, kid.

WILLY: Let me talk to you—I got nobody to talk to. Bernard, Bernard, was it my fault? Y'see? It keeps going around in my mind, maybe I did something to him. I got nothing to give him.

BERNARD: Don't take it so hard.

WILLY: Why did he lay down? What is the story there? You were his friend!

310 **BERNARD:** Willy, I remember, it was June, and our grades came out. And he'd flunked math.

WILLY: That son-of-a-bitch!

BERNARD: No, it wasn't right then. Biff just got very angry, I remember, and he was ready to enroll in summer school.

WILLY: [*surprised*] He was?

BERNARD: He wasn't beaten by it at all. But then, Willy, he disappeared from the block for almost a month. And I got the idea that he'd gone up to New England to see you. Did he have a talk with you then?

[*WILLY stares in silence.*]

BERNARD: Willy?   315

WILLY: [*with a strong edge of resentment in his voice*] Yeah, he came to Boston. What about it?

BERNARD: Well, just that when he came back—I'll never forget this, it always mystifies me. Because I'd thought so well of Biff, even though he'd always taken advantage of me. I loved him, Willy, y'know? And he came back after that month and took his sneakers—remember the sneakers with "University of Virginia" printed on them? He was so proud of those, wore them every day. And he took them down in the cellar, and burned them up in the furnace. We had a fist fight. It lasted at least half an hour. Just the two of us, punching each other down the cellar, and crying right through it. I've often thought of how strange it was that I knew he'd given up his life. What happened in Boston, Willy?

[*WILLY looks at him as at an intruder.*]

BERNARD: I just bring it up because you asked me.

WILLY: [*angrily*] Nothing. What do you mean, "What happened?" What's that got to do with anything?

BERNARD: Well, don't get sore.   320

WILLY: What are you trying to do, blame it on me? If a boy lays down is that my fault?

BERNARD: Now, Willy, don't get—

WILLY: Well, don't—don't talk to me that way! What does that mean, "What happened?"

[*CHARLEY enters. He is in his vest, and he carries a bottle of bourbon.*]

CHARLEY: Hey, you're going to miss that train. [*He waves the bottle.*]

BERNARD: Yeah, I'm going. [*He takes the bottle.*] Thanks, Pop. [*He picks up his rackets and   325
bag.*] Good-by, Willy, and don't worry about it. You know, "If at first you don't succeed . . ."

WILLY: Yes, I believe in that.

BERNARD: But sometimes, Willy, it's better for a man just to walk away.

WILLY: Walk away?

BERNARD: That's right.

WILLY: But if you can't walk away?   330

BERNARD: [*after a slight pause*] I guess that's when it's tough. [*extending his hand*] Good-by, Willy.

WILLY: [*shaking BERNARD's hand*] Good-by, boy.

CHARLEY: [*an arm on BERNARD's shoulder*] How do you like this kid? Gonna argue a case in front of the Supreme Court.

BERNARD: [*protesting*] Pop!

WILLY: [*genuinely shocked, pained, and happy*] No! The Supreme Court!   335

BERNARD: I gotta run. 'By, Dad!

CHARLEY: Knock 'em dead, Bernard!

[*BERNARD goes off.*]

WILLY: [*as CHARLEY takes out his wallet*] The Supreme Court! And he didn't even mention it!

CHARLEY: [*counting out money on the desk*] He don't have to—he's gonna do it.

340 WILLY: And you never told him what to do, did you? You never took any interest in him.

CHARLEY: My salvation is that I never took any interest in anything. There's some money—fifty dollars. I got an accountant inside.

WILLY: Charley, look . . . [*with difficulty*] I got my insurance to pay. If you can manage it—I need a hundred and ten dollars.

[*CHARLEY doesn't reply for a moment; merely stops moving.*]

WILLY: I'd draw it from my bank but Linda would know, and I . . .

CHARLEY: Sit down, Willy.

345 WILLY: [*moving toward the chair*] I'm keeping an account of everything, remember. I'll pay every penny back. [*He sits.*]

CHARLEY: Now listen to me, Willy . . .

WILLY: I want you to know I appreciate . . .

CHARLEY: [*sitting down on the table*] Willy, what're you doin'? What the hell is goin' on in your head?

WILLY: Why? I'm simply . . .

350 CHARLEY: I offered you a job. You can make fifty dollars a week. And I won't send you on the road.

WILLY: I've got a job.

CHARLEY: Without pay? What kind of job is a job without pay? [*He rises.*] Now, look, kid, enough is enough. I'm no genius but I know when I'm being insulted.

WILLY: Insulted!

CHARLEY: Why don't you want to work for me?

355 WILLY: What's the matter with you? I've got a job.

CHARLEY: Then what're you walkin' in here every week for?

WILLY: [*getting up*] Well, if you don't want me to walk in here—

CHARLEY: I am offering you a job.

WILLY: I don't want your goddam job!

360 CHARLEY: When the hell are you going to grow up?

WILLY: [*furiously*] You big ignoramus, if you say that to me again I'll rap you one! I don't care how big you are [*He's ready to fight.*]

[*Pause.*]

CHARLEY: [*kindly, going to him*] How much do you need, Willy?

WILLY: Charley, I'm strapped. I'm strapped. I don't know what to do. I was just fired.

CHARLEY: Howard fired you?

365 WILLY: That snotnose. Imagine that? I named him. I named him Howard.

CHARLEY: Willy, when're you gonna realize that them things don't mean anything? You named him Howard, but you can't sell that. The only thing you got in this world is what you can sell. And the funny thing is that you're a salesman, and you don't know that.

WILLY: I've tried to think otherwise, I guess. I always felt that if a man was impressive, and well liked, that nothing—

CHARLEY: Why must everybody like you? Who liked J. P. Morgan?° Was he impressive? In a Turkish bath he'd look like a butcher. But with his pockets on he was very well liked.

°368 *J. P. Morgan:* John Pierpont Morgan (1837–1913) was the founder of U.S. Steel and the head of a gigantic family fortune that was enlarged by his son, John Pierpont Morgan (1867–1943). Charley is probably referring to the son.

Now listen, Willy, I know you don't like me, and nobody can say I'm in love with you, but I'll give you a job because—just for the hell of it, put it that way. Now what do you say?

WILLY: I—I just can't work for you, Charley.

CHARLEY: What're you, jealous of me?   370

WILLY: I can't work for you, that's all, don't ask me why.

CHARLEY: [*angered, takes out more bills*] You been jealous of me all your life, you damned fool! Here, pay your insurance. [*He puts the money in* WILLY's *hand.*]

WILLY: I'm keeping strict accounts.

CHARLEY: I've got some work to do. Take care of yourself. And pay your insurance.

WILLY: [*moving to the right*] Funny, y'know? After all the highways, and the trains, and the   375
appointments, and the years, you end up worth more dead than alive.

CHARLEY: Willy, nobody's worth nothin' dead. [*after a slight pause*] Did you hear what I said?

[WILLY *stands still, dreaming.*]

CHARLEY: Willy!

WILLY: Apologize to Bernard for me when you see him. I didn't mean to argue with him. He's a fine boy. They're all fine boys, and they'll end up big—all of them. Someday they'll all play tennis together. Wish me luck, Charley. He saw Bill Oliver today.

CHARLEY: Good luck.

WILLY: [*on the verge of tears*] Charley, you're the only friend I got. Isn't that a remarkable   380
thing? [*He goes out.*]

CHARLEY: Jesus!

[CHARLEY *stares after him a moment and follows. All light blacks out. Suddenly raucous music is heard, and a red glow rises behind the screen at right.* STANLEY, *a young waiter, appears, carrying a table, followed by* HAPPY, *who is carrying two chairs.*]

STANLEY: [*putting the table down*] That's all right, Mr. Loman. I can handle it myself. [*He turns and takes the chairs from* HAPPY *and places them at the table.*]

HAPPY: [*glancing around.*] Oh, this is better.

STANLEY: Sure, in the front there you're in the middle of all kinds a noise. Whenever you got a party, Mr. Loman, you just tell me and I'll put you back here. Y' know, there's a lotta people they don't like it private, because when they go out they like to see a lotta action around them because they're sick and tired to stay in the house by theirself. But I know you, you ain't from Hackensack.° You know what I mean?

HAPPY: [*sitting down*] So how's it coming, Stanley?   385

STANLEY: Ah, it's a dog's life. I only wish during the war they'd a took me in the Army. I coulda been dead by now.

HAPPY: My brother's back, Stanley.

STANLEY: Oh, he come back, heh? From the Far West.

HAPPY: Yeah, big cattle man, my brother, so treat him right. And my father's coming too.

STANLEY: Oh, your father too!   390

HAPPY: You got a couple of nice lobsters?

STANLEY: Hundred per cent, big.

HAPPY: I want them with claws.

STANLEY: Don't worry. I don't give you no mice. [HAPPY *laughs.*] How about some wine? It'll put a head on the meal.

°384 *Hackensack*: a city in northeastern New Jersey; Stanley uses the name as a reference to unsophisticated visitors to New York City.

395   HAPPY: No. You remember, Stanley, that recipe I brought you from overseas? With the champagne in it?

    STANLEY: Oh, yeah, sure. I still got it tacked up yet in the kitchen. But that'll have to cost a buck apiece anyways.

    HAPPY: That's all right.

    STANLEY: What'd you, hit a number or somethin'?

    HAPPY: No, it's a little celebration. My brother is—I think he pulled off a big deal today. I think we're going into business together.

400   STANLEY: Great! That's the best for you. Because a family business, you know what I mean?—that's the best.

    HAPPY: That's what I think.

    STANLEY: 'Cause what's the difference? Somebody steals? It's in the family. Know what I mean? [*sotto voce*°] Like this bartender here. The boss is goin' crazy what kinda leak he's got in the cash register. You put it in but it don't come out.

    HAPPY: [*raising his head*] Sh!

    STANLEY: What?

405   HAPPY: You notice I wasn't lookin' right or left, was I?

    STANLEY: No.

    HAPPY: And my eyes are closed.

    STANLEY: So what's the—?

    HAPPY: Strudel's comin'.

410   STANLEY: [*catching on, looks around*] Ah, no, there's no—

[*He breaks off as a furred, lavishly dressed Girl enters and sits at the next table. Both follow her with their eyes.*]

    STANLEY: Geez, how'd ya know?

    HAPPY: I got radar or something. [*staring directly at her profile*] Oooooooo . . . Stanley.

    STANLEY: I think that's for you, Mr. Loman.

    HAPPY: Look at that mouth. Oh God. And the binoculars.

415   STANLEY: Geez, you got a life, Mr. Loman.

    HAPPY: Wait on her.

    STANLEY: [*going to the GIRL's table*] Would you like a menu, ma'am?

    GIRL: I'm expecting someone, but I'd like a—

    HAPPY: Why don't you bring her—excuse me, miss, do you mind? I sell champagne, and I'd like you to try my brand. Bring her a champagne, Stanley.

420   GIRL: That's awfully nice of you.

    HAPPY: Don't mention it. It's all company money. [*He laughs.*]

    GIRL: That's a charming product to be selling, isn't it?

    HAPPY: Oh, gets to be like everything else. Selling is selling, y'know.

    GIRL: I suppose.

425   HAPPY: You don't happen to sell, do you?

    GIRL: No, I don't sell.

    HAPPY: Would you object to a compliment from a stranger? You ought to be on a magazine cover.

    GIRL: [*looking at him a little archly*] I have been.

[*STANLEY comes in with a glass of champagne.*]

    HAPPY: What'd I say before, Stanley? You see? She's a cover girl.

430   STANLEY: Oh, I could see, I could see.

    HAPPY: [*to the GIRL*] What magazine?

°402 *sotto voce*: spoken in an undertone or "stage" whisper.

GIRL: Oh, a lot of them [*She takes the drink.*] Thank you.

HAPPY: You know what they say in France, don't you? "Champagne is the drink of the complexion"—Hya, Biff!

[*BIFF has entered and sits with HAPPY.*]

BIFF: Hello, kid. Sorry I'm late.

HAPPY: I just got here. Uh, Miss—?   435

GIRL: Forsythe.

HAPPY: Miss Forsythe, this is my brother.

BIFF: Is Dad here?

HAPPY: His name is Biff. You might've heard of him. Great football player.

GIRL: Really? What team?   440

HAPPY: Are you familiar with football?

GIRL: No. I'm afraid I'm not.

HAPPY: Biff is quarterback with the New York Giants.

GIRL: Well, that is nice, isn't it? [*She drinks.*]

HAPPY: Good health.   445

GIRL: I'm happy to meet you.

HAPPY: That's my name. Hap. It's really Harold, but at West Point they called me Happy.

GIRL: [*now really impressed*] Oh, I see. How do you do? [*She turns her profile.*]

BIFF: Isn't Dad coming?

HAPPY: You want her?   450

BIFF: Oh, I could never make that.

HAPPY: I remember the time that idea would never come into your head. Where's the old confidence, Biff?

BIFF: I just saw Oliver—

HAPPY: Wait a minute. I've got to see that old confidence again. Do you want her? She's on call.

BIFF: Oh, no. [*He turns to look at the GIRL.*]   455

HAPPY: I'm telling you. Watch this. [*turning to the GIRL*] Honey? [*She turns to him.*] Are you busy?

GIRL: Well, I am . . . but I could make a phone call.

HAPPY: Do that, will you, honey? And see if you can get a friend. We'll be here for a while. Biff is one of the greatest football players in the country.

GIRL: [*standing up*] Well, I'm certainly happy to meet you.

HAPPY: Come back soon.   460

GIRL: I'll try.

HAPPY: Don't try, honey, try hard.

[*The GIRL exits. STANLEY follows, shaking his head in bewildered admiration.*]

HAPPY: Isn't that a shame now? A beautiful girl like that? That's why I can't get married. There's not a good woman in a thousand. New York is loaded with them, kid!

BIFF: Hap, look—

HAPPY: I told you she was on call!   465

BIFF: [*strangely unnerved*] Cut it out, will ya? I want to say something to you.

HAPPY: Did you see Oliver?

BIFF: I saw him all right. Now look, I want to tell Dad a couple of things and I want you to help me.

HAPPY: What? Is he going to back you?

BIFF: Are you crazy? You're out of your goddam head, you know that?   470

HAPPY: Why? What happened?

BIFF: [*breathlessly*] I did a terrible thing today, Hap. It's been the strangest day I ever went through. I'm all numb, I swear.

HAPPY: You mean he wouldn't see you?

BIFF: Well, I waited six hours for him, see? All day. Kept sending my name in. Even tried to date his secretary so she'd get me to him, but no soap.

475 **HAPPY:** Because you're not showin' the old confidence, Biff. He remembered you, didn't he?

BIFF: [*stopping HAPPY with a gesture*] Finally, about five o'clock, he comes out. Didn't remember who I was or anything. I felt like such an idiot, Hap.

HAPPY: Did you tell him my Florida idea?

BIFF: He walked away. I saw him for one minute. I got so mad I could've torn the walls down! How the hell did I ever get the idea I was a salesman there? I even believed myself that I'd been a salesman for him! And then he gave me one look and—I realized what a ridiculous lie my whole life has been! We've been talking in a dream for fifteen years. I was a shipping clerk.

HAPPY: What'd you do?

480 **BIFF:** [*with great tension and wonder*] Well, he left, see. And the secretary went out. I was all alone in the waiting-room. I don't know what came over me, Hap. The next thing I know I'm in his office—paneled walls, everything. I can't explain it. I—Hap, I took his fountain pen.

HAPPY: Geez, did he catch you?

BIFF: I ran out. I ran down all eleven flights. I ran and ran and ran.

HAPPY: That was an awful dumb—what'd you do that for?

BIFF: [*agonized*] I don't know, I just—wanted to take something. I don't know. You gotta help me, Hap, I'm gonna tell Pop.

485 **HAPPY:** You crazy? What for?

BIFF: Hap, he's got to understand that I'm not the man somebody lends that kind of money to. He thinks I've been spiting him all these years and it's eating him up.

HAPPY: That's just it. You tell him something nice.

BIFF: I can't.

HAPPY: Say you got a lunch date with Oliver tomorrow.

490 **BIFF:** So what do I do tomorrow?

HAPPY: You leave the house tomorrow and come back at night and say Oliver is thinking it over. And he thinks it over for a couple of weeks, and gradually it fades away and nobody's the worse.

BIFF: But it'll go on forever!

HAPPY: Dad is never so happy as when he's looking forward to something!

[*WILLY enters.*]

HAPPY: Hello, scout!

495 **WILLY:** Gee, I haven't been here in years!

[*STANLEY has followed WILLY in and sets a chair for him. STANLEY starts off but HAPPY stops him.*]

HAPPY: Stanley!

[*STANLEY stands by, waiting for an order.*]

BIFF: [*going to WILLY with guilt, as to an invalid*] Sit down, Pop. You want a drink?

WILLY: Sure, I don't mind.

BIFF: Let's get a load on.

500 **WILLY:** You look worried.

BIFF: N-no. [*to STANLEY*] Scotch all around. Make it doubles.

STANLEY: Doubles, right. [*He goes.*]

WILLY: You had a couple already, didn't you?

BIFF: Just a couple, yeah.

WILLY: Well, what happened, boy? [*nodding affirmatively, with a smile*] Everything go all   505
right?

BIFF: [*takes a breath, then reaches out and grasps WILLY's hand*] Pal . . . [*He is smiling bravely, and WILLY is smiling too.*] I had an experience today.

HAPPY: Terrific, Pop.

WILLY: That so? What happened?

BIFF: [*high, slightly alcoholic, above the earth*] I'm going to tell you everything from first to last. It's been a strange day. [*Silence. He looks around, composes himself as best he can, but his breath keeps breaking the rhythm of his voice.*] I had to wait quite a while for him, and—

WILLY: Oliver?   510

BIFF: Yeah, Oliver. All day, as a matter of cold fact. And a lot of—instances—facts, Pop, facts about my life came back to me. Who was it, Pop? Who ever said I was a salesman with Oliver?

WILLY: Well, you were.

BIFF: No, Dad, I was a shipping clerk.

WILLY: But you were practically—

BIFF: [*with determination*] Dad, I don't know who said it first, but I was never a salesman for   515
Bill Oliver.

WILLY: What're you talking about?

BIFF: Let's hold on to the facts tonight, Pop. We're not going to get anywhere bullin' around. I was a shipping clerk.

WILLY: [*angrily*] All right, now listen to me—

BIFF: Why don't you let me finish?

WILLY: I'm not interested in stories about the past or any crap of that kind because the   520
woods are burning, boys, you understand? There's a big blaze going on all around. I was fired today.

BIFF: [*shocked*] How could you be?

WILLY: I was fired, and I'm looking for a little good news to tell your mother, because the woman has waited and the woman has suffered. The gist of it is that I haven't got a story left in my head, Biff. So don't give me a lecture about facts and aspects. I am not interested. Now what've you got to say to me?

[*STANLEY enters with three drinks. They wait until he leaves.*]

WILLY: Did you see Oliver?

BIFF: Jesus, Dad!

WILLY: You mean you didn't go up there?   525

HAPPY: Sure he went up there.

BIFF: I did. I—saw him. How could they fire you?

WILLY: [*on the edge of his chair*] What kind of a welcome did he give you?

BIFF: He won't even let you work on commission?

WILLY: I'm out! [*driving*] So tell me, he gave you a warm welcome?   530

HAPPY: Sure Pop, sure!

BIFF: [*driven*] Well, it was kind of—

WILLY: I was wondering if he'd remember you. [*to HAPPY*] Imagine, man doesn't see him for ten, twelve years and gives him that kind of a welcome!

HAPPY: Damn right!

BIFF: [*trying to return to the offensive*] Pop, look—   535

WILLY: You know why he remembered you, don't you? Because you impressed him in those days.

BIFF: Let's talk quietly and get this down to the facts, huh?

WILLY: [*as though BIFF had been interrupting*] Well, what happened? It's great news, Biff. Did he take you into his office or'd you talk in the waiting-room?

BIFF: Well, he came in, see, and—

540 **WILLY:** [*with a big smile*] What'd he say? Betcha he threw his arm around you.

BIFF: Well, he kinda—

WILLY: He's a fine man. [*to HAPPY*] Very hard man to see, y'know.

HAPPY: [*agreeing*] Oh, I know.

WILLY: [*to BIFF*] Is that where you had the drinks?

545 **BIFF:** Yeah, he gave me a couple of—no, no!

HAPPY: [*cutting in*] He told him my Florida idea.

WILLY: Don't interrupt. [*to BIFF*] How'd he react to the Florida idea?

BIFF: Dad, will you give me a minute to explain?

WILLY: I've been waiting for you to explain since I sat down here! What happened? He took you into his office and what?

550 **BIFF:** Well—I talked. And—and he listened, see.

WILLY: Famous for the way he listens, y'know. What was his answer?

BIFF: His answer was—[*He breaks off, suddenly angry.*] Dad, you're not letting me tell you what I want to tell you!

WILLY: [*accusing, angered*] You didn't see him, did you?

BIFF: I did see him!

555 **WILLY:** What'd you insult him or something? You insulted him, didn't you?

BIFF: Listen, will you let me out of it, will you just let me out of it!

HAPPY: What the hell!

WILLY: Tell me what happened!

BIFF: [*to HAPPY*] I can't talk to him!

[*A single trumpet note jars the ear. The light of green leaves stains the house, which holds the air of night and a dream. YOUNG BERNARD enters and knocks on the door of the house.*]

560 **YOUNG BERNARD:** [*frantically*] Mrs. Loman, Mrs. Loman!

HAPPY: Tell him what happened!

BIFF: [*to HAPPY*] Shut up and leave me alone!

WILLY: No, no! You had to go and flunk math!

BIFF: What math? What're you talking about?

565 **YOUNG BERNARD:** Mrs. Loman, Mrs. Loman!

[*LINDA appears in the house, as of old.*]

WILLY: [*wildly*] Math, math, math!

BIFF: Take it easy, Pop!

YOUNG BERNARD: Mrs. Loman!

WILLY: [*furiously*] If you hadn't flunked you'd've been set by now!

570 **BIFF:** Now, look, I'm gonna tell you what happened, and you're going to listen to me.

YOUNG BERNARD: Mrs. Loman!

BIFF: I waited six hour—

HAPPY: What the hell are you saying?

BIFF: I kept sending in my name but he wouldn't see me. So finally he . . .

[*He continues unheard as light fades low on the restaurant.*]

575 **YOUNG BERNARD:** Biff flunked math!

LINDA: No!

YOUNG BERNARD: Birnbaum flunked him! They won't graduate him!

LINDA: But they have to. He's gotta go to the university. Where is he? Biff! Biff!

YOUNG BERNARD: No, he left. He went to Grand Central.

LINDA: Grand—You mean he went to Boston!   580

YOUNG BERNARD: Is Uncle Willy in Boston?

LINDA: Oh, maybe Willy can talk to the teacher. Oh, the poor, poor boy!

[*Light on house area snaps out.*]

BIFF: [*at the table, now audible, holding up a gold fountain pen*] . . . so I'm washed up with Oliver, you understand? Are you listening to me?

WILLY: [*at a loss*] Yeah, sure. If you hadn't flunked—

BIFF: Flunked what? What're you talking about?   585

WILLY: Don't blame everything on me! I didn't flunk math—you did! What pen?

HAPPY: That was awful dumb, Biff, a pen like that is worth—

WILLY: [*seeing the pen for the first time*] You took Oliver's pen?

BIFF: [*weakening*] Dad, I just explained it to you.

WILLY: You stole Bill Oliver's fountain pen!   590

BIFF: I didn't exactly steal it! That's just what I've been explaining to you!

HAPPY: He had it in his hand and just then Oliver walked in, so he got nervous and stuck it in his pocket!

WILLY: My God, Biff!

BIFF: I never intended to do it, Dad!

OPERATOR'S VOICE: Standish Arms, good evening!   595

WILLY: [*shouting*] I'm not in my room!

BIFF: [*frightened*] Dad, what's the matter? [*He and HAPPY stand up.*]

OPERATOR: Ringing Mr. Loman for you!

WILLY: I'm not there, stop it!

BIFF: [*horrified, gets down on one knee before WILLY*] Dad, I'll make good, I'll make good. [*WILLY*   600 *tries to get to his feet. BIFF holds him down.*] Sit down now.

WILLY: No, you're no good, you're no good for anything.

BIFF: I am, Dad, I'll find something else, you understand? Now don't worry about anything. [*He holds up WILLY's face.*] Talk to me, Dad.

OPERATOR: Mr. Loman does not answer. Shall I page him?

WILLY: [*attempting to stand, as though to rush and silence the Operator*] No, no, no!

HAPPY: He'll strike something, Pop.   605

WILLY: No, no . . .

BIFF: [*desperately, standing over WILLY*] Pop, listen! Listen to me! I'm telling you something good. Oliver talked to his partner about the Florida idea. you listening? He—he talked to his partner, and he came to me . . . I'm going to be all right, you hear? Dad, listen to me, he said it was just a question of the amount!

WILLY: Then you . . . got it?

HAPPY: He's gonna be terrific, Pop!

WILLY: [*trying to stand*] Then you got it, haven't you? You got it! You got it!   610

BIFF: [*agonized, holds WILLY down*] No, no. Look, Pop. I'm supposed to have lunch with them tomorrow. I'm just telling you this so you'll know that I can still make an impression, Pop. And I'll make good somewhere, but I can't go tomorrow, see?

WILLY: Why not? You simply—

BIFF: But the pen, Pop!

WILLY: You give it to him and tell him it was an oversight!

HAPPY: Sure, have lunch tomorrow!   615

BIFF: I can't say that—

WILLY: You were doing a crossword puzzle and accidentally used his pen!

BIFF: Listen, kid, I took those balls years ago, now I walk in with his fountain pen? That clinches it, don't you see? I can't face him like that! I'll try elsewhere.

PAGE'S VOICE: Paging Mr. Loman!

620 WILLY: Don't you want to be anything?

BIFF: Pop, how can I go back?

WILLY: You don't want to be anything, is that what's behind it?

BIFF: [*now angry at WILLY for not crediting his sympathy*] Don't take it that way! You think it was easy walking into that office after what I'd done to him? A team of horses couldn't have dragged me back to Bill Oliver!

WILLY: Then why'd you go?

625 BIFF: Why did I go? Why did I go? Look at you! Look at what's become of you!

[*Off left, THE WOMAN laughs.*]

WILLY: Biff, you're going to go to that lunch tomorrow, or—

BIFF: I can't go. I've got no appointment!

HAPPY: Biff, for . . . !

WILLY: Are you spiting me?

630 BIFF: Don't take it that way! Goddammit!

WILLY: [*strikes BIFF and falters away from the table*] You rotten little louse! Are you spiting me?

THE WOMAN: Someone's at the door, Willy!

BIFF: I'm no good, can't you see what I am?

HAPPY: [*separating them*] Hey, you're in a restaurant! Now cut it out, both of you! [*The girls enter.*] Hello, girls, sit down.

[*THE WOMAN laughs, off left.*]

635 BERNARD: I guess we might as well. This is Letta.

THE WOMAN: Willy, are you going to wake up?

BIFF: [*ignoring WILLY*] How're ya, miss, sit down. What do you drink?

BERNARD: Letta might not be able to stay long.

LETTA: I gotta get up very early tomorrow. I got jury duty. I'm so excited! Were you fellows ever on a jury?

640 BIFF: No, but I been in front of them! [*The girls laugh.*] This is my father.

LETTA: Isn't he cute? Sit down with us, Pop.

HAPPY: Sit him down, Biff!

BIFF: [*going to him*] Come on, slugger, drink us under the table. To hell with it! Come on, sit down, pal.

[*On BIFF's last insistence, WILLY is about to sit.*]

THE WOMAN: [*now urgently*] Willy, are you going to answer the door!

[*THE WOMAN's call pulls WILLY back. He starts right, befuddled.*]

645 BIFF: Hey, where are you going?

WILLY: Open the door.

BIFF: The door?

WILLY: The washroom . . . the door . . . where's the door?

BIFF: [*leading WILLY to the left*] Just go straight down.

[*WILLY moves left.*]

650 THE WOMAN: Willy, Willy, are you going to get up, get up, get up, get up?

[*WILLY exits left.*]

LETTA: I think it's sweet you bring your daddy along.

MISS FORSYTHE: Oh, he isn't really your father!

BIFF: [*at left, turning to her resentfully*] Miss Forsythe, you've just seen a prince walk by. A fine, troubled prince. A hard-working, unappreciated prince. A pal, you understand? A good companion. Always for his boys.

LETTA: That's so sweet.

HAPPY: Well, girls, what's the program? We're wasting time. Come on, Biff. Gather round.   655
Where would you like to go?

BIFF: Why don't you do something for him?

HAPPY: Me!

BIFF: Don't you give a damn for him, Hap?

HAPPY: What're you talking about? I'm the one who—

BIFF: I sense it, you don't give a good goddam about him. [*He takes the rolled-up hose from his*   660
pocket and puts it on the table in front of HAPPY.] Look what I found in the cellar, for Christ's sake. How can you bear to let it go on?

HAPPY: Me? Who goes away? Who runs off and—

BIFF: Yeah, but he doesn't mean anything to you. You could help him—I can't! Don't you understand what I'm talking about? He's going to kill himself, don't you know that?

HAPPY: Don't I know it! Me!

BIFF: Hap, help him! Jesus . . . help him . . . Help me, help me, I can't bear to look at his face! [*Ready to weep, he hurries out, up right.*]

HAPPY: [*staring after him*] Where are you going?   665

MISS FORSYTHE: What's he so mad about?

HAPPY: Come on, girls, we'll catch up with him.

MISS FORSYTHE: [*as* HAPPY *pushes her out*] Say, I don't like that temper of his!

HAPPY: He's just a little overstrung, he'll be all right!

WILLY: [*off left, as* THE WOMAN *laughs*] Don't answer! Don't answer!   670

LETTA: Don't you want to tell your father—

HAPPY: No, that's not my father. He's just a guy. Come on, we'll catch Biff, and, honey, we're going to paint this town! Stanley, where's the check! Hey, Stanley!

[*They exit.* STANLEY *looks toward left.*]

STANLEY: [*calling to* HAPPY *indignantly*] Mr. Loman! Mr. Loman!

[STANLEY *picks up a chair and follows them off. Knocking is heard off left.* THE WOMAN *enters, laughing.* WILLY *follows her. She is in a black slip; he is buttoning his shirt. Raw, sensuous music accompanies their speech.*]

WILLY: Will you stop laughing? Will you stop?

THE WOMAN: Aren't you going to answer the door? He'll wake the whole hotel.   675

WILLY: I'm not expecting anybody.

THE WOMAN: Whyn't you have another drink, honey, and stop being so damn self-centered?

WILLY: I'm so lonely.

THE WOMAN: You know you ruined me, Willy? From now on, whenever you come to the office, I'll see that you go right through to the buyers. No waiting at my desk any more, Willy. You ruined me.

WILLY: That's nice of you to say that.   680

THE WOMAN: Gee, you are self-centered! Why so sad? You are the saddest, self-centeredest soul I ever did see-saw. [*She laughs. He kisses her.*] Come on inside, drummer boy. It's silly to be dressing in the middle of the night. [*As knocking is heard*] Aren't you going to answer the door?

WILLY: They're knocking on the wrong door.

THE WOMAN: But I felt the knocking! And he heard us talking in here. Maybe the hotel's on fire!

WILLY: [*his terror rising*] It's a mistake.

685 **THE WOMAN:** Then tell him to go away!

WILLY: There's nobody there.

THE WOMAN: It's getting on my nerves, Willy. There's somebody standing out there and it's getting on my nerves!

WILLY: [*pushing her away from him*] All right, stay in the bathroom here, and don't come out. I think there's a law in Massachusetts about it, so don't come out. It may be that new room clerk. He looked very mean. So don't come out. It's a mistake, there's no fire.

[*The knocking is heard again. He takes a few steps away from her, and she vanishes into the wing. The light follows him, and now he is facing* YOUNG BIFF, *who carries a suitcase.* BIFF *steps toward him. The music is gone.*]

BIFF: Why didn't you answer?

690 **WILLY:** Biff! What are you doing in Boston?

BIFF: Why didn't you answer? I've been knocking for five minutes, I called you on the phone—

WILLY: I just heard you. I was in the bathroom and had the door shut. Did anything happen home?

BIFF: Dad—I let you down.

WILLY: What do you mean?

695 **BIFF:** Dad . . .

WILLY: Biffo, what's this about? [*putting his arm around* BIFF] Come on, let's go downstairs and get you a malted.

BIFF: Dad, I flunked math.

WILLY: Not for the term?

BIFF: The term. I haven't got enough credits to graduate.

700 **WILLY:** You mean to say Bernard wouldn't give you the answers?

BIFF: He did, he tried, but I only got a sixty-one.

WILLY: And they wouldn't give you four points?

BIFF: Birnbaum refused absolutely. I begged him, Pop, but he won't give me those points. You gotta talk to him before they close the school. Because if he saw the kind of man you are, and you just talked to him in your way, I'm sure he'd come through for me. The class came right before practice, see, and I didn't go enough. Would you talk to him? He'd like you, Pop. You know the way you could talk.

WILLY: You're on. We'll drive right back.

705 **BIFF:** Oh, Dad, good work! I'm sure he'll change it for you!

WILLY: Go downstairs and tell the clerk I'm checkin' out. Go right down.

BIFF: Yes, sir! See, the reason he hates me, Pop—one day he was late for class so I got up at the blackboard and imitated him. I crossed my eyes and talked with a lithp.

WILLY: [*laughing*] You did? The kids like it?

BIFF: They nearly died laughing!

710 **WILLY:** Yeah? What'd you do?

BIFF: The thquare root of thixthy twee is . . . [WILLY *bursts out laughing;* BIFF *joins him.*] And in the middle of it he walked in!

[WILLY *laughs and* THE WOMAN *joins in offstage.*]

WILLY: [*without hesitation*] Hurry downstairs and—

BIFF: Somebody in there?

WILLY: No, that was next door.

[*THE WOMAN laughs offstage.*]

BIFF: Somebody got in your bathroom!   715
WILLY: No, it's the next room, there's a party—
THE WOMAN: [*enters, laughing. She lisps this.*] Can I come in? There's something in the bathtub, Willy, and it's moving!

[*WILLY looks at BIFF, who is staring open-mouthed and horrified at THE WOMAN.*]

WILLY: Ah—you better go back to your room. They must be finished painting by now. They're painting her room so I let her take a shower here. Go back, go back . . . [*He pushes her.*]
THE WOMAN: [*resisting*] But I've got to get dressed, Willy, I can't—
WILLY: Get out of here! Go back, go back . . . [*suddenly striving for the ordinary*] This is   720
Miss Francis, Biff, she's a buyer. They're painting her room. Go back, Miss Francis, go back . . .
THE WOMAN: But my clothes, I can't go out naked in the hall!
WILLY: [*pushing her offstage*] Get outa here! Go back, go back!

[*BIFF slowly sits down on his suitcase as the argument continues offstage.*]

THE WOMAN: Where's my stockings? You promised me stockings, Willy!
WILLY: I have no stockings here!
THE WOMAN: You had two boxes of size nine sheers for me, and I want them!   725
WILLY: Here, for God's sake, will you get outa here!
THE WOMAN: [*enters holding a box of stockings*] I just hope there's nobody in the hall. That's all I hope. [*To BIFF*] Are you football or baseball?
BIFF: Football.
THE WOMAN: [*angry, humiliated*] That's me too. G'night. [*She snatches her clothes from WILLY, and walks out.*]
WILLY: [*after a pause*] Well, better get going. I want to get to the school first thing in the   730
morning. Get my suits out of the closet. I'll get my valise. [*BIFF doesn't move.*] What's the matter? [*BIFF remains motionless, tears falling*] She's a buyer. Buys for J. H. Simmons. She lives down the hall—they're painting. You don't imagine—[*He breaks off. After a pause*] Now listen, pal, she's just a buyer. She sees merchandise in her room and they have to keep it looking just so . . . [*Pause. Assuming command*] All right, get my suits. [*BIFF doesn't move.*] Now stop crying and do as I say. I gave you an order. Biff, I gave you an order! Is that what you do when I give you an order? How dare you cry! [*putting his arm around BIFF*] Now look, Biff, when you grow up you'll understand about these things. You mustn't—you mustn't overemphasize a thing like this. I'll see Birnbaum first thing in the morning.
BIFF: Never mind.
WILLY: [*getting down beside BIFF*] Never mind! He's going to give you those points. I'll see to it.
BIFF: He wouldn't listen to you.
WILLY: He certainly will listen to me. You need those points for the U. of Virginia.
BIFF: I'm not going there.   735
WILLY: Heh? If I can't get him to change that mark you'll make it up in summer school. You've got all summer to—
BIFF: [*his weeping breaking from him*] Dad . . .
WILLY: [*infected by it*] Oh, my boy . . .
BIFF: Dad . . .
WILLY: She's nothing to me, Biff. I was lonely, I was terribly lonely.   740
BIFF: You—you gave her Mama's stockings! [*His tears break through and he rises to go.*]

WILLY: [*grabbing for* BIFF] I gave you an order!

BIFF: Don't touch me, you—liar!

WILLY: Apologize for that!

745 **BIFF:** You fake! You phony little fake! [*Overcome, he turns quickly and weeping fully goes out with his suitcase.* WILLY *is left on the floor on his knees.*]

WILLY: I gave you an order! Biff, come back here or I'll beat you! Come back here! I'll whip you!

[STANLEY *comes quickly in from the right and stands in front of* WILLY.]

WILLY: [*shouts at* STANLEY] I gave you an order . . .

STANLEY: Hey, let's pick it up, pick it up, Mr. Loman. [*He helps* WILLY *to his feet.*] Your boys left with the chippies. They said they'll see you home.

[*A* SECOND WAITER *watches some distance away.*]

WILLY: But we were supposed to have dinner together.

[*Music is heard,* WILLY's *theme.*]

750 **STANLEY:** Can you make it?

WILLY: I'll—sure, I can make it. [*suddenly concerned about his clothes*] Do I—I look all right?

STANLEY: Sure, you look all right. [*He flicks a speck off* WILLY's *lapel.*]

WILLY: Here—here's a dollar.

STANLEY: Oh, your son paid me. It's all right.

755 **WILLY:** [*putting it in* STANLEY's *hand*] No, take it. You're a good boy.

STANLEY: Oh, no, you don't have to . . .

WILLY: Here—here's some more, I don't need it any more. [*after a slight pause*] Tell me—is there a seed store in the neighborhood?

STANLEY: Seeds? You mean like to plant?

[*As* WILLY *turns,* STANLEY *slips the money back into his jacket pocket.*]

WILLY: Yes. Carrots, peas . . .

760 **STANLEY:** Well, there's hardware stores on Sixth Avenue, but it may be too late now.

WILLY: [*anxiously*] Oh, I'd better hurry. I've got to get some seeds. [*He starts off to the right.*] I've got to get some seeds, right away. Nothing's planted. I don't have a thing in the ground.

[WILLY *hurries out as the light goes down.* STANLEY *moves over to the right after him, watches him off. The other waiter has been staring at* WILLY.]

STANLEY: [*to the* WAITER] Well, whatta you looking at?

[*The* WAITER *picks up the chairs and moves off right.* STANLEY *takes the table and follows him. The light fades on this area. There is a long pause, the sound of the flute coming over. The light gradually rises on the kitchen, which is empty.* HAPPY *appears at the door of the house, followed by* BIFF. HAPPY *is carrying a large bunch of long-stemmed roses. He enters the kitchen, looks around for* LINDA. *Not seeing her, he turns to* BIFF, *who is just outside the house door, and makes a gesture with his hands, indicating "Not here, I guess." He looks into the living-room and freezes. Inside,* LINDA, *unseen, is seated,* WILLY's *coat on her lap. She rises ominously and quietly and moves toward* HAPPY, *who backs up into the kitchen, afraid.*]

HAPPY: Hey, what're you doing up? [LINDA *says nothing but moves toward him implacably.*] Where's Pop? [*He keeps backing to the right, and now* LINDA *is in full view in the doorway to the living-room.*] Is he sleeping?

LINDA: Where were you?

HAPPY: [*trying to laugh it off*] We met two girls, Mom, very fine types. Here, we brought you   765
some flowers. [*offering them to her*] Put them in your room, Ma.

[*She knocks them to the floor at* BIFF's *feet. He has now come inside and closed the door behind him.
She stares at* BIFF, *silent.*]

HAPPY: Now what'd you do that for? Mom, I want you to have some flowers—
LINDA: [*cutting* HAPPY *off, violently to* BIFF] Don't you care whether he lives or dies?
HAPPY: [*going to the stairs*] Come upstairs, Biff.
BIFF: [*with a flare of disgust, to* HAPPY] Go away from me! [*to* LINDA] What do you mean, lives
or dies? Nobody's dying around here, pal.
LINDA: Get out of my sight! Get out of here!   770
BIFF: I wanna see the boss.
LINDA: You're not going near him!
BIFF: Where is he? [*He moves into the living-room and* LINDA *follows.*]
LINDA: [*shouting after* BIFF] You invite him for dinner. He looks forward to it all day—[BIFF
appears in his parents' bedroom, looks around, and exits.]—and then you desert him there.
There's no stranger you'd do that to!
HAPPY: Why? He had a swell time with us. Listen, when I—[LINDA *comes back into the*   775
kitchen.]—desert him I hope I don't outlive the day!
LINDA: Get out of here!
HAPPY: Now look, Mom . . .
LINDA: Did you have to go to women tonight? You and your lousy rotten whores!

[BIFF *re-enters the kitchen.*]

HAPPY: Mom, all we did was follow Biff around trying to cheer him up! [*to* BIFF] Boy, what a
night you gave me!
LINDA: Get out of here, both of you, and don't come back! I don't want you tormenting him   780
any more. Go on now, get your things together! [*to* BIFF] You can sleep in his apartment.
[*She starts to pick up the flowers and stops herself.*] Pick up this stuff, I'm not your maid
any more. Pick it up, you bum, you!

[HAPPY *turns his back to her in refusal.* BIFF *slowly moves over and gets down on his knees, picking
up the flowers.*]

LINDA: You're a pair of animals! Not one, not another living soul would have had the
cruelty to walk out on that man in a restaurant!
BIFF: [*not looking at her*] Is that what he said?
LINDA: He didn't have to say anything. He was so humiliated he nearly limped when he
came in.
HAPPY: But, Mom, he had a great time with us—
BIFF: [*cutting him off violently*] Shut up!   785

[*Without another word,* HAPPY *goes upstairs.*]

LINDA: You! You didn't even go in to see if he was all right!
BIFF: [*still on the floor in front of* LINDA, *the flowers in his hand; with self-loathing*] No. Didn't.
Didn't do a damned thing. How do you like that, heh? Left him babbling in a toilet.
LINDA: You louse. You . . .
BIFF: Now you hit it on the nose! [*He gets up, throws the flowers in the wastebasket.*] The scum
of the earth, and you're looking at him!
LINDA: Get out of here!   790
BIFF: I gotta talk to the boss, Mom. Where is he?
LINDA: You're not going near him. Get out of his house!

BIFF: [*with absolute assurance, determination*] No. We're gonna have an abrupt conversation, him and me.

LINDA: You're not talking to him!

[*Hammering is heard from outside the house, off right. BIFF turns toward the noise.*]

795   **LINDA:** [*suddenly pleading*] Will you please leave him alone?

BIFF: What's he doing out there?

LINDA: He's planting the garden!

BIFF: [*quietly*] Now? Oh, my God!

[*BIFF moves outside, LINDA following. The light dies down on them and comes up on the center of the apron as WILLY walks into it. He is carrying a flashlight, a hoe, and a handful of seed packets. He raps the top of the hoe sharply to fix it firmly, and then moves to the left, measuring off the distance with his foot. He holds the flashlight to look at the seed packets, reading off the instructions. He is in the blue of night.*]

WILLY: Carrots . . . quarter-inch apart. Rows . . . one-foot rows. [*He measures it off.*] One foot. [*He puts down a package and measures off.*] Beets. [*He puts down another package and measures again.*] Lettuce. [*He reads the package, puts it down.*] One foot—[*He breaks off as BEN appears at the right and moves slowly down to him.*] What a proposition, ts, ts. Terrific, terrific. 'Cause she's suffered, Ben, the woman has suffered. You understand me? A man can't go out the way he came in, Ben, a man has got to add up to something. You can't, you can't—[*BEN moves toward him as though to interrupt.*] You gotta consider, now. Don't answer so quick. Remember, it's a guaranteed twenty-thousand-dollar proposition. Now look, Ben, I want you to go through the ins and outs of this thing with me. I've got nobody to talk to, Ben, and the woman has suffered, you hear me?

800   **BEN:** [*standing still, considering*] What's the proposition?

WILLY: It's twenty thousand dollars on the barrelhead. Guaranteed, gilt-edged, you understand?

BEN: You don't want to make a fool of yourself. They might not honor the policy.

WILLY: How can they dare refuse? Didn't I work like a coolie to meet every premium on the nose? And now they don't pay off? Impossible!

BEN: It's called a cowardly thing, William.

805   **WILLY:** Why? Does it take more guts to stand here the rest of my life ringing up a zero?

BEN: [*yielding*] That's a point, William. [*He moves, thinking, turns.*] And twenty thousand— that *is* something one can feel with the hand, it is there.

WILLY: [*now assured, with rising power*] Oh, Ben, that's the whole beauty of it! I see it like a diamond, shining in the dark, hard and rough, that I can pick up and touch in my hand. Not like—like an appointment! This would not be another damned-fool appointment, Ben, and it changes all the aspects. Because he thinks I'm nothing, see, and so he spites me. But the funeral—[*straightening up*] Ben, that funeral will be massive! They'll come from Maine, Massachusetts, Vermont, New Hampshire! All the old-timers with the strange license plates—that boy will be thunder-struck. Ben, because he never realized—I am known! Rhode Island, New York, New Jersey—I am known, Ben, and he'll see it with his eyes once and for all. He'll see what I am, Ben! He's in for a shock, that boy!

BEN: [*coming down to the edge of the garden*] He'll call you a coward.

WILLY: [*suddenly fearful*] No, that would be terrible.

810   **BEN:** Yes. And a damned fool.

WILLY: No, no, he mustn't, I won't have that! [*He is broken and desperate.*]

BEN: He'll hate you, William.

[*The gay music of the Boys is heard.*]

WILLY: Oh, Ben, how do we get back to all the great times? Used to be so full of light, and comradeship, the sleigh-riding in winter, and the ruddiness on his cheeks. And always some kind of good news coming up, always something nice coming up ahead. And never even let me carry the valises in the house, and simonizing, simonizing that little red car! Why, why can't I give him something and not have him hate me?

BEN: Let me think about it. [*He glances at his watch.*] I still have a little time. Remarkable proposition, but you've got to be sure you're not making a fool of yourself.

[*BEN drifts upstage and goes out of sight. BIFF comes down from the left.*]

WILLY: [*suddenly conscious of BIFF, turns and looks up at him, then begins picking up the packages of seeds in confusion*] Where the hell is that seed? [*Indignantly*] You can't see nothing out here! They boxed in the whole goddam neighborhood!   815

BIFF: There are people all around here. Don't you realize that?

WILLY: I'm busy. Don't bother me.

BIFF: [*taking the hoe from WILLY*] I'm saying good-by to you, Pop. [*WILLY looks at him, silent, unable to move.*] I'm not coming back any more.

WILLY: You're not going to see Oliver tomorrow?

BIFF: I've got no appointment, Dad.   820

WILLY: He put his arm around you, and you've got no appointment?

BIFF: Pop, get this now, will you? Everytime I've left it's been a fight that sent me out of here. Today I realized something about myself and I tried to explain it to you and I—I think I'm just not smart enough to make any sense out of it for you. To hell with whose fault it is or anything like that. [*He takes WILLY's arm.*] Let's just wrap it up, heh? Come on in, we'll tell Mom. [*He gently tries to pull WILLY to left.*]

WILLY: [*frozen, immobile, with guilt in his voice*] No, I don't want to see her.

BIFF: Come on! [*He pulls again, and WILLY tries to pull away.*]

WILLY: [*highly nervous*] No, no, I don't want to see her.   825

BIFF: [*tries to look into WILLY's face, as if to find the answer there*] Why don't you want to see her?

WILLY: [*more harshly now*] Don't bother me, will you?

BIFF: What do you mean, you don't want to see her? You don't want them calling you yellow, do you? This isn't your fault; it's me, I'm a bum. Now come inside! [*WILLY strains to get away.*] Did you hear what I said to you?

[*WILLY pulls away and quickly goes by himself into the house. BIFF follows.*]

LINDA: [*to WILLY*] Did you plant, dear?

BIFF: [*at the door, to LINDA*] All right, we had it out. I'm going and I'm not writing any more.   830

LINDA: [*going to WILLY in the kitchen*] I think that's the best way, dear. 'Cause there's no use drawing it out, you'll just never get along.

[*WILLY doesn't respond.*]

BIFF: People ask where I am and what I'm doing, you don't know, and you don't care. That way it'll be off your mind and you can start brightening up again. All right? That clears it, doesn't it? [*WILLY is silent, and BIFF goes to him.*] You gonna wish me luck, scout? [*He extends his hand.*] What do you say?

LINDA: Shake his hand, Willy.

WILLY: [*turning to her, seething with hurt*] There's no necessity to mention the pen at all, y'know.

BIFF: [*gently*] I've got no appointment, Dad.   835

WILLY: [*erupting fiercely*] He put his arm around . . .

BIFF: Dad, you're never going to see what I am, so what's the use of arguing? If I strike oil I'll send you a check. Meantime forget I'm alive.

WILLY: [*to* LINDA] Spite, see?

BIFF: Shake hands, Dad.

840 **WILLY:** Not my hand.

BIFF: I was hoping not to go this way.

WILLY: Well, this is the way you're going. Good-by.

[BIFF *looks at him a moment, then turns sharply and goes to the stairs.*]

WILLY: [*stops him with*] May you rot in hell if you leave this house!

BIFF: [*turning*] Exactly what is it that you want from me?

845 **WILLY:** I want you to know, on the train, in the mountains, in the valleys, wherever you go, that you cut down your life for spite!

BIFF: No, no.

WILLY: Spite, spite, is the word of your undoing! And when you're down and out, remember what did it. When you're rotting somewhere beside the railroad tracks, remember, and don't you dare blame it on me!

BIFF: I'm not blaming it on you!

WILLY: I won't take the rap for this, you hear?

[HAPPY *comes down the stairs and stands on the bottom step, watching.*]

850 **BIFF:** That's just what I'm telling you!

WILLY: [*sinking into a chair at the table, with full accusation*] You're trying to put a knife in me—don't think I don't know what you're doing!

BIFF: All right, phony! Then let's lay it on the line. [*He whips the rubber tube out of his pocket and puts it on the table.*]

HAPPY: You crazy—

LINDA: Biff! [*She moves to grab the hose, but* BIFF *holds it down with his hand.*]

855 **BIFF:** Leave it here! Don't move it!

WILLY: [*not looking at it*] What is that?

BIFF: You know goddam well what that is.

WILLY: [*caged, wanting to escape*] I never saw that.

BIFF: You saw it. The mice didn't bring it into the cellar! What is this supposed to do, make a hero out of you? This supposed to make me sorry for you?

860 **WILLY:** Never heard of it.

BIFF: There'll be no pity for you, you hear it? No pity!

WILLY: [*to* LINDA] You hear the spite!

BIFF: No, you're going to hear the truth—what you are and what I am!

LINDA: Stop it!

865 **WILLY:** Spite!

HAPPY: [*coming down toward* BIFF] You cut it now!

BIFF: [*to* HAPPY] The man don't know who we are! The man is gonna know! [*to* WILLY] We never told the truth for ten minutes in this house!

HAPPY: We always told the truth!

BIFF: [*turning on him*] You big blow, are you the assistant buyer? You're one of the two assistants to the assistant, aren't you?

870 **HAPPY:** Well, I'm practically—

BIFF: You're practically full of it! We all are! And I'm through with it. [*to* WILLY] Now hear this, Willy, this is me.

WILLY: I know you!

BIFF: You know why I had no address for three months? I stole a suit in Kansas City and I was in jail. [*to* LINDA, *who is sobbing*] Stop crying. I'm through with it.

[LINDA *turns from them, her hands covering her face.*]

WILLY: I suppose that's my fault!

BIFF: I stole myself out of every good job since high school!   875

WILLY: And whose fault is that?

BIFF: And I never got anywhere because you blew me so full of hot air I could never stand taking orders from anybody! That's whose fault it is!

WILLY: I hear that!

LINDA: Don't, Biff!

BIFF: It's goddam time you heard that! I had to be boss big shot in two weeks, and I'm   880 through with it!

WILLY: Then hang yourself! For spite, hang yourself!

BIFF: No! Nobody's hanging himself, Willy! I ran down eleven flights with a pen in my hand today. And suddenly I stopped, you hear me? And in the middle of that office building, do you hear this? I stopped in the middle of that building and I saw—the sky. I saw the things that I love in this world. The work and the food and time to sit and smoke. And I looked at the pen and said to myself, what the hell am I grabbing this for? Why am I trying to become what I don't want to be? What am I doing in an office, making a contemptuous, begging fool of myself, when all I want is out there, waiting for me the minute I say I know who I am! Why can't I say that, Willy?

[*He tries to make* WILLY *face him, but* WILLY *pulls away and moves to the left.*]

WILLY: [*with hatred, threateningly.*] The door of your life is wide open!

BIFF: Pop! I'm a dime a dozen, and so are you!

WILLY: [*turning on him now in an uncontrolled outburst*] I am not a dime a dozen! I am Willy   885 Loman, and you are Biff Loman!

[BIFF *starts for* WILLY, *but is blocked by* HAPPY. *In his fury,* BIFF *seems on the verge of attacking his father.*]

BIFF: I am not a leader of men, Willy, and neither are you. You were never anything but a hard-working drummer who landed in the ash can like all the rest of them! I'm one dollar an hour, Willy! I tried seven states and couldn't raise it. A buck an hour! Do you gather my meaning? I'm not bringing home any prizes any more, and you're going to stop waiting for me to bring them home!

WILLY: [*directly to* BIFF] You vengeful, spiteful mutt!

[BIFF *breaks from* HAPPY. WILLY, *in fright, starts up the stairs.* BIFF *grabs him*]

BIFF: [*at the peak of his fury*] Pop I'm nothing! I'm nothing, Pop. Can't you understand that? There's no spite in it any more. I'm just what I am, that's all.

[BIFF's *fury has spent itself, and he breaks down, sobbing, holding on to* WILLY, *who dumbly fumbles for* BIFF's *face.*]

WILLY: [*astonished*] What're you doing? What're you doing? [*to* LINDA] Why is he crying?

BIFF: [*crying, broken*] Will you let me go, for Christ's sake? Will you take that phony dream   890 and burn it before something happens? [*Struggling to contain himself, he pulls away and moves to the stairs.*] I'll go in the morning. Put him—put him to bed. [*Exhausted,* BIFF *moves up the stairs to his room.*]

WILLY: [*after a long pause, astonished, elevated*] Isn't that—isn't that remarkable? Biff—he likes me!

Linda Loman (Mildred Dunnock) and Happy (Cameron Mitchell) restrain Biff (Arthur Kennedy) as he reproaches his father Willy (Lee J. Cobb) in the Morosco Theatre, New York City, original production of *Death of a Salesman*, staged by Elia Kazan. ·

LINDA: He loves you, Willy!

HAPPY: [*deeply moved*] Always did, Pop.

WILLY: Oh, Biff! [*staring wildly*] He cried! Cried to me. [*He is choking with his love, and now cries out his promise.*] That boy—that boy is going to be magnificent!

[*BEN appears in the light just outside the kitchen.*]

895 **BEN:** Yes, outstanding, with twenty thousand behind him.

LINDA: [*sensing the racing of his mind, fearfully, carefully*] Now come to bed, Willy. It's all settled now.

WILLY: [*finding it difficult not to rush out of the house*] Yes, we'll sleep. Come on. Go to sleep, Hap.

BEN: And it does take a great kind of a man to crack the jungle.

[*In accents of dread, BEN's idyllic music starts up.*]

HAPPY: [*his arm around LINDA*] I'm getting married, Pop, don't forget it. I'm changing everything. I'm gonna run that department before the year is up. You'll see, Mom. [*He kisses her.*]

900 **BEN:** The jungle is dark but full of diamonds, Willy.

[*WILLY turns, moves, listening to BEN.*]

LINDA: Be good. You're both good boys, just act that way, that's all.

HAPPY: 'Night, Pop. [*He goes upstairs.*]

LINDA: [*to* WILLY] Come, dear.

BEN: [*with greater force*] One must go in to fetch a diamond out.

WILLY: [*to* LINDA, *as he moves slowly along the edge of the kitchen, toward the door*] I just want to   905
get settled down, Linda. Let me sit alone for a little.

LINDA: [*almost uttering her fear*] I want you upstairs.

WILLY: [*taking her in his arms*] In a few minutes, Linda. I couldn't sleep right now. Go on, you
look awful tired. [*He kisses her.*]

BEN: Not like an appointment at all. A diamond is rough and hard to the touch.

WILLY: Go on now. I'll be right up.

LINDA: I think this is the only way, Willy.   910

WILLY: Sure, it's the best thing.

BEN: Best thing!

WILLY: The only way. Everything is gonna be—go on, kid, get to bed. You look so tired.

LINDA: Come right up.

WILLY: Two minutes.   915

[LINDA *goes into the living-room, then reappears in her bedroom.* WILLY *moves just outside the
kitchen door.*]

WILLY: Loves me. [*wonderingly*] Always loved me. Isn't that a remarkable thing? Ben, he'll
worship me for it!

BEN: [*with promise*] It's dark there, but full of diamonds.

WILLY: Can you imagine that magnificence with twenty thousand dollars in his pocket?

LINDA: [*calling from her room*] Willy! Come up!

WILLY: [*calling into the kitchen*] Yes! Yes. Coming! It's very smart, you realize that, don't you,   920
sweetheart? Even Ben sees it. I gotta go, baby. 'By! 'By! [*going over to* BEN, *almost
dancing*] Imagine? When the mail comes he'll be ahead of Bernard again!

BEN: A perfect proposition all around.

WILLY: Did you see how he cried to me? Oh, if I could kiss him, Ben!

BEN: Time, William, time!

WILLY: Oh, Ben, I always knew one way or another we were gonna make it, Biff and I!

BEN: [*looking at his watch*] The boat. We'll be late. [*He moves slowly off into the darkness.*]   925

WILLY: [*elegiacally, turning to the house*] Now when you kick off, boy, I want a seventy-yard
boot, and get right down the field under the ball, and when you hit, hit low and hit
hard, because it's important, boy. [*He swings around and faces the audience.*] There's all
kinds of important people in the stands, and the first thing you know . . . [*suddenly
realizing he is alone*] Ben! Ben, where do I . . . ? [*He makes a sudden movement of search.*]
Ben, how do I . . . ?

LINDA: [*calling*] Willy, you coming up?

WILLY: [*uttering a gasp of fear, whirling about as if to quiet her*] Sh! [*He turns around as if to find
his way; sounds, faces, voices, seem to be swarming in upon him and he flicks at them, crying*]
Sh! Sh! [*Suddenly music, faint and high, stops him. It rises in intensity, almost to an
unbearable scream. He goes up and down on his toes, and rushes off around the house.*] Shhh!

LINDA: Willy?

[*There is no answer.* LINDA *waits.* BIFF *gets up off his bed. He is still in his clothes.* HAPPY *sits up.*
BIFF *stands listening.*]

LINDA: [*with real fear*] Willy, answer me! Willy!   930

[*There is the sound of a car starting and moving away at full speed.*]

LINDA: No!

BIFF: [*rushing down the stairs*] Pop!

[*As the car speeds off, the music crashes down in a frenzy of sound, which becomes the soft pulsation of a single cello string. BIFF slowly returns to his bedroom. He and HAPPY gravely don their jackets. LINDA slowly walks out of her room. The music has developed into a dead march. The leaves of day are appearing over everything. CHARLEY and BERNARD somberly dressed, appear and knock on the kitchen door. BIFF and HAPPY slowly descend the stairs to the kitchen as CHARLEY and BERNARD enter. All stop a moment when LINDA, in clothes of mourning, bearing a little bunch of roses, comes through the draped doorway into the kitchen. She goes to CHARLEY and takes his arm. Now all move toward the audience, through the wall-line of the kitchen. At the limit of the apron, LINDA lays down the flowers, kneels, and sits back on her heels. All stare down at the grave.*]

REQUIEM

CHARLEY: It's getting dark, Linda.

[*LINDA doesn't react. She stares at the grave.*]

BIFF: How about it, Mom? Better get some rest, heh? They'll be closing the gate soon.

[*LINDA makes no move. Pause.*]

HAPPY: [*deeply angered*] He had no right to do that. There was no necessity for it. We would've helped him.

CHARLEY: [*grunting*] Hmmm.

5   **BIFF:** Come along, Mom.

LINDA: Why didn't anybody come?

CHARLEY: It was a very nice funeral.

LINDA: But where are all the people he knew? Maybe they blame him.

CHARLEY: Naa. It's a rough world, Linda. They wouldn't blame him.

10   **LINDA:** I can't understand it. At this time especially. First time in thirty-five years we were just about free and clear. He only needed a little salary. He was even finished with the dentist.

CHARLEY: No man only needs a little salary.

LINDA: I can't understand it.

BIFF: There were a lot of nice days. When he'd come home from a trip; or on Sundays, making the stoop; finishing the cellar; putting on the new porch; when he built the extra bathroom; and put up the garage. You know something, Charley, there's more of him in that front stoop than in all the sales he ever made.

CHARLEY: Yeah. He was a happy man with a batch of cement.

15   **LINDA:** He was so wonderful with his hands.

BIFF: He had all the wrong dreams. All, all, wrong.

HAPPY: [*almost ready to fight BIFF*] Don't say that!

BIFF: He never knew who he was.

CHARLEY: [*stopping HAPPY's movement and reply. To BIFF*] Nobody dast blame this man. You don't understand. Willy was a salesman. And for a salesman, there is no rock bottom to the life. He don't put a bolt to a nut, he don't tell you the law or give you medicine. He's a man way out there in the blue, riding on a smile and a shoeshine. And when they start not smiling back—that's an earthquake. And then you get yourself a couple of spots on your hat, and you're finished. Nobody dast blame this man. A salesman is got to dream, boy. It comes with the territory.

20   **BIFF:** Charley, the man didn't know who he was.

HAPPY: [*infuriated*] Don't say that!

BIFF: Why don't you come with me, Happy?

HAPPY: I'm not licked that easily. I'm staying right in this city, and I'm gonna beat this racket! [*He looks at* BIFF, *his chin set.*] The Loman Brothers!

BIFF: I know who I am, kid.

HAPPY: All right, boy. I'm gonna show you and everybody else that Willy Loman did not die in vain. He had a good dream. It's the only dream you can have—to come out number-one man. He fought it out here, and this is where I'm gonna win it for him. 25

BIFF: [*with a hopeless glance at* HAPPY, *bends toward his mother*] Let's go, Mom.

LINDA: I'll be with you in a minute. Go on, Charley. [*He hesitates.*] I want to, just for a minute. I never had a chance to say good-by.

[CHARLEY *moves away, followed by* HAPPY. BIFF *remains a slight distance up and left of* LINDA. *She sits there, summoning herself. The flute begins, not far away, playing behind her speech.*]

LINDA: Forgive me, dear. I can't cry. I don't know what it is, but I can't cry. I don't understand it. Why did you ever do that? Help me, Willy, I can't cry. It seems to me that you're just on another trip. I keep expecting you. Willy, dear, I can't cry. Why did you do it? I search and search and I search, and I can't understand it, Willy. I made the last payment on the house today. Today, dear. And there'll be nobody home. [*A sob rises in her throat.*] We're free and clear. [*sobbing more fully, released*] We're free. [BIFF *comes slowly toward her.*] We're free . . . We're free . . .

[BIFF *lifts her to her feet and moves out up right with her in his arms.* LINDA *sobs quietly.* BERNARD *and* CHARLEY *come together and follow them, followed by* HAPPY. *Only the music of the flute is left on the darkening stage as over the house the hard towers of the apartment buildings rise into sharp focus, and The curtain falls.*]

QUESTIONS

ACT 1

1. What do you learn about Willy from the first stage direction?

2. What instances of stealing are in the play? Why do Biff and Happy steal? Where did they learn about stealing? How is stealing related to salesmanship?

3. In Act 1 Willy claims that "I never in my life told him [Biff] anything but decent things." Is this assertion true? What does it show you about Willy?

ACT 2 AND REQUIEM

4. What does Willy's difficulty with machines—especially his car, the refrigerator, and Howard's tape recorder—suggest about him? To what extent are these machines symbolic?

5. When Willy sees Bernard in Charley's office, he asks, "What—what's the secret?" What secret is he asking about? Does such a secret exist?

6. In Act 2 Willy buys seeds and tries to plant a garden at night. Why is Willy so disturbed that "nothing's planted" and "I don't have a thing in the ground"? What do this garden and having "things in the ground" mean to Willy?

7. In Act 2, speech 867, Biff claims that "we never told the truth for ten minutes in this house!" What does he mean? To what extent is he right?

8. Linda's last line in the play—"We're free . . . we're free"—seems to refer to the house mortgage. In what other ways, however, might you take it?

GENERAL QUESTIONS

1. How does Miller use lighting, the set, blocking, and music to differentiate between action in the present and "memory" action?

2. The stage directions are full of information that cannot be played. In describing Happy, for example, Miller notes that "sexuality is like a color on him." What is the function of such stage directions?

3. How is Willy's suicide foreshadowed throughout the play? To what extent does this foreshadowing create tension?

4. Which characters are "real" and which are "hallucinations" that spring from Willy's memory? What are the major differences between these two groups?

5. Which characters are symbolic and what do they symbolize?

6. Describe the character of Willy Loman. What are his good qualities? In what ways does he have heroic stature? What are his bad qualities? To what extent is his "fall" the result of his flaws, and to what extent is it caused by circumstances beyond his control?

7. How is the relationship between Charley and Bernard different from the one between Willy and his sons? Why is this difference important?

8. Discuss Linda's character and role. In what ways is she supportive of Willy? In what ways does she encourage his deceptions and self-delusions?

9. What sort of person is Happy? What has he inherited from Willy? How is he a debasement of Willy? To what degree is he successful or happy?

10. Willy claims that success in business is based not on "what you do" but on "who you know and the smile on your face! It's contacts . . . a man can end up with diamonds on the basis of being well liked." How does the play support or reject this assertion?

11. Most of Willy's memories—Ben's visit, Boston, the football game—are from 1928. Why does Willy's memory return to 1928? Why is the contrast between 1928 and the present significant for Willy and for the play as a whole?

WRITING ABOUT TRAGEDY

As you plan and write an essay about tragedy, keep in mind all the elements of drama. A full discussion of traditional approaches to these elements—plot, character, point of view, setting, language, tone, symbol, and theme—is found in Chapter 23. Review this material before you begin your essay.

Although the basic elements remain consistent in tragedy, the form requires a few special considerations. In planning to write about plot and conflict, you might explore the crisis or climax—that point at which the downfall becomes inevitable. Similarly, you might consider the degree to which the conflicts shape or accelerate the tragic action. With character, pay special attention to the tragic protagonist and the major antagonists: What is the connection between the protagonist's strengths and weaknesses? To what extent does the protagonist bring about or cooperate with his or her own destruction? What key characteristics and behavior patterns ensure both the protagonist's heroic stature and fall? In dealing with tone, consider the degree to which the play is ironic. Do you know more about what is going on than the protagonist? Than most of the characters? If so, how does your knowledge affect your understanding of the play?

Along with these considerations, all the traditional elements of drama can provide fruitful essays about tragic drama. Here, however, we introduce an additional way of writing about literature: an examination of a problem. This approach can be employed to write about prose fiction, poetry, or any type of dramatic literature. Our discussion will naturally focus on tragedy—specifically *Hamlet*—and the plays in which problem solving can generate effective essays about tragic drama.

An Essay About a Problem

A **problem** is any question put before you that you cannot answer easily and correctly. The question "Who is the major character in *Hamlet*?" is not a problem, because the obvious answer is Hamlet. Let us, however, ask another question: "Why is it *correct* to say that Hamlet is the major character?" This question is not as easy as the first, and for this reason it creates a problem. It requires that we think about our answer, even though we do not need to search very far. Hamlet is the title character. He is involved in most of the actions of the play. He is so much the center of our liking and concern that his death causes sadness and regret. To "solve" this problem has required a set of responses, all of which provide answers to the question "Why?"

More complex, however, and more typical of most problems, are questions like these: "Why does Hamlet talk of suicide in his first soliloquy?" "Why does he treat Ophelia so coarsely in the 'nunnery' scene?" "Why does he delay in avenging his father's death?" " Why does he so immediately and uncritically accept Laertes's challenge to the concluding duel?" Essays on a problem are normally concerned with such questions because they require a good deal of thought, together with a number of interpretations knitted together into an entire essay. More broadly, dealing with problems is one of the major tasks of the intellectual, scientific, social, and political disciplines. Being able to advance and then explain solutions is therefore one of the most important techniques that you can acquire.

Strategies for Organizing Ideas

Your first purpose is to convince readers that your solution is a good one. This you do by making sound conclusions from supporting evidence. In nonscientific subjects like literature, you rarely find absolute proofs, so your conclusions will not be *proved* in the way you prove triangles congruent in geometry. But your organization, your use of facts from the text, your interpretations, and your application of general or specific knowledge should all make your conclusions convincing. Thus your basic strategy is *persuasion*.

1. *Demonstrate that conditions for a solution are fulfilled.* This type of development is the most basic in writing—namely, illustration. You first explain that certain conditions need to exist for your solution to be plausible. Your central idea—really a brief answer to the question—is that the conditions do indeed exist. Your development is to show how the conditions can be found in the work.

Suppose that you are writing on the problem of why Hamlet delays revenge against Claudius. Suppose also that you make the point that Hamlet delays because he is never sure that Claudius is guilty. This is your "solution" to the problem. In your essay you support your answer by challenging the credibility of the information Hamlet receives about the crime (i.e., the two visits from the Ghost and Claudius's distress at the play within the play). Once you have "attacked" these sources of data on the grounds that they are unreliable, you have succeeded because your solution is consistent with the details of the play.

2. *Analyze words in the phrasing of the problem.* Your object in this approach is to clarify important words in the statement of the problem, then to decide how applicable they are. This kind of attention to words, in fact, might give you enough material for all or part of your essay. Thus, an essay on the problem of Hamlet's delay might focus in part on a treatment of the word *delay*: What, really, does *delay* mean? For Hamlet, is there a difference between delay that is reasonable and delay that is unreasonable? Does Hamlet delay unreasonably? Is his delay the result of a psychological fault? Would speedy revenge be more or less reasonable than the delay? By the time you have answered such pointed questions, you will also have sufficient material for your full essay.

3. *Refer to literary conventions or expectations.* With this strategy, the argument is to establish that the problem can be solved by reference to the literary mode or conventions of a work, or to the limitations of the work itself. In other words, what appears to be a problem is really no more than a normal characteristic. A problem about the artificiality of the choruses in *Oedipus the King*, for example, might be resolved by reference to the fact that choruses were a normal feature of Greek drama. In a similar manner, the knowledge that delay is a convention of all revenge tragedy might provide a key to the problem of Hamlet's apparent procrastination.

4. *Argue against possible objections.* With this strategy, you raise your own objections and then argue against them. Called **procatalepsis** or **anticipation,** this approach helps you sharpen your arguments, because *anticipating* and dealing with objections forces you to make analyses and use facts that you might otherwise overlook. Although procatalepsis can be used point by point throughout your essay, you may find it most useful at the end.

The situation to imagine is that someone is raising objections to your solution to the problem. It is then your task to show that the objections (1) are not accurate or valid, (2) are not strong or convincing, or (3) are based on unusual rather than usual conditions (on an exception and not the rule). Here are some examples of these approaches.

1. *The objection is not accurate or valid.* You reject this objection by showing that either the interpretation or the conclusions are wrong and also by emphasizing that the evidence supports your solution.

Although Hamlet's delay is reasonable, the claim might be made that his duty is to kill Claudius in revenge immediately after the Ghost's accusations. This claim is not persuasive because it assumes that Hamlet knows everything the audience knows. The audience accepts the Ghost's word that Claudius is guilty, but Hamlet has no certain reason to believe the Ghost. Would it not seem insane for Hamlet to kill Claudius, who reigns legally, and then to claim he did it because of the Ghost's words? The argument for speedy revenge is not good because it is based on an incorrect view of Hamlet's situation.

2. *The objection is not strong or convincing.* You *concede* that the objection has some truth or validity, but you then try to show that it is weak and that your own solution is stronger.

One might claim that Claudius's distress at the play within the play is evidence for his guilt and that therefore Hamlet should carry out his revenge right away. This argument has merit, and Hamlet's speech after Claudius has fled the scene ("I'll take the Ghost's word for a thousand pound") shows that the "conscience of the king" has been caught. But the king's guilty behavior is not a strong cause for killing him. Hamlet could justifiably ask for an investigation of his father's death on these grounds, but he could not justify a revenge killing. Claudius could not be convicted in any court on the testimony that he was disturbed at seeing *The Murder of Gonzago*. Even after the play within the play, the reasons for delay are stronger than for action.

3. *The objection depends on unusual rather than usual conditions.* You reject the objection on the grounds that it could be valid only if normal conditions were suspended. The objection depends on an exception, not a rule.

The case for quick action is simple: Hamlet should kill Claudius right after seeing the Ghost (1.3) or else after seeing the King's reaction to the stage murder of Gonzago (3.2) or else after seeing the Ghost again (3.4). Redress under these circumstances, goes the argument, must be both personal and extralegal. This argument wrongly assumes that due process does not exist in the Denmark of Hamlet and Claudius. Nothing in the play indicates that the Danes, even though they carouse a bit, do not value legality and the rules of evidence. Thus Hamlet cannot rush out to kill Claudius because he knows that the king has not had anything close to due process. The argument for quick action is poor because it rests on an exception being made from civilized law.

Remember that writing an essay on a problem requires you to argue a position: Either there is a solution or there is not. To develop your position requires that you show the steps to your conclusion. Your general thematic form is thus (1) to describe the conditions that need to be met for the solution you propose, and then (2) to demonstrate that these conditions exist. If you assert that there is no solution, then your form would be the same for the first part, but your second part—the development—would show that these conditions have *not* been met.

In developing your response, use one or more of the strategies described in this chapter. These are, again, (1) to demonstrate that conditions for a solution are fulfilled, (2) to analyze the words in the phrasing of the problem,

(3) to refer to literary conventions or expectations, and (4) to argue against possible objections. You might combine these. Thus, if we assume that your argument is that Hamlet's delay is reasonable, you might first consider the word *delay* (strategy 2). Then you might use strategy 1 to explain the reasons for Hamlet's delay. Finally, to answer objections to your argument, you might show that Hamlet acts promptly when he believes he is justified (strategy 4). Whatever your topic, the important thing is to use the method or methods that best help you make a good argument for your solution.

In your conclusion, try to affirm the validity of your solution in view of the supporting evidence. You might do this by reemphasizing your strongest points, or you might simply present a brief summary. Or you might think of your argument as still continuing and thus use the strategy of procatalepsis or anticipation to raise and answer possible objections to your solution, as in the last paragraph of the following illustrative essay.

Illustrative Student Essay

Underlined sentences in this paper *do not* conform to MLA style and are used solely as teaching tools to emphasize the central idea, thesis sentence, and topic sentences throughout the paper.

Rezik 1

Antonio Rezik

Professor Tomaiuolo

English 312

1 November 2008

The Problem of Hamlet's Apparent Delay°

[1]   Many readers and spectators of Shakespeare's <u>Hamlet</u> have been puzzled by the prince's apparent failure to kill Claudius quickly. Early in the play, the Ghost calls on his son to "Revenge his foul and most unnatural murder" (1341, 1.5.25). Hamlet, however, delays his vengeance until the end of the play. The problem results from why does he not act sooner. <u>The answer is that there is no unjustified delay and that in fact Hamlet acts as quickly as possible.</u>* This becomes evident

°**This play appears on page 1323–1420.**
*****Central idea.**

Rezik 2

when we examine the conventions of revenge tragedy, the actual "call to
revenge,"and the steps that Hamlet takes to achieve vengeance.[†]

     Revenge tragedy obviously requires that vengeance be delayed until the   **[2]**
closing moments of the play. Given this limitation, Shakespeare must justify
the wide gap of time between the call to revenge in Act 1 and the killing of
Claudius in Act 5. We find such justification in the unreliability of the ghost's
initial accusation, Hamlet's need for additional evidence, and the events that
occur after this evidence is obtained.

     The Ghost's accusations and demands are straightforward: he accuses his   **[3]**
brother of murdering him and he calls on his son for vengeance. Shakespeare is
careful, however, to establish that this testimony is doubtful. Horatio questions
the Ghost's truthfulness and motives, and he warns Hamlet that the spirit might
"assume some other horrible form / Which might deprive your sovereignty of
reason, / And draw you into madness" (1340, 1.4.73–75). Hamlet himself
expresses doubt about the ghost (1362, 2.2.573–79):

> The spirit that I have seen
>
> May be a devil, and the devil hath power
>
> T'assume a pleasing shape, yea, and perhaps
>
> Out of my weakness, and my melancholy,
>
> As he is very potent with such spirits,
>
> Abuses me to damn me; I'll have grounds
>
> More relative than this.

The prince thus cannot act on the unsupported word of the Ghost; he needs
more evidence.

     There is no delay at this point in the play, because Hamlet quickly begins   **[4]**
developing a plan of action. Immediately after speaking with the Ghost, he
decides to cover himself under an "antic disposition" while he gathers
information. He swears his companions to silence and warns them not to
react knowingly if he should seem to behave strangely or insanely (1385,

[†]**Thesis sentence.**

1.5.169–79). His idea is that this pose will make him less a subject of suspicion and will therefore make others less careful.

[5]   Once Hamlet has begun his plan, he takes advantage of every opportunity to carry out his vengeance. When the players come to Elsinore, he adroitly plans to test Claudius by making him publicly view a play, The Murder of Gonzago, which shows a murder just like Claudius's murder of Hamlet's father. Hamlet states that Claudius's appearance will give him the clue he needs to confirm the Ghost's information (1362, 2.2.571–573).

> I'll observe his looks,
>
> I'll tent him to the quick, if a' do blench
>
> I know my course.

Once the king breaks up the performance in great agitation, which Hamlet correctly interprets as an admission of guilt, Hamlet declares confidence in the Ghost ("I'll take the ghost's word for a thousand pound" [1375, 3.2.271–272]). Moreover, he is psychologically ready to act against the king, for he asserts that he could "drink hot blood, / And do such bitter business as the day / Would quake to look on" (1378, 3.2.367–369). Without doubt, Hamlet is only a prayer away from stabbing Claudius, for when he sees the king kneeling, his opportunity has merged with his desire and also with his promise to the Ghost. He tells the audience, "Now might I do it pat, now a' is a-praying, / And now I'll do't" (1380, 3.3.73–74).

[6]   But he does not "do't," and for this reason he is open to the accusation that he cannot act. Again, however, Shakespeare carefully justifies this hesitation. The prince does not want to send Claudius's soul to heaven by killing him at prayer. This reason is not simply an excuse for delay. Rather, Hamlet wants his revenge to match Claudius's treacherous murder of the previous King Hamlet, who died without the chance to pray and repent (1380, 3.3.88-95):

> Up sword, and know thou a more horrid hent,
>
> When he is drunk asleep, or in his rage,
>
> Or in th'incestuous pleasure of his bed,
>
> At game, a-swearing, or about some act
>
> That has no relish of salvation in't,
>
> Then trip him that his heels may kick at heaven,

Rezik 4

> And that his soul may be as damned and black
>
> As hell whereto it goes.

This deferral is in keeping with the code of personal blood vengeance, whereby the revenge must match or exceed the original crime. There is no question of Hamlet's incapacity to act, because his putting up his sword is reasonable and justifiable.

From this point on, Hamlet acts or reacts to every situation as the [7] opportunity presents itself. After he kills Polonius, Claudius initiates a counterplot to send Hamlet off to England and execution. Clearly, Hamlet's chances to kill the king are thus reduced to zero. It is not until Act 5 that Hamlet gets back to Denmark, after having decisively thwarted Claudius's murderous instructions by turning them against Rosencrantz and Guildenstern. He makes it clear to Horatio, however, that he will take the earliest opportunity, and that "the readiness is all" (1415, 5.2.205). Once the rigged fencing match is under way, the opportunity finally comes. Claudius, Hamlet learns, has not only killed his father but has poisoned his mother, and he himself is about to die from Laertes's poisoned sword. Upon such certain information, Hamlet immediately kills Claudius. When the revenge is complete, the Ghost, who began the cry for vengeance, is nowhere to be heard or seen, and four bodies lie on the stage.

Thus, we see that the issue of Hamlet's delay--and the vengeance does take [8] four acts to carry out--is really not a problem. The prince acts in accordance with the code of revenge as quickly as circumstances permit. Although the text of the play supports this solution, critics might still argue that procrastination is an issue because Hamlet twice accuses himself of delay. This objection does not take into consideration that Hamlet's perception of time and action is distorted by his eagerness for vengeance. From Hamlet's subjective point of view, any break in activity is delay. From our objective viewpoint, however, delay is not a true problem.

Rezik 5

Work Cited

William Shakespeare, The Tragedy of Hamlet, Prince of Denmark. Literature: An Introduction to Reading and Writing. Ed. Edgar V. Roberts. 9th ed. New York: Pearson Longman, 2009. 1323–1420.

Commentary on the Essay

The structure of the essay illustrates strategy 1 (p. 1487). Paragraph 2, however, makes brief use of strategy 3 in its reference to the conventions of revenge tragedy. In both paragraphs 6 and 8, the argument is carried on by use of *procatalepsis*, or strategy 4, whereby a counterargument is raised and then answered.

The introductory paragraph raises the problem of Hamlet's apparent delay and offers a brief statement of the solution (the central idea). This plan is developed in paragraphs 2–7 in exactly the same order in which the issues are raised in the introduction. Paragraph 2 deals with the meaning and requirements of revenge, and paragraph 3 takes up the issue of the Ghost's reliability. Paragraphs 4 and 5 deal with Hamlet's attempts to corroborate the Ghost's accusations, and paragraphs 6 and 7 consider the subsequent action. Note that each paragraph in the argument grows naturally out of the one that precedes it, just as all the paragraphs are linked to the introductory paragraph.

The concluding paragraph asserts that the original problem is solved; the paragraph then summarizes the steps of the solution. It also continues the argument by raising and then dealing with a possible objection.

Writing Topics About Tragedy

1. Much has been made of the contrast in *Oedipus the King* between vision and blindness. Write an essay that considers this contrast as it is related to the character of Oedipus. How are blindness and seeing reversed, with regard to his understanding about the curse on the city, his attempts to ferret out the guilty ones, his awakening perceptions of his own responsibility and guilt, and his self-blinding? How can Tiresias be compared and contrasted with Oedipus?

2. Develop an argument for one of these assertions.
   a. Oedipus's fall is the result of fate, predestination, and the gods, and it would happen no matter what kind of person he is.
   b. Oedipus's fall is the result only of his character and has nothing to do with fate or the gods.

3. Write an essay considering the degree to which Gertrude and Ophelia in *Hamlet* justify Hamlet's assertion "Frailty, thy name is woman" (1.2.146). Questions you might take into account concern the status of these women, their power to exert their own individuality and to make their own decisions, Gertrude as a royal queen and Ophelia as an aristocratic daughter, their capacity to undergo the pain of bereavement, Hamlet's own feelings about the death of his father, and so on.

4. Hamlet, Laertes, and Fortinbras are young men whose fathers have been killed and who set out to avenge these deaths. Their courses of action, however, are different. In an essay, consider these three as typical or archetypal sons. What characteristics do they share? What, in turn, makes them individual and distinct? Compare and contrast how each character deals with his father's death. Which approach seems most reasonable to you? Most emotional? Most effective? For additional directions in handling comparison and contrast, consult Chapter 30.

5. Considering *Oedipus the King* and *Hamlet* write an essay defining and explaining tragedy. Include references to the nature of the tragic protagonists, the situations they face, their solutions to their problems, their responses to the consequences of their actions, and their worthiness of character. Be sure to compare and contrast the actions and speeches of the characters in the plays as evidence.

6. Use your library or the Internet to locate materials on tragedy. Some general topics might be *ancient and modern tragedy, definitions, emotions, heroes, passions, problems,* and *questions.* You might also wish to locate specific books on Aristotle and tragedy or on *Oedipus the King* or *Hamlet.* Write a brief report on one of the books, being careful to consider topics such as the author's definitions of tragedy and the author's application of the topic to various specific plays. Try also to consider the completeness of the author's presentation of material and the persuasiveness of the author's arguments.

Chapter 25

The Comic Vision: Restoring the Balance

Comedy is the fraternal twin of tragedy. As a form was it was first created in the ancient Greek world, like tragedy, and the two forms bear many family resemblances.[1] Comedy is often filled with tragic potential, and tragedy sometimes is built on a story that is potentially comic. Indeed, tragedy can be seen as an abortive or incomplete comedy in which affairs take a negative turn, and comedy can be considered a tragedy in which the truth is discovered (or covered up), the hero saves the day, the villain is overcome, the hero and heroine are united, and equilibrium and balance are restored. The major differences are that tragedy moves toward despair or death, whereas comedy moves toward success, happiness, and marriage. Tragic diction is elevated and heroic. Comic diction can be elevated too, but often it is common or colloquial, and although it is frequently witty, it is also sometimes witless and bawdy. The primary difference is that the mask of tragedy despairs, grieves, and weeps, whereas the mask of comedy rejoices, smiles, and laughs.

The Origins of Comedy

In the *Poetics*, Aristotle states that he knows less about the origin of Athenian comedy than of tragedy because comedy "was not at first treated seriously" (V.2, p. 21).[2] He does say, however, that comedy developed as an improvisatory form (IV.12, p. 19), just as tragedy did. Most comic improvisations were an outgrowth of "phallic songs," which were bacchanalian processions that took place during the **Lenaia**, the Athenian religious festival held in January-February each year during *Gamelion*, the month of weddings, just following the winter solstice.

The word *comedy* is consistent with this explanation, for as "a *komos* song" its Greek meaning is "a song of revels" or "a song sung by merrymakers." The revels, like the tragedies, were religious in ways that the Greeks considered meaningful but that seem secular to us today. During parades or processions at the Lenaia, the merrymakers expressed their joy boisterously, traded bawdy and obscene remarks with spectators, lampooned public persons, wore ceremonial phalluses, and

---

[1] For a more detailed discussion of how drama developed within the ancient Athenian religious festivals, see Chapter 24, pages 1265–68.
[2] S. H. Butcher, *Aristotle's Theory of Poetry and Fine Art*, 4th ed. (New York: Dover, 1951) 21 (V.2). All parenthetical references to Aristotle are from this edition.

dressed in paunchy costumes suggesting feasting, fatness, fertility, friskiness, frolic, and fun. We may conclude that these *komos* processions were supported officially in the belief and hope that human ceremonies would encourage divine favor and bring about prosperity and happiness. As the form developing out of such processions, comedy began with many of these characteristics and has retained them to the present day. If one may generalize about subsequent comedies—even those that are cold sober rather than boisterous—it is clear that love, marriage, and ritualized celebrations of a happy future are usually major concerns.

The Athenians Held Competitions for Comedy, Just as for Tragedy

Tragedy originated in Athens, but the same does not appear to be true of comedy. Rather, comedy coexisted in the areas surrounding Greece called *Magna Graecia* ("Greater Greece"). Aristotle himself admitted that it was "late" when comic performances were separated from the phallic songs (V.2, p. 21); that is, comedy followed tragedy by many years. The earliest certain date for the existence of Athenian comedy is 486 BCE, when a writer named Chionides won a state-sponsored comedy competition. Although the earliest comedies apparently consisted of little more than loosely connected lampoons, they were highly enough regarded to justify regular competitions. Comedies were scheduled on each day of the festivals, following the tragedies and satyr plays.

According to Aristotle, the first writer to transform comedy by creating a thematic plot development was Crates, who won the first of his three prizes in about the mid-fifth century BCE (V.3, p. 21). It was at this time that comedies became popular enough to justify an additional state comedy competition, which was instituted in about 440 BCE. For the remainder of the century, writers of comedy as well as tragedy tried to win prizes for their new plays at both the Lenaia and the City Dionysia.

The Earliest Greek Comedy Is Called Old Comedy

The comedies of the fifth century BCE, called **Old Comedy** or **Old Attic Comedy** by later historians, followed intricate structural patterns and displayed complex poetic conventions. Nevertheless, they bore the marks of their origins in the bacchanalian *komos* processions. The actors (three or four men) and the members of the chorus (twenty-four men), each dressed in a distortingly padded costume, wore a character-defining mask and displayed a ceremonial phallus. The role of the chorus usually dictated the comedy's title (e.g., *The Frogs*, *The Wasps*). Customarily, the plot was fantastic and impossible, and the dialogue was farcical and bawdy. In the tradition of satires and tirades associated with the phallic songs and with early comedy, the comic dramatists freely lashed public persons (usually but not always without legal reprisal).

Although the most successful comedy writer of the fifth century BCE was Magnes (475–450 BCE), who won eleven times, the only writer whose works survive is Aristophanes (c. 450–385 BCE), who won four times. His plays constitute our principal firsthand knowledge of Greek Old Comedy. He wrote at least thirty-two comedies. Fortunately, eleven have survived, along with fragments of some of his other plays. His plots and actions are outrageous, his characters are funny, and his language is satirical, bawdy, and biting.

Middle Comedy Became Prominent after Aristophanes

Aristophanes lived into the next period of Greek comedy, called **Middle Comedy.** His plays *Ecclesiazusae* (*The Women at the Assembly,* c. 392 BCE) and *Plutus* (*Plutus, the God of Riches,* 388 BCE) ushered in Middle Comedy. All the Middle Comedy plays by other authors are lost, although there are many extant fragments. Middle Comedy eliminated some of the complex patterns of Old Comedy and treated more broadly international and less narrowly Athenian topics. Political criticism was abandoned, and character types such as the braggart soldier were introduced. The role of the chorus was diminished or eliminated (as with tragedy), and the exaggerated costumes were eliminated.

New Comedy, a Type of Romantic Comedy, Flourished after Middle Comedy

By the end of the fourth century BCE, Middle Comedy was supplanted by **New Comedy.** The most important of the New Comedy dramatists was Menander (342–292 BCE), who was heralded in ancient times as the greatest comic writer of them all. Everyone knows quotations from Menander, such as "I call a fig a fig, a spade a spade," "The gods first make mad those they intend to destroy," and "He who fights and runs away lives to fight another day." St. Paul quotes him in 1 Corinthians 15:33 ("Be not deceived: evil communications corrupt good manners."), but after the fifth century CE, copies of Menander's plays were no longer available and for the next fourteen centuries they were presumed totally lost. In the last hundred years, however, many Menandrian manuscripts have been discovered, mostly in the sands of Egypt. We now have Menander's *Dyscolus* (*The Grouch*) in its entirety, and near-complete versions of some of his other comedies, together with numerous fragments and passages.[3] In total, the titles of close to one hundred of his plays are known. His comedies, which are romantic rather than satirical, employ such stock characters as young lovers, stubborn fathers, clever slaves, and long-separated relatives.

Roman Comedy Was Composed Largely in the Third and Second Centuries BCE

After Menander, Greek power in the Mediterranean waned and was replaced by the might of Rome. In the third century BCE. Roman comedy began and flourished, largely through the translation and adaptation of Greek New Comedies. The significant Roman writers were Plautus (c. 254–184 BCE), with twenty surviving comedies, and Terence (c. 186–159 BCE), whose six comedies have survived from

---

[3]See David R. Slavitt and Palmer Bovie, eds., *Menander: The Grouch, Desperately Seeking Justice, Closely Cropped Locks, The Girl from Samos, The Shield* (Philadelphia: U of Pennsylvania P, 1998).

antiquity. Briefly, the comedies of Plautus are brisk, and those of Terence are more restrained. The central issue in most of the Roman comedies is the overcoming of a **blocking agent**, or obstruction to true love, which could be almost anyone or anything—a rival lover, an angry father, a family feud, an old law, a previously arranged marriage, or differences in social class. The pattern of action, traditionally called the **plot of intrigue** or **intrigue plot,** stems from the stratagems that young lovers undertake to overcome the blocking agent, so that the outcome frequently heralds the victory of youth over age and the passing of control from one generation to the next.

Comedy from Roman Times to the Renaissance

By the time the Roman Empire was established in 29 BCE, the writing of comedy had largely disappeared because pantomime entertainments and public spectacles such as chariot races and gladiatorial combat had preempted Roman dramatic creativity. Comedy thus accompanied tragedy into fifteen hundred years of obscurity—a period when the Roman Empire rose and fell, the Dark Ages descended, and the medieval period emerged. Although many comic and farcical scenes were included in the mystery cycles of late medieval times,[4] comedy as a form was not established again until the Renaissance.

Once reintroduced, comedy grew rapidly. By 1500 the six plays of Terence had been revived and were achieving wide recognition, followed by the twenty surviving plays of Plautus. When English dramatists began writing comedies, they followed Roman conventions. The English plays of the mid-sixteenth century contained five acts and observed the unities of time, place, and action, thus justifying the claim that they were "regular" (i.e., following the generally accepted regulations or "rules"). Character types from the Roman comedies, such as the intriguing couple, the fussing father, and the bragging soldier, initially predominated. Soon, more specifically English types appeared, anticipating the roisterers of Shakespeare's *Henry IV* plays and the "hempen homespuns" of *A Midsummer Night's Dream*. By the end of the sixteenth century, when Shakespeare had completed many of his comedies, English comedy was in full bloom. It has often been observed that this comedy was Latin in structure but English in character.

When the sixteenth century began, the chief obstacle to a wide public assimilation of drama had been the absence of institutionalized theaters. London authorities, maintaining that attending plays was a sinful public nuisance that took citizens away from work and responsibility, banned theaters within the city itself. Builders therefore had to construct theaters outside the London city limits. For example, the Rose and the Globe, where Shakespeare saw his plays produced from the mid-1590s to 1611, were built in Southwark across the Thames. We should realize that many people in Shakespeare's audiences got to the theater by walking over London Bridge or by being ferried across the river, and that they returned home the same way.

---

[4]For a description of the medieval mystery or Corpus Christi plays, see Chapter 23, pages 1218–20.

The Patterns, Characters, and Language of Comedy

Dictionaries sometimes give *funny* as a synonym for *comic,* but the two terms are not identical. Words like *funny, amusing, comical,* or *humorous* define our emotional conditioning to incidents, and our reactions always depend on context. We usually think it is funny or comical to see an actor in a slapstick routine falling down, being hit in the face with a cream pie, or being struck with a paddle. We laugh because we know that everything is staged and that no real harm is being done. But if we leave the theater and see some of the same things occurring on the streets, we are horrified to recognize that someone is enduring real harm and real pain. Street violence occurs randomly, with no apparent purpose, and there is nothing funny or comic about it. But onstage all actions occur as part of a governing pattern or plan leading to a satisfying outcome. It is the context that makes the difference.

Comedy Implies a Complete Narrative Pattern of Humorous Action

Comedy as a genre involves patterns of humorous or comic situations and actions that make up a complete and coherent story. Often the situations are simply ordinary; sometimes they are fantastic; sometimes they are even bizarre. But they are always resolvable and correctible (unless we are dealing with the special genre of **problem comedy** [see Chapter 28]). The patterns grow out of character and situation, and they reach a resolution in a logical or at least an understandable pattern of development. In considering comic patterns, we perceive most dialogue and activity—even serious problems and dangerous situations—as amusing, entertaining, and usually instructive.

COMEDY DRAMATIZES A PATTERN OF EDUCATION AND CHANGE.   In many comedies the principal characters benefit from learning about themselves and their commitments, about living well and loving deeply, about getting along with the people around them, and about finding their place in the world. This "education," which they receive in the play, enables them to improve, and the process of their learning reaches its height in crucial moments of illumination and change. The characters realize their past errors, are ready to amend them, and also are human and humble enough to ask forgiveness which, according to the comic pattern, is promptly granted. In many comedies, particularly those that touch on significant social and political problems, the audience is also educated, and the play's implication is that improvement should occur in the world just as it has occurred on the stage.

COMIC PROBLEMS FLOURISH AMID CHAOS AND POTENTIAL DISASTER.   Before the moments of change leading to the comic conclusion, however, comedy must introduce many of the problems and complications that could, in real life, lead not to happiness but to unhappiness and even to calamity. These problems can be personal, social, political, economic, or military; in short, they may enter every arena of human affairs. A man wants to find a place in the world and to gain his fortune, and he also wants to find love. A woman wants to find love also, but must be reserved and somewhat aloof when meeting suitors. A number of people want to succeed in a business venture. A politician is accused of corruption and thus needs help in exonerating himself. A man and woman in love become angry or disenchanted because others tell them lies about each other. Another man and woman need to overcome family hostility so that they may successfully begin their lives together with the approval of everyone around them. Still another man and woman, upon meeting for the first time, become so angry they threaten to do away with each other. Failure, though it is to be always overcome in comedy, is never far distant; it lurks over the horizon, around corners, in business rooms, in malicious telephone calls, and on the Internet, waiting to emerge and scatter uncertainty, indecisiveness, and distress.

All such situations, which might possibly lead to ruin, are the stuff of comedy. The worse things seem, and the more apparently chaotic, the better. In a good comic complication, the problems are constantly being fueled by misunderstanding, mistaken identity, misdirection, misinformed speech, errors in judgment, faults in intelligence, excessive or unreasonable behavior, and coincidences that stretch credulity.

THE COMIC CLIMAX IS THE PEAK OF CONFUSION.   Such complications lead ultimately to the comic **climax,** which is the moment or moments in the play when everything reaches the peak of confusion and when no good solution seems in sight. Misunderstanding is dominant, pressure is at a high point, and choices must be made even though solutions seem impossible. The **catastrophe**—the changing or turning point—is frequently launched by a sudden revelation in which a new fact, a misunderstood event, or a previously hidden identity is explained to characters and audience at the same time, and then things undergo a turnaround and start rushing toward improvement.

THE COMIC DÉNOUEMENT RESTORES SANITY AND CALM.   In most comedies, the events of the **dénouement** resolve the initial difficulties and allow for the comic resolution, which dramatizes how things are set right at every level of action. Errors are explained, personal lives are straightened out, people at odds with each other are reconciled, promises are made for the future, new families are formed through marriage, and a stable social order is reestablished.

Comic Characters Are More Limited Than Characters in Tragedy

Comic characters are relatively limited because they are almost necessarily representative and common rather than individual and heroic. Characters with breadth or individuality are therefore not typical of comedy. Instead, comedy gives us stock characters who represent classes, types, and generations. In Shakespeare's *A Midsummer Night's Dream* many of the characters are representative and stock figures. Egeus is a conventionally indignant and unreasonable father, and Hermia and Lysander are typical young lovers (along with Helena and Demetrius). In Henley's *Am I Blue*, Ashbe and John Polk are young people who are trying to deal with the confusion in their lives. Their meeting provides them with a stay against their own personal difficulties, but they do not reach any elevated insights.

Comic Language Is a Vital Vehicle of Humor

As in other types of literature, comic dramatists use language to delineate character, to establish tone and mood, and to express ideas and feelings. In comedy, however, language is also one of the most important vehicles for humor. Some comedies are characterized by elegant and witty language, others by puns and bawdy jokes.

Characters in comedy tend either to be masters of language or to be mastered by it. Those who are skillful with language can use a witty phrase to satirize their foes and friends alike. Those who are unskilled with language, like Bottom in *A Midsummer Night's Dream*, bungle their speeches because they misuse words and stumble into inadvertent puns. Both types of characters are amusing; we smile a knowing smile with the wits and laugh aloud at the would-be wits and the bunglers.

Types of Comedy

Differences in comic style, content, and intent that have evolved over the centuries make it possible to divide comedy into various types. The broadest of these divisions, based on both style and content, separates comic literature into *high comedy* and *low comedy*.

High Comedy Develops Mainly from Character

Ideally, **high comedy** (a term coined by George Meredith in 1877 in *The Idea of Comedy*) is witty, graceful, and sophisticated. The problems and complications are more closely related to character than to situation, even though, admittedly, they develop out of situations. The appeal of high comedy is to the intellect, for the comic resolution must come about because the characters learn enough to accept adjustments and changes in their lives. A simple change of situation alone will not do for high comedy. The types of high comedy are these:

1. *Romantic comedy focuses on problems of youthful love.* One of the major kinds of high comedy is **romantic comedy,** which views action and character from the standpoint of earnest young lovers like Hermia and Lysander in *A Midsummer Night's Dream*. Ultimately derived from Roman comedy, a romantic comedy is built on a plot of intrigue featuring lovers who try to overcome opposition (as, for example, Egeus) to achieve a successful union. The aim of such plays is amusement and entertainment rather than ridicule and reform. Although vice and folly may be exposed in romantic comedy, especially the follies of the antagonists blocking the young lovers, the dominant impulse is toleration and amused indulgence.

2. *Comedy of manners tests the strength of social customs and assumptions.* Related to romantic comedy is the **comedy of manners,** an important type from the seventeenth century to our own times. The comedy of manners examines and satirizes attitudes and customs in the light of high intellectual and moral standards. The dialogue is witty and sophisticated, and characters are often

measured according to their linguistic and intellectual powers. The love plots are serious and real, even though they share with romantic comedy the need to create intrigues to overcome opposition and impediments. The realism and seriousness in some of the manners comedies written in Restoration England (1660–1700) are so significant that one might consider them not only as plays of manners but also as plays of social and personal problems.

3. *Satiric comedy, like all satire, ridicules vices and follies.* Midway between high and low comedy is **satiric comedy,** which is based in a comic attack on foolishness and/or viciousness. The playwright of satiric comedy assumes the perspective of a rational and moderate observer measuring human life against a moderate norm that is represented by high and serious characters. Members of the audience are invited to share this viewpoint as they, along with the dramatist, heap scorn upon the vicious and laugh loudly at the eccentric and the foolish.

Low Comedy Dwells Amid the Silly and the Bumbling

In **low comedy,** emphasis is on funny remarks and outrageous circumstances. Complications develop from situation and plot rather than from character. Plays of this type are by definition full of physical humor and stage business—a character rounds his forefinger and thumb to imitate a hole in a wall, through which other characters speak; an irascible man constantly breaks furniture; a character masquerading as a doctor takes the pulse of a father to determine his daughter's medical condition; characters who have just declared their love are visited by people to whom they formerly swore love.

The quintessential type of low comedy is **farce,** which is derived from the Latin word *farsus,* meaning "stuffed." Henry Fielding, in the prologue to his 1730 play *The Author's Farce,* points out that the aim of farce "is but to make you laugh." Farces are mainly outlandish physical comedies overflowing with silly characters, unlikely happenings, wild clowning, improbable pratfalls, extravagant language, and bawdy jokes.

Another type of farce is the *commedia dell'arte,* a prototypical comic drama that developed among traveling companies in Italy and France in the sixteenth and seventeenth centuries. The broadly humorous characters of *commedia dell'arte* recurred from play to play with consistent names and characteristics. The action usually involved a plot of intrigue. The lovers were the permanently youthful and glowing *Inamorato* and *Inamorata,* who were aided by Inamorata's clever servant, the *soubrette,* to overcome *Pantaloon,* the foolish and presuming old man. The servant characters were *Harlequin* (who was invisible) and *Columbine* (his sweetheart, also invisible), who were joined in highjinks by *Pierrot* (a clown lover) and *Scaramouche* (the soldier). Other stock characters, most of whom were derived from Greek New Comedy by way of Roman comedy, have in turn become constant features of much subsequent comedy.

With characters of low comedy, of course, there is much tomfoolery and improvisation—the major qualities of the extreme form of farce, **slapstick,** which is named after the double paddles ("slap sticks") that made loud cracking noises when actors in the *commedia dell'arte* used them for striking each other. Slapstick depends heavily on exaggerated actions, poses, and facial expressions. In slapstick there is constant onstage business with objects such as paddles, pies, pails, paint, paste, or toilet paper, along with wild and silly actions such as squirming, hiding, stumbling, tripping, tumbling, falling, and flopping.

Other Kinds of Comedy Emphasize Complexity and Absurdity

Other types of modern and contemporary comedy include **ironic comedy, realistic comedy,** and **comedy of the absurd.** All of these shun the happy endings of traditional comedy. Often the blocking agents are successful, the protagonists are defeated, and the initial problem—either a realistic or an absurdist dilemma—remains unresolved. Such comedies, which began to appear in the late nineteenth century, illustrate the complexities and absurdities of modern life and the funny but futile efforts that people make when coming to grips with existence.

Many types of traditional comedies still flourish. Romantic comedies, comedies of manners, and farces can be found on innumerable stages and movie screens. They revolve about a central situation that might be quite ordinary. (Will Herman get along with a visiting business associate? Will Sue be accepted by schoolmates at her new school? Will Jim get a date for the prom?) Such situations find their ways into the huge numbers of **sitcoms** (**"situation comedies"**) that occupy prime-time television programming.

In view of the variety of comedy, it is most important to recognize that comedy is rarely a pure and discrete form. High comedies might include crude physical humor, especially with characters to be disapproved. Low comedies can sometimes contain wit and elegance. Satiric comedies might deal with successful young lovers. Romantic comedies can mock the vices and follies of weird and eccentric characters. Farce and slapstick can contain satire on social values and conventions.

Plays for Study

William Shakespeare . . . . A Midsummer Night's Dream, 1506

Molière (Jean Baptiste Poquelin) . . . . Love Is the Doctor, 1563

Anton Chekhov. . . . . The Bear, 1582

Beth Henley. . . . . Am I Blue, 1592

WILLIAM SHAKESPEARE (1564–1616)

For a brief biography and portrait, see Chapter 24, page 1322.

A Midsummer Night's Dream was written early in Shakespeare's career, in 1594 or 1595.[5] It is a romantic comedy dramatizing the idea that "the course of true love never did run smooth." This central line of action, which owes much to Roman

---

[5]See Chapter 24, pages 1318–23, for a description of Shakespeare's theater and career as a dramatist.

comedy, involves blocked love, a journey of circumvention and education that takes the lovers from the world of laws and problems into an imaginary world of chaos and transformations, and an ultimate victory back in the world of daylight and order.

The subject of *A Midsummer Night's Dream* is love. Shakespeare skillfully interweaves this topic in the play's four separate plots, four groups of characters, and four styles of language. Each plot explores the nature of love, the madness of irrational love, and the harmony needed for regenerative love.

In the *overplot*—the action that establishes the time for the play—the relationship is between the rulers, Theseus and Hippolyta, who have undergone a change from irrational war to rational peace. As such, they represent the dynastic continuity of the state, the order of the daylight world of Athens, and the rigor of law. These characters are the rulers, and they speak predominantly in blank verse (unrhymed iambic pentameter; see Chapter 17).

The two connected *middle love plots* concern the adventures of the four lovers and the actions of Oberon and Titania. The four lovers, embodying the most passionate and insistent phase of love, are from the upper class, and they speak mainly in rhymed couplets. During their long night of illusion in the woods, conjured by Oberon and his servant, Puck, their adventures drive them toward rationality, and they recognize and accept the need for faithfulness and constancy. The parallel middle plot involves the conflict between Oberon and Titania, the king and queen of the fairies, because of their mutually exclusive wishes to control a "changeling" child. Oberon is "jealous" and wants the child as an attendant, but Titania wants to keep him in her service because his mother had been Titania's attendant, friend, and confidante. With great power over Titania, Oberon humbles her, and she then reacknowledges his superiority—the proper attitude of a wife, according to Elizabethan males. Oberon and Titania, of course, are supernatural forces. Although they and the other fairies speak in both blank verse and rhymed couplets, the fairies are the only singing characters and also the only characters to speak in iambic tetrameter.

The examination of love in the subplot occurs partly in Titania's relationship with Bottom—the most hilarious instance of love's madness in the play—and partly in the play-within-a-play about Pyramus and Thisby. This play, filled with "very tragical mirth," echoes the central plot of *A Midsummer Night's Dream* and demonstrates, again, the pitfalls and unpredictability of love. It also emphasizes the happy and harmonious marriages and rapprochements that occur in both the overplot and the middle plots.

While *A Midsummer Night's Dream* is chiefly about love, it is equally concerned with the complicated relationship of perception, imagination, passion, art, and illusion. In Act 5 Theseus asserts that "The lunatic, the lover, and the poet" are alike because they all try to make reality conform with their own imaginations and desires (1.7–22). It would seem that chaos is therefore a normal human state, but, as Hippolyta concludes in response to Theseus, order and certainty somehow prevail, "howsoever" extraordinary and almost miraculous this result may seem (lines 23–27). The movement of the play is governed by these ideas that, along with the brilliant language and comic actions, are directly attributable to the genius of Shakespeare.

A Midsummer Night's Dream (1600; c. 1594)

Edited by Alice Griffin*

THE NAMES OF THE ACTORS

Theseus, *Duke of Athens*
Egeus, *father of Hermia*
Lysander, *beloved of Hermia*
Demetrius, *in love with Hermia, favoured by Egeus*
Philostrate, *Master of the Revels to Theseus*
Peter Quince, *a carpenter (Prologue)***
Nick Bottom, *a weaver (Pyramus)***
Francis Flute, *a bellows-mender (Thisby)***
Tom Snout, *a tinker (Wall)***
Snug, *a joiner (Lion)***
Robin Starveling, *a tailor (Moonshine)***
Hippolyta, *Queen of the Amazons, betrothed to Theseus*
Hermia, *daughter of Egeus, in love with Lysander*
Helena, *in love with Demetrius*
Oberon, *King of the Fairies*
Titania, *Queen of the Fairies*
Puck, *or* Robin Goodfellow
Peaseblossom
Cobweb   } *Fairies*
Moth
Mustardseed
Other Fairies attending Oberon and Titania. Attendants on Theseus and Hippolyta.

SCENE. *Athens, and a wood nearby*

ACT 1

[Scene 1. Athens. The palace of Theseus]

Enter THESEUS, HIPPOLYTA,° [PHILOSTRATE,] *with others.*

THESEUS: Now fair Hippolyta, our nuptial hour
    Draws on apace: four happy days bring in
    Another moon: but O, methinks how slow
    This old moon wanes! she lingers° my desires,
5   Like to a stepdame or a dowager,°
    Long withering out° a young man's revenue.
HIPPOLYTA: Four days will quickly steep themselves in night:
    Four nights will quickly dream away the time:

---

*Professor Griffin's text for A *Midsummer Night's Dream* is the First Quarto (edition) published in 1600, with modifications based on the Quarto edition of 1619 and the First Folio, published in 1623. Stage directions in those editions are printed here without brackets; added stage directions are printed within brackets. We have edited Griffin's notes for this text. **Characters who play in the interlude.
°0.3 S.D.: *Theseus, Hippolyta:* In Greek legend, Theseus captured the Amazon Queen Hippolyta and brought her to Athens where they were married. 4 *lingers:* delays the fulfillment of. 5 *dowager:* a widow supported by her dead husband's heirs. 6 *withering out:* (1) depleting (2) growing withered.

And then the moon, like to a silver bow
New-bent in heaven, shall behold the night   10
Of our solemnities.
THESEUS: Go Philostrate,
    Stir up the Athenian youth to merriments,
    Awake the pert° and nimble spirit of mirth,
    Turn melancholy forth to funerals:
    The pale companion° is not for our pomp.   [*Exit* PHILOSTRATE.]   15
    Hippolyta, I wooed thee with my sword,
    And won thy love doing thee injuries;
    But I will wed thee in another key,
    With pomp, with triumph,° and with revelling.

Enter EGEUS *and his daughter* HERMIA, LYSANDER *and* DEMETRIUS.

EGEUS: Happy be Theseus, our renownèd duke.   20
THESEUS: Thanks good Egeus:° what's the news with thee?
EGEUS: Full of vexation come I, with complaint
    Against my child, my daughter Hermia.
    Stand forth Demetrius. My noble lord,
    This man hath my consent to marry her.   25
    Stand forth Lysander. And my gracious duke,
    This man hath bewitched the bosom of my child.
    Thou, thou Lysander, thou hast given her rhymes,
    And interchanged love tokens with my child:
    Thou hast by moonlight at her window sung,   30
    With feigning voice, verses of feigning° love,
    And stol'n the impression of her fantasy°
    With bracelets of thy hair, rings, gauds° conceits,°
    Knacks,° trifles, nosegays, sweetmeats—messengers
    Of strong prevailment in unhardened youth.   35
    With cunning hast thou filched my daughter's heart,
    Turned her obedience, which is due to me,
    To stubborn harshness. And my gracious duke,
    Be it so° she will not here before your grace
    Consent to marry with Demetrius,   40
    I beg the ancient privilege of Athens:
    As she is mine, I may dispose of her:
        Which shall be, either to this gentleman,
        Or to her death, according to our law
        Immediately° provided in that case.   45
THESEUS: What say you, Hermia? Be advised, fair maid.
    To you your father should be as a god:
    One that composed your beauties: yea and one
    To whom you are but as a form in wax   50

°13 *pert:* lively. 15 *companion:* fellow (contemptuous). 19 *triumph:* public festival. 21 *Egeus:* (trisyllabic).
31 *feigning:* (1) deceptive (2) desirous ("faining"). 32 *stol'n . . . fantasy:* stealthily imprinted your image upon her
fancy. 33 *gauds:* trinkets. *conceits:* either (a) love poetry, or (b) love tokens. 34 *Knacks:* knick-knacks. 39 *Be it so:*
if it be that. 45 *Immediately:* precisely.

50   By him imprinted, and within his power
        To leave the figure, or disfigure it:
        Demetrius is a worthy gentleman.
HERMIA: So is Lysander.
THESEUS   In himself he is:
        But in this kind, wanting your father's voice,°
55   The other must be held the worthier.
HERMIA: I would my father looked but with my eyes.
THESEUS: Rather your eyes must with his judgment look.
HERMIA: I do entreat your grace to pardon me.
        I know not by what power I am made bold,
60   Nor how it may concern my modesty,
        In such a presence, here to plead my thoughts:
        But I beseech your grace that I may know
        The worst that may befall me in this case,
        If I refuse to wed Demetrius.
65 **THESEUS:** Either to die the death, or to abjure
        For ever the society of men.
        Therefore fair Hermia, question your desires,
        Know of your youth,° examine well your blood,°
        Whether, if you yield not to your father's choice,
70   You can endure the livery° of a nun,
        For aye° to be in shady cloister mewed,°
        To live a barren sister all your life,
        Chanting faint hymns to the cold fruitless moon.°
        Thrice blessèd they that master so their blood,
75   To undergo such maiden pilgrimage:
        But earthlier happy° is the rose distilled,°
        Than that which, withering on the virgin thorn,
        Grows, lives, and dies, in single blessedness.
HERMIA: So will I grow, so live, so die my lord,
80   Ere I will yield my virgin patent° up
        Unto his lordship, whose unwishéd yoke
        My soul consents not to give sovereignty.
THESEUS: Take time to pause, and by the next moon,
        The sealing day betwixt my love and me,
85   For everlasting bond of fellowship,
        Upon that day either prepare to die
        For disobedience to your father's will,
        Or else to wed Demetrius, as he would,
        Or on Diana's altar to protest°
90   For aye, austerity and single life.
DEMETRIUS: Relent, sweet Hermia, and Lysander, yield
        Thy crazèd° title to my certain right.
LYSANDER: You have her father's love, Demetrius:
        Let me have Hermia's: do you marry him.

°54 *in . . . voice:* in this respect, lacking your father's approval. 68 *Know . . . youth:* ask yourself as a young person. *blood:* passions. 70 *livery:* habit. 71 *aye:* ever. *mewed:* shut up. 73 *moon:* (the moon goddess Diana represented unmarried chastity). 76 *earthlier happy:* more happy on earth. *distilled:* i.e., into perfume (thus its essence is passed on, as to a child). 80 *patent:* privilege. 89 *protest:* vow. 92 *crazèd:* flawed.

EGEUS: Scornful Lysander, true, he hath my love: 95
    And what is mine, my love shall render him.
    And she is mine, and all my right of her
    I do estate° unto Demetrius.
LYSANDER: I am, my lord, as well derived° as he,
    As well possessed;° my love is more than his: 100
    My fortunes every way as fairly ranked
    (If not with vantage) as° Demetrius':
    And, which is more than all these boasts can be,
    I am beloved of beauteous Hermia.
    Why should not I then prosecute my right?   105
    Demetrius, I'll avouch it to his head,°
    Made love to Nedar's daughter, Helena,
    And won her soul: and she, sweet lady, dotes,
    Devoutly dotes, dotes in idolatry,
    Upon this spotted° and inconstant man.   110
THESEUS: I must confess that I have heard so much,
    And with Demetrius thought to have spoke thereof:
    But being over-full of self-affairs,
    My mind did lose it. But Demetrius come,
    And come Egeus, you shall go with me: 115
    I have some private schooling for you both.
    For you fair Hermia, look you arm yourself,
    To fit your fancies to your father's will;
    Or else the law of Athens yields you up
    (Which by no means we may extenuate)   120
    To death or to a vow of single life.
    Come my Hippolyta, what cheer my love?
    Demetrius and Egeus, go along:
    I must employ you in some business
    Against° our nuptial, and confer with you   125
    Of something nearly° that concerns yourselves.
EGEUS: With duty and desire we follow you.

Exeunt.° Manent° LYSANDER and HERMIA.

LYSANDER: How now my love? Why is your cheek so pale?
    How chance the roses there do fade so fast?
HERMIA: Belike° for want of rain, which I could well   130
    Beteem° them from the tempest of my eyes,
LYSANDER: Ay me, for aught that I could ever read,
    Could ever hear by tale or history,
    The course of true love never did run smooth;
    But either it was different in blood—   135
HERMIA: O cross! too high° to be enthralled to low.°

°98 *estate:* transfer. 99 *well derived:* well born. 100 *well possessed:* wealthy. 102 *with vantage, as:* better, than. 106 *avouch . . . head:* prove it to his face. 110 *spotted:* stained 125 *Against:* in preparation for. 126 *nearly:* closely. 127 S.D.: *Exeunt:* they exit. *Manent:* they remain. 130 *Belike:* likely. 131 *Beteem:* (1) pour out on (2) allow. 136 *high:* highborn. *enthralled to low:* made a slave to one of low birth.

LYSANDER: Or else misgraffed° in respect of years—
HERMIA: O spite! too old to be engaged to young.
LYSANDER: Or else it stood upon the choice of friends—
140 HERMIA: O hell! to choose love by another's eyes.
LYSANDER: Or if there were a sympathy in choice,
    War, death, or sickness did lay siege to it;
    Making it momentany° as a sound,
    Swift as a shadow, short as any dream,
145   Brief as the lightning in the collied° night,
    That, in a spleen,° unfolds both heaven and earth;
    And ere a man hath power to say "Behold,"
    The jaws of darkness do devour it up:
    So quick bright things come to confusion.
150 HERMIA: If then true lovers have been ever crossed,°
    It stands as an edict in destiny:
    Then let us teach our trial patience,°
    Because it is a customary cross,
    As due to love as thoughts and dreams and sighs,
155   Wishes and tears; poor Fancy's° followers.
LYSANDER: A good persuasion: therefore hear me, Hermia:
    I have a widow aunt, a dowager,
    Of great revenue, and she hath no child:
    From Athens is her house remote seven leagues,
160   And she respects° me as her only son:
    There gentle Hermia, may I marry thee,
    And to that place the sharp Athenian law
    Cannot pursue us. If thou lov'st me then,
    Steal forth thy father's house tomorrow night:
165   And in the wood, a league without the town,
    Where I did meet thee once with Helena
    To do observance to a morn of May,°
    There will I stay° for thee.
HERMIA: My good Lysander,
    I swear to thee, by Cupid's strongest bow,
170   By his best arrow, with the golden head,°
    By the simplicity of Venus' doves,
    By that which knitteth souls and prospers loves,
    And by that fire which burned the Carthage queen,
    When the false Troyan° under sail was seen,
175   By all the vows that ever men have broke,
    (In number more than ever women spoke)
    In that same place thou hast appointed me,
    Tomorrow truly will I meet with thee.

°137 *misgraffed:* badly joined. 143 *momentany:* momentary. 145 *collied:* black as coal. 146 *in a spleen:* impulsively, in a sudden outburst. 150 *ever crossed:* evermore thwarted. 152 *teach . . . patience:* teach ourselves to be patient. 155 *Fancy:* love (sometimes infatuation). 160 *respects:* regards. 167 *do . . . May:* celebrate May Day. 168 *stay:* wait. 170 *golden head:* (The arrow with the gold Head causes love). 173–74 *Carthage queen . . . false Troyan:* Dido, who burned herself to death on a funeral pyre when Trojan Aeneas deserted her.

LYSANDER: Keep promise love: look, here comes Helena.

Enter HELENA.

HERMIA: God speed fair Helena: whither away?   180
HELENA: Call you me fair? That fair again unsay.
    Demetrius loves your fair:° O happy fair!
    Your eyes are lodestars,° and your tongue's sweet air°
    More tuneable than lark to shepherd's ear,
    When wheat is green, when hawthorn buds appear.   185
    Sickness is catching: O were favour° so,
    Yours would I catch, fair Hermia, ere I go,
    My ear should catch your voice,° my eye your eye,°
    My tongue should catch your tongue's sweet melody.
    Were the world mine, Demetrius being bated,°   190
    The rest I'd give to be to you translated.°
    O teach me how you look, and with what art
    You sway the motion of Demetrius' heart.
HERMIA: I frown upon him; yet he loves me still.
HELENA: O that your frowns would teach my smiles such skill.   195
HERMIA: I give him curses; yet he gives me love.
HELENA: O that my prayers could such affection move.
HERMIA: The more I hate, the more he follows me.
HELENA: The more I love, the more he hateth me.
HERMIA: His folly, Helena, is no fault of mine.   200
HELENA: None but your beauty; would that fault were mine.
HERMIA: Take comfort: he no more shall see my face:
    Lysander and myself will fly this place.
    Before the time I did Lysander see,
    Seemed Athens as a paradise to me: 205
    O then, what graces in my love do dwell,
    That he hath turned a heaven unto a hell!
LYSANDER: Helen, to you our minds we will unfold:
    Tomorrow night, when Phoebe° doth behold
    Her silver visage in the wat'ry glass,°   210
    Decking with liquid pearl the bladed grass
    (A time that lovers' flights doth still° conceal)
    Through Athens gates have we devised to steal.
HERMIA: And in the wood, where often you and I
    Upon faint primrose beds were wont to lie,   215
    Emptying our bosoms of their counsel° sweet,
    There my Lysander and myself shall meet,
    And thence from Athens turn away our eyes,
    To see new friends and stranger companies.°
    Farewell, sweet playfellow: pray thou for us: 220
    And good luck grant thee thy Demetrius.

°182 *your fair*: i.e., beauty 183 *lodestars*: guiding stars. *air*: music. 186 *favour*: appearance. 188 *My ear . . . voice*: my ear should catch the tone of your voice. *my eye your eye*: my eye should catch the way you glance. 190 *bated*: subtracted, excepted. 191 *translated*: transformed. 209 *Phoebe*: Diana, the moon. 210 *wat'ry glass*: mirror of the water. 212 *still*: always. 216 *counsel*: secrets. 219 *stranger companies*: the companionship of strangers.

> Keep word Lysander: we must starve our sight
> From lovers' food,° till morrow deep midnight.
>
> **LYSANDER:** I will my Hermia.   *Exit* HERMIA.
>
>   Helena adieu:
> 225   As you on him, Demetrius dote on you.°   *Exit* LYSANDER.
>
> **HELENA:** How happy some, o'er other some, can be!
>   Through Athens I am thought as fair as she.
>   But what of that? Demetrius thinks not so:
>   He will not know what all but he do know.
> 230   And as he errs, doting on Hermia's eyes,
>   So I, admiring of his qualities.
>   Things base and vile, holding no quantity.°
>   Love can transpose to form and dignity.
>   Love looks not with the eyes, but with the mind:
> 235   And therefore is winged Cupid painted blind.
>   Nor hath Love's mind of any judgment taste:
>   Wings, and no eyes, figure° unheedy haste.
>   And therefore is Love said to be a child:
>   Because in choice he is so oft beguiled.
> 240   As waggish boys in game themselves forswear:
>   So the boy Love is perjured everywhere.
>   For ere Demetrius looked on Hermia's eyne,°
>   He hailed down oaths that he was only mine.
>   And when this hail some heat from Hermia felt,
> 245   So he dissolved, and show'rs of oaths did melt.
>   I will go tell him of fair Hermia's flight:
>   Then to the wood will he tomorrow night
>   Pursue her: and for this intelligence,°
>   If I have thanks, it is a dear expense.°
> 250   But herein mean I to enrich my pain,
>   To have his sight° thither and back again.   *Exit.*

[Scene 2. Quince's house]

Enter QUINCE *the Carpenter; and* SNUG *the Joiner; and* BOTTOM *the Weaver; and* FLUTE *the Bellows-mender; and* SNOUT *the Tinker; and* STARVELING *the Tailor.*°

QUINCE: Is all our company here?

BOTTOM: You were the best to call them generally,° man by man,
        according to the scrip.

QUINCE: Here is the scroll of every man's name which is thought
5   fit, through all Athens, to play in our interlude° before
        the duke and the duchess, on his wedding-day at night.

°223 *lovers' food:* the sight of the loved one. 225 *As . . . you:* As you dote on Demetrius, so may Demetrius also dote on you. 232 *holding no quantity:* out of proportion. 237 *figure:* symbolize. 242 *eyne:* eyes. 248 *intelligence:* information. 249 *dear expense:* costly outlay (on Demetrius' part). 250–51 *But . . . sight:* but I will be rewarded just by the sight of him. 0.2 S.D.: the low characters' names describe their work: *Quince:* quoins, wooden wedges used in building. *Snug:* fitting snugly, suiting a joiner of furniture. *Bottom:* bobbin or core on which yarn is wound. *Flute:* mender of fluted church organs and bellows. *Snout:* spout (of the kettles he mends). *Starveling:* (tailors being traditionally thin). 2 *generally:* Bottom often uses the wrong word; here he means the opposite: "severally, one by one." 5 *interlude:* short play.

BOTTOM: First good Peter Quince, say what the play treats on,
    then read the names of the actors: and so grow to a point.

QUINCE: Marry,° our play is "The most lamentable comedy, and
    most cruel death of Pyramus and Thisby."   10

BOTTOM: A very good piece of work I assure you, and a merry. Now
    good Peter Quince, call forth your actors by the scroll.
    Masters, spread yourselves.

QUINCE: Answer as I call you. Nick Bottom the weaver?

BOTTOM: Ready: name what part I am for, and proceed.   15

QUINCE: You, Nick Bottom, are set down for Pyramus.

BOTTOM: What is Pyramus? A lover, or a tyrant?

QUINCE: A lover that kills himself, most gallant, for love.

BOTTOM: That will ask some tears in the true performing of it. If I
    do it, let the audience look to their eyes: I will move   20
    storms: I will condole° in some measure. To the rest—
    yet my chief humour° is for a tyrant. I could play Ercles°
    rarely, or a part to tear a cat in, to make all split.°

        The raging rocks
        And shivering shocks,   25
        Shall break the locks
           Of prison gates,
        And Phibbus' car°
        Shall shine from far,
        And make and mar   30
           The foolish Fates.

    This was lofty. Now name the rest of the players. This is
    Ercles' vein, a tyrant's vein: a lover is more condoling.

QUINCE: Francis Flute, the bellows-mender?

FLUTE: Here Peter Quince.   35

QUINCE: Flute, you must take Thisby on you.

FLUTE: What is Thisby? A wand'ring knight?

QUINCE: It is the lady that Pyramus must love.

FLUTE: Nay faith, let not me play a woman: I have a beard
    coming.   40

QUINCE: That's all one:° you shall play it in a mask, and you may
    speak as small° as you will.

BOTTOM: And° I may hide my face, let me play Thisby too: I'll speak
    in a monstrous little voice; "Thisne, Thisne," "Ah
    Pyramus, my lover dear, thy Thisby dear, and lady   45
    dear."

QUINCE: No, no, you must play Pyramus: and Flute, you Thisby.

BOTTOM: Well, proceed.

QUINCE: Robin Starveling, the tailor?

STARVELING: Here Peter Quince.   50

QUINCE: Robin Starveling, you must play Thisby's mother. Tom
    Snout, the tinker?

°9 *Marry:* indeed (mild oath, corruption of "by the Virgin Mary). 21 *condole:* lament. 22 *humour:* inclination. *Ercles:* Hercules (typified by ranting). 23 *tear . . . split:* (terms for ranting and raging on the stage). 28 *Phibbus' car:* Phoebus Apollo's chariot. 41 *That's all one:* never mind. 42 *small:* softly. 43 *And:* if.

SNOUT: Here Peter Quince.

QUINCE: You, Pyramus' father; myself, Thisby's father; Snug the
55   joiner, you the lion's part: and I hope here is a play
        fitted.°

SNUG: Have you the lion's part written? Pray you, if it be, give
        it me: for I am slow of study.

QUINCE: You may do it extempore: for it is nothing but roaring.

60 BOTTOM: Let me play the lion too. I will roar, that° I will do any
        man's heart good to hear me. I will roar, that I will make
        the duke say "Let him roar again: let him roar again."

QUINCE: And you should do it too terribly, you would fright the
        duchess and the ladies, that they would shriek: and
65   that were enough to hang us all.

ALL: That would hang us, every mother's son.

BOTTOM: I grant you, friends, if you should fright the ladies out of
        their wits, they would have no more discretion but to
        hang us: but I will aggravate° my voice so, that I will roar
70   you as gently as any sucking dove: I will roar you and
        'twere° any nightingale.

QUINCE: You can play no part but Pyramus: for Pyramus is a
        sweet-faced man; a proper° man as one shall see in a
        summer's day; a most lovely gentleman-like man: therefore
75   you must needs play Pyramus.

BOTTOM: Well: I will undertake it. What beard were I best to play
        it in?

QUINCE: Why, what you will.

BOTTOM: I will discharge it in either your straw-colour beard, your
80   orange-tawny beard, your purple-in-grain° beard, or your
        French-crown-colour° beard, your perfit yellow.

QUINCE: Some of your French crowns° have no hair at all; and
        then you will play barefaced. But masters here are your
        parts, and I am to entreat you, request you, and desire
85   you, to con° them by tomorrow night: and meet me in the
        palace wood, a mile without the town, by moonlight;
        there will we rehearse: for if we meet in the city, we
        shall be dogged with company, and our devices° known.
        In the meantime, I will draw a bill of properties,° such
90   as our play wants. I pray you fail me not.   ·

BOTTOM: We will meet, and there we may rehearse most obscenely°
        and courageously. Take pain, be perfit: adieu.

QUINCE: At the duke's oak we meet.

BOTTOM: Enough: hold, or cut bow-strings.°   *Exeunt.*

°56 *fitted:* cast. 60 *that:* so that. 69 *aggravate:* (he means "moderate"). 70–71 *and 'twere:* as if it were. 73 *proper:*
handsome. 80 *purple-in-grain:* dyed permanently purple. 81 *French-crown-colour:* golden, like French crowns
(gold coins). 82 *French crowns:* bald heads believed to be caused by syphilis, the "French" disease. 85 *con:*
learn by heart. 88 *devices:* plans. 89 *bill of properties:* list of stage props. 91 *obscenely:* (he may mean "fittingly"
or "obscurely"). 94 *hold, or cut bow-strings:* (meaning uncertain, but equivalent to "fish, or cut bait").

ACT 2

[Scene 1. A wood near Athens]

Enter a FAIRY at one door, and ROBIN GOODFELLOW [PUCK] at another.

PUCK: How now spirit, whither wander you?
FAIRY: Over hill, over dale,
    Thorough bush, thorough brier,
    Over park, over pale,°
      Thorough flood, thorough fire: 5
    I do wander everywhere,
    Swifter than the moon's sphere:
    And I serve the Fairy Queen,
    To dew° her orbs° upon the green.
    The cowslips° tall her pensioners° be,   10
    In their gold coats, spots you see:
    Those be rubies, fairy favours.°
    In those freckles live their savours.°
    I must go seek some dewdrops here,
    And hang a pearl in every cowslip's ear.   15
    Farewell thou lob° of spirits: I'll be gone,
    Our queen and all her elves come here anon.
PUCK: The king doth keep his revels here tonight.
    Take heed the queen come not within his sight.
    For Oberon is passing fell° and wrath,   20
    Because that she, as her attendant, hath
    A lovely boy, stol'n from an Indian king:
    She never had so sweet a changeling.°
    And jealous Oberon would have the child
    Knight of his train, to trace° the forests wild.   25
    But she, perforce,° withholds the lovèd boy,
    Crowns him with flowers, and makes him all her joy.
    And now, they never meet in grove or green,
    By fountain clear, or spangled starlight sheen,
    But they do square,° that all their elves for fear   30
    Creep into acorn cups, and hide them there.
FAIRY: Either I mistake your shape and making quite,
    Or else you are that shrewd and knavish sprite
    Called Robin Goodfellow. Are not you he
    That frights the maidens of the villagery,   35
    Skim milk,° and sometimes labour in the quern,°
    And bootless° make the breathless housewife churn,
    And sometime make the drink to bear no barm,°
    Mislead night-wanderers, laughing at their harm?

°4 *pale:* enclosure. 9 *dew:* bedew. *orbs:* fairy rings (circles of high grass). 10 *cowslips:* primroses. *pensioners:* royal bodyguards. 12 *favours:* gifts. 13 *savours:* perfumes. 16 *lob:* lout, lubber. 20 *passing fell:* surpassingly fierce. 23 *changeling:* creature exchanged by fairies for a stolen baby (among the fairies, the stolen child). 25 *trace:* traverse. 26 *perforce:* by force. 30 *square:* quarrel. 36 *Skim milk:* steals the cream off the milk. *quern:* handmill for grinding grain. 37 *bootless:* without result. 38 *barm:* foamy head (therefore the drink was flat).

40   Those that Hobgoblin call you, and sweet Puck,
        You do their work, and they shall have good luck.
        Are not you he?
PUCK: Thou speakest aright;
        I am that merry wanderer of the night.
        I jest to Oberon, and make him smile,
45   When I a fat and bean-fed horse beguile,
        Neighing in likeness of a filly foal;
        And sometime lurk I in a gossip's° bowl,
        In very likeness of a roasted crab,°
        And when she drinks, against her lips I bob,
50   And on her withered dewlap° pour the ale.
        The wisest aunt, telling the saddest tale,
        Sometime for three-foot stool mistaketh me:
        Then slip I from her bum, down topples she,
        And "tailor"° cries, and falls into a cough;
55   And then the whole quire° hold their hips and laugh,
        And waxen° in their mirth, and neeze,° and swear
        A merrier hour was never wasted° there.
        But room° fairy: here comes Oberon.
FAIRY: And here, my mistress. Would that he were gone.

Enter [OBERON] *the King of Fairies, at one door with his* TRAIN, *and the* QUEEN [TITANIA], *at another, with hers.*

60 **OBERON:** Ill met by moonlight, proud Titania.
QUEEN: What, jealous Oberon? Fairy, skip hence.
        I have forsworn his bed and company.
OBERON: Tarry, rash wanton,° Am not I thy lord?
QUEEN: Then I must be thy lady; but I know
65   When thou hast stol'n away from fairyland,
        And in the shape of Corin° sat all day,
        Playing on pipes of corn,° and versing love
        To amorous Phillida.° Why art thou here
        Come from the farthest steep of India?
70   But that, forsooth, the bouncing Amazon,°
        Your buskined° mistress and your warrior love,
        To Theseus must be wedded; and you come,
        To give their bed joy and prosperity.
OBERON: How canst thou thus, for shame, Titania,
75   Glance at my credit with° Hippolyta,
        Knowing I know thy love to Theseus?
        Didst thou not lead him through the glimmering night,
        From Perigenia, whom he ravishèd?

°47 *gossip's*: old woman's. 48 *crab*: crabapple (often put into ale). 50 *dewlap*: loose skin hanging about the throat. 54 *"tailor"*: (variously explained: perhaps the squatting position of the tailor, or "tailard"—one with a tail). 55 *quire*: choir, group. 56 *waxen*: increase. *neeze*: sneeze. 57 *wasted*: spent. 58 *room*: make room. 63 *Tarry, rash wanton*: wait, headstrong one. 66–68 *Corin, Phillida*: (traditional names in pastoral literature for a shepherd and his loved one, respectively). 67 *corn*: wheat straws. 70 *Amazon*: Hippolyta. 71 *buskined*: wearing boots. 75 *Glance . . . credit with*: hint at my favors from.

And make him with fair Aegles break his faith,
With Ariadne, and Antiopa°?   80
QUEEN: These are the forgeries of jealousy:
    And never, since the middle summer's spring,°
    Met we on hill, in dale, forest, or mead,
    By pavèd° fountain, or by rushy brook,
    Or in the beachéd margent° of the sea,   85
    To dance our ringlets to the whistling wind,
    But with thy brawls° thou hast disturbed our sport.
    Therefore° the winds, piping to us in vain,
    As in revenge, have sucked up from the sea
    Contagious° fogs: which falling in the land,   90
    Hath every pelting° river made so proud,
    That they have overborne their continents.°
    The ox hath therefore stretched his yoke in vain,
    The ploughman lost his sweat, and the green corn°
    Hath rotted, ere his youth attained a beard:°   95
    The fold° stands empty in the drownèd field,
    And crows are fatted with the murrion° flock.
    The nine men's morris° is filled up with mud;
    And the quaint mazes° in the wanton green,°
    For lack of tread, are undistinguishable.   100
    The human mortals want° their winter here,
    No night is now with hymn or carol blest;
    Therefore the moon, the governess of floods,
    Pale in her anger, washes all the air,
    That rheumatic diseases do abound.   105
    And thorough this distemperature,° we see
    The seasons alter: hoary-headed frosts
    Fall in the fresh lap of the crimson rose,
    And on old Hiems'° thin and icy crown,
    An odorous chaplet° of sweet summer buds   110
    Is, as in mockery, set. The spring, the summer,
    The childing° autumn, angry winter change
    Their wonted liveries:° and the mazèd° world,
    By their increase, now knows not which is which:
    And this same progeny of evils comes   115
    From our debate, from our dissension:
    We are their parents and original.
OBERON: Do you amend it then: it lies in you.
    Why should Titania cross her Oberon?

°78–80 *Perigenia . . . Antiopa:* women that Theseus supposedly loved and deserted. 82 *middle . . . spring:* beginning of midsummer. 84 *pavèd:* with a pebbly bottom. 85 *margent:* margin, shore. 87 *brawls:* A brawl was a group dance—*branle* in French—obviously accompanied by noisy shouting and clapping. 88–117 *Therefore . . . original:* (the disturbance in nature reflects the discord between Oberon and Titania). 90 *Contagious:* spreading pestilence. 91 *pelting:* paltry. 92 *overborne their continents:* overflown the banks that contain them. 94 *corn:* grain. 95 *beard:* the tassels on ripened grain. 96 *fold:* enclosure for livestock. 97 *murrion:* dead from murrain, a cattle disease. 98 *nine men's morris:* game played on squares cut in the grass on which stones or disks are moved. 99 *quaint mazes:* intricate paths. *wanton green:* luxuriant grass. 101 *want:* lack. 106 *distemperature:* upset in nature. 109 *Hiems:* god of winter. 110 *odorous chaplet:* sweet-smelling wreath. 112 *childing:* fruitful. 113 *wonted liveries:* accustomed dress. *mazèd:* amazed.

120   I do but beg a little changeling boy,
          To be my henchman.°
QUEEN: Set your heart at rest.
          The fairy land buys not the child of me.
          His mother was a vot'ress° of my order:
          And in the spicèd Indian air, by night,
125   Full often hath she gossiped by my side.
          And sat with me on Neptune's yellow sands,
          Marking th' embarkèd traders° on the flood:
          When we have laughed to see the sails conceive,
          And grow big-bellied with the wanton° wind:
130   Which she, with pretty and with swimming gait,
          Following (her womb then rich with my young squire)
          Would imitate, and sail upon the land,
          To fetch me trifles, and return again,
          As from a voyage, rich with merchandise.
135   But she, being mortal, of that boy did die,
          And for her sake, do I rear up her boy:
          And for her sake, I will not part with him.
OBERON: How long within this wood intend you stay?
QUEEN: Perchance till after Theseus' wedding day.
140   If you will patiently dance in our round,°
          And see our moonlight revels, go with us:
          If not, shun me, and I will spare° your haunts.
OBERON: Give me that boy, and I will go with thee.
QUEEN: Not for thy fairy kingdom. Fairies away
145   We shall chide downright, if I longer stay.

                              Exeunt [TITANIA *and her* TRAIN.]

OBERON: Well, go thy way. Thou shalt not from this grove,
          Till I torment thee for this injury.
          My gentle Puck come hither: thou rememb'rest,
          Since° once I sat upon a promontory,
150   And heard a mermaid, on a dolphin's back,
          Uttering such dulcet and harmonious breath,
          That the rude° sea grew civil° at her song,
          And certain stars shot madly from their spheres,
          To hear the sea-maid's music.
PUCK: I remember.
155 OBERON: That very time, I saw (but thou couldst not)
          Flying between the cold moon and the earth,
          Cupid, all armed: a certain aim he took
          At a fair Vestal,° thronèd by the west,
          And loosed his love-shaft smartly from his bow,
160   As it should pierce a hundred thousand hearts:
          But I might see young Cupid's fiery shaft
          Quenched in the chaste beams of the wat'ry moon:

°121 *henchman:* attendant. 123 *vot'ress:* vowed and devoted follower. 127 *traders:* merchant ships. 129 *wanton:* sportive. 140 *round:* round dance. 142 *spare:* shun. 149 *Since:* when. 152 *rude:* rough. *civil:* calm. 158 *Vestal:* virgin, probable reference to Queen Elizabeth.

And the imperial vot'ress° passèd on,
In maiden meditation, fancy-free.°
Yet marked I where the bolt° of Cupid fell.   165
It fell upon a little western flower;
Before, milk-white; now purple with love's wound,
And maidens call it love-in-idleness.°
Fetch me that flow'r: the herb I showed thee once.
The juice of it, on sleeping eyelids laid,   170
Will make or man or woman madly dote
Upon the next live creature that it sees.
Fetch me this herb, and be thou here again
Ere the leviathan° can swim a league.
PUCK: I'll put a girdle round about the earth,   175
In forty minutes.   [*Exit.*]
OBERON: Having once this juice,
I'll watch Titania when she is asleep,
And drop the liquor of it in her eyes:
The next thing then she waking looks upon,   180
(Be it on lion, bear, or wolf, or bull,
On meddling monkey, or on busy° ape)
She shall pursue it, with the soul of love.
And ere I take this charm from off her sight
(As I can take it with another herb)   185
I'll make her render up her page to me.
But who comes here? I am invisible,
And I will overhear their conference.

Enter DEMETRIUS, HELENA *following him.*

DEMETRIUS: I love thee not: therefore pursue me not.
Where is Lysander and fair Hermia?   190
The one I'll slay: the other slayeth me.
Thou told'st me they were stol'n unto this wood:
And here am I, and wood° within this wood:
Because I cannot meet my Hermia.
Hence, get thee gone, and follow me no more.   195
HELENA: You draw me, you hard-hearted adamant:°
But yet you draw not iron, for my heart
Is true as steel. Leave you your power to draw,
And I shall have no power to follow you.
DEMETRIUS: Do I entice you? Do I speak you fair°?   200
Or rather do I not in plainest truth
Tell you I do not, nor I cannot love you?
HELENA: And even for that, do I love you the more:
I am your spaniel: and Demetrius,
The more you beat me, I will fawn on you.   205
Use me but as your spaniel: spurn me, strike me,

°163 *imperial vot'ress:* royal devotee (Queen Elizabeth) of Diana. 164 *fancy-free:* free from love. 165 *bolt:* arrow.
168 *love-in-idleness:* pansy. 174 *leviathan:* whale. 182 *busy:* mischievous. 193 *wood:* crazy. 196 *adamant:* (1) magnet (2) impenetrably hard lodestone. 200 *speak you fair:* speak to you in a kindly way.

Neglect me, lose me: only give me leave,
Unworthy as I am, to follow you.
What worser place can I beg in your love
210   (And yet a place of high respect with me)
Than to be usèd as you use your dog.
DEMETRIUS: Tempt not too much the hatred of my spirit,
For I am sick, when I do look on thee.
HELENA: And I am sick, when I look not on you.
215 **DEMETRIUS:** You do impeach° your modesty too much,
To leave the city and commit yourself
Into the hands of one that loves you not,
To trust the opportunity of night,
And the ill counsel of a desert° place,
220   With the rich worth of your virginity.
HELENA: Your virtue is my privilege:° for that°.
It is not night, when I do see your face,
Therefore I think I am not in the night.
Nor doth this wood lack worlds of company,
225   For you, in my respect,° are all the world.
Then how can it be said I am alone,
When all the world is here to look on me?
DEMETRIUS: I'll run from thee and hide me in the brakes,°
And leave thee to the mercy of wild beasts.
230 **HELENA:** The wildest hath not such a heart as you.
Run when you will: the story shall be changed;
Apollo flies, and Daphne° holds the chase:
The dove pursues the griffin:° the mild hind°
Makes speed to catch the tiger. Bootless° speed,
235   When cowardice pursues, and valour flies.
DEMETRIUS: I will not stay° thy questions. Let me go:
Or if thou follow me, do not believe
But I shall do thee mischief in the wood.   [*Exit* DEMETRIUS.]
HELENA: Ay, in the temple, in the town, the field,
240   You do me mischief. Fie Demetrius,
Your wrongs do set a scandal on my sex:
We cannot fight for love, as men may do:
We should be wooed, and were not made to woo.
I'll follow thee and make a heaven of hell,
245   To die upon the hand I love so well.   *Exit.*
OBERON: Fare thee well nymph. Ere he do leave this grove,
Thou shalt fly him, and he shall seek thy love.

Enter PUCK.

Hast thou the flower there? Welcome wanderer.
PUCK: Ay, there it is.

°215 *impeach:* discredit. 219 *desert:* deserted. 221 *Your . . . privilege:* your attraction is my excuse (for coming). *for that:* because. 225 *respect:* regard. 228 *brakes:* thickets. 232 *Apollo . . . Daphne:* (in Ovid, Apollo pursues Daphne, who turns into a laurel tree). 233 *griffin:* legendary beast with the head of an eagle and the body of a lion. *hind:* doe. 234 *Bootless:* useless. 236 *stay:* wait for.

OBERON: I pray thee give it me.
I know a bank where the wild thyme blows,   250
Where oxlips and the nodding violet grows,
Quite over-canopied with luscious woodbine,
With sweet musk-roses, and with eglantine:
There sleeps Titania, sometime of the night,
Lulled in these flowers, with dances and delight: 255
And there the snake throws° her enamelled skin,
Weed° wide enough to wrap a fairy in.
And with the juice of this, I'll streak her eyes,
And make her full of hateful fantasies.
Take thou some of it, and seek through this grove: 260
A sweet Athenian lady is in love
With a disdainful youth: anoint his eyes.
But do it when the next thing he espies
May be the lady. Thou shalt know the man
By the Athenian garments he hath on.   265
Effect it with some care, that he may prove
More fond° on her, than she upon her love:
And look thou meet me ere the first cock crow.

PUCK: Fear not my lord: your servant shall do so.   *Exeunt.*

[Scene 2. Another part of the wood]

Enter TITANIA *Queen of Fairies with her train.*

QUEEN: Come, now a roundel° and a fairy song:
Then, for the third part of a minute, hence—
Some to kill cankers in the musk-rose buds,
Some war with reremice° for their leathren wings,
To make my small elves coats, and some keep back   5
The clamorous owl, that nightly hoots and wonders
At our quaint° spirits. Sing me now asleep:
Then to your offices,° and let me rest.

Fairies sing.

You spotted snakes with double° tongue,
   Thorny hedgehogs be not seen,   10
Newts and blind-worms,° do no wrong,
   Come not near our Fairy Queen.
   Philomele,° with melody,
   Sing in our sweet lullaby,
Lulla, lulla, lullaby, lulla, lulla, lullaby.   15
   Never harm,
   Nor spell, nor charm,
Come our lovely lady nigh.
So good night, with lullaby.

°256 *throws:* casts off. 257 *weed:* garment. 267 *fond:* doting, madly in love. 1 *roundel:* dance in a ring. 4 *reremice:* bats. 7 *quaint:* dainty. 8 *offices:* duties. 9 *double:* forked. 11 *blind-worms:* legless lizards. 13 *Philomele:* the nightingale.

20 **First Fairy:** Weaving spiders come not here:
Hence you long-legged spinners, hence:
Beetles black approach not near:
Worm nor snail do no offence.
Philomele, with melody, &c. *She sleeps.*
25 **Second Fairy:** Hence away: now all is well:
One aloof stand sentinel. [*Exeunt fairies.*]

Enter Oberon [*and applies the flower juice to* Titania's *eyelids.*]

Oberon: What thou seest, when thou dost wake,
Do it for thy true love take:
Love and languish for his sake.
30 Be it ounce,° or cat, or bear,
Pard,° or boar with bristled hair,
In thy eye that shall appear,
When thou wak'st, it is thy dear:
Wake when some vile thing is near. [*Exit.*]

Enter Lysander *and* Hermia.

35 **Lysander:** Fair love, you faint with wand'ring in the wood:
And to speak troth° I have forgot our way.
We'll rest us Hermia, if you think it good,
And tarry for the comfort of the day.
Hermia: Be't so Lysander: find you out a bed:
40 For I upon this bank will rest my head.
Lysander: One turf shall serve as pillow for us both,
One heart, one bed, two bosoms, and one troth.°
Hermia: Nay good Lysander: for my sake, my dear,
Lie further off yet; do not lie so near.
45 **Lysander:** O take the sense, sweet, of my innocence.°
Love takes the meaning in love's conference.°
I mean that my heart unto yours is knit,
So that but one heart we can make of it:
Two bosoms interchainèd with an oath,
50 So then two bosoms and a single troth.
Then by your side no bed-room me deny:
For lying so, Hermia, I do not lie.
Hermia: Lysander riddles very prettily.
Now much beshrew° my manners and my pride,
55 If Hermia meant to say Lysander lied.
But gentle friend, for love and courtesy,
Lie further off, in human modesty:
Such separation as may well be said
Becomes a virtuous bachelor and a maid,
60 So far be distant, and good night sweet friend:
Thy love ne'er alter till thy sweet life end.

°30 *ounce:* lynx. 31 *Pard:* leopard. 36 *troth:* truth. 42 *troth:* true love. 45 *take . . . innocence:* understand the innocence of my remark. 46 *Love . . . conference:* Love enables lovers to understand each other when they converse. 54 *beshrew:* curse.

LYSANDER: Amen, amen, to that fair prayer say I,
    And then end life, when I end loyalty.
    Here is my bed: sleep give thee all his rest.
HERMIA: With half that wish, the wisher's eyes be pressed.°   65

                                          They sleep.

Enter PUCK.

PUCK: Through the forest have I gone,
    But Athenian found I none,
    On whose eyes I might approve°
    This flower's force in stirring love.
    Night and silence. Who is here?   70
    Weeds° of Athens he doth wear:
    This is he (my master said)
    Despiséd the Athenian maid:
    And here the maiden, sleeping sound,
    On the dank and dirty ground.   75
    Pretty soul, she durst not lie
    Near this lack-love, this kill-courtesy.
    Churl, upon thy eyes I throw
    All the power this charm doth owe.°
    When thou wak'st, let love forbid   80
    Sleep his seat on thy eyelid.°
    So awake when I am gone:
    For I must now to Oberon.   *Exit.*

Enter DEMETRIUS and HELENA running.

HELENA: Stay, thou kill me, sweet Demetrius.
DEMETRIUS: I charge thee hence, and do not haunt me thus.   85
HELENA: O, wilt thou darkling° leave me? Do not so.
DEMETRIUS: Stay on thy peril: I alone will go.   *Exit DEMETRIUS.*
HELENA: O, I am out of breath in this fond° chase:
    The more my prayer, the lesser is my grace.°
    Happy is Hermia, wheresoe'er she lies: 90
    For she hath blesséd and attractive eyes.
    How came her eyes so bright? Not with salt tears:
    If so, my eyes are oft'ner washed than hers.
    No, no: I am as ugly as a bear:
    For beasts that meet me run away for fear.   95
    Therefore no marvel, though Demetrius
    Do as a monster, fly my presence thus.
    What wicked and dissembling glass° of mine,

°65 *pressed:* i.e., by sleep. 68 *approve:* test. 71 *Weeds:* garments. 79 *owe:* own. 80–81 *forbid . . . eyelid:* make you sleepless (with love). 86 *darkling:* in the dark. 88 *fond:* foolishly doting. 89 *my grace:* favor shown to me. 98 *glass:* looking glass.

Made me compare with Hermia's sphery eyne°!
100　　But who is here? Lysander, on the ground?
Dead, or asleep? I see no blood, no wound.
Lysander, if you live, good sir awake.
LYSANDER: [*Wakes.*] And run through fire, I will for thy sweet sake.
Transparent° Helena, nature shows art,
105　　That through thy bosom, makes me see thy heart.
Where is Demetrius? O how fit a word
Is that vile name to perish on my sword!
HELENA: Do not say so, Lysander, say not so.
What though he love your Hermia? Lord, what though?
110　　Yet Hermia still loves you: then be content.
LYSANDER: Content with Hermia? No: I do repent
The tedious minutes I with her have spent.
Not Hermia, but Helena I love.
Who will not change a raven for a dove?
115　　The will of man is by his reason swayed:°
And reason says you are the worthier maid.
Things growing are not ripe until their season:
So I, being young, till now ripe° not to reason.
And touching now the point° of human skill,°
120　　Reason becomes the marshal to my will,
And leads me to your eyes; where I o'erlook
Love's stories, written in love's richest book.
HELENA: Wherefore° was I to this keen mockery born?
When at your hands did I deserve this scorn?
125　　Is't not enough, is't not enough, young man,
That I did never, no, nor never can,
Deserve a sweet look from Demetrius' eye,
But you must flout° my insufficiency?
Good troth you do me wrong, good sooth you do,
130　　In such disdainful manner me to woo.
But fare you well: perforce I must confess,
I thought you lord of more true gentleness.°
O, that a lady, of one man refused,
Should of another, therefore be abused!　　　　　　　　*Exit.*
135 LYSANDER: She sees not Hermia. Hermia, sleep thou there,
And never mayst thou come Lysander near.
For, as a surfeit of the sweetest things
The deepest loathing to the stomach brings:
Or as the heresies that men do leave,
140　　Are hated most of those they did deceive:
So thou, my surfeit and my heresy,
Of all be hated; but the most, of me:
And all my powers, address your love and might,
To honour Helen, and to be her knight.　　　　　　　　*Exit.*

°99 *sphery eyne:* starry eyes. 104 *Transparent:* radiant. 115 *swayed:* ruled. 118 *ripe:* mature. 119 *point:* peak. *skill:* knowledge. 123 *Wherefore:* why. 128 *flout:* mock. 132 *lord . . . gentleness:* more of a gentleman.

HERMIA: [*Wakes.*] Help me Lysander, help me: do thy best   145
    To pluck this crawling serpent from my breast.
    Ay me, for pity. What a dream was here?
    Lysander, look how I do quake with fear.
    Methought a serpent eat my heart away,
    And you sat smiling at his cruel prey.°   150
    Lysander: what, removed? Lysander, lord!
    What, out of hearing, gone? No sound, no word?
    Alack, where are you? Speak, and if you hear:
    Speak, of° all loves. I swoon almost with fear.
    No? Then I well perceive you are not nigh: 155
    Either death, or you, I'll find immediately.   *Exit.*

ACT 3

[Scene 1. The wood]

Enter the CLOWNS [QUINCE, SNUG, BOTTOM, FLUTE, SNOUT, *and* STARVELING.]

BOTTOM: Are we all met?
QUINCE: Pat, pat: and here's a marvellous convenient place for
    our rehearsal. This green plot shall be our stage, this
    hawthorn brake° our tiring-house,° and we will do it in
    action, as we will do it before the duke.   5
BOTTOM: Peter Quince?
QUINCE: What sayest thou, bully° Bottom?
BOTTOM: There are things in this Comedy of Pyramus and Thisby
    that will never please. First, Pyramus must draw a sword
    to kill himself; which the ladies cannot abide. How   10
    answer you that?
SNOUT: By'r lakin,° a parlous° fear.
STARVELING: I believe we must leave the killing out, when all is done.
BOTTOM: Not a whit: I have a device to make all well. Write me
    a prologue, and let the prologue seem to say, we will   15
    do no harm with our swords, and that Pyramus is not
    killed indeed: and for the more better assurance, tell
    them that I Pyramus am not Pyramus, but Bottom the
    weaver: this will put them out of fear.
QUINCE: Well, we will have such a prologue, and it shall be   20
    written in eight and six.°
BOTTOM: No, make it two more: let it be written in eight and
    eight.
SNOUT: Will not the ladies be afeared of the lion?
STARVELING: I fear it, I promise you.   25
BOTTOM: Masters, you ought to consider with yourselves, to bring
    in (God shield us) a lion among ladies, is a most dreadful

---

°150 *prey:* preying. 154 *of:* for the sake of. 4 *brake:* thicket. *tiring-house:* dressing room. 7 *bully:* "old pal." 12 *By'r lakin:* mild oath, "by Our Lady." *parlous:* awful, perilous. 21 *eight and six:* alternate lines of eight and six syllables (the ballad meter).

thing. For there is not a more fearful wild-fowl than
your lion living: and we ought to look to't.

30 SNOUT: Therefore another prologue must tell he is not a lion.

BOTTOM: Nay, you must name his name, and half his face must be
seen through the lion's neck, and he himself must speak
through, saying thus, or to the same defect:° "Ladies,"
or "Fair ladies—I would wish you," or "I would request

35 you," or "I would entreat you, not to fear,
not to tremble: my life for yours. If you think I come
hither as a lion, it were pity of my life. No, I am no
such thing: I am a man as other men are." And there
indeed let him name his name, and tell them plainly he

40 is Snug the joiner.

QUINCE: Well, it shall be so, but there is two hard things: that is,
to bring the moonlight into a chamber: for you know,
Pyramus and Thisby meet by moonlight.

SNOUT: Doth the moon shine that night we play our play?

45 BOTTOM: A calendar, a calendar: look in the almanac: find out
moonshine, find out moonshine.

QUINCE: Yes, it doth shine that night.

BOTTOM: Why then may you leave a casement of the great
chamber window, where we play, open; and the moon may

50 shine in at the casement.

QUINCE: Ay, or else one must come in with a bush of thorns° and
a lantern, and say he comes to disfigure,° or to present,
the person of Moonshine. Then, there is another thing;
we must have a wall in the great chamber: for Pyramus

55 and Thisby, says the story, did talk through the chink
of a wall.

SNOUT: You can never bring in a wall. What say you, Bottom?

BOTTOM: Some man or other must present wall: and let him have
some plaster, or some loam, or some rough-cast° about

60 him, to signify wall; and let him hold his fingers thus:
and through that cranny, shall Pyramus and Thisby whisper.

QUINCE: If that may be, then all is well. Come, sit down every
mother's son, and rehearse your parts. Pyramus, you
begin: when you have spoken your speech, enter into that

65 brake, and so every one according to his cue.

Enter PUCK.

PUCK: What hempen homespuns° have we swagg'ring here,
So near the cradle of the Fairy Queen?
What, a play toward°? I'll be an auditor,
An actor too perhaps, if I see cause.

70 QUINCE: Speak Pyramus. Thisby stand forth.

°33 *defect:* (he means "effect"). 51 *bush of thorns:* bundle of firewood (the man in the moon was supposed to have
been placed there as a punishment for gathering wood on Sundays). 52 *disfigure:* (he means "figure," symbolize).
59 *rough-cast:* coarse plaster of lime and gravel. 66 *hempen homespuns:* wearers of clothing spun at home from
hemp. 68 *toward:* in preparation.

PYRAMUS: Thisby, the flowers of odious savours sweet—
QUINCE: "Odorous, odorous."
PYRAMUS: —odours savours sweet,
    So hath thy breath, my dearest Thisby dear.
    But hark, a voice: stay thou but here awhile,   75
    And by and by I will to thee appear.   *Exit* PYRAMUS.
PUCK: A stranger Pyramus than e'er played here.   [*Exit.*]
THISBY: Must I speak now?
QUINCE: Ay marry must you. For you must understand he goes
    but to see a noise that he heard, and is to come again.   80
THISBY: Most radiant Pyramus, most lily-white of hue,
    Of colour like the red rose, on triumphant brier,
  Most brisky juvenal,° and eke most lovely Jew,°
    As true as truest horse, that yet would never tire,
  I'll meet thee Pyramus, at Ninny's tomb.   85
QUINCE: "Ninus' tomb,"° man: why, you must not speak that yet.
    That you answer to Pyramus. You speak all your part
    at once, cues and all. Pyramus, enter; your cue is past:
    it is "never tire."
THISBY: O—As true as truest horse, that yet would never tire.   90

Enter PYRAMUS *with the ass-head [followed by* PUCK*]*.

PYRAMUS: If I were fair, Thisby, I were only thine.
QUINCE: O monstrous! O strange! We are haunted. Pray masters,
    fly masters. Help!   *The clowns all exeunt.*
PUCK: I'll follow you: I'll lead you about a round,°
    Through bog, through bush, through brake, through brier.   95
  Sometime a horse I'll be, sometime a hound,
    A hog, a headless bear, sometime a fire,
  And neigh, and bark, and grunt, and roar, and burn,
  Like horse, hound, hog, bear, fire, at every turn.   *Exit.*
BOTTOM: Why do they run away? This is a knavery of them to   100
    make me afeared.

Enter SNOUT.

SNOUT: O Bottom, thou art changed. What do I see on thee?
BOTTOM: What do you see? You see an ass-head of your own, do
    you?   [*Exit* SNOUT.]

Enter QUINCE.

QUINCE: Bless thee Bottom, bless thee. Thou art translated.°   *Exit.* 105
BOTTOM: I see their knavery. This is to make an ass of me, to
    fright me if they could: but I will not stir from this
    place, do what they can. I will walk up and down here,
    and will sing that they shall hear I am not afraid.

°83 *brisky juvenal:* lively youth. *Jew:* diminutive of either "juvenal" or "jewel." 86 *Ninus' tomb:* (tomb of the founder of Nineveh, and meeting place of the lovers in Ovid's version of the Pyramus story). 94 *about a round:* in circles, like a round dance (round about). 105 *translated:* transformed.

110   [*Sings.*]   The woose° cock, so black of hue,
           With orange tawny bill,
           The throstle,° with his note so true,
           The wren, with little quill.°

TITANIA: What angel wakes me from my flow'ry bed?

115   BOTTOM: [*Sings.*] The finch, the sparrow, and the lark,
           The plain-song° cuckoo gray:
           Whose note full many a man doth mark,
           And dares not answer, nay.

For indeed, who would set his wit to° so foolish a bird?

120   Who would give a bird the lie,° though he cry "cuckoo"°
never so°?

TITANIA: I pray thee, gentle mortal, sing again.
     Mine ear is much enamoured of thy note:
     So is mine eye enthrallèd to thy shape

125   And thy fair virtue's force (perforce°) doth move me,
     On the first view to say, to swear, I love thee.

BOTTOM: Methinks mistress, you should have little reason for
     that. And yet, to say the truth, reason and love keep
     little company together now-a-days. The more the pity,

130   That some honest neighbours will not make them friends.
     Nay, I can gleek° upon occasion.

TITANIA: Thou art as wise as thou art beautiful.

BOTTOM: Not so neither: but if I had wit enough to get out of
     this wood, I have enough to serve mine own turn.

135   TITANIA: Out of this wood do not desire to go:
     Thou shalt remain here, whether thou wilt or no.
     I am a spirit of no common rate:°
     The summer still doth tend upon my state,°
     And I do love thee: therefore go with me.

140   I'll give thee fairies to attend on thee:
     And they shall fetch thee jewels from the deep,
     And sing, while thou on pressèd flowers dost sleep:
     And I will purge thy mortal grossness so,
     That thou shalt like an airy spirit go.

145   Peaseblossom, Cobweb, Moth,° and Mustardseed!

Enter four FAIRIES.

PEASEBLOSSOM: Ready.
COBWEB: And I.
MOTH: And I.
MUSTARDSEED: And I.
ALL: Where shall we go?

°110 *woose:* ousel, blackbird. 112 *throstle:* thrush. 113 *quill:* piping note. 116 *plain-song:* sounding a simple unvaried note. 119 *set . . . to:* match his wit against. 120 *Who . . . lie:* who could call a bird a liar. *"cuckoo":* (which sounded like "cuckold" = a deceived husband). 121 *never so:* i.e., often. 125 *perforce:* by force. 131 *gleek:* joke satirically. 137 *rate:* rank, value. 138 *still . . . state:* always serves as an attendant in my royal train. 145 *Moth:* mote (so pronounced), tiny speck.

TITANIA: Be kind and courteous to this gentleman,
    Hop in his walks and gambol in° his eyes,
    Feed him with apricocks° and dewberries,°   150
    With purple grapes, green figs, and mulberries.
    The honey-bags steal from the humblebees,°
    And for night-tapers, crop° their waxen thighs,
    And light them at the fiery glow-worm's eyes,
    To have my love to bed and to arise: 155
    And pluck the wings from painted butterflies,
    To fan the moonbeams from his sleeping eyes.
    Nod to him elves, and do him courtesies.

PEASEBLOSSOM: Hail, mortal.

COBWEB: Hail.   160

MOTH: Hail.

MUSTARDSEED: Hail.

BOTTOM: I cry your worships mercy,° heartily: I beseech your
    worship's name.

COBWEB: Cobweb.   165

BOTTOM: I shall desire you of more acquaintance, good Master
    Cobweb: if I cut my finger,° I shall make bold with you.
    Your name, honest gentleman?

PEASEBLOSSOM: Peaseblossom.

BOTTOM: I pray you commend me° to Mistress Squash,° your mother,   170
    and to Master Peascod,° your father. Good Master Peaseblossom,
    I shall desire you of more acquaintance, too.
    Your name I beseech you sir?

MUSTARDSEED: Mustardseed.

BOTTOM: Good Master Mustardseed, I know your patience well.   175
    That same cowardly giant-like ox beef hath devoured
    many a gentleman of your house. I promise you, your
    kindred hath made my eyes water ere now. I desire you
    of more acquaintance, good Master Mustardseed.

TITANIA: Come wait upon him: lead him to my bower.   180
        The moon methinks looks with a wat'ry eye:
       And when she weeps, weeps every little flower,
        Lamenting some enforcèd° chastity.
        Tie up my lover's tongue, bring him silently.   *Exeunt.*

[Scene 2. Another part of the wood]

Enter [OBERON,] King of Fairies, solus.°

OBERON: I wonder if Titania be awaked;
    Then what it was that next came in her eye,
    Which she must dote on in extremity.

Enter PUCK.

°149 *gambol in*: caper before. 150 *apricocks*: apricots. *dewberries*: blackberries. 152 *humblebees*: bumblebees. 153
crop: clip. 163 *I . . . mercy*: I respectfully beg your pardons. 167 *cut my finger*: (cobwebs were used to stop bleeding). 170 *commend me*: offer my respects. *Squash*: unripe peapod. 171 *Peascod*: ripe peapod. 183 *enforcèd*: violated.
S.D.: *solus*: alone.

Here comes my messenger. How now, mad spirit?
5   What night-rule° now about this haunted grove?
PUCK: My mistress with a monster is in love.
Near to her close and consecrated bower,
While she was in her dull° and sleeping hour,
A crew of patches,° rude mechanicals,°
10   That work for bread upon Athenian stalls,°
Were met together to rehearse a play,
Intended for great Theseus' nuptial day:
The shallowest thickskin of that barren sort,°
Who Pyramus presented in their sport,
15   Forsook his scene and entered in a brake:
When I did him at this advantage take,
An ass's nole° I fixèd on his head.
Anon° his Thisby must be answerèd,
And forth my mimic° comes. When they him spy,
20   As wild geese, that the creeping fowler° eye,
Or russet-pated choughs,° many in sort,°
Rising and cawing at the gun's report,
Sever themselves and madly sweep the sky,
So at his sight away his fellows fly:
25   And at our stamp, here o'er and o'er one falls:
He murder cries, and help from Athens calls.
Their sense thus weak, lost with their fears thus strong,
Made senseless things begin to do them wrong.
For briers and thorns at their apparel snatch:
30   Some° sleeves, some hats; from yielders, all things catch°
I led them on in this distracted° fear,
And left sweet Pyramus translated there:
When in that moment (so it came to pass)
Titania waked, and straightway loved an ass.
35 OBERON: This falls out better than I could devise.
But has thou yet latched° the Athenian's eyes
With the love-juice, as I did bid thee do?
PUCK: I took him sleeping (that is finished too)
And the Athenian woman by his side;
40   That when he waked, of force° she must be eyed.

Enter DEMETRIUS and HERMIA.

OBERON: Stand close:° this is the same Athenian.
PUCK: This is the woman: but not this the man.
DEMETRIUS: O why rebuke you him that loves you so?
Lay breath so bitter on your bitter foe.
45 HERMIA: Now I but chide: but I should use thee worse,
For thou, I fear, hast given me cause to curse.

°5 *night-rule:* diversion ("misrule") in the night. 8 *dull:* drowsy. 9 *patches:* fools. *mechanicals:* workers. 10 *stalls:* shops. 13 *barren sort:* stupid crew. 17 *nole:* head, noodle. 18 *Anon:* presently. 19 *mimic:* actor. 20 *fowler:* hunter of fowl. 21 *russet-pated choughs:* grey-headed jackdaws. *sort:* a flock. 30 *Some:* i.e., snatch. *from yielders . . . catch:* (everything joins in to harm the weak). 31 *distracted:* maddened. 36 *latched:* moistened. 40 *of force:* by necessity. 41 *close:* hidden.

If thou hast slain Lysander in his sleep,
Being o'er shoes in blood, plunge in the deep,
And kill me too.
The sun was not so true unto the day,   50
As he to me. Would he have stolen away
From sleeping Hermia? I'll believe as soon
This whole° earth may be bored,° and that the moon
May through the center creep, and so displease
Her brother's noontide with th' Antipodes.°   55
It cannot be but thou hast murdered him.
So should a murderer look; so dead,° so grim.
DEMETRIUS: So should the murdered look, and so should I,
    Pierced through the heart with your stern cruelty.
    Yet you, the murderer, look as bright, as clear   60
    As yonder Venus in her glimmering sphere.°
HERMIA: What's this to my Lysander? Where is he?
    Ah good Demetrius, wilt thou give him me?
DEMETRIUS: I had rather give his carcass to my hounds.
HERMIA: Out dog, out cur! Thou driv'st me past the bounds   65
    Of maiden's patience. Hast thou slain him then?
    Henceforth be never numbered among men.
    O, once tell true: tell true, even for my sake:
    Durst thou have looked upon him, being awake?
    And hast thou killed him sleeping? O brave touch°!   70
    Could not a worm,° an adder, do so much?
    An adder did it: for with doubler tongue°
    Than thine, thou serpent, never adder stung.
DEMETRIUS: You spend your passion on a misprised mood°
    I am not guilty of Lysander's blood: 75
    Nor is he dead, for aught that I can tell.
HERMIA: I pray thee, tell me then that he is well.
DEMETRIUS: And if I could, what should I get therefore?
HERMIA: A privilege never to see me more:
    And from thy hated presence part I so: 80
    See me no more, whether he be dead or no.   *Exit.*
DEMETRIUS: There is no following her in this fierce vein.
    Here therefore for a while I will remain.
    So sorrow's heaviness doth heavier grow
    For debt that bankrout sleep doth sorrow owe:°   85
    Which now in some slight measure it will pay,
    If for his tender° here I make some stay.°   *Lies down.*
OBERON: What hast thou done? Thou hast mistaken quite,
    And laid the love-juice on some true-love's sight.

°53 *whole:* solid. *be bored:* have a hole bored through it. 55 *Her brother's . . . Antipodes:* the noon of her brother
sun, by appearing among the Antipodes (the people on the other side of the earth). 57 *dead:* deadly. 61 *sphere:*
(in the Ptolemaic system, each planet moved in its own sphere around the earth). 70 *brave touch:* splendid stroke
(ironic). 71 *worm:* snake. 72 *doubler tongue:* (1) tongue more forked (2) more deceitful speech. 74 *on . . . mood:*
in mistaken anger. 85 *For debt . . . owe:* because sleep cannot pay the debt of repose he owes the man who is kept
awake by sorrow. 87 *tender:* offer. *stay:* pause.

90   Of thy misprision° must perforce° ensue
        Some true love turned, and not a false turned true.
PUCK: Then fate o'errules, that one man holding troth,
        A million fail, confounding° oath on oath.°
OBERON: About the wood, go swifter than the wind,
95   And Helena of Athens look thou find.
        All fancy-sick° she is, and pale of cheer,°
        With sighs of love, that costs the fresh blood dear.
        By some illusion see thou bring her here:
        I'll charm his eyes against she do appear.°
100 **PUCK:** I go, I go, look how I go.
        Swifter than arrow from the Tartar's bow.°   *Exit.*
OBERON: Flower of this purple dye,
            Hit with Cupid's archery,
            Sink in apple of his eye:
105   When his love he doth espy,
            Let her shine as gloriously
            As the Venus of the sky.
            When thou wak'st, if she be by,
            Beg of her for remedy.

Enter PUCK.

110 **PUCK:** Captain of our fairy band,
            Helena is here at hand,
            And the youth, mistook by me,
            Pleading for a lover's fee.°
            Shall we their fond pageant° see?
115   Lord, what fools these mortals be!
OBERON: Stand aside. The noise they make
            Will cause Demetrius to awake.
PUCK: Then will two at once woo one:
            That must needs be sport alone.°
120   And those things do best please me
            That befall prepost' rously.

Enter LYSANDER *and* HELENA.

LYSANDER: Why should you think that I should woo in scorn?
            Scorn and derision never come in tears.
            Look when I vow, I weep: and vows so born,
125   In their nativity all truth appears.°
            How can these things in me seem scorn to you,
            Bearing the badge° of faith to prove them true?
HELENA: You do advance your cunning more and more.
            When truth kills truth,° O devilish-holy fray!

°90 *misprision:* mistake. *perforce:* of necessity. 93 *confounding:* destroying. *oath on oath:* one oath after another. 96 *fancy-sick:* lovesick. *cheer:* face. 99 *against . . . appear:* in preparation for her appearance. 101 *Tartar's bow:* (the Tartars, who used powerful Oriental bows, were famed as archers). 113 *fee:* reward. 114 *fond pageant:* foolish spectacle. 119 *alone:* unique. 124–25 *vows . . . appears:* vows born in weeping must be true ones. 127 *badge:* (1) outward signs (2) family crest. 129 *truth kills truth:* Former true love is killed by vows of present true love.

These vows are Hermia's. Will you give her o'er?   130
Weigh oath with oath, and you will nothing weigh.
Your vows to her and me, put in two scales,
Will even weigh: and both as light as tales.
LYSANDER: I had no judgment, when to her I swore.
HELENA: Nor none, in my mind, now you give her o'er.   135
LYSANDER: Demetrius loves her: and he loves not you.
DEMETRIUS: [*Awakes.*] O Helen, goddess, nymph, perfect, divine,
To what, my love, shall I compare thine eyne!
Crystal is muddy. O, how ripe in show,
Thy lips, those kissing cherries, tempting grow!   140
That pure congealèd white, high Taurus'° snow,
Fanned with the eastern wind, turns to a crow,
When thou hold'st up thy hand. O let me kiss
This princess of pure white,° this seal of bliss.
HELENA: O spite! O hell! I see you all are bent   145
To set against me, for your merriment.
If you were civil,° and knew courtesy,
You would not do me thus much injury.
Can you not hate me, as I know you do,
But you must join in souls° to mock me too?   150
If you were men, as men you are in show,
You would not use a gentle lady so;
To vow, and swear, and superpraise my parts,°
When I am sure you hate me with your hearts.
You both are rivals, and love Hermia: 155
And now both rivals, to mock Helena.
A trim° exploit, a manly enterprise,
To conjure tears up in a poor maid's eyes
With your derision. None of noble sort
Would so offend a virgin, and extort°   160
A poor soul's patience, all to make you sport.
LYSANDER: You are unkind, Demetrius: be not so.
For you love Hermia: this you know I know.
And here, with all good will, with all my heart,
In Hermia's love I yield you up my part: 165
And yours of Helena to be bequeath,
Whom I do love, and will do to my death.
HELENA: Never did mockers waste more idle breath.
DEMETRIUS: Lysander, keep thy Hermia: I will none,°
If e'er I loved her, all that love is gone.   170
My heart to her but as guest-wise sojourned:°
And now to Helen is it home returned,
There to remain.
LYSANDER: Helen, it is not so.

°141 *Taurus:* mountain range in Asia Minor. 144 *princess . . . white:* sovereign example of whiteness (her hand). 147 *civil:* well behaved. 150 *join in souls:* agree in spirit. 153 *parts:* qualities. 157 *trim:* fine (ironic). 160 *extort:* wring. 169 *none:* have none of her. 171 *to her . . . sojourned:* visited her only as a guest.

DEMETRIUS: Disparage not the faith thou dost not know,
175   Lest to thy peril thou aby it dear.°
      Look where thy love comes: yonder is thy dear.

Enter HERMIA.

HERMIA: Dark night, that from the eye his function takes,
      The ear more quick of apprehension makes.
      Wherein it doth impair the seeing sense,
180   It pays the hearing double recompense.
      Thou art not by mine eye, Lysander, found:
      Mine ear, I thank it, brought me to thy sound.
      But why unkindly didst thou leave me so?
LYSANDER: Why should he stay, whom love doth press to go?
185 **HERMIA:** What love could press Lysander from my side?
LYSANDER: Lysander's love, that would not let him bide—
      Fair Helena: who more engilds the night
      Than all your fiery oes and eyes of light.°
      Why seek'st thou me? Could not this make thee know,
190   The hate I bare thee made me leave thee so?
HERMIA: You speak not as you think: it cannot be.
HELENA: Lo: She is one of this confederacy.
      Now I perceive they have conjoined all three,
      To fashion this false sport in spite of° me.
195   Injurious° Hermia, most ungrateful maid,
      Have you conspired, have you with these contrived
      To bait° me with this foul derision?
      Is all the counsel° that we two have shared,
      The sisters' vows, the hours that we have spent,
200   When we have chid the hasty-footed time
      For parting us; O, is all forgot?
      All schooldays' friendship, childhood innocence?
      We Hermia, like two artificial° gods,
      Have with our needles created both one flower,
205   Both on one sampler,° sitting on one cushion,
      Both warbling of one song, both in one key;
      As if our hands, our sides, voices, and minds
      Had been incorporate.° So we grew together,
      Like to a double cherry, seeming parted,
210   But yet an union in partition,
      Two lovely berries moulded on one stem:
      So with two seeming bodies, but one heart,
      Two of the first, like coats in heraldry,
      Due but to one, and crownèd with one crest.°
215   And will you rent° our ancient love asunder,
      To join with men in scorning your poor friend?

°175 *aby it dear:* buy it at a high price. 188 *oes . . . light:* stars. 194 *in spite of:* to spite. 195 *Injurious:* insulting. 197 *bait:* attack. 198 *counsel:* secrets. 203 *artificial:* skilled in art. 205 *sampler:* work of embroidery. 208 *incorporate:* in one body. 213–14 *Two . . . crest:* (the two bodies being) like double coats of arms joined under one crest (with one heart). 215 *rent:* rend, tear.

It is not friendly, 'tis not maidenly.
Our sex, as well as I, may chide you for it;
Though I alone do feel the injury.
HERMIA: I am amazèd at your passionate words: 220
    I scorn you not. It seems that you scorn me.
HELENA: Have you not set Lysander, as in scorn,
    To follow me, and praise my eyes and face?
    And made your other love, Demetrius
    (Who even but now did spurn° me with his foot)   225
    To call me goddess, nymph, divine, and rare,
    Precious, celestial? Wherefore speaks he this
    To her he hates? And wherefore doth Lysander
    Deny your love, so rich within his soul,
    And tender° me (forsooth) affection,   230
    But by your setting on, by your consent?
    What though I be not so in grace° as you,
    So hung upon with love, so fortunate,
    But miserable most, to love unloved?
    This you should pity, rather than despise.   235
HERMIA: I understand not what you mean by this.
HELENA: Ay, do. Persèver, counterfeit sad° looks:
    Make mouths upon° me when I turn my back:
    Wink each at other, hold the sweet jest up.
    This sport well carried, shall be chronicled.°   240
    If you have any pity, grace, or manners,
    You would not make me such an argument.°
    But fare ye well: 'tis partly my own fault:
    Which death or absence soon shall remedy.
LYSANDER: Stay, gentle Helena: hear my excuse,   245
    My love, my life, my soul, fair Helena.
HELENA: O excellent!
HERMIA: Sweet, do not scorn her so.
DEMETRIUS: If she cannot entreat,° I can compel.
LYSANDER: Thou canst compel no more than she entreat.
    Thy threats have no more strength than her weak prayers.   250
    Helen, I love thee, by my life I do:
    I swear by that which I will lose for thee.
    To prove° him false that says I love thee not.
DEMETRIUS: I say I love thee more than he can do.
LYSANDER: If thou say so, withdraw, and prove° it too.   255
DEMETRIUS: Quick, Come.
HERMIA: Lysander, whereto tends all this?
LYSANDER: Away, you Ethiope.°
DEMETRIUS: No, no, sir,
    Seem to break loose: take on as you would follow;
    But yet come not.° You are a tame man, go.

°225 *spurn:* kick. 230 *tender:* offer. 232 *in grace:* favored. 237 *sad:* serious. 238 *mouths upon:* faces at. 240 *chronicled:* written down in the history books. 242 *argument:* subject (of your mockery). 248 *entreat:* sway you by entreaty. 253, 255 *prove:* i.e., by a duel. 257 *Ethiope:* (because she is a brunette). 258–59 *Seem . . . not:* You only seem to break loose from Hermia and pretend to follow me to a duel, but you actually hold back.

260   LYSANDER: Hang off,° thou cat, thou burr: vile thing, let loose;
         Or I will shake thee from me like a serpent.
       HERMIA: Why are you grown so rude? What change is this,
         Sweet love?
       LYSANDER: Thy love? Out, tawny Tartar, out;
         Out, loathèd med'cine: O hated potion, hence!
       HERMIA: Do you not jest?
265   HELENA: Yes sooth: and so do you.
       LYSANDER: Demetrius, I will keep my word° with thee.
       DEMETRIUS: I would I had your bond.° For I perceive
         A weak bond holds you. I'll not trust your word.
       LYSANDER: What? Should I hurt her, strike her, kill her dead?
270   Although I hate her, I'll not harm her so.
       HERMIA: What? Can you do me greater harm than hate?
         Hate me, wherefore°? O me, what news,° my love?
         Am not I Hermia? Are not you Lysander?
         I am as fair now, as I was erewhile.°
275   Since night, you loved me; yet since night, you left me.
         Why then, you left me—O, the gods forbid—
         In earnest, shall I say?
       LYSANDER: Ay, by my life:
         And never did desire to see thee more.
         Therefore be out of hope, of question, of doubt:
280   Be certain: nothing truer: 'tis no jest
         That I do hate thee, and love Helena.
       HERMIA: O me, you juggler,° you canker blossom,°
         You thief of love: what, have you come by night,
         And stol'n my love's heart from him?
       HELENA: Fine, i' faith.
285   Have you no modesty, no maiden shame,
         No touch of bashfulness? What, will you tear
         Impatient answers from my gentle tongue?
         Fie, fie, you counterfeit, you puppet,° you.
       HERMIA: Puppet? Why so—ay, that way goes the game.
290   Now I perceive that she hath made compare
         Between our statures, she hath urged her height,
         And with her personage, her tall personage,
         Her height (forsooth) she hath prevailed with him.
         And are you grown so high in his esteem.
295   Because I am so dwarfish and so low?
         How low am I, thou painted maypole? Speak:
         How low am I? I am not yet so low,
         But that my nails can reach unto thine eyes.
       HELENA: I pray you, though you mock me, gentlemen,
300   Let her not hurt me. I was never curst:°
         I have no gift at all in shrewishness:

°260 *Hang off:* let go. 266 *keep my word:* i.e., to duel. 267 *bond:* written agreement. 272 *wherefore:* why. *what news:* what's the matter. 274 *erewhile:* a short while ago. 282 *juggler:* deceiver. *canker blossom:* worm that causes canker in blossoms. 288 *puppet:* (Hermia is short and Helena tall). 300 *curst:* bad-tempered.

I am a right maid for my cowardice:°
Let her not strike me. You perhaps may think,
Because she is something lower than myself,
That I can match her.   305
HERMIA: Lower? Hark again.
HELENA: Good Hermia, do not be so bitter with me,
    I evermore did love you Hermia.
    Did ever keep your counsels, never wronged you;
    Save that in love unto Demetrius,
    I told him of your stealth unto this wood.   310
    He followed you: for love I followed him.
    But he hath chid me hence, and threatened me
    To strike me, spurn me, nay to kill me too;
    And now, so° you will let me quiet go,
    To Athens will I bear my folly back,   315
    And follow you no further. Let me go.
    You see how simple and how fond° I am.
HERMIA: Why, get you gone. Who is't that hinders you?
HELENA: A foolish heart, that I leave here behind.
HERMIA: What, with Lysander?
HELENA: With Demetrius.   320
LYSANDER: Be not afraid: she shall not harm thee Helena.
DEMETRIUS: No sir: she shall not, though you take her part.
HELENA: O when she's angry, she is keen and shrewd.°
    She was a vixen when she went to school:
    And though she be but little, she is fierce.   325
HERMIA: "Little" again? Nothing but "low" and "little"?
    Why will you suffer her to flout° me thus?
    Let me come to her.
LYSANDER: Get you gone, you dwarf;
    You minimus,° of hind'ring knot-grass° made;
    You bead, you acorn.
DEMETRIUS: You are too officious   330
    In her behalf that scorns your services.
    Let her alone: speak not of Helena,
    Take not her part. For if thou dost intend°
    Never so little show of love to her,
    Thou shalt aby it.°   335
LYSANDER: Now she holds me not:
    Now follow, if thou dar'st, to try whose right,
    Of thine or mine, is most in Helena.°
DEMETRIUS: Follow? Nay, I'll go with thee, cheek by jowl.

                    Exeunt LYSANDER *and* DEMETRIUS.

HERMIA: You, mistress, all this coil is long of° you.
    Nay, go not back.

°302 *right . . . cowardice:* true woman in being cowardly. 314 *so:* if. 317 *fond:* foolish. 323 *keen and shrewd:* sharp
and malicious. 327 *flout:* mock. 329 *minimus:* smallest of creatures. *knot-grass:* weed believed to stunt the growth
if eaten. 333 *intend:* extend. 335 *aby it:* buy it dearly. 336–37 *try . . . Helena:* prove by fighting which of us has
most right to Helena. 339 *coil is long of:* turmoil is because of.

340 **HELENA:**   I will not trust you, I,
         Nor longer stay in your curst company
         Your hands than mine are quicker for a fray:
         My legs are longer though, to run away.   [*Exit.*]
     HERMIA: I am amazed,° and know not what to say.   *Exit.*
345 **OBERON:** This is thy negligence: still thou mistak'st,
         Or else commit'st thy knaveries wilfully.
     PUCK: Believe me, king of shadows, I mistook.
         Did not you tell me I should know the man
         By the Athenian garments he had on?
350   And so far blameless proves my enterprise,
         That I have 'nointed an Athenian's eyes:
         And so far am I glad it so did sort,°
         As this their jangling I esteem a sport.
     OBERON: Thou seest these lovers seek a place to fight;
355   Hie therefore Robin, overcast the night,
         The starry welkin° cover thou anon
         With drooping fog as black as Acheron,°
         And lead these testy° rivals so astray,
         As° one come not within another's way.
360   Like to Lysander sometime frame thy tongue:
         Then stir Demetrius up with bitter wrong:°
         And sometime rail thou like Demetrius:
         And from each other look thou lead them thus;
         Till o'er their brows death-counterfeiting sleep
365   With leaden legs and batty wings doth creep:
         Then crush this herb into Lysander's eye;
         Whose liquor hath this virtuous° property,
         To take from thence all error with his might,
         And make his eyeballs roll with wonted° sight.
370   When they next wake, all this derision°
         Shall seem a dream, and fruitless vision,
         And back to Athens shall the lovers wend,
         With league whose date° till death shall never end.
         Whiles I in this affair do thee employ,
375   I'll to my queen and beg her Indian boy:
         And then I will her charmèd eye release
         From monster's view, and all things shall be peace.
     PUCK: My fairy lord, this must be done with haste,
         For night's swift dragons cut the clouds full fast:
380   And yonder shines Aurora's harbinger,°
         At whose approach, ghosts wand'ring here and there,
         Troop home to churchyards: damnèd spirits all,
         That in crossways° and floods° have burial,
         Already to their wormy beds are gone:
385   For fear lest day should look their shames upon,

°344 *amazed:* confused. 352 *sort:* turn out. 356 *welkin:* sky. 357 *Acheron:* one of the four rivers in the underworld. 358 *testy:* irritable. 359 *As:* so that. 361 *wrong:* insult. 367 *virtuous:* potent. 369 *wonted:* (previously) accustomed. 370 *derision:* laughable interlude. 373 *date:* term. 380 *Aurora's harbinger:* the morning star heralding Aurora, the dawn. 383 *crossways:* cross-roads, where suicides were buried. *floods:* those who drowned.

They wilfully themselves exile from light,
And must for aye consort° with black-browed night.
OBERON: But we are spirits of another sort.
    I with the morning's love have oft made sport,°
    And like a forester, the groves may tread   390
    Even till the eastern gate all fiery red,
    Opening on Neptune, with fair blessèd beams,
    Turns into yellow gold his salt green streams.
    But notwithstanding, haste, make no delay:
    We may effect this business yet ere day.   *[Exit.]* 395
PUCK: Up and down, up and down,
    I will lead them up and down.
    I am feared in field and town.
    Goblin, lead them up and down.
    Here comes one.   400

Enter LYSANDER.

LYSANDER: Where art thou, proud Demetrius? Speak thou now.
PUCK: Here villain, drawn° and ready. Where art thou?
LYSANDER: I will be with thee straight.
PUCK: Follow me then
    To plainer° ground.   *[Exit LYSANDER.]*

Enter DEMETRIUS.

DEMETRIUS: Lysander, speak again.
    Thou runaway, thou coward, art thou fled?   405
    Speak: in some bush? Where dost thou hide thy head?
PUCK: Thou coward, art thou bragging to the stars,
    Telling the bushes that thou look'st for wars,
    And wilt not come? Come recreant,° come thou child,
    I'll whip thee with a rod. He is defiled   410
    That draws a sword on thee.
DEMETRIUS: Yea, art thou there?
PUCK: Follow my voice: we'll try no manhood° here.   *Exeunt.*

[Enter LYSANDER.]

LYSANDER: He goes before me and still dares me on:
    When I come where he calls, then he is gone
    The villain is much lighter-heeled than I;   415
    I followed fast: but faster he did fly,
    That fallen am I in dark uneven way,
    And here will rest me. *[Lie down.]* Come thou gentle day,
    For if but once thou show me thy grey light.
    I'll find Demetrius and revenge this spite.   *[Sleeps.]* 420

Enter PUCK and DEMETRIUS.

PUCK: Ho, ho, ho! Coward, why com'st thou not?

°387 *aye consort:* ever associate. 389 *morning's . . . sport:* hunted with Cephalus (beloved of Aurora and himself devoted to his wife Procris, whom he killed by accident; "sport" also = "amorous dalliance," and "love" = Aurora's love for Oberon). 402 *drawn:* with sword drawn. 404 *plainer:* more level. 409 *recreant:* oath-breaker, coward. 412 *try no manhood:* test no valor.

DEMETRIUS: Abide° me, if thou dar'st, for well I wot°
Thou run'st before me, shifting every place,
And dar'st not stand, nor look me in the face.
Where art thou now?
425 **PUCK:**   Come hither: I am here.
DEMETRIUS: Nay then thou mock'st me. Thou shalt buy this dear,°
If ever I thy face by daylight see.
Now go thy way. Faintness constraineth me
To measure out my length on this cold bed.
430   By day's approach look to be visited.   [*Lies down and sleeps.*]

Enter HELENA.

HELENA: O weary night, O long and tedious night,
Abate° thy hours; shine comforts° from the east,
That I may back to Athens by daylight,
From these that my poor company detest:
435   And sleep, that sometimes shuts up sorrow's eye.
Steal me awhile from mine own company.   *Sleeps.*
PUCK: Yet but three? Come one more,
Two of both kinds makes up four.
Here she comes, curst° and sad.
440   Cupid is a knavish lad,
Thus to make poor females mad.

Enter HERMIA.

HERMIA: Never so weary, never so in woe,
Bedabbled with the dew, and torn with briers:
I can no further crawl, no further go:
445   My legs can keep no pace with my desires.
Here will I rest me till the break of day.
Heavens shield Lysander, if they mean a fray.   [*Lies down and sleeps.*]
PUCK: On the ground,
Sleep sound:
450   I'll apply
To your eye,
Gentle lover, remedy.   [*Squeezes the love-juice on* LYSANDER'S *eyelids.*]
When thou wak'st,
Thou tak'st
455   True delight
In the sight
Of thy former lady's eye:
And the country proverb known,
That every man should take his own,
460   In your waking shall be shown.
Jack shall have Jill:
Naught shall go ill:
The man shall have his mare again, and all shall be well.
                    [*Exit* PUCK. *The lovers remain asleep on stage.*]

°422 *Abide:* wait for. *wot:* know. 426 *buy this dear:* pay dearly for this. 432 *Abate:* shorten. *shine comforts:* may strength, power shine. 439 *curst:* cross.

Titania, Queen of the Fairies (Juliet Mills) is entranced by the ass's-eared Bottom (Paul Hardwick) in the Royal Shakespeare Company production of *A Midsummer Night's Dream* (1959–1962) at the Aldwych Theatre, London—director, Peter Hall.

ACT 4

[Scene 1. The Wood]

Enter [TITANIA] QUEEN OF FAIRIES, and [BOTTOM] THE CLOWN, and FAIRIES, and the KING [OBERON] behind them [unseen].

TITANIA: Come sit thee down upon this flow'ry bed,
    While I thy amiable° cheeks do coy,°
  And stick musk-roses in thy sleek smooth head,
    And kiss thy fair large ears, my gentle joy.
BOTTOM: Where's Peaseblossom?   5
PEASEBLOSSOM: Ready.
BOTTOM: Scratch my head, Peaseblossom. Where's Mounsieur
  Cobweb?
COBWEB: Ready.
BOTTOM: Mounsieur Cobweb, good mounsieur, get you your weapons   10
  in your hand, and kill me a red-hipped humblebee on
  the top of a thistle: and good mounsieur, bring me the
  honey-bag. Do not fret yourself too much in the action,
  mounsieur: and good mounsieur have a care the honey-
  bag break not, I would be loath to have you overflowen   15
  with a honey bag, signior. Where's Mounsieur
  Mustardseed?

°2 *amiable:* lovely. *coy:* caress.

MUSTARDSEED: Ready.

BOTTOM: Give me your neaf,° Mounsieur Mustardseed. Pray you
20   leave your curtsy,° good mounsieur.

MUSTARDSEED: What's your will?

BOTTOM: Nothing, good mounsieur, but to help Cavalery° Cobweb
        to scratch. I must to the barber's mounsieur, for
        methinks I am marvellous hairy about the face. And I am
25   such a tender ass, if my hair do but tickle me, I must
        scratch.

TITANIA: What, will thou hear some music, my sweet love?

BOTTOM: I have a reasonable good ear in music. Let's have the tongs°
        and the bones.°

30 TITANIA: Or say, sweet love, what thou desirest to eat.

BOTTOM: Truly, a peck of provender. I could munch your good
        dry oats. Methinks I have a great desire to a bottle° of hay.
        Good hay, sweet hay, hath no fellow.

TITANIA: I have a venturous fairy that shall seek
35   The squirrel's hoard, and fetch thee new nuts.

BOTTOM: I had rather have a handful or two of dried pease. But
        I pray you, let none of your people stir me: I have an
        exposition of° sleep come upon me.

TITANIA: Sleep thou, and I will wind thee in my arms.
40   Fairies, be gone, and be all ways° away.   [*Exeunt* FAIRIES.]
        So doth the woodbine the sweet honeysuckle
        Gently entwist: the female ivy so
        Enrings the barky fingers of the elm.
        O how I love thee! how I dote on thee!   [*They sleep.*]

Enter ROBIN GOODFELLOW [PUCK.]

45 OBERON: [*Advances.*] Welcome good Robin. Seest thou this sweet sight?
        Her dotage now I do begin to pity.
        For meeting her of late behind the wood,
        Seeking sweet favours° for this hateful fool,
        I did upbraid her and fall out with her.
50   For she his hairy temples then had rounded
        With coronet of fresh and fragrant flowers
        And that same dew which sometime° on the buds
        Was wont to° swell like round and orient° pearls,
        Stood now within the pretty flowerets' eyes,
55   Like tears that did their own disgrace bewail.
        When I had at my pleasure taunted her,
        And she in mild terms begged my patience,
        I then did ask of her her changeling child:
        Which straight she gave me, and her fairy sent
60   To bear him to my bower in fairy land.

°19 *neaf:* fist. 20 *leave your curtsy:* either (a) stop bowing, or (b) replace your hat. 22 *Cavalery:* (he means "cava-lier"). 28 *tongs:* crude music made by striking tongs with a piece of metal. 29 *bones:* pieces of bone held between the fingers and clapped together rhythmically. 32 *bottle:* bundle. 38 *exposition of:* (he means "disposition to"). 40 *all ways:* in every direction. 48 *favours:* bouquets as love tokens. 52 *sometime:* formerly. 53 *Was wont to:* used to. *orient:* (where the most beautiful pearls came from).

And now I have the boy, I will undo
This hateful imperfection of her eyes.
And gentle Puck, take this transformèd scalp
From off the head of this Athenian swain;
That he awaking when the other do,   65
May all to Athens back again repair,°
And think no more of this night's accidents,°
But as the fierce vexation of a dream.
But first I will release the Fairy Queen.
     Be as thou wast wont to be: 70
     See, as thou wast wont to see.
     Dian's bud o'er Cupid's flower°
     Hath such force and blessèd power.
Now my Titania, wake you, my sweet queen.
TITANIA: My Oberon, what visions have I seen!   75
   Methought I was enamoured of an ass.
OBERON: There lies your love.
TITANIA: How came these things to pass?
   O, how mine eyes do loathe his visage now!
OBERON: Silence awhile Robin, take off this head:
   Titania, music call, and strike more dead   80
   Than common sleep of all these five the sense.°
TITANIA: Music, ho music! such as charmeth sleep.
PUCK: Now, when thou wak'st, with thine own fools' eyes peep.
OBERON: Sound music: *Music still.*°
          Come my queen, take hands with me,
   And rock the ground whereon these sleepers be.   *[Dance.]* 85
   Now thou and I are new in amity,
   And will tomorrow midnight solemnly
   Dance in Duke Theseus' house triumphantly,°
   And bless it to all fair prosperity.
   There shall the pairs of faithful lovers be   90
   Wedded, with Theseus, all in jollity.
PUCK: Fairy King, attend and mark:
     I do hear the morning lark.
OBERON: Then my queen, in silence sad,°
     Trip we after the night's shade: 95
     We the globe can compass soon,
     Swifter than the wand'ring moon.
TITANIA: Come my lord, and in our flight,
     Tell me how it came this night,
     That I sleeping here was found,   100
     With these mortals on the ground.   *Exeunt.*

Wind° horns. Enter THESEUS, HIPPOLYTA, ECEUS *and all his train.*

°66 *repair:* return. 67 *accidents:* incidents. 72 *Dian's bud . . . flower:* (Diana's bud counteracts the effects of love-
in-idleness, the pansy). 80–81 *strike . . . sense:* Make these five (the lovers and Bottom) sleep more soundly.
84.1 S.D.: *still:* continuously. 88 *triumphantly:* in celebration. 94 *sad:* serious. 101.1 S.D.: *wind:* blow, sound.

THESEUS: Go one of you, find out the forester:
     For now our observation° is performed.
     And since we have the vaward° of the day,
105   My love shall hear the music of my hounds.
     Uncouple° in the western valley, let them go:
     Dispatch I say, and find the forester.   [*Exit an* ATTENDANT.]
     We will, fair queen, up to the mountain's top,
     And mark the musical confusion
110   Of hounds and echo in conjunction.
HIPPOLYTA: I was with Hercules and Cadmus° once,
     When in a wood of Crete they bayed the bear,°
     With hounds of Sparta;° never did I hear
     Such gallant chiding. For besides the groves,
115   The skies, the fountains, every region near
     Seemed all one mutual cry. I never heard
     So musical a discord, such sweet thunder.
THESEUS: My hounds are bred out of the Spartan kind:
     So flewed, so sanded.° and their heads are hung
120   With ears that sweep away the morning dew,
     Crook-kneed, and dewlapped° like Thessalian bulls:
     Slow in pursuit; but matched in mouth like bells,
     Each under each.° A cry° more tuneable
     Was never holloa'd to, nor cheered with horn,
125   In Crete, in Sparta, nor in Thessaly.
     Judge when you hear. But soft.° What nymphs are these?
EGEUS: My lord, this is my daughter here asleep,
     And this Lysander, this Demetrius is,
     This Helena, old Nedar's Helena.
130   I wonder of their being here together.
THESEUS: No doubt they rose up early to observe
     The rite of May: and hearing our intent,
     Came here in grace° of our solemnity.
     But speak Egeus, is not this the day
135   That Hermia should give answer of her choice?
EGEUS: It is, my lord.
THESEUS: Go bid the huntsmen wake them with their horns.

Shout within: wind horns. They all start up.

     Good morrow, friends. Saint Valentine is past.
     Begin these wood-birds but to couple now?°
LYSANDER: Pardon, my lord.   [*They kneel.*]
140 THESEUS: I pray you all, stand up.
     I know you two are rival enemies.

°103 *observation:* observance of the May Day rites. 104 *vaward:* vanguard, earliest part. 106 *Uncouple:* unleash
(the dogs). 111 *Cadmus:* mythical builder of Thebes. 112 *bayed the bear:* brought the bear to bay, to its last stand.
113 *hounds of Sparta:* (a breed famous for their swiftness and quick scent) 119 *flewed, so sanded:* with hanging
cheeks, so sand-colored. 121 *dewlapped:* with skin hanging from the chin. 122–23 *matched . . . each:* with each
voice matched for harmony with the next in pitch, like bells in a chime. 123 *cry:* pack of dogs. 126 *soft:* wait. 133
grace: honor. 138–39 *Saint . . . now:* (birds traditionally chose their mates on St. Valentine's Day).

How comes this gentle concord in the world,
That hatred is so far from jealousy,°
To sleep by hate° and fear no enmity?
LYSANDER: My lord, I shall reply amazedly, 145
Half sleep, half waking. But as yet, I swear,
I cannot truly say how I came here.
But as I think—for truly would I speak,
And now I do bethink me, so it is—
I came with Hermia hither. Our intent 150
Was to be gone from Athens, where we might,
Without° the peril of the Athenian law—
EGEUS: Enough, enough, my lord: you have enough.
I beg the law, the law upon his head:
They would have stol'n away, they would, Demetrius, 155
Thereby to have defeated you and me:
You of your wife, and me of my consent:
Of my consent that she should be your wife.
DEMETRIUS: My lord, fair Helen told me of their stealth,
Of this their purpose hither, to this wood, 160
And I in fury hither followed them;
Fair Helena in fancy° following me.
But my good lord, I wot not by what power
(But by some power it is) my love to Hermia,
Melted as the snow, seems to me now 165
As the remembrance of an idle gaud,°
Which in my childhood I did dote upon:
And all the faith, the virtue of my heart,
The object and the pleasure of mine eye,
Is only Helena. To her, my lord, 170
Was I betrothed ere I saw Hermia:
But like a sickness,° did I loathe this food.
But as in health, come° to my natural taste,
Now I do wish it, love it, long for it.
And will for evermore be true to it. 175
THESEUS: Fair lovers, you are fortunately met.
Of this discourse we more will hear anon.
Egeus, I will overbear your will:
For in the temple, by and by,° with us,
These couples shall eternally be knit. 180
And for the morning now is something worn,°
Our purposed hunting shall be set aside.
Away with us to Athens. Three and three,
We'll hold a feast in great solemnity.
Come Hippolyta. 185

Exeunt DUKE [HIPPOLYTA, EGEUS] *and* LORDS.

°143 *jealousy:* suspicion. 144 *hate:* one it hates. 152 *Without:* beyond. 162 *in fancy:* out of doting love. 166 *idle gaud:* trifling toy. 172 *sickness:* sick person. 173 *come:* i.e., back. 179 *by and by:* immediately. 181 *something worn:* somewhat worn on.

DEMETRIUS: These things seem small and undistinguishable,
Like far-off mountains turned into clouds.
HERMIA: Methinks I see these things with parted° eye,
When everything seems double.
HELENA: So methinks:
190 And I have found Demetrius, like a jewel,
Mine own, and not mine own.°
DEMETRIUS: Are you sure
That we are awake? It seems to me,
That yet we sleep, we dream. Do not you think
The duke was here, and bid us follow him?
HERMIA: Yea, and my father.
195 HELENA: And Hippolyta.
LYSANDER: And he did bid us follow to the temple.
DEMETRIUS: Why then, we are awake: let's follow him,
And by the way let us recount our dreams.   *Exeunt Lovers.*
BOTTOM: [*Wakes.*] When my cue comes, call me, and I will answer.
200 My next is "Most fair Pyramus." Hey ho. Peter Quince?
Flute the bellows-mender? Snout the tinker? Starveling?
God's my life! Stol'n hence, and left me asleep? I have
had a most rare vision. I have had a dream, past the wit
of man to say what dream it was. Man is but an ass, if he
205 go about° to expound this dream. Methought I was—
there is no man can tell what. Methought I was, and
methought I had—but man is but a patched fool,° if he
will offer to say what methought I had. The eye of man
hath not heard, the ear of man hath not seen, man's hand is
210 not able to taste, his tongue to conceive, nor his
heart to report, what my dream was. I will get Peter
Quince to write a ballad of this dream: it shall be called
Bottom's Dream; because it hath no bottom: and I
will sing it in the latter end of our play, before the duke.
215 Peradventure, to make it the more gracious, I shall sing
it at her° death.   *Exit.*

[Scene 2. Athens, Quince's house]

Enter QUINCE, FLUTE, SNOUT, and STARVELING.

QUINCE: Have you sent to Bottom's house? Is he come home yet?
STARVELING: He cannot be heard of. Out of doubt he is transported.°
FLUTE: If he come not, then the play is marred. It goes not forward,
doth it?
5 QUINCE: It is not possible. You have not a man in all Athens able
to discharge° Pyramus but he.
FLUTE: No, he hath simply the best wit of any handicraft man in Athens.
QUINCE: Yea, and the best person too, and he is a very paramour
for a sweet voice.

°188 *parted:* divided (each eye seeing a separate image). 190–91 *like . . . own:* like a person who finds a jewel: the finder is the owner, but insecurely so. 205 *go about:* attempt. 207 *patched fool:* fool dressed in motley. 216 *her:* Thisby's. 2 *transported:* carried away (by spirits). 6 *discharge:* portray.

FLUTE: You must say "paragon." A paramour is (God bless us)   10
 a thing of naught.°

Enter SNUG THE JOINER.

SNUG: Masters, the duke is coming from the temple, and there
 is two or three lords and ladies more married. If our
 sport had gone forward, we had all been made men.°
FLUTE: O sweet bully Bottom. Thus hath he lost sixpence a day°   15
 during his life: he could not have 'scaped sixpence a day.
 And the duke had not given him sixpence a day for playing
 Pyramus, I'll be hanged. He would have deserved it.
 Sixpence a day in Pyramus, or nothing.

Enter BOTTOM.

BOTTOM: Where are these lads? Where are these hearts?   20
QUINCE: Bottom! O most courageous° day! O most happy hour!
BOTTOM: Masters, I am to discourse wonders: but ask me not what.
 For if I tell you, I am not true Athenian. I will tell you
 everything, right as it fell out.
QUINCE: Let us hear, sweet Bottom.   25
BOTTOM: Not a word of me. All that I will tell you is, that the
 duke hath dined. Get your apparel together, good
 strings to your beards, new ribbands to your pumps, meet
 presently° at the palace, every man look o'er his part: for
 the short and the long is, our play is preferred.° In any   30
 case, let Thisby have clean linen: and let not him that
 plays the lion pare his nails, for they shall hang out for
 the lion's claws. And most dear actors, eat no onions nor
 garlic, for we are to utter sweet breath: and I do not
 doubt but to hear them say it is a sweet comedy. No more   35
 words: away, go away.   *Exeunt.*

ACT 5

[Scene 1. The palace of Theseus]

Enter THESEUS, HIPPOLYTA, and PHILOSTRATE, and his LORDS.

HIPPOLYTA: 'Tis strange, my Theseus, that these lovers speak of.
THESEUS: More strange than true. I never may believe
 These antick° fables, nor these fairy toys.°
 Lovers and madmen have such seething brains,
 Such shaping fantasies,° that apprehend   5
 More than cool reason ever comprehends.
 The lunatic, the lover, and the poet,
 Are of imagination all compact.°

°11 *of naught:* wicked, naughty. 14 *made men:* men made rich. 15 *sixpence a day:* i.e., as a pension 21 *courageous:* (he may mean "auspicious"). 29 *presently:* immediately. 30 *preferred:* recommended (for presentation). 3 *antick:* fantastic. *fairy toys:* trivial fairy stories. 5 *fantasies:* imaginations. 8 *of . . . compact:* totally composed of imagination.

One sees more devils than vast hell can hold:
10   That is the madman. The lover, all as frantic,
Sees Helen's beauty in a brow of Egypt.°
The poet's eye, in a fine frenzy rolling,
Doth glance from heaven to earth, from earth to heaven.
And as imagination bodies forth
15   The forms of things unknown, the poet's pen
Turns them to shapes, and gives to airy nothing,
A local habitation and a name.
Such tricks hath strong imagination,
That if it would but apprehend some joy,
20   It comprehends° some bringer of that joy.
Or in the night, imagining some fear,
How easy is a bush supposed a bear.
HIPPOLYTA: But all the story of the night told over,
And all their minds transfigured so together,
25   More witnesseth than fancy's images,°
And grows to something of great constancy:°
But howsoever, strange and admirable.°

Enter LOVERS: LYSANDER, DEMETRIUS, HERMIA, and HELENA.

THESEUS: Here come the lovers, full of joy and mirth.
Joy, gentle friends, joy and fresh days of love
Accompany your hearts.
30 **LYSANDER:**   More° than to us
Wait in your royal walks, your board, your bed.
THESEUS: Come now, what masques,° what dances shall we have,
To wear away this long age of three hours
Between our after-supper° and bed-time?
35   Where is our usual manager of mirth?
What revels are in hand? Is there no play,
To ease the anguish of a torturing hour?
Call Philostrate.
PHILOSTRATE: Here, mighty Theseus.
THESEUS: Say, what abridgment° have you for this evening?
40   What masque,° what music? How shall we beguile
The lazy time, if not with some delight?
PHILOSTRATE: There is a brief° how many sports are ripe.°
Make choice of which your highness will see first.

[Gives a paper.]

THESEUS: "The battle with the Centaurs, to be sung
45   By an Athenian eunuch to the harp."
We'll none of that. That have I told my love

°11 *a brow of Egypt:* the swarthy face of a gypsy (believed to come from Egypt). 20 *comprehends:* includes. 25 *More
. . . images:* testifies that it is more than just imagination. 26 *constancy:* certainty. 27 *admirable:* to be wondered at.
30 *More:* even more (joy and love). 32, 40 *masques:* lavish courtly entertainments combining song and dance. 34
after-supper: late supper. 39 *abridgment:* either (a) diversion to make the hours seem shorter or (b) short entertainment. 40 *masque:* a light musical or non-musical drama, usually allegorical or mythological in subject, with many
dances and pantomime actions. Often the actors wore masks. 42 *brief:* list. *ripe:* ready.

In glory of my kinsman Hercules.
"The riot of the tipsy Bacchanals,
Tearing the Thracian singer in their rage."°
That is an old device: and it was played   50
When I from Thebes came last a conqueror.
"The thrice three Muses mourning for the death
Of Learning, late deceased in beggary."
That is some satire keen and critical,
Not sorting with° a nuptial ceremony.   55
"A tedious brief scene of young Pyramus
And his love Thisby; very tragical mirth."
Merry and tragical? Tedious and brief?
That is hot ice and wondrous strange snow.
How shall we find the concord of this discord?   60

PHILOSTRATE: A play there is, my lord, some ten words long,
Which is as brief as I have known a play:
But by ten words, my lord, it is too long,
Which makes it tedious: for in all the play
There is not one word apt, one player fitted.°   65
And tragical, my noble lord, it is:
For Pyramus therein doth kill himself.
Which when I saw rehearsed, I must confess,
Made mine eyes water; but more merry tears
The passion of loud laughter never shed.   70

THESEUS: What are they that do play it?

PHILOSTRATE: Hard-handed men, that work in Athens here,
Which never laboured in their minds till now:
And now have toiled their unbreathed° memories
With this same play, against° your nuptial.   75

THESEUS: And we will hear it.

PHILOSTRATE: No, my noble lord,
It is not for you. I have heard it over,
And it is nothing, nothing in the world;
Unless you can find sport in their intents,
Extremely stretched and conned° with cruel pain.   80
To do your service.

THESEUS: I will hear that play.
For never anything can be amiss,
When simpleness and duty tender° it.
Go bring them in, and take your places, ladies.   [*Exit* PHILOSTRATE.]

HIPPOLYTA: I love not to see wretchedness o'ercharged,°   85
And duty in his service perishing.

THESEUS: Why, gentle sweet, you shall see no such thing.

HIPPOLYTA: He says they can do nothing in this kind.°

THESEUS: The kinder we, to give them thanks for nothing.

°48–49 *riot . . . rage:* (The singer Orpheus of Thrace was torn limb from limb by the Maenads, frenzied female priests of Bacchus. See pages 1003–08). 55 *sorting with:* befitting. 65 *fitted:* (well) cast. 74 *unbreathed:* unpracticed, unexercised. 75 *against:* in preparation for. 80 *stretched and conned:* strained and memorized. 83 *tender:* offer. 85 *wretchedness o'ercharged:* poor fellows taxing themselves too much. 88 *in this kind:* of this sort.

90   Our sport shall be to take what they mistake.
      And what poor duty cannot do, noble respect
      Takes it in might, not merit.°
      Where I have come, great clerks° have purposèd
      To greet me with premeditated welcomes;
95   Where I have seen them shiver and look pale,
      Make periods in the midst of sentences,
      Throttle° their practised accent in their fears,
      And in conclusion dumbly have broke off,
      Not paying me a welcome. Trust me, sweet,
100   Out of this silence yet I picked a welcome:
      And in the modesty of fearful duty°
      I read as much as from the rattling tongue
      Of saucy and audacious eloquence.
      Love, therefore, and tongue-tied simplicity,
105   In° least, speak most, to my capacity.°

[*Enter* PHILOSTRATE.]

PHILOSTRATE: So please your grace, the Prologue is addressed.°
THESEUS: Let him approach.

Flourish trumpets. Enter the PROLOGUE [QUINCE].

PROLOGUE: If we offend, it is with our good will.
                That you should think, we come not to offend,
110   But with good will. To show our simple skill,
                That is the true beginning of our end.
              Consider then, we come but in despite.°
                We do not come, as minding to content you,
              Our true intent is. All for your delight,
115   We are not here. That you should here repent you,
              The actors are at hand: and by their show,
              You shall know all, that you are like to know.°
THESEUS: This fellow doth not stand upon points.°
LYSANDER: He hath rid his prologue like a rough colt: he knows
120   not the stop.° A good moral my lord: it is not enough
      to speak; but to speak true.
HIPPOLYTA: Indeed he hath played on his prologue like a child on a
      recorder:° a sound, but not in government.°
THESEUS: His speech was like a tangled chain: nothing impaired, but
125   all disordered. Who is next?

Enter PYRAMUS *and* THISBY, WALL, MOONSHINE, *and* LION.

PROLOGUE: Gentles, perchance you wonder at this show,
                But wonder on, till truth make all things plain.
              This man is Pyramus, if you would know:

°91–92 *noble . . . merit:* a noble nature considers the sincerity of effort rather than the skill of execution. 93 *clerks:* scholars. 97 *Throttle:* choke on. 101 *fearful duty:* subjects whose devotions gave them stage fright. 105 *In:* i.e., saying. *capacity:* way of thinking. 106 *addressed:* ready. 108–17 *If . . . know:* (Quince's blunders in punctuation exactly reverse the meaning). 112 *despite:* malice. 118 *stand upon points:* (1) pay attention to punctuation (2) bother about the niceties (of expression). 120 *stop:* (a) halt (b) period. 123 *recorder:* flutelike wind instrument. *in government:* well managed.

This beauteous lady, Thisby is certain.
This man, with lime and rough-cast,° doth present   130
   Wall, that vile wall which did these lovers sunder:
And through Wall's chink, poor souls, they are content
   To whisper. At the which, let no man wonder.
This man, with lantern, dog, and bush of thorn,
   Presenteth Moonshine. For if you will know,   135
By moonshine did these lovers think no scorn
   To meet at Ninus' tomb, there, there to woo:
This grisly beast (which Lion hight° by name)
The trusty Thisby, coming first by night,
Did scare away, or rather did affright: 140
And as she fled, her mantle she did fall:°
   Which Lion vile with bloody mouth did stain.
Anon comes Pyramus, sweet youth and tall,°
   And finds his trusty Thisby's mantle slain:
Whereat, with blade, with bloody blameful blade,   145
   He bravely broached° his boiling bloody breast.
And Thisby, tarrying in mulberry shade,
   His dagger drew, and died. For all the rest,
Let Lion, Moonshine, Wall, and lovers twain.
At large° discourse, while here they do remain.   150
THESEUS: I wonder if the lion be to speak.
DEMETRIUS: No wonder, my lord: one lion may, when many asses do.

             Exeunt [PROLOGUE, PYRAMUS,] LION, THISBY, MOONSHINE.

WALL: In this same interlude° it doth befall
   That I, one Snout by name, present a wall:
   And such a wall, as I would have you think,   155
   That had in it a crannied hole or chink:
   Through which the lovers, Pyramus and Thisby,
   Did whisper often, very secretly.
   This loam, this rough-cast, and this stone doth show
   That I am that same wall: the truth is so.   160
   And this the cranny is, right and sinister,°
   Through which the fearful lovers are to whisper.
THESEUS: Would you desire lime and hair to speak better?
DEMETRIUS: It is the wittiest° partition° that ever I heard discourse,
   my lord.   165

Enter PYRAMUS.

THESEUS: Pyramus draws near the wall: silence.
PYRAMUS: O grim-looked night, O night with hue so black,
        O night, which ever art when day is not:
        O night, O night, alack, alack, alack,
        I fear my Thisby's promise is forgot.   170

°130 *rough-cast:* rough plaster made of lime and gravel. 138 *hight:* is called. 141 *fall:* let fall. 143 *tall:* brave. 146 *broached:* opened (Shakespeare parodies the overuse of alliteration in the earlier bombastic Elizabethan plays). 150 *At large:* in full. 153 *interlude:* short play. 161 *right and sinister:* from right to left (he probably uses the fingers of his right and left hands to form the cranny). 164 *wittiest:* most intelligent. *partition:* (1) wall (2) section of a learned book or speech.

And thou O wall, O sweet, O lovely wall,
 That stand'st between her father's ground and mine,
Thou wall, O wall, O sweet and lovely wall,
 Show me thy chink, to blink through with mine eyne.°

[WALL *holds up his fingers.*]

175 Thanks, courteous wall. Jove shield thee well for this.
 But what see I? No Thisby do I see.
O wicked wall, through whom I see no bliss,
 Cursed be thy stones for thus deceiving me.
THESEUS: The wall methinks being sensible,° should curse again.°
180 PYRAMUS: No in truth sir, he should not. "Deceiving me" is
 Thisby's cue: she is to enter now, and I am to spy her
 through the wall. You shall see it will fall pat° as I told you:
 yonder she comes.

Enter THISBY.

THISBY: O wall, full often hast thou heard my moans,
 For parting my fair Pyramus and me.
185 My cherry lips have often kissed thy stones;
 Thy stones with lime and hair knit up in thee.
PYRAMUS: I see a voice: now will I to the chink,
190 To spy and I can hear my Thisby's face.
 Thisby?
THISBY: My love thou art, my love I think.
PYRAMUS: Think what thou wilt, I am thy lover's grace:
 And, like Limander,° am I trusty still.
THISBY: And I like Helen,° till the Fates me kill.
195 PYRAMUS: Not Shafalus to Procrus,° was so true.
THISBY: As Shafalus to Procrus, I to you.
PYRAMUS: O kiss me through the hole of this vile wall.
THISBY: I kiss the wall's hole, not your lips at all.
PYRAMUS: Wilt thou at Ninny's° tomb meet me straightway?
200 THISBY: Tide° life, tide death, I come without delay.

[*Exeunt* PYRAMUS *and* THISBY.]

WALL: Thus have I, Wall, my part dischargèd so;
 And being done, thus Wall away doth go.   *Exit.*
THESEUS: Now is the mural° down between the two neighbours.
DEMETRIUS: No remedy my lord, when walls are so wilful to hear
205 without warning.°
HIPPOLYTA: This is the silliest stuff that ever I heard.
THESEUS: The best in this kind are but shadows,° and the worst are
 no worse, if imagination amend them.
HIPPOLYTA: It must be your imagination then, and not theirs.
THESEUS: If we imagine no worse of them than they of themselves,
 they may pass for excellent men. Here come two noble
210 beasts in, a man and a lion.

Enter LION *and* MOONSHINE.

°174 *eyne:* eyes. 179 *sensible:* capable of feelings and perception. *again:* back. 182 *pat:* exactly. 193 *Limander:* (he means "Leander"). 194 *Helen:* (he means "Hero"). 195 *Shafalus to Procrus:* (he means "Cephalus" and "Procris" [see 3.2.389 n., p. 1539]). 199 *Ninny:* fool (he means "Ninus"). 200 *Tide:* come, betide. 203 *mural:* wall. 205 *without warning:* either (a) without warning the parents or (b) unexpectedly. 207 *in . . . shadows:* of this sort are only plays (or only actors).

LION: You ladies, you, whose gentle hearts do fear
  The smallest monstrous mouse that creeps on floor,
May now perchance both quake and tremble here.   215
  When lion rough in wildest rage doth roar.
Then know that I, as Snug the joiner am
  A lion fell,° nor else no lion's dam:°
For if I should as lion come in strife
Into this place, 'twere pity on my life.   220
THESEUS: A very gentle beast, and of a good conscience.
DEMETRIUS: The very best at a beast,° my lord, that e'er I saw.
LYSANDER: This lion is a very fox for his valour.
THESEUS: True: and a goose for his discretion.
DEMETRIUS: Not so my lord: for his valour cannot carry his discretion,
  and the fox carries the goose.   225
THESEUS: His discretion, I am sure, cannot carry his valour: for the
  goose carries not the fox. It is well: leave it to his discretion,
  and let us listen to the moon.
MOONSHINE: This lanthorn° doth the hornèd moon present—   230
DEMETRIUS: He should have worn the horns on his head.°
THESEUS: He is no crescent, and his horns are invisible within the
  circumference.
MOONSHINE: This lanthorn doth the hornéd moon present,
  Myself, the man i' th' moon do seem to be.   235
THESEUS: This is the greatest error of all the rest; the man should
  be put into the lanthorn. How is it else the man i'th' moon?
DEMETRIUS: He dares not come there for the candle; for you see, it
  is already in snuff.°   240
HIPPOLYTA: I am aweary of this moon. Would he would change.
THESEUS: It appears, by his small light of discretion, that he is in
  the wane: but yet in courtesy, in all reason, we must stay°
  the time.
LYSANDER: Proceed, Moon.   245
MOONSHINE: All that I have to say, is to tell you that the lanthorn is
  the moon, I the man i' th' moon, this thornbush my
  thornbush, and this dog my dog.
DEMETRIUS: Why, all these should be in the lanthorn: for all these are
  in the moon. But silence: here comes Thisby.   250

Enter THISBY.

THISBY: This is old Ninny's tomb. Where is my love?
LION: Oh!   *The* LION *roars.* THISBY *runs off.*
DEMETRIUS: Well roared, Lion.
THESEUS: Well run, Thisby.
HIPPOLYTA: Well shone, Moon. Truly, the moon shines with a good   255
  grace.

[*The* LION *shakes* THISBY'S *mantle.*]

THESEUS: Well moused,° Lion.

°218 *fell:* fierce. *nor . . . dam:* and not a lioness. 222 *best, beast:* (pronounced similarly). 230 *lanthorn:* lantern (once made of horn). 230–31 *hornèd . . . head:* (referring to the cuckold or deceived husband, who supposedly grew horns). 240 *in snuff:* (1) in need of snuffing (having a long, burnt-out wick or snuff) (2) in a temper. 243 *stay:* await. 257 *moused:* shaken, as a cat shakes a mouse.

DEMETRIUS: And then came Pyramus.

Enter PYRAMUS. [*Exit* LION.]

LYSANDER: And so the lion vanished.

260 PYRAMUS: Sweet moon, I thank thee for thy sunny beams,
    I thank thee, moon, for shining now so bright.
  For by thy gracious, golden, glittering gleams,
    I trust to take of truest Thisby sight.
  But stay: O spite!
265   But mark, poor knight,
  What dreadful dole° is here?
    Eyes, do you see!
    How can it be!
  O dainty duck, O dear!
270   Thy mantle good,
    What, stained with blood?
  Approach, ye Furies° fell:
    O Fates!° come, come:
    Cut thread and thrum.°
275   Quail,° crush, conclude, and quell.°

THESEUS: This passion, and the death of a dear friend, would go
  near to make a man look sad.

HIPPOLYTA: Beshrew° my heart, but I pity the man.

PYRAMUS: O wherefore Nature, didst thou lions frame?
280   Since lion vile hath here deflowered my dear.
  Which is—no, no—which was the fairest dame
    That lived, that loved, that liked, that looked with cheer.
    Come tears, confound:
    Out sword, and wound
285   The pap° of Pyramus:
    Ay, that left pap,
    Where heart doth hop. [*Stabs himself.*]
  Thus die, I, thus, thus, thus.
    Now am I dead,
290   Now am I fled,
  My soul is in the sky.
  Tongue lose thy light,
    Moon° take thy flight,   [*Exit* MOONSHINE.]
  Now die, die, die, die, die.   [*Dies.*]

295 DEMETRIUS: No die,° but an ace° for him. For he is but one.

LYSANDER: Less than an ace, man. For he is dead, he is nothing.

THESEUS: With the help of a surgeon, he might yet recover, and
  prove an ass.

HIPPOLYTA: How chance Moonshine is gone before Thisby comes
300   back and finds her lover?

Enter THISBY.

°266 *dole:* grief. 272 *Furies:* classical spirits of the underworld who avenged murder. 273 *Fates:* three sisters who
spun the thread of human destiny, which at will was cut with a shears. 274 *thrum:* fringelike end of the warp in
weaving. 275 *Quail:* subdue. *quell:* kill. 278 *Beshrew:* curse (meant lightly). 285 *pap:* breast. 292–93 *Tongue . . .
Moon:* (he reverses the two subjects). 295 *die:* (singular of "dice"). *ace:* a throw of one at dice.

THESEUS: She will find him by starlight. Here she comes, and her
    passion ends the play.
HIPPOLYTA: Methinks she should not use a long one for such a
    Pyramus: I hope she will be brief.
DEMETRIUS: A mote will turn the balance, which Pyramus, which   305
    Thisby, is the better: he for a man. God warr'nt° us;
    she for a woman, God bless us.
LYSANDER: She hath spied him already with those sweet eyes.
DEMETRIUS: And thus she means,° videlicet°—
THISBY: Asleep my love?   310
        What, dead, my dove?
      O Pyramus, arise,
        Speak, speak. Quite dumb?
        Dead, dead? A tomb
    Must cover thy sweet eyes.   315
        These lily lips,
        This cherry nose,
    These yellow cowslip° cheeks,
        Are gone, are gone:
        Lovers, make moan: 320
    His eyes were green as leeks.
        O Sisters Three,°
        Come, come to me,
    With hands as pale as milk,
        Lay them in gore,   325
        Since you have shore
    With shears his thread of silk.
        Tongue, not a word:
        Come trusty sword,
    Come blade, my breast imbrue°   *[Stabs herself.]*   330
        And farewell friends:
        Thus Thisby ends:
      Adieu, adieu, adieu.   *[Dies.]*
THESEUS: Moonshine and Lion are left to bury the dead.
DEMETRIUS: Ay, and Wall too.   335
BOTTOM: [*Starts up.*] No, I assure you, the wall is down that parted
    their fathers. Will it please you to see the Epilogue, or
    to hear a Bergomask° dance between two of our company?
THESEUS: No epilogue, I pray you; for your play needs no excuse.
    Never excuse: for when the players are all dead, there   340
    need none to be blamed. Marry, if he that writ it had
    played Pyramus and hanged himself in Thisby's garter,
    it would have been a fine tragedy: and so it is truly, and
    very notably discharged. But come, your Bergomask:
    let your Epilogue alone.   *[A dance.]*   345
    The iron tongue° of midnight hath told° twelve.

°306 *warr'nt:* warrant, protect. 309 *means:* laments. *videlicet:* namely. 318 *cowslip:* yellow primrose. 322 *Sisters Three:* the Fates. 330 *imbrue:* stain with gore. 338 *Bergomask:* exaggerated country dance. 346 *iron tongue:* i.e., of the bell. *told:* counted, tolled.

Lovers, to bed, 'tis almost fairy time.°
I fear we shall outsleep the coming morn,
As much as we this night have overwatched.
350 This palpable gross° play hath well beguiled
The heavy gait of night. Sweet friends, to bed.
A fortnight hold we this solemnity,
In nightly revels, and new jollity.   *Exeunt.*

Enter PUCK [*with a broom*].

PUCK: Now the hungry lion roars,
355   And the wolf behowls the moon;
     Whilst the heavy° ploughman snores,
        All with weary task fordone.°
     Now the wasted brands° do glow,
     Whilst the screech-owl, screeching loud,
360   Puts the wretch that lies in woe°
     In remembrance of a shroud.
        Now it is the time of night,
     That the graves, all gaping wide,
        Every one lets forth his sprite,°
365   In the church-way paths to glide.
        And we fairies, that do run
     By the triple Hecate's° team,°
        From the presence of the sun,
     Following darkness like a dream,
370   Now are frolic:° not a mouse
     Shall disturb this hallowed house.
     I am sent with broom before,
     To sweep the dust° behind° the door.

Enter KING *and* QUEEN OF FAIRIES, *with all their train.*

OBERON: Through the house give glimmering light,
375   By the dead and drowsy fire,
        Every elf and fairy sprite,
           Hop as light as bird from brier,
        And this ditty after me,
           Sing, and dance it trippingly.
TITANIA: First rehearse your song by rote,
380   To each word a warbling note.
     Hand in hand, with fairy grace,
     Will we sing and bless this place.   [*Song and dance.*]
OBERON: Now, until the break of day,
385   Through this house each fairy stray.
     To the best bride-bed will we,

°347 *fairy time:* (from midnight to daybreak). 350 *palpable gross:* obvious and crude. 356 *heavy:* sleepy. 357 *fordone:* worn out, "done in." 358 *wasted brands:* burnt logs. 360 *wretch . . . woe:* sick person. 364 *sprite:* spirit, ghost. 367 *triple Hecate:* the moon goddess, identified as Cynthia in heaven, Diana on earth, and Hecate in hell. *team:* dragons that pull the chariot of the night moon. 370 *frolic:* frolicsome. 373 *To sweep the dust:* (Puck often helped with household chores). *behind:* from behind.

Which by us shall blessèd be:
And the issue° there create,°
Ever shall be fortunate:
So shall all the couples three   390
Ever true in loving be:
And the blots of Nature's hand°
Shall not in their issue stand.
Never mole, harelip, nor scar,
Nor mark prodigious,° such as are   395
Despisèd in nativity,
Shall upon their children be.
With this field-dew consecrate.
Every fairy take his gait,°
And each several° chamber bless,   400
Through this palace, with sweet peace;
And the owner of its blest,
Ever shall in safety rest.
Trip away: make no stay: *Exeunt [all but* PUCK].
Meet me all by break of day.   405
PUCK: If we shadows have offended,
     Think but this, and all is mended,
     That you have but slumbered here,
     While these visions did appear.
     And this weak and idle° theme,   410
     No more yielding but° a dream,
     Gentles, do not reprehend.
     If you pardon, we will mend.°
     And as I am an honest Puck,
     If we have unearnèd luck,   415
     Now to scape the serpent's tongue,°
     We will make amends, ere long:
     Else the Puck a liar call.
     So, good night unto you all.
     Give me your hands,° if we be friends;   420
     And Robin shall restore amends.°   [*Exit.*]

QUESTIONS

Act 1

1. Describe the relationship between Theseus and Hippolyta. What does each of them represent? How does Shakespeare show us that they have different attitudes toward their marriage?

2. Characterize Hermia and Lysander. What blocks their relationship? How do they plan to circumvent these obstructions?

°388 *issue:* children. 388 *create:* created. 392 *blots . . . hand:* birth defects. 395 *mark prodigious:* unnatural birthmark. 399 *take his gait:* proceed. 400 *several:* separate. 410 *idle:* foolish. 411 *No . . . but:* yielding nothing more than. 413 *mend:* improve. 416 *serpent's tongue:* hissing of the audience. 420 *hands:* applause. 421 *restore amends:* do better in the future.

3. What are Helena's feelings about herself? About Hermia? About Demetrius? How might you account for her self-image?

4. Why have the mechanicals gathered at Quince's house? How does Shakespeare show us that Bottom is eager, ill-educated, energetic, and funny?

Act 2

5. What is Puck's job? What do you find out about his personality, habits, and pastimes in his first conversation?

6. Why are Titania and Oberon fighting with each other, and what are the specific consequences of their conflict?

7. What does Oberon plan to do to Titania? Why? What is "love-in-idleness"? What power does it have? What does it symbolize?

8. Why are Demetrius and Helena in the woods? What does Oberon decide to do to them? What error occurs? What happens to Lysander when Helena awakens him?

Act 3

9. How and why does Puck change Bottom? How is this transformation appropriate? What happens when Bottom awakens Titania? Why?

10. What does Oberon decide to do when he realizes that Puck has made a mistake? What is Puck's attitude toward the confusion he has created?

11. What happens when Helena awakens Demetrius? How does this situation reverse the one that began the play? Explain Helena's reaction to the behavior of Demetrius and Lysander.

12. What real dangers (tragic potential) do the lovers face in Act 3? How do Oberon and Puck deal with these dangers? What is their plan? How successful is it?

Act 4

13. Why does Oberon cure Titania of her infatuation with Bottom? How does the relationship between Oberon and Titania change? How is this change symbolized? Why is it significant?

14. How are the relationships among the four lovers straightened out? How does each explain his or her feelings? What does Theseus decide about the couples? Why is this significant?

Act 5

15. What momentous event occurs offstage and is briefly reported in Act 5?

16. Describe Pyramus and Thisby. What blocks their relationship? How do they plan to circumvent these obstructions? What happens to them?

17. What is the significance of the fairy masque (a combination of poetry, music, dance, and drama) that ends the play?

18. What does Puck's epilogue suggest about you as a reader or spectator? How does it reinforce the connections among dreaming, imagination, illusion, and drama?

GENERAL QUESTIONS

1. To what extent are the characters in this play conventional and representative types? What is the effect of Shakespeare's style of characterization?

2. Are any of the characters symbolic? If so, what do they symbolize? How does such symbolism reinforce the themes of the play?

3. How does Shakespeare employ language, imagery, and poetic form to define the characters in this play and differentiate among the various groups of characters?

4. To what extent do the two settings—city and woods—structure the play? Where does exposition occur? Complication and catastrophe? The comic resolution? How complete is the resolution? Why is the round-trip journey from one setting to the other necessary for the lovers? The rulers? The "hempen homespuns"?

5. What are the similarities or parallels in plot and theme between *A Midsummer Night's Dream* and "Pyramus and Thisby"? To what degree are they versions of the same play with different endings? Why do you think Shakespeare included the play-within-the-play in *A Midsummer Night's Dream*?

6. In the first soliloquy of the play, Helena discusses love. What kind of love is she talking about? What are its qualities and characteristics? How far do the relationships in the play bear out her ideas about love?

7. How well do the mechanicals understand the nature of dramatic illusion? What sorts of production problems concern them? How do they solve these?

8. What ideas about drama and the ways in which audiences respond to it does *A Midsummer Night's Dream* explore?

9. Compare the play-within-a-play in *A Midsummer Night's Dream* to the one in Act 3 of *Hamlet*. How are the internal plays and situations similar? Different? What parallels do you see in the connections between each play-within-a-play and the larger play in which each occurs?

The Life and Theater of Molière

The seventeenth century was the golden age of French neoclassical theater (called *neo* or "new" because it marked the reintroduction of Greek and Latin models). The dominant political figure of the age was the "Sun King," Louis XIV (b. 1638; r. 1643–1713), the absolute monarch of France. He and his court—a set of nobles, wits, would-be wits, and ladies- and gentlemen-in-waiting—dictated fashion to the world at large and made Paris the cultural center of Europe.

The members of this ruling class profoundly influenced the drama of the age because they were the theater's patrons and protectors. Writers of tragedy, the two most important of whom were Pierre Corneille (1606–1684) and Jean Racine (1639–1699), complimented the understanding and sympathy of the nobility by creating serious poetic dramas for them. More daring and risky was the role of the writers of comedy, who populated the stage with characters derived not so much from the nobility as from the middle classes, often mocking their appearance, customs, and tastes.

The most important of the comic writers, the acknowledged master of comedy, was Molière, the pen name of Jean Baptiste Poquelin. Born in 1622, he received a Jesuit education and took up the study of law at Orléans. His favorite reading, however, was not law, but rather the six surviving comedies of the Roman dramatist Terence.[6] In 1643 he shocked his family by abandoning both the law and his

---

[6]See page 1499 for a brief discussion of the Roman dramatists.

Molière in the character of Sganarelle

father's prosperous upholstering business and going into the theater, a career that was considered scandalous and sinful. He joined a company of actors called the Illustrious Theater, who established themselves in a playhouse, produced a tragedy, and then went bankrupt.

The acting company spent the next thirteen years touring the provinces of France, performing *commedia dell'arte* farces and short comic plays, many of them by Molière. These years gave him his real education in the theater. He soon developed into a superb actor, director, and—more important—writer.

Although the years in the provinces were not easy, the company was achieving recognition. The group returned to Paris in 1658 at the invitation of King Louis XIV. The king was pleased with Molière's comedies and publicly provided support and protection. He also gave the company the authorization to use the *Théâtre du Petit-Bourbon* at Versailles. In 1659, when the *Théâtre* was torn down, Louis provided a royal patent to use the *Palais Royale* in Paris. With the king's support, Molière spent the rest of his career at this theater as an actor, director, manager, and playwright.

Molière's personal life was a great deal more troubled than his professional life. At the age of forty he began an unhappy marriage with Armande Béjart, the twenty-year-old daughter (or sister) of his former mistress Madeleine Béjart (his enemies whispered that Armande was also *his* daughter). He endured constant ill health, but he was a fighter. He performed even on the day he died, collapsing on-stage in 1673 while acting the lead role in his *The Imaginary Invalid* and dying several hours later. Because of the suddenness of his death he was not given last rites, and he was denied burial in consecrated ground.

Despite the adversities of his life, his creative output was great. He wrote twenty-nine plays, ranging from broad farce to satirical comedies of manners. He observed the theatrical conventions of his age, and he drew his plots from Roman comedy, Italian *commedia dell'arte,* and French farce, all of which schooled him in comic character, tempo, and situation. His inspirations were the manners, morals, and customs of the French gentry and middle class.

Molière was also innovative as a dramatist. He elevated comedy to the seriousness of tragedy, as in his satiric comedies *The Ridiculous Dilettantes* (*Les Précieuses Ridicules,* 1659), *The Misanthrope* (1666), *The Miser* (1668), and *Tartuffe* (1669). What is new in these serious comedies is Molière's thoughtful and detached perspective on vices and follies. His mainspring is character, and his norm is moderation in all forms of behavior. From this point of balance, his plots mock and expose religious posturing, personal greed, social snobbery, and professional hypocrisy. In short, whatever is excessive is the subject of his satiric thrusts.

The *Théâtre Royale,* the Paris theater in which most of Molière's plays were produced, was patterned on Italian theater design of the early seventeenth century—a design that by and large has dominated theater architecture up to the present. The building was rectangular, with a proscenium stage at one end and seating in the approximate shape of a horseshoe—orchestra and balcony—for as many as six hundred spectators at the other end and both sides. Also at the sides were galleries or private boxes. There may have been space in front of the stage for special dances and ballets. A major innovation in design was the use of footlights and large chandeliers, which were essential for indoor performances. Either candles or oil lamps provided the light, and there was a constant need for attentive stage-hands and candle snuffers to forestall accidental fires.

The stage scenery could be lavish, but for economy much of it was probably used in the productions of many separate plays. Molière apparently favored sparse sets and only minimal stage properties. The actors and actresses (women were never excluded from the French stage) wore contemporary costumes. This convention made Molière's satires all the more effective. Since his performers were costumed like the social types being pictured and mocked, the comedies became images of the social scenes inhabited by his audiences.

Love Is the Doctor (*L'Amour Médecin*): A Comic Farce

Molière's *Love Is the Doctor* (*L'Amour Médecin*) was first performed in 1665 at the palace of Louis XIV at Versailles, where the king himself sometimes joined Molière's casts to indulge his own acting fantasies and to win applause from his courtiers. The play is typical of Molière's comic farces, relying heavily on pantomime, dance, and music in the *commedia dell'arte* tradition. The incidental music by Jean Baptiste Lully (1632–1687), who provided music for many other Molière plays, has survived and some parts of it are available in modern recordings.[7]

The central character in *Love Is the Doctor*, Sganarelle, appears with the same name in other Molière comedies, also in the tradition of the *commedia dell'arte*. Usually Sganarelle tries to beat others, but as often as not he is beaten himself, and therefore he is both the instigator and the butt of laughter. His function in *Love Is the Doctor* is typical: He is a wealthy businessman and a traditional paterfamilias, with the final word in family matters (like Egeus in *A Midsummer Night's Dream* and Polonius in *Hamlet*). He closely guards his daughter, Lucinda, from suitors to avoid having to pay a massive dowry to a son-in-law who, as he complains, might be a perfect stranger.

The plan by Lucinda and her suitor Clitander to marry despite Sganarelle's opposition is an example of the traditional intrigue plot, in which the father (or guardian), acting as blocking agent, chooses another man for the young woman, or, as in *Love Is the Doctor*, tries to prevent marriage entirely.[8] The *soubrette* in the play, who aids and abets the intrigue, is Lisette. Although in some intrigue plots the blocker is reconciled by the fact that the young man is independently rich, that does not happen in this play, for at the end Sganarelle is frustrated and outraged despite the surrounding merriment.

Molière's notable addition to the intrigue plot in *Love Is the Doctor* is his satiric treatment of doctors. Medical practice in the seventeenth century was based on the widely held theory that a healthy body contained a harmonious balance of the four bodily fluids or "humors"—blood, yellow bile, black bile, and phlegm. When one of the humors became excessive or "putrid," the imbalance made the patient sick. Illness, including mental illness, could also be caused by the *adust,* or burning, of a particular humor during a high fever. (The understanding of bacterial and viral causes of disease did not develop until two centuries after Molière.) When doctors made a diagnosis based on this system, their treatment was to purge the offending humor and its noxious pressures (as the doctors recommend for Lucinda many times in *Love Is the Doctor*). Depending on the humor, they employed one of four methods of purgation: (1) a lancing or "bleeding" to draw off blood, or "sanguine" (the most common purgation, but the patient, weakened by blood loss, would often die more speedily from the original disease); (2) an emetic to eliminate yellow bile, or "choler," through vomiting; (3) a laxative to purge black bile, or "melancholy"; and (4) various irritating (and sometimes poisonous) powders to eliminate "phlegm" through violent sneezing.

With such principles and treatments, doctors were open targets for satire, and *Love Is the Doctor* holds nothing back. Once Lisette reports Lucinda's illness, the play is invaded by Molière's cadre of funny physicians, who, like their real-life counterparts, were bearded men who dressed in black robes and hats. Molière satirizes his doctors on the grounds of cronyism, indifference to the condition of patients, pomposity, exploitation of gullibility, ignorance and indecision, resistance to innovation, and simple greed.

---

[7] See the recordings *L'Orchestre du Roi Soleil* (Alia Vox, 1999), and *Les Arts Florissants*, orchestra and chorus (Electra, 2002).
[8] The origins and characteristics of the intrigue plot are more fully described on page 1499.

Despite the severity of his satire, however, Molière also presents the doctors in a comic-farcical light. Both when they are summoned and when they are paid, for example, they perform dances and pantomimes. Even the blatant self-exposure of Dr. Fillpocket (Filerin) can be construed as the excess one expects of farce, and therefore honest medical practitioners in Molière's day could have claimed that the doctors in *Love Is the Doctor* represented the exception, not the rule.

Although the following version of *L'Amour Médecin* follows Molière's text faithfully, I have taken latitude in a few instances to emphasize his sharp comic intentions. For example, his introduction of the quack elixir "Orviétan" in act II, scene 6, requires explanation, which I have included as part of the dramatic text in preference to creating an extensive footnote. Because the names of the doctors are not particularly meaningful, I have given them "tag names" that I hope will be readily appreciated by today's readers. Thus Drs. Tomès, De Fonandrès, Macroton, Bahays, and Filerin are, respectively, Slicer, De Pits, Gouger, Golfer, and Fillpocket. Generally, the medical recommendations of these doctors cannot be translated into modern terms. Readers will therefore need to rely on the brief description given here about medical practice in Molière's day. Alert readers may notice some anachronisms and inconsistencies, such as the use of the words *pathological* and *psychosomatic;* these are not inadvertent, but are made in the hope that they are consistent with the comic spirit of Molière.

MOLIÈRE (JEAN BAPTISTE POQUELIN) (1622–1673)

 # Love Is the Doctor (L'Amour Médecin) (1665)

Translated by Edgar V. Roberts

CHARACTERS

Sganarelle, *a wealthy Parisian merchant, father of* Lucinda
Aminta, *his neighbor*
Lucretia, *his niece*
Mr. Williams, *his friend, a seller of tapestries*
Mr. Josse, *another friend, a jeweller*
Lucinda, *daughter of* Sganarelle, *in love with* Clitander
Lisette, *maid to* Lucinda, *a soubrette*
Champagne, *an assistant to* Sganarelle, *a dancer*
Dr. Slicer [Tomès]
Dr. De Pits [De Fonandrès]
Dr. Gouger [Macroton]   } *doctors*
Dr. Golfer [Bahays]
Dr. Fillpocket [Filerin]
Clitander, *in love with Lucinda*
A Justice
A Mountebank, *a quack, seller of the cure-all "Orviétan"*
Buffoons and Scaramouches, *assistants to the Mountebank*
The Spirit of Comedy
Musicians

Singers
Dancers
Servants, etc.

The action takes place in Paris, in the house and drawing room of SGANARELLE *[and also on a street in Paris].*

ACT 1

Scene I

Enter SGANARELLE, AMINTA, LUCRETIA, MR. WILLIAMS, *and* MR. JOSSE.

SGANARELLE: Life is strange. I agree with that great classical philosopher who said that those who have wealth also have woe,° and that misery breeds more misery. I've been married only once, and my wife is now dead.

MR. WILLIAMS: How many wives would you have liked?

SGANARELLE: Don't mock, Mr. Williams; my loss is great, and I'm still sad when I think about her. I never liked her lifestyle, and we argued a great deal, but Death, as they say, settles everything. She's dead and I'm sorry, but if she were alive we would still be fighting. Of all the children that Heaven blessed us with, only my daughter has survived, but she is my greatest sorrow because she is sad beyond belief—in a deep depression I can't get her out of. Beyond that, she won't tell me what's wrong. I'm almost beside myself, and I need your good advice. You [*to* LUCRETIA] are my niece. You [*to* AMINTA] are my neighbor. You [*to* MR. WILLIAMS *and* MR. JOSSE] are my friends and equals. What should I do?

MR. JOSSE: I believe that jewelry is what young women like best, and if I were you I would buy her some nice necklaces, brooches, or rings set with expensive diamonds, rubies, and emeralds.

5   **MR. WILLIAMS:** If I were in your position, I'd get her an elegant tapestry showing a landscape or historical scene. The sight of something like that in her room would pick up both her vision and her spirits.

AMINTA: If you ask me, I wouldn't do anything of the sort. Rather, I'd get her married off as soon as possible—maybe to the man who, they say, asked you for her hand some time ago.

LUCRETIA: I don't agree. She's not ready for marriage, and she's not strong enough to bear children. For her, having babies would be a quick way to go six feet under. She's too good for this world, and I think you should send her off to a convent, where she'll be able to do things to suit her special personality.

SGANARELLE: I appreciate your thoughts, but they seem more to your interests than mine. You are a jeweler, Mr. Josse, and your advice would probably make you a handsome profit. You, Mr. Williams, have a tapestry shop, and I think you're trying to get rid of a little excess inventory. I've heard that your boyfriend, neighbor Aminta, is carrying a torch for my daughter, and you'd therefore like to have her married off and out of circulation. And as for you, my dear niece, you know that I have no plans to consent to a marriage for my daughter—I've got my reasons—but your advice to send her to religious orders suggests that you wouldn't mind becoming the only heir to all my money. So, ladies and gentlemen, your advice is perhaps the best in the world, but, if you please, I want none of it. Please go.

[They leave, grumbling to themselves. SGANARELLE *then speaks sarcastically to the audience.]*

°1 *woe*: Ecclesiastes 2:9–11.

There you have modern, up-to-date friends, who give their impersonal advice with no hope of gain whatever.

ACT 1, SCENE 2

He remains. Enter LUCINDA.

SGANARELLE: [*Aside.*] That's my daughter taking a walk for exercise. She doesn't see me; she's sighing. Now she's raising her eyes to Heaven. [*To* LUCINDA.] Bless you, Lucinda. What's the matter? Why so sad and sorrowful? Why don't you tell me what's wrong? You can trust your dear old dad, so tell me what's on your mind. Don't worry. Give me a kiss, like a good little girl. [*Aside.*] I can't stand seeing her like this. [*To* LUCINDA.] Do you want me to die with unhappiness because of you? Won't you tell me what's troubling you? Tell me what's wrong and I'll do anything for you, I promise. Just tell me what's making you sad, because I swear on a stack of Bibles that there's nothing I won't do to make you happy. Tell me what you want. Are you jealous of any friends because they seem better dressed? I'll get you clothes that will make theirs seem like rags.—No? Does your room seem bare? I'll let you pick out the best furniture to be found anywhere.—No again? Well, maybe you want to learn music; I'll get you the best piano teacher there is.—Not that either? Maybe you're in love, and would like to be married. [LUCINDA *nods her head in agreement.*]

ACT 1, SCENE 3

They remain. Enter LISETTE.

LISETTE: Sir, you've just been chatting with your daughter. Did she tell you what's wrong?

SGANARELLE: No, she's being bitchy and it's making me mad.

LISETTE: Let me try; I'll sound her out a little.

SGANARELLE: It won't work. Since she's so stubborn, let her alone.

LISETTE: Just let me try. She may be more open with me than you. [*To* LUCINDA. *During* LISETTE'S *speech, which* SGANARELLE *also overhears, he gets increasingly irritated with his daughter.*] Now, Madam, let us know what's wrong; don't keep on like this and upset everybody. It seems to me that something really mysterious is bothering you, and if you won't tell your father, maybe you'll tell me. Do you want anything from him? You know that he'll spare no expense for you. Do you want him to give you more freedom? More promenades in the park? More presents to tempt your fancy?—No? Maybe you're angry with someone, then.—No? Well then, maybe you have a secret wish to get married, and you'd like your father's consent. [LUCINDA *nods enthusiastically.*]—Ah, that's it; why all the secrecy? Sir, the mystery is solved, and— 5

SGANARELLE: [*Interrupting her.*] Get away, you ingrate; I won't talk to you any more. Be as stubborn as you like.

LUCINDA: Father, since you want me to tell you—

SGANARELLE: No, I'm finished with you.

LISETTE: Sir, her sadness—

SGANARELLE: She's a hussy, and enjoys hurting me. 10

LUCINDA: Father, I want—

SGANARELLE: Is this the gratitude I get for bringing you up so well?

LISETTE: But, sir—

SGANARELLE: No, I'm so mad I may have a stroke.

LUCINDA: But, Father— 15

SGANARELLE: I no longer have a speck of kindness for you.

LISETTE: But—

SGANARELLE: She's a cheap wench.

LISETTE: But—

20 SGANARELLE: An ungrateful slut.

LISETTE: But—

SGANARELLE: A trollop, who won't tell me what's wrong with her.

LISETTE: It's a husband that she wants!

SGANARELLE: [*Hearing but deliberately ignoring this piece of information.*] I'll turn her out of my house.

25 LISETTE: A husband!

SGANARELLE: I detest her.

LISETTE: [*Shouting increasingly more loudly.*] A husband!

SGANARELLE: And I disown her as my daughter.

LISETTE: A husband!

30 SGANARELLE: No, don't talk to me about it.

LISETTE: A husband!

SGANARELLE: Don't talk to me about it.

LISETTE: A husband!

SGANARELLE: Don't talk to me about it.

35 LISETTE: A husband, a husband, a husband!

[*SGANARELLE stalks off.*]

ACT 1, SCENE 4

LISETTE and LUCINDA remain.

LISETTE: It's really true that none are so deaf as those who refuse to hear.

LUCINDA: [*Ironically.*] Well, Lisette, you see how wrong I was to hide my feelings, and how all I had to do was to tell my father about everything I wanted.

LISETTE: My God, he's a hard man. I swear, I'd enjoy playing some kind of trick on him to show him up. But why, Madam, did you hide your wishes from me?

LUCINDA: Alas, what would I have gained? I might just as well have kept the secret for the rest of my life. Do you think I didn't foresee what he would do? I know his temper, and I'm in despair about the refusal he gave to the envoy sent to him to propose marriage to me. I've lost hope.

5 LISETTE: [*As though recalling a forgotten incident.*] What's this? It's that stranger who arranged for the proposal, the one for whom you—

LUCINDA: Perhaps it's not right for me to speak so freely, but I confess, if I had the liberty to choose, he's the one I'd want. We've never spoken together; he's never been able to tell me he loves me. But, in all the places where he's seen me, his looks and gestures have indicated such tenderness, and his formal request for my hand has given me such a sense of his honor, that I can't help believing he loves me. No matter; you see how my father's reaction has hardened all this tenderness.

LISETTE: Well, I have to say, I think you shouldn't have kept things secret from me, but I'll still help you. You need to be certain of your determination—

LUCINDA: But what should I do against my father's authority?—And if he won't listen to my hopes—

LISETTE: Come on now, you can't let yourself be led around like a sheep. As long as you don't offend his honor, you can free yourself at least a little from him. What does he want with you? You're of age, and you're not made of stone. I say again I'll help you in this affair. Your interests are mine, and, you'll see, I know a thing or two—But I see your father; let's go in. Leave everything to me.

[*They hurry off.*]

ACT 1, SCENE 5

Enter SGANARELLE.

SGANARELLE: [*Laughing to himself.*] It's sometimes good to seem not to hear things you hear only too well. I was smart to sidestep that declaration of her hopes that I do not mean to satisfy. Is there anything more tyrannical than that custom by which marriage arrangements make paupers out of fathers?—Anything more futile and ridiculous than to spend your life grubbing and grabbing to get rich, and raising a daughter with care and love, only to be robbed of both of them at the hands of a total stranger, a nobody? No, no, I don't give a damn for that custom, and I'll keep my wealth and my daughter to myself.

ACT 1, SCENE 6

He remains. Enter LISETTE.

LISETTE: [*Pretending not to see* SGANARELLE.]—Oh unhappiness! Oh disgrace! Oh, poor Mr. Sganarelle! Where can I find him?
SGANARELLE: [*Aside.*] What's all this?
LISETTE: Oh unhappy father, what will you do when you learn about this?
SGANARELLE: [*Aside.*] What's going on?
LISETTE: My poor mistress!   5
SGANARELLE: [*Aside.*] I'm lost!
LISETTE: —Oh!
SGANARELLE: [*Running after* LISETTE.] Lisette!
LISETTE: [*Pretending not to hear him, but making sure he hears her.*] What a misfortune!
SGANARELLE: —Lisette!   10
LISETTE: [*Still pretending.*] What bad luck!
SGANARELLE: —Lisette!
LISETTE: [*Pretending yet.*] How ghastly awful!
SGANARELLE: —Lisette!
LISETTE: [*Pretending just now to have noticed him.*] Ah, Sir.   15
SGANARELLE: What's going on? What's wrong?
LISETTE: Sir, your daughter—
SGANARELLE: Oh, no!
LISETTE: Sir, sir, don't cry like that. [*Aside.*] You'll make me laugh if you keep on.
SGANARELLE: Tell me quickly.   20
LISETTE: You daughter was hurt by your words and scared by your anger. [*Dramatizing and exaggerating her following descriptions to the utmost.*] She went to her room and, in despair, she opened the window facing the river—
SGANARELLE: Oh, my God, no!
LISETTE: Then, raising her head heavenward, she said, "No, it's impossible for me to live with the anger of my father, and since he is disowning me, I want to die!"
SGANARELLE: She threw herself out?
LISETTE: No sir. She sorrowfully closed the window, and threw herself on her bed, where   25
she wept bitterly. Suddenly, her face got pale, her eyes rolled in her head, her heart seemed to stop, and she fell into my arms!
SGANARELLE: Oh, my poor daughter!
LISETTE: By slapping her face and using smelling salts, I revived her. But she's getting worse, and I don't believe she can last the day.

SGANARELLE: [*Calling to the offstage servant* CHAMPAGNE.] Champagne! Champagne! Champagne! [*Enter* CHAMPAGNE.] Quickly, go get the doctors, and as many as you can find! There can't be too many for this! Oh, my daughter, my poor daughter!

[*They leave quickly.*]

FIRST ENTR'ACTE

[CHAMPAGNE, *while dancing, knocks on the doors of four doctors, who begin dancing and then ceremoniously enter the house of the patient's father.*]

ACT 2

Scene 1

Enter SGANARELLE *and* LISETTE.

LISETTE: Why do you need four doctors, Sir? Just one alone is enough to kill you.
SGANARELLE: Be quiet. Four opinions are better than one.
LISETTE: Can't your daughter die by herself, without the help of these gentlemen?
SGANARELLE: Do you mean to say that it's the doctor who causes death, and not the disease?
5   LISETTE: Absolutely. I know a man who proved beyond doubt that we should never say, "This person died of a raging fever or a galloping consumption," but rather "That person was killed by the incompetence of two druggists and four doctors."
SGANARELLE: Stop. You'll offend these gentlemen.
LISETTE: Lord, Sir, our cat needed no drugs or treatment to recover from that jump she made from the rooftop to the street, and she didn't eat or move a muscle for three days. It's lucky for her there are no cat doctors, or they'd have wiped her out with their mindless purging and bleeding.
SGANARELLE: Will you please keep your impertinent remarks to yourself? Here they are.
LISETTE: Watch out. They'll tell you what you already know—that your daughter's sick. Only they'll bamboozle you by saying it in Latin!

ACT 2, SCENE 2

Enter DR. SLICER, DR. GOUGER, DR. DE PITS, *and* DR. GOLFER.

SGANARELLE: Welcome, gentlemen!
DR. SLICER: [*Pompously.*] We have made our diagnosis of your daughter, and she unquestionably has many impurities in her.
SGANARELLE: My daughter is impure?
DR. SLICER: You must understand that it is her body that is full of impurities—many corrupt and putrid humors.°
5   SGANARELLE: Oh, thank you, I understand.
DR. SLICER: But, we plan to consult about her.
SGANARELLE: [*To attending servants.*] Come, bring chairs for the doctors.
LISETTE: [*To* DR. SLICER.] Doctor, is that you?
SGANARELLE: How do you know Dr. Slicer?
10   LISETTE: From having seen him the other day at the home of a good friend of your niece.
DR. SLICER: How is her coachman?
LISETTE: Fabulous; he's dead.

°4 *corrupt and putrid humors:* internal illness of body fluids.

DR. SLICER: Dead?

LISETTE: Yes, dead.

DR. SLICER: That cannot be!   15

LISETTE: I don't know if it couldn't happen, but I do know that it did.

DR. SLICER: And I tell you he can't be dead.

LISETTE: And I tell you he's dead and buried.

DR. SLICER: You've made a mistake.

LISETTE: I saw it with my own eyes.   20

DR. SLICER: It's impossible. Hippocrates° says that patients don't die of this disease until the end of the second or third week, and he was sick for only six days.

LISETTE: Let Hippocrates talk all he wants; the coachman is dead.

SGANARELLE: [*To* LISETTE.] Be quiet, chatterbox; we should leave. [*To the doctors.*] Gentlemen, we will leave you in peace for your consultation. I know it's not customary to pay in advance, but I'll pay you now, before I forget.

[*He pays them, and each one, upon receiving the fee, makes a different show of thanks.* SGANARELLE *and* LISETTE *then leave.*]

ACT 2, SCENE 3

DR. SLICER, DR. GOUGER, DR. DE PITS, and DR. GOLFER remain.

DR. DE PITS: Paris is an incredibly large city, and a good medical practice requires long trips.

DR. SLICER: I have an excellent mule for that; you won't believe the distances I make him go each day.

DR. DE PITS: I have a marvelous horse; he never gets tired.

DR. SLICER: Do you know the ground my mule has covered today? I was near the Arsenal first. Then I went to the suburb of St. Germain, from there to Le Marais, and then to St. Honoré Gate; after that to St. Jacques, to the Richelieu Gate, and finally here. When I leave, I'll go to the Place Royale.

DR. DE PITS: My horse has gone to all those places today, and in addition I rode him all the   5
way to Ruel so I could see a patient.

DR. SLICER: By the way, what position do you gentlemen take in the controversy between Doctors Theophrastus and Artemius? This is a matter that's dividing the whole profession.

DR. DE PITS: I think Artemius is right.

DR. SLICER: I do too. It's true that his treatment killed the patient, and that the recommendation of Theophrastus was infinitely better, but in the circumstances, Theophrastus was wrong. He should not have ignored the recommendation of Artemius, who was, we must recognize, the senior physician in the case. What do you say about it?

DR. DE PITS: Proper procedure should always be respected. I think we would be lost without our strict order of authority.

DR. SLICER: I agree; I'm as severe about this as the devil—unless it's among friends.   10
The other day three of us were consulting with an outside physician about a patient. I stopped the whole business until we proceeded in absolute order. Meanwhile, the people of the house did their best as the illness reached a crisis, but I continued to insist

°21 *Hippocrates:* ancient Greek physician, known as the father of medicine.

Sganarelle (Didier Rousselet), concerned about his daughter's health, consults with the battery of physicians (Patricia Buignet, Paola Durant, Mikael Manoukian, Celeste Morrow) in this French language production of *Love Is the Doctor* (*L'Amour Médecin*) at the LE NEON Theater in Arlington, Virginia, in February 2003. Director: Didier Rousselet assisted by Dominique Montet. Simultaneous translations by Monica Neagoy. (Photo courtesy of LE NEON Theater, Arlington, VA)

on proper consultative procedure. Before we could end our conference, the patient died—may he rest in peace.

DR. DE PITS: Insisting on our rights like that is the best way to keep lay people in their place, and show them that we're in control.

DR. SLICER: A dead person is a dead person, and of no importance; but any neglect of standard operating procedures puts our whole profession in a bad light.

ACT 2, SCENE 4

They remain. Enter SGANARELLE.

SGANARELLE: Gentlemen, my daughter's condition is becoming serious. Please tell me at once what you have decided.

DR. SLICER: [*To DR. DE PITS.*] Sir, you speak.

DR. DE PITS: No, Sir, you speak first.

DR. SLICER: Please, Sir, don't be modest.

DR. DE PITS: No, Sir, please, after you.

5 **DR. SLICER:** Sir!

DR. DE PITS: Sir!

SGANARELLE: With all respect, gentlemen, forget your ceremony and remember our present urgency.

[*All four doctors now speak together.*]

DR. SLICER: The illness of your daughter—

10 **DR. DE PITS:** The judgment of all these gentlemen together—

Dr. Gouger: After our most exhaustive consultation—

Dr. Golfer: To consider the case step by step, we—

Sganarelle: Gentlemen, please, speak one at a time.

Dr. Slicer: Sir, we have reached a diagnosis of your daughter's illness. My opinion is that it stems from a sanguinary superabundance—too much blood, to you. So my recommendation is blood letting; as soon as possible you should let as much blood from her as you can.

Dr. De Pits: My best judgment is that her illness results from a putrefaction of humors, caused by too much repletion. So my advice—listen carefully—is that she be given an emetic. 15

Dr. Slicer: I submit that an emetic will kill her.

Dr. De Pits: And I believe that a bleeding is contra-indicated; it will bring about instant expiration—in other words, death.

Dr. Slicer: [*Huffily, to* Dr. De Pits.] You of course are a great authority.

Dr. De Pits: [*Defensively, to* Dr. Slicer] Yes, I am; I'll outshine you in any branch of medical knowledge.

Dr. Slicer: Do you recall that your wrongheaded treatment killed a man the other day? 20

Dr. De Pits: Do you recall that your bungling put a woman in her grave just three days ago?

Dr. Slicer: [*To* Sganarelle.] I've given you my opinion.

Dr. De Pits: [*To* Sganarelle.] And I've informed you of my professional judgment.

Dr. Slicer: If you don't bleed your daughter immediately, she'll be a goner. [*He leaves.*]

Dr. De Pits: And if you do bleed her, she'll die in a quarter of an hour. 25

[*He leaves.*]

ACT 2, SCENE 5

Sganarelle, Dr. Gouger, *and* Dr. Golfer *remain.*

Sganarelle: Which of the two should I believe, and what should I do with such contrary advice? Gentlemen, I ask you to understand my predicament and tell me objectively what you believe would cure my daughter.

Dr. Gouger: [*He speaks agonizingly slowly, drawing out his syllables and even stressing ordinarily silent letters.*] Sir, in these matters, we must proceed with circumspection, and, as they say, do nothing rashly, because the mistakes that we may make, according to our master, Hippocrates, may have dangerous consequences.

Dr. Golfer: [*This one speaks at breakneck speed.*] He's right; we must be careful in what we do. This is not a child's game, and when we fail, it's not easy to repair the damage and restore the dead to life: *Experimentum periculosum*: in other words, medicine is a perilous experiment that we learn from as we go along. That's why we must reason carefully, weigh the alternatives, consider individual cases, examine all the possible causes of the illness, and see what remedies we may bring to the patient.

Sganarelle: [*Aside.*] One is as slow as a turtle, the other as fast as a jackrabbit.

Dr. Gouger: [*He is the turtle.*] Therefore, Sir, to get down to the matter, I find that your daughter is sick. She has a chronic sickness which will get worse unless it gets better, for her symptoms indicate a pathological and mordant—that is to say, bad—vapor which penetrates the membranes of the brain. Now this vapor, which is called *atmos* in Greek, is caused by putrid, tenacious, and glutinous humors which are contained in the lower bowel. 5

Dr. Golfer: [*He is the jackrabbit.*] And, inasmuch as these humors were engendered there during an extended period, they have turned adust—that is, they have been overcooked, so to speak—and have produced the present pathology of the brain.

Dr. Gouger: [*Still speaking slowly.*] Therefore, in order that we may draw out, detach, withdraw, expel, and evacuate these said humors, we must recommend an aggressive treatment of purgation. But first, I find, it would not be improper to prescribe anodynes of emollients° and cleansing solutions, together with refreshing medicinal juleps and syrups to be mixed with her herbal tea and her tonic.

Dr. Golfer: After this, should come purging and bleeding, to be repeated as necessary.

Dr. Gouger: This does not mean that your daughter won't die after all this, but at least you will have done your best, and may be consoled by the realization that she died in accordance with proper procedures.

10 **Dr. Golfer:** It's much better to die by the rules than to recover in spite of them.

Dr. Gouger: We are giving you our best professional advice.

Dr. Golfer: And we have spoken to you as though you were our brother.

Sganarelle: [*To Dr. Gouger, drawing out his words.*] I thank you most humbly, Sir. [*To Dr. Golfer, as rapidly as possible.*] To you, Sir, I am infinitely obliged for the care that you have taken.

[*The doctors exit.*]

ACT 2, SCENE 6

Sganarelle, alone.

Sganarelle: Now I'm more uncertain than ever. What can I do? [*He ponders this question for a few moments.*] I've got an idea: I've heard about a medicine that can cure everything, which they make down in Orvieto, Italy. It's a marvelous new elixir called "Orviétan." The advertising says it's cured millions of people. I'll buy some for her. It's got to work.

[*He leaves.*]

ACT 2, SCENE 7

A Street. Enter Sganarelle and Mountebank, accompanied by his Buffoons and Scaramouches.

Sganarelle: Hello, Sir. Please give me a bottle of your amazing new drug, Orviétan. How much does it cost?

Mountebank: [*Singing.*]
Would the gold in the richest of mines
Be enough for this all-curing pill?
By its magic it separates the ill
From more ailments than forests have pines.
    Agues and itches,
    Fevers and twitches,
    Plagues and neuroses,
    Funks and psychoses,
    Measles, congestions,
    Strokes and depressions,
    Organs that fail you,
    All things that ail you—
All can be cured by my Orviétan, my Orviétan,
All can be cured by my Orviétan.

°7 *anodynes of emollients:* soothing lotions.

SGANARELLE: Sir, I believe that all the gold in the world is not enough to pay you for your medicine. However, here's five hundred for you.

MOUNTEBANK: [*Singing.*]

Sing my praise, for these pills, I surmise—
Such a bargain for such a small cost—
Give new strength to those lives that are tossed
By diseases the heavens devise.
　　Agues and itches,
　　Fevers and twitches,
　　Plagues and neuroses,
　　Funks and psychoses,
　　Measles, congestions,
　　Strokes and depressions,
　　Organs that fail you,
　　All things that ail you—
All can be cured by my Orviétan, my Orviétan,
All can be cured by my Orviétan.

[*Exit SGANARELLE.*]

SECOND ENTR'ACTE

A dance by the MOUNTEBANK'S BUFFOONS *and* SCARAMOUCHES.

ACT 3, SCENE 1

Enter DR. FILLPOCKET, DR. SLICER, and DR. DE PITS.

DR. FILLPOCKET: Gentlemen, as men of your experience you should be ashamed to have been so imprudent as to quarrel like young blockheads. Don't you see that such open arguments hurt us in the public eye? Isn't it enough that expert critics know all about the controversy and dissension among our authorities and ancient masters, without disclosing our humbug to the world by wrangling in front of spectators? I'm concerned that some members of our profession mismanage their public relations so badly, because lately we've been hurt, and if we're not careful we may ruin ourselves. I have nothing to lose in this, because I've already made my pile. Let it blow, rain, and hail, the dead are dead, and I'm rich enough not to fear the living. But in the long run, our squabbles and disputes don't advance the medical profession. Since Heaven has smiled on us and enabled us to hoodwink the public for centuries, let's not disabuse people by our excesses, but let us go on taking advantage of the gullible—and thereby go on making our bundles. You know we're not the only profession to prey on human vulnerability; it's the major study of half the world's population. Everyone wants to catch people in moments of weakness in order to cash in. Flatterers, for example, benefit from the human need for praise, and so they lay it on with a trowel; some people have made huge fortunes in this way. Alchemists benefit from people's greed by promising mountains of gold to fools stupid enough to invest in their phony technology about making gold out of lead. And people even pour money into those consummate fakers, the psychics, who manipulate the vanity and ambition of their victims by making rosy predictions about the future. But the greatest weakness of humanity is the love of life—yes, our instinct for self-preservation—and we, as doctors, all profit from it, even with our pompous nonsense. We reap gigantic rewards because of the worship and adoration that our profession gains from our patients' fear of death. Let us then preserve the high esteem that human fallibility has given us, and let us, in the eyes of that world of believers out there, agree to take the credit for our cures while we deceive people by convincing them to blame Nature for our blunders. Let's not go about, I say, stupidly destroying the happy continuation of this public misperception which puts bread on our tables; and from the dead, whom we put into the ground, let us raise up our boundless wealth.

DR. SLICER: [*Spellbound.*] You are so right—so very right. But our dispute arose simply from hot blood, which we cannot always control.

DR. FILLPOCKET: All right, then, gentlemen, put rancor aside, and make your apologies now.

DR. DE PITS: I agree, if my emetic can be given to our present patient then Dr. Slicer can do as he pleases with the next patient.

5   **DR. FILLPOCKET:** I couldn't say it better myself, and I'm glad to see good sense prevail.

DR. DE PITS: It's done.

DR. FILLPOCKET: Shake hands, then. [*DR. DE PITS and DR. SLICER shake hands.*] Goodbye. And next time, be more careful.

[*Exit DR. FILLPOCKET.*]

ACT 3, SCENE 2

DR. DE PITS and DR. SLICER remain. Enter LISETTE.

LISETTE: Gentlemen, how can you stand there without seeking a way of getting even for the attack that has just been made against the practice of medicine?

DR. SLICER: What do you mean?

LISETTE: A brazen fellow has just had the nerve to practice your profession without a licence; he has just wiped out another fellow with a sword clean through the body.

DR. SLICER: Listen, you can make fun of us now, but some day you'll be sick, and then we'll get you in our clutches.

5   **LISETTE:** When I'm ready, then I'll give you permission to do me in.

[*Exit the doctors.*]

ACT 3, SCENE 3

LISETTE remains. Enter CLITANDER, dressed as a doctor.

CLITANDER: Well, Lisette, what do you think of my outfit? Do you think I can fool our gentleman with it? Do I look the part of a doctor?

LISETTE: You look fine, but you're late. It's good that Heaven has made me so good-natured. I can't see two lovers sighing for each other without feeling soft myself, and wishing to satisfy their longing. Hang the consequences, I've sworn to free Lucinda from her tyranny and give her to you. I liked you from the first. I'm an authority when it comes to men, and she couldn't have made a better choice than you. True love requires great risks, and we have devised a scheme that we hope will succeed. Our plans are already moving ahead. The man we're dealing with is not one of your brightest in the world, and if we fail now, we can find a thousand other ways to reach our goal. Wait for me alone over there; I'll be right back to get you.

[*CLITANDER leaves.*]

ACT 3, SCENE 4

LISETTE remains. Enter SGANARELLE.

LISETTE: Sir, joy, joy!

SGANARELLE: What's this?

LISETTE: Rejoice.

SGANARELLE: What for?

LISETTE: And again, I say, rejoice!   5

SGANARELLE: Tell me what's going on, and then I'll rejoice—maybe.

LISETTE: No, I want you to rejoice in advance; I want you to sing and dance!

SGANARELLE: Upon what?

LISETTE: Upon my word.

SGANARELLE: Okay, then. [*He sings and dances.*] La lera la la, la lera la. What the devil!   10

LISETTE: Sir, your daughter is cured!

SGANARELLE: My daughter is cured?

LISETTE: Yes. I am bringing you a doctor, but not just any doctor. He is the most important doctor on earth, who makes miraculous cures and puts all other doctors to shame.

SGANARELLE: Where is he?

LISETTE: I'll have him come in. [*She leaves.*]   15

SGANARELLE: [*Alone.*] Let's see if this one will do better than the others.

ACT 3, SCENE 5

SGANARELLE remains. Enter LISETTE and CLITANDER in his doctor's robes.

LISETTE: [*Leading CLITANDER.*] Here he is.

SGANARELLE: This doctor has only a small growth of beard.

LISETTE: Science is not measured by a beard, and he did not get his degrees because of his chin.

SGANARELLE: Sir, I'm told that you have effective medications for regular bowel movements.

CLITANDER: Sir, my remedies are entirely unique. Other doctors use emetics, bleeding,   5
medicines, and enemas, but I cure by words, sounds, letters, signs, and mystical rings.

LISETTE: What did I tell you?

SGANARELLE: Here is a great man!

LISETTE: Sir, since your daughter is up and around, I'll get her over here.

SGANARELLE: Please do. [*LISETTE leaves.*]

CLITANDER: [*Taking SGANARELLE's pulse.*] Your daughter is indeed sick.   10

SGANARELLE: You know that from taking *my* pulse?

CLITANDER: Yes, because of the sympathetic vibrations passing between father and daughter.

ACT 3, SCENE 6

SGANARELLE and CLITANDER remain. Enter LUCINDA and LISETTE.

LISETTE: [*To CLITANDER.*] Here, Sir, take this chair. [*To SGANARELLE.*] Let's go and leave them together.

SGANARELLE: Why? I want to stay here.

LISETTE: Are you kidding? We should go; a doctor has a hundred questions that it's not right for us to hear.

[*SGANARELLE and LISETTE move to a side of the stage.*]

CLITANDER: [*Speaking to LUCINDA alone.*] Ah, Madam, I'm so overwhelmed with joy I hardly know how to begin speaking to you! When I could speak only with my eyes, I thought I had hundreds of things to say; but now that I have freedom to say what I want, I feel tongue-tied, and my happiness stifles my words.

5   LUCINDA: I feel the same thing, and like you I sense movements of joy that catch in my
        throat and prevent my speaking.
    CLITANDER: Ah, Madam, I would be so happy if you felt everything I feel, and if I could
        judge your heart by mine! But, Madam, may I believe that you were the one who
        thought of this happy stratagem that gives me such joy in your presence?
    LUCINDA: If you don't owe me the idea, at least you should know that I approved it
        eagerly.
    SGANARELLE: [*To LISETTE.*] He seems very close to her.
    LISETTE: [*To SGANARELLE.*] He's a doctor, and he's studying her facial features.
10 CLITANDER: [*To LUCINDA.*] Will you be faithful, Madam, in the promises you make to me?
    LUCINDA: And you, will you be firm in your present resolutions?
    CLITANDER: Ah, Madam, until death, and I'll demonstrate my love by what I'm now about
        to do.
    SGANARELLE: [*To CLITANDER.*] Well, our patient seems to be perking up.
    CLITANDER: That's because I've already tried one of the remedies of my great art on her.
        The mind has power over the body, and sickness often begins in the mind. My method
        is therefore to cure the spirit first before treating the body. Accordingly, I have studied
        her looks, her facial features, and the lines of her two hands; and by the science
        bestowed on me by Heaven, I have determined that her sickness is psychosomatic—
        she is sick in spirit. This disease comes entirely from her disordered imagination,
        which prompts her depraved wish to be married. My view is that there is nothing
        more extravagant or ridiculous than this wish for marriage.
15 SGANARELLE: [*Aside.*] This is indeed a man of skill!
    CLITANDER: And all my life I have had, and will continue to have, an aversion for it.
    SGANARELLE: [*Aside.*] A great physician!
    CLITANDER: But, since it's necessary to flatter the imagination of patients, and because I see
        schizophrenic tendencies in her, and also because it would be perilous not to treat her
        quickly, I have taken advantage of her weakness and told her that I came here to ask
        you for her hand in marriage. When she heard that, her appearance changed for the
        better, her complexion brightened, and her eyes sparkled. I believe that if you keep her
        in this error for several days, you will see her recover completely.
    SGANARELLE: There's nothing I want more.
20 CLITANDER: Afterwards we'll apply other remedies to cure her of this fantasy entirely.
    SGANARELLE: That will be marvellous! [*To LUCINDA.*] Well, daughter, here is a gentleman
        who wishes to marry you, and I have told him he has my blessing!
    LUCINDA: Dear me, is this possible?
    SGANARELLE: Yes.
    LUCINDA: I'm not dreaming?
25 SGANARELLE: No, you're not dreaming.
    LUCINDA: [*To CLITANDER.*] You really want to be my husband?
    CLITANDER: Yes, Madam.
    LUCINDA: And my father consents?
    SGANARELLE: Yes, daughter.
30 LUCINDA: If this is true, I couldn't be happier!
    CLITANDER: Don't doubt it, Madam. It is not just today that I began loving you and longing
        to marry you. I came here only to ask for your hand, and, if you want to know the
        whole truth exactly as it is, this doctor's costume is nothing more than a false front. I
        pretended to be a doctor only to come close to you, the more easily to realize my goal
        of marrying you.
    LUCINDA: This all shows me the proofs of your tender love. I am deeply moved by them.
    SGANARELLE: [*Aside.*] Oh, the fool! the fool! the fool!

LUCINDA: You approve of this gentleman as my husband, father, and do so willingly?

SGANARELLE: Yes. Give me your hand, and you, Sir, give me yours, too, by way of witness.   35

CLITANDER: But, Sir—

SGANARELLE: [*Stifling laughter.*] No, no, it's to—it's to ease her mind. Now, join hands. There, it's done.

CLITANDER: Accept as a token of my faith this ring that I give you. [*Speaking low, to SGANARELLE.*] It's a special ring to cure her distracted mind.

LUCINDA: Let us draw up the contract, so that everything will be complete.

CLITANDER: Certainly; I would like that, Madam. [*To SGANARELLE.*] I'll show her the man   40
who writes my prescriptions, and make her believe he's a genuine Justice.

SGANARELLE: Excellent!

CLITANDER: [*Calling offstage.*] You there, send in the Justice I brought with me!

LUCINDA: What, you brought along a Justice?

CLITANDER: Yes, Madam.

LUCINDA: I'm delighted!   45

SGANARELLE: [*Chuckling.*] Oh, the fool! the fool!

ACT 3, SCENE 7

They all remain. Enter the JUSTICE, *appropriately robed.* CLITANDER *whispers to the* JUSTICE.

SGANARELLE: [*To the* JUSTICE.] Welcome, Sir. I commission you to draft a contract for these
two young people. Please begin writing. [*While the* JUSTICE *is writing,* SGANARELLE *speaks
to* LUCINDA.] This will be a contract to end all contracts. [*To the* JUSTICE.] I give her
twenty million upon her marriage. Write that down!

LUCINDA: I'm so overwhelmingly grateful to you, father.

JUSTICE: [*Giving the contract to* SGANARELLE.] There, it's done; you need only to come
and sign.

SGANARELLE: How's that for a contract speedily finished?

CLITANDER: [*To* SGANARELLE.] At least, Sir—   5

SGANARELLE: No, no words of gratitude; say nothing, I beg you. [*Aside to* CLITANDER.] Don't
we both know what we're doing? [*To the* JUSTICE.] Come, give him the pen. [*After*
CLITANDER *signs,* SGANARELLE *gives the pen to* LUCINDA.] Come, come, sign it. Go ahead;
I'll sign too. [*He signs.*]

LUCINDA: No, no. I want to hold the contract myself.

SGANARELLE: All right, take it. [*After she has signed.*] Now, are you happy?

LUCINDA: More than you can imagine!

SGANARELLE: I'm please. I'm very pleased.   10

CLITANDER: As for the rest, I not only took the trouble to bring a Justice along, but to
celebrate the occasion I brought singers and musicians too. Send them in! These are the
people I take with me every day on my rounds; I direct them, with their harmony, to
pacify the troubled minds of my patients.

FINAL SCENE

All remain. Enter the SPIRIT OF COMEDY, DANCERS, *and* MUSICIANS.

ALL THREE [COMEDY, DANCERS, *and* MUSICIANS].
If you didn't have music and singing and dancing,
   You'd spend your life with your mind in chains;
For it's we, with our wonderful songs and our prancing,
   Who win the fight against aches and pains.

COMEDY
Do you want to break free,
In the happiest way,
From the mis'ry and grief
Of each long day?
Then sing your song
The whole day long;
Throw away your medicine,
Along with the jar it's in,
And join our throng
As we sing along.

ALL THREE
If you didn't have music and singing and dancing,
You'd spend your life with your mind in chains;
For it's we, with our wonderful songs and our prancing,
Who win the fight against aches and pains.

[*While they are singing and dancing, and amidst all the Games, Smiles, and Pleasures,* CLITANDER *leads* LUCINDA *away.*]

SGANARELLE: This is a marvelous way to cure someone! But where is my daughter, and where is the doctor?

LISETTE: They left—to complete the rest of the marriage ritual.

SGANARELLE: What are you saying? What—what marriage?

LISETTE: In truth, Sir, the game has been bagged, and what you thought was a joke turns out to be the absolute truth!

5 SGANARELLE: [*The* DANCERS *catch hold of him and bring him into the dance by force.*] What's this? The devil! Let me go! Let me go, I tell you! Still more? A plague on everything!

[*Finis.*]

QUESTIONS

Act 1

1. What does the opening scene indicate about Sganarelle's responses to other people? Describe his traits. What do you learn about his economic status? Why is this status important in the plot?

2. Describe the father–daughter relationship that is brought out in scenes 2 and 3. Why is the relationship made to seem comic and not serious?

3. Why is it important that we learn about a suitor whom Lucinda likes, and that there has been an "envoy" from him seeking to negotiate a marriage?

4. Describe Lisette. Is she flat or round, representative or individualized? Why is she important? What is her relationship with Lucinda?

5. Why does Sganarelle not want his daughter married? What do his reasons disclose about him? What effect does Sganarelle's behavior toward his daughter have on your attitude toward him at the play's conclusion?

Act 2

6. Why is Sganarelle dramatized as a person with great faith in doctors? Why is Lisette skeptical about them?

7. Study the dialogue between Lisette and Dr. Slicer (scene 2, paragraphs 8–22). Describe how character and speech here produce laughter.

8. At the end of scene 2 a stage direction describes Sganarelle's payment to the doctors. Explain how pantomime and dance might be used here to augment Moliére's satiric presentation of doctors. Be specific.

9. Though scene 3 is supposedly a medical "consultation" about the condition of Lucinda, the conversation has nothing to do with her. What does Molière achieve by introducing the topics the doctors actually discuss?

10. What treatments do the doctors prescribe for Lucinda? Though the doctors are contradictory, in what respects are some of them truthful? Why is their telling the truth comic?

11. Explain Sganarelle's role in the scenes with the doctors. What is the effect of these scenes on his seeking out the Mountebank, and also on his reception of Clitander in the next act when Clitander appears disguised as a doctor?

Act 3

12. Why does Dr. Fillpocket make such a long speech? How honest is he? Would he give this speech to anyone but fellow doctors? Is Molière's treatment of the speech comic? Serious? True? Partly true? Untrue?

13. What is the stratagem devised by Lisette and Clitander? How is it related to Sganarelle's already proven faith in doctors and medication?

14. Explain the irony of Clitander's confession to Lucinda and also of Sganarelle's responses beginning in scene 6, and extending to the revelation in the last scene. How does Molière keep the final scene light and comic?

15. How does Sganarelle react to the news that the marriage of Lucinda and Clitander is real? How is his reaction kept from seeming serious? If you were a director, what might you tell the actor playing Sganarelle to do during the concluding dance? Why?

GENERAL QUESTIONS

1. Who is the protagonist of *Love Is the Doctor?* What conflicts develop? Who and what are the antagonists? Which side is triumphant at the end?

2. A traditional topic for laughter is that the "biter gets bitten" and the "tables are turned." To what degree does Molière use this topic in the play? How successful is it as a means of developing humor?

3. The critic Harold C. Knutson has observed that in *Love Is the Doctor* we have "a particularly biting commentary on doctors and doctoring," and that one of the modes of satire is that the doctors "drop the mask and betray their callousness" and "contentiousness," and that their "concern" is not with their patients but rather with rules and formalities (*Molière: An Archetypal Approach* [Toronto: U of Toronto P, 1976], pp. 52–53). Do you agree or disagree with Professor Knutson's observations? Explain in detail.

4. Aside from the medical satire, describe the various doctors as characters. Which of the doctors are the most fully developed? Which are the most amusing? Why?

Comedy Since Shakespeare and Molière

The subject of comedy in the centuries from Shakespeare and Molière to the present is vast. In all the major European countries, and also in the United States, there were many comic dramatists. Some of them were successful in their time but are neglected today, such as Eugène Scribe in France. Some, such as Anton Chekhov in Russia, are known not only for their comedy but also for other works (such as Chekhov's many short stories). In England in the seventeenth century, dramatists such as William Wycherley (1640–1716) and William Congreve (1670–1729) created a sophisticated type of drama in the comedy-of-manners tradition that is termed "Restoration comedy" because it developed after King Charles II was reestablished on the English throne in 1660. The Restoration comedies combined and contrasted elegant and boisterous manners, and they often dealt with serious social and sexual problems. In the first part of the eighteenth century, dramatists created "sentimental" drama. Sentimental comedies showed individuals who verge on behavioral excesses but who eventually conform to morality because their goodness of heart overcomes their personal interests, feelings, and self-indulgence—hence the term "sentimental."

The first half of the eighteenth century saw the popularity of other forms such as the musical play and the burlesque play. The musical play was first known as **ballad opera;** later it was called **comic opera;** today it is called **musical comedy,** or simply a **musical.** The characteristic of a musical play is the combination of spoken dialogue and brief songs. The first such play was *The Beggar's Opera* (1728) by John Gay (1685–1732).[9] *The Beggar's Opera* was also a burlesque that satirized the Italian operas so popular in the early eighteenth century. Henry Fielding (1707–1754), best known for his later novels, wrote at least nine ballad operas in the mode of *The Beggar's Opera*, and he also wrote the best of English **burlesque** plays, *Tom Thumb* (1730, 1731). Also unique in Fielding's comic writing were a number of five-act plays dealing with serious social situations. Comic operas reached their high point in the nineteenth century with the Savoy Operas of William Gilbert (1836–1911) and Arthur Sullivan (1842–1900). The Gilbert and Sullivan operas, such as *H.M.S. Pinafore* (1878), *The Mikado* (1885), and *The Pirates of Penzance* (1879) are regularly performed today by both professionals and amateurs. In the United States during the twentieth century, the musical comedy form became a major force, as with the plays of Richard Rodgers (1902–1979) and Oscar Hammerstein II (1895–1960), and Alan Jay Lerner (1918–1986) and Frederick Loewe (1901–1988).

At the turn of the nineteenth century the major comic dramatists in addition to Chekhov were Oscar Wilde (1854–1900) and George Bernard Shaw (1856–1950), all of whose plays are still regularly revived and well attended. The twentieth century marked the appearance of numbers of important comic dramatists, including many, like Eugene O'Neill, who are better known for more serious plays. A number of writers divided their time between theater and film, such as George Kaufman (1889–1961), whose *The Man Who Came to Dinner* (1939) was successful both

---

[9]For a song from *The Beggar's Opera*, see page 767.

onstage and on the screen. For a time, Kaufman also wrote film scripts for some of the early film comedies of the Marx Brothers. Many other comic playwrights experimented with comedy. Such a writer is Arthur Kopit (b. 1937), whose *Oh Dad, Poor Dad, Mamma's Hung You in the Closet and I'm Feelin' So Sad* (1961) created a great stir when it was first performed. Of particular note is the development of the "theater of the absurd." Some significant plays in this tradition are *Waiting for Godot* (1953) by Samuel Beckett (1906–1989), *Rhinocéros* (1960) by Jean Genet (1910–1986), and *The Homecoming* (1960) by Harold Pinter (b. 1930), which has recently been revived on the New York stage. Edward Albee's *The Sandbox* (1959), a short absurdist play, is included in this book in Chapter 23 (see p. 1226).

The technology of the twentieth century has had a great influence on the development of comedy. When radio became prominent in the 1930s, a number of short radio comic dramas developed that were broadcast regionally and nationally on a daily basis, such as "Vic and Sade," written by Paul Rhymer, and "Ma Perkins," by Robert Andrews, Orvin Tovrov, and others, both of which were heard by millions who sat regularly during the day beside their radios. With the advent of television in the 1950s there was a virtual explosion of so-called "soap operas" or "soaps," and "situation comedies" or "sitcoms" in the tradition of the earlier radio shows. Some of the more prominent sitcoms among the many were "I Love Lucy," the "Jackie Gleason" show, "Frazier," "Friends," "Seinfeld," and "Mad About You." Although the shorter radio comedies were performed daily during the height of the radio years in the 1930s and 1940s, the longer television sitcoms, because of greater and more elaborate production requirements, have generally been presented weekly.

Comedy today is characterized by great variety. All the types described earlier (see pp. 1502–04) are regularly being presented. Serious plays may contain comic and farcical elements. Farcical and comic plays may introduce serious sequences and also may contain strong elements of satire. Satirical plays may contain songs to complement the onstage action and also to divert and entertain. Writers at the beginning of the twenty-first century clearly were continuing to combine the various comic forms that were brought into prominence by Shakespeare and the comic dramatists in the centuries that followed him.

ANTON CHEKHOV (1860–1904)

Anton Chekhov was born in Taganrog in southern Russia in 1860, the son of a merchant and grandson of a serf. He entered medical school in Moscow in 1879, graduating in 1884. While a student he was also obligated to help support his family, and he turned to writing stories, jokes, and potboilers for pay under a variety of pen names, one of which was "The Doctor Without Patients." The Bear *belongs to the end of this early period, ten years before Chekhov's association with the Moscow Art Theater at the end of the century.*

Chekhov tended to downplay The Bear, *referring to it as a "joke" and a "vaudeville"—both words suggesting a farcical work with little form or substance. Nevertheless the play was greatly acclaimed and financially successful, to the author's amazement and delight. Three months after its first performance in 1888, he likened* The Bear *to a "milk cow" ("cash cow") because, to his happiness, it earned him a steady income.*

The Bear is a farce, a dramatic form designed preeminently to evoke laughter, and it therefore contains extravagant language and boisterous and sudden action. But there is also an underlying seriousness that sustains the humor. In their way, both Smirnov and Mrs. Popov have been failures; they could conceivably sink into lives of depression and futility, and both are walking a very fine wire as the play begins. Chekhov makes clear that Mrs. Popov is filled with resentment at her unfaithful and now dead husband, and also that she is chafing under her self-imposed resolution to lead a life of mourning and self-denial in his memory. Smirnov is having difficulty with creditors, and he admits that his relationships with the many women he has known have ended unhappily. He is therefore both cynical and angry.

The climax of the play is the improbable and preposterous challenge to a duel that Smirnov offers Mrs. Popov, resolved by the equally preposterous outcome. Despite the improbabilities of the play, however, the actions are not impossible because they manifest the true internal needs of the main characters. Chekhov's friend Leo Tolstoy (1828–1910), who criticized some of Chekhov's late plays, laughed heartily at *The Bear,* and countless audiences and readers since then have joined him in laughter.

The Bear, A Joke in One Act (1900)

CAST OF CHARACTERS

> **Mrs. Popov,** *a widow of seven months, Mrs. Popov is small and pretty, with dimples. She is a landowner. At the start of the play, she is pining away in memory of her dead husband.*
> **Grigory Stepanovich Smirnov,** *easily angered and loud, Smirnov is older. He is a landowner, too, and a man of substance.*
> **Luka,** *Mrs. Popov's footman (a servant whose main tasks were to wait table and attend the carriages, in addition to general duties). He is old enough to feel secure in telling Mrs. Popov what he thinks.*
> **Gardener, Coachman, Workmen,** *who enter at the end.*

SCENE. *The drawing room of* MRS. POPOV's *country home.*

[MRS. POPOV, *in deep mourning, does not remove her eyes from a photograph.*]

LUKA: It isn't right, madam . . . you're only destroying yourself. . . . The chambermaid and the cook have gone off berry picking; every living being is rejoicing; even the cat knows how to be content, walking around the yard catching birds, and you sit in your room all day as if it were a convent, and you don't take pleasure in anything. Yes, really! Almost a year has passed since you've gone out of the house!

MRS. POPOV: And I shall never go out. . . . What for? My life is already ended. He lies in his grave; I have buried myself in these four walls . . . we are both dead.

LUKA: There you go again! Your husband is dead, that's as it was meant to be, it's the will of God, may he rest in peace. . . . You've done your mourning and that will do. You can't go on weeping and mourning forever. My wife died when her time came, too. . . . Well? I grieved, I wept for a month, and that was enough for her; the old lady wasn't worth a second more. [*Sighs.*] You've forgotten all your neighbors. You don't go anywhere or accept any calls. We live, so to speak, like spiders. We never see the light. The mice have eaten my uniform. It isn't as if there weren't any nice neighbors—the district is full of them . . . there's a regiment stationed at Riblov, such officers—they're like candy—you'll never get your fill of them! And in the barracks, never a Friday goes by without a dance; and, if you please, the military band plays music every day. . . . Yes, madam, my dear lady: you're young, beautiful, in the full bloom of youth—if only you took a little pleasure in life . . . beauty doesn't last forever, you know! In ten years' time, you'll be wanting to wave your fanny in front of the officers—and it will be too late.

MRS. POPOV: [*Determined.*] I must ask you never to talk to me like that! You know that when Mr. Popov died, life lost all its salt for me. It may seem to you that I am alive, but that's only conjecture! I vowed to wear mourning to my grave and not to see the light of day. . . . Do you hear me? May his departed spirit see how much I love him. . . . Yes, I know, it's no mystery to you that he was often mean to me, cruel . . . and even unfaithful, but I shall remain true to the grave and show him I know how to love. There, beyond the grave, he will see me as I was before his death. . . .

LUKA: Instead of talking like that, you should be taking a walk in the garden or have Toby   5
or Giant harnessed and go visit some of the neighbors. . . .

MRS. POPOV: Ai! [*She weeps.*]

LUKA: Madam! Dear lady! What's the matter with you! Christ be with you!

MRS. POPOV: Oh, how he loved Toby! He always used to ride on him to visit the Korchagins or the Vlasovs. How wonderfully he rode! How graceful he was when he pulled at the reins with all his strength! Do you remember? Toby, Toby! Tell them to give him an extra bag of oats today.

LUKA: Yes, madam.

[*Sound of loud ringing.*]

MRS. POPOV: [*Shudders.*] Who's that? Tell them I'm not at home!   10

LUKA: Of course, madam. [*He exits.*]

MRS. POPOV: [*Alone. Looks at the photograph.*] You will see, Nikolai, how much I can love and forgive . . . my love will die only when I do, when my poor heart stops beating. [*Laughing through her tears.*] Have you no shame? I'm a good girl, a virtuous little wife. I've locked myself in and I'll be true to you to the grave, and you . . . aren't you ashamed, you chubby cheeks? You deceived me, you made scenes, for weeks on end you left me alone . . .

LUKA: [*Enters, alarmed.*] Madam, somebody is asking for you. He wants to see you. . . .

MRS. POPOV: But didn't you tell them that since the death of my husband, I don't see anybody?

LUKA: I did, but he didn't want to listen; he spoke about some very important business.   15

MRS. POPOV: I am *not at home!*

LUKA: That's what I told him . . . but . . . the devil . . . he cursed and pushed past me right into the room . . . he's in the dining room right now.

MRS. POPOV: [*Losing her temper.*] Very well, let him come in . . . such manners! [*LUKA goes out.*] How difficult these people are! What does he want from me? Why should he disturb my peace? [*Sighs.*] But it's obvious I'll have to go live in a convent. . . . [*Thoughtfully.*] Yes, a convent. . . .

SMIRNOV: [*Enters while speaking to LUKA.*] You idiot, you talk too much. . . . Ass! [*Sees MRS. POPOV and changes to dignified speech.*] Madam, may I introduce myself: retired lieutenant of the artillery and landowner, Grigory Stepanovich Smirnov! I feel the necessity of troubling you about a highly important matter. . . .

MRS. POPOV: [*Refusing her hand.*] What do you want?   20

SMIRNOV: Your late husband, whom I had the pleasure of knowing, has remained in my debt for two twelve-hundred-ruble notes. Since I must pay the interest at the agricultural bank tomorrow, I have come to ask you, madam, to pay me the money today.

Mrs. Popov: One thousand two hundred. . . . And why was my husband in debt to you?

Smirnov: He used to buy oats from me.

Mrs. Popov: [*Sighing, to* Luka.] So, Luka, don't you forget to tell them to give Toby an extra bag of oats.

[*Luka goes out.*]

[*To* Smirnov:] If Nikolai, my husband, was in debt to you, then it goes without saying that I'll pay; but please excuse me today. I haven't any spare cash. The day after tomorrow, my steward will be back from town and I will give him instructions to pay you what is owed; until then I cannot comply with your wishes. . . . Besides, today is the anniversary—exactly seven months ago my husband died, and I'm in such a mood that I'm not quite disposed to occupy myself with money matters.

25 **Smirnov:** And I'm in such a mood that if I don't pay the interest tomorrow, I'll be owing so much that my troubles will drown me. They'll take away my estate!

Mrs. Popov: You'll receive your money the day after tomorrow.

Smirnov: I don't want the money the day after tomorrow. I want it today.

Mrs. Popov: You must excuse me. I can't pay you today.

Smirnov: And I can't wait until after tomorrow.

30 **Mrs. Popov:** What can I do, if I don't have it now?

Smirnov: You mean to say you can't pay?

Mrs. Popov: I can't pay. . . .

Smirnov: Hm! Is that your last word?

Mrs. Popov: That is my last word.

35 **Smirnov:** Positively the last?

Mrs. Popov: Positively.

Smirnov: Thank you very much. We'll make a note of that. [*Shrugs his shoulders.*] And people want me to be calm and collected! Just now, on the way here, I met a tax officer and he asked me: why are you always so angry, Grigory Stepanovich? Goodness' sake, how can I be anything but angry? I need money desperately . . . I rode out yesterday early in the morning, at daybreak, and went to see all my debtors; and if only one of them had paid his debt . . . I was dog-tired, spent the night God knows where—a Jewish tavern beside a barrel of vodka. . . . Finally I got here, fifty miles from home, hoping to be paid, and you treat me to a "mood." How can I help being angry?

Mrs. Popov: It seems to me that I clearly said: My steward will return from the country and then you will be paid.

Smirnov: I didn't come to your steward, but to you! What the hell, if you'll pardon the expression, would I do with your steward?

40 **Mrs. Popov:** Excuse me, my dear sir, I am not accustomed to such profane expressions nor to such a tone. I'm not listening to you any more. [*Goes out quickly.*]

Smirnov: [*Alone.*] Well, how do you like that? "A mood." . . . "Husband died seven months ago"! Must I pay the interest or mustn't I? I ask you: Must I pay, or must I not? So, your husband's dead, and you're in a mood and all that finicky stuff . . . and your steward's away somewhere; may he drop dead. What do you want me to do? Do you think I can fly away from my creditors in a balloon or something? Or should I run and bash my head against the wall? I go to Gruzdev—and he's not at home; Yaroshevich is hiding, with Kuritsin it's a quarrel to the death and I almost throw him out the window; Mazutov has diarrhea, and this one is in a "mood." Not one of these swine wants to pay me! And all because I'm too nice to them. I'm a sniveling idiot, I'm spineless, I'm an old lady! I'm too delicate with them! So, just you wait! You'll find out what I'm like! I won't let you play around with me, you devils! I'll stay and stick it out until she pays. Rrr! . . . How furious I am today, how furious! I'm shaking inside from rage and I can hardly catch my breath. . . . Damn it! My God, I even feel sick! [*He shouts.*] Hey, you!

LUKA: [*Enters.*] What do you want?

SMIRNOV: Give me some beer or some water! [*LUKA exits.*] What logic is there in this! A man needs money desperately, it's like a noose around his neck—and she won't pay because, you see, she's not disposed to occupy herself with money matters! . . . That's the logic of a woman! That's why I never did like and do not like to talk to women. I'd rather sit on a keg of gunpowder than talk to a woman. Brr! . . . I even have goose pimples, this broad has put me in such a rage! All I have to do is see one of those spoiled bitches from a distance, and I get so angry it gives me a cramp in the leg. I just want to shout for help.

LUKA: [*Entering with water.*] Madam is sick and won't see anyone.

SMIRNOV: Get out! [*LUKA goes.*] Sick and won't see anyone! No need to see me . . . I'll stay and   45
sit here until you give me the money. You can stay sick for a week, and I'll stay for a week . . . if you're sick for a year, I'll stay a year. . . . I'll get my own back, dear lady! You can't impress me with your widow's weeds and your dimpled cheeks . . . we know all about those dimples! [*Shouts through the window.*] Semyon, unharness the horses! We're not going away quite yet! I'm staying here! Tell them in the stable to give the horses some oats! You brute, you let the horse on the left side get all tangled up in the reins again! [*Teasing.*] "Never mind" . . . I'll give you a never mind! [*Goes away from the window.*] Shit! The heat is unbearable and nobody pays up. I slept badly last night and on top of everything else this broad in mourning is "in a mood" . . . my head aches . . . [*Drinks, and grimaces.*] Shit! This is water! What I need is a drink! [*Shouts.*] Hey, you!

LUKA: [*Enters.*] What is it?

SMIRNOV: Give me a glass of vodka. [*LUKA goes out.*] Oaf! [*Sits down and examines himself.*] Nobody would say I was looking well! Dusty all over, boots dirty, unwashed, unkempt, straw on my waistcoat. . . . The dear lady probably took me for a robber. [*Yawns.*] It's not very polite to present myself in a drawing room looking like this; oh well, who cares? . . . I'm not here as a visitor but as a creditor, and there's no official costume for creditors. . . .

LUKA: [*Enters with vodka.*] You're taking liberties, my good man. . . .

SMIRNOV: [*Angrily.*] What?

LUKA: I . . . nothing . . . I only . . .   50

SMIRNOV: Who are you talking to? Shut up!

LUKA: [*Aside.*] The devil sent this leech. An ill wind brought him. . . .[*LUKA goes out.*]

SMIRNOV: Oh how furious I am! I'm so mad I could crush the whole world into a powder! I even feel faint! [*Shouts.*] Hey, you!

MRS. POPOV: [*Enters, eyes downcast.*] My dear sir, in my solitude, I have long ago grown unaccustomed to the masculine voice and I cannot bear shouting. I must request you not to disturb my peace and quiet!

SMIRNOV: Pay me my money and I'll go.   55

MRS. POPOV: I told you in plain language: I haven't any spare cash now; wait until the day after tomorrow.

SMIRNOV: And I also told you respectfully, in plain language: I don't need the money the day after tomorrow, but today. If you don't pay me today, then tomorrow I'll have to hang myself.

MRS. POPOV: But what can I do if I don't have the money? You're so strange!

SMIRNOV: Then you won't pay me now? No?

MRS. POPOV: I can't. . . .   60

SMIRNOV: In that case, I can stay here and wait until you pay. . . . [*Sits down.*] You'll pay the day after tomorrow? Excellent! In that case I'll stay here until the day after tomorrow.

I'll sit here all that time . . . [*Jumps up.*] I ask you: Have I got to pay the interest tomorrow, or not? Or do you think I'm joking?

MRS. POPOV: My dear sir, I ask you not to shout! This isn't a stable!

SMIRNOV: I wasn't asking you about a stable but about this: Do I have to pay the interest tomorrow or not?

MRS. POPOV: You don't know how to behave in the company of a lady!

65   SMIRNOV: No, I don't know how to behave in the company of a lady!

MRS. POPOV: No, you don't! You are an ill-bred, rude man! Respectable people don't talk to a woman like that!

SMIRNOV: Ach, it's astonishing! How would you like me to talk to you? In French, perhaps? [*Lisps in anger.*] Madame, je vous prie° . . . how happy I am that you're not paying me the money. . . . Ah, pardon, I've made you uneasy! Such lovely weather we're having today! And you look so becoming in your mourning dress. [*Bows and scrapes.*]

MRS. POPOV: That's rude and not very clever!

SMIRNOV: [*Teasing.*] Rude and not very clever! I don't know how to behave in the company of ladies. Madam, in my time I've seen far more women than you've seen sparrows. Three times I've fought duels over women; I've jilted twelve women, nine have jilted me! Yes! There was a time when I played the fool; I became sentimental over women, used honeyed words, fawned on them, bowed and scraped. . . . I loved, suffered, sighed at the moon; I became limp, melted, shivered . . . I loved passionately, madly, every which way, devil take me, I chattered away like a magpie about the emancipation of women, ran through half my fortune as a result of my tender feelings; but now, if you will excuse me, I'm on to your ways! I've had enough! Dark eyes, passionate eyes, ruby lips, dimpled cheeks; the moon, whispers, bated breath—for all that I wouldn't give a good goddamn. Present company excepted, of course, but all women, young and old alike, are affected clowns, gossips, hateful, consummate liars to the marrow of their bones, vain, trivial, ruthless, outrageously illogical, and as far as this is concerned [*taps on his forehead.*], well, excuse my frankness, any sparrow could give pointers to a philosopher in petticoats! Look at one of those romantic creatures: muslin, ethereal demigoddess, a thousand raptures, and you look into her soul—a common crocodile! [*Grips the back of a chair; the chair cracks and breaks.*] But the most revolting part of it all is that this crocodile imagines that she has, above everything, her own privilege, a monopoly on tender feelings. The hell with it—you can hang me upside down by that nail if a woman is capable of loving anything besides a lapdog. All she can do when she's in love is slobber! While the man suffers and sacrifices, all her love is expressed in playing with her skirt and trying to lead him around firmly by the nose. You have the misfortune of being a woman, you know yourself what the nature of a woman is like. Tell me honestly: Have you ever in your life seen a woman who is sincere, faithful, and constant? You never have! Only old and ugly ladies are faithful and constant! You're more liable to meet a horned cat or a white woodcock than a faithful woman!

70   MRS. POPOV: Pardon me, but in your opinion, who is faithful and constant in love? The man?

SMIRNOV: Yes, the man!

MRS. POPOV: The man! [*Malicious laugh.*] Men are faithful and constant in love! That's news! [*Heatedly.*] What right have you to say that? Men are faithful and constant! For that matter, as far as I know, of all the men I have known and now know, my late

---

°67 *Madame, je vous prie*: I beg you, Madam.

husband was the best. . . . I loved him passionately, with all my being, as only a young intellectual woman can love; I gave him my youth, my happiness, my life, my fortune; he was my life's breath; I worshiped him as if I were a heathen, and . . . and, what good did it do—this best of men himself deceived me shamelessly at every step of the way. After his death, I found his desk full of love letters; and when he was alive—it's terrible to remember—he used to leave me alone for weeks at a time, and before my eyes he flirted with other women and deceived me. He squandered my money, made a mockery of my feelings . . . and, in spite of all that, I loved him and was true to him . . . and besides, now that he is dead, I am still faithful and constant. I have shut myself up in these four walls forever and I won't remove these widow's weeds until my dying day. . . .

SMIRNOV: [*Laughs contemptuously.*] Widow's weeds . . . I don't know what you take me for! As if I didn't know why you wear that black outfit and bury yourself in these four walls! Well, well! It's no secret, so romantic! When some fool of a poet passes by this country house, he'll look up at your window and think: "Here lives the mysterious Tamara, who, for the love of her husband, buried herself in these four walls." We know these tricks!

MRS. POPOV: [*Flaring.*] What? How dare you say that to me?

SMIRNOV: You may have buried yourself alive, but you haven't forgotten to powder yourself!   75

MRS. POPOV: How dare you use such expressions with me?

SMIRNOV: Please don't shout. I'm not your steward! You must allow me to call a spade a spade. I'm not a woman and I'm used to saying what's on my mind! Don't you shout at me!

MRS. POPOV: I'm not shouting, you are! Please leave me in peace!

SMIRNOV: Pay me my money and I'll go.

MRS. POPOV: I won't give you any money!   80

SMIRNOV: Yes, you will.

MRS. POPOV: To spite you, I won't pay you anything. You can leave me in peace!

SMIRNOV: I don't have the pleasure of being either your husband or your fiancé, so please don't make scenes! [*Sits down.*] I don't like it.

MRS. POPOV: [*Choking with rage.*] You're sitting down?

SMIRNOV: Yes, I am.   85

MRS. POPOV: I ask you to get out!

SMIRNOV: Give me my money . . . [*Aside.*] Oh, I'm so furious! Furious!

MRS. POPOV: I don't want to talk to impudent people! Get out of here! [*Pause.*] You're not going? No?

SMIRNOV: No.

MRS. POPOV: No?   90

SMIRNOV: No!

MRS. POPOV: We'll see about that. [*Rings.*]

[*LUKA enters.*]

Luka, show the gentleman out!

LUKA: [*Goes up to SMIRNOV.*] Sir, will you please leave, as you have been asked. You mustn't . . .

SMIRNOV: [*Jumping up.*] Shut up! Who do you think you're talking to? I'll make mincemeat out of you!

LUKA: [*His hand to his heart.*] Oh my God! Saints above! [*Falls into chair.*] Oh, I feel ill! I can't catch my breath!   95

MRS. POPOV: Where's Dasha? Dasha! [*She shouts.*] Dasha! Pelagea! Dasha! [*She rings.*]

LUKA: Oh! They've all gone berry picking . . . there's nobody at home . . . I'm ill! Water!

MRS. POPOV: Will you please get out!

SMIRNOV: Will you please be more polite?

100   MRS. POPOV: [*Clenches her fist and stamps her feet.*] You're nothing but a crude bear! A brute! A monster!

SMIRNOV: What? What did you say?

MRS. POPOV: I said that you were a bear, a monster!

SMIRNOV: [*Advancing toward her.*] Excuse me, but what right do you have to insult me?

MRS. POPOV: Yes, I am insulting you . . . so what? Do you think I'm afraid of you?

105   SMIRNOV: And do you think just because you're one of those romantic creations, that you have the right to insult me with impunity? Yes? I challenge you!

LUKA: Lord in Heaven! Saints above! . . . Water!

SMIRNOV: Pistols!

MRS. POPOV: Do you think just because you have big fists and you can bellow like a bull, that I'm afraid of you? You're such a bully!

SMIRNOV: I challenge you! I'm not going to let anybody insult me, and I don't care if you are a woman, a delicate creature!

110   MRS. POPOV: [*Trying to get a word in edgewise.*] Bear! Bear! Bear!

SMIRNOV: It's about time we got rid of the prejudice that only men must pay for their insults! Devil take it, if women want to be equal, they should behave as equals! Let's fight!

MRS. POPOV: You want to fight! By all means!

SMIRNOV: This minute!

MRS. POPOV: This minute! My husband had some pistols . . . I'll go and get them right away. [*Goes out hurriedly and then returns.*] What pleasure I'll have putting a bullet through that thick head of yours! The hell with you! [*She goes out.*]

115   SMIRNOV: I'll shoot her down like a chicken! I'm not a little boy or a sentimental puppy. I don't care if she is delicate and fragile.

LUKA: Kind sir! Holy father! [*kneels.*] Have pity on a poor old man and go away from here! You've frightened her to death and now you're going to shoot her?

SMIRNOV: [*Not listening to him.*] If she fights, then it means she believes in equality of rights and emancipation of women. Here the sexes are equal! I'll shoot her like a chicken! But what a woman! [*Imitates her.*] "The hell with you! . . . I'll put a bullet through that thick head of yours! . . . " What a woman! How she blushed, her eyes shone . . . she accepted my challenge! To tell the truth, it was the first time in my life I've seen a woman like that. . . .

LUKA: Dear sir, please go away! I'll pray to God on your behalf as long as I live!

SMIRNOV: That's a woman for you! A woman like that I can understand! A real woman! Not a sour-faced nincompoop but fiery, gunpowder! Fireworks! I'm even sorry to have to kill her!

120   LUKA: [*Weeps.*] Dear sir . . . go away!

SMIRNOV: I positively like her! Positively! Even though she has dimpled cheeks, I like her! I'm almost ready to forget about the debt. . . . My fury has diminished. Wonderful woman!

MRS. POPOV: [*Enters with pistols.*] Here they are, the pistols. Before we fight, you must show me how to fire. . . . I've never had a pistol in my hands before . . .

LUKA: Oh dear Lord, for pity's sake. . . . I'll go and find the gardener and the coachman. . . . What did we do to deserve such trouble? [*Exit.*]

SMIRNOV: [*Examining the pistols.*] You see, there are several sorts of pistols . . . there are special dueling pistols, the Mortimer with primers. Then there are Smith and Wesson revolvers, triple action with extractors . . . excellent pistols! . . . they cost a minimum of ninety rubles a pair. . . . You must hold the revolver like this . . . [*Aside.*] What eyes, what eyes! A woman to set you on fire!

MRS. POPOV: Like this?   125

SMIRNOV: Yes, like this . . . then you cock the pistol . . . take aim . . . put your head back a little . . . stretch your arm out all the way . . . that's right . . . then with this finger press on this little piece of goods . . . and that's all there is to do . . . but the most important thing is not to get excited and aim without hurrying . . . try to keep your arm from shaking.

MRS. POPOV: Good . . . it's not comfortable to shoot indoors. Let's go into the garden.

SMIRNOV: Let's go. But I'm giving you advance notice that I'm going to fire into the air.

MRS. POPOV: That's the last straw! Why?

SMIRNOV: Why? . . . Why . . . because it's my business, that's why.   130

MRS. POPOV: Are you afraid? Yes? Aahhh! No, sir. You're not going to get out of it that easily! Be so good as to follow me! I will not rest until I've put a hole through your forehead . . . that forehead I hate so much! Are you afraid?

SMIRNOV: Yes, I'm afraid.

MRS. POPOV: You're lying! Why don't you want to fight?

SMIRNOV: Because . . . because you . . . because I like you.

MRS. POPOV: [*Laughs angrily.*] He likes me! He dares say that he likes me! [*Points to the door.*]   135
Out!

SMIRNOV: [*Loads the revolver in silence, takes cap and goes; at the door, stops for half a minute while they look at each other in silence; then he approaches Mrs. Popov hesitantly.*] Listen. . . . Are you still angry? I'm extremely irritated, but, do you understand me, how can I express it . . . the fact is, that, you see, strictly speaking . . . [*He shouts.*] Is it my fault, really, for liking you? [*Grabs the back of a chair, which cracks and breaks.*] Why the hell do you have such fragile furniture! I like you! Do you understand? I . . . I'm almost in love with you!

MRS. POPOV: Get away from me—I hate you!

SMIRNOV: God, what a woman! I've never in my life seen anything like her! I'm lost! I'm done for! I'm caught like a mouse in a trap!

MRS. POPOV: Stand back or I'll shoot!

SMIRNOV: Shoot! You could never understand what happiness it would be to die under the   140
gaze of those wonderful eyes, to be shot by a revolver which was held by those little velvet hands. . . . I've gone out of my mind! Think about it and decide right away, because if I leave here, then we'll never see each other again! Decide . . . I'm a nobleman, a respectable gentleman, of good family. I have an income of ten thousand a year. . . . I can put a bullet through a coin tossed in the air . . . I have some fine horses. . . . Will you be my wife?

MRS. POPOV: [*Indignantly brandishes her revolver.*] Let's fight! I challenge you!

SMIRNOV: I'm out of my mind . . . I don't understand anything . . . [*Shouts.*] Hey, you, water!

MRS. POPOV: [*Shouts.*] Let's fight!

SMIRNOV: I've gone out of my mind. I'm in love like a boy, like an idiot! [*He grabs her hand, she screams with pain.*] I love you! [*Kneels.*] I love you as I've never loved before! I've jilted twelve women, nine women have jilted me, but I've never loved one of them as I love you. . . . I'm weak, I'm a limp rag. . . . I'm on my knees like a fool, offering you my hand. . . . Shame, shame! I haven't been in love for five years, I vowed I wouldn't; and suddenly I'm in love, like a fish out of water. I'm offering my hand in marriage. Yes or no? You don't want to? You don't need to! [*Gets up and quickly goes to the door.*]

MRS. POPOV: Wait!   145

SMIRNOV: [*Stops.*] Well?

MRS. POPOV: Nothing . . . you can go . . . go away . . . wait. . . . No, get out, get out! I hate you! But—don't go! Oh, if you only knew how furious I am, how angry! [*Throws revolver on table.*] My fingers are swollen from that nasty thing. . . .[*Tears her handkerchief furiously.*] What are you waiting for? Get out!

SMIRNOV: Farewell!

MRS. POPOV: Yes, yes, go away! [*Shouts.*] Where are you going? Stop. . . . Oh, go away! Oh, how furious I am! Don't come near me! Don't come near me!

150 SMIRNOV: [*Approaching her.*] How angry I am with myself! I'm in love like a student. I've been on my knees. . . . It gives me the shivers. [*Rudely.*] I love you! A lot of good it will do me to fall in love with you! Tomorrow I've got to pay the interest, begin the mowing of the hay. [*Puts his arm around her waist.*] I'll never forgive myself for this. . . .

MRS. POPOV: Get away from me! Get your hands away! I . . . hate you! I . . . challenge you!

[*Prolonged kiss,* LUKA *enters with an ax, the* GARDENER *with a rake, the* COACHMAN *with a pitchfork, and* WORKMEN *with cudgels.*]

LUKA: [*Catches sight of the pair kissing.*] Lord in heaven! [*Pause.*]

MRS. POPOV: [*Lowering her eyes.*] Luka, tell them in the stable not to give Toby any oats today.

CURTAIN

QUESTIONS

1. What was Mrs. Popov's life like with her late husband? What did she learn about him after his death? How has this knowledge affected her?

2. Who is Smirnov? What is he like, and how do you know? Why does he say what he does about women?

3. Why is Luka important? How do his responses highlight the emotions developing between Smirnov and Mrs. Popov?

4. What causes Mrs. Popov to call Smirnov a bear, a brute, a monster? What is his immediate response?

5. Why is Toby significant? How does he symbolize the shifting emotions of Mrs. Popov?

GENERAL QUESTIONS

1. Where did you laugh in the play? Analyze those moments and try to determine the causes of your laughter.

2. From this play, what conclusions can you draw about farce as a dramatic form? Consider the breaking chairs, the shouting, the challenge, the attitude of Smirnov about being shot, the shifting of feelings, etc.

3. How does Chekhov's presentation of the characters of Smirnov and Mrs. Popov make their reversal of feelings seem normal and logical, although sudden, unexpected, and surprising?

4. What are the major ideas or themes in *The Bear*? Consider vows made by the living to the dead, the difficulty of keeping resolutions, the nature of powerful emotions, the need to maintain conventions and expectations, and so on.

BETH HENLEY (b. 1952)

Brought up in Mississippi, Beth Henley attended Southern Methodist University, where in her sophomore year she wrote Am I Blue, *which was first produced in December 1981. She attended acting school in Illinois and went to Hollywood to take up a career as a movie actress. However, at the same time she continued to work on new plays, and it is as a writer that she has been successful. Her most notable achievement is her "Southern Gothic" play* Crimes of the Heart *(first titled* Crimes of Passion*), for which she won the Great American Play contest in 1978 and the Pulitzer Prize for Drama in 1981. She also wrote* The Wake of Jeremy Foster *(1983),* The Lucky Spot *(1986),* The Debutante Ball *(1991), and* Abundance *(1990). The year 1992 saw the publication of four collected plays* (Beth Henley: Four Plays), *including* The Miss Firecracker Contest, *a two-act play written in 1979 and first performed in 1984. Her play* Impossible Marriage *was produced off Broadway in 1998 at the Laura Pels Theater in New York. In addition, she has seen some of her shorter scripts produced as television plays. In 2002 she published* Three Plays by Beth Henley, *containing* Control Freaks *(1993),* L-Play *(1996), and* Sisters of the Winter Madrigal *(2001). She also did a documentary in 2001 titled* Intimate Portrait: Holly Hunter, *and in 2004 her "teleplay"* It Must Be Love *appeared, followed in 2006 by* Ridiculous Fraud. Crimes of the Heart *was made into a successful film in 1986, starring Diane Keaton, Jessica Lange, Sam Shepard, and Sissy Spacek.*

In many of her plays, Henley's comedic manner develops out of the eccentricity or "kookiness" of her main female characters. The comic *donnée* is that an unusual or even disturbed action is accepted as a normal event that begins a course of dramatic action. A character in one of Henley's television plays, for example, inadvertently sets a house on fire, but the outcome turns out to be fortunate because of a lucrative home insurance policy. In *Crimes of the Heart,* one of the characters, after a failed suicide attempt, explains herself by saying that she has been having "a bad day." Even in the serious play *Abundance,* the two main female characters begin their twenty-five-year friendship after they have come west in the 1860s to become mail-order brides of men they have never seen. Ashbe of *Am I Blue* is an early original in the pattern, with her liking for hot Kool-Aid and colored marshmallows, her habit of stealing ashtrays and then donating them to a fellow tenant, and her dabbling in voodoo.

Although *Am I Blue* is an amusing play, it deals with the difficulties of adjustment to adulthood, misconceptions about social roles, unfulfilled dreams, general aimlessness and indecisiveness, and the attempt to develop individuality. The larger political and historical context of the year of the supposed events of the play, 1968, is mentioned by neither Ashbe nor John Polk, but one might connect their difficulties with some of the disturbances of that year, particularly the assassinations of Robert Kennedy and Martin Luther King, Jr.; the frustrating and seemingly endless war in Vietnam; and the many antiwar demonstrations and riots, especially during the Democratic National Convention in Chicago in the summer. Henley is very specific in dating the action of *Am I Blue* on the night of November 11, 1968—in other words, after all these disturbing and destabilizing events had taken place, and also less than a week after the election that made Richard Nixon president. One might also note the irony that November 11 had before 1954 been called Armistice Day (now Veterans Day)—a holiday dedicated to peace and stability.

Am I Blue thus reflects the disturbances and disruptions of the late 1960s, even though it focuses on the individual concerns and problems of John Polk and Ashbe. Ashbe's father is an alcoholic who is absent when she needs him, and her mother has deserted the home entirely. John Polk is facing a difficult choice about his future career, and he is also trying to stay afloat in the swim of fraternity life. Unable to succeed in either situation, he seeks strength in rum instead of calling on his own inner resources. Nothing earthshaking is claimed for either John Polk or Ashbe at the play's end, but they both succeed in developing a degree of recognition—rejecting conventional behaviors and discovering their own capacities for friendship and dignity.

 ## Am I Blue° (1973; 1982)

CHARACTERS

> **John Polk Richards,** *seventeen*
> **Ashbe Williams,** *sixteen*
> **Hilda,** *a waitress, thirty-five*
> ***Street People***: Barker, Whore, Bum, Clareece

[SCENE. *A bar, the street, the living room of a run-down apartment.*]

[TIME. *Fall 1968.*]

The scene opens on a street in the New Orleans French Quarter on a rainy, blue bourbon night. Various people—a WHORE, BUM, STREET BARKER, CLAREECE—*appear and disappear along the street. The scene then focuses on a bar where a piano is heard from the back room playing softly and indistinctly "Am I Blue?"° The lights go up on* JOHN POLK, *who sits alone at a table. He is seventeen, a bit overweight and awkward. He wears nice clothes, perhaps a navy sweater with large white monograms. His navy raincoat is slung over an empty chair. While drinking John Polk concentrates on the red and black card that he holds in his hand. As soon as the scene is established,* ASHBE *enters from the street. She is sixteen, wears a flowered plastic raincoat, a white plastic rain cap, red galoshes, a butterfly barrette, and jeweled cat-eye glasses. She is carrying a bag full of stolen goods. Her hair is very curly. Ashbe makes her way cautiously to John Polk's table. As he sees her coming, he puts the card into his pocket. She sits in the empty chair and pulls his raincoat over her head.*

ASHBE: Excuse me . . . do you mind if I sit here please?

JOHN POLK: [*Looks up at her—then down into his glass.*] What are you doing hiding under my raincoat? You're getting it all wet.

ASHBE: Well, I'm very sorry, but after all it is a raincoat. [*He tries to pull off coat.*] It was rude of me I know, but look I just don't want them to recognize me.

JOHN POLK: [*Looking about.*] Who to recognize you?

5 ASHBE: Well, I stole these two ashtrays from the Screw Inn, ya know right down the street. [*She pulls out two glass commercial ashtrays from her white plastic bag.*] Anyway, I'm scared the manager saw me. They'll be after me I'm afraid.

JOHN POLK: Well, they should be. Look, do you mind giving me back my raincoat? I don't want to be found protecting any thief.

°The first New York City production was by the Circle Repertory Company. "*Am Blue?*": Music by Harry Akst (1894–1963), with lyrics by Grant Clarke (1891–1931), from the film *On With the Show* (1929).

In this first production of Henley's *Am I Blue* at the Margo Jones Experimental Theater of Southern Methodist University in Dallas, Texas, in 1973, Ashbe Williams (Marcie Glaser) enters the bar where she first meets John Polk (John Tillotson). The production was directed by Jill Christine Peters, with the set designed by John Gisondi.

ASHBE: [*Coming out from under coat.*] Thief—would you call Robin Hood a thief?

JOHN POLK: Christ.

ASHBE: [*Back under coat.*] No, you wouldn't. He was valiant—all the time stealing from the rich and giving to the poor.

JOHN POLK: But your case isn't exactly the same, is it? You're stealing from some crummy   10
little bar and keeping the ashtrays for yourself. Now give me back my coat.

ASHBE: [*Throws coat at him.*] Sure, take your old coat. I suppose I should have explained—about Miss Marcey. [*Silence.*] Miss Marcey, this cute old lady with a little hump in her back. I always see her in her sun hat and blue print dress. Miss Marcey lives in the apartment building next to ours. I leave all the stolen goods, as gifts on her front steps.

JOHN POLK: Are you one of those kleptomaniacs? [*He starts checking his wallet.*]

ASHBE: You mean when people all the time steal and they can't help it?

JOHN POLK: Yeah.

ASHBE: Oh, no. I'm not a bit careless. Take my job tonight, my very first night job, if you   15
want to know. Anyway, I've been planning it for two months, trying to decipher which

bar most deserved to be stolen from. I finally decided on the Screw Inn. Mainly because of the way they're so mean to Mr. Groves. He works at the magazine rack at Diver's Drugstore and is really very sweet, but he has a drinking problem. I don't think that's fair to be mean to people simply because they have a drinking problem—and, well, anyway, you see I'm not just stealing for personal gain. I mean, I don't even smoke.

JOHN POLK: Yeah, well, most infants don't, but then again, most infants don't hang around bars.

ASHBE: I don't see why not, Toulouse Lautrec did.

JOHN POLK: They'd throw me out.

ASHBE: Oh, they throw me out too, but I don't accept defeat. [*Slowly moves into him.*] Why it's the very same with my pickpocketing.

[*JOHN POLK sneers, turns away.*]

20   ASHBE: It's a very hard act to master. Why every time I've done it, I've been caught.

JOHN POLK: That's all I need, is to have some slum kid tell me how good it is to steal. Everyone knows it's not.

ASHBE: [*About his drink.*] That looks good. What is it?

JOHN POLK: Hey, would you mind leaving me alone—I just wanted to be alone.

ASHBE: Okay, I'm sorry. How about if I'm quiet?

[*JOHN POLK shrugs. He sips drink, looks around, catches her eye, she smiles and sighs.*]

25   ASHBE: I was just looking at your pin. What fraternity are you in?

JOHN POLK: S.A.E.

ASHBE: Is it a good fraternity?

JOHN POLK: Sure, it's the greatest.

ASHBE: I bet you have lots of friends.

30   JOHN POLK: Tons.

ASHBE: Are you being serious?

JOHN POLK: Yes.

ASHBE: Hmm. Do they have parties and all that?

JOHN POLK: Yeah, lots of parties, booze, honking horns, it's exactly what you would expect.

35   ASHBE: I wouldn't expect anything. Why did you join?

JOHN POLK: I don't know. Well, my brother . . . I guess it was my brother . . . he told me how great it was, how the fraternity was supposed to get you dates, make you study, solve all your problems.

ASHBE: Gee, does it?

JOHN POLK: Doesn't help you study.

ASHBE: How about dates? Do they get you a lot of dates?

40   JOHN POLK: Some.

ASHBE: What were the girls like?

JOHN POLK: I don't know—they were like girls.

ASHBE: Did you have a good time?

JOHN POLK: I had a pretty good time.

45   ASHBE: Did you make love to any of them?

JOHN POLK: [*To self.*] Oh, Christ . . .

ASHBE: I'm sorry . . . I just figured that's why you had the appointment with the whore . . . cause you didn't have anyone else . . . to make love to.

JOHN POLK: How did you know I had the, ah, appointment?

ASHBE: I saw you put the red card in your pocket when I came up. Those red cards are pretty familiar around here. The house is only about a block or so away. It's one of the best though, really very plush. Only two murders and a knifing in its whole history. Do you go there often?

JOHN POLK: Yeah, I like to give myself a treat.   50

ASHBE: Who do you have?

JOHN POLK: What do you mean?

ASHBE: I mean which girl. [JOHN POLK *gazes into his drink.*] Look, I just thought I might know her is all.

JOHN POLK: Know her, ah, how would you know her?

ASHBE: Well, some of the girls from my high school go there to work when they get out.   55

JOHN POLK: G.G., her name is G.G.

ASHBE: G.G. . . . Hmm, well, how does she look?

JOHN POLK: I don't know.

ASHBE: Oh, you've never been with her before?

JOHN POLK: No.   60

ASHBE: [*Confidentially.*] Are you one of those kinds that likes a lot of variety?

JOHN POLK: Variety? Sure, I guess I like variety.

ASHBE: Oh, yes, now I remember.

JOHN POLK: What?

ASHBE: G.G., that's just her working name. Her real name is Myrtle Reims, she's Kay   65
Reims' older sister. Kay is in my grade at school.

JOHN POLK: Myrtle? Her name is Myrtle?

ASHBE: I never liked the name either.

JOHN POLK: Myrtle, oh, Christ. Is she pretty?

ASHBE: [*Matter of fact.*] Pretty, no she's not real pretty.

JOHN POLK: What does she look like?   70

ASHBE: Let's see . . . she's, ah, well, Myrtle had acne and there are a few scars left. It's not bad. I think they sort of give her character. Her hair's red, only I don't think it's really red. It sort of fizzles out all over her head. She's got a pretty good figure . . . big top . . . but the rest of her is kind of skinny.

JOHN POLK: I wonder if she has a good personality.

ASHBE: Well, she was a senior when I was a freshman; so I never really knew her. I remember she used to paint her fingernails lots of different colors . . . pink, orange, purple. I don't know, but she kind of scares me. About the only time I ever saw her true personality was around a year ago. I was over at Kay's making a health poster for school. Anyway, Myrtle comes busting in, screaming about how she can't find her spangled bra anywhere. Kay and I just sat on the floor cutting pictures of food out of magazines while she was storming about slamming drawers and swearing. Finally, she found it. It was pretty garish—red with black and gold sequined G's on each cup. That's how I remember the name—G.G.

[*As* ASHBE *illustrates the placement of the G's she spots* HILDA, *the waitress, approaching.* ASHBE *pulls the raincoat over her head and hides on the floor.* HILDA *enters through the beaded curtains spilling her tray.* HILDA *is a woman of few words.*]

HILDA: Shit, damn curtain. Nuther drink?

JOHN POLK: Mam?   75

HILDA: [*Points to drink.*] Vodka coke?

JOHN POLK: No, thank you. I'm not quite finished yet.

HILDA: Napkins clean.

[ASHBE *pulls her bag off the table.* HILDA *looks at Ashbe then to* JOHN POLK. *She walks around the table, as* ASHBE *is crawling along the floor to escape.* ASHBE *runs into* HILDA'S *toes.*]

ASHBE: Are those real gold?

80 HILDA: You again. Out.

ASHBE: She wants me to leave. Why should a paying customer leave? [*Back to* HILDA.] Now
I'll have a mint julip and easy on the mint.

HILDA: This pre-teen with you?

JOHN POLK: Well, I . . . No . . . I . . .

HILDA: I.D.'s.

85 ASHBE: Certainly, I always try to cooperate with the management.

HILDA: [*Looking at* JOHN POLK'S *I.D.*] I.D., 11-12-50. Date: 11-11-68.

JOHN POLK: Yes, but . . . well, 11-12 is less than two hours away.

HILDA: Back in two hours.

ASHBE: I seem to have left my identification in my gold lamé bag.

90 HILDA: Well, boo-hoo. [*Motions for Ashbe to leave with a minimum of effort. She goes back to
table.*] No tip.

ASHBE: You didn't tip her?

JOHN POLK: I figured the drinks were so expensive . . . I just didn't . . .

HILDA: No tip!

JOHN POLK: Look, Miss, I'm sorry. [*Going through his pockets.*] Here would you like a . . . a
nickel . . . wait, wait, here's a quarter.

95 HILDA: Just move ass, sonny. You too, Barbie.

ASHBE: Ugh, I hate public rudeness. I'm sure I'll refrain from ever coming here again.

HILDA: Think I'll go in the back room and cry.

[ASHBE *and* JOHN POLK *exit.* HILDA *picks up tray and exits through the curtain, tripping again.*]

HILDA: Shit. Damn curtain.

[ASHBE *and* JOHN POLK *are now standing outside under the awning of the bar.*]

ASHBE: Gee, I didn't know it was your birthday tomorrow. Happy birthday! Don't be mad.
I thought you were at least twenty or twenty-one, really.

100 JOHN POLK: It's o.k. Forget it.

[*As they begin walking, various blues are heard coming from the nearby bars.*]

ASHBE: It's raining.

JOHN POLK: I know.

ASHBE: Are you going over to the house now?

JOHN POLK: No, not till twelve.

105 ASHBE: Yeah, the red and black cards—they mean all night. Midnight till morning.

[*At this point a street* BARKER *beckons the couple into his establishment. Perhaps he is accompanied
by a* WHORE.]

BARKER: Hey mister, bring your baby on in, buy her a few drinks, maybe tonight ya
get lucky.

ASHBE: Keep walking.

JOHN POLK: What's wrong with the place?

ASHBE: The drinks are watery rot gut, and the show girls are boys . . .

110 BARKER: Up yours, punk!

JOHN POLK: [*Who has now sat down on a street bench.*] Look, just tell me where a cheap bar is.
I've got to stay drunk, but I don't have much money left.

ASHBE: Yikes, there aren't too many cheap bars around here, and a lot of them check I.D.'s.

JOHN POLK: Well, do you know of any that don't?

ASHBE: No, not for sure.

JOHN POLK: Oh, God, I need to get drunk.　　　　　　　　　　　　　　　　　　　115

ASHBE: Aren't you?

JOHN POLK: Some, but I'm losing ground fast.

[*By this time a* BUM *who has been traveling drunkenly down the street falls near the couple and begins throwing up.*]

ASHBE: Oh, I know! You can come to my apartment. It's just down the block. We keep one bottle of rum around. I'll serve you a grand drink, three or four if you like.

JOHN POLK: [*Fretfully.*] No, thanks.

ASHBE: But look, we're getting all wet.　　　　　　　　　　　　　　　　　　　120

JOHN POLK: Sober too, wet and sober.

ASHBE: Oh, come on! Rain's blurring my glasses.

JOHN POLK: Well, how about your parents? What would they say?

ASHBE: Daddy's out of town and Mama lives in Atlanta; so I'm sure they won't mind. I think we have some cute little marshmallows. [*Pulling on him.*] Won't you really come?

JOHN POLK: You've probably got some gang of muggers waiting to kill me. Oh, all right . . .　　125
what the hell, let's go.

ASHBE: Hurrah! Come on. It's this way. [*She starts across the stage, stops, and picks up an old hat.*] Hey, look at this hat. Isn't something! Here, wear it to keep off the rain.

JOHN POLK: [*Throwing hat back onto street.*] No, thanks, you don't know who's worn it before.

ASHBE: [*Picking hat back up.*] That makes it all the more exciting. Maybe it was a butcher's who slaughtered his wife or a silver pirate with a black bird on his throat. Who do you guess?

JOHN POLK: I don't know. Anyway what's the good of guessing? I mean you'll never really know.

ASHBE: [*Trying the hat on.*] Yeah, probably not.　　　　　　　　　　　　　　　130

[*At this point* ASHBE *and* JOHN POLK *reach the front door.*]

ASHBE: Here we are.

[ASHBE *begins fumbling for her key.* CLAREECE, *a teeny-bopper, walks up to* JOHN POLK.]

CLAREECE: Hey, man, got any spare change?

JOHN POLK: [*Looking through his pockets.*] Let me see . . . I . . .

ASHBE: [*Coming up between them, giving* CLAREECE *a shove.*] Beat it, Clareece. He's my company.

CLAREECE: [*Walks away and sneers.*] Oh, shove it, Frizzels.　　　　　　　　　135

ASHBE: A lot of jerks live around here. Come on in. [*She opens the door. Lights go up on the living room of a run-down apartment in a run-down apartment house. Besides being merely run-down the room is a malicious pig sty with colors, paper hats, paper dolls, masks, torn up stuffed animals, dead flowers and leaves, dress-up clothes, etc., thrown all about.*] My bones are cold. Do you want a towel to dry off?

JOHN POLK: Yes, thank you.

ASHBE: [*She picks up a towel off the floor and tosses it to him.*] Here. [*He begins drying off, as she takes off her rain things; then she begins raking things off the sofa.*] Please do sit down. [*He sits.*] I'm sorry the place is disheveled, but my father's been out of town. I always try to pick up and all before he gets in. Of course, he's pretty used to messes. My mother never was too good at keeping things clean.

JOHN POLK: When's he coming back?

ASHBE: Sunday, I believe. Oh, I've been meaning to say . . .　　　　　　　　　140

JOHN POLK: What?

ASHBE: My name's Ashbe Williams.

JOHN POLK: Ashbe?

ASHBE: Yeah, Ashbe.

145 JOHN POLK: My name's John Polk Richards.

ASHBE: John Polk? They call you John Polk?

JOHN POLK: It's family.

ASHBE: [*Putting on socks.*] These are my favorite socks, the red furry ones. Well, here's some books and magazines to look at while I fix you something to drink. What do you want in your rum?

JOHN POLK: Coke's fine.

150 ASHBE: I'll see if we have any. I think I'll take some hot Kool-Aid myself.

[*She exits to the kitchen.*]

JOHN POLK: Hot Kool-Aid?

ASHBE: It's just Kool-Aid that's been heated, like hot chocolate or hot tea.

JOHN POLK: Sounds great.

ASHBE: Well, I'm used to it. You get so much for your dime, it makes it worth your while. I don't buy presweetened, of course, it's better to sugar your own.

155 JOHN POLK: I remember once I threw up a lot of grape Kool-Aid when I was a kid. I've hated it ever since. Hey, would you check on the time?

ASHBE: [*She enters carrying a tray with several bottles of food coloring, a bottle of rum, and a huge glass.*] I'm sorry we don't have Coke. I wonder if rum and Kool-Aid is good? Oh, we don't have a clock either.

[*She pours a large amount of rum into the large glass.*]

JOHN POLK: I'll just have it with water then.

ASHBE: [*She finds an almost empty glass of water somewhere in the room and dumps it in with the rum.*] Would you like food coloring in the water? It makes a drink all the more aesthetic. Of course, some people don't care for aesthetics.

JOHN POLK: No, thank you, just plain water.

160 ASHBE: Are you sure? The taste is entirely the same. I put it in all my water.

JOHN POLK: Well . . .

ASHBE: What color do you want?

JOHN POLK: I don't know.

ASHBE: What's your favorite color?

165 JOHN POLK: Blue, I guess.

[*She puts a few blue drops into the glass. As she has nothing to stir with, she blows into the glass turning the water blue.*]

JOHN POLK: Thanks.

ASHBE: [*Exits. She screams from kitchen.*] Come on, say come on, cat, eat your fresh, good milk.

JOHN POLK: You have a cat?

ASHBE: [*off.*] No.

170 JOHN POLK: Oh.

ASHBE: [*She enters carrying a tray with a cup of hot Kool-Aid and Cheerios and colored marshmallows.*] Here are some Cheerios and some cute, little, colored marshmallows to eat with your drink.

JOHN POLK: Thanks.

ASHBE: I one time smashed all the big white marshmallows in the plastic bag at the grocery store.

JOHN POLK: Why did you do that?

ASHBE: I was angry. Do you like ceramics?   175

JOHN POLK: Yes.

ASHBE: My mother makes them. It's sort of her hobby. She is very talented.

JOHN POLK: My mother never does anything. Well, I guess she can shuffle the bridge deck okay.

ASHBE: Actually, my mother is a dancer. She teaches at a school in Atlanta. She's really very talented.

JOHN POLK: [*Indicates ceramics.*] She must be to do all these.   180

ASHBE: Well, Madeline, my older sister, did the blue one. Madeline gets to live with Mama.

JOHN POLK: And you live with your father.

ASHBE: Yeah, but I get to go visit them sometimes.

JOHN POLK: You do ceramics too?

ASHBE: No, I never learned . . . but I have this great potholder set. [*Gets up to show him.*] See,   185
I make lots of multicolored potholders and send them to Mama and Madeline. I also make paper hats. [*Gets material to show him.*] I guess they're more creative, but making potholders is more relaxing. Here, would you like to make a hat?

JOHN POLK: I don't know, I'm a little drunk.

ASHBE: It's not hard a bit. [*Hands him material.*] Just draw a real pretty design on the paper. It really doesn't have to be pretty, just whatever you want.

JOHN POLK: It's kind of you to give my creative drives such freedom.

ASHBE: Ha, ha, ha, I'll work on my potholder set a bit.

JOHN POLK: What time is it? I've really got to check on the time.   190

ASHBE: I know. I'll call the time operator.

[*She goes to the phone.*]

JOHN POLK: How do you get along without a clock?

ASHBE: Well, I've been late for school a lot. Daddy has a watch. It's 11:03.

JOHN POLK: I've got a while yet. [*ASHBE twirls back to her chair, drops, and sighs.*] Are you a dancer, too?

ASHBE: [*Delighted.*] I can't dance a bit, really. I practice a lot is all, at home in the afternoon.   195
I imagine you go to a lot of dances.

JOHN POLK: Not really, I'm a terrible dancer. I usually get bored or drunk.

ASHBE: You probably drink too much.

JOHN POLK: No, it's just since I've come to college. All you do there is drink more beer and write more papers.

ASHBE: What are you studying for to be?

JOHN POLK: I don't know.   200

ASHBE: Why don't you become a rancher?

JOHN POLK: Dad wants me to help run his soybean farm.

ASHBE: Soybean farm. Yikes, that's really something. Where is it?

JOHN POLK: Well, I live in the Delta, Hollybluff, Mississippi. Anyway, Dad feels I should go to business school first; you know, so I'll become, well, management-minded. Pass the blue.

ASHBE: Is that what you really want to do?   205

JOHN POLK: I don't know. It would probably be as good as anything else I could do. Dad makes good money. He can take vacations whenever he wants. Sure it'll be a ball.

ASHBE: I'd hate to have to be management-minded. [*JOHN POLK shrugs.*] I don't mean to hurt your feelings, but I would really hate to be a management mind. [*She starts walking on her knees, twisting her fists in front of her eyes, and making clicking sounds as a management mind would make.*]

JOHN POLK: Cut it out. Just forget it. The farm could burn down, and I wouldn't even have to think about it.

ASHBE: [*After a pause.*] Well, what do you want to talk about?

210 **JOHN POLK:** I don't know.

ASHBE: When was the last dance you went to?

JOHN POLK: Dances. That's great subject. Let's see, oh, I don't really remember—it was probably some blind date. God, I hate dates.

ASHBE: Why?

JOHN POLK: Well, they always say that they don't want popcorn, and they wind up eating all of yours.

215 **ASHBE:** You mean, you hate dates just because they eat your popcorn? Don't you think that's kind of stingy?

JOHN POLK: It's the principle of the thing. Why can't they just say, yes, I'd like some popcorn when you ask them. But, no, they're always so damn coy.

ASHBE: I'd tell my date if I wanted popcorn. I'm not that immature.

JOHN POLK: Anyway, it's not only the popcorn. It's a lot of little things. I've finished coloring. What do I do now?

ASHBE: Now you have to fold it. Here . . . like this. [*She explains the process with relish.*] Say, that's really something.

220 **JOHN POLK:** It's kind of funny looking. [*Putting the hat on.*] Yeah, I like it, but you could never wear it anywhere.

ASHBE: Well, like what anyway?

JOHN POLK: Huh?

ASHBE: The things dates do to you that you don't like, the little things.

JOHN POLK: Oh, well, just the way they wear those false eyelashes and put their hand on your knee when you're trying to parallel park, and keep on giggling and going off to the bathroom with their girl friends. It's obvious they don't want to go out with me. They just want to go out so that they can wear their new clothes and won't have to sit on their ass in the dormitory. They never want to go out with me. I can never even talk to them.

225 **ASHBE:** Well, you can talk to me, and I'm a girl.

JOHN POLK: Well, I'm really kind of drunk, and you're a stranger . . . well, I probably wouldn't be able to talk to you tomorrow. That makes a difference.

ASHBE: Maybe it does. [*A bit of a pause and then extremely pleased by the idea she says.*] You know we're alike because I don't like dances either.

JOHN POLK: I thought you said you practiced . . . in the afternoons.

ASHBE: Well, I like dancing. I just don't like dances. At least not like . . . well, not like the one our school was having tonight . . . they're so corny.

230 **JOHN POLK:** Yeah, most dances are.

ASHBE: All they serve is potato chips and fruit punch, and then this stupid baby band plays and everybody dances around thinking they're so hot. I frankly wouldn't dance there. I would prefer to wait till I am invited to an exclusive ball. It doesn't really matter which ball, just one where they have huge, golden chandeliers and silver fountains, and serve delicacies of all sorts and bubble blue champagne. I'll arrive in a pink silk cape [*Laughing.*] I want to dance in pink!

JOHN POLK: You're mixed up. You're probably one of those people that live in a fantasy world.

ASHBE: I do not. I accept reality as well as anyone. Anyway, you can talk to me, remember. I know what you mean by the kind of girls it's hard to talk to. There are girls a lot that way in the small clique at my school. Really tacky and mean. They expect everyone to be as stylish as they are, and they won't even speak to you in the hall. I don't mind if they don't speak to me, but I really love the orphans, and it hurts my feelings when they are so mean to them.

JOHN POLK: What do you mean—they're mean to the "orpheens"? [*Giggles to himself at the wordplay.*]

ASHBE: Oh, well, they sometimes snicker at the orphans' dresses. The orphans usually   235
have hand-me-down, drab, ugly dresses. Once Shelly Maxwell wouldn't let Glinda borrow her pencil, even though she had two. It hurt her feelings.

JOHN POLK: Are you best friends with these orphans?

ASHBE: I hardly know them at all. They're really shy. I just like them a lot. They're the reason I put spells on the girls in the clique.

JOHN POLK: Spells, what do you mean, witch spells?

ASHBE: Witch spells? Not really, mostly just voodoo.

JOHN POLK: Are you kidding? Do you really do voodoo?   240

ASHBE: Sure, here I'll show you my doll. [*Goes to get doll, comes back with straw voodoo doll. Her air as she returns is one of frightening mystery.*] I know a lot about the subject. Cora, she used to wash dishes in the Moonlight Cafe, told me all about voodoo. She's a real expert on the subject, went to all the meetings and everything. Once she caused a man's throat to rot away and turn almost totally black. She's moved to Chicago now.

JOHN POLK: It doesn't really work. Does it?

ASHBE: Well, not always. The thing about voodoo is that both parties have to believe in it for it to work.

JOHN POLK: Do the girls in school believe in it?

ASHBE: Not really, I don't think. That's where my main problem comes in. I have to make   245
the clique believe in it, yet I have to be very subtle. Mainly, I give reports in English class or Speech.

JOHN POLK: Reports?

ASHBE: On voodoo.

JOHN POLK: That's really kind of sick, you know.

ASHBE: Not really. I don't cast spells that'll do any real harm. Mainly, just the kind of thing to make them think . . . to keep them on their toes. [*Blue-drink intoxication begins to take over and* JOHN POLK *begins laughing.*] What's so funny?

JOHN POLK: Nothing. I was just thinking what a mean little person you are.   250

ASHBE: Mean! I'm not mean a bit.

JOHN POLK: Yes, you are mean . . . [*Picking up color.*] . . . and green too.

ASHBE: Green?

JOHN POLK: Yes, green with envy of those other girls; so you play all those mean little tricks.

ASHBE: Envious of those other girls, that stupid, close-minded little clique!   255

JOHN POLK: Green as this marshmallow. [*Eats marshmallow.*]

ASHBE: You think I want to be in some group . . . a sheep like you? A little sheep like you that does everything when he's supposed to do it!

JOHN POLK: Me a sheep . . . I do what I want!

ASHBE: Ha! I've known you for an hour and already I see you for the sheep you are!

JOHN POLK: Don't take your green meanness out on me.   260

ASHBE: Not only are you a sheep, you are a NORMAL sheep. Give me back my colors! [*Begins snatching colors away.*]

JOHN POLK: [*Pushing colors at her.*] Green and mean! Green and mean! Green and mean!

ASHBE: [*Throwing marshmallows at him.*] That's the reason you're in a fraternity and the reason you're going to manage your mind. And dates . . . you go out on dates merely because it's expected of you even though you have a terrible time. That's the reason you go to the whorehouse to prove you're a normal man. Well, you're much too normal for me.

JOHN POLK: Infant bitch. You think you're really cute.

265 ASHBE: That really wasn't food coloring in your drink, it was poison! [*She laughs, he picks up his coat to go, and she stops throwing marshmallows at him.*] Are you going? I was only kidding. For Christ sake, it wasn't really poison. Come on, don't go. Can't you take a little friendly criticism?

JOHN POLK: Look, did you have to bother me tonight? I had enough problems without . . .

[*Phone rings. Both look at phone, it rings for the third time. He stands undecided.*]

ASHBE: Look, wait, we'll make it up. [*She goes to answer phone.*] Hello . . . Daddy. How are you? . . . I'm fine . . . Dad, you sound funny . . . What? . . . Come on, Daddy, you know she's not here. [*Pause.*] Look, I told you I wouldn't call anymore. You've got her number in Atlanta. [*Pause, as she sinks to the floor.*] Why have you started again? . . . Don't say that. I can tell it. I can. Hey, I have to go to bed now, I don't want to talk anymore, okay? [*Hangs up phone, then softly to self.*] Goddamnit.

JOHN POLK: [*He has heard the conversation and is taking off his coat.*] Hey, Ashbe . . . [*She looks at him blankly, her mind far away.*] You want to talk?

ASHBE: No, [*Slight pause.*] Why don't you look at my shell collection? I have this special shell collection. [*She shows him collection.*]

270 JOHN POLK: They're beautiful, I've never seen colors like this. [ASHBE *is silent, he continues to himself.*] I used to go to Biloxi° a lot when I was a kid . . . One time my brother and I, we camped out on the beach. The sky was purple. I remember it was really purple. We ate pork and beans out of a can. I'd always kinda wanted to do that. Every night for about a week after I got home, I dreamt about these waves foaming over my head and face. It was funny. Did you find these shells or buy them?

ASHBE: Some I found, some I bought. I've been trying to decipher their meaning. Here, listen, do you hear that?

JOHN POLK: Yes.

ASHBE: That's the soul of the sea. [*She listens.*] I'm pretty sure it's the soul of the sea. Just imagine when I decipher the language. I'll know all the secrets of the world.

JOHN POLK: Yeah, probably you will. [*Looking into the shell.*] You know, you were right.

275 ASHBE: What do you mean?

JOHN POLK: About me, you were right. I am a sheep, a normal one. I've been trying to get out of it, but now I'm as big a sheep as ever.

ASHBE: Oh, it doesn't matter. You're company. It was rude of me to say.

JOHN POLK: No, because it was true. I really didn't want to go into a fraternity, I didn't even want to go to college, and I sure as hell don't want to go back to Hollybluff and work the soybean farm till I'm eighty.

ASHBE: I still say you could work on a ranch.

280 JOHN POLK: I don't know. I wanted to be a minister or something good, but I don't even know if I believe in God.

ASHBE: Yeah.

JOHN POLK: I never used to worry about being a failure. Now I think about it all the time. It's just I need to do something that's . . . fulfilling.

ASHBE: Fulfilling, yes, I see what you mean. Well, how about college? Isn't it fulfilling? I mean, you take all those wonderful classes, and you have all your very good friends.

JOHN POLK: Friends, yeah, I have some friends.

285 ASHBE: What do you mean?

°270 *Biloxi:* city in southern Mississippi, on the Gulf of Mexico.

John Polk: Nothing . . . well, I do mean something. What the hell, let me try to explain. You see it was my "friends," the fraternity guys that set me up with G.G., excuse me, Myrtle, as a gift for my eighteenth birthday.

Ashbe: You mean, you didn't want the appointment?

John Polk: No, I didn't want it. Hey, ah, where did my blue drink go?

Ashbe: [*As she hands him the drink.*] They probably thought you really wanted to go.

John Polk: Yeah, I'm sure they gave a damn what I wanted. They never even asked me. 290
Hell, I would have told them a handkerchief, a pair of argyle socks, but, no, they have to get me a whore just because it's a cool-ass thing to do. They make me sick. I couldn't even stay at the party they gave. All the sweaty T-shirts, and moron sex stories . . . I just couldn't take it.

Ashbe: Is that why you were at the Blue Angel so early?

John Polk: Yeah, I needed to get drunk, but not with them. They're such creeps.

Ashbe: Gosh, so you really don't want to go to Myrtle's?

John Polk: No, I guess not.

Ashbe: Then are you going? 295

John Polk: [*Pause.*] Yes.

Ashbe: That's wrong. You shouldn't go just to please them.

John Polk: Oh, that's not the point anymore, maybe at first it was, but it's not anymore. Now I have go for myself . . . to prove to myself that I'm not afraid.

Ashbe: Afraid? [*Slowly, as she begins to grasp his meaning.*] You mean, you've never slept with a girl before?

John Polk: Well, I've never been in love. 300

Ashbe: [*In amazement.*] You're a virgin?

John Polk: Oh, God.

Ashbe: No, don't feel bad, I am too.

John Polk: I thought I should be in love . . .

Ashbe: Well, you're certainly not in love with Myrtle. I mean, you haven't even met her. 305

John Polk: I know, but, God, I thought maybe I'd never fall in love. What then? You should experience everything . . . shouldn't you? Oh, what's it matter, everything's so screwed.

Ashbe: Screwed? Yeah, I guess it is. I mean, I always thought it would be fun to have a lot of friends who gave parties and go to dances all dressed up. Like the dance tonight . . . it might have been fun.

John Polk: Well, why didn't you go?

Ashbe: I don't know. I'm not sure it would have been fun. Anyway, you can't go . . . alone.

John Polk: Oh, you need a date? 310

Ashbe: Yeah, or something.

John Polk: Say, Ashbe, ya wanna dance here?

Ashbe: No, I think we'd better discuss your dilemma.

John Polk: What dilemma?

Ashbe: Myrtle. It doesn't seem right you should . . . 315

John Polk: Let's forget Myrtle for now. I've got a while yet. Here have some more of this blue-moon drink.

Ashbe: You're only trying to escape through artificial means.

John Polk: Yeah, you got it. Now come on. Would you like to dance? Hey, you said you liked to dance.

Ashbe: You're being ridiculous.

John Polk: [*Winking at her.*] Dance? 320

Ashbe: John Polk, I just thought . . .

John Polk: Hmm?

Ashbe: How to solve your problem . . .

John Polk: Well . . .

325 **Ashbe:** Make love to me!

John Polk: What?!

Ashbe: It all seems logical to me. It would prove you weren't scared, and you wouldn't be doing it just to impress others.

John Polk: Look, I . . . I mean, I hardly know you . . .

Ashbe: But we've talked. It's better this way, really. I won't be so apt to point out your mistakes.

330 **John Polk:** I'd feel great, stripping a twelve-year-old of her virginity.

Ashbe: I'm sixteen! Anyway, I'd be stripping you of yours just as well. I'll go put on some Tiger Claw perfume. [*She runs out.*]

John Polk: Hey, come back! Tiger Claw perfume, Christ.

Ashbe: [*Entering.*] I think one should have different scents for different moods.

John Polk: Hey, stop spraying that! You know I'm not going to . . . well, you'd get neurotic, or pregnant, or some damn thing. Stop spraying, will you!

335 **Ashbe:** Pregnant? You really think I could get pregnant?

John Polk: Sure, it'd be a delightful possibility.

Ashbe: It really wouldn't be bad. Maybe I would get to go to Tokyo for an abortion. I've never been to the Orient.

John Polk: Sure getting cut on is always a real treat.

Ashbe: Anyway, I might just want to have my dear baby. I could move to Atlanta with Mama and Madeline. It'd be wonderful fun. Why I could take him to the supermarket, put him in one of those little baby seats to stroll him about. I'd buy peach baby food and feed it to him with a tiny golden spoon. Why I could take colored pictures of him and send them to you through the mail. Come on . . . [*Starts putting pillows onto the couch.*] Well, I guess you should kiss me for a start. It's only etiquette, everyone begins with it.

340 **John Polk:** I don't think I could even kiss you with a clear conscience. I mean, you're so small with those little cat-eye glasses and curly hair . . . I couldn't even kiss you.

Ashbe: You couldn't even kiss me? I can't help it if I have to wear glasses. I got the prettiest ones I could find.

John Polk: Your glasses are fine. Let's forget it, okay?

Ashbe: I know, my lips are too purple, but if I eat carrots, the dye'll come off and they'll be orange.

John Polk: I didn't say anything about your lips being too purple.

345 **Ashbe:** Well, what is it? You're just plain chicken, I suppose . . .

John Polk: Sure, right, I'm chicken, totally chicken. Let's forget it. I don't know how, but, somehow, this is probably all my fault.

Ashbe: You're darn right it's all your fault! I want to have my dear baby or at least get to Japan. I'm so sick of school I could smash every marshmallow in sight! [*She starts smashing.*] Go on to your skinny pimple whore. I hope the skinny whore laughs in your face, which she probably will because you have an easy face to laugh in.

John Polk: You're absolutely right, she'll probably hoot and howl her damn fizzle red head off. Maybe you can wait outside the door and hear her, give you lots of pleasure, you sadistic little thief.

Ashbe: Thief! Was Robin Hood . . . Oh, what's wrong with this world? I just wasn't made for it, is all. I've probably been put in the wrong world, I can see that now.

350 **John Polk:** You're fine in this world.

Ashbe: Sure, everyone just views me as an undesirable lump.

JOHN POLK: Who?

ASHBE: You, for one.

JOHN POLK: [*Pause.*] You mean because I wouldn't make love to you?

ASHBE: It seems clear to me.   355

JOHN POLK: But you're wrong, you know.

ASHBE: [*To self, softly.*] Don't pity me.

JOHN POLK: The reason I wouldn't wasn't that . . . it's just that . . . well, I like you too
    much to.

ASHBE: You like me?

JOHN POLK: Undesirable lump, Jesus. Your cheeks they're . . . they're . . .   360

ASHBE: My cheeks? They're what?

JOHN POLK: They're rosy.

ASHBE: My cheeks are rosy?

JOHN POLK: Yeah, your cheeks, they're really rosy.

ASHBE: Well, they're natural, you know. Say, would you like to dance?   365

JOHN POLK: Yes.

ASHBE: I'll turn on the radio. [*She turns on radio. Ethel Waters is heard singing "Honey in the
    Honeycomb." °ASHBE begins snapping her fingers.*] Yikes, let's jazz it out.

[*They dance.*]

JOHN POLK: Hey, I'm not good or anything . . .

ASHBE: John Polk.

JOHN POLK: Yeah?   370

ASHBE: Baby, I think you dance fine!

[*They dance on, laughing, saying what they want till end of song. Then a radio announcer comes on
and says the 12:00 news will be in five minutes. Billie Holiday, or Terry Pierce, begins singing, "Am
I Blue?"*]

JOHN POLK: Dance?

ASHBE: News in five minutes.

JOHN POLK: Yeah.

ASHBE: That means five minutes till midnight.   375

JOHN POLK: Yeah, I know.

ASHBE: Then you're not . . .

JOHN POLK: Ashbe, I've never danced all night. Wouldn't it be something to . . . to dance all
    night and watch the rats come out of the gutter?

ASHBE: Rats?

JOHN POLK: Don't they come out at night? I hear New Orleans has lots of rats.   380

ASHBE: Yeah, yeah, it's got lots of rats.

JOHN POLK: Then let's dance all night and wait for them to come out.

ASHBE: All right . . . but, but how about our feet?

JOHN POLK: Feet?

ASHBE: They'll hurt.   385

JOHN POLK: Yeah.

ASHBE: [*Smiling.*] Okay, then let's dance.

[*He takes her hand, and they dance as lights black out and the music soars and continues to play.*]

End.

°*"Honey in the Honeycomb"*: With music by Vernon Duke (1903–1969) and lyrics by John Latouche (1917–1956),
this song was first performed in the musical *Cabin in the Sky* (1940), which starred Ethel Waters (1896–1977).

QUESTIONS

1. What do Ashbe's actions at the start tell you about her (such as hiding under the coat, stealing and giving the stolen things away, crawling away from the waitress)? What is disclosed by her speeches?
2. Describe the circumstances of Ashbe and her family. To what degree can her character and behavior be explained by these circumstances?
3. What is Ashbe's intention in her description of G.G., or Myrtle? What does her description tell you about her? What do you learn about her from her description of the only sort of dance she would like to go to (speech 231)?
4. What personal, occupational, and social difficulties is John Polk experiencing? Why is he trying to stay drunk before going to G.G.? What are his reactions to fraternity life and to the family business?
5. Explain the effects of the arguments between Ashbe and John Polk. How does their occasionally taunting each other influence their developing relationship?
6. Why does John Polk not take up Ashbe's invitation to make love? How does this refusal suggest the development of his character? Of Ashbe's character? What may be inferred by their concluding decision to dance the night away?

GENERAL QUESTIONS

1. What is the plot of *Am I Blue?* Who is the protagonist (or protagonists)? Who or what is the antagonist? How is the plot resolved?
2. Describe and analyze the verbal comedy of the play, such as the "two murders and a knifing" (speech 49), Ashbe's description of Myrtle (speeches 71–73), and the inquiry about what to mix with rum (speech 148).
3. What is appealing (or not appealing) about Ashbe and John Polk? To what extent are you to consider them as realistic persons? How might they be seen as symbols, and what might they symbolize?
4. What are the major themes or ideas of the play? To what extent does the comic mode obscure these ideas? To what extent does it bring them out?
5. What is the effect of the setting in the New Orleans French Quarter and the characters to be found there? What is shown about Ashbe and John Polk by their brief interactions with the characters in the bar, especially Hilda, and on the street?

WRITING ABOUT COMEDY

For an essay about comedy, you can choose any of the topics discussed in this chapter, such as *plot, conflict, character, point of view, setting, style, tone, symbolism,* or *theme.* You might choose one of these, or two or more; for example, how language and action define character, how character and symbol convey meaning, or how setting may influence comic structure.

Planning and prewriting strategies for each of these conventional elements are discussed at some length in Chapter 23 (pp. 1255–57) and in other chapters on prose fiction and poetry. As you develop your essay on comedy, you will find it helpful to look at these suggestions.

For the most part, planning and writing about specific features of comedy are much like addressing the same topics in other forms of drama, short stories, and poetry. However, a few areas of consideration—such as plot, character, and language—are especially significant in comic drama and can be handled in a distinctive fashion.

Questions for Discovering Ideas

PLOT, CONFLICT, STRUCTURE. What problems, adversities, or abnormal situations are in place at the comedy's opening? How is this initial situation complicated? Do the complications spring mainly from character or from situation? If from character, what aspects of behavior or personality create the problems? If from situation, what dilemmas or troubles plague the characters? What kinds of complications dominate—misunderstandings, disagreements, mistakes in identity, situational problems, or emotional entanglements? How important is coincidence?

What problems and complications occur early? Who is the comic protagonist (or protagonists) and what is the protagonist's goal (money, success, marriage, land, freedom)? How is the protagonist blocked (fathers, rivals, laws, customs, his or her own personality)? How threatening is the obstruction? What plans are hatched to overcome the blocking agents? Are the plans sensible or silly? Who initiates and executes the plans? To what extent do plans succeed (or fail)—because of chance and good luck or because of skillful planning and manipulation?

Describe the conflicts. Which conflict is central, and whom do the conflicts involve? Do they result from personality clashes or from situations? To what degree are they related to blocking activities? How does the action reach the crisis, and which characters are involved? What choices, decisions, plans, or conclusions become necessary? What events or revelations (of character, emotion, background) produce the catastrophe, and how do these affect characters, circumstances, and relationships?

In the comic resolution, to what extent are loose ends tied up and lives straightened out? Is reasonable order restored and regeneration assured or implied? Is the resolution satisfying? Disturbing? Does it leave you happy or thoughtful, or both? Are you amused by farce, pleased by romance, or disturbed by satire? If there is to be a marriage, whom will it bring together? What will the marriage settle, or whom will it divide? Most importantly, how can you account for your responses to the resolution and the play as a whole? How do they reflect the general aims of comedy?

CHARACTER. Which characters are realistic, conventional, round, flat, changing, standing still? Who is the protagonist or lover, the antagonist or blocking agent? Which characters seem excessive, eccentric, or irrational? What is the nature of their excesses? To what extent do the excesses define the characters? How do you respond to the excessive or exaggerated characters? Does the comedy provide a "cure" for the excesses? In other words, do the characters learn and change? If so, why and how? If not, why not?

From what classes are the characters derived? What class characteristics do you find? Who are the stock or stereotyped characters, and what is their significance to the protagonist? How does the playwright bring the characters to life? Who is the choric figure or *raisonneur*, if there is one? Who is the confidant? Which character can be considered a foil (or foils)?

LANGUAGE. Does the language consist of witty turns of phrase, confusions, puns, misunderstandings, or a mixture? Which characters are masters of language and which are mastered by it? Do characters use the same type of language and level of diction consistently? To what extent does language expose a character's self-interest or hypocrisy? If the language is witty and sparkling, what devices make it work effectively? If it is garbled and filled with misunderstandings, what types of errors does the playwright put into the characters' mouths? How does the language shape your response to characters, to ideas, and to the play as a whole?

Strategies for Organizing Ideas

To develop a central idea, isolate the feature you wish to explore and consider how it affects the shape and impact of the play. For *A Midsummer Night's Dream*, for example, you might focus on Puck's character and function. You might also develop a link between Puck's conventional role as a tricky servant with his love of mischief and the chaos he creates. Remember that it is difficult to develop essays from sentences like "Puck is a comic character" or "*Am I Blue* contains dramatic satire." A more focused assertion that also reveals your thematic development is necessary, such as "Puck, modeled on the tricky servant of Roman comedy, causes most of the play's confusion," or "*Am I Blue* attacks the general indifference of people toward the situations of others."

Organize your essay by grouping related types of details together (such as observations about characters, actions, direct statements, and specific words), and choose your own order of presentation. In writing about Puck as a tricky servant and creator of chaos, for example, you might present only one kind of detail—such as direct statements—and introduce these not in their order in the play but rather as they contribute to your analysis of Puck's character.

More often than not, your supporting details will represent a variety of types of evidence—dramatic dialogue and action, individual soliloquies, special properties (such as a love potion or a disguise), or the failure or development of various plans. For example, you might support an assertion about Puck by referring to his reputation, actions, and attitudes as though each of these is equally important. Other possible strategies are to demonstrate how the topics are related according to cause and effect, to build the topics from the least to the most significant, and to trace how a common idea or image provides unity. Whatever your method of development, be sure to validate your arguments with supporting details.

A summary of key points will make your conclusion useful and effective. In addition, you can show how your conclusions in the body of the essay bear upon larger aspects of the play's meaning.

Illustrative Student Essay

Underlined sentences in this paper *do not* conform to MLA style and are used solely as teaching tools to emphasize the central idea, thesis sentence, and topic sentences throughout the paper.

Walls 1

Suzanne Walls

Professor Tompkins

English 210

6 December 2008

Setting as Symbol and Comic Structure in Shakespeare's

A Midsummer Night's Dream°

A Midsummer Night's Dream might be considered light and incon-   [1]
sequential. The changes of mind undergone by the two sets of lovers, the
placing of an ass's head on one of the characters, the presence of unrealistic
fairies, the acting of a silly sketch--all seem very far out. But the play is more
serious than that. It dramatizes the accidental and arbitrary origins of love, even
though it considers this serious subject in the good-natured medium of
comedy.* To bring out both message and merriment, Shakespeare uses two
settings--the city of Athens and the nearby forest. The play's comic structure is
governed by the movements between the order and the chaos that these two
locations represent.†

At the play's beginning, Athens is presented as a haven of daylight, order,   [2]
and law. In this setting, Duke Theseus has absolute authority, fathers are always
right, and the law permits Egeus to "dispose" of Hermia "either to this
gentleman [Demetrius], / Or to her death" ([1507] 1.1.43–44). The city is also
the place for the exposition and the beginning of complications. Here, we meet
the various groups of characters (except the fairies) and learn about the initial
problem--namely, that the relationship between Hermia and Lysander is

°This play appears on pages 1506–57.
*Central idea.
†Thesis sentence.

Walls 2

blocked by a raging father, a rival suitor, and an old law. In order to flee and then to overcome these obstructions, Lysander asks Hermia to meet him in the woods. Her agreement begins a journey from Athens to the forest that ultimately includes everyone in the play--the four lovers, Egeus, the city rulers, and the "mechanicals."

[3]   The play's second location, the woods outside Athens, is the kingdom of Oberon and Titania, the king and queen of the fairies. It is a world of moonlight, chaos, madness, and dreams, a world that symbolizes the power of imagination and passion. The disorder in this world has many sources, including Oberon's jealousy, Titania's infatuation, and Puck's delight in mischief. When the lovers and the mechanicals enter this setting, they also become disordered and chaotic.

[4]   The woods are the setting for complication, crisis, and catastrophe. Confusion dominates the action here. Puck disrupts the mechanicals' rehearsal and transforms Bottom into a monster with the head of a jackass. In addition, the passions of the lovers are rearranged several times by Oberon and Puck through the magic of "love-in-idleness," a flower that symbolizes the irrational and overwhelming power of love. Although the first two adjustments of the lovers' feelings are done to help them in their plights, each has the effect of raising the levels of complication and disorder. Puck gleefully observes that his actions are the cause of the play's confusions ([1532] 3.2.120–21):

> those things do best please me
> That befall prepost'rously.

Puck is right; his first application of love-in-idleness causes Lysander to fall wildly in love with Helena, and his second does the same to Demetrius.

[5]   The crisis and dénouement of the main plot also occur in the woods. A crisis occurs when the two lovers challenge each other and the women attack each other. At this point, complication and idiocy are at a peak, and the fairies must develop a plan to resolve the threats. Puck therefore misleads the lovers into ending their potential duel, and he adjusts their emotions one more time. The dénouement--the revelation of the newly restored emotions--occurs the

Walls 3

next morning at the edge of the woods, in the presence of Egeus, Theseus, and Hippolyta. Thus, it ends the confusing relationships occurring in the forest and begins the regularity of relationships in the more orderly world of city and society.

Resolution--the marriages and the mechanicals' production of Pyramus   [6]
and Thisby--occurs in the first setting, the city, which represents law and order. But the journey to the second setting has had a significant effect on the urban world both for Theseus and for the lovers. The law has been softened and Egeus has been overruled; the young lovers have been allowed to marry as they like, and their lives have been set right. In the end, this second setting has also become the dream world of night and the supernatural, and the fairy dance and blessings closing the play only emphasize the harmony and the regenerative implications of the comic resolutions.

Setting, symbolism, and comic pattern thus combine in *A Midsummer*   [7]
Night's Dream to produce an intricately plotted structure. Each element reinforces the others, bringing the play toward completion although time after time there seems to be no way out. The marvel of the play is that the two settings represent, realistically, two opposed states of being, and, dramatically, two distinct stages of comic structure. The journey out of Athens, into the woods, and then back to the city is also a journey from exposition and adversity, through complication, crisis, and catastrophe, and then forward to comic resolution.

Walls 4

Work Cited

William Shakespeare, A Midsummer Night's Dream. Literature: An
   Introduction to Reading and Writing. Ed. Edgar V. Roberts. 9th ed. New
   York: Pearson Longman, 2009. 1506–57.

Commentary on the Essay

This essay deals with three elements of *A Midsummer Night's Dream*: setting, symbols, and comic structure. It demonstrates the way a number of different topics can be combined in a single essay. Consequently, the essay is organized to reflect the journey from the city to the woods and then back to the city.

The body of the essay takes up the settings, their symbolic meaning, and the relationship between setting and structure. Paragraph 2 deals with Athens both as a world of law and order and as the setting for exposition and the beginnings of complication. The supporting details include circumstance, actions, and dialogue.

Paragraphs 3–5 deal with the middle of the journey and of the play. Paragraph 3 discusses the symbolic implications of the forest setting, and paragraphs 4 and 5 take up the connection between the setting and comic structure, specifically, complication, crisis, and dénouement. Again, the supporting details in these paragraphs are a mixture of actions, circumstances, and direct quotations.

Paragraph 6 deals briefly with the return to the city, linking this setting with the play's comic resolution. The concluding paragraph returns to the idea about how *A Midsummer Night's Dream* connects setting, symbol, and comic pattern.

Writing Topics About Comedy

1. Write an essay describing Shakespeare's comic technique in *A Midsummer Night's Dream*. Consider these questions: Is the basic situation serious? How does Shakespeare keep it comic? How does the boisterousness of the low characters influence your perceptions of the lovers and the courtly characters? Would the play be as interesting without Bottom and his crowd or without the fairies and their involvement? How does the comic outcome depend on the boisterousness and colorfulness provided by the players and the fairies? For research on Shakespeare as a comic dramatist, you might wish to consult Henry B. Charlton's classic study *Shakespeare's Comedies* (rpt. 1972) and/or a more recent book by Michael Mangan, *A Preface to Shakespeare's Comedies* (1996).

2. Although *Love Is the Doctor* is a farce, it deals with serious topic material—namely, a father trying to control his daughter's life, the exploitation of gullibility, and an illegal deception. How does Molière treat these topics and yet preserve the play's comic tone?

3. Write an essay that analyzes the relationship of situation to comedy in *Am I Blue*. How do the eccentricity of the characters and the improbability of their circumstances produce amusement? When you finish the play, do you believe that you have been seriously engaged? Simply entertained? Explain. For comparison with other Henley plays, you might wish to refer to *Beth Henley: Four Plays* (1992) or *Three Plays by Beth Henley* (2002) from your college library.

4. *The Bear* is one of Chekhov's most popular comedies. Read another Chekhov play (for example, *The Cherry Orchard*, *The Seagull*, *Three Sisters*, or *Uncle Vanya*) and compare it to *The Bear* (characters with characters, dialogue with dialogue, situations with situations, and so on). As you make your comparison, attempt to explain the continued popularity of *The Bear*.

5. Write an essay about the nature of comedy, using *A Midsummer Night's Dream, Am I Blue, The Bear, The Sandbox,* and *Love Is the Doctor* as material. Deal with issues such as the following: How can comic material be defined? Does the happy outcome of a serious action qualify a play as a comedy, or should no action be serious? When is a comedy no longer comic but tragic? Are jokes necessary? Is farcical action necessary? Where are the edges between comedy and farce, and absurdity, on the one hand, and comedy and tragedy on the other? For a research component for this topic, you might wish to introduce materials from books by Wylie Sypher (1956, rpt. 1982, an edition of two classic essays on the comic), G. S. Amur (1963), Robert Corrigan (1965), Robert B. Heilman (1978), T. G. A. Nelson (1990), Athene Seyler (1990), Frances Teague (1994), and Janet Suzman (1995).

6. Treat the lovers in *A Midsummer Night's Dream* and *Love Is the Doctor* as types or archetypes (see Chapter 29). What is their situation? What problems block the fulfillment of their love? How serious are these problems? What actions and ruses do they plan to make things right? How are the pairs of lovers in the two plays similar? Different?

7. Write a comic scene of your own between two people, perhaps a boy and a girl, as in *Am I Blue;* or two people who are angry with each other, as in *The Bear;* or a person under a spell and a person in normal touch with reality, as in *A Midsummer Night's Dream.* After you finish your scene, write a short essay explaining the principles on which you've written your scene, such as the reasons for your choice of material, your use of jokes (if any), straightforward dialogue, anger, outrage, amused responses, and so on.

Chapter 26

Visions of Dramatic Reality and Nonreality: Varying the Idea of Drama as Imitation

A major dimension of drama is the relationship to reality that dramatists seek to create. From Aristotle's description of the origin of tragedy, we may conclude that drama was originally considered to be an "imitation of an action"; that is, each play represents a significant and discrete series of actions that make up a complete story in the lives of the major characters. The drama focuses only on those actions and speeches that are integral to the story, and the outcome of the action is the logically necessary consequence of the conflicts and issues raised in the play. To achieve such concentration, dramatists introduce restrictions and nonrealistic conventions that aid the presentation of the story. Thus there can be no absolutely realistic drama in the sense of the straightforward duplication of life. Rather, the issue is how far drama goes either toward or away from reality.

Realism and Nonrealism in Drama

The most important difference between realistic and nonrealistic drama concerns the play's relationships to the audience, the theater, and the world at large. In **realistic drama,** the playwright seeks to create an *illusion* of reality—*verisimilitude.* The situations, problems, characters, dialogue, and other elements are all those that might genuinely exist in the real world. The play presents a self-contained action in a world that professes to imitate reality. Ideally, the illusion of reality is never compromised; the actors never drop out of character; the audience is never addressed; and the play never acknowledges that it is a play.

In **nonrealistic drama,** even the pretense to achieve realism is abandoned, and the goal instead is to present essential features of character and society through techniques that *do not* try to mirror life. Nonrealistic drama employs whatever conventions the playwright finds useful. It can be full of devices that break through the illusion on the stage (or the page) and scream out that the play is a play—a work of art, a stylized imitation of something remotely connected to life.

Nonrealistic Drama Has Prevailed During Most of Dramatic History

From ancient Greek tragedy through Victorian melodrama, plays were artificial and conventionalized. The conventions of drama changed from age to age—choruses and masks in Greek tragedy, soliloquies and blank verse in Elizabethan plays, rhymed couplets in French and much English neoclassical drama. Although these conventions were nonrealistic, audiences and readers accepted them as normal features of dramatic presentation. The enduring eloquence and power of the nonrealistic tradition can be found in plays like Sophocles' *Oedipus the King*, Shakespeare's *Hamlet*, and Miller's *Death of a Salesman*.

By the nineteenth century, artificial and romantic drama dominated the stage. These plays featured lavish sets, gorgeous costumes, flamboyant acting, conventionalized plots, and happy endings. The characters were exaggerated and idealized—heroes saving the day, heroines swooning at every opportunity, and villains twirling their mustaches and leering at the audience as they plotted to steal the hero's sweetheart and swindle him out of his money.

Realistic Drama Developed in Opposition to Unrealistic Drama

In reaction to the unrealistic tradition, and as a likely development coincidental with democratic theories of society and government, a number of nineteenth-century dramatists created plays that presented realistic characters in realistic situations and that explored the real problems of contemporary society. The rebellion began slowly, and most of these writers were Europeans; among them Émile Zola (French), Henrik Ibsen (Norwegian), Maxim Gorki (Russian), and George Bernard Shaw (Irish-English). American realists, who came to this tradition somewhat later than the Europeans, included Eugene O'Neill, Langston Hughes, and Susan Glaspell (pp. 1248, 1622, and 1231).

DRAMATIC REALISM ATTEMPTS TO EXPLORE PEOPLE'S LIVES.   In keeping with the goal of verisimilitude, realistic plays eliminate traditional but artificial dramatic conventions that do not occur in daily life, such as disguises, overheard conversations, asides, soliloquies, and verse. At its best, realistic drama is a close examination of character in conflict. The plots are straightforward and progress chronologically. The characters look, speak, and act as much as possible like real people. The settings are middle-class living rooms, the country houses of the wealthy, the squalid slums of the poor. Usually the plays explore ideas about the nature of humanity in conflict with social customs and prejudices.

REALISTIC THEATRICAL PRODUCTIONS EMPHASIZE LIFELIKE SETTINGS.   The new realism called for equally new and realistic methods of production and action. Most theaters of the nineteenth century featured a darkened auditorium, a proscenium arch separating the audience from the players, and a picture-frame stage. The spectators watched the play as though the fourth wall of a room had been removed. The illusion was that the audience was eavesdropping on private conversations and events.

The settings and stage directions for realistic drama became as detailed and lifelike as possible. When the curtain went up, the audience saw a completely furnished room or office, much like the ones in which they themselves lived or worked. Ibsen's description of the setting for Act 1 of *A Dollhouse* (1879), for example, calls for the duplication of Norwegian middle-class living and dining rooms of the late nineteenth century, complete with a piano, a coffee table, armchairs, a ceramic tile heating stove, easy chairs, a rocking-chair, and a bookcase. Lighting and costumes were equally realistic. Lighting was designed to duplicate the natural light at a particular time of day or the lamps burning in a room at night. Similarly, the lavish and beautiful costumes of nineteenth-century melodrama gave way to detailed realism in dress and makeup on the stage.

REALISTIC DRAMA REQUIRES ACTORS TO DUPLICATE THE SPEECH AND MANNERISMS OF LIVING PEOPLE. The most radical and permanent change caused by the new realism was in acting styles. In the Victorian theater, actors stood in one place, assumed a conventional stance, and declaimed their lines. In realistic drama the acting became more natural and intimate. Actors began to combine movement with dialogue and to play "within the scene" to each other rather than to the spectators.

These changes were due, in large measure, to Konstantin Stanislavsky (1863–1938), one of the founders of the Moscow Art Theater (1898) and the inventor of what we now term *method acting*. Stanislavski argued that actors had to build characterizations on a lifelong study of inner truths and motivation. He taught actors to search inwardly, within the depths of their own imaginations, for the feelings, motivations, and behavior of the characters they portray.

A New Nonrealistic Drama Was Created in Opposition to Realism

No sooner had realism taken over the stage than a new nonrealistic drama began to emerge as a reaction against realism. Many playwrights in Europe and the United States decided that realism had gone too far and that the quest for minutely realistic details had sacrificed the essence of drama—character and universal truth. Playwrights began to explore every avenue of antirealistic drama.

A CONSEQUENCE OF NONREALISTIC DRAMA WAS EXPERIMENTAL STAGING. At the same time, new types of stages and theaters began to appear. The **thrust stage,** a feature of Elizabethan theaters, was reintroduced. It projected into the audience, thus helping to destroy the fourth-wall principle of realistic drama. The **arena stage,** or **theater-in-the-round,** was developed, which also called for new concepts in drama and production.[1]

Playwrights like Luigi Pirandello (Italian, 1867–1936) and Bertolt Brecht (German, 1898–1956) wrote plays that required only minimal sets or no sets at all. In this same tradition, Edward Albee's *The Sandbox* calls for little more than suggestive sets that can be brought on stage by no more than a few stage hands. To a degree, both Miller's *Death of a Salesman* and Williams's *The Glass Menagerie* share in this tradition. Miller presents us with three rooms for his characters, together with a thrust stage in which dream sequences take place, while Williams utilizes projected images and claims that his scenes are "not realistic." Such characteristics remind us constantly that we are reading or watching a play—an illusion and an imitation—rather than real life.

---

[1]See pages 1211–14 for an additional discussion of stages.

Elements of Realistic and Nonrealistic Drama

THE TWO KINDS OF DRAMA IMPLY GREAT DIFFERENCES IN THEIR PRESENTATION OF NARRATIVE.   Because realistic plays, like life, unfold chronologically, the *story* (as opposed to the *play*) is usually nearing conclusion when the stage action begins. In Glaspell's *Trifles,* for example, the story comprises incidents from Minnie Wright's youth, her marital difficulties, and her reaction against her husband. All this, however, is presented in conversation; it all occurred *before* the play begins. Such events from the past have a profound impact on the present action in realistic drama, but the play itself presents only the last part of the story.

In nonrealistic drama, the structure of the plot is more fluid. Action shifts easily from the present to the past with little or no transition. Flashbacks are mixed with present action, and the entire play dramatizes the past through a present perspective. In Williams's *The Glass Menagerie,* recollected past action is revealed through the present memories of the narrator. Similarly, the action in Miller's *Death of a Salesman* constantly shifts between the present and memories of the past.

DRAMATIC CHARACTERS ARE SHAPED ACCORDING TO WHETHER THEY ARE CONCEIVED REALISTICALLY OR NONREALISTICALLY.   The characters in realistic drama are as much as possible like living people. They can be representative, symbolic, or even stock characters, but they must sound and act like normal human beings, with backgrounds, emotions, motivations, and last names as well as first names. There must be reasons for their actions, words, conflicts, and relationships. Most important, they must be consistent. Their responses, decisions, and characteristics must be the same as in real life. Such fidelity to life is apparent in realistic plays like Glaspell's *Trifles* and Hughes's *Mulatto.*

In modern nonrealistic drama, the characters can be nameless figures who have no background or motivation and who drop in and out of character, or who assume a number of different functions at different times, according to the dramatist's need. Tom is such a character in Williams's *The Glass Menagerie.* At various times he is a character in the action, a narrator who provides background and commentary, and a stage manager. As a character, he interacts with Laura and Amanda; as a narrator, he speaks directly to the audience; as a stage manager, he occasionally cues the technicians offstage about music and lighting.

These distinctions do not mean that realistic characters are always round and nonrealistic ones always flat. The way in which a playwright develops characters, realistically or nonrealistically, does not control the degree to which they are developed. Thus, true-to-life characters like Mr. Hale in *Trifles* or Jim O'Connor in *The Glass Menagerie* are flat. By the same token, nonrealistic characters, like Tom in *The Glass Menagerie* or Willy Loman in *Death of a Salesman,* have enough depth and scope to be considered fully round.

LANGUAGE IS A SIGN OF THE DEGREES OF REALITY OR NONREALITY.   In a realistic play, the language accurately represents the diction appropriate to the class or group of people portrayed. There is no poetry, no radical shift in style, and no direct address to the reader or speaker. In *Mulatto*, for instance, Cora and her uneducated children consistently use the vernacular speech patterns of African Americans living in the South during the 1930s. Similarly, the characters in Glaspell's *Trifles* sound like Midwestern farmers and small-town residents.

Such verisimilitude is not required in nonrealistic drama. Playwrights employ any linguistic devices that suit their needs. Some characters therefore speak in verse, clichés, or even nonsense sounds (as in *The Sandbox*). Others have two or three separate speeds of presentation, as Tom does in *The Glass Menagerie*. Dramatists are free to introduce songs or hymns into the play, and some characters speak directly to the audience. Often the characters talk as though they are in a dream, or are living through their memories, or are so preoccupied with their concerns that the other characters are incidental to them.

THE STAGE ITSELF IS A GRAPHIC GUIDE TO THE LEVEL OF REALITY.   Such differences in plot, characterization, and language are matched by differences in production techniques. Whereas the staging of a realistic drama must be true to life, as in *A Dollhouse*, nonrealistic drama is usually staged with few or no realistic effects. While the sets are based in reality, they are primarily symbolic and expressive of mood, employing lighting and a semitransparent painted cloth (called a **scrim**) to create the simultaneous effect of multiple places or times. Carefully controlled lighting indicates flashbacks, changes in mood, and shifts of location, and spotlights illuminate and emphasize objects and characters in ways that never happen in reality. In addition, the dramatist of a nonrealistic play is free to introduce music, special sound effects, words or images projected onto a wall or screen, action that flows off the stage into the auditorium, and speeches made directly to the spectators or the reader. All these and other devices break the illusion of reality and demand that we consider the play as an artistic construction. Such nonrealistic dramatic effects are described in the stage directions for both *Death of a Salesman* and *The Glass Menagerie*.

In this way, nonrealistic drama moved progressively farther away from realism throughout the latter half of the twentieth century. With the development of flexible theaters, in which the seats in certain locations are removed, with acting areas being set up throughout the house, the action of plays has moved offstage and into the space once occupied by the audience.

Paradoxically, as such drama becomes more nonrealistic, the theater itself, as a place for acting and performing, becomes the dominant reality. In the 1960s and 1970s, acting companies like the Living Theater in New York experimented with plays that began onstage, moved into the audience, and ended on the streets outside. Such productions represent the edge of drama. In the mid 1980s, the Old Vic Company in London produced *The Creation*—a series of medieval mystery plays—in which the actors mingled among the spectators, separating only when their parts were called for. Whenever new scenes were introduced, the standing spectators were (literally) swept aside to provide space, so that acting areas were being shaped by the shifting audience. A production that remained popular into this century was *Tony n' Tina's Wedding* (1988), which represented the staging of a wedding and reception (in two dif-

ferent locations, one a church and the other a restaurant).[2] Because performers
and audience were to interact, particularly at the reception, many members of
the audience took on impromptu acting and speaking roles. Every performance was therefore spontaneous and unique. An argument might be made that
such one-time performances represent superrealism, but in fact they blur the
distinction between drama and the real world to the point where art almost
ceases to be art, and all action everywhere—both real life and stage life—
seems entirely to be performance.

Most Plays Offer a Blend of Realism and Nonrealism

To this point we have been speaking as though realistic and nonrealistic drama
were always at opposite extremes, but most plays are not purely realistic or nonrealistic. Rather, the terms represent the opposite ends of a continuum, and most
plays fall somewhere between the extremes. Glaspell's *Trifles*, Wilson's *Fences*,
Hughes' *Mulatto*, and Ibsen's *A Dollhouse*, for example, are highly realistic, yet
each modifies its realism through symbolism and selective emphasis. Conversely,
the staging of *The Sandbox* is nonrealistic in most respects, yet it is based on easily
recognized characterizations of people in a strained family relationship. Both
Miller's *Death of a Salesman* and Williams's *The Glass Menagerie* fall near the middle
of the continuum; they combine realistic language and characterization with nonrealistic settings, lighting, and structure.

Plays for Study

Langston Hughes. . . . . Mulatto, 1622
Tennessee Williams . . . . The Glass Menagerie, 1644
August Wilson . . . . Fences, 1695

LANGSTON HUGHES (1902–1967)

*For a discussion of Hughes's early life and career, and his work in po-
etry, see pages 1072–76.*
   *In 1931, just before he reached the age of thirty, and while he was
still beginning his writing career, Hughes traveled to Russia. He
spent a year there, and worked on a Soviet film about racial relations in the United States. When he returned he was filled with
ideas, and his writing continued in the direction of exposing racism
and inequality in America. A major result was his first collection of
stories,* The Ways of White Folks, *which came out in 1934. This was a book in which he fic-
tionalizes his disaffection with the condition of African Americans both in the South and in the
North. One of these stories was "Father and Son," a version of the material that he turned into
his two-act play* Mulatto. *The play was produced at the Vanderbilt Theater in New York in
October 1935, and had a run of 373 performances—the record at that time for a Broadway play
by an African American dramatist.*

---

[2]*Tony n' Tina's Wedding* ran in New York for close to seventeen years and became so firmly fixed that it created
its own Web site at <www.tonylovestina.com>, a practice now common with many long-running plays. The play
was performed in eleven other American cities and also in Europe, Asia, and Australia, with as many as a hundred different performing sites worldwide.

Hughes and the African American Theater After 1920

During these years, the growing African American theater was dominated by two major themes, the first being the customs and problems of Southern blacks. The most pressing problem was the cruelty and injustice of lynching. Angelina Weld Grimke's *Rachael* (1920) and James Miller's *Never No More* (1932) openly condemned the practice. Dennis Donaghue's *Legal Murder* (1934) was an attack on the false conviction for rape of nine young black men from Scottsboro, Alabama, a topic that Hughes also treated in his early drama *Scottsboro Limited: Four Poems and a Play in Verse* (1932). The second major theme concerned the adjustments that blacks needed to make after they left the South and migrated to cities in the North. Frank Wilson's *Meek Mose* was perhaps the most optimistic of these plays, in which dispossessed blacks discover oil on their new property. More typical were Garland Anderson's *Appearances* (1925), about how a black bellhop overcomes false charges of rape, and Wallace Thurman's *Harlem* (1929), about the difficulties of a black family living in Chicago. This theme also dominates Lorraine Hansberry's *A Raisin in the Sun* (1959), the now-classic drama that marked the coming of age of post–World War II African American playwrights.

Hughes's Career as a Dramatist

Although Hughes is not thought of principally as a dramatist, he wrote plays throughout his career. In addition to the plays already mentioned, he wrote *Little Ham* (1936) and *Soul Gone Home* (1937), a short fantasy play. As the first production for the radical Suitcase Theater, which he founded after returning as a correspondent from the Spanish Civil War, he wrote *Don't You Want to Be Free* (1938). He collaborated with Arna Bontemps in *When the Jack Hollers* (1936) and with Zora Neale Hurston in *Mule Bone* (reissued in 1991). In 1948 he wrote the lyrics for the Kurt Weill and Elmer Rice musical *Street Scene*, perhaps the best known of the plays in which he was involved. In 1951 he produced a libretto, *Just Around the Corner*, and in 1957 he wrote *Simply Heavenly*, a blues-musical play featuring the character Jesse Semple, whom he had created as a character in his weekly columns for the *Chicago Defender*. Although *Simply Heavenly* (which is a musical version of an earlier play, *Semple Takes a Wife*) concludes optimistically, one can find within it the serious theme of frustration resulting from the difficulties that African Americans experience in seeking identity and recognition. Semple says, at one point:

> I'm broke, busted, and disgusted. And just spent mighty near my last nickel for a paper—and there ain't no news in it about colored folks. Unless we commit murder, robbery or rape, or are being chased by a mob, do we get on the front page, or hardly on the back. (I.5)

Hughes's interests in the last decades of his life were in the musical theater, particularly the introduction of gospel-related music and jazz. Three of his major efforts were *Black Nativity* (1961), *The Gospel Glory* (1962), and *Jericho-Jim Crow* (1964). His output as a dramatist was indeed great, even if it may be overshadowed by his preeminence as a poet and writer of fiction.

Mulatto and the Reality of the Southern Black Experience

Hughes's *Mulatto* deals with life in the South during the 1930s, a time when the system of white control over blacks was absolute and uncompromisingly harsh and brutal. Hughes's first conception of the play—a troubled relationship between father and son—is a perennial one. Colonel Tom Norwood and Robert Lewis, his mulatto son, recognize their relationship but also hate and reject each other. In *Mulatto* the realistic cause of conflict is the "color line"—the symbolic line that people of different races must cross in order to accept each other as human beings. Acceptance is an ideal goal, just as the color line is an insurmountable obstacle in the society that the play depicts. The lack of ability or will to cross the line governs the pattern of action and also the violent outcome. Colonel Norwood has lived in the same house with Cora Lewis for many years, and they do well together as long as he is not confronted with the issue of his paternity or challenged about his control over the plantation. There is no way he can recognize the four "yard blacks" on his plantation as his legitimate children, however, unless he is willing to forsake his identity as a white.

There are many other marks of dramatic realism, particularly the exploitation of black women (described in Act 1, speech 61), the front entrance of the Norwood house, Robert's complaints about Miss Gray, and his speeding with the Ford. All of his so-called "uppity" actions would not be unacceptable to white society if Robert were white, but because he is black they indicate a state of revolt. In addition, Robert's identity as half white, half black—he is called "yellow" by Colonel Tom—leaves him in an anomalous position, for he is not "white" enough to be equal or "black" enough to be subservient. The reality of his situation leads him to hate both whites and blacks alike, and the sudden eruption of his seething anger leads to his violence.

Mulatto reflects the reality of language in the South of the 1930s. Hughes's blacks, except for Robert and Sallie, use southern black vernacular (called "darky talk" by Hughes). The introduction of such speech in literature was controversial at the time. Many black intellectuals who had also been a part of the Harlem Renaissance believed that dialect should be shunned, on the principle that it reinforced negative African American stereotypes. However, Hughes believed using the vernacular was correct because it was truthful and realistic, enabling writers to demonstrate that blacks are not stereotypes, that they face human problems just like everyone else, and that they succeed and fail just like everyone else. Moreover, there were precedents for the realistic use of dialect that had been set by Mark Twain in *Tom Sawyer* and *Huckleberry Finn*, both of which are acknowledged classics of American literature.

Mulatto is one of Hughes's most important plays. In 1950 he refashioned it as a libretto, titled *The Barrier*, which was set to music by the composer Jan Meyerowitz. In addition, the play was translated into Spanish and published in South America in 1954.

Mulatto (1935)

CHARACTERS

Colonel Thomas Norwood. Plantation owner, a still vigorous man of about sixty, nervous, refined, quick-tempered, and commanding; a widower who is the father of four living mulatto children by his Negro housekeeper.

Cora Lewis. A brown woman in her forties who has kept the house and been the mistress of Colonel Norwood for some thirty years.

William Lewis. The oldest son of Cora Lewis and the Colonel; a fat, easy-going, soft looking mulatto of twenty-eight; married.

Sallie Lewis. The seventeen-year-old daughter, very light with sandy hair and freckles, who could pass for white.

Robert Lewis [Bert]. Eighteen, the youngest boy; strong and well-built; a light mulatto with ivory-yellow skin and proud thin features like his father's; as tall as the Colonel, with the same gray-blue eyes, but with curly black hair instead of brown; of a fiery, impetuous temper—immature and willful—resenting his blood and the circumstances of his birth.

Fred Higgins. A close friend of Colonel Norwood; a county politician; fat and elderly, conventionally Southern.

Sam. An old Negro retainer, a personal servant of the Colonel.

Billy. The small son of William Lewis; a chubby brown kid about five.

Talbot. The overseer.

Mose. An elderly Negro, chauffeur for Mr. Higgins.

A Storekeeper.

An Undertaker.

Undertaker's Helper. Voice offstage only.

The Mob.

ACT 1

TIME. *An afternoon in early fall.*

SETTING. *The same.*

ACTION. *The living room of the Big House on a plantation in Georgia. Rear center of the room, a vestibule with double doors leading to the porch; at each side of the doors, a large window with lace curtains and green shades; at left a broad flight of stairs leading to the second floor; near the stairs, downstage, a doorway leading to the dining room and kitchen; opposite at right of stage, a door to the library. The room is furnished in the long outdated horsehair and walnut style of the nineties; a crystal chandelier, a large old-fashioned rug, a marble-topped table, upholstered chairs. At the right there is a small cabinet. It is a very clean, but somewhat shabby and rather depressing room, dominated by a large oil painting of* NORWOOD's *wife of his youth on the center wall. The windows are raised. The afternoon sunlight streams in.*

ACTION. *As the curtain rises, the stage is empty. The door at the right opens and* COLONEL NORWOOD *enters, crossing the stage toward the stairs, his watch in his hand. Looking up, he shouts:*

NORWOOD: Cora! Oh Cora!

CORA: [*Heard above*] Yes, sir, Colonel Tom.

NORWOOD: I want to know if that child of yours means to leave here this afternoon?

CORA: [*At head of steps now*] Yes, sir, she's goin' directly. I's gettin' her ready now, packin' up an' all. 'Course, she wants to tell you goodbye 'fore she leaves.

5   NORWOOD: Well, send her down here. Who's going to drive her to the railroad? The train leaves at three—and it's after two now. You ought to know you can't drive ten miles in no time.

CORA: [*Above*] Her brother's gonna drive her. Bert. He ought to be back here most any time now with the Ford.

NORWOOD: [*Stopping on his way back to the library*] Ought to be back here? Where's he gone?

CORA: [*Coming downstairs nervously*] Why, he driv in town 'fore noon, Colonel Tom. Said he were lookin' for some tubes or somethin' 'nother by de mornin' mail for de radio he's been riggin' up out in de shed.

NORWOOD: Who gave him permission to be driving off in the middle of the morning? I bought that Ford to be used when I gave orders for it to be used, not . . .

CORA: Yes, sir, Colonel Tom, but . . .   10

NORWOOD: But what? [*Pausing. Then deliberately*] Cora, if you want that hardheaded yellow son of yours to get along around here, he'd better listen to me. He's no more than any other black buck on this plantation—due to work like the rest of 'em. I don't take such a performance from nobody under me—driving off in the middle of the day to town, after I've told him to bend his back in that cotton. How's Talbot going to keep the rest of those darkies working right if that boy's allowed to set that kind of an example? Just because Bert's your son, and I've been damn fool enough to send him off to school for five or six years, he thinks he has a right to privileges, acting as if he owned this place since he's been back here this summer.

CORA: But, Colonel Tom . . .

NORWOOD: Yes, I know what you're going to say. I don't give a damn about him! There's no nigger-child of mine, yours, ours—no darkie—going to disobey me. I put him in that field to work, and he'll stay on this plantation till I get ready to let him go. I'll tell Talbot to use the whip on him, too, if he needs it. If it hadn't been that he's yours, he'd-a had a taste of it the other day. Talbot's a damn good overseer, and no saucy, lazy Nigras stay on this plantation and get away with it. [*To* CORA] Go on back upstairs and see about getting Sallie out of here. Another word from you and I won't send your [*Sarcastically*] pretty little half-white daughter anywhere, either. Schools for darkies! Huh! If you take that boy of yours for an example, they do 'em more harm than good. He's learned nothing in college but impudence, and he'll stay here on this place and work for me awhile before he gets back to any more schools. [*He starts across the room.*]

CORA: Yes, sir, Colonel Tom. [*Hesitating*] But he's just young, sir. And he was mighty broke up when you said last week he couldn't go back to de campus. [COLONEL NORWOOD *turns and looks at* CORA *commandingly. Understanding, she murmurs*] Yes, sir. [*She starts upstairs, but turns back.*] Can't I run and fix you a cool drink, Colonel Tom?

NORWOOD: No, damn you! Sam'll do it.   15

CORA: [*Sweetly*] Go set down in de cool, then, Colonel. 'Taint good for you to be goin' on this way in de heat. I'll talk to Robert maself soon's he comes in. He don't mean nothing—just smart and young and kinder careless, Colonel Tom, like ma mother said you used to be when you was eighteen.

NORWOOD: Get on upstairs, Cora. Do I have to speak again? Get on! [*He pulls the cord of the servants' bell.*]

CORA: [*On the steps*] Does you still be in the mind to tell Sallie good-bye?

NORWOOD: Send her down here as I told you. [*Impatiently*] Where's Sam? Send him here first. [*Fuming*] Looks like he takes his time to answer that bell. You colored folks are running the house to suit yourself nowadays.

CORA: [*Coming downstairs again and going toward the door under the steps*] I'll get Sam for you.   20

[CORA *exits left.* NORWOOD *paces nervously across the floor. Goes to the window and looks out down the road. Takes a cigar from his pocket, sits in a chair with it unlighted, scowling. Rises, goes toward servants' bell and rings it again violently as* SAM *enters, out of breath.*]

NORWOOD: What the hell kind of a tortoise race is this? I suppose you were out in the sun somewhere sleeping?

SAM: No, sah, Colonel Norwood. Just tryin' to get Miss Sallie's valises down to de yard so's we can put 'em in de Ford, sah.

NORWOOD: [*Out of patience*] Huh! Darkies waiting on darkies! I can't get service in my own house. Very well. [*Loudly*] Bring me some whiskey and soda, and ice in a glass. Is that damn Frigidaire working right? Or is Livonia still too thickheaded to know how to run it? Any ice cubes in the thing?

SAM: Yes, sah, Colonel, yes, sah. [*Backing toward door left*] 'Scuse me, please sah, but [*As* NORWOOD *turns toward library*] Cora say for me to ask you is it all right to bring that big old trunk what you give Sallie down by de front steps. We ain't been able to tote it down them narrer little back steps, sah. Cora, say, can we bring it down de front way through here?

25 NORWOOD: No other way? [*SAM shakes his head*] Then pack it on through the back, quick. Don't let me catch you carrying any of Sallie's baggage out of that front door here. You-all'll be wanting to go in and out the front way next. [*Turning away, complaining to himself*] Darkies have been getting mighty fresh in this part of the country since the war. The damn Germans should've . . . [*To* SAM] Don't take that trunk out that front door.

SAM: [*Evilly, in a cunning voice*] I's seen Robert usin' de front door—when you ain't here, and he comes up from de cabin to see his mammy. [*SALLIE, the daughter, appears at the top of the stairs, but hesitates about coming down.*]

NORWOOD: Oh, you have, have you? Let me catch him and I'll break his young neck for him. [*Yelling at* SAM] Didn't I tell you some whiskey and soda an hour ago?

[*SAM exits left. SALLIE comes shyly down the stairs and approaches her father. She is dressed in a little country-style coat-suit ready for traveling. Her features are Negroid, although her skin is very fair. COLONEL NORWOOD gazes down at her without saying a word as she comes meekly toward him, half-frightened.*]

SALLIE: I just wanted to tell you goodbye, Colonel Norwood, and thank you for letting me go back to school another year, and for letting me work here in the house all summer where mama is. [*NORWOOD says nothing. The girl continues in a strained voice as if making a speech*] You mighty nice to us colored folks certainly, and mama says you the best white man in Georgia. [*Still NORWOOD says nothing. The girl continues.*] You been mighty nice to your—I mean to us colored children, letting my sister and me go off to school. The principal says I'm doing pretty well and next year I can go to Normal and learn to be a teacher. [*Raising her eyes*] You reckon I can, Colonel Tom?

NORWOOD: Stand up straight and let me see how you look. [*Backing away*] Hum-m-m! Getting kinder grown, ain't you? Do they teach you in that school to have good manners, and not be afraid of work, *and to respect white folks*?

30 SALLIE: Yes, sir, I been taking up cooking and sewing, too.

NORWOOD: Well, that's good. As I recall it, that school turned your sister out a right smart cook. Cora tells me she's got a good job in some big hotel in Chicago. I'm thinking about you going on up North there with her in a year or two. You're getting too old to be around here, and too womanish. [*He puts his hands on her arms as if feeling her flesh*]

SALLIE: [*Drawing back slightly*] But I want to live down here with mama. I want to teach school in that there empty school house by the Cross Roads what hasn't had a teacher for five years.

[*SAM has been standing with the door cracked, overhearing the conversation. He enters with the drink and places it on the table, right. NORWOOD sits down, leaving the girl standing, as SAM pours out a drink.*]

NORWOOD: Don't get that into your head, now. There's been no teacher there for years—and there won't be any teacher there, either. Cotton teaches these pickaninnies enough around here. Some of 'em's too smart as it is. The only reason I did have a teacher there once was to get you young ones o' Cora's educated. I gave you all a chance and I hope you appreciate it. [*He takes a long drink.*] Don't know why I did it. No other white man in these parts ever did it, as I know of. [*To* SAM] Get out of here! [SAM *exits left*] Guess I couldn't stand to see Cora's kids working around here dumb as the rest of these no-good darkies—need a dozen of 'em to chop one row of cotton, or to keep a house clean. Or maybe I didn't want Talbot eyeing you gals. [*Taking another drink*] Anyhow, I'm glad you and Bertha turned out right well. Yes, hum-m-m! [*Straightening up*] You know I tried to do something for those brothers of yours, too, but William's stupid as an ox—good for work, though—and that Robert's just an impudent, hardheaded, yellow young fool. I'm gonna break his damn neck for him if he don't watch out. Or else put Talbot on him.

SALLIE: [*Suddenly frightened*] Please, sir, don't put the overseer on Bert, Colonel Tom. He was the smartest boy at school, Bert was. On the football team, too. Please, sir, Colonel Tom. Let brother work here in the house, or somewhere else where Talbot can't mistreat him. He ain't used . . .

NORWOOD: [*Rising*] Telling me what to do, heh? [*Staring at her sternly*] I'll use the back of my   35 hand across your face if you don't hush. [*He takes another drink. The noise of a Ford is heard outside.*] That's Bert now, I reckon. He's to take you to the railroad line, and while you're riding with him, you better put some sense into his head. And tell him I want to see him as soon as he gets back here. [CORA *enters left with a bundle and an umbrella.* SAM *and* WILLIAM *come downstairs with a big square trunk, and exit hurriedly, left.*]

SALLIE: Yes, sir, I'll tell him.

CORA: Colonel Tom, Sallie ain't got much time now. [*To the girl*] Come on, chile. Bert's here. Yo' big brother and Sam and Livonia and everybody's all waiting at de back door to say goodbye. And your baggage is being packed in. [*Noise of another car is heard outside.*] Who else is that there coming up de drive? [CORA *looks out the window.*] Mr. Higgins' car, Colonel Tom. Reckon he's coming to see you . . . Hurry up out o' this front room, Sallie. Here, take these things of your'n [*Hands her the bundle and parasol*] while I opens de door for Mr. Higgins. [*In a whisper*] Hurry up, chile! Get out! [NORWOOD *turns toward the front door as* CORA *goes to open it*]

SALLIE: [*Shyly to her father*] Goodbye, Colonel Tom.

NORWOOD: [*His eyes on the front door, scarcely noticing the departing* SALLIE, *he motions.*] Yes, yes goodbye! Get on now! [CORA *opens the front door as her daughter exits left.*] Well, well! Howdy do, Fred. Come in, come in! [CORA *holds the outer door of the vestibule wide as* FRED HIGGINS *enters with rheumatic dignity, supported on the arm of his chauffeur,* MOSE, *a very black Negro in a slouchy uniform.* CORA *closes the door and exits left hurriedly, following* SALLIE.]

NORWOOD: [*Smiling*] How's the rheumatiz today? Women or licker or heat must've made   40 it worse—from the looks of your speed!

HIGGINS: [*Testily, sitting down puffing and blowing in a big chair*] I'm in no mood for fooling, Tom, not now. [*To* MOSE] All right. [*The* CHAUFFEUR *exits front.* HIGGINS *continues angrily.*] Norwood, that damned yellow nigger buck of yours that drives that new Ford tried his best just now to push my car off the road, then got in front of me and blew dust in my face for the last mile coming down to your gate, trying to beat me in here—which he did. Such a deliberate piece of impudence I don't know if I've ever seen out of a nigger before in all the sixty years I've lived in this country. [*The noise of the Ford is heard going out the drive, and the cries of the* NEGROES *shouting farewells to* SALLIE. HIGGINS *listens indignantly.*] What kind of crazy coons have you got on your place, anyhow? Sounds like a black Baptist picnic to me. [*Pointing to the window with his cane*] Tom, listen to that.

NORWOOD: [*Flushing*] I apologize to you, Fred, for each and every one of my darkies. [SAM *enters with more ice and another glass.*] Permit me to offer you a drink. I realize I've got to tighten down here.

CHAPTER 26 • Visions of Dramatic Reality and Nonreality

HIGGINS: Mose tells me that was Cora's boy in that Ford—and that young black fool is what I was coming here to talk to you about today. That boy! He's not gonna be around here long—not the way he's acting. The white folks in town'll see to that. Knowing he's one of your yard niggers, Norwood, I thought I ought to come and tell you. The white folks at the Junction aren't intending to put up with him much longer. And I don't know what good the jail would do him once he got in there.

NORWOOD: [*Tensely*] What do you mean, Fred—jail? Don't I always take care of the folks on my plantation without any help from the Junction's police force? Talbot can do more with an unruly black buck than your marshal.

45 HIGGINS: Warn't lookin' at it that way, Tom. I was thinking how weak the doors to that jail is. They've broke 'em down and lynched four niggers to my memory since it's been built. After what happened this morning, you better keep that yellow young fool out o' town from now on. It might not be safe for him around there—today, or no other time.

NORWOOD: What the hell? [*Perturbed*] He went in just now to take his sister to the depot. Damn it, I hope no ruffians'll break up my new Ford. What was it, Fred, about this morning?

HIGGINS: You haven't heard? Why, it's all over town already. He sassed out Miss Gray in the post office over a box of radio tubes that come by mail.

NORWOOD: He did, heh?

HIGGINS: Seems like the stuff was sent C.O.D. and got here all smashed up, so he wouldn't take it. Paid his money first before he saw the box was broke. Then wanted the money order back. Seems like the post office can't give money orders back—rule against it. Your nigger started to argue, and the girl at the window—Miss Gray—got scared and yelled for some of the mail clerks. They threw Bert out of the office, that's all. But that's enough. Lucky nothing more didn't happen. [*Indignantly*] That Bert needs a damn good beating—talking back to a white woman—and I'd like to give it to him myself, the way he kicked the dust up in my eyes all the way down the road coming out here. He was mad, I reckon. That's one yellow buck don't know his place, Tom, and it's your fault he don't—sending 'em off to be educated.

50 NORWOOD: Well, by God, I'll show him. I wish I'd have known it before he left here just now.

HIGGINS: Well, he's sure got mighty aggravating ways for a buck his color to have. Drives down the main street and don't stop for nobody, white or black. Comes in my store and if he ain't waited on as quick as the white folks are, he walks out and tells the clerk his money's as good as a white man's any day. Said last week standing out on my store front that he wasn't *all* nigger no how; said his name was Norwood—not Lewis, like the rest of his family—and part of your plantation here would be his when you passed out—and all that kind of stuff, boasting to the walleyed coons listening to him.

NORWOOD: [*Astounded*] Well, I'll be damned!

HIGGINS: Now, Tom, you know that don't go 'round these parts 'o Georgia, nor nowhere else in the South. A darkie's got to keep in his place down here. Ruinous to other niggers hearing that talk, too. All this postwar propaganda on the radio about freedom and democracy—why the niggers think it's meant for them! And that Eleanor Roosevelt,° she ought to been muzzled. She's driving our niggers crazy—your boy included! Crazy! Talking about civil rights. Ain't been no race trouble in our country for three years—since the Deekin's lynching—but I'm telling you, Norwood, you better see that that buck of yours goes away from here. I'm speaking on the quiet, but I can see ahead. And what happened this morning about them radio tubes wasn't none too good.

NORWOOD: [*Beside himself with rage*] A black ape! I—I . . .

°53 *Eleanor Roosevelt:* Eleanor Roosevelt (1884–1962), the wife of President Franklin D. Roosevelt, was an outspoken champion of minority causes.

HIGGINS: You been too decent to your darkies, Norwood. That's what's the matter with you.   55
And then the whole country suffers from a lot of impudent bucks who take lessons from
your crowd. Folks been kicking about that, too. Guess you know it. Maybe that's the reason you didn't get that nomination for committeeman a few years back.

NORWOOD: Maybe 'tis, Higgins. [*Rising and pacing the room*] God damn niggers! [*Furiously*]
Everything turns on niggers, niggers, niggers! No wonder Yankees call this the Black
Belt! [*He pours a large drink of whiskey.*]

HIGGINS: [*Soothingly*] Well, let's change the subject. Hand me my glass, there, too.

NORWOOD: Pardon me, Fred. [*He puts ice in his friend's glass and passes him the bottle.*]

HIGGINS: Tom, you get excited too easy for warm weather . . . Don't ever show black folks
they got you going, though. I think sometimes that's where you make your mistake.
Keep calm, keep calm—and then you command. Best plantation manager I ever had
never raised his voice to a nigger—and they were scared to death of him.

NORWOOD: Have a smoke. [*Pushes cigars toward* HIGGINS]   60

HIGGINS: You ought've married again, Tom—brought a white woman out here on this
damn place o' yours. A woman could help you run things. Women have soft ways, but
they can keep things humming. Nothing but blacks in the house—a man gets soft like
niggers are inside. [*Puffing at cigar*] And living with a colored woman! Of course, I
know we all have 'em—I didn't know you could make use of a white girl till I was past
twenty. Thought too much o' white women for that—but I've given many a yellow gal
a baby in my time. [*Long puff at cigar*] But for a man's own house you need a wife, not
a black woman.

NORWOOD: Reckon you're right, Fred, but it's too late to marry again now. [*Shrugging his
shoulders*] Let's get off of darkies and women for awhile. How's crops? [*Sitting down*]
How's politics going?

HIGGINS: Well, I guess you know the Republicans is trying to stir up trouble for us in
Washington. I wish the South had more men like Bilbo and Rankin° there. But, say, by
the way, Lawyer Hotchkiss wants to see us both about that budget money next week.
He's got some real Canadian stuff at his office, in his filing case, too—brought back
from his vacation last summer. Taste better'n this old mountain juice we get around
here. Not meaning to insult your drinks, Tom, but just remarking. I serve the same as
you myself, label and all.

NORWOOD: [*Laughing*] I'll have you know, sir, that this is prewar licker, sir!

HIGGINS: Hum-m-m! Well, it's got me feelin' better'n I did when I come in here—whatever   65
it is. [*Puffs at his cigar*] Say, how's your cotton this year?

NORWOOD: Doin' right well, specially down in the south field. Why not drive out that road
when you leave and take a look at it? I'll ride down with you. I want to see Talbot, anyhow.

HIGGINS: Well, let's be starting. I got to be back at the Junction by four o'clock. Promised to
let that boy of mine have the car to drive over to Thomasville for a dance tonight.

NORWOOD: One more shot before we go. [*He pours out drinks.*] The young ones must have
their fling, I reckon. When you and I grew up down here it used to be a carriage and
the best pair of black horses when you took the ladies out—now it's an automobile.
That's a good lookin' new car of yours, too.

HIGGINS: Right nice.

°63 *Bilbo, Rankin:* Theodore Bilbo (1877–1947), senator from Mississippi from 1935 to 1947, and John Eliot
Rankin (1882–1960), Mississippi representative to the House from 1921 to 1953, were both noted advocates of
white supremacy.

70 NORWOOD: Been thinking about getting a new one myself, but money's been kinder tight this year, and conditions are none too good yet, either. Reckon that's why everybody's so restless. [*He walks toward stairs calling.*] Cora! Oh, Cora! . . . If I didn't have a few thousand put away, I'd feel the pinch myself. [*As* CORA *appears on the stairs.*] Bring me my glasses up there by the side of my bed . . . Better whistle for Mose, hadn't I, Higgins? He's probably 'round back with some of his women. [*Winking*] You know I got some nice black women in this yard.

HIGGINS: Oh, no, not Mose. I got my servants trained to stay in their places—right where I want 'em—while they're working for me. Just open the door and tell him to come in here and help me out. [NORWOOD *goes to the door and calls the* CHAUFFEUR. MOSE *enters and assists his master out to the car.* CORA *appears with the glasses, goes to the vestibule and gets the* COLONEL'S *hat and cane which she hands him.*]

NORWOOD: [*To* CORA] I want to see that boy o' yours soon as I get back. That won't be long, either. And tell him to put up that Ford of mine and don't touch it again.

CORA: Yes, sir, I'll have him waiting here. [*In a whisper*] It's hot weather, Colonel Tom. Too much of this licker makes your heart upset. It ain't good for you, you know. [NORWOOD *pays her no attention as he exits toward the car. The noise of the departing motor is heard. Cora begins to tidy up the room. She takes a glass from a side table. She picks up a doily that was beneath the glass and looks at it long and lovingly. Suddenly she goes to the door left and calls toward the kitchen.*] William, you William! Com'ere, I want to show you something. Make haste, son. [*As* CORA *goes back toward the table, her eldest son,* WILLIAM *enters carrying a five-year-old boy.*] Look here at this purty doily yo' sister made this summer while she been here. She done learned all about sewing and making purty things at school. Ain't it nice, son?

WILLIAM: Sho' is. Sallie takes after you, I reckon. She's a smart little crittur, ma. [*Sighs*] De Lawd knows, I was dumb at school. [*To his child*] Get down, Billy, you's too heavy. [*He puts the boy on the floor*] This here sewin's really fine.

75 BILLY: [*Running toward the big upholstered chair and jumping up and down on the spring seat*] Gityap! I's a mule driver. Haw! Gee!

CORA: You Billy, get out of that chair 'fore I skins you alive. Get on into de kitchen, sah.

BILLY: I'm playin' horsie, grandma. [*Jumps up in the chair*] Horsie! Horsie!

CORA: Get! That's de Colonel's favorite chair. If he knows any little darkie's been jumpin' on it, he raise sand. Get on, now.

BILLY: Ole Colonel's ma grandpa, ain't he? Ain' he ma white grandpa?

80 WILLIAM: [*Snatching the child out of the chair*] Boy, I'm gonna fan your hide if you don't hush!

CORA: Shs-ss-s! You Billy, hush yo' mouth! Chile, where you hear that? [*To her son*] Some o' you all been talking too much in front o' this chile. [*To the boy*] Honey, go on in de kitchen till yo' daddy come. Get a cookie from 'Vonia and set down on de back porch. [*Little* BILLY *exits left*]

WILLIAM: Ma, you know it 'twarn't me told him. Bert's the one been goin' all over de plantation since he come back from Atlanta remindin' folks right out we's Colonel Norwood's chilluns.

CORA: [*Catching her breath*] Huh!

WILLIAM: He comes down to my shack tellin' Billy and Marybell they got a white man for grandpa. He's gonna get my chilluns in trouble sho'—like he got himself in trouble when Colonel Tom whipped him.

85 CORA: Ten or 'leven years ago, warn't it?

WILLIAM: And Bert's *sho'* in trouble now. Can't go back to that college like he could-a if he'd-a had any sense. You can't fool with white folks—an de Colonel ain't never really liked Bert since that there first time he beat him, either.

CORA: No, he ain't. Leastwise, he ain't understood him. [*Musing sadly in a low voice*] Time Bert was 'bout seven, warn't it? Just a little bigger'n yo' Billy.

WILLIAM: Yes.

CORA: Went runnin' up to Colonel Tom out in de horse stables when de Colonel was showin' off his horses—I 'members so well—to fine white company from town. Lawd, that boy's always been foolish! He went runnin' up and grabbed a-holt de Colonel and yelled right in front o' de white folks' faces, "O, papa, Cora say de dinner's ready, papa!" Ain't never called him papa before, and I don't know where he got it from. And Colonel Tom knocked him right backwards under de horse's feet.

WILLIAM: And when de company were gone, he beat that boy unmerciful.   90

CORA: I thought sho' he were gonna kill ma chile that day. And he were mad at me, too, for months. Said I was teaching you chilluns who they pappy were. Up till then Bert had been his favorite little colored child round here.

WILLIAM: Sho' had.

CORA: But he never like him no more. That's why he sent him off to school so soon to stay, winter and summer, all these years. I had to beg and plead to have him home this summer—but I's sorry now I ever got that boy back here again.

WILLIAM: He's sho' growed more like de Colonel all de time, ain't he? Bert thinks he's a real white man hisself now. Look at de first thing he did when he come home, he ain't seen de Colonel in six years—and Bert sticks out his hand fo' to shake hands with him!

CORA: Lawd! That chile!   95

WILLIAM: Just like white folks! And de Colonel turns his back and walks off. Can't blame him. He ain't used to such doings from colored folks. God knows what's got into Bert since he come back. He's acting like a fool—just like he was a boss man round here. Won't even say "Yes, sir" and "No, sir" no more to de white folks. Talbot asked him warn't he gonna work in de field this mornin'. Bert say "No!" and turn and walk away. White man so mad, I could see him nearly foam at de mouth. If he warn't yo' chile, ma, he'd been knocked in de head fo' now.

CORA: You's right.

WILLIAM: And you can't talk to him. I tried to tell him something the other day, but he just laughed at me, and said we's all just scared niggers on this plantation. Says he ain't no nigger, no how. He's a Norwood. He's half-white, and he's gonna act like it. [*In amazement at his brother's daring*] And this is Georgia, too!

CORA: I's scared to death for de boy, William. I don't know what to do. De Colonel says he won't send him off to school no mo'. Says he's mo' sassy and impudent now than any nigger he ever seed. Bert never has been like you was, and de girls, quiet and sensible like you knowed you had to be. [*She sits down*] De Colonel say he's gonna make Bert stay here now and work on this plantation like de rest of his niggers. He's gonna show him what color he is. Like that time when he beat him for callin' him "papa." He say he's gwine to teach him his place and make de boy know where he belongs. Seems like me or you can't show him. Colonel Tom has to take him in hand, or these white folks'll kill him around here and then—oh, My God!

WILLIAM: A nigger's just got to know his place in de South, that's all, ain't he, ma?   100

CORA: Yes, son. That's all, I reckon.

WILLIAM: And ma brother's one damn fool nigger. Don't seems like he knows nothin'. He's gonna ruin us all round here. Makin' it bad for everybody.

CORA: Oh, Lawd, have mercy! [*Beginning to cry*] I don't know what to do. De way he's acting up can't go on. Way he's acting to de Colonel can't last. Somethin's gonna happen to ma chile. I had a bad dream last night, too, and I looked out and seed de moon all red with blood. I seed a path o' living blood across this house, I tell you, in my sleep. Oh, Lawd, have mercy! [*Sobbing*] Oh, Lawd, help me in ma troubles. [*The noise of the returning Ford is heard outside. CORA looks up, rises, and goes to the window.*] There's de chile now, William. Run out to de back door and tell him I wants to see him. Bring him in here where Sam and Livonia and de rest of 'em won't hear ever'thing we's sayin'. I got to talk to ma boy. He's ma baby boy, and he don't know de way.

[*Exit* WILLIAM *through the door left.* CORA *is wiping her eyes and pulling herself together when the front door is flung open with a bang and* ROBERT *enters.*]

ROBERT: [*Running to his mother and hugging her teasingly*] Hello, ma! Your daughter got off, and I've come back to keep you company in the parlor! Bring out the cookies and lemonade. *Mister* Norwood's here!

105 CORA: [*Beginning to sob anew*] Take yo' hands off me, boy! Why don't you mind? Why don't you mind me?

ROBERT: [*Suddenly serious, backing away*] Why, mamma, what's the matter? Did I scare you? Your eyes are all wet! Has somebody been telling you 'bout this morning?

CORA: [*Not heeding his words*] Why don't you mind me, son? Ain't I told you and told you not to come in that front door, never? [*Suddenly angry*] Will somebody have to beat it into you? What's got wrong with you when you was away at that school? What am I gonna do?

ROBERT: [*Carelessly*] Oh, I knew that the Colonel wasn't here. I passed him and old man Higgins on the road down by the south patch. He wouldn't even look at me when I waved at him. [*Half playfully*] Anyhow, isn't this my old man's house? Ain't I his son and heir? [*Grandly, strutting around*] Am I not Mr. Norwood, Junior?

CORA: [*Utterly serious*] I believe you goin' crazy, Bert. I believes you wants to get us all killed or run away or something awful like that. I believes . . . [WILLIAM *enters left*]

110 WILLIAM: Where's Bert? He ain't come round back—[*Seeing his brother in the room*] How'd you get in here?

ROBERT: [*Grinning*] Houses have front doors.

WILLIAM: Oh, usin' de front door like de white folks, heh? You gwine do that once too much.

ROBERT: Yes, like de white folks. What's a front door for, you rabbit-hearted coon?

WILLIAM: Rabbit-hearted coon's better'n a dead coon any day.

115 ROBERT: I wouldn't say so. Besides you and me's only half-coons, anyhow, big boy. And I'm gonna act like my white half, not my black half. Get me, kid?

WILLIAM: Well, you ain't gonna act like it long here in de middle o' Georgy. And you ain't gonna act like it when de Colonel's around, either.

ROBERT: Oh, no? My stay down here'll be short and sweet, boy, short and sweet. The old man won't send me away to college no more—so you think I'm gonna stick around and work in the fields? Like fun! I might stay here awhile and teach some o' you darkies to think like men, maybe—till it gets too much for the old Colonel—but no more bowing down to white folks for me—not Robert Norwood.

CORA: Hush, son!

ROBERT: Certainly not right on my own old man's plantation—Georgia or no Georgia.

120 WILLIAM: [*Scornfully*] I hears you.

ROBERT: You can do it if you want to, but I'm ashamed of you. I've been away from here six years. [*Boasting*] I've learned something, seen people in Atlanta, and Richmond, and Washington where the football team went—real colored people who don't have to take off their hats to white folks or let 'em go to bed with their sisters—like that young Higgins boy, asking me what night Sallie was comin' to town. A damn cracker! [*To* CORA] 'Scuse me, ma. [*Continuing*] Back here in these woods maybe Sam and Livonia and you and mama and everybody's got their places fixed for 'em, but not me. [*Seriously*] Nobody's gonna fix a place for me. I'm old man Norwood's son. Nobody fixed a place for him. [*Playfully again*] Look at me. I'm a 'fay boy. [*Pretends to shake his hair back*] See these gray eyes? I got the right to everything everybody else has. [*Punching his brother in the belly*], Don't talk to me, old slavery-time Uncle Tom.

WILLIAM: [*Resentfully*] I ain't playin', boy. [*Pushes younger brother back with some force*] I ain't playin' a-tall.

CORA: All right, chilluns, stop. Stop! And William, you take Billy and go on home. 'Vonia's got to get supper and she don't like no young-uns under her feet in de kitchen. I wants to talk to Bert in here now 'fore Colonel Tom gets back. [*Exit* WILLIAM *left.* CORA *continues to* BERT] Sit down, child, right here a minute and listen.

ROBERT: [*Sitting down*] All right, ma.

CORA: Hard as I's worked and begged and humbled maself to get de Colonel to keep you   125
chilluns in school, you comes home wid yo' head full o' stubbornness and yo' mouth full o' sass for me an' de white folks an' everybody. You know can't no colored boy here talk like you's been doin' to no white folks, let alone to de Colonel and that old devil of a Talbot. They ain't gonna stand fo' yo' sass. Not only you, but I 'spects we's all gwine to pay fo' it, every colored soul on this place. I was scared to death today fo' yo' sister, Sallie, scared de Colonel warn't gwine to let her go back to school, neither, 'count o' yo' doins, but he did, thank Gawd—and then you come near makin' her miss de train. Did she have time to get her ticket and all?

ROBERT: Sure! Had to drive like sin to get there with her, though. I didn't mean to be late getting back here for her, ma, but I had a little run-in about them radio tubes in town.

CORA: [*Worried*] What's that?

ROBERT: The tubes was smashed when I got 'em, and I had already made out my money order, so the woman in the post office wouldn't give the three dollars back to me. All I did was explain to her that we could send the tubes back—but she got hot because there were two or three white folks waiting behind me to get stamps, I guess. So she yells at me to move on and not give her any of my "educated nigger talk." So I said, "I'm going to finish showing you these tubes before I move on"—and then she screamed and called the mail clerk working in the back, and told him to throw me out. [*Boasting*] He didn't do it by himself, though. Had to call all the white loafers out in the square to get me through that door.

CORA: [*Fearfully*] Lawd have mercy!

ROBERT: Guess if I hadn't-a had the Ford then, they'd've beat me half-to-death, but when   130
I saw how many crackers there was, I jumped in the car and beat it on away.

CORA: Thank God for that!

ROBERT: Not even a football man [*Half-boasting*] like me could tackle the whole junction. 'Bout a dozen colored guys standing around, too, and not one of 'em would help me— the dumb jiggaboos! They been telling me ever since I been here, [*Imitating darky talk*] "You can't argue wid whut folks, man. You better stay out o' this Juncton. You must ain't got no sense, nigger! You's a fool" . . . Maybe I am a fool, ma—but I didn't want to come back here nohow.

CORA: I's sorry I sent for you.

ROBERT: Besides you, there ain't nobody in this country but a lot of evil white folks and cowardly niggers. [*Earnstly*] I'm no nigger, anyhow, am I, ma? I'm half-white. The Colonel's my father—the richest man in the county—and I'm not going to take a lot of stuff from nobody if I do have to stay here, not from the old man either. He thinks I ought to be out there in the sun working, with Talbot standing over me like I belonged in the chain gang. Well, he's got another thought coming! [*Stubbornly*] I'm a Norwood—not a field-hand nigger.

CORA: You means you ain't workin' no mo'?   135

ROBERT: [*Flaring*] No, I'm not going to work in the fields. What did he send me away to school for—just to come back here and be his servant, or pick his hills of cotton?

CORA: He sent you away to de school because *I* asked him and begged him, and got down on my knees to him, that's why. [*Quietly*] And now I just wants to make you see some sense, if you can. I knows, honey, you reads in de books and de papers, and you knows a lot more'n I do. But, chile, you's in Georgy—and I don't see how it is you don't know where you's at. This ain't up North—and even up yonder where we hears it's so fine, yo' sister has to pass for white to get along good.

ROBERT: [*Bitterly*] I know it.

CORA: She ain't workin' in no hotel kitchen like de Colonel thinks. She's in a office type-writing. And Sallie's studyin' de typewriter, too, at de school, but yo' pappy don't know it. I knows we ain't s'posed to study nothin' but cookin' and hard workin' here in Georgy. That's all I ever done, or knowed about. I been workin' on this very place all ma life—even 'fore I come to live in this Big House. When de Colonel's wife died, I come here, and borned you chilluns. And de Colonel's been real good to me in his way. Let you all sleep in this house with me when you was little, and sent you all off to school when you growed up. Ain't no white man in this county done that with his cul-lud chilluns before, far as I can know. But you—Robert, be awful, awful careful! When de Colonel comes back, in a few minutes, he wants to talk to you. Talk right to him, boy. Talk like you was colored, 'cause you ain't white.

140 **ROBERT:** [*Angrily*] And I'm not black either. Look at me, mama. [*Rising and throwing up his arms*] Don't I look like my father? Ain't I as light as he is? Ain't my eyes gray like his eyes are? [*The noise of a car is heard outside*] Ain't this our house?

CORA: That's him now. [*Agitated*] Hurry, chile, and let's get out of this room. Come on through yonder to the kitchen. [*She starts toward the door left.*] And I'll tell him you're here.

ROBERT: I don't want to run into the kitchen. Isn't this our house? [*As CORA crosses hurriedly left, ROBERT goes toward the front door*] The Ford is parked out in front, anyway.

CORA: [*At the door left to the rear of the house*] Robert! Robert! [*As ROBERT nears the front door, COLONEL NORWOOD enters, almost runs into the boy, stops at the threshold and stares unbe-lievingly at his son. CORA backs up against the door left.*]

NORWOOD: Get out of here! [*He points toward the door to rear of the house where CORA is standing*].

145 **ROBERT:** [*Half-smiling*] Didn't you want to talk to me?

NORWOOD: Get out of here!

ROBERT: Not that way. [*THE COLONEL raises his cane to strike the boy. CORA screams. BERT draws himself up to his full height, taller than the old man and looking very much like him, pale and proud. The man and the boy face each other. NORWOOD does not strike.*]

NORWOOD: [*In a hoarse whisper*] Get out of here. [*His hand is trembling as he points.*]

CORA: Robert! Come on, son, come on! Oh, my God, come on. [*Opening the door left*]

150 **ROBERT:** Not that way, ma. [*ROBERT walks proudly out the front door. NORWOOD, in an impotent rage, crosses the room to a small cabinet right, opens it nervously with a key from his pocket, takes out a pistol, and starts toward the front door. CORA overtakes him, seizes his arm, stops him.*]

CORA: He's our son, Tom. [*She sinks slowly to her knees, holding his body.*] Remember, he's our son.

Curtain

ACT 2

Scene 1

TIME. *After supper. Sunset.*

SETTING. *The same.*

ACTION. *As the curtain rises, the stage is empty. Through the windows the late afternoon sun makes two bright paths toward the footlights. SAM, carrying a tray bearing a whiskey bottle and a bowl of ice, enters left and crosses toward the library. He stoops at the door right, listens a moment, knocks, then opens the door and goes in. In a moment SAM returns. As he leaves the library, he is heard replying to a request of NORWOOD's.*

SAM: Yes, sah, Colonel! Sho' will, sah! Right away, sah! Yes, sah, I'll tell him. [*He closes the door and crosses the stage muttering to himself.*] Six o'clock. Most nigh that now. Better tell Cora to get that boy right in here. Can't nobody else do notin' with that fool Bert but Cora. [*He exits left. Can be heard calling*] Cora! You, Cora . . .

[*Again the stage is empty. Off stage, outside, the bark of a dog is heard, the sound of Negroes singing down the road, the cry of a child. The breeze moves the shadows of leaves and tree limbs across the sunlit paths from the windows. The door left opens and* CORA *enters, followed by* ROBERT.]

CORA: [*Softly to* ROBERT *behind her in the dining room*] It's all right, son. He ain't come out yet, but it's nearly six, and that's when he said he wanted you, but I was afraid maybe you was gonna be late. I sent for you to come up here to de house and eat supper with me in de kitchen. Where'd you eat yo' vittuals at, chile?

ROBERT: Down at Willie's house, ma. After the old man tried to hit me you still want me to hang around and eat up here?

CORA: I wanted you to be here on time, honey, that's all.[*She is very nervous.*] I kinder likes to have you eat with me sometimes, too, but you ain't et up here more'n once this summer. But this evenin' I just wanted you to be here when de Colonel sent word for you, 'cause we's done had enough trouble today.

ROBERT: He's not here on time, himself, is he?   5

CORA: He's in de library. Sam couldn't get him to eat no supper tonight, and I ain't seen him a-tall.

ROBERT: Maybe he wants to see me in the library, then.

CORA: You know he don't 'low no colored folks in there 'mongst his books and things 'cept Sam. Some o' his white friends goes in there, but none o' us.

ROBERT: Maybe he wants to see *me* in there, though.

CORA: Can't you never talk sense, Robert? This ain't no time for foolin' and jokin'. Nearly   10
thirty years in this house and I ain't never been in there myself, not once, 'mongst de Colonel's papers. [*The clock strikes six.*] Stand over yonder and wait till he comes out. I's gwine on upstairs now, so's he can talk to you. And don't aggravate him no mo' for' God's sake. Agree to whatever he say. I's scared fo' you, chile, de way you been actin', and de fool tricks you done today, and de trouble about de post office besides. Don't aggravate him. Fo' yo' sake, honey, 'cause I loves you—and fo' all de po' colored folks on this place what has such a hard time when his humors get on him—agree to whatever he say, will you Bert?

ROBERT: All right, ma. [*Voice rising*] But he better not start to hit me again.

CORA: Shs-ss-s! He'll hear you. He's right in there.

ROBERT: [*Sullenly*] This was the day I ought to have started back to school—like my sister. I stayed my summer out here, didn't I? Why didn't he keep his promise to me? You said if I came home I could go back to college again.

CORA: Shs-ss-s! He'll be here now. Don't say nothin', chile, I's done all I could.

ROBERT: All right, ma.   15

CORA: [*Approaching the stairs*] I'll be in ma room, honey, where I can hear you when you goes out. I'll come down to de back door and see you 'fore you goes back to de shack. Don't aggravate him, chile.

[*She ascends the stairs. The boy sits down sullenly, left, and stares at the door opposite from which his father must enter. The clock strikes the quarter after six. The shadows of the window curtains have lengthened on the carpet. The sunshine has deepened to a pale orange, and the light paths grow less distinct across the floor. The boy sits up straight in his chair. He looks at the library door. It opens.* NORWOOD *enters. He is bent and pale. He looks across the room and sees the boy. Suddenly he straightens up. The old commanding look comes into his face. He strides directly across the room*]

*toward his son. The boy, half afraid, half defiant, yet sure of himself, rises. Now that ROBERT is stand-
ing, the white man turns, goes back to a chair near the table, right, and seats himself. He takes out a
cigar, cuts off the end and lights it, and in a voice of mixed condescension and contempt, he speaks to
his son. ROBERT remains standing near the chair.*]

NORWOOD: I don't want to have to beat you another time as I did when you were a child.
The next time I might not be able to control myself. I might kill you if I touched you
again. I been runnin' this plantation for thirty-five years, and I never had to beat a Ni-
gra as old as you are. I never had to beat one of Cora's children either—but you. The
rest of 'em had sense 'nough to keep out of my sight, and to speak to me like they
should . . . I don't have any trouble with my colored folks. Never have trouble. They do
what I say, or what Mr. Talbot says, and that's all there is to it, I give 'em a chance. If
they turn in their crops they get paid. If they're workin' for wages, they get paid. If they
want to spend their money on licker, or buy an old car, or fix up their cabins, they can.
Do what they choose long as they know their places and it don't hinder their work.
And to Cora's young ones I give all the chances any colored folks ever had in these
parts. More'n many a white child's had. I sent you all off to school. Let Bertha go on up
North when she got grown and educated. Intend to let Sallie do the same. Gave your
brother William that house he's living in when he got married, pay him for his work,
help him out if he needs it. None of my darkies suffer. Sent you to college. Would have
kept on, would have sent you back today, but I don't intend to pay for no darky, or
white boy either if I had one, that acts the way you've been acting. And certainly for no
black fool. Now I want to know what's wrong with you? I don't usually talk about
what I'm going to do with anybody on this place. It's my habit to tell people *what to do*,
not to discuss it with 'em. But I want to know what's the matter with you—whether
you're crazy or not. In that case, you'll have to be locked up. And if you aren't, you'll
have to change your ways a damn sight or it won't be safe for you here, and you know
it—venting your impudence on white women, parking the car in front of my door,
driving like mad through the Junction, and going, everywhere, just as you please. Now,
I'm going to let you talk to me, but I want you to talk right.
ROBERT: [*Still standing*] What do you mean, "talk right"?
NORWOOD: I mean talk like a nigger should to a white man.
20 ROBERT: Oh! But I'm not a nigger, Colonel Tom. I'm your son.
NORWOOD: [*Testily*] You're Cora's boy.
ROBERT: Women don't have children by themselves.
NORWOOD: Nigger women don't know the fathers. You're a bastard.

[*ROBERT clenches his fist. NORWOOD turns toward the drawer where the pistol is, takes it out, and
lays it on the table. The wind blows the lace curtains at the windows, and sweeps the shadows of
falling leaves across the paths of sunlight on the floor.*]

ROBERT: I've heard that before. I've heard it from Negroes, and I've heard it from white
folks. Now I hear it from you. [*Slowly*] You're talking about my mother.
25 NORWOOD: I'm talking about Cora, yes. Her children are bastards.
ROBERT: [*Quickly*] And you're their father. [*Angrily*] How come I look like you, if you're not
my father?
NORWOOD: Don't shout at me, boy. I can hear you. [*Half-smiling*] How come your skin is
yellow and your elbows rusty? How come they threw you out of the post office today
for talking to a white woman? How come you're the crazy young buck you are?
ROBERT: They had no right to throw me out. I asked for my money back when I saw the
broken tubes. Just as you had no right to raise that cane today when I was standing at
the door of this house where *you* live, while *I* have to sleep in a shack down the road
with the field hands. [*Slowly*] But my mother sleeps with you.

NORWOOD: You don't like it?

ROBERT: No, I don't like it.

NORWOOD: What can you do about it?

ROBERT: [*After a pause*] I'd like to kill all the white men in the world.

NORWOOD: [*Starting*] Niggers like you are hung to trees.

ROBERT: I'm not a nigger.

NORWOOD: You don't like your own race? [ROBERT *is silent*] Yet you don't like white folks   35
either?

ROBERT: [*Defiantly*] You think I ought to?

NORWOOD: You evidently don't like me.

ROBERT: [*Boyishly*] I used to like you, when I first knew you were my father, when I was a
little kid, before that time you beat me under the feet of your horses. [*Slowly*] I liked
you until then.

NORWOOD: [*A little pleased*] So you did, heh? [*Fingering his pistol*] A pickaninny calling me
"papa." I should've broken your young neck for that first time. I should've broken
your head for you today, too—since I didn't then.

ROBERT: [*Laughing scornfully*] You should've broken my head?   40

NORWOOD: Should've gotten rid of you before this. But you was Cora's child. I tried to
help you. [*Aggrieved*] I treated you decent, schooled you. Paid for it. But tonight you'll
get the hell off this place and stay off. Get the hell out of this county. [*Suddenly furious*]
Get out of this state. Don't let me lay eyes on you again. Get out of here now. Talbot
and the storekeeper are coming up here this evening to talk cotton with me. I'll tell Talbot to *see* that you go. That's all. [NORWOOD *motions toward the door, left.*] Tell Sam to
come in here when you go out. Tell him to make a light here.

ROBERT: [*Impudently*] *Ring* for Sam—I'm not going through the kitchen. [*He starts toward the
front door*] I'm not your servant. You're not going to tell me what to do. You're not going
to have Talbot run me off the place like a field hand you don't want to use any more.

NORWOOD: [*Springing between his son and the front door, pistol in hand*] You black bastard!
[ROBERT *goes toward him calmly, grasps his father's arm and twists it until the gun falls to the
floor. The older man bends backward in startled fury and pain.*] Don't you dare put your . . .

ROBERT: [*Laughing*] Why don't you shoot, papa? [*Louder*] Why don't you shoot?

NORWOOD: [*Gasping as he struggles, fighting back*] . . . black . . . hands . . . on . . . you . . .   45

ROBERT: [*Hysterically, as he takes his father by the throat*] Why don't you shoot, papa?
[NORWOOD'S *hands claw the air helplessly.* ROBERT *chokes the struggling white man until his
body grows limp*] Why don't you shoot! [*Laughing*] Why don't you shoot? Huh? Why?

[CORA *appears at the top of the stairs, hearing the commotion. She screams.*]

CORA: Oh, my God! [*She rushes down.* ROBERT *drops the body of his father at her feet in a path of
flame from the setting sun.* CORA *starts and stares in horror.*]

ROBERT: [*Wildly*] Why didn't he shoot, mama? He didn't want *me* to live. Why didn't he
shoot? [*Laughing*] He was the boss. Telling me what to do. Why didn't he shoot, then?
He was the white man.

CORA: [*Falling on the body*] Colonel Tom! Colonel Tom! Tom! Tom! [*Gazes across the corpse at
her son*] He's yo' father, Bert.

ROBERT: He's dead. The white man's dead. My father's dead. [*Laughing*] I'm living.   50

CORA: Tom! Tom! Tom!

ROBERT: Niggers are living. He's dead. [*Picks up the pistol*] This is what he wanted to kill me
with, but he's dead. I can use it now. Use it on all the white men in the world, because
they'll be coming looking for me now. [*Stuffs the pistol into his shirt*] They'll want me now.

CORA: [*Rising and running toward her boy*] Quick, chile, out that way, [*Pointing toward the
front door*] so they won't see you in de kitchen. Make for de swamp, honey. Cross de

fields fo' de swamp. Go de crick way. In runnin' water, dogs can't smell no tracks. Hurry, chile!

ROBERT: Yes, mama. I can go out the front way now, easy. But if I see they gonna get me before I can reach the swamp, I'm coming back here, mama, and [*Proudly*] let them take me out of my father's house—if they can. [*Pats the gun under his shirt*] They're not going to string me up to some roadside tree for the crackers to laugh at.

55 CORA: [*Moaning aloud*] Oh, O-o-o! Hurry! Hurry, chile!

ROBERT: I'm going, ma. [*He opens the door. The sunset streams in like a river of blood.*]

CORA: Run, chile!

ROBERT: Not out of my father's house. [*He exits slowly, tall and straight against the sun.*]

CORA: Fo' God's sake, hurry, chile! [*Glancing down the road*] Lawd have mercy! There's Talbot and de storekeeper in de drive. They sees my boy! [*Moaning*] They sees ma boy. [*Relieved*] But thank God, they's passin' him! [*CORA backs up against the wall in the vestibule. She stands as if petrified as TALBOT and the STOREKEEPER enter.*]

60 TALBOT: Hello, Cora. What's the matter with you? Where's that damn fool boy o' your'n goin', coming out the front door like he owned the house? What's the matter with you, woman? Can't you talk? Can't you talk? Where's Norwood? Let's have some light in this dark place. [*He reaches behind the door and turns on the lights. CORA remains backed up against the wall, looking out into the twilight, watching ROBERT as he goes across the field.*] Good God, Jim! Look at this! [*The Two WHITE MEN stop in horror before the sight of NORWOOD'S body on the floor.*]

STOREKEEPER: He's blue in the face. [*Bends over the body*] That nigger we saw walking out the door! [*Rising excitedly*] That nigger bastard of Cora's . . . [*Stooping over the body again*] Why the Colonel's dead!

TALBOT: That nigger! [*Rushes toward the door*] He's running toward the swamp now . . . We'll get him . . . Telephone town—there, in the library. Telephone the sheriff. Get men, white men, after that nigger.

[*The STOREKEEPER rushes into the library. He can be heard talking excitedly on the phone.*]

STOREKEEPER: Sheriff! Sheriff! Is this the sheriff? I'm calling from Norwood's plantation. That nigger, Bert, has just killed Norwood—and run, headed for the swamp. Notify the gas station at the crossroads! Tell the boys at the sawmill to head him off at the creek. Warn everybody to be on the lookout. Call your deputies! Yes! Spread a dragnet. Get out the dogs. Meanwhile we'll start after him. [*He slams the phone down and comes back into the room.*] Cora, where's Norwood's car? In the barn? [*CORA does not answer.*]

TALBOT: Talk, you black bitch!

[*She remains silent. TALBOT runs, yelling and talking, out into the yard, followed by the STOREKEEPER. Sounds of excited shouting outside, and the roar of a motor rushing down the drive. In the sky the twilight deepens into early night. CORA stands looking into the darkness.*]

65 CORA: My boy can't get to de swamp now. They's telephoned the white folks down that way. So he'll come back home now. Maybe he'll turn into de crick and follow de branch home directly. [*Protectively*] But they shan't get him. I'll make a place for to hide him. I'll make a place upstairs down under de floor, under ma bed. In a minute ma boy'll be runnin' from de white folks with their hounds and their ropes and their guns and everything they uses to kill po' colored folks with. [*Distressed*] Ma boy'll be out there runnin. [*Turning to the body on the floor*] Colonel Tom, you hear me? Our boy, out there runnin'. [*Fiercely*] You said he was ma boy—ma bastard boy. I heard you . . . but he's yours too . . . but yonder in de dark runnin'—runnin' from yo' people, from white people. [*Pleadingly*] Why don't you get up and stop 'em? He's *your* boy. His eyes is gray—like your eyes. He's tall like you's tall. He's proud like you's proud. And he's

runnin'—runnin' from po' white trash what ain't worth de little finger o' nobody what's got your blood in 'em, Tom. [*Demandingly*] Why don't you get up from there and stop 'em, Colonel Tom? What's that you say? He ain't your chile? He's ma bastard chile? My yellow bastard chile? [*Proudly*] Yes, he's mine. But don't call him that. Don't you touch him. Don't you put your white hands on him. You's beat him enough, and cussed him enough. Don't you touch him now. He is *ma* boy and no white folks gonna touch him now. That's finished. I'm gonna make a place for him upstairs under ma bed. [*Backs away from the body toward the stairs*] He's ma chile. Don't you come in ma bedroom while he's up there. Don't you come to my bed no mo'. I calls you to help me now, and you just lays there. I calls you for to wake up, and you just lays there. Whenever you called me, in de night, I woke up. When you called for me to love, I always reached out ma arms fo' you. I borned you five chilluns and now one of 'em is out yonder in de dark runnin' from yo' people. Our youngest boy out yonder in de dark runnin'. [*Accusingly*] He's runnin' from you, too. You said he warn't your'n—he's just Cora's po' little yellow bastard. But he *is* your'n, Colonel Tom. [*Sadly*] And he's runnin' from you. You are out yonder in de dark, [*Points toward the door*] runnin' our chile, with de hounds and de gun in yo' hand, and Talbot's followin' 'hind you with a rope to hang Robert with. [*Confidently*] I been sleepin' with you too long, Colonel Tom, not to know that this ain't you layin' down there with yo' eyes shut on de floor. You can't fool me—you ain't never been so still like this before—you's out yonder runnin' ma boy through de fields in de dark, runnin' ma poor little helpless Bert through de fields in de dark to lynch him . . . Damn you, Colonel Norwood! [*Backing slowly up the stairs, staring at the rigid body below her*] Damn you, Thomas Norwood! God damn you!

Curtain

Scene 2

TIME. *One hour later. Night.*

SETTING. *The same.*

ACTION. *As the curtain rises, the* UNDERTAKER *is talking to* SAM *at the outer door. All through this act the approaching cries of the man hunt are heard.*

UNDERTAKER: Reckon there won't be no orders to bring his corpse back out here, Sam. None of us ain't seen Talbot or Mr. Higgins, but I'm sure they'll be having the funeral in town. The coroner told us to bring the body into the Junction. Ain't nothin' but niggers left out here now.

SAM: [*Very frightened*] Yes, sah! Yes, sah! You's right, sah! Nothin' but us niggers, sah!

UNDERTAKER: The Colonel didn't have no relatives far as you know, did he, Sam?

SAM: No, sah. Ain't had none. No, sah! You's right, sah!

UNDERTAKER: Well, you got everything o' his locked up around here, ain't you? Too bad there   5
ain't no white folks about to look after the Colonel's stuff, but every white man that's able to walk's out with the posse. They'll have that young nigger swingin' before ten.

SAM: [*Trembling*] Yes, sah, yes, sah! I 'spects so. Yes, sah!

UNDERTAKER: Say, where's that woman the Colonel's been living with—where's that black housekeeper, Cora, that murderin's bastard's mother?

SAM: She here, sah! She's up in her room.

UNDERTAKER: [*Curiously*] I'd like to see how she looks. Get her down here. Say, how about a little drink before we start that ride back to town, for me and my partner out there with the body?

SAM: Cora got de keys to all de licker, sah!   10

UNDERTAKER: Well, get her down here then, double quick! [*SAM goes up the stairs. The UNDERTAKER leans in the front doorway talking to his partner outside in the wagon*] Bad business, a white man having saucy nigger children on his hands, and his black woman living in his own house.

VOICE OUTSIDE: Damn right, Charlie.

UNDERTAKER: Norwood didn't have a gang o' yellow gals, though, like Higgins and some o' these other big bugs. Just this one bitch far's I know, livin' with him damn near like a wife. Didn't even have much company out here. And they tell me ain't been a white woman stayed here overnight since his wife died when I was a baby. [*SAM's shuffle is heard on the stairs*] Here comes a drink, I reckon, boy. You needn't get down off the ambulance. I'll have Sam bring it out there to you. [*SAM descends followed by CORA who comes down the stairs. She says nothing. The UNDERTAKER looks up grinning at CORA*] Well, so you're the Cora that's got these educated nigger children? Hum-m! Well, I guess you'll see one of 'em swinging full of bullet holes when you wake up in the morning. They'll probably hang him to that tree down here by the Colonel's gate—'cause they tell me he strutted right out the front gate past that tree after the murder. Or maybe they'll burn him. How'd you like to see him swinging there roasted in the morning when you wake up, girlie?

CORA: [*Calmly*] Is that all you wanted to say to me?

15 **UNDERTAKER:** Don't get smart! Maybe you think there's nobody to boss you now. We gonna have a little drink before we go. Get out a bottle of rye.

CORA: I takes ma orders from Colonel Norwood, sir.

UNDERTAKER: Well, you'll take no more orders from him. He's dead out there in my wagon—so get along and get the bottle.

CORA: He's out yonder with de mob, not in your wagon.

UNDERTAKER: I tell you he's in my wagon!

20 **CORA:** He's out there with de mob.

UNDERTAKER: God damn! [*To his partner outside*] I believe this black woman's gone crazy in here. [*To CORA*] Get the keys out for that licker, and be quick about it! [*CORA does not move. SAM looks from one to the other, frightened.*]

VOICE OUTSIDE: Aw, to hell with the licker, Charlie. Come on, let's start back to town. We want to get in on some of that excitement, too. They should've found that nigger by now—and I want to see 'em drag him out here.

UNDERTAKER: All right, Jim. [*To CORA and SAM*] Don't you all go to bed until you see that bonfire. You niggers are getting besides yourselves around Polk County. We'll burn a few more of you if you don't be careful. [*He exits, and the noise of the dead-wagon going down the road is heard.*]

SAM: Oh, Lawd, hab mercy on me! I prays, Lawd hab mercy! O, ma Lawd, ma Lawd, ma Lawd! Cora, is you a fool? *Is* you a fool? Why didn't you give de mens de licker, riled as these white folks is? In ma old age is I gonna be burnt by de crackers? Lawd, is I sinned? Lawd, what has I done? [*Suddenly stops moaning and becomes schemingly calm*] I don't have to stay here tonight, does I? I done locked up de Colonel's library, and he can't be wantin' nothin'. No, ma Lawd, he won't want nothin' now. He's with Jesus— or with de devil, one. [*To CORA*] I's gwine on away from here. Sam's gwine in town to his chilluns' house, and I ain't gwine by no road either. I gwine through de holler where I don't have to pass no white folks.

25 **CORA:** Yes, Samuel, you go on. De Colonel can get his own drinks when he comes back tonight.

SAM: [*Bucking his eyes in astonishment at CORA*] Lawd God Jesus!

[*He bolts out of the room as fast as his old legs will carry him. CORA comes down stairs, looks for a long moment out into the darkness, then closes the front door and draws the blinds. She looks down at the spot where the COLONEL's body lay.*]

CORA: All de colored folks are runnin' from you tonight. Po' Colonel Tom, you too old now to be out with de mob. You got no business goin', but you had to go, I reckon. I 'members that time they hung Luke Jordon, you sent yo' dogs out to hunt him. The next day you killed all de dogs. You were kinder softhearted. Said you didn't like that kind of sport. Told me in bed one night you could hear them dogs howlin' in yo' sleep. But de time they burnt de courthouse when that po' little cullud boy was locked up in it cause they said he hugged a white girl, you was with 'em again. Said you had to go help 'em. Now you's out chasin' ma boy. [*As she stands at the window, she sees a passing figure.*] There goes yo' other woman, Colonel Tom, Livonia is runnin' from you too, now. She would've wanted you last night. Been wantin' you again ever since she got old and fat and you stopped layin' with her and put her in the kitchen to cook. Don't think I don't know, Colonel Tom. Don't think I don't remember them nights when you used to sleep in that cabin down by de spring. I knew 'Vonia was there with you. I ain't no fool, Colonel Tom. But she ain't bore you no chilluns. I'm de one that bore 'em. [*Musing*] White mens, and colored womens, and little bastard chilluns—that's de old way of de South—but it's ending now. Three of your yellow brothers yo' father had by Aunt Sallie Deal—what had to come and do your laundry to make her livin'—you got colored relatives scattered all over this county. Them de ways o' de South—mixtries, mixtries. [*WILLIAM enters left, silently, as his mother talks. She is sitting in a chair now. Without looking up*] Is that you, William?

WILLIAM: Yes, ma, it's me.

CORA: Is you runnin' from him, too?

WILLIAM: [*Hesitatingly*] Well, ma, you see . . . don't you think kinder . . . well, I reckon I   30
ought to take Libby and ma babies on down to de church house with Reverend Martin and them, or else get 'long to town if I can hitch up them mules. They's scared to be out here, my wife and her ma. All de folks done gone from de houses down yonder by de branch, and you can hear de hounds a bayin' off yonder by de swamp, and cars is tearin' up that road, and de white folks is yellin' and hollerin' and carryin' on somethin' terrible over toward de brook. I done told Robert 'bout his foolishness. They's gonna hang him sure. Don't you think you better be comin' with us, ma. That is, do you want to? 'Course we can go by ourselves, and maybe you wants to stay here and take care o' de big house. I don't want to leave you, ma, but I . . . I . . .

CORA: Yo' brother'll be back, son, then I won't be by myself.

WILLIAM: [*Bewildered by his mother's sureness*] I thought Bert went . . . I thought he run . . . I thought . . .

CORA: No, honey. He went, but they ain't gonna get him out there. I sees him comin' back here now, to be with me. I's gwine to guard him 'till he can get away.

WILLIAM: Then de white folks'll come here, too.

CORA: Yes, de Colonel'll come back here sure. [*The deep baying of the hounds is heard at a dis-*   35
tance through the night.] Colonel Tom will come after his son.

WILLIAM: My God, ma! Come with us to town.

CORA: Go on, William, go on! Don't wait for them to get back. You never was much like neither one o' them—neither de Colonel or Bert—you's mo' like de field hands. Too much o' ma blood in you, I guess. You never liked Bert much, neither, and you always was afraid of de Colonel. Go on, son, and hide yo' wife and her ma and your chilluns. Ain't nothin' gonna hurt you. You never did go against nobody. Neither did I, till tonight. Tried to live right and not hurt a soul, white or colored. [*Addressing space*] I tried to live right, Lord. [*Angrily*] Tried to live right, Lord. [*Throws out her arms resentfully as if to say, "and this is what you give me."*] What's de matter, Lawd, you ain't with me?

[*The hounds are heard howling again.*]

WILLIAM: I'm gone, ma. [*He exits fearfully as his mother talks.*]

CORA: [*Bending over the spot on the floor where the* COLONEL *has lain. She calls.*] Colonel Tom! Colonel Tom! Colonel Tom! Look! Bertha and Sallie and William and Bert, all your chilluns, runnin' from you, and you layin' on de floor there, dead! [*Pointing*] Out yonder with the mob, dead. And when you come home, upstairs in my bed on top of my body, dead. [*Goes to the window, returns, sits down, and begins to speak as if remembering a far-off dream.*] Colonel Thomas Norwood! I'm just poor Cora Lewis, Colonel Norwood. Little black Cora Lewis, Colonel Norwood. I'm just fifteen years old. Thirty years ago, you put your hands on me to feel my breasts, and you say, "You a pretty little piece of flesh, ain't you? Black and sweet, ain't you?" And I lift up ma face, and you pull me to you, and we laid down under the trees that night, and I wonder if your wife'll know when you go back up the road into the big house. And I wonder if my mama'll know it, when I go back to our cabin. Mama said she nursed you when you was a baby, just like she nursed me. And I loved you in the dark, down there under that tree by de gate, afraid of you and proud of you, feelin' your gray eyes lookin' at me in de dark. Then I cried and cried and told ma mother about it, but she didn't take it hard like I thought she'd take it. She said fine white mens like de young Colonel always took good care o' their colored womens. She said it was better than marryin' some black field hand and workin' all your life in de cotton and cane. Better even than havin' a job like ma had, takin' care o' de white chilluns. Takin' care o' you, Colonel Tom. [*As* CORA *speaks the sound of the approaching mob gradually grows louder and louder. Auto horns, the howling of dogs, the far-off shouts of men, full of malignant force and power, increase in volume.*] And I was happy because I liked you, 'cause you was tall and proud, 'cause you said I was sweet to you and called me purty. And when yo' wife died—de Mrs. Norwood [*Scornfully*] that never bore you any chilluns, the pale beautiful Mrs. Norwood that was like a slender pine tree in de winter frost . . . I knowed you wanted me. I was full with

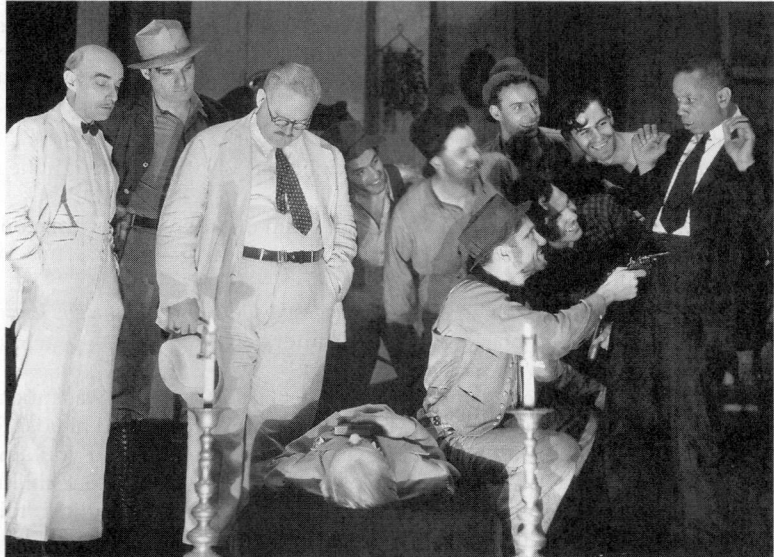

Robert, who has been apprehended here, is confronted and taunted by members of the mob as Higgins, Talbot, and the Undertaker stand beside the body of Colonel Thomas Norwood, in the original production of Hughes's *Mulatto* at the Vanderbilt Theater in New York, October 1935, produced and directed by Martin Jones. The actors are unidentified.

child by you then—William, it was—our first boy. And ma mammy said, go up there and keep de house for Colonel Tom, sweep de floors and make de beds, and by and by, you won't have to sweep de floors and make no beds. And what ma mammy said was right. It all come true. Sam and Rusus and 'Vonia and Lucy did de waitin' on you and me, and de washin' and de cleanin' and de cookin'. And all I did was a little sewin' now and then, and a little preservin' in de summer and a little makin' of pies and sweet cakes and things you like to eat on Christmas. And de years went by. And I was always ready for you when you come to me in de night. And we had them chilluns, your chilluns and mine, Tom Norwood, all of 'em! William, born dark like me, dumb like me, and then Baby John what died; then Bertha, white and smart like you; and then Bert with your eyes and your ways and your temper, and mighty nigh your color; then Sallie, nearly white, too, and smart, and purty. But Bert was yo' chile! He was always yo' child . . . Good-looking, and kind, and headstrong, and strange, and stubborn, and proud like you, and de one I could love most 'cause he needed de most lovin'. And he wanted to call you "papa," and I tried to teach him no, but he did it anyhow and [*Sternly*] you beat him, Colonel Thomas Norwood. And he growed up with de beatin' in his heart and your eyes in his head, and your ways, and your pride. And this summer he looked like you that time I first knowed you down by de road under them trees, young and fiery and proud. There was no touchin' Bert, just like there was no touchin' you. I could only love him, like I loved you. I could only love him. But I couldn't talk to him, because he hated you. He had your ways—and you beat him! After you beat that chile, then you died, Colonel Norwood. You died here in this house, and you been living dead a long time. You lived dead. [*Her voice rises above the nearing sounds of the mob.*] And when I said this evenin', "Get up! Why don't you help me?" You'd done been dead a long time—a long time before you laid down on this floor, here, with the breath choked out o' you—and Bert standin' over you living, living, living. That's why you hated him. And you want to kill him. Always, you wanted to kill him. Out there with de hounds and de torches and de cars and de guns, you want to kill ma boy. But you won't kill him! He's comin' home first. He's comin' home to me. He's comin' home! [*Outside the noise is tremendous now, the lights of autos flash on the window curtains, there are shouts and cries. CORA sits, tense, in the middle of the room.*] He's comin' home!

A MAN'S VOICE: [*Outside*] He's somewhere on this lot. 40
ANOTHER VOICE: Don't shoot, men. We want to get him alive.
VOICE: Close in on him. He must be in them bushes by the house.
FIRST VOICE: Porch! Porch! Porch! There he is yonder—running to the door!

[*Suddenly shots are heard. The door bursts open and ROBERT enters, firing back into the darkness. The shots are returned by the mob, breaking the windows. Flares, lights, voices, curses, screams.*]

VOICES: Nigger! Nigger! Nigger! Get the nigger!

[*CORA rushes toward the door and bolts it after her son's entrance.*]

CORA: [*Leaning against the door*] I was waiting for you, honey. Yo' hiding place is all ready, 45
upstairs, under ma bed, under de floor. I sawed a place there fo' you. They can't find you there. Hurry—before yo' father comes.
ROBERT: [*Panting*] No time to hide, ma. They're at the door now. They'll be coming up the back way, too. [*Sounds of knocking and the breaking of glass*] They'll be coming in the windows. They'll be coming in everywhere. And only one bullet left, ma. It's for me.
CORA: Yes, it's fo' you, chile. Save it. Go upstairs in mama's room. Lay on ma bed and rest.
ROBERT: [*Going slowly toward the stairs with the pistol in his hand*] Goodnight, ma. I'm awful tired of running, ma. They been chasing me for hours.

CORA: Goodnight, son.

[CORA *follows him to the foot of the steps. The door begins to give at the forcing of the mob. As* ROBERT *disappears above, it bursts open. A great crowd of white men pour into the room with guns, ropes, clubs, flashlights, and knives.* CORA *turns on the stairs, facing them quietly.* TALBOT, *the leader of the mob, stops.*]

50 TALBOT: Be careful, men. He's armed. [*To* CORA] Where is that yellow bastard of yours— upstairs?
CORA: Yes, he's going to sleep. Be quiet, you all. Wait. [*She bars the way with outspread arms.*]
TALBOT: [*Harshly*] Wait, hell! Come on, boys, let's go. [*A single shot is heard upstairs.*] What's that?
CORA: [*Calmly*] My boy . . . is gone . . . to sleep!

[TALBOT *and some of the men rush up the stairway,* CORA *makes a final gesture of love toward the room above. Yelling and shouting, through all the doors and windows, a great crowd pours into the room. The roar of the mob fills the house, the whole night, the whole world. Suddenly* TALBOT *returns at the top of the steps and a hush falls over the crowd.*]

TALBOT: Too late, men. We're just a little too late.

[*A sigh of disappointment rises from the mob.* TALBOT *comes down the stairs, walks up to* CORA *and slaps her once across the face. She does not move. It is as though no human hand can touch her again.*]

Curtain

QUESTIONS

Act 1

1. Throughout the act—and the play—why are the children of Colonel Norwood and Cora referred to as just Cora's children?

2. Why does the Colonel deny permission for Sallie's bags to be carried through the front door?

3. Throughout the act, what do we learn about Robert's attitudes toward his circumstances on the plantation? What do the Colonel and Higgins say about his attitude? Once Robert appears, what does he himself say about his situation?

4. What does the Colonel say about Sallie's ambition to reopen a nearby school? What does he advise her to do instead?

5. Who is Talbot? What does he represent? Why does he not appear until late in the second act?

6. What does Higgins report about how Robert has behaved in town? What does he tell Colonel Norwood to do about it?

7. As expressed in speech 61, what is Higgins's attitude toward black women? What does this attitude disclose about his character?

8. Describe the effect on both Robert and Colonel Norwood of the childhood incident when Robert called the Colonel "papa."

9. What has the Colonel decided to do about Robert? What are Cora's fears not only for Robert but for others?

Act 2, Scene 1

10. What are the issues in the confrontation between Robert and Colonel Norwood?

11. What is Robert's dilemma (speech 35)? What has the Colonel now determined to do about Robert?

12. What is Robert's response to the Colonel's display of the gun, and his threat to use it?

13. What do Talbot and the storekeeper do once they learn that Colonel Norwood is dead? What chance does Robert have to escape?

14. Why does Cora speak so extensively over the Colonel's body?

Act 2, Scene 2

15. Why are the undertaker and his companion introduced at this point? What are they like?

16. According to Cora (speech 27), what was the nature of the old "ways" of the south?

17. What is the purpose of Cora's second extensive monologue (speech 39)?

18. What finally happens to Robert? Why does Talbot slap Cora at the end?

GENERAL QUESTIONS

1. Describe *Mulatto* as a realistic play. Why is it important that the play contain many details about the plantation and the customs of the country?

2. What is the symbolism of the front door? The incident at the post office in town? Driving the Ford fast?

3. Describe Colonel Norwood. What characteristics of a Southern plantation owner does he exhibit? What is shown about him by his having sent Robert and his sisters away to school? What does Cora say about him before and after he is dead?

4. Describe the character of Robert. What are his dominant traits? How politic is he in dealing with his circumstances? To what extent does he bring about his own destruction?

5. Describe Cora. What has her life been like? To what degree has she sacrificed her individuality to stay with Colonel Norwood? How does she try to protect her children? In her two major lengthy speeches, what seems to be happening to her?

6. In light of the historical time when the play was written and produced, could there have been any other outcome?

TENNESSEE WILLIAMS (1911–1983)

Tennessee Williams (1911–1983) grew up in Mississippi and Missouri, and many of his plays reflect the attitudes and customs that he encountered in his early years. Until he was eight, his family lived in genteel poverty, mostly in Columbus, Mississippi. In 1919 the family moved to a lower-class neighborhood in St. Louis. Williams, who was sickly and bookish, tried to escape from poverty and family conflicts by writing and going to the movies. One of his few companions during those years was his shy and withdrawn sister, Rose.

He entered the University of Missouri in 1931, but the Depression and family poverty forced him to drop out and go to work in a shoe warehouse. After two years of this work, he suffered a nervous collapse, but he finally finished college at the University of Iowa. He then began wandering the country, doing odd jobs and also writing. His first full-length play, Battle of Angels, *was produced in 1940 but was unsuccessful. He continued to write, however, and was able to get* The Glass Menagerie *staged in 1945. The critical and popular success of this play marked the beginning of many good years in the theater. Along with Arthur Miller, during the 1940s and 1950s Williams dominated the American stage, going on to write many one-act plays and more than fifteen full-length dramas (many of which became successful films), including* A Streetcar Named Desire *(1947, Pulitzer Prize),* The Rose Tattoo *(1951),* Cat on a Hot Tin Roof *(1955, Pulitzer Prize),* Suddenly Last Summer *(1958), and* The Night of the Iguana *(1961).*

The Glass Menagerie, written in 1944 and produced with favorable reviews in Chicago and New York in 1945, is a largely autobiographical play that explores the family dynamics, delusions, and personalities of the Wingfields. Williams originally developed his ideas for the play in a short story called "Portrait of a Girl in Glass" and then in a screenplay for Metro-Goldwyn-Mayer titled *The Gentleman Caller.* In these treatments as well as in *The Glass Menagerie,* Laura Wingfield is modeled after his sister, Rose Williams. The least competent member of the family, she is crippled by her own insecurity and her mother's expectations. At every opportunity, Laura withdraws into a world of glass figurines and old phonograph records left by her father when he abandoned the family. Amanda Wingfield is patterned after Williams' mother. She valiantly tries to hold the family together and provide for Laura's future, but her perspectives are skewed by her romanticized memories of a gracious Southern past of plantations, formal dances, and "gentleman callers." Tom, a figure based on the playwright himself, is desperate to escape the trap of his impoverished family. He seeks to emulate the long-missing father and move out of the drab Wingfield apartment into adventure and experience.

The play offers a fascinating mixture of realistic and nonrealistic dramatic techniques. The realistic elements are the characters (excluding Tom when he narrates) and the language. This is especially true of Amanda's language, in which Williams skillfully recreates the diction and cadences characteristic of the Deep South. As he points out in his production notes and stage directions, the play's structure and staging are nonrealistic. Williams employs various devices nonrealistically—including the narrator, music, lighting, and screen projections—to underscore the emotions of his characters and to explore ideas about family and personality.

One of Williams's most effective nonrealistic techniques in *The Glass Menagerie* is its structure as "a memory play," and therefore its illustration of how a first-person narrator can be used in a drama. The characters and the action are not real and they do not exist in the present. Rather, they represent Tom's memories and feelings about events that occurred approximately five years earlier, when America was in the grip of the Great Depression, when the Spanish Civil War had resulted in the imposition of a fascist dictatorship in Spain, and when World War II was beginning in Europe. As the narrator, Tom exists at the time of the action (1944), but the events he introduces are occurring in about 1939. When Tom becomes a character in the Wingfield household, he is the Tom of this earlier period, quite distinct from his identity as the present narrator. Thus, the action in the apartment is not strictly a realistic recreation of life. Instead, even though the actions and characters seem realistic, they are exaggerated and reshaped as Tom remembers them and regrets them.

The Glass Menagerie (1945)

THE CHARACTERS

Amanda Wingfield (*the mother*)

A little woman of great but confused vitality clinging frantically to another time and place. Her characterization must be carefully created, not copied from type. She is not paranoiac, but her life is paranoia. There is much to admire in

Amanda, and as much to love and pity as there is to laugh at. Certainly she has endurance and a kind of heroism, and though her foolishness makes her unwittingly cruel at times, there is tenderness in her slight person.

Laura Wingfield (*her daughter*)

Amanda, having failed to establish contact with reality, continues to live vitally in her illusions, but Laura's situation is even graver. A childhood illness has left her crippled, one leg slightly shorter than the other, and held in a brace. This defect need not be more than suggested on the stage. Stemming from this, Laura's separation increases till she is like a piece of her own glass collection, too exquisitely fragile to move from the shelf.

Tom Wingfield (*her son*)

And the narrator of the play. A poet with a job in a warehouse. His nature is not remorseless, but to escape from a trap he has to act without pity.

Jim O'Connor (*the gentleman caller*)

A nice, ordinary, young man.

PRODUCTION NOTES[1]

Being a "memory play," *The Glass Menagerie* can be presented with unusual freedom of convention. Because of its considerably delicate or tenuous material, atmospheric touches and subtleties of direction play a particularly important part. Expressionism and all other unconventional techniques in drama have only one valid aim, and that is a closer approach to truth. When a play employs unconventional techniques, it is not, or certainly shouldn't be, trying to escape its responsibility of dealing with reality, or interpreting experience, but is actually or should be attempting to find a closer approach, a more penetrating and vivid expression of things as they are. The straight realistic play with its genuine Frigidaire and authentic ice-cubes, its characters who speak exactly as its audience speaks, corresponds to the academic landscape and has the same virtue of a photographic likeness. Everyone should know nowadays the unimportance of the photographic in art: that truth, life, or reality is an organic thing which the poetic imagination can represent or suggest, in essence, only through transformation, through changing into other forms than those which were merely present in appearance.

These remarks are not meant as a preface only to this particular play. They have to do with a conception of a new, plastic theatre which must take the place of the exhausted theatre of realistic conventions if the theatre is to resume vitality as a part of our culture.

THE SCREEN DEVICE: There is *only one important difference between the original and the acting version of the play* and that is the *omission* in the latter of the device that I tentatively included in my *original* script. This device was the use of a screen on which were projected magic-lantern slides bearing images or titles. I do not regret the omission of this device from the original Broadway production. The extraordinary power of Miss Taylor's° performance made it suitable to have the utmost simplicity in the physical production. But I think it may be interesting to some readers to see how this device was conceived. So I am putting it into the published manuscript. These images and legends, projected from behind, were cast on a section of wall between the front-room and dining-room areas, which should be indistinguishable from the rest when not in use.

The purpose of this will probably be apparent. It is to give accent to certain values in each scene. Each scene contains a particular point (or several) which is structurally the most important. In an episodic play, such as this, the basic structure or narrative line may be obscured from the audience; the effect may seem fragmentary rather than architectural. This may not be the fault of the play so much as a lack of attention in the audience. The legend

---

[1]The production notes are by Williams and are part of the play. °*Miss Taylor's:* The role of Amanda was first played by the American actress Laurette Taylor (1884–1946).

or image upon the screen will strengthen the effect of what is merely allusion in the writing and allow the primary point to be made more simply and lightly than if the entire responsibility were on the spoken lines. Aside from this structural value, I think the screen will have a definite emotional appeal, less definable but just as important. An imaginative producer or director may invent many other uses for this device than those indicated in the present script. In fact the possibilities of the device seem much larger to me than the instance of this play can possibly utilize.

5   THE MUSIC: Another extra-literary accent in this play is provided by the use of music. A single recurring tune, "The Glass Menagerie,"° is used to give emotional emphasis to suitable passages. This tune is like circus music, not when you are on the grounds or in the immediate vicinity of the parade, but when you are at some distance and very likely thinking of something else. It seems under those circumstances to continue almost interminably and it weaves in and out of your preoccupied consciousness; then it is the lightest, most delicate music in the world and perhaps the saddest. It expresses the surface vivacity of life with the underlying strain of immutable and inexpressible sorrow. When you look at a piece of delicately spun glass you think of two things: how beautiful it is and how easily it can be broken. Both of those ideas should be woven into the recurring tune, which dips in and out of the play as if it were carried on a wind that changes. It serves as a thread of connection and allusion between the narrator with his separate point in time and space and the subject of his story. Between each episode it returns as reference to the emotion, nostalgia, which is the first condition of the play. It is primarily Laura's music and therefore comes out most clearly when the play focuses upon her and the lovely fragility of glass which is her image.

THE LIGHTING: The lighting in the play is not realistic. In keeping with the atmosphere of memory, the stage is dim. Shafts of light are focused on selected areas or actors, sometimes in contradistinction to what is the apparent center. For instance, in the quarrel scene between Tom and Amanda, in which Laura has no active part, the clearest pool of light is on her figure. This is also true of the supper scene, when her silent figure on the sofa should remain the visual center. The light upon Laura should be distinct from the others, having a peculiar pristine clarity such as light used in early religious portraits of female saints or madonnas. A certain correspondence to light in religious paintings, such as El Greco's,° where the figures are radiant in atmosphere that is relatively dusky, could be effectively used throughout the play. (It will also permit a more effective use of the screen.) A free, imaginative use of light can be of enormous value in giving a mobile, plastic quality to plays of a more or less static nature.

Tennessee Williams

SCENE 1

0.1   *The Wingfield apartment is in the rear of the building, one of those vast hive-like conglomerations of cellular living-units that flower as warty growths in overcrowded urban centers of lower middle-class population and are symptomatic of the impulse of this largest and fundamentally enslaved section of American society to avoid fluidity and differentiation and to exist and function as one interfused mass of automatism.*

0.2   *The apartment faces an alley and is entered by a fire escape, a structure whose name is a touch of accidental poetic truth, for all of these huge buildings are always burning with the slow and implacable*

°5 *"The Glass Menagerie"*: Original music, including this recurrent theme, was composed for the play by Paul Bowles. 6 *El Greco:* Greek painter (c. 1548–1614) who lived in Spain; typical paintings have elongated and distorted figures and extremely vivid foreground lighting set against a murky background.

fires of human desperation. The fire escape is part of what we see—that is, the landing of it and steps descending from it.

The scene is memory and is therefore nonrealistic. Memory takes a lot of poetic license. It omits   0.3
some details; others are exaggerated, according to the emotional value of the articles it touches, for memory is seated predominantly in the heart. The interior is therefore rather dim and poetic.

At the rise of the curtain, the audience is faced with the dark, grim rear wall of the Wingfield   0.4
tenement. This building is flanked on both sides by dark, narrow alleys which run into murky canyons of tangled clotheslines, garbage cans, and the sinister latticework of neighboring fire escapes. It is up and down these side alleys that exterior entrances and exits are made during the play. At the end of Tom's opening commentary, the dark tenement wall slowly becomes transparent° and reveals the interior of the ground-floor Wingfield apartment.

Nearest the audience is the living room, which also serves as a sleeping room for LAURA, the sofa   0.5
unfolding to make her bed. Just beyond, separated from the living room by a wide arch or second proscenium with transparent faded portieres° (or second curtain), is the dining room. In an old-fashioned whatnot° in the living room are seen scores of transparent glass animals. A blown-up photograph of the father hangs on the wall of the living room, to the left of the archway. It is the face of a very handsome young man in a doughboy's° First World War cap. He is gallantly smiling, ineluctably smiling, as if to say "I will be smiling forever."

Also hanging on the wall, near the photograph, are a typewriter keyboard chart and a Gregg   0.6
shorthand diagram. An upright typewriter on a small table stands beneath the charts.

The audience hears and sees the opening scene in the dining room through both the transparent   0.7
fourth wall of the building and the transparent gauze portieres of the dining-room arch. It is during this revealing scene that the fourth wall slowly ascends, out of sight. This transparent exterior wall is not brought down again until the very end of the play, during Tom's final speech.

The narrator is an undisguised convention of the play. He takes whatever license with dramatic convention is convenient to his purposes.   0.8

Tom enters, dressed as a merchant sailor, and strolls across to the fire escape. There he stops and   0.9
lights a cigarette. He addresses the audience.

TOM: Yes, I have tricks in my pocket, I have things up my sleeve. But I am the opposite of a stage magician. He gives you illusion that has the appearance of truth. I give you truth in the pleasant disguise of illusion.

To begin with, I turn back time. I reverse it to that quaint period, the thirties, when the huge middle class of America was matriculating in a school for the blind. Their eyes had failed them, or they had failed their eyes, and so they were having their fingers pressed forcibly down on the fiery Braille alphabet of a dissolving economy.

In Spain there was revolution. Here there was only shouting and confusion. In Spain there was Guernica.° Here there were disturbances of labor, sometimes pretty violent, in otherwise peaceful cities such as Chicago, Cleveland, Saint Louis. . . . This is the social background of the play.

[*Music begins to play.*]

The play is memory. Being a memory play, it is dimly lighted, it is sentimental, it is not realistic. In memory everything seems to happen to music. That explains the fiddle in the wings.

°0.4 *transparent:* The wall is painted on a scrim, a transparent curtain that is opaque when lit from the front and transparent when lit from behind. 0.5 *portieres:* curtains hung in a doorway; in production, these may also be painted on a scrim. *whatnot:* a small set of shelves for ornaments. *doughboy:* popular name for an American infantryman during World War I. 1.3 *Guernica:* a Basque town that was destroyed in 1937 by German planes fighting on General Franco's side during the Spanish Civil War. The huge mural *Guernica*, painted by Pablo Picasso, depicts the horror of that bombardment. For a reproduction see page I–9.

I am the narrator of the play, and also a character in it. The other characters are my mother, Amanda, my sister, Laura, and a gentleman caller who appears in the final scenes. He is the most realistic character in the play, being an emissary from a world of reality that we were somehow set apart from. But since I have a poet's weakness for symbols, I am using this character also as a symbol; he is the long-delayed but always expected something that we live for.

There is a fifth character in the play who doesn't appear except in this larger-than-life-size photograph over the mantel. This is our father who left us a long time ago. He was a telephone man who fell in love with long distances; he gave up his job with the telephone company and skipped the light fantastic out of town. . . .

The last we heard of him was a picture postcard from Mazatlan, on the Pacific coast of Mexico, containing a message of two words: "Hello—Goodbye!" and no address.

I think the rest of the play will explain itself. . . .

[AMANDA's *voice becomes audible through the portieres.*]

[*Legend on screen: "Où sont les neiges."°*]

[TOM *divides the portieres and enters the dining room.* AMANDA *and* LAURA *are seated at a drop-leaf table. Eating is indicated by gestures without food or utensils.* AMANDA *faces the audience.* TOM *and* LAURA *are seated profile. The interior has lit up softly and through the scrim we see* AMANDA *and* LAURA *seated at the table.*]

AMANDA: [*calling*] Tom?
TOM: Yes, Mother.
AMANDA: We can't say grace until you come to the table!
5 TOM: Coming, Mother. [*He bows slightly and withdraws, reappearing a few moments later in his place at the table.*]
AMANDA: [*to her son*] Honey, don't *push* with your *fingers*. If you have to push with something, the thing to push with is a crust of bread. And chew—chew! Animals have secretions in their stomachs which enable them to digest food without mastication, but human beings are supposed to chew their food before they swallow it down. Eat food leisurely, son, and really enjoy it. A well-cooked meal has lots of delicate flavors that have to be held in the mouth for appreciation. So chew your food and give your salivary glands a chance to function!

[TOM *deliberately lays his imaginary fork down and pushes his chair back from the table.*]

TOM: I haven't enjoyed one bite of this dinner because of your constant directions on how to eat it. It's you that make me rush through meals with your hawklike attention to every bite I take. Sickening—spoils my appetite—all this discussion of—animals' secretion—salivary glands—mastication!
AMANDA: [*lightly*] Temperament like a Metropolitan star.°

[TOM *rises and walks toward the living room.*]

You're not excused from the table.
TOM: I'm getting a cigarette.
10 AMANDA: You smoke too much.

°1.8 S.D.: *"Où sont les neiges"*: "Where are the snows (of yesteryear)," refrain from "The Ballade of Dead Ladies" by the French poet François Villon (c. 1431–1463) 8 *Metropolitan star:* the Metropolitan Opera in New York City; opera stars are traditionally considered to be highly temperamental.

[*LAURA rises.*]

LAURA: I'll bring in the blanc mange.°

[*TOM remains standing with his cigarette by the portieres.*]

AMANDA: [*rising*] No, sister, no, sister°—you be the lady this time and I'll be the darky.
LAURA: I'm already up.
AMANDA: Resume your seat, little sister—I want you to stay fresh and pretty—for gentlemen callers!
LAURA: [*sitting down*] I'm not expecting any gentlemen callers.   15
AMANDA: [*crossing out to the kitchenette, airily*] Sometimes they come when they are least expected! Why, I remember one Sunday afternoon in Blue Mountain°—

[*She enters the kitchenette.*]

TOM: I know what's coming!
LAURA: Yes. But let her tell it.
TOM: Again?
LAURA: She loves to tell it.   20

[*AMANDA returns with a bowl of dessert.*]

AMANDA: One Sunday afternoon in Blue Mountain—your mother received—*seventeen!*—gentlemen callers! Why, sometimes there weren't chairs enough to accommodate them all. We had to send the nigger over to bring in folding chairs from the parish house.
TOM: [*remaining at the portieres*] How did you entertain those gentlemen callers?
AMANDA: I understood the art of conversation!
TOM: I bet you could talk.
AMANDA: Girls in those days *knew* how to talk, I can tell you.   25
TOM: Yes?

[*Image on screen: AMANDA as a girl on a porch, greeting callers.*]

AMANDA: They knew how to entertain their gentlemen callers. It wasn't enough for a girl to be possessed of a pretty face and a graceful figure—although I wasn't slighted in either respect. She also needed to have a nimble wit and a tongue to meet all occasions.
TOM: What did you talk about?
AMANDA: Things of importance going on in the world! Never anything coarse or common or vulgar.

[*She addresses TOM as though he were seated in the vacant chair at the table though he remains by the portieres. He plays this scene as though reading from a script.°*]

My callers were gentleman—all! Among my callers were some of the most prominent young planters of the Mississippi Delta—planters and sons of planters!

[*TOM motions for music and a spot of light on AMANDA. Her eyes lift, her face glows, her voice becomes rich and elegiac.*]

°11 *blanc mange:* a bland molded pudding or custard. 12 *sister:* In the South of Amanda's youth, the oldest daughter in a family was frequently called "sister" by her parents and siblings. 16 *Blue Mountain:* an imaginary town in northwest Mississippi modeled after Clarksville, where Williams spent much of his youth. Blue Mountain (Clarksville) is at the northern edge of the Mississippi Delta, a large fertile plain that supports numerous plantations. This is the recollected world of Amanda's youth—plantations, wealth, black servants, and gentlemen callers who were the sons of cotton planters 29.1 S.D. *script:* Here Tom becomes both a character in the play and the stage manager.

[*Screen legend: "Où sont les neiges d'antan?"*°]

> There was young Champ Laughlin who later became vice-president of the Delta Planters Bank. Hadley Stevenson who was drowned in Moon Lake and left his widow one hundred and fifty thousand in Government bonds. There were the Cutrere brothers, Wesley and Bates. Bates was one of my bright particular beaux! He got in a quarrel with that wild Wainwright boy. They shot it out on the floor of Moon Lake Casino. Bates was shot through the stomach. Died in the ambulance on his way to Memphis. His widow was also well provided-for, came into eight or ten thousand acres, that's all. She married him on the rebound—never loved her—carried my picture on him the night he died! And there was that boy that every girl in the Delta had set her cap for! That beautiful, brilliant young Fitzhugh boy from Greene County!

30 TOM: What did he leave his widow?

AMANDA: He never married! Gracious, you talk as though all of my old admirers had turned up their toes to the daisies!

TOM: Isn't this the first you've mentioned that still survives?

AMANDA: That Fitzhugh boy went North and made a fortune—came to be known as the Wolf of Wall Street! He had the Midas touch,° whatever he touched turned to gold! And I could have been Mrs. Duncan J. Fitzhugh, mind you! But—I picked your *father!*

LAURA: [*rising*] Mother, let me clear the table.

35 AMANDA: No, dear, you go in front and study your typewriter chart. Or practice your shorthand a little. Stay fresh and pretty!—It's almost time for our gentlemen callers to start arriving. [*She flounces girlishly toward the kitchenette.*] How many do you suppose we're going to entertain this afternoon?

[TOM *throws down the paper and jumps up with a groan.*]

LAURA: [*alone in the dining room*] I don't believe we're going to receive any, Mother.

AMANDA: [*reappearing airily*] What? No one?—not one? You must be joking!

[LAURA *nervously echoes her laugh. She slips in a fugitive manner through the half-open portieres and draws them gently behind her. A shaft of very clear light is thrown on her face against the faded tapestry of the curtains. Faintly the music of "The Glass Menagerie" is heard as she continues lightly:*]

> Not one gentleman caller? It can't be true! There must be a flood, there must have been a tornado!

LAURA: It isn't a flood, it's not a tornado, Mother. I'm just not popular like you were in Blue Mountain. . . .

[TOM *utters another groan.* LAURA *glances at him with a faint, apologetic smile. Her voice catches a little:*]

> Mother's afraid I'm going to be an old maid.

[*The scene dims out with the "Glass Menagerie" music.*]

SCENE 2

On the dark stage the screen is lighted with the image of blue roses. Gradually LAURA'S *figure becomes apparent and the screen goes out. The music subsides.*

°29.2 S.D. *"Où sont les neiges d'antan?"*: Where are the snows of yesteryear? See the note on page 1648.
33 *Midas touch*: In Greek mythology, King Midas was given the power to turn everything he touched into gold.

LAURA *is seated in the delicate ivory chair at the small clawfoot table. She wears a dress of soft violet material for a kimono—her hair is tied back from her forehead with a ribbon. She is washing and polishing her collection of glass.* AMANDA *appears on the fire escape steps. At the sound of her ascent,* LAURA *catches her breath, thrusts the bowl of ornaments away, and seats herself stiffly before the diagram of the typewriter keyboard as though it held her spellbound. Something has happened to* AMANDA. *It is written in her face as she climbs to the landing: a look that is grim and hopeless and a little absurd. She has on one of those cheap or imitation velvety-looking cloth coats with imitation fur collar. Her hat is five or six years old, one of those dreadful cloche hats that were worn in the late Twenties, and she is clutching an enormous black patent-leather pocketbook with nickel clasps and initials. This is her full-dress outfit, the one she usually wears to the D.A.R.° Before entering she looks through the door. She purses her lips, opens her eyes very wide, rolls them upward and shakes her head. Then she slowly lets herself in the door. Seeing her mother's expression,* LAURA *touches her lips with a nervous gesture.*

LAURA: Hello, Mother, I was—[*She makes a nervous gesture toward the chart on the wall.* AMANDA *leans against the shut door and stares at* LAURA *with a martyred look.*]

AMANDA: Deception? Deception? [*She slowly removes her hat and gloves, continuing the sweet suffering stare. She lets the hat and gloves fall on the floor—a bit of acting.*]

LAURA: [*shakily*] How was the D.A.R. meeting?

[AMANDA *slowly opens her purse and removes a dainty white handkerchief which she shakes out delicately and delicately touches to her lips and nostrils.*]

Didn't you go to the D.A.R. meeting, Mother?

AMANDA: [*faintly, almost inaudibly*]—No.—No. [*then more forcibly:*] I did not have the strength—to go to the D.A.R. In fact, I did not have the courage! I wanted to find a hole in the ground and hide myself in it forever! [*She crosses slowly to the wall and removes the diagram of the typewriter keyboard. She holds it in front of her for a second, staring at it sweetly and sorrowfully—then bites her lips and tears it in two pieces.*]

LAURA: [*faintly*] Why did you do that, Mother?   5

[AMANDA *repeats the same procedure with the chart of the Gregg Alphabet.*]

Why are you—

AMANDA: Why? Why? How old are you, Laura?

LAURA: Mother, you know my age.

AMANDA: I thought you were an adult; it seems that I was mistaken. [*She crosses slowly to the sofa and sinks down and stares at* LAURA.]

LAURA: Please don't stare at me, Mother.

[AMANDA *closes her eyes and lowers her head. There is a ten-second pause.*]

AMANDA: What are we going to do, what is going to become of us, what is the future?   10

[*There is another pause.*]

LAURA: Has something happened, Mother?

[AMANDA *draws a long breath, takes out the handkerchief again, goes through the dabbing process.*]

Mother, has—something happened?

AMANDA: I'll be all right in a minute, I'm just bewildered—[*She hesitates.*]—by life. . . .

LAURA: Mother, I wish that you would tell me what's happened!

°0.2 *D.A.R.:* Daughters of the American Revolution, a patriotic women's organization (founded in 1890) open only to women whose ancestors aided the American Revolution.

AMANDA: As you know, I was supposed to be inducted into my office at the D.A.R. this afternoon.

[*Screen image: A swarm of typewriters.*]

But I stopped off at Rubicam's Business College to speak to your teachers about your having a cold and ask them what progress they thought you were making down there.

15   LAURA: Oh. . . .

AMANDA: I went to the typing instructor and introduced myself as your mother. She didn't know who you were.

"Wingfield," she said, "We don't have any such student enrolled at the school!"

I assured her she did, that you had been going to classes since early in January.

"I wonder," she said, "if you could be talking about that terribly shy little girl who dropped out of school after only a few days' attendance?"

"No," I said, "Laura, my daughter, has been going to school every day for the past six weeks!"

"Excuse me," she said. She took the attendance book out and there was your name, unmistakably printed, and all the dates you were absent until they decided that you had dropped out of school.

I still said, "No, there must have been some mistake! There must have been some mix-up in the records!"

And she said, "No—I remember her perfectly now. Her hands shook so that she couldn't hit the right keys! The first time we gave a speed test, she broke down completely—was sick at the stomach and almost had to be carried into the wash room! After that morning she never showed up any more. We phoned the house but never got any answer"—While I was working at Famous-Barr,° I suppose, demonstrating those—

[*She indicates a brassiere with her hands.*]

Oh! I felt so weak I could barely keep on my feet! I had to sit down while they got me a glass of water! Fifty dollars' tuition, all of our plans—my hopes and ambitions for you—just gone up the spout, just gone up the spout like that.

[*LAURA draws a long breath and gets awkwardly to her feet. She crosses to the Victrola and winds it up.°*]

What are you doing?

LAURA: Oh! [*She releases the handle and returns to her seat.*]

AMANDA: Laura, where have you been going when you've gone out pretending that you were going to business college?

LAURA: I've just been going out walking.

20   AMANDA: That's not true.

LAURA: It is. I just went walking.

AMANDA: Walking? Walking? In winter? Deliberately courting pneumonia in that light coat? Where did you walk to, Laura?

LAURA: All sorts of places—mostly in the park.

AMANDA: Even after you'd started catching that cold?

25   LAURA: It was the lesser of two evils, Mother.

[*Screen image: Winter scene in a park.*]

°16.8 *Famous-Barr:* a department store in St. Louis. 16.11 S. D. *winds it up:* Laura is using a spring-powered (rather than electric) phonograph that has to be rewound frequently.

I couldn't go back there. I—threw up—on the floor!

AMANDA: From half past seven till after five every day you mean to tell me you walked around the park, because you wanted to make me think that you were still going to Rubicam's Business College?

LAURA: It wasn't as bad as it sounds. I went inside places to get warmed up.

AMANDA: Inside where?

LAURA: I went in the art museum and the bird houses at the Zoo. I visited the penguins every day! Sometimes I did without lunch and went to the movies. Lately I've been spending most of my afternoons in the Jewel Box, that big glass house where they raise the tropical flowers.

AMANDA: You did all this to deceive me, just for deception? [*LAURA looks down.*] Why?   30

LAURA: Mother, when you're disappointed, you get that awful suffering look on your face, like the picture of Jesus' mother in the museum!

AMANDA: Hush!

LAURA: I couldn't face it.

[*There is a pause. A whisper of strings is heard. Legend on screen: "The Crust of Humility."*]

AMANDA: [*hopelessly fingering the huge pocketbook*] So what are we going to do the rest of our lives? Stay home and watch the parades go by? Amuse ourselves with the glass menagerie, darling? Eternally play those worn-out phonograph records your father left as a painful reminder of him? We won't have a business career—we've given that up because it gave us nervous indigestion! [*She laughs wearily.*] What is there left but dependency all our lives? I know so well what becomes of unmarried women who aren't prepared to occupy a position. I've seen such pitiful cases in the South—barely tolerated spinsters living upon the grudging patronage of sister's husband or brother's wife!—stuck away in some little mousetrap of a room—encouraged by one in-law to visit another—little birdlike women without any nest—eating the crust of humility all their life!

Is that the future that we've mapped out for ourselves? I swear it's the only alternative I can think of! [*She pauses.*] It isn't a very pleasant alternative, is it? [*She pauses again.*] Of course—some girls *do marry.*

[*LAURA twists her hands nervously.*]

Haven't you ever liked some boy?

LAURA: Yes. I liked one once. [*She rises.*] I came across his picture a while ago.   35

AMANDA: [*with some interest*] He gave you his picture?

LAURA: No, it's in the yearbook.

AMANDA: [*disappointed*] Oh—a high school boy.

[*Screen image: JIM as the high school hero bearing a silver cup.*]

LAURA: Yes. His name was Jim. [*She lifts the heavy annual from the claw-foot table.*] Here he is in *The Pirates of Penzance.*°

AMANDA: [*absently*] The what?   40

LAURA: The operetta the senior class put on. He had a wonderful voice and we sat across the aisle from each other Mondays, Wednesdays and Fridays in the Aud. Here he is with the silver cup for debating! See his grin?

AMANDA: [*absently*] He must have had a jolly disposition.

LAURA: He used to call me—Blue Roses.

[*Screen image: Blue roses.*]

°39 *The Pirates of Penzance:* a comic light opera (1879) by W. S. Gilbert and Arthur Sullivan.

AMANDA: Why did he call you such a name as that?

45 **LAURA:** When I had that attack of pleurosis—he asked me what was the matter when I came back. I said pleurosis—he thought that I said Blue Roses! So that's what he always called me after that. Whenever he saw me, he'd holler, "Hello, Blue Roses!" I didn't care for the girl that he went out with. Emily Meisenbach. Emily was the best-dressed girl at Soldan. She never struck me, though, as being sincere. . . . It says in the Personal Section—they're engaged. That's—six years ago! They must be married by now.

AMANDA: Girls that aren't cut out for business careers usually wind up married to some nice man. [*She gets up with a spark of revival.*] Sister, that's what you'll do!

[*LAURA utters a startled, doubtful laugh. She reaches quickly for a piece of glass.*]

LAURA: But, Mother—

AMANDA: Yes? [*She goes over to the photograph.*]

LAURA: [*in a tone of frightened apology*] I'm—crippled!

50 **AMANDA:** Nonsense! Laura, I've told you never, never to use that word. Why, you're not crippled, you just have a little defect—hardly noticeable, even! When people have some slight disadvantage like that, they cultivate other things to make up for it—develop charm—and vivacity—and—*charm*! That's all you have to do! [*She turns again to the photograph.*] One thing your father had *plenty of*—was *charm*!

[*The scene fades out with music.*]

SCENE 3

[*Legend on screen: "After the fiasco—"*]

TOM speaks from the fire escape landing.]

TOM: After the fiasco at Rubicam's Business College, the idea of getting a gentleman caller for Laura began to play a more and more important part in Mother's calculations. It became an obsession. Like some archetype of the universal unconscious, the image of the gentleman caller haunted our small apartment. . . .

[*Screen image: A young man at the door of a house with flowers.*]

An evening at home rarely passed without some allusion to this image, this specter, this hope. . . . Even when he wasn't mentioned, his presence hung in Mother's preoccupied look and in my sister's frightened, apologetic manner—hung like a sentence passed upon the Wingfields!

Mother was a woman of action as well as words. She began to take logical steps in the planned direction. Late that winter and in the early spring—realizing that extra money would be needed to properly feather the nest and plume the bird—she conducted a vigorous campaign on the telephone, roping in subscribers to one of those magazines for matrons called The Homemaker's Companion, the type of journal that features the serialized sublimations of ladies of letters who think in terms of delicate cuplike breasts, slim, tapering waists, rich, creamy thighs, eyes like wood smoke in autumn, fingers that soothe and caress like strains of music, bodies as powerful as Etruscan sculpture.

[*Screen image: The cover of a glamor magazine.*

Amanda enters with the telephone on a long extension cord. She is spotlighted in the dim stage.]

AMANDA: Ida Scott? This is Amanda Wingfield! We missed you at the D.A.R. last Monday! I said to myself: She's probably suffering with that sinus condition! How is that sinus condition?

Horrors! Heaven have mercy!—You're a Christian martyr, yes, that's what you are, a Christian martyr!

Well, I just now happened to notice that your subscription to the *Companion's* about to expire! Yes, it expires with the next issue, honey!—just when that wonderful new serial by Bessie Mae Hopper is getting off to such an exciting start. Oh, honey, it's something that you can't miss! You remember how *Gone with the Wind*° took everybody by storm? You simply couldn't go out if you hadn't read it. All everybody *talked* was Scarlett O'Hara. Well, this is a book that critics already compare to *Gone with the Wind*. It's the *Gone with the Wind* of the post-World-War generation!—What?—Burning?—Oh, honey, don't let them burn, go take a look in the oven and I'll hold the wire! Heavens—I think she's hung up!

[*The scene dims out.*]

[*Legend on screen: "You think I'm in love with Continental Shoemakers?"*]

[*Before the lights come up again, the violent voices of* TOM *and* AMANDA *are heard. They are quarreling behind the portieres. In front of them stands* LAURA *with clenched hands and panicky expression. A clear pool of light is on her figure throughout this scene.*]

TOM: What in Christ's name am I—
AMANDA: [*shrilly*] Don't you use that—
TOM: —supposed to do!   5
AMANDA: —expression! Not in my—
TOM: Ohhh!
AMANDA: —presence! Have you gone out of your senses?
TOM: I have, that's true, *driven* out!
AMANDA: What is the matter with you, you—big—big—IDIOT!   10
TOM: Look!—I've got *no thing*, no single thing—
AMANDA: Lower your voice!
TOM: —in my life here that I can call my OWN! Everything is—
AMANDA: Stop that shouting!
TOM: Yesterday you confiscated my books! You had the nerve to—   15
AMANDA: I took that horrible novel back to the library—yes! That hideous book by that insane Mr. Lawrence.°

[TOM *laughs wildly.*]

I cannot control the output of diseased minds or people who cater to them—

[TOM *laughs still more wildly.*]

BUT I WON'T ALLOW SUCH FILTH BROUGHT INTO MY HOUSE! No, no, no, no, no!
TOM: House, house! Who pays rent on it, who makes a slave of himself to—
AMANDA: [*fairly screeching*] Don't you DARE to—
TOM: No, no, I mustn't say things! *I've* got to just—
AMANDA: Let me tell you—   20
TOM: I don't want to hear any more!

[*He tears the portieres open. The dining-room area is lit with turgid smoky red glow. Now we see* AMANDA; *her hair is in metal curlers and she is wearing a very old bathrobe, much too large for her*

°2.3 *Gone with the Wind*: popular novel (1936) by Margaret Mitchell (1900–1949), set in the South before, during, and after the Civil War. Scarlett O'Hara was the heroine. 16 *Lawrence*: D. H. Lawrence (1885–1930), English poet and fiction writer, popularly known as an advocate of passion and sexuality. See "The Horse Dealer's Daughter," p. 472.

slight figure, a relic of the faithless Mr. Wingfield. The upright typewriter now stands on the drop-leaf table, along with a wild disarray of manuscripts. The quarrel was probably precipitated by AMANDA's *interruption of* TOM's *creative labor. A chair lies overthrown on the floor. Their gesticulating shadows are cast on the ceiling by the fiery glow.*]

AMANDA: You *will* hear more, you—

TOM: No, I won't hear more, I'm going out!

AMANDA: You come right back in—

25 TOM: Out, out, out! Because I'm—

AMANDA: Come back here, Tom Wingfield! I'm not through talking to you!

TOM: Oh, go—

LAURA: [*desperately*]—Tom!

AMANDA: You're going to listen, and no more insolence from you! I'm at the end of my patience!

[*He comes back toward her.*]

30 TOM: What do you think I'm at? Aren't I supposed to have any patience to reach the end of, Mother? I know, I know. It seems unimportant to you, what I'm *doing*—what I *want* to do—having a little *difference* between them! You don't think that—

AMANDA: I think you've been doing things that you're ashamed of. That's why you act like this. I don't believe that you go every night to the movies. Nobody goes to the movies night after night. Nobody in their right minds goes to the movies as often as you pretend to. People don't go to the movies at nearly midnight, and movies don't let out at two A.M. Come in stumbling. Muttering to yourself like a maniac! You get three hours' sleep and then go to work. Oh, I can picture the way you're doing down there. Moping, doping, because you're in no condition.

TOM: [*wildly*] No, I'm in no condition!

AMANDA: What right have you got to jeopardize your job? Jeopardize the security of us all? How do you think we'd manage if you were—

TOM: Listen! You think I'm crazy about the *warehouse?* [*He bends fiercely toward her slight figure.*] You think I'm in love with the Continental Shoemakers? You think I want to spend fifty-five *years* down there in that—*celotex interior!* with—*fluorescent—tubes!* Look! I'd rather somebody picked up a crowbar and battered out my brains—than go back mornings! I *go!* Every time you come in yelling that God damn *"Rise and Shine!" "Rise and Shine!"* I say to myself, "How *lucky dead* people are!" But I get up. I *go!* For sixty-five dollars a month I give up all that I dream of doing and being *ever!* And you say self—*self's* all I ever think of. Why, listen, if self is what I thought of, Mother, I'd be where he is—GONE! [*He points to his father's picture.*] As far as the system of transportation reaches! [*He starts past her. She grabs his arm.*] Don't grab at me, Mother!

35 AMANDA: Where are you going?

TOM: I'm going to the *movies!*

AMANDA: I don't believe that lie!

[TOM *crouches toward her, overtowering her tiny figure. She backs away, gasping.*]

TOM: I'm going to opium dens! Yes, opium dens, dens of vice and criminals' hangouts, Mother. I've joined the Hogan Gang,° I'm a hired assassin, I carry a tommy gun in a violin case! I run a string of cat houses in the Valley! They call me Killer, Killer Wingfield, I'm leading a double life, a simple, honest warehouse worker by day, by night a dynamic *czar* of the

---

°38 *Hogan Gang:* one of the major criminal organizations in St. Louis in the 1920s and 1930s.

underworld, Mother. I go to gambling casinos, I spin away fortunes on the roulette table! I wear a patch over one eye and a false mustache, sometimes I put on green whiskers. On those occasions they call me—*El Diablo!*° Oh, I could tell you many things to make you sleepless! My enemies plan to dynamite this place. They're going to blow us all sky-high some night! I'll be glad, very happy, and so will you! You'll go up, up on a broomstick, over Blue Mountain with seventeen gentlemen callers! You ugly—babbling old—*witch*. . . .

[*He goes through a series of violent, clumsy movements, seizing his overcoat, lunging to the door, pulling it fiercely open. The women watch him, aghast. His arm catches in the sleeve of the coat as he struggles to pull it on. For a moment he is pinioned by the bulky garment. With an outraged groan he tears the coat off again, splitting the shoulder of it, and hurls it across the room. It strikes against the shelf of* LAURA'S *glass collection, and there is a tinkle of shattering glass.* LAURA *cries out as if wounded.*

Music.

Screen legend: "The Glass Menagerie."]

LAURA: [*shrilly*] My glass!—menagerie. . . . [*She covers her face and turns away.*]

[*But* AMANDA *is still stunned and stupefied by the "ugly witch" so that she barely notices this occurrence. Now she recovers her speech.*]

AMANDA: [*in an awful voice*] I won't speak to you—until you apologize!   40

[*She crosses through the portieres and draws them together behind her.* TOM *is left with* LAURA. LAURA *clings weakly to the mantel with her face averted.* TOM *stares at her stupidly for a moment. Then he crosses to the shelf. He drops awkwardly on his knees to collect the fallen glass, glancing at* LAURA *as if he would speak but couldn't.*

"The Glass Menagerie" music steals in as the scene dims out.]

SCENE 4

The interior of the apartment is dark. There is a faint light in the alley. A deep-voiced bell in a church is tolling the hour of five.

  TOM *appears at the top of the alley. After each solemn boom of the bell in the tower, he shakes a little noisemaker or rattle as if to express the tiny spasm of man in contrast to the sustained power and dignity of the Almighty. This and the unsteadiness of his advance make it evident that he has been drinking. As he climbs the few steps to the fire escape landing light steals up inside.* LAURA *appears in the front room in a nightdress. She notices that* TOM'S *bed is empty.* TOM *fishes in his pockets for his door key, removing a motley assortment of articles in the search, including a shower of movie ticket stubs and an empty bottle. At last he finds the key, but just as he is about to insert it, it slips from his fingers. He strikes a match and crouches below the door.*

TOM: [*bitterly*] One crack—and it falls through!

[LAURA *opens the door.*]

LAURA: Tom! Tom, what are you doing?
TOM: Looking for a door key.
LAURA: Where have you been all this time?
TOM: I have been to the movies.   5

———————————
°38 *El Diablo:* the devil.

LAURA: All this time at the movies?

TOM: There was a very long program. There was a Garbo° picture and a Mickey Mouse and a travelogue and a newsreel and a preview of coming attractions. And there was an organ solo and a collection for the Milk Fund—simultaneously—which ended up in a terrible fight between a fat lady and an usher!

LAURA: [*innocently*] Did you have to stay through everything?

TOM: Of course! And, oh I forgot! There was a big stage show! The headliner on this stage show was Malvolio° the Magician. He performed wonderful tricks, many of them, such as pouring water back and forth between pitchers. First it turned to wine and then it turned to beer and then it turned to whisky. I know it was whisky it finally turned into because he needed somebody to come up out of the audience to help him, and I came up—both shows! It was Kentucky Straight Bourbon. A very generous fellow, he gave souvenirs. [*He pulls from his back pocket a shimmering rainbow-colored scarf.*] He gave me this. This is his magic scarf. You can have it, Laura. You wave it over a canary cage and you get a bowl of goldfish. You wave it over the goldfish bowl and they fly away canaries. . . . But the wonderfullest trick of all was the coffin trick. We nailed him into a coffin and he got out of the coffin without removing one nail. [*He has come inside.*] There is a trick that would come in handy for me—get me out of this two-by-four situation! [*He flops onto the bed and starts removing his shoes.*]

10 LAURA: Tom—shhh!

TOM: What're you shushing me for?

LAURA: You'll wake up Mother.

TOM: Goody, goody! Pay 'er back for all those "Rise an' Shines." [*He lies down, groaning.*] You know it don't take much intelligence to get yourself into a nailed-up coffin, Laura. But who in hell ever got himself out of one without removing one nail?

[*As if in answer, the father's grinning photograph lights up. The scene dims out.*]

[*Immediately following, the church bell is heard striking six. At the sixth stroke the alarm clock goes off in* AMANDA's *room, and after a few moments we hear her calling: "Rise and Shine! Rise and Shine! Laura, go tell your brother to rise and shine!"*]

TOM: [*sitting up slowly*] I'll rise—but I won't shine.

[*The light increases.*]

15 AMANDA: Laura, tell your brother his coffee is ready.

[LAURA *slips into the front room.*]

LAURA: Tom!—It's nearly seven. Don't make Mother nervous.

[*He stares at her stupidly.*]

[*Beseechingly.*] Tom, speak to Mother this morning. Make up with her, apologize, speak to her!

TOM: She won't to me. It's her that started not speaking.

LAURA: If you just say you're sorry she'll start speaking.

TOM: Her not speaking—is that such a tragedy?

20 LAURA: Please—please!

°7 *Garbo:* Greta Garbo (1905–1990), Swedish star of American silent and early sound films. 9 *Malvolio:* the name, borrowed from a puritanical character in Shakespeare's *Twelfth Night*, means "malevolence" or "ill-will."

AMANDA: [*calling from the kitchenette*] Laura, are you going to do what I asked you to do, or do I have to get dressed and go out myself?

LAURA: Going, going—soon as I get on my coat!

[*She pulls on a shapeless felt hat with a nervous, jerky movement, pleadingly glancing at* TOM. *She rushes awkwardly for her coat. The coat is one of* AMANDA's, *inaccurately made-over, the sleeves too short for* LAURA.]

Butter and what else?

AMANDA: [*entering from the kitchenette*] Just butter. Tell them to charge it.

LAURA: Mother, they make such faces when I do that.

AMANDA: Sticks and stones can break our bones, but the expression on Mr. Garfinkel's face   25
won't harm us! Tell your brother his coffee is getting cold.

LAURA: [*at the door*] Do what I asked you, will you, will you, Tom?

[*He looks sullenly away.*]

AMANDA: Laura, go now or just don't go at all!

LAURA: [*rushing out*] Going—going!

[*A second later she cries out.* TOM *springs up and crosses to the door.* TOM *opens the door.*]

TOM: Laura?

LAURA: I'm all right. I slipped, but I'm all right.   30

AMANDA: [*peering anxiously after her*] If anyone breaks a leg on those fire-escape steps, the landlord ought to be sued for every cent he possesses! [*She shuts the door. Now she remembers she isn't speaking to* TOM *and returns to the other room.*]

[*As* TOM *comes listlessly for his coffee, she turns her back to him and stands rigidly facing the window on the gloomy gray vault of the areaway. Its light on her face with its aged but childish features is cruelly sharp, satirical as a Daumier print.°*]

The music of "Ave Maria"° is heard softly.

TOM *glances sheepishly but sullenly at her averted figure and slumps at the table. The coffee is scalding hot; he sips it and gasps and spits it back in the cup. At his gasp,* AMANDA *catches her breath and half turns. Then she catches herself and turns back to the window.* TOM *blows on his coffee, glancing sidewise at his mother. She clears her throat.* TOM *clears his. He starts to rise, sinks back down again, scratches his head, clears his throat again.* AMANDA *coughs.* TOM *raises his cup in both hands to blow on it, his eyes staring over the rim of it at his mother for several moments. Then he slowly sets the cup down and awkwardly and hesitantly rises from the chair.*]

TOM: [*hoarsely*] Mother. I—I apologize, Mother.

[AMANDA *draws a quick, shuddering breath. Her face works grotesquely. She breaks into childlike tears.*]

I'm sorry for what I said, for everything that I said, I didn't mean it.

AMANDA: [*sobbingly*] My devotion has made me a witch and so I make myself hateful to my children!

TOM: No, you *don't.*

AMANDA: I worry so much, don't sleep, it makes me nervous!   35

°31.2 S. D. *Daumier print:* Honoré Daumier (1808–1879), French painter and engraver whose prints frequently satirized his society. 31.2 S. D. *"Ave Maria":* a Roman Catholic prayer to the Virgin Mary; the musical setting called for here is by Franz Schubert (1797–1828).

Tom: [*gently*] I understand that.

Amanda: I've had to put up a solitary battle all these years. But you're my right-hand bower!° Don't fall down, don't fail!

Tom: [*gently*] I try, Mother.

Amanda: [*with great enthusiasm*] Try and you will *succeed!* [*The notion makes her breathless.*] Why, you—you're just *full* of natural endowments! Both of my children—they're *unusual* children! Don't you think I know it? I'm so—*proud!* Happy and—feel I've—so much to be thankful for but—promise me one thing, son!

40 Tom: What, Mother?

Amanda: Promise, son, you'll—never be a drunkard!

Tom: [*turns to her grinning*] I will never be a drunkard, Mother.

Amanda: That's what frightened me so, that you'd be drinking! Eat a bowl of Purina!

Tom: Just coffee, Mother.

45 Amanda: Shredded wheat biscuit?

Tom: No. No, Mother, just coffee.

Amanda: You can't put in a day's work on an empty stomach. You've got ten minutes—don't gulp! Drinking too-hot liquids makes cancer of the stomach. . . . Put cream in.

Tom: No, thank you.

Amanda: To cool it.

50 Tom: No! No, thank you, I want it black.

Amanda: I know, but it's not good for you. We have to do all that we can to build ourselves up. In these trying times we live in, all that we have to cling to is—each other. . . . That's why it's so important to—Tom, I—I sent out your sister so I could discuss something with you. If you hadn't spoken I would have spoken to you. [*She sits down.*]

Tom: [*gently*] What is it, Mother, that you want to discuss?

Amanda: *Laura!*

[*Tom puts his cup down slowly.*]

[*Legend on screen "Laura." Music: "The Glass Menagerie."*]

Tom: —Oh.—Laura . . .

55 Amanda: [*touching his sleeve*] You know how Laura is. So quiet but—still water runs deep! She notices things and I think she—broods about them.

[*Tom looks up.*]

A few days ago I came in and she was crying.

Tom: What about?

Amanda: You.

Tom: Me?

Amanda: She has an idea that you're not happy here.

60 Tom: What gave her that idea?

Amanda: What gives her any idea? However, you do act strangely.—I'm not criticizing, understand *that!* I know your ambitions do not lie in the warehouse, that like everybody in the whole wide world—you've had to—make sacrifices, but—Tom—Tom—life's not easy, it calls for—Spartan endurance! There's so many things in my heart that I cannot describe to you! I've never told you but I—*loved* your father. . . .

Tom: [*gently*] I know that, Mother.

°37 *right-hand bower* or *rightbower:* the Jack of trump in the card game 500, the second-highest card (below the joker).

AMANDA: And you—when I see you taking after his ways! Staying out late—and—well, you *had* been drinking the night you were in that—terrifying condition! Laura says that you hate the apartment and that you go out nights to get away from it! Is that true, Tom?

TOM: No. You say there's so much in your heart that you can't describe to me. That's true of me, too. There's so much in my heart that I can't describe to *you!* So let's respect each other's—

AMANDA: But, why—*why*, Tom—are you always so *restless?* Where do you *go* to, nights?   65

TOM: I—go to the movies.

AMANDA: Why do you go to the movies so much, Tom?

TOM: I go to the movies because—I like adventure. Adventure is something I don't have much of at work, so I go to the movies.

AMANDA: But, Tom, you go to the movies *entirely* too *much!*

TOM: I like a lot of adventure.   70

[AMANDA *looks baffled, then hurt. As the familiar inquisition resumes,* TOM *becomes hard and impatient again. Amanda slips back into her querulous attitude toward him.*

Image on screen: A sailing vessel with Jolly Roger.°]

AMANDA: Most young men find adventure in their careers.

TOM: Then most young men are not employed in a warehouse.

AMANDA: The world is full of young men employed in warehouses and offices and factories.

TOM: Do all of them find adventure in their careers?

AMANDA: They do or they do without it! Not everybody has a craze for adventure.   75

TOM: Man is by instinct a lover, a hunter, a fighter, and none of those instincts are given much play at the warehouse!

AMANDA: Man is by instinct! Don't quote instinct to me! Instinct is something that people have got away from! It belongs to animals! Christian adults don't want it!

TOM: What do Christian adults want, then, Mother?

AMANDA: Superior things! Things of the mind and the spirit! Only animals have to satisfy instincts! Surely your aims are somewhat higher than theirs! Than monkeys—pigs—

TOM: I reckon they're not.   80

AMANDA: You're joking. However, that isn't what I wanted to discuss.

TOM: [*rising*] I haven't much time.

AMANDA: [*pushing his shoulders*] Sit down.

TOM: You want me to punch in red° at the warehouse, Mother?

AMANDA: You have five minutes. I want to talk about Laura.   85

[*Screen legend: "Plans and Provisions."*]

TOM: All right! What about Laura?

AMANDA: We have to be making some plans and provisions for her. She's older than you, two years, and nothing has happened. She just drifts along doing nothing. It frightens me terribly how she just drifts along.

TOM: I guess she's the type that people call home girls.

AMANDA: There's no such type, and if there is, it's a pity! That is unless the home is hers, with a husband!

TOM: What?   90

°70.2 S. D. *Jolly Roger:* the traditional flag of a pirate ship—a skull and crossbones on a field of black. 84 *punch in red:* arrive late for work; the time clock stamps late arrival times in red on the time card.

AMANDA: Oh, I can see the handwriting on the wall as plain as I see the nose in front of my face! It's terrifying! More and more you remind me of your father! He was out all hours without explanation!—Then *left! Goodbye!* And me with the bag to hold. I saw that letter you got from the Merchant Marine. I know what you're dreaming of. I'm not standing here blindfolded. [*She pauses.*] Very well, then. Then *do* it! But not till there's somebody to take your place.

TOM: What do you mean?

AMANDA: I mean that as soon as Laura has got somebody to take care of her, married, a home of her own, independent—why, then you'll be free to go wherever you please, on land, on sea, whichever way the wind blows you! But until that time you've got to look out for your sister. I don't say me because I'm old and don't matter! I say for your sister because she's young and dependent.

I put her in business college—a dismal failure! Frightened her so it made her sick at the stomach. I took her over to the Young People's League at the church. Another fiasco. She spoke to nobody, nobody spoke to her. Now all she does is fool with those pieces of glass and play those worn-out records. What kind of a life is that for a girl to lead?

TOM: What can I do about it?

95   AMANDA: Overcome selfishness! Self, self, self is all that you ever think of!

[TOM *springs up and crosses to get his coat. It is ugly and bulky. He pulls on a cap with earmuffs.*]

Where is your muffler? Put your wool muffler on!

[*He snatches it angrily from the closet, tosses it around his neck and pulls both ends tight.*]

Tom! I haven't said what I had in mind to ask you.

TOM: I'm too late to—

AMANDA: [*catching his arm—very importunately; then shyly*] Down at the warehouse, aren't there some—nice young men?

TOM: No!

AMANDA: There *must* be—*some* . . .

100 TOM: Mother—[*He gestures.*]

AMANDA: Find out one that's clean-living—doesn't drink and ask him out for sister!

TOM: What?

AMANDA: For *sister!* To *meet!* Get *acquainted!*

TOM: [*stamping to the door*] Oh, my go-osh!

105 AMANDA: Will you? [*He opens the door. She says, imploringly:*] Will you?

[*He starts down the fire escape.*]

Will you? *Will* you, dear?

TOM: [*calling back*] Yes!

[AMANDA *closes the door hesitantly and with a troubled but faintly hopeful expression.*

Screen image: The cover of a glamor magazine.

The spotlight picks up AMANDA *on the phone.*]

AMANDA: Ella Cartwright? This is Amanda Wingfield! How are you honey? How is that kidney condition? [*There is a five-second pause.*] Horrors! [*There is another pause.*]

You're a Christian martyr, yes, honey, that's what you are, a Christian martyr! Well, I just now happened to notice in my little red book that your subscription to the *Companion* has just run out! I knew that you wouldn't want to miss out on the wonderful serial starting in this new issue. It's by Bessie Mae Hopper, the first thing she's written since *Honeymoon for Three.* Wasn't that a strange and interesting story? Well, this one is even lovelier, I believe. It has a sophisticated, society background. It's all about the horsey set on Long Island!

[*The light fades out.*]

SCENE 5

[*Legend on the screen: "Annunciation."*]

Music is heard as the light slowly comes on.

It is early dusk of a spring evening. Supper has just been finished in the Wingfield apartment. AMANDA *and* LAURA, *in light-colored dresses, are removing dishes from the table in the dining room, which is shadowy, their movements formalized almost as a dance or ritual, their moving forms as pale and silent as moths.* TOM, *in white shirt and trousers, rises from the table and crosses toward the fire escape.*]

AMANDA: [*as he passes her*] Son, will you do me a favor?
TOM: What?
AMANDA: Comb your hair! You look so pretty when your hair is combed!

[*Tom slouches on the sofa with the evening paper. Its enormous headline reads: "Franco Triumphs."°*]

There is only one respect in which I would like you to emulate your father.
TOM: What respect is that?
AMANDA: The care he always took of his appearance. He never allowed himself to look un-   5
tidy.

[*He throws down the paper and crosses to the fire escape.*]

Where are you going?
TOM: I'm going out to smoke.
AMANDA: You smoke too much. A pack a day at fifteen cents a pack. How much would that amount to in a month? Thirty times fifteen is how much, Tom? Figure it out and you will be astounded at what you could save. Enough to give you a night-school course in accounting at Washington U.°! Just think what a wonderful thing that would be for you, son!

[*TOM is unmoved by the thought.*]

TOM: I'd rather smoke. [*He steps out on the landing, letting the screen door slam.*]
AMANDA: [*sharply*] I know! That's the tragedy of it. . . . [*Alone, she turns to look at her husband's picture.*]

[*Dance music: "The World Is Waiting for the Sunrise!"°*]

TOM: [*to the audience*] Across the alley from us was the Paradise Dance Hall. On evenings   10
in spring the windows and doors were open and the music came outdoors. Sometimes the lights were turned out except for a large glass sphere that hung from the ceiling. It would turn slowly about and filter the dusk with delicate rainbow colors. Then the orchestra played a waltz or a tango, something that had a slow and sensuous rhythm. Couples would come outside, to the relative privacy of the alley. You could see them

---

°3.1 S. D. *"Franco Triumphs"*: Francisco Franco (1892–1975), dictator of Spain from 1939 until his death, was the general of the victorious Falangist armies in the Spanish Civil War (1936–1939). 7 *Washington U*: Washington University, a highly competitive liberal arts school in St. Louis. 9.1 S. D. *"The World . . . Sunrise"*: popular song, copyright 1919, written by Eugene Lockhart and Ernest Seitz.

kissing behind ash pits and telephone poles. This was the compensation for lives that passed like mine, without any change or adventure. Adventure and change were imminent in this year. They were waiting around the corner for all these kids. Suspended in the mist over Berchtesgaden,° caught in the folds of Chamberlain's umbrella. In Spain there was Guernica! But here there was only hot swing music and liquor, dance halls, bars, and movies, and sex that hung in the gloom like a chandelier and flooded the world with brief, deceptive rainbows. . . . All the world was waiting for bombardments!

[AMANDA *turns from the picture and comes outside.*]

AMANDA: [*sighing*] A fire escape landing's a poor excuse for a porch. [*She spreads a newspaper on a step and sits down, gracefully and demurely as if she were settling into a swing on a Mississippi veranda.*] What are you looking at?
TOM: The moon.
AMANDA: Is there a moon this evening?
TOM: It's rising over Garfinkel's Delicatessen.
15 AMANDA: So it is! A little silver slipper of a moon. Have you made a wish on it yet?
TOM: Um-hum.
AMANDA: What did you wish for?
TOM: That's a secret.
AMANDA: A secret, huh? Well, I won't tell mine either. I will be just as mysterious as you.
20 TOM: I bet I can guess what yours is.
AMANDA: Is my head so transparent?
TOM: You're not a sphinx.°
AMANDA: No, I don't have secrets. I'll tell you what I wished for on the moon. Success and happiness for my precious children! I wish for that whenever there's a moon, and when there isn't a moon, I wish for it, too.
TOM: I thought perhaps you wished for a gentleman caller.
25 AMANDA: Why do you say that?
TOM: Don't you remember asking me to fetch one?
AMANDA: I remember suggesting that it would be nice for your sister if you brought home some nice young man from the warehouse. I think that I've made that suggestion more than once.
TOM: Yes, you have made it repeatedly.
AMANDA: Well?
30 TOM: We are going to have one.
AMANDA: What?
TOM: A gentleman caller!

[*The annunciation is celebrated with music.*

AMANDA *rises.*

Image on screen: A caller with a bouquet.]

°10 *Berchtesgaden . . . Guernica:* The three names mentioned are all foreshadowings of World War II. Berchtesgaden, a resort in the Bavarian Alps, was Adolf Hitler's favorite residence. Neville Chamberlain was the British prime minister who signed the Munich Pact with Hitler in 1938, allowing Nazi Germany to occupy parts of Czechoslovakia. Chamberlain, who always carried an umbrella, declared that he had ensured "peace in our time." The bombardment of Guernica during the Spanish Civil War made the name of the town synonymous with the horrors of war, and especially the killing of civilian women and children. (See page 1647, note to 1.3 and page I–9.) 22 *sphinx:* a mythological monster with the head of a woman and body of a lion, famous for her riddles. See page 128.

AMANDA: You mean you have asked some nice young man to come over?

TOM: Yep. I've asked him to dinner.

AMANDA: You really did?   35

TOM: I did!

AMANDA: You did, and did he—*accept?*

TOM: He did!

AMANDA: Well, well—well, well! That's—lovely!

TOM: I thought that you would be pleased.   40

AMANDA: It's definite then?

TOM: Very definite.

AMANDA: Soon?

TOM: Very soon.

AMANDA: For heaven's sake, stop putting on and tell me some things, will you?   45

TOM: What things do you want me to tell you?

AMANDA: *Naturally* I would like to know when he's *coming!*

TOM: He's coming tomorrow.

AMANDA: *Tomorrow?*

TOM: Yep. Tomorrow.   50

AMANDA: But, Tom!

TOM: Yes, Mother?

AMANDA: Tomorrow gives me no time!

TOM: Time for what?

AMANDA: Preparations! Why didn't you phone me at once, as soon as you asked him, the   55
minute that he accepted? Then, don't you see, I could have been getting ready!

TOM: You don't have to make any fuss.

AMANDA: Oh, Tom, Tom, Tom, of course I have to make a fuss! I want things nice, not sloppy! Not thrown together. I'll certainly have to do some fast thinking, won't I?

TOM: I don't see why you have to think at all.

AMANDA: You just don't know. We can't have a gentleman caller in a pigsty! All my wed-
ding silver has to be polished, the monogrammed table linen ought to be laundered!
The windows have to be washed and fresh curtains put up. And how about clothes?
We have to *wear* something, don't we?

TOM: Mother, this boy is no one to make a fuss over!   60

AMANDA: Do you realize he's the first young man we've introduced to your sister? It's terrible, disgraceful that poor little sister has never received a single gentleman caller!
Tom, come inside! [*She opens the screen door.*]

TOM: What for?

AMANDA: I want to ask you some things.

TOM: If you're going to make such a fuss, I'll call it off, I'll tell him not to come!

AMANDA: You certainly won't do anything of the kind. Nothing offends people worse than   65
broken engagements. It simply means I'll have to work like a Turk! We won't be brilliant, but we will pass inspection. Come on inside.

[*TOM follows her inside, groaning.*]

Sit down.

TOM: Any particular place you would like me to sit?

AMANDA: Thank heavens I've got that new sofa! I'm also making payments on a floor lamp
I'll have sent out! And put the chintz covers on, they'll brighten things up! Of course
I'd hoped to have these walls re-papered. . . . What is the young man's name?

TOM: His name is O'Connor.

AMANDA: That, of course, means fish°—tomorrow is Friday! I'll have that salmon loaf—with Durkee's dressing! What does he do? He works at the warehouse?

70 TOM: Of course! How else would I—

AMANDA: Tom, he—doesn't drink?

TOM: Why do you ask me that?

AMANDA: Your father *did!*

TOM: Don't get started on that!

75 AMANDA: He *does* drink, then?

TOM: Not that I know of!

AMANDA: Make sure, be certain! The last thing I want for my daughter's a boy who drinks!

TOM: Aren't you being a little bit premature? Mr. O'Connor has not yet appeared on the scene!

AMANDA: But will tomorrow. To meet your sister, and what do I know about his character? Nothing! Old maids are better off than wives of drunkards!

80 TOM: Oh, my God!

AMANDA: Be still!

TOM: [*leaning forward to whisper*] Lots of fellows meet girls whom they don't marry!

AMANDA: Oh, talk sensibly, Tom—and don't be sarcastic! [*She has gotten a hairbrush.*]

TOM: What are you doing?

85 AMANDA: I'm brushing that cowlick down! [*She attacks his hair with the brush.*] What is this young man's position at the warehouse?

TOM: [*submitting grimly to the brush and the interrogation*] This young man's position is that of a shipping clerk, Mother.

AMANDA: Sounds to me like a fairly responsible job, the sort of job *you* would be in if you just had more *get-up.* What is his salary? Have you any idea?

TOM: I would judge it to be approximately eighty-five dollars a month.

AMANDA: Well—not princely, but—

90 TOM: Twenty more than I make.

AMANDA: Yes, how well I know! But for a family man, eighty-five dollars a month is not much more than you can just get by on. . . .

TOM: Yes, but Mr. O'Connor is not a family man.

AMANDA: He might be, mightn't he? Some time in the future?

TOM: I see. Plans and provisions.

95 AMANDA: You are the only young man that I know of who ignores the fact that the future becomes the present, the present the past, and the past turns into everlasting regret if you don't plan for it!

TOM: I will think that over and see what I can make of it.

AMANDA: Don't be supercilious with your mother! Tell me some more about this—what do you call him?

TOM: James D. O'Connor. The D. is for Delaney.

AMANDA: Irish on *both* sides! *Gracious!* And he doesn't drink?

100 TOM: Shall I call him up and ask him right this minute?

AMANDA: The only way to find out about those things is to make discreet inquiries at the proper moment. When I was a girl in Blue Mountain and it was suspected that a young man drank, the girl whose attentions he had been receiving, if any girl *was,* would sometimes speak to the minister of his church, or rather her father would if her

---

°69 *fish:* Amanda assumes that O'Connor is Catholic. Until the 1960s, Roman Catholics were required by the church to abstain from meat on Fridays.

father was living, and sort of feel him out on the young man's character. That is the way such things are discreetly handled to keep a young woman from making a tragic mistake!

Tom: Then how did you happen to make a tragic mistake?

Amanda: That innocent look of your father's had everyone fooled! He *smiled*—the world was *enchanted*! No girl can do worse than put herself at the mercy of a handsome appearance! I hope that Mr. O'Connor is not too good-looking.

Tom: No, he's not too good-looking. He's covered with freckles and hasn't too much of a nose.

Amanda: He's not right-down homely, though?   105

Tom: Not right-down homely. Just medium homely, I'd say.

Amanda: Character's what to look for in a man.

Tom: That's what I've always said, Mother.

Amanda: You've never said anything of the kind and I suspect you would never give it a thought.

Tom: Don't be so suspicious of me.   110

Amanda: At least I hope he's the type that's up and coming.

Tom: I think he really goes in for self-improvement.

Amanda: What reason have you to think so?

Tom: He goes to night school.

Amanda: [*beaming*] Splendid! What does he do, I mean study?   115

Tom: Radio engineering and public speaking!

Amanda: Then he has visions of being advanced in the world! Any young man who studies public speaking is aiming to have an executive job some day! And radio engineering? A thing for the future! Both of these facts are very illuminating. Those are the sort of things that a mother should know concerning any young man who comes to call on her daughter. Seriously or—not.

Tom: One little warning. He doesn't know about Laura. I didn't let on that we had dark ulterior motives. I just said, why don't you come and have dinner with us? He said okay and that was the whole conversation.

Amanda: I bet it was! You're eloquent as an oyster. However, he'll know about Laura when he gets here. When he sees how lovely and sweet and pretty she is, he'll thank his lucky stars he was asked to dinner.

Tom: Mother, you mustn't expect too much of Laura.   120

Amanda: What do you mean?

Tom: Laura seems all those things to you and me because she's ours and we love her. We don't even notice she's crippled any more.

Amanda: Don't say crippled! You know that I never allow that word to be used!

Tom: But face facts, Mother. She is and—that's not all—

Amanda: What do you mean "not all"?   125

Tom: Laura is very different from other girls.

Amanda: I think the difference is all to her advantage.

Tom: Not quite all—in the eyes of others—strangers—she's terribly shy and lives in a world of her own and those things make her seem a little peculiar to people outside the house.

Amanda: Don't say peculiar.

Tom: Face the facts. She is.   130

[*The dance hall music changes to a tango that has a minor and somewhat ominous tone.*]

Amanda: In what way is she peculiar—may I ask?

TOM: [*gently*] She lives in a world of her own—a world of little glass ornaments, Mother. . . .

[*He gets up. AMANDA remains holding the brush, looking at him, troubled.*]

She plays old phonograph records and—that's about all—[*He glances at himself in the mirror and crosses to the door.*]

AMANDA: [*sharply*] Where are you going?

TOM: I'm going to the movies. [*He goes out the screen door.*]

135 AMANDA: Not to the movies, every night to the movies! [*She follows quickly to the screen door.*] I don't believe you always go to the movies!

[*He is gone. AMANDA looks worriedly after him for a moment. Then vitality and optimism return and she turns from the door, crossing to the portieres.*]

Laura! Laura!

[*LAURA answers from the kitchenette.*]

LAURA: Yes, Mother.

AMANDA: Let those dishes go and come in front!

[*LAURA appears with a dish towel. AMANDA speaks to her gaily.*]

Laura, come here and make a wish on the moon!

[*Screen image: The Moon.*]

LAURA: [*entering*] Moon—moon?

AMANDA: A little silver slipper of a moon. Look over your left shoulder, Laura, and make a wish!

[*LAURA looks faintly puzzled as if called out of sleep. AMANDA seizes her shoulders and turns her at an angle by the door.*]

Now! Now, darling, *wish!*

140 LAURA: What shall I wish for, Mother?

AMANDA: [*her voice trembling and her eyes suddenly filling with tears*] Happiness! Good fortune!

[*The sound of the violin rises and the stage dims out.*]

SCENE 6

[*The light comes up on the fire escape landing. Tom is leaning against the grill, smoking. Screen image: The high school hero.*]

TOM: And so the following evening I brought Jim home to dinner. I had known Jim slightly in high school. In high school Jim was a hero. He had tremendous Irish good nature and vitality with the scrubbed and polished look of white chinaware. He seemed to move in a continual spotlight. He was a star in basketball, captain of the debating club, president of the senior class and the glee club and he sang the male lead in the annual light operas. He was always running or bounding, never just walking. He seemed always at the point of defeating the law of gravity. He was shooting with such velocity through his adolescence that you would logically expect him to arrive at nothing short of the White House by the time he was thirty. But Jim apparently ran into more interference after his graduation from Soldan. His speed had definitely slowed. Six years after he left high school he was holding a job that wasn't much better than mine.

[*Screen image: The Clerk.*]

He was the only one at the warehouse with whom I was on friendly terms. I was valuable to him as someone who could remember his former glory, who had seen him win basketball games and the silver cup in debating. He knew of my secret practice of retiring to a cabinet of the washroom to work on poems when business was slack in the warehouse. He called me Shakespeare. And while the other boys in the warehouse regarded me with suspicious hostility, Jim took a humorous attitude toward me. Gradually his attitude affected the others, their hostility wore off and they also began to smile at me as people smile at an oddly fashioned dog who trots across their path at some distance.

I knew that Jim and Laura had known each other at Soldan, and I had heard Laura speak admiringly of his voice. I didn't know if Jim remembered her or not. In high school Laura had been as unobtrusive as Jim had been astonishing. If he did remember Laura, it was not as my sister, for when I asked him to dinner, he grinned and said, "You know, Shakespeare, I never thought of you as having folks!"

He was about to discover that I did. . . .

[*Legend on screen: "The accent of a coming foot."*]

[*The light dims out on Tom and comes up in the Wingfield living room—a delicate lemony light. It is about five on a Friday evening of late spring which comes "scattering poems in the sky."*]

AMANDA has worked like a Turk in preparation for the gentleman caller. The results are astonishing. The new floor lamp with its rose silk shade is in place, a colored paper lantern conceals the broken light fixture in the ceiling, new billowing white curtains are at the windows, chintz covers are on the chairs and sofa, a pair of new sofa pillows make their initial appearance. Open boxes and tissue paper are scattered on the floor.

LAURA stands in the middle of the room with lifted arms while AMANDA crouches before her, adjusting the hem of a new dress, devout and ritualistic. The dress is colored and designed by memory. The arrangement of LAURA's hair is changed; it is softer and more becoming. A fragile, unearthly prettiness has come out in LAURA: she is like a piece of translucent glass touched by light, given a momentary radiance, not actual, not lasting.]

AMANDA: [*impatiently*] Why are you trembling?
LAURA: Mother, you've made me so nervous!
AMANDA: How have I made you nervous?
LAURA: By all this fuss! You make it seem so important!   5
AMANDA: I don't understand you, Laura. You couldn't be satisfied with just sitting home, and yet whenever I try to arrange something for you, you seem to resist it. [*She gets up.*] Now take a look at yourself. No, wait! Wait just a moment—I have an idea!
LAURA: What is it now?

[*AMANDA produces two powder puffs which she wraps in handkerchiefs and stuffs in LAURA's bosom.*]

LAURA: Mother, what are you doing?
AMANDA: They call them "Gay Deceivers"!
LAURA: I won't wear them!   10
AMANDA: You will!
LAURA: Why should I?
AMANDA: Because, to be painfully honest, your chest is flat.
LAURA: You make it seem like we were setting a trap.
AMANDA: All pretty girls are a trap, a pretty trap, and men expect them to be.   15

[*Legend on screen: "A pretty trap."*]

Now look at yourself, young lady. This is the prettiest you will ever be! [*She stands back to admire* LAURA.] I've got to fix myself now! You're going to be surprised by your mother's appearance!

[AMANDA *crosses through the portieres, humming gaily.* LAURA *moves slowly to the long mirror and stares solemnly at herself. A wind blows the white curtains inward in a slow, graceful motion and with a faint, sorrowful sighing.*]

AMANDA: [*from somewhere behind the portieres*] It isn't dark enough yet.

[LAURA *turns slowly before the mirror with a troubled look.*

Legend on screen: "This is my sister: Celebrate her with strings!" Music plays.]

AMANDA: [*laughing, still not visible*] I'm going to show you something. I'm going to make a spectacular appearance!

LAURA: What is it, Mother?

AMANDA: Possess your soul in patience—you will see! Something I've resurrected from that old trunk! Styles haven't changed so terribly much after all. . . . [*She parts the portieres.*] Now just look at your mother! [*She wears a girlish frock of yellowed voile with a blue silk sash. She carries a bunch of jonquils—the legend of her youth is nearly revived. Now she speaks feverishly:*] This is the dress in which I led the cotillion. Won the cakewalk twice at Sunset Hill, wore one Spring to the Governor's Ball in Jackson!° See how I sashayed around the ballroom, Laura? [*She raises her skirt and does a mincing step around the room.*] I wore it on Sundays for my gentlemen callers! I had it on the day I met your father. . . . I had malaria fever all that Spring. The change of climate from East Tennessee to the Delta—weakened resistance. I had a little temperature all the time—not enough to be serious—just enough to make me restless and giddy! Invitations poured in—parties all over the Delta! "Stay in bed," said Mother, "you have a fever!"—but I just wouldn't. I took quinine° but kept on going, going! Evenings, dances! Afternoons, long, long rides! Picnics—lovely! So lovely, that country in May—all lacy with dogwood, literally flooded with jonquils! That was the spring I had the craze for jonquils. Jonquils became an absolute obsession. Mother said, "Honey, there's no more room for jonquils." And still I kept on bringing in more jonquils. Whenever, wherever I saw them, I'd say, "Stop! Stop! I see jonquils!" I made the young men help me gather the jonquils! It was a joke, Amanda and her jonquils. Finally there were no more vases to hold them, every available space was filled with jonquils. No vases to hold them? All right, I'll hold them myself! And then I—[*She stops in front of the picture. Music plays.*] met your father! Malaria fever and jonquils and then—this—boy. . . . [*She switches on the rose-colored lamp.*] I hope they get here before it starts to rain. [*She crosses the room and places the jonquils in a bowl on the table.*] I gave your brother a little extra change so he and Mr. O'Connor could take the service car home.

20 LAURA: [*with an altered look*] What did you say his name was?

AMANDA: O'Connor.

LAURA: What is his first name?

AMANDA: I don't remember. Oh, yes, I do. It was—Jim.

[LAURA *sways slightly and catches hold of a chair.*

Legend on screen: "Not Jim!"]

°19 *Jackson:* capital of Mississippi. Amanda refers to the social events of her youth. A cotillion is a formal ball, often given for debutantes. The cakewalk is a strutting dance step. *quinine:* long used as a standard drug to control malaria.

LAURA: [*faintly*] Not—Jim!
AMANDA: Yes, that was it, it was Jim! I've never known a Jim that wasn't nice!   25

[*The music becomes ominous.*]

LAURA: Are you sure his name is Jim O'Connor?
AMANDA: Yes. Why?
LAURA: Is he the one that Tom used to know in high school?
AMANDA: He didn't say so. I think he just got to know him at the warehouse.
LAURA: There was a Jim O'Connor we both knew in high school—[*Then, with effort.*] If that   30
    is the one that Tom is bringing to dinner—you'll have to excuse me, I won't come to the
    table.
AMANDA: What sort of nonsense is this?
LAURA: You asked me once if I'd ever liked a boy. Don't you remember I showed you this
    boy's picture?
AMANDA: You mean the boy you showed me in the yearbook?
LAURA: Yes, that boy.
AMANDA: Laura, Laura, were you in love with that boy?   35
LAURA: I don't know, Mother. All I know is I couldn't sit at the table if it was him!
AMANDA: It won't be him! It isn't the least bit likely. But whether it is or not, you will come
    to the table. You will not be excused.
LAURA: I'll have to be, Mother.
AMANDA: I don't intend to humor your silliness, Laura. I've had too much from you and
    your brother, both! So just sit down and compose yourself till they come. Tom has for-
    gotten his key so you'll have to let them in, when they arrive.
LAURA: [*panicky*] Oh, Mother—*you* answer the door!   40
AMANDA: [*lightly*] I'll be in the kitchen—busy!
LAURA: Oh, Mother, please answer the door, don't make me do it!
AMANDA: [*crossing into the kitchenette*] I've got to fix the dressing for the salmon. Fuss,
    fuss—silliness!—over a gentleman caller!

[*The door swings shut, LAURA is left alone.*

Legend on screen: "Terror!"

*She utters a low moan and turns off the lamp—sits stiffly on the edge of the sofa, knotting her fingers
together.*

Legend on screen: "The Opening of a Door!"

*TOM and JIM appear on the fire escape steps and climb to the landing. Hearing their approach, LAURA
rises with a panicky gesture. She retreats to the portieres. The doorbell rings. LAURA catches her
breath and touches her throat. Low drums sound.*]

AMANDA: [*calling*] Laura, sweetheart! The door!

[*LAURA stares at it without moving.*]

JIM: I think we just beat the rain.   45
TOM: Uh-huh. [*He rings again, nervously. JIM whistles and fishes for a cigarette.*]
AMANDA: [*very, very gaily*] Laura, that is your brother and Mr. O'Connor! Will you let them
    in, darling?

[*LAURA crosses toward the kitchenette door.*]

LAURA: [*breathlessly*] Mother—you go to the door!

[AMANDA *steps out of the kitchenette and stares furiously at* LAURA. *She points imperiously at the door.*]

LAURA: Please, please!
50 AMANDA: [*in a fierce whisper*] What is the matter with you, you silly thing?
LAURA: [*desperately*] Please, you answer it, *please!*
AMANDA: I told you I wasn't going to humor you, Laura. Why have you chosen this moment to lose your mind?
LAURA: Please, please, please, you go!
AMANDA: You'll have to go to the door because I can't.
55 LAURA: [*despairingly*] I can't either!
AMANDA: *Why?*
LAURA: I'm *sick!*
AMANDA: I'm sick, too—of your nonsense! Why can't you and your brother be normal people? Fantastic whims and behavior!

[TOM *gives a long ring.*]

Preposterous goings on! Can you give me one reason—[*She calls out lyrically.*] *Coming!* Just one second!—why you should be afraid to open a door? Now you answer it, Laura!
LAURA: Oh, oh, oh . . . [*She returns through the portieres, darts to the Victrola, winds it frantically and turns it on.*]
60 AMANDA: Laura Wingfield, you march right to that door!
LAURA: *Yes—yes, Mother!*

[*A faraway, scratchy rendition of "Dardanella"*° *softens the air and gives her strength to move through it. She slips to the door and draws it cautiously open.* TOM *enters with the caller,* JIM O'CONNOR.]

TOM: Laura, this is Jim. Jim, this is my sister, Laura.
JIM: [*stepping inside*] I didn't know that Shakespeare had a sister!
LAURA: [*retreating, stiff and trembling, from the door*] How—how do you do?
65 JIM: [*heartily, extending his hand*] Okay!

[LAURA *touches it hesitantly with hers.*]

JIM: Your hand's *cold*, Laura!
LAURA: Yes, well—I've been playing the Victrola. . . .
JIM: Must have been playing classical music on it! You ought to play a little hot swing music to warm you up!
LAURA: Excuse me—I haven't finished playing the Victrola. . . . [*She turns awkwardly and hurries into the front room. She pauses a second by the Victrola. Then she catches her breath and darts through the portieres like a frightened deer.*]
70 JIM: [*grinning*] What was the matter?
TOM: Oh—with Laura? Laura is—terribly shy.
JIM: Shy, huh? It's unusual to meet a shy girl nowadays. I don't believe you ever mentioned you had a sister.
TOM: Well, now you know. I have one. Here is the *Post Dispatch*.° You want a piece of it?
JIM: Uh-huh.
TOM: What piece? The comics?

°61 S.D. *"Dardanella"*: a popular song and dance tune, copyright 1914, by Fred Fisher, Felix Bernard, and Johnny S. Black. 73 *Post Dispatch*: the *St. Louis Post Dispatch*, a newspaper.

JIM: Sports! [*He glances at it.*] Ole Dizzy Dean° is on his bad behavior.

TOM: [*uninterested*] Yeah? [*He lights a cigarette and goes over to the fire-escape door.*]

JIM: Where are *you* going?

TOM: I'm going out on the terrace.

JIM: [*going after him*] You know, Shakespeare—I'm going to sell you a bill of goods! 80

TOM: What goods?

JIM: A course I'm taking.

TOM: Huh?

JIM: In public speaking! You and me, we're not the warehouse type.

TOM: Thanks—that's good news. But what has public speaking got to do with it? 85

JIM: It fits you for—executive positions!

TOM: Awww.

JIM: I tell you it's done a helluva lot for me.

[*Image on screen: Executive at his desk.*]

TOM: In what respect?

JIM: In every! Ask yourself what is the difference between you an' me and men in the office 90
down front? Brains?—No!—Ability?—No! Then what? Just one little thing—

TOM: What is that one little thing?

JIM: Primarily it amounts to—social poise! Being able to square up to people and hold your
own on any social level!

AMANDA: [*from the kitchenette*] Tom?

TOM: Yes, Mother?

AMANDA: Is that you and Mr. O'Connor? 95

TOM: Yes, Mother.

AMANDA: Well, you just make yourselves comfortable in there.

TOM: Yes, Mother.

AMANDA: Ask Mr. O'Connor if he would like to wash his hands.

JIM: Aw, no—no—thank you—I took care of that at the warehouse. Tom— 100

TOM: Yes?

JIM: Mr. Mendoza was speaking to me about you.

TOM: Favorably?

JIM: What do you think?

TOM: Well— 105

JIM: You're going to be out of a job if you don't wake up.

TOM: I am waking up—

JIM: You show no signs.

TOM: The signs are interior.

[*Image on screen: The sailing vessel with the Jolly Roger again.*]

TOM: I'm planning to change. [*He leans over the fire escape rail, speaking with quiet exhilaration.* 110
The incandescent marquees and signs of the first-run movie houses light his face from across the
alley. He looks like a voyager.] I'm right at the point of committing myself to a future that
doesn't include the warehouse and Mr. Mendoza or even a night-school course in public speaking.

JIM: What are you gassing about?

TOM: I'm tired of the movies.

°76 *Dizzy Dean:* Jerome Herman (or Jay Hanna) Dean (1911–1974), outstanding pitcher with the St. Louis Car-
dinals during the 1930s.

JIM: Movies!

TOM: Yes, movies! Look at them—[*a wave toward the marvels of Grand Avenue*] All of those glamorous people—having adventures—hogging it all, gobbling the whole thing up! You know what happens? People go to the *movies* instead of *moving!* Hollywood characters are supposed to have all the adventures for everybody in America, while everybody in America sits in a dark room and watches them have them! Yes, until there's a war. That's when adventure becomes available to the masses! *Everyone's* dish, not only Gable's!° Then the people in the dark room come out of the dark room to have some adventures themselves—goody, goody! It's our turn now, to go to the South Sea Island—to make a safari—to be exotic, far-off! But I'm not patient. I don't want to wait till then. I'm tired of the *movies* and I am *about* to *move!*

115 JIM: [*incredulously*] Move?

TOM: Yes.

JIM: When?

TOM: Soon!

JIM: Where? Where?

[*The music seems to answer the question, while* TOM *thinks it over. He searches in his pockets.*]

120 TOM: I'm starting to boil inside. I know I seem dreamy, but inside—well, I'm boiling! Whenever I pick up a shoe, I shudder a little thinking how short life is and what I am doing! Whatever that means, I know it doesn't mean shoes—except as something to wear on a traveler's feet! [*He finds what he has been searching for in his pockets and holds out a paper to* JIM.] Look—

JIM: What?

TOM: I'm a member.

JIM: [*reading*] The Union of Merchant Seamen.

TOM: I paid my dues this month, instead of the light bill.

125 JIM: You will regret it when they turn off the lights.

TOM: I won't be here.

JIM: How about your mother?

TOM: I'm like my father. The bastard son of a bastard! Did you notice how he's grinning in his picture in there? And he's been absent going on sixteen years!

JIM: You're just talking, you drip. How does your mother feel about it?

130 TOM: Shhh! Here comes Mother! Mother is not acquainted with my plans!

AMANDA: [*coming through the portieres*] Where are you all?

TOM: On the terrace, Mother.

[*They start inside. She advances to them.* TOM *is distinctly shocked at her appearance. Even* JIM *blinks a little. He is making his first contact with the girlish Southern vivacity and in spite of the night-school course in public speaking is somewhat thrown off the beam by the unexpected outlay of social charm. Certain responses are attempted by* JIM *but are swept aside by* AMANDA's *gay laughter and chatter.* TOM *is embarrassed but after the first shock* JIM *reacts very warmly. He grins and chuckles, is altogether won over.*

Image on screen: AMANDA *as a girl.*]

AMANDA: [*coyly smiling, shaking her girlish ringlets*] Well, well, well, so this is Mr. O'Connor. Introductions entirely unnecessary. I've heard so much about you from my boy. I finally said

---

°114 *Gable:* Clark Gable (1901–1960), popular American screen actor and matinee idol from the 1930s to his death.

Amanda (Jessica Tandy) tries to charm the Gentleman Caller (John Heard) on behalf of her indifferent daughter Laura (Amanda Plummer) in the Eugene O'Neill Theater production of *The Glass Menagerie,* directed by John Dexter (1983–1984).

to him, Tom—good gracious!—why don't you bring this paragon to supper? I'd like to meet this nice young man at the warehouse!—instead of just hearing him sing your praises so much! I don't know why my son is so stand-offish—that's not Southern behavior!

Let's sit down and—I think we could stand a little more air in here! Tom, leave the door open. I felt a nice fresh breeze a moment ago. Where has it gone to? Mmm, so warm already! And not quite summer, even. We're going to burn up when summer really gets started. However, we're having—we're having a very light supper. I think light things are better fo' this time of year. The same as light clothes are. Light clothes an' light food are what warm weather calls fo'. You know our blood gets so thick during th' winter—it takes a while fo' us to *adjust* ourselves!—when the season changes. . . . It's come so quick this year. I wasn't prepared. All of sudden—heavens! Already summer! I ran to the trunk an' pulled out this light dress—terribly old! Historical almost! But feels so good—so good an' co-ol, y'know. . . .

TOM: Mother—

135 AMANDA: Yes, honey?

TOM: How about—supper?

AMANDA: Honey, you go ask Sister if supper is ready! You know that Sister is in full charge of supper! Tell her you hungry boys are waiting for it. [*To* JIM.] Have you met Laura?

JIM: She—

AMANDA: Let you in? Oh, good, you've met already! It's rare for a girl as sweet an' pretty as Laura to be domestic! But Laura is, thank heavens, not only pretty but also very domestic. I'm not at all. I never was a bit. I never could make a thing but angel-food cake. Well, in the South we had so many servants. Gone, gone, gone. All vestige of gracious living! Gone completely! I wasn't prepared for what the future brought me. All of my gentlemen callers were sons of planters and so of course I assumed that I would be married to one and raise my family on a large piece of land with plenty of servants. But man proposes—and woman accepts the proposal! to vary that old, old saying a little but—I married no planter! I married a man who worked for the telephone company! That gallantly smiling gentleman over there! [*She points to the picture.*] A telephone man who—fell in love with long-distance! Now he travels and I don't even know where! But what am I going on for about my—tribulations? Tell me yours—I hope you don't have any! Tom?

140 TOM: [*returning*] Yes, Mother?

AMANDA: Is supper nearly ready?

TOM: It looks to me like supper is on the table.

AMANDA: Let me look—[*She rises prettily and looks through the portieres.*] Oh lovely! But where is Sister?

TOM: Laura is not feeling well and she says that she thinks she'd better not come to the table.

145 AMANDA: What? Nonsense! Laura? Oh, Laura!

LAURA: [*from the kitchenette, faintly*] Yes, Mother.

AMANDA: You really must come to the table. We won't be seated until you come to the table! Come in, Mr. O'Connor. You sit over there and I'll. . . . Laura? Laura Wingfield! You're keeping us waiting, honey! We can't say grace until you come to the table!

[*The kitchenette door is pushed weakly open and* LAURA *comes in. She is obviously quite faint, her lips trembling, her eyes wide and staring. She moves unsteadily toward the table.*

Screen legend: "Terror!"

Outside a summer storm is coming on abruptly. The white curtains billow inward at the windows and there is a sorrowful murmur from the deep blue dusk.

LAURA *suddenly stumbles; she catches at a chair with a faint moan.*]

TOM: Laura!

AMANDA: Laura!

[*There is a clap of thunder.*

Screen legend: "Ah!"]

[*despairingly*] Why, Laura, you are ill, darling! Tom, help your sister into the living room, dear! Sit in the living room, Laura—rest on the sofa. Well! [*To* JIM *as* TOM *helps his sister to the sofa in the living room.*] Standing over the hot stove made her ill! I told her that it was just too warm this evening, but—

[*TOM comes back to the table.*]

Is Laura all right now?

TOM: Yes. 150

AMANDA: What is that? Rain? A nice cool rain has come up! [*She gives* JIM *a frightened look.*] I think we may—have grace—now . . . [*TOM looks at her stupidly.*] Tom, honey—you say grace!

TOM: Oh . . . "For these and all thy mercies—"

[*They bow their heads,* AMANDA *stealing a nervous glance at* JIM. *In the living room* LAURA, *stretched on the sofa, clenches her hand to her lips, to hold back a shuddering sob.*]

God's Holy Name be praised—

[*The scene dims out.*]

SCENE 7

[*It is half an hour later. Dinner is just being finished in the dining room,* LAURA *is still huddled upon the sofa, her feet drawn under her, her head resting on a pale blue pillow, her eyes wide and mysteriously watchful. The new floor lamp with its shade of rose-colored silk gives a soft, becoming light to her face, bringing out the fragile, unearthly prettiness which usually escapes attention. From outside there is a steady murmur of rain, but it is slackening and soon stops; the air outside becomes pale and luminous as the moon breaks through the clouds. A moment after the curtain rises, the lights in both rooms flicker and go out.*]

JIM: Hey, there, Mr. Light Bulb!

[AMANDA *laughs nervously.*

Legend on screen: "Suspension of a public service."]

AMANDA: Where was Moses when the lights went out? Ha-ha. Do you know the answer to that one, Mr. O'Connor?

JIM: No, Ma'am, what's the answer?

AMANDA: In the dark!

[JIM *laughs appreciatively.*]

Everybody sit still. I'll light the candles. Isn't it lucky we have them on the table? Where's a match? Which of you gentlemen can provide a match?

JIM: Here. 5

AMANDA: Thank you, Sir.

JIM: Not at all, Ma'am!

AMANDA: [*as she lights the candles*] I guess the fuse has burnt out. Mr. O'Connor, can you tell a burnt-out fuse? I know I can't and Tom is a total loss when it comes to mechanics. [*They rise from the table and go into the kitchenette, from where their voices are heard.*] Oh, be careful you don't bump into something. We don't want our gentleman caller to break his neck. Now wouldn't that be a fine howdy-do?

JIM: Ha-ha! Where is the fuse-box?

AMANDA: Right here next to the stove. Can you see anything? 10

JIM: Just a minute.

AMANDA: Isn't electricity a mysterious thing? Wasn't it Benjamin Franklin who tied a key to a kite? We live in such a mysterious universe, don't we? Some people say that science clears up all the mysteries for us. In my opinion it only creates more! Have you found it yet?

JIM: No, Ma'am. All these fuses look okay to me.

AMANDA: Tom!

TOM: Yes, Mother? 15

AMANDA: That light bill I gave you several days ago. That one I told you we got the notices about?

[*Legend on screen: "Ha!"*]

TOM: Oh—yeah.

AMANDA: You didn't neglect to pay it by any chance?

TOM: Why, I—

20   AMANDA: Didn't! I might have known it!

JIM: Shakespeare probably wrote a poem on that light bill, Mrs. Wingfield.

AMANDA: I might have known better than to trust him with it! There's such a high price for negligence in this world!

JIM: Maybe the poem will win a ten-dollar prize.

AMANDA: We'll just have to spend the remainder of the evening in the nineteenth century, before Mr. Edison made the Mazda lamp!°

25   JIM: Candlelight is my favorite kind of light.

AMANDA: That shows you're romantic! But that's no excuse for Tom. Well, we got through dinner. Very considerate of them to let us get through dinner before they plunged us into everlasting darkness, wasn't it, Mr. O'Connor?

JIM: Ha-ha!

AMANDA: Tom, as a penalty for your carelessness you can help me with the dishes.

JIM: Let me give you a hand.

30   AMANDA: Indeed you will not!

JIM: I ought to be good for something.

AMANDA: Good for something? [*Her tone is rhapsodic.*] You? Why, Mr. O'Connor, nobody, *nobody's* given me this much entertainment in years—as you have!

JIM: Aw, now, Mrs. Wingfield!

AMANDA: I'm not exaggerating, not one bit! But Sister is all by her lonesome. You go keep her company in the parlor! I'll give you this lovely old candelabrum that used to be on the altar at the Church of the Heavenly Rest. It was melted a little out of shape when the church burnt down. Lightning struck it one spring. Gypsy Jones was holding a revival at the time and he intimated that the church was destroyed because the Episcopalians gave card parties.

35   JIM: Ha-ha.

AMANDA: And how about you coaxing Sister to drink a little wine? I think it would be good for her! Can you carry both at once?

JIM: Sure. I'm Superman!

AMANDA: Now, Thomas, get into this apron!

[*JIM comes into the dining room, carrying the candelabrum, its candles lighted, in one hand and a glass of wine in the other. The door of the kitchenette swings closed on AMANDA's gay laughter; the flickering light approaches the portieres. LAURA sits up nervously as JIM enters. She can hardly speak from the almost intolerable strain of being alone with a stranger.*]

Screen legend: "I don't suppose you remember me at all!"

[*At first, before JIM's warmth overcomes her paralyzing shyness, LAURA's voice is thin and breathless, as though she had just run up a steep flight of stairs. JIM's attitude is gently humorous. While the incident is apparently unimportant, it is to LAURA the climax of her secret life.*]

JIM: Hello there, Laura.

°24 *Mazda lamp:* Thomas A. Edison (1847–1931) developed the first practical incandescent lamp in 1879.

LAURA: [*faintly*] Hello.   40

[*She clears her throat.*]

JIM: How are you feeling now? Better?
LAURA: Yes. Yes, thank you.
JIM: This is for you. A little dandelion wine. [*He extends the glass toward her with extravagant gallantry.*]
LAURA: Thank you.   45
JIM: Drink it—but don't get drunk!

[*He laughs heartily.* LAURA *takes the glass uncertainly; she laughs shyly.*]

Where shall I set the candles?
LAURA: Oh—oh, anywhere . . .
JIM: How about here on the floor? Any objections?
LAURA: No.
JIM: I'll spread a newspaper under to catch the drippings. I like to sit on the floor. Mind if I do?
LAURA: Oh, no.   50
JIM: Give me a pillow?
LAURA: What?
JIM: A pillow!
LAURA: Oh . . . [*She hands him one quickly.*]
JIM: How about you? Don't you like to sit on the floor?   55
LAURA: Oh—yes.
JIM: Why don't you, then?
LAURA: I—will.
JIM: Take a pillow!

[*Laura does. She sits on the floor on the other side of the candelabrum.* JIM *crosses his legs and smiles engagingly at her.*]

I can't hardly see you sitting way over there.
LAURA: I can—see you.   60
JIM: I know, but that's not fair, I'm in the limelight.

[LAURA *moves her pillow closer.*]

Good! Now I can see you! Comfortable?
LAURA: Yes.
JIM: So am I. Comfortable as a cow! Will you have some gum?
LAURA: No, thank you.
JIM: I think that I will indulge, with your permission. [*He musingly unwraps a stick of gum and*   65
holds it up.] Think of the fortune made by the guy that invented the first piece of chewing gum. Amazing, huh? The Wrigley Building° is one of the sights of Chicago—I saw it when I went up to the Century of Progress.° Did you take in the Century of Progress?
LAURA: No, I didn't.
JIM: Well, it was quite a wonderful exposition. What impressed me most was the Hall of Science. Gives you an idea of what the future will be in America, even more wonderful than the present time is! [*There is a pause.* JIM *smiles at her.*] Your brother tells me you're shy. Is that right—Laura?

°65 *Wrigley Building:* Finished in 1924, this was one of the first skyscrapers in the United States. *Century of Progress:* a world's fair held in Chicago (1933–1934) to celebrate the city's centennial.

LAURA: I—don't know.

JIM: I judge you to be an old-fashioned type of girl. Well, I think that's a pretty good type to be. Hope you don't think I'm being too personal—do you?

70 LAURA: [*Hastily, out of embarrassment*] I believe I *will* take a piece of gum, if you—don't mind. [*clearing her throat*] Mr. O'Connor, have you—kept up with your singing?

JIM: Singing? Me?

LAURA: Yes. I remember what a beautiful voice you had.

JIM: When did you hear me sing?

[*LAURA does not answer, and in the long pause which follows a man's voice is heard singing off-stage.*]

VOICE:

> O blow, ye winds, heigh-ho,
> A-roving I will go!
> I'm off to my love
> With a boxing glove—
> Ten thousand miles away!°

75 JIM: You say you've heard me sing?

LAURA: Oh, Yes! Yes, very often . . . I—don't suppose—you remember me—at all?

JIM: [*smiling doubtfully*] You know I have an idea I've seen you before. I had that idea soon as you opened the door. It seemed almost like I was about to remember your name. But the name that I started to call you—wasn't a name! And so I stopped myself before I said it.

LAURA: Wasn't it—Blue Roses?

JIM: [*springing up, grinning*] Blue Roses! My gosh, yes—Blue Roses! That's what I had on my tongue when you opened the door! Isn't it funny what tricks your memory plays? I didn't connect you with high school somehow or other. But that's where it was; it was high school. I didn't even know you were Shakespeare's sister! Gosh, I'm sorry.

80 LAURA: I didn't expect you to. You—barely knew me!

JIM: But we did have a speaking acquaintance, huh?

LAURA: Yes, we—spoke to each other.

JIM: When did you recognize me?

LAURA: Oh, right away!

85 JIM: Soon as I came in the door?

LAURA: When I heard your name I thought it was probably you. I knew that Tom used to know you a little in high school. So when you came in the door—well, then I was—sure.

JIM: Why didn't you *say* something, then?

LAURA: [*breathlessly*] I didn't know what to say, I was—too surprised!

JIM: For goodness' sakes! You know, this sure is funny!

90 LAURA: Yes! Yes, isn't it, though . . .

JIM: Didn't we have a class in something together?

LAURA: Yes, we did.

JIM: What class was that?

LAURA: It was—singing—chorus!

95 JIM: Aw!

LAURA: I sat across the aisle from you in the Aud.

JIM: Aw!

°74 *O blow* . . . : This is a simplified version of the refrain of "A Capital Ship" (1885), a song that Charles E. Carryl (1841–1920) wrote for the music of the early-nineteenth-century Irish sea shanty "Ten Thousand Miles Away."

LAURA: Mondays, Wednesdays, and Fridays.

JIM: Now I remember—you always came in late.

LAURA: Yes, it was so hard for me, getting upstairs. I had that brace on my leg—it clumped   100
so loud!

JIM: I never heard any clumping.

LAURA: [*wincing at the recollection*] To me it sounded like—thunder!

JIM: Well, well, well, I never even noticed.

LAURA: And everybody was seated before I came in. I had to walk in front of all those people. My seat was in the back row. I had to go clumping all the way up the aisle with
everyone watching!

JIM: You shouldn't have been self-conscious.   105

LAURA: I know, but I was. It was always such a relief when the singing started.

JIM: Aw, yes, I've placed you now! I used to call you Blue Roses. How was it that I got started calling you that?

LAURA: I was out of school a little while with pleurosis. When I came back you asked me
what was the matter. I said I had pleurosis—you thought that I said *Blue Roses*. That's
what you always called me after that!

JIM: I hope you didn't mind.

LAURA: Oh, no—I liked it. You see, I wasn't acquainted with many—people. . . .   110

JIM: As I remember you sort of stuck by yourself.

LAURA: I—I—never have had much luck at—making friends.

JIM: I don't see why you wouldn't.

LAURA: Well, I—started out badly.

JIM: You mean being—   115

LAURA: Yes, it sort of—stood between me—

JIM: You shouldn't have let it!

LAURA: I know, but it did, and—

JIM: You were shy with people!

LAURA: I tried not to be but never could—   120

JIM: Overcome it?

LAURA: No, I—I never could!

JIM: I guess being shy is something you have to work out of kind of gradually.

LAURA: [*sorrowfully*] Yes—I guess it—

JIM: Takes time!   125

LAURA: Yes—

JIM: People are not so dreadful when you know them. That's what you have to remember!
And everybody has problems, not just you, but practically everybody has got some
problems. You think of yourself as having the only problems, as being the only one
who is disappointed. But just look around you and you will see lots of people as disappointed as you are. For instance, I hoped when I was going to high school that I would
be further along at this time, six years later, than I am now. You remember that wonderful write-up I had in *The Torch*?

LAURA: Yes! [*She rises and crosses to the table.*]

JIM: It said I was bound to succeed in anything I went into!

[*LAURA returns with the high school yearbook.*]

Holy Jeez! *The Torch*!

[*He accepts it reverently. They smile across the book with mutual wonder. LAURA crouches beside
him and they begin to turn the pages. LAURA's shyness is dissolving in his warmth.*]

LAURA: Here you are in *The Pirates of Penzance*!   130

JIM: [*wistfully*] I sang the baritone lead in that operetta.

LAURA: [*raptly*] So—*beautifully!*

JIM: [*protesting*] Aw—

LAURA: Yes, yes—beautifully—beautifully!

135 JIM: You heard me?

LAURA: All three times!

JIM: No!

LAURA: Yes!

JIM: All three performances?

140 LAURA: [*looking down*] Yes.

JIM: Why?

LAURA: I—wanted to ask you to—autograph my program. [*She takes the program from the back of the yearbook and shows it to him.*]

JIM: Why didn't you ask me to?

LAURA: You were always surrounded by your own friends so much that I never had a chance to.

145 JIM: You should have just—

LAURA: Well, I—thought you might think I was—

JIM: Thought I might think you was—what?

LAURA: Oh—

JIM: [*with reflective relish*] I was beleaguered by females in those days.

150 LAURA: You were terribly popular!

JIM: Yeah—

LAURA: You had such a—friendly way—

JIM: I was spoiled in high school.

LAURA: Everybody—liked you!

155 JIM: Including you?

LAURA: I—yes, I—did, too—[*She gently closes the book in her lap.*]

JIM: Well, well, well! Give me that program, Laura.

[*She hands it to him. He signs it with a flourish.*]

There you are—better late than never!

LAURA: Oh, I—what a—surprise!

JIM: My signature isn't worth very much right now. But some day—maybe—it will increase in value! Being disappointed is one thing and being discouraged is something else. I am disappointed but I am not discouraged. I'm twenty-three years old. How old are you?

160 LAURA: I'll be twenty-four in June.

JIM: That's not old age!

LAURA: No, but—

JIM: You finished high school?

LAURA: [*with difficulty*] I didn't go back.

165 JIM: You mean you dropped out?

LAURA: I made bad grades in my final examinations. [*She rises and replaces the book and the program on the table. Her voice is strained.*] How is—Emily Meisenbach getting along?

JIM: Oh, that kraut-head!

LAURA: Why do you call her that?

JIM: That's what she was.

170 LAURA: You're not still—going with her?

JIM: I never see her.

LAURA: It was in the "Personal" section that you were—engaged!

JIM: I know, but I wasn't impressed by that—propaganda!
LAURA: It wasn't—the truth?
JIM: Only in Emily's optimistic opinion!   175
LAURA: Oh—

[*Legend: "What have you done since high school?"*]

JIM lights a cigarette and leans indolently back on his elbows smiling at LAURA with a warmth and charm which lights her inwardly with altar candles. She remains by the table, picks up a piece from the glass menagerie collection, and turns it in her hands to cover her tumult.]

JIM: [*after several reflective puffs on his cigarette*] What have you done since high school?

[*She seems not to hear him.*]

   Huh?

[*LAURA looks up.*]

   I said what have you done since high school, Laura?
LAURA: Nothing much.
JIM: You must have been doing something these six long years.
LAURA: Yes.   180
JIM: Well, then, such as what?
LAURA: I took a business course at business college—
JIM: How did that work out?
LAURA: Well, not very—well—I had to drop out, it gave me—indigestion—

[*JIM laughs gently.*]

JIM: What are you doing now?   185
LAURA: I don't do anything—much. Oh, please don't think I sit around doing nothing! My glass collection takes up a good deal of time. Glass is something you have to take good care of.
JIM: What did you say—about glass?
LAURA: Collection I said—I have one—[*She clears her throat and turns away again, acutely shy.*]
JIM: [*abruptly*] You know what I judge to be the trouble with you? Inferiority complex! Know what that is? That's what they call it when someone low-rates himself! I understand it because I had it too. Although my case was not so aggravated as yours seems to be. I had it until I took up public speaking, developed my voice, and learned that I had an aptitude for science. Before that time I never thought of myself as being outstanding in any way whatsoever! Now I've never made a regular study of it, but I have a friend who says I can analyze people better than doctors that make a profession of it. I don't claim that to be necessarily true, but I can sure guess a person's psychology. Laura! [*He takes out his gum.*] Excuse me, Laura. I always take it out when the flavor is gone. I'll use this scrap of paper to wrap it in. I know how it is to get it stuck on a shoe. [*He wraps the gum in paper and puts it in his pocket.*] Yep—that's what I judge to be your principal trouble. A lack of confidence in yourself as a person. You don't have the proper amount of faith in yourself. I'm basing that fact on a number of your remarks and also on certain observations I've made. For instance that clumping you thought was so awful in high school. You say that you even dreaded to walk into class. You see what you did? You dropped out of school, you gave up an education because of a clump, which as far as I know was practically nonexistent! A little physical defect is what you have. Hardly noticeable even! Magnified thousands of times by imagination! You know what my strong advice to you is? Think of yourself as *superior* in some way!

190 **LAURA:** In what way would I think?

JIM: Why, man alive, Laura! Just look about you a little. What do you see? A world full of common people! All of 'em born and all of 'em going to die! Which of them has one-tenth of your good points! Or mine! Or anyone else's, as far as that goes—gosh! Everybody excels in some one thing. Some in many! [*He unconsciously glances at himself in the mirror.*] All you've got to do is discover in *what!* Take me, for instance. [*He adjusts his tie at the mirror.*] My interest happens to lie in electro-dynamics. I'm taking a course in radio engineering at night school, Laura, on top of a fairly responsible job at the warehouse. I'm taking that course and studying public speaking.

LAURA: Ohhhh.

JIM: Because I believe in the future of television! [*turning his back to her*] I wish to be ready to go up right along with it. Therefore I'm planning to get in on the ground floor. In fact I've already made the right connections and all that remains is for the industry itself to get under way! Full steam—[*His eyes are starry.*] *Knowledge*—Zzzzzp! *Money*—Zzzzzp!—Power! That's the cycle democracy is built on!

[*His attitude is convincingly dynamic. LAURA stares at him, even her shyness eclipsed in her absolute wonder. He suddenly grins.*]

I guess you think I think a lot of myself!

LAURA: No—o-o-o, I—

195 **JIM:** Now how about you? Isn't there something you take more interest in than anything else?

LAURA: Well, I do—as I said—have my—glass collection—

[*A peal of girlish laughter rings from the kitchenette.*]

JIM: I'm not right sure I know what you're talking about. What kind of glass is it?

LAURA: Little articles of it, they're ornaments mostly! Most of them are little animals made out of glass, the tiniest little animals in the world. Mother calls them a glass menagerie! Here's an example of one, if you'd like to see it! This one is one of the oldest. It's nearly thirteen.

[*Music: "The Glass Menagerie." He stretches out his hand.*]

Oh, be careful—if you breathe, it breaks!

JIM: I'd better not take it. I'm pretty clumsy with things.

200 **LAURA:** Go, on, I trust you with him! [*She places the piece in his palm.*] There now—you're holding him gently! Hold him over the light, he loves the light! You see how the light shines through him?

JIM: It sure does shine!

LAURA: I shouldn't be partial, but he is my favorite one.

JIM: What kind of a thing is this one supposed to be?

LAURA: Haven't you noticed the single horn on his forehead?

205 **JIM:** A unicorn, huh?

LAURA: Mmmm-hmmm!

JIM: Unicorns—aren't they extinct in the modern world?

LAURA: I know!

JIM: Poor little fellow, he must feel sort of lonesome.

210 **LAURA:** [*smiling*] Well, if he does, he doesn't complain about it. He stays on a shelf with some horses that don't have horns and all of them seem to get along nicely together.

JIM: How do you know?

LAURA: [*lightly*] I haven't heard any arguments among them!

JIM: [*grinning*] No arguments, huh? Well, that's a pretty good sign! Where shall I set him?

LAURA: Put him on the table. They all like a change of scenery once in a while!

JIM: Well, well, well, well—[*He places the glass piece on the table, then raises his arms and stretches.*] Look how big my shadow is when I stretch!   215

LAURA: Oh, oh, yes—it stretches across the ceiling!

JIM: [*crossing to the door*] I think it's stopped raining. [*He opens the fire-escape door and the background music changes to a dance tune.*] Where does the music come from?

LAURA: From the Paradise Dance Hall across the alley.

JIM: How about cutting the rug a little, Miss Wingfield?

LAURA: Oh, I—   220

JIM: Or is your program filled up? Let me have a look at it. [*He grasps an imaginary card.*] Why, every dance is taken! I'll just have to scratch some out.

[*Waltz music: "La Golondrina"°*]

Ahh, a waltz! [*He executes some sweeping turns by himself, then holds his arms toward* LAURA.]

LAURA: [*breathlessly*] I—can't dance.

JIM: There you go, that inferiority stuff!

LAURA: I've never danced in my life!

JIM: Come on, try!   225

LAURA: Oh, but I'd step on you!

JIM: I'm not made out of glass.

LAURA: How—how—how do we start?

JIM: Just leave it to me. You hold your arms out a little.

LAURA: Like this?   230

JIM: [*taking her in his arms*] A little bit higher. Right. Now don't tighten up, that's the main thing about it—relax.

LAURA: [*laughing breathlessly*] It's hard not to.

JIM: Okay.

LAURA: I'm afraid you can't budge me.

JIM: What do you bet I can't? [*He swings her into motion.*]   235

LAURA: Goodness, yes, you can!

JIM: Let yourself go, now, Laura, just let yourself go.

LAURA: I'm—

JIM: Come on!

LAURA: —trying!   240

JIM: Not so stiff—easy does it!

LAURA: I know but I'm—

JIM: Loosen th' backbone! There now, that's a lot better.

LAURA: Am I?

JIM: Lots, lots better! [*He moves her about the room in a clumsy waltz.*]   245

LAURA: Oh, my!

JIM: Ha-ha!

LAURA: Oh, my goodness!

JIM: Ha-ha-ha!

[*They suddenly bump into the table, and the glass piece on it falls to the floor. Jim stops the dance.*]

°221 S. D. "*La Golondrina*": a popular Mexican song (1883) written by Narciso Serradel Sevilla (1843–1910). It is not a waltz.

What did we hit?

250 LAURA: Table.

JIM: Did something fall off it? I think—

LAURA: Yes.

JIM: I hope that it wasn't the little glass horse with the horn!

LAURA: Yes. [*She stoops to pick it up.*]

255 JIM: Aw, aw, aw. Is it broken?

LAURA: Now it is just like all the other horses.

JIM: It's lost its—

LAURA: Horn! It doesn't matter. Maybe it's a blessing in disguise.

JIM: You'll never forgive me. I bet that that was your favorite piece of glass.

260 LAURA: I don't have favorites much. It's no tragedy, Freckles. Glass breaks so easily. No matter how careful you are. The traffic jars the shelves and things fall off them.

JIM: Still I'm awfully sorry that I was the cause.

LAURA: [*smiling*] I'll just imagine he had an operation. The horn was removed to make him feel less—freakish!

[*They both laugh.*]

Now he will feel more at home with the other horses, the ones that don't have horns. . . .

JIM: Ha-ha, that's very funny! [*Suddenly he is serious.*] I'm glad to see that you have a sense of humor. You know—you're—well—very different! Surprisingly different from anyone else I know! [*His voice becomes soft and hesitant with a genuine feeling.*] Do you mind me telling you that?

[*LAURA is abashed beyond speech.*]

I mean it in a nice way—

[*LAURA nods shyly, looking away.*]

You make me feel sort of—I don't know how to put it! I'm usually pretty good at expressing things, but—this is something that I don't know how to say!

[*LAURA touches her throat and clears it—turns the broken unicorn in her hands. His voice becomes softer.*]

Has anyone ever told you that you were pretty?

[*There is a pause, and the music rises slightly. LAURA looks up slowly, with wonder, and shakes her head.*]

Well, you are! In a very different way from anyone else. And all the nicer because of the difference, too.

[*His voice becomes low and husky. LAURA turns away, nearly faint with the novelty of her emotions.*]

I wish that you were my sister. I'd teach you to have some confidence in yourself. The different people are not like other people, but being different is nothing to be ashamed of. Because other people are not such wonderful people. They're one hundred times one thousand. You're one times one! They walk all over the earth. You just stay here. They're common as—weeds, but—you—well, you're—*Blue Roses*!

[*Image on screen: Blue Roses. The music changes.*]

LAURA: But blue is wrong for—roses. . . .

265 JIM: It's right for you! You're—pretty!

LAURA: In what respect am I pretty?

JIM: In all respects—believe me! Your eyes—your hair—are pretty! Your hands are pretty! [*He catches hold of her hand.*] You think I'm making this up because I'm invited to dinner and have to be nice. Oh, I could do that! I could put on an act for you, Laura, and say lots of things without being very sincere. But this time I am. I'm talking to you sincerely. I happened to notice you had this inferiority complex that keeps you from feeling comfortable with people. Somebody needs to build your confidence up and make you proud instead of shy and turning away and—blushing. Somebody—ought to—*kiss* you, Laura!

[*His hand slips slowly up her arm to her shoulder as the music swells tumultuously. He suddenly turns about and kisses her on the lips. When he releases her, LAURA sinks on the sofa with a bright, dazed look. Jim backs away and fishes in his pocket for a cigarette.*

Legend on screen: "A souvenir."]

Stumblejohn!

[*He lights the cigarette, avoiding her look. There is a peal of girlish laughter from AMANDA in the kitchenette. LAURA slowly raises and opens her hand. It still contains the little broken glass animal. She looks at it with a tender, bewildered expression.*]

Stumblejohn! I shouldn't have done that—that was way off the beam. You don't smoke, do you?

[*She looks up, smiling, not hearing the question. He sits beside her rather gingerly. She looks at him speechlessly—waiting. He coughs decorously and moves a little further aside as he considers the situation and senses her feelings, dimly, with perturbation. He speaks gently.*]

Would you—care for a mint?

[*She doesn't seem to hear him but her look grows brighter even.*]

Peppermint? Life Saver? My pocket's a regular drugstore—wherever I go. . . . [*He pops a mint in his mouth. Then he gulps and decides to make a clean breast of it. He speaks slowly and gingerly.*] Laura, you know, if I had a sister like you, I'd do the same thing as Tom. I'd bring out fellows and—introduce her to them. The right type of boys—of a type to—appreciate her. Only—well—he made a mistake about me. Maybe I've got no call to be saying this. That may not have been the idea in having me over. But what if it was? There's nothing wrong about that. The only trouble is that in my case—I'm not in a situation to—do the right thing. I can't take down your number and say I'll phone. I can't call up next week and—ask for a date. I thought I had better explain the situation in case you—misunderstood it and—I hurt your feelings. . . .

[*There is a pause. Slowly, very slowly, LAURA's look changes, her eyes returning slowly from his to the glass figure in her palm. AMANDA utters another gay laugh in the kitchenette.*]

LAURA: [*faintly*] You—won't—call again?

JIM: No, Laura, I can't. [*He rises from the sofa.*] As I was just explaining, I've—got strings on me, Laura, I've—been going steady! I go out all the time with a girl named Betty. She's a home-girl like you, and Catholic, and Irish, and in a great many ways we—get along fine. I met her last summer on a moonlight boat trip up the river to Alton,° on the *Majestic*. Well—right away from the start it was—love!

°269.1 *Alton*: a city in Illinois about twenty miles north of St. Louis on the Mississippi River.

[*Legend: Love!*

LAURA *sways slightly forward and grips the arm of the sofa. He fails to notice, now enrapt in his own comfortable being.*]

Being in love has made a new man of me!

[*Leaning stiffly forward, clutching the arm of the sofa,* LAURA *struggles visibly with her storm. But* JIM *is oblivious; she is a long way off.*]

The power of love is really pretty tremendous! Love is something that—changes the whole world, Laura!

[*The storm abates a little and* LAURA *leans back. He notices her again.*]

It happened that Betty's aunt took sick, she got a wire and had to go to Centralia.° So Tom—when he asked me to dinner—I naturally just accepted the invitation, not knowing that you—that he—that I—[*He stops awkwardly.*] Huh—I'm a stumblejohn!

[*He flops back on the sofa. The holy candles on the altar of* LAURA's *face have been snuffed out. There is a look of almost infinite desolation.* JIM *glances at her uneasily.*]

I wish that you would—say something.

[*She bites her lip which was trembling and then bravely smiles. She opens her hand again on the broken glass figure. Then she gently takes his hand and raises it level with her own. She carefully places the unicorn in the palm of his hand, then pushes his fingers closed upon it.*]

What are you—doing that for? You want me to have him? Laura?

[*She nods.*]

What for?

270 **LAURA:** A—souvenir. . . .

[*She rises unsteadily and crouches beside the Victrola to wind it up.*

Legend on screen: "Things have a way of turning out so badly!" Or image: "Gentleman caller waving goodbye—gaily."

At this moment AMANDA *rushes brightly back into the living room. She bears a pitcher of fruit punch in an old-fashioned cut-glass pitcher, and a plate of macaroons. The plate has a gold border and poppies painted on it.*]

AMANDA: Well, well, well! Isn't the air delightful after the shower? I've made you children a little liquid refreshment. [*She turns gaily to* JIM.] Jim, do you know that song about lemonade?

> "Lemonade, lemonade
> Made in the shade and stirred with a spade—
> Good enough for any old maid!"

JIM: [*uneasily*] Ha-ha! No—I never heard it.
AMANDA: Why, Laura! You look so serious!
JIM: We were having a serious conversation.
275 **AMANDA:** Good! Now you're better acquainted!
JIM: [*uncertainly*] Ha-ha! Yes.

°269.8 *Centralia:* a city in Illinois about sixty miles east of St. Louis.

AMANDA: You modern young people are much more serious-minded than my generation. I was so gay as a girl!

JIM: You haven't changed, Mrs. Wingfield.

AMANDA: Tonight I'm rejuvenated! The gaiety of the occasion, Mr. O'Connor! [*She tosses her head with a peal of laughter, spilling some lemonade.*] Oooo! I'm baptizing myself!

JIM: Here—let me—   280

AMANDA: [*setting the pitcher down*] There now. I discovered we had some maraschino cherries. I dumped them in, juice and all!

JIM: You shouldn't have gone to that trouble, Mrs. Wingfield.

AMANDA: Trouble, trouble? Why, it was loads of fun! Didn't you hear me cutting up in the kitchen? I bet your ears were burning! I told Tom how outdone with him I was for keeping you to himself so long a time! He should have brought you over much, much sooner! Well, now that you've found your way, I want you to be a very frequent caller! Not just occasional but all the time. Oh, we're going to have a lot of gay times together! I see them coming! Mmm, just breathe that air! So fresh, and the moon's so pretty! I'll skip back out—I know where my place is when young folks are having a—serious conversation!

JIM: Oh, don't go out, Mrs. Wingfield. The fact of the matter is I've got to be going.

AMANDA: Going, now? You're joking! Why, it's only the shank of the evening,° Mr.   285 O'Connor!

JIM: Well, you know how it is.

AMANDA: You mean you're a young workingman and have to keep workingmen's hours. We'll let you off early tonight. But only on the condition that next time you stay later. What's the best night for you? Isn't Saturday night the best night for you workingmen?

JIM: I have a couple of time-clocks to punch, Mrs. Wingfield. One at morning, another one at night!

AMANDA: My, but you *are* ambitious! You work at night, too?

JIM: No, Ma'am, not work but—Betty!   290

[*He crosses deliberately to pick up his hat. The band at the Paradise Dance Hall goes into a tender waltz.*]

AMANDA: Betty? Betty? Who's—Betty!

[*There is an ominous cracking sound in the sky.*]

JIM: Oh, just a girl. The girl I go steady with!

[*He smiles charmingly. The sky falls.*

Legend: "The Sky Falls."]

AMANDA: [*a long-drawn exhalation*] Ohhh . . . Is it a serious romance, Mr. O'Connor?

JIM: We're going to be married the second Sunday in June.

AMANDA: Ohhh—how nice! Tom didn't mention that you were engaged to be   295 married.

JIM: The cat's not out of the bag at the warehouse yet. You know how they are. They call you Romeo and stuff like that. [*He stops at the oval mirror to put on his hat. He carefully shapes the brim and the crown to give a discreetly dashing effect.*] It's been a wonderful evening, Mrs. Wingfield. I guess this is what they mean by Southern hospitality.

AMANDA: It really wasn't anything at all.

°285 *shank of the evening:* still early, the best part of the evening.

JIM: I hope it don't seem like I'm rushing off. But I promised Betty I'd pick her up at the Wabash depot, an' by the time I get my jalopy down there her train'll be in. Some women are pretty upset if you keep 'em waiting.

AMANDA: Yes, I know—the tyranny of women! [*She extends her hand.*] Goodbye, Mr. O' Connor. I wish you luck—and happiness—and success! All three of them, and so does Laura! Don't you, Laura?

300 LAURA: Yes!

JIM: [*taking LAURA's hand*] Goodbye, Laura. I'm certainly going to treasure that souvenir. And don't you forget the good advice I gave you. [*He raises his voice to a cheery shout.*] So long, Shakespeare! Thanks again, ladies. Good night!

[*He grins and ducks jauntily out. Still bravely grimacing, Amanda closes the door on the gentleman caller. Then she turns back to the room with a puzzled expression. She and LAURA don't dare to face each other. LAURA crouches beside the Victrola to wind it.*]

AMANDA: [*faintly*] Things have a way of turning out so badly. I don't believe that I would play the Victrola. Well, well—well! Our gentleman caller was engaged to be married? [*She raises her voice.*] Tom!

TOM: [*from the kitchenette*] Yes, Mother?

AMANDA: Come in here a minute. I want to tell you something awfully funny.

305 TOM: [*entering with a macaroon and a glass of the lemonade*] Has the gentleman caller gotten away already?

AMANDA: The gentleman caller has made an early departure. What a wonderful joke you played on us!

TOM: How do you mean?

AMANDA: You didn't mention that he was engaged to be married.

TOM: Jim? Engaged?

310 AMANDA: That's what he just informed us.

TOM: I'll be jiggered! I didn't know about that.

AMANDA: That seems very peculiar.

TOM: What's peculiar about it?

AMANDA: Didn't you call him your best friend down at the warehouse?

315 TOM: He is, but how did I know?

AMANDA: It seems extremely peculiar that you wouldn't know your best friend was going to be married!

TOM: The warehouse is where I work, not where I know things about people!

AMANDA: You don't know things anywhere! You live in a dream; you manufacture illusions!

[*He crosses to the door.*]

Where are you going?

TOM: I'm going to the movies.

320 AMANDA: That's right, now that you've had us make such fools of ourselves. The effort, the preparations, all the expense! The new floor lamp, the rug, the clothes for Laura! All for what? To entertain some other girl's fiancé! Go to the movies, go! Don't think about us, a mother deserted, an unmarried sister who's crippled and has no job! Don't let anything interfere with your selfish pleasure! Just go, go, go—to the movies!

TOM: All right, I will! The more you shout about my selfishness to me the quicker I'll go, and I won't go to the movies!

AMANDA: Go, then! Go to the moon—you selfish dreamer!

[TOM *smashes his glass on the floor. He plunges out on the fire escape, slamming the door.* LAURA *screams in fright. The dance-hall music becomes louder. Tom stands on the fire escape, gripping the rail. The moon breaks through the storm clouds, illuminating his face.*

Legend on screen: "And so goodbye . . ."

TOM'S *closing speech is timed with what is happening inside the house. We see, as though through soundproof glass, that* AMANDA *appears to be making a comforting speech to* LAURA, *who is huddled upon the sofa. Now that we cannot hear the mother's speech, her silliness is gone and she has dignity and tragic beauty.* LAURA'S *hair hides her face until, at the end of the speech, she lifts her head to smile at her mother.* AMANDA'S *gestures are slow and graceful, almost dancelike, as she comforts her daughter. At the end of her speech she glances a moment at the father's picture—then withdraws through the portieres. At the close of* TOM'S *speech,* LAURA *blows out the candles, ending the play.*]

TOM: I didn't go to the moon, I went much further—for time is the longest distance between two places. Not long after that I was fired for writing a poem on the lid of a shoe box. I left Saint Louis. I descended the steps of this fire escape for a last time and followed, from then on, in my father's footsteps, attempting to find in motion what was lost in space. I traveled around a great deal. The cities swept about me like dead leaves, leaves that were brightly colored but torn away from the branches. I would have stopped, but I was pursued by something. It always came upon me unawares, taking me altogether by surprise. Perhaps it was a familiar bit of music. Perhaps it was only a piece of transparent glass. Perhaps I am walking along a street at night, in some strange city, before I have found companions. I pass the lighted window of a shop where perfume is sold. The window is filled with pieces of colored glass, tiny transparent bottles in delicate colors, like bits of a shattered rainbow. Then all at once my sister touches my shoulder. I turn around and look into her eyes. Oh, Laura, Laura, I tried to leave you behind me, but I am more faithful than I intended to be! I reach for a cigarette, I cross the street, I run into the movies or a bar, I buy a drink, I speak to the nearest stranger—anything that can blow your candles out!

[LAURA *bends over the candles.*]

For nowadays the world is lit by lightning! Blow out your candles, Laura—and so good bye. . . .

[*She blows the candles out.*]

QUESTIONS

1. What does the setting described in the opening stage direction tell you about the Wingfields? Consider especially the adjectives and the symbolism of the alley and the fire escape.
2. Who is the "fifth character" in the play, and how is his presence established? In what ways is Tom a parallel to this character?
3. What does Amanda reveal about her past in scene 1? How does Williams reveal that Amanda often dwells in the past?
4. What happened to Laura at Rubicam's Business College? How can you account for her behavior? What plan of Amanda's did she upset?
5. What new plan for Laura's future does Amanda begin to develop in scene 2? Why is the plan impracticable? Why is the image of Jim introduced here?

6. Summarize the argument between Tom and Amanda in scene 3. What does Amanda assert about Tom? What does he claim about his life? Why is Laura spotlighted throughout the argument?

7. What sort of agreement does Amanda try to reach with Tom about Laura in scene 4?

8. How do Amanda and Laura react to the news of a gentleman caller? Describe Laura's feelings toward Jim during the conversation and the dancing in scene 7. Describe how he changes after the kiss.

9. Explain the symbolism of the unicorn (both whole and broken). Why does Laura give it to Jim as a souvenir?

10. What is Tom's situation at the end? To what degree has he achieved his dreams of escape and adventure?

11. Describe Amanda's and Laura's concluding situations. Why does Laura blow out the candles? What is the future for these women?

GENERAL QUESTIONS

1. Explain the most striking nonrealistic aspects of the play. What do these contribute to the play's meaning and impact? Which aspect is the most effective? Why?

2. Which characters in the play change significantly? To what extent do the characters succeed or fail? How do they try to escape the realities they face?

3. Consider Tom as character and narrator. Explain why his language changes as he shifts between narrator and character. What does the character dream about and strive for? What does the narrator learn about these dreams and strivings?

4. Explain why Laura cannot deal with reality. What does her glass menagerie symbolize?

5. Williams says that there is much to admire, pity, and laugh at in Amanda. What aspects of her character are admirable? Pitiable? Laughable? Which reaction is dominant for you at the close of the play? Why?

6. Tom calls Jim the play's "most realistic character." In what ways is Jim realistic? How are his dreams and goals more (or less) realistic than Tom's?

7. At the opening, Tom (as narrator) mentions the "social background," and he remarks on it throughout. Discuss how this background relates to the play, especially the events occurring in Europe.

8. Discuss the play's religious allusion and imagery, especially Malvolio the Magician, the "Ave Maria," the "Annunciation," the Paradise Dance Hall, and Laura's candles. How do these references affect the play's level of reality?

AUGUST WILSON (1945–2005)

To judge from the poverty of his birth and early days, one might never have supposed that August Wilson would eventually become one of America's most celebrated dramatists. His birth name was Frederick August Kittel, the fourth of six children. His father was an immigrant German, a baker, who never spent much time with the family, and by the time Wilson was five his father and mother had separated. Wilson's mother, Daisy Wilson, was an African American, and did housecleaning. It was she who taught August how to read when he was only four. When Wilson's father died, in 1965, Wilson changed his name to

"August Wilson" to honor his mother. Daisy had remarried, and with her new husband and her family, had moved to a more prestigious neighborhood than the "hill district" where the family had previously resided. In the new school system, Wilson, the only African American student, experienced great hostility, both from fellow students and also from some of the teachers. He wrote a research paper about Napoleon, and his instructor accused him of plagiarising it. Because of such disparagement, Wilson left school, though still in ninth grade, and began a program of self education at a branch of Pittsburgh's Carnegie library. He educated himself so well that eventually the Library granted him a degree. It was just one of the special degrees he received, for he would later be granted two dozen honorary doctorates.

Wilson's young adulthood was also not auspicious, but he was slowly moving in the direction of becoming a writer. Three years before America became fully engaged in the Vietnam conflict, he signed up for a three-year hitch in the army, but somehow he was able to secure a discharge after a year, and he then began doing odd jobs for his subsistence. He bought a typewriter in 1965, and declared that he was a poet. At the age of 23, he co-founded the Black Horizon on the Hill Theater in Pittsburgh, and began haltingly to write a few plays, which were not distinguished or very successful. He moved to Minneapolis/St. Paul, and stayed there for a number of years. Later he moved to Seattle, his final home, where he became one of the founders of the Seattle Repertory Theater. When living in Minnesota, he had begun working for the Minnesota Science Museum, and was given the duty of dramatizing Native American folk tales for visiting children. It was this rather journeyman task that confirmed his decision to pursue his career in drama.

It is apparent that at some point during his years of movement from place to place, he developed the ambitious idea that would inform his major dramatic output during his lifetime career as dramatist. He planned a full cycle of ten plays, to be called "The Pittsburgh Cycle," in which he would explore the lives and times of African Americans during the twentieth century. His aim was to dramatize the "comedy and tragedy" of blacks who were the descendents of the slaves who had been granted freedom at the time of the Civil War. Each of the plays was to deal with life during one of the decades, though Wilson did not write them in the chronological order of their topic matter. The settings of all but one of the plays is the Pittsburgh "hill district"—the location where his family had lived during the early years of his life. The ten plays are the following: Gem of the Ocean (1900–1910), written 2003; Joe Turner's Come and Gone (1910–20), written 1986; Ma Rainey's Black Bottom (1920–30), written 1984; The Piano Lesson (1930-40), written 1987, Pulitzer Prize; Seven Guitars (1940–50), written 1995; Fences (1957, 1965), written 1985, Pulitzer Prize; Two Trains Running (1960–70), written 1990; Jitney (1970–80), written 1982; King Hedley, II (1980-90), written 1999; Radio Golf (1990–2000), written 2005.

Although Wilson's first forty years were both an artistic and financial struggle, his later life was characterized by great recognition and praise. Fences, one of his best-known plays, was acclaimed for the 1987 production on Broadway, directed by Lloyd Richards and starring James Earl Jones. It won a Pulitzer Prize for Drama, and was additionally distinguished with a Tony award. For Wilson, it was also financially rewarding. His play The Piano Lesson received a Pulitzer Prize in 1990, along with the New York Drama Critics' Circle Award. In Wilson's final years of life, prizes and honorary degrees almost cascaded upon him. When he succumbed to cancer in 2005, he was recognized as one of America's leading dramatists.

The Background of *Fences*

Fences, written in the mid 1980s, is about a period in the 1950s during the growth of the Civil Rights Movement under Dr. Martin Luther King, but before the advent of the Black Power movement of the 1960s. Although there was progress in the 1950s, the country was nevertheless still racist. It is important to recognize that major league baseball, after World War II, was becoming integrated, though slowly. The "Old Negro Leagues" had produced Black players with great ability, but with little public support and recognition. In the late 1940s, changes had begun to take place. Jackie Robinson became the first African American to have become a player in the National League, and Monte Irvin led the way in the American League. By the mid 1950s, there were stalwart players like Minnie Minoso (b. 1922), Ernie Banks (b. 1931), and Elston Howard (1929–1980). The last Negro League player to move to the Big Leagues was Hank Aaron, who became almost a regular yearly member of the All-Star National League teams. He went on to set the professional record of 755 home runs, which stood unchallenged until June, 2007.

In short, encouraging things were happening, and that is the backdrop of the world of baseball that is so much a part of the life and outlook of Troy Maxson (i.e., "maximum son"), August Wilson's protagonist in *Fences*. It is clear that Troy was a player who could hit the ball over fences, but it is also clear that circumstances prevented him from doing so through an entire baseball career. Wilson creates Troy as being too old to benefit from the integration of professional baseball, and also of American society, that was taking place at the time. Troy had spent the prime part of his youth in prison, and it was there that he was able to develop his baseball talents. The result is that with all his ability, he had become too old to be one of those to break baseball's "color line." This despite the fact that Satchel Paige had joined the Cleveland Indians in 1948, at the age of 42, almost exactly the same age that Wilson visualizes for Troy. Paige pitched for four major league teams, and did not finally retire until he was fifty-nine. Troy believes that he could have done just as well, and, as he says, "If you could play . . . then they ought to have let you play." Instead of excelling at hitting balls over the fence, however, he is in the process of retreat, and he is deeply unhappy about being no more than a garbage collector. The fence he builds around his house during the play is symbolically a fence of his own suspicion, anger, and cynicism, preventing him from glorying in the world where he might have conquered.

All this is important in considering the character of Troy. He is a special example of those whose lives were demonstrably marred by discrimination in the twentieth century. (Let us remember that *Fences* is a part of Wilson's chronicle of Black life during the ten decades from 1900 to 2000.) Wilson is careful to show that discrimination hurt Troy's family life during his boyhood. He was particularly afflicted by his father, who was "just as evil as he could be," as Troy tells his son Lyons. In 1.4 Troy describes the events of his leaving home at the age of 14. He had been raised on a cotton farm in the South, and his life was the "stoop labor" of endless cotton picking and cotton baling. Troy's father's attack on him underlies his hostility toward the dreams of his own son, Cory ("heart"), about going into professional football. Despite his negative attitude about Cory's hopes, however, Troy has moved beyond the narrow brutality of his own father. In 2.4, the most agitated and also the most moving scene in the play, Troy has the opportunity to swing a baseball bat at Cory, and thus he has the absolute power over Cory that his own father had exerted over him. But Troy turns away from violence, in a scene that recalls the famous "duel averted" scene in the popular eighteenth-century play *The Conscious Lovers* (1722), by Sir Richard Steele (1672–1729). Although Troy gives up his destructive power, however, he permanently alienates himself from his son.

Named after the ancient mythical city described by Homer, Troy is not only the major character of *Fences*, but he is also one of the major characters to have been created by a twentieth-century dramatist. He is a man of immense power, a leader, but by no means is he perfect. He is a drinker, he is unfaithful, and he is a man of contradictions. As he strays, he tries to justify his straying, but he is not convincing. He does not understand love, but he does understand duty, and that is his compensating strength. He somewhat resembles the biblical patriarch Jacob, who wrestles with God (Genesis 32:24–32). Troy's perception is that he has wrestled with Death. A major theme in his story is that Death will inevitably win, but that he, Troy, is confident in himself, and defiant. He announces, as though Death is listening, "I be ready for you . . . but I ain't gonna be easy." (2.4.97). Although he is imperfect, he has great inner strength, and he is, above all, memorable.

 # Fences (1985)

for Lloyd Richards,°
who adds to whatever he touches

When the sins of our fathers visit us
We do not have to play host.
We can banish them with forgiveness
As God, in His Largeness and Laws.
—August Wilson

CAST OF CHARACTERS

Troy Maxson, [fifty-three years old; a powrful man; now a garbage collector, though formerly a ballplayer and home-run hitter in the old "Negro leagues"]

Jim Bono, Troy's friend [of "thirty odd years"; acts as a conscience for Troy]

Rose, Troy's wife [of eighteen years]

Lyons, Troy's oldest son by a previous marriage

Gabriel, Troy's brother [severely injured in World War II]

Cory, Troy and Rose's son [ready to graduate from high school; an aspiring athlete]

Raynell, Troy's daughter [with Alberta; Raynell is seven in Act 2, Scene 5]

SETTING

The setting is the yard which fronts the only entrance to the Maxson household, an ancient two-story brick house set back off a small alley in a big-city neighborhood. The entrance to the house is gained by two or three steps leading to a wooden porch badly in need of paint.   0.1

A relatively recent addition to the house and running its full width, the porch lacks congruence. It is a sturdy porch with a flat roof. One or two chairs of dubious value sit at one end where the kitchen window opens onto the porch. An old-fashioned icebox stands silent guard at the opposite end.   0.2

The yard is a small dirt yard, partially fenced, except for the last scene, with a wooden saw horse, a pile of lumber, and other fence-building equipment set off to the side. Opposite is a tree from which hangs a ball made of rags. A baseball bat leans against the tree. Two oil drums serve as garbage receptacles and sit near the house at right to complete the setting.   0.3

°*Lloyd Richards:* Richards (1919–2006) is perhaps best known for his having directed Lorraine Hansberry's *A Raisin in the Sun* in 1959, making him the first African American to direct a play on Broadway. Richards was a staunch friend and supportive colleague of Wilson, and eventually he directed six Broadway productions of Wilson plays, including *Fences* in 1987.

THE PLAY

0.4   *Near the turn of the century, the destitute of Europe sprang on the city with tenacious claws and an honest and solid dream. The city devoured them. They swelled its belly until it burst into a thousand furnaces and sewing machines, a thousand butcher shops and bakers' ovens, a thousand churches and hospitals and funeral parlors and moneylenders.*

0.5   *The city grew. It nourished itself and offered each man a partnership limited only by his talent, his guile and his willingness and capacity for hard work. For the immigrants of Europe, a dream dared and won true.*

0.6   *The descendants of African slaves were offered no such welcome or participation. They came from places called the Carolinas and the Virginias, Georgia, Alabama, Mississippi, and Tennessee. They came strong, eager, searching. The city rejected them and they fled and settled along the riverbanks and under bridges in shallow, ramshackle houses made of sticks and tarpaper. They collected rags and wood. They sold the use of their muscles and their bodies. They cleaned houses and washed clothes, they shined shoes, and in quiet desperation and vengeful pride, they stole, and lived in pursuit of their own dream. That they could breathe free, finally, and stand to meet life with the force of dignity and whatever eloquence the heart could call upon.*

0.7   *By 1957, the hard-won victories of the European immigrants had solidified the industrial might of America. War had been confronted and won with new energies that used loyalty and patriotism as its fuel. Life was rich, full, and flourishing. The Milwaukee Braves won the World Series, and the hot winds of change that would make the sixties a turbulent, racing, dangerous, and provocative decade had not yet begun to blow full.*

ACT 1

Scene 1

1.1 *It is 1957.* Troy *and* Bono *enter the yard, engaged in conversation.* Troy *is fifty-three years old, a large man with thick, heavy hands; it is this largeness that he strives to fill out and make an accommodation with. Together with his blackness, his largeness informs his sensibilities and the choices he has made in his life.*

1.2   *Of the two men,* Bono *is obviously the follower. His commitment to their friendship of thirty-odd years is rooted in his admiration of* Troy's *honesty, capacity for hard work, and his strength, which* Bono *seeks to emulate.*

1.3   *It is Friday night, payday, and the one night of the week the two men engage in a ritual of talk and drink.* Troy *is usually the most talkative and at times he can be crude and almost vulgar, though he is capable of rising to profound heights of expression. The men carry lunch buckets and wear or carry burlap aprons and are dressed in clothes suitable to their jobs as garbage collectors.*

Bono: Troy, you ought to stop that lying!

Troy: I ain't lying! The nigger had a watermelon this big. [*He indicates with his hands.*] Talking about . . . "What watermelon, Mr. Rand?" I liked to fell out! "What watermelon, Mr. Rand?" . . . And it sitting there big as life.

Bono: What did Mr. Rand say?

Troy: Ain't said nothing. Figure if the nigger too dumb to know he carrying a watermelon, he wasn't gonna get much sense out of him. Trying to hide that great big old watermelon under his coat. Afraid to let the white man see him carry it home.

5 Bono: I'm like you . . . I ain't got no time for them kind of people.

Troy: Now what he look like getting mad cause he see the man from the union talking to Mr. Rand?

Bono: He come to me talking about . . . "Maxson gonna get us fired." I told him to get away from me with that. He walked away from me calling you a troublemaker. What Mr. Rand say?

TROY: Ain't said nothing. He told me to go down the Commissioner's office next Friday. They called me down there to see them.

BONO: Well, as long as you got your complaint filed, they can't fire you. That's what one of them white fellows tell me.

TROY: I ain't worried about them firing me. They gonna fire me cause I asked a question?   10
That's all I did. I went to Mr. Rand and asked him, "Why? Why you got the white mens driving and the colored lifting?" Told him, "What's the matter, don't I count? You think only white fellows got sense enough to drive a truck. That ain't no paper job! Hell, anybody can drive a truck. How come you got all whites driving and the colored lifting?" He told me "take it to the union." Well, hell, that's what I done! Now they wanna come up with this pack of lies.

BONO: I told Brownie if the man come and ask him any questions . . . just tell the truth! It ain't nothing but something they done trumped up on you cause you filed a complaint on them.

TROY: Brownie don't understand nothing. All I want them to do is change the job description. Give everybody a chance to drive the truck. Brownie can't see that. He ain't got that much sense.

BONO: How you figure he be making out with that gal be up at Taylor's all the time . . . that Alberta gal?

TROY: Same as you and me. Getting just as much as we is. Which is to say nothing.

BONO: It is, huh? I figure you doing a little better than me . . . and I ain't saying what I'm   15
doing.

TROY: Aw, nigger, look here . . . I know you. If you had got anywhere near that gal, twenty minutes later you be looking to tell somebody. And the first one you gonna tell . . . that you gonna want to brag to . . . is me.

BONO: I ain't saying that, I see where you be eyeing her.

TROY: I eye all the women. I don't miss nothing. Don't never let nobody tell you Troy Maxson don't eye the women.

BONO: You been doing more than eyeing her. You done bought her a drink or two.

TROY: Hell yeah, I bought her a drink! What that mean? I bought you one, too. What that   20
mean cause I buy her a drink? I'm just being polite.

BONO: It's all right to buy her one drink. That's what you call being polite. But when you wanna be buying two or three . . . that's what you call eyeing her.

TROY: Look here, as long as you known me . . . you ever known me to chase after women?

BONO: Hell yeah! Long as I done known you. You forgetting I knew you when.

TROY: Naw, I'm talking about since I been married to Rose?

BONO: Oh, not since you been married to Rose. Now, that's the truth, there, I can say that.   25

TROY: All right then! Case closed.

BONO: I see you be walking up around Alberta's house. You supposed to be at Taylors' and you be walking up around there.

TROY: What you watching where I'm walking for? I ain't watching after you.

BONO: I seen you walking around there more than once.

TROY: Hell, you liable to see me walking anywhere! That don't mean nothing cause you   30
see me walking around there.

BONO: Where she come from anyway? She just kinda showed up one day.

TROY: Tallahassee. You can look at her and tell she one of them Florida gals. They got some big healthy women down there. Grow them right up out the ground. Got a little bit of Indian in her. Most of them niggers down in Florida got some Indian in them.

BONO: I don't know about that Indian part. But she damn sure big and healthy. Women wear some big stockings. Got them great big old legs and hips as wide as the Mississippi River.

TROY: Legs don't mean nothing. You don't do nothing but push them out of the way. But them hips cushion the ride!

35 **BONO:** Troy, you ain't got no sense.

TROY: It's the truth! Like you riding on Goodyears!

ROSE enters from the house. She is ten years younger than TROY, her devotion to him stems from her recognition of the possibilities of her life without him: a succession of abusive men and their babies, a life of partying and running the streets, the Church, or aloneness with its attendant pain and frustration. She recognizes TROY's spirit as a fine and illuminating one and she either ignores or forgives his faults, only some of which she recognizes. Though she doesn't drink, her presence is an integral part of the Friday night rituals. She alternates between the porch and the kitchen, where supper preparations are under way.

ROSE: What you all out here getting into?

TROY: What you worried about what we getting into for? This is men talk, woman.

ROSE: What I care what you all talking about? Bono, you gonna stay for supper?

40 **BONO:** No, I thank you, Rose. But Lucille say she cooking up a pot of pigfeet.

TROY: Pigfeet! Hell, I'm going home with you! Might even stay the night if you got some pigfeet. You got something in there to top them pigfeet, Rose?

ROSE: I'm cooking up some chicken. I got some chicken and collard greens.

TROY: Well, go on back in the house and let me and Bono finish what we was talking about. This is men talk. I got some talk for you later. You know what kind of talk I mean. You go on and powder it up.

ROSE: Troy Maxson, don't you start that now!

45 **TROY:** [*puts his arm around her.*] Aw, woman . . . come here. Look here. Bono . . . when I met this woman . . . I got out that place, say, "Hitch up my pony, saddle up my mare . . . there's a woman out there for me somewhere." I looked here. Looked there. Saw Rose and latched on to her. I latched on to her and told her—I'm gonna tell you the truth—I told her, "Baby, I don't wanna marry, I just wanna be your man." Rose told me . . . tell him what you told me, Rose.

ROSE: I told him if he wasn't the marrying kind, then move out the way so the marrying kind could find me.

TROY: That's what she told me. "Nigger, you in my way. You blocking the view! Move out the way so I can find me a husband." I thought it over two or three days. Come back—

ROSE: Ain't no two or three days nothing. You was back the same night.

TROY: Come back, told her . . . "Okay, baby . . . but I'm gonna buy me a banty rooster and put him out there in the backyard . . . and when he see a stranger come, he'll flap his wings and crow. . . ." Look here, Bono, I could watch the front door by myself . . . it was that back door I was worried about.

50 **ROSE:** Troy, you ought not talk like that. Troy ain't doing nothing but telling a lie.

TROY: Only thing is . . . when we first got married . . . forget the rooster . . . we ain't had no yard!

BONO: I hear you tell it. Me and Lucille was staying down there on Logan Street. Had two rooms with the outhouse in the back. I ain't mind the outhouse none. But when that goddamn wind blow through there in the winter . . . that's what I'm talking about! To this day I wonder why in the hell I ever stayed down there for six long years. But see, I didn't know I could do no better. I thought only white folks had inside toilets and things.

ROSE: There's a lot of people don't know they can do no better than they doing now. That's just something you got to learn. A lot of folks still shop at Bella's.

TROY: Ain't nothing wrong with shopping at Bella's. She got fresh food.

55 **ROSE:** I ain't said nothing about if she got fresh food. I'm talking about what she charge. She charge ten cents more than the A&P.

TROY: The A&P ain't never done nothing for me. I spends my money where I'm treated right. I go down to Bella, say, "I need a loaf of bread, I'll pay you Friday." She give it to me. What sense that make when I got money to go and spend it somewhere else and ignore the person who done right by me? That ain't in the Bible.

ROSE: We ain't talking about what's in the Bible. What sense it make to shop there when she overcharge?

TROY: You shop where you want to. I'll do my shopping where the people been good to me.

ROSE: Well, I don't think it's right for her to overcharge. That's all I was saying.

BONO: Look here . . . I got to get on. Lucille going be raising all kind of hell.   60

TROY: Where you going, nigger? We ain't finished this pint. Come here, finish this pint.

BONO: Well, hell, I am . . . if you ever turn the bottle loose.

TROY: [*hands him the bottle.*] The only thing I say about the A&P is I'm glad Cory got that job down there. Help him take care of his school clothes and things. Gabe done moved out and things getting tight around here. He got that job. . . . He can start to look out for himself.

ROSE: Cory done went and got recruited by a college football team.

TROY: I told that boy about that football stuff. The white man ain't gonna let him get   65
nowhere with that football. I told him when he first come to me with it. Now you come telling me he done went and got more tied up in it. He ought to go and get recruited in how to fix cars or something where he can make a living.

ROSE: He ain't talking about making no living playing football. It's just something the boys in school do. They gonna send a recruiter by to talk to you. He'll tell you he ain't talking about making no living playing football. It's a honor to be recruited.

TROY: It ain't gonna get him nowhere. Bono'll tell you that.

BONO: If he be like you in the sports . . . he's gonna be all right. Ain't but two men ever played baseball as good as you. That's Babe Ruth and Josh Gibson.° Them's the only two men ever hit more home runs than you.

TROY: What it ever get me? Ain't got a pot to piss in or a window to throw it out of.

ROSE: Times have changed since you was playing baseball, Troy. That was before the war.   70
Times have changed a lot since then.

TROY: How in hell they done changed?

ROSE: They got lots of colored boys playing ball now. Baseball and football.

BONO: You right about that, Rose. Times have changed, Troy. You just come along too early.

TROY: There ought not never have been no time called too early! Now you take that fellow . . . What's that fellow they had playing right field for the Yankees back then? You know who I'm talking about, Bono. Used to play right field for the Yankees.

ROSE: Selkirk? °   75

°68 *Babe Ruth and Josh Gibson:* George Herman Ruth, "Babe" Ruth (1895–1948), had a baseball career that lasted from 1914 to 1935. During this time he set many batting records, including his number of home runs in a season in 1927 (60) and total home runs (714). In 1957, no one had surpassed either of these records, and no one was close. Ruth was one of the first men to be made a member of the Baseball Hall of Fame. His record for a single season lasted until 1961, when Roger Maris hit 61. Joshua Gibson (1911–47), a catcher, is considered as one of the greatest home run hitters in baseball history, though he never was permitted to play in the major leagues. In seventeen seasons in the Negro Leagues, and in corrolary exhibition games, he may have batted as high as .384, and may have hit more than 800 home runs. One of the claims made about him is that he was the only batter to have hit a home run out of Yankee Stadium. He was elected posthumously to Baseball's Hall of Fame in 1972. 75 *Selkirk:* George Alexander ("Twinkletoes") Selkirk (1908–87), played for the Yankees for nine seasons from 1934 to 1942. When Babe Ruth retired in 1935, Selkirk became the regular Yankee right fielder. His major league lifetime batting average was .290, and he batted .269 in 1940. He hit a total of 108 home runs during his career, with 576 rbi. After 1942, he left the Yankees to serve in World War II.

TROY: Selkirk! That's it! Man batting .269, understand? 269! What kind of sense that make? I was hitting .432 with thirty-seven home runs! Man batting .269 and playing right field for the Yankees! I saw Josh Gibson's daughter yesterday. She walking around with raggedy shoes on her feet. Now I bet you Selkirk's daughter ain't walking around with raggedy shoes on the feet! I bet you that!

ROSE: They got a lot of colored baseball players now. Jackie Robinson was the first. Folks had to wait for Jackie Robinson.°

TROY: I done seen a hundred niggers play baseball better than Jackie Robinson. Hell, I know some teams Jackie Robinson couldn't even make! What you talking about Jackie Robinson. Jackie Robinson wasn't nobody. I'm talking about if you could play ball then they ought to have let you play. Don't care what color you were. Come telling me I come along too early. If you could play . . . then they ought to have let you play.

TROY takes a long drink from the bottle.

ROSE: You gonna drink yourself to death. You don't need to be drinking like that.

80 TROY: Death ain't nothing. I done seen him. Done wrassled with him. You can't tell me nothing about death. Death ain't nothing but a fastball on the outside corner. And you know what I'll do to that! Lookee here, Bono . . . am I lying? You get one of them fastballs, about waist high, over the outside corner of the plate where you can get the meat of the bat on it . . . and good god! You can kiss it goodbye. Now, am I lying?

BONO: Naw, you telling the truth there. I seen you do it.

TROY: If I'm lying . . . that 450 feet worth of lying! [*Pause.*] That's all death is to me. A fastball on the outside corner.

ROSE: I don't know why you want to get on talking about death.

TROY: Ain't nothing wrong with talking about death. That's part of life. Everybody gonna die. You gonna die, I'm gonna die. Bono's gonna die. Hell, we all gonna die.

85 ROSE: But you ain't got to talk about it. I don't like to talk about it.

TROY: You the one brought it up. Me and Bono was talking about baseball . . . you tell me I'm gonna drink myself to death. Ain't that right, Bono? You know I don't drink this but one night out of the week. That's Friday night. I'm gonna drink just enough to where I can handle it. Then I cuts it loose. I leave it alone. So don't you worry about me drinking myself to death. 'Cause I ain't worried about Death. I done seen him. I done wrestled with him. Look here, Bono . . . I looked up one day and Death was marching straight at me. Like Soldiers on Parade! The Army of Death was marching straight at me. The middle of July, 1941. It got real cold just like it be winter. It seem like Death himself reached out and touched me on the shoulder. He touched me just like I touch you. I got cold as ice and Death standing there grinning at me.

ROSE: Troy, why don't you hush that talk.

TROY: I say . . . what you want, Mr. Death? You be wanting me? You done brought your army to be getting me? I looked him dead in the eye. I wasn't fearing nothing. I was ready to tangle. Just like I'm ready to tangle now. The Bible say be ever vigilant.° That's why I don't get but so drunk. I got to keep watch.

ROSE: Troy was right down there in Mercy Hospital. You remember he had pneumonia? Laying there with a fever talking plumb out of his head.

90 TROY: Death standing there staring at me . . . carrying that sickle in his hand. Finally he say, "You want bound over for another year?" See, just like that . . . "You want bound over for another year?" I told him, "Bound over hell! Let's settle this now!" It seem like he

°77 *Jackie Robinson:* Robinson (1919–72) led the way for equality in professional sports when he became the first African American to play major league baseball in 1947. He went on to have a sterling if brief major league career. He was made a member of the Baseball Hall of Fame in 1962. 88 *vigilant:* See I Peter, 5:8.

kinda fell back when I said that, and all the cold went out of me. I reached down and grabbed that sickle and threw it just as far as I could throw it . . . and me and him commenced to wrestling. We wrestled for three days and three nights. I can't say where I found the strength from. Everytime it seemed like he was gonna get the best of me, I'd reach way down deep inside myself and find the strength to do him one better.

ROSE: Every time Troy tell that story he find different ways to tell it. Different things to make up about it.

TROY: I ain't making up nothing. I'm telling you the facts of what happened. I wrestled with Death for three days and three nights and I'm standing here to tell you about it. [*Pause.*] All right. At the end of the third night we done weakened each other to where we can't hardly move. Death stood up, throwed on his robe . . . had him a white robe with a hood on it. He threwed on that robe and went off to look for his sickle. Say, "I'll be back." Just like that. "I'll be back." I told him, say, "Yeah, but . . . you gonna have to find me!" I wasn't no fool. I wasn't going looking for him. Death ain't nothing to play with. And I know he's gonna get me. I know I got to join his army . . . his camp followers. But as long as I keep my strength and see him coming . . . as long as I keep up my vigilance . . . he's gonna have to fight to get me. I ain't going easy.

BONO: Well, look here, since you got to keep up your vigilance . . . let me have the bottle.

TROY: Aw hell, I shouldn't have told you that part. I should have left out that part.

ROSE: Troy be talking that stuff and half the time don't even know what he be talking about.   95

TROY: Bono know me better than that.

BONO: That's right. I know you. I know you got some Uncle Remus° in your blood. You got more stories than the devil got sinners.

TROY: Aw hell, I done seen him too! Done talked with the devil.

ROSE: Troy, don't nobody wanna be hearing all that stuff.

LYONS enters the yard from the street. Thirty-four years old, TROY'S son by a previous marriage, he sports a neatly trimmed goatee, sport coat, white shirt, tieless and buttoned at the collar. Though he fancies himself a musician, he is more caught up in the rituals and "idea" of being a musician than in the actual practice of the music. He has come to borrow money from TROY, and while he knows he will be successful, he is uncertain as to what extent his lifestyle will be held up to scrutiny and ridicule.

LYONS: Hey, Pop.   100

TROY: What you come "Hey, Popping" me for?

LYONS: How you doing, Rose? [*He kisses her.*] Mr. Bono. How you doing?

BONO: Hey, Lyons . . . how you been?

TROY: He must have been doing all right. I ain't seen him around here last week.

ROSE: Troy, leave your boy alone. He come by to see you and you wanna start all that nonsense.   105

TROY: I ain't bothering Lyons. [*Offers him the bottle.*] Here . . . get you a drink. We got an understanding. I know why he come by to see me and he know I know.

LYONS: Come on, Pop . . . I just stopped by to say hi . . . see how you was doing.

TROY: You ain't stopped by yesterday.

ROSE: You gonna stay for supper, Lyons? I got some chicken cooking in the oven.

LYONS: No, Rose . . . thanks. I was just in the neighborhood and thought I'd stop by for a minute.   110

TROY: You was in the neighborhood all right, nigger. You telling the truth there. You was in the neighborhood 'cause it's my payday.

LYONS: Well, hell, since you mentioned it . . . let me have ten dollars.

TROY: I'll be damned! I'll die and go to hell and play blackjack with the devil before I give you ten dollars.

°97 *Uncle Remus:* A reference to the Uncle Remus stories (1881) of Joel Chandler Harris.

Bono: That's what I wanna know about . . . that devil you done seen.

115 **Lyons:** What . . . Pop done seen the devil? You too much, Pops.

Troy: Yeah, I done seen him. Talked to him too!

Rose: You ain't seen no devil. I done told you that man ain't had nothing to do with the devil. Anything you can't understand, you want to call it the devil.

Troy: Look here, Bono . . . I went down to see Hertzberger about some furniture. Got three rooms for two-ninety-eight. That what it say on the radio. "Three rooms . . . two-ninety-eight." Even made up a little song about it. Go down there . . . man tell me I can't get no credit. I'm working every day and can't get no credit. What to do? I got an empty house with some raggedy furniture in it. Cory ain't got no bed. He's sleeping on a pile of rags on the floor. Working every day and can't get no credit. Come back here—Rose'll tell you—madder than hell. Sit down . . . try to figure what I'm gonna do. Come a knock on the door. Ain't been living here but three days. Who know I'm here? Open the door . . . devil standing there bigger than life. White fellow . . . got on good clothes and everything. Standing there with a clipboard in his hand. I ain't had to say nothing. First words come out of his mouth was . . . "I understand you need some furniture and can't get no credit." I liked to fell over. He say, "I'll give you all the credit you want, but you got to pay the interest on it." I told him, "Give me three rooms worth and charge whatever you want." Next day a truck pulled up here and two men unloaded them three rooms. Man what drove the truck give me a book. Say send ten dollars, first of every month to the address in the book and everything will be all right. Say if I miss a payment the devil was coming back and it'll be hell to pay. That was fifteen years ago. To this day . . . the first of the month I send my ten dollars, Rose'll tell you.

Rose: Troy lying.

120 **Troy:** I ain't never seen that man since. Now you tell me who else that could have been but the devil? I ain't sold my soul or nothing like that, you understand. Naw, I wouldn't have truck with the devil about nothing like that. I got my furniture and pays my ten dollars the first of the month just like clockwork.

Bono: How long you say you been paying this ten dollars a month?

Troy: Fifteen years!

Bono: Hell, ain't you finished paying for it yet? How much the man done charged you?

Troy: Ah hell, I done paid for it. I done paid for it ten times over! The fact is I'm scared to stop paying it.

125 **Rose:** Troy lying. We got that furniture from Mr. Glickman. He ain't paying no ten dollars a month to nobody.

Troy: Aw hell, woman. Bono know I ain't that big a fool.

Lyons: I was just getting ready to say . . . I know where there's a bridge for sale.

Troy: Look here, I'll tell you this . . . it don't matter to me if he was the devil. It don't matter if the devil give credit. Somebody has got to give it.

Rose: It ought to matter. You going around talking about having truck with the devil. . . . God's the one you gonna have to answer to. He's the one gonna be at the Judgment.

130 **Lyons:** Yeah, well, look here, Pop . . . Let me have that ten dollars. I'll give it back to you. Bonnie got a job working at the hospital.

Troy: What I tell you, Bono? The only time I see this nigger is when he wants something. That's the only time I see him.

Lyons: Come on, Pop, Mr. Bono don't want to hear all that. Let me have the ten dollars. I told you Bonnie working.

Troy: What that mean to me? "Bonnie working." I don't care if she working. Go ask her for the ten dollars if she working. Talking about "Bonnie working." Why ain't you working?

LYONS: Aw, Pop, you know I can't find no decent job. Where am I gonna get a job at? You know I can't get no job.

TROY: I told you I know some people down there. I can get you on the rubbish if you want   135
to work. I told you that the last time you came by here asking me for something.

LYONS: Naw, Pop . . . thanks. That ain't for me. I don't wanna be carrying nobody's rubbish. I don't wanna be punching nobody's time clock.

TROY: What's the matter, you too good to carry people's rubbish? Where you think that ten dollars you talking about come from? I'm just supposed to haul people's rubbish and give my money to you cause you too lazy to work. You too lazy to work and wanna know why you ain't got what I got.

ROSE: What hospital Bonnie working at? Mercy?

LYONS: She's down at Passavant° working in the laundry.

TROY: I ain't got nothing as it is. I give you that ten dollars and I got to eat beans the rest of   140
the week. Naw . . . you ain't getting no ten dollars here.

LYONS: You ain't got to be eating no beans. I don't know why you wanna say that.

TROY: I ain't got no extra money. Gabe done moved over to Miss Pearl's paying her the rent and things done got tight around here. I can't afford to be giving you every pay-day.

LYONS: I ain't asked you to give me nothing. I asked you to loan me ten dollars. I know you got ten dollars.

TROY: Yeah, I got it. You know why I got it? 'Cause I don't throw my money away out there in the streets. You living the fast life . . . wanna be a musician . . . running around in them clubs and things . . . then, you learn to take care of yourself. You ain't gonna find me going and asking nobody for nothing. I done spent too many years without.

LYONS: You and me is two different people, Pop.   145

TROY: I done learned my mistake and learned to do what's right by it. You still trying to get something for nothing. Life don't owe you nothing. You owe it to yourself. Ask Bono. He'll tell you I'm right.

LYONS: You got your way of dealing with the world . . . I got mine. The only thing that matters to me is the music.

TROY: Yeah, I can see that! It don't matter how you gonna eat . . . where your next dollar is coming from. You telling the truth there.

LYONS: I know I got to eat. But I got to live too. I need something that gonna help me to get out of the bed in the morning. Make me feel like I belong in the world. I don't bother nobody. I just stay with the music cause that's the only way I can find to live in the world. Otherwise there ain't no telling what I might do. Now I don't come criticizing you and how you live. I just come by to ask you for ten dollars. I don't wanna hear all that about how I live.

TROY: Boy, your mamma did a hell of a job raising you.   150

LYONS: You can't change me, Pop. I'm thirty-four years old. If you wanted to change me, you should have been there when I was growing up. I come by to see you . . . ask for ten dollars and you want to talk about how I was raised. You don't know nothing about how I was raised.

ROSE: Let the boy have ten dollars, Troy.

TROY: [*To* LYONS.] What the hell you looking at me for? I ain't got no ten dollars. You know what I do with my money. [*To* ROSE.] Give him ten dollars if you want him to have it.

ROSE: I will. Just as soon as you turn it loose.

°139 *Passavant:* The University of Pittsburgh Medical Center Passavant, in Pittsburgh.

155 **TROY:** [*handing ROSE the money.*] There it is. Seventy-six dollars and forty-two cents. You see this, Bono? Now, I ain't gonna get but six of that back.

ROSE: You ought to stop telling that lie. Here, Lyons. [*She hands him the money.*]

LYONS: Thanks, Rose. Look . . . I got to run . . . I'll see you later.

TROY: Wait a minute. You gonna say, "Thanks, Rose" and ain't gonna look to see where she got that ten dollars from? See how they do me, Bono?

LYONS: I know she got it from you, Pop. Thanks. I'll give it back to you.

160 **TROY:** There he go telling another lie. Time I see that ten dollars . . . he'll be owing me thirty more.

LYONS: See you, Mr. Bono.

BONO: Take care, Lyons!

LYONS: Thanks, Pop. I'll see you again. [*LYONS exits the yard.*]

TROY: I don't know why he don't go and get him a decent job and take care of that woman he got.

165 **BONO:** He'll be all right, Troy. The boy is still young.

TROY: The *boy* is thirty-four years old.

ROSE: Let's not get off into all that.

BONO: Look here . . . I got to be going. I got to be getting on. Lucille gonna be waiting.

TROY: [*puts his arm around ROSE.*] See this woman, Bono? I love this woman. I love this woman so much it hurts. I love her so much . . . I done run out of ways of loving her. So I got to go back to basics. Don't you come by my house Monday morning talking about time to go to work . . . . 'cause I'm still gonna be stroking!

170 **ROSE:** Troy! Stop it now!

BONO: I ain't paying him no mind, Rose. That ain't nothing but gin-talk. Go on, Troy. I'll see you Monday.

TROY: Don't you come by my house, nigger! I done told you what I'm gonna be doing.

The lights go down to black.

ACT 1

Scene 2

The lights come up on Rose hanging up clothes. She hums and sings softly to herself. It is the following morning.

ROSE: [*sings.*]

Jesus, be a fence all around me every day
Jesus, I want you to protect me as I travel on my way.
Jesus, be a fence all around me every day.

> [*TROY enters from the house.*]

Jesus, I want you to protect me
As I travel on my way.

[*To TROY.*] Morning. You ready for breakfast? I can fix it soon as I finish hanging up these clothes.

TROY: I got the coffee on. That'll be all right. I'll just drink some of that this morning.

ROSE: That 651 hit yesterday. That's the second time this month. Miss Pearl hit for a dollar. . . . Seem like those that need the least always get lucky. Poor folks can't get nothing.

TROY: Them numbers don't know nobody. I don't know why you fool with them. You and Lyons both.

5 **ROSE:** It's something to do.

TROY: You ain't doing nothing but throwing your money away.

ROSE: Troy, you know I don't play foolishly. I just play a nickel here and a nickel there.

TROY: That's two nickels you done thrown away.

ROSE: Now I hit sometimes . . . that makes up for it. It always comes in handy when I do hit. I don't hear you complaining then.

TROY: I ain't complaining now. I just say it's foolish. Trying to guess out of six hundred ways which way the number gonna come. If I had all the money niggers, these Negroes, throw away on numbers for one week—just one week—I'd be a rich man. 10

ROSE: Well, you wishing and calling it foolish ain't gonna stop folks from playing numbers. That's one thing for sure. Besides . . . some good things come from playing numbers. Look where Pope done bought him that restaurant off of numbers.

TROY: I can't stand niggers like that. Man ain't had two dimes to rub together. He walking around with his shoes all run over bumming money for cigarettes. All right. Got lucky there and hit the numbers . . .

ROSE: Troy, I know all about it.

TROY: Had good sense, I'll say that for him. He ain't throwed his money away. I seen niggers hit the numbers and go through two thousand dollars in four days. Man bought him that restaurant down there . . . fixed it up real nice . . . and then didn't want nobody to come in it! A Negro go in there and can't get no kind of service. I seen a white fellow come in there and order a bowl of stew. Pope picked all the meat out of the pot for him. Man ain't had nothing but a bowl of meat! Negro come behind him and ain't got nothing but the potatoes and carrots. Talking about what numbers do for people, you picked a wrong example. Ain't done nothing but make a worser fool out of him than he was before.

ROSE: Troy, you ought to stop worrying about what happened at work yesterday. 15

TROY: I ain't worried. Just told me to be down there at the Commissioner's office on Friday. Everybody think they gonna fire me. I ain't worried about them firing me. You ain't got to worry about that. [*Pause.*] Where's Cory? Cory in the house? [*Calls.*] Cory?

ROSE: He gone out.

TROY: Out, huh? He gone out 'cause he know I want him to help me with this fence. I know how he is. That boy scared of work.

GABRIEL enters. He comes halfway down the alley and, hearing TROY'S voice, stops.

TROY: [*continues.*] He ain't done a lick of work in his life.

ROSE: He had to go to football practice. Coach wanted them to get in a little extra practice before the season start. 20

TROY: I got his practice . . . running out of here before he get his chores done.

ROSE: Troy, what is wrong with you this morning? Don't nothing set right with you. Go on back in there and go to bed . . . get up on the other side.

TROY: Why something got to be wrong with me? I ain't said nothing wrong with me.

ROSE: You got something to say about everything. First it's the numbers . . . then it's the way the man runs his restaurant . . . then you done got on Cory. What's it gonna be next? Take a look up there and see if the weather suits you . . . or is it gonna be how you gonna put up the fence with the clothes hanging in the yard.

TROY: You hit the nail on the head then. 25

ROSE: I know you like I know the back of my hand. Go on in there and get you some coffee . . . see if that straighten you up. 'Cause you ain't right this morning.

TROY starts into the house and sees GABRIEL. GABRIEL starts singing. TROY'S brother, he is seven years younger than TROY. Injured in World War II, he has a metal plate in his head. He carries an old trumpet tied around his waist and believes with every fiber of his being that he is the Archangel Gabriel. He carries a chipped basket with an assortment of discarded fruits and vegetables he has picked up in the strip district and which he attempts to sell.

GABRIEL: [*singing*].

> Yes, ma'am I got plums
> You ask me how I sell them
> Oh ten cents apiece
> Three for a quarter
> Come and buy now
> 'Cause I'm here today
> And tomorrow I'll be gone.

GABRIEL enters.

GABRIEL: Hey, Rose!

ROSE: How you doing Gabe?

30 GABRIEL: There's Troy . . . Hey, Troy!

TROY: Hey, Gabe. [*Exit into kitchen.*]

ROSE: [*to GABRIEL*]. What you got there?

GABRIEL: You know what I got, Rose. I got fruits and vegetables.

ROSE: [*looking in basket*]. Where's all these plums you talking about?

35 GABRIEL: I ain't got no plums today, Rose. I was just singing that. Have some tomorrow. Put me in a big order for plums. Have enough plums tomorrow for St. Peter and everybody.

TROY reenters from kitchen, crosses to steps.

[*To ROSE.*] Troy's mad at me.

TROY: I ain't mad at you. What I got to be mad at you about? You ain't done nothing to me.

GABRIEL: I just moved over to Miss Pearl's to keep out from in your way. I ain't mean no harm by it.

TROY: Who said anything about that? I ain't said anything about that.

GABRIEL: You ain't mad at me, is you?

40 TROY: Naw . . . I ain't mad at you, Gabe. If I was mad at you I'd tell you about it.

GABRIEL: Got me two rooms. In the basement. Got my own door too. Wanna see my key? [*He holds up a key.*] That's my own key! My two rooms!

TROY: Well, that's good, Gabe. You got your own key . . . that's good.

ROSE: You hungry, Gabe? I was just fixing to cook Troy his breakfast.

GABRIEL: I'll take some biscuits. You got some biscuits? Did you know when I was in heaven . . . every morning me and St. Peter would sit down by the gate and eat some big fat biscuits? Oh, yeah! We had us a good time. We'd sit there and eat us them biscuits and then St. Peter would go off to sleep and tell me to wake him up when it's time to open the gates for the judgment.

45 ROSE: Well, come on . . . I'll make up a batch of biscuits.

ROSE exits into the house.

GABRIEL: Troy . . . St. Peter got your name in the book. I seen it. It say . . . Troy Maxson. I say . . . I know him! He got the same name like what I got. That's my brother!

TROY: How many times you gonna tell me that, Gabe?

GABRIEL: Ain't got my name in the book. Don't have to have my name. I done died and went to heaven. He got your name though. One morning St. Peter was looking at his book . . . marking it up for the judgment . . . and he let me see your name. Got it in there under M. Got Rose's name . . . I ain't seen it like I seen yours . . . but I know it's in there. He got a great big book. Got everybody's name what was ever been born. That's what he told me. But I seen your name. Seen it with my own eyes.

TROY: Go on in the house there. Rose going to fix you something to eat.

50 GABRIEL: Oh, I ain't hungry. I done had breakfast with Aunt Jemimah. She come by and cooked me up a whole mess of flapjacks. Remember how we used to eat them flapjacks?

TROY: Go on in the house and get you something to eat now.

GABRIEL: I got to sell my plums. I done sold some tomatoes. Got me two quarters. Wanna see? [*He shows* TROY *his quarters.*] I'm gonna save them and buy me a new horn so St. Peter can hear me when it's time to open the gates. [GABRIEL *stops suddenly. Listens.*] Hear that? That's the hellhounds. I got to chase them out of here. Go on get out of here! Get out! [GABRIEL *exits singing.*]
Better get ready for the judgment
Better get ready for the judgment
My Lord is coming down

                      ROSE *enters from the house.*

TROY: He's gone off somewhere.
GABRIEL: [*offstage.*]
Better get ready for the judgment
Better get ready for the judgment morning
Better get ready for the judgment
My God is coming down.

ROSE: He ain't eating right. Miss Pearl say she can't get him to eat nothing.   55
TROY: What you want me to do about it, Rose? I done did everything I can for the man. I can't make him get well. Man got half his head blown away . . . what you expect?
ROSE: Seem like something ought to be done to help him.
TROY: Man don't bother nobody. He just mixed up from that metal plate he got in his head. Ain't no sense for him to go back into the hospital.
ROSE: Least he be eating right. They can help him take care of himself.
TROY: Don't nobody wanna be locked up, Rose. What you wanna lock him up for? Man go   60
over there and fight the war . . . messin' around with them Japs, get half his head blow off . . . and they give him a lousy three thousand dollars. And I had to swoop down on that.
ROSE: Is you fixing to go into that again?
TROY: That's the only way I got a roof over my head . . . cause of that metal plate.
ROSE: Ain't no sense you blaming yourself for nothing. Gabe wasn't in no condition to manage that money. You done what was right by him. Can't nobody say you ain't done what was right by him. Look how long you took care of him . . . till he wanted to have his own place and moved over there with Miss Pearl.
TROY: That ain't what I'm saying woman! I'm just stating the facts. If my brother didn't have that metal plate in his head . . . I wouldn't have a pot to piss in or a window to throw it out of. And I'm fifty-three years old. Now see if you can understand that!

TROY *gets up from the porch and starts to exit the yard.*

ROSE: Where you going off to? You been running out of here every Saturday for weeks.   65
I thought you was gonna work on this fence?
TROY: I'm gonna walk down to Taylors'. Listen to the ball game. I'll be back in a bit. I'll work on it when I get back.

He exits the yard. The lights go to black.

ACT 1

Scene 3

The lights come up on the yard. It is four hours later. ROSE *is taking down the clothes from the line.* CORY *enters carrying his football equipment.*

ROSE: Your daddy like to had a fit with you running out of here this morning without do-ing your chores.
CORY: I told you I had to go to practice.

ROSE: He say you were supposed to help him with this fence.

CORY: He been saying that the last four or five Saturdays, and then he don't never do nothing, but go down to Taylors'. Did you tell him about the recruiter?

5   ROSE: Yeah, I told him.

CORY: What he say?

ROSE: He ain't said nothing too much. You get in there and get started on your chores before he gets back. Go on and scrub down them steps before he gets back here hollering and carrying on.

CORY: I'm hungry. What you got to eat, Mama?

ROSE: Go on and get started on your chores. I got some meat loaf in there. Go on and make you a sandwich . . . and don't leave no mess in there.

CORY exits into the house. ROSE continues to take down the clothes. TROY enters the yard and sneaks up and grabs her from behind.

Troy! Go on, now. You liked to scared me to death. What was the score of the game? Lucille had me on the phone and I couldn't keep up with it.

10 TROY: What I care about the game? Come here, woman. [*He tries to kiss her.*]

ROSE: I thought you went down Taylors' to listen to the game. Go on, Troy! You supposed to be putting up this fence.

TROY: [*attempting to kiss her again.*] I'll put it up when I finish with what is at hand.

ROSE: Go on, Troy. I ain't studying you.

TROY: [*chasing after her.*] I'm studying you . . . fixing to do my homework!

15 ROSE: Troy, you better leave me alone.

TROY: Where's Cory? That boy brought his butt home yet?

ROSE: He's in the house doing his chores.

TROY: [*calling.*] Cory! Get your butt out here, boy!

ROSE exits into the house with the laundry. TROY goes over to the pile of wood, picks up a board, and starts sawing. CORY enters from the house.

TROY: You just now coming in here from leaving this morning?

20 CORY: Yeah, I had to go to football practice.

TROY: Yeah, what?

CORY: Yessir.

TROY: I ain't but two seconds off you noway. The garbage sitting in there overflowing . . . you ain't done none of your chores . . . and you come in here talking about "Yeah."

CORY: I was just getting ready to do my chores now, Pop . . .

25 TROY: Your first chore is to help me with this fence on Saturday. Everything else come after that. Now get that saw and cut them boards.

CORY takes the saw and begins cutting the boards. TROY continues working. There is a long pause.

CORY: Hey, Pop . . . why don't you buy a TV?

TROY: What I want with a TV? What I want one of them for?

CORY: Everybody got one. Earl, Ba Bra . . . Jesse!

TROY: I ain't asked you who had one. I say what I want with one?

30 CORY: So you can watch it. They got lots of things on TV. Baseball games and everything. We could watch the World Series.

TROY: Yeah . . . and how much this TV cost?

CORY: I don't know. They got them on sale for around two hundred dollars.

TROY: Two hundred dollars, huh?

CORY: That ain't that much, Pop.

35 TROY: Naw, it's just two hundred dollars. See that roof you got over your head at night? Let me tell you something about that roof. It's been over ten years since that roof was

last tarred. See now . . . the snow come this winter and sit up there on that roof like it is . . . and it's gonna seep inside. It's just gonna be a little bit . . . ain't gonna hardly notice it. Then the next thing you know, it's gonna be leaking all over the house. Then the wood rot from all that water and you gonna need a whole new roof. Now, how much you think it cost to get that roof tarred?

CORY: I don't know.

TROY: Two hundred and sixty-four dollars . . . cash money. While you thinking about a TV, I got to be thinking about the roof . . . and whatever else go wrong here. Now if you had two hundred dollars, what would you do . . . fix the roof or buy a TV?

CORY: I'd buy a TV. Then when the roof started to leak . . . when it needed fixing . . . I'd fix it.

TROY: Where you gonna get the money from? You done spent it for a TV. You gonna sit up and watch the water run all over your brand new TV.

CORY: Aw, Pop. You got money. I know you do.   40

TROY: Where I got it at, huh?

CORY: You got it in the bank.

TROY: You wanna see my bankbook? You wanna see that seventy-three dollars and twenty-two cents I got sitting up in there?

CORY: You ain't got to pay for it all at one time. You can put a down payment on it and carry it on home with you.

TROY: Not me. I ain't gonna owe nobody nothing if I can help it. Miss a payment and they   45
come and snatch it right out of your house. Then what you got? Now, soon as I get two hundred dollars clear, then I'll buy a TV. Right now, as soon as I get two hundred and sixty-four dollars, I'm gonna have this roof tarred.

CORY: Aw . . . Pop!

TROY: You go on and get you two hundred dollars and buy one if ya want it. I got better things to do with my money.

CORY: I can't get no two hundred dollars. I ain't never seen two hundred dollars.

TROY: I'll tell you what . . . you get you a hundred dollars and I'll put the other hundred with it.

CORY: All right, I'm gonna show you.   50

TROY: You gonna show me how you can cut them boards right now.

CORY *begins to cut the boards. There is a long pause.*

CORY: The Pirates won today. That makes five in a row.

TROY: I ain't thinking about the Pirates. Got an all-white team. Got that boy . . . that Puerto Rican boy . . . Clemente.° Don't even half-play him. That boy could be something if they give him a chance. Play him one day and sit him on the bench the next.

CORY: He gets a lot of chances to play.

TROY: I'm talking about playing regular. Playing every day so you can get your timing.   55
That's what I'm talking about.

CORY: They got some white guys on the team that don't play every day. You can't play everybody at the same time.

TROY: If they got a white fellow sitting on the bench . . . you can bet your last dollar he can't play! That colored guy got to be twice as good before he get on the team. That's why I don't want you to get all tied up in them sports. Man on the team and what it get him? They got colored on the team and don't use them. Same as not having them. All them teams the same.

°53 *Clemente:* Roberto Clemente (1934–72), one of the all-time best right fielders, played 18 seasons for the Pittsburgh Pirates. In 1957 he was still relatively new, and did not play full time, though Cory is correct in claiming that he was getting "lots of chances to play." Clemente eventually got 3,000 hits, and his lifetime average was .317. He was killed in a plane crash in December 1972.

CORY: The Braves got Hank Aaron and Wes Covington.° Hank Aaron hit two home runs today. That makes forty-three.

TROY: Hank Aaron ain't nobody. That what you supposed to do. That's how you supposed to play the game. Ain't nothing to it. It's just a matter of timing . . . getting the right follow-through. Hell, I can hit forty-three home runs right now!

60 CORY: Not off no major-league pitching, you couldn't.

TROY: We had better pitching in the Negro leagues. I hit seven home runs off of Satchel Paige.° You can't get no better than that!

CORY: Sandy Koufax.° He's leading the league in strikeouts.

TROY: I ain't thinking of no Sandy Koufax.

CORY: You got Warren Spahn and Lew Burdette.° I bet you couldn't hit no home runs off of Warren Spahn.

65 TROY: I'm through with it now. You go on and cut them boards. [*Pause.*] Your mama tell me you done got recruited by a college football team? Is that right?

CORY: Yeah. Coach Zellman say the recruiter gonna be coming by to talk to you. Get you to sign the permission papers.

TROY: I thought you supposed to be working down there at the A&P. Ain't you suppose to be working down there after school?

CORY: Mr. Stawicki say he gonna hold my job for me until after the football season. Say starting next week I can work weekends.

TROY: I thought we had an understanding about this football stuff? You suppose to keep up with your chores and hold that job down at the A&P. Ain't been around here all day on a Saturday. Ain't none of your chores done . . . and now you telling me you done quit your job.

70 CORY: I'm going to be working weekends.

TROY: You damn right you are! And ain't no need for nobody coming around here to talk to me about signing nothing.

CORY: Hey, Pop . . . you can't do that. He's coming all the way from North Carolina.

TROY: I don't care where he coming from. The white man ain't gonna let you get nowhere with that football noway. You go on and get your book-learning so you can work yourself up in that A&P or learn how to fix cars or build houses or something, get you a trade. That way you have something can't nobody take away from you. You go on and learn how to put your hands to some good use. Besides hauling people's garbage.

CORY: I get good grades, Pop. That's why the recruiter wants to talk with you. You got to keep up your grades to get recruited. This way I'll be going to college. I'll get a chance . . .

75 TROY: First you gonna get your butt down there to the A&P and get your job back.

CORY: Mr. Stawicki done already hired somebody else 'cause I told him I was playing football.

TROY: You a bigger fool than I thought . . . to let somebody take away your job so you can play some football. Where you gonna get your money to take out your girlfriend and whatnot? What kind of foolishness is that to let somebody take away your job?

°58 *Hank Aaron and Wes Covington:* Both were relatively new players for the Milwaukee Braves in 1957. Aaron played for the Braves for 18 seasons, and at his retirement in 1976 he was the all-time career home run champion, with 755. Covington's career was not illustrious, lasting only 10 years. 61 *Satchel Paige:* Leroy Robert (Satchel) Paige (1906–82) was a legendary pitcher in the Negro Leagues for more than 20 years, and he ultimately was inducted into Baseball's Hall of Fame. He joined the Cleveland Indians in 1948 when he was already in his forties. His major league career was consequently not outstanding, though baseball fans were enthusiastic about him whenever he pitched. During the year 1957, Paige was involved in exhibition games. His last game as a pitcher took place in 1966, when he was 60 years old. He has been considered one of the alltime best pitchers. 62 *Sandy Koufax:* Sandy Koufax (b. 1935), was in his third professional year in 1957, with the Brooklyn Dodgers. His best years were yet to come, in the 1960s, after the Dodgers moved to Los Angeles. 64 *Warren Spahn and Lew Burdette:* Both Spahn (1921–2003) and Burdette (1926–2007) were stalwart pitchers for the Milwaukee Braves during the 1950s. Spahn won 21 games in 1957, and won the Cy Young Award. He still holds the record for the greatest number of wins by a left-handed pitcher (363). Burdette won 17 games that year, and won three games in the World Series against the Yankees.

CORY: I'm still gonna be working weekends.

TROY: Naw . . . naw. You getting your butt out of here and finding you another job.

CORY: Come on, Pop! I got to practice. I can't work after school and play football too. The   80
team needs me. That's what Coach Zellman say . . .

TROY: I don't care what nobody else say. I'm the boss . . . you understand? I'm the boss
around here. I do the only saying what counts.

CORY: Come on, Pop!

TROY: I asked you . . . did you understand?

CORY: Yeah . . .

TROY: What?!   85

CORY: Yessir.

TROY: You go on down there to that A&P and see if you can get your job back. If you can't
do both . . . then you quit the football team. You've got to take the crookeds with the
straights.

CORY: Yessir. [*Pause.*] Can I ask you a question?

TROY: What the hell you wanna ask me? Mr. Stawicki the one you got the questions for.

CORY: How come you ain't never liked me?   90

TROY: Liked you? Who the hell say I got to like you? What law is there say I got to like
you? Wanna stand up in my face and ask a damn fool-ass question like that. Talking
about liking somebody. Come here, boy, when I talk to you.

*CORY comes over to where TROY is working. He stands slouched over and TROY shoves him on his
shoulder.*

Straighten up, goddammit! I asked you a question . . . what law is there say I got to like you?

CORY: None.

TROY: Well, all right then! Don't you eat every day? [*Pause.*] Answer me when I talk to you!
Don't you eat every day?

CORY: Yeah.

TROY: Nigger, as long as you in my house, you put that sir on the end of it when you talk   95
to me.

CORY: Yes . . . sir.

TROY: You eat every day.

CORY: Yessir!

TROY: Got a roof over your head.

CORY: Yessir!

TROY: Got clothes on your back.   100

CORY: Yessir.

TROY: Why you think that is?

CORY: 'Cause of you.

TROY: Ah, hell I know it's 'cause of me . . . but why do you think that is?   105

CORY: [*hesitant.*] 'Cause you like me.

TROY: Like you? I go out of here every morning . . . bust my butt . . . putting up with them
crackers every day . . . 'cause I like you? You are the biggest fool I ever saw. [*Pause.*]
It's my job. It's my responsibility! You understand that? A man got to take care of his
family. You live in my house . . . sleep you behind on my bedclothes . . . fill you belly
up with my food . . . cause you my son. You my flesh and blood. Not 'cause I like you!
'Cause it's my duty to take care of you. I owe a responsibility to you! Let's get this
straight right here . . . before it go along any further . . . I ain't got to like you. Mr.
Rand don't give me my money come payday 'cause he likes me. He gives me 'cause he
owe me. I done give you everything I had to give you. I gave you your life! Me and
your mama worked that out between us. And liking your black ass wasn't part of the

bargain. Don't you try and go through life worrying about if somebody like you or not. You best be making sure they doing right by you. You understand what I'm saying boy?

CORY: Yes sir.

TROY: Then get the hell out of my face, and get on down to that A&P.

ROSE has been standing behind the screen door for much of the scene. She enters as CORY exits.

110 ROSE: Why don't you let the boy go ahead and play football, Troy? Ain't no harm in that. He's just trying to be like you with the sports.

TROY: I don't want him to be like me! I want him to move as far away from my life as he can get. You the only decent thing that ever happened to me. I wish him that. But I don't wish him a thing else from my life. I decided seventeen years ago that boy wasn't getting involved in no sports. Not after what they did to me in the sports.

ROSE: Troy, why don't you admit you was too old to play in the major leagues? For once . . . why don't you admit that?

TROY: What do you mean too old? Don't come telling me I was too old. I just wasn't the right color. Hell, I'm fifty-three years old and can do better than Selkirk's .269 right now!

ROSE: How's was you gonna play ball when you were over forty? Sometimes I can't get no sense out of you.

115 TROY: I got good sense, woman. I got sense enough not to let my boy get hurt over playing no sports. You been mothering that boy too much. Worried about if people like him.

ROSE: Everything that boy do . . . he do for you. He wants you to say "Good job, son." That's all.

TROY: Rose, I ain't got time for that. He's alive. He's healthy. He's got to make his own way. I made mine. Ain't nobody gonna hold his hand when he get out there in that world.

ROSE: Times have changed from when you was young, Troy. People change. The world's changing around you and you can't even see it.

TROY: [*slow, methodical.*] Woman . . . I do the best I can do. I come in here every Friday. I carry a sack of potatoes and a bucket of lard. You all line up at the door with your hands out. I give you the lint from my pockets. I give you my sweat and my blood. I ain't got no tears. I done spent them. We go upstairs in that room at night . . . and I fall down on you and try to blast a hole into forever. I get up Monday morning . . . find my lunch on the table. I go out. Make my way. Find my strength to carry me through to the next Friday. [*Pause.*] That's all I got, Rose. That's all I got to give. I can't give nothing else.

TROY exits into the house. The lights go down to black.

ACT 1

Scene 4

It is Friday. Two weeks later. CORY starts out of the house with his football equipment. The phone rings.

CORY: [*calling.*] I got it! [*He answers the phone and stands in the screen door talking.*] Hello? Hey, Jesse. Naw . . . I was just getting ready to leave now.

ROSE: [*calling.*] Cory!

CORY: I told you, man, them spikes is all tore up. You can use them if you want, but they ain't no good. Earl got some spikes.

ROSE: [*calling.*] Cory!

5 CORY: [*calling to ROSE.*] Mam? I'm talking to Jesse. [*Into phone.*] When she say that? [*Pause.*] Aw, you lying, man. I'm gonna tell her you said that.

ROSE: [*calling.*] Cory, don't you go nowhere!

CORY: I got to go to the game, Ma! [*Into the phone.*] Yeah, hey, look, I'll talk to you later. Yeah, I'll meet you over Earl's house. Later. Bye, Ma.

CORY *exits the house and starts out the yard.*

ROSE: Cory, where you going off to? You got that stuff all pulled out and thrown all over your room.

CORY: [*in the yard.*] I was looking for my spikes. Jesse wanted to borrow my spikes.

ROSE: Get up there and get that cleaned up before your daddy get back in here.   10

CORY: I got to go to the game! I'll clean it up *when I get back.* [CORY *exits.*]

ROSE: That's all he need to do is see that room all messed up.

ROSE *exits into the house.* TROY *and* BONO *enter the yard.* TROY *is dressed in clothes other than his work clothes.*

BONO: He told him the same thing he told you. Take it to the union.

TROY: Brownie ain't got that much sense. Man wasn't thinking about nothing. He wait until I confront them on it . . . then he wanna come crying seniority. [*Calls.*] Hey, Rose!

BONO: I wish I could have seen Mr. Rand's face when he told you.   15

TROY: He couldn't get it out of his mouth! Liked to bit his tongue! When they called me down there to the Commissioner's office . . . he thought they was gonna fire me. Like everybody else.

BONO: I didn't think they was gonna fire you. I thought they was gonna put you on the warning paper.

TROY: Hey, Rose! [*To* BONO.] Yeah, Mr. Rand like to bit his tongue.

James Earl Jones (as Troy Maxson) sitting on a porch surrounded from left to right by Charles Brown (as Lyons) Mary Alice (as Rose) and Ray Aranha (as Jim Bono) in a 1987 stage production of *Fences* directed by Lloyd Richards at the 46th Street Theater in New York City.

TROY breaks the seal on the bottle, takes a drink, and hands it to BONO.

BONO: I see you run right down to Taylors' and told that Alberta gal.

20 **TROY:** [*calling.*] Hey Rose! [*To BONO.*] I told everybody. Hey, Rose! I went down there to cash my check.

ROSE: [*entering from the house.*] Hush all that hollering, man! I know you out here. What they say down there at the Commissioner's office?

TROY: You supposed to come when I call you, woman. Bono'll tell you that. [*To BONO.*] Don't Lucille come when you call her?

ROSE: Man, hush your mouth. I ain't no dog . . . talk about "come when you call me."

TROY: [*puts his arm around ROSE.*] You hear this, Bono? I had me an old dog used to get up-pity like that. You say, "C'mere, Blue!" . . . and he just lay there and look at you. End up getting a stick and chasing him away trying to make him come.

25 **ROSE:** I ain't studying you and your dog. I remember you used to sing that old song.

TROY: [*he sings.*]

Hear it ring! Hear it ring!
I had a dog his name was Blue.

ROSE: Don't nobody wanna hear you sing that old song.

TROY: [*sings*]. You know Blue was mighty true.

ROSE: Used to have Cory running around here singing that song.

30 **BONO:** Hell, I remember that song myself.

TROY: [*sings.*]

You know Blue was a good old dog
Blue treed a possum in a hollow log.

That was my daddy's song. My daddy made up that song.

ROSE: I don't care who made it up. Don't nobody wanna hear you sing it.

TROY: [*makes a song like calling a dog.*] Come here, woman.

ROSE: You come in here carrying on, I reckon they ain't fired you. What they say down there at the Commissioner's office?

35 **TROY:** Look here, Rose. . . . Mr. Rand called me into his office today when I got back from talking to them people down there . . . it come from up top . . . he called me in and told me they was making me a driver.

ROSE: Troy, you kidding!

TROY: No I ain't. Ask Bono.

ROSE: Well, that's great, Troy. Now you don't have to hassle them people no more.

LYONS enters from the street.

TROY: Aw hell, I wasn't looking to see you today. I thought you was in jail. Got it all over the front page of the *Courier* about them raiding Sefus's place . . . where you be hanging out with all them thugs.

40 **LYONS:** Hey, Pop . . . that ain't got nothing to do with me. I don't go down there gambling. I go down there to sit in with the band. I ain't got nothing to do with the gambling part. They got some good music down there.

TROY: They got some rogues . . . is what they got.

LYONS: How you been, Mr. Bono? Hi, Rose.

BONO: I see where you playing down at the Crawford Grill tonight.

ROSE: How come you ain't brought Bonnie like I told you? You should have brought Bonnie with you, she ain't been over in a month of Sundays.

45 **LYONS:** I was just in the neighborhood . . . thought I'd stop by.

TROY: Here he come . . .

BONO: Your daddy got a promotion on the rubbish. He's gonna be the first colored driver. Ain't got to do nothing but sit up there and read the paper like them white fellows.

LYONS: Hey, Pop . . . if you knew how to read you'd be all right.

BONO: Naw . . . naw . . . you mean if the nigger knew how to drive he'd be all right. Been fighting with them people about driving and ain't even got a license. Mr. Rand know you ain't got no driver's license?

TROY: Driving ain't nothing. All you do is point the truck where you want it to go. Driving ain't nothing.   50

BONO: Do Mr. Rand know you ain't got no driver's license? That's what I'm talking about. I ain't asked if driving was easy. I asked if Mr. Rand know you ain't got no driver's license.

TROY: He ain't got to know. The man ain't got to know my business. Time he find out, I have two or three driver's licenses.

LYONS: [*going into his pocket.*] Say, look here, Pop . . .

TROY: I knew it was coming. Didn't I tell you, Bono? I know what kind of "Look here, Pop" that was. The nigger fixing to ask me for some money. It's Friday night. It's my payday. All them rogues down there on the avenue . . . the ones that ain't in jail . . . and Lyons is hopping in his shoes to get down there with them.

LYONS: See, Pop . . . if you give somebody else a chance to talk sometimes, you'd see that I   55
was fixing to pay you back your ten dollars like I told you. Here . . . I told you I'd pay you when Bonnie got paid.

TROY: Naw . . . you go ahead and keep that ten dollars. Put it in the bank. The next time you feel like you wanna come by here and ask me for something . . . you go on down there and get that.

LYONS: Here's your ten dollars, Pop. I told you I don't want you to give me nothing. I just wanted to borrow ten dollars.

TROY: Naw . . . you go on and keep that for the next time you want to ask me.

LYONS: Come on, Pop . . . here go your ten dollars.

ROSE: Why don't you go on and let the boy pay you back, Troy?   60

LYONS: Here you go, Rose. If you don't take it I'm gonna have to hear about it for the next six months. [*He hands her the money.*]

ROSE: You can hand yours over here too, Troy.

TROY: You see this, Bono. You see how they do me.

BONO: Yeah, Lucille do me the same way.

GABRIEL is heard singing off stage. He enters.

GABRIEL: Better get ready for the Judgment! Better get ready for . . . Hey! . . . Hey! . . .   65
There's Troy's boy!

LYONS: How are you doing, Uncle Gabe?

GABRIEL: Lyons . . . The King of the Jungle! Rose . . . hey, Rose. Got a flower for you. [*He takes a rose from his pocket.*] Picked it myself. That's the same rose like you is!

ROSE: That's right nice of you, Gabe.

LYONS: What you been doing, Uncle Gabe?

GABRIEL: Oh, I been chasing hellhounds and waiting on the time to tell St. Peter to open   70
the gates.

LYONS: You been chasing hellhounds, huh? Well . . . you doing the right thing, Uncle Gabe. Somebody got to chase them.

GABRIEL: Oh, yeah . . . I know it. The devil's strong. The devil ain't no pushover. Hellhounds snipping at everybody's heels. But I got my trumpet waiting on the Judgment time.

LYONS: Waiting on the Battle of Armageddon, huh?

GABRIEL: Ain't gonna be too much of a battle when God get to waving that Judgment sword. But the people's gonna have a hell of a time trying to get into heaven if them gates ain't open.

75   LYONS: [*putting his arm around* GABRIEL.] You hear this, Pop. Uncle Gabe, you all right!

GABRIEL: [*laughing with* LYONS.] Lyons! King of the Jungle.

ROSE: You gonna stay for suppper, Gabe? Want me to fix you a plate?

GABRIEL: I'll take a sandwich, Rose. Don't want no plate. Just wanna eat with my hands. I'll take a sandwich.

ROSE: How about you, Lyons? You staying? Got some short ribs cooking.

80   LYONS: Naw, I won't eat nothing till after we finished playing. [*Pause.*] You ought to come down and listen to me play, Pop.

TROY: I don't like that Chinese music. All that noise.

ROSE: Go on in the house and wash up, Gabe . . . I'll fix you a sandwich.

GABRIEL: [*to* LYONS, *as he exits.*] Troy's mad at me.

LYONS: What you mad at Uncle Gabe for, Pop?

85   ROSE: He thinks Troy's mad at him 'cause he moved over to Miss Pearl's.

TROY: I ain't mad at the man. He can live where he want to live at.

LYONS: What he move over there for? Miss Pearl don't like nobody.

ROSE: She don't mind him none. She treats him real nice. She just don't allow all that singing.

TROY: She don't mind that rent he be paying . . . That's what she don't mind.

90   ROSE: Troy, I ain't going through that with you no more. He's over there cause he want to have his own place. He can come and go as he please.

TROY: Hell, he could come and go as he please here. I wasn't stopping him. I ain't put no rules on him.

ROSE: It ain't the same thing, Troy. And you know it. [GABRIEL *comes to the door.*] Now, that's the last I wanna hear about that. I don't wanna hear nothing else about Gabe and Miss Pearl. And next week . . .

GABRIEL: I'm ready for my sandwich, Rose.

ROSE: And next week . . . when that recruiter come from that school . . . I want you to sign that paper and go on and let Cory play football. Then that'll be the last I have to hear about that.

95   TROY: [*to* ROSE *as she exits in to the house.*] I ain't thinking about Cory nothing.

LYONS: What . . . Cory got recruited? What school he going to?

TROY: That boy walking around here smelling his piss . . . thinking he's grown. Thinking he's gonna do what he want, irrespective of what I say. Look here, Bono . . . I left the Commissioner's office and went down to the A&P . . . that boy ain't working down there. He lying to me. Telling me he got his job back . . . telling me he working weekends . . . telling me he working after school . . . Mr. Stawicki tell me he ain't working down there at all!

LYONS: Cory just growing up. He's just busting at the seams trying to fill out your shoes.

TROY: I don't care what he's doing. When he get to the point where he wanna disobey me . . . then it's time for him to move on. Bono'll tell you that. I bet he ain't never disobeyed his daddy without paying the consequences.

100 BONO: I ain't never had a chance. My daddy came on through . . . but I ain't never knew him to see him . . . or what he had on his mind or where he went. Just moving on through. Searching out the New Land. That's what the old folks used to call it. See a fellow moving around from place to place . . . woman to woman . . . called it searching out the New Land. I can't say if he ever found it. I come along, didn't want no kids. Didn't know if I was gonna be in one place long enough to fix on them right as their daddy. I figured I was going searching too. As it turned out I been hooked up with Lucille near about as long as your daddy been with Rose. Going on sixteen years.

TROY: Sometimes I wish I hadn't known my daddy. He ain't cared nothing about no kids. A kid to him wasn't nothing. All he wanted was for you to learn how to walk so he could start you to working. When it come time for eating . . . he ate first. If there was anything left over, that's what you got. Man would sit down and eat two chickens and give you the wing.

LYONS: You ought to stop that, Pop. Everybody feed their kids. No matter how hard times is . . . everybody care about their kids. Make sure they have something to eat.

TROY: The only thing my daddy cared about was getting them bales of cotton in to Mr. Lubin. That's the only thing that mattered to him. Sometimes I used to wonder why he was living. Wonder why the devil hadn't come and got him. "Get them bales of cotton in to Mr. Lubin" and find out he owe him money . . .

LYONS: He should have just went on and left when he saw he couldn't get nowhere. That's what I would have done.

TROY: How he gonna leave with eleven kids? And where he gonna go? He ain't knew how to do nothing but farm. No, he was trapped and I think he knew it. But I'll say this for him . . . he felt a responsibility toward us. Maybe he ain't treated us the way I felt he should have . . . but without that responsibility he could have walked off and left us . . . made his own way. 105

BONO: A lot of them did. Back in those days what you talking about . . . they walk out their front door and just take on down one road or another and keep on walking.

LYONS: There you go! That's what I'm talking about.

BONO: Just keep on walking till you come to something else. Ain't you never heard of nobody having the walking blues? Well, that's what you call it when you just take off like that.

TROY: My daddy ain't had them walking blues! What you talking about? He stayed right there with his family. But he was just as evil as he could be. My mama couldn't stand him. Couldn't stand that evilness. She run off when I was about eight. She sneaked off one night after he had gone to sleep. Told me she was coming back for me. I ain't never seen her no more. All his women run off and left him. He wasn't good for nobody. When my turn come to head out, I was fourteen and got to sniffing around Joe Canewell's daughter. Had us an old mule we called Greyboy. My daddy sent me out to do some plowing and I tied up Greyboy and went to fooling around with Joe Canewell's daughter. We done found us a nice little spot, got real cozy with each other. She about thirteen and we done figured we was grown anyway . . . so we down there enjoying ourselves . . . ain't thinking about nothing. We didn't know Greyboy had got loose and wandered back to the house and my daddy was looking for me. We down there by the creek enjoying ourselves when my daddy come up on us. Surprised us. He had them leather straps off the mule and commenced to whupping me like there was no tomorrow. I jumped up, mad and embarrassed. I was scared of my daddy. When he commenced to whupping on me . . . quite naturally I run to get out of the way. [Pause.] Now I thought he was mad 'cause I ain't done my work. But I see where he was chasing me off so he could have the gal for himself. When I see what the matter of if was, I lost all fear of my daddy. Right there is where I become a man . . . at fourteen years of age. [Pause.] Now it was my turn to run him off. I picked up them same reins that he had used on me. I picked up them reins and commenced to whupping on him. The gal jumped up and run him off . . . and when my daddy turned to face me, I could see why the devil had never come to get him . . . 'cause he was the devil himself. I don't know what happened. When I woke up, I was laying right there by the creek, and Blue . . . this old dog we had . . . was licking my face. I thought I was blind. I couldn't see nothing. Both my eyes were swollen shut. I laid there and cried. I didn't know what I was gonna do. The only thing I knew was the time had come for me to leave my daddy's house. And right there the world suddenly got big. And it was a long time before I could cut it down to where I could handle it. Part of that cutting down was when I got to the place where I could feel him kicking in my blood and knew that the only thing that separated us was the matter of a few years.

GABRIEL *enters from the house with a sandwich.*

110 LYONS: What you got there, Uncle Gabe?

GABRIEL: Got me a ham sandwich. Rose gave me a ham sandwich.

TROY: I don't know what happened to him. I done lost touch with everybody except Gabriel. But I hope he's dead. I hope he found some peace.

LYONS: That's a heavy story, Pop. I didn't know you left home when you was fourteen.

TROY: And didn't know nothing. The only part of the world I knew was the forty-two acres of Mr. Lubin's land. That's all I knew about life.

115 LYONS: Fourteen's kinda young to be out on your own. [*Phone rings.*] I don't even think I was ready to be out on my own at fourteen. I don't know what I would have done.

TROY: I got up from the creek and walked on down to Mobile. I was through with farming. Figured I could do better in the city. So I walked the two hundred miles to Mobile.

LYONS: Wait a minute . . . you ain't walked no two hundred miles, Pop. Ain't nobody gonna walk no two hundred miles. You talking about some walking there.

BONO: That's the only way you got anywhere back in them days.

LYONS: Shhh. Damn if I wouldn't have hitched a ride with someday!

120 TROY: Who you gonna hitch it with? They ain't had no cars and things like they got now. We talking about 1918.

ROSE: [*entering.*] What you all out here getting into?

TROY: [*to ROSE.*] I'm telling Lyons how good he got it. He don't know nothing about this I'm talking.

ROSE: Lyons, that was Bonnie on the phone. She say you supposed to pick her up.

LYONS: Yeah, okay Rose.

125 TROY: I walked on down to Mobile and hitched up with some of them fellows that was heading this way. Got up here and found out . . . not only couldn't you get a job . . . you couldn't find no place to live. I thought I was in freedom. Shhh. Colored folks living down there on the river banks in whatever kind of shelter they could find for themselves. Right down there under the Brady Street Bridge. Living in shacks made of sticks and tarpaper. Messed around there and went from bad to worse. Started stealing. First it was food. Then I figured, hell, if I steal money I can buy me some food. Buy me some shoes too! One thing led to another. Met your mama. I was young and anxious to be a man. Met your mama and had you. What I do that for? Now I got to worry about feeding you and her. Got to steal three times as much. Went out one day looking for somebody to rob . . . that's what I was, a robber. I'll tell you the truth. I'm ashamed of it today. But it's the truth. Went to rob this fellow . . . pulled out my knife . . . and he pulled out a gun. Shot me in the chest. I felt just like somebody had taken a hot branding iron and laid it on me. When he shot me I jumped at him with my knife. They told me I killed him and they put me in the penitentiary and locked me up for fifteen years. That's where I met Bono. That's where I learned how to play baseball. Got out that place and your mama had taken you and went on to make life without me. Fifteen years was a long time for her to wait. But that fifteen years cured me of that robbing stuff. Rose'll tell you. She asked me when I met her if I had gotten all that foolishness out of my system. And I told her, "Baby, it's you and baseball all what count with me." You hear me, Bono? I meant it too. She say, "Which one comes first?" I told her, "Baby, ain't no doubt it's baseball . . . but you stick and get old with me and we'll both outlive this baseball." Am I right, Rose? And it's true.

ROSE: Man, hush your mouth. You ain't said no such thing. Talking about, "Baby you know you'll always be number one with me." That's what you was talking.

TROY: You hear that, Bono. That's why I love her.

BONO: Rose'll keep you straight. You get off the track, she'll straighten you up.

ROSE: Lyons, you better get on up and get Bonnie. She waiting on you.

LYONS: [*gets up to go.*] Hey, Pop, why don't you come on down to the Grill and hear me   130
play?

TROY: I ain't going down there. I'm too old to be sitting around in them clubs.

BONO: You got to be good to play down at the Grill.

LYONS: Come on, Pop . . .

TROY: I got to get up in the morning.

LYONS: You ain't got to stay long.   135

TROY: Naw, I'm gonna get my supper and go on to bed.

LYONS: Well, I got to go. I'll see you again.

TROY: Don't you come around my house on my payday.

ROSE: Pick up the phone and let somebody know you coming. And bring Bonnie with you.
You know I'm always glad to see her.

LYONS: Yeah, I'll do that, Rose. You take care now. See you, Pop. See you, Mr. Bono. See   140
you, Uncle Gabe.

GABRIEL: Lyons! King of the Jungle! [*LYONS exits.*]

TROY: Is supper ready, woman? Me and you got some business to take care of. I'm gonna
tear it up too.

ROSE: Troy, I done told you now!

TROY: [*puts his arm around BONO.*] Aw hell, woman . . . this is Bono. Bono like family. I done
known this nigger since . . . how long I done know you?

BONO: It's been a long time.   145

TROY: I done know this nigger since Skippy was a pup. Me and him done been through
some times.

BONO: You sure right about that.

TROY: Hell, I done know him longer than I known you. And we still standing shoulder to
shoulder. Hey look here, Bono . . . a man can't ask for no more than that. [*Drinks to
him.*] I love you, nigger.

BONO: Hell, I love you too . . . I got to get home see my woman. You got yours in hand. I
got to get mine.

*BONO starts to exit as CORY enters the yard, dressed in his football uniform. He gives TROY a hard,
uncompromising look.*

CORY: What you do that for, Pop?   150

He throws his helmet down in the direction of TROY.

ROSE: What's the matter? Cory . . . What's the matter?

CORY: Papa done went up to the school and told Coach Zellman I can't play football no
more. Wouldn't even let me play the game. Told him to tell the recruiter not to come.

ROSE: Troy . . .

TROY: What you Troying me for. Yeah, I did it. And the boy know why I did it.

CORY: Why you wanna do that to me? That was the one chance I had.   155

ROSE: Ain't nothing wrong with Cory playing football, Troy.

TROY: The boy lied to me. I told the nigger if he wanna play football . . . to keep up his
chores and hold down that job at the A&P. That was the conditions. Stopped down
there to see Mr. Stawicki . . .

CORY: I can't work after school during the football season, Pop! I tried to tell you that Mr.
Stawicki's holding my job for me. You don't never want to listen to nobody. And then
you wanna go and do this to me!

TROY: I ain't done nothing to you. You done it to yourself.

160 CORY: Just cause you didn't have a chance! You just scared I'm gonna be better than you, that's all.

TROY: Come here.

ROSE: Troy . . .

CORY reluctantly crosses over to TROY.

TROY: All right! See. You done made a mistake.

CORY: I didn't even do nothing!

165 TROY: I'm gonna tell you what your mistake was. See . . . you swung at the ball and didn't hit it. That's strike one. See, you in the batter's box now. You swung and you missed. That's strike one. Don't you strike out!

Lights fade to black.

ACT 2

Scene 1

The following morning. CORY is at the tree hitting the ball with the bat. He tries to mimic TROY, but his swing is awkward, less sure. ROSE enters from the house.

ROSE: Cory, I want you to help me with this cupboard.

CORY: I ain't quitting the team. I don't care what Poppa say.

ROSE: I'll talk to him when he gets back. He had to go see about your Uncle Gabe. The police done arrested him. Say he was disturbing the peace. He'll be back directly. Come on in here and help me clean out the top of this cupboard.

CORY exits into the house. ROSE sees TROY and BONO coming down the alley.

TROY: . . . what they say down there?

5 TROY: Ain't said nothing. I give them fifty dollars and they let him go. I'll talk to you about it. Where's Cory?

ROSE: He's in there helping me clean out these cupboards.

TROY: Tell him to get his butt out here.

TROY and BONO go over to the pile of wood. BONO picks up the saw and begins sawing.

TROY: [*to BONO.*] All they want is the money. That makes six or seven times I done went down there and got him. See me coming they stick out their hands.

BONO: Yeah. I know what you mean. That's all they care about . . . that money. They don't care about what's right. [*Pause.*] Nigger, why you got to go and get some hard wood? You ain't doing nothing but building a little old fence. Get you some soft pine wood. That's all you need.

10 TROY: I know what I'm doing. This is outside wood. You put pine wood inside the house. Pine wood is inside wood. This here is outside wood. Now you tell me where the fence is gonna be?

BONO: You don't need this wood. You can put it up with pine wood and it'll stand as long as you gonna be here looking at it.

TROY: How you know how long I'm gonna be here, nigger? Hell, I might just live forever. Live longer than old man Horsely.

BONO: That's what Magee used to say.

TROY: Magee's a damn fool. Now you tell me who you ever heard of gonna pull their own teeth with a pair of rusty pliers.

BONO: The old folks . . . my granddaddy used to pull his teeth with pliers. They ain't had   15
no dentists for the colored folks back then.

TROY: Get clean pliers! You understand? Clean pliers! Sterilize them! Besides we ain't living back then. All Magee had to do was walk over to Doc Goldblum's.

BONO: I see where you and that Tallahassee gal . . . that Alberta . . . I see where you all
done got tight.

TROY: What you mean "got tight"?

BONO: I see where you be laughing and joking with her all the time.

TROY: I laughs and jokes with all of them, Bono. You know me.   20

BONO: That ain't the kind of laughing and joking I'm talking about.

CORY enters from the house.

CORY: How you doing, Mr. Bono?

TROY: Cory? Get that saw from Bono and cut some wood. He talking about the wood's too
hard to cut. Stand back there, Jim, and let that young boy show you how it's done.

BONO: He's sure welcome to it. [*CORY takes the saw and begins to cut the wood.*]
Whew-e-e! Look at that. Big old strong boy. Look like Joe Louis.° Hell, must be getting
old the way I'm watching that boy whip through that wood.

CORY: I don't see why Mama want a fence around the yard noways.   25

TROY: Damn if I know either. What the hell she keeping out with it? She ain't got nothing
nobody want.

BONO: Some people build fences to keep people out . . . and other people build fences to
keep people in. Rose wants to hold on to you all. She loves you.

TROY: Hell, nigger, I don't need nobody to tell me my wife loves me. Cory . . . go on in the
house and see if you can find that other saw.

CORY: Where's it at?

TROY: I said find it! Look for it till you find it! [*CORY exits into the house.*] What's that sup-   30
posed to mean? Wanna keep us in?

BONO: Troy . . . I done known you seem like damn near my whole life. You and Rose both.
I done know both of you all for a long time. I remember when you met Rose. When
you was hitting them baseball out the park. A lot of them old gals was after you then.
You had the pick of the litter. When you picked Rose, I was happy for you. That was
the first time I knew you had any sense. I said . . . My man Troy knows what he's doing . . . I'm gonna follow this nigger . . . he might take me somewhere.
I been following you too. I done learned a whole heap of things about life watching
you. I done learned how to tell where the shit lies. How to tell it from the alfalfa. You
done learned me a lot of things. You showed me how to not make the same mistakes . . .
to take life as it comes along and keep putting one foot in front of the other. [*Pause.*]
Rose a good woman, Troy.

TROY: Hell, nigger, I know she a good woman. I been married to her for eighteen years.
What you got on your mind, Bono?

BONO: I just say she a good woman. Just like I say anything. I ain't got to have nothing on
my mind.

TROY: You just gonna say she a good woman and leave it hanging out there like that? Why
you telling me she a good woman?

BONO: She loves you, Troy. Rose loves you.   35

°24 *Joe Louis:* Louis (1914–81), known as the "Brown Bomber," was a dominant black heavyweight who became
champion in 1937, and held the championship for 11 years. By 1957 he had long since retired from boxing, and had
become a wrestler. He retired from that in 1957 because of an injury. He was proverbial for his power in the ring.

TROY: You saying I don't measure up. That's what you trying to say. I don't measure up cause I'm seeing this other gal. I know what you trying to say.

BONO: I know what Rose means to you, Troy. I'm just trying to say I don't want to see you mess up.

TROY: Yeah, I appreciate that, Bono. If you was messing around on Lucille I'd be telling you the same thing.

BONO: Well, that's all I got to say. I just say that because I love you both.

40 TROY: Hell, you know me . . . I wasn't out there looking for nothing. You can't find a better woman than Rose. I know that. But seems like this woman just stuck onto me where I can't shake her loose. I done wrestled with it, tried to throw her off me . . . but she just stuck on tighter. Now she's stuck on for good.

BONO: You's in control . . . that's what you tell me all the time. You responsible for what you do.

TROY: I ain't ducking the responsibility of it. As long as it sets right in my heart . . . then I'm okay. 'Cause that's all I listen to. It'll tell me right from wrong every time. And I ain't talking about doing Rose no bad turn. I love Rose. She done carried me a long ways and I love and respect her for that.

BONO: I know you do. That's why I don't want to see you hurt her. But what you gonna do when she find out? What you got then? If you try and juggle both of them . . . sooner or later you gonna drop one of them. That's common sense.

TROY: Yeah, I hear what you saying, Bono. I been trying to figure a way to work it out.

45 BONO: Work it out right, Troy. I don't want to be getting all up between you and Rose's business . . . but work it so it come out right.

TROY: Ah hell, I get all up between you and Lucille's business. When you gonna get that woman that refrigerator she been wanting? Don't tell me you ain't got no money now. I know who your banker is. Mellon don't need that money bad as Lucille want that refrigerator. I'll tell you that.

BONO: Tell you what I'll do . . . when you finish building this fence for Rose . . . I'll buy Lucille that refrigerator.

TROY: You done stuck your foot in your mouth now!

TROY grabs up a board and begins to saw. BONO starts to walk out the yard.

Hey, nigger . . . where you going?

BONO: I'm going home. I know you don't expect me to help you now. I'm protecting my money. I wanna see you put that fence up by yourself. That's what I want to see. You'll be here another six months without me.

50 TROY: Nigger, you ain't right.

BONO: When it comes to my money . . . I'm right as fireworks on the Fourth of July.

TROY: All right, we gonna see now. You better get out your bankbook.

BONO exits, and TROY continues to work. ROSE enters from the house.

ROSE: What they say down there? What's happening with Gabe?

TROY: I went down there and got him out. Cost me fifty dollars. Say he was disturbing the peace. Judge set up a hearing for him in three weeks. Say to show cause why he shouldn't be recommitted.

55 ROSE: What was he doing that cause them to arrest him?

TROY: Some kids was teasing him and he run them off home. Say he was howling and carrying on. Some folks seen him and called the police. That's all it was.

ROSE: Well, what's you say? What'd you tell the judge?

TROY: Told him I'd look after him. It didn't make no sense to recommit the man. He stuck out his big greasy palm and told me to give him fifty dollars and take him on home.

ROSE: Where's he at now? Where'd he go off to?

TROY: He's gone about his business. He don't need nobody to hold his hand.   60

ROSE: Well, I don't know. Seem like that would be the best place for him if they did put him into the hospital. I know what you're gonna say. But that's what I think would be best.

TROY: The man done had his life ruined fighting for what? And they wanna take and lock him up. Let him be free. He don't bother nobody.

ROSE: Well, everybody got their own way of looking at it I guess. Come on and get your lunch. I got a bowl of lima beans and some cornbread in the oven. Come and get something to eat. Ain't no sense you fretting over Gabe.

ROSE turns to go into the house.

TROY: Rose . . . got something to tell you.

ROSE: Well, come on . . . wait till I get this food on the table.   65

TROY: Rose! [*She stops and turns around.*] I don't know how to say this. [*Pause.*] I can't explain it none. It just sort of grows on you till it gets out of hand. It starts out like a little bush . . . and the next thing you know it's a whole forest.

ROSE: Troy . . . what is you talking about?

TROY: I'm talking, woman, let me talk. I'm trying to find a way to tell you . . . I'm gonna be a daddy. I'm gonna be somebody's daddy.

ROSE: Troy . . . you're not telling me this? You're gonna be . . . what?

TROY: Rose . . . now . . . see . . .   70

ROSE: You telling me you gonna be somebody's daddy? You telling your *wife* this?

GABRIEL: [*enters from the street. He carries a rose in his hand.*] Hey, Troy! Hey, Rose!

ROSE: I have to wait eighteen years to hear something like this.

GABRIEL: Hey, Rose . . . I got a flower for you. [*He hands it to her.*] That's a rose. Same rose like you is.

ROSE: Thanks, Gabe.   75

GABRIEL: Troy, you ain't mad at me is you? Them bad mens come and put me away. You ain't mad at me is you?

TROY: Naw, Gabe, I ain't mad at you.

ROSE: Eighteen years and you wanna come with this.

GABRIEL: [*takes a quarter out of his pocket*]. See what I got? Got a brand new quarter.

TROY: Rose . . . it's just . . .   80

ROSE: Ain't nothing you can say, Troy. Ain't no way of explaining that.

GABRIEL: Fellow that give me this quarter had a whole mess of them. I'm gonna keep this quarter till it stop shining.

ROSE: Gabe, go on in the house there. I got some watermelon in the Frigidaire. Go on and get you a piece.

GABRIEL: Say, Rose . . . you know I was chasing hellhounds and them bad mens come and get me and take me away. Troy helped me. He come down there and told them they better let me go before he beat them up. Yeah, he did!

ROSE: You go on and get you a piece of watermelon, Gabe. Them bad mens is gone now.   85

GABRIEL: Okay, Rose . . . gonna get me some watermelon. The kind with the stripes on it.

GABRIEL exits into the house.

ROSE: Why, Troy? Why? After all these years to come dragging this in to me now. It don't make no sense at your age. I could have expected this ten or fifteen years ago, but not now.

TROY: Age ain't got nothing to do with it, Rose.

ROSE: I done tried to be everything a wife should be. Everything a wife could be. Been married eighteen years and I got to live to see the day you tell me you been seeing another woman and done fathered a child by her. And you know I ain't never wanted no half nothing in my family. My whole family is half. Everybody got different fathers and mothers . . . my two sisters and my brother. Can't hardly tell who's who. Can't never sit down and talk about Papa and Mama. It's your papa and your mama and my papa and my mama . . .

90 TROY: Rose . . . stop it now.

ROSE: I ain't never wanted that for none of my children. And now you wanna drag your behind in here and tell me something like this.

TROY: You ought to know. It's time for you to know.

ROSE: Well, I don't want to know, goddamn it!

TROY: I can't just make it go away. It's done now. I can't wish the circumstance of the thing away.

95 ROSE: And you don't want to either. Maybe you want to wish me and my boy away. Maybe that's what you want? Well, you can't wish us away. I've got eighteen years of my life invested in you. You ought to have stayed upstairs in my bed where you belong.

TROY: Rose . . . now listen to me . . . we can get a handle on this thing. We can talk this out . . . come to an understanding.

ROSE: All of a sudden it's "we." Where was "we" at when you was down there rolling around with some godforsaken woman? "We" should have come to an understanding before you started making a damn fool of yourself. You're a day late and a dollar short when it comes to an understanding with me.

TROY: It's just . . . She gives me a different idea . . . a different understanding about myself. I can step out of this house and get away from the pressures and problems . . . be a different man. I ain't got to wonder how I'm gonna pay the bills or get the roof fixed. I can just be a part of myself that I ain't never been.

ROSE: What I want to know . . . is do you plan to continue seeing her. That's all you can say to me.

100 TROY: I can sit up in her house and laugh. Do you understand what I'm saying. I can laugh out loud . . . and it feels good. It reaches all the way down to the bottom of my shoes. [*Pause.*] Rose, I can't give that up.

ROSE: Maybe you ought to go on and stay down there with her . . . if she's a better woman than me.

TROY: It ain't about nobody being a better woman or nothing. Rose, you ain't the blame. A man couldn't ask for no woman to be a better wife than you've been. I'm responsible for it. I done locked myself into a pattern trying to take care of you all that I forgot about myself.

ROSE: What the hell was I there for? That was my job, not somebody else's.

TROY: Rose, I done tried all my life to live decent . . . to live a clean . . . hard . . . useful life. I tried to be a good husband to you. In every way I knew how. Maybe I come into the world backwards, I don't know. But . . . you born with two strikes on you before you come to the plate. You got to guard it closely . . . always looking for the curve ball on the inside corner. You can't afford to let none get past you. You can't afford a call strike. If you going down . . . you going down swinging. Everything lined up against you. What you gonna do. I fooled them, Rose. I bunted. When I found you and Cory and a halfway decent job . . . I was safe. Couldn't nothing touch me. I wasn't gonna strike out no more. I wasn't going back to the penitentiary. I wasn't gonna lay in the streets with a bottle of wine. I was safe. I had me a family. A job. I wasn't gonna get that last strike. I was on first looking for one of them boys to knock me in. To get me home.

105 ROSE: You should have stayed in my bed, Troy.

TROY: Then when I saw that gal . . . she firmed up my backbone. And I got to thinking that if I tried . . . I just might be able to steal second. Do you understand after eighteen years I wanted to steal second.

ROSE: You should have held me tight. You should have grabbed me and held on.

TROY: I stood on first base for eighteen years and I thought . . . well, goddamn it . . . go on for it!

ROSE: We're not talking about baseball! We're talking about you going off to lay in bed with another woman . . . and then bring it home to me. That's what we're talking about. We ain't talking about no baseball.

TROY: Rose, you're not listening to me. I'm trying the best I can to explain it to you. It's not   110
easy for me to admit that I been standing in the same place for eighteen years.

ROSE: I been standing with you! I been right here with you, Troy. I got a life too. I gave eighteen years of my life to stand in the same spot with you. Don't you think I ever wanted other things? Don't you think I had dreams and hopes? What about my life? What about me? Don't you think it ever crossed my mind to want to know other men? That I wanted to lay up somewhere and forget about my responsibilities? That I wanted someone to make me laugh so I could feel good? You not the only one who's got wants and needs. But I held on to you, Troy. I took all my feelings, my wants and needs, my dreams . . . and I buried them inside you. I planted a seed and watched and prayed over it. I planted myself inside you and waited to bloom. And it didn't take me no eighteen years to find out the soil was hard and rocky and it wasn't never gonna bloom. But I held on to you, Troy. I held you tighter. You was my husband. I owed you everything I had. Every part of me I could find to give you. And upstairs in that room . . . with the darkness falling in on me . . . I gave everything I had to try and erase the doubt that you wasn't the finest man in the world. And wherever you was going . . . I wanted to be there with you. 'Cause you was my husband. 'Cause that's the only way I was gonna survive as your wife. You always talking about what you give . . . and what you don't have to give. But you take too. You take . . . and don't even know nobody's giving!

ROSE turns to exit into the house; TROY grabs her arm.

TROY: You say I take and don't give!

ROSE: Troy! You're hurting me!

TROY: You say I take and don't give!

ROSE: Troy . . . you're hurting my arm! Let go!   115

TROY: I done give you everything I got. Don't you tell that lie on me.

ROSE: Troy!

TROY: Don't you tell that lie on me!

CORY: [*enters from the house.*] Mama!

ROSE: Troy. You're hurting me.   120

TROY: Don't you tell me about no taking and giving.

CORY comes up behind TROY and grabs him. TROY, surprised, is thrown off balance just as CORY throws a glancing blow that catches him on the chest and knocks him down. TROY is stunned, as is CORY.

ROSE: Troy. Troy. No! [*TROY gets to his feet and starts at CORY.*] Troy . . . no. Please! Troy!

ROSE pulls on TROY to hold him back. TROY stops himself.

TROY: [*to CORY.*] All right. That's strike two. You stay away from around me, boy. Don't you strike out. You living with a full count. Don't you strike out.

TROY exits out the yard as the lights go down.

ACT 2

Scene 2

It is six months later, early afternoon. TROY *enters from the house and starts to exit the yard.* ROSE *enters from the house.*

ROSE: Troy, I want to talk to you.

TROY: All of a sudden, after all this time, you want to talk to me, huh? You ain't wanted to talk to me for months. You ain't wanted to talk to me last night. You ain't wanted no part of me then. What you wanna talk to me about now?

ROSE: Tomorrow's Friday.

TROY: I know what day tomorrow is. You think I don't know tomorrow's Friday? My whole life I ain't done nothing but look to see Friday coming and you got to tell me it's Friday.

5   ROSE: I want to know if you're coming home.

TROY: I always come home, Rose. You know that. There ain't never been a night I ain't come home.

ROSE: That ain't what I mean . . . and you know it. I want to know if you're coming straight home after work.

TROY: I figure I'd cash my check . . . hang out at Taylors' with the boys . . . maybe play a game of checkers . . .

ROSE: Troy, I can't live like this. I won't live like this. You livin' on borrowed time with me. It's been going on six months now you ain't been coming home.

10   TROY: I be here every night. Every night of the year. That's 365 days.

ROSE: I want you to come home tomorrow after work.

TROY: Rose . . . I don't mess up my pay. You know that now. I take my pay and I give it to you. I don't have no money but what you give me back. I just want to have little time to myself . . . a little time to enjoy life.

ROSE: What about me? When's my time to enjoy life?

TROY: I don't know what to tell you, Rose. I'm doing the best I can.

15   ROSE: You ain't been home from work but time enough to change your clothes and run out . . . and you wanna call that the best you can do?

TROY: I'm going over to the hospital to see Alberta. She went into the hospital this afternoon. Look like she might have the baby early. I won't be gone long.

ROSE: Well, you ought to know. They went over to Miss Pearl's and got Gabe today. She said you told them to go ahead and lock him up.

TROY: I ain't said no such thing. Whoever told you that is telling a lie. Pearl ain't doing nothing but telling a big fat lie.

ROSE: She ain't had to tell me. I read it on the papers.

20   TROY: I ain't told them nothing of the kind.

ROSE: I saw it right there on the papers.

TROY: What it say, huh?

ROSE: It said you told them to take him.

TROY: Then they screwed that up, just the way they screw up everything. I ain't worried about what they got on the paper.

25   ROSE: Say the government sent part of his check to the hospital and the other part to you.

TROY: I ain't got nothing to do with that if that's the way it works. I ain't made up the rules about how it work.

ROSE: You did Gabe just like you did Cory. You wouldn't sign the paper for Cory . . . but you signed for Gabe. You signed that paper.

The telephone is heard ringing inside the house.

TROY: I told you I ain't signed nothing, woman! The only thing I signed was the release form. Hell, I can't read, I don't know what they had on that paper! I ain't signed nothing about sending Gabe away.

ROSE: I said send him to the hospital . . . you said let him be free . . . now you done went down there and signed him to the hospital for half his money. You went back on yourself, Troy. You gonna have to answer for that.

TROY: See now . . . you been over there talking to Miss Pearl. She done got mad 'cause she   30
ain't getting Gabe's rent money. That's all it is. She's liable to say anything.

ROSE: Troy, I seen where you signed the paper.

TROY: You ain't seen nothing I signed. What she doing got papers on my brother anyway? Miss Pearl telling a big fat lie. And I'm gonna tell her about it too! You ain't seen nothing I signed. Say . . . you ain't seen nothing I signed.

ROSE exits into the house to answer the telephone. Presently she returns.

ROSE: Troy . . . that was the hospital. Alberta had the baby.

TROY: What she have? What is it?

ROSE: It's a girl.   35

TROY: I better get on down to the hospital to see her.

ROSE: Troy . . .

TROY: Rose . . . I got to go see her now. That's only right . . . what's the matter . . . the baby's all right, ain't it?

ROSE: Alberta died having the baby.

TROY: Died . . . you say she's dead? Alberta's dead?   40

ROSE: They said they done all they could. They couldn't do nothing for her.

TROY: The baby? How's the baby?

ROSE: They say it's healthy. I wonder who's gonna bury her.

TROY: She had family, Rose. She wasn't living in the world by herself.

ROSE: I know she wasn't living in the world by herself.   45

TROY: Next thing you gonna want to know if she had any insurance.

ROSE: Troy, you ain't got to talk like that.

TROY: That's the first thing that jumped out your mouth. "Who's gonna bury her?" Like I'm fixing to take on that task for myself.

ROSE: I am your wife. Don't push me away.

TROY: I ain't pushing nobody away. Just give me some space. That's all. Just give me some   50
room to breathe.

ROSE exits into the house. TROY walks about the yard.

[*with a quiet rage that threatens to consume him*]. All right . . . Mr. Death. See now . . . I'm gonna tell you what I'm gonna do. I'm gonna take and build me a fence around this yard. See? I'm gonna build me a fence around what belongs to me. And then I want you to stay on the other side. See? You stay over there until you're ready for me. Then you come on. Bring your army. Bring your sickel. Bring your wrestling clothes. I ain't gonna fall down on my vigilance this time. You ain't gonna sneak up on me no more. When you ready for me . . . when the top of your list say Troy Maxson . . . that's when you come around here. You come up and knock on the front door. Ain't nobody else got nothing to do with this. This is between you and me. Man to man. You stay on the other side of that fence until you ready for me. Then you come up and knock on the front door. Anytime you want. I'll be ready for you.

The lights go down to black.

ACT 2

Scene 3

The lights come up on the porch. It is late evening three days later. ROSE *sits listening to the ball game waiting for* TROY. *The final out of the game is made and* ROSE *switches off the radio.* TROY *enters the yard carrying an infant wrapped in blankets. He stands back from the house and calls.*

ROSE enters and stands on the porch. There is a long, awkward silence, the weight of which grows heavier with each passing second.

TROY: Rose . . . I'm standing here with my daughter in my arms. She ain't but a wee bittie little old thing. She don't know nothing about grownups' business. She innocent . . . and she ain't got no mama.

ROSE: What you telling me for, Troy? [*She turns and exits into the house.*]

TROY: Well . . . I guess we'll just sit out here on the porch.

He sits down on the porch. There is an awkward indelicateness about the way be handles the body. His largeness engulfs and seems to swallow it. He speaks loud enough for ROSE *to hear.*

A man's got to do what's right for him. I ain't sorry for nothing I done. It felt right in my heart. [*To the baby.*] What you smiling at? Your daddy's a big man. Got these great big old hands. But sometimes he's scared. And right now your daddy's scared cause we sitting out here and ain't got no home. Oh, I been homeless before. I ain't had no little baby with me. But I been homeless. You just be out on the road by your lonesome and you see one of them trains coming and you just kinda go like this . . . [*He sings as a lullaby.*]

Please, Mr. Engineer let a man ride the line
Please, Mr. Engineer let a man ride the line
I ain't got no ticket please let me ride the blinds.

ROSE enters from the house. TROY, *hearing her steps behind him, stands and faces her.*

She's my daughter, Rose. My own flesh and blood. I can't deny her no more than I can deny them boys. [*Pause.*] You and them boys is my family. You and them and this child is all I got in the world. So I guess what I'm saying is . . . I'd appreciate it if you'd help me take care of her.

ROSE: Okay, Troy . . . you're right. I'll take care of your baby for you . . . 'cause . . . like you say . . . she's innocent . . . and you can't visit the sins of the father upon the child. A motherless child has got a hard time. [*She takes the baby from him.*] From right now . . . this child got a mother. But you a womanless man.

ROSE turns and exits into the house with the baby. Lights go down to black.

ACT 2

Scene 4

It is two months later. LYONS *enters the street. He knocks on the door and calls.*

LYONS: Hey, Rose! [*Pause.*] Rose!

ROSE: [*from inside the house.*] Stop that yelling. You gonna wake up Raynell. I just got her to sleep.

LYONS: I just stopped by to pay Papa this twenty dollars I owe him. Where's Papa at?

ROSE: He should be here in a minute. I'm getting ready to go down to the church. Sit down and wait on him.

LYONS: I got to go pick up Bonnie over her mother's house.   5

ROSE: Well, sit it down there on the table. He'll get it.

LYONS: [*enters the house and sets the money on the table.*] Tell Papa I said thanks. I'll see you again.

ROSE: All right, Lyons. We'll see you.

LYONS starts to exit as CORY enters.

CORY: Hey, Lyons.

LYONS: What's happening, Cory? Say man, I'm sorry I missed your graduation. You know   10
I had a gig and couldn't get away. Otherwise, I would have been there, man. So what you doing?

CORY: I'm trying to find a job.

LYONS: Yeah I know how that go, man. It's rough out here. Jobs are scarce.

CORY: Yeah, I know.

LYONS: Look here, I got to run. Talk to Papa . . . he know some people. He'll be able to help get you a job. Talk to him . . . see what he say.

CORY: Yeah . . . all right, Lyons.   15

LYONS: You take care. I'll talk to you soon. We'll find some time to talk.

LYONS exits the yard. CORY wanders over to the tree, picks up the bat, and assumes a batting stance. He studies an imaginary pitcher and swings. Dissatisfied with the result, he tries again. TROY enters. They eye each other for a beat. CORY puts the bat down and exits the yard. TROY starts into the house as ROSE exits with RAYNELL. She is carrying a cake.

TROY: I'm coming in and everybody's going out.

ROSE: I'm taking this cake down to the church for the bake sale. Lyons was by to see you. He stopped by to pay you your twenty dollars. It's laying in there on the table.

TROY: [*going into his pocket*]. Well . . . here go this money.

ROSE: Put it in there on the table, Troy. I'll get it.   20

TROY: What time you coming back?

ROSE: Ain't no use in you studying me. It don't matter what time I come back.

TROY: I just asked you a question, woman. What's the matter . . . can't I ask you a question?

ROSE: Troy, I don't want to go into it. Your dinner's in there on the stove. All you got to do is heat it up. And don't you be eating the rest of them cakes in there. I'm coming back for them. We having a bake sale at the church tomorrow.

ROSE exits the yard. TROY sits down on the steps, takes a pint bottle from his pocket, opens it, and drinks. He begins to sing.

TROY: 25
    Hear it ring! Hear it ring!
    Had an old dog his name was Blue
    You know Blue was mighty true
    You know Blue as a good old dog
    Blue trees a possum in a hollow log
    You know from that he was a good old dog.

BONO: [*enters the yard.*] Hey, Troy.

TROY: Hey, what's happening, Bono?

BONO: I just thought I'd stop by to see you.

TROY: What you stop by and see me for? You ain't stopped by in a mouth of Sundays. Hell, I must owe you money or something.

BONO: Since you got your promotion I can't keep up with you. Used to see you every day.   30
Now I don't even know what route you working.

TROY: They keep switching me around. Got me out in Greentree now . . . hauling white folks' garbage.

BONO: Greentree, huh? You lucky, at least you ain't got to be lifting them barrels. Damn if they ain't getting heavier. I'm gonna put in my two years and call it quits.

TROY: I'm thinking about retiring myself.

BONO: You got it easy. You can drive for another five years.

35 **TROY:** It ain't the same, Bono. It ain't like working the back of the truck. Ain't got nobody to talk to . . . feel like you working by yourself. Naw, I'm thinking about retiring. How's Lucille?

BONO: She all right. Her arthritis get to acting up on her sometime. Saw Rose on my way in. She going down to the church, huh?

TROY: Yeah, she took up going down there. All them preachers looking for somebody to fatten their pockets. [*Pause.*] Got some gin here.

BONO: Naw, thanks. I just stopped by to say hello.

TROY: Hell, nigger . . . you can take a drink. I ain't never known you to say no to a drink. You ain't got to work tomorrow.

40 **BONO:** I just stopped by. I'm fixing to go over to Skinner's. We got us a domino game going over his house every Friday.

TROY: Nigger, you can't play no dominoes. I used to whup you four games out of five.

BONO: Well, that learned me. I'm getting better.

TROY: Yeah? Well, that's all right.

BONO: Look here . . . I got to be getting on. Stop by sometime, huh?

45 **TROY:** Yeah, I'll do that, Bono. Lucille told Rose you bought her a new refrigerator.

BONO: Yeah, Rose told Lucille you had finally built your fence . . . so I figured we'd call it even.

TROY: I knew you would.

BONO: Yeah . . . okay. I'll be talking to you.

TROY: Yeah, take care, Bono. Good to see you. I'm gonna stop over.

50 **BONO:** Yeah. Okay, Troy. [BONO *EXITS.*]

TROY: [*drinks from the bottle.*]

> *Old Blue died and I dig his grave*
> *Let him down with a golden chain*
> *Every night when I hear old Blue bark*
> *I know Blue treed a possum in Noah's Ark*
> *Hear it ring! Hear it ring!*

CORY *enters the yard. They eye each other for a beat.* TROY *is sitting in the middle of the steps.* CORY *walks over.*

CORY: I got to get by.

TROY: Say what? What's you say?

CORY: You in my way. I got to get by.

55 **TROY:** You got to get by where? This is my house. Bought and paid for. In full. Took me fifteen years. And if you wanna go in my house and I'm sitting on the steps . . . you say excuse me. Like your mama taught you.

CORY: Come on, Pop . . . I got to get by.

CORY *starts to maneuver his way past* TROY. TROY *grabs his leg and shoves him back.*

TROY: You just gonna walk over top of me?

CORY: I live here too!

TROY: [*advancing toward him.*] You just gonna walk over top of me in my own house?

60 **CORY:** I ain't scared of you.

TROY: I ain't asked if you was scared of me. I asked you if you was fixing to walk over top of me in my own house? That's the question. You ain't gonna say excuse me? You just gonna walk over top of me?

CORY: If you wanna put it like that.

TROY: How else am I gonna put it?

CORY: I was walking by you to go into the house cause you sitting on the steps drunk, singing to yourself. You can put it like that.

TROY: Without saying excuse me??? [*CORY doesn't respond.*] I asked you a question. Without   65
saying excuse me???

CORY: I ain't got to say excuse me to you. You don't count around here no more.

TROY: Oh, I see . . . I don't count around here no more. You ain't got to say excuse me to your daddy. All of a sudden you done got so grown that your daddy don't count around here no more . . . Around here in his own house and yard that he done paid for with the sweat of his brow. You done got so grown to where you gonna take over. You gonna take over my house. Is that right? You gonna wear my pants. You gonna go in there and stretch out on my bed. You ain't got to say excuse me cause I don't count around here no more. Is that right?

CORY: That's right. You always talking this dumb stuff. Now, why don't you just get out my way?

TROY: I guess you got someplace to sleep and something to put in your belly. You got that, huh? You got that? That's what you need. You got that, huh?

CORY: You don't know what I got. You ain't got to worry about what I got.   70

TROY: You right! You one hundred percent right! I done spent the last seventeen years worrying about what you got. Now it's your turn, see? I'll tell you what to do. You grown . . . we done established that. You a man. Now, let's see you act like one. Turn your behind around and walk out this yard. And when you get out there in the alley . . . you can forget about this house. See? 'Cause this is my house. You go on and be a man and get your own house. You can forget about this. 'Cause this is mine. You go on and get yours cause I'm through with doing for you.

CORY: You talking about what you did for me . . . what'd you ever give me?

TROY: Them feet and bones! That pumping heart, nigger! I give you more than anybody else is ever gonna give you.

CORY: You ain't never gave me nothing! You ain't never done nothing but hold me back. Afraid I was gonna be better than you. All you ever did was try and make me scared of you. I used to tremble every time you called my name. Every time I heard your footsteps in the house. Wondering all the time . . . what's Papa gonna say if I do this? . . . What's he gonna say if I do that? . . . What's Papa gonna say if I turn on the radio? And mama, too . . . she tries . . . but she's scared of you.

TROY: You leave your mama out of this. She ain't got nothing to do with this.   75

CORY: I don't know how she stand you . . . after what you did to her.

TROY: I told you to leave your mama out of this! [*He advances toward* CORY.]

CORY: What you gonna do . . . give me a whupping? You can't whup me no more. You're too old. You just an old man.

TROY: [*shoves him on his shoulder.*] Nigger! That's what you are. You just another nigger on the street to me!

CORY: You crazy! You know that?   80

TROY: Go on now! You got the devil in you. Get on away from me!

CORY: You just a crazy old man . . . talking about I got the devil in me.

TROY: Yeah, I'm crazy! If you don't get on the other side of that yard . . . I'm gonna show you how crazy I am! Go on . . . get the hell out of my yard.

CORY: It ain't your yard. You took Uncle Gabe's money he got from the army to buy this house and then you put him out.

85   **TROY:** [*advances on* CORY.] Get your black ass out of my yard! [TROY's *advance backs* CORY *up against the tree.* CORY *grabs up the bat.*]

CORY: I ain't going nowhere! Come on . . . put me out! I ain't scared of you.

TROY: That's my bat!

CORY: Come on!

TROY: Put my bat down!

90   **CORY:** Come on, put me out. [CORY *swings at* TROY, *who backs across the yard.*] What's the matter? You so bad . . . put me out! [TROY *advances toward* CORY.]

CORY: [*backing up.*] Come on! Come on!

TROY: You're gonna have to use it! You wanna draw that bat back on me . . . you're gonna have to use it.

CORY: Come on! . . . Come on!

CORY swings the bat at TROY *a second time. He misses.* TROY *continues to advance toward him.*

TROY: You're gonna have to kill me! You wanna draw that bat back on me. You're gonna have to kill me.

CORY, *backed up against the tree, can go no farther.* TROY *taunts him. He sticks out his head and offers him a target.*

   Come on! Come on!

CORY *is unable to swing the bat.* TROY *grabs it.*

95   **TROY:** Then I'll show you.

CORY *and* TROY *struggle over the bat. The struggle is fierce and fully engaged.* TROY *ultimately is the stronger and takes the bat from* CORY *and stands over him ready to swing. He stops himself.*

   Go on and get away from around my house.

CORY: [*stung by his defeat, picks himself up, walks slowly out of the yard and up the alley.*] Tell Mama I'll be back for my things.

TROY: They'll be on the other side of that fence. [CORY *exits.*] I can't taste nothing. Helluljah! I can't taste nothing no more. [TROY *assumes a batting posture and begins to taunt Death, the fastball on the outside corner.*] Come on! It's between you and me now! Come on! Anytime you want! Come on! I be ready for you . . . but I ain't gonna be easy.

The lights go down on the scene.

ACT 2

Scene 5

The time is 1965. The lights come up in the yard. It is the morning of TROY's *funeral. A funeral plaque with a light hangs beside the door. There is a small garden plot off to the side. There is noise and activity in the house as* ROSE, LYONS, *and* BONO *have gathered.*

   The door opens and RAYNELL, *seven years old, enters dressed in a flannel nightgown. She crosses to the garden and pokes around with a stick.* ROSE *calls from the house.*

ROSE: Raynell!

RAYNELL: Mam?

ROSE: What you doing out there?

RAYNELL: Nothing.

ROSE: [*comes to the door.*] Girl, get in here and get dressed. What you doing?   5

RAYNELL: Seeing if my garden growed.

ROSE: I told you it ain't gonna grow overnight. You got to wait.

RAYNELL: It don't look like it never gonna grow. Dag!

ROSE: I told you a watched pot never boils. Get in here and get dressed.

RAYNELL: This ain't even no pot, Mama.   10

ROSE: You just have to give it a chance. It'll grow. Now you come on and do what I told you. We got to be getting ready. This ain't no morning to be playing around. You hear me?

RAYNELL: Yes, mam.

ROSE exits into the house. RAYNELL *continues to poke at her garden with a stick.* CORY *enters. He is dressed in a Marine corporal's uniform, and carries a duffelbag. His posture is that of a military man, and his speech has a clipped sternness.*

CORY: [*to* RAYNELL.] Hi. [*Pause.*] I bet your name is Raynell.

RAYNELL: Uh huh.

CORY: Is your mama home?   15

RAYNELL: [*runs up on the porch and calls through the screen door.*] Mama . . . there's some man out here. Mama?

ROSE: [*comes to the door.*] Cory? Lord have mercy! Look here, you all!

ROSE and CORY *embrace in a tearful reunion as* BONO *and* LYONS *enters from the house dressed in funeral clothes.*

BONO: Aw, looka here . . .

ROSE: Done got all grown up!

CORY: Don't cry, Mama. What you crying about?   20

ROSE: I'm just so glad you made it.

CORY: Hey Lyons. How you doing, Mr. Bono.

LYONS: [*goes to embrace* CORY.] Look at you, man. Look at you. Don't he look good, Rose. Got them Corporal stripes.

ROSE: What took you so long?

CORY: You know how the Marines are, Mama. They got to get all their paperwork straight   25
before they let you do anything.

ROSE: Well, I'm sure glad you made it. They let Lyons come. Your Uncle Gabe's still in the hospital. They don't know if they gonna let him out or not. I just talked to them a little while ago.

LYONS: A Corporal in the United States Marines.

BONO: Your daddy knew you had it in you. He used to tell me all the time.

LYONS: Don't he look good, Mr. Bono?

BONO: Yeah, he remind me of Troy when I first met him. [*Pause.*] Say, Rose, Lucille's down   30
at the church with the choir. I'm gonna go down and get the pallbearers lined up. I'll be back to get you all.

ROSE: Thanks, Jim.

CORY: See you, Mr. Bono.

LYONS: [*with his arm around* RAYNELL.] Cory . . . look at Raynell. Ain't she precious? She gonna break a whole lot of hearts.

ROSE: Raynell, come and say hello to your brother. This is your brother, Cory. You remember Cory.

RAYNELL: No, Mam.   35

CORY: She don't remember me, Mama.

ROSE: Well, we talk about you. She heard us talk about you. [*To* RAYNELL.] This is your brother, Cory. Come on and say hello.

RAYNELL: Hi.

CORY: Hi. So you're Raynell. Mama told me a lot about you.

40 ROSE: You all come on into the house and let me fix you some breakfast. Keep up your strength.

CORY: I ain't hungry, Mama.

LYONS: You can fix me something, Rose. I'll be in there in a minute.

ROSE: Cory, you sure you don't want nothing? I know they ain't feeding you right.

CORY: No, Mama . . . thanks. I don't feel like eating. I'll get something later.

45 ROSE: Raynell . . . get on upstairs and get that dress on like I told you.

ROSE and RAYNELL exit into the house.

LYONS: So . . . I hear you thinking about getting married.

CORY: Yeah, I done found the right one, Lyons. It's about time.

LYONS: Me and Bonnie been split up about four years now. About the time Papa retired. I guess she just got tired of all them changes I was putting her through. [*Pause.*] I always knew you was gonna make something out yourself. Your head was always in the right direction. So . . . you gonna stay in . . . make it a career . . . put in your twenty years?

CORY: I don't know. I got six already, I think that's enough.

50 LYONS: Stick with Uncle Sam and retire early. Ain't nothing out here. I guess Rose told you what happened with me. They got me down the workhouse. I thought I was being slick cashing other people's checks.

CORY: How much time you doing?

LYONS: They give me three years. I got that beat now. I ain't got but nine more months. It ain't so bad. You learn to deal with it like anything else. You got to take the crookeds with the straights. That's what Papa used to say. He used to say that when he struck out. I seen him strike out three times in a row . . . and the next time up he hit the ball over the grandstand. Right out there in Homestead Field.° He wasn't satisfied hitting in the seats . . . he want to hit it over everything! After the game he had two hundred people standing around waiting to shake his hand. You got to take the crookeds with the straights. Yeah, Papa was something else.

CORY: You still playing?

LYONS: Cory . . . you know I'm gonna do that. There's some fellows down there we got us a band . . . we gonna try and stay together when we get out . . . but yeah, I'm still playing. It still helps me to get out of bed in the morning. As long as it do that I'm gonna be right there playing and trying to make some sense out of it.

55 ROSE: [*calling*]. Lyons, I got these eggs in the pan.

LYONS: Let me go on and get these eggs, man. Get ready to go bury Papa. [*Pause.*] How you doing? You doing all right?

CORY nods. LYONS touches him on the shoulder and they share a moment of silent grief. LYONS exits into the house. CORY wanders about the yard. RAYNELL enters.

RAYNELL: Hi.

CORY: Hi.

RAYNELL: Did you used to sleep in my room?

60 CORY: Yeah . . . that used to be my room.

RAYNELL: That's what Papa call it. "Cory's room." It got your football in the closet.

°52 *Homestead Field*: i.e., Forbes Field, the home field of the Homestead Grays of the Negro Leagues. The Grays played in the field from 1939 until 1948.

ROSE: [*comes to the door.*] Raynell, get in there and get them good shoes on.

RAYNELL: Mama, can't I wear these? Them other one hurt my feet.

ROSE: Well, they just gonna have to hurt your feet for a while. You ain't said they hurt your feet when you went down to the store and got them.

RAYNELL: They didn't hurt then. My feet done got bigger.   65

ROSE: Don't you give me no backtalk now. You get in there and get them shoes on. [*RAYNELL exits into the house.*] Ain't too much changed. He still got that piece of rag tied to that tree. He was out here swinging that bat. I was just ready to go back in the house. He swung that bat and then he just fell over. Seem like he swung it and stood there with this grin on his face . . . and then he just fell over. They carried him on down to the hospital, but I knew there wasn't no need . . . why don't you come on in the house?

CORY: Mama . . . I got something to tell you. I don't know how to tell you this . . . but I've got to tell you . . . I'm not going to Papa's funeral.

ROSE: Boy, hush your month. That's your daddy you talking about. I don't want hear that kind of talk this morning. I done raised you to come to this? You standing there all healthy and grown talking about you ain't going to your daddy's funeral?

CORY: Mama . . . listen . . .

ROSE: I don't want to hear it, Cory. You just get that thought out of your head.   70

CORY: I can't drag Papa with me everywhere I go. I've got to say no to him. One time in my life I've got to say no.

ROSE: Don't nobody have to listen to nothing like that. I know you and your daddy ain't seen eye to eye, but I ain't got to listen to that kind of talk this morning. Whatever was between you and your daddy . . . the time has come to put it aside. Just take it and set it over there on the shelf and forget about it. Disrespecting your daddy ain't gonna make you a man, Cory. You got to find a way to come to that on your own. Not going to your daddy's funeral ain't gonna make you a man.

CORY: The whole time I was growing up . . . living in his house . . . Papa was like a shadow that followed you everywhere. It weighted on you and sunk into your flesh. It would wrap around you and lay there until you couldn't tell which one was you anymore. That shadow digging in your flesh. Trying to crawl in. Trying to live through you. Everywhere I looked, Troy Maxson was staring back at me . . . hiding under the bed . . . in the closet. I'm just saying I've got to find a way to get rid of that shadow, Mama.

ROSE: You just like him. You got him in you good.

CORY: Don't tell me that, Mama.

ROSE: You Troy Maxson all over again.   75

CORY: I don't want to be Troy Maxson. I want to be me.

ROSE: You can't be nobody but who you are, Cory. That shadow wasn't nothing but you growing into yourself. You either got to grow into it or cut it down to fit you. But that's all you got to make life with. That's all you got to measure yourself against that world out there. Your daddy wanted you to be everything he wasn't . . . and at the same time he tried to make you into everything he was. I don't know if he was right or wrong . . . but I do know he meant to do more good than he meant to do harm. He wasn't always right. Sometimes when he touched he bruised. And sometimes when he took me in his arms he cut. When I first met your daddy I thought . . . Here is a man I can lay down with and make a baby. That's the first thing I thought when I seen him. I was thirty years old and had done seen my share of men. But when he walked up to me and said, "I can dance a waltz that'll make you dizzy," I thought, Rose Lee, here is a man that you can open yourself up to and be filled to bursting. Here is a man that can fill all them empty spaces you been tipping around the edges of. One of them empty spaces was being somebody's mother. I married your daddy and settled down to cooking his supper and keeping clean sheets on the bed. When your daddy walked through the house he was so big he filled it up. That was my first mistake. Not to make him leave some room for me. For my part in the matter. But at that time I wanted that. I wanted a house that I could sing in. And that's what your daddy gave me. I didn't know to keep up his strength I had to give up little pieces of mine. I did that. I took on his life as mine and mixed up the pieces so that you couldn't hardly tell which was which anymore. It was my choice. It was my life and I didn't have to live it like that. But that's what life offered me in the way of being a woman and I took it. I grabbed hold of it with both hands. By the time Raynell came into the house, me and your daddy had done lost touch with one another. I didn't want to make my blessing off of nobody's misfortune . . . but I took on to Raynell like she was all them babies I had wanted and never had.

The phone rings.

Like I'd been blessed to relive a part of my life. And if the Lord see fit to keep up my strength . . . I'm gonna do her just like your daddy did you . . . I'm gonna give her the best of what's in me.
RAYNELL: [*entering, still with her old shoes.*] Mama . . . Reverend Tollivier on the phone.

ROSE exits into the house.

Hi.
80 **CORY:** Hi.
RAYNELL: You in the Army or the Marines?
CORY: Marines.
RAYNELL: Papa said it was the Army. Did you know Blue?
CORY: Blue? Who's Blue?
85 **RAYNELL:** Papa's dog what he sing about all the time.
CORY: [*singing*].
   Hear it ring! Hear it ring!
   I had a dog his name was Blue
   You know Blue was mighty true
   You know Blue was a good old dog
   Blue treed a possum in a hollow log
   You know from that he was a good old dog.
   Hear it ring! Hear it ring!

RAYNELL joins in singing.

CORY AND RAYNELL:
   Blue treed a possum out on a limb
   Blue looked at me and I looked at him
   Grabbed that possum and put him in a sack
   Blue stayed there till I came back
   Old Blue's feets was big and round
   Never allowed a possum to touch the ground.
   Old Blue died and I dug his grave
   I dug his grave with a silver spade
   Let him down with a golden chain
   Any every night I call his name
   Go on Blue, you good dog you
   Go on Blue, you good dog you.

RAYNELL:
  Blue laid down and died like a man
  Blue laid down and died . . .
BOTH:
  Blue laid down and died like a man
  Now he's treeing possums in the Promised Land
  I'm gonna tell you this to let you know
  Blue's gone where the good dogs go
  When I hear old Blue bark
  When I hear old Blue bark
  Blue treed a possum in Noah's Ark
  Blue treed a possum in Noah's Ark.

ROSE: [*comes to the screen door.*] Cory, we gonna be ready to go in a minute.   90

CORY: [*to* RAYNELL]. You go on in the house and change them shoes like Mama told you so we can go to Papa's funeral.

RAYNELL: Okay, I'll be back.

RAYNELL exits into the house. CORY *gets up and crosses over to the tree.* ROSE *stands in the screen door watching him.* GABRIEL *enters from the alley.*

GABRIEL: [*calling*]. Hey, Rose!

ROSE: Gabe?

GABRIEL: I'm here, Rose. Hey Rose, I'm here!   95

ROSE: [*enters from the house.*] Lord . . . Look here, Lyons!

LYONS: See, I told you, Rose . . . I told you they'd let him come.

CORY: How you doing, Uncle Gabe?

LYONS: How you doing, Uncle Gabe?

GABRIEL: Hey, Rose. It's time. It's time to tell St. Peter to open the gates. Troy, you ready?   100
  You ready, Troy. I'm gonna tell St. Peter to open the gates. You get ready now.

GABRIEL, with great fanfare, braces himself to blow. The trumpet is without a mouthpiece. He puts the end of it into his mouth and blows with great force, like a man who has been waiting some twenty-odd years for this single moment. No sound comes out of the trumpet. He braces himself and blows again with the same results. A third time he blows. There is a weight of impossible description that falls away and leaves him bare and exposed to a frightful realization. It is a trauma that a sane and normal mind would be unable to withstand. He begins to dance. A slow, strange dance, eerie and life-giving. A dance of atavistic signature and ritual. LYONS *attempts to embrace him.* GABRIEL *pushes* LYONS *away. He begins to howl in what is an attempt at song, or perhaps a song turning back into itself in an attempt at speech. He finishes his dance and the gates of heaven stand open as wide as God's closet. That's the way that go!*

[BLACKOUT]

QUESTIONS

Act 1, Scene 1

1. Who is Troy Maxson? Who is Jim Bono? What are they doing as the play opens? What kind of complaint has Troy filed with commissioner? How is this complaint connected with the basic overall thought of the first scene?

2. Why does the discussion between Troy and Bono turn toward how Troy is behaving toward women other than his wife? Why does Troy deny any connections with "that Alberta gal"?

3. Describe Rose. How did Rose and Troy decide to wed? What seem to be their present feelings for each other?

4. Who is Lyons? What has Lyons come to see Troy about? Why does Troy tell the story of his having seen the devil? Whom has he actually seen? How is this story connected to the major themes of the play?

Act 1, Scene 2

5. Why has Rose been playing the numbers?

6. Who is Gabriel? What has happened to him? In what way is he a symbol of Troy, his family, and his race?

Act 1, Scene 3

7. Who is Cory? Whose child is he? What is his relationship to Lyons? What ambition does Cory seem to have? What does Troy want for him instead? (See also the end of 1.3.) What is the reason behind Troy's thought about Cory's athletic ability? Why is there such a conflict between the father and the son? In what way is Rose connected to Troy's discussion of how he regards his role with Cory?

8. What is the purpose of the discussion about the costs of a television set as opposed to the costs of repairing the roof?

9. Why does Troy explain his role about supporting his family? What does this explanation show about Troy? Why do Troy's words likely disappoint Cory?

Act 1, Scene 4

10. Who is Alberta? What is her relationship with Troy? Why is she mentioned so early in this scene?

11. What success has Troy had with his appeal at work? What does Troy say about not having a driver's licence? Why does he disparage the act of driving a motor vehicle? What does this discussion show about his character?

12. What is significant about Gabriel's claim that he has been chasing hellhounds?

13. What forced Troy to leave home at the age of 14? What was his attitude toward his own father? What was Troy's story after he left home? How did he learn about baseball? Why does Wilson stress that Troy would have been in his twenties before he was able to develop his baseball skills? What is the implied difference between Troy's baseball career and the careers of white players?

14. Why has Cory not been allowed to play in the football game? What is his reaction to learning that Troy has spoken to his football coach? What does Cory see as a possible outcome of this conflict?

Act 2, Scene 1

15. What is the purpose of the discussion about hard and soft woods at the beginning of this scene? Why does Troy prefer hard wood instead of soft for the outside fence?

16. What has happened to Gabriel? What has Troy done to help Gabriel? What does Troy think of the judge who has been involved in Gabriel's case? In the course of the play, what do we learn about how Troy has acquired the money to pay for the house in which he and his family live? How is this detail important in the relationship between Cory and Troy?

17. Why does Bono believe that he can speak confidentially to Troy about his extramarital affair?

18. Describe the crisis scene between Troy and Rose. How does Troy explain what has happened? How does he explain his involvement with Alberta? What is Rose's response to the situation? How is Troy's attitude toward Cory affected by what happens between him and Rose?

Act 2, Scene 2

19. What are relationships like in the Maxson house, six months after the events in scene 1?
20. What has happened to Gabriel? What has Troy had to do with it?
21. What has happened to Alberta?
22. What is the significance of Troy's speech to "Mr. Death"? How is this speech echoed at the end of the play? Why does Troy, here, resolve to complete the fence that has been under construction for virtually the entire play up to this point?

Act 2, Scene 3

23. What is the major action taking place in this scene?

Act 2, Scene 4

24. What is the significance of the fact that Lyons is paying back Troy the 20 dollars he owes?
25. What is Troy's attitude toward ministers? What changes do you perceive have taken place in Troy's character in the course of the play?

Act 2, Scene 5

26. What has happened in the eight-year interval since scene 4? What is to be the major action of scene 5? What has happened to Cory? To Lyons? Who is Raynell? What is her first response to Cory? What is happening to the family at the play's end?

GENERAL QUESTIONS

1. Explain the importance of big-league baseball in the play. What has been Troy's connection to baseball? In what way is Troy an authority on well-known baseball stars of the 1950s? Who is Josh Gibson? How does Troy come to have known Josh Gibson? In what way is Josh Gibson's career symbolic in the play?

2. Why is this play titled *Fences*? In what way are fences used symbolically by Wilson? What fences pertain to Troy? In what way is Jesus a fence around Rose? Does Jesus separate her from others, or make her special? What fences separate Troy and Cory? What fences separate Troy and Lyons? What other meanings of fences can you think of that might apply to this play?

3. What is the significance of Troy's dog "Blue"? Why is Blue regularly mentioned in the course of the play? What is the significance of the duet, about the dog, sung by Cory and Raynell? What does their singing suggest about their attitudes toward Troy?

4. How might *Fences* be considered as a play about the relationship of fathers and sons? What is the importance of Bono's story about his father? What does Troy's account of his experience with his own father tell us about Troy? About his attitude toward his own sons? Describe the relationship between Troy and Lyons. Why does antagonism verging on hatred and outright violence between Troy and Cory develop in 2.4? What is Troy trying to establish? In what way is Troy superior to his own father, when it comes to his relationship with Cory? Why does Cory tell Troy that he is no more than

"just an old man"? How does the situation escalate between Troy and Cory? How does it get resolved?

5. Explain the symbolism and meaning of Gabriel's being alone on stage at the play's end. Why is it Gabriel who is the last speaker in the play? What is the meaning of Gabriel's dance? Why does the play end as it does, with the image of Gabriel trying to blow his horn, but with no sound coming out? What is the meaning of the Gate of Heaven as the final vision? In what way is the gate also a fence?

6. What significance should one attach to the names of the play's characters: Troy, Rose, Bono, Cory, Lyons, Raynell, Gabriel? In what ways might the names be considered symbolic?

7. Describe the language, which has been called "Black English," used by the characters in *Fences*? What grammatical "rules" do the characters follow? What rules do they ignore? Is there ever any passage that is rendered obscure by the speech patterns? What difficulties, if any, does this speech offer to a modern reader? What is gained for the play by the use of this type of speech?

8. What is the relationship of the epigraph by Wilson ("As God . . . ") to the events of the play?

WRITING ABOUT REALISTIC AND NONREALISTIC DRAMA

Your essay should take into account the traditional elements of drama—plot, character, language, setting, symbol, and theme. Conventional approaches to these elements are discussed in Chapter 23 (pp. 1255–58), and you may want to review this material. As you plan your essay, your overall concern should be to determine the relative degrees of realism or nonrealism with which the elements are presented and developed. Your discoveries here will enable you to describe the ways in which the play establishes its views and ideas about life and the world. In short, how do conventional aspects of dramatic structure, together with the degree of realism or nonrealism, create a perspective that is the unique quality of the play?

Questions for Discovering Ideas

PLOT. Does the play unfold in a chronological order that imitates reality, or does it mix past and present action? Is the action true to life or stylized? Are the conflicts resolved realistically, or does the playwright employ a conventional and perhaps improbable happy (or sad) ending? How does the realistic or nonrealistic development of these aspects affect the play's meaning and impact?

CHARACTER. Are the characters realistic or symbolic, representative, or stereotyped? Are they round or flat? Are they motivated by lifelike considerations, like Amanda in *The Glass Menagerie*, who lives only in the past? Or are they motivated by the play's requirements, like the narrator, who has the artificial role of speaking directly to the audience? Are the characters consistent, or do they drop in and out of character? Is their clothing and makeup (as described in the stage directions) an imitation of real life, or is it theatrical and nonrealistic? Are all the characters developed in the same manner, or are there differences in the degree of realism you find in each? Is one character more or less realistic than any of the others? If so, why? Of what importance is this character to the play as a whole?

LANGUAGE. Look carefully at the diction, style, and patterns of the dialogue. In realistic drama, what is the nature of the speeches? Is the language colloquial, formal, low? Is it appropriate for the characters? Is the dialogue normal or natural, granted the situation? Do the characters speak loudly? Do they whisper? Shout? Why? What pattern or consistency can you discover by studying how the characters speak? Within the confines of realistic drama, what normal or realistic variations occur? (For example, a letter is read aloud; a phone conversation occurs; a character is alone onstage and speaks to characters offstage as in O'Neill's *Before Breakfast* [Chapter 23], or a character speaks to characters who do not hear.) What proportion of the dialogue is ordinary two- or three-way conversation? How much variation occurs, and what kind is it? Why do you think the dramatists have varied the normal dialogue, and how do these variations shape your perception of the play?

In nonrealistic drama, some dialogue will be realistically normal or appear so, but much of it will be shaped by the play's nonrealistic premise. How do you identify nonrealistic speech? Do you find nonrealistic devices such as verse, song, or unnatural and patterned repetition? Does any character seem to be speaking in different voices? If so, why? Which characters seem to ignore other characters and speak instead to the air or to the audience? How extensive is such direct address? Does a single character do most of this talking? If so, what is he or she like? What does the character tell you about himself or herself? About the other characters in the play? The background? Plot? Action? Setting? Staging? How accurate and objective is this character? How does this direct address shape and control your responses?

In sum, how do all aspects of language determine the extent to which the play effectively communicates ideas and emotions to you? As you deal with language, also consider the significance of other aspects of sound indicated in the stage directions, such as sound effects (as in *A Dollhouse*) or music (as in *The Sandbox*).

SETTING. To what degree do the stage directions present the setting as realistic or nonrealistic? Do the directions call for the reproduction of an actual room or place? How much specific detail is included? If less than a fully realistic setting is described, how far does the playwright go in reducing the setting to the bare stage? How much of the physical theater does the playwright indicate that he or she wants you to see or imagine? To what extent do you find symbolic, impressionistic, and nonrealistic devices, such as transparent walls? How do the stage directions describe lighting? Is the lighting used realistically, to recreate natural illumination, or nonrealistically, to spotlight and emphasize specific places, objects, characters, or actions? Most important, how does the setting and its degree of realism (or nonrealism) contribute to the impact and meaning of the play?

SYMBOLISM. Because symbols operate in life as they do in art, there is symbolism both in the realistic plays of Glaspell and Wilson and in the relatively nonrealistic dramas of Miller and Williams. Are symbols introduced through realistic or logical techniques, or do they appear illogically and nonrealistically? You can focus your exploration directly on the symbol and its meaning (the front doorway in *Mulatto*) or the nonrealistic methods through which it is established (the blue roses in *The Glass Menagerie*).

THEME. What are the important concepts in the play, and how are they conveyed? Be sure to give special consideration to significantly realistic or nonrealistic techniques. In considering a realistic play like *Trifles* or *Mulatto*, explore the ways in which realism in character, action, and setting contribute to the play's ideas. Conversely, consider how Williams employs a strikingly nonrealistic device, such as the music or the screen projections, to convey and emphasize the themes of *The Glass Menagerie*.

Strategies for Organizing Ideas

Your central idea should show how realistic or nonrealistic elements affect part or all of the play. Try to connect the topic with its effect. For example, begin with sentences such as these: (1) "Tom as a nonrealistic narrator and realistic character unifies *The Glass Menagerie* and gives the play a coherent and subjective point of view." (2) "In *A Dollhouse*, Krogstad's exposure of Nora's forgery makes Nora realize the weakness of her marriage, and thus it brings the marriage of the Helmers to a breaking point."

The supporting details can be organized in any way that produces a logical and convincing essay. If you are writing about the ways in which nonrealistic devices emphasize meaning in *The Glass Menagerie*, for example, you might organize your essay around the setting, the lighting, and the screen device. When your essay focuses on only one element, you can organize your supporting details to reflect the order in which they occur in the play.

In your conclusion you might raise larger issues than you have already raised, or you might make broader connections not only about your topics but also about the play as a whole. You might also reconsider the significance of the play's general level of realistic or nonrealistic techniques.

Illustrative Student Essay

Underlined sentences in this paper *do not* conform to MLA style and are used solely as teaching tools to emphasize the central idea, thesis sentence, and topic sentences throughout the paper.

Jhaveri 1

Deepunkhar Jhaveri

Professor Gordon

English 121

5 May 2008

Realism and Nonrealism in Tom's Triple Role in The Glass Menagerie°

In <u>The Glass Menagerie</u>, Tennessee Williams combines realistic and   [1]
nonrealistic elements to explore the personalities and conflicts of the Wingfield
family. <u>One of his most effective nonrealistic elements in the play is his use of
Tom in three different roles.</u>* As a realistic character within the action, a
nonrealistic stage manager of the action, and a nonrealistic narrator of the
entire play, Tom combines three functions that strongly shape our perceptions.†

<u>As a realistic character involved in the recollected action of the play, Tom</u>   [2]
<u>is ensnared by the economic and emotional demands of his family and his job.</u>
In the opening description of the characters, Williams explains Tom's plight:
"to escape from a trap he [Tom] has to act without pity." In addition, Tom
himself dramatically expresses his need to escape from his stifling life at home.
He discusses this need with his mother in scene 3, with Laura in scene 4, and,
above all, with Jim in scene 6. Here, we see that Tom craves not only escape but
also adventure. He tells Jim, "I'm planning a change." And he clearly expresses
his desire to move out of the prison house of the family:

> It's our turn now, to go to the South Sea Island--to make a safari--to
> be exotic, far off! But I'm not patient. I don't want to wait till then,
> I'm tired of the *movies* and I am <u>about to move</u>! (scene 6, speech 114)
> I'm starting to boil inside. I know I seem dreamy, but inside--well,
> I'm boiling! (scene 6, speech 120)

°**This play appears on pages 1644–91.**
*****Central idea.**
†**Thesis sentence.**

Jhaveri 2

These expressions of his need to escape define a major line of the realistic thought and action in The Glass Menagerie.

[3]   Tom's realism as a character is undercut by his momentary role as a stage manager in Scene 1. Here, he speaks with Amanda "as though reading from a script." In this same scene, "Tom motions for music and a spot of light on Amanda." Although this device is abandoned, the image of Tom holding an imaginary script and giving cues to the musicians and the lighting technicians breaks any possible illusions that the play is imitating real life. The role as manager emphasizes the fact that The Glass Menagerie is a play designed for the stage and for live actors carrying out conventional stage roles.

[4]   Tom's part in shaping and unifying the play is most apparent in his nonrealistic function as narrator. In this role, he stands aside from the action occurring in the Wingfield apartment, and he also speaks directly to us. He introduces the characters, provides background, and supplies an ongoing commentary. In addition, he presents his own subjective views and also personifies the play's theme of escape. As a character out of the past--the one actually involved in the play's action--he represents a yearning for freedom and adventure. As the narrator of the present action, he speaks truths that his character in its past role has not yet learned, and he thus recognizes that escape from the past is impossible. When the play closes, he tells us that he remains trapped (scene 7, speech 323), and thus he provides a final perspective on the central theme of escape.

[5]   The second striking aspect of Tom's function as narrator concerns his complete control of the play. Because he is the narrator, the action in The Glass Menagerie represents Tom's memories of events, rather than the events themselves. In the first speech of scene 1, he tells us, "The play is memory. Being a memory play, it is dimly lighted, it is sentimental, it is not realistic." Since the events from the past that occur onstage emerge from Tom's memory, it is he who provides an overriding unity and perspective. We perceive everything through his mind and from his point of view. As a nonrealistic narrator, he holds the stage action together and totally controls our responses.

Jhaveri 3

Williams thus uses Tom in three distinct ways to create unity and   [6]
perspective. As a realistic character aching to leave the confinement of home,
Tom embodies the theme of escape. As a nonrealistic stage manager, he
illustrates the artificiality of the dramatic literary form and stresses the
legendary nature of the action. As the play's narrator, he imposes a subjective
but coherent control over the action and offers thematic resolution. The
nonrealistic aspects of his roles mesh perfectly with other devices that Williams
employs nonrealistically, especially the slides, music, and lighting.

Whether realistic or unrealistic, however, The Glass Menagerie is about   [7]
life--its desires, its dreams, its need for independent action, its disappointments,
and its poignancy. If Williams did not dramatize these issues, the technique
alone would not make a great play. But he does dramatize them, and as a result
the freedom of action and character he achieves through the combination of
roles for Tom enables him to achieve a remarkable unity of topic, merging past
with present and reality with unreality. Williams's use of Tom is a major reason
for which The Glass Menagerie may be considered a great modern drama .

Jhaveri 4

Work Cited

Tennessee Williams, The Glass Menagerie. Literature: An Introduction to
    Reading and Writing. Ed. Edgar V. Roberts. 9th ed. New York: Pearson
    Longman, 2009. 1644–91.

Commentary on the Essay

This essay shows how Williams's manipulation of Tom creates artistic and thematic unity in *The Glass Menagerie*. The primary focus is on character, but a number of distinct topics are taken up in connection with this element because the essay concerns Tom as a character, stage director, and narrator.

The body of the essay (paragraphs 2–5) takes up these three roles in the order listed in the introduction. Notice that this order does not reflect the sequence in which these roles occur in the play. Rather, they are organized to reflect a progression from the most realistic to the most nonrealistic aspects of Tom's three different functions. Thus, paragraph 2 discusses Tom as a realistic character and connects him to one of the play's central themes—entrapment and the desire to escape. Paragraphs 3, 4, and 5 shift to a consideration of Tom first as stage manager and second as narrator. These paragraphs explain the nonrealistic nature of these roles and explore the effects of Tom as the nonrealistic figure.

The concluding two paragraphs (6 and 7) provide a review and summary of the three roles Tom plays and the effects each produces in connection with theme and unity. In addition, they suggest a connection between the nonrealistic aspects of Tom's roles and the play's great power.

Throughout the body, direct quotation of dialogue or action as indicated in the stage directions is employed as supporting evidence. Quotations are used to validate specific points and are documented either within parentheses or in the body of discourse itself.

Writing Topics About Dramatic Reality and Nonreality

1. Compare the families of the Wingfields in *The Glass Menagerie*, Colonel Norwood in *Mulatto*, and the Maxsons in *Fences* (to which you might wish to add the Helmers in *A Dollhouse* and the Wrights in *Trifles*). What concept of family do these plays present? What good and bad effects do the families create? Which type of effect predominates? How realistic is the internal family dissension? How serious? How essential to the various plots? What is unusual or illogical about the dissentions? How? Why?

2. Compare the set descriptions of *Fences* and *The Glass Menagerie*. What elements of realism or nonrealism are common to both? How? Why? What effects would the sets have on the audience? Why?

3. The screen device described in Williams's Production Notes (see p. 1645) is omitted from most productions of *The Glass Menagerie*. Why? Consider the advantages or disadvantages of referring to this device in the printed text. How do the screen images affect your reading?

4. Describe Hughes's symbolism in *Mulatto*. How does the symbolism bring out the black/white differences in the play? Which locations, objects, and actions are symbolic, and what do they symbolize? In what ways are the symbols realistic? If they were not realistic, would they be successful as symbols? Explain.

5. Consider any of the plays in this chapter, using a feminist approach (see Chapter 29 for a discussion of this topic). What elements of realism or nonrealism are relevant to such a discussion? To aid your discussion, you might wish to use a study by Patricia R. Schroeder, *The Feminist Possibilities of Dramatic Realism* (Madison: Fairleigh Dickinson UP, 1996).

6. Write a research essay on the concept and practice of literary realism. To begin your research, you might wish to use books like these: Hugh S. Davies, *Realism in the Drama* (Cambridge, Cambridge UP, 1934); John B. Moore, *The Comic and the Realistic in English Drama* (New York: Russell & Russell, 1965); Harold H. Kolb, *The Illusion of Life: American Realism as a Literary Form* (Charlottesville: U of Virginia P, 1969); and Joseph P. Stern, *On Realism* (Boston: Routledge, 1973).

7. Write two separate versions of a scene of your own. (Some possible topics: a woman confronts her boyfriend upon learning that he has been seeing someone else; a man has an interview with his boss and learns that he is being fired; an army lieutenant tells his platoon that they are about to be attacked; a woman realizes that she is the best salesperson in the firm.) In the first, aim for total reality; in the second, for total unreality. What differences do you think your intentions in each case require of you as a practicing dramatist? What different requirements are made on your dialogue, on your action, on your setting, and on your costuming and suggested makeup for your actors? What elements do you think are the most unrealistic in your unrealistic version, and why do you believe you make them so unrealistic? Does the lack of realism, in your judgment, make your scene either more or less dramatic? Write an introductory essay to your two versions explaining these and other principles of your dramatic composition.

Chapter 27

Dramatic Vision On Film: From the Silver Screen to the World of Digital Fantasy

Film is the word most often used for motion pictures, although other common words are *cinema, movies,* and sometimes *pics.* It is a specialized type of drama, utilizing, like drama, the techniques of dialogue, monologue, and action. Also like drama, it employs movement and spectacle. For these reasons, film can be studied for aspects such as character, plot, structure, tone, and symbolism. Unlike drama, however, film embodies many techniques from photography, film chemistry, electronic technology, sound, and editing. Because these techniques are an integral aspect of movies, they require special consideration.

A Thumbnail History of Film

Film arose out of technologies developed in the late nineteenth century. The first of these was the invention of a flexible substance—celluloid—that could accept the chemical emulsions that in the early years of photography could be applied only to glass. Other essential inventions were the motion picture camera and projector, together with a screen coated with silver paint on which the moving pictures could be projected. Once these were in place, and once producers and directors decided to use the medium for full-length dramas, movies as we know them came into existence.

Although the earliest filmmakers thought of motion pictures as private entertainment, they soon recognized that the development of large filmmaking studios, national distribution, and a system of local movie theaters could become extremely lucrative. And that is what happened. The history of film is hence just as much a history of the film business as of the art and development of film dramas and film acting. The enormous potential of the movie business was first realized with the production in 1915 of D. W. Griffith's landmark but still controversial film *Birth of a Nation,* which reaped an enormous profit on a small investment.

The first motion pictures were black and white and were silent. Producers realized that large profits required easily recognized actors with "big names," and so the "star system" made national figures out of actors such as Mary Pickford, Charlie Chaplin, and Rudolph Valentino. In 1928 the first talking picture, *Lights of New York,* was made. Filmed drama—the movie—as we know it today was substantially established in 1934 with the first Technicolor film, *La Cucaracha,* a "short subject," and in 1935 with *Becky Sharp,* a feature film. For a long time afterward, however, most movies continued in black and white, whereas color, which was more expensive to produce, was uncommon. More recently the situation has been reversed, with color now being dominant.

For the greater part of film history, movies depended exclusively on the technology of the motion picture camera, but in recent years this technology has been merged with refined electronic enhancements. Many basic visual images are being augmented by digital visual technicians, who can create virtually entire environments. An inhabited island, for example, can be re-created digitally to seem like a desert island; a costumed man actually sitting on nothing more than a sawhorse can be made to appear as a general leading a company of cavalry; and a jerry-built stairway can be transformed into an elegant staircase for richly robed royalty.

This electronic transformation has brought about a revolution in the ways in which contemporary audiences see movies. The development of videotape, DVD (*digital video disc* or *digital versatile disc*), and digital technology has enabled the private viewing of movies at home in addition to the collective viewing of films exclusively in movie theaters. There are now many movie rental outlets in shopping districts everywhere, and there are DVD film clubs that advertise and sell large selections of movies to members. Movies are normal features of television broadcasts and satellite television, and they can be regularly downloaded through the Internet. The result is that most of the movies that have ever been made are within the reach of anyone with a television screen and the proper playing equipment. Miniaturization has also occurred. People can select film offerings on personal computers, iPods, iPhones, and other electronic devices. In short, there are so many outlets for film that today's students face an embarrassment of riches. Early dramatists dreamed of filling their theaters for a number of consecutive performances, thus reaching perhaps several thousand persons. Film writers today, however, reach millions in first-run movie theaters, and they also gain audiences of additional millions through the electronic equipment in modern homes.

Stage Plays and Film

Although film is a form of drama, there are a number of important differences between film and stage productions. Plays can be produced many times, in many different places, with many different people. In bringing a play to life, the producer and director rely not only on actors but also on artists, scene designers, carpenters, painters, lighting technicians, costume makers, choreographers, music directors, and musicians. For the actual performance of a play, however, the stage itself limits what can be done. In each theater production, the actors, setting, and effects are all physically confined to the stage.

The stage for makers of film, however, is virtually infinite, and the absence of restrictions permits the inclusion of countless details—car chases, underwater adventures, flying geese following an airplane, wartime combat, legislative debates, executive discussions; scenes in living rooms, courtrooms, boxing rings, hotel rooms, football stadiums, and kitchens; and locations in cities and countrysides anywhere—domestic or foreign, modern or ancient. And if a location or setting is not readily available, technicians can dub it in by computer enhancement, as in the various Harry Potter movies that show imaginative settings together

DVD TECHNOLOGY AND FILM STUDY

Of particular importance for today's students of movies is the easy availability of DVDs, many of which are issued with extra features that provide informative background and sidelights for film study—in addition, of course, to the basic film itself. A common "extra" is a film index that permits the viewer to select individual scenes and to replay them at will. Viewers may also find voiceover commentaries by screenwriters, directors, critics, various experts, and principal members of the cast. Additional features for study are selected scenes that were reduced or omitted in the final editing, together with complete alternative "takes" of various scenes. In these respects, many DVDs provide topics and guides for study.

The release of a DVD version of a film may often be considered an event itself in the film's history. The DVD version of Welles's *Citizen Kane* contains a totally remastered edition of the movie, and in addition it features running analyses of the entire movie by both Roger Ebert, a preeminent film critic, and Peter Bogdanovich, a widely recognized film director (Turner Home Video © 2001). The DVD of Terry Gilliam's 1985 film *Brazil* includes instructive interviews about the problems and controversies that preceded and followed the film's release. Of course, not all DVDs are equally elaborate. The reissues of Charlie Chaplin's comedies, for example, contain just the films, such as *City Lights* (one of the American Film Institute's recommendation as a best "romantic" film) and *The Gold Rush*. Even some of the releases of relatively new and successful films do not contain extras.

with individual actors flying through the air at will—sometimes on broomsticks. Such computerized and digital special effects, in which filmmakers sometimes indulge too liberally, can create dramatic images that were beyond reach for the greatest part of theater, and human, history. In short, the freedom enjoyed by the filmmaker almost limitlessly exceeds the freedom of the play producer. Nothing is left to the audience's imagination.

The two types of dramatic productions—drama and film—are therefore greatly different. Each new production of a play is unlike every other production, because not only the actors but also the appurtenances of the staging are unique. Shakespeare's play *Hamlet*, for example, has been produced innumerable times since Shakespeare's actors at London's Globe Theatre first performed it at the beginning of the seventeenth century, and each subsequent production, including the various filmed versions, has been different from all the rest.[1]

Paradoxically, this same variety cannot easily occur with film. Although the filmmaker has great freedom in producing each individual movie, this freedom also imposes its own limitations. Because of high production costs and also because

---

[1]See Chapter 23, pages 1222–24, for a brief discussion of The Ghost Scene as presented in six recent DVD versions of *Hamlet*.

films reach a mass audience through wide distribution, films are generally released in only one version, perhaps with "remakes" and dubbed versions for foreign audiences. Thus Orson Welles's *Citizen Kane* (1941) is in only one form, and although it has been recently restored and reedited, it remains in this form even though it is frequently shown and seen. Interestingly, no person can ever claim to have seen all the productions of plays like *Hamlet*, but everyone who sees a film like *Citizen Kane* can claim to have seen the exact same version.

The Aesthetics of Film

To the degree that film is confined to a screen, it can be compared visually with the art of the painter and the still photographer. It uses the language of visual art, where one object in a painting can take on special relationships to others as the artist directs the eyes of the observer. A color used in one part can be balanced with the same color, or its complement, in another part. Painters and photographers can introduce certain colors and details as symbols and can suggest allegorical interpretations through the inclusion of mythical figures or universally recognized objects. Particular effects can be achieved with the use of the textures of paint or with control over shutter speed, focus, and various techniques of development. The techniques and effects are extensive.

The filmmaker is able to utilize most of the resources of the still photographer and many of those of the painter and can augment these with special electronic effects. Artistically, the most confining aspect of film is the rectangular screen, but aside from that, film is unrestricted. Based in a dramatic text called a **film script** or **shooting script,** the film uses words and their effects, but it also employs the language of visual art and especially the particular vividness and power of moving pictures. When considering film, then, you should realize that film communicates not only with words but also with various visual techniques. The visual presentation is inseparable from the medium of film itself.

The Techniques of Film

There are many techniques of film, and a full description and documentation of them can be—and has become—extensive.[2] In evaluating film, however, you need

---

[2]See, for example, David Bleiler, *TLA Film, Video, and DVD Guide 2005: The Discerning Film Lover's Guide*; Roger Ebert, *Roger Ebert's Movie Yearbook 2007* (2006); Roger Ebert, *The Great Movies* (2002, regularly revised); Louis D. Giannetti, *Understanding Movies*, 11th ed. (2008); Leslie Halliwell, *Halliwell's Film Guide, 2008*, John Walker, ed. (2008); (2002); Ephraim Katz, *The Film Encyclopedia*, 5th ed., revised by Fred Klein and Ronald Dean Nolan (2004); Leonard Maltin, *Leonard Maltin's Movie Guide 2008* (2007); James Monaco, *How to Read a Film: The World of Movies, Media, and Multimedia: Language, History, Theory*, 3rd ed. (2000); Richard Beck Peacock, *The Art of Movie Making: Script to Screen* (2001); John Pym, *Time Out Film Guide 2008*, 16th ed. (2007); Robert Sklar, *A World History of Film* (2002); and David Thomson, *The New Biographical Dictionary of Film, Expanded and Updated* (2004).

See also the Internet Movie Data Base for complete data on films of all periods, at <www.imdb.com>. In 2008, the American Film Institute declared its own recommendations for film history through the issuance of *America's 10 Greatest Films in 10 Classic Genres* (http://www.afi.com/10top10).

to familiarize yourself only with those aspects of technique that have an immediate bearing on your responses and interpretations.

Film Utilizes Special Visual Techniques

THE CAMERA IS THE BASIC TOOL OF FILM.   Each film begins with the technique of the camera—buttressed today by electronic effects—which permits great freedom in the presentation of characters and actions. In a film, the visual viewpoint can shift. Thus, a film can begin with a distant shot of the actors—a "long shot"—much like the view of actors onstage. Then the camera can zoom in to show a close-up, or zoom out to present a wide and complete panorama. Usually a speaking actor will be the subject of a close-up, but the camera view can also capture other actors' reactions in close-up. You must interpret the effects of close-ups and long shots yourself, but it should be plain that the frequent use of either—or of middle-distance views—is a means by which film directors control viewer perception of characters and situations.

The camera can also move from character to character or from character to object. In this way, film can mark a series of reactions, concentrate your attention on a character's attitude, or comment visually on a character's actions. If a man and woman are in love, for example, the photographic view can shift from the couple to flowers and trees, thus associating their love visually with objects of beauty and growth. Should the flowers be wilted and the trees leafless, however, the visual commentary might be that their love is doomed and hopeless.

The camera also lends itself to the creation of unique effects. A common technique is slow motion, which can be used to emphasize a certain aspect of a person's character. The concentrated focus on a child running happily in a meadow (as in *The Color Purple* [1985] by Steven Spielberg) suggests the joy inherent in such movement. Surprisingly, speed is sometimes indicated by slow motion, which emphasizes strong muscular effort (as in the running scenes in Hugh Hudson's *Chariots of Fire* [1981]).

Many other camera techniques bear on action and character. The focus can be sharp at one point, indistinct at another. Moving a speaking character out of focus can suggest that listeners are bored. Sharp or blurred focus can also show that a character has seen things exactly or inexactly. In action sequences, the camera can be mounted in a moving vehicle to "track" or follow running human beings or horses, speeding bicycles and cars (as in Woody Allen's *Annie Hall* [1977]), or moving sailboats, canoes, speedboats, or rowboats. A camera operator on foot can also be the tracker, or the camera may track ground movement from a helicopter, or from the top of a bridge. Movement can also be captured by a rotating focal point that follows a moving object or character. Alternatively, the camera can be fixed while a character or object moves from one side of the frame to the other.

THE IMAGES IN FILM INVOLVE LIGHT, SHADOW, AND COLOR.   As in traditional theater, the filmmaker uses light, shadow, and color to reinforce ideas and to create realistic and symbolic effects. Characters in bright light are presumably open and frank, whereas characters in shadow may be hiding something, as in Alan J. Pakula's *All the President's Men* (1976). Flashing or strobe lights might indicate a changeable or sinister character or situation. A scene in sunshine, which brings out colors, and the same scene in rain and clouds or in twilight, all of which mute colors, create different moods. An example of such contrasts is the film *From Hell* (2001), directed by Albert and Allen Hughes, in which virtually the entire action takes place in darkness, and only the final scene is filmed in full light.

Colors, of course, have much the same meaning that they have in any other artistic medium. Blue sky and clear light suggest happiness, while dimly greenish light may indicate something ghoulish. A memorable control of color occurs midway through David O. Selznick's classic film *Gone with the Wind* (1939) when Scarlett O'Hara reflects upon the devastation of her plantation home. She resolves never to be hungry again, and as she speaks she is silhouetted against a darkened orange sky—a background that suggests how totally the way of life she knew as a young woman has been burned away. As in this example, you may expect colors to complement the story of the film. Thus, lovers may wear clothing with the same or complementary colors, whereas people who are not "right" for each other may wear clashing colors.

Action Is the Essence of Film

The strength of film is direct action. Actions of all sorts—running, swimming, driving a car, fighting, embracing and kissing, or even just sitting; chases, trick effects, ambushes—all these and more create a sense of immediate reality, and all are tied (or should be) to narrative development. Scenes of action can run on for several minutes, with little or no accompanying dialogue, to carry on the story or to convey ideas about the interests and abilities of the characters.

Camera Angles and Views of the Heads, Bodies, and Movements of Actors Are Related to a Film's Content

Closely related to the portrayal of action is the way in which film shows the human body (and animal bodies) together with bodily motion and gesture (or body language). The view or perspective that the filmmaker presents is particularly important. A torso shot of a character may stress no more than the content of that character's speech. A close-up shot, however, with the character's head filling the screen, may emphasize motives as well as content. The camera can also distort ordinary expectations of reality. Using wide-angle lenses and close-ups, for example, human subjects can be made to seem bizarre or grotesque, as are the faces in the crowd in Woody Allen's *Stardust Memories* (1980). Sometimes the camera creates other bodily distortions—for example, enlarging the limbs of the forest dweller in Ingmar Bergman's *The Virgin Spring* (1959) or throwing into unnatural prominence a scolding mouth or a suspicious eye. Distortion invites interpretation: The filmmaker may be asserting that certain human beings, even supposedly normal ones, are odd, sinister, intimidating, or psychopathic.

Sound Is Integral to the Presentation and Content of a Film

DIALOGUE AND MUSIC COMPLEMENT FILM DRAMATIZATIONS. The first business of the sound track is the spoken dialogue, which is mixed in editing to be synchronized with the action. There are also many other elements in the sound track. Music, the most important, creates and augments moods. A melody in a major or minor key, or in a slow or fast tempo, can affect our perception of actions. If a character is thinking deeply, complementary music may be played by muted strings. But if the character is going insane, the music may become discordant and percussive.

Sometimes, music gives a film a special identity. Hudson's *Chariots of Fire* (1981), for example, includes music by Vangelis. Although this music is independently well known, it is always associated with the film. In addition, musical accompaniments can directly render dramatic statement, without dialogue. An example occurs in Welles's *Citizen Kane* (1941). Beginning that portion of the narrative derived from the autobiography of a character who is now dead (the scene first focuses on his statue), the musical sound track by Bernard Herrmann quotes the *Dies Irae* theme from the traditional Mass for the Dead. The instrumentation, however, makes the music funny, and we smile rather than grieve. Incidentally, Herrmann varies the *Dies Irae* theme elsewhere in the film, usually for comic effect.

FILM USES SPECIAL AND OFTEN INGENIOUS SOUND EFFECTS.   Special sound effects can also augment a film's action. The sound of a blow can be enhanced electronically to cause an impact similar to the force of the blow itself (as in the boxing scenes from the many *Rocky* films). At times some sounds—such as the noises of wailing people, squeaking or slamming doors, marching feet, or moving vehicles—are filtered electronically to create weird or ghostly effects. Often a character's words echo rapidly and sickeningly to show dismay or anguish.

Editing or Montage

A finished film is a composite, not a continuous work filmed from start to end. The putting together of the film is the process of editing, or **montage** (assemblage, mounting, construction), which at one time involved cutting and gluing, but which now takes place on specially programmed computers. Depending on the flexibility of the film-script, the various scenes of the film are planned before shooting begins, but the major task of montage is accomplished in a studio by editing specialists.

If we again compare film with a stage play, we note that a theatrical production moves continuously, with pauses only for intermissions and scene changes. Your perception of the action is caused by your distance from the stage (perhaps aided by opera glasses or binoculars). Also, even as you move your eyes from one character to another, you still perceive the entire stage. In a film, however, the directors and editors *create* these continuous perceptions for you by piecing together different parts. The editors begin with many "takes" (separately photographed scenes, including many versions of the same scenes). What they select, or "mount," will be the film, and we never see the discarded scenes (unless they appear on a DVD special edition). Thus, it is montage, or editing, that puts everything together.

MONTAGE CREATES NARRATIVE CONTINUITY.   The first use of montage, already suggested, is narrative continuity. For example, a climb up a steep cliff can be shown at the bottom, middle, and top (with backward slips and falls to show the danger of the climb and to make viewers catch their breath). All such narrative sequences result from the assembling of individual pieces, each one representing phases of the activity. A classic example of a large number of separate parts forming a narrative unit is the well-known shower murder in Alfred Hitchcock's *Psycho* (1959), where a forty-five-second sequence is made up of seventy-eight different shots (the woman in the shower, the murderer behind the curtain, the attack, the slumping figure, the running water, the dead woman's eye, the bathtub drain, etc.).

MONTAGE PROVIDES EXPLANATION OF CHARACTER AND MOTIVATION.   Montage is used in flashbacks to explain ongoing actions or characteristics; or in illustration of a character's thoughts and memories; or in brief examples from the unremembered past of a character suffering from amnesia. It also supplies direct visual explanation of character. A famous example occurs in Welles's *Citizen Kane*. The concluding scene shows overhead views of Kane's vast collection of statuary and mementos. At the very end, the camera focuses on a raging furnace, into which workmen have thrown his boyhood sled which bears the brand name "Rosebud" (we have fleetingly seen Kane playing with the sled as a boy). Because "Rosebud" is Kane's last word, and everyone in the film is trying to decipher its meaning, this final scene reveals that Kane's dying thoughts were of his lost boyhood, before he was taken away from his parents, and that his unhappy life has resulted from early rejection and personal pain. (When we first see him as a boy, he is playing in the snow with his sled.)

MONTAGE FACILITATES DIRECTORIAL COMMENTARY.   Montage is also used symbolically as commentary, as in an early sequence in Charlie Chaplin's *Modern Times* (1936) that shows a large group of workers rushing to their factory jobs. Immediately following this scene is a view of a large, milling herd of sheep. By this symbolic montage, Chaplin suggests that the men are being herded and dehumanized by modern industry. Thus, montage and editorial statement go hand in hand.

MONTAGE IS USED IN MANY OTHER WAYS.   Montage can also produce other characteristics through camera work, development, and special effects of sound and light. For example, montage editors might reverse an action to emphasize its illogicality or ridiculousness. Editing can also speed up action (which makes even the most serious things funny) or slow things down. It can also blend one scene with another or juxtapose two or more actions in quick succession to show what people are doing while they are separated. The possibilities for creativity and innovation are extensive.

It bears stressing that montage should be thought of as the finishing stage in the readying of the film for presentation. When the photographic and other technical phases of filmmaking are completed, there is often much leftover material— enough to make a movie that would run for many hours and perhaps even days. The movie is definitely not yet ready for distribution.

It is therefore the montage editors who put everything together, sitting at their machines and trying, testing, arranging. They pick and choose to create many separate but connected scenes from the abundance of material at their command. They might begin by selecting a longshot, and then they might pick out film footage that represents a closer view of the action. A character may begin a gesture as we see him or her from a distance. But by the time the gesture is completed there may be a number of closeup and semi-closeup views of that character. In addition, there may be responses of other characters to the action. Similarly, a group of people may be walking together over the countryside, and at first we see the entire group, maybe of twenty, or forty, or more. And then, through montage, the scene may focus on several characters together. And then one or two individually, and then one of them may stumble, and that in itself creates the group reactions. Then the characters may stop to have dinner. Or maybe the group may stop to rest while some of the characters seek their dinner by using fishing equipment or rifles.

In such ways, the number of separate scenes that develop from any particular event can become magnified, modified, and individualized, and the final narrative scene will have been selected and pieced together from many separate views. No movie is ever complete until a considerable amount of montage work has been done on it. And even then what seems to be a final version may still be too long to present as a workable movie, and at that point the montage editors go back to their computers to shorten some scenes and to excise others.

By the time the finished film is presented to the public, it has been through the hands of one or more montage editors who, with the director and others closely involved in the process, have made innumerable artistic decisions about the final version that we see.

Two Film Scenes for Study

Orson Welles and Herman J. Mankiewicz . . . . From Citizen Kane, 1757

Arthur Laurents . . . . From The Turning Point, 1761

ORSON WELLES (1915–1985)
AND HERMAN J. MANKIEWICZ (1897–1953)

Orson Welles (1915–1985) developed an early interest in the theater. As a youth he traveled extensively, even spending some time in Spain as a bullfighter. In 1937 he cofounded the Mercury Theater, specializing in hour-long Sunday evening radio dramatizations. He achieved early immortality in October 1938, when he directed and acted in a version of H. G. Wells's The War of the Worlds. *This program created a near panic in the nation among listeners who did not understand what they were hearing. They thought they were listening to a program mostly of music, but regular interruptions reported that an "invasion" of Martians was taking place in the United States. After this, Welles was regularly identified with this dramatization that bewildered and scared so many Americans.*

Shortly after founding the Mercury Theater, Welles, along with Herman J. Mankiewicz (1897–1953), who had participated in the writing of the filmscript for The Wizard of Oz *(1939), planned a film on a larger-than-life American figure. Their model was the newspaper magnate William Randolph Hearst. Mankiewicz produced a lengthy draft of the script, which was titled first* American, *and then, a little later,* John Citizen, USA. *Welles changed the plot, wrote a number of new sections, and edited and shortened much of the original material. It was during this process of rewriting and editing that the title* Citizen Kane *was proposed and accepted. Soon, Welles began production with many of the actors of the Mercury Theater. Hearst, who quickly learned about the forthcoming film, sought a legal restraint on it, but* Citizen Kane *was successfully completed despite his efforts. The film reached the movie theaters with massive critical acclaim, and both Welles and Mankiewicz received an Academy Award for the best screenplay as joint authors.*

In 1958 a poll of international critics listed *Citizen Kane* as one of the twelve best films ever made. Its use of a format similar to *The March of Time* (a popular news feature series that ran regularly as a "selected short subject" in movie theaters), deep-focus camera work, unusual camera angles, contrasts of light and shadow, and its employment of four distinct points of view, together with its relentless insights into the major figure, all combined to make it a pioneering work in the history of film. Today, it is one of the touchstones in any discussion of movies, and its continued recognition justifies the claim that Welles was one of the great directors. After *Citizen Kane,* however, Welles struggled with personal and financial difficulties on each of his films, and he never again reached the heights of his first attempt.

The scene included here occurs about two-thirds of the way through the film. It is vital because it is a major indicator of Kane's personal decline. At first imbued with ideals for informing and reforming society, Kane (played by Orson Welles) becomes publisher of a newspaper he has inherited, and he advances public-minded editorial policies. A high point in his career is his running for governor of the state, but he loses the election after his secret love affair is made public. The following scene occurs right after the election loss. His most loyal supporter and coworker, Jedediah Leland (Joseph Cotten), confronts him and asks for a transfer to Chicago. The unspoken issue in the scene is that both men know that their friendship has been lost not because of the election, but because of Kane's misperceptions of people and his desertion of his earlier ideals.

The scene is taken from the so-called shooting script, which in film most closely corresponds to a dramatic text, and it is the full version, with copious directions for the actors. A comparison of this "shot," or scene, with the filmed version will show that some of the dialogue has been trimmed for purposes of pacing and speed. The shortening indicates a major characteristic of film (and also the production of plays), namely, to reduce speeches to no more than the essentials in order to keep the action moving and hold the audience's attention.

Shot 71 from the Shooting Script of Citizen Kane* (1941)

RKO Radio Pictures. A Mercury Production. Producer and Director, Orson Welles. Photographer, Gregg Toland, Editor, Robert Wise. Art Director, Van Nest Polglase. Music, Bernard Herrmann. Special Effects, Vernon L. Walker.

---

*The scene is gratefully reprinted from *The Citizen Kane Book* (Boston: Little, Brown & Co., 1971, 228–31). A remastered DVD film version is available: RKO Pictures, Inc., 1941. *Orson Welles, Citizen Kane*. Original Screen Play by Herman J. Mankiewicz and Orson Welles. Direction and Production by Orson Welles. Burbank, CA: Turner Entertainment Co. and Warner Home Video. Available from Warner Home Video, 4000 Warner Blvd, Burbank, CA 91522. This DVD set includes additional features. There is extensive commentary by both Roger Ebert and Peter Bogdanovich, and there is also a separate disc containing a lengthy documentary, "The Battle Over Citizen Kane" of 1995.

Dissolve in.
71 Int. Kane's Office—"Inquirer"—Night—1916

[*KANE looks up from his desk as there is a knock on the door.*]

KANE: Come in.

[*LELAND enters.*]

KANE: [*Surprised*] I thought I heard somebody knock.
LELAND: [*A bit drunk*] I knocked. [*He looks at him defiantly*]
KANE: [*Trying to laugh it off*] Oh! An official visit of state, eh? [*Waves his hand*] Sit down, Jedediah.
5   **LELAND:** [*Sitting down angrily*] I'm drunk.
KANE: Good! It's high time—
LELAND: You don't have to be amusing.
KANE: All right. Tell you what I'll do. I'll get drunk, too.
LELAND: [*Thinks this over*] No. That wouldn't help. Besides, you never get drunk. [*Pauses*] I want to talk to you—about—about—[*He can't get it out*]
10 **KANE:** [*Looks at him sharply a moment*] If you've got yourself drunk to talk to me about Susan Alexander—I'm not interested.
LELAND: She's not important. What's much more important—[*He keeps glaring at KANE*]
KANE: [*As if genuinely surprised*] Oh! [*He gets up*] I frankly didn't think I'd have to listen to that lecture from you. [*Pauses*] I've betrayed the sacred cause of reform, is that it? I've set back the sacred cause of reform in this state twenty years. Don't tell me, Jed, *you*—

[*Despite his load,° Leland manages to achieve a dignity about the silent contempt with which he looks at KANE.*]

KANE: [*An outburst*] What makes the sacred cause of reform so sacred? Why does the sacred cause of reform have to be exempt from all the other facts of life? Why do the laws of this state have to be executed by a man on a white charger?

[*LELAND lets the storm ride over his head.*]

KANE: [*Cont'd*] [*Calming down*] But, if that's the way they want it—they've made their choice. The people of this state obviously prefer Mr. Rogers to me. [*His lips tighten*] So be it.
15 **LELAND:** You talk about the people as though they belong to you. As long as I can remember you've talked about giving the people their rights as though you could make them a present of liberty—in reward for services rendered. You remember the workingman? You used to write an awful lot about the workingman. Well, he's turning into something called organized labor, and you're not going to like that a bit when you find out it means that he thinks he's entitled to something as his right and not your gift. [*He pauses*] And listen, Charles. When your precious underprivileged really do get together—that's going to add up to something bigger—than your privilege—and then I don't know what you'll do. Sail away to a desert island, probably, and lord it over the monkeys.
KANE: Don't worry about it too much, Jed. There's sure to be a few of them there to tell me where I'm wrong.
LELAND: You may not always be that lucky. [*Pauses*] Charlie, why can't you get to look at things less personally? Everything doesn't have to be between you and—the personal note doesn't always—

°12 S. D.: *load:* i.e., a heavy amount of liquor.

Still from *Citizen Kane*.

KANE: [*Violently*] The personal note is all there is to it. It's all there ever is to it. It's all there ever is to anything! Stupidity in our government—crookedness—even just compla-cency and self-satisfaction and an unwillingness to believe that anything done by a certain class of people can be wrong—you can't fight those things impersonally. They're not impersonal crimes against the people. They're being done by actual per-sons—with actual names and positions and—the right of the American people to their own country is not an academic issue, Jed, that you debate—and then the judges retire to return a verdict—and the winners give a dinner for the losers.

LELAND: You almost convince me, almost. The truth is, Charlie, you just don't care about anything except you. You just want to convince people that you love them so much that they should love you back. Only you want love on your own terms. It's some-thing to be played your way—according to your rules. And if anything goes wrong and you're hurt—then the game stops, and you've got to be soothed and nursed, no matter what else is happening—and no matter who else is hurt!

[*They look at each other.*]

KANE: [*Trying to kid him into a better humor*] Hey, Jedediah!   20

[*LELAND is not to be seduced.*]

LELAND: Charlie, I wish you'd let me work on the Chicago paper—you said yourself you were looking for someone to do dramatic criticism there—

KANE: You're more valuable here.

[*There is silence.*]

LELAND: Well, Charlie, then I'm afraid there's nothing I can do but to ask you to accept—

KANE: [*Harshly*] All right. You can go to Chicago.

25 LELAND: Thank you.

[*There is an awkward pause.* KANE *opens a drawer of his desk and takes out a bottle and two glasses.*]

KANE: I guess I'd better *try* to get drunk, anyway.

[KANE *hands* JED *a glass, which he makes no move to take.*]

KANE: [*Cont'd*] But I warn you, Jedediah, you're not going to like it in Chicago. The wind comes howling in off the lake, and the Lord only knows if they've ever heard of lobster Newburg.

LELAND: Will a week from Saturday be all right?

KANE: [*Wearily*] Anytime you say.

30 LELAND: Thank you.

[KANE *looks at him intently and lifts the glass.*]

KANE: A toast, Jedediah—to love on *my* terms. Those are the only terms anybody knows— his own.

Dissolve

QUESTIONS

1. What do you learn about the past and present relationship of Kane and Leland in this scene? What do Leland's speeches indicate about Kane's attitudes toward people? About Kane's shortcomings?

2. Basing your conclusions on this scene, why do you think the film is named *Citizen Kane*, and not something like *The Life of an American Tycoon* or *The Perils of Wealth*?

3. This scene is one of the revolutionary ones in the film because Welles and Toland (the principal photographer) shot it from floor height, emphasizing the distance from the camera to the heads of the characters. What effect do you think this vantage point has on viewers of the film? If you have seen the film, what do you think the camera angles and the lighting contribute to your perception of the characters?

ARTHUR LAURENTS (b. 1918)

Arthur Laurents, who began his career as a writer while serving in the U.S. Army during World War II, is one of the most successful novelists, playwrights, and film writers of the post-war period. Among his achievements in film are The Snake Pit *(1948),* Anastasia *(1956), and* The Way We Were *(1973). His plays* West Side Story *(1957) and* Gypsy *(1959) had extended Broadway runs as musicals and also became successful films. In 1983 he directed the originally French play* La Cage Aux Folles, *which was a great success. Recent works by Laurents are* The Radical Mystique *(1995), and* Jolson Sings Again *(1999). His autobiography is* Original Story By, *published in 2000. He was a participant in the documentary* Broadway: The American Musical, *Episode 6: Putting It Together (2004). The Turning Point (1977), which Laurents first published as a novel, received the Golden Globe Award, the National Board of Review Best Picture, an Academy Award nomination for the best screenplay, and the Writers Guild of America Award as the best film of that year.*

The Turning Point takes place against the background of ballet and the life of professional dancers. Deedee Rodgers (Shirley MacLaine) and Emma Jacklin (Anne Bancroft) had been close friends and rivals as young dancers with the

American Ballet Theater. Deedee became pregnant and married before she had a chance to become a star, and after the birth of her daughter, Emilia, she left the stage entirely for family life. With her husband Wayne (Tom Skerrit), who had also earlier been a dancer, she moved to Oklahoma, had two more children, and established a successful ballet school.

During the following seventeen years, Deedee has believed she could have gained stardom if she had not become a mother. She has also carried a grudge against Emma for having urged her to have the baby. In this way, Deedee believes, Emma pushed her aside when the two women had competed for the once-in-a-lifetime opportunity to dance in a new ballet. Emma, who won the role, went on to become famous as the company's prima ballerina. However, she has lived her life alone, her principal companions being the three dogs she keeps in her elegant apartment.

As the film opens, the ballet company comes to perform in Oklahoma City. Deedee's first daughter, Emilia (Leslie Browne), is now a promising dancer, and with Emma's help and support she becomes a star with the company during the following summer in New York. The scene included here occurs after a gala New York performance by the company, in which Emilia has brilliantly performed her first major solo dance, and in which Emma has been featured in a solo from *Anna Karenina*, perhaps for the last time.

At the reception after the gala, Emma makes a show of acknowledging Emilia, a gesture that angers Deedee and leads her to conclude that for a number of months Emma has been trying to gain undue influence over Emilia. Shortly after this, the company's director, Adelaide (Martha Scott) asks Emma to create a new production of Tchaikowsky's *Sleeping Beauty* ballet, but *not* to dance in it. This request hits Emma with full force, for she now recognizes that she is getting old and is about to be pushed aside by dancers who, like Emilia, are young and strong. She rushes out and stops at the nearby bar, where she encounters Deedee. The scene, which is virtually a short play all by itself, then develops, as the long-pent-up frustration, apprehension, and guilt of both women emerge.

 ## A Scene from The Turning Point* (1977)

Twentieth Century Fox. Producers, Herbert Ross and Arthur Laurents. Executive Producer, Nora Kaye. Photography, Robert Surtees. Film editor, William Reynolds. Music adapter, John Lanchbery. Director, Herbert Ross.

[SCENE] INTERIOR BAR—RAINBOW ROOM

[DEEDEE *is alone at the bar, drinking champagne. As* EMMA, *on her way to the Ladies' room, comes toward her,* DEEDEE *smiles and does a half-curtsy.* EMMA *stops and smiles back. Then she tosses her evening bag onto the bar.*]

---

*Twentieth Century Fox Film Corporation. A Herbert Ross Film. *The Turning Point*, 1977. Written by Arthur Laurents. Executive Producer, Nora Kay. Produced by Herbert Ross and Arthur Laurents. Featuring Shirley MacLaine, Anne Bancroft, Leslie Browne, Tom Skerrit, Mikhail Baryshnikov, and the Artists of the American Ballet Theatre. A DVD is available of *The Turning Point* (Twentieth Century Fox Home Entertainment, 2004; distributed by Anchor Bay Entertainment, Inc. [www.anchorbayentertainment.com], 2005).

EMMA: [*to the bartender*]. Champagne, please.

[*Declaration of war accepted. During the following, they both get refills, but they do not guzzle; there is no need for them to get drunk. Emotionally, each is ready to burst anyway. They (and we) are unaware of the bartender and he is unaware of them. For despite the lines, despite what each feels underneath, they are totally charming: two smiling, lovely, delightful friends having a chat.*]

DEEDEE: Remember the fairy tales we used to take turns reading to Emilia? Like the one about the two princesses? Every time one opened her mouth, out came diamonds and rubies. Every time the other opened her mouth, out came newts and hoptoads. Newts and hoptoads—[*taps her chest*]—coming out.

EMMA: One of those little toads has already made an appearance.

DEEDEE: Really! When?

5   EMMA: In my dressing room. When you said I shouldn't have bought Emilia that dress. Twice, you said it. Just before a performance. . . . I danced better tonight than I have in years.

DEEDEE: So I heard.

EMMA: Oh, another little toad! You've kept quite a few bottled up all these years, haven't you?

DEEDEE: Ohhh—embalmed, really.

EMMA: I think not. Why don't you let them out? I don't have a performance tomorrow.

[DEEDEE *looks at her, then accepts the challenge. She puts her glass down on the bar and holds out her hands with her fists clenched.*]

10   DEEDEE: Okay. Pick.

[EMMA *puts her glass down and points to a fist.* DEEDEE *opens it.*]

DEEDEE: Ah, a tiny one. I'd practically forgotten him. [*Looks up now.*] Why'd you make your best pal doubt herself and her hubby, Emma? Why'd you take the chance of lousing up her marriage? Why'd you say: "You better have that baby. It's the only way you can hold on to Wayne." I'm just curious now.

EMMA: You have a curious memory, but don't we all? As I remember, I said if you had an abortion, you might lose Wayne.

DEEDEE: Sweet, but inaccurate. I've remembered your exact words for lo, these too many moons. I eventually figured out why you said 'em. Because you also said: "Forget Michael's ballet, there'll be others." You clever little twinkletoes! You knew a ballet like that comes once in a career. You wanted it real bad, so you lied to make sure you got what you wanted.

EMMA: I've never had to lie to get what I wanted, Deedee. I'm too good.

15   DEEDEE: Really?

EMMA: Oh, yes.

DEEDEE: Well, I suppose if you said "bullshit," you'd say it in French.

[*Close shot.*]

EMMA: If that word came as naturally to me as it does to you, I'd have used it several times by now. In English. I think it's more appropriate that you say it—to yourself. For trying to blame *me* for what you did, for example. The choice was yours. It's much too late to regret it now, Deedee.

DEEDEE: And the same to you, Emma me darlin'.

20   EMMA: I certainly don't regret mine.

DEEDEE: Then why are you trying to become a mother at your age?

EMMA: Ooh, that's not a little toad. That's a rather large bullfrog. I don't want to be anybody's mother. I think of Emilia as a friend. And one reason I tried to help—stupid
me—I thought it would make you happy if your daughter became what you wanted
to be and couldn't be.

DEEDEE: Meaning you. It's so lovely to be you.

EMMA: Obviously, you think so.

DEEDEE: Oh, no no no no no no!   25

EMMA: No no no no?

DEEDEE: No; alas. And I doubt if Emilia could become you. Oh, she's as talented. She
works as hard. But there's one thing, dearest friend, that you are that she, poor darling, is not.

EMMA: And what, pray tell, is that?

DEEDEE: A killer. You'll walk over anybody and still get a good night's sleep. That's what
got you where you are, Emma.

[*She is smiling adorably.* EMMA *smiles back, finishes her drink, pushes the glass to the bartender,
keeps smiling until it is refilled, then picks it up. They are both smiling, almost laughing as* EMMA
looks at her drink, looks at DEEDEE, *then throws the champagne in* DEEDEE'S *face. A moment. Then*
DEEDEE *sets down her glass.*]

DEEDEE: Good girl.   30

[*She picks up her evening bag and starts out of the bar toward the exit and the elevators. The cool reaction infuriates* EMMA. *She puts down her glass and starts after* DEEDEE.]

INTERIOR CORRIDOR OUTSIDE RAINBOW ROOM

[EMMA *comes through the entrance to the Rainbow Room just as* DEEDEE *steps into an elevator.*]

EMMA: Deedee!

[*She runs for the elevator and just gets in as the doors are closing.*]

INTERIOR ELEVATOR—ROCKEFELLER CENTER

EMMA: I'm sick to death of your jealousy and resentment!

DEEDEE: So am I.

EMMA: Then stop blaming your goddamn life on me! You picked it!

DEEDEE: You did. You took away the choice, you didn't give me the chance to find out if I   35
was good enough.

EMMA: I can tell you now: you weren't.

[*The elevator doors open and* DEEDEE *strides out,* EMMA *after her.*]

EXTERIOR ROCKEFELLER PLAZA—NIGHT

[EMMA *is fast after* DEEDEE, *their heels clicking on the stone.*]

EMMA. You knew it yourself. That's why you married Wayne!

DEEDEE: [*whirls around*] I loved him!

EMMA: So much that you said to hell with your career!

DEEDEE: Yes!   40

EMMA: And got pregnant to prove you meant it!

DEEDEE: Yes!

EMMA: Lie to yourself, not to me. You got married because you knew you were second-rate; you got pregnant because Wayne was a ballet dancer, and that meant queer!

DEEDEE: *He wasn't!*

45 EMMA: Still afraid someone will think he is? You were terrified then! You had to *prove* he was a man! *That's* why you had a baby!

DEEDEE: That's a goddamn lie!

EMMA: It's the goddamn truth! You saddled him with a baby and blew his career! And now she's grown up and better than you ever were and you're jealous!

DEEDEE: You're certifiable! You'll use anything for an excuse.

EMMA: What's that an excuse for?

50 DEEDEE: Trying to take away my child!

EMMA: I return the compliment: you're a liar!

DEEDEE: And you're a user. You have been your whole life! Me, Michael—pretending to love him!—Adelaide and now Emilia!

EMMA: How Emilia?!

DEEDEE: "How Emilia." That display five minutes ago: Curtsy! Applause! Embrace! For *you*, not her! You were using her so everyone'd say: "Emma's so gracious, Emma's so wonderful!"

55 EMMA: Untrue!

DEEDEE: You *are* wonderful! You're amazing! It's incredible how you keep going on. You're over the hill; you know it and *you're* terrified. All you've got are your scrapbooks and your old toe shoes and those stupid, ridiculous dogs! What are you going to fill in with, Emma? Not my daughter. You keep your goddam hands off!

EMMA: I'm better for her than you are.

DEEDEE: Like hell!

EMMA: She came to me because her mother wasn't there. Her mother was too busy screwing her head off!

60 DEEDEE: You bitch!

[*She whacks* EMMA *with her evening bag. For a moment,* EMMA *is too startled to move. But as* DEEDEE *lifts her bag again,* EMMA *blocks it with one hand and with the other whacks* DEEDEE *with her evening bag. They both go at it: rarely hitting, ducking blows, slamming out blindly with their evening bags.*]

EXTERIOR ROCKEFELLER CENTER—NIGHT

[*There they are, these two ladies in their evening gowns, each making a last pass, a last weak attempt to hit the other, and missing. They are panting, exhausted, and at last, they stop and just stand there, breathing hard.*]

[*Close shot—Their breath is coming back.* DEEDEE *smiles.*]

DEEDEE: If there'd been a photographer handy, you'd have a whole new career.

EMMA: I must look awful.

DEEDEE: No: beautiful. I don't know how you do it.

[EMMA *has taken out a mirror and is looking in it.*]

EMMA: If I can borrow your comb, I'll show you. Oh, I lost an earring.

65 DEEDEE: [*handing her a comb*] I'm sorry.

EMMA: I'm not.

DEEDEE: Really?

EMMA: Yes.

[*She returns the comb, and they start walking, looking for the lost earring. The following is very quiet:*]

DEEDEE: Jealousy is poison. Makes you a monster.
EMMA: Well, it does make one unfair. [*Smiles.*] Two.   70
DEEDEE: Two?
EMMA: Me, too.
DEEDEE: [*a second, then laughs*] Emma, you made a good joke!
EMMA: Yes, I did. . . . I'm really not so humorless.
DEEDEE: Listen, you got off some really good ones before. Oh, look!   75

[*She picks up the earring and gives it to EMMA.*]

EMMA: How did it get over here? Thank you.
DEEDEE: You also hit a couple of bull's-eyes before.
EMMA: So did you.
DEEDEE: Sit?
EMMA: Oh, please.   80

[*They sit on the rim of the fountain.*]

EMMA: I don't really remember what I said about having the baby. But I do know I would have said anything to make sure I got that ballet . . . . I had to have it, Deedee. I just had to.
DEEDEE: My God. Oh Emma. Emma, I didn't know how much all I wanted was for you to say just that . . . . Let's have a drink!
EMMA: Absolutely!

[*They get up. EMMA links her arm through DEEDEE'S as they start walking.*]

EMMA: It's good.
DEEDEE: You bet.   85
EMMA: I'm glad Wayne's coming.
DEEDEE: Me, too . . . . How's with Carter?
EMMA: Ça va . . . . *That's* bullshit in French.

[*DEEDEE laughs and walks toward the street, to a taxi. But EMMA has stopped, turned toward the entrance to the party.*]

DEEDEE: Not back to the party?
EMMA: I have to.   90
DEEDEE: [*nods, understands*] Call me when you wake up.
EMMA: If not before.

[*They smile—and walk in opposite directions.*]

QUESTIONS

1. Despite the fact that the two women carry their anger so far as to strike each other, what does the scene show about the nature of friendship? What key admissions do the women make to effect their reconciliation?

2. The film omits the last ten speeches of the script (concluding with "to say just that" in speech 82). Justify eliminating these last speeches.

3. What is the effect of the fact that the locations of this scene move from the interior bar to the exterior plaza? Granted the actions of the two women, why can the scene not be in a single location (as it would necessarily be if written for the theater)? On the basis of your answers, what conclusions can you draw about the comparative freedoms and limitations of film and theater?

4. View the film *The Turning Point*, and compare the details of the script with the final filmed version of the scene. Explain the purpose and nature of the changes in the film. If you had the freedom of a film director, what other liberties might you take in the performance? Why?

WRITING ABOUT FILM

Obviously the first requirement is to see the film, either in a movie theater, on videocassette, or on DVD. No matter how you see it, you should go through it at least twice, taking notes, because your discussion takes on value the more thoroughly you know the material. Include the names of the scriptwriter, director, composer, special effects editor, chief photographer, and major actresses and actors. If particular speeches are worth quoting, remember the general circumstances of the quotation and also, if possible, key words. Take notes on costume and color or (if the film is in black and white) on light and shade. You may need to rely on memory, but if you have a videotape or a DVD, you can easily replay important sections of the film and can verify important details.

Questions for Discovering Ideas

ACTION

- How important is action? Is there much repetition of action, say, in slow motion, or from different angles? Are actors (or animals) viewed closely or distantly? Why?
- What actions are stressed (chases, concealment, gun battles, lovemaking, etc.)? What does the type of action contribute to the film?
- What do close-ups (smiles and laughter, frowns, leers, anxious looks, etc.) show about character and motivation?
- What actions indicate seasonal conditions (e.g., cold by a character's stamping of feet, warmth by the character's removing a coat or shirt)? What connection do these actions have to the film's general ideas?
- Does the action show any changing of mood, say, from sadness to happiness or from indecision to decision?

CINEMATOGRAPHIC TECHNIQUES

- What notable techniques are used (colors, lighting, etc.)? What is their relationship to the film's characterizations and themes?

- What characterizes the use of the camera (tracking, close-ups, distant shots, camera angles, etc.)? How do the camera perspectives reinforce or detract from the film's theme and plot?
- How does the editing (the sequencing of scenes) reinforce or detract from story and theme?
- What scene or scenes best exemplify how the cinematographic techniques interact with the theme, plot, characters, setting, and so on? Why?

ACTING

- How well do the actors adapt to the medium of film? How well do they deliver their lines? How convincing are their performances?
- How well do the actors control their facial expressions and body movement? Are they graceful? Awkward?
- What does their appearance lend to your understanding of their characters?
- Does it seem that the actors are genuinely creating their roles, or are they just reading through the parts?

Strategies for Organizing Ideas

State your central idea and thesis sentence. You should include the background necessary to support points you make in the body of the essay and should also name the major creative and performing persons of the film.

Any of the organizing strategies discussed in this book's previous chapters, such as plot, structure, character, ideas, or setting, are equally valid for an essay on a film, except that you will need to consider them in a visual context. For example, if you choose to discuss the effects of a character on the plot, you need to develop your argument using the evidence of camera techniques, montage, sound effects, and the like.

When discussing film techniques, be sure to have good notes so that your supporting details are accurate. A good method is to concentrate on technique in only a few scenes. If you analyze the effects of montage, for example, you can use a videocassette or DVD to repeat seeing the scene a number of times.

In the conclusion of your essay, you might evaluate the effectiveness of the cinematic form to story and idea. Are all the devices of film used in the best possible way? Is anything overdone? Is anything underplayed? Is the film good, bad, or indifferent up to a point, and then does it change? How? Why?

Illustrative Student Essay

Underlined sentences in this paper *do not* conform to MLA style and are used solely as teaching tools to emphasize the central idea, thesis sentence, and topic sentences throughout the paper.

Leal 1

Sebastian Leal

Professor Hoover

English 222

13 February 2008

Welles's Citizen Kane:° Whittling a Giant Down to Size

[1]   Citizen Kane (1941) is a superbly crafted film in black and white. The script is by Herman Mankiewicz and Orson Welles, with photography by Gregg Toland, music by Bernard Herrmann, direction and production by Welles, and the leading role by Welles. It is the story of a wealthy and powerful man, Charles Foster Kane, who exemplifies the American Dream of economic self-sufficiency, self-determination, and self, period. The film does not explore the "greatness" of the hero, however, but rather exposes him as a misguided, unhappy person who tries to buy love and remake reality.* All aspects of the picture--characterization, structure, and technique--are focused on this goal.†

[2]   At the film's heart is the deterioration of Kane, the newly deceased newspaper magnate and millionaire who was rich beyond imagination. He begins well, but goes tragically downward. For example, the view we see of him as a child, being taken away from home, invites sympathy. When we next see him as a young man, he idealistically takes over a daily newspaper, the Inquirer. This idealism makes him admirable but also makes his deterioration tragic. As he says to Thatcher in a moment of insight, he could have been a great person if he had not been wealthy. His corruption begins when he tries to alter the world to suit himself, as in his demented attempt to make an opera star out of his second wife, Susan, and his related attempt to shape critical praise

°A scene from *Citizen Kane* appears on pages 1757–60.
*Central idea.
†Thesis sentence.

Leal 2

for her. Even though he builds an opera house for her and also sponsors many performances, he cannot change reality. This tampering with truth indicates how completely he loses his youthful integrity.

The structure is progressively arranged to bring out such weaknesses. The film flows out of the opening obituary newsreel, from which we learn that Kane's dying word was the name "Rosebud" (the brand name of his boyhood sled, which is spoken at the beginning by a person [Kane] whose mouth is shown in close-up). The newsreel director, wanting to get the inside story, assigns a reporter named Thompson to learn about "Rosebud." Thompson's search unifies the rest of the film; he goes from place to place and person to person to collect materials and conduct interviews that disclose Kane's increasing strangeness and alienation. At the end, although the camera abandons Thompson and focuses on the burning sled, he has been successful in uncovering the story of Kane's deterioration (even though he himself never learns what "Rosebud" means). Both the sled and the reporter therefore tie together the many aspects of the film.

[3]

It is through Thompson's searches that the film presents the flashback accounts of Kane's deterioration. The separate people being interviewed (including Thatcher's handwritten account) each contribute something different to the narrative because their experiences with Kane have all been different. Because of these individual points of view, the story is intricate. For example, we learn in the Bernstein section that Jedediah proudly saves a copy of Kane's declaration about truth in reporting. We do not learn in Jedediah's interview, however, that he, Jedediah (Joseph Cotten), sends the copy back to Kane as an indictment of Kane's betrayal of principle. Rather, it is in Susan's account that we learn about the return, even though she herself understands nothing about it. This subtlety, so typical of the film, marks the ways in which the biography of Kane is progressively revealed.

[4]

In addition to these perceptive structural characterizations, Citizen Kane is a masterpiece of film technique. The camera images are sharp, with clear depth of field. In keeping with Kane's disintegration and mysteriousness, the screen is rarely bright. Instead, the film makes strong use of darkness and contrasts, almost to the point at times of blurring distinctions between people. Unique in

[5]

Leal 3

Gregg Toland's camera work are the many shots taken from waist height or below, distorting the bodies of the characters by distancing their heads-- suggesting that the characters are preoccupied with their own concerns and oblivious to normal perspectives. Nowhere is this distortion better exemplified than in the scene between Kane and Jedediah in the empty rooms after the lost election, when Jedediah asks permission to leave for Chicago.

[6]   As might be expected in a film so dominated by its central figure, the many symbols create strong statements about character. The most obvious is the sled, "Rosebud," the dominating symbol of the need for love and acceptance in childhood. Another notable symbol is glass and, in one scene, ice. In the party scene, two ice statues are in the foreground of the employees of the Inquirer. In another scene, a bottle looms large in front of Jedediah, who is drunk. In another, a pill bottle and drinking glass are in front of Susan, who has just used them in her suicide attempt. The suggestion of these carefully photographed symbols is that life is brittle and temporary. Particularly symbolic is the bizarre entertainment in the party scene. Because Kane joins the dancing and singing, the action suggests that he is doing no more than taking a role in life, never being himself or knowing himself. Symbols that frame the film are the wire fence and the "No Trespassing" sign at both beginning and end. These symbols suggest that even if we understand a little about Kane, or anyone else, there are boundaries we cannot pass, depths we can never reach.

[7]   In all respects, Citizen Kane is a superb film. This is not to say that the characters are likable or that the amusing parts make it a comedy. Instead, the film pursues truth, suggesting that greatness and wealth cannot give happiness. It is relentless in whittling away at its major figure. Kane is likable at times, and he is enormously generous (as shown when he sends Jedediah $25,000 in severance pay). But these high moments show the contrasting depths to which Kane falls, with the general point being that people who are powerful and great may deteriorate even at their height. The goal of the newsreel director at the beginning is to get at the "real story" behind the public man. There is more to

Leal 4

any person than a two-hour film can reveal, but within its limits, Citizen Kane

gets at the real story, and the real story is both sad and disturbing.

Leal 5

Work Cited

Citizen Kane. Screenplay by Orson Welles and Herman R. Mankiewicz. Dir.

Orson Wells. Perf. Orson Welles. 1941. DVD. Turner Entertainment Co.

and Warner Home Video, ©2001.

Commentary on the Essay

The major point of this essay is that the film diminishes the major figure, Kane. In this respect the essay illustrates the analysis of *character* (Chapter 3), and it therefore emphasizes how film can be considered as a form of literature. Also shown in the essay are other methods of literary analysis: *structure* (Chapter 5) and *symbolism* (Chapters 7, 19). Of these topics, only the use of symbols, because they are visually presented in the film, is unique to the medium of film as opposed to the medium of words.

Any one of the topics might be developed as a separate essay. There is more than enough about the character of Susan, for example, to sustain a complete essay, and the film's structure could be extensively explored. *Citizen Kane* itself as a repository of film techniques is rich enough for an exhaustive, book-length account.

Because the essay is about a film, the unique aspect of paragraph 1 is the opening brief description (stressing the medium of black and white) and the credits to the scriptwriters, principal photographer, composer, and director. Unlike works written by a single author, film is a collaborative medium, and therefore it is appropriate to recognize the separate efforts of the principal contributors.

Paragraph 2 begins the body and carries out a brief analysis of the major character. Paragraphs 3 to 5 discuss various aspects of the film's structure (the second topic announced in the thesis sentence) as they bear on Kane. Paragraph 3 explains the unifying importance of the sled and Thompson, the reporter. Paragraph 4 focuses on the film's use of flashback as a structural technique. In paragraphs 5 and 6, the topic is film technique, the third and last topic of the thesis sentence. Paragraph 5 focuses on darkness and light, camera angles, and distortion; paragraph 6 treats visual symbols. The final paragraph, 7, restates the central idea and also relates the theme of deterioration to the larger issue of how great wealth and power affect character. Thus, as a conclusion, this paragraph not only presents a summary but also notes the film's general ideas.

Writing Topics About Film

1. Select a single film technique, such as the use of color, the control of light, or the photographing of action, and write an essay describing how it is used in a film. For best results, use a DVD or a videocassette for your study. As much as possible, try to explain how the technique is used throughout the film. Determine constant and contrasting features, the relationship of the technique to the development of story and character, and so on.

2. Write an essay explaining how all the film techniques of a particular part or section are employed (e.g., camera angles, close-ups or long shots, tracking, on-camera and off-camera speeches, lighting, depth of field). For your study, you will have to rerun the section a number of times, trying to notice elements for the first time and also reinforcing your first observations. To add a research element to this question, you might consult the works by Bleiler, Ebert, Giannetti, Halliwell, Katz, Monaco, Peacock, Sklar, and Thomson listed in the footnote on page 1751.

3. Pick out a news story and write a dramatic scene about it. Next, consider how to write the scene for a film, providing directions for actors and camera operators (e.g., "As Character A speaks, his face shows that he is lying; the camera zooms slowly in on his face, with a loss of focus," or "As Character A speaks, the camera focuses on Character B exchanging looks with Character C"). When you are done, write an explanation of how you intend your directions to bring out details about your story and characters.

Chapter 28

Henrik Ibsen and the Realistic Problem Play: *A Dollhouse*

The Norwegian playwright Henrik Johan Ibsen (1828–1906) is the acknowledged originator—the "father"— of modern drama. He deserves this recognition because of his pioneering dramatizations of challenging and sometimes shocking private and public issues. Today there are few restrictions on dramatists except success at the box office. Plays may range freely on almost any subject, such as the drug culture, sexual inclinations, AIDS, the right to commit suicide, the problems of real-estate dealers, the life of a fan dancer, violence, family dissension, homosexuality, the Vietnam war or the Kuwait war or the Afghanistan war or the Iraq war, and the aftereffects of the atrocities of 9/11/01. If one includes film as drama, there is virtually no limit to the topics that dramatists currently explore. It is well to stress that writers for the stage have not always been this free, and that Ibsen was in the forefront of the struggle for unbridled dramatic expression. A brief consideration of some of his major dramatic topics shows his originality and daring: the blinding and crippling effects of congenital syphilis, a woman's renunciation of a traditional protective marriage, suicide, the manipulations of people seeking personal benefits, the sacrifices of pursuing truth, the rejection of a child by a parent, and the abandonment of personal happiness in favor of professional interests.

Ibsen's Life and Early Work

From Ibsen's beginnings, there was little to indicate how important he was to become. He was born in Skien (*SHEE-en*), Norway, a small town just seventy miles southwest of the capital, Christiania (now Oslo). Although his parents had been prosperous, they went bankrupt when he was only seven, and in the years that followed the family suffered the miseries of poverty. When Ibsen was fifteen, he was apprenticed to a pharmacist, and he seemed headed for an undistinguished career in this profession even though he hated it. By 1849, however, when he wrote *Catiline*, his first play in verse, it was clear that the theater was to be his life. Largely through the efforts of the famous violinist Ole Bull, a new National Theater had been established in Bergen, and Ibsen was appointed its director. He stayed in Bergen for six years and then went to Christiania, where for the next five years he tried to fashion a genuine Norwegian national theater. His attempts proved fruitless, for the theater went bankrupt in 1862. After writing *The Pretenders* in 1864, he secured enough governmental travel money to enable him to leave Norway. For the next twenty-seven years he lived in Germany and Italy in what has been called a self-imposed exile.

Although this first part of Ibsen's theatrical career was devoted to many practical matters—production, management, directing, and finances—he was also constantly writing. His early plays were in verse and were mainly nationalist and romantic, as a few representative titles suggest: *Lady Inger of Oestraat* (1855), *The Feast of Solhaug* (1856), *Olaf Liljekrans* (1857). In his first ten years in Germany and Italy he finished four plays. The best known of these is *Peer Gynt* (1867), a fantasy play about a historical Norwegian hero, Peer Gynt, who is saved from spiritual emptiness by the love of the devoted heroine Solveig. Today, *Peer Gynt* is best known because of the incidental music written for it by Norway's major composer, Edvard Grieg (1843–1907). Ibsen asked Grieg to compose the music for the initial performances in 1876. Grieg's response was enthusiastic and creative, and the result is still enjoyed by millions today. Ibsen also supplied the poem for which Grieg composed one of his loveliest songs, "A Swan."

Ibsen's Major Prose Plays

During the years when Ibsen was fighting poverty and establishing his career in the theater, Europe was undergoing great political and intellectual changes. Throughout the nineteenth century, Ibsen's home country, Norway, was trying to release itself from the domination of neighboring Sweden and to establish its own territorial and national integrity. In Ibsen's twentieth year, 1848, the February Uprising in Paris resulted in the deposition of the French king and the establishment of a new French republic. This same year also saw the publication of the *Communist Manifesto* of Karl Marx (1818–1883). In 1864, the year Ibsen left Norway, Marx's first socialist International was held in London. In addition, during the time Ibsen lived in Italy and Germany, both countries were going through the tenuous political processes of becoming authentic nation-states. In short, change was everywhere.

Ibsen also was changing and growing as a thinker and dramatist, driven by the idea that a forward and creative drama could bring about deeper and more permanent changes than could be effected by soldiers and politicians. To this end he developed the realistic **problem play**—a theatrical work that posits a major personal, social, professional, or political problem that occasion the play's dramatic conflicts and tensions. Each problem is timely, topical, and realistic, as are Ibsen's characters, places, situations, and outcomes. In this vein, Ibsen wrote the twelve prose problem plays on which his reputation rests: *The Pillars of Society* (1877), *A Dollhouse* (1879), *Ghosts* (1881), *An Enemy of the People* (1882), *The Wild Duck* (1884), *Rosmersholm* (1886), *The Lady from the Sea* (1888), *Hedda Gabler* (1890), *The Master Builder* (1892), *Little Eyolf* (1894), *John Gabriel Borkman* (1896), and *When We Dead Awaken* (1899). He finished the first eight of these plays while living in Germany and Italy, the last four after returning to Norway in 1891.

In these major plays Ibsen dramatizes human beings breaking free from restrictions and inhibitions and trying to establish their individuality and freedom—freedom of self, inquiry, pursuit of truth, artistic dedication, and, above all, the freedom of love. In attempting to achieve these goals, Ibsen's dramatic characters find internal opposition in self-interest, self-indulgence, and self-denial, and external opposition in the personal and political influences and manipulations of others. Because the plays are designed to be realistic, Ibsen's characters fall short of their goals. At best they achieve a respite in their combat, as in *An Enemy of the People*, or begin a quest in new directions, as in *A Dollhouse*. They always make great sacrifices, sometimes losing life itself, as in *Hedda Gabler* and *John Gabriel Borkman*.

A Dollhouse: Ibsen's Best-Known Problem Play

A Dollhouse (*Et Dukkehjem*, 1879)[1] is representative of Ibsen's realistic problem dramas. Its scenes are realistic, including appropriate furniture, a piano, a Christmas tree, carpeting, and wall engravings. Its characters are in the process of realistically confronting overwhelming personal, marital, and economic problems. Realism extends also to the technique of presentation, particularly the exposition about the root causes of the problems that come to a head in the play itself. As *A Dollhouse* unfolds, we learn that years earlier, Nora Helmer had extended herself beyond her means to save Torvald from a near-fatal illness.

Ibsen's Symbolism In *A Dollhouse*

A Dollhouse is representative of Ibsen's realism, but it is also replete with contextual symbolism, like the major plays that came before and after it. At the end of the late play *John Gabriel Borkman*, for example, the major character freezes to death, an occurrence symbolic of what he had done to himself much earlier by denying love. In reference to *A Dollhouse*, the title itself symbolizes the dependent and dehumanized role of the wife within traditional middle-class marriages. In addition, the entire nation of Norway (cold, legal, male) is contrasted symbolically with Italy (warm, emotional, female). Ironically, the break in the Helmers' marriage is symbolically aligned with events that occur or have occurred in both locations. Other symbols in *A Dollhouse* are the Christmas tree, the children's presents, the death of Dr. Rank, and the mailbox.

A Dollhouse as a "Well-Made Play"

The plot and structure of *A Dollhouse* show Ibsen's use of the conventions of the **well-made play** (*la pièce bien faite*), a form developed and popularized in nineteenth-century France by Eugène Scribe (1791–1861) and Victorien Sardou

---

[1] Ibsen's title *Et Dukkehjem* literally means the home (*hjem*) of a doll or puppet (*dukke*). *A Doll's House*, the traditional and most common English title of the play, is not an accurate rendering of *dukkehjem*, and, in addition, it is misleading because of some of the connotations of our word *doll*. Recent translators have used *A Doll House* as the title, but this form is not in regular use. Our English word for a toy house for dolls is listed in collegiate dictionaries as *dollhouse*, a one-word compound. *A Dollhouse* is therefore preferable to the other two titles because it accurately renders *Et Dukkehjem*, and it is also the form accepted in current dictionaries.

(1831–1908). Ibsen was familiar with well-made plays, having directed many of them himself at Bergen and Christiania. The well-made play follows a rigid and efficient structure in which the drama begins at the story's climax. Usually the plot is built on a secret known by the audience and perhaps one or two of the characters. The well-made play thus begins in suspense and offers a pattern of increasing tension produced through exposition and the timely arrivals of new characters (like Krogstad) and threatening news or props like the disclosure of Nora's earlier financial transactions. In the course of action of the well-made play, the fortunes of the protagonist go from a low point, through a *peripeteia* or reversal (Aristotle's concept), to a high point at which the protagonist confronts and defeats the villain.

Although Ibsen makes use of many of the structural elements of the well-made play, he varies and departs from the pattern to suit his realistic purposes. Thus in *A Dollhouse* his variation is that Nora's confrontation with Krogstad, who is the apparent villain, does not lead to a satisfactory resolution, but rather precipitates the more significant albeit intractable confrontation with her husband. In *A Dollhouse*, just as in many other Ibsen plays, there is not a traditionally well-made victorious outcome; rather there are provisional outcomes—adjustments—in keeping with the realistic concept that as life goes on, problems continue.

The Timeliness and Dramatic Power of *A Dollhouse*

Ibsen's focus on real-life issues and problems has given his plays continued timeliness and strength. Thus *A Dollhouse* vividly portrays the totally dependent position of married women in the nineteenth century. Most notably, a woman could not borrow funds legally without a man's cosignature, and Nora had been forced to violate the law to obtain the money to restore her husband's health. The mailbox, to which Torvald has the only key, symbolizes this limitation, and the ultimate disclosure of the box's contents, rather than freeing Nora and Torvald, highlights her dependency. Today's feminism has stressed the issues of female freedom and equality, together with many other issues vital to women, but the need for feminine individuality and independence has not been more originally and forcefully dramatized than in *A Dollhouse*.

Bibliographic Studies

Because of Ibsen's importance, there have been many translations and editions of the plays. The Modern Library Giant edition of Farquharson-Sharp's translations of *Eleven Plays by Henrik Ibsen* (introduction by H. L. Mencken) has been a mainstay for many decades. Rolf Fjelde published paperback translations in 1970 and followed these up with *The Complete Major Prose Plays* in 1978 (twelve plays). Michael Meyer's translations (sixteen plays in four paperback volumes, 1986) are of major significance. Other individual and collected plays have been translated by Peter Watts, Una Ellis-Fermor, James McFarlane, Christopher Hampton, Inger Lignell, Nicholas Rudall, William Archer, Christopher Fry, and Kenneth McLeish. These names by no means constitute a complete list. A short edition of Ibsen's poetry has been translated by Michael Feingold (1987).

The major biography of Ibsen is Halvdan Hoht, *Life of Ibsen*, translated and edited by Einar Haugen and A. E. Santaniello (New York: Blom, 1971). Significant critical and biographical studies include George Bernard Shaw, *The Quintessence of Ibsenism* (1891; rpt. 1957), the pioneering work of Ibsen criticism; Rolf Fjelde, *Ibsen: A Collection of Critical Essays* (Englewood Cliffs: Prentice Hall, 1965); Michael Meyer, *Henrik Ibsen: The Farewell to Poetry 1864–1882* (London: Hart-Davis, 1971); James Hurt, *Catiline's Dream: An Essay on Ibsen's Plays* (Urbana: U of Illinois P, 1972); Clela Allphin, *Women in the Plays of Henrik Ibsen* (New York: Revisionist, 1975); Harold Clurman, *Ibsen* (New York: Macmillan, 1977); Einar Haugen, *Ibsen's Drama: Author to Audience* (Minneapolis: U of Minnesota P, 1979); David Thomas, *Henrik Ibsen* (London, Macmillan, 1983); Yvonne Shafer, ed., *Approaches to Teaching Ibsen's* A Doll House (New York: MLA, 1985); Charles R. Lyons, ed., *Critical Essays on Henrik Ibsen* (Boston: Hall, 1987); Frederick Marker and Lise-Lone Marker, *Ibsen's Lively Art* (New York: Cambridge UP, 1989); Joan Templeton, "The *Doll House* Backlash: Criticism, Feminism, and Ibsen," *PMLA* 104 (1989): 28–40; Naomi Lebowitz, *Ibsen and the Great World* (Baton Rouge: Louisiana UP, 1990); Errol Durbach, A Doll's House: *Ibsen's Myth of Transformation* (Boston: Twayne, 1991); Brian Johnston, *The Ibsen Cycle: The Design of the Plays from* Pillars of Society *to* When We Dead Awaken (University Park: Pennsylvania State UP, 1992); and James McFarlane, ed., *The Cambridge Companion to Ibsen* (Cambridge: Cambridge UP, 1994).

HENRIK IBSEN (1828–1906)

 # A Dollhouse (Et Dukkehjem) (1879)

Translated by R. Farquharson Sharp

CHARACTERS

Torvald Helmer, a lawyer and bank manager
Nora, his wife
Doctor Rank, the "greatest friend" of the Helmers
Mrs. Christine Linde, Nora's old friend, recently widowed, returning after a ten-year absence
Nils Krogstad, a lawyer and bank clerk
Ivar, Bob, and Emmy, the Helmers' three young children
Anne, their nurse
Helen, a housemaid
A Porter

The action takes place in HELMER'S *apartment.*

ACT 1

SCENE. *A room furnished comfortably and tastefully, but not extravagantly. At the back, a door to the right leads to the entrance hall, another to the left leads to* HELMER'S *study. Between the doors stands a piano. In the middle of the left-hand wall is a door, and beyond it a window. Near the window are a round table, armchairs and a small sofa. In the right-hand wall, at the farther end, another door; and on the same side, nearer the footlights, a stove, two easy chairs and a rocking-chair; between the stove and the door, a small table. Engravings on the walls; a cabinet with china and other small objects; a small book case with well-bound books. The floors are carpeted, and a fire burns in the stove. It is winter.*

A bell rings in the hall; shortly afterwards the door is heard to open. Enter NORA, *humming a tune and in high spirits. She is in outdoor dress and carries a number of parcels; these she lays on the table to the right. She leaves the outer door open after her, and through it is seen a* PORTER *who is carrying a Christmas Tree and a basket, which he gives to the* MAID *who has opened the door.*

NORA: Hide the Christmas Tree carefully, Helen. Be sure the children do not see it till this evening, when it is dressed. [*to the* PORTER, *taking out her purse.*] How much?

PORTER: Sixpence.

NORA: There is a shilling. No, keep the change. [*The* PORTER *thanks her, and goes out.* NORA *shuts the door. She is laughing to herself, as she takes off her hat and coat. She takes a packet of macaroons from her pocket and eats one or two; then goes cautiously to her husband's door and listens.*] Yes, he is in.

[*Still humming, she goes to the table on the right.*]

HELMER: [*calls out from his room*] Is that my little lark twittering out there?

5   NORA: [*busy opening some of the parcels*] Yes, it is!

HELMER: Is my little squirrel bustling about?

NORA: Yes!

HELMER: When did my squirrel come home?

NORA: Just now. [*puts the bag of macaroons into her pocket and wipes her mouth.*] Come in here, Torvald, and see what I have bought.

10   HELMER: Don't disturb me. [*A little later, he opens the door and looks into the room, pen in hand.*] Bought, did you say? All these things? Has my little spendthrift been wasting money again?

NORA: Yes, but, Torvald, this year we really can let ourselves go a little. This is the first Christmas that we have not needed to economise.

HELMER: Still, you know, we can't spend money recklessly.

NORA: Yes, Torvald, we may be a wee bit more reckless now, mayn't we? Just a tiny wee bit! You are going to have a big salary and earn lots and lots of money.

HELMER: Yes, after the New Year; but then it will be a whole quarter before the salary is due.

15   NORA: Pooh! we can borrow till then.

HELMER: Nora! [*goes up to her and takes her playfully by the ear.*] The same little feather-head! Suppose, now, that I borrowed fifty pounds to-day, and you spent it all in the Christmas week, and then on New Year's Eve a slate fell on my head and killed me, and—

NORA: [*putting her hands over his mouth*] Oh! don't say such horrid things.

HELMER: Still, suppose that happened—what then?

NORA: If that were to happen, I don't suppose I should care whether I owed money or not.

20   HELMER: Yes, but what about the people who had lent it?

NORA: They? Who would bother about them? I should not know who they were.

HELMER: That is like a woman! But seriously, Nora, you know what I think about that. No debt, no borrowing. There can be no freedom or beauty about a home life that depends on borrowing and debt. We two have kept bravely on the straight road so far, and we will go on the same way for the short time longer that there need be any struggle.

NORA: [*moving towards the stove*] As you please, Torvald.

HELMER: [*following her*] Come, come, my little skylark must not droop her wings. What is this! Is my little squirrel out of temper? [*taking out his purse.*] Nora, what do you think I have got here?

25   NORA: [*turning around quickly*] Money!

HELMER: There you are. [*gives her some money*] Do you think I don't know what a lot is wanted for housekeeping at Christmas-time?

NORA: [*counting*] Ten shillings—a pound—two pounds! Thank you, thank you, Torvald; that will keep me going for a long time.

HELMER: Indeed it must.

NORA: Yes, yes, it will. But come here and let me show you what I have bought. And all so cheap! Look, here is a new suit for Ivar, and a sword; and a horse and a trumpet for Bob; and a doll and dolly's bedstead for Emmy—they are very plain, but anyway she will soon break them in pieces. And here are dress-lengths and handkerchiefs for the maids; old Anne ought really to have something better.

HELMER: And what is in this parcel?   30

NORA: [*crying out*] No, no! you mustn't see that till this evening.

HELMER: Very well. But now tell me, you extravagant little person, what would you like for yourself?

NORA: For myself? Oh, I am sure I don't want anything.

HELMER: Yes, but you must. Tell me something reasonable that you would particularly like to have.

NORA: No, I really can't think of anything—unless, Torvald—   35

HELMER: Well?

NORA: [*playing with his coat buttons, and without raising her eyes to his*] If you really want to give me something, you might—you might—

HELMER: Well, out with it!

NORA: [*speaking quickly*] You might give me money, Torvald. Only just as much as you can afford; and then one of these days I will buy something with it.

HELMER: But, Nora—   40

NORA: Oh, do! dear Torvald; please, please do! Then I will wrap it up in beautiful gilt paper and hang it on the Christmas Tree. Wouldn't that be fun?

HELMER: What are little people called that are always wasting money?

NORA: Spendthrifts—I know. Let us do as you suggest, Torvald, and then I shall have time to think what I am most in want of. That is a very sensible plan, isn't it?

HELMER: [*smiling*] Indeed it is—that is to say, if you were really to save out of the money I give you, and then really buy something for yourself. But if you spend it all on the housekeeping and any number of unnecessary things, then I merely have to pay up again.

NORA: Oh but, Torvald—   45

HELMER: You can't deny it, my dear little Nora. [*puts his arm round her waist*] It's a sweet little spendthrift, but she uses up a deal of money. One would hardly believe how expensive such little persons are!

NORA: It's a shame to say that. I do really save all I can.

HELMER: [*laughing*] That's very true—all you can. But you can't save anything!

NORA: [*smiling quietly and happily*] You haven't any idea how many expenses we skylarks and squirrels have, Torvald.

HELMER: You are an odd little soul. Very like your father. You always find some new way of wheedling money out of me, and, as soon as you have got it, it seems to melt in your hands. You never know where it has gone. Still, one must take you as you are. It is in the blood; for indeed it is true that you can inherit these things, Nora.   50

NORA: Ah, I wish I had inherited many of papa's qualities.

HELMER: And I would not wish you to be anything but just what you are, my sweet little skylark. But, do you know, it strikes me that you are looking rather—what shall I say—rather uneasy to-day?

NORA: Do I?

HELMER: You do, really. Look straight at me.

55 NORA: [*looks at him*] Well?

HELMER: [*wagging his finger at her*] Hasn't Miss Sweet-Tooth been breaking rules in town to-day?

NORA: No; what makes you think that?

HELMER: Hasn't she paid a visit to the confectioner's?

NORA: No, I assure you, Torvald—

60 HELMER: Not been nibbling sweets?

NORA: No, certainly not.

HELMER: Not even taken a bite at a macaroon or two?

NORA: No, Torvald, I assure you really—

HELMER: There, there, of course I was only joking.

65 NORA: [*going to the table on the right*] I should not think of going against your wishes.

HELMER: No, I am sure of that! besides, you gave me your word—[*going up to her*] Keep your little Christmas secrets to yourself, my darling. They will all be revealed to-night when the Christmas Tree is lit, no doubt.

NORA: Did you remember to invite Doctor Rank?

HELMER: No. But there is no need; as a matter of course he will come to dinner with us. However, I will ask him when he comes in this morning. I have ordered some good wine. Nora, you can't think how I am looking forward to this evening.

NORA: So am I! And how the children will enjoy themselves, Torvald!

70 HELMER: It is splendid to feel that one has a perfectly safe appointment, and a big enough income. It's delightful to think of, isn't it?

NORA: It's wonderful!

HELMER: Do you remember last Christmas? For a full three weeks beforehand you shut yourself up every evening till long after midnight, making ornaments for the Christmas Tree and all the other fine things that were to be a surprise to us. It was the dullest three weeks I ever spent!

NORA: I didn't find it dull.

HELMER: [*smiling*] But there was precious little result, Nora.

75 NORA: Oh, you shouldn't tease me about that again. How could I help the cat's going in and tearing everything to pieces?

HELMER: Of course you couldn't, poor little girl. You had the best of intentions to please us all, and that's the main thing. But it is a good thing that our hard times are over.

NORA: Yes, it is really wonderful.

HELMER: This time I needn't sit here and be dull all alone, and you needn't ruin your dear eyes and your pretty little hands—

NORA: [*clapping her hands*] No, Torvald, I needn't any longer, need I! It's wonderfully lovely to hear you say so! [*taking his arm*] Now I will tell you how I have been thinking we ought to arrange things, Torvald. As soon as Christmas is over—[*A bell rings in the hall.*] There's the bell. [*She tidies the room a little.*] There's someone at the door. What a nuisance!

80 HELMER: If it is a caller, remember I am not at home.

MAID: [*in the doorway*] A lady to see you, ma'am—a stranger.

NORA: Ask her to come in.

MAID: [*to HELMER*] The doctor came at the same time, sir.

HELMER: Did he go straight into my room?

85 MAID: Yes sir.

[*HELMER goes into his room. The MAID ushers in MRS. LINDE, who is in travelling dress, and shuts the door.*]

MRS. LINDE: [*in a dejected and timid voice*] How do you do, Nora?

NORA: [*doubtfully*] How do you do—

MRS. LINDE: You don't recognise me, I suppose.

NORA: No, I don't know—yes, to be sure, I seem to—[*suddenly*] Yes! Christine! Is it really you?

MRS. LINDE: Yes, it is I.   90

NORA: Christine! To think of my not recognising you! And yet how could I—[*in a gentle voice*] How you have altered, Christine!

MRS. LINDE: Yes, I have indeed. In nine, ten long years—

NORA: Is it so long since we met? I suppose it is. The last eight years have been a happy time for me, I can tell you. And so now you have come into the town, and have taken this long journey in winter—that was plucky of you.

MRS. LINDE: I arrived by steamer this morning.

NORA: To have some fun at Christmas-time, of course. How delightful! We will have such   95
fun together! But take off your things. You are not cold, I hope. [*helps her*] Now we will sit down by the stove, and be cosy. No, take this arm-chair; I will sit here in the rocking-chair. [*takes her hands*] Now you look like your old self again; it was only the first moment—You are a little paler, Christine, and perhaps a little thinner.

MRS. LINDE: And much, much older, Nora.

NORA: Perhaps a little older; very, very little; certainly not much. [*stops suddenly and speaks seriously*] What a thoughtless creature I am, chattering away like this. My poor, dear Christine, do forgive me.

MRS. LINDE: What do you mean, Nora?

NORA: [*gently*] Poor Christine, you are a widow.

MRS. LINDE: Yes; it is three years ago now.   100

NORA: Yes, I knew; I saw it in the papers. I assure you, Christine, I meant ever so often to write to you at the time, but I always put it off and something always prevented me.

MRS. LINDE: I quite understand, dear.

NORA: It was very bad of me, Christine. Poor thing, how you must have suffered. And he left you nothing?

MRS. LINDE: No.

NORA: And no children?   105

MRS. LINDE: No.

NORA: Nothing at all, then?

MRS. LINDE: Not even any sorrow or grief to live upon.

NORA: [*looking incredulously at her*] But, Christine, is that possible?

MRS. LINDE: [*smiles sadly and strokes her hair*] It sometimes happens, Nora.   110

NORA: So you are quite alone. How dreadfully sad that must be. I have three lovely children. You can't see them just now, for they are out with their nurse. But now you must tell me all about it.

MRS. LINDE: No, no; I want to hear you.

NORA: No, you must begin. I mustn't be selfish to-day; to-day I must only think of your affairs. But there is one thing I must tell you. Do you know we have just had a great piece of good luck?

MRS. LINDE: No, what is it?

NORA: Just fancy, my husband has been made manager of the Bank!   115

MRS. LINDE: Your husband? What good luck!

NORA: Yes, tremendous! A barrister's profession is such an uncertain thing, especially if he won't undertake unsavoury cases; and naturally Torvald has never been willing to do that, and I quite agree with him. You may imagine how pleased we are! He is to take up his work in the Bank at the New Year, and then he will have a big salary and lots of commissions. For the future we can live quite differently—we can do just as we like. I feel so relieved and so happy, Christine! It will be splendid to have heaps of money and not need to have any anxiety, won't it?

MRS. LINDE: Yes, anyhow I think it would be delightful to have what one needs.

NORA: No, not only what one needs, but heaps and heaps of money.

120 MRS. LINDE: [*smiling*] Nora, Nora haven't you learnt sense yet? In our schooldays you were a great spendthrift.

NORA: [*laughing*] Yes, that is what Torvald says now. [*wags her finger at her*] But "Nora, Nora" is not so silly as you think. We have not been in a position for me to waste money. We have both had to work.

MRS. LINDE: You too?

NORA: Yes; odds and ends, needlework, crochet-work, embroidery, and that kind of thing. [*dropping her voice*] And other things as well. You know Torvald left his office when we were married? There was no prospect of promotion there, and he had to try and earn more than before. But during the first year he overworked himself dreadfully. You see, he had to make money every way he could, and he worked early and late; but he couldn't stand it, and fell dreadfully ill, and the doctors said it was necessary for him to go south.

MRS. LINDE: You spent a whole year in Italy didn't you?

125 NORA: Yes. It was no easy matter to get away, I can tell you. It was just as Ivar was born; but naturally we had to go. It was a wonderfully beautiful journey, and it saved Torvald's life. But it cost a tremendous lot of money, Christine.

MRS. LINDE: So I should think.

NORA: It cost about two hundred and fifty pounds. That's a lot, isn't it?

MRS. LINDE: Yes, and in emergencies like that it is lucky to have the money.

NORA: I ought to tell you that we had it from papa.

130 MRS. LINDE: Oh, I see. It was just about that time that he died, wasn't it?

NORA: Yes; and, just think of it, I couldn't go and nurse him. I was expecting little Ivar's birth every day and I had my poor sick Torvald to look after. My dear, kind father—I never saw him again, Christine. That was the saddest time I have known since our marriage.

MRS. LINDE: I know how fond you were of him. And then you went off to Italy?

NORA: Yes; you see we had money then, and the doctors insisted on our going, so we started a month later.

MRS. LINDE: And your husband came back quite well?

135 NORA: As sound as a bell!

MRS. LINDE: But—the doctor?

NORA: What doctor?

MRS. LINDE: I thought your maid said the gentleman who arrived here just as I did was the doctor?

NORA: Yes, that was Doctor Rank, but he doesn't come here professionally. He is our greatest friend, and comes in at least once every day. No, Torvald has not had an hour's illness since then, and our children are strong and healthy and so am I. [*jumps up and claps her hands*] Christine! Christine! it's good to be alive and happy!—But how horrid of me; I am talking of nothing but my own affairs. [*sits on a stool near her, and rests her arms on her knees*] You mustn't be angry with me. Tell me, is it really true that you did not love your husband? Why did you marry him?

140 MRS. LINDE: My mother was alive then, and was bedridden and helpless, and I had to provide for my two younger brothers; so I did not think I was justified in refusing his offer.

NORA: No, perhaps you were quite right. He was rich at that time, then?

MRS. LINDE: I believe he was quite well off. But his business was a precarious one; and, when he died, it all went to pieces and there was nothing left.

NORA: And then?—

MRS. LINDE: Well, I had to turn my hand to anything I could find—first a small shop, then a small school, and so on. The last three years have seemed like one long working-day, with no rest. Now it is at an end, Nora. My poor mother needs me no more, for she is gone; and the boys do not need me either; they have got situations and can shift for themselves.

NORA: What a relief you must feel it—   145

MRS. LINDE: No, indeed; I only feel my life unspeakably empty. No one to live for any more. [gets up restlessly] That was why I could not stand the life in my little backwater any longer. I hope it may be easier here to find something which will busy me and occupy my thoughts. If only I could have the good luck to get some regular work—office work of some kind—

NORA: But, Christine, that is so frightfully tiring, and you look tired out now. You had far better go away to some watering-place.

MRS. LINDE: [walking to the window] I have no father to give me money for a journey, Nora.

NORA: [rising] Oh, don't be angry with me.

MRS. LINDE: [going up to her] It is you that must not be angry with me, dear. The worst of a   150
position like mine is that it makes one so bitter. No one to work for, and yet obliged to be always on the look-out for chances. One must live, and so one becomes selfish. When you told me of the happy turn your fortunes have taken—you will hardly believe it—I was delighted not so much on your account as on my own.

NORA: How do you mean?—Oh, I understand. You mean that perhaps Torvald could get you something to do.

MRS. LINDE: Yes, that was what I was thinking of.

NORA: He must, Christine. Just leave it to me; I will broach the subject very cleverly—I will think of something that will please him very much. It will make me so happy to be of some use to you.

MRS. LINDE: How kind you are, Nora, to be so anxious to help me! It is doubly kind in you, for you know so little of the burdens and troubles of life.

NORA: I—? I know so little of them?   155

MRS. LINDE: [smiling] My dear! Small household cares and that sort of thing!—You are a child, Nora.

NORA: [tosses her head and crosses the stage] You ought not to be so superior.

MRS. LINDE: No?

NORA: You are just like the others. They all think that I am incapable of anything really serious—

MRS. LINDE: Come, come—   160

NORA: —that I have gone through nothing in this world of cares.

MRS. LINDE: But, my dear Nora, you have just told me all your troubles.

NORA: Pooh!—those were trifles. [lowering her voice] I have not told you the important thing.

MRS. LINDE: The important thing? What do you mean?

NORA: You look down upon me altogether, Christine—but you ought not to. You are   165
proud, aren't you, of having worked so hard and so long for your mother?

MRS. LINDE: Indeed, I don't look down on any one. But it is true that I am both proud and glad to think that I was privileged to make the end of my mother's life almost free from care.

NORA: And you are proud to think of what you have done for your brothers.

MRS. LINDE: I think I have the right to be.

NORA: I think so, too. But now, listen to this; I too have something to be proud of and glad of.

170 MRS. LINDE: I have no doubt you have. But what do you refer to?

NORA: Speak low. Suppose Torvald were to hear! He mustn't on any account—no one in the world must know, Christine, except you.

MRS. LINDE: But what is it?

NORA: Come here [*pulls her down on the sofa beside her*] Now I will show you that I too have something to be proud and glad of. It was I who saved Torvald's life.

MRS. LINDE: "Saved"? How?

175 NORA: I told you about our trip to Italy. Torvald would never have recovered if he had not gone there—

MRS. LINDE: Yes, but your father gave you the necessary funds.

NORA: [*smiling*] Yes, that is what Torvald and all the others think, but—

MRS. LINDE: But—

NORA: Papa didn't give us a shilling. It was I who procured the money.

180 MR. LINDE: You? All that large sum?

NORA: Two hundred and fifty pounds. What do you think of that?

MRS. LINDE: But, Nora, how could you possibly do it? Did you win a prize in the Lottery?

NORA: [*contemptuously*] In the Lottery? There would have been no credit in that.

MRS. LINDE: But where did you get it from, then?

185 NORA: [*humming and smiling with an air of mystery*] Hm, hm! Aha!

MRS. LINDE: Because you couldn't have borrowed it.

NORA: Couldn't I? Why not?

MRS. LINDE: No, a wife cannot borrow without her husband's consent.

NORA: [*tossing her head*] Oh, if it is a wife who has any head for business—a wife who has the wit to be a little bit clever—

190 MRS. LINDE: I don't understand it at all, Nora.

NORA: There is no need you should. I never said I had borrowed the money. I may have got it some other way. [*lies back on the sofa*] Perhaps I got it from some other admirer. When anyone is as attractive as I am—

MRS. LINDE: You are a mad creature.

NORA: Now, you know you're full of curiosity, Christine.

MRS. LINDE: Listen to me, Nora dear. Haven't you been a little bit imprudent?

195 NORA: [*sits up straight*] Is it imprudent to save your husband's life?

MRS. LINDE: It seems to me imprudent, without his knowledge, to—

NORA: But it was absolutely necessary that he should not know! My goodness, can't you understand that? It was necessary he should have no idea what a dangerous condition he was in. It was to me that the doctors came and said that his life was in danger, and that the only thing to save him was to live in the south. Do you suppose I didn't try, first of all, to get what I wanted as if it were for myself? I told him how much I should love to travel abroad like other young wives; I tried tears and entreaties with him; I told him that he ought to remember the condition I was in, and that he ought to be kind and indulgent to me; I even hinted that he might raise a loan. That nearly made him angry, Christine. He said I was thoughtless, and that it was his duty as my husband not to indulge me in my whims and caprices—as I believe he called them. Very well I thought, you must be saved—and that was how I came to devise a way out of the difficulty—

MRS. LINDE: And did your husband never get to know from your father that the money had not come from him?

NORA: No, never. Papa died just at that time. I had meant to let him into the secret and beg him never to reveal it. But he was so ill then—alas, there never was any need to tell him.

MRS. LINDE: And since then have you never told your secret to your husband?   200

NORA: Good Heavens, no! How could you think so? A man who has such strong opinions about these things! And besides, how painful and humiliating it would be for Torvald, with his manly independence, to know that he owed me anything! It would upset our mutual relations altogether; our beautiful happy home would no longer be what it is now.

MRS. LINDE: Do you mean never to tell him about it?

NORA: [*meditatively, and with a half smile*] Yes—some day, perhaps, after many years, when I am no longer as nice-looking as I am now. Don't laugh at me! I mean of course, when Torvald is no longer as devoted to me as he is now; when my dancing and dressing-up and reciting have palled on him; then it may be a good thing to have something in reserve—[*breaking off*] What nonsense! That time will never come. Now, what do you think of my great secret, Christine? Do you still think I am of no use? I can tell you, too, that this affair has caused me a lot of worry. It has been by no means easy for me to meet my engagements punctually. I may tell you that there is something that is called, in business, quarterly interest, and another thing called payment in instalments, and it is always so dreadfully difficult to manage them. I have had to save a little here and there, where I could, you understand. I have not been able to put aside much from my housekeeping money, for Torvald must have a good table. I couldn't let my children be shabbily dressed; I have felt obliged to use up all he gave me for them, the sweet little darlings!

MRS. LINDE: So it has all had to come out of your own necessaries of life, poor Nora?

NORA: Of course. Besides, I was the one responsible for it. Whenever Torvald has given me   205
the money for new dresses and such things, I have never spent more than half of it; I have always bought the simplest and cheapest things. Thank Heaven, any clothes look well on me, and so Torvald has never noticed it. But it was often very hard on me, Christine—because it is delightful to be really well dressed, isn't it?

MRS. LINDE: Quite so.

NORA: Well, then I have found other ways of earning money. Last winter I was lucky enough to get a lot of copying to do; so I locked myself up and sat writing every evening until quite late at night. Many a time I was desperately tired; but all the same it was a tremendous pleasure to sit there working and earning money. It was like being a man.

MRS. LINDE: How much have you been able to pay off in that way?

NORA: I can't tell you exactly. You see, it is very difficult to keep an account of a business matter of that kind. I only know that I have paid every penny that I could scrape together. Many a time I was at my wit's end. [*smiles*] Then I used to sit here and imagine that a rich old gentleman had fallen in love with me—

MRS. LINDE: What! Who was it?   210

NORA: Be quiet!—that he had died; and that when his will was opened it contained, written in big letters, the instruction: "The lovely Mrs. Nora Helmer is to have all I possess paid over to her at once in cash."

MRS. LINDE: But, my dear Nora—who could the man be?

NORA: Good gracious, can't you understand? There was no old gentleman at all; it was only something that I used to sit here and imagine, when I couldn't think of any way of procuring money. But it's all the same now; the tiresome old person can stay where he is, as far as I am concerned; I don't care about him or his will either, for I am free from care now. [*jumps up*] My goodness, it's delightful to think of, Christine! Free from care! To be able to be free from care, quite free from care; to be able to play and romp with the children; to be able to keep the house beautifully and have everything just as Torvald likes it! And, think of it, soon the spring will come and the big blue sky! Perhaps

we shall be able to take a little trip—perhaps I shall see the sea again! Oh, it's a wonderful thing to be alive and be happy. [*A bell is heard in the hall.*]

MRS. LINDE: [*rising*] There is the bell; perhaps I had better go.

215 NORA: No, don't go; no one will come in here; it is sure to be for Torvald.

SERVANT: [*at the hall door*] Excuse me, ma'am—there is a gentleman to see the master, and
as the doctor is with him—

NORA: Who is it?

KROGSTAD: [*at the door*] It is I, Mrs. Helmer. [*Mrs. Linde starts, trembles, and turns to the window.*]

NORA: [*takes a step towards him, and speaks in a strained, low voice*] You? What is it? What do
you want to see my husband about?

220 KROGSTAD: Bank business—in a way. I have a small post in the Bank, and I hear your husband is to be our chief now—

NORA: Then it is—

KROGSTAD: Nothing but dry business matters, Mrs. Helmer; absolutely nothing else.

NORA: Be so good as to go into the study, then. [*She bows indifferently to him and shuts the
door into the hall; then comes back and makes up the fire in the stove.*]

MRS. LINDE: Nora—who was that man?

225 NORA: A lawyer, of the name of Krogstad.

MRS. LINDE: Then it really was he.

NORA: Do you know the man?

MRS. LINDE: I used to—many years ago. At one time he was a solicitor's clerk in our town.

NORA: Yes, he was.

230 MRS. LINDE: He is greatly altered.

NORA: He made a very unhappy marriage.

MRS. LINDE: He is a widower now, isn't he?

NORA: With several children. There now, it is burning up.

[*Shuts the door of the stove and moves the rocking-chair aside.*]

MRS. LINDE: They say he carries on various kinds of business.

235 NORA: Really! Perhaps he does; I don't know anything about it. But don't let us think of
business; it is so tiresome.

DOCTOR RANK: [*comes out of HELMER's study. Before he shuts the door he calls to him.*] No, my
dear fellow, I won't disturb you; I would rather go in to your wife for a little while. [*shuts
the door and sees MRS. LINDE*] I beg your pardon; I am afraid I am disturbing you too.

NORA: No, not at all. [*introducing him*] Doctor Rank, Mrs. Linde.

RANK: I have often heard Mrs. Linde's name mentioned here. I think I passed you on the
stairs when I arrived, Mrs. Linde?

MRS. LINDE: Yes, I go up very slowly; I can't manage stairs well.

240 RANK: Ah! some slight internal weakness?

MRS. LINDE: No, the fact is I have been overworking myself.

RANK: Nothing more than that? Then I suppose you have come to town to amuse yourself
with our entertainments?

MRS. LINDE: I have come to look for work.

RANK: Is that a good cure for overwork?

245 MRS. LINDE: One must live, Doctor Rank.

RANK: Yes, the general opinion seems to be that it is necessary.

NORA: Look here, Doctor Rank—you know you want to live.

RANK: Certainly. However wretched I may feel, I want to prolong the agony as long as
possible. All my patients are like that. And so are those who are morally diseased; one
of them, and a bad case too, is at this very moment with Helmer—

MRS. LINDE: [*sadly*] Ah!

NORA: Whom do you mean?   250
RANK: A lawyer of the name of Krogstad, a fellow you don't know at all. He suffers from a
    diseased moral character, Mrs. Helmer; but even he began talking of its being highly
    important that he should live.
NORA: Did he? What did he want to speak to Torvald about?
RANK: I have no idea; I only heard that it was something about the Bank.
NORA: I didn't know this—what's his name—Krogstad had anything to do with the Bank.
RANK: Yes, he has some sort of appointment there. [*to Mrs. LINDE*] I don't know whether   255
    you find also in your part of the world that there are certain people who go zealously
    snuffing about to smell out moral corruption, and, as soon as they have found some,
    put the person concerned into some lucrative position where they can keep their eye
    on him. Healthy natures are left out in the cold.
MRS. LINDE: Still I think the sick are those who most need taking care of.
RANK: [*shrugging his shoulders*] Yes, there you are. That is the sentiment that is turning Soci-
    ety into a sickhouse.

[*NORA, who has been absorbed in her thoughts, breaks out into smothered laughter and claps her hands.*]

RANK: Why do you laugh at that? Have you any notion what Society really is?
NORA: What do I care about tiresome Society? I am laughing at something quite different,
    something extremely amusing. Tell me, Doctor Rank, are all the people who are em-
    ployed in the Bank dependent on Torvald now?
RANK: Is that what you find so extremely amusing?   260
NORA: [*smiling and humming*] That's my affair! [*walking about the room*] It's perfectly glori-
    ous to think that we have—that Torvald has so much power over so many people.
    [*takes the packet from her pocket*] Doctor Rank, what do you say to a macaroon?
RANK: What, macaroons? I thought they were forbidden here.
NORA: Yes, but these are some Christine gave me.
MRS. LINDE: What! I?—
NORA: Oh, well, don't be alarmed! You couldn't know that Torvald had forbidden them. I   265
    must tell you that he is afraid they will spoil my teeth. But, bah!—once in a way—
    That's so, isn't it, Doctor Rank? By your leave? [*puts a macaroon into his mouth*] You
    must have one too, Christine. And I shall have one, just a little one—or at most two.
    [*walking about*] I am tremendously happy. There is just one thing in the world now that
    I should dearly love to do.
RANK: Well, what is that?
NORA: It's something I should dearly love to say, if Torvald could hear me.
RANK: Well, why can't you say it?
NORA: No, I daren't; it's so shocking.
MRS. LINDE: Shocking?   270
RANK: Well, I should not advise you to say it. Still, with us you might. What is it you
    would so much like to say if Torvald could hear you?
NORA: I should just love to say—Well, I'm damned!
RANK: Are you mad?
MRS. LINDE: Nora, dear—!
RANK: Say it, here he is!   275
NORA: [*hiding the packet*] Hush! Hush! Hush!

[*HELMER comes out of his room, with his coat over his arm and his hat in his hands.*]

NORA: Well, Torvald dear, have you got rid of him?
HELMER: Yes, he has just gone.
NORA: Let me introduce you—this is Christine, who has come to town.

280 HELMER: Christine—? Excuse me, but I don't know—

NORA: Mrs. Linde, dear; Christine Linde.

HELMER: Of course. A school friend of my wife's, I presume?

MRS. LINDE: Yes, we have known each other since then.

NORA: And just think, she has taken a long journey in order to see you.

285 HELMER: What do you mean?

MRS. LINDE: No, really, I—

NORA: Christine is tremendously clever at book-keeping, and she is frightfully anxious to work under some clever man, so as to perfect herself—

HELMER: Very sensible, Mrs. Linde.

NORA: And when she heard you had been appointed manager of the Bank—the news was telegraphed, you know—she travelled here as quick as she could. Torvald, I am sure you will be able to do something for Christine, for my sake, won't you?

290 HELMER: Well, it is not altogether impossible. I presume you are a widow, Mrs. Linde?

MRS. LINDE: Yes.

HELMER: And have had some experience of book-keeping?

MRS. LINDE: Yes, a fair amount.

HELMER: Ah! well, it's very likely I may be able to find something for you—

295 NORA: [*clapping her hands*] What did I tell you? What did I tell you?

HELMER: You have just come at a fortunate moment, Mrs. Linde.

MRS. LINDE: How am I to thank you?

HELMER: There is no need. [*puts on his coat*] But to-day you must excuse me—

RANK: Wait a minute; I will come with you.

[*Brings his fur coat from the hall and warms it at the fire.*]

300 NORA: Don't be long away, Torvald dear.

HELMER: About an hour, not more.

NORA: Are you going too, Christine?

MRS. LINDE: [*putting on her cloak*] Yes, I must go and look for a room.

HELMER: Oh, well then, we can walk down the street together.

305 NORA: [*helping her*] What a pity it is we are so short of space here: I am afraid it is impossible for us—

MRS. LINDE: Please don't think of it! Good-bye, Nora dear, and many thanks.

NORA: Good-bye for the present. Of course you will come back this evening. And you too, Dr. Rank. What do you say? If you are well enough? Oh, you must be! Wrap yourself up well.

[*They go to the door all talking together. Children's voices are heard on the staircase.*]

NORA: There they are. There they are! [*She runs to open the door. The* NURSE *comes in with the children.*] Come in! Come in! [*stoops and kisses them*] Oh, you sweet blessings! Look at them, Christine! Aren't they darlings?

RANK: Don't let us stand here in the draught.

310 HELMER: Come along, Mrs. Linde; the place will only be bearable for a mother now!

[*RANK, HELMER and MRS. LINDE go downstairs. The* NURSE *comes forward with the children;* NORA *shuts the hall door.*]

NORA: How fresh and well you look! Such red cheeks!—like apples and roses. [*The children all talk at once while she speaks to them.*] Have you had great fun? That's splendid! What, you pulled both Emmy and Bob along on the sledge?—both at once?—that was good. You are a clever boy, Ivar. Let me take her for a little, Anne. My sweet little baby doll! [*takes the baby from the* MAID *and dances it up and down*] Yes, yes, mother will dance with Bob too. What! Have you been snowballing? I wish I had been there too! No, no, I will take their things off, Anne; please let me do it, it is such fun. Go in now, you look half frozen. There is some coffee for you on the stove.

[*The* NURSE *goes into the room on the left.* NORA *takes off the children's things and throws them about, while they all talk to her at once.*]

NORA: Really! Did a big dog run after you? But it didn't bite you? No, dogs don't bite nice little dolly children. You mustn't look at the parcels, Ivar. What are they? Ah, I daresay you would like to know. No, no—it's something nasty! Come, let us have a game! What shall we play at? Hide and Seek? Yes, we'll play Hide and Seek. Bob shall hide first. Must I hide? Very well, I'll hide first.

[*She and the children laugh and shout, and romp in and out of the room; at last* NORA *hides under the table, the children rush in and look for her, but do not see her; they hear her smothered laughter, run to the table, lift up the cloth and find her. Shouts of laughter. She crawls forward and pretends to frighten them. Fresh laughter. Meanwhile there has been a knock at the hall door, but none of them has noticed it. The door is half opened, and* KROGSTAD *appears. He waits a little; the game goes on.*]

KROGSTAD: Excuse me, Mrs. Helmer.

NORA: [*with a stifled cry, turns round and gets up on to her knees*] Ah! what do you want?

KROGSTAD: Excuse me, the outer door was ajar; I suppose someone forgot to shut it.   315

NORA: [*rising*] My husband is out, Mr. Krogstad.

KROGSTAD: I know that.

NORA: What do you want here, then?

KROGSTAD: A word with you.

NORA: With me?—[*to the children, gently*] Go in to nurse. What? No, the strange man won't   320
do mother any harm. When he has gone we will have another game. [*She takes the children into the room on the left, and shuts the door after them.*] You want to speak to me?

KROGSTAD: Yes, I do.

NORA: To-day? It is not the first of the month yet.

KROGSTAD: No, it is Christmas Eve, and it will depend on yourself what sort of a Christmas you will spend.

NORA: What do you want? To-day it is absolutely impossible for me—

KROGSTAD: We won't talk about that till later on. This is something different. I presume   325
you can give me a moment?

NORA: Yes—yes, I can—although—

KROGSTAD: Good. I was in Olsen's Restaurant and saw your husband going down the street—

NORA: Yes?

KROGSTAD: With a lady.

NORA: What then?   330

KROGSTAD: May I make so bold as to ask if it was a Mrs. Linde?

NORA: It was.

KROGSTAD: Just arrived in town?

NORA: Yes, to-day.

KROGSTAD: She is a great friend of yours, isn't she?   335

NORA: She is. But I don't see—

KROGSTAD: I knew her too, once upon a time.

NORA: I am aware of that.

KROGSTAD: Are you? So you know all about it; I thought as much. Then I can ask you, without beating about the bush—is Mrs. Linde to have an appointment in the Bank?

NORA: What right have you to question me, Mr. Krogstad?—You, one of my husband's   340
subordinates! But since you ask, you shall know. Yes, Mrs. Linde *is* to have an appointment. And it was I who pleaded her cause, Mr. Krogstad, let me tell you that.

KROGSTAD: I was right in what I thought, then.

NORA: [*walking up and down the stage*] Sometimes one has a tiny little bit of influence, I should hope. Because one is a woman, it does not necessarily follow that—. When anyone is in a subordinate position, Mr. Krogstad, they should really be careful to avoid offending anyone who—who—

KROGSTAD: Who has influence?

NORA: Exactly.

345 KROGSTAD: [*changing his tone*] Mrs. Helmer, you will be so good as to use your influence on my behalf.

NORA: What? What do you mean?

KROGSTAD: You will be so kind as to see that I am allowed to keep my subordinate position in the Bank.

NORA: What do you mean by that? Who proposes to take your post away from you?

KROGSTAD: Oh, there is no necessity to keep up the pretence of ignorance. I can quite understand that your friend is not very anxious to expose herself to the chance of rubbing shoulders with me; and I quite understand, too, whom I have to thank for being turned out.

350 NORA: But I assure you—

KROGSTAD: Very likely; but, to come to the point, the time has come when I should advise you to use your influence to prevent that.

NORA: But, Mr. Krogstad, I *have* no influence.

KROGSTAD: Haven't you? I thought you said yourself just now—

NORA: Naturally I did not mean you to put that construction on it. I! What should make you think I have any influence of that kind with my husband?

355 KROGSTAD: Oh, I have known your husband from our student days. I don't suppose he is any more unassailable than other husbands.

NORA: If you speak slightingly of my husband, I shall turn you out of the house.

KROGSTAD: You are bold, Mrs. Helmer.

NORA: I am not afraid of you any longer. As soon as the New Year comes, I shall in a very short time be free of the whole thing.

KROGSTAD: [*controlling himself*] Listen to me, Mrs. Helmer. If necessary, I am prepared to fight for my small post in the Bank as if I were fighting for my life.

360 NORA: So it seems.

KROGSTAD: It is not only for the sake of the money; indeed, that weighs least with me in the matter. There is another reason—well, I may as well tell you. My position is this. I daresay you know, like everybody else, that once, many years ago, I was guilty of an indiscretion.

NORA: I think I have heard something of the kind.

KROGSTAD: The matter never came into court; but every way seemed to be closed to me after that. So I took to the business that you know of. I had to do something; and, honestly, I don't think I've been one of the worst. But now I must cut myself free from all that. My sons are growing up; for their sake I must try and win back as much respect as I can in the town. This post in the Bank was like the first step up for me—and now your husband is going to kick me downstairs again into the mud.

NORA: But you must believe me, Mr. Krogstad; it is not in my power to help you at all.

365 KROGSTAD: Then it is because you haven't the will; but I have means to compel you.

NORA: You don't mean that you will tell my husband that I owe you money?

KROGSTAD: Hm!—suppose I were to tell him?

NORA: It would be perfectly infamous of you. [*sobbing*] To think of his learning my secret, which has been my joy and pride, in such an ugly, clumsy way—that he should learn it from you! And it would put me in a horribly disagreeable position—

KROGSTAD: Only disagreeable?

NORA: [*impetuously*] Well, do it, then!—and it will be the worse for you. My husband will   370
see for himself what a blackguard you are, and you certainly won't keep your post
then.

KROGSTAD: I asked you if it was only a disagreeable scene at home that you were afraid of?

NORA: If my husband does get to know of it, of course he will at once pay you what is still
owing, and we shall have nothing more to do with you.

KROGSTAD: [*coming a step nearer*] Listen to me, Mrs. Helmer. Either you have a very bad
memory or you know very little of business. I shall be obliged to remind you of a few
details.

NORA: What do you mean?

KROGSTAD: When your husband was ill, you came to me to borrow two hundred and fifty   375
pounds.

NORA: I didn't know any one else to go to.

KROGSTAD: I promised to get you that amount—

NORA: Yes, and you did so.

KROGSTAD: I promised to get you that amount, on certain conditions. Your mind was so
taken up with your husband's illness, and you were so anxious to get the money for
your journey, that you seem to have paid no attention to the conditions of our bargain.
Therefore it will not be amiss if I remind you of them. Now, I promised to get the
money on the security of a bond which I drew up.

NORA: Yes, and which I signed.   380

KROGSTAD: Good. But below your signature there were a few lines constituting your father
a surety for the money; those lines your father should have signed.

NORA: Should? He did sign them.

KROGSTAD: I had left the date blank; that is to say your father should himself have inserted
the date on which he signed the paper. Do you remember that?

NORA: Yes, I think I remember—

KROGSTAD: Then I gave you the bond to send by post to your father. Is that not so?   385

NORA: Yes.

KROGSTAD: And you naturally did so at once, because five or six days afterwards you
brought me the bond with your father's signature. And then I gave you the money.

NORA: Well, haven't I been paying it off regularly?

KROGSTAD: Fairly so, yes. But—to come back to the matter in hand—that must have been a
very trying time for you, Mrs. Helmer?

NORA: It was, indeed.   390

KROGSTAD: Your father was very ill, wasn't he?

NORA: He was very near his end.

KROGSTAD: And died soon afterwards?

NORA: Yes.

KROGSTAD: Tell me, Mrs. Helmer, can you by any chance remember what day your father   395
died?—on what day of the month, I mean.

NORA: Papa died on the 29th of September.

KROGSTAD: That is correct; I have ascertained it for myself. And, as that is so, there is a discrepancy [*taking a paper from his pocket*] which I cannot account for.

NORA: What discrepancy? I don't know—

KROGSTAD: The discrepancy consists, Mrs. Helmer, in the fact that your father signed this
bond three days after his death.

NORA: What do you mean? I don't understand—   400

KROGSTAD: Your father died on the 29th of September. But, look here; your father has
dated his signature the 2nd of October. It is a discrepancy, isn't it? [*NORA is silent.*] Can

you explain it to me? [NORA *is still silent.*] It is a remarkable thing, too, that the words "2nd of October," as well as the year, are not written in your father's handwriting but in one that I think I know. Well, of course it can be explained; your father may have forgotten to date his signature, and someone else may have dated it haphazard before they knew of his death. There is no harm in that. It all depends on the signature of the name; and *that* is genuine, I suppose, Mrs. Helmer? It was your father himself who signed his name here?

NORA: [*after a short pause, throws her head up and looks defiantly at him*] No, it was not. It was I that wrote papa's name.

KROGSTAD: Are you aware that is a dangerous confession?

NORA: In what way? You shall have your money soon.

405 KROGSTAD: Let me ask you a question; why did you not send the paper to your father?

NORA: It was impossible; papa was so ill. If I had asked him for his signature, I should have had to tell him what the money was to be used for; and when he was so ill himself I couldn't tell him that my husband's life was in danger—it was impossible.

KROGSTAD: It would have been better for you if you had given up your trip abroad.

NORA: No, that was impossible. That trip was to save my husband's life; I couldn't give that up.

KROGSTAD: But did it never occur to you that you were committing a fraud on me?

410 NORA: I couldn't take that into account; I didn't trouble myself about you at all. I couldn't bear you, because you put so many heartless difficulties in my way, although you knew what a dangerous condition my husband was in.

KROGSTAD: Mrs. Helmer, you evidently do not realise clearly what it is that you have been guilty of. But I can assure you that my one false step, which lost me all my reputation, was nothing more or nothing worse than what you have done.

NORA: You? Do you ask me to believe that you were brave enough to run a risk to save your wife's life?

KROGSTAD: The law cares nothing about motives.

NORA: Then it must be a very foolish law.

415 KROGSTAD: Foolish or not, it is the law by which you will be judged, if I produce this paper in court.

NORA: I don't believe it. Is a daughter not to be allowed to spare her dying father anxiety and care? Is a wife not to be allowed to save her husband's life? I don't know much about law; but I am certain that there must be laws permitting such things as that. Have you no knowledge of such laws—you who are a lawyer? You must be a very poor lawyer, Mr. Krogstad.

KROGSTAD: Maybe. But matters of business—such business as you and I have had together—do you think I don't understand that? Very well. Do as you please. But let me tell you this—if I lose my position a second time, you shall lose yours with me.

[*He bows, and goes out through the hall.*]

NORA: [*appears buried in thought for a short time, then tosses her head*] Nonsense! Trying to frighten me like that!—I am not so silly as he thinks. [*begins to busy herself putting the children's things in order*] And yet—? No, it's impossible! I did it for love's sake.

THE CHILDREN: [*in the doorway on the left*] Mother, the stranger man has gone out through the gate.

420 NORA: Yes, dears, I know. But, don't tell anyone about the stranger man. Do you hear? Not even papa.

CHILDREN: No, mother; but will you come and play again?

NORA: No, no—not now.

CHILDREN: But, mother, you promised us.

NORA: Yes, but I can't now. Run away in; I have such a lot to do. Run away in, my sweet lit-tle darlings. [*She gets them into the room by degrees and shuts the door on them; then sits down on the sofa, takes up a piece of needlework and sews a few stitches, but soon stops.*] No! [*throws down the work, gets up, goes to the hall door and calls out*] Helen! bring the Tree in. [*goes to the table on the left, opens a drawer, and stops again*] No, no! it is quite impossible!

MAID: [*coming in with the Tree*] Where shall I put it, ma'am?   425

NORA: Here, in the middle of the floor.

MAID: Shall I get you anything else?

NORA: No, thank you. I have all I want.

[*Exit MAID.*]

NORA: [*begins dressing the tree*] A candle here—and flowers here—. The horrible man! It's all nonsense—there's nothing wrong. The Tree shall be splendid! I will do everything I can think of to please you, Torvald!—I will sing for you, dance for you— [*HELMER comes in with some papers under his arm*] Oh! are you back already?

HELMER: Yes. Has anyone been here?   430

NORA: Here? No.

HELMER: That is strange. I saw Krogstad going out of the gate.

NORA: Did you? Oh yes, I forgot, Krogstad was here for a moment.

HELMER: Nora, I can see from your manner that he has been here begging you to say a good word for him.

NORA: Yes.   435

HELMER: And you were to appear to do it of your own accord; you were to conceal from me the fact of his having been here; didn't he beg that of you too?

NORA: Yes, Torvald, but—

HELMER: Nora, Nora, and you would be a party to that sort of thing? To have any talk with a man like that, and give him any sort of promise? And to tell me a lie into the bargain?

NORA: A lie—?

HELMER: Didn't you tell me no one had been here? [*shakes his finger at her*] My little song-   440
bird must never do that again. A song-bird must have a clean beak to chirp with—no false notes! [*puts his arm round her waist*] That is so, isn't it? Yes, I am sure it is. [*lets her go*] We will say no more about it. [*sits down by the stove*] How warm and snug it is here!

[*Turns over his papers.*]

NORA: [*after a short pause, during which she busies herself with the Christmas Tree*] Torvald!

HELMER: Yes.

NORA: I am looking forward tremendously to the fancy dress ball at the Stenborgs' the day after to-morrow.

HELMER: And I am tremendously curious to see what you are going to surprise me with.

NORA: It was very silly of me to want to do that.   445

HELMER: What do you mean?

NORA: I can't hit upon anything that will do; everything I think of seems so silly and in-significant.

HELMER: Does my little Nora acknowledge that at last?

NORA: [*standing behind his chair with her arms on the back of it*] Are you very busy, Torvald?

HELMER: Well—   450

NORA: What are all those papers?

HELMER: Bank business.

NORA: Already?

HELMER: I have got authority from the retiring manager to undertake the necessary changes in the staff and in the rearrangement of the work; and I must make use of the Christmas week for that, so as to have everything in order for the new year.

455 NORA: Then that was why this poor Krogstad—

HELMER: Hm!

NORA: [*leans against the back of his chair and strokes his hair*] If you hadn't been so busy I should have asked you a tremendously big favour, Torvald.

HELMER: What is that? Tell me.

NORA: There is no one has such good taste as you. And I do so want to look nice at the fancy-dress ball. Torvald, couldn't you take me in hand and decide what I shall go as, and what sort of a dress I shall wear?

460 HELMER: Aha! so my obstinate little woman is obliged to get someone to come to her rescue?

NORA: Yes, Torvald, I can't get along a bit without your help.

HELMER: Very well, I will think it over, we shall manage to hit upon something.

NORA: That is nice of you. [*Goes to the Christmas Tree. A short pause.*] How pretty the red flowers look—. But, tell me, was it really something very bad that this Krogstad was guilty of?

HELMER: He forged someone's name. Have you any idea what that means?

465 NORA: Isn't it possible that he was driven to do it by necessity?

HELMER: Yes; or, as in so many cases, by imprudence. I am not so heartless as to condemn a man altogether because of a single false step of that kind.

NORA: No you wouldn't, would you, Torvald?

HELMER: Many a man has been able to retrieve his character, if he has openly confessed his fault and taken his punishment.

NORA: Punishment—?

470 HELMER: But Krogstad did nothing of that sort; he got himself out of it by a cunning trick, and that is why he has gone under altogether.

NORA: But do you think it would—?

HELMER: Just think how a guilty man like that has to lie and play the hypocrite with everyone, how he has to wear a mask in the presence of those near and dear to him, even before his own wife and children. And about the children—that is the most terrible part of it all, Nora.

NORA: How?

HELMER: Because such an atmosphere of lies infects and poisons the whole life of a home. Each breath the children take in such a house is full of the germs of evil.

475 NORA: [*coming nearer him*] Are you sure of that?

HELMER: My dear, I have often seen it in the course of my life as a lawyer. Almost everyone who has gone to the bad early in life has had a deceitful mother.

NORA: Why do you only say—mother?

HELMER: It seems most commonly to be the mother's influence, though naturally a bad father's would have the same result. Every lawyer is familiar with the fact. This Krogstad, now, has been persistently poisoning his own children with lies and dissimulation; that is why I say he has lost all moral character. [*holds out his hands to her*] That is why my sweet little Nora must promise me not to plead his cause. Give me your hand on it. Come, come, what is this? Give me your hand. There now, that's settled. I assure you it would be quite impossible for me to work with him; I literally feel physically ill when I am in the company of such people.

NORA: [*takes her hand out of his and goes to the opposite side of the Christmas Tree*] How hot it is in here; and I have such a lot to do.

480 HELMER: [*getting up and putting his papers in order*] Yes, and I must try and read through some of these before dinner; and I must think about your costume, too. And it is just

possible I may have something ready in gold paper to hang up on the Tree. [*Puts his hand on her head.*] My precious little singing-bird!

[*He goes into his room and shuts the door after him.*]

NORA: [*after a pause, whispers*] No, no—it isn't true. It's impossible; it must be impossible.

[*The NURSE opens the door on the left.*]

NURSE: The little ones are begging so hard to be allowed to come in to mamma.
NORA: No, no, no! Don't let them come in to me! You stay with them, Anne.
NURSE: Very well, ma'am.

[*Shuts the door.*]

NORA: [*pale with terror*] Deprave my little children? Poison my home? [*a short pause. Then*   485
she tosses her head.] It's not true. It can't possibly be true.

ACT 2

THE SAME SCENE. The Christmas Tree is in the corner by the piano, stripped of its ornaments and with burnt-down candle-ends on its dishevelled branches. NORA's cloak and hat are lying on the sofa. She is alone in the room, walking about uneasily. She stops by the sofa and takes up her cloak.

NORA: [*drops the cloak*] Someone is coming now! [*goes to the door and listens*] No—it is no one. Of course, no one will come to-day, Christmas Day—nor tomorrow either. But, perhaps—[*opens the door and looks out*] No, nothing in the letter-box; it is quite empty. [*comes forward*] What rubbish! of course he can't be in earnest about it. Such a thing couldn't happen; it is impossible—I have three little children.

[*Enter the NURSE from the room on the left, carrying a big cardboard box.*]

NURSE: At last I have found the box with the fancy dress.
NORA: Thanks; put it on the table.
NURSE: [*doing so*] But it is very much in want of mending.
NORA: I should like to tear it into a hundred thousand pieces.   5
NURSE: What an idea! It can easily be put in order—just a little patience.
NORA: Yes, I will go and get Mrs. Linde to come and help me with it.
NURSE: What, out again? In this horrible weather? You will catch cold, ma'am, and make yourself ill.
NORA: Well, worse than that might happen. How are the children?
NURSE: The poor little souls are playing with their Christmas presents, but—   10
NORA: Do they ask much for me?
NURSE: You see, they are so accustomed to have their mamma with them.
NORA: Yes, but, nurse, I shall not be able to be so much with them now as I was before.
NURSE: Oh well, young children easily get accustomed to anything.
NORA: Do you think so? Do you think they would forget their mother if she went away al-   15
together?
NURSE: Good heavens!—went away altogether?
NORA: Nurse, I want you to tell me something I have often wondered about—how could you have the heart to put your own child out among strangers?
NURSE: I was obliged to, if I wanted to be little Nora's nurse.
NORA: Yes, but how could you be willing to do it?
NURSE: What, when I was going to get such a good place by it? A poor girl who has got into   20
trouble should be glad to. Besides, that wicked man didn't do a single thing for me.
NORA: But I suppose your daughter has quite forgotten you.

NURSE: No, indeed she hasn't. She wrote to me when she was confirmed, and when she was married.

NORA: [*putting her arms round her neck*] Dear old Anne, you were a good mother to me when I was little.

NURSE: Little Nora, poor dear, had no other mother but me.

25 NORA: And if my little ones had no other mother, I am sure you would—What nonsense I am talking! [*opens the box*] Go in to them. Now I must—. You will see tomorrow how charming I shall look.

NURSE: I am sure there will be no one at the ball so charming as you, ma'am.

[*Goes into the room on the left.*]

NORA: [*begins to unpack the box, but soon pushes it away from her*] If only I dared go out. If only no one would come. If only I could be sure nothing would happen here in the meantime. Stuff and nonsense! No one will come. Only I mustn't think about it. I will brush my muff. What, lovely gloves! Out of my thoughts, out of my thoughts! One, two, three, four, five, six—[*Screams.*] Ah! there is someone coming—

[*Makes a movement towards the door, but stands irresolute.*]

[*Enter* MRS. LINDE *from the hall, where she has taken off her cloak and hat.*]

NORA: Oh, it's you, Christine. There is no one else out there, is there? How good of you to come!

MRS. LINDE: I heard you were up asking for me.

30 NORA: Yes, I was passing by. As a matter of fact, it is something you could help me with. Let us sit down here on the sofa. Look here. To-morrow evening there is to be a fancy-dress ball at the Stenborgs', who live about us; and Torvald wants me to go as a Neapolitan fisher-girl, and dance the Tarantella that I learnt at Capri.

MRS. LINDE: I see; you are going to keep up the character.

NORA: Yes, Torvald wants me to. Look, here is the dress; Torvald had it made for me there, but now it is all so torn, and I haven't any idea—

MRS. LINDE: We will easily put that right. It is only some of the trimming come unsewn here and there. Needle and thread? Now then, that's all we want.

NORA: It *is* nice of you.

35 MRS. LINDE: [*sewing*] So you are going to be dressed up to-morrow, Nora. I will tell you what—I shall come in for a moment and see you in your fine feathers. But I have completely forgotten to thank you for a delightful evening yesterday.

NORA: [*gets up, and crosses the stages*] Well I don't think yesterday was as pleasant as usual. You ought to have come to town a little earlier, Christine. Certainly Torvald does understand how to make a house dainty and attractive.

MRS. LINDE: And so do you, it seems to me; you are not your father's daughter for nothing. But tell me, is Doctor Rank always as depressed as he was yesterday?

NORA: No; yesterday it was very noticeable. I must tell you that he suffers from a very dangerous disease. He has consumption of the spine, poor creature. His father was a horrible man who committed all sorts of excesses; and that is why his son was sickly from childhood, do you understand?

MRS. LINDE: [*dropping her sewing*] But, my dearest Nora, how do you know anything about such things?

40 NORA: [*walking about*] Pooh! When you have three children, you get visits now and then from—from married women, who know something of medical matters, and they talk about one thing and another.

MRS. LINDE: [*goes on sewing. A short silence*] Does Doctor Rank come here every day?

NORA: Every day regularly. He is Torvald's most intimate friend, and a great friend of mine too. He is just like one of the family.

MRS. LINDE: But tell me this—is he perfectly sincere? I mean, isn't he the kind of man that is very anxious to make himself agreeable?

NORA: Not in the least. What makes you think that?

MRS. LINDE: When you introduced him to me yesterday, he declared he had often heard   45
my name mentioned in this house; but afterwards I noticed that your husband hadn't the slightest idea who I was. So how could Doctor Rank—?

NORA: That is quite right, Christine. Torvald is so absurdly fond of me that he wants me absolutely to himself, as he says. At first he used to seem almost jealous if I mentioned any of the dear folk at home, so naturally I gave up doing so. But I often talk about such things with Doctor Rank, because he likes hearing about them.

MRS. LINDE: Listen to me, Nora. You are still very like a child in many things, and I am older than you in many ways and have a little more experience. Let me tell you this— you ought to make an end of it with Doctor Rank.

NORA: What ought I to make an end of?

MRS. LINDE: Of two things, I think. Yesterday you talked some nonsense about a rich admirer who was to leave you money—

NORA: An admirer who doesn't exist, unfortunately! But what then?   50

MRS. LINDE: Is Doctor Rank a man of means?

NORA: Yes, he is.

MRS. LINDE: And has no one to provide for?

NORA: No, no one; but—

MRS. LINDE: And comes here every day?   55

NORA: Yes, I told you so.

MRS. LINDE: But how can this well-bred man be so tactless?

NORA: I don't understand you at all.

MRS. LINDE: Don't prevaricate, Nora. Do you suppose I don't guess who lent you the two hundred and fifty pounds?

NORA: Are you out of your senses? How can you think of such a thing! A friend of ours,   60
who comes here every day! Do you realise what a horribly painful position that would be?

MRS. LINDE: Then it really isn't he?

NORA: No, certainly not. It would never have entered into my head for a moment. Besides, he had no money to lend then; he came into his money afterwards.

MRS. LINDE: Well, I think that was lucky for you, my dear Nora.

NORA: No, it would never have come into my head to ask Doctor Rank. Although I am quite sure that if I had asked him—

MRS. LINDE: But of course you won't.   65

NORA: Of course not. I have no reason to think it could possibly be necessary. But I am quite sure that if I told Doctor Rank—

MRS. LINDE: Behind your husband's back?

NORA: I *must* make an end of it with the other one, and that will be behind his back too. I *must* make an end of it with him.

MRS. LINDE: Yes, that is what I told you yesterday, but—

NORA: [*walking up and down*] A man can put a thing like that straight much easier than a   70
woman—

MRS. LINDE: One's husband, yes.

NORA: Nonsense! [*standing still*] When you pay off a debt you get your bond back, don't you?

MRS. LINDE: Yes, as a matter of course.

NORA: And can tear it into a hundred thousand pieces, and burn it up—the nasty dirty paper!

75 MRS. LINDE: [*looks hard at her, lays down her sewing and gets up slowly*] Nora, you are concealing something from me.

NORA: Do I look as if I were?

MRS. LINDE: Something has happened to you since yesterday morning. Nora, what is it?

NORA: [*going nearer to her*] Christine! [*listens*] Hush! there's Torvald come home. Do you mind going in to the children for the present? Torvald can't bear to see dressmaking going on. Let Anne help you.

MRS. LINDE: [*gathering some of the things together*] Certainly—but I am not going away from here till we have had it out with one another.

[*She goes into the room on the left, as* HELMER *comes in from the hall.*]

80 NORA: [*going up to* HELMER] I have wanted you so much, Torvald dear.

HELMER: Was that the dressmaker?

NORA: No, it was Christine; she is helping me to put my dress in order. You will see I shall look quite smart.

HELMER: Wasn't that a happy thought of mine, now?

NORA: Splendid! But don't you think it is nice of me, too, to do as you wish?

85 HELMER: Nice?—because you do as your husband wishes? Well, well, you little rogue, I am sure you did not mean it in that way. But I am not going to disturb you; you will want to be trying on your dress, I expect.

NORA: I suppose you are going to work.

HELMER: Yes. [*shows her a bundle of papers*] Look at that. I have just been into the bank. [*Turns to go into his room.*]

NORA: Torvald.

HELMER: Yes.

90 NORA: If your little squirrel were to ask you for something very, very prettily—?

HELMER: What then?

NORA: Would you do it?

HELMER: I should like to hear what it is, first.

NORA: Your squirrel would run about and do all her tricks if you would be nice, and do what she wants.

95 HELMER: Speak plainly.

NORA: Your skylark would chirp about in every room, with her song rising and falling—

HELMER: Well, my skylark does that anyhow.

NORA: I would play the fairy and dance for you in the moonlight, Torvald.

HELMER: Nora—you surely don't mean that request you made of me this morning?

100 NORA: [*going near him*] Yes, Torvald, I beg you so earnestly—

HELMER: Have you really the courage to open up that question again?

NORA: Yes, dear, you *must* do as I ask; you *must* let Krogstad keep his post in the Bank.

HELMER: My dear Nora, it is his post that I have arranged Mrs. Linde shall have.

NORA: Yes, you have been awfully kind about that; but you could just as well dismiss some other clerk instead of Krogstad.

105 HELMER: This is simply incredible obstinacy! Because you chose to give him a thoughtless promise that you would speak for him, I am expected to—

NORA: That isn't the reason, Torvald. It is for your own sake. This fellow writes in the most scurrilous newspapers; you have told me so yourself. He can do you an unspeakable amount of harm. I am frightened to death of him—

HELMER: Ah, I understand; it is recollections of the past that scare you.

NORA: What do you mean?

HELMER: Naturally you are thinking of your father.

NORA: Yes—yes, of course. Just recall to your mind what these malicious creatures wrote   110
in the papers about papa, and how horribly they slandered him. I believe they would
have procured his dismissal if the Department had not sent you over to inquire into it,
and if you had not been so kindly disposed and helpful to him.

HELMER: My little Nora, there is an important difference between your father and me. Your
father's reputation as a public official was not above suspicion. Mine is, and I hope it
will continue to be so, as long as I hold my office.

NORA: You never can tell what mischief these men may contrive. We ought to be so well
off, so snug and happy here in our peaceful home, and have no cares—you and I and
the children, Torvald! That is why I beg you so earnestly—

HELMER: And it is just by interceding for him that you make it impossible for me to keep
him. It is already known at the Bank that I mean to dismiss Krogstad. Is it to get about
now that the new manager has changed his mind at his wife's bidding—

NORA: And what if it did?

HELMER: Of course!—if only this obstinate little person can get her way! Do you suppose I   115
am going to make myself ridiculous before my whole staff, to let people think that I am a
man to be swayed by all sorts of outside influence? I should very soon feel the consequences of it, I can tell you! And besides, there is one thing that makes it quite impossible for me to have Krogstad in the Bank as long as I am manager.

NORA: Whatever is that?

HELMER: His moral failings I might perhaps have overlooked, if necessary—

NORA: Yes, you could—couldn't you?

HELMER: And I hear he is a good worker, too. But I knew him when we were boys. It was
one of those rash friendships that so often prove an incubus in after life. I may as well
tell you plainly, we were once on very intimate terms with one another. But this tactless fellow lays no restraint on himself when other people are present. On the contrary,
he thinks it gives him the right to adopt a familiar tone with me, and every minute it is
"I say, Helmer, old fellow!" and that sort of thing. I assure you it is extremely painful
for me. He would make my position in the Bank intolerable.

NORA: Torvald, I don't believe you mean that.   120

HELMER: Don't you? Why not?

NORA: Because it is such a narrow-minded way of looking at things.

HELMER: What are you saying? Narrow-minded? Do you think I am narrow-minded?

NORA: No, just the opposite, dear—and it is exactly for that reason.

HELMER: It's the same thing. You say my point of view is narrow-minded, so I must be so   125
too. Narrow-minded! Very well—I must put an end to this. [*Goes to the hall-door and
calls.*] Helen!

NORA: What are you going to do?

HELMER: [*looking among his papers*] Settle it. [*Enter MAID.*] Look here; take this letter and go
downstairs with it at once. Find a messenger and tell him to deliver it, and be quick.
The address is on it, and here is the money.

MAID: Very well, sir.

[*Exits with the letter.*]

HELMER: [*putting his papers together*] Now then, little Miss Obstinate.

NORA: [*breathlessly*] Torvald—what was that letter?   130

HELMER: Krogstad's dismissal.

NORA: Call her back, Torvald! There is still time. Oh Torvald, call her back! Do it for my
sake—for your own sake—for the children's sake! Do you hear me, Torvald? Call her
back!! You don't know what that letter can bring upon us.

HELMER: It's too late.

NORA: Yes, it's too late.

135 HELMER: My dear Nora, I can forgive the anxiety you are in, although really it is an insult to me. It is, indeed. Isn't it an insult to think that I should be afraid of a starving quill-driver's vengeance? But I forgive you nevertheless, because it is such eloquent witness to your great love for me. [*takes her in his arms*] And that is as it should be, my own darling Nora. Come what will, you may be sure I shall have both courage and strength if they be needed. You will see I am man enough to take everything upon myself.

NORA: [*in a horror-stricken voice*] What do you mean by that?

HELMER: Everything, I say—

NORA: [*recovering herself*] You will never have to do that.

HELMER: That's right. Well, we will share it, Nora, as man and wife should. That is how it shall be. [*caressing her*] Are you content now? There! there!—not these frightened dove's eyes! The whole thing is only the wildest fancy!—Now, you must go and play through the Tarantella and practise with your tambourine. I shall go into the inner office and shut the door, and I shall hear nothing; you can make as much noise as you please. [*turns back at the door*] And when Rank comes, tell him where he will find me.

[*Nods to her, takes his papers and goes into his room, and shuts the door after him*]

140 NORA: [*bewildered with anxiety, stands as if rooted to the spot, and whispers*] He is capable of doing it. He will do it. He will do it in spite of everything.—No, not that! Never, never! Anything rather than that! Oh, for some help, some way out of it! [*The door-bell rings.*] Doctor Rank! Anything rather than that—anything, whatever it is!

[*She puts her hands over her face, pulls herself together, goes to the door and opens it. Rank is standing without, hanging up his coat. During the following dialogue it begins to grow dark.*]

NORA: Good-day, Doctor Rank. I knew your ring. But you mustn't go in to Torvald now; I think he is busy with something.

RANK: And you?

NORA: [*brings him in and shuts the door after him*] Oh, you know very well I always have time for you.

RANK: Thank you. I shall make use of as much of it as I can.

145 NORA: What do you mean by that? As much of it as you can?

RANK: Well, does that alarm you?

NORA: It was such a strange way of putting it. Is anything likely to happen?

RANK: Nothing but what I have long been prepared for. But I certainly didn't expect it to happen so soon.

NORA: [*gripping him by the arm*] What have you found out? Doctor Rank, you must tell me.

150 RANK: [*sitting down by the stove*] It is all up with me. And it can't be helped.

NORA: [*with a sigh of relief*] Is it about yourself?

RANK: Who else? It is no use lying to one's self. I am the most wretched of all my patients, Mrs. Helmer. Lately I have been taking stock of my internal economy. Bankrupt! Probably within a month I shall lie rotting in the churchyard.

NORA: What an ugly thing to say!

RANK: The thing itself is cursedly ugly, and the worst of it is that I shall have to face so much more that is ugly before that. I shall only make one more examination of myself; when I have done that, I shall know pretty certainly when it will be that the horrors of dissolution will begin. There is something I want to tell you. Helmer's refined nature gives him an unconquerable disgust at everything that is ugly; I won't have him in my sick-room.

155 NORA: Oh, but, Doctor Rank—

RANK: I won't have him there. Not on any account. I bar my door to him. As soon as I am quite certain that the worst has come, I shall send you my card with a black cross on it, and then you will know that the loathsome end has begun.

NORA: You are quite absurd to-day. And I wanted you so much to be in a really good humour.

RANK: With death stalking beside me?—To have to pay this penalty for another man's sin! Is there any justice in that? And in every single family, in one way or another, some such inexorable retribution is being exacted—

NORA: [putting her hands over her ears] Rubbish! Do talk of something cheerful.

RANK: Oh, it's a mere laughing matter, the whole thing. My poor innocent spine has to suffer for my father's youthful amusements.   160

NORA: [sitting at the table on the left] I suppose you mean that he was too partial to asparagus and pâté de foie gras, don't you.

RANK: Yes, and to truffles.

NORA: Truffles, yes. And oysters too, I suppose?

RANK: Oysters, of course, that goes without saying.

NORA: And heaps of port and champagne. It is sad that all these nice things should take their revenge on our bones.   165

RANK: Especially that they should revenge themselves on the unlucky bones of those who have not had the satisfaction of enjoying them.

NORA: Yes, that's the saddest part of it all.

RANK: [with a searching look at her] Hm!—

NORA: [after a short pause] Why did you smile?

RANK: No, it was you that laughed.   170

NORA: No, it was you that smiled, Doctor Rank!

RANK: [rising] You are a greater rascal than I thought.

NORA: I am in a silly mood to-day.

RANK: So it seems.

NORA: [putting her hands on his shoulders] Dear, dear Doctor Rank, death mustn't take you away from Torvald and me.   175

RANK: It is a loss you would easily recover from. Those who are gone are soon forgotten.

NORA: [looking at him anxiously] Do you believe that?

RANK: People form new ties, and then—

NORA: Who will form new ties?

RANK: Both you and Helmer, when I am gone. You yourself are already on the high road to it, I think. What did that Mrs. Linde want here last night?   180

NORA: Oho!—you don't mean to say you are jealous of poor Christine?

RANK: Yes, I am. She will be my successor in this house. When I am done for, this woman will—

NORA: Hush! don't speak so loud. She is in that room.

RANK: To-day again. There, you see.

NORA: She has only come to sew my dress for me. Bless my soul, how unreasonable you are! [sits down on the sofa] Be nice now, Doctor Rank, and tomorrow you will see how beautifully I shall dance, and you can imagine I am doing it all for you—and for Torvald too, of course. [takes various things out of the box] Doctor Rank, come and sit down here, and I will show you something.   185

RANK: [sitting down] What is it?

NORA: Just look at those!

RANK: Silk stockings.

NORA: Flesh-coloured. Aren't they lovely? It is so dark here now, but to-morrow—. No, no, no! you must only look at the feet. Oh well, you may have leave to look at the legs too.

190 **RANK:** Hm!—

NORA: Why are you looking so critical? Don't you think they will fit me?

RANK: I have no means of forming an opinion about that.

NORA: [*looks at him for a moment*] For shame! [*hits him lightly on the ear with the stockings*] That's to punish you. [*folds them up again*]

RANK: And what other nice things am I to be allowed to see?

195 **NORA:** Not a single thing more, for being so naughty. [*She looks among the things, humming to herself.*]

RANK: [*after a short silence*] When I am sitting here, talking to you as intimately as this, I cannot imagine for a moment what would have become of me if I had never come into this house.

NORA: [*smiling*] I believe you do feel thoroughly at home with us.

RANK: [*in a lower voice, looking straight in front of him*] And to be obliged to leave it all—

NORA: Nonsense, you are not going to leave it.

200 **RANK:** [*as before*] And not be able to leave behind one the slightest token of one's gratitude, scarcely even a fleeting regret—nothing but an empty place which the first comer can fill as well as any other.

NORA: And if I asked you now for a—? No!

RANK: For what?

NORA: For a big proof of your friendship—

RANK: Yes, yes!

205 **NORA:** I mean a tremendously big favour—

RANK: Would you really make me so happy for once?

NORA: Ah, but you don't know what it is yet.

RANK: No—but tell me.

NORA: I really can't, Doctor Rank. It is something out of all reason; it means advice, and help, and a favour—

210 **RANK:** The bigger a thing it is the better. I can't conceive what it is you mean. Do tell me. Haven't I your confidence?

NORA: More than anyone else. I know you are my truest and best friend, and so I will tell you what it is. Well, Doctor Rank, it is something you must help me to prevent. You know how devotedly, how inexpressibly deeply Torvald loves me; he would never for a moment hesitate to give his life for me.

RANK: [*leaning towards her*] Nora—do you think he is the only one—?

NORA: [*with a slight start*] The only one—?

RANK: The only one who would gladly give his life for your sake.

215 **NORA:** [*sadly*] Is that it?

RANK: I was determined you should know it before I went away, and there will never be a better opportunity than this. Now you know it, Nora. And now you know, too, that you can trust me as you would trust no one else.

NORA: [*rises, deliberately and quietly*] Let me pass.

RANK: [*makes room for her to pass him, but sits still*] Nora!

NORA: [*at the hall door*] Helen, bring in the lamp. [*goes over to the stove*] Dear Doctor Rank, that was really horrid of you.

220 **RANK:** To have loved you as much as anyone else does? Was that horrid?

NORA: No, but to go and tell me so. There was really no need—

RANK: What do you mean? Did you know—? [*MAID enters with lamp, puts it down on the table, and goes out.*] Nora—Mrs. Helmer—tell me, had you any idea of this?

NORA: Oh, how do I know whether I had or whether I hadn't? I really can't tell you—To think you could be so clumsy, Doctor Rank! We were getting on so nicely.

RANK: Well, at all events you know now that you can command me, body and soul. So won't you speak out?

NORA: [*looking at him*] After what happened?   225

RANK: I beg you to let me know what it is.

NORA: I can't tell you anything now.

RANK: Yes, yes. You mustn't punish me in that way. Let me have permission to do for you whatever a man may do.

NORA: You can do nothing for me now. Besides, I really don't need any help at all. You will find that the whole thing is merely fancy on my part. It really is so—of course it is! [*Sits down in the rocking-chair, and looks at him with a smile*] You are a nice sort of man, Doctor Rank!—don't you feel ashamed of yourself, now the lamp has come?

RANK: Not a bit. But perhaps I had better go—for ever?   230

NORA: No, indeed, you shall not. Of course you must come here just as before. You know very well Torvald can't do without you.

RANK: Yes, but you?

NORA: Oh, I am always tremendously pleased when you come.

RANK: It is just that, that put me on the wrong track. You are a riddle to me. I have often thought that you would almost as soon be in my company as in Helmer's.

NORA: Yes—you see there are some people one loves best, and others whom one would al-   235
most always rather have as companions.

RANK: Yes, there is something in that.

NORA: When I was at home, of course I loved papa best. But I always thought it tremendous fun if I could steal down into the maid's room, because they never moralised at all, and talked to each other about such entertaining things.

RANK: I see—it is *their* place I have taken.

NORA: [*jumping up and going to him*] Oh, dear, nice Doctor Rank, I never meant that at all. But surely you can understand that being with Torvald is a little like being with papa—

[*Enter MAID from the hall*]

MAID: If you please, ma'am. [*whispers and hands her a card*]   240

NORA: [*glancing at the card*] Oh! [*puts it in her pocket*]

RANK: Is there anything wrong?

NORA: No, no, not in the least. It is only something—it is my new dress—

RANK: What? Your dress is lying there.

NORA: Oh, yes, that one; but this is another. I ordered it. Torvald mustn't know about it— 245

RANK: Oho! Then that was the great secret.

NORA: Of course. Just go in to him; he is sitting in the inner room. Keep him as long as—

RANK: Make your mind easy; I won't let him escape. [*goes into HELMER'S room*]

NORA: [*to the MAID*] And he is standing waiting in the kitchen?

MAID: Yes; he came up the back stairs.   250

NORA: But didn't you tell him no one was in?

MAID: Yes, but it was no good.

NORA: He won't go away?

MAID: No; he says he won't until he has seen you, ma'am.

NORA: Well, let him come in—but quietly. Helen, you mustn't say anything about it to any-   255
one. It is a surprise for my husband.

MAID: Yes, ma'am, I quite understand.   [*Exit*]

NORA: This dreadful thing is going to happen! It will happen in spite of me! No, no, no, it can't happen—it shan't happen!

[*She bolts the door of HELMER'S room. The MAID opens the hall door for KROGSTAD and shuts it after him. He is wearing a fur coat, high boots and a fur cap.*]

NORA: [*advancing towards him*] Speak low—my husband is at home.

KROGSTAD: No matter about that.

260 NORA: What do you want of me?

KROGSTAD: An explanation of something.

NORA: Make haste then. What is it?

KROGSTAD: You know, I suppose, that I have got my dismissal.

NORA: I couldn't prevent it, Mr. Krogstad. I fought as hard as I could on your side, but it was no good.

265 KROGSTAD: Does your husband love you so little, then? He knows that what I can expose you to, and yet he ventures—

NORA: How can you suppose that he has any knowledge of the sort?

KROGSTAD: I didn't suppose so at all. It would not be the least like our dear Torvald Helmer to show so much courage—

NORA: Mr. Krogstad, a little respect for my husband, please.

KROGSTAD: Certainly—all the respect he deserves. But since you have kept the matter so carefully to yourself, I make bold to suppose that you have a little clearer idea, than you had yesterday, of what it actually is that you have done?

270 NORA: More than you could ever teach me.

KROGSTAD: Yes, such a bad lawyer as I am.

NORA: What is it you want of me?

KROGSTAD: Only to see how you were, Mrs. Helmer. I have been thinking about you all day long. A mere cashier, a quill-driver, a—well, a man like me—even he has a little of what is called feeling, you know.

NORA: Show it, then; think of my little children.

275 KROGSTAD: Have you and your husband thought of mine? But never mind about that. I only wanted to tell you that you need not take this matter too seriously. In the first place there will be no accusation made on my part.

NORA: No, of course not; I was sure of that.

KROGSTAD: The whole thing can be arranged amicably; there is no reason why anyone should know anything about it. It will remain a secret between us three.

NORA: My husband must never get to know anything about it.

KROGSTAD: How will you be able to prevent it? Am I to understand that you can pay the balance that is owing?

280 NORA: No, not just at present.

KROGSTAD: Or perhaps that you have some expedient for raising the money soon?

NORA: No expedient that I mean to make use of.

KROGSTAD: Well, in any case, it would have been of no use to you now. If you stood there with ever so much money in your hand, I would never part with your bond.

NORA: Tell me what purpose you mean to put it to.

285 KROGSTAD: I shall only preserve it—keep it in my possession. No one who is not concerned in the matter shall have the slightest hint of it. So that if the thought of it has driven you to any desperate resolution—

NORA: It has.

KROGSTAD: If you had it in your mind to run away from your home—

NORA: I had.

KROGSTAD: Or even something worse—

290 NORA: How could you know that?

KROGSTAD: Give up the idea.

NORA: How did you know I had thought of *that?*

KROGSTAD: Most of us think of that at first. I did, too—but I hadn't the courage.

NORA: [*faintly*] No more had I.

295 KROGSTAD: [*in a tone of relief*] No, that's it, isn't it—you hadn't the courage either?

NORA: No, I haven't—I haven't.

KROGSTAD: Besides, it would have been a great piece of folly. Once the first storm at home is over—. I have a letter for your husband in my pocket.

NORA: Telling him everything?

KROGSTAD: In as lenient a manner as I possibly could.

NORA: [*quickly*] He mustn't get the letter. Tear it up. I will find some means of getting money.   300

KROGSTAD: Excuse me, Mrs. Helmer, but I think I told you just now—

NORA: I am not speaking of what I owe you. Tell me what sum you are asking my husband for, and I will get the money.

KROGSTAD: I am not asking your husband for a penny.

NORA: What do you want, then?

KROGSTAD: I will tell you. I want to rehabilitate myself, Mrs. Helmer; I want to get on; and   305
in that your husband must help me. For the last year and a half I have not had a hand in anything dishonourable, and all that time I have been struggling in most restricted circumstances. I was content to work my way up step by step. Now I am turned out, and I am not going to be satisfied with merely being taken into favour again. I want to get on, I tell you. I want to get into the Bank again, in a higher position. Your husband must make a place for me—

NORA: That he will never do!

KROGSTAD: He will; I know him; he dare not protest. And as soon as I am in there again with him, then you will see! Within a year I shall be the manager's right hand. It will be Nils Krogstad and not Torvald Helmer who manages the Bank.

NORA: That's a thing you will never see!

KROGSTAD: Do you mean that you will—?

NORA: I have courage enough for it now.   310

KROGSTAD: Oh, you can't frighten me. A fine, spoilt lady like you—

NORA: You will see, you will see.

KROGSTAD: Under the ice, perhaps? Down into the cold, coal-black water? And then, in the spring, to float up to the surface, all horrible and unrecognisable, with your hair fallen out—

NORA: You can't frighten me.

KROGSTAD: Nor you me. People don't do such things, Mrs. Helmer. Besides, what use   315
would it be? I should have him completely in my power all the same.

NORA: Afterwards? When I am no longer—

KROGSTAD: Have you forgotten that it is I who have the keeping of your reputation? [*NORA stands speechlessly looking at him.*] Well, now, I have warned you. Do not do anything foolish. When Helmer has had my letter, I shall expect a message from him. And be sure you remember that it is your husband himself who has forced me into such ways as this again. I will never forgive him for that. Good-bye, Mrs. Helmer.

[*Exit through the hall*]

NORA: [*goes to the hall door, opens it slightly and listens*] He is going. He is not putting the letter in the box. Oh no, no! that's impossible! [*opens the door by degrees*] What is that? He is standing outside. He is not going downstairs. Is he hesitating? Can he—

[*A letter drops into the box; then Krogstad's footsteps are heard, till they die away as he goes downstairs. Nora utters a stifled cry and runs across the room to the table by the sofa. A short pause.*]

NORA: In the letter-box. [*steals across to the hall door*] There it lies—Torvald, Torvald, there is no hope for us now!

[*MRS. LINDE comes in from the room on the left, carrying the dress.*]

320 MRS. LINDE: There, I can't see anything more to mend now. Would you like to try it on—?

NORA: [*in a hoarse whisper*] Christine, come here.

MRS. LINDE: [*throwing the dress down on the sofa*] What is the matter with you? You look so agitated!

NORA: Come here. Do you see that letter? There, look—you can see it through the glass in the letter-box.

MRS. LINDE: Yes, I see it.

325 NORA: That letter is from Krogstad.

MRS. LINDE: Nora—it was Krogstad who lent you the money!

NORA: Yes, and now Torvald will know all about it.

MRS. LINDE: Believe me, Nora, that's the best thing for both of you.

NORA: You don't know all. I forged a name.

330 MRS. LINDE: Good heavens—!

NORA: I only want to say this to you, Christine—you must be my witness.

MRS. LINDE: Your witness? What do you mean? What am I to—?

NORA: If I should go out of my mind—and it might easily happen—

MRS. LINDE: Nora!

335 NORA: Or if anything else should happen to me—anything, for instance, that might prevent my being here—

MRS. LINDE: Nora! Nora! you are quite out of your mind.

NORA: And if it should happen that there were someone who wanted to take all the responsibility, all the blame, you understand—

MRS. LINDE: Yes, yes—but how can you suppose—?

NORA: Then you must be my witness, that it is not true, Christine. I am not out of my mind at all; I am in my right senses now, and I tell you no one else has known anything about it; I, and I alone, did the whole thing. Remember that.

340 MRS. LINDE: I will, indeed. But I don't understand all this.

NORA: How should you understand it? A wonderful thing is going to happen.

MRS. LINDE: A wonderful thing?

NORA: Yes, a wonderful thing!—But it is so terrible, Christine; it *mustn't* happen, not for all the world.

MRS. LINDE: I will go at once and see Krogstad.

345 NORA: Don't go to him; he will do you some harm.

MRS. LINDE: There was a time when he would gladly do anything for my sake.

NORA: He?

MRS. LINDE: Where does he live?

NORA: How should I know—? Yes [*feeling in her pocket*] here is his card. But the letter, the letter—!

350 HELMER: [*calls from his room, knocking at the door*] Nora!

NORA: [*cries out anxiously*] Oh, what's that? What do you want?

HELMER: Don't be so frightened. We are not coming in; you have locked the door. Are you trying on your dress?

NORA: Yes, that's it. I look so nice, Torvald.

MRS. LINDE: [*who has read the card*] I see he lives at the corner here.

355 NORA: Yes, but it's no use. It is hopeless. The letter is lying there in the box.

MRS. LINDE: And your husband keeps the key?

NORA: Yes, always.

MRS. LINDE: Krogstad must ask for his letter back unread, he must find some pretence—

NORA: But it is just at this time that Torvald generally—

360 MRS. LINDE: You must delay him. Go in to him in the meantime. I will come back as soon as I can.

[*She goes out hurriedly through the hall door.*]

NORA: [*goes to* HELMER'S *door, opens it and peeps in*] Torvald!

HELMER: [*from the inner room*] Well? May I venture at last to come into my own room again? Come along, Rank, now you will see—[*halting in the doorway*] But what is this?

NORA: What is what, dear?

HELMER: Rank led me to expect a splendid transformation.

RANK: [*in the doorway*] I understood so, but evidently I was mistaken.   365

NORA: Yes, nobody is to have the chance of admiring me in my dress until tomorrow.

HELMER: But, my dear Nora, you look so worn out. Have you been practising too much?

NORA: No, I have not practised at all.

HELMER: But you will need to—

NORA: Yes, indeed I shall, Torvald. But I can't get on a bit without you to help me; I have   370
absolutely forgotten the whole thing.

HELMER: Oh, we will soon work it up again.

NORA: Yes, help me, Torvald. Promise that you will! I am so nervous about it—all the people—. You must give yourself up to me entirely this evening. Not the tiniest bit of business—you mustn't even take a pen in your hand. Will you promise, Torvald dear?

HELMER: I promise. This evening I will be wholly and absolutely at your service, you helpless little mortal. Ah, by the way, first of all I will just—

[*Goes towards the hall door*]

NORA: What are you going to do there?

HELMER: Only see if any letters have come.   375

NORA: No, no! don't do that, Torvald!

HELMER: Why not?

NORA: Torvald, please don't. There is nothing there.

HELMER: Well, let me look. [*Turns to go to the letter-box.* NORA, *at the piano, plays the first bars of the Tarantella.* HELMER *stops in the doorway.*] Aha!

NORA: I can't dance to-morrow if I don't practise with you.   380

HELMER: [*going up to her*] Are you really so afraid of it, dear.

NORA: Yes, so dreadfully afraid of it. Let me practise at once; there is time now, before we go to dinner. Sit down and play for me, Torvald dear; criticise me, and correct me as you play.

HELMER: With great pleasure, if you wish me to.

[*Sits down at the piano.*]

NORA: [*takes out of the box a tambourine and a long variegated shawl. She hastily drapes the shawl round her. Then she springs to the front of the stage and calls out.*] Now play for me! I am going to dance!

[HELMER *plays and* NORA *dances.* RANK *stands by the piano behind* HELMER *and looks on.*]

HELMER: [*as he plays*] Slower, slower!   385

NORA: I can't do it any other way.

HELMER: Not so violently, Nora!

NORA: This is the way.

HELMER: [*stops playing*] No, no—that is not a bit right.

NORA: [*laughing and swinging the tambourine*] Didn't I tell you so?   390

RANK: Let me play for her.

HELMER: [*getting up*] Yes, do. I can correct her better then.

[RANK *sits down at the piano and plays.* NORA *dances more and more wildly.* HELMER *has taken up a position beside the stove, and during her dance gives her frequent instructions. She does not seem to hear him; her hair comes down and falls over her shoulders; she pays no attention to it, but goes on dancing. Enter* MRS. LINDE.]

MRS. LINDE: [*standing as if spell-bound in the doorway*] Oh!—
NORA: [*as she dances*] Such fun, Christine!
395 HELMER: My dear darling Nora, you are dancing as if your life depended on it.
NORA: So it does.
HELMER: Stop, Rank; this is sheer madness. Stop, I tell you! [RANK *stops playing, and* NORA *suddenly stands still.* HELMER *goes up to her.*] I could never have believed it. You have forgotten everything I taught you.
NORA: [*throwing away the tambourine*] There, you see.
HELMER: You will want a lot of coaching.
400 NORA: Yes, you see how much I need it. You must coach me up to the last minute. Promise me that, Torvald!
HELMER: You can depend on me.
NORA: You must not think of anything but me, either to-day or to-morrow; you mustn't open a single letter—not even open the letter-box—
HELMER: Ah, you are still afraid of that fellow—
NORA: Yes, indeed I am.
405 HELMER: Nora, I can tell from your looks that there is a letter from him lying there.
NORA: I don't know; I think there is; but you must not read anything of that kind now. Nothing horrid must come between us till this is all over.
RANK: [*whispers to* HELMER] You mustn't contradict her.
HELMER: [*taking her in his arms*] The child shall have her way. But to-morrow night, after you have danced—
NORA: Then you will be free.

[MAID *appears in the doorway to the right.*]

410 MAID: Dinner is served, ma'am.
NORA: We will have champagne, Helen.
MAID: Very good, ma'am.

[*Exit.*]

HELMER: Hullo!—are we going to have a banquet?
NORA: Yes, a champagne banquet till the small hours. [*calls out*] And a few macaroons, Helen—lots, just for once!
415 HELMER: Come, come, don't be so wild and nervous. Be my own little skylark, as you used.
NORA: Yes, dear, I will. But go in now and you too, Doctor Rank. Christine, you must help me to do up my hair.
RANK: [*whispers to* HELMER *as they go out*] I suppose there is nothing—she is not expecting anything?
HELMER: Far from it, my dear fellow; it is simply nothing more than this childish nervousness I was telling you of.

[*They go into the right-hand room.*]

NORA: Well!
420 MRS. LINDE: Gone out of town.
NORA: I could tell from your face.

MRS. LINDE: He is coming home to-morrow evening. I wrote a note for him.

NORA: You should have let it alone; you must prevent nothing. After all, it is splendid to be waiting for a wonderful thing to happen.

MRS. LINDE: What is it that you are waiting for?

NORA: Oh, you wouldn't understand. Go in to them, I will come in a moment. [MRS. LINDE   425
goes into the dining-room. NORA stands still for a little while, as if to compose herself. Then she looks at her watch.] Five o'clock. Seven hours till midnight; and then four-and-twenty hours till the next midnight. Then the Tarantella will be over. Twenty-four and seven? Thirty-one hours to live.

HELMER: [from the doorway on the right] Where's my little skylark?

NORA: [going to him with her arms outstretched] Here she is!

ACT 3

THE SAME SCENE. The table has been placed in the middle of the stage, with chairs round it. A lamp is burning on the table. The door into the hall stands open. Dance music is heard in the room above. Mrs. LINDE is sitting at the table idly turning over the leaves of a book; she tries to read, but does not seem able to collect her thoughts. Every now and then she listens intently for a sound at the outer door.

MRS. LINDE: [looking at her watch] Not yet—and the time is nearly up. If only he does not—. [listens again] Ah, there he is. [Goes into the hall and opens the outer door carefully. Light footsteps are heard on the stairs. She whispers.] Come in. There is no one here.

KROGSTAD: [in the doorway] I found a note from you at home. What does this mean?

MRS. LINDE: It is absolutely necessary that I should have a talk with you.

KROGSTAD: Really? And is it absolutely necessary that it should be here?

MRS. LINDE: It is impossible where I live; there is no private entrance to my rooms. Come   5
in; we are quite alone. The maid is asleep, and the Helmers are at the dance upstairs.

KROGSTAD: [coming into the room] Are the Helmers really at a dance to-night?

MRS. LINDE: Yes, why not?

KROGSTAD: Certainly—why not?

MRS. LINDE: Now, Nils, let us have a talk.

KROGSTAD: Can we two have anything to talk about?   10

MRS. LINDE: We have a great deal to talk about.

KROGSTAD: I shouldn't have thought so.

MRS. LINDE: No, you have never properly understood me.

KROGSTAD: Was there anything else to understand except what was obvious to all the world—a heartless woman jilts a man when a more lucrative chance turns up?

MRS. LINDE: Do you believe I am as absolutely heartless as all that? And do you believe   15
that I did it with a light heart?

KROGSTAD: Didn't you?

MRS. LINDE: Nils, did you really think that?

KROGSTAD: If it were as you say, why did you write to me as you did at the time?

MRS. LINDE: I could do nothing else. As I had to break with you, it was my duty also to put an end to all that you felt for me.

KROGSTAD: [wringing his hands] So that was it, and all this—only for the sake of money!   20

MRS. LINDE: You must not forget that I had a helpless mother and two little brothers. We couldn't wait for you, Nils; your prospects seemed hopeless then.

KROGSTAD: That may be so, but you had no right to throw me over for any one else's sake.

MRS. LINDE: Indeed I don't know. Many a time did I ask myself if I had the right to do it.

KROGSTAD: [more gently] When I lost you, it was as if all the solid ground went from under my feet. Look at me now—I am a shipwrecked man clinging to a bit of wreckage.

MRS. LINDE: But help may be near.   25

KROGSTAD: It *was* near; but then you came and stood in my way.

MRS. LINDE: Unintentionally, Nils. It was only to-day that I learnt it was your place I was going to take in the Bank.

KROGSTAD: I believe you, if you say so. But now that you know it, are you not going to give it up to me?

MRS. LINDE: No, because that would not benefit you in the least.

30   KROGSTAD: Oh, benefit, benefit—I would have done it whether or no.

MRS. LINDE: I have learnt to act prudently. Life, and hard, bitter necessity have taught me that.

KROGSTAD: And life has taught me not to believe in fine speeches.

MRS. LINDE: Then life has taught you something very reasonable. But deeds you must believe in?

KROGSTAD: What do you mean by that?

35   MRS. LINDE: You said you were like a shipwrecked man clinging to some wreckage.

KROGSTAD: I had good reason to say so.

MRS. LINDE: Well, I am like a shipwrecked woman clinging to some wreckage—no one to mourn for, no one to care for.

KROGSTAD: It was your own choice.

MRS. LINDE: There was no other choice—then.

40   KROGSTAD: Well, what now?

MRS. LINDE: Nils, how would it be if we two shipwrecked people could join forces?

KROGSTAD: What are you saying?

MRS. LINDE: Two on the same piece of wreckage would stand a better chance than each on their own.

KROGSTAD: Christine!

45   MRS. LINDE: What do you suppose brought me to town?

KROGSTAD: Do you mean that you gave me a thought?

MRS. LINDE: I could not endure life without work. All my life, as long as I can remember, I have worked, and it has been my greatest and only pleasure. But now I am quite alone in the world—my life is so dreadfully empty and I feel so forsaken. There is not the least pleasure in working for one's self. Nils, give me someone and something to work for.

KROGSTAD: I don't trust that. It is nothing but a woman's overstrained sense of generosity that prompts you to make such an offer of yourself.

MRS. LINDE: Have you ever noticed anything of the sort in me?

50   KROGSTAD: Could you really do it? Tell me—do you know all about my past life?

MRS. LINDE: Yes.

KROGSTAD: And do you know what they think of me here?

MRS. LINDE: You seemed to me to imply that with me you might have been quite another man.

KROGSTAD: I am certain of it.

55   MRS. LINDE: Is it too late now?

KROGSTAD: Christine, are you saying this deliberately? Yes, I am sure you are. I see it in your face. Have you really the courage, then—?

MRS. LINDE: I want to be a mother to someone, and your children need a mother. We two need each other. Nils, I have faith in your real character—I can dare anything together with you.

KROGSTAD: [*grasps her hands*] Thanks, thanks, Christine! Now I shall find a way to clear myself in the eyes of the world. Ah, but I forgot—

MRS. LINDE: [*listening*] Hush! The Tarantella! Go, go!

60   KROGSTAD: Why? What is it?

MRS. LINDE: Do you hear them up there? When that is over, we may expect them back.

KROGSTAD: Yes, yes—I will go. But it is all no use. Of course you are not aware what steps I have taken in the matter of the Helmers.

MRS. LINDE: Yes. I know all about that.

KROGSTAD: And in spite of that have you the courage to—?

MRS. LINDE: I understand very well to what lengths a man like you might be driven by despair.   65

KROGSTAD: If I could only undo what I have done!

MRS. LINDE: You can. Your letter is lying in the letter-box now.

KROGSTAD: Are you sure of that?

MRS. LINDE: Quite sure, but—

KROGSTAD: [*with a searching look at her*] Is that what it all means?—that you want to save   70 your friend at any cost? Tell me frankly. Is that it?

MRS. LINDE: Nils, a woman who has once sold herself for another's sake, doesn't do it a second time.

KROGSTAD: I will ask for my letter back.

MRS. LINDE: No, no.

KROGSTAD: Yes, of course I will. I will wait here till Helmer comes; I will tell him he must give me my letter back—that it only concerns my dismissal—that he is not to read it—

MRS. LINDE: No, Nils, you must not recall your letter.   75

KROGSTAD: But, tell me, wasn't it for that very purpose that you asked me to meet you here?

MRS. LINDE: In my first moment of fright, it was. But twenty-four hours have elapsed since then, and in that time I have witnessed incredible things in this house. Helmer must know all about it. This unhappy secret must be disclosed; they must have a complete understanding between them, which is impossible with all this concealment and falsehood going on.

KROGSTAD: Very well, if you will take the responsibility. But there is one thing I can do in any case, and I shall do it at once.

MRS. LINDE: [*listening*] You must be quick and go! The dance is over; we are not safe a moment longer.

KROGSTAD: I will wait for you below.   80

MRS. LINDE: Yes, do. You must see me back to my door.

KROGSTAD: I have never had such an amazing piece of good fortune in my life.

[*Goes out through the outer door. The door between the room and the hall remains open.*]

MRS. LINDE: [*tidying up the room and laying her hat and cloak ready*] What a difference! what a difference! Someone to work for and live for—a home to bring comfort into. That I will do, indeed. I wish they would be quick and come—[*listens*] Ah, there they are now. I must put on my things.

[*Takes up her hat and cloak. HELMER'S and NORA'S voices are heard outside; a key is turned, and HELMER brings NORA almost by force into the hall. She is in an Italian costume with a large black shawl round her; he is in evening dress and a black domino which is flying open.*]

NORA: [*hanging back in the doorway, and struggling with him*] No, no, no!—don't take me in. I want to go upstairs again; I don't want to leave so early.

HELMER: But, my dearest Nora—   85

NORA: Please, Torvald dear—please, *please*—only an hour more.

HELMER: Not a single minute, my sweet Nora. You know that was our agreement. Come along into the room; you are catching cold standing there.

[*He brings her gently into the room, in spite of her resistance.*]

MRS. LINDE: Good evening.

NORA: Christine!

90 HELMER: You here, so late, Mrs. Linde?

MRS. LINDE: Yes, you must excuse me; I was so anxious to see Nora in her dress.

NORA: Have you been sitting here waiting for me?

MRS. LINDE: Yes, unfortunately I came too late, you had already gone upstairs; and I thought I couldn't go away without having seen you.

HELMER: [*taking off* NORA'S *shawl*] Yes, take a good look at her. I think she is worth looking at. Isn't she charming, Mrs. Linde?

95 MRS. LINDE: Yes, indeed she is.

HELMER: Doesn't she look remarkably pretty? Everyone thought so at the dance. But she is terribly self-willed, this sweet little person. What are we to do with her? You will hardly believe that I had almost to bring her away by force.

NORA: Torvald, you will repent not having let me stay, even if it were only for half an hour.

HELMER: Listen to her, Mrs. Linde! She had danced her Tarantella, and it had been a tremendous success, as it deserved—although possibly the performance was a trifle too realistic—a little more so, I mean, than was strictly compatible with the limitations of art. But never mind about that! The chief thing is, she had made a success—she had made a tremendous success. Do you think I was going to let her remain there after that, and spoil the effect? No indeed! I took my charming little Capri maiden—my capricious little Capri maiden, I should say—on my arm; took one quick turn round the room; a curtsey on either side, and, as they say in novels, the beautiful apparition disappeared. An exit ought always to be effective, Mrs. Linde; but that is what I cannot make Nora understand. Pooh! this room is hot. [*throws his domino on a chair and opens the door of his room*] Hullo! it's all dark in here. Oh, of course—excuse me—.

[*He goes in and lights some candles.*]

NORA: [*in a hurried and breathless whisper*] Well?

100 MRS. LINDE: [*in a low voice*] I have had a talk with him.

NORA: Yes, and—

MRS. LINDE: Nora, you must tell your husband all about it.

NORA: [*in an expressionless voice*] I knew it.

MRS. LINDE: You have nothing to be afraid of as far as Krogstad is concerned; but you must tell him.

105 NORA: I won't tell him.

MRS. LINDE: Then the letter will.

NORA: Thank you, Christine. Now I know what I must do. Hush—!

HELMER: [*coming in again*] Well, Mrs. Linde, have you admired her?

MRS. LINDE: Yes, and now I will say good-night.

110 HELMER: What already? Is this yours, this knitting?

MRS. LINDE: [*taking it*] Yes, thank you, I had very nearly forgotten it.

HELMER: So you knit?

MRS. LINDE: Of course.

HELMER: Do you know, you ought to embroider.

115 MRS. LINDE: Really? Why?

HELMER: Yes, it's far more becoming. Let me show you. You hold the embroidery thus in your left hand, and use the needle with the right—like this—with a long, easy sweep. Do you see?

MRS. LINDE: Yes, perhaps—

HELMER: But in the case of knitting—that can never be anything but ungraceful; look here—the arms close together, the knitting-needles going up and down—it has a sort of Chinese effect—. That was really excellent champagne they gave us.

MRS. LINDE: Well,—good-night, Nora, and don't be self-willed any more.

HELMER: That's right, Mrs. Linde. 120

MRS. LINDE: Good-night, Mr. Helmer.

HELMER: [*accompanying her to the door*] Good-night, good-night. I hope you will get home all right. I should be very happy to—but you haven't any great distance to go. Good-night, good-night. [*She goes out; he shuts the door after her, and comes in again.*] Ah!—at last we have got rid of her. She is a frightful bore, that woman.

NORA: Aren't you very tired, Torvald?

HELMER: No, not in the least.

NORA: Nor sleepy? 125

HELMER: Not a bit. On the contrary, I feel extraordinarily lively. And you?—you really look both tired and sleepy.

NORA: Yes, I am very tired. I want to go to sleep at once.

HELMER: There, you see it was quite right of me not to let you stay there any longer.

NORA: Everything you do is quite right, Torvald.

HELMER: [*kissing her on the forehead*] Now my little skylark is speaking reasonably. Did you 130
notice what good spirits Rank was in this evening?

NORA: Really? Was he? I didn't speak to him at all.

HELMER: And I very little, but I have not for a long time seen him in such good form. [*looks for a while at her and then goes nearer to her*] It is delightful to be at home by ourselves again, to be all alone with you—you fascinating, charming little darling!

NORA: Don't look at me like that, Torvald.

HELMER: Why shouldn't I look at my dearest treasure?—at all the beauty that is mine, all my very own?

NORA: [*going to the other side of the table*] You mustn't say things like that to me to-night. 135

HELMER: [*following her*] You have still got the Tarantella in your blood, I see. And it makes you more captivating than ever. Listen—the guests are beginning to go now. [*in a lower voice*] Nora—soon the whole house will be quiet.

NORA: Yes, I hope so.

HELMER: Yes, my own darling Nora. Do you know, when I am out at a party with you like this, why I speak so little to you, keep away from you, and only send a stolen glance in your direction now and then?—do you know why I do that? It is because I make believe to myself that we are secretly in love, and you are my secretly promised bride, and that no one suspects there is anything between us.

NORA: Yes, yes—I know very well your thoughts are with me all the time.

HELMER: And when we are leaving, and I am putting the shawl over your beautiful young 140
shoulders—on your lovely neck—then I imagine that you are my young bride and that we have just come from the wedding, and I am bringing you for the first time into our home—to be alone with you for the first time—quite alone with my shy little darling! All this evening I have longed for nothing but you. When I watched the seductive figures of the Tarantella, my blood was on fire; I could endure it no longer, and that was why I brought you down so early—

NORA: Go away, Torvald! You must let me go. I won't—

HELMER: What's that? You're joking, my little Nora! You won't—you won't? Am I not your husband—?

[*A knock is heard at the outer door.*]

NORA: [*starting*] Did you hear—?

HELMER: [*going into the hall*] Who is it?

RANK: [*outside*] It is I. May I come in for a moment? 145

HELMER: [*in a fretful whisper*] Oh, what does he want now? [*aloud*] Wait a minute! [*unlocks the door*] Come, that's kind of you not to pass by our door.

RANK: I thought I heard your voice, and felt as if I should like to look in. [*with a swift glance round*] Ah, yes!—these dear familiar rooms. You are very happy and cosy in here, you two.

HELMER: It seems to me that you looked after yourself pretty well upstairs too.

RANK: Excellently. Why shouldn't I? Why shouldn't one enjoy everything in this world?—at any rate as much as one can, and as long as one can. The wine was capital—

150 HELMER: Especially the champagne.

RANK: So you noticed that too? It is almost incredible how much I managed to put away!

NORA: Torvald drank a great deal of champagne tonight, too.

RANK: Did he?

NORA: Yes, and he is always in such good spirits afterwards.

155 RANK: Well, why should one not enjoy a merry evening after a well-spent day?

HELMER: Well spent? I am afraid I can't take credit for that.

RANK: [*clapping him on the back*] But I can, you know!

NORA: Doctor Rank, you must have been occupied with some scientific investigation to-day.

RANK: Exactly.

160 HELMER: Just listen!—little Nora talking about scientific investigations!

NORA: And may I congratulate you on the result?

RANK: Indeed you may.

NORA: Was it favourable, then?

RANK: The best possible, for both doctor and patient—certainty.

165 NORA: [*quickly and searchingly*] Certainty?

RANK: Absolute certainty. So wasn't I entitled to make a merry evening of it after that?

NORA: Yes, you certainly were, Doctor Rank.

HELMER: I think so too, so long as you don't have to pay for it in the morning.

RANK: Oh well, one can't have anything in this life without paying for it.

170 NORA: Doctor Rank—are you fond of fancy-dress balls?

RANK: Yes, if there is a fine lot of pretty costumes.

NORA: Tell me—what shall we two wear at the next?

HELMER: Little featherbrain!—are you thinking of the next already?

RANK: We two? Yes, I can tell you. You shall go as a good fairy—

175 HELMER: Yes, but what do you suggest as an appropriate costume for that?

RANK: Let your wife go dressed just as she is in everyday life.

HELMER: That was really very prettily turned. But can't you tell us what you will be?

RANK: Yes, my dear friend, I have quite made up my mind about that.

HELMER: Well?

180 RANK: At the next fancy dress ball I shall be invisible.

HELMER: That's a good joke!

RANK: There is a big black hat—have you never heard of hats that make you invisible? If you put one on, no one can see you.

HELMER: [*suppressing a smile*] Yes, you are quite right.

RANK: But I am clean forgetting what I came for. Helmer, give me a cigar—one of the dark Havanas.

185 HELMER: With the greatest pleasure. [*offers him his case*]

RANK: [*takes a cigar and cuts off the end*] Thanks.

NORA: [*striking a match*] Let me give you a light.

RANK: Thank you. [*She holds the match for him to light his cigar.*] And now good-bye!

HELMER: Good-bye, good-bye, dear old man!

190 NORA: Sleep well, Doctor Rank.

RANK: Thank you for that wish.

NORA: Wish me the same.

RANK: You? Well, if you want me to: sleep well! And thanks for the light.

[*He nods to them both and goes out.*]

HELMER: [*in a subdued voice*] He has drunk more than he ought.

NORA: [*absently*] Maybe. [HELMER *takes a bunch of keys out of his pocket and goes into the hall.*]   195
Torvald! what are you going to do there?

HELMER: Empty the letter-box; it is quite full; there will be no room to put the newspaper in to-morrow morning.

NORA: Are you going to work to-night?

HELMER: You know quite well I'm not. What is this? Some one has been at the lock.

NORA: At the lock—?

HELMER: Yes, someone has. What can it mean? I should never have thought the maid—.   200
Here is a broken hairpin. Nora, it is one of yours.

NORA: [*quickly*] Then it must have been the children—

HELMER: Then you must get them out of those ways. There, at last I have got it open. [*Takes out the contents of the letter-box, and calls to the kitchen.*] Helen!—Helen, put out the light over the front door. [*Goes back into the room and shuts the door into the hall. He holds out his hand full of letters.*] Look at that—look what a heap of them there are. [*turning them over*] What on earth is that?

NORA: [*at the window*] The letter—No! Torvald, no!

HELMER: Two cards—of Rank's.

NORA: Of Doctor Rank's?   205

HELMER: [*looking at them*] Doctor Rank. They were on the top. He must have put them in when he went out.

NORA: Is there anything written on them?

HELMER: There is a black cross over the name. Look there—what an uncomfortable idea! It looks as if he were announcing his own death.

NORA: It is just what he is doing.

HELMER: What? Do you know anything about it? Has he said anything to you?   210

NORA: Yes. He told me that when the cards came it would be his leave-taking from us. He means to shut himself up and die.

HELMER: My poor old friend. Certainly I knew we should not have him very long with us. But so soon! And so he hides himself away like a wounded animal.

NORA: If it has to happen, it is best it should be without a word—don't you think so, Torvald?

HELMER: [*walking up and down*] He had so grown into our lives. I can't think of him as having gone out of them. He, with his sufferings and his loneliness, was like a cloudy background to our sunlit happiness. Well, perhaps it is best so. For him, anyway. [*standing still*] And perhaps for us too, Nora. We two are thrown quite upon each other now. [*puts his arms round her*] My darling wife, I don't feel as if I could hold you tight enough. Do you know, Nora, I have often wished that you might be threatened by some great danger, so that I might risk my life's blood, and everything, for your sake.

NORA: [*disengages herself, and says firmly and decidedly*] Now you must read your letters,   215
Torvald.

HELMER: No, no; not to-night. I want to be with you, my darling wife.

NORA: With the thought of your friend's death—

HELMER: You are right, it has affected us both. Something ugly has come between us—the thought of the horrors of death. We must try and rid our minds of that. Until then—we will each go to our own room.

NORA: [*hanging on his neck*] Good-night, Torvald—Good-night!

220 HELMER: [*kissing her on the forehead.*] Good-night, my little singing-bird. Sleep sound, Nora. Now I will read my letters through.

[*He takes his letters and goes into his room, shutting the door after him.*]

NORA: [*gropes distractedly about, seizes* HELMER'S *domino, throws it round her, while she says in quick, hoarse, spasmodic whispers*] Never to see him again. Never! Never! [*puts her shawl over her head*] Never to see my children again either—never again. Never! Never!—Ah! the icy, black water—the unfathomable depths—If only it were over! He has got it now—now he is reading it. Good-by, Torvald and my children!

[*She is about to rush out through the hall, when* HELMER *opens his door hurriedly and stands with an open letter in his hand.*]

HELMER: Nora!

NORA: Ah!—

HELMER: What is this? Do you know what is in this letter?

225 NORA: Yes, I know. Let me go! Let me get out!

HELMER: [*holding her back*] Where are you going?

NORA: [*trying to get free*] You shan't save me, Torvald!

HELMER: [*reeling*] True? Is this true, that I read here? Horrible! No, no—it is impossible that it can be true.

NORA: It is true. I have loved you above everything else in the world.

230 HELMER: Oh, don't let us have any silly excuses.

NORA: [*taking a step towards him*] Torvald—!

HELMER: Miserable creature—what have you done?

NORA: Let me go. You shall not suffer for my sake. You shall not take it upon yourself.

HELMER: No tragedy airs, please. [*locks the hall door*] Here you shall stay and give me an explanation. Do you understand what you have done? Answer me? Do you understand what you have done?

235 NORA: [*looks steadily at him and says with a growing look of coldness in her face*] Yes, now I am beginning to understand thoroughly.

HELMER: [*walking about the room*] What a horrible awakening! All these eight years—she who was my joy and pride—a hypocrite, a liar—worse, worse—a criminal! The unutterable ugliness of it all! For shame! For shame! [*NORA is silent and looks steadily at him. He stops in front of her.*] I ought to have suspected that something of the sort would happen. I ought to have foreseen it. All your father's want of principle—be silent!—all your father's want of principle has come out in you. No religion, no morality, no sense of duty—. How I am punished for having winked at what he did! I did it for your sake, and this is how you repay me.

NORA: Yes, that's just it.

HELMER: Now you have destroyed all my happiness. You have ruined all my future. It is horrible to think of! I am in the power of an unscrupulous man; he can do what he likes with me, ask anything he likes of me, give me any orders he pleases— I dare not refuse. And I must sink to such miserable depths because of a thoughtless woman!

NORA: When I am out of the way, you will be free.

240 HELMER: No fine speeches, please. Your father had always plenty of those ready, too. What good would it be to me if you were out of the way, as you say? Not the slightest. He can make the affair known everywhere; and if he does, I may be falsely suspected of having been a party to your criminal action. Very likely people will think I was behind it all—that it was I who prompted you! And I have to thank you for all this—you

whom I have cherished during the whole of our married life. Do you understand now what it is you have done for me?

NORA: [*coldly and quietly*] Yes.

HELMER: It is so incredible that I can't take it in. But we must come to some understanding. Take off that shawl. Take it off, I tell you. I must try and appease him some way or another. The matter must be hushed up at any cost. And as for you and me, it must appear as if everything between us were just as before—but naturally only in the eyes of the world. You will still remain in my house, that is a matter of course. But I shall not allow you to bring up the children; I dare not trust them to you. To think that I should be obliged to say so to one whom I have loved so dearly, and whom I still—. No, that is all over. From this moment happiness is not the question; all that concerns us is to save the remains, the fragments, the appearance—

[*A ring is heard at the front-door bell.*]

HELMER: [*with a start*] What is that? So late! Can the worst—? Can he—? Hide yourself, Nora. Say you are ill.

[*NORA stands motionless. HELMER goes and unlocks the hall door.*]

MAID: [*half-dressed, comes to the door*] A letter for the mistress.

HELMER: Give it to me. [*takes the letter, and shuts the door*] Yes, it is from him. You shall not have it; I will read it myself. 245

NORA: Yes, read it.

HELMER: [*standing by the lamp*] I scarcely have the courage to do it. It may mean ruin for both of us. No, I must know. [*tears open the letter, runs his eye over a few lines, looks at a paper enclosed and gives a shout of joy*] Nora! [*She looks at him questioningly.*] Nora!—No, I must read it once again—. Yes, it is true! I am saved! Nora, I am saved!

NORA: And I?

HELMER: You too, of course; we are both saved, both you and I. Look, he sends you your bond back. He says he regrets and repents—that a happy change in his life—never mind what he says! We are saved, Nora! No one can do anything to you. Oh, Nora, Nora!—no, first I must destroy these hateful things. Let me see—. [*takes a look at the bond*] No, no, I won't look at it. The whole thing shall be nothing but a bad dream to me. [*tears up the bond and both letters, throws them all into the stove, and watches them burn*] There—now it doesn't exist any longer. He says that since Christmas Eve you—. These must have been three dreadful days for you, Nora.

NORA: I have fought a hard fight these three days. 250

HELMER: And suffered agonies, and seen no way out but—. No, we won't call any of the horrors to mind. We will only shout with joy, and keep saying "It's all over! It's all over!" Listen to me, Nora. You don't seem to realise that it is all over. What is this?—such a cold, set face! My poor little Nora, I quite understand; you don't feel as if you could believe that I have forgiven you. But it is true, Nora, I swear it; I have forgiven you everything. I know that what you did, you did out of love for me.

NORA: That is true.

HELMER: You have loved me as a wife ought to love her husband. Only you had not sufficient knowledge to judge of the means you used. But do you suppose you are any the less dear to me, because you don't understand how to act on your own responsibility? No, no; only lean on me; I will advise you and direct you. I should not be a man if this womanly helplessness did not just give you a double attractiveness in my eyes. You must not think any more about the hard things I said in my first moment of consternation, when I thought everything was going to overwhelm me. I have forgiven you, Nora; I swear to you I have forgiven you.

NORA: Thank you for your forgiveness.

[She goes out through the door to the right.]

255 HELMER: No, don't go—. *[looks in]* What are you doing in there?

NORA: *[from within]* Taking off my fancy dress.

HELMER: *[standing at the open door]* Yes, do. Try and calm yourself, and make your mind easy again, my frightened little singing-bird. Be at rest, and feel secure; I have broad wings to shelter you under. *[walks up and down by the door]* How warm and cosy our home is, Nora. Here is shelter for you; here I will protect you like a hunted dove that I have saved from a hawk's claws. I will bring peace to your poor beating heart. It will come, little by little, Nora, believe me. Tomorrow morning you will look upon it all quite differently; soon everything will be just as it was before. Very soon you won't need me to assure you that I have forgiven you; you will yourself feel the certainty that I have done so. Can you suppose I should ever think of such a thing as repudiating you, or even reproaching you? You have no idea what a true man's heart is like, Nora. There is something so indescribably sweet and satisfying, to a man, in the knowledge that he has forgiven his wife—forgiven her freely, and with all his heart. It seems as if that had made her, as it were, doubly his own; he has given her a new life, so to speak; and she has in a way become both wife and child to him. So you shall be for me after this, my little scared, helpless darling. Have no anxiety about anything, Nora; only be frank and open with me, and I will serve as will and conscience both to you—. What is this? Not gone to bed? Have you changed your things?

NORA: *[in everyday dress]* Yes, Torvald, I have changed my things now.

HELMER: But what for?—so late as this.

260 NORA: I shall not sleep to-night.

HELMER: But, my dear Nora—

NORA: *[looking at her watch]* It is not so very late. Sit down here, Torvald. You and I have much to say to one another.

[She sits down at one side of the table.]

HELMER: Nora—what is this?—this cold, set face?

NORA: Sit down. it will take some time; I have a lot to talk over with you.

265 HELMER: *[sits down at the opposite side of the table]* You alarm me, Nora!—and I don't understand you.

NORA: No, that is just it. You don't understand me, and I have never understood you either—before to-night. No, you mustn't interrupt me. You must simply listen to what I say. Torvald, this is a settling of accounts.

HELMER: What do you mean by that?

NORA: *[after a short silence]* Isn't there one thing that strikes you as strange in our sitting here like this?

HELMER: What is that?

270 NORA: We have been married now eight years. Does it not occur to you that this is the first time we two, you and I, husband and wife, have had a serious conversation?

HELMER: What do you mean by serious?

NORA: In all these eight years—longer than that—from the very beginning of our acquaintance, we have never exchanged a word on any serious subject.

HELMER: Was it likely that I would be continually and for ever telling you about worries that you could not help me to bear?

Torvald Helmer (Sam Waterston) begs Nora (Liv Ullmann) to reconsider her decision to leave home in the Joseph Papp New York Shakespeare Festival production (1995) of *A Dollhouse* (director, Tormod Skagestad).

NORA: I am not speaking about business matters. I say that we have never sat down in earnest together to try and get at the bottom of anything.

HELMER: But, dearest Nora, would it have been any good to you?   275

NORA: That is just it; you have never understood me. I have been greatly wronged, Torvald—first by papa and then by you.

HELMER: What! By us two—by us two, who have loved you better than anyone else in the world?

NORA: [*shaking her head*] You have never loved me. You have only thought it pleasant to be in love with me.

HELMER: Nora, what do I hear you saying?

NORA: It is perfectly true, Torvald. When I was at home with papa, he told me his opinion   280
about everything, and so I had the same opinions; and if I differed from him I concealed the fact, because he would not have liked it. He called me his doll-child, and he

played with me just as I used to play with my dolls. And when I came to live with you—

HELMER: What sort of an expression is that to use about our marriage?

NORA: [*undisturbed*] I mean that I was simply transferred from papa's hands into yours. You arranged everything according to your own taste, and so I got the same tastes as you—or else I pretended to, I am really not quite sure which—I think sometimes the one and sometimes the other. When I look back on it, it seems to me as if I had been living here like a poor woman—just from hand to mouth. I have existed merely to perform tricks for you, Torvald. But you would have it so. You and papa have committed a great sin against me. It is your fault that I have made nothing of my life.

HELMER: How unreasonable and how ungrateful you are, Nora! Have you not been happy here?

NORA: No, I have never been happy. I thought I was, but it has never really been so.

285 HELMER: Not—not happy!

NORA: No, only merry. And you have always been so kind to me. But our home has been nothing but a playroom. I have been your doll-wife, just as at home I was papa's doll-child; and here the children have been my dolls. I thought it great fun when you played with me, just as they thought it great fun when I played with them. That is what our marriage has been, Torvald.

HELMER: There is some truth in what you say—exaggerated and strained as your view of it is. But for the future it shall be different. Playtime shall be over, and lesson-time shall begin.

NORA: Whose lessons? Mine, or the children's?

HELMER: Both yours and the children's, my darling Nora.

290 NORA: Alas, Torvald, you are not the man to educate me into being a proper wife for you.

HELMER: And you can say that!

NORA: And I—how am I fitted to bring up the children?

HELMER: Nora!

NORA: Didn't you say so yourself a little while ago—that you dare not trust me to bring them up?

295 HELMER: In a moment of anger! Why do you pay any heed to that?

NORA: Indeed, you were perfectly right. I am not fit for the task. There is another task I must undertake first. I must try and educate myself—you are not the man to help me in that. I must do that for myself. And that is why I am going to leave you now.

HELMER: [*springing up*] What do you say?

NORA: I must stand quite alone, if I am to understand myself and everything about me. It is for that reason that I cannot remain with you any longer.

HELMER: Nora! Nora!

300 NORA: I am going away from here now, at once. I am sure Christine will take me in for the night—

HELMER: You are out of your mind! I won't allow it! I forbid you!

NORA: It is no use forbidding me anything any longer. I will take with me what belongs to myself. I will take nothing from you, either now or later.

HELMER: What sort of madness is this!

NORA: To-morrow I shall go home—I mean, to my old home. It will be easiest for me to find something to do there.

305 HELMER: You blind, foolish woman!

NORA: I must try and get some sense, Torvald.

HELMER: To desert your home, your husband and your children! And you don't consider what people will say!

NORA: I cannot consider that at all. I only know that it is necessary for me.

HELMER: It's shocking. This is how you would neglect your most sacred duties.

NORA: What do you consider my most sacred duties?   310

HELMER: Do I need to tell you that? Are they not your duties to your husband and your children?

NORA: I have other duties just as sacred.

HELMER: That you have not. What duties could those be?

NORA: Duties to myself.

HELMER: Before all else, you are a wife and a mother.   315

NORA: I don't believe that any longer. I believe that before all else I am a reasonable human being, just as you are—or, at all events, that I must try and become one. I know quite well, Torvald, that most people would think you right, and that views of that kind are to be found in books; but I can no longer content myself with what most people say, or with what is found in books. I must think over things for myself and get to understand them.

HELMER: Can you not understand your place in your own home? Have you not a reliable guide in such matters as that?—have you no religion?

NORA: I am afraid, Torvald, I do not exactly know what religion is.

HELMER: What are you saying?

NORA: I know nothing but what the clergyman said when I went to be confirmed. He told   320 us that religion was this, and that, and the other. When I am away from all this, and am alone, I will look into that matter too. I will see if what the clergyman said is true, or at all events if it is true for me.

HELMER: This is unheard of in a girl of your age! But if religion cannot lead you aright, let me try and awaken your conscience. I suppose you have some moral sense? Or—answer me—am I to think you have none?

NORA: I assure you, Torvald, that is not an easy question to answer. I really don't know. The thing perplexes me altogether. I only know that you and I look at it in quite a different light. I am learning, too, that the law is quite another thing from what I supposed; but I find it impossible to convince myself that the law is right. According to it a woman has no right to spare her old dying father, or to save her husband's life. I can't believe that.

HELMER: You talk like a child. You don't understand the conditions of the world in which you live.

NORA: No, I don't. But now I am going to try. I am going to see if I can make out who is right, the world or I.

HELMER: You are ill, Nora; you are delirious; I almost think you are out of your mind.   325

NORA: I have never felt my mind so clear and certain as to-night.

HELMER: And is it with a clear and certain mind that you forsake your husband and your children?

NORA: Yes, it is.

HELMER: Then there is only one possible explanation.

NORA: What is that?   330

HELMER: You do not love me any more.

NORA: No, that is just it.

HELMER: Nora!—and you can say that?

NORA: It gives me great pain, Torvald, for you have always been so kind to me, but I cannot help it. I do not love you any more.

HELMER: [*regaining his composure*] Is that a clear and certain conviction too?   335

NORA: Yes, absolutely clear and certain. That is the reason why I will not stay here any longer.

HELMER: And can you tell me what I have done to forfeit your love?

NORA: Yes, indeed I can. It was to-night, when the wonderful thing did not happen; then I saw you were not the man I had thought you.

HELMER: Explain yourself better—I don't understand you.

340 NORA: I have waited so patiently for eight years; for, goodness knows, I knew very well that wonderful things don't happen every day. Then this horrible misfortune came upon me; and then I felt quite certain that the wonderful thing was going to happen at last. When Krogstad's letter was lying out there, never for a moment did I imagine that you would consent to accept this man's conditions. I was so absolutely certain that you would say to him: Publish the thing to the whole world. And when that was done—

HELMER: Yes, what then?—when I had exposed my wife to shame and disgrace?

NORA: When that was done, I was so absolutely certain, you would come forward and take everything upon yourself, and say: I am the guilty one.

HELMER: Nora—!

NORA: You mean that I would never have accepted such a sacrifice on your part? No, of course not. But what would my assurances have been worth against yours? That was the wonderful thing which I hoped for and feared; and it was to prevent that, that I wanted to kill myself.

345 HELMER: I would gladly work night and day for you, Nora—bear sorrow and want for your sake. But no man would sacrifice his honour for the one he loves.

NORA: It is a thing hundreds of thousands of women have done.

HELMER: Oh, you think and talk like a heedless child.

NORA: Maybe. But you neither think nor talk like the man I could bind myself to. As soon as your fear was over—and it was not fear for what threatened me, but for what might happen to you—when the whole thing was past, as far as you were concerned it was exactly as if nothing at all had happened. Exactly as before, I was your little skylark, your doll, which you would in future treat with doubly gentle care, because it was so brittle and fragile. [*getting up*] Torvald—it was then it dawned upon me that for eight years I had been living here with a strange man, and had borne him three children—. Oh, I can't bear to think of it! I could tear myself into little bits!

HELMER: [*sadly*] I see, I see. An abyss has opened between us—there is no denying it. But, Nora, would it not be possible to fill it up?

350 NORA: As I am now, I am no wife for you.

HELMER: I have it in me to become a different man.

NORA: Perhaps—if your doll is taken away from you.

HELMER: But to part!—to part from you! No, no, Nora, I can't understand that idea.

NORA: [*going out to the right*] That makes it all the more certain that it must be done.

[*She comes back with her cloak and hat and a small bag which she puts on a chair by the table.*]

355 HELMER: Nora, Nora, not now! Wait till to-morrow.

NORA: [*putting on her cloak*] I cannot spend the night in a strange man's room.

HELMER: But can't we live here like brother and sister—?

NORA: [*putting on her hat*] You know very well that would not last long. [*puts the shawl round her*] Good-bye, Torvald. I won't see the little ones. I know they are in better hands than mine. As I am now, I can be of no use to them.

HELMER: But some day, Nora—some day?

360 NORA: How can I tell? I have no idea what is going to become of me.

HELMER: But you are my wife, whatever becomes of you.

NORA: Listen, Torvald. I have heard that when a wife deserts her husband's house, as I am doing now, he is legally freed from all obligations towards her. In any case I set you free from all your obligations. You are not to feel yourself bound in the slightest way, any more than I shall. There must be perfect freedom on both sides. See here is your ring back. Give me mine.

HELMER: That too?

NORA: That too.

HELMER: Here it is.   365

NORA: That's right. Now it is all over. I have put the keys here. The maids know all about everything in the house—better than I do. To-morrow, after I have left her, Christine will come here and pack up my own things that I brought with me from home. I will have them sent after me.

HELMER: All over! All over!—Nora, shall you never think of me again?

NORA: I know I shall often think of you and the children and this house.

HELMER: May I write to you, Nora?

NORA: No—never. You must not do that.   370

HELMER: But at least let me send you—

NORA: Nothing—nothing—

HELMER: Let me help you if you are in want.

NORA: No. I can receive nothing from a stranger.

HELMER: Nora—can I never be anything more than a stranger to you?   375

NORA: [taking her bag] Ah, Torvald, the most wonderful thing of all would have to happen.

HELMER: Tell me what that would be!

NORA: Both you and I would have to be so changed that—. Oh, Torvald, I don't believe any longer in wonderful things happening.

HELMER: But I will believe in it. Tell me? So changed that—?

NORA: That our life together would be a real wedlock. Good-bye.   380

[She goes out through the hall.]

HELMER: [sinks down on a chair at the door and buries his face in his hands] Nora! Nora! [looks round, and rises] Empty. She is gone. [A hope flashes across his mind.] The most wonderful thing of all—?

[The sound of a door slamming is heard from below.]

QUESTIONS

Act 1

1. What does the opening stage direction reveal about the Helmer family? About the time of year?

2. Explain the ways Nora and Torvald behave toward each other.

3. What does Torvald's refusal to consider borrowing and debt tell you about him (speech 22)? Where else in the play are these characteristics important?

4. What have the Helmer finances been like in the past? How is their situation about to change?

5. How are Mrs. Linde and Nora alike? Different? Why is it ironic that Nora helps Christine get a job at the bank? How will this affect Krogstad? Nora?

6. How does Ibsen show that Krogstad is a threat when he first appears?

7. Why should Nora's scene with her children in Act 1 not be cut in production? What does it show about Nora and the household?

8. What is Nora's secret "crime"? What is the explanation and justification for it? At the end of the act, what new problems does she face?

Act 2

9. What is symbolized by the stripped Christmas tree?

10. What is implied about Nora's self-perceptions when she calls herself "your little squirrel" and "your skylark"?

11. After sending Krogstad's dismissal, Torvald tells Nora that "You will see I am man enough to take everything upon myself" (speech 135). How does this speech conform to Nora's hopes? How is it ironic?

12. Why does Nora flirt with Dr. Rank? How and why does he distress her?

13. Why does Nora dance the tarantella so wildly?

14. What is the "wonderful thing" that Nora is waiting for?

Act 3

15. Explain Christine's past rejection of Krogstad. Why will she accept him now? How will their union differ from the Helmers' marriage?

16. What does Christine decide to do about Krogstad's letter? Why?

17. Explain the reactions of Torvald and Nora to the death of Dr. Rank.

18. Describe Torvald's reaction to Krogstad's first letter. How does Nora respond to Torvald? How do you respond to him? Why?

19. Explain what Nora learns about Torvald, herself, her marriage, and her identity as a woman as a result of Torvald's responses. Why does she decide to leave?

GENERAL QUESTIONS

1. Which elements and aspects of *A Dollhouse* are most and least realistic? Explain.

2. Consider Ibsen's symbolism, with reference to Dr. Rank, macaroons, the Christmas tree, the presents, the locked mailbox, the dance, Nora's black shawl, her change of clothing in Act 3, and the door slam at the play's close.

3. Is Nora a victim of circumstances or a villain who brings about problems? What is Ibsen's view? What is yours? Why?

4. Describe the "role-playing" in the Helmer marriage. Does any evidence suggest that Nora knows she is playing a role? What degree of self-awareness, if any, characterizes Torvald's role-playing?

5. When Nora asks Torvald to restore Krogstad's job, Torvald refuses on the ground that he should not give in to his wife's pressure (Act 2, speech 113). Later, he claims that their marriage is destroyed, but that they should keep up the appearance of marital stability (Act 3, speech 242). In the light of such statements, describe Torvald's character. What concerns him most about life and marriage?

6. A major theme in the play is that weakness and corruption are passed from generation to generation. Examine this theme in connection with Krogstad and his sons, Nora and her children, Nora and her father, and Dr. Rank.

7. Discuss the ideas about individual growth, marriage, and social convention in the play. How are these ideas developed and related? Which character most closely embodies Ibsen's ideas?

8. Write an essay about any or all of the following questions:

    a. Is *A Dollhouse* a comedy, a tragedy, or something in between?

    b. How do the play's characters change for the better (or worse)?

    c. How negative, or affirmative, is the conclusion? Why?

Edited Selections from Criticism of Ibsen's *A Dollhouse* and Other Plays

The following selected criticism is intended to supply details and ideas for research essays on Ibsen's *A Dollhouse*. For a more detailed bibliography, consult the "Bibliographic Studies" section (pp. 1776–77), which may be augmented with your college library catalogue and the most recent volumes of the *MLA International Bibliography* available in your library's reference section together with online references. The bracketed page numbers in these selections refer to the original pagination of the sources included here. Footnotes, original passages in Norwegian, and unnecessary references have been deleted in these selections.

1. Freedom, Truth, and Society—Rhetoric and Reality[2]

During the night of 9 January 1871, a young Dane lay awake in his hospital bed in Rome writing. He was committing to paper a poem to which he had given the title "To Henrik Ibsen." He had recently received a letter from Ibsen—a letter carrying a powerful appeal to him to put himself at the head of the "revolution of the human spirit" which the age cried out for. In the poem which formed his enthusiastic response, the young Dane—the critic Georg Brandes (1842–1927)—described how all those mendacious and authoritarian forces of the contemporary age would be brought low when "the intellectuals" made their revolt. And he raised the banner of freedom and progress with the words: "Truth and Freedom are one and the same." [68]

Time after time in the years that followed, Ibsen was himself to raise this same revolutionary banner—with truth and freedom as the central watchwords. In later years these concepts could sound both abstract and ambiguous; nevertheless, within their historical context, they served as a battle cry in the struggle against the prevailing situation. "Truth" alone—that truth of the new age such as a Brandes and an Ibsen saw it—could achieve liberation. Without truth there could be no change, no genuine "freedom." This was the ideological basis for that quartet of realistic social plays which Ibsen published in the years between 1877 and 1882: *Pillars of Society, A Doll's House, Ghosts* and *An Enemy of the People*. In both the first and the last of these plays the double-barrelled phrase "truth and freedom" is used as a rallying cry and as a definition of what in the final instance the problematic reality of the day—"society"—lacked. This was the battle-ground on which Ibsen and Brandes found each other and where they could make common cause. However unlike they may have been, one thing they were agreed on: that *they* were conducting the case for progress and the future. They did not stand alone, but they must be counted as the indisputable leaders in the campaign for a modern, radical and realistic literature in the cultural life of Scandinavia of this age. It was [69]

[2]From Bjørn Hemmer, "Ibsen and the Realistic Problem Drama," in James McFarlane, ed., *The Cambridge Companion to Ibsen* (Cambridge: Cambridge UP, 1994).

these two who most powerfully challenged the values of the existing middle-class society and who formulated the basic rights and liberties of the individual.

In November of the same year in which he wrote his poem to Ibsen, Brandes began a series of public lectures in Copenhagen on the literature of nineteenth-century Europe. These lectures provoked great attention and controversy, precisely because in them Brandes called upon writers to revolt. He did it in the light of an ideology of liberation which he himself linked directly to the ideas of freedom which underlay the French Revolution of 1789.

His main concern, Brandes declared, was not *political* opposition, for political liberty had very largely been assured. What was at stake was "liberty of the spirit," "liberty of thought and of the human condition." The entire range of "social values" would have to be changed radically by the younger generation before a new and vigorous literature could begin any new growth. But in Brandes's view it was surely the writers themselves who ought to take the lead in this work on behalf of progress.

What Brandes directs his criticism against is a conservative, stagnant society which "under the mask of liberty has all the features of tyranny." His target is Victorian society with its facade of false morality and its manipulation of public opinion. It is this same kind of society that Ibsen turns the searchlight on in his first realistic dramas. The people who live in such a society know the weight of "public opinion" and of all those agencies which keep watch over society's "law and order": the norms, the conventions and the traditions which in essence belong to the past but which continue into the present and there thwart individual liberty in a variety of ways. Not all see this as a problem. Consul Bernick, the bank manager Torvald Helmer and Pastor Manders have all accepted the premises for this kind of bourgeois living and have adapted to society's demands—without any awareness of the cost in human terms. In their own estimation, their task is to confirm the existing social structure—"pillars of society."

[70] The point that Ibsen and Brandes were making was that this kind of society could not satisfy the natural need of the individual for freedom. It all had to do with power, with status and with the role of the sexes. The repressive attitude of bourgeois society towards everything that threatened its own position of power demonstrated only too clearly how far it had moved from the standpoint of the revolutionary citizens of 1789. The question of political and spiritual liberty had been thrust into the background by what had constantly been the motivating force in the life of the individual: economic freedom. Capital gave a position of power in society; and once those positions had been won, the bourgeois individual had acquired something which had to be defended. In this way, the bourgeois individual became a defender of the status quo and a traitor to his own officially expressed values. Official rhetoric was one thing; the realities on the other hand were something else.

It is this which forms the background to Ibsen's and Brandes's criticism of contemporary society. They found in their age a clear dichotomy between ideology and practice, a contradiction between the official and the private life of the bourgeois individual. Behind the splendour of the Victorian family facade there was to be found a much murkier reality. It was precisely these contradictions, this problematical element, in the bourgeois world that Ibsen made his special field as a realistic commentator on contemporary life. Both Ibsen and Brandes wanted to make the individual the sustaining element in society and thereby dethrone the bourgeois family as the central institution of society. From the perspective of the bourgeois individual the family is a micro-society which mirrors the nature of the macro-society and which is to bear witness to its health. In *Pillars of Society* the scoundrelly Consul Bernick is praised by the young teacher Rørlund for his "exemplary family life"; and the consul's fellow-conspirator, the businessman Rummel, delivers himself of the following pronouncement: "A man's home ought to be like a showcase." But he himself recommends an *arranged* family tableau behind the glass walls.

In the spirit of liberalism, Ibsen lets the individual's status in the family stand as an illustration of his position in the wider society. The power structure within the walls of the domestic home reflects the hierarchical power structures which prevail in the wider world. But those who participate in public life also encounter other repressive forces. Consul Bernick eventually admits that he feels like an isolated tool of an uncomprehending and crippled society, controlled in all his actions.

The main social perspective in Ibsen's first realistic plays coincides with the [71] perspective of Brandes's lecture series on "Main Currents in Nineteenth Century Literature." Here Brandes had presented a well-formulated programme for a new "modern" literature. His challenge to his fellow authors was primarily that they should enter into their own times and make contemporary concrete reality the subject of their writing: "What shows a literature in our own day to be a living thing is the fact of its subjecting problems to debate . . . For a literature to submit nothing to debate is tantamount to its being in the process of losing all significance."

What sort of "problems" he had in mind is illustrated by the examples he immediately adduces: marriage, religion, property rights, the relationships between the sexes, and social conditions. The objectives of his programme seem to have been both social and aesthetic. Brandes's idea was not that literature should become an instrument of abstract debate about prevailing social problems; his intention was to point out that if literature was to have any useful function at all, it had to come to grips with those conditions which invade and determine the concrete existence of the individual. Literature—as he put it—was to deal with "our life," not with "our dreams."

If Ibsen's dramas in the period 1877 to 1882 have come to be designated as realistic *problem* plays, this has to be seen against the background of Brandes's formula-like statement. Some Ibsen scholars prefer the rubric "critical realism"; others again have chosen to apply the term "modern contemporary drama" to the whole series of works after 1877. Each of these different designations nevertheless has a bearing on one or other of the central elements in the kind of literary realism which Ibsen practised: on social problems, on critical perspective and contemporaneity. Indeed this last is often accepted as one of the defining characteristics of realism: "*Il faut être de temps.*"

Within the framework of these dramas, Ibsen concentrates on some phase in [72] the contemporary situation where a latent crisis suddenly becomes visible. In this way he was able to embody contemporary social problems through the medium of an individual's destiny. This is another of realism's main tenets in the matter of individual characterization: the particular is to throw light on the general, and from one's response to a particular individual one should be able to glimpse the socially representative type. This, according to René Wellek, is an almost universal demand in theories of realism. It marks not only a polemical break with romantic characterization, but is also linked to realism's demand for objective reality and to its implicit didactic tendency. "Truth" and "sincerity" are concepts central to Linda Nochlin's account of the realists' own definition of where they stand. It may sound paradoxical to say that the realists combined on the one hand a wish for the objective presentation of reality with a didactic purpose on the other; but the paradox is illusory. A work of realism aspires to convey a moral message of general validity, and this is why the realist has need of the socially representative type. In Ibsen this sometimes leads to a difficult balancing act between over-explicitness and caricatured characterization on the one hand, and on the other an objective evocation of plausible human types, where the author's presence is less evident. Viewed from a later standpoint in time, there are some things—particularly his treatment of selected male characters—that might prompt one to set a question mark against his "realism."

* * *

[73]   In his poetic practice, Ibsen demonstrates time after time that he conceives of truth as something individual and subjective. It is always the minority which is right. This is why he lets Nora go out into the world alone both to find out who she really is and to be able to re-assess values and concepts. Ibsen has her sweep aside any doubts about what the problem is: "I must try to discover who is right, society or me." She admits her husband is right when he says she no longer understands the society they live in. As a dramatist, Ibsen must make it evident to his audience that Nora, as the drama moves towards its close, is truer and freer than before—and that her path is one of general validity. Helmer has mobilized the rhetoric of established society to keep Nora within the framework of the community and of the family. The reaction of the public was—and possibly still is—dependent on whether Nora's (and Ibsen's) use of an alternative rhetoric carries greater weight and conviction.

Nora's situation illustrates the pattern central to Ibsen's realistic problem dramas: the individual in opposition to a hostile society. The structure of the conflict is simple—and nobody can be in any doubt as to where the author's sympathies lie. Collective aberration about which ideals or values are true and which are false means that Ibsen sets in motion a process whereby concepts which are central to the bourgeois world are subject to re-definition. It is a striking feature of, for example, *Ghosts* that the reactionary Manders and the radical Helene Alving both make use of the concept of "the ideal," despite their having totally contradictory views of the meaning of "truth" and of individual "freedom" in life. Ibsen clearly saw that the concepts of established bourgeois society needed a new content—something which he himself drew attention to in a letter to Brandes. In this same letter he writes of the need for "a revolution of the human spirit," and claimed that the 1789 rallying-cry of "Liberty, equality, fraternity" needed filling with new meaning.

Perhaps the battle-lines between the conservative bourgeoisie and the radical [74] intelligentsia in Scandinavia in this age of Ibsen and Brandes were not as clearly drawn as all this might suggest. The literary history of Northern Europe has very largely been based on the premises of radicalism. The perspective may not entirely falsify history, but it does somewhat oversimplify it. There are distinctly conservative elements to be found in Ibsen's works of social criticism; and he gave clear acknowledgement of the part he played within the society he was attacking: "One never stands totally without some share of responsibility or guilt in the society to which one belongs." This is why he defines, in one and the same breath, the writing of poetry as the passing of judgement upon one's own self. Some of the phenomena he criticized were things he well knew from his own inner life. Honest introspection—what he was inclined to call "self-anatomy"—had made it clear to him that he too bore the stamp of the Victorian society of the day. Life and learning were not always the same, as he admitted in a speech to Norwegian students in Christiania in 1874, The irony directed at those who histrionically held high the banner of the ideal at no great cost to themselves lost none of its point when applied to himself and to fellow writers.

Nevertheless he stood distanced, an outsider, from the society he was criticizing. Like Brandes, he was marginalized in respect of the collective life of his own people—not least by the concrete fact of his own twenty-seven years in exile. It was a stance which gave Ibsen both a personal freedom as an artist and also the clarifying perspective of distance—something he always claimed as a necessity for himself as a writer.

It is something of a paradox that, in this socially critical phase of his authorship, he was able to create a large and broadly based market among the wider European public for his art. What he had to offer to this bourgeois public was a successive chronicling of their own vices and lies. Granted the setting of his works was Norwegian, but the perspective on Victorian morality was international enough when he allowed it to reveal its defects.

It is not to be wondered at that Ibsen's dramas provoked scandal and outrage. [75] Yet at the same time he won a large following, including many of those whom he had attacked. Even a proportion of "the pillars of society" found it worthwhile to listen to what this author had to say. This could well imply that bourgeois society had not entirely lost its sense of its past and of its own lost ideals. Even bourgeois society was ready to acknowledge that contemporary reality might have its problems—with socially destabilizing phenomena like industrialization, positivism, liberalism, secularization, political polarization and the like. Society in the 1870s was becoming increasingly fluid. Only the most conservative forces wished to defend its "law and order" by neutralizing such "enemies of the people" as Ibsen and Brandes. But strong resistance could be found—and this gave Ibsen an adversary and the stuff of conflict for his dramas. The opposition consisted of all those who wished to withdraw within the circle of their own little community, their small township or their family—there to defend their world against the threat from the new or larger world "out there." Ibsen himself in these years was a resident of this wider and freer European cultural scene. And he wrote about Norwegian provincial life. When for his first realistic problem drama he chose as its setting "a small, Norwegian coastal town," this was clearly connected to its being a milieu he was greatly familiar with from his childhood and early years. As an observant outsider he had lived in a small community of this kind—in Grimstad in the 1840s—and it was here he had first begun his career as a writer. Patterns and tensions—social, economic and psychological—present themselves much more clearly in a small and easily surveyable community of this kind than in a larger and more pluralist society. For a dramatist, a society of this sort could nicely function as a social laboratory.

2. Ibsen's Feminist Characters[3]

[34] Anyone who claims that Ibsen thought of Nora as a silly, hysterical, or selfish woman is either ignoring or misrepresenting the plain truth, present from the earliest to the most recent biographies, that Ibsen admired, even adored, Nora Helmer. Among all his characters, she was the one he liked best and found most real. While working on *A Doll House*, he announced to Suzannah Ibsen, his wife, "I've just seen Nora. She came right over to me and put her hand on my shoulder." The quick-witted Suzannah replied at once, "What was she wearing?" In a perfectly serious tone, Ibsen answered, "A simple blue woolen dress."

[35]   After *A Doll House* had made him famous, Ibsen was fond of explaining that his heroine's "real" name was "Eleanora" but that she had been called "Nora" from childhood. Bergliot Bjornson Ibsen, the playwright's daughter-in-law, tells the story of how she and her husband, Sigurd, on one of the last occasions on which they saw Ibsen out of bed in the year he died, asked permission to name their newborn daughter "Eleanora." Ibsen was greatly moved. "God bless you, Bergliot," he said to her. He had, in fact, christened his own Nora with a precious gift, for both "Nora" and "Eleanora" were names given to the sister of Ole Schulerud, one of the few close friends of Ibsen's life, who in the early years of grinding poverty believed in Ibsen's genius and tirelessly hawked his first play to bookseller after bookseller, finally spending his small inheritance to pay for its publication.

Ibsen was inspired to write *A Doll House* by the terrible events in the life of his protégé Laura Petersen Kieler, a Norwegian journalist of whom he was extremely fond. Married to a man with a phobia about debt, she had secretly borrowed money to finance an Italian journey necessary for her husband's recovery from tuberculosis. She worked frantically to reimburse the loan, exhausting herself in turning out hackwork, and when her earnings proved insufficient, in desperation she forged a check. On discovering the crime, her husband demanded a legal separation on the grounds that she was an unfit mother and had her placed in an asylum, where she was put in the insane ward. Throughout the affair, Ibsen, her confidant and adviser, was greatly disturbed; he brooded on the wife, "forced to spill her heart's blood," as he wrote in a letter to her, and on the oblivious husband, allowing his wife to slave away on unworthy jobs, concerned neither about her physical welfare nor her work. Having done all for love, Laura Kieler was

---

[3]From Joan Templeton, "The *Doll House* Backlash: Criticism, Feminism, and Ibsen." PMLA 104 (1989): 28–40.

treated monstrously for her efforts by a husband obsessed with his standing in the eyes of the world. In Ibsen's working notes for *A Doll House* we find:

> She has committed forgery, and is proud of it; for she has done it out of love for her husband, to save his life. But this husband of hers takes his standpoint, conventionally honorable, on the side of the law, and sees the situation with male eyes.

The conflict between love and law, between heart and head, between feminine and masculine, is the moral center of *A Doll House*. But Ibsen would sharpen life's blurred edges to meet art's demand for plausibility. The heroine would be a housewife, not a writer, and the hackwork not bad novels but copying; her antagonist, the husband, would not be a cruel brute but a kind guardian: rather than put her into an asylum, he would merely denounce her as an unfit wife and mother, permitting her to receive bed and board, and then, once his reputation was safe, would offer to forgive her and take her back on the spot. The Helmers, in other words, would be "normal." And this normality would transform a sensational *fait divers* into a devastating picture of the ordinary relations between wife and husband and allow Ibsen to treat what he called, in a letter to Edmund Gosse, "the problems of married life." Moreover, he would reverse the ending: the original Nora, the career journalist, had begged to be taken back; his housewife would sadly, emphatically refuse to stay.

A year after *A Doll House* appeared, when Ibsen was living in Rome, a Scandinavian woman arrived there, who had left her husband and small daughter to run away with her lover. The Norwegian exile community considered her behavior unnatural and asked Ibsen what he thought. "It is not unnatural, only it is unusual" was Ibsen's opinion. The woman made it a point to speak with Ibsen, but to her surprise he treated her offhandedly. "Well, I did the same thing your Nora did," she said, offended. Ibsen replied quietly, "My Nora went alone."

A favorite piece of evidence in the argument that Ibsen was not interested in women's rights is his aversion to John Stuart Mill. It is popular to quote Ibsen's remark to Georg Brandes about Mill's declaration that he owed the best things in his writing to his wife, Harriet Taylor: "'Fancy!' [Ibsen] said smiling, 'if you had to read Hegel or Krause with the thought that you did not know for certain whether it was Mr. or Mrs. Hegel, Mr. or Mrs. Krause you had before you!'" But in fact, Brandes, one of Ibsen's closest associates and probably the critic who understood him best, reports this mot in a discussion of Ibsen's wholehearted support of the women's movement. He notes that Mill's assertion "seemed especially ridiculous to Ibsen, with his marked individualism," and explains that although Ibsen had at first little sympathy for feminism—perhaps, Brandes guesses, because of "irritation at some of the ridiculous forms the movement assumed"—this initial response gave way "to a sympathy all the more enthusiastic" when he saw that it was "one of the great rallying points in the battle of progress." [36]

A well-known, perhaps embarrassing fact about Ibsen, never brought up in discussions disclaiming his interest in women's rights, is that when he made the banquet speech denying that he had consciously worked for the movement, he was primarily interested in young women and annoyed by the elderly feminists who surrounded him. During the seventieth-birthday celebrations, Ibsen constantly exhibited his marked and, as Michael Meyer has it, "rather pathetic longing for young girls." He had already had several romantic friendships, including one that had caused a family scandal and threatened to wreck his marriage. In the light of this fully documented biographical information about the aging playwright, is his intention in *A Doll House* more likely to be revealed by what he said in irritation at a banquet or by what he wrote twenty years earlier in sketching out his play?

> A woman cannot be herself in the society of today, which is exclusively a masculine society, with laws written by men, and with accusers and judges who judge feminine conduct from the masculine standpoint.

A Doll House is not about Everybody's struggle to find him- or herself but, according to its author, about Everywoman's struggle against Everyman.

A Doll House is a natural development of the play Ibsen had just written, the unabashedly feminist *Pillars of Society*; both plays reflect Ibsen's extremely privileged feminist education, which he shared with few other nineteenth-century male authors and which he owed to a trio of extraordinary women: Suzannah Thoresen Ibsen, his wife; Magdalen Thoresen, his colleague at the Norwegian National Theatre in Bergen, who was Suzannah's stepmother and former governess; and Camilla Wergeland Collett, Ibsen's literary colleague, valued friend, and the founder of Norwegian feminism.

Magdalen Thoresen wrote novels and plays and translated the French plays Ibsen put on as a young stage manager at the Bergen theater. She was probably the first "New Woman" he had ever met. She pitied the insolvent young writer, took him under her wing, and brought him home. She had passed her strong feminist principles on to her charge, the outspoken and irrepressible Suzannah, who adored her strong-minded stepmother and whose favorite author was George Sand. The second time Ibsen met Suzannah he asked her to marry him. Hjordis, the fierce shield-maiden of *The Vikings at Helgeland*, the play of their engagement, and Svanhild, the strong-willed heroine of *Love's Comedy*, the play that followed, owe much to Suzannah Thoresen Ibsen. Later, Nora's way of speaking would remind people of Suzannah's.

The third and perhaps most important feminist in Ibsen's life was his friend Camilla Collett, one of the most active feminists in nineteenth-century Europe and founder of the modern Norwegian novel. Fifteen years before Mill's *Subjection of Women*, Collett wrote *Amtmandens Døtre (The Governor's Daughters)*. Faced with the choice of a masculine nom de plume or no name at all on the title page, Collett brought out her novel anonymously in two parts in 1854 and 1855, but she nonetheless became widely known as the author. Its main argument, based on the general feminist claim that women's feelings matter, is that women should have the right to educate themselves and to marry whom they please. In the world of the governor's daughters, it is masculine success that matters. Brought up to be ornaments and mothers, women marry suitable men and devote their lives to their husbands' careers and to their children. The novel, a cause célèbre, made Collett famous overnight.

Collett regularly visited the Ibsens in their years of exile in Germany, and she and Suzannah took every occasion to urge Ibsen to take up the feminist cause. They had long, lively discussions in the years preceding *A Doll House*, when feminism had become a strong movement and the topic of the day in Scandinavia. Collett was in Munich in 1877, when Ibsen was hard at work on *Pillars of Society*, and Ibsen's biographer Koht speculates that Ibsen may have deliberately prodded her to talk about the women's movement in order to get material for his dialogue. In any case, the play undoubtedly owes much to the conversations in the Ibsen household, as well as to the Norwegian suffragette Aasta Hansteen, the most notorious woman in the country. Deliberately provocative, Hansteen took to the platform wearing men's boots and carrying a whip to protect herself against the oppressor. A popular news item during the Ibsens' visit to Norway in 1874, Hansteen became the model for Lona Hessel, the shocking *raisonneuse* of *Pillars of Society.*

The play opens with a striking image of woman's place in the world: eight [37] ladies participating in what has been, since antiquity, the most quintessentially female activity in literature—they are "busy sewing"—as they listen to the town schoolmaster read aloud from *Woman as the Servant of Society.* Lona Hessel bursts in, and when the ladies ask her how she can aid their "Society for the Morally Disabled," she suggests, "I can air it out." Returning from America, where she is rumored to have sung in saloons (even for money!), lectured, and written a book, Lona is the New Woman with a vengeance who teaches the others the truth. Lona had loved Bernick, but she packed her bags when he rejected her to marry for money. Bernick turns out not to have been much of a loss, however; he has reduced his wife, Betty, to an obedient cipher and made a personal servant of his sister, Martha, a paradigm of the nineteenth-century spinster who devotes her life to a male relative. Martha's story may have had its source in *The Governor's Daughters.* Like Collett's Margarethe, Martha had once loved a young man but, too modest to declare her feelings, suffered in silence. She now lives for her brother, who is insufferable when he speaks of her; she is a "nonentity," he explains, "who'll take on whatever comes along." It is in explaining Martha's exemplary function in life that Bernick speaks the line, "People shouldn't always be thinking of themselves first, especially women." Dina Dorf, Bernick's ward, disregards this happy maxim, and though she agrees to marry, she tells her husband-to-be, "But first I want to work, become something the way you have. I don't want to be a thing that's just taken along." Dina knows beforehand what Nora learns after eight years of marriage: "I have to try to educate myself. . . . I've got to do it alone."

Pillars of Society, little known and played outside Scandinavia and Germany, is one of the most radically feminist works of nineteenth-century literature. Ibsen took the old maid, the butt of society's ridicule, a figure of pity and contempt, and made her a heroine. Rejected as unfit to be a wife, Lona Hessel refuses to sacrifice herself to a surrogate family and escapes to the New World, where she leads an independent, authentic life. As *raisonneuse,* she summarizes his point of view for Bernick and the rest: "This society of yours is a bachelors' club. You don't see women."

It is simply not true, then, that Ibsen was not interested in feminism. It is also not true that "there is no indication that Ibsen was thinking of writing a feminist play when he first began to work seriously on *A Doll House* in the summer of 1879." In the spring of that year, while Ibsen was planning his play, a scandalous incident, easily available in the biographies, took place that proves not only Ibsen's interest in women's rights but his passionate support for the movement. Ibsen had made two proposals to the Scandinavian Club in Rome, where he was living: that the post of librarian be opened to women candidates and that women be allowed to vote in club meetings. In the debate on the proposal, he made a long, occasionally eloquent speech, part of which follows:

> Is there anyone in this gathering who dares assert that our ladies are inferior to us in culture, or intelligence, or knowledge, or artistic talent? I don't think many men would dare suggest that. Then what is it men fear? I hear there is a tradition here that women are cunning intriguers, and that therefore we don't want them. Well, I have encountered a good deal of male intrigue in my time.

Ibsen's first proposal was accepted, the second not, failing by one vote. He left the club in a cold rage. A few days later, he astonished his compatriots by appearing at a gala evening. People thought he was penitent. But he was planning a surprise: facing the ballroom and its dancing couples, he interrupted the music to make a terrible scene, haranguing the celebrants with a furious tirade. He had tried to bring them progress, he shouted, but their cowardly resistance had refused it. The women were especially contemptible, for it was for them he had tried to fight. A Danish countess fainted and had to be removed, but Ibsen continued, growing more and more violent. Gunnar Heiberg, who was present, later gave this account of the event:

> As his voice thundered it was as though he were clarifying his own thoughts, as his tongue chastised it was as though his spirit were scouring the darkness in search of his present spiritual goal—his poem [*A Doll House*]—as though he were personally bringing out his theories, incarnating his characters. And when he was done, he went out into the hall, took his overcoat and walked home.

[38]

In 1884, five years after *A Doll House* had made Ibsen a recognized champion of the feminist cause, he joined with H. E. Berner, president of the Norwegian Women's Rights League, and with his fellow Norwegian writers Bjornson, Lie, and Kielland, in signing a petition to the Storting, the Norwegian parliament, urging the passage of a bill establishing separate property rights for married women. When he returned the petition to Bjornson, Ibsen wryly commented that the Storting should not be interested in men's opinions: "To consult men in such a matter is like asking wolves if they desire better protection for the sheep." He also spoke of his fears that the current campaign for universal suffrage would come to nothing. The solution, which he despaired of seeing, would be the formation of a "strong, resolute progressive party" that would include in its goals "the statutory improvement of the position of woman."

It is foolish to apply the formalist notion that art is never sullied by argument to Ibsen's middle-period plays, written at a time when he was an outspoken and direct fighter in what he called the "mortal combat between two epochs." Ibsen was fiercely his own man, refusing all his life to be claimed by organizations or campaigns of many sorts, including the Women's Rights League and the movement to remove the mark of Sweden from the Norwegian flag. And he had a deeply conservative streak where manners were concerned (except when he lost his temper), for he was acutely suspicious of show. Temperamentally, Ibsen was a loner. But he was also, as Georg Brandes declared, "a born polemist." While it is true that Ibsen never reduced life to "ideas," it is equally true that he was passionately interested in the events and ideas of his day. He was as deeply anchored in his time as any writer has been before or since. Writing to his German translator a year after the publication of *A Doll House*, Ibsen offered one of the truest self-appraisals a writer has ever made:

> Everything that I have written is intimately connected with what I have lived through, even if I have not lived it myself. Every new work has served me as emancipation and catharsis; for none of us can escape the responsibility and the guilt of the society to which we belong.

3. "A Marxist Approach to *A Doll House*"[4]

Theatrical production is a process that illuminates the dramatic text, and criticism is the tool that enables theater artists to make the most effective choices. This is the central premise of Drama 102 (Play Analysis), in which we discuss eight or so plays from a variety of critical viewpoints. Although some of the plays lend themselves more readily to a particular kind of analysis (such as a Jungian reading of *The Emperor Jones*), we point out that this affinity should not exclude additional insights that can be gained from a structuralist or feminist reading. We stress that criticism is a preamble to production and that plays are complex and multifaceted. Moreover, we discourage the theatrical sleight of hand that frequently reduces plays to a single metaphor, and we encourage our students to view drama through the lenses of differing approaches.

    In teaching *A Doll House* we first examine the text from a traditional point of view stressing historical and biographical considerations. We review Ibsen's commitment to women's rights and his interest in the career of Laura Kieler, who some critics believe was the model for Nora. Indeed, F. L. Lucas has stated that "one cannot fully understand Nora without knowing something of the strange, yet true story of Laura Kieler." By comparing the two women it is possible to watch Ibsen's heroine emerge from the despair and pain that characterized much of Kieler's life.

    Still, the historical and biographical approach is limiting, and our next step is to explore the play through another lens. (The metaphor of the "lens" we have found to be particularly effective since it implies that there are no right or wrong interpretations but rather discoveries that can be made by studying a play from more

[76]

---

[4]From Barry Witham and John Lutterbie, "A Marxist Approach to *A Doll House*," in Yvonne Shafer, ed., *Approaches to Teaching Ibsen's* A Doll House (New York: MLA, 1985).

than one vantage point.) The critical method that has stimulated many of our recent students—and that concerns us here—is a Marxist reading of the play. Marxist criticism is a complex topic, and, as the recent work of Fredric Jameson, Henri Arvon, and Raymond Williams exemplifies, critical methodologies vary widely. Moreover, many American students come to Marxist aesthetics with reluctance, conditioned partly by a distrust of all things Russian. Thus we try to emphasize specific issues on which critics agree, and we assign short readings from Terry Eagleton's *Marxism and Literary Criticism* as a point of departure.

It is important, of course, to review Marx's early writings with their humanistic focus and analysis of class structure. Notions of the dialectic and of human alienation are productive ways of introducing students to Marx since alienation seems to be a concept with which they can identify. This approach has the added value of breaking down some initial prejudices toward the subject matter. By stressing the human side of Marx's work, we can reduce student resistance and
[77] encourage a more objective view of the social analysis that follows.

We then talk about the text of the play as an objectification of the author's idea, a process that is a creative act but that in dialectical terms is imperfect because it can never completely express Ibsen's vision or totally repress unconscious ideas that shape the text. Drawing on both Terry Eagleton and Louis Althusser (*Lenin and Philosophy*), we define ideology as a false consciousness, a system of beliefs and ideas that functions to disguise the inequities of a class-based society. Using this definition to examine the play, we stress the concept that ideology is shaped by both what is in the text (Torvald's domination of Nora) and by what is "absent" (Nora's relationship with her mother). One of the primary goals of any Marxist analysis is the investigation of ideological content, and the existence of this content allows Marxist critics to argue that all works of art are political. This is a highly controversial point with many students, and the discussions often become heated as we examine its implications.

We then focus on the economic realities of Ibsen's world. *A Doll House* is especially suited to this type of examination because the bank—an obvious and blatant symbol for money—stands at the center of the play. Torvald has just been appointed manager. Mrs. Linde wants to work there, as does Krogstad. And Nora's jubilance at the beginning of the play is directly related to the financial security ensured by Torvald's new job. Moreover, an economic analysis quickly reveals how the consciousness of the characters is shaped and determined by their class and status. Even though Downs has argued that "except for three virtual supernumeraries, all the persons of the play belong to the educated middle class," it is clear that class differences do exist. Torvald stands for the moneyed elite—in this case the bank owners—while Mrs. Linde and Krogstad function as workers struggling to maintain a subsistence income.

A principal tenet of Marxist criticism is that human consciousness is a product of social conditions and that human relationships are often subverted by and through economic considerations. Mrs. Linde has sacrificed a genuine love to provide for her brothers, and Krogstad has committed a crime to support his children. Anne-Marie, the maid, has also been the victim of her economic background. Because she's "a girl who's poor and gotten in trouble," her relationship with her child has been interrupted and virtually destroyed. In each instance the need for money is linked with the ability to exist. But while the characters accept the social realities of their misfortunes, they do not appear to question how their human attitudes have been thoroughly shaped by socioeconomic considerations.

Once students begin to perceive how consciousness is affected by economics, a Marxist reading of Ibsen's play can illuminate a number of areas. Krogstad, for example, becomes less of a traditional villain when we realize that he is fighting for his job at the bank "as if it were life itself." And his realization of the senselessness of their lives is poignantly revealed when he reflects on Mrs. Linde's past, "all this simply for money." Even Dr. Rank speaks about his failing health and imminent death in entirely financial terms. "These past few days I've been auditing my internal accounts. Bankrupt! Within a month I'll probably be laid out and rotting in the churchyard." [78]

All these characters, however, serve as foils for the central struggle between Nora and Torvald and highlight the pilgrimage that Nora makes in the play. At the outset two things are clear: (1) Nora is enslaved by Torvald in economic terms, and (2) she equates personal freedom with the acquisition of wealth. The play begins joyfully not only because it is the holiday season but also because Torvald's promotion to bank manager will ensure "a safe, secure job with a comfortable salary." Nora is happy because she sees the future in wholly economic terms. "Won't it be lovely to have stacks of money and not a care in the world?"

What she learns, however, is that financial enslavement is symptomatic of other forms of enslavement—master–slave, male–female, sexual objectification, all of which characterize her relationship with Torvald—and that money is no guarantee of happiness. At the end of the play she renounces not only her marital vows but also her financial dependence because she has discovered that personal and human freedom are not measured in economic terms.

This discovery also prompts her to reexamine the society of which she is a part and leads us into a consideration of the ideology in the play. In what sense has Nora committed a criminal offense in forging her father's name? Is it indeed just that she should be punished for an altruistic act, one that cost her dearly both in terms of self-denial and the destruction of her family? Ibsen's defense of Nora is clear, of course, and his implicit indictment of a society that encourages this kind of injustice stimulates a discussion of the assumptions that created the law.

One of the striking things about *A Doll House* is how Anne-Marie accepts her alienation from her child as if it were natural, given the circumstances of class and money. It does not occur to her that laws were framed by other people and thus are capable of imperfection and susceptible to change. Nora broke a law that not only tries to stop thievery (the appropriation of capital) by outlawing forgery but also discriminates against anyone deemed a bad risk. Question leads to question as the class investigates why women were bad risks and why they had difficulty finding employment. It becomes obvious that the function of women in this society was not "natural" but artificial, a role created by their relationship to the family and by their subservience to men. In the marketplace they were a labor force expecting subsistence wages and providing an income to supplement that earned by their husbands or fathers. . . . [79]

Viewing the play through the lens of Marxist aesthetics does make one thing clear. Nora's departure had ramifications for her society that went beyond the marriage bed. By studying the play within the context of its socioeconomic structure, we can see how the ideology in the text affects the characters and how they perpetuate the ideology. The conclusion of *A Doll House* was a challenge to the economic superstructures that had controlled and excluded the Noras of the world by manipulating their economic status and, by extension, their conscious estimation of themselves and their place in society.

Chapter 28A

Writing a Research Essay on Drama

At the end of the fiction section of this book, Chapter 10A (p. 594) contains a chapter on the use of research as the basis of an essay of term-paper length on fiction. A shorter essay embodying research is included in Chapter 22A (p. 1195). Because the objects and goals of research are general, most of the materials in these research chapters are also essential for research projects in drama. It is therefore necessary to consult these earlier chapters for many relevant ways to engage in detailed research about drama as well as about both fiction and poetry.

Any of the questions and essay assignments on drama described in Chapters 23 to 28 can serve as the basic topic as a guide for you to find helpful research materials. Because of the general nature of research, research essays about drama are not markedly different from the research introduced in writing about fiction and poetry. As a help in such assignments with all the genres, there are extra materials for research in Chapter 9, on the fiction of Poe; in Chapter 21, on the poetry of Dickinson, Frost, Hughes, and Plath; and in Chapter 28, on the drama of Ibsen.

Topics to Discover in Research

Your goal in doing research on drama should always be to discover materials that have a meaningful bearing on the play or plays about which you are writing. As with both fiction and poetry, some things to look for might be these:

- *The period of time when the play was written, together with significant events.* In this section, Chapter 28A, the illustrative research essay on the Ghost in Shakespeare's *Hamlet* introduces sixteenth-century ideas about the nature of ghosts and the supernatural. If you look at the introductory material to Henley's *Am I Blue*, you will see that the play is dated very clearly in November 1968, and that particular events at that time may have a bearing on our understanding of the play.
- *Social, natural, and/or political circumstances at the time of the poem or poems.* What was the dominant political situation at the time? Who were the sorts of persons in political power? What attitudes were prevalent at the time with regard to the circumstances of nature? The characters in O'Neill's *Before Breakfast* are representative of people living close to the edge in New York's Greenwich Village in the second decade of the twentieth century, with all that this way of life implied.
- *Biographical details about a dramatist.* At what time in his or her life did the dramatist write the play? What kind of work was he or she doing at the time,

and which of his or her particular concerns might be relevant to our understanding of the play? Did the dramatist write anything about the play in personal correspondence, if any exists? What was this? Are there any results of
interviews with the dramatist that might be introduced to explain the play?
What were the dramatist's aims in creating the particular play, to the degree
that it is possible to discover these aims?

- *Specific or general thoughts by the dramatist that are relevant to the poem/poems.*
  Sometimes there might be details about a dramatist's thoughts on the thinking and reading he or she was doing, or on works of art seen, or on religious
  or philosophical musings. Sometimes these concerns must be inferred.
  Langston Hughes was deeply concerned about the circumstances of African
  Americans in the United States, and his *Mulatto* is a deeply felt play dramatizing his concerns. It is clear from *Tea Party* that Betty Keller was acutely aware
  of the difficult plight of aged people who are alone and increasingly helpless.

In planning your essay, you should aim at a normal type of essay for the play
you have chosen. Often, you might select an individual character and the importance of that character to the play's action or structure. Or, you may wish to describe the character's interests or language. Much of what you may do of course
depends on the nature of the play and what you discover about it. The section
"Writing About the Elements of Drama" in Chapter 23, beginning on page 1255,
will give you ideas for how to select and develop your topic. Of greatest importance, of course, is your integration of research discoveries into the development
of your essay. The following illustrative research essay indicates a term-paper
length treatment of the Ghost, a major character in Shakespeare's *Hamlet*. You will
observe that the essay treats the character of the Ghost, and also goes on to describe other aspects of the Ghost's significance in the play at large.

Illustrative Student Essay Written with the Aid of Research

Underlined sentences in this paper *do not* conform to MLA style and are used solely as teaching tools to
emphasize the central idea, thesis sentence, and topic sentences throughout the paper.

The Ghost in Hamlet°

Outline

**Use 1/2 inch top
margin, 1 inch
bottom and side
margin; double
space
throughout.**

I. Introduction

   A. The Importance of the Ghost in Hamlet

   B. The Ghost's Influence on the Play's Themes

°This play appears on pages 1323–1420.

II. The Ghost's Status as a Spirit

III. The Ghost's Character

IV. The Ghost's Importance in the Structure of the Play

V. The Ghost's Effect

VI. Conclusion

Kruse 1

Toni Ann Kruse

Professor Rios

English 364

10 May 2008

Center title one double space below
identifying information.

I. Introduction

A. The Importance of the Ghost in <u>Hamlet</u>

Even though the Ghost of Hamlet's father is present in only a few scenes

of Hamlet, he is a dominating presence.* He appears twice in the first scene,

and this entire scene itself is about the meaning of these and earlier

appearances. He enters again in the fourth scene of Act 1, when he beckons to

Hamlet and leads him offstage--in this way providing an early illustration of

Hamlet's courage (Edgar 257). In the fifth scene of Act 1 he speaks for the first

time, explaining how his brother Claudius murdered him, and exhorting his

son, Hamlet, to kill Claudius in retribution. Because this cry for revenge

directly or indirectly causes the rest of the play's action, it is clear, as Marjorie

Garber puts it, that "the dead man turned Ghost is more powerful than he was

when living" (304). After some words which the Ghost speaks from under the

stage, he does not enter again until the fourth scene of Act 3, in the queen's

private rooms, when he reveals himself to Hamlet--but not to Gertrude--to

reproach the Prince for not yet having killed Claudius. The Ghost is not present

at the play's end, but the actions he sets in motion are concluded there, and

hence his effect is always dominant.

In MLA style, the
header has the
student's last
name and page
number.

Put identifying
information in
upper left corner,
double space.

[1]

*Central idea.

Kruse 2

B. The Ghost's Influence on the Play's Themes

[2]

In MLA style, put only page number in parentheses when author is named in the sentence.

Not only is the Ghost dominant over actions, but he is also directly linked to many of the play's themes. William Kerrigan calls the Ghost a "nightmind" who introduces the mental darkness of evil that pervades the play (42). In addition, the Ghost intensifies the play's "interior suffering" (Paris 85). This suffering is brought out in Hamlet's anguished soliloquies and also in the pain of Ophelia, Laertes, and even Claudius himself. Another theme is shown by the Ghost's commands to Hamlet--those of responsibility, whether personal,

In MLA style, put author and page number in parentheses when author is not named in the sentence.

political, or conjugal (McFarland 15). Hamlet of course does not rush right out to kill Claudius, despite the Ghost's urgings, and hence the Ghost is indirectly responsible for the theme of hesitation--this great "Sphinx of modern Literature"--which has become one of the weaknesses cited most frequently about Hamlet's character (Jones 22). The Ghost's scary presence also poses questions about the power of superstition, terror, and fear (Campbell 211). Beyond all this, deeply within the psychological realm, the Ghost has been cited as a "confirmation" of the influence of "psychic residues in governing and shaping human life" (McFarland 34), not to mention the significance of the Oedipus complex in the development of Hamlet's character.

[3]

Because the Ghost is so important, one hardly needs to justify studying him. His importance can be traced in his spirit nature, his influence on the play's structure, and his effect on Hamlet and therefore indirectly on all the major characters.†

II. The Ghost's Status as a Spirit

[4]

When citing plays in MLA style, cite the act, scene, and line number.

The Ghost is shown as an apparition of questionable and vague status. When Hamlet first sees the Ghost, he asks whether he sees "a spirit of health, or goblin damned" (1.4.40). Horatio adds that Hamlet is "desperate with imagination" (1.4.87), thus throwing doubt on the Ghost's reality even though the vision is seen by everyone onstage. When speaking with Hamlet, the Ghost is vague about his out-of-earth location, complaining that he is suffering hellish

†Thesis sentence.

Kruse 3

fires but intimating that he will be compelled to do so only until his earthly sins are purged away. Although this description, according to Anthony Holden, indicates that "the Ghost . . . occupies an authentically Catholic version of Purgatory" (28), and Dobson and Wells state that "the Ghost seems to belong to a Catholic theology rather than a Protestant one" (182), Shakespeare's treatment is ambiguous. The Ghost says that he is allowed to walk the earth for a certain time--presumably, in the first act, only at night. But then, in Act 3, scene 4, the Ghost appears in the Queen's private room. Does this visit take place at night or during the day? This inconsistency about where and when the Ghost spends his time may have been deliberate on Shakespeare's part, for showing a ghost straight out of purgatory might have seemed dangerously close to Catholic doctrine. It was apparently safest for writers in the dominant Anglican culture to show the ghost only of a person who was "freshly dead or on the point of death" (O'Meara 15), and also to make the details vague and ambiguous.

The status and existence of Shakespeare's Ghost therefore reflects   [5]
uncertainties during the Elizabethan period. Lily Campbell offers a number of ways in which Elizabethans dealt with these uncertainties. First, James VI of Scotland, who at the time Hamlet was first performed was soon to be James I of England, wrote about departed spirits and emphasized that the devil himself could choose the shape of loved ones to deceive and corrupt living persons. It is this danger that Hamlet specifically describes. Second, as already mentioned, some Elizabethan religious thinkers held it possible for souls in purgatory to return to earth for a time and speak to the living. Third, scientifically oriented thinkers interpreted ghostly appearances as a sign of madness or deep melancholia (Campbell 121), or what O'Meara calls "sorrowful imagination" (19). There were apparently a number of "tests" that might have enabled people to determine the authenticity of ghosts. Most of these required that the spirit should show goodness of character and give comfort to the living (Campbell 123).

Kruse 4

[6]   The Ghost of Hamlet's father both passes and fails these tests. He is not totally bad (Campbell 126), but he urges Hamlet to commit murder, something that no ghost trying to reach heaven would possibly do (McFarland 36). Although the Ghost describes the pain of a soul in purgatory, he does so to create fear, not to urge Hamlet to seek salvation. Thus he is more like the devil than a spirit on the way to redemption (Prosser 133–34; Frye 22). Another sign suggesting the Ghost's devilishness is that he withholds his appearance from Gertrude when he shows himself to Hamlet in Act 3, scene 4 (Campbell 124). Hamlet creates his own test of the Ghost by getting the touring actors to perform The Murder of Gonzago. Once he sees the King's disturbance at the play, Hamlet concludes that the Ghost is real and not just a "figment of his melancholy imagination" (Harrison 883). Perhaps the best answer to the conflicting views of the Ghost is given by Lily Campbell, who suggests that the ambiguity indicates the general uncertainty about ghosts among Shakespeare's contemporaries (127). In other words, there was no unanimity about the nature and motivation of ghosts, and Shakespeare's Ghost reflected common Elizabethan understanding and attitudes.

III. The Ghost's Character

[7]   Uncertainty and theology aside, the Ghost is probably Shakespeare's rendering of what he thought a ghost would be like. Shakespeare inherited a tradition of noisy, bloodthirsty ghosts from his sources--what Harold Fisch calls a "Senecan ghost" (91). There was also a tradition of "hungry ghosts," who were spirits prowling about the earth "searching for the life they were deprived of" (Austin 93). In this tradition, Shakespeare's Ghost is bloodthirsty, although ironically not as bloodthirsty as Hamlet himself becomes during the play (Gottschalk 166). The Ghost is surrounded by awe and horror (DeLuca 147) and is frightening, both to the soldiers at the beginning of the play and also to Hamlet in Act 3, scene 4 (Charney, Style 167–68). It seems that horror is the main effect that Shakespeare wanted the Ghost to achieve.

Kruse 5

Although the Ghost is bloodthirsty and horrible, he has redeeming [8]
qualities (Alexander 30). He is toned down from a ghost in an anonymous and
lost earlier play, perhaps a first version of Hamlet by Shakespeare himself,
which was described by Shakespeare's contemporary Thomas Lodge
(1558–1625) (Bloom 383). Lodge talked about "ye ghost which cried so
miserally [pitifully, sorrowfully] at ye theator . . . Hamlet, reuenge" [sic].
Shakespeare's Ghost also cries out for vengeance, but as a former loving
husband he is still concerned for the welfare of Hamlet's mother, Gertrude,
directing his son to treat her kindly and help her (Kerrigan 54). Also, as a
former king, he voices concern about the reputation and future of Denmark
(Gottschalk 165). Paul Gottschalk points to these redeeming qualities to
indicate that the Ghost is concerned with "restoration" as well as "retaliation"
(166)--a view not shared by Norman Austin, who calls the Ghost "the spirit of
ruin" (105).

Indeed, the Ghost has many qualities of a living human being. For [9]
example, he is witty, as Maurice Charney observes about the following
interchange between the Ghost and Hamlet just at the beginning of the
revelation speeches in Act 1, scene 5, lines 6–7:

> HAMLET. Speak, I am bound to hear.
>
> GHOST. So art thou to revenge, when thou shalt hear.

In other words, even though the Ghost may have come "with . . . airs from
heaven, or blasts from hell" (1.4.41), he is still mentally alert enough to make a
pun out of Hamlet's word "bound" (Charney, Style 118). To this quickness can
be added his shrewd ability to judge his son's character. He knows that Hamlet
may neglect duty, and hence his last words in Act 1, scene 5, are "remember
me," and his first words in Act 3, scene 4 are "Do not forget." A. C. Bradley
suggests that these speeches indicate Shakespeare's master touch in the
development of the Ghost's character (126).

**When citing
dialogue between
two or more
characters, indent
the quotation one
inch (or ten
spaces) and type
each character's
name next to the
corresponding
dialogue in all
caps followed by
a period.**

Kruse 6

[10]   The Ghost also shows other human traits. He strongly feels remorse about his lifelong crimes and "imperfections" for which his sudden death did not give him time to atone. It is this awareness that has made him bitter and vengeful. Also, he has a sense of appropriateness that extends to what he wears. Thus, at the beginning he appears on the parapets dressed in full armor. This battle uniform is in keeping with the location and also with his vengeful mission (Aldus 54). The armor is intimidating, a means of enforcing the idea that the Ghost in death has become a "spirit of hatred" (Austin 99). By contrast, in the closet scene he wears a dressing gown ["in his habit as he lived," 3.4.135], as though he is prepared for ordinary palace activities of both business and leisure (Charney, Style 26).

IV. The Ghost's Importance in the Structure of the Play

[11]   Shakespeare's great strength as a dramatist is shown not only in his giving the Ghost such a round, full character but also in his integrating the Ghost fully within the play's structure. According to Peter Alexander, the Ghost is "indispensable" in the plot as the force that sets things in motion (29). The Ghost is also a director and organizer as well as an informer--a figure who keeps the action moving until there is no stopping it (Aldus 100). A careful study of his speeches shows that he is a manipulator, playing on his son's emotions to make him hurry to kill the king. In addition, the Ghost is persistent, because his return to Hamlet in Act 3, scene 4, to "whet thy almost blunted purpose" (line 111) is the mark of a manager who nervously intervenes when his directions are being neglected or delayed.

[12]   The Ghost is also significant in a major structure of the play. During the imagined period when the events at Elsinore are taking place, Denmark is undergoing a national preparation for war against Norway (Alexander 34). Structurally, the beginning and ending of Hamlet are marked by the fear of war and the political takeover by "Young Fortinbras" of Norway, who is like Hamlet because King Hamlet, now the Ghost, had killed Old Fortinbras in single combat. Young Fortinbras is therefore as much an avenger as Hamlet (Honan 283), and the cause is King Hamlet, who now as a Ghost pushes Hamlet to

Kruse 7

vengeance. So strong is the Ghost's anger against Claudius that he insists on revenge even if it means the defeat of his country in the face of impending war. Ironically, the Ghost in death brings about the passing of the political stability he courageously promoted in life.

An additional major structure also involves the Ghost. Maurice Charney observes that the Ghost is significant in the "symmetrical" poison plots in the play (Style 39). The first of these plots, the poisoning of King Hamlet, is described by the Ghost himself in Act 1, scene 5. The poisoning of the player king in Act 3, scene 2, is a reenactment of the first murder, and it occurs in approximately the middle of the action. The final poisonings--of Gertrude, Laertes, Claudius, and finally Hamlet himself--occur in Act 5, scene 2, the play's last scene. These actions have value as symbolic frames that measure the deterioration of the play's major characters. [13]

V. The Ghost's Effect

Beyond the Ghost's practical and structural importance in the action, he has profound psychological influence, mainly negative, on the characters. Roy Walker describes him as a "prologue" to the "omen" of Hamlet himself, who is the agent of the "dread purpose" of vengeance (220). Because Hamlet is already suffering depression after his father's death, this murderous mission opens the wounds of his vulnerability (Campbell 127–28). Literally, Hamlet must give up everything he has ever learned, even "the movement of existence itself," so that he can carry out the Ghost's commands (McFarland 32–33). In Harold Bloom's words, "everything in the play depends upon Hamlet's response to the Ghost" (387). Because of this malign ghostly influence, Hamlet is gripped by a melancholy that undermines his love for Ophelia, his possible friendship with Laertes, and his relationship with his mother (Kirsch 31; Kott 49). The effects are like radiating waves, with the Ghost at the center as a relentless, destructive force. No one escapes. [14]

This overwhelming ghostly force possesses Hamlet once the first encounter has occurred. This possession is shown both literally and figuratively when the Ghost goes under the stage in Act 1, scene 5, and hears Hamlet's [15]

Kruse 8

conversation with Horatio and the guards. The Ghost thus represents "dimensions of reality" beyond what we see on the stage, a mysterious world "elsewhere" that dominates the very souls of living persons (Charney, "Asides" 127). As a result of this ever-present force, which as far as Hamlet is concerned might become visible at any moment, Hamlet is denied the healing that might normally occur after the death of a parent (Kirsch 26). The steady pressure to kill Claudius disrupts any movement to mental health and creates what Kirsch calls a "pathology of depression" (26) that inhibits Hamlet's actions (Bradley 123), causes his Oedipal preoccupation with the sexuality of his parents (Kirsch 22), and brings about his desire for the oblivion of suicide (Kirsch 27).

[16]   It is, finally, this power over his son that gives the Ghost the greatest influence in the play. Once the Ghost has appeared, Hamlet is not and never can be the same. He loses the dignity and composure that he has assumed as his right as a prince of Denmark and as a student in quest of knowledge (McFarland 38). The Ghost's commands make it impossible for Hamlet to solve problems through negotiation--the way he would likely have chosen as prince and student. The commands force him instead into a plan requiring murder. What could be more normal than hesitation under such circumstances? Despite all of Hamlet's reflections, however, the web of vengeance woven by the Ghost finally closes in on all those caught in it, both the deserving and undeserving. There is no solution but the final one--real death, which is the literal conclusion of the symbolic death represented by the Ghost when he first appears on the Elsinore battlements.

VI. Conclusion

[17]   The Ghost is real in the play's action and structure. He is seen by the characters on the stage, and when he speaks we hear him. He is made round and full by Shakespeare, and his motivation is direct and clear, even though the signs of his spirit nature are presented ambiguously. But the Ghost is more. He has been made a ghost by the greed and envy of Claudius, and for this reason he becomes in the play either a conscious or an unwitting agent of the "unseen Fates or forces" of his own doom (Walker 220). What he brings is the

Kruse 9

horror that lurks within the depths of good, moral people, waiting to overwhelm them and destroy them. Once the horror is released, there is no restraining it, and those who are hurt cannot be rescued. The tragedy is that there is no way to win against these odds.

Kruse 10

Works Cited

Aldus, P. J. Mousetrap: Structure and Meaning in Hamlet. Toronto: U of Toronto P, 1977.

Alexander, Peter. Hamlet: Father and Son. Oxford: Clarendon, 1955.

Austin, Norman. "Hamlet's Hungry Ghost." Shenandoah 37.1 (1987): 78–105.

Bloom, Harold. Shakespeare: The Invention of the Human. New York: Riverhead, 1998.

Bradley, A. C. Shakespearean Tragedy. 1904. London: Macmillan, 1950.

Campbell, Lily B. Shakespeare's Tragic Heroes: Slaves of Passion. New York: Barnes, 1959.

Charney, Maurice. "Asides, Soliloquies, and Offstage Speech in Hamlet." Shakespeare and the Sense of Performance: Essays in the Tradition of Performance Criticism in Honor of Bernard Beckerman. Ed. Marvin and Ruth Thompson. Newark: U of Delaware P, 1989. 116–31.

---. Style in Hamlet. Princeton: Princeton UP, 1969.

DeLuca, Diana Macintyre. "The Movements of the Ghost in Hamlet." Shakespeare Quarterly 24 (1973): 147–54.

In MLA style, the list of sources, called the Works Cited, begins a new page. Double space throughout.

List sources in alphabetical order.

Kruse 11

Dobson, Michael, and Stanley Wells. The Oxford Companion to Shakespeare.
    Oxford: Oxford UP, 2001.

Edgar, Irving I. Shakespeare, Medicine, and Psychiatry. New York,
    Philosophical Library, 1970.

Fisch, Harold. Hamlet and the Word. New York: Ungar, 1971.

Frye, Roland Mushat. The Renaissance Hamlet: Issues and Responses in 1600.
    Princeton: Princeton UP, 1984.

Garber, Marjorie. "Hamlet: Giving Up the Ghost." William Shakespeare:
    Hamlet. Ed. Suzanne L. Wofford. Boston: Bedford, 1994. 297–331.

Gottschalk, Paul. "Hamlet and the Scanning of Revenge." Shakespeare
    Quarterly 24 (1973): 155–70.

Harrison, G. B., ed. Shakespeare: The Complete Works. 1948. New York:
    Harcourt.

Holden, Anthony. William Shakespeare: The Man Behind the Genius: A
    Biography. Boston: 1968. Little, 1999.

Honan, Park. Shakespeare: A Life. Oxford: Oxford UP, 1998.

Jones, Ernest. Hamlet and Oedipus. 1949. New York: Doubleday, 1954.

Kerrigan, William. Hamlet's Perfection. Baltimore: Johns Hopkins UP, 1994.

Kirsch, Arthur. "Hamlet's Grief." ELH 48 (1981): 17–36.

Kott, Jan. Shakespeare, Our Contemporary. Trans. Boleslaw Taborski. 1967.
    London: Methuen, 1970.

McFarland, Thomas. Tragic Meanings in Shakespeare. New York: Random,
    1966.

O'Meara, John. "Hamlet and the Fortunes of Sorrowful Imagination: A Re-
    examination of the Genesis and Fate of the Ghost." Cahiers Elisabéthains
    35 (1989): 15–25.

Paris, Jean. Shakespeare. Trans. Richard Seaver. New York: Grove, 1960.

Prosser, Eleanor. Hamlet and Revenge. 2nd ed. Stanford: Stanford UP, 1971.

Walker, Roy. "Hamlet: The Opening Scene." Shakespeare: Modern Essays in
    Criticism. Ed. Leonard F. Dean. New York: Oxford UP, 1961.

Commentary on the Essay

This essay illustrates an assignment requiring about twenty-five sources and about 2,500 words (there are actually twenty-seven sources). The sources were located through an examination of library catalogs, the *MLA Bibliography*, library bookshelves, the Internet, and the bibliographies in some of the listed books. They represent the range of materials available in a college library with a selective, but by no means exhaustive, set of holdings. Two of the sources (Austin and O'Meara) were obtained through Interlibrary Loan.

The writing itself is developed from the sources listed. Originality (see p. 605) is provided by the structure and development of the essay, additional observations not existing in the sources, and transitions. The topic outline is placed appropriately at the beginning—a pattern you can follow unless your instructor asks for a more detailed outline, or, perhaps, for no outline at all.

Because the essay is concerned with only one work—and one subject about that work—it demonstrates approach 1 (p. 594). The essay is eclectic, introducing discussions of ideas, character, style, and structure. These four topics fulfill the goal of covering the ground thoroughly within the confines of the assignment. A shorter research assignment might deal with no more than, say, the Ghost's character, ignoring other topics. A longer essay might deal further with the philosophical and theological meanings of ghosts during the Elizabethan period, or a more detailed study of all the traits of the Ghost's character, and so on.

The central idea of the essay is stressed in paragraph 1, along with an assertion that the Ghost is a major influence in the play, together with a concession that the Ghost is only a minor character in the action. The research for this paragraph is derived primarily from a reading of the play itself. Paragraph 2, continuing the exploration of the central idea, demonstrates that the Ghost figures in the major themes of *Hamlet*. Paragraph 3 is mainly functional, being used as the location of the thesis sentence.

Part II, containing paragraphs 4–6, deals with the Ghost's status as a spirit. Part III, with paragraphs 7–10 is concerned with the Ghost's human rather than spiritual characteristics. Part IV, with paragraphs 11–13, deals with the significance of the Ghost in the major structures that dominate the play. Part V, with three paragraphs, considers the Ghost's negative and overwhelming influence over the major figures of *Hamlet*, the emphasis being the character of Hamlet as the transferring agent of the Ghost's destructive revenge. The concluding paragraph (17) sums up the essay with the final idea of how the Ghost affects the tragic nature of *Hamlet*.

The list of works cited is the basis of all parenthetical references in the essay, in accordance with the *MLA Handbook for Writers of Research Papers*, 6th ed. Using these references, an interested reader can consult the sources for a more detailed development of the ideas in the illustrative essay. The works cited can also serve as a springboard for expanded research.

Part V

Special Writing Topics About Literature

Chapter 29

Critical Approaches Important in the Study of Literature

A number of critical theories or approaches for understanding and interpreting literature are available to critics and students alike.[1] Many of these were developed during the twentieth century to create a discipline of literary studies comparable with disciplines in the natural and social sciences. Literary critics have often borrowed liberally from other disciplines (e.g., history, psychology, politics, anthropology) but have primarily aimed at developing literature as a study in its own right.

At the heart of the various critical approaches are many fundamental questions: What is literature? What does it do? Is its concern primarily to tell stories, to divert attention, to entertain, to communicate ideas, to persuade, and to teach, or is it to describe and interpret reality, or to explore and explain emotions—or is it all of these? To what degree is literature an art, as opposed to a medium for imparting knowledge? What more does it do than express ideas? How does it get its ideas across? What can it contribute to intellectual, artistic, political, and social thought and history? How is literature used, and how and why is it misused? Is it private? Public? What theoretical and technical expertise may be invoked to enhance literary studies? How valuable was literature in the past, and how valuable is it now? To what degree should literature be in the vanguard of social and political change?

Questions such as these indicate that criticism is concerned not only with reading and interpreting stories, poems, and plays but also with establishing theoretical understanding. Because of such extensive aims, a full explanation and illustration of the approaches would fill the pages of a long book. The following descriptions are therefore intended as no more than brief introductions. Bear in mind that in the hands of skilled critics, the approaches are so subtle, sophisticated, and complex that they are not only critical stances but also philosophies.

Although the various approaches provide widely divergent ways to study literature and literary problems, they reflect major tendencies rather than absolute straitjacketing. Not every approach is appropriate for every work, nor are the approaches always mutually exclusive. Even the most devoted practitioners of the methods do not pursue them rigidly. In addition, some of the approaches are more "user friendly" than others for certain types of discovery. To a degree at least, most critics therefore take a particular approach but utilize methods that technically belong to one or more of the other approaches. A critic stressing the topical/historical approach, for example, might introduce the close study of a work that is associated with the method of the New Criticism.

---

[1]Some of the approaches described in this chapter are presented more simply in Part I as basic study techniques for writing about literary works.

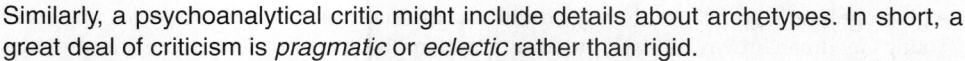

Similarly, a psychoanalytical critic might include details about archetypes. In short, a great deal of criticism is *pragmatic* or *eclectic* rather than rigid.

Ten approaches will be considered here: (1) *moral/intellectual;* (2) *topical/historical;* (3) *New Critical/formalist;* (4) *structuralist;* (5) *feminist/gender studies/queer theory;* (6) *economic determinist/Marxist;* (7) *psychological/psychoanalytic;* (8) *archetypal/ symbolic/mythic;* (9) *deconstructionist;* and (10) *reader-response.*

The object of learning about these approaches, like everything else in this book, is to help you develop your own capacities as a reader and writer. Accordingly, following each of the descriptions is a brief paragraph showing how Hawthorne's story "Young Goodman Brown" (Chapter 8) might be considered in the light of the particular approach. The illustrative paragraphs following the discussion of structuralism, for example, shows an application of the structuralist approach to Goodman Brown and his story, and so also with the feminist approach, the economic determinist approach, and the others. These paragraphs are followed by additional commentary illustrating the same approaches based on other literary works. Whenever you are doing your own writing about literature, you are free to use the various approaches as part or all of your assignment, if you believe the approach may help you.

Moral/Intellectual

The **moral/intellectual critical approach** is concerned with content, ideas, and values (see also Chapter 8). The approach is as old as literature itself, for literature is a traditional mode of inculcating thought, morality, philosophy, and religion. The concern in moral/intellectual criticism is not only to discover meaning but also to determine whether works of literature are both *true* and *significant*.

To study literature from the moral/intellectual perspective is therefore to determine whether a work conveys a lesson or a message and whether it can help readers lead better lives and improve their understanding of the world. What ideas does the work contain? How strongly does the work bring forth its ideas? What application do the ideas have to the work's characters and situations? How may the ideas be evaluated intellectually? Morally? Discussions based on such questions do not imply that literature is primarily a medium of moral and intellectual exhortation. Ideally, moral/intellectual criticism should differ from sermonizing to the degree that readers should always be left with their own decisions about whether to assimilate the ideas of a work and about whether the ideas—and values— are personally or morally acceptable.

Sophisticated critics have sometimes demeaned the moral/intellectual approach on the grounds that "message hunting" reduces a work's artistic value by treating it like a sermon or political speech; but the approach will be valuable as long as readers expect literature to be applicable to their own lives.

❧ Example: Hawthorne's "Young Goodman Brown"

"Young Goodman Brown" raises the issue of how an institution designed for human elevation, such as the religious system of colonial Salem, can be so ruinous. Does the failure result from the system itself or from the people who misunderstand it? Is what is true of religion as practiced by Brown also true of social and political institutions? Should any religious or political philosophy be given greater significance than goodwill and mutual trust? One of the major virtues of "Young Goodman Brown" is that it provokes questions like these but at the same time provides a number of satisfying answers. A particularly important one is that religious and moral beliefs should not be used to justify the condemnation of others. Another important answer is that attacks made from the refuge of a religion or group, such as Brown's Puritanism, are dangerous because the judge may condemn without thought and without personal responsibility.

Second Example: Stafford's "Traveling Through the Dark," page 1179

William Stafford's "Traveling Through the Dark" presents a moral quandary. While the speaker is driving along a narrow road at night, he comes upon the carcass of a doe. Upon investigation, he finds that the doe is pregnant with a live fawn. It is customary to throw dead animals off the side of the road in order to remove the danger of having a swerving car veer off the road. But in the present situation, the speaker "hesitates." The living fawn complicates the moral option, for now life must be taken. As the speaker hesitates, he "could hear the wilderness listen" because moral decisions are not only an individual's domain but affect all of us. "I thought hard for us all" the speaker says, but then adds "my only swerving" as if uncertain if it is presumptuous for one person to think for all people. Sometimes, however, it is a human being's responsibility to make a decision, and one may argue whether the right one was made in this instance. As if to highlight the human quandary that moral situations put us in, Stafford refers to the car as aiming its headlights, as if the car were conscious. Despite that, it is only human beings who are responsible for moral action. Nature merely "listens," and objects merely "light" the path toward decision. In "Traveling Through the Dark" Stafford, through a simple situation that might confront almost anyone, probes many of the issues raised by moral action.

READINGS

Buckley, Vincent. *Poetry and Morality: Studies in the Criticism of Matthew Arnold, T. S. Eliot, and F. R. Leavis*. London: Chato and Windus, 1959.

Else, Gerald F. *Plato and Aristotle on Poetry*. Chapel Hill: U of North Carolina P, 1986.

Farrell, James T. *Literature and Morality*. New York: Vanguard, 1947.

Foerster, Norman. *American Criticism: A Study in Literary Theory from Poe to the Present*. 1928. New York: Russell and Russell, 1962.

Gardner, John. *On Moral Fiction*. New York: Basic Books, 1978.

McCloskey, Mary A. *Kant's Aesthetic*. Basingstoke: Macmillan, 1987.

Olson, Elder. *Aristotle's Poetics and English Literature*. Chicago: U of Chicago P, 1965.

Sartre, Jean Paul. *What is Literature?* New York: Philosophical Library, 1966.

Wallis, R. T. *Neoplatonism*. London: Duckworth, 1995.

Topical/Historical

The **topical/historical critical approach** stresses the relationship of literature to its historical period, and for this reason it has had a long life. Although much literature may be applicable to many places and times, much of it also directly reflects

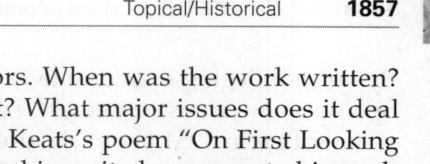

the intellectual and social worlds of the authors. When was the work written? What were the circumstances that produced it? What major issues does it deal with? How does it fit into the author's career? Keats's poem "On First Looking into Chapman's Homer" (p. 762), for example, is his excited response to his reading of one of the major literary works of Western civilization. Hardy's "Channel Firing" (page 738) is an ironically acerbic response to continued armament and preparation for war in the past, in the present, and in the future.

The topical/historical approach investigates relationships of this sort, including the elucidation of words and concepts that today's readers may not immediately understand. It may also include biographical information about the author or be informed by a sociological study. For instance, knowing that William Butler Yeats spent his summers at Coole, in County Galway, Ireland, gives resonance to his poem, "The Wild Swans at Coole" (p. 1193). Obviously, the approach requires the assistance of footnotes, dictionaries, library catalogs, histories, and handbooks.

A common criticism of the topical/historical approach is that in the extreme, it deals with background knowledge rather than with literature itself. It is possible, for example, for a topical/historical critic to describe a writer's life, the period of the writer's work, and the social and intellectual ideas of the time—all without ever considering the meaning, importance, and value of any of that writer's works themselves.

A reaction against such an unconnected use of historical details is the so-called **New Historicism.** This approach justifies the parallel reading of both literary and nonliterary works in order to bring an informed understanding of the context of a literary work. The new historicist assumes that history is not a "fixed" essence but a literary construction. As such, history is a prism through which a society views itself; a work of literature is given resonance by seeing the nonobjective context in which it was produced. This approach justifies the introduction of historical knowledge by integrating it with the understanding of particular texts. Readers of Arnold's "Dover Beach" (p. 694), for example, sometimes find it difficult to follow the meaning of Arnold's statement "The Sea of Faith / Was once, too, at the full." Historical background has a definite role to play here. In Arnold's time there developed a method of treating the Bible as a historical document rather than a divinely inspired revelation. This approach has been called the "Higher Criticism" of the Bible, and to many thoughtful people the Higher Criticism undermined the concept that the Bible was divine, infallible, and inerrant. Therefore Arnold's idea is that the "Sea of Faith" is no longer at full tide but is now rather at an ebb. Because the introduction of such historical material is designed to facilitate the reading of the poem—and also the reading of other literature of the period—the New Historicism represents an integration of knowledge and interpretation. As a principle, New Historicism entails the acquisition of as much historical information as possible because our knowledge of the relationship of literature to its historical period can never be complete. The practitioner of historical criticism must always seek new information on the grounds that it may prove relevant to the understanding of various literary works.

Cultural Study is a more recent approach that justifies the analyses of nonliterary materials such as television and radio shows, movies, brochures, and advertisements.

By not privileging literature over mass culture, Cultural Studies critics are able to open up new areas of interest. Langston Hughes' poem "Harlem," for example, was written in 1951 about possible resentment of African Americans when faced with constant discrimination. In 1985, August Wilson created his drama *Fences*, in which baseball has been a vital element in the life of the major character, Troy Maxson. Both works—the poem and the play—are made vital because they reflect the treatment of African Americans by the dominant white races in American society. It therefore becomes relevant that in 1947 Jackie Robinson became the first African American ball player to play baseball for a major league team, and that soon after, increasing numbers of black ballplayers were joining major league clubs. Reading newspaper accounts of the problems they faced provides insights into both "Harlem" and *Fences*.

❧ Example: Hawthorne's "Young Goodman Brown"

"Young Goodman Brown" is an allegorical story by Nathaniel Hawthorne (1804–1864), the major New England writer who probed deeply into the relationship between religion and guilt. His ancestors had been involved in religious persecutions, including the Salem witch trials, and he, living 150 years afterward, wanted to analyze the weaknesses and uncertainties of the sin-dominated religion of the earlier period, a tradition of which he was a resentful heir. Not surprisingly, therefore, the story about "Young Goodman Brown" takes place in Salem during Puritan times, and Hawthorne's implied judgments are those of a severe critic of how the harsh old religion destroyed personal and family relationships. Although the immediate concerns of the story belong to a vanished age, Hawthorne's treatment remains valuable because it remains timely.

❧ Second Example: Jarrell's "The Death of the Ball Turret Gunner," page 639

Juxtaposing World War II propaganda posters with Randall Jarrell's 1945 poem "The Death of the Ball Turret Gunner," gives special meaning to both. In an American poster of 1943 the words BATTLE OF GERMANY at the top and JOIN THE AIR CREW at the bottom are boldly visible. In the middle is a group of bombers flying in neat formation high above a bombed German city. All that is rising from below is smoke emanating from the site of the bombing. One gets the impression that a bombing run is an orderly operation and that the bombers are high above any danger, and immune from it. A British poster of the same year, with the words BACK THEM UP at the bottom, shows a fighter plane in close-up as it drops bombs on a German city. In the background other fighters can be seen in formation, apparently leaving the city after a successful bombing raid. While these posters imply a heroic struggle against an enemy, they only point obliquely to any danger. Jarrell's poem confronts the darker realities of war. The gunner of this poem is not consumed by his heroic duty. He seems to be born into his nightmarish situation, for he says "From my mother's sleep I fell into the State." His height above the action does not suggest safety but rather a remote detachment from the "dream of life." Describing his own death and how he was "washed . . . out of the turret with a hose," the speaker manifests the horrifying impersonality of war. This "dialogue" between World War II posters and Randell Jarell's poem gives the reader a richer understanding of the many motives and outcomes of an event so dangerous and complex as war.

READINGS

During, Simon, ed. *The Cultural Studies Reader.* New York: Routledge, 1993.

Greenblatt, Stephen. *Renaissance Self-Fashioning: From More to Shakespeare.* Chicago: U of Chicago P, 1980.

———, ed. *Repressing the English Renaissance.* Berkeley: U of California P, 1988.

Hoggart, Richard. *The Uses of Literacy: Changing Patterns in English Mass Culture.* Harmondsworth: Penguin, 1957.

LaCapra, Dominick. *History and Criticism.* Ithaca: Cornell UP, 1985.

Lindenberger, Herbert, ed. *History in Literature: On Value, Genre, Institutions.* New York: Columbia UP, 1990.

McGann, Jerome. *The Beauty of Inflections: Literary Investigations in Historical Method and Theory.* Oxford: Clarendon P, 1985.

———, ed. *Historical Studies and Literary Criticism.* Madison: U of Wisconsin P, 1985.

Said, Edward W. *Orientalism.* New York: Random House, 1978.

———. *Culture and Imperialism.* New York: Knopf, 1993.

Thomas, Brook. *The New Historicism and Other Old-Fashioned Topics.* Princeton: Princeton UP, 1991.

New Critical/Formalist

The **new critical/formalist approach** (the **new criticism**) has been a dominant force in modern literary studies. It focuses on literary texts as formal works of art, and for this reason it can be seen as a reaction against the topical/historical approach. The objection raised by new critics is that as topical/historical critics consider literary history, they evade direct contact with actual texts.

The inspiration for the new critical/formalist approach was the French practice of *explication de texte,* a method that emphasizes detailed examination and explanation. (See "Writing an Explication of a Poem," Chapter 11.) The new criticism is at its most brilliant in the formal analysis of smaller units such as entire poems and short passages. For the analysis of larger structures, the new criticism also utilizes a number of techniques that have been selected as the basis of chapters in this book. Discussions of point of view, tone, plot, character, and structure, for example, are formal ways of looking at literature that are derived from the new criticism.

The aim of the new critical study of literature is to provide readers not only with the means of explaining the content of works (what, specifically, does a work say?) but also with the insights needed for evaluating the artistic quality of individual works and writers (how well is it said?). A major aspect of new critical thought is that content and form—including all ideas, ambiguities, subtleties, and even apparent contradictions—were originally within the conscious or subconscious control of the author. There are no accidents. It does not necessarily follow, however, that today's critic is able to define the author's intentions exactly, for such intentions require knowledge of biographical details that are irretrievably lost. Each literary work therefore takes on its own existence and identity, and the critic's work is to discover a reading or readings that explain the facts of the text. It should be noted that the new critic does not claim infallible interpretations and does not exclude the validity of multiple readings of the same work.

Dissenters from the new criticism have noted a tendency by new critics to ignore relevant knowledge that history and biography can bring to literary studies. In addition, the approach has been subject to the charge that stressing the explication of texts alone fails to deal with literary value and appreciation. In other words, the new critics, in explaining the meaning of literature, sometimes neglect the reasons for which readers find literature stimulating and valuable.

Example: Hawthorne's "Young Goodman Brown"

A major aspect of Hawthorne's "Young Goodman Brown" is that the details are so vague and dreamlike that many readers are uncertain about what is happening. The action is a nighttime walk by the protagonist, Young Goodman Brown, into a deep forest where he encounters a mysterious satanic ritual that leaves him bitter and misanthropic. This much seems clear, but the precise nature of Brown's experience is not clear, nor is the identity of the stranger (father, village elder, devil) who accompanies Brown as he begins his walk. At the story's end Hawthorne's narrator states that the whole episode may have been no more than a dream or nightmare. Yet when morning comes, Brown walks back into town as though returning from an overnight trip, and he recoils in horror from his fellow villagers, including his wife Faith (paragraph 70). Could his attitude result from nothing more than a nightmare? Even at the story's end these uncertainties remain. For this reason one may conclude that Hawthorne deliberately creates the uncertainties to reveal how people like Brown build defensive walls of judgment around themselves. The story thus implies that the real source of Brown's anger is as vague as his nocturnal walk, but he doesn't understand it in this way. Because Brown's vision and judgment are absolute, he rejects everyone around him, even if the cost is a life of bitter suspicion and spiritual isolation.

Example: Robinson's "Richard Cory," page 675

Edwin Arlington Robinson's *Richard Cory* is a tightly structured poem in which all the traditional elements of verse are orchestrated to form a unified and clear meaning. The four quatrains, in iambic pentameter lines, rhyme *abab cdcd efef ghgh*, forming a predictable pattern that boldly frames the ironic ending: "And Richard Cory, one calm summer night, / Went home and put a bullet through his head." The "regal" diction describing Richard Cory, contrasted with the bland circumstances of the townspeople, lets the reader know why Cory was so envied, and the diction also carries the poem forward to its shocking conclusion. The people of the town are walking on the "pavement" and "flutter" at the sight of the neighbor they envy: Richard Cory is "a gentleman from sole to crown, /. . . and imperially slim." Each stanza is modulated by images of Cory himself, or at least as he is perceived by those around him, along with the images of the townspeople themselves. The townspeople, including the speaker who is one of them, are so envious of Cory that they "curse" their own predicament and would rather be in his place. Yet, upon close scrutiny, the reader can see how the images describing Cory are superficial, as if only the "surface" of his personality were enough to judge him. He was "slim" and "rich" and "admirably schooled," but no reference is made to his thoughts, feelings, or aspirations. By the common and unimaginative standards of the speaker, the final irony is surprising, yet by the standards of the reader it is not surprising. As in many works of art, the title of the poem is significant. Did anyone know the "heart" of Richard Cory, the "core" of his existence?

READINGS

Brooks, Cleanth. *The Well Wrought Urn: Studies in the Structure of Poetry.* New York: Reynal and Hitchcock, 1947.

Brooks, Cleanth, and Robert Penn Warren. *Understanding Poetry.* 4th ed. New York: Holt, 1938.

Empson, William. *Seven Types of Ambiguity.* London: Chatto and Windus, 1930.

Krieger, Murray. *The New Apologists for Poetry.* Minneapolis: U of Minnesota P, 1986.

Ransom, John Crowe. *The New Criticism.* Norfolk: New Directions, 1941.

Richards, I. A. *Principles of Literary Criticism.* New York: Harcourt Brace, 1924.

Wellek, Rene, and Austin Warren. *Theory of Literature.* New York: Harcourt, Brace, 1949.

Wimsatt, William K. *The Verbal Icon: Studies in the Meaning of Poetry.* Lexington: UP of Kentucky, 1954.

Structuralist

The principle of the **stucturalist critical approach** stems from the attempt to find relationships and connections among elements that appear to be separate and unique. Just as physical science reveals unifying universal principles of matter such as gravity and the forces of electromagnetism (and is constantly searching for a "unified field theory"), the structuralist critic attempts to discover the forms unifying all literature. Thus a structuralist description of Maupassant's "The Necklace" (p. 6) stresses that the main character, Mathilde, is an *active* protagonist who undergoes a *test* (or series of tests) and emerges with a victory, though not the kind she had originally hoped for. The same might be said of Mrs. Popov and Smirnov in Chekhov's *The Bear* (p. 1582). If this same kind of structural view is applied to Bierce's "An Occurrence at Owl Creek Bridge" (p. 71), the protagonist is defeated in the test. Generally, the structuralist approach applies such patterns to other works of literature to determine that certain protagonists are active or submissive, that they pass or fail their tests, or that they succeed or fail at other encounters. The key is that many apparently unrelated works reveal many common patterns or contain similar structures with important variations.

The structuralist approach is important because it enables critics to discuss works from widely separate cultures and historical periods. In this respect, critics have followed the leads of modern anthropologists, most notably Claude Lévi-Strauss (1908–1990). Along such lines, critics have undertaken the serious examination of folk and fairy tales. Some of the groundbreaking structuralist criticism, for example, was devoted to the structural analysis of themes, actions, and characters to be found in Russian folktales. The method also bridges popular and serious literature, making little distinction between the two insofar as the description of the structures is concerned. Indeed, structuralism furnishes an ideal approach for comparative literature, and the method also enables critics to consolidate genres such as modern romances, detective tales, soap operas, sitcoms, and film.

Like New Criticism, structuralism aims at comprehensiveness of description, and many critics would insist that the two are complementary and not separate. A distinction is that New Criticism is at its best in dealing with smaller units of literature, whereas structuralist criticism is best in the analysis of narratives and therefore larger units such as novels, myths, stories, plays, and films. Because structuralism shows how fiction is organized into various typical situations, the approach merges with the *archetypal* approach (see below, p. 1869), and at times it is difficult to find any distinctions between structuralist and archetypal criticism.

Structuralism, however, deals not just with narrative structures but also with structures of any type, wherever they occur. For example, structuralism makes considerable use of linguistics. Modern linguistic scholars have determined that there is a difference between "deep structures" and "surface structures" in language. A structuralist analysis of style, therefore, emphasizes how writers utilize such structures. The structuralist interpretation of language also perceives distinguishing types or "grammars" of language that are recurrent in various types of literature. Suppose, for example, that you encounter opening passages like the following:

1. Once upon a time a young prince fell in love with a young princess. He was in love so deeply that he wanted to declare his love for her, and early one morning he left his castle on his white charger, along with his retainers and servants, riding toward her castle home high in the distant and cloud-topped mountains.

2. Early that morning, Alan found himself thinking about Anne. He had thought that she was being ambiguous when she said she loved him, and his feelings about her were not certain. His further thought left him still unsure.

The words of these two passages create different and distinct frames of reference. One is a fairy tale of the past, the other a modern internalized reflection of feeling. The passages therefore demonstrate how language itself fits into predetermined patterns or structures. Similar uses of language structures can be associated with other types of literature.

Example: Hawthorne's "Young Goodman Brown"

Young Goodman Brown is a hero who is passive, not active. He is a *witness*, a *receiver* rather than a *doer*. His only action—taking his trip in the forest—occurs at the story's beginning. After that point, he no longer acts but instead is acted upon, and his reactions to what he sees around him put his life's beliefs to a test. Of course, many protagonists undergo similar testing (such as rescuing victims and overcoming particularly terrible dragons), and they emerge as heroes or conquerors. Not so with Goodman Brown. He is a responder who allows himself to be victimized by his own perceptions—or misperceptions. Despite all his previous experiences with his wife and with the good people of his village, he generalizes too hastily. He lets the single disillusioning experience of his nightmare govern his entire outlook on others, and thus he fails his test and turns his entire life into darkness.

Second Example: Jackson's "The Lottery," page 141

Shirley Jackson's story "The Lottery" is a powerful indictment of tradition for its own sake. The narrator/resident of a small town explains how a yearly lottery is held to determine who among its citizens is to be stoned. Apparently the purpose of this ritual has generally been forgotten, but the rules governing its execution are known in great detail. The plot is given resonance and predictability by following two structurally determined elements—the basic outline of a tragedy and the outlines of a contest. Like a traditional tragedy the story begins in apparent innocence and happiness and ends in definite calamity. It is a "sunny" day when the lottery is about to begin, "the flowers . . . [are] blossoming profusely," and the town folk are in a jovial mood. The tension builds with the "drawing" from the black box, and the story ends with the stoning and presumed death of the victim. The horror of the story is not to be found in an individual but rather in the collective, slavish acquiescence to a shockingly anachronistic ritual. As in tragedy, the end is the inevitable outcome, for once we know that the people accept the rules of the town lottery, the end is predictable. The townspeople do not know why they must stone someone, but they know that when they partake in the lottery and follow its rules, someone will "win" the contest and meet his or her doom. Understanding the basic elements of tragedy and reading "The Lottery" as a contest or game gives the story a comprehensible and predictable form.

READINGS

Barthes, Roland. *Writing Degree Zero.* 1953. New York: Beacon, 1970.

———. *Critical Essays.* 1964. Evanston: Northwestern UP, 1970.

———. *Mythologies.* 1957. New York: Hill and Wang, 1972.

Cassirer, Ernst. *Symbol, Myth, and Culture.* New Haven: Yale UP, 1979.

Caws, Peter. *Structuralism: The Art of the Intelligible.* Atlantic Highlands: Humanities, 1988.

Culler, Jonathan. *Structuralist Poetics.* Ithaca: Cornell UP, 1975.

Genette, Gerard. *Narrative Discourse: An Essay in Method.* Ithaca: Cornell UP, 1980.

Greimas, A. J. *Structural Semantics: An Attempt at a Method.* Lincoln: U of Nebraska P, 1984.

Lane, Michael, ed. *Structuralism: A Reader.* London: Cape, 1970.

Macksey, Richard, and Eugenio Donato, eds. *The Structuralism Controversy: The Languages of Criticism and the Sciences of Man.* Baltimore: Johns Hopkins UP, 1970.

Feminist Criticism/Gender Studies/Queer Theory

Feminism/Gender Studies/Queer Theory displays divergent interests drawing insights from many disciplines. It is a still evolving and rich field of inquiry. *Feminist Criticism* had its genesis in the women's movement of the 1960s, shares many of its concerns, and has applied them to the study of literature. One of the early aims of feminist critics was to question the traditional canon and claim a place in it for neglected women writers. Writers such as Mary Shelley, Elizabeth Gaskell, Christina Rossetti, Kate Chopin, and Charlotte Perkins Gillman—three of whom are represented in this book—have been given great critical attention as a result. Feminist critics also delineate the ways both male and female characters are portrayed in literature, looking at how societal norms about sexual difference are either enforced or subverted, and focusing partly on patriarchal structures and institutions such as marriage. As early as the beginning of the twentieth century, Virginia Woolf questioned whether there was a feminine/masculine divide in writing styles, a contentious subject among feminist critics to this day. Feminist critics are also interested in how interpreting texts differs between the sexes. For instance, in *A Map for Rereading* (1980), the critic Annette Kolodny analyzes how men and women read the same stories differently.

Gender Studies, a more recent critical approach, brings attention to gender rather than to sexual differences. Gender Studies critics see the masculine/feminine divide as socially constructed and not innate. Drawing partly on the works of the French philosopher Michel Foucault (1926–1984) such as *The History of Sexuality* and *Madness and Civilization*, which explore the way powerful institutions organize our society and way of thinking. Such critics apply Foucault's ideas to understanding patriarchal structures and their representations in literature. Many studies have also built on the insights of psychoanalysis and deconstruction (see below), questioning Freud's male-oriented categories and seeking insights into the way language is constructed and the way it affects our thinking. In the essay, *Laugh of the Medusa* (1975), Hélène Cixous applies deconstructionist insights about binary oppositions to a study of discourse about women, showing how it disparages women. Thus, while men's discourse in relation to women's may highlight such separate ways of thinking as logic/inconsistency, it is the traditional patriarchal way of thinking that values male over female experience.

A more recent critical orientation, which came to prominence in the early 1990s is *Queer Theory*, which also appropriates many of the insights of deconstruction, particularly its understanding that binary oppositions are relative and that thinking about matters such as sexual orientation is partly ideological and partly social. Many Queer theorists see the heterosexual/homosexual divide as less distinct than has commonly been believed. Queer theorists are interested in how homosexuals are portrayed in literature and whether they write or read literature differently than heterosexuals. Queer Theory has brought attention to recent literary works, dealing explicitly with lesbian and gay themes, along with attention to sometimes "veiled" references to the same themes in writers whose works make up the standard canon. Much of Queer Theory is theoretical; one example, applied to reading a particular work, is Jonathan Crewe's essay, "Queering 'The Yellow Wallpaper'? Charlotte Perkins Gilman and the Politics of Form" (*Tulsa Studies in Women's Literature* 14.2 [1995]: 273–93).

🌿 Example: Hawthorne's "Young Goodman Brown"

At the beginning of "Young Goodman Brown," Brown's wife, Faith, is seen only peripherally. In the traditional patriarchal spirit of wife-as-adjunct, she tells her new husband of her fears, and then asks him to stay at home and take his journey at some other time. Hawthorne does not give her the intelligence or dignity, however, to let her explain her concern (or might he not have been interested in what she had to say?) and she therefore remains in the background with her pink hair ribbon as her distinguishing symbol of submissive inferiority. During the mid-forest satanic ritual, she appears again and is given power, but only the power to cause her husband to go astray. Once she is led in as a novice in the practice of demonism, her husband falls right in step. Unfortunately, by following her, Brown can conveniently excuse himself from guilt by claiming that "she" had made him do it, just as Eve, in some traditional views of the fall of humankind, compelled Adam to eat the apple (Genesis 3:16–17). Hawthorne's attention to the male protagonist, in other words, permits him to neglect the independence and integrity of a female protagonist.

Second Example: Chopin's "The Story of an Hour," page 331

"The Story of an Hour" by Kate Chopin is about a woman who is told that her husband has died in a train accident. Rather than feeling devastated by this news as her family and friends expect, she feels strangely free and happy to pursue a life for herself. While the story's plot suggests obvious themes of interest for feminist critics, a closer look at many details reveals how language, institutions, and expected demeanor suppress the natural desires and aspirations of women. The protagonist of the story is referred to as "Mrs. Mallard" while her husband is called by his name, Brently Mallard, which has nothing to do with his marital status. Assuming that because of a heart condition Louise Mallard might not survive the bad news, she is told by her sister indirectly "in broken sentences:" of her husband's fate. At first she reacts predictably by weeping "with sudden, wild abandonment." Soon, however, Louise finds herself resisting a feeling that is finally identified as "freedom." In her last few moments of solitude, she imagines a life devoted only to herself, and not to being molded by the will of another. Her resistance indicates the pull of societal norms, while her anticipation of possible liberation is a sign of her true inner self. When, at the end of the story, Louise sees her husband appear, perfectly safe and unharmed, she dies of a heart attack, which is diagnosed by attending doctors as a result "of joy that kills." Since there is no indication that Brently Mallard was anything but a good husband, we may assume that it was freedom from the bonds of marriage itself and the overpowering will of a man that turned a supposedly tragic event into a liberating one. "The Story of an Hour" is a powerful commentary on the institution of marriage as it suppresses the natural desires and pursuits of women.

READINGS

Brownstein, Rachel. *Becoming a Heroine: Reading about Women in Novels*. New York: Viking, 1982.

Cameron, Deborah. *Feminism in Linguistic Theory*. London: Macmillan, 1992.

Delany, Sheila. *Writing Women: Women Writers and Women in Literature, Medieval to Modern*. New York: Schocken, 1984.

Gilbert, Sandra M., and Susan Gubar. *The Madwoman in the Attic: The Woman Writer and the Nineteenth-Century Literary Imagination*. New Haven: Yale UP, 1979.

Jacobus, Mary. *Women's Writing and Writing about Women*. New York: Barnes and Noble, 1979.

Kauffman, Linda, ed. *Gender and Theory: Dialogues on Feminist Criticism*. New York: Blackwell, 1985.

Kolodny, Annette. "Some Notes on Defining a 'Feminist Literary Criticism.'" *Critical Inquiry 2* (1975): 75–92.

Lilly, Mark, ed. *Lesbian and Gay Writing*. London: Macmillian, 1990.

Sedgwick, Eve Kosovsky. *Between Men: English Literature and Male Homosocial Desire*. New York: Columbia UP, 1985.

Showalter, Elaine. *A Literature of Their Own: British Women Novelists from Bronte to Lessing*. Princeton: Princeton UP, 1977.

Woods, Greg, *A History of Gay Literature*. New Haven: Yale UP, 1999.

Economic Determinist/Marxist

The concept of cultural and economic determinism—and its corollary, the **economic determinist/Marxist critical approach**—is one of the major political ideas of the nineteenth century. Karl Marx (1818–1883) emphasized that the primary influence on life was economic, and he saw society enmeshed in a continuous conflict between capitalist oppressors and oppressed working people. The literature that emerged from this kind of analysis often features individuals who are coping with the ill effects of economic disadvantage. Sometimes called "proletarian" literature, it focuses on persons of the lower class—the poor and oppressed who spend their lives in endless drudgery and misery, and whose attempts to rise to the top usually result in renewed oppression.

Marx's political ideas were never widely accepted in the United States and have faded still more after the political breakup of the Soviet Union, but the idea of economic determinism (and the related term *Social Darwinism*) is still credible. As a result, much literature can be judged from an economic perspective even though the economic critics may not be Marxian: What is the economic status of the characters? What happens to them as a result of this status? How do they fare against economic and political odds? What other conditions stemming from their class does the writer emphasize (e.g., poor education, poor nutrition, poor health care, inadequate opportunity)? To what extent does the work fail by overlooking the economic, social, and political implications of its material? In what other ways does economic determinism affect the work? How should readers consider the story in today's developed or underdeveloped world? Seemingly, Hawthorne's story "Young Goodman Brown," which we have used for analysis in these discussions, has no major economic implications, but an economic determinist/Marxist critical approach might take the following turns. (See also p. 1835.)

Example: Hawthorne's "Young Goodman Brown"

"Young Goodman Brown" is a fine story just as it is. It deals with the false values instilled by the skewed acceptance of sin-dominated religion, but it overlooks the economic implications of this situation. One might suspect that the real story in the little world of Goodman Brown's Salem should be about the disruption that an alienated member of society can produce. After Brown's condemnation and distrust of others forces him into his own shell of sick imagination, Hawthorne does not consider how such a disaffected character would injure the economic and public life of the town. Consider this, just for a moment: Why would the people from whom Brown recoils in disgust want to deal with him in business or personal matters? In town meetings, would they want to follow his opinions on crucial issues of public concern and investment? Would his preoccupation with sin and damnation make him anything more than a horror in his domestic life? Would his wife, Faith, be able to discuss household management with him, or to ask him about methods of caring for the children? All these questions of course are pointed toward another story—a story that Hawthorne did not write. They also indicate the shortcomings of Hawthorne's approach, because it is clear that the major result of Young Goodman Brown's selfish preoccupation with evil would be a serious disruption of the economic and political affairs of his small community.

Second Example: Miller's "Death of a Salesman," page 1424

Arthur Miller's *Death of a Salesman* is a devastating indictment of capitalism. Willy Loman is an aging salesman who is struggling to live his later life in dignity. Although his desire to live the American dream of economic security is partly shattered by his own personal inadequacies and increasing age, much of his deterioration and death can be traced to the cruel system that he accepts and in which he believes. As a salesman, Willy represents the purist form of capitalism. He is worth only what he sells, and he is selling less and less. The cost of fixing his car and home appliances weighs heavily on him. When he confronts his boss about a better job close to home, he is ignored and rejected, and he faces indigence and humiliation. His descent into irrationality stems from his confusion about the grimness of his economic reality. On the one hand he professes the importance to his adult children of being well-liked, as if personality were a substitute for the harsh realities of capitalistic economic necessity. On the other hand, referring to his own "vital" role as a salesman indicates an acceptance of the values inherent in capitalism. The problem is that he is no longer productive and is therefore of no value to his employer. At the play's end, Willy kills himself for the insurance money his wife will gain, and when the last payment on his mortgage has been made, the irony only underscores how capitalism degrades life by equating human worth with economic productivity. In *Death of a Salesman* Arthur Miller has written a powerful critique of the American economic system.

READINGS

Adorno, Theodor. *Prisms: Cultural Criticism and Society.* 1955. London: Neville Spearman, 1967.

Althusser, Louis. *For Marx.* New York: Pantheon, 1969.

Bakhtin, Mikhail. *Between Phenomenology and Marxism.* New York: Cambridge UP, 1995.

Demetz, Peter. *Marx, Engels, and the Poets: Origins of Marxist Literary Criticism.* Chicago, U of Chicago P, 1967.

Dowling, William. *Jameson, Althusser, Marx: An Introduction to the Political Unconscious.* Ithaca: Cornell UP, 1984.

Eagleton, Terry. *Criticism and Ideology: A Study in Marxist Literary Theory.* London: New Left, 1976.

Frow, John. *Marxism and Literary History.* Ithaca: Cornell UP, 1986.

Jameson, Frederic. *Marxism and Form: Twentieth Century Dialectical Theories of Literature.* Princeton: Princeton UP, 1971.

Lukacs, Georg. *Realism in Our Time: Literature and the Class Struggle.* 1957. New York: Harper and Row, 1964.

Marcuse, Herbert. *The Aesthetic Dimension: Toward a Critique of Marxist Aesthetics.* Boston: Beacon, 1978.

Psychological/Psychoanalytic

The scientific study of the mind is a product of psychodynamic theory as established by Sigmund Freud (1856–1939) and of the psychoanalytic method practiced by his followers. Psychoanalysis provided a new key to the understanding of character by claiming that behavior is caused by hidden and unconscious motives. It was greeted as a revelation with far-reaching implications for all intellectual pursuits. Not surprisingly it has had a profound and continuing effect on post-Freudian literature.

In addition, its popularity produced the **psychological/psychoanalytic approach** to criticism.[2] Some critics use the approach to explain fictional characters, as in the landmark interpretation by Freud and Ernest Jones that Shakespeare's Hamlet suffers from an Oedipus complex. Still other critics use it as a way of analyzing authors and the artistic process. For example, John Livingston Lowes's study *The Road to Xanadu* presents a detailed examination of the mind, reading, and neuroses of Coleridge, the author of "Kubla Khan" (p. 734).

Critics using the psychoanalytic approach treat literature somewhat like information about patients in therapy. In the work itself, what are the obvious and hidden motives that cause a character's behavior and speech? How much background (e.g., repressed childhood trauma, adolescent memories) does the author reveal about a character? How purposeful is this information with regard to the character's psychological condition? How much is important in the analysis and understanding of the character?

In the consideration of authors, critics utilizing the psychoanalytic model consider questions like these: What particular life experiences explain characteristic subjects or preoccupations? Was the author's life happy? Miserable? Upsetting? Solitary? Social? Can the death of someone in the author's family be associated with melancholy situations in that author's work? All eleven brothers and sisters of the English poet Thomas Gray, for example, died before reaching adulthood. Gray was the only one of the twelve to survive. In his poetry, Gray often deals with death, and he is therefore considered one of the "Graveyard School" of eighteenth-century poets. A psychoanalytical critic might make much of this connection.

❧ Example: Hawthorne's "Young Goodman Brown"

At the end of "Young Goodman Brown," Hawthorne's major character is no longer capable of normal existence. His nightmare should be read as a symbol of what in reality would have been lifelong mental subjection to the type of puritanical religion that emphasizes sin and guilt. Such preoccupation with sin is no hindrance to psychological health if the preoccupied people are convinced that God forgives them and grants them mercy. In their dealings with others, they remain healthy as long as they believe that other people have the same sincere trust in divine forgiveness. If their own faith is weak and uncertain, however, and if they cannot believe in forgiveness, then they are likely to transfer their own guilt— really a form of personal terror—to others. They remain conscious of their own sins, but they find it easy to claim that others are sinful—even those who are spiritually spotless, and even their own family, who should be dearest to them. When this process of projection or transference occurs, such people have created the rationale of condemning others because of their own guilt. The price that they pay is a life of gloom, a fate that Hawthorne designates for Goodman Brown after his nightmare about demons in human form.

---

[2]See also Chapter 3, "Characters: The People in Fiction."

Example: Browning's "My Last Duchess," page 697

"My Last Duchess" by Robert Browning is a dramatic monologue based loosely on the real-life Duke of Ferrara, Alfonso II (1533–1597). In presumably discussing a marriage proposal with an envoy, the duke reveals his jealousy, egocentrism, and greed. The duke points to a painting of his former duchess and notices her happy "countenance," which was easily aroused by strangers. From what we gather from Browning's poem about the malevolent duke, it is plausible that he had his apparently cheerful wife killed. Getting back to the business at hand, the duke escorts the envoy down the stairs, but not before pointing out a painting of Neptune "taming a seahorse." Besides indicating a love of possessions, his reference to the painting and its subject of taming also suggests a consciousness of subjugation and the desire to bend others to his will—certainly a sign of how he will treat the future duchess. While some psychological studies may point to the poet's frame of mind, "My Last Duchess" is a study of how a poem may imply a personality through a speaker's unsuspecting words.

READINGS

Bloom, Harold. *The Anxiety of Influence*. New York: Oxford UP, 1975.

Bowie, Malcolm. *Freud, Proust, and Lacan: Theory as Fiction*. New York: Cambridge UP, 1987.

Gilbert, Sandra, and Susan Gubar. *The Madwoman in the Attic*. New Haven: Yale UP, 1979.

Gilman, Sander L. ed. *Introducing Psychoanalytic Theory*. New York: Brunner/Mazel, 1982.

Holland, Norman N. *The Dynamics of Literary Response*. New York: Oxford UP, 1968.

Lacan, Jacques. *Ecrits: A Selection*. New York: Norton, 2004.

Shamdsani, Sonu, and Michael Munchow, eds. *Speculations After Freud: Psychoanalysis, Philosophy, and Culture*. New York: Routledge, 1994.

Skura, Meredith Anne. *The Literary Use of the Psychoanalytic Process*. New Haven: Yale UP, 1981.

Wright, Elizabeth. *Psychoanalytic Criticism: Theory in Practice*. New York and London: Methuen, 1984.

Archetypal/Symbolic/Mythic

The **archetypal/symbolic/mythic critical approach,** derived from the work of the Swiss psychoanalyst Carl Jung (1875–1961), presupposes that human life is built up out of patterns, or *archetypes* ("first molds" or "first patterns") that are similar throughout various cultures and historical times.[3] The approach is similar to the structuralist analysis of literature, for both approaches stress the connections that may be discovered in literature written in different times and in vastly different locations in the world.

In literary evaluation, the archetypal approach is used to support the claim that the very best literature is grounded in archetypal patterns. The archetypal critic therefore looks for archetypes such as God's creation of human beings, the

---

[3]Symbolism is also considered in Chapters 7 and 19.

sacrifice of a hero, or the search for paradise. How does an individual story, poem, or play fit into any of the archetypal patterns? What truths does this correlation provide (particularly truths that cross historical, national, and cultural lines)? How closely does the work fit the archetype? What variations can be seen? What meaning or meanings do the connections have?

The most tenuous aspect of archetypal criticism is Jung's assertion that the recurring patterns provide evidence for a "universal human consciousness" that all of us, by virtue of our humanity, still retain in our minds and in our very blood.

Not all critics accept the hypothesis of a universal human consciousness, but they nevertheless consider the approach important for comparisons and contrasts (see Chapter 30). Many human situations, such as adolescence, dawning love, the search for success, the reconciliation with one's mother and father, and the encroachment of age and death, are similar in structure and can be analyzed as archetypes. For example, the following situations can be seen as a pattern or archetype of initiation: A young man discovers the power of literature and understanding (Keats's "On First Looking into Chapman's Homer"); a man determines the importance of truth and fidelity amidst uncertainty (Arnold's "Dover Beach"); a man and woman fall in love despite their wishes to remain independent (Chekhov's *The Bear*); a woman gains strength and integrity because of previously unrealized inner resources (Maupassant's "The Necklace"). The archetypal approach encourages the analysis of variations on the same theme, as in Glaspell's "A Jury of Her Peers" (p. 189) and Faulkner's "A Rose for Emily" (p. 89) when characters choose to ignore the existence of a crime (one sort of initiation) and also, as a result, assert their own individuality and freedom (another sort of initiation).

Example: Hawthorne's "Young Goodman Brown"

In the sense that Young Goodman Brown undergoes a change from psychological normality to rigidity, the story is a reverse archetype of the initiation ritual. According to the archetype of successful initiation, initiates seek to demonstrate their worthiness to become full-fledged members of society. Telemachus in Homer's *Odyssey*, for example, is a young man who in the course of the epic goes through the initiation rituals of travel, discussion, and battle. But in "Young Goodman Brown" we see initiation in reverse, for just as there is an archetype of successful initiation, Brown's initiation leads him into failure. In the private areas of life on which happiness depends, he falls short. He sees evil in his fellow villagers, condemns his minister, and shrinks even from his own family. His life therefore becomes filled with despair and gloom. His suspicions are those of a Puritan of long ago, but the timeliness of Hawthorne's story is that the archetype of misunderstanding and condemnation has not changed. Today's headlines of misery and war are produced by the same kind of intolerance that is exhibited by Goodman Brown.

Second Example: Frost's "Birches," page 1066

Interpreting Frost's poem "Birches" symbolically gives the poem a special depth that it otherwise might not have. On the literal level the poem is about a man who describes birch trees in winter and who states his belief that a lonely boy has perhaps been swinging on them. The poem moves from the third person to the first and we come to realize that the speaker is reminiscing about his own childhood: "So I was once myself a swinger of birches." Many of the rich images of the poem are sexually suggestive. The trunks of the trees are "trailing their leaves on the ground / Like girls on hands and knees that throw their hair / Before them over their heads to dry in the sun." The speaker also describes a boy "riding" the trees "Until he took the stiffness out of them." And While hanging on the tree branches he learned "about not launching out too soon." While these images have clear suggestions about sexuality, the poem ends with the alternate yearning to ride the trees toward heaven and to return back to earth. Reading the poem symbolically thus opens up resonant avenues of interpretation. Expression is given to the dual nature of humankind—physical and spiritual release. By describing the boy swinging on birch trees Frost is expressing the desire for sexual fulfillment and spiritual release from earthly constraints. A rich, evocative poem emerges when "Birches" is read symbolically.

READINGS

Barber, C. L. *Shakespeare's Festive Comedy: A Study of Dramatic Form and Its Relation to Social Custom*. Princeton, Princeton UP, 1972.

Bloom, Harold. *Shelley's Mythmaking*. New Haven: Yale UP, 1959.

Bodkin, Maud. *Archetypal Patterns in Poetry*. London: Oxford UP, 1934.

Bush, Douglas. *Mythology and the Renaissance Tradition in English Poetry*. New York: W. W. Norton, 1963.

Chase, Richard. *Quest for Myth*. Baton Rouge: Louisiana State UP, 1949.

Frye, Northrop *Anatomy of Criticism: Four Essays*. Princeton: Princeton UP, 1957.

Hyman, Stanley Edgar. *The Tangled Bank*. New York: Atheneum, 1962.

Deconstructionist

The **deconstructionist critical approach**—which deconstructionists explain not as an approach but rather as a performance or as a strategy of reading—was developed by the French philosopher Jacques Derrida (1930–2004). In the 1970s and 1980s it became a major mode of criticism by critiquing a Western philosophical tradition known as logocentrism—the belief that speech is a direct expression of a speaker's intention, that it has a direct correspondence to reality, and that it is therefore the privileged arbiter of interpretation. By exposing what he saw as the fallacious assumptions of logocentrism, Derrida sought to undermine the basis of stable meanings derivable from language. The implications for reading and therefore for literary studies were far-reaching.

Deconstructionist critics begin literary analysis by assuming the instability of language and the impossibility of arriving at a fixed standard to anchor interpretation. The dictum, in Derrida's *Of Grammatology*, that "There is nothing outside the text" indicates the denial of any authoritative referent outside of words. Texts are always self-contradictory because they can always be reread to undermine an apparently stable interpretation. In part, this is due to how meaning is derived from binary oppositions such as speech/writing, male/female, good/evil. Each word of the pair obtains its significance by contrast with the other, so that its meaning is relative, not absolute. A female may therefore be defined as lacking male features or a male as lacking female traits. In addition, each set of opposites has been arranged hierarchically; speech, for instance, is considered more immediate and therefore closer to reality than writing and therefore speech is the privileged member of the set speech/writing. These pairings are social constructs and form part of our way of thinking, even if they do not necessarily reflect reality.

Other strategies for undermining the stability of texts are to see how they have "gaps," or missing pieces of information, or words with several meanings and connotations, that therefore "de-center" the meaning of the texts. While a poem may seem to mean one thing when our habitual, formalistic reading strategies are applied to it, it can be shown to have a completely different meaning as well. Additional readings will yield still other meanings. The text is therefore said to "deconstruct" itself as the reading strategies applied to it are merely pointing out contradictory elements that inhere in the nature of language itself.

While formalist critics aim at resolving contradictions and ambiguities to form a unified literary work, deconstructionists aim to find disunity and disruptions in the language of a text. The typical deconstructionist strategy is to start with a standard formalistic reading of a text and then undermine that interpretation in order to yield a new one. The deconstructionist does not deny that interpretations are possible, only that there is no basis for appealing to final, absolute ones. Deconstruction has yielded some new, imaginative readings of canonical literature. Some critics of deconstruction argue that the "initial" formalistic readings of the deconstructionist strategy are the most rewarding and that often deconstructionist interpretations are incoherent.

Example: Hawthorne's "Young Goodman Brown"

There are many uncertainties in the details of "Young Goodman Brown." If one starts with the stranger on the path, one might conclude that he could be Brown's father, because he recognizes Brown immediately and speaks to him jovially. On the other hand, the stranger could be the devil (he is recognized as such by Goody Cloyse) because of his wriggling walking stick. After disappearing, the stranger also takes on the characteristics of an omniscient cult leader and seer, because at the satanic celebration he knows all the secret sins committed by Brown's neighbors and the community of greater New England. Additionally, he might represent a perverted conscience whose aim is to mislead and befuddle people by steering them into the holier-than-thou judgmental attitude that Brown adopts. This method would be truly diabolical—to use religion in order to bring people to their own damnation. That the stranger is an evil force is therefore clear, but the pathways of his evil are not as clear. He seems to work his mission of damnation by reaching the souls of persons like Goodman Brown through means ordinarily attributed to conscience. If the stranger represents a satanic conscience, what are we to suppose that Hawthorne is asserting about what is considered real conscience?

Second Example: Auden's "Musée des Beaux Arts," page 998

"Musée des Beaux Arts" may be read as a poem about an indifferent universe in the face of human suffering. Auden posits the "old master" painters of the Renaissance as depicting this situation correctly: "About suffering they were never wrong." Suffering apparently takes place in the midst of the dull happenings of everyday life, the speaker asserts. The poem ends by focusing on a specific example—Breughel's depiction of the mythic Icarus, who fell into the sea because he flew too close to the sun. No notice is apparently taken by the characters in the painting of the splash made by the falling body as it enters the water. While the poem may be read as being unified around the theme of indifference to suffering, alternate interpretations arise when the poem is deconstructed. The title of the poem indicates the museum where Breughel's painting may be seen. Museums are, in part, repositories of historical events. By referring to a painting in a specific place, Auden lets the reader know that he or she may see a depiction of Icarus's suffering. While the figures in the painting turn away from the fallen Icarus, the observer of the painting—like the reader of the poem—is made conscious of Icarus' story and his suffering. While the dichotomy-event (Icarus falling)/depiction of event (painting and poem of Icarus falling) may suggest a priority to the event itself, it is ironically Auden's poem that encourages us to think of the anguish Icarus must have felt as he fell. In describing the "white legs [of Icarus] disappearing into the green / Water," Auden focuses our attention to suffering and death. "Turns" is a key word in the poem. Auden describes how everyone in the scene "turns away / Quite leisurely from the disaster." Just as something may turn away from an event, the same motion of turning may return us to the same event, in this instance, a contemplation of suffering. While indifference to suffering may be one theme of "Musée des Beaux Arts," deconstructing the poem also shows how it "pulls" in other directions. The language of the poem itself tugs the reader in different directions.

READINGS

Abrams, M. H. "The Deconstructive Angel." in *Doing Things with Texts*. New York and London: Norton, 1989.

Arac, Jonathan, Wlad Godzich, and Wallace Martin, eds. *The Yale Critics: Deconstruction in America*. Minneapolis: U of Minnesota P, 1983.

De Man, Paul. *Blindness and Insight*. New York: Oxford UP, 1971.

Derrida, Jacques. *Of Grammatology*. 1967. Baltimore: Johns Hopkins UP, 1976.

———. *Writing and Difference*. 1967. Chicago: U of Chicago P, 1978.

Hartman, Geoffrey. *Saving the Text: Literature/Derrida/Philosophy*. Baltimore: Johns Hopkins UP, 1981.

Miller, J. Hillis. *Fiction and Repetition: Seven English Novels*. Cambridge: Harvard UP, 1982.

———. *The Linguistic Moment: From Wordsworth to Stevens*. Princeton: Princeton UP, 1985.

———. *The Ethics of Reading: Kant, de Man, Eliot, Trollope, James, and Benjamin*. New York: Columbia UP, 1987.

Silverman, Hugh J., and Gary E. Aylesworth, eds. *The Textual Sublime: Deconstruction and Its Differences*. Albany: State U of New York P, 1990.

Reader-Response

The **reader-response critical approach** is rooted in *phenomenology*, a branch of philosophy that deals with the understanding of how things appear. The phenomenological idea of knowledge is based on the separation of the reality of our thoughts from the reality of the world. Our quest for truth is to be found not in the external world itself but rather in our mental *perception* and interpretation of externals. All that we human beings can know—actual *knowledge*—is our collective and personal understanding of the world and our conclusions about it.

As a consequence of the phenomenological concept, reader-response theory holds that the reader is a necessary third party in the author-text-reader relationship that constitutes the literary work. The work, in other words, is not fully created until readers make a *transaction* with it by assimilating it and *actualizing* it in the light of their own knowledge and experience. The representative questions of the theory are these: What does this work mean to me, in my present intellectual and moral makeup? How can the work improve my understanding and widen my insights? How can my increasing understanding help me understand the work more deeply? The theory is that the free interchange or transaction that such questions bring about leads toward interest and growth, so that readers can assimilate literary works and accept them as parts of their lives and as parts of the civilization in which they live.

As an initial way of reading, the reader-response method may be personal and anecdotal. In addition, by stressing response rather than interpretation, one of the leading exponents of the method (Stanley Fish) has raised the extreme question about whether texts, by themselves, have objective identity. These aspects have been cited as both a shortcoming and an inconsequentiality of the method.

It is therefore important to stress that the reader-response theory is *open*. It permits beginning readers to bring their own personal reactions to literature, but it also aims to increase their discipline and skill. The more that readers bring to literature through their interests and disciplined studies, the more "competent" and comprehensive their "transactions" will be. It is possible, for example, to explain the structure of a work not according to commonly recognized categories such as exposition and climax, but rather according to the personal reactions of representative readers. The contention is that structure, like other avenues of literary study such as tone or the comprehension of figurative language, refers to clearly definable responses that readers experience when reading and transacting with works. By such means, literature is subject not only to outward and objective analysis, but also to inward and psychological response.

The reader-response approach thus lends an additional dimension to the critical awareness of literature. If literary works imply that readers should possess special knowledge in fields such as art, politics, science, philosophy, religion, or morality, then competent readers will seek out such knowledge and utilize it in developing their responses. Also, because students experience many similar intellectual and cultural disciplines, it is logical to conclude that responses will tend not to diverge but rather to coalesce; agreements result not from personal but from cultural similarities. The reader-response theory, then, can and should be an avenue toward informed and detailed understanding of literature, but the initial emphasis is the *transaction* that readers make with literary works.

Example: Hawthorne's "Young Goodman Brown"

"Young Goodman Brown" is worrisome because it shows so disturbingly that good intentions may cause harmful results. I think that a person with too high a set of expectations is ripe for disillusionment, just as Goodman Brown is. When people don't measure up to this person's standard of perfection, they can be thrown aside as though they are worthless. They may be good people, but whatever past mistakes they have made make it impossible for the person with high expectations to endure them. Goodman Brown makes the same kind of misjudgment, expecting perfection and turning sour when he learns about flaws. It is not that he is not a good man, because he is shown at the start as a person of belief and stability. He uncritically accepts his nightmare revelation that everyone else is evil, however (including his parents), and he finally distrusts everyone because of this baseless suspicion. He cannot look at his neighbors without avoiding them like an "anathema," and he turns away from his own wife "without a greeting" (paragraph 70). Brown's problem is that he equates being human with being unworthy. By such a distorted standard of judgment, all of us fail, and that is what makes the story so disturbing.

Second Example: Roethke's "My Papa's Waltz," page 828

"My Papa's Waltz" by Theodore Roethke shows how complicated relationships between father and son may be. While it is the memory of a spirited "waltz" that the speaker, as a child, had with his father, the emotions it evokes are not so easy to pin down. On the one hand, the speaker recalls what might have seemed a happy time, with father and son romping "until the pans / slid from the kitchen shelf" and the boy danced off to bed "Still clinging to your [the father's] shirt." There is, however, a darker side to this memory as suggested by images that border on abuse. The whiskey on the father's breath "Could make a small boy dizzy." Also, the father "scraped a buckle" every time he missed a step of the dance and "beat time" on the boy's head; in addition, the speaker's memory is that his mother was an unhappy witness to this rough play. That her "countenance / Could not unfrown itself" suggests a disapproving uneasiness. The regular stanzas and short lines indicate the symmetry and balance of an orderly dance, but the more disturbing images imply violence. This double-edged emotion points to the complex nature of love and the ambivalent feelings we may have toward a parent. We might wish sometimes that our memories could be resolved into one overwhelming feeling, but "My Papa's Waltz," through its rich imagery, evokes the true nature of most relationships. They aren't easily categorized.

READINGS

Altick, Richard. *The English Common Reader: A Social History of the Mass Reading Public 1800–1900.* Chicago: U of Chicago P, 1957.

Bleich, David. *Readings and Feelings: An Introduction to Subjective Criticism.* Urbana: National Council of Teachers of English, 1975.

Booth, Wayne C. *The Rhetoric of Fiction.* 2nd ed. Chicago: U of Chicago P, 1983.

Fish, Stanley. *Is There a Text in This Class? The Authority of Interpretive Communities.* Cambridge: Harvard UP, 1980.

Holland, Norman N. *The Dynamics of Literary Response.* New York: Oxford UP, 1968.

Iser, Wolfgang. *The Implied Reader: Pattern of Communication in Prose Fiction From Bunyan to Beckett.* Baltimore: Johns Hopkins UP, 1974.

Leavis, Q. D. *Fiction and the Reading Public.* London: Chatto and Windus, 1932.

Mailloux, Steven J. *Interpretive Convections.* Ithaca: Cornell UP, 1982.

Richards, I. A. *Practical Criticism: A Study of Literary Judgment.* New York: Harcourt, Brace, 1935.

Sartre, Jean-Paul. *What Is Literature?* New York: Philosophical Library, 1966.

Suleiman, Susan, and Inge Crosman, eds. *The Reader in the Text: Essays on Audience and Interpretation.* Princeton: Princeton UP, 1980.

Chapter 30

Comparison-Contrast and Extended Comparison-Contrast: Learning by Seeing Literary Works Together

Comparison-contrast analysis is the act of putting literary works side by side—juxtaposing them, looking at them together—for a variety of purposes such as description, enhanced understanding, evaluation, and decision making. The technique underlies other important techniques, specifically (1) the analysis of causes and effects, and (2) the scientific method of constant-and-variable analysis. Significant questions may be asked about all these methods: How is *A* both like and unlike *B*? What are the causes of *A*? How does a change in *A* affect *B*? These are all questions that call into play the technique of comparison and contrast.

The educational significance of the technique is to encourage you to make connections—*one of the most important aspects of productive thinking*. As long as things *seem* different and disconnected they in fact *are* different and disconnected. In practice, they are two separate and distinct entities. But when you can demonstrate that they have similarities and connections, then you can make relationships clear. You are in a position both to stress points of likeness and also to emphasize just what makes literary works distinct and unique. For all these reasons, it is vital for you to find similarities and differences through the technique of comparison and contrast. In a very real sense, the language of comparison and contrast is also the language of active and creative thinking.

The immediate goals of a comparison-contrast essay on literary works is to compare and contrast different authors; two or more works by the same author; different drafts of the same work; or characters, incidents, techniques, and ideas in the same work or in a number of separate works. Developing a comparison-contrast analysis enables you to study works in perspective. No matter what works you consider together, the method helps you get at the essence of a work or writer. Similarities are brought out by comparison; differences are brought out by contrast. In other words, you can enhance your understanding of what a thing *is* by using comparison-contrast to determine what it *is not*.

For example, our understanding of Shakespeare's Sonnet 30, "When to the Sessions of Sweet Silent Thought" (Chapter 15) can be augmented if we compare it with Denise Levertov's poem "A Time Past" (Chapter 14). Both poems treat recollections of past experiences told by a speaker to a listener, and we as readers become, as it were, witnesses to the poems. Both poems refer to persons, dead or absent, with whom the speakers were closely involved. In these respects, the poems are comparable.

In addition to these similarities, there are significant differences. Shakespeare's speaker numbers the dead persons as friends whom he laments generally. Levertov's speaker refers to a number of vanished people, but her major focus is on one person with whom she had been in love, whose sight at one time made her joyful and happy. Levertov's topics are the sorrow of past memory and lost love, the inexorable power of change, and the causes of isolation and regret. Shakespeare refers to dead friends as a way of accounting for present sorrows, but then his speaker turns to the present and asserts that thinking about the "dear friend" being addressed enables him to restore past "losses" and end all "sorrows." In Levertov's poem, there is recognition of both past and present, but no reconciliation. Instead the speaker focuses on the unpleasantness and distastefulness of the changes that time has wrought. Both poems are similarly retrospective, but they differ widely in their conclusions about how the present has been altered by the past.

Guidelines for the Comparison-Contrast Method

The preceding example, although brief, shows how the comparison-contrast method makes it possible to identify leading similarities and distinguishing differences in two works. Frequently you can overcome the difficulties you might encounter in understanding one work by comparing and contrasting it with another work on a comparable subject. A few guidelines will help direct your efforts in writing comparison-contrast essays.

Clarify Your Intention

When planning a comparison-contrast essay, first decide on your goal, for you can use the method in a number of ways. One objective is the equal and mutual illumination of two (or more) works. For example, in an essay comparing Welty's "A Worn Path" (Chapter 1) with Hawthorne's "Young Goodman Brown" (Chapter 7) you might (1) compare ideas, characters, or methods in these stories equally, without stressing or favoring either; (2) emphasize "Young Goodman Brown," and therefore use "A Worn Path" as material for highlighting Hawthorne's story; (3) illustrate the superiority of one story over another; or (4) emphasize a method or idea that you think is especially noteworthy or appropriate.

A first task, therefore, is to decide what to emphasize. The illustrative essay on pages 1883–85 gives "equal time" to both works being considered, without claiming the superiority of either. Unless you have a different rhetorical goal, this essay provides a suitable example for most comparisons.

Find Common Grounds for Comparison

The second stage in preparing a comparison-contrast essay is to select and articulate a common ground for discussion. It is pointless to compare dissimilar things, for the resulting conclusions will not have much value. Instead, compare like with like: idea with idea, characterization with characterization, setting with setting, point of view with point of view, tone with tone. Nothing much can be learned from a comparison of Frost's view of individuality and Chekhov's view of love; but a comparison of the relationship of individuality with identity and character in Frost and Chekhov suggests common ground, with the promise of significant ideas to be developed through the examination of similarities and differences.

In seeking common ground, you will need to be inventive and creative. For instance, if you compare Maupassant's "The Necklace" (Part I) and Chekhov's *The Bear* (Chapter 25), these two works at first may seem dissimilar. Yet common ground can be discovered, such as the treatment of self-deceit, the effects of chance on human affairs, and the authors' views of women. Although other works may seem even more dissimilar than these, it is usually possible to find a common ground for comparison and contrast. Much of your success in an essay of this type depends on your finding a workable basis—a common denominator—for comparison.

Integrate the Bases of Comparison

Let us assume that you have decided on your rhetorical purpose and on the basis or bases of your comparison. You have done your reading and taken notes, and you have a rough idea of what you want to say. The remaining problem is the treatment of your material.

One method is to make your points first about one work and then about the other. Unfortunately, such a comparison makes your paper seem like two separate lumps. ("Work 1" takes up one half of your paper to make one lump, and "Work 2" takes up the other half to make a second lump.) Also, the method involves repetition because you must repeat many points when you treat the second subject.

Therefore, a better method is to treat the major aspects of your main idea and to refer to the two (or more) works as they support your arguments. Thus you refer constantly to *both* works, sometimes within the same sentence, and remind your reader of the point of your discussion. There are reasons for the superiority of this method: (1) You do not repeat your points needlessly, for you develop them as you raise them. (2) By constantly referring to the two works, you make your points without requiring a reader with a poor memory to reread previous sections.

As a model, here is a paragraph on "Natural References as a Basis of Comparison in Frost's 'Desert Places' (Chapter 18) and Shakespeare's Sonnet 73: 'That Time of Year Thou May'st in Me Behold'" (Chapter 17). The virtue of the paragraph is that it uses material from each of the poems simultaneously as the substance for the development of the ideas, as nearly as the time sequence of sentences allows. For illustration, the sentences are numbered.

(1) Both Shakespeare and Frost link their ideas to events occurring in the natural world. (2) Night as a parallel with death is common to both poems, with Frost speaking about it in his first line and Shakespeare introducing it in his seventh. (3) Along with night, Frost emphasizes the onset of winter and snow as a time of death and desolation. (4) With this natural description, Frost also symbolically refers to empty, secret, dead places in the inner spirit—crannies of the soul where bleak winter snowfalls

correspond to selfishness and indifference. (5) By contrast, Shakespeare uses the fall season, with the yellowing and falling of leaves, and the migrations of birds, to stress the closeness of real death and therefore the need to love fully during the time remaining. (6) Both poems thus share a sense of gloom because both present death as inevitable and final, just like the emptiness of winter. (7) Because Shakespeare's sonnet is addressed to a listener who is also a loved one, however, it is more outgoing than the more introspective poem of Frost. (8) Frost turns the snow, the night, and the emptiness of the universe inward in order to show the speaker's inner bleakness, and by extension, the bleakness of many human spirits. (9) Shakespeare instead uses the bleakness of night, dying fires, and changing seasons to emphasize the need for loving "well." (10) The poems thus use common and similar references for different purposes and effects.

This paragraph links Shakespeare's references to nature to those of Frost. Five sentences speak of both authors together; three speak of Frost alone and two of Shakespeare alone, but all the sentences are unified topically. This interweaving of references indicates that the writer has learned both poems well enough to consider them together, and it also enables the writing to be more pointed and succinct than if the works were separately treated.

You can learn from this example: If you develop your essay by putting your two subjects constantly together, you will write economically and pointedly (not only for essays but also for tests). Beyond that, if you digest the material as successfully as this method indicates, you demonstrate that you are fulfilling a major educational goal—the assimilation and *use* of material. Too often, because you learn things separately (in separate works and courses, at separate times), you tend also to compartmentalize them. Instead, you should always try to relate them, to *synthesize* them. Comparison and contrast help in this process of putting together, of seeing things not as fragments but as parts of wholes.

Avoid the Tennis-Ball Method

As you make your comparison, do not confuse an interlocking method with a "tennis-ball" method, in which you bounce your subject back and forth constantly and repetitively, almost as though you were hitting observations back and forth over a net. The tennis-ball method is shown in the following example from a comparison of the characters Mathilde (Maupassant's "The Necklace") and Mrs. Popov (Chekhov's *The Bear*).

> Mathilde is a young married woman; Mrs. Popov is also young but a widow. Mathilde has a limited social life, and she doesn't have more than one friend; Mrs. Popov chooses to lead a life of solitude. Mathilde's daydreams about wealth are responsible for her misfortune, and Mrs. Popov's dedication to the memory of her husband is capable of ruining her life. Mathilde is made unhappy because of her shortcomings, but Mrs. Popov is rescued despite her shortcomings. In Mathilde's case the focus is on adversity not only causing trouble but also strengthening character. Similarly, in Mrs. Popov's case the focus is on a strong person realizing her strength regardless of her conscious decision to weaken herself.

Imagine the effect of an entire essay written in this invariable 1, 2, 1, 2, 1, 2 order. Aside from the inflexible patterning of subjects, the tennis-ball method does not permit much illustrative development. You should not feel so constrained that you cannot take two or more sentences to develop a point about one writer or subject before you include comparative references to another. If you remember to interlock the two subjects of comparison, however, as in the paragraph about Frost and Shakespeare, your method will give you the freedom to develop your topics fully.

The Extended Comparison-Contrast Essay

For a longer essay about a number of works—such as a limited research paper, comprehensive exam questions, and the sort of extended essay required at the end of a semester—comparison-contrast is an essential method. You may wish to compare the works on the basis of elements such as ideas, plot, language, structure, character, metaphor, point of view, or setting. Because of the larger number of works, however, you will need to modify the way in which you employ comparison-contrast. Suppose you are dealing with not just two works but with six, seven, or more. You need first to find a common ground to use as your central, unifying idea, just as you do for a comparison of only two works. Once you establish the common ground, you can classify or group your works on the basis of the similarities and differences they exemplify with regard to the topic. The idea is to get two *groups* for comparison, not just two works.

Let us assume that three or four works treat a topic in one way but that two or three do it in another (e.g., either criticism or praise of wealth and trade, the joys or sorrows of love, the enthusiasm of youth, gratitude for life, or the disillusionment of age). In writing about these works, you might treat the topic itself in a straightforward comparison-contrast method, but use details from the works within the groupings as the material that you use for illustration and argument.

To make your essay as specific as possible, it is best to stress only a small number of works with each of your subpoints. Once you have established these points, there is no need to go into abundant detail with all the other works you are studying. Instead, you need to make no more than brief references to the other works, for your purpose should be to strengthen your points without creating more and more examples. Once you go to another subpoint, you should then use different works for illustration, so that by the end of your essay, you will have given due attention to each work in your assignment. In this way—by treating many works in small comparative groups—you can keep your essay reasonably brief, for there is no need to go into unproductive detail.

As an example, the illustrative essay on pages 1887–90 shows how this grouping may be done. In the first part of the body of this essay, six works are used comparatively to show how private needs conflict with social and public demands. The next part shows how three works can be compared and contrasted on the ways they treat the topic of public concerns as expressed through law.

🍁 CITING REFERENCES IN A LONGER COMPARISON-CONTRAST ESSAY

For the longer comparison-contrast essay, you may find a problem in making references to many different works. Generally you do not need to repeat references. For example, if you refer to Louise of Chopin's "The Story of an Hour" (Chapter 6) or to Minnie Wright of Glaspell's "A Jury of Her Peers" (Chapter 3), you should make the full references only once and then refer later just to the character, story, or author, according to your needs.

When you quote lines or passages or when you cite actions or characters in special ways, you should use parenthetical line, speech, or paragraph references, as in the illustrative essay on (p. 1887). Be guided by the following principle: If you make a specific reference that you think your reader might want to examine in more detail, supply the line, speech, or paragraph number. If you refer to minor details that might easily be unnoticed or forgotten, also supply the appropriate number. Your intention should be to include the appropriate locating numbers whenever you are in doubt about references.

WRITING A COMPARISON-CONTRAST ESSAY

In planning your essay, you should first narrow and simplify your topic so that you can handle it conveniently. If your subject is a comparison of two poets (as in the illustrative comparison-contrast essay on Lowell and Owen, p. 1883), choose one or two of each poet's poems on the same or a similar topic, and write your essay about these.

Once you have found an organizing principle, along with the relevant works, begin to refine and to focus the direction of your essay. As you study each work, note common or contrasting elements and use these to form your central idea. At the same time, you can select the most illustrative works and classify them according to your topic, such as war, love, work, faithfulness, or self-analysis.

Strategies for Organizing Ideas

Begin by stating the works, authors, characters, or ideas that you are considering; then show how you have narrowed the topic. Your central idea should briefly highlight the principal grounds of comparison and contrast, such as that both works treat a common topic, exhibit a similar idea, use a similar form, or develop an identical attitude, and also that major or minor differences help make the works unique. You may also assert that one work is superior to the other, if you wish to make this judgment and defend it.

The body of your essay is governed by the works and your basis of comparison (presentations of ideas, depictions of character, uses of setting, qualities of style and tone, uses of poetic form, uses of comparable imagery or symbols, uses of point of view, and so on). For a comparison-contrast treatment on such a basis, your goal should be to shed light on both (or more) of the works you are treating. For example, you might examine stories written in the first-person point of view (see Chapter 2). An essay on this topic might compare the ways in which each author uses point of view to achieve similar or distinct effects; or it might compare poems that employ similar images, symbols, or ironic methods. Sometimes, the process can be as simple as identifying female or male protagonists and comparing the ways in which their characters are developed. Another obvious approach is to compare the *subjects*, as opposed to the *idea*. You might identify works dealing with general subjects such as love, death, youth, race, or war. Such groupings provide a basis for excellent comparisons and contrasts.

As you develop your essay, remember to keep comparison-contrast foremost. That is, your discussions of point of view, figurative language, or whatever should not so much explain these topics *as topics* but rather should explore *similarities and differences* of the works you are comparing. If your topic is an idea, for example, you need to explain the idea, but just enough to establish points of similarity or difference. As you develop such an essay, you might illustrate your arguments by referring to related uses of elements such as setting, characterization, symbolism, point of view, or metaphor. When you introduce these new subjects, you will be on target as long as you use them in the context of comparison-contrast.

In concluding, you might reflect on other ideas or techniques in the works you have compared, make observations about similar qualities, or summarize briefly the grounds of your comparison. If there is a point you have considered especially important, you might stress that point again in your conclusion. Also, your comparison might have led you to conclude that one work—or group of works—is superior to another. Stressing that point again would make an effective conclusion.

Illustrative Student Essay (Two Works)

Underlined sentences in this paper *do not* conform to MLA style and are used solely as teaching tools to emphasize the central idea, thesis sentence, and topic sentences throughout the paper.

Mane 1

Marcelino Mane

Professor Park

English 123

11 April 2008

The Treatment of Responses to War in Amy Lowell's "Patterns"

and Wilfred Owen's "Anthem for Doomed Youth"°

Lowell's "Patterns" and Owen's "Anthem for Doomed Youth" are both   [1]

powerful and unique condemnations of war.* Owen's short poem speaks

broadly and generally about the ugliness of war and also about large groups of

sorrowful people. Lowell's longer poem focuses on the personal grief of just

one person. In a sense, Lowell's poem begins where Owen's ends, a fact that

accounts for both the similarities and the differences between the two works.

The antiwar themes can be compared on the basis of their subjects, their

lengths, their concreteness, and their use of a common metaphor.†

"Anthem for Doomed Youth" attacks war more directly than "Patterns."   [2]

Owen's opening line "What passing-bells for those who die as cattle?" suggests

that in war human beings are depersonalized before they are slaughtered, like

so much meat, and his observations about the "monstrous" guns and the "shrill,

demented" shells unambiguously condemn the horrors of war. By contrast, in

"Patterns," warfare is far away, on another continent, intruding only when the

messenger delivers the letter stating that the speaker's fiancé has been killed

(lines 63–64). A comparable situation governs the last six lines of Owen's

poem, quietly describing how those at home respond to the news that their

loved ones have died in war. Thus the antiwar focus in "Patterns" is the contrast

between the calm, peaceful life of the speaker's garden and the anguish of her

°These poems appear in Chapters 14 and 22.
*Central idea.
†Thesis sentence.

Mane 2

responses. In "Anthem for Doomed Youth," the stress is more on the external horrors of war that bring about the need for ceremonies honoring the dead.

[3]   Another major difference between the poems is their wide discrepancy in length. "Patterns" is an interior monologue or meditation of 107 lines, but it could not be shorter and still be convincing. In the poem the speaker thinks of the past and contemplates her future loneliness. Her final outburst, "Christ! What are patterns for?" could make no sense if she did not explain her situation as extensively as she does. "Anthem for Doomed Youth," however, is brief--a fourteen-line sonnet--because it is more general and less personal than "Patterns." Although Owen's speaker shows great sympathy, he or she views the sorrows of others distantly, unlike Lowell, who goes right into the mind and spirit of the grieving woman. Owen's use, in his last six lines, of phrases such as "tenderness of patient minds" and "drawing down of blinds" is a powerful representation of deep grief. He gives no further details even though thousands of individual stories might be told. In contrast, Lowell tells just one of these stories as she focuses on her solitary speaker's lost hopes and dreams. Thus the contrasting lengths of the poems are determined by each poet's treatment of the topic.

[4]   Despite these differences of approach and length, both poems are similarly concrete and real. Owen moves from the real scenes and sounds of far-off battlefields to the homes of the many soldiers who have been killed in battle, but Lowell's scene is a single place--the garden of her speaker's estate. The speaker walks on real gravel along garden paths that contain daffodils, squills, a fountain, and a lime tree. She thinks of her clothing and her ribboned shoes, and also of her fiancé's boots, sword hilts, and buttons. The images in Owen's poem are equally real but are not associated with individuals as in "Patterns." Thus Owen's images are those of cattle, bells, rifle shots, shells, bugles, candles, and window blinds. Although both poems reflect reality, Owen's details are more general and public; Lowell's are more specific and intimate.

[5]   Along with this concreteness, the poems share a major metaphor: that cultural patterns both control and frustrate human wishes and hopes. In "Patterns," this metaphor is shown in warfare itself (line 106), which is the

Mane 3

pinnacle of organized human patterns of destruction. Further examples of the metaphor are found in details about clothing (particularly the speaker's stiff, confining gown in lines 5, 18, 21, 73, and 101, and also the lover's military boots in lines 46 and 49); the orderly, formal garden paths in which the speaker is walking (lines 1 and 93); her restraint at hearing about her lover's death; and her courtesy, despite her grief, in ordering refreshment for the messenger (line 69). Within such rigid patterns, her hopes for happiness have vanished, along with the sensuous spontaneity symbolized by her lover's hope to make love with her on a "shady seat" in the garden (lines 85–89). The metaphor of the constricting pattern is also seen in "Anthem for Doomed Youth," except that in this poem, the pattern is the funeral, not love or marriage. Owen's speaker contrasts the calm, peaceful tolling of "passing-bells" (line 1) to the frightening sounds of war represented by the "monstrous anger of the guns," "the stuttering rifles' rapid rattle," and "the demented choirs of wailing shells" (lines 2–8). Thus, while Lowell uses the metaphor to reveal the irony of hope and desire being destroyed by war, Owen uses it to reveal the irony of war's negation of peaceful ceremonies.

Though in these ways the poems share topics and some aspects of treatment, they are distinct and individual. "Patterns" includes many references to visible things, whereas "Anthem for Doomed Youth" emphasizes sound (and silence). Both poems conclude on powerfully emotional although different notes. Owen's poem dwells on the pathos and sadness that war brings to many unnamed people, and Lowell's expresses the most intimate thoughts of a woman who is alone in her first agony of grief. Although neither poem attacks the usual platitudes and justifications for war (the needs to mobilize, to sacrifice, to achieve peace through fighting, and so on), the attack is there by implication, for both poems make their appeal by stressing how war destroys the relationships that make life worth living. For this reason, despite their differences, both "Patterns" and "Anthem for Doomed Youth" are parallel anti-war poems, and both are strong expressions of feeling.

[6]

Mane 4

Work Cited

Amy Lowell, "Patterns," and Wilfred Owen, "Anthem for Doomed Youth."

Literature: An Introduction to Reading and Writing. 9th ed. Ed. Edgar V.

Roberts. New York: Pearson Longman, 2009, 729 and 1149–52.

Commentary on the Essay

This essay shows how approximately equal attention can be given to the two works being studied. Words stressing similarity are *common, share, equally, parallel, both, similar,* and *also.* Contrasts are stressed by *while, whereas, different, dissimilar, contrast, although,* and *except.* Transitions from paragraph to paragraph are not different in this type of essay from those in other essays. Thus, the phrases *despite, along with this,* and *in these ways,* which are used here, could be used anywhere for the same transitional purpose.

The central idea—that the poems mutually condemn war—is brought out in paragraph 1, together with the supporting idea that the poems blend into each other because both show responses to news of battle casualties.

Paragraph 2, the first in the body, discusses how each poem brings out its attack on warfare. Paragraph 3 explains the differing lengths of the poems as a function of differences in perspective. Because Owen's sonnet views war and its effects at a distance, it is brief; but because Lowell's interior monologue views death intimately, she provides more detail and greater length.

Paragraph 4, on the topic of concreteness and reality, shows that the two works can receive equal attention without the bouncing back and forth of the tennis-ball method. Three of the sentences in this paragraph (3, 4, and 6) are devoted exclusively to details in one poem or the other; but sentences 1, 2, 5, and 7 refer to both works, stressing points of broad or specific comparison. The scheme demonstrates that the two works are, in effect, interlocked within the paragraph.

Paragraph 5, the last in the body, considers the similar and dissimilar ways in which the poems treat the common metaphor of cultural patterns.

The conclusion, paragraph 6, summarizes the central idea, and it also stresses the ways in which the poems, although similar, are distinct and unique.

Illustrative Student Essay (Extended Comparison-Contrast)

Underlined sentences in this paper *do not* conform to MLA style and are used solely as teaching tools to emphasize the central idea, thesis sentence, and topic sentences throughout the paper.

Mane 1

Marcelino Mane

Professor Park

English 123

19 May 2008

Literary Treatments of the Conflicts Between Private and Public Life

<u>The conflict between private or personal life, on the one hand, and public</u>   [1]
<u>or civic and national life, on the other, is a topic common to many literary</u>
<u>works.</u>° Authors show that individuals try to maintain their personal lives and
commitments even though they are tested and stressed by public and external
forces. Ideally, individuals should have the freedom to follow their own wishes
independently of the outside world. It is a fact, however, that living itself causes
people to venture into the public world and therefore to encounter conflicts.
Getting married, following a profession, observing the natural world, looking
at a person's possessions, taking a walk--all these draw people into the public
world in which rules, regulations, and laws override private wishes. To greater
and lesser degrees, such conflicts are found in Arnold's "Dover Beach,"
Bierce's "An Occurrence at Owl Creek Bridge," Chekhov's "The Bear,"
Glaspell's "Trifles," Chopin's "The Story of an Hour," Hardy's "Channel
Firing," Hawthorne's "Young Goodman Brown," Keats's "Bright Star," Lowell's
"Patterns," and Shakespeare's Sonnet 73: "That Time of Year Thou May'st
in Me Behold."* <u>In these works, conflicts are shown between interests of</u>
<u>individuals and those of the social, legal, and military public.</u>†

°Central idea.
*These works appear in Chapters 2, 6, 7, 13, 14, 15, 17, 22, 23, and 25.
†Thesis sentence.

Mane 2

[2]   One of the major private-public conflicts is created by the way in which characters respond to social conventions and expectations. In Chekhov's "The Bear," for example, Mrs. Popov has given up her personal life to memorialize her dead husband. She resolves to wear black, to swear eternal fidelity, and to stay in her house for an entire year. And she does all this to fulfill what she considers her public role as a grieving widow. Fortunately for her, Smirnov arrives on the scene and arouses her enough to make her give up this foolish pose. Not as fortunate is Hawthorne's Goodman Brown in "Young Goodman Brown." Brown's obligation is much less public and also more philosophical than Mrs. Popov's because his religiously inspired vision of evil fills him with lifelong gloom. Although Mrs. Popov is easily moved away from her position by the prospect of immediate life and vitality, Brown's mindless distrust locks him into a fear of evil from which not even his faithful wife can shake him. The two characters therefore go in entirely different directions--Mrs. Popov toward personal fulfillment, and Goodman Brown toward personal destruction.

[3]   A major idea in the various works is that philosophical or religious difficulties such as those of Goodman Brown force a crisis in an individual life. In Arnold's "Dover Beach" the speaker expresses regret about uncertainty and the loss of religious faith that symbolically wear away civilization just like surf beating on the stones of Dover Beach. This situation might be expected to make a person as dreary and depressed as Goodman Brown actually is. Arnold's speaker, however, in the lines "Ah, love, let us be true / To one another," finds power in personal fidelity and commitment (lines 29–30). In other words, the public world of "human misery" and the diminishing "Sea of Faith" is beyond control, and therefore all that is left is personal commitment. This is not to say that "Young Goodman Brown," as a story, is negative, for Hawthorne implies that a positive personal life lies in the denial of choices like those made by Brown and in the acceptance of choices like those made by Mrs. Popov and Arnold's speaker. It is only fair, however, to observe that Hawthorne does not state this idea directly.

[4]   To deny or to ignore the public world is a possible option that, under some circumstances, can be chosen. For example, "Dover Beach" reflects a conscious

Mane 3

decision to ignore the philosophic and religious uncertainty that the speaker finds in the intellectual and public world. Even more independent of such a public world, Shakespeare's "That Time of Year" and Keats's "Bright Star" bring out their ideas as meditations about purely personal situations. Shakespeare's speaker deals with the love between himself and the listener, whereas Keats's speaker, addressing a distant star, considers his need for steadfastness in his relationship with his "fair love." In Chopin's "The Story of an Hour" Louise embodies an interesting variation on the personal matters brought up in these two sonnets. At first, she is crushed by the news coming from the public world that her husband has been killed. Her first vision of herself is that of a grieving, private widow. As she thinks about things, however, she quickly begins to anticipate the liberation and freedom--to become free to explore the public world--that widowhood will give her. Ironically, it is the reappearance of her husband, who moves freely in the public world, that causes her sudden heart failure. What she looked forward to as the possibility of free choice to do what she wants and to go where she wishes has suddenly been withdrawn from her by her renewed status within the publicly sanctioned system of marriage, and it is her recognition of her abrupt loss of this possibility that triggers the end of her life.

    The complexity of the conflicts between private and public life is brought out in the way in which structures secure their power through law and legality. [5] With immense power, the law often acts as an arbitrary form of public judgment that disregards personal needs and circumstances. This idea is brought out on the most personal level in Glaspell's "Trifles," in which the two major characters, both women, urgently confront the conflict between their personal identification with the accused woman, Minnie, and their public obligation to the law. One of the women, Mrs. Peters, is reminded that she is "married to the law," but she and Mrs. Hale suppress the evidence that they know would condemn Minnie, even though technically--by law, that is--their knowledge is public property. Their way of resolving the conflict is therefore to reject the public demands made upon them, and to accept their own private wishes and thoughts about personal behavior.

Mane 4

[6]   It is works about warfare that especially highlight how irreconcilable the conflicts between personal and public concerns can become. A comic but nevertheless real instance is dramatized by Hardy in "Channel Firing." In this poem, set in a church graveyard, the skeleton of "Parson Thirdly" views "gunnery practice out at sea" (line 10) as evidence that his "forty year" dedication to serving his church was a waste of time. His conclusion is that he would have been better off ignoring his public role and instead sticking "to pipes and beer." Although Thirdly is disillusioned, he has not been as deeply affected personally by warfare as the speaker of Lowell's "Patterns." Her fiancé, she learns, has been killed fighting abroad; and his death leads her to question--and by implication to doubt--the external "patterns" that have suddenly destroyed her personal plans for life (line 107). Unlike both these characters, who are deeply affected by the effects of warfare, Peyton Farquhar, the main character in Bierce's "An Occurrence at Owl Creek Bridge," is actually killed by his commitment to a public concern--that of the Southern forces in the Civil War. As in "Channel Firing" and "Patterns," Farquhar's situation shows how the public world may exert absolute power over the private.

[7]   The works examined here are in general agreement that, under ideal conditions, private life should be supreme over public life. They also demonstrate that in many ways, the public world invades the private world with a wide range of effects, from making people behave foolishly to destroying them utterly. Naturally, the tone of the works is shaped by the degree of seriousness of the conflict. Chekhov's "The Bear" is good-humored and farcical because the characters overcome the social roles in which they are cast. More sober are works such as "Dover Beach" and "Young Goodman Brown," in which characters either are overcome by public commitments or deliberately turn their backs on them. In the highest range of seriousness are works such as "Patterns," and "An Occurrence at Owl Creek Bridge," in which the individual is crushed by irresistible public forces. The works compared and contrasted here show varied and powerful conflicts between public demands and personal interests.

Mane 5

Work Cited

Selected Works. Literature: An Introduction to Reading and Writing. Ed. Edgar

V. Roberts and Henry E. Jacobs. 9th ed. New York: Pearson Longman,

2009.

Commentary on the Essay

This essay, combining for discussion all three genres of fiction, poetry, and drama, is visualized as an assignment at the end of a unit of study. The expectation prompting the assignment is that a fairly large number of literary works can be profitably compared on the basis of a unifying subject, idea, or technique. For this essay, the works—five poems, three stories, and two short plays—are compared and contrasted on the common topic of private-public conflicts. It is obviously impossible to discuss all the works in detail in every paragraph. The essay therefore shows how a writer may introduce a large number of works in a straightforward comparison-contrast method without a need for detailed comparison of each work with every other work on each of the major subtopics (social, legal, military).

Thus, the first section, consisting of paragraphs 2–4, treats six of the works. In paragraph 2, however, only two works are discussed, and in paragraph 3 one of these works is carried over for comparison with only one additional work. The fourth paragraph springs out of the second, utilizing one of the works discussed there and then bringing out comparisons with three additional works.

The same technique is used in the rest of the essay. Paragraph 5 introduces only one work; paragraph 6 introduces two additional works; and paragraph 7 introduces three works for comparison and contrast. Each of the ten works is therefore discussed at least once in terms of how it contributes to the major topic. One might note that the essay concentrates on a relatively small number of the works, such as Chekhov's *The Bear* and Hawthorne's "Young Goodman Brown," but that as newer topics are introduced, the essay goes on to works that are more closely connected to these topics.

The technique of extended comparison-contrast used in this way shows how the various works can be defined and distinguished in relation to the common idea. The concluding paragraph summarizes these distinctions by suggesting a continuous line along which each of the works may be placed.

Even so, the treatment of so many texts might easily cause crowding and confusion. The division of the major topic into subtopics, as noted, is a major means of trying to make the essay easy to follow. An additional means is the introduction of transitional words and phrases such as *also, choose,* and *one of the major conflicts.*

An extended comparison-contrast essay cannot present a full treatment of each of the works. The works are unique, and there are many elements that do not yield to the comparison-contrast method. Ideas that are particularly important in Hardy's "Channel Firing," for example, are (1) that human beings need eternal rest and not eternal life, (2) that God is amused by—or indifferent to—human affairs, (3) that religious callings or vocations may be futile, and (4) that war itself is the supreme form of cruelty. All these topics could be treated in another essay, but they do not pertain to the particular goals of this particular illustrative essay. A topic compatible with the general private-public topic is needed, and the connection is readily made (paragraph 6) through the character of Hardy's Parson Thirdly. Because the essay deals with the conflicts brought out by Thirdly's comments, Hardy's poem is linked to all the other works for comparative purposes. So it is with the other works, each of which could also be the subject of analysis from many standpoints other than comparison-contrast. The effect of the comparison of all the works collectively, however, is the enhanced understanding of each of the works separately. To achieve such an understanding and to explain it are the major goals of the extended comparison-contrast method.

Writing Topics for Comparison and Contrast

1. The use of the speaker in Arnold's "Dover Beach" (p. 694) and Hardy's "Channel Firing" (p. 738).

2. The description of fidelity to love in Keats's "Bright Star" (p. 765) and Shakespeare's Sonnet 73: "That Time of Year Thou May'st in Me Behold" (p. 878), Arnold's "Dover Beach" (p. 694), or Lowell's "Patterns" (p. 1149).

3. The view of women in Chekhov's *The Bear* (p. 1582) and Maupassant's "The Necklace" (p. 6) or in Glaspell's *Trifles* (p. 1232) and O'Neill's "Before Breakfast" (p. 1249).

4. The use of descriptive scenery in Hawthorne's "Young Goodman Brown" (p. 385) and Lowell's "Patterns" (p. 1149) or in Poe's "The Masque of the Red Death" (p. 510) and Bierce's "An Occurrence at Owl Creek Bridge" (p. 71).

5. Symbols of disapproval in Hardy's "Channel Firing" (p. 738) and Frost's "Desert Places" (p. 918).

6. The treatment of loss in Lowell's "Patterns" (p. 1149) and Wagner's "The Boxes" (p. 1185).

7. Treatments of religion in "Spring" by Hopkins (p. 740) and "Batter My Heart" by Donne (p. 666).

8. Any of the foregoing topics applied to a number of separate works. Consult the Topical and Thematic Table of Contents (p. xlix) for additional ideas.

Chapter 31

Taking Examinations on Literature

Getting a good grade on a literature examination is largely a result of intelligent and skillful preparation. Preparation means that you (1) study the material assigned, in conjunction with the comments made in class by your instructor and by fellow students in discussion; (2) develop and reinforce your own thoughts; (3) anticipate exam questions by creating and answering your own practice questions; and (4) understand the precise function of the test.

You should also realize that the test is not designed either to trap you or to hold down your grade. The grade you receive is a reflection of your achievement in the course. If your grades are high, congratulations; keep doing what you have been doing. If your grades are low, however, you can improve them through diligent and systematic study. Those students who can easily do satisfactory work might do superior work if they improved their habits of study and preparation. From whatever level you begin, *you can increase your achievement by improving your study methods*.

Your instructor has three major concerns in evaluating your tests (assuming the correct use of English): (1) to assess the extent of your command over the subject material of the course (How good is your retention?); (2) to assess how well you respond to a question or deal with an issue (How well do you separate the important from the unimportant?); and (3) to assess how well you draw conclusions about the material (How well are you educating yourself?).

Answer the Questions That Are Asked

Many elements go into writing good answers on tests, but *responsiveness* is the most important. A major cause of low exam grades is that students *often do not answer the questions asked*. Does that failure seem surprising? The problem is that some students do no more than retell a story or restate an argument, but they do not zero in on the issues in the question. This problem is not uncommon. Therefore, if you are asked, "Why does . . . ?," be sure to emphasize the *why* and use the *does* primarily to exemplify the *why*. If the question is about *organization*, focus on organization. If the question is about the *interpretation* of an idea, deal with the interpretation of the idea. In short, *always respond directly to the question or instruction*. Answer what is asked. Compare the following two answers to the same question:

Question: How is the setting of Ambrose Bierce's "An Occurrence at Owl Creek Bridge" (Chapter 1) important in the story's development?

ANSWER A

The setting of Bierce's "An Occurrence at Owl Creek Bridge" is a major element in the story's development. The first scene is on a railroad bridge in northern Alabama, and the action is that a man, Peyton Farquhar, is about to be hanged. He is a southerner who has been surrounded and captured by Union soldiers. They are ready to string him up and they have the guns and power, so he cannot escape. He is so scared that his own watch seems to be slow and loud, like a cannon. He also thinks about how he might escape, once he is hanged, by freeing his hands and throwing off the noose that will soon be choking and killing him. The scene shifts to the week before, at Farquhar's plantation. A Union spy deceives Farquhar, thereby tempting him to try to sabotage the Union efforts to keep the railroad open. Because the spy tells Farquhar about the punishment, the reader assumes that Farquhar had tried to sabotage the bridge, was caught, and now is going to be hanged. The third scene is also at the bridge, but it is about what Farquhar sees and thinks in his own mind: He imagines that he has been hanged and then escapes. He thinks he falls into the creek, frees himself from the ropes, and makes it to shore, and from there he makes the long walk home. His final vision is of his wife coming out of the house to meet him, with everything looking beautiful in the morning sunshine. Then we find out that all this was just in his mind, because we are back on the bridge, from which Farquhar is swinging, hanged, dead, with a broken neck.

ANSWER B

The setting of Bierce's "An Occurrence at Owl Creek Bridge" is a major element in the story's development. The railroad bridge in northern Alabama, from which the doomed Peyton Farquhar will be hanged, is a frame for the story. The bridge, which begins as a real-life bridge in the first scene, becomes the bridge that the dying man imagines in the third. In between there is a brief scene at Farquhar's home, which took place a week before. The setting thus marks the progression of Farquhar's dying vision. He begins to distort and slow down reality—at the real bridge—when he realizes that there is no escape. The first indication of this distortion is that his watch seems to be ticking as slowly as a blacksmith's hammer. Once he is dropped from the bridge to be hanged, his perceptions slow down time so much that he imagines his complete escape before his death: falling into the water, freeing himself, being shot at, getting to shore, walking through a darkening forest, and returning home in beautiful morning sunshine. The final sentence of the story brutally restores the real situation at the railroad bridge and makes clear that Farquhar is hanging from it and is actually dead despite his imaginings. In all respects, therefore, the setting is essential to the story's development.

Answer A begins well and introduces important details of the story's setting, but it does not answer the question because it does not show how the details figure into the story's development. On the other hand, answer B focuses directly on the connection between the locations and the changes in the protagonist's perceptions. Because of this emphasis, B answers the question and is also shorter than A (288 words for A to 219 for B, according to a computerized count); with the focus directly on the issue, there is no need for irrelevant narrative details. Thus, A is unresponsive and unnecessarily long, whereas B is responsive and includes details only if they exemplify the major points.

Systematic Preparation

Your challenge is how best to prepare yourself to have a knowledgeable and ready mind at examination time. If you simply cram facts into your head for the test in the hope that you can adjust to the questions, you will likely flounder. You need a systematic approach.

Read and Reread the Material on Which You Are to Be Examined

Above all, recognize that your preparation should begin as soon as the course begins, not on the night before the exam. Complete each assignment by the date it is due, for you will understand the classroom discussion only if you know the material (see also the guides for study in Chapter 1, pp. 13–14). Then, about a week before the exam, review each assignment, preferably rereading everything completely. If particular passages were read and discussed in class, make a special point of studying the passages and referring to the notes you took at the time of the discussions. With this preparation, your study on the night before the exam will be fruitful because it is the climax of your preparation, *not your entire preparation*.

Construct Your Own Questions: Go on the Attack

To prepare yourself well for an exam, read *actively*, not passively. Read with a goal, and *go on the attack* by anticipating test conditions—creating and answering your own practice questions. Don't waste time, however, in trying to guess the questions you think your instructor might ask. Guessing correctly might happen (and wouldn't you be absolutely delighted if it did?) but do not turn your study into a game of chance. Instead, arrange the subject matter by asking yourself questions that help you get things straight.

How can you construct your own questions? It is not as hard as you might think. Your instructor may have announced certain topics or ideas to be tested on the exam, and you might develop questions from these, or you might apply general questions to the specifics of your assignments, as in the following examples:

1. *Ideas about a character and the interactions of characters* (see also Chapter 3). What is character *A* like? How does *A* grow or change in the work? What does *A* learn or not learn that brings about the conclusion? To what degree does *A* represent a type or an idea? How does character *B* influence *A*? Does a change in character *C* bring about any corresponding change in *A*?

2. *Ideas about technical and structural questions.* These can be broad, covering everything from point of view (Chapter 2) to poetic form (Chapter 18). The best guide here is to study those technical aspects that have been discussed in class, for it is unlikely that you will be asked to go beyond the levels considered in classroom discussion.

3. *Ideas about events or situations.* What relationship does episode *A* have to situation *B*? Does *C's* thinking about situation *D* have any influence on the outcome of event *E*?

4. *Ideas about a problem* (see also Chapter 24, pp. 1487–94). Why is character *A* or situation *X* this way and not that way? Is the conclusion justified by the ideas and events leading up to it?

Rephrase Your Notes as Questions

Because your classroom notes are the fullest record you have about your instructor's views, one of the best ways to construct questions is to develop them from these notes. As you select topics and phrase questions, refer to passages from the texts that were studied by the class and stressed by your instructor. If there is time, memorize as many important phrases or lines as you can from the assigned works. Plan to incorporate these into your answers as evidence to support the points you make. Remember that it is useful to work not only with main ideas from your notes but also with matters such as character, setting, imagery, symbolism, ideas, and organization.

Obviously, you cannot make questions from all your notes, and you will therefore need to select from those that seem most important. As an example, here is a short note written by a student during a classroom discussion of Shakespeare's *Hamlet*: "A study in how private problems get public, how a private assassination can produce disastrous national and international consequences." You may devise the following practice questions from this note:

1. Why may *Hamlet* be seen as a play not only about private problems but also about public ones?

2. Why should the political consequences of Claudius's murder of Hamlet's father be considered disastrous?

The principle here is that good exam questions do not ask just about *what* but rather get into the issues of *why*. Observe that both questions introduce the word *why* in the phrasing of the notes. Either question creates the need for you to study pointedly, and neither asks you merely to describe events from the play. Question 1 requires you to consider the wider political effects of Hamlet's hostility toward Claudius, including Hamlet's murder of Polonius and the subsequent madness of Ophelia. Question 2, with its emphasis on disaster, leads you to consider not only the ruination of the hopes and lives of those in the play but also the importance of young Fortinbras and the eventual establishment of Norwegian control over Denmark after Claudius and Hamlet have died. If you were to spend fifteen or twenty minutes writing practice answers to these questions, you could be confident in taking an examination on the material, for you could likely adapt, or even partially duplicate, your study answers to any exam question about the personal and political results of Claudius's murder of his brother.

Make Up Your Own Questions Even When Time Is Short

Whatever your subject, spend as much study time as possible making and answering your own questions. *Writing practice answers is one of the most important things you can do in preparing for your exam.* Remember also to work with your own remarks and the ideas you develop in the notebook or journal entries that you make when doing your regular assignments (see Part I, pp. 13–17). Many of these will give you additional ideas for your own questions, which you can practice along with the questions you develop from your classroom notes.

Obviously, with limited study time, you will not be able to create your own questions and answers indefinitely. Even so, don't neglect asking and answering your own questions. If time is too short for full practice answers, write out the main heads, or topics, of an answer. When the press of time (or the need for sleep) no longer permits you to make even such a brief outline answer, keep thinking of questions and their answers as you go to the exam. *Never read passively or unresponsively.* Always read with a creative, question-and-answer goal. Always keep thinking of *why* in addition to *what.* Consider your study as a preliminary step leading to writing.

The time you spend in this way will be valuable, for as you practice, you will develop control and therefore confidence. Often those who have difficulty with tests, or claim a phobia about them, prepare passively rather than actively. Your instructor's test questions compel responsiveness, organization, thought, and insight. But a passively prepared student is not ready for this challenge and therefore writes answers that are unresponsive and filled with summary. The grade for such a performance is low, and the student's fear of tests is reinforced. The best way to break such long-standing patterns of fear or uncertainty is to study actively and creatively.

Study with a Classmate

Often the thoughts of another person can help you understand the material to be tested. Find a fellow student with whom you can work comfortably but also productively, for both of you together can help each other individually. In view of the need for steady preparation throughout a course, regular discussions about the material are a good idea. You might also make your joint study systematic by setting aside a specific evening or afternoon for work sessions. Many students have said that they encounter problems in taking examinations because they are unfamiliar with the ways in which questions are phrased. Consequently, they waste time in understanding and interpreting the questions before they begin their answers, and sometimes they lose all their time because they misunderstand the questions entirely. If you work with a fellow student, however, and trade questions, you will be gaining experience (and confidence) in dealing with this basic difficulty about exams. Working with someone else can be extremely rewarding, just as it can also be stimulating and instructive. Make the effort, and you'll never regret it.

Two Basic Types of Questions about Literature

Generally, you should keep in mind two types of questions as you prepare for literature exams. The first type is *factual*, or *mainly objective*; and the second is *general, comprehensive, broad*, or *mainly subjective*. Except for multiple-choice questions, very few questions are purely objective in a literature course.

Anticipate the Kinds of Factual Questions That Might Be Asked

MULTIPLE-CHOICE QUESTIONS ASK YOU TO PICK THE MOST ACCURATE AND LIKELY ANSWERS.   Multiple-choice questions are almost necessarily factual. Your instructor will most likely use them for short quizzes, usually on days when an assignment is due, to make sure that you are keeping up with the reading. Multiple-choice questions test your knowledge of facts and your ingenuity in perceiving subtleties of phrasing. On literature exams, however, this type of question is rare.

IDENTIFICATION QUESTIONS ASK FOR ACCURACY, EXPLANATION, AND INTERPRETATION.   Identification questions are interesting and challenging because they require you both to know details and also to develop thoughts about them. These types of questions are frequently used as a check on the depth and scope of your reading. In fact, an entire exam could be composed of only identification questions, each requiring perhaps five minutes for you to answer. Here are some typical examples of what you might be asked to identify.

1. *A character.* To identify a character, it is necessary to describe briefly the character's position, main activity, and significance. Let us assume that "Prince Prospero" is the character to be identified. Our answer should state that he is the prince (position) who invites a thousand followers to his castle to enjoy themselves while keeping out the plague of the Red Death in Edgar Allan Poe's "The Masque of the Red Death" (main activity). Prospero's egotism and arrogance are the major causes of the action, and he embodies the story's theme that pride is vain and that death is inescapable (significance). Under the category of "significance," of course, you might develop as many ideas as you have time for, but the short example here is a general model for most identification questions.

2. *Incidents or situations.* To identify an incident or a situation (for example, "A woman mourns the death of her husband"), first describe the circumstances and the principal character involved in them (Mrs. Popov's reaction to her widowhood in Chekhov's play *The Bear*). Then, describe the importance of this incident or situation in the work. For example, in *The Bear*, Mrs. Popov is mourning the death of her husband, and in the course of the play Chekhov uses her feelings to show amusingly that life and love with real emotion are stronger than allegiance to the dead.

3. *Things, places, and dates.* Your instructor may ask you to identify a hair ribbon (Nathaniel Hawthorne's "Young Goodman Brown") or a beach (Matthew

Arnold's "Dover Beach" or Amy Clampitt's "Beach Glass"), or the date of Amy Lowell's "Patterns" (1916). For dates, you may be given a leeway of five or ten years. What is important about a date is not so much exactness as historical and intellectual perspective. The date of Lowell's "Patterns," for example, was the third year of World War I, and the poem consequently reflects a reaction against the protracted and senseless loss of life in war (even though details of the poem itself suggest an eighteenth-century war). To claim "World War I" as the date of the poem would be acceptable as an answer if it happens that you cannot remember the exact date.

4. *Quotations.* You should remember enough of the text to identify a passage taken from it, or at least to make an informed guess. Generally, you should (1) locate the quotation, if you remember it, or else describe what you think is the probable location; (2) show the ways in which the quotation is typical of the content and style of the work you have read; and (3) describe the importance of the passage. If you suffer a lapse of memory, write a reasoned and careful explanation of your guess. Even if your guess is not actually correct, the knowledge and cogency of your explanation should give you points.

TECHNICAL AND ANALYTICAL QUESTIONS AND PROBLEMS REQUIRE YOU TO RELATE KNOWLEDGE AND TECHNICAL UNDERSTANDING TO THE ISSUE. In a scale of ascending importance, the third and most difficult type of factual question brings out those matters of writing with which much of this book is concerned: technique and analysis. You might be asked to analyze the *setting, images, point of view,* or *important idea* of a work; you might be asked about the *tone and style* of a story or poem; or you might be asked to *explicate* a poem that may or may not be duplicated for your benefit (if it is not duplicated, woe to students who have not studied their assignments). Questions like these assume that you have technical knowledge, and they also ask you to examine the text within the limitations imposed by the directions.

Obviously, technical questions occur more frequently in advanced courses than in elementary ones, and the questions grow more subtle as the courses become more advanced. Instructors of introductory courses may ask about ideas and problems but will likely not use many of the others unless they state their intentions to do so in advance or unless technical terms have been studied in class.

Questions of this type are fairly long, perhaps allowing from fifteen to twenty-five minutes apiece. If you have two or more of these questions, try to space your time sensibly; do not devote eighty percent of your time to one question and leave only twenty percent for the rest.

Understand How Your Responses Will Be Judged and Graded

IDENTIFICATION QUESTIONS PROBE YOUR UNDERSTANDING AND APPLICATION OF FACTS. In all factual questions, your instructor is testing (1) your factual command and (2) your quickness in relating a part to the whole. Thus, suppose you are identifying the incident "A man kills a canary." It is correct to say that Susan Glaspell's play *Trifles* (or her story "A Jury of Her Peers") is the location of the incident, that the murdered farmer John Wright is the killer, and that the canary belonged to his wife, Minnie. Knowledge of these details clearly establishes that you know the facts. But a strong answer must go further. Even in the brief time you have for short answers, you must demonstrate your processes of thought. You should always connect the facts (1) to major causation in the work, (2) to an important idea or ideas, (3) to the development of the work, and (4) for a quotation, to the style. Time is short and you must be selective, but if you can make your answer move from facts to significance, you will always fashion superior responses. Along these lines, let us look at an answer identifying the action from *Trifles*. Because some of the details of the play and the story are slightly different, we will refer only to *Trifles* here:

> The action is from Glaspell's *Trifles*. The man who kills the bird is John Wright, the dead man, and the owner is his wife, Minnie, who, before the story begins, has been jailed on suspicion of murder. The wringing of the little bird's neck is important because it is shown as an indignity and outrage in Minnie Wright's desperate life, and it obviously has made her angry enough to put a rope around Wright's neck to strangle him in his sleep. It is thus the cause not only of the murder but also of the investigation that brings the two lawmen and their wives to the Wright kitchen. In fact, the killing of the bird makes the story possible inasmuch as it is the women who discover the dead bird's remains, and this discovery is the means by which Glaspell highlights them as the major characters of the action. Because the husband's cruelly brutal act shows how bleak the married life of Minnie Wright actually was, it dramatizes the lonely and victimized plight of women in a male-dominated way of life like that on the Wright farm. The discovery also raises the issue of legality and morality, because the women decide to conceal the evidence, therefore protecting Minnie Wright from conviction and punishment.

Any of the points in this answer could be developed as a separate essay, but the paragraph is successful as a short answer because it goes beyond fact to deal with significance. Clearly, such answers are possible at the time of an exam only if you have devoted considerable thought beforehand to the works on which you are tested. The more thinking and practicing you do before an exam, the better your answers will be. Remember this advice as an axiom: *You cannot write superior answers if you do not think extensively before the exam.* By ambitious advance study, you will be able to reduce surprise to a minimum.

LONGER FACTUAL QUESTIONS PROBE YOUR KNOWLEDGE AND YOUR ABILITY TO ORGANIZE YOUR THOUGHTS.   More extended factual questions also require more thoroughly developed organization. Remember that for these questions your skill in writing essays is important because the thought you show in your composition will determine a major share of your instructor's evaluation of your answers. It is therefore best to take several minutes to gather your thoughts before you begin to write. Remember, *a ten-minute planned answer is preferable to a twenty-five-minute unplanned answer.* You do not need to write every possible fact on each particular question. Of greater importance is the use to which you put the facts that you know and the organization and development of your answer. Use a sheet of scratch paper to jot down important facts and your ideas about them in relation to the question. Then put them together, phrase a thesis sentence, and use your facts to exemplify and support your thesis.

It is always necessary to begin your answer pointedly, using key words or phrases from the question or direction if possible, so that your answer will have thematic shape. You should *never* begin an answer with "Because" and then go on from there without referring again to the question. To be most responsive during the short time available for an exam, you should use the question as your guide for your answer. Let us suppose that you have the following question on your test: "How does Glaspell use details in *Trifles* to reveal the character of Minnie Wright?" The most common way to go astray on such a question—and the easiest thing to do also—is to concentrate on Minnie Wright's character rather than on how Glaspell uses detail to bring out her character. The word *how* makes a vast difference in the nature of the final answer, and hence a good method on the exam is to duplicate key phrases in the question to ensure that you make your major points clear. Here is an opening sentence that uses the key words and phrases (italicized here) from the question to organize thought and provide focus.

> Glaspell *uses details* of setting, marital relationships, and personal habits *to reveal the character of Minnie Wright* as a person of great but unfulfilled potential whom anger has finally overcome.

Because this sentence repeats the key phrases from the question and also because it promises to show *how* the details are to be focused on the character, it suggests that the answer to follow will be responsive.

General or Comprehensive Questions Require You to Connect a Number of Works to Broader Matters of Idea and Technique

General or comprehensive questions are particularly important on final examinations, when your instructor is testing your total comprehension of the course material and your thought about it. Considerable time is usually allowed for answering this type of question, which can be phrased in a number of ways.

1. A *direct question* asking about philosophy, underlying attitudes, main ideas, characteristics of style, backgrounds, and so on. Here are some possible questions in this category.

   What use do _____, _____, and _____ make of the topic of _____?

   Define and characterize the short story as a genre of literature, using examples from the stories of _____, _____, and _____.

   Describe the use of dialogue by _____, _____, and _____.

   Contrast the technique of point of view as used by _____, _____, and _____.

2. A *"comment" question*, often based on an extensive quotation, borrowed from a critic or written by your instructor for the occasion, asking about a broad class of writers, a literary movement, or the like. Your instructor may ask you to treat this question broadly (taking in many writers) or else to apply the quotation to a specific writer.

3. A *"suppose" question*, such as "What advice might Minnie Wright of Glaspell's *Trifles* give the speakers of Elizabeth Barrett Browning's 'How Do I Love Thee' and Keats's 'Bright Star'?" or "What might the speaker of Lowell's poem 'Patterns' say if she learned that her dead lover was actually a person like Goodman Brown of Hawthorne's 'Young Goodman Brown'?" Although "suppose" questions seem whimsical at first sight, they have a serious design and should prompt original and radical thinking. The first question, for example, might cause a test writer to bring out, from Minnie Wright's perspective, that the love expressed by both speakers overlooks the possibilities of changes in character over a long period. She would likely sympathize with the speaker of "How Do I Love Thee," a woman, but she might also say that the speaker's enthusiasm would need to be augmented by the constant exertion of kindness and mutual understanding. For the speaker of "Bright Star," a man, Mrs. Wright might say that the steadfast love he seeks should be linked to thoughtfulness and constant communication as well as passion.

Although "suppose" questions (and answers) are speculative, the need to respond to them requires a detailed consideration of the works involved, and in this respect the "suppose" question is a salutary means of learning. It is of course difficult to prepare for a "suppose" question, which you can therefore regard as a test not only of your knowledge but also of your adaptability, inventiveness, ingenuity and power of thought.

Understand How Your Responses to General and Comprehensive Questions Will Be Judged and Graded

When answering broad, general questions, you are dealing with an unstructured situation, and you must not only supply an answer but—equally important—create a *structure* within which your answer can have meaning. You might say that you make up your own specific question out of the original general question. If you were asked to consider the role of women as seen in works by Amy Lowell, Maupassant, and Glaspell, for example, you would structure the question by focusing a number of clearly defined topics. A possible way to begin answering such a question might be this.

> Amy Lowell, Maupassant, and Glaspell present a view of female resilience by demonstrating the inner control, endurance, and power of adaptation of their major characters.

With this sort of focus, you would be able to proceed point-by-point, introducing supporting data as you form your answer.

As a general rule, the best method for answering a comprehensive question is comparison-contrast (see also Chapter 30). The reason is that in dealing with, say, a general question on Lawrence, Chekhov, and Keats, it is too easy to write *three* separate essays rather than *one*. Thus, you should try to create a topic such as "the treatment of real or idealized love" or "the difficulties in male-female relationships" and then develop your answer point by point rather than writer by writer. By creating your answer in this way, you can bring in references to each or all of the writers as they become relevant. If you were to treat each writer separately, your comprehensive answer would lose focus and effectiveness, and it would also be repetitive.

Remember that in judging your response to a general question, your instructor is interested in seeing (1) how effectively you perceive and explain the significant issues in the question, (2) how intelligently and clearly you organize your answer, and (3) how persuasively you link your answer to materials from the work as supporting evidence.

Bear in mind that in answering comprehensive questions, you do not have the freedom or license to write about anything at all, whether it is relevant or not. You must stick to the questions. The freedom you do have, however, is the freedom to create your own organization and development in response to the questions that your instructor has asked you. The underlying idea of the comprehensive, general question is that you possess special knowledge and insights that cannot be discovered by more factual questions. You must therefore demonstrate your power of thinking. You need to formulate your own responses to the material and introduce evidence that reflects your own insights and command of information.

A final thought: Try to enjoy the learning experience that preparing for an exam offers you. You may surprise yourself!

Appendix I

MLA Recommendations for Documenting Sources

This appendix provides general guidelines for making source citations, and therefore it is intended to augment the section titled "Documenting Your Work" in Chapter 10A. For general information on citation recommendations by the Modern Language Association (MLA), see Joseph Gibaldi, *MLA Handbook for Writers of Research Papers,* 6th ed. (New York: MLA, 2003).

The following examples show the formats you are likely to use most often, both for nonelectronic and electronic references.

(Nonelectronic) Books, Articles, Poems, Letters, Reviews, Recordings, Programs

Book by One Author

Fitzgerald, F. Scott. The Great Gatsby. New York: Scribner, 1925.

Book with No Author Listed

The Pictorial History of the Guitar. New York: Random, 1992.

Book by Two (or Three) Authors

Clemens, Samuel L., and Charles Dudley Warner. The Gilded Age: A Tale of Today. Hartford: American, 1874.

For a Book by Four or More Authors

Guerin, Wilfred L., Earle Labor, Lee Morgan, Jeanne C. Reesman, and John R. Willingham. A Handbook of Critical Approaches to Literature. New York: Oxford UP, 2004.

or

Guerin, Wilfred L., et al. A Handbook of Critical Approaches to Literature. New York: Oxford UP, 2004.

Two Books by the Same Author

Reynolds, David S. Beneath the American Renaissance. Cambridge: Harvard UP, 1988.

———. Walt Whitman's America: A Cultural Biography. New York: Knopf, 1995.

Citing a Book

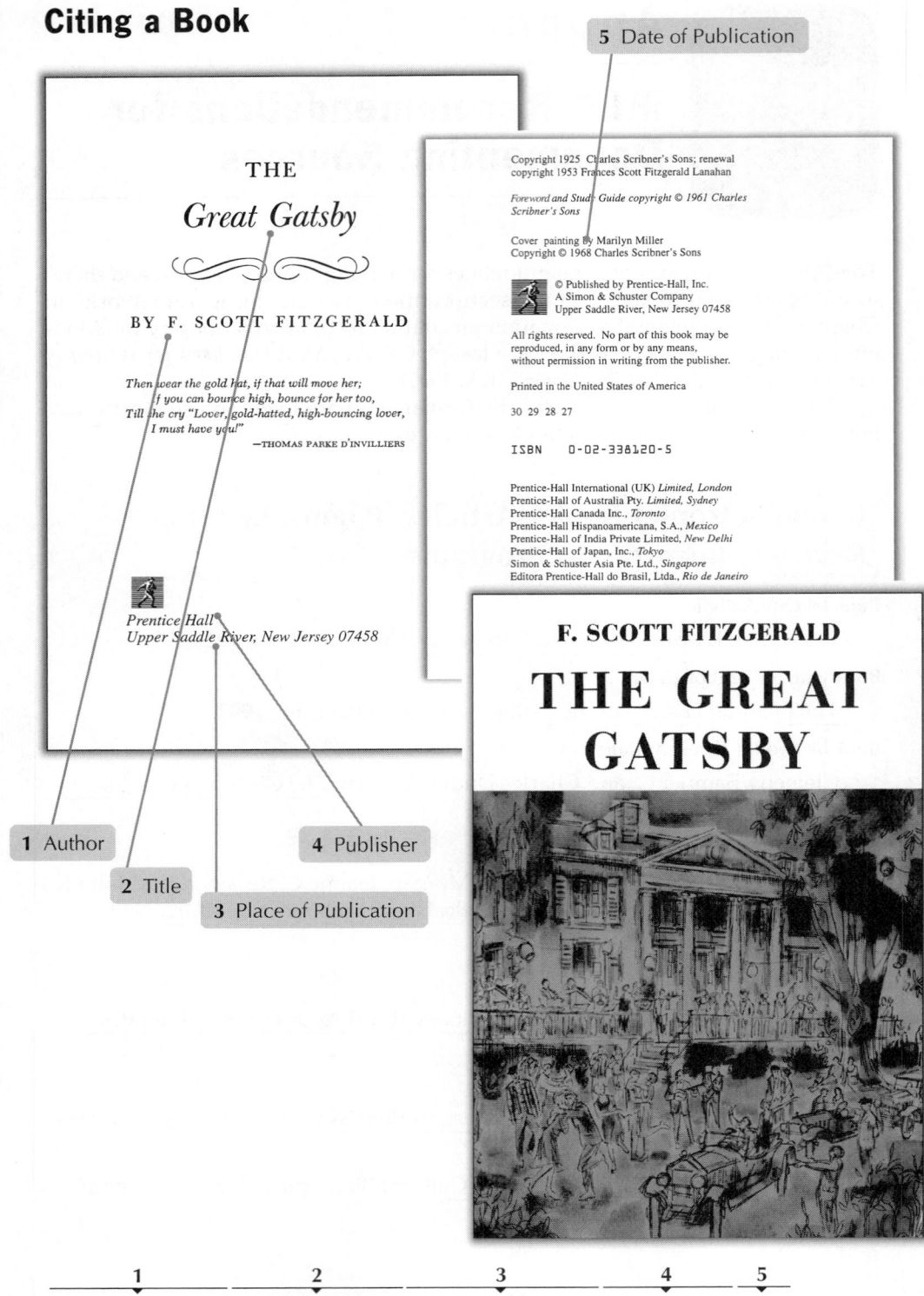

5 Date of Publication

THE

Great Gatsby

BY F. SCOTT FITZGERALD

Then wear the gold hat, if that will move her;
   If you can bounce high, bounce for her too,
Till she cry "Lover, gold-hatted, high-bouncing lover,
   I must have you!"

—THOMAS PARKE D'INVILLIERS

Prentice Hall
Upper Saddle River, New Jersey 07458

Copyright 1925 Charles Scribner's Sons; renewal
copyright 1953 Frances Scott Fitzgerald Lanahan

*Foreword and Study Guide copyright © 1961 Charles
Scribner's Sons*

Cover painting by Marilyn Miller
Copyright © 1968 Charles Scribner's Sons

© Published by Prentice-Hall, Inc.
A Simon & Schuster Company
Upper Saddle River, New Jersey 07458

All rights reserved. No part of this book may be
reproduced, in any form or by any means,
without permission in writing from the publisher.

Printed in the United States of America

30 29 28 27

ISBN   0-02-338120-5

Prentice-Hall International (UK) *Limited, London*
Prentice-Hall of Australia Pty. *Limited, Sydney*
Prentice-Hall Canada Inc., *Toronto*
Prentice-Hall Hispanoamericana, S.A., *Mexico*
Prentice-Hall of India Private Limited, *New Delhi*
Prentice-Hall of Japan, Inc., *Tokyo*
Simon & Schuster Asia Pte. Ltd., *Singapore*
Editora Prentice-Hall do Brasil, Ltda., *Rio de Janeiro*

F. SCOTT FITZGERALD

THE GREAT GATSBY

1 Author

2 Title

3 Place of Publication

4 Publisher

1	2	3	4	5

Fitzgerald, F. Scott. The Great Gatsby. Upper Saddle River: Prentice Hall, 1968.

Book with an Editor

Scharnhorst, Gary, ed. Selected Letters of Bret Harte. Norman: U of Okla-
    homa P, 1997.

Book with Two Editors

Dionne, Craig, and Steve Mentz, eds. Rogues and Early Modern English
    Culture. Ann Arbor: U of Michigan P, 2004.

Book with an Author and an Editor

De Quille, Dan. The Fighting Horse of the Stanislaus. Ed. Lawrence I.
    Berkove. Iowa City: U of Iowa P, 1990.

Translated Book

Cervantes Saavedra, Miguel de. Don Quixote de la Mancha. Trans. Charles
    Jarvis. New York: Oxford UP, 1999.

Long Poem Published as a Book

Homer. The Odyssey. Trans. Robert Fitzgerald. New York: Vintage, 1990.

Collection of Poetry Published as a Book

Mueller, Lisel. Alive Together: New and Selected Poems. Baton Rouge:
    Louisiana State UP, 1996.

Literary Work in an Anthology

Chopin, Kate. "The Storm." Fiction 100: An Anthology of Short Fiction. Ed.
    James H. Pickering. 10th ed. Upper Saddle River: Pearson, 2004. 226–29.

Introduction, Preface, Foreword, or Afterword in a Book

Pryse, Marjorie. Introduction. The Country of the Pointed Firs and Other
    Stories. By Sarah Orne Jewett. New York: Norton, 1981. v–xix.

Article in a Reference Book

Gerber, Phillip. "Naturalism." The Encyclopedia of American Literature. Ed.
    Steven Serafin. New York: Continuum, 1999. 808–09.

Article in a Journal with Continuous Paging

Rhodes, Chip. "Satire in Romanian Literature." Humor 8 (1995): 275–86.

Article in a Journal That Pages Each Issue Separately

Kruse, Horst. "The Motif of the Flattened Corpse." Studies in American
    Humor 4 (Spring 1997): 47–53.

Signed Book Review

Bird, John. Rev. of The Singular Mark Twain, by Fred Kaplan.
    Mark Twain Annual 2 (2004): 57–61.

Unsigned Book Review

Rev. of Canons by Consensus: Critical Trends and American Literature
    Anthologies, by Joseph Csicsila. Essays in Arts and Sciences 24 (2000):
    69–74.

Citing a Work in an Anthology

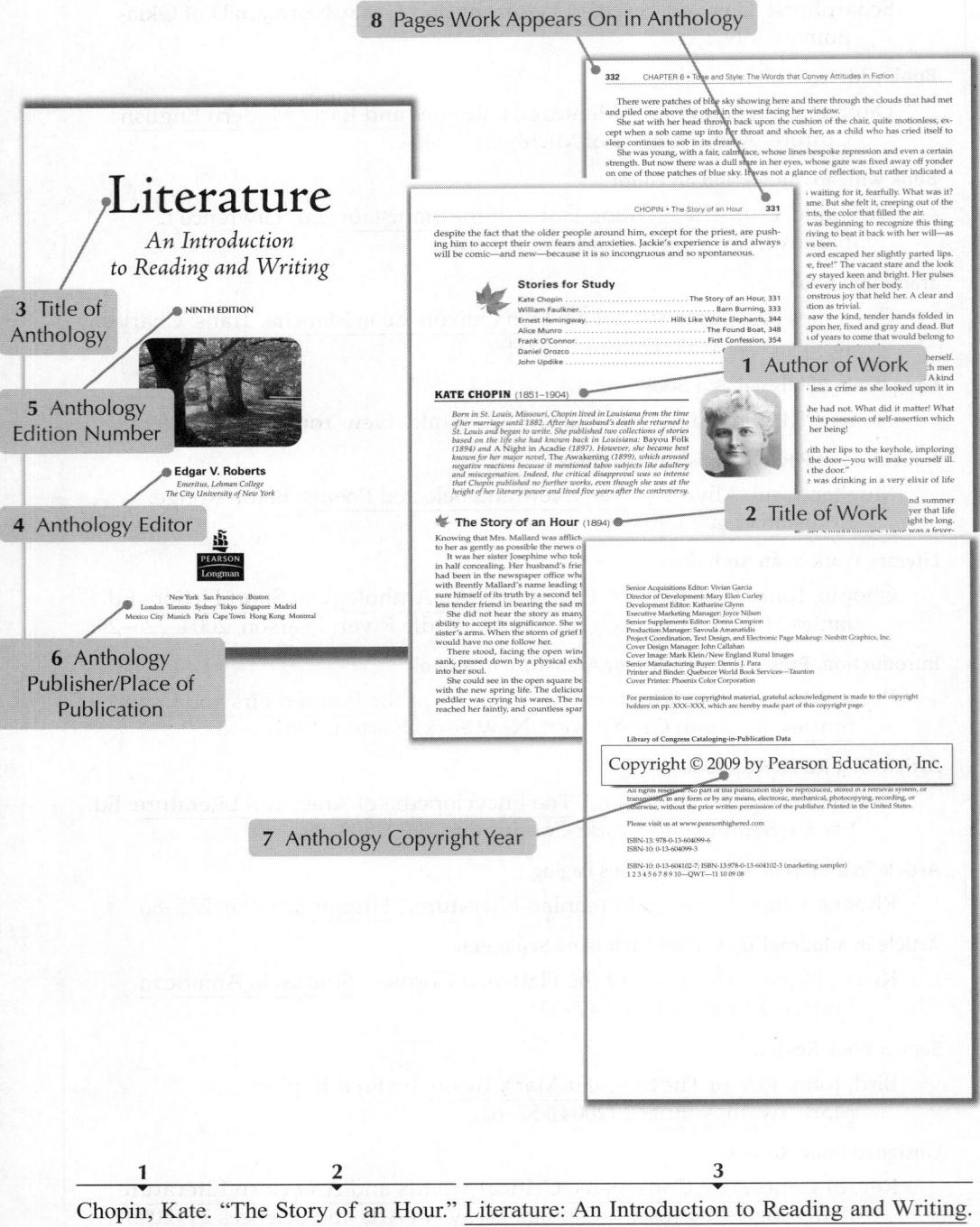

8 Pages Work Appears On in Anthology

3 Title of Anthology

5 Anthology Edition Number

4 Anthology Editor

6 Anthology Publisher/Place of Publication

7 Anthology Copyright Year

1 Author of Work

2 Title of Work

Chopin, Kate. "The Story of an Hour." Literature: An Introduction to Reading and Writing.
Ed. Edgar V. Roberts. 9th ed. New York: Pearson Longman 2009. 331–32.

Citing an Article in a Journal

2 Article Title

1 Author

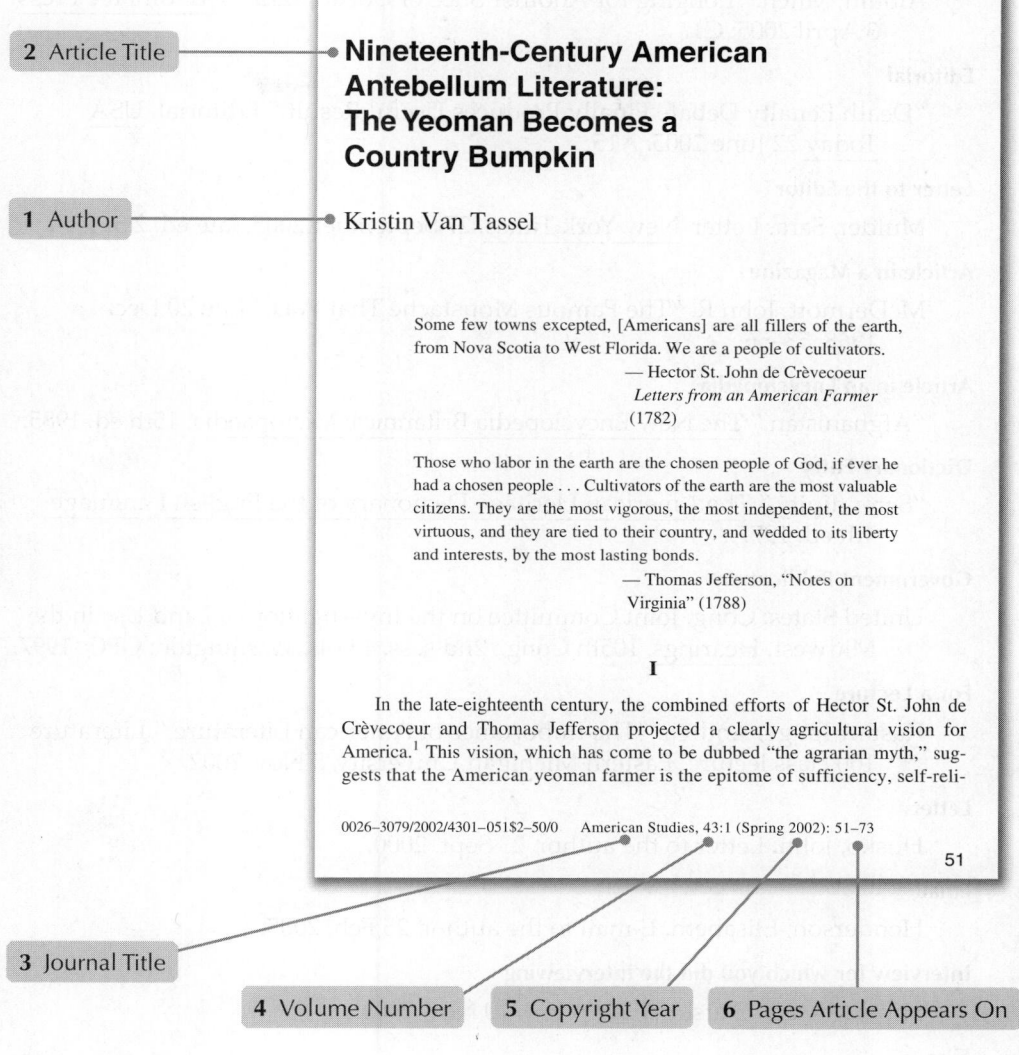

Nineteenth-Century American Antebellum Literature: The Yeoman Becomes a Country Bumpkin

Kristin Van Tassel

> Some few towns excepted, [Americans] are all fillers of the earth, from Nova Scotia to West Florida. We are a people of cultivators.
> — Hector St. John de Crèvecoeur
> *Letters from an American Farmer*
> (1782)

> Those who labor in the earth are the chosen people of God, if ever he had a chosen people . . . Cultivators of the earth are the most valuable citizens. They are the most vigorous, the most independent, the most virtuous, and they are tied to their country, and wedded to its liberty and interests, by the most lasting bonds.
> — Thomas Jefferson, "Notes on Virginia" (1788)

I

    In the late-eighteenth century, the combined efforts of Hector St. John de Crèvecoeur and Thomas Jefferson projected a clearly agricultural vision for America.[1] This vision, which has come to be dubbed "the agrarian myth," suggests that the American yeoman farmer is the epitome of sufficiency, self-reli-

0026–3079/2002/4301–051$2–50/0   American Studies, 43:1 (Spring 2002): 51–73

51

3 Journal Title

4 Volume Number   **5** Copyright Year   **6** Pages Article Appears On

Note: A scholarly article in printed form ordinarily provides all necessary information on its first page.

———— 1 ————   ———————————— 2 ————————————

Van Tassel, Kristin. "Nineteenth-Century American Antebellum Literature: The Yeoman Becomes a Country Bumpkin." American Studies 43:1 (2002): 51–73.

———— 2 cont. ————   ———— 3 ————   —— 4 —— — 5 — — 6 —

Article in a Newspaper

Album, Mitch. "Longing for Another Slice of Dorm Pizza." Detroit Free Press 3 April 2005: C1.

Editorial

"Death Penalty Debate Finally Produces Useful Result." Editorial. USA Today 22 June 2005: A15.

Letter to the Editor

Mulder, Sara. Letter. New York Times. 27 September 2005, late ed: 2:5.

Article in a Magazine

McDermott, John R. "The Famous Moustache That Was." Life 20 Dec. 1968: 53–56.

Article in an Encyclopedia

"Afghanistan." The New Encyclopedia Britannica: Micropaedia. 15th ed. 1985.

Dictionary Entry

"Serendipity." The American Heritage Dictionary of the English Language. 4th ed. 1977.

Government Publication

United States. Cong. Joint Committee on the Investigation of Land Use in the Midwest. Hearings. 105th Cong., 2nd sess. 4 vols. Washington: GPO, 1997.

For a Lecture

Kaston Tange, Andrea. "The Importance of American Literature." Literature 100 class lecture. Eastern Michigan University, 5 Nov. 2002.

Letter

Hosko, John. Letter to the author. 23 Sept. 2000.

Email

Henderson, Elisabeth. E-mail to the author. 25 Feb. 2005.

Interview for which you did the interviewing

Stipe, Michael. Personal interview. 10 Nov. 2004.

Film

Napoleon Dynamite. Dir. Jared Hess. Fox Searchlight, 2004.

Television Program

"The Parking Garage." Seinfeld. NBC. WDIV, Detroit. 23 July 1994.

Sound Recording

R.E.M. Fables of the Reconstruction. IRS Records, 1985.

Song on a Recording

R.E.M. "Life and How to Live It." Fables of the Reconstruction. IRS Records, 1985.

Citing a Newspaper

5 Edition

4 Date

3 Newspaper Name

1 Author

2 Article Title

6 Section and Page Number

```
        1                              2                          3
```
Ryzick, Melena. "Indoors and Out, Theater Is Making a Splash." The New York Times
```
        4          5        6
```
5 July 2007, late ed.: E1+.

Music Video

> Outkast. "Hey Ya." Speakerboxx/The Love Below. La Face, 2003. Music
> video. Dir. Bryan Barber. MTV. 22 Aug. 2004.

The Citation of Electronic Sources

Both students and instructors routinely take advantage of the technology available to assist in research. While many libraries offer varied databases that enable
researchers to locate information easily, the main thrust of research is now the exploration of the World Wide Web. Through the use of various search engines, such
as Google and Yahoo, you simply need to enter the name of an author, a title, or a
topic, upon which you will be linked to a host of resources from all over the
world—home pages of specific authors, literary organizations, and works on various topics by contemporary writers. You'll find a good deal of what you're
searching for in only a few seconds. An important caveat is that many sources still
remain in printed journals and magazines that may be or, more probably, may not
be on the Web. To make sure your searches are thorough, therefore, *you must never
neglect to search for information provided by traditional printed sources.*

Because the available methods of obtaining electronic information are developing so rapidly, the printed style manuals have had difficulty keeping up with
the changes. If you do a Web search looking for information on these styles,
chances are that the information you discover will vary from site to site. Therefore, you need to know the basics that are required for the citation of your
sources.

When recovering electronic sources, it is vital to type the letters, numbers,
symbols, dots, underlines, and spaces in the uniform resource locator (URL) accurately. Recovery systems are unforgiving, and mistakes or omissions of any sort
will make it impossible for you to retrieve your source. URLs are often transitory
because someone, somewhere, must maintain them (through the updating of information and the paying of fees). If the URL you have used does not turn up the material for which you are searching, you may be able to locate it simply by typing in
the name of the author or the name of the article on a search engine. You may often
rely on search engines to turn up references for you, for the autofill feature will
often complete the entire address automatically, with all the dots and other directions in the correct order.

By the same token, it is essential for you, when you are compiling your own
list of works cited, to be absolutely accurate in reproducing the URLs of your
sources. You must assume that someone reading your essay and using your list
will want to check out the sources themselves, and any errors in your transcrip-
tion may create confusion.

The style generally accepted in the cyber world, and the one recommended by
the MLA, places angle brackets (< >) before and after Internet addresses and
URLs. If you see brackets around an address you want to use, do not include them
as part of the address when you are seeking retrieval. Also, since a number of
word-processing programs now support the use of italics, you can use italics as a

regular practice. Some researchers, however, still prefer underlines, and if your programs (or typewriter) cannot produce italics, of course use underlines. If in doubt about which to use, consult your instructor.

MLA Style Guidelines for Electronic Sources

Many of the guidelines the MLA has authorized for the citation of electronic sources overlap with the MLA recommendations for printed sources, but to avoid ambiguity a number of recommendations bear repetition. Electronic materials are to be documented in basically the same style as printed sources. According to the sixth edition of the *MLA Handbook,* which illustrates virtually all the situations you can ever encounter, the following items need to be included if they are available.

1. The name of the author, editor, compiler, or translator of the source (if available and relevant), last name first, followed by an abbreviation, such as *ed.,* if appropriate.

2. If there is no author listed in the source, you should list the title first: the title of a poem, short story, article, or similar short work within a scholarly project, database, or periodical (in quotation marks); or the title of a posting to a discussion list or forum (taken from the subject line and enclosed by quotation marks), concluded by the phrase "Online posting."

3. The title of a book, underlined or italicized.

4. The name of the editor, compiler, or translator of the text (if relevant and if not cited earlier), preceded by (not followed by) any necessary abbreviations, such as *Ed.*

5. Publication information for any printed version of the source.

6. The title of the scholarly project, database, periodical, or professional or personal site, underlined or italicized; or, for a professional or personal site with no title, a description such as "Home Page."

7. The name of the editor of the scholarly project or database (if available).

8. The version number of the source (if not part of the title), or, for a journal, the volume number, issue number, or other identifying number. All numbers should be in Arabic numerals, not Roman.

9. The date of publication or posting that you find in your source. Sometimes the original date is no longer available because it has been replaced with an update; if so, cite that. Dates should be arranged by (a) day of the month, (b) month (the names of longer months may be abbreviated), and (c) year.

10. For a work from a subscription service, the name of the service (and name, city, and state abbreviation if the subscriber is a library).

11. For a posting to a discussion list or forum, the name of the list or forum.

12. The number range or total number of pages, paragraphs, or other sections, if they are numbered. If you do your own numbering, include your numbers within square brackets [ ], and be sure to indicate what you have numbered.

13. The name of any institution or organization sponsoring or associated with the Web site.

14. The date when you consulted the source. If you have looked at the site a number of times, include the most recent date of use. The principle here is that the date immediately before the URL will mark the last time you used the source.

15. The electronic address or URL of the source in angle brackets < >. Many programs now automatically include the angle brackets. If the URL is too long to fit on one line, the line break should occur at a slash (/) if possible. (Do not introduce hyphenations into the URL as these may be mistaken for actual significant characters in that address.)

Book

Shaw, Bernard. Pygmalion. 1916, 1999. Bartleby Archive. 25 Mar. 2008 <http://www.bartleby.com/138/index.html>.

Poem

Carroll, Lewis. The Hunting of the Snark. 1876. 25 Mar. 2008 <http://www.everypoet.com/archive/poetry/Lewis_Carroll/lewis_carroll_the_hunting_of_the_snark.htm>.

Play

Shakespeare, William. Hamlet. c. 1601. Project Gutenberg. 25 Mar. 2008 <http://www.novelguide.com/hamlet/hamlet.txt>.

Journal Article

Hewlett, Beth L., and Christa Ehmann Powers. "How Do You Ground Your Training? Sharing the Principles and Processes of Preparing Educators for Online Writing Instruction." Kairos 10.1 (Fall 2005). Multiple Sections. 25 Mar. 2008 <http://english.ttu.edu/kairos/10.1/binder.html?praxis/hewett/index.htm>.

Magazine Article

Jones, Kenneth. "Bill Gates and Steve Jobs Sing and Dance in New Musical, Nerds, Already a Hit in NYMF." Playbill.com September 20, 2005. 25 March 2008 <http://www.playbill.com/news/article/95180.html>.

Posting to a Discussion List

McElhearn, Kirk. "J. S. Bach: Oxford Composer Companion [A review]." Online posting. 1 Dec. 2000. Google Groups. 24 March 2008 <http://groups.google.com/group/alt.music.j-s-bach/browse_thread/thread/30524010237bd51a/488691878789a15d?lnk=st&q=%22Kirk+Mcelhearn%22&rnum=5#488691878789a15d>.

Scholarly Project

Voice of the Shuttle: Web Site for Humanities Research. Ed. Alan Liu. 23 March 2008. U of California Santa Barbara. 23 Mar. 2008 <http://vos.ucsb.edu/>.

Professional Site

> NobelMuseum. The Nobel Foundation. 25 March 2008.
> <http://nobelprize.org/index.html>.

Personal Site

> Barrett, Dan. The Gentle Giant Home Page. 19 February 2008. 25 March 2008.
> <http://www.blazemonger.com/GG/index.html>.

Citing a Professional Website

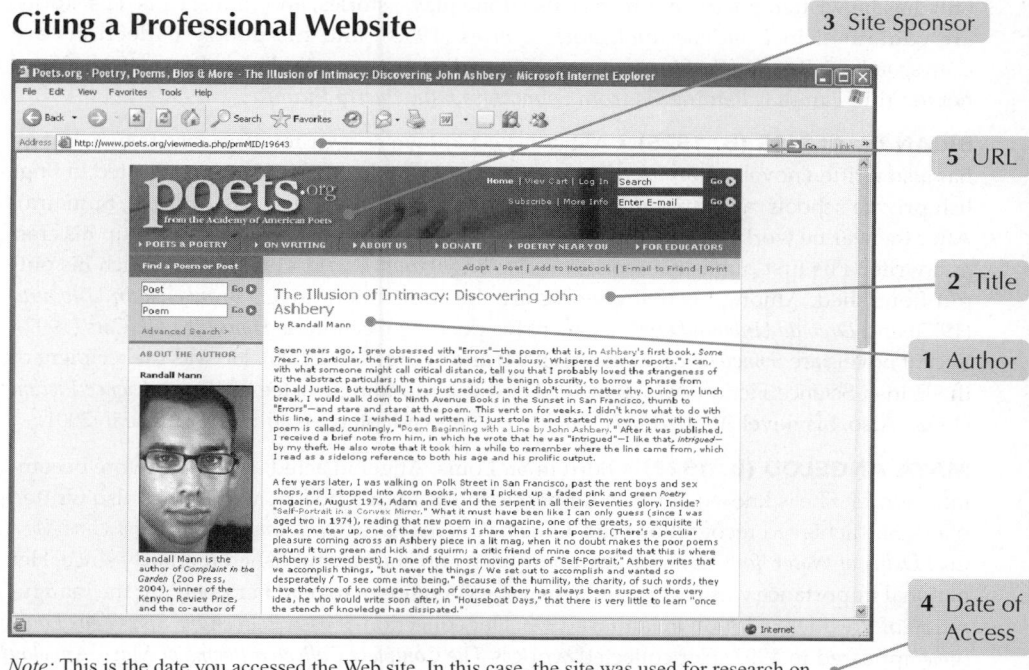

3 Site Sponsor

5 URL

2 Title

1 Author

4 Date of Access

Note: This is the date you accessed the Web site. In this case, the site was used for research on June 20, 2007.

1　　　　　　　　　2　　　　　　　　　3

Mann, Randall. "The Illusion of Intimacy: Discovering John Ashberry." Academy of American Poets
　　20 June 2007 <http://www.poets.org/viewmedia.php/prmMID/19643>.

4　　　　　　　　　5

Appendix II

Brief Biographies of the Poets in Part III

JACK AGÜEROS (b. 1934) • Agüeros, a native of New York, is a well known Latino writer. He earned a B.A. from Brooklyn College and an M.A. from Occidental College. Not only has he written poetry, but he has also done plays, stories, and film-scripts. His stories are contained in *Dominoes and Other Stories* (1993), and his poetry collections are *Correspondence Between the Stonehaulers* (1991) and *Sonnets from the Puerto Rican* (1996). "Sonnet for You, Familiar Famine" is from *Sonnets from the Puerto Rican*.

BRIAN W. ALDISS (b. 1925) • Aldiss is best known as a writer of science fiction, but he has also written novels, dramas, reviews, and considerable poetry. He was educated in English private schools, and during World War II he served in the Far East (Burma, Sumatra). After the war he worked for a time as a bookseller in Oxford, when he also took up his craft as a writer. His first published work was *The Brightfount Diaries* (1955), after which his output flourished. Among his many works are the companion novels *Frankenstein Unbound* (1973) and *Dracula Unbound* (1991). One of his poetry collections is *Homelife with Cats* (1992). Recent novels are *Somewhere East of Life* (1994) and *White Mars* (2000). He was the recipient of the British Science Fiction Award in 1972 and is a founding trustee of *World Science Fiction* (1982). Also, his novel *A.I. [Artificial Intelligence]* was adapted as a film for release in 2001.

MAYA ANGELOU (b. 1928) • Born in St. Louis, Angelou acted and sang before becoming a writer. She is known as much for her fiction as for her poetry, and she has also written plays. She achieved recognition with *I Know Why the Caged Bird Sings* (1970). *Just Give Me a Cool Drink of Water 'fore I Diiie* appeared in 1971, and she has published regularly since. Her national importance was recognized when she was chosen to read her poetry at the inauguration of President Clinton in January 1993. Her collection of essays *Even the Stars Look Lonesome* appeared in 1997. Her collected work is *The Complete Collected Poems of Maya Angelou* (1994). Recent collections are *Amazing Peace* (2005), *Mother, a Cradle to Hold Me* (2006), and *Poetry for Young People* (2007). She has also recently spoken and sung on a number of public television productions.

MATTHEW ARNOLD (1822–1888) • One of the major Victorian poets, Arnold was brought up among books and learning, and he became a professor of poetry at Oxford in 1857. In his Oxford lectures he described a loss of security and religious faith, and hence he stressed the need to recover absolutes—which to him was the major "function of criticism at the present time." "Dover Beach" is, along with "The Scholar Gypsy" and "Stanzas from the Grande Chartreuse," among his best-known poems.

MARGARET ATWOOD (b. 1939) • Atwood is one of Canada's premier and most prolific writers, having published many books of poetry, a number of novels and stories, and much criticism. In addition, she is editor of *The Oxford Book of Canadian Verse* (1982). One of her most widely recognized works is the anti-utopian novel *The Handmaid's Tale* (1986), which describes a futuristic nightmare society of fear and repression for women. This story was adapted as a movie in 1990. The stories in her collection *Wilderness Tips* (1992) reflect regret and diminished hopes, unlike the more comic topic of the poem "Siren Song." The scope of her work may be inferred from some of her later publications: *Poems* (1994), *Princess Prunella and the Purple Peanut* (1995), *Morning in the Burned House* (1995), *The Edible Woman* (1998), *Dancing Girls: And Other Stories* (1998), *Lady Oracle* (1998), *The Blind Assassin* (2000, 2001), *Oryx and Crake* (again, a futuristic novel, 2003), and *The Penelopiad: The Myth of Penelope and Odysseus* (2005).

W. H. AUDEN (WYSTAN HUGH AUDEN, 1907–1973) • Auden was born in England but became a permanent resident of the United States after 1939. A Marxist in his youth, he became a devout Christian in later years. He wrote prolifically, including collaborations with the dramatist Christopher Isherwood and the poet Louis MacNeice. Another notable collaboration is the libretto for Igor Stravinsky's opera *The Rake's Progress* (1951). He edited *The Oxford Book of Light Verse* (1938).

WENDELL BERRY (b. 1934) • One of the most popular poets in the United States, Berry is a resident of Kentucky, where he was brought up and educated, and where he taught for many years. His output as a poet, essayist, and novelist has been voluminous. He has published many separate volumes of poetry, including *The Broken Ground* (1964), *Clearing* (1977), *The Wheel* (1982), *Entries* (1997), *A Timbered Choir: The Sabbath Poems, 1979–1997* (1998), and *Given* (2005). Readers can find some of his short fiction in *Fidelity: Five Stories* (1993). His *The Memory of Old Jack* (1999) is a recent novel. An early edition of his collected verse is *Collected Poems, 1957–1982* (1985).

ELIZABETH BISHOP (1911–1979) • Bishop was brought up by an aunt in Worcester, Massachusetts. She attended private schools and Vassar College. For a time she taught at the University of Washington and then at Harvard. A good friend was Robert Lowell, who dedicated his poem "Skunk Hour" to her. During much of her life she lived in Brazil. Her first collection of poems was *North and South* (1946), which she expanded in 1955 as *North and South—A Cold Spring*, for which she received the Pulitzer Prize in Poetry in 1956.

WILLIAM BLAKE (1757–1827) • Blake was apprenticed to an engraver in London at the age of fourteen. Throughout his career he published his poems with his own engravings, and these original editions are now valuable collector's items. Blake was a revolutionary at heart who thought that humanity would flower if institutions were eliminated or at least redirected. *Songs of Experience*, from which "London" is taken, is a collection of poems on this theme, published in 1794, five years after the outbreak of the French Revolution. In this same year he published *Songs of Innocence*, from which "The Lamb" is taken.

LOUISE BOGAN (1897–1970) • Born in Maine, Bogan spent most of her life in New York, writing regular reviews for *The New Yorker*. Her first volume of poems was *Body of This Death* (1923), in which "Women" appeared. Her *Collected Poems* (1954) was awarded the Bollingen Prize. Her major critical work was *Achievement in American Poetry, 1900–1950* (1951). *Journey Around My Room* (1980) is a posthumous autobiographical work.

ARNA BONTEMPS (1902–1973) • Born in Louisiana, Bontemps by profession was a librarian (at Fisk University). In addition to poetry, he published a number of novels and works of children's fiction. *One Hundred Years of Negro Freedom* (1961) is a widely heralded historical work.

ANNE BRADSTREET (1612–1672) • Bradstreet was born in England. She married early and came to the American colonies when she was eighteen. Her career was that of wife and mother, and she bore eight children. Nevertheless she wrote poems regularly and kept them together in manuscript. In 1650 her brother-in-law had them published in London without her knowledge, and she was therefore unable to make corrections. The volume, titled *The Tenth Muse,* was the first poetic publication in England by anyone living in colonial America. A second and corrected edition was considered in about 1666, but the new edition did not appear until six years after her death.

ELIZABETH BREWSTER (b. 1922) • Brewster is a native of the United States but has spent her professional life largely in Canada. She received degrees from Radcliffe, Toronto, and Indiana. She is a Professor Emerita at the University of Saskatchewan at Saskatoon, where she taught for many years. Two of her works are *Away from Home* (1995) and *Garden of Sculpture* (1998). In 1985 she published *Selected Poems of Elizabeth Brewster,* and in 1995 she was given a Lifetime Award for Excellence in the Arts.

EMILY BRONTË (1818–1848) • The middle child of the Brontë sisters, Emily received no more than a minimum of formal education and was largely self-taught, although she spent some time in Belgium studying music and languages. Her unfortunately brief life was characterized by poverty and deprivation. She was deeply affected by the landscape near Haworth, the family home in Yorkshire in the northern part of England, and her almost mystical identification of land and character pervades her best known work, the novel *Wuthering Heights* (1847). She and her sisters published a joint collection of verse in 1846, *Poems, by Currer, Ellis, and Acton Bell* (i.e., Charlotte, Emily, and Anne). "No Coward Soul Is Mine" is considered one of her best poems, along with "The Night Is Darkening Round Me" and "Remembrance."

GWENDOLYN BROOKS (1917–2000) • Brooks was born in Chicago, where she spent most of her life. Winner of the Pulitzer Prize for Poetry in 1950 (for *Annie Allen,* 1949), she was concerned with race in both her fictional and poetic works. "We Real Cool" exemplifies this emphasis. In 1967 she began directing her work toward African American readers, and she independently published a number of her poems in pamphlet form, of which *Primer for Blacks* (1980) is one. Her last published works are *Blacks* (1991), *Maud Martha* (1993), and *Selected Poems* (1999).

ELIZABETH BARRETT BROWNING (1806–1861) • English born, Elizabeth Barrett was the first of twelve children in her family. She suffered a lifelong pulmonary illness, possibly tuberculosis. Her family considered her an invalid. Despite this adversity she had become a widely recognized poet when she married Robert Browning in 1846. Because of her condition and the English climate, the Brownings moved to Italy, where they remained until Elizabeth's death, in her husband's arms, with her head at his cheek. During her lifetime, her reputation as a poet eclipsed that of her husband. Her *Cry of the Children* (1843) was an early poetic protest against the industrial exploitation of children. In 1850 she published *Sonnets from the Portuguese,* which she presented as a gift to her husband.

ROBERT BROWNING (1812–1889) • In his twenties and early thirties, Browning wrote a number of versified plays for the stage, but these were unsuccessful, and he did not achieve fame in his native England until he was well into his fifties. Because of his experience with drama, he found his poetic voice within the medium of the dramatic monologue, which he perfected to a high degree. Both "My Last Duchess" and "Soliloquy of the Spanish Cloister" appeared in his *Dramatic Lyrics* of 1842, exactly during the time when he was also writing his plays.

WILLIAM CULLEN BRYANT (1794–1878) • Bryant was born in Massachusetts and spent his adult life in New York. Early in his career he practiced law, which he disliked, and after ten years of that he was pleased to take up literature and editorial work. He was a newspaper editor and owner for fifty years, and at the time of his death he was one of the most beloved writers in the United States. His best known work was *Thanatopsis* (1817), which he wrote when still a boy. He published many collections of poems and also did successful translations of Homer's *Iliad* and *Odyssey*. Quotations from his poem "The Song of Marion's Men" (1832) may be found in Paredes's "The Hammon and the Beans" in Chapter 8.

ROBERT BURNS (1759–1796) • The best-known and most loved poet of Scotland, Burns gave up farming and taught himself to read and write English, French, and Latin. He published his first volume, *Scots Poems Chiefly in the Scottish Dialect*, in 1786. His use of the down-to-earth idiom of Scots peasants, together with joyous irreverence and frank lustiness, made him instantly famous.

GEORGE GORDON, LORD BYRON (1788–1824) • One of the major English Romantic poets, Byron created the so-called Byronic hero, a driven and solitary figure who is misunderstood by his fellow human beings. He published his semi-autobiographical poem "Childe Harolde's Pilgrimage" in 1811. In 1815 he published *Hebrew Melodies* (1815), in which "The Destruction of Sennacherib" appeared. That year, he left England and never returned. He continued writing poetry as he traveled, including the 16,000-line unfinished poem *Don Juan*. He died at Missolonghi, in Greece, while serving in the cause of Greek independence. It was Byron's "Childe Harolde's Pilgrimage" that inspired the French composer Hector Berlioz (1803–1869) to create his orchestral work with viola solos, *Harold in Italy* (1834), a work that is perennially popular on concert stages throughout the world.

LEWIS CARROLL (1832–1898) • Carroll is the pen name of the English writer Charles L. Dodgson, who is famous for *Alice's Adventures in Wonderland* and *Through the Looking-Glass*. Carroll was also a mathematician, lecturer, logician, and photographer. "Jabberwocky," from *Through the Looking-Glass*, stems out of his interest in words. The word *chortle,* which he created in this poem (a blending of *chuckle* and *snort*), is now standard English.

HAYDEN CARRUTH (1921–2008) • Carruth was a native of Connecticut and received degrees at the Universities of North Carolina and Chicago. In World War II he served for two years in Italy. After the war he taught, among other schools, at Syracuse and Bucknell. He was an editor of *Poetry* and served as poetry editor of *Harper's*. He was the author of more than two dozen poetry collections, including the recent *Doctor Jazz: Poems, 1996–2000* (2001) and *Toward the Distant Islands: New and Selected Poems* (2006). Among his many distinctions he received the Harriet Monroe Poetry Prize, a Guggenheim Fellowship, an NEA grant, and the National Book Award of 1996 for his collection *Scrambled Eggs and Whiskey: Poems: 1991–1995* (1996).

JIMMY CARTER (b. 1924) • James Earl Carter was born in Plains, Georgia, which is still his home. He graduated from the U.S. Naval Academy (1946), served in the Navy, became a peanut farmer, was governor of Georgia (1971–1975), and became the thirty-ninth president of the United States (1977–1981). Since his presidency he has distinguished himself in many national and international causes, such as creating the Carter Foundation, serving with the International Negotiation Network, and working closely with Habitat for Humanity. He has been the recipient of devoted recognition and many honorary degrees, but despite his national and international standing he has frequently been seen on TV house-building programs serving as a worker, along with other volunteers, on Habitat projects. He has sawed wood and driven many nails. His continued work for peace was recognized in 2002, when he received the Nobel Peace Prize. His varied list of published works is extensive, and he has even co-written, with his daughter Amy, a children's book. In 1995 he published *Always a Reckoning and Other Poems*, from which "I Wanted to Share My Father's World" is selected.

AMY CLAMPITT (1920–1994) • Clampitt was a native of Iowa, receiving her education at Grinnell College and later at Columbia University. For many years she worked in the publishing field and also for the National Audubon Society. Although she wrote poetry during most of her lifetime, she was not published until she was in her sixties, her first volume being *The Kingfisher* (1983). During the remainder of her life she published regular volumes of poems, completing *What the Light Was Like* (1985), *Archaic Figure* (1987), and *Westward* (1990). In 1994, the last year of her life, she published her final collection, *A Silence Opens*.

LUCILLE CLIFTON (b. 1936) • Clifton was born and educated in New York. Her productivity as a writer began in the 1970s and has been strong ever since. One of her earliest poetry collections was *An Ordinary Woman* (1974). Later she published *Next: New Poems* (1987) and *Good Woman: Poems and a Memoir, 1969–1980* (1987). In addition to her poetry, she has written a number of stories and poems for children, such as *All Us Come Cross the Water* (1973), *The Book of Light* (1993), *Everett Anderson's Christmas Coming* (1993), and *The Lucky Stone* (1999). A collection of her poems is *Blessing the Boats: New and Selected Poems, 1988–2000* (2000).

ARTHUR HUGH CLOUGH (1819–1861) • Clough's father was a businessman who often worked in the United States, and for a period of five years as a boy Arthur lived with his family in South Carolina. Returning to England, he attended Rugby, a famous public (i.e., private) school, and became a favorite in the household of Dr. Thomas Arnold, the headmaster. Though Clough had a good deal of academic promise, his achievement did not measure up, and he felt that he had failed in his academic goals. He was fond of giving his poems titles in foreign languages, such as "Qua Cursum Ventus" (the wind creates the course [of the ship]), "Wen Gott Betrügt, Ist Wohl Betrogen" ([the person] whom God deceives is well deceived), "Sehnsucht" (longing), and "Tò Kalón" (the beautiful). His "Say Not the Struggle Nought Availeth" is one of his famous poems, along with the satiric "The Latest Decalogue." After Clough died in Florence in 1861, his good friend Matthew Arnold commemorated his life in the monody "Thyrsis" (1866), one of the best-known elegies in the English language.

JUDITH COFER. See *Judith Ortiz Cofer*.

LEONARD COHEN (b. 1934) • Cohen is a native of Montreal, and he received his education at McGill University and also at Columbia. He traveled widely, spending years in Greece, England, New York, and California. He began writing poetry early. His first collections were *Let Us Compare Mythologies* (1956) and *The Spice Box of Earth* (1961). He also published two successful novels, *The Favorite Game* (1963) and *Beautiful Losers* (1966). Today he is best known for his having become a member of the Rock and Roll of Fame (in 2008), for his featured television concerts, and also for the many record albums and compact disc collections of his songs and music. Among the most recent of these are *Cohen Live* (1994) and *Ten New Songs* (2001). An anthology of his work is *The Concise Leonard Cohen* (1999).

SAMUEL TAYLOR COLERIDGE (1772–1834) • Coleridge was born in Devon, in southern England, and studied at Cambridge University but did not earn a degree. After a short stint as a soldier, he fell into dire financial straits, from which he was rescued by the Wedgwood brothers of ceramic fame, who provided him with an annuity so that he could devote himself to poetry. Wordsworth and he together published the *Lyrical Ballads* of 1798, a collection that is the benchmark of the English Romantic movement. Coleridge contributed "The Rime of the Ancient Mariner," his most famous poem, and also "Kubla Khan." After 1802 he wrote little poetry, but his *Biographia Literaria* of 1817 is one of the major works of literary criticism of the early nineteenth century.

BILLY COLLINS (b. 1941) • A native of New York, Collins received degrees at Holy Cross and the University of California at Riverside. He lives in New York State and is a Distinguished Professor of English at Lehman College. Among his collections of poetry are *The Apple That Astonished Paris* (1989), which includes "Schoolsville"; *Questions about Angels* (1991), a winner in the National Poetry Series competition; *The Art of Drowning* (1996); *Picnic, Lightning* (1998); *Sailing Around the Room: New and Selected Poems* (2001), *Nine Horses* (2002), and *The Trouble with Poetry and Other Poems* (2005), and *Ballistics* (2008). In 2001 he was named American Poet Laureate for 2001–2002, and the next year he was reappointed. One of his major projects as Poet Laureate was to emphasize the daily reading of poetry in the schools, and to this goal he published a significant collection of verse, *Poetry 180: A Turning Back to Poetry* (2003). He was named New York State Poet for 2004, and edited *The Best American Poetry 2006* (2006).

FRANCES CORNFORD (1886–1960) • Cornford, a granddaughter of Charles Darwin, lived most of her life in Cambridge, England. She published only a few volumes of verse, and her *Collected Poems* was published in 1954.

WILLIAM COWPER (1731–1800) • Cowper is universally recognized because of his lines "God moves in a mysterious way / His wonders to perform." He received his education at an English private ("public") school, an institution that he attacked in his *Tirocinium* in 1785. He was qualified to practice law but never made a career of it. Although throughout his life he was troubled with depression and he made at least two suicide attempts, he wrote a considerable amount of prose and much poetry. His most widely recognized long poem is *The Task* (1785), and his best lyric poems are found in the *Olney Hymns* (1775), which contain "God Moves in a Mysterious Way" and "Oh, for a Closer Walk with God."

STEPHEN CRANE (1871–1900) • For a brief biography, see Chapter 10, page 548.

ROBERT CREELEY (1926–2005) • A native of Massachusetts, Creeley received his master's degree from the University of New Mexico. He achieved wide recognition and many honors, including a Bollingen Prize and the appointment as New York State Poet for 1989–1991. He was closely associated with the "Black Mountain Poets," a group that in the immediate post–World War II years was connected with Black Mountain College in North Carolina. This group advocated a minimalist approach to expression and believed that poetic form should be a consequence of content. On this principle, poetry has no preconceptions, and each poem evolves freely and spontaneously as the poet writes it. Creeley authored numerous books of poetry, together with short stories, essays, and correspondence. Some of his recent collections were *Thinking* (2000), *For Friends* (2000), *Just in Time: Poems, 1984–1994* (2001), and *If I Were Writing This* (2003). "Do You Think . . ." (1972) is taken from his *Selected Poems* of 1991.

E. E. CUMMINGS (1894–1962) • Cummings studied at Harvard, receiving a master's degree there. During World War I, he served in the Ambulance Corps in France and, as a result of false charges of treason, was imprisoned—an experience he wrote about in his first work, *The Enormous Room* (1922). He began publishing poetry shortly thereafter and continued doing so throughout his life. His collected poetry, consisting of more than a thousand poems, was published in 1992.

PETER DAVISON (1928–2004) • Davison was born in New York City but grew up in Colorado. He received degrees at Harvard and Cambridge and served as a lecturer and also as an editor with a number of leading publishers. His first poetry collection was *The Breaking of the Day and Other Poems* (1964). Among his numerous collections since then were *Praying Wrong: New and Selected Poems* (1985), *The Poems of Peter Davison, 1957–1995* (1995), and *Breathing Room: New Poems* (2000). "Delphi" is selected from *The Breaking of the Day and Other Poems*.

CARL DENNIS (b. 1939) • Dennis is a native of St. Louis, and received degrees from the University of Minnesota and the University of California, Berkeley. He has taught for many years at the University of Buffalo. A few of his many poetry collections are *A House of My Own* (1974), *Signs and Wonders*, (1979), and *Practical Gods* (2001). "The God Who Loves You" is from *Practical Gods*, the collection for which Dennis was awarded the Pulitzer Prize for Poetry in 2002.

EMILY DICKINSON (1830–1886) • For a brief biography, see page 1023.

JOHN DONNE (c. 1572–1631) • Donne was born into a Roman Catholic family at a time when the Protestant reign of Elizabeth I was firmly established in England. In 1591 he enrolled at Lincoln's Inn in London to study science, philosophy, law, languages, and literature. So that he might rise in English aristocratic circles, he changed his religion to Anglicanism. His hopes for preference were ended in 1601, however, because of his elopement with Ann More, whose uncle accused him of a clandestine marriage (then a crime if the woman was an heiress) and had him jailed. Although the marriage was recognized in 1602, Donne could not regain political favor, and he and Ann struggled until he took a doctorate of divinity in 1616 (Ann died in 1617). He found favor and rose quickly to become Dean of St. Paul's Cathedral in London, where his sermons were well attended by "nobility and gentry." He became widely known, publishing more than 130 of the sermons he delivered during his decade as dean. His poems, both religious and love poems, were not published during his lifetime but were circulated only privately in manuscript. They were first published two years after his death. For two centuries he was neglected, but in our times he has earned recognition as one of the greatest of English poets.

JOHN DRYDEN (1631–1700) • Poet Laureate from 1668 to 1688, Dryden was one of the foremost English poets and dramatists of the seventeenth century. Dr. Johnson considered him the father of English literary criticism. Dryden's major poetic achievement was to fine-tune the heroic or neoclassic couplet, which he used for "To the Memory of Mr. Oldham." He is best known for his verse satires *Mac Flecknoe* (1676, 1682) and *Absalom and Achitophel*

(1681), both in rhymed couplets. Nevertheless, he used blank verse for his best play, *All for Love* (1677), which deals with the same material as Acts 4 and 5 of Shakespeare's *Antony and Cleopatra*. In 1688 he lost his official positions because he had been a supporter of King James II, who had been deposed. During the last twelve years of his life, therefore, Dryden was forced to support himself mainly with poetic translations, providing his contemporaries with versions of Virgil, Ovid, Juvenal, and Chaucer.

PAUL LAURENCE DUNBAR (1872–1906) • Dunbar was born in Ohio, the son of former slaves. During his brief life he rose to prominence as a poet, dramatist, and novelist. His first two collections of poems, *Oak and Ivy* (1893) and *Majors and Minors* (1895), in which "Sympathy" appeared, were favorably reviewed by William Dean Howells. His collected poems were published posthumously in 1913.

STEPHEN DUNN (b. 1939) • Born in New York, Dunn received a master's degree from Syracuse in 1960. He is perhaps the only Pulitzer Prize winner in poetry to have played professional basketball. He has taught at a number of schools, including the University of Michigan and Stockton State College in New Jersey. Some of his collections are *Five Impersonations* (1971), *Looking for Holes in the Ceiling* (1974), *Between Angels* (1989), and *Loosestrife* (1996). It was for *Different Hours* (2000) that he received the Pulitzer Prize. "Hawk" is taken from *Between Angels*.

RICHARD EBERHART (1904–2005) • Eberhart was a man of great longevity. The recipient of many awards, including the Pulitzer Prize in Poetry in 1966, he was born in Minnesota and received his higher education at Dartmouth and Cambridge. His many works included *Maine Poems* (1988) and *Collected Poems* of 1930, 1976, and 1988. In addition, *Long Reach: Uncollected Poems, 1948–1983* appeared in 1984; *New and Selected Poems: 1930–1990*, in 1990; and *Collected Poems 1930–1976: Including 43 New Poems* in 2001. From 1959 to 1961 he was the consultant in poetry (a position now titled Poet Laureate) at the Library of Congress, and in 1982 the governor of New Hampshire, Eberhart's home state, proclaimed a Richard Eberhart Day in his honor.

BART EDELMAN (b. 1951) • Edelman is a native of New Jersey. He received degrees at Hofstra University and now teaches at Glendale College. In addition to his collections of poetry (*Crossing the Hackensack* [1993], *Under Damaris' Dress* [1996], *The Alphabet of Love* [1999], *The Gentle Man* [2001], and *The Last Mojito* [2005]), he has served as the editor of *Eclipse*, has been awarded a number of significant grants and fellowships, and has done considerable research abroad. Additional information can be obtained on his Website at bartedelman.com.

T. S. ELIOT (1888–1965) • Born in Missouri, Thomas Stearns Eliot moved to England in 1914 and became a British citizen in 1927. With *The Waste Land* in 1922, he electrified the literary world because of his poetic use of colloquial speech and frank subject matter. Though he is considered a hyper-serious poet, his lighter side is shown in *Old Possum's Book of Practical Cats* (1939). These poems achieved popular fame in 1981 in the Broadway musical *Cats*, which then began a record run of nineteen consecutive years, not closing until 2000.

ELIZABETH TUDOR, QUEEN ELIZABETH I (1533–1603) • Queen of England from 1558 to 1603, Elizabeth was famed for her eloquence and wit. She is perhaps best remembered today for the support she gave to Shakespeare and the acting company at the Globe Theatre. She wrote a number of translations and left a small number of poems. Some other poems attributed to her are of doubtful authorship. Her works were edited and published in 1964.

JAMES EMANUEL (b. 1921) • Emanuel was born in Nebraska and attended Howard University. He earned his Ph.D. at Columbia in 1962 and joined the faculty of English at the City College of New York. Throughout his career, he has regularly written poetry, publishing poems in journals such as *Phylon* and *Negro Digest*. An early collection of his poems is *Panther Man* (1970). Other collections are *Black Man Abroad: The Toulouse Poems* (1978), *A Chisel in the Dark* (1980), *The Broken Bowl* (1983), *Deadly James and Other Poems* (1987), and *Jazz: From the Haiku King* (1999). In 1967 he published a biography of Langston Hughes for the Twayne Series of American Authors.

LYNN EMANUEL (b. 1949) • Emanuel is a native of New York and for a number of years directed the University of Pittsburgh's writing program. She earned degrees from Bennington, the City College of New York, and the University of Iowa Writer's Workshop. Her first two collections of poetry are *Hotel Fiesta* and *The Dig*, which have been reprinted together by the University of Illinois Press. A recent poetry collection is *Then, Suddenly* (1999).

RALPH WALDO EMERSON (1803–1882) • Emerson, known in his time as the Sage of Concord, was born in Massachusetts and studied to be a minister. His first profession was indeed the ministry, but conscientiously he could not continue when he found it impossible to maintain the orthodoxy that was demanded of his chosen faith. Increasingly he turned to philosophy and became the acknowledged leader of the Transcendental movement, the ideas of which he enunciated in his seminal book *Nature* (1836). His belief in the power of the human mind led him naturally into his involvement with the equal rights of women and also with the abolitionist movement prior to the Civil War. His literary output was enormous. "The American Scholar" (1837) is one of his major essays, as is "Self Reliance" (1841). His reputation as a poet was established by *Poems* in 1846 and *May-Day* in 1867. He has been called one of the most significant of all American thinkers.

ABBIE HUSTON EVANS (1881–1983) • Evans was perhaps the longest-lived of all American or British poets, dying in 1983 at the age of 102. She began receiving recognition in the 1930s and was granted an honorary Litt.D. degree from Bowdoin College in 1961. Her collections of poems are *Outcrop* (1928), *The Bright North* (1938), and *Fact of Crystal* (1961). The University of Pittsburgh Press published her *Collected Poems* in 1970. "The Iceberg Seven-eighths Under" was first published in *Fact of Crystal*.

MARI EVANS (b. 1923) • Evans has written fiction and criticism in addition to a major collection of poems, *I Am a Black Woman* (1970). *JD* (1975) is a collection of four stories about a young boy living in an urban housing project. Her *Black Women Writers (1950–1980): A Critical Evaluation* appeared in 1984, and *A Dark and Splendid Mass* was published in 1992. Interest in social matters prompted *Dear Corinne: Tell Somebody*, a fictional work about child abuse (1999). A collection of children's verse is *Sing My Black: Alternative Nursery Rhymes for Children* (1998).

JOHN CHIPMAN FARRAR (1896–1974) • Farrar was a native of Vermont. He began studies at Yale but his education was interrupted by his military service during World War I. After returning from the war he completed his degree in 1919. He became the author of a number of books but he is best known as a publisher, one of the founding partners of the still flourishing house of Farrar, Straus, & Giroux. Another of his achievements was his involvement in the beginning of the Breadloaf Writer's Conference. The poem "Song for a Forgotten Shrine to Pan" was published in 1919 and was included in the *Yale Younger Poets Anthology* (1998).

EDWARD FIELD (1924–1994) • A native of Brooklyn, Field attended New York University and also, for a time, studied method acting at the Moscow Art Theatre. "Icarus" is taken from his first collection of poems, *Stand Up, Friend, with Me* (1963). Other collections are *A Full Hearth* (1977), *Stars in My Eyes* (1979), and *New and Selected Poems* (1987). In 1990 he edited *Head of a Sad Angel,* stories by Alfred Chester, his long-time friend, with an introduction by Gore Vidal.

CAROLYN FORCHÉ (b. 1950) • Forché is a native of Detroit. After her first volume of poems in the Yale Younger Poets series (*Gathering the Tribes* [1976]) she spent two years in El Salvador as a journalist for Amnesty International. In 1982 she translated Claribel Alegria's *Flowers for the Volcano* in an English-Spanish edition. Her next volume of poetry was *The Country Between Us* in 1982. The section of this collection entitled "In Salvador, 1978–80" contains "The Colonel." In 1993 she published *Against Forgetting: Twentieth-Century Poetry of Witness*, an anthology of poems protesting against repression and genocide. In 1995 she published a long poem, *The Angel of History*, followed in 2003 by her poetry collection *Blue Hour*.

ROBERT C. FRANCIS (1901–1987) • Francis received his higher education at Harvard and lived most of his life in Amherst, Massachusetts, not far from the home of Emily Dickinson. Some of his collections are *The Orb Weaver* (1980*), Come Out into the Sun* (1965), *Like Ghosts of Eagles* (1974), and *Butter Hill and Other Poems* (1984). His collected verse appeared in *Collected Poems 1936–1976* (1976). He received a number of distinctions, among them the Brandeis University Creative Arts Award in 1974.

ROBERT FROST (1874–1963) • For a detailed biography, see page 1058.

ISABELLA GARDNER (1915–1981) • Isabella Gardner was born in Massachusetts. She was a niece of the Isabella Stewart Gardner who left an art museum to the City of Boston, and she was a cousin of Robert Lowell. During her lifetime, she acted, edited *Poetry* magazine (1952–1956), taught, published four volumes of poems, and gave frequent poetry readings. She declared herself "a poet who is woman first and poet second." Two years before her death, she published much of her poetry in *Isabella Gardner: The Collected Poems.*

JOHN GAY (1685–1732) • English poet and playwright John Gay was born in the same year as J. S. Bach and George Frideric Handel, and he was educated in Devon. As a young boy he was apprenticed to a silk mercer but freed himself to become a writer in London. For a time in the late 1720s, he was a gentleman-in-waiting to the young Duke of Cumberland, for whom he wrote his *Fables*, which were among the most popular poems in the eighteenth century. His most famous play is *The Beggar's Opera* (1728), which at a stroke created "ballad opera"—a form featuring spoken dialogue and songs sung to popular music. "Let Us Take the Road" is from this play, and the music is the "March" in the opera *Rinaldo* (1711) by Handel.

DAN GEORGAKAS (b. 1938) • A native of Detroit, Georgakas received degrees at Wayne State University and the University of Michigan. He lectures widely throughout the United States, and teaches at New York University. His publications are varied, dealing with the film industry, radical American publications, the International Workers of the World, and American Indians. His poetry collection *Happy Man* (1968) includes "Hiroshima Crewman." Among his other works are *Z: An Anthology of Revolutionary Poetry* (1968), *Detroit: I Do Mind Dying* (1975), and *Encyclopedia of the American Left* (1992).

CHIEF DAN GEORGE (1899–1981) • In the early part of his life, George took many jobs unrelated to writing. In 1947 he became chief of the Tse-lal-Watt Sioux tribe, holding this post until 1959. In the 1960s he launched himself on an acting and writing career. His greatest success as an actor was in the film *Little Big Man* (1970), for which he received an Oscar nomination as best supporting actor. After this time he appeared in a number of films and television shows, and he spent much time campaigning for more Native American involvement in the film industry. His autobiography *You Call Me Chief* appeared in 1981, the last year of his life. His poem "My Heart Soars" is from *Sannichtoni* (1974).

ALLEN GINSBERG (1926–1997) • One of the major voices of the "beat generation" of the 1950s and 1960s, Ginsberg was born in New Jersey and lived in San Francisco for a time. For many years he was Distinguished Professor of English at Brooklyn College, and held that position at the time of his death. His landmark poetry collection was *Howl and Other Poems* (1956), which occasioned a court case when certain persons sued, unsuccessfully, to suppress it on the grounds of obscenity. Ironically, his collection of 1973, *The Fall of America: Poems of These States*, received a National Book Award. Among his later publications were *Cosmopolitan Greetings: Poems 1986–1992* (1994) and a four-CD/cassette box set entitled *Holy Soul Jelly Roll: Poems and Songs 1949–1993* (available from Rhino Word Beat).

NIKKI GIOVANNI (YOLANDE CORNELIA GIOVANNI JR., b. 1943) • Giovanni, a poet whose reputation has coincided with the development of African American consciousness and pride, was born in Tennessee. She has written poems for children and has also published interviews with James Baldwin and Alice Walker. Among her early collections of poetry are *Black Feeling, Black Talk* (1968), *Black Judgment* (1968), and *Cotton Candy on a Rainy Day* (1978). More recent works are *Those Who Ride the Night Winds* (1983), *Sacred Cows—and Other Edibles* (1988), *The Selected Poems of Nikki Giovanni* (1996), *Love Poems* (1997), *Blues: For All the Changes: New Poems* (1999), *Quilting the Black-Eyed Pea: Poems and Not Quite Poems* (2002), and *Rosa* (2005), the story of Rosa Parks.

LOUISE GLÜCK (b. 1943) • A native of New York, Glück received her higher education at Sarah Lawrence and Columbia. She currently lives in Vermont and teaches at Williams College. Recent poetry collections are *Ararat* (1990), *The Wild Iris* (1992), *Meadowlands* (1996), *Vita Nova: Poems* (1999), *The Seven Ages* (2001), and *Averno* (2006). In 1985 she received the National Book Critics Circle Award. Her collection *The Garden* earned her the Pulitzer Prize for Poetry in 2003. She served as Poet Laureate of the United States from 2003 to 2004.

JORIE GRAHAM (b. 1951) • A person of international credentials, Graham is a native of New York but was brought up in Italy and studied in Paris. She received a degree in film from New York University. Later she studied writing at the University of Iowa, where she is a faculty member; she is also on the faculty of Harvard University. Her poetry is thoughtful—a number of critics have said difficult—as well as reflective and challenging. Among her collections are *The End of Beauty* (1987), *Region of Unlikeness* (1991), *Materialism* (1993, 1998), *The Dream of the Unified Field* (1995), *The End of Beauty* (1998), *Swarm* (2000), *Never* (2002), and *Overlord* (2005).

ROBERT GRAVES (1895–1985) • Graves fought in the British army in World War I and was badly wounded. His early autobiographical memoir, *Good-Bye to All That* (1929), deals in part with his war experiences. He became famous in the 1970s, when the BBC and PBS dramatized his historical novels about the life and times of the Roman Emperor Claudius. His studies of mythology, *The White Goddess* (1947) and *The Greek Myths* (1955), have explained the meaning of ancient religion to a generation of students.

THOMAS GRAY (1716–1771) • Gray was a professor of history at Cambridge University. His poetic output was small, but nevertheless in 1757 he was offered the honor of the Poet Laureateship, which he refused. The "Elegy Written in a Country Churchyard" has been called one of the most often quoted poems of the English language. Another of Gray's frequently quoted poems is the "Ode on a Distant Prospect of Eton College," which concludes with the familiar lines "Where ignorance is bliss / 'Tis folly to be wise."

SUSAN GRIFFIN (b. 1943) • Griffin is a native of California, and received her B.A. and M.A. degrees from San Francisco State. During her career she has served as an editor, teacher, playwright, and writer, and she is a leading feminist and activist critic. She received a number of grants and distinctions, and holds an honorary Ph.D. Among her poetry volumes are *Dear Sky* (1971), *Like the Iris of an Eye* (1976), *Unremembered Country: Poems* (1987), and *Bending Home: Selected and New Poems, 1967–1998* (1998). She is also the author of many volumes of nonfiction.

MARILYN HACKER (b. 1942) • Hacker, a native of New York City, has been the recipient of a National Book Award (1975) and a Guggenheim Fellowship. Her collections of poems include *Presentation Piece* (1974); *Separations* (1976); *Taking Notice* (1980), which includes "Sonnet Ending with a Film Subtitle"; and *Selected Poems* (1994). The year 1990 saw the publication of the collection *Going Back to the River*, and in the same year she included new and selected poems in *The Hang-Glider's Daughter*. Other collections are *Selected Poems: 1965–1990* (1995) and *Love, Death, and the Changing of the Seasons* (1995). *Squares and Courtyards* (2000) is a recent collection. In 1989 the composer Dennis Riley set five of her poems to music for soprano and chamber ensemble. In 1995 she was awarded the Lenore Marshall Poetry Prize for her eighth book of poems, *Winter Numbers* (1994). Recently she has published *Desesperanto: Poems, 1999–2002* (2003), and *Essays on Departure: New and Selected Poems* (2006).

DANIEL HALPERN (b. 1945) • Halpern was born and raised in New York and is a professor in the graduate writing program of Columbia University. He has lived on both the East and West Coasts and also has a residence in Morocco. He has produced a number of poetry volumes, including *Traveling on Credit* (1972), *Seasonal Rights* (1982), *Foreign Neon* (1991), *Selected Poems* (1994), and *Something Shining: Poems* (1999). He has also done work in editing and translating and is editor of *The Art of the Story: An International Anthology of Contemporary Short Stories* (2000). Uniquely interesting about him is that he has coauthored a cookbook, *The Good Food: Soups, Stews, and Pastas* (1985). He has also written a tourist's guide, *Guide to the Essential Restaurants of Italy* (1990).

H. S. ("SAM") HAMOD (b. 1936) • Hamod is a Lebanese American who was born in Indiana. He received a Ph.D. from the Writer's Workshop of the University of Iowa and has served as director of the National Communications Institute in Washington, D.C. He has published a large number of poetic volumes, including *Dying with the Wrong Name* (1980), from which "Leaves" is selected. In 1980 he received a nomination for the Pulitzer Prize for Poetry.

THOMAS HARDY (1840–1928) • For a brief biography, see page 287.

JOY HARJO (b. 1951) • Harjo, who is Creek, Cherokee, and French, was born in Oklahoma. She received her B.A. from the University of New Mexico and her M.F.A. at the University of Iowa, and has taught at a number of schools, including Arizona State University. In 1990 she received the American Indian Distinguished Achievement Award, and in 1991 she received the Josephine Miles Award for excellence in literature. She enjoys playing the saxophone and has done some musical recordings. Her poetry collections are *The Last Song* (1975), *What Moon Drove Me to This?* (1980), *She Had Some Horses* (1983), *Secrets from the Center of the World* (1989), *In Mad Love and War* (1990), *The Woman Who Fell from the Sky* (1996, 1998), *A Map to the Next World: Poems and Tales* (2000), and *How We Became Human: New And Selected Poems* (2002). She was a coeditor of *Reinventing the Enemy's Language: North American Native Women's Writing* (1997).

FRANCES E. W. HARPER (1825–1911) • Although Harper was a native of Maryland, a slave state in 1825, she was born free. She ensured her continued freedom by eventually moving to the free state of Pennsylvania. Before the Civil War she lectured extensively against slavery and supported the Underground Railroad. Early collections of her work were *Forest Leaves* (1845), *Eventide* (1854), and *Poems on Miscellaneous Subjects* (1854), the last containing a preface by William Lloyd Garrison. Her novel, *Iola Leroy, or Shadows Uplifted* (1892), was well received and was included as part of a collection of fiction by African-American writers. One of her better-known poetry collections is *Atlanta Offering: Poems* (1895). In 1970 and 1988 her reputation as a poet was permanently secured with the publication of complete editions of her poems.

MICHAEL S. HARPER (b. 1938) • Born in Brooklyn, the American poet Michael S. Harper should not be confused with the English writer Michael Harper. Harper has held distinguished visiting professorships at Carlton College and at Colgate, and has received both a Guggenheim Fellowship and a National Endowment for the Arts Creative Writing Award. He was the first person to be distinguished as Poet Laureate of the state of Rhode Island. He received degrees from California State University and the University of Iowa. He has taught for a number of decades at Brown University. Some of his collections of poems are *Dear John, Dear Coltrane* (1970, 1985), *Images of Kin* (1977), *Nightmare Begins Responsibility* (1975), *Healing Song for the Inner Ear* (1984), and *Honorable Amendments* (1995). He is the editor, with Anthony Walton, of *Every Shut Eye Ain't Asleep: An Anthology of Poetry by African Americans Since 1945* (1994). "Called" is from *Nightmare Begins Responsibility*.

ROBERT HASS (b. 1941) • A native of California, Hass is one of America's most distinguished poets. He was educated at Stanford. He taught at St. Mary's College and then became poet resident at the University of California at Berkeley. His first collection of poems, *Field Guide* (1973), received the Yale Series of Younger Poets Award. Among his many later collections are *Praise* (1979), *Twentieth Century Pleasures* (1984), *Human Wishes* (1989), and *Sun Under Wood* (1996). He has recently published a number of translations of the work of Czeslaw Milosz. In 1995 he was made United States Poet Laureate.

ROBERT HAYDEN (1913–1980) • Born in Detroit and educated at the University of Michigan, Hayden became a professor of English at both Fisk and Michigan. His earliest collection of poems was *Heart-Shape in the Dust* (1940). He received a special prize for *A Ballad of Remembrance* at the World Festival of Negro Arts held in Senegal in 1962. His *Words in the Mourning Time* (1970) included laments for the assassinated leaders Martin Luther King and Robert Kennedy, together with poems opposing the Vietnam War.

SEAMUS HEANEY (b. 1939) • Heaney lives in Northern Ireland, and has written broadly on many topics. Among his collections of verse are *Wintering Out* (1972), *Field Work* (1979), *Seamus Heaney: Selected Poems, 1966–1987* (1990), *The Spirit Level* (1996) and *Opened Ground: Selected Poems 1966–1996* (1999). His verse translation (1999) of the Old English poem

Beowulf was well accepted both critically and commercially. His *Finders Keepers: Selected Prose 1971–2001* was published in 2002. The highlight of his many awards and distinctions is the Nobel Prize in Literature in 1995.

WILLIAM ERNEST HENLEY (1849–1903) • Born in 1849, Henley contracted tuberculosis when still a boy. A major and lamentable result was that he suffered the amputation of a leg. During his recuperation he began writing poetry and became immediately recognized for the depth and range of his poetic vision. While still in his thirties he collaborated with Robert Louis Stevenson on four dramas, which were well received. His poetry collections were *The Song of the Sword* (1892), *London Voluntaries* (1893), *Collected Poems* (1898), and *In Hospital* (1903), in which he included his well known "Invictus." He was also a critic and editor, being one of the editors of the poetry of Robert Burns, and also of the works of Henry Fielding.

GEORGE HERBERT (1593–1633) • Herbert, whose brother was an English lord, became a priest in 1630 after a career in government service. He died in 1633, leaving his poems to a friend, Nicholas Ferrar, who had them printed in 1633 as *The Temple*. The intricacy of Herbert's thought, illustrated in poems like "The Pulley," "The Collar," and "Colossians III. 3" (Our Life is Hid With Christ in God), has caused later critics to classify him as a "metaphysical" poet. In the twentieth and twenty-first centuries a large number of church-music composers have set many of his lyrics as choral anthems, and through this medium his poetry has reached untold numbers of churchgoers.

ROBERT HERRICK (1591–1674) • Herrick attended Cambridge and became an Anglican priest in 1627. During the English Civil War, he remained loyal to King Charles I, for which he was removed from service in 1647, but he resumed his duties after the Restoration of Charles II in 1660. His major collection of poems was *Hesperides*, published in 1648. A number of people expressed disapproval because of his frank subject matter, but, as he said, though his muse was jocund, his spirit was chaste. "To the Virgins, to Make Much of Time" is one of the better-known poems in the *carpe diem* tradition.

WILLIAM HEYEN (b. 1940) • Heyen's father came to the United States from Germany in 1928. Two uncles who remained in Germany joined the Nazi party and were killed in combat when serving in the German army in World War II. Heyen's concern with the Holocaust is thus a complex product of his ethnic ties and his anxiety and anguish over Nazi atrocities. "The Hair: Jacob Korman's Story" was published in *Erika: Poems of the Holocaust* (1984). Among his volumes of poems are *The City Parables* (1980), *Pterodactyl Rose: Poems of Ecology*, and *Ribbons: The Gulf War*. A collection of his poems titled *The Host: Selected Poems, 1965–1990* was published in 1994. This collection is also available in cassette form. A more recent collection is *Crazy Horse in Stillness: Poems* (1996). In 2002 he was the editor of *September 11, 2001: American Writers Respond*, a collection of works on the topic of the Al Qaeda attacks against the United States.

EDWARD HIRSCH (b. 1950) • Hirsch is originally from Illinois, and he received degrees from Grinnell College and the University of Pennsylvania. His collections of poetry began with *For the Sleepwalkers* (1981), and continued with *Wild Gratitude* (1986) *The Night Parade* (1990), *Earthly Measures* (1994), and *Lay Back the Darkness* (2004). He has written regularly about poetry for the *Washington Post*, and one of his particularly noteworthy achievements is *How to Read a Poem and Fall in Love with Poetry* (2000). Among his many distinctions are an

NEA fellowship, a Guggenheim fellowship, a MacArthur Fellowship, the Rome Prize, and an endowed professorship at the University of Houston, where he taught for eighteen years. Since 2002 he has been President of the Guggenheim Memorial Foundation.

JANE HIRSHFIELD (b. 1953) • Hirshfield was born in New York and took her undergraduate degree at Princeton. Her honors and her work in poetry have been prolific. Her collections of poetry are *Alaya* (1982), *Of Gravity and Angels* (1988), *The October Palace* (1994), *The Lives of the Heart* (1997), *Given Sugar, Given Salt* (2001), and *After* (2006). She has also written a study of poetry and has translated and published collections of Japanese poetry. She has taught at the University of California at Berkeley, the University of San Francisco, the University of Cincinnati, and Bennington. Among her distinctions are fellowships from the Guggenheim Foundation, the Rockefeller Foundation, the Academy of American Poets, and the NEA.

JOHN HOLLANDER (b. 1929) • Born in New York, Hollander received his Ph.D. from the University of Indiana and has taught at Hunter College and Yale University. He is a remarkably energetic and diversified poet, writing shaped verse (such as "Swan and Shadow"), children's verse, and nonsense verse. His musical-critical study *The Untuning of the Sky: Ideas of Music in English Poetry, 1500–1700* appeared in 1961. In 1967 he published *Jiggery-Pokery: A Compendium of Double Dactyls*, in collaboration with Anthony Hecht. His *Rhyme's Reason* (1981) is a guide to the various forms of English verse, which he illustrates with his own examples. *Figurehead and Other Poems*, a recent collection, was published in 1999.

A. D. HOPE (ALEC DERWENT HOPE, 1907–2000) • Hope was an Australian whose lyrics were praised for their traditionalism, their clarity and directness, their satire, and their search for redemption in love, literature, and art. His collections of poetry are *Collected Poems* (1966), *Collected Poems, 1930–1970* (1972), *Antechinus: Poems 1975–1980* (1981), and *Selected Poems* (1992). A play, *Ladies from the Sea*, appeared in 1987. The Australian National University recognized Hope by granting him an honorary Litt.D. degree in 1972. *A. D. Hope*, a study of Hope by Robert Darling, was published in 1997 in the Twayne's English Authors Series.

GERARD MANLEY HOPKINS (1844–1889) • Hopkins was an English poet gifted not only in poetry but also in music and art. At the age of twenty-two, under the pastoral care of John Henry Cardinal Newman, he converted to Roman Catholicism. He studied for the priesthood and was ordained as a priest in 1877. Although he published the long poem *The Wreck of the Deutschland* in 1875, his religious poems linking his devotion to nature, on which his reputation now rests, were not published until early in the twentieth century. The *Poetical Works of Gerard Manley Hopkins*, edited by N. H. Mackenzie, was published in 1990.

CAROLINA HOSPITAL (b. 1957) • Hospital was born in Cuba in 1957 and was brought to the United States as a child of four, two years after the Castro revolution. She thus received an American education, and she earned an M.A. from the University of Florida in 1984. She included "Dear Tia" in her collection *Cuban American Writers: Los Atrevidos* (1988). Her *The Child of Exile: A Poetry Memoir* appeared in 2004. Using the *nom de plume* C. C. Medina, she published the novel *A Little Love* in 2000.

A. E. HOUSMAN (1859–1936) • Housman was a professor of classics at Cambridge University. He created one major book of verse, *A Shropshire Lad* (1896), a collection of poems stressing the brevity and fragility of youth and love. His major scholarly pursuit was a study of the ancient Latin writer Manilius, whose works he edited. His *More Poems* was published posthumously, and his *Complete Poems* was published in 1956.

LANGSTON HUGHES (1902–1967) • For a brief biography in two parts, see page 1072 and also page 1619.

DAVID IGNATOW (1914–1997) • Ignatow did not come to poetry through traditional academic degrees. Instead, he began his adult life as a worker, and only later did poetry become the rock of his life. Eventually he published twenty-two collections, and received the distinction of two Guggenheim scholarships. He taught at a number of schools, but his base was the New York City area. His first collection was named simply *Poems* (1948), and his final collection, published posthumously, was *Living Is What I Wanted: Last Poems* (1999). Robert Bly wrote the following tribute to him: "I find him a great poet and a friend of the soul."

JOHN HALL INGHAM (1860–c.1920) • Ingham's principal literary efforts took place in the 1890s and the early years of the twentieth century. His major work of poetry was *Pompeii of the West and Other Poems* (1903). In *An American Anthology* (1900), Clarence Steadman published "George Washington," together with two other Ingham poems, "A Summer Sanctuary" and "Genesis." In 1919, the composer Frances McCollin set Ingham's poem "The Midnight Sea" to voice with accompanying piano.

JOSEPHINE JACOBSEN (1908–2003) • Jacobsen, a Canadian by birth, did not receive a higher education because her parents believed that she, as a young woman, would gain no benefit from it. Despite such discouragement, she began writing poetry in 1940 with *Let Each Man Remember*, and she continued to write voluminously, both poetry and fiction, after that time. Her collection *The Shade-Seller: New and Selected Poems* appeared in 1974, and *In the Crevice of Time* was published in 1995. Among her many distinctions and honors were a Consultantship in Poetry (later the Poet Laureatship) to the Library of Congress and an award from the American Academy of Arts and Letters.

RANDALL JARRELL (1914–1965) • Jarrell was born in Tennessee. He received his B.A. and M.A. degrees from Vanderbilt University. He wrote poetry, criticism, a novel, and children's fiction. His 1945 collection of poems, *Little Friend, Little Friend*, which includes "The Death of the Ball Turret Gunner," resulted from his service in the Army Air Corps during World War II. He published a number of other verse collections, including *Selected Poems* (1955) and *The Woman at the Washington Zoo* (1960).

ROBINSON JEFFERS (1887–1962) • Jeffers was born in Pittsburgh and spent most of his life in California. He used negative and often brutal subject matter in his poetry, for example, fratricide in *Give Your Heart to the Hawks* (1933), betrayal in *Dear Judas, and Other Poems* (1929), and infidelity in *Thurso's Landing, and Other Poems* (1932). His adaptation of Euripides' *Medea* (1947), starring Judith Anderson in the title role, won him wide national recognition. "The Answer" and "The Purse-Seine" appeared in his *Selected Poetry* (1938).

BEN JONSON (1573–1637) • Born during the reign of Queen Elizabeth I, Jonson was raised in the household of his stepfather, a bricklayer, and young Ben began his working life in that trade. He was able to free himself to attend the Westminster School, where he began acquiring his immense store of knowledge. After brief service as a soldier, he embarked on a career as poet and playwright. After Shakespeare retired in 1611, Jonson was, in effect, the major practicing dramatist in England. In 1616 he published his nondramatic poems, *Epigrams*—from which his elegiac poem on the deaths of his daughter is taken—and *The Forrest*. In 1619, he became England's first Poet Laureate.

DONALD JUSTICE (1925–2004) • Born in Florida, Justice graduated from the University of Miami in 1945. He received his Ph.D. from the University of Iowa, and became a member of the faculty there and at other schools. His collections of poetry include *The Summer Anniversaries* (1959); *Departures* (1973); *Selected Poems* (1979), for which he was awarded the Pulitzer Prize in 1980; *The Sunset Maker* (1987); *New and Selected Poems* (1995); and *Collected Poems* (2004, published posthumously). In 1991 he was the recipient of a Bollingen Prize. A generous selection of his work has been included in *A Donald Justice Reader* 1991).

JOHN KEATS (1795–1821) • Keats is one of the major English Romantic poets. Both his parents died when he was still a child, and at the age of fifteen he was apprenticed to an apothecary-surgeon. In 1816 he received his license to practice medicine, but almost immediately he gave up that career in order to become a full-time poet. In the following five years he created a magnificent body of poetry. Mortally afflicted with tuberculosis, he went to Rome, where he took rooms in a building adjoining the Spanish Steps. He died in Rome at the age of twenty-six and is buried in the English Cemetery in Rome near the Pyramid of Sestius Sextus.

HENRY KING (1592–1669) • King became Bishop of Chichester in 1642 and held this position for the rest of his life. He had been a friend of John Donne and was likely one of Donne's early editors. During his lifetime he published two volumes of his own verse, one a poetic rendering of the Psalms and the other an edition of *Poems, Elegies, Paradoxes, and Sonnets* (1657). His collected poems were published in 1965.

GALWAY KINNELL (b. 1927) • Kinnell was born in Rhode Island and received degrees from Princeton and the University of Rochester. During his career he has taught at many schools, including the Universities of Grenoble in France, Teheran in Iran (on a Fulbright Fellowship), and Hawaii. Among his many distinctions, he was awarded the National Book Award for Poetry and the Pulitzer Prize in Poetry, both in 1983, for *Selected Poems* (1982). He was also the recipient of the prestigious MacArthur Fellowship. He has published a great number of poetry collections, including *What a Kingdom It Was* (1960) and *A New Selected Poems* (2000). "After Making Love We Hear Footsteps" was included in *Mortal Acts, Mortal Words* (1980).

CAROLYN KIZER (b. 1925) • Born in Spokane, Washington, Kizer studied at the University of Washington with Theodore Roethke. During much of her life she has lived in California. One of her specialties is the adaptation of poems from China and Japan. "Night Sounds," from *Mermaids in the Basement* (1984), is an example. Since 1959 she has regularly published poetry collections, some of which are *Knock Upon Silence* (1965), *Midnight Was My Cry* (1971), *The Nearness of You* (1986), *Harping On: Poems 1985–1995* (1996), and *Cool Calm & Collected* (2000). In 1985 her collection of poems *Yin* (1984) received the Pulitzer Prize in Poetry.

YUSEF KOMUNYAKAA (b. 1947) • Komunyakaa was born in Louisiana, and received degrees from the University of Colorado at Colorado Springs and also at the University of California at Irvine. He served in the U.S. Army during the Vietnam War, and his knowledge of Vietnamese underlay the title of his poetry collection *Dien Cai Dau* ("this crazy head") in 1993. He taught at Indiana and Princeton, and presently is the senior poet at New York University. Some of his poetry collections are *Neon Vernacular* (1994), for which he was awarded the Pulitzer Prize, *Pleasure Dome* (2001), and *Taboo: The Wishbone Trilogy* (2004). Among his distinctions was a fellowship from the National Endowment of the Arts. He was guest editor of *The Best of American Poetry* 2003 (2003).

TED KOOSER (b. 1939) • Kooser is a native of Iowa. If anyone can lay claim to being a midwest poet, it is he. He was educated at Iowa State and the University of Nebraska, and he has taught at Nebraska. In 2004 he was appointed the thirteenth Poet Laureate of the United States. Among his other honors are fellowships from the NEA, a Pushcart Prize, and the Stanley Kunitz Prize. He has published ten collections of poetry, including *Sure Signs* (1980), *One World at a Time* (1985), *Weather Central* (1994), *Delights and Shadows* (2004), *Flying at Night: Poems 1965–1985* (2005), *The Poetry Home Repair Manual: Practical Advice For Beginning Poets* (2005), and *Valentines* (2008).

PHILIP LARKIN (1922–1985) • A novelist, editor, and reviewer as well as a poet, Larkin was born in northern England and attended Oxford. His first collection of verse was *The North Ship* (1946), followed nine years later by *The Less Deceived*, in which "Next, Please" was printed. In 1964 he published *The Whitsun Weddings*, and in 1974 *High Windows*.

KATHERINE LARSON (b. 1977) • Larson graduated from the University of Arizona with a B.S. in Ecology and Evolutionary Biology and a B.A. in Creative Writing. She received her M.F.A. at the University of Virginia as a Henry Hoyns Fellow. She is the recipient of *Poetry* magazine's Ruth Lilly Fellowship (2003) and The Union League Civic and Arts Foundation Poetry Prize (2006). She currently works as a research specialist in pediatric genetics at the University of Arizona.

DORIANNE LAUX (b. 1952) • Laux is a native of Maine, and before receiving a degree from Mills College in 1988 she supported herself by odd jobs such as managing a gas station, cooking for a sanatorium, doing housework as a maid, and cutting holes in doughnut dough. Since then she has published four volumes of poetry: *Awake* (1990), *What We Carry* (1994), *Smoke* (2000), and *Facts About the Moon* (2005). With Kim Addonizio, she published *The Poet's Companion: A Guide to the Pleasures of Writing Poetry* (1997). She has received a fellowship from the NEA, and teaches at the University of Oregon.

IRVING PETER LAYTON (1912–2005) • Although he was born in Romania, Layton became one of Canada's major poets, publishing more than fifty poetry collections, including selected poetry in 1966, 1972, and 1986. A comprehensive selection of his poems, *A Wild Peculiar Joy: Selected Poems 1945–1982*, was published in 1983. *The Love Poems of Irving Layton* and *Dance with Desire: Love Poems* were published in 1984 and 1986. A new edition of *The Love Poems of Irving Layton* appeared in 2003. In 1982 and 1983 he was a nominee for the Nobel Prize in Literature.

EMMA LAZARUS (1849–1887) • Lazarus was born in New York before the Civil War, and was a member of the New York aristocracy. She began writing early, not only her own poetry but also translations of writers such as Goethe and Heine. Aroused by the plight of European Jewry, she wrote articles on the need for a Jewish homeland, and also translated the poems of many Jewish writers. A few years before the dedication of the Statue of Liberty in 1886, she wrote "The New Colossus" as a celebration of immigrants coming to the United States. In 1903, sixteen years after her death, the entire sonnet was embossed on a large metal plate which was affixed to the base of the Statue. It is still there, for all visitors to read.

LI-YOUNG LEE (b. 1957) • Lee, whose parents were Chinese, was born in Indonesia. Because of fear of Indonesian anti-Chinese discrimination, Lee's parents fled the country and moved from place to place throughout Asia before they came to the United States in 1964. Lee was educated at Pittsburgh and Arizona, and also at SUNY Brockport, and he has taught at both Northwestern University and the University of Iowa. Among his honors are grants from the National Endowment for the Arts and the Guggenheim Foundation. His major collections are *Rose* (1986), *The City in Which I Love You* (1990, the Lamont Poetry Selection for 1990), *Book of My Nights* (2001), and *Behind My Eyes* (2008). In 1995 he published *The Winged Seed: A Remembrance*, an autobiographical memoir.

DAVID LEHMAN (b. 1948) • A native of New York, Lehman attended Columbia in New York and Cambridge in England. He teaches at Bennington and also the New School for Social Research. His poetry collections are *An Alternative to Speech* (1986), *Operation Memory* (1990), *Valentine Place* (1996), *The Daily Mirror: A Journal in Poetry* (2000), *The Evening Sun* (2002), and *When a Woman Loves a Man* (2005). He is a highly creative and productive writer. He originated *The Best American Poetry* series, which has been published each September since 1988. He has also written extensive criticism on the topic of poetry, and has perhaps amazed people by sustaining the habit of writing a poem a day for a number of years. He is also interested in mystery writers, and received an Edgar Award from the Mystery Writers of America for his study of detective novels, *The Perfect Murder* (1989). He has received grants from the NEA and the Guggenheim Foundation.

DENISE LEVERTOV (1923–1997) • Levertov was a native of England whose parents were Welsh and Jewish. She was educated at home and served as a nurse in World War II. After the war she married an American and left England to live in the United States. She began publishing poems in her twenties. Since her first poetry collection, *The Double Image*, which appeared in 1946, she published at least two collections each decade. In the 1970s she published four. Her collections ranged from personal topics to deeply political ones, particularly *Light Up the Cave* (1981), which contains a number of poems on the Vietnam War. Some of her last poetry collections were *The Double Image* (1991), *Evening Train* (1992), and *Sands of the Well* (1996). In 1995 the Academy of American Poets awarded her an Academy Fellowship. *The Great Unknowing: Last Poems* (1999) a posthumous collection of her poetry.

PHILIP LEVINE (b. 1928) • Levine's parents were Russian-Jewish immigrants who settled in Detroit. He was educated there, and for higher education he stayed in Detroit and attended Wayne University (now Wayne State University), but later he went to the University of Iowa. For a long time he took industrial jobs, living in a number of cities before he became a professor at Fresno State in California. He is noted for his use of plain language and straightforward, simple syntax, in keeping with his pronounced sympathies for ordinary, working-class people. He has published many collections of poetry, including *They Feed, They Lion* (1972) and *The Names of the Lost* (1976), which were reprinted together in 1999. Other collections are *One for the Rose* (1981), *A Walk with Tom Jefferson* (1988), *What Work Is Like* (1991), *The Simple Truth* (1994; Pulitzer Prize for Poetry, 1995), *New Selected Poems* (1995), and *Breath* (2004). He has been honored with the American Book Award and the National Book Award, and has twice received fellowships from the Guggenheim Foundation.

ALAN P. LIGHTMAN (b. 1948) • Lightman, a faculty member of the Massachusetts Institute of Technology, is a native of Tennessee. He received degrees from Princeton and the California Institute of Technology, and his basic training is in theoretical physics. He is well known for his scientific writings, such as *Great Ideas in Physics* and *Time for the Stars*. More recently he has written *The Inflationary Universe: The Quest for a New Theory of Cosmic Origins* (1998) and *A Sense of the Mysterious: Science and the Human Spirit* (2005). He is, however, a writer who bridges the scientific and the humanist worlds through the writing of fiction and poetry. His novel *Good Benito* (1994), for example, describes the life and tribulations of a young scientist. Recent novels are *The Diagnosis* (2002) and *Reunion* (2004).

ABRAHAM LINCOLN (1809–1865) • Lincoln served as President of the United States, the sixteenth, from 1861 until his assassination in 1865. He was born in Kentucky in 1809 and with his family moved to southwestern Indiana in 1816. Because the area was still wild, Lincoln, though a child, was needed in helping his father clear the land and in performing the many duties needed for life on the frontier. There was virtually no time for him to attend school. Eventually he rose to be the partner in a successful law firm in Illinois, and then he went into state politics. In 1844, before he stood for any national office and when he was campaigning for Henry Clay (1777–1852) for the presidency, he returned to Indiana, and it was then that he wrote "My Childhood's Home," one of his three surviving poems. He is perhaps the most often quoted of American presidents, but it is for his many memorable speeches, especially the Gettysburg Address, that he is best known today.

LIZ LOCHHEAD (b. 1947) • In addition to her poetry, Lochhead also writes plays, translations, and television scripts. She is a native of Scotland and has taught at the Glasgow School of Art and the University of Glasgow. Her poetry collection *Memo for Spring* (1972) earned her a fellowship award from the Scottish Arts Council (1973). Some of her other poetry collections are *The Grimm Sisters* (1981), *Dreaming Frankenstein and Collected Poems* (1984), and *Bagpipe Muzak* (1991). She is a featured poet in the collection *Three Scottish Poets* of 1992, and in another collection, *Four Women Poets* (1996). Later works are *Perfect Days*, a play (2000); *Medea*, a translation/version of the *Medea* of Euripides (2001); and *Miseryguts/Taruffe*, translations of two Molière plays (2002).

HENRY WADSWORTH LONGFELLOW (1807–1882) • Longfellow was acknowledged in his own time as one of the great American poets. He was so popular, and his poetry sold so well, that he was able to live on the proceeds of his writing. After graduating from Bowdoin College in 1825, he began mastering Spanish, French, Italian, German, and the Scandinavian languages. This mastery equipped him to accept a professorship in languages at Harvard in 1836. His translation of Dante's *Divine Comedy* appeared in 1867, and at this same time he composed a number of sonnets that he published in 1867 and 1875. Some of his best-known works are *Ballads and Other Poems* (1842), *Evangeline* (1847), *The Song of Hiawatha* (1855), *The Children's Hour* (1860), and *Paul Revere's Ride* (1863).

AUDRE LORDE (1934–1992) • Lorde was a New Yorker whose parents were immigrants from Jamaica. She was educated at the National University of Mexico, Hunter College, and Columbia. Some of her poetry collections are *Chosen Poems Old and New* (1982), *Our Dead Behind Us* (1986), and *Undersong* (1992). *The Marvelous Arithmetics of Distance: Poems 1987–1992* (1993) is a posthumous collection.

AMY LOWELL (1874–1925) • Lowell was a member of the Lowell family of Massachusetts, which also included Robert Lowell. She was a proponent of the imagist school of poetry in the early twentieth century. Her first collection of poems was *A Dome of Many-Colored Glass* (1912). Later collections were *Sword Blades and Poppy Seed* (1914) and

Legends (1921). "Patterns" appeared in her collection *Men, Women, and Ghosts* (1916), just a year before the United States entered World War I.

ROBERT LOWELL (1917–1977) • Robert Lowell was a member of the Lowell family, which included Amy Lowell and traced its origins back to the earliest days of the republic. He has been called one of the "Boston Brahmins" for this reason. He was a conscientious objector during World War II, and served five months of a prison term because of his beliefs. During the Vietnam era, he marched with other war protestors. During his lifetime he regularly published poetry collections, being awarded the Pulitzer Prize twice for his work. A few of his collections are *For the Union Dead* (1964), *Life Studies* (1959), *Selected Poems* (1976), and the posthumous *Collected Poems* (2003). He has been closely identified with the confessional school of poetry, and two of his students were Sylvia Plath and Anne Sexton. He has been recognized as one of the most influential of all twentieth-century poets.

THOMAS LUX (b. 1946) • A winner of the Kingsley Tufts Poetry Award, Lux was educated at the University of Iowa and has taught at Sarah Lawrence College for many years. His poetry has been characterized as an "ironic mingling of humor and sincerity." Some of his collections are *The Land Sighted* (1970), *The Drowned River: New Poems* (1990), *Pecked to Death by Swans* (1993), *Split Horizon* (1994), *The Blind Swimmer: Selected Early Poems, 1970–1975* (1996), *New and Selected Poems 1975–1995* (1997), and *The Street of Clocks* (2001).

ANDREW MARVELL (1621–1678) • One of the major metaphysical poets of the seventeenth century, Marvell was active during the unsettled period of the English Civil Wars of 1642–1649, the Commonwealth, and the Protectorate of Oliver Cromwell. The Restoration of King Charles II (1660) ushered in a period of relative calm in Marvell's life. During his long career, which he began as a tutor in an aristocratic household, he assisted Milton (who served as Latin Secretary for the English Commonwealth), and he also was a Member of Parliament. His poems were not published until three years after his death. A modern edition of his *Poems and Letters* was published in 1971.

JOHN MASEFIELD (1878–1967) • The English poet John Masefield, though not an academic, was a compulsive reader and writer. In his youth he was a merchant seaman and worker at odd jobs in the United States. Eventually he published fifty volumes of poems, together with many plays and novels, and he became Poet Laureate of England in 1930. Today, his two best-known poems are "I Must Go Down to the Sea Again," included in *Salt-Water Ballads* (1902), and "Cargoes," which appeared in *Ballads and Poems* (1910).

HEATHER McHUGH (b. 1948) • McHugh, whose parents were Canadian, is a native Californian who received her B.A. from Radcliffe and her M.A. from Denver University. She has taught in Washington, North Carolina, and Iowa, and has received grants from the NEA and the Guggenheim Foundation. Her poetry was first collected in *Dangers* (1977) and *A World of Difference* (1981). Recent collections are *Broken English: Poetry and Partiality* (1993), *Hinge and Sign: Poems, 1968–1993* (1994), *The Father of the Predicaments* (1999, 2001), and *Eyeshot* (2003). She was guest editor of *The Best American Poetry 2007* (2007).

CLAUDE McKAY (1890–1948) • One of the important voices in the Harlem Renaissance of the 1920s, McKay was born in Jamaica, emigrated to the United States in 1912, and settled in Harlem in 1914. He wrote a number of novels, including *Home to Harlem* (1928), and short stories, published in *Gingertown* (1932). His poems were collected in *Songs of Jamaica* (1911), *Spring in New Hampshire and Other Poems* (1920), and *Harlem Shadows* (1922), where we find "In Bondage" and "The White City."

HERMAN MELVILLE (1819–1891) • Melville is best known as the author of *Moby Dick* (1851), which has been called the greatest of all American novels. Born in New York, he left school at the age of fifteen to take up clerical work, an experience on which he based his famous short story "Bartleby the Scrivener" (1856). He spent a number of years as a seaman, which gave him the experience to write *Typee* (1846), *Omoo* (1847), *Mardi* (1849), *Redburn* (1849), *White-Jacket* (1850), and *Billy Budd* (1888, 1924), in addition to *Moby-Dick*. He wrote an extensive poem based on his visit to the Near East, *Clarel* (1876), and collected his poems in *Battle-Pieces and Aspects of the War* (1866, containing "Shiloh"), *John Marr and Other Sailors* (1888), *Timoleon* (1891), and the posthumous *Weeds and Wildings, with a Rose or Two* (1924).

W. S. MERWIN (WILLIAM STANLEY MERWIN, b. 1927) • Merwin was born in New York and raised in New Jersey and Pennsylvania. He currently lives in Hawaii. He published *Selected Translations 1948–1968* in 1968 and was distinguished by a PEN translation prize for this work. In 1988 he published two collections of poems: *The Rain in the Trees* and *Selected Poems*. In 1996 he published *The Vixen*, a collection of poems about people and life in the southern part of France. Also in 1996 he published *Flower and Hand: Poems 1977–1983*. Three long poems make up his *The River Sound* (1999). In 2001 he published *The Pupil: Poems*. He was awarded the Pulitzer Prize in Poetry for *The Carriers of Ladders* (1970). "Odysseus" appeared in one of his early collections, *The Drunk in the Furnace* (1960).

JOHN MILTON (1608–1674) • Milton is acknowledged as one of the greatest English poets. His fame rests largely on the epic poem *Paradise Lost*, which he wrote in 1667, long after he became blind. He led a varied career and wrote extensively in both prose and verse, including many poems in Latin. His most important political position was as Latin Secretary to Oliver Cromwell during the Interregnum (1649–1660). Latin at that time was the language of diplomacy, and a good Latinist like Milton was essential to the government. Milton's *Poems* was published in 1645, and he issued a second edition in 1673.

EDNA ST. VINCENT MILLAY (1892–1950) • Known as a free spirit at Vassar, Millay matured quickly, receiving the Pulitzer Prize for Poetry—the first woman to be so honored—for *The Harp Weaver and Other Poems* (1923), which contained "What Lips My Lips Have Kissed." Her maturing concerns were reflected in *Make Bright the Arrows* (1940) and especially *The Murder of Lidice* (1942), which she wrote for radio presentation after the Nazi extermination of that Czech village. She published her *Collected Sonnets* in 1941. *Edna St. Vincent Millay: Collected Poems*, a centenary edition, was published in 1993.

JUDITH MINTY (b. 1937) • Of Finnish, Irish, and Mohawk descent, Minty has done a variety of things in addition to writing poetry, including working as a speech therapist, selling cosmetics, and introducing poetry to prisoners. She lives in Michigan, but has taught at many colleges and universities, including the University of Alaska. Among her poetry collections are *Lake Songs and Other Fears* (1974), *In the Presence of Mothers* (1981), *Counting the Losses* (1986), and *Dancing the Fault* (1991). A recent poetry collection is *Walking with the Bear* (2000).

N. SCOTT MOMADAY (b. 1934) • A member of the Kiowa tribe, Momaday was educated at the University of New Mexico and Stanford University. He has taught at Stanford and the University of Arizona. His reputation as a writer was gained by his *House Made of Dawn* (1968) and *The Way to Rainy Mountain* (1969). Despite his success as a novelist, he considers himself a poet. Some of his collections are *Angle of Geese and Other Poems* (1974), *The Gourd Dancer* (1976), and *In the Presence of the Sun: Stories and Poems 1961–1991* (1992).

EUGENIO MONTALE (1896–1981) • The poet and critic Eugenio Montale is often associated with *hermeticism*, a movement associated with other Italian poets writing in the early part of the twentieth century, particularly Umberto Saba, Giuseppe Ungaretti, and Salvatore Quasimodo (q.v.). Its main tenets are a deliberate obscurity, a bare style and a deeply personal symbolism. Some have suggested that Fascist censors during the dictatorship of Benito Mussolini may have led Montale to "disguise" his meanings in difficult language and allusion, but his poetry undoubtedly has a literary rationale as well and has influenced poets outside the Italian tradition. For many poets, the "hermetic model" reflects the complexity of modern life and the inability to reach absolute conclusions about the human condition. "English Horn" reflects the thoughts of an adolescent girl, and indeed she may be a girl from any time and place. Although the images of the wind, earth, light and the sky resonate throughout many of Montale's poems, and have deeply personal associations for him, a careful reader of "English Horn" can understand the meanings of these major images apart from any knowledge of other Montale poems. Montale was awarded the Nobel Prize for Literature in 1975.

MARIANNE MOORE (1887–1972) • Born in Missouri, Moore was raised by her grandfather, a Presbyterian minister. She studied typing, which was unfortunately the only avenue of education for her as a girl. She did, however, matriculate at Bryn Mawr, and graduated in 1909, after which she taught for a period of six years at the Carlisle Indian Industrial School at a time when Jim Thorpe was starring as an All-America football player. Coming to New York, she worked in the New York Public Library as what was called an "assistant." She was writing poetry during these years, and with the encouragement of poets like William Carlos Williams and Wallace Stevens, she developed her poetic skills. She became the editor of *Dial* magazine, an early outlet for American poetic talent, and in this way she encouraged many other poets. Her first publication, entitled simply *Poems*, was arranged by H. D. (1886–1961) without Moore's knowledge, and was carried out by an English publisher. In the subsequent years her poetic output was considerable. Her *Collected Poems* of 1951 earned her a Pulitzer Prize. She became known as something of a character, but maintained a friendship with Muhammed Ali, the heavyweight boxing champion, and the New York Yankees. After suffering a series of crippling strokes, she died in 1972. *The Complete Poems of Marianne Moore* was published in 1967. A posthumous collection of her poetry was *Complete Poems* (1982).

PAT MORA (b. 1942) • Mora received her B.A. from Texas Western College in 1963, and her M.A. from the University of Texas at El Paso in 1967. In addition, she holds an honorary Doctorate of Letters from the State University of New York at Buffalo, and has received many distinctions, such as the National Hispanic Cultural Center Literary Award for 2006. Mora has championed the causes of both children's literature and bilingualism. Some of her works are *My Own True Name: New and Selected Poems for Young Adults* (1999), *Aunt Carmen's Book of Practical Saints* (1999), *Adobe Odes* (1999), and *Tomás and the Library Lady* (2005). She currently lives in Santa Fe, New Mexico.

LISEL MUELLER (b. 1924) • Lisel Neumann Mueller came to this country from Germany in 1939, just as World War II was intensifying in Europe. She studied at the University of Indiana and taught at Goddard College. Even though English is not her first language, she mastered the craft of English poetry and has made English translations of works by Marie Luise Kaschnitz. Her poetry volumes are *Dependencies* (1965), *The Private Life* (1976), *The*

Need to Hold Still (1980), *Second Language: Poems* (1986), and *Waving from Shore: Poems* (1989). Her Pulitzer Prize-winning *Alive Together: New and Selected Poems* (1996) includes poems from each of these collections and adds a number of new poems.

OGDEN NASH (1902–1971) • Nash is most closely associated with *The New Yorker*, where he served as an editor for many years. Wit, humor, and satire characterize his verse, with an emphasis on original and clever rhymes and rhythms. Students of music may remember his voice on a 1950s recording of Camille Saint-Saëns's *Carnival of the Animals*. His many poetry collections include *Free Wheeling* (1931), *The Bad Parents' Garden of Verse* (1936), *You Can't Get There from Here* (1957), *Everyone But Thee and Me* (1962), and *Bed Riddance* (1970).

HOWARD NEMEROV (1920–1991) • Nemerov graduated from Harvard and served in World War II. After the war he taught at a number of colleges and began publishing his many essays, stories, plays, and poems. His poetry collections include *The Image and the Law* (1947), *The Western Approaches: Poems 1973–1975* (1975), and *Inside the Onion* (1985). The Library of Congress honored him as Poet Laureate of the United States from 1986 to 1988.

PABLO NERUDA (1904–1973) • Chilean poet and diplomat Pablo Neruda was the *nom de plume* of Naftali Ricardo Reyes Basoalto. Throughout his life, Neruda was devoted to leftist causes, and he served the Chilean government as a diplomat as long as the party favoring him was in power. During turbulent times of political unrest in Chile, he was forced to live underground, and at one point he fled Chile on horseback and spent three years in exile. He was attracted by the political philosophy of the Soviet Union, and favored the Republican forces in Spain during the Spanish Revolution in the 1930s. He began writing poetry early in his life, and his first collection was *The Book of Twilights* in 1923. The next year saw the appearance of his *Twenty Poems of Love and a Song of Despair*, from which "Every Day You Play" is excerpted. This collection is his best-known work, which has been translated into many languages and read by millions of readers throughout the world. Neruda was the winner of the Nobel Prize for Literature in 1971. Upon his death, his three homes in Chile became national shrines, which are open to the public.

JIM NORTHRUP (b. 1943) • Northrup is a Chippewa Indian and lives with his family on the Fond du Lac Reservation in Minnesota. He has published a number of stories, and his poems have been published mainly in magazines and journals. His major poetry collection, which also contains short stories, is *Walking the Rez Road* (1993). Another collection of his poetry, *The Rez Road Follies*, was published in 1997. More recently he has published poems in *Nitaawichige: Selected Poetry and Prose by Four Anishinaabe Writers* (2002). He writes a syndicated column and also works as an artist.

NAOMI SHIHAB NYE (b. 1952) • Nye, a Palestinian-American, is a native of Missouri but has lived for a time in Jerusalem. She is not only a poet but also a writer of children's books and, interestingly, a folk singer (with recordings to her credit). In her work as a teacher she has taught at the University of Hawaii and the University of Texas at Austin. She has published her poetry in a number of collections, including *Tattooed Feet* (1977), *Different Ways to Pray* (1980), *Hugging the Jukebox* (1982), *Yellow Glove* (1986), *Texas Poets in Concert: A Quartet* (1990, as one of four poets), *Red Suitcase* (1994), *The Words Under the Words: Selected Poems* (1995), *Fuel* (1998), *Come with Me: Poems for a Journey* (2000), and *19 Varieties of Gazelle: Poems of the Middle East* (2002). A collection of her essays, *Never in a Hurry*, was published in 1996. She recently published *The Space between Our Footsteps: Poems and*

Paintings from the Middle East (1998). *Habibi* (1997) is an autobiographical novel for young people. In 2005 she published *A Maze Me: Poems for Girls.*

JOYCE CAROL OATES (b. 1938) • For a brief biography, see page 150.

SHARON OLDS (b. 1942) • Born in San Francisco, Olds received her Ph.D. from Columbia in 1972 and has taught at New York University, Sarah Lawrence, Brandeis, and Columbia. In 1998 she was named New York State Poet. Her early poetry collections are *Satan Says* (1980) and *The Dead and the Living* (1984). Recent collections are *The Gold Cell* (1987), *The Father* (1992), *The Wellspring* (1996), *Blood, Tin, Straw* (1999), *The Unswept Room* (2002), and *Strike Sparks: Selected Poems 1980–2002* (2004). Although her poems are often physical and deeply personal, she remains, at heart, a private person. Several years ago, members of the Academy of American Poets most often named her as their favorite contemporary American poet.

MARY OLIVER (b. 1935) • A native of Cleveland, Oliver received her higher education at Ohio State University and Vassar College. She is a longtime resident of Provincetown, Massachusetts, and is on the faculty of Bennington College. Her poetry collections have been regular and numerous, including *No Voyage and Other Poems* (1963), *Sleeping in the Forest* (1978), *American Primitive* (1983), *New and Selected Poems* (1992), *White Pine: Poems and Prose Poems* (1994), *Blue Pastures* (1995), *West Wind* (1997), and *Winter Hours: Poetry, Prose, and Essays* (1999). She is also the author of *A Poetry Handbook* (1994) and *Rules for the Dance: A Handbook for Writing and Reading Metrical Verse* (1998). She received the National Book Award and the Shelley Memorial Award, and in 1984 she was honored with the Pulitzer Prize in Poetry for *American Primitive.*

SIMON ORTIZ (b. 1941) • Ortiz, of the Acoma Pueblo Indian Nation, was born in New Mexico. He attended the universities of New Mexico and Iowa. His first volume of poetry was *Naked in the Wind* (1971). In 1991 he published the collection *After and Before the Lightning. Woven Stone*, a three-in-one volume of poems containing a memoir, appeared in 1992, and *From Sand Creek: Rising in This Heart Which Is Our America (Sun Tracks)*, a combination of prose and poetry, was published in 2000. His best-known collection of stories is *Howbah Indians* (1978). A recent collection of stories is *Men on the Moon: Collected Short Stories* (1999). Recently he published *Out There Somewhere* (2002).

JUDITH ORTIZ COFER (b. 1952) • Ortiz Cofer's mother was a Puerto Rican who did not know English, and her father was a career member of the U.S. Navy. She spent her early life being moved back and forth between New Jersey, where her father was stationed, and Puerto Rico. Although she is bilingual, her education was mainly in English. She received her B.A. from Augusta College in 1974, and her M.A. from Florida Atlantic College in 1977. At present she teaches at the University of Georgia. She has written novels and memoirs, and her two collections of poems are *Terms of Survival* (1987) and *Peregrina* (1986). She stated that she had originally written "Latin Women Pray," one of her very first publications, as a personal joke. She extended the title *Latin Women Pray* to a three-act play in 1984.

WILFRED OWEN (1893–1918) • A native of Shropshire, England, Owen became a British Army officer and at the age of twenty-five was killed in France in 1918, just a week before the Armistice on November 11. He published only four poems in his lifetime, but after his death Siegfried Sassoon issued a collection of twenty-four poems (1920). Benjamin Britten used a number of Owen's poems, including "Anthem for Doomed

Youth," as texts for his *War Requiem* (1962). The band "10,000 Maniacs" recorded versions of both "Anthem for Doomed Youth" and "Dulce et Decorum Est" on their album *Hope Chest* (Elektra 9-60962-2).

DOROTHY PARKER (1893–1967) • Parker became legendary because of her many witty "one-liners" and also because of her often caustic book and drama reviews for *The New Yorker* in the period between the World Wars I and II. Her first volume of poetry was *Enough Rope* (1926). "Penelope" was included in her comprehensive collection *Not So Deep as a Well* (1936). She wrote many short stories and served as a correspondent during the Spanish Civil War in the late 1930s.

LINDA PASTAN (b. 1932) • Pastan was born in New York. She received a B.A. from Radcliffe and an M.A. from Brandeis. Among her many volumes of verse are *A Perfect Circle of Sun* (1971), *Setting the Table* (1980), *Waiting for My Life* (1981), *PM/AM: New and Selected Poems* (1983), *A Fraction of Darkness* (1985), *An Early Afterlife* (1996), *Carnival Evening: New and Selected Poems 1968–1998* (1998), and *The Last Uncle* (2002).

MOLLY PEACOCK (b. 1947) • Peacock was born in Buffalo, New York, and received a master's degree with honors from Johns Hopkins University. The first of her many collections of poetry was *And Live Apart* (1980). Recent collections are *Paradise, Piece by Piece* (1998), and *Cornucopia: New and Collected Poems* (2002). "Desire" is selected from *Raw Heaven* (1984). She is known as a poet who deals with the "pain and joy of living," and she has been praised for her fearless and uninhibited treatment of subjects that many consider taboo, even for personal and confessional poets. A major project of hers was "Poetry in Motion," which was designed to put poetry in buses and subway cars. She has been honored by the National Endowment for the Humanities and the Woodrow Wilson Fund.

MARGE PIERCY (b. 1936) • A native of Detroit, Piercy now lives in Wellfleet, on Cape Cod, in Massachusetts. She received her B.A. from the University of Michigan (1957) and M.A. from Northwestern (1958). Among her novels are *Braided Lives* (1980) and *Fly Away Home* (1984). The first of her many poetry collections was *Breaking Camp* (1968). Others are *The Moon Is Always Female* (1980); *Circles on the Water: Selected Poems* (1982), including "A Work of Artifice"; and *Available Light* (1988). Her most recent poetic volumes are *What Are Big Girls Made Of?* (1996), *Early Grrrl: The Early Poems of Marge Piercy* (1999), and *The Art of Blessing the Day: Poems with a Jewish Theme* (1999).

ROBERT PINSKY (b. 1940) • Poet, scholar, and translator, Pinsky was educated in his home state of New Jersey and also at Stanford. He has taught at the University of California, Boston University, and Harvard. Some of his poetry collections are *Sadness and Happiness* (1975), *An Explanation of America* (1979), *The Want Bone* (1990), and *The Figured Wheel: New and Collected Poems 1966–1996* (1996). His *Explanation of America* (1979) is a book-length poem. For a time he was poetry editor of *The New Republic*. In the 1990s he became Poet Laureate of the United States for three successive terms, the only person to be so honored. He used the prestige of his position advantageously. He brought out a short book (*The Sounds of Poetry: A Brief Guide* [1998]), and he also did much to put poetry before the public eye, appearing regularly on national television to read poems and to comment extensively on poetry. In this capacity he became the most widely recognized person to serve as U.S. Poet Laureate. One of his important efforts for poetry was the development of the Favorite Poem Project. The result, on which he worked in collaboration with many persons from all walks of life, is *Americans' Favorite Poems* (1999). With Maggie Dietz, he published *Poems to Read* in 2002. "Dying" is taken from his collection *History of My Heart* (1984, 1998).

SYLVIA PLATH (1932–1963) • For a brief biography, see page 1085.

EDGAR ALLAN POE (1809–1849) • For a brief biography, see page 493.

ALEXANDER POPE (1688–1744) • Pope is the eminent eighteenth-century English poet, the acknowledged master of the neoclassic couplet. A childhood accident deformed his spine and retarded his physical growth, but it did not hinder his poetic gifts. Because his family was Roman Catholic, he was not sent to school but was educated at home. By the age of 23 he had completed *An Essay on Criticism* (1711), the leading English work of criticism in poetic form. After 1725 he devoted himself principally to writing satire, producing *The Dunciad* (1728, rev. 1743), *Moral Essays* (1731–35), *An Epistle to Dr. Arbuthnot* (1735), and other satiric works, including the *Epilogues to the Satires* in dialogue form (1738). One of his life's plans was to publish a major philosophic work in poetry, but the only part he completed was *An Essay on Man* (1734).

EZRA POUND (1885–1972) • A native of Idaho, Pound was educated at the University of Pennsylvania and spent most of his life in Europe. He was the leading exponent of poetic imagism (see also *Amy Lowell*). During World War II he broadcast pro-Axis propaganda from Rome. After the war he was prosecuted for this but was exonerated on the grounds of insanity. Pound is as much known for his influence on other poets as for his own poetry (T. S. Eliot acknowledged him as "the better maker" in the dedication to *The Waste Land*). He published many poetry collections, such as *Exultations* (1909), *Canzoni* (1911), and *Cathay* (1915), which contained his versions of Chinese poems. His major work was the *Cantos*, which he worked on throughout his life after publishing the first portion in 1925.

WYATT PRUNTY (b. 1947) • Prunty was born in Tennessee and grew up in Georgia. He graduated from Sewanee: The University of the South and then went into the Navy, where he served as a gunnery officer. After leaving the service he took advanced degrees at Johns Hopkins and Louisiana State. Among his seven poetry collections are *The Times Between* (1982), *What Women Know, What Men Believe* (1986), and *Unarmed and Dangerous: New and Selected Poems* (2003). Prunty teaches at Sewanee. He is editor of the Sewanee Writer's Series, and also directs the Sewanee Writers' Conference.

SALVATORE QUASÍMODO (1901–1968) • A native of Italy, Quasímodo's early work was part of the so-called Italian "hermetic" period prior to World War II. (See *Eugenio Montale*.) That is, his poetry was highly imagistic, personal, and nonpolitical. During the war he became militantly antifascist, and for this reason the government of Benito Mussolini sent him to prison. After the war he became deeply concerned with the conditions of common people. In addition, he translated many works into Italian. He was the recipient of the Nobel Prize in Literature in 1959. His *Complete Poems* was published in 1984.

MIKLÓS RADNÓTI (1909–1944) • Radnóti has been called one of the major Hungarian poets of the twentieth century. His earliest book of poems was *Pagan Salute*, published in 1930. Because he had converted to Catholicism, although he was originally Jewish, he was conscripted into a labor unit that was forced to mine copper in Serbia during the 1940s. As the Yugoslavian Partisan forces under Josef Broz Tito advanced into the area where the labor group was working, the men were banded into a forced march, with Hungary being their destination. On this march, when he could, Radnóti kept a small notebook on which he wrote poems about his experiences. After a number of days without nourishment, and without respite, Radnóti was shot and thrown into a mass grave. It was not until late in 1945 that his body was exhumed, and his poetry was rescued. These poems mark one of a small number of works that actually survived the Holocaust.

SIR WALTER RALEGH (c. 1552–1618) • Ralegh was a courtier, explorer, and adventurer who alternately pleased and displeased Queen Elizabeth I, who reigned until 1603. During the reign of James I (1603–1625) he was imprisoned for thirteen years in the Tower of London. He was released to go on an expedition to South America, which proved disastrous. In 1618 he was executed on charges of treason. Like many aristocrats, he wrote extensively but circulated his poetry mostly in manuscript, with rare exceptions such as "The Nymph's Reply to the Shepherd." His collected poems were edited and published in 1951.

DUDLEY RANDALL (1914–2000) • A native of Washington, D.C., Randall spent five years working in the foundry at the Ford River Rouge plant, near Detroit, in Michigan. He became a librarian after that and went on to the position of head librarian. In 1965 he founded the Broadside Press, an important and valuable publisher for African American writers. One of the first poems from the press was "Ballad of Birmingham," which had earlier (1963) been set to music and made popular by the folk singer Jerry Moore. Randall's major poetry collections are *More to Remember: Poems of Four Decades* (1971) and *A Litany of Friends: New and Selected Poems* (1981, 1983).

JOHN CROWE RANSOM (1888–1974) • Along with Robert Penn Warren, Alan Tate, and Cleanth Brooks, Ransom was one of the important exponents of the New Criticism (see Chapter 29). He founded the *Kenyon Review* and edited it for twenty years. His major poetry collections are *Chills and Fever* (1924), *Two Gentlemen in Bonds* (1927), and *Selected Poems* (1945, revised in 1963 and 1969).

HENRY REED (1914–1986) • Reed was English and received a degree from the University of Birmingham. During the 1950s he became well known in England for his translations and radio dramas for the BBC. His major book of poems was *A Map of Verona* (1946), which contains "Naming of Parts." Five of his radio plays in verse were published as *The Streets of Pompeii* (1971), and four of his comedies in prose were published in *Hilda Tablet and Others* (1971).

ANNE BARBARA RIDLER (1912–2001) • Ridler was a writer not only of poems but also of plays, film scripts, songs, and translations. She was an editor at the Oxford University Press, which published some of her poems, and also at Faber and Faber, where T. S. Eliot was an editor. She published her first collection of poems, *Poems*, in 1939. Following collections were *A Dream Observed and Other Poems* (1941), *The Golden Bird and Other Poems* (1951), *Selected Poems* (1961), *Some Time After and Other Poems* (1972), *New and Selected Poems* (1988), *Collected Poems* (1994), and *Anne Ridler: Collected Poems* (1997). She edited many collections, including an anthology of ghost stories. Most notable among her many other writings are English translations of the libretti of Mozart's operas *The Marriage of Figaro* and *Cosi fan Tutte*.

RAINER MARIA RILKE (1875–1926) • Rilke, a friend of both Leo Tolstoy and Auguste Rodin, has been called the greatest twentieth-century German poet, and his work is deeply admired today by most students of literature. He was born in Prague, but although he traveled constantly, he spent the most satisfactory years of his life in France. During World War I he was compelled to leave France, and lived in Munich for the duration of the conflict. Two of his early collections of poetry were *Life and Songs* (1894) and *New Poems* (1907). A major novel, *The Notebooks of Malte Laurids Brigge*, appeared in 1910. His poetic reputation rests on two major collections, *The Duinese Elegies* (1923) and the *Sonnets to Orpheus* (1923). In the 1920s he contracted leukemia and died of that disease in 1926. Today there are a number of significant translations of his work. His *Selected Poems* appeared in English translation in 1981. His *Selected Letters* was published in 1960.

ALBERTO RÍOS (b. 1952) • A native of Arizona, Rios received degrees from the University of Arizona in 1974 and 1979. Among his collections of poems are *Teodora Luna's Two Kisses: Poems*(1990); *The Lime Orchard Woman: Poems* (1988); *Five Indiscretions: A Book of Poems* (1985), and *The Smallest Muscle in the Human Body* (2002). He has been widely anthologized, and has been distinguished by grants from the National Endowment for the Arts and the Guggenheim Foundation. He currently teaches at Arizona State University.

EDWIN ARLINGTON ROBINSON (1869–1935) • Robinson began his career inauspiciously with various jobs in New York City. The publication of *The Children of the Night* (1897) and *Captain Craig* (1902) impressed President Theodore Roosevelt, who arranged a position for him as clerk in the New York Customs House. After publication of *The Town Down the River* in 1910, he was able to support himself with his poetry. "Tilbury Town," where many of his poetic characters reside, is modeled on Gardiner, Maine, the town where he grew up. He is particularly notable because he received the first Pulitzer Prize in Poetry ever to be awarded (1922). He received the prize twice more, in 1924 and 1928. In 1976 A. R. Gurney wrote a drama, *Who Killed Richard Cory?*, which played at the Circle Repertory Theatre in New York. Simon and Garfunkel, in their early years together, created a song telling the tale of Richard Cory (available on CD).

THEODORE ROETHKE (1908–1963) • Roethke was born in Saginaw, Michigan, where his father operated a successful greenhouse. After graduating from the University of Michigan he taught at a number of schools, primarily at the University of Washington. His first book was *Open House* (1941), and his second was *The Lost Son and Other Poems* (1948), which included "My Papa's Waltz." His collection *The Waking* (1953) received the Pulitzer Prize for Poetry for 1954. His *Collected Poems* was published posthumously in 1966. When he died in 1963 he had achieved wide recognition and acclaim. In addition to distinguishing himself, he was also the teacher of other poets, numbering James Wright among his students at the University of Washington.

CHRISTINA ROSSETTI (1830–1894) • English-born Christina Rossetti's religious lyrics and ballads have made her a favorite with composers such as Gustav Holst and John Rutter. Painters of the Pre-Raphaelite Brotherhood, of whom her brother Dante Gabriel Rossetti was a leading figure, frequently called upon her to pose for their paintings. Ill health forced her to forsake a career as a governess, and after 1874 she became a virtual invalid. Some of her poetry collections are *Goblin Market and Other Poems* (1862), *The Prince's Progress and Other Poems* (1866), and *A Pageant and Other Poems* (1872). A modern edition of her *Complete Poems* was published in 1979.

MURIEL RUKEYSER (1913–1980) • A *poète engagée*, Rukeyser was arrested in Alabama in the 1930s for demonstrating in favor of the Scottsboro Nine (see also the introduction to *Mulatto* by Langston Hughes in Chapter 26). Later, she wrote on behalf of an imprisoned Korean poet in *The Gates* (1976). She published many collections, including *Theory of*

Flight (1935), *Beast in View* (1944), *Body of Waking* (1958), and *Collected Poems* (1979). Among other academic positions, she taught for a time at Sarah Lawrence College in Bronxville, New York.

GEORGE WILLIAM RUSSELL ("Æ") (1867–1935) • Russell used the *nom de plume* which is rendered either as "Æ " or "A.E." He was a native of Ireland and became an activist in the cause of Irish nationalism. For more than twenty-five years he was an editor, and he is considered an important figure in the Irish literary renaissance of the early twentieth century. He was a friend of both Yeats and Joyce. An early collection of his verse, noted for its spiritualism, was *Homeward: Songs by the Way* (1894), and a later collection was *Selected Poems* (1935).

LUIS OMAR SALINAS (b. 1937) • Salinas was born in Texas. He attended Fresno State University from 1967 to 1972 and made his home in California. His first volume of poems was *Crazy Gypsy* (1970). In 1973 he edited *From the Barrio: A Chicano Anthology*, and in 1975 he was one of four poets included (along with Gary Soto) in *Entrance: Four Chicano Poets*. Since then he has been regularly productive. One of his major volumes was *The Sadness of Days: Selected and New Poems*, which appeared in 1987.

SONIA SANCHEZ (b. 1934) • Sanchez was born in Alabama. She received a B.A. from Hunter College in 1955, and for a time after that she worked for the Congress of Racial Equality. Her major teaching position was at Temple University. Early volumes of poetry were *Homecoming* (1969) and *We a BaddDDD People* (1970). Later she published *homegirls and handgrenades* (1984), *Under a Soprano Sky* (1987), and more recently *Does Your House Have Lions* (1997), *Wounded in the House of a Friend* (1997), *Like the Singing Coming Off of Drums: Love Poems* (1999), *Shake Loose My Skin: New and Selected Poems* (1999, 2000), *Ash* (2001), and *Bum Rush the Page: A Def Poetry Jam* (2001).

CARL SANDBURG (1878–1967) • It is fair to say that Sandburg "knocked around" a good deal in his youth before working his way through Knox College (then Lombard College) in Galesburg, Illinois, his hometown. He published a volume of poetry in 1904 but did not gain recognition until 1914, when *Poetry* printed some of his poems. Later he published *Chicago Poems* (1916), *Smoke and Steel* (1920), *Selected Poems* (1926), and *Good Morning, America* (1928). He received the Pulitzer Prize for History (1939) for his biography of Abraham Lincoln and the Pulitzer Prize for Poetry (1951) for his *Complete Poems* of 1950.

MAY SARTON (1912–1995) • Eleanor May Sarton was born in Belgium and at the age of four came to the United States with her parents. Eventually she taught at both Harvard University and Wellesley College. Her first poetry volume, *Encounter in April*, appeared in 1937, and she published regularly after that, her final volume (*Coming into Eighty*) appearing in 1994, the year before her death. Her *Collected Poems, 1930–1970*, was published in 1974. An anthology of her work in all literary genres was edited by Bradford Daziel and published in 1991 as *Sarton Selected*.

SIEGFRIED SASSOON (1886–1967) • Sassoon served as an officer in World War I, was wounded twice, and was awarded two medals for bravery (one of which he threw away as a symbol of protest against war). He is most widely recognized for his antiwar collections *The Old Huntsman* (1917) and *Counter-Attack and Other Poems* (1918), which contains "Dreamers." Neither of these books was well received. Later, Sassoon turned to spiritual subjects, as shown in *Vigils* (1935) and *Sequences* (1956). His *Collected Poems* was published in 1961.

GJERTRUD CECILIA SCHNACKENBERG (b. 1953) • Originally from Washington State, Schnackenberg now lives in Boston. She achieved great critical acclaim with the publication of her first volume of poems, *Portraits and Elegies* (1982). She later published *The Lamplit Answer* (1985), *A Gilded Lapse of Time* (1992, 1994), *Supernatural Love: Poems 1978–1992* (2000), and *The Throne of Labdacus* (2001). She won the Rome Prize in literature for 1983–1984 and received an honorary doctorate from Mount Holyoke College, her alma mater, in 1985. She was honored with a Los Angeles Book Award for *The Throne of Labdacus*.

VIRGINIA SCOTT (b. 1937) • Canadian born, Scott received her degrees at Boston University and Wisconsin. She created, edited, and managed the Sunbury Press, a small press, and received a national award for this work in 1980. She has published poetry widely in journals. Her collected poems appear in *The Witness Box* (1985) and *Toward Appomattox* (1992). She taught at Lehman College for many years.

ALAN SEEGER (1886–1916) • Seeger was born in New York and was educated at Harvard. When World War I began, he joined the French Foreign Legion, and at the age of thirty he was killed in combat during the Battle of the Somme in 1916. His war poems were published in his posthumous *Poems* (1916).

BRENDA SEROTTE (b. 1946) • Serotte's Sephardic-Jewish grandparents came to the United States from Turkey in 1918. Born and educated in New York, she worked as a secretary, but after receiving a Bachelor's degree she taught English at a Bronx junior high school. She received her M.A. in literature in 1992, and then was a James A. Michener fellow in creative writing at the University of Miami, where she earned her Master of Fine Arts in 1997. She is an adjunct professor at Nova Southwestern University in Fort Lauderdale, Florida, and her first book of poetry, *The Blue Farm*, is published by Ginninderra Press (2005). Serotte's memoir, *The Fortune Teller's Kiss* (University of Nebraska Press, 2006), is about growing up Sephardic in the Bronx.

ANNE SEXTON (1928–1974) • Massachusetts born, Sexton is one of the more personal confessional poets. *To Bedlam and Part Way Back* (1960), for example, developed out of a nervous breakdown, and her posthumous *The Awful Rowing Toward God* (1975) describes some of the feelings leading to her suicide in 1974. Her collection *Live or Die* (1966) was awarded the Pulitzer Prize for Poetry in 1967.

WILLIAM SHAKESPEARE (1564–1616) • For a brief biography, see page 1322.

KARL SHAPIRO (1913–2000) • Shapiro was born in Baltimore, and lived in Nebraska and California. He was recognized early in his distinguished career as a poet and critic—his *V-Letter and Other Poems* (1944) receiving the 1945 Pulitzer Prize. Among his many poetry collections are *Essay on Rime* (1945), *Poems of a Jew* (1958), *Selected Poems* (1968), *Selected Poems: 1940–1977* (1978), and *The Wild Card: Selected Poems Early and Late* (1998). He edited *Poetry* magazine for five years and *Prairie Schooner* for ten.

PERCY BYSSHE SHELLEY (1792–1822) • Shelley is one of the major English Romantic poets. He was by nature a revolutionary, and he suffered expulsion from Oxford as a result of an early pamphlet titled *The Necessity of Atheism*. He married before he was twenty but within three years left his wife and went to Italy with Mary Godwin (1797–1851), the author of *Frankenstein*. The two were married in 1816. Throughout these years Shelley was writing his best-known short poems. He was working on his long philosophic poem *The Triumph of*

Life in 1822 when he was drowned during a storm at sea near the coast of Italy. He is buried in the English Cemetery in Rome, near the grave of John Keats. There are many excellent modern editions of his works, including the Houghton-Mifflin Cambridge edition and the Oxford edition.

JANE SHORE (b. 1947) • Shore was born in New Jersey and received her M.A. from the University of Iowa in 1971. She teaches at George Washington University. Her poems have been widely circulated in journals and magazines, and the general merit of her work is shown by frequent prizes and awards, including a grant from the National Endowment for the Arts. Her poetry collections are *Lying Down in the Olive Press* (1969), *Eye Level* (1977), *The Minute Hand* (1987), *This Time, for Always* (1990), *Music Minus One: Poems* (1996, 1997), and *Happy Family* (1999, 2000).

LESLIE MARMON SILKO (b. 1948) • A Native American, Silko was brought up in Laguna Pueblo, New Mexico. She has taught at the University of Arizona and also at the University of New Mexico, and she has been honored with a MacArthur Foundation Fellowship. The topic in most of her works is the tradition of the Navajo people, which she treats with great love and understanding, as in "Where Mountain Lion Lay Down with Deer," which connects the individual with the past, the land, and Nature. Recent publications are *Rain* (1996), *Love Poem and Slim Man Canyon* (1996) and *Gardens in the Dunes* (1999, 2000).

STEVIE SMITH (FLORENCE MARGARET SMITH, 1902–1971) • Smith was a native of Hull, in Yorkshire. During her life she worked in publishing, and in addition she became well known as a radio personality because of her many poetry readings for the BBC. Some of her poetry collections were *A Good Time Was Had by All* (1937) and *Not Waving But Drowning* (1957). Posthumous collections of her work are *Scorpion and Other Poems* (1972) and *Collected Poems* (1975).

GARY SNYDER (b. 1930) • Although Snyder is often associated with the beat generation poets of the 1960s, he is actually a multitalented thinker who defies easy description. During his earliest years, when his family was living in Washington, he became a voracious reader, and the universality of his concerns is perhaps his most dominant characteristic. In his youth he did a variety of jobs, including those of seaman and trail worker. He received his B.A. from Reed College and went to graduate school in Indiana, but he gave that up after one semester. He has been interested in preserving the environment—an idea that he particularly associated with Western Indian tribes. Another major concern was his interest in Zen Buddhism, and he spent twelve years in Japan, learning more and more about Eastern philosophies. Eventually he became a member of the English Department at the University of California at Davis, where he is currently a Professor Emeritus. His list of publications is extensive. Of particular interest for students of poetry are *Riprap and Cold Mountain Poems* (1969), *No Nature: New and Selected Poems* (1992), and *The Gary Snyder Reader: Prose, Poetry, and Translations* (1999). In 2008 he was the winner of the Ruth Lilly Poetry Prize.

GARY SOTO (b. 1952) • Soto is a native of Fresno, California, and was educated in California. Since 1985 he taught at Berkeley and also at Riverside. Because of his native city, he has sometimes been grouped with a "Fresno" school of poets. His first book of poetry was *The Elements of San Joaquin* (1977). Later collections are *The Tale of Sunlight* (1978), *Where Sparrows Work Hard* (1981), *Home Course in Religion* (1991), *Canto Familiar/Familiar Song* (1994), *New and Selected Poems* (1995), *Junior College: Poems* (1997), and *A Natural Man* (1999). Soto is a prolific writer with many different interests, including works for young people. His book *Baseball in April* (1990), for example, was named a Best Book for Young Adults in 1990.

STEPHEN SPENDER (1909–1995) • Sir Stephen Spender, along with W. H. Auden, Christopher Isherwood, and Louis Macneice, was one of the poets known as the "Oxford Poets" during the late 1920s and early 1930s. After leaving Oxford, Spender lived for a time in Germany. He believed firmly in the need for poets to be politically engaged, and he joined the Communist Party for a few weeks in the 1930s, although he later renounced this affiliation (in *The God That Failed* [1950]). Along with editing journals and writing many prose works, he, with John Lehmann, wrote a five-act poetic play *Trial of a Judge*, based on circumstances in Germany at the time of Hitler. Spender's first poems were collected in a small book titled *Twenty Poems* in 1930. Later collections were *Poems of Dedication* (1947), *Edge of Being: Poems* (1949), and *Collected Poems 1928–1953* (1955). He was knighted in 1962.

WILLIAM E. STAFFORD (1914–1993) • Stafford, who published more than two dozen volumes of verse, was born in Kansas. He received his Ph.D. from Iowa State in 1955. In 1975 he was named Poet Laureate of Oregon, and at his death in 1993 he was a professor emeritus at Lewis and Clark College. For *Traveling through the Dark* (1962), his second volume of poetry, he won the National Book Award for Poetry in 1963. Among his many poetry collections are *Wyoming* (1985) and *An Oregon Message* (1987). With Marvin Bell, he published *Segues* in 1983. *Down in My Heart* (1994) is his autobiography of the years he spent in an internment camp for conscientious objectors in World War II.

GERALD STERN (b. 1925) • Stern was born in Pittsburgh and became a faculty member of the University of Iowa's Writer's Workshop. He was honored by three grants from the National Endowment for the Arts and by a Guggenheim Fellowship. His *Lucky Life* (1977), which contains "Burying an Animal," received the Lamont Prize in Poetry in 1977. Most recently he published *Leaving Another Kingdom: Selected Poems* (1990), *Bread Without Sugar* (1992), *Odd Mercy* (1995), *This Time* (1998), and *Last Blue* (2000).

WALLACE STEVENS (1879–1955) • Stevens spent his professional life in business rather than academia. He wrote most of his poems after the age of fifty, but he included "The Emperor of Ice-Cream" and "Disillusionment of Ten O'clock," both earlier poems, in the first edition of *Harmonium* in 1923. Some of his poetic collections are a second version of *Harmonium* (1931) and also *The Auroras of Autumn* (1950) and *Collected Poems* (1954).

MARK STRAND (b. 1934) • Strand was born in Prince Edward Island, Canada. He studied at Antioch, Yale, and the University of Iowa, and he taught at the University of Utah. He has received many honors, including the particularly prized MacArthur Foundation Fellowship. In 1990 he was named U.S. Poet Laureate. His collections include *Selected Poems* (1990), *The Continuous Life* (1990, 1992), and *Blizzard of One* (1999, 2000), for which he was awarded the Pulitzer Prize for Poetry.

MAY SWENSON (1919–1989) • Born in Utah, Swenson was of Swedish ancestry. She experimented constantly in her poetry, not only in content but also in form, as is shown in her shaped-verse poems. Her *Iconographs* (1970) was a collection of formed poetry. The formed poem "Women" was included in her collection *New and Selected Things Taking Place* (1978). She also translated poetry from Swedish, as represented by *Windows and Stones* (1972).

JONATHAN SWIFT (1667–1745) • Swift was born in Ireland. He became Dean of St. Patrick's Cathedral in Dublin, a position in which he served for thirty-one years. His most famous prose works are *A Tale of a Tub* (1704), *Gulliver's Travels* (1726), and *A Modest Proposal* (1729). Throughout his life, however, he constantly wrote poetry, and he devoted himself almost exclusively to poetry after 1730. His poems were edited by Harold Williams and published in three volumes in 1937.

JAMES TATE (b. 1943) • Tate was born in Kansas City, earning degrees from the universities of Kansas and Iowa. He taught English at the University of Massachusetts. Since his first collection, *The Lost Pilot*, published when he was only twenty-three, he has published a dozen volumes of verse. More recent works include *Viper Jazz* (1976); *Riven Doggeries* (1979); *Reckoner* (1986); *Distance from Loved Ones* (1990); *Selected Poems* (1991), for which he received the Pulitzer Prize for Poetry in 1992; *Shroud of the Gnome* (1997, 1999); *Memoir of the Hawk: Poems* (2001), *Lost River: A Chapbook* (2003), *Return to the City of White Donkeys* (2004), and *Ghost Soldiers* (2008). In 1994 he received the National Book Award for his collection *Worshipful Company of Fletchers*. In 1995 he was awarded the Tanning Prize—the largest annual literary prize in the United States—for his achievement as a poet. He was selected to edit *The Best American Poetry 1997* (1997).

ALFRED, LORD TENNYSON (1809–1892) • One of the most popular of the Victorian poets, Tennyson became English Poet Laureate in 1850. His earliest verse was published in collaboration with his brother Charles in *Poems by Two Brothers* (1827). Some of his other collections were *Poems* (1842), *Locksley Hall* (1842), *The Princess* (1847), *Maud, and Other Poems* (1855), and *Idylls of the King* (1857–1891). He wrote *In Memoriam*, in which the well-known phrase "nature red in tooth and claw" appears, from 1833 to 1850. A new collected and annotated edition of his poetry was published in 1969, but there are also many other useful editions.

ELAINE TERRANOVA (b. 1939) • Terranova was born in Pennsylvania and received an MFA degree from Goddard College in 1977. Among her distinctions is a National Endowment for the Arts fellowship in poetry and a Pew Fellowship in the Arts for 2006. She has published poems in many significant journals. Among her collections are *The Cult of the Right Hand* (1991) and *Damages* (1995, 1996), from which "Rush Hour" is selected. Her latest collection of poems, *NOT TO: New and Selected Poems* (2003) received a nomination for the Pulitzer Prize for Poetry.

DYLAN THOMAS (1914–1953) • A native of Wales, Thomas published his first collection, *Eighteen Poems*, in 1934. After World War II he became immensely popular in America as a speaker and lecturer because of the incantatory power with which he read his own poems. Fortunately, many of his readings survive on records and CDs. Thomas's *Collected Poems 1934–1952* was published in 1952 and was a commercial success. *The Poems of Dylan Thomas*, a definitive edition, was published in 1971. In the 1980s, the musician John Cale set "Do Not Go Gentle" to music as part of his *Falklands Suite* (found on Cale's *Words for the Dying*, Opal/Warner Bros. 9-26024-2).

DANIEL TOBIN (b. 1958) • Tobin received his doctorate from the University of Virginia and is the author of four books of poems: *Where the World is Made* (1998); *A Double Life* (2004); *The Narrows* (2005); and *Second Things* (2009). He has written *Passage to the Center: Imagination and the Sacred in the Poetry of Seamus Heaney* (1999), a critical study. He edited *The Book of Irish American Poetry from the Eighteenth Century to the Present* (2007), together with writing a number of essays on poetry. Among his numerous honors are the Robert Penn Warren Award and a fellowship from the National Endowment for the Arts. Currently he is Chair of the Department of Writing, Literature, and Publishing at Emerson College.

JEAN TOOMER (1894–1967) • Toomer was born in Washington, D.C., studied at five colleges, and eventually settled in the African American community in Sparta, Georgia. An important voice in the Harlem Renaissance, Toomer published his only book, *Cane*, a grouping of stories, poems, and a play, in 1923. A collection of his works is found in *The Wayward and the Seeking* (1980).

CHASE TWICHELL (b. 1950) • Twichell, born in Connecticut, and presently a resident of New York, received her B.A. from Trinity College in Hartford and her M.A. from the University of Iowa. For a time she did editorial work, and she is the founder of her own publishing company, the Ausable Press, which specializes in the publication of poetry. She taught at the University of Alabama and Hampshire College, among other schools. She received a Guggenheim Fellowship and also a grant from the National Endowment for the Arts. Her five poetry collections are *Northern Spy* (1981), *The Odds* (1986), *Perdido* (1991), *The Ghost of Eden* (1995, 1998), and *The Snow Watcher* (1998).

PETER ULISSE (b. 1944) • Ulisse lives in Connecticut, where he has chaired the Humanities Department of Housatonic Community Technical College, where he has also served as a dean. He has written many poetry reviews for *Small Pond of Literature* and was also the editor of the *Connecticut River Review*. His first major poetry collection was *Vietnam Voices* (1990). In 1995 he published *Memory Is an Illusive State*, which includes "Odyssey: 20 Years Later."

JOHN UPDIKE (b. 1932) • For a brief biography, see page 363.

MONA VAN DUYN (1921–2004) • Mona Jane Van Duyn was a native of Iowa and received her college degrees there. She taught at the universities of Iowa and Louisville, and in 1950 she and her husband went to Washington University in St. Louis, where she taught until her retirement. Among her poetry collections are *Valentines to the Wide World* (1959), *Merciful Disguises* (1973), *Near Changes* (1990, 1992), *Firefall* (1994), and *Selected Poems* (2002). She received numerous distinctions. In 1990 she received the Pulitzer Prize for her collection *Near Changes*, and in the following year she was distinguished as the first woman to be the U.S. Poet Laureate.

JUDITH VIORST (b. 1931) •A native of New Jersey, Viorst received degrees from Rutgers and the Washington Psychoanalytic Institute. She is known for her wry humor. Her first major volume was *It's Hard to Be Hip over Thirty and Other Tragedies of Married Life* in 1968. Among later works are *Necessary Losses* (1986), *Forever Fifty and Other Negotiations* (1989, 1996), and *Suddenly Sixty, and Other Shocks of Later Life* (2000). She has also written a considerable amount of fiction for young people.

ELLEN BRYANT VOIGT (b. 1943) • Voigt lives in Vermont, where she held the position of state poet from 1999 to 2003. She teaches at Warren Wilson College. She has written a number of poetry volumes, including *Claiming Kin* (1976), *The Lotus Flowers* (1987), *Two Trees* (1992), *Shadow of Heaven* (2002), and *Messenger: New and Selected Poems* (2007). Her distinctions are numerous, including fellowships from the Academy of American Poets, from the Guggenheim Foundation, and the National Endowment for the Arts. Since 2003 she has served as a chancellor of the Academy of American Poets.

SHELLY WAGNER (b. 1948) • A native of Virginia, Wagner received her B.A. from Old Dominion University, after which she worked as an interior designer and social worker. In July 1984, her younger son Andrew, then five, accidentally drowned in the river at the back of the family's property. It was not until five years later that she began her cycle of elegiac poems, *The Andrew Poems*, including "Boxes," which was published in 1994. Before this she had published poetry in publications such as *American Poetry Review* and *Poetry East*.

DAVID WAGONER (b. 1926) • Wagoner was born in Ohio and studied at Pennsylvania State University and the University of Indiana. In 1954 he began teaching at the University of Washington, where he was a colleague, and later an editor, of Theodore Roethke. He has been extremely productive both as poet, having published seventeen poetry collections, and writer of fiction, having published ten novels. One of his works was adapted for a film (*The Escape Artist*, 1982) produced through Francis Ford Coppola's Zoetrope Studios. Wagoner's many poetry collections include *Dry Sun, Dry Wind* (1953), *Staying Alive* (1966), *Collected Poems* (1976), *Landfall* (1981), *Through the Forest: New and Selected Poems* (1987), and *Walt Whitman Bathing* (1996), *The House of Song: Poems* (2002), and *Good Morning and Good Night* (2005).

ALICE WALKER (b. 1944) • For a brief biography, see page 108.

EDMUND WALLER (1606–1687) • Waller, whom John Dryden constantly praised for the quality and originality of his poetic couplets, was a Royalist during the English Civil Wars of 1642–1649, and for his efforts he was forced into exile. He returned in 1651 after swearing loyalty to Oliver Cromwell. During the Restoration, he supported King Charles II. His major collections of poetry were *Poems* (1645) and *Divine Poems* (1685).

CHARLES HARPER WEBB (b. 1952) • Webb is a native of Pennsylvania but grew up in Texas. He received degrees at Rice University, the University of Washington, and the University of Southern California. For fifteen years he was a rock guitarist and singer, but since then he has changed his career orientation. He is now a licenced psychotherapist, and he has become director of the creative writing program at California State University at Long Beach. Some of his books are *Everyday Outrages* (1989), *Poetry That Heals* (1991), *A Webb for All Seasons* (1992), *Hot Popsicles* (2005), and *Amplified Dog* (2006). He has also published a novel, *The Wilderness Effect* (1982).

PHYLLIS WEBB (b. 1927) • Webb is a native of British Columbia, and presently lives there. She was educated at the University of British Columbia and also at McGill University. During her career she worked with the Canadian Broadcasting Company both as a program planner and a producer; she has also taught in various Canadian colleges and universities as a guest lecturer and professor. A major concern in her poetry has been the problem of maintaining personal integrity amid a world of "hate and broken things," to quote from one of her poems in *Trio* (1954). One of her interests has been to experiment with a form of Persian poetry, the *ghazal*, which consists of five couplets. Among her poetry collections are *Wilson's Bowl* (1980), *The Vision Tree* (1982), *Selected Poems* (1982), *Water and Light: Ghazals and Anti Ghazals* (1984), and *Hanging Fire* (1990).

BRUCE WEIGL (b. 1949) • Weigl, who teaches at Penn State, was born in Ohio. He took his B.A. at Oberlin (1974) and his Ph.D. at the University of Utah (1979). His poetry collections include *Like a Sack Full of Old Quarrels* (1976), *Executioner* (1977), *A Romance* (1979), *The Monkey Wars* (1984), *Song of Napalm* (1988), *What Saves Us* (1992), and *Sweet Lorain* (1996). His most recent collections are *Archaeology of the Circle: New and Selected Poems* (1998, 1999), *After the Others* (1999), *The Unraveling Strangeness* (2002), and *Declension in the Village of Chung Luong* (2006).

PHILLIS WHEATLEY (c. 1753–1784) • Born in Africa, Wheatley was captured by slave traders and sold to John Wheatley, a Boston merchant, who treated her virtually as a daughter and saw to it that she was educated. When she published her *Poems on Various Subjects, Religious and Moral* (1773), however, the temper of the times made it necessary to include prefaces by Massachusetts men verifying that she was qualified to write poetry and that she had indeed written the poems in the collection. Although she wrote a second volume of poetry, she could not find a publisher for it during her lifetime. Her collected works were published in 1988.

WALT WHITMAN (1819–1892) • Whitman, who became a legend during his lifetime, is one of America's major poets. He was born in New York and lived with his family in both Long Island and Brooklyn. At various times he worked as a printer, teacher, reporter, and government bureaucrat. In addition, he served as a nurse during the Civil War. His major work was *Leaves of Grass*, which he first published as a collection of twelve poems in 1855, and to which he added as time went on. Many editions were published in his lifetime, the last one in 1892. *Drum Taps*, poems based on his Civil War experiences, was published in 1865; a second edition contained "When Lilacs Last in the Dooryard Bloom'd," his poem on the death of President Abraham Lincoln.

JOHN GREENLEAF WHITTIER (1807–1892) • Whittier was born in Massachusetts of Quaker stock. He was not formally educated and was trained to be a shoemaker. However, he was a compulsive reader and at the age of nineteen he wrote a poem that was accepted by William Lloyd Garrison for publication in the Newburyport Press. From that point Whittier went on to become one of America's best known poets and writers. Joining the abolitionist movement, he worked diligently in that cause, and for a brief period he served in the Massachusetts Legislature. The best way to describe his poetic output is that it was voluminous, and with his publication of *Snow-Bound* in 1866 and *Poetical Works* in 1869 he became financially secure. A particularly notable achievement was his being part of the group that founded the *Atlantic Monthly* in 1857.

CORNELIUS WHUR (1782–1853) • Whur was a Methodist minister in Suffolk, England. In 1837 he published a poetry collection, *Village Musings on Moral and Religious Subjects*, which included "The First-Rate Wife." In his obituary notice he was recognized not only as a "distinguished" poet but also as an accomplished gardener.

RICHARD WILBUR (b. 1921) • Wilbur was born in New York. He has published a number of poetry collections, including *New and Collected Poems* (1988, 1989), for which he was awarded the Pulitzer Prize for Poetry. He has also made a number of well-received translations of French drama and has published collections for children, such as *The Pig in the Spigot* (2000). In 1988 he was distinguished as the second U.S. Poet Laureate (the first being Robert Penn Warren), and for his *New and Collected Poems* (1988), he received his second Pulitzer Prize. Recent collections are *Mayflies: New Poems and Translations* (2000), and *Collected Poems, 1943–2004* (2004).

C. K. WILLIAMS (CHARLES KENNETH WILLIAMS, b. 1936) • Williams is a native of New Jersey who graduated from Bucknell and the University of Pennsylvania. He taught at a number of schools and colleges and has become a permanent resident of France. He is known for his discursively long lines in the manner of Walt Whitman. Among his many volumes of poems are *Tar* (1983); *Flesh and Blood* (1987), for which he was awarded the 1987

National Book Critics Circle Award; *Poems, 1963–1983* (1988); *A Dream of the Mind* (1992); and *Repair* (1999). Recently he has undertaken translations of Greek drama. "Dimensions" is taken from *Lies*, his collection of 1969.

WILLIAM CARLOS WILLIAMS (1883–1963) • Williams spent his career as a practicing pediatrician, but he early became friendly with the poets Ezra Pound and Hilda Doolittle (H. D.). He developed a second career as a writer, producing poems, plays, stories, novels, and essays. At the age of thirty he began publishing poems, beginning with *Poems* (1913) and *Tempers* (1913) and ending with *Pictures from Brueghel* (1963), for which he was posthumously awarded the Pulitzer Prize.

DAVID WOJAHN (b. 1953) • A native of Minnesota, Wojahn received degrees from the universities of Minnesota and Arizona. He teaches at Virginia Commonwealth University, where he directs the creative writing program. His first volume of verse was *Icehouse Lights* (1981), which was distinguished by the Yale Series of Younger Poets Award. More recently he published *Mystery Train* (1990), which contains "It's Only Rock and Roll, But I Like It," *Late Empire* (1994), *The Falling Hour* (1997), *Spirit Cabinet* (2002), and *Interrogation Palace: New and Selected Poems, 1982–2004* (2006).

WILLIAM WORDSWORTH (1770–1850) • Along with Coleridge, Wordsworth was the first of the English Romantic poets. In 1798 the two men published *Lyrical Ballads*, a landmark poetry collection that emphasizes the importance of imagination in revealing the significance of events in the lives of (mainly) ordinary people. One of Wordsworth's major ideas was that poetry grows from "emotion recollected in tranquility," and he also believed that poetic diction should consist of everyday language that the poet chooses as a result of looking steadily at the poetic subject. Throughout much of his adult life Wordsworth wrote and revised his long poem *The Prelude*, which was intended to show how the exalted but mysterious "wisdom and spirit of the universe" reached him through his imagination and brought out his power as a poet. He became English Poet Laureate in 1843.

JAMES WRIGHT (1927–1980) • Wright was born in Martins Ferry, Ohio, and received his Ph.D. at the University of Washington, where he was a student of Theodore Roethke. In 1966 he began teaching at Hunter College, and he remained there until his death in 1980. His first poetry collection, *The Green Wall*, appeared in 1957, and after that he published collections regularly, receiving the 1972 Pulitzer Prize in Poetry for his *Collected Poems* (1971). *This Journey* was published posthumously in 1982, and *Above the River: The Complete Poems* appeared in 1990. Each year, in Martins Ferry, a celebration is held to commemorate Wright's work and career.

SIR THOMAS WYATT (c. 1503–1542) • Wyatt was a courtier in the service of King Henry VIII. He is credited with introducing the sonnet form into English as a result of his translations of the sonnets of the Italian sonneteer Petrarch. He circulated his poems in manuscript, although a number of them were anthologized after his death in *The Court of Venus* (1542) and *Seven Penitential Psalms* (1549). Modern editions of his poems were published in 1969, 1975, and 1978.

WILLIAM BUTLER YEATS (1865–1939) • The foremost Irish poet of the twentieth century, Yeats was instrumental in the founding of the Abbey Theatre in Dublin in 1899. An unorthodox thinker, he developed his poems out of his vast reading and his special interest in spiritualism. He published many volumes of poems, including *The Green Helmet* (1910), *The*

Wild Swans at Coole (1917), *The Winding Stair* (1929), and *The Collected Poems* (1932). He was awarded the Nobel Prize in Literature in 1923.

PAUL ZIMMER (b. 1934) • Zimmer, whose sister was the science-fiction writer Marion Zimmer Bradley (1930–1999), was born in Canton, Ohio, and received his B.A. from Kent State University. In the 1950s, he was among those servicemen who were assigned to view nuclear explosions, and his reactions were duly recorded by those who were conducting these experiments. When Zimmer became a career editor and poet, he managed bookstores and university presses, including the University of Iowa Press. He now lives in retirement in Wisconsin. Among his many volumes of poems are *A Seed on the Wind* (1960), *The Ribs of Death* (1967), *Family Reunion* (1983), and *Big Blue Train* (1993, 2007). His "Zimmer" poems are collected in *The Zimmer Poems* (1976), *Earthbound Zimmer* (1983), *The American Zimmer* (1984), *The Great Bird of Love* (1989), *Crossing to Sunlight: Selected Poems* (1996), and *Crossing to Sunlight Revisited* (2007). Recently he has published *After the Fire: A Writer Finds His Place* (2002) and *Trains in the Distance* (2004).

A Glossary of Important Literary Terms

This glossary presents brief definitions of terms and concepts that are boldfaced in the text. Page references indicate where readers may find additional detail and illustration, together with discussions about how the concepts can be utilized in studying and writing about literature. Generally, words italicized as parts of various definitions are also separately glossed in their own right.

abstract diction Language describing qualities that are rarefied and theoretical (e.g., "good," "interesting," "neat," and so on); distinguished from *concrete diction*. 326, 653

absurd See *comedy of the absurd*.

accent or beat The heavy *stresses* or accents in lines of *poetry*. Because heavy stresses are paired with *light stresses* to compose metrical *feet*, the numbers of accents or beats in a *line* usually govern the meter of the line (five beats in a *pentameter* line, four in a *tetrameter* line, etc.). 844

accented syllable A syllable receiving a major, or heavy, *stress* or *accent*. 844

actions or incidents The events or occurrences in a work. 4, 1207

actors Persons who perform as characters in a play. 1211

allegory A complete *narrative* that may also be applied to a parallel set of moral, philosophical, political, religious, or social situations. 69, 70, 375–431, 1210, 1211

alliteration The repetition of identical consonant sounds (most often the sounds beginning words) in close proximity (e.g., "*pensive poets,*" "*somewhere safe to sea,*" "*gracious, golden, glittering gleams,*" "*And death once dead, there's no more dying then*"). 843, 851

allusion Unacknowledged references and quotations that authors make while assuming that readers will recognize the original sources and relate their meanings to the new context. Allusions are hence compliments that the author pays to readers for their perceptiveness, knowledge, and awareness. 379, 940–82

amphibrach A three-syllable foot consisting of a light, heavy, and light stress, as in *I'm SING – ing*. 848

amphimacer or cretic A three-syllable foot consisting of a heavy, light, and heavy stress, as in *SING – ing SONGS*. 848

anagnorisis or recognition Aristotle's term describing that point in a play, usually the *climax*, when a character experiences understanding. 1272

analysis See *commentary*.

analytical sentence outline A scheme or plan for an essay, arranged according to topics (A, B, C, etc.) and with the topics expressed in sentences. 35

anapest Sometimes spelled *anapaest*. A three-syllable *foot* consisting of two light *stresses* climaxed by a heavy stress, as in *ear-ly LIGHT*. 847

anaphora ("to carry again or repeat") The repetition of the same word or phrase throughout a work or section of a work. The effect is to lend weight and emphasis. 764

ancillary characters   *Characters* in a story or play who set off or highlight the protagonist and who provide insight into the action. The *foil*, *choric figure*, and *raisonneur* are all ancillary characters. 1206

antagonist   One who struggles against. The person, idea, force, or general set of circumstances opposing the *protagonist*; an essential element of *plot*. 61, 178, 1205

anticipation   See *procatalepsis*.

antimetabole   See *chiasmus*.

antithesis   A rhetorical device of opposition in which one idea or word is established, and then the opposite idea or word is expressed, as in "I *burn* and *freeze*" and "I *love* and *hate*." 658, 898

apostrophe   The addressing of a discourse to a real or imagined person who is not present; also a speech to an abstraction. 765

apron or **thrust stage**   A stage that projects into the auditorium area, thus increasing the space for action; a characteristic feature of Elizabethan as well as contemporary theaters. 1212

archetypal/symbolic/mythic critical approach   The explanation of literature in terms of archetypal patterns (e.g., God's creation of human beings, the search for paradise, the sacrifice of a hero, the initiation or "test" of a young person). 1869

archetype   A character, action, or situation that is a prototype or pattern of human life generally; a situation that occurs over and over again in literature, such as a quest, an initiation, or an attempt to overcome evil. Many *myths* are archetypes. 986

archon, eponymous archon   In ancient Athens, the Eponymous Archon, or Archon Eponymous, was a leading magistrate, after whom the year was named. He made arrangements for the tragedies and comedies to be performed at the yearly festivals in honor of the God Dionysus. 1268

arena stage, or **theater-in-the-round**   A theater arrangement, often outdoors, in which the audience totally surrounds a *platform stage*, with all actors entering and exiting along the same aisles used by the audience. 1616

argument   The development of a pattern of interpretation or thought with an intent to persuade. In most writing about literature, the persuasive situation is to show the validity of a particular idea or circumstance in a story, poem, or play. More broadly, the term *argument* applies to any situation about which there may be disagreement. Although sometimes argumentative discourse may become disputatious, one should never forget that true arguments should stem from the reasonable interpretation of correct and accurate data. 31, 42

aside   A speech, usually short and often witty or satirical, delivered by a character to the audience or to another character, the convention being that only the intended characters can hear it, along, of course, with the audience. A more extensive speech that is delivered only to the audience when the character is alone on stage is a *soliloquy*. 1321

assertion   A sentence putting an *idea* or *argument* (the subject) into operation (the predicate); necessary for both developing and understanding the idea. 432

assonance   The repetition of identical vowel sounds in different words in close proximity, as in the d*ee*p gr*ee*n s*ea*. 843

atmosphere or **mood**   The emotional aura invoked by a work. 227, 1210

audience or **intended reader** or **listener**   (1) The people attending a theatrical production. (2) The intended group of readers for whom a writer writes, such as a group of religious worshippers, or a group of rocket scientists. 1214

auditory images   References to sounds. 729

authorial symbol   See *contextual symbol*.

authorial voice   The *voice* or *persona* used by authors when seemingly speaking for themselves. The use of the term makes it possible to discuss a narration or presentation without assuming that the ideas are necessarily those of the author in his or her own person. See also *speaker*, *point of view*, and *third-person point of view*. 133

bacchius or **bacchic** A three-syllable foot consisting of a light stress followed by two heavy stresses, as in "*a NEW SONG*" or "*the OLD WAYS.*" 848, 875

ballad, ballad measure A narrative poem, originally a popular form, composed of quatrains in *ballad measure*; that is, a pattern of iambic tetrameter alternating with iambic trimeter and rhyming *x-a-x-a*. 4, 633, 856, 902

ballad opera An eighteenth-century comic drama, originated by John Gay (1685–1732) in *The Beggar's Opera* (1728), featuring lyrics written for existing and usually well-known tunes, such as "Greensleeves." See also *comic opera*. 1580

beast fable A narrative, usually short, attributing human characteristics to animals. 379

beat A *heavy stress* or *accent* in a line of poetry. The number of beats in a line dictates the *meter* of the line, such as five beats to a line of *iambic pentameter*, or three beats to a line of *trimeter*. See also *accent*. 844

blank verse Unrhymed *iambic pentameter*. Most of the poetry in Shakespeare's plays is blank verse, as is the poetry of Milton's *Paradise Lost*. 4, 897

blocking In the performance of a play, the director's plan for the grouping and movement of characters on stage. 1211

blocking agent A person, circumstance, or attitude that obstructs the plans of various characters, such as the parental denial of permission to marry, as in Shakespeare's *A Midsummer Night's Dream*. 1499

box set In the modern theater, the *realistic* setting of a single room from which the "fourth wall" is missing, so that the stage resembles a picture. 1213

brainstorming The exploration, discovery, and development of details to be used in a composition. 20

breve In poetic *scansion*, a mark in the shape of a bowl-like half circle (˘) to indicate a light stress or unaccented syllable. 844

business or **stage business** The gestures, expressions, and general activity (beyond *blocking*) of *actors* onstage. Usually, business is designed to create laughter. It is often done spontaneously by actors. 1211

buskins Elegantly laced boots (*kothorni* or *cothurni*) worn by actors in ancient Greek *tragedy*. Eventually the buskins became elevator shoes to stress the royal status of actors by making them seem especially tall. 1279

cacophony Meaning "bad sound," but by no means bad, *cacophony* refers to words combining sharp or harsh sounds and rhythms, as in Pope's "When Ajax strives some rock's vast weight to throw." Cacophony is the opposite of *euphony*. 852

cadence group A coherent word group spoken as a single rhythmical unit, such as a prepositional phrase ("of human events") or noun phrase ("our sacred honor"). 850

caesura, (plural **caesurae**) The pause(s) or juncture(s) separating words and phrases within lines of poetry, as in Pope's line "Trees, where you sit, shall crowd into a shade" (*Second Pastoral*, "Summer," line 74), in which there is a caesura after "Trees" and also after "sit." In poetic *scansion* the caesura is marked by a double *virgule* (/ /). The control of caesurae is a vital aspect of poetic *rhythm*. 848, 852

catastrophe The "overturning" of the dramatic *plot*, the fourth stage in the structure immediately following the *climax*; the *dénouement* of a play, in which things are explained and put into place. 1208, 1501

catharsis (purgation)   Aristotle's concept that *tragedy*, by arousing pity and fear (*eleos* and *phobos*), regularizes and shapes human emotions, and that therefore tragedy, like literature and art generally, is essential in civilized society. 1271

central idea or **central argument**   (1) The *thesis* or main idea of an essay. (2) The *theme* of a literary work. 29

character   An extended verbal representation of a human being, the inner self that determines thought, speech, and behavior. 173–221, 1205

character, comic   Comic characters tend to be characters who are unrealistic and sometimes exaggerated, representing classes, types, and generations. 4, 60, 1501

chiasmus or **antimetabole**   A rhetorical pattern in which words (and also ideas) are repeated in the sequence *a b b a*, as in "I lead the life I love; I love the life I lead," and "When the issue deteriorates to violence, violence becomes the issue." 658

choragos or **choregus**   The sponsor or financial backer of a classical Athenian dramatic production. Often the Athenians honored the choragos by selecting him to serve as the leader (*koryphaios*) of the chorus. 1377

choree   See *trochee*.

choric figure   A character who remains somewhat outside the dramatic *action* and who provides commentary when appropriate. See also *raisonneur*. 1206

chorus   In ancient Athenian drama, the chorus was composed of young men—fifteen in tragedies and twenty-four in comedies—who chanted or sang, probably in unison, and who performed dance movements to a flute accompaniment. The chorus was, in effect, a major (and also collective) character in the *drama*. 1277–79

chronology (the **"logic of time"**)   The sequence of events in a work, with emphasis on the complex intertwining of cause and effect. 1207

City Dionysia   See *Dionysia*.

clerihew   A comic and often satiric closed-form poem in four lines, rhyming *a b a b*, usually on the topic of a famous real or literary person. 904

cliché rhyme   An overly used and particularly easy rhyme, such as *moon* and *June* or *trees* and *breeze*. 853

climax (from the Greek word for *ladder*)   The high point of *conflict* and tension preceding the *resolution* or *dénoument* of a *story* or *play*; the point of decision, of inevitability and no return. The climax is sometimes equated with the *crisis* in the consideration of dramatic and narrative *structure*. 276, 1201, 1501

closed-form poetry   Poetry written in specific and traditional patterns produced through control of *rhyme*, *meter*, line-length, and line groupings. 897

close reading   The detailed study of a poem or passage, designed to explain characters, motivations, similarities and contrasts of sound, situations, ideas, style, organization, word selections, settings, etc. 647

close-up (film)   A camera view of an actor's head and upper body, designed to emphasize the psychological makeup and reactions of the character being portrayed; contrasted with *long shot*. 1752

comedy   A literary genre which, like *tragedy*, originated in the *Dionysia* festivals of ancient Athens. Derived from the Greek *komos* songs or "songs of merrymakers," the first comedies were wildly boisterous. Later comedies became more subdued and realistic. In typical comedies today, confusions and doubts are resolved satisfactorily if not happily, and usually comedies are characterized by smiles, jokes, and laughter. 1215, 1496–1614

comedy of the absurd   A modern form of comedy dramatizing the apparent pointlessness, ambiguity, uncertainty, and absurdity of human existence. 1504

comedy of manners A form of comedy, usually a *regular play* (in five acts or three acts), in which attitudes and customs are examined and satirized in the light of high intellectual and moral standards. The *dialogue* is witty and sophisticated, and characters are often measured according to their linguistic and intellectual powers. 1502

comic action A pattern of action, including funny situations and language, that is solvable and correctible, and therefore satisfying. 1500

comic opera An outgrowth of eighteenth-century *ballad opera*, but different because the music in comic opera is composed for the lyrics. 1580

commedia dell'arte Broadly humorous farce that was developed in sixteenth-century Italy, featuring *stock characters*, stock situations, and much improvised *dialogue*. 1503

commentary, analysis, or **interpretation** Passages of explanation and reflection about the meaning of actions, thoughts, dialogue, historical movements, and so on. 70

commentator See *raisonneur*.

common ground of assent Those interests, concerns, and assumptions that the writer assumes in common with readers so that an effective and persuasive *tone* may be maintained. 803

common measure A closed poetic quatrain, rhyming *a b a b*, in which lines of iambic tetrameter alternate with iambic trimeter. See also *ballad measure* and *hymnal measure*. 903

comparison-contrast A technique of analyzing two or more works in order to determine similarities and differences in topic, treatment, and quality. 1876–92

complete, completeness The second element in Aristotle's definition of *tragedy*, emphasizing the logic and entirety of the play. 1273

complication A stage of narrative and dramatic structure in which the major

conflicts are brought out; the *rising action* of a *drama*. 276, 1208

compound-complex sentence A potentially complicated sentence built not only from two simple sentences but also, theoretically, from three or more. There may be a number of subordinate clauses, and possibly also one or more of the clauses may have a noun clause as subject of one or more of the basic compounded sentences. 325

concrete diction Words that describe exact and particular conditions or qualities, such as *cold*, *sweet*, and *creamy* in reference to an ice-cream sundae. These words are *concrete*, while the application of *good* or *neat* to the sundae is *abstract*. See also *abstract diction*. 326, 653

concrete poetry See *visual poetry*.

conflict Opposition between two characters, between large groups of people, or between *protagonists* and larger forces such as natural objects, ideas, modes of behavior, public opinion, and the like. Conflict may also be internal and psychological, involving choices facing a *protagonist*. The resolution of conflict is the essence of *plot*. 61, 120

connotation The meanings that words suggest; the overtones of words beyond their bare dictionary definitions or denotations, as with "leave," "get away," "depart," "turn tail," and "vamoose," which have the same meaning, but differing connotations. 328, 659

consonant sounds or **consonant segments** Sounds that accompany ["con"] the (vowel) sound ["sonant"]). They are produced as a result of the touching or close proximity of the tongue or the lips in relation to the teeth or palate (e.g., *m, n, p, f, sh, ch*); to be compared and contrasted with *vowel sounds*. 842

contextual, private, or **authorial symbol** A symbol that is derived within the context of an individual work, not from common historical, cultural, or religious materials. See also *cultural symbol*. 69, 376, 941, 1210

convention   An accepted feature of a genre, such as the *point of view* in a story, the *form* of a *poem* (e.g., *sonnet, ode*), the competence or brilliance of the detective in detective fiction, the impenetrability of disguise and concealment in a Shakespearean play, or the *chorus* in Greek *drama*. 28

Corpus Christi play   A type of medieval drama that enacts events from the Bible, such as the killing of Abel by Cain, the domestic problems of Noah, the jealous anger of Herod, and so on. The word is derived from the religious festival of Corpus Christi ("Christ's body"), held in the spring of each year, mainly during the fourteenth century. Also called *mystery plays* because they were performed by individual craft guilds, or *misteries*. See also *cycle*. 1218

cosmic irony (irony of fate)   *Situational irony* that is connected to a pessimistic or fatalistic view of life. 1275

costumes   The clothes worn by *actors*, designed to indicate historical periods, social status, economic levels, etc. 1214

cothurni   See *buskins*.

couplet   Two lines that may be unified by *rhyme* or, in biblical poetry, by content. 4, 856, 898

creative nonfiction   A type of literature that is technically nonfiction, such as diaries, journals, and news features, but that nevertheless involves a high degree of imaginative and literary skill. 5

crisis   The point of uncertainty and tension in a literary work—the turning point—that results from the *conflicts* and difficulties brought about through the *complications* of the plot. The crisis leads to the *climax*—that is, to the decision made by the protagonist to resolve the conflict. Sometimes the crisis and the climax are considered as two elements of the same stage of *plot* development. 276, 1208

cultural (universal) context   See *topical/ historical context approach*.

cultural or **universal symbol**   A symbol that is recognized and shared as a result of a common political, social, and cultural heritage. See also *contextual symbol*. 69, 376, 941, 1210

cycle   (1) A group of closely related works. (2) In medieval religious drama, the complete set of plays performed during the *Corpus Christi* festival, from the creation of the world to the resurrection. As many as forty plays could make up the cycle. During those times when not many people were able to read, a complete cycle was one of the means by which stories of the Bible were brought to a wider audience. See also *Corpus Christi play*. 1219

dactyl   A three-syllable foot consisting of a heavy stress followed by two lights, as in the words QUOT-a-ble and SYN-the-sis. 847

dactylic rhyme   Rhyming dactyls, such as *spillable* and *syllable* or *mortify* and *fortify*. 854–56

deconstructionist critical approach   An interpretive literary approach that rejects absolutes, but that stresses ambiguities and contradictions. 1871

decorum   The convention or expectation that words and subjects should be exactly appropriate—*high* or *formal* words for serious subjects (e.g., *epic poems, tragedy*), and *low* or *informal* words for low subjects (e.g., *limericks, farce*). 657

denotation   The standard, minimal meaning of a word, without implications and connotations. See also *connotation*. 327, 659

dénouement (untying) or **resolution**   The final stage of *plot development*, in which mysteries are explained, characters find their destinies, lovers are united, sanity is restored, and the work is completed. Usually the dénouement is done as speedily as possible, for it occurs after all *conflicts* are ended, and little that is new can then be introduced to hold the interest of the audience. 276, 1201, 1209, 1501

description   The exposition of scenes, actions, attitudes, and feelings. 68

developing character   See *round character*.

device   A *figure of speech*, such as a *metaphor* or a *simile*. 760

deus ex machina   ("A god out of the machine"; *theos apo mechanes* in Greek, a phrase attributed to the ancient Greek playwright Menander). In ancient Athenian drama, the entrance of a god to unravel the problems in a *play*. Today, the phrase *deus ex machina* refers to the artificial and illogical solution of problems. 1277

dialect   Language characteristics—involving pronunciation, unique words, and vocal rhythms—particular to regions such as New England or the South, or to separate nations such as Britain and Australia. 655

dialogue   The speeches of two or more characters in a *story*, *play*, or *poem*. 4, 68, 1204

diction   Word choice, types of words, and the level of language. 325

diction, formal or **high**   Proper, elevated, elaborate, and often polysyllabic language. 325, 654

diction, informal or **low**   Relaxed, conversational, and familiar language, utilizing contractions and elisions, and sometimes employing *slang* and grammatical errors. 326, 655

diction, neutral or **middle**   Correct language characterized by directness and simplicity. 325, 654

dilemma   A situation, particularly in tragedy, presenting a character with two choices, either one of which is unacceptable, dangerous, or even lethal. 120

dimeter   A *line* of two metrical feet. 845

Dionysia (also **City Dionysia**)   The religious festivals of ancient Athens held to celebrate the god Dionysus. *Tragedy* developed as part of the Great, or City Dionysia in March–April, and *comedy* developed as part of a shorter festival, the Lenaea (in February). 1265

diphthong   A meaningful vowel segment (a phoneme) that begins with one sound and changes to another, with which it ends. Three examples in English are found in the words h*ou*se, c*oi*l, and f*i*ne. 842

dipody, dipodic foot, or **syzygy**   A strong *beat* that creates a single *foot* out of two normal feet—usually *iambs* or *trochees*—so that a "galloping" or "rollicking" *rhythm* results. 848

director   The person in charge of guiding and instructing all persons involved in a dramatic production. 1212

discursive poetry   Non-narrative *poetry* dealing primarily with ideas and personal, social, or political commentary. 4

discursive writing   Distinguished from imaginative writing, discursive writing is concerned with factual presentation and the development of reasonable and logical conclusions. 4

dithyramb   An ancient Athenian poetic form sung by choruses during the earliest *Dionysia*. The first *tragedies* originated as part of the dithyrambs. 1215, 1266

documentation   Granting recognition to the ideas and words of others, either through textual, parenthetical, or footnote references. 607

donnée (French for "given")   The given action or set of assumptions on which a work of literature is based, such as the unpredictability of love, the bleakness and danger of a postwar world, or the inescapability of guilt. See also *postulate* or *premise*. 59

double duple   See *dipody*.

double entendre ("double meaning")   Deliberate ambiguity, usually comic, and often sexual. 329

double rhyme   See *trochaic rhyme*.

double take   A structural device whereby a concluding event or "surprise" brings about a new and more complex understanding of the previous material. 277

drama   An individual play; also plays considered as a group; one of the three major genres of *imaginative literature*. 4, 1204–1852

dramatic irony   A special kind of *situational irony* in which a character perceives his or her plight in a limited way while the audience and one or more of the other characters understand it entirely. 1210, 1276

dramatic monologue   A type of *poem* in which a speaker addresses an internal listener or the reader. Often the speaker includes detail reflecting the listener's unrecorded responses. The form is related to the *soliloquy* and the *aside* in drama. 690

dramatic or **objective point of view**   A *third-person narration* reporting speech and *action*, but excluding commentary on the actions and thoughts of the *characters*. 133

dying rhyme   See *falling rhyme*.

dynamic character   A character who recognizes, changes with, and tries to adjust to circumstances. Such changes may be shown in (1) an action or actions, (2) the realization of new strength and therefore the affirmation of previous decisions, (3) the acceptance of new conditions and the need for making changes, (4) the discovery of unrecognized truths, or (5) the reconciliation of the character with adverse conditions. In a *short story*, there is usually only one dynamic character, whereas in a *novel* there may be many. 178, 1206

echoic words   Words echoing the actions they describe, such as *buzz, bump*, and *slap*; important in the device of *onomatopoeia*. 852, 879

economic determinist/Marxist critical approach   An interpretive literary approach based on the theories of Karl Marx (1818–1883), stressing that literature is to be judged from the perspective of economic and social inequality and oppression. 1868

editing (film)   See *montage*.

elegy   A *poem* of lamentation about a death. Often an elegy takes the form of a *pastoral*. 4, 901

enclosing setting   See *framing* or *enclosing setting*.

end-stopped line   A poetic line ending in a full pause, usually marked by a period or semicolon. 850

English (Shakespearean) sonnet   A sonnet form developed by Shakespeare, in *iambic pentameter*, composed of three *quatrains* and a *couplet*, with seven rhymes in the pattern *a b a b, c d c d, e f e f, g g*. 900

epic   A long *narrative poem* elevating *character, speech*, and *action*. 56

epigram   A short and witty *poem*, often in *couplets*, that makes a humorous or satiric point. 903

episode or *episodia*   (1) An acting *scene* or section of Greek tragedy. Divisions separating the episodes were called *stasima*, or sections for the chorus. (2) A self-enclosed portion of a work, such as a section, or a passage of particular narration, dialogue, or location. 1280

epitaph   A short comment or description marking someone's death. Also, a short, witty, and often satiric poem about death. 903

essay   A short and tightly organized written composition dealing with a topic such as a character, setting, or point of view. Essays also deal more broadly with any and all conceivable topics. 29, *passim*

euphony ("good sound")   Word groups containing consonants that permit an easy and pleasant flow of spoken sound. See also *cacophony*. 852

exact rhyme   Also called *perfect rhyme*; the placement of rhyming words in which both the vowel and concluding consonant sounds, if any, are identical, as in "done" and "run," and "see" and "be." It is important to judge rhymes on the basis of *sound* rather than spelling, as in these examples. Words do not have to be spelled the same way to be exact rhymes. 853

exam, examination A written or oral test or inquiry designed to discover a person's understanding and capacity to deal with a particular topic or set of topics. 1893–1903

exodos The final episode in a Greek tragedy, occurring after the last choral ode. 1280

explication A detailed analysis of a work of literature, often word by word and line by line; a close reading. 647

exposition The stage of dramatic or narrative structure that introduces all things necessary for the development of the plot. 275, 1208

eye rhyme or **sight rhyme** Words that seem to rhyme because parts of them are spelled identically but pronounced differently (e.g., *bear, fear; fury, bury; stove, shove; wonder, yonder*). 855

fable A brief *story* illustrating a moral truth, most often associated with the ancient Greek writer Aesop. See also *beast fable*. 56, 379

falling action See *catastrophe*.

falling rhyme Trochaic rhymes, such as *often* and *soften,* and also multisyllabic rhymes, such as *flattery* and *battery, listening* and *glistening.* 854

fantasy The creation of events that are dreamlike or fantastic, departing from ordinary understanding of *reality* because of apparently illogical *setting,* movement, causality, and *chronology.* 59

farce (from the Latin word *farsus,* meaning "stuffed") An outlandish physical *comedy* overflowing with silly characters, improbable happenings, wild clowning, extravagant language, and bawdy jokes. 1503

feet See *foot*.

feminist critical approach A critical approach designed to raise consciousness about the importance and unique nature of women in literature. See also *gender studies* and *queer theory.* 1863

fiction *Narratives* based in the imagination of the author, not in literal, reportorial facts; one of the three major genres of imaginative literature. 55–622

figurative devices See *figures of speech*.

figurative language See *figures of speech*.

figure of speech An organized pattern of comparison that deepens, broadens, extends, illuminates, and emphasizes meaning, and also that conforms to particular patterns or forms such as *metaphor, simile,* and *parallelism.* 760–99

film Motion pictures, movies. 1748–72

film script The written dramatic text on which a film is based, including directions for movement and expression. 1751

first-person point of view The use of a first-person *speaker* or *narrator* who tells about things that he or she has seen, done, spoken, heard, thought, and also learned about in other ways. 131, 135

flashback Also called *selective recollection*. A method of *narration* in which past events are introduced into a present action. 277

flat character A character, usually minor, who is not individual, but rather useful and structural, static and unchanging; distinguished from *round character*. 178, 1206

foil A character, usually minor, designed to highlight qualities of a major character. 1206

foot, feet A poetic foot consists of the measured combination of heavy and light *stresses*, such as the *iamb*, which contains a light stress followed by a heavy stress (e.g., *"of YEAR"*). In poetic scansion, one separates feet with a *virgule* or single slash mark (/), as in Shakespeare's "That TIME / of YEAR / thou MAY'ST / in ME / be - HOLD." 844

form, poetic The various shapes and organizational modes of poetry. 897–939

formal diction See *diction, formal* or *high*.

formalist critical approach See *New Critical/formalist critical approach*.

formal substitution   See *substitution*.

framing or **enclosing setting**   The same features of topic, technique, or setting used at both the beginning and ending of a work so as to "frame" or "enclose" the work. 227

free verse   *Poetry* based on the natural *rhythms* of phrases and normal pauses, not *metrical feet*. See *open-form poetry*. 905

freewriting   See *brainstorming*.

Freytag pyramid   A diagram graphically showing the stages of dramatic *structure*. *Complication* and emotional intensity go upward on the side of the pyramid rising to its peak or point. Once the high point is reached, intensity begins to decrease just as the other side of the pyramid descends to its base. 1207

gallery   The upper seats at the back and sides of a *theater*. 1212

general language   Words referring to broad classes of persons, objects, or phenomena; distinguished from *specific language*. 326, 653

gender studies   A critical approach that brings attention to gender rather than to sexual differences, based on the concept that the masculine/feminine divide is socially constructed and not innate. See also *feminist critical approach* and *queer theory*. 1863

genre   One of the major types of literature, such as *fiction* and *poetry*. Also, a type of work, such as detective fiction, epic poetry, tragedy, etc. 3

Globe Theatre   The outdoor theater built at the end of the sixteenth century just south of the Thames, where many of Shakespeare's plays were originally performed. The Globe was rebuilt in the 1990s to its original appearance, and once again is a flourishing theater close to where it was at the time of Shakespeare. 1319–21 See I.15, I.16 for photos of the modern Globe.

graph, graphics   The writing of words on the page; the spelling of words, as opposed to their actual sounds. For example, the *sh* sound may be spelled—or graphed—in many different ways, such as *ship*, na*ti*on, *oc*ean, fi*ss*ion, and fu*chs*ia. 843

graphic narrative, graphic novel   A narrative composed of connected artistic or cartoon panels. The essential quality of graphic narrative is the combination of picture and dialogue to convey a story from beginning to end. 63–66

gustatory images   References to impressions of taste. 730

haiku   A verse form derived from Japanese poetry, traditionally containing three lines of 5, 7, and 5 syllables, in that order, and usually treating a topic derived from nature. 4, 903

half rhyme   See *inexact rhyme*.

hamartia   The Greek word for "error or frailty," indicating the tragic flaw that brings about the downfall or suffering of a protagonist. The same Greek word is translated as "sin" in the New Testament. 1274

heavy-stress rhyme or **rising rhyme**   A *rhyme*, such as rhyming *iambs* or *anapests*, ending with a *strong stress*. The rhymes may be produced with one syllable words, like *SKY* and *FLY*, or with multisyllabic words in which the accent falls on the last syllable, such as *de-CLINE* and *con-FINE*. 844, 854

heptameter or **"the septenary"**   A line consisting of seven metrical *feet*. 845

hero, heroine   The major male and female *protagonists* in a *narrative* or *drama*. The terms are often used to describe leading characters in adventures and romances. 178

heroic couplet   Also called the *neoclassic couplet*. Two successive rhyming lines of *iambic pentameter*, a characteristic of much *poetry* written between 1660 and 1800. Five-stress couplets are often called "heroic" regardless of their topic matter and the period in which they were written. 898

hexameter A line consisting of six metrical *feet*. 845

high comedy Elegant *comedies* characterized by wit and sophistication, in which the complications grow not out of *situation* but rather out of *character*. See also *comedy of manners*. 1502

historical critical approach See *topical/ historical critical approach*.

hovering accent See *spondee*.

hubris or **hybris** ("Insolence, contemptuous violence") The pride and attitudes that lead tragic figures to commit their mistakes or offenses. 1266

humor In literature, those features of a *situation* or expression that provoke laughter and amusement. 1500

hymn A hymn is a religious *song*, consisting of one and usually many more replicating rhythmical *stanzas*. 903

hymnal measure The hymnal stanza, in iambics, consists of four lines of four stresses or else of four lines of alternating four and three stresses, rhyming *x a x a* or *a b a b*. See also *ballad measure* and *common measure*. 903

hyperbole See *overstatement*.

hypocrites (pronounced hip-pock-rih-TAYSS, meaning "one who plays a part") The ancient Greek word for *actor*. Yes, our modern word "hypocrite" is derived from this word. 1267

iamb A two-syllable *foot* consisting of a light *stress* followed by a heavy stress (e.g., *the WINDS, have FELT, of MAY*). The iamb is the most common metrical foot in English poetry because it closely resembles natural speech while it also follows measured poetic accents. 845

iambic pentameter A line consisting of five *iambic feet*, as in Shakespeare's "Shall I compare thee to a summer's day?" 845

iambic rhyme A *heavy-stress rhyme* that is built from rhyming *iambs* such as "the WEST" and "in REST," or from rhyming two-syllable words such as "ad-MIRE" and "de-SIRE." 845

idea or **theme** A concept, thought, opinion, or belief; in literature, a unifying, centralizing conception or *motif*. 61, 432–92

idiom (private or personal language) Usage that produces unique words and phrases within regions, classes, or groups; e.g., standing *on* line or *in* line; carrying a *pail* or a *bucket*; drinking *pop* or *soda*. Also, the habits and structures of particular languages. 655

image, imagery References that trigger the mind to fuse together memories of sights (*visual*), sounds (*auditory*), tastes (*gustatory*), smells (*olfactory*), sensations of touch (*tactile*), and perceptions of motion (*kinetic, kinesthetic*). "Image" refers to a single mental creation, "imagery" to images throughout a work or works of a writer or group of writers. Images may be *literal* (descriptive and pictorial) and *metaphorical* (figurative and suggestive). 4, 726–59

imaginative literature *Literature* based in the imagination of the writer; the genres of imaginative literature are *fiction, poetry*, and *drama*. 3, *passim*

imitation The theory that literature is derived from life and is an imaginative duplication of experience; closely connected to *realism* and *verisimilitude*. 226

imperfect foot A *metrical foot* consisting of a single syllable, either heavily or lightly stressed, as the *er* in "a joy forever." There is nothing imperfect about an imperfect foot. It is so named because, having only one syllable, it does not fit into the patterns of the other poetic feet. Some analysts of prosody explain the absence of a syllable within an established poetic foot as a *catalexis*. 847

incidents See *actions*.

incongruity A discrepancy between what is ordinarily or normally expected and what is actually experienced. The resulting gap is often, under the right circumstances, a cause of laughter. 330

inexact rhyme Rhymes that are created from words with similar but not identical sounds. In most of these instances, either the vowel segments are different while the consonants are the same, or vice versa. This type of rhyme is variously called *slant rhyme, near rhyme, half rhyme, off rhyme, analyzed rhyme,* or *suspended rhyme.* 855

informal diction   See *diction, informal or low.*

intellectual critical approach   See *moral/intellectual critical approach.*

internal rhyme   The occurrence of rhyming words within a single line of verse, as Poe's "Can ever dissever" in "Annabel Lee." 853

interpretation   See *commentary.*

intrigue plot   The dramatic rendering of how a young woman and her lover, often aided by a maidservant or *soubrette,* usually foil a *blocking agent* (usually a parent or guardian). 1499

invention   The process of discovering and determining materials to be included in a composition, whether an *essay* or an imaginative work; a vital phase of planning and developing a composition. 59

ironic comedy   A form of comedy in which characters seem to be in the grips of uncontrollable, cosmic forces. The dominant tone is therefore ironic. 1504

irony   Broadly, a means of indirection. *Verbal irony* is language that states the opposite of what is intended. *Dramatic irony* describes the condition of characters who do not know the nature, seriousness, and extent of their circumstances. See also *situational irony.* 69, 328, 804

irony of fate   See *cosmic irony.*

irony of situation   See *situational irony.*

issue   An assertion or idea to be debated, disputed, or discussed. Sometimes refers to a problematic or questionable circumstance. 62, 432

Italian or **Petrarchan sonnet**   An *iambic pentameter* poem of fourteen lines, divided between the first eight lines (the *octave*) and the last six (the *sestet*).

An Italian sonnet uses five rhymes, unlike the *Shakespearean sonnet,* which has seven rhymes. 900

jargon   Language exclusively used by particular groups, such as doctors, lawyers, astronauts, computer operators, and football players. 656

journal   A notebook or word-processor file for recording responses and observations that, for purposes of writing, may be used in the development of *essays.* 12–17

kinesthetic images   Words describing human or animal motion and activity. 730

kinetic images   Words describing general motion. 730

kothorni   See *buskins.*

Lenaia   The ancient Athenian early spring festival for which comedy as a form was first created. 1278

lighting   The general word describing the many types, positions, directions, and intensities of artificial lights used in the theater. 1213

light stress   In speech and in metrical scansion, the less emphasized syllables, as in Shakespeare's "That TIME of YEAR," in which *that* and *of* are pronounced less emphatically than *time* and *year.* 844

limerick   A brief poem with preestablished line lengths and rhyming patterns, designed to be comic. More often than not, limericks are risqué. 4, 904

limited point of view or **limited third-person point of view** or **limited-omniscient point of view**   A third-person narration in which the actions and thoughts of the protagonist are the primary focus of attention. 134, 136

line   The basic unit of length of a poem, appearing as a row of words or sometimes, as a single word or even part of a word occupying the space of a line, and cohering grammatically through phrases and sentences. Lines in *closed-form poetry* are composed of determinable numbers of *metrical feet*; lines in *open-form poetry* are variable, depending on content and rhythmical speech patterns. 897

listener (internal audience)   A character or characters imagined as the audience to whom a poem or story is spoken, and as a result one of the influences on the content of the work, as in Browning's "My Last Duchess." Although the listener is usually silent, the listener's imagined reactions may affect what the speaker says and the manner in which he or she says it. Using a listener therefore enables the author to make the narrative, or poem, both personal and dramatic. 689

literary research   See *research.*

literature   Written or oral compositions that tell stories, dramatize situations, express emotions, and analyze and advocate ideas. Literature is designed to engage readers emotionally as well as intellectually, with the major genres being *fiction, poetry, drama,* and *nonfiction prose,* and with many separate sub-forms. 1, 3, *passim*

low comedy   Crude, boisterous, and physical *comedies* and *farces,* characterized by sight gags, bawdy jokes, and outrageous situations. 1503

low diction   See *diction, informal or low.*

lyric   (1) A short *poem* or *song* written in a fixed stanzaic form. If the lyric is set to music for performance, each new stanza is usually sung to the original melody. (2) The Aristotelian term for the "several kinds of artistic ornament," such as strophes and antistrophes, that are to be used appropriately in a tragedy. 4, 901, 1274

magnitude   The third element in Aristotle's definition of *tragedy,* emphasizing that a *play* should be neither too long nor too short, so that artistic balance and proportion can be maintained. 1273

main plot   The central and major line of causality and action in a literary work. 1207

major mover   A major participant in a work's action who either causes things to happen or who is the subject of major events. If the first-person narrator is also a major mover, such as the *protagonist,* that fact gives first-hand authenticity to the narration. 128

makeup   The materials, such as cosmetics, wigs, and padding, applied to an actor to change appearance for a specific role, such as a youth, an aged person, or a hunchback. 1214

malapropism   The comic use of an improperly pronounced word, so that what comes out is a real but also incorrect word. Examples are *odorous* for *odious* (Shakespeare) or *pineapple* for *pinnacle* (Sheridan). The new word must be close enough to the correct word so that the resemblance is immediately recognized, along with the error. See also *pun.* 330

Marxist critical approach   See *economic determinist/Marxist critical approach.*

masks   Face coverings worn by ancient Athenian actors to illustrate and define dramatic characters such as youths, warriors, old men, and women. 1279

meaning   That which is to be understood in a work; the total combination of ideas, actions, descriptions, and effects. 432–92

mechanics of verse   See *prosody.*

melodrama   A sentimental dramatic form with an artificially happy ending. 1221

melos   See *lyric.*

metaphor ("carrying out a change")   A *figure of speech* that describes something as though it actually were something else, thereby enhancing understanding and insight. One of the major qualities of poetic language. 4, 68, 760

metaphorical language   See *figure of speech.*

meter   The number of *feet* within a line of traditional verse, such as *iambic pentameter* referring to a line containing five *iambs.* 845

metonymy   A *figure of speech* in which one thing is used as a substitute for another with which it is closely identified, such as when a speaker says "Dear Hearts" to refer to an audience. 766

metrical foot   See *foot.*

metrics   See *prosody.*

middle comedy   The Athenian comedies written in the first two-thirds of the fourth century BCE Middle comedy lessened or eliminated the *chorus*, and did away with the exaggerated costumes of the *old comedy.* No complete middle comedies have survived from antiquity. 1498

middle diction   See *diction, neutral or middle.*

mimesis or **representation**   Aristotle's idea that *drama (tragedy)* represents rather than duplicates history. 1272

miracle play   A late medieval play dramatizing a miracle or miracles performed by a saint. An outgrowth of the earlier medieval *Corpus Christi play.* 1220

monologue   A long speech spoken by a single character to himself or herself, to the audience, or to an off-stage character. See also *aside, soliloquy.* 1204

monometer   A line consisting of one metrical *foot.* 845

montage or **editing (film)**   The editing or assembling of the various camera "takes," or separately filmed scenes, to make a continuous film. 1754

mood   See *atmosphere.*

moral/intellectual critical approach   An interpretive literary approach that is concerned primarily with content and values. 1855

morality play   A type of medieval and early Renaissance play that dramatizes how to live a pious life. The best-known morality play is the anonymous *Everyman.* 1220

motif ("something that moves")   Sometimes used in reference to a main *idea* or *theme* in a single work or in many works, such as a *carpe diem* theme, or a comparison of lovers to little worlds. See also *archetype.* 433

motivation   The ideas and impulses that propel characters to a particular act or course of action. Motivation is the hallmark quality of a *round character.* 1206

multiple plot or **double plot**   A development in which two or more stories are both contrasted and woven together, as in Shakespeare's *A Midsummer Night's Dream.* 1207

musical comedy   A modern prose play integrated with lyrics—and also dances—set to specially composed music. Usually, musical comedies are elaborately and expensively produced. The form is in a line of development from *ballad opera* and *comic opera.* 1580

music of poetry   See *prosody.*

muthos   Aristotle's word for plot, from which our word *myth* is derived. 983

mystery play   See *Corpus Christi play.*

myth, mythology, mythos   A *myth* is a story that deals with the relationships of gods to humanity or with battles among heroes in time past. A myth may also be a set of beliefs or assumptions among societies. *Mythology* refers collectively to all the stories and beliefs, either of a single group or number of groups. A system of beliefs and religious or historical doctrines is a *mythos.* 4, 56, 379, 983–1022, 1272

mythical reader   See *audience.*

mythic critical approach   See *archetypal/symbolic/mythic critical approach.*

mythopoeic   The propensity to create *myths* and to live in terms of them. 984

narration, narrative fiction   The relating or recounting of a sequence of events or actions. Whereas a narration may be reportorial and historical, *narrative fiction* is primarily creative and imaginative. See also *prose fiction* and *creative nonfiction.* 4, 56, 62

narrative ballad   A poem in *ballad measure* telling a story and also containing dramatic speeches. 633

narrator See *speaker.*

nasal A meaningful continuant consonant in which the sound is released through the nose. The nasals in English are *n, m,* and *ng.* 843

naturalistic setting A stage *setting* designed to imitate, as closely as possible, the everyday world, often to the point of emphasizing poverty and dreariness. 1213

near rhyme See *inexact rhyme.*

neoclassic couplet See *heroic couplet.*

neutral diction See *diction, neutral* or *middle.*

new comedy Athenian comedy that developed at the end of the fourth century BCE, stressing wit, romanticism, and twists of plot. The most famous of the new comedy writers was Menander (342–292 BCE). His plays were long considered lost, but a small number have luckily come to light in the last hundred years. 1498

New Critical/formalist critical approach An interpretive literary approach based on the French practice of *explication de texte,* stressing the form and details of literary works. 1859

new historicism A type of literary criticism that emphasizes the integration of literature with historical background and culture. 1857

nonfiction prose A *genre* consisting of essays, articles, and books about real as opposed to fictional occurrences and objects; one of the major *genres* of literature. 5

nonrealistic character An undeveloped and often *symbolic character* without full motivation or individual identity. 1206

nonrealistic drama Dreamlike, fantastic, symbolic, and otherwise artificial plays that make no attempt to present an imitation of everyday reality. 1614–1747

novel A long work of prose fiction. 4, 57

objective point of view See *dramatic point of view.*

octave The first eight *lines* of an *Italian sonnet,* unified by topic, rhythm, and *rhyme.* In practice, the first eight lines of any sonnet. 900

ode A variable stanzaic poetic *form* (usually long, to contrast it with the *song*) with varying line lengths and sometimes intricate *rhyme* schemes. 4, 901

Old Comedy or **Old Attic Comedy** The Athenian comedies of the fifth century BCE, featuring song, dance, ribaldry, satire, and invective. The most famous writer of the old comedy is Aristophanes, eleven of whose plays have survived from antiquity. 1497

olfactory imagery *Images* referring to smell. 730

omniscient point of view A *third-person narrative* in which the *speaker* or *narrator,* with no apparent limitations, may describe intentions, actions, reactions, locations, and speeches of any or all of the characters, and may also describe their innermost thoughts (when necessary for the development of the *plot*). 67, 133, 136

open-form poetry Poems that avoid traditional structural patterns, such as *rhyme* or *meter,* in favor of other methods of organization. 905

orchestra (a part of a **theater**) (1) In ancient Greek theaters, the *orchestra,* or "dancing place," was the circular area at the base of the amphitheater where the chorus performed. (2) In modern theaters, the word "orchestra" now refers to the ground floor or first floor where the audience sits. 1277

organic unity The interdependence of all elements of a work, including character, actions, speeches, descriptions, thoughts, and observations. The concept of organic unity is attributed to Aristotle. 61

outline See *analytical sentence outline.*

overstatement or **hyperbole** or **overreacher.** A rhetorical *figure of speech* in which emphasis is achieved through exaggeration. 329, 767

parable   A short *allegory* designed to illustrate a religious truth, often associated with Jesus as recorded in the Gospels, primarily Luke. 379

parados   (1) A *parados* was either of the two front aisles leading from the sides to the *orchestra* in ancient Greek amphitheaters, along which the performers could enter or exit. (2) The entry and first lyrical ode of the *chorus* in Greek tragedy, after the *prologue*. 1280

paradox   A *figure of speech* embodying a contradiction that is nevertheless true. 764

parallelism   A *figure of speech* in which the same grammatical forms are repeated. 658, 898

paranomasia   See *pun*.

paraphrase   A brief restatement, in one's own words, of all or part of a literary work; a *précis*. 645

pastoral   A traditional poetic form with topic material drawn from the usually idealized vocabulary of rural and shepherd life. Famous English pastorals are Milton's "Lycidas," Arnold's "Thyrsis," Pope's *Pastorals*, and Spenser's *The Shepherd's Calendar*. 901

pathos   The "scene of suffering" in tragedy, which Aristotle defines as "a destructive or painful action, such as death on the stage, bodily agony, wounds, and the like." It is the scene of suffering that is intended to evoke the response of pity (*eleos*) from the audience. 1273

pentameter   A line of five metrical *feet*. 845

perfect rhyme   See *exact rhyme*.

performance   An individual production of a play, either for an evening or for an extended period, comprising acting, movement, lighting, sound effects, staging and scenery, ticket sales, and the accommodation of the audience. 1211

peripeteia or **reversal**   Aristotle's term for a sudden reversal, when the action of a work, particularly a play, veers around quickly to its opposite. 1272

persona   See *speaker*.

personification   A *figure of speech* in which human characteristics are attributed to nonhuman things or abstractions. 766

perspective, dramatic   The *point of view* in drama, the way in which the dramatist focuses on major characters and on particular problems. 1209

Petrarchan sonnet   See *Italian sonnet*.

phonetic, phonetics   The actual pronunciation of sounds, as distinguished from spelling or *graphics*. 844

picture poetry   See *visual poetry*.

plagiarism   A writer's use of the language and ideas of another writer or writers without proper acknowledgment. Plagiarism is an exceedingly serious breach of academic honor; some call it intellectual theft, and others call it an academic crime. 612

platform stage   A raised stage surrounded by seats for an *arena theater* or *theater-in-the-round*. 1212

plausibility   See *probability*.

play   See *drama*.

plot   The plan or groundwork for a *story* or a *play*, with the *actions* resulting from believable and authentic human responses to a *conflict*. It is causality, conflict, response, opposition, and interaction that make a plot out of a series of *actions*. Aristotle's word for plot is *muthos*, from which the word *myth* is derived. 119, 1207

plot of intrigue   See *intrigue plot*.

poem, poet, poetry   A variable literary genre that is, foremost, characterized by the rhythmical qualities of language. While poems may be short (including *epigrams* and *haiku* of just a few lines) or long (*epics* of thousands of lines), the essence of poetry is compression, economy, and force, in contrast with the expansiveness and logic of prose. There is no bar to the topics that poets may consider, and poems may range from the personal and lyric to the public and discursive. A *poem* is one poetic work.

A *poet* is a person who writes poems. *Poetry* may refer to the poems of one writer, to poems of a number of writers, to all poems generally, or to the aesthetics of poetry considered as an art. 4, 624–1201, *passim*.

point of view The *speaker, voice, narrator,* or *persona* of a work; the position from which details are perceived and related; a centralizing mind or intelligence; not to be confused with *opinion* or *belief.* 67, 127–72

point-of-view character The central figure or *protagonist* in a *limited-point-of-view narration,* the character about whom events turn, the focus of attention in the narration. 134

postulate or **premise** The assumption on which a work of literature is based, such as a level of absolute, literal *reality,* or as a dreamlike, fanciful set of events. See also *donnée.* 59

private or **contextual symbol** See *cultural symbol.*

probability or **plausibility** The standard that literature should be concerned with what is likely, common, normal, and usual. 179

problem A question or issue about the interpretation or understanding of a work. 1486

problem play A type of *play* dealing with a *problem,* whether personal, social, political, environmental, philosophical, or religious. 1500

procatalepsis or **anticipation** A rhetorical strategy whereby the writer raises an objection and then answers it; the goal is to strengthen an argument by dealing with possible objections before a dissenter can raise them. Procatalepsis is thus a writer's way of taking the wind out of an objector's sails. 1488

producer The person in charge of practical matters connected with a stage production, such as securing finances, arranging for theater use, furnishing materials, renting or making costumes and properties, guaranteeing payments, and so on. 1212

prologue In ancient Athenian *tragedy,* the introductory action and speeches before the *parados,* or first entry of the *chorus.* 1279

props or **properties** The furniture, draperies, and the like used on stage during a play. 1213

proscenium, proscenium stage An arch or frame that delineates a box set and holds the curtain, thus creating the invisible fourth wall through which the audience sees the action of the play. See also *proskenion.* 1212

prose fiction *Imaginative* prose narratives (*short stories* and *novels*) that focus on one or a few *characters* who undergo a change or development as they interact with other characters and deal with their problems. 4, 57–60

prose poem A short work, laid out to look like prose, but employing the methods of verse, such as rhythm and imagery, for poetic ends. 906

proskenion A raised stage built in front of the *skene* in ancient Greek theaters to separate the *actors* from the *chorus* and to make them more prominent. 1277

prosody Metrics and versification; the *sounds, rhythms, rhymes,* and general physical qualities of *poetry;* the relationships between content and sound in poetry. 4, 841–96

protagonist The central *character* and focus of interest in a *narrative* or *drama.* 61, 178, 1205

psychological/psychoanalytic critical approach An interpretive literary approach stressing how psychology may be used in the explanation of both authors and literary works. 1867

public mythology See *universal mythology.*

pun, or **paranomasia** Witty wordplay based on the fact that certain words with different meanings have nearly identical or even identical sounds. See also *malapropism.* 766

purgation See *catharsis.*

pyrrhic A *substitute* metrical *foot* consisting of two unaccented *syllables,* as in the words "on their" in this line from Pope's *Pastorals*: "Now sleeping flocks on their soft fleeces lie." 847

quatrain   (1) A four-line *stanza* or poetic unit. (2) In an *English* or *Shakespearean sonnet*, a group of four *lines* united by *rhyme*. 4, 856, 900

queer theory   An interpretive literary approach based on the idea that sexual orientation is partly ideological and partly social. Many queer theorists see the heterosexual/homosexual divide as less distinct than has traditionally been understood. 1863

raisonneur   A character who remains somewhat detached from the dramatic action and who provides reasoned commentary; a *choric figure*. 1206

reader-response critical approach   An interpretive literary approach based on the proposition that literary works are not fully created until readers make *transactions* with them by *actualizing* them in the light of their particular knowledge and experience. 1873

realism or **verisimilitude**   The use of true, lifelike, or probable situations and concerns. Also, the theory underlying the depiction of reality in literature. 226

realistic character   The accurate *imitation* of individualized men and women. 1206

realistic comedy   See *ironic comedy*.

realistic drama   The dramatic presentation of *action*, thoughts, and *character* that are designed to give the illusion of *reality*. 1614–1747

realistic setting   A *setting* designed to resemble places that actually exist or that might exist. The setting of Wilson's *Fences* is realistic. 1208

recognition   See *anagnorisis*.

regular play   A play conforming to the traditional *rules* of drama, particularly the *three unities*. Usually a regular play contains five acts (as in the Renaissance up through much of the nineteenth century). More recent regular plays

contain three acts, although there is nothing hard and fast about this number. See *rules of drama*. 1281

reliable narrator   A *speaker* who has nothing to hide by making misstatements and who is untainted by self-interest. This speaker's *narration* is therefore to be accepted at face value; contrasted with an *unreliable narrator*. 132

repetition   See *anaphora*.

representation   See *mimesis*.

representative character   A *flat character* with the qualities of all other members of a group (i.e., clerks, cowboys, detectives, etc.); a *stereotype*. 179, 1272

research, literary   The systematic use of primary and secondary sources for assistance in studying a literary *problem*. 594, 1202, 1839

resolution   See *dénouement*.

response   A reader's intellectual and emotional reactions to a literary work. 1873

Restoration Comedy   English *high comedies* written mainly between 1660 and 1700, dealing realistically with personal, social, and sexual issues. 1503

revenge tragedy   A popular type of English Renaissance drama, developed by Thomas Kyd, in which a person is called upon (often by a ghost) to avenge the murder of a loved one. Shakespeare's *Hamlet* is in the tradition of revenge tragedy. 1322

reversal   See *peripeteia*.

rhetoric   The art of persuasive writing; broadly, the art of all effective writing. 658

rhetorical figure   See *figure of speech*.

rhetorical substitution   See *substitution*.

rhyme   The repetition of identical or closely related sounds in the syllables of different words, almost always in concluding syllables at the ends of lines, such as Shakespeare's *DAY* and *MAY* (Sonnet 18) and Swinburne's *forEVER, NEVER,* and *RIVER* ("The Garden of Proserpine"). 852

rhyme scheme   A pattern of *rhyme*, usually indicated in prosodic analysis by the assignment of a letter of the alphabet to each rhyming sound, as in *a b b a a b b a* as the rhyming pattern of the octave of an *Italian* or *Petrarchan sonnet*. 856

rhythm   The varying speed, intensity, elevation, pitch, loudness, and expressiveness of speech, especially *poetry*. 844

rising action   The action in a *play* before the climax. See *Freytag pyramid*. 1208

romance   (1) Lengthy Spanish and French *stories* of the sixteenth and seventeenth centuries. (2) Modern formulaic *stories* describing the growth of an impulsive, passionate, and powerful love relationship. 4, 57

romantic comedy   Sympathetic *comedy* that presents the adventures of young lovers trying to overcome opposition and achieve a successful union. 1502

round character   A literary character, usually but not necessarily the *protagonist* of a story or play, who is three-dimensional, rounded, authentic, memorable, original, and true to life. A round character is the center of our attention, and is both individual and unpredictable. A round character profits from experience, and in the course of a story or play undergoes change or development. 177, 1206

rules of drama   An important concept of dramatic composition among Renaissance and eighteenth-century critics. The rules were based on ancient practice and theory, particularly the use of the five-act pyramidal (Freytag) structure and the embodiment of the *three unities* of action, place, and time. Sophocles followed the rules carefully; indeed, the rules were at least partially derived from his example. Shakespeare observed the *unity of action*, but in the interests of *probability* he apparently saw no reason to observe the others. See also *regular play*. 1281

satire   An attack on human follies or vices, as measured positively against a normative religious, moral, or social standard. 807

satiric comedy   A form of *comedy* designed to correct social and individual behavior by ridiculing human vices and follies. 1503

satyr play   A comic and burlesque *play* submitted by the ancient Athenian tragic dramatists along with their groups of three *tragedies*. On each day of tragic performances, the satyr play was performed after the three tragedies. See also *trilogy*. 1268

scan, scansion   The act of determining the prevailing *rhythm* and poetic characteristics of a *poem*. 844

scene   In a *play*, a part or division (of an act, as in *Hamlet*, or of an entire play, as in *Fences*) in which there is a unity of subject, *setting*, and *actors*. 1213

scenery   The artificial environment created onstage to produce the illusion of a specific or generalized place and time. 1212

schwa (from Hebrew)   A middle, minimal vowel sound that in prosodic scansion occupies unstressed positions, even though the sound may be spelled as *a, e, i, o*, or *u*. The schwa is the most commonly pronounced vowel sound in English. 842

scrim   A stage curtain that becomes transparent when illuminated from upstage, permitting action to take place under various lighting conditions. 1214, 1618, 1647

second-person point of view   A *narration* in which a second-person listener ("you") is the *protagonist* and the speaker is someone (e.g., doctor, parent, rejected lover) with knowledge that the protagonist does not possess or understand about his or her own actions. 132, 136

segment   The smallest meaningful unit of sound, such as the *l, uh*, and *v* sounds (phonemes) making up the word "love." Segments are to be distinguished from spellings. Thus, the *oo* segment may be spelled as *ui* in "fruit," *u* in "flute," *oo* in "foolish," *o* in "lose," *uu* in "vacuum," or *ou* in "troupe." 843, 870

selective recollection   See *flashback*.

sentimental comedy   A type of comedy dramatizing how good nature and morality enable characters to overcome their character flaws, which otherwise seem problematic or even incorrigible. 1580

septenary   See *heptameter*.

sequence   The following of one thing upon another in time or chronology. It is the *realistic* or true-to-life basis of the cause-and-effect arrangement necessary in a *plot*. 61

seriousness   The first element in Aristotle's definition of *tragedy*, demonstrating the most elevated and significant aspects of human character. 1273

sestet   (1) A six-line stanza or unit of *poetry*. (2) The last six lines of an *Italian sonnet*. 900

sets   The physical scenery and properties used in a theatrical production. 1212

setting   The natural, manufactured, and cultural environment in which characters live and move, including all their possessions, homes, ways of life, and assumptions. 224–74

Shakespearean sonnet   See *English sonnet*.

shaped verse   See *visual poetry*.

short story   A compact, concentrated work of *narrative fiction* that may also contain description, dialogue, and commentary. Poe used the term "brief prose tale" before the term "short story" was created, and he emphasized that the form should create a powerful and unified impact. 4, 58

simile   A *figure of speech*, using "like" with nouns and "as" with clauses, as in "the trees were bent by the wind *like actors bowing after a performance*." 761

simple sentence   A complete sentence containing only one subject and one verb, together with modifiers and complements. 326

sitcom   A serial type of modern television comedy dramatizing the circumstances, assumptions, and actions of a fixed number of characters (hence "situation comedy" or "sitcom"). 1504

situation   The given circumstances of a *story*, *poem*, or *play*; a *donnée*. 4

situational irony or **irony of situation**   A type of *irony* emphasizing that human beings are enmeshed in forces beyond their comprehension and control. 69, 805, 1210

skene ("tent," "hut")   In ancient Greek theaters, a building in front of the *orchestra* that contained front and side doors from which actors could make entrances and exits. It served a variety of purposes, including the storage of *costumes* and *props*. The word has given us our modern word *scene*. 1277

slang   Informal diction and substandard vocabulary. Some slang is a permanent part of the language (e.g., phrases like "I'll be damned," "That sucks," and our many four-letter words). Other slang is spontaneous, rising within a group (*jargon*), and often then being replaced when new slang emerges. 656

slapstick comedy   A type of low *farce* in which the humor depends almost entirely on physical actions and sight gags. 1503

social drama   A type of *problem play* that deals with current social issues and the place of individuals in society. 1221

soliloquy   A speech made by a character, alone on stage, directly to the *audience*, the convention being that the character is revealing his or her inner thoughts, feelings, hopes, and plans. A soliloquy is to be distinguished from an *aside*, which is made to the audience (or confidentially to another character) when other characters are present. 1321

song   See *lyric*.

sonnet   A poem of fourteen lines (originally designed to be spoken and not sung) in *iambic pentameter*. See *Italian sonnet* and *English sonnet*. 4, 900

sound   The phonetics of language, separately and collectively considered. See also *prosody*. 841–45

speaker   The *narrator* of a *story* or *poem*, the *point of view,* often an independent *character* who is completely imagined and consistently maintained by the author. In addition to narrating the essential events of the work (justifying the status of *narrator*), the speaker may also introduce other aspects of his or her knowledge, and may express judgments and opinions. Often the character of the speaker is of as much interest in the story as the *actions* or *incidents*. 127

specific language   Words referring to objects or conditions that may be perceived or imagined; distinguished from *general language*. 653

speeches   See *dialogue*.

spondee   A two-syllable *foot* consisting of successive, equally stressed words or syllables (e.g., SLOW TIME, MEN'S EYES). 846

sprung rhythm or **accentual rhythm**   A method of accenting, developed by Gerard Manley Hopkins, in which major stresses are "sprung" from the poetic line, as in "DAP - ple - DAWN - DRAWN FALcon, in his RID - ing . . ." from "The Windhover." 849

stage business   See *business*.

stage convention   See *convention*.

stage directions   A playwright's instructions concerning *blocking*, movement, *action*, tone of voice, entrances and exits, *lighting*, *scenery*, and the like. 1204

stanza   A group of *poetic lines* corresponding to paragraphs in prose; stanzaic *meters* and *rhymes* are usually repeating and systematic. 856

stasimon (plural **stasima**)   A *choral ode* separating the *episodes* in Greek tragedies. Because of the word's derivation, it would seem that the chorus remained stationary in the orchestra and watched during

the episodes, and then stood before speaking or chanting its designated odes. 1280

static character   A character who undergoes no change, a *flat character*; contrasted with a *dynamic character*. 178

stereotype   A character who is so ordinary and unoriginal that he or she seems to have been cast in a mold; a *representative character*. 179, 1206

stichomythy   In ancient Greek drama, dialogue consisting of one-line speeches designed for rapid interchanges between characters. 1280

stock character   A *flat character* in a standard role with standard *traits*, such as the irate police captain, the bored hotel clerk, or the sadistic criminal; a *stereotype*. 179, 1206

story   A *narrative*, usually fictional, and short, centering on a major character, and rendering a complete action. 58

stress   The emphasis given to a syllable, either strong or light. See also *accent*. 844

strong-stress rhythm   See *heavy-stress rhyme* or *rising rhyme*.

structuralist critical approach   An interpretive literary approach that attempts to find relationships and similarities among elements that might originally appear to be separate and discrete. 1861

structure   The arrangement and placement of materials in a work. 61, 275–323, 374, 1207

style   The manipulation of language; the placement of words in the service of content. 324–74

subject   The topic that a literary work addresses, such as love, marriage, war, death, and social inequality. 1211

subplot   A secondary line of action in a literary work that often comments directly or obliquely on the main plot. See also *multiple plot*. 1207

substitution   A variant poetic *foot* within a poem in which a particular metrical foot is dominant. *Formal substitution* is the use of an actual variant foot within a line, such as an *anapest* being used in place of an *iamb*. *Rhetorical substitution* is the manipulation of the caesura to create the effect of a series of differing *feet*. 848

suspended rhyme   See *inexact rhyme.*

syllable   A separately pronounced part of a word (e.g., the *sing* and *ing* parts of "singing"; the *sub*, *sti*, *tu*, and *tion* parts of "substitution"). Some words consist of only one syllable (e.g., *a, an, man, girl, the, when, screeched*), and other words have many syllables (*antidisestablishmentarianism, Aldeborontiphoscophornio*). 843

symbol, symbolism   A specific word, idea, or object that may stand for ideas, values, persons, or ways of life. 68, 69, 375–431, 940–82, 1206, 1210

symbolic character   A character whose primary function is symbolic, even though the character also retains normal or *realistic* qualities. 1206

symbolic critical approach   See *archetypal approach.*

synecdoche   A *figure of speech* in which a part stands for a whole, or a whole for a part. 766

synesthesia   A *figure of speech* uniting or fusing separate sensations or feelings; the description of one type of perception or thought with words that are appropriate to another. 767

syntax   Word order and sentence structure. A mark of style is a writer's syntactical patterning (regular patterns and variations), depending on the rhetorical needs of the literary work. 656

syzygy   See *dipody.*

tactile imagery   *Images* of touch and responses to touch. 730

tenor (figure of speech)   The ideas conveyed in a *metaphor* or *simile.* See also *vehicle.* 763

tense   Besides embodying reports of actions and circumstances, verbs possess altering forms—*tenses*—that signify the times when things occur,

whether past, present, or future. Perfect and progressive tenses indicate completed or continuing activities. Tense is an important aspect of *point of view* because the notation of time influences the way in which events are perceived and expressed. Narratives are usually told in the past tense, but many recent writers of fiction prefer the present tense for conveying a sense of immediacy. No matter when a sequence of actions is presumed to have taken place, the introduction of *dialogue* changes the action to the present. See *point of view.* 134

tercet or **triplet**   A three-line unit or stanza of *poetry*, usually rhyming *a a a, b b b*, etc. 4, 899

terza rima   A three-line *stanza* form with the interlocking rhyming pattern *a b a, b c b, c d c*, etc. 899

tetrameter   A *line* of four metrical *feet.* 845

theater   In ancient Athens a theater was a "place for seeing." Today it is the name given to the building in which plays and other dramatic productions are performed. It is also a generic name for local or national drama in all its aspects, as in "Tonight we're going to the theater," and "This play is the best of the New York theater this year." 1212

Theater of Dionysus   The ancient Athenian outdoor amphitheater at the base of the Acropolis, where Greek drama began. 1276

theater-in-the-round   See *arena stage* and *platform stage.*

theme   (1) The major or central idea of a work. (2) An essay, a short composition developing an interpretation or advancing an argument. (3) The main point or idea that a writer of an essay asserts and illustrates. 61, 432, 1211

theos apo mechanes   See *deus ex machina.*

thesis sentence or **thesis statement**   An introductory sentence that names the topics and ideas to be developed in the body of an *essay.* 31

third-person objective point of view   See *dramatic point of view.*

third-person point of view   A third-person method of *narration* (i.e., *she, he, it, they, them*, etc.), in which the *speaker* or *narrator* is not a part of the story, unlike the involvement of the narrator of a *first-person point of view*. Because the third-person speaker may exhibit great knowledge and understanding, together with other qualities of *character*, he or she is often virtually identified with the author, but this identification is not easily decided. See also *authorial voice, omniscient point of view*. 133, 136

three unities   Traditionally associated with Aristotle's descriptions of drama as expressed in the *Poetics*, the three unities are those of action, place, and time. The unities are a function of *verisimilitude*—the creation of literary works that are as much like reality as possible. Therefore a play should dramatize a single major *action* that takes place in a single place during the approximate time it would take for completion, from beginning to end. During the Renaissance, some critics considered the unities to be essential aspects, or *rules*, of *regular drama*. Later critics considered the unity of action important, but minimized the unities of place and time. See also *regular play*. 1281

thrust stage   See *apron stage*.

tiring house   An enclosed area in an Elizabethan theater in which *actors* changed *costumes* and awaited their cues, and in which stage *properties* were kept. The word *tiring* is derived from *attire* (e.g., clothing or costumes). 1320

tone   The techniques and modes of presentation that reveal or create attitudes. 69, 324–74, 800–40, 1210

topic sentence   The sentence determining or introducing the subject matter of a paragraph. 32

topical/historical critical approach   An interpretive literary approach that stresses the relationship of literature to its historical period. 1856

tragedy   A drama or other literary work that recounts the fall or misfortune of an individual who, while undergoing suffering, deals responsibly with the situations and dilemmas that he or she faces, and who thus demonstrates the value of human effort and human existence. 1265–1495

tragic flaw   See *hamartia*.

tragicomedy   A literary work—*drama* or *story*—containing a mixture of *tragic* and *comic* elements. 1220

trait   A typical mode of behavior; the study of major traits provides a guide to the description of *character*. 173

trilogy   A group of three literary works, usually related or unified. For the ancient Athenian festivals of Dionysus, each competing tragic dramatist submitted a trilogy (three *tragedies*), together with a *satyr play*. 1268

trimeter   A line of three metrical *feet*, as in "To-DAY / I WENT / to SCHOOL." 845

triplet   See *tercet*.

trochaic (double) rhyme   Rhyming trochees such as *FLOWER* and *TOWER*. 846

trochee, trochaic   A two-syllable *foot* consisting of a heavy *stress* followed by a light stress (e.g., *RUN-ning, SING-ing, EAT-ing*). Sometimes called a *choree*. 846

trope   A short dramatic dialogue inserted into the church mass during the early Middle Ages. 1216

Tudor interlude   Tragedies, comedies, or historical plays performed by both professional actors and students during the reigns of Henry VII and Henry VIII (i.e., the first half of the sixteenth century). The Tudor interludes sometimes featured abstract and allegorical characters and provided opportunities for both music and farcical action. 1319

unaccented syllable   A syllable receiving a *light stress*. 844

unchanging character   See *flat character*.

understatement   A *figure of speech* by which details and ideas are deliberately underplayed or undervalued in order to create emphasis—a form of *irony*. 329, 768

unit set   A series of platforms, rooms, stairs, and exits that form the locations for all of a play's actions. A unit set enables scenes to be changed rapidly, without the drawing of a curtain and the placement of new sets. 1213

unities   See *three unities*.

universal (public) mythology   Widely known mythic systems that have been well established over a long period of time, such as Greco-Roman mythology and Germanic mythology. 987

universal symbol   See *cultural symbol*.

unreliable narrator   A speaker who through ignorance, self-interest, or lack of capacity may tell lies and distort details. Locating the truth in an unreliable narrator's story requires careful judgment and not inconsiderable skepticism. 132

unstressed syllable   See *light stress*.

value, values   The attachment of worth, significance, and desirability to an *idea* so that the idea is judged not only for its significance as thought but also for its importance as a goal, ideal, or standard. 433

vehicle   The image or reference of figures of speech, such as a *metaphor* or *simile*; it is the vehicle that carries or embodies the *tenor*. See also *tenor*. 763

verbal irony   Language stressing the importance of an idea by stating the opposite of what is meant. 69, 328, 805

verisimilitude (i.e., "like truth")   A characteristic whereby the *setting*, circumstances, *characters*, *dialogue*, *actions*, and outcomes in a work are designed to seem true, lifelike, real, plausible, and probable. See also *realism*. 179, 226

versification   See *prosody*.

villanelle   A *closed-form* poem of nineteen lines, composed of five *tercets* and a concluding *quatrain*. The form requires that whole lines be repeated in a specific order and that only two rhyming sounds occur throughout. See also *tercet*. 4, 900

virgule   A slash mark (/) used in poetic *scansion* to mark the boundaries of poetic *feet*. A double virgule (//) is commonly used to indicate the placement of a *caesura*. 845, 850

visual imagery   Language describing visible objects and situations. 727

visual poetry   Poetry written so that the lines form a recognizable shape, such as a pair of wings or a geometrical figure. Also called *concrete poetry* or *shaped verse*. 907, 909

voice   See *point of view* and *speaker*.

voiced and **voiceless sounds**   Consonants that are voiced are made with the full vibration of the vocal chords, as in *b*, *z* and *v*. Consonants that are voiceless are made without the use of the vocal chords, as in *p*, *s* and *f*. These two sets of consonants are formed identically, the only difference being that one set is *voiced* whereas the other is *voiceless*, or whispered. Normally, all vowels are voiced. 842

vowel rhyme   The use of nonrhyming vowel sounds in rhyming positions, as in *DAY* and *SKY*, or *KEY* and *PLAY*. 856

vowel sounds or **vowel segments**   Meaningful sounds produced by the continuant resonation of the voice in the space between the tongue and the top of the mouth, such as the *ee* in "feel," the *eh* in "bet," and the *oo* in "cool." 841

well-made play (*la pièce bien faite*)   A form developed and popularized in nineteenth-century France by Eugène Scribe (1791–1861) and Victorien Sardou (1831–1908). Typically, the well-made play is built on both secrets and the timely arrivals of new characters and threats. The protagonist faces adversity and ultimately overcomes it. Ibsen's *A Dollhouse* exhibits many characteristics of the well-made play. 1775

words   The spoken and written signifiers of thoughts, objects, and actions—the building blocks of language. 653–85

Credits

TEXT

Jack Agüeros, "Sonnet for You, Familiar Famine" is reprinted from SONNETS FROM THE PUERTO RICAN, © 1996 by Jack Agüeros, by permission of Hanging Loose Press.

Edward Albee, *The Sandbox*. Copyright © 1959, renewed 1987 by Edward Albee. Reprinted by permission of William Morris Agency, Inc. on behalf of the Author.

Brian Aldiss, "Flight 063." Copyright © 1984 by Brian W. Aldiss. First published in Isaac Asimov's Science Fiction Magazine in December 1984. Reprinted by permission of the Author and his agent, Robin Straus Agency, Inc., New York.

Maya Angelou, "My Arkansas" from AND STILL I RISE. Copyright © 1978 by Maya Angelou. Reprinted with the permission of Random House, Inc.

Margaret Atwood, "Variations on the Word 'Sleep'," from SELECTED POEMS II, 1976–1986 by Margaret Atwood. Copyright © 1987 by Margaret Atwood. Reprinted by permission of Houghton Mifflin Harcourt Publishing Company. All rights reserved.

W. H. Auden, "The Unknown Citizen," copyright 1940 and copyright renewed 1968 by W. H. Auden, from COLLECTED POEMS by W. H. Auden. Used by permission of Random House, Inc. "Musee des Beaux Arts" copyright 1940 and renewed © 1968 by W. H. Auden, from COLLECTED POEMS by W. H. Auden. Used by permission of Random House, Inc.

James Baldwin, "Sonny's Blues" © 1957 by James Baldwin was originally published in Partisan Review. Copyright renewed. Collected in GOING TO MEET THE MAN, published by Vintage Books. Reprinted by arrangement with the James Baldwin Estate.

Toni Cade Bambara, "The Lesson," copyright © 1972 by Toni Cade Bambara, from GORILLA, MY LOVE by Toni Cade Bambara. Used by permission of Random House, Inc.

Wendell Berry, "Another Descent" from COLLECTED POEMS: 1957–1982 by Wendell Berry. Copyright © 1985 by Wendell Berry. Reprinted by permission of North Point Press, a division of Farrar, Straus and Giroux, LLC.

Elizabeth Bishop, "The Fish" and "One Art" from COMPLETE POEMS: 1927–1979 by Elizabeth Bishop. Copyright © 1979, 1983 by Alice Helen Methfessell. Reprinted by permission of Farrar, Straus and Giroux, LLC.

Louise Bogan, "Women" from THE BLUE ESTUARIES: POEMS 1923–1968 by Louise Bogan. Copyright © 1968 by Louise Bogan. Copyright renewed 1996 by Ruth Limmer. Reprinted by permission of Farrar, Straus and Giroux, LLC.

Arna Bontemps, "A Black Man Talks of Reaping" from PERSONALS. Copyright © 1963 by Arna Bontemps. Reprinted with the permission of Harold Ober Associates, Incorporated.

Elizabeth Brewster, "Where I Come From" by Elizabeth Brewster is reprinted from SELECTED POEMS OF ELIZABETH BREWSTER, 1944–84 by permission of Oberon Press.

Gwendolyn Brooks, "We Real Cool" and "The Mother." Reprinted By Consent of Brooks Permissions.

Hayden Carruth, "An Apology for Using the Word 'Heart' in Too Many Poems" from COLLECTED SHORTER POEMS 1946–1991. Copyright © 1992 by Hayden Carruth. Reprinted with the permission of Copper Canyon Press, www.coppercanyonpress.org.

Jimmy Carter, "I Wanted to Share My Father's World" from ALWAYS A RECKONING AND OTHER POEMS by Jimmy Carter, copyright © 1995 by Jimmy Carter. Used by permission of Times Books, a division of Random House, Inc.

Raymond Carver, "Neighbors" from WILL YOU PLEASE BE QUIET, PLEASE. Copyright © 1989 by Tess Gallagher. Reprinted with the permission of International Creative Management, Inc. "Cathedral," from CATHEDRAL by Raymond Carver, copyright © 1981, 1982, 1983 by Raymond Carver. Used by permission of Alfred A. Knopf, a division of Random House, Inc.

John Chioles, "Before the Firing Squad" by John Chioles. Copyright 1983 by John Chioles; first printed in The Available Press/PEN Short Story Collection (Ballantine, 1985) by permission of the PEN Syndicated Fiction Project. Reprinted by permission of the author.

Sandra Cisneros, "The House on Mango Street" from THE HOUSE ON MANGO STREET. Copyright © 1984 by Sandra Cisneros. Published by Vintage Books, a division of Random House, Inc., New York and in hardcover by Alfred A. Knopf in 1994. Reprinted by permission of Susan Bergholz Literary Services, New York, NY. All rights reserved.

Amy Clampitt, "Beach Glass" from THE KINGFISHER by Amy Clampitt, copyright © 1983 by Amy Clampitt. Used by permission of Alfred A. Knopf, a division of Random House, Inc. "Berceuse," from THE KINGFISHER by Amy Clampitt. Copyright © 1983 by Amy Clampitt. Used by permission of Alfred A. Knopf, a division of Random House, Inc.

Lucille Clifton, "homage to my hips" copyright © 1999 by Lucille Clifton. First appeared in TWO-HEADED WOMAN, published by University of Massachusetts Press. Reprinted by permission of Curtis Brown, Ltd.

Leonard Cohen, "The Killers" from STRANGER MUSIC by Leonard Cohen © 1993. Published by McClelland & Stewart. Used with permission of the publisher.

Anita Scott Coleman, "Unfinished Masterpieces." The editor wishes to thank The Crisis Publishing Co., Inc., the publisher of the magazine of the National Association for the Advancement of Colored People, for authorizing the use of this work published in the March 1927 issue of *The Crisis*.

James Wright, "A Blessing" from THE BRANCH WILL NOT BREAK (Hanover, New Hampshire: Wesleyan University Press, 1963). Copyright © 1963 by James Wright. Reprinted with the permission of University Press of New England.

W. B. Yeats, "The Second Coming" is reprinted with the permission of Scribner, an imprint of Simon & Schuster Adult Publishing Group, from THE COLLECTED WORKS OF W. B. YEATS, VOLUME 1: THE POEMS, REVISED, edited by Richard J. Finneran. Copyright © 1924 by The Macmillan Company; copyright renewed © 1952 by Bertha Georgie Yeats. All rights reserved.

PHOTOS

5 Getty Images/Time Life Pictures; 65 King Features Syndicate; 66 Random House, Inc.; 71 Culver Pictures, Inc. 77 AP Wide World Photos; 89 Corbis/Bettmann; 95 Jerry Bauer; 105 Getty Images Inc./Hulton Archive Photos; 108 AP Wide World Photos; 114 AP Wide World Photos; 137 Marion Ettlinger; 140 Magnum Photos, Inc.; 146 Joyce Ravid; 150 Murdo McLeod; 174 National Gallery of Art, Washington, DC; 202 Getty Images Inc./Hulton Archive Photos; 205 Corbis/Bettmann; 213 Corbis/Bettmann; 228 AP Wide World Photos; 230 Getty Images Inc./Hulton Archive Photos; 253 Joanne Greenberg; 262 Corbis/Bettmann; 266 Raines and Raines; 278 Getty Images/Time Life Pictures; 287 Corbis/Bettmann; 300 Getty Images, Inc./Agence France Presse; 313 Corbis/NY; 331 Missouri Historical Society; 344 Corbis/Bettmann; 347 Jerry Bauer; 354 Dublin Writers Museum and Shaw Birthplace; 363 AP Wide World Photos; 380 Picture Desk, Inc./Kobal Collection; 385 Corbis/Bettmann; 393 The Granger Collection; 399 The Granger Collection; 400 AP Wide World Photos; 405 Corbis/Bettmann; 411 Corbis/Bettmann; 438 Getty Images Inc./Hulton Archive Photos; 457 Random House, Inc.; 471 Corbis/Bettmann; 482 Benson Latin American Collection; 493 Corbis/Bettmann; 543 John Chioles; 548 Corbis/Bettmann; 563 AP Wide World Photos; 566 Culver Pictures, Inc.; 576 AP Wide World Photos; - 586 Feminist Press; 591 Getty Images; 624 AP Wide World Photos; 638 Getty Images Inc./Hulton Archive Photos; 639 Corbis/Bettmann; 640 The Granger Collection; 642 James McGoon Photography; 661 Corbis/Bettmann; 662 Corbis/Bettmann; 663 The New York Public Library; 664 University of Pennsylvania; 665 Corbis/Bettmann; 666 Corbis/Bettmann; 667 Susan Cisco; 668 Library of Congress; 670 Corbis/Bettmann; 671 Corbis/Bettmann; 672 AP Wide World Photos; 675 Miller Library; 676 Bentley Historical Library; 677 Corbis/Bettmann; 678 Culver Pictures, Inc.; 694 Corbis/Bettmann; 697 Corbis/Bettmann; 699 Corbis/Bettmann; 700 AP Wide World Photos; 711 Library of Congress; 712 Art Resource/The British Museum Great Court Ltd.; 717 University of Pennsylvania; 734 Corbis/Bettmann; 735 Corbis/Bettmann; 740 Getty Images Inc./Hulton Archive Photos; 747 Corbis/Bettmann; 762 Corbis/Bettmann; 785 AP Photo; 786 Corbis/Bettmann; 790 Corbis/Bettmann; 811 Corbis/Bettmann; 822 Corbis/Bettmann; 824 Courtesy of the Library of Congress; 825 Hulton Archive/Getty Images; 830 The Granger Collection; 833 North Wind Picture Archives; 857 Corbis/Bettmann; 863 Corbis/Bettmann; 866 Corbis/Bettmann; 867 Corbis/Bettmann; 881 Photolibrary.com; 914 Corbis/Bettmann; 920 Nikki Giovanni; 930 Corbis/Bettmann; 931 Corbis/Bettmann; 932 Corbis/Bettmann; 961 Corbis/Bettmann; 966 Getty Images Inc./Hulton Archive Photos; 971 Lescher & Lescher Ltd.; 973 Corbis/Bettmann; 985 Center for Creative Photography; 993 Corbis/Bettmann; 998 Corbis/Bettmann; 1010 Corbis/Bettmann; 1011 Art Resource, NY; 1023 Amherst College Library; 1024 The Emily Dickinson Museum; 1058 Corbis/Bettmann; 1072 Getty Images Inc./Hulton Archive Photos; 1085 Corbis/Bettmann; 1143 Art Resource, NY; 1172 Corbis/Bettmann; 1224 Larry Riley/Miramax/Picture Desk, Inc./Kobal Collection; 1225 (top) © Universal International Pictures/Photofest; 1225 (bottom) Aurora Photos, Inc.; 1232 AP Wide World Photos; 1234 Art Resource/The New York Public Library for the Performing Arts; 1237 University of Alaska Fairbanks; 1245 Betty C. Keller; 1247 Meriwether Publishing Ltd.; 1249 Corbis/Bettmann; 1251 Roger Hanna; 1277 Art Resource, NY; 1278 Benaki Museum; 1281 Art Resource, NY; 1322 Stock Montage, Inc./Historical Pictures Collection; 1371 Photofest; 1407 Picture Desk, Inc./Kobal Collection; 1423 Art Resource/The New York Public Library for the Performing Arts; 1424 AP Wide World Photos; 1482 Photofest; 1560 Library of Congress; 1570 Photo courtesy LE NEON Theater, Arlington, VA; 1581 Corbis/Bettmann; 1591 Neal Preston/Corbis; 1593 Southern Methodist University; 1619 Getty Images Inc./Hulton Archive Photos; 1640 Art Resource/The New York Public Library Photographic Services; 1643 Art Resource/The New York Public Library Photographic Services; 1675 Photofest; 1692 Newscom; 1713 Photofest; 1759 Corbis/Bettmann; 1773 Corbis/Bettmann; 1819 Photofest; I-1 Art Renewal Center; I-2 Museum of Fine Arts, Boston; I-3 Art Resource, NY; I-4 (top) Art Resource/The Metropolitan Museum of Art; I-4 (bottom) Art Resource, NY; I-5 Art Resource, NY; I-6 (top) Des Moines Art Center; I-6 (bottom) Manchester City Art Galleries; I-7 Art Resource, NY; I-8 (top) Art Resource, NY; I-8 (bottom) Art Resource/Philadelphia Museum of Art/Artists Rights Society, Inc.; I-9 Art Resource, NY; I-10 Art Resource/The Metropolitan Museum of Art; I-11 Art Resource, NY; I-12 Art Resource, NY; I-13 Art Resource, NY; I-14 Art Resource, NY; I-15 (top) Michael Holford Photographs; I-15 (bottom) April E. Roberts; I-16 (top) April E. Roberts; I-16 (bottom) April E. Roberts.

Index of Authors, Titles, and First Lines

The names of authors are printed in **bold type**, *titles in italic type*, and first lines in Roman type.

A & P, 363
A balloon of gauze around us, 710
A doe stands at the roadside, 941
A noiseless patient spider, 972
A poem should be palpable and
   mute, 1152
A speck that would have been beneath my
   sight, 1071
A sudden blow; the great wings beating still,
   988
A.U.C. 334: about this date, 1138
Abortions will not let you forget, 634
About suffering they were never
   wrong, 998
According to Brueghel, 1002
Acquainted with the Night, 1069
Advice to Young Ladies, 1138
Æ (George William Russell)
   Continuity, 929
Aesop
   The Fox and the Grapes, 380
After great pain, a formal feeling
   comes –, 1029
After Great Pain, a Formal Feeling Comes, 1029
After Making Love We Hear Footsteps, 1144
After the storm, after the rain stopped pound-
   ing, 1188
Agüeros, Jack
   Sonnet for You, Familiar Famine, 768
Albee, Edward
   The Sandbox, 1224
Aldiss, Brian
   Flight 063, 997
Alive Together, 629
All crying, "We will go with you,
   O Wind!," 1069
All over America, 1133
All we need is fourteen lines, well,
   thirteen now, 917
Always the setting forth was the same, 992
Always too eager for the future,
   we, 966
Am I Blue, 1592
And another regrettable thing about
   death, 1183
And Sarah Laughed, 253

Angelou, Maya
   My Arkansas, 1106
Annabel Lee, 869
Anne Bradstreet
   To My Dear and Loving Husband, 1111
Anonymous
   Bonny George Campbell, 687
Anonymous (Navajo)
   *Healing Prayer from the Beautyway
      Chant*, 1106
Anonymous
   Lord Randal, 1107
Anonymous
   The Myth of Atalanta, 381
Anonymous
   Sir Patrick Spens, 631
Anonymous (twentieth century)
   Spun in High, Dark Clouds, 903
Anonymous
   *The Visit to the Sepulcher (The Quem Quaeritis
      Trope)*, 1217
Anonymous
   Western Wind, 687
Another Descent, 1109
Answer, The, 1141
Anthem for Doomed Youth, 729
*Apology for Using the Word "Heart" in Too Many
   Poems, An*, 644
April 5, 1974, 1192
Araby, 262
Are ligneous, muscular, chemical, 669
Ariel, 1090
Arnold, Matthew
   Dover Beach, 694
Ars Poetica, 1152
*Arthur: Idylls of the King: The Passing of Arthur
   (lines 344–93)*, 881
As virtuous men pass mildly away, 771
Atalanta: The Myth of Atalanta, 381
At a Summer Hotel, 863
Atwood, Margaret
   Variation on the Word Sleep, 1106
Auden, W. H.
   Musée des Beaux Arts, 996
   The Unknown Citizen, 1109
Auschwitz, 825

Auto Wreck, 1176
Autumn: To Autumn (Keats), 778

Back in a yard where ringers groove a ditch, 965
Bad Man, 1076
Bagel, The, 818
Baldwin, James, *Sonny's Blues*, 438
Ballad of Birmingham, 927
Bambara, Toni Cade
 The Lesson, 457
Barn Burning, 333
Bartholdi Statue, The, 1192
Batter my heart, three–personed God;
 for You, 666
Battle Royal, 278
Beach Glass, 950
Bear, The (Chekhov), 1581
Bear, The (Momaday), 1155
Beat! Beat! Drums!, 1189
Beat! beat! drums!—blow! bugles!
 blow!, 1189
Beauty of the Trees, The, 1130
Because I Could Not Stop for Death, 635
Because I could not stop for Death –, 635
Before Breakfast, 1248
Before the Firing Squad, 543
Behold her, single in the field, 832
Bells, The, 870
Bells for John Whiteside's Daughter, 1166
Bent double, like old beggars under sacks, 802
Berceuse, 1009
Berry, Wendell
 Another Descent, 1109
Bierce, Ambrose
 An Occurrence at Owl Creek Bridge, 71
Birches, 1066
Bishop, Elizabeth
 The Fish, 730
 One Art, 916
"Bist du Jude? Bist du Jude?" the SS, 1182
Black Cat, The, 513
Black Man Talks of Reaping, A, 1110
Blackness, 1111
Black reapers with the sound of steel
 on stones, 931
Blake, William
 The Lamb, 661
 London, 695
 On Another's Sorrow, 809
 The Tyger, 769
Blessing, A, 717
Blue Winds Dancing, 313
Blurry Cow, 1183
Body my house, 1180
Bogan, Louise
 Women, 1110
Bonny George Campbell, 687
Bontemps, Arna
 A Black Man Talks of Reaping, 1110
Boxes, The, 1185
Bradstreet, Anne
 To My Dear and Loving Husband, 1111

Brewster, Elizabeth
 Where I come from, 696
Bright star! would I were steadfast as
 thou art—, 765
Bright Star, 765
Brontë, Emily
 No Coward Soul Is Mine, 948
Brooks, Gwendolyn
 The Mother, 634
 Primer for Blacks, 1111
 We Real Cool, 857
Browning, Elizabeth Barrett
 Sonnets from the Portuguese, No. 14:
  If Thou Must Love Me, 733
 Sonnets from the Portuguese, No. 43: How Do I
  Love Thee?, 1113
Browning, Robert
 My Last Duchess, 697
 Porphyria's Lover, 858
 Soliloquy of the Spanish Cloister, 1113
Bryant, William Cullen
 To Cole, the Painter, Departing for
  Europe, 1115
Buffalo (Buffalo), 744
Buffalo Bill's Defunct, 908
Buffalo Bill's, 908
Burns, Robert
 A Red, Red Rose, 770
 Green Grow the Rashes, O, 662
Burying an Animal on the Way to New York, 1179
Bustle in a House, The, 1030
Busy old fool, unruly Sun, 860
But, as he walked, King Arthur panted
 hard, 881
By the roots of my hair some god got hold
 of me, 1096
By the rude bridge that arched the
 flood, 863
Byron: George Gordon, Lord Byron
 She Walks in Beauty, 1116
 The Destruction of Sennacherib, 1116

Call the roller of big cigars, 1180
Called, 1135
Can I see another's woe, 809
Canonization, The, 952
Cargoes, 728
Carroll, Lewis
 Jabberwocky, 663
Carruth, Hayden
 An Apology for Using the Word "Heart"
  in Too Many Poems, 664
Carter, Jimmy
 I Wanted to Share My Father's World, 810
Carver, Raymond
 Cathedral, 180
 Neighbors, 137
Cask of Amontillado, The, 519
Catch, 636
Cathedral, 180
Celestial Music, 956
Channel Firing, 738

Chekhov, Anton
  The Bear, 1586
  The Lady with the Dog, 462
Chemistry Experiment, 667
Chicago, 1172
Chief Dan George
  The Beauty of the Trees, 1130
childhood remembrances are always a drag, 920
Chioles, John
  Before the Firing Squad, 543
Choose [Take] Something like a Star, 1072
Choosing, The, 1148
Chopin, Kate
  The Story of an Hour, 331
Christmas Carol, A, 712
Chrysanthemums, The, 411
Cisneros, Sandra
  The House on Mango Street, 228
Citizen Kane (Shot 71 of Citizen Kane), 1756
Clampitt, Amy
  Beach Glass, 949
  Berceuse, 1009
Clifton, Lucille
  homage to my hips, 811
Clough, Arthur Hugh
  *Say Not the Struggle Nought
    Availeth,* 950
Cohen, Leonard
  'The killers that run . . .', 1117
Coleman, Anita Scott
  Unfinished Masterpieces, 382
Coleridge, Samuel Taylor
  Kubla Khan, 734
Collage of Echoes, 955
Collar, The, 959
Collins, Billy
  Days, 1118
  The Names, 812
  Schoolsville, 624
  Sonnet, 917
Colonel, The, 915
*Colossians III.3 (Our Life Is Hid with Christ
    in God),* 909
Colossus, The, 1091
Come, live with me and be my love
    (Ginsberg), 699
Come live with me and be my love
    (Lewis), 707
Come live with me and be my love
    (Marlowe), 709
Come to me in the silence of the night, 877
Come to me, Pan, with your wind-wild
    laughter, 1015
Concord Hymn, 863
Conjoined, 783
Conrad, Joseph
  The Secret Sharer, 253
Consider Icarus, pasting those sticky
    wings on, 1001
Considerable Speck, A, 1071
Continuity, 929
Convergence of the Twain, The, 775

Cornford, Frances
  *From a Letter to America on a Visit to
    Sussex: Spring, 1942,* 1118
Cousins, The, 150
Cowper, William
  The Poplar Field, 699
Crane, Stephen
  The Open Boat, 548
  *Do Not Weep, Maiden, for War Is
    Kind,* 1119
Crazy, he stumbles, flops, gets up, and trudges
    on again, 748
Creeley, Robert
  "Do you think . . .", 1120
Cross, 1077
Cummings, E. E.
  Buffalo Bill's Defunct, 908
  if there are any heavens, 1121
  in Just-, 1014
  next to of course god america i, 665
  she being Brand / -new, 813
Curse, The, 563
Cut, 1092

Daddy, 1093
*Daffodils (I Wandered Lonely as
    a Cloud),* 678
Dance, The, 932
Delphi, 951
Danticat, Edwidge
  Night Talkers, 77
Davison, Peter
  Day Zimmer Lost Religion, The, 1194
Day-Long Day, 1184
Days, 1118
Dead in There, 1077
Dear Tia, 1140
Death of a Salesman, 1424
Death of the Ball Turret Gunner, The, 639
Death Be Not Proud (Holy Sonnet 10), 1123
Death, be not proud, though some have callèd
    thee, 1123
Delphi, 951
Dennis, Carl
  The God Who Loves You, 1121
Description of the Morning, A, 830
Desert Places, 918
Design, 1070
Desire, 1163
Destruction of Sennacherib, The, 1116
Dickinson, Emily
  After Great Pain, a Formal Feeling Comes, 1029
  Because I Could Not Stop for Death, 635
  The Bustle in a House, 1030
  The Heart Is the Capital of the Mind, 1030
  I Cannot Live with You, 1030
  I Died for Beauty – but Was Scarce, 1031
  I Dwell in Possibility, 1032
  I Felt a Funeral in My Brain, 1032
  I Heard a Fly Buzz – When I Died, 1033
  I Like to See It Lap the Miles, 1033
  I'm Nobody! Who Are You?, 1033

I Never Lost as Much But Twice, 1034
I Taste a Liquor Never Brewed, 1034
Much Madness Is Divinest Sense, 1034
My Life Closed Twice Before Its Close, 1035
My Triumph Lasted Till the Drums, 1035
One Need Not Be a Chamber – To Be Haunted, 1035
Safe in Their Alabaster Chambers, 1036
Some Keep the Sabbath Going to Church, 1036
The Soul Selects Her Own Society, 1037
Success Is Counted Sweetest, 1037
Tell All the Truth but Tell It Slant, 1037
There's a Certain Slant of Light, 1037
To Hear an Oriole Sing, 859
Wild Nights – Wild Nights!, 1038
Didja ever hear a sound, 1158
Digging the grave, 1135
Dimensions, 831
Dirge for Two Veterans, 1190
Disillusionment of Ten O'Clock, 677
Diving Into the Wreck, 1167
Doctor, you say there are no halos, 1156
Do Not Go Gentle Into That Good Night, 930
Do not go gentle into that good night, 930
Do Not Weep, Maiden, for War Is Kind, 1119
Do not weep, maiden, for war is kind, 1119
Do you know what I was, how I lived? You know, 700
"Do you think . . .", 1120
Do you think that if, 1120
Dollhouse, A, 1775
Dolor, 676
Donne, John
   The Canonization, 952
   The Good Morrow, 1122
   Holy Sonnet 10: Death Be Not Proud, 1123
   Holy Sonnet 14: Batter My Heart, Three–Person-ed God, 666
   A Hymn to God the Father, 1123
   The Sun Rising, 860
   A Valediction: Forbidding Mourning, 771
Don't flinch when you come across a dead animal lying on the road, 1179
Dover Beach, 694
Dreamers, 1172
Dream On, 750
Dream Variations, 1078
Dressing for work, 1174
Drink to Me, Only, with Thine Eyes, 689
Drink to me, only, with thine eyes, 689
Droning a drowsy syncopated tune, 1084
Dryden, John
   A Song for St. Cecilia's Day, 772
   To the Memory of Mr. Oldham, 918
Dubus, Andre
   The Curse, 563
Dulce et Decorum Est, 802
Dunbar, Paul Laurence
   Sympathy, 1124
Dunn, Stephen
   Hawk, 954

Dusk, 912
Dying, 823

Each one *is* a gift, no doubt, 1118
Eagle Poem, 638
Eagle, The, 899
Earth Tremors Felt in Missouri, 789
Easter Wings, 910
Eating Poetry, 677
Eberhart, Richard
   The Fury of Aerial Bombardment, 667
Echo, 877
Edelman, Bart
   Chemistry Experiment, 667
   Trouble, 814
Edge, 1095
Elegy Written in a Country Churchyard, 701
Eliot, T. S.
   The Love Song of J. Alfred Prufrock, 1124
   Macavity: The Mystery Cat, 861
   Preludes, 735
Elizabeth: Queen Elizabeth I
   On Monsieur's Departure, 788
Ellison, Ralph
   Battle Royal, 278
Emanuel, James
   The Negro, 1128
Emanuel, Lynn
   Like God, 1128
Emerson, Ralph Waldo
   Concord Hymn, 863
English Horn (Corno Inglese), 672
Emperor of Ice Cream, The, 1180
Epigram from the French, 807
Epigram, Engraved on the Collar of a Dog which I gave to his Royal Highness, 808
Epilogue to the Satires (Pope): From *Epilogue to the Satires, Dialogue I, Lines 137–72*, 824
Essay on Man (Pope): From *An Essay on Man, Epistle I, lines 17–90*, 873
Ethics, 1162
Evans, Abbie Huston
   The Iceberg Seven-eighths Under, 774
Evans, Mari
   I Am a Black Woman, 815
Every Day You Play, 746
Every day you play with the light of the universe, 746
Every Traveler Has One Vermont Poem, 1149
Everyday Use, 108
Everything pointed to trouble, 814

Face like a chocolate bar, 1082
Facing It, 819
Facing West from California's Shores, 790
Facing west from California's shores, 790
Fall of the House of Usher, The, 499
Far from the Vistula, along the northern plain, 825
Farewell, too little and too lately known, 918
Farrar, John Chipman
   Song for a Forgotten Shrine to Pan, 1015

Faulkner, William
  Barn Burning, 333
  A Rose for Emily, 89
Fences, 1695
Field, Edward
  Icarus, 999
Fifteen miles, 1170
Final Thing, A, 1146
Fire and Ice, 1068
First Confession, 354
First having read the book of
    myths, 1167
First-Rate Wife, The, 801
Fish, The (Bishop), 730
Fish, The (Moore), 745
Five years have past; five summers, with the
    length, 714
Flight 063, 997
For Godsake hold your tongue, and let me love,
    952
For I can snore like a bullhorn, 1144
For me, the naked and the nude, 660
Forced March, 748
Forché, Carolyn
The Colonel, 915
Found Boat, The, 347
Fox and the Grapes, The, 380
Francis, Robert
  Catch, 636
*From a Letter to America on a Visit to Sussex:
    Spring, 1942*, 1118
From *An Essay on Man, Epistle I, lines 17–90*, 873
From *Epilogue to the Satires, Dialogue I, Lines
    137–72*, 824
From harmony, from heavenly harmony, 772
From my mother's sleep I fell into the
    State, 639
Frost, Robert
  Acquainted with the Night, 1069
  Birches, 1066
  A Considerable Speck, 1071
  Desert Places, 918
  Design, 1070
  Fire and Ice, 1068
  The Gift Outright, 1071
  Mending Wall, 1065
  Misgiving, 1069
  Nothing Gold Can Stay, 1069
  "Out, Out—", 1067
  The Oven Bird, 1068
  Pan With Us, 1015
  The Road Not Taken, 1067
  The Silken Tent, 1070
  *Stopping by Woods on a Snowy
    Evening*, 637
  *Take [Choose] Something like a
    Star*, 1072
  The Tuft of Flowers, 1063
Full of Life Now, 1191
Full of life now, compact, visible, 1191
Further Proposal, A, 699
Fury of Aerial Bombardment, The, 667

García Márquez, Gabriel
  *A Very Old Man with Enormous
    Wings*, 401
Gardner, Isabella
  At a Summer Hotel, 863
  Collage of Echoes, 955
Gather ye rosebuds while ye may, 1137
Gay, John
  Let Us Take the Road, 767
Geese, The, 957
Georgakis, Dan
  Hiroshima Crewman, 955
George, Chief Dan
  The Beauty of the Trees, 1130
George Washington, 865
Ghosts, 1159
Gift Outright, The, 1071
Gilman, Charlotte Perkins
  The Yellow Wallpaper, 567
Ginsberg, Allen
  A Further Proposal, 699
  A Supermarket in California, 919
Giovanni, Nikki
  Nikki-Rosa, 920
  Poetry, 1131
  Woman, 1130
Glancing over my shoulder at the
    past, 624
Glaspell, Susan
  A Jury of Her Peers, 189
  Trifles, 1233
Glass Menagerie, The, 1643
Glory be to God for dappled things—, 1139
Glück, Louise
  Celestial Music, 956
  Penelope's Song, 991
  Snowdrops, 700
Go, Lovely Rose, 1187
Go, lovely rose!, 1187
God's Grandeur, 864
God Who Loves You, The, 1121
Good Man Is Hard to Find, A, 576
Good Morrow, The, 1122
Graham, Jorie
  The Geese, 957
*Granny Weatherall: The Jilting of Granny
    Weatherall*, 405
Graves, Robert
  The Naked and the Nude, 660
Gray, Thomas
  Elegy Written in a Country Churchyard, 701
  Sonnet on the Death of Richard West, 668
Grecian Urn: Ode on a Grecian Urn
    (Keats), 1142
Green Grow the Rashes, O, 662
Greenberg, Joanne
  And Sarah Laughed, 253
Griffin, Susan
  *Love Should Grow up like a Wild Iris in the
    Fields*, 737
G–r–r—there go, my heart's
    abhorrence!, 1113

Gusting, a sweet inferno channeled, 744
The gutteral stammer of the chopper
    blades, 751

Hacker, Marilyn
    *Sonnet Ending with a Film
        Subtitle*, 1132
Had he and I but met, 637
Had we but world enough, and time, 968
Hair, The: Jacob Korman's Story, 1138
Halpern, Daniel
    Snapshot of Hué, 1132
    Summer in the Middle Class, 1133
Hamlet, 1322
Hammon and the Beans, The, 482
Hamod, H. S. (Sam)
    Leaves, 1134
Hanging Man, The, 1096
Hardy, Thomas
    Channel Firing, 738
    In Time of "The Breaking of Nations," 958
    The Convergence of the Twain, 775
    The Man He Killed, 637
    The Ruined Maid, 704
    The Three Strangers, 287
    The Workbox, 805
Harjo, Joy
    Eagle Poem, 638
    Remember, 777
Harlem, 1078
Harper, Frances E. W.
    She's Free!, 1135
Harper, Michael S.
    Called, 1135
Hass, Robert
    Museum, 921
    Spring Rain, 1136
Have you noticed?, 1159
Hawk, 954
Hawthorne, Nathaniel
    Young Goodman Brown, 385
Hayden, Robert
    Those Winter Sundays, 1137
He clasps the crag with crooked hands, 899
He jumped me while I was asleep, 1167
He might compare you to a summer's day, 971
He said he would be back and we'd drink wine
    together, 1000
He tried to convince us, but his billiard ball, 830
He was found by the Bureau of Statistics to be,
    1109
Healing Prayer from the Beautyway Chant, 1106
Heaney, Seamus
    Mid-Term Break, 817
Hear the sledges with the bells—, 870
Heart Is the Capital of the Mind, The, 1030
Hemingway, Ernest
    Hills Like White Elephants, 344
Henley, Beth
    Am I Blue, 1591
Henley, William Ernest
    When You Are Old, 817

Herbert, George
    The Collar, 959
    *Colossians III.3 (Our Life Is Hid with Christ in
        God)*, 909
    The Pulley, 740
    Easter Wings, 910
    Virtue, 922
Here a Pretty Baby Lies, 627
Here a pretty baby lies, 627
Here lies, to each her parents' ruth, 640
Herrick, Robert
    Here a Pretty Baby Lies, 627
    To the Virgins, to Make Much of Time,
        1137
    Upon Julia's Voice, 864
He's a *boom a blat* in the uniform, 882
Heyen, William
    The Hair: Jacob Korman's Story, 1138
    Mantle, 913
High upon Highlands, 687
Hills Like White Elephants, 344
Hiroshima Crewman, 955
Hirsch, Edward
    The Swimmers, 1004
Hirshfield, Jane
    The Lives of the Heart, 669
Hog Butcher for the World, 1171
Hollander, John
    Swan and Shadow, 912
*Holy Sonnet 10: Death Be Not
    Proud*, 1123
*Holy Sonnet 14: Batter My Heart, Three-
    Personed God*, 666
homage to my hips, 811
Homes where children live exude a
    pleasant rumpledness, 642
Hope, 626
Hope, A. D.
    Advice to Young Ladies, 1138
Hopkins, Gerard Manley
    God's Grandeur, 864
    Pied Beauty, 1139
    Spring, 740
    The Windhover, 1140
Horse Dealer's Daughter, The, 472
Hospital, Carolina
    Dear Tia, 1140
House on Mango Street, The, 228
Housman, A. E.
    Loveliest of Trees, 670
    On Wenlock Edge, 741
How do I love thee? Let me count the
    ways, 1113
How say that by law we may torture and
    chase, 1135
How simply violent things, 1118
How to Become a Writer, 146
Hughes, Langston
    Bad Man, 1076
    Cross, 1077
    Dead in There, 1077
    Dream Variations, 1078

Hughes, Langston (*continued*)
  Harlem, 1078
  Let America Be America Again, 1078
  Madam And Her Madam, 1080
  Mulatto, 1619
  Negro, 1081
  The Negro Speaks of Rivers, 1082
  125th Street, 1082
  Po' Boy Blues, 1082
  Silhouette, 1083
  Subway Rush Hour, 1083
  Theme for English B, 1083
  The Weary Blues, 1084
Hunger Artist, A, 393
Hunting the Phoenix, 1009
Hymn to God the Father, A, 1123

I, 1169
I Am a Black Woman, 815
I am a black woman, 815
I am a Negro, 1081
I am here with my bountiful womanful
    child, 863
I am his Highness' dog at Kew, 808
I am silver and exact. I have no
    preconceptions, 1099
I am sorry to speak of death again, 931
I am that last, that, 1146
I battled Trojans with Odysseus, 996
I cannot live with You –, 1030
I Cannot Live with You, 1030
I caught a tremendous fish, 730
I caught this morning morning's minion,
    king-, 1140
I climb the black rock mountain, 1176
I Died for Beauty – but Was Scarce, 1031
I died for Beauty – but was scarce, 1031
I do not want a plain box, I want a
    sarcophagus, 1098
I do not write, 1140
I dwell in Possibility –, 1032
I Dwell in Possibility, 1032
I Felt a Funeral in My Brain, 1032
I felt a Funeral in my Brain, 1032
I Find No Peace, 791
I find no peace, and all my war is done, 791
I found a dimpled spider, fat and
    white, 1070
I grieve and dare not show my
    discontent, 788
I hated the fact that they had planned me, she
    had taken, 822
I have a friend who still believes in
    heaven, 956
I have a rendezvous with Death, 1173
I Have a Rendezvous with Death, 1173
I have been one acquainted with the
    night, 1069
I have done it again, 1096
I have known the inexorable sadness of
    pencils, 676
I have no promises to keep, 955

I have sown beside all waters in my day, 1110
I Hear America Singing, 1191
I hear America singing, the varied carols I
    hear, 1191
I Heard a Fly Buzz – When I Died, 1030
I heard a Fly buzz – when I died –, 1030
I know this happiness, 672
I know what the caged bird feels,
    alas!, 1124
I like to see it lap the Miles –, 1133
I Like to See It Lap the Miles, 1133
I met a traveller from an antique land, 929
I'm a bad, bad man, 1076
I'm a riddle in nine syllables, 1099
I'm Nobody! Who Are You?, 1033
I'm Nobody! Who are you?, 1033
I Never Lost as Much But Twice, 1034
I never lost as much but twice, 1034
I sat all morning in the college sick
    bay, 817
I shall never get you put together entirely, 1091
I Stand Here Ironing, 586
I stopped to pick up the bagel, 818
I struck the board, and cry'd, "No more;, 959
I taste a liquor never brewed –, 1034
I Taste a Liquor Never Brewed, 1034
*I Think Continually of Those Who Were Truly
    Great*, 676
I think continually of those who were truly
    great, 676
I, too, dislike it: there are things that are impor-
    tant beyond all this fiddle, 1155
I've known rivers, 1082
I wake to sleep, and take my waking
    slow, 928
I walk down the garden paths, 1149
I wander thro' each charter'd street, 695
I wandered lonely as a cloud, 678
I want you to know, 784
I Wanted to Share My Father's World, 810
I was born in war, WW Two, 642
I went to turn the grass once after one, 1063
I will not toy with it nor bend an inch, 1153
I worked for a woman, 1080
I wonder, by my troth, what thou and I, 1122
I would be wandering in distant fields, 925
I would like to watch you sleeping, 1108
Ibsen, Henrik
  A Dollhouse (Et Dukkehjem), 1777
Icarus (Field), 999
Iceberg Seven–eighths Under, The, 774
Idylls of the King: The Passing of Arthur (lines
    344–93), 881
If all the world and love were young, 711
If ever two were one, then surely we, 1111
If the moon smiled, she would resemble
    you, 1100
if there are any heavens my mother will (all by
    herself) have, 1121
if there are any heavens, 1121
If Thou Must Love Me, 733
If thou must love me, let it be for nought, 733

If You Forget Me, 784
If you love for the sake of beauty, O never love me!, 749
If You Love for the Sake of Beauty, 749
Ignatow, David
   The Bagel, 818
In a Farmhouse, 1170
In a solitude of the sea, 775
In a Station of the Metro, 747
In Bondage, 925
In Brueghel's great picture, The Kermess, 925
In Computers, 1147
In ethics class so many years ago, 1162
in Just-, 1014
in Just-, 1014
In New York we defy, 967
In the bleak mid-winter, 712
In the magnets of computers will, 1147
In the pathway of the sun, 993
In Time of "The Breaking of Nations," 958
In vain to me the smiling mornings shine, 668
In Xanadu did Kubla Khan, 734
Ingham, John Hall
   George Washington, 865
Ink runs from the corners of my mouth, 677
It doesn't speak and it isn't schooled, 1163
It hovers in dark corners, 626
It is true love because, 1185
It little profits that an idle king, 994
It must be troubling for the god who loves you, 1121
It was an adventure much could be made of: a walk, 1005
It was many and many a year ago, 869
Its quick soft silver bell beating, beating, 1175
*"It's Only Rock and Roll, But I Like It":
   The Fall of Saigon*, 751

Jabberwocky, 663
Jackson, Shirley
   The Lottery, 140
Jacobsen, Josephine
   Tears, 960
Jarrell, Randall
   The Death of the Ball Turret Gunner, 639
Jeffers, Robinson
   The Answer, 1141
   The Purse-Seine, 961
Jilting of Granny Weatherall, The, 405
Jonson, Ben
   Drink to Me, Only, with Thine Eyes, 689
   On My First Daughter (Epigram 22), 640
   To the Reader, 690
Joyce, James
   Araby, 262
Jury of Her Peers, A, 189
Just off the highway to Rochester, Minnesota, 717
Justice, Donald
   On the Death of Friends in Childhood, 1141

Kafka, Franz
   A Hunger Artist, 393

Keats, John
   Bright Star, 765
   La Belle Dame Sans Merci: A Ballad, 963
   Ode on a Grecian Urn, 1142
   Ode to a Nightingale, 923
   *On First Looking into Chapman's
      Homer*, 762
   To Autumn, 778
Keller, Betty
   Tea Party, 1244
Kennedy, X. J.
   Old Men Pitching Horseshoes, 965
Kenny, Maurice
   Legacy, 779
Kenyon, Jane
   Let Evening Come, 780
"killers that run . . . , The," 1117
Kincaid, Jamaica
   What I Have Been Doing Lately, 300
King, Henry
   Sic Vita, 781
Kinnell, Galway
   After Making Love We Hear Footsteps, 1144
Kizer, Carolyn
   Night Sounds, 671
Komunyakaa, Yusef
   Facing It, 819
Kooser, Ted
   Year's End, 973
Kubla Khan, 734

La Belle Dame Sans Merci: A Ballad, 963
La Migra, 821
Lady Lazarus, 1096
Lady with the Dog, The, 462
Lamb, The, 661
Landscape with the Fall of Icarus, 1002
Larkin, Philip
   Next, Please, 966
Larson, Katherine
   Statuary, 1144
Last Words, 1098
Latin Women Pray, 673
Latin women pray, 673
Laurents, Arthur
   A Scene from *The Turning Point*, 1761
Laux, Dorianne
   The Life of Trees, 705
Lawrence, D. H.
   The Horse Dealer's Daughter, 472
Layton, Irving
   Rhine Boat Trip, 1145
Lazarus, Emma
   The New Colossus, 640
Leaf through discolored manuscripts, 1009
Leaves, 1134
Leda, 989
Leda and the Swan, 988
Lee, Li-Young
   A Final Thing, 1146
Legacy, 779

Lehman, David
  Venice Is Sinking, 967
Lesson, The, 457
Let America Be America Again, 1078
Let America be America again, 1078
Let Evening Come, 780
Let me not to the marriage of true minds, 904
Let's play *La Migra*, 821
Let the light of late afternoon, 780
Let us go then, you and I, 735
Let Us Take the Road, 767
Let us take the road, 767
Letter Sent to Summer, A, 713
Letter to America on a Visit to Sussex: Spring, 1942, A, 1118
Levertov, Denise
  A Time Past, 742
  Hunting the Phoenix, 1009
  Of Being, 672
Levine, Philip
  A Theory of Prosody, 866
Lewis, C. Day
  Song, 707
Life Cycle of Common Man, 1157
Life has its nauseating ironies, 1132
Life of Trees, The, 705
Lightman, Alan P.
  In Computers, 1147
Like God, 1128
Like to the falling of a star, 781
Lines (McHugh), 1153
Lines Composed a Few Miles above Tintern Abbey, 714
Lincoln, Abraham
  My Childhood's Home, 820
Listen to Gieseking playing a Berceuse, 1010
Listen, 1154
Listen, 1154
Little Lamb, who made thee?, 661
Little soul, little perpetually undressed one, 991
Lives of the Heart, The, 669
Lochhead, Liz
  The Choosing, 1148
London, 1802 (Wordsworth), 795
London (Blake), 695
Long afterward, Oedipus, old and blinded, walked the, 1012
Longfellow, William Wadsworth
  The Sound of the Sea, 866
Looking at Each Other, 786
Lord Randal, 1107
Lord, who createdst man in wealth and store, 910
Lorde, Audre
  Every Traveler Has One Vermont Poem, 1149
Lottery, The, 140
Love Is the Doctor (L'Amour Médecin), 1563
Love Should Grow up like a Wild Iris in the Fields, 737
Love should grow up like a wild iris in the fields, 737
Love Song of J. Alfred Prufrock, The, 1124

Loveliest of Trees, 670
Loveliest of trees, the cherry now, 670
Loving, 710
Lowell, Amy
  Patterns, 1149
Lowell, Robert
  Memories of West Street and Lepke, 707
  Skunk Hour, 781
Luck, 213
Luke (St. Luke)
  The Parable of the Prodigal Son, 399
Lux, Thomas
  The Voice You Hear when You Read Silently, 743
Lycidas (first 24 lines), 902

Macavity: The Mystery Cat, 861
Macavity's a Mystery Cat: he's called the Hidden Paw—, 861
MacLeish, Archibald
  Ars Poetica, 1152
MacNeice, Louis
  Snow, 641
Madam and Her Madam, 1080
Man He Killed, The, 637
Mankiewicz, Herman J., and Orson Welles
  Shot 71 from the Shooting Script of Citizen Kane, 1757
Mansfield, Katherine
  Miss Brill, 202
Mantle ran so hard, they said, 913
Mantle, 913
March, 875
March for a One-Man Band, 882
Marks, 1162
Marlowe, Christopher
  The Passionate Shepherd to His Love, 709
Marvell, Andrew
  To His Coy Mistress, 968
Masefield, John
  Cargoes, 728
Masque of the Red Death, The, 510
Maupassant, Guy de
  The Necklace, 5
McHugh, Heather
  Lines, 1153
McKay, Claude
  In Bondage, 925
  The White City, 1153
Melville, Herman
  Shiloh: A Requiem, 867
Memories of West Street and Lepke, 707
Mending Wall, 1065
Merwin, W. S.
  Listen, 1154
  Odysseus, 992
Metaphors, 1099
Midsummer Night's Dream, A, 1504
Mid-Term Break, 817
Millay, Edna St. Vincent
  What Lips My Lips Have Kissed, and Where, and Why, 1154
Miller, Arthur
  Death of a Salesman, 1424

Milton, John
  Lycidas (first 24 lines), 902
  On His Blindness, 926
Milton by Firelight, 970
Milton, thou should'st be living at this hour, 790
Mingled, 1083
Miniver Cheevy, 876
Miniver Cheevy, child of scorn, 876
Minty, Judith
  Conjoined, 783
Mirror, 1099
Misgiving, 1069
Miss Brill, 202
Molière (Jean Baptiste Poquelin)
  Love Is the Doctor (L'Amour Médecin), 1563
Momaday, N. Scott
  The Bear, 1155
Monet Refuses the Operation, 1156
Montale, Eugenio
  Buffalo (Buffalo), 744
  English Horn (Corno Inglese), 672
Moore, Lorrie
  How to Become a Writer, 146
Moore, Marianne
  The Fish, 745
  Poetry, 1155
Mora, Pat
  La Migra, 821
Mother, The, 634
Mother dear, may I go downtown, 927
Much have I travell'd in the realms of gold, 762
Much Madness is divinest Sense –, 1034
Much Madness Is Divinest Sense, 1034
Mueller, Lisel
  Alive Together, 692
  Hope, 626
  Monet Refuses the Operation, 1156
Mulatto, 1619
Munro, Alice
  The Found Boat, 347
Musée des Beaux Arts, 998
Museum, 921
Music, when soft voices die, 644
My Arkansas, 1106
My black face fades, 819
My Childhood's Home, 820
My childhood's home I see again, 820
My face is grass, 779
My father, who works with stone, 1161
My heart aches, and a drowsy numbness
    pains, 923
My hips are a desk, 1163
My husband gives me an A, 1162
My Last Duchess, 697
My Life Closed Twice Before Its Close, 1035
My life closed twice before it's close, 1035
*My Mistress' Eyes Are Nothing Like the
    Sun*, 749
My mistress' eyes are nothing like the
    sun, 749
My Mother's Face, 1174
My old man's a white old man, 1077
My Papa's Waltz, 828

My Physics Teacher, 831
My Triumph Lasted Till the Drums, 1035
My Triumph lasted till the Drums, 1035
My Uncle's Watch, 1182
My words and thoughts do both express this
    notion, 909
Myth, 1012
Myth of Atalanta, The, 381

Naked and the Nude, The, 660
Names, The, 812
Naming of Parts, 674
Nash, Ogden
  Very Like a Whale, 868
Nature's first green is gold, 1069
Nautilus Island's Hermit, 781
Necklace, The, 5
Negro (Hughes), 1081
Negro, The (James Emanuel), 1128
Negro Speaks of Rivers, The, 1082
Neighbors, 137
Nemerov, Howard
  Life Cycle of Common Man, 1157
Neruda, Pablo
  Every Day You Play, 746
  If You Forget Me, 784
Never saw him, 1128
Never until the mankind making, 1181
New Colossus, The, 640
Next, Please, 966
next to of course god america i, 665
next to of course god america i, 665
Night Sounds, 671
Night Talkers, 77
Nightingale: Ode to a Nightingale
    (Keats), 923
Nikki-Rosa, 920
Nobody heard him, the dead man, 1177
Nobody's waiting for any apocalypse to meet
    you, Famine!, 768
Noiseless Patient Spider, A, 972
Northrup, Jim
  Ogichidag, 642
  wahbegan, 1158
No coward soul is mine, 948
No Coward Soul Is Mine, 948
No sign is made while empires pass, 929
Not even for a moment. He knew, for one thing,
    what he was, 989
Not like the brazen giant of Greek
    fame, 640
Not Marble, Nor the Gilded Monuments, 643
Not marble, nor the gilded
    monuments, 643
Not Waving But Drowning, 1177
Nothing Gold Can Stay, 1069
Nothing Is Lost, 827
Nothing is lost, 827
Nothing is so beautiful as Spring—, 740
Nothing to be said about it, and
    everything—, 823
Now hardly here and there a hackney-
    coach, 830

Now the rain is falling, freshly, in the intervals between sunlight, 1136
Now the seasons are closing their files, 965
Now winter downs the dying of the year, 973
Nye, Naomi Shihab
  Where Children Live, 642
Nymph's Reply to the Shepherd, The, 711

"O Hell, what doe mine eyes with grief behold?," 740
"O 'melia, my dear, this does everything crown!," 704
O my luve's like a red, red rose, 770
O Star (the fairest one in sight), 1072
O what can ail thee, knight at arms, 963
O wild West Wind, thou breath of Autumn's being, 878
O'Brien, Tim
  The Things they Carried, 95
O'Connor, Flannery
  A Good Man Is Hard to Find, 576
O'Connor, Frank
  First Confession, 354
O'Neill, Eugene
  Before Breakfast, 1248
Oates, Joyce Carol
  The Cousins, 150
  Loving, 710
  Where Are You Going, Where Have You Been?, 302
Occurrence at Owl Creek Bridge, An, 71
Odd, the baby's scabbed face peeking over, 744
Ode on a Grecian Urn, 1142
Ode to a Nightingale, 923
Ode to the West Wind, 878
Odysseus, 992
Odyssey: 20 Years Later, 996
Oedipus slew his father near this muddy field, 1012
Oedipus the King, 1281
Of Being, 672
Ogichidag, 642
Oh summer if you would only come, 713
Oh, where have you been, Lord Randal, my son?, 1107
Old Men Pitching Horseshoes, 965
Oldham: To the Memory of Mr. Oldham, 918
Olds, Sharon
  The Planned Child, 822
Oliver, Mary
  Ghosts, 1159
  Wild Geese, 969
Olsen, Tillie
  I Stand Here Ironing, 586
On Another's Sorrow, 809
On Being Brought from Africa to America, 1189
On First Looking into Chapman's Homer, 762
On His Blindness, 926
On Monsieur's Departure, 788
On My First Daughter (Epigram 22), 640

On the ashes of this nest, 1010
On the Death of Friends in Childhood, 1141
On the morning of the Käthe Kollwitz exhibit, a young man and woman come into, 921
On the Way to Delphi, 1012
On Wenlock Edge, 741
On Wenlock Edge the wood's in trouble, 741
Once upon a midnight dreary, 1164
One Art, 916
One need not be a Chamber – to be Haunted –, 1035
One Need Not Be a Chamber – To Be Haunted, 1035
One thing that literature would be greatly the better for, 868
125th Street, 1082
Only a man harrowing clods, 958
Only Teaching on Tuesdays, book-worming, 707
Only the feathers floating around the hat, 999
Open Boat, The, 548
Oranges, 1178
Orientation, 359
Orozco, Daniel
  Orientation, 359
Orpheus. The Sonnets to Orpheus: 1.19 (Rilke), 1004
Orpheus Alone, 1005
Ortiz, Simon
  A Story of How a Wall Stands, 1161
Ortiz Cofer, Judith
  Latin Women Pray, 673
Our sardine fishermen work at night in the dark of the moon; daylight or moonlight, 961
Out of the East, Beauty has come home, 1106
"Out, Out—", 1067
Oven Bird, The, 1068
Owen, Wilfred
  Anthem for Doomed Youth, 729
  Dulce et Decorum Est, 802
Ozick, Cynthia
  The Shawl, 266
Ozymandias, 929

Pan came out of the woods one day, 1015
Pan With Us, 1015
Paperweight, The, 1173
Parable of the Prodigal Son, The, 399
Parédes, Americo
  The Hammon and the Beans, 482
Parker, Dorothy
  Penelope, 993
  Résumé 1162
Parure, La (The Necklace), 5
Passing of Arthur: Idyls of the King: The Passing of Arthur (lines 344–93), 881
Passionate Shepherd to His Love, The, 709
Pastan, Linda
  Ethics, 1162
  Marks, 1162
  The Suitor, 993
Patterns, 1149

Peacock, Molly
  Desire, 1163
Penelope, 993
Penelope's Song, 991
People are made of places. They carry
    with them, 696
Perfection Wasted, 1183
Petronius (Gaius Petronius Arbiter)
  The Widow of Ephesus, 591
Phoenix Again, The, 1010
Pied Beauty, 1139
Piercy, Marge
  The Secretary Chant, 1163
  A Work of Artifice, 785
Pinsky, Robert
  Dying, 823
Pirandello, Luigi
  War, 105
Planned Child, The, 822
Plath, Sylvia
  Ariel, 1090
  The Colossus, 1091
  Cut, 1092
  Daddy, 1093
  Edge, 1095
  The Hanging Man, 1096
  Lady Lazarus, 1096
  Last Words, 1098
  Metaphors, 1099
  Mirror, 1099
  The Rival, 1100
  Song for a Summer's Day, 1100
  Tulips, 1101
Po' Boy Blues, 1082
Poe, Edgar Allan
  Annabel Lee, 869
  The Bells, 870
  The Black Cat, 513
  The Cask of Amontillado, 519
  The Fall of the House of Usher, 524
  The Masque of the Red Death, 527
  The Raven, 1164
Poetics Against the Angel of Death, 931
Poetry (Giovanni), 934
Poetry (Marianne Moore), 1155
Poor soul, the center of my sinful
    earth, 1175
Pope, Alexander
  Epigram from the French, 807
  *Epigram, Engraved on the Collar of a Dog
    which I gave to his Royal Highness*,
    808
  From *Epilogue to the Satires, Dialogue I, Lines
    137–72*, 824
  From *An Essay on Man, Epistle I, lines 17–90*,
    873
Poplar Field, The, 699
Porphyria's Lover, 858
Porter, Katherine Anne
  The Jilting of Granny Weatherall, 405
Pound, Ezra
  In a Station of the Metro, 747

Pray thee, take care, that tak'st my book
    in hand, 690
Preludes, 735
Primer for Blacks, 1111
Prodigal Son; The Parable of the Prodigal Son, 399
*Prufrock: The Love Song of J. Alfred
    Prufrock*, 1124
Prunty, Wyatt
  March, 875
Pulley, The, 740
Purse-Seine, The, 961

Quasímodo, Salvatore
  Auschwitz, 825
Queen Elizabeth I
  On Monsieur's Departure, 788
Question, 1180
Quinquereme of Nineveh from distant
    Ophir, 728

Radnóti, Miklós
  Forced March, 748
Ralegh, Sir Walter
  The Nymph's Reply to the Shepherd, 711
Randall, Dudley
  Ballad of Birmingham, 927
Ransom, John Crowe
  Bells for John Whiteside's Daughter, 1166
Raven, John
  Assailant, 1167
Raven, The, 1164
Reapers, 931
Reconciliation, 906
Red Wheelbarrow, The, 1193
Red, Red Rose, A, 770
Reed, Henry
  Naming of Parts, 674
*Refusal to Mourn the Death, by Fire, of a Child in
    London, A*, 1181
Remember, 777
Remember the sky that you were born
    under, 777
Revolutionary Petunias, 1186
Rhine Boat Trip, 1145
Rich, Adrienne
  Diving Into the Wreck, 1167
Richard Cory, 675
Ridler, Anne
  Nothing Is Lost, 827
Rilke, Rainer Maria
  *The Sonnets to Orpheus, 1.19
    (Though the world changes fast)*, 1004
Rios, Alberto
  The Vietnam Wall, 1169
rite on: white america, 1171
Rival, The, 1100
Road Not Taken, The, 1067
Robinson, Edwin Arlington
  Miniver Cheevy, 876
  Richard Cory, 675
Roethke, Theodore
  Dolor, 676

Roethke, Theodore (*continued*)
  My Papa's Waltz, 828
  The Waking, 928
Rose for Emily, A, 89
Rossetti, Christina
  A Christmas Carol, 712
  Echo, 877
Roughly figured, this man of moderate
  habits, 1157
Rückert, Friedrich
  If You Love for the Sake of Beauty, 749
Ruined Maid, The, 704
Rukeyser, Muriel
  Looking at Each Other, 786
  Myth, 1012
  Waiting for Icarus, 1000
Rush Hour, 1083
Russell, George William ("Æ")
  Continuity, 929

Safe in their Alabaster Chambers –, 1036
Safe in Their Alabaster Chambers, 1036
Salinas, Luis Omar
  In a Farmhouse, 1170
Sammy Lou of Rue, 1186
Sanchez, Sonia
  rite on: white america, 1171
Sandbox, The, 1224
Sandburg, Carl
  Chicago, 1172
Sarton, May
  The Phoenix Again, 1010
Sassoon, Siegfried
  Dreamers, 1172
Say first, of God above, or man below, 873
Say Not the Struggle Nought Availeth, 950
Say not the struggle nought availeth, 950
Schnackenberg, Gjertrud
  The Paperweight, 1173
Schoolsville, 624
Scott, Virginia
  Snow, 941
Season of mists and mellow fruitfulness!, 778
Second Coming, The, 974
Secretary Chant, The, 1163
Secret Sharer, The, 253
See, here's the workbox, little wife, 805
Seeger, Alan
  I Have a Rendezvous with Death, 1173
Seeing the March rain flood a field, 875
Sennacherib: The Destruction of Sennacherib, 1116
Serotte, Brenda
  My Mother's Face, 1174
Sexton, Anne
  *To a Friend Whose Work Has Come to
    Triumph*, 1001
Shakespeare, William
  Hamlet, 1322
  A Midsummer Night's Dream, 1506
  *Sonnet 18: Shall I Compare Thee to a Summer's
    Day?*, 787
  *Sonnet 29: When in Disgrace with Fortune and
    Men's Eyes*, 1175

  *Sonnet 30: When to the Sessions of Sweet Silent
    Thought*, 787
  *Sonnet 55: Not Marble, Nor the Gilded Monu-
    ments*, 643
  *Sonnet 73: That Time of Year Thou May'st in Me
    Behold*, 878
  *Sonnet 116: Let Me Not to the Marriage of True
    Minds*, 904
  Sonnet 130: My Mistress' Eyes, 749
  *Sonnet 146: Poor Soul, the Center of My Sinful
    Earth*, 1175
Shall I compare thee to a summer's
  day?, 787
Shape of History, The, 911
Shapiro, Karl
  Auto Wreck, 1176
Shawl, The, 266
she being Brand / -new, 813
she being Brand, 813
She is as in a field a silken tent, 1070
She Walks in Beauty, 1116
She walks in beauty, like the night, 1116
she wanted to be a blade, 1130
She's Free!, 1135
Shelley, Percy Bysshe
  Ode to the West Wind, 878
  Ozymandias, 929
  To —— [Music, when soft voices die], 644
Shiloh: A Requiem, 867
Shore, Jane
  A Letter Sent to Summer, 713
Shot 71 from the Shooting Script of Citizen Kane,
  1756
Sic Vita, 781
Silhouette, 1083
Silken Tent, The, 1070
Silko, Leslie Marmon
  *Where Mountain Lion Lay Down with
    Deer*, 1176
Sir *Patrick Spens*, 631
Sir, I admit your general rule, 807
Skimming lightly, wheeling still, 867
Skunk Hour, 781
Smith, Stevie
  Not Waving But Drowning, 1177
Snapshot of Hué, 1132
Snow (MacNeice), 641
Snow (Scott), 941
Snow falling and night falling fast, oh,
  fast, 941
Snowdrops, 700
Snyder, Gary
  Milton by Firelight, 970
so much depends, 1193
So smooth, so sweet, so silv'ry is thy
  voice, 864
Soldiers are citizens of death's grey
  land, 1172
Soliloquy of the Spanish Cloister, 1113
Solitary Reaper, The, 832
Some are waiting, some can't wait, 1153
Some Keep the Sabbath Going to Church, 1036
Some keep the Sabbath going to Church –, 1036

Some people go their whole lives, 750
Some say the world will end in fire, 1068
Something Like a Star: *Take [Choose] Something Like a Star*, 1072
Something there is that doesn't love a wall, 1065
Sometimes, 1077
Somewhere in California, 955
Song (Lewis), 707
Song and Story, 1007
Song for a Forgotten Shrine to Pan, 1015
Song for a Summer's Day, 1100
Song for St. Cecilia's Day, A, 772
Song of Napalm, 1188
Sonnet (Collins), 917
Sonnet 18: Shall I Compare Thee to a Summer's Day?, 787
Sonnet 29: When in Disgrace with Fortune and Men's Eyes, 1175
Sonnet 30: When to the Sessions of Sweet Silent Thought, 787
Sonnet 55: Not Marble, Nor the Gilded Monuments, 643
Sonnet 73: That Time of Year Thou May'st in Me Behold, 878
Sonnet 116: Let Me Not to the Marriage of True Minds, 904
Sonnet 130: My Mistress' Eyes, 749
Sonnet 146: Poor Soul, the Center of My Sinful Earth, 1175
Sonnet Ending with a Film Subtitle, 1132
Sonnet for You, Familiar Famine, 768
Sonnet on the Death of Richard West, 668
Sonnets from the Portuguese, No 14: If Thou Must Love Me, 733
Sonnets from the Portuguese: No. 43: How Do I Love Thee?, 1113
Sonnets to Orpheus: 1.19, The, 1004
Sonny's Blues, 438
Sophocles
  Oedipus the King, 1281
Soto, Gary
  Oranges, 1178
Soul Selects Her Own Society, The, 1037
Sound of the Sea, The, 866
Southern gentle lady, 1083
Speaking of marvels, I am alive, 692
Spender, Stephen ·
  I Think Continually of Those Who Were Truly Great, 676
Spikes of lavender aster under Route 91, 1149
Spring, 740
Spring Rain, 1136
Spun in High, Dark Clouds, 903
Spun in high, dark clouds, 903
Stafford, William
  Traveling Through the Dark, 1179
Stasis in darkness, 1090
Statuary, 1144
Steinbeck, John
  The Chrysanthemums, 411
Stern, Gerald
  Burying an Animal on the Way to New York, 1179

Stevens, Wallace
  Disillusionment of Ten O'Clock, 677
  The Emperor of Ice Cream, 1180
  Stopping by Woods on a Snowy Evening, 1069
Story of an Hour, The, 331
Story of How a Wall Stands, A, 1161
Strand, Mark
  Eating Poetry, 677
  Orpheus Alone, 1005
Subway Rush Hour, 1083
Success is counted sweetest, 1037
Success is counted sweetest, 1037
Suitor, The, 993
Summer in the Middle Class, 1133
Sun Rising, The, 860
Sundays too my father got up early, 1137
Supermarket in California, A, 919
Swan and Shadow, 912
Sweet day, so cool, so calm, so bright, 922
Swenson, May
  Question, 1180
  Women, 1110
Swift, Jonathan
  A Description of the Morning, 830
Swimmers, The, 1004
Sympathy, 1124

Take [Choose] Something Like a Star, 1072
Tan, Amy
  Two Kinds, 206
Tate, James
  Dream On, 750
Tea Party, 1244
Tears, 960
Tears leave no mark on the soil, 960
Tell All the Truth but Tell It Slant, 1037
Tell all the Truth but tell it slant, 1037
Ten kilometers from Warsaw, 1138
Tennyson, Alfred, Lord
  The Eagle, 899
  Idylls of the King: The Passing of Arthur (lines 344–93), 881
  Ulysses, 994
Terranova, Elaine
  Rush Hour, 644
That night your great guns, unawares, 738
That time of year thou may'st in me behold, 878
That's my last Duchess painted on the wall, 697
The air was soft, the ground still cold, 1192
The apparition of these faces in the crowd, 747
The art of losing isn't hard to master, 916
The Assyrian came down like the wolf on the fold, 1116
The beauty of the trees, 1130
The bonsai tree, 785
The Bustle in a House, 1030
The buzz saw snarled and rattled in the yard, 1067
The castles on the Rhine, 1145
The crackle of parched grass bent by wind, 951
The curfew tolls the knell of parting day, 701

The first Sunday I missed Mass on purpose, 1194
The first time I walked, 1178
The girl strapped in the bare mechanical crib, 1007
The Heart is the Capital of the Mind –, 1030
The houses are haunted, 677
The instructor said, 1083
The intent wind that plays tonight, 672
The killers that run, 1117
The king sits in Dumferline town, 631
The land, that, from the rule of kings, 1191
The land was ours before we were the land's, 1071
The last sunbeam, 1090
The late cranes throwing, 1144
The moonlight on my bed keeps me awake, 671
The old wooden steps to the front door, 742
The onion in my cupboard, a monster, actually, 783
The pines rub their great noise, 705
The poplars are felled, farewell to the shade, 699
The quake last night was nothing personal, 789
The rain set early in to-night, 858
The room was suddenly rich and the great bay-window was, 641
The scene within the paperweight is calm, 1173
The sea awoke at midnight from its sleep, 866
The sea is calm tonight, 694
The Soul selects her own Society –, 1037
The trees are in their autumn beauty, 1193
The tulips are too excitable, it is winter here, 1101
The Voice You Hear when You Read Silently, 743
The whiskey on your breath, 828
The winter evening settles down, 735
The woman is perfected, 1095
The world is charged with the grandeur of God, 864
Theme for English B, 1083
Then what is the answer?—Not to be deluded by dreams, 1141
Theory of Prosody, A, 866
There is a deep brooding, 1106
There is a singer everyone has heard, 1068
There is a world somewhere else that is unendurable, 831
There is always a story, 993
There was such speed in her little body, 1166
There's a Certain Slant of Light, 1037
There's a certain Slant of light, 1037
There's naught but care on ev'ry han, 662
these hips are big hips, 811
They are riding bicycles on the other side, 1132
Thine eyes shall see the light of distant skies, 1115
Things They Carried, The, 95
Third-generation timetable, 1184

This brief effusion I indite, 801
this country might have, 1171
This is a pain I mostly hide, 810
This was the man God gave us when the hour, 865
Thomas, Dylan
  Do Not Go Gentle Into That Good Night, 930
  A Refusal to Mourn the Death, by Fire, of a Child in London, 1181
Those Winter Sundays, 1137
Thou still unravish'd bride of quietness, 1142
Though the world changes fast, 1004
Through fen and farmland walking, 1100
Through the Weeks of Deep Snow, 1109
Time Past, A, 742
Tintern Abbey Lines: Lines Composed a Few Miles above Tintern Abbey, 714
To —— [Music, when soft voices die], 644
To a Friend Whose Work Has Come to Triumph, 1001
To Autumn, 778
Tobin, Daniel
  My Uncle's Watch, 1182
To Cole, the Painter, Departing for Europe, 1115
To fling my arms wide, 1078
To Hear an Oriole Sing, 857
To hear an Oriole sing, 857
To His Coy Mistress, 968
To My Dear and Loving Husband, 1111
To pray you open your whole self, 638
To the Memory of Mr. Oldham, 918
To the Reader, 690
To the Virgins, to Make Much of Time, 1137
Today as I hang out the wash I see them again, a code, 957
To-day we have naming of parts. Yesterday, 674
Today's paper is crammed full of news: pages and pages on the Somalia, 911
Tonight, Sally and I are making stuffed, 1134
Toomer, Jean
  Reapers, 931
Traveling through the dark I found a deer, 1179
Traveling Through the Dark, 1179
Trifles, 1233
Trouble, 814
True Love, 1185
Tudor, Elizabeth: Queen Elizabeth I
  On Monsieur's Departure, 788
Tuft of Flowers, The, 1063
Tulips, 1101
Turning and turning in the widening gyre, 974
Turning Point, The (film), *A Scene from The Turning Point*, 1761
Twain, Mark
  Luck, 213
Twas brillig, and the slithy toves, 663
'Twas mercy brought me from my *Pagan* land, 1189
Twichell, Chase
  Blurry Cow, 1183
Two boys uncoached are tossing a poem together, 636

Two cows stand transfixe 1183
Two Kinds, 205
Two roads diverged in a llow wood, 1067
Tyger! Tyger! burning brilt, 769
Tyger, The, 769

Ulisse, Peter
    Odyssey: 20 Years Later)6
Ulysses, 994
Under the sky at night, sined by our guesses,
    774
Unfinished Masterpieces, 3
Unknown Citizen, The, 11(
Updike, John
    A & P, 363
    On the Way to Delphi, 1
    Perfection Wasted, 1183
Upon Julia's Voice, 864

Valediction: Forbidding Ming, A, 771
Van Duyn, Mona
    Earth Tremors Felt in Mri, 789
    Leda, 988
*Variation on the Word Sle*108
Venice Is Sinking, 967
Very Like a Whale, 868
Very Old Man with EnorWings, A, 401
Vietnam Wall, The, 1169
Villanueva, Tino
    Day-Long Day, 1184
Viorst, Judith
    True Love, 1185
    A Wedding Sonnet for xt Generation, 971
Virtue, 922
Virtue may choose the h low
    degree, 824
Visit to the Sepulcher, TheQuem
    Quaeritis Trope), 12
Voice You Hear when Yousilently, The, 743
Voigt, Ellen Bryant
    Song and Story, 1007

Wade, 745
Wagner, Shelly
    The Boxes, 1185
Wagoner, David
    March for a One-Man 32
    My Physics Teacher, 8
Wahbegan, 1158
Waiting for Icarus, 1000
Waking, The, 928
Walker, Alice
    Everyday Use, 108
    Revolutionary Petunia
Waller, Edmund
    Go, Lovely Rose, 1187
War, 105
We listened intently to ssor, 667
We Real Cool, 857
We real cool. We, 857
We shall not ever meeturded in
    heaven, 1141

We warbled on the muddy banks, 1004
We were first equal Mary and I, 1148
Weary Blues, The, 1084
Webb, Charles Harper
    The Shape of History, 911
Webb, Phyllis
    Poetics Against the Angel of Death, 931
Wedding Sonnet for the Next Generation,
    A, 971
Weigl, Bruce
    Song of Napalm, 1188
Welles, Orson, and Herman J. Mankiewicz
    Shot 71 from the Shooting Script of Citizen Kane,
    1757
Welty, Eudora
    A Worn Path, 114
Western Wind, 687
Western wind, when wilt thou blow?, 687
We warbled on the muddy banks, 1004
What a needy, desperate thing, 954
What a thrill—, 1092
What does it mean? Lord knows; least
    of all I, 664
What happens to a dream deferred?, 1078
What I Have Been Doing Lately, 300
What Lips My Lips Have Kissed, and Where, and
    Why, 1154
What lips my lips have kissed, and where, and
    why, 1154
What passing-bells for these who die as
    cattle?, 729
What ruse of vision, 1155
What thoughts I have of you tonight, Walt
    Whitman, for, 919
What you have heard is true, 915
Wheatley, Phillis
    On Being Brought from Africa to America, 1189
When God at first made man, 740
When I consider how my light is spent, 926
When I see birches bend to left and right, 1066
When I told the police I couldn't find you, 1185
When Nellie, my old pussy, 866
When to the sessions of sweet silent
    thought, 787
When, in disgrace with Fortune and men's
    eyes, 1175
When You Are Old (William Ernest Henley), 817
When You Are Old (William Butler Yeats), 833
When you are old and grey, and full of
    sleep, 833
When you are old, and I am passed away, 817
Whenever Richard Cory went down town, 875
Where Are You Going, Where Have You Been?, 302
Where Children Live, 642
Where I Come From, 697
Where Mountain Lion Lay Down with
    Deer, 1177
While you walk the water's edge, 949
White City, The, 1153
Whitecloud, Tom
    Blue Winds Dancing, 313
Whitman, Walt
    Beat! Beat! Drums!, 1189

Whitman, Walt (*continued*)
Dirge for Two Veterans, 1190
Facing West from California's Shores, 790
Full of Life Now, 1191
I Hear America Singing, 1191
A Noiseless Patient Spider, 972
Reconciliation, 906
Whittier, John Greenleaf
The Bartholdi Statue, 1192
Whose woods these are I think I know, 637
Whur, Cornelius
The First-Rate Wife, 801
Why always speak of Icarus' fall?—, 997
Widow of Ephesus, The, 591
Wilbur, Richard
April 5, 1974, 1192
Year's End, 973
Wild Geese, 969
Wild Nights – Wild Nights!, 1038
Wild Nights – Wild Nights!, 1038
Wild Swans at Coole, The, 1193
Williams, C. K.
Dimensions, 831
Williams, Tennessee
The Glass Menagerie, 1643
Williams, William Carlos
The Dance, 932
Landscape with the Fall of Icarus, 1002
The Red Wheelbarrow, 1193
Wilson, August
Fences, 1695
Wilt Thou forgive that sin where I begun, 1123
Windhover, The, 1140
Wojahn, David
"It's Only Rock and Roll, But I Like It": The Fall of Saigon, 751
Woman (Giovanni), 1130
Women (Bogan), 1110
Women (Swenson), 914

Women have no wildeness in them, 1110
Women   Or they, 914
Word over all, beautif as the sky, 906
Wordsworth, William
Daffodils (I Wander Lonely as a Cloud), 678
Lines Composed a Fe Miles above Tintern Abbey, 714
London, 1802, 790
The Solitary Reaper,
Work of Artifice, A, 785
Workbox, The, 805
Worn Path, A, 114
Wright, James
A Blessing, 717
Wyatt, Sir Thomas
I Find No Peace, 791

Year's End (Kooser), 965
Year's End (Wilbur), 97
Yeats, William Butler
Leda and the Swan, 9
The Second Coming,
When You Are Old, 8
The Wild Swans at C 1193
Yellow Wallpaper, The,
Yesterday, I lay awake e palm of the night, 812
Yes, we were looking h other, 786
Yet once more, O ye la, and once more, 902
You do not do, you d do, 1093
You do not have to be, 969
you hover above the taring, 1128
You would think the ff aerial bombardment, 6
Young Goodman Brown

Zimmer, Paul
The Day Zimmer Lo ion, 1194